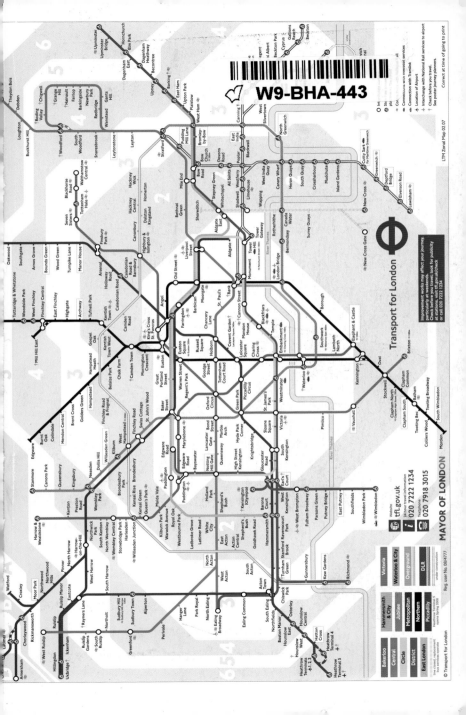

W9-BHA-443

Transport for London

MAYOR OF LONDON

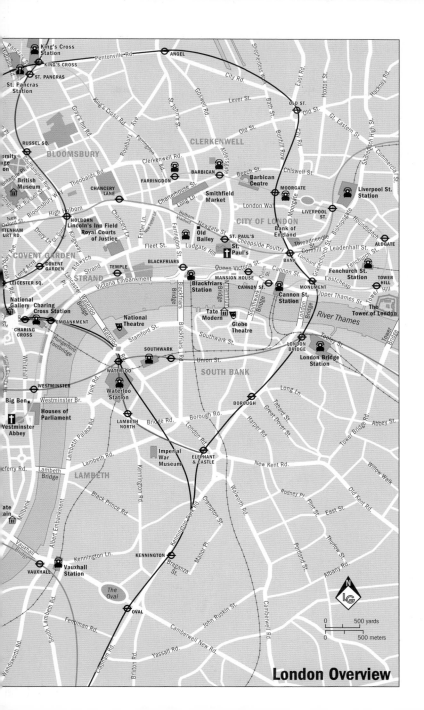

**London Overview**

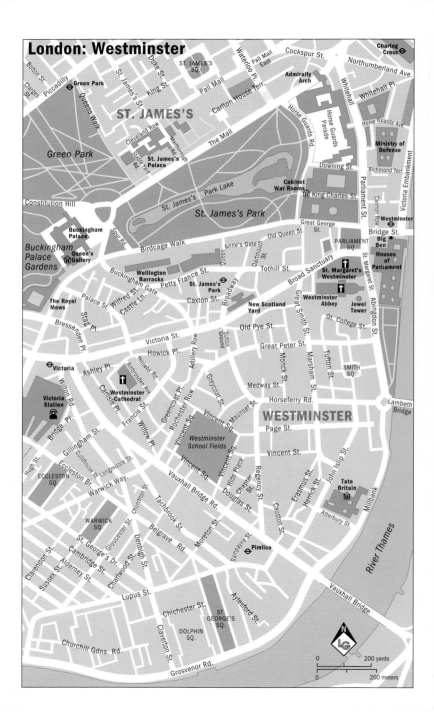

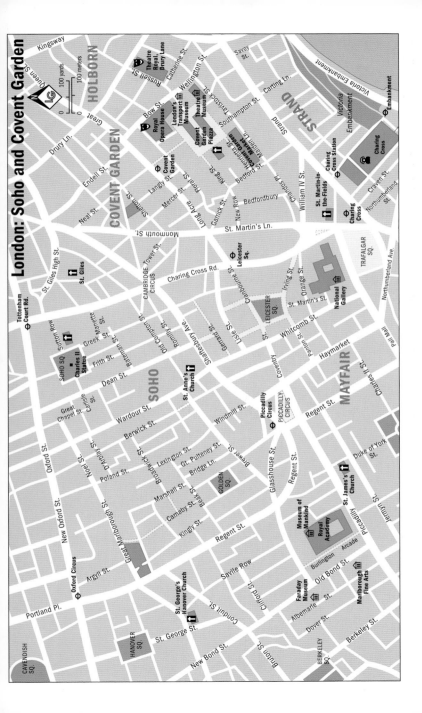

# London: Soho and Covent Garden

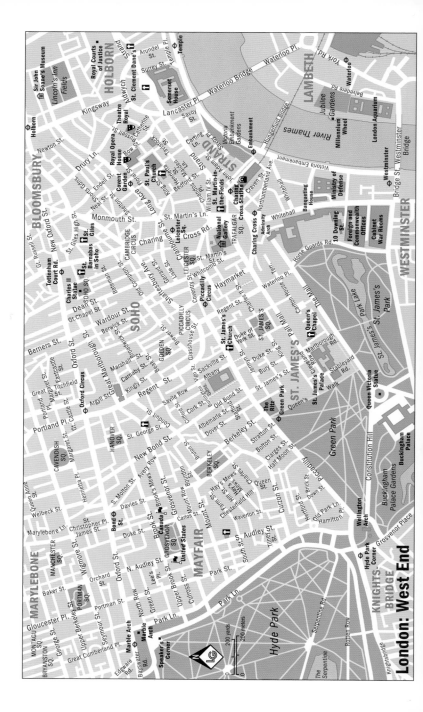

London: West End

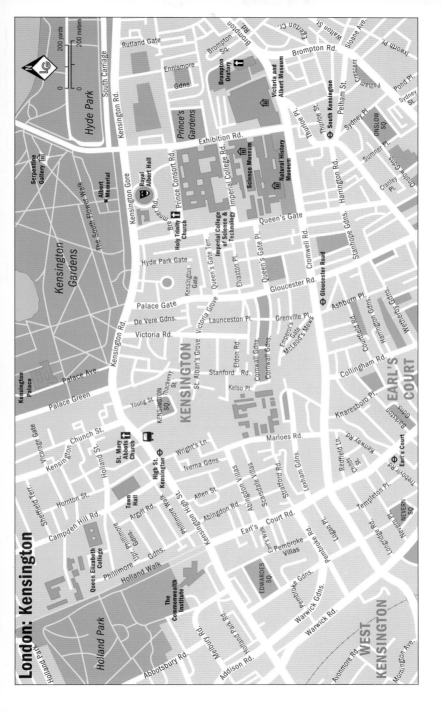

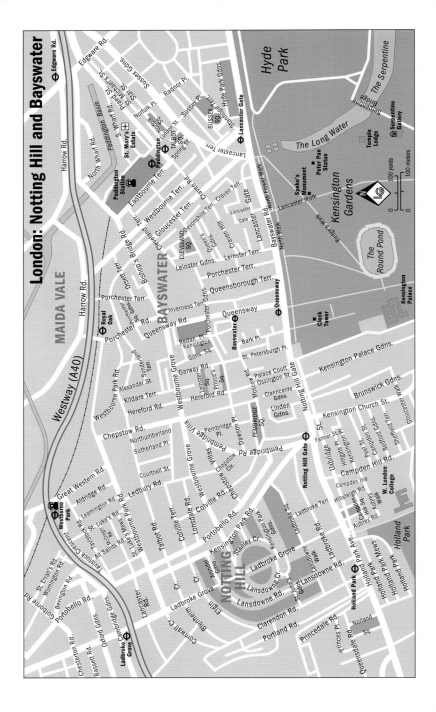

# London: Notting Hill and Bayswater

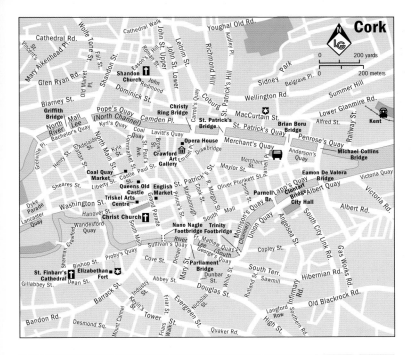

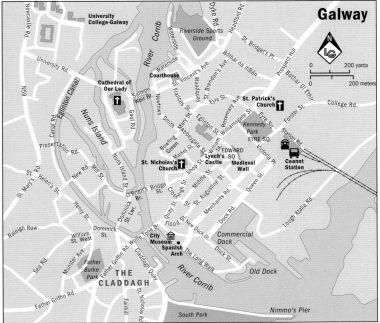

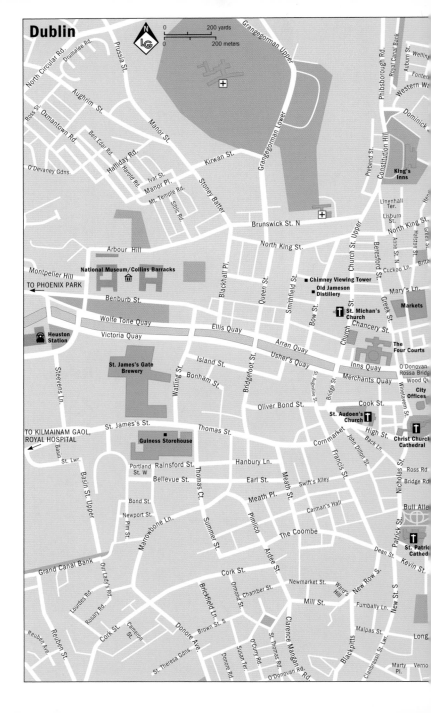

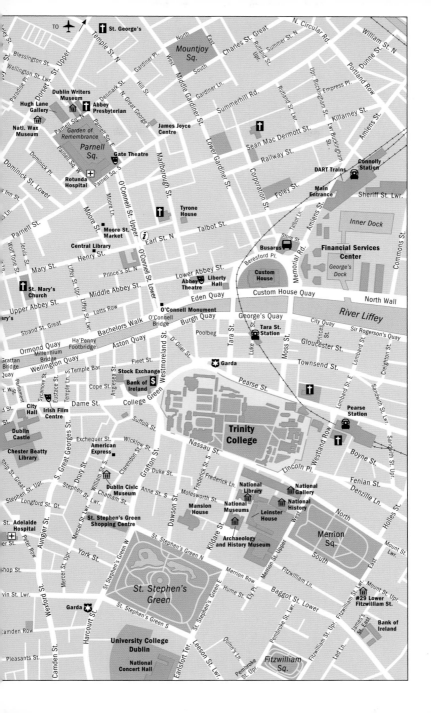

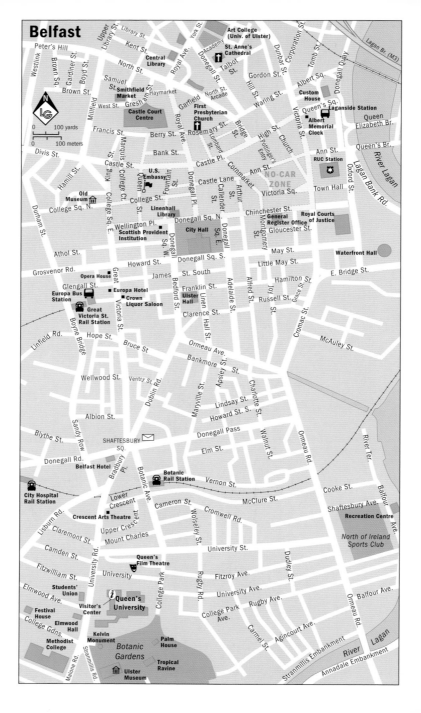

# Belfast

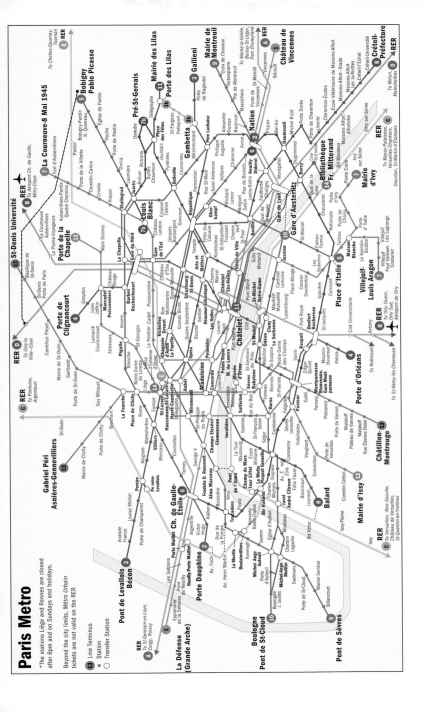

# Paris: Overview and Arrondissements

Bois de Boulogne

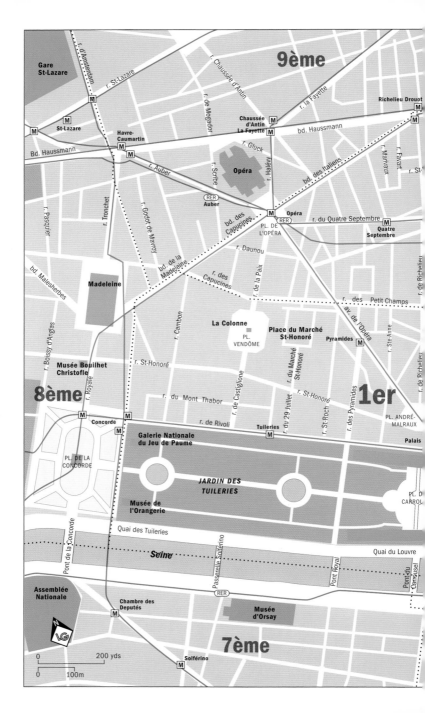

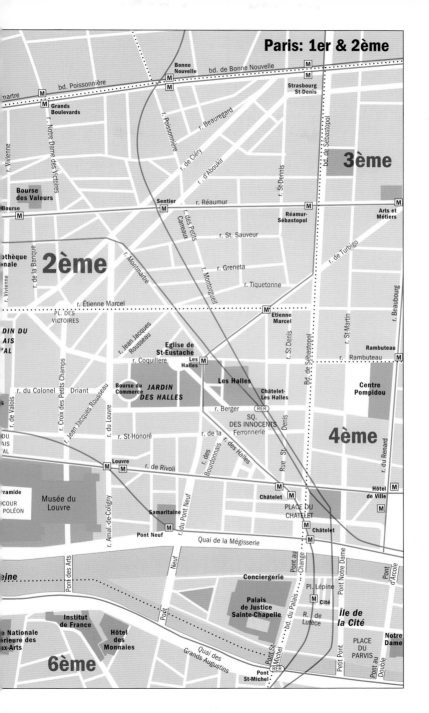

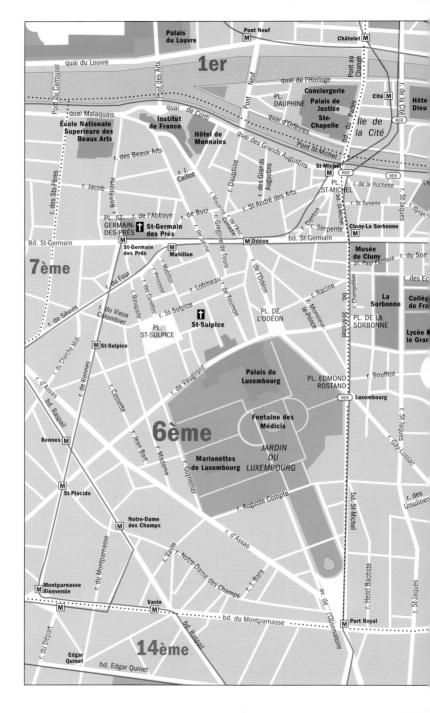

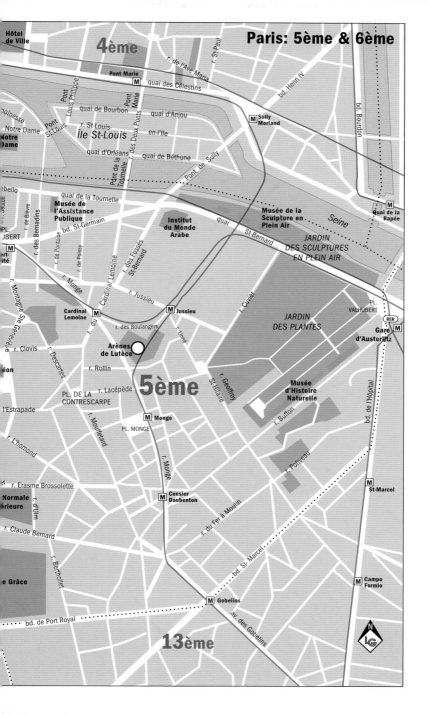

# Paris: 5ème & 6ème

**Hôtel de Ville**

**4ème**

r. de l'Ave Maria

r. St-Paul

**Pont Marie** M

quai des Célestins

bd. Henri IV

...oinesse

quai de Bourbon

quai d'Anjou

M **Sully Morland**

Pont Louis Philippe

Pont Marie

Pont des Deux Ponts

bd. Bourdon

Notre Dame

Pont St-Louis

r. St-Louis-

**Île St-Louis**

en-l'Île

**Dame**

quai d'Orléans

quai de Béthune

Pont de la Tournelle

Pont de Sully

...bello

quai de la Tournelle

**Musée de l'Assistance Publique**

bd. St-Germain

**Institut du Monde Arabe**

quai

**Musée de la Sculpture en Plein Air**

Seine

M **Quai de la Rapée**

St-Bernard

**JARDIN DES SCULPTURES EN PLEIN AIR**

PL. ...BERT

r. des Bernardins

r. de Bièvre

r. de Pontoise

r. de Poissy

r. des Fossés St-Bernard

Cardinal Lemoine

r. Jussieu

...rté- ...té M

r. Monge

r. du

r. Cuvier

PL. VALHUBERT

r. Montagne Ste Geneviève

**Cardinal Lemoine** M

M **Jussieu**

r. des Boulangers

r. Linné

**JARDIN DES PLANTES**

RER

**Gare d'Austerlitz** M

r. Clovis

r. Descartes

**Arènes de Lutèce** ○

...éon

r. Rollin

r. Lacépède

**5ème**

r. Geoffroy St-Hilaire

**Musée d'Histoire Naturelle**

bd. de l'Hôpital

PL. DE LA CONTRESCARPE

l'Estrapade

r. Mouffetard

M **Monge**

PL. MONGE

r. Buffon

r. L'homond

r. Monge

r. Poliveau

r. Erasme Brossolette

**Normale ...érieure**

r. d'Ulm

M **Censier Daubenton**

M **St-Marcel**

r. Claude Bernard

r. du Fer à Moulin

r. Berthollet

bd. St-Marcel

M **Campo Formio**

...e Grâce

M **Gobelins**

bd. de Port Royal

av. des Gobelins

**13ème**

N

LG

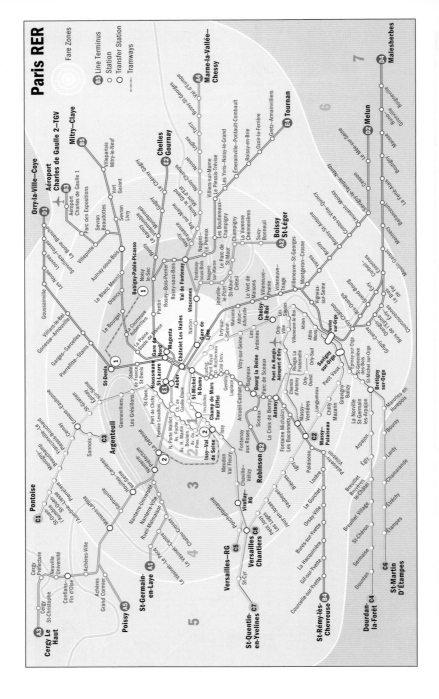

# Paris RER

# Berlin Transit

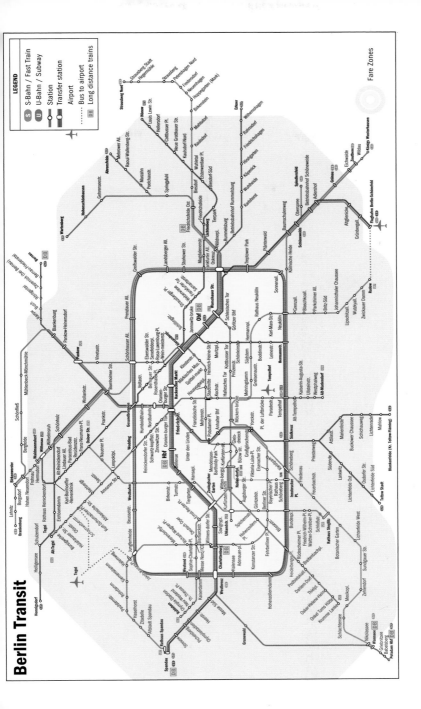

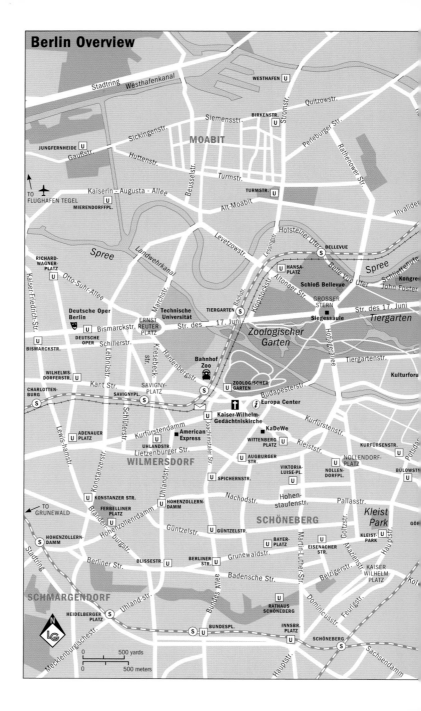

# Berlin Overview

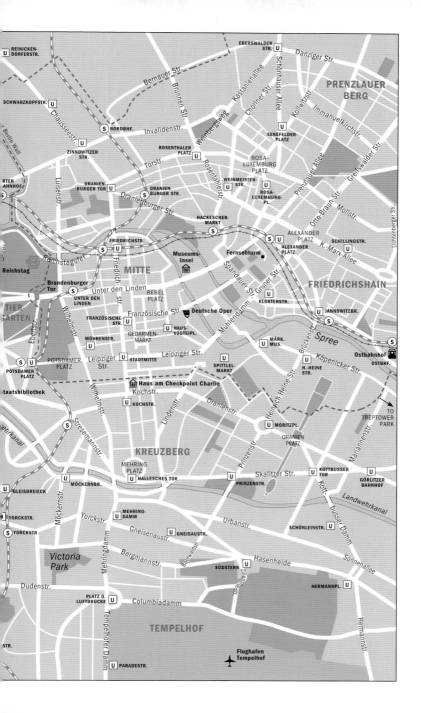

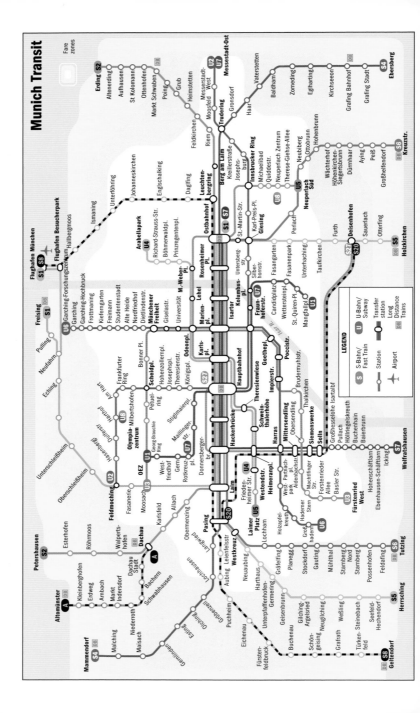
Munich Transit

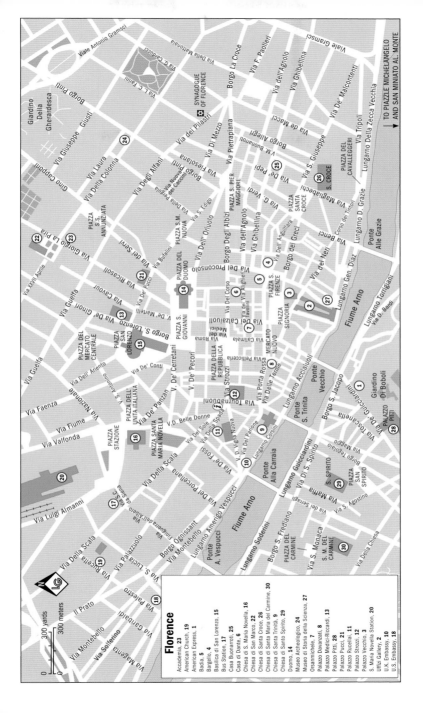

**Florence**

Accademia, **23**
American Church, **19**
American Express, **1**
Badia, **5**
Bargello, **4**
Basilica di San Lorenzo, **15**
Bus Station, **17**
Casa Buonarroti, **25**
Casa di Dante, **6**
Chiesa di S. Maria Novella, **16**
Chiesa di San Marco, **22**
Chiesa di Santa Croce, **26**
Chiesa di Santa Maria del Carmine, **30**
Chiesa di Santa Trinità, **9**
Chiesa di Santo Spirito, **29**
Duomo, **14**
Museo Archeologico, **24**
Museo di Storia della Scienza, **27**
Orsanmichele, **7**
Palazzo Davanzati, **8**
Palazzo Medici-Riccardi, **13**
Palazzo Pitti, **28**
Palazzo Pucci, **21**
Palazzo Rucellai, **11**
Palazzo Strozzi, **12**
Palazzo Vecchio, **2**
S. Maria Novella Station, **20**
Uffizi Gallery, **10**
U.K. Embassy, **2**
U.S. Embassy, **18**

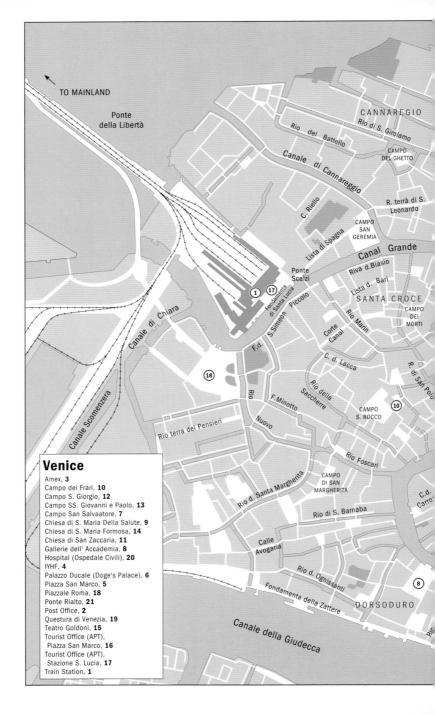

TO MAINLAND

Ponte
della Libertà

CANNAREGIO

Rio del Battello

Rio di S. Girolamo

Canale di Cannareggio

CAMPO
DEL GHETTO

C. Riello

R. terrà di S.
Leonardo

Lista di Spagna

CAMPO
SAN
GEREMIA

Canal Grande

Ponte
Scalzi

Riva d.Biasio

Fondamenta di Santa Lucia

Lista d. Bari

SANTA CROCE

F.d. S.Simeon Piccolo

Rio Marin

CAMPO
DEI
MORTI

Canale di Chiara

Corte
Canal

C. d. Lacca

R. di San Polo

Canale Scomenzera

Rio della Saccherre

CAMPO
S. ROCCO

F.Minotto

Rio

Nuovo

Rio terra dei Pensieri

Rio Foscari

Rio d. Santa Margherita

CAMPO
DI SAN
MARGHERITA

C. d.
Carro

Rio di S. Barnaba

Calle
Avogaria

Rio d. Ognissanti

Fondamenta della Zattere

DORSODURO

Canale della Giudecca

## Venice

Amex, **3**
Campo dei Frari, **10**
Campo S. Giorgio, **12**
Campo SS. Giovanni e Paolo, **13**
Campo San Salvaatore, **7**
Chiesa di S. Maria Della Salute, **9**
Chiesa di S. Maria Formosa, **14**
Chiesa di San Zaccaria, **11**
Gallerie dell' Accademia, **8**
Hospital (Ospedale Civili), **20**
IYHF, **4**
Palazzo Ducale (Doge's Palace), **6**
Piazza San Marco, **5**
Piazzale Roma, **18**
Ponte Rialto, **21**
Post Office, **2**
Questura di Venezia, **19**
Teatro Goldoni, **15**
Tourist Office (APT),
  Piazza San Marco, **16**
Tourist Office (APT),
  Stazione S. Lucia, **17**
Train Station, **1**

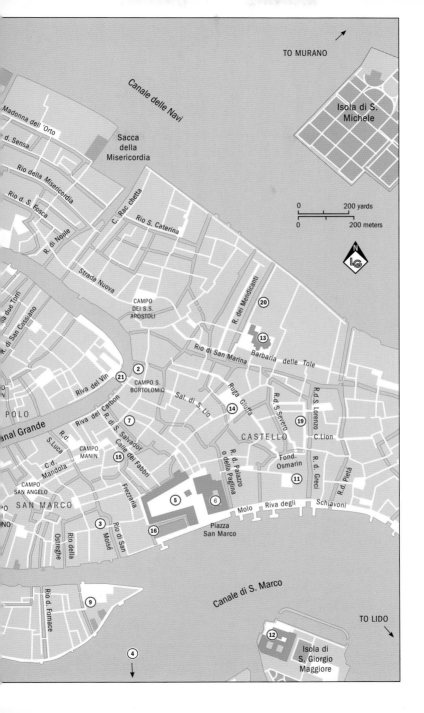

TO MURANO

Isola di S.
Michele

Canale delle Navi

Madonna dell 'Orto

d. Sensa

Sacca
della
Misericordia

Rio della Misericordia

Rio d. S. Fosca

R. di Noale

C. Rachetta

Rio S. Caterina

0        200 yards
0        200 meters

N
LG

Strada Nuova

CAMPO
DEI S.S.
APOSTOLI

R. dei Mendicanti

20

13

a due Torri

R. di San Cassiano

Rio di San Marina

Barbaria  delle  Tole

21  2

CAMPO S.
BORTOLOMIO

Riva del Vin

Sal. di S. Lio

Ruga Giuffa

14

R.d.S.Severo

R.d.S.Lorenzo

19

POLO

Riva del Carbon

R. di S. Salvador

7

R. d.
S. Luca

CAMPO
MANIN

Calle dei Fabbri

CASTELLO

C.Lion

Canal Grande

C. d.
Mandola

15

R. d. Palazzo
o della Paglina

Fond.
Osmarin

R. d. Greci

R. d. Pietá

CAMPO
SAN ANGELO

SAN MARCO

11

NO

Frezzaria

5

6

Molo  Riva degli  Schiavoni

3

Rio di San

Moisé

16

Piazza
San Marco

Rio della
Ostreghe

Rio d. Fornace

9

Canale di S. Marco

TO LIDO

4

12

Isola di
S. Giorgio
Maggiore

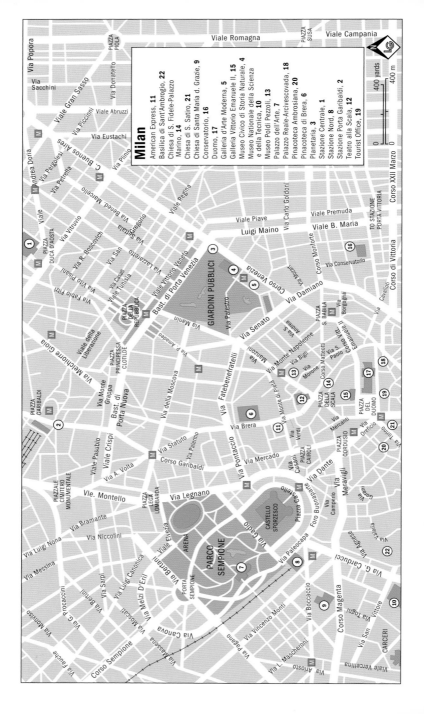

**Milan**

American Express, **11**
Basilica di Sant'Ambrogio, **22**
Chiesa di S. Fidele-Palazzo
Marino, **14**
Chiesa di S. Satiro, **21**
Chiesa di Santa Maria d. Grazie, **9**
Conservatorio, **16**
Duomo, **17**
Galleria d'Arte Moderna, **5**
Galleria Vittorio Emanuele II, **15**
Museo Civico di Storia Naturale, **4**
Museo Nazionale della Scienza
e della Tecnica, **10**
Museo Poldi Pezzoli, **13**
Palazzo dell'Arte, **7**
Palazzo Reale-Archivescovada, **18**
Pinacoteca Ambrosiana, **20**
Pinacoteca di Brera, **6**
Planetaria, **3**
Stazione Centrale, **1**
Stazione Nord, **8**
Stazione Porta Garibaldi, **2**
Teatro alla Scala, **12**
Tourist Office, **19**

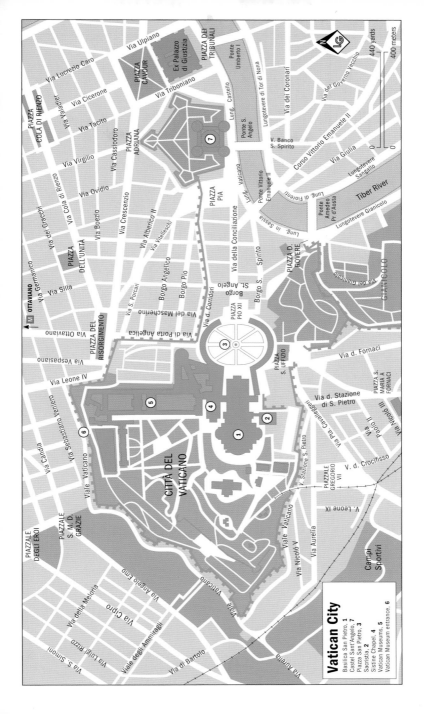

# Vatican City

Basilica San Pietro, **1**
Castel Sant'Angelo, **7**
Piazza San Pietro, **3**
Sacrista, **2**
Sistine Chapel, **4**
Vatican Museums, **5**
Vatican Museum entrance, **6**

# Rome Mass Transit

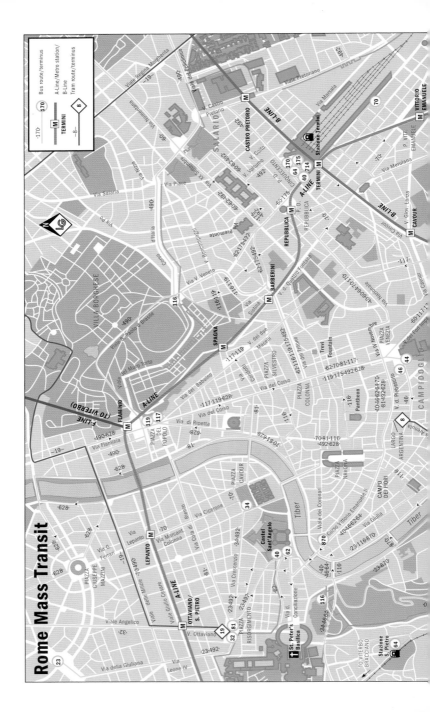

Bus route/terminus
A-Line/Metro station/ A-Line
B-Line
Tram route/terminus

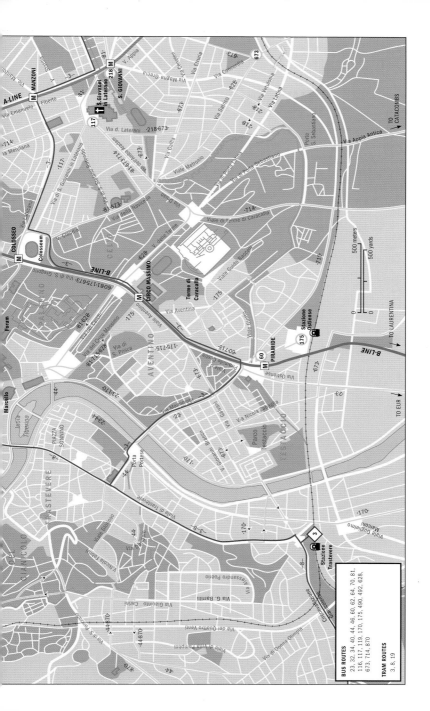

BUS ROUTES
23, 32, 34, 40, 44, 46, 60, 62, 64, 70, 81,
116, 117, 119, 170, 175, 490, 492, 628,
673, 714, 870

TRAM ROUTES
3, 8, 19

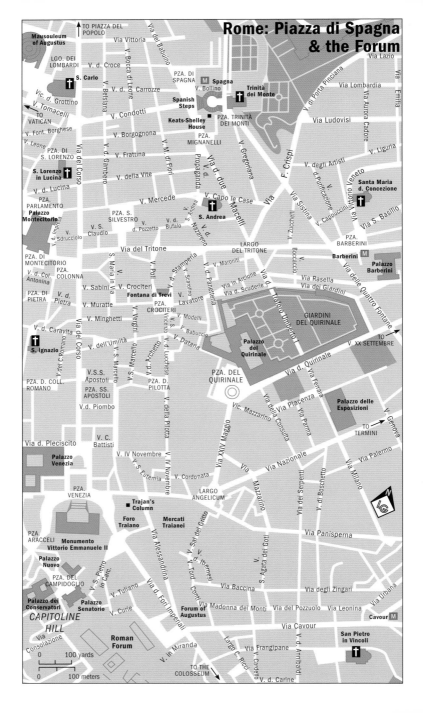

# Rome: Piazza di Spagna & the Forum

TO PIAZZA DEL POPOLO

Mausouleum of Augustus

LGO. DEI LOMBARDI

S. Carlo

Via Vittoria

Via del Babuino

V. d. Croce

V. d. Bocca di Leone

V. Belsiana

V. d. Carrozze

Vic. d. Grottino

V. Tomacelli

TO VATICAN

V. Font. Borghese

V. Leone

PZA. DI S. LORENZO

S. Lorenzo in Lucina

V. d. Lucina

PZA. PARLAMENTO

Palazzo Montecitorio

V. d. Impresa

V. Sdrucciolo

PZA. DI MONTECITORIO

V. d. Col. Antonina

PZA. COLONNA

PZA. DI PIETRA

V. d. Pietra

V. d. Caravita

S. Ignazio

PZA. D. COLL. ROMANO

V. del Corso

V. del Gambero

V. d. Gambero

V. Condotti

V. Borgognona

V. Frattina

V. della Vite

V. Mercede

PZA. DI SPAGNA

V. Bollino

Spanish Steps

Keats-Shelley House

PZA. MIGNANELLI

V. d. due Macelli

V. d. Propaganda

V. M. di Fiori

V. d. Nazareno

S. Maria in Via

V. Sabini

V. Crociteri

Fontana di Trevi

V. Murratte

V. Minghetti

V. Vergini

V. dell'Umiltà

V.S.S. Marcello

V.S.S. Apostoli

PZA. SS. APOSTOLI

V.d. Piombo

Spagna

Trinità dei Monte

PZA. TRINITÀ DEI MONTI

V. Gregoriana

V. d. Propaganda

S. Andrea

V. d. Pozzetto

V. d. Bufalo

V. S. Claudio

PZA. S. SILVESTRO

Via del Tritone

V. Poli

Stamperia

V. Scarmino

V. Panetteria

PZA. CROCITERI

V. Lavatore

V. Modelli

V. Babuccio

V. Vincenzo

V. Datania

V. d'Archetto

V. Lucchese

V. della Pilotta

PZA. D. PILOTTA

V. Capo le Case

LARGO DEL TRITONE

V. Maroniti

V. in Arcione

V. d. Scuderie

Trafioro Umberto I

Palazzo del Quirinale

PZA. DEL QUIRINALE

Vic. Mazzarino

V. della Consulta

V. d. Quirinale

V. Ferrara

V. della Placenza

V. Parma

V. F. Crispi

V. Sistina

V. Zucchelli

V. Cappuccini

V. d. Purificazione

Via Vittorio Veneto

Santa Maria d. Concezione

Via S. Basilio

PZA. BARBERINI

Barberini

Palazzo Barberini

Via Rasella

Via dei Giardini

Via delle Quattro Fontane

GIARDINI DEL QUIRINALE

TO V. XX SETTEMBRE

Palazzo delle Esposizioni

TO TERMINI

TO PIAZZA DEL POPOLO

Via Lazio

Via Lombardia

Via di Porta Pinciana

Via Ludovisi

Via Aurora Cadore

V. Emilia

V. Liguria

V. degli Artisti

V. Genova

V. C. Battisti

Via d. Pleciscito

Palazzo Venezia

PZA. VENEZIA

PZA. ARACCELI

Monumento Vittorio Emmanuele II

Palazzo Nuovo

PZA. DEL CAMPIDOGLIO

Palazzo dei Conservatori

Palazzo Senatorio

CAPITOLINE HILL

Via Consolazione

Roman Forum

V. C. Battisti

V. IV Novembre

V. S. Eutemia

V. IV Novembre

Trajan's Column

Foro Traiano

Mercati Traianei

V. Alessandrina

V. Cordonata

LARGO ANGELICUM

V. XXIV Maggio

V. dei Fori Imperiali

V. S. Pietro in Carc.

V. S. Tord

V. d. Tulliano

V. Curie

V. in Miranda

Forum of Augustus

Largo C. Ricci

V. Frangipane

V. Cardello

V. d. Carine

Via Nazionale

V. Mazzarino

V. dei Serpenti

V. di Boschetto

V. Milano

V. Palermo

Via Panisperna

V. San del Grillo

V. d. Ibernesi

V. Conti

S. Agata dei Goti

Via Baccina

Via degli Zingari

Via Madonna dei Monti

Via del Pozzuolo

Via Leonina

Via Cavour

Cavour

San Pietro in Vincoli

TO THE COLOSSEUM

V. Urbana

0   100 yards

0   100 meters

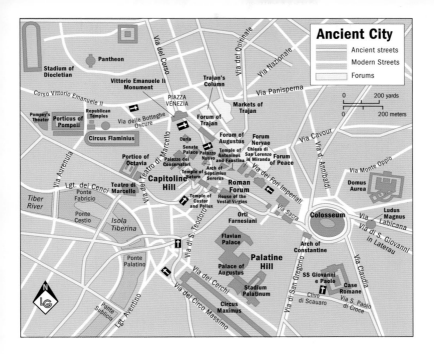

## Ancient City

- Ancient streets
- Modern Streets
- Forums

0 — 200 yards
0 — 200 meters

Stadium of Diocletian

Pantheon

Via del Corso

Via del Quirinale

Via Nazionale

Vittorio Emanuele II Monument

Trajan's Column

Corso Vittorio Emanuele II

PIAZZA VENEZIA

Via Panisperna

Pompey's Theater

Republican Temples

Porticus of Pompeii

Via delle Botteghe Oscure

Markets of Trajan

Forum of Trajan

Via Cavour

Circus Flaminius

Curia

Forum of Augustus

Forum Nervae

Senate Palace

Chiesa di San Lorenzo in Miranda

Via d. Annibaldi

Portico of Octavia

Palazzo Nuovo

Temple of Antoninus and Faustina

Forum of Peace

Via Monte Oppio

Teatro di Marcello

Palazzo dei Conservatori

Temple of Saturn

Arch of Septimius Severus

Domus Aurea

Lgt. dei Cenci

Ponte Fabricio

Capitoline Hill

Via dei Fori Imperiali

Ludus Magnus

Tiber River

Via Aurenula

Ponte Cestio

Temple of Castor and Pollux

House of the Vestal Virgins

Roman Forum

Via Sacra

Colosseum

Via di S. Giovanni in Laterau

Isola Tiberina

Via di S. Teodoro

Orti Farnesiani

Arch of Constantine

Via Claudia

Ponte Palatino

Flavian Palace

Palatine Hill

Via dei Cerchi

Palace of Augustus

Via del Circo Massimo

Stadium Palatinum

SS Giovanni e Paolo

Case Romane

Via S. Paolo di Croce

Ponte Sublicio

Lgt. Aventino

Circus Maximus

Clivo di Scauaro

Via San Gregorio

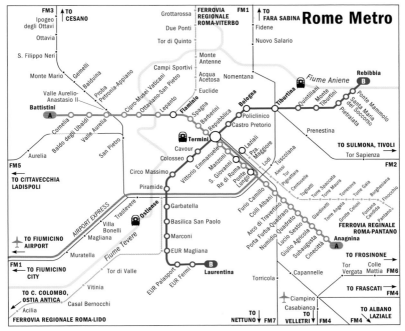

## Rome Metro

FM3 TO CESANO

Ipogeo degli Ottavi

Ottavia

S. Filippo Neri

Monte Mario

Valle Aurelio-Anastasio II

Battistini

Cornelia

Baldo degli Ubaldi

Valle Aurelia

San Pietro

Aurelia

FM5 TO CITTAVECCHIA LADISPOLI

Gemelli

Balduina

Proba Petronia

Appiano

Cipro-Musei Vaticani

Ottaviano-San Pietro

Lepanto

Grottarossa

Due Ponti

Tor di Quinto

Campi Sportivi

Monte Antenne

Acqua Acetosa

Euclide

Flaminio

Spagna

Barberini

Nomentana

FERROVIA REGIONALE ROMA-VITERBO

Fidene

Nuovo Salario

FM1 TO FARA SABINA

Bologna

Repubblica

Policlinico

Castro Pretorio

Termini

Cavour

Colosseo

Circo Massimo

Piramide

Vittorio Emanuele

Manzoni

S. Giovanni

Re di Roma

Ponte Lungo

Laziali

Pza. Maggiore

Lodi

Tuscolana

Tiburtina

Quintiliani

Monte Tiburtini

Fiume Aniene

Rebibbia B

Ponte Mammolo

Santa Maria del Soccorso

Pietralata

Prenestina

TO SULMONA, TIVOLI

Tor Sapienza

FM2

AIRPORT EXPRESS

Trastevere

Ostiense

Villa Bonelli

Magliana

TO FIUMICINO AIRPORT

Muratella

FM1 TO FIUMICINO CITY

Fiume Tevere

Tor di Valle

Vitinia

TO C. COLOMBO, OSTIA ANTICA

Casal Bernocchi

Acilia

FERROVIA REGIONALE ROMA-LIDO

Garbatella

Basilica San Paolo

Marconi

EUR Magliana

EUR Palasport

EUR Fermi

Laurentina B

Furio Camillo

Colli Albani

Arco di Travertino

Porta Furba-Quadraro

Numidio Quadrato

Lucio Sestio

Giulio Agricola

Subaugusta

Cinecittà

Capannelle

Torricola

Ciampino

Casabianca

TO NETTUNO FM7

TO VELLETRI FM4

Alessi

Tor Pignattara

Centocelle

Togliatti

Tor Spaccata

Tor Maura

Giardinetti

Torre Angela

Torrenova

Grotte Celoni

Fontana Candida

Torre Gaia

Borghesiana

Finocchio

Pantano

FERROVIA REGIONALE ROMA-PANTANO

Anagnina A

TO FROSINONE

Tor Vergata

Colle Mattia FM6

TO FRASCATI FM4

TO ALBANO LAZIALE

FM4

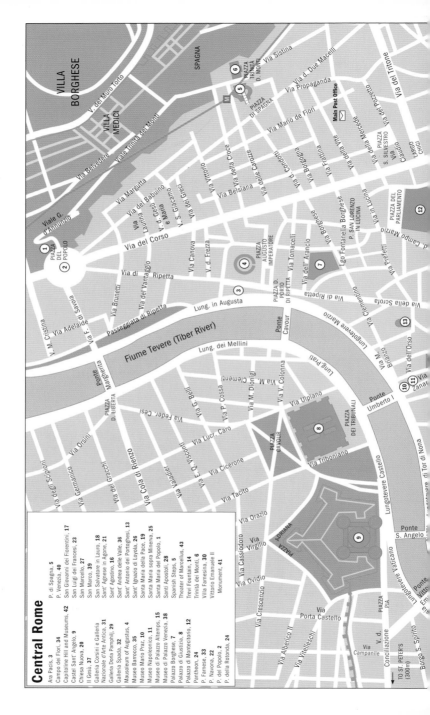

# Central Rome

Ara Pacis, **3**
Campo dei Fiori, **34**
Capitoline Hill and Museums, **42**
Castel Sant' Angelo, **9**
Chiesa Nuova **20**
Il Gesù **37**
Galleria Corsini e Galleria
  Nazionale d'Arte Antica, **31**
Galleria Doria Pamphilj, **29**
Galleria Spada, **32**
Mausoleum of Augustus, **4**
Museo Barocco, **35**
Museo Mario Praz, **10**
Museo Napoleonico, **11**
Museo di Palazzo Altemps, **15**
Museo di Palazzo Venezia, **38**
Palazzo Borghese, **7**
Palazzo di Giustizia, **8**
Palazzo di Montecitorio, **12**
Pantheon, **24**
P. Farnese **33**
P. Navona, **22**
P. del Popolo, **2**
P. della Rotonda, **24**

P. di Spagna, **5**
P. Venezia, **40**
San Giovanni dei Fiorentini, **17**
San Luigi dei Francesi, **23**
San Marcello, **27**
San Marco, **39**
San Salvatore in Lauro, **18**
Sant' Agnese in Agone, **21**
Sant' Agostino, **16**
Sant' Andrea delle Valle, **36**
Sant' Antonio dei Portoghesi, **13**
Sant' Ignazio di Loyola, **26**
Santa Maria della Pace, **19**
Santa Maria sopra Minerva, **25**
Santa Maria del Popolo, **1**
Santi Apostoli, **28**
Spanish Steps, **5**
Theater of Marcellus, **43**
Trevi Fountain, **14**
Trinità dei Monti, **6**
Villa Farnesina, **30**
Vittorio Emanuele II
  Monument, **41**

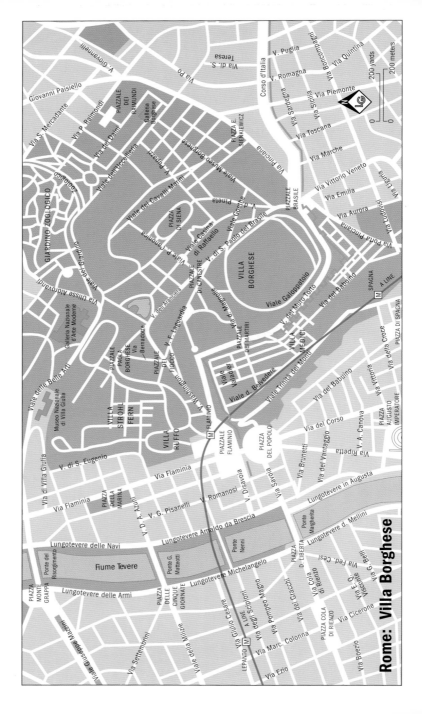

# Rome: Villa Borghese

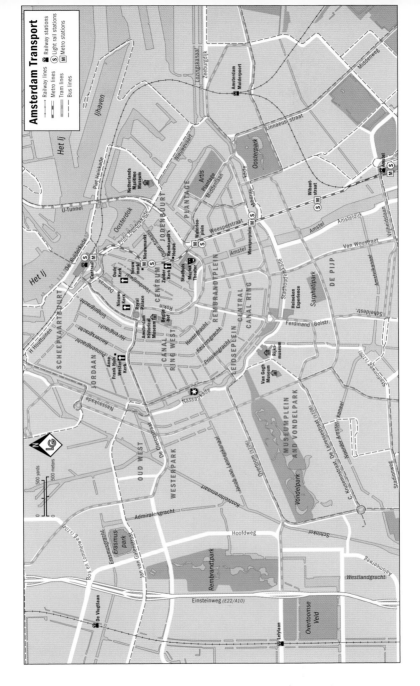

# Amsterdam Overview

- 🚆 Railway stations
- Ⓣ Light rail stations
- Ⓜ Metro stations

0 200 yards
0 200 meters

Het Ij

Sumatrakade
Javakade

Piet Heinkade

Dijksgracht

II Tunnel

Oosterdok

Scheep-
vaart-
museum 🏛

Kattenburgerstr.
Kattenburgerkade
Kattenburger vaart
Wittenburgervaart

Prins Hendrikkade

Kattenburgergracht
Wittenburgergracht
Oostenburgergracht
Oostenburgervaart

Binnenkant
Eilandsgracht

Oosterdokskade
Oosterdoksgade

e Ruijterkade

Ⓜ

STATIONS
IN
t

Geldersekade

Nieuwe Uilenburgergracht

Foeliestr.

Hoogte Kadijk

Laagte Kadijk

Entrepotdok

Nieuwevaart

Zeeburgerstr.

Czaar Peterstr.

Oude Schans

Rapenburgerstr.

Anne Frankstr.

Plantage Parklaan
Henri Polaklaan

Plantage Doklaan

Zuider-
kerk

Jodenbreestr.

Valkenburgerstr.

Rapenburgerstr.

Herengracht

Wertheim Park

Artis Zoo

Museum
Rembrandt

MR VISSER-
PLEIN Ⓣ

Muiderstr.

Jewish Historical 🏛
Museum

Plantage Middenlaan

jhuis

uziek-
eater 🎭

Waterlooplein

Nieuwe
Amstel

Nieuwe
Hortus
Botanicus

Hortus Plantsoen

Plantage Muidergracht

Plantage Muidergracht

ALEXANDER-
PLEIN Ⓣ

Von Zesenstr.

Dappelstr.

Ⓜ

Weesperstr.

Keizersgracht

Nieuwe Keizersgracht

Commelinstr.

Ⓣ

Nieuwe Prinsengracht

Tropenmuseum 🏛

Wagenaarstr.

Nieuwe Kerkstr.

Nieuwe Prinsengracht

Nieuwe Achtergracht

1e van Swindenstr.

Binnen Amstel

Lepelstr.

Roetersstr.

WEESPER-
PLEIN Ⓣ Ⓜ

Sarphatistr.

Mauritskade

Limnaeusstr.

Achtergracht

Ⓣ

Spinoza str.

's Gravesandestr.

Oosterpark

Ⓣ Wittenbachstr.

Domselaerstr.

Rhijnspoorplein

Andrea Bonnstr.

Boer Campenstr.

Ⓣ

adhouderskade

Swammerdamstr.

Wibautstr.

Ruyschstr.

Oosterparkstr.

2e Oosterparkstr.

ionylaan

Amsteldijk

Weesperzijde

3e Oosterparkstr.

Vrolikstr.

Hemonystr.

Amstel

Populierenweg

Ⓣ

Ceintuurbaan

1e Oosterparkstr.

Tuigelaweg

Retiefstr.

STEVE
BIKO
PLEIN

Woustr.

Pretoriusstr.

Transvaalstr.

Ringvaart

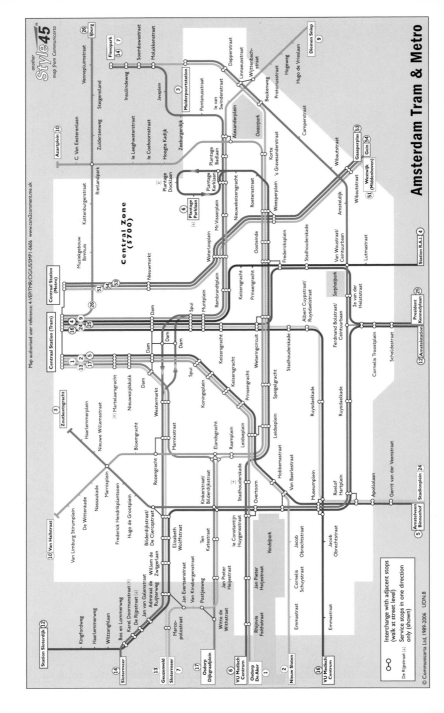

# Amsterdam Tram & Metro

another **Style45** map from Communicarta

Map authorised user reference: 4-VEP/TMR/CIG/US/MPI-0606  www.care2comment.me.uk

© Communicarta Ltd. 1989–2006  UDN.8

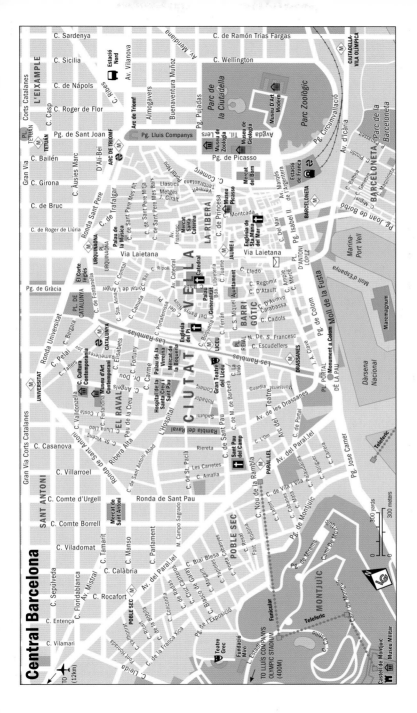

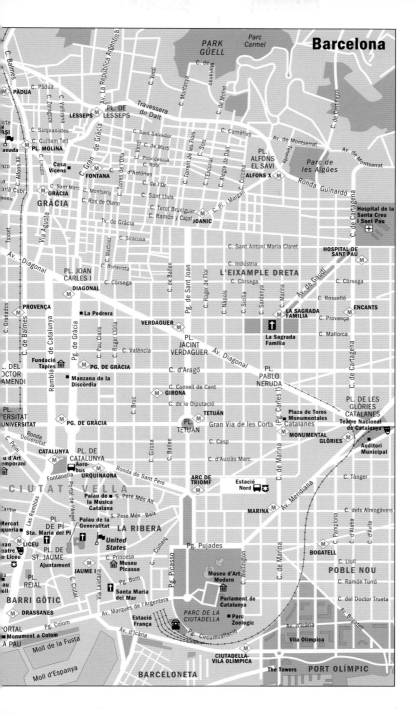

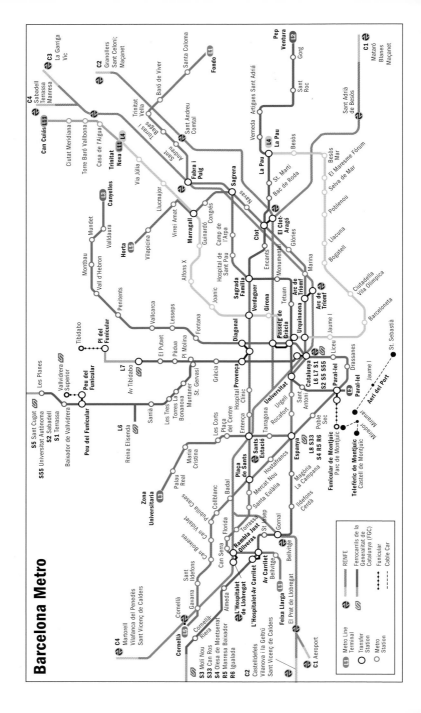

# Barcelona Metro

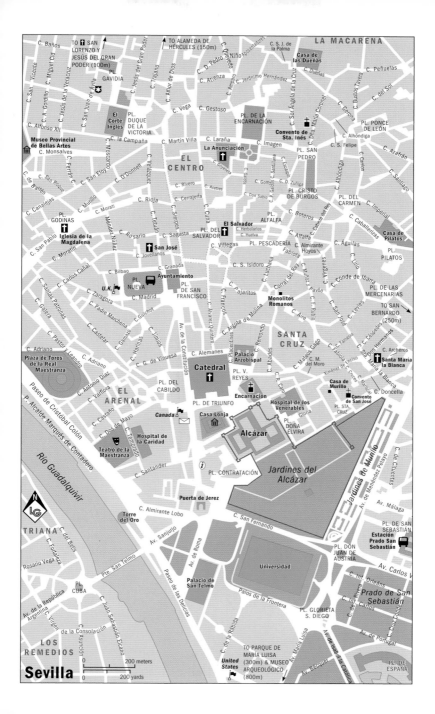

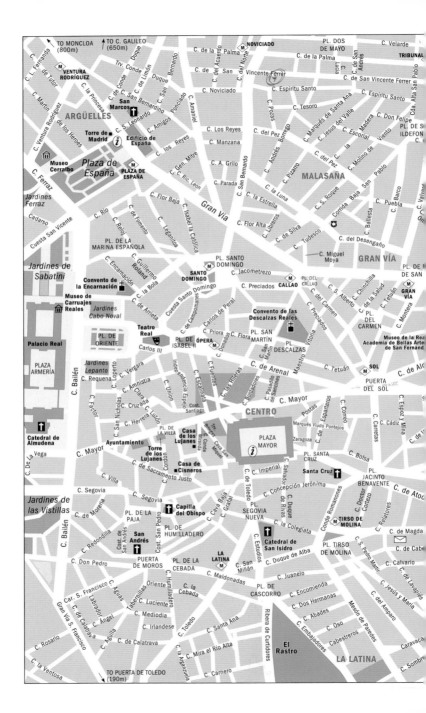

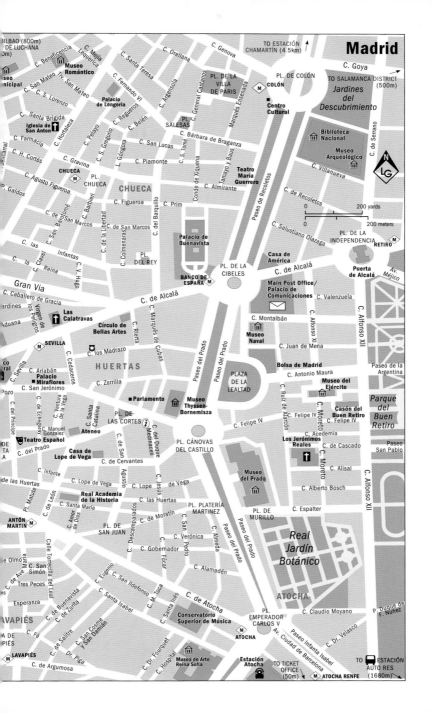

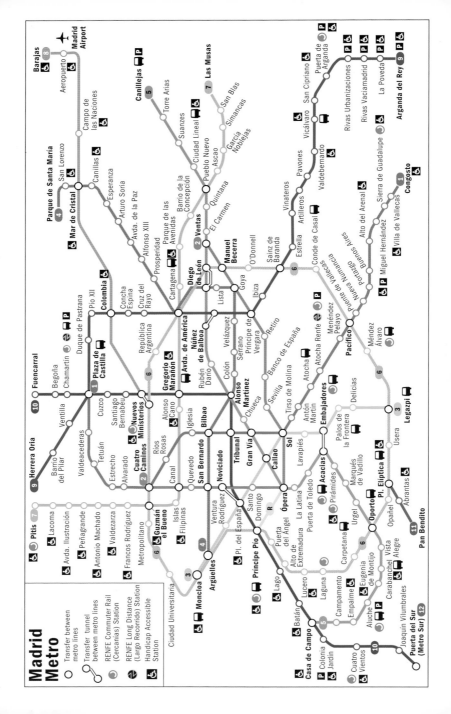

# Madrid Metro

# LET'S GO

## ■ PAGES PACKED WITH ESSENTIAL INFORMATION

"Value-packed, unbeatable, accurate, and comprehensive."

*—The Los Angeles Times*

"The guides are aimed not only at young budget travelers but at the independent traveler; a sort of streetwise cookbook for traveling alone."

*—The New York Times*

"Unbeatable; good sight-seeing advice; up-to-date info on restaurants, hotels, and inns; a commitment to money-saving travel; and a wry style that brightens nearly every page."

*—The Washington Post*

## ■ THE BEST TRAVEL BARGAINS IN YOUR BUDGET

"All the dirt, dirt cheap."

*—People*

"Let's Go follows the creed that you don't have to toss your life's savings to the wind to travel—unless you want to."

*—The Salt Lake Tribune*

## ■ REAL ADVICE FOR REAL EXPERIENCES

"The writers seem to have experienced every rooster-packed bus and lunar-surfaced mattress about which they write."

*—The New York Times*

"[Let's Go's] devoted updaters really walk the walk (and thumb the ride, and trek the trail). Learn how to fish, haggle, find work—anywhere."

*—Food & Wine*

"A world-wise traveling companion—always ready with friendly advice and helpful hints, all sprinkled with a bit of wit."

*—The Philadelphia Inquirer*

## ■ A GUIDE WITH A SPIRIT AND A SOCIAL CONSCIENCE

"Lighthearted and sophisticated, informative and fun to read. [Let's Go] helps the novice traveler navigate like a knowledgeable old hand."

*—Atlanta Journal-Constitution*

"The serious mission at the book's core reveals itself in exhortations to respect the culture and the environment—and, if possible, to visit as a volunteer, a student, or a teacher rather than a tourist."

*—San Francisco Chronicle*

# LET'S GO PUBLICATIONS

## TRAVEL GUIDES

Australia 9th edition
Austria & Switzerland 12th edition
Brazil 1st edition
Britain 2008
California 10th edition
Central America 9th edition
Chile 2nd edition
China 5th edition
Costa Rica 3rd edition
Eastern Europe 13th edition
Ecuador 1st edition
Egypt 2nd edition
Europe 2008
France 2008
Germany 13th edition
Greece 9th edition
Hawaii 4th edition
India & Nepal 8th edition
Ireland 13th edition
Israel 4th edition
Italy 2008
Japan 1st edition
Mexico 22nd edition
New Zealand 8th edition
Peru 1st edition
Puerto Rico 3rd edition
Southeast Asia 9th edition
Spain & Portugal 2008
Thailand 3rd edition
USA 24th edition
Vietnam 2nd edition
Western Europe 2008

## ROADTRIP GUIDE

Roadtripping USA 2nd edition

## ADVENTURE GUIDES

Alaska 1st edition
Pacific Northwest 1st edition
Southwest USA 3rd edition

## CITY GUIDES

Amsterdam 5th edition
Barcelona 3rd edition
Boston 4th edition
London 16th edition
New York City 16th edition
Paris 14th edition
Rome 12th edition
San Francisco 4th edition
Washington, D.C. 13th edition

## POCKET CITY GUIDES

Amsterdam
Berlin
Boston
Chicago
London
New York City
Paris
San Francisco
Venice
Washington, D.C.

# LET'S GO

# WESTERN EUROPE

# 2008

**INÉS PACHECO** EDITOR

ASSOCIATE EDITORS

**LAUREN CARUSO**     **CAROLINE CORBITT**

**BRIANNA GOODALE**     **JAKE SEGAL**

**NICHOLAS TRAVERSE**

RESEARCHER-WRITERS

**JULIAN ARNI**          **DANIEL NORMANDIN**

**DAVID PALTIEL**          **JOANNA PARGA**

**VALENTINE QUADRAT**     **RAVI RAMCHANDANI**

**THOMAS MACDONALD BARRON** MAP EDITOR
**RACHEL NOLAN** MANAGING EDITOR

ST. MARTIN'S PRESS ✠ NEW YORK

Maps by David Lindroth copyright © 2008 by St. Martin's Press.

Distributed outside the USA and Canada by Macmillan.

ISBN-13: 978-0-312-37458-7
ISBN-10: 0-312-37458-5
First edition
10 9 8 7 6 5 4 3 2 1

**Let's Go: Western Europe** is written by Let's Go Publications, 67 Mount Auburn St., Cambridge, MA 02138, USA.

**Let's Go®** and the LG logo are trademarks of Let's Go, Inc.

# CONTENTS

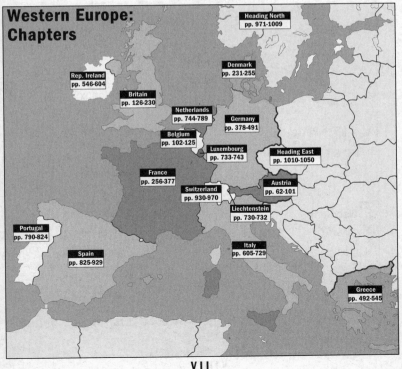

**Western Europe: Chapters**

Heading North pp. 971-1009

Rep. Ireland pp. 546-604

Britain pp. 126-230

Denmark pp. 231-255

Netherlands pp. 744-789

Belgium pp. 102-125

Germany pp. 378-491

Luxembourg pp. 733-743

Heading East pp. 1010-1050

France pp. 256-377

Switzerland pp. 930-970

Austria pp. 62-101

Liechtenstein pp. 730-732

Portugal pp. 790-824

Spain pp. 825-929

Italy pp. 605-729

Greece pp. 492-545

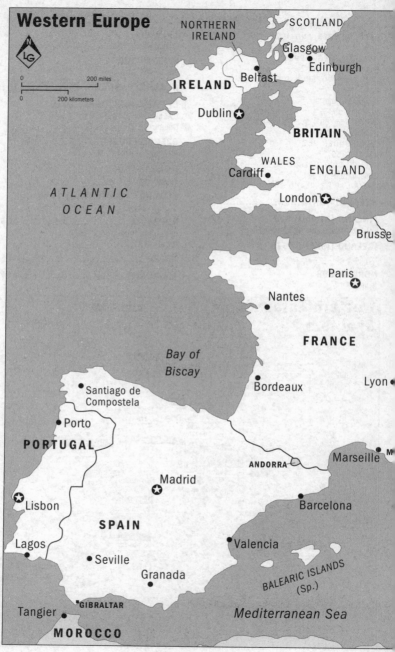

# Western Europe

N

200 miles

200 kilometers

SCOTLAND

NORTHERN IRELAND

Glasgow

Edinburgh

Belfast

IRELAND

Dublin ⭐

BRITAIN

WALES

ENGLAND

Cardiff

London ⭐

Brusse

ATLANTIC OCEAN

Paris ⭐

Nantes

FRANCE

Bay of Biscay

Bordeaux

Lyon

Santiago de Compostela

Porto

PORTUGAL

ANDORRA

Marseille

M

Madrid ⭐

Lisbon ⭐

Barcelona

SPAIN

Lagos

Valencia

Seville

BALEARIC ISLANDS (Sp.)

Granada

Mediterranean Sea

GIBRALTAR

Tangier

MOROCCO

# RESEARCHER-WRITERS

### Julian Arni
*Belgium, Denmark, and Luxembourg*

This Brazil native sauntered through unpredictable weather, conquered tricky transportation schedules, and even soldiered on through sickness. Not letting total technological meltdown or booked-solid accommodations get him down, he persevered through it all, producing clear and concise copy. Julian kept his cool, took his time, and enjoyed Europe.

### Daniel Normandin
*Switzerland and Germany*

Clad in his new Swiss jeans, Dan tackled the bewitched Black Forest, a cloud-covered Matterhorn, multiple chocolate museums, and the seductive Lorelei maiden. Along the way, he paraglided above Interlaken and got up-close-and-personal with Charlemagne. Disdaining gaudy tourist traps, Dan found many new local spots. His pun-filled and well-crafted prose, as well as his consistently cheerful attitude, kept his editors very happy.

### David Paltiel
*Austria, Germany, and Liechtenstein*

After kickin' it with the kangaroos for *LG: Australia* last year, David outwitted a dying laptop, a runaway wheelchair, and Austrian escalators this summer. He paraded through salt mines in Hallstatt, swung from cable cars in Malbun, and philosophized in Vienna. This map macdaddy won his editors' admiration with nose-to-the-grindstone dedication and attention to detail, but still made time to mingle with Bavarian monks and call home daily.

### Joanna Parga
*Iceland and Norway*

It's tough traveling in the north, with indecipherable bus schedules and menacing *huldufolk*. There's also the polar bear issue. Despite challenges, Jo toured the region like an all-star with a keen eye for sights, filling her copy with the scoop on that Icelandic lake you can't miss or that glacier that just isn't that cool. She scaled Norway's peaks, sailed the fjords, and even caught a few drunken mine stories in Svalbard after a day of dog sledding. Jealous yet?

### Valentine Quadrat
*Finland and Sweden*

Val emerged from her journey through Finland and Sweden as a master reindeer lassoer and ice sculptor. As if that weren't impressive enough, she was also an expert researcher. She cruised through the region, working continuously and earning the admiration of fellow travelers and hostel proprietors. We eagerly awaited her pristine copy with legendary tales of midnight sun hikes in Sweden and office hours with Santa Claus in Finland.

### Ravi Ramchandani
*London, Netherlands, and Germany*

The word "savior" comes to mind. With skill and dedication, Ravi traveled across Western Europe, working for four different Let's Go books. He skirted hipsters and pub grub in the Soho night scene and braved the world's largest flower trading floor, before arcing across the *Deutsche* heartland into beerhalls and *Schnitzel* stands. Rushing through the Nieuwe Zijd or relaxing in Hanover's palatial gardens, Ravi was unshakable. He was—and is—the man.

# REGIONAL EDITORS AND RESEARCHER-WRITERS

XII

## CONTRIBUTING WRITERS

**Leanna Boychenko** *Excavating in Athens*

Leanna Boychenko majored in Classics at Harvard College. She was the Associate Editor of *Let's Go: Greece 2005* and the Editor of *Let's Go: New Zealand*, 7th ed.

**Simon Schama** *Britain: A Ruinous State*

Simon Schama is University Professor of Art History at Columbia University. His most recent book is *Rough Crossings: Britain, the Slaves, and the American Revolution* (Ecco, May 2006).

**Clem Wood** *A Dead Language Lives*

Clem Wood will graduate from Harvard in the spring of 2008 with an A.B. in Classics and plans to return to Italy for further adventures and studies in the near future.

**Jane Yager** *Berlin*

Jane Yager is a Let's Go alum living in Berlin. She was a Researcher-Writer for *Let's Go: Europe*, 11th ed. and *Let's Go: Thailand*, 3rd ed., and the Editor of *Let's Go: Eastern Europe*, 12th ed.


**Editor**
Inés Pacheco
**Associate Editors**
Lauren Caruso, Caroline Corbitt, Brianna Goodale, Jake Segal, Nicholas Traverse
**Managing Editor**
Rachel Nolan
**Map Editor**
Thomas MacDonald Barron
**Typesetter**
Alexandra Hoffer

# LET'S GO

**Publishing Director**
Jennifer Q. Wong
**Editor-in-Chief**
Silvia Gonzalez Killingsworth
**Production Manager**
Victoria Esquivel-Korsiak
**Cartography Manager**
Thomas MacDonald Barron
**Editorial Managers**
Anne Bensson, Calina Ciobanu, Rachel Nolan
**Financial Manager**
Sara Culver
**Business and Marketing Manager**
Julie Vodhanel
**Personnel Manager**
Victoria Norelid
**Production Associate**
Jansen A. S. Thurmer
**Director of E-Commerce & IT**
Patrick Carroll
**Website Manager**
Kathryne A. Bevilacqua
**Office Coordinators**
Juan L. Peña, Bradley J. Jones

**Director of Advertising Sales**
Hunter McDonald
**Senior Advertising Associate**
Daniel Lee

**President**
William Hauser
**General Managers**
Bob Rombauer, Jim McKellar

# ACKNOWLEDGMENTS

**TEAM WESTERN EUROPE THANKS:** ◪Our RWs. ◪EEUR for sick summer jams, friendship, and general hilarity. ◪RaNo for followership, jorts, and something serious. ◪Tom for being dreamy and making life easy. ◪Vicki for teaching us to tame Frame. The ◪crunch teams: snap crackle pop! You rock. The fine folks at Post, for 216 boxes of HBO. Calina for being a podmate. ◪Silvia for mad skillz. Mmm Denly's ◪. No thanks to Mississippi or Widener Circulation. ◪Boom!

**INÉS THANKS:** L, C, B, J, and N: I could not have asked for a funnier, more dedicated, or generally balla team. RaNo, for everything. S&J, for leading the way. Ingrid & Co. for the Europod. My Ma Go family, for support, late-nights, drinks, and caffeine. Serge, for helping me up. 6Ex for MTV and Esopus. Sam, Jana, Clarie, I owe you my meninges. Stephen, for always. Mama, Papa, and Belly, for Paris.

**LAUREN THANKS:** Inés for leading with style. RaNo for glorious MEdits. Bri for nicknames like lucky Lauren. Caroline for slicing and dicing. Jake for answering my questions. Nick for keeping it real. Tom for hours of map party fun. ITA for jokes. IRE for putting up with me. Jeff for walks to work. And Scoow, my travel buddy, for being my Shmiku. Thanks MDMJMLPT. ◪For Joanna and her family.

**CAROLINE THANKS:** Inés, for back pats and making every day fun; Bri, for conversations and chick flicks; Jake, for niceness and irreverence; Lauren, for sly jokes and good humor; Nick, for being a fantastic neighbor; Rachel, for being crazy brilliant; Dan, who it was a pleasure to get to know; Portugal, for the laughs; EEUR, Tom, and Team S&P; Mom, Dad, and my friends, for your love and support.

**BRI THANKS:** Inés for the ABCs and bidding high; RaNo for worldy insight; Jake for an Acton home and pick-up soccer; Nick for Santa's workshop and Nick-names; Caroline for Dawson's Creek and Diet Coke; Lauren for Denly's and patience; GCE, FRA, & Mapland; David for an easy job; DGs for Th ice cream; Coop for Su picnics; the IPFA for breaking-in Boston; Mom, Dad, and Cort for showing me the world◪.

**JAKE THANKS:** iners, for alphabetizing and potato; bri, for beasting; machete, for unexpectedness; nick, trip to santa's kingdom?; tornado, see you at denly's; Rizzle B. McNizzle, for witticisms; the fam, for resweek dins and fam fun; ◪cec, for everything ever, and then some; ◪; the lemon song; dan, for hilarity and late-night kengriffs; coop, for lovin' (and dinners). albert, we always knew you'd go wrong.

**NICK THANKS:** To team awesome: Inés, Bri-Bri, Caroline, Lauren, Jake, I've never had more fun working. Much <3. RaNo, for choosing my future career. See you in Svalbard. Pat, Jen, and team Britain: YOLO! Tom: woo woo! Jo and Val, for the best Scandinavia coverage yet. EEUR, for Ra-ra-rasputin. Eva, for everything, and putting up with my hours. Dad, Ben, Hannah, and my friends for the love. To the *huldufolk*: I can see you, you bastards. Denly's ◪. Santa: time to go back to the Pole.

**RACHEL THANKS:** Inés for making my job easy. Caroline, Nick, Bri, Lauren, and Jake: hone your rifle skills for Svalbard 2008. The MEs for a great year. Amy for supplying the world's best editing buddy. Mom, dad, grandma, and Laura—as always.

**TOM THANKS:** Inés, Caroline, Nick, Bri, Jessica, and Jake for being the best EUR team in recent memory. Sheena and fake sheena for solid companionship, and 2008 ME team for always holding it down. Mum, Dad, Kay, Jamil, and Mia for all the love.

# PRICE RANGES WESTERN EUROPE

Our researchers list establishments in order of value from best to worst; our favorites are denoted by the Let's Go thumbs-up (📖). Since the best value is not always the cheapest price, however, we have also incorporated a system of price ranges, based on a rough expectation of what you will spend. For **accommodations,** we base our range on the cheapest price for which a single traveler can stay for one night. For **restaurants** and other dining establishments, we estimate the average amount a traveler will spend. The table below tells you what you will *typically* find in Western Europe at the corresponding price range; keep in mind that no system can allow for every individual establishment's quirks.

| ACCOMMODATIONS | WHAT YOU'RE *LIKELY* TO FIND |
|---|---|
| ❶ | Camping; most dorm rooms, such as HI or other hostels or university dorm rooms. Expect bunk beds and a communal bath; you may have to provide or rent towels and sheets. |
| ❷ | Upper-end hostels or small hotels. You may have a private bathroom, or there may be a sink in your room and communal shower in the hall. |
| ❸ | A small room with a private bath. Should have decent amenities, such as phone and TV. Breakfast may be included in the price of the room. |
| ❹ | Similar to 3, but may have more amenities or be in a more touristed area. |
| ❺ | Large hotels or upscale chains. If it's a 5 and it doesn't have the perks you want, you've paid too much. |

| FOOD | WHAT YOU'RE *LIKELY* TO FIND |
|---|---|
| ❶ | Mostly street-corner stands, falafel and shawarma huts, or fast-food joints. Most of the Dutch snack food, including *tostis* and *broodjes*. Desserts like *stropwafels* and *pannekoeken*. Soups and simple noodle dishes in minimalist surroundings. You may have the option of sitting down or getting take-out. |
| ❷ | Sandwiches, appetizers at a bar, or low-priced entrees and *tapas*. Ethnic eateries and pan-Asian noodle houses. Takeout is less frequent; generally a sit-down meal, sometimes with servers, but only slightly more upscale decor. |
| ❸ | Mid-priced entrees, seafood and exotic pasta dishes. More upscale ethnic eateries. Tip'll bump you up a couple dollars, since you will have a waiter. |
| ❹ | A somewhat fancy restaurant or a steakhouse. Either way, you'll have a special knife. Few restaurants in this range have a dress code, but some may look down on t-shirt and jeans. |
| ❺ | Food with foreign names and a decent wine list. Slacks and dress shirts may be expected. Don't order PB&J. |

# HOW TO USE THIS BOOK

It all started with a ⬛. With one fiery breath from his fearsome jowls, the great continent that is ⬛**Europe** was born. Yes, dear reader, there are many mysteries in this Old World. That is why you have come to us. We will be your Virgil, teaching you the art of the budget travel. We will guide you through Genoa's labyrinthine *vicoli* and Granada's *Alhambra*. We will be a less-than-comfortable pillow on long train rides. First bit of wisdom: Western Europe is awesome. From Santa's Workshop deep in northern Finland to strangely perched rocks in Salisbury, this half of a continent—like a coffee shop in Amsterdam—has it. And our gritty, dutiful researchers have fanned out to Irish shoals and Kreuzberg wine bars, between Greece's pirate party ships and Austria's posh ski towns, to bring you the freshest, most comprehensive budget travel guide ever produced. Here's how to use it:

**COVERING THE BASICS.** The first chapter is **Discover** (p. 1). Read it before you go. Its purpose is to help you find the best this chunk o' earth has to offer. If you like people telling you what to do (or just want some ideas), check out this chapter's **suggested itineraries.** The **Essentials** (p. 12) section gets down to the nitty-gritty, detailing the info you'll need to get around and stay safe on your journey. The **Transportation** (p. 41) section will help you get to and around Europe, while the **Beyond Tourism** (p. 54) chapter suggests ways to work and vounteer your way across the Continent. Then we get to the meat of the book: 33 jam-packed **country chapters,** organized alphabetically. The **Appendix** (p. 1051) has a weather chart for major cities and a handy dandy phrasebook with nine languages to help you say "I'm lost," land a bed, or find your way to a bathroom no matter where you are.

**TRANSPORTATION INFO.** Because you've told *Let's Go* you're traveling on budget airlines, we've created a new transportation format to help you navigate getting to where you really want to go from that random town an hour away: **Let's Go To...,** listed at the end of some major cities (for instance, Let's Go to Milan: Bergamo). We've also collected info on bus, ferry, and train routes; these range from rock-solid Spanish AVE schedules to, well, any transportation in Romania.

**RANKINGS AND FEATURES.** Our researchers list establishment in order of value from best to worst, with absolute favorites denoted by the *Let's Go* thumbpick ⬛. Since the lowest price does not always mean the best value, we've incorporated a system of price ranges (❶-❺) for food and accommodations. Tipboxes come in a variety of flavors: warnings (🚹), helpful hints and resources (🔳), insider deals (🔳), cheap finds (🔳), and then a smattering of stuff you should know (🔳, 🔳, 🔳).

**AWESOMENESS.** From ☎ codes to avoiding scams, from the best borscht to the boldest brews, we'll guide you through the souvenir-cluttered jungle of the old-school Europa to the most authentic food, craziest nightlife, and most mind-bendingly beautiful landscapes around. Start in Brussels, in Stockholm, in Bucharest. Open this bad boy up, and choose your own adventure.

---

# DISCOVER WESTERN EUROPE

Some things never change. Aspiring writers still spin romances in Parisian garrets; a cool glass of sangria in the Plaza Mayor tastes sweeter than ever; and iconic treasures, from the inside-out architecture of the Pompidou Center to the hulking slabs of Stonehenge, continue to inspire wonder in new generations of wayfarers. And yet, sights that used to lie on the fringes of Western Europe have come into prominence: the ice-covered fjords of Norway, the bright Blue Lagoon of Iceland, and the quaint fishing villages of the Basque country. With this new focus, the old and the very old unfold before enterprising travelers as they fan out across the Continent, reshaping the Old World's venerable culture to fit an increasingly international world.

As the European Union expanded from a small clique of Atlantic nations trading coal and steel to a 27-member commonwealth with a parliament and a central bank, suddenly Amsterdam and Madrid have found themselves competing with Budapest and Kraków for global attention. Still, "Old Europe's" niche as a destination has been aided by the proliferation of small airlines, clearing the way for a new era of budget globetrotting. Whether it's Dublin's pubs, Lyon's upscale bistros, or Croatia's dazzling beaches that call to you, *Let's Go: Western Europe 2008* will help keep you informed and on-budget.

## TACKLING WESTERN EUROPE

Anyone who tells you that there is any one "best way" to see Europe should be politely ignored. This book is designed to facilitate all varieties of travel, from a few days in Paris to a breathless continent-wide summer sprint to a leisurely year (or two) abroad. This chapter is made up of tools to help you create your own itinerary: **themed categories** let you know where to find your museums, your mountains, and your madhouses, while **suggested itineraries** outline various paths across Western Europe. Look to chapter introductions for country-specific itineraries and for more detailed information.

## WHEN TO GO

While summer sees the most tourist traffic in Western Europe, the best mix of value and accessibility comes in late spring and early fall. To the delight of skiing and ice-climbing enthusiasts, traveling during the low season (mid-Sept. to June) brings cheaper airfares and accommodations, in addition to freedom from hordes of fannypack toting tourists. On the flip side, many attractions, hostels, and tourist offices close in the winter, and in some rural areas local transportation dwindles or shuts down altogether. Most of Europe's best **festivals** (p. 5) also take place in summer. For more advice on the best time to visit, see the **Weather Chart** on p. 1058 and the **Essentials** section at the beginning of each chapter.

# WHAT TO DO

## 🏛 MUSEUMS

DISCOVER

Western Europe has kept millennia worth of artistic masterpieces close to home in strongholds like the Louvre, the Prado, and the Vatican Museums. European museums do not merely house art, however. They also have exhibits on erotica, leprosy, marijuana, marzipan, puppets, secret police, and spirits both literal and figurative—in short, whatever can be captioned. A trip across Europe qualifies as little more than a stopover without an afternoon among some of its paintings and artifacts—whether they include the pinnacles of Western culture, or more risqué fare.

| THE CLASSY | THE SASSY |
|---|---|
| ■ **AUSTRIA: ÖSTERREICHISCHE GALERIE** (p. 82). Venetian paintings, an Egyptian burial chamber, and medieval arms in the world's 4th-largest art collection impress the history nerd in all of us. | ■ **DENMARK: LOUISIANA MUSEUM OF MODERN ART** (p. 247). This well-rounded museum's name honors the three wives of the estate's original owner—all of them were named Louisa. |
| ■ **BRITAIN: THE BRITISH MUSEUM** (p. 158). Holding world artifacts like Egypt's Rosetta Stone or Iran's Oxus Treasure, the British Museum contains almost nothing British at all. | ■ **FRANCE: MUSÉE DU TEMPS** (p. 322). This whirring and ticking museum exhibits clocks from Galileo's time to the present day, along with offbeat games and hands-on experiments. |
| ■ **BRITAIN: TATE MODERN** (p. 157). Organized thematically, this former power station turned modern and contemporary art powerhouse is as much a work of art as any of the pieces in its galleries. | ■ **GERMANY: SCHOKOLADENMUSEUM** (p. 438). This chocolate museum, detailing the chocolate-making process, has gold fountains that spurt out samples and other edible displays. |
| ■ **FRANCE: THE LOUVRE** (p. 286). Six million visitors come each year to see 35,000 works of art, including Da Vinci's surprisingly small painting of art's most famous face, the *Mona Lisa*. | ■ **HUNGARY: SZAMOS MARZIPAN MUSEUM (p. 1045)**. Only one statuette on display at this museum is not composed of marzipan: an 80kg white chocolate effigy of Michael Jackson. |
| ■ **GERMANY: GEMÄLDEGALERIE** (p. 412). With over 1000 works from the 13th to 18th centuries by the likes of Bruegel and Raphael, it's no wonder this is one of the most visited museums in Germany. | ■ **ITALY: PALERMO CATACOMBS (p. 725)**. The withered faces and mostly empty eye sockets of 8000 posing corpses gaze enviously at living spectators in Europe's creepiest underground tomb. |
| ■ **GREECE: NATIONAL ARCHAEOLOGICAL MUSEUM** (p. 510). Athens itself may be museum enough for some, but this building collects what's too small to be seen with a placard on the street. | ■ **THE NETHERLANDS: CANNABIS COLLEGE** (p. 769). Cannabis College is just like college, except there are no libraries, no lectures, no studying, no liquor, no dorms, and no full-time students. |
| ■ **ITALY: GALLERIA BORGHESE (p. 639)**. Vivid paintings and graceful sculpture by Bernini, Caravaggio, Rubens, and Titian are a sight for sore eyes after staring at miles of Renaissance canvases. | ■ **NORWAY: VIGELANDPARKEN** (p. 993). Not quite a museum, but with enough art to be one, this park contains over 200 of Gustav Vigeland's controversial sculptures. Each depicts a stage of human life. |
| ■ **ITALY: VATICAN MUSEUMS (p. 639)**. Look for the *School of Athens* here; the painting crowns a mindblowing amount of Renaissance and other art, including the incredible Raphael Rooms. | ■ **PORTUGAL: OCEANÁRIO** (p. 809). Europe's largest oceanarium, with interactive exhibits exploring the four major oceans, allows visitors to get within a meter of sea otters and penguins. |
| ■ **THE NETHERLANDS: RIJKSMUSEUM** (p. 770). Renovations shouldn't deter visitors who come to see the pinnacles of the Dutch Golden Age, including Rembrandts and Vermeers, that line the walls. | ■ **SPAIN: TEATRE-MUSEU DALÍ** (p. 910). Dalí's final resting place has works like *Napoleon's Nose Transformed into a Pregnant Woman Strolling Her Shadow with Melancholic amongst Original Ruins*. |
| ■ **SPAIN: MUSEO DEL PRADO (p. 850)**. It's an art-lover's heaven to see hell, as painted by Hieronymus Bosch. Velázquez's famous 10½ by 9 ft. painting of *Las Meninas* is as luminous as it is tall. | ■ **SWITZERLAND: VERKEHRSHAUS DER SCHWEIZ** (p. 952). The Swiss Transport Museum, with an IMAX theater and a wide array of cool contraptions, isn't nearly as dorky as its name implies. |

# ■ ARCHITECTURE

European history lives on through the tiled roofs and soaring arches of the continent's architecture. Royal lines from the early Welsh dynasties and Greek ruling families to the Bourbons, Habsburgs, and Romanovs have all been outlasted by the emblems of their magnificence. Monarchs were careless of expense, and jealous of each other; Louis XIV's palace at Versailles (p. 297), a byword for opulence, whetted the ambition of rival monarchs and spurred the construction of other palaces. No expense was spared for God, either, as the many cathedrals, monasteries, synagogues, and mosques rising skyward from their cityscapes attest. Córdoba's Mezquita (p. 867) and Budapest's Great Synagogue (p. 1042) are among the finest of their kind, while Chartres's Cathédrale de Notre Dame (p. 297) and Cologne's Dom (p. 438) are pinnacles—pun intended—of the Gothic style.

| ROYAL REAL ESTATE | SACRED SITES |
|---|---|
| ■ AUSTRIA: SCHLOß SCHÖNBRUNN (p. 81). If the palace isn't impressive enough, check out the classical gardens that extend behind for four times the length of the structure. | ■ BRITAIN: WESTMINSTER ABBEY (p. 148). Royal weddings and coronations take place in the sanctuary; nearby, poets and politicians from the earliest kings to Winston Churchill rest in peace. |
| ■ BRITAIN: BUCKINGHAM PALACE (p. 148). Britain's royal family has lived in Buckingham Palace since 1832, guarded by everybody's favorite stoic, puffy-hatted guards. | ■ CZECH REPUBLIC: ST. VITUS'S CATHEDRAL (p. 1030). This spectacular Gothic cathedral, inside the walls of the Prague Castle, was completed in 1929—it took 600 years to build. |
| ■ DENMARK: EGESKOV SLOT (p. 251). This idyllic castle seems to be floating in a lake. Its moat seems straight out of a fairy tale, with imaginative gardens and hedge mazes to match. | ■ FRANCE: CHARTRES CATHEDRAL (p. 297). The world's finest example of early Gothic architecture has intact stained-glass windows from the 12th century and a crypt from the 9th. |
| ■ FRANCE: VERSAILLES (p. 297). Once home to the entire French court, the lavish palace, manicured gardens, and impressive hall of mirrors epitomize Pre-Revolutionary France's regal extravagance. | ■ GERMANY: KÖLNER DOM (p. 438). With a 44m ceiling and 1350 sq. m of stained glass illuminating the interior with particolored sunlight, Cologne's cathedral is Germany's greatest. |
| ■ GERMANY: NEUSCHWANSTEIN (p. 477). A waterfall, an artificial grotto, a byzantine throne room, and a Wagnerian opera hall deck out the inspiration for Disney's Cinderella Castle. | ■ GREECE: THE PARTHENON (p. 508). Keeping vigil over Athens from the Acropolis, the Parthenon, civilization's capital since the 5th century BC, is a necessary pilgrimage for any humanist. |
| ■ ITALY: PALAZZO DUCALE (p. 681). The home of the Venetian Doge (mayor) could pass as a city unto itself, complete with on-site prisons that miscreants once entered via the Bridge of Sighs. | ■ HUNGARY: THE GREAT SYNAGOGUE (p. 1042). Europe's largest synagogue can hold 3000. Inscribed leaves of a metal tree in the courtyard commemorate the victims of the Holocaust. |
| ■ LUXEMBOURG: CHÂTEAU DE VIANDEN (p. 742). Though its displays of armor, furniture, and tapestries are run-of-the-mill, the expansive views from the hills make the castle a must-see. | ■ ITALY: SISTINE CHAPEL (p. 637). Each fresco on its famous ceiling depicts a scene from Genesis. Michelangelo painted himself as a flayed human skin hanging between heaven in hell. |
| ■ PORTUGAL: QUINTA DA REGALEIRA (p. 812). An eccentric millionaire owner turned this stunning palace into a fantasy land in the early 20th century. It has "Dantesque" caves below the main sights. | ■ SPAIN: MEZQUITA (p. 867). Córdoba's Mezquita, one of the most important Islamic monuments in the West, is supported by 850 pink and blue marble and alabaster columns. |
| ■ SPAIN: THE ALHAMBRA (p. 881). The Spanish say, "Si mueres sin ver la Alhambra, no has vivido." ("If you die without seeing the Alhambra, you have not lived.") They know what they're talking about. | ■ SPAIN: SAGRADA FAMILIA (p. 902). Though it looks like it's already melting, Antoni Gaudí's cathedral isn't even finished. The most visited construction site in the world, it should be finished in 2026. |
| ■ SWEDEN: KUNGLIGA SLOTTET (p. 1006). Still the official residence of the Swedish royal family, the Kungliga Slottet (Royal Palace) recently hosted lavish festivities for the Crown Princess's 30th birthday. | ■ SWITZERLAND: THE ABBEY PRECINCT (p. 953). It's hard to say what is more elaborate: the collectino of rare books and illuminated manuscripts or the dramatic Rococo library that houses them. |

# ▲ OUTDOORS

As the seat of modern Western civilization, Europe's museums and ruins tend to draw more people than its mountains and rivers. But for any traveler, budget or otherwise, solo or companioned, expert or neophyte, an excursion outdoors can round off (or even salvage) any journey. Mountains crowned with trees or icy glaciers continue to challenge mankind and dwarf the manmade, just as they did when civilization began.

| CRUISING... | ...FOR A BRUISING? |
|---|---|
| ■ **AUSTRIA: THE HOHE TAUERN NATIONAL PARK** (p. 94). Filled with glaciers, mountains, lakes, and endangered species, Europe's largest park offers mountain paths once trod by Celts and Romans. | ■ **AUSTRIA: INNSBRUCK** (p. 95). The free Club Innsbruck membership is one of the best deals in Western Europe for avid skiers. When skiing becomes old hat, adventures opt for paragliding. |
| ■ **BRITAIN: LAKE DISTRICT NATIONAL PARK** (p. 199). Four million sheep have cast their votes for the loveliest park in England—an equal number of summertime tourists seem to agree. | ■ **BRITAIN: NEWQUAY** (p. 175). Believe it or not, the best surfing in Europe may just be at this little city—dubbed "the new California"—at Fistral and Tolcarne Beaches on the Cornish coast. |
| ■ **CROATIA: THE DALMATIAN COAST** (p. 1011). Touted as the new French Riviera, the Dalmatian Coast has some of the cleanest and clearest waters in the Mediterranean. | ■ **FRANCE: MONT BLANC** (p. 334). The tallest mountain in Europe (4807m), Mont Blanc has vertigo-inducing slopes and is a haven for international bikers, hikers, snowboarders, and skiers. |
| ■ **DENMARK: ÆRØSKØBING** (p. 251). Economic stagnation and recent conservation efforts have successfully fossilized the 19th-century lifestyle and charm of this tiny island town. | ■ **GERMANY: DER SCHWARZWALD** (p. 458). The eerie darkness pervading this tangled evergreen, once the inspiration of the Brothers Grimm, lures hikers and skiers instead of red-caped little girls. |
| ■ **GREECE: MYRTOS BEACH** (p. 529). Myrtos's snowy white pebbles, lucent waters, and location against the cliffs make it one of the most heart-stirring beaches in all of Europe. | ■ **ITALY: CINQUE TERRA** (p. 660). An outdoorsman's paradise, the hiking trails of Cinque Terra have opportunities for cliff diving, horseback riding, and kayaking between villages. |
| ■ **ICELAND: THERMAL POOLS** (p. 985). Iceland may be expensive, but freeloaders can find naturally occuring "hot pot" outside of Reykjavík. Each thermal pool maintains its distinct character. | ■ **ITALY: MT. VESUVIUS** (p. 721). The only active volcano on the Continent is overdue for another eruption. Scientists say the explosion will be more violent than the one that buried Pompeii in AD 79. |
| ■ **IRELAND: KILLARNEY NATIONAL PARK** (p. 579). Glacial activity during the Ice Age shaped Ireland's best park, which has pristine lakes, forested mountains, and an elusive herd of 850 red deer. | ■ **NORWAY: FJÆRLAND** (p. 997). At the base of the Jostedalsbreen glacier, is at the end of the Fjærlandfjord, is a perfect rest from serious, year-round hiking and camping through Norway's fjords. |
| ■ **ITALY: THE AMALFI COAST** (p. 723). The azure waters that lap the coastline south of Naples are second only to the gravity-defying, jagged rocks that overlook them. | ■ **PORTUGAL: SAGRES** (p. 823). Once considered the edge of the world, the windy town of Sagres now plays host to more windsurfers than it does to would-be navigators. |
| ■ **THE NETHERLANDS: HOGE VELUWE NATIONAL PARK** (p. 786). Wild boars and red deer inhabit the 13,500 acres of forestry, while the park's museum houses works by Picasso and van Gogh. | ■ **SPAIN: PAMPLONA** (p. 913). While not outdoorsy in the traditional sense, the Running of the Bulls in Pamplona attracts runners and adrenaline junkies from all over the world. |
| ■ **SPAIN: SITGES** (p. 911). One of the many destinations vying for the title "Jewel of the Mediterranean," Sitges holds its own with prime tanning and nightlife almost as hot as the beaches. | ■ **SWITZERLAND: INTERLAKEN** (p. 941). Thanks to its mild climate and pristine landscape, Interlaken is Europe's adventure sports capital, with every adrenaline-inducing opportunity imaginable. |

# ❄ FESTIVALS 2008

| COUNTRIES | APR. – JUNE | JULY – AUG. | SEPT. – MAR. |
|---|---|---|---|
| **AUSTRIA AND SWITZERLAND** | **Vienna Festwochen** (early May to mid-June) | **Salzburger Festspiele** (late July-Aug.) | **Escalade** (Geneva; Dec. 12-14) **Fasnacht** (Basel; Feb. 11-13) |
| **BELGIUM** | **Festival of Fairground Arts** (Wallonie; late May) | **Gentse Feesten** (Ghent; mid- to late July) | **International French Language Film Festival** (Namur; late Sept.) |
| **BRITAIN AND IRELAND** | **Bloomsday** (Dublin; June 16) **Wimbledon** (London; late June-early July) | **Fringe Festival** (Edinburgh; Aug.) **Edinburgh Int'l Festival** (mid-Aug. to early Sept.) | **Matchmaking Festival** (Lisdoonvarna; Sept.) **St. Patrick's Day** (Mar. 17) |
| **CZECH REPUBLIC** | **Prague Spring Festival** (May-June) | **Int'l Film Festival** (Karlovy Vary; July) | **Int'l Organ Festival** (Olomouc; Sept.) |
| **FRANCE** | **Cannes Film Festival** (May 14-25) | **Festival d'Avignon** (July-Aug.) **Bastille Day** (July 14) | **Carnevale** (Nice, Nantes; Jan. 25-Feb. 5) |
| **GERMANY** | **May Day** (Berlin; May 1) **Christopher St. Day** (late June) | **Rhine in Flames Festival** (various locations in the Rhine Valley; throughout summer) | **Oktoberfest** (Munich; Sept. 20-Oct. 5) **Fasching** (Munich; Feb. 1-5) |
| **HUNGARY** | **Danube Festival** (Budapest; June) | **Golden Shell Folklore** (Siófok; June) **Sziget Rock Festival** (Budapest; Aug.) | **Éger Vintage Days** (Sept.) **Festival of Wine Songs** (Pécs; Sept.) |
| **ITALY** | **Maggio Musicale** (Florence; May to mid-June) | **Il Palio** (Siena; July 2 and Aug. 16) **Umbria Jazz Festival** (July) | **Carnevale** (late Feb.) **Scoppio del Carro** (Florence; Easter Su) |
| **THE NETHERLANDS** | **Queen's Day** (Apr. 30) **Holland Festival** (June) | **Gay Pride Parade** (Aug.) | **Flower Parade** (Aalsmeer; early Sept.) **Cannabis Cup** (Amsterdam; Nov.) |
| **PORTUGAL** | **Burning of the Ribbons** (Coimbra; early May) | **Lisbon Beer Festival** (July) | **Carnaval** (early Mar.) **Semana Santa** (Mar. 14-Mar. 23) |
| **SCANDINAVIA** | **Midsummer** (June 19-25) **Festspillene** (Bergen; late May-early June) | **Savonlinna Opera Festival** (July) **Quart Music Festival** (Kristiansand; early July) | **Helsinki Festival** (late Aug.-early Sept.) **Tromsø Film Festival** (mid-Jan.) |
| **SPAIN** | **Feria de Abril** (Sevilla; mid-Apr.) | **San Fermines** (Pamplona; early to mid-July) | **Las Fallas** (Valencia; Mar.) **Carnaval** (Mar.) |

# THE GRAND TOUR — WESTERN EUROPE

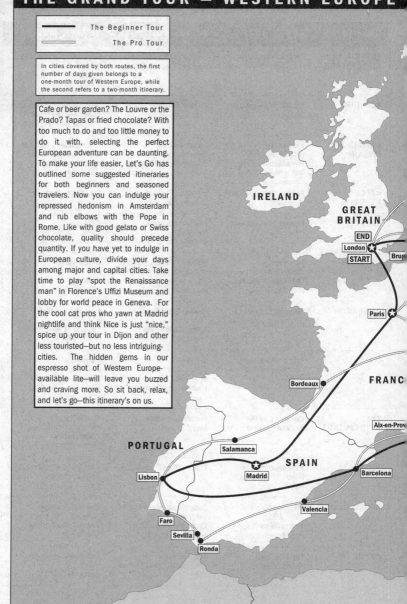

———— The Beginner Tour

====== The Pro Tour

In cities covered by both routes, the first number of days given belongs to a one-month tour of Western Europe, while the second refers to a two-month itinerary.

Cafe or beer garden? The Louvre or the Prado? Tapas or fried chocolate? With too much to do and too little money to do it with, selecting the perfect European adventure can be daunting. To make your life easier, Let's Go has outlined some suggested itineraries for both beginners and seasoned travelers. Now you can indulge your repressed hedonism in Amsterdam and rub elbows with the Pope in Rome. Like with good gelato or Swiss chocolate, quality should precede quantity. If you have yet to indulge in European culture, divide your days among major and capital cities. Take time to play "spot the Renaissance man" in Florence's Uffizi Museum and lobby for world peace in Geneva. For the cool cat pros who yawn at Madrid nightlife and think Nice is just "nice," spice up your tour in Dijon and other less touristed—but no less intriguing-cities. The hidden gems in our espresso shot of Western Europe-available lite—will leave you buzzed and craving more. So sit back, relax, and let's go—this itinerary's on us.

DISCOVER

## THE BEST OF THE MEDITERRANEAN

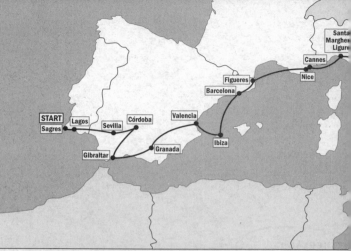

## CHANNEL JUMPING

Start your tour in the Emerald Isle's capital, **Dublin** (p. 557). Move on to the scenic **Ring of Kerry** (p. 580) and north to Galway (p. 584), Ireland's leading musical city. Hop over to **Belfast** (p. 591), and step (now safely) into the heart of The Troubles. Head to Great Britain, stopping in the jewel of Scotland, **Edinburgh** (p. 214). Leave the urban hustle behind to tour the **Lake District** (p. 199) before continuing south to **Liverpool** (p. 190), one of the EU's 2008 Cultural Capitals, and **Manchester** (p. 188). Take a breather from all things modern—hang out with grazing sheep in **The Cotswolds** (p. 183) and soak in **Bath's** (p. 172) springs. A trip to England wouldn't be complete without experiencing **Oxford's** (p. 177) binge studying and diligent drinking. Make **London** (p. 139) your final stop in England and swim down to France, landing at Dieppe. After a few days in **Paris** (p. 267), stay in the **Loire Valley** (p. 298) for spectacular cathedrals and manors. Wrap up your Anglo-centric tour with **Brittany** (p. 302), the Celtic side of France.

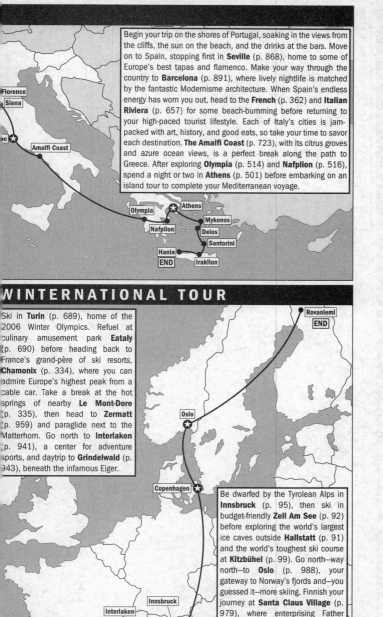

Florence
Siena

Amalfi Coast

Begin your trip on the shores of Portugal, soaking in the views from the cliffs, the sun on the beach, and the drinks at the bars. Move on to Spain, stopping first in **Seville** (p. 868), home to some of Europe's best tapas and flamenco. Make your way through the country to **Barcelona** (p. 891), where lively nightlife is matched by the fantastic Modernisme architecture. When Spain's endless energy has worn you out, head to the **French** (p. 362) and **Italian Riviera** (p. 657) for some beach-bumming before returning to your high-paced tourist lifestyle. Each of Italy's cities is jam-packed with art, history, and good eats, so take your time to savor each destination. **The Amalfi Coast** (p. 723), with its citrus groves and azure ocean views, is a perfect break along the path to Greece. After exploring **Olympia** (p. 514) and **Nafplion** (p. 516), spend a night or two in **Athens** (p. 501) before embarking on an island tour to complete your Mediterranean voyage.

Olympia    Athens

Mykonos
Nafplion    Delos
Santorini
Hania
**END**    Iraklion

# INTERNATIONAL TOUR

Rovaniemi
**END**

Ski in **Turin** (p. 689), home of the 2006 Winter Olympics. Refuel at culinary amusement park **Eataly** (p. 690) before heading back to France's grand-père of ski resorts, **Chamonix** (p. 334), where you can admire Europe's highest peak from a cable car. Take a break at the hot springs of nearby **Le Mont-Dore** (p. 335), then head to **Zermatt** (p. 959) and paraglide next to the Matterhorn. Go north to **Interlaken** (p. 941), a center for adventure sports, and daytrip to **Grindelwald** (p. 943), beneath the infamous Eiger.

Oslo

Copenhagen

Be dwarfed by the Tyrolean Alps in **Innsbruck** (p. 95), then ski in budget-friendly **Zell Am See** (p. 92) before exploring the world's largest ice caves outside **Hallstatt** (p. 91) and the world's toughest ski course at **Kitzbühel** (p. 99). Go north—way north—to **Oslo** (p. 988), your gateway to Norway's fjords and—you guessed it—more skiing. Finnish your journey at **Santa Claus Village** (p. 979), where enterprising Father Christmas holds daily office hours and oversees an empire of gift shops.

Innsbruck

Interlaken

Chamonix    Zermatt    Zell
Am See
Turin **START**

DISCOVER

# THE TREE-HUGGER'S TOUR

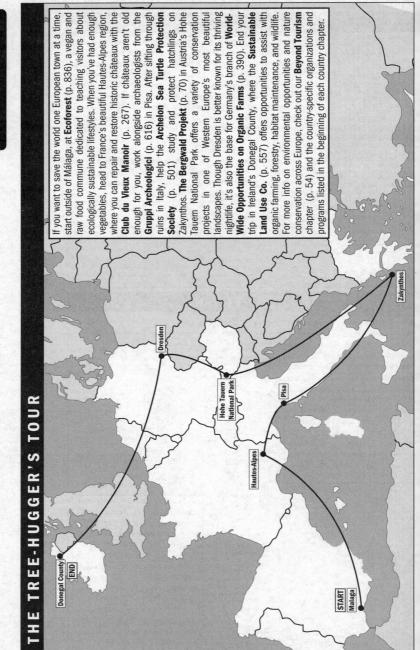

If you want to save the world one European town at a time, start outside of Málaga, at **Ecoforest** (p. 836), a vegan and raw food commune dedicated to teaching visitors about ecologically sustainable lifestyles. When you've had enough vegetables, head to France's beautiful Hautes-Alpes region, where you can repair and restore historic châteaux with the **Club du Vieux Manoir** (p. 267). If châteaux aren't old enough for you, work alongside archaeologists from the **Gruppi Archeologici** (p. 616) in Pisa. After sifting through ruins in Italy, help the **Archelon Sea Turtle Protection Society** (p. 501) study and protect hatchlings on Zakynthos. **The Bergwald Projekt** (p. 70) in Austria's Hohe Tauern National Park offers a variety of conservation projects in one of Western Europe's most beautiful landscapes. Though Dresden is better known for its thriving nightlife, it's also the base for Germany's branch of **World-Wide Opportunities on Organic Farms** (p. 390). End your trip in Ireland's Donegal County, where the **Sustainable Land Use Co.** (p. 557) offers opportunities to assist with organic farming, forestry, habitat maintenance, and wildlife. For more info on environmental opportunities and nature conservation across Europe, check out our **Beyond Tourism** chapter (p. 54) and the country-specific organizations and programs listed in the beginning of each country chapter.

Zakynthos

Dresden

Hohe Tauern
National Park

Pisa

Hautes-Alpes

Donegal County
**END**

**START**
Málaga

# THE ULTIMATE PUB CRAWL

It's not called **Publin** (p. 546) for nothing. Start your debaucherous journey in this pub-filled city, before moving on to party with the best and brightest in **Oxford** (p. 177). After spending a few nights in **London** (p. 139), hop over to **Amsterdam** (p. 752), for its infamous coffeehouse scene and the best GLBT nightlife in Europe. Pre-game in **Cologne** (p. 434), **Hamburg** (p. 425), and **Dresden** (p. 482), but finish your travels through Germany in **Munich** (p. 460), the city that brought the world Oktoberfest and the *Biergarten*. Hang out with students in the university towns of **Zürich** (p. 944) and **Grenoble** (p. 332) on your way to sleepless Spain. See the sun come up in **Barcelona** (p. 891), **Salamanca** (p. 860), and **Granada** (p. 878) before finishing your Ultimate Pub Crawl in **Lagos**, Portugal (p. 821).

# ESSENTIALS

## PLANNING YOUR TRIP

**BEFORE YOU GO.**
**Passport** (p. 12). Required for all non-EU citizens traveling in Europe.
**Visa** (p. 13). Not required for citizens of Australia, Canada, Ireland, New Zealand, the UK, and the US for stays shorter than 90 days in a 6-month period in most European countries.
**Work Permit** (p. 13). Required for all non-EU citizens planning to work in any European country.
**Vaccinations** (p. 22). Visitors to Europe should be up to date on vaccines, especially for diphtheria, hepatitis A, hepatitis B, and mumps. Visitors to Eastern Europe should also be vaccinated for measles, rabies, and typhoid.

## EMBASSIES AND CONSULATES

### CONSULAR SERVICES

Information about European consular services abroad and foreign consular services in Europe is located in individual country chapters; it can also be found at **www.embassiesabroad.com, www.embassyworld.com,** and **www.tyzo.com/planning/embassies.html.**

### TOURIST OFFICES

Information about national tourist boards in Europe is located in individual country chapters; it can also be found at **www.towd.com.**

## DOCUMENTS AND FORMALITIES

### PASSPORTS

#### REQUIREMENTS
Citizens of Australia, Canada, Ireland, New Zealand, the UK, and the US need valid passports to enter European countries and to re-enter their home countries. Most countries do not allow entrance if the holder's passport expires within six months. Returning home with an expired passport is illegal and may result in a fine.

#### NEW PASSPORTS
Citizens of Australia, Canada, Ireland, New Zealand, the UK, and the US can apply for a passport at any passport office and most post offices and courts of law. New passport or renewal applications must be filed at least two months before the departure date, though most passport offices offer rush services for a very steep fee. Be warned that even "rushed" passports can take up to two weeks to arrive. Citizens living abroad who need a passport or renewal should contact the nearest passport office or consulate of their home country.

↘ **ONE EUROPE.** European unity has come a long way since 1958, when the European Economic Community (EEC) was created to promote European solidarity and cooperation. Since then, the EEC has become the European Union (EU), a mighty political, legal, and economic institution. On May 1, 2004, 10 South, Central, and Eastern European countries—Cyprus, the Czech Republic, Estonia, Hungary, Latvia, Lithuania, Malta, Poland, Slovakia, and Slovenia—were admitted to the EU, joining 15 other member states: Austria, Belgium, Denmark, Finland, France, Germany, Greece, Ireland, Italy, Luxembourg, the Netherlands, Portugal, Spain, Sweden, and the UK.

What does this have to do with the average non-EU tourist? The EU's policy of **freedom of movement** means that border controls between the first 15 member states (not including Ireland and the UK, but including Norway and Iceland) have been abolished, and visa policies have been harmonized. Under this treaty, formally known as the **Schengen Agreement,** you're still required to carry a passport (or government-issued ID card for EU citizens) when crossing an internal border, but once you've been admitted into one country, you're free to travel to other participating states. On June 5, 2005, Switzerland ratified the treaty, and will become fully participant by 2007. The 10 newest member states of the EU are anticipated to implement the policy after 2006. Ireland and the UK have also formed a **common travel area,** abolishing passport controls between the UK and the Republic of Ireland. For more important consequences of the EU for travelers, see The Euro (p. 16) and Customs in the EU (p. 15).

## PASSPORT MAINTENANCE

Photocopy the page of your passport with your photo, as well as your visas, traveler's check serial numbers, and any other important documents. Carry one set of copies in a safe place, apart from the originals, and leave another set at home. Consulates also recommend that you carry an expired passport or an official copy of your birth certificate in a part of your baggage separate from other documents. If you lose your passport, immediately notify the local police and the nearest embassy or consulate of your home government. To expedite its replacement, you must show ID and proof of citizenship. In some cases, a replacement may take weeks, and it may be valid only for a limited time. Any visas stamped in your old passport will be irretrievably lost. In an emergency, ask for immediate temporary traveling papers that will permit you to re-enter your home country.

# VISAS, INVITATIONS, AND WORK PERMITS

### VISAS

As of August 2007, citizens of Australia, Canada, Ireland, New Zealand, the UK, or the US did not need a visa to visit the following countries for fewer than 90 days: Austria, Belgium, Britain, Croatia, the Czech Republic, Denmark, Estonia, Finland, France, Germany, Greece, Hungary, Iceland, Ireland, Italy, Latvia, Liechtenstein, Luxembourg, the Netherlands, Norway, Poland, Portugal, the Slovak Republic, Slovenia, Spain, Sweden, and Switzerland. For travelers planning to spend more than 90 days in any European country, visas cost US$35-200 and typically allow six months in that country. Visas can usually be purchased at a consulate. Double-check entrance requirements at the nearest embassy or consulate of **your destination** for up-to-date info before departure. US citizens can consult http://travel.state.gov/foreignentryreqs.html.

**WORK PERMITS**

Admission as a visitor does not include the right to work, which is authorized only by a work permit. Entering a country in Europe to study typically requires a special study visa, though many study-abroad programs are able to subsidize it. For more information, see **Beyond Tourism,** p. 54.

# IDENTIFICATION

When you travel, always carry at least two forms of identification on your person, including a photo ID; a passport and a driver's license or birth certificate is usually adequate. Never carry all of your IDs together; split them up in case of theft or loss, and keep photocopies of all of them in your luggage and at home.

## STUDENT, TEACHER, AND YOUTH IDENTIFICATION

The **International Student Identity Card (ISIC),** the most widely accepted form of student ID, provides discounts on some sights, accommodations, food, and transportation; access to a 24hr. emergency helpline; and insurance benefits for US cardholders (see **Insurance,** p. 22). Applicants must be full-time secondary or post-secondary school students. Because of the proliferation of fake ISICs, some services (particularly airlines) require additional proof of student identity.

The **International Teacher Identity Card (ITIC)** offers teachers the same insurance coverage as the ISIC and similar but limited discounts. For travelers who are under 26 years old but are not students, the **International Youth Travel Card (IYTC)** also offers many of the same benefits as the ISIC.

Each of these identity cards costs US$22. ISICs and ITICs are valid until the new year unless purchased between September and December, in which case they are valid until the beginning of the following new year. IYTCs are valid for one year from the date of issue. To learn more about ISICs, ITICs, and IYTCs, try www.myisic.com. Many travel agencies issue the cards; for more info, see the **International Student Travel Confederation (ISTC)** website (www.istc.org).

The **International Student Exchange Card (ISE Card)** is a similar identification card available to students, faculty, and youths aged 12 to 26. The card provides discounts, medical benefits, access to a 24hr. emergency helpline, and the ability to purchase student airfares. An ISE Card costs US$25; for more info, call in the US ☎ 800-255-8000, or visit www.isecard.com.

# CUSTOMS

When you enter a European country, you must declare certain items from abroad and pay a duty on the value of those articles if they exceed a set allowance. Note that goods purchased at **duty-free** shops are not exempt from duty or sales tax; "duty-free" merely means that you need not pay a tax in the country of purchase. Duty-free allowances were abolished for travel between EU member states, but still exist for those arriving from outside the EU. Upon returning home, you must likewise declare all articles acquired abroad and pay a duty on the value of articles in excess of your home country's allowance. In order to expedite your return, make a list of any valuables brought from home and register them with customs before traveling abroad, and be sure to keep receipts for all goods acquired abroad.

**CUSTOMS IN THE EU.** In addition to the freedom of movement of people within the EU (p. 13), travelers in the 15 original EU member countries (Austria, Belgium, Denmark, Finland, France, Germany, Greece, Ireland, Italy, Luxembourg, the Netherlands, Portugal, Spain, Sweden, and the UK) can also take advantage of the freedom of movement of goods. This means that there are no customs controls at internal EU borders (i.e., you can take the blue customs channel at the airport), and travelers are free to transport whatever legal substances they like as long as it is for their own personal (non-commercial) use— up to 800 cigarettes, 10L of spirits, 90L of wine (including up to 60L of sparkling wine), and 110L of beer. Duty-free allowances were abolished on June 30, 1999 for travel between the original 15 EU member states; this now also applies to Cyprus and Malta. However, travelers between the EU and the rest of the world still get a duty-free allowance when passing through customs.

ESSENTIALS

# MONEY

## CURRENCY AND EXCHANGE

The currency chart below is based on August 2007 exchange rates between the euro (€) and Australian dollars (AUS$), Canadian dollars (CDN$), New Zealand dollars (NZ$), British pounds (UK£), and US dollars (US$). Check the currency converter on websites like www.xe.com or www.bloomberg.com, or a large newspaper, for the latest exchange rates.

| EURO (€) | | |
|---|---|---|
| AUS$1 = €0.62 | | €1 = AUS$1.61 |
| CDN$1 = €0.69 | | €1 = CDN$1.45 |
| NZ$1 = €0.55 | | €1 = NZ$1.80 |
| UK£1 = €1.47 | | €1 = UK£0.68 |
| US$1 = €0.73 | | €1 = US$1.38 |

As a general rule, it's cheaper to convert money in Europe than at home. While currency exchange will probably be available in your arrival airport, it's wise to bring enough currency to last for the first 24-72hr. of your trip. When exchanging money abroad, try to go only to banks or official exchange establishments that have at most a 5% margin between their buy and sell prices. Because you lose money with every transaction, **convert large sums** (unless the currency is depreciating rapidly), but **no more than you'll need.** If you use traveler's checks or bills, carry some in small denominations (the equivalent of US$50 or less) for times when you are forced to exchange money at disadvantageous rates, but bring a range of denominations, as charges may be levied per check cashed. Store your money in a variety of forms; ideally, at any given time you will be carrying some cash, some traveler's checks, and an ATM and/or credit card. All travelers should also consider carrying some US dollars (about US$50 worth), which are sometimes preferred by local tellers. Euro (€) may also be accepted even in European nations with their own currency.

## CREDIT, ATM, AND DEBIT CARDS

Where they are accepted, credit cards often offer superior exchange rates—up to 5% better than the retail rate used by banks and other currency exchange establishments. Credit cards may also offer services such as insurance or emergency help, and are sometimes required when reserving hotel rooms or rental cars. **Mas-**

**THE EURO.** The official currency of 13 members of the European Union—Austria, Belgium, Finland, France, Germany, Greece, Ireland, Italy, Luxembourg, the Netherlands, Portugal, Slovenia, and Spain—is now the euro. The currency has some important—and positive—consequences for travelers hitting more than one euro-zone country. For one thing, money-changers across the euro-zone are obliged to exchange money at the official, fixed rate, and at no commission (though they may still charge a small service fee). Second, euro-denominated traveler's checks allow you to pay for goods and services across the euro-zone, again at the official rate and commission-free.

terCard (a.k.a. **EuroCard** or **Access** in Europe) and **Visa** (a.k.a. **Carte Bleue** or **Barclaycard**) are the most widely accepted; **American Express** cards work at some ATMs and at AmEx offices and most major airports. A **debit card** can be used wherever its associated credit card company (usually MasterCard or Visa) is accepted, and the money is withdrawn directly from the holder's checking account. Debit cards also often function as ATM cards and can be used to withdraw cash from associated banks and ATMs throughout Europe. Ask your bank about obtaining one.

The use of ATM cards is widespread in Europe. Depending on the system that your home bank uses, you can most likely access your personal bank account from abroad. ATMs get the same wholesale exchange rate as credit cards, but there is often a limit on the amount of money you can withdraw per day (usually around US$500). There is typically also a surcharge of US$1-5 per withdrawal.

**PINS AND ATMS.** To use a debit or credit card to withdraw money from a cash machine (ATM) in Europe, you must have a 4-digit **Personal Identification Number (PIN).** If your PIN is longer than 4 digits, ask your bank whether you can just use the first 4, or whether you'll need a new one. **Credit cards** don't usually come with PINs, so if you intend to hit up ATMs in Europe with a credit card to get cash advances, call your credit card company to request one before leaving. Travelers with alphabetic, rather than numerical, PINs may also be thrown off by the lack of letters on European cash machines. The following are the corresponding numbers to use: QZ=1; ABC=2; DEF=3; GHI=4; JKL=5; MNO=6; PRS=7; TUV=8; and WXY=9. Note that if you mistakenly punch the wrong code into the machine 3 times, it will swallow your card for good.

The two major international money networks are **MasterCard/Maestro/Cirrus** (for ATM locations ☎ 800-424-7787; www.mastercard.com) and **Visa/PLUS** (for ATM locations ☎ 800-847-2911; www.visa.com).

# TRAVELER'S CHECKS

Traveler's checks are one of the safest means of carrying funds, though not the most convenient. American Express and Visa are the most recognized brands. Many banks and agencies sell them for a small commission. Check issuers provide refunds if the checks are lost or stolen, and many provide additional services, such as toll-free refund hotlines, emergency message services, and assistance with lost and stolen credit cards or passports. Traveler's checks are readily accepted in most of Western Europe. Ask about toll-free refund hotlines and the location of refund centers when purchasing checks. Always carry emergency cash.

**American Express:** Checks available with commission at select banks, at all AmEx offices, and online (www.americanexpress.com; US residents only). AmEx cardholders can also purchase checks by phone (☎ 800-528-4800). AmEx also offers the Travelers

Cheque Card, a prepaid reloadable card. Cheques for Two can be signed by either of 2 people traveling together. For purchase locations or more information, contact AmEx's service centers: Australia ☎800 688 022, Canada ☎866-296-5198, US ☎800-221-7282, New Zealand ☎050 855 5358, UK ☎0800 587 6023.

**Travelex:** Thomas Cook MasterCard and Interpayment Visa traveler's checks available. For information about Thomas Cook MasterCard in Canada and the US call ☎800-223-7373, UK ☎0800 622 101; elsewhere, call UK collect ☎44 1733 318 950. For information about Interpayment Visa in Canada and the US ☎800-732-1322, in the UK ☎0800 515 884; elsewhere, call UK collect ☎44 1733 318 949. For more information, visit www.travelex.com.

**Visa:** Checks available (generally with commission) at banks worldwide. For the location of the nearest office, call the Visa Travelers Cheque Global Refund and Assistance Center: in the UK ☎0800 895 078, US 800-227-6811; elsewhere, call UK collect ☎44 2079 378 091. Visa also offers TravelMoney, a pre-paid debit card that can be reloaded online or by phone. For more information on Visa travel services, see http://usa.visa.com/personal/using_visa/travel_with_visa.html.

# GETTING MONEY FROM HOME

The easiest and cheapest solution for running out of money while traveling is to have someone back home make a deposit to the bank account linked to your credit card or ATM card. Failing that, consider one of the options below. The online **International Money Transfer Consumer Guide** (http://international-money-transfer-consumer-guide.info) may also be of help.

## WIRING MONEY

It is possible to arrange a **bank money transfer,** which means asking a bank back home to wire money to a bank in Europe. This is the cheapest way to transfer cash, but it's also the slowest, usually taking several days or more. Note that some banks may only release your funds in local currency, potentially sticking you with a poor exchange rate; inquire about this in advance. Money transfer services like **Western Union** are faster and more convenient than bank transfers, but also much pricier. Western Union has locations worldwide. To find one, visit www.westernunion.com, or call: Australia ☎800 173 833, Canada and US 800-325-6000, UK 0800 833 833. To wire money using a credit card (Discover, MasterCard, or Visa), call in Canada and the US ☎800-225-5227, UK 0800 833 833. Money transfer services are also available to **American Express** cardholders and at selected **Thomas Cook** offices.

## US STATE DEPARTMENT (US CITIZENS ONLY)

In serious emergencies only, the US State Department will forward money within hours to the nearest consular office. If you wish to use this service, you must contact the Overseas Citizens Service division of the US State Department (☎202-501-4444, toll-free 888-407-4747).

# COSTS

The cost of your trip will vary depending on where you go, how you travel, and where you stay. The most significant expenses will probably be your round-trip (return) **airfare** to Europe (see **Getting to Europe: By Plane,** p. 41) and a **rail pass** or **bus pass** (see **Getting around Europe,** p. 45).

## STAYING ON A BUDGET

Your daily budget will vary greatly from country to country. A bare-bones day in Europe would include camping or sleeping in hostels and buying food in supermarkets. A slightly more comfortable day would include sleeping in hostels or guesthouses and the occasional budget hotel, eating one meal per day at a restau-

TOP TEN LIST

## OP TEN WAYS TO SAVE N WESTERN EUROPE

**1.** Always ask about discounts. If under 26, you should rarely go a ull day without being rewarded or your youth and inexperience.

**2.** Be aware that room prices tend o shoot up and transportation is a hassle on **festival dates** and during local holidays.

**3.** Consider purchasing the combination transportation and sights **discount passes** offered by many city tourist offices; they often pay or themselves many times over.

**4.** Get **out** of the city. A day hiking or beach-lounging provides relief or both you and your wallet.

**5. Travel early;** trains, buses, and erries leaving early in the day or on weekdays (as opposed to weekends) are generally cheaper han those leaving at other times.

**6.** Don't expect to eat out every meal in Europe. **Street markets** are excellent places to find cheap fruits and vegetables, and most hostels have kitchens.

**7.** In major cities, make your base on the **outskirts** of the town, where food and beds tend to be both cheaper and less touristed.

**8.** Bring a **sleepsack** to avoid the occasional linens rental charge.

**9.** Clubbing is expensive enough without depending on overpriced mojitos; start the night off with a **market-purchased booze.**

**10.** Be your own tour guide; sightseeing is best—and free—on your own with your **Let's Go.**

rant, and going out at night. For a luxurious day, the sky's the limit. In any case, be sure to factor in emergency reserve funds (at least US$200) when planning how much money you'll need.

### TIPS FOR SAVING MONEY

Some simple ways to save include searching out free entertainment, splitting accommodation and food costs with trustworthy fellow travelers, and buying food in grocery stores. Full- or multi-day local transportation passes can also save you valuable pocket change. Bring a **sleepsack** (p. 19) to save at hostels that charge for linens, and do your **laundry** in the sink (unless you're explicitly prohibited from doing so). Museums often have certain days when admission is free. If you are eligible, consider getting an ISIC or an IYTC; many sights and museums offer reduced admission to students and youths. Renting a bike is cheaper than renting a moped or scooter. Purchasing drinks at bars and clubs quickly becomes expensive; it's cheaper to buy alcohol at a supermarket and drink before going out. Remember, though, that while staying within your budget is important, don't do so at the expense of your health or a great travel experience.

## TIPPING AND BARGAINING

In most European countries, a 5-10% gratuity is included in the food service bill. Additional tipping is not expected, but an extra 5-10% for good service is not unusual. Where gratuity is not included, 10-15% tips are standard and rounding up to the next unit of currency is common. Many countries have their own unique tipping practices with which you should familiarize yourself before visiting; for example, in Germany, the tip is handed directly to the server instead of being left on the table. In general, tipping in bars and pubs is unnecessary and money left on the bar may not make it into the bartender's hands. For other services such as taxis or hairdressers, a 10-15% tip is usually recommended. As a general rule, watch other customers to gauge what is appropriate. Bargaining is useful in Greece and in outdoor markets across Europe. See individual country chapters for more specific information.

## TAXES

The EU imposes a **value added tax (VAT)** on goods and services, usually included in the sticker price. Non-EU citizens visiting Europe may obtain a refund for taxes paid on retail goods, but not for taxes paid on services. As the VAT is 15-25%, it might be worthwhile to file for a refund. To do so, you must obtain Tax-Free Shopping Cheques, available from shops sporting the Europe Tax-Free Shopping logo, and save your receipts. Upon leaving the EU, present your **goods, invoices,** and **passport** to customs and have your checks stamped. Then, go to an ETS cash refund office on site or file for a refund once back home. Keep in mind that goods must be taken out of the country within three months of purchase, and that most countries require minimum purchase amounts per store to be eligible for a refund. See www.globalrefund.org for more info and downloads of relevant forms.

# PACKING

**Pack lightly.** Lay out only what you absolutely need, then take half the clothes and twice the money. The Travelite FAQ (www.travelite.org) is a good resource for tips on traveling light. The online **Universal Packing List** (http://upl.codeq.info) will generate a customized list of suggested items based on your trip length, the expected climate, your planned activities, and other factors. If you plan to do a lot of hiking, also consult **The Great Outdoors,** p. 33.

**Luggage:** If you plan to cover most of your itinerary by foot, a sturdy **frame backpack** is unbeatable. (For backpack basics, see p. 34.) Toting a **suitcase** or **trunk** is fine if you plan to live in 1 or 2 cities, but not a great idea if you plan to move around frequently. In addition to your main piece of luggage, a **daypack** (a small backpack or courier bag) is useful.

**Clothing:** No matter when you're traveling, it's a good idea to bring a warm jacket or wool sweater, a rain jacket (Gore-Tex® is both waterproof and breathable), sturdy shoes or hiking boots, and thick socks. Waterproof sandals are a must-have for grubby hostel showers. You may also want one outfit for going out, and maybe a nicer pair of shoes. If you plan to visit religious or cultural sites, remember that to dress modestly.

**TIP**  **DISPOSABLES.** If you're tight on space and plan to give your clothes a good workout, consider buying a pack of simple cotton undershirts. A pack of plain T-shirts is cheap and light, and you won't feel bad throwing them away when they get covered in backpacker grime.

**Sleepsack:** Some hostels require that you either provide your own linens or rent from them. Save cash by making your own sleepsack: fold a full-size sheet in half the long way, then sew it closed along the long side and one of the short sides.

**Adapters and Converters:** In Europe, electricity is 230V AC, enough to fry any 120V North American appliance. Americans and Canadians should buy an adapter (changes the shape of the plug; US$10-30) and a converter (changes the voltage; US$10-30); don't use an adapter without a converter unless appliance instructions explicitly state otherwise. Australians and New Zealanders, who use 230V, won't need a converter, but will need adapters. For more info, check out http://kropla.com/electric.htm.

**Toiletries:** Toothbrushes, towels, soap, talcum powder (to keep feet dry), deodorant, razors, tampons, and condoms are available, but it may be difficult to find your preferred brand, so bring extras. Also, be sure to bring enough extra contact lenses and solution for your entire trip. Bring your glasses and a copy of your prescription, too, in case you need an emergency replacement. If you use heat disinfection, either switch temporarily to a chemical disinfection system (check first to make sure it's safe with your brand of lenses), or buy a converter to 220/240V.

**First Aid:** For a basic first-aid kit, pack bandages, a pain reliever, antibiotic cream, a thermometer, a pocket knife, tweezers, decongestant, motion-sickness remedy, diarrhea or upset-stomach medication, an antihistamine, sunscreen, insect repellent, and burn ointment. If you will be in remote regions of less-developed Eastern European

> **TIP** **KEEP IT CLEAN.** Multi-purpose liquid soaps will save space and keep you from smelling like last night's fish and chips. Dr. Bronner's® and Campsuds® both make soap that you can use as toothpaste, shampoo, laundry detergent, dishwashing liquid, and more. Plus, they're biodegradable.

countries, consider a syringe for emergencies (get an explanatory letter from your doctor). Leave all sharp objects in your checked luggage.

**Film:** Digital cameras can be a more economical option and less of a hassle than regular cameras, just be sure to bring along a large enough **memory card** and extra (or rechargeable) **batteries.** Less serious photographers may want to bring a disposable camera or two. Despite disclaimers, airport security X-rays can fog film, so buy a **lead-lined** pouch at a camera store or ask security to hand-inspect it. Always pack film in your carry-on luggage, as higher-intensity X-rays are used on checked luggage.

**Other Useful Items:** For safety, bring a **money belt** and a small **padlock.** Basic **outdoors equipment** (water bottle, compass, waterproof matches, pocketknife, sunglasses, sunscreen, hat) may also prove useful. Make quick repairs with a needle and thread; also consider electrical tape for patching tears. To do laundry by hand, bring detergent, a small rubber ball to stop up the sink, and string for a makeshift clothesline. Extra **plastic bags** are crucial for storing food, dirty shoes, and wet clothes, and for keeping liquids from exploding all over your clothes. Other items include an umbrella, a battery-powered **alarm clock,** safety pins, rubber bands, a flashlight, a utility pocketknife, earplugs, garbage bags, and a small calculator. A **mobile phone** can be a lifesaver on the road; see p. 27 for information on acquiring one that will work at your destination.

**Important Documents:** Don't forget your passport, traveler's checks, ATM and/or credit cards, adequate ID, and photocopies of all of the aforementioned. Other documents you may wish to have include: a hostelling membership card (p. 29); a driver's license (p. 14); travel insurance forms (p. 22); an ISIC (p. 14); a rail or bus pass (p. 46).

# SAFETY AND HEALTH

## GENERAL ADVICE

In any type of crisis situation, the most important thing to do is **stay calm.** Your country's embassy abroad (p. 12) is usually your best resource when things go wrong; registering with that embassy upon arrival in the country is often a good idea. Consulates can can provide information on the services they offer their citizens in case of emergencies abroad. Let's Go lists consulates in the **Practical Information** section of large cities.

**DRUGS AND ALCOHOL.** Drug and alcohol laws vary widely throughout Europe. In the Netherlands "soft" drugs are available on the open market, while in much of Eastern Europe drug possession may lead to a heavy prison sentence. If you carry **prescription drugs,** you must carry both a copy of the prescriptions themselves and a note from a doctor, especially at border crossings. **Public drunkenness** is culturally unacceptable, unsafe, and against the law in many countries.

**TERRORISM AND CIVIL UNREST.** In the wake of September 11 and the war in Iraq, exercise increased vigilance near embassies and be wary of big crowds and demonstrations. Keep an eye on the news, pay attention to travel warnings, and comply with security measures.

Overall, risks of civil unrest tend to be localized and rarely directed toward tourists. Tensions remain in Northern Ireland, especially around July "marching season," which reaches its height July 4-12. Notoriously violent separatist movements include the ETA, a Basque group that operates in southern France and Spain, and FLNC, a Corsican separatist group in France. The November 17 group in Greece is known for anti-Western acts, though they have not targeted tourists, to date.

**TRAVEL ADVISORIES.** The following government offices provide travel information and advisories by telephone, by fax, or via the web:

**Australian Department of Foreign Affairs and Trade:** ☎ 612 6261 1111; www.dfat.gov.au.

**Canadian Department of Foreign Affairs and International Trade (DFAIT):** ☎ 800-267-8376; www.dfait-maeci.gc.ca. Call for their free booklet, *Bon Voyage...But*.

**New Zealand Ministry of Foreign Affairs:** ☎ 044 398 000; www.mfat.govt.nz.

**United Kingdom Foreign and Commonwealth Office:** ☎ 020 7008 1500; www.fco.gov.uk.

**US Department of State:** ☎ 888-407-4747; http://travel.state.gov. Visit the website for the booklet *A Safe Trip Abroad*.

# PERSONAL SAFETY

## EXPLORING AND TRAVELING

To avoid unwanted attention, try to blend in as much as possible. Respecting local customs (in many cases, dressing more conservatively than you would at home) may placate would-be hecklers. Familiarize yourself with your surroundings before setting out, and carry yourself with confidence. Check maps in shops and restaurants rather than on the street. If you are traveling alone, be sure someone at home knows your itinerary, and never tell anyone you meet that you're by yourself. When walking at night, stick to busy, well-lit streets and avoid dark alleyways. If you ever feel uncomfortable, leave the area as quickly and directly as you can.

There is no sure-fire way to avoid all the threatening situations you might encounter while traveling, but a good **self-defense course** will give you concrete ways to react to unwanted advances. **Impact, Prepare,** and **Model Mugging** can refer you to local self-defense courses in Australia, Canada, Switzerland and the US. Visit the website at www.modelmugging.org for a list of nearby chapters.

If you are using a **car,** learn local driving signals and wear a seatbelt. Children under 40 lbs. should ride only in specially designed carseats, available for a small fee from most car rental agencies. Study route maps before you hit the road, and if you plan on spending a lot of time driving, consider bringing spare parts. For long drives in desolate areas, invest in a cellular phone (p. 27) and a roadside assistance program (p. 51). Park your vehicle in a garage or well-traveled area, and use a steering wheel locking device in larger cities. **Sleeping in your car** is very dangerous, and it's also illegal in many countries. For info on the perils of **hitchhiking,** see p. 53.

## POSSESSIONS AND VALUABLES

Never leave your belongings unattended; crime occurs in even the most safe-looking hostel or hotel. Bring your own padlock for hostel lockers, and don't ever store valuables in a locker. Be particularly careful on **buses** and **trains;** horror stories abound about determined thieves who wait for travelers to fall asleep. Carry your bag or purse in front of you where you can see it. When traveling with others, sleep in alternate shifts. When alone, use good judgment in selecting a train compartment: never stay in an empty one, and use a lock to secure your pack to the luggage rack. Use extra caution if traveling at night or on overnight trains. Try to sleep on top bunks with your luggage stored above you (if not in bed with you), and keep important documents and other valuables on you at all times.

There are a few steps you can take to minimize the financial risk associated with traveling. First, **bring as little with you as possible.** Second, buy a few combination **padlocks** to secure your belongings either in your pack or in a hostel or train station locker. Third, **carry as little cash as possible.** Keep your traveler's checks and ATM/credit cards in a **money belt**—not a "fanny pack"—along with your passport and ID cards. Fourth, **keep a small cash reserve separate from your primary stash.** This should be about US$50 (US$ or euro are best) sewn into or stored in the depths of your pack, along with your traveler's check numbers and photocopies of your passport, your birth certificate, and other important documents.

In large cities **con artists** often work in groups and may involve children. Beware of certain classics: sob stories that require money, rolls of bills "found" on the street, mustard spilled (or saliva spit) onto your shoulder to distract you while they snatch your bag. **Never let your passport and your bags out of your sight.** Hostel workers will sometimes stand at bus and train station arrival points to try to recruit tired and disoriented travelers to their hostel; never believe strangers who tell you that theirs is the only hostel open. Beware of **pickpockets** in city crowds, especially on public transportation. Also, be alert in public telephone booths: If you must say your calling card number, do so very quietly; if you punch it in, make sure no one can look over your shoulder.

If you will be traveling with electronic devices, such as a laptop computer or a PDA, check whether your homeowner's insurance covers loss, theft, or damage when you travel. If not, you might consider purchasing a low-cost separate insurance policy. **Safeware** (☎ 800-800-1492; www.safeware.com) specializes in covering computers. State rates vary, but average US$200 for global coverage up to $4000.

# PRE-DEPARTURE HEALTH

In your **passport,** write the names of any people you wish to be contacted in case of a medical emergency, and list any allergies or medical conditions. Matching a prescription to a foreign equivalent is not always easy, safe, or possible, so if you take prescription drugs, consider carrying up-to-date prescriptions or a statement from your doctor stating the medication's trade name, manufacturer, chemical name, and dosage. While traveling, be sure to keep all medication with you in your carry-on luggage. For tips on packing a **first-aid kit** and other health essentials, see p. 19.

## INSURANCE

Travel insurance covers four basic areas: medical/health problems, property loss, trip cancellation/interruption, and emergency evacuation. Though regular insurance policies may well extend to travel-related accidents, you may consider purchasing separate travel insurance if the cost of potential trip cancellation, interruption, or emergency medical evacuation is greater than you can absorb. Prices for independent travel insurance generally run about US$50 per week for full coverage, while trip cancellation/interruption may be purchased separately at a rate of US$3-5 per day depending on length of stay.

**Medical insurance** (especially university policies) often covers costs incurred abroad; check with your provider. **Australians** traveling in Finland, Ireland, Italy, the Netherlands, Sweden, or the UK are entitled to many of the services that they would receive at home as part of the Reciprocal Health Care Agreement. **Homeowners' insurance** often covers theft during travel and loss of travel documents (passport, plane ticket, rail pass, etc.) up to US$500.

**ISIC** and **ITIC** (p. 14) provide basic insurance benefits to US cardholders, including US$100 per day of in-hospital sickness for up to 100 days and US$10,000 of accident-related medical reimbursement (see www.isicus.com for details). Cardholders have access to a toll-free 24hr. helpline for medical, legal, and financial emergencies. **American Express** (☎ 800-338-1670) grants most cardholders automatic collision and theft insurance on car rentals made with the card.

## USEFUL ORGANIZATIONS AND PUBLICATIONS

The American **Centers for Disease Control and Prevention** (CDC; ☎ 877-FYI-TRIP; www.cdc.gov/travel) maintains an international travelers' hotline and an informative website. Consult the appropriate government agency of your home country for consular information sheets on health, entry requirements, and other issues for various countries (see the listings in the box on **Travel Advisories**, p. 21). For quick information on health and other travel warnings, call the **Overseas Citizens Services** (M-F 8am-8pm from US ☎ 888-407-4747, from overseas 202-501-4444), or contact a passport agency, embassy, or consulate abroad. For information on medical evacuation services and travel insurance firms, see the US government's website at http://travel.state.gov/travel/abroad_health.html or the **British Foreign and Commonwealth Office** (www.fco.gov.uk). For general health information, contact the **American Red Cross** (☎ 202-303-4498; www.redcross.org).

# STAYING HEALTHY

Common sense is the simplest prescription for good health while you travel. Drink lots of fluids to prevent dehydration and constipation, and wear sturdy, broken-in shoes and clean socks.

**COMES IN HANDY.** A small bottle of liquid hand cleanser, a stash of moist towelettes, or even a package of baby wipes can keep your hands and face germ-free and refreshed on the road. The hand cleanser should have an alcohol content of at least 70% to be effective.

## ONCE IN WESTERN EUROPE

### ENVIRONMENTAL HAZARDS

**Heat exhaustion and dehydration:** Heat exhaustion leads to nausea, excessive thirst, headaches, and dizziness. Avoid it by drinking plenty of fluids, eating salty foods (e.g., crackers), abstaining from dehydrating beverages (e.g., alcohol and caffeinated beverages), and wearing sunscreen. Continuous heat stress can eventually lead to heatstroke, characterized by a rising temperature, severe headache, delirium and cessation of sweating. Victims should be cooled off with wet towels and taken to a doctor.

**Sunburn:** Always wear sunscreen (SPF 30 or higher) when spending time outdoors. If you get sunburned, drink more fluids than usual and apply an aloe-based lotion. Severe sunburns can lead to sun poisoning, a condition that can cause fever, chills, nausea, and vomiting. Sun poisoning should always be treated by a doctor.

**Hypothermia and frostbite:** A rapid drop in body temperature is the clearest sign of overexposure to cold. Victims may also shiver, feel exhausted, have poor coordination or slurred speech, hallucinate, or suffer amnesia. *Do not let hypothermia victims fall asleep.* To avoid hypothermia, keep dry, wear layers, and stay out of the wind. When the temperature is below freezing, watch out for frostbite. If skin turns white or blue, waxy,

**ESSENTIALS**

and cold, do not rub the area. Drink warm beverages, stay dry, and slowly warm the area with dry fabric or steady body contact until a doctor can be found.

**High Altitude:** Allow your body a couple of days to adjust to less oxygen before exerting yourself. Note that alcohol is more potent and UV rays are stronger at high elevations.

## INSECT-BORNE DISEASES

Many diseases are transmitted by insects—mainly mosquitoes, fleas, ticks, and lice. Be aware of insects in wet or forested areas. Especially while hiking and camping, wear long pants and long sleeves, tuck your pants into your socks, and use a mosquito net. **Ticks**—which can carry Lyme and other diseases—can be particularly dangerous in rural and forested regions.

**Tick-borne encephalitis:** A viral infection of the central nervous system transmitted during the summer by tick bites (primarily in wooded areas) or by consumption of unpasteurized dairy products. The risk of contracting the disease is relatively low, especially if precautions are taken against tick bites.

**Lyme disease:** A bacterial infection carried by ticks and marked by a circular bull's-eye rash of 2 in. or more. Later symptoms include fever, headache, fatigue, and aches and pains. Antibiotics are effective if administered early. Left untreated, Lyme can cause problems in joints, the heart, and the nervous system. If you find a tick attached to your skin, grasp the head with tweezers as close to your skin as possible and apply slow, steady traction. Removing a tick within 24hr. greatly reduces the risk of infection. Do not try to remove ticks with petroleum jelly, nail polish remover, or a hot match. Ticks usually inhabit moist, shaded environments and heavily wooded areas. If you are going to be hiking in these areas, wear long clothes and DEET.

**Other insect-borne diseases: Lymphatic filariasis** is a roundworm infestation transmitted by mosquitoes. Infection causes enlargement of extremities and has no vaccine. **Leishmaniasis,** a parasite transmitted by sand flies, can occur in rural areas of Western Europe. Common symptoms are fever, weakness, and swelling of the spleen, as well as skin sores. There is a treatment, but no vaccine.

## FOOD- AND WATER-BORNE DISEASES

Prevention is the best cure: be sure that your food is properly cooked and the water you drink is clean. If the region's tap water is known to be unsanitary, peel fruits and vegetables before eating them and avoid tap water (including ice cubes and anything washed in tap water, like salad). Watch out for food from markets or street vendors that may have been cooked in unhygienic conditions. Other culprits are raw shellfish, unpasteurized milk, and sauces containing raw eggs. Buy bottled water, or purify your own water by bringing it to a rolling boil or treating it with **iodine tablets;** note, however, that some parasites such as *giardia* have exteriors that resist iodine treatment, so boiling is more reliable. Always wash your hands.

**Giardiasis:** Transmitted through parasites and acquired by drinking untreated water from streams or lakes. Symptoms include diarrhea, cramps, bloating, fatigue, weight loss, and nausea. If untreated, it can lead to severe dehydration. Giardiasis occurs worldwide.

**Hepatitis A:** A viral infection of the liver acquired through contaminated water or shellfish from contaminated water. Symptoms include fatigue, fever, loss of appetite, nausea, dark urine, jaundice, vomiting, aches and pains, and light stools. The risk is highest in rural areas and the countryside, but it is also present in urban areas. Ask your doctor about the Hepatitis A vaccine or an injection of immune globulin.

**Traveler's diarrhea:** Results from drinking fecally contaminated water or eating uncooked and contaminated foods. Symptoms include nausea, bloating, and urgency. Try quick-energy, non-sugary foods with protein and carbohydrates to keep your strength up. Over-the-counter anti-diarrheals (e.g., Imodium) may counteract the problem. The most dangerous side effect is dehydration; drink 8 oz. of water with ½ tsp. of sugar or honey and a pinch of salt, try uncaffeinated soft drinks, or eat salted crackers. If you develop a fever or your symptoms don't go away after 4-5 days, consult a doctor. Consult a doctor immediately for treatment of diarrhea in children.

**Sexually transmitted infections (STIs):** Gonorrhea, chlamydia, genital warts, syphilis, herpes, HPV, and other STIs are easier to catch than HIV and can be just as serious. Though condoms may protect you from some STIs, oral or even tactile contact can lead to transmission. If you think you may have contracted an STI, see a doctor immediately.

# OTHER HEALTH CONCERNS

## MEDICAL CARE ON THE ROAD

While healthcare systems in Western Europe tend to be quite accessible and of high quality, medical care varies greatly across Eastern and Southern Europe. Major cities such as Prague have English-speaking medical centers or hospitals for foreigners. In general, medical service in these regions is not up to Western standards; though basic supplies are usually there, specialized treatment is not. Tourist offices may have names of local doctors who speak English. In the event of a medical emergency, contact your embassy for aid and recommendations. All EU citizens can receive free or reduced-cost first aid and emergency services by presenting a **European Health Insurance Card.**

If you are concerned about obtaining medical assistance while traveling, you may wish to employ special support services. The *MedPass* from **GlobalCare, Inc.,** 6875 Shiloh Rd. East, Alpharetta, GA 30005, USA (☎800-860-1111; www.globalcare.net), provides 24hr. international medical assistance, support, and medical evacuation resources. The **International Association for Medical Assistance to Travelers (IAMAT;** US ☎716-754-4883, Canada 519-836-0102; www.iamat.org) has free membership, lists English-speaking doctors worldwide, and offers detailed info on immunization requirements and sanitation. If your regular **insurance** policy does not cover travel abroad, you may wish to purchase additional coverage (see p. 22).

Those with medical conditions (such as diabetes, severe allergies, or epilepsy) may want to obtain a **MedicAlert** membership (US$40 per year), which includes among other things a stainless steel ID tag and a 24hr. collect-call number. Contact the MedicAlert Foundation International, 2323 Colorado Ave., Turlock, CA 95382, USA (☎888-633-4298, outside US ☎209-668-3333; www.medicalert.org).

## WOMEN'S HEALTH

Women traveling in unsanitary conditions are vulnerable to **urinary tract infections** (including bladder and kidneys). Over-the-counter medicines can sometimes alleviate symptoms, but if they persist, see a doctor. **Vaginal yeast infections** may flare up in hot and humid climates. Wearing loose-fitting trousers or a skirt and cotton underwear will help, as will over-the-counter remedies. Bring supplies if you are prone to infection, as it may be difficult to find the brands you prefer on the road. **Tampons, pads,** and **contraceptive devices** are widely available in most of Western Europe, but can be hard to find in areas of Eastern Europe—bring supplies with you. **Abortion** laws also vary from country to country. In much of Western Europe, abortion is legal during at least the first 10-12 weeks of pregnancy, but remains illegal in Ireland, Monaco, and Spain, except in extreme circumstances.

# KEEPING IN TOUCH

## BY EMAIL AND INTERNET

Email is popular and easily accessible in most of Europe. Though in some places it's possible to forge a remote link with your home server, in most cases this is a much slower (and more expensive) option than taking advantage of free **web-based email accounts** (e.g., www.gmail.com or www.hotmail.com). **Internet cafes** and the occasional free Internet terminal at a public library or university are listed in the **Practical Information** sections of major cities, and hostels frequently offer Internet access. For lists of additional cybercafes in Europe, check www.cybercaptive.com or www.cybercafe.com.

Increasingly, travelers find that taking their **laptops** on the road with them can be a convenient option for staying connected. Laptop users can call an Internet service provider via a modem using long-distance phone cards specifically intended for such calls. Another option is **Voice over Internet Protocol (VoIP).** A particularly popular VoIP provider, **Skype**, allows users to contact other users for free, and to call landlines and cell phones for an additional fee. Some Internet cafes allow travelers to connect their laptops, and those with Wi-Fi-enabled computers may be able to take advantage of an increasing number of Internet "hot spots," where they can get online for free or for a small fee. For info on insuring your laptop while traveling, see p. 22.

**WARY WI-FI.** Wireless hot spots make Internet access possible in public and remote places. Unfortunately, they also pose **security risks.** Hot spots are public, open networks that use unencrypted, unsecured connections. They are susceptible to hacks and "packet sniffing"—ways of stealing passwords and other private information. To prevent problems, disable ad hoc mode, turn off file sharing, turn off network discovery, encrypt your e-mail, turn on your firewall, beware of phony networks, and watch for over-the-shoulder creeps. Ask the establishment whose Wi-Fi you're using for the name of the network so you know you're on the right one. If you are in the vicinity and do not plan to access the Internet, turn off your wireless adapter.

## BY TELEPHONE

### CALLING HOME FROM EUROPE

You can usually make **direct international calls** from pay phones, but if you aren't using a phone card, you will need to feed the machine regularly. **Prepaid phone cards are a common and relatively inexpensive means of calling abroad.** Each one comes with a Personal Identification Number (PIN) and a toll-free access number. You call the access number and then follow the directions for dialing your PIN. To purchase prepaid phone cards, check online for the best rates; **www.calling-cards.com is a good place to start. Online providers generally send your access number and PIN via email, with no actual "card" involved.** You can also call home with prepaid phone cards purchased in Europe (see **Calling Within Europe**, p. 27). Keep in mind that phone cards can be very country-specific, so buying an international phone card once you arrive will probably save you a headache.

Another option is to purchase a **calling card,** linked to a major national telecommunications service in your home country. Calls are billed collect or to your account. To obtain a calling card, contact the appropriate company listed below.

**PLACING INTERNATIONAL CALLS.** All international dialing prefixes and country codes for Europe are shown in a chart on the **Inside Back Cover** of this book. To place international calls, dial:

1. The **international dialing prefix.** To call from **Australia,** dial 0011; **Canada** or the **US,** 011; **Ireland, New Zealand,** or the **UK,** 00.

2. The **country code** of the country you want to call. To call **Australia,** dial 61; **Canada** or the **US,** 1; **Ireland,** 353; **New Zealand,** 64; the **UK,** 44.

3. The **city/area code.** *Let's Go* lists the city/area codes for cities and towns in Europe opposite the city or town name, next to a ☎. If the 1st digit is a zero (e.g., 020 for London), omit it when calling from abroad (e.g., dial 20 from Canada to reach London).

4. The **local number.**

Where available, there are often advantages to purchasing calling cards online, including better rates and immediate access to your account. Companies that offer calling cards include: **AT&T Direct** (US ☎ 800-364-9292; www.att.com); **Canada Direct** (☎ 800-561-8868; www.infocanadadirect.com); **MCI WorldPhone** (US ☎ 800-777-5000; consumer.mci.com); **Telecom New Zealand Direct** (www.telecom.co.nz); **Telstra Australia** (☎ 1800 676 638; www.telstra.com). To call home with a calling card, contact the local operator for your service provider by dialing the appropriate toll-free access number. Placing a **collect call** through an international operator can be expensive, but may be necessary in case of an emergency. You can frequently call collect without even possessing a company's calling card just by calling its access number and following the instructions. *Let's Go* lists access numbers in the Essentials sections of each chapter.

## CALLING WITHIN EUROPE

The simplest way to call within a country is to use a public pay phone. However, much of Europe has switched to a **prepaid phone card** system, and in some countries you may have a hard time finding coin-operated phones. **Prepaid phone cards** (available at newspaper kiosks and tobacco stores), which carry a certain amount of phone time depending on the card's denomination, usually save time and money in the long run. The phone will tell you how much time, in units, you have left on your card. Another kind of prepaid phone card comes with a PIN and a toll-free access number. Instead of inserting the card into the phone, you call the access number and follow the directions on the card. These cards can be used to make international as well as domestic calls. Phone rates typically tend to be highest in the morning, lower in the evening, and lowest on Sunday and late at night.

## MOBILE PHONES

Cell phones are an increasingly popular option for travelers calling within Europe. In addition to greater convenience and safety, mobile phones often provide an economical alternative to expensive landline calls. Virtually all of Western Europe has excellent coverage, and the use of the **Global System for Mobiles (GSM)** allows one phone to function in multiple countries. To make and receive calls in Europe, you need a **GSM-compatible phone** and a **subscriber identity module (SIM) card,** a country-specific, thumbnail-sized chip that gives you a local phone number and plugs you into the local network. Many SIM cards are **prepaid,** meaning that they come with calling time included and you don't need to sign up a contract. Incoming calls are free. When you use up the prepaid time, you can buy additional cards (usually available at convenience stores) to "top up" your phone. For more information on GSM phones, check out www.orange.co.uk, www.roadpost.com, www.planetomni.com, www.telestial.com, or www.virginmobile.com.. Companies like **Cellular Abroad** (www.cellularabroad.com) rent cell phones for a variety of destinations, providing a simpler option than picking up a phone in-country.

 **GSM PHONES.** Just having a GSM phone doesn't mean you're necessarily good to go when you travel abroad. The majority of GSM phones sold in the United States operate on a different **frequency** (1900) than international phones (900/1800) and will not work abroad. Tri-band phones work on all three frequencies (900/1800/1900) and will operate through most of the world. Additionally, some GSM phones are **SIM-locked** and will only accept SIM cards from a single carrier. You'll need a **SIM-unlocked** phone to use a SIM card from a local carrier when you travel.

## TIME DIFFERENCES

All of Europe falls within 3hr. of Greenwich Mean Time (GMT). For more info, consult the time zone chart on the **Inside Back Cover.** GMT is 5hr. ahead of New York time, 8hr. ahead of Vancouver and San Francisco time, 10hr. behind Sydney time, and 12hr. behind Auckland time. Iceland is the only country in Europe to ignore Daylight Saving Time; fall and spring switchover times vary in countries that do observe Daylight Saving. For more info, visit www.worldtimeserver.com.

# BY MAIL

## SENDING MAIL HOME FROM EUROPE

**Airmail** is the best way to send mail home from Europe. From Western Europe to North America, delivery time averages about seven days. **Aerogrammes,** printed sheets that fold into envelopes and travel via airmail, are available at post offices and are the cheapest types of mail. Write "airmail" or "par avion" (or *por avión, mit Luftpost, via aerea,* etc.) on the front. **Surface mail** is by far the cheapest and slowest way to send mail. It takes one to two months to cross the Atlantic and one to three to cross the Pacific—good for heavy items you won't need for a while, such as souvenirs that you've acquired along the way. Check the **Essentials** section of each chapter for country-specific postal info.

## SENDING MAIL TO EUROPE

To ensure timely delivery, mark envelopes "airmail" in both English and the local language. In addition to standard postage systems, **Federal Express** (Australia ☎ 13 26 10, Canada and the US 800-463-3339, Ireland 1800 535 800, New Zealand 0800 733 339, the UK 08456 070 809; www.fedex.com) handles express mail services from most countries to Europe.

There are several ways to arrange pick-up of letters sent to you while you are abroad. Mail can be sent via **Poste Restante** (General Delivery; *Lista de Correos, Fermo Posta, Postlagernde Briefe,* etc.) to almost any city or town in Europe with a post office, though it can be unreliable in Eastern Europe. See individual country chapters for more info on addressing *Poste Restante* letters. The mail will go to a special desk in a town's central post office, unless you specify a post office by street address or postal code. It's best to use the largest post office, since mail may be sent there regardless. It's usually safer and quicker, though more expensive, to send mail express or registered. Bring your passport for pick-up; there may be a small fee. If the clerks insist that there is nothing for you, ask them to check under your first name as well. *Let's Go* lists post offices in the **Practical Information** section for each city and most towns.

**American Express's** travel offices throughout the world offer a free **Client Letter Service** (mail held up to 30 days and forwarded upon request) for cardholders who contact them in advance. Some offices provide these services to non-cardholders (especially AmEx Travelers Cheque holders), but call ahead to make sure. *Let's Go* lists AmEx locations for most large cities in **Practical Information** sections; for a complete list, call ☎ 800-528-4800 or visit www.americanexpress.com/travel.

# ACCOMMODATIONS

## HOSTELS

Many hostels are laid out dorm-style, often with large single-sex rooms and bunk beds, although private rooms sleeping two to four are becoming more common. They sometimes have kitchens and utensils, bike or moped rentals, storage areas, airport transportation, breakfast and other meals, laundry facilities, and Internet access. There can be drawbacks: some hostels close during certain daytime "lock-out" hours, have a curfew, don't accept reservations, impose a maximum stay, or—less frequently—require that you do chores. In Western Europe, a hostel dorm bed will average around US$15-30 and a private room around US$30-50.

> **A HOSTELER'S BILL OF RIGHTS.** There are certain standard features that we do not include in our hostel listings. Unless we state otherwise, you can expect that every hostel has free hot showers, no lockout, no curfew, some system of secure luggage storage, and no key deposit.

## HOSTELLING INTERNATIONAL (HI)

Joining the youth hostel association in your own country (listed below) automatically grants you membership privileges in **Hostelling International (HI),** a federation of national hosteling associations. Non-HI members may be allowed to stay in some hostels, but will have to pay extra. HI hostels are scattered throughout Western Europe and are typically less expensive than private hostels. HI's umbrella organization's website (www.hihostel.com), which lists the web addresses and phone numbers of all national associations, can be a great place to begin researching hosteling in a specific region. Other comprehensive hosteling websites include www.hostels.com and www.hostelplanet.com.

Most HI hostels also honor **guest memberships**—you'll get a blank card with space for six validation stamps. Each night you'll pay a nonmember supplement (one-sixth the membership fee) and earn one guest stamp; get six stamps and you're a member. In some countries you may need to remind the hostel reception. A new membership benefit is the **FreeNites** program, which allows hostelers to gain points toward free rooms. Most student travel agencies (see p. 14) sell HI cards, as do all of the national hosteling organizations listed below. All prices listed below are valid for **one-year memberships** unless otherwise noted.

**Australian Youth Hostels Association (AYHA),** 422 Kent St., Sydney, NSW 200 (☎ 02 9261 1111; www.yha.com.au). AUS$52, under 18 AUS$19.

**Hostelling International-Canada (HI-C),** 205 Catherine St. Ste. 400, Ottawa, ON K2P 1C3 (☎ 613-237-7884; www.hihostels.ca). CDN$35, under 18 free.

**An Óige (Irish Youth Hostel Association),** 61 Mountjoy St., Dublin 7 (☎ 830 4555; www.irelandyha.org). EUR€20, under 18 EUR€10.

**Hostelling International Northern Ireland (HINI),** 22-32 Donegall Rd., Belfast BT12 5JN (☎ 02890 32 47 33; www.hini.org.uk). UK£15, under 25 UK£10.

**Scottish Youth Hostels Association (SYHA),** 7 Glebe Cres., Stirling FK8 2JA (☎ 01786 89 14 00; www.syha.org.uk). UK£8, under 18 £4.

**Youth Hostels Association (England and Wales),** Trevelyan House, Dimple Rd., Matlock, Derbyshire DE4 3YH (☎08707 708 868; www.yha.org.uk). UK£16, under 26 UK£10.

**Hostelling International-USA,** 8401 Colesville Rd., Ste. 600, Silver Spring, MD 20910 (☎301-495-1240; www.hiayh.org). US$28, under 18 free.

> ⌂ **BOOKING HOSTELS ONLINE.** One of the easiest ways to ensure you've got a bed for the night is by reserving online. Click to the **Hostelworld** booking engine through **www.letsgo.com,** and you'll have access to bargain accommodations from Argentina to Zimbabwe with no added commission.

# HOTELS, GUESTHOUSES, AND PENSIONS

In Western Europe, **hotel singles** cost about US$30 (€23) per night, doubles US$40 (€30). You'll typically share a hall bathroom; a private bathroom and hot showers may cost extra. Some hotels offer "full pension" (all meals) and "half pension" (no lunch). Smaller **guesthouses** and **pensions** are often cheaper than hotels. If you make **reservations** in writing, note your night of arrival and the number of nights you plan to stay. After sending you a confirmation, the hotel may request payment for the first night. Often it's easiest to reserve over the phone with a credit card.

# OTHER TYPES OF ACCOMMODATIONS

## YMCAS AND YWCA

**Young Men's Christian Association (YMCA)** and **Young Women's Christian Association (YWCA)** lodgings are usually cheaper than a hotel but more expensive than a hostel. Not all locations offer lodging; those that do are often located in urban downtowns. Many YMCAs accept women and families; some will not lodge those under 18 without parental permission. **World Alliance of YMCAs,** 12 Clos Belmont, 1208 Geneva, SWI (☎41 22 849 5100; www.ymca.int), has more info and a register of Western European YMCAs with housing options.

**YMCA of the USA,** 101 North Wacker Dr., Chicago, IL 60606 (☎800-872-9622; www.ymca.net). Provides a listing of the nearly 1000 Ys across the US and Canada, as well as info on prices and services.

**European Alliance of YMCAs (YMCA Europe),** Na Porici 12, CZ-110 30 Prague 1, Czech Republic (☎420 22 487 20 20; www.ymcaeurope.com). Maintains listings of European Ys with opportunities to volunteer abroad.

## BED & BREAKFASTS (B&BS)

For a cozy alternative to impersonal hotel rooms, B&Bs (private homes with rooms available to travelers) range from acceptable to sublime. Rooms generally cost about €35 for a single and €70 for a double in Western Europe. Any number of websites provide listings for B&Bs. Check out **InnFinder** (www.inncrawler.com), **InnSite** (www.innsite.com), or **BedandBreakfast.com** (www.bedandbreakfast.com).

## UNIVERSITY DORMS

Many **colleges** and **universities** open their residence halls to travelers when school is not in session; some do so even during term-time. Getting a room may take a couple of phone calls and require advanced planning, but rates tend to be low and many offer free local calls and Internet. Where available, university dorms are listed in the **Accommodations** section of each city.

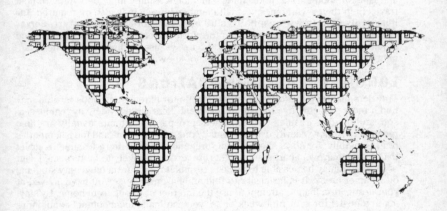

## PRIVATE ROOMS

In some Western European countries like Greece, the only accommodations in a backpacker's price range are rooms in **private houses** or **apartments.** Tourist offices will often know of owners seeking to rent their rooms to visitors. In larger towns and cities there are agencies that book private rooms. If renting directly from the owner, feel free to negotiate prices, and don't agree to anything before you see the room. This practice is illegal in some areas; check **local laws** before you rent a private room and always exercise caution when doing so.

## HOME EXCHANGES AND HOSPITALITY CLUBS

**Home exchange** offers the traveler various types of homes (houses, apartments, condominiums, villas, even castles), plus the opportunity to live like a native and to cut down on accommodation fees. For more info, contact HomeExchange.com Inc., P.O. Box 787, Hermosa Beach, CA 90254, USA (☎310 798 3864 or toll free 800-877-8723; www.homeexchange.com), **or** Intervac International Home Exchange (www.intervac.com; see site for phone listings by country).

**Hospitality clubs** link their members with individuals or families abroad who are willing to host travelers for free or for a small fee to promote cultural exchange and general good karma. In exchange, members usually must be willing to host travelers in their own homes; a small membership fee may also be required. **The Hospitality Club** (www.hospitalityclub.org) is a good place to start. **Servas** (www.servas.org) is an established, more formal, peace-based organization, and requires a fee and an interview to join. As always, use common sense when planning to stay with or host someone you do not know.

## LONG-TERM ACCOMMODATIONS

Travelers planning to stay in Western Europe for extended periods of time may find it most cost-effective to rent an **apartment.** Rent varies widely by region, season, and quality. Besides the rent itself, prospective tenants usually are also required to front a security deposit (usually one month's rent) and the last month's rent. Generally, for stays shorter than three months, it is more feasible to **sublet** than lease your own apartment. Sublets are also more likely to be furnished. Out of session, it may be possible to arrange to sublet rooms from university students on summer break. It is far easier to find an apartment once you have arrived at your destination than to attempt to use the Internet or phone from home. By staying in a hostel for your first week or so, you can make local contacts and, more importantly, check out your new digs before you commit.

## CAMPING

With Europe's vast terrain encompassing beaches, mountains, and plains, camping always has some new adventure to offer. Furthermore, you can explore nature for prices refreshingly easy on the wallet. Most towns have several campgrounds within walking distance, occasionally offering a cheap shuttle service to reach them. Even the most rudimentary **campings** (campgrounds) provide showers and laundry facilities, though almost all forbid campfires. In addition to tent camping, other patrons opt to drive RVs across Europe. Campgrounds usually charge a flat fee per person (usually around €4-6) plus a few euro extra for electricity, tents, cars, or running water. Most larger campgrounds also operate on-site general stores or cafes perfect for a quick, cheap bite. In some countries, it is illegal to pitch your tent or park your RV overnight along the road; look for designated camping areas within national parks, recognized campgrounds, or ask landowners permission before setting up residency on private property. In Sweden, Finland, and Norway, the right of public access permits travellers to tent one night in Scandinavia's forests and wilderness for free; for more info, see **Heading North**, p. 971.

If planning on using campgrounds as your go-to accommodation, consider buying a **International Camping Carnet (ICC,** US$45). Available through the association of Family Campers and RVers (☎800-245-9755; www.fcrv.org), the card entitles holders to discounts at some campgrounds and may save travelers from having to leave their passport as a deposit. National tourist offices offer more info on country-specific camping. Additionally, check out **Interhike** (www.interhike.com) which lists campgrounds by region. First-time campers may also want to peruse **KarmaBum Cafe** (www.karmabum.com) for suggested itineraries, packing lists, blogs, and camping recipes. For more info on outdoor activities in Western Europe, see **The Great Outdoors,** below.

# THE GREAT OUTDOORS

Camping can be a great way to see Europe on the cheap. There are organized **campgrounds** outside most cities. Showers, bathrooms, and a small restaurant or store are common; some sites have more elaborate facilities. Prices are low, usually US$5-15 per person plus additional charges for tents and cars. While camping is a cheaper option than hosteling, the cost of transportation to and from campgrounds can add up. Some parks and public grounds allow **free camping,** but check local laws. Many areas have additional park-specific rules. The **Great Outdoor Recreation Pages** (www.gorp.com) provides excellent general info.

**LEAVE NO TRACE.** Let's Go encourages travelers to embrace the "Leave No Trace" ethic, minimizing their impact on natural environments. Trekkers should set up camp on durable surfaces, use cookstoves instead of campfires, bury human waste away from water supplies, bag trash and carry it out with them, and respect wildlife and natural objects. For more detailed information, contact the **Leave No Trace Center for Outdoor Ethics,** P.O. Box 997, Boulder, CO 80306 (☎800-332-4100 or 303-442-8222; www.lnt.org).

# USEFUL RESOURCES

A variety of publishing companies offer hiking guidebooks to meet the educational needs of the novice or the expert. For information about biking, camping, and hiking, write or call the publishers listed below to receive a free catalog. Campers heading to Europe should consider buying an **International Camping Carnet.** Similar to a hostel membership card, it's required at a few campgrounds and provides discounts at others. It is available in North America from the **Family Campers and RVers Association** (www.fcrv.org) and in the UK from **The Caravan Club** (see below).

**Automobile Association,** Contact Centre, Carr Ellison House, William Armstrong Dr., Newcastle-upon-Tyne NE4 7YA, UK (☎08706 000 371; www.theaa.com). Publishes *Caravan and Camping Europe* and *Britain & Ireland* (UK£10) as well as road atlases for Europe as a whole and for Britain, France, Germany, Ireland, Italy, and Spain.

**The Caravan Club,** East Grinstead House, East Grinstead, West Sussex RH19 1UA, UK (☎01342 326 944; www.caravanclub.co.uk). For UK£35, members get access to campgrounds, insurance services, equipment discounts, maps, and a magazine.

**Sierra Club Books,** 85 2nd St., 2nd fl., San Francisco, CA 94105, USA (☎415-977-5500; www.sierraclub.org). Publishes general resource books on hiking and camping.

**The Mountaineers Books,** 1001 SW Klickitat Way, Ste. 201, Seattle, WA 98134, USA (☎206-223-6303; www.mountaineersbooks.org). Over 600 titles on hiking, biking, mountaineering, natural history, and conservation.

# WILDERNESS SAFETY

Staying **warm, dry,** and **well hydrated** are the keys to a happy and safe wilderness experience. Before any hike, prepare yourself for an emergency by packing a first-aid kit, a reflector, a whistle, high-energy food, extra water, raingear, a hat, mittens, and several **extra pairs of socks.** For warmth, wear wool or insulating synthetic materials designed for the outdoors. Cotton is a bad choice as it takes a ridiculously long time to dry and loses its insulating effect when wet.

Check **weather forecasts** often and pay attention to the skies when hiking, as weather patterns can change suddenly, especially in mountainous areas. Always let someone—a friend, your hostel staff, a park ranger, or a local hiking organization—know when and where you are going. Know your physical limits and do not attempt a hike beyond your ability.

# CAMPING AND HIKING EQUIPMENT

## WHAT TO BUY

Good camping equipment is both sturdy and light. North American suppliers tend to offer the most competitive prices.

**Sleeping Bags:** Most sleeping bags are rated by season; "summer" means 30-40°F (around 0°C) at night; "four-season" or "winter" often means below 0°F (-17°C). Bags are made of **down** (warm and light, but expensive, and miserable when wet) or of **synthetic** material (heavy, durable, and warm when wet). Prices range US$50-250 for a summer synthetic and US$200-300 for a good down winter bag. **Sleeping bag pads** include foam pads (US$10-30), air mattresses (US$15-50), and self-inflating mats (US$30-120). Bring a **stuff sack** to store your bag and keep it dry.

**Tents:** The best tents are free-standing (with their own frames and suspension systems), set up quickly, and only require staking in high winds. Low-profile dome tents are the best all-around. 2-person tents start at US$100, 4-person tents US$160. Make sure your tent has a rain fly and seal its seams with waterproofer. Other useful accessories include a **battery-operated lantern,** a plastic **groundcloth,** and a nylon **tarp.**

**Backpacks: Internal-frame** packs mold to your back, keep a lower center of gravity, and flex to allow you to hike difficult trails, while **external-frame packs** are more comfortable for long hikes over even terrain, as they carry weight higher and distribute it more evenly. Make sure your pack has a hip-belt to transfer weight to your legs. Any serious backpacking requires a pack of at least 4000 cu. in. (16,000cc), plus 500 cu. in. for sleeping bags in internal-frame packs. Sturdy backpacks cost anywhere from US$125 to 420—your pack is an area where it doesn't pay to economize. On your hunt for the perfect pack, fill up each prospective model with something heavy, strap it on, and walk around the store to get a sense of how the model distributes weight. Either buy a **rain cover** (US$10-20) or store your belongings in plastic bags inside your pack.

**Boots:** Be sure to wear hiking boots with good **ankle support.** They should fit snugly and comfortably over 1-2 pairs of **wool socks** and a pair of thin **liner socks.** Break in boots over several weeks before you go to spare yourself from blisters.

**Other Necessities: Synthetic layers,** like those made of polypropylene or polyester, and a pile jacket will keep you warm even when wet. A **space blanket** (US$5-15) will help you to retain body heat, and doubles as a groundcloth. Plastic **water bottles** are vital; look for shatter- and leak-resistant models. Carry **water-purification tablets** for when you can't boil water. Virtually every organized campground in Europe forbids fires or the gathering of firewood, so you'll need a **camp stove** (the classic Coleman starts at US$50) and a propane-filled **fuel bottle** to operate it. Also bring a **first-aid kit, pocket-knife, insect repellent,** and **waterproof matches** or a **lighter.**

## WHERE TO BUY IT

The online and mail-order companies listed below offer lower prices than many retail stores. A visit to a local camping or outdoors store will give you a good sense of the look and weight of certain items before you buy.

**Campmor,** 28 Parkway, P.O. Box 700, Upper Saddle River, NJ 07458, USA (☎800-525-4784; www.campmor.com).

**Cotswold Outdoor,** Unit 11 Kemble Business Park, Crudwell, Malmesbury Wiltshire SN16 9SH, UK (☎08704 427 755; www.cotswoldoutdoor.com).

**Discount Camping,** 833 Main North Rd., Pooraka, SA 5095, Australia (☎08 8262 3399; www.discountcamping.com.au).

# ORGANIZED ADVENTURE TRIPS

Organized adventure tours offer another way of exploring the wild. Activities include hiking, biking, skiing, canoeing, kayaking, rafting, climbing, photo safaris, and archaeological digs. Organizations that specialize in camping and outdoor equipment like REI and EMS (see above) are also a good source for info. **Specialty Travel Index** lists organized tour opportunities throughout Europe (from the US ☎888-624-4030, from elsewhere 415-455-1643; www.specialtytravel.com.)

# SPECIFIC CONCERNS

## SUSTAINABLE TRAVEL

As the number of travelers on the road rises, the detrimental effect they can have on natural environments becomes an increasing concern. With this in mind, Let's Go promotes the philosophy of **sustainable travel.** Through sensitivity to issues of ecology and sustainability, today's travelers can be a powerful force in preserving as well as restoring the places they visit.

**Ecotourism,** a rising trend in sustainable travel, focuses on the conservation of natural habitats and their use in building an economy without exploitation or overdevelopment. Travelers can make a difference by doing research in advance and by supporting organizations and establishments that pay attention to their impact on their natural surroundings and that strive to be environmentally friendly. **International Friends of Nature** (www.nfi.at) has info about sustainable travel options in Europe. For more information, see **Beyond Tourism,** p. 54.

**ECOTOURISM RESOURCES.** For more information on environmentally responsible tourism, contact one of the organizations below:

**Conservation International,** 2011 Crystal Dr., Ste. 500, Arlington, VA 22202, USA (☎800-406-2306 or 703-341-2400; www.conservation.org).

**Green Globe 21,** Green Globe vof, Verbenalaan 1, 2111 ZL Aerdenhout, The Netherlands (☎31 23 544 0306; www.greenglobe.com).

**International Ecotourism Society,** 1333 H St. NW, Ste. 300E, Washington, D.C. 20005, USA (☎202-347-9203; www.ecotourism.org).

**United Nations Environment Program,** 39-43 Quai André Citroën, 75739 Paris Cedex 15, FRA (☎33 1 44 37 14 50; www.uneptie.org/pc/tourism).

## RESPONSIBLE TRAVEL

The impact of tourist money on the destinations you visit should not be underestimated. The choices you make during your trip can have potent effects on local communities—for better or for worse. Travelers who care about the destinations they explore should become aware of the social, cultural, and political implications of the choices they make when they travel. Simple decisions such as buying local products instead of globally available ones, paying fair prices for products or services, and attempting to say a few words in the local language can have a strong, positive effect on the community.

**Community-based tourism** aims to channel tourist money into the local economy by emphasizing tours and cultural programs run by members of the host community and that benefit disadvantaged groups. This type of tourism also benefits the tourists themselves, as it often takes them beyond the traditional tours of the region. The *Ethical Travel Guide* (UK£13), a project of **Tourism Concern** (☎+44 020 7133 3330; www.tourismconcern.org.uk), is an excellent resource for info on community-based travel with a directory of 300 establishments in 60 countries.

# TRAVELING ALONE

Benefits to traveling alone include independence and a greater opportunity to connect with locals. However, solo travelers are more vulnerable to harassment and street theft. If traveling alone, look confident, try not to stand out as a tourist, and be careful in deserted or crowded areas. Avoid poorly lit areas. If questioned, never admit that you are traveling alone. In Eastern Europe, be particularly careful about train travel; some travelers find it safer to ride in more crowded compartments and to avoid traveling at night. Maintain regular contact with someone at home who knows your itinerary, and always research your destination before traveling. For more tips, pick up *Traveling Solo* by Eleanor Berman (Globe Pequot Press, US$18), visit www.travelaloneandloveit.com, or subscribe to **Connecting: Solo Travel Network,** 689 Park Rd., Unit 6, Gibsons, BC V0N 1V7, Canada (☎604-886-9099; www.cstn.org; membership US$30-48).

# WOMEN TRAVELERS

Women traveling on their own face some additional safety concerns, but it's easy to be adventurous without taking undue risks. If you are concerned, consider staying in hostels that offer single rooms that lock from the inside or rooms for women only. Stick to centrally located accommodations and avoid solitary late-night treks or metro rides. Always carry extra money for a phone call, bus, or taxi. **Hitchhiking** is never safe for lone women, or even for two women traveling together. Look as if you know where you're going, and approach older women or couples for directions if you're lost or uncomfortable. Generally, the less you look like a tourist, the better off you'll be. Dress modestly, especially in rural areas. Wearing a conspicuous **wedding band** sometimes helps prevent unwanted advances.

Your best answer to verbal harassment is no answer at all; feigning deafness, pretending you don't understand the language, or staring straight ahead will usually do the trick. The extremely persistent can sometimes be dissuaded by a firm, loud "Go away!" in the appropriate language. Seek out a police officer or a passerby if you are being harassed. Memorize the emergency numbers in places you visit, and consider carrying a whistle on your keychain. A self-defense course will both prepare you for a potential attack and raise your level of awareness (see **Self Defense,** p. 22).

# GLBT TRAVELERS

Attitudes toward gay, lesbian, bisexual, and transgendered (GLBT) travelers are particular to each region in Europe. On the whole, countries in Northern and Western Europe tend to be queer-friendly, while Eastern Europe harbors enclaves of tolerance in cities amid stretches of cultural conservatism. Countries like Romania that outlawed homosexuality as recently as 2002 are becoming more liberal today, and can be considered viable destinations for GLBT travelers. **Out and About** (www.planetout.com) has a newsletter and website addressing gay travel concerns. The online newspaper **365gay.com** (www.365gay.com/travel/travelchannel.htm) has a travel section, while the French-language site **netgai.com** (http://netgai.com/international/Europe) includes links to country-specific resources.

**Gay's the Word,** 66 Marchmont St., London WC1N 1AB, UK (☎020 72 78 76 54; http://freespace.virgin.net/gays.theword/). The largest gay and lesbian bookshop in the UK, with both fiction and non-fiction titles. Mail-order service available.

**Giovanni's Room,** 345 S. 12th St., Philadelphia, PA 19107, USA (☎215-923-2960; www.queerbooks.com). An international lesbian and gay bookstore with mail-order service (carries some of the publications listed below).

**International Lesbian and Gay Association (ILGA),** Avenue des Villas 34, 1060 Brussels, BEL (☎32 25 02 24 71; www.ilga.org). Provides political information, such as homosexuality laws of individual countries.

**ADDITIONAL RESOURCES.**
*Spartacus International Gay Guide 2006.* Bruno Gmunder Verlag and Briand Bedford (US$33).
*The Damron Men's Travel Guide 2006.* Gina M. Gatta, Damron Co. (US$20).
*The Gay Vacation Guide: The Best Trips and How to Plan Them.* Mark Chesnut, Kensington Books (US$15).

# TRAVELERS WITH DISABILITIES

European countries vary in accessibility to travelers with disabilities. Some tourist boards, particularly in Western and Northern Europe, provide directories on the accessibility of various accommodations and transportation services. If these services are not available, contact establishments directly. Be sure to inform airlines and hostels of any pertinent disabilities when making reservations; some time may be needed to prepare special accommodations. Guide **dog owners** should inquire as to the quarantine policies of each destination country.

   **Rail** is the most convenient form of travel for disabled travelers in Europe: many stations have ramps, and some trains have wheelchair lifts, special seating areas, and special toilets. All Eurostar, some InterCity (IC), and some EuroCity (EC) trains are wheelchair accessible. CityNightLine trains, French TGV (high speed), and Conrail trains feature special compartments. In general, the countries with the most **wheelchair-accessible rail networks** are: Denmark (IC and Lyn trains), France (TGVs and other long-distance trains), Germany (ICE, EC, IC, and IR trains), Ireland (most major trains), Italy (EC and IC trains), the Netherlands (most trains), Sweden (X2000s, most IC and IR trains), and Switzerland (all IC, most EC, and some regional trains). Austria, Poland, and the UK offer accessibility on selected routes. Bulgaria, the Czech Republic, Greece, Hungary, Slovakia, and Spain's rail systems have limited wheelchair accessibility. For those who wish to rent cars, some major **car rental** agencies (e.g., Hertz) offer hand-controlled vehicles.

## USEFUL ORGANIZATIONS

   **Access Abroad,** www.umabroad.umn.edu/access. A website devoted to making study abroad available to students with disabilities. The site is maintained by Disability Services, University of Minnesota, 230 Heller Hall, 271 19th Ave. S., Minneapolis, MN 55455, USA (☎612-626-7379).

**Accessible Journeys,** 35 W. Sellers Ave., Ridley Park, PA 19078, USA (☎800-846-4537; www.disabilitytravel.com). Designs tours for wheelchair users and slow walkers. The site has tips and forums for all travelers.

**Flying Wheels,** 143 W. Bridge St., P.O. Box 382, Owatonna, MN 55060, USA (☎507-451-5005; www.flyingwheelstravel.com). Specializes in escorted trips to Europe for people with physical disabilities; plans custom trips worldwide.

**The Guided Tour, Inc.,** 7900 Old York Rd., Ste. 114B, Elkins Park, PA 19027, USA (☎800-783-5841; www.guidedtour.com). Organizes travel programs for persons with developmental and physical challenges in Ireland, Italy, Spain, and the UK.

**Society for Accessible Travel and Hospitality (SATH),** 347 5th Ave., Ste. 610, New York, NY 10016, USA (☎212-447-7284; www.sath.org). An advocacy group that publishes free online travel information and the travel magazine *Open World* (annual subscription US$13, free for members). Annual membership US$45, students and seniors US$30.

# MINORITY TRAVELERS

In general, minority travelers will find a high level of tolerance in large cities; small towns and the countryside are less predictable. The increasingly mainstream reality of anti-immigrant sentiments means that travelers of African or Arab descent (regardless of their citizenship) may be the object of unwarranted assumptions and even hostility. The September 11 terrorist attacks on the United States and the July 7 attacks on the London Tube corresponded with an upsurge in anti-Muslim sentiments in Europe, while anti-Semitism also remains a very real problem in many countries, especially in France, Austria, and much of Eastern Europe. Discrimination is particularly forceful against Roma (gypsies) throughout much of Eastern Europe. Jews, Muslims, and other minority travelers should keep an eye out for skinheads, who have been linked to racist violence in Central and Eastern Europe, and elsewhere. The European Monitoring Centre on Racism and Xenophobia, Rahlgasse 3, 1060 Vienna, AUT (☎43 15 80 30; http://eumc.eu.int), publishes a wealth of country-specific statistics and reports. Travelers can consult **United for Intercultural Action, Postbus 413, 1000 AK, Amsterdam, NTH** (☎31 20 6834778; www.unitedagainstracism.org), for a list of over 500 country-specific organizations that work against discrimination. For more resources, contact **Youth United Against Racism in Europe,** P.O. Box 858, London, E11 1YG, UK (☎020 8558 7947).

# DIETARY CONCERNS

Vegetarians will find no shortage of meat-free dining options throughout most of Northern and Western Europe, although vegans may have a trickier time away from urban centers, where eggs and dairy can dominate traditional cuisine. The cuisine of Eastern Europe still tends to be heavy on meat and gravy, although major cities often boast surprisingly inventive vegetarian and ethnic fare.

The travel section of The Vegetarian Resource Group's website, at www.vrg.org/travel, has a comprehensive list of organizations and websites that are geared toward helping vegetarians and vegans traveling abroad. The website for the **European Vegetarian Union (EVU),** at www.europeanvegetarian.org, includes links to organizations in 26 European countries. For more information, consult *The Vegetarian Traveler: Where to Stay if You're Vegetarian, Vegan, Environmentally Sensitive,* by Jed and Susan Civic (Larson Publications; US$16), *Vegetarian Europe,* by Alex Bourke (Vegetarian Guides; US$17), and the indispensably multilingual *Vegan Passport* (The Vegan Society; US$5), along with the websites www.vegdining.com, www.happycow.net, and www.vegetariansabroad.com.

Those looking to keep kosher will find abundant dining options across Europe; contact synagogues in larger cities for information, or consult www.kashrut.com/

travel/Europe for country-specific resources. **Hebrew College Online** also offers a searchable database of kosher restaurants at www.shamash.org/kosher. Another good resource is the *Jewish Travel Guide*, edited by Michael Zaidner (Vallentine Mitchell; US$18). Travelers looking for halal groceries and restaurants will have the most success in France and Eastern European nations with substantial Muslim populations; consult www.zabihah.com for establishment reviews. **Keep in mind that** if you are strict in your observance, you may have to prepare your own food.

# OTHER RESOURCES

## TRAVEL PUBLISHERS AND BOOKSTORES

**The Globe Corner Bookstore,** 90 Mt. Auburn St., Cambridge, MA 02138 (☎617-492-6277; www.globecorner.com). The Globe Corner sponsors an Adventure Travel Lecture Series and carries a vast selection of guides and maps to every imaginable destination. Online catalog includes atlases and monthly staff picks of outstanding travel writing.

**Hippocrene Books,** 171 Madison Ave., New York, NY 10016 (☎718-454-2366; www.hippocrenebooks.com), publishes foreign-language dictionaries and learning guides, along with ethnic cookbooks and a smattering of guidebooks.

**Rand McNally,** 8255 N. Central Park, Skokie, IL 60076 (☎800-275-7263, outside the US 847-329-6656; www.randmcnally.com), sells its own country maps (US$10), along with maps from well-respected companies including Michelin, PopOut, and StreetWise.

## WORLD WIDE WEB

In 10min. at the keyboard, you can make a hostel reservation, get advice on travel hot spots from other intrepid travelers, or find out how much a train ride from Geneva to Nice costs. Listed here are some regional and travel-related sites to start off your surfing; other relevant websites are listed throughout the book. Because website turnover is high, use search engines to strike out on your own.

 **WWW.LETSGO.COM.** Our website features extensive content from our guides; a community forum where travelers can connect with each other, ask questions or advice, and share stories and tips; and expanded resources to help you plan your trip. Visit us to browse by destination and find information about ordering our titles!

**Backpacker's Ultimate Guide:** www.bugeurope.com. Tips on packing, transportation, and where to go. Also tons of country-specific travel information.

**BootsnAll.com:** www.bootsnall.com. Numerous resources for independent travelers, from planning your trip to reporting on it when you get back.

**How to See the World:** www.artoftravel.com. A compendium of great travel tips, from cheap flights to self defense to interacting with local culture.

**Travel Intelligence:** www.travelintelligence.net. A large collection of travel writing by distinguished travel writers.

**Travel Library:** www.travel-library.com. A fantastic set of links for general information and personal travelogues.

## INFORMATION ABOUT WESTERN EUROPE

**BBC News:** http://news.bbc.co.uk/europe. The latest coverage from one of Europe's most reputable sources for English-language news, for free.

**CIA World Factbook:** www.odci.gov/cia/publications/factbook/index.html. Tons of vital statistics on countries' geography, government, economy, and people.

**EUROPA:** http://europa.eu.int/index_en.htm. English-language gateway to the European Union, featuring news articles and a citizen's guide to EU institutions.

# a dead language lives

## a young classicist experiences italy yesterday and today

Although I had heard of Father Reginald Foster as a child, it was only seven years later as a Classics major that I

## "I wasn't studying a 'dead language' and tuning out the living city around me"

made the pilgrimage to Rome to study with Fr. Reggie, one of the Vatican's chief Latinists. I had traveled to Italy several times before and thought I would immerse myself exclusively in the old *lingua franca*. But I soon found that the more I read and spoke Latin, the more I came to understand and appreciate the modern Italian language and culture around me.

Since class did not begin until 2pm, I spent the mornings wandering. The irresistible scents wafting from the bakery on a side street off Vle. di Trastevere, the midday street festival in the Jewish Ghetto, or the cats prowling around the Mausoleum of Augustus are the city's best attractions—and are conveniently free.

In the afternoon, I journeyed back to the basement schoolroom at the top of the Gianicolo Hill. Fr. Reggie teaches Latin as if it were a living lanuage. He often began with musings—in Latin, naturally—on his arduous commute to work in the Vatican that morning in the face of the two-week-long taxi strike or on the intricacies of the national rail service. He devoted a portion of class every week to translating *acta diurna* (headlines) from English-language news magazines into Latin. We read everything from Thomas More to 1999 Papal marriage court decisions.

After three 1½hr. sessions, we would break for an evening of casual Latin conversation or reading *sub arboribus* (under the trees) in the garden of the Carmelite monastery.

Because of the length and pace of the course, I engaged Rome as a resident rather than as a tourist. Every day, during the break after the first class, I would wander down the street to the Star Café, where Remo, the jovial owner, would give me an espresso with an extra cookie. I spent the second recess selecting fruits from the neighborhood vendor. I got to know my neighborhood, Trastevere, through regular excursions to the nearby cheese shop and Standa supermarket and morning runs up the slopes of the Gianicolo hill and through the Doria Pamphilj Gardens. This routine helped ensure that I was not just studying a "dead language" and insulating myself from the very living city.

My Latin and Italian experiences came together while watching the final match of the World Cup with 200,000 fans in the Circus Maximus, the old Roman racetrack. The triumphant march of the *azzurri* through the tournament fostered a camaraderie that manifested itself in distinctly Italian ways. With gleeful grins, the owners of a local pizzeria not far from Fr. Reggie's class carved up watermelons and offered them *gratis* to us after the semifinal win over Germany. The victory over France even inspired T-shirts with a Latin slogan—a welcome sight despite a grammatical error.

A traveler to Rome armed with knowledge of Latin can unlock mysteries of the Eternal City that would remain otherwise indecipherable. Latin inscriptions everywhere tell stories of ceremony, betrayal, victory, and defeat. Engaging the language in Fr. Reggie's way—as a living embodiment of a humanistic tradition—gives the traveler a sense of how Italy has evolved into what it is today. It doesn't take long to realize that Rome is a city with an amazing past; Latin and its connection to Italian bridges that gap between the Rome of Caesar and chariots and the Rome of Prodi and Vespas.

*Clem Wood has spent summers in both Florence and Rome. He will graduate from Harvard in the spring of 2008 with an A.B. in Classics and plans to return to Italy for further adventures and studies in the near future.*

## A DIFFERENT PATH

# TRANSPORTATION

## GETTING TO WESTERN EUROPE

### BY PLANE

When it comes to airfare, a little effort can save you a bundle. Courier fares are the cheapest for those whose plans are flexible. Tickets sold by consolidators and standby seating are also good deals, but last-minute specials, airfare wars, and charter flights often beat these fares. The key is to hunt around, be flexible, and ask about discounts. Students, seniors, and those under 26 should never pay full price for a ticket.

### AIRFARES

Airfares to Western Europe peak between mid-June and early September; holidays are also expensive. The cheapest times to travel are November to mid-December and January to March. Midweek (M-Th morning) round-trip flights run US$50-100 cheaper than weekend flights, but they are generally more crowded and less likely to permit frequent-flier upgrades. Not fixing a return date ("open return") or arriving in and departing from different cities ("open jaw") can be pricier than buying a round-trip flight. Flights between Western Europe's capitals or regional hubs (Amsterdam, Berlin, London, Madrid, Paris) tend to be cheaper.

If your Western European destinations are part of a more extensive globe-hop, consider a round-the-world (RTW) ticket. Tickets usually include at least five stops and are valid for about a year; prices range US$1200-5000. Try **Northwest Airlines/KLM** (☎800-225-2525; www.nwa.com) or **Star Alliance** (www.staralliance.com), a consortium of 16 airlines including United.

### BUDGET AND STUDENT TRAVEL AGENCIES

While agents specializing in flights to Western **Europe** can make your life easy, they may not spend the time to find you the lowest possible fare—they get paid on commission. Travelers holding **ISICs** and **IYTCs** (p. 14) qualify for big discounts from student travel agencies. Most flights from budget agencies are on major airlines, but in peak season some may sell seats on less reliable chartered aircrafts.

**STA Travel,** 5900 Wilshire Blvd., Ste. 900, Los Angeles, CA 90036, USA (24hr. reservations and info ☎800-781-4040; www.statravel.com). A student and youth travel organization with over 150 offices worldwide, including US offices in many college towns. Ticket booking, travel insurance, rail passes, and more. Walk-in offices are located throughout Australia (☎03 92 07 59 00), New Zealand (☎09 309 9723), and the UK (☎08 701 630 026).

**Travel CUTS (Canadian Universities Travel Services Limited),** 187 College St., Toronto, ON M5T 1P7, Canada (☎888-592-2887; www.travelcuts.com). Offices across Canada and the US including Los Angeles, New York, Seattle, and San Francisco.

**USIT,** 19-21 Aston Quay, Dublin 2, Ireland (☎01 602 1904; www.usit.ie), Ireland's leading student/budget travel agency has 20 offices throughout Northern Ireland and the Republic of Ireland. Offers programs to work, study, and volunteer worldwide.

### COMMERCIAL AIRLINES

Commercial airlines' lowest regular offer is the **APEX** (Advance Purchase Excursion) fare, which provides confirmed reservations and allows "open-jaw" tickets.

✈ **FLIGHT PLANNING ON THE INTERNET.** The Internet may be the budget traveler's dream when it comes to finding and booking bargain fares, but the array of options can be overwhelming. Many airline sites offer special last-minute deals online, though some require membership logins or email subscriptions. Try www.airfrance.com, www.britishairways.com, www.icelandair.com, and www.lufthansa.de. **STA** (www.sta.com) and **StudentUniverse** (www.studentuniverse.com) provide quotes on student tickets, while **Expedia** (www.expedia.com), **Orbitz** (www.orbitz.com), and **Travelocity** (www.travelocity.com) offer full travel services. **Priceline** (www.priceline.com) lets you specify a price, and obligates you to buy any ticket that meets or beats it; **Hotwire** (www.hotwire.com) offers bargain fares but won't reveal the airline or flight times until you buy. Other sites that compile deals include www.bestfares.com, www.flights.com, www.lowestfare.com, www.onetravel.com, and www.travelzoo.com. There are tools available to sift through multiple offers; **Booking Buddy** (www.bookingbuddy.com), **SideStep** (www.sidestep.com), and **Kayak** (www.kayak.com) let you enter your trip information once and search multiple sites. Spain-based **eDreams** (www.edreams.com) is convenient to book budget flights within Europe. The **Air Traveler's Handbook** (www.faqs.org/faqs/travel/air/handbook), has comprehensive listings of everything you should know before boarding a plane.

Generally, reservations must be made seven to 21 days ahead of departure, with seven- to 14-day minimum stay and 90-day maximum stay restrictions. These fares carry hefty cancellation and change penalties (fees rise in summer). Reserve peak-season APEX fares early. Use **Expedia** or **Travelocity** to get an idea of the lowest published fares, then use the resources listed here to try to beat those fares. Low-season fares should be appreciably cheaper than the **high-season** ones listed here.

### TRAVELING FROM NORTH AMERICA

Basic round-trip fares to Western **Europe** range from roughly US$200-750: to **Frankfurt,** US$350-750; **London,** US$250-550; **Paris,** US$300-700. Standard commercial carriers like **American** (☎800-433-7300; www.aa.com), **United** (☎800-538-2929; www.ual.com), and **Northwest** (☎800-225-2525; www.nwa.com) will probably offer the most convenient flights, but they may not be the cheapest. Check **Lufthansa** (☎800-399-5838; www.lufthansa.com), **British Airways** (☎800-247-9297; www.britishairways.com), **Air France** (☎800-237-2747; www.airfrance.us), and **Alitalia** (☎800-223-5730; www.alitaliausa.com) for cheap tickets from destinations throughout the US to all over Western Europe.

### TRAVELING FROM THE UK AND IRELAND

Because of the many carriers flying from the British Isles to the continent, we only include discount airlines or those with cheap specials here. The **Air Travel Advisory Bureau** in London (☎870 737 0021; www.atab.co.uk) provides referrals to travel agencies and consolidators that offer discounted airfares out of the UK. **Cheapflights** (www.cheapflights.co.uk) publishes airfare bargains. For more info on budget airlines like Ryanair, see p. 44.

**Aer Lingus:** Ireland ☎08 18 36 50 00; www.aerlingus.com. Round-trip tickets from Cork, Dublin, and Shannon to destinations across Western Europe (€15-300).

**bmibaby:** UK ☎08 712 240 224; www.bmibaby.com. Departures from throughout the UK to destinations across Western Europe. Fares from UK£25.

**KLM:** UK ☎08 705 074 074; www.klmuk.com. Cheap round-trip tickets from 17 UK cities to destinations across Western Europe.

## TRAVELING FROM AUSTRALIA AND NEW ZEALAND

**Air New Zealand:** New Zealand ☎0800 73 70 00; www.airnz.co.nz. Auckland to London.

**Qantas Air:** Australia ☎13 13 13, New Zealand 800 00 14 00 14; www.qantas.com.au. Flights from Australia to London for around AUS$2000.

**Singapore Air:** Australia ☎13 10 11, New Zealand 0800 808 909; www.singaporeair.com. Flies from Adelaide, Auckland, Brisbane, Christchurch, Melbourne, Perth, Sydney, and Wellington to Western Europe.

**Thai Airways:** Australia ☎13 00 65 19 60, New Zealand 09 377 3886; www.thaiair.com. Auckland; Melbourne; Perth; Sydney to Amsterdam, Frankfurt, and London.

# AIR COURIER FLIGHTS

Those who travel light should consider courier flights. Couriers help transport cargo on international flights by using their checked luggage space for freight. Generally, couriers are limited to carry-ons and must deal with complex flight restrictions. Most flights are round-trip only, with short fixed-length stays (usually one week) and a limit of a one ticket per issue. Most of these flights also operate only out of major gateway cities, mostly in North America. Round-trip courier fares from the US to Western Europe run about US$200-500. Most flights leave from L.A., Miami, New York, or San Francisco in the US; and from Montreal, Toronto, or Vancouver in Canada. Generally, you must be over 18 (in some cases 21). In summer, the most popular destinations usually require an advance reservation of about two weeks (you can usually book up to two months ahead). Super-discounted fares are common for "last-minute" flights (3-14 days ahead).

**Air Courier Association,** 1767A Denver West Blvd., Golden, CO 80401, USA (☎800-461-8556; www.aircourier.org). Departure cities throughout Canada and the US to **Western Europe** (US$150-650). 1-year membership US$39, plus some monthly fees.

**International Association of Air Travel Couriers** (IAATC; www.courier.org). Courier and consolidator fares from North America to Europe. 1-year membership US$45.

**Courier Travel** (www.couriertravel.org). Searchable online database. 6 departure points in the US to various European destinations. Membership US$40 per household.

# STANDBY FLIGHTS

Traveling standby requires considerable flexibility in arrival and departure dates and cities. Companies dealing in standby flights sell vouchers rather than tickets, along with the promise to get you to your destination (or near your destination) within a certain window of time (typically 1-5 days). You call in before your specific window of time to hear your flight options and the probability that you will be able to board each flight. You can then decide which flights you want to try to make, show up at the right airport at the appropriate time, present your voucher, and board if space is available. Vouchers can usually be bought for both one-way and round-trip travel. You may receive a refund only if every available flight within your date range is full; if you opt not to take an available (but less convenient) flight, you can only get credit toward future travel. Read agreements carefully with any company offering standby flights, as tricky fine print abounds. To check on a company's service record in the US, contact the **Better Business Bureau** (☎703-276-0100; www.bbb.org). It is difficult to receive refunds, and clients' vouchers will not be honored when an airline fails to receive payment in time.

# TICKET CONSOLIDATORS

Ticket consolidators, also known as **"bucket shops,"** buy unsold tickets in bulk from commercial airlines and sell them at discounted rates. Look for tiny ads in the Sunday travel section of any major newspaper; call quickly, as availability is almost always extremely limited. Not all bucket shops are reliable, so insist on a receipt that gives full details of flight restrictions, refund policies, and tickets, and pay by credit card (in spite of the 2-5% fee) so you can stop payment on your purchase if you don't receive your tickets. For more info, see www.travel-library.com/air-travel/consolidators.html.

## CHARTER FLIGHTS

Tour operators contract charter flights with airlines to fly extra loads of passengers during peak season. Charter flights fly less frequently than major airlines, make refunds particularly difficult, and are almost always fully booked. Schedules and itineraries may also change or be cancelled at the last moment (as late as 48hr. before the trip, and without a full refund). Check-in, boarding, and baggage claim are often much slower; however, charter flights can also be cheaper. Discount clubs and fare brokers offer members savings on last-minute charter and tour deals. Study contracts closely; you don't want to end up with an unwanted overnight layover. **Travelers Advantage** (☎ 800-548-1116; www.travelersadvantage.com; US$10 monthly fee includes discounts and cheap flight directories) specializes in **European** travel and tour packages.

✈ **BEFORE YOU BOOK.** The emergence of no-frills airlines has made hop-scotching around Western Europe by air increasingly affordable. Many budget airlines save money by flying out of smaller, regional airports. A flight billed as Paris to Barcelona might in fact be from Beauvais (80km north of Paris) to Girona (104km northeast of Barcelona). For a more detailed list of these airlines by country, check out www.whichbudget.com.

**easyJet:** UK ☎ 0871 244 2366; www.easyjet.com. 72 destinations in Belgium, Czech Republic, Denmark, Estonia, France, Germany, Greece, Hungary, Italy, Latvia, the Netherlands, Poland, Portugal, Slovakia, Slovenia, Spain, Switzerland, and the UK.

**Ryanair:** Ireland ☎ 0818 303 030, UK 0871 246 00 00; www.ryanair.com. Serves 120 destinations in Austria, Belgium, the Czech Republic, France, Germany, Ireland, Italy, Latvia, the Netherlands, Poland, Portugal, Scandinavia, Spain, and the UK.

**Sterling:** Denmark ☎ 70 10 84 84, UK ☎ 870 787 8038. The first Scandinavian-based budget airline. Connects Denmark, Norway, and Sweden to 33 cities across Europe.

**Wizz Air:** Hungary ☎ 01 470 9499, Poland ☎ 22 351 9499; www.wizzair.com. 47 destinations in Belgium, Bulgaria, Croatia, France, Germany, Greece, Hungary, Ireland, Italy, the Netherlands, Norway, Poland, Romania, Slovenia, Spain, Sweden, and the UK.

You'll have to buy shuttle tickets to reach the airports of many of these airlines, and add an hour or so to your travel time. After round-trip shuttle tickets and fees for checked luggage and other services that might come standard on other airlines, that €0.01 sale fare can suddenly jump to €20-100. Prices vary dramatically; shop around, book months ahead, pack light, and stay flexible to nab the best fares.

# GETTING AROUND WESTERN EUROPE

## BY PLANE

A number of European airlines offer discount coupon packets. Most are only available as add-ons for transatlantic passengers, but some are stand-alone offers. Most must be purchased before departure. **Europe by Air's** *FlightPass* allows non-EU residents to country-hop to over 150 European cities for US$99 or $129 per flight, plus tax. (☎888-321-4737; www.europebyair.com.) **Iberia's** *Europass* allows passengers flying from the US to Spain to add a minimum of two destinations in Western Europe for $139 per trip. (US ☎800-772-4642; www.iberia.com.)

# BY TRAIN

Trains in Western Europe are comfortable, convenient, and reasonably fast, although quality varies by country. Second-class compartments, which seat two to six, are great places to meet fellow travelers. However, trains can be unsafe. For safety tips, see p. 21. For long trips, make sure you are on the correct car, as trains sometimes split at crossroads. Towns listed in parentheses on European train schedules require a switch at the town listed immediately before the parentheses.

You can either buy a **rail pass,** which allows you unlimited travel within a particular region for a given period of time, or rely on buying individual **point-to-point** tickets as you go. Almost all countries give students or youths (usually defined as anyone under 26) direct discounts on regular domestic rail tickets, and many also sell a student or youth card that provides 20-50% off all fares for up to a year.

> **※TIP※** **GOING MY WAY, SAILOR?** In Europe, fares are listed as either **single** (one-way) or **return** (round-trip). "Period returns" require you to return within a specific number of days; "day return" means you must return on the same day. Round-trip fares on trains and buses in Western Europe are simply twice the one-way fare. Unless stated otherwise, Let's Go always lists single fares.

**RESERVATIONS.** While seat reservations are required only for selected trains (usually on major lines), you are not guaranteed a seat without one (usually US$5-30). You should strongly consider reserving in advance during peak holiday and tourist seasons (at the very latest, a few hours ahead). You will also have to purchase a **supplement** (US$10-50) or special fare for high-speed or high-quality trains such as Spain's AVE, Switzerland's Cisalpino, Finland's Pendolino, Italy's ETR500 and Pendolino, Germany's ICE, and certain French TGVs. InterRail holders must also purchase supplements (US$3-20) for trains like EuroCity, InterCity, Sweden's X2000, and many French TGVs; supplements are often unnecessary for Eurail Pass and Europass holders.

**OVERNIGHT TRAINS.** On night trains, you won't waste valuable daylight hours traveling and you can avoid the hassle and expense of staying at a hotel. However, the main drawbacks include discomfort, sleepless nights, and the lack of scenery. The risk of theft also increases dramatically at night. **Sleeping accommodations** on trains differ from country to country, but typically you can either sleep upright in your seat (supplement about $2-10) or pay for a separate space. **Couchettes** (berths) typically have four to six seats per compartment (supplement about US$10-50 per person); **sleepers** (beds) in private sleeping cars offer more privacy and comfort, but are considerably more expensive (supplement US$40-150). If you are using a rail pass valid only for a restricted number of days, inspect train schedules to maximize the use of your pass: an overnight train or boat journey often uses up only one of your travel days if it departs after 7pm.

**SHOULD YOU BUY A RAIL PASS?** Rail passes were conceived to allow you to jump on any train in Europe, go wherever you want whenever you want, and change your plans at will. In practice, it's not so simple. You still must stand in line to validate your pass, pay for supplements, and fork over cash for seat and couchette reservations. More importantly, rail passes don't always pay off. Estimate the point-to-point cost of each leg of your journey; add them up and

TRANSPORATION

compare the total with the cost of a rail pass. If you are planning to spend a great deal time on trains, hopping between big cities, a rail pass will probably be worth it. But in many cases, especially if you are under 26, point-to-point tickets may prove a cheaper option.

In Scandinavia, where distances are long and rail prices are high, a **Scanrail Pass** is often your best bet. A rail pass won't always pay for itself in Belgium, Greece, Ireland, Italy, Luxembourg, the Netherlands, Portugal, or Spain, where train fares are reasonable, distances short, or buses preferable. If, however, the total cost of your trips nears the price of the pass, the convenience of avoiding ticket lines may be worth the difference.

## MULTINATIONAL RAIL PASSES

**EURAIL PASSES.** Eurail is valid in most of Western Europe: Austria, Belgium, Denmark, Finland, France, Germany, Greece, Hungary, Italy, Luxembourg, the Netherlands, Norway, Portugal, the Republic of Ireland, Romania, Spain, Sweden, and Switzerland. It is **not valid** in the UK. **Eurail Global Passes,** valid for a number of consecutive days, are best for those planning on spending extensive time on trains every few days. Other types of global passes are valid for any 10 or 15 (not necessarily consecutive) days within a two-month period, and are more cost-effective for those traveling longer distances less frequently. **Eurail Pass Saver** provides first-class travel for travelers in groups of two to five (prices are per person). **Eurail Pass Youth** provides parallel second-class perks for those under 26. Passholders receive a timetable for major routes and a map with details on bike rental, car rental, hotel, and museum discounts. Passholders often also receive reduced fares or free passage on many boat, bus, and private railroad lines.

The **Eurail Select Pass** is a slimmed-down version of the Eurail Pass: it allows five to 15 days of unlimited travel in any two-month period within three, four, or five bordering European countries. **Eurail Select Passes** (for individuals) and **Eurail Select Pass Saver** (for people traveling in groups of two to five) range from US$429/365 per person (5 days) to US$949/805 (15 days). The **Eurail Select Pass Youth** (second-class), for those ages 12-25, costs US$279-619. You are entitled to the same **freebies** afforded by the Eurail Pass, but only when they are within or between countries that you have purchased.

| EURAIL GLOBAL PASSES | 15 DAYS | 21 DAYS | 1 MONTH | 2 MONTHS | 3 MONTHS |
|---|---|---|---|---|---|
| Eurail Pass Adult | US$675 | US$879 | US$1089 | US$1539 | US$1899 |
| Eurail Pass Saver | US$569 | US$745 | US$925 | US$1309 | US$1615 |
| Eurail Pass Youth | US$439 | US$569 | US$709 | US$999 | US$1235 |

| OTHER GLOBAL PASSES | 10 DAYS IN 2 MONTHS | 15 DAYS IN 2 MONTHS |
|---|---|---|
| Eurail Pass Adult | US$799 | US$1049 |
| Eurail Pass Saver | US$679 | US$895 |
| Eurail Pass Youth | US$519 | US$679 |

**SHOPPING AROUND FOR A EURAIL.** Eurail Passes can be bought only by non-Europeans from non-European distributors. These passes must be sold at uniform prices determined by the EU. However, some travel agents tack on a US$10 handling fee, and others offer certain bonuses with purchase, so shop around. Also, keep in mind that pass prices rise annually, so if you're planning to travel early in the year, you can save cash by purchasing before January 1 (you have 3 months from the purchase date to validate your pass in Europe). It's best to buy a Eurail before leaving; only a few places in major cities sell them, and at a marked-up price. You can get a replacement for a lost pass only if you have purchased insurance on it under the **Pass Security Plan** (US$14). Eurail Passes are available through travel agents, student travel agencies like **STA** (p. 41), and **Rail Europe** (Canada ☎ 800-361-7245, US 877-257-2887; www.raileurope.com). It's also possible to buy directly from **Eurail's** website, www.eurail.com. Shipping is free to North America, Australia, New Zealand, and Canada.

**OTHER MULTINATIONAL PASSES.** If you have lived for at least six months in one of the European countries where InterRail Passes are valid, they are an economical option. The **InterRail Pass** allows travel within 30 European countries (excluding the passholder's country of residence). The **Global Pass** is valid for a given number of days (not necessarily consecutive) within a 10 day to one-month period. (5 days within 10 days, adult 1st class €329, adult 2nd class €249, youth €159; 10 days within 22 days €489/359/239; 1 month continuous €809/599/399.) The One Country Pass limits travel within one European country (€33 for 3 days). Passholders receive free admission to many museums, as well as discounts on accommodations, food, and many ferries to Ireland, Scandinavia, and the rest of Europe. Passes are available at www.interrailnet.com, from travel agents, at major train stations in Europe, and through online vendors (www.railpassdirect.co.uk).

# DOMESTIC RAIL PASSES

If you are planning to spend a significant amount of time within one country or region, a national pass—valid on all rail lines of a country's rail company—may be more cost-effective than a multinational pass. Many national passes are limited and don't provide the free or discounted travel on private railways and ferries that Eurail does. Some of these passes can be bought only in Europe, some only outside Europe; check with a rail pass agent or with national tourist offices.

**NATIONAL RAIL PASSES.** The domestic analogs of the Eurail pass, national rail passes are valid either for a given number of consecutive days or for a specific number of days within a given time period. Usually, they must be purchased before you leave. Though they will usually save travelers some money, the passes may actually be a more expensive alternative to point-to-point tickets. For more info, check out www.raileurope.com/us/rail/passes/single_country_index.htm.

**RAIL-AND-DRIVE PASSES.** In addition to rail passes, many countries (as well as Eurail) offer rail-and-drive passes, which combine car rental with rail travel—a good option for travelers who wish both to visit cities accessible by rail and to travel in the surrounding areas. Prices range US$301-2376, depending on the type of pass, type of car, and number of people included. Children under the age of 11 cost US$102-500, and adding more days costs US$72-105 per day (see **By Car**, p. 48).

**FURTHER READING & RESOURCES ON TRAIN TRAVEL.**
**Info on rail travel and rail passes:** www.raileurope.com or www.eurail.com.
**Point-to-point fares and schedules:** www.raileurope.com/us/rail/fares_schedules/index.htm. Allows you to calculate whether buying a rail pass would save you money.
**Railsaver:** www.railpass.com/new. Uses your itinerary to calculate the best rail pass for your trip.
**European Railway Server:** www.railfaneurope.net. Links to rail servers throughout Europe.
**Thomas Cook European Timetable,** updated monthly, covers all major and most minor train routes in Europe. Buy directly from Thomas Cook (www.thomascooktimetables.com).

## BY BUS

In some cases, buses prove a better option than train travel. In Britain and Hungary, the bus and train systems are on par; in Greece, Ireland, Spain, and Portugal, bus networks are more extensive, efficient, and often more comfortable; in Iceland and parts of northern Scandinavia, bus service is the only ground transportation available. In the rest of Europe, bus travel is more of a gamble. Scattered offerings from private companies are often cheap, but sometimes unreliable. Amsterdam, Athens, London, Munich, and Oslo are centers for lines that offer long-distance rides across Western Europe. **International bus passes** allow unlimited travel on a hop-on, hop-off basis between major European cities, often at cheaper prices than rail passes.

**Eurolines,** offices in 19 countries (UK ☎15 82 40 45 11; www.eurolines.co.uk or www.eurolines.com). The largest operator of Europe-wide coach services. Unlimited 15-day (high season €329, under 26 €279; low season €199/169) or 30-day (high season €439/359; low season €299/229) travel passes offer unlimited transit among 40 major European cities. Discount passes €29 or €39.

**Busabout,** 258 Vauxhall Bridge Rd., London, SW1V 1BS, UK (☎020 7950 1661; www.busabout.com). Offers 4 interconnecting bus circuits. 1 loop US$579; 2 loops US$890; 3 loops US$1319. Flexipass with 6 stops $475; additional stops $59. Also sells discounted international SIM cards (US$9; from US$0.29 per min.)

## BY CAR

Cars offer speed, freedom, access to the countryside, and an escape from the town-to-town mentality of trains. Although a single traveler won't save by renting a car, four usually will. If you can't decide between train and car travel, you may benefit from a combination of the two; RailEurope and other rail pass vendors offer rail-and-drive packages. Fly-and-drive packages are also often available from travel agents or airline/rental agency partnerships. Before setting off, know the laws of the countries in which you'll be driving (e.g., both seat belts and headlights must be on at all times in **Scandinavia,** and remember to keep left in **Ireland and the UK**). For an informal primer on European road signs and conventions, check out www.trav-lang.com/signs. The **Association for Safe International Road Travel (ASIRT)** can provide more specific information about road conditions (☎301-983-5252; www.asirt.org). ASIRT considers road travel (by car or bus) to be relatively **safe** in Denmark, Ireland, the Netherlands, Norway, Sweden, Switzerland, and the UK, and relatively **unsafe** in Turkey and many parts of Eastern Europe. Western Europeans use **unleaded gas** almost exclusively, but it's not available in many gas stations in Eastern Europe.

### RENTING A CAR

Cars can be rented from a US-based firm (Alamo, Avis, Budget, or Hertz) with European offices, from a European-based company with local representatives (Europcar), or from a tour operator (Auto Europe, Europe By Car, or Kemwel Holiday Autos) that will arrange a rental for you from a European company. Multinationals offer greater flexibility, but tour operators often strike better deals. Ask airlines about special fly-and-drive packages; you may get up to a week of free or discounted rental. See **Costs and Insurance,** p. 50, for more info. Minimum age requirements vary but tend to fall in the range of 21-25, with some as low as 18. There may be an additional insurance fee for drivers under 25. At most agencies, to rent a car, you'll need a driver's license from home with proof that you've had it for a year or an International Driving Permit (p. 51). Car rental in Europe is available through the following agencies:

TRANSPORTATION

**Auto Europe** (Canada and the US ☎ 888-223-5555; www.autoeurope.com).

**Avis** (Australia ☎ 13 63 33, Canada and the US 800-331-1212, New Zealand 0800 655 111, UK 08700 100 287; www.avis.com).

**Budget** (Australia ☎ 1300 36 28 48, Canada ☎ 800-268-8900, New Zealand ☎ 0800 283 438, UK 87 01 56 56 56, US 800-527-0700; www.budgetrentacar.com).

**Europcar International** (UK ☎ 18 70 607 5000; www.europcar.com).

**Europe by Car** (US ☎ 800-223-1516; www.europebycar.com).

**Hertz** (Canada and the US 800-654-3001; www.hertz.com).

### COSTS AND INSURANCE

Expect to pay US$200-600 per week, plus tax (5-25%), for a tiny car with a manual transmission; automatics can double or triple the price. Larger vehicles and 4WD will also raise prices. Reserve and pay in advance if at all possible. It is less expensive to reserve a car from the US than from Europe. Rates are generally lowest in Belgium, Germany, the Netherlands, and the UK, higher in Ireland and Italy, and highest in Scandinavia and Eastern Europe. Some companies charge fees for traveling into Eastern Europe. National chains often allow one-way rentals, with pickup in one city and drop-off in another. There is usually a minimum hire period and sometimes an extra drop-off charge of several hundred dollars.

Many rental packages offer unlimited kilometers, while others offer a fixed distance per day with a per-kilometer surcharge after that. Be sure to ask whether the price includes **insurance** against theft and collision. Remember that if you are driving a conventional vehicle on an **unpaved road** in a rental car, you are almost never covered by insurance; ask about this before leaving the rental agency. Always check if prices quoted include tax and collision insurance; some credit card companies provide insurance, allowing their customers to decline the collision damage waiver. Ask about discounts and check the terms of insurance, particularly the size of the deductible. Beware that cars rented on an **American Express** or **Visa/Mastercard Gold or Platinum** credit cards in Europe might not carry the automatic insurance that they would in some other countries. Check with your credit card company. Insurance plans almost always come with an **excess** (or deductible) for conventional vehicles; excess is usually higher for younger drivers and for 4WD. This provision means you pay for all damages up to the specified sum, unless they are the fault of another vehicle. The excess you will be quoted applies to collisions with other vehicles; other collisions ("single-vehicle collisions") will cost you even more. The excess can often be reduced or waived for an additional charge. Remember to return the car with a **full tank** of gas to avoid high fuel charges. Gas prices vary by country, and are generally highest in Scandinavia. Throughout Europe, fuel tends to be cheaper in cities than in outlying areas.

## LEASING A CAR

Leasing can be cheaper than renting, especially for more than 17 days. It is often the only option for those aged 18 to 21. The cheapest leases are agreements to buy the car and then sell it back to the manufacturer at a prearranged price. Leases generally include insurance coverage and are not taxed. The most affordable ones usually originate in Belgium, France, or Germany. Expect to pay US$1000-2000 for 60 days. **Renault Eurodrive** leases new cars in a tax-free "all-inclusive" package to qualifying non-EU citizens (Australia ☎ 9299 33 44, Canada ☎ 450-461-1149, New Zealand ☎ 0800 807 778, US ☎ 212-730-0676; www.renault-eurodrive.com).

## BUYING A CAR

If you're brave and know what you're doing, buying a used car or van in Europe and selling it just before you leave can provide the cheapest wheels for long trips. Check with consulates for import-export laws concerning used vehicles, registration, and safety and emission standards.

## ON THE ROAD

**Road conditions** and **regional hazards** are variable throughout Europe. Steep, curvy mountain roads may be closed in the winter. Road conditions in Eastern Europe are often poor as a result of maintenance issues and inadequately enforced traffic laws; many travelers prefer public transportation. Western European roads are generally excellent, but each area has its own dangers. In Scandinavia, for example, drivers should be on the lookout for moose and elk; on the Autobahn, the threat may come from cars speeding by at 150kph. In this book, region-specific hazards are listed in country introductions. Carry emergency equipment with you (see **Driving Precautions,** below) and know what to do in case of a breakdown. Car rental companies often have phone numbers for emergency services.

> **!** **DRIVING PRECAUTIONS.** When traveling in summer, bring **water** ( 5L per person per day) for drinking and for the radiator. For long drives to unpopulated areas, register with police before beginning the trip, and again upon arrival at the destination. Check with the local automobile club for details. Make sure tires are in good repair and have enough air, and get good maps. A **compass** and a **car manual** can also be very useful. Always carry a **spare tire** and **jack, jumper cables, extra oil, flares,** a **flashlight** (torch), and **heavy blankets** (in case your car breaks down at night or in the winter). A **cell phone** may help in an emergency. If you don't know how to change a tire, learn before heading out, especially if you're traveling in deserted areas. Blowouts on dirt roads are very common. If the car breaks down, stay with your car to wait for help.

## DRIVING PERMITS AND CAR INSURANCE

**INTERNATIONAL DRIVING PERMIT (IDP).** To drive a car in **Europe**, you must **be over 18 and** have an International Driving Permit (IDP), though certain countries (such as the UK) allow travelers to drive with a valid American or Canadian license for a limited number of months. It may be a good idea to get an IDP anyway, in case you're in a situation (e.g., you get in an accident or become stranded in a small town) where the police do not know English; information on the IDP is printed in 11 languages, including French, German, Italian, Portuguese, Russian, Spanish, and Swedish.

Your IDP, valid for one year, must be issued in your home country before you depart. An application for an IDP usually requires one or two photos, a current local license, an additional form of identification, and a fee of around US$20. To apply, contact your country's automobile association (such as the AAA in the US or the CAA in Canada). Be wary of buying IDPs from unauthorized online vendors.

**CAR INSURANCE.** If you rent, lease, or borrow a car, you will need an International Insurance Certificate, or Green Card, to certify that you have liability insurance and that it applies abroad. Green Cards can be obtained at car rental agencies, car dealerships (for those leasing cars), some travel agents, and some border crossings. Rental agencies may require you to purchase theft insurance in countries they consider to have a high risk of auto theft.

## BY CHUNNEL FROM THE UK

Traversing 27 mi. under the sea, the Chunnel is undoubtedly the fastest, most convenient, and least scenic route from England to France.

**BY TRAIN. Eurostar,** Eurostar House, Waterloo Station, London SE1 8SE (UK ☎ 08 705 186 186; www.eurostar.com) runs frequent trains between London and the continent. Ten to 28 trains per day run to 100 destinations including Paris (4hr., US$75-400, 2nd class), Disneyland Paris, Brussels, Lille, and Calais. Book online, at major rail stations in the UK, or at the office above.

**BY BUS.** Eurolines provides bus-ferry combinations (see p. 48).

**BY CAR. Eurotunnel,** Customer relations, P.O. Box 2000, Folkestone, Kent CT18 8XY (UK ☎ 08 705 353 535; www.eurotunnel.co.uk) shuttles cars and passengers between Kent and Nord-Pas-de-Calais. Return fares for vehicle and all passengers range from UK£223-253 with car. Same-day return costs UK£19-34, two- to five-day return for a car UK£123-183. Book online or via phone. Travelers with cars can also look into sea crossings by ferry (see below).

# BY BOAT

Most long-distance ferries are quite comfortable; the cheapest ticket typically includes a reclining chair or couchette. Fares jump sharply in July and August. Ask for discounts; ISIC holders can often get student fares, and Eurail Pass holders get reductions and sometimes free trips. You'll occasionally have to pay a port tax (around US$10). The fares below are **one-way** for **adult foot passengers** unless otherwise noted. Though standard round-trip fares are usually twice the one-way fare, **fixed-period returns** (usually within 5 days) may be cheaper. Ferries run **year-round** unless otherwise noted. Bringing a **bike** costs up to US$15 in high season.

## FERRIES FROM BRITAIN AND IRELAND

Ferries are frequent and dependable. The main route across the English Channel from Britain to France is Dover-Calais. The main ferry port on England's southern coast is Portsmouth, with connections to France and Spain. Ferries also cross the Irish Sea, connecting Northern Ireland with Scotland and England, and the Republic of Ireland with Wales. See the directory at www.seaview.co.uk/ferries.html.

**Brittany Ferries:** UK ☎ 08709 076 103, France ☎ 825 828 828, Spain ☎ 942 360 611; www.brittany-ferries.com. **Cork** to **Roscoff, FRA** (14hr.); **Plymouth** to **Roscoff, FRA** (6hr.) and **Santander, SPA** (18hr.); **Poole** to **Cherbourg, FRA** (4¼hr.); **Portsmouth** to **St-Malo** (10¾hr.) and **Caen, FRA** (5¾hr.).

**DFDS Seaways:** UK ☎ 0871 522 9955; www.dfdsseaways.co.uk. **Harwich** to **Cuxhaven** (19½hr.) and **Esbjerg, DEN** (18hr.); **Newcastle** to **Amsterdam, NTH** (16hr.), **Kristiansand, NOR** (18¼hr.), and **Gothenburg, SWE** (26hr.).

**Irish Ferries:** Nothern Ireland ☎ 353 818 300 400; Republic of Ireland ☎ 08 18 30 04 00, Great Britain ☎ 87 05 17 17 17; www.irishferries.ie. **Rosslare** to **Pembroke** (3¾hr.) and **Cherbourg** or **Roscoff, FRA** (18hr.). **Holyhead** to **Dublin, IRE** (2-3hr.).

**P&O Ferries:** UK ☎ 08 705 980 333; www.posl.com. **Dover** to **Calais, FRA** (1¼hr., 25 per day, UK £10-20); **Hull** to **Rotterdam, NTH** (10hr.) and **Zeebrugge, BEL** (12½hr.).

**SeaFrance:** France ☎ 03 21 17 70 33, UK ☎ 08 705 71 17 11; www.seafrance.com. **Dover** to **Calais** (1½hr., 15 per day, UK£12).

## MEDITERRANEAN AND AEGEAN FERRIES

Mediterranean ferries may be the most glamorous, but they can also be the most turbulent. Ferries run from Spain to Morocco, from Italy to Tunisia, and from France to both Morocco and Tunisia. Reservations are recommended, especially in July and August. Schedules are erratic, with varying prices for similar routes. Shop around, and beware of small companies that don't take reservations.

Ferries traverse the Adriatic from Ancona, ITA to Split, CRO and from Bari, ITA to Dubrovnik, CRO. Ferries also cross the Aegean, from Ancona, ITA to Patras, GCE and from Bari, ITA to Igoumenitsa and Patras, GCE. **Eurail** is valid on certain ferries between Brindisi, ITA and Corfu, Igoumenitsa, and Patras, GCE. Countless ferry companies operate on these routes; see country chapters for more info.

# BY MOPED AND MOTORCYCLE

**Motorized bikes** and **mopeds** don't use much gas, can be put on trains and ferries, and are a good compromise between costly car travel and the limited range of bicycles. However, they're uncomfortable for long distances, dangerous in the rain, and unpredictable on rough roads. Always wear a helmet, and never ride with a backpack. If you've never ridden a moped before, a twisting Alpine road is not the place to start. Expect to pay about US$20-35 per day; try auto repair shops, and remember to bargain. **Motorcycles** are more expensive and normally require a license, but are better for long distances. Before renting, ask if the price includes tax and insurance, or you may be hit with an unexpected fee. Avoid handing your passport over as a deposit; if you have an accident or mechanical failure you may not get it back until you cover all repairs. Pay ahead of time instead.

# BY THUMB

> **!** Let's Go strongly urges you to consider the risks before you choose to hitch. We do not recommend hitchhiking, and none of the information presented here is intended to do so.

No one should hitch without careful consideration of the risks involved. Hitching means entrusting your life to a unknown person and risking theft, assault, sexual harassment, and unsafe driving. However, some travelers report that hitchhiking in Europe allows them to meet locals and travel in areas where public transportation is sketchy. **Britain** and **Ireland** are probably the easiest places in Western Europe to get a lift. Hitching in **Scandinavia** is slow but steady. Long-distance hitching in the developed countries of northwestern Europe demands close attention to expressway junctions, rest stop locations, and destination signs. Hitching in southern Europe is generally mediocre. In some Eastern European countries, the line between hitching and taking a taxi is virtually nonexistent.

Hitchhiking at night can be particularly dangerous; experienced hitchers stand in well-lit places. For women traveling alone or even two women traveling together, hitching is simply too dangerous. A man and a woman are a safer combination, two men will have a harder time, and three will go nowhere. Experienced hitchers pick a spot outside of built-up areas, where drivers can stop, return to the road without causing an accident, and have time to look over potential passengers as they approach. Hitching (or even standing) on super-highways is usually illegal: one may only thumb at rest stops or at the entrance ramps to highways. Finally, success often depends on appearance.

Most Western European countries have ride services that pair drivers with riders; fees vary according to destination. **Eurostop** (www.taxistop.be/index_ils.htm), Taxistop's ride service, is one of the largest in Europe. Also try **Allostop** in France (French-language website www.allostop.net) and **Verband der Deutschen Mitfahrzentralen** in Germany (German-language website www.mitfahrzentrale.de). Not all organizations screen drivers and riders.

# BEYOND TOURISM

## A PHILOSOPHY FOR TRAVELERS

**HIGHLIGHTS OF BEYOND TOURISM IN WESTERN EUROPE**

**EXCAVATE** old skulls and castles in **France** (p. 267) and **Germany** (p. 390).

**PROTECT** hatchling sea turtles on the coasts of **Greece** (p. 501).

**POLITICK** as an intern at NATO in **Belgium** (p. 108).

**TEACH** English to European campers across **Italy** (p. 616).

As a tourist, you are always a foreigner. While hostel-hopping and sightseeing can be fun, you may want to consider going *beyond* tourism. Experiencing a foreign place through studying, volunteering, or working can help reduce that stranger-in-a-strange-land feeling. With this Beyond Tourism chapter, *Let's Go* hopes to promote a better understanding of Europe and to provide suggestions for those who want more than a photo album out of their travels.

There are several options for those who seek to participate in Beyond Tourism activities. Opportunities for **volunteering** with both local and international organizations are limitless. **Studying** in a new environment can be enlightening, whether through direct enrollment in a local university or an independent research project. **Working** is a way to immerse yourself in local culture while financing your travels.

As a **volunteer** in Western Europe, you can participate in projects from castle-cleaning in France to protecting endangered Loggerhead turtles in Greece, either on a short-term basis or as the main component of your trip. **Studying** at a college or in a language program is another option. Those who choose to study abroad in Western Europe often find the immersion in the region's educational environment to be much more rewarding and genuine than the backpacker trail alone. Many travelers also structure their trips by the **work** available to them along the way, ranging from odd jobs on-the-go to full-time, long-term stints in cities. The availability and legality of temporary work varies widely across Western Europe. If you are interested in working your way across the continent, we recommend picking up *Let's Go* city and country guides.

# VOLUNTEERING

Volunteering can be a powerful and fulfilling experience, especially when combined with the thrill of traveling in a new place. Whether your passion is for ecological, political, or social work, Western Europe can channel your energies. Most people who volunteer in Western Europe do so on a short-term basis at organizations that make use of drop-in or once-a-week volunteers. The best way to find opportunities that match your interests and schedule may be to check with local or national volunteer centers. Those looking for longer, more intensive volunteer experiences usually choose to go through a parent organization that takes care of logistical details and often provides a group environment and support system—for a fee. There are two main types of organizations—religious and secular—although there are rarely restrictions on participation in either.

**WHY PAY MONEY TO VOLUNTEER?** Many volunteers are surprised to learn that some organizations require large fees or "donations." While this may seem ridiculous, such fees often keep the organization afloat, in addition to covering airfare, room, board, and administrative expenses for the volunteers. (Other organizations must rely on private donations and government subsidies.) If you're concerned about how a program spends its fees, request an annual report or finance account. A reputable organization won't refuse to inform you of how volunteer money is spent.

Pay-to-volunteer programs might be a good idea for young travelers who are looking for more support and structure (such as pre-arranged transportation and housing), or anyone who would rather not deal with the uncertainty implicit in creating a volunteer experience from scratch.

## ONLINE DIRECTORIES: VOLUNTEERING

**www.alliance-network.org.** Umbrella website that brings together various international service organizations.

**www.idealist.org.** Provides extensive listings of service opportunities.

**www.worldvolunteerweb.org.** Lists organizations and events around the world.

## COMMUNITY DEVELOPMENT

If working closely with locals and helping in a hands-on fashion appeals to you, check out community development options. Many returning travelers report that working among locals was one of their most rewarding experiences.

**Global Volunteers,** 375 E. Little Canada Rd., St. Paul, MN 55109, USA (☎800-487-1074; www.globalvolunteers.org). A variety of 1- to 3-week volunteer programs throughout Europe. Fees range US$50-3000, including room and board but not airfare.

**Habitat for Humanity,** 121 Habitat St., Americus, GA 31709, USA (☎229-924-6935; www.habitat.org). A Christian non-profit organization coordinating 9- to 14-day service trips in Britain, Germany, Greece, Hungary, Ireland, the Netherlands, Poland, Portugal, and Switzerland. Participants aid local families in constructing future homes. Program costs fluctuate around US$1300-2200.

**Service Civil International Voluntary Service (SCI-IVS),** 5505 Walnut Level Rd., Crozet, VA 22932, USA (☎206-350-6585; www.sci-ivs.org). Arranges placement in 2- to 3-week outdoor service camps, or "workcamps," or 3-month teaching opportunities throughout Europe. 18+. Registration fee US$195, including room and board but not travel expenses.

**Volunteer Abroad,** 7800 Point Meadows Dr., Ste. 218 Jacksonville, FL 32256, USA (☎720-570-1702; www.volunteerabroad.com/search.cfm). Offers a variety of programs in Western Europe.

## CONSERVATION

As more people realize that long-cherished habitats and structures are in danger, diverse programs have stepped in to aid the concerned in lending a hand.

**Club du Vieux Manoir,** Ancienne Abbaye du Moncel, 60700 Pontpoint, FRA (☎33 03 44 72 33 98; http://cvmclubduvieuxmanoir.free.fr). Offers year-long and summer programs restoring castles and churches throughout France. €15 annual membership and insurance fee. Costs €14 per day, including food and tent.

BEYOND TOURISM

**Earthwatch Institute,** 3 Clock Tower Pl., Ste. 100, P.O. Box 75, Maynard, MA, 01754, USA (☎800-776-0188; www.earthwatch.org). Arranges 2-day to 3-week programs promoting the conservation of natural resources. Fees vary based on program location and duration. Costs range US$400-4000, including room and board but not airfare.

**The National Trust,** P.O. Box 39, Warrington, WA5 7WD, UK (☎44 0870 458 4000; www.nationaltrust.org.uk/volunteers). Arranges numerous volunteer opportunities, including Working Holidays. Working Holidays from £60 per week, including room and board but not travel expenses.

**World-Wide Opportunities on Organic Farms (WWOOF),** WWOOF Administrator, Moss Peteral, Brampton CA8 7HY, England, UK (www.wwoof.org). Arranges volunteer work with organic and eco-conscious farms around the world. Must become a member of WWOOF in the country in which you plan to work; prices vary by country.

# HUMANITARIAN AND SOCIAL SERVICES

Western Europe's complex, war-torn history has provided many opportunities to help rebuild. Numerous peace programs often prove to be fulfilling for those interested in humanitarian work.

**Brethren Volunteer Service (BVS),** 1451 Dundee Ave., Elgin, IL 60120, USA (☎800-323-8039; www.brethrenvolunteerservice.org). Peace and social justice based programs in various Western European countries. Min. commitment of 2 yr., must be 21 to serve overseas. US$75 fee for background check and additional US$500 fee for international volunteers.

**Simon Wiesenthal Center,** 1399 South Roxbury Dr., Los Angeles, CA 90035, USA (☎800-900-9036; www.wiesenthal.org). Fights anti-Semitism and Holocaust denial throughout Europe. Small, variable donation required for membership.

**Volunteers for Peace,** 1034 Tiffany Rd., Belmont, VT 05730, USA (☎802-259-2759; www.vfp.org). Arranges placement in camps throughout Europe. US$30 membership required for registration. Programs average US$250-500 for 2-3 weeks.

# STUDYING

**VISA INFORMATION.** Different countries have different requirements for study-abroad students. Ask the local consulate for info about acquiring a visa. Generally, applicants must be able to provide a passport, proof of enrollment, insurance, and financial support before their visa can be issued.

Study-abroad programs range from basic language or culture courses to college-level classes. To choose a program best fitting your needs, research as much as possible before making your decision. Determine costs and duration, as well as what kind of students participate and what accommodations are provided.

In programs with large groups of students who speak the same language, there is a trade-off. You may feel more comfortable, but you will not have the same opportunity to practice a foreign language or to befriend other international students. For accommodations, dorm life provides a better opportunity to mingle with fellow students, but there is less of a chance to experience the local scene. If you live with a family, there is a potential to build lifelong friendships and to experience day-to-day life in more depth, but famial conditions can vary greatly.

# UNIVERSITIES

Most university-level study-abroad programs are conducted in the local language, although many programs offer classes in English and beginner- and lower-level language courses. Those who are relatively fluent in a foreign language may find it cheaper to enroll directly in a university abroad, although getting college credit may be more difficult. You can search www.studyabroad.com for various semester-abroad programs that meet your criteria, including your desired location and focus of study. Where applicable, we note region specific programs. The following resources can help place students in university programs abroad or have their own branch in Western Europe.

## ONLINE DIRECTORIES: STUDY ABROAD

These websites are good resources for finding programs that cater to your particular interests. Each has links to various study-abroad programs broken down by a variety of criteria, including desired location and focus of study.

**www.petersons.com/stdyabrd/sasector.html.** Lists summer and term-time study-abroad programs at accredited institutions that usually offer cross credits.

**www.studyabroad.com.** A great starting point for finding college- or high-school-level programs in foreign languages or specific academic subjects. Also includes information for teaching and volunteering opportunities.

**www.westudyabroad.com.** Lists language courses and college-level programs in a number of European countries.

## AMERICAN PROGRAMS

The following is a list of organizations that can either help place students in university programs abroad or that have their own branch in Western Europe.

**American Institute for Foreign Study,** College Division, River Plaza, 9 W. Broad St., Stamford, CT 06902, USA (☎800-727-2437; www.aifsabroad.com). Organizes programs for high-school and college study in universities in Austria, Britain, the Czech Republic, France, Hungary, Ireland, Italy, Russia, and Spain. Summer programs US$5200-6500; Semester-long programs US$11,000-16,000. Scholarships available.

**Council on International Educational Exchange (CIEE),** 7 Custom House St., 3rd fl., Portland, ME, 04101, USA (☎800-407-8839; www.ciee.org/study). Sponsors work, volunteer, academic, and internship programs in Belgium, Britain, the Czech Republic, France, Hungary, Ireland, Italy, the Netherlands, Spain and Turkey for around US$10,000 per semester. Also offers volunteer opportunities across Europe. US$30 application fee.

**International Association for the Exchange of Students for Technical Experience (IAESTE),** 10400 Little Patuxent Pkwy. Ste. 250, Columbia, MD 21044, USA (☎410-997-3068; www.iaeste.org). Offers 8- to 12-week internships in Europe for college students who have completed 2 years' study in a particular trade.

**School for International Training, College Semester Abroad,** Kipling Rd., P.O. Box 676, Brattleboro, VT 05302, USA (☎888-272-7881 or 802-258-7751; www.sit.edu/studyabroad). Semester-long programs in Europe cost around US$12,900-16,000. Also runs **The Experiment in International Living** (☎800-345-2929; fax 802-258-3428; www.usexperiment.org), 3- to 5-week summer programs that offer high school students cross-cultural homestays, community service, ecological adventure, and language training in Europe for US$1900-5000.

## LANGUAGE SCHOOLS

Language schools can be independently run international or local organizations or divisions of foreign universities. Rarely offering college credit, they are a good alternative to university study for a deeper focus on a language or a less rigorous courseload. These programs are also good for younger high school students who might not feel comfortable in a university program. Worthwhile programs include:

BEYOND TOURISM

**Association of Commonwealth Universities (ACU),** Woburn House, 20-24 Tavistock Sq., London WC1H 9HF, UK (☎020 7380 6700; www.acu.ac.uk). Publishes information about Commonwealth Universities, including those in Cyprus and the UK.

**Eurocentres,** Seestr. 247, CH-8038 Zürich, SWI (☎41 1 485 50 40; www.eurocentres.com). Language programs for beginning to advanced students with homestays in Britain, France, Germany, Ireland, Italy, Spain, and Switzerland.

**Language Immersion Institute,** SCB 106, State University of New York at New Paltz, 1 Hawk Dr., New Paltz, NY 12561, USA (☎845-257-3500; www.newpaltz.edu/lii). 2-week summer language courses and some overseas courses in French, German, Greek, Hungarian, Italian, Polish, Portugese, Spanish, and Swedish. Around US$1000 for a 2-week course, not including accommodations.

**Sprachcaffe Languages Plus,** 413 Ontario St., Toronto, ON M5A 2V9, CAN (☎888-526-4758; www.sprachcaffe.com). Language classes in France, Germany, Italy, the Netherlands, and Spain for US$200-600 per week. Homestays available. Also offers French and Spanish language and travel programs for teenagers.

# WORKING

As with volunteering, work opportunities tend to fall into two categories: long-term jobs that allow travelers to integrate into a community or short-term jobs to finance the next leg of their travels. In Western Europe, people who want to work long-term might find success where their language skills are in demand, such as in teaching or working with tourists. Employment opportunities for those who want short-term work may be more limited and are generally contingent upon the city or region's economic needs. In addition to local papers, international English-language newspapers, such as the *International Herald Tribune* (www.iht.com), often list job opportunities in their classified sections. If applicable, travelers should also consult federally run employment offices. Note that working abroad often requires a special work visa; see the box below for info about obtaining one.

> **VISA INFORMATION. EU Citizens:** The EU's 2004 and 2007 enlargements led the 15 previous member states (EU-15) to fear waves of Eastern European immigrants would flood their labor markets. This fear caused some members of the union to institute a transition period of up to 7 years during which citizens of the new EU countries may still need a visa or permit to work. EU-15 citizens generally have the right to work in the pre-enlargement countries for up to 3 months without a visa; longer-term employment usually requires a work permit. By law, all EU-15 citizens are given equal consideration for jobs not directly related to national security.
> **Everyone else:** Getting a work visa in Europe is difficult for non-EU citizens. Different countries have different laws for employing foreigners; ask at your local embassy for specific info. The process is invariably time-consuming and frustrating. Having a job lined up before braving the bureaucratic gauntlet can speed up the process, as employers can perform much of the administrative leg-work.

# LONG-TERM WORK

If you're planning to spend more than three months working in Western Europe, search for a job well in advance. International placement agencies are often the easiest way to find employment abroad, especially for those interested in teaching English. Although often only available to college students, **internships** are a good way to segue into working abroad; although they are often un- or underpaid, many say the experience is well worth it. Be wary of advertisements for companies claiming to be able get you a job abroad for a fee—often the same listings are available online or in newspapers. Some organizations include:

**Escapeartist.com** (http://jobs.escapeartist.com). International employers post directly to this website; various European jobs advertised.

**International Cooperative Education,** 15 Spiros Way, Menlo Park, CA, 94025, USA (☎ 650-323-4944; www.icemenlo.com). Finds summer jobs in Belgium, Britain, Germany, and Switzerland. $200 application fee and a $600 placement fee.

**StepStone** (www.stepstone.com, branches across Europe listed at www.stepstone.com/EN/Company/Locations). Database covering international employment in Austria, Belgium, Britain, Denmark, France, Germany, Italy, the Netherlands, Norway, Portugal, and Sweden. Several search options and a constantly updated list of openings.

## TEACHING ENGLISH

Teaching jobs abroad are rarely well-paid, although some private American schools offer competitive salaries. Volunteering as a teacher in lieu of getting paid is a popular option; even then, teachers often receive some sort of a daily stipend to help with living expenses. Almost always, you must have at least a bachelor's degree to be a full-fledged teacher, though college undergraduates can often get summer positions teaching or tutoring. The difficulty of finding teaching jobs varies by country; EU countries often give EU applicants priority. Many schools require teachers to have a **Teaching English as a Foreign Language (TEFL)** certificate. Not having this certification does not necessarily exclude you from finding a teaching job, but certified teachers often find higher-paying positions. Native English speakers working in private schools are most often hired for English-immersion classrooms where the local language is not spoken. Those teaching in poorer public schools are more likely to be working in both English and the native tongue. Placement agencies or university programs are the best resources for finding jobs. The alternative is to contact schools directly or to try your luck once you get there. The best time to look for the latter is several weeks before the school year starts. The following organizations are helpful in placing teachers in Europe:

**International Schools Services (ISS),** 15 Roszel Rd., P.O. Box 5910, Princeton, NJ 08543, USA (☎ 609-452-0990; www.iss.edu). Hires teachers for more than 200 international and American schools around the world; candidates should have 2 years teaching experience and/or teacher certification. 2-year commitment expected.

**Teaching English as a Foreign Language (TEFL),** TEFL Professional Network Ltd., 72 Pentyla Baglan Rd., Port Talbot, SA12 8AD, UK (www.tefl.com). Maintains the most extensive database of openings throughout Europe. Offers job training and certification.

## AU PAIR WORK

Au pairs, typically women (although sometimes men) aged 18-27, work as live-in nannies, caring for children and doing light housework in foreign countries in exchange for room, board, and a small spending allowance or stipend. One perk of the job is that it allows you to get to know a country without the high expenses of traveling. Drawbacks, however, can include mediocre pay and long hours. Au pairs in Western Europe typically work 25-40hr. per week and receive US$300-450 per month. Much of the au pair experience depends on the family with whom you are placed. The agencies below are a good starting point for looking for employment.

**Childcare International, Ltd.,** Trafalgar House, Grenville Pl., London NW7 3SA (☎ 44 020 8906 3116; www.childint.co.uk). Offers au pair and nanny placement in Austria, Belgium, Britain, the Czech Republic, Denmark, Finland, France, Germany, Greece, Holland, Hungary, Iceland, Italy, Luxembourg, the Netherlands, Norway, Poland, Portugal, Spain, Sweden, and Switzerland.

**InterExchange,** 161 6th Ave., New York, NY, 10013, USA (☎ 212-924-0446; www.interexchange.org). Au pair, internship, and short-term work placement in France, Germany, the Netherlands, and Spain. US$495-600 placement fee.

**Sunny AuPairs** (☎ 44 020 8144 1635, in US 503-616-3026; www.sunnyaupairs.com). Online, worldwide database connecting au pairs with families. Free registration. No placement fee.

# SHORT-TERM WORK

Traveling for long periods of time can be hard on the finances; therefore, many travelers try their hand at odd jobs for a few weeks at a time to help pay for another month or two of touring. The legality of short-term work varies by country. Contact the consulate of the country you'll be traveling in for more information. Another popular option is to work several hours a day at a hostel in exchange for free or discounted room and/or board. Most often, these short-term jobs are found by word of mouth, or by expressing interest to the owner of a hostel or restaurant. Due to high turnover in the tourism industry, many places are eager for help, even if it is only temporary. *Let's Go* lists temporary jobs of this nature whenever possible; check out the practical information section of larger cities.

### FURTHER READING ON BEYOND TOURISM.

*Alternatives to the Peace Corps: A Guide of Global Volunteer Opportunities,* by Paul Backhurst. Food First Books, 2005 (US$12).

*The Back Door Guide to Short-Term Job Adventures: Internships, Summer Jobs, Seasonal Work, Volunteer Vacations, and Transitions Abroad,* by Michael Landes. Ten Speed Press, 2005 (US$22).

*Green Volunteers: The World Guide to Voluntary Work in Nature Conservation,* ed. Fabio Ausenda. Universe, 2007 (US$15).

*How to Get a Job in Europe,* by Cheryl Matherly and Robert Sanborn. Planning Communications, 2003 (US$23).

*How to Live Your Dream of Volunteering Overseas,* by Joseph Collins, Stefano DeZerega, and Zahara Heckscher. Penguin Books, 2002 (US$20).

*International Job Finder: Where the Jobs Are Worldwide,* by Daniel Lauber and Kraig Rice. Planning Communications, 2002 (US$20).

*Live and Work Abroad: A Guide for Modern Nomads,* by Huw Francis and Michelyne Callan. Vacation-Work Publications, 2001 (US$16).

*Overseas Summer Jobs 2002.* Peterson's Guides and Vacation Work, 2002 (US$18).

*Volunteer Vacations: Short-Term Adventures That Will Benefit You and Others,* by Doug Cutchins, Anne Geissinger, and Bill McMillon. Chicago Review Press, 2006 (US$18).

*Work Abroad: The Complete Guide to Finding a Job Overseas,* by Clayton Hubbs. Transitions Abroad Publishing, 2002 (US$16).

*Work Your Way Around the World,* by Susan Griffith. Vacation-Work Publications, 2007 (US$22).

# excavating in athens

Arriving in a new country alone, late at night, with no knowledge of the native language is a nerve-wracking experience. Things get even more complicated when the sites you're planning

## "A toothbrush is very useful when cleaning shards of pottery."

on visiting haven't seen daylight in a couple thousand years. So needless to say, I was a little anxious when my plane landed in Athens. I had arrived just in time to get a few hours of sleep before starting a summer of volunteer work on an archaeological dig, and luckily the famous Greek hospitality helped me safely find my way to my apartment. For the next two months, I would be helping dig at the ancient Athenian Agora with the American School of Classical Studies.

At first, I was in awe. At 7am the morning after my arrival, we met at the site and got a tour of the ancient marketplace. I wondered how I could ever go on vacation to destinations that didn't have amazing artifacts like the Acropolis looming over them. Although I got accustomed to walking by the waterclock of the Roman Agora every day on my way to work and eating lunch under the shadow of the Hephaestion, the ruins never ceased to impress me.

Yet my digging summer wasn't all gawking at towering monuments. It became immediately apparent that the term "digging" would more accurately be described as "slowly scraping away." Excavating is far too delicate a process to just pull out a shovel and go—I never saw one the entire time I was there. We used the blunt end of miniature picks to steadily work away at the dirt, and our main instrument was a trowel, something I had once thought was only used for laying the mortar on bricks. I came to realize that a tiny speck of green in the dust can be

incredibly exciting—it could be a coin, you see—and that a toothbrush is very useful when cleaning shards of pottery.

There were disappointments, of course, like the time I watched as a potential tomb turned out to be maybe a latrine. The possibilities, however, were limitless. Working on a dig in which something fantastic could be discovered any second gave a constant adrenaline rush. One day, the entire site stopped work and watched as a large statue head was pulled out of the ground. Another time, I myself was lowered into the dark ground, sitting on a rope while two other workers cranked me down into a 2m deep well. It was there that I found a loom weight, one of my four personal discoveries of the summer (I also found three coins).

I had time on weekends to take short trips to other areas of Greece. I went to see the oracle of Delphi, the monasteries of Meteora, the sacred island of Delos, and Milos's volcanic sands. I also got to experience modern Athenian culture, sipping Nescafé, going to nightclubs where nobody was dancing, and visiting the city's museums.

## "Working on a dig gave a constant adrenaline rush."

Living and working in Athens, I was able to see and do much more than the casual tourist. I touched and helped uncover ancient sites, and I got used to the cries of "*malaka*" by angry residents upset that archaeologists took down modern buildings. I became accustomed to the locals' perplexed looks when I walked through their ritzy neighborhoods covered in dirt. Now, at least, I can always introduce myself as an amateur archaeologist, as long as I don't get too specific—for all they know I spent my summer in Greece becoming a swashbuckling adventurer.

*Leanna Boychenko majored in Classics at Harvard College. She was the Associate Editor of* Let's Go: Greece 2005 *and the Editor of* Let's Go: New Zealand 2006.

**A DIFFERENT PATH**

# AUSTRIA (ÖSTERREICH)

With Vienna's high culture and the Alps's high mountains, Austria offers different extremes of beauty. Many of the world's most famous composers and thinkers, including Mozart and Freud, called Austria home. Today, its small villages brim with locally brewed beer, jagged peaks draw hikers and skiers, and magnificent palaces, museums, and concerts are omnipresent. Stroll along the blue Danube River or relax in a Viennese coffeehouse and listen for a strain of the waltz.

## 🌐 DISCOVER AUSTRIA: SUGGESTED ITINERARIES

**THREE DAYS.** Spend all three days in Vienna (p. 70), the Imperial headquarters. From the stately Stephansdom to the majestic Hofburg Palace, Vienna's many attractions will leave you with enough sensory stimulation to last until your next trip.

**ONE WEEK.** Begin in Kitzbühel (1 day; p. 99) to take advantage of its hiking and skiing opportunities. Stop in Salzburg (2 days; p. 85) to see the home of Mozart and the Salzburger Festspiele (**p. 90**). Move on to the Salzkammergut region to spelunk in the Dachstein Ice Caves (1 day; p. 92). End your trip by basking in the glory of **Vienna** (3 days).

**TWO WEEKS.** Start in Innsbruck, where museums and mountains meet (2 days; p. 95), then swing by Zell am See and the Krimml Waterfalls (1 day; p. 92). Spend another two days wandering Hohe Tauern National Park (p. 94), visiting the Pasterze Glacier and Großglockner Hochalpenstraße. Next, tour Hallstatt and its nearby ice caves (2 days; p. 91). Follow your ears to Salzburg (2 days), then head to Graz (1 day; p. 91) for its throbbing nightlife. Finally, make your way to Vienna for a grand finale of romance, waltzes, and coffeehouse culture (4 days).

# LIFE AND TIMES

## HISTORY

**HOLY ROMANS AND HABSBURGS (800-1740).** Austria has been both a barrier between and a meeting point for Eastern and Western Europe ever since the Holy Roman Emperor **Charlemagne** conquered the Bavarians in AD 794. The German king **Otto I** took control of the Holy Roman Empire after Charlemagne's death and named **Leopold of Babenberg** ruler of much of the territory of present-day Austria.

The last Babenberg died childless in the 13th century, and **Rudolf of Habsburg** established his dynasty in the resulting power vacuum. Six centuries of Habsburg kings proved the wedding vow an able companion to the sword. **Maximilian I,** who became ruler of the Netherlands through his wife in 1477, is credited with the adaptation of Ovid's couplet, "Let other nations go to war; you, happy Austria, marry." His son **Philip** married into Spanish royalty, endowing his grandson, **Charles V,** with an empire that covered wide swaths of Europe and parts of the Americas. The vast fortunes of the Habsburgs left behind many monuments and castles in Austria; the Hofburg (p. 80) and Schloß Ambras (p. 98) palaces still dazzle with Habsburgian grandeur.

Despite Austria's vast territory, Martin Luther's **Protestant Reformation** shook the reins of the Habsburgs in the 16th and 17th centuries. Peasants left the Catholic Church en masse, and Protestant nobles doggedly fought the Catholic Habsburgs in the **Thirty Years' War** (1618-1648). Soon after, the Ottoman Turks besieged Vienna until Prince **Eugene of Savoy** drove them out. The plucky Eugene would triumph

Austria

again, this time over the French in the **War of Spanish Succession** (1701-1714). His palace, Schloß Belvedere (p. 82), now houses a superb art collection.

**CASTLES CRUMBLE (1740-1914).** When **Maria Theresa,** daughter of Charles VI, ascended the throne in 1740, her neighbors were eager to infringe on the Habsburg domain. Aware of this, she forged an alliance with France by marrying her daughter **Marie Antoinette** to the future **Louis XVI.** The decapitation of Marie Antoinette during the **French Revolution** turned relations between the two nations less than friendly; after the Revolution, **Napoleon Bonaparte** conquered many Austrian territories. French troops invaded Vienna, where Napoleon took up residence in Maria Theresa's favorite palace, Schönbrunn (p. 81), and married her granddaughter.

Ironically, Napoleon's temporary success led to the establishment of a consolidated Austrian empire that could defend itself against the imperial aggressions of France. In 1804, Franz II renounced his claim to the defunct Holy Roman crown and proclaimed himself **Franz I,** Emperor of Austria. During the **Congress of Vienna** (1814-1815), which redrew the map of Europe, Chancellor **Klemens von Metternich** renewed Austria's power base. He was able to do so because of the unity between the enemies of Napoleon. Calm prevailed until the spring of 1848, when the French philosophy of **bourgeois revolution** reached Austria. Students and workers revolted, seizing the palace and demanding a constitution and freedom of the press. The movement was divided and the rebellions quashed. Nevertheless, the emperor was eventually pressured to abdicate in favor of his nephew, **Franz Josef I,** whose 68-year reign remains the second-longest in the recorded history of Europe.

Austria's political status continued to shift throughout Franz Josef's reign. Prussia, Austria's powerful northern neighbor, dominated European politics under **Otto von Bismarck** and defeated Austria in 1866. The Austrian fall from power continued in 1867, when Franz Josef was outmaneuvered by Hungarian nobles and agreed to end the Austrian Empire and form the dual **Austro-Hungarian Empire.** Non-German speakers were marginalized within the new empire until 1907, when the government ceded basic civil rights to its peoples and instituted universal male suffrage. These concessions to the empire's Slavic minority came too late. Burgeoning nationalist sentiments, especially among the South Slavs in the Balkans, led to severe divisions within the empire.

**MODERNITY APPROACHES (1914-2000).** The Austro-Hungarian Empire was wracked by ethnic tension and locked into a web of alliances at the turn of the 20th century. The assassination of Austrian archduke and heir to the throne **Franz Ferdinand** by a Serbian nationalist in Sarajevo in June 1914 sparked **World War I:** Austria's declaration of war against Serbia set off a chain reaction that spread throughout Europe. Franz Josef died in 1916, leaving the throne to his reluctant grandnephew Karl I, who struggled in vain to preserve the empire. On November 11, 1918, Karl finally surrendered, and the 640-year-old Habsburg dynasty was snuffed out by the subsequent establishment of the **First Republic of Austria.**

Between 1918 and 1938, Austria experienced its first taste of parliamentary democracy. Immediately after the war, the Republic suffered massive inflation, unemployment, and near economic collapse, but it stabilized by the mid-1920s. In 1933, the weak coalition government gave way when **Engelbert Dollfuss,** the Austrian chancellor, declared martial law and abolished freedom of the press. Two years later, Dollfuss was assassinated by Austrian **Nazis,** who hoped for an alliance between Germany and Austria that Dollfuss had opposed. In 1938, Austrian Nazis got their wish when Germany annexed Austria in the **Anschluß.** While **World War II** raged, tens of thousands of Austrian Jews, political dissidents, disabled people, Roma (gypsies), and homosexuals were sent to Nazi concentration camps.

After Soviet troops "liberated" Vienna in 1945, Allied troops divided Austria into four zones of occupation. During the occupation, the Soviets tried to make Austria a Communist state, but had to settle for stripping it of any moveable infrastructure and an agreement that the nation would be permanently neutral. As in much of Western Europe, the American **Marshall Plan** helped jump-start the economy, laying the foundation for Austria's present prosperity.

The **Federal Constitution** (1945) and the **Austrian State Treaty** (1955) established Austrian sovereignty and formed the basis for the current Austrian nation, often referred to as the **Second Republic.** Today, Austria is led by a president, elected for six-year terms, and a chancellor, usually the majority party's leader. A bicameral parliamentary legislature and strong provincial governments perform the main work of governance. Historically, the government has been dominated by a coalition of two parties: the socialist **Social Democratic Party (SPÖ)** and the Christian-conservative **People's Party (ÖVP).** Together, the two parties have built one of the world's most successful economies, with low unemployment and inflation rates.

During the 1990s, the country moved toward stronger unification with Europe, finally joining the European Union (EU) in 1995. Austria faced European criticism, however, when its far-right **Freedom Party (FPÖ)** claimed 27% of the vote in the November 1999 national elections. Founded by the infamous **Jörg Haider,** the FPÖ maintained a strong anti-immigrant stance; Haider has made remarks that some have interpreted as neo-Nazi in sentiment. Several hundred thousand protestors turned out on the day that members of the FPÖ were to be sworn in to parliament, and several EU countries ceased cooperation with the government until 2000.

# TODAY

**EUROSKEPTIC.** Beginning in 2002, the popularity of the Freedom Party began to fall precipitously; a splinter group of the Freedom Party, the **Alliance for the Future of Austria (BZÖ),** enjoyed popularity for a few subsequent years. **Heinz Fischer,** a member of the SPÖ, is Austria's current president, although the role of Federal President is largely ceremonial, with political parties and their leaders holding most of the power. The Chancellor of Austria is **Alfred Gusenbauer,** also a member of the SPÖ. Austria has become known as one of the most "euroskeptic" members of the EU, consistently opposing measures such as the free movement of labor from Eastern Europe and the entry of Turkey into the Union. Pundits argue that such skepticism stems from lingering resentment in Austria over its political ostracization by other EU nations in the 90s.

# PEOPLE AND CULTURE

**DEMOGRAPHICS.** Although almost 90% of Austria's eight million people identify as German, nearly all have ties to other ethnic groups that belonged to the former empire. The 10% of the population that does not identify as German is made up mostly of recent immigrants. An emphasis on education is responsible for sky-high literacy rates (over 98%). Unemployment is around 5%.

**LANGUAGE.** German is the nation's official language. Austrians often add a diminutive *"-erl"* (instead of the High German *"-chen"* or *"-lein"*) to words. Also, Austrians don't greet each other with the standard *Guten Tag,* but instead opt for *Servus* (ZERvus) or *Grüß Gott* (grOOs got). For basic German words, see p. 1054.

# THE ARTS

## LITERATURE

One of the earliest and most impressive works of Austrian literature is the German-language heroic epic *Song of the Nibelungs* (c. 1200), whose author is unknown. In the 19th century, **Johann Nestroy** wrote biting comedies and satires like *The Talisman* (1840), lampooning social follies. **Adalbert Stifter** wrote around the same time, but concerned himself with stories about coming-of-age and nature. His short stories and novels, such as *The Condor* (1840) and *Indian Summer* (1857), represent the height of Austria's classical style. Beginning around 1890, a growing recognition within Austria of the nation's *fin-de-siècle* social turmoil transformed Austrian literature. **Karl Kraus** unmasked the crisis, **Arthur Schnitzler** dramatized it, **Hugo von Hofmannsthal** penned its eulogy, and **Georg Trakl** commented in feverish verse. Meanwhile, the world's most famous psychoanalyst, **Sigmund Freud,** developed his theories of sexual repression and the subconscious. His former home in Vienna now houses a museum (p. 82).

Many of Austria's literary titans, such as **Franz Kafka** and **Marie von Ebner-Eschenbach,** lived in the Habsburg protectorate of Bohemia. Kafka often traveled to Vienna to drink coffee at the Herrenhof Café and swap ideas with other writers. His surrealist style is most famously demonstrated by *The Metamorphosis* (1915), in which the narrator comes to terms with his unexpected transformation into a cockroach. Ebner-Eschenbach is often called the greatest female Austrian writer for her vivid individual portraits and her defense of women's rights. The **Austrian School of Economics** began developing libertarian economic theories in 1871, the **Vienna Circle** championed logical positivism in the early 20th century, and **Ludwig Wittgenstein** published *Tractatus Logico-Philosophicus* (1921), which he believed solved all of philosophy's problems.

When the Austro-Hungarian monarchy suddenly gave way to democracy, novelists **Robert Musil** and **Joseph Roth** charted the transformation. **Ingeborg Bachmann's** novels told stories of personal transformation, while **Thomas Bernhard** critiqued Austrian society. **Peter Handke** has written many experimental novels and co-wrote the screenplay for Wim Wenders's *Wings of Desire* (1987). The wildly popular crime novels of **Wolf Haas** have been adapted into films, including *Komm, süßer Tod* ("Come, Sweet Death"; 1998, film 2000) and *Silentium!* (1999, film 2004).

## MUSIC

The first major Viennese composer was **Josef Haydn,** who created a variety of new musical forms that led to the sonata and the symphony. **Wolfgang Amadeus Mozart,** a prodigy and brilliant composer, produced such pieces as *Eine Kleine Nachtmusik* (A Little Night Music) and the unfinished *Requiem.* Mozart's birthplace in Salzburg is now a museum (p. 89), and the Salzburger Festspiele (p. 90) carries on his musical tradition. **Ludwig van Beethoven** lived in Vienna for much of his life and composed some of his most famous works there. The expressive lines of **Franz**

**Schubert** gave rise to the Romantic Movement, music characterized by swelling emotion and storytelling. Mainly self-taught, Schubert began his *Unfinished Symphony* in 1822. Later in the 19th century, **Johannes Brahms** reintroduced Classical forms into Romanticism. Between **Johann Strauss the Elder** and his son, creatively named **Johann Strauss the Younger,** the Strauss family's waltzes kept Vienna on its toes for much of the century, their new, exhilarating style. **Arnold Schönberg** rejected tonal keys at the turn of the 20th century, producing a highly abstracted sound. **Anton Webern** and **Alban Berg** were both students of Schönberg and suffered under Nazi occupation in the 1940s for their "degenerate art."

## VISUAL ARTS

Helped by the Habsburg Empire's extensive patronage, Austria has maintained a rich artistic tradition. The flowering of Austrian architecture is represented in the cherub-covered facades of the **Baroque** style, exhibited exquisitely in the **Schönbrunn** (p. 98) and **Hofburg** (p. 98) palaces. The **Ringstraße** (p. 71), a broad boulevard encircling Vienna, is an example of Austria's 19th-century **Modernism.** Modern Austrian art began in the 20th century with the works of **Gustav Klimt,** who founded the **Secession** movement. **Oskar Kokoschka** and **Egon Schiele** were other artists who worked at the same time as Klimt and were tangentially involved with the Secessionists. Also around 1900, Modernist architects took issue with the Viennese Academy's conservatism. This gave rise to the **Jugendstil** movement (Art Nouveau), which formulated an ethic of functional buildings with artistic touches in the smallest details, an idea embraced by **Otto Wagner.** Travelers can still see Jugendstil apartments near Stephanspl. in Vienna (p. 80). In the 1920s and early 1930s, the Social Democratic administration built thousands of apartments in large **municipal projects** in a style reflecting the assertiveness of workers' movements and the ideals of **urban socialism.**

# HOLIDAYS AND FESTIVALS

**Holidays:** Just about everything closes on public holidays, so plan accordingly. New Year's Day (Jan. 1); Epiphany (Jan. 6); Good Friday (Mar. 21); Easter (Mar. 23-24); Labor Day (May 1); Ascension (May 1); Corpus Christi (May 22); Assumption (Aug. 15); Austrian National Day (Oct. 26); All Saints' Day (Nov. 1); Immaculate Conception (Dec. 8); Christmas (Dec. 25); Boxing Day (Dec. 26).

**Festivals:** Vienna celebrates Fasching (Carnival) from New Year's until the start of Lent. Austria's most famous summer music festivals are the Wiener Festwochen (early May to mid-June; www.festwochen.at) and the Salzburger Festspiele (late July-late Aug.).

# ADDITIONAL RESOURCES

*German Survival Guide: The Language and Culture You Need to Travel With Confidence in Germany and Austria,* by Elizabeth Bingham. World Prospect Press (2001). Offers an overview of the do's and don't's of Austrian society, with some language instruction.

*The Metamorphosis,* by Franz Kafka. Bantam Classics (1972). An overworked man transforms into a giant cockroach in this symbolic story of industrialization.

*Fin-de-siècle Vienna: Politics and Culture,* by Carl Schorske. Vintage (1980). This work of intellectual history chronicles the birth of modernism in the Austro-Hungarian Empire.

# ESSENTIALS

## WHEN TO GO

Between November and March, prices in western Austria double and travelers need reservations months in advance. The situation reverses in the summer, when the eastern half of the country fills with tourists. Accommodations are cheaper

**FACTS AND FIGURES**

**Official Name:** Republic of Austria.

**Capital:** Vienna.

**Major Cities:** Graz, Innsbruck, Salzburg.

**Population:** 8,200,000.

**Land Area:** 82,400.

**Time Zone:** GMT +1.

**Language:** German.

**Religions:** Roman Catholic 74%, Protestant 5%, Muslim 4%, Other/None 17%.

**Adjusted Gross of the 1965 film version of** *The Sound of Music:* **$937,093,200.**

and less crowded in the shoulder seasons (May-June and Sept.-Oct.). Cultural opportunities also vary with the seasons: the Vienna State Opera, like many other theaters, has no shows in July or August, while the Vienna Boys' Choir only performs April-June and September-October.

## DOCUMENTS AND FORMALITIES

**EMBASSIES.** Foreign embassies in Austria are in Vienna (p. 70). Austrian embassies abroad include: **Australia,** 12 Talbot St., Forrest, Canberra, ACT, 2603 (☎02 6295 1533; www.austriaemb.org.au); **Canada,** 445 Wilbrod St., Ottawa, ON, K1N 6M7 (☎613-789-1444; www.austro.org); **Ireland,** 15 Ailesbury Ct., 93 Ailesbury Rd., Dublin, 4 (☎01 269 45 77); **New Zealand,** Level 2, Willbank House, 57 Willis St., Wellington, 6001 (☎04 499 63 93); **UK,** 18 Belgrave Mews West, London, SW1X 8HU (☎020 7344 3250; www.bmaa.gv.at/london); **US,** 3524 International Ct., NW, Washington, D.C., 20008 (☎202-895-6700; www.austria.org).

**VISA AND ENTRY INFORMATION.** EU citizens do not need a visa. Citizens of Australia, Canada, New Zealand, and the US do not need a visa for stays of up to 90 days, beginning upon entry into any of the countries in the EU's freedom-of-movement zone. For more info, see p. 16. For stays longer than 90 days, all non-EU citizens need visas, available at Austrian embassies. For American citizens, visas are $82 but free of charge for students studying abroad.

## TOURIST SERVICES AND MONEY

**EMERGENCY**    Ambulance: ☎ 144. Police: ☎ 133. Fire: ☎ 122.

**TOURIST OFFICES.** For general info, contact the **Austrian National Tourist Office,** Margaretenstr. 1, A-1040 Vienna (☎ 158 86 60; www.austria.info). All tourist offices are marked by signs with a green "i"; most brochures are available in English.

**MONEY.** The **euro (€)** has replaced the **schilling** as the unit of currency in Austria. As a general rule, it's cheaper to exchange money in Austria than at home. Railroad stations, airports, hotels, and most travel agencies offer exchange services, as do banks. If you stay in hostels and prepare most of your own food, expect to spend €30-60 per day. Accommodations start at about €12 and a basic sit-down meal usually costs around €8. Menus will say whether service is included (*Preise inklusive* or *Bedienung inklusiv*); if it is, a tip is not expected. If not, 10% will do. Austrian restaurants expect you to seat yourself, and servers will not bring the bill until you ask them to do so. Say *"Zahlen bitte"* (TSAHL-en BIT-uh) to settle your accounts, and give tips directly to the server. Don't expect to bargain except at street markets.

Austria has a 20% **value added tax (VAT),** a sales tax applied to most purchased goods (p. 18). The prices given in *Let's Go* include VAT. In an airport upon exiting the EU, non-EU citizens can claim a refund on the tax paid for goods purchased at participating stores. In order to qualify for a refund in a store, you must spend at least €75; make sure to ask for a refund form when you pay. For more info on qualifying for a VAT refund, see p. 18.

**AUSTRIA**

**BUSINESS HOURS.** Businesses are generally open M-Th 8am-6pm, F 8am-3pm. Government offices are open M-F 9am-3pm, and most shops M-F 9am-6pm, Sa 9am-5pm. Banks are open M-F 8am-4pm, but smaller ones may close for lunch.

# TRANSPORTATION

**BY PLANE.** The only major international airport is Vienna's **Schwechat-Flughafen (VIE).** Other airports are in Innsbruck, Graz, Linz, and Salzburg. From London-Stansted, **Ryanair** (☎3531 249 7791; www.ryanair.com) flies to the latter three. For more info on flying to Austria, see p. 41.

**BY TRAIN.** The **Österreichische Bundesbahn** (**ÖBB;** www.oebb.at), Austria's state railroad, operates an efficient system with fast and comfortable trains. **Eurail** and **InterRail** passes are valid in Austria, but they do not guarantee a seat without a reservation. The **Austrian Rail pass** allows three to eight days of travel within any 15-day period on all rail lines. It also entitles holders to 40% off bike rentals at train stations (2nd-class US$107; each additional day US$15).

**BY BUS.** The Austrian bus system consists mainly of **PostBuses,** which cover areas inaccessible by train for comparably high prices. Buy tickets at the station or from the driver. For info, call ☎43 17 11 01 from abroad or ☎0810 222 333 within Austria from 7am-8pm.

**BY CAR.** Driving is a convenient way to see the more isolated parts of Austria, but gas is costly, an international license is required, and some small towns prohibit cars. The roads are well maintained and well marked, and Austrian drivers are quite careful. **Mitfahrzentralen** (ride-share services) in larger cities pair drivers with riders for a small fee. Riders then negotiate fares with the drivers. Be aware that not all organizations screen their drivers or riders; ask ahead.

**BY BIKE.** Bicycles are a great way to get around Austria, as roads in the country are generally smooth and safe. Many train stations rent bikes and allow you to return them to any participating station.

# KEEPING IN TOUCH

| **PHONE CODES** | **Country code: 43. International dialing prefix: 00** (for Vienna, dial 00 431). For more info on how to place international calls, see **Inside Back Cover.** |
| --- | --- |

**EMAIL AND THE INTERNET.** It's easy to find Internet cafes (€2-6 per hr.) in Austria, especially in larger cities. In small towns, however, cafes are less frequent and may charge more. Ask a hostel or tourist office receptionist for suggestions.

**TELEPHONES.** Wherever possible, use a calling card for international phone calls, as long-distance rates for national phone services are often exorbitant. Prepaid phone cards and major credit cards can be used for direct international calls but are still less cost-efficient. For info on mobile phones, see p. 27. The most popular companies are A1, One, and T-mobile. Direct-dial access numbers for calling out of Austria include: **AT&T Direct** (☎0800 200 288); **British Telecom** (☎0800 200 209); **Canada Direct** (☎0800 200 217); **MCI WorldPhone** (☎0800 999 762); **Sprint** (☎0800 200 236); **Telecom New Zealand** (☎0800 200 222); **Telstra Australia** (☎0800 200 202).

**MAIL.** Letters take one or two days within Austria. Airmail (€1.25) to North America takes four to seven days, and up to nine days to Australia and New Zealand. Mark all letters and packages *"mit Flugpost"* (airmail). Aerogrammes are the cheapest option. To receive mail in Austria, have mail delivered **Poste Restante.** Mail will go to the main post office unless you specify a subsidiary by street address. Address mail to be held according to the following example: LAST NAME, First name, *Postlagernde Briefe*, Postal code City, AUSTRIA.

## ACCOMMODATIONS AND CAMPING

| AUSTRIA | ❶ | ❷ | ❸ | ❹ | ❺ |
|---|---|---|---|---|---|
| ACCOMMODATIONS | under €16 | €16-26 | €27-34 | €35-55 | over €55 |

Always ask if your lodging provides a **guest card** (*Gästekarte*), which grants discounts on activities, museums, and public transportation. The **Österreichischer Jugendherbergsverband-Hauptverband (ÖJH)** runs the over 80 **HI hostels** in Austria. Because of the rigorous standards of the national organization, these are usually very clean and orderly. Most charge €18-25 per night for dorms, with a €3-5 HI discount. **Independent hostels** vary in quality, but often have more personality and foster a lively backpacking culture. Slightly more expensive **Pensionen** are similar to American and British B&Bs. In small to mid-sized towns, singles will cost about €20-30, but expect to pay twice as much in big cities. **Hotels** are expensive (singles over €35; doubles over €48). Cheaper options have "*Gasthof*," "*Gästehaus*," or "*Pension-Garni*" in the name. Renting a **Privatzimmer** (room in a family home) is an inexpensive option. Contact the tourist office about rooms (€16-30). **Camping** in Austria is less about getting out into nature than having a cheap place to sleep; most sites are large plots glutted with RVs and are open in summer only. Prices run €10-15 per tent site and €5-8 per extra person. In the high Alps, hikers and mountaineers can retire to the well-maintained system of **Hütten** (mountain huts) where traditional Austrian fare and a good night's rest await them. Reserve ahead.

**HIKING AND SKIING.** Almost every town has hiking trails in its vicinity; consult the local tourist office. Trails are marked with either a red-white-red marker (only sturdy boots and hiking poles necessary) or a blue-white-blue marker (mountaineering equipment needed). Because of snow, most mountain hiking trails and mountain huts are open only from late June to early September. Western Austria is one of the world's best skiing regions; the areas around Innsbruck and Kitzbühel are full of runs. High season runs from November to March.

## FOOD AND DRINK

| AUSTRIA | ❶ | ❷ | ❸ | ❹ | ❺ |
|---|---|---|---|---|---|
| FOOD AND DRINK | under €5 | €5-10 | €11-16 | €17-25 | over €25 |

Loaded with fat, salt, and cholesterol, traditional Austrian cuisine is bad for your skin, your heart, and your figure—enjoy! *Wienerschnitzel* is a breaded meat cutlet (usually veal or pork) fried in butter. Natives nurse their sweet tooths with *Sacher Torte* (a rich chocolate cake layered with marmalade) and *Linzer Torte* (a light yellow cake with currant jam). Austrian beers are outstanding—try Stiegl, a Salzburg brew; Zipfer, from Upper Austria; and Styrian Gösser.

**EAT YOUR VEGGIES.** Vegetarians should look on the menu for *Spätzle* (noodles), *Eierschwammerl* (yellow mushrooms), or anything with "*Vegi*" in it.

## BEYOND TOURISM

Austria caters more to tourism than volunteerism; there are only limited opportunities to give back, so your best bet is to find them through a placement service. Opportunities for short-term work abound at hotels, ski resorts, and farms. For more info on opportunities across Europe, see **Beyond Tourism,** p. 54.

AUSTRIA

**Actilingua Academy,** Glorietteg. 8, A-1130 Vienna (☎431 877 6701; www.actilingua.com). Study German in Vienna (from €419) for 2 to 4 weeks, with accommodation in dorms, apartments or with a host family.

**Bergwald Projekt/Mountain Forest Project,** Hauptstr. 24, 7014 Trin (☎081 630 4145; www.bergwaldprojekt.ch). Organizes week-long conservation projects in Austria, Germany, and Switzerland.

**Concordia,** Heversham House, 2nd fl., 20-22 Boundary Rd., East Sussex, BN2 3HJ, UK (☎012 7342 2218; www.concordia-iye.org.uk). British volunteer organization that directs community projects in Austria, which have in the past included renovating historic buildings and parks and directing a youth drama project.

# VIENNA (WIEN) ☎01

War, marriage, and Habsburg maneuvering transformed Vienna (pop. 1,800,000) from a Roman camp along the Danube into Europe's political linchpin. Beethoven and Mozart made Vienna an everlasting arbiter of high culture; the tradition continues today with the city's prestigious orchestras and world-class museums. With dozens of coffeehouses, Vienna radiates artistic, intellectual energy. On any given afternoon, cafes turn the sidewalks into a sea of umbrellas while bars and clubs pulse with experimental techno and indie rock until dawn.

# ✈ INTERCITY TRANSPORTATION

**Flights:** The **Wien-Schwechat Flughafen (VIE;** ☎700 70), 18km from the city center, is home to **Austrian Airlines** (☎517 89; www.aua.com). The cheapest way to reach the city, the S-Bahn (☎65 17 17) stops at **Wien Mitte** (30min., 2-3 per hr., €3). The Vienna Airport Lines **bus** (☎930 00 23 00) takes 20min. to reach Südbahnhof and 40min. to Westbahnhof (2 per hr.; €6, round-trip €11). The **City Airport Train** (**CAT;** ☎252 50; www.cityairporttrain.com) takes only 16min. to reach Wien Mitte (2 per hr. 6:05am-11:35pm; purchased online €8, round-trip €15; from a ticket machine €9, round-trip €16; on board €10; Eurail not valid.)

**Trains:** Vienna has 2 main train stations with international connections. Call ☎05 17 17 (24hr.) or check www.oebb.at for general train info. Ticket counters and machines generally take AmEx/MC/V.

**Westbahnhof,** XV, Mariahilferstr. 132. Info counter open daily 7:30am-9pm. Trains go to: **Amsterdam, NTH** (12hr., 4 per day, €135); **Berlin, GER** (9-11hr., 1 per 2hr., €100-130); **Budapest, HUN** (3hr., 17 per day, €36); **Hamburg, GER** (9-12hr., 6 per day, €80); **Innsbruck** (4½-5hr., 7 per day, €54); **Munich, GER** (5hr., 10 per day, €72); **Paris, FRA** (14-24hr., 2 per day, €70-160); **Salzburg** (2½-3hr., 1 per hr., €43); **Zürich, SWI** (9hr., 3 per day, €88).

**Südbahnhof,** X, Wiener Gürtel 1a. Info counter open daily 7am-8pm. Trains go south and east to: **Graz** (2½hr., 1 per hr., €30); **Kraków, POL** (7hr., 4 per day, €46); **Prague, CZR** (4-5hr., 8 per day, €44); **Rome, ITA** (13-18hr., 2 per day, €75-100); **Venice, ITA** (7-11hr., 6 per day, €50-70).

**Buses:** Buses in Austria are rarely cheaper than trains; compare prices before buying a ticket. **Postbus** (☎517 17; www.postbus.at) provides regional bus service and **Eurolines** (☎798 29 00; www.eurolines.at) connects to international destinations. Buses leave from the city stations at Erdberg, Floridsdorf, Heiligenstadt, Hütteldorf, Kagran, Reumannpl., and Wien Mitte/Landstr.

**Hitchhiking:** Some travelers report riding tram #67 to the last stop and waiting at the roundabout near Laaerberg. Those headed for Salzburg take U4 to Hütteldorf; the highway is 10km farther. Let's Go does not recommend hitchhiking.

# ⚒ ORIENTATION

Vienna is divided into 23 **Bezirke** (districts). The first is **Innenstadt** (city center), defined by the **Ringstraße** (ring road) on three sides and the Danube Canal on the fourth. At the center of the Innenstadt lies **Stephansplatz** and much of the pedestrian district. The best way to reach Innenstadt is to take the U-bahn to Stephanspl. (U1, U3) or **Karlsplatz** (U1, U2, U4); **Schwedenplatz** (U1, U4) is close to the city's nightlife. Tram lines 1 and 2 circle the Innenstadt on the Ringstr., with line 2 heading clockwise and 1 counterclockwise.

The Ringstraße consists of different segments, such as Opernring or Kärntner Ring. Many of Vienna's major attractions are in District I and immediately around the Ringstr. Districts II-IX spread out from the city center following the clockwise traffic of the Ring. The remaining districts expand from yet another ring road, the **Gürtel** (Belt). Similar to the Ring, this major thoroughfare has numerous segments, including Margaretengürtel, Neubaugürtel, and Währinger Gürtel. Like Vienna's street signs, *Let's Go* indicates the district number in Roman or Arabic numerals before the street and number.

# ▚ LOCAL TRANSPORTATION

**Public Transportation: Wiener Linien** (general info ☎ 790 91 00; www.wienerlinien.at.) The **U-Bahn** (subway), **Straßenbahn** (tram), **S-Bahn** (elevated tram), and **bus** lines operate on a 1-ticket system, so you can transfer between types of transportation without having to buy a new ticket. Purchase tickets at a counter, machine, on board, or at a tobacco shop. A **single fare** (€1.70 in advance, €2.20 on board) lets you travel to any destination in the city and switch from bus to U-Bahn to tram to S-Bahn in any order, provided your travel is uninterrupted. Other ticket options include a **1-day pass** (€5.70), **1-day "shopping" pass** (M-Sa 8am-8pm, €4.60), **3-day rover ticket** (€13.60), **7-day pass** (€14; valid M 9am to the next M 9am), and an **8-day pass** (€28; valid any 8 days, not necessarily consecutive; can be split between several people travelling together, but must be validated for each person). The **Vorteilscard** (Vienna Card; €19) allows for 72hr. of travel and discounts at museums and sights. To avoid a €60 fine from plainclothes inspectors, **validate your ticket** by punching it in the machine. Tickets do not need to be restamped when switching trains. Regular trams and subway cars do not run midnight-5am. **Night buses** run 2 per hr., 12:30-4:30am, along most routes; "N" signs designate night bus stops. A night bus schedule and discount passes are available from Wiener Linien information offices (open M-F 6:30am-6:30pm, Sa-Su 8:30am-4pm) in the Karlspl., Stephahnspl., Westbahnhof, and some other U-Bahn stations, as well as at the tourist office (p. 71).

**Taxis:** ☎ 313 00, 401 00, 601 60, or 814 00. Stands at Südbahnhof, Karlspl. in the city center, Westbahnhof, and by the Bermuda Dreieck. Accredited taxis have yellow-and-black signs on the roof. Base rate M-Sa €2.80, €0.20 per 0.2km; base rate Su 11pm-6am €3; holidays slightly more expensive. €2 surcharge for calling a taxi.

**Car Rental: Hertz** (☎ 700 73 26 61), at the airport. Open M-F 7am-11:30pm, Sa 8am-8pm, Su 7am-11:30pm. **Europcar** (☎ 700 73 26 99), at the airport. Open M-F 7:30am-11pm, Sa 8am-7pm, Su 7am-11pm.

**Bike Rental: Pedal Power,** II, Ausstellungsstr. 3 (☎ 729 72 34; www.pedalpower.at). €17 per 4hr., €27 per day. Delivery available. Guided tours (€23) daily May-Sept. Vienna Card and student discounts. Open daily May-Sept. 8am-7pm; Mar.-Apr. and Oct. 8am-6pm. **Citybike** (www.citybikeien.at) has automated rental stations at 50 locations. €2 per day, €1 per 1st 2hr., then €4 per hr. thereafter. MC/V.

# ▨ PRACTICAL INFORMATION

## TOURIST AND FINANCIAL SERVICES

**Main Tourist Office:** I, Albertinapl. on the corner of Maysederg. (☎ 245 55; www.vienna.info). Follow Operng. up 1 block from the Opera House. Books rooms for a €2.90 fee. Open daily 9am-7pm.

AUSTRIA

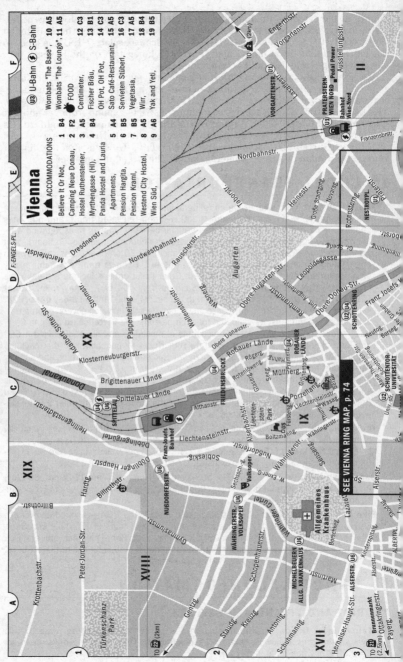

# Vienna

| ▲ ACCOMMODATIONS | | |
|---|---|---|
| Believe It Or Not, | 1 | B4 |
| Camping Neue Donau, | 2 | F2 |
| Hostel Ruthensteiner, | 3 | A5 |
| Myrthengasse (HI), | 4 | B4 |
| Panda Hostel and Lauria | | |
| Apartments, | 5 | A4 |
| Pension Hargita, | 6 | B5 |
| Pension Kraml, | 7 | B5 |
| Westend City Hostel, | 8 | A5 |
| Wien Süd, | 9 | A6 |

| Ⓤ U-Bahn Ⓢ S-Bahn | | |
|---|---|---|
| Wombats "The Base", | 10 | A5 |
| Wombats "The Lounge", | 11 | A5 |
| ● FOOD | | |
| Centimeter, | 12 | C3 |
| Fischer Bräu, | 13 | B1 |
| OH Pot, OH Pot, | 14 | C3 |
| Sato Café-Restaurant, | 15 | A5 |
| Servieten Stüberl, | 16 | C3 |
| Vegetasia, | 17 | A5 |
| Wirr, | 18 | B4 |
| Yak and Yeti, | 19 | B5 |

SEE VIENNA RING MAP, p. 74

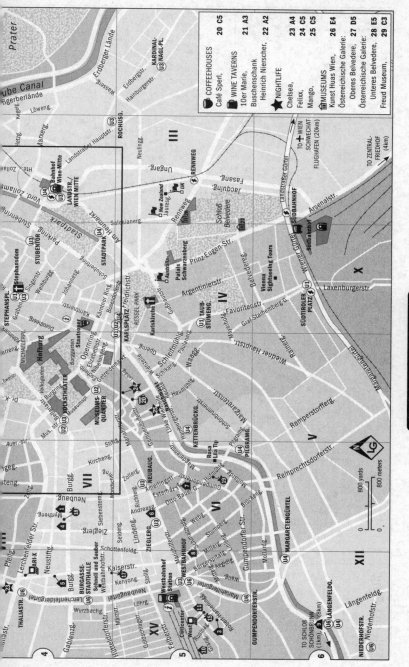

AUSTRIA

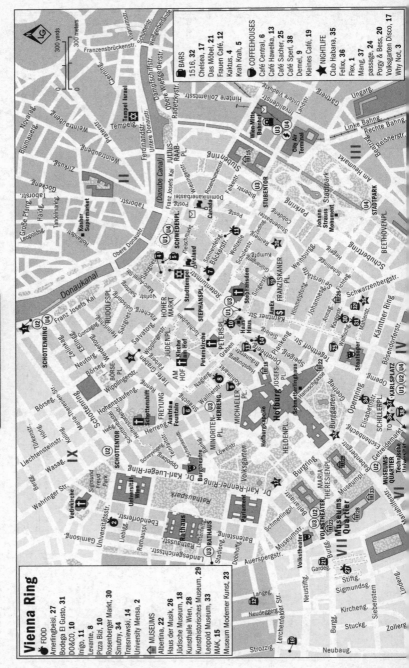

**Vienna Ring**

● FOOD
Ameringbeisi, 27
Bodega El Gusto, 31
DO&CO, 10
Inigo, 11
Levante, 8
Pizza Bizi, 10
Rosenberger Markt, 30
Smutny, 34
Trzesniewski, 14
University Mensa, 2

🏛 MUSEUMS
Albertina, 22
Haus der Musik, 26
Jüdische Museum, 18
Kunsthalle Wien, 28
Kunsthistorisches Museum, 29
Leopold Museum, 33
MAK, 15
Museum Moderner Kunst, 23

🍷 BARS
1516, 32
Chelsea, 17
Das Möbel, 21
Frauen Café, 12
Kaktus, 4
Krah Krah, 5

☕ COFFEEHOUSES
Café Central, 6
Café Hawelka, 13
Café Sacher, 25
Café Sperl, 38
Demel, 9
Kleines Café, 19

★ NIGHTLIFE
Club Habana, 35
Felix, 36
Flex, 1
Mang, 37
passage, 24
Porgy & Bess, 20
Volksgarten Disco, 17
Why Not, 3

**Embassies and Consulates: Australia,** IV, Mattiellistr. 2-4 (☎50 67 40). Open M-F 8:30am-4:30pm. **Canada,** I, Laurenzerberg 2 (☎531 38 30 00) M-F 8:30am-12:30pm and 1:30-3:30pm. **Ireland,** I, Rotenturmstr. 16-18, 5th fl. (☎715 42 46). Open M-F 9:30-11am and 1:30-4pm. **New Zealand,** III, Salesianerg. 15 (☎318 85 05). **UK,** III, Jaurèesg. 10 (☎716 13 53 33, after hours for UK nationals in emergencies only 0676 569 40 12). Open M-F 9:15am-12:30pm and 2-3:30pm. **US,** X, Boltzmanng. 16 (☎31 33 90). Open M-F 8-11:30am. 24hr. emergency services.

**Currency Exchange and Banks: ATMs** are your best bet. Nearly all accept Cirrus/MC/V. **Banks** generally give the best available exchange rate. Most open M-W and F 8am-3pm, Th 8am-5:30pm. **Train station** exchanges have long hours (daily 7am-10pm at the Westbahnhof), but charge 1% with a €6 min. fee. Stay away from the 24hr. bill-exchange machines in Innenstadt, as they generally charge outrageous fees.

**American Express Travel Agency:** I, Kärntnerstr. 21-23 (☎51 51 10), between Himmelpfortg. and Weinburgg. Cashes travelers checks (€5 min. commission for up to €250, then 2%). Open M-F 9am-5:30pm, Sa 9am-1pm.

## LOCAL SERVICES

**Luggage Storage:** Lockers available at all train stations. €2-3.50 per 24hr.

**English-language Bookstores: British Bookshop,** I, Weihburgg. 24 (☎512 19 45). Extensive travel section. Open M-F 9:30am-6:30pm, Sa 9:30am-6pm. AmEx/MC/V.

**GLBT Resources:** Pick up the *Vienna Gay Guide* (www.gaynet.at/guide), *Coxx,* or *Xtra* from any tourist office or gay bar, cafe, or club. **Rosa Lila Tip,** VI, Linke Wienzeile 102 (lesbians ☎586 51 50, gay men 585 43 43; www.villa.at), is a knowledgeable resource and social center. English spoken. Take the U4 to Pilgramg. and look for the pink house on the left bank. Open M, W, F 5-8pm.

**Laundromat: Schnell und Sauber,** VII, Westbahnhofstr. 60. U6: Burgg./Stadthalle. Wash €4.50, dry €1 per 20min. Detergent included. Open 6am-11pm.

## EMERGENCY AND COMMUNICATIONS

**Emergency:** ☎141.

**24hr. Pharmacy:** ☎15 50. Consulates have lists of English-speaking doctors.

**Hospital: Allgemeines Krankenhaus,** IX, Währinger Gürtel 18-20 (☎40 40 00).

**Internet Access: C@llCenter West,** XV, Mariahilferstr. 149. €1.40 per 30min., €2.50 per hr. Open daily 9am-midnight. **ARI-X,** VII (☎9911 151 612), corner of Kaiserstr. and Lerchenfelderstr. €1 per hr. Open M-Sa 9am-11pm, Su noon-11pm.

**Post Office: Hauptpostamt,** I, Fleischmarkt 19 (☎0577 677 10 10). Open daily 6am-10pm. Branches throughout the city and at the train stations; look for yellow signs with a trumpet logo. **Postal Codes:** A-1010 (1st district) through A-1230 (23rd district).

# ⌂ ⛺ ACCOMMODATIONS AND CAMPING

Hunting for cheap rooms in Vienna during high season (June-Sept.) can be unpleasant; call for reservations at least five days ahead. For info on camping near Vienna, visit www.campingwien.at.

## HOSTELS

▨ **Hostel Ruthensteiner,** XV, Robert-Hamerlingg. 24 (☎893 42 02; www.hostelruthen-steiner.com). Knowledgeable staff, spotless rooms, kitchen, and a secluded courtyard. Breakfast €2.50. Linens €2. Internet €2 per 40min. Key deposit €10. Reception 24hr. 32-bed summer dorm €13; 8-bed dorms €15; singles €30; doubles €48, with bath €54; quads €68/76. AmEx/MC/V; €0.40-0.80 per day surcharge. ❶

▨ **Wombats City Hostel,** (☎897 23 36; www.wombats-hostels.com) offers 2 separate locations. **"The Lounge"** (XV, Mariahilferstr. 137). Exit Westbahnhof and turn right on

Mariahilferstr. The bright walls and leather couches add a modern touch to the college dorm atmosphere. Popular and loud bar in the basement vault. **"The Base"** (XV, Grang. 6). Continue on Mariahilferstr., turn right on Rosinag., and left on Grang. Farther from the train station and a quieter street, this wildly colorful hostel compensates with an in-house pub, guided tours, and nightly English-language movies. Breakfast €3.50 daily 7:30-10am. Internet €2 per hr. Laundry €4.50. Dorms €21; doubles €50. MC/V. ❷

**Westend City Hostel,** VI, Fügerg. 3 (☎597 67 29; www.westendhostel.at), near West-bahnhof. A rose-filled courtyard and plain dorms provide respite. Breakfast included. Internet €6 per hr. Reception 24hr. Check-out 10:30am. Lockout 10:30am-2pm. Open mid-Mar. to Nov. Dorms €18-21; singles €50-63; doubles €60-78. Cash only. ❷

**Myrthengasse (HI),** VII, Myrtheng. 7 (☎523 63 16; www.jugendherberge.at). Take U6 to Burgg./Stadthalle, then bus #48A (dir.: Ring) or U3 to Neubaug. Backtrack on Burgg. 1 block. Turn right on Myrtheng. Simple rooms in an unassuming neighborhood. Breakfast included. Laundry €4. Internet €2.60 per 30min., €4.40 per hr. Max. 6-night stay when full. Reception 24hr. Dorms €21; doubles €47. €3.50 HI discount. AmEx/MC/V. ❷

**Panda Hostel** and **Lauria Apartments,** VII, Kaiserstr. 77, Apt. #8 (☎522 53 53, 522 25 55; www.panda-vienna.at, www.lauria-vienna.at). 10 beds pack Panda Hostel's dorm room. Lauria Apartments's doubles, triples, and quads, while a little roomier, still lack laundry facilities and common areas. Min. stay 2 nights. Reception 8am-1pm. Phone check-in by 11:30pm. Dorms, ages 17-30, €15; doubles with bunks €38, with queen €48; triples €51/66; quads €84. MC/V; over €150. ❶

**Believe It Or Not,** VII, Myrtheng. 10, Apt. #14 (☎526 46 58). Converted apartments. Key deposit €50 or credit card number. Min. 2-night stay. Reception 8:15am-noon. Lockout 10am-noon. 4- to 8-bed dorms €14-16. Cash only. Ages 18-30 only. ❶

## PENSIONS

**Pension Hargita,** VII, Andreasg. 1 (☎526 19 28; www.hargita.at). U3: Zieglerg. Exit on Andreasg. Hungarian decorations in the halls and immaculately clean hardwood floors accompany blue-and-white furniture and bedding. Breakfast €5. Reception 8am-mid-night. Singles €38, with shower €45, with shower and toilet €55; doubles €52/58/66; triples with shower €73, with shower and toilet €80. MC/V. ❹

**Pension Kraml,** VI, Brauerg. 5 (☎587 85 88; www.pensionkraml.at). U3: Zieglerg. Exit on Otto-Bauer-G., take 1st left onto Königsegg., then 1st right. Plush rooms in rich red and a lounge with cable TV. Breakfast included. Reception 24hr. Singles €30; doubles €50, with shower €60, with shower and toilet €70; triples €70/80. 3- to 5-person apartment with bath €95-125. Cash only. ❸

## CAMPING

**Camping Neue Donau,** XXII, Am Kleehäufel 119 (☎202 40 10; www.campingwien.at/nd). U1: Kaisermühlen. Take the Schüttaustr. exit, cross the street and then take bus #91a to Kleehäufel. 4km from the city center and adjacent to Neue Donau beaches, though not directly on the water. Boat and bike rental available. Kitchen, showers, and supermarket. Laundry €4.50. Reception 8am-12:30pm and 3-6:15pm. Open Easter-Sept. €6-7 per person, €10-12 per tent. AmEx/MC/V. ❶

**Wien Süd,** XXIII, Breitenfurter. Str. 269 (☎867 36 49; www.campingwien.at/ws). U6: Philadelphiabrücke, and bus #62A to Wien Süd. 27 sq. km of woods and fields, a cafe, playground, and supermarket comprise this former imperial park. Laundry €5. Reception 8am-8pm. Open May-Sept. €6-7 per person, €10-12 per tent. AmEx/MC/V. ❶

# ◘ FOOD

Viennese food is linked to meat: *Tafelspitz* (boiled beef), *Gulasch* (goulash; rich stew of beef, potatoes, and other vegetables), or *Wiener Schnitzel* (deep-fried, breaded veal or pork cutlet) constitute a traditional meal. The city boasts intricate sweets, including *Mohr in Hemd* (chocolate and hazelnut soufflé draped in hot chocolate sauce) and the renowned *Sacher Torte*. Restaurants that call themselves *Stüberl* ("little sitting room") or advertise *Schmankerl* serve Viennese fare.

Innenstadt restaurants are expensive. The neighborhood north of the university, where Universitätsstr. and Währingerstr. meet (U2: Schottentor), is more budget-friendly. Affordable restaurants line **Burggasse** in District VII and the area around Rechte and Linke Wienzeile near Naschmarkt (U4: Kettenbrückeng). The

---

**TIP**

**B.Y.O.B.** When shopping at Austrian supermarkets, it's a good idea to bring your own bag: most supermarkets charge €0.05-0.20 per bag. Many supermarkets also close early M-Sa at around 6:30-7pm, and often aren't open Su.

---

**Naschmarkt** itself hosts Vienna's biggest market of fresh (if pricey) produce. Its many eateries provide cheap, quick meals. (Open M-F 6am-6:30pm, Sa 6am-2pm.) The **Brunnenmarkt** (XVI, U6: Josefstädterstr.) has Turkish flair. A **kosher** supermarket is at II, Hollandstr. 10. (☎216 96 75. Open M-Th 8:30am-6:30pm, F 8am-2pm.)

## INSIDE THE RING

▓ **Trzesniewski,** I, Dorotheerg. 1 (☎512 32 91), from Stephansdom, 3 blocks down on the left side of the Graben. Once Kafka's favorite, this stand-up establishment has been serving open-faced mini-sandwiches (€0.90) for over 100 years. Toppings are mainly egg- and cucumber-based, but can also include salmon, onion, paprika, and herring. Open M-F 8:30am-7:30pm, Sa 9am-5pm. Cash only. ❶

▓ **Smutny,** I, Elisabethstr. 8 (☎587 13 56; www.smutny.com), U6: Karlspl. A traditional Viennese restaurant serving *Wiener schnitzel* (€14) and *Fiakergulash* (goulash with beef, egg, potato, and sausage; €11). M-F lunch *Menü* €8 (soup and entree), Sa-Su €10, includes dessert. M-F daily special €5. Open daily 10am-midnight. AmEx/MC/V. ❷

**Inigo,** I, Bäckerstr. 18 (☎512 74 51; www.inigo.at). Founded by a Jesuit priest, Inigo aids the long-term unemployed by hiring them as cooks. Hearty entrees served with a complimentary salad. Vegetarian entrees €8-10. Soups €4. Salads €2-7. Open M-Sa 9:30am-midnight, Su 10am-4pm. AmEx/MC/V. ❷

**Pizza Bizi,** I, Rotenturmstr. 4 (☎513 37 05), 1 block up Rotenturmstr. from Stephanspl. One of the best deals in the city, this self-serve restaurant serves big slices of pizza (€2.50), pasta (€5-6), and salads (€3-5). Open daily 10:30am-11:30pm. Cash only. ❷

**Levante,** I, Wallnerstr. 2 (☎533 23 26; www.levante.at). Walk down Graben away from Stephansdom, turn left on Kohlmarkt and right onto Wallnerstr. Easily a meal for two, Greek pizza (€5-7.50) comes on a doughy golden crust. Other Greek and Turkish dishes €7-13. Vegetarian options. Open daily 11am-11pm. AmEx/MC/V. ❷

**Bodega El Gusto,** I, Mahlerstr. 7 (☎512 06 73), off Kärntnerstr. This cozy restaurant serves tapas (€3-7) and Spanish entrees (€4-20). Open M-Sa noon-1am. MC/V. ❸

**DO&CO,** I, Stephanspl. 12, 7th fl. (☎535 39 69; www.doco.com). Gourmet Austrian and international fare served amid spires and towers in the Haas Haus. Entrees €10-24. Sushi €11-15. Reserve ahead. Open daily noon-3pm and 6pm-midnight. V. ❹

**Rosenberger Markt,** I, Mayserderg. 2 (☎512 34 58), off Kärntnerstr. A cafeteria offering everything from salad to waffles. They charge by the size of your plate, not by weight, so pile high. Entrees €2-9. Open daily 10:30am-11pm. AmEx/MC/V. ❶

## OUTSIDE THE RING

▓ **Centimeter,** IX, Liechtensteinstr. 42 (☎470 06 06; www.centimeter.at). Tram D to Bauernfeldpl. This chain offers huge portions of greasy Austrian fare (€5.50-7) and hot or cold open-faced sandwiches for €0.10-0.15 per cm. Open M-F 10am-midnight, Sa-Su 11am-midnight. AmEx/MC/V. ❶

**AUSTRIA**

## ON THE MENU

### COFFEE CULTURE

Vienna is the world's coffee capital, but for those used to *mocha lattes* or half-caff lite soys, understanding the jumble of German words on the *Kaffeehaus* menu can be daunting. Here's a cheatsheet for deciphering the menu:

A **Mokka** or a **Schwarzer** is strong, pure black espresso and nothing more. The **Kleiner Brauner** ("small brown") lightens the espresso with milk or cream, while the **Verlängerter** lowers the stakes yet again with weaker coffee. The quintessential Viennese cafe drink, a **Mélange** melds black espresso with steamed milk, sometimes capping it with a dollop of whipped cream. The **Kapuziner** ("the monk") also consists of espresso with gently foamed milk but is more commonly known by its Italian name, "cappuccino." The **Einspanner** is a strong black coffee heaped with whipped cream and sometimes a dash of chocolate shavings. **Eiskaffee**, or hot coffee with vanilla ice cream, is a refreshing jolt on hot summer days.

Vienna's specialty coffee drinks combine espresso with a variety of liqueurs for caffeine with a punch. Some cafes serve the **Maria-Theresia**, with orange liqueur, or the **Pharisär**, with rum and sugar. Other liqueurs include **Marillen** (apricot) and **Kirsche** (cherry). Or, for a protein boost, try the milk-less mocha **Kaisermelange**, stirred with brandy and an egg yolk. Be prepared to shell out €6-7 for an indulgent delight.

**Yak and Yeti**, VI, Hofmühlg. 21 (☎595 54 52; www.yakundyeti.at). U3: Zieglerg. This Himalayan restaurant serves *momos* (Nepalese dumplings; €10-11) and other ethnic specialties. Eat under the prayer flags in their lush garden. Lunch buffet €6.50. Entrees €7-13. Open May-Sept. M-Sa 11:30am-10:30pm; Oct.-Apr. M-F 11:30am-2:30pm and 6-10:30pm, Sa 11:30am-10:30pm. Cash only. ❸

**Amerlingbeisl**, VII, Stiftg. 8 (☎526 16 60). U3: Neubaug. Amid a cluster of cafes, the grapevine-covered courtyard is a perfect backdrop for Mediterranean-influenced buffet entrees (€7-12). Vegetarian options €6-7. Breakfast until 3pm €4-8; Sa-Su brunch buffet 9am-3pm €9.50. Open daily 9am-2am. Kitchen open until 1am. AmEx/MC/V. ❷

**Sato Café-Restaurant**, XV, Mariahilferstr. 151 (☎897 58 54). U3 or U6: Westbahnhof. Near the Ruthensteiner and Wombats hostels. Free baskets of fluffy Turkish bread accompany the homestyle dishes. Vegetarian options available. Entrees €5-9. Delicious breakfast omelettes €3-4. Open daily 8am-midnight. Cash only. ❶

**Fischer Bräu**, XIX, Billrothstr. 17 (☎369 59 49; www.fischerbraeu.at). U6: Nußdorfer Str. Try the homebrewed beer (0.3L, €2-3) and black bread (€3-5). Austrian fare €5-11. Jazz brunch Su 11am. Open M-Sa 4pm-1am, Su 11am-1am. Cash only. ❷

**Wirr**, VII, Burgg. 70 (☎929 40 50). U3: Neubaug. With hippies plopped down in worn sofas and neckties hanging from the ceiling, Wirr serves a relaxing breakfast (€2-10) until 2pm. At night, the club downstairs hosts electronica and funk bands. Entrees €6-14. Open M-Sa 10am-4am, Su 10am-2am. Kitchen open until 11pm. AmEx/MC/V. ❷

**Servieten Stüberl**, IX, Servieteng. 7 (☎317 53 36; www.servietenstueberl.at). U4: Roßauer Lände. In the Servientenkirche's shadow, this family-run restaurant serves its own wine and Austrian entrees (€8-13). Open daily 10am-11pm. MC/V. ❸

**OH Pot, OH Pot**, IX, Währingerstr. 22 (☎319 42 59; www.ohpot.at). U2: Schottentor, then tram #40A or walk up Währingerstr. This restaurant's specialty is filling "pots," stew-like veggie or meat concoctions with influences from Ethiopia to Brazil (€6.50-8.50). Lunch special offers soup or salad, any pot and dessert for €6.50 (M-F 11am-3pm, Sa noon-3pm). Sunday buffet 11am-5pm €11. 10% student discount. Open daily 11am-midnight. Kitchen open until 9pm. AmEx/MC/V. ❷

**Vegetasia**, VII, Kaiserstr. 45 (☎523 10 91; www.vegetasia.at). U3 or 6: Westbahnhof. This Taiwanese restaurant transforms *seitan* and soy into "meat." Entrees €7-10. Vegan options. Open daily 11:30am-3pm and 5:30-11:30pm. AmEx/MC/V. ❷

**University Mensa,** IX, Universitätsstr. 7, on the 7th fl. of the more modern university building. U2: Schottentor. Take a thrilling conveyor-belt ▓**elevator** to the top. Entree plus salad or dessert for €4. Adjoining snack bar offers more choices (€4-5) and a self-serve salad bar (€2.90). Snack bar open M-F Sept.-June 8am-6pm; July-Aug. 8am-3pm. University Mensa open Sept.-June M-F 11am-2pm. Cash only. ❶

# ▓ COFFEEHOUSES

For years these venerable establishments have been havens for artists, writers, and thinkers: Vienna's cafes watched Franz Kafka brood about solitude, Theodor Herzl plan a Zionist Israel, and Freud ponder the human mind. The most important dictate of coffeehouse etiquette is that you linger; the waiter *(Herr Ober)* will serve you when you sit down, then will leave you to sip your *Mélange* (half coffee and half steamed milk), read, and contemplate life's great questions. When you're ready to leave, ask to pay (*"Zahlen bitte"*).

▓ **Kleines Café,** I, Franziskanerpl. 3. Escape from the busy pedestrian streets with a *Mélange* (€3) and conversation on a leather couch in the relaxed interior, or by the fountain in the square. Sandwiches €3-5. Open daily 10am-2am. Cash only.

▓ **Café Central,** I, Herreng. 14 (☎ 533 37 63; www.palaisevents.at), at the corner of Strauchg. With green-gold arches and live music (M-Sa 3pm-9pm, Su 10am-6pm), this luxurious coffeehouse deserves its status as mecca of the cafe world. *Mélange* €3.50. Open M-Sa 7:30am-10pm, Su 10am-10pm. AmEx/MC/V.

**Café Hawelka,** I, Dorotheerg. 6 (☎ 512 82 30). A Viennese institution since 1939, this cafe has a long history as an artist's meeting place. The waiters move quickly between the tables and sofas, carrying plates of *Buchteln* (cake with plum marmalade; €3) and *mélange* (€3.20). Open M, W-Sa 8am-2am, Su 10am-2am. Cash only.

**Demel,** I, Kohlmarkt 14 (☎ 535 17 10). 5min. from the Stephansdom, down Graben. The most lavish *konditorei* (confectioner) in Vienna, Demel once served its creations to the imperial court. The chocolate is made fresh every morning, and the desserts are legendary. *Mélange* €3.80. Tortes €4. Open daily 10am-7pm. AmEx/MC/V.

**Café Sperl,** VI, Gumpendorferstr. 11. (☎ 586 41 58) U2: Museumsquartier. Marble tables and crystal chandeliers adorn one of Vienna's oldest, most elegant cafes. Very busy during peak hours. Sept.-June Su live piano 3:30-5:30pm. Open Sept.-June Ma-Sa 7am-11pm, Su 10am-8pm; July-Aug. M-Sa 7am-11pm. AmEx/MC/V.

**Café Sacher,** I, Philharmonikerstr. 4 (☎ 512 14 87), behind the opera house. This historic site serves the original world-famous *Sacher Torte* (€4.80). Cafe open daily 8am-11:30pm. Bakery open daily 9am-11:30pm. AmEx/MC/V.

# ▓ WINE TAVERNS (HEURIGEN)

Marked by a hanging evergreen branch, *Heurigen* serve *Heuriger* (wine) and Austrian delicacies, often in a relaxed outdoors setting. The wine is from the most recent harvest; good *Heuriger* is white, fruity, and full-bodied. Open in summer, *Heurigen* cluster in the Viennese suburbs where the grapes grow. Tourist buses head to the most famous region, **Grinzing,** in District XIX; you'll find better atmosphere in the hills of **Sievering, Neustift am Walde** (both in District XIX), and **Neuwaldegg** (in XVII). True *Heuriger* devotees make the trip to **Gumpoldskirchen.**

▓ **Buschenschank Heinrich Nierscher,** XIX, Strehlg. 21 (☎ 440 21 46). U6: Währingerstr. Tram #41 to Plötzleinsdorf (the last stop); then take bus #41A to Plötzleinsfriedhof (the 2nd stop) or walk up Pötzleinsdorfer Str. which becomes Khevenhüller Str.; go right on Strehlg. Enjoy a glass of *Heuriger* (€2.20) in the oversized country kitchen or the backyard overlooking the vineyards. Select a tray of meat, cheese, and bread for a light supper (€3-5). Open M, Th-Su 3pm-midnight. Cash only.

**10er Marie**, XVI, Ottakringerstr. 222-224 (☎489 46 47). U3: Ottakring, turn left on Thaliastr., then right onto Johannes-Krawarik. Locals frequent the large garden behind the yellow house. 0.25L of wine €2. Open M-Sa 3pm-midnight. MC/V.

# ◎ SIGHTS

Vienna's contrasting streets are by turns stately, residential, and decaying. To wander on your own, grab the brochure *Vienna from A to Z* (€3.60) from the tourist office, which also leads themed English-language walkings tours (€12); ask for the brochure *Walks in Vienna*. Contact **Pedal Power,** II, Ausstellungsstr. 3 (☎729 72 34; www.pedalpower.at), for **cycling tours** (€23). **Bus tours** (€35) are given by **Vienna Sightseeing Tours,** IV, Goldegg. 29 (☎712 46 83; www.viennasightseeing.at).

## INSIDE THE RING

A stroll in District I, Vienna's social and geographical center, is a feast for the senses. Cafe tables spill out into the cobblestone streets lined by Romanesque arches, Gothic portals, and Jugendstil apartments. The constant flow of people is interrupted by musicians and performers who attract circles of onlookers in the square just outside the modern **Haas Haus**.

**STEPHANSDOM AND GRABEN.** In the heart of the city, the massive **Stephansdom** is one of Vienna's most treasured landmarks. For a view of the old city, take the elevator up the North Tower or climb the 343 steps of the South Tower. *(☎515 52 35 26. North Tower open daily Apr.-June and Sept.-Oct. 8:30am-5:30pm; Nov.-Mar. 8:30am-5pm; July-Aug. 9am-5pm. South Tower open daily 9am-5:30pm. North Tower €4. South Tower €3.)* Downstairs, skeletons of plague victims fill the **catacombs.** The **Gruft** (vault) stores urns containing the Habsburgs' innards. *(Tours M-Sa 2 per hr. 10-11:30am and 1:30-4:30pm, Su and holidays 1:30-4:30pm. €4.)* From Stephanspl., follow Graben for Jugendstil architecture, including Otto Wagner's red marble **Grabenhof** and the underground public toilet complex designed by **Adolf Loos.**

**HOFBURG PALACE.** Previously a medieval castle, this imperial palace was the Habsburgs' home until 1918. Wing by wing, it was expanded over 800 years. Now containing the President's office and a few small museums, its grandest assets are in the **royal treasury.** The palace can best be admired from its **Michaelplatz** and **Heldenplatz** grand entrances. *(☎525 24 ext. 69 03; www.khm.at. U3: Herreng. Open Tu-W and F-Su 10am-6pm, Th 10am-9pm,. €10, students €7.50. Open M, W-Su 10am-6pm.)*

**HOHER MARKT AND STADTTEMPEL.** Once both a market and an execution site, **Hoher Markt** was home to the Roman encampment, **Vindobona.** Roman ruins lie beneath the shopping arcade across from the fountain. *(Open Tu-Su 9am-1pm and 2-5pm. €2, students €1.)* The biggest draw is the 1914 Jugendstil **Ankeruhr** (clock), whose figures—from Marcus Aurelius to Maria Theresa—rotate past the Viennese coat of arms accompanied by the tunes of their times. *(1 figure per hr. All figures appear at noon.)* Hidden on Ruprechtspl. is the **Stadttempel,** the only synagogue in Vienna to escape destruction during Kristallnacht. *(Seitenstetteng. 4. Mandatory guided tours M and Th at 11:30am, 2pm. €2, students €1.)*

**AM HOF AND FREYUNG.** Having served as a medieval jousting square, Am Hof now houses the **Kirche am Hof** (Church of the Nine Choirs of Angels) and **Collalto Palace,** where Mozart gave his first public performance. Just west of Am Hof is Freyung, the square with the **Austriabrunnen** (Austria Fountain) in the center. Medieval fugitives took asylum in the **Schottenstift** (Monastery of the Scots), giving rise to the name *Freyung,* or "sanctuary." Today, the annual **Christkindl market** fills the plaza with baked goods and holiday cheer (Dec. 1-24).

## OUTSIDE THE RING

Some of Vienna's most famous modern architecture is outside the Ring, where 20th-century designers found space to build. This area is also home to a number of Baroque palaces and parks that were once beyond the city limits.

**SCHLOß SCHÖNBRUNN.** Schönbrunn began as a humble hunting lodge, but Maria Theresa's ambition transformed it into a splendid palace. The **Imperial Tour** passes through the dazzling **Hall of Mirrors,** where six-year-old Mozart played. The longer **Grand Tour** also visits Maria Theresa's exquisite 18th-century rooms, including the ornate **Millions Room.** *(Schönbrunnerstr. 47. U4: Schönbrunn.* ☎ *811 132 39; www.schoenbrunn.at. Open daily July-Aug. 8:30am-6pm; Apr.-June and Sept.-Oct. 8:30am-5pm; Nov.-Mar. 8:30am-4:30pm. Imperial Tour 22 rooms; 35min.; €9.50, students €8.50. Grand Tour 40 rooms; 50min.; €13/12. English-language audio tour included.)* As impressive as Schönbrunn itself, the **gardens** behind the palace contain a **labyrinth** and a profusion of manicured greenery, flowers, and statuettes. *(Park open daily 6am-dusk. Labyrinth open daily July-Aug. 9am-7pm; Apr.-June and Sept. 9am-6pm; Oct. 9am-5pm; Nov. 9am-3:30pm. Park free. Labyrinth €2.90, students €2.40.)*

**KARLSKIRCHE.** Situated in Karlspl., **Karlskirche** (the Church of St. Borromeo) is an eclectic masterpiece. Under restoration in 2007, it combines a Neoclassical portico with a Baroque dome and Trajan-inspired columns. Save your money, as the church may be best viewed from the outside. *(IV, Kreuzherreng. 1. U1, 2, or 4 to Karlspl.* ☎ *504 61 87. Open M-Sa 9am-12:30pm and 1-7pm, Su 1-7pm. €6, students €4.)*

**ZENTRALFRIEDHOF.** The Viennese describe the Central Cemetery as half the size of Geneva but twice as lively. **Tor II** (Gate 2) contains the tombs of Beethoven, Brahms, Schubert, Strauss, and an honorary monument to Mozart, whose true resting place is an unmarked pauper's grave in the **Cemetery of St. Marx,** III, Leberstr. 6-8. **Tor I** (Gate 1) holds the old **Jewish Cemetery,** where many headstones are cracked and neglected. To navigate through the 2.5 million graves, pick up a map at the information desk just inside Tor II. *(XI, Simmeringer Hauptstr. 234. Tram #71 from Schwarzenbergpl. or Simmering.* ☎ *76 04 10. Open daily May-Aug. 7am-8pm; Apr. and Sept. 7am-7pm; Mar. and Oct. 7am-6pm; Nov.-Feb. 8am-5pm. Free.)*

# 🏛 MUSEUMS

With a museum around almost every corner, Vienna could exhaust any zealous visitor. The **Vienna Card** (€19), available at the tourist office, large U-bahn stops, and most hostels, entitles holders to museum and transit discounts for 72hr.

## INSIDE THE RING

**HAUS DER MUSIK AND RELIGIOUS MUSEUMS.** At the **Haus de Musik,** science meets music. Relax in the prenatal listening room, experience the physics of sound, learn about famous Viennese composers, and have a go at conducting an orchestra. *(I, Seilerstätte 30, near the opera house.* ☎ *51 64 80; www.hdm.at. Open daily 10am-10pm. €10, students €8.50. ½-price Tu after 5pm.)* After satiating your auditory senses, treat your eyes to the beautiful paintings at the **Albertina Museum.** First an Augustinian monastery and then part of Hofburg Palace, it now houses the Collection of Graphic Arts. Past exhibits featured Picasso, Monet, and various Pop artists. The *Prunkräume* (state rooms) display some of Albrecht Dürer's finest prints, including the famous praying hands. *(I, Albertinapl. 1.* ☎ *534 835 40; www.albertina.at. Open M-Tu and Th-Su 10am-6pm, W 10am-9pm. €9, students €7.)* The **Jüdisches Museum** (Jewish Museum) explores Jewish culture and history through holograms and traditional displays. The top floor has an accessible depository with thousands of seder plates, kiddush cups, and menorahs. *(I, Dorotheerg. 11, off Graben.* ☎ *535 04 31. Open M-F and Su 10am-6pm. €6.50, students €4.)*

## OUTSIDE THE RING

**▩ÖSTERREICHISCHE GALERIE (AUSTRIAN GALLERY).** The grounds of **Schloß Belvedere** houses the Österreichische Galerie's two museums. Home to *The Kiss* and other works by Klimt, the **Oberes Belvedere** supplements its magnificent collection of 19th- and 20th-century art with rotating exhibits. *(III, Prinz-Eugen-Str. 27. Walk from the Südbahnhof or take tram D from Schwarzenbergpl. to Schloß Belvedere. €9.50, students €6.)* The **Unteres Belvedere** contains the Austrian Museum of Baroque Art and the Austrian Museum of Medieval Art. *(Unteres Belvedere, III, Rennweg 6. Tram #71 from from Schwarzenbergpl. to Unteres Belvedere. €7.50, students €4.50. Both Belvederes ☎ 79 55 70. Open daily 10am-6pm. Combo ticket €13, students €8.50.)*

**▩KUNST HAUS WIEN.** Artist-environmentalist Friedenreich Hundertwasser built this museum without straight lines—even the floor bends. Arboreal "tree tenants" grow from the windowsills and the top floor. *(III, Untere Weißgerberstr. 13. U1 or 4 to Schwedenpl., then tram N to Radetzkypl. ☎ 712 04 91; www.kunsthauswien.at. Open daily 10am-7pm. Each exhibit €9, both €12; students €7/9. M €4.50/6, except holidays.)*

**▩ÖSTERREICHISCHES MUSEUM FÜR ANGEWANDTE KUNST (MAK).** This intimate, eclectic museum is dedicated to design, examining Thonet bentwood chairs' smooth curves, Venetian glass' intricacies, and modern architecture's steel heights. *(I, Stubenring 5. U3: Stubentor. ☎ 71 13 60; www.mak.at. Open Tu 10am-midnight, W-Su 10am-6pm. €7.90, students €5.50. Sa and holidays free.)*

**KUNSTHISTORISCHES MUSEUM (MUSEUM OF FINE ARTS).** One of the world's largest art collections features Italian paintings, Classical art, and an Egyptian burial chamber. The main building contains works by the Venetian and Flemish masters and across the street, in the Neue Burg wing of the Hofburg Palace, the **Ephesos Museum** exhibits findings from excavations in Turkey. The **Sammlung alter Musikinstrumente** includes Beethoven's harpsichord and Mozart's piano. *(U2: Museumsquartier. Across from the Burgring and Heldenpl., to the right of Maria Theresienpl. ☎ 525 24 41; www.khm.at. Main building open Tu-W, F-Su 10am-6pm, Th 10am-9pm; Ephesos and Sammlung open M and W-Su 10am-6pm. €10, students €7.50. English-language audio tour €3.)*

**MUSEUMSQUARTIER.** Central Europe's largest collection of modern art, the **Museum Moderner Kunst (MUMOK),** highlights Classical Modernism, Fluxus, Photo Realism, Pop Art, and Viennese Actionism in a building made from basalt lava. *(Open M-W and F-Su 10am-6pm, Th 10am-9pm. €9, students €7.)* The **Leopold Museum** has the world's largest Schiele collection, plus works by Egger-Lienz, Gerstl, Klimt, and Kokoschka. *(Open M-W and F-Su 10am-6pm, Th 10am-9pm. €9, students €6.)* Themed exhibits of contemporary artists fill **Kunsthalle Wien.** *(U2: Museumsquartier. ☎ 52 57 00; www.mqw.at. Open M-W, F-Su 10am-7pm, Th 10am-10pm. Exhibition Hall 1 €7.50; students M €5, Tu-Su €6. Exhibition Hall 2 €6/3.50/4.50. Both €11/7/9. "Art" ticket admits visitors to all three museums; €22. "Duo" ticket admits to Leopold and MUMOK; €17, students €11.)*

**FREUD MUSEUM.** Freud's former home has bric-a-brac that includes his report cards and circumcision certificate. *(IX, Bergg. 19. U2: Schottentor. ☎ 319 15 96; www.freud-museum.at. Open daily July-Sept. 9am-6pm; Oct.-June 9am-5pm €7, students €4.50.)*

# ⚠ GARDENS AND PARKS

**ALONG THE RING.** The **Stadtpark** (City Park) was the first municipal park outside the former city walls. The oft-photographed **Johann Strauss** monument is in the center of the park. *(U4: Stadtpark.)* Clockwise up the Ring, the gorgeous greenhouses of **Burggarten** (Palace Garden) were reserved for the imperial family until 1918. The **Schmetterlinghaus,** or Butterfly House, is found here. *(☎ 533 85 70. Open Apr.-Oct. M-F 10am-4:45pm, Sa-Su 10am-6:15pm; Nov.-Mar. M-Sa 10am-3:45pm.)* The romantic **Volksgarten** (People's Garden) is best viewed at sunset.

**AUGARTEN.** Northeast of downtown is Augarten, Vienna's oldest public park. In 1775, Kaiser Josef II gave the former formal French garden a Baroque face-lift and opened Augarten to the public. The WWII anti-aircraft towers now dominating the park's center detract from its previous beauty. *(Tram #31 from Schotten-ring or tram N to Obere Augartenstr. and head left down Taborstr. Open sunrise to sunset.)*

# 🎵 ENTERTAINMENT

Many of classical music's greats lived, composed, and performed in Vienna. Beethoven, Haydn, and Mozart wrote their best-known masterpieces here; a century later, Berg, Schönberg, and Webern refreshed the music scene. Today, Vienna hosts many budget performances, though in summer prices rise. The **Bundesthe-aterkasse,** I, Hanuschg. 3, sells tickets for the Staatsoper, the Volksoper, and the Burgtheater. (☎514 44 78 80. Open June to mid-Aug. M-F 10am-2pm; mid-Aug. to June M-F 8am-6pm, Sa-Su 9am-noon; Sa during Advent 9am-5pm.)

> **Staatsoper,** I, Opernring 2 (☎514 44 22 50; www.wiener-staatsoper.at). Vienna's premier opera performs nearly every night Sept.-June. No shorts. Seats €5-254. 500 standing-room tickets go on sale 80min. before every show (1 per person; €2-3.50); arrive 2hr. before curtain. Box office in the foyer open M-F 9am until 1hr. before curtain, Sa 9am-noon; 1st Sa of each month and during Advent 9am-5pm.

> **Wiener Philharmoniker Orchestra** (Vienna Philharmonic Orchestra; ☎505 65 25; www.wienerphilharmoniker.at). Plays in the **Musikverein,** Austria's premier concert hall. To purchase tickets, visit the box office, Bösendorferstr. 12, well ahead.

> **Wiener Sängerknaben** (Vienna Boys' Choir; ☎533 99 27) sings during mass every Su at 9:15am (mid-Sept. to late June) in the **Hofburgkapelle** (U3: Herreng.). Despite rumors to the contrary, standing room is free; arrive before 8am. Tickets €5-29.

# 🎭 NIGHTLIFE

With one of the highest bar-to-cobblestone ratios in the world, Vienna is a great place to party. Take U1 or 4 to Schwedenpl., which will drop you within blocks of the **Bermuda Dreieck** (Bermuda Triangle), an area packed with crowded clubs. If you make it out, head down **Rotenturmstraße** toward Stephansdom or walk around the areas bounded by the synagogue and Ruprechtskirche. Slightly outside the Ring, the streets off **Burggasse** and **Stiftgasse** in District VII and the **university quarter** in Districts XIII and IX have outdoor courtyards and hip bars. Viennese nightlife starts late, often after 11pm. For listings, pick up the indispensable *Falter* (€2.60).

## BARS

> ▨ **Das Möbel,** VII, Burgg. 10. U2 or 3: Volkstheater. (☎524 94 97; www.das-moebel.at). An artsy crowd chats and reads amid metal couches and Swiss-army tables, all created by designers and available for sale. Don't leave without seeing the bathroom. Internet free for 1st 15min., €0.90 per 15min. thereafter. Open daily 10am-1am. Cash only.

> **Chelsea,** VIII, Lerchenfeldergürtel 29-31. U6: Thaliastr. or Josefstädterstr. (☎407 93 09; www.chelsea.co.at), under the U-Bahn, between the two stops. Austrian and international bands rock this underground club twice a week, while weekend DJs spin techno-pop. 0.5L beer €3.30. Cover €6-12 for band performances, entrance to bar free. Happy hour 4-5pm. Open M-Sa 6pm-4am, Su 4pm-3am. Cash only.

> **Krah Krah,** I, Rabensteig. 8 (☎533 81 93; www.krah-krah.at). A Bermuda Dreieck bar, Krah Krah has over 50 beer varieties and many lesser-known Austrian brews. Try the Kulmbach Kulminator 28, the "world's strongest beer" (0.3L, €4.60). Happy hour M-F 3:30-5:30pm; 0.4L of Krah brew €1.50. Open M-Sa 11am-2am, Su 11am-1am. MC/V.

> **1516,** I, Schwarzenbergstr. 2 (☎961 15 16; www.1516brewingcompany.com), on the corner of Krugerstr. Old-fashioned ceiling fans and beer barrels turned into tables give

1516 a surprisingly pleasant warehouse feel. Home-brewed beer €2, Russian and Czech imports €4. Food €3-12. Open daily 11am-2am. AmEx/MC/V.

**Kaktus,** I, Seitenstetteng. 5 (☎0676 670 44 96; www.kaktusbar.at), in the heart of the Bermuda Triangle. Packed with twentysomethings and dripping with alcohol. Mostly mainstream music. 0.5L beer €3.40. Dress to impress. Happy hour M-W, F-Sa 7-10pm; drinks ½-price. Open M-Th and Su 7pm-3am, F-Sa 7pm-4am. Cash only.

## CLUBS

**Flex,** I, Donaulände (☎533 75 25; www.flex.at), near the Schottenring U-Bahn station (U2 or U4) down by the Danube. Dance, grab a beer or bring your own, and sit by the river with everyone else. DJs start spinning techno, reggae, house, ska, or electronic at 11pm. Beer €4. Cover €2-10, free after 3:30am. Open daily 8pm-4am. Cash only.

**Volksgarten Disco,** I, Burgring 1 (☎532 42 41; www.volksgarten.at). U2: Volkstheater. A fountain, palms, and a hot young crowd makes this one of Vienna's trendiest clubs. M tango, all levels welcome. Th alternative and house. F hip-hop. Sa house. Cover €5-10. Open June-Aug. M 8pm-2am, Th 8pm-4am, F 11pm-6am, Sa 9pm-6am; Sept.-May M 8pm-2am, Th 8pm-4am, F 11pm-6am, Sa 11pm-6am. MC/V; min. €70.

**passage,** I, the corner of Burgring. and Babenbergerstr. (☎961 88 00; www.sun-shine.at). What used to be an underground walkway is now a collection of small, but fashionable, nightclubs. Club Cosmopolitan plays soul music, Club Fusion spins house, and disco blares from the Bachelor Club. Open daily 10pm-late. Cash only.

**Club Habana,** I, Mahlerstr. 11 (☎513 20 75; www.clubhabana.at). This salsa-fest will add some Latin fire to your mood. All levels welcome. M Cuban band. Mixed drinks €8. Cuban cigars €2-26. Open M-Th and Su 10pm-4am, F-Sa 10pm-6am. AmEx/MC/V.

**Porgy & Bess,** I, Riemerg. 11 (☎512 88 11; www.porgy.at). U1: Stubentor. The best jazz club in Vienna. Show prices vary—generally €15-20. Open M-Th, Su 9pm-2am, F-Sa 9pm-4am. Box office open M-Sa 3-8pm, Su 5-8pm. MC/V.

## GLBT

**Mango,** VI, Laimgrubeng. 3 (☎587 44 48; www.mangobar.at). U2: Museumsquartier. Mango draws gay men with its casual climate, golden walls, and pop music. Mixed drinks €6.50. Open daily 9pm-4am. Cash only.

**Why Not,** I, Tiefer Graben 22 (☎920 47 14; www.why-not.at). Gays and lesbians dance late into the night in Vienna's only GLBT disco. Drinks from €3. Cover F after midnight and Sa €8; includes 2 drink tickets. Open F-Sa 10pm-4am or later. Cash only.

**Felixx,** Gumpendorferstr. 5 (☎920 47 14). U2: Museumsquartier. On the way to Mango. A classy bar and restaurant for people of all orientations. Beer €2.80-3.50. Wine from €2. Mixed drinks €5-6.50. Open daily 7pm-3am. Kitchen open until 11pm. Cash only.

**Frauen Café,** VIII, Lange Gasse 11 (☎406 37 54; www.frauencafe.com). U2 or 3: Volk-steater. This laid-back, women-only establishment boasts lively conversation. Open Tu-Th 7pm-midnight, F-Sa 7pm-2am. Cash only.

# ▨ FESTIVALS

Vienna hosts several important festivals, mostly musical. The **Wiener Festwochen** (early May to mid-June) has a diverse program of concerts, exhibitions, and plays. (☎58 92 20; www.festwochen.or.at.) In May, over 4000 people attend **Lifeball,** Europe's largest AIDS charity event and Vienna's biggest gay celebration. With the Lifeball Style Police threatening to dispose of underdressed guests (make-up and hair-styling are musts), come looking like you deserve to mix and mingle with Bill Clinton, Elton John, and other celebrities. (☎595 56 77; www.lifeball.org. €75-135). Democrats host the late June **Danube Island Festival,** which celebrates with fireworks and concerts (☎535 35 35; www.donauinselfest.at; free). The Staat-

ansnumbercntrtandre

soper and Volkstheater host the **Jazzfest Wien** (☎503 56 47; www.viennajazz.org) during the first weeks of July. Also in July, the annual **Film Festival** (www.wien-event.at), in Rathauspl., features nightly exhibitions of music films. From mid-July to mid-August, the **ImPulsTanz Festival** (☎523 55 58; www.impulstanz.com) attracts some of the world's greatest dance troupes and offers seminars to enthusiasts. The city-wide film festival, **Viennale** (www.viennale.at), kicks off in mid-October.

**EURO CUP 2008.** The **2008 European Football Championship** (June 7-29) will be held in Austria and Switzerland. Innsbruck, Klagenfurt, Salzburg, and Vienna will host matches. Expect crowds and unrestrained merrymaking. Visit www.uefa.com for more info. For venues in Switzerland, see p. 956.

### ⚑ LET'S GO TO VIENNA: BRATISLAVA, SLK ☎(0)2

Home to the **M.R. Štefánik International Airport** (**BTS;** ☎48 57 11 11; www.letiskobratislava.sk), Bratislava (pop. 500,000) often serves as a gateway to Western Europe. In addition to domestic flights from Slovakia, budget airlines **SkyEurope** (☎48 50 11 11; www.skyeurope.com) and **Ryanair** (www.ryanair.com; see **Transportation,** p. 44) run **shuttle buses** to and from Vienna (1-1¼hr., 7-8 per day, 363Sk). Vienna-bound **trains** (☎20 29 11 11; www.zsr.sk) depart from **Bratislava Hlavná Stanica,** at the end of Predstani̇né nám., hourly (1hr., round-trip 283Sk). **Buses** make a similar journey, leaving from Mlynské nivy 31 (1½hr., 1 per hr., 400Sk). Another option is to sail to Vienna (1¾hr., 2 per day, 150Sk) with **Lodná osobná doprava,** Fajnorovo nábr. 2 (☎52 93 22 26; www.lod.sk; open daily 8:30am-5:30pm). For overnight accommodations, food listings, and more info on Bratislava, see p. 1046.

# SALZBURGER LAND AND HOHE TAUERN REGION

Salzburger Land's precious white gold, *Salz* (salt), drew the first settlers more than 3000 years ago. Modern travelers instead prefer to seek the shining lakes and rolling hills of the Salzkammergut, where Salzburg and Hallstatt are among the more enticing destinations.

# SALZBURG ☎0662

As its Baroque architecture attests, Salzburg was Austria's ecclesiastical center in the 17th and 18th centuries. This golden age fostered a rich musical culture that lives on today in elaborate concert halls and impromptu folk performances in public squares. The city's love for its native genius, Mozart, climaxes in summer during the Salzburg Festival, when fans the world over come to pay their respects.

## ⬛ TRANSPORTATION

**Trains** leave from **Hauptbahnhof,** in Südtirolerpl. (☎05 17 17) for: Graz (4hr., 1 per hr. 8am-6:30pm, €40); Innsbruck (2hr., 11 per day, €34); Munich, GER (2-3hr., 30 per day, €27); Vienna (3½hr., 26 per day, €44); Zürich, SWI (6hr., 7 per day, €73). **Buses** depart from the depot in front of the train station. Single tickets (€1.80) available at automatic machines or from the drivers. Books of 5 tickets (€8), day passes (€4.20), and week passes (€11) are available at machines. Punch your ticket when you board or risk a €36 fine. Buses stop running 10:30-11:30pm.

## ⬛ ⚑ ORIENTATION AND PRACTICAL INFORMATION

Three hills and the **Salzach River** delineate Salzburg, located just a few kilometers from the German border. The **Neustadt** is north of the river, and the beautiful **Alts-**

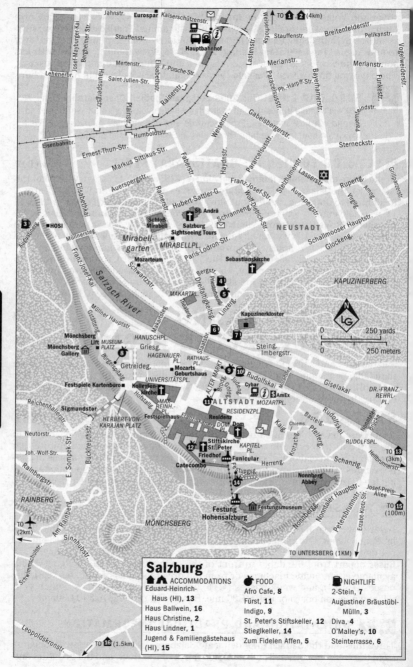

**Salzburg**

**⛺⛺ ACCOMMODATIONS**
Eduard-Heinrich-
  Haus (HI), **13**
Haus Ballwein, **16**
Haus Christine, **2**
Haus Lindner, **1**
Jugend & Familiengästehaus
  (HI) **15**

**🍎 FOOD**
Afro Cafe, **8**
Fürst, **11**
Indigo, **9**
St. Peter's Stiftskeller, **12**
Stieglkeller, **14**
Zum Fidelen Affen, **5**

**🍺 NIGHTLIFE**
2-Stein, **7**
Augustiner Bräustübl-
  Mülln, **3**
Diva, **4**
O'Malley's, **10**
Steinterrasse, **6**

AUSTRIA

**tadt** squeezes between the southern bank and the **Mönchsberg** hill. The Hauptbahnhof is on the northern side of town beyond the Neustadt; bus #1 connects it to **Hanuschplatz**, the *Altstadt's* main public transportation hub, by the river near Griesg. and the Staatsbrücke. Buses #3, 5, and 6 run from the Hauptbahnhof to Rathaus and Mozartsteg, also in the *Altstadt*. Neustadt hubs include **Mirabellplatz, Makartplatz**, and **Mozartsteg**, the pedestrian bridge leading across the Salzach to Mozartpl. To reach the *Altstadt* on foot, turn left out of the station onto Rainerstr. and follow it straight under the tunnel and on to Mirabellpl.; continue to Makartplatz and turn right to cross the **Makartsteg** bridge.

**Tourist Office:** Mozartpl. 5 (☎88 98 73 30), in the *Altstadt*. Books rooms (€2.20 fee and 10% deposit) and offers tours of the city (daily 12:15pm, €8). It also sells the **Salzburg Card**, which grants admission to all museums and sights and unlimited public transportation 1-day pass €23, 2-day €31, 3-day €36. Open daily 9am-6pm. Branch at the Hauptbahnhof.

**Currency Exchange:** Banks offer better rates for cash than AmEx offices but often charge higher commissions. Banking hours M-F 8am-12:30pm and 2-4:30pm. Train station exchange open M-F 7am-9pm.

**American Express:** Mozartpl. 5 (☎80 80). Cashes AmEx cheques (free for cheques in US dollars; €5 fee otherwise) and books tours. Open M-F 9am-5:30pm, Sa 9am-noon.

**Luggage Storage:** 24hr. lockers at the train station €2-3.50.

**GLBT Resources: Homosexual Initiative of Salzburg (HOSI)**, Müllner Hauptstr. 11 (☎43 59 27; www.hosi.or.at), hosts workshops and offers a free guide to Salzburg. Open sporadically, but the HOSI-run bar next door is open regularly W 7pm-midnight, F-Sa 8pm-midnight. Phone staffed F 7-9pm.

**Pharmacies:** Pharmacies in the city center open M-F 8am-6pm, Sa 8am-noon. 3 pharmacies rotate being open 24hr.; ask for a calendar at any pharmacy or check the list on the door of a closed one.

**Internet Access: Isis**, at the train station. €1 per 15min., €1.50 per 30min. Open daily 8am-midnight. In the *Altstadt*, **Cybar**, Mozartpl. 5 (☎84 48 22), to the left of the tourist office. €2 per 10min. Open daily July-Aug. 9am-midnight; Sept.-June 10am-11pm.

**Post Office:** At the train station (☎88 30 30). Open M-F 7am-6pm, Sa 8am-2pm, Su 1-6pm. **Postal Code:** A-5020.

# ◤ ACCOMMODATIONS

Within the city itself, budget hotels are few and far between. Instead, try looking for accommodations outside Salzburg still accessible by public transportation. For the best deal, check out *Privatzimmer* (rooms in a family home), usually located on the city's outskirts, with welcoming hosts and bargain prices. Reservations are recommended, especially in summer. For a complete list of *Privatzimmer* and booking help, see the tourist office.

**Eduard-Heinrich-Haus (HI)**, Eduard-Heinrich-Str. 2 (☎62 59 76; www.hostel-ehh.at). Spacious rooms overlook the garden and forest. Breakfast included. Laundry €6. Internet €2.60 per 20min. Key deposit €20 or ID. Reception 7-10am and 5pm-midnight. Dorms €18; singles €27, with shower and toilet €31; doubles €41/47; triples €47/55; quads €62/78. €3 HI discount. Reserve ahead in summer. AmEx/MC/V. ❶

**Jugend & Familiengästehaus (HI)**, Josef-Preis-Allee 18 (☎84 26 700; www.jfgh.at). Take bus #5 (dir.: Birkensiedlung) to Justizgebäude, close to the *Altstadt*. Kids pack this family-friendly hostel in May and June when school orchestras descend on Salzburg. Tight, poorly ventilated dorms. Breakfast included. Laundry €3. Internet €3 per 40min. Reception 7am-12:30am. 8-bed dorms €21; doubles €47, with shower and toilet €62. €1.50 HI discount. €3 discount for 2 or more nights. AmEx/MC/V. ❷

**Haus Ballwein**, Moosstr. 69a (☎82 40 29; www.privatvermieter.com/haus-ballwein), south of the city. Take a bus to Makartpl., then south-bound bus #21 to Gsengerweg.

## HOW DO YOU SOLVE A PROBLEM LIKE MARILLE?

By baking a strudel 50m long, of course.

During the *Alles Marille* ("Everything Apricot") festival in Krems, the fuzzy fruit appears in every form imaginable, from apricot schnapps to apricot ice cream to apricot dumplings to apricot spritzer. The *pièce de résistance*, however, is Café Hagmann's 50m long *Marillenstrudel*, which stretches down Taglisher Markt street. Everyone in town can get a piece of the action from this perpetual pastry, laden with fluffy apricot cream and sugared almonds (€3 per 30min. tasting). A traditionally dressed folk band serenades the town with Austrian favorites from under an awning festooned with apricot balloons, while revelers sun themselves and imbibe all things apricot. All of Krems turns out for the fun—including the mayor himself—creating the closest thing to traffic the town gets. To top it all off, Saturday ends with a huge party down by the *Schiffstation*, where the *Marillen* schnapps and punch flow like milk and honey. So as you bike, drive, or walk along the Danube and see the trees laden with their precious golden goods, drop into Krems and indulge with the locals in a lavish fruit fest.

*July 17-20, 2008. ☎2732 82676. For more info, check www.alles-marille.at.*

Rooms with colorful curtains, natural wood paneling, and braided rugs. Bike rental €5 per day. Breakfast included. Singles €25, with shower €35; doubles €48/50-55; triples with bath €75; 4-person apartment €80. Cash only. ❷

**Haus Lindner,** Panoramaweg 5 (☎45 66 81; www.haus-lindner.at), north of the city in Kasern Berg. Take the S2 train to Salzburg Kasern (6min.; 2 per hr.; €1.60, Eurail valid). Walk uphill on Bergstr. and turn left on Panormaweg. Some of the tastefully furnished rooms have balconies. Breakfast included. Call for pickup from the station. Doubles €32-36; triples €48, with shower €56; quads €56. Cash only. ❷

**Haus Christine,** Panoramaweg 3 (☎45 67 73; www.haus-christine.org), next to Haus Lindner. Spacious, clean rooms with a country motif. Breakfast served on a glass-enclosed patio overlooking the countryside—the best view on the block. Doubles €36; triples €48; quads €64. MC/V with 5% charge. ❶

## ▶ FOOD

Countless beer gardens and pastry-shop patios make Salzburg a great place for outdoor dining. Local specialties include *Salzburger nockerl* (egg whites, sugar, and raspberry filling baked into three mounds that represent the hills of Salzburg) and the world-famous *Mozartkugel* (hazelnuts coated in pistachio marzipan, nougat, and chocolate). **Supermarkets** cluster on the Mirabellpl. side of the river. **Open-air markets** in Universitätspl. sell fresh fruits and veggies, giant pretzels, meats, and cheeses. (Open M-F 6am-7pm, Sa 6am-1pm.)

**Indigo,** Rudolfskai 8 (☎84 34 80), to the left of the Staatsbrücke when facing the *Altstadt*. This tiny corner eatery draws a local crowd with delicious salads, bowls of steaming Asian noodles, and sushi (€4.50-5). Salads €1.20 per 100g. Noodles €5. Sushi €0.55-1.65. Open June-Aug. M-W 10am-10pm, Th-Sa 10am-midnight; Sept.-May M-Sa 10am-10pm. Cash only. ❶

**Zum Fidelen Affen,** Priesterhausg. 8 (☎87 73 61), off Linzerg. Hearty Austrian food keeps everyone coming back to Zum Fidelen Affen ("The Faithful Ape"). Try the toasted black bread with various toppings (€5-7), the farmer's salad (€9), or the Monkey Steak (roasted pork with bacon, mushrooms, and tomatoes; €10). Vegetarian options available. Open M-Sa 5pm-midnight. AmEx/MC/V. ❷

**St. Peter's Stiftskeller,** St-Peter-Bezirk 1-4 (☎84 12 68). At the foot of the cliffs next to St. Peter's Monastery. The oldest restaurant in Central Europe, established in AD 803. The innovative cuisine is anything but archaic, with options like quail. Entrees €10-23. Open M-F 11am-midnight. AmEx/MC/V. ❸

**Stieglkeller,** Festungsg. 10 (☎84 26 81). A short walk up the Festungsg. from the bottom of the Festungsbahn. A Salzburg favorite since 1492. Seating for 1600: outside under shady trees or inside under high ceilings and mounted antlers. Menu includes *Schweinsbraten* (roast pork with sauerkraut and dumpling; €10) and Bratwurst with sauerkraut and potatoes (€7.60). Open daily May-Sept. 10:30am-11pm. MC/V. ❸

**Afro Cafe,** Bürgerspitalpl. 5 (☎84 48 88; www.afrocoffee.com). With pink walls and pretzel-shaped chairs, this laid-back java shop serves tapas (€4-8), ostrich burgers (€10), and couscous (€9) to hip young professionals. At night, the cafe becomes a bar, serving shots (€3) and exotic mixed drinks (€4.50-7) like the Kinshas Kiwi (kiwi juice, lime juice, rum, and gingko; €7). Open daily 9am-11pm. Cash only. ❷

**Fürst,** Brodg. 13 (☎843 7590). Home to the original Mozartkugel (€.90), this popular cafe has satisfied sweet tooths and caffeine cravings for 120 years. The *hauskaffe* (€3.40), the house specialty, comes with two chocolates, foamed milk, and whipped cream. *Mélange* €2.80. Open M-Sa 8am-9pm, Su 9am-9pm. AmEx/MC/V. ❶

# 🔍 SIGHTS

**FESTUNG HOHENSALZBURG.** Built between 1077 and 1681 by the ruling archbishops, the imposing Hohensalzburg Fortress, which looms over Salzburg from atop Mönchsberg, is the largest completely preserved castle in all of Europe—partly because it was never successfully attacked. The **Festungsmuseum** inside the fortress has side-by-side histories of Salzburg, the fortress, and the world. An audio tour (30min., 4 per hr.) leads visitors up the **watch-tower** for an unmatched panorama of the city and to an organ nicknamed the "Bull of Salzburg" for its off-key snorting. (*☎8424 3011. Take the trail or the Festungsbahn funicular up to the fortress from Festungsg. Funicular May-Aug. 9am-10pm; Sept. 9am-9pm; Oct-Apr. 9am-5pm. Open daily July-Aug. 9am-7pm; Sept. and May-June 9am-6pm; Oct.-Apr. 9am-5pm. Last museum entry 30min. before closing. €10; includes round-trip funicular ride.*)

**MOZARTS GEBURTSHAUS.** Mozart's oversivited birthplace holds a collection of the child genius' belongings, including his first violin and keyboard instruments. Arrive before 11am to avoid the crowd. (*☎84 43 13. Getreideg. 9. Open daily July-Aug. 9am-7pm; Sept.-June 9am-6pm. Last entry 30min. before closing. €6, students €5.*)

**STIFTSKIRCHE, CATACOMBS, AND THE DOM.** The **Monastery of St. Peter** rests against the Mönchsberg cliffs. **Stiftskirche St. Peter,** a church within the monastery, features a marble portal from 1244. In the 18th century, the building was remodeled in Rococo style. (*☎844 5760. Open daily 9am-12:15pm and 2:30-6:30pm.*) To the right of the church's entrance is the monastery's **Friedhof** (cemetery). Tiger lilies and ivy embellish the fanciful curls of the wrought-iron crosses. The entrance to the **catacombs** is on the far right, against the Mönchsberg. (*Monastery open May-Sept. Tu-Su 10:30am-5pm; Oct.-Apr. W-Th 10:30am-3:30pm, F-Su 10:30am-4pm. €1, students €0.60. Cemetery open Apr.-Sept. 6:30am-7:30pm; Oct.-Mar. 6:30am-6pm. Free.*) The exit at the other end of the cemetery leads to the immense Baroque **Dom** (cathedral), where Mozart was christened in 1756 and later worked as concertmaster and court organist. The square in front of the cathedral, **Domplatz,** features a statue of the Virgin Mary and figures representing Wisdom, Faith, the Church, and the Devil.

**RESIDENZ.** Home of the later Salzburg princes, this palace once boasted 180 rooms of Renaissance, Baroque, and Classical art. Most of the building is now used by the University of Salzburg, but the second floor staterooms—the **Prunkräume**—still contain their original ornate furnishing. (*☎804 226 90. Residenzpl. 1. Open daily 10am-5pm. Last entry 4:30pm. €5.20, students €4.20; includes audio tour.*)

**KOLLEGIENKIRCHE.** In Mozart's backyard stands one of the largest Baroque chapels on the continent. Sculpted clouds coat the nave, while pudgy cherubim frolic over the church's immense apse. (*Open daily 9am-5pm; hours vary. Free.*)

AUSTRIA

**MIRABELL PALACE AND GARDENS.** Mirabellpl. holds the marvelous **Schloß Mirabell,** which the supposedly celibate Archbishop Wolf Dietrich built for his mistress and their 15 children in 1606. *(Open daily 7am-9pm. Free.)* Behind the palace is the **Mirabellgarten,** an ornate, well-maintained maze of flower beds and fountains that contains the moss-covered **Zauberflötenhäuschen** ("Magic Flute Little House") where Mozart purportedly composed *The Magic Flute.*

**THE SOUND OF MUSIC.** The hills may not really be alive with the sound of music, but tour companies bid eager visitors to relive all the scenes of the 1965 movie. Stops along the 4hr. tour include: **Leopoldskron Palace;** the Von Trapp home where the children fall into the lake; the meadows of **Saint Gilgen,** and **Lake Wolfgang; Lustschloß Hellbrunn,** home of the glass gazebo; and the Mirabell Gardens, where the children sing "Do re mi." **Salzburg Sightseeing Tours** runs the trip for €35. *(☎88 16 16. Mirabellpl. 2. Tours 9:30am and 2pm. Free pickup from hotel or hostel.)*

## 🎭 ENTERTAINMENT

During the **Salzburger Festspiele** (July-Aug.), operas, plays, films, concerts, and tourists overrun every available public space; expect room prices to rise accordingly and plan ahead. Info and tickets for *Festspiele* events are available through the **Festspiele Kartenbüro** (ticket office) and **Direkt Verkauf** (daily box office) at Karajanpl. 11, against the mountain and next to the tunnel. (☎804 5500; www.salzburgfestival.at. Open mid-Mar. to June M-F 9:30am-3pm, through the end of *Festspiele* daily 9:30am-6pm. Tickets €15-360.) In other months, head to a concert organized by the **Mozarteum.** Their **Mozartwoche,** a week-long celebration of Mozart, during which his sacred works are performed, occurs at the end of January. (Jan. 25-Feb. 5. ☎87 31 54; www.mozarteum.at.) The **Dom** has a concert program in July, August, and early October. (☎88 46 23 45. €20, students €7.) From May to September, the Mirabell Gardens hosts **outdoor performances** including concerts, folk singing, and dancing. The tourist office has leaflets on scheduled events, but an evening stroll through the park might answer your questions equally as well. **Mozartplatz** and **Kapitelplatz** are popular stops for street musicians and school bands. For more info, visit www.salzburg-festivals.com.

## 🍺 BARS AND BEER GARDENS

Munich may be the world's beer capital, but much of its liquid gold flows south to Austria's pubs and *Biergärten* (beer gardens). These lager oases cluster in the city center along the **Salzach River.** The more boisterous revelers stick to **Rudolfskai,** between the Staatsbrücke and Mozartsteg. Elsewhere, especially along **Chiemseegasse** and around **Anton-Neumayr-Platz,** you can throw back a few drinks in a reserved *Beisl* (pub). Refined bars with middle-aged patrons can be found along **Steingasse** and **Giselakai** on the other side of the river.

🏆 **Augustiner Bräustübl-Mülln,** Augustinerg. 4 (☎43 12 46). Although the monks are gone, the *Bäukloster* they founded in 1621 continues to turn out home-brewed beer by the barrel. Follow the long halls to the end to reach the *Biergärten.* Beer 0.3L €2.10, 0.5L €2.60. Open M-F 3-11pm, Sa-Su 2:30-11pm; last call 10:30pm. Cash only.

**2-Stein,** Giselakai 9 (☎87 71 79). The go-to place for Salzburg's gay and lesbian scene. Mixed drinks from €5. Open M-W and Su 6pm-4am, Th-Sa 6pm-5am. MC/V.

**Steinterrasse,** Giselakai 3-5 (☎88 20 70), on the 7th fl. of the Stein Hotel. This hip cafe-bar knows that a lofty rooftop panorama doesn't have to mean equally lofty prices. A young crowd comes to flirt while admiring the lights of the *Altstadt.* Beer €2-6. Mixed drinks €4-11. Open daily 9am-1am. AmEx/MC/V.

**Diva,** Priesterhausg. 22 (☎43 15 31; www.divabar.at). On warm summer nights, a gay clientele fills out the tables in front of this cafe-bar. The dark purple interior blends chic mood lighting and relaxed lounges. Beer and wine €2-3.40. Mixed drinks €3.50-12. Open M-Th and Su 6pm-2am, F-Sa 6pm-4am. MC/V.

**O'Malley's,** Rudolfskai 16 (☎84 92 65; www.omalleyssalzburg.com). Multiple bars ensure you'll always have a drink (€3-8) in hand. Happy hour 6-8pm. Open M-Th and Su 4pm-2am, F-Sa 4pm-4am. MC/V; min. €30.

**⚡ DAYTRIP FROM SALZBURG: UNTERSBERG.** On the German border south of Salzburg, Untersberg is a popular **hike** with the locals. On clear days, you can see the lakes of the Salzburg district below and snow-covered peaks on the horizon. The 3hr. climb from the base isn't difficult, but a **Seilbahn** (cable car) drops passengers off just a gentle 20-30min. hike from Hochthron's summit. From there, an 1½hr. of steeper climbing leads to ⚡**Schnellenberger Eishöhle,** Germany's largest ice cave with 60,000 cubic meters of ice. Intrepid alpinists can continue around the mountain, but should pick up a trail map from a cable car station or the Toni-Lenz Hütte, near the ice cave. (☎06246 724 77. Bus #25 from Hanuschpl. Cable car runs 2 per hr. daily July-Sept. 8:30am-5:30pm; Mar.-June and Oct. 8:30am-5pm; Nov-Feb. 9am-4pm. Up €11, students €10; down €10/9; round-trip €18/16. Ice caves open daily June-Sept. 10am-4pm; Oct. 10am-3pm. Mandatory tours 1 per hr., €5. July-Aug. come early to avoid crowds.)

# HALLSTATT
☎ 06134

Easily the Salzkammergut's most striking, touristed lakeside village, tiny Hallstatt (pop. 960) teeters on the Hallstattersee's banks. The town's salt-rich earth has helped preserve its archaeological treasures—so extensive that one era in Celtic studies (800-400 BC) is dubbed "the Hallstatt era." Back when Rome was still a village, the "white gold" from the salt mines made Hallstatt a world-famous settlement. Above Hallstatt, the 2500-year-old **Salzbergwerk** is the world's oldest salt mine. Take the 1hr. guided tour and zip down a wooden mining slide to an eerie lake deep inside the mountain. Ride the **Salzbergbahn funicular** (open daily 9am until 1hr. after last tour; one-way €8.50, with Salzbergbahn €5.10. Round-trip €8.50/5.10) or follow the footpath from town 1hr. to reach Salzbergwerk. (☎200 24 00; www.salzwelten.at. €16, students €9.30; with funicular €21/13. English-language tours June 4 per hr. 9am-3pm; July-Sept. 14 4 per hr. 9am-4pm; Apr. 26-May and Sept. 15-Oct. 26 1 per 2hr. 9am-3pm.) Hallstatt is also the site of an immense, well-preserved Iron Age archaeological find. **The Charnel House** next to St. Michael's Chapel is an ossuary filled with the painted bones of over 1200 villagers dating from as early as the 18th century; the latest skull was added in 1995. From the ferry dock, follow the signs marked **Katholische Kirche.** (☎82 79. Open daily June-Sept. 10am-6pm; May and Oct. 10am-4pm; Nov.-Apr. call for an appointment.) The tourist office has a great English-language **hiking** guide (free) suggesting 50 day hikes and 10 multi-day traverses, as well as bike trail maps (€7). The easy **Waldbachstrub Waterfall hike** (1¾-2hr. round-trip) in the Echental Valley follows a glacial stream up to a waterfall. From the bus stop, follow the brown Malerweg signs near the supermarket until you reach a gazebo (about 30min.), which marks the trailhead. At the bridge before the waterfall, the path branches off to the left up to the **Gletschergarten,** a series of small glacial-stream waterfalls. The more difficult **Gangsteig** trail (look to the right just before the falls for a slippery stairway carved into a cliff), requires sturdy shoes for the tough climb. Hikers will have to derive pleasure from the trek itself—there is no rewarding view at the end.

To reach **Gästehaus Zur Mühle ❶,** Kirchenweg 36, from the tourist office, walk uphill and head for a short tunnel at the upper right corner of the square; it's at the end of the tunnel by the waterfall. (☎48 13. Locker deposit €15. Linens €3. Reception 11am-2pm and 4-10pm. Dorms €12. MC/V.) Enjoy a glorious view of the lake from the beachside lawn at **Frühstückspension Sarstein ❷,** Gosamühlstr. 83, where friendly owners make guests feel at home. From the ferry, turn right on Seestr. and walk 10min. (☎82 17; www.pension-sarstein.com. Breakfast included. Showers €1

**AUSTRIA**

per 10min. Doubles €44-50, with shower and toilet €60-66; holiday quads for 3 or more days €60-80. Reserve ahead in summer. Cash only.) **Camping Klausner-Höll ❶**, Lahnstr. 201, lies in the shadow of the mountains and at the trail head of valley hikes. To get there, turn right out of the tourist office and follow Seestr. for 10min.; from the bus stop, make a left down Lahnstr. (☎83 22; www.campingwelt.com/klausner-hoell. Kitchen available. Laundry €6. Reception 8am-noon and 4-8pm. Lockout daily noon-3pm and 10pm-7:30am. Open Apr. 15-Oct. 15. €6.50 per person, €11 per tent. Discounts Apr. 15-June and Sept.-Oct. 15. AmEx/MC/V.) The cheapest eats are at **Konsum** supermarket, Kernmagazinpl. 8, across from the bus stop, where the butcher prepares sandwiches on request. (☎82 26. Open M-F 7:30am-noon and 3-6pm, Sa 7:30am-noon. Cash only.) The meat shop **Karl Forstinger ❶**, Seestr. 139, between the tourist office and the bus stop, grills a wide variety of fresh regional *Wurst*. (☎0676 788 72 99. *Wurst* and roll €2-3. Open M-F 10am-5pm, Sa 10am-4pm, Su 11am-4pm. Cash only.) Though most of Hallstatt's dining options are expensive and geared to tourists, try the lakeside **Bräu Gasthof ❸**, Seestr. 120, where beer and an unbeatable view have been served since 1476. (☎206 73; www.brauhaus-lobisser.com. Entrees €6-19. Vegetarian options available. Open daily noon-10pm. Cash only.)

**Trains** leave Hallstatt for Salzburg (2½hr., 1 per hr., €21) via Attnang-Puchheim and Graz (3hr., 1 per 2hr., €31) via Stainach-Irdning. **Postbus** #150 runs from Salzburg to Hallstatt (30min., 1 per hr. 7am-6pm, €3.40) via Bad Ischl (1½hr., 1 per hr., €10). A **ferry**, synced with the train schedule, runs between Hallstatt and the train station across the lake (€2). Turn left at the ferry terminal to reach the **tourist office**, Seestr. 169. (☎82 08. Open July-Aug. M-F 9am-noon and 2-5pm; Nov.-May M-F 9am-noon.) **Local buses** to neighboring towns leave from **Lahn**, at the far end of town. The **post office** is at Seestr. 169 (open M-Tu and Th-F 8am-4pm, W 8am-6pm) and shares a building with **Rent a Bike** (☎82 01; open M-F 8am-noon and 2:30-5pm; city bikes €5 per 2hr., €12 per day; mountain bikes €9/18.) **Postal Code:** A-4830.

**⚡DAYTRIP FROM HALLSTATT: DACHSTEIN ICE CAVES.** Above Obertraun, across the lake from Hallstatt, the famed **Rieseneishöhle** (Giant Ice Cave) is part of the largest system of ice caves in the world. Frozen waterfalls and curtains of ice transport visitors to a chilly wonderland. The Rieseneishöhle and mammoth **Mammuthöhle** rock caves are up on the mountain near the *Schönbergalm* cable car station. German-language tours, required, run 2 per hr.; groups are assigned at the top station of the Schönbergalm. (☎84 00; www.dachsteinhoehlen.at. *Rieseneishöhle and Mammuthöhle open daily May to mid-Sept 9am-4pm. Each cave €24; both €29. Ticket includes round-trip ride on Schönbergalm.*) **Koppenbrüllerhöhle,** a giant spring, is located in the valley below. *(Take a bus to Koppenbrullerhohle and walk 15min., or walk 45min. along a wooded path from the base of the Schönbergalm. Open June-July; tours 2 per 3hr. 10:30am-3pm. €8.)* The cave temperatures are near freezing, so bring warm clothes. **Buses** from Hallstatt go to Obertraun Dachsteinseilbahn (15min., 1 per 1-2hr., €1.60).

# ZELL AM SEE                            ☎ 06542

Surrounded by a ring of green and white mountains and cradling a broad turquoise lake, Zell am See (pop. 10,000) is a year-round resort for mountain-happy European tourists. Not far away, the 30 surrounding peaks of the Hohe Tauern range add further splendor to this tiny, budget-friendly lake town.

**▐▟ TRANSPORTATION AND PRACTICAL INFORMATION.** Leaving the station at the intersection of Bahnhofstr. and Salzmannstr., **trains** run to: Innsbruck (1½-2hr., 1 per hr., €24); Kitzbühel (45min., 1 per 2hr., €10); Vienna (5hr., €47) via Salzburg (1hr., 1 per hr., €13). The **bus station** is on Postpl. at Gartenstr. and Schulstr. Buy tickets on board or at the kiosk. (☎54 44. Kiosk open M-F 7:45am-1:45pm.) Buses go to Franz-Josefs-Höhe (#651; mid-June to mid-Sept. 2 per day, €11),

Krimml (#670; 1¼hr., €8), and Salzburg (2hr., 1 per 2hr., €11). For **bike rentals,** head to **Intersport,** Bahnhofstr. 13. (☎72 606. €2 per hr., €15 per day; mountain bikes €3/25 Open M-Sa 8:30am-6pm, Su 8:30am-noon and 4-6pm.) The **tourist office,** Brucker Bundesstr. 1a, posts English-language **weather** reports. (☎770; www.europasportregion.info. Open June-Sept. and Nov.-Apr. M-F 9am-6pm, Sa 9am-noon and 2-6pm, Su 10am-noon; May and Oct. M-F 9am-6pm, Sa 9am-noon.) For **mountain rescue,** call ☎140. The **post office** is at Postpl. 4. (☎73 791. Open mid-Sept. to Dec. 25 and Mar. 23-June M-F 7:30am-6pm, Sa 8am-6:30pm; July to mid-Sept. and Dec. 25-Easter M-F 7:30am-6pm, Sa 8am-11am.) **Postal Code:** A-5700.

**▛▟ ACCOMMODATIONS AND FOOD.** Ask at your hostel or hotel for a free **guest card,** which provides discounts throughout the city. ▓**Haus der Jugend (HI)** ❷, Seespitzstr. 13, equipped with a terrace on the lake, brings luxury to budget housing. From the station, take the exit facing the lake ("Zum See") and turn right on the lakeside footpath. When the path ends, turn left on Seespitzstr. (☎571 85; www.jungehotels.at/seespitzstrasse. Breakfast included. Lockers €1 deposit. Internet €1 per 12min. Reception 7:30-10am and 4-10pm. Dorms €18-22; doubles with bath €44. AmEx/MC/V.) Closer to town, **Junges Hotel (HI)** ❷, Schmittenstr. 27, has enormous rooms and new facilities. From the train station, head left and up the hill. Take the first right on Brucker Bundesstr., then left on Schmittenstr. (☎470 36; www.jungehotels.at/schmittenstrasse. Breakfast included. €21-24 per person. AmEx/MC/V.) **Camping Seecamp** ❶, Thumersbacherstr. 34, in Prielau, can be reached by taking PostBus #660 (dir.: Thumersbach; 2 per hr. 6:15am-7:15pm, €1.50) and requesting a stop at Seecamp. By foot, walk clockwise around the lake for 30min. Squeezed between the lake shore and a busy road, this campground fills quickly when the weather is nice. Kayaking, sailing, and biking are nearby. (☎721 15; www.seecamp.at. Wash €4, dry €1 per 30min. Wi-Fi €2 per hr. Reception 8am-noon and 2-8pm. Check-out 11am. €7.90 per person, €13-20 per tent. 20% discount May-June and Sept.-Dec. AmEx/MC/V.)

In the *Altstadt,* **Ristorante Giuseppe** ❷, Kircheng. 1, serves personal pizzas (€6-10) and pastas (€6.50-11). From the station, walk right on Bahnhofstr. past the church and go straight. (☎723 730; www.ristorante-giuseppe.at. Open daily 11:30am-11:30pm. MC/V; €40 min.) The **SPAR** supermarket is at Brucker Bundeßtr. 4. (☎700 19. Open M-Th 7:30am-6:30pm, F 7:30am-7pm, Sa 7:30am-6pm.)

**▟ HIKING AND ADVENTURE SPORTS.** The **Schmittenhöhebahn** cable car leads to many hikes. (Lift runs daily 2 per hr. 9am-5pm. Up €16, down €12, round-trip €20. Guest card discounts available.) To reach the lift, walk 20min. up Schmittenstr. or take PostBus #661 (5min., 1 per 1-2hr., €2). The moderately strenuous **Pinzgauer Spaziergang** begins at the top of the Schmittenhöhebahn and levels off high in the Kitzbüheler Alps. The trail is marked "Alpenvereinsweg" #19 or 719. Most hikers devote an entire day to it, taking a side path to one of the valley towns west of Zell, where buses return to Zell am See. For a faster-paced experience, **Outdo,** Schmittenstr. 8 (☎701 65; www.outdoadventures.com) leads a variety of trips, including **rafting** (5hr., €45), **canyoning** (6hr., €50), and **mountain biking** (4-5hr., €29) tours. In winter, they offer group **ski** lessons (3-day €125, 4-day €140, 5-day €150) and **snowboarding** classes (1-day €50, 3-day €110, 4-day €125).

**▟ SKIING.** Winter ski season lasts from late November until mid-April. The **Zell/Kaprun Ski Pass** covers both the Schmittenhöhe and Kitzsteinhorn ski areas (2-day pass €73, ages 16-18 €58; prices cheaper Nov. and Apr.). During ski season, a bus runs between Schmittenhöhe and Kitzsteinhorn (1-3 per hr., free with a ski pass and equipment). **Intersport,** on the glacier and in town on Bahnhofstr. 13, rents snowboard and ski gear (€21-29 per day). Intersport also has several other shops open in winter, including one near the top of Kitzsteinhorn. (☎72 606; www.servicenetwork.at. Open M-Sa 8:30am-6pm, Su 8:30am-noon and 4-6pm.)

**☑ DAYTRIP FROM ZELL AM SEE: KRIMML.** Plunging 380m, the **Krimml Waterfalls** kick up a mighty spray that showers the 400,000 yearly visitors who climb the steep, zigzagging 4km (1hr.) **Wasserfallpanoramaweg** to see all three waterfalls. The **Krimml Kees** glacier feeds the **Krimml Ache** river, which winds through Alpine pastures before descending into the valley. The well-trodden-tourist path hugs the river and has a number of scenic outlooks over the falls. For those low on time or energy, the first waterfall is just beyond the ticket booth and quite impressive on its own. Take PostBus #670 to the last stop, cross the highway and go left following the signs to the falls (1½hr., 2 per hr., round-trip €17). There's a National Parks office at the falls. (☎ 06564 72 12. *Office open May-Sept. M-F 11am-4pm. Falls open 24hr., year-round. Mid-Apr. to Oct. daily 8am-6pm. €2.*)

> **THE REAL DEAL.** Feel your euro cascading away? Visit Krimml from September to mid-April and enjoy the same misty shower as other patrons without the nasty charge. Alternatively, if the summer heat has got you beat, arrive before the ticket window opens (8am) and enter the 24hr. park for free.

# HOHE TAUERN NATIONAL PARK

The enormous Hohe Tauern range, part of the Austrian Central Alps and forming the largest nature reserve in central Europe, encompasses 246 glaciers and 304 mountains over 3000m. Preservation is the park's primary goal, so no large campgrounds or recreation areas are permitted. *Experiencing Nature: Walking Destinations*, available at park centers and most area tourist offices, plots and describes 54 different hikes, ranging from pleasant ambles to challenging mountain ascents. At the center of the park lies **Franz-Josefs-Höhe,** the most visited section, and the **Pasterze Glacier,** which hovers above the town of Heiligenblut.

**▐ TRANSPORTATION.** Hohe Tauern National Park sits at the meeting point of the provinces of Salzburger Land, Tyrol, and Kärnten. The heart of the park is best reached by the highway, **☑Großglockner Hochalpenstraße.** As the zigzagging road climbs high into the mountains, it passes mesmerizing vistas of jagged peaks and plunging valleys, high Alpine meadows, and glacial waterfalls. **PostBus** #651 goes from Zell am See to Franz-Josefs-Höhe (1½-2½hr., departs 9:20am and 12:20pm, returns 11:45am and 3pm; €11). The road is open from May to mid-June and mid-September to November 6am-8:30pm; mid-June to mid-September 5am-10pm. Snow chains are required in snow. (Car toll €28.)

**▟ FRANZ-JOSEFS-HÖHE.** An endless number of buses, cars, and motorcycles climb the Großglockner Hochalpenstraße to this tourist mecca above the edge of the **Pasterze Glacier.** Once out of the parking area, the Panoramaweg affords a great view of **Großglockner** (3798m). On the ridge above the information center, the **Swarovski Observation Tower** provides free telescope use. (Open daily 10am-4pm.)

**▟ HEILIGENBLUT.** The closest town to Austria's highest mountain is a great starting point for hikes. Reach Heiligenblut by **bus** from Franz-Josefs-Höhe (30min., 3-9 per day, €4) or Lienz (1hr., 2-6 per day, €6). The **tourist office** is at Hof 4, up the street from the bus stop. (☎ 04824 20 01 21; www.heiligenblut.at. Open July-Aug. M-F 9am-6pm, Sa 9am-noon and 4-6pm; Sept.-June M-F 9am-noon and 2-6pm, Sa 9am-noon and 4-6pm.) Across the street, the **National Park office** provides hiking info and books hut stays. (☎ 04824 27 00. Open daily late June-Sept. 10am-5pm.) To reach the **Jugendgästehaus (HI) ❷,** Hof 36, take the path down from the wall behind the bus stop parking lot. (☎ 04824 22 59; www.hiyou.at. Breakfast included. Reception daily July-Aug. 7-11am and 5-10pm; Sept.-June 7-10am and 5-9pm. Lockout 10am-4pm. Dorms €21; singles €26; doubles €44. €3 HI discount.)

**⊠ HIKING.** Pick up a free hiking map from the National Park or tourist office. A detailed topographic map (€10-15) is necessary for prolonged hikes in the area. From the Franz-Josefs-Höhe parking lot, the initially steep **Pasterze Gletscherweg** (3hr.) descends to the edge of the retracting Pasterze Glacier and then continues through the valley and around the Stausee Margaritze to the **Glocknerhaus Alpine Center;** stay on the well-marked path. A free shuttle bus runs between Franz-Josefs-Höhe and Glocknerhaus. Ask the Glocknerhaus staff to call for it.

Many hikes in the Großglockner area of the national park start at **Heiligenblut,** from the Retschitzbrücke parking area outside of town via Gemeindestr. The easy **Gößnitzfall-Kachlmoor** trail (round-trip 2hr.) leads through the Kachlmoor swamp to the Gößnitz Waterfalls at the head of the Gößnitz Valley. The rewarding but long **Gößnitztal-Langtalseen** hike (round-trip 10-12hr.) continues through Alpine pastures and valleys. Spend the night in the **Elberfelder Hütte ❶.** (Floor space €11; beds €21.) In the morning, pass three gleaming lakes before heading back to Heiligenblut via the Wirtsbauer Alm.

# TYROL (TIROL)

With its celestial peaks, Tyrol has become a celebrated mountain playground for hikers and winter sport enthusiasts alike. Craggy summits in the northeast and south cradle the pristine Ötzal and Zillertal valleys while the mighty Hohe Tauern mountain range marches across eastern Tyrol. In the region's center, stylish Innsbruck flaunts bronze statues and Baroque facades.

# INNSBRUCK                    ☎0512

After hosting the 1964 and 1976 winter Olympics, the mountain city of Innsbruck (pop. 118,000) rocketed to international recognition. Colorful architecture and relics from the Habsburg Empire pepper the tiny cobblestone streets of the *Altstadt* (Old Town), while the nearby Tyrolean Alps await skiers and hikers.

## ▐▪▋ TRANSPORTATION AND PRACTICAL INFORMATION

**Trains: Hauptbahnhof,** Südtirolerpl. (☎517 17). To: **Graz** (6hr., 2 per day, €48); **Salzburg** (2½hr., 1 per hr., €34); **Vienna** (5-6hr., 1 per hr., €54); **Munich, GER** (2hr., 1 per hr., €35); **Zürich, SWI** (4hr., 8 per day, €48).

**Public Transportation:** The **IVB** Office, Stainerstr. 2 (☎530 7500; www.ivb.at), off Marktgraben, has bus schedules and route maps. Open M-F 7:30am-6pm. Single fare €1.70, 24hr. pass €3.80, week €12. Discounts for students under 20. Most buses stop around 11:30pm; 4 **Nachtbus** lines run 1 per hr. midnight-5am; most pass Maria-Theresien-Str., the train station, and Landesmuseum. IVB's **Sightseer** bus is the easiest way to visit Innsbruck's far-flung attractions. Single fare €2.80, round-trip €4.40, day pass €8.80. May-Oct. 2 per hr. 9am-6:30pm; Nov.-Apr. 1 per hr. 10am-6pm. Tickets for all buses and trams can be bought on board, at a kiosk, or from the tourist office.

**Bike Rental: Neuner Radsport,** Maximilianstr. 23 (☎56 15 01). Mountain bikes €16 per ½-day, €20 per day. Open M-F 9am-6pm, Sa 9am-noon.

**Tourist Office: Innsbruck Tourist Office,** Burggraben 3 (☎598 50; www.innsbruck.info), off Museumstr. Sells the **Innsbruck Card,** with unlimited public transport and entry to most sights (1-day €24, 2-day €29, 3-day €34). Maps €1. Open daily 9am-6pm.

**Laundromat: Bubblepoint Waschsalon,** Brixnerstr. 1 (☎56 50 07 50). Wash €4 per 7kg, soap included; dry €1 per 10min. Internet €1 per 10min. Open M-F 8am-10pm, Sa-Su 8am-8pm.

**Mountain Rescue:** ☎140.

AUSTRIA

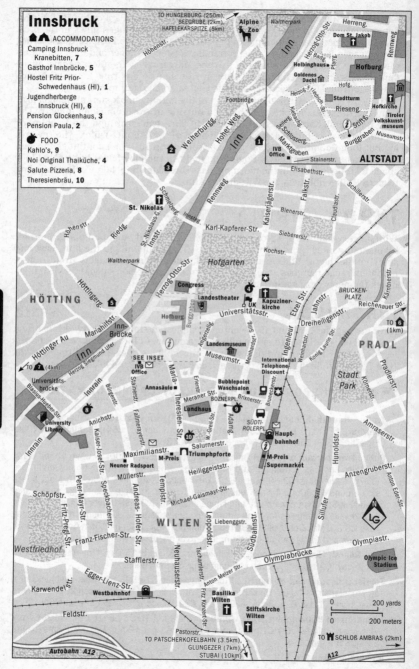

# Innsbruck

## ♠♠ ACCOMMODATIONS

Camping Innsbruck
  Kranebitten, **7**
Gasthof Innbrücke, **5**
Hostel Fritz Prior-
  Schwedenhaus (HI), **1**
Jugendherberge
  Innsbruck (HI), **6**
Pension Glockenhaus, **3**
Pension Paula, **2**

## 🍎 FOOD

Kahlo's, **9**
Noi Original Thaiküche, **4**
Salute Pizzeria, **8**
Theresienbräu, **10**

TO HUNGERBURG (250m),
SEEGRUBE (2km),
HAFELEKARSPITZE (5km)

**Alpine Zoo**

Höhenstr.

Weiherburg.

Hoher Weg

Footbridge

Inn

Rennweg

Innstr.

**St. Nikolas**

St.-Nikolaus-G.

Schmelzg.

Höhenstr.

Riedg.

Waltherpark

Höttingerg.

Herzog-Otto-Str.

Karl-Kapferer-Str.

Elisabethstr.

Kaiserjägerstr.

Falkstr.

Schillerstr.

Bienerstr.

Claudiastr.

Sieberestr.

Kochstr.

**Hofgarten**

**HÖTTING**

Mariahilfstr.

Inn-
Brücke

**5**

**Congress**

**Landestheater**

Hofburg

Burggraben

**UK**

**Kapuziner-kirche**

Etzel-Str.

Jahnstr.

**BRUCKEN-PLATZ**

Reichenauer Str.

Kärntnerstr.

TO **6**
(1km)

**PRADL**

Höttinger Au

TO **7** (4km)

Inn

Herzog Siegmund Ufer

**SEE INSET**

**IVB Office** ✉

Universitäts-
brücke

Innrain

Burgerst.

Stainerstr.

Maria-
Theresien-
Str.

Erlerstr.

Angerzellg.

Museumstr.

**Landesmuseum**

Meinhardtstr.

Wilhelm-Greil-Str.

Ing.-Etzel-Str.

International
Telephone
Discount

König Laurin Str.

**Stadt Park**

Pradlerstr.

Körnerstr.

**Annasäule**

Meraner Str.

**Landhaus**

Bubblepoint
Waschsalon

BOZNERPL.

Brixnerstr.

Brunecker-str.

Adamg.

**9**

SÜDTI-
ROLERPL.

**Hauptbahnhof**

ⓘ

Amraserstr.

Sillufer

Sill

Salurnerstr.

**10**

**University Library**

Innrain

**8**

Anichstr.

Kaiser-Josef-Str.

Fallmerayerstr.

**Maximilianstr.**

**Neuner Radsport**

M-Preis

Müllerstr.

**Triumphpforte**

Heiliggeiststr.

**M-Preis Supermarkt**

Anzengruberstr.

Anton Eder Str.

Schöpfstr.

Peter-Mayr-Str.

Speckbacherstr.

Andreas-Hofer-Str.

Templstr.

Michael-Gaismayr-Str.

Leopoldstr.

Liebenggstr.

Südbahnstr.

**WILTEN**

Fritz-Pregl-Str.

Franz-Fischer-Str.

Stafflerstr.

Neuhauserstr.

Tschamlerstr.

Anton Melzer Str.

Fritz Konzert Str.

Olympiastr.

Olympiabrücke

**Olympic Ice Stadium**

**LG**

*Westfriedhof*

Karwendel Str.

Egger-Lienz-Str.

**Westbahnhof**

Feldstr.

Pastorstr.

TO PATSCHERKOFELBAHN (3.5km),
GLUNGEZER (7km),
STUBAI (10km)

**Basilika Wilten**

**Stiftskirche Wilten**

| 0 | | 200 yards |
| --- | --- | --- |
| 0 | | 200 meters |

TO 🏰 SCHLOß AMBRAS (2km)

*Autobahn A12*

A12

**AUSTRIA**

### ALTSTADT (inset)

Waltherpark

Inn

Herzog-Otto-Str.

Herreng.

Rennweg

Herzog Friedrich Str.

Pfarrg.

**Dom St. Jakob** ✝

Herr. Badg.

**Helbinghaus**

**Goldenes Dachl** 🏛

**Hofburg**

Hofg.

**Stadtturm**

Rieseng.

Seilerg.

Kiebachg.

Schlosserg.

Markt-graben

Riesengasse

**Hofkirche**

**Tiroler Volkskunst-museum**

Museumstr.

ⓘ Stift's

Burggraben

Stainerstr.

**IVB Office** ■

**1**

**Internet Access: International Telephone Discount,** Südtirolerpl. 1 (☎282 3690). Go right from the Hauptbahnhof. €0.07 per min. Open daily 9am-11pm.

**Post Office:** Maximilianstr. 2 (☎0577 677 6010). Open M-F 7am-9pm, Sa 7am-3pm, Su 10am-7:30pm. **Postal Code:** A-6010.

# ACCOMMODATIONS AND CAMPING

Options for budget accommodations are limited in June, when some hostels close, although student dorms open to travelers in July and August. Request a free **Club Innsbruck** card from your hotel or hostel for discounts on hiking, skiing, and tours.

**Hostel Fritz Prior-Schwedenhaus (HI),** Rennweg 17b (☎58 58 14). From the station, take bus #4 to Handelsakademie, continue to the end and cross Rennweg. By the river, this hostel has comfortable rooms with bath. Breakfast 7-8am €5. Linen €1.50. Laundry €5.40. Reception 7-9am and 5-10:30pm. Lockout 9am-5pm. Open July-Aug. Dorms €13; singles €23; doubles €38; triples €49. Cash only. ❶

**Gasthof Innbrücke,** Innstr. 1 (☎28 19 34; www.gasthofinnbruecke.at). From the Altstadt, cross the Innbrücke. In a narrow building, this 582-year-old inn has a downstairs bar and restaurant. Breakfast included. Reserve ahead. Singles €31, with shower €39; doubles €50/67. MC/V. ❸

**Jugendherberge Innsbruck (HI),** Reichenauer Str. 147 (☎34 61 79; www.youth-hostel-innsbruck.at). From the train station, take tram #3 to Museumstr. and bus O to Jugendherberge. This former Olympic athlete housing turned hostel has clean rooms. Bike rental €11 per day. Breakfast included. Laundry €3.30. Internet €1 per 10min. Reception July-Aug. 7am-1pm and 3-11pm; Sept.-June 7am-1pm and 5-11pm. Dorms €16-21 1st night, €14-16 thereafter; singles €33; doubles €50. Cash only. ❷

**Pension Glockenhaus,** Weiherburgg. 3 (☎28 65 15; www.hostelnikolaus.at). Take bus D to Schmelzerg. and head uphill to the yellow house on the left, right before the castle. Cozy rooms in a former cannon and bell factory. Reception 8am-2pm and 5-11pm. Check-out 9am. Dorms €17; singles €34; doubles €51. MC/V. ❷

**Pension Paula,** Weiherburgg. 15 (☎29 22 62; www.pensionpaula.at). Take bus D to Schmelzerg. Simple rooms with TV overlooking the valley. Breakfast included. Singles €24, with shower €34, with shower and toilet €37; doubles €50/55/60; triples €78; quads €89. Cash only. ❷

**Camping Innsbruck Kranebitten,** Kranebitter Allee 214 (☎28 41 80; www.camping-innsbruck.at). Take bus O to Technik and then bus LK (1hr., 2 per hr. until 8:30pm) to Klammstr. Walk downhill and to the right. Lush lawn in the shadow of a mountain. Bike rental €5 per ½-day, €10 per day. Laundry €7. Reception 8am-noon and 2-9pm; after 9pm, find a site and check in the next morning. €5.40 per person, €8.80 per tent site. Tent rental €8-10. MC/V. ❶

# FOOD

The Altstadt cafes on Maria-Theresien-Str. are good but overpriced. **M-Preis** supermarket is at Maximilianstr. 3 (☎580 5110; open M-F 7:30am-7pm, Sa 7:30am-5pm) and inside the train station (☎58 07 30; open daily 6am-9pm).

**Theresienbräu,** Maria-Theresien-Str. 51-53 (☎58 75 80). Built around giant copper brewing kettles. Try the golden brown house lager (0.5L €3.10) or Tyrolean specialties (€6-7). Open M-W 10am-1am, Th-Sa 10am-2am, Su 10am-midnight. MC/V. ❷

**Noi Original Thaiküche,** Kaiserjägerstr. 1 (☎58 97 77). This tiny Thai kitchen packs a powerful punch with its spicy soups (€5-16) and noodles (€7-10). Lunch specials €8-9. Open M-F 11:30am-2:30pm and 6-11pm, Sa 6-11pm. Cash only. ❷

**Salute Pizzeria,** Innrain 35 (☎58 58 18). Students come for good, cheap pizza (€3.20-8.20). Pasta €4.70-7.10. Open daily 11am-midnight. Cash only. ❶

AUSTRIA

**Kahlo's,** Boznerpl. 6 (☎ 567 330; www.kahlos.com), serves spicy Mexican fare in a setting filled with cacti, strings of chilis, and Kahlo's famous unibrow paintings. Enchiladas and burritos €9-12. Fajitas €12-15. Open daily 11:30am-11pm. AmEx/MC/V. ❷

# 👁 SIGHTS

▨ **SCHLOß AMBRAS.** Ferdinand II transformed this hunting lodge into a castle and filled it with his collection of art, arms, and trinkets. While the faces in the **Habsburg Portrait Gallery** may start to look identical, giant stuffed sharks and paintings of the incredibly hirsute Petrus and Madleine Gonzalez in the **Kunst-und Wunderkammer** (Cabinet of Curiosities) are guaranteed to stand out. Don't miss the famous **Spanische Saal** (Spanish Hall), the **trompe-l'oeil frescoes** in the courtyard, or the peacocks strutting in the garden. *(Schloßstr. 20. ☎ 0525 24 4802; www.khm.at/ambras. Sightseer bus or tram #3 stops at the bottom of the hill, leaving a 15min. walk. Open daily Aug. 10am-7pm; Sept.-Oct. and Dec.-July 10am-5pm. Portrait gallery open daily Aug. 10am-7pm; Sept.-Oct. and May-July 10am-5pm. May-Oct. €8, students €6; Dec.-Apr. €4.50/3. Tours €2; reservations required for English-language tours.)*

**THE OLD TOWN.** The greens and pinks of Innsbruck's *Altstadt* stand out brilliantly against the surrounding mountains' earth tones. The Old Town centers around the **Goldenes Dachl** (Golden Roof), Herzog-Friedrich-Str. 15. The 16th-century gold-shingled balcony honors Maximilian I, Innsbruck's favorite Habsburg emperor. The nearby **Helbinghaus** is graced with pale-green floral detail and intricate stucco work. Church domes and shopping boutiques line Innsbruck's most distinctive street, **Maria-Theresien-Straße,** which runs south from the edge of the *Altstadt.* At its far end stands the **Triumphpforte** (Triumphal Arch), built in 1765 after the betrothal of Emperor Leopold II. In the middle, the **Annasäule** (Anna Column) commemorates the Tyroleans' 1703 victory over the Bavarians.

**DOM ST. JAKOB.** High Baroque ornamentation fill this pink-and-white marble cathedral. Make sure to check out its most prized possession, the small altar painting of *Our Lady of Succor* by Lukas Cranach the Elder. *(1 block behind the Goldenes Dachl. Open Apr.-Sept. M-Sa 8am-7:30pm, Su 12:30-7:30pm; Oct.-Mar. M-Sa 10am-6:30pm, Su 12:30-6:30pm. Free. Mass M-Sa 9:30am; Su 10, 11:30am.)*

**HOFBURG.** This imperial palace, originally built in 1460, was completely remodeled under Maria Theresa, who made it her "little Schönbrunn of the Alps." *(Rennweg 1. In front of Dom St. Jakob. ☎ 58 71 8612; www.hofburg-innsbruck.at. Open daily 9am-5pm. Last entry 4:30pm. €5.50, students €4. English-language guidebook €1.80.)*

**HOFKIRCHE.** Larger-than-life bronze statues of Kaiser Maximilian I's ancestors and heroes encircle his tomb. Marble reliefs of his life decorate the sarcophagus. *(Universitätsstr 8. In the Volkskunstmuseum building. ☎ 594 895 10. Open July-Aug. M-Sa 9am-5:30pm, Su 12:30-5pm; Sept.-June M-Sa 9am-5pm, Su 12:30-5pm. €3, students €2.)*

**ALPINE ZOO (ALPENZOO).** Europe's highest-altitude zoo has every vertebrate species indigenous to the Alps: bears, pine martens, a bearded vulture with a 3m wingspan, and Alpine farm animals. *(Weiherburgg. 37. ☎ 29 23 23. Bus W from Marktpl. or the Sightseer bus. Open daily Apr.-Sept. 9am-6pm; Oct.-Mar. 9am-5pm. €7, students €5.)*

# 🏔 🎿 HIKING AND SKIING

A ▨**Club Innsbruck** membership (free; see **Accommodations,** p. 97) lets you in on one of Austria's best deals. The club's popular **hiking** program around Innsbruck and its surrounding villages provides free guides, transportation, and equipment. Moderate 3-5hr. group hikes from Innsbruck meet in front of the Congress Center (early June to early Oct. daily 9am; return around 4-5pm). Free 1hr. nighttime **lantern hikes** to Heiligwaßer near Igls leave Tuesday at 7:45pm and culminate in a hut party with traditional Austrian song and dance. For the early birds, the club also offers Friday **sunrise hikes** to Rangger Köpfl. leaving at 4:50am; reserve ahead. For self-guided hikes, take the J bus to **Patscherkofel Seilbahnen** (20min.). The lift provides access to moderately difficult 1½-5hr. hikes near the 2246m bald summit of the Patscherkofel. (Open July-Aug. 9am-5pm; June and Sept. M-F 9am-4:30pm, Sa-Su 9am-5pm. €11, round-trip €17.) For more challenging climbs, ride the lifts up to the **Nordkette** mountains. Take the J bus to Hungerburg and catch the cable car to Seegrube (1905m) or continue on to Hafelekarspitze (2334m). Both stops lead to several hiking paths along jagged ridges and around rocky peaks, but be prepared: they are neither easy nor well-marked. (☎29 33 44. Hungerburg to Seegrube €11, under 20 €9; to Hafelekar €12/10; Seegrube to Hafelekar €2.70/2.20) To view Innsbruck from above, Mountain Fly offers a €95 tandem **paragliding** package, including transport and equipment (☎ 0664 282 8968).

For Club-led **ski excursions,** take the complimentary ski shuttle (schedules at the tourist office) to any cable car. The **Innsbruck Gletscher Ski Pass** (available at the tourist office) is valid for all 60 lifts in the region (with Club Innsbruck membership: 3-day €90, 6-day €155). Individual lift passes are available for Nordpark-Seegrube (☎29 33 44; www.nordpark.com), Patscherkofel (☎598 50; www.patscherkofelbahnen.at), and Glungezer (☎0552 378 321; www.glungezerbahn.at; €21). One day of skiing on **Stubai glacier** costs about €35. Stubai is also the only slope for summer skiing; packages (bus, lift, and rental) start at €50.

# KITZBÜHEL
☎05356

During ski season, everyone in Kitzbühel is merely catching his breath before the next run; the town's ski area, the **Ski Circus,** is one of the world's best and is home to the most venerable downhill course in the world—the legendary **Hahnenkamm.** A one-day **ski pass** (€34-39) or a three- or six-day summer **vacation pass** (€38/52) include all lifts and the buses that connect them; purchase either at any lift. In summer, tourists meander the town's streets or one of the 87 **hiking trails** that snake up the mountains; trail maps are free at the tourist office. To reach the town's **Fußgängerzone** (pedestrian zone) from the Hauptbahnhof, head straight down Bahnhofstr. and turn left at the main road (Joseph-Pirchlstr.). At the traffic light, turn right and follow the road past the two churches.

Noise from passing cars may disrupt light sleepers at **Pension Hörl ❷,** Joseph-Pirchlstr. 60, but down comforters will ensure a cozy night. From Hotel Kaiser, turn left onto Joseph-Pirchlstr. (☎631 44. Satellite TV. Breakfast included. €23-30 per person. Cash only.) **Huberbräu-Stüberl ❷,** Vorderstadt 18, has a variety of pleasing *Schnitzel* (€6.80-14) and *Tirolean Gröstl* (€6.50). (☎65 677. Open mid-June to mid-May M-Sa 8am-midnight, Su 9am-midnight. Cash only.) A **SPAR** supermarket is on the corner of Ehrenbachg. and Bichlstr. (☎740 52. Open M-Th 7:30am-6:30pm, F 7:30am-7pm, Sa 7:30am-5pm; low season M-Th 7:30am-6:30pm, F 7:30am-7pm, Sa 7:30am-1pm.) **Trains** leave from the Hauptbahnhof for Innsbruck (1hr., 1 per 2hr., €14) and Vienna (6hr., €50) via Salzburg (2½hr., 1 per day, €24). The **tourist office,** Hinterstadt 18, is near the Rathaus in the pedestrian zone. (☎777; www.kitzbuehel.com. Open July-Aug. and Dec. 26 to mid-Mar. M-F 8:30am-6pm, Sa 9am-6pm, Su 10am-6pm; Nov.-Dec. 25 and mid-Mar. to June M-F 8:30am-12:30pm and 2:30-6pm, Sa 9am-1pm.) Pension and hotels offer free **guest cards,** entitling holders to English-language city tours (Tu 10am), guided hikes (June-Oct. M-F 8:45am), and equipment rental discounts. **Postal Code:** A-6370.

# STYRIA (STEIERMARK)

Many of southern Austria's folk traditions live on in the emerald hills and sloping pastures of Styria, where even the largest city—Graz—remains calm and relatively untouristed. While the crumbling medieval strongholds and Lipizzaner stallions are among the region's notable attractions, the easygoing atmosphere and Styrian vineyards convince many visitors to linger.

## GRAZ ☎ 0316

Graz, Austria's second-largest city (pop. 290,000), is the nation's best-kept secret. The under-touristed *Altstadt* (Old Town), with picturesque red-tiled roofs and Baroque domes, feels unhurried: people lounge in outdoor cafes atop Schloßberg Mountain or rock climb the cliffs along the Danube. Darkness rouses 45,000 university students from their books to participate in the city's energetic nightlife.

**TRANSPORTATION AND PRACTICAL INFORMATION. Trains** run to: **Innsbruck** (6-7hr., 7 per day, €48); **Munich, GER** (6¼hr., 3 per day, €72); **Salzburg** (4¼hr., 1 per 2hr., €43); **Vienna** Südbahnhof (2½hr., 1 per hr., €30); **Zürich, SWI** (10hr., 3 per day, €83). To reach the city center take **tram** #1, 3, 6, or 7 (€1.70, day pass €3.70). By foot, exit right from the train station, then turn left onto Annenstr. Follow it to the main bridge and cross to reach **Hauptplatz.** Five minutes away is **Jakominiplatz,** the public transportation system's hub. **Herrengasse,** a pedestrian street lined with cafes and boutiques, connects the two squares. The **tourist office,** Herreng. 16, gives an English-language walking tour of *Altstadt* (2hr.; Apr.-Oct. daily 2:30pm, Jan.-Mar. and Nov. Sa 2:30pm; €9.50) and books rooms for free. (☎807 50; www.graztourismus.at. July-Aug. M-F 10am-7pm, Sa-Su 10am-6pm; Apr.-June, Sept.-Oct., and Dec. M-Sa 10am-6pm, Su 10am-4pm; Jan.-Mar. and Nov. M-F 10am-5pm, Sa-Su 10am-4pm.) **Postal Code:** A-8010.

**ACCOMMODATIONS AND FOOD.** Most accommodations in Graz are pricey and far from the city center. To reach the family-oriented **Jugendgästehaus Graz (HI) ❷,** Idlhofg. 74, from the station, cross the street, head right on Eggenberger Gürtel, turn left on Josef-Huber-G., then take the first right; the hostel complex is through the parking lot on your right. Buses #31, 32, and 33 run from Jakominipl. Be cautious in the neighborhood, especially at night. (☎708 3210; www.jfgh.at. Breakfast included. Laundry €4. Internet €1.50 per 20min. Reception 7am-11pm. Curfew 1am; night-key deposit €20. Dorms €24; singles €40; doubles €66. €1.10 HI discount. MC/V.) **Hotel Strasser ❹**, Eggenberger Gürtel 11, fills its bright rooms with abstract art. Exit the train station, cross the street, and head right for 5min. on Eggenberger Gürtel. The traffic on Eggenberger Gürtel can be noisy at night. (☎71 39 77; www.hotel-strasser.at. Breakfast included. Reception 24hr. Singles €35-50; doubles €60-76; triples €90-99. AmEx/MC/V.) On **Hauptplatz,** concession stands sell sandwiches and *Wurst* (€2-3). Situated in the shadow of Schloßberg, the cheery **Alte Münze ❷**, Schloßbergpl. 8, serves a local crowd Styrian specialties. (☎82 91 51. Entrees €7-15, vegetarian €7-12. Open mid-Mar. to Dec. Tu-Sa 8am-11:30pm; June-Sept. Tu-Sa 8am-11:30pm, Su 11am-10pm. Cash only.) The candle-lit **Continuum ❶**, Sporg. 29, dishes up pizza for €1.50-7.50. (☎81 57 78. Sa-Su brunch buffet 10am-2pm €5. Open M-F 3pm-2am, Sa-Su 10am-2am. MC/V.) A **SPAR** supermarket is in the train station. (Open daily 6am-9pm.)

🎫 🍴 **SIGHTS AND NIGHTLIFE.** North of Hauptpl., the wooded **Schloßberg** (Castle Mountain) rises above Graz. Climb the zigzagging stone steps of the **Kriegsteig,** built by Russian prisoners during WWI, to the city's emblem, the **Uhrturm** (clock tower), for sweeping views of Graz and the vast Styrian plain. The **Schloßbergbahn** (funicular), part of Graz's tram and bus network, runs from Kaiser-Franz-Josef-Kai to the **Glockenturm** (bell tower), where **Liesl**, a bell cast in 1587, chimes 101 times daily at 7am, noon, and 7pm—much to the consternation of late-risers and the hungover. The **Landhaushof** features architecture in the Lombard style, remodeled by architect Domenico dell'Allio in 1557. Most of Graz's museums are part of the **Landesmuseum Joanneum.** One ticket (1-day pass €5.50, students €3; 2-day pass €12/5) allows entrance into all participating museums. (☎80 17 96 60; www.museumjoanneum.at.) To the left of the tourist office, the **Landeszeughaus** (Provincial Armory), Herreng. 16, details the history of Ottoman attacks on the arsenal and has enough spears, muskets, and armor to outfit 28,000 mercenaries. (☎80 17 98 10. Open Apr.-Oct. M-W and F-Su 10am-6pm, Th noon-8pm; Nov.-Mar. Tu-Su 10am-3pm.) The newest additions to the Graz riverscape are the futuristic "friendly alien ship" building of the modern art museum **Kunsthaus,** Lendkai 1, at the Hauptbrücke (☎80 17 92 00; www.kunsthausgraz.at. Open Tu-Su 10am-6pm. Part of Landesmuseum Joanneum) and the mussel shell-shaped **Murinsel** in the center of the river, housing a chic cafe, open-air theater, and playground. Also included in a Landesmuseum Joanneum ticket is access to **Schloß Eggenberg,** a 17th-century castle built in the Spanish Escorial style, where the ornate **Planetensaal** (Planet Hall) is covered with paintings of the zodiac. (Tram #1 from Jakominipl. or Hauptpl. State rooms open by tour only Mar. 16-Nov. hourly 10am-4pm. Garden open May-Oct. daily 10am-6pm; Apr. and Nov.-Dec. daily 10am-4pm.) The palace also contains the **Alte Galerie,** a collection of Renaissance and Baroque art. (Open Tu-Su Apr.-Oct. 10am-6pm; Nov.-March 10am-5pm.) The modern steel sculpture at the corner of Opernring and Burgg. beckons to the magnificent **Opernhaus,** Franz-Josef-Pl. 10, which stages high-quality performances undeservedly overshadowed by those of Vienna. The hub of after-hours activity is the so-called **Bermuda Triangle,** an area of the old city behind Hauptpl. and bordered by Mehlpl., Färberg., and Prokopig. Close to the university district, at **Kulturhauskeller,** Elisabethstr. 30, dance music beats all night. (T live bands. W karaoke. 19+. Cover €3 after 11pm. Open Tu-Sa 9pm-5am. MC/V.)

AUSTRIA

# BELGIUM
# (BELGIQUE, BELGIË)

Surrounded by France, Germany, and The Netherlands, Belgium is a convergence of different cultures. Appropriately, the small country attracts an array of travellers: chocoholics, Europhiles, and art-lovers all come together to worship in Belgium. Sweet-toothed foreigners flock to Brussels, the home of filled chocolate, to nibble confections from one of 2000 cocoa-oriented specialty shops and to brush shoulders with diplomats en route to European Union and NATO headquarters. In Flanders, Gothic towers surround cobblestone squares, while visitors below admire Old Masters' canvases and guzzle monk-brewed ale. Wallonie has less tourist infrastructure, but the caves of the Lesse Valley and the forested hills of the Ardennes compensate with their stunning natural beauty.

## DISCOVER BELGIUM: SUGGESTED ITINERARY

Plan for at least two days in **Brussels** (p. 108), the capital whose **Grand-Place** Victor Hugo called "the most beautiful square in the world." Head north to the elegant boulevards of **Antwerp** (p. 119) and historic **Ghent** (p. 120), then go west to the winding streets and canals of romantic **Bruges** (p. 115). Visit **Liège** (p. 123), a university town and transit hub, or take your time exploring the leafy Ardennes, using **Namur** (p. 124) as a base for hikes into Belgium's rural south.

## LIFE AND TIMES

### HISTORY

**Charlemagne** ruled Belgium as part of his **Holy Roman Empire** around AD 800, but squabbles among grandsons following his death divided the country into separate regions: **Flanders** (p. 115), the Flemish-speaking province in the north, and **Wallonie** (p. 123), the French-speaking province in the south. From the 15th century on, conquering powers—including Austria, Denmark, and France—attempted to unite and rule Belgium, but none could quell the area's aversion to foreign occupation. In the early 1800s, the people of the north and south provinces cooperated to launch a rebellion against the Dutch king who controlled the country. They cited religious differences between Protestant rulers and the Catholic population as well as competing economic ideologies regarding trade to support their coup. In 1831, the Belgians emerged victorious as rulers of a new, independent country committed to tariff-protected trade, albeit one with intact regional divisions.

The new **constitutional monarchy,** presided over by the Belgian **Leopold I,** spent its first year fending off Dutch invaders craving a rematch. However, France stepped in, forcing the Dutch to back off. By 1839, all major European powers recognized Belgium as sovereign and neutral, the latter becoming crucial to its history. Under the rule of Leopold I and **Leopold II,** who rose to power in 1865, Belgium became a major industrial power as well as an imperial international player. In 1885, Belgium acquired the **Congo Free State,** which Leopold II governed as personal property. He proved a grossly negligent ruler, brutally oppressing and slaughtering the

BELGIUM

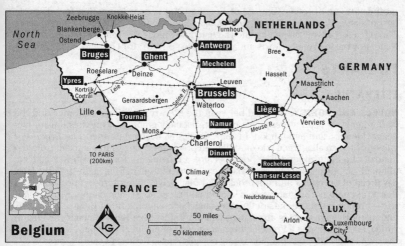

Belgium

native Congolese. Conversely, in Europe, rather than ruling as a tyrant, Leopold instituted progressive reforms by introducing universal male suffrage.

German armies invaded Belgium during both **World Wars,** upsetting the country's neutrality. During WWI, **King Albert I** and his army spent four years in the trenches trying to repel the invaders. The town of **Ypres** (p. 122) memorializes Belgium's sacrifices in that war. When the Nazis invaded in 1940, **King Leopold III** surrendered almost immediately. Post-war criticism of this move made Leopold unpopular, forcing him to hand power to his son **Baudouin** in 1951. Following WWII, Belgium shed much of its former neutrality by joining **NATO,** which is headquartered in Brussels, and the **Benelux** economic union with the Netherlands and Luxembourg. Baudouin, who ruled until 1993, continued this trend with Belgium's entrance into the European Coal and Steel Community, the predecessor to the **European Union.**

# TODAY

Under the Belgian Constitution of 1831, the Belgian king, currently **Albert II,** is the official head of state, accountable to the democratically elected parliament. The prime minister, currently **Guy Verhofstadt,** conducts day-to-day affairs. He is appointed by the monarch but must come from the majority party, which currently is the **Flemish Liberals and Democrats** party. Internal divisions fall along language lines: constitutional amendments in 1994 made Belgium a federal state with local governments centered in Flemish-speaking Flanders, French-speaking Wallonie, and bilingual **Brussels.** Even the powerful political parties, the **Socialists** on the left, the **Christian Democrats** in the center, and the **Liberals** on the right, organize through separate Flemish- and French-speaking branches. Since the late 1970s, Belgium's far-right parties, such as Flemish **Vlaams Belang** and Walloon **Front National,** have won votes on nationalist and anti-immigrant platforms.

# PEOPLE AND CULTURE

**LANGUAGE.** Belgium's three official languages are each associated with a particular region and a fierce regional sentiment. The 60% of Belgians who speak Flemish—a variation of Dutch—live in Flanders, the northern part of the country, while the 31% of citizens conversing in French dialects, like Walloon Brabant, make their home in Wallonie, the southern region. German, the third official language, is the mother tongue of fewer than 1% of Belgians and is heard only in a few districts east of Liège. Brussels, officially bilingual, is home to nearly 10% of the population. Though many Flemish speak some English, knowledge of French is helpful in Wallonie. For basic French words and phrases, see p. 1052; for German, see p. 1054.

# THE ARTS

## LITERATURE

**NOVELS AND POETRY.** Wedged between the literary traditions of France and the Netherlands, Belgian writers have characteristically grappled with questions of language, identity, and nationhood. In 1867, **Charles de Coster** published *The Legend of Ulenspiegel*, an allegorical tale of a Flemish prankster trying to free himself from the control of a Spanish king. The book became a rallying cry for Flemish regionalism, although no one missed the irony that the tale was written in French. In 1937, the **Monday Group** of Surrealist authors proclaimed that Belgian literature did not exist, and that Francophone Belgian writers should embrace the French canon. *Francophonie*—French literature outside France—has been a theme of Belgian literature, and many Belgian writers are expatriates. Surrealist poet **Henri Michaux** traveled in Africa, even becoming a French citizen at the end of his life. Fictionalized versions of her own forays into Asia pervade young novelist **Amélie Nothomb's** satirical stories.

**COMIC STRIPS AND MYSTERIES.** In the 20th century, Belgian talent made its presence known in comic strips and detective novels. Perhaps it was British writer Agatha Christie's tribute to this tradition that her famous moustached detective, **Hercule Poirot,** was Belgian. In Brussels, museums are dedicated to the history of cartooning (p. 113), specifically to the work of **Georges Remi,** better known as Hergé, creator of **Tintin,** and to **Peyo,** papa of the **Smurfs.** The enigmatic **Georges Simenon** wrote a 76-novel mystery series around the cunning **Commissaire Maigret.**

## VISUAL ARTS

**ARCHITECTURE.** The 14th-century cathedrals of Bruges and Ghent exemplify Gothic architecture. Belgium's own contribution came later, when **Victor Horta,** a native of Ghent, reacted against Classicism's heavy formality to champion a lighter Art Nouveau style in the late 19th century. Enthusiasm for Horta's trademark curvy, asymmetrical lines waned by World War I, and many of his buildings were demolished. Exhibits at the **Musée Horta** in Brussels (p. 113) reflect Horta's style.

**ON THE CANVAS.** As a member of the Flemish Primitive school of painting, **Jan van Eyck** excelled beyond his peers and transformed the art of oil painting, lavishing minute detail on his canvases without sacrificing the tenderness of his presentation. His best-known painting, the 1432 *Adoration of the Mystic Lamb,* adorns the altarpiece of St-Baafskathedraal in Ghent (p. 120). **Pieter Bruegel the Elder** is known as "peasant Bruegel" for his non-sacred works, as depicted in pieces like the 1567 *Peasant Wedding Feast.* **Peter Paul Rubens** remains Antwerp's artistic hero. In the early 17th century, he represented the female body in his Italian Renaissance-style canvases, establishing a specific and enduring ideal of beauty. In the 20th century, **René Magritte** gained fame with his **Surrealist** paintings that portrayed jarring juxtapositions of everyday objects. His most famous painting, *The Betrayal of Images* (1929), pairs the image of a pipe with the caption, *ceci n'est pas une pipe* ("this is not a pipe").

# ADDITIONAL RESOURCES

*Fear and Trembling* and *Loving Sabotage,* by Amélie Nothomb. St. Martin's Griffin (2002) and New Directions Press (2000). Satirical writing by a contemporary author.

*King Leopold's Ghost,* by Adam Hochschild. Mariner Books (1999). The history of King Leopold II's rule in the Congo.

# HOLIDAYS AND FESTIVALS

**Holidays:** New Year's Day (Jan. 1); Epiphany (Jan. 6); Good Friday (Mar. 21); Easter (Mar. 23-24); Ascension (May 1); Labor Day (May 1); Pentecost (May 11-12); Corpus Christi (May 22); Flemish Community Day (July 11); National Day (July 21); Assumption (Aug. 15); French Community Day (Sept. 27); All Saints' Day (Nov. 1); Armistice Day (Nov. 11); Christmas (Dec. 25-26).

**Festivals:** Ghent hosts Gentse Feesten (July 19-28; www.gentsefeesten.be), which brings *al fresco* theater, puppet performances, the 10 Days Off (www.10daysoff.be) dance festival, and free music and food to the city's streets. Antwerp runs films, circuses, plays, and concerts in its Zomer van Antwerpen festival (mid-July to mid-August; www.zva.be). Bruges's Cactus Festival (mid-July; www.cactusfestival.be) draws alt-pop and hip-hop acts for a weekend with nearby camping available. Eastern Belgium's Pukkelpop (mid-Aug.; www.pukkelpop.be) is a festival for the alternative music set.

# ESSENTIALS

## FACTS AND FIGURES

**Official Name:** Kingdom of Belgium.
**Capital:** Brussels.
**Major Cities:** Antwerp, Ghent, Liège.
**Population:** 10,392,000.
**Land Area:** 30,500 sq. km.
**Time Zone:** GMT +1.

**Languages:** Dutch (60%), French (40%).
**Religions:** Roman Catholic (75%), Protestant (25%).
**French Fries:** Invented in Belgium during the 18th century, despite what the name suggests. Served with mayonnaise.
**Varieties of beer:** Over 500. Bottoms up!

# WHEN TO GO

May, June, and September are the best months to visit Belgium, with temperatures around 18-22°C (64-72°F) in Brussels and Antwerp, and approximately 6°C (10°F) higher in Liège and Ghent. July and August tend to be rainy and hotter. Winters are cool, with temperatures of 2-7°C (36-45°F), somewhat colder in the Ardennes.

# DOCUMENTS AND FORMALITIES

**EMBASSIES AND CONSULATES.** Foreign embassies in Belgium are in Brussels. Belgian embassies abroad include: **Australia and New Zealand,** 19 Arkana St., Yarralumla, ACT 2600 (☎02 62 73 25 02; www.diplomatie.be/canberra); **Canada,** 360 Albert St., Ste. 820, Ottawa, ON, K1R 7X7 (☎613-236-7267; www.diplomatie.be/ottawa); **Ireland,** 2 Shrewsbury Rd., Ballsbridge, Dublin, 4 (☎01 205 71 00; www.diplomatie.be/dublin); **UK,** 17 Grosvenor Crescent, London, SW1X 7EE (☎020 7470 3700; www.diplomatie.be/london); **US,** 3330 Garfield St., NW, Washington, D.C., 20008 (☎202-333-6900; www.diplobel.us).

**VISA AND ENTRY INFORMATION.** EU citizens do not need a visa. Citizens of Australia, Canada, New Zealand, and the US do not need a visa for stays of up to 90 days, beginning upon entry into any of the countries in the EU's freedom-of-movement zone. For more info, see p. 13. For stays longer than 90 days, all non-EU citizens need visas (around US$85), available at Belgian consulates. Visit www.diplobel.us. For US citizens, visas are usually issued a few weeks after application submission.

BELGIUM

# TOURIST SERVICES AND MONEY

| **EMERGENCY** | **Ambulance:** ☎100. **Fire:** ☎100. **Police:** ☎101. |
| --- | --- |

**TOURIST OFFICES. Bureaux de Tourisme,** marked by green-and-white or blue signs labeled "i," are supplemented by **Infor Jeunes/Info-Jeugd,** info centers that help people find work and secure accommodations in Wallonie and Flanders, respectively. The **Belgian Tourist Information Center (BBB),** Grasmarkt 63, Brussels (☎025 04 03 90), has national tourist info. The weekly English-language *Bulletin* (www.thebulletin.be; €2.80 at newsstands) includes cultural events, movie listings, and news.

**MONEY.** The **euro (€)** has replaced the Belgian **franc** as the unit of currency in Belgium. For more info, see p. 15. **ATMs** generally offer the best exchange rates. A bare-bones day in Belgium might cost €35, while a more comfortable day runs about €50-65. Tipping is not common, though rounding up is. Restaurant bills usually include a service charge, although outstanding service warrants an extra 5-10% tip. Give bathroom attendants €0.25 and movie and theater attendants €0.50.

Belgium has a 21% **value added tax (VAT)**, a sales tax applied to most goods and services. Restaurant and taxi prices usually include VAT; at restaurants, this may be listed as *service comprise* or *incluse*. The prices given in *Let's Go* include VAT. In the airport upon exiting the EU, non-EU citizens can claim a refund on the tax paid for goods bought at participating stores. In order to qualify for a refund, you must spend at least €125 on a single item; make sure to ask for a refund form when you pay. For more info on qualifying for a VAT refund, see p. 18.

**BUSINESS HOURS. Banks** are generally open Monday through Friday 9am-4pm but often close for lunch midday. **Stores** are open Monday through Saturday 10am-5pm or 6pm; stores sometimes close on Mondays, but may be open Sundays in summer. Most **sights** are open Sundays but closed Mondays; in Bruges and Tournai, museums close Tuesdays or Wednesdays.

# TRANSPORTATION

**BY PLANE.** Most international flights land at **Brussels International Airport** (BRU; ☎27 53 87 98; www.brusselsairport.be), located roughly 20min. away from Brussels. Budget airlines, like **Ryanair** and **easyJet,** fly out of **Brussels South Charleroi Airport** (CRL; ☎71 25 12 11; www.charleroi-airport.com), approximately 1hr. south of Brussels, and Brussels International Airport. The Belgian national airline, **Brussels Airlines** (☎070 35 11 11, US ☎516-740-5200, UK ☎087 0735 2345; www.brusselsairlines.com), flies into Brussels from most major European cities. For more info on traveling by plane around Europe, see p. 41.

**BY TRAIN AND BUS.** The extensive and reliable **Belgian Rail** (www.b-rail.be) network traverses the country. **Eurail** is valid in Belgium. A **Benelux Tourrail Pass** (US$207, under 26 US$158) allows five days of unlimited train travel in a one-month period in Belgium, the Netherlands, and Luxembourg. Travelers with time to explore Belgium's nooks and crannies might consider the **Rail Pass** (€69) or **Go Pass** (under 26 only; €45), both of which allow 10 single trips within the country over a one-year period and can be transferred among travelers. Because trains are widely available, **buses** are used primarily for local transport. Single tickets are €1.50, and cheaper when bought in packs.

**BY FERRY. P&O Ferries** (☎070 70 77 71, UK ☎087 0598 03 33; www.poferries.com) from **Hull, BRI** to **Zeebrugge,** north of Bruges (12½hr., 7pm, from €150).

**BY CAR, BIKE, AND THUMB.** Belgium honors drivers' licenses from Australia, Canada, the EU, and the US. **New Zealanders** must contact the New Zealand Automobile Association (☎0800 822 422; www.aa.co.nz) for an International Driving

Permit. **Speed limits** are 120kph on motorways, 90kph on main roads, and 50kph elsewhere. **Biking** is popular, and many roads in Flanders have bike lanes. Wallonie has started to convert old railroad beds into bike paths. Hitchhiking is illegal and uncommon in Belgium. Let's Go does not recommend hitchhiking.

# KEEPING IN TOUCH

| **PHONE CODES** | **Country code: 32. International dialing prefix:** 00. For more info on how to place international calls, see **Inside Back Cover**. |
| --- | --- |

**EMAIL AND THE INTERNET.** There are cybercafes in all of the larger towns and cities in Belgium. Expect to pay €2-3 per 30min. In smaller towns, Internet is generally available in hostels for €5-6 per hr.

**TELEPHONE.** Most pay phones require a **phone card** (from €5), available at post offices, supermarkets, and newsstands. Whenever possible, use a calling card for international phone calls, as long-distance rates for national phone services are often very high. Calls are cheapest 6:30pm-8am and weekends. Mobile phones are an increasingly popular and economical option. Major mobile carriers include **Vodafone, Base,** and **Mobistar.** When dialing within a city, the city code must still be dialed. For operator assistance within Belgium, dial ☎ 12 07; for international, dial ☎ 12 04 (€0.25). Direct-dial access numbers for calling out of Belgium include: **AT&T** (☎ 0800 100 10); **British Telecom** (☎ 0800 100 24); **Canada Direct** (☎ 0800 100 19); **Telecom New Zealand** (☎ 0800 100 64); **Telstra Australia** (☎ 0800 100 61).

**MAIL.** Most post offices are open Monday to Friday 9am-5pm, with a midday break. Sent within Belgium, a postcard or letter (up to 50g) costs €0.46 for non-priority and €0.52 for priority. Within the EU, costs are €0.70/0.80, and for the rest of the world €0.75/0.90. Additional info is available at www.post.be.

# ACCOMMODATIONS AND CAMPING

| BELGIUM | ❶ | ❷ | ❸ | ❹ | ❺ |
| --- | --- | --- | --- | --- | --- |
| **ACCOMMODATIONS** | under €10 | €10-20 | €21-30 | €31-40 | over €40 |

**Hotels** in Belgium are fairly expensive, with rock-bottom singles from €30 and doubles from €40-45. Belgium's 31 **HI youth hostels** are run by the Flemish Youth Hostel Federation (www.vjh.be) in Flanders and Les Auberges de Jeunesses (www.laj.be) in Wallonie. Expect to pay around €18 per night, including linen, for modern, basic hostels. **Private hostels** cost about the same but are usually nicer, although some charge separately for linen. Most receptionists speak some English. Reservations are a good idea, particularly in summer and on weekends. **Campgrounds** charge about €4 per night, and are common in Wallonie but not in Flanders. An **International Camping Card** is not needed in Belgium.

# FOOD AND DRINK

| BELGIUM | ❶ | ❷ | ❸ | ❹ | ❺ |
| --- | --- | --- | --- | --- | --- |
| **FOOD** | under €5 | €5-8 | €9-12 | €13-18 | over €18 |

Belgian cuisine, acclaimed but expensive, fuses French and German styles. An evening meal may cost as much as a night's accommodations. Fresh seafood appears in *moules* or *mosselen* (steamed mussels) and *moules frites* (steamed mussels with french fries), the national dishes, which are often tasty and reasonably affordable (€14-20). *Frites* (french fries) are ubiquitous and budget-friendly; Belgians eat them dipped in mayonnaise. Look for *friekots* ("french fry shacks") in

Belgian towns. Belgian **beer** is a source of national pride, its consumption a national pastime. More varieties—over 500, ranging from ordinary pilsners (€1) to Trappist ales (€3) brewed by monks—are produced here than in any other country. Leave room for chocolate **pralines** from Leonidas or Neuhaus and Belgian **waffles** *(gaufres)*, sold on the street and in cafes.

# BEYOND TOURISM

Volunteer *(benévolat)* and work opportunities in Belgium focus on its strong international offerings, especially in Brussels, which is home to both NATO and the EU. Private-sector short- and long-term employment is listed at www.jobs-in-europe.net. A selection of public-sector job and volunteer opportunities is listed below. For more info on opportunities across Europe, see **Beyond Tourism**, p. 54.

**Amnesty International,** r. Berckmans 9, 1060 Brussels (☎02 538 8177; www.amnesty-international.be). One of the world's foremost human rights organizations has offices in Brussels. Paid positions and volunteer work available.

**The International School of Brussels,** Kattenberg-Botisfort 19, Brussels (☎02 661 42 11; www.isb.be). The ISB hires teachers for positions lasting more than 1yr. Must have permission to work in Belgium.

**North Atlantic Treaty Organization (NATO),** bd. Leopold III, 1110 Brussels (www.nato.int). Current students and recent graduates (within 1yr.) who are nationals of a NATO member state and fluent in 1 official NATO language (English or French), with a working knowledge of the other, can apply for 6-month internships. Requirements and application details available at www.nato.int/structur/interns/index.html. Application deadlines are far ahead of start dates.

# BRUSSELS (BRUXELLES, BRUSSEL)    ☎02

The headquarters of NATO and the European Union, Brussels (pop. 1,200,000) is often identified by its population of officials. Yet these civil servants aren't the only ones who speak for Belgium's capital; beneath the drone of parliamentary procedure bustles the spirited clamor of local life. These voices echo throughout the city's intricate architecture, alternately Gothic and Art Nouveau, and they jabber in both French and Flemish late into the Brussels night.

**◪ TRANSPORTATION**

**Flights: Brussels Airport (BRU;** ☎753 42 21, specific flight info 090 07 00 00, €0.45 per min.; www.brusselsairport.be) is 14km from the city and accessible by train. **South Charleroi Airport (CRL;** ☎71 25 12 11; www.charleroi-airport.com) is 46km outside the city, between Brussels and Charleroi, and services a number of European airlines, including **Ryanair.** From the airport, **Bus A** runs to the Charleroi-SUDT train station where you can catch another train to Brussels (€11). There is also a bus service which goes from the airport to Brussels's Gare du Midi (1hr., buy tickets on board).

**Trains:** (☎555 2555; www.sncb.be). All international trains stop at **Gare du Midi;** most also stop at **Gare Centrale** or **Gare du Nord.** Trains run to: **Amsterdam, NTH** (3hr.; €32, under 26 €24); **Antwerp** (45min., €6.10); **Bruges** (45min., €12); **Cologne, GER** (2¾hr.; €41, under 26 €29); **Liège** (1hr. €13); **Luxembourg City, LUX** (1¾hr., €28.80); **Paris, FRA** (1½hr., €54). **Eurostar** goes to **London, BRI** (2¾hr., €79-224), with Eurail or Benelux pass from €75, under 26 from €60.

**Public Transportation:** The **Société des Transports Intercommunaux Bruxellois (STIB;** ☎090 01 03 10, €0.45 per min.; www.stib.irisnet.be) runs the **Métro (M),** buses, and **trams** daily 5:30am-12:30am. 1hr. ticket €1.50, 1-day pass €4, 3-day pass €9, 5 trips €7, 10 trips €11.

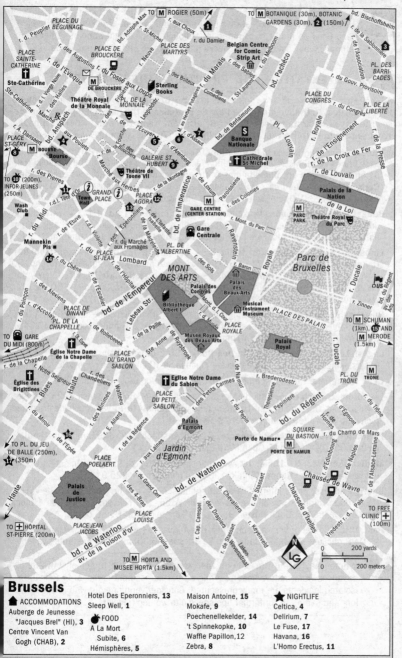

# Brussels

**ACCOMMODATIONS**
Auberge de Jeunesse "Jacques Brel" (HI), **3**
Centre Vincent Van Gogh (CHAB), **2**
Hotel Des Eperonniers, **13**
Sleep Well, **1**

**FOOD**
A La Mort Subite, **6**
Hémisphères, **5**
Maison Antoine, **15**
Mokafe, **9**
Poechenellekelder, **14**
't Spinnekopke, **10**
Waffle Papillon, **12**
Zebra, **8**

**NIGHTLIFE**
Celtica, **4**
Delirium, **7**
Le Fuse, **17**
Havana, **16**
L'Homo Erectus, **11**

**BELGIUM**

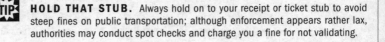

**TIP** **HOLD THAT STUB.** Always hold on to your receipt or ticket stub to avoid steep fines on public transportation; although enforcement appears rather lax, authorities may conduct spot checks and charge you a fine for not validating.

## ORIENTATION AND PRACTICAL INFORMATION

Most major attractions are clustered around **Grand-Place**, between the **Bourse** (Stock Market) to the west and the **Parc de Bruxelles** to the east. One **Métro** line circles the city and another bisects it, while efficient **trams** run north-south. Signs list street names in both French and Flemish; *Let's Go* lists all addresses in French.

**Tourist Office:** The **Brussels International Tourism and Congress** (**BITC;** ☎513 8940; www.brures.com). M: Bourse. On Grand-Place in the Town Hall, BITC is the official tourist office. It books accommodations in the city for no charge and sells the **Brussels Card,** which provides free public transport and access to 30 museums for 1, 2, or 3 days (€20/28/33). Open Easter-Dec. daily 9am-6pm; Jan.-Easter M-Sa 9am-6pm.

**Budget Travel: Infor-Jeunes Bruxelles,** 155 r. Van Artevelde (☎514 4111 ; www.inforjeunes-bxl.be). M: Bourse. Offers budget travel info for students over 18 and helps them find jobs and apartments. Free Internet for students. Open M-F 11:30am-5pm.

**Embassies and Consulates: Australia,** 6-8 r. Guimard (☎286 0500; www.austemb.be). **Canada,** 2 av. Tervuren (☎741 0611; www.international.gc.ca/brussels). **Ireland,** 50 r. Wiertz (☎235 6676). **New Zealand,** 1 sq. de Meeus (☎512 1040). **UK,** 85 r. d'Arlon (☎287 6211; www.british-embassy.be). **US,** 27 bd. du Régent (☎508 2111; www.brussels.usembassy.gov).

**Currency Exchange:** Many exchange booths near Grand-Place are open until 11pm. Most charge a commission to cash checks. Try **Travelex,** 4 Grand-Place (☎513 2845). Open M-F 10am-5pm, Sa 10am-7pm, Su 10am-4pm.

**English-Language Bookstore: Sterling Books,** 38 r. du Fossé aux Loups (☎223 6223; www.sterlingbooks.be). M: De Brouckère. Open M-Sa 10am-7pm, Su noon-6:30pm. MC/V.

**GLBT Resources:** The tourist office offers the *Safer Guide* to gay nightlife.

**Laundromat: Wash Club,** 68 r. du Marché au Charbon. M: Bourse. Wash €3.50 per 8kg, €7 per 18kg. Open daily 7am-10pm, or take your laundry to 71 van Arteveldestraat and pick it up after a few hours (☎478 23 18 30).

**Pharmacy: Neos-Bourse Pharmacie,** 61 bd. Anspach at r. du Marché aux Poulets (☎218 0640). M: Bourse. Open M-Sa 8:30am-6:30pm.

**Medical Services: St. Luc's,** 10 av. Hippocrate (☎764 1111), convenient to Grand-Place. **Clinique St Etienne Kliniek,** 100 r. du Meridien (☎ 225 9111).

**Internet Access:** Some Internet cafes with phone booths can be found on ch. de Wavre. M: Porte de Namur. They charge €1-2 per hr. **Axen,** 179 r. Royale, is located 1 block from the Centre Van Gogh Hostel. Open daily 9am-midnight. €1.50 per hr.

**Post Office:** Corner of bd. Anspach and r. des Augustins (☎226 9700; www.laposte.be). M: De Brouckère. Open M-F 8am-7pm, Sa 10:30am-6:30pm. Poste Restante available.

**!** Women navigating Brussels on their own are often the target of unwanted advances from male admirers. While sexual harassment is illegal in Belgium, isolated incidents are rarely prosecuted. Consider venturing out with a companion, and see p. 36 for further tips specific to women travelers.

# ACCOMMODATIONS

Lodging can be difficult to find, especially on weekends in summer. Overall, accommodations are well-kept and centrally located. The BITC (see **Practical Information,** p. 110) books rooms for no fee, sometimes at discounts up to 50%.

**Sleep Well,** 23 r. du Damier (☎218 5050; www.sleepwell.be). M: Rogier. The bar, pool table, lounge, and colorful common spaces contribute to this accommodation's appeal. "Star" service is similar to staying in a hotel; visitors get rooms with private bath and TV, while "non-Star" service is like being in a hostel. Breakfast and linens included. Free storage is not locked. Laundry €2.50. Lockout for non-Star 11am-3pm. Non-star dorms €17-28; singles €29; doubles €52; triples €69. Star singles €40; doubles €58. €4 discount after 1st night for all non-Star rooms except singles. MC/V. ●

**Centre Vincent Van Gogh (CHAB),** 8 r. Traversière (☎217 0158; www.chab.be). M: Botanique. Spartan rooms and inconveniently located bathrooms are countered with a laid-back environment, kitchen, TV, courtyard, and sunroom with pool table. Ages 18 to 35 only. Breakfast included. Storage room; bring a lock. Linens €3.80. Laundry €4.50. Internet €1 per 15min. Reception 24hr. Lockout 10am-2pm. Dorms €18-21; singles €33; doubles €42; triples €68. Prices reduced by €4 after 1st night. AmEx/MC/V. ●

**Les Auberges de Jeunesse "Jacques Brel" (HI),** 30 r. de la Sablonnière (☎218 0187). M: Botanique. Spacious rooms surround a courtyard with a picturesque fountain. Breakfast and linens included. Bring lock for storage. Laundry €8. Free Internet 7pm-midnight. Reception 8am-1am. Lockout noon-3pm. Dorms €19-21; singles €34; doubles €52; triples and quads €63-84. €3 HI discount. MC/V. ●

**Hotel des Eperonniers,** 1 r. des Eperonniers (☎513 5366). M: Gare Centrale. Choose between basic singles and spacious studios for up to 6 people, just around the corner from Grand-Place. Prices vary depending on amenities. Breakfast €3.75. Reception 7am-midnight. Singles €27-57; doubles €45-73. AmEx/MC/V. ●

# FOOD

Brussels has earned its reputation as one of the culinary capitals of Europe, although the city's restaurants are often more suited to the five-star port-wine-reduction set than to the budget traveler. Inexpensive eateries cluster outside **Grand-Place.** Vendors along **Rue du Marché aux Fromages** to the south hawk cheap Greek and Middle Eastern food until late at night, while **maîtres d'** along **Rue des Bouchers** noisily promote their shellfish and paella. An **AD Delhaize** supermarket is on the corner of bd. Anspach and r. du Marché aux Poulets. (M: Bourse. Open M-Th and Sa 9am-8pm, F 9am-9pm, Su 9am-6pm.)

**'t Spinnekopke,** 1 pl. du Jardin aux Fleurs (☎511 8695). M: Bourse. Locals "inside the spider's head" savor the authentically Belgian menu. Cozy, yet elegant setting. Entrees €15-25. Open M-F noon-3pm, 6pm-midnight, Sa 6pm-midnight. AmEx/MC/V. ●

**Poechenellekelder,** 5 r. du Chêne (☎511 9262). If the ongoing trickle of water from *Manneken Pis* makes your throat parched, head across the street for a drink amid hanging marionettes. Beer (€3.20-4) is supplemented by a limited menu of *tartines* (open-faced sandwiches; €4-7) and *pâté* (€8). Open Tu-Su 11am-2am. Cash only. ●

**Hémisphères,** 65 r. de l'Ecuyer (☎513 9370; www.hemispheres-resto.be). This restaurant, art gallery, and "intercultural space" serves Middle Eastern, Indian, and Asian fare. Couscous with veggies or meat (€11-15). Entrees €7-15. Concerts 1 Sa

## ON THE MENU

### LETTIN' GO OF THE EGGO

At the base of the budget tourist's food pyramid in Belgium lies an auspicious dietary group: the waffle (*gaufre* in French, *wafel* in Dutch). There are two type of Belgian waffles, both made on such particular waffle irons that they can not be made well elsewhere.

**Brussels** waffles are flat and more or less rectangular. They're light and airy, and bear some resemblance to ones eaten in the US (the kind served at diner brunches, not the ones that emerge from the freezer, pop out of the toaster, and beg to be drowned in high fructose corn syrup). Belgian recipes tend to use beaten egg whites and yeast as leavening agents, which give them their light, crisp texture. **De Lièges** waffles, ubiquitous on Belgian streets, are generally smaller, sweeter, and denser than their counterparts, and have a crunchy caramelized-sugar crust.

Pause at a cafe for a Brussels waffle, and savor it with a knife and fork. Approach a street vendor for a hand-held Liège waffle and continue to wander (in search of your next waffle?). Both can be topped with chocolate, fruit, or ice cream, or dusted with powdered sugar. Waffles generally cost about €1.50, though prices mount with the toppings.

Since you can't visit Belgium without sampling its waffles, you might as well indulge.

per month. Open M-F noon-3pm and 6:30-10:30pm, Sa 6:30pm-midnight. MC/V. ❹

**Mokafe,** in Galeries Royals St. Hubert (☎511 7870). Give your feet a rest and pause at this coffee shop while watching others walk by. Crepes (€2.80-5.60), waffles (€2.80-4.90), salads, and omelettes are among the light fare offered. Indoor and outdoor seating. Open daily 8am-11pm. ❷

**Zebra,** 31 pl. St-Géry. (☎513 5116) M: Bourse. Known for its mixed drinks, this centrally located cafe and bar also serves juices and light but filling sandwiches (€3). Open M-Th and Su 11:45am-1am, F-Sa 11:45am-2am. Kitchen closes at 11pm. MC/V. ❶

**A La Mort Subite,** 7 r. Montagne-aux-Herbes-Potagères (☎513 1318; www.alamortsubite.com). M: Gare Centrale or De Brouckère. Across from Galeries Royals St. Hubert. Feel classy—but not out of place—while ordering an omelette (€4.20-8.30) at this restaurant with original 1928 decor. Open M-Sa 11am-1am, Su 1-11pm. MC/V. ❷

**Maison Antoine,** 1 pl. Jourdan. M: Schuman. After 58 years frying, the Maison makes the best *frites* (€1.90-2.10) in town—and they only improve with a side of flavored mayo (€0.50). Open Su-Th 11:30am-1am, F-Sa 11:30am-2am. ❶

**Waffle Papillon,** Pl. Agora. Of Brussels's abundant waffle stands, this one is distinctive. Gorge on waffles topped with homemade ice cream (€1.50-5.50) or choose to add chocolate, whipped cream, strawberries, or bananas (€1.50-4.20). Cash only. ❶

## ◎ SIGHTS

**GRAND-PLACE AND ENVIRONS.** Three blocks behind the town hall, on the corner of r. de l'Étuve and r. du Chêne, is Brussels's most giggled-at sight, the **Mannekin Pis,** a tiny fountain shaped like a boy who seems to be peeing continuously. Legend claims it commemorates a young Belgian who defused a bomb destined for the Grand-Place. In reality, the fountain was installed to supply the neighborhood with water during the reign of Albert and Isabelle. Locals have created hundreds of outfits for him, each with a strategically placed hole. To even the gender gap, a statue of a squatting girl *(Jeanneken)* now pees down an ally off r. des Bouchers. Victor Hugo once called the statued and gilded Grand-Place "the most beautiful square in the world." During the day, be sure to visit **La Maison du Roi** (King's House), now the city museum whose most riveting exhibit is the collection of clothes worn by *Mannekin Pis*, and the town hall where 40min. guided tours reveal over-the-top decorations and an impressive collection of paintings. *(La Maison du Roi ☎ 279 4350. Open Tu-Su 10am-5pm. €3. Town Hall ☎ 548 0445. English-language tours Tu-W 3:15pm, Su 10:45am and 12:15pm; arrive early. €3, students €2.50.)* You'll find a brief introduction to Belgium's famed beers at the **Belgian Brewer's Museum.** *(10 Grand-Place. 2 buildings left of the town hall. ☎ 511 4987; www.beerparadise.be. Open daily 10am-5pm. €5, includes 1 beer.)* Nearby, the **Museum of Cocoa and Chocolate** tells of Belgium's other renowned edible export. Cacao fruits grow on display and the smell of chocolate permeates the air. *(11 r. de la Tête d'Or. ☎ 514 2048; www.mucc.be. Open July-Aug. and holidays daily 10am-4:30pm; Sept.-June Tu-Su 10am-4:30pm. €5, students €4.)* In the skylit **Galeries Royals St-Hubert** arcade, one block behind Grand-Place, a long covered walkway is lined with shops whose wares range from haute couture to marzipan frogs. Just north of Gare Centrale, the **Cathédrale St-Michel et Ste-Gudule** hosts royal affairs under its soaring ribbed vaults. At times, music—pipe organ or carillon—serenade visitors. *(Pl. Ste-Gudule. Open M-F 7am-6pm, Sa-Su 8:30am-6pm. Free.)*

**MONT DES ARTS.** The ▓**Musées Royaux des Beaux-Arts** encompass the **Musée d'Art Ancien,** the **Musée d'Art Moderne,** several contemporary exhibits, and the **Musée Magritte,** opening in 2008. Together, the museums steward a huge collection of Belgian art, including Bruegel's famous *Landscape with the Fall of Icarus* and pieces by Rubens and Brussels native René Magritte. Other masterpieces on display include David's *Death of Marat* and paintings by Delacroix, Gauguin, Seurat, and van Gogh. The great hall itself is a work of architectural beauty; the panoramic view of Brussels from the fourth floor of the 19th-century wing alone justifies the admission fee. *(3 r. de la Régence. M: Parc. ☎ 508 3211; www.fine-arts-museum.be. Open Tu-Su 10am-5pm. Some wings close noon-2pm. €9, students €3.50. 1st W of each month 1-5pm free. Audio tour €2.50.)* The **Musical Instrument Museum (MIM)** houses over 1500 instruments; stand in front of one and your headphones automatically play a sample of its music. *(2 r. Montagne de la Cour. ☎ 545 0130; www.mim.fgov.be. Open Tu-F 9:30am-4:45pm, Sa-Su 10am-5pm. €5, students €4. 1st W of each month 1-5pm free.)*

**BELGIAN CENTER FOR COMIC STRIP ART.** Comic strips *(les BD)* are serious business in Belgium. Today, a restored warehouse designed by famous architect Victor Horta pays tribute to what Belgians call the Ninth Art. Amusing displays document comic strip history, the museum library makes thousands of books available to scholarly researchers, and Tintin and the Smurfs make several appearances. *(☎ 214 0140. R. des Sables. M: Rogier. Open Tu-Su 10am-6pm, students with ISIC €6.)*

**OTHER SIGHTS.** The eerily illuminated Treasure Room and the Greco-Roman collection are the main attractions at the enormous Musées Royaux d'Art et d'Histoire, set in a beautiful park, while the Gothic Room and the Chinese draw-loom exhibits are quirkily enjoyable. *(10 Parc du Cinquantenaire. ☎ 741 7211. M: Mérode. Open Tu-F 9:30am-5pm, Sa-Su 10am-5pm. Ticket office closes at 4pm. €5, students €4. 1st W of each month 1-5pm free.)* The out-of-the-way **Musée Horta,** home of 20th-century master architect Victor Horta, gracefully applies his Art Nouveau style to a domestic setting. *(25 r. Américaine. M: Horta. Take a right out of the stop, walk 7min. uphill on ch. de Waterloo, then turn left onto ch. de Charleroi and right onto r. Américaine. ☎ 543 0490; www.hortamuseum.be. Open Tu-Su 2-5:30pm. €7, students €3.50.)*

# ♫ 📷 ENTERTAINMENT AND NIGHTLIFE

The weekly *What's On*, part of the *Bulletin* newspaper and available free at the tourist office, contains info on cultural events. The **Théâtre Royal de la Monnaie,** on pl. de la Monnaie, is renowned for its opera and ballet. *(M: De Brouckère. ☎ 229 1200, box office 70 39 39; www.lamonnaie.be. Tickets from €8, ½-price tickets go on sale 20min. prior to the event.)* The **Théâtre Royal de Toone VII,** 66 r. du Marché-aux-herbes, stages marionette performances, a distinctly Belgian art form, and houses an intimate bar with marionettes hanging from the ceiling. (☎513 5486; www.toone.be for show times and prices. Shows generally in French; English available for groups upon request. F 8:30pm, Sa 4pm and 8:30pm, occasionally Tu-Th. €10, students €7.) **Nova,** 3 r. d'Arenberg, screens foreign and independent films, both contemporary and historic. Live performances take place downstairs. The website lists future festivals. The theater holds a free "Open Screen" on the last Thursday of every month at 8:30pm, in which any filmmaker can screen a 15min. piece. (☎511 2477; www.nova-cinema.com. €5, students €3.50.)

On summer nights, live concerts on Grand-Place and the Bourse bring the streets to life. The *All the Fun* pamphlet, available at the tourist office, lists the newest clubs and bars. On **Place St-Géry,** patios are jammed with a laid-back crowd of students and backpackers. **Zebra** (p. 111) and a host of other bars are lively until late. **O'Reilly's Irish Pub,** pl. de la Bourse, nearby, is packed with travelers and TVs—a comforting spot for the homesick. It has large breakfast, lunch, and dinner menus, plus lots of beer. (☎25 521 0481. Open M-Th and Su 11am-1am, F-Sa, 11am-4am. Free Wi-Fi. AmEx/MC/V.) Choose from over 2000 beers at ▨**Delirium,** 4A impasse de la Fidélité, where the carefree environment makes late-night hours fly. (☎251 4434; www.deliriumcafe.be. Jam session Th and Su 11pm. Open daily 10am-4am.) **Celtica,** 55 r. aux Poulets, might have the world's longest Happy hour: throbbing techno accompanies €2 drafts 1pm-midnight. The bar downstairs is more relaxed, but a DJ spins upstairs. (☎514 3253; www.celticpubs.com. Bar open daily 1pm-late. Disco open Th-Sa 10pm.) More techno blares amid the crowd of beautiful people at **Le Fuse,** 208 r. Blaes. (☎511 9789; www.fuse.be. Cover €5 before midnight, €8 after. Open Sa 10pm-late.) **Havana,** 4 r. de l'Epee, plays everything from salsa to techno. (☎502 1224; www.havana-brussels.com. Open W-Su 7pm-late. Live music on W, F, and Sa. AmEx/MC/V.) **GBLT nightlife** centers on r. des Pierres and r. du Marché au Charbon, next to Grand-Place. **L'Homo Erectus,** 57 r. des Pierres, is extremely popular. (☎514 7493; www.lhomoerectus.com. Open daily 3pm-3am.)

## ▶ DAYTRIP FROM BRUSSELS: MECHELEN (MALINES)

The residents of Mechelen (pop. 78,000) are nicknamed the "Moon Extinguishers" for once mistaking fog and a red moon for a fire in the tower of **St-Rombouts Tower and Cathedral.** Today, the tower holds two 49-bell carillons and is home to the world's foremost bell-ringing school. In summer, you can hear recitals from anywhere in Grote Markt on Monday and Saturday at 11:30am and Sunday at 3pm. (☎20 47 92; www.beiaardschool.be.) A 1½-2hr. ▨**Cathedral tour** departs from the tourist office and heads up the 513 steps to the top to see the bells and the view. *(Tours Easter-Sept. Sa-Su 2:15pm, July-Aug. daily 2:15pm. €5.)* To reach St-Rombouts from Centraal station, walk down Hendrick Consciencestr., which becomes Graaf van Egmonstr., then Brul, to the pedestrian Grote Markt. *(Cathedral open daily Easter-Oct. 8:30am-5:30pm; Nov.-Easter 8:30am-4:30pm.)* Nearby, the 15th-century **St. John's Church** boasts Rubens's magnificent triptych *The Adoration of the Magi.* From the Grote Markt, walk down Fr. de Merodestr. and turn left onto St-Janstr. *(Open Tu-Su Easter-Oct. 1:30-5:30pm; Nov.-Easter 1:30-4:30pm.)* To reach the ▨**Jewish Museum of Deportation and Resistance,** 153 Goswin de Stassartstr., follow Wollemarkt from behind St-Rombouts until it becomes Goswin de Stassart, then enter the apartment building on your left when the streets end at the canal. The museum is in 18th-century barracks that were once used as a holding area for 25,257 Jews en route to Auschwitz-Birkenau. *(☎29 06 60; www.cicb.be. Open Su-Th 10am-5pm, F 10am-1pm. Free.)* Just off Grote Markt is **Adagio ❸,** 16 Ijzerenleen, a cheaper alternative to the cafes in the Markt itself. *(☎20 88 17. Entrees €7-12. Open M, Th-F 10am-10pm, Sa 8am-10pm, Su noon-10pm. AmEx/MC/V.)* **Trains** go to Antwerp (20min., 4 per hr., €3.70) and Brussels (20min., 4-5 per hr., €3.70). The **tourist office,** 2-6 Hallestr., is in the Grote Markt.

(☎070 22 28 00; www.inenuitmechelen.be. Open Apr.-Sept. M 9:30am-7pm, Tu-F 9:30am-5:30pm, Sa-Su 10am-4:30pm; Oct.-Mar. M-F 9:30am-4:30pm, Sa-Su 10:30am-3:30pm.)

 **THE REAL DEAL.** Skip the boring trip to Waterloo, the location of the famous battle. Hordes of tourists bear down on the site's unimaginatively displayed artifacts. If you really must see Waterloo, take Bus W from the Gare du Midi (1hr., 2 per hr., €2.40-3). The tourist office is at 218 ch. de Bruxelles. (☎354 99 10; www.waterloo-tourisme.be. Open daily Apr.-Sept. 9:30am-6:30pm; Oct.-Mar. 10:30am-5pm.)

# FLANDERS (VLAANDEREN)

## BRUGES (BRUGGE)                                        ☎50

Bruges (pop. 116,000) is arguably Belgium's most romantic city. Canals carve their way through rows of stone houses and cobblestone streets en route to the breathtaking Gothic Markt. The city remains one of the best-preserved examples of Northern Renaissance architecture. Don't let the swarms of tourists deter you from visiting—a trip to Belgium is incomplete without a stop in Bruges.

### TRANSPORTATION

**Trains** leave from the **Stationsplein**, a 15min. walk south of the city. (Open daily 4:30am-11pm. Info desk open daily 8am-7pm.) Trains head to: Antwerp (1¾hr., 2 per hr., €13); Brussels (1hr., 1-3 per hr., €12); Ghent (20min., 3 per hr., €5.40); Knokke (30min., 2 per hr., €3); Ostend (15min., 3 per hr., €3.30).

### ORIENTATION AND PRACTICAL INFORMATION

Bruges is enclosed by a circular canal, with the train station, Stationsplein, just beyond its southern extreme. The historic district is entirely accessible by foot, while bikes are popular for countryside visits. The dizzying **Belfort** looms high over the center of town, presiding over the handsome **Markt**. The windmill-lined **Kruisvestraat** and serene **Minnewater Park** are the most beautiful spots in Bruges.

**TIP** **WATCH THAT BIKE!** In Bruges, as in many Flemish cities, bike lanes are marked in red. To forestall cyclists' ire, pedestrians should avoid these areas.

**Tourist Office: In and Uit,** 't Zand 34 (☎44 46 46; www.brugge.be). From the train station, head left to 't Zand and walk for 10min.; it's in the red concert hall. Books rooms for a €2.50 fee and €20 deposit, and sells **maps** (€0.50) and **info guides** (€1). (Open M-W and F-Su 10am-6pm, Th 10am-8pm.) Branch at the train station. (Open Apr.-Sept. Tu-Su 10am-1pm and 2-6pm; Oct.-Mar. Tu-Sa 9:30am-noon and 1-5pm.)

**Tours:** 5 companies offer 30min. **boat tours** of Bruges's canals. Vessels glide by otherwise inaccessible city corners (Mar.-Nov., 2-4 per hr., €6); inquire at tourist office. **QuasiMundo Tours** has 3 different **bike tours** of Bruges and the countryside (3-4hr.). Tours depart daily at 10am and 7pm from Bruges, 1pm from the countryside. (☎33 07 75; www.quasimundo.com. Tours Mar.-Oct. €20, under 26 €18; includes free drink.) **Pink Bear Bicycle Company** leads 2 tours; both leave at 10:30am from the Belfry in the Markt. (☎61 66 86; www.pinkbear.freeservers.com. €19, under 26 €17.) Both companies advise calling ahead.

**Currency Exchange: Goffin,** Steenstraat 2, is near the Markt, and charges no commission on cash exchange (☎34 04 71. Open M-Sa 9am-5:30pm).

BELGIUM

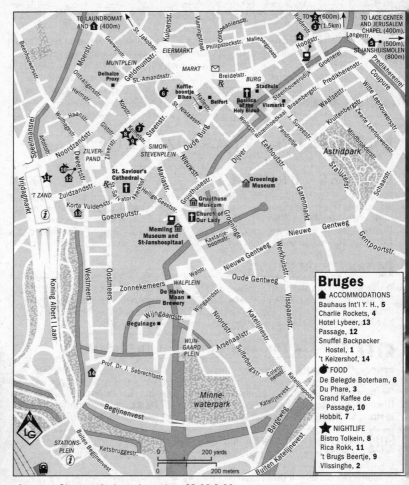

**Bruges**

**▲ ACCOMMODATIONS**
Bauhaus Int'l Y. H., **5**
Charlie Rockets, **4**
Hotel Lybeer, **13**
Passage, **12**
Snuffel Backpacker
   Hostel, **1**
't Keizershof, **14**

**● FOOD**
De Belegde Boterham, **6**
Du Phare, **3**
Grand Kaffee de
   Passage, **10**
Hobbit, **7**

**★ NIGHTLIFE**
Bistro Tolkein, **8**
Rica Rokk, **11**
't Brugs Beertje, **9**
Vlissinghe, **2**

**Luggage Storage:** At the train station. €2.60-3.60.

**Laundromat: Belfort,** Ezelstr. 51. Wash €3-6, dry €1. Open daily 7am-10pm.

**Bike Rental:** At the train station (☎30 23 28). Passport required. €6.50 per day. **Koffie-boontje,** Hallestr. 4 (☎33 80 27; www.adventure-bike-renting.be), to the right of the Belfort. €7 per 4hr.; €10 per day, students €7 per day. Open daily 9am-10pm.

**Police:** Hauwerstr. 7 (☎44 89 30).

**Hospitals: A. Z. St-Jan** (☎45 21 11; not to be confused with Oud St-Janshospitaal, a museum). **St-Lucas** (☎36 91 11). **St-Franciscus Xaveriuskliniek** (☎47 04 70).

**Internet Access: Teleboutique Brugge,** Predikherenstr. 48, is one of the cheaper options. €2 per hour. Open daily 10am-10pm. Cash only.

**Post Office:** Markt 5. Open M and W-F 9am-6pm, Sa 9:30am-12:30pm. Poste Restante available.

# ⌂ ACCOMMODATIONS

**Snuffel Backpacker Hostel,** Ezelstr. 47-49 (☎33 31 33; www.snuffel.be). Take bus #3 or 13 (€1.30) from the station to the stop after Markt, then take the 1st left. Colorful rooms decorated by local artists. Helpful staff leads free walking tours every other day. The on-site bar's Happy hour is so cheap, even locals frequent it (9-10pm, beer €1). Guests also get a free Bruges card, which gives access to museums and many discounts. Kitchen. Bike rental €6 per day. Breakfast €3. Lockers available; bring your own lock or rent one. Linens included. Internet €2 per hr.; free Wi-Fi. Key deposit €5. Reception 7:30am-midnight. Dorms €14; doubles €36; quads €60-64. AmEx/MC/V. ❷

**Passage,** Dweersstr. 26 (☎34 02 32; www.passagebruges.com). Old-world, refined hostel-hotel-cafe in an ideal location. Safes available. Breakfast €5; included in private rooms. Internet €4 per hr. Reception 9am-midnight. Open mid-Feb. to mid-Jan. Dorms €14; singles €25-45; doubles €45-60; triples and quads €75-90. AmEx/MC/V. ❷

**Hotel Lybeer,** Korte Vuldersstr. 31 (☎33 43 55; www.hostellybeer.com). Charming and well situated. Breakfast and linens included. Free Internet. Reception 7:30am-11pm. Dorms €14-24; singles €23-38; doubles €43-65; triples €70-80. AmEx/MC/V. ❸

**Bauhaus International Youth Hostel and Hotel,** Langestr. 133-137 (☎34 10 93; www.bauhaus.be). Take bus #6 or 16 from the station; ask to stop at the hostel. A giant candelabra and popular bar lead the way to airy rooms. Bike rental €9 per day. Breakfast and linens included. Lockers €1.50. Internet €3 per hr. Reception 8am-midnight. Dorms €14-15; singles from €26; doubles from €40; triples from €57. AmEx/MC/V. ❷

**Charlie Rockets,** Hoogstr. 19 (☎33 06 60; www.charlierockets.com). Americans might feel at home at this wannabe Charlie Rockets in a converted movie theatre, equipped with pool tables, darts, and, of course, 50s decor. Breakfast €3. Lockers €3. Linens included. Internet €2 per 20min. Dorms €16. MC/V. ❷

**'t Keizershof,** Oostmeers 126 (☎33 87 28; www.hotelkeizershof.be). Pretty, sunlit rooms on a quiet street. Breakfast included. Reception 8:30am-6pm; call ahead for arrivals after 6pm. Singles €25; doubles €40; triples €62; quads €72. Cash only. ❸

# ▣ FOOD

Inexpensive restaurants can be hard to find in Bruges. Seafood lovers should splurge at least once on the city's famous *mosselen* (mussels; €15-22) found at the **Vismarkt,** near the Burg. (Open Tu-Sa 8am-1pm.) Grab groceries at **Delhaize Proxy,** Noordzandstr. 4, near the Markt. (Open M-Sa 9am-7pm.)

**Grand Kaffee de Passage,** Dweersstr. 26-28 (☎34 02 32). Next to the Passage hostel. Traditional Belgian cuisine in a candlelit setting. Try the excellent Flemish stew (€11). Open daily 6-11pm. Closed from mid-Jan. to mid-Feb. AmEx/MC/V. ❸

**Du Phare,** Sasplein 2 (☎34 35 90; www.duphare.be). From the Burg, walk down Hoogstr. and turn left at the canal onto Verversdijk, crossing to the right side at the second bridge. Follow the canal for 20min. to Sasplein. Bus #4 stops right outside. This jazz and blues bistro serves international fare (€11-20). Open M and W 11:30am-2:30pm and 7pm-midnight, Tu and F-Sa 11:30am-2:30pm and 6:30pm-midnight, Su 11:30am-midnight. Reservations recommended F-Sa. AmEx/MC/V. ❸

**Hobbit,** Kemelstr. 8-10 (☎33 55 20; www.hobbitgrill.be). Order filling meats and pastas from clever newsprint menus. Entrees €7-11. Open daily 6pm-1am. AmEx/MC/V. ❷

**BELGIUM**

**De Belegde Boterham,** Kleine St-Amandsstr. 5 (☎34 91 31). Health-conscious spot serves sandwiches (€7-8) and innovative salads (€11) in its chic interior or on endearingly mismatched tables outside. Open M-Sa noon-4pm. Cash only. ❷

# 🗗 SIGHTS

Filled with Gothic and neo-Gothic buildings and crisscrossed by canals, picturesque Bruges is best experienced on foot. Avoid visiting Bruges on Mondays, when museums are closed. If you plan to visit many museums, consider a cost-saving combination ticket (€15, includes admission to 5 museums).

**MARKT AND BURG.** The medieval **Belfort** (belfry) looms over the Markt; climb its 366 steep steps for a phenomenal view. *(Belfort open Tu-Su 9:30am-5pm. Last entry 4:15pm. €5. Bell concerts mid-June to Sept. M, W, and Sa 9pm, Su 2:15pm; Oct. to mid-June W and Sa-Su 2:15pm.)* Behind the Markt, the Burg is dominated by the finely detailed facade of the **Stadhuis** (Town Hall). Inside, wander through the gilded **Gothic Hall,** where residents of Bruges still get married. *(☎44 81 10. Open Tu-Su 9:30am-4:30pm. €2.50, under 26 €1.50. Audio tour included.)* This ticket will also get you into **Liberty of Bruges Museum,** which contains an ornate fireplace. *(Open M-Sa 9:30am-12:30pm and 1:30-5pm).* Tucked away in a corner of the Burg next to the Stadhuis, the **Basilica of the Holy Blood** supposedly holds the blood of Christ in a spectacularly ornate sanctuary upstairs; its disappointing museum has paintings and clerical garments. *(Basilica open daily Apr.-Sept. 9:30-noon and 2-6pm; Oct.-Mar. 10am-noon and 2-4pm; closed W afternoon. Holy Relic can be viewed at 11am and 2-4pm. Museum €1.50.)*

**MUSEUMS.** From the Burg, follow Wollestr. left and then head right on Dijver and walk through the garden to reach the **Groeninge Museum;** small for its price, its highlights are works by Jan van Eyck and Hans Memling. *(Dijver 12. ☎44 87. Open Tu-Su 9:30am-5pm. €8, under 26 €6. Audio tour included.)* Formerly a palace, the nearby **Gruuthuse Museum** houses a large collection of 16th- and 17th-century tapestries. *(Dijver 17. ☎44 87 62. Open Tu-Su 9:30am-5pm. €6, students €4. Audio tour included.)* Continue on Dijver as it becomes Gruuthusestr. and walk under the stone archway to enter the **Memling Museum,** in Oud St-Janshospitaal, a brick building that was a hospital in medieval times. The museum reconstructs everyday life in the hospital and has several paintings by its namesake, Hans Memling. *(Mariastr. 38. ☎44 87 71. Open Tu-Su 9:30am-5pm, ticket office closes 4:30pm. €8, under 26 €5. Audio tour included.)* To get to the **Lace Center,** Peperstr. 3A, walk down Hoogstr. from the Burg. Take a left onto Molenmeers after the canal. The center shares a gate with the **Jerusalem Chapel.** Lace-making demonstrations by a troop of wrinkled octogenarians are surprisingly fun to watch. *(☎33 00 72; www.kantcentrum.com. Open M-F 10am-noon and 2-6pm, Sa-10am-noon and 2-5pm. €2.50, under 26 €1.50 for both Lace Center and Chapel.)*

**OTHER SIGHTS.** The 14th-century **Church of Our Lady,** at Mariastr. and Gruuthusestr., contains Michelangelo's *Madonna and Child. (Open Tu-F 9:30am-5pm, Sa 9:30am-4:45pm, Su 12:30-5pm; last entry 4:30pm. Church free. Tomb viewing €2.50, students €1.50. Ticket for the tomb included in Gruuthuse Museum ticket.)* Beer aficionados will enjoy the samples at 150-year-old **De Halve Maan,** a beer museum and brewery. *(Welplein 26. ☎33 26 97; www.halvemaan.be. 45min. tours Apr.-Sept. 1 per hr. M-F 11am-4pm, Sa-Su 11am-5pm; Oct.-Mar. tours M-F 11am and 3pm, Sa-Su 1 per hr. 11am-4pm. €5, includes beer.)* For God-sanctioned fun, wander the grounds of the **Beguinage,** home to nuns who share their tree-covered yard with passersby. The Beguine's house displays furnishings typical of medieval Flemish households. *(From Simon Stevinplein, follow Mariastr., and turn right on Wijngaardstr.; at the canal, turn right and cross the footbridge. ☎33 00 11. Open Mar.-Nov. daily 10am-noon and 1:45-5pm; gate open 6:30am-6:30pm. Garden free; house €2, under 26 €1.)* Walk along the river to see the windmills; to enter, go down to 235-year-old windmill **St-Janshuismolen,** which still gives occasional flour-grinding demonstrations in summer when the wind is right. (☎ *33 00 44. Open May-Sept. daily 9:30am-12:30pm and 1:30-5pm. €2, under 26 €1.*)

##  FESTIVALS AND NIGHTLIFE

Bruges plays host to the **Cactusfestival** (☎ 33 20 14; www.cactusfestival.be. €25 per day, €63 for 3 days), a series of alt-pop and hip-hop concerts the first full weekend in July. The city also sponsors **Klinkers,** an open-air music and film series that's free to the public during July and August (☎ 33 20 14; www.klinkers-brugge.be). At **'t Brugs Beertje,** Kemelstr. 5, off Steenstr., sample some of the 250 varieties of beer. (☎ 33 96 16. Open Su-M and Th 4pm-12:30am, F-Sa 4pm-2am.) Next door, the candlelit **Bistro Tolkien,** Kemelstr. 9, pours fruity *jenever* (€2), a flavored Dutch gin. (☎ 34 24 21. Entrees €6-16. Open M and W-Sa noon-2pm and 6pm-11pm.) For a quieter night, try Bruges's oldest pub, **Vlissinghe,** Blekersstr. 2, established in 1515. From the Burg, take Hoogstr. and turn left onto Verversdijk immediately before the canal. Cross the second bridge onto Blekersstr. (☎ 34 37 37. Open W-Sa 11am-midnight, Su 11am-7pm.) Steer clear of the tourist clubs behind the Markt. Belgian students tend to prefer the dance floor of **Rica Rokk,** 't Zand 6, where shots are €3 and a meter of beer starts at €19. (☎ 33 24 34; www.maricarokk.com. Open daily 9:30am-5am.) The tourist office has a list of **GLBT establishments.**

> ⚡**TIP** **THE LONG ARM OF THE LAW.** If you're wobbling back to your hostel with a bellyful of beer, think twice before yielding to nature's call en route. Police will fine you up to €152 if they catch you urinating in public. Keep €0.30 handy for the public toilets, although many of these stalls close at 8pm.

# ANTWERP (ANTWERPEN, ANVERS)  ☎ 03

While Antwerp (pop. 455,000) used to be known for its avant-garde fashion and jet-setting party hoppers, the hipster scene has since calmed. But an afternoon window-shopping in the city's diamond quarter or along the Meir reveals that Antwerp still holds as much an attraction for the fashionista as the backpacker.

**TRANSPORTATION AND PRACTICAL INFORMATION.** Antwerp has two train stations: **Berchem,** which handles most international traffic, and **Centraal,** the domestic station. Centraal's soaring arches make it a tourist destination in its own right. **Trains** go from Berchem to: Amsterdam, NTH (2hr., 1 per hr., €21-29); Brussels (45min., 4 per hr., €6.10); and Rotterdam, NTH (1hr., 1 per hr., €13-18). Centraal ticket office is open daily 6am-10pm. Lockers are available in Centraal. The **tourist office** is downstairs in Centraal. To get to the Grote Markt from Berchem, take tram #8 (€1.20, €1.50 on board) to Groenpl. From Centraal take tram #2 (dir.: Linkeroever) or walk down Meir, the main pedestrian thoroughfare, to Groenpl. (☎ 232 0103. Open M-Sa 9am-5:45pm, Su 9am-4:45pm. English-language historical city tour from Grote Markt 13 Sa-Su 11am. €5.) **Postal Code:** 2000.

**ACCOMMODATIONS AND FOOD.** The well-worn **New International Youth Hotel ❷,** Provinciestr. 256, is a 15min. walk from Centraal Station, on the corner of De Boeystr. and Provinciestr. Turn left out of the station onto Pelikaanstr., which becomes Simonsstr.; turn left on Plantin en Moretus, walk under the bridge, then turn right onto Provinciestr. (☎ 230 0522. Breakfast included. Reception 8am-midnight. Dorms €19-21, under 26 with sleeping bag €15; singles €34; doubles €49-61; triples €70-79. MC/V.) Take the metro to Groenpl. for **Guesthouse 26 ❺,** Pelgrimsstr. 26, in the heart of the city. Inventive decor keeps guests returning, even as prices rise. (☎289 3995; www.guesthouse26.be. Breakfast included. Reserve ahead. Singles €55-75; doubles €65-85. AmEx/MC/V.) **Da Giovanni ❷**, Jan Blomstr. 8, just off Groenpl., serves hearty pizzas (€5-16) and tries to bring Italy to Belgium. (☎226 7450; www.dagiovanni.be. Open daily 11am-midnight. 20% student discount. AmEx/MC/V.) More than 400 religious figurines accompany your meal at **'t Elfde Gebod ❹**, Torfburg 10. (☎289 3466. Entrees €8-20. Open daily noon-2am. Kitchen open noon-10:30pm. MC/V.) A **Super GB** supermarket is in the Grand Shopping Bazaar. (Open M-Th and Sa 8:30am-8pm, F 8:30am-9pm. MC/V.)

**◙ SIGHTS.** Antwerp's main promenades, **De Keyserlei** and the **Meir**, draw crowds to their elegant department stores and avant-garde boutiques. On the western edge of the shopping district, the **Cathedral of Our Lady**, Groenpl. 21, holds Rubens's *Descent from the Cross*. (www.dekathedraal.be. Open M-F 10am-5pm, Sa 10am-3pm, Su 1-4pm. Tours 1-3 per day. €2.) Take in the busy exterior of the nearby **Stadhuis** (city hall), then hop on tram #11 (dir.: Eksterlaar) to see the wildly opulent mansions that line **Cogels Osylei**. A stroll by the Schelde River leads to the 13th-century **Steen Castle**, Steenplein 1, which houses the collections of the **National Maritime Museum** in **Maritime Park**. (☎201 9340. Museum open Tu-Su 10am-5pm. Park open Easter-Oct. 10am-5pm. €4.) The **Museum Voor Schone Kunsten** (KMSKA; Royal Museum of Fine Arts), Leopold De Waelpl. 1-9, possesses one of the world's finest collections of Flemish paintings. (☎238 7809; www.kmska.be. Open Tu-Sa 10am-5pm, Su 10am-6pm. €6, under 19 free.) The **Mayer van den Bergh Museum**, Lange Gasthuisstr. 19, showcases Bruegel's apocalyptic *Mad Meg*, along with other 14th- to 16th-century works. Most captions are in Flemish. (☎232 4237. Open Tu-Su 10am-5pm. €4, students €3. V.) The **RubensHuis**, Wapper 9, off the Meir, was home to Baroque artist Peter Paul Rubens, and its intact rooms are filled with his works, including *The Annunciation*. (☎201 1555. Open Tu-Su 10am-4:45pm. €6, under 26 €4.) The **Diamant Museum**, Kon. Astridplein 19-23, chronicles Antwerp's historic importance in the diamond industry through interesting audiovisual displays. (☎202 4890. Open M-Tu and Th-Su 10am-5:30pm. €6, students €4.)

**◪ NIGHTLIFE.** The palatial club **Café d'Anvers**, Verversrui 15, north of Grote Markt in the red-light district, features popular DJs and caters to a younger crowd. (☎226 3870; www.cafe-d-anvers.com. Open F-Sa 11pm-7am.) Bars behind the cathedral and in the trendy neighborhood around the Royal Museum of Fine Arts offer an alternative to the club scene. For daily live jazz, hole up in the loft of **De Muze**, Melkmarkt 15, or else sip Grimbergen Abbey beer at one of the tables outside. (Open daily 11am-4am.) Step into the 15th-century cellars for a candlelit dinner at **Pelgrom**, Pelgrimstr. 15, before sampling the local *elixir d'Anvers* (a strong herbal liqueur; €5) doled out by bartenders in traditional dress. (☎234 0809. Open daily noon-late.) Gay nightlife clusters around **Van Schoonhovenstraat**, north of Centraal Station. Head to the **Gay and Lesbian Center**, Dambruggestr. 204, for more info.

# GHENT (GENT)                                                    ☎09

Once the heart of Flanders's textile industry, modern Ghent (pop. 228,000) still celebrates the memory of its medieval greatness and its more recent industrial past with awe-inspiring buildings in the city's main square. The Gentse Feesten brings performers, carnival rides, and flowing *jenever* (flavored gin) to the city center. (July 12-21 2008. ☎269 4600; www.gentsefeesten.be.) Ghent's museums close on Mondays, and most of the city shuts down for two weeks after the festival.

**◧◪ TRANSPORTATION AND PRACTICAL INFORMATION. Trains** run from St-Pietersstation (accessible by tram #1) to Antwerp (50min., 2 per hr., €11), Bruges (25min., 3 per hr., €8), and Brussels (35min., 5 per hr., €7.40). The **tourist office**,

Botermarkt 17A, in the crypt of the belfry, books rooms for no fee and leads walking tours. (☎266 5232; www.visitgent.be. Open daily Apr.-Oct. 9:30am-6:30pm; Nov.-Mar. 9:30am-4:30pm. Tours Nov.-Apr. daily 2:30pm; buy tickets by 2pm. €7.) At the tourist office and most museums, you can buy a pass for 15 museums and monuments in Ghent (€12.50). **Use-It**, St-Pietersnieuwstr. 21, is a great resource for young, budget-conscious backpackers, with quirky maps for self-guided tours and free **Internet**. Search their website for available rooms around town. (☎324 3906; www.use-it.be. Open M-F 1-6pm.) **Postal Code:** 9000.

**⌖◖ ACCOMMODATIONS AND FOOD.** To reach **De Draecke (HI) ❷**, St-Widostr. 11, from the station, take tram #1 (€1.20, €1.50 on board) to Gravensteen (15min.). Facing the castle, head left over the canal, then right on Gewad and right on St-Widostr. (☎233 7050; www.vjh.be. Breakfast and linens included. Internet €2 per 30min. Reception 7:30am-11pm. Dorms €20; doubles €50. €3 HI discount. AmEx/MC/V.) To get to **Camping Blaarmeersen ❶**, Zuiderlaan 12, take bus #9 from St-Pietersstation toward Mariakerke and get off at Europabrug (Watersportbaan); cross the street and hop on bus #38 or 39 to Blaarmeersen. Take the first street on the left to its end. (☎266 8160. Laundry available and restaurant. Open Mar. to mid-Oct. €4.50 per person, €4.50 per tent; low season €3.50/3.50.) **St-Pietersnieuwstraat**, by the university, has inexpensive kebab and pita joints that stay open until around midnight. **Magazijn ❷**, Penitentenstr. 24, has filling fare (€8.50-16), including many vegetarian options. (☎234 0708. Kitchen open Tu-F noon-2pm and 6-11pm, Sa 6-11pm. Bar open until late. Cash only.) For groceries, stop by the **Contact GB** at Hoogpoort 42. (☎225 0592. Open M-Sa 8:30am-6pm. MC/V.)

**◪ SIGHTS.** The **Leie canal** runs through the city and wraps around the **Gravensteen** (Castle of Counts), St-Veerlepl. 11, a partially restored medieval fortress. (☎225 9306. Open daily Apr.-Sept. 9am-6pm; Oct.-Mar. 9am-5pm. €6, under 26 €1.20.) Nearby is the historic **Partershol** quarter, with well-preserved 16th- to 18th-century houses. From Gravensteen, head down Geldmunt, make a right on Lange Steenst., and then turn right into the Old Town. From the Partershol, follow the river toward Groenten Markt and Korenmarkt. Stroll down along the **Graslei**, on the way to **St-Michielshelling**, lined with handsome guild houses. Walk across St-Michielshelling for the best view of Ghent's skyline. From here, you can take a 45min. boat tour (Mar.-Nov. 4 per hr., 5). St-Michielshelling connects two majestic cathedrals. Facing the bridge with Graslei behind you, **St-Niklaaskerk** is on your right. Built with bluish-gray limestone drawn from quarries in nearby Tournai, the cathedral's unique interior is a testament to the rich merchants who worshipped here in the 13th through 15th centuries. (☎225 3700. Open M 2:30-5pm, Tu-Su 10am-5pm. Free.) On the left, on Limburgstr., the elaborately decorated **St-Baafskathedraal** holds Flemish brothers Hubert and Jan van Eyck's *Adoration of the Mystic Lamb* and Rubens's *St. Bavo's Entrance into the Monastery of Ghent*. (Cathedral and crypt open daily Apr.-Oct. 8:30am-6pm; Nov.-Mar. 8:30am-5pm. *Mystic Lamb* exhibit open Apr.-Oct. M-Sa 9:30am-5pm, Su 1-5pm; Nov.-Mar. M-Sa 10:30am-4pm, Su 1-4pm. Cathedral and crypt free. *Mystic Lamb* exhibit €3.) The **belfry**, not far from here, has an elevator that takes you to views of the city. (Open mid-Apr. to mid-Nov. daily 10am-5:30pm. €3, students €2.50.) The eclectic **Design Museum**, Jan Breydelstr. 5, across the street and to the right of the Graslei, has two sections: the old part displays 17th- and 18th-century furniture, while the stylish new section exhibits a great deal of Art Deco, Art Nouveau, and contemporary works. (☎267 9999; design.museum.gent.be. Open Tu-Su 10am-6pm. €2.50, students €1.20.) **Stedelijk Museum voor Actuele Kunst (SMAK)**, in Citadel Park, a 30min. walk from the tourist office, or a shorter ride on the #1 tram from Korenmarkt (dir.: Flanders Expo; €1.20, €1.50 on tram), regularly rotates its collection of cutting-edge modern art. (☎221 1703; www.smak.be. Open Tu-Su 10am-6pm. €5, students €3.80. Free 1st F of each month 6-10pm.)

**BELGIUM**

■ **NIGHTLIFE. Korenmarkt** and **Vrijdagmarkt** are filled with restaurants and pubs. Use-It's (p. 120) guide to nightlife can direct you to live music options. One popular haunt is the dimly lit **Charlatan,** Vlasmarkt 6, which features a nightly DJ. (☎224 2457; www.charlatan.be. Live bands Th and Su. Open Tu-Su 7pm-late.) To sit down and have a drink, try **K27,** in the Vrijdag Markt at the corner of Baudelost. (Beer €2-3. Mixed drinks €5. Open M-F noon-late, Sa 2pm-late.) For GLBT nightlife, consult Use-It's Ghent Gay Map or head to the **Foyer Casa Rosa,** Kammerstr. 22/Belfortstr. 39, an info center and bar. (☎269 2812; www.casarosa.be. Bar open M-F 3pm-1am, Sa-Su 3pm-2am; info center open M 6-9pm, W 3-9pm, Sa 3-6pm.)

## YPRES (IEPER)                                                                                        ☎57

Famous for its fields filled with poppies and lined with tombstones of fallen soldiers, Ypres (pop. 35,000) and its environs continue to bear witness to the city's role in WWI. It was here the Germans realized that their anticipated quick victory would instead become an entrenched and bitter stalemate. Once a medieval textile center, Ypres was completely destroyed by four years of combat, but was impressively rebuilt as a near-perfect replica of its former self. Today, the town is surrounded by over 150 **British cemeteries** and filled with memorial sites. The **In Flanders Field Museum,** Grote Markt 34, documents the gruesome history of the Great War. (☎23 92 20; www.inflandersfields.be. Open Apr.-Sept. daily 10am-6pm, last entry 5pm; Oct.-Mar. Tu-Su 10am-5pm. €7.50. MC/V.) Behind the museum is **St. Martin's Cathedral,** rebuilt using pre-war plans and furnished with a rose window given to Belgium by the British military. (☎20 80 04. Open daily 9am-noon and 2-6pm. Free.) Cross the street in front of St. Martin's and head right to reach **St. George's Memorial Church,** Elverdingsestr. 1 (☎21 56 85). Each brass plaque and kneeling pillow in the church commemorates a particular military group. (Open daily Apr.-Oct. 9:30am-8pm; Nov.-Mar. 9:30am-4pm. Free.) Across the Markt, the names of 54,896 of the 100,000 British soldiers whose bodies were never found are inscribed on the **Menin Gate.** Every night at 8pm, the **Last Post** bugle ceremony honors those who defended Ypres (www.lastpost.be). With Menin Gate behind you, go right and take the **Rose Coombs Walk** to visit **Ramparts Cemetery,** where tombstones line the river. The battlefields are a long walk from town; **car tours** are the way to go. **Salient Tours,** Meenestr. 5 (☎21 46 57; www.salienttours.com; tours 10am and 2:30pm; €28-35), and **Flanders Battlefield Tours** (☎36 04 60; www.ypres-fbt.be; tours Apr.-Oct. 10am and 1pm, Nov.-Mar. 1pm; €30-35) offer English-language tours. A thriftier option is to **bike** the 3-4km journey to the first cemetery or to make a daytrip out of the nearly 40km ride necessary to see them all.

B&Bs are the cheapest accommodations in Ypres, and though there are many of them, call ahead to ask about availability and arrival times. **B&B Zonneweelde ❸,** Masscheleinlann 18, has TVs in every room and is not far from Grote Markt. (☎20 27 23. Singles €25; doubles €50; triples €75.) The modern **B&B Nooit Gedacht ❸,** Ligywijk 129, is also a good bet. (☎20 84 00. Free Internet. Singles €27; doubles €45; triples €65. Cash only.) The huts at **Camping Jeugdstadion ❶,** Bolwaerkstr. 1, are less refined. (☎21 72 82; www.jeugdstadion.be. Bike rental €10 per day. Reception Mar. to mid-Nov. 8am-noon and 4-7:30pm. €3 per person, €1.50 per tent site. 4-bed huts with kitchenette €32.) Restaurants line the Grote Markt; the crowded **Taverne Central Tea Room ❸,** Grote Markt 12, is a safe bet. (Entrees €6-15. Open daily 9am-10pm. AmEx/MC/V.) Free chocolate samples are handed out in the square; they are especially rich at **Vandaele,** Grote Markt 9. (☎20 03 87. Open Tu-Su 9:30am-7pm. MC/V.) Groceries are at **Super GB,** Vandepeereboompl. 15. (☎20 29 35. Open M-Th and Sa 8:30am-7pm, F 8:30am-8pm.) **Trains** run to Bruges (2hr., 1 per hr., €11), Brussels (1¾hr., 1 per hr., €15), and Ghent (1¼hr., 1 per hr., €9.50). The **tourist office,** Grote Markt 34, is inside Cloth Hall; with the station behind you, head straight down Stationsstr., turn left on

Tempelstr., then right on Boterstr. (☎23 92 20; www.ieper.be. Open Apr.-Sept. M-Sa 9am-6pm, Su 10am-6pm; Oct.-Mar. daily 9am-5pm.) **Postal Code:** 8900.

# WALLONIE

## LIÈGE (LUIK)                                                          ☎04

Liège (lee-AJH; pop. 200,000), the largest city in Wallonie, is often dismissed as a mere transportation hub for eastbound travelers, but its cutting-edge art scene and night-owl student hangouts temper the city's industrial character. The **Coeur Historique** is a pleasantly quaint area knotted with cobblestone streets. There by the river, you'll find the **Musée de L'Art Wallon,** 86 Féronstrée, a collection of Belgian art dating back to the Renaissance. (☎221 9231. Open Tu-Sa 1-6pm, Su 11am-4:30pm. €3.80, students €2.50.) Parallel to Féronstrée is **Hors Château,** a street lined with pleasant restaurants, cafés, and bars. Turn onto r. de Bueren and climb the steps of the **Montagne de Bueren** for an expansive view of the city. Take a right and climb a few more steps to find the peaceful gardens of the **Coteaux de la Citadelle.** From Féronstrée, turn left onto r. Léopold and right onto r. de la Cathédrale; after 10min. you will reach the Gothic naves and sparkling gold treasure of the **Cathédrale de St-Paul.** (☎232 6131. Cathedral open daily 8am-5pm. Treasure room open Tu-Su 2-5pm. Tour 3pm. Cathedral free. Treasure room €4, students €2.50.) In between the banks of the river, a large island makes up the working-class neighborhood of Outremeuse and is home to the ▧**Musée d'Art Moderne et d'Art Contemporain (MAMAC),** 3 Parc de la Boverie, which showcases minor works by Gauguin, Chagall, Rodin, and one piece each by Monet and Picasso. The museum's beautiful building and lovely surrounding park are across the river and to the right from the Coeur Historique and St. Paul's (20min.). Take bus #17 (€1.30) to reach MAMAC from the station. (☎343 0403; www.mamac.be. Open Tu-Sa 1-6pm, Su 11am-4:30pm. €3.80, students €2.50.) At night, students from the University of Liège pack the streets of **Le Carré,** a pedestrian area with narrow, bar-lined streets bisected by r. du Pot-d'Or.

To reach the modern **Auberge Georges Simenon de Jeunesse de Liège (HI) ❷,** 2 r. Georges Simenon, walk across the Pont des Arches from the Coeur Historique, or take bus #4 and ask to get off at Auberge Simenon. (☎344 5689. Breakfast and linens included. Internet €0.60 per 15min. Reception 7:30am-1am. Lockout 10am-3pm. Dorms €20; singles €32; doubles €48. €3 HI discount. MC/V.) **Newave à la Passerelle ❷,** 13 bd. Saucy, serves big *panini* (€3.20-3.50) and couscous (€6-16) to a hungry crowd. (☎341 1566. Open Tu-Su noon-10pm. Cash only.) Down the road, **Chez Alberte ❶,** offers quick Belgian fare. (fries €2-2.50, sandwiches €3-5). Pick up groceries a block from the hostel at **Colruyt,** r. Gaston Grégoire. (Open M-F 9am-8pm, Sa 9am-7pm.) **Trains** run to Brussels (1hr., 2-5 per hr., €13). The **tourist office,** 92 Féronstrée, is just a couple doors down from the Musée de L'Art Wallon. (☎221 9221; www.liege.be. Open M-F 9am-5pm, Sa 10am-4:30pm, Su 10am-2:30pm.) Across the Pont des Arches from the hostel, **Cyberman,** 48 r. Léopold, has **Internet** access. (☎87 60 56 95. Open daily 10am-11pm. €1 per hr.)

## TOURNAI (DOORNIK)                                                     ☎069

The first city liberated from the Nazis by Allied forces, Tournai (pop. 68,000) was once the capital of Gaul. The city's most spectacular sight is the world's only five-steepled cathedral, 800-year-old **Cathédrale Notre-Dame.** A 1999 tornado left the landmark in need of renovations, and though half of the building is inaccessible, visitors are still welcome. (Open daily June-Oct. 9:15am-noon and 2-6pm; Nov.-May 9:15am-noon and 2-5pm. Free.) Climb the 257 steps of the nearby **belfry,** the oldest in Belgium, for a stunning view. (Open Mar.-Oct. Tu-Sa 10am-1pm and 2-5:30pm, Su 11am-

1pm and 2-6:30pm; Nov.-Feb. Tu-Sa 10am-noon and 2-5pm, Su 2-5pm. €2, under 20 €1.) Two blocks away, next to the hostel, Victor Horta's **Musée des Beaux-Arts**, Enclos St-Martin, houses a small collection of Belgian and Dutch paintings. (Open Apr.-Oct. M and W-Su 9:30am-12:30pm and 2-5:30pm; Nov.-Mar. M and W-Sa 10am-noon and 2-5pm, Su 2-5pm. €3, first Su of each month free.) To reach the convenient **Auberge de Jeunesse (HI)** ❷, 64 r. St-Martin, continue up the hill from the tourist office. (☎21 61 36; www.laj.be. Breakfast and linens included. Reception 8am-noon and 5-10pm; varies in low season. Reserve ahead. Open Feb.-Nov. Dorms €18-20; singles €33; doubles €49. €3 HI discount. MC/V.) Grab a bite at **En Cas de Faim** ❸, 50 r. des Chapeliers, right by the belfry. (☎56 04 84. Entrees €6-13. Open M-Th noon-2:30pm, F-Sa noon-2:30pm and 7-9:30pm. AmEx/MC/V). Get groceries at **Super GB** on r. de la Tête D'Or. (Open M-Sa 8am-8pm.) **Trains** leave pl. Crombez for Brussels (1hr., 1 per hr., €11) and Namur (2hr., 1 per hr., €15). The **tourist office** is at 14 Vieux Marché aux Poteries. (☎22 20 45; www.tournai.be. Open Apr.-Sept. M-F 8:30am-6pm, Sa 9:30am-noon and 2-5pm, Su 10am-noon and 2:30-6pm; Oct.-Mar. M-F 8:30am-5:30pm, Sa 10am-noon and 2-5pm, Su 2:30-6pm.) **Internet** is at **CyberCenter**, 6 r. Soil de Morialme. (☎23 66 36. Open M-F 11am-11pm, Sa-Su 2pm-midnight. €3 per hr.) **Postal Code:** 7500.

# NAMUR                                                          ☎081

Namur, capital of Wallonie (pop. 110,000), is the last sizable outpost before the wilderness of the Ardennes, and a gateway for **hiking, biking, caving,** and **kayaking** in Belgium's mountainous regions. In September, Namur hosts a multicultural crowd at the **International French Language Film Festival** (☎24 12 36; www.fiff.be). The town's foreboding **citadel** (☎65 45 00; www.citadelle.namur.be) remained an active Belgian military base until 1978. To get there take bus #3 (1 per hr., dir.: Citadel). The free *Storming the Citadel!*, at the tourist office, lists five historical walking tours (1-1¾hr.). Trails thread through the surrounding **Parc de Champeau.** Flocks of geese daily near the homey 🏚 **Auberge Félicien Rops (HI)** ❷, 8 av. Félicien Rops. Take bus # 4, 17, 30 or 31 from the train station. (☎22 36 88; www.laj.be. Breakfast and linens included. Kitchen available. Laundry €6.50. Free Internet. Reception 8am-11pm. Lockout 10am-4pm. Dorms €18-20. €3 HI discount. MC/V.) To camp at **Les Trieux** ❶, 99 r. des Tris, 6km away, take bus #6. (☎44 55 83; www.campinglestrieux.be. Open Apr.-Oct. €3.50 per person, €4-5 per tent.) To reach the **tourist office,** on the Sq. de l'Europe Unie, turn left out of the train station onto r. de la Gare. (☎24 64 49; www.namurtourisme.be. Open daily 9:30am-6pm.) Rent bikes at **La Maison des Cyclistes,** 2B pl. de la Station. (☎81 38 48. Open M-W and F 10am-1pm and 2-4pm. €4 per hr., €9 per day.) **Trains** link Namur to Brussels (1hr., 2 per hr., €7.40) and Dinant (30min., 1 per hr., €4).

# DINANT                                                         ☎082

Razed by the German army in 1914, Dinant (pop. 13,000) has managed to reinvent itself as a tourist destination. Dinant's **citadel** towers over the Meuse River. To see the spectacular view, you have to pay the €6.50 entrance fee and take a required 1hr. tour detailing Dinant's bloody history. Buy tickets at 3-5 pl. Reine Astrid. (☎22 36 70. Tour in German and French. Open Apr.-Oct. daily 10am-6pm; Nov.-Dec. and Feb.-Mar. M-Th and Sa-Su 10am-5pm; Jan. Sa-Su 10am-5pm.) Descend into the beautiful depths of the **Grotte Merveilleuse,** 142 rte. de Phillipeville, 600m from the train station, for a witty 45min. tour of the cave's limestone formations. With the train station behind you, take a right and follow signs to Phillipeville and La Grotte. Bring a jacket to avoid underground chills. (☎22 22 10; www.dinantourism.com. Open July-Aug. daily 10am-6pm; Apr.-June and Sept.-Oct. daily 11am-5pm; Dec.-Mar. Sa-Su 1-4pm. Tours 1 per hr., usually in English. €6.) Rooms in Dinant tend to be pricey, so try accommodations in nearby towns. **Café Leffe** ❸, 2 r. Sax, named after the famous beer originally brewed in an abbey in Dinant, is past the bridge from the tourist office, on the left (☎22 23 72; www.leffe.be. Entrees €7-13. Open daily 11am-11pm.

MC/V.) Get set up to **kayak** on the Meuse at **Anseremme**. (☎22 43 97; www.lessekay-aks.be. Kayaks €17-26.) To get to the **tourist office** from the train station, turn right, take the first left, and take another immediate left by the river. (☎22 28 70; www.dinant-tourisme.be. Open M-F 8:30am-6pm, Sa 9:30am-5pm, Su 10am-4:30pm; low season reduced hours.) Rent bikes at **Raid Mountain-Bike**, 15 r. du Vélodrome (☎21 35 35. €16-20 per day). **Trains** run to Brussels (1½hr., 1 per hr., €12) and Namur (30min., 1 per hr., €4). The bike ride from Namur is 28km.

---

**HOW NOT TO BE A CAVE MAN.** Small tips (€0.50-1) are considered courteous on cave tours, even though it is not customary to tip in restaurants.

---

## HAN-SUR-LESSE AND ROCHEFORT ☎084

Despite the flocks of tourists who visit Han-sur-Lesse each weekend, the town is worth visiting for its impressive caves, which are larger than the more famous ones in neighboring Dinant. Only 5km away, Rochefort (pop. 12,000) is a pleasant town with more options for shopping and dining.

At the **Domaine Des Grottes de Han**, 2 r. J. Lamotte (☎37 72 13; www.grotte-de-han.be), across from the church, purchase tickets to explore the striking ancient rock formations of Han's caves (€8.75) or take a 1½hr. guided ◪**cave journey** (€10.75). Other attractions include the **Museum of the Subterranean World** with objects from the caves (€3.50) and the **Speleogame**, a new 4D interactive film/ride (€6). Combo tickets start at €12. The caves are open daily; call for specific departure times and hours as the schedules vary. Rent **bikes** in Han at **Cycle Sport**, 59 r. de Behogne (☎21 32 55; www.cyclesport.be. €5 per hr., €20 per day. Open Tu-Sa 9:30am-noon and 1:30-6:30pm, Su 9:30am-noon). With your back to the Domaine, turn right and take your first left. On the right, next to a flower shop, is the B&B **Tagnon ❸**, 15 r. de Chasseurs Ardennais, with its spacious rooms (☎37 70 68. Breakfast included. Singles €30; doubles €40. Cash only.) Get groceries at **Spar**, pl. du Baty, down the hill from the tourist office. (Open M 1-7pm, Tu-Sa 9am-7pm, Su 9am-noon. MC/V.) To reach Han and Rochefort, take the **train** from Namur toward Luxembourg to Jemelle (40min., 1 per hr., €7.40) and bus #29 from the Jemelle train station (7min. to Rochefort, €1.30; 15min. to Han-sur-Lesse, €1.90). Han's **tourist office**, across from the Domaine at 3 pl. Théo Lannoy, sells maps of Han's six hiking trails. Each can be walked in under 2½hr. (☎37 75 96. Open M-F 10am-4pm; increased hours during high season.) Rochefort's **tourist office**, 5 r. de Behogne (☎ 34 51 72; www.valdelesse.be), sells hiking maps (€7.50) and has **Internet** access. (€1 per 30min. Open Easter-Oct. daily 8:30am-noon and 1-5pm; Oct.-Easter M-F 8:30am-noon and 1-5pm.)

**BELGIUM**

# GREAT BRITAIN

Having colonized two-fifths of the globe, spearheaded the Industrial Revolution, and won every foreign war in its history but two, Britain seems intent on making the world forget its tiny size. It's hard to believe that the rolling farms of the south and the rugged cliffs of the north are only a day's train ride apart, or that people as diverse as clubbers, miners, students, and monks all occupy a land area roughly the size of the state of Oregon. Beyond the fairytale cottages and sheep farms of "Merry Olde England," today's Britain is a high-energy destination driven by international influence. Though the sun may have set on the British Empire, a colonial legacy survives in multicultural urban centers and a dynamic arts and theater scene. Brits now eat kebabs and curry as often as they do scones, and dance clubs in post-industrial settings draw as much attention as elegant country inns.

## DISCOVER BRITAIN: SUGGESTED ITINERARIES

**THREE DAYS.** Spend it all in **London** (p. 139), the city of tea, royalty, and James Bond. After a stroll through **Hyde Park,** head to **Buckingham Palace** for the changing of the guard. Check out the renowned collections of the **British Museum** and the **Tate Modern.** Stop at famed **Westminster Abbey** and catch a play at Shakespeare's **Globe Theatre** before grabbing a drink in the **East End.**

**ONE WEEK.** Begin, of course, in **London** (3 days), then visit academia at the colleges of **Oxford** (1 day; p. 177). Travel to Scotland for a day in the museums and galleries of **Glasgow** (p. 222) and finish off with pubs and parties in lively **Edinburgh** (2 days; p. 214).

**THREE WEEKS.** Start in **London** (4 days), to explore the museums, theaters, and clubs. Tour the college greens in **Cambridge** (2 days; p. 185) and **Oxford** (2 days), then amble through the rolling hills of the **Cotswolds** (1 day; p. 183). Don't miss Shakespeare's hometown, **Stratford-upon-Avon** (1 day; p. 182), or that of The Beatles, **Liverpool** (1 day; p. 190). Head to **Manchester** for its nightlife (1 day; p. 188) before moving on to **Glasgow** (1 day) and nearby **Loch Lomond** (1 day; p. 226). Energetic **Edinburgh** (4 days) will keep you busy, especially during festival season. Finally, enjoy the beautiful **Lake District** (2 days; p. 199) and historic **York** (1 day; p. 193).

# LIFE AND TIMES

## HISTORY

**THE ANCIENT ISLE (3200 BC TO AD 450).** Britain's prehistoric residents left little but stones and mysteries in their wake. These relics of the past gave way to **Roman** occupation of "Britannia" (England and Wales) by the end of the 1st century AD. You can still see remnants of their rule in the resort spa they built at **Bath** (p. 172) and in the coast-to-coast fortification of **Hadrian's Wall,** built during the early 1st century to ward off invaders from ancient Scotland. The 5th century AD saw the decline of the Roman Empire, leaving Britannia vulnerable to raids. The **Angles,** after whom England was named, and **Saxons** flooded in from Denmark and Germany to establish their own kingdoms in the south.

**Great Britain**

Cape Wrath

Orkney Islands

0 — 100 miles
0 — 100 kilometers

ATLANTIC OCEAN

*Lewis*
Stornoway
Tarbert · *Harris*
*Skye*
**Inverness**
**Kyleakin**
Loch Ness
Spey R.
Aberdeen
**Ft. William**
SCOTLAND
Ben Nevis 1343m
LOCH LOMOND AND THE TROSSACHS N.P.
Perth
**St. Andrews**
**Stirling**
**Glasgow**
**Edinburgh**
Tweed R.
North Sea
TO BERGEN, NORWAY (830km)

Ayr
Dumfries
Hadrian' Wall
**Newcastle-upon-Tyne**
· Derry
NORTHERN IRELAND
Stranraer
Carlisle
Tyne R.
Durham
North Channel
LAKE DISTRICT N.P.
TO AMSTERDAM, NETHERLANDS (600km)
Belfast
Isle of Man

IRELAND

*Irish Sea*
Aire R.
**York**
Dublin
Holyhead
**Liverpool**
ENGLAND
**Conwy**
**Manchester**
Lincoln
**Caernarfon**
Chester
Peak District N.P.
**Llanberis**
Mt. Snowdon 1085m
**Harlech**
SNOWDONIA N.P.
Aberystwyth
**Birmingham**
Norwich
Peterborough
**Cambridge**
**Stratford-upon-Avon**
Ipswich
Rosslare
WALES
Hereford
Cheltenham
Severn R.
Fishguard
BRECON BEACONS N.P.
**Oxford**
Windsor
Tenby
**Tintern**
**London**
Swansea
**Chepstow**
Avebury
Thames R.
**Canterbury**
**Cardiff**
Bristol
**Bath**
Avebury
Stonehenge
Dover
**Chunnel**
**Glastonbury**
Folkestone
Calais
**Salisbury**
**Winchester**
Exeter
**Portsmouth**
**Brighton**
Boulogne
Chichester
**Newquay**
Weymouth
Strait of Dover
St. Ives
Plymouth
*English Channel*
**Penzance** · Falmouth
TO CHANNEL ISLANDS
Cherbourg
TO LE HAVRE, FRANCE (185km)
FRANCE

**CHRISTIANITY AND THE NORMANS (450-1066).** Christianity came to Britain in AD 597 when **Augustine** converted King Æthelbert and founded England's first Catholic church at **Canterbury** (p. 167). The religion continued to flourish during the reign of **Edward the Confessor,** the last Anglo-Saxon king, and through that of the man who captured his throne, a bastard Norman named William. Better known as "The Conqueror," **William I** invaded from northern France in 1066 and defeated the Anglo-Saxons at the pivotal **Battle of Hastings,** seizing the crown. He made French the language of the educated elite and introduced **feudalism,** doling out vast tracts of land to the royals and subjugating English tenants to French lords.

**BLOOD AND DEMOCRACY (1066-1509).** The Middle Ages were a time of conquest and infighting until 1215, when noblemen forced **King John** to sign the **Magna**

Carta (p. 170), the document that inspired modern English democracy. The first "modern" parliament convened 50 years later. While English kings expanded the nation's boundaries, the **Black Death** ravaged its population, killing up to one-third of all Britons between 1349 and 1361. Many more fell in the **Hundred Years' War** (1337-1453), a squabble over the French throne in which England lost most of its holdings in France. Following this defeat, England turned its attention back home for the **War of the Roses** (1455-1485), a lengthy crisis of royal succession between the Houses of Lancaster and York. The conflict ended when Richard of York put his nephew, boy-king **Edward V,** in the **Tower of London** (p. 151) for "safe-keeping." When Edward conveniently disappeared, his uncle was crowned **Richard III.**

**REFORMATION, RENAISSANCE, AND REVOLUTION (1509-1685).** In a desperate effort to produce a male heir, England's most infamous king, **Henry VIII,** married six women. The marriages ended in disaster, with two of his wives facing execution. Stymied by the Pope's refusal to allow him to divorce, Henry rejected Catholicism and established the **Church of England** in 1534. His daughter, **Elizabeth I,** later inherited the throne and cemented the success of the **Protestant Reformation.** The first union of England, Wales, and Scotland took place in 1604, when James VI of Scotland ascended the throne as **James I** of England.

In a move to eliminate royal power, the monarchy was abolished during the **English Civil War** (1639-1651), and the first British Commonwealth was founded with **Oliver Cromwell** as its hopelessly despotic Lord Protector. To the relief of the masses, the Republic collapsed under the lackluster leadership of Cromwell's son **Richard,** but the restoration of **Charles II** to the throne in 1660 did not cure England's troubles. Debates over whether to bar Charles' Catholic brother **James II** from the throne established the first political parties: the **Whigs,** who supported reform, and the **Tories,** who backed hereditary succession.

**PARLIAMENT AND THE CROWN (1685-1783).** James II took the throne in 1685, but lost it just three years later to his son-in-law, Dutch Protestant **William of Orange,** in the bloodless **Glorious Revolution.** Supporters of James II (called Jacobites) remained a threat until 1745, when James II's grandson Charles, commonly known as **Bonnie Prince Charlie,** failed in his attempt to recapture the throne. William and his wife Mary issued a **Bill of Rights,** ushering in a more liberal age. By the end of Britain's victory over France in the **Seven Years' War** (1756-1763), the island nation had risen to great economic and political prominence, with extensive colonial holdings across the Atlantic. Meanwhile, Parliament prospered thanks to the ineffectual leadership of **Georges I, II,** and **III.** The office of Prime Minister soon eclipsed the monarchy as the true seat of power.

**EMPIRE AND INDUSTRY (1783-1832).** During the 18th and 19th centuries, Britain came to rule more than one-quarter of the world's population and two-fifths of its land, despite the loss of the American colonies in 1783, becoming an empire on which "the sun never set." The **Napoleonic Wars** (ca. 1800-1815) revived the rivalry with France and added to Britain's colonial holdings. The **Industrial Revolution** also fueled Britain as a world power and saw many cities, such as **Manchester** (p. 54), flourish as farmers shifted to urban factories. The **gold standard,** adopted by Britain in 1821, stimulated international trade and solidified the value of the pound.

**THE VICTORIAN ERA (1832-1914).** During the long, stable rule of **Queen Victoria** (1837-1901), a series of **Factory** and **Reform Acts** dealt with social difficulties, many of them stemming from rapid industrialization. The legislation limited child labor, capped the average work day, and increased male voting rights. Trade unions, also a product of progressive reform during the 19th century, found a political voice in the **Labour Party** by 1906. Yet pressures to alter the position of other marginalized groups proved ineffectual as the rich embraced *fin-de-siècle* decadence.

**THE WORLD WARS (1914-1945).** The **Great War** (1914-1918), as **World War I** was known until 1939, scarred the national spirit with the loss of a generation of young men, and dashed Victorian dreams of a peaceful, progressive society. The 1930s brought **depression** and mass unemployment. Tensions in Europe escalated once again with Germany's reoccupation of the Rhineland and subsequent invasion of Poland. Britain declared war on Germany on September 3, 1939. However, even the Great War had failed to prepare the British Isles for the utter devastation of **World War II.** German air raids began with the **Battle of Britain** in the summer of 1940 as the **Luftwaffe** devastated many English cities. The fall of France in 1940 precipitated the creation of a war cabinet, led by the eloquent **Winston Churchill.** In 1944, Britain and the Allied Forces launched the **D-Day Invasion** of Normandy, shifting the tide of the war and leading to the defeat of Germany and its allies in May 1945.

**THE POST-WAR YEARS (1945-1990).** Post-war Britain faced economic hardship with enormous war debt and non-existent infrastructure. Increasing immigration from former colonies and a growing rift between rich and poor worsened social tensions. Britain joined the **European Economic Community (EEC)** in 1971, a move that received a lukewarm approbation from many Britons; the relationship between Britain and the Continent remains a contentious issue today. When unemployment and economic unrest culminated in a series of public service strikes in 1979, the nation grasped for change, electing "Iron Lady" **Margaret Thatcher** prime minister. Thatcher dismantled vast segments of the welfare state, bringing dramatic prosperity to many but sharpening the class divide. Aggravated by her resistance to the EEC, the Conservative Party conducted a vote of no confidence that led to Thatcher's 1990 resignation and the appointment of **John Major.**

**THE NEW MILLENNIUM (1990-2005).** After the British pound fell out of the EEC's monetary regulation system in 1993, Major and the Conservative Party became less popular. Under the leadership of **Tony Blair,** the Labour Party refashioned itself into the moderate alternative for middle-class voters and garnered two landslide electoral victories in 1997 and 2001. Blair nurtured relations with the **European Union** and maintained inclusive, moderate economic and social positions. The British government's support of American foreign policy on the **Kosovo** crisis (and again in the wake of the **September 11** attacks) earned Blair the moniker of "little Clinton." Blair was often compared to the American politician and criticized for lackeyism. His government also initiated domestic **devolution** in Scotland and Wales, a move toward local governance that delegated some power to the Scottish Parliament and the Welsh National Assembly—both inaugurated in 1999. The **Good Friday Agreement** (1998) was a watershed moment and a first step toward Northern Irish autonomy. In July 2005 the **Irish Republican Army (IRA)** announced a permanent ceasefire. In April 2007, the **Ulster Volunteer Force (UVF)** announced a matching disarmament, officially ending the conflict.

# TODAY

**RULE BRITANNIA.** Since the 1700s, the monarch (currently **Elizabeth II**) has served a symbolic role, leaving real power to **Parliament,** which consists of the **House of Commons,** with its elected Members of Parliament (MPs), and the **House of Lords,** most of whom are government-appointed Life Peers. All members of the executive branch, which includes the **prime minister** and the **cabinet,** are also MPs. This fusion of legislative and executive functions—called the "efficient secret" of the British government—ensures the swift passage of the majority party's programs into bills. The prime minister is never directly elected to the post. Rather, the MPs of the ruling party choose a leader who then becomes prime minister. The two main parties are **Labour** and **Conservative** (Tory), roughly representing the left and right. A current point of contention involves Labour's support of the war in Iraq, which the Conservatives oppose.

**CURRENT EVENTS.** In the May 2005 general election, Labour maintained control of Parliament, giving Blair a third term, although its majority in the House of Com-

GREAT BRITAIN

mons dropped. Blair's continued support of US foreign policy and his political alliance with President George W. Bush has caused discontent in Britain, particularly since the war in Iraq. In February 2003, nearly one million people gathered in London to protest military intervention in Iraq. Blair's political positions remain controversial after a series of **terrorist attacks** in July 2005. Four suicide bombs detonated on public transport in London on the morning of July 7, killing 52, less than a day after the city earned the right to host the **2012 Summer Olympics;** a failed second attack occurred two weeks later. The July 7 bombings marked the deadliest attack in London since WWII. Blair's critics also point to the Prime Minister's stance on the **euro.** Blair's position on the euro—that Britain will convert to the currency when the economy is ready—has been seen by some as an equivocation and a political maneuver. The fate of the pound and Britain's participation in the EU remain heated issues, and British opinion remains, as ever, distrustful of integration with the rest of Europe. In late 2006, Blair announced that he would not seek a fourth term. He stepped down from his post as Prime Minister on June 27, 2007, passing power on to fellow Labour Party colleague **Gordon Brown.** The reinvigorated Conservative (Tory) Party opposition is led by **David Cameron.**

**A ROYAL MESS.** The world mourned the death of the "People's Princess," **Diana,** in a Paris car crash in 1997. Queen Elizabeth II—a matronly, practical character—earned praise when she began paying income tax in 1993 and threw a year-long Golden Jubilee for the 50th year of her reign in 2002. **Prince Charles** and his paramour **Camilla Parker-Bowles** married in April 2005 after a 35-year romance; the Queen did not attend the service. A quick visit to a drug rehab clinic in 2002 heralded the onset of adult celebrity—and tabloid notoriety—for **Prince Harry,** the younger of Charles and Diana's sons. Before his entry into the British military as an officer, Harry offended the British public by dressing as a Nazi soldier for a costume party. In 2007, Harry featured in news stories again when British military officers prevented him from serving in Iraq, against the Prince's wishes. Harry's increasing fame, however, still does not detract from the rapt attention devoted to second-in-line **Prince William.** Having earned a degree in geography from the University of St. Andrews, "His Royal Sighness" is seen by some as a reluctant future successor to his father; he has also joined the military.

---

**█TIP◀** **IT'S ALL BRITISH TO ME.** The United Kingdom is a political union of England, Northern Ireland, Scotland, and Wales. This is also referred to as Britain, not to be confused with the island of Great Britain, which only includes England, Scotland, and Wales. *Let's Go* uses United Kingdom and Britain interchangeably. This chapter covers Great Britain. For Northern Island, see p. 590.

---

# PEOPLE AND CULTURE

**CUSTOMS AND ETIQUETTE.** The United Kingdom is home to 60 million Britons, a dynamic and varied population made up of local subcultures. Stiff upper-lipped public schoolboys and post-punk Hoxton rockers sit next to Burberry-clad football hooligans ("chavs") on the eerily quiet Tube. There is little that a traveler can do that will inadvertently cause offense. That said, the English do place weight on proper decorum, including **politeness** ("thanks" comes in many varieties, including "cheers"), **queueing** (that is, lining up—never, *ever* cut the line or otherwise disrupt the queue), and keeping a certain **respectful distance.** You'll find, however, that the British **sense of humor**—fantastically wry, explicit, even raunchy—is somewhat at odds with any notion of their coldness or reserve.

**FOOD AND DRINK.** Historically, England has been derided for its horrific cuisine. But do not fear the gravy-laden, boiled, fried, and bland traditional nosh! Britain's cuisine is in the midst of a gourmet revolution, and even travelers on a backpacker's budget can taste the benefits. In the spring of 2005, a panel of more than 600 chefs, food critics, and restaurateurs voted 14 British restaurants into the world's top 50; the **Fat Duck** in Berkshire was named the world's best. Popular television chef **Jamie Oliver** led a well-publicized and successful campaign to increase the British government's spending on school lunches. Still, the best way to eat in Britain is to **avoid British food.** Thanks to its colonial legacy, ethnic food is ubiquitous and Britain offers some of the best **tandoori** and **curry** outside India.

# THE ARTS

## LITERATURE
**Geoffrey Chaucer** tapped into the spirited side of Middle English. His *Canterbury Tales* (1387) is among the best comedic works of all time. Under Elizabeth I, English drama flourished with the appearance of the first professional playwrights, among them **William Shakespeare,** the son of a glove-maker from **Stratford-upon-Avon** (p. 182). The British Puritans of the late 16th and early 17th centuries produced a huge body of obsessive and brilliant literature, including **John Milton's** epic *Paradise Lost* (1667). In 1719, **Daniel Defoe** started the era of the English novel with his popular, island-bound *Robinson Crusoe.* By the end of the century, **Jane Austen** satirized the modes and manners of her time in novels like *Pride and Prejudice* (1813). Victorian poverty and social change spawned the sentimental novels of **Charles Dickens.** The Romantic movement of the early 1800s found its greatest expression in poetry. The watershed *Lyrical Ballads* (1798) by **William Wordsworth** and **Samuel Taylor Coleridge** included classics like "The Rime of the Ancient Mariner." In the early 20th century, **Virginia Woolf** spoke up on behalf of female writers. She and the Irish expatriate **James Joyce** were among the groundbreaking practitioners of **Modernism** (ca. 1910-1990). One of the movement's poetic champions was **T.S. Eliot;** his influential poem "The Waste Land" (1922) portrays London as a fragmented, barren desert awaiting redemption. **D.H. Lawrence** explored tensions in the British working-class family while **E.M. Forster's** half-Modernist, half-Romantic novels like *A Passage to India* (1924) reveal a disillusionment with imperialism. The end of the empire and the growing gap between the classes splintered British literature in several directions. Postcolonial voices like **Salman Rushdie's** and **Zadie Smith's** have become an important literary force.

Britain has also produced some enduring volumes of children's literature, like **Lewis Carroll's** *Alice's Adventures in Wonderland* (1865), **C.S. Lewis's** *Chronicles of Narnia* (1950-1956), and **Roald Dahl's** *Charlie and the Chocolate Factory* (1964). In **J.R.R. Tolkien's** grandiose epics *The Hobbit* (1937) and *The Lord of the Rings* (1954-56), elves, wizards, men, and little folk go to battle over the fate of Middle Earth. Recently, **J.K. Rowling** has won over readers around the world with her tales of juvenile wizardry in the **Harry Potter** series.

## MUSIC
During the Renaissance, English ears were tuned to cathedral anthems, psalms, madrigals, and the occasional lute performance. **Henry Purcell** rang in the **Baroque** era with England's first great opera, *Dido and Aeneas* (1689). Today's audiences are familiar with the operettas of **W.S. Gilbert** and **Arthur Sullivan.** The pair were rumored to hate each other, but nonetheless managed to produce gems like *The Pirates of Penzance* (1879). A renaissance of more serious music began under **Edward Elgar,** whose *Pomp and Circumstance* (1901) is most often heard at graduation ceremonies. World Wars I and II provoked **Benjamin Britten's** heartbreaking *War Requiem* (1962). Later 20th-century trends, including the wildly popular musicals of **Sir Andrew Lloyd Webber,** were toward commercial music.

The British Invasion groups of the 1960s infiltrated the world with daring, controversial sound. **The Beatles,** fresh out of Liverpool (p. 190), were the ultimate trendsetters, still influential nearly four decades after their break-up. The edgier lyrics and grittier sound of the **Rolling Stones** shifted teens's thoughts from "I Want To Hold Your Hand" to "Let's Spend the Night Together." Over the next 20 years, England imported the urban "mod" sound of **The Who** and guitar gurus **Eric Clapton** of **Cream** and **Jimmy Page** of **Led Zeppelin.** In the mid-1970s, British rock split, as the theatrical excesses of glam rock performers like **Queen, Elton John,** and **David Bowie** contrasted with the conceptual, album-oriented art rock popularized by **Pink Floyd.** Punk rock bands including **The Sex Pistols** and **The Clash** emerged from Britain's industrial centers in the 1970s.

British bands continue to achieve popular success on both sides of the Atlantic thanks to the 1980s advent of America's MTV. **Dire Straits, Duran Duran,** the **Eurythmics, Boy George, Tears for Fears,** and the **Police** have all enjoyed many top-10 hits. England's influence on dance music comes from the **Chemical Brothers** and **Fatboy Slim,** among others. **Oasis** embodied a dramatically indulgent breed of rock 'n' roll stardom, while the tremendous popularity of American grunge rock inspired then-wannabes **Radiohead,** who have since been hailed as one of the most creative and influential British rock bands since The Beatles. The UK also produced some brilliantly awful pop, including **Robbie Williams** (survivor of the bubblegummy **Take That**), who continues to be a stadium-filling force. Sadly, the **Spice Girls** have not enjoyed the same longevity.

These days, socially-conscious **Coldplay** is still one of the UK's best-selling rock exports. Modern post-punk and New Wave bands like **Bloc Party** and **Franz Ferdinand** enjoy indie credit and impressive fan bases. A product of instant Internet success, **Lily Allen** has established herself as a major player in the world of commercial pop, winning audiences with an upbeat sound and sassy attitude. Similarly, **Amy Winehouse** smooths over her rough-and-tumble personality with deep and soulful jazz vocals. Formed in 2005, **The Kooks** have exploded out of Brighton to climb the charts with catchy pop rock tunes.

The British have also created a new genre: bands like **The Streets** and **Dizzee Rascal** play **UK Garage,** or **grime,** a blend of skittering beats, heavy bass, and urban rapping, which is now the official sound of every UK club.

## VISUAL ARTS

**ARCHITECTURE.** Houses of worship began as stone churches, but gave way to cathedrals like **Winchester** (p. 170). The Normans introduced the round arches and thick walls of **Romanesque** architecture, erecting squat castles such as the **Tower of London** (p. 151). The **Gothic** period ushered in the more intricate **Salisbury Cathedral** (p. 170) and **King's College Chapel** in Cambridge (p. 187). **Christopher Wren's** dome on **St. Paul's Cathedral** (p. 151) and sumptuous Tudor homes like Henry VIII's **Hampton Court** attest to the capabilities of **Renaissance** architecture. During the Victorian period, British nostalgia gave us the neo-Gothic **Houses of Parliament** (p. 149) and the Neoclassical **British Museum** (p. 158). Today, **Richard Rogers,** architect of London's **Millennium Dome,** and **Norman Foster,** architect of distinctive skyline landmark **30 St Mary Axe,** vie for bragging rights as England's most influential architects, dotting London with a host of Millennium constructions. A team of architects designed the **London Eye,** the largest observation wheel in the world and one of the city's most popular attractions.

**FILM.** British film has a checkered past marked by cycles of relative independence from Hollywood, followed by increasing drains of talent to America. The Royal Shakespeare Company has produced such heavyweights as **Dame Judi Dench** and **Sir Ian McKellen,** who both then made the transition to film. Earlier Shakespeare impresario **Laurence Olivier** worked both sides of the camera in *Henry V* (the 1944 brainchild of government-sponsored WWII propaganda), and his *Hamlet* (1948) is still the hallmark Dane. Master of suspense **Alfred Hitchcock** snared audiences with films produced in both Britain and the US, and Scotsman **Sean Connery** downed the first of many martinis as James Bond in *Dr. No* (1962). During the early 1980s, two British films, *Chariots of Fire* (1981) and *Gandhi* (1983) earned high accolades during a period dominated by major American productions (some of which, interestingly, were partially filmed in British studios, including 1980's *Star Wars: The Empire Strikes Back*). **Kenneth Branagh** has focused his talents on adapting Shakespeare for the screen, with glossy, acclaimed works like *Hamlet* (1996). Around the turn of the century, British films including *The Full Monty* (1997), *Billy Elliot* (2000), *Bend it Like Beckham* (2002), and *Love Actually* (2003) achieved massive success across the pond. The *Harry Potter* film franchise, which kicked off in 2001, continues to break box-office records. Films such as *The History Boys* (2006) and Academy Award-nominated *The Queen* (2006) are recent landmarks in British cinema.

**ON THE CANVAS.** Britain's early religious art shifted to secular patronage and court painters. Portrait artist **Thomas Gainsborough** (1727-88) propagated an interest in landscape painting, which peaked in the 19th century with the Romanticism of **J. M. W. Turner** and **John Constable.** The Victorian era saw movements like **Dante Gabriel Rossetti's** (1828-82) Italian-inspired pre-Raphaelite school. Modernist trends like Cubism and Expressionism were picked up by painter **Wyndham Lewis** (1882-1957) and sculptor **Henry Moore** (1898-1986). WWII inspired experimental works by painters **Francis Bacon** (not to be confused with the Renaissance thinker of the same name) and **Lucian Freud.** The precocious **Young British Artists** of the 1990s include sculptor **Rachel Whitbread** and multimedia artist **Damien Hirst.** From the late 1990s into the early 2000s, the creations of acclaimed anonymous graffiti artist and stencilist **Banksy** have appeared in cities around the world.

# HOLIDAYS AND FESTIVALS

**Holidays:** New Year's Day (Jan. 1); Epiphany (Jan. 6); Good Friday (Mar. 21); Easter (Mar. 23-24); Ascension (May 1); May Day (May 1); Pentecost (May 11-12); Corpus Christi (May 22); Bank Holidays (May 26 and Aug. 25); Assumption (Aug. 15); All Saints' Day (Nov. 1); Christmas (Dec. 25); Boxing Day (Dec. 26).

**Festivals:** Scotland's New Year's Eve celebration, Hogmanay, takes over the streets in Edinburgh and Glasgow. The National Eisteddfod of Wales (Aug. 2-9) has brought Welsh writers, musicians, and artists together since 1176. One of the largest music and theater festivals in the world is the Edinburgh International Festival (Aug. 8-31); also highly recommended is the Edinburgh Fringe Festival (Aug.). Manchester's Gay Village hosts Manchester Pride (www.manchesterpride.com) in August, and London throws a huge street party at the Notting Hill Carnival (Aug. 24-25). Bonfires and fireworks abound on England's Guy Fawkes Day (Nov. 5) in celebration of a conspirator's failed attempt to destroy the Houses of Parliament in 1605.

# ADDITIONAL RESOURCES

*A History of Britain* series, by Simon Schama. BBC Books (2000-2002). Best-selling author writes accessible, engaging history.

*Time Out.* Universal House, 251 Tottenham Court Rd, London, W1T 7AB (☎ 020 7813 3000; www.timeout.com). The absolute best weekly guide to what's going on in London and Edinburgh. The magazine is sold at every newsstand in those cities, and the website is a virtual hub for the latest on dining, discounts, and entertainment.

GREAT BRITAIN

# ESSENTIALS

## FACTS AND FIGURES

**Official Name:** United Kingdom of Great Britain and Northern Ireland.

**Capital:** London.

**Major Cities:** Cardiff, Edinburgh, Glasgow, Liverpool, Manchester.

**Population:** 60,776,000.

**Land Area:** 244,800 sq. km.

**Time Zone:** GMT.

**Language:** English; also Welsh and Scottish Gaelic.

**Religions:** Christian: Protestant and Catholic (72%), Muslim (3%).

**Harry Potter Books Sold:** More than the populations of Britain, France, Germany, and Italy combined: 325,000,000.

## WHEN TO GO

It's wise to plan around the high season (June-Aug.). Spring and fall are better times to visit; the weather is still reasonable and flights are cheaper, though there may be less transportation to rural areas. If you plan to visit the cities and stick to museums and theaters, the low season (Nov.-Mar.) is most economical. Keep in mind, however, that sights and accommodations often close or have reduced hours. In Scotland, summer light lasts almost until midnight, but in winter, the sun may set as early as 3:45pm. Regardless of when you go, it will rain—always.

## DOCUMENTS AND FORMALITIES

**EMBASSIES AND CONSULATES.** Foreign embassies in Britain are in London (p. 139). British embassies abroad include: **Australia,** Commonwealth Ave., Yarralumla, ACT 2600 (☎02 62 70 66 66; http://bhc.britaus.net); **Canada,** 80 Elgin St., Ottawa, ON, K1P 5K7 (☎613-237-1530; www.britainincanada.org); **Ireland,** 29 Merrion Rd., Ballsbridge, Dublin, 4 (☎01 205 3700; www.britishembassy.ie); **New Zealand,** 44 Hill St., Thorndon, Wellington, 6011 (☎04 924 2888; www.britain.org.nz); **US,** 3100 Mass. Ave. NW, Washington, D.C., 20008 (☎900-255-6685; www.britainusa.com).

**VISA AND ENTRY INFORMATION.** EU citizens do not need a visa. Citizens of Australia, Canada, New Zealand, and the US do not need a visa for stays of up to 6 months. Students planning to study in the UK for six months or more must obtain a student visa (around US$90). For more info, call your British embassy or visit www.ukvisas.gov.uk.

## TOURIST SERVICES AND MONEY

| **EMERGENCY** | **Ambulance, Fire,** and **Police:** ☎999. |
| --- | --- |

**TOURIST OFFICES.** Formerly the British Tourist Authority, **Visit Britain** (☎020 88 46 90 00; www.visitbritain.com) is an umbrella organization for regional tourist boards. Tourist offices in Britain are listed under **Practical Information** for each city and town. They stock maps and provide info on sights and accommodations.

 **IT'S JUST A TIC.** Tourist offices in Britain are known as Tourist Information Centres, or TICs. Britain's National Parks also have National Park Information Centres, or NPICs. This chapter refers to all offices as TICs and NPICs.

**MONEY.** The British unit of currency is the **pound sterling (£),** plural pounds sterling. One pound is equal to 100 pence, with standard denominations of 1p, 2p, 5p, 10p, 20p, 50p, £1, and £2 in coins, and £5, £10, £20, and £50 in notes. Quid is slang for pounds. Scotland has its own bank notes, which can be used interchangeably with English currency, though you may have difficulty using Scottish £1 notes outside Scotland. As a rule, it's cheaper to exchange money in Britain than at home. **ATMs** offer the best exchange rates. Many British department stores, such as Marks & Spencer, also offer excellent exchange services. **Tips** in restaurants are often included in the bill, sometimes as a "service charge." If gratuity is not included, tip your server 12%. A 10% tip is common for taxi drivers, and £1-3 is usual for bellhops and chambermaids. To the relief of budget travelers from the US, tipping is not expected at pubs and bars in Britain. Aside from open-air markets, don't expect to bargain. For more info on money in Europe, see p. 15.

The UK has a 17.5% **value added tax (VAT),** a sales tax applied to everything but food, books, medicine, and children's clothing. The tax is **included** in the amount indicated on the price tag. The prices stated in *Let's Go* include VAT. In the airport upon exiting the EU, non-EU citizens can claim a refund on the tax paid for goods purchased at participating stores. You can obtain refunds only for goods you take out of the country. Participating shops display a "Tax-Free Shopping" sign. They may have a purchase minimum of £50-100 before they offer refunds, and the complex procedure is probably only worthwhile for large purchases. To apply for a refund, fill out the form that you are given in the shop and present it with the goods and receipts at customs upon departure—look for the Tax-Free Refund Desk at the airport. At peak times, this process can take an hour. You must leave the UK within three months of your purchase to claim a refund, and you must apply for the refund before leaving. For more info on qualifying for a VAT refund, see p. 18. For VAT info specific to the UK, visit http://customs.hmrc.gov.uk.

| BRITISH POUND(£) | | |
|---|---|---|
| AUS$1 = £0.420 | £1 = AUS$2.38 | |
| CDN$1 = £0.466 | £1 = CDN$2.15 | |
| EUR€1 = £0.674 | £1 = EUR€1.48 | |
| NZ$1 = £0.375 | £1 = NZ$2.66 | |
| US$1 = £0.492 | £1 = US$2.03 | |

# TRANSPORTATION

**BY PLANE.** Most international flights land at London's **Heathrow (LHR; ☎0870 000 0123; www.heathrowairport.com) or Gatwick (WSX; ☎0870 000 2468; www.gatwickairport.com) airports; Manchester (MAN)** and **Edinburgh (EDI)** also have international airports. Budget airlines, like **Ryanair** and **easyJet,** fly out of many locales, including **Stansted Airport Luton Airport,** (see **Let's Go to London,** p. 166). The national airline, **British Airways** (☎0870 850 9850, US ☎800-247-9297; www.britishairways.com), offers discounted youth fares for those under 24. For more info on traveling by plane around Europe, see p. 41.

**BY TRAIN.** Britain's main carrier is **National Rail Enquiries** (☎08457 484 950). The country's train network is extensive, criss-crossing the length and breadth of the island. Prices and schedules often change; find up-to-date information from National Rail Enquiries website (www.nationalrail.co.uk/planmyjourney) or **Network Rail** (www.networkrail.co.uk; schedules only). **Eurostar** trains run to Britain from the Continent through the **Chunnel** (p. 51). The **BritRail Pass,** sold only outside Britain, allows unlimited travel in England, Scotland, and Wales (www.brit-

GREAT BRITAIN

rail.net). In Canada and the US, contact **Rail Europe** (Canada ☎800-361-7245, US ☎888-382-7245; www.raileurope.com). **Eurail passes are not valid in Britain.** Rail discount cards (£20), available at rail stations and through travel agents, grant 33% off most point-to-point fares and are available to those ages 16-25 or over 60, full-time students, and families. In general, traveling by train costs more than by bus. For more info on traveling by train around Europe, see p. 45.

**BY BUS.** The British distinguish between **buses,** which cover short routes, and **coaches,** which cover long distances; *Let's Go* refers to both as buses. **National Express** (☎08705 808 080; www.nationalexpress.com) is the main operator of long-distance bus service in Britain, while **Scottish Citylink** (☎08705 505 050; www.citylink.co.uk) has the most extensive coverage in Scotland. The **Brit Xplorer Pass** offers unlimited travel on National Express buses (7-day £79, 14-day £139, 28-day £219). **NX2** cards (£10), available online for ages 16-26, reduce fares by up to 30%. For those who plan far ahead, the cheapest rides are National Express's **funfares,** available only online (limited number of seats on buses out of London from £1).

**BY CAR.** To drive, you must be 18 and have a valid license from your home country; to rent, you must be over 21. Britain is covered by a high-speed system of **motorways** (M-roads) that connect London to other major cities. Visitors may not be accustomed to **driving on the left,** and automatic transmission is rare in rental cars. Roads are generally well maintained, but **gasoline** (petrol) prices are high. In London, driving is restricted during weekday working hours, with charges imposed in certain congestion zones; parking can be similarly nightmarish.

**BY FERRY.** Several ferry lines provide service between Britain and the Continent. Ask for discounts; ISIC holders can sometimes get student fares, and Eurail passholders are eligible for reductions and free trips. **Seaview Ferries** (www.seaview.co.uk/ferries.html) has a directory of UK ferries. In summer, it's a good idea to book ahead. For more info on boats to Ireland and the Continent, see p. 52.

**BY BIKE AND BY FOOT.** Much of the British countryside is well suited to **biking.** Many cities and villages have rental shops and route maps. Large-scale **Ordnance Survey** maps, often available at TICs, detail the extensive system of long-distance **hiking** paths. TICs and NPICs can provide extra information about routes.

**BY THUMB. Hitchhiking** or standing on M-roads is illegal. Despite this, hitchhiking is fairly common in rural parts of Scotland and Wales (England is tougher) where public transportation is spotty. Let's Go does not recommend hitchhiking.

# KEEPING IN TOUCH

| PHONE CODES | **Country code: 44. International dialing prefix:** 00. Within Britain, dial city code + local number, even when dialing inside the city. For more info on how to place international calls, see **Inside Back Cover.** |
| --- | --- |

**EMAIL AND THE INTERNET.** Internet access is ubiquitous in big cities, common in towns, and sparse in rural areas. **Internet cafes** or public terminals can be found almost everywhere; they usually cost £2-6 per hour, but you often pay only for the time used. For more info, see www.cybercafes.com. Public **libraries** usually have free or inexpensive Internet access, but you might have to wait or make an advance reservation. Many coffee shops, particularly chains such as Caffe Nero and Starbucks, offer Wi-Fi for a fee.

**TELEPHONE.** Most public pay phones in Britain are run by **British Telecom (BT).** Public phones charge at least 30p and don't accept 1, 2, or 5p coins. A BT Chargecard bills calls to your credit card, but most pay phones now have readers where you can swipe credit cards directly (generally AmEx/MC/V). The number for the operator in Britain is ☎100, the international operator ☎155. Whenever possible, use a calling card for international phone calls, as long-distance rates for national phone services are often very high. Mobile phones are an increasingly popular and economical option. Major mobile carriers include **T-Mobile, Vodafone,** and **O₂.** Direct-dial access numbers for calling out of Britain include: **AT&T Direct** (☎0800 89 0011); **British Telecom** (☎0800 14 41 44); **Canada Direct** (☎0800 096 0634 or 0800 559 3141); **Telecom New Zealand Direct** (☎0800 8900 64); **Telstra Australia** (☎0800 856 6161). For more info on calling home from Europe, see p. 26.

**MAIL. Royal Mail** has tried to standardize their rates around the world. To check shipment costs, use the Postal Calculator at www.royalmail.com. From Britain, it costs £0.24 to send a postcard domestically, £0.48 within Europe, and £0.54 to the rest of the world. Airmail letters up to 20g cost £0.24 domestically, £0.48 within Europe, and £0.78 elsewhere. Remember to write "Par Avión—Airmail" on the top left corner of your envelope or stop by any post office to get a free airmail label. Letters sent via Airmail should be delivered within three working days to European destinations and five working days worldwide. To receive mail in the UK, have mail delivered **Poste Restante.** Mail will go to the main post office unless you specify a subsidiary by street address. Address mail to be held according to the following example: First Name, Last Name, Poste Restante, post office address, Postal Code, UK. Bring a passport to pick up your mail; there may be a small fee.

## ACCOMMODATIONS AND CAMPING

| BRITAIN | ❶ | ❷ | ❸ | ❹ | ❺ |
|---|---|---|---|---|---|
| ACCOMMODATIONS | under £15 | £15-20 | £21-30 | £31-40 | over £40 |

**Hostelling International (HI)** hostels are prevalent throughout Britain. They are run by the **Youth Hostels Association of England and Wales (YHA;** ☎0870 770 8868; www.yha.org.uk), the **Scottish Youth Hostels Association (SYHA;** ☎01786 89 14 00; www.syha.org.uk), and the **Hostelling International Northern Ireland (HINI;** ☎28 9032 4733; www.hini.org.uk). Dorms cost around £11 in rural areas, £14 in larger cities, and £15-25 in London. You can book **B&Bs** by calling directly, or by asking the local TIC to help you. TICs usually charge a flat fee of £1-5 plus 10% deposit, deductible from the amount you pay the B&B proprietor. **Campgrounds** tend to be privately owned and cost £3-10 per person per night. It is illegal to camp in national parks.

## FOOD AND DRINK

| BRITAIN | ❶ | ❷ | ❸ | ❹ | ❺ |
|---|---|---|---|---|---|
| FOOD | under £6 | £6-10 | £11-15 | £16-20 | over £20 |

A pillar of traditional British fare, the cholesterol-filled, meat-anchored **English breakfast** is still served in most B&Bs across the country. **Beans on toast** or toast smothered in **Marmite** (the most acquired of tastes—a salty, brown spread made from yeast) are breakfast staples. The best native dishes for lunch or dinner are **roasts**—beef, lamb, and Wiltshire hams—and **Yorkshire pudding,** a type of popover drizzled with meat juices. Despite their intriguing names, **bangers and mash** and **bubble and squeak** are just sausages and potatoes and cabbage and potatoes, respectively. Pubs serve savory meat pies like **Cornish pasties** (PASS-tees) or **ploughman's lunches** consisting of bread, cheese, and pickles. **Fish and chips** (french fries) are traditionally drowned in malt vinegar and salt. **Crisps,** or potato chips, come in an astonishing variety, with flavors like prawn cocktail. Britons make their **desserts** (often called "puddings" or "afters") exceedingly sweet and gloopy. Sponges, trifles, tarts, and the ill-named spotted dick

**GREAT BRITAIN**

# a ruinous state

The British thrive on ruin. The delight in the physical remnants of the past, shared by all classes and passed from generation to generation, is one of those cultural tics which makes Britain truly singular among nations. This desire to commune with times long gone, to wax wistful about the ambitions of ages past brought low by history's pratfalls, is as British as milky tea and cow parsley in country lanes.

It's possible to experience the great British romance of ruins at many of the most celebrated piles of stones. The shell of **Tintern Abbey,** near the River Avon, marks the spot where Word-

## "Head to the lesser known and commune with bumble-bees and fellow pilgrims."

sworth made introspection a national poetic pastime. But the danger of sampling the obvious sites is, of course, the buzzing business of the present—so many tourist coaches, so much bad ice cream, so many postcards. Better to head to the lesser known and commune with bumblebees and the occasional wandering fellow pilgrim.

Go, for instance, to Northamptonshire to see what's left of **Lyveden New Bield,** the late 16th-century oratory of the Anglo-Catholic Thomas Tresham and a ruin almost as soon as it was constructed. The oratory was supposed to be a place where the Elizabethan gentleman, who tried to be loyal to both his Queen and his Church, could practice his devotions safe from the prying eyes of Protestant authorities. Tresham ran out of money and time to finish the structure, and was jailed for failing to pay the recusancy fines imposed for not subscribing to the official church. The entire building was left exposed to the elements, and visitors must now wade through knee-high meadowland to see the delicate frieze of the stations of the cross that adorns its exterior walls.

However, most of the ruins in Britain are the work of sudden disaster rather than the slow crumblings of time. **Corfe**

**Castle** in Dorset bears the charred scars of Oliver Cromwell's besieging army during the Second Civil War of 1647-1648. And some of the imposing Iron Age "brochs" of **Orkney** and **Shetland** look as brutal as they do because at some point they failed to hold back the oncoming waves of invaders and local rivals. Stunning, sandstone-red **Lindisfarne,** on the Northumbrian shore, was twice ravaged, first by Vikings who sacked the place and slaughtered the monks. The monastery was hit again during the Protestant Reformation, when it was predictably emptied of its community and treasures. Equally sudden was the end of the spectacular **Binham Priory** in southern Norfolk. The enforcers of the Reformation under Henry VIII and Edward VI turned what had been one of the most palatial Benedictine foundations into a sparse parish church. Miraculously, the Reformation's erasure of the painted screen separating the nave from the choir have themselves become ruins, peeling away to reveal some of the most astonishing church paintings that survived from the world of Roman Catholic England.

Some of the most commanding ruins are also the most modern. A little way from the center of Dublin stands Kilmainham Gaol, a working prison until 1924. Now a historical museum, the Gaol reveals the complications of crime and punishment in nationalist Ireland. The exterior is just standard-issue prison. But the interior is a cathedral of incarceration; simultaneously shocking and operatically grand, with its iron staircase and rat-hole cells where ancient pallets and fragments of anonymous rags gather grime. The effect is as powerful as it is challenging, but this is how ruins are supposed to get you. Not with a cheap rush of sentiment, much less a pang of nostalgia, but with the tender inspection of ancient scars, which linger to remind us of the resilience and redeeming vulnerability of the human condition.

## A CLOSER LOOK

*Simon Schama is University Professor of Art History at Columbia University. He writes for* The New Yorker *and was the writer and host of the BBC's* History of Britain. *His most recent book is* Rough Crossings: Britain, the Slaves, and the American Revolution *(Ecco, May 2006).*

(spongy currant cake) will satiate the sweetest tooth. To escape English food, try Chinese, Greek, or Indian cuisine. British "tea" refers to both a drink, served strong and milky, and to a social ritual. A **high tea** might include cooked meats, salad, sandwiches, and pastries, while the oft-stereotyped **afternoon tea** comes with finger sandwiches, scones with jam and clotted cream (a sinful cross between whipped cream and butter), and small cakes. **Cream tea,** a specialty of Cornwall and Devon, includes scones or crumpets, jam, and clotted cream.

## BEYOND TOURISM

There are many opportunities for **volunteering, studying,** and **working** in Britain. As a volunteer, you can participate projects ranging from archaeological digs to lobbying for social change. Explore your academic passions at the country's prestigious institutions or pursue an independent research project. Paid work opportunities include Parliament internships and teaching, among others. For more info on opportunities across Europe, see **Beyond Tourism,** p. 54.

**The National Trust,** National Trust Central Volunteering Team, The National Trust, Heelis, Kemble Dr., Swindon SN2 2NA (☎0870 609 5383; www.nationaltrust.org.uk/volunteering). Arranges numerous volunteer opportunities, including working holidays.

**The Teacher Recruitment Company,** Pennineway Offices (1), 87-89 Saffron Hill, London EC1N 8QU (☎0845 833 1934; www.teachers.eu.com). International recruitment agency lists positions and provides information on jobs in the UK.

**University of Oxford,** College Admissions Office, Wellington Sq., Oxford OX1 2JD (☎0186 528 8000; www.ox.ac.uk). Large range of summer programs (£900-4000) and year-long courses (£8880-11,840).

# ENGLAND

A land where the stately once prevailed, England is now a youthful, hip, and forward-looking nation on the cutting edge of art, music, and film. But traditionalists can rest easy; for all the moving and shaking in large cities, just around the corner scores of ancient towns, opulent castles, and comforting cups of tea still abound.

# LONDON                                                    ☎020

London offers visitors a bewildering array of choices: Leonardo at the National Gallery or Hirst at the Tate Modern; Rossini at the Royal Opera or *Les Misérables* at the Queen's; Bond Street couture or Camden cutting-edge—you could spend your entire stay just deciding what to do. London is often described not as a unified city but rather a conglomeration of villages, whose heritage and traditions are still alive and evolving. Thanks to the feisty independence and diversity of each area, the London "buzz" is continually on the move.

## ✈ INTERCITY TRANSPORTATION

**Flights: Heathrow (LON;** ☎08700 000 123) is London's main airport. The **Piccadilly Line** heads from the airport to central London (1hr., 20 per hr., £4-10). **Heathrow Connect** runs to Paddington (20min., 2 per hr., £10), as does the more expensive **Heathrow Express** (15min.; 4 per hr.; £14.50, round-trip £27). From **Gatwick Airport (LGW;** ☎08700 002 468), the **Gatwick Express** heads to Victoria (30min.; 4 per hr., round-trip £24). See **Let's Go to London** (p. 166) for info on budget airline hubs.

GREAT BRITAIN

# Central London

● SIGHTS

| | |
|---|---|
| Apsley House, 1 | C4 |
| Barbican Hall, 2 | E3 |
| British Library, 4 | D2 |
| British Museum, 5 | D3 |
| Buckingham Palace, 6 | C4 |
| Cabinet War Rooms, 7 | D4 |
| Chinatown, 9 | D4 |

| | |
|---|---|
| Courtauld Institute, 10 | D4 |
| The Houses of Parliament, 14 | D4 |
| Kensington Palace, 17 | B4 |
| London Eye, 18 | D4 |
| Marble Arch, 20 | C3 |
| Millennium Bridge, 21 | E4 |
| Monument, 22 | F4 |
| Museum of London, 23 | E3 |
| National Gallery, 24 | D4 |
| National Portrait Gallery, 25 | D4 |

| | |
|---|---|
| Natural History Museum, 26 | B5 |
| Royal Courts of Justice, 29 | E3 |
| The Royal Mews, 31 | C4 |
| St. Martin-in-the-Fields, 38 | D4 |
| St. Mary-le-Bow, 39 | E3 |
| St. Pancras Chambers, 40 | D2 |
| St. Paul's Cathedral, 41 | E3 |
| Science Museum, 43 | B5 |
| Shakespeare's Globe Theatre, 44 | E4 |

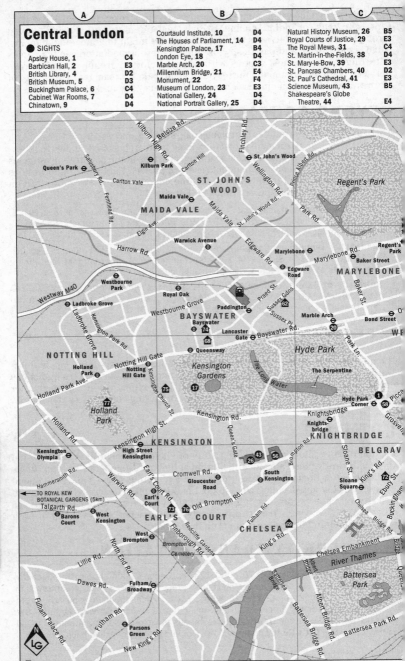

GREAT BRITAIN

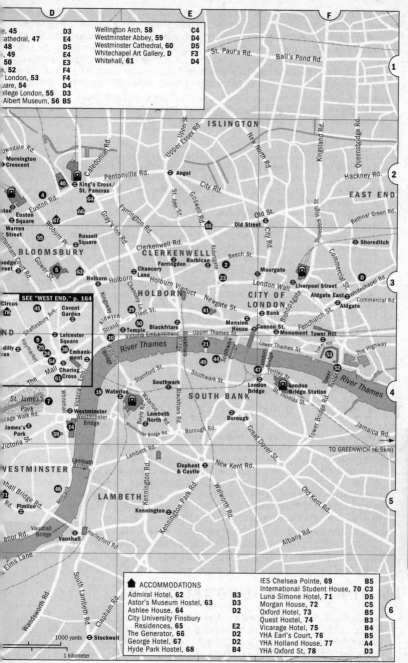

e, 45 **D3**
athedral, 47 **E4**
48 **D5**
, 49 **E4**
50 **E3**
e, 52 **F4**
London, 53 **F4**
uare, 54 **D4**
ollege London, 55 **D3**
Albert Museum, 56 **B5**

Wellington Arch, 58 **C4**
Westminster Abbey, 59 **D4**
Westminster Cathedral, 60 **D5**
Whitechapel Art Gallery, D **F3**
Whitehall, 61 **D4**

SEE "WEST END," p. 164

**GREAT BRITAIN**

## ACCOMMODATIONS

| | |
|---|---|
| Admiral Hotel, 62 | **B3** |
| Astor's Museum Hostel, 63 | **D3** |
| Ashlee House, 64 | **D2** |
| City University Finsbury Residences, 65 | **E2** |
| The Generator, 66 | **D2** |
| George Hotel, 67 | **D2** |
| Hyde Park Hostel, 68 | **B4** |
| IES Chelsea Pointe, 69 | **B5** |
| International Student House, 70 | **C3** |
| Luna Simone Hotel, 71 | **D5** |
| Morgan House, 72 | **C5** |
| Oxford Hotel, 73 | **B5** |
| Quest Hostel, 74 | **B3** |
| Vicarage Hotel, 75 | **B4** |
| YHA Earl's Court, 76 | **B5** |
| YHA Holland House, 77 | **A4** |
| YHA Oxford St, 78 | **D3** |

1000 yards ⊖ Stockwell

1 kilometer

**Trains:** London has 8 major train stations: **Charing Cross** (southern England); **Euston** (the northwest); **King's Cross** (the northeast); **Liverpool Street** (East Anglia); **Paddington** (the west and south Wales); **St. Pancras** (the Midlands and the northwest); **Victoria** (the south); **Waterloo** (the south, the southwest, and the Continent). All stations are linked by the subway, referred to as the Underground or Tube (⊖). Itineraries involving a change of stations in London usually include a cross-town transfer by Tube. Get information at the station ticket office or from the **National Rail Enquiries Line** (☎ 08457 484 950; www.britrail.com).

**Buses:** Long-distance buses (**coaches**) arrive in London at **Victoria Coach Station,** 164 Buckingham Palace Rd. ⊖Victoria. National Express (☎ 08705 808 080; www.nation-alexpress.com) is the largest operator of intercity services.

# ■ ORIENTATION

The **West End,** stretching east from Park Lane to Kingsway and south from Oxford St. to the River Thames, is the heart of London. In this area you'll find aristocratic **Mayfair,** the shopping streets near **Oxford Circus,** the clubs of **Soho,** and the boutiques of **Covent Garden.** Heading east of the West End, you'll pass legalistic **Holborn** before hitting the ancient **City of London** ("the City"), the site of the original Roman settlement and home to Tower Bridge and the Tower of London. The City's eastern border encompasses the ethnically diverse, working-class **East End.**

**Westminster** encompasses the grandeur of **Trafalgar Square** and extends south along the Thames; this is the location of both royal and political London, with the Houses of Parliament, Buckingham Palace, and Westminster Abbey. Farther west lies rich, snooty **Chelsea.** Across the river, the **South Bank** has an incredible variety of entertainment and museums. To the south, **Brixton** is one of the hottest nightlife spots in town, besides touristy Leicester Square and Piccadilly Circus. The huge expanse of **Hyde Park** lies west of the West End; along its southern border are chic **Knightsbridge** and posh **Kensington.** North of Hyde Park is the media-infested **Notting Hill** and the B&B- and hostel-filled **Bayswater.** Bayswater, Mayfair, and **Marylebone** meet at Marble Arch, on Hyde Park's northeast corner; from there, Marylebone stretches west to meet academic **Bloomsbury,** north of Soho and Holborn. **Camden Town, Islington, Hampstead,** and **Highgate** lie to the north of Bloomsbury and the City. A good street atlas is essential. ▨**London A to Z** (£6) is available at newsstands and bookstores.

# ■ LOCAL TRANSPORTATION

**Public Transportation:** Run by **Transport for London (TfL;** 24hr. info ☎ 7222 1234; www.thetube.com). The **Underground** (a.k.a. the **Tube**) is divided into 6 concentric zones; fares depend on the number of zones crossed. Buy your ticket before you board and pass it through automatic gates at both ends of your journey. Runs approximately 5:30am-midnight. See Tube map in the front of this guide. **Buses** are divided into 4 zones. Zones 1-3 are identical to the Tube zones. Buses run 5:30am-midnight, after which a network of **Night Buses,** prefixed by "N," take over. Fares £1. **Travelcard** valid on all TfL services. 1-day Travelcard from £6.20 (Zones 1-2).

**Licensed Taxicabs:** An illuminated "taxi" sign on the roof of a black cab signals availability. Tip 10%. For pickup (min. £2 extra charge), call **Taxi One-Number** (☎ 08718 718 710).

**Minicabs:** Private cars. Cheaper but less reliable—stick to a reputable company. **London Radio Cars** (☎ 8905 0000; www.londonradiocars.com) offers 24hr. pickup.

# ■ PRACTICAL INFORMATION

**Tourist Information Centre: Britain Visitor Centre,** 1 Regent St. (www.visitbritain.com). ⊖Piccadilly Circus. Open M 9:30am-6:30pm, Tu-F 9am-6:30pm, Sa-Su 10am-4pm. **London Information Centre,** 1 Leicester Pl. (☎ 7930 6769; www.londoninformation-centre.com). ⊖Leicester Sq. Open M-F 8am-midnight, Sa-Su 9am-6pm.

**Tours:** The **Big Bus Company,** 35-37 Grosvenor Gardens (☎7233 7797; www.big-bus.co.uk). ✚Victoria. Multiple routes and buses every 5-15min. 1hr. walking tours and Thames cruise. Buses start at central office and at hubs throughout the city. £20. £2 discount for online purchase. AmEx/MC/V. **Original London Walks** (☎7624 3978, recorded info 7624 9255; www.walks.com) offers themed walks, from "Haunted London" to "Slice of India." Most 2hr. £6, students £5, under 16 free.

**Embassies: Australia,** Australia House, Strand (☎7379 4334). ✚Temple. Open M-F 9am-5pm. **Canada,** MacDonald House, 1 Grosvenor Sq. (☎7258 6600). ✚Bond St. Open M-F 9am-5pm. **Ireland,** 17 Grosvenor Pl. (☎7235 2171). ✚Hyde Park Corner. Open M-F 9:30am-1pm and 2:15-5pm. **New Zealand,** New Zealand House, 80 Haymarket (☎7930 8422). ✚Piccadilly Circus. Open M-F 9am-5pm. **US,** 24 Grosvenor Sq. (☎7499 9000). ✚Bond St. Open M-F 8:30am-5:30pm.

**Currency Exchange:** Banks, such as **Barclays, HSBC, Lloyd's,** and **National Westminster** (NatWest) have the best rates. **Branches** open M-F 9:30am-4:30pm. Call ☎0895 456 6524 for the nearest **American Express** location.

**GLBT Resources:** London Lesbian and Gay Switchboard (☎7837 7324; www.queery.org.uk). 24hr. helpline and information service.

**Police:** London is covered by 2 police forces: the **City of London Police** (☎7601 2222) for the City and the **Metropolitan Police** (☎7230 1212) for the rest. At least 1 station in each of the 32 boroughs is open 24hr. Call ☎7230 1212 to find the nearest station.

**Pharmacies:** Most pharmacies open M-Sa 9:30am-5:30pm; a "duty" chemist in each district opens Su; hours may be limited. Late-night and 24hr. chemists are rare. **Zafash Pharmacy,** 233-235 Old Brompton Rd. (☎7373 2798), ✚Earl's Ct., is 24hr. **Bliss Chemist,** 5-6 Marble Arch (☎7723 6116), ✚Marble Arch, is open daily 9am-midnight.

**Hospitals: Charing Cross,** Fulham Palace Rd. (☎8846 1234), entrance on St. Dunstan's Rd., ✚Hammersmith. **Royal Free,** Pond St. (☎7794 0500), ✚Belsize Park. **St. Thomas's,** Lambeth Palace Rd. (☎7188 7188), ✚Waterloo. **University College London Hospital,** Grafton Way (☎0845 155 500), ✚Warren St.

**Internet Access:** Don't pay more than £2 per hr. Try the ubiquitous **easyInternet** (☎7241 9000; www.easyeverything.com). Locations include 9-16 Tottenham Ct. Rd. (✚Tottenham Ct. Rd.); 456/459 Strand (✚Charing Cross); 358 Oxford St. (✚Bond St.); 160-166 Kensington High St. (✚High St. Kensington). Prices vary with demand, but they're usually around £1.60 per hr. Min. 50p-£1.

**Post Office:** When sending mail to London, be sure to include the full postal code. The largest office is the **Trafalgar Square Post Office,** 24-28 William IV St. (☎7484 9305), ✚Charing Cross. Open M and W-F 8:30am-6:30pm, Tu 9:15am-6:30pm, Sa 9am-5:30pm.

# ▞ ACCOMMODATIONS

The best deals in town are student residence halls, which rent out rooms over the summer and sometimes Easter vacations. "B&B" encompasses accommodations of wildly varying quality, personality, and price. Be aware that in-room showers are often prefabricated units jammed into a corner. Linens are included at all YHAs, but towels are not; buy one from reception ($3.50). YHAs also sell discount tickets to theaters and major attractions.

## BAYSWATER

**Quest Hostel,** 45 Queensborough Terr. (☎7229 7782; www.astorhostels.com). ✚Bayswater. Night Bus #N15, 94, 148. Co-ed hostel with a chummy staff. Continental breakfast included. Internet £1 per hr. Dorms £18-23; doubles £30. MC/V. ❶

**Hyde Park Hostel,** 2-6 Inverness Terr. (☎7229 5101; www.astorhostels.com). ✚Bayswater. Night Bus #N15, 94, 148. Jungle-themed basement bar and dance space hosts DJs and parties (open W-Th and Su 7pm-2am, F-Sa 7pm-3am). Laundry, TV lounge, secure luggage room. Breakfast included. Reception 24hr. Reserve 2 weeks ahead in summer. Dorms £11-18; doubles £25. Ages 16-35 only. MC/V. ❶

**Admiral Hotel,** 143 Sussex Gardens (☎ 7723 7309; www.admiral-hotel.com). ⊖Paddington. Night Bus #N15, 94, 148. Recently redecorated rooms with bath, hair dryer, satellite TV, and kettle. English breakfast included. Free Wi-Fi. Singles £40-50; doubles £58-75; triples £75-90; quads £88-110; quints £100-130. MC/V. ❸

## BLOOMSBURY

Many B&Bs and hostels are on busy roads, so be wary of noise levels. The area becomes seedier closer to King's Cross.

■ **The Generator,** Compton Pl. (☎ 7388 7666; www.generatorhostels.com), off 37 Tavistock Pl. ⊖Russell Sq. or King's Cross St. Pancras. Night Bus #N19, 35, 38, 41, 55, 91, 243. The ultimate party hostel. 18+. Breakfast included. Internet 50p per 10min. Reserve 1 week in advance for Sa-Su. Online booking. Credit card required with reservation. 12- to 14-bed dorms M-W and Su £13; singles £30/35; doubles £40/44; triples £54/60; quads £60/68. Discounts for long stays. Under 18 not allowed unless part of a family group. MC/V. ❶

■ **Ashlee House,** 261-265 Gray's Inn Rd. (☎ 7833 9400; www.ashleehouse.co.uk). ⊖King's Cross St. Pancras. Night Bus #N10, 63, 73, 91, 390. A friendly, "designer" budget accommodation fit for the most discerning of backpackers. Private rooms include table, sink, and kettle. Breakfast and linens included; towels £1. Internet £1 per hr. Apr.-Oct. dorms £9-20; singles £37; doubles £50. MC/V. ❶

**Astor's Museum Hostel,** 27 Montague St. (☎ 7580 5360; www.astorhotels.com). ⊖Tottenham Court Rd., Russell Sq., or Goodge St. Night Bus #N19, 35, 38, 41, 55, 91, 243. Plain but friendly. Under 35 only. Free DVD rental. English breakfast and linens included. Towels £5. Reserve ahead. Dorms £19-23; doubles £66. AmEx/MC/V. ❷

**George Hotel,** 58-60 Cartwright Gardens (☎ 7387 8777; www.georgehotel.com). ⊖Russell Sq. Night Bus #N10, 73, 91, 390. Meticulously kept rooms with satellite TV, kettle, alarm clock, phone, and sink. Breakfast included. Free Internet. Reserve 3 weeks ahead in summer. Singles £50, with shower £75; doubles £69/75, with bath £89; triples £79/89/99; basic quad £89. Discount for stays over 4 days. MC/V. ❸

## KENSINGTON AND EARL'S COURT

■ **YHA Holland House,** Holland Walk (☎ 7937 0748; www.hihostels.com). ⊖High St. Kensington or Holland Park. Night Bus #N27, 94, 148. 17th-century mansion with TV room, laundry, and kitchen. Breakfast included. Internet 50p per 7min. Reception 24hr. Reserve 2-3 wks. ahead in summer, although there are frequent last-minute vacancies. Dorms £22, under 18 £17. £3 discount with student ID. AmEx/MC/V. ❶

**Vicarage Hotel,** 10 Vicarage Gate (☎ 7229 4030; www.londonvicaragehotel.com). ⊖High St. Kensington. Night Bus #N27, 28, 31, 52. Immaculately maintained Victorian house. All rooms have wood furnishings, kettle, and hair dryer. Rooms with private bath have TV. Full English breakfast included. Best to reserve 2 months in advance with 1 night's deposit; personal checks accepted for deposit with at least 2 months notice. Singles £50, with private bathroom £85; doubles £85/110; triples £105/140; quads £112/155. MC/V. ❸

**Oxford Hotel,** 24 Penywern Rd. (☎ 7370 1161; www.the-oxford-hotel.com). ⊖Earl's Court. Night Bus #N31, 74, 97. Fun fact: Sir William Ramsey, the physicist who discovered helium, once lived in a section of this hotel—guests would often hear high-pitched voices coming from his room. Mid-sized, bright rooms, all with shower and some with full bath. Minimal but generally high-quality furnishings: comfortable beds, TV, kettle, and safe. Continental breakfast included. Reception 24hr. Reserve 2-3 weeks ahead for June. Singles with shower £45, with bath £58; doubles £65/75; triples with bath £83; quads £92/100; quints £120. MC/V. ❸

**YHA Earl's Court,** 38 Bolton Gdns. (☎ 7373 7083; www.hihostels.com). ⊖Earl's Court. Night Bus #N31, 74, 97. Rambling Victorian townhouse considerably better-equipped than most

YHAs. Bright, tidy, single-sex dorms (4-10 people) have wooden bunks, lockers (bring your own lock), and sink. Features a small garden, spacious communal kitchen, 2 TV lounges, and luggage storage. Breakfast included for private rooms; otherwise £4. Linens included. Coin laundry and Internet access available. Max. 2-week stay. 24hr. cancellation policy; £5 cancellation charge. Book private rooms at least 24hr. in advance. Dorms £20, under 18 £18; doubles £60; quads £82. £3 added charge per night if not a YHA member. MC/V. ●

## OTHER NEIGHBORHOODS

**YHA Oxford Street (HI),** 14 Noel St. (☎7734 1618; www.yha.org.uk), in the West End. ⊖Oxford Circus. More than 10 Night Buses run along Oxford St., including #N7, 8, and 207. Small, clean, sunny rooms with limited facilities but an unbeatable location for nightlife. Towels £3.50. Internet terminal and Wi-Fi available. 3- to 4-bed dorms £25, under 18 £21; 2-bed dorms £27. Oct.-Mar. £24/19/26. MC/V. ●

**City University Finsbury Residences,** 15 Bastwick St. (☎7040 8811; www.city.ac.uk/ems/accomm/fins.html), in Clerkenwell. ⊖Barbican. Night Bus #N35 and 55 stop at the corner of Old St. and Goswell Rd. Open early June to early Sept. Singles £21. ❷

**Luna Simone Hotel,** 47-49 Belgrave Rd. (☎7834 5897; www.lunasimonehotel.com), in Westminster. ⊖Victoria or Pimlico. Night Bus #N2, 24, 36. Overachieving staff and lovely rooms. Breakfast included. Free Internet access. Reserve at least 3 weeks ahead. Singles £40, with bath £60; doubles with bath £90; triples with bath £110; quads with bath £130. 10-20% discount in low season. MC/V. ❸

**IES Chelsea Pointe,** (☎7808 9200; www.iesreshall.com), in Chelsea, on the corner of Manresa Rd. and King's Rd.; entrance on Manresa Rd. ⊖Sloane Sq., then bus #11, 19, 22, 319; ⊖South Kensington, then bus #49. Night Bus #N11, 19, 22. Unheard-of prices in Soho. Rooms have bath, data ports, phone, kitchen, and laundry. 20 rooms wheelchair-accessible. Reserve ahead. Singles £285 per week; doubles £375 per week. AmEx/MC/V. ❸

**Morgan House,** 120 Ebury St. (☎7730 2384; www.morganhouse.co.uk), in Knightsbridge and Belgravia. ⊖Victoria. A neighborhood standout: stylish rooms all have sink, TV, and kettle, and some have fireplaces. Breakfast included. Reserve 2-3 months ahead. Singles with sink £52; doubles with sink £72, with bath £92; triples £92/112; quad (1 double bed and bunk beds) with bath £132. MC/V. ❸

**International Student House,** 229 Great Portland St. (☎7631 8310; www.ish.org.uk), in Marylebone. ⊖Great Portland St. Night Bus #N18. Most rooms have sink and fridge; some have bath. Bar, cafeteria, and fitness center £6 per day. Continental breakfast included except for dorms (£2.30); English breakfast £3. Internet £2 per hr. Key deposit £20. Dorms £12; singles £34; doubles £52; triples £62; quads £76. 10% discount on singles, doubles, and triples with ISIC. MC/V. ●

# ◨ FOOD

Any restaurant charging under £10 for a main course is relatively inexpensive; add drinks and service and you're nudging £15. It *is* possible to eat cheaply—and well—in London. For the best and cheapest **ethnic restaurants,** head to the source: **Whitechapel** for Bangladeshi *baltis*, **Chinatown** for dim sum, **South Kensington** for French pastries, **Edgware Road** for shawarma. The cheapest places to get your own ingredients are **street markets** (see **Shopping,** p. 162). To get all your food under one roof, try supermarket chains **Tesco, Safeway, Sainsbury's,** or **Marks & Spencer.**

## BAYSWATER

**Levantine,** 26 London St. (☎7262 1111; www.levant.co.uk). ⊖Paddington. Lebanese restaurant with loads of vegetarian options, nightly belly-dancing, and *shisha* (hooka). Lunch *menu* £7 noon-5:30pm. Open daily noon-12:30am. MC/V. ❷

**La Bottega del Gelato,** 127 Bayswater Rd. (☎7243 2443). ⊖Queensway. The handmade, creamy gelato is ideal after a hard day of sightseeing. 1-3 scoops £2-4. Open daily 11am-10pm. ●

## BLOOMSBURY

🖾 **ICCo (Italiano Coffee Company),** 46 Goodge St. (☎ 7580 9688). ⊖Goodge St. To-die-for thin-crust 11 in. pizzas for an eye-popping £3. Pasta from £2. Sandwiches and baguettes ½-price after 4pm. Take-out available. Pizzas available after noon. Open daily 7am-11pm. AmEx/MC/V. ❶

**Navarro's Tapas Bar,** 67 Charlotte St. (☎ 7637 7713; www.navarros.co.uk). ⊖Goodge St. Authenticity. Superb tapas £3.50-11; 2-3 per person is plenty. Min. £7.50 per person. Open M-F noon-3pm and 6-10pm, Sa 6-10pm. AmEx/MC/V. ❸

**Newman Arms,** 23 Rathbone St. (☎ 7636 1127). ⊖Tottenham Court Rd. or Goodge St. A pub with a famous upstairs pie room and restaurant. Connoisseurs at 10 sought-after tables dig into homemade meat pies. Seasonal game fillings most popular; vegetarian and fish options available. Pie with potatoes and veggies on the side £9. Pints start at £3. Book in advance or face a hungry wait. Pub open M-F 11am-11pm. Restaurant open M-Th noon-3pm and 6-9pm, F noon-3pm. ❷

## CHELSEA

🖾 **Buona Sera,** at the Jam, 289a King's Rd. (☎ 7352 8827). ⊖Sloane Sq., then Bus #19 or 319. The "bunk" tables here are stacked high into the air. Pasta, fish, and steak entrees £7-12. Open M 6pm-midnight, Tu-F noon-3pm and 6pm-midnight, Sa-Su noon-midnight. Reservations recommended F-Sa. AmEx/MC/V. ❸

**Chelsea Bun,** 9a Limerston St. (☎ 7352 3635). ⊖Sloane Sq., then bus #11 or 22. Spirited and casual. Extensive vegetarian and vegan options. Sandwiches, pasta, and burgers £2.80-8. Early-bird specials M-F 7am-noon (£2.20-3.20). Sandwiches (£2.80-7) and breakfast (from £4) served until 6pm. Min. £3.50 per person during lunch, £5.50 dinner. Open M-Sa 7am-midnight, Su 9am-7pm. MC/V. ❸

## THE CITY OF LONDON

**Café Spice Namaste,** 16 Prescot St. (☎ 7488 9242; www.cafespice.co.uk). ⊖Tower Hill or DLR: Tower Gateway. The menu helpfully explains each Goan and Parsee specialty. Meat entrees are pricey (from £15), but vegetarian meals (from £4.75) are affordable. Open M-F noon-3pm and 6:15-10:30pm, Sa 6:30-10:30pm. AmEx/MC/V. ❸

**Futures,** 8 Botolph Alley (☎ 7623 4529; www.futures-vta.net), between Botolph and Lovat Ln. ⊖Monument. London's workforce beseiges this tiny takeaway joint during the lunch hour. Vegetarian soups, salads, and entrees (£2.20-5.20) change weekly. Open M-F 8-10am and 11:30am-2:30pm. ❶

## CLERKENWELL AND HOLBORN

🖾 **Anexo,** 61 Turnmill St. (☎ 7250 3401; www.anexo.co.uk). ⊖Farringdon. This funky Spanish restaurant and bar serves up Iberian dishes, including authentic paella (£7.50-9). Happy hour M-Sa 5-7pm. Open M-F 10am-11pm, Sa 6-11:30pm, Su 4:30-11pm. Bar open 11am-2am. AmEx/MC/V. ❷

🖾 **Bleeding Heart Tavern,** corner of Greville St. and Bleeding Heart Yard (☎ 7242 2056; www.bleedingheart.co.uk). ⊖Farringdon. Highlights include the roast suckling pig with delicately spiced apple slices (£12). Open M-F 7-10:30am, noon-2:30pm, 6-10:30pm. Upstairs pub open M-F 11:30am-11pm. AmEx/MC/V. ❸

## EAST LONDON

🖾 **Café 1001,** Dray Walk (☎ 7247 9679; www.cafe1001.co.uk). ⊖Aldgate East. Off Brick Ln. 20-somethings lounge in the smoky, spacious upstairs and numerous outdoor tables. Fresh cakes (£2 per slice), pre-made salads (£3), sandwiches (£2.50), and outdoor barbecue, weather permitting. Nightly DJs or bands 7pm-close. Open M-W and Su 7am-11:30pm, Th-Sa 7pm-midnight. ❶

**Yelo,** 8-9 Hoxton Sq. (☎ 7729 4626; www.yelothai.com). ⊖Old St. Hip and comfortable. Pad thai, curry, and stir-fry (£5) make for familiar fare, but the industrial lighting, exposed brick, and house music shake things up. For a more formal affair, call to book a "proper" table downstairs. Wheelchair-accessible. Take-out and delivery available. Open daily noon-3pm and 6-11pm. ❶

## MARYLEBONE AND REGENT'S PARK

**Mandalay,** 444 Edgware Rd. (☎ 7258 3696). ⊖Edgware Rd. Burmese entrees with good vegetarian items (£4-7.90). Lunch specials are great deals. Open M-Sa noon-2:30pm and 6-10:30pm. Dinner reservations recommended. AmEx/MC/V. ❶

**Patogh,** 8 Crawford Pl. (☎ 7262 4015). ⊖Edgware Rd. This tiny but charming Persian hole-in-the-wall serves large portions of sesame-seed flatbread (£2) and freshly prepared starters (£2.50-6). Take-out available. Open daily noon-midnight. Cash only. ❷

## NORTH LONDON

**Gallipoli,** 102 Upper St. (☎ 7359 0630; www.gallipolicafe.com), **Gallipoli Again,** 120 Upper St. (☎ 7359 1578), **Gallipoli Bazaar,** 107 Upper St. (☎ 7226 5333). ⊖Angel. Lebanese, North African, and Turkish delights. 2-course lunch £7. Open M-Th 10:30am-11pm, F-Sa 10:30am-midnight. Reservations recommended F-Sa. MC/V. ❷

**La Crêperie de Hampstead,** 77 Hampstead High St. (www.hampsteadcreperie.com), metal stand on the side of the King William IV. ⊖Hampstead. A neighborhood fixture. French-speaking cooks take your order and leave you to anticipate your crepe (£3-4). Open M-Th 11:45am-11pm, F-Su 11:45am-11:30pm. Cash only. ❶

## THE WEST END

▨ **Masala Zone,** 9 Marshall St. (☎ 7287 9966; www.realindianfood.com). ⊖Oxford Circus. South Indian favorites (£6-8), in addition to small bowls of "street food" (£3.40-5.50), and large *thali* (sampler platters; £7.50-12). Open M-F noon-2:45pm and 5:30-11pm, Sa 12:30-11pm, Su 12:30-3:30pm and 6-10:30pm. MC/V. ❷

▨ **Rock and Sole Plaice,** 47 Endell St. (☎ 7836 3785). ⊖Covent Garden. Self-proclaimed "master fryer" (qualifications unclear) delivers fish and chips for £9-11. Samosas (£4.50). Open M-Sa 11:30am-11:30pm, Su 11:30am-10 pm. MC/V. ❷

## OTHER NEIGHBORHOODS

▨ **George's Portobello Fish Bar,** 329 Portobello Rd. (☎ 8969 7895), in Notting Hill. ⊖Ladbroke Grove. George opened up here in 1961, and the fish 'n' chips are still as good as ever (from £7). Another specialty is the barbecue ribs (£7), whose secret recipe is closely guarded. Open M-F 11am-midnight, Sa 11am-9pm, Su noon-9:30pm. ❷

**Jenny Lo's Teahouse,** 14 Eccleston St. (☎ 7259 0399), in Knightsbridge. ⊖Victoria. This small cafe bustles on weekdays, but the delicious *cha shao* (pork noodle soup; £6.50) and the selection of Asian noodles, from Vietnamese to Beijing style (£6.50-8), make eating here well worth the wait. Vegetarian options. Takeaway and delivery available (min. £5). Open M-F noon-3pm and 6-10pm, Sa 6-10pm. Cash only. ❷

**Cantina del Ponte,** 36c Shad Thames, Butlers Wharf (☎ 7403 5403), in the South Bank. ⊖Tower Hill or London Bridge. Lunch *menu* is a bargain at 2 courses for £10, 3 for £14 (available M-F noon-3pm). Pizzas from £5. Entrees from £8.50. Wheelchair-accessible. Open M-Sa noon-3pm and 6-10:45pm, Su noon-3pm and 6-9:45pm. AmEx/MC/V. ❸

# ◉ SIGHTS

## WESTMINSTER

The City of Westminster, now a borough of London, has been the seat of British power for over a thousand years. William the Conqueror was crowned in

## QUEEN'S GUARD

*Let's Go got the scoop on a London icon. Corporal of Horse Simon Knowles is an 19-year veteran of the Queen's Guard.*

**LG:** What sort of training did you undergo?

**A:** In addition to a year of basic military camp, which involves mainly training on tanks and armored cars, I was also trained as a gunner and radio operator. Then I joined the service regiment at 18 years of age.

**LG:** So it's not all glamor?

**A:** Not at all. That's a common misconception. After armored training, we go through mounted training on horseback in Windsor for six months where we learn the tools of horseback riding, beginning with bareback training. The final month is spent in London training in full state uniform.

**LG:** Do the horses ever act up?

**A:** Yes, but it's natural. During the Queen's Jubilee Parade, with three million people lining the Mall, to expect any animal to be fully relaxed is absurd. The horses rely on the rider to give them confidence. If the guard is riding the horses confidently and strongly, the horse will settle down.

**LG:** Your uniforms look pretty heavy. Are they comfortable?

**A:** They're not comfortable at all.

Westminster Abbey on Christmas Day, AD 1066, and his successors built the Palace of Westminster that today houses Parliament.

■**WESTMINSTER ABBEY.** Founded as a Benedictine monastery, Westminster Abbey has evolved into a house of kings and queens both living and dead. Almost nothing remains of St. Edward's Abbey: Henry III's 13th-century Gothic reworking created most of the grand structure you see today. A door off the east cloister leads to the **Chapter House,** the original meeting place of the House of Commons. Next door to the Abbey (through the cloisters), the lackluster **Abbey Museum** is in the Norman undercroft. Just north of the Abbey, **St. Margaret's Church** enjoys a peculiar status: as a part of the Royal Peculiar, it is not under the jurisdiction of the diocese of England nor the archbishop of Canterbury. Since 1614, it's been the official worshipping place of the House of Commons. *(Parliament Sq. Access Old Monastery, cloister, and garden from Dean's Yard, behind the Abbey. ⊖Westminster. Abbey ☎ 7654 4900, Chapter House 7222 5152; www.westminster-abbey.org. No photography. Abbey open M-Tu and Th-F 9:30am-3:45pm, W 9:30am-7pm, Sa 9:30am-1:45pm, Su open for services only. Museum open daily 10:30am-4pm. Partially wheelchair-accessible. Abbey and Museum £10, students and children 11-17 £7, families of 4 £24. Services free. 1½hr. tours £5 Apr.-Oct. M-F 10, 10:30, 11am, 2, 2:30pm, Sa 10, 10:30, 11am; Oct.-Mar. M-F 10:30, 11am, 2, 2:30pm, Sa 10:30, 11am. Audio tours £4 available M-F 9:30am-3pm, Sa 9:30am-1pm. AmEx/MC/V.)*

**BUCKINGHAM PALACE.** The Palace is open to visitors from the end of July to the end of September every year. Don't expect to find any insights into the Queen's personal life—the **State Rooms** are the only rooms on view, and they are used only for formal occasions. "God Save the Queen" is the rallying cry at the **Queens Gallery,** dedicated to changing exhibits of jaw-droppingly valuable items from the Royal Collection. Detached from the palace and tour, the **Royal Mews** acts as a museum, stable, riding school, and working carriage house. The main attraction is the Queen's collection of coaches, including the Cinderella-like "Glass Coach" used to carry royal brides, including Diana, to their weddings, and the State Coaches of Australia, Ireland, and Scotland. Another highlight is the four-ton **Gold State Coach,** which can occasionally be seen wheeling around the streets in the early morning on practice runs for major events. To witness the Palace without the cost, attend a session of **Changing of the Guard.** Show up well before 11:30am and stand in front of the Palace in view of the morning guards, or use the steps of the Victoria Memorial as a vantage point. *(At the end of the Mall, between Westminster, Belgravia, and Mayfair.* ⊖*St. James's Park, Victoria, Green Park, or Hyde Park Corner.* ☎ *7766 7324; www.the-royal-collection.com. Palace open late July to late Sept. daily 9:30am-6:30pm, last admission 4:15pm. £15, students £14, children 6-17 £8.50, under 5 free, families of 5 £67. Advance booking is recommended; required for disabled visitors. Queens Gallery open daily 10am-5:30pm, last admission 4:30pm. Wheelchair-accessible. £8, students £7, families £22. Royal Mews open late July to late Sept. daily 10am-5pm, last admission 4:15pm; Mar.-July and late Sept. to late Oct. M-Th and Sa-Su 11am–4pm, last admission 3:15pm. Wheelchair-accessible. £7, seniors £6, children under 17 £4.50, families £19. Changing of the Guard Apr. to late July daily, Aug.-Mar. every other day, excepting the Queen's absence, inclement weather, or pressing state functions. Free.)*

**PARLIAMENTARY PROCEDURE.** Arrive early in the afternoon to minimize waiting, which often exceeds 2hr. Keep in mind that the wait for Lords is generally shorter than the wait for Commons. To sit in on Parliament's "question time" (40min.; M-W 2:30pm, Th-F 11am) apply for tickets several weeks in advance through your embassy in London.

**THE HOUSES OF PARLIAMENT.** The Palace of Westminster has been home to both the House of Lords and the House of Commons (together known as Parliament) since the 11th century, when Edward the Confessor established his court here. Standing guard on the northern side of the building, the **Clock Tower** is famously nicknamed **Big Ben,** after the robustly proportioned Benjamin Hall, a former Commissioner of Works. "Big Ben" actually refers only to the 14-ton bell that hangs inside the tower. **Victoria Tower,** at the south end of the palace building, contains copies of every Act of Parliament since 1497. Sir Charles Barry rebuilt the tower in the 1850s after it burned down in 1834; his design won an anonymous competition, and his symbol, the portcullis, still remains the official symbol of the Houses of Parliament. A flag flying from the top indicates that Parliament is in session. When the Queen is in the building, a special royal banner is flown instead of the Union flag. *(Parliament Sq., in Westminster. Queue for both Houses forms at St. Stephen's entrance, between Old and New Palace Yards.* ⊖*Westminster.* ☎ *08709 063 773; www.parliament.uk/visiting/visiting.cfm. "Line of Route" Tour: includes both Houses. UK residents can contact their MPs for tours year-round, generally M-W mornings and F. Foreign visitors may tour Aug.-Sept. Book online, by phone, or in person at Abingdon Green ticket office (open mid-July) across from Palace of Westminster. Open Aug. M-*

They were designed way back in Queen Victoria's time, and the leather trousers and boots are very solid. The uniform weighs about 3 stone [about 45 lb.].

**LG:** How do you overcome the itches, sneezes, and bees?

**A:** Discipline is instilled in every British soldier during training. We know not to move a muscle while on parade no matter what the provocation or distraction—unless, of course, it is a security matter. But our helmets are akin to wearing a boiling kettle on your head; to relieve the pressure, sometimes we use the back of our sword blade to ease the back of the helmet forward.

**LG:** How do you make the time pass while on duty?

**A:** The days are long. At Whitehall the shift system is derived upon inspection in Barracks. Smarter men work on horseback in the boxes in shifts from 10am-4pm; less smart men work on foot from 7am-8pm. Some guys count the number of buses that drive past. Unofficially, there are lots of pretty girls around here, and we are allowed to move our eyeballs.

**LG:** What has been your funniest distraction attempt?

**A:** One day a taxi pulled up, and out hopped four Playboy bunnies, who then posed for a photo shoot right in front of us. You could call that a distraction if you like.

*Tu and F-Sa 9:15am-4:30pm, W-Th 1:15-4:30pm; Sept. M and F-Sa 9:15am-4:30pm, Tu-Th 1:15-4:30pm. 75min. tours depart every few min. £12, students £8, families of 4 £30. MC/V.)*

**ST. JAMES'S PARK AND GREEN PARK.** The streets leading up to Buckingham Palace are flanked by two sprawling expanses of greenery: St. James's Park and Green Park. In the middle of St. James's Park is the **St. James's Park Lake**—the lake and the surrounding grassy area are a waterfowl preserve. Across the Mall, the Green Park is the creation of Charles II, connecting Westminster and St. James. *(The Mall. ⊖St. James's Park or Green Park. Open daily 5am-midnight. Lawn chairs available, weather permitting, Mar.-Oct. 10am-6pm; June-Aug. 10am-10pm £2 for 2hr., student deal £30 for the season. Last rental 2hr. before close. Summer walks in the park some M 1-2pm, including tour of Guard's Palace and Victoria Tower Gardens. Book in advance by calling ☎ 7930 1793.)*

**WESTMINSTER CATHEDRAL.** Following Henry VIII's divorce from the Catholic Church, London's Catholic community remained without a cathedral until 1884, when the Church purchased a derelict prison on a former monastery site. The Neo-Byzantine building looks somewhat like a fortress and is now one of London's great religious landmarks. An elevator, well worth the fee, carries visitors up the striped 273 ft. bell tower for a panoramic view of Westminster, the river, and Kensington. *(Cathedral Piazza, off Victoria St. ⊖Victoria. ☎ 7798 9055; www.westminstercathedral.org.uk. Open daily 8am-7pm. Free; suggested donation £2. Bell tower open daily 9:30am-12:30pm and 1-5pm. Organ recitals Su 4:45pm.)*

**WHITEHALL.** Whitehall refers to the stretch of road connecting Trafalgar Sq. with **Parliament Square** and is synonymous with the British civil service. Toward the north end of Whitehall, **Great Scotland Yard** marks the former headquarters of the Metropolitan Police. Nearer Parliament Sq., heavily guarded gates mark the entrance to **Downing Street.** In 1735, No. 10 was made the official residence of the First Lord of the Treasury, a position that soon became permanently identified with the Prime Minister. The Chancellor of the Exchequer traditionally resides at No. 11 and the Parliamentary Chief Whip at No. 12. When Tony Blair's family was too big for No. 10, he switched with Gordon Brown, a move that proved convenient when Brown was appointed Prime Minister in 2007. The street is closed to visitors, but if you wait, you may see the PM going to or coming from work. *(Between Trafalgar Sq. and Parliament Sq. ⊖Westminster, Embankment, or Charing Cross.)*

# CHELSEA

**ROYAL HOSPITAL.** The environs of the Royal Hospital—including a chapel, a small museum detailing the hospital's history, and a retirement home—house the Chelsea Pensioners, who have tottered around the grounds since 1692. The main draw is the once ritzy **Ranelagh Gardens.** They're a quiet oasis for picnics and park-playing—except during the **Chelsea Flower Show** in late May, when members of the Royal Horticultural Society descend en masse. *(2 entrance gates on Royal Hospital Rd. ⊖Sloane Sq., then Bus #137. ☎7881 5200; www.chelsea-pensioners.co.uk. Museum, Great Hall, and chapel open daily 10am-noon and 2-4pm; museum closed Su Oct.-Mar. Grounds open Nov.-Mar. M-Sa 10am-4:30pm, Su 2-4:30pm.; Apr. daily 10am-7:30pm, May-Aug. daily 10am-8:30pm, Sept. daily 10am-7pm, Oct. daily 10am-5pm. Wheelchair-accessible. Flower show: www.rhs.org.uk; tickets must be purchased well in advance. Admission to Royal Hospital free.)*

**CHELSEA PHYSIC GARDEN.** Founded in 1673 to provide medicinal herbs to locals, the Physic Garden remains a carefully ordered living repository of useful, rare, or just plain interesting plants. It has also played an important historical role, serving as the staging post from which tea was introduced to India and cotton to America. Today, the garden is a quiet place for picnics, teas, and scenic walks. You can purchase flora on display. *(66 Royal Hospital Rd.; entrance on Swan Walk. ⊖Sloane Sq., then Bus #137. ☎7352 5646; www.chelseaphysicgarden.co.uk. Open early Apr.-Oct. W* *noon-9pm, Th-F noon-6pm, Su noon-6pm; during Chelsea Flower Show (late May) and Chelsea Festival (mid-June) M-F noon-5pm. Tea served daily from 12:30pm, Su from noon. Call in advance for wheelchair access. £7, students and children under 16 £4.)*

# THE CITY OF LONDON

**ST. PAUL'S CATHEDRAL.** Christopher Wren's masterpiece is the 5th cathedral to occupy this site. After three designs were rejected by the bishops, Wren, with Charles II's support, started building. Sneakily, he had persuaded the king to let him make "necessary alterations" as work progressed, and the building that emerged in 1708 bore little resemblance to what Charles II had approved. The **Nave** can seat 2500 worshippers. The tombs, including those of Nelson, Wellington, and Florence Nightingale, are downstairs in the **crypt.** Christopher Wren lies beneath the epitaph *"Lector, si monumentum requiris circumspice"* ("Reader, if you seek his monument, look around"). To see the inside of the second-tallest freestanding **dome** in Europe (after St. Peter's in the Vatican), climb the 259 steps to the **Whispering Gallery.** From here, 119 more steps lead to the **Stone Gallery,** on the outer base of the dome, and it's another 152 to the summit's **Golden Gallery.** *(St. Paul's Churchyard.* ⊖*St. Paul's.* ☎*7246 8350;*

> **ST. PAUL'S FOR POCKET CHANGE.** To gain access to the Cathedral's nave for free, attend an Evensong service (M-Sa 5pm, 45min.). Arrive at 4:50pm to be admitted to seats in the quire.

*www.stpauls.co.uk. Open M-Sa 8:30am-4pm; last entry 3:45pm. Dome and galleries open M-Sa 9:30am-4pm. Open for worship daily 7:15am-6pm. Partially wheelchair-accessible. Admission £9.50, students £8.50, children 7-16 £3.50; worshippers free. Group of 10 or more 50p discount per ticket. "Supertour" M-F 11, 11:30am, 1:30, 2pm; £3, students £2.50, children 7-16 £1; English only. Audio tour in many languages daily 9am-3:30pm; £3.50, students £3.*

**THE TOWER OF LONDON.** The turrets and towers of this multi-functional block—serving as palace, prison, royal mint, and living museum over the past 900 years—are impressive not only for their appearance but also for their integral role in England's history. A popular way to get a feel for the Tower is to join one of the animated and theatrical **Yeoman Warders' Tours.** Queen Anne Boleyn passed through Traitor's Gate just before her death, but entering the Tower is no longer as perilous as it used to be. St. Thomas's Tower begins the self-guided tour of the Medieval Palace. At the end of the **Wall Walk**—a series of eight towers—is **Martin Tower,** which houses an exhibit that traces the history of the British Crown. It is also home to a fascinating collection of retired crowns (without the gemstones that have been recycled into the current models); informative plaques are much better here than in the Jewel House, where the crown jewels are held. With the exception of the Coronation Spoon, everything dates from after 1660, since Cromwell melted down the original booty. The centerpiece of the fortress is White Tower, which begins with the first-floor **Chapel of St. John the Evangelist.** Outside, Tower Green is a lovely grassy area—not so lovely, though, for those once executed there. *(Tower Hill, next to Tower Bridge, within easy reach of the South Bank and the East End.* ⊖*Tower Hill or DLR: Tower Gateway.* ☎*0870 751 5175, ticket sales 0870 756 6060; www.hrp.org.uk. Open Mar.-Oct. M 10am-6pm, Tu-Sa 9am-6pm, Su 10am-6pm; buildings close at 5:30pm, last entry 5pm; Nov.-Feb. all closing times 1hr. earlier. Tower Green open only by Yeoman tours, after 4:30pm, or for daily services. Admission £16, students £13, children 5-15 £9.50, children under 5 free, families of 5 £45. Tickets also sold at Tube stations; buy them in advance to avoid long queues at the door. Tours: "Yeoman Warders' Tours" meet near entrance; 1hr., every 30min. M and Su 10am-3:30pm, Tu-Sa 9:30am-3:30pm. Audio tours £3.50, students £2.50.)*

# THE MILLENNIUM MILE

**Time:** 8-9hr.

**Distance:** 2.5 mi. (4km)

**When To Go:** Begin at 8am.

**Start:** ⊖Tower Hill

**Finish:** ⊖Westminster

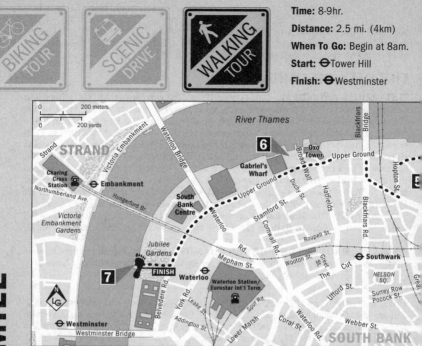

A stroll along the South Bank is a trip through history and back again. Across the river you will pass th[e] timeless monuments of London's past, like the Tower of London and St. Paul's Cathedral, while next t[o] you the round glass sphere of City Hall and the converted power facility of the Tate provide a stark, mo[d]ern contrast. Whether it's a search for Shakespeare and Picasso that brings you to the South Bank, o[r] just a hankering for a nice walk, you will find yourself rewarded.

**1 TOWER OF LONDON.** Begin your trek to the Tower **early** to avoid the crowds. Tours given by th[e] Yeomen Warders meet every 1½hr. near the entrance. Listen as they expertly recount tales of royal con[-] spiracy, treason, and murder. See the **White Tower,** once a fortress and residence of kings. Shiver a[t] the executioner's stone on the tower green and pay your respects at the Chapel of St. Peter ad Vincu[-] lum, holding the remains of three queens. First, get the dirt on the gemstones at **Martin Tower,** the[n] wait in line to see the **Crown Jewels.** The jewels include such glittering lovelies as the First Star of Africa[,] the largest cut diamond in the world (p. 151). Time: 2hr.

**2 TOWER BRIDGE.** An engineering wonder that puts its plainer sibling, the London Bridge, t[o] shame. Marvel at its beauty, but skip the Tower Bridge Experience. Better yet, call in advance t[o] inquire what times the Tower drawbridge is lifted (p. 154). Time: no need to stop walking; tak[e] in the mechanics as you head to the next sight.

**3 DESIGN MUSEUM.** On Butler's Wharf, let the Design Museum introduce you to the lates[t] innovations in contemporary design. See what's to come in the forward-looking Review Gallery o[r] hone in on individual designers and products in the Temporary Gallery. From the museum, wal[k] along the **Queen's Walk.** To your left you will find the **HMS Belfast,** which was launched in 193[8] and led the landing for D-Day, 1944. Time: 1hr.

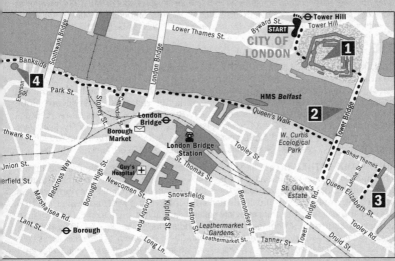

**1 SHAKESPEARE'S GLOBE THEATRE** "I hope to see London once ere I die," says Shakespeare's Davy in *Henry IV*. In time, he may see it from the beautiful recreation of The Bard's most famous theater. Excellent exhibits demonstrate how Shakespearean actors dressed and the secrets of stage effects, and tell of the painstaking process of rebuilding of the theater almost 400 years after the original burned down (p. 154). You might be able to catch a matinee performance if you time your visit right. Call in advance for tour and show times. Time: 1hr. for tour; 3hr. for performance.

**2 TATE MODERN** It's hard to imagine anything casting a shadow over the Globe Theatre, but the massive former Bankside Power Station does just that. One of the world's premier Modern art museums, the Tate promises a new spin on well-known favorites and works by emerging British artists. Be sure to catch one of the informative docent tours and don't forget to check out the rotating installation in the Turbine Room (p. 157). Time: 2hr.

**3 GABRIEL'S WHARF** Check out the cafes, bars, and boutiques of colorful **Gabriel's Wharf**. If you missed the top floor of the Tate Modern, go to the public viewing gallery on the 8th fl. of the **OXO Tower Wharf.** On your way to the London Eye, stop by the **South Bank Centre.** Established as a primary cultural center in 1951, it now exhibits a range of music from Philharmonic extravaganzas to low-key jazz. You may even catch one of the free lunchtime or afternoon events. Call in advance for dates and times. Time: 1½hr. for schmoozing and dinner.

**4 LONDON EYE** The London Eye has firmly established itself as one of London's top attractions, popular with locals and tourists alike. The Eye offers amazing 360° views from its glass pods; you may be able to see all of London lit up at sunset. Book in advance to minimize queue time (p. 154). Time: 1hr.

**TOWER BRIDGE.** Not to be mistaken for its plainer sibling, **London Bridge,** Tower Bridge is the one you know from all the London-based movies. Historians and technophiles will appreciate the **Tower Bridge Exhibition,** which combines scenic 140 ft. glass-enclosed walkways with videos of a bells-and-whistles history of the bridge. *(Entrance to the Tower Bridge Exhibition is through the west side (upriver) of the North Tower. ❷ Tower Hill or London Bridge. ☎ 7403 3761, for lifting schedule 7940 3984; www.tower-bridge.org.uk. Open daily Apr.-Sept. 10am-6:30pm, last entry 5:30pm; Oct.-Mar. 9:30am-6pm, last entry 5pm. Wheelchair-accessible. £6, students £4.50, children 5-16 £3.)*

# THE SOUTH BANK

■ **SHAKESPEARE'S GLOBE THEATRE.** This incarnation of the Globe is faithful to the original, thatch roof and all. The first Globe burned down in 1613 after a 14-year run as the Bard's preferred playhouse. Today's reconstruction had its first full season in 1997 and is now the cornerstone of the International Shakespeare Globe Centre. For info on performances, see p. 161. *(Bankside, close to Bankside pier. ❷ Southwark or London Bridge. ☎ 7902 1400; www.shakespeares-globe.org. Open daily Apr.-Sept. 9am-noon for exhibit and tours and 12:30-5pm for exhibit only; Oct.-Apr. 10am-5pm (exhibit and tours). Wheelchair-accessible. £9, students £7.50, children 5-15 £6.50, families of 5 £20.)*

**SOUTHWARK CATHEDRAL.** A site of worship since AD 606, the cathedral has undergone numerous transformations in the last 1400 years. Shakespeare's brother Edmund is buried here. In the rear of the nave, there are four smaller chapels; the northernmost Chapel of St. Andrew is specifically dedicated to those living with and dying from HIV/AIDS. Near the center, the **archaeological gallery** is actually a small excavation of a first-century Roman road. *(Montague Close. ❷ London Bridge. ☎ 7367 6700; www.south-wark.anglican.org/cathedral. Open M-F 8am-6pm, Sa-Su 9am-6pm. Wheelchair-accessible. Admission free, suggested donation £4. Groups are asked to book in advance; group rates available. Audio tours £5; students £4, children 5-15 £2.50. Camera permit £2; video permit £5.)*

**LONDON EYE.** Also known as the Millennium Wheel, the British Airways London Eye is the biggest observational wheel in the world at 135m. The ellipsoidal glass "pods" give uninterrupted views throughout each 30min. revolution. *(Jubilee Gardens, between County Hall and the Festival Hall. ❷ Waterloo. ☎ 087 990 8883; www.ba-london-eye.com. Open daily Oct.-May 10am-8pm, June-Sept. 10am-9pm. Wheelchair-accessible. Buy tickets at the corner of County Hall before joining the queue at the Eye. Booking in advance recommended, but check the weather. £15, students £11, children under 16 £7.25.)*

 **THE REAL DEAL.** While the London Eye does offer magnificent views (particularly at night), the queues are long, and it's expensive. For equally impressive sights in a quieter atmosphere, head to Hampstead Heath (p. 142).

# BLOOMSBURY AND MARYLEBONE

Marylebone's most famous resident (and address) never existed. 221b Baker St. was the fictional home of Sherlock Holmes, but 221 Baker St. is actually the headquarters of the Abbey National Bank. Bloomsbury's intellectual reputation was bolstered in the early 20th century when Gordon Sq. resounded with the philosophizing and womanizing of the **Bloomsbury Group,** a set of intellectuals including John Maynard Keynes, Bertrand Russell, Lytton Strachey, and Virginia Woolf.

■ **REGENT'S PARK.** This is perhaps London's most attractive, most popular park, with landscapes ranging from football-scarred fields to Italian-style formal plantings. It's all very different from John Nash's vision of wealthy villas hidden among exclusive gardens; fortunately for us common folk, Parliament intervened in 1811 and guaranteed the space would remain open to all. (⊖*Baker St., Regent's Park, Great Portland St., or Camden Town.* ☎ *7486 7905, police 7706 7272;* www.royalparks.org. Open daily 5am-dusk. Free.)

**BRITISH LIBRARY.** Criticized during its long construction by traditionalists for being too modern and by modernists for being too traditional, the completed British Library building is unequivocally impressive. The heart of the library is underground, with 12 million books on 200 mi. of shelving. The brick building aboveground is home to cavernous reading rooms and an engrossing ▧**exhibition gallery.** *(96 Euston Rd.* ⊖*Euston Sq. or King's Cross St. Pancras.* ☎ *7412 7332; www.bl.uk. Open M 9:30am-6pm, Tu 9:30am-8pm, W-F 9:30am-6pm, Sa 9:30am-5pm, Su 11am-5pm. Tours of public areas M, W, F 3pm; Sa 10:30am and 3pm. Tours including one of the reading rooms Su and bank holidays 11:30am and 3pm. Reservations recommended. Wheelchair-accessible. To use reading rooms, bring 2 forms of ID—1 with a signature and 1 with a home address. Free. Tours £8, students £6.50. Audio tours £3.50, students £2.50.)*

**OTHER BLOOMSBURY SIGHTS.** A co-founder and key advisor of **University College London**—the first in Britain to ignore race, creed, and politics in admissions and, later, the first to allow women to sit for degrees—social philosopher Jeremy Bentham still watches over his old haunts; his body has sat on display in the South Cloister since 1850, wax head and all. *(Main entrance on Gower St. South Cloister entrance through the courtyard.* ⊖*Euston.* ☎ *7679 2000; www.ucl.ac.uk. Quadrangle gates close at midnight; access to Jeremy Bentham ends at 6pm. Wheelchair-accessible. Free.)* Next to the British Library are the soaring Gothic spires of **St. Pancras Chambers.** Formerly housing the Midland Grand Hotel, today the gorgeous red brick building is a hollow shell being developed as apartments and a five-star hotel. *(Euston Rd. just west of the King's Cross St. Pancras Tube station.* ⊖*King's Cross St. Pancras.)*

# CLERKENWELL AND HOLBORN

Although mostly off-limits to tourists, Clerkenwell is full of lovely buildings. The **Clerkenwell Historic Trail** passes many of them. Maps are available at **3 Things Coffee Room.** (53 Clerkenwell Close. ⊖Farringdon. ☎ 7125 37438. Open daily 8am-8pm.)

▧**THE TEMPLE.** South of Fleet St., the land upon which this labyrinthine compound rests belonged to the crusading Knights Templar in the 13th century. The only remnant is the round **Temple Church.** *(☎ 7353 3470. Hours vary depending on the week's services and are posted outside the door of the church for the coming week. Organ recitals W 1:15-1:45pm; no services Aug.-Sept.)* According to Shakespeare's *Henry VI,* the red and white flowers that served as emblems in the Wars of the Roses were plucked in **Middle Temple Garden,** south of the hall. *(Open May-Sept. M-F noon-3pm.)*

**ROYAL COURTS OF JUSTICE.** Straddling the official division between the City of Westminster and the City of London, this neo-Gothic structure encloses courtrooms and the Great Hall (home to Europe's largest mosaic floor) amid elaborate passageways. All courtrooms are open to the public during trials. *(Where the Strand becomes Fleet St.; rear entrance on Carey St.* ⊖*Temple or Chancery Ln.* ☎ *7947 6000, tours 7947 7684. Open M-F 9am-4:30pm; cases are heard 10:30am-1pm and 2-4pm. Wheelchair-accessible. Be prepared to go through a security checkpoint with metal detector. Free. Tours £6.)*

# KENSINGTON AND EARL'S COURT

Nobody took much notice of Kensington before 1689, when the newly crowned William III and Mary II moved into Kensington Palace. In 1851, the Great Exhibition brought in enough money to finance museums and colleges. Now that the neighborhood is home to expensive stores like Harrods and Harvey Nichols, it's hard to imagine the days when the area was known for taverns and highwaymen.

■ **HYDE PARK AND KENSINGTON GARDENS.** Surrounded by London's wealthiest neighborhoods, Hyde Park has served as the model for city parks around the world, including Central Park in New York and Paris's Bois de Boulogne. **Kensington Gardens,** contiguous with Hyde Park and originally part of it, was created in the late 17th century when William and Mary set up house in Kensington Palace. *(Framed by Kensington Rd., Knightsbridge, Park Ln., and Bayswater Rd. ⊖ Queensway, Lancaster Gate, Marble Arch, Hyde Park Corner, or High St. Kensington. ☎ 7298 2100; www.royalparks.org.uk. Park open daily 6am-dusk. Admission free. "Liberty Drive" rides available Tu-F 10am-5pm for seniors and the disabled; call ☎ 077 6749 8096. A full program of music, performance, and children's activities takes place during the summer; see park notice boards for details.)* In the middle of the park is the **Serpentine,** officially known as the "Long Water West of the Serpentine Bridge." Dog-paddling tourists, rowers, and pedal boaters have made it London's busiest swimming hole. Nowhere near the water, the **Serpentine Gallery** holds contemporary art, and is open to the public from 10am-6pm daily. *(⊖ Hyde Park Corner. Boating: ☎ 7262 1330. Open daily Apr.-Sept. 10am-5pm, 6pm or later in good weather. £4 per person per 30min., £6 per hr.; children £1.50/2.50. Deposit may be required for large groups. Swimming at the Lido, south shore; ☎ 7706 3422. Open daily June-early Sept. 10am-5:30pm. Lockers and sun lounges available. £3.50, £2.80 after 4pm, students £2.50/1.60, children 80p/60p, families £8. Gallery open daily 10am-5pm. Free.)* At the northeast corner of the park, near **Marble Arch,** you can see free speech in action as proselytizers, politicos, and flat-out crazies dispense wisdom to bemused tourists at **Speaker's Corner** on Sundays, the only place in London where demonstrators can assemble without a permit.

**KENSINGTON PALACE.** Remodeled by Christopher Wren for William and Mary, parts of the palace are still a royal residence. Diana lived here until her death. The **Royal Ceremonial Dress Collection** features 19th-century court costumes along with the Queen's demure evening gowns and some of Diana's sexier numbers. *(Western edge of Kensington Gardens; enter through the park. ⊖ High St. Kensington, Notting Hill Gate, or Queensway. ☎ 7937 9561; www.royalresidences.com. Open daily 10am-6pm, last entry 5pm. Wheelchair-accessible. £12, students £10, children 5-15 £6, families of 5. No more than 2 people over 15. £33. Combo passes with Tower of London or Hampton Court available. MC/V.)*

## KNIGHTSBRIDGE AND BELGRAVIA

■ **APSLEY HOUSE AND WELLINGTON ARCH.** Apsley House, with the convenient address of "No. 1, London," was bought in 1817 by the Duke of Wellington, defeater of Napoleon. On display is his outstanding art collection, much of it given by grateful European royalty following the Battle of Waterloo. The majority of the paintings hang, fittingly, in the **Waterloo Gallery.** *(Hyde Park Corner. ⊖ Hyde Park Corner. ☎ 7499 5676; www.english-heritage.org.uk/london. Open Apr.-Oct. Tu-Su 10am-5pm; Nov.-Mar. Tu-Su 10am-4pm. Wheelchair-accessible. £5.30, students £4, children 5-18 £2.70. Joint ticket with Wellington Arch £6.90/5.20/3.50. Audio tour free. MC/V.)* Across from Apsley House, the **Wellington Arch** was dedicated to the Duke of Wellington in 1838. Later, to the horror of its architect, a huge statue of the Duke was placed on top. *(Hyde Park Corner. ⊖ Hyde Park Corner. ☎ 7930 2726; www.english-heritage.org.uk/london. Open W-Su Apr.-Oct. 10am-5pm, Nov.-Mar. 10am-4pm. Wheelchair-accessible. £3.20, students with ISIC £2.40, children 5-16 £1.60. Joint tickets with Apsley House available. MC/V.)*

## THE WEST END

■ **TRAFALGAR SQUARE.** John Nash first suggested laying out this square in 1820, but it took almost 50 years for London's largest roundabout to take on its current appearance. The square is named in commemoration of the defeat of Napoleon's navy at Trafalgar, considered England's greatest naval victory. It has traditionally been a site for public rallies and protests. Towering over the square is the 51m granite **Nelson's Column,** which used to be one of the world's tallest displays of pigeon droppings. Now, thanks to a deep-clean sponsored by the mayor, this monument to hero Lord Nelson sparkles once again. *(⊖Charing Cross.)*

**ST. MARTIN-IN-THE-FIELDS.** The 4th church to stand here, James Gibbs's 1726 creation is instantly recognizable: the rectangular portico building supporting a soaring steeple made it the model for countless Georgian churches in Ireland and America. Handel and Mozart both performed here, and the church still hosts frequent concerts. In order to support the cost of keeping the church open, a large cafe, book shop, and art gallery dwell in the Crypt. *(St. Martin's Ln., northeast corner of Trafalgar Sq.; crypt entrance on Duncannon St. ⊖Leicester Sq. or Charing Cross. ☎7766 1100; www.smitf.org. Call or visit website for hours and further information.)*

**SOHO.** Soho is one of London's most diverse areas. **Old Compton Street** is the center of London's GLBT culture. In the 1950s, immigrants from Hong Kong began moving to the blocks just north of Leicester Sq., near **Gerrard Street** and grittier **Lisle Street,** now **Chinatown.** Gaudy, brash, and world-famous, **Piccadilly Circus** is made up of four of the West End's major arteries (Piccadilly, Regent St., Shaftesbury Ave., and the Haymarket). In the middle of all the glitz stands Gilbert's famous **Statue of Eros.** *(⊖Piccadilly Circus.)* Lined with tour buses, overpriced clubs, fast-food restaurants, and generic cafes, **Leicester Square** is one spot Londoners go out of their way to avoid. *(⊖Piccadilly Circus or Leicester Sq.)* A calm in the storm, **Soho Square** is a scruffy, green patch popular with picnickers. *(⊖Tottenham Court Rd. Park open daily 10am-dusk.)*

# 🏛 MUSEUMS AND GALLERIES

Centuries spent as the capital of an empire, together with a decidedly English penchant for collecting, have given London a spectacular set of museums. Art lovers, history buffs, and amateur ethnologists won't know which way to turn. And there's even better news for museum lovers: since 2002, admission to all major collections is free indefinitely in celebration of the Queen's Golden Jubilee.

## MAJOR COLLECTIONS

**▩TATE MODERN.** Sir Giles Gilbert Scott's mammoth building, formerly the Bankside power station, houses the second half of the national collection (the earlier set is held in the National Gallery). The Tate Modern is probably the most popular museum in London, as well as one of the most famous modern art museums in the world. The public galleries on the 3rd and 5th floors are divided into four themes. The collection is enormous while gallery space is limited—works rotate frequently. If you are dying to see a particular piece, head to the museum's computer station on the 5th floor to browse the entire collection. The 7th floor has unblemished views of the Thames and north and south of London. *(Main entrance on Bankside, on the South Bank; 2nd entrance on Queen's Walk. ⊖Southwark or Blackfriars. From the Southwark tube, turn left up Union, then left on Great Suffolk, then left on Holland. ☎7887 8000; www.tate.org.uk. Open M-Th and Su 10am-6pm, F-Sa 10am-10pm. Free; special exhibits can be up to £10. Free tours meet on the gallery concourses: Level 3 11am and noon, Level 5 2 and 3pm. 5 types of audio tours include highlights, collection tour, architecture tour, children's tour, and the visually impaired tour; £2. Free talks M-F 1pm; meet at the concourse on the appropriate level. Wheelchair-accessible on Holland St.)*

**▩NATIONAL GALLERY.** The National Gallery was founded by an Act of Parliament in 1824, with 38 pictures displayed in a townhouse; over the years it has grown to hold an enormous collection of Western European paintings, ranging from the 1200s to the 1900s. Numerous additions have been made, the most recent (and controversial) being the massive modern Sainsbury Wing—Prince Charles described it as "a monstrous carbuncle on the face of a much-loved and elegant friend." The Sainsbury

Wing holds almost all of the museum's large exhibitions as well as restaurants and lecture halls. If pressed for time, head to **Art Start** in the Sainsbury Wing, where you can design and print out a personalized tour of the paintings you want to see. Themed audio guides and family routes also available from the info desk. (*Main Portico Entrance on north side of Trafalgar Sq. ⊖Charing Cross or Leicester Sq. ☎ 7747 2885; www.nationalgallery.org.uk. Wheelchair-accessible at Sainsbury Wing on Pall Mall East, Orange St., and Getty Entrance. Open M-Tu and Th-Su 10am-6pm, W 10am-9pm. Special exhibitions in the Sainsbury Wing occasionally open until 10pm. Free; some temporary exhibitions £5-10, seniors £4-8, students and children ages 12-18 £2-5. 1hr. tours start at Sainsbury Wing information desk. Tours M-F and Su 11:30am and 2:30pm, Sa 11:30am, 12:30, 2:30, 3:30pm. Audio tours free, suggested donation £4. AmEx/MC/V for ticketed events.*)

■**NATIONAL PORTRAIT GALLERY.** The Who's Who of Britain began in 1856 and has grown to be the place to see Britain's freshest new artwork as well as centuries-old portraiture. It was recently bolstered by the addition of the sleek Ondaatje Wing. New facilities include an IT Gallery, with computers to search for pictures and print out a personalized tour, and a third-floor restaurant offering an aerial view of London—although the inflated prices (meals around £15) will limit most visitors to coffee. To see the paintings in historical order, take the escalator in the Ondaatje Wing to the top floor. The Tudor Gallery is especially impressive, but the paintings done since 1990 are also worth a visit. (*St. Martin's Pl., at the start of Charing Cross Rd., Trafalgar Sq. ⊖Leicester Sq. or Charing Cross. ☎ 7312 2463; www.npg.org.uk. Wheelchair-accessible on Orange St. Open M-W and Sa-Su 10am-6pm, Th-F 10am-9pm. Free; some special exhibitions free, others up to £6. Audio tours £2. Lectures Tu 3pm free, but popular events require tickets, available from the information desk. Some evening talks Th 7pm free, others up to £3. Live music F 6:30pm free.*)

**BRITISH MUSEUM.** With 50,000 items from all corners of the globe, the magnificent collection is expansive and, although a bit difficult to navigate, definitely worth seeing. Most people don't even make it past the main floor, but they should—the galleries upstairs and downstairs are some of the best. Must-sees include the Rosetta stone, which was the key in deciphering ancient Egyptian hieroglyphs, and the ancient mummies. (*Great Russell St. ⊖Tottenham Court Rd., Russell Sq., or Holborn. ☎ 7323 8299; www.thebritishmuseum.ac.uk. Great Court open Su-W 9am-6pm, Th-Sa 9am-11pm (9pm in winter); galleries open daily 10am-5:30pm, selected galleries open Th-F 10am-8:30pm. Free 30-40min. tours daily starting at 11am from the Enlightenment Desk. "Highlights Tour" daily 10:30am, 1, 3pm; advanced booking recommended. Wheelchair-accessible. Free; £3 suggested donation. Temporary exhibitions around £5, students £3.50. "Highlights Tour" £8, students £5. Audio tours £3.50, family audio tours for 2 adults and up to 3 children £10. MC/V.*)

**VICTORIA AND ALBERT MUSEUM.** As the largest museum of decorative (and not-so-decorative) arts and design in the world, the V&A has over nine and a half miles of corridors open to the public, and is twice the size of the British Museum. It displays "the fine and applied arts of all countries, all styles, all periods." Unlike the British Museum, the V&A's documentation is consistently excellent. Interactive displays, hi-tech touch points, and engaging activities ensure that the exhibits won't become boring. Some of the most interesting areas of the museum are the Glass Gallery, the Japanese and Korean areas with suits of armor and kimonos, and the Indian Gallery. Themed itineraries (£5) available at the desk can help streamline your visit, and **Family Trail** cards suggest kid-friendly routes through the museum. (*Main entrance on Cromwell Rd., wheelchair-accessible entrance on Exhibition Rd. ⊖South Kensington. ☎ 7942 2000; www.vam.ac.uk. Open M-Th and Sa-Su 10am-5:45pm, F 10am-10pm. Wheelchair-accessible. Free tours meet at rear of main entrance; daily 10:30am, 11:30am, 1:30pm, 3:30pm, plus W 4:30pm. British gallery tours daily 12:30, 2:30pm. Talks and events meet at rear of main entrance. Free gallery talks Th 1pm and Su 3pm, 45-60min. Admission free; additional charge for some special exhibits.*)

**TATE BRITAIN.** Tate Britain is the foremost collection on British art from 1500 to the present, including pieces from foreign artists working in Britain and Brits working abroad. There are four Tate Galleries in England; this is the original Tate, opened in 1897 to house Sir Henry Tate's collection of "modern" British art and later expanded to include a gift from famed British painter J.M.W. Turner. Turner's donation of 282 oils and 19,000 watercolors can make the museum feel like one big tribute to the man. The annual and always controversial **Turner Prize** for contemporary visual art is still given here. Four contemporary British artists are nominated for the $40,000 prize; their short-listed works go on show from late October through late January. The Modern British Art Gallery, featuring works by Vanessa Bell and Francis Bacon, is also worth a look. *(Millbank, near Vauxhall Bridge, in Westminster. ⊖Pimlico. Information ☎ 7887 8008, M-F exhibition booking 7887 8888; www.tate.org.uk. Open daily 10am-5:50pm, last admission 5pm. Wheelchair-accessible via Clore Wing. Free; special exhibitions £7-11. Audio tours free. Free tours: "Art from 1500-1800" 11am, "1800-1900" M-F noon; "Turner" M-F 2pm; "1900-2005" M-F 3pm; "1500-2005" Sa-Su noon, 3pm. Regular events include "Painting of the Month Lectures" (15min.) M 1:15pm and Sa 2:30pm; occasional "Friday Lectures" F 1pm.)*

## OTHER MUSEUMS AND GALLERIES

▨ **Courtauld Institute,** Somerset House, Strand, Clerkenwell and Holborn (☎ 7420 9400; www.courtauld.ac.uk). ⊖Charing Cross. Small, outstanding collection. 14th- to 20th-century abstractions, focusing on Impressionism. Cézanne's *The Card Players,* Manet's *A Bar at the Follies Bergères,* and van Gogh's *Self Portrait with Bandaged Ear.* Open daily 10am-6pm. £6.50, students £6. Free M 10am-2pm.

▨ **Cabinet War Rooms,** Clive Steps, Westminster (☎ 7930 6961; www.iwm.org.uk). ⊖Westminster. Churchill and his strategists lived and worked underground here from 1939 to 1945. Highlights include the room with the top-secret transatlantic hotline—the official story was that it was Churchill's personal toilet. Open daily 9:30am-6pm. £10, students £8. MC/V.

**British Library Galleries,** 96 Euston Rd. (☎ 7412 7332; www.bl.uk). ⊖King's Cross. A stunning display of texts from the 2nd-century *Unknown Gospel* to The Beatles' hand-scrawled lyrics. Other highlights include a Gutenberg Bible, Joyce's handwritten *Finnegan's Wake,* and pages from da Vinci's notebooks. Open M and W-F 9:30am-6pm, Tu 9:30am-8pm, Sa 9:30am-5pm, Su 11am-5pm. Wheelchair-accessible. Free. Audio tours £3.50, students £2.50.

**Science Museum,** Exhibition Rd., Kensington (☎ 08708 704 868; www.sciencemuseum.org.uk.). ⊖South Kensington. A mix of state-of-the-art interactive displays and priceless historical artifacts, encompassing all forms of technology. Daily demonstrations and workshops in the basement galleries and IMAX theater. Open daily 10am-6pm. Free.

**Natural History Museum,** on Cromwell Rd., Kensington (☎ 7942 5000; www.nhm.ac.uk). ⊖South Kensington. The Natural History Museum is home to an array of minerals and stuffed animals. Highlights include a suspended blue whale and the colossal dinosaur gallery. Open M-Sa 10am-5:50pm, Su 11am-5:50pm. Free.

**Museum of London,** London Wall, The City of London (☎ 0870 444 3851; www.museumoflondon.org.uk). ⊖Barbican. Enter through the Barbican. The collection traces the history of London from its foundations to the present day, cleverly incorporating adjacent ruins. Open M-Sa 10am-5:50pm, Su noon-5:50pm. Free.

**Whitechapel Art Gallery,** Whitechapel High St. (☎ 7522 7888; www.whitechapel.org). ⊖Aldgate East. At the forefront of the East End's art scene, Whitechapel hosts excellent, often controversial, shows of contemporary art. Th nights bring music, poetry readings, and film screenings. Open Tu-W and F-Su 11am-6pm, Th 11am-9pm. Wheelchair-accessible. Gallery may close between installations; call ahead. Free.

# 🎵 ENTERTAINMENT

Although West End ticket prices are sky high and the quality of some shows questionable, the city that brought the world Shakespeare, the Sex Pistols, and Andrew Lloyd Webber still retains its originality and theatrical edge. London is a city of immense talent, full of up-and-comers, experimental writers, and undergrounders.

## CINEMA

**Leicester Square** holds premieres a day before movies hit the city's chains. The dominant cinema chain is **Odeon** (☎08712 241 999; www.odeon.co.uk). Tickets to West End cinemas cost £9-13; weekday matinees are cheaper. For less mainstream offerings, try the ▧**Electric Cinema,** 191 Portobello Rd., for the combination of baroque stage splendor and the buzzing effects of a big screen. (⊖Ladbroke Grove. ☎7908 9696; www.the-electric.co.uk. Front 3 rows M £5, Tu-Su £10; regular tickets M £7.50, Tu-Su £13; 2-seat sofa M £20, Tu-Su £30. Double bills Su 2pm £5-20. Wheelchair-accessible. Box office open M-Sa 9am-8:30pm, Su 10am-8:30pm. MC/V.) **Riverside Studios,** Crisp Rd., shows a wide range of excellent foreign and classic films. (⊖Hammersmith. ☎8237 1111; www.riversidestudios.co.uk. £6.50, students £5.50.) The **National Film Theatre (NFT)** screens a mind-boggling array of films—six movies hit the three screens every evening, starting around 6pm (South Bank, underneath Waterloo Bridge. ⊖Waterloo, Embankment, or Temple. ☎7928 3232; www.bfi.org.uk/nft. £7.50, students £5.70.)

## COMEDY

Summertime visitors should note that London empties of comedians in **August,** when most head to Edinburgh for the annual festivals (p. 221). **July** brings comedians trying out material; check *TimeOut* or a newspaper. ▧**Comedy Store,** 1a Oxendon St., is the UK's top comedy club and sower of the seeds that gave rise to *Ab Fab, Whose Line is it Anyway?,* and *Blackadder.* (⊖Piccadilly Circus. ☎7839 6642, tickets 08700 602 340; www.thecomedystore.biz. Tu "Cutting Edge" (current events-based satire), W and Su Comedy Store Players improv, Th-Sa standup. Shows daily 8pm, plus F-Sa midnight. 18+. Tu "Cutting Edge," W and Su Comedy Store Players improv, Th-Sa standup. Shows Su-Th 8pm, F-Sa 8pm and midnight. 18+. Tu-W, F midnight, Su £13, students £8. Th-F early show and Sa £15. Box office open Tu-Th and Su 6:30-9:30pm, F-Sa 6:30pm-1:30am. M hours vary. AmEx/MC/V.) North London's **Canal Cafe Theatre,** Delamere Terr., above the Bridge House pub, is one of the few venues to specialize in sketch, as opposed to stand-up. (⊖Warwick Ave. ☎7289 6054; www.canalcafetheatre.com Shows W-Sa 7:30, 9:30pm; £5, students £4. Newsrevue £9, students £7. £1 membership included in price.)

## MUSIC

### CLASSICAL

**Barbican Hall,** Silk St. (☎0845 1216827; www.barbican.org.uk), in City of London. ⊖Barbican or Moorgate. A multi-function venue, the hall is home to a library, theater, and art gallery. The resident **London Symphony Orchestra** plays here frequently; the hall also hosts concerts by international orchestras, jazz artists, and top musicians. Call ahead for tickets, especially for popular events. The online and phone box office sometimes have good last-minute options. Orchestra tickets £10-35. AmEx/MC/V.

**English National Opera,** London Coliseum, St. Martin's Ln. (☎7632 8300; www.eno.org), in Covent Garden. ⊖Charing Cross or Leicester Sq. All performances in English. Box office open M-Sa 10am-8pm. Discounted tickets available 3hr. before show; balcony (£8-10), upper circle (£10), or dress circle (£20). Call to verify daily availability; however, tickets are usually available. Wheelchair-accessible. AmEx/MC/V.

**Holland Park Theatre,** Holland Park (box office ☎08452 309 769; www.operahollandpark.com), in Kensington and Earl's Court. ⊖High St. Kensington or Holland Park. Outdoor performance space in the ruins of Holland House. Performances June-early Aug. Tu-Sa 7:30pm. Box office in the Old Stable Block; open late Mar.-early Aug. M-Sa 10am-6pm or 30min. after curtain. Tickets £21, £38 (£35 for students during select performances), and £43. Special allocation of tickets for wheelchair users. MC/V.

## JAZZ

▨ **Spitz,** 109 Commercial St. (☎7392 9032; www.spitz.co.uk), in East London. ⊖Liverpool St. Fresh range of music, from klezmer and jazz to rap. Profits to charity. Cover free to £15. Open M-W 10:30am-midnight, Th-Sa 10:30am-1am, Su 4-10:30pm. MC/V.

▨ **Jazz Café,** 5 Parkway (☎7344 0044; www.jazzcafe.co.uk), in North London. ⊖Camden Town. Shows can be pricey, but with a top roster of jazz, hip-hop, funk, and Latin performers (9pm, £15-30). DJs spin F-Sa after shows to 2am. Wheelchair-accessible. Cover F-Sa after show £11, with flyer £6. Open daily 7pm-2am. AmEx/MC/V.

**Ronnie Scott's,** 47 Frith St. (☎7439 0747; www.ronniescotts.co.uk), in **Soho.** ⊖Tottenham Court Rd. or Leicester Sq. London's oldest and most famous jazz club, having hosted everyone from Dizzy Gillespie to Jimi Hendrix. Table reservations essential for big-name acts, though there's limited unreserved standing room at the smoky bar; if it's sold out, try coming back at the end of the main act's first set, around midnight. Box office open M-F 11am-6pm, Sa noon-6pm. Club open M-Sa 6pm-3am, Su 6pm-midnight. Tickets generally £26. AmEx/MC/V.

## POP AND ROCK

▨ **The Water Rats,** 328 Grays Inn Rd., in Bloomsbury. (☎7837 7269; www.plummusic.com for the music gigs). ⊖King's Cross St. Pancras. Cafe by day, stomping ground for top new talent by night (from 8pm). Crowd varies with the music. Cover £5-6, with band flyer £4-5. Music M-Sa 8pm-late; headliner 9:45pm. AmEx/MC/V; min. £7.

**Carling Academy, Brixton,** 211 Stockwell Rd. (☎7771 3000, tickets 0870 771 2000; www.brixton-academy.co.uk), in South London. ⊖Brixton. Named *TimeOut's* "Live Venue of the Year" in 2004, and was *NME's* "Best Live Venue" in 2005. Order tickets online, by phone, or go to the Carling Academy, Islington box office. (16 Parkfield Street, Islington. Open M-Sa noon-4pm.) Tickets generally £5-30. AmEx/MC/V.

**London Astoria (LA1),** 157 Charing Cross Rd. (☎7434 9592, 24hr. ticket line 0870 060 3777; www.londonastoria.com), in Soho. ⊖Tottenham Ct. Rd. Formerly a pickle factory, strip club, and music hall, this varied venue now caters to rock fans and gay clubbers. The 2000-person venue is best known for its G-A-Y club nights M and Th-Sa (p. 166). Box office open M-F 10am-6pm, Sa 10am-5pm. MC/V.

# THEATER

London's West End is dominated by musicals and plays that run for years, if not decades. For a list of shows and discount tickets, head to the **tkts** booth in Leicester Sq. (⊖Leicester Sq. www.tkts.co.uk. Most shows £20-30; up to £2.50 booking fee per ticket. Open M-Sa 10am-7pm, Su noon-3pm. MC/V.)

## REPERTORY

▨ **Shakespeare's Globe Theatre,** 21 New Globe Walk (☎7401 9919; www.shakespearesglobe.org), in the South Bank. ⊖London Bridge. Stages plays by Shakespeare and his contemporaries. Choose from 3 covered tiers of wooden benches or brave the elements as a "groundling." Wheelchair-accessible. Performances mid-May to early Oct. Tu-Sa 7:30pm, Su 6:30pm; June-Sept. also often Tu-Sa 2pm, Su 1pm. Box office open M-Sa 10am-6pm, 8pm on performance days. Seats from £12, students from £10; yard (standing) £5.

**National Theatre,** South Bank (info ☎ 7452 3400, box office 7452 3000; www.nationaltheatre.org.uk), in the South Bank. ⊖Waterloo. Laurence Olivier founded the National Theatre in 1976, and it has been at the forefront of British theater ever since. Wheelchair-accessible. Box office open M-Sa 10am-7:45pm. Complicated pricing scheme; contact box office for details. Tickets typically start at £10. AmEx/MC/V.

### "OFF-WEST END"

▩ **The Almeida,** Almeida St. (☎ 7359 4404; www.almeida.co.uk), North London. ⊖Angel or Highbury and Islington. Top fringe theater in London. Wheelchair-accessible. Shows M-F 7:30pm, Sa 3 and 7:30pm. Tickets from £10. Student tickets available. MC/V.

**Donmar Warehouse,** 41 Earlham St. (☎ 08700 606 624; www.donmarwarehouse.com), in Covent Garden. ⊖Covent Garden. Artistic director Sam Mendes transformed this gritty space into one of the best theaters in England. Tickets £13-29; student standby 30min. before curtain, £12 (when available); £7.50 standing-room tickets available day of, once performance sells out. Box office open M-Sa 10am-7:30pm. AmEx/MC/V.

**Royal Academy of Dramatic Arts (RADA),** 62-64 Gower St. (☎ 7636 7076; www.rada.org), entrance on Malet St.; in Bloomsbury. ⊖Goodge St. Britain's most famous drama school has 3 on-site theaters. Wheelchair-accessible. £3-10, students £2-7.50. Regular Foyer events during the academic year including plays, music, and readings M-Th 7 or 7:30pm (some free, others up to £4). Box office open M-F 10am-6pm, on performance nights 10am-7:30pm. AmEx/MC/V.

# ⌐ SHOPPING

London has long been considered one of the fashion capitals of the world. Unfortunately, the city features as many underwhelming chain stores as it does one-of-a-kind boutiques. The truly budget-conscious should forget buying altogether and stick to window-shopping in **Knightsbridge** and on **Regent Street.** Vintage shopping in **Notting Hill** is also a viable alternative; steer clear of **Oxford Street,** where so-called vintage clothing was probably made in 2002 and marked up 200%.

## DEPARTMENT STORES

**Harrods,** 87-135 Brompton Rd. (☎ 7730 1234; www.harrods.com), in Knightsbridge and Belgravia. ⊖Knightsbridge. The only thing bigger than the store is the mark-up on the goods—no wonder only tourists and oil sheikhs actually shop here. Wheelchair-accessible. Open M-Sa 10am-8pm, Su noon-6pm. AmEx/MC/V.

**Harvey Nichols,** 109-125 Knightsbridge (☎ 7235 5000; www.harveynichols.com), in Knightsbridge. ⊖Knightsbridge. Rue St-Honoré and Fifth Ave. rolled into 5 fl. of fashion. Wheelchair-accessible. Open M-Sa 10am-8pm, Su noon-6pm. AmEx/MC/V.

**Selfridges,** 400 Oxford St. (☎ 0870 837 7377; www.selfridges.com), in the West End. ⊖Bond St. The total department store covers everything from traditional tweeds to space-age clubwear. Massive Jan. and July sales. Wheelchair-accessible. Open M-F 10am-8pm, Sa 9:30am-8pm, Su noon-6pm. AmEx/MC/V.

**Liberty,** 210-220 Regent St. (☎ 7734 1234; www.liberty.co.uk), in the West End. ⊖Oxford Circus. The focus on top-quality design and handcrafts makes it more like a giant boutique than a department store. Famous for custom fabric prints. Wheelchair-accessible. Open M-W and F-Sa 10am-7pm, Th 10am-8pm, Su noon-6pm. AmEx/MC/V.

**Fortnum & Mason,** 181 Piccadilly (☎ 7734 8040; www.fortnumandmason.co.uk), in the West End. ⊖Green Park or Piccadilly Circus. Gourmet department store provides quality foodstuffs fit for a queen. Wheelchair-accessible. Open M-Sa 10am-6:30pm, Su noon-6pm (food hall and patio restaurant only). AmEx/MC/V.

## STREET MARKETS

Better for people-watching than hardcore shopping, street markets may not bring you the big goods but are a much better alternative to a day on Oxford St. **Portobello Road Markets** includes foods, antiques, secondhand clothing, and jewelry. In order to see it all, come Friday or Saturday when everything is sure to be open. (❸Notting Hill Gate; also Westbourne Park and Ladroke Grove. Stalls set their own times. General hours Th 8am-1pm, F 9am-5pm, and Sa 6:30am-5pm.) ▧**Camden Passage Market** is more for looking than for buying—London's premier antique shops line these charming alleyways. (Islington High St., in North London. ❸Angel. Turn right from the Tube; it's the alleyway that starts behind "The Mall" antiques gallery on Upper St. Stalls open W 7:30am-6pm and Sa 9am-6pm; some stores open daily, but W is the best day to go.) Its overrun sibling **Camden Markets** (☎ 7969 1500) mostly includes cheap clubbing gear and tourist trinkets; avoid the canal areas. The best bet is to stick with the **Stables Market,** farthest north from the Tube station. (Make a sharp right out of the Tube station to reach Camden High St., where most of the markets start. All stores are accessible from ❸Camden Town. Many stores open daily 9:30am-6pm; Stables open F-Su.) **Brixton Market** has London's best selection of Afro-Caribbean fruits, vegetables, spices, and fish. It is unforgettably colorful, noisy, and fun. (Along Electric Ave., Pope's Rd., and Brixton Station Rd., and inside markets in Granville Arcade and Market Row; in South London. ❸Brixton. Open M-Tu and Th-Sa 7am-7pm, W 7am-3:30pm.) Formerly a wholesale vegetable market, ▧**Spitalfields** has become the best of the East End markets. On Sundays, the food shares space with rows of clothing by 25-30 independent local designers. (Commercial St., in East London. ❸Shoreditch (during rush hour), Liverpool St., or Aldgate East. Crafts market open M-F 11am-3:30pm, Su 10am-5pm. Antiques market open Th 9am-5pm. Organic market open F and Su 10am-5pm.) **Petticoat Lane Market** is Spitalfield's little sister market, just down the road. Located on Petticoat Ln., off of Commercial St., it sells everything from clothes to crafts, and is open M 8am-2pm and Tu-F 9am-4pm. Crowds can be overwhelming; head to the **Sunday (Up) Market** for similar items in a calmer environment. (☎ 7770 6100; www.bricklanemarket.com. Housed in a portion of the old Truman Brewery just off Hanbury St., in East London. ❸Shoreditch or Aldgate East. Open Su 10am-5pm.)

## ▧ NIGHTLIFE

First-time visitors may initially head directly to the **West End,** drawn by the flashy lights and pumping music of Leicester Sq. Be warned, though, that like much of the West End, nightlife here is not the definitive voice of Londoners who like to rock out; for a more authentic experience, head to the **East End** or **Brixton.** Soho's **Old Compton Street** is the center of GLBT nightlife. Before heading out for the evening, make sure to plan **Night Bus** travel. Listings open past 11pm include local Night Bus routes. Night Buses in the West End are ubiquitous—head to Trafalgar Sq., Oxford St., or Piccadilly Circus.

## PUBS

▧ **Fitzroy Tavern,** 16 Charlotte St. (☎ 7580 3714), in Bloomsbury. ❸Goodge St. A perfect pub for sunny days and sipping beer on the street outside, this place attracts artists, writers, locals, and students in droves. W 8:30pm comedy night (£5). Open M-Sa 11am-11pm, Su noon-10:30pm. MC/V.

**The Jerusalem Tavern,** 55 Britton St. (☎ 7490 4281; www.stpetersbrewery.co.uk), in Clerkenwell. ❸Farringdon. A broad selection of specialty ales (£2.40), including grapefruit, cinnamon, and apple, rewards the brave. Open M-F 11am-11pm. AmEx/MC/V.

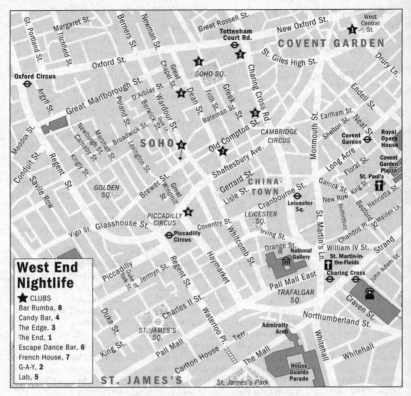

**West End Nightlife**

★ CLUBS
Bar Rumba, **8**
Candy Bar, **4**
The Edge, **3**
The End, **1**
Escape Dance Bar, **6**
French House, **7**
G-A-Y, **2**
Lab, **5**

**The Golden Eagle,** 59 Marylebone Ln. (☎ 7935 3228), in Marylebone. ⊖Bond St. The quintessence of "olde worlde"—both in clientele and in charm. Sidle up to this local-filled bar and enjoy authentic pub sing-alongs (Tu 8:30-10:30pm, Th-F 8:30-11pm) around the piano in the corner. Limited menu—sausage rolls (£1.50) and pasties (£2.20). Sandwiches (£3.50) available M-F noon-3pm. Open M-Sa 11am-11pm, Su noon-7pm. MC/V.

**French House,** 49 Dean St. (☎ 7437 2799). ⊖Leicester Sq. or Piccadilly Circus, in Soho. This small Soho landmark used to be frequented by personalities such as Maurice Chevalier, Charlie Chaplin, Salvador Dali, and Dylan Thomas before it became the unofficial gathering place of the French Resistance during World War II. Enjoy beer or an extensive wine selection (available by the glass) and hob-nob with some of the most interesting characters in Soho. Wheelchair-accessible. Open M-W noon-11pm, Th-Sa noon-midnight, Su noon-11pm. Restaurant on 1st fl. open daily noon-3pm and 5:30-11pm. AmEx/MC/V.

**Ye Olde Cheshire Cheese,** Wine Office Court. (☎ 7353 6170; www.yeoldecheshire-cheese.com), in Holborn. By 145 Fleet St., not to be confused with The Cheshire Cheese on the other side of Fleet St. Entrance in alleyway. ⊖Blackfriars or St. Paul's. Dating from 1667, the Cheese was once a haunt of Samuel Johnson, Charles Dickens, Mark Twain, and Theodore Roosevelt. Open M-Sa 11am-11pm, Su noon-6pm. Cellar Bar open M-Th noon-2:30pm and 5:30-11pm, F noon-2:30pm. Chop Room open M-F noon-9:30pm, Sa noon-2:30pm and 6-9:30pm, Su noon-5pm. Johnson Room open M-F noon-2:30pm and 7-9:30pm. AmEx/MC/V.

**Ye Olde Mitre Tavern,** 1 Ely Court (☎ 7405 4751), off #8 Hatton Garden, in Holborn. ⊖Chancery Ln. Look for the street lamp on Hatton Garden bearing a sign of a mitre; the pub is in the nearby alley. This classic pub fully merits the "ye olde"—it was built in 1546 by the Bishop of Ely. With oak beams and spun glass, the 2 rooms are perfect for nestling up to a bitter, and the winding courtyard outside is ideal in nice weather. Hot meals subject to availability (about £4), with bar snacks and superior sandwiches (£1.50) served until 9:30pm. Open M-F 11am-11pm. AmEx/MC/V.

# BARS

▨ **Lab,** 12 Old Compton St. (☎ 7437 7820; www.lab-townhouse.com), in the West End. ⊖Leicester Sq. or Tottenham Court Rd. With restrooms for "bitches" and "bastards," the only thing this cocktail bar takes seriously is its stellar drink menu. DJs spin house and funk from 8pm nightly. Open M-Sa 4pm-midnight, Su 4pm-10:30pm. AmEx/MC/V.

**Bar Kick,** 127 Shoreditch High St. (☎ 7739 8700), in East London. ⊖Old St. The dozens of flags on the ceiling add international flavor to the European-style food and music. Wheelchair-accessible. Open M-W noon-11pm, Th-Sa noon-midnight, Su noon-7pm. Kitchen open M-F noon-3:30pm and 6-10pm, Sa-Su all day. AmEx/MC/V.

**Vibe Bar,** 91-95 Brick Ln. (☎ 7247 3479; www.vibe-bar.co.uk), in East London. ⊖Aldgate East or Liverpool St. Night Bus: hub at Liverpool St. Station. Dance to hip-hop, soul, acoustic, and jazz. Pint £3. DJs spin M-Sa from 7pm, Su from 6pm. Cover F-Sa after 8pm £3.50. Open Su-Th 11am-11:30pm, F-Sa 11am-1am. Cash only; ATM in bar.

**Filthy MacNasty's Whiskey Café,** 68 Amwell St. (☎ 7837 6067; www.filthymacnastys.com), in North London. ⊖Angel or King's Cross. Night Bus #N10, 63, 73, 91, 390. This laid-back semi-Irish pub is known for having hosted jam sessions by Shane MacGowan, et. al. Open M-Sa noon-11pm, Su noon-10:30pm. MC/V.

# CLUBS

▨ **Ministry of Sound,** 103 Gaunt St. (☎ 7378 6528; www.ministryofsound.co.uk), in the South Bank. ⊖Elephant and Castle; take the exit for South Bank University. Night Bus #N35, 133, 343. Mecca for serious clubbers worldwide. Dress code casual, but famously unsmiling door staff make it prudent to err on the side of smartness. Cover F £12, Sa £15.

**The End,** 16a West Central St. (☎ 7419 9199; www.endclub.com), in the West End. ⊖Tottenham Ct. Rd. Cutting edge clubbers' Eden; theme nights online. Wheelchair-accessible. Cover M £6; W £5-6; Th £6-8; F £10-13; Sa £16. Open M 10pm-3am, W 10:30pm-3am, Th-F 10pm-4am, Sa 6pm-7am. AmEx/MC/V.

**Fabric,** 77a Charterhouse St. (☎ 7336 8898; www.fabriclondon.com), in Clerkenwell. ⊖Farringdon. Night Bus #242. This club, deep underground, has 5 bars and 3 rooms. F "Fabriclive"; Su "DTPM Polysexual Night" (☎ 7749 1199; www.blue-cube.net). Wheelchair-accessible. Get there before 11pm on Sa to avoid lines. Cover F £12; Sa after 11pm £15. Open F 9:30pm-5am, Sa 10pm-7am, Su 10pm-5am. AmEx/MC/V.

**Notting Hill Arts Club,** 21 Notting Hill Gate (☎ 7598 5226; www.nottinghillartsclub.com), in Notting Hill. ⊖Notting Hill Gate. Night Bus #N94, 148, 207, 390. Unlabeled and unmarked (but right next to the Tex-Mex Tapas Bar). Not touristy and very chill. Later in the night 1-in, 1-out policy. Cover Th-Sa after 8pm £5-7. Open M-F 6pm-2am, Sa 4pm-2am, Su 4pm-1am. MC/V.

**Bar Rumba,** 36 Shaftesbury Ave. (☎ 7287 6933; www.barrumba.co.uk), in the West End. ⊖Piccadilly Circus. The Rumba crowd makes good use of the industrial-strength interior for dancing, mostly in R&B. Cover nightly £5-10; W women free before midnight, students £3 all night. Open M and W 9pm-3am, Tu 6pm-3am, Th 8pm-3:30am, F 6pm-3:30am, Sa 9pm-4am, Su 8:30pm-2:30am. MC/V.

GREAT BRITAIN

## GLBT NIGHTLIFE

Many venues have Gay and Lesbian nights on a rotating basis. Check **TimeOut** and look for flyers/magazines floating around Soho: **The Pink Paper** (free from newsagents) and **Boyz** (www.boyz.co.uk; free at gay bars and clubs.)

▨ **The Edge,** 11 Soho Sq. (☎ 7439 1313; www.edge.uk.com), in the West End. ⊖Oxford Circus or Tottenham Court Rd. A chill, friendly gay and lesbian drinking spot. Piano bar Tu-Sa, DJs and dancing Th-Sa. Cover Th-Sa after 10pm £2. Open M-Sa noon-1am, Su noon-11pm. MC/V.

▨ **The Black Cap,** 171 Camden High St. (☎ 7428 2721; www.theblackcap.com), in North London. ⊖Camden Town. North London's most popular gay bar and cabaret is always buzzing. Mixed crowd. Cover for downstairs M-Th and Su before 11pm £2, 11pm-close £3; F-Sa before 11pm £3, 11pm-close £4. Open M-Th noon-2am, F-Sa noon-3am, Su noon-1am. Kitchen open noon-10pm.

**Escape Dance Bar,** 10A Brewer St. (☎ 7731 2626; www.kudosgroup.com), in the West End. ⊖Leicester Sq. Dance to the latest pop hits in an enjoyably cramped space. A video DJ plays tunes with big, bright screens from 8pm to 3am daily. Open Tu-Sa 4pm-3am. AmEx/MC/V.

**Candy Bar,** 4 Carlisle St. (☎ 7494 4041; www.thecandybar.co.uk), in the West End. ⊖Tottenham Court Rd. or Oxford Circus. This drinking spot is the place for lesbian entertainment. Stripteases, DJs, and popular dance nights. W karaoke. Cover F-Sa after 9pm £5. Open M-Th 5-10:30pm, F-Sa 3pm-2am, Su 3-10:30pm. MC/V.

**G-A-Y,** 157 Charing Cross Rd. (☎ 7434 9592; www.g-a-y.co.uk), in the West End. ⊖Tottenham Court Rd. London's biggest gay and lesbian night. Commercial-dance DJs and live pop shows rock Sa G-A-Y night. Wheelchair-accessible. Cover M and Th with flyer or ad (available at most gay bars) £1, students 50p; F with flyer or ad £2, after midnight £3; Sa depending on performer £8-15. Open M and Th-F 11pm-4am, Sa 10:30pm-5am. Cash only.

### ▓ LET'S GO TO LONDON: LUTON AND STANSTED

**London Luton Airport** (**LTN;** ☎ 1582 405 100; www.london-luton.co.uk), 50km north of London, is a budget airline hub for **easyJet, Ryanair,** and **Wizz Air.** First Capital Connect (☎ 0845 026 4700; www.firstcapitalconnect.co.uk) and Midland Mainline (☎ 0870 010 1296; www.midlandmainline.com) run **trains** between London King's Cross and Luton (30min.-1hr., 3-4 per hr., £10-20). Easybus (www.easybus.co.uk) and National Express (☎ 08705 808 080; www.nationalexpress.com) operate **buses** between London Victoria and Luton (1¼hr., 2-3 per hr., from £2).

**London Stansted Airport** (**STN;** ☎ 0870 000 0303; www.stanstedairport.com), 48km northeast of London, is the main hub for **Ryanair** and also serves **easyJet** and **Wizz Air.** The Stansted Express (☎ 0845 600 7245; www.website.com) train shuttles between London Liverpool and Stansted (45min., 4 per hr., £15-24). Easybus runs buses between London Baker St. and Stansted and National Express runs from London Victoria (1hr., 3-6 per hr., from £2).

## ▐ DAYTRIPS FROM LONDON

▨ **ROYAL BOTANICAL GARDENS, KEW.** In the summer of 2003, UNESCO announced the Royal Botanical Gardens as a World Heritage site. The 250-year-old Royal Botanical Gardens, about an hour's Tube ride outside of central London, extend with a green English placidity in a 300-acre swath along the Thames. The three conservatories are at the center of the collection. The steamy Victorian Palm House boasts *Encephalartos Altensteinii*, "The Oldest Pot Plant In The World"; while the Princess of Wales Conservatory houses 10 different climate zones, from rainforest to desert, including two devoted entirely to orchids. Low-season visitors will not be disappointed—the Woodland Glade is renowned for displays of autumn color. Close to the Thames in the northern part of the gardens, newly renovated Kew Palace is a modest red-brick affair used by royalty on Garden visits, and which is now open to the public for the first time in 200 years. On the hill behind and to the right of the palace, 17th-century medicinal plants flourish in the stunning Queen's Garden. *(Kew, on the south bank of the Thames. Main entrance and Visitors Center are at Victoria Gate, nearest the Tube. Go up the white stairs that go above the station tracks, and walk straight down the road. ⊖ Kew Gardens (zone 3). ☎ 8332 5000; www.kew.org. Open Apr.-Aug. M-F 9:30am-6:30pm, Sa-Su 9:30am-7:30pm; Sept.- Oct. daily 9:30am-6pm; Nov.-Jan. daily 9:30am-4:15pm. Last admission 30min. before close. Glasshouses close Apr.-Oct. 5:30pm; Nov.-Feb. 3:45pm. £12.25, students £10.25, children under 17 free; 45min. before close £10.25. Free 1hr. walking tours daily 11am and 2pm start at Victoria Gate Visitors Center. "Explorer" hop-on, hop-off shuttle makes 40min. rounds of the gardens; 1st shuttle daily 11am, last 4pm; £3.50, children under 17 £1. Free 1hr. "Discovery Bus" tours for mobility-impaired daily 11am and 2pm; booking required; free.)*

**HAMPTON COURT PALACE.** Although a monarch hasn't lived here for 250 years, Hampton Court still exudes regal charm. Cardinal Wolsey built the first palace here in 1514, showing the young Henry VIII how to act the part of a powerful ruler. Henry learned the lesson all too well, confiscating Hampton in 1528 and embarking on a massive building program. In 1689, William and Mary employed Christopher Wren to bring the Court up to date, but less than 50 years later George II abandoned it for good. The **palace** is divided into six 20min.-1hr. tour routes, all starting at **Clock Court,** where you can pick up a program of the day's events and an audio guide. In ◾**Henry VIII's State Apartments,** only the massive Great Hall and exquisite Chapel Royal hint at past magnificence. A costumed guide leads the Henry VIII tour. Below, the **Tudor Kitchens** offer insight into how Henry ate himself to a 54 in. waist. Predating Henry's additions, the 16th-century **Wolsey Rooms** are complemented by Renaissance masterpieces. Wren's **King's Apartments** were restored to their original appearance after a 1986 fire. The **Queen's Apartments** weren't completed until 1734, postponed by Mary II's death. The **Georgian Rooms** were created by William Kent for George II's family. No less impressive are the **gardens,** with Mantegna's *Triumphs of Caesar* paintings secreted away in the Lower Orangery. North of the palace, the **Wilderness,** a pseudo-natural area earmarked for picnickers, holds the ever-popular **maze,** planted in 1714. Its small size belies a devilish design. *(45min. from Waterloo by train; round-trip £5.60. 3-4hr. by boat; daily 10:30, 11am, noon, 2pm; £14, round-trip £20; students £9/13; children £6.75/9.75. Westminster Passenger Cruises ☎ 7930 4721; www.thamesriverboats.co.uk. Palace ☎ 08707 527 777; www.hamptoncourtpalace.org.uk. Open daily late Mar. to late Oct. 10am-6pm; late Oct. to late Mar. 10am-4:30pm. Last admission 45min. before close. Palace and gardens £13, students £11, children 5-15 free. Admission free for worshippers at Chapel Royal; services Su 11am and 3:30pm. Audio and guided tours included.)*

# SOUTHERN ENGLAND

History and myth shroud Southern England. Cornwall, the alleged birthplace of King Arthur, was the last stronghold of the Celts in England, but traces of even older Neolithic communities linger in the stone circles their builders left behind. In WWII, German bombings uncovered long-buried evidence of an invasion by Caesar, whose Romans dotted the countryside with settlements. William the Conqueror left his mark in the form of awe-inspiring castles and cathedrals. Apart from this pomp and circumstance is another, less palpable, presence: the voices of British literati such as Jane Austen, Geoffrey Chaucer, Charles Dickens, and E. M. Forster still seem to echo above the sprawling pastures and seaside cliffs.

## CANTERBURY ☎ 01227

Archbishop Thomas Becket met his demise at ◾**Canterbury Cathedral** in 1170 after an irate Henry II asked, "Will no one rid me of this troublesome priest?" Later, in his famed *Canterbury Tales*, Chaucer caricatured the pilgrims who traveled the road from London to England's most famous execution site. (☎762 862; www.canterbury-cathedral.org. Cathedral open Easter-Sept. M-Sa 9am-6:30pm, Su 12:30-2:30pm and 4:30-5:30pm; Oct.-Easter M-Sa 9am-5pm, Su 12:30-2:30pm and 4:30-5:30pm. 3 1¼hr. tours per day M-Sa; check nave or welcome center for times. Evensong M-F 5:30pm, Sa-Su 3:15pm. £6.50, students £5. Tours £4/3. 40min. audio tour £3.50/2.50.) The skeletons of arches and crumbling walls are all that remain of **Saint Augustine's Abbey,** outside the city wall near the cathedral. St. Augustine is buried under a humble pile of rocks. (☎767 345. Open Apr.-Sept. daily 10am-6pm; Oct.-Mar. W-Su 10am-4pm. £4, students £3.) England's first Franciscan friary, **Greyfriars,** 6A Stour St., has quiet riverside gardens. (☎462 395. Open Easter-Sept. M-Sa 2-4pm. Free.) **The Canterbury Tales,** on St. Margaret's St., recreates Chaucer's medieval England in scenes complete with ambient lighting and wax characters. The smell isn't the guy next you—the facility pipes in the "authentic" stench of sweat, hay, and grime to help bring you back in time. Audio tours take you through the scenes in a 45min. abbreviation of Chaucer's bawdy masterpiece. (☎479 227; www.canterburytales.org.uk. Open daily July-Aug. 9:30am-5pm; Mar.-June and Sept.-Oct. 10am-5pm; Nov.-Feb. 10am-4:30pm. £7.30, students £6.30.)

**B&Bs** are around **High Street** and on **New Dover Road.** Ten minutes from the city center, **Kipps Independent Hostel ❶,** 40 Nunnery Fields, is a century-old townhouse with modern amenities. (☎786 121. Kitchen available. Laundry £3. Internet £2 per hr. If there are no vacancies, ask to set up a tent in the garden. Key deposit £10. Dorms £14; singles £19; doubles £33. MC/V.) Share sizzling steak fajitas (£22) and grab your own margarita (£6) at **Cafe des Amis du Mexique ❷,** St. Dunstan's St., home to inspired Mexican dishes in a funky cantina setting. (☎464 390. Entrees £5-10. Open M-Sa noon-10:30pm, Su noon-9:30pm. AmEx/MC/V.) The **Safeway** supermarket, St. George's Center, St. George's Pl., is a 4min. walk from the town center. (☎769 335. Open M-F 8am-9pm, Sa 8am-8pm, Su 11am-5pm.) **Coffee & Corks,** 13 Palace St., is a cafe-bar with a cool, bohemian feel. (☎457 707. Tea £1.50. Mixed drinks £4. Wine £10 per bottle. Free Wi-Fi. Open daily noon-midnight. MC/V.) **Trains** run from East Station, off Castle St., to London Victoria (1¾hr., 2 per hr., £20) and Cambridge (3hr., 2 per hr., £33). Trains from West Station, Station Rd. W, off St. Dunstan's St., go to Central London (1½hr., 1 per hr., £17) and Brighton (3hr., 3 per hr., £16). National Express **buses** (☎08705 808 080) run from St. George's Ln. to London (2hr., 2 per hr., £14). The **TIC,** 12-13 Sun St., in the Buttermarket, books rooms for a £2.50 fee plus 10% deposit. (☎378 100; www.visitcanterbury.co.uk. Open Easter-Christmas M-Sa 9:30am-5pm, Su 10am-4pm; Christmas-Easter M-Sa 10am-4pm.) **Postal Code:** CT1 2BA.

# BRIGHTON ☎01273

Brighton (pop. 250,000) has been one of Britain's largest seaside resorts for the last three centuries. King George IV came to the city in 1783 and enjoyed the anything-goes atmosphere so much that he made it his headquarters for debauchery (the Royal Pavilion). The rumpus continues, and today, Brighton is still the unrivaled home of the "dirty weekend," sparkling with a tawdry luster all its own. The extravagant **Royal Pavilion,** on Pavilion Parade, next to Old Steine, is a touch of the Far East in the heart of England with Taj Mahal-style architecture. (☎292 880. Open daily Apr.-Sept. 9:30am-5:45pm; Oct.-Mar. 10am-5:15pm. Tours daily 11:30am and 2:30pm; £1.60. Pavilion £6, students £4.30.) Around the corner on Church St. stands the **Brighton Museum and Art Gallery,** showcasing Art Nouveau and Art Deco pieces, and an exhibit that thoroughly explains the phrase "dirty weekend." (☎292 882. Open Tu 10am-7pm, W-Sa 10am-5pm, Su 2-5pm. Free.) Before heading to the **beach** and piers, visit the novelty shops and cafes of the **North Laines,** off Trafalgar St.

West of West Pier along King's Rd. Arches, ▨**Baggies Backpackers ❶,** 33 Oriental Pl., is a social hostel where spontaneous parties on "Baggies Beach" are common. Book ahead, especially on weekends. (☎733 740. Co-ed bathrooms. Dorms £13; 1

double £35. Cash only.) **Food for Friends ❷,** 17a-18a Prince Albert St., serves inventive vegetarian dishes and a decadent afternoon tea (£5.50). Entrees (£8-11) draw on Indian and East Asian cuisines. (☎202 310. Open M-Th and Su noon-10pm, F-Sa noon-10:30pm. AmEx/MC/V.) A stand-out among the many Indian restaurants in Brighton, **Deli India ❷,** 81 Trafalgar St., offers mouth-watering vegetarian and meat *thalli* (£6.50-7.50) along with a teashop and delicatessen. (☎699 985. Open M-F 10am-7:30pm, Sa 10am-6pm, Su noon-3pm. MC/V.) Buy groceries at **Somerfield,** 6 St. James's St. (☎570 363. Open M-Sa 8am-10pm, Su 11am-5pm.)

■**Fortune of War,** 157 King's Rd. Arches, is a beachfront bar shaped like a 19th-century ship hull. (☎205 065. Pints £3.10. Open daily noon until they feel like closing.) **The Fish Bowl,** 73 East St., is a student hot spot that's cool without trying to be. (☎777 505. Open M-Sa 11am-11pm, Su noon-10:30pm.) Most **clubs** are open Monday through Saturday 9pm-2am; after they close, the party moves to the waterfront. **Audio,** 10 Marine Parade, is the city's nightlife fixture, with two floors of debauchery and a mix of music. (☎606 906; www.audiobrighton.com. Cover M-Th £3-4, F £5, Sa £7. Open M-Sa 10pm-2am.) **The Beach,** 171-181 King's Rd. Arches, is always packed with weekenders dancing to an eclectic mix of hits. (☎722 272. Cover £10, students £8. Open M and W-Th 10pm-2am, F-Sa 10pm-3am.) **Charles St.,** 8-9 Marine Parade, is a gay-friendly club with live DJs spinning dance tracks. The anything-goes atmosphere is conducive to anything-goes dancing. (☎624 091. Cover M £1.50, Th £3, Sa £5-8. Open M 10:30pm-2am, Th-Sa 10:30pm-3am.) **Trains** (☎08457 484 950) leave from the northern end of Queen's Rd. for London Victoria (1hr., 2 per hr., £19) and Portsmouth (1½hr., 2 per hr., £14). National Express **buses** (☎08705 808 080) leave from Preston Park for London Victoria (2-2½hr., 1 per hr., £9.30). The **TIC** is at Royal Pavilion Shop, 4-5 Pavilion Buildings. (☎09067 112 255; www.visitbrighton.com. Open June-Sept. M-F 9am-5pm, Sa 10am-5pm, Su 10am-4pm; Oct.-May M-F 9:30am-5pm, Sa 10am-5pm.) **Postal Code:** BN1 1BA.

# PORTSMOUTH
☎02392

Sailing enthusiasts and history buffs will wet themselves at this waterfront destination, a famous naval port since Henry V set sail for France in 1415. Portsmouth's Victorian seaside setting and its 900-year history of prostitutes, drunkards, and cursing sailors give the city a compelling, gritty history. Portsmouth sprawls along the coast for miles—**Portsmouth, Old Portsmouth** (near the Portsmouth and Southsea train station and Commercial Rd.), and the resort community of **Southsea** (stretching to the east) can seem like entirely different cities. Major sights cluster at Old Portsmouth, **The Hard,** and Southsea's **Esplanade.** Armchair admirals will want to plunge head-first into the ■**Portsmouth Historic Dockyard,** in the Naval Yard, which houses some of Britain's most storied ships: Henry VIII's *Mary Rose*, Nelson's HMS *Victory*, and the HMS *Warrior*. The entrance is next to the TIC on The Hard. (Ships open daily Apr.-Oct. 10am-5:30pm, last entry 4:30pm; Nov.-Mar. 10am-5pm, last entry 4pm. Each ship £10. Combo ticket £16.) The ■**D-Day Museum,** on Clarence Esplanade in Southsea, has life-size dioramas of the 1944 invasion. (☎9282 7261. Open daily Apr.-Sept. 10am-5:30pm; Oct.-Mar. 10am-5pm. £6, students £3.60.)

Moderately priced **B&Bs** (around £25) clutter Southsea, 2.5km southeast of The Hard along the coast. Take any Southsea bus from Commercial Rd. and get off at the Strand to reach the **Portsmouth and Southsea Backpackers Lodge ❶,** 4 Florence Rd. This hostel attracts a pan-European crowd with accommodating owners, lounge, satellite TV, and grocery counter. (☎832 495. Kitchen available. Laundry £2. Internet £2 per hr. Dorms £13; doubles £30, with bath £34. Cash only.) **Britannia Guest House ❸,** 48 Granada Rd., has spotless rooms decorated with the owner's art. (☎814 234. Breakfast included. Singles £25; doubles £45-50. MC/V.) **Agora Cafe-Bar and Restaurant ❷,** 9 Clarendon Rd., serves English breakfasts (£3-5), light fare by day, and Turkish and Greek cuisine (£7-10) by night. (☎822 617. Open daily 9am-4pm and 5:30-11:30pm. Student discount. MC/V; £10 min.) Pick up groceries at **Tesco,** 56-61 Elm Grove. (☎08456 269

090. Open daily 6am-midnight.) Pubs near The Hard provide galley fare and grog, while those on **Albert Road** cater to students. **One Eyed Dog,** at the corner of Elm Grove and Victoria Rd. S, is a trendy pub popular with students. (☎827 188. Mixed drinks £2-3. M night cheap beer. Open M-Th 4-11pm, F-Sa 1-11pm, Su 5-10:30pm. Cash only.) **Trains** (☎08457 484 950) run from Commercial Rd., in the city center, to London Waterloo (1¾hr., 4 per hr., £23) and Salisbury (1hr., 1 per hr., £13). National Express **buses** (☎08705 808 080) run from the Hard Interchange, The Hard, next to Harbour Station, to London Victoria (2½hr., 1 per hr., £21) and Salisbury (1½hr., 1 per day, £8.30). The **TIC,** which books rooms for a £2 fee plus 10% deposit, is on The Hard, near the historic ships. (☎826 722; www.visitportsmouth.co.uk. Open daily Apr.-Sept. 9:30am-5:45pm; Oct.-Mar. 9:30am-5:15pm.) **Postal Code:** PO1 1AA.

## WINCHESTER                                              ☎01962

Once the center of William the Conqueror's kingdom, Winchester's (pop. 32,000) residents revel in the town's history. At 169m, **Winchester Cathedral,** 5 The Close, is Europe's longest medieval cathedral. Jane Austen is entombed beneath a stone slab in the northern aisle, while the 12th-century Winchester Bible resides in the library. (☎857 200; www.winchester-cathedral.org.uk. Open M-Sa 8:30am-6pm, Su 8:30am-5:30pm; east end closes 5pm. Free 1hr. tours on the hr. 10am-3pm. £4, students £2.50.) William the Conqueror built **Winchester Castle,** at the end of High St. atop Castle Hill, in 1067, but unyielding forces (time and Cromwell) have all but destroyed the fortress. The remaining Great Hall contains an imitation—or legendary, according to locals—Arthurian Round Table. Henry VIII tried to pass the table off as authentic to Holy Roman Emperor Charles V, but the repainted "Arthur," resembling Henry himself, fooled no one. (Open daily Mar.-Oct. 10am-5pm; Nov.-Feb. 10am-4pm. Free.) The **Buttercross,** 12 High St., a statue portraying King Alfred and other greats, gets its name from the shadow it cast over the 15th-century market that kept the butter cool. It's a good starting point for several walking routes detailed in *The Winchester Walk,* available at the TIC. From 1809 to 1817, Jane Austen lived in the village of **Chawton,** about 25km north of Winchester. In a **cottage** here, she perfected *Emma* and *Pride and Prejudice,* among others. Take Hampshire **bus** X64 (40min., M-Sa 11 per day, round-trip £6), or London and Country bus #65 (Su) from Winchester; ask to be let off at the Chawton roundabout, and follow the brown signs. (☎01420 832 62. Cottage open June-Sept. daily 10am-5pm; Mar.-May and Oct.-Dec. daily 11am-4:30pm; Jan.-Feb. Sa-Su 11am-4:30pm. £4.50, students £3.50.)

The rooms at **Mrs. P. Patton ❹,** 12 Christchurch Rd., down the road from the train station, are in a Victorian mansion. (☎854 272. Singles £35-40; doubles £45-50. Cash only.) Housed in a 16th-century rectory, **The Eclipse Inn ❶,** The Square, is one of Winchester's smallest, most popular pubs. Grub (£3-7) attracts regulars and supposedly a ghost or two. (☎865 676. Open M-Sa 11am-11pm, Su noon-11pm. Kitchen open daily noon-3pm. MC/V.) There is an **open-air market** (open W-Sa 8am-6pm) and a **Sainsbury's** supermarket on Middle Brook St., off High St. (☎861 792. Open M-Sa 7am-8pm, Su 11am-5pm.) **Trains** (☎08547 484 950) go from Station Hill to: Brighton (1½hr., 1 per hr., £20); London Waterloo (1hr., 3-4 per hr., £22); Portsmouth (1hr., 1 per hr., £9); Salisbury (1hr., 2 per hr., £12). National Express **buses** (☎08705 808 080) run from the station on Broadway to London via Heathrow (1½hr., 7 per day, £14) and Oxford (2½hr., 2 per day, £10). Wilts and Dorset (☎001722 336 855) buses go to Salisbury (#68; 1¼hr., 6 per day, £5). The **TIC,** The Guildhall, Broadway, is across from the bus station. (☎840 500; www.visitwinchester.co.uk. Open May-Sept. M-Sa 9:30am-5pm, Su 11am-3:30pm; Oct.-Apr. M-Sa 10am-4:30pm.) **Postal Code:** SO23 8WA.

## SALISBURY                                              ☎01722

Salisbury (pop. 37,000) centers on 13th-century ◙**Salisbury Cathedral.** Its spire was the tallest in medieval England, and the bases of its marble pillars bend inward under 6400 tons of stone. If you hear a cracking sound, you should probably run as far away as possible. (☎555 120. Open June-Aug. M-Sa 7:15am-8pm, Su 7:15am-6:15pm; Sept.-May daily 7:15am-6:15pm. Call ahead. Suggested donation £4, students £3.50. Cathedral tours free. Roof and tower tours £4.50, students £3.50.) A well-preserved copy of the **Magna Carta** rests in the nearby **Chapter House.** (Open June-Aug. M-Sa 9:30am-5:30pm, Su noon-5:30pm; Sept.-May daily 9:30am-5:30pm. Free.) The **YHA Salisbury (HI) ❷**, Milford Hill House, on Milford Hill, offers basic, comfortable dorms with a TV lounge and kitchen. (☎327 572. Breakfast included. Laundry £3. Internet £4.20 per hr. Reserve ahead. Dorms £18, under 18 £14. MC/V.) **Farthings B&B ❸**, 9 Swaynes Close, 10min. from the city center, is a comfortable, homey retreat. (☎330 749; www.farthingsbandb.co.uk. Breakfast included. Singles £25-32; doubles £46-56. Cash only.) At ◪**Harper's "Upstairs Restaurant" ❷**, 6-7 Ox Rd., Market Sq., inventive English dishes (£7-10) make hearty meals. (☎333 118. Early Bird 2-course special before 8pm £7.50. Open M-F noon-2pm and 6-9:30pm, Sa noon-2pm and 6-10pm, Su 6-9pm; Oct.-May closed Su. AmEx/MC/V.) **Trains** run from South Western Rd., west of town across the River Avon, to London Waterloo (1½hr., 2 per hr., £27), Portsmouth (1½hr., 2 per hr., £13), and Winchester (1hr., 2 per hr., £12). National Express **buses** (☎08705 808 080) go from 8 Endless St. to London (3hr., 3 per day, £14). Wilts and Dorset buses (☎336 855) run to Bath (X4; 1 per hr., £4.20) and Winchester (#68; 1¾hr., 8 per day, £4.50). An **Explorer** ticket is good for one day of travel on Wilts and Dorset buses (£6.50). The **TIC** is on Fish Row, in back of the Guildhall in Market Sq. (☎334 956; www.visitsalisbury.com. Open June-Sept. M-Sa 9:30am-6pm, Su 10:30am-4:30pm; Oct.-May M-Sa 9:30am-5pm.) **Postal Code:** SP1 1AB.

## ◪ DAYTRIP FROM SALISBURY: STONEHENGE AND AVEBURY.

A ring of colossal stones amid swaying grass and indifferent sheep, Stonehenge has been battered for millennia by winds whipping at 80km per hour and visited by legions of people for over 5000 years. The monument, which has retained its present shape since about 1500 BC, was once a complete circle of 6.5m tall stones weighing up to 45 tons each. Though the construction of Stonehenge has been attributed to builders as diverse as Merlin and extraterrestrials, the more plausible explanation—Neolithic builders using still unknown methods—is perhaps the most astonishing of all. Sensationalized religious and scientific explanations for Stonehenge's purpose add to its intrigue. Some believe the stones are oriented as a calendar, with the position of the sun on the stones indicating the time of year. Admission to Stonehenge includes a 30min. audio tour. The effect may be more haunting than the rocks themselves—a bizarre march of tourists who stop suddenly to silently devote their attention to black handsets. Ropes confine the throngs to a path around the outside of the monument. From the roadside or from Amesbury Hill, 2km up the A303, you can get a free, if distant, view of the stones. There are also many walks and trails that pass by; ask at the Salisbury TIC. (☎01980 624 715. Open daily June-Aug. 9am-7pm; mid-Mar. to May and Sept. to mid-Oct. 9:30am-6pm; mid-Oct. to mid-Mar. 9:30am-4pm. £6, students £4.40.)

▪TIP▪ **RUIN YOUR DAY.** Early risers can see Stonehenge, Avebury, and Old Sarum, an ancient settlement, in one day. Head to Stonehenge on the 8:45 or 9:45am bus (buy the Explorer ticket; see above), then catch the 11:10am or 12:20pm bus to Amesbury and transfer to an Avebury bus. Take the 2 or 3pm bus back from Avebury and stop off in Old Sarum before you reach Salisbury.

A wonder for the world: why is **Avebury's** stone circle, larger and older than its favored cousin Stonehenge, often so lonely during the day? Avebury gives an up-close and largely untouristed view of its 98 stones, dated to 2500 BC and standing in a circle with a 300m diameter. Wilts and Dorset **buses** (☎336 855) run daily service from the Salisbury train station and bus station (#3, 5, and 6; 30min.-2hr.; round-trip £4-8). The first bus leaves Salisbury at 9:45am, and the last leaves Stonehenge at 4:05pm. Check a schedule before you leave; intervals between drop-offs and pickups are at least 1hr. Wilts and Dorset also runs a **tour** bus from Salisbury (3 per day, £7.50-15). The closest lodgings are in **Salisbury** (see above).

# BATH                                               ☎01225

Perhaps the world's first tourist town, Bath (pop. 90,000) has been a must-see for travelers since AD 43, when the Romans built an elaborate complex of baths to house the town's curative waters. In 1701, Queen Anne's trip to the springs re-established the city as a prominent meeting place for artists, politicians, and intellectuals; it became a social capital second in England only to London. No longer an upper-crust resort, today Bath plays host to crowds of tourists eager to appreciate its historic sites and well-preserved elegance.

**⚏⛭ TRANSPORTATION AND PRACTICAL INFORMATION. Trains** leave from Dorchester St. for: Birmingham (2hr., 1 per hr., £33); Bristol (15min., 3 per hr., £6); London Paddington (1½hr., 2 per hr., £46); London Waterloo (2½hr., 2 per day, £34). National Express **buses** (☎08705 808 080) run from Manvers St. to London (3½hr., 1 per 1½hr., £17) and Oxford (2¼hr., 1 per day, £9.20). The train and bus stations are near the south end of Manvers St. Walk toward the town center and turn left on York St. to reach the **TIC,** in Abbey Chambers. (☎08704 446 442; www.visitbath.co.uk. Open May-Sept. M-Sa 9:30am-6pm, Su 10am-4pm; Oct.-Apr. M-Sa 9:30am-5pm, Su 10am-4pm.) **Postal Code:** BA1 1AJ.

**⛭⛶ ACCOMMODATIONS AND FOOD. B&Bs** line **Pulteney Rd.** and **Pulteney Gardens.** Conveniently located **Bath Backpackers ❶,** 13 Pierrepont St., is a laid-back backpackers' lair with music-themed dorms, TV lounge, and "dungeon" bar. (☎446 787; www.hostels.co.uk/bath. Kitchen available. Internet £2 per hr., free Wi-Fi. Luggage storage £2 per bag. Reception 8am-11pm. Check-out 10:30am. Reserve ahead in summer. Dorms £15; doubles £35; triples £53. MC/V.) **St. Christopher's Inn ❷,** 16 Green St., has clean rooms and a downstairs pub. (☎481 444; www.st-christophers.co.uk. Internet £3 per hr. Dorms £14-22. Discount for online booking. MC/V.) **Riverside Cafe ❶,** below Pulteney Bridge, serves light dishes and delicious coffee. Patrons have a gorgeous view of the River Avon. (☎480 532. Sandwiches and soups £3-8. Open daily in summer 9am-9:30pm, winter 9am-4:30pm. MC/V.) Try the exotic vegetarian dishes, or the superb chocolate fudge cake (£5.25) at **Demuths Restaurant ❸,** 2 N. Parade Passage. (☎446 059; www.demuths.co.uk. Entrees £11-16. *Prix-fixe* lunch £8. Open M-F and Su 10am-5pm and 6-10pm, Sa 9:30am-5:30pm and 6-11pm. Reserve ahead in summer. MC/V.) Next to Green Park Station is a **Sainsbury's** supermarket. (☎444 737. Open M-F 8am-10pm, Sa 7am-10pm, Su 10am-4pm.)

**◧ SIGHTS.** In 1880, sewer diggers uncovered the first glimpse of an extravagant feat of Roman engineering. For 400 years, the Romans harnessed Bath's bubbling springs, where nearly 1,000,000L of 47°C (115°F) water flow every day. The ⯃**Roman Baths Museum,** Stall St., shows the complexity of Roman architecture and engineering, which included central heating and internal plumbing. (☎447 785; www.romanbaths.co.uk. Open daily July-Aug. 9am-9pm; Sept.-Oct. and Mar.-June 9am-6pm; Nov.-Feb. 9:30am-5:30pm. £11, students £8.50. Joint ticket with Museum of Costume £13/11. Audio tour included.) Next to the baths, the towering **Bath Abbey** meets masons George and William Vertue's oath to build "the goodliest vault in all England and France." (☎422 462; www.bathabbey.org. Open Apr.-Oct. M-Sa 9am-6:30pm, Su 8am-6pm; Nov.-Mar. M-Sa 9am-4pm, Su between services.

Requested donation £2.50.) Walk up Gay St. to **The Circus,** a classic Georgian block where painter Thomas Gainsborough and 18th-century prime minister William Pitt lived. Near The Circus, the **Museum of Costume,** on Bennett St., has a dazzling parade of 400 years of fashions, from 17th-century silver tissue garments to J. Lo's racy Versace jungle-print ensemble. (☎477 785; www.museumofcostume.co.uk. Open daily Mar.-Oct. 11am-6pm; Nov.-Feb. 11am-5pm. £6.50, students £5.50.)

## GLASTONBURY                                    ☎01458

The reputed birthplace of Christianity in England, an Arthurian hot spot, and home to England's biggest summer music festival, Glastonbury (pop. 8800) is a quirky intersection of mysticism and pop culture. Legend holds that Joseph of Arimathea founded **Glastonbury Abbey,** on Magdalene St., in AD 63. Though the abbey was destroyed during the English Reformation, the colossal pile of ruins and accompanying museum evoke the abbey's original grandeur. (☎832 267; www.glastonbury-abbey.com. Open daily June-Aug. 9am-6pm; Sept.-Nov. and Mar.-May 9:30am-dusk; Dec.-Feb. 10am-dusk. £4.50, students £4.) For Arthurians, **Glastonbury Tor** is a must-see. The 160m tower offers great views and is supposedly where King Arthur sleeps until his country needs him. To reach the Tor between April and October, take the bus from St. Dunstan's Car Park (£2), or turn right at the top of High St. onto Lambrook, which becomes Chilkwell St.; turn left on Wellhouse Ln. and follow the public footpath up the hill, looking out for cow dung. (Open year-round. Free.) The annual **Glastonbury Festival** (tickets ☎834 596; www.glastonburyfestivals.co.uk) is the biggest and best of Britain's summer music festivals. The week-long concert series (June 27-29, 2008) and has featured top bands, with recent headliners including The Killers, The Who, and Radiohead.

**Glastonbury Backpackers ❶,** 4 Market Pl., at the corner of Magdalene and High St., has spacious rooms and a cafe-bar in a superb central location. (☎833 353; www.glastonburybackpackers.com. Kitchen available. Internet £5 per hr. Reception until 11pm. Check-in 4pm. Check-out 11:30am. Dorms £14; doubles £34. MC/V.) The vegetarian and whole-food menu at **Rainbow's End ❶,** 17a High St., includes soups, salads, and quiches for £3-7. (☎833 896. Open M-Sa 10am-5pm, Su 11am-4pm. Cash only.) **Heritage Fine Foods,** 32-34 High St., stocks groceries and discounted beer. (☎831 003. Open M-W 7am-9pm, Th-Sa 9am-10pm, Su 8am-9pm.) First Badgerline **buses** (☎08706 082 608, fare info 08456 064 446) run from town hall to Bristol (#375 or 376; 1hr., £5.10) via Wells. Travel to Yeovil on #376 (1hr., 1 per hr.) to connect to destinations in the south, including Lyme Regis and Dorchester. From the bus stop, turn right on High St. to reach the **TIC,** the Tribunal, 9 High St. (☎832 954; www.glastonburytic.co.uk. Open Apr.-Sept. M-Th and Su 10am-5pm, F-Sa 10am-5:30pm; Oct.-Mar. M-Th and Su 10am-4pm, F-Sa 10am-4:30pm.) **Postal Code:** BA6 9HG.

# CHANNEL ISLANDS

Jersey, Guernsey, and seven smaller islands constitute the Channel Islands. Situated 128km south of England and 64km west of France, the islands offer a mix of cultures and a touch of expensive elegance. Fortifications built during the islands' WWII occupation by the Germans lie in rocky coves, while in town, cafes, shops, and tourists make the islands feel like a perpetual holiday.

◢ **FERRIES.** Condor high-speed **ferries** (☎01202 207 216; www.condorferries.com) run one early and one late ferry per day from Poole and Weymouth, as well as St-Malo, FRA, docking at St. Peter Port, Guernsey (2hr.), and Elizabeth Harbor at St. Helier, Jersey (3½-3¾hr.). The season and tides affect frequency and ticket prices. Call ☎0845 124 2003 or visit the website for schedules. ISIC holders are eligible for a 20% discount; ask before purchasing a ticket. Daytrips can be the most affordable, with round-trip tickets to Jersey and Guernsey from £25.

**JERSEY.** Jersey, the largest Channel Island, is notorious for both its landscape-altering tides and its budget-altering high prices. Avoid the latter by breaking free from trendy clubs, eateries, and shops in the port of **Saint Helier** and escaping to the island's countryside, where you'll experience the region's beguiling blend of British sensibility and French *joie de vivre*. The 13th-century **■Mont Orgueil Castle** on Gorey Pier was built in the 13th century to protect the island from the French. The top of the castle yields spectacular views of land and sea. (☎01534 853 292. Open daily Apr.-Oct. 10am-6pm; Nov.-Mar. 10am-dusk. Last entry 1hr. before closing. £9, students £8.20.) Across from Liberation Sq. by St. Helier Marina, the **Maritime Museum** contains a nautical hodgepodge of exhibits on the island's surrounding seas. (☎01534 811 043. Open daily Apr.-Oct. 10am-5pm; Nov.-Mar. 10am-4pm. £6.50, students £5.70.) The **Jersey War Tunnels,** Les Charrieres Malorey, St. Lawrence, provide a history lesson about life in Jersey under Nazi occupation. (☎01534 860 808; www.jerseywartunnels.com. Open mid-Feb. to mid-Dec. daily 10am-6pm. Last entry 4:30pm. £9.30, students £6.30.) In October, Jersey plays host to **Tennerfest,** challenging local restaurants to come up with the best £10 menu. Check out www.jersey.com for more on festivals throughout the year.

---

**THE REAL DEAL.** Though part of the UK, Jersey and Guernsey are essentially self-governing states. The British pound is the official currency, but ATMs dish out Jersey or Guernsey pounds. These local pounds are on par with their British counterparts, but are not accepted outside the Channel Islands; you will have to exchange them upon returning to the mainland. Toward the end of your stay in the islands, make sure to ask local merchants to give you change in British pounds. Also keep in mind that your mobile phone carrier may think you are in France (or not recognize you at all) and charge accordingly.

---

Cheaper lodging options than the B&Bs on Havre de Pas are east in coastal St. Martin. To reach the island's only hostel, **YHA Jersey ❸,** Haut de la Garenne, La Rue de la Pouclée et des Quatre Chemins, St. Martin, take bus #3A from St. Helier (20min., 1 per hr.), get off before Ransoms Garden Centre, and walk 180m; after 5:45pm take #1 to Gorey (last bus 11pm), walk up the hill, cross the road, and turn left up the larger hill. (☎0870 770 6130. Breakfast included. Reception 7-10am and 5-11pm. Open Feb.-Nov. daily; Dec.-Jan. F-Sa. Dorms £22, under 18 £15. MC/V.) Jersey offers a range of restaurants with fare from Asian to seafood. Visit **Beach House ❷,** on Gorey Pier, for chic furnishings and ample people-watching. (☎01534 859 902. Open M 11am-6pm, Tu-Su 12:30-3:30pm and 6:30-9:30pm. Kitchen open until 30min. before closing. MC/V.) Pass through the bright red door of **Rojo ❷,** 10 Bond St., for filling £3 tapas. (☎01534 729 904. Express-lunch discount noon-2pm. Open noon-3pm and 6pm-10pm. MC/V.) Connex **buses** leave from the Weighbridge Terminal in St. Helier and travel all over the island. (☎01534 877 772; www.mybus.je. £1-1.60.) Island Explore offers a hop-on, hop-off **tour** service from Weighbridge. (☎01534 876 418. M-F and Su. 1-day Explorer ticket £7.50, 3-day £18, 5-day £23.) From the harbor, follow the pedestrian signs along the pier toward the **TIC** at Liberation Sq. (☎01534 448 800; www.jersey.com. Open M-Sa 8:30am-5:30pm, Su 8:30am-2:15pm; winter hours vary.)

**GUERNSEY.** Smaller than Jersey in size but not in charm, Guernsey flaunts its French roots—cultural fusion is evident in its architecture, cuisine, and locals' speech. Pull yourself away from Guernsey's wildflowers and beaches long enough to tour **■Hauteville House,** St. Peter Port. The house remains virtually unaltered since Victor Hugo lived here and penned *Les Misérables* during his exile from France. Hauteville is full of hidden inscriptions and mantles built by Hugo from recycled furniture. (☎01481 721 911. Open May to early Oct. M-Sa 10am-4pm; Apr.

M-Sa noon-4pm. £4, students £2, under 20 free.) For lodgings near town with views of Sark and Herm Islands, try **St. George's Guest House ❹**, St. George's Esplanade, St. Peter Port. (☎01481 721 027. Breakfast included. £33-35. MC/V.) **Christies ❸**, Le Pollet, has an airy French bistro serving local seafood salads and sandwiches, and a more expensive restaurant in back. (☎01481 726 624. Lunch entrees £4.50-15. Open daily noon-2:30pm and 6-10:30pm. MC/V.) Island Coachways (☎01481 720 210; www.buses.gg) **buses** operate throughout the island and offer **tours** from May to September; call the office for fares and info. Routes #7 and 7a circle the coast (1 per hr., £0.60). To reach the **TIC** on North Esplanade, take a left at the end of the ferry landing at St. Julian's pier. *Naturally Guernsey* is a helpful guide to the island. (☎01481 723 552; www.visitguernsey.com. Open in summer M-Sa 9am-6pm, Su 9am-1pm; in winter M-F 9am-5pm, Sa 9am-4pm.)

# THE CORNISH COAST

With cliffsides stretching out into the Atlantic, Cornwall's terrain doesn't feel English. Years ago, the Celts fled westward in the face of Saxon conquest. Today, the migration to Cornwall continues in the form of artists, surfers, and vacationers. Though the Cornish language is no longer spoken, the area remains protective of its distinctive past and its ubiquitous pasties.

**THAT'S EMBARRASSING.** Cornwall's famous pasties (PAH-stees) are pie-like pastries usually filled with diced meat and vegetables. Not to be confused with the pasties (PAY-stees) you might find in a lingerie shop.

## NEWQUAY ☎01637

Known as the "new California," Newquay (NEW-key; pop. 20,000) is a slice of surfer culture in Cornwall. Strong Atlantic winds descend on **Fistral Beach,** creating what most consider the best surfing in Europe. Visit **Sunset Surf Shop,** 106 Fore St., for equipment and lessons. (☎877 624. Boards £5-10 per day, £12-25 per 3 days, £25-40 per week. Wetsuits or bodyboards £4-5/10-12/20. Open Apr.-Oct. daily 9am-6pm.) On the bay side, there are four beaches: tamer waters at **Towan Beach** and **Great Western Beach,** smack dab in the middle of town, lure sunbathers and novice surfers, while spotless **Tolcarne Beach** and **Lusty Glaze Beach** are privately owned. Many **hostels** and surf lodges (£12-16) line **Headland Road** and **Tower Road,** near Fistral Beach. In low season, wander up the road from the beach and take your pick. Reserve ahead. **Fistral Backpackers ❷**, 18 Headland Rd., seconds from Fistral beach, has everything you could need, from great advice to a warm bed. (☎873 146; www.fistralbackpackers.co.uk. Reception 24hr. Dorms £10-19.) Newquay specializes in low cost takeout; sit-down food tends to be pricey. For cheap eats, head to pubs, pizza and kebab shops, or the **Somerfield** supermarket at the end of Fore St. (☎876 006. Open July-Aug. M-Th and Sa 8am-9pm, F 8am-10pm, Su 11am-4pm; Sept.-June M-Th and Sa 8am-8pm, F 8am-9pm, Su 11am-4pm.) The town teems with sun-kissed surfers and visitors ready to drink, dance, and drink some more. Watch out for stag and hen parties, and head toward the shore for more relaxed nightlife venues. **On The Rocks,** 14 The Crescent, has eclectic live music, pool tables, and big-screen TVs playing bodacious surfing footage. (☎872 897; www.ontherocksbar.co.uk. W beer £1. Open daily 10:30am-2am.) **Trains** (☎08457 484 950) depart from Cliff Rd. and pass through Par (50min, 5-8 per day, £4.50), connecting to Penzance (1½hr., 12 per day, £11) and Plymouth (50min., 15 per day, £7). National Express **buses** (☎08705 808 080) leave Manor Rd. for London (7hr., 4-7 per day, £36). The **TIC** is on Marcus Hill, a few blocks toward the city center from the train station. (☎854 020; www.newquay.co.uk. Open June-Sept. M-Sa 9:30am-5:30pm, Su 9:30am-3:30pm; Oct.-May M-F 9:30am-4:30pm, Sa 9:30am-12:30pm.)

## PENZANCE
☎ 01736

Penzance was once a model English pirate town; it appears, though, that Disney has since moved all the pirates to the Caribbean. The only ones here are in murals or made of wax. What Penzance lacks in swashbucklers it makes up for in galleries, quirky stores, and sunsets. A former Benedictine monastery, **St. Michael's Mount,** on a hill that becomes an island at high tide, marks the spot where St. Michael is believed to have appeared in AD 495. The interior has a champagne-cork model of the island and views from the top are well worth the 30-story climb. (☎710 507, ferry and tide info 710 265. Open Apr.-Oct. M-F and Su 10:30am-5:30pm; Nov.-Mar. by tour only, appointment necessary. Last entry 4:45pm. ₤6.40; with private garden ₤9.40.) Penzance contains an impressive number of art galleries; pick up the *Cornwall Galleries Guide* (₤1) at the TIC. Walk 20min. from the train or bus station, or take First bus #5 or 6 from the bus station to the Pirate Pub and walk 10min. up Castle Horneck Rd. to reach the **YHA Penzance (HI) ❶,** Castle Horneck. Housed in an 18th-century mansion, this hostel has spacious dorms. (☎362 666. Internet ₤0.07 per min. Lockout 10am-noon. Dorms ₤16, under 18 ₤13; doubles ₤35. Tent sites ₤7. MC/V.) ◪**Admiral Benbow,** 46 Chapel St., has the town's liveliest pub scene and is decorated with paraphernalia from local shipwrecks. (☎363 448. Pints ₤2.20. Open M-Sa 11am-11pm, Su noon-10:30pm.) **Trains** leave Wharf Rd., at the head of Albert Pier, for London (5½hr., 7 per day, ₤69), Newquay (3hr., 8 per day, ₤7), and St. Ives via St. Erth (40-55min., 1 per hr., ₤4.80). **Buses** also leave Wharf Rd. for London (8½hr., 7 per day, ₤36). The **TIC** is between the train and bus stations on Station Rd. (☎362 207; www.penwith.gov.uk. Open May-Sept. M-F 9am-5pm, Sa 10am-4pm, Su 9am-2pm; Oct.-Apr. M-F 9am-5pm, Sa 10am-1pm.)

## ST. IVES
☎ 01736

Medieval St. Ives (pop. 11,400), bordered by beaches and azure waters, has attracted visitors for centuries. Many painters and sculptors arrived in the 20s, and their legacy fills the windows of countless local art galleries. The energy of the Atlantic at St. Ives charmed Virginia Woolf; *To the Lighthouse* is thought to refer to the Godrevy Lighthouse, visible in the distance. The *Cornwall Galleries Guide* (₤1) will help you navigate the dozens of galleries, but St. Ives's real attractions are its beaches, far less overrun with surfers than those in Newquay. ◪**Porthminster Beach,** downhill from the train station, is a magnificent stretch of golden sand and tame waves. To escape the sunbathing crowds, head for quieter **Porthgwidden Beach.** Below the Tate Gallery, **Porthmeor Beach** attracts surfers, but has less appealing sands. Farther east, **Carbis Bay,** 2km from Porthminster, is less crowded and easily accessible. Take the train one stop toward St. Erth or bus #17 (M-Sa) or 17B (Su). **St. Ives International Backpackers ❶,** The Stennack, has bright murals and a cavernous lounge. (☎799 444; www.backpackers.co.uk. Internet ₤1 per 15min. July-Aug. min. 7-night stay for advance bookings. Dorms ₤11-16; doubles ₤26-36. MC/V.) Takeout and pasty shops line **Fore Street.** For local seafood at reasonable prices, the trendy **Seafood Cafe ❸,** 45 Fore St., is unbeatable. Choose your fish raw from the display area (₤8.50-17) and select garnishes. (☎794 004. Open daily noon-3pm and 5:30-11pm. MC/V.) Buy groceries at **Co-op,** Royal Sq. (☎796 494. Open daily M-Sa 8am-11pm, Su 8am-10:30pm.) **Trains** (☎08457 484 950) to St. Ives pass through or change at St. Erth (15min., 1 per hr., ₤1.70). First **buses** run to Newquay (#301; 1¾hr., July-Aug. 4 per day, ₤4.70) and Penzance (#16, 16B, 17B; 40min., 2 per hr., round-trip ₤3). **DayRover** tickets allow unlimited travel on First buses for ₤5.50. From the stations, walk to the foot of Tregenna Hill and turn right to reach the **TIC,** in the Guildhall on Street-an-Pol. (☎796 297. Open July-Sept. M-F 9am-5pm, Sa 10am-4pm, Su 10am-2pm; May-June M-F 9am-5pm, Sa 10am-4pm; Oct.-Apr. M-F 9am-5pm, Sa 10am-1pm.)

# EAST ANGLIA AND THE MIDLANDS

The rich farmland and watery flats of East Anglia stretch northeast from London, cloaking the counties of Cambridgeshire, Norfolk, Suffolk, and parts of Essex. Mention of The Midlands inevitably evokes grim urban images, but there is a unique heritage and quiet grandeur to this smokestacked landscape. Even Birmingham, the region's much-maligned center, has its saving graces, among them a lively nightlife scene and the Cadbury chocolate empire.

# OXFORD ☎ 01865

Sprawling college grounds and 12th-century spires mark this Holy Grail of British academia. Nearly a millennium of scholarship at Oxford (pop. 145,000) has included the education of world leaders, including 25 British prime ministers. Despite the tourist crowds, Oxford has an irrepressible grandeur and pockets of tranquility: the basement room of Blackwell's Bookshop, the galleries of the Ashmolean, and the perfectly maintained quadrangles of the university's 39 colleges.

**🖪🔢 TRANSPORTATION AND PRACTICAL INFORMATION. Trains** (☎ 08457 484 950) run from Botley Rd., down Park End, to: Birmingham (1¼hr., 2 per hr., £20); Glasgow (5-7hr., 1 per hr., £70); London Paddington (1hr., 2-4 per hr., £9.50-19); Manchester (3hr., 1-2 per hr., £21-42). Stagecoach **buses** (☎ 772 250; www.stagecoachbus.com) run to: Cambridge (3hr., 2 per hr., £6); London (1¾hr.; 3-5 per hr.; £12, students £10). National Express (☎ 08705 808 080) runs to: Birmingham (1½hr., 5 per day, £15); Cambridge (3hr., 2 per hr., £9); Stratford-upon-Avon (1hr., 2 per day, £8.50). Oxford Bus Company (☎ 785 400; www.oxfordbus.co.uk) runs to: London (1¾hr.; 3-5 per hr.; £12, students £10); Gatwick (2hr., 1 per hr. 8am-9pm, £20); Heathrow (1¼hr., 3 per hr., £15). The **TIC,** 15-16 Broad St., books rooms for a £4 fee plus 10% deposit. (☎ 726 871; www.visitoxford.org. Open M-Sa 9:30am-5pm; Easter-June and Aug.-Oct. also Su 10am-3:30pm; June-July also Su 10am-4pm.) **Internet** is available at **Oxford Central Library,** Queen St. near the Westgate Shopping Center. (☎ 815 549. Open M-Th 9:15am-7pm, F-Sa 9:15am-5pm. Free.) **Postal Code:** OX1 1ZZ.

**🔓🔲 ACCOMMODATIONS AND FOOD.** Book at least a week ahead in summer, especially for singles. If it's late, call the **Oxford Association of Hotels and Guest Houses** (East Oxford ☎ 721 561, West Oxford 862 138, North Oxford 244 691, South Oxford 244 268). The newest hostel in town, 🖪**Central Backpackers ❷,** 13 Park End St., has spacious rooms and a popular rooftop terrace perfect for summertime barbecues. (☎ 242 288. Kitchen available. Free luggage storage. Free Internet. Reception 8am-11pm. Check-out 11am. 4-bed dorms £18; 6-bed female or 8-bed mixed dorms £16; 12-bed dorms £14. MC/V.) Turn right from the train station to reach the superbly located **YHA Oxford (HI) ❷,** 2a Botley Rd., which features quiet rooms and a kitchen. (☎ 727 275. Full English breakfast included. Lockers £1. Laundry £3. Internet £4.20 per hr. 4- and 6-bed dorms £21, under 18 £16; doubles £46. £3 student discount. MC/V.) The **Oxford Backpackers Hostel ❶,** 9a Hythe Bridge St., between the bus and train stations, fosters a lively social scene with an inexpensive bar, pool table, and constant music. (☎ 721 761. Laundry £2.50. Internet £2 per hr. Dorms £14; quads £64. MC/V.)

Look for after-hours **kebab vans,** usually at Broad, High, Queen, and St. Aldate's St. Students and residents alike flock to 🖪**The Alternative Tuck Shop ❶,** 24 Holywell St., for their famous panini and a slew of delicious made-to-order sandwiches, all for under £3. (☎ 792 054. Open daily 8:30am-6pm. Cash only.) For a

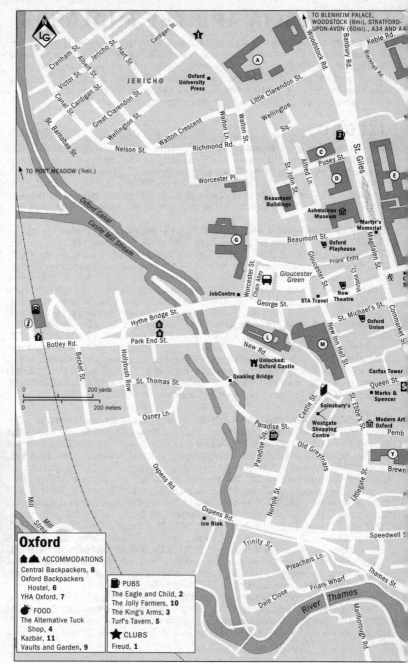

TO BLENHEIM PALACE,
WOODSTOCK (8mi), STRATFORD-
UPON-AVON (60mi)., A34 AND A4

TO PORT MEADOW (¾mi.)

JERICHO

Oxford
University
Press

Beaumont
Buildings

Ashmolean
Museum

Martyr's
Memorial

Beaumont St.

Oxford
Playhouse

Friars' Entry

Gloucester
Green

JobCentre

STA Travel

New
Theatre

George St.

Oxford
Union

Hythe Bridge St.

Park End St.

Botley Rd.

Carfax Tower

Queen St.

Marks &
Spencer

New Rd.

Unlocked:
Oxford Castle

Quaking Bridge

St. Thomas St.

Osney Ln.

Sainsbury's

Westgate
Shopping
Centre

Modern Art
Oxford

Paradise St.

Paradise
Sq.

Old Greyfriars

Oxpens Rd.

Oxpens Rd.
Ice Rink

Trinity St.

Preachers Ln.

Friars Wharf

Dale Close

River Thames

Speedwell St.

**GREAT BRITAIN**

# Oxford

🏠🏠 ACCOMMODATIONS
Central Backpackers, **8**
Oxford Backpackers
  Hostel, **6**
YHA Oxford, **7**

🍴 FOOD
The Alternative Tuck
  Shop, **4**
Kazbar, **11**
Vaults and Garden, **9**

🍺 PUBS
The Eagle and Child, **2**
The Jolly Farmers, **10**
The King's Arms, **3**
Turf's Tavern, **5**

⭐ CLUBS
Freud, **1**

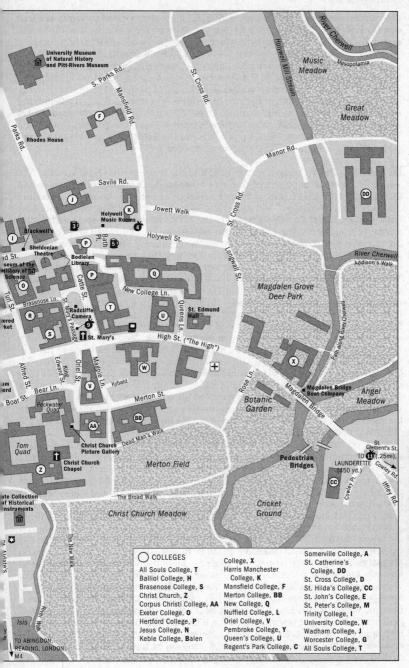

University Museum
of Natural History
and Pitt-Rivers Museum

S. Parks Rd.

St. Cross Rd.

Holywell Mill Stream

Music
Meadow

Mesopotamia

River Cherwell

Great
Meadow

Mansfield Rd.

Parks Rd.

Rhodes House

Manor Rd.

F

DD

Savile Rd.

J

Jowett Walk

K

Holywell
Music Rooms

River Cherwell

Addison's Walk

St. Cross Rd.

3

4

Holywell St.

Blackwell's

I

Sheldonian
Theatre

P

5

Bath Pl.

Magdalen Grove
Deer Park

Bodleian
Library

O

Catte St.

Q

New College Ln.

Museum of the
History of
Science

Longwall St.

Brasenose Ln.

St. Mary's Passage

Radcliffe
Camera

9

St. Mary's

T

U

Queen's Ln.

St. Edmund
Hall

R

S

High St. ("The High")

Turl St.

Covered
Market

Path along River Cherwell

X

Alfred St.

King Edward St.

Oriel St.

Magpie Ln.

W

Kybald

Rose Ln.

Magdalen Bridge
Boat Company

Angel
Meadow

Ashmolean
Museum of
Oxford

Boar St.

Bear Ln.

V

Merton St.

Magdalen Bridge

Peckwater
Quad

AA

BB

Botanic
Garden

St.
Clement's St.

Tom
Quad

Christ Church
Picture Gallery

Dead Man's Walk

Pedestrian
Bridges

TO 11 (.25mi).

LAUNDERETTE
(450 yd.)

Cowley Rd.

Iffley Rd.

Christ Church
Chapel

Z

Merton Field

CC

Cowley Pl.

Pitt Collection
of Historical
Instruments

The Broad Walk

Christ Church Meadow

Cricket
Ground

St. Aldate's

The New Walk

Isis

River Walk

TO ABINGDON,
READING, LONDON,
M4

○ COLLEGES

All Souls College, **T**
Balliol College, **H**
Brasenose College, **S**
Christ Church, **Z**
Corpus Christi College, **AA**
Exeter College, **O**
Hertford College, **P**
Jesus College, **N**
Keble College, **B**

College, **X**
Harris Manchester
　College, **K**
Mansfield College, **F**
Merton College, **BB**
New College, **Q**
Nuffield College, **L**
Oriel College, **V**
Pembroke College, **Y**
Queen's College, **U**
Regent's Park College, **C**

Somerville College, **A**
St. Catherine's
　College, **DD**
St. Cross College, **D**
St. Hilda's College, **CC**
St. John's College, **E**
St. Peter's College, **M**
Trinity College, **I**
University College, **W**
Wadham College, **J**
Worcester College, **G**
All Souls College, **T**

delectable homemade meal made with local ingredients, head to **Vaults and Garden ❷**, Radcliffe Square, under St. Mary's Church. Cozy booths line the inside and outdoor tables in the garden, which overlooks the iconic Radcliffe Camera. (☎ 279 112. Open daily 9am-5:30pm. Cash only.) Visit **Kazbar ❶**, 25-27 Cowley Rd., for a Mediterranean tapas bar with Spanish-style decor. (☎ 202 920. Tapas £2.20-4.75. Free tapas with drink M-F 4-7pm. Open M-F 4-11pm, Sa-Su noon-midnight. AmEx/MC/V.) Students fed up with college food and perpetual tourists are easily seduced by a bevy of budget options in Oxford. If you're cooking, try **Gloucester Green Market,** behind the bus station. (Open W 8am-3:30pm.) The **Covered Market** between Market St. and Carfax has fresh produce and deli goods. (Open M-Sa 7am-8pm, Su 11am-5pm.) Pick up groceries at the **Sainsbury's** in Westgate Shopping Center. (Open M-Sa 7am-8pm, Su 11am-5pm.)

◙ **SIGHTS.** The TIC sells a map (£1.25) and the *Welcome to Oxford* guide (£1), which lists the visiting hours of Oxford's **colleges.** Don't bother trying to sneak in after hours; even after hiding your pack and copy of *Let's Go*, bouncers, affectionately known as "bulldogs," will squint and kick you out. Just down St. Aldate's St. from Carfax, **Christ Church College** has Oxford's grandest quad and most distinguished alumni, including 13 past prime ministers. The dining hall and Tom Quad are also shooting locations for the *Harry Potter* movies. The **Christ Church Chapel** functions as the university's cathedral. It was here that the Rev. Charles Dodgson (better known as Lewis Carroll) first met Alice Liddell, the dean's daughter; the White Rabbit is immortalized in the hall's stained glass. **Tom Quad** takes its name from Great Tom, the seven-ton bell in Tom Tower that has faithfully rung 101 (the original number of students) strokes at 9:05pm (the original undergraduate curfew) every evening since 1682. (☎ 286 573; www.chch.ox.ac.uk. Open M-Sa 9am-5:30pm, Su 1-5:30pm. Chapel services M-F 6pm; Su 8, 10, 11:15am, 6pm. £4.70, students £3.70.) J.R.R. Tolkien lectured at **Merton College,** Merton St., whose library houses the first printed Welsh Bible. Nearby **St. Alban's Quad** has some of the university's best gargoyles. (☎ 276 310; www.merton.ox.ac.uk. Open M-F 2-4pm, Sa-Su 10am-4pm. Free.) Soot-blackened **University College,** High St., was built in 1249 and vies with Merton for the title of oldest, claiming Alfred the Great as its founder. Percy Bysshe Shelley was expelled for writing the pamphlet *The Necessity of Atheism*, but was later immortalized in a prominent monument located to the right as you enter. Bill Clinton also spent his Rhodes scholar days here. (☎ 276 602; www.univ.ox.ac.uk. Open to tours only.)

South of Oriel, **Corpus Christi College,** the smallest of Oxford's colleges, surrounds a sundialed quad. The garden gate was built for visits between Charles I and his queen, who lived nearby during the Civil Wars. (☎ 276 700; www.ccc.ox.ac.uk. Open daily 1:30-4:30pm.) The prestigious **All Souls College,** at the corner of High and Cattle St., admits only the best scholars and stores only the best wine in its cellar. (☎ 279 379; www.all-souls.ox.ac.uk. Open Sept.-July M-F 2-4pm. Free.) At **Queen's College,** High St., a boar's head graces the table at Christmas to honor a student who, attacked by a boar on the outskirts of Oxford, choked the animal to death with a volume of Aristotle. (☎ 279 120; www.queens.ox.ac.uk. Open to tours only.) With extensive grounds, flower-edged quads, and a deer park, **Magdalen College** (MAUD-lin), on High St. near the Cherwell, is considered Oxford's handsomest. Oscar Wilde is among the distinguished alumni. (☎ 276 000; www.magd.ox.ac.uk. Open daily Oct.-Mar. 1pm-dusk; Apr.-June 1-6pm; July-Sept. noon-6pm. £3, students £2.) Founded in 1555, **Trinity College,** Broad St., has a Baroque chapel with a limewood altarpiece, cedar lattices, and cherubim-spotted pediments. (☎ 279 900; www.trinity.ox.ac.uk. Open M-F 10am-noon and 2-4pm, Sa-Su 2-4pm; during vacations also Sa-Su 10am-noon. £1.50, students £0.75.) Students at **Balliol College** preserve a semblance of tradition by hurling abuse over the wall at their conservative Trinity College rivals. The interior gates of the college bear lingering scorch marks from the executions of 16th-century Protestant martyrs. (☎277 777; www.balliol.ox.ac.uk. Open daily 2-5pm. £1, students free.) Indira Gandhi and Margaret Thatcher attended **Somerville College,** Oxford's most famous former women's-only college. Women were not granted degrees until 1920—Cambridge held out until 1948. Today, all but one of Oxford's colleges are coed; **St. Hilda's** remains women-only, but will start to admit men in 2008. From Carfax, head down Cornmarket St., which becomes Magdalen St., St. Giles, and finally Woodstock Rd. (☎270 600; www.some.ox.ac.uk. Open daily 9am-5pm. Free.)

The grand **Ashmolean Museum,** on Beaumont St., houses works by da Vinci, Matisse, Michelangelo, Monet, and van Gogh. Opened in 1683, the Ashmolean was Britain's first public museum and still holds one of the country's finest collections. The museum is undergoing extensive renovations until 2009, but continues to show an exhibit of "treasures"—more than 200 artifacts from its galleries—including the lantern carried by Guy Fawkes in the Gunpowder Plot of 1605 and the deerskin mantle of Powhatan, father of Pocahantas. (☎278 000. Open Tu-Sa 10am-5pm, Su noon-5pm; in summer open Th until 7pm. Free. Tours £2.) **Bodleian Library,** on Broad St., is Oxford's main reading and research library with over five million books and 50,000 manuscripts. It receives a copy of every book printed in Great Britain, but no one has ever been allowed to check one out. (☎277 000; www.bodley.ox.ac.uk. Library open M-F 9am-10pm, Sa 9am-1pm; summer M-F 9am-7pm, Sa 9am-1pm. Tours leave from the Divinity School in the main quad M-Sa 2-4 per day. Tours £4, audio tour £2.) A teenage Christopher Wren designed the **Sheldonian Theatre,** next door on Broad St. Graduation ceremonies, conducted in Latin, take place in the theatre, as do opera performances. (☎277 299. Open M-Sa 10am-12:30pm and 2-4:30pm; in winter until 3:30pm; in July and Aug. also Su 11am-4pm. £2, students £1.) With 10km of bookshelves, **Blackwell's Bookstore,** 53 Broad St., is Oxford's largest bookshop and is famous for letting patrons read undisturbed. (☎792 792. Open M and W-Sa 9am-6pm, Tu 9:30am-6pm, Su 11am-5pm.)

🃏🎴 **ENTERTAINMENT AND NIGHTLIFE.** **Punting** on the River Thames, known in Oxford as the "Isis," or on the River Cherwell (CHAR-wul), is a traditional pastime. Punters propel their small wooden vessels using a tall pole and oar. **Magdalen Bridge Boathouse,** just under Magdalen Bridge, rents boats. (☎202 643. Open daily Mar.-Oct. 10am-dusk. £12 per hr.; £30 deposit and ID required. Cash only.) Bring wine for a floating toast. Music and drama at Oxford are cherished arts. The **City of Oxford Orchestra,** Oxford's professional symphony orchestra, plays at the Sheldonian and in college chapels during summer. (☎744 457. Tickets £16-18.) The **Oxford Playhouse,** 11-12 Beaumont St. (☎305 305; www.oxfordplayhouse.com), stages amateur and professional plays, and music and dance performances. *This Month in Oxford* and *Daily Information* (www.daily-info.co.uk), both available for free at the TIC, list upcoming events.

**Pubs** outnumber colleges in Oxford. Many are so small that a single band of students will squeeze out other patrons. Luckily, there's usually another place just around the corner, so be ready to crawl. 🔲**Turf's Tavern,** 4 Bath Pl., off Holywell St., is a popular 13th-century student pub tucked in an alley off an alley. Bob Hawke, former prime minister of Australia, downed a yard of ale here (over 2½ pints) in a record time of 11 seconds during his time as a student. (☎243 235. Open M-Sa 11am-11pm, Su noon-10:30pm. Kitchen closes 7:30pm. AmEx/MC/V.) Merry masses head to the back rooms at **The King's Arms,** 40 Holywell St., considered to be Oxford's unofficial student union. Plenty of space and large tables make getting a seat possible, even when it's busy. (☎242 369. Open M-Sa 10:30am-11pm, Su 10:30am-10:30pm. MC/V.) *The Hobbit* and *The Chronicles of Narnia* were first read aloud at **The Eagle and Child,** 49 St. Giles, the favored haunt of their authors, J.R.R. Tolkien and C.S. Lewis. (☎302 925. Open M-Sa 11am-11pm, Su noon-10:30pm. Kitchen closes M-F 10pm, Sa-Su 9pm.) **The Jolly Farmers,** 20 Paradise St., one of Oxfordshire's first gay and lesbian pubs, often finds itself crowded with twentysomethings. (☎763 759; www.jollyfarmers.com. Open M-Sa noon-11pm, Su noon-10:30pm.) After Happy hour, head to clubs at **Walton Street** or **Cowley Road.** In a former church, **Freud,** 119 Walton St., is a cafe by day and bar by night. (☎311 171. Open Su-Tu 11am-midnight, W 11am-1am, Th-Sa 11am-2am. MC/V.)

# STRATFORD-UPON-AVON                    ☎01789

Shakespeare was born here, and this fluke of fate has made Stratford-upon-Avon a major stop on the tourist superhighway. Proprietors tout the dozen-odd properties linked, however remotely, to the Bard and his extended family; shops and restaurants devotedly stencil his prose and poetry on their windows and walls. But, behind the sound and fury of rumbling tour buses and chaotic swarms of daytrippers, there lies a town worth seeing for the beauty of the Avon and for the riveting performances in the Royal Shakespeare Theatre.

**⬛🔢 HENCE, AWAY!** Trains (☎08457 484 950) arrive at Station Rd., off Alcester Rd., and run to: Birmingham (50min., 2 per hr., £5.60); London Paddington (2¼hr., 2 per hr., £42); Warwick (25min., 9 per day, £3.70). National Express **buses** (☎08705 808 080) go to: London (3hr., 5 per day, £17); Oxford (1hr., 2 per day, £9.50). Local Stratford Blue bus #X20 stops at Wood and Bridge St., and goes to Birmingham (1¼hr., 1 per hr., £4). The **TIC**, Bridgefoot, is across Warwick Rd. (☎0870 160 7930. Open Apr.-Oct. M-Sa 9am-5:30pm, Su 10am-4pm; Nov.-Mar. M-Sa 9am-5pm.) Surf the **Internet** at **Cyber Junction,** 28 Greenhill St. (☎263 400. £4 per hr. Open M-F 10am-6pm, Sa 10:30am-5:30pm.) **Postal Code:** CV37 6PU.

**🔢🔳 TO SLEEP, PERCHANCE TO DREAM.** B&Bs line **Evesham Place, Evesham Road, Grove Road,** and **Shipston Road,** but reservations are a must. **⬛Carlton Guest House ❸,** 22 Evesham Pl., has spacious rooms and spectacular service. (☎293 548. Singles £20-26; doubles £40-52; triples £60-78. Cash only.) To reach **YHA Stratford (HI) ❷,** Wellsbourne Rd., follow B4086 from the town center (35min.), or take bus #X18 or 77 from Bridge St. (10min., 1 per hr., £2). This isolated hostel caters mostly to school groups and families and is a solid, inexpensive option for longer stays. (☎297 093. Breakfast included. Internet £4.20 per hr. Dorms £24, under 18 £15. £3 HI discount. MC/V.) The pristine white linens and pastel walls will make you feel like you've been whisked to the seaside at **The Marlyn Hotel ❸,** 3 Chestnut Walk, a classy new B&B near the RSC theater. (☎293 752. Full English breakfast included. Singles £30; doubles £45. AmEx/MC/V.)

Classy yet cozy, **The Oppo ❸,** 13 Sheep St., receives rave reviews from locals. (☎269 980. Entrees from £9. Open daily for lunch noon-2pm; dinner M-Th 5:30-9:30pm, F-Sa 5-11pm, and Su 6-9:30pm. MC/V.) **Hussain's ❷,** 6a Chapel St., a favorite of Ben Kingsley, offers Stratford's best Indian menu, featuring tandoori with homecrushed spices. (☎276 506. 3-course lunch £6. Entrees from £6.75. Open daily 12:30-2:30pm and 5pm-midnight. AmEx/MC/V.) A **Somerfield** supermarket is in Town Sq. (☎292 604. Open M-W 8am-7pm, Th-Sa 8am-8pm, Su 10am-4pm.)

**◉🎭 THE PLAY'S THE THING.** Stratford's Will-centered sights are best seen before 11am, when daytrippers arrive, or after 4pm, when crowds disperse. Fans can buy the **All Five Houses** ticket for admission to all official Shakespeare properties: Anne Hathaway's Cottage, Mary Arden's House, Hall's Croft, New Place and Nash's House, and Shakespeare's Birthplace. (Tickets available at all houses. £14, students £12.) The **Three In-Town Houses** pass covers the latter three sights. (£11, students £9.) **Shakespeare's Birthplace,** on Henley St., is part period re-creation and part exhibit of Shakespeare's life and works. (☎201 822. Open in summer M-Sa 9am-5pm, Su 9:30am-5pm; mid-season daily 10am-5pm; winter M-Sa 10am-4pm, Su 10:30am-4pm. £7, students £5.50.) **New Place,** on Chapel St., was Stratford's finest home when Shakespeare bought it in 1597; now only the foundation remains, the house itself destroyed by a disgruntled 19th-century owner to spite Bard tourists. New Place can be viewed from **Nash's House,** on Chapel St., which belonged to the first husband of Shakespeare's granddaughter. **Hall's Croft** and **Mary Arden's House** also capitalize on connections to Shakespeare's extended family and provide exhibits on Elizabethan daily life. Pay homage to the Bard's **grave** in the **Holy Trinity Church,** Trinity St. (☎266 316. Open Apr.-Sept. M-Sa 8:30am-6pm, Su noon-5pm; Mar. and Oct. M-Sa 9am-5pm, Su noon-5pm; Nov.-Feb. M-Sa 9am-4pm, Su noon-5pm. Last entry 20min. before close. Requested donation £1.)

The ◪**Royal Shakespeare Company** sells well over one million tickets each year. The **Royal Shakespeare Theatre** and the **Swan Theatre,** the RSC's more intimate neighbor, are currently undergoing a £100 million renovation and will re-open in 2010. The company will continue to perform shows down the road at **The Courtyard Theatre.** Visitors can get backstage tours and a glimpse at the high-tech stage to be installed at the Royal Shakespeare Theatre. Tickets are sold through the box office in the foyer of the Courtyard Theatre. (☎0870 800 1110; www.rsc.org.uk. Open M and W-Sa 9:30am-8pm, Tu 10am-8pm. Tickets £5-40. Students and those under 25 receive half-price tickets for M-W evening performances in advance, otherwise by availability on performance days. Standby tickets in summer £15; winter £12. Disabled travelers should call ahead to advise the box office of their needs; some performances feature sign language interpretation or audio description.) The Shakespeare Birthplace Trust hosts a **Poetry Festival** every Sunday evening in July and August. Past participants include Seamus Heaney, Ted Hughes, and Derek Walcott. (☎292 176. Tickets £7-10.) Theater crowds abound at the ◪**Dirty Duck Pub,** 66 Waterside, where RSC actors make appearances almost nightly. (☎297 312. Open M-Sa 11am-11pm, Su noon-10:30pm.)

🞂 **DAYTRIP FROM STRATFORD: WARWICK CASTLE.** From the towers of 14th-century ◪**Warwick Castle,** the countryside unfolds like a medieval kingdom. This spectacular castle, one of England's finest, has dungeons with life-sized wax soldiers preparing for battle, while wax "knights" and "craftsmen" discuss their trades in the festival village. Events include summer jousting tournaments, storytelling, and live concerts. Ask at the TIC in Stratford-upon-Avon about discounted tickets. (☎0870 442 2000; www.warwick-castle.co.uk. Open daily Apr.-Sept. 10am-6pm; Oct.-Mar. 10am-5pm. £14-17, seniors £10-13, children £8-11, families £43-46. Audio tours £3.) **Trains** arrive at the station off Coventry Rd. and run to Birmingham (40min., 2 per hr., £5.20), London Marylebone (2hr., 3 per hr., £15-41), and Stratford (25min., 1 per 1½hr., £3.40). Local **buses** #16 and 18 also stop at Market Pl. from Stratford (20min., 3-4 per hr., £2.60-2.90).

# THE COTSWOLDS

The Cotswolds have deviated little from their etymological roots: "Cotswolds" means "sheep enclosures in rolling hillsides." Despite the sleepy moniker, the Cotswolds are filled with rich history and traditions—like cheese-rolling—that reach back to Roman and Saxon times. While it may seem that classic English hedgerows outnumber people, the more urban towns of Gloucester, Cirencester, and Cheltenham supply both shoppers and hikers in the region.

🞂 **TRANSPORTATION AND PRACTICAL INFORMATION.** Public transit to and in the Cotswolds is scarce; planning ahead is a must. Useful gateway cities are Bath, Bristol, Cheltenham, Oxford, and Stratford-upon-Avon. **Moreton-in-Marsh,** one of the larger villages, runs **trains** to London (1½hr., every 1-2hr., £30) via Oxford (30min., £9.50). It's easier to reach the Cotswolds by **bus.** The Cheltenham **TIC** (Municipal Offices, 77 The Promenade. ☎522 878) offers the free *Getting There* pamphlet, which has detailed bus information. *Explore the Cotswolds by Public Transport*, available for free at village TICs, has bus frequency and routes. Pulham's Coaches #801 (☎01451 820 369) runs from Chelten-ham to Moreton-in-Marsh (1hr., M-Sa 7 per day, £1.75) via Bourton-on-the-Water (35min., £1.65) and Stow-on-the-Wold (50min., £1.75).

For a comprehensive look at the region, try the **Cotswold Discovery Tour,** a full-day bus tour that starts in Bath and visits five of the most scenic and touristed villages. (☎09067 112 000; www.madmax.abel.co.uk. Apr.-Oct. Tu, Th, Su 9am-5:15pm. £25.) Local roads are ideal for **biking,** the best way to explore the Cotswolds. Rent bikes at **The Toy Shop** on High St. in Moreton-in-Marsh, where you can also find maps and route suggestions. (☎01608 650 756. £12 per ½-day, £14 per day. Open M, W-Sa 9am-1pm and 2-5pm.) Visitors can also see the Cotswolds as the English have for centuries by treading the paths from village to village. The **Cotswold Way,** spanning 160km from Bath to Chipping Camden, can be done in a week and passes through pasturelands and the ruins of ancient settlements. The **National Trails Office** (☎01865 810 224) has details on this and other trails. Town TICs offer help-ful walking and cycling guides and the free *Cotswold Events* booklet, which lists music festivals, antique markets, cheese-rolling events, and woolsack races.

**WINCHCOMBE, MORETON-IN-MARSH, STOW-ON-THE-WOLD, AND BOUR-TON-ON-THE-WATER.** Ten kilometers north of Cheltenham on A46, **Sudeley Castle,** once the manor of King Ethelred the Unready, crowns the town of **Winchcombe.** Today, the castle is home of Lord and Lady Ashcombe and has pristine gardens and exhibits on Tudor life. (☎01242 602 308; www.sudeleycas-tle.co.uk. Open daily Mar.-Oct. 11am-5pm. £7.20, students £6.20.) The Winch-combe **TIC** is on High St., next to Town Hall. (☎01242 602 925. Open Apr.-Oct. M-Sa 10am-5pm, Su 10am-4pm; Nov.-Mar. Sa-Su 10am-4pm.)

With a train station, frequent bus service, and a bike shop, **Moreton-in-Marsh** is a convenient base for exploring the region. **Warwick House B&B ❸,** London Rd., has an energetic owner and many perks, including four-poster beds, Wi-Fi, and ample breakfasts. Follow A44 east out of town toward Oxford for 10min.; the B&B is on the left. (☎01608 650 733; www.snoozeandsizzle.com. Free pickup from train sta-tion. £30-35 per person. Cash only.) Grab tea and lunch at **Tilly's Tea Room ❶,** High St., and choose from a host of homemade cakes and jams to enjoy their garden. (☎01608 650 000. Tea and scone £4.35. Cash only.) The **TIC** is in the District Council Building on High St. (☎01608 650 881. Open M 8:45am-4pm, Tu-Th 8:45am-5:15pm, F 8:45am-4:45pm, Sa 10am-1pm; low season reduced hours.)

The hyphenation paradise continues in **Stow-on-the-Wold,** the self-proclaimed "Heart of the Cotswolds" and home to many inns and taverns. The **YHA hostel (HI) ❷,** next to the TIC in The Square, offers rooms with village views and bath. (☎01451 830 497. Laundry available. Reception 8-10am and 5-10pm. Lockout 10am-5pm. Curfew 11pm. Reserve 1 month ahead. Dorms £18, under 18 £15. £3 HI dis-count. MC/V.) A **Tesco** supermarket is on Fosse Way. (Open M-F 6am-midnight, Sa 6am-10pm, Su 10am-4pm.) The **TIC** is in Hollis House on The Square. (☎01451 831 082. Open Easter-Oct. M-Sa 9:30am-5:30pm; Nov.-Easter M-Sa 9:30am-4:30pm.)

**Bourton-on-the-water** is acclaimed as the Cotswolds' most beautiful village. The footbridge-straddled River Windrush runs along the main street, giving the town the moniker "Venice of the Cotswolds." The region is home to many trailheads, including those for the **Oxford, Warden's, Heart of England, Windrush,** and **Gloucester-shire Ways.** The **Cotswold Perfumery,** Victoria St., offers a factory tour and a make-your-own perfumery course, but a mere visit to the shop is an olfactory experi-ence. (☎01451 820 698; www.cotswold-perfumery.co.uk. Open M-Sa 9:30am-5pm, Su 10:30am-5pm. £5, students £3.50. Call ahead for a tour; usually 1-2 per day.)

# BIRMINGHAM                                                          ☎0121

Birmingham (pop. 1,000,000), second to London in population, has a long-standing reputation as a grim, industrial metropolis. To counter this bleak stereotype, the city has revitalized its central district with a visitor magnet: **shopping**—and lots of it. The epic **Bullring,** Europe's largest retail establishment, is the foundation of Birmingham's material-world makeover. Recognizable by the wavy, scaled Selfridges department store, the center has more than 140 shops and cafes. (☎632 1500; www.bullring.co.uk. Open M-F 9:30am-8pm, Sa 9am-8pm, Su 11am-5pm.) Twelve minutes south of town by rail or bus lies ⚑**Cadbury World,** a cavity-inducing celebration of the famed chocolate empire. Take a train from New St. to Bournville, or bus #84 from the city center. (☎451 4159. Open Mar.-Oct. daily 10am-3pm; Nov.-Feb. Tu-Th and Sa-Su 10am-3pm. Reserve ahead. £12.50, students £10.) The **Birmingham International Jazz Festival** brings over 200 performers to town during the first two weeks of July. (☎454 7020; www.birminghamjazzfestival.com.)

**Hagley Road** has several budget B&Bs—the farther away from downtown, the lower the prices (and standards). Take bus #9, 109, 126, or 139 from Colomore Row to Hagley Rd. Near the bus stop, **Birmingham Central Backpackers ❷,** 58 Coventry St., is a recently renovated pub now sporting tidy dorm rooms and a TV lounge. The full bar also stocks plenty of snacks and simple items for dinner. (☎643 0033; www.birminghambackpackers.com. Breakfast included. Laundry and Internet available for a small donation to the Oxfam International charity. Beds from £16. AmEx/MC/V.) Slightly farther out, **The Merry Maid ❷,** 263 Moseley Rd., offers standard dorm-style rooms and a knowledgeable staff. (☎440 6126; www.birminghambackpackers.com. Beds from £16. MC/V.) **Canalside Cafe ❶,** 35 Worcester Bar, serves baguettes and hearty specials like chili. (☎441 9862. Most sandwiches £3-5. Open daily 9am-5pm, with occasional evening openings. Cash only.) Get groceries from **Sainsbury's,** Martineau Pl., 17 Union St. (☎236 6496. Open M-Sa 7am-8pm, Su 11am-5pm.) **Broad Street,** with trendy cafe-bars and clubs, gets rowdy on weekends; as always, exercise caution at night. Pick up the bimonthly *What's On* to discover Birmingham's latest hot spots. ⚑**The Yardbird,** Paradise Pl., is an excellent alternative to the club scene. No dress code, no cover, no pretense—just good music, big couches, and drinks with friends. DJs spin beats on Friday, with live music on Saturdays. (☎212 2524. Open M-W and Su 11am-midnight, Th-Sa 11am-2am.) A popular bar at the heart of city nightlife, **Rococo Lounge,** 260 Broad St., has a large outdoor patio and retro-modern furnishings. It's near similar venues if you get bored with or kicked out of another. (☎207 0283. Open Su-W 9am-1am, Th-Sa 9am-2am.) A gay-friendly scene centers around **Lower Essex Street.** At **Nightingale,** Essex House, Kent St., a predominantly gay clientele enjoys two dance floors, five bars, a jazz lounge, and a billiard room. (☎622 1718; www.nightingaleclub.co.uk. Cover varies. Open Tu-Th 9pm-2am, F 7pm-4am, Sa 7pm-6am, Su 7pm-2am.)

Birmingham is at the center of train and bus lines between London, central Wales, southwest England, and all northern destinations. **Trains** run from New St. Station (☎08457 484 950) to: Liverpool Lime St. (1½hr., 1 per hr., £20); London Euston (1½hr., 2 per hr., £28); Manchester Piccadilly (2hr., 2 per hr., £19); Oxford (1¼hr., 1 per hr., £19). National Express **buses** (☎08705 808 080) leave from Digbeth Station for: Cardiff (1½hr., 4 per day, £19.40); Liverpool (1hr., 5 per day, £13); London Heathrow (3hr., 1 per hr., £14); Manchester (2½hr., 1 per 2hr., £11). The **TIC,** The Rotune, 150 New St., books rooms for a 10% deposit and offers listings and flyers for budget accommodations. (☎202 5099; www.beinbirmingham.com. Branch at the junction of New and Corporation St. Open M-Sa 9:30am-5:30pm, Su 10:30am-4:30pm.) **Postal Code:** B2 4TU.

# CAMBRIDGE ☎01223

Unlike museum-oriented, metropolitan Oxford, Cambridge is a town for students before tourists. It was here that Newton's gravity, Watson and Crick's model of DNA, Byron and Milton's poetry, and Milne's Winnie the Pooh were born. No longer the exclusive academy of upper-class sons, the university feeds the minds of female, international, and state-school pupils alike. At exams' end, Cambridge explodes in Pimm's-soaked glee, and May Week is a swirl of parties and balls.

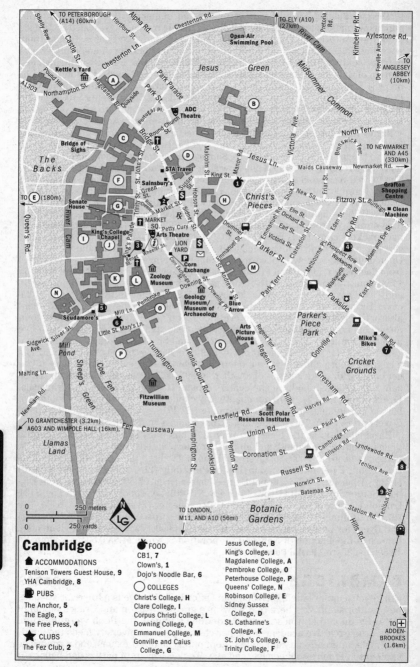

# Cambridge

🏠 **ACCOMMODATIONS**
Tenison Towers Guest House, **9**
YHA Cambridge, **8**

🍴 **FOOD**
CB1, **7**
Clown's, **1**
Dojo's Noodle Bar, **6**

📦 **PUBS**
The Anchor, **5**
The Eagle, **3**
The Free Press, **4**

⭐ **CLUBS**
The Fez Club, **2**

◯ **COLLEGES**
Christ's College, **H**
Clare College, **I**
Corpus Christi College, **L**
Downing College, **Q**
Emmanuel College, **M**
Gonville and Caius
    College, **G**

Jesus College, **B**
King's College, **J**
Magdalene College, **A**
Pembroke College, **O**
Peterhouse College, **P**
Queens' College, **N**
Robinson College, **E**
Sidney Sussex
    College, **D**
St. Catharine's
    College, **K**
St. John's College, **C**
Trinity College, **F**

**🖃🔢 TRANSPORTATION AND PRACTICAL INFORMATION. Trains** (☎ 08457 484 950) run from Station Rd. to London King's Cross (45min., 3 per hr., £18) and Ely (20min., 3 per hr., round-trip £3.50). National Express **buses** (☎ 08705 808 080) run from Drummer St. Station to London Victoria (3hr., 1 per hr., £10), Gatwick (4hr., 1 per hr., £30), Heathrow (2½hr., 2 per hr., £25), and Stansted (1hr., 1 per hr., £10). Stagecoach Express buses (☎ 01604 676 060) go to Oxford (3hr., 1 per hr., from £6.50). **Bicycles** are the main mode of transportation in Cambridge. Rent at **Mike's Bikes,** 28 Mill Rd. (☎ 312 591. £10 per day plus £35 deposit. Open M-Sa 9am-6pm, Su 10am-4pm. MC/V.) The **TIC,** south of Market Sq. on Wheeler St., books rooms for £3 plus 10% deposit and sells the Cambridge Visitors Card (£2.50), which gives city-wide discounts. (☎ 09065 862 526; www.visitcambridge.org. Open Easter-Oct. M-F 10am-5:30pm, Sa 10-5pm, Su 11am-4pm; Nov.-Easter M-F 10am-5:30pm, Sa 10am-5pm.) **Postal Code:** CB2 3AA.

**🖃🖸 ACCOMMODATIONS AND FOOD.** John Maynard Keynes, who studied and taught at Cambridge, tells us that low supply and high demand usually means one thing: high prices. **B&Bs** are around **Portugal Street** and **Tenison Road** outside the city center. Book ahead in summer and check the guide to accommodations (£0.50) at the TIC. **YHA Cambridge (HI) ❷,** 97 Tenison Rd., close to the train station, has a relaxed, welcoming character with popular TV lounges and a well-equipped kitchen. (☎ 354 601. Breakfast included. Lockers £1. Laundry £3. Internet £0.50 per 7min. Reception 24hr. Dorms £19, under 18 £15. MC/V.) **Tension Towers Guest House ❹,** 148 Tension Rd., two blocks from the train station, has freshly baked muffins and impeccable rooms. (☎ 363 924; www.cambridgecitytenisontowers.com. Singles £35; doubles £55. Cash only.) South of town, **Hills Road** and **Mill Road** are full of budget restaurants popular with the college crowd. **🖾Clown's ❶,** 54 King St., serves huge portions (£2.50-6.50) of pasta and dessert. (☎ 355 711. Set menu with drink, salad, small pasta, and cake £6.50. Open M-Sa 8am-midnight, Su 8am-11pm. Cash only.) The walls are crammed with books at **CB1 ❶,** 32 Mill Rd., a decidedly chill student-hangout coffee shop. (☎ 576 306. Free Wi-Fi. Coffee £1-1.50. Open M-F 8am-8pm, Sa-Su 10am-8pm. Cash only.) **Dojo's Noodle Bar ❶,** 1-2 Mill Rd., whips up enormous plates of Asian noodles for less than £7. (☎ 363 471; www.dojonoodlebar.co.uk. Open M-Th noon-2:30pm and 5:30-11pm, F noon-4pm and 5:30-11pm, Sa-Su noon-11pm. MC/V.) **Market Square** has pyramids of fruits and vegetables. (Open M-Sa 9:30am-4:30pm.) Students buy their Pimm's and baguettes at **Sainsbury's,** 44 Sidney St. (☎ 366 891. Open M-Sa 8am-10pm, Su 11am-5pm.)

**🖸 SIGHTS.** Cambridge packs some of England's most breathtaking architecture into three square kilometers. Soaring **King's College Chapel** and St. John's **Bridge of Sighs** are sightseeing staples, while more obscure college courts veil largely undiscovered gardens and courtyards. The **University of Cambridge** has three eight-week terms: Michaelmas (Oct.-Dec.), Lent (Jan.-Mar.), and Easter (Apr.-June). Many of its colleges close to sightseers during Easter term, and virtually all are closed during exams (mid-May to mid-June); your best bet is to call ahead for hours. Porters (bowler-wearing former servicemen) guard the gates. Travelers that look like undergrads (no backpack, camera, or Cambridge sweatshirt) can often wander freely through the grounds after hours. The fastest way to blow your cover is to trample the sacred grass of the courtyards, a privilege reserved for the elite.

If you only have time for a few colleges, visit Trinity, King's, St. John's, and Queens's. Sir Isaac Newton originally measured the speed of sound by timing the echo in the cloisters along the north side of the Great Court at **Trinity College,** on Trinity St. Also the alma mater of Vladimir Nabokov, Ernest Rutherford, and Alfred Lord Tennyson, Trinity houses the stunning **Wren Library,** with A. A. Milne's handwritten manuscript of *Winnie the Pooh* and the original copy of Newton's *Principia.* (☎ 338 400. Chapel and courtyard open daily 10am-5pm. Library open

M-F noon-2pm. Easter-Oct. £2.20, students £1.30; Nov.-Easter free.) **King's College,** south of Trinity on King's Parade, is E. M. Forster and Salman Rushdie's alma mater. Peter Paul Reubens's *Adoration of the Magi* hangs behind the altar of its Gothic chapel. (☎331 100. Open M-Sa 9:30am-5pm, Su 10am-5pm. Tours arranged through the TIC. £4.50, students £3.) Established in 1511 by Henry VIII's mother, **St. John's College,** on St. John's St., is one of seven colleges founded by women. It boasts the 12th-century School of Pythagoras, thought to be the oldest complete building in Cambridge, a replica of the Bridge of Sighs, and the longest room in the city—the Fellows' Room in Second Court spans 28m. (☎338 600. Open daily 10am-5:30pm. £2.50, students £1.50.) **Queens' College,** Silver St., has the only unaltered Tudor courtyard in Cambridge. Despite rumors to the contrary, its Mathematical Bridge is supported by screws and bolts, not just by mathematical principle. (☎335 511. Open Mar.-Oct. M-F 10am-5pm, Sa-Su 9:30am-5pm. £1.30.) A break from academia, the ✠**Fitzwilliam Museum,** on Trumpington St., displays Egyptian, Greek, and Asian treasures as well as works by Brueghel, Monet, and Reubens. (☎332 900. Open Tu-Sa 10am-5pm, Su noon-5pm. Suggested donation £3.)

🎵🎭 **ENTERTAINMENT AND NIGHTLIFE. May Week** is in June—you would think those bright Cambridge students could understand a calendar. An elaborate celebration of the end of the term, the week is crammed with concerts, plays, and balls followed by recuperative riverside breakfasts and 5am punting. ✠**Punting** (p. 181) on the River Cam is a favorite pastime in Cambridge. Beware of punt-bombers: jumping from bridges into the river alongside a punt, thereby tipping its occupants into the Cam, has evolved into an art form. Touristy? Maybe, but it's still a blast. **Scudamore's,** Silver St. Bridge, rents boats. (☎359 750; www.scudamores.com. M-F £14 per hr. plus £70 deposit, Sa-Su £16 per hr. MC/V.) **King Street** has a diverse collection of pubs. At **The Anchor,** Silver St., a crowded undergrad watering hole, you can have a beer in the same spot that Pink Floyd's Syd Barrett drew his inspiration. Savor a pint outdoors and scoff at colliding amateur punters. (☎353 554. Open M-Sa 10am-11pm, Su 11am-10:30pm. Food served M-Sa noon-9:30pm, Su noon-9pm.) Popular with locals, **The Free Press,** Prospect Row, has no pool table, no cell phones, and no loud music—just good beer and conversation. (☎368 337. Open M-F noon-2:30pm and 6-11pm, Sa noon-3pm and 6-11pm, Su noon-3pm and 7-10:30pm.) When Watson and Crick ran into **The Eagle,** 8 Benet St., to announce their discovery of DNA, the barmaid insisted they settle their 4-shilling tab before she'd serve them. Cambridge's oldest pub also has a Royal Airforce room, where WWII pilots stood on each other's shoulders to burn their initials into the ceiling. (☎505 020. Open M-Sa 11am-11pm, Su noon-10:30pm.) **The Fez Club,** 15 Market Passage, draws students to its Moroccan setting with Latin and trance. (Cover £2-8. M and W students ½-price. Open daily 9pm-3am.)

# NORTHERN ENGLAND

The north's major cities grew out of the wool and coal industries, and bear the 19th-century scars to prove it, but their reinvigorated city centers have embraced post-industrial hipness with fresh youth culture. The region's innovative music and arts scenes are world-famous: Liverpool and Manchester alone have produced four of *Q Magazine*'s 10 biggest rock stars of the 20th century. When you need a break from frenetic urbanity, find respite in the Peak or Lake District.

## MANCHESTER ☎0161

Teeming with electronic beats and post-industrial glitz, Manchester (pop. 430,000) has risen from factory soot to savor a reputation as one of England's hippest spots. In 1996, the IRA bombed the city center, sparking urban renewal that has given

Manchester a sleek modern look. The city is a hive of activity, from the shopping districts and museums to the wild nightlife and preeminent football team.

**TRANSPORTATION AND PRACTICAL INFORMATION. Flights** arrive at **Manchester International Airport** (**MAN**; ☎ 489 3000). **Trains** leave Piccadilly Station on London Rd., for: Birmingham (1¾hr., 1 per hr., £23); Edinburgh (4hr., 5 per day, £45); Liverpool (50min., 2 per hr., £9); London Euston (2½-3hr., 1 per hr., £59); York (40min., 2 per hr., £18). Trains from Victoria Station on Victoria St. go to Liverpool (50min., 2 per hr., £9). National Express **buses** (☎ 08705 808 080) go from Chorlton St. to Liverpool (1hr., 1 per hr., £6) and London (4-6hr., 1 per hr., £22). Nearly 50 local bus routes stop at Piccadilly Gardens (1-day bus pass £3.30); route maps are available at the TIC. **Manchester Visitor Centre,** in the Town Hall Extension on Lloyd St., books rooms for a £2.50 free plus 10% deposit. (☎ 234 3157; www.visitmanchester.com. Open M-Sa 10am-5:30pm, Su 10:30am-4:30pm.) Free **Internet** is available at **Central Library,** St. Peter's Sq. (☎ 234 1900. Open M-Th 9am-8pm, F-Sa 9am-5pm.) **Postal Code:** M2 1BB.

**ACCOMMODATIONS AND FOOD.** Browse the free *Where to Stay* (at the TIC) for listings. Book ahead in summer. **Hilton Chambers ❷,** 15 Hilton St., has a helpful staff and large, clean rooms, topped off with a grill-equipped roof deck. (☎ 236 4414; www.hattersgroup.com. Laundry £5. Free Wi-Fi. Reception 24hr. Dorms £15-21; doubles £28-35. MC/V.) Around the corner, **The Hatters Tourist Hostel ❷,** 50 Newton St., housed in a renovated hat factory, has clean but crowded rooms and friendly service. (☎ 236 9500; www.hattersgroup.com. Breakfast included. Laundry £1.50. Reception 24hr. Dorms £14-18; doubles £45; triples £60. MC/V.) Take the metro to G-Mex Station or bus #33 (dir.: Wigan) from Piccadilly Gardens to Deansgate to reach the spacious **YHA Manchester (HI) ❸,** Potato Wharf, Castlefield. (☎ 0870 770 5950; www.yhamanchester.org.uk. Breakfast included. Laundry £1.50. Internet £0.70 per min. Reception 24hr. Dorms £21; doubles £45. MC/V.)

Restaurants in **Chinatown** can be pricey, but most offer a reasonable, multi-course "Businessman's Lunch" (M-F noon-2pm; £4-8). Better yet, visit **Curry Mile,** a stretch of affordable Asian restaurants on Wilmslow Rd. For delicious food with unique character, stop at ⬛**Trof ❷,** 2a Landcross Rd, a bohemian cafe, bar, and restaurant. Wash down a bacon and brie sandwich (£4.25) with one of 45 international beers. (☎ 224 0476; www.trof.co.uk. Open daily 9am-midnight. MC/V.) **Soup Kitchen ❶,** 31-33 Spear St., serves homemade soups and pies. Arrive early—the soups of the day are usually gone by 2pm. (☎ 236 5100; www.soup-kitchen.co.uk. Lunch special £4. Open M-F 9am-4pm. Cash only.) **Tampopo Noodle House ❷,** 16 Albert Sq., is a Manchester favorite, serving noodles from Indonesia, Japan, Malaysia, Thailand, and Vietnam. (☎ 819 1966; www.tampopo.co.uk. Noodles £6-11. Open daily noon-11pm. AmEx/MC/V.) Pick up groceries at **Tesco,** 58-66 Market St. (☎ 911 9400. Open M-F 6am-midnight, Sa 6am-10pm, Su 11am-5pm.)

**SIGHTS AND ENTERTAINMENT.** The ⬛**Manchester Art Gallery,** Nicholas St., features interactive exhibits (try to make one of the paintings burp) and an art restoration gallery. The pre-Raphaelite collection is impressive. (☎ 235 8888. Open Tu-Su and bank holidays 10am-5pm. Free.) Don't miss the exploration of modern urban culture and art at the **Urbis** museum, Cathedral Gardens. The awe-inspiring museum is itself a sculpture, covered in 2200 plates of glass beneath a "ski-slope" copper roof. (☎ 605 8200; www.urbis.org.uk. Open Tu-Su 10am-6pm. Free.) The **Museum of Science and Industry,** Liverpool Rd., in Castlefield, displays working looms and steam engines in an illustration of Britain's industrialization. (☎ 832 2244. Open daily 10am-5pm. Free. Special exhibits £3-5.) **Central Library,** behind the Town Hall Extension, is one of the largest municipal libraries in Europe, holding a music and theater library, a language and literature library, and the UK's second-largest Judaica collection (☎ 234 1900). The **John Rylands Library,** 150 Deansgate,

GREAT BRITAIN

keeps rare books. Its most famous holding is the St. John Fragment, a piece of New Testament writing from the 2nd century. (☎275 3764; www.library.manchester.ac.uk. Open M and W-Sa 10am-5m, Tu and Su noon-5pm. Free.)

Loved and reviled in equal proportion, Manchester United is one of England's top football teams. From Old Trafford Metrolink stop, follow the signs up Warwick Rd. to the **Manchester United Museum and Tour Centre,** Sir Matt Busby Way, at the Old Trafford football stadium. Memorabilia from the club's 1878 inception to its recent trophy-hogging success may just convert you into a fanatic. (☎0870 442 1994. Open daily 9:30am-5pm. Tours 6 per hr. except on match days. Reserve ahead. ₤9.) The **Royal Exchange Theatre** has returned to St. Ann's Sq. after an IRA bomb destroyed the original building in 1996. The theater stages Shakespearean productions and premieres original works. (☎833 9333; www.royalexchange.co.uk. Box office open M-Sa 9:30am-7:30pm. Tickets ₤7.25-26. M under 25 ₤5.) The Gay Village (see **Nightlife**) hosts a number of festivals, most notably **Manchester Pride** (Aug. 2-4; ☎230 2624; www.manchesterpride.com), which raises money for GLBT organizations and AIDS relief.

> ❗ Streets in the **Northern Quarter** are dimly lit at night. If you're crossing from Piccadilly to Swan St. or Great Ancoats St., use Oldham St., where the neon-lit clubs provide reassurance. There's no shame in short taxi trips at night.

■ **NIGHTLIFE.** At night, many of Manchester's lunchtime spots turn into pre-club drinking venues or become clubs themselves. At **Thirsty Scholar,** off Oxford St., the students crowd into a small, dark bar underneath a railroad bridge. On weekend nights, the thud of overhead trains is drowned out by the music of local DJs. (☎236 6071. M and Th acoustic nights. F-Su DJ. Open M-Th 11am-2am, F-Sa 11am-2:30am, Su 11am-1am.) **The Temple,** 100 Great Bridgewater, makes for a one-of-a-kind experience, serving German beer in a Victorian public-toilet-turned-pub. (☎278 1610. Open daily 1pm-1am.) Centered around **Oldham Street,** the **Northern Quarter** is the city's youthful outlet for live music. Partiers head to **Oxford Street** for late-night clubbing. At **Cord,** 8 Dorsey St., corduroy meets chic. No, really. The small venue makes for a subdued, exclusive drink. (Open Su-Th noon-10:30pm, F-Sa noon-1am.) Gay and lesbian clubbers should check out the **Gay Village,** northeast of Princess St. Evening crowds fill the bars lining **Canal Street,** but the area is also lively during the day. **Queer,** 4 Canal St., has huge booths and flatscreen TVs. When the weather's warm, sit outside with the rest of Manchester. (☎228 1360; www.queer-manchester.com. Open M-Sa 11am-2am, Su 11am-12:30am.)

# LIVERPOOL ☎0151

Many Brits still scoff at once-industrial Liverpool, but Scousers—as Liverpudlians are colloquially known, in reference to a local stew dish—have watched their metropolis undergo a cultural face-lift, trading in working-class grit for offbeat vitality. Several free museums, two deified football teams, and top-notch nightlife helped earn the city the title of **European Capital of Culture 2008.** Oh, yeah—some fuss is made over The Beatles.

■ **TICKET TO RIDE. Trains** (☎08457 484 950) leave Lime St. Station for: Birmingham (1¾hr., M-Sa 1 per hr., ₤28); London Euston (3hr., 1 per hr., ₤60); Manchester Piccadilly (1hr., 2-4 per hr., ₤8.50). National Express **buses** (☎08705 808 080) run from Norton St. Station to: Birmingham (3hr., 4 per day, ₤14); London (4½-5½hr., 2 per hr., ₤22); Manchester (1hr., 1-3 per hr., ₤6). The Isle of Man Steam Packet Company (☎08705 523 523; www.steam-packet.com) runs **ferries** from Princess Dock to the Isle of Man. P&O Irish Ferry service (☎870 2424 777; www.poirishsea.com) runs to Dublin. The **TIC,** 08 Pl., has the free, handy brochure *Visitor Guide to Liverpool, Merseyside, and England's Northwest*, and books rooms for a 10% fee. (☎233 2008; www.visitliverpool.com. Open M and W-Sa 9am-6pm, Tu 10am-6pm, Su 11am-4pm.) Expert guide Phil Hughes runs personalized 3-4hr. Beatles tours leave from Strawberry Fields and Eleanor Rigby's grave (☎228 4565; £13). Surf the **Internet** for free or peruse a helpful scale model of the city at the Central **Library** on William Brown St. (☎233 5817. Open M-F 9am-6pm, Sa 9am-5pm, Su noon-4pm.) **Postal Code:** L1 1AA.

**▛▟ GOLDEN SLUMBERS AND STRAWBERRY FIELDS FOREVER.** Budget hotels are located around **Lord Nelson Street,** next to the train station, and **Mount Pleasant,** one block from Brownlow Hill. ▊**Embassie Backpackers ❷**, is a first-rate, comfortable hostel. (☎707 1089; www.embassie.com. Free laundry. Free Internet. Reception 24hr. Dorms £15 first night, £14 thereafter. Cash only.) Housed in a former Victorian warehouse, **International Inn ❷**, 4 South Hunter St., is clean and fun, with a lounge and adjoining Internet cafe. (☎709 8135; www.internation-alinn.co.uk. Free coffee, tea, and toast. Internet £3 per hr. Dorms Su-Th £15, F-Sa £20; doubles £36/45. AmEx/MC/V.) **YHA Liverpool (HI) ❷**, 25 Tabley St., off The Wapping, is a tidy place with Beatles-themed rooms. (☎0870 7705 924. Kitchen available. Breakfast included. Dorms from £18, under 18 £16. Members only. MC/V.) Trendy cafes and budget-friendly kebab stands line **Bold** and **Hardman Streets.** Many of the fast-food joints on **Berry** and **Leece Streets** stay open late. At ▊**Tabac ❶**, 126 Bold St., sleek, trendy decor belies affordable food. Sandwiches (from £3.50) on freshly baked foccaccia are served all day. (☎709 9502. Breakfast from £2. Dinner specials £5.50-8. Open M-F 9am-11pm, Sa 9am-midnight, Su 10am-11pm. MC/V.) The **Granary Sandwich Bar ❶**, Drury Lane, has outrageously low prices. (☎236 0509. Open M-F 7:30am-2:30pm. Cash only.) **Hole in the Wall ❶**, 37 School Ln., offers a variety of barms (sandwiches) and quiches (from £4) for eat-in or take-out. (☎709 7733. Open M-Sa 10am-4:30pm. Cash only.) Pick up groceries at the **Tesco Metro** in Clayton Sq., across from St. John's Shopping Centre. (Open M-F 6am-midnight, Sa 6am-10pm, Su 11am-5pm.)

**▣ MAGICAL MYSTERY TOUR.** The TIC's **Beatles Map** (£3) leads visitors through the city's Beatles-themed sights including **Strawberry Fields** and **Penny Lane.** At Albert Dock, ▊**The Beatles Story** traces the rise and fall of the band through Hamburg, the Cavern Club, and a pseudo-shrine to John's legacy of love. (☎709 1963; www.beatlesstory.com. Open daily 10am-6pm. £10, students £7.) The Liverpool branch of the **Tate Gallery**, also on Albert Dock, contains a collection of 19th- and 20th-century art. (☎702 7400; www.tate.org.uk/liverpool. Open Tu-Su 10am-5:50pm. Suggested donation £2. Special exhibits £5, students £4.) The **Walker Art Gallery** focuses on British artists, from the 1700s to today. (☎709 1963; www.thewalker.org.uk. Open daily 10am-5pm. Free.) Completed in 1978, the Anglican **Liverpool Cathedral,** on Upper Duke St., boasts the highest Gothic arches and the heaviest bells in the world. Climb the tower for a view that extends to Wales. (☎709 6271; www.liverpoolcathedral.org.uk. Cathedral open daily 8am-6pm. Tower open daily Mar.-Sept. 11am-5pm; Oct.-Feb. 11am-4pm. Cathedral free, tower £4.25.) Neon-blue stained glass casts a glow over the controversially modern interior of the **Metropolitan Cathedral of Christ the King,** on Mt. Pleasant. (☎709 9222. Open in summer M-Sa 8am-6pm, Su 8am-5pm; reduced hours in winter. Free.) The **Liverpool** and **Everton football clubs**—intense rivals—offer tours of their grounds. Bus #26 runs from the city center to Liverpool F.C.'s Anfield. Bus #19 from the city center to Everton's Goodison Park. (Liverpool ☎260 6677; tour £10, students £6. Everton ☎330 2277; tour £8.50, students £5. Reserve ahead.)

**▛ A HARD DAY'S NIGHT.** Consult the *Liverpool Echo* (£0.35), sold daily by street vendors, for the most up-to-date information on city nightlife. The down-town **Ropewalks** area—especially **Matthew, Church,** and **Bold Streets**—overflows with clubbers on weekends. Fabulous **Society,** 64 Duke St., draws decadent crowds and posh VIPs to its steamy dance floor. (☎707 3575. Cover F and Su £5, Sa £10. Open F 10:30pm-2am, Sa 10:30pm-4am, Su 10:30pm-1am.) **The Cavern Club,** 10 Matthew St., where the Fab Four gained prominence, draws live bands, who hope history will repeat itself. (☎236 9091. Cover £2 on DJ nights, varies for live bands. Pub open M-Sa from 11am, Su noon-11:30pm. Club open M-Tu 11am-6pm, W-Sa 11am-2am, Su noon-12:30am.) **BaaBar,** 43-45 Fleet St., draws a youthful crowd and offers 35 varieties of shots (£1) with nearly nightly specials. (☎708 8673. Open M-Th 5pm-2am, F-Sa 5pm-3am, Su 5pm-1am. MC/V.)

# PEAK DISTRICT NATIONAL PARK

The Peak District isn't home to any true mountains, but its 1400 sq. km offer a bit of almost everything else. Surrounded by industrial giants Manchester, Nottingham, and Sheffield, the Peak District is a sanctuary of deep gullies, green pastures, and rocky hillsides, with picturesque villages and historic manors set against some of Britain's best scenery. Transportation is easiest in the south and near outlying cities, but hikers should head north for a more isolated escape.

**🖪🖌 TRANSPORTATION AND PRACTICAL INFORMATION.** The invaluable *Peak District Timetables* (£0.80), available at TICs, has accommodation and **bike** rental info, maps, and transit routes. Two **train** lines (☎08457 48 49 50) start in Manchester and enter the park at New Mills. One stops at Buxton, near the park's edge (1hr., 1 per hr., £6.70). The other crosses the park via Edale (50min., 12 per day, £7.70), Hope, and Hathersage (both 1hr., 12 per day, £7.85), ending in Sheffield (1½hr., 1 per hr., £12.90). **Buses** make a noble effort to connect scattered Peak towns; **Traveline** (☎0870 608 2608; www.traveline.org.uk) is a vital resource. **Transpeak** makes the 3hr. journey between Buxton, Bakewell, and Matlock (continuing to Manchester in one direction and Nottingham in the other), stopping at towns along the way (15 per day). Bus #173 runs from Bakewell to Castleton (1hr., 3-4 per day). Bus #200 runs from Castleton to Edale (20min., M-F 3 per day). The **Derbyshire Wayfarer** ticket, available at Manchester train stations and **NPICs,** allows one day of unlimited train and bus travel through Peak District as far north as Sheffield and as far south as Derby (£8, students £4).

The NPICs at Bakewell, Buxton, Castleton, and Edale offer walking guides. **YHA Hostels ❶** operates 15 locations in the park (reserve ahead; dorms £13-16). For Buxton, Castleton, and Edale, see below. For the park's nine **YHA Camping Barns (HI) ❶,** book at the **YHA Camping Barns Department,** Trevelyan House, Dimple Rd., Matlock, Derbyshire, DE4 3YH. (☎0870 770 8868; £6 per person.) The park has three **Cycle Hire Centres** (£14 per day); the free *Cycle Derbyshire*, available at NPICs, includes contact info, hours, locations, and a trail map.

**BAKEWELL AND EDALE.** The town of **Bakewell,** 50km southeast of Manchester, is the best base for exploring the region. Several scenic walks through the **White Peaks** begin nearby. **The Garden Room ❹,** 1 Park Rd., is a 5min. walk from the town center. (☎81 42 99. Singles £45. Cash only.) A **Midlands Co-op** sells groceries at the corner of Granby Rd. and Market St. (Open M-Sa 8am-10pm, Su 10am-4pm.) Bakewell's **NPIC** is in Old Market Hall, on Bridge St. (☎0870 444 7275. Open daily Mar.-Oct. 9:30am-5:30pm; Nov.-Feb. 10am-5pm.) The northern Dark Peak area contains some of the wildest, most rugged hill country in England, including the spectacular peat marshes around **Edale.** For details on shorter **trails** nearby, check out the National Park Authority's *8 Walks Around Edale* (£1.40). Edale itself offers little more than a church, cafe, pub, school, and the nearby **YHA Edale (HI) ❶,** Rowland Cote. (☎0870 770 5808. Dorms £15, under 18 £11. MC/V.)

**CASTLETON.** Castleton's main attraction is ■**Treak Cliff Cavern** and its purple seams of Blue John, a unique semi-precious mineral. (☎01433 62 05 71; www.blue-johnstone.com. Open daily Mar.-Oct. 10am-4:20pm; Nov.-Feb. 10am-3:20pm. 40min. tours 2-4 per hr. ₤6.80, students and YHA members ₤5.80.) The **NPIC** is on Buxton Rd. (☎01629 81 65 58. Open daily Easter-Oct. 9:30am-5:30pm; Nov.-Easter 10am-5pm.) **YHA Castleton (HI)** ❷ is in the heart of town. It may be unavailable in July and August, when it hosts children's camps. (☎0870 770 5758. Kitchen available. Reserve 2-3 weeks ahead. Open Feb.-Dec. Dorms ₤14, under 18 ₤10. MC/V.)

**BUXTON.** A main hub for Peak travel, the spa town of Buxton, highly reminiscent of Bath, is a picture of Georgian elegance. Just outside of town in the Buxton Country Park is the spectacular **Poole's Cavern,** a large cave that has drawn tourists for centuries; legend has it that Mary, Queen of Scots, once visited. (☎01298 269 78; www.poolescavern.co.uk. Open daily Mar.-Oct. 10am-5pm. 45min. tours every 30min. ₤6.75, students ₤5.50. Dress warmly.) The **TIC** is located in The Crescent, a large Georgian-style building at the center of town. (☎01298 251 06; www.visitbuxton.com. Open daily Mar.-Oct. 9:30am-5pm; Nov.-Feb. 10am-4pm.) **Roseleigh Hotel** ❸, Broad Walk overlooking Pavilion Gardens, has a reading parlor with shelves of travel and adventure books; the hosts are former tour guides. (☎01298 249 04; www.roseleighhotel.co.uk. ₤31-33 per person. MC/V.) **Co-op**, spring Gardens, sells groceries (☎278 44; open daily 8am-11pm), while **The Slopes Bar** ❶, also on Spring Gardens, offers light meals and cafe fare in a swanky bistro setting. (☎01298 238 04. Open 9:30am-midnight; hot food served noon-5pm. MC/V.)

# YORK ☎01904

With a history rife with conflict, York (pop. 137,000) is known as the "most haunted city in the world." Despite the lore—or because of it—the city remains one of England's top destinations. Once impenetrable to outsiders, the crumbling medieval walls of York are now defenseless against hordes of travelers. Brandishing cameras in place of swords, visitors come to ogle Britain's largest Gothic cathedral and down a pint at one of the city's many pubs.

▊▐ **TRANSPORTATION AND PRACTICAL INFORMATION. Trains** (☎08457 484 950) leave Station Rd. for: Edinburgh (2½hr., 2 per hr., ₤67); London King's Cross (2hr., 2 per hr., ₤74); Manchester Piccadilly (1½hr., 3 per hr., ₤18); Newcastle (1hr., 4 per hr., ₤21). National Express **buses** (☎08705 808 080) depart from 20 Rougier St.; Exhibition Sq.; the train station, Piccadilly; and the Stonebow for: Edinburgh (6hr., 1 per day, ₤31); London (5½hr., 15 per day, ₤23); and Manchester (3hr., 15 per day, ₤12). Take Station Rd. to Museum St., cross the bridge, and go left on St. Leonard's Pl. for the **TIC**, Exhibition Sq. (☎550 099; www.visityork.org. Open Apr.-Oct. M-Sa 9am-6pm, Su 10am-5pm; Nov.-Mar. M-Sa 9am-5pm, Su 10am-4pm.) **York Central Library**, Museum St., has **Internet** (☎655 631. ₤2 per hr.). **Postal Code:** YO1 8DA.

▐▌ **ACCOMMODATIONS AND FOOD. B&Bs** (from ₤30) are usually outside the city walls and scattered along **Blossom, Bootham,** and **Clifton Streets,** and **Bishopthorpe Road.** Reserve weeks ahead in summer. ■**Foss Bank Guest House** ❸, 16 Huntington Rd., has elegant, bright rooms with Wi-Fi, and a guest lounge. (☎635 548. Singles ₤29; doubles ₤60. Cash only.) **YHA York International** ❷, Water End, Clifton, 3km from the train station, has clean rooms, a bar (beer ₤2), and restaurant. Follow the river path "Dame Judi Dench" off Water End. (☎653 147. Kitchen available. Breakfast included. Dorms ₤20, under 18 ₤15; singles ₤28; doubles ₤52-55. AmEx/MC/V.) **York Backpackers** ❷, 88-90 Micklegate, is a Georgian mansion with a kitchen, TV lounge, and 24hr. "dungeon" bar. (☎627 720; www.yorkbackpackers.co.uk. Breakfast included. Laundry £3. Dorms £15; doubles £38. Ask about working in exchange for accommodation. MC/V; £0.50 surcharge.)

At ■ **El Piano** ❶, 15 Grape Ln., Mexican flavors infuse veggie dishes. Meals are served in 3 sizes: *chica* (£2.95), tapas (£4.25), and *ración* (£6) in this laid-back eatery. (☎ 610 676. Open M-Sa 10am-midnight, Su noon-5pm. MC/V.) If you can part the crowds, find a seat on the patio of local favorite **Oscar's Wine Bar and Bistro** ❷, 8 Little Stonegate, for epic portions. (☎ 652 002. Meals run from £6-8. Happy hour M 4-11pm, Tu-F 5-7pm, Su 4-10:30pm. Open M-Sa 11:30am-11pm, Su noon-10:30pm. MC/V). **Victor J's Artbar** ❶, 1 Finkle St., serves huge sandwiches and burgers in a casual bistro. (☎ 541 771. Open M-W 10am-midnight, Th-Sa 10am-1am, Su 11am-6pm. MC/V.) Opt to eat street-side and try sausages (£2), burgers (£2), and fresh squeezed lemonade (£2) from stands in **St. Sampson's Square.** For authentic York grub, visit one of the city's pubs, or find cheap eats at the many Indian restaurants outside the city gates. Greengrocers have peddled for centuries at **Newgate Market** between Parliament St. and the Shambles. (Open Apr.-Dec. M-Sa 9am-5pm, Su 9am-4:30pm; Jan.-Mar. M-Sa 9am-5pm.) **Sainsbury's** grocery is at the intersection of Foss Bank and Heworth Green. (☎ 643 801. Open M-Sa 8am-8pm, Su 11am-5pm.)

🖸 **SIGHTS.** A 4km walk along the **medieval walls** is the best introduction to York. Beware the tourist stampede, which only wanes in the morning and just before the walls and gates close at dusk. The **Association of Voluntary Guides** (☎ 621 756) offers free 2hr. **walking tours** at 10:15am, 2:15, and 6:45pm in summer and 10:15am in winter. ◪**York Minster** is the largest Gothic cathedral outside of Italy. It's estimated that half of the medieval stained glass in England lines this cathedral's walls. The Great East Window depicts the beginning and end of the world in over 100 scenes. Nearby, see if you can spot the statue of Archbishop Thomas Lamplugh. (☎ 557 216; www.yorkminster.org. Open daily 7am-6:30pm. Evensong M-Sa 5pm, Su 4pm. Combined ticket with Undercroft, Treasury, and Crypt £7.50; students £4.50. Free 1hr. tours when volunteers are available, daily Apr.-Sept. 9:30am-3:30pm; Oct.-Mar. 10am-2pm. £5.50) The cathedral also has other sights, like the **Chapter House,** which displays grotesque medieval carvings of everything from roguish demons to a three-faced woman. Look for the Virgin Mary on the right upon entering, a carving so small that it went unnoticed by Cromwell's idol-smashing thugs. (Open daily 9am-6pm. Free.) The **Central Tower** offers views of York's rooftops. Ascents are only permitted during a 5min. period every half-hour—the narrow staircase won't allow passing traffic. (Open daily Apr.-Sept. 9:30am-6pm; Oct.-Mar. 10am-4pm. £4.) After making your way down from the heights of the Minster, venture to its depths. The **Undercroft, Treasury,** and **Crypt** are filled with priceless treasures, including the spot where Constantine the Great was proclaimed Roman Emperor, and the 12th-century **Doomstone** upon which the cathedral was built. (Open daily Apr.-Sept. 9:30am-5pm; Oct.-Mar. 10am-5pm. £4, students £3. 45min. audio tour included.)

The ◪**York Castle Museum,** between Tower St. and Piccadilly, is arguably Britain's premier museum of daily life. Rooms include Kirkgate, a reconstructed Victorian shopping street, and Half Moon Court, its Edwardian counterpart. (☎ 687 687; www.yorkcastlemuseum.org.uk. Open daily 9:30am-5pm. £6.50, students £5.) **Clifford's Tower,** Tower St., is one of the last remaining pieces of **York Castle** and a chilling reminder of the worst outbreak of anti-Jewish violence in English history. In 1190, Christian merchants tried to erase their debts to Jewish bankers by annihilating York's Jewish community. One hundred fifty Jews took refuge in the tower where, faced with the prospect of starvation or butchery, they committed mass suicide. (☎ 646 940. Open daily Apr.-Sept. 10am-6pm; Oct. 10am-5pm; Nov.-Mar. 10am-4pm. £3, students £2.30.) The **Jorvik Viking Centre,** on Coppergate, is one of the busiest attractions in York; arrive early or late to avoid lines, or reserve a day ahead. Visitors float in "time cars" through the York of AD 948, past artifacts, life-like mannequins, and painfully accurate smells. (☎ 543 402 for advance book-

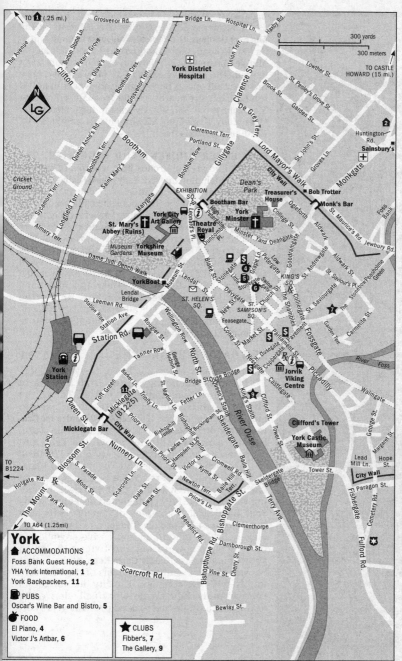

TO ☗ (.25 mi.)

Grosvenor Rd.

Bridge Ln.

Hospital Ln.

Harby Rd.

Lowther St

0      300 yards

0      300 meters

TO CASTLE
HOWARD (15 mi.)

The Avenue

Clifton

Button Stone Ln.

St. Peter's Grove

St. Olave's Rd.

Bootham Cres.

Grosvenor Terr.

Bootham Terr.

Union Terr.

St. Penley's Grove St.

Brook St.

Garden St.

St. John's St.

Groves Ln.

Huntington Rd.

2

Sainsbury's

Queen Anne's Rd.

Bootham Terr.

Saint Mary's

Bootham

Claremont Terr.

Portland St.

Gillygate

De Grey Terr.

Clarence St.

Lord Mayor's Walk

City Wall

Monkgate

Foss Bank

York District Hospital

Cricket Ground

Sycamore Terr.

Longfield Terr.

Almery Terr.

Marygate

Bootham Row

York City Art Gallery

EXHIBITION SQ.

Dean's Park

Treasurer's House

Bob Trotter

Monk's Bar

Ogleforth

St. Maurice's Rd.

Jewbury Rd.

St. Mary's Abbey (Ruins)

Museum Gardens

Yorkshire Museum

Bootham Bar

York Minster

High Petergate

College St.

Minster Yard

Deangate

Aldwark

St. Andrewgate

Aldwark St.

Dame Judi Dench Walk

YorkBoat

Lendal Bridge

Leeman Rd.

Station Rise

Museum St.

Lendal

ST. HELEN'S SQ.

Blake St.

Stonegate

Low Petergate

Little Stonegate

4

5

S

6

Swinegate

Grape Ln.

S

KING'S SQ.

St. Saviourgate

St. Saviour's Pl.

Peasholme Green

The Stonebow

Garden Terr.

Carmelite St.

7

Station Rd.

Station Ave.

Rougier St.

Tanner Row

George Hudson St.

Wellington Row

North St.

Davygate

New St.

SAMPSON'S SQ.

ST. SAMPSON'S SQ.

Feasegate

Coney St.

Market St.

Church St.

The Shambles

Colliergate

Fossgate

River Foss

Walmgate

York Station

Barker Ln.

Trinity Ln.

Fetter Ln.

St. Martin's Ln.

Bridge St.

Ouse Bridge

Queen's Staith

King's Staith

Parliament St.

Nessgate

Coppergate

Pavement

Piccadilly

Jorvik Viking Centre

Castlegate

Queen St.

Toft Green

11

Micklegate (B1225)

Priory St.

Bishophill Junior

Fairfax St.

Buckingham St.

Bishophill Senior

Skeldergate

River Ouse

Clifford St.

Tower St.

Clifford's Tower

York Castle Museum

George St.

Margaret St.

Micklegate Bar

City Wall

Nunnery Ln.

Blossom St.

TO B1224

Holgate Rd.

The Mount

Park St.

Moss St.

Scarcroft Ln.

Dale St.

Swan St.

Hampden St.

Victor St.

Kyme St.

Newton Terr.

Price's Ln.

St. Benedict Rd.

Baile Hill Terr.

Bishophorpe Rd.

Darnborough St.

Cherry St.

Vine St.

Skeldergate Bridge

Terry Ave.

Lead Mill Ln.

Hope St.

Paragon St.

City Wall

Cemetery Rd.

Fishergate

Fulford Rd.

TO A64 (1.25mi.)

Clementhorpe

Scarcroft Rd.

Bewlay St.

Tower St.

**York**

☗ **ACCOMMODATIONS**
Foss Bank Guest House, **2**
YHA York International, **1**
York Backpackers, **11**

🍺 **PUBS**
Oscar's Wine Bar and Bistro, **5**

🍎 **FOOD**
El Piano, **4**
Victor J's Artbar, **6**

★ **CLUBS**
Fibber's, **7**
The Gallery, **9**

GREAT BRITAIN

## A REALLY COLD WAR

Despite the perpetual and divisive intra-Continental conflicts of the 20th century, Europe has unified. Today, Icelanders and Greeks and everyone in between live in economic and political cooperation. Everyone, that is, except for the citizens of Russia and of the small English village of Berwick-upon-Tweed.

Due to an unfortunate accident of semantics, Berwick-upon-Tweed has been at war with Russia for 153 years. In a 1502 treaty, Berwick was described as being "of" the Kingdom of England, rather than "in" it; Berwick received special mention in every ensuing royal proclamation. Nothing came of this inconvenience until 1853, when Queen Victoria signed a declaration of war on Russia, in the name of "Victoria, Queen of Great Britain, Ireland, Berwick-upon-Tweed, and the British Dominions beyond the sea." In the peace treaty ending the war, no mention of Berwick appeared.

Sources vary on what happened next. Some say the matter was cleared up by Tsarist Russia in 1914. Others assert a Soviet official signed a peace treaty in 1966 with the mayor of Berwick, who then said, "please tell the Russian people that they can sleep peacefully in their beds." Either way, no official documents have surfaced that can resolve the debate. Berwick, for its part, appears to have no intention of backing down.

ings; www.vikingjorvik.com. Open daily 10am-5pm. £7.75, students £6.60.) Set on the 10 acres of the **Museum Gardens,** the **Yorkshire Museum** houses Anglo-Saxon, Roman, and Viking artifacts, as well as the Middleham Jewel (c. 1450), an opulent sapphire set in gold. The haunting ruins of **St. Mary's Abbey,** once the most influential Benedictine monastery in northern England, are nearby. (Enter from Museum St. or Marygate. ☎ 687 687; www.yorkshiremuseum.org.uk. Open daily 10am-5pm. £5, students £4, families £14. Gardens and ruins free.)

🎵🎭 **ENTERTAINMENT AND NIGHTLIFE.** The Minster and area churches host a series of **summer concerts,** including the **York Early Music Festival.** (☎ 658 338; www.ncem.co.uk. Mid-July.) The *What's On* guide, available at the TIC, publishes info on current cultural events. In the evening, barbershop quartets fill **King's Square** and **Stonegate** along with jugglers and magicians. There are more pubs in York than gargoyles on the Minster's wall. York's dressy club, **The Gallery,** 12 Clifford St., has two hot dance floors and six bars. (☎ 647 947. Cover £3.50-10. Open Su-Th 10pm-2am, F-Sa 10pm-3am.) Hear up-and-coming bands nightly at **Fibber's,** Stonebow House, the Stonebow, followed by DJs after 10:30pm. (☎ 651 250; www.fibbers.co.uk. Cover £5, students £3 before 11:30pm. Live music 8-10:30pm.)

# NEWCASTLE-UPON-TYNE ☎ 0191

The largest city in the northeast, Newcastle (pop. 278,000) has taken many forms, from a medieval fortress town to an industrial center. Today, the city is a frontrunner in architecture, fashion, music, and modern art. The ■**BALTIC Centre for Contemporary Art,** housed in a renovated grain warehouse, rises seven stories above the Tyne and showcases a cutting-edge collection. (☎ 478 1810; www.balticmill.com. Open Su-Tu and Th-Sa 10am-6pm, W 10am-8pm. Free.) The BALTIC Centre is one of a trio of new buildings on the river, including the Norman Foster designed steel-and-glass **Sage Gateshead,** a complex of concert halls, and the **Gateshead Millennium Bridge,** a pedestrian and bicycle bridge that, in an impressive engineering feat, swivels upward once or twice per day to allow ships to pass. **Castle Garth Keep,** at the foot of St. Nicholas St., is all that remains of the 12th-century New Castle complex. The city did not get its name from the New Castle—it actually derives its name from a castle that existed over 100 years earlier. (☎ 232 7938. Open daily Apr.-Sept. 9:30am-5:30pm; Oct.-Mar. 9:30am-4:30pm. £1.50, students £0.50.) Theater buffs can treat themselves to an evening at the **Theatre Royal**, 100 Grey St., northern England's premier stage. (☎ 0870 905 5060; www.theatreroyal.co.uk. Student tickets half-price on performance day when not sold out.)

Book accommodations well ahead for weekends, when stag- and hen-night parties fill Newcastle's budget options. ▓**Albatross Backpackers ❷**, 51 Grainger St., has secure, modern facilities, two minutes from the train station and adjacent to major nightlife. (☎ 233 1330; www.albatrossnewcastle.com. Reception 24hr. 2- to 10-bed dorms £17-23. MC/V.) To get to the small but welcoming **YHA Newcastle (HI) ❷**, 107 Jesmond Rd., take the metro to Jesmond and turn left on Jesmond Rd. (☎ 0870 770 5972. Internet £5 per hr. Reception 7-11pm. Curfew 11pm. Closed mid-Dec. to mid-Jan. Dorms £18, under 18 £14. AmEx/MC/V.) **University of Northumbria ❸**, Sandyford Rd., offers dorms near the city center. Take the metro to Haymarket. (☎ 227 3215; www.unn.ac.uk. Breakfast and linens included. Open mid-June to Aug. Singles M-Th £25 F-Su £30. MC/V.) **Pani's Cafe ❷**, 61 High Bridge St., has Italian dishes (£5-10) and a boisterous vibe. (☎ 232 4366; www.paniscafe.com. Open M-Sa 10am-10pm. MC/V.) Pick up groceries at the downtown **Safeway** on Clayton St. (☎ 261 2805. Open M-Sa 8am-7pm, Su 11am-5pm.)

As home of the nectar known as brown ale, Newcastle has a fittingly legendary party scene. *The Crack* (free at record stores) is the best source for nightlife listings. Rough and rowdy **Bigg Market** features the highest concentration of pubs in England, while neighboring **Quayside** attracts herds to its packed clubs. Catch up-and-coming bands nightly at **The Cluney,** 36 Lime St., Newcastle's premier underground music venue. (☎ 230 4474. Open daily 11am-late, food served until 9pm.) **The Head of Steam,** 2 Neville St., near the train station, features funk, jazz, reggae, soul, and occasional local DJs. (☎ 230 4236. Open M-Sa noon-1am, Su noon-midnight.) A state-of-the-art sound system keeps things pumping through the wee hours at **Digital,** Time Square, which attracts Britain's top DJs to Saturday night's "Shindig." (☎ 261 9755. Cover £3-12. Open M-Tu and Th 10:30pm-2:30am, F-Sa 10:30pm-4am.) Newcastle's **Pink Triangle** of gay bars and clubs is just west of the Centre for Life along Westmoreland Rd., St. James Blvd. and Marlborough Cres. No matter what your plans are, be sure to finish the night Newcastle-style with a kebab and extra chili sauce. **Trains** leave from Central Station for Edinburgh (1½hr., £40) and London King's Cross (3hr., 2 per hr., £103.) National Express **buses** (☎ 08705 80 80 80) leave St. James Blvd. for Edinburgh (3hr., 4 per day, £15) and London (7hr., 4 per day, £27). The **TIC** is at 27 Market St. in the Central Arcade. (☎ 277 8000. Open M-F 9:30am-5:30pm, Sa 9am-5:30pm.) **Postal Code:** NE1 7AB.

# HADRIAN'S WALL

In AD 122, Roman Emperor Hadrian ordered the construction of a wall to guard Britannia's border, hoping to prevent those uncouth blue-tattooed barbarians to the north from infiltrating his empire. The wall is Britain's most important Roman monument, stretching 117km from Carlisle in the west to Newcastle in the east. West from Newcastle or north from Hexham, the **Chesters** cavalry fort is along the wall near Chollerford. The well-preserved bath house remains show how seriously the Romans took hygiene. (☎ 01434 681 379. Open daily Apr.-Sept. 9:30am-6pm; Oct. 10am-5pm; Nov.-Mar. 10am-4pm. £3.80, students £3.) Continuing west, **House-steads,** on a scenic ridge 1km from the road, has one of the best-preserved wall sections. (☎ 01434 344 363. Open daily Apr.-Sept. 10am-6pm; Oct. 10am-5pm; Nov.-Mar. 10am-4pm. £3.80, students £3.) Just 1.5km from Once Brewed Hostel (see

## GIVING BACK

### ROAMIN' RUINS

Vindolanda is a fascinating Roman fort and settlement lying just south of Hadrian's Wall. Recent excavations have uncovered numerous buildings and some of the most unusual and best-preserved artifacts from the Roman world. In the superb site museum, set in charming gardens, you can see Roman boots, shoes, armor, jewelry, and coins.

From April to August each year, the excavations are open to any enthusiastic digger who doesn't mind getting his or her hands dirty. Archaeologists predict that it will take at least another 100 years to unearth all the site's secrets, so they need all the help they can get. The recommended stay is two weeks, but volunteers can work for a week or longer by arrangement.

Excavations take place Monday through Friday and on Sunday. A typical work day involves 4½hr. of digging, with breaks and meals in between. The closest accommodation is at YHA Once Brewed Hostel, only 2.4km from the site. There are also B&Bs in the nearby towns of Haltwhistle, Bardon Mill, or Haydon Bridge.

*The program costs £55. Applicants must be at least 16 years old and physically fit. For more information visit www.vindolanda.com or call Andrew Birley at ☎01434 345 277.*

below), archaeologists unearth artifacts daily at ▨**Vindolanda** fort and settlement. An on-site museum displays finds from the area. (☎01434 344 277; www.vindolanda.com. Open daily Apr.-Sept. 10am-6pm; mid-Feb. to Mar. and Oct. to mid-Nov. 10am-5pm. £5, students £4.10; combo ticket with Roman Army Museum £6.50/5.50.) Built from stones "borrowed" from the wall, the **Roman Army Museum** is at Carvoran, 1.5km northeast of Greenhead Hostel (see below) and five stops from Vindolanda on the AD122. (☎01697 747 485. Open daily Apr.-Sept. 10am-6pm; Feb.-Mar. and Oct.-Nov. 10am-5pm. Last entry 30min. before close. £4, students £3.50.)

**Birdoswald Roman Fort**, 25km east of Carlisle, offers views of walls, turrets, and milecastles. (☎01697 747 602. Open daily Apr.-Sept. 10am-5:30pm; Mar. and Oct. 10am-4pm. Museum and wall £3.80, students £3.) West of Carlisle, on the cliffs of Maryport, the **Senhouse Museum** houses Britain's oldest antiquarian collection, with exhibits on Roman religion and warfare. (☎01900 816 168; www.senhousemuseum.co.uk. Open July-Oct. daily 10am-5pm; Apr.-June Tu and Th-Su 10am-5pm; Nov.-Mar. F-Su 10:30am-4pm. £2.50.) **Hadrian's Wall National Trail** is an 135km, six-day route from coast to coast. Guides and information are available at TICs. The recently opened **Hadrian's Cycleway** provides access to all the wall's main attractions following minor roads and cycle paths.

Carlisle and Hexham have many **B&Bs** and make good bases for daytrips to the wall. Two hostels lie along the Hadrian's Wall Bus route. **YHA Greenhead** ❷, 26km east of Carlisle near the Greenhead bus stop, is in a converted chapel near the wall. (☎08707 705 842. Breakfast £4. Reception 8-10am and 5-10pm. Curfew 11pm. Dorms £13, under 18 £9.50. MC/V.) The AD122 stops at the **YHA Once Brewed** ❷, Military Rd., Bardon Mill, 1km from the wall. (☎08707 705 980. Breakfast £4. Laundry £1. Internet £2.50 per 30min. at the pub next door. Reception 8-10am and 2-10pm. Open Feb.-Nov. Dorms £15, under 18 £10. MC/V.)

Although traveling by **car** is the easiest option, ▨**Hadrian's Wall Bus AD122** (who knew public transportation had a sense of humor?) provides reliable service, occasionally with a guide on board. The bus runs between Carlisle and Newcastle, stopping at historical sights. Buy the **DayRover** ticket, available from TICs and bus drivers, to get the most out of AD122. (2¼hr., Apr.-Oct. 7-8 per day, £7.) **Bus** #685 runs between Newcastle and Carlisle via Greenhead, Hexham, and other wall towns (2hr., 1 per hr.). **Trains** (☎08457 484 950) run between Carlisle and Newcastle (1½hr., 1 per hr., £11). Stations are roughly 2½km from the wall. The Hexham **TIC** is at the bottom of the hill from the abbey on Hallgate Rd., and the **NPIC** is in Once Brewed, on Military Rd. (☎01434 344 396. Open Apr.-Oct. daily 9:30am-5pm; Nov.-Mar. Sa-Su 10am-3pm.) Pick up the free and invaluable **Hadrian's Wall Bus AD122 Bus & Rail Timetables,** available from any area TIC or bus. For general info, call the **Hadrian's Wall Information Line** (☎01434 322 002; www.hadrians-wall.org).

# LAKE DISTRICT NATIONAL PARK

Blessed with some of the most stunning scenery in England, the Lake District owes its beauty to a thorough glacier-gouging during the Ice Age. The district's jagged peaks and glassy lakes form a giant playground for bikers, boaters, and hikers, who in summer nearly equal sheep in number—and with four million sheep, that's quite a feat. Yet there's always some lonely hill or quiet cove where you will seem the sole visitor. Use the villages of Ambleside, Grasmere, Keswick, and Windermere as bases for exploring the region's hills—the farther west you go from A591, the more countryside you'll have to yourself.

**⊞ ⊞ TRANSPORTATION AND PRACTICAL INFORMATION. Trains** (☎08457 484 950) run from Oxenholme, the primary gateway for the lakes, to: Birmingham (2hr., 1 per hr., £47); Edinburgh (2hr., 5-10 per day, £33); London Euston (3½hr., 7-9 per day, £108); Manchester Piccadilly (1½hr., 4-10 per day, £20). Trains also run from Windermere to Oxenholme (20min., 1 per hr., £3.50) and Manchester Piccadilly (1¾hr., 1-5 per day, £20). National Express **buses** (☎08705 808 080) arrive in Windermere from Birmingham (4½hr., 1 per day, £31) and London (8hr., 1 per day, £29), continuing north through Ambleside and Grasmere to Keswick. Stagecoach in Cumbria (☎0870 608 2608) is the primary bus service in the region; a complete timetable, *The Lakesrider,* is available for free at TICs and on buses. An **Explorer ticket** offers unlimited travel on all area Stagecoach buses (1-day £9; 4-day £19; 7-day £28). YHA Ambleside offers a convenient **minibus** service (☎015394 323 04) between hostels (2 per day, £2.50) and service from the Windermere train station to hostels in Windermere and Ambleside (7 per day, 1st ride free, £2 thereafter).

The **NPIC** is in **Brockhole,** halfway between Windermere and Ambleside. (☎015394 466 01; www.lake-district.gov.uk. Open Apr.-Oct. daily 10am-5pm.) NPICs book accommodations and dispense free information and maps. Though B&Bs line every street in every town and there's a hostel around every bend, lodgings fill up in summer; reserve ahead.

**WINDERMERE AND BOWNESS.** Windermere and its sidekick Bowness-on-Windermere fill to the gills with vacationers in summer, when sailboats swarm the lake. The short climb to **Orrest Head** (round-trip 2.5km) is moderately difficult, but offers one of the best views in the Lake District. It begins opposite the TIC on the other side of A591. To get to the spacious **YHA Windermere (HI) ❶,** Bridge Ln., 3.2km north of Windermere off A591, catch the YHA shuttle from the train station. This hostel offers panoramic views of the lake and rents **bikes.** (☎015394 435 43. Breakfast, packed lunch, and dinner available with advance notice for £3.50-5.50 per meal. Internet £5 per hr. Open Feb.-Nov. daily; early Dec. F-Sa only. Dorms £13-16, under 18 £9-11.) In Windermere, **Lake District Backpackers ❶** is a hostel well-suited to independent travelers—they won't coddle you, but they'll give you a warm bed. (☎015394 463 74; www.lakedistrictbackpackers.co.uk. Dorms £10-13. MC/V.) To camp at **Park Cliffe ❷,** Birks Rd., 7km south of Bowness, take bus #618 from Wind-

**TOP TEN RULES AT WORDSWORTH'S GRAMMAR SCHOOL**

**10. School is to be held in session from 6am until 5pm.** Bet morale was delightful by 4pm.

**9. School holidays are three weeks at Christmas and three weeks at Easter only.** How do they put up with all that school?

**8. Only three pints of beer are permitted to be drunk.** Oh. That's how they put up with it.

**7. Tobacco is permitted only at lunchtime. It is both fashionable and medicinal.** In your face, smoking ban.

**6. Missed sermons are punishable by 20 lashes of the rod.** Yikes.

**5. Any student can be expelled after three missed sermons.** They do take church seriously.

**4. Greek or Latin must be spoken during all hours.** English, Latin—it's all Greek to me.

**3. No student may attend taverns.** Good thing I'd get all my drinking done during school, then.

**2. Girls may not attend Hawkshead Grammar School.** With over 100 grimy boys crammed into that tiny building, what girl would want to be locked up in there?

**1. Each student is to be issued a penknife, which he is to use to sharpen his writing quill.** Or, he could use it to carve 18th-century graffiti into the desk.

*Hawkshead Grammar School is 10km south of Grasmere. (☎015394 367 35. Open Apr.-Oct. M-Sa 10am-5pm, Su 1-5pm. £2.)*

take bus #618 from Windermere. (☎015395 313 44; www.parkcliffe.co.uk. Tent sites £11-12. MC/V.) **Windermere Lake Cruises** (☎015394 433 60), at the northern end of Bowness Pier, sends boats to Waterhead Pier in Ambleside (30min., round-trip £7.50) and south to Lakeside (40min., round-trip £7.80). The Lakeland Experience **bus** #599 (3 per hr., £1.60) leaves for Bowness pier from the train station in Windermere. The **TIC** is near the train station. (☎015394 464 99. Open Easter-Aug. M-Sa 9am-5:30pm, Su 10am-5pm.) The local **NPIC**, on Glebe Rd., is beside Bowness Pier. (☎015394 428 95. Open daily Apr.-Oct. 9:30am-5:30pm; Nov.-Mar. 10am-4pm.)

**AMBLESIDE.** Set in a valley 1.5km north of Lake Windermere, Ambleside is an attractive village with convenient access to the southern lakes. **Hiking** trails extend in all directions. The top of **Loughrigg**, a moderately difficult climb (round-trip 11km), has splendid views of high fells. The lovely **Stockghyll Force** waterfall is an easy 1.5km from town. Lakeslink bus #555 stops in front of ⬛**YHA Ambleside (HI)** ➋, 1.5km south of Ambleside and 5km north of Windermere, a magnificent former hotel with great food, refurbished rooms, and swimming. (☎015394 323 04. Bike rental £1.50 per hr. Internet £5 per hr. Dorms £20, under 18 £15.) Pick up fruits and veggies at **Granny Smith's** in Market Pl. (☎015394 331 45. Open M-F 8am-5pm, Sa 8am-6pm, Su 9am-4pm. Cash only.) **Bus** #555 (☎015394 322 31) leaves from Kelsick Rd. for Grasmere, Keswick, and Windermere (1 per hr., £2-6.50). The **TIC** is in the Central Building on Market Cross. (☎015394 325 82. Open daily 9am-5pm.)

**GRASMERE.** The peace that William Wordsworth enjoyed in the village of Grasmere is still palpable on quiet mornings. Guides provide 30min. tours of the early 17th-century **Dove Cottage**, 10min. from the center of town, where the poet lived from 1799 to 1808. The cottage is almost exactly as he left it. Next door is the outstanding **Wordsworth Museum.** (☎015394 355 44. Both open daily mid-Feb. to mid-Jan. 9:30am-5pm. Cottage and museum £6.40, students and HI members £5. Museum only £5.) The 10km **Wordsworth Walk** circumnavigates the two lakes of the Rothay River, passing the cottage, the poet's **grave** in St. Oswald's churchyard, and **Rydal Mount**, where he lived until his death in 1850. (Rydal ☎015394 330 02. Open Mar.-Oct. daily 9:30am-5pm; Nov. and Feb. M and W-Su 10am-4pm. £5, students £3.75.) **YHA Butharlyp Howe (HI)** ➋, on

Easedale Rd., is a large Victorian house. (☎015394 353 16. Free Internet. Dorms £16, under 18 £11. MC/V.) The famous gingerbread at ◪**Sarah Nelson's Grasmere Gingerbread Shop ❶**, in Church Cottage, outside St. Oswald's Church, is a bargain at £0.33 per piece. (☎015934 354 28; www.grasmereginger-bread.co.uk. Open Easter-Sept. M-Sa 9:15am-5:30pm, Su 12:30-5:30pm; Oct.-Easter M-Sa 9:30am-4:30pm, Su 12:30-5:30pm.) **Bus** #555 stops in Grasmere every hour on its way south to Ambleside or north to Keswick.

**KESWICK.** Between Skiddaw peak and the northern edge of Lake Derwentwater, Keswick (KEZ-ick) rivals Windermere as the Lake District's tourist capital. A stand-out 6km dayhike from Keswick culminates with the eerily striking **Castlerigg Stone Circle**, a 5000-year-old Neolithic henge. Another short walk leads to the beautiful **Friar's Crag**, on the shore of Derwentwater, and **Castlehead**, a viewpoint encompass-ing the town, the lakes, and the peaks beyond. Both of these walks are fairly easy, with only a few strenuous moments. The riverside ◪**YHA Keswick (HI) ❷** has modern facilities near the town center. (☎0870 770 5894. Breakfast included. Dorms £20, under 10 £15. MC/V.) Farther out, the **YHA Derwentwater (HI) ❶**, Barrow House, Bor-rowdale, is a 200-year-old house with its own waterfall. Take bus #79 (1 per hr.) 3km south out of Keswick. (☎017687 772 46. Open Mar.-Oct. daily; Nov.-Feb. F-Sa only. Dorms £14, under 18 £10. MC/V.) The **NPIC** is in Moot Hall, Market Sq. (☎017687 726 45. Open Apr.-Oct. daily 9:30am-5:30pm.)

# ISLE OF MAN ☎01624

Wherever you go on this Irish Sea islet, you'll come across an emblem: three legs joined together like the spokes of a wheel. It's the Three Legs of Man, the symbol of Manx pride and independence. Its accompanying motto translates to "Which-ever Way You Throw Me, I Stand." This speaks to the predicament of the island over the last few millennia, during which it's been thrown around between English, Scots, and Vikings. Today, Man controls its own affairs while remaining a crown possession, although it is technically not part of the UK or the EU.

## ✈ GETTING THERE

**Ronaldsway Airport (IOM; ☎**821 600; www.gov.im/airport) is 16km southwest of Douglas on the coast road. Buses #1, 1C, 2A, and 2 connect to Douglas (25min., 1-3 per hr.), while others stop around the island. British Airways (☎0845 773 3377; www.britishairways.com), British European (☎01232 824 354; www.flybe.com), Manx2 (☎0870 242 2226; www.manx2.com), and Euromanx (☎0870 787 7879; www.euromanx.com) **fly** to the Isle. **Ferries** dock at the Douglas Sea Terminal at the southern end of town, where North Quay and the Promenade meet near the bus station. The Isle of Man Steam Packet Company (☎661 661 or 08705 523 523; www.steam-packet.com) runs to Belfast (2¾hr., 2 per week), Dublin, IRE (3hr.; Jun.-Aug. 2 per week, Sept.-May 1-2 per month), Heysham, Lancashire (3½hr., 2 per day), and Liverpool (2½hr., 1-4 per day). Fares are highest in summer and on weekends (£15-32, round-trip £30-64). Book online for cheaper fares.

## DOUGLAS

The Isle's capital and largest city, Douglas (pop. 27,000), a useful gateway for Isle exploration, sprawls along the eastern side of Man. The city's broad promenade bordered with pastel-colored rowhouses gives it the feeling of a Victorian resort.

GREAT BRITAIN

**▐ TRANSPORTATION.** Isle of Man Transport (☎662 525; www.iombusand-rail.info) runs public **buses** and **trains**. The **Travel Shop**, on Lord St. next to the bus station, has bus maps and schedules. (☎663 366. Open M 8am-12:30pm and 1:30-5:45pm, Tu-F 8am-5:45pm, Sa 8am-12:30pm and 1:30-3:30pm.) The Travel Shop and the Douglas TIC sell **Island Explorer Tickets,** which provide unlimited travel on most buses, trains, and horse trams (1-day £12, 3-day £24, 5-day £35). **Protours,** Summer Hill, buses travelers from Douglas for ½- and full-day Isle tours. (☎676 105. W and Su 8:30am. £11-18). The island's small size makes it easy to navigate by **bike.** Try Eurocycles for rentals. (☎624 909. £15 per day. ID deposit. Open M-Sa 9am-5pm.)

**◼▐ ORIENTATION AND PRACTICAL INFORMATION.** Douglas stretches 3km along the shore, from **Douglas Head** to the **Electric Railway** terminal. Douglas Head is separated from town by the **River Douglas.** Ferry and bus terminals lie just north of the river. The **Promenade** curves from the ferry terminal to the Electric Railway terminal along the beach, dividing the coastline from the shopping district with a line of Victorian rowhouses. Shops and cafes line **The Strand,** a pedestrian thoroughfare that begins near the bus station and runs parallel to the Promenade, turning into Castle St. and ending at a taxi queue near the Gaiety Theatre. The **TIC** is in the Sea Terminal Building just outside the ferry departure lounge. (☎686 766; www.visitisleofman.com. Open Easter-Sept. M-Sa 8am-7pm, Su 9am-3pm; Oct.-Easter M-F 9:15am-5:30pm.) **Internet** is at Feegan's Lounge, 8 Victoria St. (☎619 786; www.feegan.com; £1 per 20min.; open M-Sa 8:30am-6pm). **Postal Code:** IM1 2EA.

> **◣ YOU DA (ISLE OF) MAN.** The Isle of Man sets itself apart from other lesser isles. The island has its own Manx language (a cousin of Irish and Scottish Gaelic), tailless Manx cat, multi-horned Manx Loghtan sheep, and a local delicacy—kipper (herring smoked over oak chips).

**Manx currency** is equivalent in value to British pounds, but it's not accepted outside the Isle. If you use an ATM on the island, it will likely give you Manx currency. Notes and coins from England, Scotland, and Northern Ireland can be used in Man. Some Manx shops accept euro—look for signs. When preparing to leave, you will generally be successful asking for your change in UK tender. Post offices and newsstands sell Manx Telecom **phonecards.** Mobile phone users on plans from elsewhere in Britain will likely incur surcharges. The Isle shares Britain's **international dialing code,** ☎44. In an **emergency,** dial ☎999 or 112. It's wise to rely on phone cards and landlines for a short stay, although more long-term visitors should probably invest in a **Manx prepay SIM card,** available at the shop on Victoria St. in Douglas for £15. These allow access to the only official service, **Manx Pronto.**

**▐▐ ACCOMMODATIONS AND FOOD.** Douglas is awash with **B&Bs** and **hotels.** For TT weeks, they fill a year ahead and raise their rates. The **Devonian Hotel ❷,** 4 Sherwood Terr., on Broadway, is a Victorian-style townhouse just off the Promenade. (☎674 676; www.thedevonian.co.uk. All rooms have TV. Breakfast included. Singles £25-28; doubles from £44. Cash only.) Next door, **Athol House Hotel ❸,** 3 Sherwood Terr. on Broadway, features elegant rooms with bath and TV. (☎629 356; www.atholhouse.net. From £26. Cash only.) TICs list 11 **campgrounds ❶.**

Grill and chip shops line **Duke, Strand,** and **Castle Streets,** while many hotels along the **Promenade** have elegant restaurants. **Copperfield's Olde Tea Shoppe and Restaurant ❸,** 24 Castle St., holds Viking Feasts and Edwardian Extravaganzas, and serves classically British fare. (☎613 650. Open in summer M-F 11am-8pm, Sa 11am-6pm; winter M-Sa 10am-4pm. MC/V, with a £0.50 charge.) Guinness posters and traditional music at **Brendann O'Donnell's ❶**, 16-18 Strand St., remind patrons of the Man's proximity to Ireland. (☎621 566. Open M-Th and Su noon-11pm, F-Sa noon-midnight. Cash only.) The **Food For Less** grocery is on Chester St., behind The Strand. (Open M-W and Sa 8am-8pm, Th-F 8am-9pm, Su 9am-6pm.)

**⬛🏞 SIGHTS AND HIKING.** From the shopping district, signs point to the Chester St. parking garage next to Food For Less; an elevator ride to the 8th-floor roof leads to a footbridge to the **Manx Museum**. The museum covers the geology and history of Man, with the artistic side displayed at the **Manx National Gallery of Art**. Don't miss exhibits about the island's days as a Victorian getaway, when it was unofficially known as the Isle of Woman due to its attractive seasonal population. (☎648 000. Open M-Sa 10am-5pm. Free.) The museum and gallery are part of the island-wide **Story of Mann**, a collection of museums and exhibits focused on island heritage, including sites in Ballasalla, the former capital Castletown, Peel, and Ramsey. A **Heritage Pass** (£11), available at all museums, grants admission to any four sites, which otherwise cost £3.30-5.50. (☎648 000; www.storyofmann.com).

**Raad ny Foillan** (Road of the Gull) is a 135km path around the island marked with blue seagull signs. The spectacular ⬛**Port Erin to Castletown Route** (20km) offers the best of the island's beaches, cliffs, surf, and wildlife. **Bayr ny Skeddan** (The Herring Road), once used by Manx fishermen, covers the less thrilling 23km land route between Peel in the west and Castletown in the east. Appropriately, signs with her-ring pictures mark the trail. It overlaps the **Millennium Way,** which runs 45km from Castletown to Ramsey along the 14th-century Royal Highway, ending 1½km from Ramsey's Parliament Sq. *Walks on the Isle of Man* (free), available at the TIC, gives a cursory description of 11 walks. Free pamphlets also list dozens of routes. Eleven **campsites,** listed at the TIC, dot the isle.

**🌺🎶 FESTIVALS AND NIGHTLIFE.** TICs stock a calendar of events; ask for *What's On the Isle of Man* or check out www.isleofman.com or www.visitisleof-man.com. During the two weeks from late May to early June, Man turns into a motorcycle mecca for the **Tourist Trophy (TT) Races** as the population doubles and 10,000 bikes flood the island (www.iomtt.com). The races were first held on Man in 1907 because restrictions on vehicle speed were less severe (read: nonexistent) on the island than on mainland Britain. The circuit consists of 60km of hairpin turns that top racers navigate at speeds over 120 mph. The **World Tin Bath Champi-onships,** a race across the harbor in tin tubs in August, and a **Darts Festival** in March invite Manx natives and visitors alike to revel in idiosyncrasy.

**Pubs** in Douglas are numerous and boisterous, especially during the TT Races. Pass through the subway-like turnstile at **Quids Inn,** on the Promenade, where drinks cost £1-1.50. Prepare to drink standing up on weekends. (☎611 769. Hours vary.) Most of the **clubs** in Douglas are 21+ and some have free entrance until 10 or 11pm, with a £2-5 cover thereafter. Relax at **Colours,** on Central Promenade, in the Hilton. A spacious sports bar gives way to live cover bands and dance music as the night goes on. (☎662 662. Open daily noon-3:30am. £5 cover after 10pm.)

**🚩 DAYTRIP FROM DOUGLAS: PEEL.** Long ago, this "cradle of Manx heritage" played host to the Vikings. The Quayside maintains a rough-and-tumble sailor's edge (and holds a miniature Viking longhouse), while ⬛**ruins** across the harbor are set against western sunsets. The most prominent relics are the stone towers of

**Peel Castle,** which share the skyline of **St. Patrick's Isle** with the stone arches of **St. German's Cathedral** and the an excavated Viking tomb. The audio tour, included in the admission price, informs visitors about the history of the ruins. The site is on a cliff overlooking Peel, accessible by pedestrian causeway from the Quay. *(Open daily Easter-Oct. 10am-5pm. Last entry 1hr. before close. £3.30, children £1.70.)* **Moore's Traditional Curers,** Mill Rd., is supposedly the only kipper factory of its kind left in the world. Informal tours let visitors watch kippering in action and even climb up the interior of one of the smoking chimneys. Free kipper samples are available. *(☎843 622; www.manxkippers.com. Shop open M-Sa 10am-5pm. Tours Apr.-Oct. M-Sa 3:30pm. £2, children free.)* Outside of Peel at Ballacraine Farm, **Ballacraine Quad Bike Trails** leads 1½hr. trail rides, including training and refreshments. *(☎801 219. £40 per person.)* **Buses** (☎ 662 525) arrive and depart across the street from the Town Hall on Derby Rd., going to Douglas (#4, 4B, 5A, 6, 6B, X5; 35min.; 1-2 per hr.; £2) and Port Erin (#8; 55min., M-Sa 4 per day, £2). The **TIC** is a window in the Town Hall, Derby Rd. *(☎842 341. Open M-Th 8:45am-4:45pm, F 8:45am-4:30pm.)* **Postal Code:** IM5 1AA.

# WALES (CYMRU)

If many of the nearly three million Welsh people had a choice, they would float away from the English. Ever since England solidified control over Wales with the murder of Prince Llywelyn ap Gruffydd in 1282, Wales has attempted to assert its national identity. The country clings steadfastly to its Celtic heritage, and the Welsh language endures in conversation, commerce, and literature. As mines faltered in the mid-20th century, Wales turned from heavy industry to tourism. Travelers today come for dramatic beaches, castles, cliffs, and mountains.

## CARDIFF (CAERDYDD)   ☎029

Cardiff calls itself "Europe's Youngest Capital" and seems eager to meet the title, with a metropolitan renaissance alongside rich history. Next to traditional monuments are landmarks of a different tenor: a new riverside stadium and cosmopolitan dining and entertainment venues. At the same time, local pride, shown in the red dragons on flags and in windows, remains as strong as ever.

**⊞⊟ TRANSPORTATION AND PRACTICAL INFORMATION. Trains** (☎08457 484 950) leave Central Station, Central Sq., for: Bath (1-1½hr., 1-3 per hr., £14); Birmingham (2hr., 2 per hr., £32); Edinburgh (7-7½hr., 3 per day, £100); London Paddington (2hr., 2 per hr., £53). National Express **buses** (☎08705 808 080) leave from Wood St. for Birmingham (2¼hr., 8 per day, £21), London (3½hr., 9 per day, £20), and Manchester (6hr., 8 per day, £39). Pick up a free *Wales Bus, Rail, and Tourist Map and Guide* at the TIC. Cardiff Bus (Bws Caerdydd), St. David's House, Wood St. (☎2066 6444), runs green and orange city buses in Cardiff and surrounding areas. (Service ends M-Sa 11:20pm, Su 11pm. £1-1.60, week pass £13.) The **TIC** is at Old Library, The Hayes. (☎2022 7281; www.visit-cardiff.info. Open M-Sa 9:30am-6pm, Su 10am-4pm.) The public **library,** on Bute St. just past the rail bridge, offers free **Internet** in 30min. slots. (☎2038 2116. Open M-W and F 9am-6pm, Th 9am-7pm, Sa 9am-5:30pm.) **Postal Code:** CF10 2SJ.

**⊡⊟ ACCOMMODATIONS AND FOOD.** Budget lodgings are hard to find in Cardiff. The cheapest B&Bs (from £20) are on the city outskirts. ◼**Cardiff International Backpacker ❷,** 98 Neville St., is a backpacker's dream, with Happy hours (Su-

Th 7-9pm) and a rooftop patio with hammocks. (☎2034 5577; www.cardiffbackpacker.com. Breakfast included. Internet £2 per hr. Su-Th curfew 2:30am. Dorms £18; singles £24; doubles £38; triples £48. Credit card required for reservations. MC/V.) **Nos Da ❷**, 53-59 Despenser St., has charming, new common spaces, a restaurant, and a nightclub. (☎388 741; www.nosda.co.uk. Kitchen available. Free Wi-Fi. Dorms £19-20; singles £36-42. MC/V.) **Acorn Camping and Caravaning ❶**, near Rosedew Farm, Ham Ln. South, Llantwit Major, is 1hr. by bus X91 from Central Station and a 15min. walk from the Ham Ln. stop. (☎01446 794 024. £3.80 per person; £6.80 per tent site, £9 per 2 tent sites. Electricity £3. AmEx/MC/V.)

At **Europa Cafe ❶**, 25 Castle St., across from the castle, near the river, stone walls hung with abstract art combine with couches to create a trendy yet comfortable feel. Upcoming performers and theme nights are chalked on the wall. Sip a big mocha (£2.50) as you thumb through one of their books. (☎667 776. Sandwiches

£3.70. Open daily 10am-3:30pm. Cash only.) **Pancake House ❶**, Old Brewery Quarter, housed in a glass cube, serves specialty crepes, such as bacon, avocado, and sour cream (£3.80), at low prices. (☎644 954. Open M-Th 10am-10pm, F 10am-11pm, Sa 9am-11pm, Su 9am-10pm. AmEx/MC/V.) Budget travelers looking for food on the go can scavenge the stalls of **Central Market**, between St. Mary St. and Trinity St., for produce, bread, and raw meat. (Open daily 10am-4pm.) **Mill Lane** is a popular destination with pubs, chains, and British fare. **Caroline Street** is a surefire post-club hot spot, with curried or fried goodies at shops that stay open until 3 or 4am.

**◧◨ SIGHTS AND NIGHTLIFE.** From a Roman legionary outpost to a Norman keep, medieval stronghold, and finally a Victorian neo-Gothic curiosity, extravagant ▨**Cardiff Castle**, Castle St., has seen some drastic changes in its 2000-year existence. (☎2087 8100. Open daily Mar.-Oct. 9:30am-6pm; Nov.-Feb. 9:30am-5pm. £7.50, students £6.) The **Civic Centre**, in Cathays Park, includes Alexandra Gardens, City Hall, and the **National Museum and Gallery**. The museum's exhibits range from a room of Celtic crosses to a walk-through display of Wales's indigenous flora and fauna. (☎2039 7951. Open Tu-Su 10am-5pm. Free.)

After 11pm, many of Cardiff's downtown pubs stop serving alcohol and the action migrates to nearby clubs, most located on or around **St. Mary Street**. For nightlife info, check the free *Buzz* guide or the *Itchy Cardiff Guide* (£3.50), available at the TIC. Three worlds collide at **Clwb Ifor Bach**, 11 Womanby St. The ground floor plays cheesy pop, especially on Wednesday student nights, the middle floor bar has softer music, and the top rocks out to live bands or trance. Cover is £3-4, but up to £10 for popular bands. (☎232 199;

www.clwb.net. Drink specials nightly. Open Su-W until 2am, Th-Sa until 3 am. Call ahead for opening hours.) **Club X**, 35 Charles St., attracts a mixed gay and straight crowd with techno, live bands, and a beer garden. The club keeps the latest hours in Cardiff. (☎ 400 876; www.club-x-cardiff.co.uk. Cover £3-7. Open W 9pm-4am, F-Sa 10pm-6am.)

**⚄ DAYTRIPS FROM CARDIFF: CAERPHILLY CASTLE AND THE MUSEUM OF WELSH LIFE.** Visitors to ▧**Caerphilly Castle,** 13km north of Cardiff, may find the 30-acre grounds easy to navigate today, but 13th-century warriors had to contend with pivoting drawbridges, trebuchets, crossbows, and catapults (replicas of which are now displayed) when attacking this stronghold, the most technologically advanced fortification of its time. Take the train (20min., M-Sa 2 per hr., £3.30) or bus #26 from Central Station. (☎ 2088 3143. Open June-Sept. daily 9:30am-6pm; Apr.-May daily 9:30am-5pm; Oct.-Mar. M-Sa 9:30am-4pm, Su 11am-4pm. £3.50, students £3.) The open-air **Museum of Welsh Life,** 6km west of Cardiff, is home to over 40 buildings from all parts of Wales reassembled into an interactive display of the nation's history. Take advantage of the guides and craftsmen around the park. (☎ 2057 3500. Open daily 10am-5pm. Free. Guidebook £2.) Buses #32 and 320 run to the museum from Central Station (20min., 1-2 per hr., £2.60).

# WYE VALLEY

William Wordsworth mused on the tranquility and pastoral majesty of the once-troubled Welsh-English border territory around Wye Valley. As the *Afon Gwy* (Wye River) winds through the surrounding abbeys, castles, farms, and trails, much of the landscape seems untouched by human hands and the passage of time.

**▟ TRANSPORTATION.** Chepstow is the best entrance to the valley. From Chepstow, **trains** (☎ 08457 484 950; www.nationalrail.com) go to Cardiff (40min., 1-2 per hr., £6). National Express (☎ 08705 808 080; www.nationalexpress.com) **buses** go to Cardiff (50min., 13 per day, £4.60) and London (2½hr., 7 per day, £20). TICs offer the free *Monmouthshire Local Transport Guide* and *Discover the Wye Valley by Foot and by Bus* (£0.50). **Hiking** is a great way to explore the region. The 220km **Wye Valley Walk** treks north from Chepstow, through Hay-on-Wye, and on to Prestatyn. **Offa's Dyke Path** has 285km of hiking and biking paths along the Welsh-English border. For info, call the Offa's Dyke Association (☎ 01547 528 753).

## CHEPSTOW ☎ 01291

Chepstow's position at the mouth of the river and the base of the English border made it an important Norman fortification. Flowers spring from the ruins of **Castell Casgwent,** Britain's oldest dateable stone castle (c. 1070), which offers stunning views of the Wye from its tower walls. (☎ 624 065. Open daily 9:30am-6pm. £3.50, students £3.) The **First Hurdle Guest House ❹,** 9-10 Upper Church St., has comfortable rooms near the castle. (☎ 622 189. Singles £40; doubles £60. AmEx/MC/V; £1.50 charge.) An eclectic array of pubs and Chinese restaurants can be found near the town center. **Kreation Coffee Lounge ❶,** above Kreation Gift Shop on St. Mary's St., offers traditional tea fare and hot sandwiches for around £2. (☎ 621 711. Open M-Sa 9:30am-4:30pm, Su noon-6pm.) Pick up groceries at **Tesco** on Station Rd. (Open M 8am-midnight, Tu-F 24hr., Sa midnight-10pm, Su 10am-4pm.) **Trains** arrive on Station Rd.; buses stop in front of Somerfield supermarket. Buy tickets at **The Travel House,** 9 Moor St. (☎ 623 031. Open M-Sa

9am-5:30pm.) The **TIC** is on Bridge St. (☎ 623 772; www.chepstow.co.uk. Open daily Apr.-Oct. 10am-5:30pm; Nov.-Mar. 10am-3:30pm.) **Postal Code:** NP16 5DA.

# TINTERN                                                    ☎ 01291

Eight kilometers north of Chepstow on A466, the Gothic arches of ◼Tintern Abbey "connect the landscape with the quiet of the sky," as described by Wordsworth. (☎ 689 251. Open June-Sept. daily 9:30am-6pm; Apr.-May and Oct. daily 9:30am-5pm; Nov.-Mar. M-Sa 9:30am-4pm, Su 11am-4pm. £3.50, students £3. 45min. audio tour £1.) A 3km hike along **Monk's Trail** leads to **Devil's Pulpit**, from which Satan is said to have tempted the monks as they worked in the fields. **YHA St. Briavel's Castle (HI) ❶**, 6km northeast of Tintern across the English border, occupies a 13th-century fortress. While a unique experience—it was formerly King John's hunting lodge—it's somewhat remote, and should only be booked by those prepared for a 3km uphill hike. From A466 (bus #69 from Chepstow; ask to be let off at Bigsweir Bridge) or Offa's Dyke, follow signs from the edge of the bridge. (☎ 01594 530 272. Lockout 10am-5pm. Curfew 11:30pm. Dorms from £17. MC/V.) Campers can use the **field ❶** next to the old train station (£2). Try **The Moon and Sixpence ❷**, on High St., for classic pub grub with great views of the Wye. (☎ 689 284. Kitchen open noon-2:30pm and 6:30-9:30pm. Open daily noon-11pm.)

# BRECON BEACONS NATIONAL PARK

The Parc Cenedlaethol Bannau Brycheiniog encompasses 1340 sq. km of sandstone crags, forests, and waterfalls. The park has four main regions: Brecon Beacons, where King Arthur's fortress supposedly stood; Fforest Fawr, with the spectacular waterfalls of Ystradfellte; the eastern, Tolkien-esque Black Mountains; and the remote, western, and oddly named Black Mountain—a region, not a single peak. Brecon, on the park's edge, is the best base for touring.

◨ **TRANSPORTATION. Trains** (☎ 08457 484 950) run from London Paddington via Cardiff to Abergavenny, at the park's southeastern corner, and to Merthyr Tydfil, on the southern edge. National Express (☎ 08705 808 080) **bus #509** runs once per day from Brecon, on the northern side of the park, to Cardiff (1hr., £3.60) and London (5 hr., £23). Stagecoach Red and White (☎ 01685 388 216) buses cross the park en route to Brecon from Abergavenny (X43; 50min., 6 per day). The free *Brecon Beacons: A Visitor's Guide*, available at most TICs, details bus coverage and lists walks accessible by public transportation.

**BRECON (ABERHONDDU).** Most hikers start at the northern edge of the park in Brecon. Lodgings fill up for the **Jazz Festival** (mid-Aug.); book early. The nearest **YHA hostel** is **Brecon (Ty'n-y-Caeau) ❶** (tin-uh-KAY-uh), a Victorian house 5km from town with kitchen. From Brecon, walk down The Watton to the A40-A470 roundabout, follow the Abergavenny branch of the A40, and take the path to the left of Groesffordd. Turn left on the main road and continue 10-15min. before bearing left at the fork; the hostel is on the right. (☎ 01874 665 270. Dorms £14, under 18 £10. MC/V.) Camp at **Pencelli Castle Caravan and Camping Park ❶**, 3.2km from Brecon on the Taff Trail. (☎ 01874 665 451. £7.50-8.50 per person.) **Buses** arrive at the **Bulwark** in the central square. National Express bus #509 runs to London (6hr., 1 per day, £23) via Cardiff (1¼hr., 1 per day, £3.60). The **TIC** is in the Cattle Market parking lot; walk through Bethel Square off Lion St. (☎ 01874 622 485. Open M-Sa 9:30am-5:30pm, Su 9:30am-4pm.)

**THE BRECON BEACONS.** These peaks at the center of the park lure hikers with grassy slopes and impressive vistas on clear days. The most convenient—and

GREAT BRITAIN

crowded—route to the top begins at **Storey Arms** (a parking lot and bus stop on A470) and offers views of **Llyn Cwm Llwch** (HLIN koom hlooch), a 600m deep glacial pool. For trail recommendations, consult guides at the **NPIC** in Brecon or Abergavenny, Monmouth Rd., across from the bus station. (☎01873 857 588; www.abergavenny.co.uk. Open daily Apr.-Oct. 9:30am-5:30pm; Nov.-Mar. 10am-4pm.)

**FFOREST FAWR.** Sixteen kilometers of trails run through Fforest Fawr and the waterfall district, enroute to the somewhat touristy **Dan-yr-Ogof Showcaves.** (☎01639 730 284. Open Apr.-Oct. daily 10am-3pm. £11, children £6.50.) Moss and ferns fill the woods around the spectacular falls near **Ystradfellte** (uh-strahd-VELTH-tuh), about 11km southwest of the Beacons. Stagecoach Red and White **bus** #63 (1½hr., 3 per day, £3-4) stops at the caves en route from Brecon to Swansea.

**THE BLACK MOUNTAINS.** In the easternmost section of the park, the Black Mountains are a group of long, lofty ridges offering 200 sq. km of solitude and ridge-walks. **Crickhowell,** on A40 and Roy Brown's Coaches route between Abergavenny and Builth Wells (#82; 25min., 1 per Tu), is one of the best starting points for forays into the area. Another option is to travel the eastern boundary along **Offa's Dyke Path,** which is dotted with impressive ruins. On Sundays and bank holidays from May to September, Offa's Dyke Flyer **bus** (3 per day) runs from Hay-on-Wye to Llanfihangel Crucorney and stops at access points to the Black Mountains along the way (☎01873 853 254; www.visitbreconbeacons.com).

# SNOWDONIA NATIONAL PARK

Amid Edward I's impressive 13th-century manmade battlements in Northern Wales lies the 2175 sq. km natural fortress of Snowdonia National Park. The region's craggy peaks, the highest in England and Wales, yield diverse terrain—pristine blue lakes dot rolling grasslands, while slate cliffs slope into wooded hills.

**🖅🔁 TRANSPORTATION AND PRACTICAL INFORMATION. Trains** (☎08457 484 950) stop at larger towns on the park's outskirts, including Conwy (p. 210). The Conwy Valley Line runs across the park from Llandudno through Betws-y-Coed to Blaenau Ffestiniog (1hr., 2-7 per day). There, it connects with the Ffestiniog Railway (p. 209), which runs through the mountains to Porthmadog, meeting the Cambrian Coaster line to Llanberis and Aberystwyth. **Buses** run to the park interior from Conwy and Caernarfon; consult the *Gwynedd Public Transport Maps and Timetables* and *Conwy Public Transport Information,* free in all regional **TICs.** The **NPIC** is in Penrhyndeudraeth, Gwynedd (☎01766 770 274; www.eryri-npa.gov.uk or www.gwynedd.gov.uk).

**🥾 HIKING.** The highest peak in England and Wales, **Mount Snowdon** (1085m) is the park's most popular destination. Its Welsh name is *Yr Wyddfa* (the burial place)—local lore holds that Rhita Gawr, a giant cloaked with the beards of the kings he slaughtered, is buried here. Six paths of varying difficulty wind their way up Snowdon; pick up *Ordnance Survey Landranger Map #115* (£6.50) and *Outdoor Leisure Map #17* (£7.50), as well as individual trail guides, at TICs and NPICs. No matter how beautiful the weather is below, it will be cold, wet, and unpredictable high up—dress accordingly. Contact **Mountaincall Snowdonia** (☎09068 500 449) for local forecasts and ground conditions or visit an NPIC.

## LLANBERIS                                                            ☎01286

Llanberis owes its outdoorsy bustle to the appeal of nearby Mt. Snowdon. The popular and pricey **Snowdon Mountain Railway** has helped visitors ascend the summit since 1896. (☎0870 458 0033; www.snowdonrailway.co.uk. Open daily Mar.-early Nov. 9am-5pm. Mar.-May trains stop halfway to the summit. £11, round-trip £15.) From the bus station, walk uphill past the railway station and the Victoria Hotel. Around the bend to the left is lovely ◼Snowdon Cottage ❸, which offers a garden with castle view and a gracious hostess. (☎872 015. £25 per person. Discount for longer stays. Cash only.) KMP (☎870 880) bus #88 runs to and from Caernarfon (25min.; 1-2 per hr.; £1.50, round-trip £2). The TIC is at 41B High St. (☎870 765. Open Easter-Oct. daily 9:30am-5pm; Nov.-Easter M and F-Su 11am-4pm.)

# HARLECH                                                      ☎01766

Harlech Castle is part of the "iron ring" of fortresses built by Edward I to quell Welsh troublemakers, but it later served as the insurrection headquarters of Welsh rebel Owain Glyndŵr. (☎780 552. Open June-Sept. daily 9:30am-6pm; Apr.-May and Oct. daily 9:30am-5pm; Nov.-Mar. M-Sa 9:30am-4pm, Su 11am-4pm. £3.50, students £3.) Enjoy spacious rooms and castle views at ◼Arundel ❷, Stryd Fawr. If the steep climb from the train station isn't appealing, call ahead for a ride. (☎780 637. £16. Cash only.) The Weary Walker's Cafe ❶, on Stryd Fawr near the bus stop, has sandwiches and baguettes for £2-3. (☎780 751. Open in summer daily 9:30am-5pm; low season 10:30am-4pm. Cash only.) Harlech lies midway on the Cambrian Coaster line; Arriva Cymru train T5 (☎08457 484 950) arrives from and runs to Porthmadog (20min., 3-9 per day, £2.40) and connects to other towns on the Llyn Peninsula. The Day Ranger pass allows unlimited travel on the Coaster line for one day (£7, children £3.50, families £14). The TIC and NPIC are on Stryd Fawr. (☎780 658. Open daily Easter-Oct. 9:30am-12:30pm and 1:30-5:30pm.) Postal Code: LL46 2YA.

# LLYN PENINSULA                                               ☎01766

The tranquility of the Llyn Peninsula has humbled visitors since the Middle Ages, when pilgrims crossed it on their way to Bardsey Island. Today, sun worshippers make the pilgrimage to beaches on the southern coast. Porthmadog, on the southeastern part of the peninsula, is the main gateway. This travel hub's main attraction is the Ffestiniog Railway, which offers a bumpy, scenic ride from Harbour Station, High St., into Snowdonia. (☎516 000; www.festrail.co.uk. Round-trip 3hr.; 2-10 per day; £17, students £16.) The birthplace of Lawrence of Arabia, ◼Snowdon Lodge ❶ is a great option in nearby Tremadog, 15min. down High St. from Porthmadog. (☎515 354; www.snowdonlodge.co.uk. Breakfast included. Laundry £2. Dorms £15; doubles £35-38; family rooms £65. AmEx/MC/V.) The northern end of the Cambrian Coaster train (☎08457 489 450) runs from Aberystwyth or Birmingham to Porthmadog (2hr., 3-8 per day) via Machynlleth. Express Motors (☎01286 881 108) bus #1 stops in Porthmadog on its way from Blaenau Ffestiniog to Caernarfon (1hr., 1 per hr., £2.60). The TIC is on High St. by the harbor. (☎512 981. Open daily Easter-Oct. 9:30am-5:30pm; Nov.-Easter 10am-5pm.) Postal Code: LL9 9AD.

# CAERNARFON                                                   ☎01286

Majestic and fervently Welsh, the walled city of Caernarfon (car-NAR-von) has a world-famous castle at its prow and mountains in its wake. Edward I started building ◼Caernarfon Castle in 1283 to contain and intimidate the rebellious Welsh, but it was left unfinished when he ran out of money. The castle is nonetheless an architectural feat; its walls withstood a rebel siege in 1404 with only 28 defenders. (☎677 617. Open June-Sept. daily 9:30am-6pm; Apr.-May and Oct. daily 9:30am-5pm; Nov.-Mar. M-Sa 9:30am-4pm, Su 11am-4pm. £5, students £4.50.) Totter's Hostel ❶, 2 High St., has spacious rooms and terrific owners. (☎672 963; www.totters.co.uk. Dorms £14. MC/V.) Charming Hole-in-the-Wall Street offers bistros, cafes,

and restaurants. Try Welsh lamb (£15) at **Stones Bistro ❸**, 4 Hole-in-the-Wall St. (☎671 152. Open Tu-Sa 6-11pm. Reserve ahead. AmEx/MC/V.) Arriva Cymru (☎08706 082 608) **buses** #5 and 5X leave the city center at Penllyn for Conwy (1¾hr., 1-3 per hr.). National Express (☎08705 808 080) buses run to London (9hr., 1 per day, £28). The **TIC** is on Castle St. (☎672 232. Open Apr.-Oct. daily 9:30am-4:30pm; Nov.-Mar. M-Sa 9:30am-4:30pm.) **Postal Code:** LL55 2ND.

# CONWY ☎01492

The central attraction of this tourist mecca is the imposing, 13th-century ▨**Conwy Castle** and its impressive **town walls** (free). Try to get on "celebrity" guide Neville Hortop's tour; his ferocious approach to history is very entertaining. (☎592 358. Open June-Sept. daily 9:30am-6pm; Apr.-May and Oct. daily 9:30am-5pm; Nov.-Mar. M-Sa 9:30am-4pm, Su 11am-4pm. £4.50, students £4. Tours £1.) Enjoy comfortable rooms (some with quay views) at ▨**Swan Cottage ❷**, 18 Berry St., a bed and breakfast in a renovated 16th-century building near the center of town. (☎596 840; myweb.tiscali.co.uk/swancottage. Singles £25; doubles £45. Cash only.) **Pen-y-Bryn Tea Rooms ❶**, on High St., offers great tea (Welsh tea £4.50) and 16th-century timbered nooks. (☎596 445. Sandwiches from £3.50. Open M-F 10am-5pm, Sa-Su

10am-5:30pm. Cash only.) Arriva Cymru **buses** (☎08706 082 608) #5 and 5X stop in Conwy on their way to Caernarfon from Llandudno (1¼hr., 2-4 per hr., £5). The **TIC** is at the castle entrance. (☎592 248. Open daily June-Sept. 9:30am-6pm; May and Oct.-Nov. 9:30am-5pm; Dec.-Apr. 9:30am-4pm.) **Postal Code:** LL32 8H7.

# SCOTLAND

Half the size of England with only one-tenth of its population, Scotland has open spaces and natural splendor unrivaled by its southern neighbor. The craggy, heathered Highlands and the mists of the Hebrides elicit awe, while farmlands and fishing villages harbor a gentler beauty. Scotland at its best is a world apart from the rest of the UK, and its people revel in a culture all their own. The Scots defended their independence for hundreds of years before reluctantly joining England in 1707. While the kilts, bagpipes, and souvenir clan paraphernalia of the big cities may grow tiresome, a visit to Scotland's less touristed areas will allow you to rub elbows with the inheritors of many cherished traditions: a B&B owner speaking Gaelic to her children, a crofter cutting peat, or a fisherman setting out in his skiff.

## ✈ GETTING TO SCOTLAND

**Buses** from London (8-12hr.) are generally the cheapest option. National Express (☎08705 808 080; www.nationalexpress.com) connects England and Scotland via Edinburgh and Glasgow. **Trains** are faster but more expensive. From London, **GNER** runs trains (☎08457 225 225; www.gner.co.uk) to Edinburgh and Glasgow (4½-6hr, £27-100). Book online for discounts. **British Airways** (☎0870 8509 850; www.ba.com) sells round-trip England-to-Scotland tickets from £85. **easyJet** (☎08706 000 000; www.easyjet.com) flies to Edinburgh and Glasgow from London Gatwick, Luton, and Stansted. The fares are web-only; book far ahead and fly for as little as £5. **Ryanair** (☎08712 460 000; www.ryanair.com) flies to Edinburgh and to Glasgow Prestwick (1hr. from the city) from Dublin and London.

## ⌸ TRANSPORTATION

In the **Lowlands** (south of Stirling and north of the Borders), train and bus connections are frequent. In the **Highlands,** Scotrail and GNER **trains** snake slowly on a few routes, bypassing the northwest almost entirely. Many stations are unstaffed—buy tickets on board. A great money-saver is the **Freedom of Scotland Travelpass,** which allows unlimited train travel and transportation on most **Caledonian MacBrayne** ("CalMac") ferries, with discounts on other ferry lines. Purchase the pass before traveling to Britain at any BritRail distributor (p. 135). **Buses** tend to be the best way to travel. **Traveline Scotland** has the best information on all routes and services (☎0871 200 2233; www.travelinescotland.com). Scottish Citylink (☎08705 505 050) runs most intercity routes. **Postbuses** (Royal Mail customer service ☎08457 740 740) are a British phenomenon. Red mail vans pick up passengers and mail once or twice a day in the most remote parts of the country, typically charging £2-5 (and sometimes nothing). Many travelers believe them to be a reliable way to get around the Highlands. **HAGGIS** (☎0131 558 3738; www.haggisadventures.com) and **Mac-**

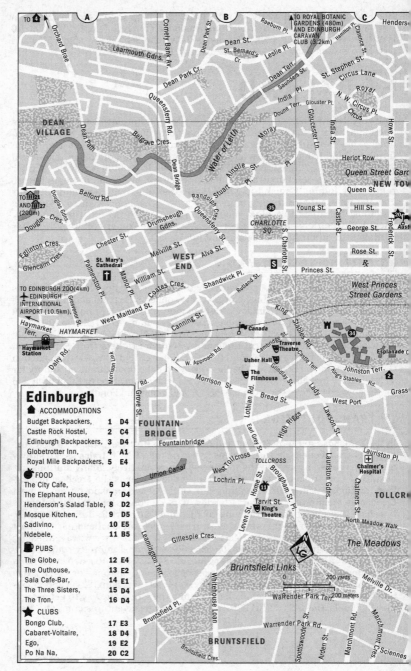

# Edinburgh

**⌂ ACCOMMODATIONS**

| | | |
|---|---|---|
| Budget Backpackers, | **1** | **D4** |
| Castle Rock Hostel, | **2** | **C4** |
| Edinburgh Backpackers, | **3** | **D4** |
| Globetrotter Inn, | **4** | **A1** |
| Royal Mile Backpackers, | **5** | **E4** |

**🍎 FOOD**

| | | |
|---|---|---|
| The City Cafe, | **6** | **D4** |
| The Elephant House, | **7** | **D4** |
| Henderson's Salad Table, | **8** | **D2** |
| Mosque Kitchen, | **9** | **D5** |
| Sadivino, | **10** | **E5** |
| Ndebele, | **11** | **B5** |

**🍺 PUBS**

| | | |
|---|---|---|
| The Globe, | **12** | **E4** |
| The Outhouse, | **13** | **E2** |
| Sala Cafe-Bar, | **14** | **E1** |
| The Three Sisters, | **15** | **D4** |
| The Tron, | **16** | **D4** |

**★ CLUBS**

| | | |
|---|---|---|
| Bongo Club, | **17** | **E3** |
| Cabaret-Voltaire, | **18** | **D4** |
| Ego, | **19** | **E2** |
| Po Na Na, | **20** | **C2** |

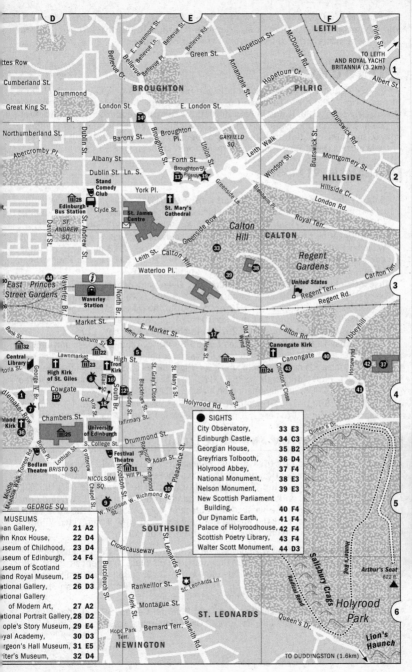

**GREAT BRITAIN**

| ● SIGHTS | |
|---|---|
| City Observatory, | **33 E3** |
| Edinburgh Castle, | **34 C3** |
| Georgian House, | **35 B2** |
| Greyfriars Tolbooth, | **36 D4** |
| Holyrood Abbey, | **37 F4** |
| National Monument, | **38 E3** |
| Nelson Monument, | **39 E3** |
| New Scottish Parliament | |
| Building, | **40 F4** |
| Our Dynamic Earth, | **41 F4** |
| Palace of Holyroodhouse, | **42 F4** |
| Scottish Poetry Library, | **43 F4** |
| Walter Scott Monument, | **44 D3** |

| MUSEUMS | |
|---|---|
| ...an Gallery, | **21 A2** |
| ...hn Knox House, | **22 D4** |
| ...useum of Childhood, | **23 D4** |
| ...useum of Edinburgh, | **24 F4** |
| ...useum of Scotland | |
| ...and Royal Museum, | **25 D4** |
| ...tional Gallery, | **26 D3** |
| ...tional Gallery | |
| ...of Modern Art, | **27 A2** |
| ...tional Portrait Gallery, | **28 D2** |
| ...ople's Story Museum, | **29 E4** |
| ...yal Academy, | **30 D3** |
| ...rgeon's Hall Museum, | **31 E5** |
| ...iter's Museum, | **32 D4** |

**Backpackers** (☎ 01315 589 900; www.macbackpackers.com) cater to the young and adventurous, with many tours departing from Edinburgh. Both run hop-on, hop-off excursions that let you travel at your own pace.

# EDINBURGH ☎ 0131

A city of elegant stone amid rolling hills and ancient volcanoes, Edinburgh (ED-in-bur-ra; pop. 500,000) is the jewel of Scotland. Since David I granted it *burgh* (town) status in 1130, it has been a hotbed for forward-thinking artists and intellectuals. The tradition lives on today as new clubs emerge beneath its medieval spires. In August, Edinburgh becomes a mecca for the arts, drawing talent and crowds across the globe to its wild International and Fringe Festivals.

## ◖ TRANSPORTATION

**Flights: Edinburgh International Airport** (**EDI**; ☎ 0870 040 0007) is 11km west of the city. Lothian **Airlink** (☎ 555 6363) shuttles between the airport and Waverley Bridge (25min.; 4-6 per hr., 1 per hr. after midnight; £3, round-trip £5; children £2/3.)

**Trains: Waverley Station** (☎ 08457 484 950), between Princes St., Market St., and Waverley Bridge. Trains to: **Aberdeen** (2½hr.; M-Sa 1 per hr., Su 8 per day; £34); **Glasgow** (1hr., 4 per hr., £10); **Inverness** (3½hr., 1 per 2hr., £32); **London King's Cross** (4¾hr., 1 per hr., £103); **Stirling** (50min., 2 per hr., £6.10).

**Buses: Edinburgh Bus Station**, St. Andrew Sq. Open daily 6am-midnight. Ticket office open daily 8am-8pm. National Express (☎ 08705 808 080) to **London** (10hr., 4 per day, £21). Scottish Citylink (☎ 08705 505 050) to: **Aberdeen** (4hr., 1 per hr., £18), **Glasgow** (1hr., 2-4 per hr., £4), and **Inverness** (4½hr., 8-10 per day, £17). A bus-ferry route goes to **Belfast** (2 per day, £20) and **Dublin, IRE** (1 per day, £27).

**Public Transportation: Lothian** buses (☎ 555 6363; www.lothianbuses.com) provide most services. Exact change required (£1 flat fare, children £0.60). **Daysaver** ticket (£2.30, children £2) available from any driver. **Night buses** cover select routes after midnight (£2). **First Edinburgh** (☎ 0870 872 7271) also operates locally. **Traveline** (☎ 0870 608 2608) has information on all area public transport.

**Bike Rental: Biketrax,** 11 Lochrin Pl. (☎ 228 6633; www.biketrax.co.uk). Mountain bikes £12 per ½-day, £16 per day. Open M-Sa 9:30am-5:30pm, Su noon-5pm.

## ✱ 🛈 ORIENTATION AND PRACTICAL INFORMATION

Edinburgh is a perfect city for walking. **Princes Street** is the main thoroughfare in **New Town,** the northern section of the city. From there you can view the impressive stone facade of the towering **Old Town** to the south. The **Royal Mile** (Castle Hill, Lawnmarket, High St., and Canongate) is the major road in the Old Town and connects **Edinburgh Castle** in the west to the **Palace of Holyroodhouse** in the east. **North Bridge, Waverley Bridge,** and **The Mound** connect Old and New Town. Two kilometers northeast, **Leith** is the city's seaport on the Firth of Forth.

**Tourist Information Centre:** Waverley Market, 3 Princes St. (☎ 0845 225 5121), on the north side of Waverley Station. Books rooms for £3 plus 10% deposit; sells bus, museum, theater, and tour tickets. Open July-Aug. M-Sa 9am-8pm, Su 10am-8pm; May-June and Sept. M-Sa 9am-7pm, Su 10am-7pm; Apr. and Oct. M-Sa 9am-6pm, Su 10am-6pm; Nov.-Mar. M-Sa 9am-5pm, Su 10am-5pm.

**GLBT Services: Edinburgh Lesbian, Gay, and Bisexual Centre,** 58a-60 Broughton St. (☎ 478 7069), inside Sala Cafe-Bar, or visit **Gay Edinburgh** at www.visitscotland.com.

**Police:** Headquarters at Fettes Ave. (☎311 3901; www.lbp.police.uk).

**Hospital: Royal Infirmary,** 51 Little France Cr. (☎536 1000, emergencies 536 6000).

**Internet Access:** Free at the **Central Library** (☎242 8000) on George IV Bridge. Open M-Th 10am-8pm, F 10am-5pm, Sa 9am-1pm. **easyInternet Cafe,** 58 Rose St. (☎220 3577), inside Caffe Nero. £2 per hr. Open M-Sa 7am-10pm, Su 9am-10pm.

**Post Office:** (☎556 9546.) In the St. James Centre beside the bus station. Open M-Sa 9am-5:30pm. **Postal Code:** EH1 3SR.

# ACCOMMODATIONS

Edinburgh's accommodations cater to every kind of traveler. Hostels and hotels are the only city-center options, while B&Bs and guesthouses begin on the periphery. It's a good idea to reserve ahead in summer, and essential to be well ahead of the game at New Year's and during festival season (late July-early Sept.).

**Budget Backpackers,** 37-39 Cowgate (☎226 2351; www.budgetbackpackers.co.uk). A modern inner city hostel, renowned for its pub crawls (M-Sa). Spacious 2- to 12-bed rooms; women-only dorms available. Free daily city tour. Breakfast £2. Lockers free. Internet £0.15 per 30min. Reception 24hr. Ages 18+ only. Rooms £9-24. MC/V. ❶

**Globetrotter Inn,** 46 Marine Dr. (☎336 1030; www.globetrotterinns.com). 15min. from Waverley train station and Edinburgh International Airport. This hostel feels like a world of its own on large grounds next to the Firth of Forth. An hourly shuttle service runs to and from the city, though a bar, gym, hot tub, shop, and TV room make it tempting to stay put. Curtained bunks offer maximum privacy. Light breakfast included. Free lockers. Key card access. Dorms £9.50-19; doubles with bath £23. MC/V. ❶

**Castle Rock Hostel,** 15 Johnston Terr. (☎225 9666). Just steps from the castle, this friendly hostel has a party atmosphere and a top-notch cinema room. Nightly movies. Ask about their haircut offer: £10 with a free shot of vodka. 8- to 16-bed dorms £13-15; doubles and triples £15-17. AmEx/MC/V. ❷

**Royal Mile Backpackers,** 105 High St. (☎557 6120). A well-kept hostel with a community aura. As a branch of Scotland's Top Hostels, guests have access to Mac-Backpackers Tours of Scotland, run by the same branch. Amenities, such as free Wi-Fi, at nearby High St. Hostel. 8-bed dorms £13-15. AmEx/MC/V. ❶

## TOP TEN LIST

### TOP TEN WAYS TO CLOG YOUR ARTERIES

Edinburgh is famous for its fried foods. Here are the greasiest options:

**10. Deep-Fried Cheeseburger:** Patty and cheese are deep fried, then placed on the bun and enjoyed as usual.

**9. Deep-Fried Sausage:** Tastes a bit like a corn dog, looks a bit like—well, never mind.

**8. Deep-Fried Haggis:** The traditional Scottish favorite. Improved upon? Opinions differ.

**7. Deep-Fried Steak:** This is no filet mignon. Think deep fried burger, minus the bun.

**6. Deep-Fried Skittles:** How do they not lose the Skittles through the holes in the bottom of the fryer? More importantly, who was the first person who thought, "Hey, these Skittles are good. You know what would make them even better? Dousing them in a pan of hot lard."

**5. Deep-Fried Pizza:** With your choice of toppings.

**4. Deep-Fried Black Pudding:** The only way to improve upon a sausage made from pig's blood is to throw it in a deep fat fryer.

**3. Deep-Fried White Pudding:** Like black pudding, but white.

**2. Deep-Fried Mars Bar:** 

**1. Deep-Fried Hospitality:** Many chip shops will deep fry anything you want, if you bring it to the shop and ask nicely. Be creative!

**Edinburgh Backpackers,** 65 Cockburn (CO-burn) St. (☎220 1717; www.hoppo.com). A clean, energetic hostel with a hotel-like feel. Common areas, pool table, and TV. 15% discount at the downstairs cafe. Laundry and Internet access. Reception 24hr. Check-out 10am. 8- to 16-bed co-ed dorms £14-19; private rooms from £45. MC/V. ❷

# FOOD

Scotland's capital features an exceptionally wide range of cuisines and restaurants. For a traditional taste of the country, Edinburgh offers everything from haggis to creative "modern Scottish." Many pubs offer student and hosteler discounts in the early evening. Take-out shops on **South Clerk Street, Leith Street,** and **Lothian Road** have reasonably priced Chinese and Indian food. Buy groceries at **Sainsbury's,** 9-10 St. Andrew Sq. (☎225 8400. Open M-Sa 7am-10pm, Su 10am-8pm.)

▨ **The City Cafe,** 19 Blair St. (☎220 0125), right off the Royal Mile behind the Tron Kirk. This popular Edinburgh institution is a cafe by day and a flashy pre-club by night. Try the herb chicken and avocado melt (£6) or their incredible milkshakes. Street-side seating ideal for people-watching. Happy hour daily 5-8pm. Open daily 11am-1am; during festival 11am-3am. Kitchen open M-Th 11am-11pm, F-Su 11am-10pm. MC/V. ❷

▨ **The Mosque Kitchen,** 50 Potterrow. In the courtyard of Edinburgh's central mosque, a jumble of mismatched chairs and long tables make up an outdoor cafeteria. Popular with students. Their heaping plates of curry (£3) are unbeatable. Open M-Th and Sa-Su noon-7pm; F noon-1pm and 1:45-7pm. Cash only. ❶

**The Elephant House,** 21 George IV Bridge (☎220 5355). *Harry Potter* and Hogwarts were conceived here on hastily scribbled napkins. A perfect place to chill, chat, or start a best-selling book series. Teas, coffees, and the best shortbread in the universe. Selections from scrumptious pastries (£1.25) to sandwiches, panini, and pizzas (from £5.30). Turns into a sit-down restaurant with live music Th 8pm. Great views of the castle. Happy hour daily 8-9pm. Open daily 8am-11pm. MC/V. ❶

**Sadivino,** 52 West Richmond St. (☎667 7719). This friendly sidewalk cafe fills up during lunch. Everything from panini to more substantial Italian fare is under £4. Most entrees £3. Open M-F 11am-6pm, Sa noon-6pm. Cash only. ❶

**Henderson's Salad Table,** 94 Hanover St. (☎225 2131). The founding member of Edinburgh's vegetarian scene, Henderson's has dished up seriously good salads (£4) for as long as anyone can remember. Feel healthy while drunk: the wine bar offers a range of organic and vegan beers, spirits, and wines. Open M-Su 7:30am-10:30pm. MC/V. ❶

**Ndebele,** 57 Home St., Tolcross (☎221 1141; www.ndebele.co.uk). An African deli 1km south from the west end of Princes St. Grab an ostrich and mango chutney sandwich (£2.60) and some chocolate chili cheesecake (£2) for a Meadows picnic. Extensive selection of South African wines, beers, and spirits. Open M-Sa 9am-6pm, Su noon-5pm. MC/V. ❶

# SIGHTS

Among the boggling array of tours touting themselves as "the original," ▨**Edinburgh Literary Pub Tour** is the most worthwhile. Led by professional actors, this 2hr. crash course in Scottish literature meets outside the Beehive Inn on Grassmarket. (☎226 6665; www.edinburghliterarypubtour.co.uk. Tours June-Sept. daily 7:30pm; Mar.-May and Oct. Th-Su 7:30pm; Nov.-Feb. F 7:30pm. £7, students £6. Discount for online booking.) The **City of the Dead Tour** is a popular exploration of

Edinburgh's grisly past. (☎225 9044; www.blackhart.uk.com. Nightly Easter-Oct. 31 8:30, 9:15, 10pm; Oct. 31-Easter 7:30 and 8:30pm. £8.50, students £6.50.)

## THE OLD TOWN AND THE ROYAL MILE

Edinburgh's medieval center, the fascinating Royal Mile, defines the Old Town. Once lined with narrow shopfronts and slums towering a dozen stories high, this famous strip is now a playground for hostelers and locals alike, buzzing with bars, attractions, and the inevitable cheesy souvenir shops.

**■ EDINBURGH CASTLE.** Dominating the Edinburgh skyline from atop a (thankfully) extinct volcano, Edinburgh Castle is a testament to the city's past strategic importance. Today's castle is the product of centuries of renovation and rebuilding, the most recent of which hail from the 1920s. The **One O'Clock Gun** fires Monday through Saturday. *(You can't miss it. ☎225 9846; www.historic-scotland.gov.uk. Open daily Apr.-Oct. 9:30am-6pm; Nov.-Mar. 9:30am-5pm. £11, students £9; includes guided tour.)*

**CASTLE HILL AND LAWNMARKET AREA.** The Scotch Whisky Experience at the **Scotch Whisky Heritage Centre** provides a Disney-style tour through the "history and mystery" of Scotland's most famous export. *(354 Castle Hill. ☎220 0441. Open daily June-Sept. 9:45am-5:30pm; Oct.-May 10am-5pm. £9, students £7. Tours 4 per hr.)* Staffed with knowledgeable guides, **Gladstone's Land** (c. 1617) is the oldest surviving house on the Royal Mile. *(477B Lawnmarket. ☎226 5856. Open daily July-Aug. 10am-7pm; Apr.-June and Sept.-Oct. 10am-5pm. £5, students £4.)* Nearby, **Lady Stair's House** contains the **Writer's Museum,** featuring memorabilia of three of Scotland's greatest literary figures: Robert Burns, Sir Walter Scott, and Robert Louis Stevenson. *(Lawnmarket. ☎529 4901. Open M-Sa 10am-5pm; during Festival daily 2-5pm. Free.)*

**HIGH STREET AND CANONGATE AREA.** At the **■ High Kirk of St. Giles** (St. Giles Cathedral), Scotland's principal church, John Knox delivered the fiery Presbyterian sermons that drove Catholic Mary, Queen of Scots, into exile. Most of today's structure was built in the 15th century, but parts date as far back as 1126. The Kirk hosts free concerts throughout the year. *(Where Lawnmarket becomes High St. ☎225 9442; www.stgilescathedral.org.uk. Suggested donation £1.)* The **Canongate Kirk,** on the hill at the end of the Royal Mile, is the resting place of Adam Smith; royals worshiped here when in residence. *(Both kirks open daily M-Sa 9am-5pm, Su 1-5pm.)*

**THE PALACE OF HOLYROODHOUSE.** This Stewart palace, at the base of the Royal Mile beside Holyrood Park, is Queen Elizabeth II's Scottish residence. Only parts of the interior are open to the public. The ruins of **Holyrood Abbey** sit on the grounds, built by David I in 1128 and ransacked during the Reformation. Most of the ruins date from the 13th century. The **Queen's Gallery,** in a renovated 17th-century schoolhouse near the palace entrance, displays pieces from the royal art collection. *(☎556 5100. Open Apr.-Sept. daily 9:30am-6pm; Nov.-Mar. M-Sa 9:30am-4:30pm. Last entry 1hr. before closing. No entry while royals are in residence, often June-July. Palace £9.50, students and seniors £8.50, under 17 £5.50, families £25, under 5 free. Queen's Gallery £5.50/5/3.50/14. Joint ticket £13/12/7.50/33.50. Audio tour free.)*

**OTHER SIGHTS IN THE OLD TOWN.** South of the George IV Bridge on Chambers St., the **■ Museum of Scotland** houses Scottish artifacts. Check out the working **Corliss Steam Engine** and the **Maiden,** Edinburgh's pre-French-Revolution guillotine. The nearby **Royal Museum** has a mix of European art and ancient Roman and Egyptian artifacts. *(☎247 4422; www.nms.ac.uk. Both museums open daily 10am-5pm. Free.)* Across the street, a statue of Greyfriar's pooch marks the entrance to the 17th-century **Highland Kirk,** ringed by a haunted churchyard. *(Off Candlemaker Row. ☎225 1900. Open Apr.-Oct. M-F 10:30am-4:30pm, Sa 10:30am-2:30pm; Nov.-Mar. Th 1:30-3:30pm. Free.)*

GREAT BRITAIN

## THE NEW TOWN

Don't be fooled by the name. Edinburgh's New Town, a masterpiece of Georgian design, has few buildings younger than a century or two old. James Craig, a 23-year-old architect, won the city-planning contest in 1767; his rectangular grid of three parallel streets (**Queen, George,** and **Princes**) linking two large squares (**Charlotte** and **St. Andrew**) reflects the Scottish Enlightenment's love of order.

■**ROYAL YACHT BRITANNIA.** Northeast of the city center floats the Royal Yacht *Britannia.* Used by monarchs from 1953 to 1997, *Britannia* sailed around the world on state visits and royal holidays before settling in Edinburgh for permanent retirement. *(Entrance on the Ocean Terminal's 3rd fl. Take bus #22 from Princes St. or #35 from the Royal Mile to Ocean Terminal; £1. ☎ 555 5566; www.royalyachtbritannia.co.uk. Open daily Mar.-Oct. 9:30am-4pm; Nov.-Feb. 10am-4:30pm. £9, students £7. Audio tour free.)*

**THE WALTER SCOTT MONUMENT AND THE GEORGIAN HOUSE.** The ■**Walter Scott Monument** is a "steeple without a church"; climb to the top for views of Princes St., the castle, and the surrounding city. *(Princes St. between The Mound and Waverley Bridge. ☎ 529 4068. Open Apr.-Sept. M-Sa 9am-6pm, Su 10am-6pm; Oct.-Mar. M-Sa 9am-3pm, Su 10am-3pm. £2.50.)* **Georgian House** gives a fair picture of how Edinburgh's elite lived 200 years ago. *(7 Charlotte Sq. ☎ 226 3318. Open daily July-Aug. 10am-7pm; Apr.-June and Sept.-Oct. 10am-5pm; Mar. and Nov. 11am-3pm. £5, students £4.)*

**THE NATIONAL GALLERIES.** Edinburgh's National Galleries of Scotland form an elite group, with excellent collections housed in stately buildings connected by a free shuttle *(1 every 45min.)* The flagship is the superb ■**National Gallery of Scotland,** on The Mound, which has works by Renaissance, Romantic, and Impressionist masters. Don't miss the octagonal room with Poussin's entire *Seven Sacraments.* The **Scottish National Portrait Gallery,** 1 Queen St., north of St. Andrew Sq., features the faces of famous men and women who have shaped Scotland's history. The gallery also hosts contemporary art exhibits. Take the free bus #13 from George St., or walk to the **Scottish National Gallery of Modern Art,** 75 Belford Rd., west of town, to see works by Braque, Matisse, and Picasso. The landscaping out front uses dirt and greenery to represent the concept of chaos theory. The **Dean Gallery,** 73 Belford Rd., is dedicated to Dadaist and Surrealist art. *(☎ 624 6200; www.nationalgalleries.org. All open daily 10am-5pm; during Festival 10am-6pm. Free.)*

## GARDENS AND PARKS

Off the eastern end of the Royal Mile, the oasis of **Holyrood Park** is a natural wilderness. ■**Arthur's Seat** is the park's highest point; the walk to the summit takes about 45min. Located in the city center and offering great views of the Old Town and the castle, the **Princes Street Gardens** are on the site of the drained Nor'Loch, where Edinburghers used to drown accused witches. On summer days, it seems all of Edinburgh eats lunch here. The **Royal Botanic Gardens** are north of the city center. Tours go across the grounds and through greenhouses. *(Inverleith Row. Take bus #23 or 27 from Hanover St. ☎ 552 7171. Open daily Apr.-Sept. 10am-7pm; Mar. and Oct. 10am-6pm; Nov.-Feb. 10am-4pm. Parks free. Greenhouses £3.50, students £3, children £1, families £8.)*

## ♫ ENTERTAINMENT

The summer sees a joyful string of events—music in the gardens, plays and films, and *ceilidhs* (KAY-lee; traditional Scottish dances). In winter, shorter days and the crush of students promote nightlife shenanigans. For up-to-date info on what's going on, check out *The List* (£2.50), available from newsstands. The **Festival Theatre,** 13-29 Nicholson St., stages ballet and opera, while the **King's Theatre,** 2 Leven St., hosts comedy, drama, musicals, and opera. *(☎ 529 6000. Box office open M-Sa 10am-6pm. Tickets £5-55.)* **The Stand Comedy Club,** 5 York Pl., has nightly acts.

(☎558 7272. Tickets £1-10.) The **Filmhouse,** 88 Lothian Rd., shows arthouse, European, and Hollywood cinema. (☎228 2688. Tickets £3.50-5.50.) Edinburgh has a vibrant live music scene. Enjoy live jazz at **Henry's Jazz Cellar,** 8 Morrison St. (☎538 7385. £5. Open daily 8pm-3am.) **Whistle Binkie's,** 4-6 South Bridge, off High St., is a subterranean pub with live bands every night. (☎557 5114. Open daily until 3am.) **The Royal Oak,** 1 Infirmary St., hosts live traditional music nightly at 7pm. (☎557 2976. Tickets £3. Open M-F 10am-2am, Sa 11am-2am, Su 12:30pm-2am.)

## 🎭🎭 NIGHTLIFE

### PUBS
Students and backpackers gather nightly in the Old Town. Pubs on the Royal Mile attract a mixed crowd, while casual pub-goers move to live music on **Grassmarket, Candlemaker Row,** and **Victoria Street.** Historic pubs New Town line **Rose Street,** parallel to Princes St. Depending on where you are, you'll hear last call sometime between 11pm and 1am or 3am during festival season.

🏆 **The Tron,** 9 Hunter Sq. (☎226 0931), behind the Tron Kirk. Friendly student bar. Downstairs is a mix of alcoves and pool tables. Frequent live music. Burger and a pint £4.50. W night £1 pints can't be beat. Open M-Sa noon-1am, Su 12:30pm-1am; during Festival daily 8:30am-3am. Kitchen open M-Sa noon-9pm, Su 12:30-9pm.

**The Outhouse,** 12a Broughton St. (☎557 6668). Hidden up an alley off Broughton St., this bar is well worth seeking out. More stylish than your average pub but just as cheap, with one of the best beer gardens in the city. Open daily 11am-1am.

**The Globe,** 13 Niddry St. (☎557 4670). This hole-in-the-wall is recommended up and down the Royal Mile. DJs, international sports, karaoke, and quiz nights. Open M-F 4pm-1am, Sa noon-1am, Su 12:30pm-1am; during Festival until 3am.

**The Three Sisters,** 139 Cowgate (☎622 6801). Loads of space for dancing, drinking, and lounging with 3 bars (Irish, Gothic, and American). Beer garden and barbecue. Open daily 9am-1am. Kitchen open M-F 9am-9pm, Sa-Su 9am-8pm.

### CLUBS
Club venues are constantly closing down and reopening under new management; consult *The List* for updated info. Many clubs are around the historically disreputable **Cowgate,** downhill from and parallel to the Royal Mile. Most venues close at 3am, 5am during the Festival. The Broughton St. area of the New Town (better known as the **Broughton Triangle**) is the center of Edinburgh's gay community.

🏆 **Cabaret-Voltaire,** 36-38 Blair St. (☎220 6176; www.thecabaretvoltaire.com). With a wide range of art, dance, and live music, this club throws a great party. M cheap drinks. W huge 'We Are Electric' party. Cover up to £12. Open daily 10pm-3am.

**Bongo Club,** 14 New St. (☎558 7604). Students and backpackers flock to the long-running and immensely popular Messenger (reggae) and Headspin (funk and dance) nights, each 1 Sa per month. Cover up to £7. Cafe during the day with free Internet. Open Su-W 10am-midnight, Th-Sa 10am-3am.

**Po Na Na,** 43B Frederick St. (☎226 2224), below Cafe Rouge. Moroccan-themed with parachute ceilings, red velvet couches, and an eclectic mix of music. Cover £2.50-6. Open Su-M and Th 11pm-3am, F-Sa 10pm-3am.

**Ego,** 14 Picardy Pl. (☎478 7434; www.clubego.co.uk). Not strictly a GLBT club, but hosts several gay nights within its elegantly paneled interior. Open Su-W 10pm-1am, Th-Sa 11pm-3am; check *The List* for gay night dates. Cover £3-10.

GREAT BRITAIN

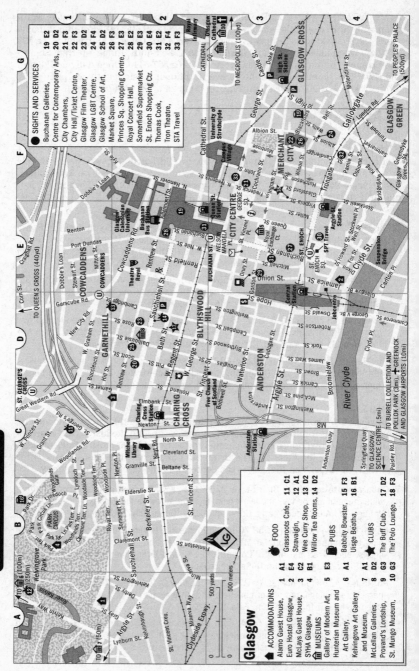

## ❋ FESTIVALS

In August, Edinburgh is *the* place to be in Europe. What's commonly referred to as "the Festival" actually encompasses several independent events. For more info, check out www.edinburghfestivals.co.uk. The **Edinburgh International Festival** (www.eif.co.uk; Aug. 8-31), the largest of them all, features a kaleidoscopic program of art, dance, drama, and music. Tickets (£7-58, students £3.50-29) are sold beginning in April, but a limited number of £5 tickets are available 1hr. before every event. Bookings can be made by mail, phone, fax, web, or in person at **The HUB** (☎473 2000), Edinburgh's Festival center, on Castle hill. A less formal ✖**Fringe Festival** (www.edfringe.com; Aug. 3-25) has grown around the established festival. Anyone who can afford the small registration fee can perform, guaranteeing many great to not-so-good independent acts and an absolutely wild month. Pick up a free copy of *The Fringe Programme*, distributed throughout the city, for a complete listing of events. The **Edinburgh Jazz and Blues Festival** is in late July. (www.jazzmusic.co.uk. Tickets on sale in June.) The **Military Tattoo** (Aug. 1-23) is a spectacle of military bands, bagpipes, and drums in front of the castle. For tickets (£9-31), contact the Tattoo Ticket Sale Office, 33-34 Market St. (☎08707 555 118; www.edintattoo.co.uk). The **Edinburgh International Film Festival** arrives during the last two weeks of August at The Filmhouse. (www.edfilmfest.org.uk. Tickets on sale starting late July.) The fun doesn't stop in winter. ✖**Hogmanay,** the traditional New Year's Eve festival, is a serious street party with a week of associated events (www.edinburghshogmanay.org).

## ▶ DAYTRIP FROM EDINBURGH: ST. ANDREWS

If you love golf, play golf, or think that you might ever want to play golf, this is your town. The game originated here centuries ago and its presence is still felt at yearly tournaments on its courses. Mary, Queen of Scots supposedly played at the **Old Course** just days after her husband was murdered. Nonmembers must present a handicap certificate or letter of introduction from a golf club. Reserve at least a year ahead, enter your name into a near-impossible lottery by 2pm the day before you hope to play, or get in line before dawn by the caddie master's hut as a single. (☎*01334 466 666. Apr.-Oct. £80-120 per round; Nov.-Mar. £56.)* The lovely budget option is the nine-hole **Balgove Course** (£10). Next to the Old Course on Bruce Embankment, the **British Golf Museum** covers the origins of the game for dedicated fans. (☎*01334 460 046. Open Mar.-Oct. M-Sa 9:30am-5:30pm, Su 10am-5pm; Nov.-Mar. daily 10am-4pm. £5.30, students £4.30.)* The ruins of St. **Andrews Castle** hold medieval siege tunnels and dungeons. (☎*01334 477 196. Open daily Apr.-Sept. 9:30am-6:30pm; Oct.-Mar. 9:30am-4:30pm. £5.)* Founded in 1410, St. **Andrews University,** between North St. and The Scores, maintains a well-heeled student body (including recent alumnus Prince William). Tours go through placid quads and include tales of the school's many traditions, from polar bear swims to commencement quirks. (☎*01334 462 245. Buy tickets from the Admissions Reception, Butts Wynd, beside St. Salvator's Chapel Tower on North St. 1hr. £5.50, students £4.50. Tours mid-June to Aug. M-F 11am and 2:30pm.)* **Trains** (☎*08457 484 950)* stop 8km away in Leuchars, where buses #94 and 96 depart for St. Andrews (£1.85). **Buses** (☎*01383 621 249)* run from City Rd. to Edinburgh (#X60; 2hr., M-Sa 1-2 per hr., £7). To get from the bus station to the **TIC,** 70 Market St., turn right on City Rd. and take the first left. Ask for the free *St. Andrews Town Map and Guide.*

(☎ 01334 472 021. Open July-Sept. M-Sa 9:30am-7pm, Su 9:30am-5pm; Apr.-June M-Sa 9:30am-5:30pm, Su 11am-4pm; Oct.-Mar. M-Sa 9:30am-5pm.)

# GLASGOW ☎ 0141

Glasgow (pop. 580,000), Scotland's largest city, has reinvented itself many times and retains the mark of each transformation. Stately architecture recalls Queen Victoria's reign, while cranes littering the River Clyde bear witness to its past as an industrial hub. By day, world-class museums give Glasgow a thriving energy, but the city truly comes alive at night, fueled by its football-crazed locals.

**▨ ⁊ TRANSPORTATION AND PRACTICAL INFORMATION. Flights** land at **Glasgow International Airport** (**GLA**; ☎ 08700 400 0008; www.baa.co.uk/glasgow). Citylink bus #905 connects to Buchanan Station (25min., 6 per hr., £3.30). From **Glasgow Prestwick International Airport** (**PIK**; ☎ 08712 230 700; www.gpia.co.uk), 52km away, express bus #X99 runs to Buchanan Station (50min., 1 per hr., £7) and trains leave for Central Station (30min.; 2 per hr.; £5.20, with Ryanair receipt £2.60). **Trains** run from Central Station, Gordon St. (U: St. Enoch), to: London King's Cross (6hr., 1 per hr., £91); Manchester (4hr., 1 per hr., £40). From Queen St. Station, George Sq. (U: Buchanan St.), trains go to: Aberdeen (2½hr., M-Sa 1 per hr., Su 7 per day, £34); Edinburgh (50min., 4 per hr., £8.20); Inverness (3¼hr., 4-7 per day, £34). Bus #88 (£0.50) connects the two stations, but it's only a 10min. walk. Scottish Citylink (☎ 08705 505 050; www.citylink.co.uk) **buses** leave Buchanan Station, on Killermont St., for Aberdeen (4hr., 1 per hr., £18), Edinburgh (1¼hr., 4 per hr., £4.20), and Inverness (3½hr., 1 per hr., £18). National Express (☎ 08705 808 080) travels to London (8½hr., 3 per day, £18). Local transport includes the **Underground (U)** subway line (☎ 08457 484 950; www.spt.co.uk. M-Sa 6:30am-11pm, Su 11am-5:30pm; prices vary depending on final stop). A **Discovery Ticket** (£1.90) allows one day of unlimited travel on the U (valid M-Sa after 9:30am, Su all day). The **TIC** is at 11 George Sq. (☎ 204 4400; www.seeglasgow.com. U: Buchanan St. Open July-Aug. M-Sa 9am-8pm, Su 10am-6pm; June and Sept. M-Sa 9am-7pm, Su 10am-6pm; Oct.-May M-Sa 9am-6pm.) Surf the **Internet** at **EasyInternet Cafe,** 57-61 Vincent St. (☎ 222 2365. £1 per 30min. Open daily 7am-10:45pm.) **Postal Code:** G2 5QX.

**▨ ▢ ACCOMMODATIONS AND FOOD.** Reserve ahead for B&Bs and hostels, especially in summer. B&Bs are along either side of **Argyle Street,** near the university, and near **Renfrew Street.** The former residence of a nobleman, **▧SYHA Glasgow (HI) ❶,** 7-8 Park Terr., is now the best hostel in town. (☎ 332 3004. U: St. George's Cross. Laundry available. Basement coffeehouse offers Internet £1 per hr. and light eats. June-Sept. dorms £16, under 18 £12. Oct.-May rates vary, from £12. MC/V.) Conveniently located **Alamo Guest House ❸,** 46 Gray St., has a family feel and newly refurbished rooms. (☎ 339 2395. www.alamoguesthouse.com. Breakfast included. Free Wi-Fi. Singles from £26; doubles from £48. MC/V.) The **Euro Hostel Glasgow ❷,** at the corner of Clyde St. and Jamaica St., features quiet, clean rooms, and a bar, all near some of Glasgow's hippest clubs. (☎ 222 2828; www.euro-hostels.com. U: St. Enoch. Breakfast included. Laundry £2. Free Wi-Fi. Computer access £1 per 15min. Wheelchair-accessible. Dorms £15; singles £40. MC/V.) Posh **McLays Guest House ❸,** 264-276 Renfrew St., feels like a hotel with its elegant dining room. Satellite TV and phones in each room. (☎ 332 4796; www.mclays.com. Breakfast included. Singles from £28, with bath £36; doubles £48/56. AmEx/MC/V.)

Glasgow is often called the curry capital of Britain, and for good reason. The city's West End brims with kebab and curry joints, and fusion cuisine is all the rage. Throughout town, Italian and Thai eateries provide alternatives to traditional Scottish pub fare. **Byres Road** and tiny, parallel **Ashton Lane** overflow with affordable, trendy cafes. The **◩Willow Tea Rooms ❷**, 217 Sauchiehall St., upstairs from Henderson Jewellers, are a cozy Glasgow landmark. (☎332 0521; www.willowtearooms.co.uk. U: Buchanan St. Tea £2 per pot. 3-course high tea £11. Salads and sandwiches £4-7. Open M-Sa 9am-5pm, Su 11am-4:45pm. MC/V.) Find Glasgow's best vegetarian food and creative organic dishes at the happening **Grassroots Cafe ❷**, 97 St. George's Rd. (☎333 0534. U: St. George's Cross. Handmade pastas from £6.80. Open daily 10am-9:45pm. AmEx/MC/V.) **The Wee Curry Shop ❶**, 7 Buccleuch St., is the best deal in a town full of pakora and poori. (☎353 0777. U: Cowcaddens. Entrees £5.80-10. Seats 25; reservations are a must. Open M-Sa noon-2:30pm and 5:30-10:30pm. Cash only. Branch at 23 Ashton Ln. ☎357 5280. U: Hillhead. MC/V.) Find first-rate traditional Scottish fare at **Stravaigin ❹**, 28 Gibson St. (☎334 2665; www.stravaigin.com. U: Kelvinbridge. Entrees £14-26. Open for breakfast M-F 9:30am-noon, Sa-Su 11am-4pm; dinner Tu-Th and Su 5-11pm, F-Sa noon-2:30pm and 5-11pm. AmEx/MC/V.)

**◩ SIGHTS.** Glasgow is a budget traveler's paradise, with many free cathedrals and museums. *The List* (www.list.co.uk; £2.50), available at newsstands, is an essential review of exhibitions, music, and nightlife. Your first stop should be the Gothic **◩Glasgow Cathedral,** Castle St., the only full-scale cathedral spared by the 16th-century Scottish Reformation. (☎552 6891. Open Apr.-Sept. M-Sa 9:30am-6pm, Su 1-5pm; Oct.-Mar. M-Sa 9:30am-4pm, Su 1-4pm. Organ recitals and concerts July-Aug. Tu 7:30pm, £7. Ask for free personal tours.) Behind the cathedral is the **Necropolis,** where tombstones lie aslant. Climb to the top of the hill for city views. (Open 24hr. Free.) **St. Mungo Museum of Religious Life and Art,** 2 Castle St., surveys religions from Islam to Yoruba, and displays Dalí's *Christ of St. John's Cross*. (☎553 2557. Open M-Th and Sa 10am-5pm, F and Su 11am-5pm. Free.) Built in 1471, **Provand's Lordship,** 3-7 Castle St., is the oldest house in Glasgow. (☎552 8819. Open M-Th and Sa 10am-5pm, F and Su 11am-5pm. Free.)

In the West End, wooded **Kelvingrove Park** lies on the banks of the River Kelvin. In the southwestern corner of the park, at Argyle and Sauchiehall St., the magnificent **Kelvingrove Art Gallery and Museum** features works by van Gogh, Monet, and Rembrandt. (☎276 9599; www.glasgowmuseums.com. U: Kelvinhall. Open M-Th and Sa 10am-5pm, F and Su 11am-5pm. Free.) Farther west are the Gothic edifices of the **University of Glasgow.** The main building is on University Ave., which runs into Byres Rd. On campus, stop by the **Hunterian Museum,** home to the Blackstone chair, used until 1858, where all students sat for oral examinations while timed by an overhead hourglass. The **◩Hunterian Art Gallery,** across the street, displays a large Whistler collection and a variety of Rembrandts and Pissaros. (☎330 4221; www.hunterian.gla.ac.uk. U: Hillhead. Both open M-Sa 9:30am-5pm. Free.) Take bus #45, 47, 48, or 57 from Jamaica St. (15min., £1.20) to reach the famous **◩Burrell Collection,** in Pollok Country Park. Once the private stash of ship magnate William Burrell, the collection includes works by Cézanne and Degas, medieval tapestries, and fine china. (☎287 2550. Open M-Th and Sa 10am-5pm, F and Su 11am-5pm. Tours daily 11am and 2pm. Free.) Also in the park is the less spectacular **Pollok House,** a Victorian mansion with a small collection of paintings, some by El Greco and Goya. (☎616 6410. Open daily 10am-5pm. £5, students £3.80. Nov.-Mar. free.)

GREAT BRITAIN

🅰️🅱️ **ENTERTAINMENT AND NIGHTLIFE.** Glaswegians have a reputation for partying hard. The infamous **Byres Road** pub crawl slithers past the University area, running from Tennant's Bar toward the River Clyde. For Scottish grub and ambience, you can't beat 🅱️**Babbity Bowster,** 16-18 Blackfriars St. (☎ 552 5055. Entrees ₤4-8. Open M-Sa 11am-midnight, Su 10am-midnight. MC/V.) **Uisge Beatha** (ISH-ker VAH), 232 Woodlands Rd., is Gaelic for "water of life," a.k.a. whisky in Scotland— choose from over 100 varieties. (☎ 564 1596. U: Kelvinbridge. Whisky from ₤2. Open M-Sa noon-midnight, Su 12:30pm-midnight.) 🅱️**The Buff Club,** 142 Bath Ln., with a pub and two dance floors, is *the* after-hours club scene in Glasgow. (☎ 248 1777; www.thebuffclub.com. Cover ₤3-6, free with receipt from local bar; ask at the door for details. Open M-Th and Su 11pm-3am, F-Sa 10:30pm-3am.) **The Polo Lounge,** 58 Wilson St., is Glasgow's largest gay and lesbian club. (☎ 553 1221. Cover ₤5. Open M-Th 5pm-1am, F-Sa 5pm-3am.)

## STIRLING                                              ☎ 01786

It was once said that "he who controls Stirling controls Scotland." The third point of a strategic triangle completed by Glasgow and Edinburgh, Stirling has historically presided over north-south travel in the region. 🅱️**Stirling Castle** is decorated with prim gardens that belie its turbulent history. **Argyll's Lodging,** a 17th-century mansion below the castle, is considered one of the most important surviving Renaissance mansions in Scotland. (☎ 450 000. Castle and Lodging open daily Apr.-Oct. 9:30am-6pm; Nov.-Mar. 9:30am-5pm. Castle ₤9, students ₤7. Lodging ₤4, students ₤3; free with castle admission. Free castle 30min. guided tours.) At the 1297 Battle of Stirling Bridge, William Wallace (of *Braveheart* fame) overpowered the English army, enabling Robert the Bruce to finally overthrow the English at **Bannockburn,** 3km south of town. (Take bus #51 or 52 from Murray Pl. in Stirling. Visitor's Center open Mar.-Oct. daily 10am-4pm. Battlefield open year-round.) The **National Wallace Monument,** on Hillfouts Rd., 2.5km from town, offers unbelievable views. On the way up its narrow 246 steps, stop to catch your breath and gawk at William Wallace's 1.6m sword. Take the City Sightseeing bus or #62/63 from Murray Pl. (☎ 472 140; www.nationalwallacemonument.com. Open daily July-Aug. 9:30am-6pm; low season reduced hours. ₤6.50, students ₤4.90.)

A fun vibe prevails in the vivaciously decorated rooms of 🅱️ **Willy Wallace Hostel ❶,** 77 Murray Pl., near the train station. (☎ 446 773. Internet ₤1 per hr. Dorms ₤10-14. MC/V.) **Cisco's ❶,** 70 Port St., serves every sandwich combination (₤1.35-4) under the sun. (☎ 445 900. Open M-Sa 10am-4pm. MC/V.) **The Greengrocer,** 81 Port St., has fresh produce. (☎ 479 159. Open M-Sa 9am-5:30pm.) **Trains** (☎ 08457 484 950) run from Goosecroft Rd. to: Aberdeen (2hr.; M-Sa 1 per hr., Su 6 per day; ₤35); Edinburgh (50min., 2 per hr., ₤6.20); Glasgow (40min., 1-3 per hr., ₤5.90); Inverness (3hr., 3-4 per day, ₤54); London King's Cross (5½hr., 1 per day, ₤124). Scottish Citylink **buses** (☎ 0870 505 050) also leave from Goosecroft Rd. and run to: Edinburgh (1¼hr., 1 per hr., ₤4.30); Fort William (2¾hr., 1 per day, ₤16); Glasgow (40min., 1 per hr., ₤4.30); Inverness via Perth (3¾hr., 4-6 per day, ₤16). The **TIC** is at 41 Dumbarton Rd. (☎ 475 019. Open M-Sa 9am-7pm, Su 10am-4pm; reduced hours low season.) **Postal Code:** FK8 2BP.

🅰️ **DAYTRIP FROM STIRLING: DOUNE CASTLE.** Above a bend in the River Teith, impressive Doune Castle is a well-preserved 14th-century fortress. Many of the castle's original rooms are entirely intact, notably the towering great hall and the kitchen, with a fireplace large enough to roast a cow. Today, well-versed medieval scholars share the castle with those well-versed in Monty Python, as many scenes from *Monty Python and the Holy Grail* were filmed here. The ticket desk kindly provides coconut shells for re-enactors. *(From Stirling, First bus #59 stops in Doune on its way to Callander; 25min., 1 per hr. The castle is a 5min. walk from town; ask the bus driver for directions. ☎ 01786 841 742. Open daily Apr.-Sept. 9:30am-6:30pm; Oct.-Mar. 9:30am-4:30pm. £3.70, students £2.50, children £1.50.)*

# THE TROSSACHS   ☎ 01877

The most accessible tract of Scotland's wilderness, the mountains and misty lochs of the Trossachs (from Scottish Gaelic for "bristly country") are popular for their moderate hikes and unbeatable beauty. The Trossachs and Loch Lomond constitute Scotland's first national park, established in 2002, where the highlands meet the lowlands. You'll find long bike routes winding through dense forest, peaceful loch-side walks, and some of Scotland's more manageable peaks.

**▉ TRANSPORTATION.** Access to the Trossachs is easiest from Stirling. First **buses** (☎ 01324 613 777) connect to the region's two main towns, running from Stirling to Aberfoyle (#11; 45min., 4 per day, £2.50) and Callander (#59; 45min., 12 per day, £3). Scottish Citylink also runs a bus from Edinburgh to Callander (1¾hr., 1 per day, £9.60) via Stirling. In summer, the useful Trossachs Trundler (☎ 01786 442 707) **ferries** between Aberfoyle, Callander, and the Trossachs Pier at Loch Katrine; one daily trip begins and ends in Stirling. (July-Sept. M-Th 4 per day; Day Rover £5, students £4, children £1.75; including travel from Stirling £8/6/2.50.)

**CALLANDER.** Along the quiet River Teith, Callander is a good base for exploring the Trossachs. Dominating the horizon, **Ben Ledi** (880m) provides a strenuous but manageable trek. A trail up the mountain (9km) begins just north of town along A84. A number of excellent walks depart from Callander itself. **The Crags** (10km) heads up through the woods to the ridge above town, while the popular walk to **Bracklinn Falls** (8km) wanders through a picturesque glen. **Cyclists** can join the **Lowland Highland Trail,** which runs north to Strathyre along an old railway line. Passing through the forest and beside Loch Lubnaig, a sidetrack from the route runs to **Balquhidder,** where Rob Roy, Scotland's legendary patriot, and his family find peace under a stone which reads, "MacGregor Despite Them"—an act of defiance since his surname, MacGregor, had been banned by King James VI of Scotland in 1603. Callander's **Rob Roy and Trossachs Visitor Centre,** Main St., is a combination **TIC** and exhibit on the 17th-century hero. (☎ 330 342. Open daily June-Sept. 10am-6pm; Mar.-May and Oct. 10am-5pm; Nov.-Feb. 11am-4pm. Exhibit £3.60, students £2.40.) Walkers should grab the *Callander Walks and Fort Trails* pamphlet; cyclists can consult *Rides around the Trossachs* (both £2). Rent bikes at **Cycle Hire Callander,** Ancaster Sq., beside the TIC. (☎ 331 052. £7 per ½-day, £10 per day. Open daily 9am-6pm. MC/V.) The hidden gem of the region's lodgings is ◪**Trossachs Backpackers ❷,** Invertrossachs Rd., 0.8km south of Callander. The owners will often pick up guests from Callander. (For hostel ☎ 331 200, for bike rental ☎ 331 100. Bikes £13 per day, £8 per ½-day. Breakfast included. Laundry included. Dorms £15. MC/V.) In Callander itself, **White Shutters B&B ❷,** 6 S. Church St., is just steps from the main road. The great prices and an included hot breakfast make up for the lack of rooms with bath. (☎ 330 442. £18 per person. Cash only.)

**ABERFOYLE AND LOCH KATRINE.** Aberfoyle, another springboard into the wild, is at the heart of the **Queen Elizabeth Forest Park,** established in 1953 to celebrate her Majesty's coronation. The park covers a vast territory from the shore of Loch Lomond to the slopes of the Strathyre Mountains. For more info on **trails,**

visit the **Trossachs Discovery Centre** in town. (☎382 352. Open July-Aug. daily 9:30am-6pm; Apr.-June and Sept.-Oct. daily 10am-5pm; Nov.-Mar. Sa-Su 10am-5pm.) Keep an eye out for visiting foxes at **Corrie Glen B&B ❺**, Manse Rd. (☎382 427. Open Mar.-Nov. Singles from $30; doubles from $50. Cash only.)

The A821, named the **Trossachs Trail**, winds through the heart of the Trossachs between Aberfoyle and Callander. This scenic drive passes near majestic Loch Katrine, the Trossachs' original attraction and the setting of Sir Walter Scott's "The Lady of the Lake." The **SS Sir Walter Scott** cruises the loch from Trossachs Pier, stopping at Stronachlachar, on the northwestern bank. (☎376 316. Apr.-Oct. M-Tu and Th-Su 11am, 1:45, 3:15pm; W 1:45 and 3:15pm. 45min. tour $6.50; 1hr. tour $7.50.) At the pier, rent bikes from **Katrinewheelz.** (☎376 284. $14 per day.) For a daytrip, take the ferry to Stronachlachar and then walk or ride back along the 22km wooded shore road to the pier. Above the loch hulks **Ben A'an** (460m), a reasonable 3km ascent that begins from a parking lot 1.5km along A821.

## LOCH LOMOND                                                 ☎01389

Immortalized by a famous ballad, the Loch Lomond's wilderness continues to awe visitors. Britain's largest loch has some 38 islands. Given their proximity to Glasgow, parts of these bonnie banks can get crowded, especially in summer when daytrippers pour into **Balloch,** the area's largest town. Hikers adore the **West Highland Way,** which snakes along the eastern side of the loch and stretches north 150km from Milngavie to Fort William. The *West Highland Way* guide ($15) includes maps for the route. The **Loch Lomond Shores** visitor complex and shopping mall in Balloch includes an aquarium, a **NPIC**, a **TIC**, and bike and canoe rentals. (☎722 406. Open daily June-Sept. 10am-6pm; Oct.-May 10am-5pm.) Departing from Loch Lomond Shores and the Balloch TIC on the River Leven, **Sweeney's Cruises** provides excellent 1hr. introductions to the area. (☎752 376; www.sweeneyscruises.com. 1 per hr. 10:30am-4:30pm. $5.50, children $3, families $19.50.) Two daily 2hr. cruises also sail around the loch. Relax with a drink and chuckle at all your paddle-boating peers on one of Sweeney's evening tours (1½hr; 7:30pm; $9.50, children $5, families $26).

The ■**SYHA Loch Lomond (HI) ❷**, 3km north of town, is in a 19th-century mansion. Looking for an adrenaline rush after a day of hiking? Ask for the haunted room. From the train station, follow the main road west for 1km, turn right at the roundabout, continue 2.5km, and follow signs to the hostel. Citylink buses to Oban and Campbelltown stop right outside, as do buses #305 and 306 from Balloch. (☎850 226. Internet $5 per hr. Open Mar.-Oct. Dorms $15, under 18 $11. MC/V.) **Trains** (☎08457 484 950) leave Balloch Rd. for Glasgow (45min., 2 per hr., $3.80). Scottish Citylink (☎08705 505 050) **buses** also serve Glasgow (45min., 7 per day, $4.30). The **TIC,** Balloch Rd., is in the Old Station Building. (☎753 533. Open daily July-Aug. 9:30am-6pm; June 9:30am-5:30pm; Sept. 10am-5:30pm; May 10am-5pm.)

## INVERNESS AND LOCH NESS                          ☎01463

The only city in the Highlands, Inverness has an appealing mix of Highland hospitality and urban hustle. Split by the River Ness, the city is a base for exploring the region. Its amenities and proximity to Loch Ness ensure a constant stream of tourists in summer. ■**Loch Ness,** 8km south of Inverness, draws crowds captivated by tales of its legendary inhabitant. In AD 565, St. Columba repelled a savage sea beast as it attacked a monk. Whether prehistoric leftover, giant sea snake, or product of a saintly imagination, the monster and its lair remain a mystery. The easiest way to see the loch is with a tour group, departing from the Inverness TIC. **Jacobite Cruises,** Tomnahurich Bridge, Glenurquhart Rd., whisk you around on coach or boat trips. (☎233 999; www.jacobite.co.uk. £9-20, includes admission to Urquhart Castle. Student discounts available.) South on A82 sits the ruined **Urquhart Castle** (URK-hart), one of the largest in Scotland before it was blown up in 1692 to prevent Jacobite occupation. Today it's a popular viewing area for hopeful Nessie watchers. (☎450 551. Open Apr.-Sept. daily 9:30am-6:30pm; Oct.-Mar. M-Sa 9:30am-4:30pm. £6.50, students £5.) Made famous by its role in Shakespeare's *Macbeth*, **Cawdor Castle** is the stuff of fairy tales, complete with humorous placards describing the castle's sights. Take Highland Country bus #7 (30min., 1 per hr., £5), leaving from the Inverness post office at 14-16 Queensgate. (☎01667 404 401; www.cawdorcastle.com. Open May-Oct. daily 10am-5pm. £7, students £6.)

Riverside ■**Inverness Student Hotel ❶,** 8 Culduthel Rd., is a sociable hangout with quiet rooms. (☎236 556. Breakfast £2. Laundry £2.50. Internet £0.80 per 30min., £1 per hr. Dorms £12-14. MC/V.) Behind the bus station, the **Inverness Tourist Hostel ❶,** 34 Rose St., has swank leather couches and TV. (☎241 962. Dorms £11-14. MC/V). **Hootananny,** 67 Church St., is a feisty bar complete with Scottish song and dance and a mouth-watering, if slightly out of place, Thai restaurant downstairs (entrees £5-6). Groove to live bands in the club upstairs. (☎233 651; www.hootananny.com. Restaurant open daily noon-1am. Club open W-Th 8pm-1am, F-Sa 8pm-3am. MC/V.) Try the Thai soup (£3) or cakes (£2) at the **Lemon Tree ❶,** 18 Inglis St. (☎241 114. Open M-Sa 8:30am-5:30pm. Cash only.) **Trains** (☎08457 484 950) run from Academy St. in Inverness's Station Sq. to: Edinburgh (3½hr., 8 per day, £37); Glasgow (3½hr., 8 per day, £37); Kyle of Lochalsh (2½hr., 4 per day, £16.50); London (8-11hr., 1 per day, £133). **Buses** run from Farraline Park, off Academy St., to: Edinburgh (4½hr., 1 per hr., £20.20); Glasgow (4hr., 1 per hr., £20.20); Kyle of Lochalsh (2hr., 2 per day, £15); London (13hr., 1 per day, £39). The **TIC** is at Castle Wynd; from the stations, turn left on Academy St., right on Union St., and left on Church St. (☎234 353. Internet £1 per 20min., £2.50 per hr. Open mid-June to Aug. M-Sa 9am-6pm, Su 9:30am-4pm; Sept. to mid-June M-Sa 9am-5pm, Su 10am-4pm.)

## FORT WILLIAM AND BEN NEVIS ☎01397

In 1654, General Monck founded Fort William among Britain's highest peaks to keep out "savage clans and roving barbarians." His scheme backfired: today, thousands of Highlands-bound hikers invade Fort William, a base for exploring some of Scotland's impressive wilderness. Just outside of town, beautiful **Glen Nevis** runs southeast into Britain's tallest mountain. **Ben Nevis** (1343m) offers a challenging but manageable hike. One trail starts at the **Glen Nevis Visitor Centre,** where hikers stock up on maps and useful advice. (☎705 922. Open Easter-Oct. daily 9am-5pm.) The ascent (13km; 6-8hr. round-trip) is difficult more in its length than in its terrain, but harsh conditions near the summit can be treacherous for the unprepared. Bring plenty of water and warm, waterproof clothes, and be sure to inform someone of your route. For those not intent on tackling Ben Nevis, a journey into the glen provides spectacular views of gorges, mountains, and waterfalls. Try the popular **Nevis Gorge and Steall Falls** trail (5km) starting from the end of Glen Nevis Rd. The ■**West Coast Railway's** Jacobite steam train rose to stardom as the Hogwarts Express in the *Harry Potter* films. The route, connecting Fort William and Mallaig, passes some of Scotland's finest scenery. (☎01463 239 026; www.westcoast-trailway.co.uk. 2hr.; Runs June and Sept.-Oct. M-F; July-Aug. M-F and Su. Departs Fort William at 10:20am. £20, round-trip £27.)

GREAT BRITAIN

Lodgings fill quickly in summer. From the train station, turn left on Belford Rd. and right on Alma Rd., bear left at the fork, and vault into a top bunk at ⬛**Fort William Backpackers ❶,** 6 Alma Rd., a fun, welcoming hostel with facilities geared toward hikers. (☎700 711; www.scotlandstophostels.com. Breakfast £2. Laundry £2.50. Internet £1 per 20min. Reception 7-11am and 5-11pm. Curfew 2am. Dorms £13-14. AmEx/MC/V.) On the less touristed side of the glen, **Achintee Farm B&B and Hostel ❶,** Achintee Farm, across the river from the Glen Nevis Visitor Centre, is ideal for exploring Glen Nevis, with a kitchen and large, comfortable rooms. From town, walk 3km down Glen Nevis Rd. or call ahead for a lift. (☎702 240; www.achinteefarm.com. Dorms £12-14; singles £30. MC/V.) Before hitting the trails, pick up a packed lunch (£3) at the **Nevis Bakery ❶,** 49 High St., across from the TIC. (☎704 101. Open M-F 8am-5pm, Sa 8am-4pm. Cash only.) Buy groceries at **Tesco,** at the north end of High St. (☎902 400. Open M-Sa 8am-9pm, Su 9:30am-6pm.) Follow the sounds of merriment down an underground alleyway to **Maryburgh Inn,** 26 High St., a popular local pub. (Open M-W and Su 9am-midnight, F-Sa 9am-1am. Karaoke Th, F, and Sa nights.)

**Trains** (☎08457 484 950) depart from the station north of High St. for Glasgow Queen St. (3¾hr., 2-3 per day, £20). The Caledonian sleeper train runs to London Euston (12hr., 1 per day, £99). **Buses** arrive next to Morrison's grocery store by the train station. Scottish Citylink (☎08705 505 050) travels to: Edinburgh (4hr., 3 per day, £21); Glasgow (3hr., 4 per day, £15); Inverness (2hr., 7-8 per day, £9.20); Kyle of Lochalsh (2hr., 3 per day, £14). The **TIC** is in Cameron Sq. (☎703 781. Open July-Aug. M-Sa 9am-7pm, Su 9:30am-5pm; Sept.-Oct. and Apr.-June M-Sa 9am-6pm, Su 10am-4pm; Nov.-Mar. M-Sa 9am-5pm.) **Internet** (30min., free) is available at the **Fort William Library,** High St., across from Nevisport (open M and Th 10am-8pm, Tu and F 10am-6pm, W and Sa 10am-1pm). **Postal Code:** PH33 6AR.

# ISLE OF SKYE

Mountains extend into the clouds on the Isle of Skye, whose hills, peninsulas, and seaside walks hold many secrets for the savvy traveler. Small towns provide glimpses into highland culture and Gaelic tradition. Because visitors tend to stick to major roads, many of Skye's most unique landscapes lay undisturbed, a far cry from the island's revived castles and their summer crowds.

🄴 **TRANSPORTATION. Skye Bridge** links Kyleakin, on the island, to mainland Kyle of Lochalsh. Pedestrians can take the bridge's 2.5km **footpath** or the **shuttle bus** (1 per hr., £0.70). **Trains** (☎08457 484 950) run from Kyle to Inverness (2½hr., 2-4 per day, £16). Scottish Citylink **buses** #915 and 917 travel to Fort William (2hr., 3 per day, £12), Glasgow (6hr., 3 per day, £22), and Inverness (2hr., 3 per day, £12). Buses on Skye are infrequent and expensive; grab the handy *Public Transport Map: The Highlands, Orkney, Shetland and Western Isles* at any TIC. From Portree, Highland Country **buses** run to most island sights (M-Sa 3-8 per day).

**KYLE OF LOCHALSH AND KYLEAKIN.** Kyle of Lochalsh ("Kyle" for short) and Kyleakin (Ky-LOCK-in) serve as hubs for travelers to and from the isle. ⬛**Mac-Backpackers Skye Trekker Tour,** departing Skye Backpackers hostel in Kyleakin, offers a one-day tour emphasizing the mystical, historical side of the island. (☎01599 534 510; www.macbackpackers.com. Weekly departure Sa 7:30am. £18.) Several kilometers east of Kyle near Dornie, **Eilean Donan Castle** is the restored 13th-century seat of the MacKensie family, and offers one of the country's best castle tours. (☎01599 555 202; www.eileandonancastle.com. Open Apr.-Oct. daily

10am-5:30pm. £5, students £4.) The laid-back staff and humorously themed rooms at Kyleakin's **Skye Backpackers** ❶ create a social starting point for any trip to Skye. (☎01599 534 510; www.skyebackpackers.com. Laundry £2.50. Internet £0.80 per 30min. Curfew M-Th and Su 12:30am, F-Sa 1:30am. Dorms £11-14. AmEx/MC/V.) **Cu'chulainn's** ❶ offers upscale Kyle seafood and great vegetarian options in its beer garden. (☎01599 534 492. Open M-Sa 11am-12:45am. Kitchen open 11am-8pm. MC/V.) By the pier in Kyle, **Hector's** ❶ serves homemade ice cream and sweets. (☎01599 534 248. Open M-Sa noon-10pm, Su noon-9pm.) In Kyleakin, **Saucy Mary's**, named after a Norse seductress, packs in pints, crowds, and occasional live music. (Open M-Th 5pm-midnight, F 5pm-1am, Sa 5-11:30pm, Su 5-11pm.) The large **King Haakon Bar,** at the east end of the village green, serves delicious seafood in a room ripe for dancing. (☎01599 534 164. Open M-Th 12:30pm-midnight, F 12:30pm-1am, Sa 12:30pm-12:30am, Su 12:30-11:30pm. 18+ after 8:30pm. Food served 12:30-8:30pm. MC/V.) The **TIC** is by the pier in Kyle. (Open May-Oct. M-F 9:30am-5pm, Sa-Su 10am-4pm.) Free **Internet** is available at the **Kyle Library.** (☎01599 534 146. Open Tu 12:30-3:30pm and 4:30-8pm.)

**PORTREE.** The island's festive harbor capital is a hub for culture and transportation. Off A850, **Dunvegan Castle,** seat of the MacLoed clan, is the longest-inhabited Scottish castle, occupied since the 13th century. Highland Country bus #56 (M-Sa 2 per day) runs from Portree to the castle. (☎01470 521 206; www.dunvegancastle.com. Open daily mid-Mar. to Oct. 10am-5:30pm; Nov. to mid-Mar. 11am-4pm. £7, students £6. Gardens only £5/3.50.) The **Portree Independent Hostel** ❶, in the center of town, has many amenities, including a well-stocked kitchen. (☎01478 613 737. Dorms £12-13. MC/V.) Scottish Citylink and Highland Country **buses** travel from Somerled Sq. to Kyle and Kyleakin (5-10 per day). To reach the **TIC,** Bayfield Rd., from the square, face the Bank of Scotland, turn left down the lane, and left again onto Bridge Rd. (☎01478 612 137. Open July-Aug. M-Sa 9am-6pm, Su 10am-4pm; Sept.-Oct. and Apr.-June M-F 9am-5pm, Su 10am-4pm; Nov.-Mar. M-Sa 9am-4pm.)

**▨TROTTERNISH PENINSULA.** Many cliffs, waterfalls, and ancient standing stones on Trotternish remain virtually untouched. A steep hike (1hr. round-trip) leads to the **Old Man of Storr,** a 165 ft. basalt stone at the top of the highest peak in Trotternish (2358 ft.), located north of Portree on the A855. Start your ascent at the car park. North of Staffin, a footpath leads through the **Quirang** rocks, some of the world's most striking geological formations (3hr. round-trip). Nearby **Staffin Bay** has Jurassic fossils and pottery remains from more recent settlers. South of Staffin, **Kilt Rock** has pleated lava columns above a rocky base crumbling into the sea. Climb to the top of nearby **Mealt Falls** (300 ft.) for the best view of the formation. Take the Staffin bus from Portree and ask to be let off. (☎552 212. Internet access £1 per 30min. Dorms £12.50. Camping £6 per person. Cash only.)

# ISLE OF LEWIS (LEODHAS)                              ☎01851

Fantastic hiking, biking, surfing, and historic sites attract travelers to Lewis, the most populous of the Outer Hebridean Islands. The small city of **Stornoway** (pop. 5600) adds a splash of urban life to the otherwise rural island. Many of Lewis's natural and historical attractions line its west coast along A858 and are accessible by the W2 bus from Stornoway (M-Sa 4-6 per day in either direction). Alternatively, travel with **Out and About Tours** (☎612 288; personalized group tours from £67 per ½-day, £102 per day) in the untouched moorland and half-cut fields of peat. Second only to Stonehenge in grandeur and less overrun with tourists, the gargantuan **▨Callanish Stones** are 22km west of Stornoway on A858. Archaeologists have dated the formation to 2000 BC and believe that prehistoric people used Callanish and two nearby circles to track the movements of the heavens. Lewis is also home to crashing waves and consistent surf. Warm currents and long daylight hours draw **surfers** to the popular **Dalmor Beach,** near the village of **Dalbeg,** which has hosted several competitions (take the W2 bus from Stornoway).

The immaculate ▨**Heb Hostel ❷,** 25 Kenneth St., offers exceptional facilities. (☎709 889. Internet £1 per 30min. £15 per person. Cash only.) Feast on classic dishes in the green-curtained glow of the ▨**Thai Cafe ❷,** 27 Church St., which serves mouth-watering entrees (£4-6) by candlelight. (☎701 811. Open M-Sa noon-2:30pm and 5-11pm. MC/V.) Buy groceries at the **Co-op** on Cromwell St. (☎702 703. Open M-Sa 8am-8pm.) CalMac **ferries** sail to Ullapool (2¾hr.; M-Sa 2-3 per day; £15, 5-day round-trip £26; car £73/125). **Lewis Car Rentals** is at 52 Bayhead St. (☎703 760. 21+. £25-45 per day. Open M-Sa 9am-6pm. AmEx/MC/V.) Rent bikes at **Alex Dan's Cycle Centre,** 67 Kenneth St. (☎704 025. £12 per day, £38 per week. Open M-Sa 9am-6pm.) Western Isles **buses** depart from Stornoway's Beach St. station; pick up a free *Lewis and Harris Bus Timetable* for destinations. Be aware that the only things running on Sundays are planes and churchgoers late for services. The **TIC** is at 26 Cromwell St. From the ferry terminal, turn left onto South Beach, then right on Cromwell St. (☎703 088. Open Apr.-Oct. daily 9am-6pm and 8-9pm; Nov.-Mar. M-F 9am-5pm.) **Internet** is free at the **Stornoway Library.** (☎708 631. Open M-W and Sa 10am-5pm, Th-F 10am-6pm.) **Postal Code:** HS1 2AA.

# DENMARK (DANMARK)

 Straddling the border between Scandinavia and continental Europe, Denmark packs majestic castles, pristine beaches, and thriving nightlife onto the compact Jutland peninsula and its network of islands. Vibrant Copenhagen boasts the busy pedestrian thoroughfare of Strøget and the world's tallest carousel in Tivoli Gardens, while beyond the city, fairytale lovers can tour Hans Christian Andersen's home in rural Odense. In spite of the nation's historically homogenous population, its Viking past has given way to a dynamic multicultural society that draws in visitors as it turns out Legos and Skagen watches.

## DISCOVER DENMARK: SUGGESTED ITINERARIES

**THREE DAYS.** Start off in the capital of **Copenhagen** (p. 237), soaking up some sun on a **bike tour** (p. 244) of the city or waiting out showers in the medieval ruins beneath **Christianborg Slot.** Channel the Bard at Kronborg Slot in **Helsingør** (p. 247), where the real-life Hamlet slept.

**BEST OF DENMARK, 12 DAYS.** Begin your journey in **Copenhagen** (3 days), then castle-hop to Frederiksborg Slot in nearby **Hillerød** (1 day; p. 247). The best way to explore the beautiful beaches,

farmlands, and forests of **Bornholm** (2 days; p. 249) is to bike around the island. After returning to the mainland, head west to **Odense** (1 day; p. 250) for celebrations of Hans Christian Andersen's birth. Discover the museums and nightlife of little-known **Århus** (2 days; p. 251) before indulging your inner child at Legoland in **Billund** (1 day; p. 253). Finish your journey at the northern tip of Jutland, where the yellow houses of **Skagen** (2 days; p. 254) look out on the Baltic Sea.

# LIFE AND TIMES

## HISTORY

The Danes evolved from nomadic hunters to farmers during the Stone Age before taking to the water as **Vikings**, sacking everything from the English coast to Constantinople and ruling the North Sea. Denmark—then called Jutland—was unified and Christianized in the 10th century by **King Harold Bluetooth.** Under the rule of Harold's descendants, the empire grew to include all of modern Norway, Iceland, and England. Various disputes plagued the Danish throne until 1282 when the **Danehof,** a council composed of high nobles and church leaders, established control over state affairs. In 1397, Denmark united with Norway and Sweden under the rule of **Queen Margrethe I,** until Sweden seceded from the union in the 1520s after a violent conflict. During the 16th century, the **Protestant Reformation** swept through Denmark, and **Lutheranism** was established as the national religion. Over several centuries, the **Thirty Years' War** (1618-1648), the **Napoleonic Wars** (1799-1815), the **War of 1864,** and a series of squabbles with Sweden resulted in severe financial and territorial losses. Denmark's policy of neutrality during **WWI** proved fiscally beneficial, allowing the country to profit from trade with the warring nations. During **WWII**, Nazi forces occupied Denmark, but the underground **Danish Resistance Movement** safely evacuated most of the nation's 8000 Jewish citizens to Sweden. After the war, Denmark took its place on the international stage, becoming a founding member of **NATO** in 1949 and joining the **European Union** in 1973.

**Denmark**

Skagen
Hirtshals
Gothenburg
Skagerrak
Frederikshavn
Hanstholm
Aalborg
Læsø
Varberg
Kattegat
Limfjorden
North Sea
Holstebro
Viborg
Anholt
Gudenå R.
Grenaa
SWEDEN
JUTLAND
Silkeborg
Århus
Herning
Ry
Horsens
Samsø
Helsingør
Helsingborg
Hillerød
Billund
Vejle
Hov
Humlebæk
Rungsted
Klampenborg
Esbjerg
Kolding
Fredericia
Kalundborg
Roskilde
Copenhagen
Malmö
Fanø
Bramming
Odense
Great Belt
Ishøj
Køge
Ribe
FUNEN
ZEALAND
Ystad
Rønø
Kværndrup
Trelleborg
Tønder
Svendborg
Langeland
Tåsinge
Møn
TO BORNHOLM
(SEE INSET BELOW)
Ærøskøbing
Vordingborg
Møns Klint
Allinge and Sandvig
GERMANY
Ærø
Stege
LOLLAND
Rødby
Falster
Rønne
Kiel
Kiel Bay
Baltic Sea
Bornholm

## TODAY

Prime Minister **Anders Fogh Rasmussen** leads Denmark's unicameral legislature, the Folketing, while **Queen Margrethe II** remains the nominal head of state. Support for the European Union has been underwhelming; the country rejected the EU's common defense policy as well as the euro. Periodic economic setbacks have increased support for conservative groups, and the far-right **Danish People's Party** has garnered an increasing share of the vote since 1996. In response to the party's lobbying, the government passed a controversial anti-immigration bill in 2002 that imposed stringent citizenship requirements and limited spouses' rights of entry. The bill led many native Copenhageners to cross the Øresund Bridge—nicknamed the "Love Bridge"—into neighboring Sweden to remain with their foreign partners.

In recent years, several high-profile incidents in Denmark have highlighted tensions with Muslims, who make up about 2% of the population. In 2005, the Danish Supreme Court upheld the firing of a Muslim resident for her refusal to remove her headscarf at work. Later that year, Danish newspaper *Jyllands-Posten* published a series of controversial cartoons of the prophet Muhammad, some of which were reprinted in newspapers around the world. Clerics in Denmark and leaders of Islamic nations organized protests, and over 130 people were killed in violent demonstrations worldwide. In response to the conflict, **Naser Khader**, a Muslim member of the Danish Parliament, founded the **Democratic Muslims Network** and organized a job fair that resulted in Danish companies hiring hundreds of Muslims.

# PEOPLE AND CULTURE

**DEMOGRAPHICS AND LANGUAGE.** Denmark has traditionally been home to a homogenous population of Scandinavian descent. Immigration increased steadily during the last decades of the 20th century, but the influx of foreigners has declined since the passage of new restrictions in 2002. Today immigrants make up about 8% of the population. Danish is the official language of Denmark, although natives of Greenland and the Faroe Islands speak local dialects. The Danish add *æ* (pronounced like the "e" in egg), *ø* (pronounced "euh"), and *å* (sometimes written *aa;* pronounced "oh" with tightly pursed lips) to the end of the alphabet; thus Århus would follow Skagen in an alphabetical listing of cities. *Let's Go* indexes these under "ae," "o," and "a." Nearly all Danes speak flawless English, but for basic Danish words and phrases, see **Phrasebook: Danish,** p. 1051.

# THE ARTS

Denmark's wide cultural influence ranges from fairy tales to philosophy. Hans Christian Andersen's famous tales, including "The Little Mermaid" and "The Ugly Duckling," have delighted children around the world since their initial publication in 1835. Nineteenth-century philosopher and theologian Søren Kierkegaard developed the term "leap of faith," the idea that religious belief is beyond the bounds of human reason. Karen Blixen gained fame under the pen name Isak Dinesen, detailing her experiences in Kenya in *Out of Africa* (1937). Carl Nielsen composed six symphonies with unique tonal progressions that won him international recognition by the early 20th century. Director Carl Dreyer explored complex religious themes in films including *The Passion of Joan of Arc* (1928).

# HOLIDAYS AND FESTIVALS

**Holidays:** New Year's Day (Jan. 1); Easter (Mar. 23); Queen's Birthday (Apr. 16); Worker's Day (May 1); Whit Sunday and Monday (May 11-12); Constitution Day (June 5); Midsummer's Eve (June 23); Christmas (Dec. 24-26).

**Festivals:** In February before the start of Lent, Danish children assault candy-filled barrels with birch branches on *Fastelavn* (Shrovetide), while adults take to the streets for carnivals. Guitar solos ring out over Roskilde during the Roskilde Festival (July 3-6), just before Copenhagen and Århus kick off their annual jazz festivals in mid- to late July.

# ADDITIONAL RESOURCES

*A History of Denmark,* by Knud J.V. Jespersen. Palgrave Macmillan (2004). A good introduction to Danish history.

*Conquered, Not Defeated: Growing Up in Denmark During the German Occupation of World War II,* by Peter H. Tveskov. Hellgate (2003). A poignant first-hand account of life during the Nazi occupation.

*Fairy Tales,* by Hans Christian Andersen. Andersen's original stories are surprisingly dark, especially compared to their cartoon and storybook interpretations.

# ESSENTIALS

## WHEN TO GO

Denmark is best between May and September, when days are usually sunny and temperatures average 10-16°C (50-61°F). Winter temperatures average 0°C (32°F). Although temperate for its northern location, Denmark can turn rainy or cool at a moment's notice; pack a sweater and an umbrella, even in summer.

DENMARK

**FACTS AND FIGURES**

**Official Name:** Kingdom of Denmark.
**Capital:** Copenhagen.
**Major Cities:** Aalborg, Århus, Odense.
**Population:** 5,468,000.
**Land Area:** 42,400 sq. km.

**Time Zone:** GMT +1.
**Languages:** Danish. Pockets of Faroese, Greenlandic, and German. English is nearly universal as a second language.
**Tallest Lego Tower:** Constructed in 2003 at Billund's Legoland (p. 253); 27.22m.

# DOCUMENTS AND FORMALITIES

**EMBASSIES AND CONSULATES.** All foreign embassies are in Copenhagen (p. 238). Danish embassies abroad include: **Australia,** Gold Fields House, Level 14, 1 Alfred St., Circular Quay, Sydney, NSW, 2000 (☎02 92 47 22 24; www.gksydney.um.dk/en); **Canada,** 47 Clarence St., Ste. 450, Ottawa, ON, K1N 9K1 (☎613-562-1811; www.ambottawa.um.dk/en); **Ireland,** Harcourt Road, 7th floor, Block E, Iveagh Court, Dublin 2 (☎01 475 6404; www.ambdublin.um.dk/en); **New Zealand,** Forsyth Barr House, Level 7, 45 Johnston Street, P.O. Box 10-874, Wellington, 6036 (☎04 471 0520; www.danishconsulatesnz.org.nz); **UK,** 55 Sloane St., London, SW1X 9SR (☎020 73 33 02 00; www.amblondon.um.dk/en); **US,** 3200 Whitehaven St., NW, Washington, D.C., 20008 (☎202-234-4300; www.denmarkemb.org).

**VISA AND ENTRY INFORMATION.** EU citizens do not need a visa. Citizens of Australia, Canada, New Zealand, and the US do not need a visa for stays of up to 90 days, beginning upon entry into any of the countries in the EU's freedom-of-movement zone. For more info, see p. 13. For stays longer than 90 days, non-EU citizens need a residence or work permit. More info is available at www.um.dk/en.

# TOURIST SERVICES AND MONEY

**EMERGENCY** | **Ambulance, Fire,** and **Police:** ☎112.

**TOURIST OFFICES.** The Danish Tourist Board has offices in most cities throughout the country, with its main office in Copenhagen at Islands Brygge 43 (☎3288 9900; www.visitdenmark.dt.dk). The website offers a wealth of info as well as an online booking tool for accommodations.

**MONEY.** The Danish unit of currency is the **krone (kr)**, plural **kroner**. One krone is equal to 100 **øre**. The easiest way to get cash is from ATMs; cash cards are widely accepted, and many machines give advances on credit cards. Money and traveler's checks can be exchanged at most banks for a fee of 30kr. Denmark has a high cost of living, which it passes along to visitors; expect to pay 100-150kr for a hostel bed, 450-800kr for a hotel room, 80-130kr for a day's groceries, and 50-90kr for a cheap restaurant meal. A bare-bones day might cost 250-350kr, and a slightly more comfortable one 400-600kr. There are no hard and fast rules for tipping. In general, service at restaurants is included in the bill, but it's always polite to round up to the nearest 10kr, and to leave an additional 10-20kr for good service.

Denmark has a 25% **value added tax** (VAT), a sales tax applied to most goods and services. The prices given in *Let's Go* include VAT. In the airport upon exiting the EU, non-EU citizens can claim a refund on the tax paid for goods purchased at participating stores. In order to qualify for a refund in a store, you must spend at least 300kr; make sure to ask for a refund form when you pay. For more info on qualifying for a VAT refund, see p. 18.

**BUSINESS HOURS.** Shops are normally open Monday to Thursday from about 9 or 10am to 6pm and Friday until 7 or 8pm; they are always open Saturday morn-

| DANISH KRONER (KR) | | |
|---|---|---|
| AUS$1 = 4.41KR | 10KR = AUS$2.27 | |
| CDN$1 = 5.22KR | 10KR = CDN$1.92 | |
| EUR€1 = 7.44KR | 10KR = EUR€1.34 | |
| NZ$1 = 3.83KR | 10KR = NZ$2.61 | |
| UK£1 = 10.93KR | 10KR = UK£0.91 | |
| US$1 = 5.52KR | 10KR = US$1.81 | |

ings and in Copenhagen, they stay open all day Saturday. Regular banking hours are Monday to Wednesday and Friday 10am-4pm, Thursday 10am-6pm.

# TRANSPORTATION

**BY PLANE.** International flights arrive at **Kastrup Airport** in Copenhagen (**CPH;** ☎3231 3231; www.cph.dk). Flights from Europe also arrive at **Billund Airport,** outside Århus (**BLL;** ☎7650 5050; www.billund-airport.dk). Smaller airports in Århus and Esbjerg serve as hubs for budget airline **Ryanair** (☎353 12 49 77 91; www.ryanair.com). **SAS** (Scandinavian Airlines; Denmark ☎70 10 20 00, UK 0870 60 72 77 27, US 800-221-2350; www.scandinavian.net), the national airline company, offers youth discounts to some destinations.

**BY TRAIN AND BY BUS.** The state-run rail line in Denmark is **DSB;** their helpful route planner is online at www.rejseplanen.dk. **Eurail** is valid on all state-run routes. The **ScanRail pass** (p. 46) is good for rail travel through Denmark, Finland, Norway, and Sweden, as well as many discounted ferry and bus rides. Remote towns are typically served by buses from the nearest train station. **Buses** are reliable and can be less expensive than trains.

> **TIP** **RAIL SAVINGS.** ScanRail passes purchased outside Scandinavia may be cheaper, depending on the exchange rate, and they are also more flexible. Travelers who purchase passes within Scandinavia can only use three travel days in the country of purchase. Check www.scanrail.com for more info.

**BY FERRY.** Several companies operate ferries to and from Denmark. **Scandlines** (☎33 15 15 15; www.scandlines.dk) arrives from Germany and Sweden and also operates domestic routes. **Color Line** (Norway ☎47 81 00 08 11; www.color-line.com) runs ferries between Denmark and Norway. **DFDS Seaways** (UK ☎08715 229 955; www.dfdsseaways.co.uk) sails from Harwich, BRI to Esbjerg and from Copenhagen to Oslo, NOR. For more info, check www.aferry.to/ferry-to-denmark-ferries.htm. Tourist offices help sort out the dozens of smaller ferries that serve Denmark's outlying islands. For more info on connections from Bornholm to Sweden, see p. 249; for connections from Jutland to Norway and Sweden, see p. 254.

**BY CAR.** Denmark's only toll roads are the **Storebæltsbro** (Great Belt Bridge; 205kr) and the **Øresund Bridge** (245kr). Speed limits are 50kph (30 mph) in urban areas, 80kph (50 mph) on highways, and 110-130kph (65-80 mph) on motorways. **Gas** averages 9-11kr per liter. Watch out for bikes, which have the right-of-way. High parking prices and numerous one-way streets make driving something of a nightmare in cities. For more info on driving, contact the **Forenede Danske Motorejere,** Firskovvej 32, Box 500, 2800 Kgs. Lyngby (☎70 13 30 40; www.fdm.dk).

**BY BIKE AND BY THUMB.** With its flat terrain and well-marked bike routes, Denmark is a cyclist's dream. You can rent bikes (50-80kr per day) from designated shops as well as some tourist offices and train stations. The **Dansk Cyklist Forbund** (☎3332 3121; www.dcf.dk) provides info about cycling in Denmark and investing in long-term rentals. Pick up *Bikes and Trains* at any train station for info on

DENMARK

bringing your bike on a train, which can cost up to 50kr. **Hitchhiking** on motorways is illegal and uncommon. Let's Go does not recommend hitchhiking.

# KEEPING IN TOUCH

| **PHONE CODES** | **Country code: 45. International dialing prefix:** 00.<br>For more info on how to place international calls, see **Inside Back Cover.** |
|---|---|

**EMAIL AND THE INTERNET.** In Copenhagen and other cities, you can generally find at least one Internet cafe; expect to pay 20-40kr per hr. DSB, the national railroad, maintains Internet cafes in some stations as well. In smaller towns, access at public libraries is free, although you typically have to reserve a slot in advance.

**TELEPHONE.** Pay phones accept both coins and phone cards, available at post offices or kiosks in 100kr denominations. Mobile phones (p. 27) are a popular and economical alternative. For domestic directory info, dial ☎118; for international info, dial ☎113. International direct dial numbers include: **AT&T Direct** (☎8001 0010); **Canada Direct** (☎8001 0011); **MCI WorldPhone** (☎8001 0022); **Sprint** (☎8001 0877); **Telecom New Zealand** (☎8001 0064); **Telstra Australia** (☎8001 0061).

**MAIL.** Mailing a postcard or letter to Australia, Canada, New Zealand, or the US costs 8kr; to elsewhere in Europe costs 7kr. Domestic mail costs 4.50kr.

# ACCOMMODATIONS AND CAMPING

| **DENMARK** | ❶ | ❷ | ❸ | ❹ | ❺ |
|---|---|---|---|---|---|
| **ACCOMMODATIONS** | under 100kr | 100-160kr | 161-220kr | 221-350kr | over 350kr |

Denmark's hotels are uniformly expensive, so **youth hostels** *(vandrehjem)* tend to be mobbed by budget travelers of all ages. HI-affiliated **Danhostels** are the most common, and are often the only option in smaller towns. Facilities are clean, spacious, and comfortable, often attracting families as well as backpackers. Eco-conscious tourists can choose from one of the six Danhostels that have earned a **Green Key** (www.green-key.org) for their environmentally friendly practices. Room rates vary according to season and location; dorms range from 100 to 200kr per night, with a 35kr HI discount. Linens cost 40-60kr; sleeping bags are not permitted. Reserve ahead, especially in summer and near beaches. Danhostel check-in times are usually a non-negotiable 3-4hr. window. For more info, contact the Danish Youth Hostel Association (☎3331 3612; www.danhostel.dk). **Independent hostels,** found mostly in cities and larger towns, draw a younger crowd and tend to be more sociable, although their facilities are rarely as nice as those in Danhostels. Most tourist offices book rooms in private homes (150-250kr).

Denmark's 496 **campgrounds** (about 60kr per person) range from one star (toilets and drinking water) to three stars (showers and laundry) to five stars (swimming, restaurants, and stoves). Info is available at **DK-Camp** (☎7571 2962; www.dk-camp.dk). You'll need a **Camping Card Scandinavia** (125kr for 1yr. membership; available at www.camping.se; allow at least 3 weeks for delivery), valid across Scandinavia and sold at campgrounds as well as through the Danish Youth Hostel Association. Campsites affiliated with hostels generally do not require a card. If you plan to camp for only a night, you can buy a 24hr. pass (20kr). The **Danish Camping Council** *(Campingradet)*, Mosedalvej 15, 2500 Valby (☎39 27 88 44; www.campingraadet.dk) sells passes and the *Camping Denmark* handbook (95kr). Sleeping in train stations, in parks, or on public property is illegal.

# FOOD AND DRINK

| DENMARK | ❶ | ❷ | ❸ | ❹ | ❺ |
|---|---|---|---|---|---|
| FOOD | under 40kr | 40-70kr | 71-100kr | 101-150kr | over 150kr |

A "danish" in Denmark is a *wienerbrød* (Viennese bread), found in bakeries alongside other flaky treats. Traditionally, Danes have favored open-faced sandwiches called *smørrebrød* for a more substantial meal, although today these delicacies are rarely found in restaurants. Herring is served in various forms, usually pickled or raw with onions or curry mayonnaise. For cheap eats, look for lunch specials *(dagens ret)* and all-you-can-eat buffets. National beers include Carlsberg and Tuborg; bottled brews tend to be cheaper than drafts. A popular alcohol is *snaps* (or *aquavit*), a clear liquor flavored with fiery spices, usually served chilled and unmixed. Many vegetarian *(vegetarret)* options are the result of Indian and Mediterranean influences, and salads and veggies *(grønsager)* can be found on most menus. Expect to pay around 120kr for a sit-down meal at a restaurant, while cheaper eats can be found in cafes and ethnic takeaways for 40-80kr.

# BEYOND TOURISM

For short-term employment in Denmark, check www.jobs-in-europe.net. For more info on opportunities across Europe, see **Beyond Tourism**, p. 54.

**The American-Scandinavian Foundation (AMSCAN),** 58 Park Ave., New York, NY, 10016, USA (☎212-879-9779; www.amscan.org/jobs/index.html). Volunteer and job opportunities throughout Scandinavia. Limited number of fellowships for study in Denmark available to Americans.

**Vi Hjælper Hinanden (VHH),** Aasenv. 35, 9881 Bindslev, DEN, c/o Inga Nielsen (☎98 93 86 07; www.wwoof.dk). For 50kr, the Danish branch of World-Wide Opportunities on Organic Farms (WWOOF) provides a list of farmers currently accepting volunteers.

# COPENHAGEN (KØBENHAVN)  ☎33, 35

The center of Europe's oldest monarchy, Copenhagen (pop. 1,800,000) embodies a laid-back spirit. The Strøget, the city's famed pedestrian thoroughfare, now bustles with Middle Eastern restaurants and cybercafes, and neon signs glimmer next to angels in the architecture. The up-and-coming districts of Vesterbro and Nørrebro reverberate with some of Europe's wildest nightlife, while the hippie paradise of Christiania swings to a more downbeat vibe.

## ▆ TRANSPORTATION

**Flights: Kastrup Airport (CPH;** ☎3231 3231; www.cph.dk). **Trains** connect the airport to København H (13min., 6 per hr., 29kr or 2 clips). Ryanair flies into nearby **Sturup Airport** in Malmö, SWE **(MMX;** ☎40 613 1000; www.sturup.com) at low rates.

**Trains: København H** (Hovedbanegården or Central Station; domestic travel ☎7013 1415, international 7013 1416; www.dsb.dk). Trains run to: **Berlin, GER** (8hr., 9 per day, 803kr); **Hamburg, GER** (5hr., 5 per day, 537kr); **Malmö, SWE** (25min., every 20min., 71kr); **Oslo, NOR** (8hr., 2 per day, 821kr); **Stockholm, SWE** (5hr., 1 per 1-2hr., 1040kr). For international trips, fares depend on seat availability and can drop to as low as 50% of the quotes listed above; ▆**book at least 2 weeks in advance.**

**Public Transportation:** Copenhagen has an extensive public transportation system. **Buses** (☎3613 1415; www.hur.dk) run daily 5:30am-12:30am; maps are available on any bus. **S-togs** (subways and suburban trains; ☎3314 1701) run M-Sa 5am-12:30am, Su 6am-12:30am. The **metro** (☎7015 1615; www.m.dk) is small but efficient. All 3 types of public transportation operate on a zone system. To travel any distance, a 2-zone **ticket** is required (19kr; additional zones 9.50kr), which covers most of Copenhagen. For extended stays, the best deal is the **rabatkort** (rebate card; 120kr), available from supermarkets, corner stores, and kiosks, which offers 10 2-zone tickets at a discount. The **24hr. pass** (120kr), available at train stations, grants unlimited bus and train transport in the Northern Zealand region, as does the **Copenhagen Card** (see **Orientation and Practical Information**, p. 238). **Night buses,** marked with an "N," run 12:30-5:30am on limited routes and charge double fare; they accept the 24hr. pass.

 **TAKE A RIDE.** Tickets on the S-togs are covered by Eurail, ScanRail, and Inter Rail passes. So ride away!

**Taxis: Københavns Taxa** (☎3535 3535) and **Hovedstadens Taxi** (☎3877 7777) charge a base fare of 35kr for arranged pickups and 23kr otherwise, plus 10kr per km during the day and 13kr at night. From København H to Kastrup Airport costs around 200kr.

**Bike Rental: City Bike** (www.bycyklen.dk/engelsk) lends bikes mid-Apr. to Nov. from 110 racks all over the city for a 20kr deposit. Anyone can return your bike and claim your deposit, so keep an eye on it. **Københavns Cyklebørs,** Gothersg. 157 (☎3314 0717; www.cykelborsen.dk) rents bikes for 60kr per day, 270kr per week; 200kr deposit. Open M-F 8:30am-5:30pm, Sa 10am-1:30pm. MC/V.

# ◼✦ ◼ ❼ ORIENTATION AND PRACTICAL INFORMATION

Copenhagen lies on the east coast of the island of **Zealand** (Sjælland), across the Øresund Sound from Malmö, Sweden. The 28km **Øresund Bridge,** which opened July 1, 2000, established the first "fixed link" between the two countries. Copenhagen's main train station, København H, lies near the city center. Just north of the station, **Vesterbrogade** passes **Tivoli** and **Rådhuspladsen,** the main square, then cuts through the city center as **Strøget** (STROY-yet), the world's longest pedestrian thoroughfare. As it heads east, Strøget goes through a series of names: **Frederiksberggade, Nygade, Vimmelskaftet, Amagertorv,** and **Østergade.** The city center is bordered to the west by five **lakes,** outside of which are the less touristed communities of **Vesterbro, Nørrebro,** and **Østerbro.** Vesterbro and Nørrebro are home to many of the region's immigrants, while some of Copenhagen's highest-income residents live on the wide streets of Østerbro.

**Tourist Offices: Copenhagen Right Now,** Vesterbrog. 4A (☎7022 2442; www.visit-copenhagen.com). From København H, cross Vesterbrog. toward the Axelrod building. Open July-Aug. M-Sa 9am-8pm, Su 10am-6pm; May-June M-Sa 9am-6pm; Sept.-Apr. M-F 9am-4pm, Sa 9am-2pm. Sells the **Copenhagen Card** (1-day 199kr; 3-day 429kr), which grants free or discounted admission to most sights and unlimited travel throughout Northern Zealand; however, cardholders will need to keep up an almost manic pace to justify the cost. ▨**Use It,** Rådhusstr. 13 (☎3373 0620; www.useit.dk), has indispensable info and services for budget travelers. Offers *Playtime,* a comprehensive budget guide to the city. Provides daytime luggage storage, has free **Internet** (max. 20min.), holds mail, and finds lodgings for no charge. Open mid-June to mid-Sept. daily 9am-7pm; mid-Sept. to mid-June M-W 11am-4pm, Th 11am-6pm, F 11am-2pm.

**Budget Travel: STA Travel,** Fiolstr. 18 (☎3314 1501). Open M-Th 9:30am-5:30pm, F 10am-5:30pm. **Kilroy Travels,** Skinderg. 28 (☎7015 4015). Open M-F 10am-5:30pm, Sa 10am-2pm. **Wasteels Rejser,** Skoubog. 6 (☎3314 4633). Open M-F 9am-5pm.

**Embassies and Consulates: Australia,** Dampfærgev. 26, 2nd fl. (☎7026 3676). **Canada,** Kristen Bernikowsg. 1 (☎3348 3200). **Ireland,** Østbaneg. 21 (☎3542 3233).

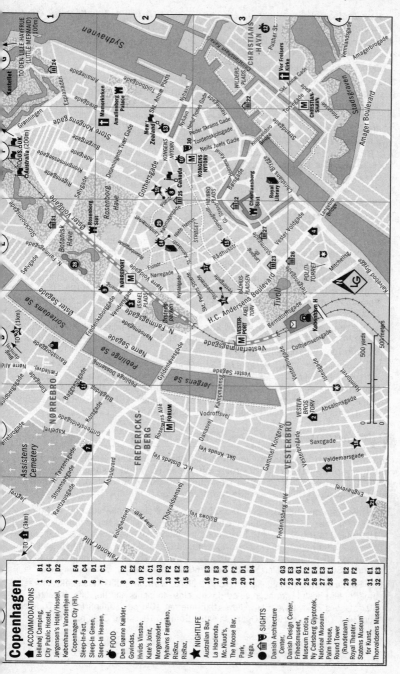

# Copenhagen

## ▲ ACCOMMODATIONS

| | |
|---|---|
| Bellahøj Camping, | 1 B1 |
| City Public Hostel, | 2 C4 |
| Jørgensen's Hotel/Hostel, | 3 D2 |
| København Vandrerhjem | |
| Copenhagen City (HI), | 4 E4 |
| Sleep-In-Fact, | 5 C4 |
| Sleep-In Green, | 6 D1 |
| Sleep-In Heaven, | 7 C1 |

## ◆ FOOD

| | |
|---|---|
| Den Grønne Kælder, | 8 F2 |
| Govindas, | 9 E2 |
| Hviids Vinstue, | 10 F2 |
| Kate's Joint, | 11 C1 |
| Morgenstedet, | 12 G3 |
| Nyhavns Færgekro, | 13 F1 |
| RizRaz, | 14 E2 |
| RizRaz, | 15 E3 |

## ★ NIGHTLIFE

| | |
|---|---|
| Australian Bar, | 16 E3 |
| La Hacienda, | 17 E3 |
| Mc.Kluud's, | 18 F2 |
| The Moose Bar, | 19 C4 |
| Park, | 20 D1 |
| Vega, | 21 B4 |

## ● 🏛 SIGHTS

| | |
|---|---|
| Danish Architecture | |
| Center, | 22 G3 |
| Danish Design Center, | 23 E3 |
| Frihedsmuseet, | 24 G1 |
| Museum Erotica, | 25 F2 |
| Ny Carlsberg Glyptotek, | 26 E4 |
| National Museum, | 27 E3 |
| Palm House, | 28 E1 |
| Round Tower | |
| (Rundetaarn), | 29 E2 |
| Royal Theater, | 30 F2 |
| Statens Museum | |
| for Kunst, | 31 E1 |
| Thorvaldsens Museum, | 32 E3 |

**New Zealand,** Store Strandst. 21, 2nd fl. (☎3337 7702). **UK,** Kastelsv. 36-40 (☎3544 5200). **US,** Dag Hammarskjölds Allé 24 (☎3341 7100).

**Currency Exchange: Forex,** in København H. 20kr commission for cash exchanges, 10kr per traveler's check. Open daily 8am-9pm.

**Luggage Storage:** Free at **Use It** (p. 239) and most hostels.

**Laundromats:** Look for **Vascomat** and **Møntvask** chains. Locations at Borgerg. 2, Vendersg. 13, and Istedg. 45. Wash and dry each 40-50kr. Most open daily 7am-9pm. At the ▓ **Laundromat Café,** Elmeg. 15 (☎3535 2672), bus 3A or 80N, you can pick up a used book, check email on the free Wi-Fi, or enjoy a meal while you wait for your laundry. Brunch 68-110kr. Wash 32kr, dry 1kr per min. Open M-Th 8am-midnight, F-Sa 8am-2am, Su 10am-midnight. MC/V.

**GLBT Resources: Landsforeningen for Bøsser og Lesbiske (LBL),** Teglgårdstr. 13 (☎3313 1948; www.lbl.dk). Open M-F noon-2:30pm and 3-4:30pm. The monthly *Out and About,* which lists nightlife options, is available at gay clubs and the tourist office. Other resources include www.copenhagen-gay-life.dk and www.gayguide.dk.

**Police:** ☎3325 1448. Headquarters at Halmtorvet 20.

**24hr. Pharmacy: Steno Apotek,** Vesterbrog. 6C (☎3314 8266), across from the Banegårdspl. exit of København H. Ring the bell at night. Cash only.

**Medical Services: Doctors on Call** (☎7027 5757). Emergency rooms at **Amager Hospital,** Italiensv. 1 (☎3234 3234), **Frederiksberg Hospital,** Nordre Fasanv. 57 (☎3816 3816), and **Bispebjerg Hospital,** Bispebjerg Bakke 23 (☎3531 3531).

**Internet Access:** Free at **Use It** and **Copenhagen Hovedbibliotek** (Central Library), Krystalg. 15 (☎3373 6060). Coffee shop on 1st fl. Open M-F 10am-7pm, Sa 10am-2pm. **Boomtown,** Axeltorv. 1-3 (☎3332 1032; www.boomtown.net), across from the Tivoli entrance. 30kr per hr. Open 24hr.

**English-Language Bookstore: Arnold Busck International Boghandel,** Købmagerg. 49 (☎3373 3500; www.arnoldbusck.dk). Open M 10am-6pm, Tu-Th 9:30am-6pm, F 9:30am-7pm, Sa 10am-4pm. MC/V.

**Post Office:** In København H. Open M-F 8am-9pm, Sa-Su 10am-4pm. Address mail to be held as follows: LAST NAME First name, Post Denmark, Hovedbanegårdens Posthus, Hovedbanegården, 1570 Copenhagen V, DENMARK. **Use It** also holds mail for 2 months. Address mail to be held as follows: First name LAST NAME, *Poste Restante,* Use It, Rådhusstr. 13, 1466 Copenhagen K, DENMARK.

# ▓▓ ACCOMMODATIONS AND CAMPING

Comfortable and inexpensive accommodations can be hard to find near the city center, but pedestrian-friendly streets and the great public transportation system ensure that travelers are never far from the action. Many hostels are also dynamic social worlds unto themselves. Reserve well ahead in summer.

▓ **Sleep-In Heaven,** Struenseeg. 7 (☎3535 4648; www.sleepinheaven.com), in Nørrebro. M: Forum. Take bus #250S from the airport or from København H. (dir.: Buddinge; every 10-20min.) to H.C. Ørsteds V. Take your 1st right on Kapelvej, then take a left into the alley just after Kapelvej 44. Guests chat around the pool table or on the outdoor patio. Breakfast 40kr. Linens for dorms 40kr. Free Wi-Fi. Reception 24hr. Under age 35 only. Dorms 130-160kr; doubles 500kr; triples 600kr. AmEx/MC/V; 5% surcharge. ❷

▓ **City Public Hostel,** Absalonsg. 8 (☎3331 2070; www.city-public-hostel.dk), in Vesterbro. Popular hostel with huge co-ed dorms, close to sights and nightlife. Breakfast 20-30kr. Linens 35kr, towel 5kr, pillow 10kr. Internet 10kr per 20min.; free Wi-Fi. Reception 24hr. Check-out 10am. Open May-Aug. Dorms 110-140kr. Cash only. ❷

**Sleep-In Green,** Ravnsborgg. 18, Baghuset (☎3537 7777). M: Nørreport. Eco-friendly hostel. Breakfast 40kr. Linens included; pillow 10kr, blanket 20kr. Free Internet. Reception 24hr. Lockout noon-4pm. Open June-Oct. 10. 30-bed dorms 120kr. Cash only. ❶

**Jørgensen's Hostel/Hotel Jørgensen,** Rømersg. 11 (☎3313 8186; www.hoteljoergensen.dk). M: Nørreport. The hostel is in the basement of the hotel and offers cozy rooms in a convenient location. Breakfast included. Linens 30kr. Max. 5-night stay. Dorm lockout 11am-3pm. Dorms under age 35 only. 6- to 14-bed dorms 150kr; singles 500-600kr; doubles 600-725kr. Cash only for dorms; AmEx/MC/V for private rooms. ❷

**København Vandrerhjem Copenhagen City (HI),** H.C. Andersens Bvd. 50 (☎3311 8585; www.danhostel.dk/copenhagencity). This 15-story hostel provides sleek accommodations just 5min. from the city center. Bike rental 100kr per day. Breakfast 50kr. Linens 60kr. Internet 39kr per hr. Reception 24hr. Check-in 2-5pm. Reserve ahead. Dorms 165-200kr; private rooms 555-695kr. 35kr HI discount. AmEx/MC/V. ❷

**Sleep-In-Fact,** Valdemarsg. 14 (☎3379 6779; www.sleep-in-fact.dk), in Vesterbro. Spacious, modern factory-turned-hostel. Bike rental 50kr per day. Breakfast included. Linens 30kr. Internet 20kr per 30min. Reception 7am-noon and 3pm-3am. Lockout noon-3pm. Curfew 3am. Open July-Aug. 10- to 30-bed dorms 100-120kr. Cash only. ❷

**Bellahøj Camping,** Hvidkildev. 66 (☎3810 1150; www.bellahoj-camping.dk). Take bus #2A from København H. (dir.: Tingbjerg; 15min., 6-12 per hr.) all the way to Hulgårdsv. Backtrack from there and turn left on Hulgårdsv., stay left of the church, and then make another left. Basic campground 5km from the city center. Reception 24hr. Open June-Aug. Tent sites 65kr. Electricity 25kr. Showers included. Cash only. ❶

# ◘ FOOD

Good, inexpensive food is plentiful in central Copenhagen. **Strøget** is lined with all-you-can-eat pizza, pasta, and Indian buffets. Around **Kongens Nytorv,** elegant cafes serve filling *smørrebrød* (open-faced sandwiches) and herring meals. **Open-air markets** provide fresh fruits and veggies; a popular one is at **Israel Plads** near Nørreport Station. (Open M-Th 9am-5:30pm, F 9am-6:30pm, Sa 9am-3pm. Cash only.) Greengrocers line the main streets in **Vesterbro** and **Nørrebro,** and **Fakta** and **Netto** supermarkets are common around Nørrebro (M: Nørreport).

▓ **Morgenstedet,** Langgaden, Bådsmandsstr. 43 (☎3295 7770; www.morgenstedet.dk), in Christiania. Walk down Pusher St. and take a left at the end, leaving Cafe Nemoland to your right. Then take a right up the concrete ramp at the bike shop and left before the bathrooms; it will be on your right. This unassuming restaurant serves cheap organic meals. Soup 45kr. Entrees 60kr, with salad 70kr. Open Tu-Su noon-9pm. Cash only. ❷

▓ **RizRaz,** Kompagnistr. 20 (☎3315 0575). M: Kongens Nytorv. Also at Store Kannikestr. 19 (☎3332 3345). Vegetarian buffet with Mediterranean and Middle Eastern specials. Lunch buffet 69kr. Dinner 79kr. Open daily 11:30am-midnight. AmEx/MC/V. ❸

**Den Grønne Kælder,** Pilestr. 48 (☎3393 0140). M: Kongens Nytorv. Vegetarian and vegan dining in a cozy basement cafe. Takeout available. Sandwiches 40kr. Lunch 65kr. Dinner 95kr. Open M-Sa 11am-10pm. Cash only. ❷

**Nyhavns Færgekro,** Nyhavn 5 (☎3315 1588; www.nyhavnsfaergekro.dk). M: Kongens Nytorv. Upscale cafe along the canal with lunch bargains. Try 10 styles of herring at the all-you-can-eat lunch buffet (109kr) or pick just one (45kr). Dinners from 164kr. Kitchen open daily 11:30am-11:30pm. Lunch served daily 11:30am-5pm. MC/V. ❹

**Govindas,** Nørre Farimagsg. 82 (☎3333 7444). M: Nørreport. Hare Krishnas serve vegetarian and vegan fare. Not much atmosphere, but great deals. All-you-can-eat lunch buffet 55kr, dinner buffet 75kr. Open M-F noon-9pm, Sa 1-7pm. Cash only. ❷

**Kate's Joint,** Blågårdsg. 12 (☎3537 4496), in Nørrebro. Bus: 5A. Rotating menu of pan-Asian cuisine with African and Middle Eastern influences. Entrees 62-90kr. Stir-fry, tofu, other appetizers 50-69kr. Open daily 5:30-10:30pm. MC/V. ❷

**Hviids Vinstue,** Kongens Nytorv 19 (☎3315 1064). M: Kongens Nytorv. Copenhagen's oldest pub. Lunch special includes 3 varieties of *smørrebrød* and a Danish beer. Open M-Th 10am-1am, F-Sa 10am-2am, Su 10am-10pm. AmEx/MC/V. ❷

# 🗓 SIGHTS

Flat Copenhagen lends itself to exploration by **bike** (p. 244). **Walking tours** are detailed in *Playtime* (available at **Use It,** p. 238). Window-shop down pedestrian **Strøget** until you reach Kongens Nytorv; opposite is the picturesque **Nyhavn,** where Hans Christian Andersen penned his first fairy tale. On a clear day, take the 6.4km walk along the five **lakes** on the western border of the city center. Wednesday is the best day to visit museums; most are free and some have extended hours.

**CITY CENTER.** Near the train station, ▓**Tivoli Gardens,** the famous 19th-century amusement park, features old-fashioned and new rides, shimmering fountains, and a world-class **Commedia dell'arte** variety show. **Tivoli Illuminations,** an evocative light show, is staged on Tivoli Lake each night 30min. before closing. (☎3315 1001; www.tivoligardens.com. Open mid-June to mid-Aug. Su-Th 11am-midnight, F-Sa 11am-12:30am; mid-Aug. to mid-June reduced hours. Admission 79kr. Rides 10-60kr. Admission with unlimited rides 279kr. AmEx/MC/V.) Across the street, the beautiful **Ny Carlsberg Glyptotek** is home to an excellent collection of Impressionist and Danish art. Tickets for free guided tours go quickly. (Dantes Pl. 7. ☎3341 8141. Open Tu-Su 10am-4pm. 40kr. Su free. Tours mid-June to Aug. W 2pm. MC/V.) Nearby, the **Danish Design Center** showcases trends in Danish fashion and lifestyles. The Flow Market exhibition downstairs lets visitors purchase items. (H.C. Andersens Bvd. 27. ☎3369 3369; www.ddc.dk. Open M-Tu and Th-F 10am-5pm, W 10am-9pm, Sa-Su 11am-4pm. 50kr, students 25kr. W after 5pm free. AmEx/MC/V.) To reach the ▓**National Museum** from H.C. Andersens Bvd., turn onto Stormg., take a right on Vester Volg., and go left on Ny Vesterg. Its vast collections include several large rune stones, examples of ancient Viking art, and the fabulous permanent ethnographic exhibit, "People of the Earth." (Ny Vesterg. 10. ☎3313 4411; www.natmus.dk. Open Tu-Su 10am-5pm. Free.)

**Christiansborg Slot,** the home of Parliament *(Folketing)* and the royal reception rooms, displays vivid modernist tapestries that were designed by Bjørn Nørgård and presented to the Queen on her 50th birthday. Visitors can tour the subterranean ruins underneath the Slot. (Prins Jørgens Gård 1. ☎3392 6494; www.ses.dk/christrainsborg. Ruins open May-Sept. daily 10am-4pm; Oct.-Apr. Tu-Su 10am-4pm. Call ☎3392 6492 for English-language castle tours, May-Sept. daily 11am, 1, 3pm; Oct.-Apr. Tu, Th, and Sa-Su 3pm. Ruins 40kr, students 30kr. Castle tour 60/50kr.) Nearby, the **Thorvaldsens Museum** has colorfully painted rooms with works by Danish sculptor Bertel Thorvaldsen, including some original plaster models. Head upstairs to see the collection of Etruscan and Egyptian artifacts. (Bertel Thorvaldsens Pl. 2. ☎3332 1532; www.thorvaldsensmuseum.dk. Open Tu-Su 10am-5pm. 20kr. W free.) Sixteenth-century astronomer Tycho Brahe once observed the stars from the top of the **Round Tower** (Rundetaarn), which provides a sweeping view of the city. (Købmagerg. 52A. ☎3373 0373; www.rundetaarn.dk. Open June to mid-Aug. M-Sa 10am-8pm, Su noon-8pm; Sept. to mid-Oct. and Apr.-May M-Sa 10am-5pm, Su noon-5pm; mid-Oct. to Mar. M and Th-Sa 10am-5pm, Tu-W 10am-5pm and 7-10pm, Su noon-5pm. 25kr. AmEx/MC/V.) Down the street, the **Museum Erotica** celebrates all things carnal; the videos from the Porn Room can be purchased at the front desk. (Købmagerg. 24.

☎ 3312 0311; www.museumerotica.dk. Open May-Sept. daily 10am-11pm; Oct.-Apr. Su-Th 11am-8pm, F-Sa 11am-10pm. 109kr with guidebook. AmEx/MC/V.)

**CHRISTIANSHAVN.** In 1971, a few dozen flower children established the "free city" of **Christiania** in an abandoned Christianshavn fort. Today, the thousand-odd residents continue the tradition of artistic expression and unconventionality. Vendors sell clothing and jewelry, while spots like **Woodstock Cafe** and **Cafe Nemoland** have cheap beer and diverse crowds. Recent government crackdowns have driven **Pusher Street's** once open drug trade underground, and arrests for possession have become commonplace. A large sign warns passersby not to take pictures on Pusher St. (Main entrance on Prinsesseg. Take bus #66 from København H.) **Vor Frelsers Kirke** (Our Savior's Church) has recently reopened its gold-accented interior to the public. (Sankt Annæg. 9. M: Christianshavn or bus #66. Turn left onto Prinsesseg. ☎ 3257 2798; www.vorfrelserskirke.dk. Spire ☎ 3254 1573. Church free. Spire 20kr. Cash only.) The **Danish Architecture Center** hosts elegantly presented exhibits. (Strandg. 27B. ☎ 3257 1930; www.dac.dk. Open daily 10am-5pm. 40kr, students 25kr. MC/V.)

**FREDERIKSTADEN.** Northeast of the city center, Edvard Eriksen's tiny **Little Mermaid** (Lille Havfrue) statue at the mouth of the harbor honors Hans Christian Andersen's beloved tale. (S-tog: Østerport. Turn left out of the station, go left on Folke Bernadottes Allé, bear right on the path bordering the canal, go left up the stairs, and then head right along the street.) Head back along the canal and turn left across the moat to reach **Kastellet,** a rampart-enclosed 17th-century fortress that's now a park. (Open daily 6am-10pm.) On the other side of Kastellet, the **Frihedsmuseet** (Museum of Danish Resistance) documents the German occupation of 1940-1945, when the Danes helped over 7000 Jews escape to Sweden. (At Churchillparken. ☎ 3313 7714. Open May-Sept. Tu-Su 10am-5pm; Oct.-Apr. Tu-Su 10am-3pm. English-language tours July-Sept. Tu and Th 11am. Free.) Walk south down Amalieng. to reach **Amalienborg Palace,** a complex of four enormous mansions that serve as the winter residences of the royal family. Several apartments are open to the public, including the studies of 19th-century Danish kings. The changing of the guard takes place at noon on the vast plaza. (☎ 3312 0808; www.rosenborgslot.dk. Open May-Oct. daily 10am-4pm; Nov.-Apr. Tu-Su 11am-4pm. 50kr, students 30kr. Combined ticket with Rosenborg Slot 80kr. MC/V.) The imposing 19th-century **Marmorkirken** (Marble Church), opposite the palace, features an ornate interior under Europe's third-largest dome. (Fredriksg. 4. ☎ 3315 0144; www.marmorkirken.dk. Open M-Tu and Th 10am-5pm, W 10am-6pm, F-Sa noon-5pm. English-language tours to the top of the dome mid-June to Aug. daily 1 and 3pm; Oct. to mid-June Sa-Su 1 and 3pm. Church free. Tours 25kr. Cash only.)

The **Statens Museum for Kunst** (State Museum of Fine Arts) displays an eclectic collection of Danish and international art in two buildings linked by a glass-roof gallery. (Sølvg. 48-50. S-tog: Nørreport. Walk up Øster Voldg. ☎ 3374 8494; www.smk.dk. Open Tu and Th-Su 10am-5pm, W 10am-8pm. English-language tours July-Aug. Sa-Su 2pm. Permanent collection free. Special exhibits 50kr, students 30kr. W free. AmEx/MC/V.) Opposite the museum, the Baroque **Rosenborg Slot,** built by King Christian IV in the 17th century as a summer residence, shows off the crown jewels and the opulent **Unicorn Throne,** which legend holds is constructed from unicorn horns. (Øster Voldg. 4A. M: Nørreport. ☎ 3315 3286; www.rosenborgslot.dk. Open June-Aug. daily 11am-5pm; May and Sept. daily 10am-4pm; Oct. daily 11am-3pm; Nov.-Apr. Tu-Su 11am-2pm. 50kr, students 40kr. AmEx/MC/V.) About 13,000 plant species thrive in the ■Botanisk Have (Botanical Gardens); tropical and subtropical plants mingle happily in the iron-and-glass **Palm House.** (Gardens open May-Sept. daily 8:30am-6pm; Oct.-Apr. Tu-Su 8:30am-4pm. Palm House open May-Dec. daily 10am-3pm; Jan.-Apr. Tu-Su 10am-3pm. Free.)

**DENMARK**

**TIME:** 4hr. With visits to Rosenbo[rg]
Slot and Christiansborg Slot, 6hr.

**DISTANCE:** About 6km.

**SEASON:** Year-round, althou[gh]
Rosenborg Slot has reduced ho[urs]
Nov.-Apr.

The *Copenhagen Post* estimates that there may be more bikes than Danes in Denmark, and [the]
city of Copenhagen leads the way as one of Europe's most bike-friendly capitals this side [of]
Amsterdam. Rentals from **City Bike** (p. 238) are the most convenient way to go, although t[he]
rules require that you only ride the bikes in the city center. The eastern banks of the five wes[t]
lakes are fair game, but if you cross over to the other side of the lakes, you'll face a 1000kr f[ine.]

When biking through the city, you should avoid pedestrian thoroughfares like Strøget, unl[ess]
you're in the mood for slaloming around strolling couples and scampering children. If you w[ant]
to ride out into the countryside, ask your hostel about rental bikes. You can take your b[ike]
onto an S-tog for 10kr. In Denmark you are legally required to use lights when riding at ni[ght,]
and police are not shy about handing out 400kr fines to enforce this law. Helmets are stro[ngly]
recommended, but not mandatory.

This tour starts and ends at the **Rådhus.** Begin by carefully making your way down busy H[ans]
Christian Andersens Boulevard.

**1. BOTANISK HAVE** Take a right onto Nørre Voldg. and follow it until you see the gates lead[ing]
into the University of Copenhagen's lush **Botanical Gardens** (p. 243). Wander along paths li[ned]
with more than 13,000 species of plants, or hone in on the **Palm House** to view its extrava[gant]
orchids, cycads, and other tropical rarities.

**2. STATENS MUSEUM FOR KUNST AND ROSENBORG SLOT** Turn left out of the gard[en]
onto Øster Voldg. At the intersection with Sølvg., you'll see the gates of the **Statens Muse[um]
for Kunst** (State Museum of Fine Arts; p. 243) to the north and the spires of **Rosenborg S[lot]**
(p. 243) to the south. The latter served as the 16th-century summer house of King Christian[ IV,]
and the royal family took refuge here in 1801 when the British navy was shelling Copenhag[en.]
Lock up your bike and pop inside for a look at the Sculpture Street in the museum or D[en]
mark's crown jewels in the Slot's treasury.

**3. ROUND TOWER** Backtrack down Øster Voldg. and turn left onto Gothersg. Make a right o[nto]
Landemærket and then hop off again to scale the heights of the **Round Tower** (p. 242), a o[ld-]
time royal observatory that still affords a sweeping view of the city.

**4. AMALIENBORG PALACE** Head back up to Gothersg. and turn right. Pass by **Kong[ens]
Nytorv,** the 1670 "new square" that turns into a skating rink each winter, and take a left o[nto]
Bredg. Keep your eyes peeled for the gilded dome of the **Marmorkirken** (Marble Church; p. 2[43)]
on your left, and then turn right to enter the octagonal plaza of **Amalienborg Palace** (p. 243[), a]
set of four Rococo mansions that the queen and her family call home.

**5. NYHAVN.** Continue on through the plaza, turn right on Toldbodg., and then right before [the]
bridge onto Nyhavn. Part of the city's old waterfront, Nyhavn was known for centuries as a se[edy]
strip for sailors to find grog, women, and a tattoo artist sober enough to wield a firm needle. O[ver]
the past 30 years, Copenhagen has embarked on a clean-up campaign, and today you're m[ore]
likely to find an upscale deli serving *smørrebrod* than a tumbledown soup kitchen. Wheneve[r a]
scrap of sunshine can be found, the good people of Copenhagen are soaking it up along [the]
wharf, joined by Swedes from Malmö in search of cheap Danish beer.

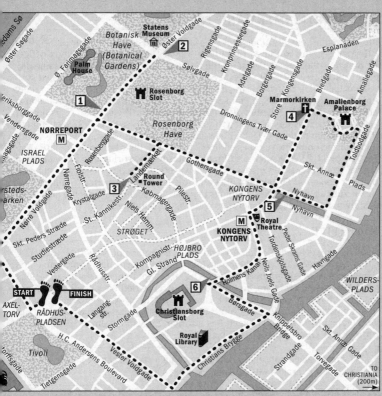

**CHRISTIANBORG SLOT** Walk your bike through Kongens Nytorv, and then thread your ⸱ between the **Royal Theater** (p. 246) and the metro station down Neils Juels G. Turn right ⸱ Holmens Kanal and cross the bridge to reach **Christiansborg Slot** (p. 242), seat of the ⸱ish Parliament. Look for the 103m tower; it's difficult to miss. If you arrive before ⸱pm, try to catch a tour of the **Royal Reception Rooms,** or head down into the ruins of ⸱ four previous castles underneath the present-day building. The first castle was demol-⸱ed to make way for a larger one, the next two burned down in fires, and the Hanseatic ⸱gue dismantled the fourth castle stone by stone after they captured the city in 1369.

**SLIDING INTO HOME.** You're in the home stretch. Head east toward the **Knippelsbro** ⸱dge and **Christiania** (p. 243), taking in the industrial skyline before lugging your bike ⸱n the steps to Christians Brygge below. Turn right and bike along the canal. Keep ⸱ch for the Black Diamond annex of the **Royal Library,** built in 1996 from black marble ⸱orted from Zimbabwe. Make a quick stop to check your email at one of the two free ⸱ninals inside. Make a right onto Vester Voldg. and coast back up to the Rådhus. ⸱'ve earned the right to call it a day.

##  ENTERTAINMENT AND FESTIVALS

For info on events, consult *Copenhagen This Week* or ask at Use It (see p. 238). The **Royal Theater** is home to the world-famous Royal Danish Ballet. The box office, August Bournonville Pass. 1, is just off the Konges Nytorv metro and sells same-day half-price tickets. (☎3369 6969. Open M-Sa 10am-6pm.) The **Tivoli ticket office,** Vesterbrog. 3, has half-price tickets for the city's other theaters. (☎3315 1012. Open daily mid-Apr. to mid-Sept. 11am-8pm; mid-Sept. to mid-Apr. 9am-5pm.) Tickets are also available online at www.billetnet.dk. Relaxed **Kulkaféen,** Teglgårdsstr. 5, is a great place to see live performers and listen to stand-up comedy. (☎3332 1777. Cover up to 50kr. Open M 11am-midnight, Tu-Sa 11am-2am. MC/V.) In late March and early April, international and domestic releases compete for Danish distribution deals at the **Nat-Film Festival** (☎3312 0005; www.natfilm.dk). During the world-class ◪**Copenhagen Jazz Festival** (early July 2008; ☎3393 2013; www.festival.jazz.dk), the city teems with free outdoor concerts. Throughout July and August, **Zulu Sommerbio** (Summer Cinema; www.zulu.dk) holds free screenings in parks and squares across the city. Movies are shown in their original languages with Danish subtitles.

##  NIGHTLIFE

In Copenhagen, weekends begin on Wednesday, and clubs pulse with activity late enough to serve breakfast with their martinis. On Thursdays, many bars and clubs have cheaper drinks and reduced covers. The streets of the city center, as well as those of **Nørrebro** and **Vesterbro,** are lined with hip, crowded bars. Look for fancier options along Nyhavn, where laid-back Danes bring their own beer and sit on the pier; open containers are legal within the city limits. Unless otherwise noted, all bars and clubs are 18+. Copenhagen has a thriving gay and lesbian scene; check out *Playtime* or *Out and About* for listings.

> **!** The areas behind København H, the central train station, can be unsafe, especially at night. Explore with caution, and bring a friend.

◪**Vega,** Enghavev. 40 (☎3326 0954; www.vega.dk), in Vesterbro. Bus: 80N, 84N. Copenhagen's largest nightclub, 2 concert venues, and a popular bar. Come before 1am to avoid paying cover and party all night with the glitterati. Bar 18+; club 20+. Club cover 60kr after 1am. Bar open F-Sa 7pm-5am. Club open F-Sa 11pm-5am. MC/V.

◪**The Moose Bar,** Sværtev. 5 (☎3391 4291). M: Kongens Nytorv. Rowdy local spirit dominates in this popular bar, famous for its cheap beer and its jukebox playing classic rock hits. Beer 24kr, 2 for 32kr. 2 mixed drinks 30-35kr. Reduced prices Tu, Th, and Sa 9pm-close. Open M and Su 1pm-3am, Tu-F 1pm-6am. AmEx/MC/V.

**The Australian Bar,** Vesterg. 10 (☎2024 1411). M: Nørreport. This bar boasts cheap drinks, a smoke machine, and a dance-club playlist. Beer 20kr. Mixed drinks 30kr. Reduced prices Th. Cover 40kr. Open Su-W 4pm-2am, Th-Sa 4pm-5am. MC/V.

**Park,** Østerbrog. 79 (☎3525 1661; www.park.dk). Bus 85N. Far from the center, this club has a live music hall, lavish lounges, and a rooftop patio. Beer 45kr. Dress to impress. F 20+, Sa 22+. Cover Th-Sa 50-70kr. Restaurant open Tu-Sa 11am-10pm. Club open Su-Tu 11am-midnight, W 11am-2am, Th-Sa 11am-5am. AmEx/MC/V.

**Mc.Kluud's,** Istedg. 126 (☎3331 6383; www.mckluud.dk), in Vesterbro. Bus: 10, 84N. Artists and students come to sample the cheap beer at this Wild West bar inspired by the American TV show *McCloud.* Beer 15-17kr. Open daily 2pm-2am. Cash only.

**La Hacienda/The Dance Floor,** Gammel Torv 8 (☎3311 7478; www.la-hacienda.dk). M: Nørreport. Choose between **La Hacienda,** a laid-back lounge playing soul and hip hop, and **The Dance Floor,** a 2-story trance-driven club. Cover for men 150kr, women

130kr, 75kr before midnight; includes 1 champagne and 1 beer. Open F 11pm-8am, Sa 11pm-10am. AmEx/MC/V.

## DAYTRIPS FROM COPENHAGEN

Copenhagen's **S-togs** and other regional lines can whisk travelers away from the urban din to castles, countryside scenery, museums, and well-trodden beaches. It's significantly cheaper and more flexible for travelers to buy cards and stamp them with clips rather than purchasing one-way tickets.

**HILLERØD.** Hillerød is home to ■**Frederiksborg Slot,** one of Denmark's most impressive castles. Close to 90 rooms are open to the public, including the Chapel, the Rose Room, the Great Hall, and the Baroque gardens. From the train station, cross the street onto Vibekev. and continue straight along the path until you can follow the signs; at the Torvet (main plaza), walk to the pond and bear left, following its perimeter to reach the castle entrance. *(Hillerød is at the end of S-tog lines A and E. 40min., 6 per hr., 67kr or 4 clips. ☎ 4826 0439; www.frederiksborgmuseet.dk. Gardens open May-Aug. daily 10am-9pm; Sept.-Apr. reduced hours. Castle open daily Apr.-Oct. 10am-5pm; Nov.-Mar. 11am-3pm. Gardens free. Castle 60kr, students 50kr. AmEx/MC/V.)*

**STOP THAT TRAIN!** In much of Denmark, especially rural areas, trains do not stop at every station on the line. Be sure to check at the ticket counter to find out which train to take, and ask whether you need to sit in a particular car.

**HELSINGØR.** Helsingør sits at a strategic entrance to the Baltic Sea, just 5km from Sweden. Originally built to levy taxes on passing ships, the majestic 16th-century **Kronborg Slot** is better known as **Elsinore,** the setting for Shakespeare's *Hamlet.* A statue of Viking chief Holger Danske sleeps in the dank, forbidding ■**dungeon;** legend holds that he will awake to defend Denmark in its darkest hour. *(☎ 4921 3078; www.kronborg.dk. Book tours ahead. Open May-Sept. daily 10:30am-5pm; Apr. and Oct. Tu-Su 11am-4pm; Nov.-Mar. Tu-Su 11am-3pm. 85kr. AmEx/MC/V.)* In early August, the **Hamlet Sommer Festival** *(www.hamletsommer.dk)* brings Hamlet's ghost back to life in a series of performances in the castle's commons. The **tourist office,** Havnepl. 3, is in the Kulturhus, across from the station. *(☎ 4921 1333; www.visithelsingor.dk. Open July M-F 10am-5pm, Sa 10am-2pm; Aug. to June M-F 10am-4pm, Sa 10am-1pm. Helsingør is at the end of the northern train line from Malmö, SWE via Copenhagen. 1hr., 3 per hr., 67kr or 4 clips.)*

**HUMLEBÆK AND RUNGSTED.** The ■**Louisiana Museum of Modern Art,** 13 Gl. Strandv., in Humlebæk, honors the three wives (all named Louisa) of the estate's original owner. It rounds out its permanent collection—including works by Lichtenstein, Picasso, and Warhol—with several major exhibits each year. Landscape architects have lavished attention on the seaside sculpture garden and the sloping lake garden. From the Humlebæk station, follow signs for 10min. or catch bus #388. *(From Copenhagen, take a Helsingør-bound train. 45min., 3 per hr., 63kr or 4 clips. ☎ 4919 0719; www.louisiana.dk. Open M-Tu and Th-Su 10am-5pm, W 10am-10pm. 80kr, students with ISIC 70kr. AmEx/MC/V.)* Near the water in Rungsted stands the house where Karen Blixen wrote her autobiographical 1937 novel *Out of Africa* under the pseudonym Isak Dinesen. The **Karen Blixen Museum,** Rungsted Strandv. 111, provides a chronicle of the author's life. The grounds are home to 40 species of birds. Follow the street leading out of the train station and turn right on Rungstedv., then right again on Rungsted Strandv., or take bus #388. *(From Copenhagen, take a Nivå-bound train. 30min., 3 per hr., 67kr or 4 clips. ☎ 4557 1057. Open May-Sept. Tu-Su 10am-5pm; Oct.-Apr. W-F 1-4pm, Sa-Su 11am-4pm. 45kr. AmEx/MC/V.)*

## MØN                                                                    ☎ 55

Hans Christian Andersen once called the isle of Møn the most beautiful spot in Denmark. The sheer white **Møns Klint** (Chalk Cliffs), which plunge straight into calm blue waters, can be viewed from the rocky beaches below or the densely forested hiking trails above. The **Liselund Slot** (Doll Castle) looks more like a country house than a castle. The main attraction is the surrounding park, with peacocks and thatched-roof farmhouses. Walking away from the castle, you'll reach a path that becomes a ▨**hiking trail,** which snakes 3km through a lush forest before arriving at the cliffs. Buses to Møn arrive in **Stege,** the island's largest town, across the island from the castle and cliffs. From Stege, take bus #52 to Busene (1 per 1-2hr., 13kr) and walk 10min. to the cliffs. Between mid-June and late August, bus #632 runs from Stege to the parking lots at the cliffs (30min., 3 per day, 13kr). Another way to see Møn is by renting a **bike** in Klintholm Havn, the last stop on bus #52.

Orchids line the trail of the 143m **Aborrebjerg** (Bass Mountain) near the island's youth hostel, lakeside **Møns Klint Vandrerhjem (HI) ❷,** Langebjergv. 1. Between late June and mid-August, take bus #632 from Stege to the campground stop, then continue in the direction of the bus and take the first right. In low season, take bus #52 to Magleby and walk left 2.5km down the road. (☎81 20 30. Breakfast 50kr. Linens 45kr. Laundry 30kr. Reception 8-10:30am and 4-7pm. Open May-Sept. Dorms 185kr; singles and doubles 335-370kr. 35kr HI discount. MC/V; 5% surcharge.) **Stege Camping ❶,** Flacksvej 5, is just a 5min. walk from the Stege bus stop. (☎81 84 04. Reception 9am-10pm. Open May to mid-Oct. 50kr per tent site. Hot water 20kr. Cash only.) To get to Møn, take the **train** from Copenhagen to Vordingborg (1½hr., 108kr), then bus #62 to Stege (45min., 39kr). The info center, **Feriepartner Møn,** Storeg. 2, is next to the Stege bus stop. (☎86 04 00; www.feriepartnermoen.dk. Open M-F 9:30am-5pm, Sa 9am-6pm.)

## ROSKILDE ☎46

Once the capital of the Danish Empire, Roskilde (pop. 53,000) is an easy daytrip from Denmark's modern-day capital. Each summer, music fans arrive in droves to hear performances by artists such as The Who and Red Hot Chili Peppers at the ▨**Roskilde Music Festival** (July 3-6, 2008; www.roskilde-festival.dk), northern Europe's largest outdoor concert. Stunning sarcophagi hold the remains of generations of Danish royalty in the red-brick church, **Roskilde Domkirke,** off the Stændertorvet. Head left out of the train station, go right on Herseg., and left onto Alg. (☎35 16 24; www.roskildedomkirke.dk. Open Apr.-Sept. M-Sa 9am-5pm, Su 12:30-5pm; Oct.-Mar. Tu-Sa 10am-4pm, Su 12:30-4pm. English-language tours mid-June to mid-Aug. M-F 11am and 2pm, Sa-Su 2pm depending on church services. 25kr, students 15kr. Tours 20kr.) On the harbor next to the hostel, the ▨**Viking Ship Museum,** Vindeboder 12, displays five ships unearthed from the Roskilde Fjord. The museum also includes a shipyard where volunteers build vessels using Viking methods. Some of the ships are available for sailing. (☎30 02 53; www.vikingeskibsmuseet.dk. Open daily 10am-5pm. Call for a schedule of English-language tours. May-Sept. 80kr, students 70kr; Oct.-Apr. 50/40kr. AmEx/MC/V.)

**Roskilde Vandrerhjem (HI) ❸,** Vindeboder 7, has bright rooms harborside. Reserve ahead during the music festival. (☎35 21 84; www.danhostel.dk/roskilde. Breakfast 45kr. Linens 45kr. Reception 7am-10pm. Dorms 185kr. 35kr HI discount. AmEx/MC/V.) To reach **Roskilde Camping ❶,** Baunehøjv. 7, take bus #603 (dir.: Veddelev; 15kr) to Veddelev Byg. (☎75 79 96; www.roskildecamping.dk. Open Apr. to mid-Sept. Reception 8am-9pm. 70kr per tent site, 350-450kr per cabin. Electricity 30kr. Showers 6kr per 4min. MC/V; 5% surcharge.) Restaurants line **Algade** and **Skomagergade** in the town center. **Memos ❶,** Jernbanegade 8, serves pita sandwiches (25-35kr) and has an **Internet** cafe (15kr per hr.) downstairs. (☎32 70 76. Open M-Th 11am-8pm, F-Sa 11am-4am.) **Trains** depart for Copenhagen (25-30min., 4 per hr., 66kr) and Odense (1¼hr., 3 per hr., 181kr). The **tourist office,** Gullandsstr. 15, books rooms for a 25kr fee and 10-15% deposit. Walk through the Stændertorvet with the Domkirke on your right, turn left on Allehelgensgade, and follow the signs. (☎31 65 65. Open late June-late Aug. M-F 10am-5pm, Sa 10am-1pm; low season reduced hours.)

# BORNHOLM

Residents of the island of Bornholm like to say that when Scandinavia was created, God saved the best piece for last and dropped it into the Baltic Sea. After a day or two in Bornholm, you might be inclined to agree. The undulating farmlands of the south are ideal for bikers, while nature lovers will favor the dramatic, rocky landscape of the north. The central forest is one of the largest in Denmark, and the sandiest beaches are at Dueodde, on the island's southern tip.

**▣ TRANSPORTATION.** The cheapest way to get to Bornholm from Copenhagen is by a **bus** and **ferry** combination. Bornholmerbussen #866 leaves from København H for Ystad, SWE, where passengers can transfer to the ferry. (☎4468 4400. 3hr., 5 per day, 225kr.) A **train** and **ferry** combo runs from Copenhagen to Rønne by way of Ystad. (Train ☎7013 1415; www.dsb.dk; 1¼hr., 5-6 per day. Ferry ☎5695 1866; www.bornholmferries.dk; 80min. Combination 200-251kr.) A discount "red ticket" (224kr, low season 150kr) for the ferry is available online a week in advance, but the combo ticket is cheaper for travelers coming from Copenhagen. Overnight ferries from Køge (S-tog: A+, E, Ex), south of Copenhagen, leave at 11:30pm and arrive in Rønne at 6:30am (244kr, 281kr for a bed).

Bornholm has an efficient BAT **local bus** service; buses run less frequently on weekends. (☎5695 2121. 36-45kr, bikes 22kr; 24hr. pass 140kr.) Bus #7 makes a circuit of the coastline, heading from Rønne to Hammershus and stopping at most of the island's towns and attractions along the way. Bus #3 from Rønne passes by Østerlars Church on its way to Gudhjem, where the ferry departs for Christiansø, a small island to the north of Bornholm. There are well-marked **bike** paths between all the major towns; pick up a guide (40kr) at Rønne's tourist office. The ride from Rønne to either Sandvig in the north or Dueodde in the southeast is about 30km.

**RØNNE.** Rønne (pop. 14,000), on Bornholm's southwestern coast, is the principal port of entry. **Rønne Vandrerhjem (HI) ❷**, Arsenalv. 12, is in a peaceful, wooded area. From the ferry, head toward the tourist office and turn right on Munch Petersens V. Bear left up the hill on Zahrtmannsv., follow it to the left at the top of the hill, and turn right at the roundabout onto Søndre Allé; Arsenalv. is 100m up on the right. (☎5695 1340; www.danhostel-roenne.dk. Breakfast 45kr. Linens 50kr. Wash 30kr, dry 50kr. Reception 8am-noon and 4-5pm. Open Apr.-Oct. Dorms 185kr; singles 370kr. 35kr HI discount. Cash only.) **Galløkken Camping ❶**, Strandvejen 4, is 15min. south of the town center, near the beach. Follow directions to the hostel, but continue down Søndre Allé until it becomes Strandvejen; the campground is on the right. (☎5695 2320; www.gallokken.dk. Bike rental 60kr per day. Reception 8am-noon and 5-7pm. Open May-Aug. 64kr per tent site. Electricity 25kr. Scandinavian Camping Card required; available for purchase at reception, 100kr. MC/V; 5% surcharge.) **Sam's Corner ❷**, St. Torv 2, is a basic burger and pizza joint with low prices (45-75kr) and large portions. (☎5695 1523. Open daily in summer 10am-10pm; in winter 10am-9pm. Cash only.) Get groceries at **Kvickly,** opposite the tourist office. (☎5695 1777. Open mid-June to Aug. daily 9am-8pm; Sept. to mid-June M-F 9am-8pm, Sa 9am-5pm, Su 10am-4pm. Cash only.) The **tourist office** is at Ndr. Kystv. 3. Turn right out of the ferry terminal, pass the BAT bus terminal, and cross toward the gas station; look for the green flag. (☎5695 9500. Open mid-June to mid-Aug. daily 9am-5pm; mid-Aug. to mid-June reduced hours. MC/V.)

**ALLINGE AND SANDVIG.** These seaside villages are excellent starting points for hikes and bike rides through Bornholm's northern coast. Many trails originate in Sandvig. The rocky area around **Hammeren,** northwest of the town, is a beautiful 2hr. walk that can be covered only on foot. Just outside Sandvig is the lakeside **Sandvig Vandrerhjem (HI) ❷**, Hammershusv. 94. Get off the bus one stop past Sandvig Gl. Station and follow the signs. (☎5648 0362. Breakfast 45kr. Linens 50kr. Laundry 40kr. Reception 9-10am and 4-6pm. Open May-Sept. Dorms 150kr; singles

275kr; doubles 400kr. 35kr HI discount. Cash only.) **Riccos ❷**, Strandg. 8, in Sand-vig, is a pleasant cafe in a private home near the sea and has free **Internet.** (☎5648 0314. Open daily 7am-10pm. MC/V.) The **tourist office** is at Kirkeg. 4 in Allinge. (☎5648 0001. Open June-Aug. M-F 10am-4pm, Sa 10am-1pm; Oct.-May M-F 11am-4pm.) Rent **bikes** at the **Sandvig Cykeludlejning,** Strandvejen 121. (☎2145 6013. Open May-Sept. M-F 9am-3:30pm, Sa 9am-1pm, Su 10am-1pm. 60kr per day. Cash only.)

# FUNEN (FYN)

Nestled between Zealand to the east and the Jutland Peninsula to the west, the island of Funen attracts cyclists and fairytale fans. Isolated in the time of golden son Hans Christian Andersen, this once-remote breadbasket has since been con-nected to Zealand by the magnificent Storebæltsbro bridge and tunnel.

## ODENSE                                                      ☎63, 65, 66

The legacy of Hans Christian Andersen draws most tourists to Odense (OH-den-suh; pop. 200,000), Denmark's third-largest city. While fairy tales still reign supreme in the writer's hometown, a thriving nightlife and music scene also make Odense a destination for the young and trendy.

**⌨🔁 TRANSPORTATION AND PRACTICAL INFORMATION. Trains** run to Copenhagen (1½hr., 2 per hr., 214kr). **Buses** depart from behind the train station. The **tourist office,** in the Rådhuset, offers free **Internet** and bike maps. Turn left out of the train station, make a right on Thomas Thriges G. at the second light, then go right on Vesterg. (☎66 12 75 20; www.visitodense.com. Open July-Aug. M-F 9:30am-6pm, Sa 10am-3pm, Su 11am-2pm; Sept. to mid-June M-F 9:30am-4:30pm, Sa 10am-1pm.) The library in the station also has free Internet. (☎65 51 44 21. Open Apr.-Sept. M-Th 10am-7pm, F 10am-4pm, Sa 10am-2pm; low season extended hours.) Rent **bikes** at **City Cykler,** Vesterbro 27. Continue down Vesterg. from the tourist office for 10min.; it will be on the right. (☎66 13 97 83. 99kr per day, with 750kr deposit. Open M-F 10am-5:30pm, Sa 10am-1pm.) **Postal Code:** 5000.

**🔲🔳 ACCOMMODATIONS AND FOOD. Danhostel Odense City (HI) ❸,** next to the train station, has excellent facilities. (☎63 11 04 25; www.cityhostel.dk. Break-fast 50kr. Linens 60kr. Laundry 45kr. Internet 10kr per 15min. Reception 8am-noon and 4-8pm. Dorms 185kr; singles 400kr; doubles 550kr; triples 585kr; quads 617kr. 35kr HI discount. MC/V; 4% surcharge.) To reach **DCU-Camping Odense ❷,** Odensev. 102, take bus #21-24 (dir.: Højby; 14kr) 4km from town. (☎66 11 47 02; www.camp-ing-odense.dk. Reception mid-June to mid-Aug. 7:30am-noon and 2-10pm; low sea-son 7:30am-noon and 4-10pm. 108kr per tent site; low season 86kr. 4-person cabin with stove 390kr. Electricity 25-30kr. AmEx/MC/V.) **Vestergade,** a long pedestrian street, has ethnic restaurants and cafes. Don't overlook the alleys off Vesterg., including **Brandts Passage,** filled with hip cafes, and the more low-key **Vintapper-stræde.** Get groceries at **Aktiv Super,** Nørreg. 63, at the corner of Nørreg. and Skulk-enborgg. (☎66 12 85 59. Open M-F 9am-7pm, Sa 9am-4pm. Cash only.)

**🔳🔲 SIGHTS AND NIGHTLIFE.** At **Hans Christian Andersen Hus,** Bangs Boder 29, visitors can learn about the author's eccentricities and see the home where he grew up. Enjoy free performances of his timeless stories in a mix of Danish, English, and German. From the tourist office, walk right on Vesterg., turn left on Thomas Thriges G., and go right on Hans Jensens Str. (☎65 51 46 01; www.museum.odense.dk. Open June-Aug. daily 9am-6pm; Sept.-May Tu-Su 10am-4pm. 60kr. Summer performances 11am, 1, 3pm.) Music wafts through the halls of the **Carl Nielsen Museum,** Claus Bergs G. 11, which depicts the life of the Danish composer. (Open Th-F 4-8pm, Su noon-4pm. 25kr.) Down Vesterg., near the tourist office, **St. Knud's Cathedral** has a magnificent triptych by Claus Berg. Inside, view the skeleton of St. Knud, murdered at the altar of the church that previously stood on the site. (☎66 12 03 92. Open daily Apr.-Oct. 10am-5pm; low season 10am-4pm.)

On weekend evenings, the area around Vesterg. is packed with people of all ages drinking and listening to live bands. After 11pm, the club and bar scene takes over. *What's On?*, available at the tourist office, provides nightlife info. **Crazy Daisy**, Klingenberg 14, Skt. Knuds Kirkestr. just past Radhuspl., has six bars on three floors. (☎66 14 67 88. Cover 50kr. Open F-Sa 11pm-6am.) A young crowd moves to the beats of Odense's best DJs at **Boogie Dance Cafe**, Norreg. 21. (☎66 14 00 39. Cover Th 20kr; F-Sa 40kr after midnight. Open Tu-Sa 10:30pm-5:30am. MC/V.)

**◪ DAYTRIP FROM ODENSE: KVÆRNDRUP.** ▨**Egeskov Slot**, 25min. south of Odense in Kværndrup, is a magnificent castle that appears to float on the lake. The grounds include imaginative gardens, hedge mazes, and small museums. *(☎62 27 10 16. Castle open July M-Tu and Th-Su 10am-7pm, W 10am-11pm; May-June and Aug.-Sept. daily 10am-5pm. Grounds open daily July 10am-8pm; June and Aug. 10am-6pm; May and Sept. 10am-5pm. Grounds, mazes, and museums 110kr; with castle 165kr. MC/V.)* Take the Svendborg-bound **train** (25min., 51kr) that leaves 35min. past the hour from Odense. In Kværndrup, turn right out of the station and walk up to Bøjdenv., where you can catch **bus** #920 (1 per hr., 16kr), or turn right and walk 20min. to the castle. From mid-June to mid-August, you can take FynBus #801 from Odense directly to the castle (1hr., 3-8 per day, 44kr).

## ▨ ÆRØ ☎62

The wheat fields, harbors, and hamlets of Ærø (EH-ruh), a small island off the southern coast of Funen, use modern technology to preserve an earlier era of Danish history. Almost 80% of the island is powered by renewable energy sources, keeping the air pristine. The town of **Ærøskøbing** (pop. 3900) serves as a gateway to the island. Hollyhocks and half-timbered houses line the cobblestone streets, and one-lane roads and picturesque windmills lure vacationing Danes into exploring the rest of the island by bicycle. Several **trains** running from Odense to Svendborg are timed to meet the ferry to Ærøskøbing. (2hr., 5-6 per day, 153kr. Cash only.) On the island, **bus** #990 travels among the towns of Ærøskøbing, Marstal, and Søby (23kr, day pass 75kr). Ærøskøbing's **tourist office**, Havnen 4, has **Internet** for 25kr per 15min. (☎52 13 00; www.arre.dk. Open M-F 10am-2pm.) **Postal Code:** 5970.

# JUTLAND (JYLLAND)

Jutland's sandy beaches and historic houses complement its sleek wind turbines and contemporary art. Vikings once journeyed to the trading centers on the western half of the peninsula, but now the coast attracts windsurfers in search of prime waves. Cyclers and canoers enjoy the vast open spaces of the central lakes region, while the cities of Århus and Aalborg have emerged as cultural havens in the east.

# ÅRHUS ☎86-89

Pedestrian walkways wind through the impressive museums, crowded nightclubs, and well-developed art scene of Århus (OR-hoos; pop. 280,000), Denmark's second-largest city. Copenhagen may draw more tourists, but Århus tempers urban sophistication with a dose of Jutland practicality.

**▣◪ TRANSPORTATION AND PRACTICAL INFORMATION. Flights** arrive at **Århus airport** (**AAR;** ☎8775 7000), 45km from the city center. **Airport buses** leave from the front of the main terminal building for Århus (45min., 85kr). Some budget air-

**DENMARK**

lines fly also fly to **Billund** (p. 253). **Trains** run to Aalborg (1½hr., 2 per hr., 153kr), Copenhagen (3hr., 2 per hr., 302kr), and Frederikshavn (2¾hr., 1 per hr., 199kr). **Buses** leave from outside the train station. From May to October, **free bikes** are available to borrow from stands across the city with a 20kr deposit. **MM Cykler Værksted,** Mejlg. 41, rents bikes for 85kr per day. (☎8619 2927. Open M-F 9am-5pm.) To get to the **tourist office,** Banegårdspl. 20, head left after exiting the train station. The office sells the **24hr. Tourist Ticket** (55kr), which offers unlimited use of the city's extensive bus system. The **Århus pass** (1-day 119kr, 2-day 149kr, 1-week 206kr) includes admission to most museums and sights as well as unlimited public transit. (☎87 31 50 10; www.visitaarhus.com. Open mid-June to early Sept. M-F 9:30am-6pm, Sa 9:30am-5pm, Su 9:30am-1pm; low season reduced hours.) The main public **library,** Mølleg. 1 in Mølleparken, offers free **Internet.** (☎89 40 92 55. Open May-Sept. M-Th 10am-7pm, F 10am-5pm, Sa 10am-2pm; Oct.-Apr. M-Th 10am-8pm, F 10am-6pm, Sa-Su 10am-3pm.) **Postal Code:** 8000.

**🖪🖫 ACCOMMODATIONS AND FOOD.** The popular ■**Århus City Sleep-In ❷,** Havneg. 20, is near the city's nightlife. From the train station, turn right and follow Ny Banegårdsg., then turn left onto Havneg. when the street forks in front of the train tracks. (☎86 19 20 55; www.citysleep-in.dk. Breakfast 48-55kr. Linens 48kr, 50kr deposit. Laundry 30kr. Internet 20kr per hr. Key deposit 50kr. Reception 24hr. Dorms 120-125kr; doubles 380-460kr. MC/V; 5% surcharge.) The quieter **Århus Vanderhjem (HI) ❸,** Marienlundsv. 10, is 5min. north of the city in a public park near the beach. Take bus #1, 6, 9, or 16 to Marienlunds. (☎86 21 21 20; www.aarhus-danhostel.dk. Breakfast 50kr. Linens 45kr. Free Wi-Fi. Reception Apr.-Oct. 8am-noon and 4-8pm, Nov.-Mar. 8am-noon and 4-7pm. Dorms 175kr; private rooms 483kr. 35kr HI discount. MC/V; 2.3% surcharge.) **Blommehaven Camping ❷,** Ørneredev. 35, is 4km south of the city. In summer, bus #19 goes there directly; in low season, take bus #6 to Hørhavev., continue down the street, and turn right on Ørneredev. (☎86 27 02 07; blommehaven@dcu.dk. Reception 8am-noon and 2-10pm. Open mid-Mar. to late Oct. 68kr per person, 86-108kr per tent site. AmEx/MC/V.)

Ethnic restaurants and pizzerias line **Skolegade,** which becomes Mejlg. just behind City Sleep-In. **Pinden's Restaurant ❷,** Skoleg. 29, serves traditional Danish food. (☎8612 1102. Entrees 42-86kr. Open daily 11:30am-9pm. AmEx/MC/V.) Pick up groceries at **Netto,** in St. Knuds Torv; take Ryeseg. from the station and turn right into the square across from the church. (☎8612 3112. Open M-Th 5-10pm, F-Sa noon-10pm. Cash only.)

**🖪🖫 SIGHTS AND ENTERTAINMENT.** The exceptional ■**Århus Kunstmuseum (ARoS),** Aros Allé 2, off Vester Allé, features eight levels of galleries that hold multimedia exhibits and modern art. Highlights include Ron Mueck's *Boy,* a colossal 5m statue of a crouching boy. (☎87 30 66 00; www.aros.dk. Open Tu and Th 10am-5pm, W 10am-10pm. 90kr, students 75kr.) The nation's tallest cathedral, **Århus Domkirke,** Skoleg. 17, is near the harbor. (☎86 20 54 00; www.aarhus-domkirke.dk. Open May-Sept. M-Sa 9:30am-4pm, Oct.-Apr. M-Sa 10am-3pm. Free.) At ■**Den Gamle By,** Viborgvej 2, actors bring to life a medieval village with authentic houses transported from all over Denmark. (☎86 12 31 88; www.dengamleby.dk. Open daily mid-June to mid-Sept. 9am-6pm; low season reduced hours.) The **Moesgård Museum of Prehistory,** Moesgård Allé 20, 15min. south of town, features the mummified **Grauballe Man.** Take bus #6 from the train station to the end. (☎89 42 11 00; www.moesmus.dk. Open Apr.-Sept. daily 10am-5pm; Oct.-Mar. Tu-Su 10am-4pm. 45kr, students 35kr. AmEx/MC/V.) The 3km ■**Prehistoric Trail** behind the museum reconstructs Danish forests from different ages and leads to a popular **beach.** In summer, bus #19 returns from the beach to the train station.

Every year in mid-July, Århus hosts its acclaimed **International Jazz Festival** (www.jazzfest.dk). The **Århus Festuge** (☎89 40 91 91; www.aarhusfestuge.dk), a rollicking celebration of theater, dance, and music, is held from late August through early September. ▨**The Social Club,** Klosterg. 34, has three bars on two levels with loud music. (☎85 19 42 50; www.socialclub.dk. Beer and liquor 20kr. Cover after 2am Th 20kr; F-Sa 40kr. 11pm-midnight entrance only with student ID; one free beer and no cover. Open Th-Sa 11pm-6am.) **Train,** Tolbodg. 6, has reinvented a dockside warehouse as a club and concert hall. (☎86 13 47 22; www.train.dk. Concerts all ages, club 23+. Club open F-Sa 11pm-late.)

## ▨ LET'S GO TO LEGOLAND: BILLUND      ☎75, 76

Budget airlines like **Iceland Express, Ryanair,** and **Sterling** serve **Billund's airport** (**BLL;** ☎76 50 50 50). Buses leave the airport for Århus (1½hr., 8-9 per day, 180kr) and Legoland (10min., 1-2 per hr.).

Tourists are drawn to Billund not just for its airport. The city is home to ▨**Legoland,** an amusement park with sprawling Lego sculptures made from over 50 million of the candy-colored blocks. The **Power Builder** ride will convert any skeptic. (☎75 33 13 33; www.legoland.com. Open daily Apr.-Oct. 10am-6pm with extended hours during the summer; check website for detailed schedule. Day pass 229kr. Free 30min. before rides close.) If not flying, take the **train** from Århus to Vejle (45min., 1 per hr., 88kr), then **bus** #244 (dir.: Grinsted; 46kr).

## RIBE      ☎75, 76

Denmark's oldest settlement, Ribe (pop. 18,000) is a well-preserved medieval town near Jutland's west coast. The tower of the 12th-century **Domkirke** offers a sweeping view of the town's red-shingled roofs. (☎75 42 06 19. Open July to mid-Aug. M-Sa 10am-5:30pm, Su noon-5:30pm; May-June and mid-Aug. to Sept. M-Sa 10am-5pm, Su noon-5pm; low season reduced hours. 12kr.) Near the **Torvet** (Main Square), the **Old Town Hall,** on Von Støckens Pl., houses a former debtors' prison where artifacts of Ribe's medieval "justice" system are displayed. (☎76 88 11 22. Open June-Aug. daily 1-3pm; May and Sept. M-F 1-3pm. 15kr.) A singing ▨**night watchman** leads entertaining walking tours, beginning in the Torvet. (40min. June-Aug. 8 and 10pm; May and Sept. 10pm. Free.) The no-frills **Ribe Vandrerhjem (HI) ❷,** Sct. Pedersg. 16, has a knowledgeable staff that relates tidbits of Ribe's history. The hostel rents bikes (60kr per day) and provides guests with a free **Ribe Pass,** which grants discounts around the city. From the station, cross the parking lot, bear right, walk to the end of Sct. Nicolajg., then turn right on Saltg. and immediately left. (☎75 42 06 20; www.danhostel-ribe.dk. Breakfast 50kr. Linens 50kr. Laundry 45kr. Internet 10kr per 15min. Reception 8am-noon and 4-6pm. Check-in 4-6pm. Open Feb.-Nov. Dorms 135-185kr; singles 320-535kr; doubles 350-535kr. 35kr HI discount. AmEx/MC/V.) **Overdammen,** which begins at the Torvet, has inexpensive cafes and pizzerias, while supermarkets are on **Seminarievej.** Nightlife in Ribe is nearly nonexistent, though after hours a handful of locals and tourists loll in the town's few bars. At the **Strygejernet Pub Café,** Dagmarsg. 1, locals enjoy cheap beer (20kr) and watch sports. (☎75 41 13 51. Open Tu-Th 3pm-midnight, F-Sa 1pm-5am. Cash only.) **Trains** go to Århus (3½hr., 1 per 1-2hr., 218kr) via Fredricia. The **tourist office** is at Torvet 3. From the train station, walk down Dagmarsg.; the office is in the main square. (☎75 42 15 00; www.visitribe.dk. Open July-Aug. M-F 9am-6pm, Sa 10am-5pm, Su 10am-2pm; June and Sept. M-F 9am-5pm, Sa 10am-1pm; Jan.-May and Oct.-Dec. M-F 9:30am-4:30pm, Sa 10am-1pm.)

## AALBORG      ☎96, 98, 99

A laid-back haven for university students by day, Aalborg (OLE-borg; pop. 162,000) heats up at night. At the corner of Alg. and Molleg., an elevator descends from outside the Salling Department Store to the half-excavated ruins of a **Franciscan friary.** (☎96 31 04 10. Open Tu-Su 10am-5pm; elevator closes at 4:30pm. Elevator 20kr per 2-3 people, up to 250kg.) North of town, the solemn grounds of **Lindholm Høje,** Vendilav. 11, hold 700 ancient Viking graves and a museum of arti-

DENMARK

facts. Take bus #2C, which departs near the tourist office. (☎99 31 74 40; www.nordjyllandshistoriskemuseum.dk. Grounds open 24hr. Museum open Apr.-Oct. daily 10am-5pm; Nov.-Mar. Tu 10am-4pm, Su 11am-4pm. English-language tours in July W 2pm. Grounds free. Museum 30kr, students 15kr. MC/V.) After a day of dusty antiquarianism, head to **Jomfru Ane Gade,** a pedestrian strip of bars and clubs that's packed with students. For an even wilder time, hit up Aalborg the last weekend in May for **Karneval i Aalborg** (May 17-24, 2008; www.karnevaliaalborg.dk), when the city celebrates spring with Northern Europe's largest carnival.

Cozy private cabins double as dorms at **Aalborg Vandrerhjem and Camping (HI) ❸,** Skydebanev. 50, alongside the Lim Fjord. Take bus #13 (dir.: Fjordparken, 2 per hr.) to the end of the line. (☎98 11 60 44. Breakfast 50kr. Linens 36kr. Laundry 35kr. Free Internet. Reception mid-June to mid-Aug. 8am-11pm; low season 8am-noon and 4-9pm. Reserve ahead in summer. Dorms 195kr; singles 325-525kr; doubles 385-555kr. 35kr HI discount. 70-82kr per tent site. Camping electricity 28kr. MC/V; 4% surcharge.) Enjoy street performances at the outdoor tables of **Café Ministeriet ❷,** Møllesplads, which serves a lunch plate of three types of *smørrebrød* for 52kr. (☎98 19 40 50; www.cafeministeriet.dk. Open M-Th 10am-midnight, F-Sa 10am-2am, Su 10am-5pm. MC/V.) **Føtex supermarket,** Slotsg. 8-14, is just past Boomtown on Nytorv. (☎99 32 90 00. Open M-F 9am-8pm, Sa 8am-5pm. Cash only.)

**Trains** run to Århus (1½hr., 1 per hr., 153kr) and Copenhagen (5hr., 2 per hr., 338kr). Within the city, **buses** cost 16kr, including 1hr. transfers. To find the **tourist office,** Østeråg. 8, head out of the train station, cross JFK Pl., and turn left on Boulevarden, which becomes Østeråg. (☎99 30 60 90; www.visitaalborg.com. Open July M-F 9am-5:30pm, Sa 10am-4pm; late June and Aug. M-F 9am-5:30pm, Sa 10am-1pm; Sept. to mid-June M-F 9am-4:30pm, Sa 10am-1pm.) The public **library,** Rendsburgg. 2, near the end of Nytorv., has free **Internet.** (☎99 31 43 00. Open June-Aug. M-Th 10am-7pm, F 10am-6pm, Sa 10am-2pm; Sept.-May M-Th 10am-7pm, F 10am-6pm, Sa 10am-3pm, Su noon-4pm.)

# FREDERIKSHAVN
☎96, 98, 99

Since its days as a fishing village and naval base, Frederikshavn (fred-riks-HOW-n; pop. 35,000) has evolved into a transportation hub for Scandinavian ferry lines. **Stena Line** ferries (☎96 20 02 00; www.stenaline.com) leave for Gothenburg, SWE (3¼hr.; from 160kr, 30% ScanRail discount) and Oslo, NOR (8½hr.; from 180kr, 50% ScanRail discount). **Color Line** (☎99 56 19 77; www.colorline.com) sails to Larvik, NOR (6¼hr., from 120kr). To get from the station to the **Frederikshavn Vandrerhjem (HI) ❷,** Buhlsv. 6, walk right on Skipperg. for 10min., turn left onto Nørreg., and take a right on Buhlsv. (☎98 42 14 75; www.danhostel.dk/frederikshavn. Breakfast 50kr. Linens 45kr. Laundry 40kr. Reception 8am-noon and 4-8pm. Dorms 120kr; singles 285kr; doubles 440kr. 35kr HI discount. Cash only.) Restaurants and shops cluster along **Søndergade** and **Havnegade;** Rådhus Allé has several grocery stores. To get to the commercial area from the train station, turn left and cross Skipperg. A church, the Frederikshavn Kirke, with a huge anchor on its front lawn, will be on the left. Walk up one block to Danmarksg., the main pedestrian thoroughfare, and turn left. Danmarksg. becomes Sønderg. and intersects with Havneg.

# SKAGEN
☎98

Located on Denmark's northernmost tip, Skagen (SKAY-en; pop. 10,000) is bordered by long stretches of white sand dunes that descend to ice-blue water. Brightly painted "Skagen yellow" houses topped by red-tiled roofs welcome fishermen home from sea. Danish tourists discovered Skagen's colorful charms long ago, but international visitors are just beginning to venture to this out-of-the-way spot. The **Skagens Museum,** Brøndumsv. 4, features 19th- and 20th-century works by local artists. From the train station, walk left down Sct. Laurentii V. and turn right on Brøndumsv. (☎44 64 44; www.skagensmuseum.dk. Open Apr.-Sept. Tu.-

Su. 10am-5pm; Oct.-Mar. W-Su 10am-3pm. 70kr. AmEx/MC/V.) At nearby **Grenen,** the currents of the North and Baltic Seas collide in striking rhythm. Unlike the 60km of beach in other areas of Skagen, Grenen is strictly off-limits for swimming because of life-threatening tides. Take the bus from the Skagen station (15kr; last return 7:30pm) or walk 5km down Fyrv. About 13km south of Skagen is the enormous ▨**Råberg Mile** (ROH-bayrg MEE-leh), a sand dune formed by a 16th-century storm. The dune resembles a vast moonscape and migrates 15m east each year. Take bus #99 or the train from Skagen to Hulsig, then walk 4km down Kandestedv. Each July, the town welcomes Irish fiddlers and Scandinavian troubadours for the ▨**Skagen Folk Music Festival** (☎ 44 40 94; www.skagenfestival.dk; early July).

Reserve ahead at the popular **Skagen Ny Vandrerhjem ❸,** Rolighedsv. 2. From the station, turn right on Chr. X's V., which becomes Frederikshavnv., then go left on Rolighedsv. (☎ 44 22 00; www.danhostelnord.dk/skagen. Breakfast 50kr. Linens 50kr. Reception 9am-noon and 4-6pm. Open Feb.-Nov. Dorms 185kr; singles 335-535kr; doubles 385-635kr. 35kr HI discount. Cash only.) To reach the campgrounds at **Poul Eeg Camping ❶,** Batterivej 21, turn left out of the train station, walk 3km straight down Sct. Laurentii V., and go left on Batterivej. (☎ 44 14 70. Bike rental 60kr per day. Tent sites 67-78kr. Cash only.) Turn right out of the station onto Sct. Laurentii V. to get to an area of restaurants near **Havnevej.** In the town center, **Orchid Thai Restaurant ❶,** Sct. Laurentii V. 60, offers authentic, cheap, and filling lunch boxes for 35kr. (☎ 44 60 44. Open daily 11am-10pm. MC/V.) Pick up picnic supplies at **Super Brugsen,** Sct. Laurentii V. 28. (☎ 44 17 00. Open daily 9am-10pm.)

**Trains** run from Skagen to Frederikshavn (40min., 1 per hr., 48kr). Despite the wind, **biking** is the best way to experience the region. Rent bikes at **Cykelhandler,** Kappelborgv. 23; from the station, turn right onto Sct. Laurentii V., right on to Havnev., and right again. (☎ 44 25 28. 20kr per hr., 60kr per day. Open M-F 8am-5:30pm, Sa 9:30am-noon. Cash only.) The **tourist office** is in the station. (☎ 44 13 77; www.skagen-tourist.dk. Open July M-Sa 9am-6pm, Su 10am-4pm; June and Aug. M-Sa 9am-5pm, Su 10am-2pm; low season reduced hours.) The **library,** Sct. Laurentii V. 23, has free **Internet.** (☎ 44 28 22; www.skagen.dk/skagbib. Open M and Th 10am-6pm, Tu-W and F 1-6pm, Sa 10am-1pm.)

# FRANCE

With its lavish châteaux, lavender fields, medieval streets, and sidewalk cafes, France conjures up any number of postcard-ready scenes. To the proud French, it is only natural that outsiders flock to their history-steeped and art-rich homeland. Although France may no longer manipulate world events, the vineyards of Bordeaux, the museums of Paris, the beaches of the Riviera, and many other attractions draw more tourists than any other nation in the world. Centuries-old farms and churches share the landscape with inventive, modern architecture; street posters advertise jazz festivals as well as Baroque concerts. The country's rich culinary tradition rounds out a culture that cannot be sent home on a four-by-six.

## DISCOVER FRANCE: SUGGESTED ITINERARIES

**THREE DAYS.** Don't even think of leaving **Paris,** the City of Light (p. 267). Explore the shops and cafes of the **Latin Quarter,** then cross the Seine to reach **Île de la Cité** to admire **Sainte Chapelle** and the **Cathédrale de Notre Dame.** Visit the wacky **Centre National d'Art et de Culture Georges Pompidou** before swinging through **Marais** for food and fun. The next day, stroll down the **Champs-Elysées,** starting at the **Arc de Triomphe,** meander through the **Jardin des Tuileries,** and over to the **Musée d'Orsay.** See part of the **Louvre** the next morning, then spend the afternoon at **Versailles.**

**ONE WEEK.** After three days in **Paris,** go to **Tours** (1 day; p. 300), a great base for exploring the châteaux of the **Loire Valley** (1 day; p. 312). Head to **Rennes** for medieval sights and modern nightlife (1 day; p. 303), then to the dazzling island of **Mont-St-Michel** (1 day; p. 311).

**BEST OF FRANCE, THREE WEEKS.** Begin with three days in **Paris,** with a daytrip to the royal residences at **Versailles.** Whirl through the **Loire Valley** (2 days) before traveling to the wine country of **Bordeaux** (1 day; p. 340). Check out the rose-colored architecture of **Toulouse** (1 day; p. 344) and the medieval walls of **Carcassonne** (1 day; p. 346) before sailing through **Avignon** (p. 346), **Aix-en-Provence** (p. 357), and **Nîmes** (p. 361) in sunny Provence (3 days). Let loose in **Marseille** (2 days; p. 362), and bask in the glitter of the Riviera in **Nice** (2 days; p. 362). Then show off your tan in the Alps as you travel to **Lyon** (2 days; p. 324) and **Chamonix** (1 day; p. 334). Spice it up with a mustard tour in **Dijon** (1 day; p. 315), and finish your trip with some German flavor in **Strasbourg** (1 day; p. 317), where trains will whisk you away to your next European adventure.

# LIFE AND TIMES

## HISTORY

**FROM GAULS TO GOTHS (25,000 BC-AD 900).** The first Frenchmen appeared in 25,000 BC, covering the caves of the **Dordogne Valley** (p. 340) with graffiti. By 4500 BC Neolithic people carved the famous stone monoliths *(menhirs)* at **Carnac,** which were admired by the Celtic **Gauls,** who arrived from the east around 600 BC to trade with Greek colonists in **Marseille** (p. 362). Fierce resistance from the Gauls and their leader **Vercingétorix** kept the Romans out of their territory until **Julius Caesar's** victory at Alesia in 52 BC. When Rome fell in AD 476, **Gothic** tribes plundered the area and moved on,

France

BRITAIN
Dover
Folkestone
Dunkerque
BELGIUM
Portsmouth
Calais
★ Brussels
Plymouth
Boulogne-sur-Mer
Lille
Arras
LUX.
English Channel
(La Manche)
Somme R.
Amiens
GERMANY
Channel
Islands
Cherbourg
Le Havre
Rouen
Reims
Metz
Roscoff
Bayeux
Caen
Seine R.
Marne R.
Épernay
Nancy
Strasbourg
Sélestat
Brest
St-Malo
Mont-St-Michel
Paris ★
Colmar
Quimper
Dinan
Chartres
Troyes
Mulhouse
Rennes
Le Mans
Orléans
Fontainebleau
Besançon
Angers
Blois
Loire R.
Dijon
SWITZ.
Belle Ile
Tours
Amboise
Beaune
Pontarlier
★ Bern
Nantes
Saumur
Indre R.
Bourges
Nevers
Lake
Geneva
ATLANTIC
OCEAN
Ile d'Yeu
Poitiers
Vienne R.
HAUT-JURA
MTS.
Geneva
120 miles
Vichy
Cluny
Annecy
ALPS
0    120 kilometers
La Rochelle
Limoges
Clermont-
Ferrand
Lyon
Chamonix
Gironde R.
Cognac
Angoulême
Montignac
Le-Mont-Dore
Mont Blanc
4810m
ITALY
Bay of Biscay
Périgueux
Les Eyzies-
de-Tayac
LE PUY DE
SANCY
Grenoble
TGV Line
Bordeaux
Sarlat
Dordogne R.
Castelnaud-La-Chapelle
CEVENNES
MTS.
Rhône R.
MONACO
Menton
Garonne R.
Avignon
Nice
Cap Corse
Bastia
Biarritz
Bayonne
Toulouse
Nîmes
Aix-en-
Provence
Antibes
Cannes
CÔTE
D'AZUR
Calvi
CORSICA
Corte
Montpellier
Arles
St-Raphaël
St-Tropez
Ajaccio
St-Jean-
Pied-de-Port
Lourdes
Carcassonne
Marseille
Toulon
Porto-
Vecchio
Cauterets
Perpignan
Golfe du Lion
TO CORSICA
Bonifacio
PYRENEES
SARDINIA
(ITALY)
SPAIN
ANDORRA
Mediterranean Sea

leaving the **Franks** in control of Gaul (now France). The Frankish king, **Clovis,** founded the Merovingian dynasty and was baptized in AD 507. Later, **Charlemagne,** who began the Carolingian dynasty, expanded his domain, the **Holy Roman Empire,** into Austria. The **Treaty of Verdun** in AD 843 resolved territorial squabbles after Charlemagne's death, dividing the empire between his three grandsons.

**ENGLISH INTERFERENCE.** After the death of the last Carolingian king, the noble-elected **Hugh Capet** consolidated power. When **Eleanor of Aquitaine,** the former queen of Capet's descendant Louis VII, married into the English Plantagenet dynasty in the 12th century, a swath of land stretching from the Channel to the Pyrénées became English territory. This opened the door for England's **Edward III** to claim the French throne, triggering the **Hundred Years' War** in 1337. French defeat seemed imminent when England crowned **Henry VI** king of France 90 years later, but salvation arrived in the form of a 17-year-old peasant, **Jeanne d'Arc** (Joan of Arc). Leading the French army disguised as a man, she won a string of victories and swept the English off the continent before she was burned at the stake for heresy in **Rouen** (p. 306) in 1431.

**POPES AND PROTESTANTS.** Hoping to wrest Jerusalem from the Saracens, **Pope Urban II** declared the First Crusade in 1295 from **Clermont,** convincing thousands to take up arms. In the 16th century, religious conflict between **Huguenots** (French Protestants) and **Catholics** initiated the Wars of Religion. After orchestrating a marriage between her daughter and Protestant prince **Henri de Navarre** in 1572, Catholic queen **Catherine de Médici** inadvertently set off a series of events culminating in the **St. Bartholomew's Day Massacre.** While over 3000 Parisian Huguenots died, Henri survived, converted to Catholicism, and rose to the throne as the first **Bourbon** monarch. His 1598 **Edict of Nantes** granted tolerance for Protestants and quelled religious warfare for a century.

**BOURBON ON THE ROCKS.** The power of the Bourbon dynasty peaked in the 17th century as **Louis XIII's** ruthless minister, **Cardinal Richelieu,** consolidated power for the monarchy by creating the centralized, bureaucratic administration characteristic of France to this day. The king was succeeded by the five-year-old **Louis XIV,** who later proclaimed himself "Sun King" and uttered the famous statement: *"l'état, c'est moi"* (I am the state). He brought the nobility to **Versailles** (p. 297) to keep watch over them and avoid any unpleasant uprisings.

Despite such precautions, Louis's successors felt resentment against them grow. In 1789, **Louis XVI** called a meeting of the **Estates-General** with representatives from the three classes of society: the aristocracy, the clergy, and the revolutionary **Third Estate,** wealthy merchants representing the rest of the people. The Third Estate's delegates broke away and began to draft their own constitution. Meanwhile, a Parisian mob stormed the **Bastille** on July 14, freeing seven prisoners and gaining ammunition. Despite the principles of *liberté, égalité,* and *fraternité* set forth in its new **Declaration of the Rights of Man and the Citizen,** the Revolution took a radical turn under the **First Republic** in 1792. **Maximilien Robespierre** gained control and inaugurated the **Reign of Terror.** He guillotined the king, France's much-maligned queen, **Marie-Antoinette,** and other perceived rivals. When Robespierre met the guillotine himself in 1794, power was entrusted to a five-man **Directory.**

**THE LITTLE DICTATOR.** Meanwhile, **Napoleon Bonaparte,** a young Corsican general from Ajaccio, swept through northern Italy into Austria with his army. Riding a wave of public support, he overthrew the Directory, and crowned himself Emperor in 1804. After a disastrous invasion of Russia, Napoleon lost the support of a war-weary nation. In return for his 1814 abdication, he was given the Mediterranean island of **Elba.** Restless "ruling" just one small island, Napoleon left Elba and landed with an army at Cannes in March 1815. King **Louis XVIII** fled to England as Napoleon marched north. His ensuing **Hundred Days'** rule ended on the battlefield at **Waterloo,** where combined Prussian and British forces triumphed over him. Napoleon was banished again, this time to remote **St. Helena** in the south Atlantic, where he died in 1821.

**WAR, PEACE, AND MORE WAR.** Concerned about the changing balance of power in Europe after Germany's 1871 unification, France, Britain, and Russia forged the **Triple Entente** to counter Germany, Italy, and the Austro-Hungarian Empire's **Triple Alliance.** When **WWI** erupted in 1914, German armies swarmed into France, but hit impenetrable trenches along the length of the country. The war ended in 1918, but not before 1.3 million Frenchmen had died. The 1930s found France ill-equipped to deal with Hitler's mobilization across the Rhine. In May 1940, Germany swept through Belgium and invaded France from the north, seizing it by June. With the north under German occupation, WWI hero **Maréchal Pétain's** puppet state ruled the rest of the country from **Vichy** and answered to the Germans. Those who escaped joined the French government-in-exile under **General Charles de Gaulle.** At his insistence, French troops led the **Liberation of Paris** on August 25, 1944.

**FOURTH REPUBLIC AND POST-COLONIAL FRANCE.** While drafting the Fourth Republic's constitution, de Gaulle's provisional government established female suffrage and nationalized energy companies. De Gaulle's 1946 retirement left the Republic without a strong leader. Twenty-five different governments ruled France over the next 14 years until de Gaulle returned to power in 1958. Concurrently, the remnants of France's 19th-century **colonial empire** were crumbling. The 1950s witnessed the systematic and sometimes bloody dismantling of the remaining colonies. In 1958, with a new constitution in hand, the nation declared itself the **Fifth Republic.** In May 1968, student protest grew into a full-scale revolt, and 10 million state workers went on strike in support of social reform. The government responded by deploying tank and commando units, and another revolution seemed inevitable. Crisis was averted only with the return of the Gaullists. The aging de Gaulle had lost his magic touch, however, and he resigned following a referendum defeat in 1969.

**THE 1980S AND BEYOND.** In 1981, **François Mitterrand** became France's first Socialist president, helping his party gain a majority in the **Assemblée Nationale.** Far-reaching social programs implemented early in the administration gave way to compromise with the right, and Mitterrand was forced to appoint the Conservative **Jacques Chirac** as prime minister. In an unprecedented power-sharing relationship called "cohabitation," Mitterrand controlled foreign affairs, leaving domestic power to Chirac. The French elected Chirac president in 1995. The 2002 presidential elections shocked the world when far-right nationalist **Jean-Marie Le Pen,** leader of the **Front National (FN),** beat out left-wing candidate **Lionel Jospin** in the preliminary elections. He was defeated by Chirac, who was reelected in an 82% landslide amid protest against Le Pen's anti-immigration policies, reputed racism, and dismissive remarks about the Holocaust.

# TODAY

Facing an increasingly global society, France continues to negotiate tradition and modernity. In February 2004, the National Assembly sparked controversy by backing a bill enforcing *laïcité,* the strict separation between church and state. The new law banned all religious symbols, most notably **Muslim headscarves,** in public schools. While some view the bill as discriminating against Muslims, then-Prime Minister **Jean-Pierre Raffarin** affirmed it would maintain the long-standing secular tradition of French public education. **Gay rights** have also been a point of controversy in recent years. In 1999, the **Civil Solidarity Pact (PACS)** made France the first Catholic country to legally recognize homosexual unions. In foreign policy, France's opposition to the US-led **war in Iraq** made headlines in 2003. Although Franco-German cooperation has played a central role in the **European Union's** economic policies, integration has met with resistance from the French, who worry about losing their autonomy and national character. In May 2005, the French voted against the adoption of the EU constitution, fearing unemployment and the disintegration of the welfare system. Chirac consequently named the more conservative **Dominique de Villepin** as prime minister in order to boost public confidence. In October 2005, riots erupted across France after two teenage immigrants were killed in an altercation with the police in a low-income suburb of Paris. Thousands of cars were torched in nearly 300 towns in protest of France's intolerance before the violence stopped. Only a few months later, more riots paralyzed the country when students protested a new labor law that they feared would erode job stability. In France's 2007 presidential elections, the Socialist party's **Ségolène Royal** faced off against **Nicolas Sarkozy,** who represented the **Union for a Popular Movement (UMP).** Sarkozy, promising immigration reform and more jobs for the unemployed, beat Royal by only five points.

# PEOPLE AND CULTURE

**LANGUAGE AND POLITESSE.** Even if your French is near-perfect, waiters and salespeople who detect the slightest accent will often respond in English. If your language skills are good, continue to speak in French; more often than not, the person will revert to French. The French put a premium on pleasantries. Always say *"bonjour Madame/Monsieur"* when you come into a business, restaurant, or hotel, and *"au revoir"* upon leaving. If you bump into someone on the street, always say *"pardon."* When meeting someone for the first time, a handshake is

FRANCE

**FEATURED ITINERARY: WINE TASTING IN FRANCE**

Start your tour in **Paris** (p. 267), and preview some of France's most distinctive vintages at **La Belle Hortense,** an egghead wine bar in the Marais. Then set out for **Reims** (p. 313), where the folks at **Champagne Pommery** offer tours of cellars that hold magnums of the bubbly stuff. Spend a night in **Epernay** (p. 314), and saunter down the avenue de Champagne for wine tastings at blue-blood **Moët & Chandon** and the more populist **Mercier.** Then head for **Strasbourg** (p. 317), the northernmost point on Alsace's legendary **Route du Vin** (p. 319). Frequent trains will whisk you south to touristy **Colmar** (p. 321), the site of a ten-day wine festival or ride to **Dijon**—just to the south lies **Beaune** (p. 316), surrounded by the **Côte de Beaune** vineyards. Don't pass up a visit to **Patriarche Père et Fils,** where a tour of the byzantine cellars includes tasting 13 regional wines. Then dart back to Paris, or extend your itinerary to explore the **Médoc** region around **Bordeaux** (p. 340) and the vineyards at **Sélestat** (p. 320).

**TIP**

**SAY WHAT?!** French youngsters have developed a very particular—but decipherable—form of slang, called *verlan*. It is based on the idea of reversing the order of syllables: the word Verlan itself is a reversed form of *l'envers*, which means backwards. One syllable words such as *femme* (woman) or *mère* (mother) are reversed to form what is pronounced as 'mef' or 'rem.' Two syllable words such as *crayon* are broken up according to syllable, and the order is changed, to make words like 'yoncré.' So when you hear an unfamiliar word, don't assume it's brand-new to your vocab; try deciphering it first—it could be *verlan*. Try this: *cainri*—it comes from *ricain,* an abbreviated form of *américain.*

appropriate. However, friends and acquaintances greet each other with a kiss on each cheek. For some useful French, see **Phrasebook: French** (p. 1052).

**TABLE MANNERS.** Bread is served with every meal, and it is perfectly polite to use a piece to wipe your plate. Etiquette dictates hands above the table, not in the lap, and discourages resting elbows on the table. In a restaurant, waiters will not bring the check until you ask (*"l'addition, s'il vous plaît"*). Asking the waitstaff to wrap up leftovers at the end of a meal will usually result in a scornful look or refusal. It's best to buy food from establishments that advertise meals *à emporter* (to go) if you are in a rush. And no matter what movies would suggest, waiters should never be addressed as *"garçon,"* (boy) but as *"Monsieur"* (or *"Madame"*).

# THE ARTS

## ARCHITECTURE

Long before the "civilizing" Greek and Roman invasions, Frenchmen were leaving their own impressive mark. The prehistoric murals of **Lascaux** (p. 339) and **Les Eyzies-de-Tayac** (p. 339) testify to the presence of ancient and well-established peoples. No such monuments remain from the Gauls, whose legacy was swept away by Roman conquerors. Rome's architectural influence is most visible in the arena and temple at **Nîmes** (p. 361). **Romanesque** churches, like the **Basilique St-Sernin** in Toulouse (p. 344), were designed to accommodate large crowds of worshippers. **Gothic** houses of worship include spectacular medieval cathedrals like the 12th- to 14th-century **Notre Dame de Paris** (p. 280). In the mid-1600s, Louis XIV commissioned the world's largest royal residence, **Versailles** (p. 297), filled with crystal, mirrors, and gold, and surrounded by formal gardens in keeping with the **Baroque** style. Modern engineering burst onto the architectural scene in the late 19th century; **Gustave Eiffel** built the famed **Eiffel tower** (p. 282) in 1889 and writer **Guy de Maupassant** took to dining every day in its lower level restaurant so he wouldn't have to look at the damn thing. Between the world wars, Charles-Edouard Jean-neret (a.k.a. **Le Corbusier**) developed the architectural use of reinforced concrete. In the 1980s, Mitterrand poured 15 billion francs into **les Grands Projets,** giving Paris the **Musée d'Orsay** (p. 285) and **I.M. Pei's** glass pyramid at the **Louvre** (p. 286).

## FILM

Before WWI, Paris dominated the nascent world of cinema, producing both main-stream films and experimental works like **Luis Buñuel** and **Salvador Dalí's** *An Andalu-sian Dog.* French cinema in the 1960s highlighted French talent, including **Catherine Deneuve** *(Belle de jour),* **Isabelle Adjani** *(La Reine Margot),* and the omnipresent **Gérard Depardieu** *(Cyrano de Bergerac* and *My Father the Hero).* **François Truffaut's** *The 400 Blows,* **Jean-Luc Godard's** *Breathless,* and **Alain Resnais's** *Hiroshima, Mon Amour* paved the way for the **New Wave** film movement that dominated French cinema through the 70s. Late 20th-century French cinema classics include **Claude Berri's** *Jean de Florette* and **Krzysztof Kieslowski's** *Three Colors* trilogy, *Bleu, Blanc,* and *Rouge.* Several recent French films have explored the issue of gay identity, including Belgian **Alain Berliner's** gender-bending tragicomedy *Ma vie en rose.* Jean-Pierre Jeunet's *Le Fabuleux Destin d'Amélie Poulain,* nominated for five Oscars in 2002, made lead actress **Audrey Tautou** an international sweetheart. **Cinéma Beur,** a movement exploring second-generation North Africans coming to terms with life in Parisian housing projects, has produced several explosive films, including **Mathieu Kassovitz's** *Hate.* Sweeping five categories including best picture at the 2007 *Césars* (France's equiva-lent to the Oscars), **Lady Chatterley,** directed by **Pascale Ferran,** recreates the sensuous romance between a married noblewoman and her gamekeeper. Based on **D.H. Lawrence's** 1928 novel *Lady Chatterley's Lover,* this adaptation explores earthly nature in addition to human sexuality. Documenting the more modern *vie quotidi-enne* (daily life) of both French citizens and Parisian tourists, *Paris, Je t'aime* (2006) combines the theatrical genius of several renowned directors including the **Cohen Brothers, Gus Van Sant, Alexander Payne, and Oliver Assayas.**

## LITERATURE AND PHILOSOPHY

During the 13th century, popular **fabliaux** (satirical stories) celebrated the bawdy with tales of cuckolded husbands, saucy wives, and shrewd peasants. **John Calvin's** human-ist treaties of the mid-1500s criticized the Catholic Church and opened the road to the ill-fated Protestant Reformation in France. Rationalist **René Descartes's** *Discourse on Method* (1637) ushered in intellectual modernity with his catchy deduction, "I think, therefore I am." **La Fontaine's** *Fables* taught readers about right and wrong. **Molière,** providing the 17th century's comic relief, satirized the social pretensions of his age. His actors later initiated the great **Comédie Française.** Informed by advances in the sci-ences, the French held the torch for the **Enlightenment** and aimed at the promotion of reason and tolerance in an often backward and bigoted world. As **Denis Diderot** com-piled the first encyclopedia (1751), **Jean-Jacques Rousseau's** *Social Contract* (1763) laid the foundations for modern democracy, and **Voltaire** refuted the claim that "all is for the best in the best of all possible worlds" in *Candide* (1759). Realist novelists like **Stendhal** (1783-1842) and **Balzac** (1799-1850) represented the emotional reaction against Enlightenment rationality, but it was **Victor Hugo** (1802-1885) who dominated the **Romantic** age. The heroine of **Gustave Flaubert's** *Madame Bovary* (1857) spurned provincial life for sensuality. Though **Charles Baudelaire** gained a reputation for liter-ary obscenity, his collection *Les Fleurs du Mal* (1861) contained many of the 19th century's most influential poems. **Marcel Proust's** *Remembrance of Things Past* (1913) captured turn-of-the-century decadence and snobbery. **Jean-Paul Sartre** expounded his philosophy of **existentialism** in the 1940s, finding that *"L'enfer, c'est les autres"* ("Hell is other people"). His contemporaries include absurdist **Albert Camus** *(The Stranger,* 1942) and **Simone de Beauvoir,** whose *The Second Sex* inspired a gen-eration of second-wave **feminists** in the 50s, 60s, and 70s. Exploring gender identity, **Marguerite Duras** *(The Lover,* 1984) further sparked feminist movements.

## VISUAL ARTS

The 11th-century **Bayeux tapestry** (p. 309) unraveled a 70m long narrative of the Battle of Hastings (see BRI, p. 127). Stained glass and stone facades, like those at **Chartres** (p. 297) and **Reims** (p. 313), served as large Biblical reproductions in medieval times. In 1516, **Leonardo da Vinci,** with the smiling **Mona Lisa** in tow, moved from Florence to his final home in **Amboise** (p. 300). During the French Revolution, painters depicted heroic scenes from their own time, like neo-Classicist **Jacques-Louis David's** *Death of Marat* and **Eugène Delacroix's** *Liberty Leading the People.* **Edouard Manet** facilitated the transition to **Impressionism** by flattening the fine shading and sharp perspectives of academic art and turning his focus to texture and color. **Claude Monet, Camille Pissarro,** and **Pierre-Auguste Renoir** also began to explore Impressionist techniques in the 1860s. Monet's garden at **Giverny** (p. 297), which inspired his monumental *Water Lilies* series, remains a popular daytrip from Paris. Impressionism also inspired **Edgar Dégas'** ballerinas and **Auguste Rodin's** romantic sculptures. Post-Impressionist **Paul Cézanne** created still lifes, portraits, and geometric landscapes using bold blocks of color. **Georges Seurat** took fragmentation a step further with **Pointillism** (divisionism), merging thousands of tiny dots into a coherent picture. **Henri de Toulouse-Lautrec's** dynamic posters capture 19th-century Paris's lascivious nightlife. The **Fauvist** rich colors and thick contours of **Henri Matisse** anticipated and rivaled those of **Georges Braque** and Spanish-born **Pablo Picasso,** who developed **Cubism.** By reducing everyday objects to a composition of shaded planes, Picasso became the most influential artist of the 20th century; his career is chronicled at the **Musée Picasso** (p. 287) in Paris and at the seaside **Musée Picasso** in **Antibes** (p. 371). The loss and disillusionment that pervaded Europe after WWI prompted artists to reject the bourgeois culture they believed caused the war and resulted in the **Surrealist** and **Dada** movements, led by **Marcel Duchamp.** Their work can be seen at the **Centre Pompidou** (p. 286) in Paris.

# HOLIDAYS AND FESTIVALS

**Holidays:** New Year's Day (Jan. 1); Good Friday (Mar. 21); Easter (Mar. 23-24); Labor Day (May 1); Ascension Day (May 1); Victory Day (May 8); Pentecost (May 11-12); Whit Monday (May 12); Bastille Day (July 14); Assumption (Aug. 15); All Saints' Day (Nov. 1); Armistice Day (Nov. 11); Christmas (Dec. 25-26).

**Festivals:** Many cities celebrate a pre-Lenten *Carnaval*—for the most over-the-top festivities, head to Nice (Jan. 25-Feb. 5). The Cannes Film Festival (May 14-25; www.festival-cannes.com) caters to the rich, famous, and creative. In 2008, the Tour de France will start with a straight stage in Brittany (p. 302), the first time in more than 40 years (begins July 5; www.letour.fr). The Festival d'Avignon (July-Aug.; www.festival-avignon.com) is famous for its theater productions.

# ADDITIONAL RESOURCES

*A History of the French New Wave Cinema,* by Richard Neupert. University of Wisconsin Press (2007). Looks into the 1950s birth of a daring French movement.

*A Year in Provence,* by Peter Mayle. Knopf Publishing Group (1991). The charming travel memoirs of a couple that decide to escape to the south of France for 12 months.

*Americans in Paris: A Literary Anthology,* edited by Adam Gopnik. Library of America (2004). Compiles American writings thematically linked by their Parisian inspiration.

*The Road from the Past: Traveling through History in France,* by Ina Caro. Harvest Books (1996). A portrait of France from Roman ruins to Versailles through a tourist's eyes.

# ESSENTIALS

## FACTS AND FIGURES

**Official Name:** French Republic.
**Capital:** Paris.
**Major Cities:** Lyon, Marseille, Nice.
**Population:** 60,880,000.
**Land Area:** 547,000 sq. km.

**Time Zone:** GMT+1.
**Language:** French.
**Religion:** Roman Catholic (88%), Muslim (9%), Protestant (2%), Jewish (1%).
**Number of Cheese Varieties:** Over 500.

## WHEN TO GO

In July, Paris starts to shrink; by August it is devoid of Parisians, animated only by tourists and the pickpockets who love them. The French Riviera fills with Anglophones from June to September. During these months, French natives flee to other parts of the country, especially the Atlantic coast. Early summer and fall are the best times to visit Paris—the city has warmed up but not completely emptied out. The north and west have cool winters and mild summers, while the less-crowded center and east have a more temperate climate. From December through April, the Alps provide some of the world's best skiing, while the Pyrénées offer a calmer, if less climatically dependable, alternative.

## DOCUMENTS AND FORMALITIES

**EMBASSIES AND CONSULATES.** Foreign embassies in France are in Paris (p. 270). French embassies abroad include: **Australia,** 6 Perth Av., Yarralumla, Canberra, ACT 2600 (☎02 62 16 01 00; www.ambafrance-au.org); **Canada,** 42 Sussex Dr., Ottawa, ON, K1M 2C9 (☎613-789-1795; www.ambafrance-ca.org); **Ireland,** 36 Ailesbury Rd., Ballsbridge, Dublin, 4 (☎00 353 1 227 5000; www.ambafrance.ie); **New Zealand,** 34-42 Manners St., Wellington (☎64 384 25 55; www.ambafrance-nz.org); **UK,** 58 Knightsbridge, London, SW1X 7JT (☎44 207 073 1000; www.ambafrance-uk.org); **US,** 4101 Reservoir Rd., NW, Washington, D.C., 20007 (☎202-944-6195; www.ambafrance-us.org).

**VISA AND ENTRY INFORMATION.** EU citizens do not need a visa. Citizens of Australia, Canada, New Zealand, and the US do not need a visa for stays of up to 90 days, beginning upon entry into any of the countries in the EU's freedom-of-movement zone. For more info, see p. 13. For stays longer than 90 days, all non-EU citizens need Schengen visas (around US$81), available at French consulates and online at www.consulfrance-washington.org.

## TOURIST SERVICES AND MONEY

| EMERGENCY | Ambulance: ☎15. Fire: ☎18. Police: ☎17. General Emergency: ☎112. |
|---|---|

**TOURIST OFFICES.** The **French Government Tourist Office** (**FGTO;** www.franceguide.com), also known as **Maison de la France,** runs tourist offices (called *syndicats d'initiative* or *offices de tourisme*) and offers tourist services to travelers abroad. In smaller towns, the **mairie** (town hall) may also distribute maps and pamphlets, help travelers find accommodations, and suggest sights and excursions.

**MONEY.** The **euro (€)** has replaced the **franc** as the unit of currency in France. For more info, see p. 16. As a general rule, it's cheaper to exchange money in France than at home. Be prepared to spend at least €40-60 per day and considerably more in Paris. **Tips** are generally included in meal prices at restaurants and cafes, as well as in drink prices at bars and clubs; ask or look for the phrase *service compris* on the menu. If service is not included, tip 15-20%. Even when service is included, it is polite to leave a *pourboire* of up to 5% at a cafe, bistro, restaurant, or bar. Workers such as concierges may expect at least a €1.50 tip for services beyond the call of duty; taxi drivers expect 10-15% of the metered fare. Tipping tour guides and bus drivers €1.50-3 is customary.

France has a 19.6% **value added tax (VAT; TVA** in French), a sales tax applied to a wide range of goods and services. The prices included in *Let's Go* include VAT. In the airport upon exiting the EU, non-EU citizens can claim a refund on the tax paid for goods purchased at participating stores. In order to qualify for a refund in a store, you must spend at least €175; make sure to ask for a refund form when you pay. For more info on qualifying for a VAT refund, see p. 18.

# TRANSPORTATION

**BY PLANE.** Most transatlantic flights to Paris land at **Roissy-Charles de Gaulle (CDG;** ☎01 48 62 22 80). Many continental and charter flights use **Orly (ORY;** ☎01 49 75 15 15). **Aéroports de Paris** (www.aeroportsdeparis.fr) has info about both airports. **Paris Beauvais Tillé (BVA;** ☎38 92 68 20 66; www.aeroportbeauvais.com) caters to budget travelers, servicing discount airlines like **Ryanair** (☎38 92 68 20 73; www.ryanair.com). For more info on flying to France, see p. 41. Once in France, most people prefer alternative travel modes unless heading to Corsica (p. 374).

**BY TRAIN.** The French national railway company, **SNCF** (☎08 36 35 35 35; www.sncf.fr), manages one of Europe's most efficient rail networks. Among the fastest in the world, **TGV** (www.tgv.com) trains (*train à grande vitesse;* high-speed) now link many major French cities, as well as some European destinations, including Brussels, Geneva, Lausanne, and Zürich. **Rapide** trains are slower. Local **Express** trains are, strangely enough, the slowest option. French trains offer discounts of 25-50% on tickets for travelers under 26 with the **Carte 12-25** (€52; good for 1yr.). Locate the **guichets** (ticket counters), the **quais** (platforms), and the **voies** (tracks), and you will be ready to roll. Terminals can be divided into **banlieue** (suburb) and the bigger **grandes lignes** (intercity trains). While only some select trains require reservations, you are not guaranteed a seat without one (usually US$5-30). Reserve ahead during peak holiday and tourist seasons.

If you are planning to spend a great deal of time on trains, a rail pass might be worthwhile, but in many cases—especially if you are under 26—point-to-point tickets may be cheaper. **Eurail** is valid in France. Standard **Eurail Passes,** valid for a given number of consecutive days, are best for those traveling long distances. **Flexipasses,** valid for any 10 or 15 (not necessarily consecutive) days within a two-month period, are more cost-effective for those traveling longer distances less frequently. **Youth Passes** and **Youth Flexipasses** provide the same second-class perks for those under 26. It is best to purchase a pass before going to France. For prices and more info, contact student travel agencies, **Rail Europe** (Canada ☎800-361-7245, US 877-257-2887; www.raileurope.com), or **DER Travel Services** (☎800-782-2424; www.der.com).

 **VALIDATE=GREAT.** Be sure to validate *(composter)* your ticket! Orange validation boxes lie around every station, and you must have it stamped with the date and time by the machine before boarding the train.

**BY BUS.** Within France, long-distance buses are a secondary transportation choice, as service is relatively infrequent. However, in some regions buses are indispensable for reaching out-of-the-way towns. Bus services operated by **SNCF** accept rail passes. *Gare routière* is French for "bus station."

**BY FERRY.** Ferries across the English Channel *(La Manche)* link France to England and Ireland. The shortest and most popular route is between Dover, BRI and Calais (1-1½hr.) and is run by **P&O Stena Line** (☎0870 598 0333; www.poferries.com) and **SeaFrance** (☎0871 663 2546; www.seafrance.com). **Norfolkline** (☎44 0870 870 1020; www.norfolkline-ferries.com) provides an alternative route from Dover, BRI to Dunkerque (1¾hr.). **Brittany Ferries** (France ☎0825 82 88 28, UK 0870 9 076 103; www.brittany-ferries.com) travels from Portsmouth to Caen (4¾-6¾hr.), Cherbourg (4hr.) and St-Malo (7¾-11¾hr.). For more info on English Channel ferries, see p. 52. For info on ferries to Corsica, see p. 374.

**BY CAR.** Drivers in France visiting for fewer than 90 days must be 18 years old and carry either an **International Driving Permit (IDP)** or a valid EU-issued or American driving license. You need to also have the vehicle's registration, national plate, and current insurance certificate on hand; French car rental agencies provide necessary documents. Agencies require renters to be 20 and most charge those aged 21-24 an additional insurance fee (€20-25 per day). If you don't know how to drive stick, you may have to pay a hefty premium for a car with automatic transmission. French law requires that both drivers and passengers wear seat belts. The almost 1,000,000km of French roads are usually in great condition, due in part to expensive tolls paid by travelers. Check www.francetourism.com/practicalinfo for more info on domestic travel and car rentals.

**BY BIKE AND BY THUMB.** Of Europeans, the French alone may love cycling more than football. Renting a bike (€8-19 per day) beats bringing your own if you're only touring one or two regions. Hitchhiking is illegal on French highways, although some people describe the French's ready willingness to lend a ride. Let's Go does not recommend hitchhiking.

## KEEPING IN TOUCH

| **PHONE CODES** | **Country code: 33. International dialing prefix: 00.**<br>When calling within a city, dial 0 + city code + local number.<br>For more info on how to place international calls, see **Inside Back Cover.** |
| --- | --- |

**EMAIL AND THE INTERNET.** Internet access is readily available throughout France. Only the smallest villages lack Internet cafes, and in larger towns Internet cafes are well equipped and widespread, though often pricey. In addition to the locations suggested here, check out www.cybercaptive.com for more options.

**TELEPHONE.** Whenever possible, use a calling card for international phone calls, as long-distance rates for national phone services are often very high. Publicly owned **France Télécom** pay phones charge less than their privately owned counterparts. They accept stylish **Télécartes** (phonecards), available in 50-unit (€7.50) and 120-unit (€15) denominations at newspaper kiosks and *tabacs*. Mobile phones are an increasingly popular and economical option. Major mobile carrieres include Orange, Bouyges Telecom, and SFR. *Décrochez* means pick up; you'll then be asked to **patientez** (wait) to insert your card; at *numérotez* or *composez*, you can dial. The number for general info is ☎12; for an international operator, call ☎00 33 11. International direct dial numbers include: **AT&T Direct** ☎0 800 99 00 11; **Canada Direct** ☎0 800 99 00 16 or 99 02 16; **MCI WorldPhone** ☎0 800 99 00 19; **Telecom New Zealand** ☎0 800 90 42 80; **Telstra Australia** ☎0 800 99 00 61.

**MAIL.** Send mail from **La Poste** offices throughout France (www.laposte.net. Open M-F 9am-7pm, Sa 9am-noon). Airmail between France and North America takes five to 10 days; writing "prioritaire" on the envelope should ensure delivery in four to five days at no extra charge. To send a 20g airmail letter or postcard within France or from France to another EU destination costs around €0.50, to a non-EU European country €0.75, and to Australia, Canada, New Zealand, or the US €0.90. To receive mail in France, have it delivered **Poste Restante.** Mail will go to the main post office unless you specify a subsidiary by street address. Address mail to be held as follows: Last name, First name, *Poste Restante*, postal code, city, France. Bring a passport to pick up your mail; there may be a small fee.

## ACCOMMODATIONS AND CAMPING

| FRANCE | ❶ | ❷ | ❸ | ❹ | ❺ |
|---|---|---|---|---|---|
| **ACCOMMODATIONS** | under €15 | €15-27 | €28-38 | €39-55 | over €55 |

The French Hostelling International (HI) affiliate, **Fédération Unie des Auberges de Jeunesse** (**FUAJ**; ☎01 44 89 87 27; www.fuaj.org), operates 150 hostels within France. A dorm bed in a hostel averages €10-15. Some hostels accept reservations through the International Booking Network (www.hostelbooking.com). Two or more people traveling together can save money by staying in cheap hotels rather than hostels. The French government employs a four-star hotel rating system. *Gîtes d'étapes* are rural accommodations for cyclists, hikers, and other amblers in less-populated areas. After 3000 years of settlement, true wilderness in France is hard to find, and it's illegal to camp in most public spaces, including national parks. Instead, look for organized **campings** (campgrounds), replete with vacationing families and programmed fun. Most have toilets, showers, and electrical outlets, though you may have to pay €2-5 extra for such luxuries; you'll often need to pay a fee for your car, too (€3-8). In total, expect to pay €8-15 per site.

## FOOD AND DRINK

| FRANCE | ❶ | ❷ | ❸ | ❹ | ❺ |
|---|---|---|---|---|---|
| **FOOD** | under €7 | €7-12 | €13-18 | €19-33 | over €33 |

French chefs cook for one of the world's most finicky clienteles. The largest meal of the day is **le déjeuner** (lunch) while a light croissant with or without **confiture** (jelly) characterizes **le petit déjeuner** (breakfast). A complete French meal includes an **apéritif** (drink), an **entrée** (appetizer), a **plat** (main course), salad, cheese, dessert, fruit, coffee, and a **digestif** (after-dinner drink). The French drink wine with virtually every meal; *boisson comprise* entitles you to a free drink (usually wine) with your food. France's legal drinking age is 16. Most restaurants offer a **menu à prix fixe** (fixed-price meal) that costs less than ordering *à la carte*. The *formule* is a cheaper, two-course version for the hurried luncher. Odd-hour cravings between lunch and dinner can be satisfied at *brasseries* or *crêperies*, the middle ground between cafes and restaurants. *Service compris* means the tip is included in **l'addition** (the check). It's easy to get a satisfying dinner for under €10 with staples such as cheese, pâté, wine, bread, and chocolate. For a picnic, get fresh produce at a **marché** (outdoor market) and then hop between specialty shops. Start with a **boulangerie** (bakery) for bread, proceed to a **charcuterie** (butcher) for meats, and then **pâtisseries** (pastry shops), and **confiseries** (candy shops) to satisfy a sweet tooth. When choosing a cafe, remember that major boulevards provide more expensive venues than smaller places on side streets. Prices are also cheaper at the **comptoir** (counter) than in the **salle** (seating area). For supermarket shopping, look for the chains **Carrefour, Casino,** and **Monoprix.**

## BEYOND TOURISM

As the most visited nation in the world, France benefits economically from the tourism industry. Yet the country's popularity has adversely affected some French communities and their natural life. Throw off the *touriste* stigma and advocate for immigrant communities, restore a crumbling château, or educate others about the importance of environmental issues while exploring France. For more info on opportunities across Europe, see **Beyond Tourism,** p. 54.

**Care France,** CAP 19, 13 r. Georges Auric, 75019 Paris (☎01 53 19 89 89; www.care-france.org). An international organization providing volunteer opportunities, from combating AIDS to promoting education.

**Club du Vieux Manoir,** Ancienne Abbaye du Moncel, 60700 Pontpoint (☎03 44 72 33 98; cvmclubduvieuxmanoir.free.fr). Year-long and summer work restoring castles and churches. €14 membership and insurance fee; €12.50 per day, plus food and tent.

**International Partnership for Service-Learning and Leadership,** 815 Second Av., Ste. 315, New York, NY 10017, USA (☎212-986-0989; www.ipsl.org). Matches volunteers with host families, provides intensive French classes, and requires 10-15hr. per week of service for a year, semester, or summer. Ages 18-30. Based in Montpellier. Costs range US$7200-US$23,600.

# PARIS

☎01

Paris (pah-ree; pop. 2,153,600), a cultural and commercial center for over 2000 years, draws millions of visitors each year, from students who come to study at the Sorbonne to tourists who wonder why the French ignore so many consonants. The City of Light, Paris is a source of inspiration unrivaled in beauty. Art emanates from its world-class museums and history from every Roman ruin, medieval street, Renaissance hotel, and 19th-century boulevard. A vibrant political center, Paris blends the spirit of revolution with a reverence for tradition, devoting as much energy to preserving conventions as it does to shattering them.

## ◼ INTERCITY TRANSPORTATION

**Flights:** Some budget airlines fly into **Aéroport de Paris Beauvais Tillé (BVA)** about 1hr. outside of Paris (p. 264). **Aéroport Roissy-Charles de Gaulle (CDG, Roissy;** ☎3950; www.adp.fr), 23km northeast of Paris, serves most transatlantic flights. 24hr. English-speaking info center. The **RER B** (one of the Parisian commuter rail lines) runs to central Paris from Terminals 1 and 2. (30-45min.; €8.20, under 18 €5.80). **Aéroport d'Orly (ORY;** ☎49 75 15 15), 18km south of Paris, used by charters and continental flights.

**Trains:** Paris has 6 major train stations: **Gare d'Austerlitz** (to the Loire Valley, southwestern France, Portugal, and Spain); **Gare de l'Est** (to Austria, eastern France, Czech Republic, southern Germany, Hungary, Luxembourg, and Switzerland); **Gare de Lyon** (to southern and southeastern France, Greece, Italy, and Switzerland); **Gare du Nord** (to Belgium, Britain, Eastern Europe, northern France, northern Germany, the Netherlands, and Scandinavia); **Gare Montparnasse** (to Brittany and southwestern France on the TGV); **Gare St-Lazare** (to Normandy). All are accessible by Métro.

**Buses: Gare Routière Internationale du Paris-Gallieni,** 28 av. du Général de Gaulle, outside Paris. Ⓜ Gallieni. **Eurolines** (☎49 72 57 80, €0.34 per min.; www.eurolines.fr) sells tickets to most destinations in France and bordering countries.

## ◼ ORIENTATION

The **Seine River** (SEHN) flows from east to west through Paris with two islands, **Ile de la Cité** and **Ile St-Louis,** situated in the city's geographical center. The Seine splits Paris in half: the **Rive Gauche** (REEV go-sh; Left Bank) to the south and the **Rive Droite** (REEV dwaht; Right Bank) to the north. Modern Paris is divided into **20 arrondissements** (districts) that spiral clockwise outward from the center of the city. Each *arrondisse-*

FRANCE

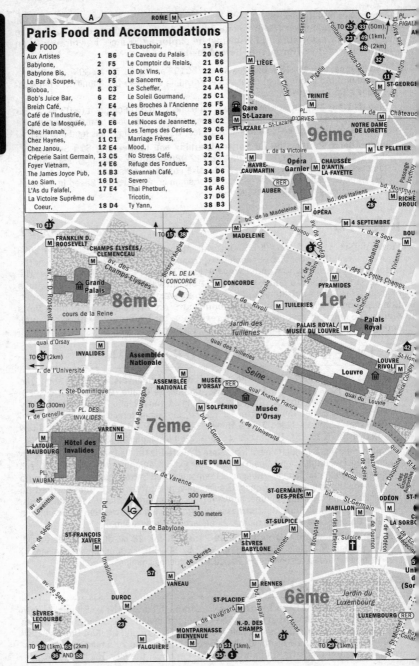

# Paris Food and Accommodations

● FOOD

| | | |
|---|---|---|
| Aux Artistes | 1 | B6 |
| Babylone, | 2 | F5 |
| Babylone Bis, | 3 | D3 |
| Le Bar à Soupes, | 4 | F5 |
| Bioboa, | 5 | C3 |
| Bob's Juice Bar, | 6 | E2 |
| Breizh Café, | 7 | E4 |
| Café de l'Industrie, | 8 | F4 |
| Café de la Mosquée, | 9 | E6 |
| Chez Hannah, | 10 | E4 |
| Chez Haynes, | 11 | C1 |
| Chez Janou, | 12 | E4 |
| Crêperie Saint Germain, | 13 | C5 |
| Foyer Vietnam, | 14 | E6 |
| The James Joyce Pub, | 15 | B3 |
| Lao Siam, | 16 | D1 |
| L'As du Falafel, | 17 | E4 |
| La Victoire Suprême du Coeur, | 18 | D4 |
| L'Ebauchoir, | 19 | F6 |
| Le Caveau du Palais, | 20 | C5 |
| Le Comptoir du Relais, | 21 | B6 |
| Le Dix Vins, | 22 | A6 |
| Le Sancerre, | 23 | C1 |
| Le Scheffer, | 24 | A4 |
| Le Soleil Gourmand, | 25 | C1 |
| Les Broches à l'Ancienne | 26 | F5 |
| Les Deux Magots, | 27 | B5 |
| Les Noces de Jeannette, | 28 | C2 |
| Les Temps des Cerises, | 29 | C6 |
| Marriage Frères, | 30 | E4 |
| Mood, | 31 | A2 |
| No Stress Café, | 32 | C1 |
| Refuge des Fondues, | 33 | C1 |
| Savannah Café, | 34 | D6 |
| Severo, | 35 | B6 |
| Thai Phetburi, | 36 | A6 |
| Tricotin, | 37 | D6 |
| Ty Yann, | 38 | B3 |

FRANCE

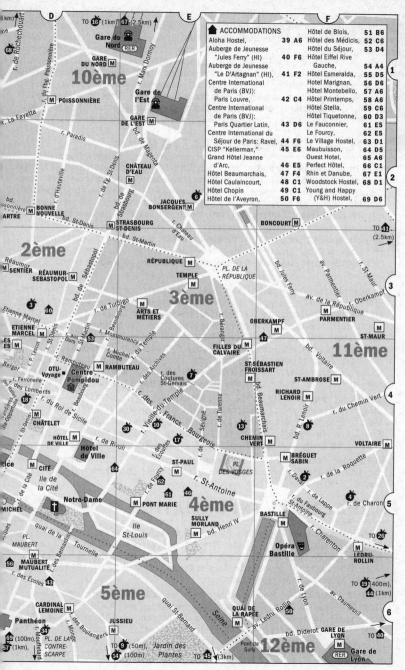

| ACCOMMODATIONS | | Hôtel de Blois, | **51 B6** |
| Aloha Hostel, | **39 A6** | Hôtel des Médicis, | **52 C6** |
| Auberge de Jeunesse | | Hôtel du Séjour, | **53 D4** |
| "Jules Ferry" (HI) | **40 F6** | Hôtel Eiffel Rive | |
| Auberge de Jeunesse | | Gauche, | **54 A4** |
| "Le D'Artagnan" (HI), | **41 F2** | Hôtel Esmeralda, | **55 D5** |
| Centre International | | Hotel Marignan, | **56 D6** |
| de Paris (BVJ): | | Hôtel Montebello, | **57 A6** |
| Paris Louvre, | **42 C4** | Hôtel Printemps, | **58 A6** |
| Centre International | | Hôtel Stella, | **59 C6** |
| de Paris (BVJ): | | Hôtel Tiquetonne, | **60 D3** |
| Paris Quartier Latin, | **43 D6** | Le Fauconnier, | **61 E5** |
| Centre International du | | Le Fourcy, | **62 E5** |
| Séjour de Paris: Ravel, | **44 F6** | Le Village Hostel, | **63 D1** |
| CISP "Kellerman," | **45 E6** | Maubuisson, | **64 D5** |
| Grand Hôtel Jeanne | | Ouest Hotel, | **65 A6** |
| d'Arc, | **46 E5** | Perfect Hôtel, | **66 C1** |
| Hôtel Beaumarchais, | **47 F4** | Rhin et Danube, | **67 E1** |
| Hôtel Caulaincourt, | **48 C1** | Woodstock Hostel, | **68 D1** |
| Hôtel Chopin, | **49 C1** | Young and Happy | |
| Hôtel de l'Aveyron, | **50 F6** | (Y&H) Hostel, | **69 D6** |

*ment* is referred to by its number (e.g. the Third, the Sixteenth). Sometimes it is helpful to orient yourself around central Paris's major monuments: on Rive Gauche, the sprawling Jardin du Luxembourg lies in the southeast; the Eiffel Tower, visible from many points in the city, stands in the southwest; moving clockwise and crossing the Seine to Rive Droite, the Champs Elysées and Arc de Triomphe occupy the northwest and the Sacre-Coeur stands high in the northeast. *Let's Go: Europe* splits Paris into four sections according to geographical grouping of *arrondissements*: the city center (1*er*, 2*ème*, 3*ème*, and 4*ème*); Left Bank East (5*ème*, 6*ème*, and 13*ème*); Left Bank West (7*ème*, 14*ème*, and 15*ème*); Right Bank East (10*ème*, 11*ème*, 12*ème*, 18*ème*, 19*ème*, and 20*ème*); Right Bank West (8*ème*, 9*ème*, 16*ème*, and 17*ème*).

# ▣ LOCAL TRANSPORTATION

**Public Transportation:** The **Métro** (Ⓜ) runs 5:30am-1:20am. Lines are numbered and are generally referred to by their number and final destinations; connections are called *correspondances*. Single-fare tickets within the city cost €1.40; carnet of 10 €10.90. Buy extras for when ticket booths are closed (after 10pm) and hold onto your ticket until you exit. The **RER (Réseau Express Régional),** the commuter train to the suburbs, serves as

> **!** The following stations can be dangerous at night: Anvers, Barbès-Rochechouart, Château d'Eau, Châtelet, Châtelet-Les-Halles, Gare de l'Est, Gare du Nord, and Pigalle. If concerned, take a taxi, or sit near the driver on a *Noctilien* bus.

an express subway within central Paris. **Keep your ticket:** changing to and getting off the RER requires sticking your validated ticket into a turnstile. Watch the signboards next to the RER tracks and check that your stop is lit up before riding. **Buses** use the same €1.40 tickets (validate in the machine by the driver). Buses run 7am-8:30pm, *Autobus de Nuit* until 1:30am, and *Noctambus* 1 per hr. 12:30-5:30am at stops marked with a blue "N" inside a white circle, with a red star on the upper right-hand side. The **Mobilis** pass covers the Métro, RER, and buses (€5.50 for a 1-day pass in Zones 1 and 2). A **Carte Orange** weekly pass *(carte orange hebdomadaire)* costs €16 and expires on Su; photo required. Refer to the front of the book for **color maps** of Paris's transit network.

**Taxis: Alpha Taxis** (☎45 85 85 85). **Taxis Bleus** (☎08 25 16 24 24). Taxis take 3 passengers (4th passenger €2-3 surcharge). *Tarif A,* daily 7am-7pm (€0.62 per km). *Tarif B,* M-Sa 7pm-7am, Su 24hr., and from the airports and immediate suburbs (€1.06 per km). *Tarif C,* from the airports 7pm-7am (€1.24 per km). In addition, there is a €2 base fee and min. €5 charge. It is customary to tip 15% and polite to add €1 extra.

**Bike Rental: Paris-Vélo,** 2 r. de Fer-à-Moulin, 5*ème* (☎43 37 59 22). Ⓜ Censier-Daubenton. €14 per day. Open Apr.-Sept. M-Sa 10am-7pm, Su 10am-2pm and 5-7pm; Oct.-Mar. M-Sa 10am-6pm, Su 10am-2pm and 5-7pm.

# ▣ PRACTICAL INFORMATION

**Tourist Office: Bureau Pyramides,** 25 r. des Pyramides, 1*er* (☎08 92 68 30 00). Ⓜ Pyramides. Open June-Oct. daily 9am-7pm; Nov.-May M-Sa 10am-7pm, Su 11am-7pm. **Bureau Gare de Lyon,** 20 bd. Diderot, 12*ème* (☎08 92 68 30 00). Ⓜ Gare de Lyon. Open M-Sa 8am-6pm. **Montmartre Tourist Office,** 21 pl. du Tertre, 18*ème* (☎42 62 21 21). Ⓜ Anvers. Open daily 10am-7pm.

**Embassies: Australia,** 4 r. Jean-Rey, 15*ème* (☎40 59 33 00; www.france.embassy.gov.au). Open M-F 9am-5pm. **Canada,** 35 av. Montaigne, 8*ème* (☎44 43 29 00; www.international.gc.ca/canada-europa/france). Open daily 9am-noon and 2-5pm. **Ireland,** 12 av. Foch, 16*ème* (☎44 17 67 00; www.embassyofirelandparis.netfirms.com). Open M-F 9:30am-noon. **New Zealand,** 7ter r. Léonard de Vinci, 16*ème* (☎45 01 43 43; www.nzembassy.com/france). Open July-Aug. M-Th 9am-1pm and 2-4:30pm, F 9am-2pm; Sept.-June

M-Th 9am-1pm and 2-5:30pm, F 9am-1pm and 2-4pm. **UK,** 18bis r. d'Anjou, 8ème (☎44 51 31 02; www.amb-grandebretagne.fr). Open M-F 9:30am-12:30pm and 2:30-4:30pm. **US,** 2 av. Gabriel, 8ème (☎43 12 22 22; www.amb-usa.fr). Open M-F 9am-12:30pm.

**American Express:** 11 r. Scribe, 9ème (☎47 77 79 28). ⓜ Opéra or Auber. Open M-Sa 9am-6:30pm.

**GLBT Resources: Centre Gai et Lesbien,** 3 r. Keller, 11ème (☎43 57 21 47). ⓜ Ledru-Rollin or Bastille. Open M-F 4-8pm.

**Laundromats:** Laundromats are everywhere, especially in the 5ème and 6ème.

**Crisis Lines: Rape, SOS Viol** (☎08 00 05 95 95). Open M-F 10am-7pm. **SOS Help!** (☎46 21 46 46). Confidential English-speaking crisis hotline. Open daily 3-11pm.

**Pharmacies:** Look for the neon green crosses that indicate pharmacies all over the city. Call the police for the *pharmacies de garde,* the rotating pharmacies in different *arrondissements* that handle emergencies.

**Hospitals: American Hospital of Paris,** 63 bd. Hugo, Neuilly (☎46 41 25 25). ⓜ Port Maillot, then bus #82 to the end of the line. **Hôpital Franco-Britannique de Paris** (Hertford British Hospital), 3 r. Barbès, in the Levallois-Perret suburb (☎46 39 22 22). ⓜ Anatole France. Some English-speaking doctors.

**Internet Access:** Internet is not hard to find in Paris; cheap Internet, however, is scarce. Most establishments charge about €0.10-0.15 per min. or €2-6 per hr. Hotels and hostels charge more because of the convenience. McDonald's customers can access its free Wi-Fi network for as long as they wish at most locations. Many cafes have Wi-Fi as well.

**Post Office: Poste du Louvre,** 52 r. du Louvre, 1er (☎40 28 20 40). ⓜ Louvre. Open 24hr. Address mail to be held: LAST NAME First name, *Poste Restante,* 52 r. du Louvre, 75001 Paris, FRANCE. **Postal Codes:** 750xx, where "xx" is the *arrondissement* (e.g., 75003 for any address in the 3ème).

# █ ACCOMMODATIONS

Accommodations in Paris are expensive—you don't need *Let's Go* to tell you that. At the absolute minimum, expect to pay at least €20 for a hostel dorm-style bed and €28 for a hotel single. Hostels are a better option for single travelers, whereas staying in a hotel is more economical for groups. Paris's hostels skip many standard restrictions (e.g., curfews) and tend to have flexible maximum stays. In cheaper hotels, few rooms have private baths. Rooms fill quickly after morning check-out; arrive early or reserve ahead. Most hostels and *foyers* include the **taxe de séjour** (€0.10-2 per person per day) in listed prices.

## CITY CENTER

▨ **Hôtel des Jeunes,** 4ème (**MIJE;** ☎42 74 23 45; www.mije.com). Books beds in 3 small hostels in beautiful old Marais residences recognized as historical 17th-century monuments. No smoking. English spoken. Breakfast, private shower, and linens included. Internet €0.10 per min. with €0.50 initial connection fee. Lockers €1 deposit. Max. 7-night stay. Reception 7am-1am. Check-in noon. Lockout noon-3pm. Curfew 1am. Quiet hours after 10pm. 4- to 9-bed dorms €28; singles €43; doubles €66; triples €87; quads €108. MIJE membership required (€2.50). Cash only. ❸

**Maubuisson,** 12 r. des Barres, ⓜ Hôtel de Ville or Pont Marie, is a half-timbered former girls' convent on a silent street by the St-Gervais monastery. Accommodates more individuals than groups.

**Le Fourcy,** 6 r. de Fourcy, ⓜ St-Paul or Pont Marie, surrounds a large, social courtyard—think Tuileries in miniature—ideal for outdoor picnicking. Le Fourcy's restaurant offers a main course with drink (€8.50, lunch only) and a 3-course "hosteler special" (€11).

**Le Fauconnier,** 11 r. de Fourcy, ⓜ St-Paul or Pont Marie. Ivy-covered, sun-drenched building just steps away from the Seine and Île St-Louis.

**Centre International de Paris (BVJ): Paris Louvre,** 20 r. Jean-Jacques Rousseau, 1er (☎53 00 90 90; www.bvjhotel.com). ⓜ Louvre or Palais-Royal. Bright, dorm-style rooms with 2-8 beds per room. Guests must be ages 18-35. English spoken. Breakfast

FRANCE

and showers included. Lockers €2. Internet €1 per 10min. Reception 24hr. Reserve ahead. Dorms €27, doubles €29. Cash only. ❷

**Hôtel Tiquetonne,** 6 r. Tiquetonne, 2ème (☎42 36 94 58; fax 42 36 02 94). ⓜ Etienne-Marcel. Small, simple rooms a stone's throw from the sex shops on r. St-Denis and the r. Montorgueil market. Elevator. Breakfast €6. Showers €6. Closed Aug. and late Dec. Reserve ahead. Singles €30, with shower €40; doubles €50. AmEx/MC/V. ❷

**Grand Hôtel Jeanne d'Arc,** 3 r. de Jarente, 4ème (☎48 87 62 11; www.hoteljeanne-darc.com). ⓜ St-Paul. Gorgeous rooms with shower, toilet, and TV. Wheelchair-accessible ground floor double. English spoken. Breakfast €6. Reserve 3 months in advance by calling with credit card. Singles €60-84; doubles €84-97; triples €116; quads €146. MC/V. ❺

**Hôtel du Séjour,** 36 r. du Grenier St-Lazare, 3ème (☎48 87 40 36). ⓜ Etienne-Marcel. 1 block from Les Halles and Centre Pompidou. Family-run hotel offers 20 clean rooms and a warm welcome. Showers €4. Reception 7:30am-10:30pm. Reserve ahead. Singles €35; doubles €47, with shower and toilet €58; extra person €22. Cash only. ❸

## LEFT BANK EAST

🏨 **Young and Happy (Y&H) Hostel,** 80 r. Mouffetard, 5ème (☎47 07 47 07; www.youngandhappy.fr). ⓜ Monge. A funky, friendly hostel. Laid-back staff and clean (if basic) rooms. A few rooms have showers and toilets. English spoken. Kitchen. Breakfast included. Linens €2.50 with €5 deposit, towels €1. Internet €2 per 30min. Lockout 11am-4pm. Apr.-Dec. 4- to 10-bed dorms €23; doubles €52. Jan.-Mar. €21/24. ❷

🏨 **Hôtel Stella,** 41 r. Monsieur-le-Prince, 6ème (☎40 51 00 25; http://site.voila.fr/hotel-stella). ⓜ Odéon. Centuries-old woodwork takes the exposed-beam look to a whole new level. Huge rooms with high ceilings, some with pianos. Reserve ahead. Singles €35-45; doubles €55-65; triples €75-85; quads €85-95. ❸

**Hôtel Marignan,** 13 r. du Sommerard, 5ème (☎43 54 63 81; www.hotel-marignan.com). ⓜ Maubert-Mutualité. Clean, freshly decorated rooms. English-speaking owner combines hotel privacy with hostel-like friendliness. Kitchen. Breakfast and laundry included. Hall showers open until 10:45pm. Internet. Reserve ahead. Singles €45-60; doubles €55-85; triples €75-110; quads €85-135; quints €90-150. Cash only. ❹

**Hôtel Esmeralda,** 4 r. St-Julien-le-Pauvre, 5ème (☎43 54 19 20; fax 40 51 00 68). ⓜ St-Michel. Antique wallpaper, ceiling beams, and red velvet create an ambience both rustic and Victorian. The location is truly outstanding—adjacent to a small park, less than a block from the Seine, and within earshot of Notre Dame's bells. Breakfast €6. Singles €35, with shower and toilet €65; doubles €85-120; triples €110. ❸

**Hôtel des Médicis,** 214 r. St-Jacques, 5ème (☎43 54 14 66). RER Luxembourg. Turn right on r. Guy-Lussac and left on r. St-Jacques. Jim Morrison slummed in room #4 for 3 weeks in 1971. You get what you pay for—peeling paint, broken furniture, and a dose of raggedy charm. 1 shower and toilet per fl. Some rooms with balcony. Reception 24hr. Singles €30; doubles €31; triples €45. ❷

**Centre International du Séjour de Paris: CISP "Kellerman,"** 17 bd. Kellerman, 13ème (☎44 16 37 38; www.cisp.asso.fr). ⓜ Porte d'Italie. This large hostel resembles a retro spaceship on stilts. Breakfast included; cafeteria open daily noon-1:30pm for lunch and 6:30-9:30pm for dinner. Reception 6:30am-1:30am. Reserve 1 month ahead. 8-bed dorms €19; 2- to 4-bed dorms €26; singles with bath €39; doubles with bath €28. MC/V. ❷

**Centre International de Paris (BVJ): Paris Quartier Latin,** 44 r. des Bernardins, 5ème (☎43 29 34 80; fax 53 00 90 91). ⓜ Maubert-Mutualité. Boisterous hostel with big down-stairs cafeteria. In-room microwave, shower, TV, and message service. 100 beds. English spoken. Breakfast included. Lockers €2. Internet €1 per 10min. Reception 24hr. Reserve at least 1 week ahead. 10-bed dorms €28; singles €40; doubles €60; quads €120. ❸

## LEFT BANK WEST

🏨 **Hôtel Montebello,** 18 r. Pierre Leroux, 7ème (☎47 34 41 18; hmontebello@aol.com). ⓜ Vaneau. Sparsely furnished but exceptionally clean rooms with a helpful and welcoming English-speaking staff. A bit far from the 7ème's sights, but unbeatable rates for this upscale neighborhood. Breakfast 7:30-9:30am; €4. Reserve ahead. Singles €25-42; doubles €40-49. Extra bed €10. Cash only. ❸

**Aloha Hostel,** 1 r. Borromée, 15ème (☎42 73 03 03; www.aloha.fr). ⓜ Volontaires. Colorful hostel fills with international backpackers sharing travel tips over drinks at its cafe. No outside alcohol allowed. Breakfast included. Safe deposit boxes. Linens €3. Towels €3. Internet €2 per 30min.; free Wi-Fi. Reception 7am-2am. Lockout 11am-5pm. Curfew 2am. Reserve ahead. Apr.-Oct. dorms €25; doubles €50. Nov.-Mar. €19/46. ❷

**Hôtel Eiffel Rive Gauche,** 6 r. du Gros Caillou, 7ème (☎45 51 24 56; www.hotel-eiffel.com). ⓜ École Militaire. On a quiet street, this family-run hotel is refreshingly open and filled with light. Rooms have cable TV, Internet jacks, and full bath; some have Eiffel Tower views. Breakfast €10. Safe deposit box €3. Singles €75-115; doubles €75-125; triples €95-145; quads €105-175. Rates fluctuate with demand. Extra bed €10. MC/V. ❺

**Hôtel de Blois,** 5 r. des Plantes, 14ème (☎45 40 99 48; www.hoteldeblois.com). ⓜ Mouton-Duvernet. One of the best deals in Paris. Lushly carpeted rooms have hair dryer, phone, and TV. Laundromat and public pool nearby. Breakfast €6.30. Reserve ahead. Singles or doubles with shower €60-65, with bath €65-82. AmEx/MC/V. ❹

**Ouest Hôtel,** 27 r. de Gergovie, 14ème (☎45 42 64 99). ⓜ Pernety. A modest hotel decorated in 70s bling. Owner keeps a lending library with books left by previous guests. Breakfast €5. Showers €5. Doubles €22-28, with shower €37-39. MC/V. ❷

**Hôtel Printemps,** 31 r. du Commerce, 15ème (☎45 79 83 36; www.hotelprintemps15.com). ⓜ La Motte-Picquet-Grenelle. In a busy neighborhood, this 52-room hotel is a relatively clean option. Breakfast €5. Curfew 2:30am. Reserve ahead. Singles and doubles €37, with shower €43, with bath €46. MC/V. ❸

# RIGHT BANK WEST

**Woodstock Hostel,** 48 r. Rodier, 9ème (☎48 78 87 76; www.woodstock.fr). ⓜ Anvers. From the Metro, walk against traffic on pl. Anvers, turn right on av. Trudaine and left on rue Rodier. A VW bug hanging from the ceiling and a serious case of Beatles-worship contribute to the Woodstock's fun, can-do atmosphere. English spoken. Breakfast included. Linens €2.50. Towels €1. Internet €2 per 30min. Max. 2-week stay. Lockout 11am-3pm. Curfew 2am. Basic 4- or 6-bed dorms €22; doubles €50. ❷

**Perfect Hôtel,** 39 r. Rodier, 9ème (☎42 81 18 86; www.paris-hostel.biz). ⓜ Anvers. Lives up to its name with hotel-quality rooms at hostel prices, some with balconies. English-speaking staff. Beer vending machine (€1.50). Breakfast included. Reserve ahead. Singles €44, with toilet €60; doubles €50/60. MC/V. ❷

**Hôtel Chopin,** 10 bd. Montmartre, 9ème (☎47 70 58 10; fax 42 47 00 70). ⓜ Grands Boulevards. Mostly new, clean rooms with fan, phone, and TV by request. Breakfast €7. Reserve 2-3 months ahead. Singles with toilet €61, with shower or bath €68-76; doubles with shower or bath €81-92; triples €109. MC/V. ❺

# RIGHT BANK EAST

**Auberge de Jeunesse "Le D'Artagnan" (HI),** 80 r. Vitruve, 20ème (☎40 32 34 56; www.hihostels.com). ⓜ Porte de Bagnolet. Well-lit, generously sized rooms. Neon lights and funky decorations. Breakfast 7-11am. Lockers €2 per day. Linens included. Towel €2.50. Laundry €4. Internet €2 per 30min. Restaurant, bar, and a small cinema (free films, nightly at 6:30pm). Max. 8-night stay. Reception 8am-1am. Lockout noon-3pm. Reservations by fax or email required. 9-bed dorms €20; 3-, 4-, 5-bed dorms €22; 2-bed dorm €26. Children under 10 ½-price, under 5 free. ❷

**Auberge de Jeunesse "Jules Ferry" (HI),** 8 bd. Jules Ferry, 11ème (☎43 57 55 60; auberge@micronet.fr). ⓜ République. A party atmosphere in a great location next to a park and pl. de la République. 100 beds. Modern, clean rooms with mirrors, sinks, and tiled floors. Breakfast, linens, and showers included. Lockers €2. Laundry €5. Internet

€1 per 10min. Max. 1-week stay. Reception 24hr. Lockout 10:30am-2pm. Arrive 8-11am to ensure a room. 4- to 6-bed dorms €21; doubles €42. MC/V. ❷

**Centre International du Séjour de Paris: CISP "Ravel,"** 6 av. Maurice Ravel, 12ème (☎44 75 60 00; www.cisp.asso.fr). Ⓜ Porte de Vincennes. The price makes the hike to Paris' main attractions worth it. Large, clean rooms and an enormous outdoor pool (€3-4). Cafeteria open daily 7:30-9:30am, noon-1:30pm, and 7-10:30pm; meals €11. Breakfast, linens, and towels included. Free Internet. Reception 24hr. Curfew 1:30am; arrange with the night guard to be let in later. Reserve ahead. 8-bed dorms €19; 2- to 4-bed dorms €25; singles with bath €37; doubles with bath €54. AmEx/MC/V. ❷

**Hôtel Caulaincourt,** 2 sq. Caulaincourt, 18ème (☎46 06 46 06; www.caulain-court.com). Ⓜ Lamarck-Caulaincourt. Turn right on r. Caulaincourt. Formerly artists' studios, the simple rooms, all with phone and TV, have wonderful views of Montmartre and the Paris skyline. Breakfast €5.50. Free Internet. Reserve 1 month ahead. Singles €25, with shower €50, with bath €60; doubles €63-76; triples with shower €89. MC/V. ❸

**Rhin et Danube,** 3 pl. de Rhin et Danube, 19ème (☎42 45 10 13; fax 42 06 88 82). Ⓜ Danube; or bus #75 from M: Châtelet (30min.). With spacious but not fancy suites, the R&D is a real deal. Many rooms look onto a quaint *place* and each has fridge, kitchen, phone, shower, toilet, and satellite TV. Reserve ahead. Singles €46; doubles €61; triples €73; quads €83; quints €92. MC/V. ❹

**Hôtel Beaumarchais,** 3 r. Oberkampf, 11ème (☎53 36 86 86; www.hotelbeaumar-chais.com). Ⓜ Oberkampf. With some of Paris's best nightlife at its doorstep, this spacious hotel is worth the extra money. Suites include A/C and TV room. Breakfast €10. Reserve 2 weeks ahead. Singles €75-90; doubles €110-130; suites €150-170; triples €170-190. Baby cribs €16. AmEx/MC/V. ❺

**Le Village Hostel,** 20 r. d'Orsel, 18ème (☎42 64 22 02). Ⓜ Anvers. Though in the midst of the Sacré-Coeur tourist traffic, Le Village is cheap, clean, and comfortable. Breakfast included. Linens €2.50. Towel €1. Max. 1-week stay. Lockout 11am-4pm. 4- to 8-bed dorms €24; singles €27; doubles €60; triples €81. Cash only. ❷

**Hôtel de l'Aveyron,** 5 r. d'Austerlitz, 12ème (☎43 07 86 86, fax 43 07 85 20). Ⓜ Gare de Lyon. On a quiet street, with 30 small, thoughtfully-decorated rooms. Eager, English-speaking staff. Breakfast €5. 1 wheelchair-accessible room. Sept.-Oct. and Mar.-Apr. reserve 2-3 months ahead. Singles with shower €55; doubles with shower €59, with bath €65; triples €70; quads €100. MC/V. ❹

# 🍴 FOOD

When in doubt, spend your money on food in Paris. Skip the museum, sleep in the dingy hotel, but 🔲**eat well.** Paris's culinary scene has been famous for centuries, and eating in the City of Light remains as exciting today as it was when Sun King Louis XIV made feasts an everyday occurrence. Beyond the traditional assortment of French cuisine, the city offers delicious international dishes. Avoid a pricey sit-down meal and stop into an *épicerie* to create a picnic to eat in Luxembourg Gardens, Parc Buttes Chaumont, or on the steps at Sacré-Coeur. *Bon Appetit!*

## RESTAURANTS

### CITY CENTER

🔲 **Chez Janou,** 2 rue Roger Verlomme (☎42 72 28 41). M: Chemin-Vert. Hidden in a quiet section of the 3ème, this bistro is lauded for its inexpensive, gourmet food. Shady terrace is superb for summer dining. *Plats* €15. Open daily noon-3pm and 7pm-midnight. Reserve ahead, as this local favorite is packed every night of the week. Cash only. ❷

**Bioboa,** 3 r. Danielle Casanova, 1er (☎42 61 17 67). Ⓜ Pyramides. Cheap, delicious, organic lunches in a bright, trendy atmosphere. Prepared foods available for those in a hurry. Hot panini with *chèvre* and grilled vegetables €7. Fruit smoothies €5-7. Open daily 11am-6pm. MC/V. ❶

**Breizh Café,** 109 r. Vieille du Temple, 4*ème* (☎42 72 13 77; www.breizhcafe.com). Ⓜ St-Sebastien. While Parisian crepes aren't hard to find, inexpensive, inventive crepes made with the highest quality ingredients (raw milk cheese and organic veggies) are rare. Crepe with potatoes, herring, *crème fraiche*, and caviar €10.50. Wide selection of regional ciders and Breton beers €3.50. Open M and W-Su noon-11:30pm. MC/V. ❷

**La Victoire Suprême du Coeur,** 41 r. des Bourdonnais, 1*er* (☎40 41 93 95). Ⓜ Châtelet. Vegetarian dishes like *escalope de seitan à la sauce champignon* (scallops in mushroom sauce; €14) highlight a health-conscious menu. Relaxed, with a breezy decor, this is one of the area's best lunches. Vegan meals available. Smoothies €5.50. 2-course *menu* €13. Open M-F 11:45am-10pm, Sa noon-10pm. AmEx/MC/V. ❸

**Le Caveau du Palais,** 19 pl. Dauphine, 1*er* (☎43 26 04 28). Ⓜ Cité. Serves up hearty French fare under timbered ceilings. Well-heeled locals crowd the terrace in the summertime. The meat-heavy menu is pricey but worth the splurge. Entrees €17-50. Desserts €8-9. Reserve ahead. Open daily 12:15-2:30pm and 7:15-10:30pm. AmEx/MC/V. ❹

**Chez Hannah,** 54 r. des Rosiers, 4*ème* (☎42 74 74 99). Ⓜ St-Paul. L'As du Falafel's ever-so-slightly resentful younger brother serves up an almost identical menu and much more manageable lines. Some believe the falafel special (€8.50, €4 takeout) here is better than its more celebrated counterpart. Open Tu-Su noon-midnight. ❶

**L'As du Falafel,** 34 r. des Rosiers, 4*ème* (☎48 87 63 60). Ⓜ St-Paul. Recommended by Lenny Kravitz, this always-packed kosher falafel stand and restaurant rocks the falafel world. Wash down their incredible falafel special (€6.50, takeout €4) with a glass of the house lemonade (€4). Open M-Th and Su 11am-midnight, F 11am-6pm. MC/V. ❶

**Babylone Bis,** 34 r. Tiquetonne, 2*ème* (☎42 33 48 35). Ⓜ Etienne-Marcel. With zebra skin on the walls, banana leaves on the ceiling, and loud *zouk* music blasting from the speakers, this eatery cooks up Antillean and African cuisine including delicious *aloko* (fried bananas; €5.50) and stuffed crab (€9). Previous patrons include Snoop Dogg, Stevie Wonder, and Marvin Gaye. Open daily 8pm-8am. MC/V. ❸

**Les Noces de Jeannette,** 14 r. Favart and 9 r. d'Amboise, 2*ème* (☎42 96 36 89). Ⓜ Richelieu-Drouot. This elegant, diverse bistro will impress your date (or your mom). *Menu du Jeanette* (€27) includes salad entrees, grilled meat, roasted fish and duck *plats*, as well as fabulous desserts. *Kir* included with meal. Reservations recommended. Open daily noon-1:30pm and 7-9:30pm. Cash only. ❹

## LEFT BANK EAST

🎗 **Le Comptoir du Relais,** 9 carrefour de l'Odeon, 6*ème* (☎44 27 07 97). Ⓜ Odeon. With no weak link on its menu, this locals-heavy, hyper-crowded bistro loves all things meat. Try *foie gras* on toast (€11) or beef stew with noodles, onions, and refreshing hints of lemon (€16). Open M-F noon-6pm and 8:30-10pm, Sa-Su noon-10pm. Reservations strongly recommended for M-Th dinner, not accepted F-Su. MC/V. ❹

**Foyer Vietnam,** 80 r. Monge, 5*ème* (☎45 35 32 54). Ⓜ Place Monge. This local favorite serves big portions without big prices. Start the 2-course lunch *menu* (€7 with student ID) with the tasty phô before trying the *porc au caramel*. Other dishes include duck with bananas (€9) and lychees in syrup (€3). Open M-Sa noon-2pm and 7-10pm. ❷

**Café de la Mosquée,** 39 r. Geoffroy-St-Hilaire, 5*ème* (☎43 31 38 20). Ⓜ Censier-Daubenton. In the Mosquée de Paris. With fountains, white marble floors, and an outdoor terrace, this cafe deserves a visit. Persian mint tea €2.50. *Maghrebain* pastries €2.50. Couscous €9-25. Open daily 9am-11pm. MC/V. ❷

**Tricotin,** 15 av. de Choisy, 13*ème* (☎45 84 74 44). Ⓜ Porte de Choisy. 6 chefs prepare delicious food from Cambodia, Thailand, and Vietnam, including *vapeur* (dim sum) options like steamed shrimp ravioli (€3.50). Open daily 9:30am-11:30pm. MC/V. ❶

## TOP TEN WEIRD ANIMAL PARTS TO EAT IN FRANCE

While contemporary French cuisine is renowned for its sophistication, the roots of French cooking can be found in some not-so-sophisticated parts of nature's most delicious creatures.

**1. Pied de Porc** (pig's feet). They're usually chopped, seasoned, and delicately fried.

**2. Tête de Veau** (calf's head). Rolled up, sliced, and served to the applause of French diners everywhere. A national favorite.

**3. L'Os à moelle** (bone marrow). Served on its own with salt, parsley, and eaten with a spoon.

**4. Boudin** (blood sausage). Mentioned as far back as Homer's *Odyssey*. Now you too, sitting "beside a great fire," can "fill a sausage with fat and blood and turn it this way and that."

**5. Foie Gras** ("fatty" goose liver). Some American cities have banned *foie gras*'s sale, but the French hold fast to their tradition.

**6. Whole Fish.** The best meat on any fish is behind the eye. So when the whole thing arrives on a plate, *carpe diem!*

**7. Tripe** (stomach). It's pretty meta—your intestines are digesting intestines.

**8. Tail.** Can be eaten on its own, in a stew, or you name it.

**9. Groin.** In French, pigs say "groin," not "oink." So when you order this, you're also imitating it.

**10. Filet** (muscle). So weird!

**Savannah Café,** 27 r. Descartes, 5ème (☎43 29 45 77). Ⓜ Cardinal Lemoine. This cheerful restaurant serves Lebanese food including eggplant caviar, taboule, and a selection of pasta dishes. *Plats* €13-15. Open M-Sa 7-11pm. MC/V. ❸

**Crêperie Saint Germain,** 33 r. St-André-des-Arts, 6ème (☎43 54 24 41), Ⓜ St-Michel, serves filling buckwheat crepes, like the Chihuahua (chicken cooked with peppers, tomatoes, and onions; €9), and dessert crepes like the Zanzibar (pear ice cream, raspberries, chocolate sauce, and *chantilly;* €7.50). M-F noon-3pm *menu* (€9) includes 2 crepes and a *cidre* or soda. Open daily noon-midnight. AmEx/MC/V. ❷

**Le Temps des Cerises,** 18 r. de la Butte-aux-Cailles, 13ème (☎45 89 69 48). Ⓜ Place d'Italie. A local cooperative, all of Le Temps's workers have shared restaurant ownership since 1976. Classic French dishes like *andouillette* (€14) are house specialties. Lunch *menu* €9.50, anytime *menus* €15-23. Open M-F 11:45am-2:15pm and 7:30-11:45pm, Sa 11:45am-2:15pm. Reserve ahead. AmEx/MC/V. ❹

### LEFT BANK WEST

🍽 **Thai Phetburi,** 31 bd. de Grenelle, 15ème (☎40 58 14 88; www.phetburi-paris.com). Ⓜ Bir-Hakeim. Try the award-winning *tom yam koung* (shrimp soup with lemongrass; €7.30). Vegetarian options. Open M-Sa noon-2:45pm and 7-11pm. AmEx/MC/V. ❷

**Le Dix Vins,** 57 r. Falguière, 15ème (☎43 20 91 77). Ⓜ Pasteur. Follow Pasteur away from the rails and make a left onto r. Falguière. This intimate bistro has a *menu* (€20-24) that, while not exactly cheap, offers a classic meal with a *nouvelle cuisine* twist. Open M-F noon-2:30pm and 8-11pm. MC/V. ❹

**Severo,** 8 r. des Plantes, 14ème (☎45 40 40 91). Ⓜ Mouton Duvernet. Consider its out-of-the-way location a blessing in disguise: a *New York Times* shout-out hasn't altered its local following. The owner, a former butcher, serves some of the city's best meat. While splurging on expensive cuts is worth your while, an inexpensive meal is both possible and delicious. Entrees with *frites* €14-29. *Mousse au chocolat* €6. Open M-F noon-2:30pm and 7:30-10:30pm. MC/V. ❸

**Aux Artistes,** 63 r. Falguière, 15ème (☎43 22 05 39). Ⓜ Pasteur. Its hectic cover-every-inch-of-the-wall decor draws artists, professionals, and students. Lunch *menu* €10. Dinner *menu* €13. Open M-F noon-2:30pm and 7:30pm-midnight, Sa 7:30pm-midnight. ❷

### RIGHT BANK WEST

🍽 **Ty Yann,** 10 r. de Constantinople, 8ème (☎40 08 00 17). Ⓜ Europe. The chef-owner, M. Yann, cheerfully prepares outstanding, inexpensive *galettes* (€7-10)

FRANCE

and crepes in the restaurant decorated with his mother's pastoral paintings. Create your own crepe (€5.50-6.50) for lunch. Takeout discount 15%. Open M-F noon-2:30pm and 7-10:30pm, Sa 7-10:30pm. MC/V. ❷

**No Stress Café,** 2 pl. Gustave Toudouze, 9ème (☎48 78 00 27). Ⓜ St-Georges. A French crowd comes for American-sized salads: giant piles of veggies and enthusiastically seasoned meats (€13-16). Onion rings with a spicy sauce €5. Vegetarian options. W-Sa massages 9pm-2am. Su brunch noon-3:30pm. Open Tu-Su 11am-2am. MC/V. ❸

**The James Joyce Pub,** 71 bd. Gouvion St-Cyr, 17ème (☎44 09 70 32). Ⓜ Porte Maillot (exit at Palais de Congrès). Stained-glass windows depicting Joyce's novels brighten the upstairs restaurant and downstairs bar, both of which serve as informal tourist offices for Anglophone expats. Traditional Irish meals from €9.50. Free "Funky Maps" listing English-speaking bars and pubs in Paris. F nights live Irish rock music at 9:30pm, except in summer. Open daily 11am-2am. Kitchen open noon-9pm. AmEx/MC/V. ❷

**Le Scheffer,** 22 r. Scheffer, 16ème (☎47 27 81 11). Ⓜ Trocadero. From the sounds of clattering pans to the red-checkered tablecloths, Le Scheffer is an unpretentious bastion of traditional French cuisine and a local favorite. Lunchtime service can be slow. Appetizers €6-7.50. *Steak tartare* (raw ground beef with mustard, capers, and other ingredients) €14. Open M-Sa 10:30am-11pm. ❸

**Mood,** 114 av. des Champs-Elysées and 1 r. Washington, 8ème (☎42 89 98 89). Ⓜ George V. A Japanese fusion restaurant. Dine on the *prix-fixe* lunch (€20) in the upper dining room, or indulge your hedonistic side on the lower level's plush red beds at night. Appetizers €9-17.50. *Plats* €12-16. Mixed drinks €9-11. Live music and DJ in the evening. Restaurant open daily 10am-4am, lounge open 10pm-4am. Reservations recommended for the restaurant and required for the lounge. AmEx/MC/V. ❸

**Chez Haynes,** 3 r. Clauzel, 9ème (☎48 78 40 63). Ⓜ St-Georges. Opened in 1949 and famous for its New Orleans soul food and complimentary cornbread, this was Paris's first African-American-owned restaurant. A former hangout of Louis Armstrong, James Baldwin, and Richard Wright. Most entrees under €16. F-Sa nights live music; cover €5. Su Brazillian dishes. Open Tu-Su 7pm-midnight. AmEx/MC/V. ❸

## RIGHT BANK EAST

▨ **Lao Siam,** 49 r. de Belleville, 19ème (☎40 40 09 68). Ⓜ Belleville. Even before your food arrives, you'll be impressed by this Chinese and Thai favorite. A unique Thai-dried calamari salad (€6.30) makes for a light preamble to the *poulet royal au curry* (€8.40) or *filet du poisson* with "hip-hop" sauce (€8.60). Wash it down with a *citron pressé* (lemonade, €2.30) and finish it off with kumquats (€2.80). Open daily noon-3pm and 7-11pm. MC/V. ❶

▨ **Le Bar à Soupes,** 33 r. Charonne, 11ème (☎43 57 53 79; www.lebarasoupes.com). Ⓜ Bastille. Featuring—you guessed it—big bowls of tasty soup (€5.50). The €10 lunch *menu* comes with a roll, salad, or cheese plate, soup, and wine or coffee. Try gooey *gateau chocolat* (€3) for dessert. Open M-Sa noon-3pm, 6:30-11pm. MC/V. ❶

 **SAVE YOUR WALLET, HAVE A PICNIC.** As a major tourist attraction, Montmartre has inevitably high prices. Save a couple euro by avoiding its touristy cafes, and picnic over Paris. Buy a *croque monsieur* or ham sandwich *à emporter,* and eat on the church's steps.

**Bob's Juice Bar,** 15 r. Lucien-Sampaix, 10ème (☎06 82 63 72 74; www.bobsjuice-bar.com). Ⓜ Jacques Bonsergent. This vegetarian eatery serves freshly made juices (€3-4.50), pancakes (€2), salads, sandwiches, and soups. A large communal table gives it a social character, and the cool indie tunes add style points. Over a dozen *formules* (€5-9). Open Tu-F 7:30am-6pm, Sa-Su 7:30am-4pm. Cash only. ❶

**Babylone,** 21 r. Daval, 11ème (☎47 00 55 02). Ⓜ Bastille. In an area full of cheap sandwich shops and crepe stands, this *Shawarma* and falafel spot stands out. Flickering neon sign and a checkered tile floor exude a 50s diner vibe. Falafel €4. *Shawarma* €5. Falafel and *Shawarma* sandwich €5. Open M 10am-7pm, Tu-Sa 10am-12:30am. Cash only. ❶

**Le Soleil Gourmand,** 10 r. Ravignan, 18ème (☎42 51 00 50). Ⓜ Abbesses. Local favorite serves light *Provençale* fare in a cheerful, half-underground dining room. Try the *bricks* (grilled stuffed filo dough; €11) or the 5-cheese *tartes* with salad (€11). Vegetarian options like the *assiette sud* (grilled and marinated vegetables; €13). Open daily 12:30-2:30pm and 7:30-11pm. ❷

**Les Broches à l'Ancienne,** 21 r. St-Nicolas, 12ème (☎43 43 26 16). Ⓜ Ledru-Rollin. Follow your nose: the meats are slow-cooked over flames in a stone oven. Dark wood sets the tone for serious food at surprisingly low prices. Shoulder of lamb with *frites* €18. Appetizers €5-9. Some F nights jazz at 8pm; dinner and performance about €25. Open late Aug.-early Aug. Open M-Sa noon-2:30pm and 7-10:30pm. AmEx/MC/V. ❸

**L'Ebauchoir,** 45 r. de Citeaux, 12ème (☎43 42 49 31). Ⓜ Faidherbe-Chaligny. Funky decorations and a stainless steel fan give L'Ebauchoir a fun, informal character. 3-course lunch *menu* €14. *Plats* from €15. Open M 8-11pm, Tu-Sa noon-11pm. Kitchen open noon-2:30pm and 8-11pm. MC/V. ❹

**Refuge des Fondues,** 17 r. des Trois Frères, 18ème (☎42 55 22 65). Ⓜ Abbesses. Only 2 main dishes: *fondue bourguignonne* (meat fondue) and *fondue savoyarde* (cheese fondue). *Menu* with wine, *amuse-gueule* (light appetizer), fondue, and dessert €16. Open Sept.-June daily 5pm-2am; July-Aug. Tu-Sa 5pm-2am. Kitchen open Sept.-June daily 7pm-12:30am; July-Aug. Tu-Sa 7pm-12:30am. Reserve ahead. ❸

**Le Sancerre,** 35 r. des Abbesses, 18ème (☎42 58 08 20). Ⓜ Abbesses. A modernized cafe with a topless mermaid on the ceiling and simple, delicious dishes like tomato and mozzarella salad (€7). Wines €3-5. Beer €4-6. *Apéritifs* €4-8. Open daily 7am-2am. MC/V. ❶

## SALONS DU THÉ (TEA ROOMS)

▨**Café de l'Industrie,** 15-17 r. St-Sabin, 12ème (☎47 00 13 53). Ⓜ Breguet-Sabin. A happening, cozy cafe frequented by funky 20-somethings. l'Industrie may be the only restaurant in Paris to straddle a street. Diverse menu includes tagliatelle with pesto (€10). Marlin €14. Coffee €2.50. *Vin chaud* (warm wine) €4.50. Popular fruit-filled brunch Sa-Su €18. Open daily 10am-2am. Lunch served noon-2pm. MC/V. ❸

**Mariage Frères,** 30 r. du Bourg-Tibourg, 4ème (☎42 72 28 11). Ⓜ Hôtel-de-Ville. Started by 2 brothers who found British tea shoddy, this salon offers 500 varieties of tea (€7-15). While the clientele contribute to the salon's refined aura, it's the waiters in cream-colored linen suits that really seal the deal. Tea *menu* includes sandwiches, pastries, and tea (€30). Classic brunch *menu* (brioche, eggs, tea, cakes) €30-36. Snob Salad piled high with *foie gras* and smoked salmon €24. For brunch, reserve ahead. Also at 13 r. des Grands Augustins, 6ème (☎40 51 82 50) and at 260 r. du Faubourg St-Honoré, 8ème (☎46 22 18 54). Open daily 10:30am-7:30pm; lunch M-Sa noon-3pm; afternoon tea 3-6:30pm; Su brunch 12:30-6:30pm. AmEx/MC/V. ❹

## SPECIALTY SHOPS

Food shops, particularly *boulangeries* (bakeries) and *pâtisseries* (pastry shops), are on virtually every street in Paris, or at least it seems like it. Your gustatory experiences, particularly when buying breads or pastries, will vary depending on how recently your food has left the oven.

▨**Amorino,** 47 r. St-Louis-en-l'Île, 4ème (☎44 07 48 08). Ⓜ Pont Marie. With a selection of 20 *gelati* and *sorbetti* flavors (more in summer), Amorino serves amazing concoctions in more generous portions than its better known neighborhood rivals. Ask for as many flavors as you want at no extra charge. Your cone (€3-5.50) or cup (€3-8.50) will look like a work of art. ❶

▨**La Fournée d'Augustine,** 31 r. des Batignolles, 17ème (☎48 89 91 54). Ⓜ Rome. This closet-sized *pâtisserie* bakes an absolutely fantastic baguette (€1). With lunchtime lines out the door, it's hard to miss. Sandwiches (€3-4), made with fresh bread, range from light to more substantial. Grab a *pain au chocolat* (€1) or a *congolais* (individually sized coconut cake; €2). Open M-Sa 7am-8pm. MC/V, min. €10. ❶

**Gusto Italia,** 199 r. de Grenelle, *7ème* (☎45 55 00 43). ⓜ École Militaire. This unassuming spot sells a small selection of cheeses, meats, and wines. Authentic Italian lasagna or pizza big enough to share €11. Lunch served daily noon-3pm. ❷

**Berthillon,** 31 r. St-Louis-en-l'Île, *4ème* (☎43 54 31 61). ⓜ Cité or Pont Marie. Berthillon plays up its own celebrity so well—it's reputed to have Paris's best ice cream—you may trick yourself into believing your tiny scoop was worth €2. Look for stores nearby that sell Berthillon indulgences. The wait is shorter, they usually offer a wider selection of flavors, and they're open in late July and Aug. Single scoop €2; double €3; triple €4. Open Sept. to mid-July W-Su 10am-8pm. Closed 2 weeks in Feb. and Apr. ❶

# MARKETS

▨ **Saxe-Breteuil Outdoor Market,** 15*ème*. ⓜ Ségur. Exit the Metro and walk against traffic on r. Perignon to the market. With the Eiffel tower poised gracefully in the distance, Saxe-Breteuil backs up its impeccable style with an incredible selection of produce, seafood, and cheese, including even a falafel stand. A wine vendor frequently hands out samples of the day's stock if you ask nicely. It's best to arrive before noon, after which vendors begin to run low on produce. Open Sa 7am-3pm.

**Davoli,** 32 r. Cler, *7ème* (☎45 51 23 41). ⓜ École Militaire. Gourmet paradise Davoli is a tiny food-market with a celebrity pedigree (sightings include Catherine Deneuve and Jeanne Moreau). Perfect for budget travelers caught in a rich neighborhood, Davoli has a selection of meats, cheeses, baked goods, and prepared foods sure to be a guaranteed hit. Try their quiche lorraine (€2.20 for one) or go out on a limb with *escargots de bourgogne* (€8.20 per dozen).

**Belleville Outdoor Market,** 20*ème*. ⓜ Belleville. Produce, spices, sneakers, belts, and everything else you can think of squeezed onto bd. de Belleville. Not for the faint of heart; vendors behind the tables bellow at anyone who walks by. Strong Middle Eastern influence. Look out for pickpockets. Open Tu and F 7:30am-2:30pm.

# ◉ SIGHTS

While it would take weeks to see all of Paris's monuments, museums, and gardens, the city's small size makes sightseeing easy and enjoyable. In a few hours, you can walk from the Bastille in the east to the Eiffel Tower in the west, passing most major monuments along the way. A solid day of wandering will show you how close the medieval Notre Dame is to the modern Centre Pompidou and the funky Latin Quarter to the royal Louvre—the diversity of Paris is all the more amazing for the compact area in which it unfolds.

## CITY CENTER

In the 3rd century BC, Paris consisted only of the **Île de la Cité,** inhabited by the Parisii, a Gallic tribe of merchants and fishermen. Today, all distance-points in France are measured from *kilomètre zéro*, a sundial in front of Notre Dame. On the far west side of the island is the **Pont Neuf** (New Bridge), actually Paris's oldest bridge—and now the city's most popular make-out spot. (ⓜ *Pont Neuf.*) To the east of Île de la Cité is the tiny **Île Saint-Louis.** Rue Saint-Louis-en-l'Île rolls down the center, and is a welcome distraction from busy Parisian life. There's a wealth of ice cream parlors, upscale shops, and boutique hotels, but not much to see. (ⓜ *Pont Marie.*) On right bank, the **Marais** is home to some of Paris's best falafel (p. 275), museums, bars, as well as much of Paris's Orthodox Jewish community. At the end of **rue des Francs-Bourgeois** sits the magnificent **place des Vosges,** Paris's oldest public square. Molière, Racine, and Voltaire filled the grand parlors with their *bon* *mots*, while seven-year-old Mozart played a concert here. Victor Hugo lived at no. 6, which is now a museum devoted to his life. (Ⓜ *Chemin Vert or St-Paul.*)

**CATHÉDRALE DE NOTRE DAME DE PARIS.** This 12th- to 14th-century cathedral, begun under Bishop Maurice de Sully, is one of the world's most famous and beautiful examples of medieval architecture. After the Revolution, the building fell into disrepair—it was even used to shelter livestock—until Victor Hugo's 1831 novel *Notre Dame de Paris* (a.k.a. *The Hunchback of Notre Dame*) inspired citizens to lobby for the cathedral's restoration. The apocalyptic facade and seemingly weightless walls—effects produced by Gothic engineering and optical illusions—are inspiring even for the most church-weary. The cathedral's biggest draws are its enormous stained-glass rose windows that dominate the transept's northern and southern ends. A staircase inside the towers leads to a perch from which gargoyles survey the city. The best time to view the Cathedral is late at night, when you can see the full facade without mobs blocking the view. (Ⓜ *Cité.* ☎ *42 34 56 10. Cathedral open daily 7:45am-7pm. Towers open July-Aug. M-F 10am-6:30pm, Sa-Su 10am-11pm; Apr.-June and Sept. daily 10am-6:30pm; Oct.-Mar. daily 10am-5:30pm. English-language tours W-Th noon, Sa 2:30pm; free. Cathedral and towers €7.50, 18-25 €5, under 18 free.*)

**STE-CHAPELLE, CONCIERGERIE, AND PALAIS DE JUSTICE.** The **Palais de la Cité** contains three vastly different buildings. ◤**Ste-Chapelle** remains the foremost example of flamboyant Gothic architecture and a tribute to the craft of medieval stained glass. On sunny days, light pours through the Upper Chapel's windows, illuminating frescoes of saints and martyrs. Around the corner is the **Conciergerie**, one of Paris's most famous prisons; Marie-Antoinette and Robespierre were incarcerated here during the Revolution. (*6 bd. du Palais.* Ⓜ *Cité.* ☎ *53 40 60 93. Open daily Mar.-Oct. 9:30am-6pm; Nov.-Feb. 9am-5pm. Last entry 30min. before closing. €7.50, seniors and 18-25 €4.80, under 18 free. Combo ticket with Conciergerie €9.50/7/free.*) Built after the great fire of 1776, the **Palais de Justice** houses France's district courts. (*4 bd. du Palais.* Ⓜ *Cité.* ☎ *44 32 51 51. Courtrooms open M-F 9am-noon and 1:30-end of last trial. Free.*)

**MÉMORIAL DE LA DÉPORTATION.** Commemorating the 200,000 French victims of Nazi concentration camps, the museum includes a tunnel lined with 200,000 quartz pebbles that reflects the Jewish custom of placing stones on graves. (Ⓜ *Cité. At the very tip of the island on pl. de l'Île de France. Open daily Apr.-Sept. 10am-noon and 2-7pm; Oct.-Mar. 10am-noon and 2-5pm. Last entry 10min. before closing. Free.*)

**HÔTEL DE VILLE.** Paris's grandiose city hall dominates a large square filled with fountains and *Belle Époque* lampposts. The present edifice is a 19th-century replica of the original medieval structure, a meeting hall for the cartel that controlled traffic on the Seine. (*29 r. de Rivoli.* Ⓜ *Hôtel-de-Ville.* ☎ *42 76 43 43. Open M-F 9am-7pm when there is an exhibit, 9am-6pm otherwise.*)

# LEFT BANK EAST

The **Latin Quarter,** named for the prestigious universities that taught in Latin until 1798, lives for its ever-vibrant student population. Since the student riots in May 1968, many artists and intellectuals have migrated to the cheaper outer *arrondissements*, and the *haute bourgeoisie* have moved in. The 5*ème* still presents the most diverse array of bookstores, cinemas, and jazz clubs in the city. Designer shops and edgy art galleries are found around **St-Germain-des-Prés** in the 6*ème*. Farther east, the residential 13*ème* doesn't have much to attract the typical tourist, but its diverse neighborhoods offer an authentic view of Parisian life.

◤**JARDIN DU LUXEMBOURG.** Parisians sunbathers flock to these formal gardens. A Roman residential area, the site of a medieval monastery, and later home to 17th-century French royalty, the gardens were liberated during the Revolution. (*6ème.* Ⓜ *Odéon or RER: Luxembourg. Main entrance on bd. St-Michel. Open daily dawn-dusk.*)

**ODÉON.** The **Cour du Commerce St-André** is one of the most picturesque walking areas in the 6*ème*, with cobblestone streets, centuries-old cafes (including **Le Procope**), and outdoor seating. Just south of bd. St-Germain, the **Carrefour de l'Odéon,** a favorite Parisian hangout, has more bistros and cafes. (Ⓜ *Odéon.*)

**ÉGLISE ST-GERMAIN-DES-PRÉS.** Paris's oldest standing church, Église de St-Germain-des-Prés was the centerpiece of the Abbey of St-Germain-des-Prés, the crux of Catholic intellectual life until it was disbanded during the Revolution. Worn away by fire and even a saltpetre explosion, the abbey's exterior looks appropriately world-weary. Its interior frescoes, redone in the 19th century, depict the life of Jesus in striking maroon, green, and gold. (3 pl. St-Germain-des-Prés. Ⓜ *St-Germain-des-Prés.* ☎ 55 42 81 18. Open daily 8am-7:45pm. Info office open M 2:30-6:45pm, Tu-F 10:30am-noon and 2:30-6:45pm, Sa 3-6:45pm.)

**PLACE ST-MICHEL AND ENVIRONS.** At the center of the Latin Quarter, bd. St-Michel, which divides the 5*ème* and 6*ème*, is filled with bookstores, boutiques, cafes, and restaurants. Tourists pack pl. St-Michel, where the 1871 Paris Commune and the 1968 student uprising began. You can find many traditional bistros on nearby r. Soufflot, the street connecting the Luxembourg Gardens to the Pantheon, and smaller restaurants on r. des Fossés St-Jacques. (Ⓜ *St-Michel.*)

**LA SORBONNE.** The Sorbonne is one of Europe's oldest universities, founded in 1253 by Robert de Sorbon as a dormitory for 16 theology students. Nearby **place de la Sorbonne,** off bd. St-Michel, is flooded with cafes, bookstores, and during term-time, students. The **Chapelle de la Sorbonne**, which usually houses temporary exhibits on arts and letters, is undergoing renovations through 2009. (45-47 r. des Écoles. Ⓜ *Cluny-La Sorbonne or RER: Luxembourg.*)

**PANTHÉON.** Though it looks like a religious monument, the Pantheon, occupying the Left Bank's highest point, celebrates France's great thinkers. The crypt houses the tombs of Marie and Pierre Curie, Victor Hugo, Jean Jaurès, Rousseau, Voltaire, and Émile Zola. On the main level, **Foucault's Pendulum** confirms the rotation of the earth. Outside (Pl. du Panthéon. Ⓜ *or RER: Cardinal Lemoine.* ☎ 44 32 18 04. Open daily Apr.-Sept. 10am-6:30pm; Oct.-Mar. 10am-6pm. Last entry 45min. before closing. €7.50, 18-25 €5, under 18 and Oct.-Mar. 1st Su of each month free.)

**RUE MOUFFETARD.** South of pl. de la Contrescarpe, r. Mouffetard plays host to one of Paris's busiest **street markets,** drawing a mix of Parisians and visitors. The stretch of r. Mouffetard past pl. de la Contrescarpe and onto r. Descartes and r. de la Montagne Ste-Geneviève is the quintessential Latin Quarter stroll. (Ⓜ *Cardinal Lemoine, Pl. Monge, or Censier Daubenton.*)

**MOSQUÉE DE PARIS.** The **Institut Musulman** houses the Persian gardens, elaborate minaret, and shady porticoes of the Mosquée de Paris, a beautiful mosque constructed in 1920 by French architects to honor North African countries' role in WWI. Travelers can relax in the Turkish baths at the exquisite *hammam* or sip mint tea in the relaxing cafe. (39 r. St-Hilaire. Ⓜ *Censier Daubenton. Walk down r. Daubenton and turn left on r. Georges Desplas; the mosque is on the right.* ☎ 43 31 38 20; www.la-mosquee.com. Open daily 10am-noon and 2-5:30pm. Tour €3, students €2. Hammam open for men Tu 2-9pm, Su 10am-9pm; women M, W-Th, Sa 10am-9pm, F 2-9pm. €15.)

**JARDIN DES PLANTES.** Opened in 1640 to grow medicinal plants for King Louis XIII, the garden now features science museums, rosaries, and a zoo, which Parisians raided for food during the Prussian siege of 1871. (Ⓜ *Gare d'Austerlitz, Jussieu, or Censier-Daubenton.* ☎ 40 79 37 94. Jardin and rosarie open daily in summer 7:30am-8pm; in winter 8am-5:30pm. Free. Zoo open daily Apr.-Sept. 10am-6pm; Oct.-Mar. 10am-5:30pm. Last entry 30min. before closing. €6, students €4.)

**BIBLIOTHÈQUE NATIONALE DE FRANCE: SITE FRANÇOIS MITTERRAND.** The complex that many Parisians refer to as "the ugliest building ever built" is the result of the last, most expensive of Mitterrand's *Grands Projets*. Its L-shaped towers of Dominique Perrault's controversial design resemble open books. Its rotating art, literary, and photography exhibits are a welcome break from the city center's packed sights. Avoid going around opening hours, especially during university exam season, when students line up around the block to get a desk. (*Q. F. Mauriac. ☎ 53 79 59 79; www.bnf.fr. Ⓜ Q. de la Gare or Bibliothèque François Mitterand. Reception M 2-7pm, Tu-Sa 9am-7pm, Su 1-7pm; closed Su Sept. 16+. €3.50. MC/V.*)

**CHINATOWN (QUARTIER CHINOIS).** Paris's Chinatown is bound by r. de Tolbiac, bd. Masséna, av. de Choisy, and av. d'Ivry. It is home to large Chinese, Vietnamese, Thai, and Cambodian communities and a host of Asian restaurants and shops. (*Ⓜ Pl. d'Italie, Porte de Choisy, Tolbiac, or Maison Blanche.*)

**QUARTIER DE LA BUTTE-AUX-CAILLES.** Historically a working-class neighborhood, the old-fashioned Butte-aux-Cailles (Quail Knoll) Quarter now attracts trend-setters, artists, and intellectuals. Funky new restaurants and galleries have cropped up in recent years. **Rue de la Butte-aux-Cailles** and **rue des Cinq Diamants** share duties as the quartier's main drags. (*Ⓜ Corvisart. Exit onto bd. Blanqui and turn onto r. Barrault, which will meet r. de la Butte-aux-Cailles.*)

# LEFT BANK WEST

**▨ EIFFEL TOWER.** Gustave Eiffel wrote of his tower: "France is the only country in the world with a 300m flagpole." Designed in 1889 as the tallest structure in the world, the Eiffel Tower was conceived as a modern monument to engineering that would surpass the Egyptian pyramids in size and notoriety. Critics dubbed it a "metal asparagus" and a "Parisian tower of Babel." Writer Guy de Maupassant ate lunch every day at its ground-floor restaurant—the only place in Paris, he claimed, from which he couldn't see the offensive thing. Nevertheless, when it was inaugurated in March 1889 as the centerpiece of the World's Fair, the tower earned Parisians' love: nearly two million people ascended it during the fair. Some still criticize its glut of tourists, trinkets, and vagrants, but don't believe the anti-hype—the tower is worth seeing. (*Ⓜ Bir-Hakeim or Trocadéro. ☎ 44 11 23 23; www.toureiffel.fr. Open daily mid-June to Aug. 9am-midnight; Sept. to mid-June 9:30am-11pm; stairs 9:30am-6pm. Last access to top 30min. before closing. Elevator to 1st fl. €5, under 12 €2.30, to 2nd fl. €8/4.30, to top €12/6.30. Stairs to 1st and 2nd fl. €3.50. Under 3 free.*)

**CHAMPS DE MARS.** The Champs de Mars, a tree-lined expanse stretching from the École Militaire to the Eiffel Tower, is named, appropriately enough, after the Roman god of war. Close to the 7ème's monuments and museums, the field was a drill ground for the École Militaire during Napoleon's reign. Today, despite frolicking children and a monument to international peace, the Champs can't quite hold a candle to Paris's many spectacular public parks and gardens. (*Ⓜ La Motte Picquet-Grenelle or École Militaire. From the av. de la Motte-Picquet, walk toward École Militaire.*)

**INVALIDES.** The gold-leaf dome of the **Hôtel des Invalides,** built by Napoleon as a hospital for crippled and ill soldiers, shines at the center of the 7ème. The grassy **Esplanade des Invalides** runs from the *hôtel* to the **Pont Alexandre III,** a bridge with gilded lampposts from which you can catch a great view of the Invalides and the Seine. Both housed inside the Invalides complex, the **Musée de l'Armée** and **Musée de l'Ordre de la Libération,** documenting the Free France movement under General de Gaulle, are worth a look; the real star, however, is the ▨**Musée des Plans-Reliefs,** which features dozens of enormous, detailed models of French fortresses and towns, all made around 1700. **Napoleon's tomb** is also here, resting in the **Église St-Louis.** (*127 r. de Grenelle. Ⓜ Invalides. Enter from either pl. des Invalides or pl. Vauban and av. de Tourville. Open daily Apr.-Sept. 10am-6pm; Oct.-Mar. 10am-5pm.*)

**CATACOMBS.** Originally excavated to provide stone for building Paris, the Catacombs were converted into a mass grave in 1785 when the stench of the city's public cemeteries became unbearable. Built twice as far underground as the Metro, Paris's "municipal ossuary" now has dozens of winding tunnels and hundreds of thousands of bones. *(1 av. du Colonel Henri Rol-Tanguy. Ⓜ Denfert-Rochereau. Exit to pl. Denfert-Rochereau and cross av. du Colonel Henri Roi-Tanguy. ☎ 43 22 47 63. 45min. tours. Open Tu-Su 10am-4pm. €7, over 60 €5.50, 14-26 €3.50, under 14 free. MC/V; min. €15.)*

**BOULEVARD DU MONTPARNASSE.** In the early 20th century, avant-garde artists like Chagall, Duchamp, Léger, and Modigliani moved to Montparnasse. Soviet exiles Lenin and Trotsky talked strategy over cognac in cafes like **Le Dôme, Le Sélect,** and **La Coupole.** After WWI, Montparnasse attracted American expats like Calder, Hemingway, and Henry Miller. Chain restaurants and tourists crowd the now heavily commercialized street. Classic cafes like pricey **La Coupole** still hold their own, however, providing a wonderful place to sip coffee, read Apollinaire, and daydream away. *(Ⓜ Montparnasse-Bienvenüe or Vavin.)*

**ⓂPARC ANDRÉ CITROËN.** The futuristic Parc André Citroën was created by landscapers Alain Provost and Gilles Clément in the 1990s. Hot-air balloon rides launch from the central garden and offer spectacular aerial views of Paris. *(Ⓜ Javelor Balard. ☎ 44 26 20 00; www.aeroparis.com. Park open 24hr. Balloon rides M-F 7am-9:30pm, Sa-Su 9am-9:30pm. Sa-Su and holidays 10min. rides €12, 12-17 €10, 3-11 €6, under 3 free; M-F €10/9/5/free.)*

# RIGHT BANK WEST

**OPÉRA GARNIER.** The exterior of the Opéra Garnier—with its newly restored multi-colored marble facade, sculpted golden goddesses, and ornate columns and friezes—is as impressive as it is kitschy. It's no wonder that Oscar Wilde once swore he saw an angel floating on the sidewalk. Inside, Chagall's whimsical ceiling design contrasts with the gold and red that dominate the theater. For shows, see **Entertainment,** p. 288. *(Ⓜ Opéra. ☎ 08 92 89 90 90; www.operadeparis.fr. Concert hall and museum open daily mid-July to Aug. 10am-5:30pm; Sept. to mid-July 10am-4:30pm. Concert hall closed during rehearsals; call ahead. €8, students and under 25 €4. English-language tours daily 11:30am and 2:30pm; €12, seniors €10, students €9, under 10 €6.)*

**PLACE DE LA CONCORDE.** Paris's most infamous public square, built between 1757 and 1777, is the eastern terminus of the Champs-Élysées at its intersection with the Jardin des Tuileries. During the Revolution and Reign of Terror, the area became known as the **place de la Révolution,** site of the guillotine that severed the heads of 1343 aristocrats, including Louis XVI, Marie Antoinette, and Robespierre. In 1830, the square was optimistically renamed *concorde* (peace) and the 3200-year-old **Obélisque de Luxor,** given to Charles X by the Viceroy of Egypt, replaced the guillotine. *(Ⓜ Concorde.)*

**AVENUE DES CHAMPS-ELYSÉES.** Extending from the Louvre, Paris's most famous thoroughfare was a piecemeal project begun under the reign of Louis XIV. The center of Parisian opulence in the early 20th century, with flashy mansions towering above exclusive cafes, the Champs has since undergone a bizarre kind of democratization. Shops along the avenue now range from designer fashion to low-budget tchotchkes. While it may be an inelegant spectacle, the Champs offers some of the city's best people-watching—tourists, wealthy bar-hoppers, even authentic Parisians crowd its broad sidewalks throughout the week. *(Ⓜ Charles de Gaulle-Étoile. Runs from the pl. Charles de Gaulle-Étoile southeast to the pl. de la Concorde.)*

**ⓂARC DE TRIOMPHE.** Napoleon commissioned the Arc, at the western end of the Champs-Elysées, in 1806 to honor his Grande Armée. In 1940, Parisians were brought to tears by the sight of Nazis goose-stepping through the Arc. At the end of the German occupation, a sympathetic Allied army made sure that a French general would be the first to drive under the arch. The terrace at the top has a fabulous view. The **Tomb of the Unknown Soldier** has been under the Arc

FRANCE

since November 11, 1920 while an eternal flame has been burning since 1921. *(Pl. Charles de Gaulle. Ⓜ Charles-de-Gaulle-Étoile. ☎ 43 80 31 31. Open daily Apr.-Sept. 10am-11pm; Oct.-Mar. 10am-10:30pm. €8, 18-25 €5, under 18 free.)*

**CATHÉDRALE ALEXANDRE-NEVSKY.** The onion-domed Cathédrale Alexandre-Nevski, also known as the **Église Russe**, is Paris's primary Russian Orthodox church and unofficial Russian cultural center. The spectacular and recently restored interior, lavishly decorated with icons, was painted by artists from St. Petersburg in gold, deep reds, blues, and greens—classic Byzantine style. *(12 r. Daru. Ⓜ Ternes. ☎ 42 27 37 34. Open Tu, F, Su 3-5pm. Services in French and Russian: Sa 6-8pm, Su 10am-12:30pm, other times posted on church calendar.)*

**TROCADÉRO.** In the 1820s, the Duc d'Angoulême built a memorial to his victory in Spain at Trocadéro. For the 1937 World's Fair, Jacques Carlu created the **Palais de Chaillot**, which features two white stone wings and an imposing, austere veranda. The terrace, flanked by two theaters, offers brilliant views of the Eiffel Tower. Be wary of pickpockets and traffic, however, as you gaze upward. *(Ⓜ Trocadéro.)*

**BOIS DE BOULOGNE.** By day, this 2000-acre park, with several gardens, stadiums, and two lakes, is a popular picnicking, jogging, and bike-riding spot. By night, the *bois* becomes a bazaar of crime, drugs, and prostitution. *(On the western edge of the 16ème. Ⓜ Porte Maillot, Sablons, Pont de Neuilly, or Porte Dauphine or Porte d'Auteil.)*

**🔳 LA DÉFENSE.** Outside the city limits, west of the 16*ème*, the skyscrapers and modern architecture of La Défense make up Paris's newest (unofficial) *arrondissement*, a playground for many of Paris's biggest corporations. Its centerpiece is hard to miss: the **Grande Arche de la Défense** stretches 35 stories into the air and is shaped like a hollow cube. The roof of this unconventional office covers one hectare—Notre Dame could fit in its concave core. *(1 parvis de la Défense, 92040 Paris-La Défense. Ⓜ or RER: La Défense. ☎ 49 07 27 57; www.paris.org/Monuments/Defense. Open daily 9am-8pm. Winter reduced hours. €8, students and under 18 €6.)*

# RIGHT BANK EAST

**PLACE DE LA BASTILLE.** This busy intersection was once home to the famous Bastille Prison, stormed on July 14, 1789, sparking the French Revolution. Two days later, the National Assembly ordered the prison demolished, but the ground plan of the prison's turrets remains embedded in the road near r. Saint-Antoine. At the center of the square is a monument of the winged Mercury holding a torch of freedom, symbolizing France's movement towards democracy. *(Ⓜ Bastille.)*

**OPÉRA DE LA BASTILLE.** One of Mitterrand's *Grands Projets*, the Opéra opened in 1989 to loud protests over its unattractive design. It has been described as a huge toilet because of its resemblance to the city's coin-operated *pissoirs*. The opera has not struck a completely sour note, though, as it has helped renew local interest in the arts. The guided tour offers a behind-the-scenes view of the world's largest theater. *(130 r. de Lyon. Ⓜ Bastille. Look for the words "Billeterie" on the building. ☎ 08 92 89 90 90; www.opera-de-paris.fr. Open daily 10am-6pm. Last entry 30min. before closing. 1hr. French-language tours usually 2 per day; call ahead; English-language tours for groups of 10 or more. €12, students and under 25 €9, under 10 €6.)*

**BAL DU MOULIN ROUGE.** Along bd. de Clichy and bd. de Rochechouart, you'll find many Belle Époque cabarets and nightclubs, including the Bal du Moulin Rouge, immortalized by Toulouse-Lautrec's paintings, Offenbach's music, and Baz Luhrmann's 2001 Hollywood blockbuster. The crowd consists of tourists out for an evening of sequins, tassels, and skin. The revues are still risqué, but the real shock is the price of admission. *(82 bd. de Clichy. Ⓜ Blanche. ☎ 53 09 82 82; www.moulin-rouge.com. Shows daily 7, 9, 11pm. Tickets €89-175; includes champagne.)*

■**BASILIQUE DU SACRÉ-COEUR.** This ethereal basilica, with its signature shining white onion domes, was commissioned to atone for France's war crimes in the Franco-Prussian War. During WWII, 13 bombs were dropped on Paris, all near the structure, but miraculously no one was killed. This inspired fervent devotion made Sacré-Coeur an even holier site. *(35 r. du Chevalier-de-la-Barre. ⓜ Anvers or Abbesses. ☎ 53 41 89 00. Open daily 6am-11pm. Wheelchair-accessible. Free. Dome open daily 9am-6pm. €5. Crypt open periodically.)*

■**CIMITIÈRE PÈRE LACHAISE.** This cemetery holds the remains of such famous Frenchmen as Balzac, Bernhardt, Colette, David, Delacroix, Piaf, La Fontaine, Haussmann, Molière, Proust, and Seurat within its peaceful paths and elaborate sarcophagi. Foreigners buried here include Chopin, Modigliani, Gertrude Stein, and Oscar Wilde, though the most frequently visited grave is that of Jim Morrison. French Leftists make a ceremonial pilgrimage to the **Mur des Fédérés** (Wall of the Federals), where 147 *communards* were executed in 1871. *(16 r. du Repos. 20ème. ⓜ Père Lachaise. ☎ 55 25 82 10. Open Mar.-Oct. M-F 8am-6pm, Sa 8:30am-6pm, Su and holidays 9am-6pm; Nov.-Feb. M-F 8am-5:30pm, Sa 8:30am-5:30pm, Su and holidays 9am-5:30pm. Last entry 15min. before closing. Free. Call ☎ 40 71 75 60 for tour times and fares.)*

**PARC DES BUTTES-CHAUMONT.** In the south of the 19*ème*, Parc des Buttes-Chaumont is a mix of manmade topography and transplanted vegetation; previously a lime quarry and gallows, Napoleon III commissioned Baron Haussman to redesign the space in 1862. Today's visitors walk the winding paths surrounded by lush greenery and dynamic—sometimes exhausting—hills, enjoying a great view of the *quartier* from the Roman temple atop cave-filled cliffs. *(ⓜ Buttes-Chaumont or Botzaris. Open daily May-Sept. 7am-10:15pm; Oct.-May 7am-8:15pm. Some gates close early.)*

**PARC DE LA VILLETTE.** Previously a meatpacking district, La Villette is the product of a successful urban renewal project. Inaugurated by President Mitterrand in 1985 as "the place of intelligent leisure," it now contains museums, libraries, and concert halls in the Cité des Sciences and the Cité de la Musique. Every July and August, La Villette holds a free open-air film festival. The Zénith concert hall hosts major rock bands, and the Trabendo jazz and modern music club holds an extraordinarily popular annual jazz festival. *(ⓜ Porte de Pantin. General info ☎ 40 03 75 03. Info office open daily 9:30am-6:30pm. Promenade des Jardins open 6am-1am. Free.)*

# 🏛 MUSEUMS

No visitor should miss Paris's museums, which are universally considered to be among the world's best. Cost-effective for visiting more than three museums or sights daily, the **Carte Musées et Monuments** offers admission to 65 museums in greater Paris. It is available at major museums, tourist office kiosks, and many Metro stations. A pass for one day is €15, for three days €30, for five days €45. Students with art or art history ID can get into art museums free. Most museums, including the **Musée d'Orsay,** are closed on Mondays.

■**MUSÉE D'ORSAY.** If only the *Académiciens* who turned the Impressionists away from the Louvre could see the Musée d'Orsay. Now considered masterpieces, these "rejects" are well worth the pilgrimage to this mecca of modernity. The collection, installed in a former railway station, includes painting, sculpture, decorative arts, and photography from 1848 until WWI. On the ground floor, Clas-

**CROWDLESS CULTURE.** Orsay's undeniably amazing collection draws massive crowds, marring an otherwise enjoyable museum. A Sunday morning or Thursday evening visit will avoid the tourist throngs.

sical and Proto-Impressionist works are on display, including Manet's *Olympia*, a painting that caused scandal when it was unveiled in 1865. Other highlights include Monet's *Poppies*, Renoir's *Bal au moulin de la Galette*, Dégas's *La classe de danse*, and paintings by Cézanne, Gauguin, Seurat, and Van Gogh. The top floor offers one of the most comprehensive collections of Impressionist and Post-Impressionist art in the world. In addition, the exterior and interior balconies offer supreme views of the Seine and the jungle of sculptures below. Don't miss Rodin's imperious *Honoré de Balzac*, or Pompon's adorably big-footed *Ours Blanc*. (*62 r. de Lille, 7ème. Ⓜ Solférino, RER: Musée d'Orsay. Visitor's entrance off 1 r. de la Légion d'Honneur. ☎ 40 49 48 14; www.musee-orsay.fr. Wheelchair-accessible. Open mid-June to mid-Sept. Tu-W and F-Sa 9:30am-6pm, last ticket sales 5pm; Th 10am-9:45pm, last ticket sales 9:15pm; Su 9am-6pm, last ticket sales 5pm. Mid-Sept. to mid-June Tu-W and F-Su 9:30am-6pm, Th 10am-9:45pm. Bookstore open Tu-W and F-Su 9:30am-6:30pm, Th 10am-9:30pm. €7.50, Tu-W and F-Sa 4:15pm, Th after 8pm, and Su €5.50, 18-25 €5, under 18 free. English-language tours 1hr. Tu-Sa 11:30am and 2:30pm, call ahead to confirm; €6.50/5/free. AmEx/MC/V.*)

■ **MUSÉE DU LOUVRE.** No visitor has ever allotted enough time to thoughtfully ponder every display at the Louvre, namely because it would take weeks to read every caption of the over 30,000 items in the museum. Its masterpieces include Hammurabi's Code, Jacques-Louis David's *The Oath of the Horatii* and *The Coronation of Napoleon*, Delacroix's *Liberty Leading the People*, Vermeer's *Lacemaker*, da Vinci's *Mona Lisa*, the classically sculpted Winged Victory of Samothrace, and the Venus de Milo. Enter through I. M. Pei's stunning glass Pyramid in the Cour Napoléon, or skip the line by entering directly from the Métro. The Louvre is organized into three different wings: Denon, Richelieu, and Sully. Each is divided according to the artwork's date, national origin, and medium. (*1er. Ⓜ Palais-Royal/Musée du Louvre. ☎ 40 20 53 17; www.louvre.fr. Open M, Th, Sa 9am-6pm, W and F 9am-10pm. Last entry 45min. before closing. €8.50, W and F after 6pm €6, under 18 free, under 26 F after 6pm free, 1st Su of each month free. MC/V.*)

■ **CENTRE POMPIDOU.** This inside-out building has inspired debate since its 1977 opening. Whatever its aesthetic merits, the exterior's chaotic colored piping provides an appropriate shell for the Cubist, Conceptual, Fauvist, and Pop works inside. The **Musée National d'Art Moderne** is the Centre Pompidou's main attraction. (*Pl. Georges-Pompidou, r. Beaubourg, 4ème. Ⓜ Rambuteau or Hôtel-de-Ville. ☎ 44 78 12 33; www.centrepompidou.fr. Centre open M and W-Su 11am-9:50pm. Museum open M, W-Su 11am-8:50pm, last ticket sales 8pm. €10, under 26 €8, under 18, and 1st Su of each month free.*)

■ **MUSÉE RODIN.** The 18th-century Hôtel Biron holds hundreds of sculptures by Auguste Rodin, including the *The Thinker*, *Bourgeois de Calais*, and *La Porte d'Enfer*. Bring a book and relax amid the gracious gestures of bending flowers and flexing sculptures. (*79 r. de Varenne, 7ème. Ⓜ Varenne. ☎ 44 18 61 10; www.musee-rodin.fr. Open Tu-Su Apr.-Sept. 9:30am-5:45pm; Oct.-Mar. 9:30am-4:45pm. Last entry 30min. before closing. Ground floor and gardens wheelchair-accessible. €6, 18-25 €4, under 18 and 1st Su of the month free; special exhibits €7/5/free. Audio tour €4 for permanent or temporary exhibits; combo ticket €6. Touch tours for the blind available, call ☎ 44 18 61 24. MC/V.*)

■ **MUSÉE JACQUEMART-ANDRÉ.** The 19th-century mansion of Nélie Jacquemart and her husband contains a world-class collection of Renaissance art, including *Madonna and Child* by Botticelli and *St. George and the Dragon* by Ucello. (*158 bd. Haussmann, 8ème. Ⓜ Miromesnil. ☎ 45 62 11 59. Open daily 10am-6pm. Last entry 30min. before closing. €9.50, students and 7-17 €7, under 7 free. 1 free youth 7-17 ticket with every 3 purchased by the same family. Audio tour included. AmEx/MC/V; min. €10.*)

■ **MUSÉE DE CLUNY.** The Musée de Cluny, housed in a monastery built atop Roman baths, holds one of the world's finest collections of medieval art. Works include ■**La Dame et La Licorne** (The Lady and the Unicorn), a striking 15th-century tapestry series. *(6 pl. Paul Painlevé, 5ème. ⓜ Cluny-La Sorbonne. ☎ 53 73 78 00. Open M and W-Sa 9:15am-5:45pm. €7.50, 18-25 and 1st Su of each month €5.50, under 18 free.)*

**▨ EXPLORA SCIENCE MUSEUM.** Dedicated to bringing science to young people, the Explora Science Museum is the star attraction of La Villette, in the complex's Cité des Sciences et de l'Industrie. The building's impressive, futuristic architecture only hints at the close to 300 exhibits waiting inside. *(30 av. Corentin-Cariou, 19ème. ⓜ Porte de la Villette. ☎ 40 05 80 00; www.cite-sciences.fr. Open Tu-Sa 10am-6pm, Su 10am-7pm. Last entry Tu-Sa 5:30pm, Su 6pm. €8, under 25 or families of 5+ €6, under 7 free.)*

**MUSÉE PICASSO.** When Picasso died in 1973, his family paid the French inheritance tax in artwork. The French government put this collection, which includes work from his Cubist, Surrealist, and Neoclassical years, on display in 1985 in the 17th-century Hôtel Salé. *(5 r. de Thorigny, 3ème. ⓜ Chemin Vert. ☎ 42 71 25 21; www.musee-picasso.fr. Open M and W-Su Apr.-Sept. 9:30am-6pm; Oct.-Mar. 9:30am-5:30pm. Last entry 45min. before closing. €7.70, 18-25 €5.70, under 18 and 1st Su of each month free.)*

**INSTITUT DU MONDE ARABE (IMA).** Housing 3rd- through 18th-century Arabesque art, the IMA building was designed to look like the ships that carried North African immigrants to France. Its southern face is comprised of ▨**240 mechanized portals** which automatically open and close depending on how much light is needed to illuminate the interior. *(1 r. des Fossés St-Bernard, 5ème. ⓜ Jussieu. ☎ 40 51 38 38; www.imarabe.org. Open Tu-Su 10am-6pm. €5, under 26 €4, under 12 free.)*

**FONDATION CARTIER POUR L'ART CONTEMPORAINE.** This gallery of contemporary art looks like a futuristic indoor forest, with a stunning glass facade surrounding natural greenery. *(261 bd. Raspail, 14ème. ⓜ Raspail. ☎ 42 18 56 50; www.fondation.cartier.com. Open Tu-Su noon-8pm. €8, students and seniors €6, under 10 free.)*

**MUSÉE CARNAVALET.** Housed in Mme. de Sévigné's 16th-century *hôtel particulier,* this museum presents room after room of historical objects and curiosities from Paris's origins through the present day. *(23 r. de Sévigné, 3ème. ⓜ Chemin Vert. Take r. St-Gilles, which turns into r. de Parc Royal, and turn left on r. de Sévigné. ☎ 44 59 58 58. Open Tu-Su 10am-6pm. Last entry 5pm. Free.)*

**MAISON DE BALZAC.** Honoré de Balzac hid from bill collectors in this three-story hillside mansion, his home from 1840-1847. Here in this tranquil retreat, he wrote a substantial part of *La Comédie Humaine;* today's visitors can see his original manuscripts, along with his beautifully embroidered chair and desk at which he purportedly wrote and edited for 17hr. a day. *(47 r. Raynouard, 16ème. ⓜ Passy. Walk up the hill and turn left onto r. Raynouard. ☎ 55 74 41 80; www.paris.fr/musees/balzac. Open Tu-Su 10am-6pm. Last entry 30min. before closing. Free. Tours €4.50, students and seniors €4.)*

**PALAIS DE TOKYO.** Recently refurbished, this large warehouse contains the **site création contemporaine,** exhibiting today's hottest (and most controversial) art, as well as the ▨**Musée d'Art Moderne de la Ville de Paris.** The museum's unrushed atmosphere and spacious architecture provide a welcome relief from the maelstrom of the Louvre and Musée d'Orsay. *(☎ 53 67 40 00; www.mam.paris.fr. Open Tu and Th-Su 10am-6pm, W 10am-10pm. Permanent collections free; call ahead for temporary exhibit prices.)* The Palais is outfitted to host prominent avant-garde sculptures, video displays, and multimedia installations. Exhibits change every two or three months; be on the lookout for each exhibit's *vernissage* (premiere party) for free entrance and refreshments. *(11 av. du Président Wilson, 16ème. ⓜ Iéna. Follow av. du Président-Wilson with the Seine on your right. ☎ 47 23 38 86; www.palaisdetokyo.com. Open Tu-Su noon-midnight. Wheelchair-accessible. €6, students under 26 €4.50.)*

**MUSÉE D'ART ET D'HISTOIRE DU JUDAÏSME.** Housed in the **Hôtel de St-Aignan,** once a tenement populated by Jews fleeing Eastern Europe, this museum displays a history of Jews in Europe, France, and North Africa. The collection includes extensive and interesting relics from the end of the 19th-century Dreyfus affair, in which Captain Alfred Dreyfus, a French Jew, was wrongfully accused of treason. *(71 r. de Temple, 3ème.* Ⓜ *Rambuteau.* ☎ *53 01 86 60; www.mahj.org. Open M-F 11am-6pm, Su 10am-7pm. Last entry 30min. before closing. €7, 18-26 €4.50, under 18 free. MC/V; min. €12.)*

**MUSÉE D'HISTOIRE NATURELLE.** The Jardin des Plantes is home to the three-part Natural History museum, comprised of the modern **Grande Galerie de l'Evolution,** the **Musée de Minéralogie,** and the ghastly 🖾**Galeries de Paléontologie et d'Anatomie Comparée.** *(57 r. Cuvier, 5ème.* Ⓜ *Gare d'Austerlitz or Jussieu.* ☎ *40 79 32 16; www.mnhn.fr. Grande Galerie de l'Evolution open M and W-Su 10am-6pm. €8, 4-14 and students under €6. Musée de Minéralogie and Galeries de Paléontologie et d'Anatomie Comparée open Apr.-Sept. M and W-F 10am-5pm, Sa-Su 10am-6pm; Oct.-Mar. M and W-Su 10am-5pm. Each museum €6, students €4. Weekend pass for the 3 museums €20, students €15.)*

**MUSÉE DE L'EROTISME.** Paris's Museum of Erotic Art celebrates sex across all media and cultures. Look for King Alfonso XIII of Spain's porno collection and a cigar tray resembling a vagina. Despite the museum's scholarly nature, it is not advised to bring children here. *(72 bd. de Clichy, 18ème.* Ⓜ *Blanche.* ☎ *42 58 28 73; www.musee-erotisme.com. Open daily 10am-2am. €8, students and groups €6.)*

# 🎵 ENTERTAINMENT

Pick up one of the weekly bibles of Parisian entertainment, *Pariscope* (€0.40) and *Figaroscope* (€1), at any newsstand or *tabac. Pariscope* includes an English-language section. For concert listings, check the free magazine *Paris Selection*, available at tourist offices. Free concerts are often held in churches and parks, especially during summer festivals. They are extremely popular, so plan to arrive early. FNAC (p. 291) sells concert tickets.

## OPERA AND THEATER

**La Comédie Française,** pl. Collette, 1er (☎ 44 58 15 15; www.comedie-francaise.fr). Ⓜ Palais-Royal. Founded by Molière, this is the granddaddy of all French theaters. Expect wildly gesticulated slapstick farce. Tickets €11-35. Rush tickets available 1hr. before show. AmEx/MC/V.

**Opéra Garnier,** pl. de l'Opéra, 9ème (☎ 08 92 89 90 90; www.operadeparis.fr). Ⓜ Opéra. Beautiful building (p. 283) hosts ballet and symphonies, as well as operas. Tickets usually available 2 weeks before shows. Box office open M-Sa 10am-6:30pm. Rush tickets on sale 1hr. before showtime. Tickets €5-200. AmEx/MC/V.

**Opéra Comique,** 5 r. Favart, 2ème (☎ 42 44 45 46; www.opera-comique.com). Ⓜ Richelieu-Drouot. Operas on a lighter scale. Upcoming shows include *Porgy and Bess* (June). Box office open M-Sa 9am-9pm. Tickets €6-95. Cheapest tickets (limited visibility) usually available until curtain.

**Opéra de la Bastille,** pl. de la Bastille, 12ème (☎ 08 92 89 90 90; www.operade-paris.fr). Ⓜ Bastille. Opera and ballet with a modern spin. Subtitles in French. Tickets can be purchased by Internet, mail, phone (M-Th 9am-6pm, Sa 9am-1pm), or in person (M-Sa 10:30am-6:30pm). Rush tickets for students under 25 and over 65 15min. before show. For wheelchair access or those with hearing/sight disabilities, call 2 weeks ahead (☎ 40 01 18 50). Tickets €5-160. AmEx/MC/V.

**Marionnettes du Luxembourg,** in the Jardin du Luxembourg, 6ème (☎ 43 26 46 47, groups 43 29 50 97). Ⓜ Vavin. The best *guignol* (puppets) in Paris. This theater has played the same classics since its opening in 1933, including *Little Red Riding Hood* and *The Three Little Pigs*. Performances in summer W 4pm, Sa-Su 11am and 4pm. €4.

## JAZZ AND CABARET

🖾 **Le Baiser Salé,** 58 r. des Lombards (☎ 42 33 37 71; www.lebaisersale.com). Ⓜ Châtelet. Cuban, African, and Antillean music featured with modern jazz and funk in a welcoming, mellow space. Beer €6.50-11.50. Mixed drinks €9. Month-long African music festival in July. Jazz concerts 10pm-2:30am. Cover €12-18. Happy hour 5-8:30pm. Open daily 5pm-6am. AmEx/MC/V.

**Au Duc des Lombards,** 42 r. des Lombards, 1er (☎42 33 22 88; www.ducdeslombards.fr). ⓜ Châtelet. One of France's premier jazz spots. Newly renovated for 2008. Cover €19-23; in advance students €12, couples €30. Beer €7-10. Mixed drinks €10. Music 10pm-1:30am. Open M-Sa 5pm-2am. MC/V.

**Au Lapin Agile,** 22 r. des Saules, 18ème (☎46 06 85 87). ⓜ Lamarck-Coulaincourt. Apollinaire, Picasso, Renoir, and Verlaine hung out here during Montmartre's heyday; now mainly tourists crowd in for comical poems and songs. Drinks €6-7. Shows Tu-Su 9pm-2am. €24, includes 1 drink; students M-F and Su €17.

**Aux Trois Mailletz,** 56 r. Galande, 5ème (☎43 54 00 79; before 5pm 43 25 96 86). ⓜ St-Michel. Walk along the Seine on the Quai St-Michel; turn right on r. du Petit Pont and left on r. Galande. Basement cafe features world music and jazz vocals. Well-dressed students and fortysomethings pack the upper floor. Grog €9. Mixed drinks €13. Club cover Sa-Su €20-25; bar free. Club open daily 10pm-dawn. Bar open daily 5pm-dawn.

## CINEMA

There are many cinemas in Paris, especially in the Latin Quarter and on the Champs-Elysées. The big theater chains—**Gaumont** and **UGC**—offer discounts for five visits or more. Most cinemas offer student, senior, family, and matinee discounts. On Monday and Wednesday, prices drop by about €1.50. Check *Pariscope* or *l'Officiel des Spectacles* for film schedules, prices, and reviews. English-language films in V.O. are shown in English; screenings in V.F. are dubbed into French.

**✉ Accattone,** 20 r. Cujas, 5ème (☎46 33 86 86). ⓜ Luxembourg. Sets the gold-standard for art-house ambience with a carefully selected line-up. Antonioni, Dalí, and Eisenstein are deities here. All in V.O. €6.50, students €5.50.

**Musée du Louvre,** 1er (☎40 20 53 17; www.louvre.fr). ⓜ Louvre. Art films and silent movies. Some English-language films. Open Sept.-June. Free.

**Les Trois Luxembourg,** 67 r. Monsieur-le-Prince, 6ème (☎46 33 97 77). ⓜ Cluny. Turn left on bd. St-Michel, right on r. Racine, and left on r. M-le-Prince. High-quality independent, classic, and foreign films, all in V.O. €7, students and seniors €5.50.

**La Pagode,** 57bis r. de Babylone, 7ème (☎45 55 48 48). ⓜ St-François-Xavier. An 1895 Japanese pagoda re-opened as a cinema in 2000, La Pagode screens independent and classic French films, as well as the occasional American new release (in English, *bien sûr*). Tickets €8; over 60, under 21, students, and M and W €6.50. MC/V.

## FROLICSOME FIREMEN

You know Bastille Day is approaching when two things occur: French flags go up around the city, and all Parisians escape to the countryside. The weekend is the most extravagant and fun of the year, but expats find themselves enjoying the festivities with a large proportion of other tourists. Despite the prevalence of the English language, Bastille "Day" provides an action-packed weekend of fun. For a truly unusual patriotic experience, be sure not to miss **Les Saupeurs Pompiers.**

Paris celebrates the night of July 13th and 14th with huge parties in fire stations called "Fireman's Balls." Makes sense, *n'est-ce pas? Les Saupeurs Pompiers* open the courtyards of their *caserne* (stations) to the public for a night of flowing alcohol, loud music, and, yes, firemen. Doors open at around 9pm, depending on the station, and lines can be very long with waits up to an hour. Show up early or late for shorter queues. The parties go until 4am, but time flies as you dance, drink, and are entertained by shows—not all G-rated—put on by the *pompiers*. Entrance is free and drinks are cheap, usually €2-5.

*For more festival info, see p. 262.* Check online at www.pompiersparis.fr for a list of participating stations and addresses.

# SHOPPING

In a city where Hermès scarves serve as slings for broken arms and department store history stretches back to the mid-19th century, shopping is nothing less than an art form. Shopping is as diverse as the citzens are, from the wild club wear sold near r. Etienne-Marcel to the off-the-beaten path boutiques in the **18ème** or the **Marais**. The great **soldes** (sales) of the year begin after New Year's and at the very end of June, with the best prices at the beginning of February and the end of July. If at any time of year you see the word *braderie* (clearance sale) in a store window, enter without hesitation.

**PARIS COUTURE FOR POCKET CHANGE.** A *stock* is the French version of an outlet store, selling big name clothing for less—often because it has small imperfections or dates from last season. Many are on rue d'Alésia in the 14ème (M: Alésia), including **Cacharel Stock,** no. 114 (☎45 42 53 04; open M-Sa 10am-7pm; AmEx/MC/V); **S.R. Store** (Sonia Rykiel) at no. 112 and no. 64 (☎43 95 06 13; open Tu 11am-7pm, W-Sa 10am-7pm; MC/V); and **Stock Patrick Gerard,** no. 113 (☎40 44 07 40). A large **Stock Kookaï** bustles at 82 rue Réamur, 2ème (☎45 08 17 91; open M 11:30am-7:30pm, Tu-Sa 10:30am-7pm); **Apara Stock** sits at 16 rue Etienne Marcel (☎40 26 70 04); and **Haut-de-Gomme Stock,** with names like Armani, Christian Dior, and Dolce & Gabbana, has 2 locations: 9 rue Scribe, 9ème (M: Opéra; ☎40 07 10 20; open M-Sa 10am-7pm) and 190 rue de Rivoli, 1er (M: Louvre-Rivoli; ☎42 96 97 47; open daily 11am-7pm).

## CLOTHING

**Colette,** 213 r. St-Honoré, 1er (☎55 35 33 90; www.colette.fr). Ⓜ Pyramides. This multi-level boutique has an uncanny knack for knowing what you want before you know you want it. Offering T-shirts, dresses, handbags, jeans, sneakers, art books, DVDs, perfumes, CDs, and stylish gadgets from around the world, with a water bar on the lower level. An extremely wide range of prices makes this a destination for too-cool-for-school kids with some extra cash as well as tried-and-true fashionistas. T-shirts from €50. Pants from €180. Open M-Sa 11am-7pm. AmEx/MC/V.

**Espace Kiliwatch,** 64 r. Tiquetonne, 2ème (☎42 21 17 37). Ⓜ Etienne-Marcel. Walk east down r. Etienne-Marcel and turn right onto r. Tiquetonne. One of Paris's coolest, most popular shops offers secondhand shirts from around €20 and pants from €30. Open M 2-7pm, Tu-Th 11am-7pm, F-Sa 11am-8:30pm. MC/V.

**Alternatives,** 18 rue du Roi de Sicile, 4ème (☎42 78 31 50). M: St-Paul. This upscale secondhand shop sells an eclectic collection, including reasonably priced designer digs. Pants under €100. Christian Louboutin heels as cheap as €50. Only a few customers allowed at a time to ensure quality service. Open Tu-Sa 1-6:30pm. MC/V.

## BOOKS AND MUSIC

**Abbey Bookshop,** 29 r. de la Parcheminerie, 5ème (☎46 33 16 24; www.abbeybookshop.net). Ⓜ St-Michel or Cluny. Located on a road steeped in literary history, the shop overflows with new and used English-language titles. A good selection of travel books. Canadian ex-pat Brian occasionally gives out cups of the best coffee in Paris for free, complete with a dollop of maple syrup. Ask about the Canadian club's author events and Su hikes. Open M-Sa 10am-7pm, sometimes later.

**Shakespeare & Co.,** 37 r.de la Bucherie, 5ème (☎43 25 40 93; www.shakespeareco.org). Ⓜ St-Michel. Terrific English-language bookshop. Scenes from the film *Before Sunset* were shot here. Open daily noon-midnight. MC/V.

**Galignani,** 224 r. de Rivoli, 1er (☎42 60 76 07). Ⓜ Tuileries. Opened in 1810, this was continental Europe's first English-language bookshop. Today has both French and English-language books and magazines. Open M-Sa 10am-7pm. AmEx/MC/V.

**FNAC (Fédération Nationale des Achats et Cadres;** www.fnac.com), the big Kahuna of Parisian chains, has 9 branches throughout the city, including the Champs-Elysées (74 av. des Champs-Elysées), Bastille (4 pl. de la Bastille), and Châtelet-les-Halles (Centre Commercial Forum Les Halles). Comprehensive selections of music, stereo equipment, and books in some branches. Purchase tickets to nearly any show at the **ticket desk.** Most open M-Sa 10am-7:30 or 8pm. Champs-Elysées branch closes midnight. MC/V.

## GIFTS AND MISCELLANY

**Kusmi Tea,** 56 r. de Seine, 6ème (☎46 34 29 06; www.kusmitea.com). Ⓜ Mabillon. Founded in 1867, Kusmi once produced the teas consumed by the Tsars of Russia. The sleek white decor and gorgeous tins hint at its luxurious tea. Try the Prince Wladimir (black tea flavored with citrus and vanilla). 125g tins from €9.50. Open daily 11am-8pm.

**Pylônes,** 57 r. St-Louis-en-l'Île, 1er (☎46 34 05 02). Ⓜ Pont Marie. Sells all the crazy items you never really need but always want. Open daily 10:30am-7:30pm. Also at 13 r. Ste-Croix-de-la-Brettonnerie, 4ème. AmEx/MC/V.

**Florent Monestier,** 47bis av. Bosquet, 7ème (☎45 55 03 01). Ⓜ École Militaire. All manner of nostalgic bric-a-brac to perfect that cluttered, shabby-chic look. Has everything from a hand-labeled bottle of bubble bath (€28) to an enormous ceramic rooster (€40). Open M-Sa 10:30am-7pm.

## DEPARTMENT STORES

**Galeries Lafayette,** 40 bd. Haussmann, 9ème (☎42 82 34 56). Ⓜ Chaussée d'Antin. Chaotic, it can be difficult to find a middle ground between high-end labels and ultra-edgy here. The top fl. cafeteria has amazing views of the Eiffel Tower and the Opéra, and a wine/soda fountain. Open M-W and F-Sa 9:30am-7:30pm, Th 9:30am-9pm. AmEx/V.

**Le Bon Marché,** 24 r. de Sèvres, 7ème (☎44 39 80 00). Ⓜ Sèvres-Babylone. Paris's oldest department store, Le Bon Marché has it all, from scarves to smoking accessories, designer clothes to home furnishings. Don't be fooled by its name—*bon marché* means cheap—this is Paris's most expensive department store. Make sure to try the dried or freshly baked goods at its food annex, **La Grande Epicerie de Paris,** 38 r. de Sèvres, across the street. Store open M-W and F 9:30am-7pm, Th 10am-9pm, Sa 9:30am-8pm. La Grande Epicerie open M-Sa 8:30am-9pm. AmEx/MC/V.

#  NIGHTLIFE

In the **5ème** and **6ème,** bars draw French and foreign students, while Paris's young and hip, queer and straight swarm the **Marais,** the center of Paris's GLBT life. Great neighborhood spots are springing up in the Left Bank's outlying areas, particularly in the **13ème** and **14ème.** A slightly older crowd congregates around **Les Halles,** while the outer *arrondissements* cater to locals. The **Bastille,** another central party area, is more suited to pounding vodka shots than sipping Bordeaux.

---

**TIP** **PILLOW TALK.** The French often mock English-speakers for their unwitting sexual references. Here are a couple of common expressions to avoid:

*Je suis excité(e)* might be an attempt to express excitement at a new museum or film but actually means "I am sexually aroused."

*Je suis plein(e)* may seem to translate to "I am full (of food)," but for a girl, this means "I have been sexually satisfied."

*Oh my God!* This English expression may seem harmless, but in French, *godde* means vibrator, so what you're really saying is "Oh my vibrator!"

FRANCE

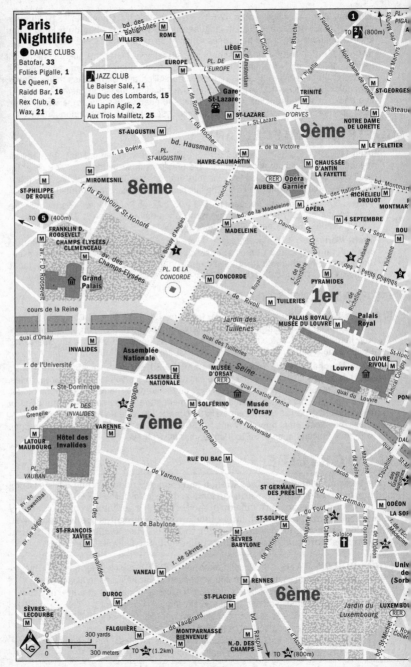

**Paris Nightlife**

● DANCE CLUBS
Batofar, **33**
Folies Pigalle, **1**
Le Queen, **5**
Raidd Bar, **16**
Rex Club, **6**
Wax, **21**

■ JAZZ CLUB
Le Baiser Salé, **14**
Au Duc des Lombards, **15**
Au Lapin Agile, **2**
Aux Trois Mailletz, **25**

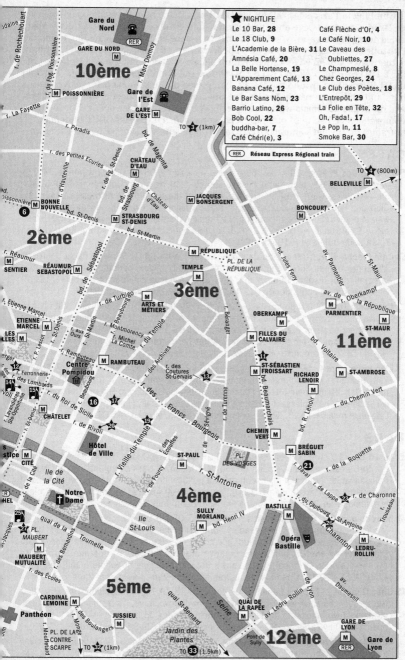

★ NIGHTLIFE

| | |
|---|---|
| Le 10 Bar, **28** | Café Flèche d'Or, **4** |
| Le 18 Club, **9** | Le Café Noir, **10** |
| L'Academie de la Bière, **31** | Le Caveau des |
| Amnésia Café, **20** | Oubliettes, **27** |
| La Belle Hortense, **19** | Le Champmeslé, **8** |
| L'Apparement Café, **13** | Chez Georges, **24** |
| Banana Café, **12** | Le Club des Poètes, **18** |
| Le Bar Sans Nom, **23** | L'Entrepôt, **29** |
| Barrio Latino, **26** | La Folie en Tête, **32** |
| Bob Cool, **22** | Oh, Fada!, **17** |
| buddha-bar, **7** | Le Pop In, **11** |
| Café Chéri(e), **3** | Smoke Bar, **30** |

**RER** Réseau Express Régional train

FRANCE

Clubbing in Paris is less about hip DJs' beats than about dressing up and getting in. Drinks are expensive and clubbers consume little beyond the first round. Many clubs accept reservations, so come early to assure entry on busy nights. Bouncers like tourists because they generally spend more money, so speaking English might actually give you an edge. Clubs heat up between 2 and 4am. Tune in to *Radio FG* (98.2 FM) or *Radio Nova* (101.5 FM) to find out about upcoming events. Parisian GLBT life centers around the **Marais**, comprised of the 3*ème* and 4*ème*. Numerous bars and clubs line **rue du Temple, rue Ste-Croix de la Bretonnerie, rue des Archives,** and **rue Vieille du Temple** while the 3*ème* boasts a lively lesbian scene. For the most comprehensive listing of organizations, consult *Illico* (free at GLBT bars and restaurants) or Zurban's annual *Paris Gay and Lesbian Guide* (€5 at any kiosk).

## CAFES

▨ **Le Club des Poètes,** 30 r. de Bourgogne, 7*ème* (☎47 05 06 03; www.poesie.net). Ⓜ Varenne. In 1961, Jean-Pierre Rosnay started "making poetry contagious and inevitable—*vive la poésie!*" Now his son has inherited the tradition. A restaurant by day, Le Club des Poètes is transformed Tu, F, and Sa nights at 10pm. If arriving after 10pm, wait to enter until you hear clapping or a break in the performance. Drinks €7.50. Lunch *menu* €15. Dinner €20. Open Sept.-July Tu-Sa noon-3pm and 8pm-1am. Kitchen open Tu-Sa noon-3pm and 8-10pm. MC/V.

▨ **Café Flèche d'Or,** 102bis r. de Bagnolet, 20*ème* (☎44 64 01 02; www.flechedor.fr). Ⓜ Alexandre Dumas. In a defunct train station, this bar/cafe/performance space serves internationally inspired fare. Try the "New York," a bacon cheddar cheeseburger (€15). Nightly entertainment. *Menus* €12-15. Kitchen open 8pm-midnight. MC/V.

**Café Chéri(e),** 44 bd. de la Villette, 19*ème* (☎42 02 02 05). Ⓜ Belleville. With cheap drinks and attractive artsy kids on the outdoor seating, this is quickly becoming one of the hottest spots in the 19*ème*. Beer starts at €3 and comes with free potato chips, and those looking for a mixed drink will not be disappointed by the creative menu. Nightly DJ starts around 10pm. Open daily 8am-2am.

**L'Apparement Café,** 18 r. des Coutures St-Gervais, 3*ème* (☎48 87 12 22). Ⓜ Chemin Vert. Beautiful wood lounge with games and a chill, young crowd. Those looking for a momentary escape from Marais's thumping beats will be happy to find only the murmur of conversation and a pleasant clattering of dishes here. Displays local paintings, all for sale. Late-night meals €12-15. Kitchen open until 11:30pm. Mixed drinks €9.

## BARS

▨ **Le 10 Bar,** 10 r. de l'Odéon, 6*ème* (☎43 26 66 83). Ⓜ Odéon. Walk against traffic on bd. St-Germain and make a left on rue de l'Odéon. A classic student hangout, where Parisian youth indulge in philosophical and political discussion. After several glasses of their famous spiced sangria (€3.50), you might feel inspired to join in. Jukebox plays everything from Édith Piaf to Aretha Franklin. Open daily 6pm-2am.

▨ **buddha-bar,** 8 r. Boissy d'Anglas, 8*ème* (☎53 05 90 00; www.buddha-bar.com). Ⓜ Madeleine or Concorde. The legendary buddha-bar has to be the most glamorous drinking hole in the world. A giant buddha watches over the expensive ground-floor restaurant while an elegant bar serves creative mixed drinks (€15) upstairs to the elite clientele (Madonna drops by when she's in town) lounging on intimate couches. Beer €8-9. Wine €10-12. Open M-F noon-3pm and 6pm-2am, Sa-Su 6pm-2am.

▨ **Chez Georges,** 11 r. des Canettes, 6*ème* (☎43 26 79 15). Ⓜ Mabillon. Upstairs, Chez Georges is a small wine bar with a diverse crowd; downstairs, it's a smoky, candlelit cellar packed with students drinking and dancing. Beer €3.50-4. Wine €1.50-4. Upstairs open Sept.-July Tu-Sa noon-2am. Cellar open Sept.-July Tu-Sa 10pm-2am.

**La Belle Hortense,** 31 r. Vieille du Temple, 4*ème* (☎48 04 71 60). Ⓜ St-Paul. Books lining the walls, wannabe philosophers lining the bar, and mellow music to go with the merlot. Frequent readings, signings, lectures. and discussions in its leather-couch-filled rooms. Wine from €4 per glass, €8 per bottle. Open daily 5pm-2am. MC/V.

**L'Entrepôt,** 7-9 r. Francis de Pressensé, 14ème (☎45 40 07 50; www.lentrepot.fr). ⓜ Pernety. Proving that intellectualism and good times can go together, this establishment offers a quadruple combo: a 3-screen independent cinema; a restaurant with a garden patio; a modern art gallery; and a trendy bar that features live jazz, Latin, and world music. You may need to come a few times to see it all. Jazz and poetry readings Th 9:30pm €5-7. Su Ciné-Philo (a screening, lecture, and discussion cafe; €8; 2:20pm) or improv theater (free; 6:30pm). World music concerts F-Sa; cover €5-7. Check website for other events. Beer €3.50. Su brunch noon-3pm €22. Open M-Sa 11am-1am or later, Su 11am-midnight. Kitchen open daily noon-3pm and 8-11pm.

**L'Academie de la Bière,** 88bis bd. Port Royal, 5ème (☎43 54 66 65; www.academie-biere.com). RER: Port Royal. With 12 on tap and over 300 bottled beers, this bar does not mess around. Fortunately, there's not a weak link on the menu. Beer €6.50-8.50. Happy hour daily 3:30-7:30pm. Open M-Th 10am-2am, F-Sa 10am-3am.

**Le Caveau des Oubliettes,** 52 r. Galande, 5ème (☎46 34 23 09). ⓜ St-Michel. Previously a caveau des oubliettes (cave of the forgotten ones) where criminals were locked up and forgotten, Le Caveau is now 2 scenes in 1. The upstairs bar (La Guillotine) has sod carpeting, ferns, and a real guillotine, while the downstairs cellar is an outstanding jazz club. Free soirée boeuf (jam session) Su-Th 10pm-1:30am. F-Sa free concerts. Beer from €4. Mixed drinks from €4.50. Happy hour 5-9pm. Open daily 5pm-2am.

**La Folie en Tête,** 33 r. de la Butte-aux-Cailles, 13ème (☎45 80 65 99). ⓜ Corvisart. Exotic instruments line the walls of this beaten-up neighborhood hangout. Sept.-June Sa night concerts, usually Afro-Caribbean music (€8). Beer €3. Ti punch €5.50. Happy hour 6-8pm. Open M-Sa 6pm-2am; last call 1:30am. MC/V.

**Le Pop In,** 105 r. Amelot, 11ème (48 05 56 11). ⓜ St-Sebastien Froissart. Living a double life as both neighborhood bar and rock club, this crowded spot is a favorite among Paris's carefully bedraggled youth and Anglophone study abroaders. Nightly concerts in their tiny basement. Plays pop and rock. Beer €2.50-5. Open Tu-Su 6:30pm-1:30am.

**Le Café Noir,** 65 r. Montmartre, 2ème (☎40 39 07 36). ⓜ Sentier. With a leopard-skin bike in the window and bartenders leaping onto the bar to perform comedy, one of Paris's least predictable bars mixes locals and Anglophones. Beer €2.50-3.50. Open M-F 8am-2am, Sa 4pm-2am. MC/V.

**Le Bar Sans Nom,** 49 r. de Lappe, 11ème (☎48 05 59 36). ⓜ Bastille. Stands out for its dim, fantastically cluttered decor. Famed mixed drinks (€9) are listed on oversized wooden menus and consumed by a subdued crowd. Beer €5-6.20. Shots €6.20. Free tarot-card reading Tu 5:30pm. Open Tu-Th 6pm-2am, F-Sa 6pm-4am. MC/V; min. €16.

**Barrio Latino,** 46-48 r. du Faubourg St-Antoine, 11ème (☎55 78 84 75; www.buddha-bar.com). ⓜ Bastille. Same swanky owners as buddha-bar. No wallflowers on this Latin dance floor, and not an empty barstool on weekends. To avoid bouncer troubles, ditch the flip-flops and T-shirt. Potent mixed drinks €12. Su brunch noon-4pm €28; includes a salsa lesson. DJ 10pm-2am. Open daily noon-2am. AmEx/MC/V.

**Bob Cool,** 15 r. des Grands Augustins, 6ème (☎46 33 33 77). ⓜ Odéon. One of Paris's best expat hangouts, Bob Cool has a laid-back clientele and friendly vibe. The music veers from salsa to The Corrs to Buddy Holly. Happy hour 5-9pm. Pints €4.50. Mixed drinks €5-6. Open daily 5pm-2am.

**Smoke Bar,** 29 r. Delambre, 14ème (☎43 20 61 73). ⓜ Vavin. Local bar filled with lively regulars and cheap drinks that undercut Paris prices. Su open mic. Beer €2.30-3. Mixed drinks €5-7. Open M-F noon-2am. Sa 6pm-2am. MC/V.

# DANCE CLUBS

**Batofar,** facing 11 q. François-Mauriac, 13ème (☎53 60 17 42). ⓜ Q. de la Gare. This 45m long, 520t barge/bar/club has made it big with the electronic music crowd. Live

## GAY OLD TIME

Boasting a substantial GLBT population and the first openly gay mayor of a major European city, Paris is bursting at the seams with queer-friendly entertainment and resources. Most notably, the City of Light participates in a campaign of marches across France to celebrate and raise awareness for queer communities. The highlight of Paris is its annual **Gay Pride Festival,** held on the last Saturday of June.

Nearly all of Paris's vibrant queer communities turn out for this exuberant parade. The festive din can be heard from several Metro stops away; attendance is only partially optional if you're within the city limits, but that's for the best. A fabulous Carnaval scene greets visitors as they reach the festival. Drag queens in feathered costumes pose daintily next to scantily clad dancers bumping, grinding, and shimmying on floats.

This might be the only time the Communist Party, the Socialist Party, and the UMP (Sarkozy's right-wing party) root for the same cause. A sense of organized chaos ensues as the crowds and floats wiggle and bob from Montparnasse to the Bastille, dancing, chanting, and waving banners. While there is a hint of political consciousness, it hardly distracts from the parade's glittery, muscled, and celebratory mood.

*For more info, visit www.gaypride.fr.*

artists and DJs daily. Su "Electronic brunch." Cover €8-15; usually includes 1 drink. Open M-Th 11pm-6am, F-Su 11pm-dawn; hours may vary. MC/V.

**Rex Club,** 5 bd. Poissonnière, 2ème (☎42 36 10 96; www.rexclub.com). Ⓜ Bonne-Nouvelle. A non-selective club that presents the most selective of DJ line-ups. Cutting-edge techno, jungle, and house fusion from international DJs. Beer €7.50-8. Mixed drinks €9-10. Cover up to €13. Open W-Th 11:30pm-6am, F-Sa midnight-6am.

**Wax,** 15 r. Daval, 11ème (☎48 05 88 33). Ⓜ Bastille. In a concrete bunker with retro couches, this mod bar/club gets crowded at night. Beer €5.50-7. Mixed drinks €9.50. W and Su disco/funk, Th R&B, F-Sa house. Open daily 9pm-dawn. MC/V; min. €15.

## GLBT NIGHTLIFE

▨ **Raidd Bar,** 23 r. du Temple, 3ème. Ⓜ Hôtel de Ville. The hippest GLBT club in the Marais and perhaps Paris, with the most muscular bartenders. Watch performers strip for the clients in a glass shower cubicle built into the wall (yes, they take it all off at 11pm, midnight, 1, and 2am). Beer €4. Tu disco night, W 80s and house and Su 90s.

▨ **Le Champmeslé,** 4 r. Chabanais, 2ème (☎42 96 85 20). Ⓜ Pyramides. This lesbian bar is Paris's oldest and most famous; everyone is welcome. Beer €4-5. Mixed drinks €8. Th cabaret show 10pm. Free drink on your birthday. Open M-Sa 3pm-dawn.

▨ **Le 18 Club,** 18 r. du Beaujolais, 1er (☎42 97 52 13; www.club18.fr). Ⓜ Pyramides. Paris's oldest gay club draws a mostly male crowd to its small bar and dance floor. Mixed drinks €6-9. Cover €10; includes 1 drink. Open W 7pm-3am, F-Sa midnight-6am.

**Oh Fada!,** 35 r. Ste-Croix de la Bretonnerie, 4ème (☎40 29 44 40) Ⓜ Hotel de Ville. With its outstanding musical taste and self-deprecating sense of fun ("This bar kills me" is written on a wall), Oh Fada! is the Marais' most likeable GLBT spot. Mostly gay men, but women and straight men welcome. Drinking gives way to dancing later at night. Beer €4-6. Open M-W and Su 5pm-2am, Th-Sa 5pm-4am.

**Banana Café,** 13 r. de la Ferronerie, 1er (☎42 33 35 31; www.bananacafeparis.com). Ⓜ Châtelet. Take r. Pierre Lescot to r. de la Ferronerie. This *très branché* (way cool) evening arena is the most popular GLBT bar in the 1er, and it draws an extremely mixed group. Beer €4-5.50. Mixed drinks €8.50. Th-Sa Go-Go Boys. Happy hour 6-9pm. Cover F-Sa €10; includes 1 drink. Open daily 5:30pm-6am. AmEx/MC/V.

**Le Queen,** 102 av. des Champs-Elysées, 8ème (☎53 89 08 90; www.queen.fr). Ⓜ George V. Where drag queens, superstars, tourists, and go-go boys get down to the mainstream rhythms of a 10,000-gigawatt sound system. Women have better luck with the bouncer if at least 1 man accompanies her. All drinks €10. M disco, Th-Sa house, Su 80s. Cover Su-Th €15, F-Sa €20; includes 1 drink. W Ladies' Night. Bring an ID and avoid coming in large groups. Open daily noon-dawn. AmEx/MC/V.

**Folies Pigalle,** 11 pl. Pigalle, 9ème (☎48 78 55 25; www.folies-pigalle.com). Ⓜ Pigalle. The largest, wildest club in the sleazy Pigalle *quartier*—not for the faint of heart. A former strip joint, the Folies is popular with both GLBT and straight clubbers. 1st M of each month *Soirées Transsexuelles*. Open M-Th and Su midnight-dawn, F-Sa midnight-noon. Drinks €10. Cover €20; includes 1 drink. AmEx/MC/V.

**Amnésia Café,** 42 r. Vieille du Temple, 4ème (☎42 72 16 94). Ⓜ St-Paul or Hôtel de Ville. A largely queer crowd comes to lounge on plush sofas in Amnésia's sleek interior. 1st fl. cafe, 2nd fl. lounge, and basement club with music beginning 9pm. *Kir* €4. Mixed drinks €7.50-10. Open daily 11am-2am. MC/V.

# DAYTRIPS FROM PARIS

🔳**VERSAILLES.** Louis XIV, the Sun King, built and held court at Versailles's extraordinary palace, 12km west of Paris. The château embodies the Old Regime's extravagance, especially in the newly renovated **Hall of Mirrors,** the ornate **State Apartments,** and the fountain-filled **gardens.** Arrive as soon as the château opens to avoid horrendous crowds. The line to buy tickets is to the left of the courtyard, while the line to get into the château is to the right; skip the former line by buying a day pass at the Versailles **tourist office,** 2bis av. de Paris, or skip the latter line by buying a combo guided tour and entrance ticket to the right of the château ticket office. (☎30 83 78 00. *Château open Tu-Su Apr.-Oct. 9am-6:30pm; Nov.-Mar. 9am-5:30pm. Gardens open daily Apr.-Oct. 7:30am-8:30pm, Nov.-Mar. 8am-6pm. Day pass including entrance to château, gardens, and Trianons €20, during Grandes Eaux €25, under 18 free. Château only €14, 2½hr. before closing €10, under 18 free. Gardens Apr.-Sept. Sa-Su €7, students and under 18 €5.50, M-F free; Oct.-Mar. daily free. 1½hr. guided tour and château €22, under 18 €5.50. Audio tour €6.)* A **shuttle** (round-trip €6, 11-18 €4.50) runs through the gardens to Louis XIV's pink marble hideaway, the **Grand Trianon,** and Marie-Antoinette's **Petit Trianon,** including her pseudo-peasant **Hameau,** or hamlet. *(Grand Trianon open daily Apr.-Oct. noon-6:30pm, Nov.-Mar. noon-5:30pm. Petit Trianon open daily Apr.-Oct. noon-6pm. Marie-Antoinette's gardens open Apr.-Oct. noon-7:30pm, Nov.-Mar. 9am-5:30pm. All 3 €9, after 4pm €5, under 18 free.)* Take the **RER C5 train** from Ⓜ Invalides to the Versailles Rive Gauche station (30-40min., 4 per hr., round-trip €5.60). Make sure you keep your RER (not Metro) ticket to exit at the Versailles station.

🔳**CHARTRES.** Chartres's phenomenal cathedral is one of the most beautiful surviving creations of the Middle Ages. Arguably the finest example of early Gothic architecture in Europe, the cathedral retains nearly all of its original 12th- and 13th-century stained-glass windows, many featuring the stunning "Chartres blue." Climb the spiral staircase to the top of the 16th-century Flamboyant Gothic left tower **(Tour Jehan-de-Beauce),** built 300 years after the rest of the cathedral, for dizzying views. (☎02 37 21 75 02; www.diocese-chartres.com/cathedrale. *Open daily 8:30am-7:30pm. Tower open May-Aug. M-Sa 9:30am-12:30pm and 2-6pm, Su 2-6pm; Sept.-Apr. M-Sa 9:30am-12:30pm and 2-5pm, Su 2-5pm. Last entry 30min. before closing. Cathedral free. Tower €6.50, 18-25 €4.50. Nov.-May 1st Su of month free.)* Trains run from Paris's Gare Montparnasse (1¼hr., 1 per hr., round-trip €26). The cathedral towers are visible to the left from outside the station.

**GIVERNY.** Monet's house and gardens in Giverny have become the **Fondation Claude Monet.** From April to July, Giverny overflows with water lilies that seem to be plucked straight from Monet's paintings. The artist's house, with a pink crushed-brick facade and green shutters, holds his collection of 18th- and 19th-century Japanese prints. *(84 r. Claude Monet. ☎ 02 32 51 28 21; www.fondation-monet.com. Open Apr.-Oct. Tu-Su 9:30am-6pm. €5.50, students €4. Only gardens €4.)* The accompanying **Musée d'Art Américain** houses temporary exhibits of late 18th- to early 19th-century American art. *(99 r. Claude Monet. ☎ 02 32 51 94 65; www.maag.org. Open Apr.-Oct. Tu-Su 10am-6pm. €5.50, students and seniors €4, free 1st Su of each month.)* **Trains** run regularly from Paris-St-Lazare to Vernon, the station near Giverny (40min., 13 per day, round-trip €24). April through October, shuttle buses run between the Vernon station and Giverny in sync with the train schedule (20min., Tu-Su 6-7 per day, round-trip €4.)

**DISNEYLAND PARIS.** It's a small world after all, and Disney is hellbent on making it even smaller. Celebrations for the park's 15th anniversary continue through March 2008, including extended hours and new rides. *(www.disneylandparis.com. Open mid-July to Aug. daily 10am-11pm; Sept. and May to mid-July M-F 10am-7pm, Sa-Su 10am-10pm; Oct. M-F 10am-7pm, Sa-Su 10am-9pm. Hours subject to change. Buy tickets at the Disneyland Hotel, online, Paris tourist office kiosks, or A line RER stations. 1-day 1 park ticket €46, 3-11 €38; 1-day 2 parks €56/48; 2-day 2 parks €103/84; 3-day 2 parks €128/105.)* Order ahead online to receive discount tickets. From Paris, take RER A4 Marne-la-Vallée to Marne-la-Vallée-Chessy (35min., 2 per hr., round-trip €11); the last train back is at 12:20am, arriving in Paris after the Métro closes. Eurailers can take the TGV (10min., 26 per day, €15-29) from Roissy-Charles de Gaulle Airport.

# LOIRE VALLEY (VAL DE LOIRE)

The Loire, France's longest and most celebrated river, meanders toward the Atlantic through a valley containing the fertile soil of vineyards that produce some of France's best wines. It's hardly surprising that a string of French (and English) kings chose to station themselves in opulent châteaux by these waters rather than in the commotion of their capital cities.

## ▐ TRANSPORTATION

Faced with such widespread grandeur, many travelers plan overly ambitious itineraries—two châteaux per day is a reasonable goal. The city of **Tours** (p. 300) is the region's best **rail** hub. However, train schedules are often inconvenient, and many châteaux aren't accessible by train. **Biking** is the best way to explore the region. Many stations distribute the invaluable *Châteaux pour Train et Vélo* booklet with train schedules and bike and **car** rental info.

## ORLÉANS ☎ 02 38

A gateway from Paris into the Loire, Orléans (pop. 113,000) cherishes its historical connection to **Joan of Arc**, who marched triumphantly past the **rue de Bourgogne** in 1429 after liberating the city from a seven-month British siege. Most of Orléans's highlights are near **place Ste-Croix**. With towering buttresses and stained-glass windows that depict Joan's story, the ▧**Cathédrale Sainte-Croix**, pl. Ste-Croix, is Orléans's crown jewel. (Open daily July-Aug. 9:15am-7pm; Sept.-June reduced hours.) The **Hôtel Groslot d'Orléans**, pl. de l'Étape, to the left of the Musée des Beaux Arts, was the king's country residence for two centuries and Orléans's city hall until the 1970s. Joan of Arc memorabilia fills the first room while another hosts the final resting place of François II, who died in disgrace in 1560. (☎ 79 22 30; hotelgroslot@ville-orleans.fr. Open July-Sept. Su-F 9am-7pm, Sa 5-8pm; Oct.-June Su-F 10am-noon and 2-6pm. Contact tourist office for available tours. For English guides, call ahead. Brochure €1. Garden open daily Apr.-Sept. 7:30am-8pm; Oct.-Mar. 8am-5:30pm.) One block from the train station, ▧**Hôtel de L'Abeille ●**, 64 r. Alsace-Lorraine, has been owned by the same family since 1919. Thirty-one comfortable rooms with antique furniture and fireplaces (albeit non-functional) are worth the price. (☎53 54 87; www.hoteldelabeille.com. Breakfast €7, in bed €8. Singles with shower €42-52, with bath €59; doubles €45-58/89; triples €59/89; quads €75. AmEx/MC/V.) **Rue de Bourgogne** and **rue Ste-Catherine** have a variety of cheap buffets and a lively bar scene at night. At ◼**Mijana ❸**, 175 r. de Bourgogne, a charming Lebanese couple prepares gourmet cuisine. (☎62 02 02; www.mijanaresto.com. Sandwiches €4-6. Falafel €7. Lunch €18. *Plats* from €12. Vegetarian options. Open M-Sa noon-1:30pm and 7-10pm. AmEx/MC/V.) Find groceries at **Carrefour**, in the mall at pl. d'Arc. (Open M-Sa 8:30am-9pm. AmEx/MC/V.)

**Trains** leave from the Gare d'Orléans on pl. Albert I for Blois (30min., 15 per day, €9.50), Paris (1¼hr., 1 per hr., €17), and Tours (1½hr., 2 per hr., €16). To reach the **tourist office**, 2 pl. de l'Étape, exit the train station onto r. de la République and continue straight until pl. du Martroi. Turn left onto r. d'Escures and continue to pl. de l'Étape. (☎24 05 05; www.tourisme-orleans.com. Open July-Aug. 9:30am-7pm; June 9:30am-1pm and 2-6:30pm; May and Sept. Tu-Sa 9:30am-1pm and 2-6pm; Oct.-Apr. reduced hours.) **Postal Code:** 45000.

# BLOIS
☎02 54

Awash in a rich regal history, Blois (pop. 50,000) is one of the Loire's most charming, popular cities. Once home to monarchs Louis XII and François I, Blois's gold-trimmed ◼**Château** was the Versailles of the late 15th and early 16th centuries. Housed within are well-preserved collections and historical museums with excellent temporary exhibits. While the royal apartments showcase extravagant and elegant pieces, the **Musée des Beaux-Arts** features a gallery of 16th- to 19th-century portraits, and the **Musée Lapidaire** exhibits sculptures from nearby châteaux. (☎90 33 33. Open daily Apr.-Sept. 9am-6:30pm; Jan.-Mar. and Oct.-Dec. 9am-noon and 2-5:30pm. €6.50, students under 25 €5.) The most enjoyable attractions in Blois are, however, its hilly streets and ancient staircases. Bars and bakeries on r. St-Lubin and r. des Trois Marchands tempt those en route to the 12th-century **Abbaye St-Laumer**, also called the **Église St-Nicolas**. (Open daily 9am-6:30pm. Su Mass 9:30am.) The winding streets east of r. Denis Papin and the view at the top of the staircase bearing the same name are especially beautiful. Five hundred years of expansions to **Cathédrale St-Louis**, one of Blois's architectural jewels, endowed it with an eclectic mix of styles. (Open daily 7:30am-6pm; crypt open June-Aug.) A spectacular view from the ◼**Jardin de l'Evêché**, behind the cathedral, runs past the rooftops and winding alleys of the old quarter, stretching along the brilliant Loire. ◼**Hôtel du Bellay ❷**, 12 r. des Minimes, is at the top of porte Chartraine, 2min. above the city center. It offers comfortable rooms with colorful decor. (☎78 23 62; http://hoteldubellay.free.fr. Breakfast €5. Reservations recommended. Singles and doubles €25, with toilet €27, with shower €28, with bath €37; triples or quads €54-62. MC/V.) Fragrant pâtisseries entice visitors on **rue Denis Papin**, while **rue St-Lubin, place Poids du Roi,** and **place de la Résistance** offer more dining options. An **Inter-marché** supermarket is at 16 av. Gambetta. (Open M-Sa 9am-7pm.) At night, the château's *"Son et Lumiere"* light show brightens Blois. Move from the cafes of pl. de la Résistance to the **Velvet Jazz Lounge**, 15 r. Haute, an ex-abbey turned into a classy, laid-back bar with occasional live jazz and a medieval atmosphere. (☎78 36 32. Beer €3; cocktails €6.50-8. Open Tu-Su 3pm-2am.)

**Trains** leave pl. de la Gare for Orléans (30-50min., 14 per day, €9), Paris (1¾hr., 8 per day, €23), and Tours (40min., 8-13 per day, €8.75). Transports Loir-et-Cher (TLC; ☎58 55 44; www.TLCinfo.net) sends **buses** from the station to nearby châteaux (35min., May 15-Sept. 2 per day; €11.25, students €9). Rent a **bike** from **Bike in Blois**, 8 r. Henri Drussy near pl. de la Résistance. (☎56 07 73; www.locationdevelos.com. 1st day €14, tandem €38, discount thereafter. Open M-Sa 9:15am-1pm and 3-6:30pm, Su 10:30am-1pm and 3-6:15pm. Cash only.) The **tourist office** is on pl. du Château. (☎90 41 41; www.bloispaysdechambord.com. Open Apr.-Sept. M-Sa 9am-7pm, Su 10am-7pm; Oct.-Mar. reduced hours.) **Postal Code:** 41000.

FRANCE

## ⚡ DAYTRIPS FROM BLOIS

**CHAMBORD.** Built between 1519 and 1545 to satisfy François I's egomania, **Chambord** is the largest and one of the most extravagant of the Loire châteaux. With 426 rooms, 365 chimneys, and 77 staircases, the castle could accommodate up to 10,000 people. To cement his claim, François stamped 200 of his trademark stone salamanders throughout the "hunting lodge," which also features a spectacular double-helix staircase thought to be designed by Leonardo da Vinci. (☎50 40 00. *Open daily Apr.-June 9am-6:15pm; July-Aug. 9am-7:30pm; Sept. 9am-6:15pm; Oct.-Mar. reduced hours. €9.50, 18-25 €6:50, under 17 free.)* Take the TLC **bus** from Blois (35min.; 3 per day; €11.25, students €9) or **bike** south from Blois for 2-3km until St.-Gervais-la-foret, then turn left on D33 (1hr.). **Postal Code:** 41330.

**CHEVERNY.** This castle with a tumultuous past has been privately owned since 1634 by the Hurault family, whose members have served as financiers and officers to French kings. The château's magnificent furnishings include elegant tapestries, delicate vases, and royal portraits. Fans of Hergé's *Tintin* books may recognize Cheverny's Renaissance facade as the inspiration for Marlinspike, Captain Haddock's mansion. The kennels hold 120 mixed English-Poitevin hunting hounds whose impressive dinner manners can be observed daily at 5pm. (☎79 96 29. *Open daily July-Aug. 9:15am-6:45pm; Apr.-June and Sept. 9:15am-6:15pm; Oct.-Mar. reduced hours. €7, students €5.)* Cheverny is 45min. south of Blois by bike and also on the TLC bus route. **Postal Code:** 41400.

## AMBOISE                                                ☎02 47

Amboise (pop. 12,000) is guarded by the parapets of the 15th-century château that six French kings called home. In the **Logis du Roi**—where the kidnapping of the Dauphin king was plotted—intricate 16th-century Gothic chairs stand over 2m tall to prevent attacks from behind. The jewel of the grounds is the unassuming **Chapelle St-Hubert,** the final resting place of **Leonardo da Vinci.** (☎57 00 98. Open daily July-Aug. 9am-6:30pm; Sept.-June reduced hours. €8.50, students €7.) **Clos Lucé,** 400m farther north, is where da Vinci spent his last three years. One of the manor's main attractions is a collection of 40 machines realized from da Vinci's visionary designs, including the world's first machine gun. (☎57 00 73. Open daily July-Aug. 9am-8pm; Apr.-June and Sept.-Oct. 9am-7pm; Nov.-Dec. 9am-6pm; Jan. 10am-5pm. €12, students €9.50. Sept.-June €9/7.) The **Centre International de Séjour Charles Péguy (HI) ❶**, sits on Île d'Oran, an island in the Loire. Follow r. Jules Ferry from the station, cross the first bridge on your left, and head downhill to the right immediately after the bridge. (☎30 60 90; www.mjcamboise.fr. Breakfast €3. Linens €3. Reception M-F 10am-noon and 2-8pm. Dorms €12. Cash only.) Try the local favorite **Chez Hippeau ❸**, 1 r. François 1er, for delicious regional treats on its classy terrace or cool interior. The staff will be happy to guide you through the menu options. (☎57 26 30. *Menu* €15-24. Large salads €7-15. Open daily noon-3:30pm and 7-10:30pm. MC/V.)

**Trains** leave 1 r. Jules-Ferry for: Blois (20min., 10 per day, €6); Orléans (1hr., 2 per 3hr., €13); Paris (2¼hr., 1 per hr., €26); Tours (20min., 24 per day, €5). To reach the **tourist office,** take a left from the station and follow r. Jules-Ferry, taking a right at the end of the street, crossing the first bridge to your left, and passing the residential Île d'Or. After crossing the second bridge, turn right immediately; the office is 30m down in a circular building on quai du Général de Gaulle, on the river bank. (☎57 09 28; www.amboise-valdeloire.com. Open M-Sa 9am-1pm and 2-6pm, schedules change frequently). **Postal Code:** 37400.

## TOURS                                                ☎02 47

On the surface, Tours (pop. 137,000) sparkles with the shops and bars of a modern metropolis. Yet behind its store-lined streets loom magnificent towers, ancient buildings, and cathedrals. Home to 30,000 students, abundant restaurants, and a booming nightlife, Balzac's birthplace is a comfortable base for château-hopping. The **Cathédrale St-Gatien,** off of r. Lavoisier, first erected in the AD 4th century, combines Romanesque columns, Gothic carvings, and two Renaissance spires into an intricate facade. (Cathedral open daily 9am-7pm. Cloister open May-Sept. M-Sa 9:30am-12:30pm and 2-6pm; Oct.-Mar. Th-Sa 9:30am-12:30pm and 2-5pm. Cathedral free. Cloister €3, under 18 and art students free.) Jutting up from modern commercial streets, the imposing **Tour de l'Horloge** and **Tour de Charlemagne,** on r. Descartes, are a ruinous testimony to the impressive proportions of the old basilique, destroyed after the 1789 Revolution. The **Nouvelle Basilique St-Martin** is an ornate church designed by Victor Laloux, architect of the Tours railway station and of Paris's Musée d'Orsay (p. 285). (Open daily 8am-8pm. Mass daily 11am.) **Musée des Compagnons,** 8 r. Nationale, showcases the masterpieces of France's best craftsmen and explains the decade-long traditional training of the *Compagnonage*—allegedly in place since King Solomon gathered workers to build the temple of Jerusalem. (☎21 62 20. €4.90, students and seniors €2.90, children under 12 free. Open M and W-Su mid-Sept. to mid-June 9am-noon and 2-6pm; mid-June to mid-Oct. 9am-12:30pm and 2-6pm).

The **Association Jeunesse et Habitat ❷,** 16 r. Bernard Palissy, houses workers, students, and backpackers in spacious rooms with private baths. When exiting the tourist office, turn right on r. Bernard Palissy. (☎60 51 51. Free Internet. Singles with shower €18; doubles with bath €26.) A large converted student dorm, **AJ "Vieux Tours" (HI) ❶,** 5 r. Bretonneau, offers TV lounges and kitchens on every floor while private balconies adorn each room. (☎37 81 58. Breakfast and linens included. Internet €1.50 per 15min. Reception daily 8am-noon and 5-11pm. Singles €18. AmEx/MC/V). Try **place Plumereau** and **rue Colbert** for bustling restaurants, cafes, and bars. Cheese-lovers converge for the delicious selection of dishes at ▨**La Souris Gourmande ❷,** 100 r. Colbert, where the variety of bovine decor almost overshadows the food. (☎47 04 80. Fondue €13-14, min. 2 people. Crepes and omelettes €8-9. Open Tu-Sa noon-2pm and 7-10:30pm. MC/V.) At night, the elegant **place Plumereau** blossoms with animated bars. The friendly staff and quirky interior at **Au Temps des Rois,** 3 pl. Plumereau, make it popular among a mixed crowd. (☎05 04 51. Beer €2.50-5. Open daily 8:30am-2am. AmEx/MC/V.) **Trains** leave pl. du Général Leclerc for Bordeaux (2½hr., 1 per hr., €44) and Paris (3hr., 14 per day, €29; TGV 1hr., 1 per hr., €53). To reach the **tourist office,** 78-82 r. Bernard Palissy, from the station, walk through pl. du Général Leclerc. Across the street, the office's neon sign will be in plain sight. (☎70 37 37; www.ligeris.com. Open mid-Apr. to mid-Oct. M-Sa 8:30am-7pm, Su 10am-12:30pm and 2:30-5pm; mid-Oct. to mid-Apr. M-Sa 9am-12:30pm and 1:30-6pm, Su 10am-1pm.) **Postal Code:** 37000.

## ▌◢ DAYTRIPS FROM TOURS

▨**CHENONCEAU.** Nicknamed the *château des dames* (castle of the ladies), Chenonceau owes its beauty to the series of women who designed it: first Katherine Bohier, the wife of a 16th-century tax collector; then Henri II's lover, Diane de Poitiers; and finally Henri's widowed wife, Catherine de Médici. The part of the château bridging the Cher River marked the border between occupied and Vichy France during WWII. (☎23 90 07. Open daily mid-Mar. to mid-Sept. 9am-7pm. Low season reduced hours. €9, students €7.50.) Trains from Tours stop at the station in front of the castle (30min., 8 per day, €5.70). Fil Vert buses also run from Amboise (25min., M-Sa 2 per day, €1.50) and Tours (1hr., M-Sa 2 per day, €1.50).

**AZAY-LE-RIDEAU.** Atop an island in the Indre, the flamboyant château at Azay-le-Rideau stands on the ruins of an earlier fortress. Seized by Francois I in the early 16th century, the castle still bears his royal insignia: crownless salamanders slinking above external doors. Azay's furniture and the ornate Italian second-floor staircase carved with the faces of 10 Valois monarchs reflect the Renaissance style. Gothic influence appears in the *grande salle* (grand drawing room), in which balls and festivals were once held and where tapestries from the 1500s still hang. (☎ 45 45 04. Open daily July-Aug. 9:30am-7pm; Apr.-June and Sept. 9:30am-6pm; Oct.-Mar. 9:30am-12:30pm and 2-5:30pm. Last entry 45min. before closing. Light show daily early July 9:45pm; mid-July to mid-Aug. 10pm. Château €7.50, show €9, both €12; age 18-25 €4.80/5/7, under 18 free. Gardens €3. Guided tour €4, students €3; audio tour €4.) Trains run from Tours to the town of Azay-le-Rideau (25min.; M-F 9 per day, Sa 5 per day, Su 3 per day; €5). Buses run from Tours train station to the tourist office (50min., 3 per day, €6).

## ANGERS

Angers (pop. 156,000) has grown into a sophisticated city, building on its illustrious aristocratic origins. From behind the arresting stone walls of the **Château d'Angers,** pl. Kennedy, the medieval Dukes of Anjou ruled the surrounding area, including Great Britain across the Channel. Inside the château hangs the 14th-century ■**Tapisserie de l'Apocalypse,** famous for its graphic portrayal of the universal battle between good and evil. (☎ 86 48 77. Open daily May-Aug. 9:30am-6:30pm; Sept.-Apr. 10am-5:30pm. €7.50, students €4.80.) Angers's other woven masterpiece is the 1950s **Chant du Monde** (Song of the World), in the **Musée Jean Lurçat,** 4 bd. Arago. Next door, the **Musée de la Tapisserie Contemporaine** surprises visitors with its unconventional art forms. (☎ 24 18 45. Open June-Sept. daily 10am-7pm; Oct.-May Tu-Su 10am-noon and 2-6pm. Both museums €4, students €3.) Maker of the famous *liqueur* since 1849, the **Musée Cointreau** offers tours of its factory and free tastings. Take bus #7 from the train station to Cointreau. (☎ 31 50 50; www.cointreau.com. Open daily July-Aug. 10:30am-6:30pm; Sept.-June reduced hours. €5.50.) **Royal Hôtel ❸,** 8 bis pl. de la Visitation, offers spacious rooms with double beds, big windows, and cable TV. (☎ 88 30 25. Breakfast €5. Free Internet. Reception M-F 6:45am-midnight, Sa-Su reduced hours. Singles €30-41; doubles €32-51, with shower or bath €49; triples €56; quads €65. AmEx/MC/V.) **Hôtel de l'Univers ❸,** 2 pl. de la Gare, across the street from the train station, has simple but well-kept rooms. (☎ 88 43 58; fax 86 97 28. Breakfast €7. Singles and doubles with sink €31, with shower €42-44, with bath €53-58; quads €66-73. AmEx/MC/V.) Relatively cheap restaurants flourish along **rue St-Laud** and **rue St-Aubin.** Grab groceries in **Monoprix,** pl. de la Republique, on the ground floor of Les Halles. (Open M-Sa 8:30am-9pm). From the station on pl. de la Gare, **trains** leave for Paris (2-3hr., 15 per day, €39-46) and Tours (1hr., 10 per day, €16). **Buses** run from the Esplanade de la Gare, in front of the train station, to Rennes (3hr., 2 per day, €14). To get from the station to the **tourist office** on pl. Kennedy, exit straight onto r. de la Gare, turn right at pl. de la Visitation on r. Targot, and turn left on bd. du Roi-René; the office is on the right, across from the château. (☎ 23 50 00; www.angersloiretourisme.com. Open May-Sept. M-Sa 9am-7pm, Su 10am-7pm; Oct.-Apr. reduced hours.) **Postal Code:** 49100.

# BRITTANY (BRETAGNE)

Despite superficially French *centre villes*, châteaux, and creperies, Brittany reveres its pre-Roman Celtic roots. After 800 years of Breton settlement, the province became part of France in 1491 when the duke's daughter married two successive French kings. Black-and-white *Breizh* (Breton) flags still decorate buildings, however, and the Celtic language *Brezhoneg* remains on street signs.

# RENNES

☎ **02 99**

The cultural capital of Brittany, Rennes (pop 212,000) flourishes from September to June. Ethnic eateries, colorful nightspots, and crowds of university students enliven the cobblestone streets and half-timbered houses of the *vieille ville*.

**TRANSPORTATION AND PRACTICAL INFORMATION. Trains** leave pl. de la Gare for: Caen (3hr., 4 per day, €30); Paris (2hr., 1 per hr., €53-65); St-Malo (1hr., 15 per day, €12); Tours (3hr., 4 per day, €37) via Le Mans. **Buses** go from 16 pl. de la Gare to Angers (2½hr., 2 per day, €14) and Mont-St-Michel (1½hr., 4 per day, €10). Local buses run Monday through Saturday 5:15am-12:30am and Sunday 7:25am-midnight. The **metro** line uses the same ticket (€1.10, day pass €4, *carnet* of 10 €10). To get from the train station to the **tourist office**, 11 r. St-Yves, follow av. Jean Janvier to q. Chateaubriand. Turn left and walk along the river, through pl. de la République, turn right on r. George Dottin, and right again on r. St-Yves. (☎67 11 11; www.tourisme-rennes.com. Open July-Aug. M-Sa 9am-7pm, Su 11am-1pm and 2-6pm; Sept.-June M 1-6pm, Tu-Sa 10am-6pm, Su 11am-1pm and 2-6pm.) Surf the **Internet** at **Neurogame**, 2 r. de Dinan. (☎65 53 85. €3 per hr. Open Sept.-June M noon-midnight, Tu-F 10am-midnight, Sa 2pm-midnight, Su 2-10pm; mid-July to mid-Aug. M-F noon-midnight, Sa 2pm-midnight, Su 2-10pm.) **Postal Code:** 35000.

**ACCOMMODATIONS AND FOOD.** The **Auberge de Jeunesse (HI) ❶**, 10-12 Canal St-Martin, has simple dorms, a TV room, and a cafeteria. Take the metro (dir.: Kennedy) to Ste-Anne. Follow r. de St-Malo downhill onto r. St-Martin; the hostel will be on the right after the bridge. (☎33 22 33; rennes@fuaj.org. Breakfast and linens included. Reception 7am-11pm. Dorms €16. MC/V.) **Hôtel Maréchal Joffre ❷**, 6 r. Maréchal Joffre, has small, cheerful, and quiet rooms above a tiny lunch counter in the center of town. (☎79 37 74. Breakfast €5. Reception M-Sa 24hr., Su midnight-1pm and 8pm-midnight. Singles €25-34; doubles €25-38; triples €40-44. AmEx/MC/V.) **Rue St-Malo** has many ethnic restaurants, while the *vieille ville* contains more traditional *brasseries*, and cheap kebab stands around **place Ste-Anne**. Organic vegetarian *plats* (€10) and *menus* (€14-18) attract tree-huggers to ▓**Le St-Germain des Champs (Restaurant Végétarien-Biologique) ❸**, 12 r. du Vau St-Germain. (☎79 25 52. Open M-Sa noon-2:30pm. MC/V.) A **Champion** supermarket is in the mall at 20 r. d'Isly. (Open M-Sa 9:30am-8pm.)

**SIGHTS AND ENTERTAINMENT.** Medieval architecture peppers Rennes's *vieille ville*, particularly **rue de la Psalette** and **rue St-Guillaume.** At the end of r. St-Guillaume, turn left onto r. de la Monnaie to visit the **Cathédrale St-Pierre,** a 19th-century masterpiece with a solid, Neoclassical facade and frescoed, gilded interior. Hidden in a side chapel, an intricately carved altarpiece depicts the life of the Virgin Mary. (Open daily 9:30am-noon and 3-6pm.) Across the street, the **Portes Mordelaises** are last vestiges of Rennes's medieval walls. The **Musée des Beaux-Arts,** 20 q. Émile Zola, houses an excellent collection including Baroque and Breton masterpieces but few famous works. (☎02 23 62 17 45; www.mbar.org. Open Tu 10am-6pm, W-Su 10am-noon and 2-6pm. €5, students €2.20, under 18 free; with special exhibits €5.40/2.70/free.) Across the river and up r. Gambetta is the lush ▓**Jardin du Thabor,** one of the most beautiful gardens in France. Concerts are often held here and a gallery on the northern side exhibits local artwork on a rotating basis. (☎28 56 62. Open daily June-Aug. 7:30am-8:30pm; Sept.-June 7:30am-6:30pm.)

With enough bars for a city twice its size and clubs that draw students from Paris and beyond, Rennes is a partygoer's dream, especially during term time.

Look for action in place Ste-Anne, **place St-Michel, place de Lices,** and the surrounding streets. The young and beautiful pack two floors and four bars at ◼**Le Zing,** 5 pl. des Lices. (☎79 64 60. Mixed drinks €8-9. Open daily 3pm-3am. MC/V.) **Delicatessen,** 7 impasse Rallier du Baty, around the corner from pl. St-Michel in a former prison, has swapped jailhouse bars for heavy beats to become one of Rennes's hottest clubs. (Drinks €6-10. Cover €5-15. Open Tu-Sa midnight-5am.) **La Cité d'Ys,** 31 r. Vasselot, has Celtic decor and a mythical vibe. (☎78 24 84. Beer €2.40-3.20. Open daily noon-1am. AmEx/MC/V.)

## ST-MALO                                                                    ☎02 99

St-Malo (pop. 52,000) merges all the best of northern France: miles of sandy beaches, imposing ramparts guarding a walled *vieille ville*, and festivals enhancing an already active cultural scene. East of the walled city is **Grande Plage de Sillon,** the town's largest and longest beach. The slightly more sheltered **Plage de Bon Secours** lies to the west and features the curious (and free) **Piscine de Bon Secours,** three cement walls that hold in a deep pool of salt water even when the tide recedes. The best view of St-Malo is from the **château's** watchtower, part of the **Musée d'Histoire,** which houses artifacts from St-Malo's naval past. (☎40 71 57. Open Apr.-Sept. daily 10am-12:30pm and 2-6pm; Oct.-Mar. reduced hours. €5, students €3.) All entrances to the city have stairs leading up to the old **ramparts;** the view from the north side reveals a sea speckled with islands, including the **Grand Bé**—where French author **Chateaubriand** is buried—and the **Fort National,** both of which can be reached on foot at low tide.

The **"Centre Patrick Varangot" (HI) ❶,** 37 av. du Révérend Père Umbricht, has 242 beds near the beach. From the train station, take bus #5 (dir.: Croix Désilles) or #10 (dir.: Cancale). By foot from the station (30min.), turn right and go straight at the roundabout onto av. de Moka. Turn right on av. Pasteur, which becomes av. du Révérend Père Umbricht. (☎40 29 80; www.centrevarangot.com. Breakfast included. Luggage storage €2. Linens included. Laundry €4. Free Internet and Wi-Fi. Reception daily 8am-11pm. Dorms €15-19; singles €25-29. MC/V.) The best eateries lie farther from the walls of the *vieille ville.* For a real treat, head to ◼**Le Sanchez ❶,** 9 r. de la Vieille Boucherie at pl. du Pilori, an ice cream counter that serves gluttonous scoops of exotic *gelato.* Get it to go—you'll get more ice cream for less money.(☎56 67 17. 1 scoop €2, 2 scoops €3. Super Sanchez; 3-scoop sundae; €4.80. Open mid-June to mid-Sept. daily 8:30am-midnight; Apr. to mid-June daily 8:30am-7:30pm; mid-Sept to Mar. M-Tu, Th-Su 8:30am-7:30pm. MC/V; min. €15 charge.) Also try the delicious, if slow-serving, **La Brigantine ❶,** 13 r. de Dinan. (☎56 82 82. *Galettes*; savory crepes; €2-9. Open July-Aug. daily noon-3pm and 7-11pm; Sept.-June M, Th-Su noon-3pm and 7-11pm. MC/V.) **Marché Plus,** 10bis r. Ste-Barbe, is near the Porte St-Vincent entrance within the city walls. (Open M-Sa 7am-9pm, Su 9am-1pm.) **Trains** run to Dinan (1½hr., 5 per day, €8), Paris (4hr., 14 per day, €59-73), and Rennes (1hr., 14 per day, €12). To get to the **tourist office** from the station, turn right, then left at the roundabout onto av. Jean Jaurès. Turn left onto r. de l'Astrolabe, then right and follow av. Louis Martin to esplanade St-Vincent, near the *vieille ville*'s entrance. (☎08 25 13 52 00. Open July-Aug. M-Sa 9am-7:30pm, Su 10am-6pm; Sept.-June reduced hours.) **Postal Code:** 35400.

## DINAN                                                                      ☎02 96

Perhaps the best-preserved medieval town in Brittany, Dinan (pop. 11,000) has cobblestone streets lined with 15th-century houses inhabited by traditional sculptors and painters. On the ramparts, the 13th-century **Porte du Guichet** is the original entrance to the **Château de Dinan.** Once a military stronghold, ducal residence, and prison, its two towers are now a museum. The **donjon** (keep) displays local art and artifacts, while the 15th-century **Tour de Coëtquen's** basement stores funerary sculptures. (Open June-Sept. daily 10am-6:30pm; Oct.-May reduced hours. €4.25, ages 12-18 €1.70.) A long, picturesque walk down the steep r. du Jerzual and left along the river leads to the **Maison d'Artiste de la Grande Vigne,** 103 r. du Quai. This former home of painter Yvonne Jean-Haffen (1895-1993) is a work of art, with murals adorning the walls and a beautiful hillside garden. (☎87 90 80. Open mid-May to Sept. daily 2-6:30pm. €2.80, students €1.75.) To reach the **Auberge de Jeunesse (HI) ❶,** in Vallée de la Fontaine-des-Eaux, turn left from the station, cross the tracks, then turn right and head downhill for 2km before turning right again for another 2km. (☎39 10 83; dinan@fuaj.org. Breakfast €3.50. Linens included. Free Internet. Reception July-Aug. 8am-noon and 5-9pm; Sept.-June 9am-noon and 5-8pm. Dorms €12. HI members only. MC/V.) Creperies, *brasseries*, and bars sit along **rue de la Cordonnerie** and **place des Merciers.** A **Monoprix** supermarket is at 7 pl. du Marchix. (Open M-Sa 9am-7pm.) **Trains** run from pl. du 11 Novembre 1918 to Paris (3hr., 6 per day, €59) and Rennes (1hr., 8 per day, €13). The **tourist office** is at 9 r. du Château. (☎87 69 76. Open July-Aug. M-Sa 9am-7pm, Su 10am-12:30pm and 2:30-6pm; Sept.-June reduced hours.) **Postal Code:** 22100.

# QUIMPER                                                         ☎02 98

With flower-adorned footbridges crisscrossing its central waterway, Quimper (kam-PAIR; pop. 63,000) has irrepressible charm to fuel its fierce Breton pride. At **Faïenceries de Quimper HB-Henriot,** r. Haute, guides lead visitors through studios where artists hand-paint the town's renowned earthenware. (☎90 09 36; www.hb-henriot.com. Open July-Aug. M-Sa 9:30-11:45am and 2-5:15pm; Sept.-June M-F 9:30-11:15am and 2-4:15pm. Mandatory French- or English-language tours every 45min. €4, 8-14 €2, under 8 free.) The twin windowed spires of the **Cathédrale St-Corentin,** built between the 13th and 15th centuries, rise over the Old Town. Inside the light-filled church, a bent choir supposedly mimics the angle of Jesus's head drooping from the cross. (Open May-Oct. daily 8:30am-noon and 1:30-6:30pm; Nov.-Apr. M-Sa 9am-noon and 1:30-6pm, Su 1:30-6pm. Hours may vary.) The **Musée Départemental Breton,** 1 r. du Roi Gradlon, through the cathedral garden, has exhibits on Breton history and culture, including displays of traditional clothing and carved furniture. (☎95 21 60. Open daily June-Sept. 9am-6pm; Oct.-May Tu-Sa 9am-noon and 2-5pm, Su 2-5pm. €3.80, students and 18-26 €2.50, under 18 free.)

To reach the no-frills **Auberge de Jeunesse (HI) ❶,** 6 av. des Oiseaux, take bus #1 (dir.: Kermoysan; last bus 7:30pm) from pl. de la Résistance to Chaptal; the hostel will be up the street on the left. (☎64 97 97; quimper@fuaj.org. Breakfast €3.50. Linens included. Reception 8-11am and 5-8pm. Lockout 11am-5pm. Open Apr.-Sept. Dorms €11.50; single €14. Cash only. HI members only.) Next to the hostel, **Camping Municipal ❶,** 4 av. des Oiseaux, offers forested sites 15min. from the town center. (☎ 55 61 09; camping-municipal@quimper.fr. Reception June-Sept. M 1-7pm; Tu, Th 8-11am and 3-8pm; W 9am-noon; F 9-11am and 3-8pm; Sa 8am-noon and 3-8pm; Su 9-11am. Oct.-May M-Tu, Th 9-11:30am and 3:30-7:30pm; F 9:30-10:30am and 3:30-7:30pm; Sa 9:30-11:30am and 4:30-6:30pm. €3.30 per adult, €1.70 per child under 7, €0.80 per tent, €1.70 per car, €1.50 per RV. Electricity €2.90.) The **Les Halles market,** on r. St-François off r. Kéréon, has cheese, meat, produce, and seafood. (Open daily 9am-7pm, but hours may vary.) At night, head to the cafes near the cathedral, or to **An Poitín Still,** 2 av. de la Liberation by the train station, where live Irish music plays Friday nights at 10pm. (Beer €2-5. Open M-Sa 3pm-1am, Su 5pm-1am. AmEx/MC/V.) **Trains** go from av. de la Gare to Brest (1¼hr., 6 per day, €10) and Rennes (2½hr., 14 per day, €30-36). From the train station, go right onto av. de la Gare and follow it, with the river on your right, as it becomes bd. Dupleix and leads to pl. de la Résistance. The **tourist office,** 7 r. de la Déesse, is on the left. (☎53 04 05; www.quimper-tourisme.com. Open July-Aug. M-Sa 9am-7pm, Su 10am-1pm and 3-5:45pm; Sept.-June reduced hours.) **Postal Code:** 29000.

# NANTES                                                         ☎02 40

With broad boulevards, relaxing public parks, and great bistros, Nantes (pop. 280,000) knows how to take life easy. The massive **Château des Ducs de Bretagne,** built to safeguard Breton independence in the late 15th century, now holds the excellent **Musée d'Histoire de Nantes** in 32 rooms. While at the museum's exhibits, look for the elaborate graffiti carved into the walls by former prisoners. Surrounding the castle's moat are neatly trimmed lawns ideal for picnics. The **Harnachement,** across the château courtyard from the museum, holds temporary exhibits on the history of Brittany. (Château grounds open daily mid-May to mid-Sept. 9am-8pm; mid-Sept. to mid-May 10am-7pm. Museum open mid-May to mid-Sept. 9:30am-7pm; mid-Sept. to mid-May 10am-6pm. Grounds free. Exhibits each €5, 18-26 €3; both €8/4.80.) Gothic vaults soar 39m in the bright **Cathédrale St-Pierre.** A complete restoration of the interior has undone the ravages of time, though it could not salvage the stained glass shattered during WWII. Only one original window remains, in the right transept above the beautifully sculpted 16th-century tomb of François II, the last Duke of Brittany. (Open daily Apr.-Oct. 8am-7pm, Nov.-Mar. 8am-6pm.) The **Musée des Beaux-Arts,** 10 r. Georges Clemenceau, features a wide range of European masterpieces on the second floor. The ground floor has temporary exhibits on contemporary French art. Nearby **Chapelle de l'Oratoire** displays more temporary collections. (☎02 51 17 45 00. Open M, W, F-Su 10am-6pm, Th 10am-8pm. €3.50, students €2, under 18, Th 6-8pm, and 1st Su of each month free; €2 daily after 4:30pm.)

A 15min. walk from the train station, **Auberge de Jeunesse "La Manu" (HI) ❶,** 2 pl. de la Manu, once a tobacco factory, still has an industrial feel. (☎29 29 20; nanteslamanu@fuaj.org. Breakfast and linens included. Luggage storage €1.50. Internet €1 per 40min. Reception daily July-Aug. 8am-noon and 4-11pm; Sept.-June 8am-noon and 5-11pm. Lockout July-Aug. 10am-4pm, Sept.-June 10am-5pm. Open Jan. to mid-Dec. 3- to 6-bed dorms €16. HI members only. MC/V.) To reach **Camping du Petit Port ❶,** 21 bd. du Petit Port, from pl. du Commerce, take tram #2 (dir.: Orvault Grand Val) to Morrhonnière, cross the street and head right. (☎74 47 94; www.nge-nantes.fr. Reception July-Aug. 8am-9pm; Sept.-June 9am-7pm. In summer, reserve ahead. June-Sept. €3.30 per adult, €2.10 per child under 10, €4.40 per tent, €6.40 per tent and car, €8.60 per RV, €2.30 per extra car; Oct.-May €2.70/ 1.70/3.60/5.20/6.80/1.90. Electricity €3. MC/V.) Plenty of reasonably-priced eateries—from crepe stands to sit-down venues—are between **place du Bouffay** and **place du Pilori.** One of France's most beautiful bistros, ▨**La Cigale ❸,** 4 pl. Graslin, is filled with painted tiles, huge mirrors, and wall sculptures. The exquisite food and excellent service deserve equal acclaim. (☎02 51 84 94 94; www.lacigale.com. *Plats* €10-25. 2-course lunch *menus* €13-24; 3-course dinner *menus* €17-27. Breakfast €10. Open daily 7:30am-12:30am. AmEx/MC/V.) There's a supermarket on the bottom floor of the **Galeries Lafayette,** 2-20 r. de la Marne (open M-Sa 9am-8pm). For nightlife, the **Ste-Croix area,** near **place du Bouffay,** has bars and cafes in abundance. **Trains** leave from 27 bd. de Stalingrad for Bordeaux (4hr., 5 per day, €42), Paris (2-4hr., 1 per hr., €54-69), and Rennes (1¾hr., 7-15 per day, €21). The **tourist office** is at 3 cours Olivier de Clisson. (☎08 92 46 40 44; www.nantes-tourisme.com. Open M-W and F-Sa 10am-6pm, Tu 10:30am-6pm.) **Postal Code:** 44000.

# NORMANDY (NORMANDIE)

Rainy, fertile Normandy is a land of fields, fishing villages, and cathedrals. Invasions have twice secured the region's place in military history: in 1066, William of Normandy conquered England; on D-Day, June 6, 1944, Allied armies returned the favor, liberating France from Normandy's beaches.

## ROUEN                                                                ☎02 35

Madame Bovary—literature's most famous desperate housewife—may have criticized Rouen (pop. 106,000), but Flaubert's hometown is no provincial hamlet. Historically important as the capital of Normandy and the city where Joan of Arc burned at the stake in 1431, Rouen today boasts splendid Gothic cathedrals and buzzing urban energy. The most famous of Rouen's "hundred spires" belong to the ▣**Cathédrale de Notre-Dame,** pl. de la Cathédrale. The central spire, standing at 151m, is the tallest in France. Art lovers may also recognize the cathedral's facade from Monet's celebrated studies of light. (Open Apr.-Oct. M 2-7pm, Tu-Sa 7:30am-7pm, Su 8am-6pm; Nov.-Mar. M 2-7pm, Tu-Sa 7:30am-noon and 2-6pm, Su 8am-6pm.) Combining the disparate themes of Flaubert, who was raised on the premises, and the history of medicine, the **Musée Flaubert et d'Histoire de la Médicine,** 51 r. de Lecat, down r. de Crosne from pl. de Vieux-Marché, houses a large collection of bizarre paraphernalia on both subjects. (☎ 15 59 95; www.chu-rouen.fr. Open Tu 10am-6pm, W-Sa 10am-noon and 2-6pm. €3, 18-25 €1.50, under 18 free.) The **Musée des Beaux-Arts,** Esplanade Marcel Duchamp, off sq. Verdrel, houses a notable collection of 16th to 20th century art, including works by Caravaggio and Monet. (☎ 71 28 40. Open M and W-Su 10am-6pm. €3, 18-25 €2, under 18 free.)

**Hotel des Arcades** ❸, 52 r. de Carmes, is down the street from Notre-Dame. (☎ 70 10 30; www.hotel-des-arcades.fr. Breakfast €6.50. Singles €29-36, with shower €40-46; doubles €30-37/41-47; triples with shower €53. AmEx/MC/V.) Cheap eateries surround **place du Vieux-Marché** and the **Gros Horloge** area. **Chez Wam** ❶, 67 r. de la République, near l'Abbatiale St-Ouen, serves delicious *kebab-frites* (gyros with fries; €3-4), ideal for picnics in the **Jardins de l'Hôtel de Ville** across the street. (☎ 15 97 51. Open daily 11am-2am. AmEx/MC/V.) Buy groceries at the **Monoprix** supermarket, r. du Gros Horloge. (Open M-Sa 8:30am-9pm.) Trains leave r. Jeanne d'Arc, on pl. Bernard Tissot, for Lille (3hr., 3 per day, €29) and Paris (1½hr., 1 per hr., €19). From the station, walk down r. Jeanne d'Arc and turn left on r. du Gros Horloge to reach the **tourist office,** 25 pl. de la Cathédrale. (☎ 02 32 08 32 40; www.rouentourisme.com. Open May-Sept. M-Sa 9am-7pm, Su 9:30am-12:30pm and 2-6pm; Oct.-Apr. M-Sa 9:30am-6:30pm.) **Postal Code:** 76000.

# HONFLEUR ☎ 02 31

Miraculously unharmed by WWII, the harbor town of Honfleur (on-FLER; pop. 6000) hosts a close-knit artist community, members of which often set up their easels in the streets. Middle-aged and elderly tourists flock to Honfleur in summer, mostly to browse local galleries and sample regional *liqueurs*. Named after the town's most famous artist, the **Musée Eugène Boudin,** pl. Erik Satie, off r. de l'Homme de Bois, emphasizes artists—especially Boudin—who were born or worked in Honfleur. (☎ 89 54 00. Open mid-Mar. to Sept. M and W-Su 10am-noon and 2-6pm; Oct. to mid-Mar. M and W-F 2:30-5pm, Sa-Su 10am-noon and 2:30-5pm. €5, students and under 18 €3, under 10 free. Cash

## THE LOCAL STORY

### PARDON ME, ST-ROMAIN

Every year since 1156, on Ascension Day, a prisoner is brought before Rouen's parliament. Without a judge, jury, or trial, he is set free. By this annual act of mercy, Rouen celebrates the most famous miracle of its patron saint, St-Romain: his defeat of a dragon aided by a convict.

While serving as Bishop of Rouen in the 7th century, St-Romain lived a life of quiet piety; it was not until well after his death in 641 that his fame as a dragon-slayer began to spread. When the saint's remains were moved within Rouen's walls in the 10th century, they were interred in a flood-prone part of town that subsequently stopped flooding. With this new miracle attributed to St-Romain, the old legend of his run-in with a river dragon recaptured popular imagination.

As the story goes, one day a dragon emerged from the Seine and sent a flood over Rouen. St-Romain tried to recruit villagers to stop the beast, but only one man—a prisoner—answered his plea. The two entered the dragon's cave, St-Romain made the sign of the cross, and the beast collapsed.

To honor their legendary patron saint and the lone convict who aided him, the people of Rouen began to annually pardon a prisoner. Improbable as it may seem, this millennium-old tradition continues to this day.

only.) A giant winged pear greets visitors to **Maisons Satie,** 67 bd. Charles V, an interactive museum housed in the birthplace of prolific composer and musician Erik Satie. (☎89 11 11. Open M and W-Su May-Sept. 10am-7pm; Oct.-Dec. and mid-Feb. to Apr. 11am-6pm. €6, students and seniors €4, under 10 free.) Past the **public gardens,** on Jetée de l'Ouest, the **Jardin des Personalités** (Garden of Fame) features busts of Honfleur-related celebrities including Charles Baudelaire, Claude Monet, and Erik Satie.

Extravagant hotels hoping to attract stuffed wallets fill Honfleur. **Les Cascades** ❸, 17 pl. Thiers, across from the tourist office, offers relatively inexpensive, airy rooms, some with skylights. At the elegant seafood restaurant below, *plats* cost €10-14 and *menus* run €13-30. (☎89 05 83. Breakfast €6. Open Feb.-Nov. Singles and doubles with shower €32-40, with shower and TV €45-56, with bath €50. AmEx/MC/V.) Many pricey, indistinguishable restaurants along **quai Ste-Catherine** and on **place Hamelin** provide a taste of local seafood. One of the most affordable options near the water, **Le Bistrot à Crêpes** ❶, 1 q. de Passagers, serves *crêpes* for €3-8 and *galettes* for €3-10. (☎89 74 96. Open daily noon-3pm and 6:30-10pm; hours vary. Cash only.) For dessert, try one of the bizarre but delicious ice cream flavors at **Pom'Cannelle** ❶, 60 q. Ste-Catherine. (☎89 55 25. 1 scoop €2, 2 scoops €3.80. Open in high season daily 9am-11pm; in low season 2-7pm; hours vary. MC/V.) Wednesday mornings (8am-1pm), there is a **Marché Bio** (organic produce market) on pl. Ste-Catherine, beside the church. The regular market is held there Saturday mornings. **Bus Verts** (☎08 10 21 42 14) depart the *gare routière* at the end of q. Lepaulmier for Caen (2hr.; 9-15 per day; €7, under 26 €6). To get to the **tourist office,** take a right out of the bus station and follow q. Lepaulmier two blocks. (☎89 23 30; www.ot-honfleur.fr. Open July-Aug. M-Sa 10am-7pm, Su 10am-5pm; Easter-June and Sept. M-Sa 10am-12:30pm and 2-6:30pm, Su 10am-5pm; Oct. to mid-Apr. M-Sa 10am-12:30pm and 2-6pm.) **Postal Code:** 14600.

# CAEN                                   ☎02 31

Although Allied bombing leveled three-quarters of its buildings during WWII, Caen (pop. 114,000) has successfully rebuilt itself into an active university town. Its strength and endurance would make even its 1050 founder, infamous William the Conqueror, proud.

**▨▨ TRANSPORTATION AND PRACTICAL INFORMATION. Trains** run to: Paris (2¼hr., 11 per day, €28); Rennes (3hr., 2 per day, €30); Rouen (1½hr., 9 per day, €21); Tours (3hr., 3 per day, €31). Bus Verts **buses** (☎08 10 21 42 14) cover the beaches and the rest of Normandy. Twisto, operating local buses and **trams,** has comprehensive schedules at its office on 15 r. de Gêole. (☎15 55 55; www.twisto.fr; €1.20, *carnet* of 10 €10.) The **tourist office** is in pl. St-Pierre. (☎27 14 14; www.caen.fr/tourisme. Open July-Aug. M-Sa 9am-7pm, Su 10am-1pm and 2-5pm; Mar.-June and Sept. M-Sa 9:30am-6:30pm, Su 10am-1pm; Oct.-Feb. M-Sa 9:30am-1pm and 2-6pm, Su 10am-1pm.) **Postal Code:** 14000.

**▨▨ ACCOMMODATIONS AND FOOD.** The cheap and spacious four-bed dorms at **Auberge de Jeunesse (HI), Résidence Robert Rème,** ❶ 68 r. Eustache Restout, make its distance from town (3km) worth the trek. Take bus # 5, dir. Fleury Cimetière, to Lycée Fresnel (15min.); go back half a block in the direction the bus came from, then take a right on r. Restout and the hostel will be on your left. (☎52 19 96; fax 84 29 49. Breakfast €2. Linens €2.50. Laundry wash €3, dry €1.50. Free Wi-Fi. Reception 5-9pm. Check-out 10am. Open daily June-Sept. Dorms €11. HI members only. Cash only.) In the center of town, **Hôtel de la Paix** ❷, 14 r. Neuve-St-Jean, off av. du 6 Juin, is a stone's throw from the château and offers simple, clean rooms that come with a TV and firm beds. (☎86 18 99; fax 38 20 74. Breakfast €5. Reception 24hr. Singles €26, with shower €29, with toilet €32; doubles €29/35/37; triples €37/43/45; quads with shower €53. Extra bed €8.

AmEx/MC/V.) Ethnic restaurants, creperies, and brasseries can be found near the château and around **Place Courtonne** and **Église St-Pierre.** Buy your groceries at **Monoprix,** 45 bd. du Maréchal Leclerc. (Open M-Sa 8:30am-8:30pm.)

**SIGHTS AND NIGHTLIFE.** Caen's biggest (and priciest) draw is the ▓**Mémorial de Caen,** which powerfully, tastefully, and creatively explores WWII, from the "failure of peace" to modern prospects for global harmony. Take bus #2 dir: Mémorial/La Folie to Mémorial. (☎06 06 44; www.memorial-caen.fr. Open mid-Feb. to mid-Nov. daily 9am-7pm; mid-Nov. to mid-Feb. Tu-Su 9:30am-6pm. €17-18; students, seniors, and 10-18 €15-16, under 10 free. Prices vary by season.) The ruins of William the Conqueror's enormous **château,** ramparts open for visiting (free), sprawl above the center of town. The **Musée de Normandie,** within the château grounds on the left, traces the cultural evolution of people living on Norman soil from the beginning of civilization to the present. (☎30 47 60; www.musee-de-normandie.caen.fr. Open June-Sept. daily 9:30am-6pm; Oct.-May M and W-Su 9:30am-6pm. Free.) The **Musée des Beaux-Arts de Caen,** inside the château to the right, houses European works from the 16th century to the present. (☎30 47 70; www.ville-caen.fr/mba. Open M and W-Su 9:30am-6pm. Free.) The **Église St-Etienne,** whose facade and nave date back to the 11th century, contains William the Conqueror's tomb. Pillagers during the Wars of Religion ravished his grave, however, so that only the monarch's left femur remains today. (Open M-Sa 8:30am-12:30pm and 1:30-7:30pm, Su 8:30am-12:30pm and 2:30-7:30pm, except during services.) At night, Caen's already busy streets turn boisterous; well-attended bars and clubs populate the area around **rue de Bras, rue des Croisiers,** and **rue St-Pierre.** Begin your quest by checking out the medieval decor of **Vertigo,** 14 r. Ecuyère, just past the intersection with r. St-Pierre. (☎85 43 12. Beer €2.20-2.70. Mixed drinks €2.70-3. Open M-Sa 10am-1am.) Later, head over to lively **Le Semaphore,** 44 r. le Bras, whose loud music, neon lights, and sleek leather bar stools set the mood. (☎39 08 57. Beer €2.20-3.50. Mixed drinks €3-4.50. Happy hour 7-9pm. Open M-Sa 7pm-4am. MC/V.)

# BAYEUX
☎02 31

Relatively unharmed by WWII, beautiful Bayeux (pop. 15,000) is an ideal base for exploring nearby D-Day beaches, especially in summer when more buses run. Visitors should not miss the 900-year-old ▓**Tapisserie Bayeux,** 70m of embroidery depicting William the Conqueror's invasion of England. The tapestry is displayed in the **Centre Guillaume le Conquérant,** on r. de Nesmond. (Open daily May-Aug. 9am-7pm; mid-Mar. to Apr. and Sept.-Oct. 9am-6:30pm; Nov. to mid-Mar. 9:30am-12:30pm and 2-6pm. €7.70, students €3.80.) Close by, **Cathédrale Notre-Dame** was the tapestry's original home. (Open daily July-Sept. 8:30am-7pm; Oct.-Dec. 8:30am-6pm; Jan.-Mar. 9am-5pm; Apr.-June 8am-6pm. French-language tours of the Old Town, including access to the labyrinth and treasury: 5 tours per day July-Aug., €4.) The **Musée de la Bataille de Normandie,** bd. Fabian Ware, recounts the D-Day landing and subsequent 76-day struggle for northern France. (☎51 46 90. Open daily May-Sept. 9:30am-6:30pm; Oct.-Apr. 10am-12:30pm and 2-6pm. English-language film about every 2hr. €6.50, students €3.80.) **Le Maupassant ❸,** 19 r. St-Martin, in the center of town, has cheerful, clean rooms above a *brasserie.* (☎92 28 53; h.lemaupassant@orange.fr. Breakfast €6. Singles €29; doubles with shower €40; quads with bath €69. Extra bed €10. MC/V.) To reach **Camping Municipal ❶,** bd. d'Eindhoven, a 12min. walk from the tourist office, take r. Genas Duhomme to the right off r. St-Martin. Continue straight on av. de la Vallée des Prés before turning right on bd. d'Eindhoven. (☎92 08 43. Office open July-Aug. 7am-9pm; Sept. and May-June 8-10am and 5-7pm. Lockout 10pm-7am. Open May-Sept. €3.20 per adult, €1.70 per child under seven, €3.90 per campsite including car and tent or car and RV. Electricity €3.30. Showers free. 10% discount for stays of five days or more. AmEx/MC/V.) Get groceries at **Marché Plus,** just down the street from the tourist office on r. St-Jean. (Open M-Sa 7am-9pm, Su 8:30am-12:30pm.)

**Trains** leave pl. de la Gare for Caen (20min., 11 per day, €5) and Paris (2½hr., 7 per day, €31). To reach the **tourist office,** r. St-Jean, turn left on bd. Sadi-Carnot, go right at the roundabout, bear right up r. Larcher past the cathedral, then turn right on r. St-Jean. (☎51 28 28; www.bayeux-bessin-tourism.com. Open July-Aug. M-Sa 9am-7pm, Su 9am-1pm and 2-6pm; Sept.-June reduced hours.) **Postal Code:** 14400.

### ⚑ DAYTRIP FROM BAYEUX: D-DAY BEACHES.

On June 6, 1944, more than a hundred thousand Allied soldiers invaded Normandy's beaches, leading to France's liberation and the downfall of Nazi Europe. Reminders of that devastating battle can be seen in the somber gravestones, remnants of German bunkers, and pockmarked landscapes. Army Rangers scaled 30m cliffs under heavy fire at the ⚑**Pointe du Hoc,** between **Utah** and **Omaha Beaches,** to capture a strongly fortified German naval battery. Having achieved their objective, the Army Rangers held the battery against counterattacks for two days past their anticipated relief. Of the 225 men in the division, only 90 survived. The ground is still churned and littered with fragments of reinforced concrete bunkers up to 5m thick.

Often referred to as "bloody Omaha," Omaha Beach, next to Colleville-sur-Mer and east of the Pointe du Hoc, is the most famous D-Day beach. On June 6, Allied preparatory bombings missed the German positions due to fog, while the full-strength German bunkers inflicted an 85% casualty rate on the first waves of Americans; ultimately, over 800 soldiers died on the beach. The 9387 graves at the **American Cemetery** stretch throughout expansive grounds on the cliffs overlooking the beach. (Open daily 9am-6pm.) To Omaha's east and just west of **Gold Beach** is **Arromanches,** a small town where the ruins of the Allies' temporary **Port Winston** lie in a giant semi-circle off the coast. The **Arromanches 360° Cinéma** combines images of modern Normandy and 1944 D-Day. (Open daily June-Aug. 9:40am-6:40pm; Sept.-May reduced hours. €4, students €3.50.)

Reaching the beaches can be difficult without a car. Some sites are accessible by **Bus Verts** from Caen on lines #1, 3, and 4 and from Bayeux on lines 70 and 74; more buses run in July-Aug., including a special D-Day line from Bayeux and Caen to Omaha Beach (€1.50-10, 1-day pass €12.) **Normandy Sightseeing Tours,** based in Bayeux, runs half-day and full-day guided tours with English-speaking guides. (☎51 70 52; www.normandywebguide.com. Reservations required. ½-day tour €40-45, students €35-40; full-day tour €75/65. Pick-up at train station, pl. du Québec, or your hotel. MC/V.) **Vélos Location** in

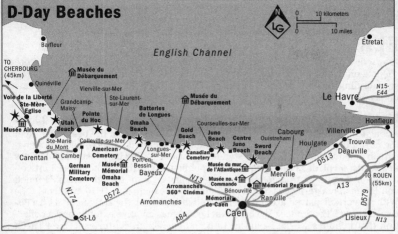

## D-Day Beaches

*English Channel*

Bayeux rents bikes, 5 r. Larcher, near the tourist office. (☎92 89 16. €10 per ½-day, €15 per day, €90 per week. Passport deposit required.)

## MONT-ST-MICHEL                                                    ☎02 33

Once regarded as a paradise, the fortified island of Mont-St-Michel is a medieval wonder. Stone and half-timbering enclose the town's narrow main street which leads steeply up to the **abbey's** twisting stairs. Adjacent to the abbey church is **La Merveille** (the Marvel), a 13th-century Gothic monastery, while four crypts support the church and keep it balanced on the hilltop. (Open daily May-Aug. 9am-7pm; Sept.-Apr. 9:30am-6pm. €8, 18-25 €5.) Hotels on Mont-St-Michel are expensive, starting at €50 per night. Pontorson, 9km away by bus, has **Camping Haliotis ●**, chemin des Soupirs and r. du Général Patton, a mini-resort offering cabins as well as campsites. (☎68 11 59; www.camping.haliotis-mont-saint-michel.com. Amenities include bar, heated pool, jacuzzi, playground, sauna, tennis and volleyball courts. Breakfast €5. Laundry €5. Reception 7:30am-10pm. Open Apr.-Nov. €4.50-6 per adult, €2-3.50 per child, €5-7 per tent or caravan and car or RV; cabins from €25. Electricity €3. MC/V.) Cheap beds are only 1.8km away at the **Camping du Mont-St-Michel ●**, rte. du Mont-St-Michel (☎60 22 10; www.le-mont-saint-michel.com. Laundry €6. Free Wi-Fi at adjoining Hôtel Motel Vert. Reception 24hr. Check-out 2pm. Gates closed 11pm-6am. Open Feb.-Nov. €4-5 per adult, €2-3 per child, €5-9 per tent site; dorms €8.60. MC/V). Courriers

> **! DON'T BE CAUGHT ADRIFT.** Visitors hoping to see the Mont illuminated at night should plan ahead. Evening transportation off the island does not exist, and walking across the 1km of sand during low tide is extremely dangerous.

Bretons (☎02 99 19 70 70), runs **buses** from Mont-St-Michel to Rennes (1¼hr., 2-3 per week, €2.50). The **tourist office** is to the left of the entrance. (☎60 14 30; www.ot-mont-saintmichel.com. Open July-Aug. daily 9am-7pm; Sept. and Apr.-June M-Sa 9am-12:30pm and 2-6:30pm, Su 9am-noon and 2-6pm; Oct.-Dec. and

Feb.-Mar. M-Sa 9am-noon and 2-6pm, Su 10am-noon and 2-5pm; Jan. M-Sa 9am-noon and 2-5:30pm, Su 10am-noon and 2-5pm.) **Postal Code:** 50170.

# FLANDERS AND PAS DE CALAIS

Every day, thousands of tourists pass through the channel ports of the Côte d'Opale on their way to Britain, yet few manage more than a quick glimpse at the surrounding regions, leaving Flanders, Picardy, and the coastal Pas de Calais undiscovered. When fleeing the ferry ports, don't miss the area's hidden gems.

## LILLE                                                                                ☎03 20

A long-time international hub with rich Flemish ancestry and the best nightlife in the north, Lille (pop. 220,000) has abandoned its industrial days to become a stylish, diverse metropolis with two stand-out museums. The impressive ▓**Palais des Beaux-Arts,** on pl. de la République (M: République), has the second-largest art collection in France, with a comprehensive display of 15th- to 20th-century French and Flemish masterpieces. (Open M 2-6pm, W-Su 10am-6pm. €10, students €7.) With artwork displayed around a renovated indoor pool, the aptly named ▓**La Piscine,** 23 r. de L'Espérance (M: Gare Jean Lebas), has creative exhibits and a collection that includes works from the 19th and early 20th centuries. (Open Tu-Th 11am-6pm, F 11am-8pm, Sa-Su 1-6pm. €3.50, F students free.) Dating from the 15th century, the **Vieille Bourse** (Old Stock Exchange), pl. Général de Gaulle, is now home to regular book markets. (Open Tu-Su 9:30am-7:30pm.)

To reach the affable **Auberge de Jeunesse (HI) ❶**, 12 r. Malpart, from the train station, circle left around the station, then turn right on r. du Molinel, left on r. de Paris, and right on r. Malpart. (☎57 08 94; lille@fuaj.org. Breakfast and linens included. Reception 24hr. Lockout 11am-3pm. Open late Jan. to mid-Dec. 3- to 6-bed dorms €20. €3 HI discount. MC/V.) The garden-themed ▓**La Pâte Brisée ❷**, 65 r. de la Monnaie, in *vieux* Lille, has seating along a quiet cobblestone street. (☎74 29 00. *Menus* €8-18. Open M-F noon-10:30pm, Sa-Su noon-11pm. MC/V.) At night, students swarm the pubs on **rue Solférino** and **rue Masséna,** while *vieux* Lille has a trendier bar scene. Energetic mobs and beer connoisseurs flock to **Pub Mac Ewan's,** 8 pl. Sébastopol, for its 140 cheap beers. (☎42 04 42. Beer from €2. Mixed drinks from €2.20. Open M-Th 11am-2am, F-Sa 11am-3am. MC/V.) Open only to locals on weekends, **Le Network Café,** 15 r. Faisan, offers weeknight revelers lots of drinking and dancing. (☎40 04 91. Open Tu-Su 10:30pm-8am. MC/V.)

**Trains** leave from Gare Lille Flandres, on pl. de la Gare (M: Gare Lille Flandres), for Paris (1hr., 20 per day, €37-50) and Brussels, BEL (1¾hr., 1-3 per day, €18-24). Gare Lille Europe, on r. Le Corbusier (M: Gare Lille Europe), sends Eurostar trains to Brussels, BEL (40min., 15 per day, €18-24) and London, BRI (1¾hr., 15 per day, €110-175), and TGVs to Paris (1¼hr., 6 per day, €37-50). Eurolines **buses** (☎78 18 88) also leave there for: Amsterdam, NTH (5hr., 2 per day, round-trip €47), Brussels, BEL (3 per day, 1½hr., round-trip €22), and London, BRI (5½hr., 2 per day, round-trip €61). From Gare Lille Flandres, walk straight down r. Faidherbe and turn left through pl. du Théâtre and pl. Général de Gaulle; turn right at the Théâtre du Nord. Offering bus, bike, Segway, and mobile phone tours, the **tourist office,** pl. Rihour (M: Rihour), is inside the Palais Rihour. (☎21 94 21; www.lilletourism.com. Open M-Sa 9:30am-6:30pm, Su 10am-noon and 2-5pm.) **Postal Code:** 59000.

## BOULOGNE-SUR-MER                                            ☎03 21

Boulogne-sur-Mer (pop. 46,000) is by far the most attractive, vigorous Channel port. Its huge aquarium, ▓**Le Grand Nausicaä,** on bd. Ste-Beuve next to the **beach,** capitalizes on the town's main source of commerce and nutrition and emphasizes ocean conservation. (Open daily July-Aug. 9:30am-7:30pm; Sept.-June 9:30am-6:30pm. €15-17, students €10-11.) The **Château-Musée,** r. de Bernet, contains France's second-largest collection of Greek urns—550 to be exact, second only to the Louvre's 25,000—and an eclectic collection of relics discovered by Boulogne natives. (☎ 10 02 20. Open M and W-Sa 10am-12:30pm and 2-5pm, Su 10am-12:30pm and 2:30-5:30pm. €1, under 18 free. English-language audio tour €2.) The **Auberge de Jeunesse (HI) ❶**, pl. Rouget de Lisle, offers tidy two- to four-bed rooms. (☎ 99 15 30; fax 99 15 39. Breakfast included. Reception Mar.-Sept. daily 8am-midnight; Oct.-Dec. M-F 9am-11pm, Sa-Su 9am-noon and 5-11pm. Dorms €21, 4-11 €12; private rooms €26, 4-11 €17. €3 HI discount. MC/V.) Restaurants are clustered at **place Dalton** and on **rue de Lille** in the *vieille ville*. **Champion** supermarket is on bd. Daunou, in the Centre Commercial de la Liane. (Open M-Sa 8:30am-8pm.) **Trains** leave Gare Boulogne-Ville, bd. Voltaire, to Calais (30min., 13 per day, €8), Lille (2½hr., 11 per day, €21; TGV 1hr., 2-3 per day, €24), and Paris (2-3hr., 11 per day, €31-58). To get to the **tourist office,** 24 q. Gambetta, from the station, turn right on bd. Voltaire, left on bd. Daunou, and continue to pl. de France past the roundabout. (☎ 10 88 10; www.tourisme-boulognesurmer.com. Open M-Sa 9:30am-12:30pm and 1:45-6:30pm, Su 10am-1pm and 3-6pm.) **Postal Code:** 62200.

## CALAIS ☎ 03 21

Calais (pop. 80,000) is a relaxing Channel port where people speak English as often as French. Rodin's famous sculpture **The Burghers of Calais** stands in front of the Hôtel de Ville, at bd. Jacquard and r. Royale, though most visitors come for the big, blue watery attraction down the road and the wide, sandy 🌊**beaches** on its edge. Exceptionally clean and pleasant 🌊**Centre Européen de Séjour/Auberge de Jeunesse (HI) ❶**, av. Maréchal Delattre de Tassigny, is less than a block from the beach and offers a bar and library. (☎ 34 70 20; www.auberge-jeunesse-calais.com. Singles €26; doubles €21. €3 HI discount. AmEx/MC/V.) Open-air morning **markets** are on pl. Crèvecoeur (Th and Sa) and pl. d'Armes (W and Sa). **Match** supermarket is at 50 pl. d'Armes. (☎ 34 33 79. Open July-Aug. M-Sa 9am-7:30pm, Su 9-11:45am; Sept.-June M-Sa 9am-7:30pm.) For more info on **ferries** to Dover, BRI see p. 52. During the day, free **buses** connect the ferry terminal and Gare Calais-Ville on bd. Jacquard, where **trains** leave for Boulogne (30min., 11 per day, €8), Lille (1¼hr., 16 per day, €16), and Paris (3¼hr., 6 per day, €30-60). To reach the **tourist office,** 12 bd. Clemenceau, turn left from the station and cross the bridge; it's on the right. (☎ 96 62 40; www.ot-calais.fr. Open June-Aug. M-Sa 10am-1pm and Su 10am-1pm and 2-6:30pm; Sept.-May 10am-1pm.) **Postal Code:** 62100.

# CHAMPAGNE AND BURGUNDY

Legend has it that when Dom Perignon first tasted champagne, he exclaimed, "Come quickly! I am drinking stars!" Few modern-day visitors need further convincing as they flock to the wine cellars in Reims and Epernay, where champagne is produced from regional grapes according to a rigorous, time-honored method. To the east, Burgundy's abbeys and cathedrals bear witness to the Middle Ages's religious fervor. Today, the region draws epicureans with its fine wines and delectable dishes like *coq au vin* and *bœuf bourguignon*.

## REIMS ☎ 03 26

From the 26 monarchs crowned in its cathedral to the bubbling champagne of its famed *caves* (cellars), everything Reims (pop. 191,000) touches turns to gold. The 🌊**Cathédrale de Notre-Dame,** built with golden limestone taken from the medieval city walls, features sea-blue stained-glass windows by Marc Chagall, hanging chandeliers, and an impressive royal history. (☎ 47 55 34. Open daily 7:30am-7:30pm. Free. English-language audio tour €5.) The adjacent **Palais du Tau,** 2 pl. du Cardinal Luçon, houses original statues from the cathedral's facade alongside majestic 16th-century tapestries. Charles X's ornate and enormous coronation robes are equally impressive. (☎47 81 79. Open May-Aug. Tu-Su 9:30am-6:30pm; Sept.-Apr. 9:30am-12:30pm and 2-5:30pm. €6.50, 18-25 €4.50, under 18 free.) ▒**Champagne Pommery,** 5 pl. du Général Gouraud, gives the best tours of Reims's champagne *caves.* Its 75,000L *tonneau* (vat) is one of the largest in the world; it, along with the maison's modern art exhibits, can be viewed in the lobby free of charge. (☎61 62 56; www.pommery.com. Tours by reservation only, €10-17.) For champagne bargains, look for sales on local brands. Good bottles start at €10. The small map-covered schoolroom where Germany surrendered to the Allies during WWII is now the **Musée de la Reddition,** 12 r. Franklin Roosevelt, a potent time capsule for the momentous event it witnessed. (☎47 84 19. Open M and W-Su 10am-noon and 2-6pm, Tu 2-6pm. €3 pass includes Musée-Abbaye St-Rémi, Foujita Chapel, Musée de Beaux-Arts, and the planetarium; students free.) In July, Reims kicks off the **Flâneries Musicales d'Eté,** with over 80 concerts in six weeks. (☎77 45 12. Tickets free-€12, students free-€10.)

> ❗ **STEER CLEAR.** Many of the roads in Reims's *centre-ville* are under serious construction until 2010. If you plan to drive in the city, be prepared for confusing detours and bring an up-to-date roadmap. The sidewalks remain open, so if you are on foot the only inconveniences will be aesthetic.

The ▒**Centre International de Séjour/Auberge de Jeunesse (HI) ❶,** chaussée Bocquaine, has clean rooms next to a park. (☎40 52 60; fax 47 35 70. Breakfast €4. Reception 24hr. 4- to 5-bed dorms €19, with toilet and shower €22; singles €28/41; doubles €21/28; triples with shower €22. €3 HI discount. MC/V.) A **Monoprix** supermarket is at 21 r. Chativesle. (Open M-Sa 9am-8pm.) Cafes, restaurants, and bars crowd **place Drouet d'Erlon,** Reims's choice nightspot. **Trains** leave bd. Joffre for Epernay (20min., 11 per day, €4.80) and Paris (1½hr., 11 per day, €21). To get to the **tourist office,** 2 r. Guillaume de Machault, follow the right curve of the roundabout to pl. Drouet d'Erlon, turn left onto r. de Vesle, and right on r. du Trésor; the office, in an old, stone ruin, is on the left before the cathedral. (☎77 45 00; www.reims-tourisme.com. Open mid-Apr. to mid-Oct. M-Sa 9am-7pm, Su 10am-6pm; mid-Oct. to mid-Apr. M-Sa 9am-6pm, Su 11am-6pm.) **Postal Code:** 51100.

# EPERNAY
☎03 26

Champagne's showcase town, Epernay (pop. 26,000) is rightly lavish and seductive. Palatial mansions, lush gardens, and swanky champagne companies distinguish the aptly named ▒**avenue de Champagne.** Here you'll find ▒**Moët & Chandon,** 20 av. de Champagne, producers of the king of all champagnes: **Dom Perignon.** (☎51 20 20; www.moet.com. Open daily 9:30-11:30am and 2-4:30pm. Tours with several tasting options for those 18+ €11-23, 10-18 €6.70, under 10 free.) Ten minutes away is **Mercier,** 70 av. de Champagne, producers of the self-proclaimed "most popular champagne in France." Tours are in roller-coaster-style cars that tell the story of its Willy-Wonka-like founder, Eugène Mercier. (☎51 22 22. Open mid-Mar. to mid-Nov. daily 9:30-11:30am and 2-4:30pm; mid-Nov. to mid-Dec. and mid-Feb. to mid-Mar. M and Th-Su 9:30-11:30am and 2-4:30pm. 30min. tour €7-15.)

Budget hotels are rare in Epernay, but ▒**Hôtel St-Pierre ❷,** 1 r. Jeanne d'Arc, offers spacious, antique-furnished rooms at unbeatable prices. (☎54 40 80; fax 57 88 68. Breakfast €6. Reception 7am-10pm. Singles €21, with shower €30; doubles €24/36. MC/V.) Ethnic food options, as well as pricier Champagne-soaked cuisine, line **rue Gambetta,** near the tourist office. Bakeries and delis dot the area around **place des Arcades** and **place Hugues Plomb.** A **Marché Plus** supermarket is at 17 pl. Hugues Plomb. (Open M-Sa 7am-9pm, Su 9am-1pm.)**Trains** leave Cours de la Gare for Paris (1¼hr., 18 per day, €19) and Strasbourg (3½hr., 3 per day, €40). From the station, walk straight ahead through pl. Mendès France, go one block up r. Gambetta to pl. de la République, and turn left on av. de Champagne to reach the **tourist** office, 7 av. de Champagne. (☎53 33 00; www.ot-epernay.fr. Open Mar. 23 to mid-Oct. M-Sa 9:30am-12:30pm and 1:30-7pm, Su 11am-4pm; mid-Oct. to Easter M-Sa 9:30am-12:30pm and 1:30-5:30pm.) **Postal Code:** 51200.

# TROYES                                                     ☎03 25

Although the city plan resembles a champagne cork, little else links Troyes (pop. 60,000) with its grape-crazy northern neighbors. Troyes features Gothic churches, 16th-century mansions, and an abundance of museums that complement an energy and social scene equal to cities many times its size. The enormous ▧**Cathédrale St-Pierre et St-Paul,** pl. St-Pierre, down r. Clemençeau past the town hall, is a flamboyant Gothic church with ornate detail and flying buttresses. Its stained glass, in the unique Troyes style, has survived several fires, bombings, and other disasters. (Open Tu-Sa 10am-1pm and 2-6pm, Su 10am-noon and 2-5pm. Free.) The **Musée d'Art Moderne,** just next door on pl. St-Pierre, houses over 2000 works by French artists, including Degas, Rodin, and Seurat, in a former Episcopal palace. (☎76 26 80. Open Tu-Su 10am-1pm and 2-6pm. €5, students and under 18 free. 1st Su of each month free.) Troyes is also home to the intriguing **Maison de l'Outil de la Pensée Ouvrière,** 7 r. de la Trinité, which houses over 8000 tools elaborately arranged in complicated geometric patterns. (☎73 28 26. Open M 1-6pm, Tu-Su 10am-6pm. €6.50, families €16, students under 25 free.) The fresh-water **Grands Lacs** dot the Forêt d'Orient region around Troyes. The **Comité Départemental du Tourisme de l'Aube,** 34 q. Dampierre, provides info on fishing, waterskiing, and windsurfing. (☎42 50 00. Open M-F 9:30am-12:30pm and 1:30-6pm.)

   ▧**Les Comtes de Champagne ❸,** 56 r. de la Monnaie, is in a 16th-century mansion with large, airy rooms. (☎73 11 70; www.comtesdechampagne.com. Reception 7am-10pm. Singles from €32; doubles from €38; triples from €61; quads from €67. AmEx/MC/V.) To reach **Camping Municipal ❶,** 2km from Troyes on N60, take bus #1 (dir.: Pont St-Marie) and ask to be let off at the campground. (☎81 02 64. Open Apr. to mid-Oct. Tent sites €6, €4.40 per person. MC/V.) Creperies and inexpensive eateries lie near **rue Champeaux,** in *quartier* St-Jean, and on **rue Général Saussier,** in *quartier* Vauluisant. **Aux Crieurs de Vin ❷,** 4-6 pl. Jean Jaurès, compensates for a tiny menu of *plats* with an elaborate selection of wines. A meal with wine runs about €13. (☎40 01 01. Open Tu-Sa noon-2pm and 7:30-10pm. MC/V.) Get groceries at **Monoprix** supermarket, 78 r. Émile Zola. (Open M-Sa 8:30am-8pm.) Lining Champeaux and **rue Molé** near **place Alexandre Israël,** cafes and taverns draw locals on warm nights. **Trains** run from av. Maréchal Joffre to Paris (1½hr., 16 per day, €22). The **tourist office,** 16 bd. Carnot, is one block from the station. (☎82 62 70; www.ot-troyes.fr. Open Nov.-Mar. M-Sa 9am-12:30pm and 2-6:30pm, Su 10am-1pm; Apr.-Oct. M-Sa 9am-12:30pm and 2-6:30pm.) **Postal Code:** 10000.

# DIJON                                                     ☎03 80

Dijon (pop. 150,000) isn't just about the mustard. The capital of Burgundy, once home to dukes who wielded a power unmatched by the French monarchy, counters its historic grandeur with a modern irreverence. The diverse ▧**Musée des Beaux-Arts** occupies the east wing of the colossal **Palais des Ducs de Bourgogne,** on pl. de la Libération, at the center of the *vieille ville.* (☎74 52 70. Open M and W-Su May-Oct. 9:30am-6pm; Nov.-Apr. 10am-5pm. Free. Temporary exhibits €2, students €1.) Built in only 20 years, the **Église Notre-Dame,** pl. Notre Dame, is one of France's most famous churches. Its 11th-century statue of the Black Virgin is credited with having liberated the city on two occasions: in 1513 from a Swiss siege and in 1944 from the German occupation. (☎41 86 76; www.notre-dame-dijon.net.) The brightly tiled towers of **Cathédrale St-Bénigne,** on pl. St-Bénigne, are visible from anywhere in town. Inside, the church features a spooky, circular crypt. (☎30 39 33. Open daily 9am-7pm. Crypt €1.) Next door, the **Musée Archéologique,** 5 r. Dr. Maret, displays Côte d'Or artifacts, including prehistoric jewelry and 17th-century mustard crocks. Its courtyard is a popular picnic spot. (☎30 88 54. Open W-Su mid-May to Sept. 9am-6pm; Oct. to mid-May 9am-12:30pm and 1:30-6pm. Free.) Dijon's **Estivade** (☎74 53 33; tickets under €8) brings dance, music, and theater to the city throughout July. In late summer, the week-long **Fêtes de la Vigne** and **Folkloriades Internationales** (☎30 37 95; www.fetesdelavigne.com; tickets €10-46) celebrate the grape harvest with dance and music from around the world.

◪**Hotel Le Jacquemart ❸**, 32 r. Verrerie, offers tidy, florally decorated rooms and a gorgeous old-fashioned staircase. (☎60 09 60. Breakfast €5.75. Reception 24hr. Singles €29-53; doubles €32-63. AmEx/MC/V.) Find cheap, colorless dorm rooms in **Foyer International d'Étudiants ❷**, 6 r. Maréchal Leclerc, which also serves as university housing. Take bus #3 from the station (dir.: St-Apollinaire la Fleuriée/Val Sully) to Billardon; r. Maréchal Leclerc is one block down. (☎71 70 00. Cafeteria open daily Oct.-early June; entrees €6. Reception 24hr. Singles €16; doubles €22. MC/V.) **Rue Amiral Boussin** has charming cafes, while reasonably priced restaurants line **rue Berbisey, rue Monge, rue Musette,** and **place Émile Zola.** Fend for yourself at the supermarket in the basement of the **Galeries Lafayette** department store, 41 r. de la Liberté. (Open M-Sa 9:15am-8pm.) From the station at cours de la Gare, **trains** run to Lyon (2hr., 14 per day, €25), Nice (6-8hr., 6-8 per day, €88), and Paris (1¾-3hr., 15-19 per day, €52). The **tourist office**, in pl. Darcy, is straight down av. Maréchal Foch from the station. (☎08 92 70 05 58; www.dijon-tourism.com. Open daily May to mid-Oct. 9am-7pm; mid-Oct. to Apr. 10am-6pm.) **Postal Code:** 21000.

# BEAUNE
☎03 80

Wine has poured out of the well-touristed town of Beaune (pop. 23,000), just south of Dijon, for centuries. Surrounded by the famous Côte de Beaune vineyards, the town itself is packed with middle-aged American tourists and wineries offering free *dégustations* (tastings). The largest of the *caves* (KAHVES; cellars), a 5km labyrinth of corridors with over four million bottles, belongs to **Patriarche Père et Fils,** 5-7 r. du Collège. (☎24 53 78. Open daily 9:30-11:30am and 2-5:30pm. €10; all proceeds to charity.) Oenophiles thirsting for knowledge can learn more about wine-making on the Côte at the **Musée du Vin,** r. d'Enfer, off pl. Général Leclerc. (☎22 08 19. Open Apr.-Nov. daily 9:30am-6pm; Dec.-Mar. W-Su 9:30am-5pm. €5.40, students €3.50.) Beaune is also home to the ◪**Hôtel-Dieu,** 2 r. de l'Hôtel-Dieu, one of France's architectural icons. A hospital built in 1443 to help the city's poor recover from the famine following the Hundred Years' War, the building is now a breathtaking museum. (☎24 45 00. Open daily late Mar. to mid-Nov. 9am-7:30pm; mid-Nov. to late-Mar. 9-11:30am and 2-6:30pm. Last entry 1hr. before closing. €5.60, students €4.80.) At **La Moutarderie Fallot,** 31 Faubourg Bretonnière, professional guides, cartoon films, and audio tours help explain the mustard-making process. (☎26 21 33; www.fallot.com. Guided 1hr. tour M-Sa at 10 and 11:30am. Extra afternoon visits July-Aug.; call the tourist office for times and ticket sales. €10.)

**Hôtel le Foch ❷**, 24 bd. Foch, across the ramparts from the train station, has bright blue rooms featuring large windows. (☎24 05 65. Singles and doubles €25, with shower €33-38; triples €45; quads €48. MC/V.) Cheap accommodations are hard to come by in Beaune, so staying in Dijon (p. 315) may be a better option. ◪**Relais de la Madeleine ❷**, 44 pl. Madeleine, features large portions of specialties like duck pâté with pistachio, peppered trout, and a wonderful *mousse au chocolat*—all of which can be sampled in a four-course €16 *menu.* (☎22 07 47. *Menus* from €13. Open M-Tu and F-Su noon-2pm and 7-10pm, Th noon-2pm. AmEx/MC/V.) Rent a bike at **Bourgogne Randonées,** 7 av. du 8 Septembre, near the station, and follow their route to the *caves.* (☎22 06 03. €4 per hr., €17 per day, €32 per 2 days, €90 per week. Credit card deposit required. Open M-Sa 9am-noon and 1:30-7pm, Su 10am-noon and 2-7pm. MC/V.) **Trains** go to Dijon (20-35min., 26 per day, €7-9), Lyon (1½-2hr., 10 per day, €21), and Paris (2-2½hr., 11 per day, €45-55). The **tourist office** is at 1 r. de l'Hôtel-Dieu. (☎26 21 30; www.ot-beaune.fr. Open late June to late Sept. M-Sa 9am-7pm, Su 9am-6pm; late Sept. to late June reduced hours.) **Postal Code:** 21200.

# ALSACE-LORRAINE AND FRANCHE-COMTÉ

Heavily influenced by its tumultuous past, the region's fascinating blend of French and German surfaces in local dialects, cuisine, and architecture. Alsatian towns display half-timbered Bavarian houses, crooked streets, and canals, while Lorraine's wheat fields are interspersed with elegant, well-planned cities. The Jura mountains in Franche-Comté offer some of France's finest cross-country skiing in winter and challenging hiking and biking trails in summer.

## STRASBOURG                                    ☎ 03 88

Just a few kilometers from the Franco-German border, Strasbourg (pop. 270,000) is a city with true international character. *Winstubs* (wine-bar restaurants specializing in local dishes) sit peacefully beside *pâtisseries* in the *vieille ville*, while German and French conversations mingle in the street. Hordes of visitors from across the continent come to relish Strasbourg's rich sights and soak up the city's old-world beauty. It's no wonder the EU placed its parliament here—Strasbourg seems to represent a more coherent European community.

> **TIP**  **BIG BUCKS FOR BIGWIGS.** Strasbourg's prices rise during EU plenary sessions. To take in the city's sights without breaking the bank, avoid visiting (in 2008) Jan. 14-17, Feb. 18-21, Mar. 10-13, Apr. 21-24, May 19-22, June 16-19, July 7-10, Sept. 1-4 and 22-25, Oct. 20-23, Nov. 17-20, and Dec. 15-18.

**TRANSPORTATION AND PRACTICAL INFORMATION.** Strasbourg is a major rail hub. **Trains** go to: **Frankfurt, GER** (2-4hr., 13 per day, €52); **Luxembourg** (2-3hr., 10 per day, €33); **Paris** (4hr., 24 per day, €47; TGV 2½hr., €63); **Zürich, SWI** (3hr., 4 per day, €40-47). The **tourist office** is at 17 pl. de la Cathédrale. (☎52 28 28; www.ot-strasbourg.fr. Open daily 9am-7pm.) There's also a branch at pl. de la Gare, near the train station. (☎32 51 49. Open M-Sa 9am-12:30pm and 1:45-7pm.) Go online at **Net.sur.cour,** 18 q. des Pêcheurs. (☎35 66 76. €1 per 30min. Open M-Sa 9:30am-8:30pm and Su 1:30-7:30pm.) **Postal Code:** 67000.

**ACCOMMODATIONS AND FOOD.** High-quality, inexpensive hotels are all over the city, especially around the train station. Wherever you stay, make reservations early, particularly in summer. Hotel prices often drop on weekends and when the EU Parliament is not in session. **Hôtel le Grillon ❷**, 2 r. Thiergarten, near the train station, offers the best value, with a young staff, soft comforters, color-themed floors, and dark wooden furnishings. (☎32 71 88; www.grillon.com. Breakfast €7.50. Internet €1 per 15min; Wi-Fi free. Reception 24hr. Singles €33, with shower €43-58; doubles €40/50-65. Extra bed €13. MC/V.) The **Centre International d'Accueil de Strasbourg (CIARUS) ❷**, 7 r. Finkmatt, has a friendly staff and clean, bright rooms complete with shower and toilet. From the train station, take r. du Maire-Kuss to the canal, turn left, and follow q. St-Jean. Turn left on r. Finkmatt; the hotel will be on your left. (☎15 27 88; www.ciarus.com. Breakfast included; other cafeteria meals €5-7. Free Wi-Fi. When parliament is in session 6- to 8-bed dorms €24; 3- to 4-bed dorms €28; 2-bed dorms €31; singles €47; family rooms €24 per person. When parliament is out of session 6- to 8-bed dorms €21; 3- to 4-bed dorms €25; 2-bed dorms €28; singles €44; family rooms €21 per person. MC/V.) A spacious riverside campground, **Camping la Montagne Verte ❶**, 2 r. Robert Forrer, offers tennis courts, basketball, and a bar, but no privacy. (☎30 25 46. Reception 7am-10pm. Car curfew 10pm. €4.80 per person, €2 per child, €5.50 per site. Open mid-Mar. to Oct. and late Nov.-early Jan. Electricity €4.30. MC/V.) The

FRANCE

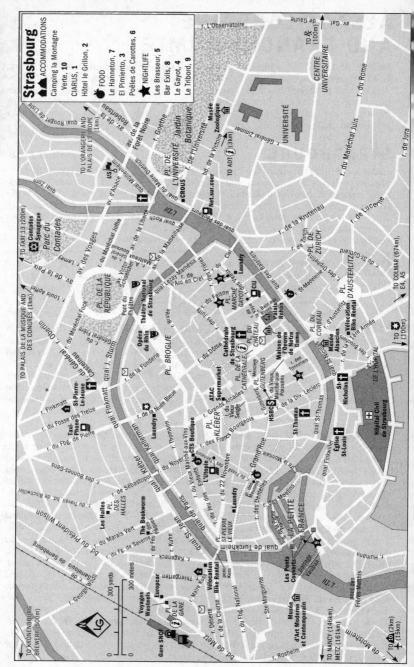

### Strasbourg

**▲▲ ACCOMMODATIONS**
Camping la Montagne Verte, **10**
CIARUS, **1**
Hôtel le Grillon, **2**

**● FOOD**
Le Hanneton, **7**
El Pimiento, **3**
Poêles de Carottes, **6**

**★ NIGHTLIFE**
Les Brasseur, **5**
Bar Exils, **8**
Le Gayot, **4**
Le Tribord, **9**

scenic ■La Petite France neighborhood, especially along r. des Dentelles, is full of informal *winstubs* with Alsatian specialties such as *choucroute garnie* (spiced sauerkraut with meats). Explore **place de la Cathédrale, rue Mercière,** or **rue du Vieil Hôpital** for restaurants, and **place Marché Gayot,** off r. des Frères, for cafes. Friends gobble down Alsatian specialties by candelabra light at ■**Le Hanneton (Chez Denis) ❸,** 5 r. Ste. Madeleine, a relatively untouristed *winstub* with a ceiling full of traditional Alsacian *sorcières* (witch dolls) and only seven tables. (☎36 93 76. Open Tu 7-11pm, W-Su noon-2pm and 7-11pm. MC/V.) **El Pimiento ❷,** 52 r. du Jeu des Enfants, a chile-themed tapas joint, serves both traditional favorites and creative variations. (☎21 94 52. Most tapas €2.30-5.90. Sangria €3.10. Open M-Sa 11:30am-2:30pm and 6:30pm-midnight. AmEx/MC/V.) On the outskirts of La Petite France, **Poêles de Carottes ❷,** 2 pl. des Meuniers, offers a plethora of healthful (and yummy) vegetarian dishes in a canary-yellow dining room decorated with seed packets. (☎32 33 23. Pizzas, *gratins,* and huge salads €7-11. €3 course lunch *menu* €11. Open Tu-Sa noon-3pm and 7-10:30pm. MC/V.) For groceries, swing by **ATAC,** 47 r. des Grandes Arcades, off pl. Kléber. (Open M-Sa 8:30am-8:30pm. MC/V.)

◨ ▨ **SIGHTS AND NIGHTLIFE.** The tower of the Gothic ■**Cathédrale de Strasbourg** stretches 142m skyward; young Goethe scaled its 332 steps regularly to cure his fear of heights. Inside, the **Horloge Astronomique** demonstrates 16th-century Swiss clockmaking wizardry. While you wait for the clock to strut its stuff—apostles parade out of the clock face and a cock crows to greet St. Peter daily at 12:30pm—check out the **Pilier des Anges** (Angels' Pillar), a depiction of the Last Judgment. (Cathedral open M-Sa 7-11:40am and 12:40-7pm, Su 12:45-6pm. Tower open daily July-Aug. 8:30am-7pm; Apr.-June and Sept. 9am-6pm; Mar. and Oct. 9am-5:30pm; Nov.-Feb. 9am-4:30pm. Clock tickets sold at the northern entrance to the Cathedral; €1. Tower €4.40, students €2.20.) **Palais Rohan,** 2 pl. du Château, houses three small but excellent museums. The **Musée des Beaux-Arts** displays 14th- to 19th-century art, including works by Botticelli, Giotto, Goya, Raphaël, and Rubens. The **Musée des Arts Décoratifs,** refurbished for Napoleon in 1805, features pistachio-green rooms encrusted with gold and marble, including the emperor's bedroom and library. The **Musée Archéologique** illustrates Alsace's history through old tools, relics, and a slew of skeletons. (All open M and W-Su 10am-6pm. €4 each, students €2; free 1st Su of every month.) Take bus #6 (dir.: pl. des Sports) from pl. des Halles to **L'Orangerie,** the city's most spectacular park, complete with a zoo and stork farm. In summer, the **Pavilion Joséphine** hosts free concerts.

Strasbourg, home to an international university, has bars everywhere. ■**Bar Exils,** 28 r. de l'Ail, offers over 40 beers, leather couches, and an upbeat spirit that buzzes into the early morning. (☎35 52 70. Beer from €2; after 10pm €2.50. Open M-F noon-4am, Sa-Su 2pm-4am. MC/V; min. €6.) Rock all night at **Le Tribord,** Ponts Couverts, a lively gay and lesbian club situated in a small boat. From pl. du Quartier Blanc, make a right onto the footpath by the canal in front of the Hotel du Département, following it to the waterside. The club is inside the well-marked first boat on the right. (☎36 22 90. Beer from €2.50. Mixed drinks from €4. Open Th-Sa 10pm-4am). Students pack the microbrewery **Les Brasseurs,** 22 r. des Veaux, enjoying its home brews, late-night food, and weekly concerts. (☎36 12 13. Beer from €2; after 9:30pm €2.40. Live music F-Sa 9:30pm. Happy hour 5-7pm; 2-for-1 beers. Open daily 11:30am-1am. MC/V.) **Le Gayot,** 18 r. des Frères, attracts a slightly older crowd, and is a perfect place to enjoy a leisurely drink during summer. (☎36 31 88. Beer €3.10. Mixed drinks from €6.10. Mojito €8.50. Open June-Aug. daily 11am-2am; Sept.-May M-Sa 11am-1am. MC/V; min. €8.)

# LA ROUTE DU VIN

The vineyards of Alsace flourish in a 150km corridor along the foothills of the Vosges from Strasbourg to Mulhouse—a region known as the *Route du Vin.* The

FRANCE

Romans were the first to ferment Alsatian grapes, and today Alsatians sell over 150 million bottles annually. Picture-book houses and free *dégustations* draw hordes of wine-loving and largely middle-aged tourists to the medieval villages along the route. Though an abundance of spirits characterize towns along *la Route du Vin*, different mediums for enjoying regional produce distinguish each village; some offer tours through of massive vineyards while others are geared toward sipping wine sophisticatedly over dinner. Consider staying in **Colmar** (p. 321) or **Sélestat** (p. 320), larger towns that anchor the southern Route, and daytripping to the smaller (and pricier) towns. The best source of info on regional *caves* is the **Centre d'Information du Vin d'Alsace**, 12 av. de la Foire aux Vins, at the Maison du Vin d'Alsace in Colmar. (☎03 89 20 16 20. Open M-F 9am-noon and 2-5pm.) Tourist offices in Strasbourg (p. 317) or along the Route dispense helpful advice, including the *Alsace Wine Route* brochure.

## ⌐ TRANSPORTATION

**Buses,** the most inexpensive option, run frequently from Colmar to surrounding towns, though smaller northern towns prove difficult to reach. **Car rental** from Strasbourg or Colmar expensively resolves transportation problems. Despite well marked trails and turn-offs, only those with stamina should **bike** the lengthy and often hilly roads from Colmar. **Trains** connect Sélestat, Molsheim, Barr, Colmar, and Mulhouse. Minimal sidewalks make country roads difficult to walk along.

## SÉLESTAT                                                    ☎03 88

Sélestat (pop. 17,500), between Colmar and Strasbourg, is a haven of good wines and good vibes often overlooked by tourists on their way to more "authentic" Route cities. Founded in 1452, the ◨**Bibliothèque Humaniste**, 1 r. de la Bibliothèque, contains a fascinating collection of illuminated manuscripts and meticulously handwritten books produced during Sélestat's 15th-century Humanist heyday. The library is considered one of Alsace's greatest treasures. (Open July-Aug. M and W-F 9am-noon and 2-6pm, Sa 9am-noon and 2-5pm, Su 2-5pm; Sept.-June M-F 9am-noon and 2-6pm, Sa 9am-noon. €3.70, students €2.15.) Nearby, on r. du Sel, the **Maison du Pain** reveals the history of bread-making from 12,500 BC to the present. View models of ancient and modern bakeries before taking history into your own hands: a workshop in the ground-floor *pâtisserie* allows visitors to twist and bake their own pretzels. (Open Dec. daily 10am-7pm; Jan. and Mar.-Nov. Tu-F 9:30am-12:30pm and 2-6pm, Sa 9am-12:30pm and 2-6pm, Su 9am-12:30pm and 2:30-6pm. Closed Dec. 25-Jan. 7 and mid-Jan to Feb. €4.60, students €3.80.)

**Hôtel de l'Ill ❸,** 13 r. des Bateliers, has 15 cheerfully colored rooms with shower and TV. (☎92 91 09. Breakfast €5. Reception 7am-9pm. Check-out 10am. Singles €30; doubles €40; triples €50. AmEx/MC/V.) A local favorite, **JP Kamm ❶,** 15 r. des Clefs, has outdoor dining and a large selection of mouthwatering desserts. (☎92 11 04. Pizzas and quiches €3.50-4.70. Ice cream from €4.60; cheaper if ordered to go. Open Tu and Th-F 8am-7pm, W 8:30am-7pm, Sa 8am-6pm, Su 8am-1pm. Terrace service Tu-F until 6:30pm, Sa until 5:30pm. MC/V; min. €8.) An enormous **market** fills the town center, offering bread, meat, and produce, as well as clothing, books, toys and other knick-knacks. (Open Tu 8am-noon.) From pl. de la Gare, **trains** run to Colmar (15min., 38 per day, €4) and Strasbourg (30min., 54 per day, €7). The **tourist office,** bd. Général Leclerc, in the Commanderie St-Jean rents **bikes** (€13 per day). From the train station, go straight on av. de la Gare, through pl. du Général de Gaulle, to av. de la Liberté. Turn left onto bd. du Maréchal Foch, which becomes bd. Général Leclerc. The tourist office is on the left, past the restaurant L'Improviste. (☎58 87 20; www.selestat-tourisme.com. Open July-Aug. M-Sa 9:30am-12:30pm and 1:30-6:45pm, Su 10:30am-3pm; Sept.-June reduced hours.) **Postal Code:** 67600.

# COLMAR ☎03 89

A great base for exploring smaller Route towns, Colmar (pop. 68,000) is defined by its pastel facades and crowds of tourists. The **Musée Unterlinden,** 1 r. d'Unterlinden, centered around a beautiful courtyard, has a collection ranging from Romanesque to Renaissance, including Grünewald's *Issenheim Altarpiece*, an Alsatian treasure. (Open May.-Oct. daily 9am-6pm; Nov.-Apr. W-M 9am-noon and 2-5pm. €7, students €5. MC/V; min. €8.) The **Église des Dominicains,** pl. des Dominicains, is a bare-bones showroom for Colmar's other masterpiece, Schongauer's ornate *Virgin in the Rose Bower*. (Open June-Oct. Su-Th 10am-1pm and 3-6pm, F-Sa 10am-6pm; Apr.-May and Nov.-Dec. daily 10am-1pm and 3-6pm. €1.50, students €1.) The 10-day **Foire aux Vins d'Alsace** is the region's largest wine fair, with concerts, free tastings, and exhibitions. (Mid-Aug. ☎03 90 50 50 50; www.foire-colmar.com. 11:30am-1:30pm €1, 1:30pm-5pm €3, after 5pm €5. Concerts €20-43.)

To reach the **Auberge de Jeunesse (HI) ❶,** 2 r. Pasteur, take bus #4 (dir.: Europe) to Pont Rouge. The hostel offers dorm rooms at bargain prices. (☎80 57 39. Breakfast €4. Linens €4. Reception Nov. to mid-Dec. and mid-Jan. to Feb. 7-10am and 5-11pm; Apr.-Sept. 7-10am and 5pm-10:30pm. Lockout 10am-5pm. Curfew midnight, in winter 11pm. Open mid-Jan. to mid-Dec. Dorms €12; singles €17; doubles €26. HI discount €3. MC/V.) **La Pergola et sa Taverne ❷,** 28 r. des Marchands, has regional cuisine in a cozy restaurant full of toy pigs and puppets. (☎41 36 79. *Tartes flambées* and pan-fried potato-and-cheese *roestis* €8.50-13. Open M-W, F-Su noon-2:30pm and 6-10pm. MC/V.) A **Monoprix** supermarket is on pl. Unterlinden. (Open M-Sa 8am-8pm. AmEx/MC/V.) **Trains** depart pl. de la Gare for Lyon (4½-5½hr., 9 per day, €42), Paris (5¼hr., 2 per day, €52), and Strasbourg (30min., 12 per day, €10). To get to the **tourist office,** 4 r. d'Unterlinden, from the train station, turn left on av. de la République, which becomes r. Kléber, and follow it to the right to pl. Unterlinden. (☎20 68 92; www.ot-colmar.fr. Open July-Aug. M-Sa 9am-7pm, Su 10am-1pm; Sept.-June reduced hours.) **Postal Code:** 68000.

# NANCY ☎03 83

Nancy (pop. 106,000) combines classical beauty with innovation in everything from its museums to its architecture. The city that spawned the Art Nouveau "Nancy School" in 1901 is the artistic and intellectual heart of modern Lorraine. The works on display at the ◼Musée de L'École de Nancy, 36-38 r. du Sergent Blandan, reject straight lines, instead using organic forms to recreate aspects of the natural landscape. Take bus #122 (dir.: Villers Clairlieu) or 123 (dir.: Vandoeuvre Cheminots) to Painlevé. (☎40 14 86; www.ecole-de-nancy.com. Open W-Su 10:30am-6pm. €6, students €4. W students free. €8 pass to all museums.) The recently renovated ◼place Stanislas houses three Neoclassical pavilions, including **place de la Carrière,** a former jousting ground that Stanislas Leszczynski—Duke of Lorraine from 1737 to 1766—refurbished with Baroque architecture, golden angel sculptures, and wrought-iron ornaments. The *place*'s beauty can be absorbed over a large cup of coffee at one of its many cafes. The collection in the **Musée des Beaux-Arts,** 3 pl. Stanislas, features works dating from the 14th century to the present, including gems by Delacroix, Monet, Picasso, Rodin, and stunning glasswork by Daum. (☎85 30 72. Open M, W-Su 10am-6pm. €6, students €4. W students free.) Roses lead into the aromatic **Roserie,** in the relaxing **Parc de la Pépinière,** just north of pl. de la Carrière. Look for Rodin's famous sculpture of **Claude Gellée (Le Lorrain)**

## GIVING BACK

### HELPING THROUGH HUMOR

At the age of 26, Michel Colucci adopted the name Coluche and—like so many before him with only one appellation—embarked on a career in entertainment. Sure enough, the man with the razor-sharp political wit quickly became one of France's most beloved comedians. He ran for president in 1981—"I'll quit politics when politicians quit comedy"—but dropped out of the race when polls showed that he actually had a chance of winning. Before a motorcycle accident ended his life in 1986, Coluche founded the charity **Restos du Coeur** (restaurants of the heart), leaving a permanent mark on France.

Restos du Coeur comprises a network of soup kitchens and other volunteer activities. Their emphasis on fostering personal relationships between those who volunteer and those who receive aid, as well as on good humor—would a comedian have it any other way?—has set them apart as a uniquely positive force of goodwill. Volunteers can work the kitchens, provide face-to-face companionship, or help combat illiteracy, but they have to be able to do it for a few months.

*Paris office: 4 cité d'Hauteville (☎53 24 98 00; www.restosducoeur.org). Meals distributed daily in different regions of the city.*

near the entrance. (Open daily June-Aug. 6:30am-10:30pm; Sept.-Oct. and Apr.-May 6:30am-9pm; Nov.-Mar. 6:30am-8pm. Free.)

Don't let the shabby exterior of **Hôtel de L'Académie ❷**, 7 r. des Michottes, deter you; it has large, clean rooms in a convenient location. (☎35 52 31. Breakfast €3.50. Reception 7am-11pm. Singles €20-28; doubles €28-39. AmEx/MC/V.) Cheaper **Château de Remicourt (HI) ❶**, 149 r. de Vandœuvre, is in Villiers-les-Nancy, 4km away. From the Nancy station, take bus #126 to St-Fiacre (dir.: Villiers Clairlieu; 2 per hr.); head downhill from the stop and turn right on r. de la Grange des Moines, which turns into r. de Vandoeuvre and follow the hostel's signs. (☎27 73 67. Reception M-Sa 9:30am-9pm, Su 5:30-9pm. Dorms €15; 2-bed dorm €17. AmEx/MC/V.) Immerse yourself (or your bread) in the cheesy delights of ◪**Le Bouche à Oreille ❷**, 42 r. des Carmes (☎35 17 17. Fondues €14-15. Lunch *menu* €11. Dinner *menu* €17. Open M, Sa 7-10:30pm, Tu-F noon-1:30pm and 7-10:30pm. AmEx/MC/V.). Restaurants also line **rue des Maréchaux, place Lafayette**, and **place St-Epvre**. A **Shopi** supermarket is at 26 r. St-Georges. (Open M-F 9am-8pm, Sa 9am-7:30pm. MC/V.) **Rue Stanislas** and **Grand Rue** are great places to grab a drink. ◪**Blitz**, 76 r. St-Julien, is smoky red-velvet suave at its best. (Beer from €2.20. Mixed drinks from €5. Open M 5:30pm-2am, Tu- Sa 2pm-2am. AmEx/MC/V; min. €7 charge.) **Trains** depart from the station at 3 pl. Thiers for Paris (3½ hr., 27 per day, €42-50) and Strasbourg (1¼hr., 20 per day, €23). The new **TGV Est line** also connects Nancy to Paris (1½hr.). To reach the **tourist office**, head through pl. Thiers, turn left on r. Mazagran, pass through a stone archway on the right, and continue straight. (☎35 22 41; www.ot-nancy.fr. Open Apr.-Oct. M-Sa 9am-7pm, Su 10am-5pm; Nov.-Mar. M-Sa 9am-6pm, Su 10am-1pm.) **Postal Code:** 54000.

## BESANÇON                    ☎03 81

Bounded by the Doubs River on three sides and a steep bluff on the fourth, Besançon (pop. 123,000) hosts a slew of world-class museums and an active student population. Julius Caesar conquered the vulnerable city in 58 BC, unaware that Vauban's 17th-century enormous **citadelle,** at the end of r. des Fusilles de la Résistance, would one day make Besançon completely impenetrable. More daunting than pretty, Besançon's mountaintop fortresses require an intense uphill climb to reach but reward visitors with emotionally moving displays. Within the *citadelle*, the deeply touching ◪**Musée de la Résistance et de la Déportation** chronicles the Nazi rise to power and the events of WWII from a French perspective. (☎87 83 33; www.citadelle.com. Open daily July-Aug. 9am-7pm, Sept.-June reduced hours. In summer €7.80, students €6.50; in winter €7.20/6.) The whirring and ticking ▓Musée du Temps, 96 Grand Rue, exhibits clocks from Galileo's era to the present day with quirky games and hands-on experiments. (☎87 81 53. Open Tu-Sa 9:15am-noon and 2-6pm, Su 10am-6pm. Tu-F €5, Sa €2.50, Su free; students free.) The Musée des Beaux-Arts et d'Archéologie, on pl. de la Révolution, houses an exceptional collection ranging from ancient Egyptian mummies to works by Matisse, Picasso, and Renoir. (☎87 80 49. Open M and W-F 9:30am-noon and 2-6pm, Sa-Su 9:30am-6pm. €5; Su, students, and under 18 free.)

To reach the Foyer Mixte de Jeunes Travailleurs (HI) ❷, 48 r. des Cras, take a left from the train station onto r. de la Viotte, the first right onto r. de l'Industrie, then a right on r. de Belfort to pl. de la Liberté. Take bus #5 or night line A (dir.: Orchamps, 3-5 per hr., €1.05) to the Les Oiseaux stop. The hostel offers clean single rooms with private bathrooms and free Internet in the lobby. (☎40 32 00. Breakfast included. Open Apr.-Sept. Singles €23, 2nd night €18. AmEx/MC/V.) Hôtel du Nord ❸, 8 r. Moncey, is a fully outfitted hotel in a quiet, central location. (☎81 34 56. Breakfast €4.80. Free Wi-Fi. Singles and doubles with shower or bath €38-51, triples and quads with shower €51-59. AmEx/MC/V.) Rue Claude-Pouillet and rue des Granges have the cheapest dining options and the best nightlife. Like a friend's cozy kitchen, ▓Au Gourmand ❷, 5 r. Megevand, serves hearty meat and potato dishes. (☎81 40 56. Entrees €6-8. Open Tu-F 11:30am-1:45pm and 6:45-8:30pm, Sa 6:45-8:30pm. Reservations recommended. MC/V.) Carpe Diem, 2 pl. Jean Gigoux, brings together all ages and creeds for genial conversation and idea-swapping (☎83 11 18. Beer from €2. Regular events, films, and concerts. Open M-Th 9am-1am, F-Sa 9am-2am, Su 9am-11pm. MC/V over €16).

Trains (☎08 36 35 35 35) leave av. de la Paix for Dijon (1hr., 34 per day, €13), Paris (2½hr., 9 per day, €49), and Strasbourg (3hr., 9 per day, €30). Monts Jura buses, with an office in the train station (☎08 25 00 22 44), go to Pontarlier (1hr., 8 per day, €7.50). From the station, walk downhill; follow av. de la Paix as it turns into av. Maréchal Foch and continue to the left as it becomes av. de l'Helvétie before the river. Once you reach pl. de la 1ère Armée Française, the *vieille ville* is across the pont de la République. The tourist office, 2 pl. de la 1ère Armée Française, is in the park to the right. (☎80 92 55; www.besancon-tourisme.com. Open June-Sept. M 10am-7pm, Tu-Sa 9:30am-7pm, Su 10am-5pm; Oct.-May reduced hours.) Postal Code: 25000.

# PONTARLIER AND THE HAUT-JURA MOUNTAINS ☎03 81

The sedate town of Pontarlier (pop. 18,400) is a good base from which to explore the oft-overlooked Haut-Jura Mountains. The Jura are best known for cross-country skiing; nine trails cover every skill level. (Day pass available at the Le Larmont and Le Malmaison trails; €6, under 17 €3.50.) Le Larmont is the closest Alpine ski area (☎46 55 20). In summer, fishing, hiking, and mountain biking are popular. There's a mountain bike departure point to the north just off r. Pompée, and another to the south, about 2km west of Forges. Hikers can choose between the GR5, an international 262km trail accessible from Le Larmont, and the GR6, which leads to a narrow valley and dramatic château. To get to Camping du Larmont ❶, on r. du Tolombief, from the station, turn right onto Rocade Georges Pompidou, cross the river, and bear left on r. de l'Industrie. Take the first right onto av. de Neuchâtel and follow the signs. (☎46 23 33; www.camping-pontarlier.fr. Reception July-Aug. daily 8am-10pm, Sept.-June M-Sa 9am-noon and 5-8pm, Su 9am-noon. July-Aug. €3.20 per adult, €2 per child, €7.50 per tent and car; Sept.-June €3.20/2/6.50. 2-person chalets July-Aug. €60 per day, €405 per week; Sept.-June €53/315. Extra person €5 per night. 6-person max. Electricity Sept.-June €6; July-Aug. €4. MC/V.) Monts Jura buses (☎ 39 88 80) run to Besançon (1hr., 5 per day, €8). The **tourist office** is at 14bis r. de la Gare. (☎ 46 48 33; www.pontarlier.org. Open July-Aug. M-Sa 9am-7pm, Su 10am-noon; Sept.-June M-Sa 9am-12:30pm and 1:30-6pm.) **Postal Code:** 25300.

# RHÔNE-ALPES AND MASSIF CENTRAL

Nature's architecture is the Alps' real attraction. The curves of the Chartreuse Valley rise to rugged crags in the Vercors range and crescendo at Europe's highest peak, Mont Blanc (4807m). From bases like Chamonix, winter skiers enjoy some of the world's most challenging slopes. In summer, hikers take over the mountains, seeking pristine vistas and clear air.

## LYON ☎ 04 78

Ultra-modern, ultra-friendly, and undeniably gourmet, Lyon (pop. 453,000) elicits cries of "Forget Paris!" from backpackers. Its location—at the confluence of the Rhône and Saône rivers and along an Italian road—earned Lyon (then Lugdunum) its place as Roman Gaul's capital. One of the major stops on the inaugural TGV line from Paris to Marseille, the city continues to be a major transportation and trading hub while shedding its longstanding reputation as a gritty industrial city. Lyon is now better known for its beautiful parks, modern financial center, well-preserved Renaissance quarter, and fantastic restaurants. If the way to your heart is through your stomach, Lyon will have you at *"bon appetit."*

## ▐ TRANSPORTATION

**Flights:** Aéroport Lyon-Saint-Exupéry (☎ 08 26 80 08 26). Satobuses/Navette Aéroport (☎ 72 68 72 17) **shuttles** to Gare de la Part-Dieu, Gare de Perrache, and subway stops Grange-Blanche, Jean Macé, and Mermoz Pinel (every 20min., €8.60). **Air France,** 10 q. Jules Courmont, 2ème (☎ 08 20 32 08 20), has 10 daily flights to Paris's Orly and Charles de Gaulle airports (from €118). Open M-Sa 9am-6pm.

**Trains:** The more convenient **TGV,** which stops at the airport, is cheaper than daily flights to Paris. Trains passing through Lyon stop at **Gare de la Part-Dieu,** 5 pl. Béraudier (M: Part-Dieu), on the Rhône's east bank. Info desk open daily 5am-12:45am. Ticket window open M-Th and Sa 5:15am-11pm, F and Su 5:15am-midnight. Trains terminating in Lyon continue to **Gare de Perrache,** pl. Carnot (M: Perrache). Open daily 4:45am-12:30am. Ticket window open M 5am-10pm, Tu-Sa 5:30am-10pm, Su 7am-10pm. SNCF trains go from both stations to: **Dijon** (2hr., 1 per hr., €26); **Grenoble** (1½hr., 1 per hr., €18); **Marseille** (1½hr., 1 per hr., €44); **Nice** (6hr., 3 per day, €62); **Paris** (2hr., 17 per day, €60); **Strasbourg** (5½hr., 6 per day, €49); **Geneva, SWI** (4hr., 6 per day, €23). The **SNCF Boutique,** 2 pl. Bellecour, is near the tourist office. Open M-F 9am-6:45pm, Sa 10am-6:30pm.

**Buses:** On the Gare de Perrache's lowest level and at Gorge de Loup in the 9*ème.* (☎ 72 61 72 61) It's almost always cheaper, faster, and simpler to take the train. Domestic companies include **Philibert** (☎ 72 75 06 06). **Eurolines** (☎ 72 56 95 30; www.eurolines.fr) travels out of France; office on the main floor of Perrache open M-Sa 9am-9pm.

**Local Transportation: TCL** (☎ 08 20 42 70 00; www.tcl.fr) has info offices at both bus stations and all major metro stops. *Plan de Poche* (pocket map) available from any TCL branch. Tickets valid for all forms of mass transport, including **metro, buses,** and **trams.** Tickets €1.50, *carnet* of 10 €13; student discount includes 10 passes valid for 1 month €10.80. Pass valid 1hr. in 1 dir., connections included. *Ticket Liberté* day pass (€4.40) is a great deal for short-term visitors. The clean, efficient **metro** runs 5am-12:20am, as do **buses** and **trams,** which have 2 different lines; T1 connects Part-Dieu to Perrache directly. A night *navette* (shuttle bus) runs between pl. Tarreaux and local universities; Th-Sa 1 per hr. 1-4am. **Funiculars** swing between the Vieux Lyon metro stop, pl. St-Jean, and the top of Fourvière and St-Just until midnight. €2.20.

## ORIENTATION AND PRACTICAL INFORMATION

Lyon is divided into nine **arrondissements** (districts). The 1*er*, 2*ème*, and 4*ème* lie on the **presqu'île** (peninsula), which juts toward the **Saône** River to the west and the **Rhône** to the east. Starting in the south, the 2*ème* (the *centre ville*) includes the **Gare de Perrache** and **place Bellecour**. The nocturnal **Terreaux** neighborhood, with its sidewalk cafes and student-packed bars, makes up the 1*er*. Farther north, the *presqu'île* widens into the 4*ème* and the famous **Croix-Rousse**. The main pedestrian roads on the *presqu'île* are **rue de la République** and **rue Victor Hugo**. West of the Saône, **Fourvière Hill** and its basilica overlook **Vieux Lyon** (5*ème*). East of the Rhône (3*ème* and 6-8*ème*) lie the **Gare de la Part-Dieu** and most of the city's population.

**Tourist Office:** In the **Pavilion** at pl. Bellecour, 2*ème* (☎04 72 77 69 69; www.lyon-france.com). M: Bellecour. The **Lyon City Card** authorizes unlimited public transport along with admission to museums, tours, and river boat cruises. 1-day pass €19; 2-day €29; 3-day €39. Open June-Sept. M-Sa 9:30am-6:30pm, Su 10am-5:30pm; Oct.-May M-Sa 10am-5:30pm. MC/V.

**Police:** 47 r. de la Charité (☎42 26 56). M: Perrache.

**Hospital: Hôpital Hôtel-Dieu,** 1 pl. de l'Hôpital, 2*ème*, near q. du Rhône, is the most central. City hospital line ☎08 20 69.

**Internet Access: Raconte Moi la Terre** (☎92 60 23), at the intersection of r. Grolee and r. Thomassin, 2*ème*. €4 per hr. Open M noon-7:30pm, Tu-Sa 10am-7:30pm. Free Wi-Fi at **McDonald's.**

**Post Office:** pl. Antonin Poncet, 2*ème* (☎04 72 40 65 22), near pl. Bellecour. **Postal Code:** 69001-69009; last digit indicates *arrondissement*.

## ACCOMMODATIONS AND CAMPING

September is Lyon's busiest month; it's easier and cheaper to find a place in summer but still wise to reserve ahead. A room less than €30 is rare. Low-end hotels are east of **place Carnot.** There are inexpensive options north of **place des Terraux.** Watch out for budget-breaking accommodations in *vieux* Lyon.

**Auberge de Jeunesse (HI),** 41-45 montée du Chemin Neuf, 5*ème* (☎15 05 50). M: Vieux Lyon. A grassy terrace and bar draw international backpackers. English-speaking staff. Breakfast and linens included. Laundry €4.05. Internet €5 per hr. Max. 6-night stay. Reception 24hr. Reserve ahead in summer. Dorms €17. HI members only. MC/V. ❶

**Hôtel Iris,** 36 r. de l'Arbre Sec, 1*er* (☎39 93 80; www.hoteliris.freesurf.fr). M: Hôtel de Ville. This convent-turned-hotel has a tranquil feel in a prime location near Terreaux. Creatively decorated rooms demonstrate its owner's artistic eye. Breakfast €5.50. Reception 8am-8:30pm. Reserve 2 weeks ahead in summer. Singles and doubles with sink €40-42, with toilet and shower €48-50. MC/V. ❸

**Hôtel d'Ainay,** 14 r. des Remparts d'Ainay, 2*ème* (☎42 43 42; fax 04 72 77 51 90). M: Ampère-Victor Hugo. Offers spacious rooms with private bath in a great location between Perrache and Bellecour. Breakfast €4.50. Reception 24hr. Singles €27, with shower €42; doubles €32/48. Extra bed €8. MC/V. ❸

**Hôtel de la Marne,** 78 r. de la Charité, 2*ème* (☎37 07 46). M: Perrache. 2min. from Gare de Perrache. This recently renovated hotel lets quiet rooms with A/C and spacious bathrooms. The potpourri and abstract art in each room create a homey, modern aura. Breakfast €6. Reception 24hr. Singles €47; doubles €53-63. MC/V. ❸

**Hôtel de Paris,** 16 r. de la Platière, 1*er* (☎28 00 95; www.hoteldeparis-lyon.com). M: Hôtel de Ville. Offering small, no-frills rooms, Hôtel de Paris has clean, recently reno-

**FRANCE**

FRANCE

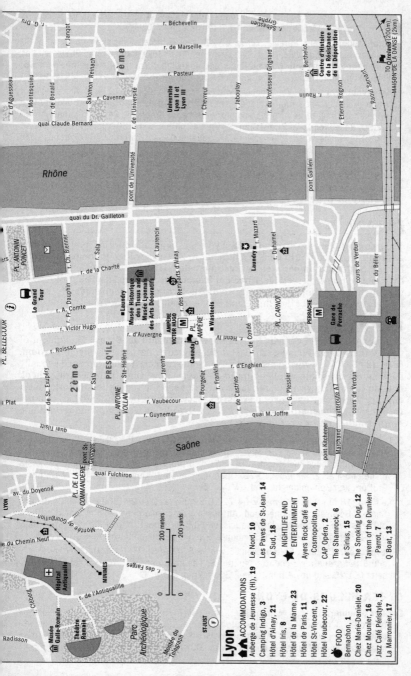

**Lyon**

🏠 **ACCOMMODATIONS**
Auberge de Jeunesse (HI), **19**
Camping Indigo, **3**
Hôtel d'Ainay, **21**
Hôtel Iris, **8**
Hôtel de la Marne, **23**
Hôtel de Paris, **11**
Hôtel St-Vincent, **9**
Hôtel Vaubecour, **22**
🍴 **FOOD**
Bernachon, **1**
Chez Marie-Danielle, **20**
Chez Mounier, **16**
Jazz Café Péristyle, **5**
La Marronnier, **17**

Le Nord, **10**
Les Paves de St-Jean, **14**
Le Sud, **18**
⭐ **NIGHTLIFE AND ENTERTAINMENT**
Ayers Rock Café and Cosmopolitan, **4**
CAP Opéra, **2**
The Shamrock, **6**
Le Sirius, **15**
The Smoking Dog, **12**
Tavern of the Drunken Parrot, **7**
Q Boat, **13**

vated bathrooms and balconies in many rooms. Elevator. Breakfast €6.50. Reception 24hr. Singles €45-50; doubles €54-74; triples €84. MC/V. ❹

**Hôtel St-Vincent,** 9 r. Pareille, 1er (☎27 22 56; www.hotel-saintvincent.com), off q. St-Vincent. M: Hôtel de Ville. On a quiet street near the banks of the Saône, St-Vincent has comfortable rooms with wooden floors and sparkling clean bathrooms. Breakfast €6. Reception 24hr. Reserve ahead. Singles €50; doubles €60; triples €70. MC/V. ❸

**Hôtel Vaubecour,** 28 r. Vaubecour, 2ème (☎37 44 91; fax 42 90 17). M: Ampère-Victor Hugo. High-ceilinged rooms hidden away on the 3rd fl. of an antique building. Low prices help negate its less-than-comfortable beds. Breakfast €4. Communal shower €2.50. Reception M-Sa 7am-10pm, Su 7am-12:30pm and 6:30-10pm. Reserve ahead June-Aug. Singles €28, with shower €37; doubles €35/45; triples €48-55; quads €70; quints €90. Extra bed €15. MC/V. ❸

**Camping Indigo,** 10km from Lyon (☎35 64 55; www.camping-indigo.com). Take Metro line D to Gare de Vaise, then bus #89 (dir: Dardilly) to Gargantua. Offers bar with terrace, game room, pool, shady sites, and TV. Jul.-Aug. €16 for 2 people, car, and tent; €4 per extra person, €3 per extra child; Sept.-June €13/3.10/2.40. ❶

## ▪ FOOD

The galaxy of Michelin stars adorning Lyon's restaurants confirms its status as the gastronomic capital of France. It's difficult to go wrong when it comes to cuisine here, though most dinner *menus* don't dip below €16. Equally appealing alternatives can be found on **rue St-Jean, rue des Marronniers,** and **rue Mercière** for less during lunchtime. Ethnic restaurants center near **rue de la République.** There are **markets** on the quais of the Rhône and Saône (open Tu-Su 8am-1pm).

## THE PRIDE OF LYON

The pinnacle of the Lyonnais food scene is **Restaurant Paul Bocuse** ❺, 4km out of town, where the menus (€120-195) definitely cost more than your hotel room. (☎04 72 42 90 90; www.bocuse.fr. MC/V.) Some of these restaurants occasionally have more accessible weekend buffet brunches hovering around €30-40; check outside or call. However, gourmands need not sell their souls to enjoy Bocusian cuisine; the master has several █spin-off restaurants in Lyon, themed around the four corners of the earth: *Le Nord, Le Sud, L'Est* and *L'Ouest.* Whether heading north, south, east, or west, reserve ahead.

▨ **Le Sud,** 11 pl. Antonin Poncet, 2ème (☎04 72 77 80 00). M: Bellecour. Specializing in "la cuisine du soleil," *Le Sud* serves up Mediterranean fare in a casual dining room decorated with a huge metal sun. A seafood dish (from €15) is worth the splurge. Pasta dishes from €12. *Menus* €19-22. Open daily noon-2:30pm and 7-11pm, F-Sa noon-2:30pm and 7pm-midnight. AmEx/MC/V. ❹

**Le Nord,** 18 rue Neuve, 2ème (☎04 72 10 69 69; fax 04 72 10 69 68). M: Cordeliers. Sample Bocuse's traditional food. An upscale ambience pervades the famed century-old *brasserie.* Try the specialty, *saucisson* (€7) for a treat. *Menus* €20-28. Open daily noon-2:30pm and 7-11pm, F-Sa noon-2:30pm and 7pm-midnight. AmEx/MC/V. ❹

**Bernachon,** 42 cours F. Roosevelt, 6ème (☎52 23 65). M: Foch. Don't come to this grand *pâtisserie* for a cheap baguette. Serves up expensive, extremely delicious desserts (€1.20 and up). Open Tu-Sa 8:30am-7pm. MC/V. ❷

## OTHER FLEURS-DE-LYON

▨ **Chez Mounier,** 3 r. des Marronniers, 2ème (☎37 79 26). M: Bellecour. Despite small portions, a friendly staff, top-notch cuisine, and great prices make this small restaurant a good choice. Afternoon *menu* €8. 4-course *menus* €11-20. Open Tu-Sa noon-2pm and 7-11pm, Su noon-1:30pm. MC/V. ❸

**Chabert et Fils,** 11 r. des Marronniers, 2ème (☎37 01 94). M: Bellecour. A well-known, well-loved *bouchon*, 1 of 4 on r. des Marroniers run by the same family. *Museau de bœuf* (cow tongue) is one of many unique *lyonnais* concoctions on the €18 *menu*. For dessert, try the exquisite, creamy *guignol* (rich, rum-soaked cake with slight orange flavoring; €5.70). Lunch *menus* €8-13. Dinner *menus* €18-34. Open daily noon-2pm and 7-11pm, F-Sa until 11:30pm. MC/V. ❸

**Chez Marie-Danielle,** 29 r. des Remparts d'Ainay (☎37 65 60). M: Ampère-Victor Hugo. Award-winning chef Marie-Danielle makes guests feel at home as she whips up superb *lyonnais* fare in her intimate eatery. Lunch *menu* €15. Dinner *menu* €22. Open M-F noon-2pm and 7:30-10pm. MC/V. ❹

**Les Paves de St-Jean,** 23 r. St-Jean. 6ème (☎42 24 13). M: Vieux Lyon. Offers excellent value and savory meat dishes but discourages lingering. *Menu* €13-20. MC/V. ❸

**La Marronnier,** 5 r. des Marronniers, 2ème (☎37 30 09). M: Bellecour. A *bouchon* featuring filling *plats* of delicious local specialties like black pudding with apples and potatoes (€9). Lunch *menu* €12. 3-course *menu* €15-20. Open M-Sa noon-2pm and 7-11pm. ❸

**Jazz Café Péristyle,** under the arches of the opera house, is the place to go to enjoy cool jazz with a salad, sandwich, or drink. Frequent live performances. Call for schedule. *Menu du jour* €10. Open M-Sa 9am-11pm. ❷

## 👁 SIGHTS

### VIEUX LYON

Stacked against the Saône at the foot of the Fourvière hill, *vieux* Lyon's narrow streets are home to lively cafes, hidden passageways, and magnificent medieval and Renaissance homes. The striking *hôtels particuliers*, with their delicate carvings and ornate turrets, sprang up between the 15th and 18th centuries when Lyon was the center of Europe's silk and printing industries.

**TRABOULES.** The distinguishing features of *vieux* Lyon townhouses are their **traboules,** tunnels connecting parallel streets through a maze of courtyards, often with vaulted ceilings and exquisite spiral staircases. Although their original purpose is debated, the *traboules* were often used to transport silk safely from looms to storage rooms. During WWII, the passageways proved invaluable as info-gathering and escape routes for the Resistance. Many are open to the public, especially in the morning. A 2hr. tour beginning at the tourist office is the ideal way to see them. The tourist office has a list of open *traboules* and their addresses. *(English-language tours in summer every few days at 2:30pm; in winter hours vary. €9, students €5.)*

**CATHÉDRALE ST-JEAN.** The cathedral's soaring columns dominate the southern end of *Vieux Lyon*. Paris might have been worth a Mass, but Lyon got the wedding cake; it was here that Henri IV met and married Maria de Médici in 1600. While many of the older stained-glass windows depict Bible stories, some of the newer geometric ones replaced those destroyed during the Nazis' hasty retreat in 1944. Inside, every hour between noon and 4pm, mechanical angels pop out of the 14th-century ▨**astronomical clock** in a reenactment of the Annunciation. *(Open M-F 8am-noon and 2-7:30pm, Sa-Su 8am-noon and 2-7pm. Free.)*

### FOURVIÈRE AND ROMAN LYON

Fourvière Hill, the nucleus of **Roman Lyon,** towers above the old city and is accessible via the rose-lined **Chemin de la Rosaire** (garden open daily 6am-9:30pm) and, for non-walkers, **la ficelle** (funicular), which leaves from the *vieux* Lyon Metro station. For panoramas views of the city, visit the Notre-Dame de Fouvrière's **Tour de l'Observatoire,** or the **esplanade Fourvière,** next to the basilica. On a clear day, search for Mont Blanc, about 200km to the east. *(Tower accessible June-Sept. daily 2:30 and 4pm; Apr.-May W and Su 2:30 and 4pm. Elevator €2, under 15 €1.)*

■**BASILIQUE NOTRE-DAME DE FOURVIÈRE.** During the Franco-Prussian War, the people of Lyon and their archbishop prayed fervently to the Virgin Mary for protection; afterward, they erected this magnificent basilica in her honor. Locals maintain that the building's octagonal turrets makes it look like *"un éléphant renversé"* (upside-down elephant). Inside, colorful mosaics depict the life of Mary and other religious scenes, such as Joan of Arc at Orléans. *(Behind the esplanade at the top of the hill. Chapel open daily 7am-7pm. Basilica open daily 8am-7pm.)*

**MUSÉE GALLO-ROMAIN.** Taking up five mostly underground floors, this surprisingly expansive museum educates and fascinates. History buffs and novices alike will appreciate a vast collection of mosaics and statues, and unique items such as a bronze tablet inscribed with a speech by Lyon's favorite son, Emperor Claudius. Artifacts are mostly labeled in English and French. *(☎72 38 81 90; www.musees-galloromains.com. Open Tu-Su 10am-6pm. €3.80, students €2.30; under 18 and Th free.)*

**PARC ARCHÉOLOGIQUE.** While the Musée Gallo-Romain provides a wonderful collection of artifacts, the Roman experience in Lyon isn't complete without a walk through this ancient park. Next to the Minimes/Théâtre Romain funicular stop, the Parc holds the well-restored 2000-year-old **Théâtre Romain** and the **Odéon,** discovered when modern developers dug into the hill. Visitors are free to explore most of the hilltop ruins on their own. On summer evenings, relax and enjoy the show; the **Nuits de Fourvière** festival (see p. 331) plays in both venues. *(Open daily mid-Apr. to mid-Sept. 7am-9pm; mid-Sept. to mid-Apr. 7am-7pm. Free.)*

## LA PRESQU'ÎLE AND LES TERREAUX

Monumental squares, statues, and fountains are the *presqu'île's* trademarks. At its heart, **place Bellecour** links Lyon's two main pedestrian arteries. Boutique-lined **rue Victor Hugo** runs south. To the north, crowded **rue de la République,** or "la Ré," is Lyon's urban aorta. It continues through **place de la République,** ending at **place Louis Pradel** in the 1*er,* at the tip of the Terreaux district. Once a marshy wasteland, this area was filled with soil, creating a neighborhood of dry *terreaux* (terraces) where today chic bars, cafes, and clubs keep things hopping long into the night.

**MUSÉE DES BEAUX-ARTS.** This converted palace takes visitors on a whirlwind tour through diverse exhibits: an archaeological wing displays Egyptian sarcophagi and Roman busts while distinguished Dutch, French, and Spanish paintings including works by Monet, Renoir, and Picasso line the third-floor walls. Other highlights include a fascinating Islamic art display and an unbelievably large French, Greek, and Roman coin collection. *(20 pl. des Terreaux. ☎04 72 10 17 40; www.mairie-lyon.fr. Open M and W-Su 10am-6pm. Sculptures and antiques closed noon-2:15pm; paintings closed 1-2:15pm. €6, under 26 €4, students free. MC/V.)*

## LA CROIX-ROUSSE AND THE SILK INDUSTRY

Though mass silk manufacturing is based elsewhere today, Lyon is proud of its historical dominance of the industry in Europe. The city's Croix-Rousse district, a steep, uphill walk from pl. Terreaux, houses the vestiges of its silk-weaving days; Lyon's few remaining silk workers still create delicate handiwork, reconstructing and replicating rare patterns for museum and château displays.

■**LA MAISON DES CANUTS.** The silk industry lives on at this Croix-Rousse workshop, which provides the best intro to Lyon's *canuts* (silk weavers). The weavers specialize in two methods of embroidery—both impossible to automate—and still use 19th-century looms. Scarves cost €32 or more, but silk enthusiasts can purchase a handkerchief for €9. *(10-12 r. d'Ivry, 4ème. ☎28 62 04. Open Tu-Sa 10am-6:30pm. €5, students €2.50, under 12 free. English-language tours daily at 11am and 3:30pm.)*

**MUSÉE HISTORIQUE DES TISSUS.** Clothing and textile fanatics will enjoy the rows of extravagant 18th-century dresses and 4000-year-old Egyptian tunics displayed here. Other highlights include scraps of Byzantine cloth and silk wall-hangings resembling stained glass. The neighboring **Musée des Arts Décoratifs,** housed in an 18th-century *hôtel* has rooms showcasing clocks, furniture, painted plates, and silverware from the Renaissance to the present. *(34 r. de la Charité, 2ème. M: Ampère Victor Hugo. ☎ 38 42 00. Tissus open Tu-Su 10am-5:30pm. Arts Décoratifs open Tu-Su 10am-noon and 2-5:30pm. €5, students €3.50, under 18 free; includes both museums.)*

## EAST OF THE RHÔNE AND MODERN LYON

Lyon's newest train station and monstrous space-age mall form the core of the ultra-modern Part-Dieu district. Locals call the commercial **Tour du Crédit Lyonnais** *"le Crayon"* for its unintentional resemblance to a giant pencil standing on end. Next to it, the shell-shaped **Auditorium Maurice Ravel** hosts major cultural events.

**CENTRE D'HISTOIRE DE LA RÉSISTANCE ET DE LA DÉPORTATION.** Housed in a building where Nazis tortured detainees during the Occupation, the museum presents documents, photos, and films about Lyon's role in the Resistance. Audio tours lead visitors through displays of heartbreaking letters and inspiring biographies. *(14 av. Berthelot, 7ème. M: Jean Macé. ☎ 72 23 11. Open W-F 9am-5:30pm, Sa-Su 9:30am-6pm. €4, students €2, under 18 free; includes audio tour in 3 languages.)*

**MUSÉE D'ART CONTEMPORAIN.** This extensive mecca of modern art, video, and high-tech installations resides in the futuristic **Cité International de Lyon,** a supermodern complex with shops, theaters, and Interpol's world headquarters. All of its exhibits are temporary—even the walls are rebuilt for each display. *(Q. Charles de Gaulle, next to Parc de la Tête d'Or, 6ème. Take bus #4 from M: Foch. ☎ 04 72 69 17 17; www.moca-lyon.org. Open W-Su noon-7pm. €5, students €2, under 18 free.)*

**INSTITUT LUMIÈRE.** A must-see for film buffs, the small museum chronicles the exploits of the brothers Lumière, who invented the motion picture in 1895. Housed in the Lumière family villa, the Institut exposes little-known facts about the brothers. Its complex also includes a movie theater, "Le Hangar du Premier-Film." *(25 r. du Premier-Film, 8ème. M: Monplaisir Lumière. ☎ 78 18 95; www.institut-lumiere.org. Open Tu-Su 11am-6:30pm. €6.50, students €5.50. groups of 4 or more €4.50 per person.)*

**PARC DE LA TÊTE D'OR.** Named for a golden head of Jesus supposedly buried on its grounds, the park is one of Europe's largest at over 259 acres. Visitors wander the 60,000-bush rose garden, paddle boats dot the artificial lake, and African animals fill the free zoo. *(M: Charpennes or tram T1 from Perrache, dir.: IUT-Feyssine. ☎ 89 02 03. Open daily mid-Apr. to mid-Oct. 6:30am-10:30pm; mid-Oct. to mid-Apr. 6:30am-8:30pm.)*

## 🎵 📷 ENTERTAINMENT AND NIGHTLIFE

At the end of June, the two-week **Festival Jazz à Vienne** welcomes jazz masters to Vienne, a sleepy river town south of Lyon, accessible by bus or train. (www.jazzavienne.com. Tickets free-€30.) In June and July, **Les Nuits de Fourvière** music festival features classical concerts, dance, movies, plays, and popular performers in the ancient Théâtre Romain and Odéon. (☎ 04 72 32 00 00; www.nuitsdefourviere.fr. Tickets and info at the Théâtre Romain and the FNAC shop on r. de la République. Tickets from €12.) Nightlife in Lyon is fast and furious; the city's vast array of anglophone pubs, GLBT establishments, riverboat nightclubs, and student bars make going out an adventure. The best, most accessible late-night spots are a strip of **riverboat dance clubs** docked by the east bank of the Rhône. Students buzz in and out of tiny, intimate bars on **rue Ste-Catherine** (1er) until 1am, before hitting up the clubs. For a more mellow (and expensive) evening, head to the **jazz and piano bars** on the streets off **rue Mercerie.** *Lyon Libertin* (€2) lists hot nightlife venues. For superb tips about gay nightlife, pick up *Le Petit Paumé.*

🏞 **Ayers Rock Café,** 2 r. Désirée, 1er (☎ 08 20 32 02 03). M: Hôtel de Ville. This Aussie bar is a cacophony of loud rock music and wild bartenders drumming on the hanging lights for twentysomethings. Bouncers can be selective when the bar is crowded, usually during rugby matches. Open daily 9pm-3am. Next door and with the same owners, slightly more chic **Cosmopolitan,** 4 r. Désirée (☎08 20 32 02 03) serves New York-themed drinks, like the "Taxi Driver" and "Greenwich Village." Both bars shots €3; mixed drinks from €7. Tu student nights; happy hour 8pm-3am. Open M-Sa 8pm-3am. MC/V.

**Le Sirius,** across from 4 q. Auganeur, 3ème (☎71 78 71; www.lesirius.com). M: Guillotière. A young, international crowd packs the lower-level dance floor and bar of this cargo ship-themed riverboat. Open Tu-Sa 6pm-3am.

**Q Boat,** across from 17 q. Auganeur, 3ème (☎04 72 84 98 98). M: Guillotière. Formerly Le Fish, club plays electronic and house music on a swanky boat. Chic Europeans crowd its 2 bars and top-floor deck. Dress well; admission at bouncer's discretion. Open W-Sa 5pm-5am; Su 2pm-5am. AmEx/MC/V.

**The Shamrock,** 15 r. Ste-Catherine, 1er (☎04 72 07 64 96). M: Hôtel de Ville. Black lights illuminate this happening Irish pub's smoky wooden interior while a young crowd knocks back €5.20 pints to the beat of live concerts W-Su (9pm). W night jam sessions. Open daily 6pm-1am. Happy hour 6-9pm; €4 pints. AmEx/MC/V.

**The Smoking Dog,** 16 r. Lainerie, 5ème (☎28 38 27). M: Vieux Lyon. The English-speaking bartenders serve €5 mixed drinks and €4.50 pints to loosen up patrons for Tu night's legendary "quiz night" (9pm). Guests can study up by browsing the bookshelves that ring the entire pub. Open daily 2pm-1am. MC/V.

**Tavern of the Drunken Parrot,** 18 r. Ste-Catherine, 1er (☎06 85 29 51 11). M: Hôtel de Ville. Get sloshed with potent rum drinks (€2) in 28 flavors. Open daily 6pm-1am.

**CAP Opéra,** 2 pl. Louis Pradel, 1er. A popular gay pub, with red lights to match the Opéra next door. A mellow early evening crowd spills onto the lively stairs outside as night descends. Occasional *soirées à thème.* Open daily 9am-3am. Cash only.

# GRENOBLE ☎04 76

Young scholars from all corners of the globe including sizable North and West African populations meet in Grenoble (pop. 168,000), a dynamic city whose surrounding snow-capped peaks are cherished by both athletes and aesthetes.

**█▓ TRANSPORTATION AND PRACTICAL INFORMATION. Trains** leave pl. de la Gare for: Lyon (1½hr., 30 per day, €18); Marseille (4-5½hr., 15 per day, €37); Nice (5-6½hr., 5 per day, €57); Paris (3hr., 9 per day, €70). **Buses** leave from left of the train station for Geneva, SWI (3hr., 1 per day, €26). From the station, turn right into pl. de la Gare, take the third left on av. Alsace-Lorraine, and follow the tram tracks on r. Félix Poulat and r. Blanchard to reach the **tourist office,** 14 r. de la République. (☎42 41 41; www.grenoble-isere.info. Open M-Sa 9am-6:30pm, Su 10am-1pm and 2-5pm.) **Celciuscafe.com,** 11 r. Gutéal, has **Internet.** (☎46 43 36. €2.50 per hr. Open daily 9am-11pm.) **Postal Code:** 38000.

**▐▐ ACCOMMODATIONS AND FOOD.** From the tourist office, follow pl. Ste-Claire to pl. Notre-Dame and take r. du Vieux Temple on the right to reach **◙Le Foyer de l'Étudiante ❶,** 4 r. Ste-Ursule. This stately building serves as a student dorm during most of the year, but opens its large, modern rooms to co-ed travelers from June to August. (☎42 00 84. Laundry €2.20. Free Wi-Fi. Singles €15; doubles €24.) Well-furnished rooms with tall windows turn **Hôtel de la Poste ❷,** 25 r. de la Poste, in the pedestrian zone, into a home away from home. (☎46 67 25. Reception 24hr. Singles €33; doubles €43-45. Cash only.) *Grenoblaise* restaurants cater to locals around **place de Gordes,** while Italian eateries and cheap pizzerias line **quai Perrière** across the river. *Pâtisseries* and North African joints center around **rue**

**Chenoise** and **rue Lionne,** between the pedestrian area and the river. Cafes and smaller bistros cluster around **place Notre-Dame** and **place St-André,** in the heart of the *vieille ville.* The seven-table gem **Tête à l'Envers ❸,** 12 r. Chenoise, serves a creative melange of international cuisine. Guess 5 of the 6 exotic flavors on the dessert platter for a free coffee or *digestif.* (☎51 13 42. *Plat du jour* €11. Dessert platter €9.50. Open Tu-F noon-3pm and 7:30pm-1am, Sa 7:30pm-1am. MC/V.) Try West African specialties like honey- and almond-saturated Tunisian pastries (€1-2.50) or couscous (€7-13) at **Mosaique Patisserie ❶,** 3 r. Chenoise (☎01 91 28. Open daily 8am-10pm. MC/V.) Buy groceries at **Marché Plus,** 22 cours Jean Jaurès, near the Alsace-Lorraine tram stop. (☎12 91 44. Open M-Sa 7am-9pm, Su 8am-noon.)

**◼ ♫ SIGHTS AND ENTERTAINMENT. Téléphériques** (cable cars) depart from q. Stéphane-Jay every 10min. for the 16th-century **Bastille,** a fort perched 475m above the city. (Open July-Aug. M 11am-12:15am, Tu-Su 9:15am-12:15am; Sept.-June reduced hours. €4, students €3.30; round-trip €5.80/4.70.) After enjoying the views from the top, you can walk down the **Parc Guy Pape,** through the other end of the fortress, to the **Jardin des Dauphins** (1hr.). Cross the Pont St-Laurent and go up Montée Chalemont to reach the **Musée Dauphinois,** 30 r. Maurice Gignoux, which displays exhibits on the people of the Alps and the history of skiing. (Open M and W-Su June-Sept. 10am-7pm; Oct.-May 10am-6pm. Free.) The ◼**Musée de Grenoble,** 5 pl. de Lavelette, houses one of France's most prestigious art collections. (☎63 44 44; www.museedegrenoble.fr. Open daily 10am-6:30pm. €5, students €2.) Another attractive aspect of Grenoble is its proximity to slopes. The biggest and most developed **ski areas** are to the east in **Oisans;** the **Alpe d'Huez** has 250km of trails. (Tourist office ☎11 44 44, ski area 80 30 30.) The **Belledonne** region, northeast of Grenoble, has a lower elevation and lower prices; its most popular ski area is **Chamrousse.** (Tourist office ☎89 92 65. Lift tickets €26 per day, €149 per week.) Only 30min. from Grenoble by bus, the resort also makes a great destination for summer **hiking.** Whether you've spent your day in the museums or on the slopes, Grenoble's funky cafes, college bars, and hopping clubs will liven up your night. Most hotspots are between **place St-André** and **place Notre-Dame.** International students and twentysomethings mix it up at **Le Couche-Tard,** 1 r. du Palais, a small bar whose walls are covered in patrons' humorous messages. (Mixed drinks €2.50. Happy hour M-W 7-11pm, Th-Sa 7-9pm. Open M-Sa 7pm-2am. AmEx/MC/V.) **London Pub,** 11 r. Brocherie,

## LOST IN TRANSLATION

Hollywood movies and American TV may have captivated an enthusiastic French market, but there's often little rhyme or reason regulating the translation of their titles:

**Lolita in Spite of Myself** (*Mean Girls*): Nabokov and Lindsay Lohan: the perfect pop culture union.

**The Counter Attack of the Blondes** (*Legally Blond*): Perhaps a little aggressive for a movie about Reese Witherspoon and handbags?

**Sexy Dance** (*Step Up*): If broken toenails and tortured soles (souls?) define your foot fetish, then sure, poor players stumbling over pirouettes is erotic.

**The Little Champions** (*Mighty Ducks*): From the Flying V to the quack chant, doesn't the *canard* hold this movie together?

**Rambo** (*Rambo*): Some words just transcend linguistic and cultural lines.

**The Man who would Murmur at the Ears of Horses** (*The Horse Whisperer*): Just in case there was any ambiguity in the original title.

**A Day with No End** (*Groundhog Day*): If you don't get the Groundhog Day reference, this is going to be a long movie.

**Lost in Translation** (*Lost in Translation*): Apparently this one wasn't.

*–Vinnie Chiappini*

gets loud and rowdy as the night progresses, with crowds of French teens and international students turning the pub into a dance floor. (Happy hour daily 6-9pm; pints from €3. Open M-Sa 6pm-1am.)

## ANNECY                                    ☎ 04 50

With narrow cobblestone streets, romantic canals, and a turreted castle, Annecy (pop. 53,000), the "Venice of the Alps," seems more like a fairy tale than a modern city. A 13th-century château in the *vieille ville*, the **Palais de l'Isle** served as a prison for WWII Resistance fighters. (☎ 33 87 30. Open June-Sept. daily 10:30am-6pm; Oct.-May M, W-Su 10am-noon and 2-5pm. €3.30, students €1.) The award-winning floral displays in the shaded **Jardin de l'Europe** are Annecy's pride and joy. In summer, the crystalline **lake** is a popular spot for windsurfing and kayaking, particularly along the **plage d'Albigny**. Annecy's Alpine forests have excellent hiking and biking trails. One of the best hikes begins within walking distance of the *vieille ville* at the **Basilique de la Visitation**, near the hostel, while a scenic 30km *piste cyclable* (bike route) hugs the lake's eastern shore.

Reach the clean ⛄**Auberge de Jeunesse "La Grande Jeanne" (HI)** ❷, rte. de Semnoz, via the *ligne d'été* bus in summer (dir.: Semnoz; €1) from the train station, or take bus #6 (dir.: Marquisats) from the station to Hôtel de Police, turn right on av. du Tresum, and follow signs to Semnoz. (☎ 45 33 19; annecy@fuaj.org. Breakfast and linens included. Internet €2 per 20min. Reception 7am-11pm. Open mid-Jan. to Nov. 4- and 5-bed dorms with showers €18. MC/V.) **Camping le Belvédère** ❶, 8 rte. de Semnoz, up the road from the hostel, has a small grocery store, ping-pong, *pétanque* (similar to bocce and lawn bowling), TV, and extensive hiking trails nearby. (☎ 45 48 30; camping@ville-annecy.fr. Bike rental €6 per ½-day, €10 per day. Laundry €8.40. Open early Apr. to mid-Oct. €11-14 per 1-2 people and car, €5 per extra person, €2-3 per tent. Electricity €2.60. MC/V.) **Place Ste-Claire** has morning **markets** (Tu, F, Su 8am-noon) and some of the city's most charming restaurants. At **La Bastille** ❸, 4 q. des Vieilles Prisons, sample savoyard specialties like *tartiflette* (cheese, meat, and potato dish; €9) while relaxing on the beautiful canalside terrace. (☎ 45 09 37. *Plats* €9-14. *Menus* €14-19. Open M-F 11am-2:30pm and 6-10:30pm, Sa-Su 11am-2:30pm and 6-11pm. MC/V.) A Monoprix **supermarket** is at pl. de Notre-Dame. (Open M-Sa 8:30am-7:50pm.) **Trains** run from pl. de la Gare to: Chamonix (2½hr., 7 per day, €20); Grenoble (€1½hr., 8 per day, €16); Lyon (2½hr., 8 per day, €22); Nice (7-9hr., 6 per day, €86); Paris (4hr., 7 per day, €85). Autocars Frossard **buses** (☎ 45 73 90) leave from next to the station for Geneva, SWI (1¼hr., 2-3 per day, €10). From the train station, walk one block down r. de la Gare, turn left on r. Vaugelas for four blocks, and enter the Bonlieu shopping mall to reach the **tourist office**, 1 r. Jean Jaurès, in pl. de la Libération. (☎ 45 00 33; www.lac-annecy.com. Open June-Aug. M-Sa 9am-6:30pm, Su 9am-12:30pm and 1:45-6:30pm; Sept. to mid-Oct. and Mar.-May daily 9am-12:30pm and 1:45-6pm.; late Oct.-Feb. M-Sa 9am-12:30pm and 1:45-6pm.) **Postal Code:** 74000.

## CHAMONIX                                  ☎ 04 50

The site of the first Winter Olympics in 1924 and home to Europe's highest peak (**Mont Blanc;** 4807m), Chamonix (pop. 10,000) draws outdoor enthusiasts from around the world. Whether you've come to climb its mountains or ski down them, be cautious—steep grades and potential avalanches make the slopes challenging and dangerous. The pricey ⛄**Aiguille du Midi téléphérique** (cable car) offers a knuckle-whitening ascent over snowy forests and cliffs to a needlepoint peak, revealing a fantastic panorama from 3842m. (☎ 08 92 68 00 67. Round-trip €37.) Bring your passport to continue via gondola to **Helbronner, ITA** for views of three countries, the **Matterhorn** and Mont Blanc. (Open May-Sept. Round-trip €54; includes Aiguille du Midi.) South of Chamonix, **Le Tour-Col de Balme** (☎ 54 00 58; day pass €37), above the village of **Le Tour,** draws beginner and intermediate skiers, while **Les Grands Montets** (☎54 00 71; day pass €37), to the north, is the *grande dame* of Chamonix skiing, with advanced terrain and **snowboarding** facilities. Chamonix has 350km of **hiking;** the tourist office has a map (€4) with departure points and estimated duration of all trails, though some are accessible only by cable car.

Chamonix's *gîtes* (mountain hostels) are cheap, but fill up fast; call ahead. From the train station, walk down av. Michel Croz and turn on r. du Docteur Paccard for **Gîte le Vagabond ❶**, 365 av. Ravanel le Rouge, where a young group of Brits provide rustic bunk rooms with stone walls and a popular bar. (☎53 15 43; www.gitevagabond.com. Climbing wall and kitchen available. Breakfast €5. Linens €5. Free Wi-Fi. Dorms €15. Credit card deposit. MC/V.) Turn left from the base of the Aiguille du Midi and go past the main roundabout to camp at **L'Île des Barrats ❶**, 185 chemin de l'Île des Barrats, off rte. des Pélerins. (☎53 51 44. Laundry €8. Reception July-Aug. 8am-noon and 2-8pm; May-June and Sept. 9am-noon and 4-7pm. Open May-Sept. €7 per person, €6 per tent, €3 per car. Electricity €4. Cash only.) Restaurants and nightlife center around **Rue du Docteur Paccard** and **Rue des Moulins.** Buy groceries at **Super U**, 117 r. Joseph Vallot. (Open M-Sa 8:15am-7:30pm, Su 8:30am-noon.) **Trains** leave pl. de la Gare (☎35 36) and usually connect through St-Gervais to: Annecy (1½hr., 8 per day, €13); Lyon (3½hr., 7 per day, €29); Paris (5-8hr., 6 per day, €75-95); Geneva, SWI (4½hr., 2 per day, €51). Société Alpes Transports **buses** (☎53 01 15) leave the train station for Geneva, SWI (1½hr., 1-5 per day, €35). Local buses (€1.50) connect to ski slopes and hiking trails. From the station, follow av. Michel Croz, turn left on r. du Dr. Paccard, and take the first right to reach the **tourist office**, 85 pl. du Triangle de l'Amitié. (☎53 00 24; www.chamonix.com. Free Wi-Fi. Open daily 8:30am-7pm.) Find **Internet** at **Shop 74**, 16 cours du Bartavel, near the cinema. (☎90 73 17. €6 per hr. Free Wi-Fi with drink purchase. Open Sept.-June 24hr.; July-Aug. daily 10am-1pm and 3-7:30pm. MC/V.) **Postal Code:** 74400.

# LE MONT-DORE ☎04 73

Le Mont-Dore ("luh mohn dohr;" pop. 1700), sits at the foot of a dormant volcano in an isolated valley. Le Puy de Sancy, Central France's highest peak, is only 3.5km from the *centre ville*, making the town a premier winter ski resort and a year-round hiking mecca. Le Mont-Dore brims with mountain *chalets* and natural luxury; its famous *thermes* have, for centuries, attracted summer visitors seeking rejuvenation from the mineral-rich hot waters that seep through cracks in the lava.

**▊▊ TRANSPORTATION AND PRACTICAL INFORMATION. Trains** and SNCF **buses** (☎65 00 02) run from pl. de la Gare to Paris (6hr., 2 per day, €57). For a **taxi**, call ☎65 09 32. Rent **bikes** and **skis** at **Bessac Sports**, r. de Maréchal Juin. (☎65 02 25. Bikes €12 per ½-day, €18 per day. Ski packages €13-27 per day. Snowboard pack €16-21. ID deposit. Open daily May-Sept. 9am-noon and 2-7pm; early to mid-Dec. and mid-Jan to Apr. 9am-noon and 1:30-7pm; mid-Dec. to mid-Jan. 8:30am-7pm. MC/V.) From the station, head up av. Michel Bertrand, through pl. Charles de Gaulle and on r. Meynadier. Take a right on allée Georges Lagaye; the **tourist office**, av. de la Libération, is on the far side of the ice-skating rink. (☎65 20 21. Open July-Aug. M-Sa 9am-7pm, Su 10am-noon and 2-6pm; May-June and Sept. M-Sa 9am-12:30pm and 2-6pm, Su 10am-noon and 2-6pm; Oct. M-Sa 9am-noon and 2-6pm.) The **post office** is in pl. Charles de Gaulle. (☎65 37 10. Open M-F 8:30am-noon and 2-5:30pm, Sa 8:30am-noon.) **Postal Code:** 63240.

**▊▊ ACCOMMODATIONS AND FOOD. Hôtel Artense ❷**, 19 av. de la Libération, near the tourist office, has clean, comfortable rooms. (☎65 03 43; www.artense-hotel.com. Breakfast €5. Reception 8am-7pm. Open Dec.-Oct. Singles and doubles €20-40; triples with bath €40-45; quads €43-53. MC/V.) The most convenient of Le Mont-Dore's campsites is **Des Crouzets ❶**, av. des Crouzets, across from the train station. Its non-landscaped sites are well-kept but lack privacy-providing hedges.

(☎65 21 60. Reception M-Sa 9am-noon and 3-6:30pm, Su 9:30am-noon and 4-6pm. Open mid-Dec. to mid.-Oct. €3 per person, €3.10 per tent. Electricity €3.50-3.90.)

Restaurants take a back seat to outdoor pursuits in Le Mont-Dore. You can find St-Nectaire cheese, flavored dry sausage, and other regional specialties at one of the street side shops between **place de la Republique** and **place du Pantheon**. Many restaurants are affiliated with a hotel and give discounts to guests. ■**Café de Paris** ❷, 8 r. Jean Moulin, evokes the Jazz Age in a classy 1920s salon that hosts frequent concerts. (☎65 01 77. Omelettes €6. *Truffade* (potatoes with melted cheese) €13. Open Dec.-Oct. daily 8am-8pm. Kitchen open noon-3pm. Cash only.)

◙ **SIGHTS.** During the May-October thermal season, *curistes* descend upon **Établissement Thermal**, 1 pl. du Panthéon, a tradition which has sustained the town for hundreds of years. The Romans originally channeled the eight springs used today, discovering that the water did wonders for their horses' sinuses. Today, a French-language tour of the *thermes* ends with a dose of *douche nasale gazeuse*, a tiny blast of carbon and helium that ■evacuates sinuses more effectively than any sneeze. (☎65 05 10. Tours late Apr.-late Oct. M-Sa 4 per day; €3.20.) Bikers and drivers should visit the calm volcanic lakes, which pool in nearby craters. Most have small beaches suitable for windsurfing, sailing, and swimming.

◪◭ **HIKING AND SKIING.** Over 650km of trails lace the region's dormant volcanic mountains. Those planning an extended hike should review their route with the tourist office, which sells hiking maps (€7), and leave a multi-day itinerary with the *peloton de montagne* (mountain police; ☎65 04 06), on r. des Chasseurs or at the base of Puy de Sancy. While some popular trails feature yellow signs indicating distance and direction to nearby destinations, others are unmarked and often little more than foot-wide dirt paths or muddy ditches. Be sure to check weather reports—mist in the valley often signifies hail or snow in the peaks.

For all the views without all the exertion, the **téléphérique** runs from the base by the hostel to a station just below the Puy de Sancy; a 10min. climb up steep wooden stairs leads to the summit. (☎08 20 82 09 48. 5 per hr. €5.50, child €4.10; round-trip €7.20/5.60. MC/V.) Farther north, the **funicular** departs from near the tourist office to Salon des Capucins, a rocky outcropping high above town. (3 per hr. €3.30, under 10 €2.70; round-trip €4.20/3.30. MC/V.) Both the funicular and the *téléphérique* can be used as launching points for many hikes.

The following distances and times given are for round-trips from the trailhead. The hike to ■**La Grande Cascade** (4km, 1½hr., 222m ascent) starts from the center of town and ends above the area's largest falls (30m) on the *Plateau de Durbise*, a grassy plain overlooking the town. During the summer, large, flat rocks at the base of the falls make an ideal setting for picnics or afternoon sunbathing, while ice-climbers scale the frozen falls in winter. The ascent to the Massif's highest peak, the **Puy de Sancy** (6.2km, 3hr., 555m vertical), is simply spectacular. The 360° view from the platform on the summit on clear days includes the entire Auvergne region. Begin the hike at the base of the Puy de Sancy and ascend the mountain via *Val de Courre*, a picturesque cow pasture. The trail begins a few hundred meters to the right of *téléphérique* #2. Hikers should be careful on the trail's upper section, especially on wet days, as the path borders steep drop-offs. Experienced hikers may consider a scenic 8.9km hike along  a **chain of peaks** between Sancy and La Grande Cascade. Because of the hike's difficulty, it offers amazing views and is less crowded. Most of the trek lies along the GR4, but the trail branches off at many points along the way. An easy, flat hike through a forest leads to two beautiful waterfalls, **Cascade de Queureuilh** and **Cascade de Rossignolet** (5km, 1-2hr., 60m vertical). Queureuilh, arguably the more spectacular one, falls from a steep 30m cliff face. To reach them, follow the same staircase as to La Grand Cascade, but turn left at the top onto chemin de Melchi-Rose. After emptying out onto av. de Clermont, turn left onto chemin de

Montieyroux, then left right onto rte. des Cascades. Signs mark the trailhead, which begins a few hundred meters up on the right at Prends-Toi-Garde.

Skiers and snowboarders will encounter smaller crowds (and shorter lift lines) than elsewhere in France. A network of ski trails covers much of the Massif du Sancy; skiers can also venture down the other side of the valley into ritzy Super-Besse on clear days. **Ski-rental** shops fill the main village; rental packages usually cost €10-26 per day. Lift tickets for the entire Mont-Dore and Super-Besse area cost €19 per ½-day and €24 per day. At the base of the Puy de Sancy lifts is a **ski school** (☎ 65 07 43). The area features an extensive network of **cross-country skiing** trails; ask at the tourist office or call the central cross-country resort (☎ 21 54 32) for info.

# DORDOGNE AND LIMOUSIN

A lack of large population centers, waterfronts, and well-known attractions has kept this region from the fame it deserves. Most of the sights are relatively undis-covered, offering a welcome respite from the ceaseless crowds at the Loire châ-teaux. The Dordogne river cuts through the region's rolling hillsides, creating a spectacular backdrop for the many castles and hilltop cities. Nearby Périgord—where green countryside is splashed with yellow sunflowers, steep and chalky limestone cliffs, and ducks paddling down shady rivers—boasts exceptional his-torical remnants of the Neolithic, Roman, and medieval periods.

## BOURGES                                              ☎ 02 48

Once France's capital, Bourges (pop. 75,000) attracts visitors with its Gothic archi-tecture, half-timbered houses, and shop-filled medieval streets. Bourges's wealth originated in 1433, when **Jacques Cœur,** Charles VII's financier, chose the humble city as the site for his palatial home. Secluded châteaux, tucked away into thick forests and rolling vineyards, fill the region around the city. Bourges is also a con-venient base for daytrips to the beautiful villages of **Charité-sur-Loire** (by train: 1½-3½hr., €14 via Nevers) and **Mehun-sur-Yèvre** (by train: 10-15min., €4).

During the long French-language tour, you'll see more of the unfurnished **Palais Jacques Coeur,** 10bis r. Jacques Cœur, than Cœur ever did, since he was impris-oned for embezzlement before its completion. (Open July-Aug. 9:30am-noon and 2-7pm; Sept.-June reduced hours. €6.50, 18-25 €4.50, under 18 free.) Ask at the tour-ist office about excursions to 13 other châteaux along the **Route Jacques Cœur;** most are accessible only by car or bike. **Cathedral St-Étienne's** complex stained-glass scenes, tremendous size, and infinitely intricate facade make it Bourges's most impressive sight. (Open M-Sa Apr.-Sept. 8:30am-7:15pm; Oct.-Mar. 9am-5:45pm. Closed Su morning for mass. Free. Crypt and tower €7, students €4.50.)

To get from the station to the well-kept **Auberge de Jeunesse (HI) ❶,** 22 r. Henri Sell-ier, bear right on r. du Commerce onto r. des Arènes, which becomes r. Fernault; and cross to r. René Ménard, then turn left onto r. Henri Sellier. (☎ 24 58 09. HI members only. Breakfast €3.50. Reception 8-10am and 6-10pm. Dorms €13. Cash only.) **Place Gordaine** and **rue des Beaux-Arts** are lined with cheap eateries, while the restaurants on **rue Bourbonnoux** and **rue Girard** feature regional menus in a more elegant atmosphere. A **Leclerc** supermarket is on r. Prado off bd. Juraville. (Open M-Sa 8:30am-7:20pm. MC/V.) **Trains** leave from pl. du Général Leclerc (☎ 08 92 35 35 35) for Paris (2hr., 8 per day, €28) and Tours (1½hr., 4 per day, €20). From the station, follow av. H. Laudier as it turns into av. Jean Jaurès; bear left on r. du Commerce, which becomes r. Moyenne and leads to the **tourist office,** 21 r. Victor Hugo. (☎ 23 02 60. Open Apr.-Sept. M-Sa 9am-7pm, Su 10am-6pm; Oct.-Mar. reduced hours.) **Postal Code:** 18000.

## PÉRIGUEUX                                            ☎ 05 53

Périgueux (pop. 65,000) rests on the hills high above the Isle River. Rich with tradi-tion and gourmet cuisine, the lovely old quarters of Périgueux preserve architec-

### QUIET RIOT

During the first week of August, a hush falls over the town of Périgueux. In no way mournful, it announces the arrival of **Mimos,** an annual international mime festival. Week-long festivities transform Périgueux into a whirlwind of silent performances and welcome entertainers from three continents. Forget silent men donning black and white bodysuits; this mime festival features a much more diverse, circus-oriented array of performances. Shows take place throughout the city, in concert halls, parks, and squares, as mime companies and individuals compete for prizes awarded by the Mimos Jury.

Spectators watch performers display their talents in everything from acrobats to physical theater to juggling. Shows, which range from innocent, clownish gags and visual humor to sensual modern dance reenactments of ancient myths. Also noteworthy but more somber, the Korean mime spectacle depicts the separation of the Korean peninsula. Contemporary and engaging, the festival offers a unique deviation from the jazz and wine events common in the southwest region.

*Buy tickets at Le Théâtre, Esplanade de Théâtre. ☎05 53 53 18 71; www.mimos.fr. Tickets €8-15.*

ture from medieval and Gallo-Roman times. Périgueux's **Cathédrale St-Front,** the largest cathedral in southwestern France, is a massive Greek cross crowned by five immense Byzantine cupolas next to a belfry. The interior features beautiful chandeliers, an impressive organ, and a spectacular wooden altarpiece. (Open daily 8am-noon and 2:30-7pm.) Just down r. St-Front, the **Musée du Périgord,** 22 cours Tourny, houses one of France's most important collections of prehistoric artifacts, including a set of 2m mammoth tusks. (☎06 40 70. Open Apr.-Sept. M and W-F 10:30am-5:30pm, Sa-Su 1-6pm; Oct.-Mar. M and W-F 10am-5pm. €4, students €2, under 18 free.) The **⊠Musée Gallo-Romain,** r. Claude Bertrand, has a walkway over the excavated ruins of the Domus de Vésone, once the home of a wealthy Roman merchant. (☎05 65 60. Open July 5-Sept. 2 daily 10am-7pm; Apr.-July 4 and Sept. 3-Nov. 11 Tu-Su 10am-12:30pm and 2-6pm; Nov. 12-Jan. 6 and Feb. 7-Mar. Tu-Su 10am-12:30pm and 2-5:30pm. €5.70, under 12 €3.70. French-language tours daily July-Aug. €1. English-language audio tour €1.) Across from the train station, the welcoming owners of **Les Charentes ❷,** 16 r. Denis Papin, offer clean rooms and plenty of info about Périgord. (☎53 37 13. Breakfast €5. Reception 7am-10pm. Open early Jan.-late Dec. Reserve ahead in summer. Singles with shower €25, with TV €30, with toilet €35; doubles €30/35/40. Extra person €5. AmEx/MC/V.) **Les Barris ❹,** 2 r. Pierre Magne, a comfortable riverside hotel close to the center of town, commands spectacular views of the cathedral and *vieille ville.* (☎53 04 05; www.hoteldesbarris.com. Breakfast €6. Wi-Fi available. Singles €44; doubles €49; triples €54; quads €59; quints €64. MC/V.) **⊠Au Bien Bon ❷,** 15 r. de l'Aubergerie, serves *magret* (duck steak; €14) and other regional specialties. (☎09 69 91. *Plats* €9-14. Lunch *menus* €10-14. Open Tu-F noon-1:30pm and 7:30-9:30pm, Sa 7:30-9:30pm, M noon-1:30pm. MC/V.) **Monoprix** supermarket is on pl. Bugeaud. (Open M-Sa 8:30am-8pm.) **Trains** leave r. Denis Papin for: Bordeaux (1½hr., 12 per day, €18); Lyon (6-8hr., 2 per day, €51); Paris (4-6hr., 13 per day, €57); Toulouse (4hr., 12 per day, €32-44). The **tourist office** is at 26 pl. Francheville. From the train station, turn right on r. Denis Papin, bear left on r. des Mobiles-de-Coulmierts, which becomes r. du Président Wilson, and take the next right after the Monoprix; the office will be on the left. (☎53 10 63; www.tourisme-perigueux.fr. Open June-Sept. M-Sa 9am-6pm, Su 10am-1pm and 2-6pm; Oct.-May M-Sa 9am-1pm and 2-6pm.) **Postal Code:** 24000.

## SARLAT ☎05 53

Sarlat (pop. 11,000), best used as a base for exploring the **Caves of Lascaux** and the Dordogne Valley (see below), merits attention for its gorgeous medieval *centre-ville*. Accommodations have become quite expensive since the town's only hostel closed. Your best bet is to book a room at one of the nearby *chambres d'hôtes* (rooms €25-50; visit the tourist office for a complete list) or rough it overnight at a nearby camping. The campground **Maisonneuve ❶**, 11km from Sarlat and a few hundred meters from Castlenaud on D57, provides an exceptional base from which to explore Castlenaud, La Roque Gageac, Château des Millandes, and Domme (p. 340). It has billiards, a cafe, a *gîte* (a restored onsite farmhouse that sleeps ten), grocery store, mini-golf, ping-pong, pool, and a riverside swimming hole. (☎29 51 29; www.campingmaisonneuve.com. Reception 9am-8pm. Open Apr.-Oct. and July-Aug. €5.30 per adult, €3.60 per child under 7, €7.20 per tent and vehicle. *Gîte* €10 per person. Electricity €3.60. 10-30% discount Sept.-Oct. and Apr.-June. MC/V.) Next to Maisonneuve, **MultiTravel** bike rentals makes countryside excursions even easier. Buy groceries at **HyperChampion,** along av. de Selves. (Open M-Sa 9am-8pm, Su 9am-12:30pm.) The strings of sausages hanging from the ceiling of ◨**Chez le Gaulois ❷,** 3 r. Tourny, near the tourist office, hint at the restaurant's emphasis on generous portions of excellent cuts of meat. (☎59 50 64. *Plats* €9.50-11. Open July-Aug. daily noon-2pm and 7-10pm; Sept.-June Tu-Sa 11:30am-2:30pm and 6:30-9:30pm. V.) **Trains** go from av. de la Gare to Bordeaux (2½hr., 5-8 per day, €23) and Périgueux (3hr., 3 per day, €14). Trans-Périgord **buses** run from pl. Pasteur to Périgueux (1½hr., 1 per day, €9). The **tourist office** is off r. Tourny in the *centre ville*. (☎31 45 45; www.sarlat-tourisme.com. Open July-Aug. M-Sa 9am-7pm, Su 10am-noon and 2-6pm; Sept.-June reduced hours.) **Postal Code:** 24200.

# THE VÉZÈRES VALLEY                                    ☎05 53

Arguably the most spectacular cave paintings ever discovered line the **Caves of Lascaux,** "the Sistine Chapel of prehistory," near the town of **Montignac,** 25km north of Sarlat. Uncovered in 1940 by four teenagers, the caves were closed to the public in 1963 when algae and mineral deposits—nourished by the breathing of countless visitors per year—threatened to ruin the paintings. **Lascaux II** replicates the original cave exactly: modern artists painted the designs with the same pigments used 17,000 years ago. Although the Lascaux II drawings lack ancient mystery, the new caves—replete with paintings of 5m bulls, horses, and bison—manage to inspire a wonder all their own. The ticket office (☎51 96 23) shares a building with Montignac's **tourist office** (☎51 82 60), on pl. Bertrand-de-Born. (Ticket office open 9am until sold out. Reserve 1 week ahead. €8.) The **train** station nearest Montignac is at Le Lardin, 10km away. From there, you can call a **taxi** (☎50 86 61). During the academic year, CFTA (☎05 55 59 01 48) runs **buses** from Périgueux and Sarlat; call or check the stations for times and prices. Numerous **campgrounds** dot the Vézères Valley near Montignac; the tourist office has a complete list.

At the **Grotte de Font-de-Gaume,** 1km east of **Les Eyzies-de-Tayac** on D47, 15,000-year-old friezes are still open for viewing. (☎06 86 00; www.leseyzies.com/grottes-ornees. Open mid-May to mid-Sept. Su-F 9:30am-5:30pm; mid-Sept. to mid-May daily 9:30am-12:30pm and 2-5:30pm. English-language tours 1hr. Reserve 2-4 weeks in advance. €6.50, 18-25 €4.50.) Rooms tend to be expensive—consider staying in **Périgueux** or check out quiet, clean, and well-located ◨**Demaison Chambre d'Hôte ❷,** rte. de Sarlat, 3min. outside of Les Eyzies-de-Tayac on the edge of the forest. From the train station, follow signs to Sarlat; the house is past the laundromat on the right. (☎06 91 43. Breakfast €5. Reserve ahead. Singles and doubles €25-36; triples and quads €48. Cash only.) The **tourist office** is on pl. de la Mairie in Les Eyzies-de-Tayac. (☎06 97 05; www.leseyzies.com. Open July-Aug. M-Sa 9am-7pm, Su 10am-noon and 2-6pm; Sept. and Apr.-June M-Sa 9am-noon and 2-6pm, Su 10am-noon and 2-5pm; Oct.-Mar. M-Sa 9am-noon and 2-6pm.) From Les Eyzies, **trains** go to Paris (4-6hr., 4 per day, €59), Périgueux (30min., 6 per day, €7), and Sarlat (1hr., 2 per day, €8).

## THE DORDOGNE VALLEY ☎ 05 53

Steep, craggy cliffs tower over the slow-moving waters of the Dordogne River, 12km south of Sarlat. The nearby town of ◪**Castelnaud-La-Chapelle,** along the D57, overlooks the Dordogne from its hillside stoop. At the summit is its spectacular **château,** which houses a museum on medieval warfare. (☎31 30 00; www.castelnaud.com. Open July-Aug. daily 9am-8pm; low season reduced hours. €7.20.) The town of **Domme** was built by King Philippe III in 1281 as a defensive stronghold. In 1307, Phillippe IV imprisoned and tortured over 70 Knights Templar in the **Porte des Tours.** Their graffiti, scrawled upon the walls with their bare hands and teeth, remains today. Across from the tourist office, tours descend underneath the city into the ◪**Grottes de la Halle,** a cathedral-like network of caves with stalactites and stalagmites. (☎31 71 00. French-language tours with English-language captions July-Aug. 2-3 per hr. 10:15am-7pm; Apr.-June and Sept. 1 per hr. 10:15am-noon and 2-6pm; Feb.-Mar. and Oct. 1 per hr. 2-5pm. €6.50, students €5.50.) Visit the **tourist office,** pl. de la Halle, for tickets and more info on exploring the region. (☎31 71 00. Open daily July-Aug. 9:30am-12:30pm and 2-6pm; Sept.-Mar. 10am-12:30pm and 2-5:30pm.) To get to and around the valley, you'll need to rent a **car** (p. 265) or be prepared for strenuous **bike** rides. Many outfits along the Dordogne rent **canoes** and **kayaks** including **Canoës-Loisirs,** at the Pont de Vitrac, near Domme. (☎31 22 92). Most activities in the area work well as daytrips from **Sarlat** (p. 338).

# AQUITAINE AND PAYS BASQUE

At the geographical edge of France and Spain, Aquitaine (AH-kee-tenn) and the Pays Basque (PAY-ee bahss-kuh) are diverse in landscape and culture. In Aquitaine, sprawling vineyards abound and in Pays Basque, closer to the Spanish border, the clinking of cowbells mixes with the scent of seafood. When locals aren't out enjoying the beach or mountain trails, they're relishing the regional cuisine.

## BORDEAUX ☎ 05 56

Though its name is synonymous with wine, the city of Bordeaux ("bohr-doh;" pop. 235,000) has more to offer than most lushes would expect. Everyone from punks to tourists gather on the elegant streets of the shop- and cafe-filled city center, while in the surrounding countryside, the vineyards of St-Emilion, Médoc, Sauternes, and Graves draw international renown. The city is filled with history, drenched in culture, and animated with student nightlife.

◪▨ **TRANSPORTATION AND PRACTICAL INFORMATION. Trains** leave Gare St-Jean, r. Charles Domercq, for: Lyon (8-10hr., 7 per day, €61-154); Marseille (6-7hr., 10 per day, €73); Nice (9-12hr., 2 per day, €105); Paris (3hr., 15-25 per day, €55); Toulouse (2-3hr., 10 per day, €32). From the train station, take tramway line C to pl. Quinconces (€1.30) and cross the street to reach the **tourist office,** 12 cours du 30 juillet, which arranges winery tours. (☎00 66 00; www.bordeaux-tourisme.com. Open July-Aug. M-Sa 9am-7:30pm, Su 9:30am-6:30pm; May-June and Sept.-Oct. M-Sa 9am-7pm, Su 9:30am-6:30pm; Nov.-Apr. M-Sa 9am-6:30pm, Su 9:45am-4:30pm.) **Postal Code:** 33000.

◪▨ **ACCOMMODATIONS AND FOOD.** A favorite among backpackers, ◪**Hôtel Studio ❷,** 26 r. Huguerie, has tiny, relatively clean rooms with bath, phone, and TV. (☎48 00 14; www.hotel-bordeaux.com. Breakfast €5. Reserve ahead. Singles €19-28; doubles €25-35. AmEx/MC/V.) Shiny metal and bright colors characterize rooms at the popular **Auberge de Jeunesse Barbey (HI) ❷,** 22 cours Barbey, four blocks from the Gare St-Jean in the run-down red light district. Visitors, especially those traveling alone, should exercise caution at night. (☎33 00 70; fax 33 00 71. Breakfast and linens included. Free Internet. Max. 3-night stay. Lockout 10am-4pm. Curfew 2am. 2- to 6-bed dorms €21. MC/V.)

The Bordelais's flair for food rivals their vineyard expertise. Hunt around **rue St-Remi** and **place St-Pierre** for regional specialties: oysters, *foie gras*, and *lamproie à la bordelaise* (eel braised in red wine). Busy ☒**L'Ombrière ❸**, 13 pl. du Parlement, serves perfectly prepared French cuisine in one of the city's most beautiful squares. (*Menu* €15-20. Open daily noon-2pm and 7-11pm. MC/V.) Overload on cow decor in tiny **La Fromentine ❷**, 4 r. du Pas St-Georges, near pl. du Parlement, serving *galettes* (€6-8) with imaginative names. (☎79 24 10. 3-course *menu* €10-15. Open M-F noon-2pm and 7-10pm, Sa 7-10pm. MC/V.) **Cassolette Café ❷**, 20 pl. de la Victoire, cultivates its amicable climate with unique style and cheap prices, offering *cassolette* (€2.50-7) and 30 other French staples. (☎92 94 96; www.cassolettecafe.com. *Menu* €10-12. Open daily noon-midnight. MC/V.) A **Marché Plus** supermarket is at 268 r. Ste Catherine. (Open M-Sa 7am-9pm, Su 9am-noon.)

🎦 🎵 **SIGHTS AND ENTERTAINMENT.** Nearly nine centuries after its consecration, the **Cathédrale St-André**, in pl. Pey-Berland, sits at the heart of Gothic Bordeaux. Its bell tower, the **Tour Pey-Berland,** rises 66m. (Cathedral open M 2-7pm, Tu-F 7:30am-6pm, Sa 9am-7pm, Su 9am-6pm. Tower open June-Sept. daily 10am-1:15pm and 2-6pm; Oct.-May Tu-Su 10am-12:30pm and 2-5:30pm. €5, 18-25 and seniors €3.50, under 18 with an adult free.) For the best cityscape of Bordeaux, look down from the 114m bell tower of the **Église St-Michel.** (Open June-Sept. daily 2-7pm. €2.50, under 12 free.) Back at ground level, a lively flea market sells anything from Syrian *narguilas* (hookahs) to African specialties. (Open daily 9am-1pm.) Note that this area, like around the train station, should not be frequented alone at night. On pl. de Quinconces, the elaborate **Monument aux Girondins** commemorates guillotined Revolutionary leaders from towns bordering the Gironde. Bordeaux's opera house, the **Grand Théâtre,** conceals a breathtaking interior behind its Neoclassical facade and houses concerts, operas, and plays in fall and winter. (☎00 85 95; www.opera-bordeaux.com. Tours M-Sa 11am-6pm. Concert tickets from €8. Opera tickets up to €80. 50% discount for students and under 26.)

Bordeaux has a varied, vibrant nightlife. For an overview, check out the free *Clubs and Concerts* brochure at the tourist office. Year-round, students and visitors pack the bars in **Place de la Victoire, Place Gambetta,** and **Place Camille Julian.** Popular but cheesy **El Bodegon,** on pl. de la Victoire, draws students with cheap drinks, theme nights, and weekend giveaways. (Beer €3. Happy hour 6-8pm. Open M-Sa 7am-2am, Su 2pm-2am.) Decorated with flashing lights and mirrors, the fashionable gay bar **BHV,** 4 r. de l'Hôtel de Ville, is almost always full. (Beer €4. W theme night. Open daily 6pm-2am.) Gauze curtains, soft cushions, and exotic drinks greet guests in **Le Namasthé,** 8 r. de la devise. Tall *chichas* (hookahs; €9) available in a dozen flavors complete the relaxing experience. (☎81 08 68. *Lassi* €5. Beer €5. Reserve ahead. Open in summer M-F 7pm-1:30am, Sa-Su 4pm-1:30am; in winter Tu-F 7pm-1:30am, Sa-Su 4pm-1:30am. MC/V.)

# BIARRITZ ☎05 59

Once a playground for 19th-century aristocrats, Biarritz (pop. 29,000) can still make a dent in your wallet. Luckily, its sparkling beaches are free for rich and budget travelers alike. In summer, thousands of bodies soak up the sun at **Grande Plage,** while thrill-seekers surf the waves. **Plage Miramar,** just to the north, is less crowded. Facing away from Plage Miramar, turn left along av. de l'Impératrice to reach the **Pont St-Martin** for a fantastic view. Take bus #2 (dir.: Gare SNCF) to Francis Jammes or #9 (dir: Labourd) to Bois de Boulogne to reach the ☒**Auberge de Jeunesse (HI) ❷**, 8 r. de Chiquito de Cambo, offering a welcoming staff and lakefront location. (☎41 76 00; aubergejeune.biarritz@wanadoo.fr. Internet €3 per hr.

Reception 8:30am-12:30pm and 6-10pm. Dorms €18. AmEx/MC/V.) **Rue Mazagran** and **Rue du Port Vieux** have cheap, filling crepes and sandwiches. **Shopi** supermarket, 2 r. du Centre, is off r. Gambetta. (Open M-Sa 9am-12:40pm and 3-7:10pm, Su 9am-12:30pm.) **Trains** leave from Biarritz-la-Négresse (☎50 83 07), 3km from town, for Bayonne (10min.; 29 per day; €2.50, TGV €4), Bordeaux (2hr.; 14 per day; €29, TGV €26), and Paris (5hr., 12 TGV per day, €79). The **tourist office** is on pl. d'Ixelles. (☎22 37 10; www.biarritz.fr. Open July-Aug. daily 8am-8pm; Sept.-June M-F 9am-6pm, Sa-Su 10am-5pm.) **Postal Code:** 64200.

# BAYONNE
☎05 59

In Bayonne (pop. 42,000), the self-proclaimed chocolate capital of France, visitors wander along the Nive River's narrow banks and admire the small bridges, petite streets, and colorful shutters before heading to the nearest *chocolaterie*. The ▨**Musée Bonnat**, 5 r. Jacques Laffitte, showcases works by Bayonnais painter Léon Bonnat alongside others by Degas, van Dyck, Goya, Rembrandt, and Reubens. (Open May-Oct. W-M 10am-6:30pm; July-Aug. Th-Tu 10am-6:30pm, W 10am-9:30pm; Nov.-Apr. daily 10am-12:30pm and 2-6pm. €5.50, students €3; Sept.-June free 1st Su of the month and July-Aug. free W 6:30-9:30pm.) The 13th-century **Cathédrale Ste-Marie** endured fires and Revolution-related destruction, but renovations have since restored it to its former glory. (Open M-Sa 10-11:45am and 3-5:45pm, Su 3:30-6pm. Free.) Starting the first Wednesday in August, locals let loose for five days during the **Fêtes Traditionnelles** (Aug. 6-10; www.fetes-de-bayonne.com).

The ▨**Hôtel Paris-Madrid ❷**, pl. de la Gare, has clean rooms at rock-bottom prices and knowledgeable proprietors. (☎55 13 98. Breakfast €4. Reception Sept.-June daily 6:15am-1am; Oct.-May M-Sa 6:15am-1am, Su 6:15am-noon and 6pm-1am. Singles €19, with shower €27, with shower and toilet €34-49; doubles €24/28/34-49; triples and quads with bath €49-59. MC/V.) A **Monoprix** supermarket is at 8 r. Orbe. (Open M-Sa 8:30am-8pm.) **Trains** depart from pl. de la Gare for: Biarritz (10min.; 36 per day; €2.20, TGV €4); Bordeaux (2hr., 28 per day, €28); Paris (5hr., 10 TGV per day, €81); San Sebastián, SPA via Hendaye (30min., 15 per day, €8); Toulouse (4hr., 5 per day, €37). Local STAB **buses** (☎59 04 61) depart from the Hôtel de Ville for Biarritz (buses #1, 2, and 6 run M-Sa 6:30am-8pm, Lines A and B run Su 6:30am-7pm. €1.50). From the train station, take the middle fork onto pl. de la République, veer right over pont St-Esprit, pass through pl. Réduit, cross pont Mayou, and turn right on r. Bernède, which becomes av. Bonnat. The **tourist office,** pl. des Basques, is on the left. (☎42 64 64; www.bayonne-tourisme.com. Open July-Aug. M-Sa 9am-7pm, Su 10am-1pm; Sept.-June M-F 9am-6:30pm, Sa 10am-6pm.) **Postal Code:** 64100.

# LOURDES
☎05 62

Lourdes (pop. 16,300) attracts six million pilgrims annually. They visit the **Grotte de Massabielle,** where in 1858, 14-year-old Bernadette Soubirous saw the first of 18 visions of the Virgin Mary. Follow av. de la Gare from the train station, turn left on bd. de la Grotte, and follow it to the right and across the River Gave to reach the Grotte de Massabielle. Visitors whisper prayers, receive blessings, and carry home water from the spring where Bernadette washed her face. (No shorts or tank tops. Open 24hr., *Grotte* open daily 11am-3:30pm and 4pm-6am.) The **Basilique du Rosaire** and the **Upper Basilica** were built double-decker style above the *Grotte.* The **Basilique St-Pius X,** a huge concrete echo chamber designed to resemble an overturned ship, is hidden underground. (Basilicas open daily Easter-Oct. 6am-7pm; Nov.-Easter 8am-6pm.) Processions depart daily from the **Église St. Bernadette** (5pm) and the *Grotte* (9pm). In 2008, the sesquicentennial of Bernadette's vision, 9pm processions will continue Friday and Saturday throughout the winter.

**Hôtel Lutétia ❷,** 19 av. de la Gare, is in an Art-Nouveau building to the right of the train station. Clean, comfortable rooms sport a sink and telephone, while more upscale rooms have TVs. (☎94 22 85; www.lutetialourdes.com. Free parking.

Singles €18, with toilet €25, with shower €32; doubles €25-64; triples €58. Students receive free room upgrade. MC/V.) The cheapest eateries are near the tourist office and on bd. de la Grotte. Stock up at the **market** at Les Halles, pl. du Champ Commun. (Open M-F 6:30am-1:30pm, Sa 5:30am-1:30pm, Su 6:30am-1:30pm.) **Trains** leave 33 av. de la Gare for: Bayonne (2hr., 5 per day, €20); Bordeaux (3hr., 7 per day, €32); Paris (6-7hr., 5 TGV per day, €84); Toulouse (2½hr., 8 per day, €23). To reach the **tourist office,** on pl. Peyramale, turn right on av. de la Gare, bear left on av. Maransin, cross the bridge above bd. du Lapacca, and continue straight. (☎42 77 40; www.lourdes-infotourisme.com. Open July-Aug. M-Sa 9am-7pm, Su 10am-6pm; Oct.-Jan. M-Sa 9am-noon and 2-6pm; Mar.-June and Sept. M-Sa 9am-6:30pm, Su 10am-12:30pm.) **Postal Code:** 65100.

# PARC NATIONAL DES PYRÉNÉES

Punctuated by sulfurous springs and unattainable peaks, the Pyrénées change dramatically with the seasons, never failing to impress visitors. To get a full sense of the mountains' breadth, hikers should experience both the lush French and barren Spanish sides of the Pyrénées (a 4- to 5-day round-trip hike from Cauterets).

## CAUTERETS                                          ☎05 62

Nestled in a narrow valley on the edge of the **Parc National des Pyrénées Occidentales** is tiny Cauterets (pop. 1300). Its sulfuric *thermes* (hot springs) have long been instruments of healing. **Thermes de César,** av. du Docteur Domer, still offers treatments. (☎92 51 60. Open Sept.-June M-Sa 4-8pm and some Su; June-Sept. M-Sa 5-8pm. Hours may vary.) Most visitors come to Cauterets to **ski** and hike. Multiple half-day **hikes** depart from a trailhead behind the Thermes de César; for more info, talk to the Parc National des Pyrénées (p. 343). **Hotel le Chantilly ❸,** 10 r. de la Raillère, one street away from the town center, is owned by a charming Irish couple. (☎92 52 77; www.hotel-cauterets.com. Breakfast €6. Reception 7am-10pm. Open late Dec. to Oct. July-Sept. singles and doubles €34, with shower €38; triples from €42. Oct.-June €30/34/38. MC/V.) SNCF **buses** run from pl. de la Gare to Lourdes (1hr., 8 per day, €6.50). Rent **bikes** at Le Grenier, 4 av. du Mamelon Vert. (☎92 55 71. €17-23 per ½ day, €22-32 per day. Open daily 9am-7pm.) The **tourist office** is in pl. Foch. (☎92 50 50; www.cauterets.com. Open July-Aug. M-Sa 9am-12:30pm and 2-7pm, Su 9am-noon and 3-6pm; Sept.-June reduced hours.) **Postal Code:** 65110.

## ▚ OUTDOOR ACTIVITIES

The **Parc National des Pyrénées Occidentales** shelters hundreds of endangered species in its snow-capped mountains and lush valleys. Touch base with the friendly **Parc National Office,** Maison du Parc, pl. de la Gare, in Cauterets, before braving the park's **ski** paths or 14 **hiking** trails. (☎92 52 56; www.parc-pyrenees.com. Open July-Aug. M-F 9:30am-noon and 2:30-7pm; Sept.-June M-F 9:30am-noon and 3-6pm. Maps €7-9.) Appropriate for a variety of skill levels, the trails begin and end in Cauterets. From there, the **GR10** (a.k.a. **circuit de Gavarnie),** which intersects most other hikes in the area, winds through Luz-St-Saveur, over the mountain, and then on to Gavarnie, another day's trek up the valley. One of the most spectacular trails follows the GR10 past the turquoise **Lac de Gaube** to the end of the glacial valley (2hr. past the *lac*), where you can spend the night at the **Refuge des Oulettes ❶.** (☎92 62 97. Open June-Sept. Dorms €19.) Other *gîtes* (shelters) in the park, usually located in towns along the GR10, cost about €11 per night.

# LANGUEDOC-ROUSSILLON

With reasonable prices all over, Languedoc-Rousillon provides a great opportunity for travelers to see the south of France on a budget. Though it has been part of

France since the 12th century, Languedoc preserves its rebellious spirit and its *joie de vivre* shows up in impromptu street performances and large neighborhood parties. Between the Mediterranean coast and the peaks of the Pyrénées, Roussillon inspired Matisse and Picasso and now attracts a mix of sunbathers and backpackers. The region was historically part of Catalunya, not France, and many inhabitants of Roussillon identify more with Barcelona than with Paris. Architecture, food, and nightlife all bear the zest of Spanish neighbors.

# TOULOUSE
☎ 05 61

Vibrant, zany Toulouse (pop. 390,000) is known as *la ville en rose* (the pink city). It's the place to visit when all French towns begin to look alike. Exuberant yet laid-back, clean yet gritty, Toulouse is a university town that graduating students don't want to leave. Numerous museums and concert halls makes France's fourth-largest city the southwest's cultural capital. Family-owned art galleries, independent theaters, and a diverse music scene continue Toulouse's free-thinking tradition.

**TRANSPORTATION AND PRACTICAL INFORMATION. Trains** leave Gare Matabiau, 64 bd. Pierre Sémard, for: Bordeaux (2-3hr., 14 per day, €33); Lyon (4½hr., 7 per day, €70); Marseille (4hr., 10 per day, €50); Paris (6hr., 12 per day, €90). The ticket office is open daily 7am-9:10pm. Eurolines, 68-70 bd. Pierre Sémard, sends **buses** to major European cities. (☎ 26 40 04; www.eurolines.fr. Open M-F 9:30am-12:30pm and 2-6:30pm, Sa 9:30am-12:30pm and 2-5pm.) To get from the train station to the **tourist office**, r. Lafayette, in pl. Charles de Gaulle, head straight down r. de Bayard. Veer left, keeping pl. Jeanne d'Arc on your right, and continue on r. d'Alsace-Lorraine; after turning right onto r. Lafayette, the office is on the left. (☎ 11 02 22; www.ot-toulouse.fr. Open June-Sept. M-Sa 9am-7pm, Su 10:30am-12:30pm and 2-5:15pm; Oct.-May M-Sa 9am-6pm, Su 10:30am-12:30pm and 2-5pm.) Surf the **Internet** at **Feeling Copies**, 3 r. Valade. (€1 per hr. Open M-F 9am-7pm.) **Postal Code:** 31000.

> **NOTHING TOU-LOUSE.** Those visiting Toulouse for longer than a day or two should pick up a *Carte Privilège* at the tourist office. For a mere €13, cardholders get 30% discounts at museums and participating hotels. As a final bonus, cardholders receive free *apéritifs* at many Toulouse restaurants. The tourist office has a list of participating hotels, museums, and restaurants.

**ACCOMMODATIONS AND FOOD.** A member of the French League of Youth Hostels, **Residence Jolimont ❶**, 2 av. Yves Brunaud, doubles as a long-term *résidence sociale* for 18-25 year-olds. A basketball court, billiards, and ping-pong tables bring excitement to large, plain double rooms. (☎ 05 34 30 42 80; www.residence-jolimont.com. Breakfast M-F €2. Dinner daily €8. Linens included. Reception 24hr. Doubles €16. €1 HI member discount. AmEx/MC/V.) **Hôtel Beauséjour ❷**, 4 r. Caffarelli, near the station, has clean, bright rooms with new beds, making it a great value. (☎/fax 62 77 59. Free Wi-Fi. Reception 7am-11pm. Singles €30, with bath €32; doubles €37/39; triples €42/44. MC/V.) Take bus #59 (dir.: Fenouillet) from pl. Jeanne d'Arc to camp at **Pont de Rupé ❶**, 21 ch. du Pont de Rupé, at av. des États-Unis along N20 north. (☎ 70 07 35. €13 for 2 adults and a tent, €2.80 per additional person. MC/V.) Cheap eateries on **rue du Taur**, in the student quarter, serve meals for €5.50-10. Markets (open Tu-Su 6am-1pm) line **place des Carmes, place Victor Hugo,** and **place Saint-Cyprien.** Neighborhood favorite **Jour de Fête ❷**, 43 r. du Taur, is a relaxed *brasserie* with tastes as creative as the local art decorating its brick walls. (☎ 23 36 48. *Plat du jour* €7. Open daily noon-midnight. Cash only.) Part restaurant, part art gallery, and part small theater, **La Faim des Haricots ❸**, r. du Puits Vert, between pl. Capitole and the

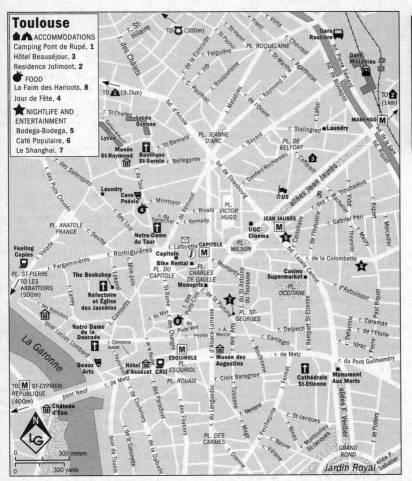

**Toulouse**

🏠🏕 ACCOMMODATIONS
Camping Pont de Rupé, **1**
Hôtel Beauséjour, **3**
Residence Jolimont, **2**

🍎 FOOD
La Faim des Haricots, **8**
Jour de Fête, **4**

⭐ NIGHTLIFE AND
ENTERTAINMENT
Bodega-Bodega, **5**
Café Populaire, **6**
Le Shanghai, **7**

student quarter, is a vegetarian's heaven. It offers a fresh and filling selection of pasta, *tartes*, and ingeniously combined veggies. *Menus* (€10-13) let you pick up to five choices from the unlimited salad, *tarte*, soup, and dessert bars. (☎22 49 25. Open M-W noon-2:30pm, Th-Sa noon-2:30pm and 7-10:30pm. MC/V.) There's a **Monoprix** supermarket at 39 r. d'Alsace-Lorraine. (Open M-Sa 9am-10pm.)

🎨🌙 **SIGHTS AND NIGHTLIFE.** The **Capitole,** a brick palace next door to the tourist office, is Toulouse's most prominent monument. The building was home to the bourgeois *capitouls* (unofficial city magistrates) in the 12th century. (Open daily 9am-7pm. Free.) Rue du Taur leads to the **Basilique St-Sernin,** the longest Romanesque structure in the world. Its **crypt** houses holy relics from the time of Charlemagne. (☎21 80 45. Church open July-Sept. daily 8:30am-6:30pm; Oct.-June daily 8:30-noon and 2-6pm. Crypt open July-Sept. M-Sa 10am-5pm, Su 11:30am-5pm; Oct.-June M-Sa 10-11:30am and 2:30-5pm, Su 11:30-5pm. €2.) The 13th-century southern Gothic **Jacobin church,** 69 r. Pargaminières, entrance on r. Lakanal, houses the remains of St. Thomas Aquinas in an elevated tomb. (☎22 21 92; www.jacobins.mairie-toulouse.fr. Open daily 9am-7pm.) Just across the river, **Les Abbatoirs,** 76 allées Charles-de-Fitte, previously an old slaughterhouse, presents intermittent exhibits by up-and-coming artists. Don't skip the basement, which houses the eight by thirteen meter curtain Picasso painted for the premier of Romain Rolland's play "14 Juillet." (☎51 10 60. Open Tu-Su 11am-7pm. €6, students €3.) The huge **Musée des Augustins,** 21 r. de Metz, bristles with Romanesque and Gothic sculptures, including 15 howling gargoyles, in a renovated monastery. (☎22 21 82. Open M-Tu and Th-Su 10am-6pm, W 10am-9pm. €3, students free. Temporary exhibits €7, students €5.) The restored **Hôtel d'Assézat,** at pl. d'Assézat on r. de Metz, displays the **Fondation Bemberg,** a modest collection of Bonnard, Gauguin, and Pissarro. From mid-March to mid-June 2008, the museum will host an exhibit of distinguished monochromatic painting, featuring Rubens, Boucher, and Doré, among others. (☎12 06 89. Open Tu-W and F-Su 10am-12:30pm and 1:30-6pm, Th 10am-12:30pm. €4.60, students €2.75.)

Toulouse has something to please almost any nocturnal whim, although nightlife generally caters to students. Young people crowd the streets at all hours, creating the feeling of a large city in the small, concentrated downtown. Numerous cafes flank **place St-Georges, place St-Pierre,** and **place du Capitole,** and late-night bars line **rue de la Colombette** and **rue des Filatiers.** For cheap drinks and a rambunctious atmosphere, try **Café Populaire,** 9 r. de la Colombette, where you can polish off 13 glasses of beer for only €20, €13 on Mondays 9:30pm-12:45am. (☎63 07 00. Happy hour 7:30-8:30pm. Every 13th of the month beer €1. Open M-F 11am-2am, Sa 2pm-4am. Cash only.) The best dancing is at the spacious, wildly touristy two-story **Bodega-Bodega,** 1 r. Gabriel Péri, just off bd. Lazare Carnot. (Beer €3. Mixed drinks €6. Tapas €5-10. Th-Sa cover €6 after 11:30pm. Open M-F and Su 7pm-2am, Sa 7pm-6am. AmEx/MC/V.) For GLBT-friendly nightlife, try **Le Shangai,** 12 r. de la Pomme, a sleek club that draws a mixed crowd. (☎23 37 80. Mixed drinks €8. Cover €8. Open daily midnight-7am. Cash only.)

## CARCASSONNE                                                    ☎04 68

Walking over the drawbridge and through the stone portals into Carcassonne's *La Cité* (pop. 46,000) is like stepping into a fairy tale; the first-century ramparts still seem to resound with the clang of armor. However, the only battles raging today are between camera-wielding visitors vying for space on the narrow streets. Built as a palace in the 12th century, the **Château Comtal,** 1 r. Viollet-le-Duc, became a citadel after the royal takeover in 1226. (☎11 70 77. 45min. tours in English, French, and Spanish. Open daily Apr.-Sept. 10am-6:30pm; Oct.-Mar. 9:30am-5pm. €7.50, under 25 €4.80.) In the summer, Agglo'Bus runs **shuttles** from the bus stop across the canal from the train station to the citadel gates (☎47 82 22. Daily mid-June to mid-Sept. 9:30am-noon and 1:30-7:30pm, 4 per hr., round-trip €1.50.) Converted into a fortress after the city was razed during the Hundred Years' War, the Gothic **Cathédrale St-Michel,** r. Voltaire, in the Bastide St-Louis, still has fortifications on its southern side. (Open M-Sa 7am-noon and 2-7pm, Su 9am-1pm.) Nestled in an alley in the heart of *La Cité,* the ◪**Auberge de Jeunesse (HI) ❷,** r. de Vicomte Trencavel, offers affordable comfort. (☎25 23 16; carcassonne@fuaj.org. Breakfast included. Laundry €5. Internet €3 per hr. Reception 24hr. Lockout 10am-3pm. Reservations recommended. Dorms €20; €3 HI discount. MC/V.) ◪**Maison de la Blanquette de Limoux 3,** pl. Marcou, is the best place to enjoy *cassoulet* (white bean stew; €11-13). A three-course menu, including *apéritif, cassoulet,* and wine costs €14. (☎71 66 09. Open July-Aug. daily 9am-midnight; Apr.-June and Sept. to mid-Nov. Th-M 9am-midnight, Tu 9am-5pm; closed Nov. 15-Apr. 1. MC/V.) Save room for crepes and other desserts offered around **place Marcou.** While Carcassonne has effervescent nightlife during the year, the city quickly falls asleep in summer when most of the regulars go to the beach. Nonetheless, several bars on **place Verdun,** in the lower city, stay open past midnight. **Le Bar à Vins,** 6 r. du Plô, where wine bar meets beer garden, remains popular and crowded throughout the summer. (☎47 38 38. Beer €2.80-5. Wine €2 per glass. Open Feb.-Nov. daily 9am-2am; hours may vary Mar.-May and Oct. MC/V.) Down a pint of Guinness (€6) at **O'Sheridans,** 13 r. Victor Hugo, off pl. Carnot, a convivial Irish pub. (☎72 06 58. Live music Sept.-June every other Th 10pm. Happy hour 6-8pm; whiskey half price. Open daily 5pm-2am. MC/V.)

**Trains** (☎71 79 14) depart behind Jardin A. Chenier for: Marseille (3hr., 4 per day, €42); Nice (6hr., 4 per day, €63); Nîmes (2hr., 10 per day, €28); Toulouse (1hr., 10 per day, €13). Shops, hotels, the cathedral, and the train station are in the **Bastide St-Louis,** once known as the *basse ville* (lower city). From the station, walk down av. de Maréchal Joffre, which becomes r. Clemençeau; after pl. Carnot, turn left on r. de Verdun to reach the **tourist office,** 28 r. de Verdun. (☎10 24 30; www.carcassonne-tourisme.com. Open July-Aug. daily 9am-7pm; Sept.-June M-Sa 9am-6pm, Su 9am-1pm.) **Postal Code:** 11000.

# PERPIGNAN                                            ☎04 68

A few kilometers from the Mediterranean, 27km from Spain, and 30km from the Pyrénées, Perpignan (pear-peen-yohn; pop. 117,000) is a daytripper's paradise. Free week-long regional bus passes give access to the remarkable, and otherwise unaffordable, towns of Céret, Villefranche-de-Conflent, and Collioure.

■ **TRANSPORTATION AND PRACTICAL INFORMATION.** Budget airline **Ryanair** (www.ryanair.com) flies out of **Aéroport de Perpignan-Rivesaltes (PGF;** ☎ 52 60 70; aeroport@perpignan.cci.fr), 6km northwest of the city center along D117, to London, BRI (1¼hr., 1 per day). **Trains** leave Rue Courteline for: Carcassonne (1½hr., 3-7 per day, €17) via Narbonne; Lyon (4-5½hr., 5 per day, €62); Marseille (4½-6hr., 3 per day, €38) via Narbonne; Montpellier (1½-2hr., 8-11 per day, €21) via Narbonne; Paris (5hr., 1-4 per day, €101); Toulouse (2½-3hr., 2-7 per day, €26) via Narbonne. The **Compagnie Transports Perpignan Mediterranée (CTPM),** 27 bd. Clemenceau, runs intercity **buses.** ( ☎61 01 13. Tickets €1.10, round-trip €2, *carnet* of 10 €8. Office open M-F 7:30am-12:30pm and 1:30-6:30pm, Sa 9am-noon and 2:30-5pm.) The regional **tourist office, place de Catalogne,** and **place de Catalogne** mark the triangular area of Perpignan's *vieille ville.* Avoid **Quartier St-Jacques,** near bd. Jean Bourrat and bd. To reach the **tourist office,** Palais des Congrès, pl. Armand Lanoux, from the train station, follow av. de Gaulle to pl. de Catalogne, then take bd. Clémenceau to pl. de la Résistance. Veer left on cours Pamarole and continue along Promenade des Plantanes (☎66 30 30; www.perpignantourisme.com. Open mid-June to mid-Sept. M-Sa 9am-7pm, Su 10am-4pm; mid-Sept. to mid-June M-Sa 9am-6pm, Su 10am-1pm.) Anatole France, at night. **Cyber Espace,** 45bis av. du Général Lecler, facing the *gare routière* has **Internet.** (☎35 36 29. €2 per 30min., €3 per hr.; ½-price 8-10am. Open July-Aug. M-Sa noon-1am, Su 1-8pm; Sept.-June M-F 8am-1am, Sa noon-1am, Su 1-8pm.) **Postal Code:** 66000.

**TIP** **FREE-FOR-ALL.** Bring your passport and photo to the tourist office to obtain a free tourist pass, entitling holders to a week of **free regional bus rides.**

■ **ACCOMMODATIONS AND FOOD.** Perpignan's cheapest hotels are near the train station on **avenue du Général de Gaulle,** although even they are not amazing bargains. The **Avenir Hôtel ❷,** 11 r. de l'Avenir, off av. Général de Gaulle, sports colorful—though stuffy—rooms and decorations painted by the owner but beware the communal shower's steep price. (☎34 20 30; www.avenirhotel.com. Breakfast €4.50. Communal shower €3.20 per room per day. Reception M-Sa 8am-11pm, Su 8am-noon and 6-11pm. Reserve ahead. Singles and doubles €18-24, with toilet

€27, with shower €30, with bath €36; triples €39; quads €42. Extra bed €6. AmEx/MC/V.) Take bus #15 (dir: Bompas) to Lidl (15min., 1-4 per hr., €1.10) to reach **Camping Le Catalan ❶**, rte. de Bompas, which offers 94 sites, hot showers, laundry facilities, a playground, and a seasonal pool. (☎63 16 92. Wheelchair-accessible. Open Apr. to mid-Oct. July-Aug. €18 for 2 people and car, €5 per extra person; Sept.-Oct. and Mar.-June €14/4. Electricity €3.50. MC/V.)

Perpignan's specialities include local *charcuterie*, Catalan *pâté*, and *escargots* with garlic, as well as *tourron* nougat in flavors like caramel or almond. **Place Arago, place de la Loge, place de la République,** and **place de Verdun** in the *vieille ville* remain lively at night. Pricier options and candlelit tables line **quai Vauban** along the canal, while av. du Général de Gaulle has as many kebab shops as it does Internet cafes. A variety of fresh produce can be found at the open-air markets on **place Cassanyes** (open daily 7am-1pm) and place de la République (open Tu-Su 7am-1pm). ◪**Casa Sansa ❸**, r. des Fabriques Couvertes, serves outstanding Catalan food on a tiny street near the Castille. The trick is to order from the illustrated tapas menu (€3-7) and create a feast for only €10-15. (☎34 21 84. *Plats* €13-20. *Menu* €19. Open daily 11:30am-3pm and 6-11pm. AmEx/D/MC/V.) On a hot day, try the air-conditioned **Peace 'n' Love ❶**, 40 r. de la Fusterie, a vegetarian restaurant that will also satisfy budget meat-eaters. Try the cumin vegetable curry. (☎06 08 33 67 84. Entrees €6.50. Desserts €3-5. Open M-W noon-2:30pm, Th-Sa noon-2:30pm and 7-10:30pm. Cash only.) A huge **Casino** supermarket is on bd. Félix Mercader. (☎51 56 00. Open M-Sa 8:30am-8pm, Su 8:30am-12:30pm.)

🎥 🎵 **SIGHTS AND ENTERTAINMENT.** An uphill walk across the *vieille ville* brings you to the 15th-century Spanish **citadel's** red-rock walls. Concealed inside is the **Palais des Rois de Majorque**, where the kings of the Majorcan Dynasty (1272-1344) settled. The marble facade of the **Ste-Croix chapel** reveals French, Italian, and Moorish architecture. The palace's large courtyard serves as a concert hall in July, hosting a variety of plays and musical (mostly jazz) performances. (Enter from av. G. Brutus. Open daily June-Sept. 10am-6pm; Oct.-May 9am-5pm. Last ticket sale 45min. before closing. €4, students €2, under 12 free. Concerts €5-10; available at Fnac. 1hr. French-language tours July-Aug. 2 per hr.; Sept.-June 2 per day.) Partly supported by a pillar depicting John the Baptist's severed head, the **Cathédrale St-Jean** is a paragon of Gothic architecture. Begun in 1324 and consecrated in 1509, it sports an 80m long nave, the third-largest in the world. (☎51 33 72. Open M 7:30am-noon and 3-7pm, Tu-Su 7:30am-7pm. Mass Su 8, 10:30am, 6:30pm.) Guarding the entrance to the city's center, **Le Castillet,** built in 1368 by the Spanish, was intended to repel French invaders. The Castillet now holds the **Casa Pairal,** a museum of Catalan domestic ware, farm equipment, and religious relics. (☎35 42 05. Open M and W-Su May-Sept. 10am-6:30pm; Oct.-Apr. 11am-5:30pm. French-language tours in summer 2 per month. €4, students and under 15 €2.) Back in the *vieille ville*, the **Musée Hyacinthe Rigaud,** 16 rue de l'Ange, contains a collection of Gothic paintings by 13th-century Catalan and Spanish masters, as well as canvases by Ingres, Miró, Picasso, and Rigaud. (☎35 43 40. Open M and W-Su May-Sept. noon-7pm; Oct.-Apr. 11am-5:30pm. Wheelchair-accessible. €4, students and 15-18 €2, under 15 free.)

Though Perpignan is not known for its nightlife, a few—albeit expensive—bars lie scattered around the Castillet. ◪**L'Ubu,** 40 pl. Rigaud, a literary café, has live jazz most nights. Grab a beer (€2.30) and listen to the music or take advantage of the free Internet access. (☎34 27 74; www.ubujazz.com. Open M-Sa 10am-2am. AmEx/MC/V.) The clubs lining the beaches at nearby **Canet-Plage** provide the wildest nightlife, but getting back to Perpignan means paying €20-25 for a taxi. On Saturday nights, a **bus service** runs between Perpignan and the Canet clubs. (Buses leave Sa from the Castillet at 11:45pm, 12:45, 2:10am and return from Canet-Plage 12:10, 1, 4, 5am. Call ☎06 09 49 89 27 or check www.route-66.fr for up-to-date schedules. Unlimited bus rides for a year €1.)

In July and August, beginning after Bastille Day (July 14), Perpignan hosts free musical performances and traditional Catalan dancing for the **Jeudis de Perpignan** (Th 7:30-11:30pm). A sacred fire permanently lit at Mt. Canigou is brought back to Perpignan on June 23 for the **Fête de St-Jean.** Known as the **Festa Major** (☎ 35 07 60), the two weeks surrounding the celebrated day are filled with concerts, food tasting, and traditional dancing, culminating in a sound-and-light show. At the end of June, Perpignan gets a little jollier for **La Fête des Vins,** when stands hand out wine samples between bd. Wilson and cours Palmarole. (☎ 51 59 99. Empty glass €3.) Throughout July, the **Estivales de Perpignan** brings world-renowned theater and dance to town. (☎ 86 08 51; www.estivales.com. Buy tickets online or at the Palmarium, next to the tourist office annex. Open daily mid-June to mid-Sept. 10am-6:30pm; Oct.-May 10am-5:30pm. Prices vary; student discounts available.) The city's most important festival, **Visa Pour l'Image** celebrates photojournalism during the first two weeks in September (☎ 62 38 00; www.visapourlimage.com).

## ◪ DAYTRIPS FROM PERPIGNAN

**VILLEFRANCHE-DE-CONFLENT.** A village-in-a-fortress, Villefranche (pop. 230), lies deep in the Conflent mountains. Constructed by Vauban in 1681 to protect Catalonia from the Spanish army, ■**Fort Liberia,** 734 underground steps above Villefranche offers a stunning view of Mt. Canigou. (☎ 93 34 01. Open daily July-Aug. 9am-8pm; May-June and Sept. 10am-7pm; Mar.-Apr. 10am-6pm; Nov.-Feb. 10am-5pm. €6, students €5, 5-11 €3.) A navette (shuttle bus) runs from the Villefranche train station or the two gates' parking lot to the Fort (10min.; July-Aug. 2 per hr., Sept.-June request at the St-Jacques info desk; €7, 5-11 €4.10; ticket includes fort entry). Alternatively, walk 30min. along the road that begins on the far side of the train station. The magnificent **Grandes Canalettes** contain water-carved galleries, stalactite-filled grottoes, and underground lakes. (☎ 96 23 11; www.grotte-grandes-canalettes.com. Open daily mid-June to mid-Sept. 10am-6pm; mid-Sept. to Oct. and Apr. to mid-June daily 10am-5:30pm; Nov.-Mar. Su 2-5pm. €8, 5-12 €4; 2 caves €12/6. AmEx/MC/V.) Running 63km through the Pyrénées, the **petit train jaune** (little yellow train) departs from the train station and stops at 20 small towns. The train also carts **skiers** to the first-rate **Font-Romeu** (2hr., 3-8 per day, €11). Arrive at the petit train jaune station in the early morning or at least 1-2hr. ahead. (☎ 30 60 61. Day pass €28; includes navette. €4 student discount.) Celebrated throughout Catalonia around June 23, the **Fête des Feux de la St-Jean** lights up Villefranche. Runners carry a sacred flame from Canigou's summit to the Castillet in Perpignan, and locals celebrate by dancing the traditional Sardane, drinking wine, and leaping over bonfires. **Trains** (☎ 96 63 62) connect Perpignan to the Villefranche train station (1hr., 6-7 per day, €7.50), while **Couriers Catalans Buses** (☎ 35 29 02) run directly to Villefranche's gates (1hr.; 5-6 per day; €9.60, free with tourist pass).

**CÉRET.** Tucked into the foothills of the Pyrénées, Céret blossoms in the spring. Each season the President of France receives the first cérises (cherries) from its orchards. Famous for more than its fruit, Céret was also the stomping ground of Chagall, Herbin, Manolo, and Picasso. As a result, the **Musée d'Art Moderne,** 8 bd. Maréchal Joffre, uphill from the tourist office, is one of France's best. (☎ 87 27 76; www.musee-ceret.com. Open July to mid-Sept. daily 10am-7pm; May-June and late Sept. daily 10am-6pm; Oct.-Apr. M and W-Su 10am-6pm. Wheelchair-accessible. €5.50, students €3.50, under 12 free. Temporary summer exhibits €8/6/free.) According to legend, the **pont du Diable** (Bridge of the Devil), which links the town center to its outskirts, couldn't be built until the devil agreed to aid in its construction in exchange for the first soul to cross the bridge. The villagers tried to outwit Satan by sending a sacrificial black cat across, but the devil took revenge by removing one of the bridge's stones. The pont du Diable remains one brick away from "completion" to this day. The **tourist office,** 1 av. Georges Clemenceau, provides a free Les Petits Guides

*Rando Pyrénées Roussillon* guide to regional hikes. (☎87 00 53; www.ot-ceret.fr. Open July-Sept. M-Sa 9am-1pm and 2-7pm, Su 10am-1pm; Oct.-June M-F 9am-noon and 2-5pm, Sa 9:30am-12:30pm.) A quick **hike** (round-trip 2½hr. from Céret's center; #3 in *Les Petits Guides Rando Pyrénées*) takes visitors through cherry fields, into the hills and ends at **L'Ermitage St-Férréol**, the site of a festive meal during the **Festa Major de Sant Férriol** (☎87 00 53) on September 18. From May 31-July 1, Céret celebrates the **Grande Fête de la Cérise** and the **Festival de Bandas** with two days of cherry markets and Catalonian music. The city's most raucous *féria*, **Céret de Toros**, occurs every year for three days in the middle of July, during which the town hosts two *corridas* (bullfights) and a *novillada*, a bull fight with an uncertified fighter. (☎87 47 47; www.ceret-de-toros.com. Corridas €35-86. Novillada €27-56.) **Buses** run from Perpignan's train station and *gare routière* to Céret's center (45min., 8-11 per day, €4.40). Most return buses stop outside Perpignan at Pont or r. du 19 Mars.

## MONTPELLIER                                                    ☎04 67

Occasional live music brings each street corner to life in Montpellier (pop. 225,000), southern France's most lighthearted city. The gigantic, beautifully renovated ◾**Musée Fabre,** 39 bd. Bonne Nouvelle, holds one of the largest collections of 17th- to 19th-century paintings outside Paris, with works by Delacroix, Ingres, and Poussin. The museum will host a temporary Courbet exhibit in winter 2007 and spring 2008. (☎14 83 00. Open Tu, Th-F, and Su 10am-6pm, W 1-9pm, Sa 11am-6pm. €6, with temporary exhibits €7; students €4/5.) Boulevard Henri IV leads to the **Jardin des Plantes,** France's first botanical garden. (☎63 43 22. Open Tu-Su June-Sept. noon-8pm; Oct.-Mar. noon-6pm. Free.)

The friendly owner of **Hôtel des Etuves** ❷, 24 r. des Etuves, keeps 13 plain, comfortable rooms, all with toilet and shower. (☎60 78 19; www.hoteldesetuves.fr. Breakfast €5. Reception M-Sa 6:30am-11pm, Su 7am-noon and 6-11pm. Reserve 1 week ahead. Singles €23, with TV €33; doubles €37; singles and doubles with bath €42. Cash only.) Standard French cuisine dominates Montpellier's *vieille ville*, while a number of Indian and Lebanese restaurants are on **rue des Écoles Laïques.** Behind the Crédit Lyonnaise on pl. de la Comédie, **Crêperie le Kreisker** ❶, 3 passage Bruyas, serves 80 kinds of crepes (€1.90-6.60) topped with everything from buttered bananas to snails. (☎60 82 50. Open M-Sa 11:30am-3pm and 6:30-11pm. AmEx/MC/V.) Get groceries at **INNO,** in the basement of the Polygone commercial center, just past the tourist office. (Open M-Sa 8:30am-8:30pm. MC/V.) At dusk, **rue de la Loge** fills with vendors, musicians, and stilt-walkers. The liveliest bars are in **place Jean-Jaurès,** which lights up at night. **Cubanito Cafe,** 13 r. de Verdun, just off pl. de la Comédie, overflows with twentysomethings who dance to Latin beats (Su-M) and hip-hop (Tu-Sa) in the back. (☎92 65 82. Mixed drinks €5. Open daily July-Aug. noon-2am; Sept.-June noon-1am. AmEx/MC/V.) Prominent gay nightlife is centered around **place du Marché aux Fleurs.**

**Trains** leave pl. Auguste Gibert (☎08 92 35 35 35) for: Avignon (1hr., 13 per day, €14); Marseille (1¾hr., 11 per day, €26); Nice (4hr., 2 per day, €48); Paris (3½hr., 12 per day, €93); Toulouse (2½hr., 13 per day, €33). The **tourist office** is at 30 allée Jean de Lattre de Tassigny. (☎60 60 60; www.ot-montpellier.fr. Open July-Sept. M-F 9am-7:30pm, Sa 10am-6pm, Su 9:30am-1pm and 2:30-6pm; Oct.-June M-F 9am-6:30pm, Sa 10am-6pm, Su 10am-1pm and 2-5pm.) Surf the web at **Cybercafé www,** 12bis r. Jules Ferry, across from the train station. (€1.50 per hr. Open M-Sa 10am-10pm.) **Postal Code:** 34000.

# PROVENCE

If Paris boasts world-class paintings, it's only because Provence inspired them. Fierce mistral winds cut through olive groves in the north, while pink flamingoes, black bulls, and unicorn-like white horses gallop freely in the marshy south. From

**Provence**

TO THE ARDECHE VALLEY
TO LYON (220km)
Vaison-la-Romaine
Die
Séguret
DENTELLES DE MONTMIRAIL
Bagnols
Orange
Nyons
Mt. Ventoux 1909m
Alès
Uzès
Châteauneuf-du-Pape
Carpentras
VAUCLUSE PLATEAU
Villeneuve-lès-Avignon
L'Isle-sur-la-Sorgue
Fontaine de Vaucluse
Abbaye de Sénanque
Roussillon
Pont du Gard
**Avignon**
Gordes
Apt
Village des Bories
Lacoste
**Nimes**
Cavaillon
Oppède-le-Vieux
Ménerbes
Bonnieux
Tarascon
St-Rémy-de-Provence
MONTAGNE DU LUBERON
Lourmarin
Pertuis
Les Baux-de-Provence
Durance
Abbaye de Montmajour
**Arles**
Salon-de-Provence
Vauvenargues
Aigues-Mortes
THE CAMARGUE
Vaccarès Lagoon
Fos-sur-Mer
Berre Lagoon
**Aix-en-Provence**
*Golfe du Lion*
Stes-Maries-de-la-Mer
Martigues
Marignane
*Golfe de Fos*
TO NICE AND THE CÔTE D'AZUR (210km)
**Marseille**
Château d'If
*MEDITERRANEAN SEA*
Les Calanques
TO CORSICA
Cassis

0    10 kilometers
0    10 miles

the Roman arena and cobblestone elegance of Arles to Cézanne's lingering foot-steps in Aix-en-Provence, Provence provides a taste of *La Vie en Rose*.

# MARSEILLE    ☎ 04 91

Dubbed "the meeting place of the entire world" by Alexandre Dumas, Marseille (pop. 800,000) is a jumble of color and commotion. A walk through its side streets is punctuated by the vibrant hues of West African fabrics, the sounds of Arabic music, and the smells of North African cuisine. A true immigrant city, Marseille offers visitors a taste of multiple Mediterranean cultures, some long gone.

## ▗ TRANSPORTATION

**Flights: Aéroport Marseille-Provence (MRS; ☎ 04 42 14 14 14; www.marseille.aeroport.fr).** Flights to: **Corsica, Lyon** and **Paris.** Shuttle buses run to Gare St-Charles (3 per hr.; €8.50). Taxis from the *centre-ville* to airport cost €40-50.

**Trains: Gare St-Charles,** pl. Victor Hugo (☎08 92 35 35 35). To **Lyon** (1½hr., 21 per day, €55), **Nice** (2¾hr., 21 per day, €31), and **Paris** (3hr., 18 per day, €94).

**Buses: Gare Routière,** pl. Victor Hugo, near the train station. M: Gare St-Charles. To **Aix-en-Provence** (2-6 per hr., €4.60), **Cannes** (2¼-3hr., 4 per day, €18-25), and **Nice** (2¾hr., 1 per day, €18-26). Ticket windows open M-F 6:15am-7:30pm, Sa 6:30am-6:30pm, Su 7:30am-noon and 12:45-6pm.

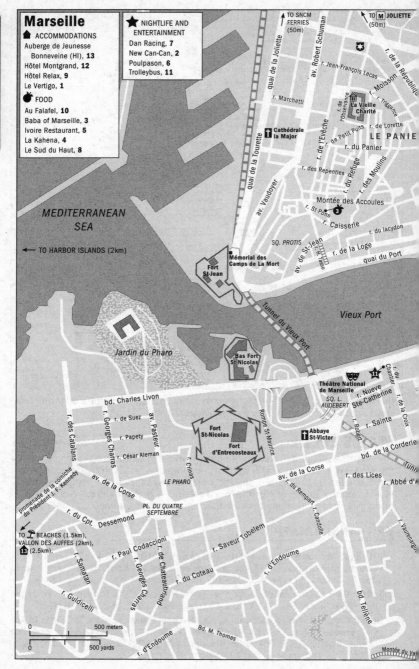

# Marseille

**ACCOMMODATIONS**
Auberge de Jeunesse
  Bonneveine (HI), **13**
Hôtel Montgrand, **12**
Hôtel Relax, **9**
Le Vertigo, **1**

**FOOD**
Au Falafel, **10**
Baba of Marseille, **3**
Ivoire Restaurant, **5**
La Kahena, **4**
Le Sud du Haut, **8**

★ NIGHTLIFE AND
  ENTERTAINMENT
Dan Racing, **7**
New Can-Can, **2**
Poulpason, **6**
Trolleybus, **11**

TO SNCM
FERRIES
(50m)

TO M JOLIETTE
(50m)

quai de la Joliette

av. Robert Schuman

r. de la Républiqu

r. Jean-François Lecas

r. Marchetti

r. Moisson

r. Tiggance

r. de
l'observance

La Vieille
Charité

r. de la Tourette

Cathédrale
la Major

r. de Petit Puits

r. de Lorette

r. de l'Evêché

LE PANIE

r. du Panier

av. Vaudoyer

r. des Repenties

r. du Refuge

r. des Moulins

Montée des Accoules

r. St-Pons

r. Caisserie

r. du lacydon

MEDITERRANEAN
SEA

SQ. PROTIS

av. de St-Jean

r. de la Loge

← TO HARBOR ISLANDS (2km)

Mémorial des
Camps de La Mort

quai du Port

Fort
St-Jean

Tunnel du Vieux Port

Vieux Port

Jardin du Pharo

Bas Fort
St-Nicolas

Théâtre National
de Marseille

r. du
Chantier

r. Nueve

SQ. L.
AUDEBERT

Ste-Catherine

r. de la Croix

bd. Charles Livon

Fort
St-Nicolas

Rampe St-Maurice

Abbaye
St-Victor

r. Robert

r. Sainte

r. des Catalans

r. de Suez

av. Pasteur

r. Georges Charras

r. Papety

r. César Aleman

r. Crinas

Fort
d'Entrecosteaux

av. de la Corse

bd. de la Corderie

r. des Lices

Tunn

promenade de la corniche
du Président J. F. Kennedy

av. de la Corse

LE PHARO

r. du Rempart

r. Abbé d'

r. du Cpt. Dessemond

PL. DU QUATRE
SEPTEMBRE

r. Candolle

r. Vaurenargu

TO BEACHES (1.5km),
VALLON DES AUFFES (2km),
(2.5km),

r. Paul Codaccioni

r. de Chateaubriand

r. Saveur Tobelem

r. d'Endoume

r. du Coteau

r. Samatan

r. Georges
Charras

bd. Tellene

r. Guldicelli

0        500 meters

0        500 yards

r. d'Endoume

Bd. M. Thomas

Montée du Val

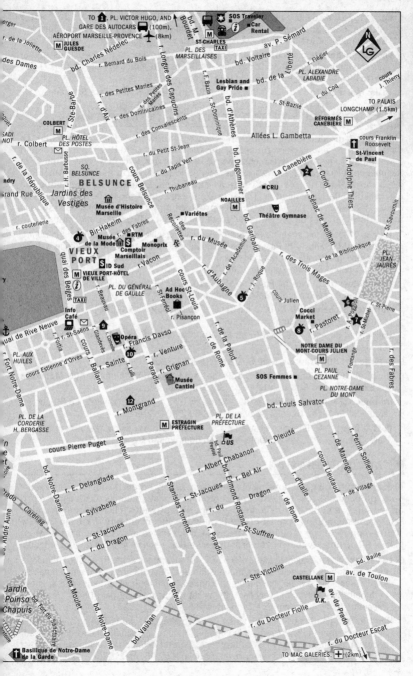

FRANCE

TO 1, PL. VICTOR HUGO, AND
GARE DES AUTOCARS (100m),
AÉROPORT MARSEILLE-PROVENCE ✈ (8km)

bd. M. Bourdet
SOS Traveler
Car Rental
av. P. Sémard

M JULES GUESDE
bd. Charles Nédelec
r. Bernard du Bois
ST-CHARLES TAXI
PL. DES MARSEILLAISES
bd. Voltaire
av. P. Sémard

erger
r. de la Joliette
des Dames

r. des Petites Maries
r. des Dominicaines
r. d'Aix
r. des Petites Maries
r. E. Bazin
r. St-Dominique
bd. d'Athènes
Lesbian and Gay Pride ■
bd. de la Liberté
r. Fléger
PL. ALEXANDRE LABADIE
r. du Coq
cours J. Thierry

Ste-Barbe
COLBERT M
PL. HÔTEL DES POSTES
r. des Convalescents
r. du Petit St-Jean
r. Tapis Vert
r. Thubaneau
bd. Dugommier
r. St-Bazile
RÉFORMÉS CANEBIÈRE M
TO PALAIS LONGCHAMP (1.5km)
Allées L. Gambetta
cours Franklin Roosevelt
St-Vincent de Paul

SADI
NOT
r. Colbert
r. de la République
rand Rue
ndry
r. H. Barbusse
SQ. BELSUNCE
BELSUNCE
Jardins des Vestiges
Musée d'Histoire Marseille
cours Belsunce
NOAILLES M
La Canebière
CRIJ
r. Sénac de Meilhan
r. Curiol
r. Adolphe Thiers
r. St-Savournin

r. coutellerie
Bir-Hakeim
Musée de la Mode
RTM
Comptoir Marseillais
Monoprix
r. des Fabres
r. des Récolettes
Variétés
Théâtre Gymnase
r. du Musée
r. d'Académie
r. des Trois Mages
r. de la Bibliothèque
PL. JEAN JAURÈS

VIEUX PORT
ID Sud
VIEUX PORT-HÔTEL DE VILLE
quai des Belges
PL. DU GÉNÉRAL DE GAULLE
Ad Hoc Books
cours St-Louis
r. Pisançon
r. d'Aubagne
r. J. Roque
cours Julien
Cocci Market
r. Pastoret
r. St-Pierre
r. St-Michel

Info Café
quai de Rive Neuve
r. St-Saëns
r. Fortia
cours J. Ballard
r. Glandeves
r. Corneille
Opéra
r. Francis Davso
r. Lulli
r. Sainte
r. Venture
r. Paradis
r. Grignan
r. de la Palud
r. de Rome
NOTRE DAME DU MONT-COURS JULIEN M
PL. PAUL CEZANNE
r. Fontange
r. des Fabres

Fort Notre-Dame
PL. AUX HUILES
cours Estienne d'Orves
Musée Cantini
SOS Femmes
PL. NOTRE-DAME DU MONT

r. Montgrand
ESTRANGIN PRÉFECTURE M
PL. DE LA PRÉFECTURE
bd. Louis Salvator

PL. DE LA CORDERIE H. BERGASSE
cours Pierre Puget
r. Breteuil
bd. Paul Peytral
BUS
r. Dieudé
r. de Perrin Solliers
r. de Marengo

n
e
t
oire
bd. Notre-Dame
r. E. Delanglade
r. Sylvabelle
r. Albert Chabanon
r. Edmond Rostand
r. Bel Air
r. Dragon
r. d'Italie
r. de Village

Prado
Carénas
André Aune
r. St-Jacques
r. du Dragon
r. Stanislas Torrents
r. St-Jacques
r. du
r. de Rome
r. St-Suffren
r. Paradis

Jardin Poinso Chapuis
r. Jules Moulet
r. Breteuil
bd. Notre-Dame
bd. Vauban
r. Ste-Victoire
CASTELLANE M
U.K.
bd. Baille
av. de Toulon
av. du Prado

Basilique de Notre-Dame de la Garde
r. du Docteur Fiolle
TO MAC GALERIES, ✈ (2km)
r. du Docteur Escat

**Ferries: SNCM,** 61 bd. des Dames (☎08 25 88 80 88; www.sncm.fr). To **Corsica** (11½hr.; €35-53, students €20-40) and **Sardinia** (14½hr., €59-69/50-65). Open M-F 8am-6pm, Sa 8:30am-noon and 2-5:30pm. Prices higher June-Sept.

**Local Transportation: RTM,** 6 r. des Fabres (☎91 92 10; www.rtm.fr). Tickets sold at bus and metro stations (€1.70, day pass €4.50, 5- to 10-ride Carte Liberté €6-12). The **Metro** runs M-Th 5am-9pm, F-Su 5am-12:30am.

**Taxis: Marseille Taxi** (☎02 20 20). 24hr. €20-30 to hostels from Gare St-Charles.

## ▣ ⁊ ORIENTATION AND PRACTICAL INFORMATION

Marseille is divided along major streets into 16 *quartiers* (neighborhoods). **La Canebière** is the main artery, funneling into the **vieux port** (Old Port) to the west and becoming urban sprawl to the east. North of the *vieux port* and west of **rue de la République** lies **Le Panier,** the city's oldest neighborhood. Surrounding La Canebière are several *Maghreb,* or North African and Arabic communities, including the market-filled **Belsunce quartier.** The area around **rue Curiol** should be avoided late at night. Marseille's two quick metro lines provide limited service. The bus system is more thorough but complex—a map from the tourist office helps enormously.

**Tourist Office:** 4 la Canebière (☎13 89 00; www.marseille-tourisme.com) M: Vieux Port. Sells the **Marseille City Pass,** which includes an RTM day pass, tourist office walking tours, the ferry to Île d'If, and admission to 14 museums (€20 for 1 day, €27 for 2 days). Open M-Sa 9am-7pm, Su 10am-5pm.

**Consulates: UK,** 24 av. du Prado (☎15 72 10). **US,** 12 bd. Paul Peytral (☎54 92 00). Both open by appointment M-F 9am-noon and 2-4pm.

**Currency Exchange: ID SUD,** 3 pl. Général de Gaulle (☎13 09 00). Open M-F 9am-6pm, Sa 9am-5pm. Also at the post office.

**Police:** 2 r. du Antoine Becker (☎39 80 00). Also in the train station on esplanade St-Charles (☎04 96 13 01 88).

**Emergency: SOS Traveler,** Gare St-Charles (☎62 12 80).

**Hospital: Hôpital Timone,** 246 r. St-Pierre (☎38 00 00). M: Timone. **SOS Médecins** (☎52 91 52) and **SOS Dentist** (☎85 39 39). Doctors on call.

**Internet Access: Info Café,** 1 q. Rive Neuve (☎33 74 98). M: Noailles. €3.80 per hr., students €3 per hr. Open M-Sa 9am-10pm, Su 2:30-7:30pm.

**Post Office:** 1 pl. Hôtel des Postes (☎15 47 00). **Currency exchange** at main branch only. Open M-F 9:30am-12:30pm and 1:30-6pm. **Postal Code:** 13001.

## ▮ ACCOMMODATIONS

Marseille has a range of housing options, from pricey hotels throughout the *vieux port* to Belsunce's less reputable but temptingly cheap lodgings. Listings here prioritize safety and location. The tourist office also provides a list of recommended safe accommodations. The HI hostel is quiet but inconveniently far from the city center—particularly in light of infrequent bus service and early curfews. Most places fill up quickly on weekends and in summer; reserve at least a week ahead.

**☒ Le Vertigo,** 42 r. des petites Maries (☎91 07 11; www.hotelvertigo.fr). About 100m from the train station, this newcomer combines the best of youth hostel and small hotel. Its English-speaking owners, hand-painted wooden furniture, inviting beds, and spotless bathrooms make it worth every cent. Breakfast €5. Internet €1 per 30min.; free Wi-Fi. Reception 24hr. 4-bed dorms €24; doubles €50-60. MC/V. ❷

**Hôtel Relax,** 4 r. Corneille (☎33 15 87; www.hotelrelax.fr). M: Vieux Port. Just around the corner from the *vieux port,* this charming hotel offers small, clean rooms at fair prices. Amenities include A/C, bath, phone, TV, and soundproof windows. Breakfast €6. Free Wi-Fi. Reception 6am-midnight. Doubles €50-55. AmEx/MC/V. ❷

**Hôtel Montgrand,** 50 r. Montgrand (☎00 35 20; www.hotel-montgrand-marseille.com). M: Estragin-Préfecture. Quiet, recently renovated rooms near the *vieux port*. A/C. Breakfast €5. Singles €42-49; family-size rooms €54-62. Extra person €8. MC/V. ❸

**Auberge de Jeunesse Bonneveine (HI),** impasse Bonfils (☎17 63 30). M: Rond-Point du Prado. Take bus #44 to pl. Bonnefon, backtrack toward the roundabout, turn left at av. J. Vidal, then go left onto impasse Bonfils. Despite its discouraging concrete exterior and bare garden, the Auberge is a well-organized hostel with an international crowd. Max. 3-night stay. Reception 7am-12:45pm, 1:30-8pm, and 8:45pm-1am. Open mid-Jan. to mid-Dec. Apr.-Aug. doubles €18; dorms €21. Mid-Jan. to Mar. and Sept. to mid-Dec. doubles €17; dorms €20. €3 HI discount. MC/V. ❷

## ◖ FOOD

Marseille's restaurants are as diverse as its inhabitants. African eateries and kebab stands line **cours St-Louis**, while outdoor cafes pack the streets around the *vieux port*. **Cours Julien** has a wonderful, eclectic collection of restaurants. Buy groceries at the **Monoprix** on bd. de la Canebière. (Open M-Sa 8:30am-9pm.)

▨ **Ivoire Restaurant,** 57 r. d'Aubagne (☎33 75 33). M: Noailles. Loyal patrons come to this no-frills restaurant for authentic African cuisine and helpful advice from its exuberant owner, Mama Africa. The Côte d'Ivoire specialties include *maffé* (a meat dish with peanut sauce; €8) and *jus de gingembre* (a refreshingly spicy ginger drink and West African natural aphrodisiac; €3). *Plats* €8-11. Open daily 11am-2am. Cash only. ❷

**Le Sud du Haut,** 80 cours Julien (☎92 66 64). M: Cours Julien. Inviting décor, spacious outdoor seating, and creative *provençal* cuisine make this the ideal place for a leisurely meal. The ▨**lunch formule** (€11) includes a *plat*, coffee, and dessert. Entrees €8-11. *Plats* €13-19. Rotating menu. Open M-Sa noon-2:30pm and 8-10:30pm. MC/V. ❸

**La Kahena,** 2 r. de la République (☎90 61 93). M: Vieux Port. Offers tasty couscous dishes (€9-15) garnished with fresh fish and traditional African ingredients and speedy service. Open daily noon-2:30pm and 7-10:30pm. MC/V. ❸

**Au Falafel,** 5 r. Lulli (☎54 08 55). M: Vieux Port. Warm, soft pita bread is the primary reason to visit this Israeli restaurant, which also offers first-class hummus, falafels, and *shawarma* (€10-16). Try the *Assiette Israelienne Falafel* (€7); though it's listed as an appetizer, it will satisfy all but the hungriest travelers. Open M-Th and Su noon-midnight, F noon-4pm. AmEx/MC/V. ❸

**Baba of Marseille,** 14 r. St-Pons (☎90 66 36). M: Vieux Port. Baba's generous portions of delicious *provençal* dishes spiced according to the season inspire its loyal clientele. Photos of past diners as well as paper lanterns, glass chandeliers, and local art give this restaurant a homey feel. Salads €8-9. Entrees €9-20. *Plats* €10-20. Open W-Sa noon-2:30pm for salads only and 8pm-midnight for dinner. ❹

## ◔ SIGHTS

A walk through the city's streets tops any sights-oriented itinerary, providing glimpses of active African and Arabic communities amid ancient Roman ruins and 17th-century forts. Check www.museum-paca.org for info on museums. Unless otherwise noted, all the museums listed below have the same hours: June-Sept. Tu-Su 11am-6pm; Oct.-May Tu-Su 10am-5pm.

▨**BASILIQUE DE NOTRE DAME DE LA GARDE.** A stunning view of the city, surrounding mountains, and island-studded bay make this a must-see. During the WWII liberation, the Resistance fought to regain the basilica, which remains pocked with bullet holes and shrapnel scars. Towering nearly 230m above the city, the church's statue of Madonna is regarded by many as the symbol of Marseille. (*Take bus #60, dir.: Notre Dame.* ☎ 13 40 80. *Open daily in summer 7am-8pm; in winter 7am-7pm. Free.*)

**HARBOR ISLANDS.** Resembling a child's sandcastle, the **Château d'If** guards the city from its rocky perch outside the harbor. Its dungeon, immortalized in Dumas's *Count of Monte Cristo*, once held a number of hapless Huguenots. Nearby, the **Île Frioul** was only marginally successful in isolating plague victims when an outbreak in 1720 killed half of the city's 80,000 citizens. A handful of small shops and restaurants, combined with popular swimming inlets, make the islands a convenient escape from the city. *(Boats depart from q. des Belges for both islands. Round-trip 1hr.; 1 island €10, both €15. Château €5, 18-25 €3.50, under 18 accompanied by an adult free.)*

**ABBAYE ST-VICTOR.** Fortified against pirates and Saracen invaders, this medieval abbey's ▓**crypt**—still holding the remains of two 3rd-century martyrs—is one of Europe's oldest Christian sites. Its 5th-century construction brought Christianity to the pagan *Marseillais*. The abbey hosts a concert festival each year from September to December. *(On r. Sainte at the end of q. de Rive Neuve. ☎04 96 11 22 60. Festival info ☎05 84 48. Open daily 9am-7pm. Crypt €2. Festival tickets €32, students €13.)*

**MUSÉE CANTINI.** This memorable museum chronicles the region's 20th-century artistic successes, with major Cubist, Fauvist, and Surrealist collections, including works by Matisse and Signac. *(19 r. Grignan. M: Estragin-Préfecture. ☎54 77 75. €2, students €1, over 65 and under 10 free.)*

**PALAIS LONGCHAMP.** Constructed in 1838 to honor the completion of a canal which brought fresh water to the plague-ridden city, the complex now houses a museum, observatory, and park. The **Musée de l'Histoire Naturelle** holds temporary exhibits on subjects like dinosaurs, milk, and human speech. *(M1: Cinq Avenues Longchamps. ☎14 59 50. Open Tu-Su 10am-5pm. €3, students €1.50, seniors and under 10 free.)*

**MÉMORIAL DES CAMPS DE LA MORT.** This small museum is located in a blockhouse built by the Germans during their occupation of Marseille. Sobering exhibits recall the death camps of WWII and the deportation of thousands of Jews from the *vieux port* in 1943. Unsettling quotes from Anne Frank, Primo Levi, and Elie Wiesel and a collection of ashes are on display. *(Q. de la Tourette. M: Vieux Port. ☎90 73 15. Open Tu-Su June-Aug. 11am-6pm; Sept.-May 10am-5pm. Free.)*

**LA VIEILLE CHARITÉ.** A formidable example of 17th-century local architecture by Pierre Puget, La Charité was built to house the hundreds of beggars congesting the entrances to Marseille's churches. Now a national monument and home to many of the city's cultural organizations, it also houses the anthropological collections of the **Musée des Arts Africains, Océaniens et Amérindiens.** *(2 r. de la Charité. M: Vieux Port or Joliette. ☎14 58 80. €2, students €1. Temporary exhibits €5/2.)*

**OTHER SIGHTS.** The **Musée de la Mode's** rotating exhibits feature international clothing from different eras. *(Espace Mode Méditerranée, 11 La Canebière. M: Vieux Port-Hôtel de Ville. ☎04 96 17 06 00. €3, students €2, seniors free.)* At the nearby **Musée d'Histoire de Marseille,** Greek, Phoenician, and modern artifacts reveal Marseille's rich past. A museum ticket also gives access to the adjacent **Jardin des Vestiges,** marked by crumbling medieval foundations. *(Enter through the Centre Bourse mall's lowest level. ☎90 42 22. Open M-Sa noon-7pm. €2, students €1, under 10 free.)* Bus #83 (dir.: Rond-Point du Prado) goes from the *vieux port* to Marseille's main **public beaches.** Get off the bus just after it rounds the David statue (20-30min.). Both the north and south **plages du Prado** offer views of Marseille's surrounding cliffs.

## ▚ NIGHTLIFE

Late-night restaurants and a few nightclubs center around **place Thiers,** near the *vieux port*. On weekends, tables from the bars along the **quai de Rive Neuve** spill out into the sidewalk. A more counter-cultural crowd unwinds along the **cours Julien.** Tourists should exercise caution at night, particularly in Panier and Belsunce, and near the Opera on the *vieux port*. Night buses are scarce, taxis are expensive, and the metro closes early (Su-Th 9pm, F-Sa 12:30am).

**Trolleybus,** 24 q. de Rive Neuve. M: Vieux Port. A mega-club in an 18th-century warehouse with 3 separate rooms for pop-rock, techno, and soul-funk-salsa. Prize-winning French and international DJs have been spinning here for 15 years. Beer from €5. Mixed drinks €4-8. Cover Sa €10; includes 1 drink. Open July-Aug. W-Sa 11pm-6am; Sept.-June Th-Sa 11pm-6am. MC/V.

**Dan Racing,** 17 r. André Poggiol. M: Cours Julien. Let your inner rock star run wild at this fun, casual bar, where W clubbers can jam on stage using any one of the 20 guitars, 2 drum sets, and other provided instruments. Auto- and bike-racing decor adds to the club's character. Drinks €2-5. Th-Sa concerts 9pm. Open W-Sa 9pm-2am.

**Poulpason,** 2 r. André Poggioli. M: Cours Julien. DJs spin hip hop, funk, jazz, reggae, and electro-house while a giant octopus stretches out from the wall. Drinks €3-5. Cover on specially featured DJ nights €3-10. Open M-Sa 10pm-2am. MC/V.

**New Can-Can,** 3 r. Sénac de Meilhan. M: Noailles. A perpetual party for the city's GLBT community. Swanky club set-up with full-length mirrors, a small stage, and leather couches. Drinks €9. Cover F 11pm-midnight €10, €15 after midnight. Open daily 11pm-dawn. AmEx/MC/V.

# AIX-EN-PROVENCE    ☎ 04 42

Famous for festivals, fountains, and former residents Paul Cézanne and Émile Zola, Aix-en-Provence ("X"; pop. 170,000) caters to tourists without being ruined by them. The large art collection—nearly 600 works—at the **Musée Granet,** pl. Saint-Jean de Matte, emphasizes 17th- to 19th-century French painters and includes one room displaying nine oil paintings by Cézanne. (☎ 52 87 97; www.museegranet-aixenprovence.fr. Open Tu-Su June-Sept. 11am-7pm; Oct.-May noon-6pm. €4, students €2, under 18 free.) The **chemin de Cézanne,** 9 av. Paul Cézanne, features a 2hr. self-guided tour that leads to the artist's birthplace and favorite cafes. (Open daily July-Aug. 10am-6pm; Apr.-June and Sept. 10am-noon and 2-6pm; Oct.-Mar. 10am-noon and 2-5pm. €5.50, students €2.) The **Fondation Vasarely,** av. Marcel-Pagnol, in nearby Jas-de-Bouffan, is a must-see for Op-Art fans. (Open Apr.-Oct. M-Sa 10am-6pm; Nov.-Mar. Tu-Sa 10am-6pm. €7, students €4.) A mix of Romanesque, Gothic, and Baroque, the **Cathédrale St-Sauveur,** r. Gaston de Saporta, fell victim to misplaced violence during the Revolution; angry *Aixois* mistook the apostle statues for statues of royalty and defiantly chopped off their heads. The statues were recapitated in the 19th century, but remain sans neck. (Open daily 8am-noon and 2-6pm.) In June and July, famous performers and rising stars descend on Aix for the **Festival d'Aix-en-Provence,** a series of opera and orchestral performances. (☎ 16 11 70; www.festival-aix.com. Tickets from €8.)

Aix has few cheap hotels; July travelers should reserve rooms in March. **Hôtel Paul ❸,** 10 av. Pasteur, has relatively cheap, clean rooms and serves breakfast in a quiet garden. (☎ 23 23 89; hotel.paul@wanadoo.fr. Breakfast €5. Check-in before 6pm. Singles and doubles with bath €40, with garden-facing windows €50; triples €62; quads €72. Cash only.) Well-lit rooms at the **Hôtel du Globe ❸,** 74 cours Sextius, are spacious. (☎ 26 03 58; www.hotelduglobe.com. Oct.-May singles €36, with shower €39; doubles with bath €65-69; triples €89; quads €95. June-Sept prices €4-6 higher. AmEx/MC/V.) To camp at **Arc-en-Ciel ❶,** on rte. de Nice, take bus #3 from La Rotonde to Trois Sautets. (☎ 26 14 28. Reception 8:30-11am and 3-8pm. €6.10 per person, €5.60 per tent. Electricity €3.10.) Charming restaurants pack **rue Verrerie** and the roads north of **cours Mirabeau.** There's a **Petit Casino** supermarket at 3 cours d'Orbitelle. (Open M-Sa 8am-1pm and 4-8pm.) **Rue Verrerie,** off r. des Cordiliers, has bars and clubs. **IPN,** 42 cours Sextius, hosts international students in a friendly, cave-like bar. (Open Tu-Sa 6pm-4am.)

**Trains,** at the end of av. Victor Hugo, run to Marseille (45min., 27 per day, €7), Nice (3-4hr., 25 per day, €35), and Paris (TGV 3hr., 10 per day, €77-131). **Buses**

FRANCE

> **TIP** Don't take the "train" from Aix to Marseille or vice-versa; you'll end up on a SNCF bus that takes twice as long as the *navette* from the *Gare Routière*, which costs €2 less, runs every 10min., and makes no stops.

(☎08 91 02 40 25) leave av. de l'Europe for Marseille (30min., 6 per hr., €5). From the train station, follow av. Victor Hugo, bearing left at the fork, until it feeds into La Rotonde. On the left is the **tourist office**, 2 pl. du Général de Gaulle. (☎16 11 61; www.aixenprovencetourism.com. Open July-Aug. M-Sa 8:30am-9pm, Su 10am-8pm; Sept.-June M-Sa 8:30am-8pm, Su 10am-1pm and 2-6pm.) **Postal Code:** 13100.

## AVIGNON
☎04 90

Temporary home to the papacy 700 years ago, Avignon (pop. 89,500) now hosts Europe's most prestigious theater festival. For three weeks in July, the ⊠**Festival d'Avignon** holds theatrical performances in at least 30 venues, from cloisters to factories to palaces. (☎14 14 14; www.festival-avignon.com. Reservations accepted from mid-June. Tickets free-€45, under 25 50% discount.) The more experimental **Festival OFF**, also in July, is almost as well established. (☎25 24 30; www.avignon-off.org. Tickets under €16. 30% discount with €10 Carte OFF.) The golden ⊠**Palais des Papes,** Europe's largest Gothic palace, is a reminder of the city's brief stint as the center of the Catholic Church. Although revolutionary looting stripped the interior of its lavish furnishings and fires erased its medieval murals, its vast chambers and few remaining frescoes are still remarkable. (☎27 50 00. Open daily Aug. 9am-9pm; July and Sept. 9am-8pm; Oct. and Apr.-June 9am-7pm; Nov.-Mar. 9:30am-5:45pm. €10.) The French children's song "Sur le pont d'Avigon" has immortalized the 12th-century bridge **Pont St-Bénézet.** Despite its supposedly divinely ordained location, the bridge has suffered from warfare and the once-turbulent Rhône. It now extends only partway across the river. (☎27 51 16. €4. Free audio tour. Open daily Aug. 9am-9pm; July and Sept. 9am-8pm; Apr.-June and Oct. 9am-7pm; Nov.-Mar. 9:30am-5:45pm.) Farther downstream, **Pont Daladier** makes it all the way across, offering free views of the broken bridge and the Palais.

Avignon's accommodations fill up three to four months before festival season; reserve ahead or stay in Arles (p.360) or Nîmes (p.361). Rooms with many amenities, including A/C and TV, make **Hôtel Mignon ❸,** 12 r. Joseph Vernet, a good deal despite its small, inconvenient bathrooms. (☎82 17 30; www.hotel-mignon.com. Breakfast included. Free Internet and in-room Wi-Fi. Reception 7am-11pm. Singles €38-€49, during festival €45-62; doubles €55-60/62-73; triples €66/80; quads €86/100. AmEx/MC/V.) Sleep for cheap at **Camping du Pont d'Avignon ❶,** 10 chemin de la Barthelasse, and enjoy its jacuzzi, laundry facilities, pool, restaurant, hot showers, supermarket, and tennis and volleyball courts. (☎80 63 50; www.camping-avignon.com. Internet €4 per hr. Reception July-Aug. 8am-10pm; Sept. and June 8:30am-8pm; Oct. and Mar.-May 8:30am-6:30pm. Open Mar.-Oct. 1-person tent site €15; 2-person €22; extra person €6. Electricity €2.60-3.10. MC/V.) Restaurants group on **rue des Teinturiers.** For good food at a great price, try **Citron Pressé ❷,** 38 r. Carreterie. This small restaurant serves French fare with Lebanese and Indian touches. (☎86 09 29. 3-course *menu* with wine €12. *Plats* €3-7. Open M-Th noon-2:30pm, F-Sa noon-2pm and 7:30pm-11:30pm; during festival daily noon-2am. Cash only.) A **Marché Plus** supermarket is at 7 r. Portail Matheron. (Open M-Sa 7am-9pm, Su 9am-12:30pm. AmEx/MC/V.) During July festivals, free theatrical performances spill into the streets at night, and many eateries stay open until 2 or 3am. **Place des Corps Saints** has a few bars that remain busy year-round.

**Trains** (☎27 81 89) run from bd. St-Roch to: Arles (20min., 1-2 per hr., €9); Lyon (2hr., 7 per day, €31); Marseille (1¼hr., 1 per hr., €28); Nîmes (30min., 14 per day, €9); Paris (TGV 3-4hr., 13 per day, €97). Exit the train station and turn right for **buses,** which go to Arles (1½hr., 5 per day, €8) and Marseille (2hr., 1 per day, €19). Walk straight through porte de la République to reach the **tourist office,** 41

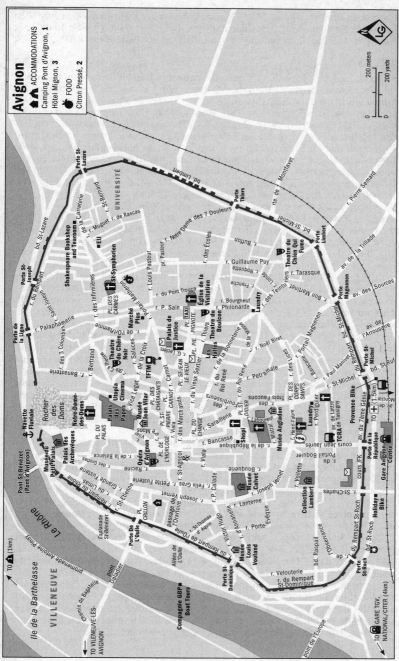

**Avignon**

▲ ACCOMMODATIONS
Camping Pont d'Avignon, **1**
Hôtel Mignon, **3**

● FOOD
Citron Pressé, **2**

FRANCE

0    200 meters
0    200 yards

cours Jean Jaurès. (☎ 04 32 74 32 74; www.avignon-tourisme.com. Open July M-Sa 9am-7pm, Su 10am-5pm; Apr.-June and Aug.-Oct. M-Sa 9am-5pm, Su 10am-5pm; Nov.-Mar. M-F 9am-6pm, Sa 9am-5pm, Su 10am-noon.) **Postal Code:** 84000.

# ARLES                                                                  ☎04 90

All roads in Arles (pop. 35,000), once the capital of Roman Gaul, seem to meet at the great Roman arena. Built in the AD first century to seat 20,000 spectators, **Les Arènes** is still used for bullfights. (☎49 36 86. Open daily May-Sept. 9am-6pm; Oct. and Mar.-Apr. 9am-5:30pm; Nov.-Feb. 10am-4:30pm. €5.50, students and children €4. Bullfight tickets from €12, children €6.) The appealing small streets of the *vieille ville* harbor a remarkable number of museums and monuments worth visiting. *Provençal* daily life and folklore are displayed at the **Muséon Arlatan,** 29 r. de la République. Ongoing renovations have led to discounted admission and the closure of three-quarters of the museum's exhibits through 2009, when the entire sight will temporarily shut down. (Open July-Aug. daily 9:30am-1pm and 2-6:30pm; June Tu-Su 9:30am-1pm and 2-6:30pm; Sept. daily 9:30am-12:30pm and 2-6pm; Apr.-May Tu-Su 9:30am-12:30pm and 2-6pm; Oct.-Mar. Tu-Su 9:30am-12:30pm and 2-5pm.) The excellent **Musée de l'Arles Antique,** on av. de la 1*er* D. F. L., only a 10min. walk from the center of town, recreates the city's Roman past. (Open daily Apr.-Oct. 9am-7pm; Nov.-Mar. 10am-5pm. €5.50, students €4.) The contemporary **Musée Réattu,** 10 r. du Grand Prieuré, houses 57 Picasso drawings inspired by Arles. (Open daily July-Sept. 10am-7pm; Mar.-June and Oct. 10am-12:30pm and 2-6pm; Nov.-Feb. 1-6pm. €4, students €3; during photography festival €6/4.50.) The annual three-week-long **Fête d'Arles,** beginning on summer solstice, brings traditional costumes, *Provençal* dancing, and bullfights to town. Once every three years, during the **Fête des Gardians** (May 1), the city elects the Queen of Arles and her six ladies, who represent the city's language, customs, and history at local and international events. The next election will occur in 2008. At the annual ▧**Rencontres Internationales de la Photographie,** in the first week of July, undiscovered photographers court potential agents while established artists hold nightly slide shows (€8-12). When the five-day festival crowd departs, the remarkable exhibits are left behind until mid-September (€3.50 per exhibit; all exhibits €28, students €22, under 16 free). For info, contact **Rencontres d'Arles,** 10 rond-point des Arènes (☎96 76 06; www.rencontres-arles.com). During the festival, buy tickets in one of the many *billeteries* scattered through the city center. If you plan to stay in Arles during the photography festival, make sure to reserve a room at least two months ahead.

To get from the train station to the **Auberge de Jeunesse (HI) ❶,** 20 av. Maréchal Foch, walk along bd. Émile Zola before taking a left on av. du Maréchal Foch. Simple, comfortably arranged single-sex dorms and individual lockers await. (☎96 18 25. English-speaking staff. Breakfast and linens included. Reception 7-10am and 5-11pm. Lockout 10am-5pm. Curfew in summer midnight, winter 11pm. 8-bed dorms €15. MC/V.) The *brasseries* on **place du Forum** are pricey but popular, while the cafes on **place Voltaire** have cheaper, though less elegant, fare. A **Monoprix** supermarket is on pl. Lamartine on the way to the train station. (Open M-Th 8:30am-7:30pm, F-Sa 8:30am-8pm. AmEx/MC/V.) **Trains** leave av. P. Talabot for: Avignon (20min., 12-20 per day, €7); Marseille (50min., 18-27 per day, €15); Montpellier (1hr., 5-8 per day, €16); Nîmes (20min., 8-11 per day, €10). **Buses** depart near the train station and from bd. Georges Clemenceau for Nîmes (1hr., 4 per day, €5.50). To get to the **tourist office,** esplanade Charles de Gaulle on bd. des Lices, turn left outside the train station and walk to the roundabout. Veer clockwise, going left after the Monoprix onto bd. Émile Courbes. At the intersection by the city tower, take a right on bd. des Lices. (☎18 41 20; www.arlestourisme.com. Open daily Apr.-Sept. 9am-6:45pm; Oct.-Mar. 9am-4:45pm.) **Postal Code:** 13200.

**⊠ DAYTRIP FROM ARLES: THE CAMARGUE.** Flamingos, bulls, and famous white Camargue horses roam this protected expanse of wild marshland stretching between Arles and the Mediterranean coast. The **Parc Ornithologique de Pont de Gau**, along D570, presents 60 hectares of the *Camarguaise* landscape. (☎97 82 62. *Park open daily Apr.-Sept. 9am-sunset; Oct.-Mar. 10am-sunset. Tours €9, under 10 €4.*) The best way to see the Camargue is on horseback; call the **Association Camarguaise de Tourisme Equestre** for more info. (☎97 10 40; www.parc-camargue.fr. *€13-16 per hr., €26-30 per 2hr., €35-40 per day.*) Other options include jeep safaris from **Le Gitan** (17 av. de la République, Stes-Maries; ☎97 89 33; legitansafari@libertysurf.fr; open Apr.-Nov. daily 9am-7pm) and boat trips by **Le Camargue**, 5 r. des Launes (☎97 84 72; www.bateau-camargue.com; 1½hr., 2-3 per day, €10). Trail maps are available from the **tourist office** in the region's largest town, **Stes-Maries-de-la-Mer**, 5 av. van Gogh. (☎97 82 55; www.santesmaries.com. *Open daily July-Aug. 9am-8pm; Apr.-June and Sept. 9am-7pm; Mar. and Oct. 9am-6pm; Nov.-Feb. 9am-5pm.*) **Buses** from Arles run to Stes-Maries-de-la-Mer (1hr., 4-5 per day, €5.20). Visitors to the Camargue will find that, though plentiful, accommodations are expensive; it is cheaper to stay in Arles.

# NÎMES

☎04 66

Southern France flocks to Nîmes (pop. 135,000) for its *férias*, celebrations with bullfights, flamenco dancing, and other hot-blooded festivities (mid-Sept. and May 7-12, 2008). Every Thursday night in summer, art and musical performances fill the squares of the Old Town. **Les Arènes** is a well-preserved first-century **Roman amphitheater** that still holds bullfights and concerts. (☎21 82 56. Open daily June-Aug. 9am-7pm; Mar.-May and Sept.-Oct. 9am-6pm; Nov.-Feb. 9:30am-5pm. Closed during *férias* or concerts; call ahead. €8, students €6.) North of the arena stands the **Maison Carrée**, a rectangular temple built in the first century BC. Today, visitors can enjoy a 3D film retracing the town's Roman past. (Open daily June-Aug. 9am-7:30pm; Apr.-May and Sept. 10am-7pm; Mar. and Oct. 10am-6:30pm; Jan.-Feb. and Nov.-Dec. 10am-1pm and 2-5pm. Film 2 per hr. €4.50, students €3.60.) Across the square, the **Carrée d'Art** displays traveling exhibits of contemporary art. (Open Tu-Su 10am-6pm. Last entry at 5:30pm. €5, students €3.70.) Near the mouth of the canals enjoy the spacious grounds, *pétanque* (similar to *bocce* and lawn bowling) courts, and luscious woods of the **Jardins de la Fontaine.** A steep hike through the park brings you to the Roman ruins of the **Tour Magne.** (Garden open daily mid.-Mar. to mid-Oct. 7:30am-10pm; mid-Oct. to mid-Mar. 7:30am-6:30pm. Tower open daily June-Aug. 9:30am-7pm; Apr.-May and Sept. 9:30am-6:30pm; Mar. and Oct. 9:30am-1pm and 2-4:30pm. Garden free. Tower €2.70, students €2.30.)

To get to the newly renovated ⊠**Auberge de Jeunesse (HI) ❶**, 257 ch. de l'Auberge de Jeunesse, take bus I (dir.: Alès) from the train station to Stade, rte. d'Alès and follow the signs uphill. With jovial staff and a beautiful courtyard garden, this comfortable hostel is worth the 45min. trek from the train station. (☎68 03 20. Breakfast €3.40. Internet €1 per 15min; free Wi-Fi. Reception 7:30am-1am. Open Mar.-Sept. Camping €3.90. €3 HI discount. MC/V.) **Camping Domaine de La Bastide ❶**, rte. de Générac, 5km south of the train station, has a restaurant and laundry in addition to tent sites. Take bus D (dir.: La Bastide, last bus 8pm) to its terminus. (☎62 05 82. €9.50 per person, €13 for 2 people. MC/V; €15 min.) For groceries, head to the **Monoprix**, 3 bd. Admiral Courbet, near Esplanade Charles de Gaulle. (Open M-Sa 8:30am-8:30pm, Su 9am-noon. AmEx/MC/V.) **Trains** go from bd. Talabot to: Arles (25min., 8 per day, €10); Marseille (1¼hr., 9 per day, €22); Montpellier (30min., 31-46 per day, €8); Toulouse (3hr., 17 per day, €38). **Buses** (☎29 52 00) depart from behind the train station for Avignon (1½hr., 3-5 per day, €8.30). The **tourist office,** is at 6 r. Auguste. (☎58 38 00; www.ot-nimes.fr. Open July-Aug. M-W and F 8:30am-8pm, Th 8:30am-9pm, Sa 9am-7pm, Su 10am-6pm; Sept.-June reduced hours.) **Postal Codes:** 30000; 30900.

# FRENCH RIVIERA (CÔTE D'AZUR)

Between Marseille and the Italian border, sun-drenched beaches and warm Mediterranean waters combine to form the fabled playground of the rich and famous. Chagall, F. Scott Fitzgerald, Matisse, Picasso, and Renoir all flocked to the French Riviera in its heyday. Now, the coast is a curious combination of high-rolling millionaires and low-budget tourists. In May, high society makes its yearly pilgrimage to the Cannes Film Festival and the Monte-Carlo Grand Prix, while Nice's February *Carnaval* and summer jazz festivals draw budget travelers.

## NICE ☎ 04 93

Classy, colorful Nice ("NIECE"; pop. 340,000) is the Riviera's unofficial capital. Its non-stop nightlife, top-notch museums, and packed beaches are tourist magnets. During February **Carnaval**, visitors and *Niçois* alike ring in spring with costumes and revelry. When visiting Nice, prepare to have more fun than you'll remember.

### ⌐ TRANSPORTATION

**Flights: Aéroport Nice-Côte d'Azur** (NCE; ☎08 20 42 33 33). **Air France,** 10 av. de Verdun (☎08 02 80 28 02). To: **Bastia, Corsica** (€116; under 25, over 60, and couples €59) and **Paris** (€93/50). **Buses** on the Ligne d'Azur (€4, 3-4 per hr.) leave for the airport from the train station (#98) and the bus station (#99), or before 8am, take bus #23 (€1.30, 3-4 per hr.).

**Trains: Gare SNCF Nice-Ville,** av. Thiers (☎14 82 12). Open daily 5am-12:30am. To: **Cannes** (40min., 3 per hr., €5.60); **Marseille** (2½hr., 16 per day, €27); **Monaco** (15min., 2-6 per hr., €3.10); **Paris** (5½hr., 9 per day, €94).

**Buses:** 5 bd. Jean Jaurès (☎85 61 81). Info booth open M-F 8:30am-5:30pm, Sa 9am-4pm. To **Cannes** (2hr., 2-3 per hr., €6) and **Monaco** (1hr., 3-6 per hr., €1.30).

**Ferries: Corsica Ferries** (☎04 92 00 42 93; www.corsicaferries.com). Bus #1 or 2 (dir.: Port) from pl. Masséna. To **Corsica** (€20-40, bikes €10, cars €40-57). MC/V.

**Public Transportation: Ligne d'Azur,** 10 av. Félix Faure (☎93 13 53 13; www.lignedazur.com), near pl. Leclerc. Buses run daily 7am-8pm. Tickets €1.30, 1-day pass €4, 8-ticket *carnet* €8.30, 5-day pass €13, 1-week pass €17. Purchase tickets and day passes on board the bus; *carnet,* 5-day, and 1-week passes from the office. **Noctambus** (night service) runs 4 routes daily 9:10pm-1:10am.

**Bike and Scooter Rental: Holiday Bikes,** 34 av. Auber (☎16 01 62; nice@holiday-bikes.com), near the train station. Bikes €16 per day, €70 per week; €230 deposit. Scooters €35/175; €500 deposit. Open M-Sa 9am-6:30pm. AmEx/MC/V.

### ◢▐ ORIENTATION AND PRACTICAL INFORMATION

**Avenue Jean Médecin,** on the left as you exit the train station, and **boulevard Gambetta,** on the right, run directly to the beach. **Place Masséna** is 10min. down av. Jean Médecin. On the coast, **promenade des Anglais** is a people-watcher's paradise. To the southeast, past av. Jean Médecin and toward the bus station, is **vieux Nice.** Women should not walk alone after dark, and everyone should exercise caution at night, around the train station, in *vieux* Nice, and on promenade des Anglais.

**Tourist Office:** av. Thiers (☎08 92 70 74 07; www.nicetourisme.com), next to the train station. The free *Le Pitchoun* (www.pitchoun.com) offers insight on local venues. Open June-Sept. M-Sa 8am-8pm, Su 10am-5pm; Oct.-May M-Sa 8am-7pm, Su 9am-6pm.

**Consulates: Canada,** 10 r. Lamartine (☎92 93 22; cancons.nce@club-internet.fr). Open M-F 9am-noon. **US,** 7 av. Gustave V (☎88 89 55). Open M-F 9-11:30am and 1:30-4:30pm.

**Currency Exchange: Office Provençal,** 17 av. Thiers (☎88 56 80), opposite the train station. 4% commission on euro-denominated traveler's checks. Open M-F 7:30am-8pm, Sa-Su 7:30am-7:30pm.

**Laundromat: Lavomatique,** 7 r. d'Italie (☎85 88 14). Wash €3.50, dry €1 per 18min. Open daily 7am-9pm.

**Police:** 1 av. Maréchal Foch (☎04 92 17 22 22), opposite end from bd. Jean Médecin.

**24hr. Pharmacy:** 7 r. Masséna (☎87 78 94).

**Hospital: St-Roch,** 5 r. Pierre Dévoluy (☎04 92 03 33 75).

**Internet Access: Royal Com,** 23 r. d'Angleterre (☎97 20 10 79). €2 per hr. Open daily 7:30am-midnight. **Cyber Internet,** 9 r. Masséna. €4 per hr. Open daily 10am-11pm.

**Post Office:** 23 av. Thiers (☎82 65 22), near the station. Open M-F 8am-7pm, Sa 8am-noon. **Postal Code:** 06033.

# ACCOMMODATIONS

Make reservations before visiting Nice; it can be hard to find beds, particularly in summer. The city has two clusters of budget accommodations: near the train station and near *vieux* Nice. Those by the station are newer but more remote; the surrounding neighborhood has a deservedly rough reputation, so exercise caution at night. Hotels closer to *vieux* Nice are more convenient but less modern.

**Hôtel Belle Meunière,** 21 av. Durante (☎88 66 15), opposite the train station. Relaxed backpackers fill 4- to 5-bed co-ed dorms in a former mansion. Showers €2. Laundry from €5.50. Reception 7:30am-midnight. Dorms €15, with shower €20; 2-person apartment, min. 3-night stay, €36; doubles €50; triples €60; quads €80. MC/V. ❷

**Auberge de Jeunesse Les Camélias (HI),** 3 r. Spitalieri (☎62 15 54; nice-camelias@fuaj.org), behind the Centre Commerical Nice Étoile. A new hostel with plain, clean bathrooms. Breakfast included. Laundry €6. Internet €5 per hr. Reception 24hr. Lock-out 11am-3pm. Dorms €20. MC/V. ❷

**Hôtel Petit Trianon,** 11 r. Paradis (☎87 50 46; hotel.nice.lepetittrianon@wanadoo.fr). The caring owner looks after guests in 8 comfortable rooms near pl. Masséna. Breakfast €5. Free beach towel loan. Laundry €10 per 5kg. Free Internet and Wi-Fi. Reserve ahead. Mid-June to mid-Sept. singles €30, with bath €35; doubles €40-42/50-53; triples €60-75; quads €76-96. Mid.-Sept. to mid-June prices €2-5 less. MC/V. ❸

**Villa Saint-Exupéry,** 22 av. Gravier (☎0800 307 409; www.vsaint.com), 5km from the city center. Take bus #1, 2, or 23 to Gravier, Noisetiers B or Place St-Maurice; call for free pickup. Internationally renowned, this large, Aussie-staffed hostel attracts young travelers. Some rooms with balconies or private baths. Breakfast included. Free Internet and Wi-Fi. Dorms €22-24; singles €35-39; doubles €58-70; triples €81-93. MC/V. ❷

**Star Hôtel,** 14 r. Biscarra (☎85 19 03; www.hotel-star.com), in a quiet area between the train station and *vieux* Nice. Spacious pastel rooms with A/C, TV, and soundproof windows. Open Dec.-Oct. Singles €52-57; doubles with shower €62-67, with bath €70; triples with bath €79. Sept.-May €10-15 discount. MC/V. ❹

**Auberge de Jeunesse Mont Boron (HI),** rte. Forestière du Mont-Alban (☎89 23 64; www.hihostels.com), 4km from city center. From the bus station, take bus #14 (dir.: Mont Boron) to "l'Auberge" or, from the train station, bus #17 and switch to 14 at "Ligne d'Azur." Ultra-clean 6-bed dorms have individual lockers. Breakfast included. Linens €2.70. Reception 7am-midnight. Lockout noon-5pm. Dorms €19. MC/V. ❶

# FOOD

Mediterranean spices flavor *Niçois* cuisine. Try crusty *pan bagnat*, a round loaf of bread topped with tuna, sardines, vegetables, and olive oil, or *socca*, a thin, olive-oil-flavored chickpea bread. Famous *salade niçoise* combines tuna, olives,

FRANCE

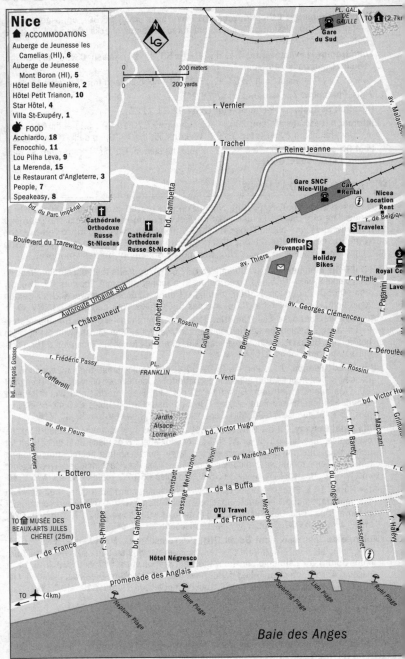

## Nice

### ▲ ACCOMMODATIONS
Auberge de Jeunesse les
  Camelias (HI), **6**
Auberge de Jeunesse
  Mont Boron (HI), **5**
Hôtel Belle Meunière, **2**
Hôtel Petit Trianon, **10**
Star Hôtel, **4**
Villa St-Exupéry, **1**

### ● FOOD
Acchiardo, **18**
Fenocchio, **11**
Lou Pilha Leva, **9**
La Merenda, **15**
Le Restaurant d'Angleterre, **3**
People, **7**
Speakeasy, **8**

PL. GAL. DE GAULLE
TO ① (2.7kr
Gare du Sud

r. Vernier

r. Trachel

r. Reine Jeanne

av. Malauss

Gare SNCF Nice-Ville
Car Rental
Nicea Location Rent
ⓘ

bd. du Parc Impérial

✝ Cathédrale Orthodoxe Russe St-Nicolas

✝ Cathédrale Orthodoxe Russe St-Nicolas

Boulevard du Tzarewitch

r. de Belgiqu

$ Travelex

Office Provençal $
Holiday Bikes
2

av. Thiers

r. d'Italie

Royal Co

r. Paganini
Lavo

3

Autoroute Urbaine Sud

r. Châteauneuf

r. Rossini

av. Georges Clémenceau

r. Déroulè

bd. François Grosso

r. Frédéric Passy

bd. Gambetta

r. Guigila

r. Berlioz

r. Gounod

av. Auber

av. Durante

r. Rossini

r. Caffarelli

PL. FRANKLIN

r. Verdi

bd. Victor Hu

av. des Fleurs

Jardin Alsace Lorraine

bd. Victor Hugo

r. Dr. Barety

r. Macarani

r. Grimau

r. des Potiers

r. de Rivoli

r. du Maréchal Joffre

r. Bottero

r. Cronstadt
passage Merianzone

r. de la Buffa

r. Meyerbeer

r. du Congrès

r. C

r. Dante

OTU Travel
r. de France

r. Massenet

r. Halévy

TO 🏛 MUSÉE DES
BEAUX-ARTS JULES
CHÉRET (25m)

r. St-Philippe

bd. Gambetta

r. de France

Hôtel Négresco

ⓘ

TO ✈ (4km)

promenade des Anglais

Sporting Plage
Lido Plage
Ruhl Plage

Neptune Plage

Blue Plage

*Baie des Anges*

0    200 meters
0    200 yards

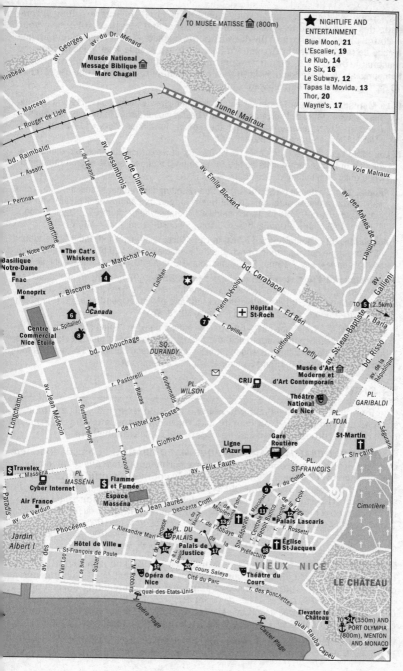

TO MUSÉE MATISSE ⋔ (800m)

★ NIGHTLIFE AND ENTERTAINMENT
Blue Moon, **21**
L'Escalier, **19**
Le Klub, **14**
Le Six, **16**
Le Subway, **12**
Tapas la Movida, **13**
Thor, **20**
Wayne's, **17**

av. Georges V
av. du Dr. Ménard

Musée National
Message Biblique
Marc Chagall

r. Marceau
r. Rouget de Lisle

Tunnel Malraux

Voie Malraux

bd. Raimbaldi
r. Assalit

r. Pertinax

r. Lamartine

av. de l'Épanie
av. Desambrois
bd. de Cimiez

av. Emile Bieckert

av. des Arènes de Cimiez

av. Notre Dame
■The Cat's
Whiskers

Basilique
Notre-Dame
■Fnac

av. Maréchal Foch

bd. Carabacel

av. Gallieni

Monoprix
r. Biscarra

r. Callian

r. Pierre Dévoluy

Hôpital
St-Roch

r. Ed Béri

TO 5 (2.5km)

r. St-Jean-Baptiste
r. Barla

6 ▫Canada

Centre
Commercial
Nice Étoile
av. Spitalien
8

bd. Dubouchage

7
r. Deille

r. Gioffredo
r. Defly

bd. Risso
av. de la République

SQ.
DURANDY

Musée d'Art ⋔
Moderne et
d'Art Contemporain

PL.
GARIBALDI

r. Pastorelli
r. Blacas

PL.
WILSON

CRIJ ▯

Théâtre
National
de Nice

r. Gubernatis

PL.
J. TOJA

St-Martin ✝

r. Longchamp
av. Jean Médecin
r. Gustave Deloye

r. de l'Hôtel des Postes

r. Gioffredo
r. Chauvain

Ligne
d'Azur

Gare
Routière

PL.
ST-FRANCOIS

r. Sincaire

Cimetière

S Travelex
r. Masséna

PL.
MASSÉNA

S Flamme
et Fumée

av. Félix Faure

r. du Collet

Cyber Internet

Air France
av. de Verdun

Espace
Masséna

bd. Jean Jaurès

Descente Crotti

9

r. de la Loge
r. de la Croix

11
Palais Lascaris
12
r. Rossetti

Phocéens

r. Alexandre Mari

PL. DU
PALAIS
15

r. du Moulin
r. de l'Abbaye
r. Centrale
r. Benoît Bunico

Église
St-Jacques

Jardin
Albert I

Hôtel de Ville
r. St-François de Paule

16
Palais de
Justice
17

r. Ste-Réparate
18
r. Préfecture

r. M. Robbins
19
Opéra de
Nice
20 cours Saleya
Cité du Parc

Théâtre du
Cours

VIEUX NICE

quai des Etats-Unis
r. des Ponchettes

LE CHÂTEAU

Opéra Plage

Elevator to
Château

quai Rauba Capeu

TO 21 (350m) AND
PORT OLYMPIA
(800m), MENTON
AND MONACO

Castel Plage

eggs, potatoes, tomatoes, and a spicy mustard dressing. The eateries along promenade des Anglais and av. Masséna are expensive and unremarkable. Save your euro for olives, cheese, and produce from the **markets** at **cours Saleya** and **avenue Maché de la Libération** (both open Tu-Su 7am-1pm). **Avenue Jean Médecin** features reasonable *brasseries*, panini vendors, and kebab stands. Load up on groceries at **Monoprix**, av. Jean Médecin, next to the centre commercial Nice Étoile. (☎04 92 47 72 62. Open M-Sa 8:30am-8:50pm. AmEx/MC/V.)

■ **La Merenda**, 4 r. de la Terrasse. Behind a stained-glass exterior and a beaded curtain, this intimate restaurant serves some of the best regional dishes in the city. Seatings at 7 and 9pm only; reserve in person in the morning for dinner. *Plats* €11-16. Open M-F noon-1:30pm and 7-9pm. Cash only. ❷

■ **Lou Pilha Leva**, 10-13 r. du Collet (☎13 99 08), in *vieux* Nice. At lunch and dinnertime, the line of locals and tourists hungry for cheap *Niçois* fare extends around the corner. Open daily 8am-midnight. Cash only. ❶

**People**, 12 r. Pastorelli (☎85 08 43). A trendy setting for traditional cuisine, with stone walls and a stainless steel bar. Try the trendy *magret de canard* (duck steak) with *foie gras* (€18). *Plats* €7.50-17. Lunch *menu* €13; dinner *menus* from €21. Open M noon-2:30pm, Tu-F noon-2:30pm and 5:30-11pm, Sa 5:30-11pm. AmEx/MC/V.

**Acchiardo**, 38 r. Droite (☎85 51 16), in *vieux* Nice. Long, crowded, family-style tables fill with simple but appetizing French and Italian dishes served up by a quick, dedicated staff. Open M-F July 7-10pm; Sept.-June noon-1:30pm and 7-10pm. Cash only. ❶

**Le Restaurant d'Angleterre**, 25 r. d'Angleterre (☎88 64 49), near the train station. Frequented by a loyal crowd of locals who come for traditional French favorites. The €14 *menu* includes salad, *plat*, side dish, dessert, and *digestif*. Open Tu-Sa 11:45am-2pm and 6:45-9:55pm, Su 11:45am-2pm. AmEx/MC/V. ❸

**Speakeasy**, 7 r. Lamartine (☎85 59 50). The stiffest drink you'll find at this tiny hole-in-the-wall is freshly made carrot juice, the perfect complement to the delectable vegan menu. All customers share 3 wooden tables. 2 courses and dessert €12-14. Open M-F noon-2:15pm and 7-9:15pm, Sa noon-2:15pm. Cash only. ❸

## 👁 SIGHTS

One look at Nice's waves and you may be tempted to spend your entire stay stretched out on the sand. As the city with the second-most museums in France, however, Nice offers more than azure waters and topless sunbathers.

■ **MUSÉE NATIONAL MESSAGE BIBLIQUE MARC CHAGALL.** Chagall founded this extraordinary museum to showcase an assortment of biblically themed pieces that he gave to the French State in 1966. Twelve of these colorful canvases illustrate the first two books of the Old Testament. The museum also includes an auditorium with stained-glass panels depicting the creation story. The auditorium hosts concerts; ask at the entrance for program info. (*Av. du Dr. Ménard. Walk 15min. north of the station, or take bus #15, dir.: Rimiez, to Musée Chagall.* ☎53 87 20; www.musee-chagall.fr. Open M and W-Su July-Sept. 10am-6pm; Oct.-June 10am-5pm. €6.70, students 18-25 €5.20, under 18 and 1st and 3rd Su of each month free. MC/V.)

■ **MUSÉE MATISSE.** Henri Matisse visited Nice in 1916 and never left. His 17th-century Genoese villa, this museum contains a small collection of paintings and a dazzling exhibit of Matisse's three-dimensional work, including dozens of cut paper tableaux. (*164 av. des Arènes de Cimiez. Bus #15, 17, 20, 22, or 25 to Arènes. Free bus between Musée Chagall and Musée Matisse.* ☎81 08 08; www.musee-matisse-nice.org. Open M and W-Su 10am-6pm. €4, students €1.50, 1st and 3rd Su of each month free. MC/V.)

**VIEUX NICE.** Hand-painted awnings and beautiful churches await at every turn in *vieux* Nice. Though filled with the inevitable slew of souvenir shops, *vieux*

Nice, southeast of bd. Jean Jaurès, remains the city's historical heart. Bilingual street signs introduce you to *Niçard*, a subdialect of the Occitan language still spoken by half a million Frenchmen. **Rue Droite** has various handmade furniture stores and mosaic studios. **Fenocchio**, on pl. Rosetti, Nice's best-loved ice cream shop, offers over 54 flavors including avocado, black olive, beer, tomato basil, and thyme. *(1 scoop €2, 2 scoops €3.50. Open daily 10:30am-2am. MC/V.)*

**MUSÉE D'ART MODERNE ET D'ART CONTEMPORAIN.** An impressive glass facade welcomes visitors to exhibits of French New Realists and American pop artists like Lichtenstein and Warhol. Minimalist galleries enshrine the avant-garde pieces, including statues by Niki de St-Phalle and color field pieces by Yves Klein. *(Promenade des Arts, at the intersection of av. St-Jean Baptiste and Traverse Garibaldi. Bus #5, dir.: St-Charles, to Musée Promenade des Arts. ☎ 62 61 62; www.mamac-nice.org. Open Tu-Su 10am-6pm. €7, 1st and 3rd Su of each month free. Cash only.)*

**MUSÉE DES BEAUX-ARTS JULES CHARET.** The former villa of Ukraine's Princess Kotschoubey has been converted into a celebration of French and Italian painting. Raoul Dufy, a local Fauvist painter, celebrated his city's spontaneity with sensational pictures of the town at rest and at play. *(33 av. Baumettes. Bus #38 to Musée Chéret or #12 to Grosso. ☎ 04 92 15 28 28; www.musee-beaux-arts-nice.org. Open Tu-Su 10am-6pm. €4, students €2.50, under 18 and 1st and 3rd Su of each month free.)*

**CATHÉDRALE ORTHODOXE RUSSE ST-NICOLAS.** Also known as the **Église Russe,** the cathedral was commissioned by Empress Marie Feodorovna in memory of her husband, Tsar Nicholas Alexandrovich, who died in Nice in 1865. Soon after its 1912 dedication, the cathedral's gold interior became a haven for exiled Russian nobles. *(17 bd. du Tzarewitch, off bd. Gambetta. ☎ 96 88 02. Open M-Sa 9am-noon and 2:30-6pm, Su 2:30-5:30pm. Closed during mass. €2.50, students €2.)*

**LE CHÂTEAU.** At the eastern end of promenade des Anglais, the remains of an 11th-century fort mark the city's birthplace. The château itself was destroyed by Louis XIV in 1706, but it still provides a spectacular ◙**view** of Nice and the sparkling Baie des Anges. In summer, an outdoor theater hosts orchestral and vocal musicians. *(☎ 85 62 33. Park open daily June-Aug. 9am-8pm; Sept. 10am-7pm; Oct.-Mar. 8am-6pm; Apr.-May 8am-7pm. Free walk to the top. Elevator daily June-Aug. 9am-8pm; Apr.-May and Sept. 10am-7pm; Oct.-Mar. 10am-6pm. €0.70, round-trip €1.)*

**JARDIN ALBERT I.** The city's oldest park, Jardin Albert I, below pl. Masséna, has plenty of benches, fountains, and palm trees. The outdoor **Théâtre de Verdure** presents concerts in summer. Contact the tourist office for info. Unfortunately, the park is one of Nice's most dangerous spots after dark. Tourists should avoid crossing the park at night. *(Between av. Verdun and bd. Jean Jaurès, off promenade des Anglais. Box office open daily 10:30am-noon and 3:30-6:30pm. MC/V.)*

**OTHER SIGHTS.** Named by the rich English community that commissioned it, the **promenade des Anglais,** a palm-lined seaside boulevard, is filled with ice-cream eating tourists and jogging locals. **Hôtel Négresco** presents the best of *Belle Époque* luxury with coffered ceilings, crystal chandeliers, and a large collection of valuable artwork. The seashore between bd. Gambetta and the Opéra alternates **private beaches** with crowded **public strands,** but a large section west of bd. Gambetta is public. Many travelers are surprised to find that stretches of rock—not soft sand—line the Baie des Anges; bring your beach mat.

# 🎵 📷 ENTERTAINMENT AND NIGHTLIFE

Nice's **Jazz Festival,** at the Parc et Arènes de Cimiez, attracts world-famous performers. (mid-July; ☎ 08 20 80 04 00; www.nicejazzfest.com. €33.) The ◙**Carnaval** gives Rio a run for its money with three weeks of confetti, fireworks, parades, and parties. (Feb. 16-Mar. 2, 2008. ☎ 04 92 14 46 46; www.nicecarnaval.com.)

Bars and nightclubs around **rue Masséna** and **vieux Nice** pulsate with dance and jazz but have a strict dress code. Many clubs will turn revelers away for wearing shorts, sandals, or baseball caps. To experience Nice's nightlife without spending a euro, head down to the **promenade des Anglais,** where street performers, musicians, and pedestrians fill the beach and boardwalk. Hard to find student-produced French-language *Le Pitchoun* provides the lowdown on trendy bars and clubs (free; www.lepitchoun.com). Exercise caution after dark; men have a reputation for harassing lone women on the promenade, in the Jardin Albert I, and near the train station, while the beach sometimes becomes a gathering place for prostitutes and thugs. Travelers should walk in groups if possible, and take only prominent, well-lit avenues when returning to their accommodations.

## BARS

**Thor,** 32 cours Saleya (☎62 49 90). Svelte bartenders pour pints for a youthful clientele amid war shields, long wooden oars, and glasses shaped like Viking horns in this raucous faux-Scandinavian pub. Daily live bands blare rock starting at 10pm. Happy hour 6-9pm; pints €4.50. Open daily 6pm-2:30am. MC/V.

**Wayne's,** 15 r. de la Préfecture (☎13 46 99; www.waynes.fr). A laid-back crowd drinks at tables by the bar while the rowdier crew finds its way downstairs to the noticeably darker dance floor. Patrons dance on tables and each other. Pints €6.10. Mixed drinks €6.50. Su karaoke. Happy hour noon-9pm; all drinks €3.50. Open daily noon-2am.

**Tapas la Movida,** 3 r. de l'Abbaye (☎62 27 46). This hole-in-the-wall bar attracts a young, alternative crowd. Figure out how to crawl home before attempting the *bar-o-mètre* (a meter-long box of shots; €15). M-F live reggae, rock, and ska (€2). F-Sa DJ and theme parties. Open July-Aug. daily 9pm-12:30am; Sept.-June M-Sa 9pm-12:30am. Cash only.

**L'Escalier,** 10 r. de la Terrasse (☎92 64 39). DJs spin R&B, funk, and hip hop for a mix of locals late into the night. The real party starts around 1am when other bars close. Cover 1-5am €10; includes 1 drink. Open daily 10pm-5am. MC/V.

**Le Six,** 6 r. Bosio (☎62 66 64). Halfway between a nightclub and a piano bar, Le Six draws a mixed crowd that dances to Top 40 songs interpreted by a local singer. Reasonably priced drinks served in an original decor, complete with a high 18th-century ceiling. Beer €7. Mixed drinks €5-10. Open T-Su 10pm-2am. MC/V.

## CLUBS

■ **Blue Moon,** 26 q. Lunel (☎26 54 79). Hip fashionistas flash their threads before a backdrop of white vinyl stools and bare tile walls. Cover €15. Open Th-Sa midnight-5am.

**Le Klub,** 6 r. Halévy (☎16 87 26). Nice's most popular gay klub attracts a large krew of men and women to its sleek lounge and active dance floor. Mixed drinks €6-10. Cover €11-14; includes 1 drink. Open W-Su midnight-5am. AmEx/MC/V.

**Le Subway,** 19 r. Droite (☎80 56 27), in *vieux* Nice. Locals and tourists dance to metal, pop, and rock, creating an unpretentious, electric mood. Drinks €3-7. Cover €8, women free after midnight; includes 1 drink. Open Th-Sa 11:30pm until dawn.

# MONACO AND MONTE-CARLO ☎04 93

In 1297, François Grimaldi of Genoa established his family as Monaco's rulers, staging a coup aided by henchmen disguised as *monaco* (Italian for monk). The tiny principality has since jealously guarded its independence. Monaco (pop. 7100) proves its tax-free wealth with ubiquitous surveillance cameras, high-speed luxury cars, multi-million-dollar yachts, and Monte-Carlo's famous casino.

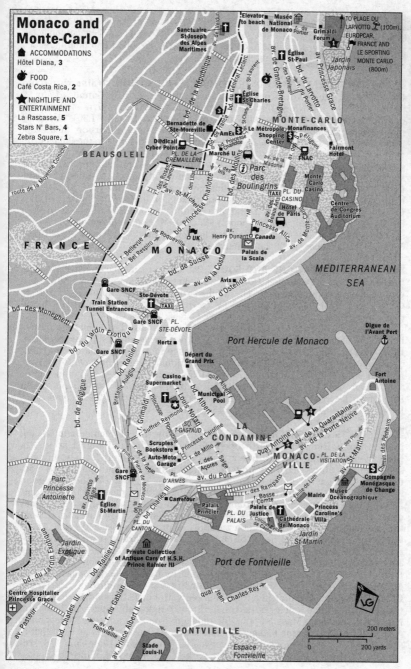

**Monaco and Monte-Carlo**

**ACCOMMODATIONS**
Hôtel Diana, **3**

**FOOD**
Café Costa Rica, **2**

**NIGHTLIFE AND ENTERTAINMENT**
La Rascasse, **5**
Stars N' Bars, **4**
Zebra Square, **1**

FRANCE

| CALLING TO AND FROM MONACO | Monaco's country code is 377. To call Monaco from France, dial 00377, then the eight-digit Monaco number. To call France from Monaco, dial 0033 and drop the first zero of the French number. |
| --- | --- |

**🖅 🔽 TRANSPORTATION AND PRACTICAL INFORMATION. Trains** run from **Gare SNCF,** pl. Ste-Dêvote, to Antibes (1hr., 2 per hr., €6.10), Cannes (1¼hr., 2 per hr., €7.70), and Nice (25min., 2 per hr., €3.10). **Buses** (☎85 64 44) leave bd. des Moulins and av. Princesse Alice for Nice (45min., 4 per hr., €1.30). The enormous **Rocher de Monaco** (Rock of Monaco) looms over the harbor. At its top, **Monaco-Ville**—the city's historical and legislative heart—is home to the Palais Princier, the Cathédrale de Monaco, and narrow cafe-lined pedestrian avenues. **La Condamine** quarter, Monaco's port, sits below Monaco-Ville, with a morning market, spirited bars, and lots of traffic. Monaco's famous glitz is concentrated in **Monte-Carlo,** whose casino draws international visitors. Bus #4 links the Ste-Dêvote train station entrance to the casino; buy tickets on board (€1.50, *carnet* of 4 €3.60). The **tourist office** is at 2A bd. des Moulins. (☎04 92 16 61 16. Open M-Sa 9am-7pm, Su and holidays 10am-noon.) **FNAC,** Le Métropole Shopping Center, 17 av. des Spélugues, offers 20min. of free **Internet.** (☎10 81 81. Open M-Sa 10am-5:30pm.) **Postal Code:** MC 98000 Monaco.

**🖅 🗋 ACCOMMODATIONS AND FOOD.** Rather than stay in expensive Monaco, the nearby town of **Beausoleil, FRA,** only a 10min. walk from the casino, offers several budget accommodations. The modest rooms at **Hôtel Diana ❸,** 17 bd. du Général Leclerc, come with A/C and TV. (☎78 47 58; www.monte-carlo.mc/hotel-diana-beausoleil. Singles €40-48; doubles €35-65; triples €67-70. AmEx/MC/V.) Unsurprisingly, Monaco has little in the way of cheap fare. Try the narrow streets behind the **place du Palais** for affordable sit-down meals, or fill a picnic basket at the **market** on pl. d'Armes at the end of av. Prince Pierre. (Open daily 6am-1pm.) The bright, merry **Café Costa Rica ❷,** 40 bd. des Moulins, serves *bruschetta*, salads, and other flavorful Italian staples. (☎25 44 45. Pasta €8-11. Tea and crepes after 3pm. Open Sept.-June daily 8am-7pm; July and late Aug. M-F 8am-7:30pm, Sa-Su 8am-3pm. Closed Aug. 1-15. V.) Buy groceries at **Marché U,** 30 bd. Princesse Charlotte. (☎50 68 60. Open M-Sa 8:30am-7:15pm. MC/V.)

**🎰 🎵 SIGHTS AND ENTERTAINMENT.** At the notorious ▨**Monte-Carlo Casino,** pl. du Casino, Richard Burton wooed Elizabeth Taylor and Mata Hari shot a Russian spy. Optimists tempt fate at blackjack, roulette (daily from noon), and slot machines (July-Aug. daily from noon; Sept.-June M-F from 2pm, Sa-Su from noon). French games like *chemin de fer* and *trente et quarante* begin at noon in the exclusive **salons privés.** (Cover €10. Coat and tie required.) Next door, relaxed **Café de Paris** opens at 10am and has no cover. All casinos have **dress codes** at night (no sandals, shorts, sneakers, or jeans). Guards are strict about the age requirement (18+); bring a passport as proof. On a seaside cliff, **Palais Princier** is the occasional home of Monaco's tabloid-darling royal family. Visitors curious about royal life can tour the small but lavish palace. (Open daily June-Sept. 9:30am-6pm; Oct. 10am-5pm. €6, students €3.) The venue for Prince Rainier and Grace Kelly's 1956 wedding, nearby **Cathédrale de Monaco,** pl. St-Martin, is the burial site for 35 generations of the Grimaldi family. Princess Grace lies behind the altar in a tomb marked with her Latinized name, "Patritia Gracia," with Prince Rainier buried on her right. (Open daily Mar.-Oct. 8am-7pm; Nov.-Feb. 8am-6pm. Mass Sa 6pm, Su 10:30am. Free.) The **Private Collection of Antique Cars of His Serene Highness Prince Rainier III,** les Terraces de Fontvieille, showcases 100 of the sexiest cars ever made. (Open daily 10am-6pm. €6, students €3.) Though Monaco hardly seems like a desert locale, multiple species of imported cacti thrive in the **Jardin Exotique**, 62 bd. du Jardin Exotique. (Open daily mid-May to mid-Sept. 9am-7pm; mid-Sept. to mid-May 9am-sunset. €7, students €4.) The **Musée Océanographique**, av. St-Martin, has a 90-tank aquarium full of exotic sea life. (www.oceano.mc. Open daily July-Aug. 9:30am-7:30pm; Apr.-June and Sept. 9:30am-7pm; Oct.-Mar. 10am-6pm. €11, students €6.)

Monaco's nightlife offers fashionistas a chance to see and be seen. Speckled with cheaper venues, **La Condamine**, near the port, caters to a young clientele while glitzy trust-funders frequent pricier spots near the casino. Vintage decor, video games, and the latest pop and techno beats draw young, international masses to **Stars N' Bars**, 6 q. Antoine 1. (☎04 97 97 95 95; www.starsnbars.com. Open June-Sept. daily 11am-3am; Oct.-May Tu-Su 11am-3am.) **La Rascasse**, 1 q. Antoine 1, hosts live music nightly at 11pm (☎25 56 90; www.larascasse.mc. Beer €5-8. Mixed drinks €12-13. Happy hour M-F 6-9pm; drinks half-price. Open daily 10am-5am. AmEx/MC/V). Gaze out wistfully over the ocean horizon while sipping mixed drinks (€9-14) with an older crowd at **Zebra Square**, 10 av. Princesse Grace, on top of the Grimaldi Forum. (☎04 99 99 25 50; www.zebrasquare.com. Club open daily M-F 6pm-2am, Sa-Su 6pm-3am; terrace open July-Aug. daily 6-9pm. AmEx/MC/V).

# ANTIBES ☎ 04 93

Blessed with beautiful beaches and a charming *vieille ville*, Antibes (pop. 80,000) is less touristy than Nice and more relaxed than St-Tropez. It provides much-needed middle ground on the glitterati-controlled coast. The ▨**Musée Picasso**, in the Château Grimaldi on pl. Mariejol, which displays works by the former Antibes resident and his contemporaries, is closed for renovations through early 2008. The two main public beaches in Antibes, **plage du Ponteil** and neighboring **plage de la Salis**, are crowded all summer. Cleaner and slightly more secluded, the rocky beaches on **Cap d'Antibes** have white cliffs and blue water perfect for snorkeling.

For the cheapest accommodations in Antibes, grab a bunk with a rowdy crowd of yacht-hands at **The Crew House** ❷, 1 av. St-Roch. From the train station, walk down av. de la Libération; just after the roundabout, make a right onto av. St-Roch. (☎04 92 90 49 39; workstation_fr@yahoo.com. Internet €4.80 per hr. Reception M-F 9am-7pm, Sa-Su 10am-6pm. Dorms Apr.-Oct. €20; Nov.-Mar. €15. MC/V.) A variety of restaurants set up outdoor tables along **boulevard d'Aguillon**, behind the *vieux port*. For cheaper eats, you're better off at **place Nationale**, a few blocks away. The **Marché Provençal**, on cours Masséna, is one of the best fresh produce markets on the Côte d'Azur. (Open Tu-Su 6am-1pm.) Boutiques generally remain open until midnight, cafes until 2am, discothèques until 5am, and bars past dawn.

Come summer, the young and hip neighboring town **Juan-les-Pins** is synonymous with wild nightlife. **Pam Pam Rhumerie**, 137 bd. Wilson, is a hot Brazilian sit-down bar. Bikinied showgirls take the stage at 9:30pm to dance and down flaming drinks. (☎61 11 05. Open daily mid-Mar. to early Nov. 2pm-5am.) In psychedelic **Whisky à Gogo**, 5 r. Jacques Leonetti, water-filled columns lit with blacklights frame a young crowd on the intimate dance floor. (Cover €16, students €8; includes 1 drink. Open July-Aug. daily midnight-5am; Apr.-June and Sept.-Oct. Th-Sa midnight-5am.) Frequent **buses** (10min., 2 per hr., €1) and **trains** (5min., 1-2 per hr., €1.20) run from Antibes, although walking between the two towns along bd. Wilson is also an option. **Taxis** usually wait at the Jardin de la Pinède or outside the train station and carry passengers to Antibes for €12-15. (☎04 92 93 07 07.) Although touristy, the **petit train** (☎06 03 35 61 35) leaves r. de la République and serves as both a guided tour of Antibes and a means of transportation to Juan-les-Pins. (30min.; 1 per hr. July-Aug. 10am-11pm, May-Oct. 10am-7pm. Round-trip €8, 3-10 €3.50. Buy tickets on board. Cash only.)

**Trains** leave pl. Pierre Semard in Antibes, off av. Robert Soleau, for Cannes (15min., 23 per day, €2.30), Marseille (2¼hr., 12 per day, €25), and Nice (15min., 25 per day, €3.60). RCA **buses** leave pl. de Gaulle for Cannes (20min.)

## FROM THE ROAD

### FRENCH 101:
### A CRASH COURSE

Traveling through France, you will undoubtedly encounter familiar words on signs and menus. Though these cognates will appear to help in your struggle to comprehend *le monde francophone*, beware! Some can also lead you astray. Here are some *faux amis* (false cognates; literally, "false friends") to watch out for:

*Blesser* has nothing to do with spirituality (or sneezing). It means **to hurt**, not to bless.

*Pain* is anything but misery for the French: it's their word for **bread**.

*Bras* is not a supportive undergarment, it's an **arm**.

*Rage* is not just regular anger, it's **rabies**.

*Rabais*, it follows, is not the disease you can catch from a dog, but a **discount**.

A *sale* is not an event with a lot of *rabais*; it means **dirty**.

*Draguer* means **to hit on**, not to drag, unless you encounter an overly aggressive flirt.

*Balancer* is **to swing**, not to steady oneself.

A *peste* is slightly more serious than a bothersome creature. It is a **plague**.

*Puéril* is not grave danger, just **childhood**.

*Preservatif* is not something found in packaged food, but it can be found in other packages, so to speak. This is the French word for **condom**.

*Crayon* means **pencil**, not crayon, and *gomme* is not for

and Nice (45min.). All buses depart every 20min. and cost €1.30. From the train station, turn right on av. Robert Soleau and follow the signs to the **tourist office,** 11 pl. de Gaulle. (☎04 97 23 11 11; www.antibesjuanlespins.com. Open July-Aug. daily 9am-7pm; Sept.-June M-F 9am-12:30pm and 1:30-5pm.) **Postal Code:** 06600.

## CANNES                     ☎04 93

Stars compete for camera time at Cannes's annual, world-famous—and invite only—■**Festival International du Film** (May 14-25, 2008). During the rest of the year, Cannes (pop. 67,000) rolls up the red carpet—save its most famous one, still at the Palais for your tacky photographic pleasure—and becomes the most accessible of all the Riviera's glam towns. A palm-lined boardwalk, sandy beaches, and numerous boutiques draw the wealthy as well as the young. Of the town's three **casinos,** the least exclusive is **Le Casino Croisette,** 1 Lucien Barrière, next to the Palais des Festivals. (No shorts, jeans, or T-shirts. Jackets required for men. 18+. Cover €10. Open daily 10am-4am; table games 8pm-4am.)

Hostels are 10-20min. farther from the beach than other lodgings, but are the cheapest options in town. **Hotel Mimont ❸,** 39 r. de Mimont, is Cannes's best budget hotel. English-speaking owners maintain basic, clean rooms two streets behind the train station. (☎39 51 64; canneshotelmimont65@wanadoo.fr. Free Wi-Fi. Singles €34-40; doubles €40-47; triples €58. Prices about 15% higher July-Aug. Ask about €30 petites chambres for *Let's Go* travelers. AmEx/MC/V.) Run by a young, English-speaking couple, **Hostel Les Iris ❷,** 77 bd. Carnot, was converted from an old hotel into a bright hostel with sturdy bunks and a Mexican-themed terrace restaurant. (☎68 30 20; www.iris-solola.com. Dorms €23. AmEx/MC/V.) The pedestrian zone around **rue Meynadier** has inexpensive restaurants. Find groceries at **Champion,** 6 r. Meynadier. (Open M-Sa 8:30am-7:30pm. MC/V.) Cafes and bars near the waterfront stay open all night and are a great alternative to the expense of gambling and posh clubs. Nightlife thrives around **rue Dr. G. Monod.** Try ■**Morrison's,** 10 r. Teisseire, for casual company in a literary-themed pub. (☎04 92 98 16 17. Beer from €5. Happy hour 5-8pm. Open daily 5pm-2am. MC/V.) Coastal **trains** depart from 1 r. Jean Jaurès for: Antibes (15min., €2.30); Marseille (2hr., 6:30am-11:03pm, €24); Monaco (1hr., €7.50); Nice (40min., €5.50); St-Raphaël (25min., €5.70). **Buses** go to Nice (1½hr., 3 per hr., €6) from the pl. de l'Hôtel de Ville (☎48 70 30) and Grasse (50min., 1 per hr., €4) from the train station. The **tourist office** is at 1 bd. de la Croisette. (☎39

24 53; www.cannes.fr. Open July-Aug. daily 9am-8pm; Sept.-June M-F 9am-7pm.) Get **Internet** at **Cap Cyber,** 12 r. 24 Août. (€3 per hr. Open in summer 10am-11pm; in winter 10am-10pm. MC/V.) **Postal Code:** 06400.

# ST-TROPEZ
☎ 04 94

Hollywood stars, corporate giants, and curious backpackers congregate on the spotless streets of St-Tropez (pop. 5400), where the Riviera's glitz and glamor shines brightest. The young, beautiful, and restless flock to this "Jewel of the Riviera" to flaunt tans and designer clothing on notorious **beaches** and in posh nightclubs. The best beaches are difficult to reach without a car, but the **navette municipale** (shuttle) leaves pl. des Lices for **Les Salins,** a secluded sunspot, and **plage Tahiti** (Capon-Pinet stop), the first of the famous **plages des Pampelonne.** (M-Sa 5 per day, €1. Tourist office has schedule.) Take a break from the sun at the **Musée de l'Annonciade,** pl. Grammont, which showcases Fauvist and neo-Impressionist paintings. (Open M and W-Su June-Sept. 10am-noon and 2-6pm; Oct.-May 10am-1pm and 4-7pm. €4.60, students €2.30.)

Budget hotels do not exist in St-Tropez. **Camping** is the cheapest option, but is only available outside the city. Prices remain shockingly high, especially in July and August. To reach **Les Prairies de la Mer** ❸, a social campground on the beach, take a *bateau vert* (☎49 29 39) from the *vieux port* to Port Grimaud (Apr.-early Oct., 5min., 1 per hr., round-trip €11). Bowling, supermarkets, tennis courts and other facilities are available. (☎79 09 09; www.riviera-villages.com. Bike rental €7 per day. Open early Apr.-early Oct. July to mid-Aug. €6 per person, €42 per tent; Apr.-June and late Aug. €5/25; Sept. to mid-Oct. €5/18-25. Free electricity. MC/V.) Pricey restaurants line the streets behind the waterfront and the *vieux port.* To create your own cheap meal, shop at **Monoprix,** 9 av. du Général Leclerc (open daily July-Aug. 8am-10pm; Sept.-June 8am-8:20pm), or stop by the snack stands and cafes near **place des Lices,** the center of St-Tropez's wild nightlife. Shell out €25,000 for a bottle of Cristal at **Les Caves du Roy,** av. Paul Signac, in the **Hotel Byblos,** or if things look shaky on the trust-fund front, settle for the €25 gin and tonic. (☎56 68 00. Open July-Aug. daily 11pm-5am; June and Sept. F-Sa 11:30pm-4am. AmEx/MC/V.)

Sodetrav **buses** (☎97 88 51) leave av. Général Leclerc for St-Raphaël (2hr., 10-14 per day, €9.50). **Ferries** (☎95 17 46; www.tmr-saintraphael.com), at the *vieux port,* serve St-Tropez from St-Raphaël (1hr., 4-5 per day, €12). The **tourist office** is on q. Jean Jaurès. (☎97 45 21. Open daily July-Sept.

chewing, unless you like the taste of rubber—it is an **eraser.**

An *extincteur* is not some sort of bazooka. It is a **fire extinguisher.**

*Fesses* is not a colloquial term for "coming clean"; it means **buttocks.**

*As* is not another way to say *fesses* or even an insult. This is a French compliment, meaning **ace** or **champion.**

*Ranger* is neither a woodsman nor a mighty morpher. This means **to tidy up.**

A *smoking* has little to do with tobacco (or any other substance). It is a **tuxedo** or **dinner suit.**

*Raisins* are juicy **grapes,** not the dried-up snack food. Try *raisins-secs* instead.

*Prunes* are plums. *Pruneaus* are the dried fruit.

*Tampons* are stamps (for documents), not the feminine care item. If you are looking for those, ask for a *tampon hygiénique* or *napkins.* To wipe your mouth, you would do better with a *serviette.*

The *patron* is the **boss,** not the customer.

A *glacier* does translate literally, meaning glacier, but you are more likely to see it around town on signs for **ice cream vendors;** *glace* does not mean glass, but a frozen summer treat.

If the French language seems full of deception, think again. Deception in French actually means **disappointment.**

*—Jack Pararas*

9:30am-8pm; Sept.-Oct. and mid-Mar. to June 9:30am-12:30pm and 2-7pm; early
Nov. to mid-Mar. 9:30am-12:30pm and 2-6pm.) **Postal Code:** 83990.

 CORSICA (LA CORSE)     ☎ 04 95

Bathed in turquoise Mediterranean waters, Corsica (COHR-sih-kuh; pop. 279,000)
was dubbed *Kallysté* (the most beautiful) by the Greeks. Fiercely defensive of its
identity, Corsica has long resisted foreign rule. Despite centuries of invasions by
Phoenicia, Carthage, Rome, Pisa, and Genoa, the island has guarded its culture.

> **TIP** **ÇA VA?** Perhaps more than their mainland compatriots, Corsicans appreciate
> a little chit-chat before getting down to business. Ask how people are doing—a
> few minutes' conversation may result in more helpful answers to your questions.

Natives remain divided over the issue of allegiance to France, and often reject the
French language in favor of Corse. Most of Corsica's visitors come for its
unspoiled landscapes, easily accessible from major towns. Nearly one-third of the
island is a protected nature reserve, and over 100 summits pierce Corisca's sunny
sky—it only rains 55 days of the year. An unbroken coastlines beckons to kayakers,
windsurfers, sailors, and sunbathers alike.

## ▐ TRANSPORTATION

**Air France** and its subsidiary **Compagnie Corse Méditerranée (CCM)** fly to Ajaccio and
Bastia from Marseille (€88, students €71), Nice (€85/68), and Paris (€112/109).
The Air France/CCM office is at 3 bd. du Roi Jérôme, Ajaccio (☎08 20 82 08 20).
**Ferries** between the mainland and Corsica can be rough, and aren't much cheaper
than planes. Hydrofoils (3½hr.) run from Nice, while overnight ferries depart from
Marseille (10hr.). The Société National Maritime Corse Méditerranée (SNCM; ☎08
91 70 18 01; www.sncm.fr) sends ferries from Marseille (€40-58, under 25 €25-45)
and Nice (€35-47, under 25 €20-35) to Ajaccio and Bastia. Corsica Ferries (☎08 25
09 50 95; www.corsicaferries.com) has similar destinations and prices. SAREMAR
(☎04 95 73 00 96) and Moby Lines (☎04 95 73 00 29) go from Santa Teresa, ITA to
Bonifacio. (2-5 per day, €14-15, cars €26-52). Moby Lines (€16-28) and Corisca
Ferries (€16-32) cross from Genoa and Livorno, ITA to Bastia.

    The Marquis de Sade and Machiavelli are rumored to have collaborated on the
design of Corsica's transportation system. **Train** service in Corsica is slow, limited to
destinations north of Ajaccio, and doesn't accept rail passes. Eurocorse Voyages
**buses** (☎04 95 21 06 30) serve the whole island, but be prepared for twisting roads.
**Hiking** is the best way to explore Corsica's mountainous interior. The GR20 is a difficult 12- to 15-day, 180km hiking trail that spans from Calenzana to Conca. The popular Mare e Monti (7-10 days), Mare a Mare Sud (4-6 days), Mare a Mare Nord (12
days), and Mare a Mare Centre (7 days) trails are shorter and easier. The **Parc Naturel
Régional de la Corse,** 2 Sargent Casalonga, in Ajaccio, has a guide to *gîtes d'étape*
(rest houses) and maps. (☎04 95 51 79 00; www.parc-naturel-corse.com.)

## AJACCIO (AIACCIU)

Napoleon must have insisted on the best from the very beginning: the little dictator couldn't have picked a better place to call home. Brimming with more energy
than most Corsican towns, Ajaccio (pop. 60,000) has excellent museums and, in
summer, nightlife to complement its palm-lined boulevards, sunlit buildings, and
white-sand beaches. Inside the ▓**Musée Fesch,** 50-52 r. Cardinal Fesch, cavernous
rooms hold an impressive collection of 14th- to 19th-century Italian paintings gathered by Napoleon's art-collecting uncle. Also within the complex is the **Chapelle**

**Impériale,** the final resting place of most of the Bonaparte family, though Napoleon himself is buried in Paris. (Open July-Aug. M 2-6pm, Tu-Th 10:30am-6pm, F 2-9:30pm, Sa-Su 10:30am-6pm; Sept.-June reduced hours. Museum €5.35, students €3.80. Chapel €1.50/0.75.) Napoleon's childhood home is now the **Musée National de la Maison Bonaparte,** r. St-Charles, (entrance on r. Bonaparte), a warehouse of memorabilia. (Open Apr.-Sept. Tu-Su 9am-noon and 2-6pm; Oct.-Apr. M 2-4:45pm, Tu-Su 10am-noon and 2-4:45pm. €5, under 26 €3.50.)

Although Ajaccio has many hotels, rates soar and vacancies plummet from June through August. The welcoming **Pension de Famille Tina Morelli ❹,** 1 r. Major Lambroschini, fills up quickly. (☎ 21 16 97. Breakfast included. Singles €50, with half-pension €72; doubles €70/124. Cash only.) To camp at **Barbicaja ❶,** take bus #5 from av. Dr. Ramaroni to Barbicaja and walk straight ahead. (☎52 01 17. Open mid-Apr. to mid-Oct. €5.70 per person, €2.50 per tent, €2.50 per car. Electricity €2.40. Cash only.) Though Ajaccio has no shortage of restaurants, your best option is the 🖼**morning market** on pl. du Marché. (Open Tu-Su 8am-1pm.) Pizzerias, bakeries, and panini shops can be found on **rue Cardinal Fesch;** at night, patios on the festive dock offer affordable seafood and pizza. Get groceries at **Monoprix,** 31 cours Napoléon. (Open July-Sept. M-Sa 8:30am-8pm; Oct.-June 8:30am-7:20pm.) **Boulevard Pascal Rossini,** near the casino, is home to Ajaccio's busiest strip of bars. TCA bus #8 (€4.50) shuttles passengers from the bus station at q. l'Herminier to **Aéroport Campo dell'Oro (AJA;** ☎ 23 56 56), where flights serve Lyon, Marseille, Nice, and Paris. **Trains** (☎23 11 03) leave pl. de la Gare for Bastia (3-4hr., 4 per day, €24) and Corte (2½hr., 4 per day, €13). Eurocorse Voyages **buses** (☎21 06 30) go to Bastia (3hr., 2 per day, €18), Bonifacio (3hr., 2 per day, €21), and Corte (1¾hr., 2 per day, €11). The **tourist office** is at 3 bd. du Roi Jérôme. (☎51 53 03; www.ajaccio-tourisme.com. Open July-Aug. M-Sa 8am-8:30pm, Su 9am-1pm and 4-7pm; Sept.-June reduced hours.) **Postal Code:** 20000.

# CORTE (CORTI)

Corte (pop. 6800) possesses unforgettable plunging cliffs, jagged snow-capped summits, and quaint cobblestone streets. The geographical, intellectual, and political heart of Corsica, Corte harbors unparalleled pride in its heritage. It is also home to the island's only university, whose students boost the town's population by 4000 during termtime. The town's *vieille ville,* with its steep streets and 15th-century stone **citadel,** has long been a bastion of Corsican patriotism. The citadel, at the top of r. Scolisca, now houses the **Musée de la Corse,** which displays historical island artifacts. (Open daily June-Sept. 10am-8pm; Nov.-May reduced hours. €5.30, students €3.) Corte's mountains offer great **hiking, biking,** and **horseback riding.** Ride horses at **Ferme Equestre Albadu,** 1.5km from town on N193. (☎46 24 55. €14 per hr., €75 per day with picnic.)

At the no-frills **Hôtel-Residence Porette ❷,** 6 allée du 9 Septembre, across from the stadium, functional, clean rooms and a pleasant garden hide behind an austere cement facade. (☎45 11 11. Breakfast buffet €6. Laundry €7. Reserve ahead. Singles €25-30, with bath €42; doubles €30-32/42; triples and quads €65. AmEx.) Small streets behind **place Paoli** have sandwich and pizza joints, while **rue Scolisca** and the side streets off **cours Paoli** offer cheap local fare. Find groceries at the **SPAR** supermarket, in the *haute ville.* (Open M-Sa 8:30am-8pm, Su 8:30am-noon.) **Trains** (☎00 80 17) leave from the roundabout at av. Jean Nicoli and N193 for Ajaccio (2½hr., 3 per day, €13) and Bastia (2hr., 4 per day, €12). Eurocorse Voyages (☎31 73 76) runs **buses** to Ajaccio (1¾hr., M-Sa 2 per day, €11) and Bastia (1¼hr., M-Sa 2 per day, €10). From the town center, turn left onto pl. Paoli before climbing the stairs of r. Scolisca and entering the citadel's walls to reach the **tourist office.** (☎46 26 70; www.corte-tourisme.com. Open July-Aug. M and Sa 10am-5pm, Tu-F 9am-7pm, Su 10am-6pm; Sept.-June reduced hours.) **Postal Code:** 20250.

## BASTIA

Bastia (pop. 40,000), Corsica's second-largest city, is one of the island's most trampled gateways, with connections to the French mainland and to more remote villages and vacation spots. Its enormous 14th-century **citadel,** also called **Terra Nova,** is impressively intact, with ramparts reaching down the hill toward the *vieux port,* dwarfing nearby shops and bakeries. The tiny **Eco-Musée,** in the citadel's old powder magazine (ammunition storehouse), contains a detailed replica of a traditional Corsican village, complete with miniature houses and authentic vegetation. (Open Apr.-Oct. M-Sa 9am-noon and 2-6pm. €3.50, students €3.) On the other side of the *vieux port,* the 17th-century **Église St-Jean Baptiste,** pl. de l'Hôtel de Ville, is Corisca's largest church. Its gilded walls and ornate altars were constructed with funds raised by local fishermen. The **Oratoire de l'Imaculée Conception,** on r. Napoléon, contains elaborate Baroque ceilings and red and gold walls. (Open daily 8am-7pm.) While there are no true budget hotels in Bastia, **Hôtel Posta Vecchia ❹,** 8

**MIND THE MEDUSAS.** Bays on Cap Corse can be filled with jellyfish for an entire week but be *méduse*-free the next. Crowded beaches and empty water are signs you should rethink skinny-dipping. Ask park employees at the Sentier des Douaniers whether the waters are clear. They can also help if you get stung.

r. Posta-Vecchia, has a few small rooms that remain reasonably priced during high season (☎32 32 38; www.hotel-postavecchia.com. Breakfast €6. July-Sept. singles €45, doubles €55-90, triples €90-100; Oct.-Feb. €40/53-75/80-86; Mar.-June €40/45-70/70-80. AmEx/MC/V.) To reach **Camping Les Orangers ❶,** take bus #4 from the tourist office to Licciola-Miomo. (☎33 24 09. Restaurant and snack bar. Open May to mid-Oct. €5 per person, €3 per tent, €2.60 per car. Electricity €3.50.) Inexpensive cafes crowd **place St-Nicolas.** Find groceries at **SPAR** supermarket, 14 r. César Campinchi. (Open M-Sa 8am-12:30pm and 4-8:30pm, Su 8am-noon. MC/V.) Though Bastia nightlife is less dynamic than other Corsican towns, young people find their way to **Port de Plaisance de Toga.** Shuttle buses (30min., €8) leave from the *préfecture,* across from the train station, for the **Bastia-Poretta Airport** (**BIA;** ☎54 54 54). Flights go to Marseille, Nice, and Paris. **Trains** (☎32 80 61) run from pl. de la Gare to Ajaccio (4hr., 3-5 per day, €24) and Calvi (3hr., 2 per day, €19). Eurocorse **buses** (☎21 06 31) leave from rte. du Nouveau Port for Ajaccio (3hr., 1-2 per day, €20). The **tourist office** is in pl. St-Nicolas. (☎54 20 40; www.bastia-tourisme.com. Open daily July-Aug. 8am-8pm; Sept.-June 8:30am-noon and 2-6pm.) **Postal Code:** 20200.

## CAP CORSE

North of Bastia stretches the Cap Corse peninsula, a necklace of tiny former fishing villages strung together by a narrow road traveling perilous curves, windswept valleys, and oceanside cliffs. The Cap is a hiker's dream; every forest lays claim to some decaying Genoese tower or hilltop chapel. The coastal trail **Sentier des Douaniers** (Custom Officers Route; 8hr.) connects Macinaggio in the east with Centuri in the west, offering 19km of unbelievable vistas and secluded beaches. The free *Cap Corse Guide Pratique,* available from Bastia's tourist office, lists campsites. The best way to reach the Cap is by renting a car in Bastia. **Bus #4** (☎04 95 31 06 65) also goes from pl. St-Nicolas in Bastia to Erbalunga (20min., 1-2 per hr., €2), Macinaggio (50min., 3 per day, €7), or Sisco (30min., 1 per hr., €2.30). Ask politely and the driver will drop you off wherever you feel like exploring. Most buses serve coastal towns only; you'll have to hike to discover villages further inland.

# BONIFACIO (BONIFAZIU)

At the southern tip of Corsica, the stone ramparts of Bonifacio (pop. 2660), atop 70m limestone cliffs, present an imposing visage to miles of empty turquoise sea. Bonifacio's fantastic **boat tours** reveal multicolored cliffs, coves, and stalactite-filled grottoes. Ferries also run to the pristine sands of **Îles Lavezzi,** a nature reserve with beautiful reefs perfect for **scuba diving.** Book tours with **Les Vedettes.** (☎06 86 34 00 49. Grottes-Falaises-Calanques tour 2 per hr. 9am-6:30pm; €17. Îles Lavezzi tour 5 departures per day, last return 5:30pm; €25. Cash only.) To explore the *haute ville*, head up the steep, broad steps of the **montée Rastello,** located halfway down the port, from where excellent views of the hazy cliffs to the east can be seen. Continue up montée St-Roch to the lookout at **Porte des Gênes,** a drawbridge built by invaders, then walk to the **Poste du Gouvernail** at the southern tip of the *haute ville*, where an underground tunnel leads to grottoes carved out by Italians and Germans during WWII and to a lookout point 10m above the sea.

Finding affordable rooms is virtually impossible in summer; avoid visiting in August when prices soar. **Hôtel des Étrangers ❹,** av. Sylvère Bohn, offers spotless white rooms, most with A/C and TV. (☎73 01 09. Breakfast €5. Reception 24hr. Reservations recommended July-Aug. Open Apr.-late Oct. Mid.-July to mid-Sept. singles and doubles €48-76; triples €72-76; quads €82-84. Late Sept. and mid-May to mid-July singles €42-65; doubles €62-66; triples €72-76. Oct. and Apr. to mid-May singles €35-47; doubles €52-57; triples €62-65. MC/V.) Camping is by far the cheapest option. **L'Araguina ❶,** av. Sylvère Bohn, is at the entrance to town between Hôtel des Étrangers and the port. (☎73 02 96. Open Apr. to mid-Oct. €6.10 per person, €2.40 per tent, €2.40 per car. Electricity free. Laundry €5. Cash only.) A few supermarkets dot the port, including **SPAR,** at the start of rte. de Santa Manza. (Open daily July-Aug. 8am-8:30pm; Sept.-June reduced hours.) Eurocorse Voyages (☎21 06 30) sends **buses** to Ajaccio (3½hr., 1-3 per day, €21). To reach the main **tourist office,** at the corner of av. de Gaulle and r. F. Scamaroni, walk along the port and climb the stairs right before the *gare maritime*. A second branch is next to the *Capitainerie*. (☎73 11 88. Open July-Aug. daily 9am-8pm; May-June and Sept. daily 10am-7pm; Oct.-Apr. M-F 9am-noon and 2-6pm.) **Postal Code:** 20169.

# GERMANY
# (DEUTSCHLAND)

Encounters with history are unavoidable on visits to Germany, as changes in outlook, policy, and culture are manifest in the country's architecture, landscape, and customs. Streamlined glass skyscrapers rise from former concrete wastelands; towns crop up from fields and forests, interspersed with medieval castles and industrial structures. World-class music rings out from sophisticated city centers, while a grittier youth culture flourishes in quite different neighborhoods. Such divisions echo the entrenched Cold War separation between East and West. Today, nearly 20 years after the fall of the Berlin Wall, Germans have fashioned a new identity for themselves. Visitors will find flowing beer and wondrous sights from the darkest corners of the Black Forest to the shores of the Baltic Sea.

## DISCOVER GERMANY: SUGGESTED ITINERARIES

**THREE DAYS.** Enjoy two days in **Berlin** (p. 390): stroll along **Unter den Linden** and the **Ku'damm,** gape at the **Brandenburger Tor** and the **Reichstag,** and explore the **Tiergarten.** Walk along the **East Side Gallery** and visit **Checkpoint Charlie** for a history of the Berlin Wall, then pass an afternoon at **Schloß Sanssouci** (p. 422). Overnight it to **Munich** (p. 460) for a Stein-themed last day.

**ONE WEEK.** After scrambling through **Berlin** (3 days), head north to racy **Hamburg** (1 day; p. 425). Take in the cathedral of **Cologne** (1 day; p. 449) before slowing down in the bucolic **Lorelei Cliffs** (1 day; p. 451). End your trip Bavarian-style with the beer gardens, castles, and cathedrals of **Munich** (1 day).

**THREE WEEKS.** Begin in **Berlin** (3 days). Party in **Hamburg** (2 days), then zip to **Cologne** (1 day) and the former West German capital, **Bonn** (1 day; p. 449). Contrast the Roman ruins at **Trier** (1 day; p. 452) with glitzy **Frankfurt** (1 day; p. 445), then visit Germany's oldest university in **Heidelberg** (2 days; p. 454). Lose your way in the fairy-tale **Black Forest** (2 days; p. 458), before finding it again in **Munich** (2 days). Marvel at **Neuschwanstein** (1 day; p. 477) and see the beauty of the **Romantic Road** (2 days; p. 476). Get cultured in Goethe's **Weimar** (1 day; p. 479)—then dramatize your learnings in Faust's cellar in **Leipzig** (1 day; p. 489). End your trip in the reconstructed splendor of **Dresden** (1 day; p. 482).

## LIFE AND TIMES

### HISTORY

**EARLY HISTORY AND THE FIRST REICH (UNTIL 1400).** Germany's recent history has been one of cyclical unity and fracture, and its early history was no different. The **Roman Empire** conquered the tribes that had occupied the area; Roman ruins can still be seen in **Trier** (p. 452) and **Cologne** (p. 439). After the collapse of the empire, the Germanic tribes separated again, only to be reunified in the AD 8th century by **Charlemagne** (Karl der Große) into what is now known as the **First Reich,** or first empire. Charlemagne established his capital at **Aachen** (p. 449), where his remains still reside. After his death, the former empire disintegrated into

a system of decentralized **feudalism**. Visit **Rothenburg** (p. 478) for a glimpse into a medieval walled city typical of the period.

**THE NORTHERN RENAISSANCE (1400-1517).** Inspired by the new ideas of the Italian Renaissance, northern philosophers developed their own tradition of **humanism,** with a particular focus on religious reform and a return to classical authors. **Johannes Gutenberg** paved the way for widespread dissemination of ideas by inventing the **printing press** in Mainz (p. 451). Rapid production of books led to increased literacy, putting info—and power—into the hands of laypeople.

**RELIGION AND REFORM (1517-1700).** On All Saints' Day, 1517, **Martin Luther** nailed his *95 Theses* to the door of Wittenberg's church (p. 491). His treatises, which condemned the extravagances of the Catholic hierarchy, sparked the Protestant Reformation, and his translation of the Bible into German crystallized the various German dialects into a standard literary form and allowed ordinary people

## FEATURED ITINERARY: THE CASTLES OF GERMANY

Tour the pristine grounds and surrounding museums of the monumental **Schloß Charlottenburg** (p. 408) in Berlin before departing to Potsdam's **Schloß Sanssouci** (p. 422), Friedrich the Great's answer to Versailles. From there, head north to Schleswig for **Schloß Gottorf** (p. 424), now a museum complex. Alternatively, skip that port excursion and head straight for the castle heartland. In Kassel, the intact, hillside **Schloß Wilhelmshöhe** (p. 449) counterpoints a second, nearby castle in ruins. Budget travelers to Bacharach can stay in **Jugendherberge Stahleck** (p. 451) overlooking the Rhine.

If you tire of the view, duck into the underground passages of St. Goar's **Burg Rheinfels** (p. 451). Martin Luther translated the Bible into German in Eisenach's **Wartburg Fortress** (p. 481). Farther south, the cellar of beautiful **Heidelberger Schloß** (p. 456) contains the largest wine barrel ever used. In the foothills of the Alps, Füssen neighbors the famed **Neuschwanstein** (p. 477), which Ludwig II built, as well as the lesser-known **Hohenschwangau** (p. 477), where he summered as a child. End the journey with Ludwig I's scandalous portrait gallery of beauties in Munich's **Schloß Nymphenburg** (p. 468).

to access the text without mediation. Tensions brewing between Catholics and Protestants across the continent eventually led to the **Thirty Years' War** (1618-1648), which dissolved Germany into small, independent fiefdoms ruled by local princes.

**RISE OF BRANDENBURG-PRUSSIA (1700-1862) AND THE SECOND REICH (1862-1914).** The 18th and early 19th centuries saw the rise of Prussian power, the conquest of Germany by **Napoleon Bonaparte**, and, after Napoleon's fall, the formation of the Austrian-led **German Confederation.** The relative peace following the establishment of the Confederation came to an end when worldly aristocrat **Otto von Bismarck** was named chancellor of Prussia in 1862. A great practitioner of *Realpolitik* ("the ends justify the means"), Bismarck worked to consolidate the disunited German states through a complex series of political and military maneuvers. These efforts culminated in the **Franco-Prussian War** in 1870, in which the technologically superior Prussians swept through France. After the German victory, the king of Prussia, **Wilhelm I,** crowned himself **Kaiser of the German Reich** at Versailles. Bismarck's unification of Germany under an authoritarian ruler made it a formidable and ambitious neighbor. Anxiety over Germany's rising power soon caused Britain, France, and Russia to band together in the **Triple Entente.**

**WORLD WAR I (1914-1918).** The growing polarization of Europe resulted in war when, in 1914, a Serbian nationalist assassinated Archduke **Franz Ferdinand,** heir to the Austrian throne. Russia's loyalty to Serbia and Germany's to Austria led this obscure act to plunge the entire continent into the **First World War.** After four agonizing years of trench warfare, Germany and its allies were defeated.

**THE WEIMAR REPUBLIC (1918-1933).** The harsh peace agreement in the **Treaty of Versailles** drastically reduced the size of the German army and required Germany to make staggering reparation payments. The defeated nation had little choice but to accept. The constitution for a new republic was written in **Weimar** (p. 479); its parliament met in the **Reichstag** in Berlin (p. 405). Outstanding war debts and the burden of reparations produced staggering hyperinflation from 1922 to 1923 during which paper money was worth more as fuel in the fireplace than as currency. Already suffering from the Treaty of Versailles, Germany needed any sort of change, which the charismatic Austrian **Adolf Hitler** seemed to promise. His party, the National Socialists (or **Nazis**), offered an über-nationalist platform.

Hitler's first attempt to seize power, the 1923 **Beer Hall Putsch** in Munich, failed and ended in his arrest. As hardship worsened, however, Nazi promises of prosperity and community appealed to more Germans, and by 1930, party membership exceeded one million. Hitler failed in his 1932 presidential bid against the nearly senile war hero **Paul von Hindenburg,** but since Hitler's party won a legislative majority, Hindenburg reluctantly appointed Hitler chancellor on January 30, 1933.

**UNDER THE THIRD REICH (1933-1939).** Hitler's platform, set out clearly in his early book **Mein Kampf** (My Struggle), used the Jews as a scapegoat for Germany's defeat in WWI. His government instituted a boycott of Jewish enterprises and expelled Jews from professional and civil service. Rival parties were outlawed or dissolved, and after Hindenburg's death in 1934, Hitler appropriated presidential powers. That year also saw the first **Nuremberg Laws,** depriving Jews of German citizenship and preventing intermarriage between Jewish and Aryan residents. Nazis destroyed Jewish businesses, burned synagogues, and killed and deported thousands of Jews on the **Kristallnacht** (Night of Broken Glass), November 9, 1938. With the help of **Joseph Goebbels,** his minister of propaganda, Hitler consolidated his power by saturating media with Nazi ideology. The Nazis burned books by Jewish and other "subversive" authors at Bebelplatz in Berlin (p. 405), banned American art, and destroyed "degenerate" art in favor of propagandist paintings and statues.

Hitler expanded beyond attacking his own country and began invading others. In 1938, he annexed Austria in an infamous maneuver known as the **Anschluß.** Other nations, hoping to avert another world war, next sanctioned his invasion of the Sudetenland, now part of the Czech Republic, at the **Munich Accords.**

**WORLD WAR II (1939-1945).** Despite Hitler's promises at Munich that he would not seek to acquire further territories, German tanks rolled into Poland on September 1, 1939. Britain and France immediately declared war on Germany, dragging most of the world into conflict. Germany's **Blitzkrieg** (lightning war) overwhelmed Poland; Belgium, Denmark, France, the Netherlands, and Norway were soon swallowed up as well.

Soon the Nazis had opened two fronts, attacking westward with an airborne offensive in the **Battle of Britain** and eastward with the invasion of the USSR, which had not yet joined the Allies. Daily air raids spurred the British to fight back tooth and nail, and the *Blitzkrieg* on the eastern front faltered in the Russian winter; Hitler sacrificed thousands of his soldiers by refusing to retreat. The bloody **Battle of Stalingrad** (1942-1943), won by the Soviets, marked a critical turning point on the eastern front. The western front was punctured by the Allied landing in Normandy on **D-Day** (June 6, 1944) and followed by an arduous advance eastward. The Soviet Army finally took Berlin in April 1945. The Third Reich, which Hitler had boasted would endure for 1000 years, had lasted only 12.

**THE HOLOCAUST.** At the center of Nazi ideology was **genocide,** Hitler's "final solution" to the "Jewish question." By 1940, Jews had lost all rights and had to wear yellow Star of David patches. By 1945, nearly six million Jews—two-thirds of those living in Europe—had been gassed, shot, starved, worked to death. Six death camps carried out this mass extermination; dozens of "labor" camps, including **Dachau** (p. 472), held Jews and other undesirables. Millions of others, including other religious minorities, prisoners of war, Slavs, Roma (gypsies), homosexuals, mentally disabled, and political dissidents, also died in Nazi camps.

**OCCUPATION AND DIVISION (1945-1949).** In July 1945, the United States, Great Britain, and the Soviet Union met at **Potsdam** (p. 422) to partition Germany into zones of occupation. The East went to the Soviets and the West to the British and Americans; Berlin was likewise divided. Despite rising Western animosity toward the Soviets, their plan of democratization, demilitarization, and de-Nazification proceeded apace. In 1948, the Allies welded their zones into a single economic unit, and, with huge infusions of cash granted by the

American **Marshall Plan,** they began to rebuild a market economy in Western Germany. Afterward, and especially after the Allies' introduction of the **Deutschmark,** Germany's twin halves became increasingly disparate.

**THE FEDERAL REPUBLIC OF GERMANY (1949-1989).** Western Germany established the Federal Republic of Germany *(Bundesrepublik Deutschland)* as its provisional government on May 23, 1949. Its **Basic Law** safeguarded individual rights and established a system of freely elected parliamentary assemblies. One of its most visionary paragraphs established a **Right of Asylum,** guaranteeing refuge to any person fleeing persecution.

As the only party untainted by the Third Reich, the **Social Democratic Party (SDP)** seemed poised to dominate postwar politics, but the **Christian Democratic Union (CDU)** was able to gain power in the new Federal Republic by uniting Germany's historically fragmented conservatives and centrists under one platform. Helmed by former Cologne mayor **Konrad Adenauer,** the CDU won a small majority of seats in the Federal Republic's first general election. As chancellor, Adenauer tirelessly worked to integrate Germany into a unified Europe. West Germany aligned in 1955 with the **North Atlantic Treaty Organization (NATO)** and soon became a charter member of the European Coal and Steel Community, precursor to the **European Union (EU).** Speedy fiscal recovery consolidated the position of the CDU. In 1982, the CDU's **Helmut Kohl** became chancellor and pursued a policy of tight monetary policy and military cooperation with the US.

**THE GERMAN DEMOCRATIC REPUBLIC (1949-1989).** Despite pledges to the contrary, the Soviets ended free elections in their sector in 1949. On October 7, they established the **German Democratic Republic** with Berlin as its capital. Constitutional promises of civil liberties and democracy were empty: East Germany became a satellite of the Soviet Union. The **Stasi,** or secret police, strove to monitor every citizen from their Berlin headquarters (p. 390) using spy networks—one in seven East Germans was a paid informant.

Many chose to escape oppression by immigrating to West Germany. By 1961, more than three million had crossed the border illegally, and the East German government decided to stop the exodus of young skilled workers. Overnight on August 12, the first foundations of the **Berlin Wall** were laid; barbed wire and guns dissuaded further attempts to escape.

**REUNIFICATION (1989).** Following his policy of **glasnost** (openness), Soviet President **Mikhail Gorbachev** announced in October 1989 that the USSR would not interfere with East Germany's domestic affairs. Citizens began to demand free elections and freedom of press and of travel. The entire East German government resigned on November 8, 1989, and the next day the Central Committee announced all borders open to the West. Both West and East Germans began climbing over and dismantling the Berlin Wall in what become the symbolic end of the Cold War.

On September 12, 1990, the two halves and the four occupying powers signed the **Four-Plus-Two Treaty,** which spelled the **end of a divided Germany.** On October 3, Germany became a united sovereign nation for the first time in 45 years. East and West Germany did not come together on equal terms, however. The collapse of East Germany's inefficient industries brought with it massive unemployment in the East and ushered in the West's worst-ever recession. Many Westerners resented the inflation and taxes brought on by reunification, while Easterners missed the generous social benefits associated with communism. Economic frustrations led to the scapegoating of foreigners, especially immigrant workers and asylum-seekers from Eastern Europe, leading Germany to abolish its uncategorical right to asylum. Germany has recently begun to implement economic and social reforms that seek to address this issue.

# TODAY

After the demolition of the Berlin Wall in 1989, Helmut Kohl and his CDU party seemed invincible, scoring a stunning victory in the first all-German elections. Kohl had difficulties managing the reunification, however, and his popularity plummeted to the point that Easterners pelted him with eggs during campaign visits. In 1998, left-wingers ousted the CDU and elected **Gerhard Schröder** chancellor.

Given the past, many continue to be uneasy about Germany's participation in military operations. Germans have recently promoted peace, however, with a hand in peacekeeping missions in Yugoslavia and flood relief operations in Africa. Germany was also initially an outspoken critic of aggressive Anglo-American foreign policy after the terrorist attacks of September 11, 2001. Rioters greeted American President George W. Bush's visit to Berlin in May 2002 with protests significant enough to necessitate the largest police presence since the end of WWII. Relations, however, have recently improved; in February 2004, Schröder issued a joint statement with Bush on "The German-American Alliance for the 21st Century." Ties to America were strengthened with the election of Germany's current and first female chancellor, CDU-affiliated **Angela Merkel**—so strengthened that US President George W. Bush felt the urge to give her an impromptu shoulder rub at a 2006 G-8 Summit. Merkel has also made waves for having the highest approval rating recorded for a German chancellor since 1949, although the failure of her plan to reform national healthcare in 2007 has lowered her popularity.

In recent years, major symbols have marked Germany's reconciliation with its other WWII antagonists. Schröder attended the 60th anniversary of the D-Day invasion in France in 2004 and was present at the opening of Berlin's **Holocaust Memorial** (p. 404) in 2005. Even German architecture shows signs of the nation's healing: the cross now atop Dresden's Frauenkirche was built by the son of a RAF pilot who took part in the Allied firebombing of the city.

# PEOPLE AND CULTURE

**CUSTOMS AND ETIQUETTE.** Although Germans may seem reserved or even unfriendly, they are not as standoffish as they may first appear. Germans are simply more formal than Americans and Australians. Unless you're addressing fellow students, friends, or children, remember to use the formal *Sie* for "you," as in the question *Sprechen Sie Englisch?* Addressing a woman as *Fräulein* is inappropriate in most instances; address all women as *Frau* (followed by a name). Remember at least two phrases: **bitte** (BIT-tuh; please and you're welcome) and **danke** (DAHNK-uh; thank you).

Germany is an extremely law-abiding nation, and **jaywalking** and **littering** are only two of the petty offenses that will mark you as a foreigner (and subject you to fines). Many tourists also do not realize that the **bike lanes** marked in red between the sidewalk and the road are strictly off-limits for pedestrians. The drinking age is 16 for beer and wine and 18 for hard liquor, although reportedly neither is strictly enforced, and it is not uncommon to see young teenagers in a store picking up a bottle of wine for the family dinner. Driving under the influence, however, is an extremely severe offense. **Drug** use has yet to become publicly acceptable, even where penalties are more relaxed.

**DEMOGRAPHICS AND RELIGION.** Germany is home to roughly 82 million people. Most of Germany's population growth in recent years has come from a rise in immigration. The group of Turkish immigrants is the largest, followed by groups from various Southern and Eastern European countries; together, these groups account for nearly 10% of the population. In terms of religion, Germany has developed as a Christian country, with the Protestant North and the Roman Catholic South each currently representing about one-third of the country's inhabitants.

The total Jewish population in Germany today has risen to approximately 100,000; the largest Jewish congregations are in Berlin and Frankfurt. A small Islamic community has developed as a result of Turkish and Bosnian immigration.

**LANGUAGE.** Younger Germans often speak some English, and residents of Western Germany are usually proficient as well. Recent spelling reforms didn't eliminate the letter **ß** (the *ess-tset*), although they reduced its use; it is equivalent to a double "s" in English. For some basic German , see **Phrasebook: German,** p. 1054.

# THE ARTS

## ARCHITECTURE

The robust arches and elaborate towers of **Romanesque** cathedrals can be found along the Rhine at Trier (p. 452) and Mainz (p. 451); the Romanesque period, which combined Early Christian and Roman architectural forms, spanned the years AD 800 to 1300. The Gothic style, characterized by pointed rib vaulting, replaced the Romanesque style in the 14th century. Among these stained-glass wonders, the best known is the **Gothic** cathedral in Cologne (p. 438). Secular architecture at the end of the Middle Ages was dominated by the **Fachwerk** (half-timbered) houses visible in the *Altstadt* (Old Town) areas of many German cities. Baroque ostentation bloomed late in the 17th century; see the Zwinger (p. 486) in Dresden for a magnificent example. **Rococo** style then appeared, with ornate buildings like Schloß Sanssouci (p. 422). A more minimalist movement, Neoclassicism reacted to frou-frou Rococo facades; the Brandenburger Tor (p. 404) and the buildings along Unter den Linden in Berlin recall the splendor of classical Greece. In 1919, Weimar birthed the boxy **Bauhaus** style, in which form follows function.

## LITERATURE

**NOVELS AND POETRY.** German literature before Romanticism is largely a wasteland, notably excepting the 13th-century epic **Nibelungenlied** and **Hans J. C. von Grimmelshausen's** near-inauguration of the German novel with his roguish series *Simplicissimus*, written during the Thirty Years' War. By the late 18th century, however, High German literature was flourishing. **Johann Wolfgang von Goethe** penned his masterpiece *Faust* in two parts (its writing spanned his career) and left an indelible mark on his town of residence, Weimar (p. 479). The **Brothers Grimm** transformed folklore from an oral tradition into a vibrant, if often dark, literature. Political realism predominated in the turbulent mid-19th century; **Heinrich Heine,** satirist and poet, was among the period's finest writers.

In the wake of WWI, the **Weimar era** was a period of active artistic production. **Hermann Hesse** experimented with Eastern motifs in *Siddhartha* (1922); **Erich Maria Remarque's** *All Quiet on the Western Front* (1929), a blunt account of the horrors of war, became an international best-seller. With his "epic theater," **Bertolt Brecht** introduced a socially conscious aesthetic to the stage in the 1920s and 30s. **Thomas Mann** penned one of the grandest novels of the century in *The Magic Mountain* (1924) and later helped to inaugurate post-WWII literature with *Doctor Faustus* (1947). In the same year, several writers, including **Günter Grass** and poet **Paul Celan,** formed **Gruppe 47,** which coined the term *Nullstunde* (Zero Hour) to signify that, after WWII, culture had to begin anew. Much of German literature since then has preoccupied itself with the pall of the country's Nazi past and with the division and reunification of Germany. Novels by Nobel laureates Grass and **Heinrich Böll,** as well as the poetry of **Hans Magnus Enzensberger,** turn a critical eye on governmental repression. Since the fall of the Berlin Wall, Grass has been openly critical of reunification. More recently, the expatriate novelist **W.G. Sebald** has devoted himself to the theme of personal and cultural memory.

**PHILOSOPHY.** Germany has one of the most influential philosophical traditions in the world. In 1517, **Martin Luther's** *95 Theses* denied papal infallibility, claiming that only scripture was holy and advocating a direct relationship with God. **Gottfried Wilhelm Leibnitz** thought of God as a watchmaker who set the individual's body and soul in motion like two synchronized clocks. During the **Enlightenment,** the watchword was Reason: **Immanuel Kant** argued that ethics and the existence of God could be deduced rationally from nature; **Georg W. F. Hegel** proposed that world history and the development of the individual consciousness could be understood as part of an ongoing struggle, one with a fixed "end of history."

Certain thinkers of the 19th century forged philosophies that influenced the course of events in the 20th century. **Karl Marx,** who asserted that class conflict was the driving force of all history, indirectly inspired the Russian Revolution in 1917. **Friedrich Nietzsche** developed the idea of the *Übermensch*, an "over-man" so self-mastered that he could live his life over again eternally; later the Nazis would claim a bastardized version of his ideas as an intellectual wellspring. German thought continued to break new ground in the 20th century, when sociologist **Max Weber** pinpointed the "Protestant Ethic" of work as salvation. Later, **Martin Heidegger** was a principal exponent of **Existentialism;** his seminal work *Being and Time* (1927) examines philosophical crises in a world of technological advancement. After the fall of the Third Reich, thinkers **Theodor Adorno** and **Max Horkheimer** authored *The Dialectic of Enlightenment* (1947), suggesting that bourgeois culture logically culminates in Fascism. More recently, **Jürgen Habermas** has criticized German national reunification as being dangerous and culturally unaware.

## MUSIC

During the Baroque period in the 17th century, the intricate harmonies of **Johann Sebastian Bach** graced churches in Leipzig (p. 489) while the music of **Georg Friedrich Händel** echoed in concert halls across Europe. The theme-and-variation pattern of their music laid the groundwork for the classical tradition and remains powerful in its own right: Bach's music has become standard fare for solo musicians and small ensembles, and Händel's *Messiah* (1741) is still widely performed.

The 19th century witnessed an unprecedented musical outpouring in Germany. **Ludwig van Beethoven's** symphonies and sonatas revolutionized the world of classical music, complicating the clear forms of Classicism with dramatic new harmonies. His impressive *Fifth* and *Ninth Symphonies* (1808 and 1824, respectively) have become part of the modern musical canon; you can visit Beethoven's birthplace in Bonn (p. 449). **Felix Mendelssohn-Bartholdy,** one of the first Romantic composers, wrote impressionistic music that includes the ethereal overture to *A Midsummer Night's Dream* (1826). Later in the century, **Johannes Brahms** imbued Classical forms with Romantic emotion, while Brahms's rival, the highly nationalistic **Richard Wagner** revolutionized German opera with works like *Tristan and Isolde* (1859) and *Lohengrin* (1850). Bavarian composer **Richard Strauss** wrote lush operas around the turn of the century; his shimmering orchestrations and lyrical lines carried the last strains of Romanticism into the 20th century, just before the advent of modern classical music. Today, Germany is still home to some of the best orchestras and operas in the entire world. The **Berlin Philharmonic** (p. 414) is internationally renowned for its rich sound and dynamic musical interpretations, and the various city operas around the country are also exceptional.

Germany's popular music scene has been mostly transnational since WWII, particularly dominated by American pop. Germany itself is best known internationally for pioneering techno with bands like **Kraftwerk.** The most popular bands in Germany include the pop group **Wir sind Helden** and rockers **Sportfreunde Stiller** and **Silbermond.**

## VISUAL ARTS

During the Renaissance, **Albrecht Dürer** emerged as a master of engraving, drafts-manship, and painting; his *Self-Portrait at 20* (1500) was one of the first portraits in Europe. In the 19th century, **Caspar David Friedrich** painted dramatic mountain scenes and billowing landscapes in a Romantic style distinguished by its crystal-line lines and sharp detail. It was in the 20th century, however, that German art truly came into its own. The anti-realism of **German Expressionism** intensified color and representation to project deeply personal emotions onto the canvas. In the darker Weimar period, artists turned their brushes to political subjects in reaction to the rise of fascism. **Max Beckmann** painted expressively elongated figures whose gestures and symbolism communicated a tortured view of mankind, and **Max Ernst** started a **Dadaist** group in Cologne, conveying artistic nihilism through collage. During the Nazi era, almost all art was controlled by the state, and idealized the image of Aryan workers and soldiers. Postwar, **Josef Beuys's** innovative art objects and performances challenge convention.

## HOLIDAYS AND FESTIVALS

**Holidays:** New Year's Day (Jan. 1); Epiphany (Jan. 6); Good Friday (Mar. 21); Easter (Mar. 23-24); Ascension (May 1); Pentecost (May 11-12); Corpus Christi (May 22); Assumption (Aug. 15); German Unity Day (Oct. 3); All Saints' Day (Nov. 1); Christmas (Dec. 25-26).

**Festivals:** Check out the pre-Lenten bacchanalia during *Fasching* in Munich and *Karneval* in Cologne (Feb. 1-5); international film in the Berlinale Film Festival (Feb. 7-17; p. 415); gay pride parades on Christopher Street Day in major cities (early June); vanishing kegs during Oktoberfest in Munich (Sept. 20-Oct. 5; p. 471); and the Christ-mas Market in Nuremberg (Nov. 28-Dec. 24).

## ADDITIONAL RESOURCES

*Germany: Unraveling an Enigma,* by Greg Nees. Intercultural Press (2000). Provides an overview of German culture and etiquette, particularly in comparison with the US.

*All Quiet on the Western Front,* by Erich Maria Remarque. Ballantine Books (1987). This story of the disillusionment of a German young solider describes the bloody trenches of WWI with a moving and unmistakably pacifist message.

*Germany: A New History,* by Hagen Schulze. Harvard University Press (2001). Covers 2000 years of Germany history in detail.

# ESSENTIALS

## WHEN TO GO

Germany's climate is temperate. The cloudy, mild months of May, June, and Sep-tember are the best time to go, as there are fewer tourists and the weather is pleas-ant. In July, Germans head en masse to summer spots. Winter sports gear up from November to April; ski season takes place from mid-December to March.

## DOCUMENTS AND FORMALITIES

**EMBASSIES.** All foreign embassies are in Berlin (p. 390). German embassies abroad include: **Australia,** 119 Empire Circuit, Yarralumla, Canberra, ACT 2600 (☎02 6270 1911; www.germanembassy.org.au); **Canada,** 1 Waverly St., Ottawa, ON, K2P OT8 (☎613-232-1101; www.ottawa.diplo.de); **Ireland,** 31 Trimleston Ave., Booterstown, Blackrock, Co. Dublin (☎01 269 3011; www.dublin.diplo.de); **New**

## FACTS AND FIGURES

**Official Name:** Federal Republic of Germany.

**Capital:** Berlin.

**Major Cities:** Cologne, Frankfurt, Hamburg, Munich.

**Population:** 82,401,000.

**Land Area:** 349,200 sq. km.

**Time Zone:** GMT +1.

**Religions:** Protestant (34%), Roman Catholic (34%), Muslim (2%).

**Percentage of European Beer Production:** 26.5%.

**Beer Consumed Annually:** 9,200,000L.

**Per Capita:** 111.6L (a whole lot of beer).

**Zealand,** 90-92 Hobson St., Thorndon, Wellington 6001 (☎04 473 6063; www.wellington.diplo.de); **UK,** 23 Belgrave Sq., London, SW1X 8PZ (☎020 7824 1300; www.london.diplo.de); **US,** 4645 Reservoir Rd. NW, Washington, D.C., 20007 (☎202-298-4000; www.germany-info.org).

**VISA AND ENTRY INFORMATION.** EU citizens do not need a visa. Citizens of Australia, Canada, New Zealand, and the US do not need a visa for stays of up to 90 days, beginning upon entry into any of the countries in the EU's freedom-of-movement zone. For more info, see p. 13. For stays longer than 90 days, all non-EU citizens need visas (around €100), available at Germany consulates.

# TOURIST SERVICES AND MONEY

**EMERGENCY** **Ambulance** and **Fire:** ☎112. **Police:** ☎110.

**TOURIST OFFICES.** The **National Tourist Board** website (www.germany-tourism.de) links to regional info and provides dates of national and local festivals. Every city in Germany has a tourist office, usually near the *Hauptbahnhof* (main train station) or *Marktplatz* (central square). All are marked by a sign with a thick lowercase *"i,"* and many book rooms for a small fee.

**MONEY.** The **euro (€)** has replaced the **Deutschmark (DM)** as the unit of currency in Germany. For more info, see p. 16. As a general rule, it's cheaper to exchange money in Germany than at home. Costs for those who stay in hostels and prepare their own food may range anywhere from €25-50 per person per day. **Tipping** is not practiced as liberally in Germany as elsewhere—most natives just round up €1. Tips are handed directly to the server with payment of the bill—if you don't want any change, say *"Das stimmt so"* (das SHTIMMT zo; "so it stands"). Germans rarely bargain except at flea markets. Germany has a 19% **value added tax (VAT),** a sales tax applied to most goods and services. The prices given in *Let's Go* include VAT. In the airport upon exiting the EU, non-EU citizens can claim a refund on the tax paid for goods purchased at participating stores. In order to qualify for a refund in a store, you must spend at least €25; make sure to ask for a refund form when you pay. For more info on qualifying for a VAT refund, see p. 18.

**BUSINESS HOURS.** Offices and stores are open from 9am-6pm, Monday through Friday, often closing for an hour lunch break. Stores may be open on Saturday in cities or shopping centers. Banks are also open from approximately 9am-6pm, and close briefly in the late afternoon but may stay open late on Thursday nights. Many museums are closed on Monday.

# TRANSPORTATION

**BY PLANE.** Most international flights land at **Frankfurt Airport** (**FRA;** ☎069 6900; www.airportcity-frankfurt.com); **Berlin (BML), Munich (MUC),** and **Hamburg (HAM)** also have international airports. **Lufthansa,** the national airline, is not always the best-priced option. Often it is cheaper to travel domestically by plane than by train; check out **Air Berlin** (www.airberlin.com), among other options.

**BY TRAIN.** The **Deutsche Bahn** (**DB;** www.bahn.de) network is Europe's best—and one of its most expensive. Luckily, all trains have clean and comfy second-class compartments, and there are a wide variety of train lines to choose from. **Regional-Bahn (RB)** trains include rail networks between neighboring cities and connects to **RegionalExpress (RE)** lines. **InterRegioExpress (IRE)** trains, covering larger networks between cities, are speedy and comfortable. **S-Bahn** trains run locally within large cities and high density areas. Some S-Bahn stops also service speedy **StadtExpress (SE)** trains, which directly connects city centers. **EuroCity (EC)** and **InterCity (IC)** trains zoom between major cities every 1-2hr. **InterCityExpress (ICE)** trains approach the luxury and kinetics of airplanes, barreling along the tracks at speeds up to 300kph, and service international destinations including Austria, Belgium, the Netherlands, and Switzerland. For overnight travel, choose between the first-class **DB Autozug** or cheaper **DB Nachtzug** lines.

   **Eurail** is valid in Germany. The **German Rail Pass** allows unlimited travel for four to 10 days within a one-month period, including Basel, SWI and Salzburg, AUT. Non-EU citizens can purchase German Rail Passes at select major train stations in Germany (5- or 10-day passes only) or through travel agents (2nd class 4-day pass €169, 10-day €289; under 26 €139/199). A **Schönes-Wochenende-Ticket** (€33) gives up to five people unlimited travel on any of the slower trains (RE or RB) from 12:01am Saturday or Sunday until 3am the next day; single travelers often find larger groups who will share their ticket.

**BY BUS.** Bus service runs from the local **ZOB** (*Zentralomnibusbahnhof*), usually close to the main train station. Buses are usually slightly more expensive than trains. Rail Passes are not valid on buses except for a few run by Deutsche Bahn.

**BY CAR AND BY BIKE.** Given generally excellent road conditions, Germans drive fast. The rumors are true: the *Autobahn* does not have a speed limit, only a recommendation of 130kph (80 mph). Watch for signs indicating the right-of-way (usually a yellow triangle). Signs with an "A" denote the *Autobahn;* signs bearing a "B" accompany secondary highways, which typically have a 100kph (60mph) speed limit. In cities and towns, speed limits hover around 30-60kph (20-35 mph). For a small fee, **Mitfahrzentralen,** and their women-only counterparts, **Frauenmitfahrzen-tralen,** agencies pair up drivers and riders, who then negotiate trip payment between themselves. Seat belts are mandatory, and police strictly enforce driving laws. Germany has designated lanes for **bicycles.** *Germany by Bike*, by Nadine Slavinski (Mountaineers Books, 1994), details 20 tours throughout Germany.

**BY THUMB.** Hitchhiking or even standing on the Autobahn is illegal. In some parts of Germany, hitchhiking does occur. Let's Go does not recommend hitchhiking.

# KEEPING IN TOUCH

| **PHONE CODES** | **Country code: 49. International dialing prefix: 00.** <br> For more info on how to place international calls, see **Inside Back Cover.** |
| --- | --- |

**EMAIL AND THE INTERNET.** Almost all German cities, as well as a surprising number of smaller towns, have at least one Internet cafe with web access for about €2-10 per hour. Wi-Fi is often available in bigger cities; in Berlin's new Sony Center (p. 405), the Wi-Fi is completely, blissfully free. Some German universities have Internet in their libraries intended for student use.

**TELEPHONE.** Most public phones will accept only a phone card *(Tele-fonkarte)*, available at post offices, kiosks, and some Deutsche Bahn counters. **Mobile phones** are an increasingly popular and economical alternative (p. 27). Phone numbers have no standard length. Direct-dial access numbers for calling out of Germany include: **AT&T USADirect** (☎0800 225 5288); **Canada Direct** (☎0800 888 0014); **MCI WorldPhone** (☎0800 888 8000); **Telecom New Zealand** (☎0800 080 0064); and **Telstra Australia** (☎0800 080 0061); most of these services require a calling card or credit card. For more info, see p. 26.

**MAIL.** Airmail *(Luftpost* or *par avion)* usually takes three to six days to Ireland and the UK, four to 10 days to Australia and North America. *Let's Go* lists addresses for mail to be held **Poste Restante** *(Postlagernde Briefe)* in the **Practical Information** sections of big cities. Mail will go to the main post office unless you specify a subsidiary by street address. Most post offices are open between 9am and 6pm. Address mail to be held according to the following example: First name Last name, *Postlagernde Briefe*, Postal code, City, GERMANY.

## ACCOMMODATIONS AND CAMPING

| GERMANY | ❶ | ❷ | ❸ | ❹ | ❺ |
|---|---|---|---|---|---|
| **ACCOMMODATIONS** | under €15 | €15-25 | €26-33 | €34-50 | over €50 |

Germany currently has more than 600 **youth hostels**—more than any other nation. Official hostels in Germany are overseen by **DJH** *(Deutsches Jugendherberg-swerk)*, Bismarckstr. 8, D 32756 Detmold, Germany (☎05231 740 10; www.jugendherberge.de). A growing number of **Jugendgästehäuser** (youth guest-houses) have more facilities than hostels and attract slightly older guests. DJH publishes *Jugendherbergen in Deutschland*, a guide to federated German hostels. Most charge €15-25 for dorms. The cheapest **hotel-style** accommodations are places with *Pension, Gasthof,* or *Gästehaus* in the name. Hotel rooms start at €20 for singles and €30 for doubles; in large cities, expect to pay nearly twice as much. *Frühstück* (breakfast) is almost always available, if not included. The best bet for a cheap bed is often a **Privatzimmer** (room in a family home), where a basic knowledge of German is very helpful. Prices can be as low as €15 per person. Reservations are made through the local tourist office or through a *Zimmervermit-tlung* (private booking office), sometimes for a small fee. Over 2500 **campsites** dot the German landscape. Bathrooms, a restaurant or store, and showers generally accompany a campground's well-maintained facilities. Camping costs €3-12 per tent site and €4-6 per extra person, with additional charges for tent and vehicle rental. Blue signs with a black tent on a white background indicate official sites.

> **TIP** **CHILDREN, CHILDREN, EVERYWHERE.** Schools in Germany often take students on week-long trips at the end of May and throughout June. As a result, hostels tend to be booked on weekdays—make reservations early!

## FOOD AND DRINK

| GERMANY | ❶ | ❷ | ❸ | ❹ | ❺ |
|---|---|---|---|---|---|
| **FOOD AND DRINK** | under €4 | €4-8 | €9-12 | €13-20 | over €20 |

A typical breakfast *(Frühstück)* consists of coffee or tea with rolls *(Brötchen)*, **cold sausage** *(Wurst)*, and **cheese** *(Käse)*. Germans' main meal, lunch *(Mittages-sen)*, includes soup, broiled sausage or roasted meat, potatoes or dumplings, and a salad or vegetable. Dinner (*Abendessen* or *Abendbrot*) is a reprise of breakfast, with beer in place of coffee and a wider selection of meats and cheeses. Many older Germans indulge in a daily ritual of coffee and cake *(Kaffee und Kuchen)* at 3 or 4pm. To eat cheaply, stick to a restaurant's daily menu *(Tagesmenü)*, buy food in supermarkets, or head to a **university cafeteria** *(Mensa)*. Fast-food stands *(Imbiß)* also offer cheap, often foreign eats—try a *Döner kebab*. The average German beer is maltier and more "bread-like" than Czech or American beers; a common nickname for German brew is liquid bread *(flüßiges Brot)*.

# BEYOND TOURISM

Germany's volunteering opportunities often involve environmental preservation—working on farms or in forests and educating people on protecting the environment—though opportunities for civil service and community building still exist, especially in eastern Germany. For more info on opportunities across Europe, see **Beyond Tourism**, p. 54.

**World-Wide Opportunities on Organic Farms (WWOOF)**, Postfach 210259, 01263 Dresden, Germany (www.wwoof.de). €18 membership in WWOOF gives you room and board at a variety of organic farms in Germany in exchange for chores.

**Open Houses Network,** Goethepl. 9B, D-99423 Weimar (☎03 643 502 390; www.openhouses.de). A group dedicated to restoring and sharing public space (mostly in Eastern Germany), providing lodging in return for work.

# BERLIN     ☎030

Berlin is bigger than Paris, up later than New York, and wilder than Amsterdam. Dizzying and electric, this city of 3.4 million has an increasingly diverse population, and it can be hard to keep track of which *Bezirk* (neighborhood) is currently the trendiest. Traces of the past century's Nazi and Communist regimes remain etched in residents' minds, and a psychological division between East and West Germany—the problem dubbed *Mauer im Kopf* ("wall in the head")—still exists nearly two decades after the Berlin Wall's destruction. Restless and contradictory, Germany's capital shows no signs of slowing down its self-reinvention, and the Berlin of next year may be radically different from the Berlin of today.

## ✈ INTERCITY TRANSPORTATION

**Flights:** The city is now transitioning from 3 airports to 1 (Flughafen Schönefeld will become the Berlin-Brandenburg International Airport), but at least until 2011, **Flughafen Tegel (TXL)** will remain West Berlin's main international airport. For info on all 3 of Berlin's airports, call ☎0180 500 0186 (www.berlin-airport.de). Take express bus #X9 from Bahnhof Zoo, bus #109 from Jakob-Kaiser-Pl. on U7, bus #128 from Kurt-Schumacher-Pl. on U6, or bus TXL from Potsdamer Pl. or Bahnhof Zoo. **Flughafen Schönefeld (BER),** southeast of Berlin, is used for intercontinental flights and travel to developing countries. Take S9 or 45 to Flughafen Berlin Schönefeld, or ride the Schönefeld Express train, which runs 2 per hr. through most major S-Bahn stations, including Alexanderpl., Bahnhof Zoo, Friedrichstr., *Hauptbahnhof*, and *Ostbahnhof*. **Flughafen Tempelhof (THF)** is slated to close October 31, 2008, but remains open until then for European flights. Take U6 to Pl. der Luftbrücke.

**Trains:** Berlin's massive new **Hauptbahnhof,** which opened in time for the 2006 World Cup, is the city's major transit hub, with some international and domestic trains continuing to **Ostbahnhof** in the East. Hauptbahnhof currently connects only to the S-Bahn, but a U55 line is scheduled to open in late 2007. **Bahnhof Zoologischer Garten** (a.k.a. **Bahnhof Zoo**), formerly the West's main station, now connects only to regional destinations. Many trains also connect to **Schönefeld** airport. A number of U- and S-Bahn lines stop at **Oranienburg, Potsdam,** and **Spandau.** Trains in the Brandenburg regional transit system tend to stop at all major stations, as well as Alexanderpl. and Friedrichstr.

**Buses: ZOB** (☎301 03 80), the "central" bus station, is actually at the western edge of town, by the Funkturm near Kaiserdamm. U2 to Kaiserdamm or S41/42 to Messe Nord/ICC. Open M-F 6am-9pm, Sa-Su 6am-3pm. **Gullivers,** at ZOB (☎311 0211; www.gullivers.de), Hardenbergpl. 14 (☎0800 48 55 48 37), and **Berlin Linien Bus** (030 851 9331, www.berlinlinienbus.de) often have good deals on bus fares. Open in summer daily 8am-9:30pm; in winter reduced hours.

**Mitfahrzentralen: Citynetz,** Joachimstaler Str. 17 (☎194 44), has a computerized rideshare database. U9 or 15 to Kurfürstendamm. To **Hamburg** or **Hanover** (€18) and **Frankfurt** (€31). Open M-F 9am-8pm, Sa-Su 10am-6pm. Other ride share bulletins at www.mitfahrzentrale.de and www.mitfahrgelegenheit.de. Check *030, Tip,* and *Zitty* for addresses and phone numbers.

# ✈ ORIENTATION

Berlin's landmarks include the **Spree River,** which flows through the city from west to east, and the narrower **Landwehrkanal Canal** that dumps into the Spree from the south. The vast central park, **Tiergarten,** stretches between the waterways. Two radio towers loom above the city: the pointed **Funkturm,** in the west, and the globed **Fernsehturm,** rising above **Alexanderplatz** in the east. In the west, the major thoroughfare **Kurfürstendamm** (a.k.a. Ku'damm) is lined with department stores and leads to the **Bahnhof Zoologischer Garten,** West Berlin's transportation hub. Nearby is the elegant wreck of the **Kaiser-Wilhelm Gedächtniskirche,** as well as one of Berlin's few real skyscrapers, the **EuropaCenter.** Tree-lined **Straße des 17. Juni** runs

> **!** Berlin is by far the most tolerant city in Germany, with thriving minority communities. However, minorities, gays, and lesbians should exercise caution in the outlying eastern suburbs, especially at night. If you see people wearing dark combat boots (especially with white laces)—a potential sign of neo-Nazis—exercise caution but do not panic, and avoid drawing attention to yourself.

east-west through the Tiergarten, ending at the **Brandenburger Tor,** the park's eastern border gate. The **Reichstag** (Parliament) is north of the gate; several blocks south, **Potsdamer Platz** bustles beneath the glittering Sony Center and the headquarters of the Deutsche Bahn. Heading east, Straße des 17. Juni becomes **Unter den Linden** and travels past most of Berlin's imperial architecture. In the east, **Karl-Marx-Allee, Prenzlauer Allee,** and **Schönhauser Allee** fan out from the Alexanderplatz.

Berlin's short streets change names often; addresses often climb higher and higher and then wrap around to the other side of the street, placing the highest- and lowest-numbered buildings across from one another. Well-indexed maps are invaluable. Berlin is rightly considered a collection of towns, not a homogeneous city; each neighborhood has a strong sense of its individual history. **Mitte** is currently its commercial heart. The neighboring eastern districts of **Friedrichshain** and **Prenzlauer Berg** are the city's liveliest and most youthful, while Kreuzberg is the outpost of counterculture in the west. **Charlottenburg** in the west has a more staid, upscale character, while **Schöneberg** is right in between **Kreuzberg** and Charlottenburg, both in geography and in spirit.

GERMANY

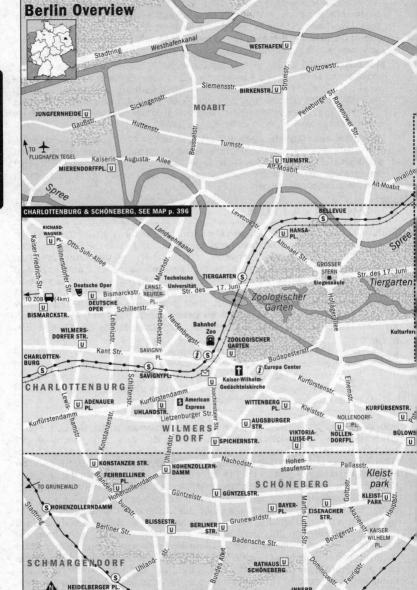

# Berlin Overview

Stadtring
Westhafenkanal
WESTHAFEN U
Quitzowstr.
Stromstr.
Siemensstr.
BIRKENSTR. U
Perleburger Str.
Rathenower Str.
MOABIT
JUNGFERNHEIDE U
Sickingenstr.
Gaußstr.
Huttenstr.
Beusselstr.
Turmstr.
TO
FLUGHAFEN TEGEL
Kaiserin– Augusta– Allee
U TURMSTR.
Alt-Moabit
MIERENDORFFPL. U
Alt-Moabit
Invalide
Spree
Levetzowstr.
BELLEVUE S
Spree

CHARLOTTENBURG & SCHÖNEBERG, SEE MAP p. 396

Landwehrkanal
RICHARD-WAGNER-PL. U
Otto-Suhr-Allee
Wilmersdorfer Str.
Altonaer Str.
U HANSA-PL.
GROSSER STERN
Siegessäule
Str. des 17. Juni
Tiergarten
Kaiser-Friedrich-Str.
Deutsche Oper U
Marchstr.
Technische Universität
TIERGARTEN S
Str. des 17. Juni
Hofjägerallee
Bismarckstr.
ERNST-REUTER-PL. U
DEUTSCHE OPER
Schillerstr.
Knesebeckstr.
Zoologischer Garten
TO ZOB (4km)
BISMARCKSTR. U
Leibnizstr.
Hardenbergstr.
Bahnhof Zoo
Kulturforu
WILMERS-DORFER STR. U
Kant Str.
SAVIGNY-PL.
ZOOLOGISCHER GARTEN U
CHARLOTTEN-BURG S
Schlüterstr.
SAVIGNYPL. S
i S
Budapester Str.
i Europa Center
CHARLOTTENBURG
Lewis- hamstr.
Kurfürstendamm
Konstanzerstr.
Kurfürstendamm
Joachimstaler Str.
Kaiser-Wilhelm-Gedächtniskirche
Kurfürstenstr.
Einemstr.
Por
S American Express
UHLANDSTR. U
Lietzenburger Str.
WITTENBERG PL. U
Kleiststr.
KURFÜRSTENSTR. U
ADENAUER PL. U
Uhlandstr.
WILMERS-DORF
U AUGSBURGER STR.
NOLLENDORF-PL. U
NOLLEN-DORFPL. U
BÜLOWS U
U SPICHERNSTR.
VIKTORIA-LUISE-PL.
U KONSTANZER STR.
FEHRBELLINER PL. U
U HOHENZOLLERN-DAMM
Nachodstr.
Hohen-staufenstr.
Pallasstr.
Kleist-park
TO GRUNEWALD
Branden- burgstr.
Hohenzollerndamm
Güntzelstr.
U GÜNTZELSTR.
SCHÖNEBERG
Martin-Luther-Str.
Goltzstr.
KLEIST-PARK U
S HOHENZOLLERNDAMM
Stadtring
Berliner Str.
BLISSESTR. U
BERLINER STR. U
Grunewaldstr.
BAYER-PL.
EISENACHER STR. U
Akazienstr.
Hauptstr.
Uhland- str.
Badensche Str.
Belziger str.
KAISER WILHELM PL.
SCHMARGENDORF
Bundes Allee
RATHAUS SCHÖNEBERG U
Dominicusstr.
Feurigstr.
HEIDELBERGER PL. S
INNSBR. PL. U
S U BUNDESPL.
SCHÖNEBERG S
Hauptstr.
Sachsendamm
Mecklenburgischestr.

0                    1 mile
0          1 kilometer

GERMANY

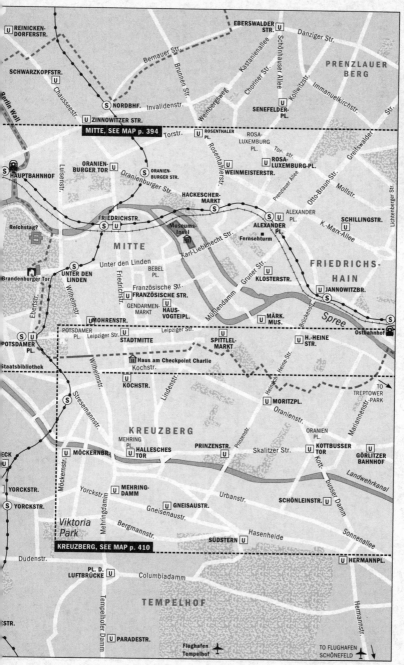

GERMANY

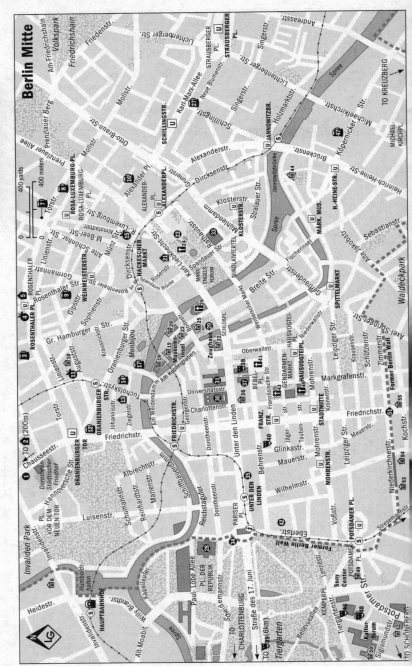

Berlin Mitte

# Berlin Mitte

**ACCOMMODATIONS**
Circus, **5**
BaxPax Downtown Hostel, **13**
CityStay Hostel, **21**
BaxPax Mitte, **2**

**FOOD & DRINK**
Beth Cafe, **11**
Dolores, **15**
Gorki Park, **4**

**ENTERTAINMENT**
Berliner Philharmoniker, **46**
Deutsche Oper Berlin, **39**
Deutsche Staatsoper, **38**
Komische Oper, **40**
Konzerthaus, **48**

**BARS & NIGHTLIFE**
2BE-Club, **14**
b-flat, **9**
Cafe Moskau, **27**
Kaffee Burger, **8**
Strandbar Mitte, **17**
Tacheles, **12**
Tresor, **47**
Weekend, **16**
White Trash Fast Food, **7**
Z-bar, **3**

**CHURCHES**
Berliner Dom, **26**
Deutscher Dom, **45**
Französischer Dom, **43**
Marienkirche, **24**
St.-Hedwigs-
    Kathedrale, **41**

**MUSEUMS**
Alte Nationalgalerie, **20**
Altes Museum, **25**
Bodemuseum, **18**
Deutsche Guggenheim
    Berlin, **36**
Deutsches Hist. Museum, **32**
Filmmuseum Berlin, **49**
Gemäldegalerie, **50**
Hamburger Bahnhof, **6**
Haus am Checkpoint
    Charlie, **55**
Kunst-Werke Berlin, **10**
Märkisches Museum, **44**
Martin-Gropius-Bau, **53**
Neue Nationalgalerie, **52**
Neues Museum, **22**
Pergamonmuseum, **19**
Topographie des Terrors, **54**

**SIGHTS**
Alte Bibliothek, **37**
Berliner Rathaus, **33**
Bertolt-Brecht-Haus, **1**
Brandenburger Tor, **34**
Checkpoint Charlie, **51**
Denkmal für die ermordeten
    Juden Europas, **42**
Deutsche Staatsbibliothek, **30**
Fernsehturm, **23**
Humboldt-Universität, **31**
Lustgarten, **29**
Reichstag, **28**
Russian Embassy, **35**

**GERMANY**

# ◰ LOCAL TRANSPORTATION

**Public Transportation:** The **BVG** (www.bvg.de) is one of the world's most efficient transportation systems. The extensive **Bus, Straßenbahn** (streetcar or tram), **U-Bahn** (subway), and **S-Bahn** (surface rail) networks will get you to your destination quickly. Almost all the reconstruction and expansion of the pre-war transit grid has been completed; service disruptions are rare, causing at most an extra 20min. wait.

**Orientation and Basic Fares:** Berlin is divided into 3 transit zones. **Zone A** encompasses central Berlin, including Flughafen Tempelhof. The rest of Berlin is in **Zone B** while **Zone C** consists of the outlying areas, including Potsdam and Oranienburg. An AB ticket is the best deal, as you can buy extension tickets for the outlying areas. An **Einzelfahrausweis** (1-way ticket) is good for 2hr. after validation. Zones A and B €2.10; B and C €2.40; A, B, and C €2.70. Under 6 free with an adult; children under 14 reduced fare. Within the validation period, the ticket may be used on any S-Bahn, U-Bahn, bus, or tram. A **Tageskarte** (1-day unlimited ticket; €6.10) is the best deal if you're planning to travel a lot in a single day.

**Night Transport:** U- and S-Bahn lines generally don't run M-F 1-4am. On F-Sa nights, all trains except for the U4, S45, and S85 continue but less frequently. An extensive system of approximately 70 **night buses** runs 2-3 per hr. and tends to follow major transit lines; pick up the free Nachtliniennetz map at a Fahrscheine und Mehr office. The letter N precedes night bus numbers. Trams continue to run at night.

**Taxis:** ☎080 02 63 00 00. Call at least 15min. ahead. Women can request female drivers. Trips within the city cost up to €21. Request a *Kurzstrecke* to travel up to 2km in any direction for a flat €3 fee.

**Car Rental:** Most companies have counters at the airports and around Bahnhof Zoo, Friedrichstr., and Ostbahnhof stations. Offices are also in EuropaCenter, with entrances at Budapester Str. 39-41. Rates around €65 for a car. 19+. **Hertz** (☎261 10 53). Open M-F 7am-8pm, Sa 8am-4pm, Su 9am-1pm.

 **LIFE (OR, UH, DEATH) IN THE FAST LANE.** When you're walking on Berlin's sidewalks, make sure you don't step onto a bike path. Lanes usually run through the middle of walkways and are marked by subtle, reddish lanes. Bikers usually don't tolerate wandering tourists well, so stay clear.

GERMANY

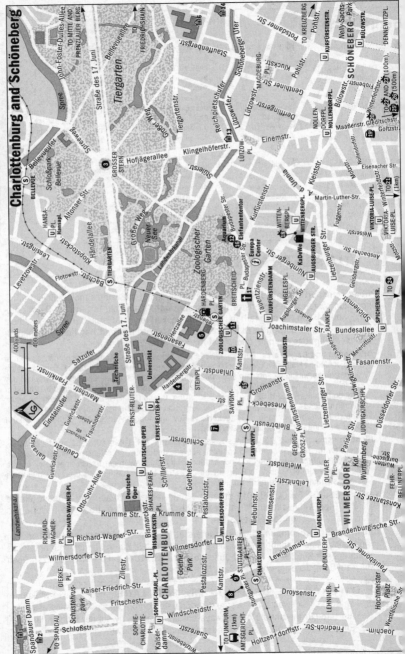

Charlottenburg and Schöneberg

## Charlottenburg and Schöneberg

▲ ACCOMMODATIONS
A&O Hostel, 11
Berolina Backpacker, 8
Frauenhotel Artemisia, 21
Jugendgästehaus am Zoo, 4

🍸 BARS AND ⭐ NIGHTLIFE
A-Trane, 7
Mister Hu, 25
Quasimodo, 10
Slumberland, 19

🏛 MUSEUMS
Bauhaus-Archiv Museum Für
   Gestaltung, 13
Gemäldegalerie, 6
Neue Nationalgalerie, 14
Museum Berggruen, 2
Schloß Charlottenburg, 1

🍎 FOOD & DRINK
Baharat Falafel, 23
Cafe Berio, 20
Cafe Bilderbuch, 26
Die Feinbäckerei, 22
Orchidee Sushi
   Restaurant, 9
Schwarzes Cafe, 15
Witty's, 18

● SIGHTS
Aquarium, 12
Bahnhof Zoologischer
   Garten, 5
Elefantententor, 16
Grunewald, 24
Kaiser-Wilhelm-
   Gedächtiskirche, 17
Siegessäule, 3

GERMANY

**Bike Rental: Fahrradstation,** Dorotheenstr. 30 (☎20 45 45 00; www.fahrradsta-tion.de), near the Friedrichstr. S-Bahn station. Turn in at the parking lot next to STA. €15 per day. Open in summer daily 8am-8pm; winter M-F 8am-7pm, Sa 10am-3pm. Less central **Orange Bikes,** Kollwitzstr. 35, is a youth community project. Bikes €2.50 per 3hr., €5 per day. Open M-F 2:30-7pm, Sa 10am-7pm. **Deutsche Bahn Call-A-Bike** (☎0700 522 5522; www.callabike.de) operates all over the city. After signing up (€5), call to unlock a bike. €0.07 per min.; up to €15 per day. €60 per week.

# 🔢 PRACTICAL INFORMATION

**Tourist Offices: Euraide** (www.euraide.com), in the *Hauptbahnhof*. Sells phone cards, rail- and walking-tour tickets. Arrive early—the office is often packed and doesn't accept phone calls. Open June-Oct. daily 8am-noon and 1-6pm; Nov.-May M-F 8am-noon and 1-4:45pm. **Berlin Tourismus Marketing (BTM),** in the EuropaCenter, on Budapester Str., in Charlottenburg. Reserves rooms (€3). Open M-Sa 10am-7pm, Su 10am-6pm. Branches at Brandenburger Tor and Alexanderpl. Fernsehturm.

**City Tours:** The guides at 🔲**Terry Brewer's Best of Berlin** (www.brewersberlintours.com) are legendary for their vast knowledge and engaging personalities. 8hr. tours (€12) and shorter free tours leave daily at 10:30am from in front of the Bandy Brooks shop on Friedrichstr. (S5, 7, 9, or 75 or U6 to Friedrichstr.). **Berliner Unterwelten** (www.ber-liner-unterwelten.de) earns praise for their Berlin Underground tours, which explore the spaces underneath the city (1½hr., 1-2 per day, €9). English-language tours leave from Brunnenstr. 108a (U or S to Gesundbrunnen); check website for tour times.

**Embassies and Consulates: Australia,** Mitte, Wallstr. 76-79 (☎880 0880; www.austra-lian-embassy.de). U2: Märkisches Museum. Open M-Th 8:30am-5pm, F 8:30am-4:15pm. **Canada,** Mitte, Leipziger Pl. 17 (☎20 31 20; www.canada.de). S1, 2 or U2: Potsdamer Pl. Open M-F 8:30am-12:30pm and 1:30-5pm. **Ireland,** Mitte, Friedrichstr. 200 (☎22 07 20; www.botschaft-irland.de). U2 or 6: Stadtmitte. Open M-F 9:30am-12:30pm and 2:30-4:45pm. **New Zealand,** Mitte, Friedrichstr. 60 (☎20 62 10; www.nzembassy.com). U2 or 6: Stadtmitte. Open M-Th 9am-1pm and 2-5:30pm, F 9am-1pm and 2-4:30pm. **UK,** Mitte, Wilhelmstr. 70-71 (☎20 45 70; www.britische-botschaft.de). S1-3, 5, 7, 9, 25, or 75, or U6: Friedrichstr. Open M-F 9am-5:30pm. **US,** Clayallee 170 (☎832 9233; fax 83 05 12 15). U1: Oskar-Helene-Heim. After a long debate over the security of proposed locations, the US Embassy will move to a spot next to the Brandenburg Gate by 2008. Open M-F 8:30am-noon. Telephone advice available M-F 2-4pm; after hours, call ☎830 50 for emergencies.

**Boat Tours:** The city's extensive canal system makes boat tours a popular option. **Reederei Heinz Riedel,** Planufer 78, Kreuzberg (☎693 4646; U8 Schönleinstr.). Tours €7-16. Open Mar.-Sept. M-F 6am-9pm, Sa 8am-6pm, Su 10am-3pm; Oct.-Feb. M-F 8am-4pm. **Stern & Kreisschiffahrt** (☎536 3600; www.sternundkreis.de), Puschkinallee 15, Treptow. Crusies from €5 (1hr. mini-tour). Open M-Th 9am-4pm, F 9am-2pm.

**Currency Exchange:** The best rates are usually found in large squares, at most major train stations, and at exchange offices with **Wechselstube** signs outside. **ReiseBank,** at the *Hauptbahnhof* (open M-Sa 8am-10pm), at Bahnhof Zoo (☎881 7117; open daily 7:30am-10pm) and at Ostbahnhof (☎296 4393; open M-F 7am-10pm, Sa 8am-8pm, Su 8am-noon and 12:30-4pm), is conveniently located, but has poor rates.

**American Express: Main Office,** Bayreuther Str. 37-38 (☎21 47 62 92). U1 or 2 to Wittenbergpl. Holds mail and offers banking services. No commission for cashing American Express Travelers Cheques. Expect long lines F-Sa. Open M-F 9am-7pm, Sa 10am-2pm. Branch at Friedrichstr. 172 (☎204 5572). U6 to Französische Str.

**Luggage Storage:** In **DB Gepack Center,** in the *Hauptbahnhof.* €3 for up to 3 bags. In **Bahnhof Zoo.** Lockers €3-5 per day. Max 72hr. Open daily 6:15am-10:30pm. Lockers, accessible 24hr., also at **Ostbahnhof** and **Alexanderpl.,** as well as the bus station.

**English-language Bookstores:** Berlin has a wealth of English-language bookstores, many of which also host events. **Marga Schöler Bücherstube,** Knesebeckstr. 33 (☎881 1112), at Mommsenstr., between Savignypl. and the Ku'damm. S5, 7, 9, or 75 to Savignypl. Off-beat, contemporary English reading material. Open M-W 9:30am-7pm, Th-F 9:30am-8pm, Sa 9:30am-4pm. **St. George's Bookstore,** Wörther Str. (☎81 79 83 33). Tram M2 to Marienburger Str. Open M-F 1-8pm, Sa 1-6pm.

**Crisis Lines: American Hotline** (☎0177 814 1510). **Berliner Behindertenverband,** Jägerstr. 63D (☎204 3847), has advice for the disabled. Open M-F 8am-4pm. **Frauenkrisentelefon** (☎611 0333) is a women's crisis line. Open M, W noon-2pm, Th 2-4pm.

**Pharmacies:** *Apotheken* (pharmacies) list a rotating schedule of 24hr. service.

**Medical Services:** The American and British embassies list English-speaking doctors. **Emergency doctor:** ☎31 00 31. **Emergency dentist:** ☎89 00 43 33. Both 24hr.

**Internet Access:** Free Internet access with admission to the **Deutsche Staatsbibliothek** (p. 404). Cheap Internet cafes cluster on Oranienstr. in Kreuzberg and around U-Bahn Ebeswalder Str. in Prenzlauer Berg. **Netlounge,** Auguststr. 89 (☎24 34 25 97; www.netlounge-berlin.de). U-Bahn to Oranienburger Str. €2.50 per hr. Open noon-midnight. **WLAN** stickers indicate free or charge-based **Wi-Fi** access.

**Post Offices:** Joachimstaler Str. 7 (☎88 70 86 11), down Joachimstaler Str. from Bahnhof Zoo and near the Kantstr. intersection. Open M-Sa 9am-8pm. Branches: **Tegel Airport,** open M-F 8am-6pm, Sa 8am-noon; **Ostbahnhof,** open M-F 8am-8pm, Sa-Su 10am-6pm. **Postal Code:** 10706.

# ▛ ACCOMMODATIONS

Longer stays are most conveniently arranged through one of Berlin's many **Mitwohnzentrale,** which can set up house-sitting gigs or sublets (from €250 per month). **Home Company Mitwohnzentrale,** Joachimstaler Str. 17, has a useful placement website. (☎194 45; www.homecompany.de. U9 or 15 to Ku'damm. Open M-Th 9am-6pm, F 9am-5pm, Sa 11am-2pm. MC/V.)

## MITTE

▨ **BaxPax Downtown Hostel/Hotel,** Ziegelstr. 28 (☎251 5202; www.baxpax-downtown.de). S1, 2, or 25 to Oranienburger Str. or U6 to Oranienburger Tor. This well-known hostel offers its young, party-happy crowd an unmatched array of hangout spaces.

There are two inflatable pools; one is on the roof terrace. Rooms are spotless and bright, but don't opt for the 30-bed K-Studio unless you're sure you want the round-the-clock company of 29 roommates. Wheelchair-accessible. Breakfast €4.50. Laundry €5-8. Internet €3 per hr.; Wi-Fi €1.50 per hr. K-Studio €13; dorms €16-21; singles €30-45; doubles €59-88; triples €66; quads €88. MC/V. ❸

**CityStay Hostel**, Rosenstr. 16 (☎23 62 40 31; www.citystay.de). S5, 7, 9, or 75 to Hackescher Markt or U2, 5, or 8 to Alexanderpl. CityStay could not be more central, but it's still on a quiet side street. Individual showers, organic breakfast made to order, and a tasteful color scheme a cut above the hostel norm. Occasional BBQs. All-night bar serves dinner 6-10pm. Breakfast €4. Linens €2.50. Laundry €5. Internet €3 per hr.; free Wi-Fi. Dorms €17-21; singles €34-45; doubles €50-64; quads €84. Cash only. ❸

**Circus**, Weinbergsweg 1A (☎28 39 14 33; www.circus-berlin.de). U8 to Rosenthaler Pl. Clean, modern, and well run. Wheelchair-accessible. Breakfast €2-5. Internet €0.50 per 10min; free Wi-Fi. Reception and bar 24hr. Dorms €17-19; singles €33, with shower €45; doubles €50; triples €63; apartments with balcony €77. MC/V. ❷

**BaxPax Mitte** (formerly Mitte's Backpacker Hostel), Chausseestr. 102 (☎28 39 09 65). U6 to Zinnowitzer Str. Walk up Chausseestr. on the left. Affiliated with BaxPax Downtown, but with a worn-in, old-school backpacker feel. Large, sometimes smoky lounge area with matching bar. Bike rental €10 per day. Linens €2.50. Laundry €7. Internet €6 per hr. Reception 24hr. Dorms €15-18; singles €30; doubles €43-56; triples €60-63; quads €76-80. Low season reduced rates. AmEx/MC/V. ❷

## TIERGARTEN

**Jugendherberge Berlin International (HI)**, Kluckstr. 3 (☎257 998 08; www.jh-berlin-international.de). U1 to Kurfürstenstr. Berlin's only HI hostel has a summer-camp feel—cafeteria breakfast and kids included—but features a big-screen TV, table tennis, and large common room. Bike rental €10 per day. Breakfast included; other meals €5. Internet €3 per hr. Reception and cafe 24hr. Dorms €24, under 27 €21; doubles €28/24. Backyard camping €16. MC/V. ❷

## CHARLOTTENBURG

**Berolina Backpacker**, Stuttgarter Pl. 17 (☎32 70 90 72; www.berolinabackpacker.de). S3, 5, 7, 9, or 75 to Charlottenburg. Quiet hostel with an ivy-laced facade has print art in its bunk-free dorms and daisies on the breakfast table. The quiet residential surroundings and proximity to the S-Bahn make up for its removed location. Breakfast €6. Reception 24hr. Check-out 11am. May-Sept. dorms €14-17; singles €35; doubles €46; triples €48. Nov.-Apr. €4 discount. AmEx/MC/V. ❶

**Jugendgästehaus am Zoo**, Hardenbergstr. 9A (☎312 9410; www.jgh-zoo.de), opposite the Technical University Mensa. U2 Ernst-Reuter-Platz or U to Zoo. Tucked away on the 4th fl. of an elegant *Jugendstil* building. 85 beds in simple rooms. Reception 24hr. Check-out 10am. Lockout 10am-2pm. 4- to 8-bed dorms €21, under 27 €18; singles €29/26; doubles €49/46. Cash only. ❸

**Frauenhotel Artemisia**, Brandenburgische Str. 18 (☎873 8905; www.frauenhotel-berlin.de). U7 to Konstanzer Str. Women-only hotel with terrace features art by a different Berlin-based female artist in each of its 12 rooms. Serves drinks 5-10pm. Breakfast included. Reception 9am-10pm. Free Wi-Fi. Singles €54, with bath €64-74; doubles €78/98-108. Extra bed €20. AmEx/MC/V. ❺

**A&O Hostel**, Joachimstaler Str. 1-3 (☎0800 222 5722; www.aohostels.com), 30m from Bahnhof Zoo. Conveniently located, reliably cheap dorms. Bar, lobby, and rooftop terrace are packed at night. Breakfast €5, included for private rooms. Linens €3. Internet €3 per hr. Reception 24hr. 16-bed dorm from €10; smaller dorms €13-17, with showers €20-24; singles €30-76; doubles €44-86. Low season reduced rates. MC/V. Branches in Mitte and Friedrichshain. ❷

## SCHÖNEBERG AND WILMERSDORF

**Jugendhotel Berlincity,** Crellestr. 22 (☎78 70 21 30; www.jugendhotel-berlin.de). U7 to Kleistpark. Airy, stylish common rooms cause this small hotel to fill up fast; reserve ahead. Breakfast included. Singles €35-40, with bath €45-55; doubles €55-65/60-79; triples €84/99; quads €108/118. Discounted rates for extended stays. MC/V. ❸

**Meininger City Hostel,** Meininger Str. 10 (☎0800 634 6464, from abroad 666 361 00; www.meininger-hostels.de). U4 or bus #146 to *Rathaus* Schöneberg. 1 branch of a Berlin hostel chain, Meininger's has formulaic splashy colors and unfailing cleanliness. Bar and beer garden compensate for less-than-ideal location. Breakfast included. Linens deposit €5. Internet €3 per hr. Reception 24hr. Dorms €14-16; singles €31; doubles €41; quads €68. 10% *Let's Go* discount on 1st night. MC/V. ❶

**JetPAK,** Pücklerstr. 54 (☎83 26 011; www.jetpak.de). U3 to Fehrbelliner Platz, then bus #115 (dir.: Neuruppiner Str.) to Pücklerstr. Housed in an old military complex. Breakfast €3. Linens €3. Free Internet. Dorms €14-16; singles €25; doubles €40. Cash only. ❷ Also runs the new Charlottenburg **JetPAK City Hostel,** Pariserstr. 58 (784 43 60). U3/U9 to Spichernstr. ❶

## KREUZBERG

**Bax Pax,** Skalitzer Str. 104 (☎69 51 83 22; www.baxpax.de). U1 or 15 to Görlitzer Bahnhof. Offers a pool table, shared balcony for barbecues, and a funky, low-key common area. Each room has a different country theme; the Germany room (#3) features a bed inside a VW Bug. Linens €3. Internet €3 per hr. Reception 24hr. Dorms €16; singles €30; doubles €46; triples €60. Nov.-Feb €1-2 discount. AmEx/MC/V. ❷

**Hostel X Berger,** Schlesische Str. 22 (☎695 1863; www.hostelxberger.com). U1 to Schlesisches Tor or night bus #N65 to Taborstr. Opened in 2006, this hostel provides access to one of the most up-and-coming areas in Kreuzberg. Spacious, plain dorms off hallways painted with bright blocks of color. Kitchen facilities in a small common area. Women-only dorms available. Linens €2. Free Internet. Reception 24hr. Dorms €12-16; singles €26; doubles €36; triples €48; quads €56. Cash only. ❶

**Die Fabrik,** Schlesische Str. 18 (☎611 7116; www.diefabrik.com). U1 to Schlesisches Tor. A renovated factory with spacious rooms but few amenities. Close to nightlife. Internet €3 per hr.; free Wi-Fi. Reception 24hr. Dorms €18; singles €38; doubles Su-Th €52, Sa €58, with private bath €54/62; triples €69/78; quads €84/92. Cash only. ❷

**Hotel Transit,** Hagelberger Str. 53-54 (☎789 0470; www.hotel-transit.de). U6 or 7; bus #119, 219, or 140; or night bus N4, 6, 19, 76 to Mehringdamm. Hip, gay-friendly hotel is open to everyone. All rooms with bath. Breakfast included. Internet €6 per hr. Reception 24hr. Check-in 2pm. Check-out noon. Dorms €21; singles €62; doubles €72; 3- to 6-bed rooms €30 per person. AmEx/MC/V. ❷ Affiliated **Transit Loft** in Prenzlauer Berg, Greifswalder Str 219 (48 49 37 73; www.transit-loft.de). U2 to Senefelder Pl. ❷

**Pension Kreuzberg,** Großbeerenstr. 64 (☎251 1362; www.pension-kreuzberg.de). U6 or 7 or night bus N19 to Mehringdamm. Cheery breakfast room, elegant staircases, and antique iron stoves. Breakfast included. Reception 8am-10pm. Dorms €24, with bath 26; singles €41/60; doubles €55/68. Cash only. ❷

## FRIEDRICHSHAIN

**Globetrotter Hostel Odyssee,** Grünberger Str. 23 (☎29 00 00 81; www.globetrotterhostel.de). U1 to Warschauer Str. or U5 to Frankfurter Tor. Gothic statues and candlelit tables give the lobby a funky feel, while the tattooed staff keep everything spotless. Bar open until dawn. Breakfast €3. Linens deposit €3. Internet €0.50 per 10min.; free Wi-Fi. Reception 24hr. Check-in 4pm. Check-out noon. Reserve ahead. Dorms €14-22; singles €36-39; doubles €54-57; triples €66; quads €80. MC/V. ❷

**Schlafmeile,** Weichselstr. 25 (☎965 14676; www.schlafmeile.de). S to Ostbahnhof and then bus 240 to Boxhagener/Holteistr., or S to Ostkreuz. Beside a park in a residential neighborhood. This family business adds the personal touch missing from the slicker Mitte hostels. Attached cafe serves Kiwi food. Wheelchair-accessible. Kitchen facilities. Linens included. Internet €1 per hr. Dorms €14-20; doubles €39-57; apartment with kitchen €120. Discounts for longer stays. Cash only. ❷

**Eastern Comfort Hostelboat & Lounge,** Mühlenstr. 73-77 (☎66 76 38 06; www.eastern-comfort.com). U or S to Warschauerstr. Moored in the Spree, the entrance to this hostelboat is in the middle of the East Side Gallery (p. 409). Clean cabins offer spectacular views of the Oberbaumbrücke, but—as this is a boat—low-ceilings small quarters. The **Floating Lounge** on the top floor—popular with both guests and Anglophone expats—offers plenty of space to stretch out. Breakfast €4. Linens €5. Internet €2 per hr. Dorms €16-21; singles €46-60; doubles €54-76; triples €63; quads €72. MC/V. ❶

## PRENZLAUER BERG

▨ **East Seven,** Schwedter Str. 7 (☎93 62 22 40; www.eastseven.de). U2 to Senefelderpl. Hip, sophisticated hostel on a quiet street in trendy Prenzlauer Berg. From the classy decor to the garden and Italian coffee served at breakfast, East 7 is unbeatable. Stag and hen party groups are banned here. Free tours. Kitchen facilities. Linens €3. Laundry €4. Internet €0.50 per 20min.; free Wi-Fi. Dorms €15-17; singles €35; doubles €48; triples €63; quads €76. Low season reduced rates. MC/V. ❶

**Lette'm Sleep Hostel,** Lettestr. 7 (☎44 73 36 23; www.backpackers.de). U2 to Eberswalder Str. The big kitchen with its comfy red couches is the social nexus of this homey 48-bed hostel overlooking a park in the fashionable Helmholzplatz neighborhood. Beer garden in the back. Wheelchair-accessible. Linens included. Free Internet. Dorms €17-20; doubles €49; new apartments with bath €68. Low season reduced rates. 10% discount for stays over 3 nights. AmEx/MC/V. ❷

# ▐ FOOD

Berlin's cuisine is quite diverse thanks to its Middle Eastern and Southeast Asian populations. Seasonal highlights include the beloved *Spargel* (white asparagus) in early summer, Pfifferling mushrooms in late summer, and *Federweiße* (young wine) in September. Perhaps the dearest culinary tradition is breakfast; Germans love to wake up late over a *Milchkaffee* (bowl of coffee with foamed milk) and a sprawling brunch buffet. Vendors of Currywurst or Bratwurst supply a quick bite, or find a 24hr. Turkish *Imbiß* (snack food stand) to satisfy a midnight craving.

**Aldi, Edeka, Penny Markt,** and **Plus** are the cheapest supermarket chains (all typically open M-F 9am-8pm, Sa 9am-4pm). An exception to Sunday closing laws is made for stores at Ostbahnhof. Almost every neighborhood has an **open-air market;** Bahnhof Zoo market, on Winterfeldtpl., is particularly busy on Saturday mornings. In Kreuzberg along Maybachufer, on the Landwehrkanal, the **Turkish market** sells cheap veggies and huge wheels of Fladenbrot every Tuesday and Friday. Take U8 to Schönleinstr. Also popular is the more upscale, largely **organic market** that takes over Prenzlauer Berg's Kollwitz Pl. on Thursday and Friday. (U2 to Senefelder Pl).

## MITTE

Cheap eats in Berlin are better almost anywhere outside Mitte. Mitte's food scene is made of almost entirely of either posh restaurants or predatory tourist traps, with only a few exceptions. The former are generally outside the range of the budget eater's wallet; the latter tend to serve mediocre food at inflated prices, with the possibility of strange or hidden charges on the side. Yum!

**Gorki Park,** Weinbergsweg 25 (☎448 7286; www.gorki-park.de). U8 to Rosenthaler Pl. Nobody does borscht, *bliny, wareniki,* or *pelmeni* like this feisty little Russian cafe; serious devotees of Russian food can also find dishes like *intelligenz* (chopped herring, apple, egg, and salt pickle, served with or without vodka). Russian weekend brunch is a break from the standard Berlin version. Outdoor seating available. Entrees €4-10. Brunch €8.50. Open M-Sa 9:30am-2am, Su 10am-2am. Cash only. ❷

**Dolores,** Rosa-Luxembourg-Str. 7. U or S to Alexanderplatz. Simple, tasty, and affordable. The ingredients at this California-style burrito bar are as fresh as the cherry-and-lime color scheme. Choose one of 7 basic burritos and pile it high with treats like black beans, lime rice, and what may be the only authentic guacamole in Berlin. Vegetarian-friendly. Burritos €3.60-4.70. Open M-F 10am-9pm, Sa 12:30pm-late. Cash only. ❷

**Beth Cafe,** Tucholskystr. 40 (☎281 3135), off Auguststr. S1, 2, or 25 to Oranienburger Str. Come for the tranquil garden seating in a historic *Hinterhof.* The kosher menu features favorites like bagels with lox and cream cheese (€2.50). Vegetarian options available. Entrees €6-11. Cake slices €1.70. Open in summer Su-Th 11am-10pm, F 11am-5pm; in winter Su-Th 11am-10pm, F 11am-3pm. AmEx/MC. ❷

## CHARLOTTENBURG

**Schwarzes Cafe,** Kantstr. 148 (☎313 8038). S3, 5, 7, 9, or 75 to Savignypl. Labyrinthine institution of bohemian Berlin is both loud and romantic, with candlelit tables and a 24hr. breakfast menu (€5-8). Open 24hr. except Tu closed 3-11am. Cash only. ❸

**Orchidee Sushi Restaurant,** Stuttgarter Pl. 13 (☎31 99 74 67; www.restaurantorchidee.de). S to Charlottenburg. Though it touts its sushi, this pan-Asian cafe serves outstanding Vietnamese cuisine. Lunch special 11am-5pm; ½-price sushi or free appetizer with €5-11 entree. Open M-Sa 11am-midnight, Su 3pm-midnight. Cash only. ❸

**Witty's,** Wittenbergplatz, facing KaDeWe. U to Wittenbergplatz. Perhaps Berlin's best *Imbiß.* An organic beer accompanies the Pommes's organic potatoes and the Currywurst's organic meat well. Open daily 11am-1am. Cash only. ❶

## SCHÖNEBERG

🏅 **Cafe Bilderbuch,** Akazienstr. 28 (☎78 70 60 57; www.cafe-bilderbuch.de). U7 to Eisenacher Str. Relax in the Venetian library or the airy courtyard of the "Picturebook Cafe." Known for daily breakfasts named after fairy tales (€7-8), the menu comes with a monthly literature magazine. Open M-Th 9am-1am, F-Sa 9am-2am, Su 10am-1am. Kitchen open M-Sa 9am-11pm, Su 10am-11pm. Cash only. ❸

🏅 **Cafe Berio,** Maaßenstr. 7 (☎216 1946; www.cafe-berio.de). U1, 2, 3, or 4 to Nollendorfpl. Always jam-packed with locals savoring late-afternoon breakfast, this subtly retro 2-fl. Viennese-style cafe tempts passersby with its unbeatable breakfast menu (€3.50-8.50) and perfect people-watching location. Open daily 8am-1am. Cash only. ❷

**Die Feinbäckerei,** Vorbergstr. 2 (☎81 49 42 40; www.feinbaeck.de). U7 to Kleistpark or Eisenacher. Neighborhood bistro has unassuming Swabian fare. Amazing *Spätzle* (noodles; €7). Lunch special M-F 10am-5pm €5. Open daily noon-midnight. Cash only. ❷

**Baharat Falafel,** Winterfeldtstr. 37 (☎216 8301). U1, 2, 3, or 4 to Nollendorfpl. This is no greasy *Döner* stand—it's all about falafel. 3 or 5 chick-pea balls in a fluffy pita, with veggies and heavenly chili sauce, mango, or sesame sauce (€3-4). Fresh-squeezed *Gute-Laune Saft* (good mood juice; €1-3.50). Open daily noon-2am. Cash only. ❶

## KREUZBERG

**Café V,** Lausitzer Pl. 12 (☎612 4505). U1 to Görlitzer Bahnhof. Vegan and fish entrees served in the romantic interior of Berlin's oldest vegetarian cafe. Top-of-the-line German and Middle Eastern entrees (€6-8). Open daily 10am-2am. Cash only. ❸

**Pagode,** Bergmannstr. 88 (☎691 2640). U7 to Gneisenaustr. One of Berlin's best Thai restaurants, Pagode is staffed by Thai women who churn out excellent curries and soups in record time. The ground floor can look crowded, but there's extra basement seating beside a giant aquarium. Entrees €4-9. Open daily noon-midnight. Cash only. ❷

**Wirtshaus Henne,** Leuschnerdamm 25 (☎614 7730; www.henne-berlin.de). U1 to Kottbusser Tor. Just about the only thing on the menu at this beer garden is Berlin's best *Brathänchen* (fried chicken; €6). Reserve ahead. Open Tu-Su 7pm-late. Cash only. ❷

**Restaurant Rissani,** Spreewaldplatz 4-6 (☎61 62 49 33). U1 to Görlitzer Bahnhof. The best Middle Eastern food in a neighborhood known for its Middle Eastern food. Moroccan and Lebanese specialties like an absurdly good lamb with rice (€5) and cheap, delicious *Falafel im Brot* (€2). Open Su-Th noon-3am, F-Sa noon-5am. Cash only. ❷

**Melek Bäckerei,** Oranienstr. 28 (☎61 20 19 58). U1 or 8 to Kottbusser Tor. Popular shop sells Turkish pastries. Baklava €0.75 per 100g. Open 24hr. Cash only. ❶

**Kreuzburger,** Oranienstr. 190 (☎80 57 53 98). U1 or 8 to Kotbusser Tor. Down-to-earth, no-frills burger bar puts its energy into the patties, including a number of veggie options. Burgers €2.50-4.30. Open daily 11:30am-3am. Cash only. 2nd branch to open soon in Prenzlauer Berg. ❶

**Eisdiele Aldemir,** Falckensteinstr. 7 (☎611 8368). U1 to Schlesisches Tor. Berlin's most popular ice cream stand has 40 homemade varieties, from chili-chocolate to sesame-honey. €0.80 per scoop. Open Mar.-Sept. daily 10am-midnight. Cash only. ❶

**Cafe Ohio,** Schlesische Str. 35a (☎15 20 88 19 681). U1 to Schlesische Str. Run by an American expat, this laid-back cafe serves excellent chili (€4) and sandwiches (€3). At night, live performances draw Anglophones. Open daily 8:30am-midnight. Cash only. ❶

## FRIEDRICHSHAIN AND PRENZLAUER BERG

**I Due Forni,** Schönhauser Allee 12 (44 01 73 33). Locals swear by the stone-oven pizza at this hilltop pizzeria run by Italian rocker dudes. Waits can be long in summer, when front and back gardens strain the capacity of the kitchen; be entertained by the lively graffiti on the walls. Pizzas €5.40-8.50; if you're feeling adventurous, try the one featuring *Pferdefleisch* (horse meat). Open daily noon-1am. Cash only. ❶

**Babel,** Kastanienallee 33 (☎44 03 13 18). U2 to Eberswalder Str. Locals and tourists obsessed with Babel's falafel (€3-5) keep this neighborhood Middle Eastern joint busy at all hours. Open daily 11am-midnight. Cash only. ❶

**Prater Biergarten,** Kastanienallee 7-9 (☎448 5688; www.pratergarten.de). U2 to Eberswalder Str. Berlin's oldest beer garden is a summertime institution. Heaping plates of old-school German food. Outdoor theater and big-screen TV for watching sports. Bratwurst €2. Entrees €5.70-15. Beer €2.20-3.10. Open in good weather Apr.-Sept. M-Sa 6pm-late, Su noon-late. Cash only. ❶

**Asian Deli,** Lychener Str. 28 (☎44 04 89 20). U2 to Eberswalder Str. A neighborhood crowd scarfs down Thai, Vietnamese, and Malaysian standards at this cheap Helmholzkiez cafe. Kitchen stays open late. The Kuakunyilkan fish soup (€3) is particularly good. Entrees €4-7. Outdoor seating available. Open daily 11:30am-midnight. Cash only. ❷

**Cafe Schönbrunn,** Am Schwanenteich, in Volkspark Friedrichshain (☎46 79 38 93). Take bus #200 to the fountainside setting in Volkspark Friedrichshain. The Schönbrunn complex includes an upscale Austrian restaurant indoors (entrees €9-20), a more affordable cafe marked by cow statues on its roof (currywurst €2.50; organic Bioburger €4.50), and an even cheaper snack bar under the "kiosk" sign. All share scenic outdoor seating amid pink rosebushes. Open M-F 10am-1am, Sa-Su 10am-2am. V. ❶

**Intimes,** Boxhagener Str. 107 (☎29 66 64 57). U5 to Frankfurter Tor. This Turkish and Mediterranean cafe is the perfect start to an evening, with large portions and numerous vegetarian options. Adjoining cinema plays European indie flicks. Entrees €6-11. Su brunch 10am-4pm €8. Open daily 10am-late. Kitchen closes midnight. Cash only. ❸

**Volkswirtschaft,** Krossener Str. 17 (☎29 00 46 04). U or S-Bahn to Warschauer Str. or U5 to Samaritenstr. This Friedrichshain favorite offers a changing daily menu of organic, primarily German dishes, with a wide array of vegetarian and vegan options.

The vegetarian Su brunch receives special praise. Entrees €5-14. Open M-W 6pm-midnight, Th-Sa 1pm-midnight, Su 11am-late. Cash only. ❷

# ◎ SIGHTS

Most of central Berlin's major sights lie along the route of **bus #100**, which runs every 5min. from Bahnhof Zoo to Prenzlauer Berg. It passes the **Siegessäule** (p. 405), **Brandenburger Tor** (p. 404) and **Unter den Linden,** the **Berliner Dom** (p. 406), and **Alexanderplatz** (p. 406). Remnants of the **Berlin Wall** still survive in only a few places: in **Potsdamer Platz** (p. 405); near the **Haus Am Checkpoint Charlie** (p. 409); in **Prenzlauer Berg,** next to the sobering **Documentation Center** (p. 411); and in altered form at the **East Side Gallery** (p. 409) in Friedrichshain.

## MITTE

Mitte was once the heart of Berlin, but the wall split it down the middle, and much of it languished in disrepair under the GDR. The wave of revitalization that swept Berlin after the collapse of communism came to Mitte first: the area received a few new coats of polish and has been getting increasingly upscale ever since. It's becoming ever harder to find war wrecks squeezed in among the glittering modern buildings, swank galleries, and stores so hyper-hip that they only sell one thing, like messenger bags, acid-tone sweaters, or rugs with words on them.

### UNTER DEN LINDEN

One of Europe's best-known boulevards, Unter den Linden was the spine of imperial Berlin. During the Cold War it was known as the "Idiot's Mile" because it was often all that visitors to the East saw, and it gave them little idea of what the city was like. Beginning in Pariser Pl. in front of Brandenburger Tor, the street extends east through Bebelpl. and the Lustgarten, punctuated by dramatic squares. *(S1, 2, or 25 to Unter den Linden. Bus #100 runs the length of the boulevard; 10-15 per hr.)*

▨**BRANDENBURGER TOR.** Built as a tribute to 18th century peace, this gate at the heart of Pariser Pl. came to symbolize the city's division: facing the Berlin Wall, it became a barricaded gateway to nowhere. After serving as the memorable backdrop for the fall of the Berlin Wall, the gate is now the most powerful emblem of reunited Germany. Visitors can reflect in the **Room of Silence** at the northern end.

**DENKMAL FÜR DIE ERMORDETEN JUDEN EUROPAS (MEMORIAL TO THE MURDERED JEWS OF EUROPE).** Filling a block just south of Pariser Pl., this new and controversial monument consists of 2711 concrete columns of various heights and angles, all set on an undulating surface. The viewer is meant to experience this disorienting space by walking through it. There's an info center on the southeast corner. *(Cora-Berliner-Str. 1.)*

**RUSSIAN EMBASSY.** One of the most striking buildings along Unter den Linden is this monstrous Stalinist-style 1950s edifice that once demonstrated the might of the Soviet Union. Berlin's largest embassy, it covers almost an entire city block. Now, it draws visitors who gaze from behind a cast-iron fence and speculate on the rumor that there's a swimming pool inside with a giant mosaic of Lenin on the bottom. *(Unter den Linden 55.)*

**DEUTSCHE STAATSBIBLIOTHEK AND HUMBOLDT-UNIVERSITÄT.** This stately library's ivy-covered courtyard, complete with lounging intellectuals, provides a pleasant respite from the urban rush. (Unter den Linden 8. ☎ 26 60. Free Internet. Library open M-F 9am-9pm, Sa 9am-5pm. €0.50.) Beyond the Staatsbibliothek lies **Humboldt-Universität,** which over the years has been home to Bismarck, Einstein, the Brothers Grimm, Hegel, and Marx. If you have a student ID, grab a bite to eat at the **Mensa der Humboldt-Universität** at the back of the main building. It's a cafeteria, but you can't beat the €2-3 meals. *(Unter den Linden 6.)*

**BEBELPLATZ.** In this square on May 10, 1933, Nazi students burned nearly 20,000 books by communist, Jewish, and pacifist authors including Heinrich Heine and Sigmund Freud, both of Jewish descent. Today, a small window in the ground reveals empty bookcases beneath and a quote from Heine: "Wherever they burn books, eventually they will burn people too." On the western side of Bebelpl., the building with a curved facade is the **Alte Bibliothek;** once the royal library, it's now home to the law faculty of Humboldt-Universität. On the eastern side is the **Deutsche Staatsoper,** one of Berlin's three opera houses, fully rebuilt after the war based on the original sketches. The blue dome at the end of the square belongs to **St.-Hedwigs-Kathedrale,** the first Catholic church built in Berlin after the Reformation. Modeled on the Roman Pantheon and completed in 1773, it was destroyed by Allied bombers in 1943. The church was rebuilt in the 1950s in a more modern style. *(Open M-Sa 10am-5pm, Su 1-5pm. Organ concerts W 3pm. Cathedral free.)*

## TIERGARTEN

Once a hunting ground for Prussian monarchs, the lush Tiergarten (Animal Park) is now the eye of Berlin's metropolitan storm. From Bahnhof Zoo to the Brandenburger Tor, the vast landscaped park is frequented by bikers, joggers, and more than a few nude sunbathers. Straße des 17. Juni bisects the park from west to east. Near S-Bahnhof Tiergarten, is the open-air gas lantern museum (Gaslaternen Freilichtmuseum), which takes on a magical quality at dusk.

**▧ THE REICHSTAG.** Today home to the *Bundestag*, Germany's governing body, the Reichstag was central to one of the most critical moments in history. When it mysteriously burned down in 1933, Hitler declared a state of emergency and seized power. Today, a glass dome offers visitors 360° views of the city as they climb the spiral staircase inside. Go before 8am or after 8pm to avoid long lines. *(☎ 22 73 21 52; www.bundestag.de. Open daily 8am-midnight; last entrance 10pm. Free.)*

**SIEGESSÄULE.** This column above the Tiergarten commemorates Prussia's victory over France in 1870. The goddess of victory on the top is made of melted French cannons. Climb the 285 steps for a panoramic look at the city. *(Großer Stern. Take bus #100 or 187 to Großer Stern or S5, 7, or 9 to Tiergarten and walk 5min. down Straße des 17. Juni. Accessible via the stairs at the West corners around the traffic circle. ☎ 391 2961. Open Apr.-Nov. M-F 9:30am-6:30pm, Sa-Su 9:30am-7pm; Dec.-Mar. M-F 10am-5pm, Sa-Su 10am-5:30pm. €2.20, students €1.50.)*

**POTSDAMER PLATZ.** Originally designed to allow the rapid mobilization of troops under Friedrich Wilhelm I, Potsdamer Pl. now strives to reclaim its former role as Berlin's commercial center. During the 1990s, the city sunk a fortune into rebuilding what was mostly an empty lot, and the resulting style has met mixed reviews. Though most of the new office space is empty, the central complex includes Berlin's Film Museum, the towering headquarters of the Deutsche Bahn, and the glitzy **▧ Sony Center,** where travelers can watch a movie, enjoy free Wi-Fi, or window-shop under a retractable steel-and-glass roof. *(U2, S1, 2, or 25 to Potsdamer Pl.)*

**GENDARMENMARKT.** Several blocks south of Unter den Linden, this gorgeous square was considered the French Quarter in the 18th century, when it became the main settlement for Protestant Huguenots fleeing persecution by "Sun King" Louis XIV. During the last week of June and the first week of July, the square transforms into a stage for classical concerts. *(U6 to Französische Str. or U2 or 6 to Stadtmitte.)*

**DEUTSCHER DOM.** Gracing the southern end of the square, the Dom is not currently used as a church but instead houses **Wege Irrwege Umwege** ("Milestones, Setbacks, Sidetracks"), an exhibition tracing German political history from despotism to democracy. *(Gendarmenmarkt 1. ☎ 22 73 04 31. Little English-language info. Open Tu-Su June-Aug. 10am-7pm; Sept.-May 10am-6pm. Free.)*

**FRANZÖSISCHER DOM.** Built in the early 18th century by French Huguenots, the still-active church now holds a restaurant and small museum on the Huguenot diaspora. The tower offers a sweeping view of the city. *(Gendarmenmarkt 5. At the opposite end of the square from the Deutscher Dom. ☎ 229 1760. Museum open Tu-Su noon-5pm. Tower open daily 9am-7pm. Museum €2, students €1. Tower €2/1.50.)*

## MUSEUMSINSEL AND ALEXANDERPLATZ

After crossing the Spree, Unter den Linden becomes Karl-Liebknecht-Str. and cuts through the Museumsinsel (Museum Island), home to five major museums and the **Berliner Dom.** Karl-Liebknecht-Str. then continues onward to Alexanderpl. Take S3, 5, 7, 9, or 75 to Hackescher Markt, or bus #100 to Lustgarten.

**BERLINER DOM.** Berlin's most recognizable landmark, this multi-domed cathedral proves that Protestants can be as dramatic as Catholics. Built during the reign of Kaiser Wilhelm II, the Dom suffered damage in a 1944 air raid and only recently emerged from three decades of restoration. Inside, keep an eye out for the likenesses of Protestant luminaries Calvin, Luther, and Zwingli, or enjoy the glorious view of Berlin from the tower. In the crypt, check out the nearly 100 Hohenzollern sarcophagi. *(Open M-Sa 9am-8pm, Su noon-8pm, closed during services 6:30-7:30pm. Free organ recitals W-F 3pm. Frequent concerts in summer; buy tickets in the church or call ☎ 20 26 91 36. Combined admission to crypt, Dom, galleries, and tower €5, students €3.)*

**AQUADOM AND SEA LIFE CENTER BERLIN.** More than 2000 fish swim through the waters of the world's largest cylindrical aquarium; a glass elevator in the center of the tank lets visitors feel like they're swimming, too. Visitors begin with local fish of the Spree and moved outward through Wannsee, Hamburg Harbor, the North Sea, before exhibits on the Atlantic Ocean. *(Spandauer Str. 3. ☎ 99 28 00; www.sealife.de. Open daily Apr.-Aug. 10am-7pm; Sept.-Mar. 10am-6pm. €14, students €13.)*

**ALEXANDERPLATZ.** This plaza formed the heart of Berlin in the Weimar era, but it is now overwhelmed by construction and overgrown grass. Socialist relics like the 1950s-style Weltzeituhr, a clock showing the time around the former communist world, share space with capitalist add-ons like the department store **Kaufhof.**

 **NO DANCING IN THIS REVOLUTION.** *Let's Go* uses GDR to refer to the German Democratic Republic, more commonly known as former East Germany. In German, it's DDR, for **Deutsche Demokratische Republik.**

**MARIENKIRCHE.** After several centuries of additions to the original structure, the church is Gothic, the altar and pulpit Rococo, and the tower Neo-Romantic. Relatively undamaged during the war, this little church still holds relics from nearby churches that used it as a bomb shelter. Knowledgeable guides explain the artifacts, as well as the painting collection, including works from the Dürer and Cranach schools. *(☎ 242 4467. Open daily in summer 10am-6pm, winter 10am-4pm.)*

**FERNSEHTURM.** Berlin's tallest structure (368m), this bizarre TV tower was built to prove East Germany's technological capabilities—even though Swedish engineers helped construct it. The Swedes left a controversial surprise known as the "Papsts Rache" (Pope's Revenge): a crucifix appears when the sun hits the dome, defying the GDR's attempt to rid the city of religious symbols. An elevator whisks tourists up to a magnificent view from the spherical node 203m above the city. A cafe one floor up serves international meals for €1117. *(☎ 242 3333. Open daily Mar.-Oct. 9am-11pm; Nov.-Feb. 10am-midnight. €8.50, under 16 €4.)*

**BERLINER RATHAUS (CITY HALL).** This building is called the *Rotes Rathaus* (Red City Hall) for its brick color, not for the politics of the government that used it in the GDR days. Now the seat of Berlin's municipal government, the hall is often mobbed by schoolchildren who come on field trips to watch legislation in action. *(Rathausstr. 1. Open M-F 9am-6pm. Call ☎ 90 26 25 23 for guided tours. Free.)*

**SCHEUNENVIERTEL.** Northwest of Alexanderpl. is the Scheunenviertel, once the center of Berlin's Orthodox Jewish community. Prior to WWII, Berlin didn't have ghettos; assimilated Jews lived in Western Berlin, while Orthodox Jews from Eastern Europe settled here. The district shows a few traces of Jewish life back to the 13th century but is now known mainly for its street prostitutes and touristy Indian restaurants. *(S1, 2, or 25 to Oranienburger Str. or U6 to Oranienburger Tor.)*

**NEUE SYNAGOGE.** This synagogue was used for worship until 1940, when the Nazis occupied it and used it for storage. Amazingly, the building survived *Kristallnacht* (Night of the Broken Glass)—even though the SS torched it, a local police chief managed to bluff his way past SS officers and order that the fire be extinguished. The building no longer holds services; instead, it houses small exhibits on the history of Berlin's Jews. *(Oranienburger Str. 29. ☎ 88 02 83 00. Open May-Aug. Su-M 10am-8pm, Tu-Th 10am-6pm, F 10am-5pm; Sept.-Apr. M-Th and Su 10am-6pm, F 10am-2pm. A series of security checks is required to enter. €3, students €2.)*

## OTHER SIGHTS IN MITTE

**BERTOLT-BRECHT-HAUS.** If anyone personifies Berlin's maelstrom of political and aesthetic contradictions, it is **Bertolt Brecht,** who lived and worked in this house from 1953 to 1956. "There is a reason to prefer Berlin to other cities," the playwright once said, "because it is constantly changing. What is bad today can be improved tomorrow." The **Literaturforum im Brecht-Haus** on the second floor sponsors exhibits and lectures on artistic and literary subjects. *(Chausseestr. 125. U6 to Oranienburger Tor or Zinnowitzer Str. ☎ 283 057 044. Mandatory German-language tours Tu-Sa 2 per hr., Su 1 per hr.; max. 8 people. Open Tu-W and F 10-11:30am, Th 10-11:30am and 5-6:30pm, Sa 9:30am-1:30pm, Su 11am-6pm. €3, students €1.50.)*

# CHARLOTTENBURG

Originally a separate town huddled around Friedrich I's imperial palace, Charlottenburg is now home to one of Berlin's main shopping streets, the Ku'damm. The area's sights can be expensive; budget travelers come mostly to explore the attractions near Bahnhof Zoo.

## IN RECENT NEWS

### WHO PUTS A BEAR ON A DIET?

It's a familiar story. When he was young and cute, he got all the attention—screaming fans and his likeness on Vanity Fair covers and billboards across Berlin. But then things started to slide, like they always do. No, it wasn't a DUI, and—thank god—it wasn't cocaine. No, for Knut, the first polar bear cub to survive childhood in the Berlin Zoo for three decades, it had to do with the waistline.

It all started with a troubled childhood. Abandoned by his mother on the rocks of his shelter, Knut ("kah-noot") was rescued by a zoo worker. Weak, living in an incubator, he survived due to the careful ministrations of his keeper, Thomas Doerflein. Cuddly and playful, "Cute Knut" soon became a star both at the zoo and beyond, his fame spread worldwide in magazines and on the Internet. Since his debut, Berlin Zoo attendance has doubled.

That was eight months ago. Today, though, Knut is just a little less cute. At 130 pounds, he's starting to look a little—how do we say?—full-figured. All of which has prompted the young polar bear to go South Beach. "Extras like croissants will need to be dropped," zoo veterinarian Andreas Ochs told the Associated Press.

It goes to show that, even for a polar bear, the life of a celebrity can be tough.

**AROUND BAHNHOF ZOO.** Former West Berlin centered on Bahnhof Zoo, the station that inspired U2's "Zoo TV" tour. In the surrounding area, peepshows mingle with department stores, souvenir shops and other G-rated attractions. The **Zoologischer Garten,** one of the world's largest and oldest zoos, gained international attention in early 2007 as the home of celebrity polar bear **Knut.** Now that the fuss has died down, there's more room to take in the zoo's open-air habitats, attractive landscaping, and large collection of endangered species. At the second entrance across from EuropaCenter is the famous **Elefantentor,** a pagoda of pachyderms. *(Budapester Str. 34. Open daily May-Sept. 9am-6:30pm; Mar.-Apr. 9am-5:30pm; Oct.-Feb. 9am-5pm. €11, students €8.)* Within the zoo walls but independently accessible, an **aquarium** contains insects, reptiles, and kilometers of fish tanks. *(Budapester Str. 32. Open daily 9am-6pm. €11, students €8. Combo ticket with zoo €17/13.)*

**KAISER-WILHELM-GEDÄCHTNISKIRCHE.** Nicknamed *hohler Zahn* ("the hollow tooth"), this shattered church has been left in its jagged state as a reminder of WWII. The church houses an exhibit of photos contrasting its condition before and after Allied bombings. The exterior is most impressive by night. In summer, Berlin's salesmen, street performers, and youth gather in front to hang out, hawk their wares, and play bagpipes and sitars. *(☎218 5023. www.gedaechtniskirche.com. Church open daily 9am-7pm. Exhibit open M-Sa 10am-4pm.)*

**SCHLOẞ CHARLOTTENBURG.** This monumental Baroque palace occupies a park in northern Charlottenburg and contains more 18th-century French paintings than any other location outside of France. Its pristine grounds include: the beautifully furnished **Altes Schloß;** the **Belvedere,** which houses the royal family's porcelain collection; the marbled receiving rooms of the **Neuer Flügel,** the **Neuer Pavillon,** and the palace **Mausoleum.** Leave time to stroll the **Schloßgarten** behind the main buildings, a paradise of footbridges, fountains, and small lakes. *(Bus #145 from Bahnhof Zoo to Luisenpl./Schloß Charlottenburg or U2 to Sophie-Charlotte Pl. Walk 10-15min. up Schlosstr. ☎320 92 75. Altes Schloß open Tu-F 9am-5pm, Sa-Su 10am-5pm. Mandatory German-language tour €8, students €5; upper floor €2/1.50. Neuer Flügel open Tu-F 10am-6pm, Sa-Su 11am-6pm. €5/4. Neuer Pavillon open Tu-Su 10am-5pm. €2/1.50. Mausoleum open Apr.-Oct. Tu-Su 10am-noon and 1-5pm. €1. Belvedere open Apr.-Oct. Tu-Su 10am-5pm; Nov.-Mar. Tu-F noon-4pm, Sa-Su noon-5pm. €2/1.50. Schloßgarten open Tu-Su 6am-10pm. Free. Combo ticket includes admission to everything except the Altes Schloß €9/7.)*

**OLYMPIA-STADION.** At the western edge of Charlottenburg, the Olympic Stadium is one of the major surviving examples of Nazi architecture. An overhaul for the 2006 World Cup has put a roof over the whole complex, but traces of the Nazi aesthetic remain. It was erected for the 1936 Olympic Games, in which African-American Jesse Owens won four gold medals. Hitler refused to congratulate Owens because of his skin color; now, there's a Jesse-Owens-Allee to the south of the stadium. Film buffs will recognize the complex from Leni Riefenstahl's controversial 1938 film *Olympia.* The **Glockenturm** (bell tower) provides a great lookout point and holds an exhibit on the history of German athletics. *(S5 or 7 or U2 to Olympia-Stadion. For Glockenturm, take S5 or 7 to Pichelsburg, then turn left onto Schirwindter Allee and left again onto Passenheimerstr. Open Apr.-Oct. 9am-6pm. €3.)*

# SCHÖNEBERG

South of the Ku'damm, Schöneberg is a residential district notable for its laid-back cafes and good restaurants. In spirit as well as geography, it lies between posh Charlottenburg to the west and funky Kreuzberg to the east. In **Nollendorfplatz,** the nexus of Berlin's gay community, rainbow flags drape even the military store.

**GRUNEWALD.** In summer, this 745-acre birch forest—the dog-walking turf of many a Berliner and large enough to maintain a population of wild boars—provides an ideal retreat from the heat and chaos of the city. About 1km into the forest, on the edge of the Grunewaldsee, the **Jagdschloß,** a restored 16th-century royal hunting lodge, houses paintings by Cranach, Graff, and other German artists. Also worth seeing is the **Teufelsberg,** a man-made mountain built from the rubble of wartime Berlin, carried here by railroad. The top of the mountain offers spectacular views and holds an abandoned American listening post from the Cold War. *(Am Grunewaldsee 29. U3 or 7 to Fehrbelliner Pl., or S45 or 46 to Hohenzollerndamm, then bus #115, dir.: Neuruppiner Str., to Pücklerstr. ☎813 3597. Open May 15-Oct. 15 Tu-Su 10am-5pm; Oct.-16-May 14 Sa-Su tours only at 11am, 1, 3pm. €2, students €1.50; with tour €3/2.50.)*

# KREUZBERG

Kreuzberg was once the most countercultural place in West Germany, home to artists, draft dodgers, and Turkish guest workers. Most of the punk *Hausbesetzer* (squatters) who long occupied the area are gone now, following 1980s government evictions, but the district retains its distinctive spirit. Protests are still frequent and intense; the most prominent is an annual demonstration on Labor Day that nearly always escalates into rioting. The eastern half of the district, Kreuzberg 36, is the center of Berlin's Turkish population and fashionable nightlife (around Schlesische Str.), while Kreuzberg 61 to the west is more ritzy.

**HAUS AM CHECKPOINT CHARLIE.** A strange mix of eastern sincerity and glossy western salesmanship, Checkpoint Charlie documents the history of the Berlin Wall and the dramatic escapes that once centered there. The museum showcases artwork, newspaper clippings, and photographs of the Wall, as well as a collection of contraptions used to get over, under, or through it. Out on the street, the checkpoint itself is overshadowed by staged photos of two soldiers, one American and one Russian, each symbolically keeping watch. The surrounding area is given over to vendors hawking Cold War memorabilia. *(Friedrichstr. 43-45. U6 to Kochstr. ☎253 7250; www.mauer-museum.de. Museum open daily 9am-10pm. German-language films with English subtitles 1 per 2hr. €9.50, students €5.50. Audio tour €3.)*

**ORANIENSTRAßE.** This colorful mix of bars, cafes, and stores also plays host to a more radical element: May Day parades, which start on Oranienpl. and usually becomes riotous by nightfall. Revolutionaries jostle with Turkish families, while an anarchist punk faction and a boisterous gay and lesbian population shake things up after hours. *(U1 to Kottbusser Tor or Görlitzer Bahnhof.)*

# FRIEDRICHSHAIN AND LICHTENBERG

As the alternative scene follows low rents eastward, **Friedrichshain** is becoming the new hallowed ground of the unpretentiously hip. The district hasn't been extensively renovated since reunification, so it retains old pre-fab apartments and large stretches of the Wall. **Simon-Dach-Straße** is filled with outdoor cafes and a crowd of twentysomethings. The grungier area surrounding **Rigärstraße** is one of the strongholds of Berlin's legendary alternative scene, home to squatter bars, makeshift clubs, and lounging grounds for punks.

**■ EAST SIDE GALLERY.** The longest remaining portion of the Wall, this 1.3km stretch of cement slabs and asbestos also serves as the world's largest open-air art gallery, unsupervised and open at all hours. The murals are not remnants of Cold War graffiti, but instead the efforts of an international group of artists who gathered here in 1989 to celebrate the end of the city's division. It was expected that the wall would be destroyed soon after and the paintings lost, but in 2000, with this portion still standing, many of the artists reconvened to repaint their work, covering others' scrawlings. Unfortunately, the new paintings are being rapidly eclipsed by graffiti. Keep in mind that this art project is in no way meant to show what the wall actually looked like during GDR times—only on the western side was it graf-

GERMANY

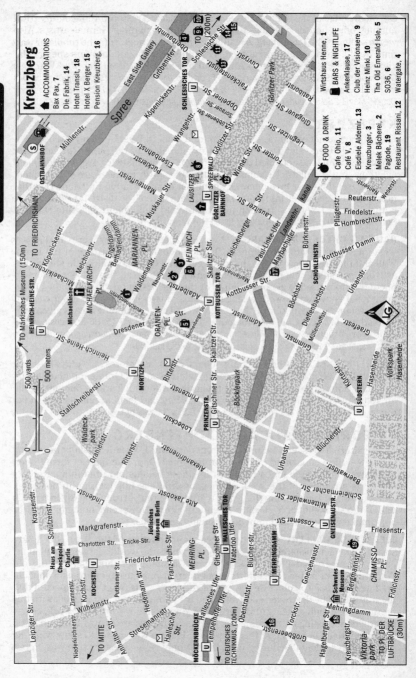

**Kreuzberg**

▲ ACCOMMODATIONS
Bax Pax, **7**
Die Fabrik, **14**
Hotel Transit, **18**
Hotel X Berger, **15**
Pension Kreuzberg, **16**

🍴 FOOD & DRINK
Cafe Ohio, **11**
Café v, **8**
Eisdiele Aldemir, **13**
Kreuzburger, **3**
Melek Bäckerei, **2**
Pagode, **19**
Restaurant Rissani, **12**

🍸 BARS & NIGHTLIFE
Ankerklause, **17**
Club der Visionaere, **9**
Heinz Minki, **10**
The Old Emerald Isle, **5**
SO36, **6**
Watergate, **4**
Wirtshaus Henne, **1**

fitied. *(Along Mühlenstr. Take U1 or 15 or S3, 5-7, 9, or 75 to Warschauer Str. or S5, 7, 9, or 75 to Ostbahnhof and walk back toward the river. www.eastsidegallery.com.)*

**FORSCHUNGS- UND GEDENKSTÄTTE NORMANNENSTRAßE.** The Lichtenberg suburb harbors the most feared building of the GDR regime: the headquarters of the **secret police** (*Staatssicherheit*, or *Stasi*). During the Cold War, the Stasi kept dossiers on six million East Germans. Spy aficionados will enjoy the exhibits of the Stasi's many varieties of bugging devices. Communist kitsch also has strong presence here, as in a showcase of busts of Lenin. *(Ruschestr. 103, Haus 1. U5 to Magdalenenstr. From the station, walk up Ruschestr. and take the 1st right into the complex of buildings. Haus #1 is straight ahead; a sign on Ruschestr. marks the turn. ☎ 553 6854; www.stasimuseum.de. Exhibits in German. Helpful English-language info booklet €3. Open M-F 11am-6pm, Sa-Su 2-6pm. €3.50, students €2.50.)*

# PRENZLAUER BERG

Everything in Prenzlauer Berg used to be something else. Brunches unfold in what were once butcher shops, furniture exhibits bring domestic grace to a former power plant, and kids cavort in breweries-turned-nightclubs. Relics of the Bezirk's past life are disappearing, but cafe owners know shabby chic when they see it—plenty of cabbage ads and mismatched sofas remain, and old graffiti remains on Prenzlauer Berg's increasingly trendy buildings. Now reputed to have the highest birth rate in Europe, Prenzlauer Berg is perhaps most striking for—no joke—the sheer number of fashionably dressed babies swarming its parks and sidewalks.

**DOKUMENTATIONSZENTRUM BERLINER MAUER.** Nowhere else is the full structure of the Wall—two concrete barriers separated by the open **Todesstreife** (death strip)—preserved as it is here. The center assembles film clips, historic photos, and sound bites from the Wall's history in order to display it as authentically as possible. Ascend the spiral staircases for the full, desolate effect. *(Bernauer Str. 111. ☎ 464 1030; www.berliner-mauer-dokumentationszentrum.de. U8 to Bernauer Str. Open Tu-Su Apr.-Oct. 10am-6pm; Nov.-Mar. 10am-5pm. Free.)*

**KOLLWITZPLATZ.** A triangle of greenery at the nexus of Prenzlauer Berg's cafe scene, Kollwitzpl. centers on a statue of artist **Käthe Kollwitz**. Locals have painted and repainted the statue time and again in acts of affectionate vandalism, once with pink polka-dots. *(U2 to Senefelderpl. Kollwitzstr. forks right off Schönhauser Allee and runs along one side of Kollwitzpl.)*

**JÜDISCHER FRIEDHOF.** Prenzlauer Berg was once one of the major centers of Jewish Berlin, especially during the 19th and early 20th centuries. In the ivy-covered **Jewish cemetery** on Schönhauser Allee are the graves of composer Giacomo Meyerbeer and painter Max Liebermann. *(Open M-Th 8am-4pm, F 8am-1pm. Closed Jewish holidays. Men must cover their heads before entering.)* Nearby stands the **Synagoge Rykestraße,** Rykestr. 53, one of Berlin's loveliest, spared on *Kristallnacht* thanks to its inconspicuous courtyard location. *(Under construction as of August 2007.)*

# 🏛 MUSEUMS

Berlin is one of the world's great museum cities, with over 170 museums that include collections from every epoch in world history. The *Berlin Programm* (€1.60) lists them all.

## SMB MUSEUMS

**Staatliche Museen zu Berlin (SMB)** runs over 20 museums in four major areas of Berlin—the **Museumsinsel, Tiergarten-Kulturforum, Charlottenburg,** and **Dahlem**—and elsewhere in Mitte and the Tiergarten. All museums sell single-admission tickets (€8, students €4) and the three-day card (Drei-Tage-Karte; €15, students €7).

Admission is free the first Sunday of every month and on Thursdays after 6pm. Unless otherwise noted, all SMB museums are open Tuesday through Sunday 10am-6pm and Thursday 10am-10pm. All offer free English-language audio tours.

## MUSEUMSINSEL (MUSEUM ISLAND)

Germany's greatest cultural treasures reside in five separate museums, separated from the rest of Mitte by two arms of the Spree. The **Neues Museum** is undergoing renovation and scheduled to reopen in late 2008. (S3, 5, 7, 9, or 75 to Hackescher Markt or bus #100 to Lustgarten. ☎ 20 90 55 55.)

■ **PERGAMONMUSEUM.** One of the great ancient history museums, displaying almost an entire ancient city reconstructed in Berlin. Pergamonmuseum is named for the Turkish city from which the enormous **Altar of Zeus** (180 BC) was taken. The collection of artifacts from the ancient Near East includes the colossal blue **Ishtar Gate of Babylon** (575 BC) and the Roman **Market Gate of Miletus**. *(Bodestr. 1-3. ☎ 20 90 55 77. €10, students €5.)*

**ALTE NATIONALGALERIE (OLD NATIONAL GALLERY).** This museum of 19th-century art reopened after extensive renovations. The gallery presents everything from German Realism to French Impressionism; Manet, Monet, Degas, and Renoir are just a few names in an all-star cast. Enjoy a drink at the outdoor Sage Bar under the columns overlooking the water. *(Lustgarten. ☎ 20 90 58 01.)*

**ALTES MUSEUM.** At the far end of the Lustgarten, the Altes Museum's galleries are surprisingly untouristed. Unless you're craving ancient Greco-Roman (especially Etruscan) decorative art, go to the Pergamon first. *(Lustgarten. ☎ 266 36 60.)*

**BODEMUSEUM.** Reopened in October 2006 after major renovation, the Bodemuseum displays Byzantine art, medieval sculptures, and one of the world's largest collections of ancient coins *(Bodestr. 1-3. ☎ 20 90 56 01.)*

## TIERGARTEN-KULTURFORUM

The Tiergarten-Kulturforum, a complex of museums at the eastern end of the Tiergarten near the Staatsbibliothek and Potsdamer Pl., is a good place to find fine-arts students and local aficionados. *(Take S1, 2, or 25, or U2 to Potsdamer Pl. Look for Matthäikirchpl. on the right. ☎ 20 90 55 55.)*

■ **GEMÄLDEGALERIE.** One of Germany's best-known museums, the Gemäldegalerie displays over 1000 masterpieces by Dutch, Flemish, German, and Italian masters from the 13th to 18th centuries, including works by Botticelli, Dürer, Raphael, Rembrandt, Titian, and Vermeer. *(Stauffenbergstr. 40. ☎ 266 2951. Open Tu, W-Su 10am-6pm, Th 10am-10pm. €8, students €4, Tu 6-10pm free.)*

■ **HAMBURGER BAHNHOF/MUSEUM FÜR GEGENWART.** North of the Tiergarten, Berlin's foremost contemporary art collection occupies 10,000 sq. m of this former train station. Its artist roster includes Beuys, Kiefer, and Warhol. The museum hosts outrageous sculptures and attention-grabbing temporary exhibits. *(Invalidenstr. 50-51. S3, 5, 7, 9, or 75 to Hauptbahnhof, or U6 to Zinnowitzer Str. ☎ 39 78 34 11. Open Tu-F 10am-6pm, Sa 11am-8pm, Su 11am-6pm. €8, students €4, Th 2-6pm free.)*

**NEUE NATIONALGALERIE.** Designed by Mies van der Rohe, this sleek building hosts temporary exhibits of modern art and the occasional work from its permanent collection—which includes Beckmann, Kirchner, Munch, and Warhol. Check www.smb.museum to see current displays. *(Potsdamer Str. 50, past the Kulturforum. ☎ 266 2662. Open Tu-W 10am-6pm, Th 10am-10pm, F-Su 10am-8pm. €10-12, students €5-6.)*

## CHARLOTTENBURG

Many excellent museums surround **Schloß Charlottenburg.** Take bus #145 from Bahnhof Zoo to Luisenpl./Schloß Charlottenburg, or take U2 to Sophie-Charlotte-Pl. and walk 10-15min. up the tree-lined Schloßstr.

**MUSEUM BERGGRUEN.** Subtitled "Picasso and His Time," the three-story Museum Berggruen explores the work of the groundbreaking 20th-century artist and the movements that sprung up around him. Picasso's influences, which include African masks and late paintings by Matisse, occupy the bottom floor. On the top floor are the elongated sculptures of Giacometti and paintings by Klee. *(Schlosstr. 1. ☎32 69 58 11. Open Tu-Su 10am-6pm. €6, students €3.)*

## DAHLEM

■**ETHNOLOGISCHES MUSEUM.** It's worth the trek to Dahlem to see the ancient Central American stonework and boats from the South Pacific, among many other stunning exhibits displayed in the **Ethnologisches Museum.** In the same building, the smaller Museum für Indische Kunst (Museum of Indian Art) has ornate shrines and murals. The Museum für Ostasiatisches Kunst (Museum of East Asian Art) houses extremely long tapestries. *(U3 to Dahlem-Dorf; follow the "Museen" signs. ☎830 1438. Open Tu-F 10am-6pm, Sa-Su 11am-6pm. Th 2-6pm free. 3-day ticket €15.)*

# INDEPENDENT (NON-SMB) MUSEUMS

**JÜDISCHES MUSEUM BERLIN.** Daniel Libeskind designed this museum so that no facing walls run parallel. Jagged hallways end in windows overlooking "the void." Wander through the labyrinthine **Garden of Exile** or shut yourself in the **Holocaust Tower,** a room nearly devoid of light and sound. End with the incredibly exhaustive exhibit on the last millennium of German Jewish history. *(Lindenstr. 9-14. U6 to Kochstr., or U1, 6, or 15 to Hallesches Tor. ☎308 785 681; www.jmberlin.de. Open M 10am-10pm, Tu-Su 10am-8pm. €5, students €2.50. Special exhibits €4.)*

**FILMMUSEUM BERLIN.** This interactive new museum chronicles German film's development, with a focus on older films and multimedia exhibits devoted to superstars including Leni Riefenstahl and Marlene Dietrich. *(Potsdamer Str. 2, 3rd and 4th fl. of the Sony Center. S1, 2, 25 or U2 to Potsdamer Pl. ☎300 9030; www.filmmuseum-berlin.de. Open Tu-W and F-Su 10am-6pm, Th 10am-8pm. €6, students €4, children €2.50.)*

**DEUTSCHE GUGGENHEIM BERLIN.** In a renovated building across from the Deutsche Staatsbibliothek, the Deutsche Bank and the Guggenheim Foundation's joint venture is relatively small, featuring exhibits on modern and contemporary art. *(Unter den Linden 13-15. S1, 2, or 25 to Unter den Linden. ☎202 0930; www.deutsche-guggenheim.de. Open M-W and F-Su 11am-8pm, Th 11am-10pm. €4, students €3, M free.)*

**KUNST-WERKE BERLIN.** Under the direction of Mitte art luminary Klaus Biesenbach, this former margarine factory houses artists' studios, rotating modern exhibits, and a garden cafe in a glass cube. *(Auguststr. 69. U6 to Oranienburger Tor. ☎243 4590; www.kw-berlin.de. Open Tu-W and F-Su noon-7pm, Th noon-9pm. €6, students €4.)*

**BAUHAUS-ARCHIV MUSEUM FÜR GESTALTUNG.** Designed by Walter Gropius, founder of the Bauhaus design movement, this museum exhibits furniture, sculptures, and paintings from the Bauhaus workshop. *(Klingelhöferstr. 14. Bus #100, 187, 200, or 341 to Nordische Botschaften/Adenauer-Stiftg. or U1, 2, 3, or 4 to Nollendorf Platz. ☎254 0020. Open M and W-Su 10am-5pm. M and Sa-Su €7, students €4; W-F €6/3.)*

**TOPOGRAPHIE DES TERRORS.** On the grounds of the former Gestapo headquarters, outdoor exhibits with documents, photographs, and text-heavy captions detail the Nazis' rise to power and their wartime atrocities. Along the its perimeter stands a remaining 200m of the Berlin Wall. Part of the exhibit is in German only. *(Behind the Martin-Gropius-Bau, at the corner of Niederkirchnerstr. and Wilhelmstr. S1 or 2, or U2 to Potsdamer Pl. ☎ 25 48 67 03. Open daily May-Sept. 10am-8pm; Oct.-Apr. 10am-dark. Free.)*

# 🎵 ENTERTAINMENT

Berlin has one of the world's most vibrant cultural scenes. Numerous festivals celebrating everything from Chinese film to West African music enrich the regular offerings; posters advertising special events plaster the city well in advance. Despite recent cutbacks, the city still generously subsidizes its art scene, and tickets are usually reasonably priced. Most theaters and concert halls offer up to 50% off for students who buy at the *Abendkasse* (evening box office), which generally opens 1hr. before shows. Other ticket outlets charge 15-18% commissions and do not offer student discounts. The **KaDeWe** (p. 416) has a ticket counter. (☎217 7754. Open M-F 10am-8pm, Sa 10am-4pm.) Theaters generally accept credit cards, but many ticket outlets do not. Most theaters and operas close from mid-July to late August. The monthly pamphlets *Konzerte und Theater in Berlin und Brandenburg* (free) and *Berlin Programm* (€1.75) list concerts, film, and theater info, as do the biweekly *030*, *Kultur!news*, *Tip*, and *Zitty*.

## CONCERTS, DANCE, AND OPERA

Berlin reaches its musical zenith in September, during the fabulous **Berliner Festwochen,** which draws the world's best orchestras and soloists. The **Berliner Jazztage** in November features top jazz musicians. For tickets (which sell out months ahead) and more info for both festivals, call **Berliner Festspiele** (☎25 48 90; www.berlinerfestspiele.de). In mid-July, the **Bachtage** feature an intense week of classical music, while every Saturday night in August the **Sommer Festspiele** turns the Ku'damm into a multi-faceted concert hall with folk, punk, and steel-drum groups competing for attention.

The programs for many theaters and opera houses are listed on huge posters in U-Bahn stations. Tickets for the *Philharmonie* and the *Oper* are nearly impossible to get without writing months in advance; you can try standing outside before performances with a small sign saying *"Suche Karte"* (seeking ticket)—people often try to sell tickets at the last moment, usually at outrageous prices.

🎭 **Berliner Philharmoniker,** Herbert Von Karajanstr. 1 (☎25 48 81 32; www.berlin-philharmonic.com). Take S1, 2, or 25 or U2 to Potsdamer Pl. It may look bizarre, but this yellow building, designed by Scharoun in 1963, is acoustically perfect: every audience member hears the music exactly as it is meant to sound. The Berliner Philharmoniker, led by Sir Simon Rattle, is one of the world's finest orchestras. It is practically impossible to get a seat; check 1hr. before concert time, write at least 8 weeks ahead, or check their website. Open mid-Sept. to mid-June. Box office open M-F 3-6pm, Sa-Su 11am-2pm. Standing room from €7, seats from €13. AmEx/MC/V.

**Konzerthaus (Schauspielhaus am Gendarmenmarkt),** Gendarmenmarkt 2 (☎20 30 90; www.konzerthaus.de). U2 or 6 to Stadtmitte. Berlin Symphony's opulent home, with 3 concert spaces. Last-minute tickets are somewhat easier to come by. Performances Sept. to mid-July. Box office open M-Sa 11am-7pm, Su noon-4pm. AmEx/MC/V.

**Deutsche Oper Berlin,** Bismarckstr. 35 (☎0700 67 37 23 75 46; www.deutscheoper-berlin.de). U2 to Deutsche Oper. Berlin's youngest opera, featuring newly commissioned works as well as German and Italian classics. Open Sept.-June. Box office open M-Sa 11am until 1hr. before performance, Su 10am-2pm. ½-price evening tickets available 1hr. before performances. €10-115, students €7.50-€87. AmEx/V.

**Deutsche Staatsoper,** Unter den Linden 7 (☎20 35 45 55; www.staatsoper-berlin.de). U6 to Französische Str., or bus #100, 157, or 348 to Deutsche Staatsoper. East Berlin's top opera company, led by Daniel Barenboim. A big budget yields grandiose productions. Occasional ballet and classical music performances. Open Sept. to mid-July. Box office open M-F 11am-7pm, Sa-Su 2-7pm, and 1hr. before shows. €5-120, 1hr. before shows students under 30 €12 and ½-price on €7-43 seats. AmEx/MC/V.

**Komische Oper,** Behrenstr. 55-57 (☎47 99 74 00; www.komische-oper-berlin.de). U6 to Französische Str., or S1, 2, 25 to Unter den Linden. Started in 1947 by zany post-war director Walter Felsenstein and now under the direction of Andreas Homoki, the comic opera is known for fresh versions of the classics, often sung in German to make them more easily accessible. Program ranges from Mozart to Gilbert and Sullivan. Box office open M-Sa 11am-7pm, Su 1-4pm. €8-93. 25% student discounts almost always available 1hr. before performances. AmEx/MC/V.

## THEATER

Theater listings can be found on the yellow and blue posters in most U-Bahn stations and in the monthly pamphlets listed above. In addition to the world's best German-language theater, Berlin also has a strong English-language scene; look for listings in *Zitty* or *Tip* that say *"in englischer Sprache"* (in English). A number of privately run companies called Off-Theaters also occasionally feature English-language plays. As with concert halls, virtually all theaters are closed in July and August, indicated by the words *Theaterferien* or *Sommerpause.*

**Deutsches Theater,** Schumannstr. 13A (☎28 44 12 25; www.deutsches-theater.berlin.net). U6 or S1, 2, 5, 7, 9, 25, or 75 to Friedrichstr. Even former West Berliners admits it: the one-time East German state theater is Germany's best. Made great by Max Reinhardt 100 years ago, it now produces innovative takes on classics and newer works from Büchner to Ibsen. The **Kammerspiel** (☎28 44 12 26) stages smaller, provocative productions. Box office for both open M-Sa 11am-6:30pm, Su 3-6:30pm. Tickets for Deutsches Theater €5-43, for Kammerspiel €12-30; students €8. AmEx/MC/V.

**HAU,** Hallesches Ufer 32 (☎25 90 04 27; www.hebbel-theater.de). U1, 6, or 15 to Hallesches Tor. The most avant of Berlin's avant-garde theaters, this consortium of 3 theaters on the Landwehrkanal draws innovative talent from the world over. Committed to original-language production, it brings in the original playwrights to work with actors. Order tickets from the box office (open daily noon-7pm) on Hallesches Ufer, by phone, or show up 1hr. before performances. €10-15, students €6. AmEx/MC/V.

**Volksbühne,** Rosa-Luxembourg-Pl (☎247 6772; www.volksbuehne-berlin.de). U2 to Rosa-Luxembourg-Pl. The "people's stage," a major GDR landmark, now hosts cutting-edge productions by international theater companies and resident director Frank Castorf. Also home to the Roter and Grüner Salons, music venues with palpable Ostalgie. Try to get the ushers to allow you into the classically East Berlin actors' *Kantine* after the show. Box office open daily noon-6pm. €10-30, students €5-15. AmEx/MC/V.

**English Theater Berlin,** Fidicinstr. 40 (☎691 1211; www.thefriends.de). U6 Platz der Luftbrücke. Smaller theater formerly known as The Friends of Italian Opera is hub of Berlin's lively English-language theater scene. Program includes a number of staged readings and workshop performances. €6-15. Cash only.

## FILM

On any given night you can choose from over 150 different films. O.F. next to a movie listing means original version; O.m.U. means original version with German subtitles. Mondays through Wednesdays are *Kinotage* days at most theaters, with reduced prices. In summer, *Freiluftkino* (open-air cinemas) show movies in the city's parks; winter brings the international **Berlinale** film festival (Feb. 7-17, 2008).

**Arsenal,** in the Filmhaus, Potsdamer Pl. (☎26 95 51 00). U2 or S1, 2, or 25 to Potsdamer Pl. Run by the Berlinale's founders, Arsenal showcases an eccentric program of cult favorites, indie films, and international classics. Frequent appearances by guest directors make the theater popular with Berlin filmmakers. €7, students €5.

**Filmkunsthaus Babylon,** Rosa-Luxemburg-Str. 30 (☎242 5969; www.babylonberlin.de). U2 to Rosa-Luxemburg-Pl. Shows classics like *Goodfellas* in the main theater and international art films in the **Studiokino** (entrance on Hirtenstr.). Main theater M €4.50, Tu-W €5.50, Th-Su €6.50. Studiokino €5.50.

**Odeon,** Hauptstr. 116 (☎78 70 40 19; www.yorck.de). U4 to Innsbrucker Pl. One of Berlin's 1st English-language theaters, Odeon shows mainstream American and British flicks, generally with German subtitles. Th-Su €7.50, students €7; Tu-W €6, M €5.

# 📷 SHOPPING

When West Berlin was a lonely outpost in the Eastern Bloc's consumer wilderness, its residents had no choice but to buy local. Consequently, the city amassed a mind-boggling array of things for sale. The high temple of consumerism is the dazzling, pricey seven-story **KaDeWe department store** on Wittenbergpl. at Tauentzienstr. 21-24, continental Europe's largest department store. The name is a German abbreviation of *Kaufhaus des Westens* (Department Store of the West); for the tens of thousands of product-starved East Germans who flooded Berlin in the days after the Berlin Wall's fall, KaDeWe was the West. (☎212 10. Open M-F 10am-8pm, Sa 9:30am-8pm.) The sidewalks of the 3-kilometer-long **Kurfürstendamm,** near Bahnhof Zoo, have at least one big store from every mega-chain you can name. Upscale shopping also lines Friedrichstr. south of Unter den Linden. Near Hackescher Markt and Alte Schönhauser Str., the art galleries of Mitte give way to clothing galleries with similar price tags. The flea market on Str. des 17. Juni has a better selection but higher prices than other markets. (Take S5, 7, 9, or 75 to Tiergarten. Open Sa-Su 11am-5pm.) **Winterfeldtplatz,** near Nollendorfpl., overflows with food, flowers, and people crooning Bob Dylan tunes over acoustic guitars. (Open W and Sa 8am-1pm.) On Sundays a massive second-hand market takes over Prenzlauer Berg's **Mauerpark,** with everything from food to furniture. Other major markets are around Ostbahnhof in Friedrichshain near Erich-Steinfurth-Str. (S3, 5, 7, 9, or 75 to Ostbahnhof; open Sa 9am-3pm, Su 10am-5pm), on **Am Weidendamm** in Mitte (S-Bahn or U6 to Friedrichstr; open Sa-Su 11am-5pm), and on **John-F.-Kennedy-Pl.** in Schöneberg (U4 to Rathaus Schöneberg; open F-Su 8am-4pm).

# 🎵 NIGHTLIFE

Berlin's nightlife is absolute madness. Bars typically open around 6pm and get going around midnight, just as clubs begin opening their doors. The bar scene winds down anywhere between 1 and 6am; meanwhile, clubs fill up and don't empty until well after dawn, when they pass the baton to after-parties and 24hr. cafes. Between 1 and 4am, take advantage of the **night buses** and **U-Bahn** 9 and 12, which run all night on Friday and Saturday. Info about bands and dance venues can be found in the pamphlets *Tip* (€2.50) and *Zitty* (€2.30), available at newsstands, or in *030* (free), distributed in bars, cafes, and hostels.

Berlin's most touristed bar scene sprawls down pricey, packed **Hackescher Markt** and **Oranienburger Straße** in Mitte. Prices fall only slightly around yuppie **Kollwitzplatz** and **Kastanienallee** in Prenzlauer Berg, but areas around Schönhauser Allee and **Danziger Straße** still harbor a somewhat edgier scene. The most serious clubbing takes place near the river in Friedrichshain, with a growing presence on the Kreuzberg side of the river. Bars line Simon-Dach-Straße, **Gabriel-Max-Straße,** and **Schlesiche Straße.** Businessmen and middle-aged tourists drink at bars along the Ku'damm. Gay nightlife centers on Nollendorfplatz, in the west, and lesbian nightlife has its stronghold in Kreuzberg.

# BARS AND CLUBS

## MITTE

**Weekend,** Alexanderpl. 5 (www.week-end-berlin.de), on the 12th fl. of the building with the neon "Sharp" sign. A touch on the posh side, with a fashionable crowd, Weekend is a must-see for its panoramic rooftop terrace. The music is danceable and the DJs prominent, but the real attraction here is watching the sun rise over the block-housing of East Berlin. Wheelchair-accessible. Cover €6-10. Open Th-Sa 11pm-late. Cash only.

**Cafe Moskau,** Karl-Marx-Allee 34. U5 to Schillingstr. The varied spaces tucked into this steel-and-glass GDR edifice play host to events from hip-hop and electronic nights to fashion shows. Also home to the too-cool-for-a-name bar known by its address, KMA 36. Beer €3. Su gay night. Cover €7-13. Open Sa 11pm-6am, Su 10pm-5am. Cash only.

**2BE-Club,** Ziegelstr. 23 (☎89 06 84 10; www.2be-club.de). U6 to Oranienburger Tor. Hip-hop and occasional reggae in a huge space with 2 dance floors and a tented courtyard; crowd is young and energetic. Cover €7.50-8; Sa until midnight women free. Open F-Sa and sometimes W 11pm-late. Cash only.

**Kaffee Burger,** Torstr. 60 (☎28 04 64 95; www.kaffeeburger.de). U2 to Rosa-Luxemburg-Pl. A true Berlin institution, this worn-in and comfortable bar/club has cheap drinks and a tinge of GDR-era retro. Nightly parties, especially bi-monthly "Russian Disco" night. Th live bands 10pm. Cover Su-Th €1, F-Sa €2-6. Open Su-Th 7pm-late, F 8pm-late, Sa 9pm-late. Cash only.

**Tresor,** Köpernickerstr. 59-71 (www.tresor-club.de). U8 to Heinrich-Heine-Str. A renovated power plant is home to what was once the most renowned techno club in Berlin. No longer draws the old-school Berlin crowd it once did, but this imposing, starkly industrial space is for people very serious about their electronic music. Cover €10. Open F-Sa 11pm-late. Cash only.

**Z-bar,** Bergstr. 2 (☎28 38 91 21; www.z-bar.de). U8 to Rosenthaler Pl. This intimate, artsy bar with flickering candlelight hosts a packed schedule of concerts, films, and literary readings. Occasional cover €2-6. Open daily 6pm-late. Cash only.

**White Trash Fast Food,** Schönhauser Allee 6-7 (www.whitetrashfastfood.com). U2 to Senefelderpl. Liquor-and-irony-drenched bastion of Anglophone expats is brash, loud, and hard-partying. Multiple floors host nightly DJs, frequent live bands, and a restaurant serving American food. Occasional "face control" at the door, and occasional cover €3-8. Open daily 4pm-late. Cash only.

**Strandbar Mitte,** Monbijoustr. 3 (☎28 38 55 88). S3, 5, 7, 9, or 75 to Hackescher Markt. Enter from Oranienburgerstr. through the center of Monbijoupark. This canal-side beach bar, dotted with beach chairs and potted palm trees, has a great view of the illuminated Museumsinsel and the passing S-Bahn. Mainstream crowd and steep drink prices. Beer €3.50. Mixed drinks €4-7. Open in summer daily 10am-late. Cash only.

**Tacheles,** Oranienburger Str. 54-56 (☎282 6185; www.tacheles.de). U6 to Oranienburger Tor, S1, 2, or 25 to Oranienburger Str., or night buses N6 or 84. Once a massive squat housed in a bombed-out department store, this complex has definitely lost its edge. What remains is an outdoor space littered with scrap-metal artwork and a labyrinth of rooms leading to art galleries, movie theaters, and balcony bars. Opening times for the theater and galleries vary, as do rave dates; check website. **Cafe Zapata** open daily noon-4am. **Offen Bar Konzept** on the top floor open 8pm-late. Cash only.

**b-flat,** Rosenthaler Str. 13 (☎28 38 68 35, tickets 283 3123; www.b-flat-berlin.de). U8 to Weinmeister, or S3, 5, 7, 9, or 75 to Hackescher Markt. Nightly live jazz and acoustic. Cover M-Tu, Th-Su €8-12. Open daily 8pm-late. Cash only.

GERMANY

## I EAT BEATS FOR BREAKFAST

So proclaims the T-shirt of the boy bopping arhythmically in front of me at Maria am Bahnhof, a hot spot in the Friedrichshain club scene. Yes, I am at a techno concert—my first—and am trying to learn the particularities of dancing to something that has neither lyrics nor a recognizable melody (not that I can dance under any circumstances, to be fair).

More difficult, even, than learning the nuances of moving to electronic music is knowing what its various sub-categories even mean. As I researched Berlin, I would frequently learn that a club played, say, "drum 'n' bass" on Fridays and "electro" on Saturdays. I would give a confident nod and record this information while secretly having no idea what these terms meant, my own taste being generally confined to faux-obscure indie pop. So for those who are looking to test the waters of Berlin nightlife but are equally clueless about its fiendish electronic music culture, I can offer some info, if not some dance moves:

**Drum 'n' Bass**—Also called "dnb," this form is mostly a product of British rave culture. The quick drum beats and complex bass lines are the most prominent sonic elements. Influenced by hip-hop, it is usually mid-tempo and can involve samples or synthesized bass lines.

## TIERGARTEN

**Schleusenkrug,** Müller-Breslau-Str./Unterschleuse (☎313 9909; www.schleusenkrug.de). U2 to Ernst-Reuter-Platz. Berlin's most scenic beer garden, strung with colored overhead lights, sits canalside. Also has an indoor bar with a nautical retro look. Full food menu. Open daily 10am-late. Cash only.

## CHARLOTTENBURG (SAVIGNYPLATZ)

**Quasimodo,** Kantstr. 12A (www.quasimodo.de). U2 or S5, 7, 9, or 75 to Zoologischer Garten. Beneath a cafe, this cozy venue showcases mostly jazz with occasional R&B and soul. Concert tickets available from 5pm at the cafe upstairs or through the Kant-Kasse ticket service (☎313 4554). Concerts 11pm. Cover €8-20. Call or check website for schedules. Reserve ahead for cheaper tickets. Open daily noon-late. Cash only.

**A-Trane,** Bleibtreustr. 1 (☎313 2550; www.a-trane.de). S5, 7, 9, or 75 to Savignypl. Jazz fans are here for the music, not to chat. Cover €7-15, students with ID €5-13. Open daily 9pm-late. Closed some Su. Cash only.

## SCHÖNEBERG

**Slumberland,** Goltzstr. 24 (☎216 5349). U1, 2, 3, or 4, to Nollendorfpl. Quirky, pink space with African art, palm trees, a sand floor and tantalizing mixed drinks encourages jamming to the reggae music. Open Su-F 6pm-late, Sa 11am-late. Cash only.

**Mister Hu,** Goltzstr. 39 (☎217 2111; www.misterhu-berlin.de). U1, 2, 3, or 4 to Nollendorfpl. This bar made of rocky tiles serves creative drinks that the relaxed crowd enjoys indoor or out on the sidewalk patio. Happy hour M-Sa 5-8pm, Su 6pm-2am; mixed drinks €4.50. Open Su-Th 6pm-2am, F-Sa 6pm-4am. Cash only.

## KREUZBERG

🖾 **Club der Visionaere,** Am Flutgraben 1 (☎69 51 89 44; www.clubdervisionaere.de). U1 to Schlesisches Tor or night bus #N65 to Heckmannufer. From the many languages drifting through the air to the people settled on ground-cushions, canal-side Club der Visionaere gives off a backpacker vibe. Drift on a raft attached to the terrace. DJ spins house inside. Beer €3. Open M-F 4pm-late, Sa-Su noon-late. Cash only.

**Watergate,** Falckensteinstr. 49 (☎61 28 03 96; www.water-gate.de). U1 to Schlesisches Tor. Hugging the river, this stylish 2 fl. club has windows opening onto the water with spectacular views of the Oberbaumbrücke. Features different DJs on each floor, mostly spinning electronic and house. Often packed, with a energetic, sophisticated crowd. €6-10 cover. Open W, F-Sa 11pm-late, occasionally open Tu and Th. Cash only.

**SO36,** Oranienstr. 190 (☎ 61 40 13 06; www.SO36.de). U1 to Görlitzer Bahnhof or night bus #N29 to Heinrichpl. A staple of Berlin's club scene, with a punk feel. Named for the local postal code, the club has a dark, massive dance floor and a stage for concerts (€7-25). Diverse array of music. Cover €4-8. Cash only.

**Heinz Minki,** Vor dem Schlesischen Tor 3 (☎ 695 337 66; www.heinzminki.de). U1 to Schlesisches Tor or night bus #N65 to Heckmannufer. A beer garden sandwiched between two canals. Patrons pound down beers (0.5L €3.10) at long tables under hanging colored lights, surrounded by trees and shrubs. Gourmet pizza €2.60. Open daily in summer noon-late; in winter reduced hours. Cash only.

**Ankerklause,** Kottbusser Damm 104 (☎ 693 5649; www.ankerlause.de). U1 or 8 or night bus #N8 to Kottbusser Tor. Patrons spill out onto the curb or sip their beers in diner-style booths at this canal-side bar. Features an impressive jukebox collection of classic rock and indie. Terrace overlooking the water provides a mellow alternative to the dance floor. 0.5L Pilsner €3. Th parties; cover €2. Open 9am-late. Cash only.

**The Old Emerald Isle,** Erkelenzdamm 49 (☎ 615 6917; www.old-emerald-isle.de). U1 or 8 to Kottbusser Tor. A continental rarity: an Irish pub that is in no way a tourist trap. Authentic pub food, British football on TV, draught Guinness, and Th bilingual quiz night draw an expat crowd. Cozy in winter. Open S-Th noon-2am, F-Sa noon-4am. Cash only.

## FRIEDRICHSHAIN

**Rosi's,** Revaler Str. 29 (www.rosis-berlin.de). U/S to Warshauerstr. An unpretentious warren of bars, clubs, and outdoor lounges strung across a former industrial space. Art markets and exhibitions round out the roster of DJs and live bands. There's something for everyone, from pubbers to clubbers to people who just want to lie around on couches. Nightly music runs the gamut from indie to drum-and-bass to reggae. Open Th-Sa 8pm-late, Su 2pm-late. Occasional daytime events. Cash only.

**Habermeyer,** Gartnerstr. 6 (☎ 29 77 18 87; www.habermeyer-bar.de). U5 to Samariterstr. Quintessential Friedrichshain DJ bar with retro stylings and soft red lighting to complement the nostalgic New Wave tunes favored by the DJ. Mixed drinks €5.40-6.80. Open daily 7pm-late. Cash only.

**Matrix,** Warschauer Pl. 18 (☎ 29 36 99 90; www.matrixclub.de). U1 or S3, 5, 7, 9, or 75 to Warschauer Str. The pounding sound of the bass from underneath the station isn't only in your head—4 dance floors and multiple bars extend through the caverns under the tracks. Draws a young, mainstream crowd for mixed drinks (€4.50-7.50) by the pool in the VIP lounge. Cover €3-6. 18+; bring ID. Open M-Sa 10pm-late. Cash only.

**Electro** - Shorthand for "electro funk." This brand of electronic hip-hop, sometimes traced all the way back to German stalwarts Kraftwerk, relies heavily on drum machines, synthetic bass lines, and elaborate sonic reverberations. It often takes on futuristic themes. Lyrics are digitially remastered in order to make the voices sound mechanical.

**House** - A form of electronic dance music in which the 4/4 beat is heavily accentuated by the drum. It tends to have a Latin influence and often tries to approximate the experience of live music, sampling everything from pop to jazz. Although the drum accents vary in their placement, the uptempo beat structure stays relatively consistent.

**Techno** - Techno employs computerized sequences that layer different rhythms and syncopations. Generally more melodic than its counterparts, it tends to use exclusively inorganic sounds.

**Trance** - Using the high degree of repetition common to melodic song structures, trance often builds up a steady crescendo using recurring synthesizer phrases. A bass drum catches the down beats while minor scales add variety. Occasionally, though not often, vocal layers are added to the mix.

*—Amelia Atlas*

**Astro-Bar,** Simon-Dach-Str. 40. DJ bar dripping with retro kitsch, from the plastic robots lining the bar to the 70s-futuristic control panel collage in the back room. DJs spin anything from "60s wildbunch" to "bubblegum and Tiki sounds." Mixed drinks €4.50-5.50. Open daily 6pm-late. Cash only.

## PRENZLAUER BERG

**Intersoup,** Schliemannstr. 31 (☎23 27 30 45; www.intersoup.de). U2 to Eberswalder Str. This bar eschews big-name drink brands and popular music in favor of worn 70s furniture, soup specials (€4.50-5), and retro floral wallpaper. Downstairs, the small club **Undersoup** has live music (most W and Sa), karaoke Th, films, and even puppet theater (M-Tu). DJs most nights. Club cover max. €3. Open daily 4pm-late. Cash only.

**Morgenrot,** Kastanienallee 85. U2 to Eberswalder Str. A last outpost of punk spirit on increasingly upscale Kastanienallee. Candy-print wallpaper and funky print art are the backdrop for frosty vodka shots (€3.20). Vegetarian brunch buffet Th-Su 11am-4pm, €3-7. *Volksküche* dinner Tu €2. Open Tu-Th 10am-1am, F 10am-3am, Sa 11am-3am, Su 11am-1am. Cash only.

**Wohnzimmer,** Lettestr. 6 (☎445 5458; www.wohnzimmer.de). U2 to Eberswalder Str. The name means "living room," and they aren't kidding. With wood-beam floors and a bar that resembles an old-fashioned kitchen, you'll feel right at home as you settle into a velvet armchair for a mixed drink (€4-5). Arguably the best mojitos in town. Open daily 10am-4am. Cash only.

**8mm,** Schönhauser Allee 177B (☎40 50 06 24; www.8mmbar.com). U2 to Senefelderpl. Entrance unmarked; look for the house number. In a small, dark room with film projections on the wall, an unassuming indie crowd knocks back the hard stuff until sunrise. Open daily 9pm-late. Cash only.

**Dr. Pong,** Ebersawlder Str. 21 (www.drpong.de). Exuberant ping-pong bar run by an American expat where players in varied states of drunkenness—some good at ping-pong, some very bad—circle around a single table. DJs spin in the sparse back room. Picks up after midnight. €5 deposit for paddles. Open daily 8pm-late. Cash only.

**KulturBrauerei,** Knaackstr. 97 (☎441 9269; www.kulturbrauerei.de). U2 to Eberswalder Str. A dauntingly massive party space in an old East German brewery, housing the popular clubs **Soda** (www.soda-berlin.de), **Kesselhaus** (www.kesselhaus-berlin.de), and **nbi,** along with a beer garden, a cinema, upscale cafes, and much more. Cover and hours vary between venues. Cash only.

## TREPTOW

**Insel,** Alt-Treptow 6 (☎20 91 49 90; www.insel-berlin.net). S4, 6, 8, or 9 to Treptower Park, then bus #265 or N65 from Puschkinallee to Rathaus Treptow. Enter through the park at the corner of Alt-Treptow. Located on an island in the Spree River, the club is a winding 3-story tower crammed with gyrating bodies, multiple bars, an open-air movie theater, and riverside chairs. Depending on the night, the top 2 fl. spin hip hop, house, reggae, and ska—sometimes all at once—while a techno scene dominates the basement. Cover Th-Sa €4-6. Open F-Sa from 10 or 11pm-late, some W 7pm-late. Cafe open in summer daily 2pm-late; winter Th 2-7pm, Sa-Su 2pm-late. Cash only.

# GLBT NIGHTLIFE

Berlin is one of Europe's most gay-friendly cities. Thousands of homosexuals flocked to Berlin during the Cold War to take part in the city's left-wing activism and avoid West Germany's *Wehrpflicht* (mandatory military service). **Akazienstraße, Goltzstraße, Schöneberg,** and **Winterfeldtstraße** have mixed bars and cafes, while the **"Bermuda Triangle"** of Eisenacherstr., Fuggerstr., and Motzstr. is more exclusively gay. *Gay-yellowpages, Sergej,* and *Siegessäule* have GLBT entertainment listings. **Mann-o-Meter,** Bülowstr. 106, at the corner of Else-Lasker-Schüler-Str., provides counseling, info on gay nightlife, and long-term accommodations, in addition to **Internet** access. (☎216 8008; www.mann-o-meter.de. Open M-F 5-10pm, Sa-Su 4-10pm.) **Spinnboden-Lesbenarchiv,** Anklamer Str. 38, has hip lesbian offerings, including exhibits, films, and other cultural info. Take U8 to Bernauer Str. (☎448 5848. Open W and F 2-7pm.) The **Christopher Street Day (CSD)** parade, a 6hr. street party with ecstatic, champagne-soaked floats, draws over 250,000 participants annually in June. Nollendorfl. hosts the **Lesbisch-schwules Stadtfest** (Lesbian-Gay City Fair) the weekend before the parade.

## SCHÖNEBERG

**Hafen,** Motzstr. 19 (www.hafen-berlin.de). U1-4 to Nollendorfpl. The owners of "Harbor" created its nautical decor. A fashionable—mostly gay male—crowd in summer. 1st M of each month English-language pub quiz 10pm. Open daily 8pm-late. Cash only.

**Heile Welt,** Motzstr. 5 (☎21 91 75 07). U1, 2, 3, or 4 to Nollendorfpl. Bar-goers spill out into the street: 2 sitting rooms in the back offer a quieter ambience for conversation. Mostly gay male crowd during "prime time," mixed in the early evening and latest hours of the night. Open daily 6pm-4am, sometimes later. Cash only.

**Neues Ufer,** Hauptstr. 157. U7 to Kleistpark. With nice artwork and a mellow mood, this long-running gay cafe has become *Neues Ufer* ("the new shore"). Open daily 8am-2am.

## KREUZBERG

**Rose's,** Oranienstr. 187 (☎615 6570). U1 or U8 to Kottbusser Tor or U1 to Görlitzer Bahnhof. Marked only by a sign over the door reading "Bar." A friendly, mixed clientele packs this claustrophobic party spot at all hours. The campy dark-red interior is filled with hearts, glowing lips, furry ceilings, feathers, and glitter. Vodka tonic €5 and absolutely "no fucking cocktails." Open daily 10pm-6am. Cash only.

**SchwuZ,** Mehringdamm 61 (☎629 0880; www.schwuz.de). U6 or 7 to Mehringdamm. Enter through Sundström. An underground lair lined with pipes and disco lights. Boisterous disco features 2 small dance floors and a lounge area with its own DJ. Music varies but usually pop. Cover €5 before midnight, €6 after. Open F-Sa 11pm-late. Cash only.

**Barbie Deinhoff's,** Schlesisches Str. 18 (www.bader-deinhoff.de). U1 to Schlesisches Tor or night bus #N65 to Heckmannufer. Crowds pour onto the sidewalk at this neighborhood lesbian bar. Inside, you'll find flashy pink decor, friendly bartenders, a drink menu jokingly advertising phone sex, and rotating art exhibits. Shots €2-2.50. Open M-Th 6pm-2am, F-Sa 6pm-6am. Cash only.

## FRIEDRICHSHAIN AND PRENZLAUER BERG

🎖 **Das Haus B,** Warschauer Pl. 18 (☎296 0800; www.dashausb.de). U1 or S3, 5-7, 9, or 75 to Warschauer Str. East Berlin's most famous disco in the GDR era is still a color-saturated haven for dancers, spinning techno, Top 40, and German Schlager to a mixed crowd. Cover €2-6. Open W 10pm-5am, F-Sa 10pm-7am. Cash only.

**Cafe Amsterdam,** Gleimstr. 24 (☎448 0792). S8, 41, 42, or 85 or U2 to Schönhauser Allee. Romantic and quieter than some of its overflowing neighbors, with gilt-framed paintings and sweet, creamy cocoa. Gay-friendly. Pasta dishes (€6-10) until 11:30pm. Su brunch from 10am. Open daily 3pm-1:30am. Cash only.

# 🔲 DAYTRIPS FROM BERLIN

**KZ SACHSENHAUSEN.** Just north of Berlin, the small town of Oranienburg was the setting for the Nazi concentration camp Sachsenhausen, where more than 100,000 homosexuals, Jews, Roma (gypsies), and political opponents of the Nazi regime were killed between 1933 and 1945. **Gedenkstätte und Museum Sachsenhausen,** Str. der Nationen 22, a memorial preserving the partially restored camp remains, opened in 1961 under the GDR. Today, a series of exhibits is housed in buildings scattered across the grassy expanse of the camp grounds. Visitors can view some of the original barracks, the cell block where "dangerous" prisoners were kept in solitary confinement and tortured, and a pathology wing where Nazis experimented on inmates. The chilling remnants of **Station Z,** the extermination block, stand beside a mass grave that holds the ashes of victims. The museum complex also includes memorials to the more than 10,000 prisoners who died here between 1945 and 1950, when the camp served as a Soviet political prison. Although exhibits are informative and well organized, the layout of the place can make it difficult to navigate; the audio tour, available in English, is very helpful. To get there, take S1 (dir.: Oranienburg) to the end (45min. from Mitte), then follow the well-marked signs for "Gedenkstätte Sachsenhausen" (20min.). Bus transport on the infrequently running lines #804 and 821 to Gedenkstätte is unlikely to be faster than walking. Following the signs, turn right on Bernauer Str., left on Str. der Einheit, and right on Str. der Nationen. (☎033 012 000; www.stiftung-bg.de. Open daily Mar. 15-Oct. 14 8:30am-6pm; Oct. 15-Mar. 14 8:30am-4:30pm. Museums closed M. Free. Audio tour €3.)

**POTSDAM.** Potsdam offers visitors the kind of attractions most conspicuously absent from Berlin: royal palaces, a quaint Old Town, and manicured formal gardens. Today the capital of the state of Brandenburg, Potsdam was long the summer residence of the ruling Hollenzollern family. The Prussian royals collected palaces in every conceivable style, from mock-Tudor to Neoclassical. These buildings are scattered among lakes and parks in a bucolic landscape whose sprawling scale makes bicycling, whether alone or in a tour group, the best way to take in the sights. On the S-Bahn platform at the Potsdam *Hauptbahnhof* station, ■**Potsdam Per Pedales** rents bikes and provides maps and tours of the sights. (☎748 0057; www.potsdam-per-pedales.de. Open May-Sept. daily 9:30am-7pm. Branch at Griebnitzsee S-Bahn station.) The **tourist office,** Brandenburger Str. 3, leads 3½hr. English-language walking tours. (☎508 8838. Tours Apr.-Oct. Tu-Su at 11am €26. Open Apr.-Oct. M-F 9am-6pm, Sa-Su 9:30am-4pm; Nov.-Mar. M-F 10am-6pm, Sa-Su 10am-2pm.)

Spread over 600 acres, ■**Park Sanssouci** is Potsdam's leading tourist attraction, and it's usually packed on summer weekends. (Open daily dawn-dusk.) **Schloß Sanssouci,** the "Prussian Versailles" of Friedrich the Great, overlooks terraced gardens and custom-built artificial ruins. German-language tours leave every 20min.; the final tour at 5pm usually sells out hours earlier. The tourist office leads English-language tours of the main *Schloß* only. (☎969 4190. Open Tu-Su Apr.-Oct. 9am-5pm; Nov.-Mar. 9am-4pm. Mandatory tours €12, students €9.) Next door, the **Bildergalerie,** included in tours of Schloß Sanssouci, displays works by Caravaggio, Rubens, and van Dyck. (☎03 31 96 94 181. Open mid-May to mid-Oct. Tu-Su 10am-5pm.) Less crowded and more opulent, the 200-chamber Neues Palais, the largest of the park's four palaces, is at the park's western end. Highlights include the royal chambers and the palace theater. (Open M-Th and Sa-Su Apr.-Oct. 9am-5pm; Nov.-Mar. 9am-4pm. €5, students €4. Summer tours €1.) The gold-plated **Chinesisches Haus,** adorned with gold-plated 18th-century European visions of "the Chinese"—complete with a rooftop Buddha carrying a parasol—contains 18th-century porcelain. (Open May-Oct. Tu-Su 10am-5pm. €2.)

Potsdam's second park, the **Neuer Garten,** occupies one shore of the Heiliger See, while the villas of German celebrities line the opposite shore. The park contains several royal residences. **Schloß Cecilienhof,** built in the 1910s in the style of an English Tudor manor, documents the Potsdam Treaty, which was signed here in 1945. It would have been the "Berlin Treaty" if the capital hadn't been too bombed-out for the Big Three. (Open Tu-Su Apr.-Oct. 9am-5pm; Nov.-Mar. 9am-4pm. €5, students €4. Summer tours €1.) The garden also contains the neoclassical marble **Marmorpalais** and numerous small, eccentric monuments such as a faux Egyptian pyramid. (Marmorpalais open Apr.-Oct. Tu-Su 10am-5pm; Nov.-Mar. Sa-Su 10am-4pm. €4, students €3. Tours

€1.) To get to Potsdam, take the S7 S-Bahn line (45min. from Friedrichstraße) or the RE1 regional express (30min.) to Potsdam *Hauptbahnhof.*

# NORTHERN GERMANY

Schleswig-Holstein, Germany's gateway to Scandinavia, gains its livelihood from the trade generated at its port towns. Between the North Sea's western coast and the Batic's eastern coast, the velvety plains are populated primarily by sheep and bales of hay. Farther south in Lower Saxony, cities begin to appear, straddling rivers or sprawling through the countryside. The huge, less idyllic Hamburg is notoriously rich and radical, while the small city of Hanover charms visitors with its orderly English gardens and flourishing culture.

## LÜBECK                                                           ☎ 0451

Lübeck (pop. 215,000), a UNESCO World Cultural Heritage Site, is easily Schleswig-Holstein's most beautiful city. Massive churches and winding alleys feature architecture of every style from Medieval and Renaissance on down—you'd never guess it was mostly razed in WWII. In its heyday, Lübeck controlled Northern European trade. No longer a center of commercial or political influence, today the city is a merchant of delicious marzipan and red-blond Dückstein beer, as well as a gateway to the Baltics. Between the station and the *Altstadt* stands the massive **Holstentor,** one of Lübeck's four 15th-century defensive gates and the city's symbol. The small museum inside deals equally in trade and torture, focusing on the history of the city and the role the building played in the town's defenses. (Open Apr.-Sept. daily 10am-5pm; Oct.-Mar. Tu-Su 10am-5pm. €5, students and seniors €2.50, families €9.) The twin brick towers of the **Marienkirche,** a gigantic church that houses the largest mechanical organ in the world, dominate the skyline. Make sure to check out the remains of two bells that came crashing to the ground during a 1942 British bombing raid. (☎39 77 01 80. Open daily in summer 10am-6pm; in winter 10am-4pm. Suggested donation €2. Free tours May-Oct. W 12:15pm. Tours of church and its tower June-Sept. W 3:15pm, Apr. and Dec. Sa 3:15pm. €4, students €3.) Next to Marienkirche sits Lübeck's **Rathaus** (town hall). Built over several centuries, this impressive building features a hodge-podge of different styles, with the oldest portions dating back to the 13th century. Built in 1173 and guarded by a lion statue, the **Dom** (cathedral) on Domkirchhof shelters a huge crucifix and features Gothic, Renaissance, and Romanesque architecture. (Open daily 10am-6pm. Organ concerts July-Aug. F 5pm. Cathedral free. Concerts €6, students €4.) For a sweeping view of the spire-studded *Altstadt*, take the elevator to the top of **Petrikirche.** (☎39 77 30. Church open Tu-Su 11am-4pm. Tower open daily Apr.-Oct. 9am-7pm, Nov.-Mar. 10am-7pm. Church suggested donation €2. Tower €3, students €2.) The **Theaterfigurenmuseum,** Kolk 14, displays 1200 holdings from the world's largest private puppet collection (over 40,000). Be sure to ask for the English-language guide at the reception desk. (☎786 26. Open daily 10am-6pm. €4, students €3, children €2.)

To reach **Rucksack Hotel ❷,** Kanalstr. 70, take bus #1, 11, 21, or 31 to Katharineum and turn right at the church on Glockengießerstr and continue until you reach the water. This popular hostel is a member of a collective of eco-friendly shops in a former glass factory. Stay in bright, clean, and colorful rooms decorated in motifs like "Australia" and "Denmark." (☎70 68 92; www.rucksack-hotel-luebeck.de. Breakfast €3. Linens €3. Reception 10am-1pm and 5-9pm. 6- to 8-bed dorms €13; doubles €34, with bath €40; quads €60/68. Cash only.) Stop by the famous confectionery **I.G. Niederegger Marzipan Café ❶,** Breitestr. 89, for

## THE BEST *WURST*

So you're finally in Germany and itching to sink your teeth into your first authentic German *Wurst*. With over 1500 varieties, you'll have plenty of choices. All have one thing in common: German law mandates that sausages can only be made of meat and spices. If it has cereal filling, it's not *Wurst*.

**Bockwurst:** This tasty sausage is common roasted or grilled at street stands, and is served dripping with ketchup and mustard in a *Brötchen* (roll). Although *Bock* means billy-goat, this *Wurst* is made of ground veal with parsley and chives. Complement your *Bockwurst* with some *Bock* beer.

**Thüringer Bratwurst:** Similar to the *Bockwurst*, the *Bratwurst* also has pork, plus ginger and nutmeg.

**Frankfurter:** Unlike the American variety, the German *Frankfurter* can only have this name if it is made in Frankfurt. It's made of lean pork ground into a paste and then cold smoked, which gives it its orange-yellow coloring.

**Knockwurst:** Shorter and plumper, this sausage is served with *sauerkraut*. It's made of lean pork and beef, with a healthy dose of garlic.

**Weißwurst:** Cream and eggs give this "white sausage" its pale coloring. *Weißwurst* goes with rye bread and mustard.

**Currywurst:** A great late-night snack, this pork *Bratwurst* is smothered in tomato sauce and sprinkled with paprika and curry.

marzipan, a delicious treat made of almonds, rosewater, and sugar. Lübeck's specialty is created in the shape of fruit, fish, and even the town gate. (☎530 1126. Open M-F 9am-7pm, Sa 9am-6pm, Su 10am-6pm. AmEx/MC/V.) ◧**Café Affenbrot ❷,** Kanalstr. 70, on the corner of Glockengießerstr., is a vegetarian cafe and *Biergarten;* it is also part of the same cooperative as Rucksack Hostel. Sit at tables crafted from antique sewing machines and indulge in a variety of light organic dinners (€4-8), or enjoy breakfast (€3.50-9) with the masses. (☎721 93; www.cafeaffenbrot.de. Open Apr.-Sept. daily 9am-midnight; Oct.-May M-Sa 9am-noon, Su 9am-10pm. Kitchen closes 11pm. Cash only.)

**Trains** run to Berlin (2½ hr., 1 per hr., €49-71) and Hamburg (50min., 1 per hr., €15). Lübeck's **tourist office,** Holstentorpl. 1, books rooms for no fee. The **Happy Day Card** provides unlimited access to public transportation and museum discounts. The tourist office also provides German-language tours of the town at 11am and 2pm for €6. (☎88 22 33. Open June-Sept. M-F 9:30am-7pm, Sa 10am-3pm Su 10am-2pm; Jan.-May and Oct.-Nov. M-F 9:30am-6pm, Sa 10am-3pm; Dec. M-F 9:30am-6pm, Sa 10am-3pm.) **Postal Code:** 23552.

## SCHLESWIG ☎04621

With its sailboat-filled harbor and cafe-lined shores, Schleswig has held the Schlei River in its horseshoe embrace since AD 800. By the harbor, the outstanding 18th-century ◧**Schloß Gottorf** and surrounding buildings comprise the **Landesmuseen.** It contains six individual museums with enough Danish, Dutch, and German art, armor, silver, and weaponry to fill 20. Don't miss the full Viking boat. Unfortunately, few captions are in English. The surrounding park is a **sculpture garden,** and in the back of the grounds there is a baroque garden. (Open Apr.-Oct. daily 10am-6pm; Nov.-Mar. Tu-F 10am-4pm, Sa-Su 10am-5pm. Combo ticket €6, students €3.) Scale the 240 steps of the **St. Petri Dom** for a bird's-eye view of town, or just marvel at the intricately carved altar. (Open May-Sept. M-Sa 9am-5pm, Su 1:30-5pm; Oct.-Apr. M-Sa 10am-4pm, Su 1:30-4pm. Tower €1, children €0.50.) From St. Petri, continue down Suderdomstr. to see the old section of town. Check out **Rathausmarkt,** which contains the town hall—a former Franciscan Friary—in its northeast corner, before continuing on. Turn right onto Topferstr. and you'll soon reach a quiet cemetery surrounded by small, beautiful houses that were once home to the town's fishermen. Finally, continue straight on Am St. Johanniskloster to see **St. Johannis-Kloster,** a former Benedictine convent.

To get to **Jugendherberge (HI) ❶,** Spielkoppel 1, near the city center, take bus #1501-1503, 1505, or

1506 from the train station to the bus station, and then take a cab (€5-7). Ask for a room in the newer part of the building. (☎238 93; www.jugendher-berge.de/jh/schleswig. Breakfast included. Reception 7am-noon and 5-10pm. Grab a key to get in after 11pm. Dorms €15-23, under 27 €12-20; singles €23, with shower €26; doubles €39/46. Cash only.) **Hotel Schleiblick ❸**, Hafengang 4, has rooms and a restaurant that overlook the harbor. (☎234 68. Free bike rental. Breakfast included. Reception 8am-1pm and 6-9pm. Singles €40; doubles €70. Low season reduced prices. Cash only.) Nurse cloudy beers at **Asgaard-Brauerei ❸**, Königstr. 27, a popular brewery-restaurant. (Meals €8-15. Open M-Th 5pm-midnight, F 5pm-2am, Sa 10am-2am, Su 11am-midnight. Cash only.) Schleswig centers around its bus terminal. Single rides in town cost €1.20, day passes €3.80. Buses #1501-1503, 1506, and 1507 run 15min. south of the *Altstadt* to the train station. **Trains** go to Hamburg (2hr., 1 per hr., €21-26). The **tourist office**, Plessenstr. 7, is up the street from the harbor. They run guided tours of the city in German (€8) and book rooms for a 10% fee. (☎85 00 56. Open June-Sept. M-F 9:30am-6:30pm, Sa 10am-2pm; Oct. and Mar.-May M-F 10am-5pm, Sa-Su 10am-2pm; Nov.-Feb. M-F 10am-4pm. **Postal Code:** 24837.

# HAMBURG                                            ☎040

Germany's largest port city and the second largest in Europe, Hamburg (pop. 1,800,000) radiates an inimitable recklessness. Its skyline is punctuated by ancient church towers, modern skyscrapers, and the masts of ships carrying millions of containers of goods. It gained the status of Free Imperial City in 1618 and now retains its autonomy as one of Germany's 16 federal states, making it one of only three German city-states. Riots and restorations defined the post-WWII landscape. Today, Hamburg is a haven for contemporary artists, intellectuals, and partygoers who live it up in Germany's self-declared "capital of lust."

## ⊏ TRANSPORTATION

**Trains:** The **Hauptbahnhof** has hourly connections to: **Berlin** (1½hr., €62); **Copenhagen, DEN** (5hr., €78); **Frankfurt** (3½hr., €98); **Hanover** (1½hr., €38); **Munich** (6hr., €119). **DB Reisezentrum** ticket office open M-F 5:30am-10pm, Sa-Su 7am-10pm. The **Dammtor** train station is near the university; **Harburg** station is south of the Elbe; **Altona** station is to the west of the city; and **Bergedorf** is to the southeast. **Lockers** (€2.50-5 per day, €7.50-15 per 3 days) are available at stations.

**Buses:** The **ZOB** is on Steintorpl. across from the *Hauptbahnhof*, just past the Museum für Kunst und Gewerbe. Open Su-Th 5am-10pm, F-Sa 5am-midnight. **Autokraft** (☎280 8660) runs to **Berlin** (3¼hr., 10-12 per day, €25). **Gulliver's** (☎280 048 35) runs to **Paris, FRA** (12hr., 1 per day, €66). Student discounts available.

**Public Transportation:** **HVV** operates an efficient U-Bahn, S-Bahn, and bus network. One-way tickets within the downtown area cost €2.60; prices vary with distance and network. 1-day pass €6, after 9am or Sa-Su €5.10; 3-day pass €15. Buy tickets at *Automaten* (machines), or consider buying a **Hamburg Card** (p. 428).

**Bike Rental: Fahrradstation Dammtor/Rothebaum**, Schlüterstr. 11 (☎41 46 82 77), rents bikes for just €3 per day. Open M-F 9am-6:30pm. **Fahrradladen St. Georg**, Schmilinskystr. 6 (☎24 39 08), is off Lange Reihe toward the Außenalster. €8 per day, €56 per week with €50 deposit. Open M-F 10am-7pm, Sa 10am-1pm.

## ✳❼ ORIENTATION AND PRACTICAL INFORMATION

Hamburg's city center sits between the **Elbe River** and two lakes, **Außenalster** and **Binnenalster**. Bisecting the downtown, the **Alsterfleet** canal separates the *Altstadt*

GERMANY

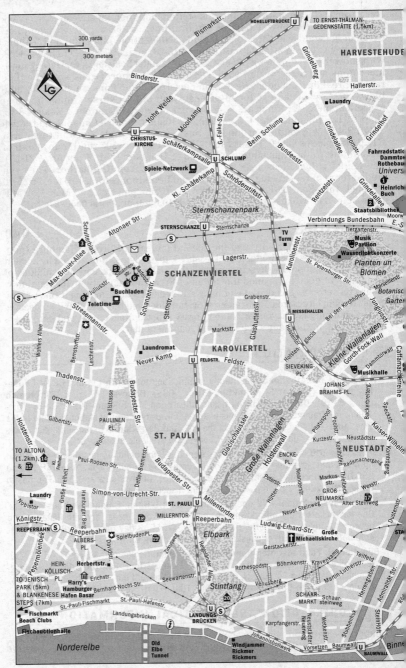

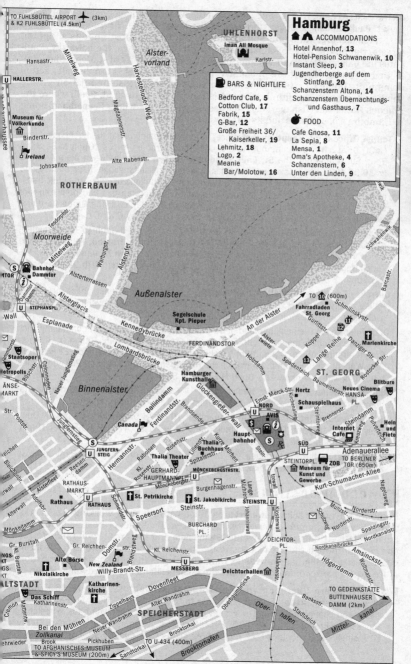

## Hamburg

### 🏠🏠 ACCOMMODATIONS
Hotel Annenhof, **13**
Hotel-Pension Schwanenwik, **10**
Instant Sleep, **3**
Jugendherberge auf dem
  Stintfang, **20**
Schanzenstern Altona, **14**
Schanzenstern Übernachtungs-
  und Gasthaus, **7**

### 🛏 BARS & NIGHTLIFE
Bedford Cafe, **5**
Cotton Club, **17**
Fabrik, **15**
G-Bar, **12**
Große Freiheit 36/
  Kaiserkeller, **19**
Lehmitz, **18**
Logo, **2**
Meanie
  Bar/Molotow, **16**

### 🍴 FOOD
Cafe Gnosa, **11**
La Sepia, **8**
Mensa, **1**
Oma's Apotheke, **4**
Schanzenstern, **6**
Unter den Linden, **9**

GERMANY

on the eastern bank from the *Neustadt* on the west. Most major sights lie between the **St. Pauli Landungsbrücken** port area in the west and the *Hauptbahnhof* in the east. **Mönckebergstraße** and **Spitalerstraße,** Hamburg's most famous shopping streets, run all the way to **Rathausmarkt.** North of downtown, the **university** dominates the **Dammtor** area and sustains an animated community of students and intellectuals. To the west of the university, the **Schanzenviertel** is a politically active community home to artists, squatters, and a sizable Turkish population. At the south end of town, an entirely different atmosphere reigns in **St. Pauli,** where the raucous **Fischmarkt** (fish market) is surpassed only by the wilder **Reeperbahn,** home to Hamburg's best discos and its infamous sex trade.

**Tourist Offices:** The **Hauptbahnhof** office, in the Wandelhalle near the Kirchenallee exit (☎30 05 12 01; www.hamburg-tourism.de), books rooms for €4. Open M-Sa 8am-9pm, Su 10am-6pm. The **St. Pauli Landungsbrücken** office, between piers 4 and 5 (☎30 05 12 03), is less crowded. Both supply free English-language maps and a guide to the city and sell the **Hamburg Card,** which provides unlimited access to public transportation, reduced admission to museums, and discounts on bus and boat tours for small groups with children. 1-day card €8, 3-day €18, 5-day €33. The **Group Card** provides the same benefits for up to 5 people. 1-day €12, 3-day €30, 5-day €51.

**Consulates: Canada,** Ballindamm 35 (☎460 0270). S- or U-Bahn to Jungfernstieg; between Alstertor and Bergstr. Open M-F 9:30am-12:30pm. **Ireland,** Feldbrunnenstr. 43 (☎44 18 61 13). U1 to Hallerstr. Open M-F 9am-1pm. **New Zealand,** Domstr. 19, Zürich-Haus, Cout C, 3rd fl. (☎442 5550). U1 to Messberg. Open M-Th 9am-1pm and 2-5:30pm, F 9am-1pm and 2-4:30pm.

**Currency Exchange: ReiseBank,** on the 2nd fl. of the *Hauptbahnhof* near the Kirchenallee exit (☎32 34 83), has Western Union services, cashes traveler's checks, and exchanges currency for a 4-5% fee. Open daily 7:30am-10pm.

**GLBT Resources:** The neighborhood of St. Georg is the center of the gay community. Pick up the free *Hinnerk* magazine and *Friends: The Gay Map* from **Café Gnosa** (p. 430) or from the tourist office. Organizations include **Hein und Fiete,** Pulverteich 21 (☎24 03 33). Walk down Steindamm away from the *Hauptbahnhof,* turn right on Pulverteich; it's a building with a rainbow flag. Open M-F 4-9pm, Sa 4-7pm.

**Pharmacy: Senator-Apotheke,** Hachmannpl. 14 (☎32 75 27). Turn right from the station's Kirchenallee exit. English spoken. Open M-F 7am-8pm, Sa 8am-8pm.

**Internet Access: Internet Cafe,** Adenauerallee 10 (☎28 00 38 98). €1 per hr. Open daily 10am-11:55pm. **Teletime,** Schulterblatt 39 (☎41 30 47 30). €0.50 per 15min. Open M-F 10am-10pm, Sa-Su 10am-7pm.

**Post Office:** At the Kirchenallee exit of the *Hauptbahnhof.* Open M-F 8am-6pm, Sa 8:30am-12:30pm. **Postal Code: 20099.**

# ACCOMMODATIONS

Hamburg's dynamic **Schanzenviertel** area, filled with students, working-class Turks, and left-wing dissenters, houses two of the best backpacker hostels in the city. Small, relatively cheap pensions line **Steindamm** and the area around the *Hauptbahnhof,* although the area's prostitutes and wannabe mafiosi detract from its charm. **Lange Reihe** has equivalent lodging options in a cleaner neighborhood. More expensive accommodations line the **Binnenalster** and eastern **Außenalster.**

■ **Schanzenstern Übernachtungs- und Gasthaus,** Bartelsstr. 12 (☎439 8441; www.schanzenstern.de). S21 or 31, or U3 to "Sternschanze." Near St. Pauli, bright, clean, and comfortable rooms in a renovated pen factory, most with bath. Wheelchair-accessible. Breakfast €4.30-6.30. Reception 7am-1:30am. Reserve ahead. Dorms €19; singles €38; doubles €53; triples €63; quads €77; quints €95. Cash only. ❷

▨ **Instant Sleep,** Max-Brauer-Allee 277 (☎ 43 18 23 10; www.instantsleep.de). S21 or 31 or U3 to "Sternschanze." Helpful, bilingual staff—as well as an improvised library and communal kitchen—contribute to a family feel at this backpacker hostel. Close to the S-Bahn, making it convenient and sometimes noisy. Lockers €5 deposit. Linens €2. Internet €1 per 30min. Reception 8am-2am. Check-out 11am. Dorms €16; singles €30; doubles €23 per person; triples €21 per person. Cash only. ❷

**Jugendherberge auf dem Stintfang (HI),** Alfred-Wegener-Weg 5 (☎ 31 34 88). S1, S3, or U3 to Landungsbrücke. The hostel is above the Landungsbrücke station—look for stairs on the left side. Newly renovated and expanded, this huge hostel has an incredible view of the harbor. Bunks, checkered curtains, and views of the nearby woods contribute to a camp feel. Breakfast and linens included. Reception 24hr. Check-out 10am. Lockout 10am-1pm. Dorms €23-25, under 27 €19-21. HI members only, although membership can be purchased at the hostel for €3.10 per night. MC/V. ❸

**Schanzenstern Altona,** Kleiner Rainstr. 24-26 (☎ 39 91 91 91; www.schanzenstern-altona.de). Just as nice as its counterpart in the Schanzenviertel, with brightly colored walls and art. All rooms have bath. Close to the Altona station with frequent S-Bahn service. Wheelchair-accessible. Dorms €19; singles €43; doubles €58-68; triples €73; quads €83. Cash only. ❸

**Hotel-Pension Schwanenwik,** Schwanenwik 29 (☎ 220 0918; www.hotel-schwanenwik.de). Bus #6 to Mundsburger Brücke, cross the street, walk down Hartwicusstr., and turn right on Schwanenwik. Beautiful rooms near the lake with TVs, and most with bathrooms. Breakfast included. Wi-Fi available. Singles €48, with shower €78; doubles €68/98. AmEx/MC/V. ❹

**Hotel Annenhof,** Lange Reihe 23 (☎ 24 34 26; www.hotelannenhof.de). Around the corner from the *Hauptbahnof*. Turn left out of the train station's Kirchenallee exit, pass the Schauspielhaus, then turn right on Lange Reihe. Built in 1901, high ceilings, moldings, brightly colored walls and hardwood floors make inviting rooms, some with shower. Reception M-F 8am-8pm, Sa-Su 9am-6pm. Singles €40; doubles €70. Cash only. ❹

# ▐ FOOD

Seafood is common in the port city of Hamburg. In Schanzenviertel, avant-garde cafes and Turkish falafel stands entice hungry passersby. **Schulterblatt, Susannenstraße,** and **Schanzenstraße** are home to funky cafes and restaurants, while cheaper establishments crowd in the **university** area, especially along **Rentzelstraße, Grindelhof,** and **Grindelallee.** In **Altona,** the pedestrian zone approaching the train station is packed with food stands and produce shops. The Portuguese community gives its take on seafood in the area between the Michaelskirche and the river.

▨ **La Sepia,** Schulterblatt 36 (☎ 432 2484; www.lasepia.de). This Portuguese-Spanish restaurant serves some of the city's most reasonably priced seafood. For your pocketbook's sake, come for lunch (11am-5pm), when €5 gets you a big plate of grilled tuna with sauteed and scalloped carrots and potatoes, a basket of fresh bread, and a bowl of soup. Lunch €3.50-6. Dinner €7.50-22. Open daily noon-3am. AmEx/MC/V. ❷

**Schanzenstern,** Bartelsstr. 12 (☎ 43 29 04 09; www.schanzenstern.de). Organic masterpieces are served in the Schanzenstern Übernachtungs und Gasthaus hostel. Breakfast €4.30-9.40. Lunch €4-11.50. Daily lunch special €6.20. Dinner €8-12.50. Open M 3pm-1am, Tu-Sa 10:30am-1am, Su 11am-midnight. Cash only. ❷

**Unter den Linden,** Juliusstr. 16 (☎ 43 81 40). Read complimentary German papers over *Milchkaffee* (coffee with foamed milk; €2.90-3.40), breakfast (€4.60-7.30), or salad and pasta (€3.70-6.90) in a relaxed atmosphere underneath, as the name suggests, the linden trees. Open daily 10am-1am. Cash only. ❷

**Oma's Apotheke,** Schanzenstr. 87 (☎ 43 66 20). Old-style ambience and large portions, popular with students. German, Italian, and American cuisine. *Schnitzel* €7.50. Hamburger with 1lb. fries €6.60. Open Su-Th 9am-1am, F-Sa 9am-2am. Cash only. ❷

**Mensa,** Von-Melle-Park 5 (☎41 90 22 02). S21 or 31 to Dammtor, then bus #4 or 5 to Staatsbibliothek (1 stop). Cafeteria food and listings of university events. Meals €2.50-3.95, student €1.55-3.35. Open M-Th 10am-4pm, F 10am-3:30pm. Cash only. ❶

**Cafe Gnosa,** Lange Reihe 93 (☎24 30 34; www.gnosa.de). A mixed crowd eats at this gay-friendly cafe that serves delicious breakfast and pastries all day, as well as lunch and dinner entrees. Breakfast €3.50-7. For a splurge, try the champagne breakfast for two (€35). Drinks €2-5. Open Su-Th 10am-1am, F-Sa 10am-2am. Cash only. ❶

## 👁 SIGHTS

## ALTSTADT

**GROßE MICHAELSKIRCHE.** The 18th-century Michaelskirche is the symbol of Hamburg, and with good reason. Named for the Archangel Michael, who stands guard over the main entrance, the church was destroyed successively by lightning, accidents, and Allied bombs. It was finally rebuilt after the Cold War. Its fate, essentially, has kept in tandem with the city's. Restored in 1996, the scalloped walls of the interior recall the space of a concert hall. A panoramic view of Hamburg awaits those who climb the 462 stairs of the spire (or those who opt for the elevator). In the crypt, a multimedia presentation on the history of the church screens on weekends. (U-Bahn to Baumwall, S-Bahn to Stadthausbrücke. ☎37 67 81 00. Church open daily 9am-8pm. Crypt open June-Oct. daily 11am-4:30pm; Nov.-May Sa-Su 11am-4:30pm. Screenings M-Sa 1 per hr. 12:30-3:30pm, Su 2 per hr. 11:30am-3:30pm. Church suggested donation €2. Crypt €1.50. Screenings €2.50. Tower €3.)

**RATHAUS.** Built between 1886 and 1897, the city's town hall is one of the *Altstadt*'s most impressive buildings. The city and state governments both convene amid the intricate mahogany carvings and two-ton chandeliers. Its 647 stunning and varied rooms should not be missed. In front, the **Rathausmarkt** hosts festivities ranging from political demonstrations to medieval fairs. (☎428 312 470. English-language tours every 2hr. or more often depending on popularity. M-Th 10:15am-3:15pm, F-Su 10:15am-1:15pm. Building open daily 8am-6pm. €1.50, under 14 €0.50.)

**NIKOLAIKIRCHE.** The spire of this neo-Gothic ruin, bombed in 1943, serves as a memorial for victims of war and persecution. The church itself, built first in 1195, took nearly 700 years to complete, with the construction of its tower in 1874. A glass elevator takes visitors up 76m, and a small documentation center details "Operation Gomorrah," the 1943 bombing of Hamburg. (U3 to Rödingsmarkt. Church open daily Nov.-Mar. 10:30am-5:30pm; Apr.-May and Sept.-Oct. 10am-7pm; June-Aug. M-Th and Su 9:30am-8pm, F-Sa 9:30am-8pm, F-Sa 9:30am-10pm. Document center open M-F 10:30am-5:30pm. Tower €3, students €1.50, children €1. Document Center €1.60. Combined ticket €4.)

**MÖNCKEBERGSTRAßE.** Two spires punctuate Hamburg's shopping zone, which stretches from the *Rathaus* to the *Hauptbahnhof*. Closest to the *Rathaus* is **St. Petrikirche,** the oldest church in Hamburg, dating back to 1195. (☎325 7400. Open M-Tu and Th-F 10am-4:30pm, W 10am-7pm, Sa 10am-5pm, Su 9am-9pm. Frequent free concerts.) The other, **St. Jakobikirche,** is known for its 17th-century Arp-Schnittger organ with almost 4000 pipes. (☎303 7370. Open M-Sa 10am-5pm.) The buildings along **Trostbrücke** sport huge copper models of clipper ships on their spires, testiments to Hamburg's sea-trade wealth. (Just south of the Rathaus, off Ost-West-Str.)

## BEYOND THE ALTSTADT

**PLANTEN UN BLOMEN.** West of the Außenalster, this huge expanse of manicured flower beds and trees includes the largest Japanese garden in Europe, complete with a teahouse built in Japan. *(S21 or 31 to Dammtor. www.plantenunblomen.hamburg.de. Open May-Sept. daily 7am-11pm, Oct.-Apr. 7am-8pm. Free.)* In summer, performers in the outdoor **Musikpavillon** range from Irish step-dancers to Hamburg's police choir. *(May-Sept. Most performances 3pm. See garden website for details.)* At night, opt for the **Wasserlichtkonzerte,** with a choreographed play of fountains and underwater lights. *(May-Aug. daily 10pm; Sept. 9pm.)* To the north, the tree-lined paths bordering the two **Alster lakes** provide refuge from the city crowds.

**ST. PAULI LANDUNGSBRÜCKEN.** The harbor lights up at night with ships from all over the world. Look for the 426m **Elbtunnel,** completed in 1911 and still active. *(Free for pedestrians. Behind Pier 6 in the building with the copper cupola.)* At the **Fischmarkt,** vendors hawk fish, produce, and other goods. *(S1, S3, or U3 to Landungsbrücken or S1 or S3 to Königstr. or Reeperbahn. Open Su Apr.-Oct. 5-10am; Nov.-Mar. 7-10am.)*

**KZ NEUENGAMME.** An idyllic agricultural village east of Hamburg provided the backdrop for the Neuengamme concentration camp, where Nazis killed 55,000 prisoners through slave labor. Neuengamme was the main concentration camp for northwestern Germany until 1945. It was then used as an internment camp for British prisoners; from 1953-2005, large portions of the former camp served as a penal facility. In 1989, the Hamburg Senate built a memorial on the site; since then, the facility has expanded to cover most of the original camp. A mile-long path begins at the **Haus des Gedenkens,** a memorial building containing banners inscribed with the names and death dates of the victims. The path eventually leads to the former **Prisoners' Block,** which contains a detailed exhibit on the history of the camp, including the recorded testimony of survivors in English, French, German, and Russian. Keep an eye out for special exhibits. *(Jean-Doldier-Weg 39. S21 to Bergedorf, then bus #227 or 327, about 1hr. from city. Buses runs from Bergedorf M-Sa 3-4 per hr., Su 1 per hr. ☎ 428 131 500; www.kz-gedenkstaette-neuengamme.de. Museum and memorial open May-Sept. M-F 9:30am-4pm, Sa-Su noon-7pm; Oct.-Mar. daily noon-5pm. Path open 24hr.)*

**GEDENKSTÄTTE BULLENHUSER DAMM UND ROSENGARTEN.** Surrounded by warehouses, this schoolhouse is a memorial to 20 Jewish children who were subjected to medical experimentation while in Auschwitz and murdered by the SS in an attempt to destroy evidence only hours before Allied troops arrived. Visitors are invited to plant a rose for the children in the flower garden behind the school, where memorial plaques line the fence. *(Bullenhuser Damm 92. S21 to Rothenburgsort. Follow the signs to Bullenhuser Damm along Ausschläger Bildeich to the intersection with Grossmannstr.; the garden is on the far left; the school is 200m farther. ☎ 428 131 500. Rose garden open 24hr. Exhibit open Su 10am-5pm, Th 2-8pm. Free.)*

# 🏛 MUSEUMS

The **Hamburg Card** provides free or discounted access to all museums except the Deichtorhallen and the Hafen Basar. *Museumswelt Hamburg,* a free newspaper available at tourist offices, lists exhibits and events. Most museums are closed on Monday. Usually, musuems also house a "Kultur Kompact," a small kiosk or display that contains info and brochures to most other museums in the city.

**HAMBURGER KUNSTHALLE.** It would take many days to see every work in this sprawling fine-arts museum. The oldest building presents the Old Masters and extensive special exhibits, including a large number of Impressionist works by the likes of Degas, Monet, and Renoir. In the connected four-level **Galerie der Gegenwart,** contemporary art takes a stand in a mix of temporary and permanent exhibits. *(Glockengießerwall 1. Turn right from the Spitalerstr. City exit of the Hauptbahnhof and cross the street. ☎ 428 131 200; www.hamburger.kunsthalle.de. Open Tu-W and F-Su 10am-6pm, Th 10am-9pm. €8.50, students €5, families €14.)*

**MUSEUM FÜR KUNST UND GEWERBE.** Handicrafts, china, and furnishings from all corners of the earth fill this arts and crafts museum. A huge exhibit chronicles the evolution of the modern piano with dozens of the world's oldest harpsichords, clavichords, and *Hammerklaviers*. Be sure to visit the **Hall of Mirrors,** a beautiful reconstruction of a room in the home of a Hamburg banker. *(Steintorpl. 1., 1 block south of the Hauptbahnhof. ☎428 542 732; www.mkg-hamburg.de. Open Tu-W and F-Su 10am-6pm, Th 10am-9pm. €8, students, Hamburg Card holders, and seniors €5, under 18 free.)*

**DEICHTORHALLEN HAMBURG.** Hamburg's contemporary art scene thrives inside these two former fruit markets, with painting, photography, and video displays. Their vaulted halls rotate exhibits seasonally. *(Deichtorstr. 1-2. U1 to Steinstr. Follow signs from the metro. ☎31 10 31 40; www.deichtorhallen.de. Open Tu-Su 11am-6pm. Each building €7, students €5, families €9.50. Combo ticket to both halls €13/8.50/17.)*

**HARRY'S HAMBURGER HAFEN BASAR.** After sailing the world and collecting many oddities along the way, Harry dropped anchor and set up this cavernous museum-shop displaying everything from statues to idols, masks, and gourds. Collectors will be glad to know that everything except the shrunken heads and the stuffed leopard is for sale. *(Balduinstr. 18. S1 or S3 to Reeperbahn or U3 to St. Pauli. ☎31 24 82; www.hafenbasar.de. Open Tu-Su noon-6pm. €2.50, 6-12 €1.50.)*

## 🎵 ENTERTAINMENT

The **Staatsoper,** Große Theaterstr. 36, houses one of the best **opera** companies in Germany; the associated **ballet** is one of the nation's best. (U2 to Gänsemarkt. ☎35 68 68. Open M-Sa 10am-6:30pm and 1½hr. before performances.) **Orchestras** include the Philharmonie, the Norddeutscher Rundfunk Symphony, and Hamburg Symphonia, which all perform at the **Musikhalle** on Johannes-Brahms-Pl. (U2 to Gänsemarkt. ☎34 69 20; www.musikhalle-hamburg.de. Box office open M-F 10am-4pm.) Live music also prospers in Hamburg. Superb traditional jazz swings at the **Cotton Club** (p. 433) and **Indra** (Große Freiheit 64). Early on Sundays, musicians talented and otherwise play at the **Fischmarkt.** The **West Port Jazz Festival** runs in mid-July; for info, call the *Konzertkasse* (ticket office; ☎32 87 38 54).

## 🎵 NIGHTLIFE

Hamburg's unrestrained nightlife scene heats up in the **Schanzenviertel** and **St. Pauli** areas. The infamous **Reeperbahn** runs through the heart of St. Pauli; lined with sex shops, strip joints, and peep shows, it's also home to the city's best bars and clubs. Though the Reeperbahn is generally safe, women may want to avoid adjacent streets. Parallel to the Reeperbahn lies **Herbertstraße,** Hamburg's official prostitution strip, where licensed sex entrepreneurs flaunt their flesh. Herbertstr. is open only to those over the age of 18; potential patrons should be warned that engaging with streetwalkers in the city involves playing a game of venereal Russian roulette. Students head north to the streets of the Schanzenviertel, where cafes create an atmosphere more leftist than lustful. The **St. Georg** district, near Berliner Tor and along Lange Reihe, is the center of Hamburg's **gay scene.** In general, clubs open and close late, with some techno and trance clubs remaining open all night. *Szene* (€3), available at newsstands, lists events.

🎵 **Große Freiheit 36/Kaiserkeller,** Große Freiheit 36 (☎317 7780). Everyone from Ziggy Marley to Prince to Matchbox 20 has performed on the big stage and dance floor upstairs. Live music or DJs usually 10pm-4am. F-Sa club nights cover €3-6. Concerts usually at 7pm; €10-30, with higher prices for bigger names. Often free until 11pm.

**Fabrik,** Barnerstr. 36 (☎39 10 70; www.fabrik.de). From Altona station, head toward Offenser Hauptstr. and go right on Bahrenfelderstr. This former weapons factory now cranks out raging beats. For years, crowds have packed this 2 fl. club to hear big-name rock acts and an eclectic mix of other bands, with styles ranging from Latin to punk. Music nearly every night at 9pm. Cover for live music €5-30. Every 2nd Sa of the month, "Gay Factory" attracts a mixed crowd. Live DJ 10pm most Sa; cover €7-8. Cash only.

**Meanie Bar/Molotow,** Spielbudenpl. 5 (☎31 08 45; www.molotowclub.com), parallel to the Reeperbahn. The Molotow, in the basement of the retro Meanie Bar, has 70s decor and alternative music, great bands, and good dancers that keep this small club rocking. The bar upstairs has a more relaxed atmosphere, decked out with old-school recliners. Meanie Bar open daily from 9pm. No cover. Molotow cover for club nights and other events €3-4, live bands €8-15. Open from 8pm when there are concerts, and from 11pm F-Sa for disco. Cash only.

**Bedford Cafe,** Schulterblatt 72 (☎43 18 83 32), on the corner of Schulterblatt and Suzannensstr; look for the "Pascucci" sign. One of the most crowded bars in the Schanzenviertel, and known to locals as the "no-name bar," the Bedford is a fashionable hangout. Beer €2.50-3.40. Mixed drinks €5.50-6.50. Open daily 10am-late. Cash only.

**Logo,** Grindelallee 5 (☎36 26 22; www.logohamburg.de). U-Bahn to Stephanspl., or S21 or 31 to Dammtor. Educates the college crowd with its live folk, hip-hop, rock, and samba. Cover €5-15. Live music from 9pm. Cash only.

**G-Bar,** Lange Reihe 81 (☎28 00 46 90). Young male waiters could be models at this clean-cut gay bar. Beer €2-3. Mixed drinks €5-7. Open daily 7pm-2am. Cash only.

**Cotton Club,** Alter Steinweg 10 (☎34 38 78; www.cotton-club.de). U3 to Rödingsmarkt. With the same owner since 1959, this subterranean club features New Orleans dixie, swing, blues, and Big Band jazz in a warmly lit setting. Cover €5 for Hamburg bands, around €10 for guest bands. Shows 8:30pm. Open M-Th 8pm-midnight, F-Sa 8pm-1am; Sept.-Apr. also open Su 11pm-3am. AmEx/MC/V.

**Lehmitz,** Reeperbahn 22 (☎31 46 41; www.lehmitz.de). Friendly students, metal rockers, and hardcore punks gather around the wrap-around bar for €2 beers in the heart of the Red Light district. W, Th, F and Sa live thrash music. Open 2pm-late. Cash only.

# HANOVER (HANNOVER)                                             ☎0511

Despite its relatively small size, Hanover (pop. 515,000) has the art, culture, and landscape to rival any larger European city. Hanover's highlights are the three bountiful ◪**Herrenhausen gardens.** The largest, **Großer Garten,** is one of Europe's most beautiful Baroque gardens, featuring geometric shrubbery and the **Große Fontäne,** one of Europe's highest-shooting fountains. To get there from the train station, walk to the far end of the lower shop level and take the U4 or 5 to Herrenhauser Garten. (Fountain spurts Apr.-Oct. M-F 11am-noon and 3-5pm, Sa-Su 11am-noon and 2-5pm. Garden open daily Apr. 9am-7pm; May-Aug. 9am-8pm; Sept. 9am-7pm; early Oct. 9am-6pm. Entrance €4, including admission to *Berggarten.* Concerts and performances June-Aug.; ☎16 84 12 22 for schedule.) On the outskirts of the *Altstadt* is the **Neues Rathaus,** the impressive town hall built between 1901 and 1913. The building features scale models of Hanover from 1689, 1939, 1945 and the present day. Take the elevator up the tower for a lovely view year-round or ascend to the dome on a summer evening. (Open May-Sept. M-F 9am-6pm, Sa-Su 10am-6pm. Free. Elevator M-F 9:30am-6pm, Sa-Su 10am-6pm. €2.50, students €2.) A combo ticket can be purchased for Hanover's three major museums (€10, students €5). Nearby, a first-rate contemporary art museum, the ◪**Sprengel Museum,** Kurt-Schwitters-Pl., hosts work from some of the 20th century's greatest artists, including works by Kandinsky, Leger, and Picasso. (Open Tu 10am-8pm, W-Su 10am-6pm. €7, students €4.) **Kestner-Museum,** Trammpl. 3, is a small, somewhat

GERMANY

lackluster museum that showcases decorative arts, with a special focus on ancient art. (☎16 84 21 20; www.kestner-museum.de. Open Tu and Th-Su 11am-6pm, W 11am-8pm. €4; students €3.) The **Niedersachsisches Landesmuseum Hannover,** Willy-Brandt-Allee 5, features small collections on art, ethnology, and natural history from the Middle Ages to the Impressionist period. On Leibnizufer, North of Fried-erikenplatz, is the **Sculpture Mile,** a 1.5km stretch of sculpture and art exhibits.

◪ **Hotel Flora ❸,** Heinrichstr. 36, is located in the center of town 10min. from the station. Take the back exit and continue straight ahead onto Berliner Allee, cross the street, then turn left on Heinrichstr, a quiet street close to the *Hauptbanhof.* Rooms come with carpeting, framed Monet prints, and TVs. (☎38 39 10; www.hotel-flora-hannover.de. Breakfast included. Reception 8am-8pm. Singles €37-49, doubles €64-75, triples €84-96. Dogs €7.50. AmEx/MC/V.) **Jugendherberge Hannover (HI) ❷,** Ferdinand-Wilhelm-Fricke-Weg 1, is situated outside the city center, but worth the trek: balconies in the sun-filled rooms overlook a park. Ask for a room in the new wing. Take the U3 or 7 to Fischerhof. From the stop, backtrack 10m, turn right, and cross the tracks; continue until the next stoplight at Lodeman-nweg, then turn right and follow the path as it curves and cross Stammestr. Turn right after going over the red footbridge. (☎131 7674. Wheelchair-accessible. Break-fast included. Reception 7:30am-1am. After 1am, doors open on the hr. Check-out 9am. Internet €0.10 per min. Dorms €22-28. €3 discount under 27. MC/V.) **Holland-ische Kakaostube ❷,** Standehausstr. 2-3 (☎30 41 00), features a dozen different award-winning hot chocolates (€3.70) and a gorgeous assortment of cakes. Try the *Mohrenkof,* a merengue filled with hazelnuts and enrobed in chocolate (€2.10). The classy gold-accented dining room features old-world elegance; those who can't bear to part with the dainty china sets on which the desserts are served can purchase a set to keep. (Open M-F 9am-7:30pm and Sa 8:30am-6pm. Cash only.) Relaxed students fill the chic garden at **The Loft,** Georgstr. 50a, off the main shopping road. (☎363 1376. Happy hour M-Th, Su 8-10pm, F-Sa 8-9pm and midnight-1am; mixed drinks ½-price. Open W-Sa from 8pm. Cash only.)

**Trains** leave at least every hour for: Berlin (2hr., €45-56); Frankfurt (3hr., €75); Hamburg (1½hr., €38); Munich (4½hr., €110); Amsterdam, NTH (4½-5hr., €60-80). To reach the **tourist office,** Ernst-August-Pl. 8, in the Spardabank building across the street from the station. (☎12 34 51 11. Open Oct.-Mar. M-F 9:30am-6:30pm, Sa 9am-2pm; Apr.-Sept. also Su 9am-2pm.) The office leads bus tours of the city (2½hr.; 1:30pm; €15) and sells the **Hannover Card** (1-day €9; 3-day €15; group ticket for up to 5 people €17/29), which covers transportation costs and reduces museum and sightseeing tour prices. **Postal Code:** 30159.

# CENTRAL AND WESTERN GERMANY

*Niedersachsen* (Lower Saxony), which stretches from the North Sea to the hills of central Germany, comprises agricultural plains and foggy marshland. Just south, North Rhine-Westphalia—the most economically powerful area in Germany—is so densely populated that it's nearly impossible to travel through the countryside without glimpsing the next hamlet, metropolis, or village ahead.

# COLOGNE (KÖLN)                    ☎0221

Although 90% of inner historic Cologne (pop. 968,000) crumbled to the ground during WWII, the magnificent Gothic *Dom* amazingly survived 14 bombings and remains one of Germany's main attractions. Today, the city is the largest in North Rhine-Westphalia, offering first-rate museums, theaters, and nightlife.

# ☐ TRANSPORTATION

**Flights:** Planes depart from **Köln-Bonn Flughafen (CGN)**. Flight info ☎ 022 03 40 40 01 02; www.koeln-bonn-airport.de. Airport shuttle S13 leaves the train station M-F 3-6 per hr., Sa-Su 2 per hr. Shuttle to **Berlin** 24 per day 6:30am-8:30pm.

**Trains:** Cologne's **Hauptbahnhof** is one of Germany's rail hubs. Trains leave for **Berlin** (4-5hr., 1-2 per hr., €82-100); **Düsseldorf** (30min., 5-6 per hr., €10-17); **Frankfurt** (1¼-2hr., 2-3 per hr., €42-60); **Hamburg** (4hr., 1-2 per hr., €70-84); **Munich** (4½-5hr., 1-2 per hr., €90-120); **Amsterdam, NTH** (2½-3½hr., 1 per 2hr., €42-55); **Paris, FRA** (4hr., 5-6 per day, €87-120).

**Ride Share: Citynetz Mitfahrzentrale,** Krefelderst. 21 (☎ 194 44). Turn left from the back of the train station, left at the intersection onto Eigelstein, then another left onto Weidengasse, which becomes Krefelderst. Open M-F 9am-8pm, Sa-Su 10am-6pm.

**Public Transportation:** KVB offices have free maps of the S- and U-Bahn, bus, and street-car lines; branch downstairs in the *Hauptbahnhof*. Major terminals include the **Hauptbahnhof, Neumarkt,** and **Appellhofplatz.** Single-ride tickets €1.40-2.30, depending on distance. Day pass €6.40. The Minigruppen-Ticket (from €9.50) allows up to 5 people to ride M-F 9am-midnight and all day Sa-Su. Week tickets €14-20.

**Bike Rental: Radstation,** in Breslauerpl. behind the Hauptbahnhof. (☎ 139 7190). €5 per 3hr., €10 per day, €20 per 3 days, €40 per week. Open M-F 5:30am-10:30pm, Sa 6:30am-8pm, Su 8am-8pm.

# ☒ ☐ ORIENTATION AND PRACTICAL INFORMATION

Cologne extends across the Rhine, but the city center and nearly all sights are located on the western side. The *Altstadt* splits into **Altstadt-Nord,** near the **Hauptbahnhof,** and **Altstadt-Süd,** just south of the **Severinsbrücke** bridge.

**Tourist Office: KölnTourismus,** Unter Fettenhennen 19 (☎ 22 13 04 10; www.koelntourismus.de), across from the main entrance to the *Dom* books rooms for a €3 fee and sells the **Welcome Card** (€9), which provides a day's worth of free public transportation and museum discounts. Open daily M-Sa 9am-8pm, Su 10am-5pm.

**Currency Exchange: Reisebank,** in the train station. Open M-Sa 9am-8pm.

**Internet: Telepoint Callshop & Internet C@fe,** Komödenstr. 19 (☎ 250 9930), by the *Dom.* €1.50 per hr. Open M-F 8:30am-midnight, Sa-Su 9am-midnight. **Branch** at Fleischmengerg. 33 (☎ 397 5246), near Neumarkt. €1 per hr. Open M-F 8:30am-midnight, Sa-Su 10am-midnight.

**Laundromat: Waschsalon,** at the corner of Händelst. and Richard-Wagner-St. Take U1, 7, 12, 15, 16, or 18 to Rudolfpl. Open M-Sa 6am-11pm.

**Post Office:** At the corner of Breitestr. and Tunisstr. in the WDR-Arkaden shopping gallery. Open M-F 9am-7pm, Sa 9am-2pm. **Postal Code:** 50667.

# ☐ ☒ ACCOMMODATIONS AND CAMPING

Conventions fill hotels in spring and fall, and Cologne's hostels often sell out. If you're staying over a weekend in summer, reserve at least two weeks ahead.

▨ **Station Hostel for Backpackers,** Marzellenstr. 44-56 (☎ 912 5301; www.hostel-cologne.de). From the station, walk down Dompropst-Ketzer-Str., and take the 1st right on Marzellenstr. Large dorms without bunks and an ideal location attract crowds of backpackers. Breakfast price varies. Free Wi-Fi. Reception 24hr. 4- to 6-bed dorms €17-21; singles €30-37; doubles €45-52; triples €72. Cash only. ❷

**GERMANY**

▨ **Meininger City Hostel & Hotel,** Engelbertst. 33-35 (☎92 40 90; www.meininger-hostels.de). U1, 7, 12, 15, 16, or 18 to Rudolfpl., then turn left on Habsburgerst., right on Lindenst., and left on Engelbertst. A bar and lounge as well as proximity to Rudolpl. and Zülpicherpl. nightlife keep things hopping. Breakfast included. Reception 24hr. Dorms €17-24; singles €43-49; doubles €58-68; triples €72-81. Cash only. ❷

**Pension Jansen,** Richard-Wagner-Str. 18 (☎25 18 75; www.pensionjansen.de). U1, 6, 7, 15, 17, or 19 to Rudolfpl. Family-run with beautiful, high-ceilinged rooms and colorful walls. Breakfast included. Singles €30-42; doubles €62. Cash only. ❸

**Das Kleine Stapelhäus'chen,** Fischmarkt 1-3 (☎272 7777; www.koeln-altstadt.de/stapelhaeuschen). From the Rathaus, cross the Altenmarkt and take Lintg. to the Fischmarkt. An old-fashioned, richly decorated inn overlooking the Rhine. Breakfast included. Singles €39-51, with bath €53-85; doubles €67-90/90-148. MC/V. ❹

**Jugendherberge Köln-Deutz (HI),** Siegesstr. 5A (☎81 47 11; www.koeln-deutz.jugendherberge.de), just over the Hohenzollernbrücke. Take U1 or 7-9 to Deutzer Freiheit, then turn right from the pedestrian walkway onto Siegesst. 7-story, 506-bed hostel with shop boasts immaculate rooms, all with shower and toilet. Breakfast included. Internet €4 per hr. Reception 24hr. Reserve ahead. Dorms €27; singles €44; doubles €60-67. €3.10 HI discount. MC/V. ❸

**Jugendgästehaus Köln-Riehl (HI),** An der Schanz 14 (☎76 70 81; www.djh.de/jugendherbergen/koeln-riehl). U18 (dir.: Thielenbruch) or U19 (dir.: Buchheim) to Boltensternstr.; exit station and follow the signs. Features rooms with bath and a tree-lined location on the Rhine. Breakfast included. Laundry €3. Reception 24hr. Reserve ahead. Dorms €26; singles €43-48; doubles €63-71. HI discount €3.10. MC/V. ❸

**Hotel am Rathaus,** Bürgerstr. 6 (☎257 7624; www.hostel-am-rathaus-koeln.de). Standing on the porch of the *Rathaus,* head right down Bürgerstr. Rooms are simple and mostly unadorned, but centrally located in the *Altstadt.* Breakfast included. Singles €40, with bath €45; doubles €60/65; triples €80. AmEx/MC/V. ❹

**Campingplatz Poll,** Weidenweg (☎83 19 66). U16 (dir.: Bonn) to Heinrich-Lübke-Ufer, then cross the Rodenkirchener Brücke. Reception 8am-noon and 5-8pm. Open mid-Apr. to Oct. €5.50 per person, €3.50-4.50 per tent. MC/V. ❶

## ☕ FOOD

The *Kölner* diet includes *Rievekoochen* (fried potato dunked in applesauce) and the city's trademark smooth *Kölsch* beer. Cheap restaurants converge on **Zülpicherstraße** to the southeast and **Eigelstein** and **Weidengasse** in the Turkish district. Ethnic restaurants line the perimeter of the *Altstadt,* particularly from **Hohenzollernring** to **Hohenstaufenring.** German eateries surround **Domplatz.** An **open-air market** on Wilhelmspl. fills the Nippes neighborhood. (Open M-Sa 8am-1pm.)

▨ **Päffgen-Brauerei,** Friesenstr. 64. Take U3-5, 12, 16, or 18 to Friesenpl. A local favorite since 1883. *Kölsch* (€1.40) is brewed on the premises, consumed in cavernous halls and in the 600-seat beer garden, and refilled until you put your coaster on top of your glass. Entrees €7-15. Open daily 10am-12:30am. Cash only. ❸

▨ **Café Orlando,** Engelbertstr. 7 (☎23 75 23; www.cafeorlando.de). U8 or 9 to "Zülpicher Pl." Free Wi-Fi and an assortment of newspapers create a Sunday morning atmosphere any time of day. Complete breakfasts (€3.10-6), omelettes and salads (€5.50-8), pasta (€5-7), and mixed drinks (€3.50-4.80) draw a devoted following of students who squeeze. Open daily 9am-11pm. Cash only. ❷

**Restaurant Magnus,** Zülpicherstr. 48 (☎24 14 69). Take U8, 9, 12, 15, 16, or 18 to Zülpicher Pl. Locals flock to this crowded cafe for funky tunes, artfully prepared meals (mostly Italian) from €4, and many vegetarian options (€5-8). Open M-Th 8am-3am, F-Sa 8am-4am, Su 8am-1am. Cash only. ❷

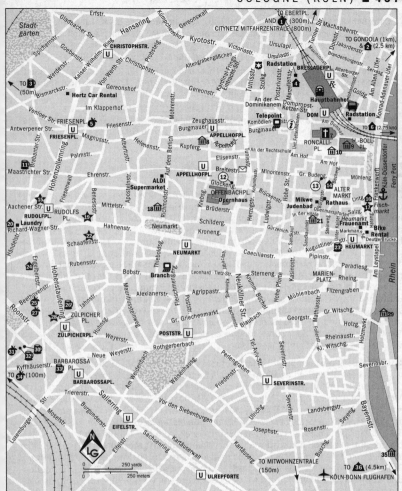

GERMANY

# Cologne (Köln)

**🏕️🏠 ACCOMMODATIONS**

Campingplatz Poll, **36**
Das Kleine Stapelhäus'chen, **16**
Hotel am Rathaus, **14**
Jugendgästehaus Köln-Riehl, **2**
Jugendherberge Köln-Deutz, **6**
Meininger Hostel & Hotel, **24**
Pension Jansen, **20**
Station Hostel for
　Backpackers, **4**

**🍺⭐ BARS & NIGHTLIFE**

Brauerei Weiß, **19**
Cent Club, **28**
Cubana Bar, **32, 33**
Das Ding, **26**
Hotel Timp, **23**
Iron, **22**
M20, **11**
Papa Joe's Jazzlokal, **17**
Roxy, **15**
Stadtgarten, **3**
Stiefel, **30**

**🍴 FOOD**

Café Orlando, **25**
Café Schmitz, **1**
Engelbät, **27**
Mensa, **34**
Päffgen-Brauerei, **5**
Restaurant Magnus, **31**

**🏛️⛪〇 CHURCHES,
MUSEUMS, AND SITES**

Dom, **7**
House #4711, **12**
Imhoff-Stollwerck-
　Museum, **35**

Käthe-Kollwitz-
　Museum, **18**
Museum Ludwig, **9**
NS-Dokumentations-
　Zentrum, **8**
Römisch-Germanisches
　Museum, **10**
Römisches Praetorium
　und Kanal, **13**
Schokoladen-
　museum, **29**
Wallraf-Richartz
　Museum, **21**

**Café Schmitz,** Hansaring 98. (☎ 139 7733). Turn left from the back of the train station, head right on Eigelstein at the intersection and walk to the gate, then turn left on Lübeckerst. Features a large bar and an extensive breakfast menu (€3-7). Try the Nutella-rich Sweet Sue breakfast (€5.80). Open daily from 9am-11:30pm. Cash only. ❶

**Engelbät,** Engelbertst. 7. (☎ 24 69 14). U8 or 9 to Zülpicher Pl. The best place for plentiful crepes, vegetarian and otherwise (€4-7.50). Breakfast (€1.50-3.50) served daily until 3pm. Open daily 11am-midnight. Cash only. ❶

**Mensa,** Zülpicherstr. 70. Take U8 or 9 to Dasselstr./Bahnhof Süd. Walk away from the bridge; it's 50m ahead on the right side. Cheap food (€2-5) in a huge cafeteria. Open during the semester M-F 11:30am-2:15pm and 5:30-9pm; summer and holidays M-F 11:30am-2:15pm. Cash only. ❶

# ◉ SIGHTS

🏛 **DOM.** Germany's greatest cathedral, the *Dom*, is a perfect realization of High Gothic style. Built over the course of six centuries, it was finally finished in 1880 and miraculously escaped destruction during WWII. Today, its colossal spires define the skyline of Cologne. A chapel on the inside right houses a 15th-century **triptych** depicting the city's five patron saints. Behind the altar in the center of the choir is the **Shrine of the Magi,** the cathedral's most sacred compartment, which allegedly holds the remains of the Three Kings and was once a pilgrimage site for monarchs. Before exiting the choir, stop in the **Chapel of the Cross** to admire the 10th-century **Gero crucifix,** which is the oldest intact sculpture of a crucified Christ. It takes about 15min. to scale the 509 steps of the **Südturm** (south tower); catch your breath at the **Glockenstube,** a chamber with the tower's nine bells, three-quarters of the way up. *(Cathedral open daily 6am-7:30pm. 45min. English-language tours M-Sa 10:30am and 2:30pm, Su 2:30pm. Tower open daily May-Sept. 9am-6pm; Nov.-Feb. 9am-4pm; Mar.-Apr. and Oct. 9am-5pm. Cathedral free. Tour €4, children €2. Tower €2, students €1.)*

**MUSEUMS.** Gourmands will want to head straight for the 🍫**Schokoladenmuseum,** which is best described as Willy Wonka's factory made real. It presents every step of chocolate production, from the rainforests to the gold fountain that spurts streams of free samples. *(Rheinauhafen 1A, near the Severinsbrücke. ☎ 931 8880; www.schokoladenmuseum.de. From the train station, head for the Rhine, and walk to the right along the river; go under the Deutzer Brücke, and take the 1st footbridge. Open Tu-F 10am-6pm, Sa-Su 11am-7pm. €6.50, students €4.)* Masterpieces from the Middle Ages to the Post-Impressionist period are gathered in the **Wallraf-Richartz Museum.** *(Martinstr. 39. From the Heumarkt, take Gürzenichstr. 1 block to Martinstr. ☎ 276 94; www.museenkoeln.de/wrm. Open Tu 10am-8pm, W-F 10am-6pm, Sa-Su 11am-6pm. €5.80, students €3.30.)* The collection of the **Museum Ludwig** focuses on 20th-century and contemporary art. *(Bischofsgartenstr. 1, behind the Römisch-Germanisches Museum. ☎ 22 12 61 65. Open Tu-Su 10am-6pm, 1st F of each month 10am-10pm. €7.50, students €5.50.)* The **Römisch-Germanisches Museum** displays a large array of artifacts documenting the daily lives of Romans in ancient Colonia. *(Roncallipl. 4, beside the Dom. Open Tu-Su, W 10am-8pm. €4.50, students €2.70.)* The chilling **NS-Dokumentations-Zentrum,** Appellhofpl. 23-25, includes a former Gestapo prison with inmates' wall graffiti intact. *(☎ 22 12 63 32. U3-6 or 19 to Appelhofpl. Open Tu-F 10am-4pm, Sa-Su 11am-4pm. €2.50, students €1.)* The **Käthe-Kollwitz-Museum** houses the world's largest collection of sketches, sculptures, and prints by the 20th-century artist-activist. *(Neumarkt 18-24. On the top fl. in the Neumarkt-Passage. Take U1, 3-4, 6-9, or 19 to Neumarkt. ☎ 227 2363. Open Tu-F 10am-6pm, Sa-Su 11am-6pm. German-language tours Su 3pm. €3, students €1.)*

**HOUSE #4711.** The fabled **Eau de Cologne,** once prescribed as a drinkable curative, earned the town worldwide recognition. Today, the house of its origin, labeled #4711 by a Napoleonic system that abolished street names, is a boutique where a fountain flows with the scented water. Visit the gallery upstairs for a history of the fragrance. *(On Glockeng. near the intersection with Tunisstr. From Hohe Str., turn right on Brückenstr., which becomes Glockeng. Open M-F 9am-7pm, Sa 9am-6pm. Free.)*

**RÖMISCHES PRAETORIUM UND KANAL.** The ruins of the former Roman military headquarters display remains of Roman idols and an array of rocks left by early inhabitants—walk through the old sewer for a particularly intimate look at ancient life. *(From the Rathaus, turn right toward the cluster of hotels along Bürgerstr. and then left onto Kleine Budeng. ☎ 223 94. Open Tu-Su 10am-5pm. €1.50, students €0.75.)*

## 🎵 🎭 ENTERTAINMENT AND NIGHTLIFE

Cologne explodes in celebration during 🎭**Karneval** (late Jan. to early Feb. 2008), a week-long pre-Lenten festival made up of 50 neighborhood processions. **Weiberfastnacht** (Jan. 31, 2008) is the first major to-do: the mayor mounts the platform at Alter Markt and surrenders leadership to the city's women, who then hunt down their husbands at work and chop off their ties. The weekend builds to the out-of-control parade on **Rosenmontag** (Rose Monday; Feb. 4, 2008), when thousands of merry participants sing and dance their way through the city center while exchanging *Bützchen* (kisses on the cheek). While most revelers nurse their hangovers on Shrove Tuesday, pubs and restaurants set fire to the straw scarecrows hanging out their windows. For more info, pick up the Karneval booklet at the tourist office. For summer visitors, Cologne offers the huge **C/O Pop Festival** in mid-August, a multi-day event that draws some 200 electronic and independent musicians for 40 shows. (www.c-o-pop.de. €49.)

Roman mosaics dating back to the 3rd century record the wild excesses of the city's early residents; they've toned it down only a bit since. The monthly *Kölner* (€1), sold at newsstands, lists clubs, parties, and concerts. The closer to the Rhine or *Dom* you venture, the faster your wallet will empty. After dark in **Hohenzollernring**, crowds of people move from theaters to clubs and finally to cafes in the early morning. The area around **Zülpicherpl.** is a favorite of students and the best option for an affordable good time. Radiating westward from Friesenpl., the **Belgisches Viertel** (Belgian Quarter) has slightly more expensive bars and cafes.

🎷 **Papa Joe's Jazzlokal,** Buttermarkt 37 (☎257 7931). Papa Joe has a legendary reputation for providing good jazz and good times. Add your business card or expired ID to the collage that adorns the bar. *Kölsch* (€3.60) in 0.4L glasses, not the usual 0.2L. Live jazz M-Sa 10:30pm-12:30am. Open daily 7pm-1am, F-Sa 7pm-3am. Cash only.

🎷 **Cent Club,** Hohenstaufenring 25-27 (www.centclub.de). Near Zülpicher Pl. Take U8 or 9 to Zülpicher. This student disco features more dance (R&B, pop, dance classics) and less talk, with the appeal of low-priced drinks. Shots €0.50. Beer €1-2. Mixed drinks €3. Cover W-Sa €5. Open M-Sa 9pm-late.

**M20,** Maastrichterstr. 20 (☎51 96 66; www.m20-koeln.de). U1, 6, or 7 to Rudolfpl. DJs deliver some of the city's best drum 'n' bass and punk to a local crowd. Beer €1.50-3.20. Open Su-Th 10pm-2am, F-Sa 10pm-4am. Cash only.

**Stadtgarten,** Venloerstr. 40 (☎95 29 94 33). Take U3, 5, 6, or 12 to Friesenpl. An outdoor beer garden and 2 indoor clubs. Downstairs hosts parties playing everything from soul to techno, while the upper concert hall is renowned for its jazz recordings and performances. Cover €5-8. Open M-Th 9pm-1am, F-Sa 9pm-3am. Cash only.

**Das Ding,** Hohenstaufenring 30 (☎240 7019; www.dingzone.de). U8 or 9 to Zülpicherpl. Smoky and very noir, this popular student bar and disco has varied music and dirt-cheap drink specials (€1). Cover €5. Open Tu, Th, Su 9pm-3am; W 9pm-2am; F-Sa 9pm-4am. Cash only.

**Roxy,** Aachenerst. 2. U1, 7, 12, 15-16, or 18 to Rudolfpl. The place to go in the wee hours of the night. Beer €1.60-3. Open daily from midnight. Cash only.

**Cubana Bar,** Barbarossapl. 5 (☎216 0280). Take U6, 12, 15-16, or 18 to Barbarossapl. This cocktail lounge and bar with an extensive Latin American drink list and alternating *reggaetón* and salsa playlist proudly features blown-up portraits of Che Guevara on its walls and awning. Branch at Zülpicherstr. 36 (U8 or 9 to Zülpicherpl.). Open daily 6pm-late. Cash only.

**Stiefel,** at the corner of Zülpicherstr. and Heinsbergst., holds to a definite grunge ethic. Graffiti-covered concrete walls and rough wooden tables host a mellow crowd of students. Beer €1.40-3. Cash only.

## GLBT-FRIENDLY

Gay nightlife thrives in Cologne, centering on the **Bermuda-Dreieck** (Bermuda Triangle), around Rudolfpl., and also in the area running up Matthiasstr. to Mühlenbach, Hohe Pforte, Marienpl., and the Heumarkt neighborhood by **Deutzer Brücke.** *Ric*, offered at gay bars, and *Out in Cologne*, published by the tourist office, offers recommendations for gay events, festivals, and nightlife. The **Cologne Pride** festival (late June to early July), centered in Rudolfpl., culminates in the massive **Christopher Street Day Parade,** which draws up to a million visitors.

**⛎ Hotel Timp,** Heumarkt 25 (☎258 1409; www.timp.de). Across from the U-Bahn stop. This club and hotel has become an institution in Cologne for travesty theater. Gay and straight crowds come here for the gaudy and glitter-filled cabarets. Drag shows daily 1-4am. No cover. 1st drink Su-Th €8, F-Sa €13. Open daily 11am-late. AmEx/MC/V.

**Brauerai Weiß,** Hahnenst. 22. U1, 7, 12, 15-16, or 18 to Rudolfpl. Once one of the few gay brewhouses in town, this restaurant and bar features an extensive menu (€6-14). Open daily 11am-late. MC/V.

**Iron,** Schaafenst. 45 (☎801 4095). This sleek bar and hangout is in the center of the Rudolfpl. gay scene. Classic dance tracks and a disco ball add to the energetic mood. Beer €2-5. Open Su and Tu-Th 8pm-2am, F-Sa 8pm-4am. Cash only.

# BONN ☎0228

While the residence of Chancellor Konrad Adenauer, Bonn (pop. 305,000) served as the West German capital—and was derided as *"Hauptdorf,"* or "capital village." The *Bundestag* moved to Berlin in 1999, but Bonn remains a center of international diplomacy. The city capitalizes on its most famous native: Beethoven.

**▐▜ TRANSPORTATION AND PRACTICAL INFORMATION. Trains** go to Berlin (5hr., 4 per day, €87-100) and Cologne (30min., 4-5 per hr., €9-15). The **tourist office** is at Windeckstr. 1, off Münsterpl.; follow Poststr. from the station. (☎77 50 00; www.bonn.de. Open M-F 9am-6:30pm, Sa 9am-4pm, Su 10am-2pm.) The **post office** is at Münsterpl. 17. (Open M-F 9am-8pm, Sa 9am-4pm.) **Postal Code:** 53111.

**▐▐ ACCOMMODATIONS AND FOOD. ⛎Deutsches Haus ❸,** Kasernenstr. 19-21, is on a quiet residential street within easy walking distance of the *Altstadt* and has a decadent included breakfast. (☎63 37 77; info@hotel-deutscheshaus.net. Reception 7am-11pm. Singles €32, with bath €55-70; doubles €65-77; triples €66-99. AmEx/MC/V.) For the spacious but distant **Jugendherberge Bonn (HI) ❷,** Haager Weg 42, take bus #621 (dir.: Ippendorf Altenheim) to Jugendgästehaus. (☎28 99 70; bonn@jugendherberge.de. Reception 7am-1am. Wheelchair-accessible. Breakfast and linens included. Laundry €4. Curfew 1am. Dorms €26; singles €42; doubles €64. MC/V.) The **market** on Münsterpl. teems with haggling vendors and customers. Prices plummet at the end of the day. (Open M-Sa 8am-6pm.) Take a break from meaty German fare at ◼**Cassius-Garten ❷**, Maximilianstr. 28D, near the train station, which serves 50 kinds of salad, pasta, and whole-grain baked goods, all for €1.50 per 100g. (☎65 24 29; www.cassiusgarten.de. Open M-F 11am-8pm.)

◼◼ **SIGHTS AND NIGHTLIFE.** Bonn's pedestrian zone has many historic nooks. ◼**Beethovenhaus,** Bonng. 20, Ludwig van Beethoven's birthplace, houses a fantastic collection of the composer's personal effects, from his first viola to his primitive hearing aids—even some of his hair. The Digital Archives Studio offers recordings and scores of all of his works. (☎981 7525; www.beethoven-haus-bonn.de. Open Apr.-Oct. M-Sa 10am-6pm, Su 11am-6pm; Nov.-Mar. M-Sa 10am-5pm, Su 11am-5pm. €5, students €4.) Forty thousand students study in the huge 18th-century palace now serving as the center of **Friedrich-Wilhelms-Universität.** To reach Bonn's "other" palace, stroll down Poppelsdorfer Allee to **Poppelsdorfer Schloß,** which has a French facade, an Italian courtyard, and beautifully manicured botanical gardens; check out the world's largest water lilies in the greenhouses. (Gardens open Apr.-Oct. Su-F 9am-6pm; Oct.-Mar. M-F 9am-4pm.) Five museums line the *Museumsmeile* near the banks of the Rhine, though they're not within walking distance; take U16, 63, 66, 67, 68 to the Heussallee/Museumsmeile stop. Around 7,000 interactive exhibits examine post-WWII Germany at the ◼**Haus der Geschichte,** Willy-Brandt-Allee 14. (☎916 50. Open Tu-Su 9am-7pm. Free.) One block away, the immense **Kunstmuseum Bonn,** Friedrich-Ebert-Allee 2, houses a superb collection of 20th-century German art. (☎77 62 60. Open Tu and Th-Su 11am-6pm, W 11am-9pm. €5, students €2.50.) The **Bundeshaus** once earned the title of "least prepossessing parliament building" in the world; take bus #610 to "Bundeshaus" if so inclined. *Schnüss* (€1), sold at newsstands, has club and concert listings. ◼**The Jazz Galerie,** Oxfordstr. 24, is a mostly jazz-less bar and disco popular with swanky youths. (☎63 93 24. Cover Th €5, F-Sa €8; includes 1 drink. Open Tu and Th 9pm-3am, F-Sa 10pm-5am. Cash only.) **Balustrade,** Heerstr. 52, has a huge TV screen and monthly theme nights that include beach, snowball, and jungle parties. (Beer €2-2.50. Open M-Th 7pm-1am, F-Sa 7pm-late. Cash only.) **Pantheon,** Bundeskanzlerpl. 2-10, hosts concerts, stand-up comedy, and art exhibits. (☎21 25 21; www.pantheon.de. Cover €6.50. Disco open 11pm-late. MC/V.)

## AACHEN ☎0241

Easygoing Aachen (pop. 246,000), Germany's westernmost city, was once "Roma secunda," the 8th-century capital of Charlemagne's enormous Frankish empire. The legacy of the medieval superstar is ubiquitous—even local pharmacies use him as their namesake. For a glimpse of Aachen's former splendor, visit the three-tiered dome, octagonal interior, and blue-gold mosaics of the ◼**Dom,** in the city center. Charlemagne's remains are housed in the ornate reliquary behind the altar. (Open M-Sa 7am-7pm, Su 1-7pm, except during services.) Around the corner is the **Schatzkammer,** Klosterpl. 2, considered the most important ecclesiastical treasury north of the Alps. A silver bust of Charlemagne containing the emperor's skull is just one of several priceless artifacts. (☎47 70 91 27. Open M 10am-1pm, Tu-W and F-Su 10am-6pm, Th 10am-9pm. €4, students €3.) Aachen's earliest settlers were scared off by the natural springs that run through the area, believing that they came from hell. The Romans were indifferent to satanic connections and constructed the city's first **mineral baths.** These baths are now the luxurious **Carolus Thermen,** Passstr. 79, with eight pools and numerous themed saunas. Take bus #51 from the Normaluhr bus stop on Theaterst. to Carolus Thermen. (☎18 27 40; www.carolus-thermen.de. 2½hr. soak €10, with sauna €20; day-long soak €15, sauna €29. Open daily 9am-11pm. Cash only.) The **Ludwigforum für Internationale**

GERMANY

**Kunst,** Jülicherstr. 97-109, houses international exhibits and a rotating collection of cutting-edge art. (☎180 7104; www.ludwigforum.de. Open Tu-W and F noon-6pm, Th noon-8pm, Sa-Su 11am-6pm. €5, students €2.50.)

**Hotel Cortis ❸,** Krefelderstr. 52, is an small B&B with cable TV in each room. Take bus #34 (dir.: Kohlscheid Banhof) from the Normaluhr bus stop to Carolus Thermen, then take bus #51 to Rolandstr. Turn left on Krefelderstr. (☎997 4110; www.hotel-cortis.de. Breakfast included. Singles €30; doubles €53-58, with bath €62. MC/V.) **Euroregionales Jugendgästehaus (HI) ❷,** Maria-Theresia-Allee 260, has clean, bright rooms about a 20min. bus ride from the city center. Take bus #2 (dir.: Preusswald) from the Misereor bus stop to Ronheide. (☎71 10 10; aachen.jugendherberge.de. Breakfast included. Curfew 1am. Dorms €25; singles €39; doubles €61. €3.10 HI discount. MC/V.) **Sausalitos ❸,** Markt 47, is a Mexican restaurant with a huge cocktail bar. Red lighting and a central location makes this bar a haunt of the young and trendy. (☎234 9200; www.sausolitos.de. Entrees €6-14. Open Su-Th noon-1am, F-Sa noon-2am. Cash only.) The **pedestrian zone** and **Pontstraße,** off Marktpl., have a number of restaurants that are easy on the wallet. **Trains** go to Brussels, BEL (2hr., 1 per hr., €25-30), Cologne (1hr., 2 per hr., €13-19), and Paris, FRA (3hr., 6-7 per day, €126). The **tourist office** is on Friedrich-Wilhelm-Pl. in the Atrium Elisenbrunnen. From the station, head up Bahnhofstr., turn left onto Theaterstr., which becomes Theaterpl., and then turn right onto Kapuzinergraben, which becomes Friedrich-Wilhelm-Pl. (☎180 2960. Open M-F 9am-6pm, Sa 9am-2pm, Su 10am-2pm; Closed Su Christmas-Easter.) **Postal Code:** 52062.

# DÜSSELDORF ☎0211

Düsseldorf (pop. 571,000), the nation's *"Hautstadt"*—a pun on the German *"Hauptstadt"* (capital)—is a stately metropolis with an *Altstadt* (Old Town) that features stellar nightlife and pricey shopping. In addition to glitz and glamour, Düsseldorf has an internationally recognized art school and top-notch museums.

**▣⚡ TRANSPORTATION AND PRACTICAL INFORMATION. Trains** run to: **Amsterdam, NTH** (2hr., 1 per 2hr., €32-42); **Berlin** (4½hr., 1-2 per hr., €94-96); **Frankfurt** (2hr., 2 per hr., €45-70); **Hamburg** (4hr., 1-2 per hr., €68-80); **Munich** (5-6hr., 2 per hr., €93-121). Düsseldorf's S-Bahn is integrated into the regional **VRR** *(Verkehrsverbund Rhein-Ruhr)* system, which links most nearby cities and is the cheapest way to get to Aachen and Cologne. On the **public transportation** system, single tickets cost €1.10-2.10. *Tagestickets* (€11-18) allow up to five people to travel for 24hr. on any line. To reach the **tourist office,** Immermannstr. 65, head out of the train station and to the right; look for the Immermannhof building. It books rooms for free, except during trade fairs. (☎172 0228. Open M-F 9:30am-6:30pm, Sa 9am-2pm.) The **post office** is on Konrad-Adenauer-Pl. to the right of the tourist office. (Open M-F 8am-8pm, Sa 9am-2pm.) **Postal Code:** 40210.

**▟▞ ACCOMMODATIONS AND FOOD.** Düsseldorf's hotels and hostels often double their prices during trade fairs, which take place from August to April. Close to the center of town, ▩**Backpackers Düsseldorf ❷,** Fürstenwall 180, has carpeted floors, colorful beds, and a common room equipped with leather sofas, a TV, and a DVD player. Take bus #725 (dir.: Hafen/Lausward) from the station, and get off at Kirchpl. (☎302 0848; www.backpackers-duesseldorf.de. Kitchen available. Breakfast, lockers, linens, and towel included. Free Internet and Wi-Fi. Reception 8am-9pm. Reserve ahead F-Sa in summer. Dorms €22. MC/V.) The modern **Jugendgästehaus Düsseldorf (HI) ❷,** Düsseldorfer Str. 1, is just over the Rheinkniebrücke from the Altstadt. Take U70 or 74-77 to Luegpl., then walk 500m down Kaiser-Wilhelm-Ring. Or, get off at Belsenpl., and take bus #835 or 836 to the Jugendherberge stop.

GERMANY

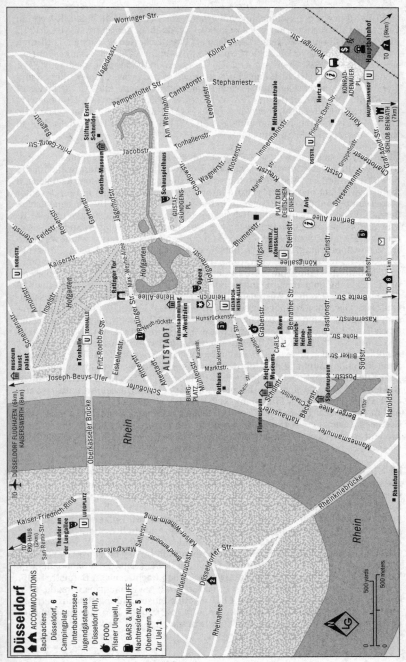

**Düsseldorf**

**▲▲ ACCOMMODATIONS**

Backpackers
  Düsseldorf, **6**
Campingplatz
  Unterbachersee, **7**
Jugendgästehaus
  Düsseldorf (HI), **2**

**♦ FOOD**
Pilsner Urquell, **4**

**■ BARS & NIGHTLIFE**
Nachtresidenz, **5**
Oberbayern, **3**
Zur Uel, **1**

Worringer Str.

Vagedesstr.

Prinz-Georg-Str.

Stiftung Ernst Schneider

Jacobstr.

Goethe-Museum

Pempelforter Str.

Kölner Str.

Stephaniestr.

Cantadorstr.

Leopoldstr.

Am Wehrhahn

Tonhallenstr.

Klosterstr.

Wagnerstr.

Schadowstr.

Immermannstr.

Mitwohnzentrale

Konrad-Adenauer-Pl.

Hertz

Friedrich-Ebert-Str.

Hauptbahnhof

TO 7 (9km)

TO HAUPTBAHNHOF (7km)

SCHLOB BENRATH

Ostst.

Graf-Adolf-Str.

Corneliusstr.

Gruppelostr.

Charlottenstr.

Marien str.

Kreuzstr.

Stresemannstr.

Berliner Allee

Avis

PLATZ DER DEUTSCHEN EINHEIT

STEINSTR. / KÖNIGSALLEE

Steinstr.

Grünstr.

Bahnstr.

TO 6 (1km)

Blumenstr.

Königstr.

Königsallee

Schauspielhaus

GUSTAF-GRÜNDGENS-PL.

Jägerhofstr.

Hofgarten

Max-Weyhe-Allee

Ratinger Tor

Hofgarten

Heine-Allee

Opera

Kunstsammlung N.-Westfalen

Heinrich-Heine-Allee

HEINRICH-HEINE-ALLEE

Hunsrückenstr.

Benrather Str.

Bastionstr.

Breite Str.

Kasernenstr.

Hohe Str.

Heinrich-Heine-Institut

CARLS-PL.

Flinger str.

Grabenstr.

Rewe

Bolkerstr.

Wallstr.

Kurzestr.

Rathaus

BURG-PLATZ

Müllenstr.

Marktstr.

Altestr.

Rittestr.

Fritz-Roeber-Str.

Eiskellerstr.

Schlöbufer

Joseph-Beuys-Ufer

Rhein str.

Rathausufer

Filmmuseum

Hetjens Museum

Schulstr.

Bäckerstr.

Citadellstr.

Stadtmuseum

Berger Allee

Postst.

Bilker Str.

Südstr.

Kartfor.

Haroldstr.

Mannesmannufer

**Rhein**

Oberkasseler Brücke

TO DÜSSELDORF FLUGHAFEN (6km), KAISERSWERTH (3km)

TO DÜSSELDORF FLUGHAFEN

museum kunst palast

Tonhalle

TONHALLE

TONHALLE

NORDSTR.

Kaiserstr.

Sternstr.

Inselstr.

Feldstr.

Rosenstr.

Gartenstr.

Arnoldstr.

Neubrückstr.

Ratinger Str.

**ALTSTADT**

Rheinkniebrücke

**Rhein**

Rheinturm

TO EKO-HAUS (2km)

Kaiser-Friedrich-Ring

San-Remo-Str.

Theater an der Luegallee

LUEGPLATZ

Markgrafenstr.

Sällerstr.

Brend'amourstr.

Kaiser-Wilhelm-Ring

Düsseldorfer Str.

Wildenbruchstr.

Rheinallee

500 yards

500 meters

LG

(☎55 73 10; www.duesseldorf-jugendherberge.de. Breakfast included. Reception 7am-1am. Curfew 1am. Dorms €26; singles €42; doubles €60; quads €93. €3.10 HI discount. Cash only.) To reach **Campingplatz Unterbachersee ❶,** Kleiner Torfbruch 31, take any S-Bahn to Düsseldorf Geresheim, then bus #735 (dir.: Stamesberg) to Seeweg. (☎899 2038. Open Apr.-Oct. €5 per person, €10 per tent. Cash only.) For a cheap meal, the *Altstadt* can't be beat; rows of pizzerias, Chinese diners, and *Döner,* waffle, and crepe stands reach from Heinrich-Heine-Allee to the banks of the Rhine. The local outlet of the Czech brewery **Pilsner Urquell ❷,** Grabenstr. 6, specializes in Eastern European fare. (☎868 1411. Entrees €5-13. Beer €2.50-4.10. Open M-Sa 11am-1pm, Su 4pm-midnight. MC/V.) **Rewe** supermarket is in Carlspl. in the *Altstadt.* (Open M-Sa 7am-8pm.)

◙ **SIGHTS. Königsallee** ("the Kö"), just outside the *Altstadt,* embodies the vitality of wealthy Düsseldorf. To reach the Kö from the train station, walk 10min. down Graf-Adolf-Str. Midway up the street is the marble-and-copper **Kö-Galerie,** a mall showcasing one haughty store after another. Better deals in non-designer stores can be found along Flingerstr. in the *Altstadt.* To get to the Baroque **Schloß Benrath,** Benrather Schloßallee 104, in the suburbs of Düsseldorf, take tram #701. The *Schloß* was originally built as a pleasure palace and hunting grounds for Elector Karl Theodor. Strategically placed mirrors and false exterior windows make the castle appear larger than it is, but the enormous French gardens still dwarf it. (☎899 3832; www.schloss-benrath.de. Open Tu-Su mid-Apr. to Oct. 10am-6pm; Nov. to mid-Apr. 11am-5pm. Tours 1 per hr. €5, students €3.50.) At the upper end of the Kö is the **Hofgarten,** the oldest public park in Germany. To its west, the **K20 Kunstsammlung Nordrhein-Westfalen,** Grabbepl. 5, has various works by Expressionists, Surrealists, and former Düsseldorf resident Paul Klee. (U70 or 75-79 to Heinrich-Heine-Allee, and walk two blocks north. ☎838 1130; www.kunstsammlung.de. Open Tu-F 10am-6pm, Sa-Su 11am-6pm. €6.50, students €4.50.) To the north at Ehrenhof 4-5, the works of the **museum kunst palast** emphasize the Düsseldorf school; there's also an extensive collection of glass artwork. (U74-77 to Kulturzentrum Ehrenhof/Tonhalle and follow the signs. ☎899 2460; www.museum-kunst-palast.de. Open Tu-Su 11am-6pm. €6, students €4.50.) The **Heinrich-Heine-Institut,** Bilker Str. 12-14, is a shrine to the melancholic poet and Düsseldorf native. (☎899 5571. Open Tu-F and Su 11am-5pm, Sa 1-5pm. €3, students €1.50.) At the eastern end of the Hofgarten, the 18th-century **Schloß Jägerhof,** Jakobistr. 2, houses the **Goethe-Museum,** a collection of memorabilia relating to all aspects of the writer's life and work. Take streetcar #707 or bus #752 to Schloß Jägerhof. (☎899 6262. Open Tu-F and Su 11am-5pm, Sa 1-5pm. €3, students €1.50.)

▣ **NIGHTLIFE.** It's said that Düsseldorf's 500 pubs make up the longest bar in the world. By nightfall, it's nearly impossible to see where one pub ends and the next begins in the packed *Altstadt.* **Bolkerstraße** is jam-packed with street performers. The newsletter *Prinz* (€3) gives tips on the entertainment scene; some youth hostels have it for free. The spacious **Oberbayern,** Bolkerstr. 37, draws a young crowd to its flashy, frenetic dance floor and mellow bar. (☎854 9070; www.oberbayern-duesseldorf.de. Mixed drinks €2-4.50. Open W-Su 7pm-5am. Cash only.) **Zur Uel,** Ratinger Str. 16, is a restaurant by day and a rowdy German pub by night. (☎32 53 69. Beer €2-3. Open Su-Th 9am-2am, F-Sa 9am-3am. MC/V.) Sleek clubs, such as the half-lounge, half-disco **Nachtresidenz,** Bahnstr. 13-15, are located farther from the *Altstadt.* (☎136 5755; www.nachtresidenz.de. 21+. Open F-Sa 10pm-5am. Cash only.) **GLBT nightlife** clusters along Bismarckstr., at the intersection with Charlottenstr. *Facolte* (€2), a gay and lesbian nightlife magazine, is available at most newsstands in the city.

# FRANKFURT AM MAIN ☎069

International offices, shiny skyscrapers, and expensive cars can be found at every intersection in Frankfurt (pop. 660,000), nicknamed "Mainhattan" for its location on the Main River and its glitzy vitality. Both people and money are constantly in motion in this transport hub, which is also home to the central bank of the EU.

## ▐ TRANSPORTATION

**Flights:** The busy **Flughafen Rhein-Main** (☎01805 37 24 36) is connected to the *Hauptbahnhof* by S-Bahn trains S8 and 9 (2-3 per hr.). Buy tickets (€3.55) from the green machines marked *Fahrkarten* before boarding. Taxis to the city center cost around €20.

**Trains:** Trains run from the **Hauptbahnhof** to: **Amsterdam, NTH** (4hr., 1 per 2hr., €150); **Berlin** (4hr., 2 per hr., €87-104); **Cologne** (1½hr., 1 per hr., €38-60); **Hamburg** (3½-5hr., 1 per hr., €78-98); **Munich** (3hr., 1 per hr., €64-81). Call ☎01805 19 41 95 for schedules, reservations, and info.

**Public Transportation:** Frankfurt's public transportation system runs daily 4am-1:30am. Single-ride tickets (€2) are valid for 1hr. in 1 dir. **Eurail** is valid only on S-Bahn trains. The **Tageskarte** (day pass; €5.40) provides unlimited transportation on the S-Bahn, U-Bahn, streetcars, and buses, and can be purchased from machines in any station (€5.40). Ticketless passengers can be fined €40.

**Ride share:** Stuttgarter Str. 12 (☎23 64 44). Take a right on Baseler Str. at the side exit of the *Hauptbahnhof* (track 1) and walk 2 blocks. Arranges rides to **Berlin** (€30), **Munich** (€23), and elsewhere. Open M-F 6:30am-9pm, Sa 8am-9pm, Su 9am-8pm.

**Taxis:** ☎23 00 01, ☎23 00 33, or ☎25 00 01. €1.50-1.75 per km.

**Bike Rental: Deutsche Bahn (DB)** runs the citywide service **Call a Bike** (☎0700 05 22 55 22; www.callabike.de). Bikes marked with the red DB logo can be found throughout the city. To rent one, call the service hotline. €0.10 per min., €15 per day.

## ▐ ▐ ORIENTATION AND PRACTICAL INFORMATION

Frankfurt's *Hauptbahnhof* opens onto the city's red-light district; from the station, the *Altstadt* is a 20min. walk down Kaiserstr. or Münchenerstr. The tourist heavy **Römerberg** square is just north of the Main River, while the city's commercial center lies farther north along **Zeil**. Cafes and services cluster near the university in **Bockenheim** (U6 or 7 to Bockenheimer Warte). Across the river, the **Sachsen-hausen** area draws pub-crawlers and museum-goers (U1, 2, or 3 to Schweizer Pl.).

**Tourist Office:** in the *Hauptbahnhof* (☎21 23 88 00; www.frankfurt-tourismus.de). Books rooms for a €3 fee; free if you call ahead. Sells the **Frankfurt Card** (1-day €8, 2-day €12), which allows unlimited use of public transportation and provides discounts on many sights. Open M-F 8am-9pm, Sa-Su and holidays 9am-6pm. **Branch** in Römer-berg square (open M-F 9:30am-5:30pm, Sa-Su 10am-4pm).

**Currency Exchange:** At the **Reise Bank** in the *Hauptbahnhof* (open daily 7:30am-9pm), though cheaper exchange rates can be found outside the train station.

**Laundromat: Miele Wash World,** Moselstr. 17; walk straight on Kaiserstr. from the Hauptbanhof and turn right after 1 block. Wash €4, dry €1 per 15min. **Waschsalon,** Wallstr. 8, near the youth hostel in Sachsenhausen. Wash €3, dry €0.50 per 15min. Detergent included. Open daily 6am-11pm.

**Internet Access:** In the basement of the train station. €2 per hr. Open M-Sa 8:30am-1am. Internet cafes are on Kaiserstr., across from the *Hauptbahnhof*.

**Post Office:** Goethe Pl. Walk 10min. down Taunusstr. from the *Hauptbahnhof,* or take the U- or S-Bahn to Hauptwache and walk south to the square. Open M-F 9:30am-7pm, Sa 9am-2pm. **Postal Code:** 60313.

## 🏠🏠 ACCOMMODATIONS AND CAMPING

Deals are rare and trade fairs make rooms scarce; reserve at least two to three weeks ahead. The **Westend/University** area has a few cheap options.

**🏠 Frankfurt Hostel,** Kaiserstr. 74 (☎247 5130; info@frankfurt-hostel.com). Near the *Hauptbahnhof* (and the red-light district), this convenient, sociable hostel with airy rooms organizes free city tours and F night "club crawls." Luggage storage and laundry included. Internet €1 per hr. Dorms €18-22; singles €50; doubles €60; triples €66. Higher rates during trade fairs. MC/V. ❷

**Haus der Jugend (HI),** Deutschherrnufer 12 (☎610 0150; www.jugendherberge-frank-furt.de). Bus #46 (dir.: Mühlberg) from the station to Frankensteiner Pl., or take tram #16 (dir.: Offenbach Stadtgrenze) to *Lokalbahnhof* and walk back up Dreicherstr., turn-ing left on Deutschherrnufer. Great location along the Main and in front of Sachsen-hausen's pubs and cafes. Some private baths. Breakfast and linens included. Check-in 1pm. Check-out 9:30am. Curfew 2am. Dorms from €25, under 27 €20; singles €39/43; doubles €56-68/66-76. €3.10 HI discount. MC/V. ❷

**Hotel-Pension Bruns,** Mendelssohnstr. 42, 2nd fl. (☎74 88 96; www.brunsgallus-hotel.de). U4: Festhalle. Exit onto Beethovenstr. and turn left. At the traffic circle, con-tinue on Mendelssohnstr.; the hotel is on the right. In the wealthy but quiet Westend area, Bruns has 9 Victorian rooms with cable TV. Breakfast-in-bed included. Singles €40-45; doubles €50-55; triples €65-70; quads €88-95. Cash only. ❹

**City Camp Frankfurt,** An der Sandelmühle 35B (☎57 03 32; www.city-camp-frank-furt.de). U1-3: Heddernheim. Take a left at the Kleingartnerverein sign and continue until you reach the Sandelmühle sign. Cross the stream, turn left, and follow signs to the campground. Reception Mar.-Oct. 9am-1pm and 4-8pm; Nov.-Feb. 4-8pm. €6 per person, €3.50 per tent. Showers €1 per 4min. Cash only. ❶

## 🍴 FOOD

The most reasonably priced meals can be found near the university in **Bockenheim,** and many **Sachsenhausen** pubs serve food at decent prices. Just blocks from the HI hostel is a well-stocked **Rewe** supermarket, Dreieichstr. 56. (Open M-Sa 8am-10pm.) **Alim Markt,** Münchener Str. 37, is near the *Hauptbahnhof.* (Open M-F 8:30am-7:30pm, Su 8am-2pm.) **🏠Kleinmarkthalle,** on Haseng. between Berlinerstr. and Töngesg., is a three-story warehouse with bakeries, butchers, and fruit, nuts, cheese, and vegetable stands. (Open M-F 8am-6pm, Sa 8am-4pm.)

**🍴 Mozart Cafe,** Töngesg. 23-25 (☎29 19 54). Lauded by locals, this cafe serves famously huge breakfasts (€5-12) and a wide selection of pastas (€7.20-8), salads (€9.50-11.50), and desserts (€3-6). Open daily 8am-9pm. MC/V. ❷

**Da Rosario,** Ottostr. 17 (☎24 24 81 82). Go left out of the *Hauptbahnhof,* take the first left on Poststr., and go right on Ottostr. This small pizzeria is endearingly hectic. Pizzas from €4. Open M-F 11:30am-3pm and 6-11:30pm, Sa-Su 3-11:30pm. Cash only. ❷

**Cantina Mescal,** at the corner of Schweizerstr. and Textorstr. (☎61 99 23 12). Head south across the Untermainbrücke and continue down Schweizerstr. for 10min. This vi-brant, colorful restaurant and bar offers tacos (€8.90-9.40), enchiladas (€8.90-9.60), and other Mexican specialties. Open daily 10am-midnight. AmEx/MC/V.

GERMANY

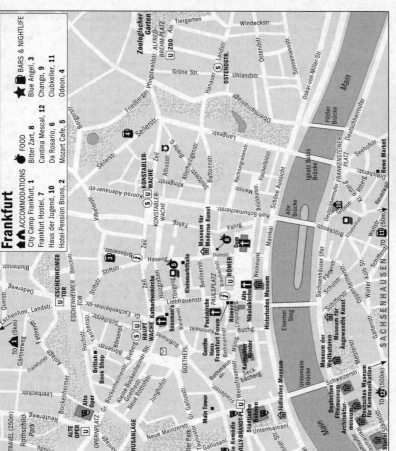

## Frankfurt

**♦ ACCOMMODATIONS**
City Camp Frankfurt, **1**
Frankfurt Hostel, **7**
Haus der Jugend, **10**
Hotel-Pension Bruns, **2**

**● FOOD**
Bitter Zart, **8**
Cantina Mescal, **12**
Da Rosario, **6**
Mozart Cafe, **5**

**★ BARS & NIGHTLIFE**
Blue Angel, **3**
Chango, **9**
Clubkeller, **11**
Odeon, **4**

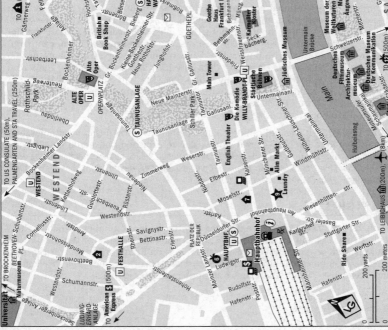

**Bitter Zart,** Domstr. 5 (☎94 94 28 46). This famous sweets shop sells some of the best chocolates and *gelee früchte* (from €3.80 per 100g) in the city. The hot chocolate (€7.90-15) suits any season. Open M-F 10am-7pm, Sa 10am-4pm. Cash only. ❷

## ◉ SIGHTS

Allied bombing in 1944 destroyed everything but Frankfurt's cathedral, so the city's historic splendor survives mostly in memories and reconstructed, sometimes tacky, monuments. The **Museum Bank** along the southern side of the Main includes some of the city's most vital cultural institutions. If you plan on touring them, consider buying a **Frankfurt Card** (p. 445).

▧ **STÄDEL.** The *Städel's* impressive collection comprises seven centuries of art and includes notable works by Old Masters, Impressionists, and Modernists. *(Schaumainkai 63, between Dürerstr. and Holbeinstr. ☎605 0980; www.staedelmuseum.de. Open Tu and F-Su 10am-6pm, W-Th 10am-9pm. €10, students €8, under 12 and last Sa of each month free. English-language audio tour €4, students €3.)*

▧ **MUSEUM FÜR MODERNE KUNST.** Dubbed "slice of cake," this triangular building displays European and American art from the 1960s to the present, including works by Lichtenstein, Johns, and emerging talents. *(Domstr. 10. ☎21 23 04 47; www.mmk-frankfurt.de. Open Tu and Th-Su 10am-5pm, W 10am-8pm. €6, students €3.)*

**RÖMERBERG.** This square, buried between modern structures, is essentially Frankfurt's entire *Altstadt;* its obviously reconstructed half-timbered homes appear on most postcards of the city. The **Statue of Justice** in the center of the square once spouted wine in celebration of the 13 imperial coronations held in Frankfurt; unfortunately, she has since sobered up. Across from the Römerberg, **Paulskirche** (St. Paul's Church), the birthplace of Germany's 19th-century attempt at constitutional government, now memorializes the trials of German democracy and displays an acclaimed mural. *(☎21 23 85 26. Open daily 10am-5pm. Free.)* At the west end of the Römerberg, the gables of **Römer** have marked the site of Frankfurt's city hall since 1405. Upstairs, the **Kaisersaal** is a former imperial banquet hall adorned with portraits of 52 German emperors, from Charlemagne to Franz II. *(Entrance from Limpurgerg. Open daily 10am-1pm and 2-5pm. €2.)* Emperors were once crowned in the red sandstone **Dom,** the lone survivor of the WWII bombings. An attached museum features large paintings and elaborate altar-pieces. *(Church open M-Th and Sa-Su 9am-noon and 2:30-6pm. Museum open Tu-F 10am-5pm and Sa-Su 11am-5pm. Church free. Museum €2, students €1.)*

**GOETHE-HAUS.** It was in Frankfurt that Goethe was born, began his studies, and penned some of his best-known works. The refurbished house and neighboring museum will appeal to his fans. *(Großer Hirschgraben 23-25, northwest of the Römer. ☎13 88 00. Open M-Sa 10am-6pm, Su 10am-5:30pm; last Sa of the month 10am-8pm. Audio tour in German or English €2. €4, students €2.50.)*

## ◈ NIGHTLIFE

Though Frankfurt lacks one centralized nightlife scene, a number of techno clubs lie between **Zeil** and **Bleichstraße.** Wait until midnight or 1am for things to really heat up. Visit www.nachtleben.de for more info on Frankfurt's clubs. For drinks, head to the cobblestone streets of the **Sachsenhausen** district, between Brückenstr. and Dreieichstr., where there are rowdy pubs and beer gardens.

**Odeon,** Seilerstr. 34 (☎28 50 55). It's out of the way, but few clubs are in a medieval villa. M hip-hop, Th student night, F 27+, Sa Wild Card. M and Th-F drinks ½-price until midnight. Cover €5, Th students €3. Open M-Sa 10pm-late. Cash only.

**Clubkeller,** Textorstr. 26 (☎66 37 26 97; www.clubkeller.com). A small bar and club with low brick-arched ceilings, a fun-loving clientele, diverse theme nights, and cheap beer (€2.50-3.50). Cover €3. Open M-Sa 9pm-late. Cash only.

**Chango,** Münchener Str. 57 (☎27 22 08 07; www.latinpalace-chango.de). A lively influx of Latin fire right next to the very German *Hauptbahnhof*. Hip-hop, meringue, and salsa predominate. Cover €7. Open F-Sa 10pm-6am. AmEx/MC/V.

# KASSEL ☎0561

Grandiose monuments and sweeping green vistas surround Kassel (pop. 194,000). The city's park, the 🔲**Wilhelmshöhe,** is famed throughout Germany. To reach the park, take tram #1 from Banhof Wilhelmshöhe (dir.: Wilhelmshöhe) to the last stop. Inside, **Schloß Wilhelmshöhe** is a dressed-down version of the Residenz in Würzburg (p. 478); the palace houses art from the classical era to the 1700s, including an impressive collection of Rembrandts. (☎31 68 00. Open Tu-Su March-Oct. 10am-5pm; Nov.-Feb. 10am-4pm. €6, students €2.) Wilhelm IX built **Schloß Löwenburg** in the 18th century with stones deliberately missing so it would resemble a crumbling medieval castle—he was obsessed with the year 1495 and imagined himself a knight. (☎31 68 02. Open Tu-Su Mar.-Oct. 10am-5pm; Nov.-Feb. 10am-4pm. Required tours 1 per hr.; €3.50, students €2.50.) Park paths lead to the statue of **Herkules** (Hercules), Kassel's emblem. A viewing pedestal provides stunning views of the park. (Pedestal open mid-Mar. to mid-Nov. Tu-Su 10am-5pm. €2, students €1.25.) To the east lies the city itself, whose historic sights were destroyed in WWII. The **Brüder-Grimm-Museum,** Schöne Aussicht 2, displays a handwritten copy of The Brothers Grimm's *Children's and Household Tales.* (☎787 2033; www.grimms.de. Open daily 10am-5pm. €1.50.)

To reach the flower-filled **Jugendherberge und Bildungsstätte Kassel (HI) ❷,** Schenkendorfstr. 18, located in a residential neighborhood, take streetcar #4 from the Wilhelmshöhe station to Querallee, then turn left on Querallee, which becomes Schenkendorfstr. (☎77 64 55; www.djh-hessen.de/jh/kassel. Breakfast included. Linens €3. Internet €2 per hr., €15 per day. Reception 8am-11:30pm. Curfew 12:30am. Floor mattresses €15; dorms €23; singles €33; doubles €38. €3.10 HI discount. Cash only.) The cozy, peaceful **Hotel Garni Kö78 ❸,** Kölnische Str. 78, has a lovely garden in back, as well as cable TV and phones. (☎716 14; www.koe78.de. Breakfast included. Reception 6am-10pm. Singles €34, with toilet €43-48; doubles €53/64-78. Prices rise about €5 in summer. AmEx/MC/V.) **Friedrich-Ebert-Straße,** the upper part of **Wilhelmshöher Allee,** and the area around **Königsplatz** all have supermarkets, takeout stands, and cafes among clothing stores. 🔲**Limerick ❷,** Wilhelmshöher Allee 116, has a pan-European menu boasting 237 entrees and appetizers. The pizza list (over 60 total, €3-8) is broken down into meat, vegetarian, poultry, and seafood categories. The 25 beers on tap (€2-3) attract loyal crowds to its spacious dining room and garden. (☎77 66 49; www.restaurant-limerick.de. Open M-Sa 11am-1am, Su 11am-11pm. Cash only.) Kassel has two **train** stations, Bahnhof Wilhelmshöhe and the *Hauptbahnhof*, but most trains stop only at Wilhelmshöhe. **Trains** run to: Berlin (3hr., 2 per hr., €78); Düsseldorf (3hr., 1 per 2hr., €44-80); Frankfurt (2hr., 3-4 per hr., €35-45); Hamburg (2½hr., 3 per hr., €65); Munich (4hr., 2-3 per hr., €89). The **tourist office** is in Bahnhof Wilhelmshöhe. (☎70 77 07; www.kassel-tourist.de. Open M-Sa 9am-6pm.) **Postal Code:** 34117.

# SOUTHWESTERN GERMANY

The Rhine and Mosel River Valleys are filled with much to be seen and drunk. Along river banks, medieval castles loom over vineyards that produce the best wines in Germany. Farther south, modern cities fade slowly into the beautiful hinterlands of the Black Forest.

## KOBLENZ        ☎ 0261

A menacing fortress high above the city of Koblenz (pop. 107,000) overlooks the confluence of two of Germany's major rivers, the Rhine and the Mosel. Koblenz has long been a strategic hot spot; in the two millennia since its birth, the city has hosted every empire seeking to conquer Europe. Koblenz centers around the **Deutsches Eck** (German Corner), at the intersection of the rivers. The **Mahnmal der Deutschen Einheit** (Monument to German Unity) is a tribute to Kaiser Wilhelm I. The **Ludwig Museum,** Danziger Freiheit 1, features mostly contemporary French art. (☎30 40 40; www.ludwigmuseum.org. Open Tu-Sa 10:30am-5pm, Su 11am-6pm. €2.50, students €1.50.) Head across the river to the **Festung Ehrenbreitstein,** the fortress at the city's highest point. It contains a youth hostel, numerous museums, and rotating historical exhibits. (Non-hostel guests €1.10, students €0.60.)

**Jugendherberge Koblenz (HI) ❷,** in the fortress, has spacious dorms and views of the rivers. Take bus #8 or 9 from the bus station to Ehrenbreitstein. From there, walk left along the main road for 100m, take the path to your right, and climb up the hill for 20min. (☎97 28 70; www.diejugendherbergen.de. Breakfast included. Reception 7:15am-10pm. Curfew midnight. Dorms €17; doubles €45. €3.10 HI discount. MC/V.) The **Hotel Jan von Werth ❷,** Von-Werth-Str. 9, has a great location near the center of town. From the station, walk left on Bahnhofstr. to the market district, and take a right on Von-Werth-Str. (☎365 00. Breakfast included. Reception 7am-10pm. Singles from €24, with bath €43; doubles €50/64; triples €60. MC/V.) Ferries (€0.80) cross the Mosel from the Deutsches Eck area to **Campingplatz Rhein-Mosel ❶,** Am Neuendorfer Eck. (☎827 19. Reception 8am-10pm. Open Apr.-Oct. 15. €4.50 per person, €2.50-3.50 per tent site.) At Markitst. 8 near the *Altstadt*, **Cafe Extra Blatt ❶** serves cheap pizza (€4-10), pasta (€6-7), and salads (€2.50-7) to a young crowd. (Open M-F 8am-midnight; Sa-Su 9am-1am. Cash only.) **Trains** run to: Bonn (30min., 2-3 per hr., €9-15); Cologne (1½hr., 2 per hr., €16-21); Frankfurt (1½hr., 1 per hr., €20-24); Mainz (1hr., 2-3 per hr., €15-19); Trier (1½hr., 1 per hr., €18-22). Across from the station is the **tourist office,** Bahnhofpl. 17, which gives out maps and books rooms at no charge. (☎100 4399. Open May-Oct. daily 9am-7pm; Nov.-Apr. M-F 9am-6pm.) **Postal Code:** 65068.

# RHINE VALLEY (RHEINTAL)

The Rhine River carves its way through the 80km stretch of the Rhine Valley, flowing north from Mainz to Bonn. According to German folklore, this region of medieval castles and jagged cliffs is enchanted.

## ▐ TRANSPORTATION

Two different **train** lines traverse the Rhine Valley, one on each bank; the line on the western side stays closer to the water and has better views. It's often tricky to switch banks, as train and ferry schedules don't always match up. **Boats** are the best way to see the sights; the **Köln-Düsseldorfer (KD) Line** and **Bingen Rüdesheim Line** cover the Mainz-Koblenz stretch three to four times per day in summer (€20-40).

## MAINZ
☎ 06131

The pastel-colored buildings in the *Altstadt* (Old Town) of Mainz (pop. 190,000) contain many bookstores, one reminder among many that this was the birthplace and home of famed printer Johannes Gutenberg. The city was also once the most powerful Catholic diocese north of the Alps, as attested to by the **Martinsdom,** a colossal sandstone 10th-century cathedral. (☎ 25 34 12. Open Mar.-Oct. M-F 9am-6:30pm, Sa 9am-4pm, Su 1-2:45pm and 4-6:30pm; Nov.-Feb. M-F 9am-5pm, Sa 9am-4pm, Su 12:45-3pm and 4-5pm. Free.) On a hill south of the *Dom*, the Gothic **Stephanskirche** on Stephansberg is inlaid with stunning stained-glass windows by Russian exile Marc Chagall. (Open M-F 10am-noon and 2-5pm, Sa 2-5pm. Free.) The advent of movable type in AD 1455 is immortalized at the **Gutenberg Museum,** Liebfrauenpl. 5, across from the Dom, which has a replica of Gutenberg's original press. (Open Tu-Sa 9am-5pm, Su 11am-3pm. €5, students €3.)

To reach the plain but comfortable rooms and downstairs bistro of the **Jugendgästehaus (HI)** ❷, Otto-Brunfels-Schneise 4, take bus #62 (dir.: Weisenau) or 63 (dir.: Laubenheim) to Viktorstift/Jugendherberge, and follow the signs. (☎ 853 32; www.diejugendherbergen.de. Breakfast included. Reception 7:30am-9:30pm. 4- to 6-bed dorms €18; doubles €47. MC/V.) **Der Eisgrub-Bräu** ❷, Weißlilieng. 1A, on the edge of the *Altstadt*, serves breakfast and lunch buffets (€3.50/5.30) as well as its house beer in its cellar-like interior. (Open Su-Th 9am-1pm, F-Sa 9am-2pm. MC/V.) **Trains** run to Cologne (1¾hr., 2-3 per hr., €27-50); Frankfurt (40min., 4 per hr., €10-15); Hamburg (6hr., 1 per hr., €84-100); Koblenz (1hr., 3-5 per hr., €15-21). KD **ferries** (☎ 23 28 00; www.k-d.com) depart from the wharfs on the other side of the *Rathaus* (City Hall). The **tourist office,** in Brückenturm by the river in the *Altstadt*, conducts English-language tours. From the station, walk straight down Schottstr., turn right onto Kaiserstr., and continue straight for 10min. until you reach Ludwigstr.; turn left and follow the green signs beginning at the cathedral. (☎ 28 62 10; www.info-mainz.de/tourist. Open M-F 9am-6pm, Sa 10:30am-2pm. 2hr. English-language tours May-Oct. W and F-Sa 2pm; Nov.-Apr. Sa 2pm. €5.) **Postal Code:** 55001.

## BACHARACH
☎ 06743

Bacharach (Altar of Bacchus; pop. 2000) lives up to its wine-god namesake, with *Weinkeller* (wine cellars) tucked between every other half-timbered house. Try some of the Rhine's best wines (from €2) and cheeses (€3-7) at **Die Weinstube,** Oberstr. 63. (Open M-F from 1pm, Sa-Su from noon. Cash only.) On the path to the hostel is the 14th-century **Wernerkapelle,** the remains of a red sandstone chapel that took 140 years to build but only hours to destroy during the 1689 Palatinate War of Succession. At the height of hostel greatness, **Jugendherberge Stahleck (HI)** ❷ is in a converted 12th-century castle with a panoramic view of the Rhine Valley. The steep 15min. hike to the hostel is worth every step. Make a right out of the station, turn left at the stairs between the tourist office and the Peterskirche, and follow signs up the hill. (☎ 12 66; www.diejugendherbergen.de. Breakfast included. Reception 7:30am-7:30pm. Curfew 10pm. Reserve ahead. Dorms €17; doubles €45. MC/V.) A friendly German couple serves three-course meals of regional fare (€6-11) at **Café Restaurant Rusticana** ❷, Oberstr. 40A. (☎ 17 41. Open May-Oct. daily noon-9pm. Cash only.) **Trains** run to Koblenz (40min., 2-3 per hr., €7.90) and Mainz (40min., 2-3 per hr., €7.20). The **tourist office,** Oberstr. 45, near the town center, offers **Internet** access (€1 per 30min.). (☎ 91 93 03. Open Apr.-Oct. M-F 9am-5pm, Sa-Su 10am-3pm; Nov.-Mar. M-F 9am-noon.) **Postal Code:** 55422.

## LORELEI (LORELEY) CLIFFS AND CASTLES
☎ 067

The mythological Lorelei maiden once lured sailors to their deaths on the cliffs of the Rhine. Now it's tourists who come in spades, entranced by romantic villages, slanting vineyards, and dramatic castles. Tiny **St. Goarshausen** and larger **St. Goar**, towns on either side of the Rhine, host the spectacular **Rhein in Flammen** (Rhine Ablaze) fireworks celebration in mid-September. St. Goarshausen, on the east bank, provides access by foot to a statue of the Lorelei and the cliffs. Directly above the town, the dark **Burg Katz** (Cat Castle) eternally stalks its prey, the smaller **Burg Maus** (Mouse Castle) downstream. While these castles are mostly closed to visitors, Burg Maus offers daily falconry demonstrations at 11am and 2:30pm from May to early October. (Face the river, turn right, and follow the signs. ☎71 76 69. €6.50, children €5.50.) Towering over St. Goar, **Burg Rheinfels** is a sprawling castle in ruins with underground passages. Take the red tourist trolley from St. Goar's center or follow the red signs for Fußweg Burg Rheinfels up the hill. (Open mid-Mar. to mid-Oct. daily 9am-6pm; mid-Oct. to Nov. daily 9am-5pm; Dec. to mid-Mar. Sa-Su 11am-5pm. €4, families €10.)

The family-oriented **Loreley-Jugendherberge (HI) ❶** sits directly beneath Burg Rheinfels. Follow the signs from St. Goar's main street. (☎413 88. Breakfast included. Reception 7-9am and 5-10pm. Dorms €14; doubles €35. MC/V.) **Reblaus Keller ❶** offers meaty dishes (€2-4) and plentiful beer (from €1.60); head left out of St. Goarhausen's station. (Open daily 3-10pm. Cash only.) **Trains** run from St. Goarshausen to Koblenz (30min., 2 per hr., €6) and Mainz (1½hr., 2 per hr., €10.60) and from St. Goar to Koblenz (30min. 2 per hr., €6) and Mainz (1hr., 2 per hr., €9.60). The Loreley VI **ferry** connects St. Goarshausen and St. Goar (M-F 6am-11pm, Sa-Su 8am-11pm. €1.30). For St. Goarhausen's **tourist office,** Bahnhofstr. 8, make a left out of the train station and follow the signs. (☎71 91 00; www.loreley-touristik.de. Open M-F 9am-1pm and 2-5pm, Sa 10am-noon.) St. Goar's **tourist office,** Heerstr. 86, is a 5min. walk from the ferry dock. (☎413 83; www.st-goar.de. Open M-F 9am-12:30pm and 1:30-6pm, Sa 10am-noon.) **Postal Code:** 56329.

# TRIER                                                                    ☎ 0651

The oldest town in Germany, Trier (pop. 100,000) has weathered more than two millennia in the western end of the Mosel Valley. An inscription at Trier's Hauptmarkt (Main Market) reads: "Trier stood one thousand and three hundred years before Rome." Founded by the Gallo-Celtic Treveri tribe and seized by the Romans during the reign of Augustus, Trier reached its zenith in the early 4th century, when it served as the capital of the Western Roman Empire and was a major center of Christianity in Europe. Today, Trier hums with students pondering life's questions in the tradition of the town's most famous son, Karl Marx.

**⌨⁊ TRANSPORTATION AND PRACTICAL INFORMATION. Trains** run to Koblenz (1½hr., 1-2 per hr., €18-22) and Luxembourg City, LUX (45min., 1 per hr., €13-17). From the station, walk down Theodor-Haus-Allee, and turn left under the Porta Nigra to reach the **tourist office.** (☎97 80 80; www.trier.de/tourismus. Open May-Oct. M-Th 9am-6pm, F-Sa 9am-7pm, Su 10am-5pm; Mar.-Apr. and Nov.-Dec. M-Sa 9am-6pm, Su 10am-3pm; Jan.-Feb. M-Sa 10am-5pm, Su 10am-1pm. 2hr. English-language city tour Sa 1:30pm; 1hr. German- and English-language coach tour daily 1pm. Both tours €7, students €6.) A **Trier Card,** available at the tourist office, offers free intracity bus fare and discounts on sites over a three-day period (€9, students €6.50). **Postal Code:** 54290.

**⌗⌨ ACCOMMODATIONS AND FOOD.** With its large, comfortable beds and prime location near all the major sights, the joint hostel and guest house **Warsberger Hof ❶**, Dietrichstr. 42, is the best deal in town. Head straight through the Porta Nigra down Simeonst. to the Hauptmarkt, then turn right on Dietrichstr. (☎97 52 50; www.warsberger-hof.de. Dorms €19; singles €23-27; doubles €45; tri-

ples €65. Reception 8am-11pm. Check-in 2:30pm. Reserve ahead. MC/V.)
**Jugendgästehaus Trier (HI) ❷,** An der Jugendherberge 4, is far from town, but its riverside location is ideal for promenades. Take buses #12 or 87 from the train station to Zurlaubenerufer, then walk 10min. downstream. (☎14 66 20; www.diejugendherbergen.de. Breakfast included. Laundry €5. Dorms €18; doubles €47. €3.10 HI discount. MC/V.) Moderately priced restaurants line the pedestrian path along the river between the youth hostel and the Kaiser-Wilhelm-Brücke. **Astarix ❷,** Karl-Marx-Str. 11, attracts a young crowd with generous portions of pasta and pizza served in a relaxed environment. It can be reached from the Trier Theater area or by walking down Brückenstr. toward the river. (Salads €3-6.50. Pasta and pizza €2.50-5. Open daily 1am-11pm.) **Plus** supermarket, Brotstr. 54, is near the Hauptmarkt. (Open M-F 8:30am-8pm, Sa 8:30am-6pm.)

◪ **SIGHTS.** A one-day **combination ticket** (€6.20, students €3.10) provides access to all of the city's Roman monuments. The most famous is the massive 2nd-century ▨**Porta Nigra** (Black Gate), which travelers can climb for a view of Trier. (Open daily Apr.-Sept. 9am-6pm; Oct. and Mar. 9am-5pm; Nov.-Feb. 9am-4pm. €2.10, students €1.60.) The enormous **Dom** nearby shelters the **Tunica Christi** (Holy Robe of Christ) and the tombs of archbishops. Amazingly, the original 4th-century church was four times larger. The adjoining **Church of Our Lady** adds some Gothic flair to the complex. (Both open daily Apr.-Oct. 6:30am-6pm; Nov.-Mar. 6:30am-5:30pm. Free.) The 4th-century **Basilika,** originally Emperor Constantine's throne room, is the largest single surviving room from antiquity. (Open Easter-Oct. M-Sa 10am-6pm, Su noon-6pm; Nov.-Easter Tu-Sa 11am-noon and 3-4pm, Su noon-1pm. Free.) Near the southeast corner of the city walls are the 4th-century **Kaiserthermen** (Emperor's Baths), with underground passages that once served as Roman sewers. A 10min. walk uphill along Olewiger Str. leads to the **amphitheater.** Once a gladiatorial arena, it's now a stage for city productions. (Baths and amphitheater open daily Apr.-Sept. 9am-6pm; Oct. and Mar. 9am-5pm; Nov.-Feb. 9am-4pm. Both €2.10, students €1.60.) The **Karl Marx Haus,** Brückenstr. 10, presents a biography of the philosopher in the house where he was born and grew up. (Open Apr.-Oct. M 1-6pm, Tu-Su 10am-6pm; Nov.-Mar. M 2-5pm, Tu-Su 10am-1pm. Free.)

# STUTTGART                                                         ☎0711

Daimler-Benz, Porsche, and a host of other corporate thoroughbreds keep Stuttgart (pop. 591,000) speeding along in the fast lane. In the heart of the Stuttgart lies the **Schloßplatz,** a 19th-century grassy square framed by an ornate palace and graced by the "Jubilee Column," which supports a statue of the goddess Concordia. The city's amazing **Mineralbäder** (mineral baths), fueled by Western Europe's most active mineral springs, draw young and old to their healing waters. The health-care facility **Mineralbad Leuze,** Am Leuzebad 2-6, has indoor and outdoor thermal pools. Take U1, U2, or U14 to Mineralbäder. (☎216 4210. Open M-Th 6am-8pm, F-Sa 6am-9pm, Su 6am-5pm. Entrance to mineral baths €6.50, students €3.50. Day pass for thermal baths and sauna €14, students €11. Cash only.) The superb ▨**Staatsgalerie Stuttgart,** Konrad-Adenauer-Str. 30-32, displays Dalí, Kandinsky, and Picasso in its new wing, as well as paintings from the Middle Ages to the 19th century in its old wing. (☎47 04 00; www.staatsgalerie.de. Open Tu-W and F-Su 10am-6pm, Th 10am-9pm. €7, students €5.50, W free.) The sleek, modern **Mercedes-Benz Museum,** Mercedesstr. 100, is a must for car-lovers. Take S1 (dir.: Plochingen) to Gottlieb-Daimler-Stadion and follow the signs. (☎173 0000; www.mercedes-benz.com/museum. Open Tu-Su 9am-6pm. €8, students €4.)

An international clientele crashes in hip rooms with funky wall paintings at ▨**Alex 30 Hostel ❷,** Alexanderstr. 30. Take tram #15 (dir.: Ruhbank) to Olgaeck.

(☎838 8950; www.alex30-hostel.de. Breakfast €6. Linens €3. Dorms €22; singles €34; doubles €54, with shower €64. MC/V.) The comfortable rooms at the hillside **Jugendherberge Stuttgart International (HI)** ❷, Haufmanstr. 27, have spectacular views of the city. Take tram #15 (dir.: Ruhbank) to Eugenspl., walk up the hill, and turn left on top of the second incline. (☎66 47 470; www.jugendherberge-stuttgart.de. Breakfast and linens included. Reception 24hr. Dorms €27-24; singles €32; doubles €37. €3.10 HI discount. Reduced rates for stays over one night. MC/V.) Look for mid-range restaurants in the pedestrian zone between Pfarrstr. and Charlottenstr. **San's Sandwich Bar** ❷, Eberhardstr. 47, serves sandwiches (€2.70-3.50) with plenty of vegetarian options. The brownies and muffins are heavenly. (☎410 1118; www.sans-stuttgart.de. Open M-F 8:30am-10pm, Sa 10am-7pm. Cash only.) The basement of the **Kaufhof Galeria**, Königstr. 6, has a **supermarket.** (Open M-W 9:30am-8pm, Th 9:30am-9pm, F 9:30am-8pm, Sa 9am-8pm. AmEx/MC/V.)

Stuttgart's club scene doesn't pick up until after midnight, and when it does, **Eberhardstraße, Rotebühlplatz,** and **Theodor-Heuss-Straße** are the most popular areas. **Suite 212,** Theodor-Heuss-Str. 15, is a popular bar and lounge featuring DJs and video-mixing on weekends. (☎253 6113; www.suite212.org. Beer €2.50-3. Mixed drinks €6.50-8. Open Su-Th 11am-2am, F-Sa 11am-5am. Cash only.) The monthly magazine *Schwulst* (www.schwulst.de) has info on gay and lesbian nightlife. **Trains** run to: Berlin (6hr., 1 per hr., €118); Frankfurt (1½hr., 2 per hr., €36-52); Munich (2½hr., 2 per hr., €33-49); Paris, FRA (8hr., 6 per day, €120-150). The **tourist office,** Königstr. 1A, is across from the train station. (☎222 80. Open M-F 9am-8pm, Sa 9am-6pm, Su 11am-6pm.) The **post office,** Arnulf-Klett-Pl. 2, is in the train station. (Open M-F 8:30am-6pm, Sa 8:30am-12:30pm.) **Postal Code:** 70173.

# HEIDELBERG                                             ☎06221

Heidelberg (pop. 142,000) has been one of Germany's top attractions ever since the Romantics waxed poetic about its crumbling castle and beautiful setting above the Neckar River. Today, legions of visitors fill the length of *Hauptstraße*, where postcards sell like hotcakes and every sign is posted in four languages. Fortunately, Heidelberg maintains university town charm in spite of the crowds.

## TRANSPORTATION AND PRACTICAL INFORMATION

**Trains** run to Frankfurt (1¼hr., 1-2 per hr., €14-24), Hamburg (7hr., 1 per hr., €87-101), and Stuttgart (1¼hr., 1-2 per hr., €18-33). Within Heidelberg, single-ride **bus** tickets cost around €2; day passes €5 are available on board. **Rhein-Neckar-Fahrgastschifffahrt** (☎201 81; www.rnf-schifffahrt.de), in front of the *Kongresshaus*, runs **ferries** all over Germany and cruises up the Neckar to Neckarsteinach (3hr. round-trip, Easter-late Oct. 1 per hr., €10.50). Rent **bikes** at **Eldorado**, Neckarstaden 52, near the Alte Brücke. Take bus #41 or 42 from the *Hauptbahnhof* to Marstallstraße and continue for 100m. (☎654 4460; www.eldorado-hd.de. Open Tu-F 9am-noon and 2-6pm, Sa 10am-6pm, Su 2-6pm. €5 per hour, €15 per day.) Heidelberg's attractions lie mostly in the eastern part of the city, along the south bank of the Neckar. From the train station, take any bus or streetcar to Bismarckpl., then walk east down **Hauptstraße**, the city's main thoroughfare, to the *Altstadt.* The **tourist office,** in front of the station, books room for a €3 fee. (☎138 8121. Open Apr.-Oct. M-Sa 9am-7pm, Su 10am-6pm; Nov.-Mar. M-Sa 9am-6pm.) The office sells the **Heidelberg Card,** which includes unlimited public transit and admission to most sights. (1-day card €10, 2-day €14, 4-day €20.) The **post office** is at Sofienstr. 8-10. (Open M-F 9:30am-6pm, Sa 9:30am-1pm.) **Postal Code:** 69115.

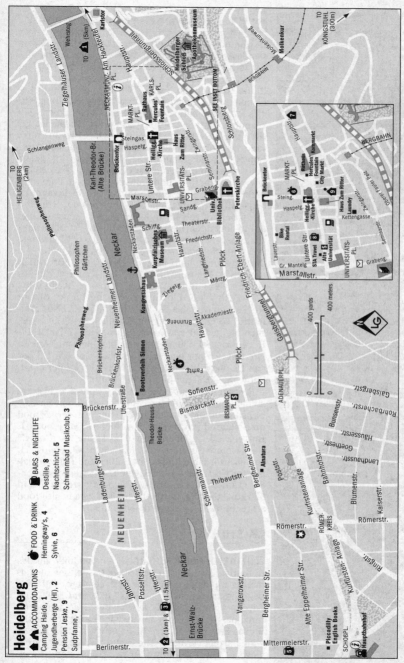

# Heidelberg

**ACCOMMODATIONS**
Camping Haide, **1**
Jugendherberge (HI), **2**
Pension Jeske, **9**
Sudpfanne, **7**

**FOOD & DRINK**
Hemingway's, **4**
Sylvie, **6**

**BARS & NIGHTLIFE**
Destille, **8**
Nachtschicht, **5**
Schwimmbad Musikclub, **3**

## UNIVERSITY POLITICS

The University of Heidelberg, Germany's oldest, has proudly held to its democratic traditions and autonomy from local authorities for centuries. So it came as a shock to many when the spread of Nazism in the early 1930s managed to engulf even this vanguard of independent thought.

Spurred by the influence of a few far-right-wing professors—most notably Philipp Lenard, head of the physics department, Nobel Prize winner, and vehement anti-Semite who once criticized the theory of relativity as "Jewish physics"—the university expelled all "undesirables" from its faculty. This included both Jews and many liberal thinkers. The Weimar Republic era had been one of educational freedom in Heidelberg; now, Nazi propaganda was expounded in the lecture halls. The sign in Universitätsplatz that read "To the Living Spirit" soon proclaimed, "To the German Spirit." Most dramatically, forced labor was used to construct Thingstätte, a huge amphitheatre on top of Heiligenberg hill across the Neckar River. Built on an ancient Celtic site, it was used to profess Nazi ideology to the local masses.

Today, the amphitheater is abandoned, hollow, and decrepit. But it remains Heidelberg's most tangible memory of a period so dark that it managed to corrupt one of Germany's leading educational institutions.

## ACCOMMODATIONS AND FOOD

In summer, reserve accommodations ahead. ☑**Pension Jeske ❸**, Mittelbadg. 2, offers the area's friendliest lodgings, with a perfect location next to the Marktpl. Take bus #33 (dir.: Ziegelhausen) to Rathaus/Bergbahn. (☎237 33; www.pension-jeske-heidelberg.de. Reception 11am-1pm and 5-7pm. Singles €25, with bath €35; doubles €40/60; triples €60/75; quints with bath €100. Cash only.) **Sudpfanne ❷**, Hauptstr. 223, has spare but congenial rooms next to its restaurant in the *Altstadt*. Take bus #33 (dir.: Köpfel) to Nekcarmünzplatz, walk up Leyergasse to your right, and turn left on Hauptstr. (☎16 36 36; www.heidelberger-sudpfanne.de. Check-in 3pm-midnight. Dorms €20. Cash only.) For the **Jugendherberge (HI) ❷**, Tiergartenstr. 5, take bus #32 from the Hauptbahnof to Chirurgische Klinik, then take bus #31 to Jugendherberge. Next to one of Europe's largest zoos, this hostel also teems with wild species, including *Schoolchildus germanus*, and features a discotheque in its basement. (☎65 11 90. Breakfast included. Reception until 2am. Reserve ahead. Dorms €24, under 27 €21; singles €29; doubles €34. MC/V.) For camping on the banks of the Neckar, go to **Haide ❶**. Take bus #35 (dir.: Neckargmünd) to Orthopädisches Klinik, cross the river, turn right, and walk for 20min. (☎062 23 21 11. Reception 8-11:30am and 4-8pm. Open mid-Apr to late-Oct. €5 per person, €3 per tent or RV, €2 per car. Cabins €13. Cash only. Electricity €2 per night. Showers €0.50 per 5min. Cash only)

Restaurants near Hauptstr. are expensive; historic student pubs outside the center are cheaper. **Hemingway's Bar-Café-Meeting Point ❷**, Fahrtg. 1, serves food on a shaded patio near the Neckar. (☎16 50 331. Entrees €5-12. Open daily 9am-11pm. Cash only.) Near Untere Str. in the *Altstadt*, **Sylvie ❷**, Steing. 11, serves affordable Italian specialties and regional salads for €6-12. (☎65 90 90. Open Su-Th 11am-1am, F-Sa 11am-2am. Cash only.) Grocery stores are in Marktpl. **Alnatura**, Bergheimer 59-63, is a health-food store. (☎61 86 34. Open daily 9am-8pm.)

## SIGHTS

☑**HEIDELBERGER SCHLOß.** Every summer, hordes of tourists lay siege to **Heidelberg Castle**, one of Germany's top attractions. The 14th-century castle has been destroyed twice by war (1622 and 1693) and once by lightning (1764), leaving it with a unique, battered beauty. The cool, musty wine cellar houses the **Großes Faß;** with a 221,726L capacity, it is the largest wine barrel ever used. The castle **gardens** offer great views of the city below; they're always open, so trek up at night to enjoy the city's lights. (☎ 53 84 21. Castle grounds open daily 8am-6pm; last entry 5:30pm. English-language audio tour €3.50. English-language tours 1 per hr. M-F 11:15am-4:15pm, Sa-Su 10:15am-4:15pm; €4, students €2. Schloß, Großes Faß, and Pharmaceutical Museum €3, students €1.50.) Reach the castle by the uphill path (10min.) from the Kornmarkt or by the **Bergbahn,** one of Germany's oldest cable cars. (Take bus #33, dir.: Köpfel, to Rathaus/Bergbahn. Cable cars leave from the parking lot next to the bus stop daily Mar.-Oct. 6 per hr. 9am-8pm; Nov.-Feb. 3 per hr. 9am-6pm. Round-trip €5.)

**UNIVERSITÄT.** Heidelberg is home to Germany's oldest (est. 1386) and most prestigious university. Over 20 Nobel laureates have been part of the faculty, and the university launched the field of sociology. The oldest remaining buildings border the stone lion fountain of the Universitätspl. The **Museum der Universität Heidelberg** traces the institution's tumultuous history; in the same building is the **Alte Aula,** the school's oldest auditorium. (Grabeng. 1. ☎ 54 21 52.) Before 1914, students were exempt from prosecution by civil authorities due to a code of academic freedom, so the faculty tried crimes from plagiarism to pig-chasing. View the irreverent, colorful graffiti of guilty students in the ▓**Studentkarzer** jail. (Augustinerg. 2. ☎ 54 35 54. Museum, auditorium, and jail open Apr.-Sept. Tu-Su 10am-6pm; Oct.-Mar. Tu-Sa 10am-4pm. €3, students €2.50.)

**PHILOSOPHENWEG.** On the opposite side of the Neckar from the *Altstadt*, the steep Philosophenweg (Philosopher's Path) offers unbeatable views of the city. Famed thinkers Goethe, Ludwig Feuerbach, and Ernst Jünger once strolled here. Follow signs to the top of **Heiligenberg** (Holy Mountain), where you'll find the ruins of the 9th-century **St. Michael Basilika,** the 11th-century **Stefanskloster,** and **Thingstätte,** an amphitheater built by the Nazis using forced labor on the site of an ancient Celtic gathering place. (To get to the path, use the steep, stone-walled footpath 10m west of the Karl-Theodor-Brücke.)

**ALTSTADT.** At the center of the *Altstadt* is the cobblestoned **Marktplatz,** where alleged witches and heretics were burned at the stake in the 15th century. Two of Heidelberg's oldest structures border the square. The 14th-century **Heiliggeistkirche** (Church of the Holy Spirit) is now used for Protestant worship; its tower offers great views of the city and mountains. (Open M-Sa 11am-5pm, Su 1-5pm. Church free. Tower €1.) The 16th-century inn **Haus Zum Ritter** is opposite the church. East of the Marktplatz, the **Kornmarkt** offers great views of the looming castle above. The twin domes of the **Brückentor** loom over the 18th-century *Alte Brücke*.

## ⚜ ▣ FESTIVALS AND NIGHTLIFE

The **Schlossbeleuchtung** (castle lighting) occurs on the first Saturday in June, the second Saturday in July, and the first Saturday in September. The ceremony begins after nightfall with the "burning" of the castle, which commemorates the three times it was ravaged by fire. Meanwhile, fireworks are set off over the *Altstadt* from the Alte Brücke. Head to Neuenheim or the Philosophenweg across the river for the best views. Heidelberg's traditional **Christmas Market** runs daily from November 24 to December 22 in the Kornmarkt, Marktpl., and Universitätspl.

Most popular nightspots fan out from the Marktpl. On the Neckar side of the Heiliggeistkirche, **Untere Straße** has the densest collection of bars in the city, and revelers fill the narrow way until 1 or 2am. **Steingasse,** off the Marktpl. toward the Neckar, also attracts crowds and Hauptstr. harbors a number of higher-end venues. **Schwimmbad Musikclub,** Tiergartenstr. 13, near the youth hostel, attracts a crowd with four levels of live music, dancing, and movies—not to mention a pool. From the Jugendherberge bus stop, walk forward another 500m. (☎ 47 02 01; www.schwimmbad-musik-club.de. Open Th 9pm-3am, F-Sa 9pm-4am. Cover varies; students often free. Cash only.) At **Nachtschicht,** in the Landfried-Komplex near the train station, university students dance in a basement resembling an old factory. (☎ 43 85 50; www.nachtschicht.com. Cover €3.50; M and F students €1.50.

Open W 10pm-3am, Th-F 10pm-4am, Sa 10pm-5am. Cash only.) A giant tree grows in the center of the forest-themed bar **Destille**, Unterstr. 16, which serves quirky shots. (☎228 08. Open Su-Th noon-2am, F-Sa noon-3am. Cash only.)

### ▶ DAYTRIP FROM HEIDELBERG: NECKARSTEINACH

This fishing village boasts four 12th- and 13th-century castles. The two to the west abide in picturesque dilapidation, while the two to the east are privately occupied and closed to visitors. All lie within 3km of one another on the Neckar's north bank and can be reached by foot via the **Burgenweg** (castle path). From the train station, turn right onto Bahnhofstr., take a left on Hauptstr., and continue to the brick *Schloßsteige* (castle stairs) on the right, which lead up to the *Burgenweg*. Fireworks set the sky ablaze during the **Vierburgenbeleuchtung** (four-castle lighting), on the second Saturday after Pentecost in June and on the last Saturday in July. From Heidelberg, take the S-Bahn RheinNeckar **train** S1 or S2 to Neckarsteinach (20min., 2-3 per hr.). The **tourist office**, Hauptstr. 15, has lists of private rooms in the area. (☎06229 920 00; www.neckarsteinach.com. Open M-Tu and Th-F 9am-12:30pm and 2:30-6pm, W 9am-12:30pm, Sa 9am-1:30pm.) **Postal Code:** 69239.

## BLACK FOREST (SCHWARZWALD)

The eerie darkness of the Black Forest has inspired a host of German fairy tales, most notably Hansel and Gretel. Today, the trees lure hikers and skiers with their grim beauty. The gateway to the forest is Freiburg, accessible by train from Basel and Stuttgart. Visitors tend to favor exploring the area by bike or by car, as public transportation is sparse. Rail lines encircle the forest, but only two cut through. Bus service is more thorough, but slow and infrequent.

**FREIBURG IM BREISGAU AND TRIBERG.** Tucked into the western edge of the Black Forest, **Freiburg** (pop. 210,000) is home to Germany's second oldest university and a renowned jazz house. The city's centerpiece, though, is its ▣**Münster,** a 13th- to 16th-century stone cathedral that amazes from every angle; historian Jacob Burkhardt considered it Christianity's most impressive monument. (☎0761 298 59 63. Open M-Sa 9:30am-5pm, Su 1-5pm. Tours M-F 2-3pm, Sa-Su 2:30-3:30pm. Tower €1.50, students €1.) For an excellent view of the city, head to Schloßbergring across from Hermannstr. and make the 20min. climb up the **Schloßberg.** You can also take a shuttle up from the Stadtgarten at Leopoldring; take tram #2 to Stadtgarten. Shuttles leave every 20min. from 11:30am to 6:50pm (€2.50). With all the well-marked **hiking** and **mountain biking** trails on the surrounding hills, you won't need bread crumbs; buy maps at the tourist office (€3.50-6). Rent **bikes** from **Mobile,** Wentzingerstr. 15, in the round building to the left behind the station. (☎0761 292 7998. €9.50 per 6hr., €13 per day. Open daily 24hr.)

The congenial **Black Forest Hostel ❷**, Kartäuserstr. 33, is as hip as the Black Forest gets; enjoy its enormous common room and large, comfortable dorms. Take tram #1 (dir.: Littenweiler; €2) to Oberlinden, go through the gate ahead, and turn left down Kartäuserstr. (☎0761 881 7870; www.blackforest-hostel.de. Linens €3. Reception 7am-1am. Dorms €13-21; singles €28; doubles €46. Cash only.) Stalls at the **Freiburger Markthalle ❶**, Grünwaldst. 4 (next to the Martinstor), serve ethnic cuisine for €3-7. Open M-F 7am-7pm, Sa 7am-4pm.) **Brennessel ❷**, Eschholzstr. 17, a few blocks behind the train station, stuffs patrons with everything from pancakes to ostrich steak. (☎0761 28 11 87. Entrees €4-14. Open M-Sa 6pm-1am, Su and holidays 5pm-1am. Cash only.) **Trains** run to Basel, SWI (1hr., 2-4 per hr., €10.50-18), Berlin (6½hr., 1 per 2hr., €119), and Cologne (3hr., 1 per 2hr., €77-97). The **tourist office**, Rathauspl. 2-4, is housed in the Rathaus;

head straight down Eisenbahnstr. from the station, turn left on Rotteckring, and follow the signs. The office books private rooms for €3. (☎0761 388 1880; www.freiburg.de. Open June-Sept. M-F 9:30am-8pm, Sa 9:30am-5pm, Su 10am-noon; Oct.-May M-F 9:30am-6pm, Sa 9:30am-2pm, Su 10am-noon.)

Tourists flock in summer to the tiny village of **Triberg** (pop. 5000) to see the world's two largest **cuckoo clocks** or hike to the **Gutacher Wasserfall**, a series of cascades tumbling 163m down moss-covered rocks. Renowned as the highest waterfall in Germany, Gutacher draws a half-million visitors each year. (Park open 24hr.; admission 9am-7pm. €2.50, under 18 €2.) Signs for "Wallfahrtskirche" lead to the pilgrimage church, **Maria in der Tanne**, where, according to legend, the pious have been miraculously cured since the 17th century. (☎0772 245 66. Service Sa 9am.) Triberg's **tourist office**, Wallfahrtsstr. 4, is connected to the **Schwarzwald Museum,** across from the entrance to the waterfalls. From the station, turn right on Bahnhofstr. and follow the signs. (☎0772 286 6490; www.triberg.de. Open daily 10am-6pm.) Triberg is accessible by train from Freiburg via Offenburg. (1¾hr., 3 per hr., €20.) **Postal Code:** 79098.

# CONSTANCE (KONSTANZ)    ☎07531

Located on the **Bodensee** (Lake Constance) and ranking among Germany's most popular vacation spots, Constance (pop. 29,000) has river promenades and narrow streets that wind around beautiful Baroque and Renaissance facades. Since part of the city extends into neutral Switzerland, Constance emerged unscathed from Allied bombs during WWII; however, a small monument reminds visitors that the Holocaust was not so discerning. The **Münster** (Cathedral) in the town center displays ancient religious relics and dark tunnels beneath its soaring 76m Gothic spire. (Open M-F 10am-5pm, Sa-Su 12:30-5:30pm.) Wander down **Seestraße**, near the yacht harbor on the lake, or **Rheinsteig**, along the Rhine. Constance boasts a number of **public beaches;** all are free and open from May to September. Take bus #5 to **Freibad Horn,** which is the largest and most crowded beach and has a nude sunbathing section enclosed by hedges.

Reserve accommodations a month ahead in summer. In the center of town, **Pension Gretel ❸,** Zollernstr. 6-8, offers clean rooms at surprisingly low prices, considering the steep hotel fares elsewhere in Constance. (☎45 58 23; www.hotel-gretel.de. Breakfast included. Singles €45; doubles €60-78; triples €96; quads €120; extra bed €18. Nov.-Mar. around €10 discount per person. Cash only.) Formerly a water

## LOCAL LEGEND

### TREASURES AND TRYST

If the *Nibelungenlied* (Song of the Nibelungs) can be trusted, budge backpackers in Southwestern Germany need look no further than the nearby Rhine to replenish their supply of cash: the medieval epic claims that the greatest treasure ever known is still buried beneath the river.

According to the legend Worms, a town near Heidelberg, was home to the Burgundian princess Kriemhild and her elder brother Günther. Several versions of the narrative exist, but most agree that Siegfried, slayer of the dragon Fafnir and owner of the *Nibelungenschatz* (a treasure of unsurpassed worth), set out to court Kriemhild after hearing of her equally unsurpassed beauty. Günther consented to the marriage only after Siegfried helped him beguile Brünhild, the Queen of Iceland. Much later, when the men and their wives reunited Brünhild learned that it was Siegfried, not Günther, who bested her in combat and won her hand. Afraid that his deception would become public knowledge Günther had Siegfried assassinated. The treasure was thrown into the Rhine outside of Worms, and both Günther and Kriemhild perished in subsequent attempts to recover it. The story was later made famous in Wagner's four opera "Ring" cycle, and also influenced Tolkien's *The Lord of the Rings* trilogy.

tower, **Jugendherberge Otto-Möricke-Turm (HI) ❷**, Zur Allmannshöhe 18, has a terrific view, though it isn't within walking distance of the city center. Take bus #4 from the train station to Jugendherberge; turn back and head uphill on Zur Allmannshöhe. (☎322 62; www.jugendherberge-konstanz.de. Breakfast included. Dinner €4.50, mandatory for stays over 1 night. Linens €3.10. Reception Apr.-Oct. 8am-noon and 3-6pm; Nov.-Mar. 8am-noon and 5-10pm. Lockout 9:30am-noon. Curfew 10pm, house key with €20 deposit. Dorms €27; under 27 €24; additional nights €23/20. AmEx/MC/V.) Fall asleep to lapping waves at **DKV-Campingplatz Brudehofer ❶**, Fohrenbühlweg 50. Take bus #1 to Staad and walk for 10min. with the lake to your left. The campground is on the waterfront. (☎313 88; www.campingkonstanz.de. Showers €1. Reception closed noon-2:30pm. €3.50 per person, €2 per child, €3.10-4.50 per tent, €2.60 per car, €7 per RV, €0.50 per bike. Cash only.) **Cafe Restaurant Antrik ❶**, on Hussenst. about 5min. from the cathedral, offers cheap yet bountiful meals (€4-7, beer or wine €2-3) in both its friendly downstairs area and in the slightly fancier cafe upstairs. Groceries are in the basement of the **Lago** shopping center on Augustinerpl. and Blätzlepl. by the train station. (☎12 31 58. Open M-F 9:30am-8pm, Sa 9:30am-7pm.)

**Trains** run from Constance to most cities in southern Germany; a short hop to neighboring Kreuzlingen connects you to destinations in Switzerland. **BSB ferries** leave hourly for ports around the lake. Buy tickets on board or in the building behind the train station, Hafenstr. 6. (☎364 0389; www.bsb-online.com. Open Apr.-Oct. M-Th 8am-noon and 1-4pm, F 8am-noon and 1-5pm.) The **tourist office,** Bahnhofspl. 13, to the right of the train station, finds private rooms for a €2.50 fee. (☎13 30 30; www.konstanz.de. Open Apr.-Oct. M-F 9am-6:30pm, Sa 9am-4pm, Su 10am-1pm; Nov.-Mar. M-F 9:30am-12:30pm and 2-6pm.) **Postal Code:** 78462.

# BAVARIA (BAYERN)

Bavaria is the Germany of Teutonic myth and Wagnerian opera, shielded by mountains and cradled by lakes. Most foreign notions of Germany are tied to this land of *Biergärten* and *Lederhosen;* from the Baroque cities along the Danube to mad King Ludwig's castles high in the Alps, the region attracts more tourists than any other part of the country. Life runs slowly here, especially on Sundays. Those journeying into the green countryside will encounter the rural *Bayerisch* dialect and centuries-old traditions. Local authorities still use the proper name *Freistaat Bayern* to refer to their area, a testament to the region's fierce pride and independence—residents have always been Bavarians first, Germans second.

## MUNICH (MÜNCHEN) ☎089

Bavaria's capital and cultural center, Munich (pop. 1,300,000) is a sprawling, liberal metropolis where world-class museums, handsome parks, colossal architecture, and a genial population create a thriving city. *Müncheners* party zealously during **Fasching** (Mardi Gras; Jan. 7-Feb. 5, 2008), shop with abandon during the **Christkindlmarkt** (Christ Child Market; Dec. 1-23), and chug unfathomable quantities of beer during the legendary **Oktoberfest** (Sept. 20-Oct. 5, 2008).

### ▶ TRANSPORTATION

**Flights: Flughafen München** (MUC; ☎97 52 13 13). S1 and 8 run from the airport to the *Hauptbahnhof* and Marienpl. (40min., 3 per hr., €8 or 8 strips on the *Streifenkarte*). Buy a **Gesaskamtnetz** day pass that covers all zones (€10). The **Lufthansa** shuttle bus goes to the *Hauptbahnhof* (40min., 3 per hr., €10).

**Trains:** Munich's **Hauptbahnhof** (☎118 61) is the hub of southern Germany with connections to: **Berlin** (5¾-6½hr., 1-2 per hr., €105-119); **Cologne** (6hr., 2-4 per hr., €88-121); **Frankfurt** (3-4½hr., 1-2 per hr., €64-81); **Füssen** (2hr., 1 per hr., €21); **Hamburg** (5¾-6½hr., 1-2 per hr., €104-119); **Amsterdam, NTH** (7-11hr., 17 per day, €134-144); **Budapest, HUN** (7½-9½hr., 8 per day, €98); **Copenhagen, DEN** (11-15hr., 8 per day, €156); **Paris, FRA** (8-10hr., 9 per day, €124-152); **Prague, CZR** (6-8¼hr., 9 per day, €49-84); **Rome, ITA** (10-11hr., 5 per day, €126); **Salzburg, AUT** (1½-2hr., 2 per hr., €21-27); **Venice, ITA** (7-10hr., 6 per day, €92); **Vienna, AUT** (4¼-6hr., 1-2 per hr., €69-85); **Zürich, SWI** (4¼-5½hr., 20 per day, €50-102). Purchase a **Bayern-Ticket** (single €21, 2-5 people €27) for unlimited train transit M-Sa 9am-3am, Su midnight-3am the next day in Bavaria and to Salzburg. **EurAide,** in the station, sells tickets. **Reisezentrum** ticket counters at the station are open daily 7am-9:30pm.

**Car Rental:** Agencies at the *Hauptbahnhof.* Most open M-F 7am-9pm, Sa-Su 9am-5pm.

**Ride Share: Mitfahrzentrale,** Lämmerstr. 6 (☎194 40; www.mifaz.de/muenchen). Arranges intercity rides with drivers going the same way. See **Transportation,** p. 387.

**Public Transportation:** MVV (☎41 42 43 44; www.mvv-muenchen.de) operates buses, trains, the S-Bahn (underground trains), and the U-Bahn (subway). Most run M-Th 5am-12:30am, F-Sa 5am-2am. S-Bahn trains go until 2 or 3am daily. Night buses and trams ("N") serve Munich's dedicated clubbers. Eurail, Inter Rail, and German rail passes valid on the S-Bahn but not on buses, trams, or the U-Bahn.

**Tickets:** Buy tickets at the blue vending machines and validate them in the blue boxes before entering the platform or risk a €40 fine.

**Prices: Single-ride** tickets €2.20 (valid 2hr.). **Kurzstrecke** (short-trip) tickets €1.10 (1hr. or 2 stops on the U- or S-Bahn, 4 stops on a tram or bus). A **Streifenkarte** (10-strip ticket; €10) can be used by more than 1 person. Cancel 2 strips per person for a normal ride, or 1 strip for a short trip; for rides beyond the city center, cancel 2 strips per zone. A **Single-Tageskarte** (single-day ticket; €5) for *Innenraum* (the city's central zone) is valid until 6am the next day; the **partner** day pass (€9) is valid for up to 5 people. **3-day** single pass €13; 5-person pass €21. The **XXL Ticket** (single €6.70, partner €12) gives day-long transit in Munich's 2 innermost zones, white and green. Single **Gesamtnetz** (day ticket for all zones) €10; 5-person pass €18.

**Taxis: Taxi-München-Zentrale** (☎216 10 or 194 10).

**Bike Rental:** ◨**Mike's Bike Tours,** Bräuhausstr. 10 (☎25 54 39 87; after hours 0172 852 0660). €12 per 1st day; €9 per day thereafter. 50% discount with tour (below). Open daily mid.-Apr. to mid-Oct. 10am-8pm; Mar. to mid-Apr. and mid-Oct. to mid-Nov. 10:30am-1pm and 4:30-5:30pm. **Radius Bikes** (☎59 61 13), in the *Hauptbahnhof,* behind the lockers opposite tracks 30-36. €3-4 per hr., €15-18 per day. €50 deposit. Open daily mid-Apr. to mid-Oct. 9:30am-6pm. 10% student or Eurail Pass discount.

**Hitchhiking:** Munich hitchhikers scan bulletin boards in the **Mensa,** Leopoldstr. 13, or try near the Autobahn on-ramps. However, it is illegal for cars to stop on the on-ramps, and anyone hitching on the Autobahn where there is a blue sign with a white auto symbol faces **fines.** Hitchhikers to Salzburg, AUT take U1 or 2 to Karl-Preis-Pl. For Nuremberg and Berlin, take U6 to Studentenstadt and walk 500m to the Frankfurter Ring. For the Bodensee and Switzerland, take U4 or 5 to Heimeranpl., then bus #33 to Siegenburger Str. Let's Go does not recommend hitchhiking.

# ◪ ORIENTATION

Downtown Munich is split into quadrants by thoroughfares running east-west and north-south. These intersect at Munich's central square, **Marienplatz,** and link the traffic rings at **Karlsplatz** (called Stachus by locals) in the west, **Isartorplatz** in the east, **Odeonsplatz** in the north, and **Sendlinger Tor** in the south. In the east beyond the Isartor, the Isar River flows north-south. The *Hauptbahnhof* is beyond Karlspl., to the west of the ring. To get to Marienpl. from the station, take any east-

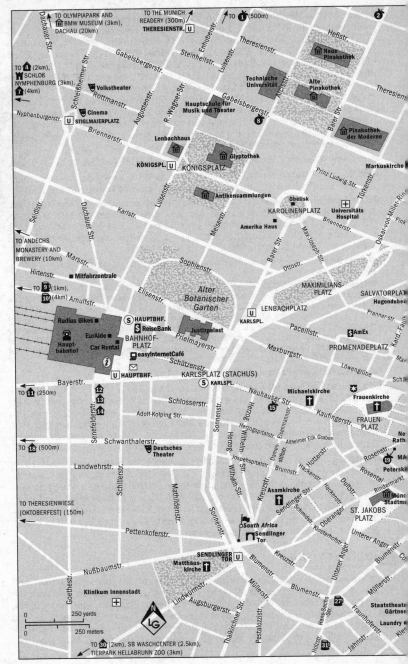

TO OLYMPIAPARK AND
BMW MUSEUM (3km),
DACHAU (20km)

TO THE MUNICH
READERY (300m)
THERESIENSTR. U

TO ⓵ (500m)

❷

Dachauer Str.

Heßstr.

Theresienstr.

Neue
Pinakothek

Gabelsbergerstr.

Steinheilstr.

Enhuberstr.

Luisenstr.

Theresienstr.

Technische
Universität

Alte
Pinakothek

Theresiens

TO 🏠 (2km),
SCHLOß
NYMPHENBURG (3km),
ⓖ (4km)

Schleißheimer Str.

Volkstheater

Rottmanstr.

Augustenstr.

R. Wagner-Str.

Gabelsbergerstr.

Barer Str.

Nyphenburgerstr.

Cinema
STIGLMAIERPLATZ U

Briennerstr.

Hauptschule für
Musik und Theater
ⓧ

Pinakothek
der Moderne

Markuskirche

Lenbachhaus

Glyptothek

Prinz-Ludwig-Str.

Türkenstr.

Oskar-von-Miller-Ring

Fink

KÖNIGSPL. U  KÖNIGSPLATZ

Seidlstr.

Dachauer Str.

Karlstr.

Luisenstr.

Meiserstr.

Antikensammlungen

KAROLINENPLATZ

Obelisk

Universitäts
Hospital

Briennerstr.

Amerika Haus

Barer Str.

Max-Joseph-Str.

TO ANDECHS
MONASTERY AND
BREWERY (10km)

Marsstr.

Hirtenstr.

Mitfahrzentrale

Sophienstr.

Ottostr.

MAXIMILIANS-
PLATZ

SALVATORPLAT

Hugendube

TO ⓽ (1km),
⓾ (4km)

Arnulfstr.

Elisenstr.

Alter
Botanischer
Garten

LENBACHPLATZ

Pranner-str.

Radius Bikes

S HAUPTBHF.

U KARLSPL.

Pacellistr.

S AmEx

PROMENADEPLATZ

Kard-Faulh

Mari

Hauptbahnhof

EurAide

Car Rental

S ReiseBank

Justizpalast

Prielmayerstr.

Maxburgstr.

Löwengrube

Scha

easyInternetCafé

✉

U HAUPTBHF.

Schützenstr.

KARLSPLATZ (STACHUS)

S KARLSPL.

Neuhauser Str.

Michaelskirche

Frauenkirche

FRAUEN-
PLATZ

Ne
Rath

Bayerstr.

TO ⓫ (250m)

⓬
⓭
⓮

Senefelderstr.

Schlosserstr.

Adolf-Kolping Str.

Sonnenstr.

Herzog-Wilhelm-Str.

Herzogspitalstr.

Eisenmannstr.

Damenstiftstr.

Altheimer Eck  Graben

Kaufingerstr.

Hotterstr.

⓯

Rosenstr.

⓳ MA

Peterski

Schwanthalerstr.

Deutsches
Theater

Jospehspitalstr.

Brunnstr.

Hackenstr.

Rosental

Rindermarkt

Münc
Stadtm

TO ⓲ (500m)

Landwehrstr.

Mathildenstr.

Wilhelm-Str.

Kreuzstr.

Asamkirche

Sendlinger Str.

Schmidstr.

Hackenstr.

Duftstr.

Oberanger

ST. JAKOBS
PLATZ

TO THERESIENWIESE
[OKTOBERFEST] (150m)

Schillerstr.

Pettenkoferstr.

Sonnenstr.

South Africa
Sendlinger
Tor

Klosterhofstr.

Unterer Anger

Unterer Anger

Blumenstr.

Co

Goethestr.

Nußbaumstr.

Klinikum Innenstadt

Matthäus-
kirche

SENDLINGER
TOR U

Blumenstr.

Kreuzstr.

Blumenstr.

Müllerstr.

Lindwurmstr.

Augsburgerstr.

Thalkirchner Str.

Pestalozzistr.

Hans-Sachs-Str.

⓲⓻

Staatstheate
Gärtner

Laundry

Fraunhoferstr.

Kle

0    250 yards
0    250 meters

N

TO ③⓪ (2km), SB WASCHCENTER (2.5km),
TIERPARK HELLABRUNN ZOO (3km)

Jahnstr.

Holtstr.

③⓵

GERMANY

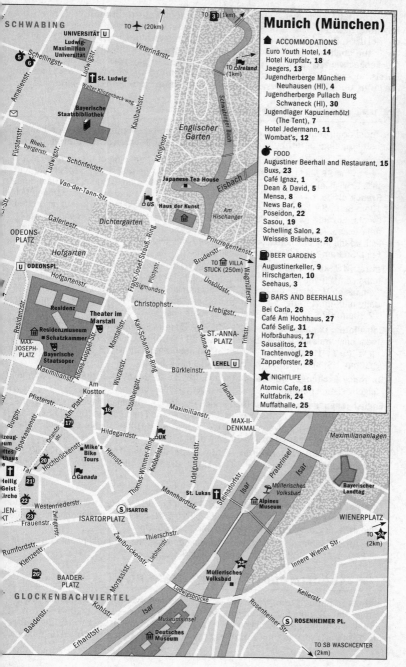

**GERMANY**

## Munich (München)

### 🏠 ACCOMMODATIONS
Euro Youth Hotel, **14**
Hotel Kurpfalz, **18**
Jaegers, **13**
Jugendherberge München
  Neuhausen (HI), **4**
Jugendherberge Pullach Burg
  Schwaneck (HI), **30**
Jugendlager Kapuzinerhölzl
  (The Tent), **7**
Hotel Jedermann, **11**
Wombat's, **12**

### 🍴 FOOD
Augustiner Beerhall and Restaurant, **15**
Buxs, **23**
Café Ignaz, **1**
Dean & David, **5**
Mensa, **8**
News Bar, **6**
Poseidon, **22**
Sasou, **19**
Schelling Salon, **2**
Weisses Bräuhaus, **20**

### 🍺 BEER GARDENS
Augustinerkeller, **9**
Hirschgarten, **10**
Seehaus, **3**

### 🍻 BARS AND BEERHALLS
Bei Carla, **26**
Café Am Hochhaus, **27**
Café Selig, **31**
Hofbräuhaus, **17**
Sausalitos, **21**
Trachtenvogl, **29**
Zappeforster, **28**

### ⭐ NIGHTLIFE
Atomic Cafe, **16**
Kultfabrik, **24**
Muffathalle, **25**

bound S-Bahn or use the main exit and make a right on Bahnhofpl., a left on Bayerstr. heading east through Karlspl., and continue straight. The **university** is to the north amid the **Schwabing** district's budget restaurants; to the east of Schwabing is the **English Garden** and to the west, **Olympiapark**. South of downtown is the **Glockenbachviertel**, filled with nightlife hot spots and gay bars. A seedy area with hotels and sex shops surrounds the *Hauptbahnhof*. Oktoberfest takes place on the large, open **Theresienwiese**, southeast of the train station on the U4 and 5 lines.

## 7 PRACTICAL INFORMATION

The most comprehensive list of services, events, and museums can be found in the English-language monthly *Munich Found*, available for free at the tourist office.

**Tourist Offices: Main office** (☎23 39 65 55), on the front side of the *Hauptbahnhof*, next to the SB-Markt on Bahnhofpl. Books rooms for free with a 10-15% deposit, and sells English-language city maps (€0.30). Open M-Sa 9:30am-6:30pm, Su 10am-6pm. **Branch office**, on Marienpl. at the entrance to the Neues Rathaus tower, is open M-F 10am-8pm, Sa 10am-4pm and accepts MC/V. Books tickets for concerts and other events. **EurAide** (☎59 38 89), room #2 along track 11 of the *Hauptbahnhof*, books train tickets for free, English-language city tours, and explains public transportation. Pick up the free brochure *Inside Track*. Open June-Sept. M-Sa 7:45am-12:45pm and 2-6pm, Su 8am-noon; Oct.-May reduced hours.

**Tours:** ■ **Mike's Bike Tours**, Bräuhausstr. 10 (☎25 54 39 87; www.mikesbike-tours.com). If you only have 1 day in Munich, take this tour. Starting from the Altes Rathaus on Marienpl., the 4hr., 6.5km city tour includes a *Biergärten* break. Tours leave daily mid-Apr. to Aug. 11:30am and 4pm; Sept. to mid-Nov. and Mar. to mid-Apr. 12:30pm. €24. Look for €6 coupons at youth hostels.

**Consulates: Canada,** Tal 29 (☎219 9570). Open M-F 9am-noon; 2-4pm by appointment only. **Ireland,** Dennigerstr. 15 (☎20 80 59 90). Open M-F 9am-noon. **UK,** Möhlstr. 5 (☎21 10 90). Open M-Th 8:30am-noon and 1-5pm, F 8:30am-noon and 1-3:30pm. **US,** Königinstr. 5 (☎288 80). Open M-F 1-4pm.

**Currency Exchange: ReiseBank** (☎551 0813), at the front of the *Hauptbahnhof*. Slightly cheaper than other banks. Open daily 7am-10pm.

**English-language Bookstores: The Munich Readery,** Augustenstr. 104 (☎12 19 24 03; www.readery.de). U2 to Theriesenstr. Cheap pre-owned paperbacks. Open M-Sa 11am-8pm. **Hugendubel,** Salvatorpl. 2 (☎018 01 48 44 84) has a large selection of new English-language titles. Open M-Sa 8am-8pm.

**Laundromat: SB Waschcenter,** Lindwurmstr. 124. Wash €3.50, dry €0.60 per 10min. Soap €0.30. Open daily 7am-11pm. **Branch** at Untersbergstr. 8 (U2, 7, or 8 to Untersbergstraße) has free Wi-Fi.

**Medical Emergency:** ☎192 22.

**Internet Access: easyInternetCafé,** on Bahnhofpl. next to the post office. Over 400 PCs. Prices depend on demand (around €2.20-2.40 per hr.); rates are cheapest after midnight, dropping as low as €1.70. 24hr. pass €5. Open 24hr.

**Post Office:** Bahnhofpl. In the yellow building opposite the *Hauptbahnhof* exit. Open M-F 7:30am-8pm, Sa 9am-4pm. **Postal Code:** 80335.

## ACCOMMODATIONS AND CAMPING

Lodgings in Munich tend to be either seedy, expensive, or booked solid. In midsummer and Oktoberfest, rooms are hard to find and prices jump 10% or more. In summer, it's usually necessary to book at least a week ahead or start calling before noon. Don't rely on catching shuteye in public areas, as police patrol all night long.

**OH, TO BE YOUNG AND BROKE.** HI-affiliated hostels in Bavaria usually do not admit guests over 26, except families or adults with young children.

## HOSTELS AND CAMPING

**Euro Youth Hotel,** Senefelderstr. 5 (☎ 59 90 88 11; www.euro-youth-hotel.de), near the *Hauptbahnhof*. The fun and colorful travelers' bar serves *Augustinerbräu* (€2.80) daily 6pm-4am, lending the laid-back hostel an energetic atmosphere at night. Happy hour 6-9pm; beer €2. Breakfast €3.90. Laundry €4.10. Internet €1 per 30min.; free Wi-Fi. Reception 24hr. In summer dorms €20; 3- to 5-bed dorms €24; singles €45; doubles €60, with breakfast, shower, and TV €75. In winter €10/13/45/60/75. Cheapest beds available online. MC/V. ❷

**Jugendlager Kapuzinerhölzl (The Tent),** In den Kirschen 30 (☎ 141 43 00; www.the-tent.de). Tram #17 from the *Hauptbahnhof* (dir.: Amalienburgstr.) to Botanischer Garten (15min.). Follow the signs straight. The Tent is on the right. Join 250 international "campers" under a gigantic tent on a wooden floor. Evening campfires. W morning free German- and English-language city tours. Kitchen and laundry available. Free lockers; no lock provided. Internet €1 per 30min. Key deposit €25 or passport. Reception 24hr. Open June 15-Oct. 15. €7.50, includes breakfast, foam pad, and wool blankets; beds €11, linens not included; camping €5.50 per person, €5.50 per tent. Cash only. ❶

**Wombat's,** Senefelderstr. 1 (☎ 59 98 91 80; www.wombats.at/munich-hostel/index.php). Unusual touches include a glass-enclosed winter garden and a free welcome drink. Breakfast €4. Internet €1 per 20min. Reception 24hr. Dorms €24; private rooms €68. MC/V. ❷

**Jaegers,** Senefelderstr. 3 (☎ 55 52 81; www.jaegershostel.de). Modern, colorful hostel with a mellow lounge by day and a boisterous bar by night. Breakfast included. Internet €1 per 20min.; free Wi-Fi. Laundry €4. Reception 24hr. 40-bed dorms €20; smaller dorms €23-25; singles €55; doubles with bath €79. Rates may vary. AmEx/MC/V. ❷

**Jugendherberge Pullach Burg Schwaneck (HI),** Burgweg 4-6 (☎ 74 48 66 70; www.burgschwaneck.de), in a castle 12km outside the city center. S7 (dir.: Wolfratshausen) to Pullach (20min.). From the train platform, turn right towards the football field, then cross the tracks and follow the signs down Margarethenstr. (10min.). Caters largely to an under-18 crowd. Bowling €25. Breakfast and linens included. Meals €4.30-4.80. Reception 7:30am-12:45pm and 1:30-5:30pm. Curfew 11:30pm. 10-bed dorms €17; 4- to 6-bed dorms €19; singles €28; doubles €50. MC/V. ❷

**Jugendherberge München Neuhausen (HI),** Wendl-Dietrich-Str. 20 (☎ 13 11 56.). U1 (dir.: Westfriedhof) to Rotkreuzpl. Go down Wendl-Dietrich-Str. past the Galeria Kaufhof; the entrance is 2 blocks ahead on the right. The most "central" of the HI hostels (3km from the city center). Bike rental €10. Free safes. Breakfast and linens included. Dinner €5.40. Laundry €4.10. Key deposit €15. Reception 24hr. 33-bed dorms €23-27; 6-bed dorms €26-30; singles €30-34; doubles €58-62. €3 HI discount. MC/V. ❷

## HOTELS AND PENSIONS

**Hotel Jedermann,** Bayerstr. 95 (☎ 54 32 40; www.hotel-jedermann.de). Take the *Hauptbahnhof* to Bayerstr. or tram #19 (dir.: Freiham Süd) to Hermann-Lingg-Str. Family-owned hotel offers inviting common areas and beautiful rooms with TV. Breakfast included. Free Internet. Singles from €49; doubles from €67. Extra bed €15. MC/V. ❹

**Hotel Kurpfalz,** Schwanthaler Str. 121 (☎ 540 9860; www.kurpfalz-hotel.de). Take the *Hauptbahnhof* to Bayerstr. or tram #19 to Holzapfelstr. Each colorfully decorated room has phone, private bath, and satellite TV. Breakfast included. Laundry service available. Reception 24hr. Reserve ahead; prices increase steeply as availability decreases. Singles from €40; doubles from €60. Extra bed €15. Cash only. ❹

↳ *Great Hotel!*

GERMANY

## ◻ FOOD

For a typical Bavarian lunch, spread a *Brez'n* (pretzel) with *Leberwurst* (liverwurst) or cheese. *Weißwürste* (white veal sausages) are a specialty. Don't eat the skin; slice them open instead. *Leberknödel* are liver dumplings.

Just south of Marienpl., vendors gather in the **Viktualienmarkt** to sell flowers, meats, fresh veggies, and specialty dishes, but don't expect budget groceries. (Open M-F 10am-8pm, Sa 8am-4pm.) Off **Ludwigstraße**, the university district supplies students with inexpensive, filling meals. Many reasonably priced restaurants and cafes cluster on **Schellingstraße, Amalienstraße,** and **Türkenstraße** (U3 or 6 to Universität). Munich is also the place where someone first connected the separate concepts of "beer" and "garden" to create the **Biergärten** (beer garden; p. 467).

### IN THE CENTER

**Weisses Bräuhaus,** Tal 7 (☎290 1380). This 500-year-old tavern provides traditional Bavarian fare. Adventurous eaters can pass on the roast pork dishes (€12-16), favoring *Münchener Voressen* (calf and pig lungs; €7.90). Entrees €10-20. Large daily specials menu. Open daily 8am-midnight. MC/V. ❹

**Buxs,** Frauenstr. 9 (☎291 9550). This vegetarian restaurant serves artful pastas, salads, and soups. Self-serve, with a weight-based charge (€2.20 per 100g). Takeout available. Open M-F 11am-6:45pm, Sa 11am-3pm. Cash only. ❷

**Sasou,** Marienpl. 28 (☎26 37 01; www.sasou.de). This pan-Asian restaurant attracts hordes of locals with its noodles, soups, and sushi. For a snack, stick to the finger food: fresh and lightly salted edamame €3.60. Open M-Sa 11am-10pm. Cash only. ❸

**Augustiner Beerhall and Restaurant,** Neuhauser Str. 27 (☎23 18 32 57). This restaurant, between Marienpl. and the train station, offers Bavarian specialties and *Maß* (Augustiner brew; €6). English menu. Entrees €4-13.50. Open daily 10am-midnight. ❸

**Poseidon,** Westenriederstr. 13 (☎29 92 96). Bowls of *bouillabaisse* with bread (€10) in a bustling fish-market atmosphere. Join Müncheners in the know for the special sushi menu on Th (€20). Other seafood dishes €4-13. Open M-W 8am-6:30pm, Th-F 8am-7pm, Sa 8am-4pm. Cash only. ❸

### SCHWABING AND THE UNIVERSITY DISTRICT

▨ **Dean & David,** Schellingstr. 13 (☎33 09 83 18; www.deananddavid.com). U3 or U6 to Universität. Curries and fresh salads (from €3) in an airy, modern setting. Entrees €5-7. Free Wi-Fi. Open M-F 8am-9pm, Sa 10am-7pm. Cash only. ❷

**Café Ignaz,** Georgenstr. 67 (☎271 6093). U2 to Josephspl., then take Adelheidstr. 1 block north and turn right on Georgenstr. Dinners range from crepes to stir-fry dishes (€5-9) at this eco-friendly vegetarian cafe. Breakfast buffet M and W-F 8-11:30am (€7); lunch buffet M-F noon-2pm (€6.50); brunch buffet Sa-Su 9am-1:30pm (€8). Open M and W-F 8am-10pm, Tu 11am-10pm, Sa-Su 9am-10pm. AmEx. ❷

**News Bar,** Amalienstr. 55 (☎28 17 87). U3 or U6 to Universität. Trendy cafe teeming with students. Large portions at reasonable prices. Breakfast €3-9. Wide assortment of salads, sandwiches, and pasta €5-10. Open daily 7:30am-2am. AmEx/MC/V. ❸

**Mensa,** Arcisstr. 17 (☎86 46 62 51; www.studentenwerk.mhn.de). U2 or U8 to Königspl. Students from the Technical University hit the cafeteria on the ground floor for light meals (€0.70-2). At the Mensa upstairs, servers in hairnets scoop large portions of German "fare" (€2-4) onto trays. At least 1 vegetarian dish. To eat here, get a "Legic-Karte" in the library (€6 deposit and student ID required). Open M-Th 8am-4:30pm, F 8am-2:30pm; reduced hours during vacations. 7 other cafeterias in Munich. Cash only. ❶

**Schelling Salon,** Schellingstr. 54 (☎272 0788). U3 or U6 to Universität. Bavarian billiards and *Knödel* (potato or dried bread dumpling) since 1872. Rack up at tables where Lenin, Rilke, and Hitler once played (€7 per hr.). Breakfast €3-5.10. German entrees €4-11. Open M and Th-Su 6:30am-1am. Kitchen open M and Th-Su 6:30am-midnight. A free **billiard museum** covers the history of pool dating back to the Pharaohs; open by advance request. Cash only. ❸

## BEER GARDENS (BIERGÄRTEN)

Munich has six great beer labels: *Augustiner*, *Hacker-Pschorr*, *Hofbraü*, *Löwenbraü*, *Paulaner*, and *Spaten-Franziskaner.* Most establishments have chosen sides and only serve one brewery's beer, in four varieties: *Helles* (light), *Dunkles* (dark), *Weißbier* (cloudy blond wheat beer), and *Radler* ("biker's brew"; half beer, half lemon soda). To order a *Maß* (liter; €4-6), you need only say, *"Ein Bier, bitte."* Specify for a *halb-Maß* (half-liter; €3-4) or a *Pils* (0.3L; €2-3).

 **GARDEN PARTY ETIQUETTE.** Despite serving similar drinks, beer gardens and beer halls offer very different experiences. *Biergärtens*, removed from the city center, often have outdoor patios on which patrons recline in the afternoon sun, surrounded by bright flowers and chirping birds. In contrast, beer halls tend to be noisier, more closely resembling a bar.

**Augustinerkeller,** Arnulfstr. 52 (☎59 43 93), at Zirkus-Krone-Str. S1-8 to Hackerbrücke. From the station, make a right on Arnulfstr. Founded in 1824, Augustiner is viewed by many as Munich's finest *Biergärten*, with enormous *Brez'n* and dim lighting beneath 100-year-old chestnut trees. Don't miss the delicious, sharp Augustiner beer (*Maß* €6.50). Open daily 10am-1am. Kitchen open 10am-10:30pm. AmEx/MC/V.

**Hirschgarten,** Hirschgarten 1 (☎17 25 91). Tram #17 (dir.: Amalienburgstr.) to Romanpl. Walk south to the end of Guntherstr. Europe's largest *Biergärten* (seats 9000) is boisterous and always crowded. Families come for the carnival rides, grassy park, on-site deer, and flea market. Entrees €5-15. *Maß* €5.50. Open daily 9am-midnight. Kitchen open 9am-10pm. Cash only.

**Seehaus,** Kleinhesselohe 3 (☎381 6130). U6 to Dietlindenstr., then bus #144 (dir.: Giesing) to Osterwaldstr. Directly on the Kleinhesseloher See in the Englischer Garten. Watch the sun set over the water as you enjoy a *Maß* (€6.60) and a pretzel (€3.20) from this cafeteria-style eatery. Open daily 10am-midnight. Cash only.

## ⊙ SIGHTS

**RESIDENZ.** Down the pedestrian zone from Odeonspl., the richly decorated state rooms and apartments of the Residenz, home to the Wittelsbach dynasty from 1623 to 1918, represent Neoclassical, Baroque, and Rococo styles. Highlights of the **Residenzmuseum** include the painting-packed **Antiquarium**, the royal **family portraits** in the ancestral gallery, and the lavish **papal chambers.** The adjacent **Schatzkammer** (treasury) contains crowns, crucifixes, reliquaries, and swords. Out back, the manicured **Hofgarten** shelters the lovely temple of Diana. *(Max-Joseph-Pl. 3. U3-6 to Odeonspl. ☎29 06 71. Open daily Apr. to mid-Oct. 9am-6pm; mid-Oct. to Mar. 10am-4pm. Half of the Residenz is open in the morning until 1:30pm and the other half is open after 1:30pm. Each €6, students €5; both €9/8. Garden free. Free audio tour.)*

 Be wary when passing through Marienpl. With all the tourists looking upward at the Glockenspiel, pickpockets have a field day.

**MARIENPLATZ.** The **Mariensäule,** a 1683 monument to the Virgin Mary, commemorates Munich's survival of the Thirty Years' War. At the **Neues Rathaus,** the **Glockenspiel** chimes, pleasing tourists with jousting knights and dancing coopers. *(Daily in summer at 11am, noon, 3pm, 5pm; in winter 11am, noon, 3pm.)* At 9pm, a mechanical watchman marches out and the Guardian Angel escorts the *Münchner Kindl*

(Munich Child) to bed. Adorning the **Altes Rathaus** tower, at the end of Marienpl., are all of Munich's coats of arms but one: the swastika emblem of the Nazi era.

**PETERSKIRCHE AND FRAUENKIRCHE.** Across from the Neues Rathaus, the 12th-century **Peterskirche** is the city's oldest parish church. Scale over 300 steps up the tower for a spectacular view. *(Open M-Tu and Th-Su 7:30am-7pm. Tower €1.50, students €1.)* From Marienpl., take Kaufingerstr. toward the *Hauptbahnhof* to the onion-domed towers of the 15th-century **Frauenkirche**—one of Munich's most notable landmarks and a city emblem. *(Frauenpl. 1. Open daily 7am-7pm. €3.50, students €1.50.)*

**ENGLISCHER GARTEN.** More expansive than New York's Central Park or London's Hyde Park, the Englischer Garten is Europe's largest metropolitan public park. On sunny days, the city turns out to bike, play badminton, or ride horses. The garden includes a Chinese pagoda, classic *Biergärten*, Greek temple, and Japanese tea house. FKK *(Frei Körper Kultur;* free body culture) on signs and park maps designates nude sunbathing areas. Daring *Müncheners* raft, surf, or swim the rapids of the Eisbach, which flows through the park.

**SCHLOß NYMPHENBURG.** After a decade of trying for an heir, Ludwig I celebrated his son's 1662 birth by building an elaborate summer playground northwest of Munich. Modeled after Versailles, the palace's most unusual asset is its **Gallery of Beauties,** a collection of portraits of noblewomen and commoners whom the king fancied. In the landscaped gardens, the **Amalienburg, Badenburg,** and **Pagodenburg** manors housed exclusive parties. See royal carriages, as well as portraits of Ludwig's favorite horses, in the **Marstallmuseum.** *(Tram #17, dir.: Amalienburgstr., to Schloß Nymphenburg. ☎ 17 90 80. Complex open daily Apr. to mid-Oct. 9am-6pm; mid-Oct. to Mar. 10am-4pm. Badenburg and Pagodenburg closed mid-Oct. to Mar. Schloß €5, students €4; audio tour €3. Manors each €2/1. Marstallmuseum €4/3. Entire complex €10/8; in winter €8/6.)*

**OLYMPIAPARK.** Built for the 1972 Olympic Games, Olympiapark contains the shimmering, tent-like **Olympia Zentrum** and the **Olympiaturm** (tower), Munich's highest building (291m). For a superb view, visitors can take an elevator to the top or—more daringly—explore the Olympiastadion by rope and hook during a roof climb tour. In summer, the stadium hosts events from concerts to flea markets to bungee jumping. *(U3 to Olympiazentrum. ☎ 30 67 24 14, tower 30 67 27 50. Olympia Zentrum open M-F 10am-6pm, Sa 10am-3pm. Olympiaturm open daily 9am-midnight. Olympia Zentrum free. Olympiaturm €4. Roof climb Apr.-Oct. daily 2:30pm; €35, students €25.)*

# 🏛 MUSEUMS

Many of Munich's museums would require days to explore completely. All state-owned museums, including the three **Pinakotheken,** are €1 on Sunday.

**▓ PINAKOTHEKEN.** Designed by *Münchener* Stephan Braunfels, the beautiful **Pinakothek der Moderne** is four museums in one. Subgalleries display architecture, design, drawings, and paintings by artists ranging from Picasso to contemporary masters. *(Barerstr. 40. U2 to Königspl or tram #27 to Pinakotheken. ☎ 23 80 53 60. Open Tu-W and Sa-Su 10am-5pm, Th-F 10am-8pm. €9.50, students €6. Audio guide €2.)* Commissioned in 1826 by King Ludwig I, the **Alte Pinakothek** houses 500 years of art, including works by Leonardo da Vinci, Rembrandt, and Rubens. *(Barerstr. 27. ☎ 23 80 52 16; www.alte-pinakothek.de. Open Tu 10am-8pm, W-Su 10am-6pm. €5.50, students €4.)* Next door, the **Neue Pinakothek** exhibits artists of the 19th and 20th centuries, including Cézanne, Monet, and van Gogh. *(Barerstr. 29. ☎ 23 80 51 95; www.neue-pinakothek.de. Open M and Th-Su 10am-5pm, W 10am-8pm. €5.50, students €4; includes audio tour.)*

**▓ DEUTSCHES MUSEUM.** Even if you don't know (or care) how engines power a Boeing 747, the Deutsches Museum's over 50 departments on science and technology will keep you entertained and educated. Exhibits include one of the first telephones and a recreated subterranean labyrinth of mining tunnels, as well as realistic models of medieval alchemist labs and international musical instruments. *(Museuminsel 1. S1-8 to Isartor or tram #18 to Deutsches Museum.* ☎ *217 91; www.deutsches-museum.de. Open daily 9am-5pm. €9, students €3. English-language guidebook €4.)*

**LENBACHHAUS.** Artwork in 19th-century painter Franz von Lenbach's villa chronicles Wassily Kandinsky's move to abstraction and the *Blaue Reiter* movement that he founded. The gallery also features works by modern artists like Paul Klee and Gabriele Münter. The nearby **Kunstbau**, in the U-bahn station, has rotating exhibitions on contemporary artists. *(Luisenstr. 33. U2 to Königspl.* ☎ *23 33 20 02. Open Tu-Su 10am-6pm. €6, students €3. Free tour Su 11am. Audio tour €3.)*

**BMW MUSEUM.** This driving museum displays past, present, and future BMW products. The main building is closed for renovation until spring 2008; in the meantime, the museum has a temporary home nearer to the Olympiaturm. *(Main building at Petuelring 130. U3 to Olympiazentrum, take the Olympiaturm exit, and walk a block up Lerchenauer Str.; the museum will be on your left.* ☎ *38 22 56 52; www.bmw-museum.de. Open daily 10am-8pm. €2, students €1.50. Check website for post-renovation prices and hours.)*

**GLYPTOTHEK AND ANTIKENSAMMLUNGEN (SCULPTURE AND ANTIQUITIES MUSEUMS).** Sketch artists camp out in these neighboring classical art museums. Both have small, but magnificent collections, including exquisite Roman vases and sculptures. *(Königspl. 1-3. U2 to Königspl.* ☎ *28 61 00. Open Tu-W and F-Su 10am-5pm, Th 10am-8pm. Each €3.50, students €2.50; both €5.50/3.50.)*

**SPIELZEUGMUSEUM (TOY MUSEUM).** Housed in the Altes Rathaus, this tiny toy-themed museum plays host to rotating exhibits like "100 Years of Teddy Bears." Check website for latest exhibition. *(Marienpl. 15. In the Altes Rathaus.* ☎ *29 40 01; www.toymuseum.de. Open daily 10am-5:30pm. €3, under 15 €1, families €6.)*

# 🎭 ENTERTAINMENT

Munich deserves its reputation as a world-class cultural center. Sixty theaters are scattered throughout the city; venues range from dramatic classics at the **Residenztheater** and **Volkstheater** to comic opera at the **Staatstheater am Gärtnerplatz** to experimental works at the **Theater im Marstall.** Munich's numerous fringe theaters, cabaret stages, and art cinemas in **Schwabing** reveal its bohemian spirit. *Monatsprogramm* (€1.50) and *Munich Found* (free at the tourist office) list schedules for festivals, museums, and performances. In July, a magnificent **opera festi-**

val arrives at the **Bayerische Staatsoper** (Bavarian National Opera), Max-Joseph-Pl. 2. (☎21 85 01; www.bayerische.staatsoper.de. U3-6 to Odeonspl. or tram #19 to Nationaltheater.) For €10, students can buy tickets for performances marked "Young Audience Program" two weeks in advance. Or, snag leftover tickets—if there are any—at the evening box office, Max-Joseph-Pl. 2, near the theater, for €10. (Opens 1hr. before curtain.) Standing-room tickets are half-price and can be purchased at any time. The daytime box office is at Marstallpl. 5. (☎21 85 19 20. Open M-F 10am-6pm, Sa 10am-1pm. No performances Aug. to mid-Sept.)

## 🎭 NIGHTLIFE

Munich's nightlife is a mix of Bavarian *Gemütlichkeit* (coziness) and chic. A typical odyssey begins at a beer hall, which usually closes around midnight. Cafes and bars shutting off tap at 1am (later on weekends) while discos and dance clubs, sedate before midnight, throb until 4am. Trendsetters head to **Leopoldstraße** in **Schwabing** or **Glockenbachviertel,** near Garnterpl. Many venues require partiers to attempt the hipster look, i.e., something besides shorts and a T-shirt.

### BARS AND BEER HALLS

🍺 **Zappeforster,** Corneliusstr. 16 (☎20 24 52 50). U1-3 or 6 to Sendlinger Tor. Students and young hipsters huddle around the tables on Gärtner Platz or bop along to the alternative beats in the no-frills interior. During the day, *Müncheners* lounge on cushions for coffee and conversation. Beer 0.3L €2.50. Open daily 9am-1am. Cash only.

🍺 **Trachtenvogl,** Reichenbachstr. 47 (☎201 5160; www.trachtenvogl.de). U1-2 or 7-8 to Frauenhofer. Enjoy 1 of their 32 types of hot chocolate—some with alcohol, of course—in a cozy living room with chic lamps. F live bands. Su chocolate fondue; reservations required. Happy hour daily 6-7pm; Astra beer €1.60. Jäger hour daily 9-10pm; Jägermeister drinks ½-price. Open Su-Th 10am-1am, F-Sa 10am-3am. Cash only.

**Hofbräuhaus,** Platzl 9 (☎290 1360), 2 blocks from Marienpl. Come for the full beer hall experience: this is as jolly, as festive, and as loud as it gets. Go in the early afternoon to avoid tourists. *Maß* €6.20. *Weißwürste* €4.20. Open daily 9am-midnight. Cash only.

**Café Am Hochhaus,** Blumenstr. 29 (☎89 05 81 52; www.cafeamhochhaus.de). U1-3 or 6 to Sendlinger Tor. Sometimes a dance party, sometimes a relaxed cafe, the mood at the popular Café Am Hochhaus changes nightly with the crowd. Beer 0.5L €3.20. Mixed drinks €7-8. Open M-W and Su 10pm-3am, Th-Sa 10pm-5am. Cash only.

**Sausalitos,** Im Tal 16 (☎24 29 54 94). U3 or S1-8 to Marienpl. Walk past the Heilig Geist Kirche; the bar is on your right. Mexican bar and hopping restaurant with crowds of backpackers. Drinks €6-9. Entrees, including vegetarian options, €9-13. Happy hour daily 5-8pm. Open Su-Th 11am-1am, F-Sa 11am-2:30am. MC/V.

### CLUBS

🎶 **Muffathalle,** Zellstr. 4 (☎45 87 50 10; www.muffathalle.de), in Haidhausen. S1-8 to Rosenheimerpl. or tram #18 (dir.: St. Emmeram) to Deutsches Museum. This former power plant generates hip-hop, jazz, spoken word, techno, and dance performances. Features a non-traditional *Biergärten*. Cover from €5. Open M-Th 5pm-late, F-Su noon-late. Buy tickets online or through München Ticket.

🎶 **Kultfabrik,** Grafingerstr. 6 (☎49 00 90 70; www.kultfabrik.info). Take U5 or S1-8 to Ostbahnhof, turn right on Friedenstr., then left on Grafingerstr. With 23 clubs crammed into 1 complex, Kultfabrik attracts Munich's dedicated partygoers for all-night revelry. The Russian-themed **Club Kalinka** is 1 of the more rowdy spots, popular with young locals and backpackers. Most doors open around 10pm and close late.

**Atomic Café,** Neuturmstr. 5 (☎228 3052), around the corner from the Hofbräuhaus, is the Bavarian take on late-60s mod glory. Sticks to its 60s and 70s beats but avoids mainstream disco. Young audiences come for the live Britpop, R&B, reggae, and ska. Beer 0.5L €3.70. Cover €3-7. Happy hour 9-10pm; mixed drinks €6. Open Tu-Th 10pm-3am, F-Sa 10pm-5am. Cash only.

## GLBT NIGHTLIFE

Despite Bavaria's reputation for being more conservative than the rest of Germany, gay nightlife thrives in Munich. The gay scene centers in the **Glockenbachviertel,** stretching from south of Sendlinger Tor through the Viktualienmarkt/Gärtnerpl. area to the Isartor. Look for the *Gay Guide to Munich, GayTimer,* or *Leo* for nightclub and event listings, available at most gay venues.

■ **Café Selig,** Hans-Sachs Str. 3 (☎23 88 88 78; www.einfachselig.de). U1 or 2 to Frauenhofer Str. Join the diverse crowd (mixed by day, mostly gay Sa-Su and by night) at this unpretentious cafe and bar with homemade cakes, international coffees, and strudel (€5-7). Open M and W 9pm-1am, F 9am-3am, Sa-Su 9am-late. AmEx/MC/V.

**Bei Carla,** Buttermelcherstr. 9 (☎22 79 01). S1-8 to Isartor. This friendly lesbian bar is one of Munich's best-kept secrets. Women in their 20s and 30s flock here for pleasant conversation, mixed drinks, and a round or 2 of darts. Limited menu. Open M-Sa 4pm-2am, Su 6pm-2am. Cash only.

## ■ OKTOBERFEST

Every fall, hordes of tourists make an unholy pilgrimage to Munich to drink and be merry in true Bavarian style. From the penultimate Saturday of September through early October (Sept. 20-Oct. 5, 2008), beer consumption prevails. The numbers for this festival have become truly mind-boggling: participants chug five million liters of beer, but only on a full stomach of 200,000 *Würste*. What began in 1810 as a celebration of the wedding of Ludwig I has become the world's largest folk festival. Representatives from all over Bavaria met outside the city gates, for a week of horse racing on fields they named **Theresienwiese** in honor of Ludwig's bride (U4 or U5 to Theresienwiese). The bash was such fun that Munich's citizens have repeated the revelry (minus the horses) ever since. An agricultural show, inaugurated in 1811, is still held every three years.

Festivities begin with the "Grand Entry of the *Oktoberfest* Landlords and Breweries," a **parade** ending at noon with the ceremonial drinking of the first keg, to the cry of "*O'zapft is!*" or "it's tapped!" by the Lord Mayor of Munich. Other highlights include international folklore presentations, a costume and rifleman's parade, and an open-air concert. Each of Munich's breweries set up tents in the Theresienwiese. Arrive early (by 4:30pm) to get a table; you must have a seat to be served alcohol. Drinking hours are fairly short, from 9am to 10:30pm, depending on the day; fairground attractions and sideshows are open slightly later. Those sharing a love of alcohol with their kin will appreciate the reduced prices of family days.

## ■ DAYTRIPS FROM MUNICH *Good to see*

**DACHAU.** *Arbeit Macht Frei* (Work Will Set You Free) was the first message prisoners saw as they passed through the **Jourhaus** gate into Dachau, where over 206,000 "undesirables" were interned between 1933 and 1945. The Third Reich's first concentration camp, Dachau was primarily a work rather than a death camp like Auschwitz; knowing the Allies would not bomb prisoners, the SS reserved it for the construction of armaments. Restored in 1962, the crematorium, gates, and walls now form a **memorial** to the victims. *(Open Tu-Su 9am-5pm. Free.)* In former administrative buildings, the ■**museum** examines pre-1930s anti-Semitism, the rise of Nazism, the establishment of the concentration camp system, and the lives of prisoners. A short **English-language film** (22min., free) screens at 11:30am, 2, and 3:30pm. Displays in the , the former prison and torture chamber, chronicle prisoners' lives and SS guards' barbarism. A 2½hr. English-language **tour** covers the entire camp. *(May-Sept. Tu-F at 1:30pm, Sa-Su at noon and 1:30pm; Oct.-Apr. Th-Su at 1:30pm. €3.)* A brief **introduction** (30min.) gives an overview of the complex. *(May-Sept. Tu-F 12:30pm, Sa-Su 11am and 12:30pm; Oct.-Apr. Th-Su 12:30pm. €2.)* Or, purchase the worthwhile audio tour (€3, students €2) for a self-tour of the camp. Food and beverages are not available at Dachau; pack your own. Take the S2 (dir.: Petershausen) to Dachau (20min.), then bus #726 (dir.: Saubachsiedlung) to KZ-Gedenkstätte (10min.); a €6.70 XXL day pass covers the trip.

**ANDECHS MONASTERY AND BREWERY.** Andechs has been the destination of pilgrimages since the Middle Ages, though it's debatable whether the faithful came for the collection of precious reliquaries or the beer. **Brewery** tours take place Tuesday, Wednesday, and Sunday at 11am (€4). Andechs beer is crisp and uniquely strong; the *Helles* has an alcoholic content of 11.5%, and *Doppelbock Dunkles* reaches a dizzying 18.5%. Join locals on the terrace or in the beer garden at the **Bräustüberl ❷**. The beer is cheaper than in Munich (*Maß* €4.80), and the fresh-baked pretzels (€2.60) are enormous and fluffy. *(☎08152 37 62 61. Leberkäse and Wurst €1-3 per 100g. Open daily 10am-8:45pm; low season 10am-8pm. Kitchen closes 6:30pm. Cash only.)* Take S5 to Herrsching (45min.; use a €10 *Gesamtnetz* day pass). From Herrsching, walk 1hr. following the signs "nach Andechs" or take a bus (10min., about 1 per hr., fare covered by day pass).

# GARMISCH-PARTENKIRCHEN                    ☎ 08821

The two united villages of Garmisch and Partenkirchen lie at the foot of the **Zugspitze** (2964m), Germany's highest peak. The climb should only be attempted in fair weather. To reach the summit, take the **cog train** from the Zugspitzbahnhof, behind the main train station, to Eibsee (30min., 1 per hr. 8:15am-2:15pm), and continue on the **Eibsee Seilbahn.** To descend, you can follow the alternative route, riding the **Gletscherbahn** to Zugspitzplatt, where the cog train will bring you back to town (1¼hr., 1 per hr. 9:30am-4:30pm). Tickets cost the same, regardless of your transportation preference (round-trip €47, ages 16-18 €33). Only very experienced hikers should skip the railways and make the two-day (10-12hr.) trek.

On the edge of the forest in Partenkirchen is the backpacker-friendly **Naturfreundehaus ❶**, Schalmeiweg 21. From the station, walk straight on Bahnhofstr. as it becomes Ludwigstr. Follow the bend to the right, turn left on Sonnenbergstr., left on Prof.-Michael-Sachs-Str., then left on Schalmeiweg. *(☎43 22. Breakfast €5. Reception 6-8pm. Dorms €11-13. Cash only.)* Along Ludwigstr. in Partenkirchen, a string of *Stüberl* (sitting rooms) serve traditional Bavarian fare. In the more multi-ethnic Garmisch side of town, head to **Saigon City ❶**, Am Kurpark Pl. 17A, for a bowl of soup (€2.80) or €7 egg-fried noodles. *(☎96 93 15. Entrees €6-11. Open Tu-Su 11am-2:30pm and 5-10:30pm. Cash only.)* **Trains** run to Munich (1½hr., 1 per hr.) and Innsbruck, AUT (1½hr., 1 per hr., €15). **Bus** #9606 goes to Füssen (2hr., 6-7 per day, €7). To reach the **tourist office,** Richard-Strauss-Pl. 2, turn left on Bahnhofstr. from the train station and left on Von-Brug-Str. *(☎18 07 00; www.garmisch-partenkirchen.de. Open M-Sa 8am-6pm, Su 10am-noon.)* **Postal Code:** 82467.

# BERCHTESGADEN                    ☎ 08652

The high mountain peaks and glacial lakes of Berchtesgaden National Park are a nirvana for hikers, cyclists, and skiers. The trails meander through alpine meadows and up steep rock faces. The nearby town of Berchtesgaden (pop. 8000) provides easy access to day hikes and plenty of local charm.

Drawn by Berchtesgaden's natural beauty, Hitler built his **Kehlsteinhaus,** dubbed the "Eagle's Nest" by the Allies, as a high mountain retreat here. A switchback road up the cliff, a bunker-like tunnel, and a brass-mirrored elevator lead to this unsettling "teahouse" and its stunning view. Take bus #838 or 849 to Dokumentation (15min., 2-3 per hr. 8am-2pm) for €2. (☎96 70. Open daily May-Oct., except in heavy snow. €15.) Across from the bus stop, the **Dokumentation Obersalzberg,** one of the Führer's forbidden areas, now contains an exhibit on the rise of Nazism and its machinery of terror and murder. (☎947 960; www.obersalzberg.de. Open Apr.-Oct. daily 9am-5pm; Nov.-Mar. Tu-Su 10am-3pm. €3, students free.) A 20min. walk from Berchtesgaden, the **Jugendherberge (HI) ❷,** Gebirgsjägerstr. 52, rewards those who make the climb with striking mountaintop views. Turn right out of the station onto Ramsauer Str., then right again on Gmundbrücke, and left up the gravel path; otherwise, take bus #39 (dir.: Strub Kaserne) from the train station. (☎943 70. Breakfast and linens included. Reception 7-9am and 5-7pm. Curfew midnight; low season 10pm. Closed Nov.-Dec. 26. Dorms €22, under 26 €18. MC/V.) **Gasthof Goldener Bär ❸,** Weihnactsschützenpl. 4, serves Bavarian favorites like roast pork with dumplings and cabbage for €9.50. (☎25 90. Entrees €8-14. Open daily 9am-10pm. Cash only.) For cheap Italian fare, check out **Dalmacija ❶,** Maktpl. 5. (☎976 027. Personal pizzas €4.50-6. Pasta €3-6.50. Open daily noon-10pm. Cash only.) Across the Markpl. from Dalmacija is a **Tengelmann** supermarket. (Open M-F 8am-7pm, Sa 8am-5pm.) **Trains** run hourly to Berchtesgaden from Munich (2-3hr., €27) and Salzburg, AUT (1hr., €7). The info desk at the train station is open M-Tu 6am-4:30pm, W-F 7am-4:30pm, Sa 7am-3pm. Across the roundabout from the train station, the **tourist office** is at Königßeerstr. 2. (☎96 70; www.berchtesgadenerland.com. Open mid-June to Sept. M-F 8:30am-6pm, Sa 9am-5pm, Su 9am-3pm; Nov. to mid-June M-F 8:30am-5pm, Sa 9am-noon.) The center of town lies on the other side of the train tracks on top of the cliff; turn right out of the train station and follow the sign "Zum Markt" up the stairs. **Postal Code:** 83471.

■☀ **HIKING AND SKIING.** With dozens of trails and *alpenhütte* (huts), **Berchtesgaden National Park** is a joy for day-hiking explorers. The **info center** Nationalpark-Haus is at Franziskanerpl. 7, in Berchtesgaden. (☎643 43; www.nationalpark-berchtesgaden.de. Open daily 9am-5pm.) There are also five info centers inside the park, near most trailheads. Pick up the free brochure *A National Park for Everyone,* which includes a map and scenic hike info.

One of the more popular day hikes goes to the snowy peaks and pine forests that encircle the crystal-clear waters of **Königßee.** The 5.5km hike from Berchtesgaden is nearly as serene as the lake itself, and winds through quiet meadows and woods accompanied by the music of a *bach* (brook). From the train station, head counter-clockwise around the roundabout to the parking lot behind Pizza-Pazza and follow the signs for Königßee. Once at the lake, ferries loop to **St. Bartholomä,** home to a 17th-century chapel, and **Salet.** The pristine **Obersee** lake is only 15min. from the Salet ferry stop. Another 30min. leads to the **Fischunkel Alm,** a farm that sells fresh milk and cheese in summer. Hike 30min. more to the stunning **Röthbach waterfall,** but be sure to check the time of the last ferry back. (Ferries ☎96 360; www.seenschifffahrt.de. 1hr., 2 per hr., €15.) Bus #41 leaves the bus station for Königssee (20min., 1 per hr., €2.30) and returns hourly until 7pm.

In winter, tourists glide down cross-country ski trails and sled runs or ice skate on the Hintersee. Reach the **Jenner,** the largest ski slope, via the Jennerbahn (☎958 10; www.jennerbahn.de; day pass €24, 6-14 €14) or ask at the Berchtesgaden tourist office for a list of ski and snowboard schools, most of which rent equipment.

# PASSAU                                                      ☎0851

Baroque arches cast shadows across the alleys of Passau (pop. 51,000), a two-millennium-old city situated at the confluence of the Danube, Ilz, and Inn rivers. Passau's main attraction is the Baroque **Stephansdom,** Dompl., which has the world's

## THE PROPER PROST

It is a universally acknowledged truth that a European traveler in possession of a dry throat must be in want of a German *Bier*. Careless drinkers be warned: German drinking protocol is simple, but strictly enforced.

Bavarian custom requires each drinker to wait until everyone has received his beverage before any glass is touched. Once the whole party has been served, everyone greets each other with a hearty "Prost" (cheers). Failure to make eye contact with the person whose glass you're clinking is rude at best, and at worst is supposed to result in seven years of bad sex. (Let's Go, however, believes that readers are responsible for the quality of their own sex life.) After glasses have been tapped all the away around, everyone hits his Stein to the table before taking the first sip.

This final tap is said to date back to King Ludwig I, who sent the political and social pressures of ruling Munich and Bavaria straight to his belly, growing quite fat in his old age. When he would *Prost* his companions at the dinner table, he would be so exhausted from holding up his *Maß* that he had to set it down again before he could muster up the energy to drink.

So channel the spirit of Ludwig, get ready for some eye-contact, and *Prost* with heartfelt drunken pride. And enjoy sex for the next seven years of your life.

largest church organ. Its 17,974 pipes and multiple keyboards accommodate five organists. (Open daily in summer 6:30am-7pm; winter 6:30am-6pm. Church free. Organ concerts May-Oct. and Dec. 27-31 M-F noon and Th 7:30pm. €4, students €2; evening concerts €5-8/3-4.) Behind the cathedral, the **Residenz** is home to the **Domschatz**, a grand collection of tapestries and gold. Enter through the back of the Stephansdom, to the right of the altar. (☎39 33 74. Open May 2-Oct. M-Sa 10am-4pm. €2, students €1.) Several floods—the most recent in 2002—left high-water marks on the outer wall of the 13th-century Gothic **Rathaus** (town hall). A bus runs every 30min. between the *Rathaus* and the former palace of the bishopric **Veste Oberhaus**, which now houses the **Kulturhistorisches** (Cultural History) **Museum**. (☎49 33 50; www.oberhausmuseum.de. Open mid-Apr. to mid-Nov. M-F 9am-5pm, Sa-Su 10am-6pm; mid-Nov. to mid-Mar. Tu-Su 9am-5pm. €5, students €4.)

**Fahrrad Pension ❶**, Bahnhofstr. 33, has cheap beds over an aromatic bakery. From the train station, walk 100m to the left and look for the blue "Bäckerei" sign. (☎347 84; www.fahrrad-pension.com. 4-bed dorms €8; singles €18. Cash only.) Possibly the most oddly shaped hotel you'll ever stay in, the **Rotel Inn ❸**, Hauptbahnhof/Donauufer, is built like a sleeping man, with tiny rooms just wide enough to fit a bed. From the train station, cross the street and head down the stairs; it's right on the Danube. (☎951 60; www.rotel-inn.de. Breakfast €5. Reception 24hr. Dorms €20; singles €25; doubles €30. Cash only.) **Sensasian ❷**, Heuwinkel 9, between Ludwigstr. and Rindermarkt, dishes up pan-Asian cuisine with plenty of vegetarian options. Hungry students grab a table outside or dine in the sleek, all-white interior. (☎989 0152. Ramen €6-8. Open M-Sa 10am-11pm, Su 11am-11pm. Cash only.) There is an **open-air market** in the Dompl. (Tu and F mornings). The free German-language magazine *Pasta* lists the hottest nightlife venues.

**Trains** depart for: Frankfurt (4¼hr., 1 per 2hr., €72); Munich (2¼-3hr., 1-2 per hr., €28-34); Nuremberg (2-4hr., 1 per hr., €31-38); Regensburg (1½-1¾hr., 1 per hr., €19). To get to the **tourist office**, Rathauspl. 3, follow Bahnhofstr. from the train station to Ludwigspl., then bear left downhill to Ludwigstr., which becomes Rindermarkt, Steinweg, and finally Große Messerg.; continue straight on Schusterg. and turn left on Schrottg. (☎95 59 80. Open Easter to mid-Oct. M-F 8:30am-6pm, Sa-Su 9am-4pm; mid-Oct. to Easter M-Th 8:30am-5pm, F 8:30am-4pm.) A second branch is at Bahnhofstr. 36. (Open Easter to mid-Oct. M-F 9am-noon and 12:30-5pm; mid-Oct. to Easter M-Th 9am-5pm, F 9am-4pm.) **Postal Code:** 94032.

## REGENSBURG ☎**0941**

Students swarm Regensburg (pop. 144,000), justifying the town's profusion of bars and restaurants catering to twentysomethings. Brilliant stained glass dazzles visitors to the **Dom St. Peter,** Dompl. 5. Begun in 1276, construction on the cathedral's twin spires finished under King Ludwig I in the 19th century. (☎298 6278. Open daily Apr.-Oct. 6:30am-6pm; Nov.-Mar. 6:30am-5pm. Free.) Inside, the **Domschatz** displays golden crosses, sparkling chalices, and jewel-encrusted reliquaries. (☎576 45. Open Apr. to mid-Jan. Tu-Sa 10am-5pm, Su noon-5pm; mid-Jan. to Mar. F-Sa 10am-4pm, Su noon-4pm. €2, children €1.) Close to the train station and above a convenience store, **Brook Lane Hostel ❶**, Obere Bachg. 21, has wooden furniture and pastel walls. (☎690 0966; www.hostel-regensburg.de. Linens €2.50. 10-bed dorms €15; 4-bed dorms €18; doubles €40. AmEx/MC/V.) Gaze at the Danube while sipping a brew (0.5 L €2.90) at ◪**Historische Wurstküche ❷**, Thundorfer Str. 3, an 850-year-old beer garden. (☎466 210. *Würste* 6 for €6.30. Open daily Apr.-Oct. 8am-7pm; Nov.-Mar. 8am-3pm. Cash only.) Crowded **Cafe Felix ❸**, Fröhliche Türkenstraße 6, specializes in huge salads (€8-10) with ingredients like pineapples and prawns. (☎590 59; www.cafefelix.de. Breakfast M-Sa 9am-3pm, Su 10am-3pm €3-12. Open M-Sa 9am-1am, Su 10am-1am. Cash only.) **Trains** go to Munich (1½-1¾hr., 1 per hr., €22), Nuremberg (1-1¼hr., 1-3 per hr., €16-22), and Passau (1½-1¾hr., 1 per hr., €19). The **tourist office** is in the *Altes Rathaus*, which was home to the Holy Roman Empire's parliament until 1803. From the station, walk down Maximilianstr., turn left on Grasg., continue straight onto Obermünsterstr., then go right on Obere Bachg for five blocks. (☎507 4410; www.regensburg.de. Open M-F 9:15am-6pm, Sa 9:15am-4pm, Su 9:30am-2:30pm.) **Postal Code:** 93047.

# NUREMBERG (NÜRNBERG) ☎**0911**

Before it witnessed the fanaticism of Hitler's Nazi rallies, Nuremberg (pop. 491,000) hosted Imperial Diets (parliamentary meetings) in the first Reich. Today, the remnants of both regimes draw visitors to the city, which new generations have rechristened *Stadt der Menschenrechte* (City of Human Rights).

**🖪🖪 TRANSPORTATION AND PRACTICAL INFORMATION. Trains** go to: Berlin (4.5hr., 1 per hr., €83); Frankfurt (2-3½hr., 2 per hr., €33-45); Munich (1½hr., 2-4 per hr., €29-45); Stuttgart (2¼-3hr., 1 per hr., €29-35). Walk through the tunnel from the train station to the *Altstadt* and take a right to reach the **tourist office,** Königstr. 93. (☎233 6132. Open M-Sa 9am-7pm.) A second office is in the Hauptmarkt. (Open M-Sa 9am-6pm.) **Internet** is available at **Sonia Call Shop,** on the underground level of the train station. (€1.50 per hr. Open M-Sa 8am-2am, Su 10am-2am.) **Postal Code:** 90402.

**🖪🖸 ACCOMMODATIONS AND FOOD.** ◪**Jugendgästehaus (HI) ❷**, Burg 2, sits in a castle above the city. From the tourist office, follow Königstr. over the bridge to the Hauptmarkt, head diagonally across to the fountain, and continue up Burgstr. (☎230 9360. Reception 7am-1am. Curfew 1am. Dorms €20-21; singles €39; doubles €46. MC/V.) The quirkily-named, spacious rooms—like "Wrong Room" and "Right Room"—of **Lette'm Sleep ❷**, Frauentormauer 42, are only a short walk away from the train station. Take the first left after entering the *Altstadt* through Königpl. (☎992 8128. Linens €3. Free Internet. Reception 24hr. Dorms €16; singles €30; doubles €48-52. MC/V.) **Zum Gulden Stern ❷**, Zirkelschmiedg. 26, is the world's oldest *Bratwürst* kitchen. (☎205 9298. 6 for €7.80. Entrees €5-10. Open daily 11am-10pm. AmEx/MC/V.) **Bratwursthäusle ❶**, Rathauspl. 1, has cheaper fare like three *Rostbratwurst* in a *Weckla* (roll) for €1.80, six *Würste* with kraut for €3.70, and *Spargel* (white asparagus) for €4. (☎22 76 95. Entrees €3-8. Open daily 10am-11pm. Cash only.) **Super Markt Straub,** Hauptmarkt 12, is near the Frauenkirche. (Open M-Sa 8am-6pm.) **Hauptmarkt** vendors sell cheese, sandwiches, pastries, and produce from early morning to dusk.

**SIGHTS AND ENTERTAINMENT.** Allied bombing destroyed most of old Nuremberg, but its castle and some other buildings have been reconstructed. The walled-in **Handwerkerhof** near the station is a tourist trap disguised as a history lesson; head up Königstr. for the real sights. Take a detour to the left for the pillared **Straße der Menschenrechte** (Avenue of Human Rights) as well as the gleaming glass **Germanisches Nationalmuseum,** Kartäuserg. 1, which chronicles German art since prehistoric times. (☎133 10. Open Tu-Su 10am-6pm, W 10am-9pm. Last entry 1hr. before closing. €6, students €4, W 6-9pm free.) Across the river is the **Hauptmarktplatz,** site of the annual **Christmas market** (Nov. 30-Dec. 24, 2007; Nov. 28-Dec. 24, 2008). Hidden in the fence of the **Schöner Brunnen** (Beautiful Fountain), in the Hauptmarkt, is a seamless, spinning golden ring, thought to bring good luck. Atop the hill, the **Kaiserburg** (Fortress of the Holy Roman Emperor) looms symbolically over Nuremberg. Climb the **Sinwellturm** for the best views of the city. (Open daily 9am-6pm. €6, students €5.) The ruins of **Reichsparteitagsgelände,** where the Nazi Party held Congress rallies, remind visitors of the city's darker days. On the far side of the lake is the **Zeppelintribüne,** the grandstand where Hitler addressed the masses. The Fascination and Terror exhibit, in the ■**Kongresshalle** at the north end of the park, covers the Nazi era. (☎231 5666. Open M-F 9am-6pm, Sa-Su 10am-6pm. €5, students €2.50; includes audio tour.) Tram #9 from the train station stops directly at Kongresshalle (Dokumentationszentrum stop). To reach the Zeppelintribüne, walk clockwise (10min.) around the lake. Nazi leaders faced Allied judges during the Nuremberg trials in Room 600 of the **Justizgebäude,** Fürtherstr. 110. (U1 to Bärenschanze. English-language tours Sa-Su 1 per hr. 1-4pm. €3, students €2.)

Most of Nuremberg's nightlife thrives in the *Altstadt*, especially by the river in the west. **Cine Città,** Gewerbemuseumspl. 3, U-Bahn to Wöhrder Wiese, packs 16 bars and cafes, 17 German-language cinemas, an IMAX theater, and a disco inside one complex. (☎20 66 60. Open Su-Th until 2am, F-Sa until 3am.) The large club **Hirsch,** Vogelweiherstr. 66, has multiple bars and a *Biergärten* out front. (Take nightbus #5 to Vogelweiherstr. www.der-hirsch.de. Mixed drinks €5.50. M-Th frequent concerts. Cover €3-15. Open M-Th 8pm-2am, F-Sa 10pm-5am. Cash only.) **Cartoon,** An der Sparkasse 6, is a popular gay bar near Lorenzpl. (☎22 71 70. Shots €3.80. Mixed drinks €6-7. Open M-Th 11am-1am, F-Sa 11am-3am, Su 2pm-1am.)

# ROMANTIC ROAD

Groomed fields of sunflowers, vineyards, and hills checker the landscape between Würzburg and Füssen. Officially christened *Romantische Straße* (the Romantic Road) in 1950, the road is dotted with almost a hundred castles, helping to make it one of the most traversed routes in Germany.

## ▐ TRANSPORTATION

Train travel is the most flexible, economical way to visit the Romantic Road. **Deutsche Bahn** operates a bus route along the Romantic Road, shuttling tourists from Frankfurt to Munich (13¼hr., €99), stopping in Würzburg (2hr., €22), Rothenburg (4¾hr., €35), and Füssen (11¾hr., €80). A **Castle Road** route connects Rothenburg with Nuremburg (3hr., €14). Both buses run once a day in each direction. For reservations and more info, see www.romanticroadcoach.de. There is a 10% student and under 26 discount and a 60% Eurail and German Rail Pass discount.

> **TIP** **A GOOD REASON TO SLEEP IN.** Try to take trains after 9am so you
> can use the Bayern Ticket (€21), which offers unlimited travel within Bavaria
> and parts of Austria on weekdays between 9am and 3am the following day, and
> on weekends between midnight and 3am the following day. Find other travelers
> going your way to use the €27 Bayern Ticket, which covers two to five people.

## FÜSSEN ☎ 08362

Füssen ("feet") seems an apt name for a little town at the foot of the Romantic Road. Füssen's main attraction is its proximity to Ludwig's famed **Königsschlößer** (p. 477), best seen as a daytrip. Above the pedestrian district, the town's own **Hohes Schloß** (High Castle) features *trompe-l'oeil* windows in its inner courtyard. (☎90 31 64. Open Tu-Su Apr.-Oct. 11am-4pm; Nov.-Mar. 2-4pm. €2.50, students €2.) The **Annakapelle,** which commemorates bubonic plague victims, has paintings depicting everyone swept up in the dance of death. Entry to the Annakapelle is included in a ticket to the **Museum der Stadt** (City Museum), which details Füssen's history as a manufacturing center. (☎90 31 46. Open Tu-Su Apr.-Oct. 10am-5pm; Nov.-Mar. 1-4pm. €2.50, students €2.)

Although Füssen's best accommodations are pensions, the tourist office keeps a list of *privatzimmer* with vacant rooms. **Jugendherberge (HI) ❷,** Mariahilfer Str. 5, lies in a residential area 15min. from the town center. Turn right from the station and follow the railroad tracks. (☎77 54. Laundry €3.60. Reception daily Mar.-Sept. 7am-noon and 5-10pm; Oct. and Dec.-Apr. 5-10pm. Lockout 11pm-6:30am. Dorms €18. MC/V.) Bakeries, butcher shops, and *Imbiße* (snack bars) stand among the pricey cafes on **Reichenstraße,** particularly off the **Luitpold Passage.** The **Plus** supermarket is on the right toward the rotary from the station. (Open M-Sa 8:30am-8pm.) **Trains** run to Augsburg (1¾hr., 1 per hr., €17) and Munich (2hr., 1 per hr., €21). To reach the **tourist office,** Kaiser-Maximilian-Pl. 1, from the train station, walk the length of Bahnhofstr. and head across the roundabout to the big yellow building on your left. (☎938 50; www.fuessen.de. Open June-Sept. M-F 9am-6pm, Sa 10am-2pm; Oct.-May M-F 9am-5pm, Sa 10am-noon.) **Postal Code:** 87629.

■ **DAYTRIP FROM FÜSSEN:** ■**KÖNIGSSCHLÖßER.** King Ludwig II, a frenzied visionary, built fantastic castles soaring into the alpine skies. In 1886, a band of nobles and bureaucrats deposed Ludwig, declared him insane, and imprisoned him; three days later, the king was mysteriously discovered dead in a lake. The fairy-tale castles that Ludwig created and the enigma of his death captivate tourists. The glitzy **Schloß Neuschwanstein** inspired Disney's Cinderella Castle and is one of Germany's iconic attractions. Its chambers include an artificial grotto and an immense Wagnerian opera hall. Hike 10min. to the **Marienbrücke,** a bridge that spans the gorge behind the castle. Climb the mountain on the other side of the bridge for enchantment minus the crowds. Ludwig spent his summers in the bright yellow **Schloß Hohenschwangau** across the valley. Don't miss the night-sky frescoes in the king's bedroom. Separate paths lead uphill to the castles. (☎08362 93 08 30. Both castles open daily Apr.-Sept. 9am-6pm, ticket windows open 8am-5pm; Oct.-Mar. castles 10am-4pm, tickets 9am-3pm. Mandatory tours of each castle €9, students €8; 10 languages available. Combination ticket €17/15.) From the Füssen train station, take **bus** #73 or 78, marked "Königsschlößer" (10min.; 1-2 per hr.; €1.70, round-trip €3.20). Tickets for both castles are sold at the **Ticket-Service Center,** about 100m uphill from the bus stop. Arrive before 10am to escape long lines.

## ROTHENBURG OB DER TAUBER ☎ 09861

Possibly the only walled medieval city without a single modern building, Rothen-burg (pop. 12,000) is *the* Romantic Road stop. After the Thirty Years' War, without money to modernize, the town remained unchanged for 250 years. Tourism later brought economic stability and another reason to preserve the medieval *Altstadt*. The English-language tour led by the **night watchman** gives a fast-paced and enter-taining introduction to Rothenburg history. (Starts at the *Rathaus* on Marktpl. Easter-Dec. 25 daily 8pm. €6, students €4.) A long climb up the narrow stairs of the 60m **Rathaus Tower** leads to a panoramic view of the town's red roofs. (Open Apr.-Oct. daily 9:30am-12:30pm and 1:30-5pm; Dec. daily noon-3pm; Nov. and Jan.-Mar. Sa-Su noon-3pm. €1.) According to local lore, during the Thirty Years' War, the conquering Catholic general Johann Tilly offered to spare the town from destruction if any local could chug a keg containing 3.25L (almost a gallon) of wine. Mayor Nusch successfully met the challenge, passed out for several days, then lived to a ripe old age. His saving **Meistertrunk** (Master Draught) is reenacted with great fanfare each year (May 9-12, Sept. 7, Oct. 4 and 11, 2008).

For private rooms unregistered at the tourist office (€15-45), look for the *Zimmer frei* (free room) signs in restaurants and stores. The 500-year-old ▧**Pension Raidel ❷,** Wengg. 3, will make you feel like you're sleeping in the past. (☎31 15; www.romanticroad.com/raidel. Breakfast included. Singles €24, with bath €39; doubles €45/59. Cash only.) Dine on sinfully good food at **Zur Höll ❷,** Burgg. 8. Originally built as a home in AD 980, Zur Höll ("To Hell") still serves Franconian fare (€4-18) by dim candlelight. (☎42 29. Bratwurst with sauerkraut €6. Open daily 5pm-midnight. Cash only.) **Trains** run to Steinach (15min., 1 per hr., €1.80), which has transfers to Munich (€32) and Würzburg (€12). The **Europabus** leaves from the *Busbahnhof* by the train station. The **tourist office,** Marktpl. 2, offers 15min. of free **Internet.** From the train station, head left before taking a right on Bacherstr. (☎404 800. Open May-Oct. M-F 9am-noon and 1-6pm, Sa-Su 10am-3pm; Nov.-Apr. M-F 9am-noon and 1-5pm, Sa 10am-1pm.) **Postal Code:** 91541.

## WÜRZBURG ☎ 0931

Surrounded by vineyards, the university town of Würzburg retains its medieval feel, although its bars and students keep the *Altstadt* humming with energy. The Main River flows through town; visit the stone bridge at sunset for a luminous view of the Gothic steeples and spires high above. The **Fortress Marienburg** houses the 11th-century **Marienkirche,** the 40m Bergfried **watchtower,** and the **Fürstengarten,** built to resemble a ship. Outside the fortress, the castle arsenal now hosts the **Mainfränkisches Museum,** featuring a collection of wooden sculptures by Gothic master Tilman Riemenschneider. (Bus #9 from Residenzpl. to Festung, or a 30min. walk up the hill. ☎20 59 40. Open Tu-Su Apr.-Oct. 10am-5pm; Nov.-Mar. 10am-4pm. €4, students €2. Audio guides €3.) The **Residenz** has one of the world's largest ceiling frescoes, by Giovanni Tiepolo of Venice, as well as Rococo stuc-coed ornamentation and plump cherubs. To the right of the *Residenz* lie the **Hof-garten** (court gardens) and the pink marble of the **Residenzhofkirche.** (*Residenz* open daily Apr.-Oct. 9am-6pm; Nov.-Mar. 10am-4:30pm. Last entry 30min. before closing. English-language tours 2 per day. €5, students €4. *Hofgarten* open daily dawn to dusk. Church open daily 9am-6pm. *Hofgarten* and church free.)

Unbeatable for its convenience, ▧**Babelfish Hostel ❷,** Prymstr. 3, offers airy dorms and comfortable beds. With your back to the train station, turn left on Hau-gering and walk about 7min. (☎304 0430; www.babelfish-hostel.de. Linens €3. Laundry €8. Free Internet and Wi-Fi. Key deposit €10. Reception 7am-11pm. Cur-few 11pm. 4- to 10-bed dorms €16-18; doubles €45. Cash only.) Across the river from the Altstadt, the **Jugendgästehaus (HI) ❷,** Burkarderstr. 44, is an enormous villa with great views. Take streetcar #3 or 5 to Löwenbrücke and backtrack 300m. (☎ 425 90; www.wuerzburg.jugendherberge.de. Breakfast included. Check-in 3-6pm and 7-10pm. Dorms €20-27. €3 HI discount. MC/V.) Würzburg has many cheap eats. Find crepes, sandwiches, and vegetarian dishes (€4-8) at **Le Clochard ❷**, Neubaustraße 20. (Open M-Tu 5pm-1am, W-Su 10am-1am. AmEx/MC/V.) Living up to its name, **Auflauf ❷**, Peterpl. 5, specializes in *Auflauf* (casseroles) with creative ingredients. (Lunch specials M-F noon-2:30pm €5.60. Student discounts. Open M-F noon-2:30pm and 5:30pm-midnight, Sa-Su noon-midnight. MC/V.)

**Trains** run to: Frankfurt (2hr., 3 per hr., €22-30); Munich (2-3hr., 1-3 per hr., €37-59); Nuremberg (1hr., 3 per hr., €16-24); Rothenburg (1¼hr., 1 per hr., €11). The **tourist office** is on Marktpl. (☎ 37 23 98. Open May-Oct. M-F 10am-6pm, Sa-Su 10am-2pm; Apr. and Nov.-Dec. M-F 10am-6pm, Sa 10am-2pm; Jan.-Mar. M-F 10am-4pm, Sa 10am-1pm.) **Postal Code:** 97070.

# EASTERN GERMANY

Saxony *(Sachsen)* and Thuringia *(Thüringen)*, the most interesting regions in eastern Germany outside of Berlin, encompass Dresden, Leipzig, and Weimar. The architecture of the area is defined by contrasts: castles surrounding Dresden attest to Saxony's one-time decadence, while boxy GDR-era buildings recall the socialist aesthetic. Cultural contrasts are also evident in eastern Saxony, where the Sorbs—Germany's only national minority—bring a Slavic influence to the small towns.

## WEIMAR                                                   ☎ 03643

The writer Goethe once said of Weimar (pop. 62,000), "Where else can you find so much that is good in a place that is so small?" Indeed, Weimar's diverse cultural attractions, lustrous parks, and rich history make the city a UNESCO World Heritage site and a worthwhile stop on any tour of eastern Germany. Weimar's history is not entirely a happy one, however, and a visit here is incomplete without a stop to nearby Buchenwald (p. 481).

While German towns leap at any excuse to build a memorial *Goethehaus*, Weimar has the authentic goods. The **Goethehaus** and **Goethe-Nationalmuseum,** Frauenplan 1, preserve the chambers where the poet wrote, entertained guests, and, after a half-century in Weimar, died. Expect a wait on summer weekends. Consider getting an audio tour (€1) to supplement the limited info provided. (Open Apr.-Sept. Tu-F and Su 9am-6pm, Sa 9am-7pm; Oct. Tu-Su 9am-6pm; Nov.-Mar. Tu-Su 9am-4pm. €6.50, students €5. Museum €3/2.50.) The multi-talented Goethe landscaped the serene **Park an der Ilm,** Corona-Schöfer-Str., which contains his first Weimar residence as well as the small but pleasant **Gartenhaus,** a retreat he owned until his death. (Open daily Apr.-Oct. 10am-6pm, Nov.-Mar. 10am-4pm. €3.50, students €2.50.) South of the town center is the less touristed **Historischer Friedhof** cemetery, where Goethe and Schiller rest together in the crypt of the **Fürstengruft** (Ducal Vault). Schiller, who died during an epidemic, was originally buried in a mass grave; Goethe later combed through the remains until he found Schiller and had him interred in a tomb. Behind and attached to the crypt is a small, beautiful **Russian Orthodox Church** built for the Grand Duchess Maria Pavlovna, a daughter of Czar Paul III and wife of Grand Duke Carl Friedrich. (Cemetery open daily Mar.-Sept. 8am-9pm; Oct.-Feb. 8am-6pm. Tomb and church open daily Apr.-Oct. 10am-6pm; Nov.-Mar. 10am-4pm. Tomb €2.50, students €2.) With the Medieval Palace Tower out front, the **Schloßmuseum** (Palace Museum), Burgplatz 4, is one of the city's most impressive sites. Rebuilt in 1803 after a fire, the former palace of the Dukes of Sachsen-Weimer-Eisenach now houses a museum featuring works from the Middle Ages to the Impressionist period, with a focus on

## THE LOCAL STORY

## A MEMORABLE MUSEUM

Weimar's newest museum isn't one dedicated to a classical German author or a noteworthy Grand Duke.

This museum features a plant.

The ginkgo tree—the beloved plant of the city's most noted residents, Johann Wolfgand von Goethe—was brought from Asia, where it had been used for centuries for its medicinal effects, in the 18th century. It was first cultivated in Europe in the Netherlands during the 1730s. It began to appear in Weimar in the early 1800s, most likely thanks to Goethe, who included a poem titled "Gingko Biloba" extolling the plant in his 1815 collection of poems, "East-West Divan." A short walk from Markt, behind the Prince's Palace on the Plaz de Demokratie, you can see the oldest Gingko tree in Weimar, planted in 1813.

The Gingko Museum, on Windischenstr., right off Markt, sells everything Ginko in the shop on its first floor. On the second floor, there are a few small exhibits dedicated to the plant, its unique character, its medicinal effects (one of which is to enhance memory), and its use in artistic expression.

*Planet Weimar Gingko Museum and Gallery. Windischenstr. 1. ☎80 54 52; www.planet-weimar.de. Open M-F 10am-5pm. Sa-Su 10am-3:30pm.*

Weimar artists. Though there is almost no info in English, the museum's second floor, displaying the grand rooms of the former palace, is well worth a visit. (Open Apr.-Oct. Tu-Su 10am-6pm; Nov.-Mar. Tu-Su 10am-4pm. €3.50, students €2.50.) Weimar's small **Bauhaus Museum** on Theaterpl. will appeal to anyone with an interest in architecture, art, or design. It showcases furniture, sculpture, weavings, and even coffee pots that illuminate the Bauhaus philosophy. (Open daily 10am-6pm. €4.50, students €3.50.) The **Former School of Fine Arts**, Geschwister-School-Straße 8, and the **Former School of Arts and Crafts**, Geschwister-School-Straße 7, were both built in the Bauhaus tradition and feature striking murals and reliefs on their walls. (Both open M-F 8am-9pm, Sa 8am-3pm. Both free.)

Relax in front of the piano at the **Hababusch Hostel ❶**, Geleitstr. 4, a bohemian hostel run by art students. The prices can't be beat. To get there, follow Geleitstr. from Goethepl. After a sharp right, you'll come to a statue on your left; the entrance is behind it. (☎ 85 07 37; www.hababusch.de. Linens €2.50. Key deposit €10. Reception 9am-9pm. Dorms €10; singles €20; doubles €30. Cash only.) **Jugendherberge Germania (HI) ❷**, Carl-August-Allee 13, is close to the train station but a 15min. walk from the city center. Small but comfortable beds at good prices make this hostel one of the best deals in town. (☎85 04 90; www.djh-thueringen.de. Breakfast included. 1st night €24, under 27 €21; €22/19 thereafter. Cash only.) Enjoy one of the excellent, filling savory or sweet crepes at **Crêperie du Palais ❷**, Am Palais 1, near Theaterpl. and down the street from the Hababusch hostel. (Open daily M-F 10am-midnight. Cash only.) Both a cafe and a gallery, **ACC ❷**, Burgpl. 1, serves creative daily specials (€5-6.50), screens art films in the hallway, and offers free Internet and Wi-Fi to its clientele. (Open daily May-Sept. 10am-1am; Oct.-Apr. 11am-1am. AmEx/MC/V.) A **market** is on Marktpl. (Open M-Sa 7am-5pm.)

**Trains** run to Dresden (2hr., 1 per hr., €49), Frankfurt (3hr., 1 per hr., €51), and Leipzig (1hr., 1 per hr., €23). To reach **Goetheplatz,** a bus hub at the center of the Altstadt, from the station, follow Carl-August-Allee downhill to Karl-Liebknecht-Str. (15min.). The efficient **Weimar Information,** Markt 10, is across from the *Rathaus.* (☎74 50; www.weimar.de. Maps €0.20. City guide €0.50. Books rooms for 10% fee.) They also sell the **Wiemar Card,** which provides free admission to the *Goethehaus* and the *Schloßmuseum* and discounts to most other sights in the city, as well as free public transportation within Weimar. Two-hour German-language **walking tours** (€6, with Weimar Card €3, students €4, under 11 free) leave the office daily at 10am and 2pm. (Open Apr.-Oct. M-Sa 9:30am-7pm, Su 9:30am-3pm; Nov.-Mar. M-F 9:30am-6pm, Sa-Su 9:30am-2pm.)

**⬛ DAYTRIP FROM WEIMAR: BUCHENWALD.** During WWII, the Buchenwald camp interred 250,000 prisoners, including communists, homosexuals, Jews, Roma (gypsies), and other political dissidents. Although Buchenwald was not built as an extermination camp, over 50,000 died here from malnutrition, medical experimentation, or abominably harsh treatment by the SS. The **Nationale Mahnmal und Gedenkstätte Buchenwald** (Buchenwald National Monument and Memorial) has two principal sites. The **KZ-Lager** is what remains of the camp, where a former storehouse now hosts a detailed exhibit documenting the history of Buchenwald from 1937 to 1945. Next door, a smaller room displays artistic responses to imprisonment in the camp. A monument, built by the former East German government, is on the other side of the hill. To reach the memorial, go up the main road that bisects the two large parking lots or take the footpath uphill from the old Buchenwald train station and continue on the main road. Camp **archives** are open to anyone searching for records of family and friends between 1937 and 1945; schedule an appointment with the curator. (*Archives ☎ 43 01 54. Outdoor camp area open daily sunrise-sunset.*) Sadly, the suffering at Buchenwald did not end with liberation. Soviet authorities later used the site as an internment camp, **Special Camp No. 2**, where more than 28,000 Germans—mostly Nazi war criminals and opponents of communism—were held until 1950. To get to the exhibit on this period, follow the signs and walk from the camp into the woods beyond the exhibition buildings.

The best way to reach the camp is by **bus** #6 from Weimar's train station or from Goethepl. Check the schedule carefully; some #6 buses go to Ettersburg rather than Gedenkstätte Buchenwald. (*20min.; 1-2 per hr.*) Ask at Buchenwald's **info center** for bus times back to Weimar. The hourly bus picks up at the KZ-Lager parking lot and at the road by the *Glockenturm* (bell tower). Be sure to watch the info center's video (English-language subtitles; 30min., 1 per hr.), and consider investing in an audio tour (€3 at the info center) or an audio-visual tour featuring an audio tour and photos documenting the camp's history (€5 at the info center). Both help the limited written info outside the main exhibits. (*☎ 43 00; www.buchenwald.de. Open daily Apr.-Oct. 10am-6pm; Nov.-Mar. 10am-4pm.*)

# EISENACH ☎ 03691

Eisenach (pop. 44,000), the picturesque city Martin Luther once called "my dear town," is best known as home to ⬛**Wartburg Fortress,** which protected Luther in 1521 after his excommunication. It was here, disguised as a bearded noble named Junker (Squire) Jörg, that Luther famously fought an apparition of the devil with an inkwell. After renovations, much of the castle's interior is no longer authentically medieval, but Wartburg is still evocative. Make sure to check out the spectacular view from the southern tower. To reach Wartburg, walk along Schloßberg and follow the signs, take bus #10 from the station, or catch a shuttle bus (€2.50) from one of the Wartburg parking lots along Mariental. (Open daily Mar.-Oct. 8:30am-5pm; Nov.-Feb. 9am-3:30pm. Mandatory tours €6.50, students €3.50. English-language tour 1:30pm.) Eisenach is also the birthplace of composer **Johann Sebastian Bach.** Although his exact place of birth is unknown, local legend holds that Bach was born in 1685 in the **Bachhaus**, Frauenplan 21, a museum that spills out of the old patrician townhouse into a sleek modern building next door. Roughly every hour, a guide plays several of the museum's period keyboard instruments and provides historical context in German. (Open daily 10am-6pm. €5, students €3. English translations available.) Martin Luther served as a choir-boy and Bach was baptized at the 800-year-old **Georgenkirche,** off the Markt, where members of Bach's family were organists for 132 years. Check out the huge statue of Bach in the entryway. (Open M-Sa 10am-12:30pm and 2-5pm, Su 11:30am-12:30pm and 2-5pm.) Up the street is the latticed **Lutherhaus,** Lutherpl. 8, where Luther lived during his school days and one of the city's oldest buildings. The museum details Luther's life from his schoolboy days to his revolutionary ones. (English-language info available. Open daily 10am-5pm. €3, students €1.50.)

The **Residenz Haus ❷,** Auf der Esplanade, next to the tourist office, offers nicely decorated, spacious rooms off an 18th-century tower. (☎21 41 33; www.residenzhaus-eisenach.de. Shared baths. Breakfast €6. Singles, doubles, and 4- and 6-person rooms €20 per person, students €15. Cash only.) To reach the renovated **Jugendherberge Arthur Becker (HI) ❷,** Mariental 24, take bus #3 or 10 (dir.: Mariental) to Liliengrund Parkpl., or call a taxi (€6). To make the 35min. walk, take Bahnhofstr. from the station to Wartburger Allee, which runs into Mariental. Though far from town, the hostel is close to the Wartburg. (☎74 32 59; ww.djh-thueringen.de. Breakfast included. Reception M-F 7am-10pm, Sa-Su 7-10am and 3-10pm. Dorms €21, under 27 €18. MC/V.) **La Fontana ❶,** Georgenstr. 22, with a large fountain in front, is the best deal in town. (☎74 35 39. Pizza and pasta €3-4. Open Su-Th 11:30am-2:30pm and 5-11pm, F-Sa 11:30am-2:30pm and 5-11:30pm. Cash only.) For groceries, head to **Edeka** on Johannispl. (Open M-F 7am-7pm, Sa 7am-2pm.)

**Trains** run to and from Weimar (1hr., 1 per hr., €13-21). The **tourist office,** Markt 9, runs city tours in German (Apr.-Oct. daily 2pm; Nov.-Mar. Sa 2pm; €5). From the train station, follow Bahnhofstr. through the tunnel and veer left, then take a right onto the pedestrian Karlstr. (☎792 30. Open Apr.-Oct. M-F 10am-6pm, Sa 10am-4pm, Su 10am-4pm; Nov.-Mar. M-F 10am-6pm, Sa 10am-4pm.) **Postal Code:** 99817.

# WITTENBERG ☎03491

Martin Luther inaugurated the Protestant Reformation here in 1517 when he nailed his 95 Theses to the door of the **Schloßkirche;** Wittenberg (pop. 48,000) has been fanatical about its native heretic ever since. All major sights surround **Collegienstraße** (which becomes **Schloßstraße** toward the church). The ▨**Lutherhaus,** Collegienstr. 54, chronicles the Reformation through art, artifacts, letters, and texts. (☎420 3118. Open Apr.-Oct. daily 9am-6pm; Nov.-Mar. Tu-Su 10am-5pm. €5, students €3.) Down Schloßstr., the *Schloßkirche* allegedly holds Luther's body and a copy of the Theses; its tower has a sumptuous view of the *Altstadt,* the countryside, and the Elbe. (Tower ☎40 25 85. Church open daily 10am-6pm. Tower open Easter-Oct. Tu-Su 10am-noon and 2-4pm. Church free. Tower €2, students €1.) The **Jugendherberge (HI) ❷,** Schloßstr. 14/15, is the white building next to the church. Find the incongruously glassy entrance in the courtyard to the left after the main entrance. (☎40 32 55. Breakfast included. Linens €3.50. Reception 8am-10pm. Check-out 9:30am. Curfew 10pm. Dorms €20, under 27 €17. HI members only. MC/V.) Look for cheap meals along the Collegienstr.-Schloßstr. strip. People, potatoes, and a very strange ceiling converge at the **Wittenberger Kartoffelhaus,** Schloßstr. 2. (☎41 12 00. Entrees €3.50-13. Open daily 11am-1am. V.) **Trains** leave for Berlin (45min., 1 per hr., €21) and Leipzig (1hr., every 2hr., €10). Follow the "City" and *"Altstadt"* signs out of the station to the red brick path, which leads to Collegienstr., the start of the pedestrian zone. The **tourist office,** Schloßpl. 2, opposite the church, provides maps (€0.50), books rooms, gives audio tours (€6) in eight languages. (☎49 86 10. Open Mar.-Oct. M-F 9am-6:30pm, Sa-Su 10am-4pm; Nov.-Feb. M-F 10am-4pm, Sa 10am-2pm, Su 11am-3pm.) **Postal Code:** 06886.

# DRESDEN ☎0351

The buildings that form the skyline of Dresden's magnificent *Altstadt* look ancient, but most of them are newly reconstructed—the Allied firebombings in February 1945 that claimed over 40,000 lives also destroyed 75% of the city center.

Long-delayed healing has accompanied the city's reconstruction, and today, its Baroque architecture, dazzling views of the Elbe River, world-class museums, and thriving *Neustadt* nightlife earn small Dresden (pop. 479,000) celebrity status. Backpackers traveling from Berlin to Prague won't want to miss it.

# ▐ TRANSPORTATION

**Flights:** Dresden's **airport** (**DRS;** ☎ 881 3360; www.dresden-airport.de) is 9km from the city. S2 runs there from both train stations (13min. from *Neustadt*, 23min. from the *Hauptbahnhof;* 2 per hr. 4am-11:30pm; €1.80).

**Trains:** Nearly all trains stop at both the **Hauptbahnhof** in the *Altstadt* and **Bahnhof Dresden Neustadt** across the Elbe. Trains run to: **Berlin** (3hr., 1 per hr., €33-55); **Frankfurt am Main** (4½hr., 1 per hr., €80); **Leipzig** (1½hr., 1-2 per hr., €25); **Munich** (6hr., 1-2 per hr., €93); **Budapest, HUN** (11hr., 2 per day, €81); **Prague, CZR** (2½hr., 9 per day, €20). Tickets are available from the machines in the station main hall, but are cheaper at the *Reisezentrum* desk.

**Public Transportation:** Much of Dresden is accessible on foot, but **streetcars** cover the whole city. 1hr. ticket €1.80. Day pass €4.50. The €6 **Family Card,** good for 2 passengers until 4am, is probably the best deal. Weekly pass €17. Tickets are available from *Fahrkarte* dispensers at major stops and on streetcars. For info and maps, go to one of the **Service Punkt** stands in front of the *Hauptbahnhof* (open M-F 8am-7pm, Sa 8am-6pm, Su 9am-6pm) or at Postpl. (open M-F 8am-7pm, Sa 8am-6pm). Most major lines run hourly after midnight until 4am—look for the moon sign marked **Gute-Nacht-Linie.**

**Taxis:** ☎ 21 12 11 and 88 88 88 88.

**Ride-Share: Mitfahrzentrale,** Dr.-Friedrich-Wolf-Str. 2 (☎ 194 40; www.mf24.de). On Slesischen Pl., across from *Bahnhof Neustadt.* Open M-F 9am-8pm, Sa-Su 10am-2pm. Non-German speakers may require assistance from their hostels in order to book.

# ▐ ❷ ORIENTATION AND PRACTICAL INFORMATION

The **Elbe** River bisects Dresden 60km northwest of the Czech border, dividing the city into the **Altstadt** in the south (where the *Hauptbahnhof* is located) and the **Neustadt** in the north. Many of Dresden's attractions lie in the *Altstadt* between **Altmarkt** and the Elbe. Nightlife centers in the *Neustadt* to the north by **Albertplatz.**

**Tourist Office:** 2 main branches: Prager Str. 2A, near the *Hauptbahnhof* (open M-F 9:30am-6:30pm, Sa 9:30am-6pm), and Theaterpl. in the Schinkelwache, a small building directly in front of the Semper-Oper (open M-Th 10am-6pm, F 10am-7pm, Sa-Su 10am-5pm). 2 cards provide transportation and free or reduced admission to Dresden museums: the **Dresden City-Card,** valid for 48hr. of transport in the city-zone (€21), and the **Dresden Regio-Card,** good for 72hr. in the Oberelbe region, including Meißen and Saxon Switzerland (€32). Call the city hotlines for general info (☎ 49 19 21 00), room reservations (☎ 49 19 22 22), and tours and advance tickets (☎ 49 19 22 33).

**Currency Exchange: ReiseBank** (☎ 471 2177), in the main hall of the *Hauptbahnhof.* €5 commission for cash; 1-1.5% commission to cash **traveler's checks.** Western Union money transfers. Open M-F 8am-7:30pm, Sa 9am-noon and 12:30-4pm, Su 9am-1pm.

**ATMs:** The **Deutsche Bank** and Sparkasse bank at the corner of Königsbrücker Str. and Stetzscherstr. have 24hr. ATMs, as do many central *Neustadt* and *Altstadt* banks.

**Luggage Storage:** At all train stations. Lockers €2-2.50 for 24hr.

**Laundromat: Eco-Express,** Königsbrücker Str. 2. Wash €1.90 6-11am, €2.40 11am-11pm. Dry €0.50 per 10min. Open M-Sa 6am-11pm. Also try **"Crazy" Waschsalon,** 6 Louisenstr. Wash €2.50-2.70. Dry €0.50 per 10min. Open M-Sa 7am-11pm.

**24hr. Pharmacy:** Notdienst signs outside most pharmacies list 24hr. pharmacies.

**Dresden Altstadt**

🏠🏕 ACCOMMODATIONS
Jugendgastehaus Dresden (HI), **3**

🍴 FOOD & DRINK
Cafe Aha, **2**
Rauschenbach, **1**

**Internet Access: Mobile Call Shop & Internet Cafe,** Alaunstr. 70 (☎ 646 518 946). €2 per hr. Open M-Th 11am-11pm, F-Sa 11am-midnight, Su 11am-10pm.

**Post Office: The Hauptpostamt,** Königsbrücker Str. 21/29 (☎ 819 1373), in the *Neustadt.* Open M-F 9am-7pm, Sa 10am-1pm. Branch in the *Altstadt* on Weberg. at the Altmarkt Galerie. Open daily 9:30am-9pm. **Postal Code:** 0351.

# 🏠 ACCOMMODATIONS

In Dresden's *Neustadt*, high-quality hostels with late check-out times neighbor countless clubs and bars. In the *Altstadt*, quieter hostels and pricier hotels are closer to the sights. Reservations are a good idea from April through November.

🏅 **Hostel Mondpalast,** Louisenstr. 77 (☎ 563 4050; www.mondpalast.de). Settle down in a comfy bed in large and clean rooms, some with TV, after a night hanging out in the lively bar downstairs. Bike rental €5 per 3hr., €7 per day. Breakfast €5. Linens €2. Internet €2 per hr. Reception 24hr. Dorms €14-17; singles €29-34, with bath €39-44; doubles €37-44/50-52; quads €74-78. AmEx/MC/V. ❶

**Hostel Louise 20,** Louisenstr. 20 (☎ 889 4894; www.louise20.de). Above the restaurant Planwirtschaft. Walk through a courtyard to this luxurious hostel, where a winding staircase leads up to modern rooms with wooden furniture. Breakfast €5. Linens €2.50.

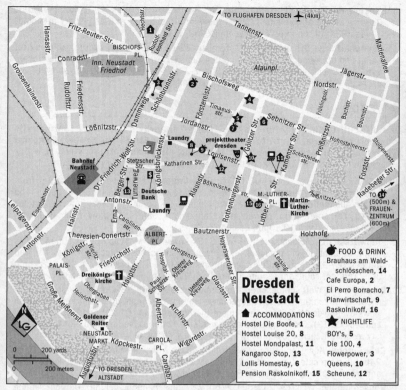

**Dresden Neustadt**

🏠 ACCOMMODATIONS
Hostel Die Boofe, 1
Hostel Louise 20, 8
Hostel Mondpalast, 11
Kangaroo Stop, 13
Lollis Homestay, 6
Pension Raskolnikoff, 15

🍎 FOOD & DRINK
Brauhaus am Wald-
schlösschen, 14
Cafe Europa, 2
El Perro Borracho, 7
Planwirtschaft, 9
Raskolnikoff, 16

⭐ NIGHTLIFE
BOY's, 5
Die 100, 4
Flowerpower, 3
Queens, 10
Scheune, 12

Reception 7am-11pm. Check-out noon. Dorms €16-17; singles €29-32; doubles €39-43; triples €51; quads €68; quints €80. Free linens with ISIC. MC/V. ❶

**Kangaroo-Stop,** Erna-Berger-Str. 8-10 (☎314 3455; www.kangaroo-stop.de). From the *Neustadt* station, take Antonstr. toward Albertpl. and turn left onto Erna-Berger-Str. A young staff runs this Outback-themed backpackers' hostel with co-ed dorms and hammocks in a quiet corner of the Neustadt near the train station. Breakfast €4.90. Linens €2.20. Free Internet. Reception 8am-10pm. Check-in 2pm. Check-out 11am. 10-bed dorms €13, 5- to 6-bed €14-15, 4-bed €15-16, 3-bed €16-17; singles €27-29; doubles €36-38. 10% ISIC discount on rooms and breakfast. Cash only. ❶

**Lollis Homestay,** Görlitzer Str. 34 (☎81 08 45 58; www.lollishome.de). This hostel reproduces the relaxed feel of a student flat, with free coffee, tea, and a book exchange. Old bikes available to borrow. Breakfast €3. Linens €2. Laundry €3. Internet €2.50 per hr. Dorms €13-16; singles €27-38; doubles €36-42; triples €48-57; quads €60-72. 10% ISIC discount. MC/V; €2.50 surcharge. ❶

**Hostel Die Boofe,** Hechtstr. 10 (☎801 3361; www.boofe.de). This funky hostel has a sauna in the basement. Wheelchair-accessible. Breakfast €5.50. Internet €1 per hr. Reception 7am-midnight. Check-in 2pm. Check-out 11am. Dorms €17, with shower €19; singles €29-34; doubles €41/50. 10% discount with 3-night stay. Cash only. ❷

GERMANY

**Pension Raskolnikoff,** Böhmische Str. 34 (☎804 5706; www.raskolnikoff.de). Reserve ahead at this small, stylish pension. Restaurant and art gallery attached. Singles €34-42; doubles €44-52. AmEx/MC/V. ❸

**Jugendherberge Dresden (HI),** Maternistr. 22 (☎49 26 20; www.djh-sachsen.de). Clean and bunk-free. Breakfast included. Linens €1.50. Internet €0.10 per min. Reception 24hr. Check-in 4pm. Check-out 9:30am. 2- to 4-bed dorms €22, with shower €27, under 27 €19/24. €1 winter discount. Cash only. ❷

## 🍴 FOOD

It's difficult to find anything in the *Altstadt* that does not target tourists; the cheapest eats are at the *Imbiß* stands along **Prager Straße** and around **Postplatz.** The area in the *Neustadt* between **Albertplatz** and **Alaunplatz** spawns a new bar every few weeks and is home to many quirky, student-friendly restaurants.

🍴 **Cafe Aha,** Kreuzstr. 7 (☎496 0673; www.ladencafe.de), across the street from Kreuzkirche in the *Altstadt*. Often exotic, always delicious, Cafe Aha introduces food from a different developing country each month. Abundant vegetarian options. Entrees €5-11. Fair trade shop located in the basement. Cafe open daily 10am-midnight. Kitchen open 10am-10:30pm. Cash only. ❶

🍴 **Planwirtschaft,** Louisenstr. 20 (☎801 3187; www.planwirtschaft.de). German dishes with ingredients fresh from local farms. Inventive soups, crisp salads (€4.30-8.40), and entrees (€7-11) from stuffed eggplant to fresh lake fish. Breakfast buffet (€8) until 3pm. Outdoor courtyard seating. Open Su-Th 9am-1am, F-Sa 9am-2am. MC/V. ❸

**Brauhaus am Waldschlösschen,** Am Brauhaus 8B (☎652 3900; www.waldschloesschen.de). Take tram #11 to Waldschlösschen or walk 25min. up Baunitzerstr. Beautiful views overlooking the Elbe complement the house brews (€1.90) and classic German entrees (€8-13). Order from the garden cafeteria or be served by barmaids in the touristy restaurant inside. Open daily 11-1am. AmEx/MC/V. ❸

**Cafe Europa,** Königsbrücker Str. 68 (☎804 4810; www.cafe-europa-dresden.de). Open 24hr., this hip cafe draws a crowd of locals of all ages with tons of drinks, soups (€3), and traditional entrees (€6-10). Free Wi-Fi. AmEx/MC/V. ❷

**Rauschenbach,** Weisseg. 2 (☎821 2760; www.rauschenbach-deli.de). Outdoor seating is a place to see and be seen. Tapas and sandwiches €2.90-4.20. Reserve ahead. Open Su-Th 9am-1am, F-Sa 9am-3am. AmEx/MC/V. ❷

**El Perro Borracho,** Alaunstr. 70 (☎803 6723; www.elperro.de). In the Kunsthofpassage—a courtyard complex filled with quirky shops, restaurants, and even a ballet school—this near-hidden restaurant, where flowing Spanish wines, sangria, and tasty tapas (all €2.90) make Dresdeners happy. Entrees €8-13. Open M 4pm-2am, Tu-F 11:30am-2am, Sa-Su 10am-3am. Tapas M-F 6pm-2am, Sa-Su 3pm-3am. Cash only. ❸

**Raskolnikoff,** Böhmische Str. 34 (☎804 5706; www.raskolnikoff.de). A Dostoyevskian haunt in a pre-war building. Savory fare from every corner of the world (€3.50-12). Open daily 10am-2am. AmEx/MC/V. ❸

## 🔆 SIGHTS

Saxony's electors once ruled nearly all of central Europe from the banks of the majestic Elbe. Despite the *Altstadt*'s demolition in WWII and only partial reconstruction during Communist times, the area remains an impressive cultural center.

**SEMPER-OPER.** Dresden's opera house echoes the splendor of the Zwinger's (p.p. 488) north wing. Painstaking restoration has returned the building to its pre-war state. (*Theaterpl. 2. ☎491 1496. Tours usually M-Sa 2 per hr., but times vary each week; check at the entrance or the ticket office in the Schinkelwache building. €7, students €3.50.*)

**RESIDENZSCHLOß.** Once the home of August the Strong, the Polish king who built most of the Dresden area's castles, this palace shelters the ▓Grünes Gewölbe (Green Vault). Re-opened in 2006, the **Historisches Grünes Gewölbe** presents items from August's treasury in original Baroque treasure rooms as impressive as the objects on display. From the mind-blowing collection of rare medieval chalices to lavish jewels, the vault dazzles with some of Europe's finest metal and gem work. The **Neues Grünes Gewölbe** presents even more objects from the collections, including a stunning green diamond and a bejeweled diorama of the court of the Mughal Emperor Aurangzeb. (☎ 49 14 20 00. *Historisches Grünes open M and W-Su 10am-7pm. €10; includes audio tour. Neues Grünes open M and W-Su 10am-6pm. €8, students €2.50. Audio tour €2.*) In a quiet tower of the palace, the 100m **Hausmannsturm** hosts a collection of sobering photographs of the city after the firebombings that, combined with the 360° view from the tower, convey the enormity of the reconstruction project. (*Open Apr.-Sept. M and W-Su 10am-6pm. €3, students €2.*) To view the curiously irresponsible rulers of Saxony from 1123 to 1904, stop by the **Fürstenzug** (Procession of Electors) along Augustsstr., a 102m mural made of 24,000 tiles of Meißen china.

**FRAUENKIRCHE.** The product of a legendary 10-year reconstruction effort after crumbling to the ground on February 13, 1945, the Frauenkirche re-opened on Oct. 31, 2005, completing Dresden's skyline with its regal silhouette. The cathedral's completion has brought floods of German tourists into Dresden to gaze at the circular ascending balconies, golden altar, and magnificent cupola. Crowds are smallest on weekday afternoons. Expect a wait on the weekend. (*Neumarkt.* ☎ 498 1131. *Open M-F 10am-noon and 1-6pm, Sa-Su hours vary, check the church's info center in the Kulturpalast across Neumarkt or pick up a free copy of the German-language Leben in der Frauenkirche at the tourist office and look for "Offene Kirche." English-language audio tour €2.50.*)

**KREUZKIRCHE.** After it was leveled three times—by fire in 1669 and 1897 and by the Seven Years' War in 1760—the Kreuzkirche survived WWII, despite the flames that ruined its interior. Its tower offers a bird's-eye view of downtown. (*An der Kreuzkirche 6.* ☎ 496 5807; *www.dresdner-kreuzkirche.de. Open Apr.-Oct. M-F 10am-5:30pm, Sa 10am-4:30pm, Su noon-5:30pm; Nov.-Mar. M-Sa 10am-3:30pm, Su noon-4:30pm. Church free. Tower €2.*) The world-class **Kreuzchor** boys' choir has sung here since the 13th century. (☎ 315 3560; *www.kreuzchor.de. Concerts 6pm on some Sa in winter.*)

**GOLDENER REITER.** A shiny, gold-plated statue of August the Strong stands across the Augustusbrücke on Hauptstr. August's epithet has two sources: his physical strength, to which a thumbprint (miraculously imprinted after his death) on the Brühlische Terasse supposedly attests, and his remarkable virility; legend has it he fathered 365 children, though the official tally is 15.

**DIE GLÄSERNE MANUFAKTUR.** The nearly transparent Volkswagen factory is architecturally bold. Phaetons in various stages of assembly are stacked in plain view. The tour includes an amazingly realistic virtual test drive. Unfortunately, the production process is not shown from mid-July to mid-August. German-language tours available; English-language tours must be scheduled ahead. (*Lennestr. 1.* ☎ 01 80 58 96 268; *www.glaesernemanufaktur.de. Tours daily 8am-8pm by appointment.*)

## ▥ MUSEUMS

After several years of renovations, Dresden's museums are once again ready to compete with the best in Europe. If you plan on visiting more than one in a day, consider a **Tageskarte** (€10, students €6), which grants one-day admission to the Schloß, most of the Zwinger, and more. The **Dresden City-Card** and **Dresden Regio-Card** (see **Practical Information,** p. 483) include museum admission. Info about all the museums is at www.skd-dresden.de. Most museums close on Mondays.

**ZWINGER.** The extravagant collection of Saxon elector August the Strong occupies the magnificent Zwinger palace. A glorious example of Baroque design, Zwinger narrowly escaped destruction in the 1945 bombings. Gottfried Semper, revolutionary activist and master architect, designed the north wing. The palace now hosts Dresden's finest museums. Through the archway from the Semper-Oper, ⬛**Gemäldegalerie Alte Meister** has a world-class collection of Dutch and Italian paintings from 1400 to 1800, including Cranach the Elder's luminous *Adam and Eve*, Giorgione's *Sleeping Venus*, and Raphael's enchanting *Sistine Madonna*. *(☎ 49 14 20 00. Open Tu-Su 10am-6pm. €6, students €3.50; includes entry to the Rüstkammer.)* The ⬛**Rüstkammer** shows the deadly toys of the Wettin princes in one of the greatest collections of armory in Europe: ivory-inlaid guns, chain mail, and toddler-sized armor. *(Open Tu-Su 10am-6pm. €3, students €2.)* With over 20,000 pieces from Europe, China, and Japan, the **Porzellansammlung** has the largest collection of porcelain in Europe. *(Open Tu-Su 10am-6pm. €6, students and seniors €3.40.)* Europe's oldest science museum, the **Mathematisch-Physikalischer Salon**, contains stylish 16th- to 19th-century scientific instruments. *(Open Tu-Su 10am-6pm. €3, students €2. English-language audio tour €1.50 with a €10 deposit.)*

**STADTMUSEUM.** Artifacts of Dresden's early history, which begins in the 13th century, pale before the museum's fascinating 20th-century memorabilia, including a People's Gas Mask *(Volksgasmask)* and a 1902 replica firefighter with a helmet-sprinkler. The museum also includes temporary exhibits highlighting contemporary artists from the city. *(Wilsdruffer Str. 2. ☎ 65 64 80. Open Tu-Th and Sa-Su 10am-6pm, F noon-8pm. €3, students €2.)*

**DEUTSCHES HYGIENEMUSEUM.** The world's first public health museum focuses on the "Transparent Man," a see-through human model with illuminated organs. Most exhibits are hands-on and kid-friendly. Ask for info in English. *(Lingnerpl. 1, enter from Blüherstr. ☎ 484 6600. Open Tu-Su 10am-6pm. €6, students €3.)*

## 🎵 ENTERTAINMENT

Dresden has long been a focal point of music, opera, and theater. Most theaters break from mid-July to early September, but open-air festivals bridge the gap. Outdoor movies screen along the Elbe during **Filmnächte am Elbufer** in July and August. (Office at Alaunstr. 62. ☎ 89 93 20. Movies show around 9pm. Tickets €6.) The **Zwinger** has classical concerts in summer at 6:30pm.

**Sächsische Staatsoper (Semper-Oper),** Theaterpl. 2 (☎ 491 1705; www.semper-oper.de). Some of the world's finest opera. Tickets can sell out; call ahead. Tickets €4.50-160. Box office at Schinkelwache open M-F 10am-6pm, Sa-Su 10am-4pm, and 1hr. before performances.

**Kulturpalast,** Schloßstr. 2, in Altmarkt (☎ 486 1866; www.kulturpalast-dresden.de). Home to the **Dresdner Philharmonie** (☎ 486 6306; www.dresdnerphilharmonie.de) and a variety of performances. Open M and W-F 10am-6pm, Tu 10am-7pm, Su 10am-2pm.

**Staatsoperette Dresden,** Pirnär Landstr. 131 (☎ 20 79 90; www.staatsoperette-dresden.de). Musicals and operettas from Nicolai to Sondheim. €11-28. Box office open M 11am-4pm, Tu-Th 10am-7pm, F 11am-7pm, Sa 4-7pm, Su 1hr. before shows.

**projekttheater dresden,** Louisenstr. 47 (☎ 810 7610; www.projekttheater.de). Cutting-edge, international experimental theater in the heart of the *Neustadt*. Tickets €11, students €9. Shows start 8 or 9pm. Box office open 1hr. before shows.

## 🌃 NIGHTLIFE

It's as if the entire *Neustadt* spends the day anticipating nightfall. A decade ago, the area north of Albertpl. was a maze of gray streets and crumbling buildings;

since then, an alternative community has thrived in bars on **Louisenstraße, Königs-brücker straße, Bischofsweg, Kamenzerstraße,** and **Albertplatz.** The German-language *Dresdener Kulturmagazin,* free at *Neustadt* hostels, describes every bar.

**Scheune,** Alaunstr. 36 (☎804 38; www.scheune.org). The granddaddy of the *Neustadt* scene, this huge bar and cafe is a starting point for hipsters. Entrees €4.50-10. Club opens 8pm and hosts a variety of events including live music. Cover €5-20. Cafe open M-Th 5pm-1am, F 5pm-2am, Sa 10am-2am, Su 10am-1am. Cash only.

**Flowerpower,** Eschenstr. 11 (☎804 9814; www.flower-power.de). Over-the-top decor from the 60s and 70s attracts a dedicated crowd of 20-somethings. M student night; discounts on beer and wine. Th Karaoke. F club night. Open daily 8pm-5am. Cash only.

**Die 100,** Alaunstr. 100 (☎801 3957). The candlelit interior and intimate stone court-yard of this laid-back, well-stocked wine cellar provide an escape from the social flurry elsewhere. Wine from €3 per glass. Open daily 5pm-3am. Cash only.

**BOY's,** Alaunstr. 80, just beyond the Kunsthof Passage. A half-clad devil mannequin guards one of Dresden's popular gay-friendly bars. Drinks €1.90-5. Open Tu-Th 8pm-3am, F-Su 8pm-5am. MC/V.

**Queens,** Görlitzer Str. 3 (☎810 8108; www.queens-dresden.de). Unpretentious and relaxed. While BOY's may be more hip, this gay bar and disco is known for its fun, relaxed vibe. Su-Th 8pm-5am, F-Sa 9pm-late.

## ◼ DAYTRIP FROM DRESDEN: MEIßEN

In 1710, the Saxon elector contracted a severe case of the porcelain bug, and he turned the city's defunct castle into Europe's first porcelain factory. To prevent competitors from learning its techniques, the building was once extremely tightly guarded; today, anyone can tour the **Staatliche Porzellan-Manufaktur Meißen,** Talstr. 9, and observe the craftsmen in action. You can look through finished products in the *Schauhalle,* but the real fun is in the *Schauwerkstatt* (demonstration show-room), where you can watch porcelain artists paint petal-perfect flowers before your disbelieving eyes. (☎0352 146 8208. Open daily May-Oct. 9am-6pm; Nov.-Apr. 9am-5pm. €8.50, students €4.50. English-language audio tour €3.) Cutesy souvenir-lined alley-ways snake up to the castle, cathedral, and beery eateries of ▨**Albrechtsburg** (www.albrechtsburg-meissen.de). To get there from the train station, walk straight on Bahnhofstr. and follow it over the Elbbrücke. Cross the bridge, con-tinue straight to the Markt, and turn right on Burgstr. Follow the signs up the hill, then look for a long staircase hugging a wall to your right; this leads to the castle. (Open daily Mar.-Oct. 10am-6pm; Nov.-Feb. 10am-5pm. Last entry 15min. before closing. €3.50, students €2.50. English-language audio tour €2.) Next door looms the **Dom zu Meißen,** a Gothic cathedral featuring four 13th-century statues by the Naumburg Master, an amazing 13th-century stained-glass window, and a triptych by Cranach the Elder. (Open daily Apr.-Oct. 9am-6pm; Nov.-Mar. 10am-4pm. €2.50, students €1.50.) **Trains** run to Meißen from Dresden (40min., €5.10). The **tourist office,** Markt 3, across from Frauenkirche, finds private rooms. (☎419 40. Open Apr.-Oct. M-F 10am-6pm, Sa-Su 10am-43pm; Nov.-Mar. M-F 10am-5pm, Sa 10am-3pm.) **Postal Code:** 01662.

# LEIPZIG
☎0341

Leipzig (pop. 493,000) is known as the city of music, and indeed, it's hard to walk more than a few blocks without being serenaded by a classical quartet, wooed by a Spanish guitar, or riveted by the choir music wafting from the Thomaskirche. Large enough to have a life outside its university, but small enough to feel the influence of its students, Leipzig boasts world-class museums and corners packed with cafes, cabarets, and second-hand stores.

**▣⚑ TRANSPORTATION AND PRACTICAL INFORMATION.** Leipzig lies on the Berlin-Munich line. **Trains** run to: Berlin (1½hr., 2 per hr., €39); Dresden (2hr., 2 per hr., €27); Frankfurt (3½hr., 1 per hr., €65); Munich (5hr., 1 per hr., €81). To find the **tourist office,** Richard-Wagner-Str. 1, cross Willy-Brandt-Pl. in front of the station and hang a left on Richard-Wagner-Str. (☎710 4265. Open Mar.-Oct. M-F 9:30am-6pm, Sa 9:30am-4pm, Su 9:30am-3pm; Nov.-Feb. M-F 10am-6pm.) The **Leipzig Card** is good for free public transport and discounted museums and tours. (1-day, until 4am, €9; 3-day €19.) **Postal Code:** 04109.

**▣▢ ACCOMMODATIONS AND FOOD.** To reach ⊠**Hostel Sleepy Lion ❶**, Käthe-Kollwitz-Str. 3, take streetcar #1 (dir.: Lausen) to Gottschedstr., or, from the station, turn right and walk along Trondlinring, then left on Goerdelering and continue straight on Käthe-Kollwitz-Str. Run by young locals, it draws an international crowd with its spacious lounge, foosball table, and separate non-smoking area. (☎993 9480; www.hostel-leipzig.de. All rooms with bath. Bike rental €5 per day. Breakfast €3.50. Linens €2.50. Internet €2 per hr. Reception 24hr. Dorms €14-16; singles €30; doubles €42; quads €68. Winter reduced rates. AmEx/MC/V.) **Central Globetrotter ❶**, Kurt-Schumacher-Str. 41, fills its wildly spray-painted rooms with young backpackers and church choir groups. Take the west exit and turn right onto Kurt-Schumacher-Str. (☎149 8960; www.globetrotter-leipzig.de. Communal showers. Breakfast €4. Linens €2. Internet €2 per hr. Dorms €13-14; singles €24; doubles €36; quads €60. AmEx/MC/V.)

*Imbiß* stands, bistros, and bakeries line **Grimmaischestraße** in the Innenstadt. Outside the city center, cafes, bars, and *Döner* stands pack **Karl-Liebknecht-Straße** (streetcar #10 or 11 to Südpl.). The hip cafe **Bellini's ❷**, Barfußgäßchen 3-5 (☎961 7681), serves salads, and pasta (€3.80-11) in the heart of the Markt. (Open daily noon-late. MC/V.) Designed in the imaginatively whimsical style of Friedrich Hundertwasser, **100-Wasser Cafe ❷**, Barfußg. 15, serves generous pastas and other dishes. (☎215 7927. Entrees €5.50-13. Open daily 9am-2am. Cash only.) **Zur Pleißenburg ❷**, Ratfreischulstr. 2, down Burgstr. from the Thomaskirche, serves German fare at reasonable prices. (☎960 2653. Open daily 9am-5am. Cash only.) There is a **market** on Richard-Wagner-Pl. at the end of the Brühl. (Open Tu and F 9am-5pm.)

**◪ SIGHTS.** The heart of Leipzig is the **Marktplatz,** a cobblestone square guarded by the slanted 16th-century **Altes Rathaus** (town hall). Head down Grimmaischestr. to the **Nikolaikirche,** a church ornamented in the classicist style with carved columns and ceilings, where massive weekly demonstrations accelerated the fall of the GDR. (Open M-Sa 10am-6pm, Su 9:30am-6pm. Free tours Tu and Th-F at 5pm, Sa at 11am. Organ concerts Sa 5pm; tickets €10, students €7.) Backtrack to the *Rathaus* and follow Thomasg. to the **Thomaskirche.** Bach spent his last 27 years here as cantor; his grave is in front of the altar. (☎960 2855. Open daily 9am-6pm. Free.) Just behind the church is the small **Johann-Sebastian-Bach-Museum,** Thomaskirchhof 16, with exhibits on the composer's life, an annual Bach **festival** (June 13-22, 2008), and many fall concerts. (Open daily 10am-5pm. €4, students €2. Free English-language audio tour.) Head back to Thomasg., turn left, then turn right on Dittrichring to reach Leipzig's fascinating ⊠**Museum in der "Runden Ecke,"** Dittrichring 24, situated in a former police building with blunt exhibits on the GDR-era *Stasi* (secret police). Ask in the office for a €0.50 English-language brochure. (☎961 2443; www.runde-ecke-leipzig.de. Open daily 10am-6pm. Free.) Outside the city ring, the ziggurat-like **Völkerschlachtdenkmal,** built in 1913, memorializes the centennial of the 1813 Battle of Nations, when the combined forces of Austria, Prussia, Russia, and Sweden defeated Napoleon near Leipzig. Climb the 364 steps for an impressive view of the city. (Tram #15 from the station to Völkerschlacht-denkmal. Open daily Apr.-Oct. 10am-6pm; Nov.-Mar. 10am-4pm. €5, students €3.) Leipzig's **Gewandhaus-Orchester,** Augustuspl. 8, has housed a major international

GERMANY

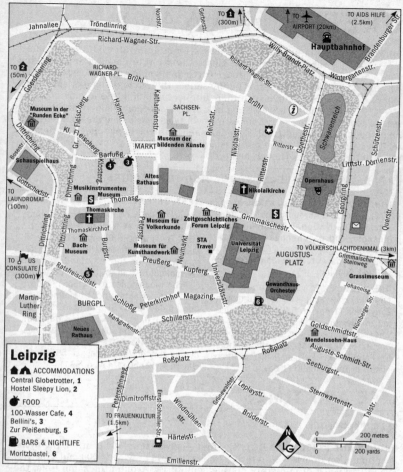

**Leipzig**

🏠🏠 **ACCOMMODATIONS**
Central Globetrotter, **1**
Hostel Sleepy Lion, **2**

🍴 **FOOD**
100-Wasser Cafe, **4**
Bellini's, **3**
Zur Pleißenburg, **5**

🍸 **BARS & NIGHTLIFE**
Moritzbastei, **6**

orchestra since 1843. (☎ 127 0280. Open M-F 10am-6pm, Su 10am-2pm, and 1hr. before performances. Tickets €10-65.)

🎭 **NIGHTLIFE.** The free magazines *Frizz* and *Blitz* have nightlife info, as does *Kreuzer* (€2 at newsstands). **Barfußgäßchen**, a street off the Markt, is the place to see and be seen for the student and young professional crowd. A slightly younger crowd and slightly louder music lie across Dittrichring on **Gottschedstraße** and **Bosestraße**. Leipzig university students spent eight years excavating a series of medieval tunnels so they could get their groove on in the 🎭**Moritzbastei**, Universitätsstr. 9, a massive cave with bars, a cafe, and multi-level dance floors under vaulted brick ceilings. "All You Can Dance" club nights take place on Wednesdays and Saturdays; other nights, there are film screenings and live performances—see website for details. (☎ 70 25 90; www.moritzbastei.de. Cover W €4, students €2.50; Sa €4.50/3. Cafe open M-F 10am-midnight, Sa noon-midnight, Su 9am-midnight. Club open W 10am-6am, Sa noon-6am. Cash only.)

# GREECE (ΈΛΛΑς)

With sacred monasteries as mountainside fixtures, standard three hour seaside siestas, and circle dancing and drinking until daybreak, Greece revels in its epic past. Renaissance men long before the Renaissance, the ancient Greeks sprung to prominence with their intellectual and athletic mastery. The modern lifestyle is a mix of high speed and sun-inspired loung-ing, as old men hold lively debates in town *plateias*, teenagers zoom around on mopeds, and unpredictable schedules teach travelers patience and flexibil-ity. Let Hermes, ancient god of travel, guide your feet as you wander the birth-place of the Olympics, Homer, and *gyros*.

## DISCOVER GREECE: SUGGESTED ITINERARIES

**THREE DAYS.** Spend it all in **Athens** (p. 501). Roam the **Acropolis,** gaze at trea-sures in the **National Archaeological Museum,** and pay homage at the **Par-thenon.** Visit the ancient **Agora**, then take a trip down to **Poseidon's Temple** at Cape Sounion.

**ONE WEEK.** Begin your sojourn in **Ath-ens** (3 days). Scope out sea turtles in **Zakynthos** (1 day; p. 530) before sprint-ing to **Olympia** (1 day; p. 514) to see where the games began. Sail to **Corfu** (1 day; p. 528) and peer into Albania from Mt. Pantokrator. Lastly, soak up Byzantine history in **Thessaloniki** (1 day; p. 518).

**BEST OF GREECE, THREE WEEKS.** Explore **Athens** (4 days) before visiting the mansions of **Nafplion** (1 day; p. 516). Race west to **Olympia** (1 day) and take a ferry to the beaches of **Corfu** (2 days). Back on the mainland, wander **Thessaloniki** (2 days), then climb to the cliffside monasteries of **Meteora** (1 day; p. 526). Consult the gods at **Mount Olym-pus** (1 day; p. 523) and the Oracle of **Delphi** (1 day). On **Crete** (3 days; p. 537), hike Europe's largest gorge. Seek rest on **Santorini** (1 day; p. 536), debauchery on **Ios** (1 day; p. 535), and sun on **Mykonos** (1 day; p. 531).

# LIFE AND TIMES

## HISTORY

**BRONZE AGE (3200-1150 BC).** The first Aegean island civilization, the **Cycla-dic** population flourished on the Cyclades (p. 531) between 3000 and 1100 BC, leaving a legacy of miniature marble sculptures. Around the same time, the seafaring **Minoans** of Crete (p. 537) created grand palaces and a syllabic writing system before they disappeared around 1500 BC, presumably in a volcanic eruption in Santorini. On the mainland, the warring **Mycenaean** princes allied for the storied attack on Troy and further developed Linear B, a written lan-guage based on Minoan hieroglyphs. The Mycenaean civilization ended abruptly around 1150 BC when the Dorians invaded from the north, causing three centuries of archaeological silence and cultural decline.

**THE RISE OF THE CITY-STATE (800-500 BC).** Around 800 BC, a discernibly Greek culture coalesced, unified by the Greek language and religious rites. The **polis**, or city-state, emerged as the major Greek political structure. At the heart of each city was the **acropolis**, a fortified citadel and religious center atop the highest point, and the **agora**, the marketplace and center of commercial and social life. Greek unity grew during the **Persian Wars** (490-449 BC), when Athens and Sparta led the Greeks

Greece

GREECE

against overwhelming odds to defeat the Persians in the legendary battles at Marathon, Plataea, and Salamis. The victories ushered in the Classical period: a time of unprecedented prosperity as well as artistic, commercial, and political success.

**CLASSICAL GREECE (479-323 BC).** Following the Persian Wars, Athens created the **Delian League** of Greek states to defend against Persian aggression. The league established Athens as a colonial power by requiring all members to pay dues and swear loyalty to Athens. This expansion brought the city, which prided itself on its commercial, democratic, and cultural achievements, into direct conflict with the agricultural, monarchical, and martial Sparta for control of Greece. During the **Peloponnesian War** (431-404 BC), the Athenians proved no match for the military prowess of the Spartans, whose soldiers entered the army at age seven. A 403 BC Athenian revolt weakened but failed to dislodge Sparta's power completely. Classical Greece dissolved as bickering between warring poli became more heated.

**MACEDONIAN RULE (323-20BC).** After the Peloponnesian War, Macedonia's **King Philip II** took advantage of the weakened city-states and invaded from the north in 338 BC. His later assassination left his 20-year-old son Alexander in command. The young king spent the rest of his life at war, establishing a stranglehold on the Greek city-states before sweeping into Persia and Egypt. At the time of his sudden death, **Alexander the Great,** 33, ruled much of the known world, having widely spread Greek culture and language. His extensive empire's dissolution restored some independence to the Greek city-states, but self-rule did not last long. The Romans invaded in 146 BC; by 20 BC Greece was part of the Roman Empire, which borrowed from Greek architecture, art, religion, and scholarship.

**ROMAN EMPIRE: EAST SIDE (20 BC-1000 AD).** As Rome slowly declined, competing halves began to dominate the empire: an eastern half, centered in Anatolia, the Levant, and Greece, and a western half, centered in Rome. This unusual political arrangement ended in a scramble for power won by **Constantine** in AD 312. He later legalized Christianity, already a powerful force in Greece, and gave the Roman Empire a new capital in AD 324 with the founding of **Constantinople,** built over the ancient city of Byzantium in modern-day Turkey. While Western Europe was overrun by barbarian invaders, the eastern **Byzantine Empire** became an unrivaled center of learning, trade, and influence. During the 6th century, **Emperor Justinian's** battles against the Sassanians of Persia weakened the Byzantine army. Power waned under the strain of repeated Slavic and Mongolian raids.

**NASTY NEIGHBORS (1000-1800 AD).** From 1200 to 1400, the Byzantine Empire was plagued by crusaders, including the Venetians, who conquered and looted Constantinople in 1204 and imposed Catholicism upon the city. In 1453, the Ottoman Turks overran the much-reduced city, renaming it İstanbul. The Muslim Turkish rulers treated their Greek subjects as members of a *millet*—a separate community ruled by its own religious leaders. The Greek Orthodox church became the moderator of culture and the foundation of Greek autonomy. By the 19th century, Greeks were pushing for independence from the Ottoman Empire.

**GREEK NATIONALIST REVOLT (1800-1833 AD).** In 1821, **Bishop Germanos** of Patras raised a Greek flag at the monastery of Agia Lavra, sparking an empire-wide rebellion. Disorganized but impassioned guerrillas on the Peloponnese and in the Aegean Islands waged war sporadically on the Turkish government for nearly a decade, although the revolt never gained the hoped-for support from the peasants. Finally, in 1829, with help from various European powers, Greece won its **independence.** The borders of the new Greece were narrow, including only a fraction of the six million Greeks living under Ottoman rule. For the next century, Greek politics centered around the **Megali Idea** (Great Idea): freeing İstanbul from the Turks and uniting all Greeks into one sovereign state. Although Greece gained back territory over the next century, it never realized these ambitious goals.

**A GREECEY SITUATION (1833-1923 AD).** In 1833, after the assassination of **Ioannis Kapodistrias,** the first democratically elected Greek president, the European powers intervened, declared Greece a monarchy, and handed the crown to a succession of Germanic princes. Democracy prevailed in 1864, however, when the constitution established an elected prime minister as the head of state. **Eleftherios Venizelos,** elected in 1910, employed these powers to expand Greece's territory to **Crete** (p. 537), **Thessaloniki** (p. 518), **Epirus,** and a portion of **Macedonia** on the Aegean coast. Despite the Ottoman Empire's defeat in WWI, Greece did not receive land in Asia Minor, and in 1919 Venizelos ordered an invasion of Turkey. A young Turkish general, Mustafa Kemal, later called **Atatürk,** crushed the invasion and ordered the slaughter of ethnic Greeks along the Turkish coast. This continued until the **Treaty of Lausanne** (1923) enacted a population exchange that brought one and a half million Greeks from Asia Minor to Greece and sent 400,000 Turkish Muslims from Greece to Turkey, effectively ending the *Megali Idea.*

**WORLD WAR II AND THE MODERN GREEK STATE (1923-1980 AD).** The 1930s were rocked by political turmoil as brief intervals of democracy gave way to a succession of monarchies and military rule. The extreme nationalist General John Metaxas succeeded Venizelos as prime minister, notably rejecting Mussolini's request to bring Italian troops through neutral Greece with a resounding "Oci!"

(No!). Greeks now celebrate Okhi Day on October 28. Although they drove back the Italians who invaded anyway, Greece fell to the Axis in 1941 and endured four years of bloody and brutal occupation, during which 65,000 Greek Jews perished in Nazi camps. Resistance was split between the popular communist-led movement and the US-backed royalist movement. This struggle for influence turned violent in 1944 as the devastating Greek Civil War, marked by purges and starvation, became one of the early battles in the Cold War. The left-wing, Soviet-backed Democratic Army finally lost to the anti-communist coalition in 1949. The US played a visible role in Greek politics through the subsequent decades of turmoil. A new constitution was drawn up in 1975, establishing the current parliamentary government with a ceremonial president appointed by the country's legislature.

## TODAY

On January 1, 1981, Greece became the European Union's 10th member. The nation's Prime Minister throughout the 1980s and mid-1990s, **Andreas Papandreou**, founded the leftist **Panhellenic Socialist Movement (PASOK)** and pioneered the passage of women's rights legislation. **Costas Simitis** succeeded him, successfully pursuing economic reforms. Under his guidance, Greece finally met the qualifying standards for adoption of the **euro (€)** in January 2001. In the same month, foreign minister **George Papandreou** traveled to Turkey, the first such visit in 37 years. Officially, Greece supports Turkey's bid for EU membership but Cyprus remains a stumbling block in Greco-Turkish relations. A UN-sponsored plan to reunify the Greek and Turkish areas of the island passed in the Turkish North in 2004 but was voted down in the Greek region. Regardless, Greek Cyprus was admitted into the EU later that year. National power shifted back to the right-wing New Democracy party following the 2004 parliamentary elections. Prime Minister **Kostas Karmanlis**, new to office, finished preparing Athens for the 2004 Summer Olympics. His ascension returned PASOK to the opposition. Greece's Communist Party (KKE) forms a vocal minority, occasionally channeling passionate anti-Americanism.

## PEOPLE AND CULTURE

**CUSTOMS AND ETIQUETTE.** Greek hospitality is legendary and the invitations genuine; it's impossible to spend any length of time in the country and not have some friendly interactions with locals. Greet new acquaintances with *kalimera* (good morning) or *kalispera* (good evening). As a general rule, when offered food or drink, take it—it's almost always considered rude to refuse. Coffee is usually offered upon arriving at someone's home. Wine drinkers should be aware that glasses are filled only halfway and constantly replenished; it's considered bad manners to empty your glass. When eating dinner at a restaurant, the bill is usually paid by the host rather than split amongst the diners. Never offer money in return for an invitation to dine in someone's home. A small gift, such as a toy for the host's children, is a welcome token of gratitude.

**LANGUAGE.** To the non-Greek speaker, the language's intricate levels of nuance, idiom, irony, and poetry can present a seemingly impenetrable wall barring understanding. Greek (Ελληνικά, eh-lee-nee-KAH) is one of the most difficult languages for English speakers to learn fluently, but learning enough to order a meal, send a postcard, or get to the airport is surprisingly easy. Greek is highly phonetic; though a cursory knowledge of the Greek alphabet (p. 1053) does not always help with the double consonants and double vowels, all multisyllabic words come with a handy accent called a *tonos*, which marks the emphasized syllable. Greeks are famously welcoming of foreigners who try their hand at the language, but many Greeks—and certainly most working in the tourist industry—understand English. For useful phrases, see **Phrasebook: Greek,** p. 1053.

# THE ARTS

## ARCHITECTURE

The earliest Greek artifacts are pottery vessels used for storage, covered with geometric patterns that developed from abstract Mycenaean decorations. During the **Archaic period** (c. 700-500 BC), vessel art increasingly depicted scenes from mythology and everyday life. Throughout the **Archaic period** (c. 700-500 BC), architecture standardized the **Doric** and **Ionic** orders and artists created life-sized human sculptures of the nude male *(kouros)* and draped female *(kore)*, whose rigid poses and stylized features resemble Egyptian statues.

The arts flourished as Athens reached the apex of its power during the **Classical period** (480-323 BC). The peerless Athenian **Acropolis** (p. 508) was built during this era; its crowning glory, the **Parthenon** (p. 508) was dedicated to Athena and demonstrates the Greek aesthetic of the golden ratio, or perfect proportions. The **Severe Style** catalyzed the Greek tradition of making a sculpture intended to be seen from all sides and led to international dominance in representations of the human form.

After the death of Alexander the Great, the flamboyant **Hellenistic period** (323-31 BC) rose from the ashes of Classical Greece. Scuttling the simpler Doric and Ionic styles, eastern Greeks designed ornate, flower-topped **Corinthian** columns. Hellenistic architects worked on a monumental scale, building huge complexes of temples and palaces. Astoundingly precise acoustics graced enormous amphitheaters like the one at **Epidavros** (p. 517); a coin dropped onstage is audible from the most distant seat. Sculptures **Venus de Milo** and **Nike of Samothrace** are two of the most famous pieces created during this period. With the arrival of the Roman Empire, styles shifted to suit the imperial and more reserved tastes of the Romans.

The Byzantine and Ottoman empires, politically dominating Greece through the early 19th century, ruled Grecian art as well. Religious Byzantine artistry saw the creation of magnificent mosaics, iconography, and church architecture. Mosaics, like those in the churches of **Thessaloniki** (p. 518) and **Meteora** (p. 526), were composed of **tesserae,** small cubes of stone, glass-covered ceramic, or metallic foil.

However, upon gaining autonomy in 1831, Greeks denounced Byzantine influence on their art. King Otto encouraged young artists to study their craft in Munich, before later establishing the **Ethnicon Metsovion Polytechnion,** Greece's first modern art school, in 1836. While sculptors still looked to Classical Greece for inspiration, the first wave of post-independence painters showed strong evidence of their German training. Many 20th-century Greek artists assimilated European trends, including Impressionism, Expressionism, and Surrealism. Volos-born **Giorgio de Chirico** (1888-1978), student of art in both Munich and Athens, painted faceless mannequins and bizarre still lifes admired all across Europe. Other painters, however, rejected foreign influences, among them the much-adored **Theophilos Chatzimichael** (1873-1934). Modern Greek artists worth noting include **Yiannis Psychopedis** (1945-), who belongs to the Critical Realism movement, and the painter **Opy Zouni** (1941-), whose geometric art has won international acclaim.

## LITERATURE AND DRAMA

The first written Greek did not appear until after 800 BC, but the Greek literary tradition began long before with poetry and myths passed down from storyteller to storyteller. The most famous is the mysterious **Homer**, credited with composing the **Iliad** and the **Odyssey** in the mid-8th century BC. Homer's contemporary **Hesiod** composed the **Theogony,** an account of the gods' sensational entanglements and the world's creation. On Lesvos (p. 544) during the late 7th century BC, lyric poet **Sappho,** ancient Greece's only known female poet, earned the title of 10th muse.

Greek drama probably began with *tragodoi* (goat songs) sung by men in competitions where a goat was awarded to the victor. These performances transformed over the years into festivals in honor of **Dionysus,** where the chorus interacted with one actor. **Aeschylus,** who composed the *Oresteia* (458 BC), introduced the idea of two actors and thus brought dialogue to the theater. **Aristophanes, Sophocles,** and **Euripides** were other highly influential playwrights.

**Dionysios Solomos,** whose 1823 *Hymn to Liberty* became the national anthem, is still referred to as the National Poet. **Odysseas Elytis,** winner of the 1979 Nobel Prize in Literature, integrated the French Surrealist style with Greek nationalist themes. The best known modern Greek author, **Nikos Kazantzakis,** wrote *Zorba the Greek* and *The Last Temptation of Christ,* both of which became successful films. Modern playwrights like **Iakovos Kambanellis** have wooed audiences with portrayals of 20th-century Greek life, but Classical theater still dominates the **Athens Festival** (p. 511) and the **Epidavros Festival** (p. 517).

## MUSIC

Since the Bronze Age, Greeks have played musical instruments like the **lyre** and the double-reeded **aulo** in accompaniment to sung or chanted poetry, partly to help poets remember lengthy **epics.** During the Classical period, appreciation of music came to be considered an essential part of education, and the mark of a good musician was one who could convey virtue through his music. An integral part of Greek drama, music also graced most other social gatherings, from rowdy festivals to the sacred Oracle of Delphi.

In the 1920s, gritty, urban **rembétika,** which gets its name from the Turkish word meaning "of the gutter," appeared in Greece. It used traditional Greek and Turkish instruments to sing about the ugly side of modern life: drugs, crime, and poverty. Interest in traditional *rembétika* has resurfaced, and musicians strumming *bouzouki* (a Greek instrument similar to the mandolin) can be found in several clubs.

Greece's hottest pop stars include Cypriot siren **Anna Vissi,** pole vaulter **Sakis Rouvas,** and Swedish-born **Elena Paparizou.** The trendiest venues' playlists are saturated with Europop and American hits from the 70s and 80s.

# HOLIDAYS AND FESTIVALS

**Holidays:** Feast of St. Basil/New Year's Day (Jan. 1); Epiphany (Jan. 6); Clean Monday (Mar. 10); Independence Day (Mar. 25); St. George's Day (Apr. 23); Orthodox Good Friday (Apr. 25); Orthodox Easter (Apr. 27-28); Labor Day (May 1); Pentecost (May 11-12); Day of the Holy Spirit (June 16); Assumption (Aug. 15); Feast of St. Demetrius (Oct. 26); Okhi Day (Oct. 28); All Saints' Day (Nov. 1); Christmas (Dec. 25-26).

**Festivals:** Three weeks of Carnival feasting and dancing (Feb. 18-Mar. 10) precede Lenten fasting. April 23 is St. George's Day, when Greece honors the dragon-slaying knight with horse races, wrestling matches, and dances. The Feast of St. Demetrius (Oct. 26) is celebrated with particular enthusiasm in Thessaloniki.

# ADDITIONAL RESOURCES

*Mythology,* by Edith Hamilton. Back Bay Books (1999). The standard introduction to Greek mythology.

*Colossus of Maroussi,* by Henry Miller. New Directions Publishing Co. (1975). A zealous account of Miller's travels in Greece at the start of WWII.

*Cambridge Illustrated History of Ancient Greece,* edited by Paul Cartledge. Cambridge University Press (2002). A well-written, thorough look at all aspects of ancient Greece.

*Zorba The Greek,* directed by Michael Cacoyannis (1964). An exuberant film about Grecian love of life, based on the novel by Nikos Kazantzakis. Won 3 Academy Awards.

# ESSENTIALS

### FACTS AND FIGURES

**Official Name:** Hellenic Republic.
**Capital:** Athens.
**Major Cities:** Thessaloniki, Patras.
**Population:** 10,688,000.
**Land Area:** 131,900 sq. km.

**Time Zone:** GMT +2.
**Language:** Greek.
**Religion:** Eastern Orthodox (98%).
**Highest Peak:** Mt. Olympus (2917m).
**Length of National Anthem:** 158 verses.

## WHEN TO GO

July through August is high season; it is best to visit in May, early June, or September, when smaller crowds enjoy the gorgeous weather. Visiting during low season ensures lower prices, but many sights and accommodations have shorter hours or close altogether. Transportation runs less frequently, so plan accordingly.

## DOCUMENTS AND FORMALITIES

**EMBASSIES.** Foreign embassies in Greece are in Athens (p. 501). Greek embassies abroad include: Australia, 9 Turrana St., Yarralumla, Canberra, ACT, 2600 (☎62 7330 11); Canada, 80 MacLaren St., Ottawa, ON, K2P 0K6 (☎613-238-6271; www.greekembassy.ca); Ireland, 1 Upper Pembroke St., Dublin, 2 (☎31 676 7254, ext. 5); New Zealand, 5-7 Willeston St., 10th fl., Wellington (☎4 473 7775, ext. 6); UK, 1a Holland Park, London, W11 3TP (☎020 72 21 64 67; www.greekembassy.org.uk); US, 2217 Massachusetts Ave., NW, Washington, D.C., 20008 (☎202-939-1300; www.greekembassy.org).

**VISA AND ENTRY INFORMATION.** EU citizens do not need a visa. Citizens of Australia, Canada, New Zealand, and the US do not need a visa for stays of up to 90 days, beginning upon entry into any of the countries in the EU's freedom-of-movement zone. For more info, see p. 13. For stays longer than 90 days, all non-EU citizens need Schengen visas, available at Greek embassies and online at www.greekembassy.org. Processing a tourist visa takes approximately 20 days.

## TRANSPORTATION

**BY PLANE.** Most international flights land in Athens International Airport (**ATH**; ☎21035 30 000; www.aia.gr), though some also serve Corfu (**CFU**), Iraklion (**HER**), Kos (**KSG**), and Thessaloniki (**SKG**). **Olympic Airlines,** 96 Syngrou Ave., Athens, 11741 (☎21092 691 11; www.olympicairlines.com), offers extensive domestic service. A 1hr. flight from Athens (€60-100) can get you to almost any Grecian island.

**BY TRAIN.** Greece is served by a number of international train routes that connect Athens and Thessaloniki to most European cities. Train service within Greece, however, is limited and sometimes uncomfortable. The new air-conditioned, intercity express trains, while slightly more expensive and less frequent, are worth the price. **Eurail Passes** are valid on all Greek trains. **Hellenic Railways Organization** (OSE; ☎1110; www.osenet.gr) connects Athens to major Greek cities.

**BY BUS.** Few buses run directly from any European city to Greece, except for chartered tour buses. Domestic bus service is extensive and fares are cheap. **KTEL** (www.ktel.org) operates most domestic buses; always check with an official source about scheduled departures, as posted schedules are often outdated.

**BY FERRY.** Boats travel from Bari, ITA, to Corfu, Durres, Igoumenitsa, Patras, and Sami and from Ancona, ITA, to Corfu, Igoumenitsa, and Patras. Ferries also run from Greece to various points on the Turkish coast. There is frequent ferry service to the Greek islands, but schedules are irregular and incorrect information is common. Check schedules posted at the tourist office, at the port police, or at www.ferries.gr. Make reservations and arrive at least 1hr. before your departure time. In addition to conventional service, **Hellenic Seaways** (☎21041 99 000; www.hellenicseaways.gr) runs high-speed vessels between the islands at twice the cost and speed of ferries. Student and children receive reduced fares; additionally, travelers buying tickets up to 15 days before intended departure date receive a 15% Early Booking Discount on ferries leaving Tuesday through Thursday.

**BY CAR AND MOPED.** You must be 18 to drive in Greece, and 21 to rent a car; some agencies require renters to be at least 23 or 25; most rental cars start at €35. Rental agencies may quote low daily rates that exclude the 18% tax and **collision damage waiver (CDW)** insurance. Foreign drivers must have an **International Driving Permit** and an **International Insurance Certificate**. The **Automobile and Touring Club of Greece (ELPA),** Messogion 395, Athens, 15343, provides help and offers reciprocal membership to members of foreign auto clubs like AAA. (☎21060 68 800, 24hr. emergency roadside assistance 104, infoline 174; www.elpa.gr.) Mopeds, while great for exploring, are extremely dangerous—wear a helmet.

# TOURIST SERVICES AND MONEY

| EMERGENCY | Ambulance: ☎166. Fire: ☎199. Police: ☎100. General Emergency: ☎112. |
|---|---|

**TOURIST OFFICES.** Two national organizations oversee tourism in Greece: **Greek National Tourist Organization (GNTO;** known as the **EOT** in Greece) and the **tourist police** *(touristiki astinomia)*. The GNTO, Tsoha 7, Athens, supplies general info about Grecian sights and accommodations. (☎2108 70 70 00; www.gnto.gr. Open M-F 8am-3pm.) In addition to the "Tourist Police" insignia decorating their uniforms, white belts, gloves, and cap bands help identify the tourist police. The **Tourist Police Service** and **General Police Directorate,** P. Kanellopoulou 4, Athens (☎2106 92 8510, 24hr. general emergency 171) deal with local and immediate problems concerning bus schedules, accommodations, and lost passports. Offices are open long hours and are willing to help, but their staff's English may be limited.

**MONEY.** The **euro (€)** has replaced the **Greek drachma** as the unit of currency in Greece. For more info, see p. 16. It's generally cheaper to change money in Greece than at home. When changing money in Greece, try to go to a bank (τράπεζα; TRAH-peh-za) with at most a 5% margin between its buy and sell prices. A barebones day in Greece costs €40-60. A day with more comforts runs €55-75. While all restaurant prices include a 15% **gratuity,** tipping an additional 5-10% for the assistant waiters and busboys is considered good form. **Taxi** drivers do not expect tips although patrons generally round their fare up to the nearest euro. Generally, **bargaining** is expected for street wares and at other informal venues, but when in doubt, wait and watch to avoid offending merchants. Bargaining for cheaper *domatia* (rooms to let) and at small hotels, as well as for unmetered taxi rides is also common. For more info on money in Europe, see p. 16.

Greece has a 19% **value added tax (VAT)**, a sales tax applied to goods and services sold in mainland Greece and 13% VAT on the Aegean islands. Both are included in the listed price. The prices given in *Let's Go* include VAT. The prices given in *Let's Go* include VAT. In the airport upon exiting the EU, non-EU citizens can claim a refund on the tax paid for goods purchased at participating stores. In order to qualify for a refund in a store, you must spend at least €120; make sure to ask for a refund form when you pay. For more info on qualifying for a VAT refund, see p. 18.

# KEEPING IN TOUCH

| **PHONE CODES** | **Country code: 30. International dialing prefix:** 00. For more info on how to place international calls, see **Inside Back Cover.** |
|---|---|

**EMAIL AND THE INTERNET.** The availability of the Internet in Greece is rapidly expanding. In all big cities, most small cities and large towns, and on most islands, you'll be able to find Internet cafes. Expect to pay €2-6 per hr.

**TELEPHONE.** Whenever possible use a calling card for international phone calls, as long-distance rates for national phone services are often very high. Pay phones in Greece use prepaid phone cards, sold at *peripteros* (streetside kiosks) and OTE offices. Mobile phones are an increasingly popular, economical option. Major mobile carriers include **Q-Telecom, Telestet,** and **Vodaphone.** Direct-dial access numbers for calling out of Greece include: **AT&T Direct** (☎ 00 800 1311); **British Telecom** (☎ 00 800 4411); **Canada Direct** (☎ 00 800 1611); **Sprint** (☎ 00 800 1411); **NTL** (☎ 00 800 4422); **Telstra Australia** (☎ 00 800 6111). For more info on calling home from Europe, see p. 26.

**MAIL. Airmail** is the best way to send mail home from Greece. To send a letter (up to 20g) anywhere from Greece costs €0.65. To receive mail in Greece, have it delivered **Poste Restante.** Mail will go to the main post office unless you specify a subsidiary by street address. Address mail to be held as follows: First name LAST NAME, Town Post Office, Island, Greece, Postal Code, POSTE RESTANTE. Bring a passport to pick up your mail; there may be a small fee.

# ACCOMMODATIONS AND CAMPING

| GREECE | ❶ | ❷ | ❸ | ❹ | ❺ |
|---|---|---|---|---|---|
| **ACCOMMODATIONS** | under €17 | €17-27 | €28-37 | €38-70 | over €70 |

Local tourist offices usually maintain lists of inexpensive accommodations. A bed in a **hostel** averages €15-30. Those not endorsed by HI are in most cases still safe and reputable. In many areas, **domatia** are a good option; you may be approached by locals offering cheap lodging as you enter town, a practice that is common but illegal. It's usually a better bet to go to an official tourist office. Prices vary; expect to pay €15-35 for a single and €25-45 for a double depending on the city. Always see the room and negotiate with *domatia* owners before settling on a price; never pay more than you would for a hotel room. If in doubt, ask the tourist police; they may set you up with a room and conduct the negotiations themselves. **Hotel** prices are regulated, but proprietors may push you to take the most expensive room. Budget hotels start at €20 for singles and €30 for doubles. Check your bill carefully, and threaten to contact the tourist police if you think you are being cheated. Greece has plenty of official **campgrounds,** which cost €2-3 per tent plus €4-8 per person. Camping on public beaches—sometimes illegal—is common in summer but may not be the safest option.

## FOOD AND DRINK

| GREECE | ❶ | ❷ | ❸ | ❹ | ❺ |
|--------|-----|-----|-----|-----|-----|
| FOOD | under €5 | €5-9 | €10-15 | €16-25 | over €25 |

Penny-pinching carnivores will thank Zeus for lamb, chicken, or pork **souvlaki,** stuffed into a pita to make **gyros** (YEE-ros). Vegetarians can also find cheap eateries; options include **horiatiki** (Greek salad), savory pastries like **tiropita** (cheese pie) and **spanakopita** (spinach and feta pie). Frothy iced coffee milkshakes take the edge off the summer heat. **Ouzo** (a powerful licorice-flavored spirit) is served with **mezedes** (snacks of octopus, cheese, and sausage). Breakfast, served only in the early morning, is generally very simple: a piece of toast with **marmelada** or a pastry. Lunch, a hearty and leisurely meal, can begin as early as noon but is more likely eaten sometime between 2 and 5pm. Dinner is a drawn-out, relaxed affair served late. Greek restaurants are known as **tavernas** or **estiatorios;** a grill is a **psistaria.**

## BEYOND TOURISM

Doing more than just sightseeing on a trip to Greece is as easy (and as challenging) as offering some of one's own time. Though considered wealthy by international standards, Greece has an abundance of aid organizations to combat the nation's very real problems. From preserving storied remnants of the past to ensuring the survival of wildlife species in the future, plenty of opportunities exist to give back. For more info on opportunities across Europe, see **Beyond Tourism,** p. 54.

**American School of Classical Studies at Athens (ASCSA),** 54 Souidias St., GR-106 76 Athens (☎21072 36 313; www.ascsa.edu.gr). Provides study abroad opportunities in Greece for students interested in archaeology and the classics. US$2950-17,000 including tuition, room, and partial board.

**Anglo-Hellenic Teacher Recruitment,** 45 Kyprou St., 20100 Corinth (☎27410 53 511; www.anglo-hellenic.com). Provides TEFL training, employment, and support for English teachers in Greece.

**Archelon Sea Turtle Protection Society,** Solomou 57, Athens 10432 (☎/fax 21052 31 342; www.archelon.gr). Non-profit group devoted to studying and protecting sea turtles on the beaches of Zakynthos, Crete, and the Peloponnese. Opportunities for seasonal field work and year-round work at the rehabilitation center. €100 participation fee.

**Conservation Volunteers Greece,** Veranzerou 15, 10677 Athens (☎21038 25 506; www.cvgpeep.gr; phones answered M-F 9am-2pm). Offers 2- to 3-week summer programs in environmental and cultural conservation, as well as courses in leadership and First Aid. Participants must be over 18, under 30 and speak English. €120 participation fee.

**Seaturtle Rescue Center,** on the Third Marina, Glyfada (☎21089 82 600). Volunteer at Athens's only turtle hospital. Open daily 5-8pm. No participation fee.

# ATHENS Αθήνα ☎210

An illustrious past invigorates modern Athens. The ghosts of antiquity peer down from its hilltops, instilling citizens and visitors with a sense of the city's historic

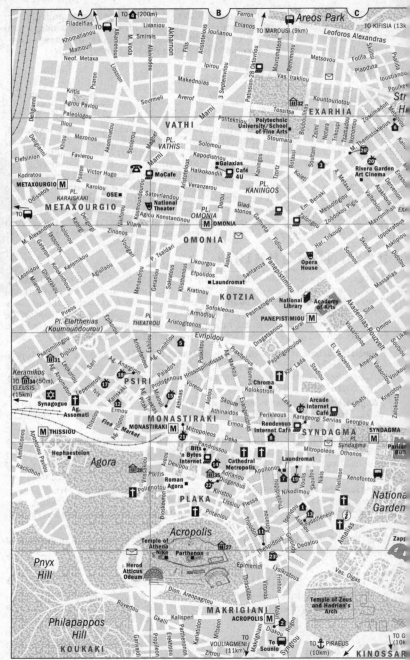

# thens

| ACCOMMODATIONS | | |
|---|---|---|
| opolis House, | 1 | C5 |
| ens Backpackers, | 2 | B6 |
| Exarcheion, | 3 | C2 |
| stel Aphrodite (HI), | 4 | A1 |
| el Cecil, | 5 | B4 |
| el Dryades, | 6 | C2 |
| el Kimon, | 7 | B5 |
| el Metropolis, | 8 | B4 |
| el Orion, | 9 | C2 |
| gration Athens | | |
| outh Hostel, | 10 | F6 |
| a Inn, | 11 | B5 |
| edra Hotel, | 12 | A4 |
| dent and | | |
| raveller's Inn, | 13 | C5 |

| FOOD | | |
|---|---|---|
| Attalos Restaurant, | 14 | B5 |
| Bean, | 15 | B4 |
| Chroma, | 16 | C4 |
| Gelatomania, | 17 | A4 |
| Mandras, | 18 | A4 |
| Noodle Bar, | 19 | C5 |
| O Barba Giannis, | 20 | C2 |
| Savvas, | 21 | B4 |
| Taverna Platanos, | 22 | B5 |

| NIGHTLIFE | | |
|---|---|---|
| Bretto's, | 23 | B6 |
| Flower, | 24 | F2 |
| The Daily, | 25 | E3 |
| Wunderbar, | 26 | C2 |

| MUSEUMS | | |
|---|---|---|
| Acropolis Museum, | 27 | B5 |
| Agora Museum, | 28 | A5 |
| Byzantine & | | |
| Christian Museum, | 29 | D4 |
| Goulandris Museum, | 30 | D4 |
| Benaki Museum of | | |
| Islamic Art, | 31 | A4 |
| National Archaeolgical | | |
| Museum, | 32 | C1 |
| National Gallery, | 33 | E4 |
| Oberlaender Museum, | 34 | A4 |
| Popular Musical | | |
| Instruments Museum, | 35 | B5 |

GREECE

importance. Its fiercely patriotic residents—6 million to be exact, half of Greece's population—pushed their capital into the 21st century with massive clean-up and building projects before the 2004 Olympic Games. Creative international menus, hipster bars, and large warehouse performance spaces crowd among Byzantine churches, traditional *tavernas*, and toppled columns.

## ▐ TRANSPORTATION

**Flights: Eleftherios Venizelou (ATH;** ☎353 0000; www.aia.gr). Greece's international airport operates as 1 massive yet navigable terminal. Arrivals are on the ground floor, departures on the 2nd. The **Suburban Rail** services the airport from the city center in 30min. 4 bus lines run to Athens, Piraeus, and Rafina. Budget airlines **SkyEurope** (www.skyeurope.com) and **Wizz Air** (www.wizzair.com) fly to Athens.

**Trains: Hellenic Railways (OSE),** Sina 6 (☎21036 24 402; www.ose.gr). **Larisis Train Station** (☎529 8837) serves northern Greece. Ticket office open daily 5am-midnight. Trolley #1 from El. Venizelou in Pl. Syndagma (5 per hr., €0.50) or the Metro to Sepolia. Trains go to **Thessaloniki** (7hr., 5 per day, €14; express 5½hr., 6 per day, €28).

**Buses: Terminal A,** Kifissou 100 (☎512 4910). Take blue bus #051 from the corner of Zinonos and Menandrou near Pl. Omonia (4 per hr., €0.50). Buses to: **Corfu** (10hr., 4 per day, €30); **Corinth** (1½hr., 2 per hr., €7); **Patras** (3hr., 2 per hr., €16; express 2½hr., 20 per day); **Thessaloniki** (6hr., 11 per day, €32). **Terminal B,** Liossion 260 (☎831 7153). Take blue bus #024 from Amalias, outside the National Gardens (45min., 3 per hr., €0.50). Buses to **Delphi** (3hr., 6 per day, €13).

**Ferries:** Most leave from the Piraeus port. Ferry schedule changes daily; check ahead at the tourist office, in the *Athens News,* or over the phone (☎14 40). Ferries sail directly to all major Greek islands except for the Sporades and Ionians. To Crete: **Hania** (11hr., €22); **Iraklion** (11hr., €24); **Rethymno** (11hr., €24). Others to: **Ios** (7½hr., €22); **Kos** (13½hr., €36); **Lesvos** (12hr., €26); **Milos** (7hr., €20); **Mykonos** (6hr., €20); **Naxos** (6hr., €24); **Paros** (5hr., €24); **Patmos** (8hr., €30); **Rhodes** (14hr., €43); **Samos** (10hr., €27); **Santorini** (9hr., €28). International ferries head to **Turkey** (€30).

**Public Transportation:** Yellow KTEL **buses** travel all around Attica from orange bus stops around the city. Other buses around Athens and its suburbs are blue and designated by 3-digit numbers. Electrical antennae distinguish **trolleys** from buses. Buy bus and trolley tickets at any street kiosk. Hold on to your ticket or face a €18-30 fine. A standard bus/trolley ticket costs €0.50. The modern Athens **metro** consists of 3 lines running 5am-midnight. The green **M1** line runs from northern Kifisia to Piraeus, the red **M2** from Ag. Antonios to Ag. Dimitrios, the blue **M3** from Doukissis Plakentias to Monastiraki in central Athens. Buy tickets (€0.70) in any station.

**Taxis:** Companies include **Ikaros** (☎51 52 800); **Ermis** (☎41 15 200); **Kosmos** (☎1300). Base fare €0.85; €0.30 per km, midnight-5am €0.53 per km. €3 surcharge from airport, €0.80 surcharge for trips from bus and railway terminals, plus €0.30 for each piece of luggage over 10kg. Call for pickup (€1.50-2.50 extra).

**Car Rental:** Agencies on **Syngrou.** €35-50 for car with 100km mileage (includes tax and insurance); €200-350 per week. Prices higher in summer. Up to 50% student discount.

## ▐ ▐ ORIENTATION AND PRACTICAL INFORMATION

Most travelers hang around the **Acropolis** and **Agoras,** while guide-bearing foreigners pack central **Plaka.** Marked by the square and flea market, **Monastiraki** (Little Monastery) is a hectic, exciting neighborhood where packed *tavernas* and Psiri's trendy bars keep pedestrian traffic flowing late into the night. In the heart of Athens, **Syndagma** square is the center of transportation. On the opposite side of Stadiou, **Omonia** square bursts with ethnic and ideological diversity. A short walk north on **Emmanuil Benaki** leads to the student-filled neighborhood of **Exarhia,** packed with thrift shops and record stores. The **Larissa** train station is to the northwest of town, while most museums are on **Vas Sofias** to the east. The neighborhood of **Kolonaki** is under Lycavittos Hill. Take the M1 (green) south to its end or bus #040 from Filellinon and Mitropoleos, in Syndagma (4 per hr.) to reach Athens's port city, **Piraeus.** The metro also travels east to several beaches. If you get lost, just look for Syndagma or the Acropolis, Athens's clearest reference points.

**Tourist Office: Information Office,** Amalias 26 (☎331 0392; www.gnto.gr). Open M-F 10am-6pm, Sa-Su 10am-3pm.

**Budget Travel: STA Travel,** Voulis 43 (☎21032 11 188). Open M-F 9am-5pm, Sa 10am-2pm. **Consolas Travel,** Aiolou 100 (☎21032 19 228), on the 9th fl. above the post office. Open M and Sa 9am-2pm, Tu-F 9am-5pm.

**Bank: National Bank,** Karageorgi Servias 2 (☎21033 40 500), in Pl. Syndagma. Open M-Th 8am-2:30pm, F 8am-2pm; open for **currency exchange** M-F 3:30-5pm, Sa 9am-2pm, Su 9am-1pm. Commission about 5%. 24hr. currency exchange at the airport, but commissions there are usually exorbitant.

**Laundromat:** Most *plintirias* (laundromats) have English signs. **National,** Apollonos 17, Syndagma (☎323 2226). Laundry €5 per kg. Open M, W 8am-4pm, Tu and Th-F 8am-8pm.

**Emergencies: Poison control** ☎779 3777. **AIDS Help Line** ☎722 2222.

**Tourist Police:** Dimitrakopoulou 77 (☎171). English spoken. Open 24hr.

**Pharmacies:** Check *Athens News* for a current list of 24hr. pharmacies.

**Hospitals:** *Athens News* lists emergency hospitals. Free emergency health care for tourists. **Geniko Kratiko Nosokomio (Y. Gennimatas; Public State Hospital),** Mesogion 154 (☎777 8901). **Aeginitio,** Vas. Sofias 72 (☎722 0811) and Vas. Sofias 80 (☎777 0501), are closer to Athens's center. Near Kolonaki is the public hospital **Evangelismos,** Ypsilantou 45-47 (☎720 1000).

**Internet Access:** Athens has numerous Internet cafes. Expect to pay around €3 per hr. **Bits'n Bytes Internet,** Kapnikareas 19 (☎382 2545; www.bnb.gr), in Plaka. 9am-midnight €5 per hr., midnight-9am €3 per hr. Open 24hr. 2nd location in Exarhia, Akadamias 78 (☎522 7717). **Rendez-Vous Cafe,** Voulis 18 (☎322 3158), in Syndagma. €3 per hr.; min. €1. Open M-F 7:30am-9pm, Sa 7:30am-6pm.

**Post Offices:** For customer service call the **Greek National Post Office (ELTA;** ΕΛΤΑ) at ☎80011 82 000. **Syndagma** branch (☎622 6253), on the corner of Mitropoleos. **Omonia** branch, Aiolou 100 (☎325 3586). Open M-F 7:30am-8pm, Sa 7:30am-2pm. **Exarhia** branch, at the corner of Zaimi and K. Deligiani. Open M-F 7:30am-2pm. **Postal Codes:** 10300 (Syndagma); 10200 (Omonia); 10022 (Exarhia); 11702 (Plaka).

# ACCOMMODATIONS

Many budget accommodations exist in Athens, but prices generally increase toward the city center at Syndagma Square. The **Greek Youth Hostel Association,** Damareos 75, in Pangrati, lists cheap hostels throughout Greece (☎751 9530; www.grhotels.com). The **Hellenic Chamber of Hotels,** Stadiou 24, in Syndagma, lists all hotels in Greece, but does not make reservations. Call for info in several languages. The office is on the 7th fl. to the left. (☎323 7193. Open M-F 8am-2pm.)

**Athens Backpackers,** Makri 12 (☎922 4044; www.backpackers.gr), in Plaka. Near the metro and most Athenian sights, this popular place provides cold beer (€2) and a nightly terrace party in summer atop their rooftop bar under the Acropolis. Free luggage storage and Wi-Fi. Laundry €5. 6- or 8-bed dorms €18-25. AmEx/MC/V. ❷

■ **Pagration Athens Youth Hostel,** Damareos 75 (☎751 9530; www.athens-yhostel.com), in Pangrati. From Omonia or Pl. Syndagma, take trolley #2 or 11 to Filolaou. Only the number 75 and a green door—no sign—mark this cheery, family-owned hostel. Large common spaces make up for the 20-25min. walk to the city center. TV lounge and full kitchen. Bring a sleeping bag to stay on the roof (€10). Hot showers €0.50. Linens included. Laundry €7. Quiet hours 2:30-5pm and 11:30pm-7am. Dorms €10-12. Low season reduced rates. Cash only. ❶

■ **Hostel Aphrodite (HI),** Einardou 12 (☎881 0589; www.hostelaphrodite.com), in Omonia. Welcoming place with clean, basic rooms and basement bar. Breakfast €4-5. Safe deposit box available. Free luggage storage. Laundry €8. Free Internet. 8-bed dorms €15; doubles €44; triples €57; quads €68. Low season reduced rates. Cash only. ❶

**Phaedra Hotel,** Kodrou 3 (☎324 9737), in Plaka. The amiable family owners keep their 21 plain rooms spic and span. Bonus: the enormous rooftop garden offers a side view of the nearby Acropolis. Singles €50-60; doubles €60-70; triples €75-85. ❹

**Hotel Cecil,** Athinas 39 (☎321 7079), on the border of Psiri, 4 blocks from the Monastiraki metro. Wood-floored, high-ceilinged rooms with A/C, spotless, private baths, and TV. Roof bar with Acropolis view. Breakfast included. Free luggage storage. Singles €50-70; doubles €79-99; triples €120-140; quads €145. AmEx/MC/V. ❹

**The Exarcheion,** Themistokleous 55 (☎380 0731), in Exarhia, near a string of *tavernas* and a 5min. walk from the Omonia metro. Its rooms, though sparse and unadorned, retain a retro, 70s appeal. Breakfast €5. Internet €3 per hr. Reserve ahead. Singles €35-40; doubles €45-50; triples €60-70; apartments €80. 10% *Let's Go* discount. ❸

**Pella Inn,** Karaiskaki 1 (☎325 0598; www.pellainn.gr), 2 blocks west of the Monastiraki metro. Despite its less-than-friendly staff, Pella offers a rooftop terrace, amazing views of the Acropolis, and old rooms with clean, shared baths. Breakfast included with private rooms, €3 with dorms. Free luggage storage. Laundry €6. Dorms €15; doubles €40-50; triples €60; quads €80. Low season prices negotiable. Cash only. ❶

**Hotel Orion,** Em. Benaki 105 (☎330 2387; www.orion-dryades.com), in Exarhia. A 10min. walk up the hill on Em. Benaki. University students intent on experiencing Athens away from the tourist machine fill Orion. Offers fully furnished rooftop lounge, complete with kitchen, TV, and a clear view of the Acropolis. Breakfast €6. Laundry €3. Internet €2 per hr. Singles €25-30; doubles €45-55; triples €60-65. MC/V. ❷

**Hotel Metropolis,** Mitropoleos 46 (☎321 7469; www.hotelmetropolis.gr), in Syndagma. Balconies with excellent views of the square or the Acropolis make this otherwise simple hotel distinct. Elevator and A/C. Free luggage storage. Laundry €10. Free Wi-Fi. Singles €55-70; doubles €60-80; triples €75-90. AmEx/MC/V. ❹

**Student and Traveller's Inn,** Kydatheneon 16 (☎324 4808; www.studenttravellersinn.com), in central Plaka. Clean hostel with 24hr. cyber cafe and garden bar (open daily until midnight). Breakfast €4-5.50. Free Wi-Fi. Reception 24hr. The "dungeon" (windowless, downstairs co-ed dorm) €12; co-ed dorms €25-27; doubles €55-65, with bath €60-70; triples €75-85; quads €88-100. V. ❷

**Hotel Kimon,** Apollonos 27 (☎331 4658), in Syndagma. This 17-room hideaway boasts an Acropolis view from its rooftop garden and sizable rooms, some with balconies and all with A/C, TV, and private bath. A marble staircase, iron bedsteads, and colorful walls add verve to insipid decor. Doubles €55-80; triples €80-100. Cash only. ❹

**Hotel Dryades,** Dryadon 4 (☎382 7116). Next to Hotel Orion. Orion's sister is one of Athens's nicest mid-level accommodations, with large rooms and baths. Full kitchen and TV lounge. Breakfast €5. Internet €2 per hr. Singles €40-45; doubles €50-60. ❹

**Acropolis House,** 6-8 Koudro (☎322 2344), across from Adonis Hotel, in Plaka. The same family has run this 19th-century mansion-turned-guesthouse since 1965. While some rooms are small or could use slight refurbishing, high ceilings and Neoclassical architecture add charm. A/C. Breakfast included. Doubles €67-87. ❹

# FOOD

Athens offers a mix of fast-food stands, open-air cafes, side-street *tavernas*, and intriguing restaurants. On the streets, vendors sell dried fruits and nuts or fresh coconut (€1-2), and you can find *spanakopita* (spinach and cheese pies) at any local bakery (€1.50-2). The area around **Syndagma** serves cheap food. Places in **Plaka** tend to advertise "authentic Greek for tourists." If you really want to eat like a local, head to the simple *tavernas* uphill on **Emmanuil Benaki** in Exarhia.

☒ **O Barba Giannis,** Em. Benaki 94 (☎382 4138), in Exarhia. With tall green doors, "Uncle John's" is informal—just how the Athenian students, CEOs, and artists who consider themselves regulars like it. Entrees €5-10. Open M-Sa noon-1:30am. Cash only. ❸

☒ **Chroma,** Lekka 8 (☎331 7793), in Syndagma. Dine on fancy leather couches while listening to lounge music in this modern cafe, which morphs into a bar at night. Entrees €6-14. Open Su-F 8am-2am, Sa 8am-10pm. Kitchen open Su-F 1pm-midnight, Sa 1pm-10pm. MC/V. ❸

**Noodle Bar,** Apollonos 11 (☎318 585), in Syndagma. Greek salads please even the feta-phobic. Lighter fare includes mango salad (€5) and Thai chicken coconut soup (€4.10). Open M-Sa 11am-midnight, Su 5:30pm-midnight. ❷

**Mandras,** Ag. Anargiron 8 (☎321 3765), at Taki. Live, modern Greek music plays for a young, buzzing crowd of locals in this attractive brick building in the heart of Psiri. *Pleurotous* (mushrooms grilled with oil and vinegar; €6.20) makes a great light meal. Spicy grilled chicken €9.20. Open daily 8am-4am. Music 2pm-4am. ❸

**Savvas,** Mitropoleos 86 (☎324 5048), right off of Pl. Monastiraki, across from the flea market. Cab drivers and kiosk vendors recommend this famous *souvlaki* joint as the best in town. Save money by eating on the fly; restaurant prices for gyros (€6-9) shrink to €1.50-1.80 for take-out orders. Open daily 10am-3am. Cash only. ❶

**Taverna Platanos,** Diogenous 4 (☎322 0666), in Plaka. Just meters from the hustle of Adrianou and Kydatheon, Platanos offers authentic, traditional fare in a plant-draped patio or cozy taverna. Tomato salad €3. Lamb with string beans €7. Vegetarian options. Open M-Sa noon-4:30pm and 7:30pm-midnight, Su noon-4:30pm. Cash only. ❷

**Gelatomania,** Taki 21 (☎323 001), on the corner of Aisopou, in Monastiraki. Heaping displays of homemade ice cream tempt patrons with flavors like rum raisin and honeyed cherry peach. Stick with 1 scoop to go (€1.50). Prices rise dramatically when you sit down. Open daily 10am-2am, later on F and Sa. ❶

**Bean,** Em. Benaki 45 (☎330 0010), in Exarhia. Modern decor belies the menu's *taverna* flavor. Hanging lamps and small white lights illuminate this simple venue. Daily specials. Pastas €5-6. Italian salads €4-5.50. Open M-Sa 1pm-midnight. ❷

**Attalos Restaurant,** Adrianou 9 (☎321 9520), in Monastiraki. On the edge of the Agora and the Temple of Hephaestus. Outdoor tables have excellent views. Large white umbrellas and yellow tablecloths make the restaurant bright and inviting. The menu ranges from mussels *saganaki* (€6.20) to a vegetarian's dream plate of zucchini, eggplant, and tomato croquettes (serves 2-4; €8). Open daily 10am-1am. ❷

**Pak Indian Restaurant,** Menandrou 13 (☎321 9412), in Omonia. Indian lanterns and pungent scents may make you wonder if you've stepped into a land where *souvlaki* joints are just an idle dream. Veggie samosa €1.50. Lamb *rogan josh* (with ginger, onions, tomato, and spices) €10. Open daily 2pm-midnight. MC/V. ❸

GREECE

**Healthy Food Vegetarian Restaurant and Grocery Store,** Panepistimiou 57-58 (☎381 8021), in Omonia. This meatless kitchen makes different daily specials (€5-7), including tofu *souvlaki,* soy *pastitsio,* and freshly squeezed fruit juices. Its adjacent sister store sells produce. Open M-F 8am-9:30pm, Sa 8am-8pm, Su 8am-4pm. ❷

## 🔎 SIGHTS

### ACROPOLIS

The Acropolis has loomed over the heart of Athens since the 5th century BC. Although each Greek *polis* had an *acropolis* (high point), the buildings atop Athens's peak outshone their imitators and continue to awe visitors. Visit as early in the day as possible to avoid crowds and the broiling midday sun. *(Enter on Dionissiou Areopagitou or Theorias. ☎321 0219. Open daily in summer 8am-7:30pm; in winter 8am-2:30pm. Admission includes access to the Acropolis, the Agora, the Roman Agora, the Olympian Temple of Zeus, and the Theater of Dionysos, within a 48hr. period; purchase tickets at any of the sights. €12, students and EU seniors over 65 €6, under 19 free. Cash only.)*

▨ **PARTHENON.** The **Temple of Athena Parthenos** (Athena the Virgin), commonly known as the Parthenon, watches over Athens. Ancient Athenians saw their city as the capital of civilization; the **metopes** (scenes in the spaces above the columns) on the sides of the temple celebrate Athens's rise. The architect Iktinos integrated the Golden Mean, about a four-to-nine ratio, in every aspect of the temple.

▨ **ACROPOLIS MUSEUM.** Currently under extensive renovations that were supposed to have finished before the 2004 Olympic games, the museum houses a superb collection of statues, including five of the original **Caryatids** that supported the southern side of the Erechtheion. The carvings of a lion devouring a bull and of a wrestling match between Herakles and a sea monster display the Ancient mastery of anatomical and emotional detail. Notice the empty space where room has been left for the British to return the missing Elgin marbles. *(Open during renovations daily 8am-7:30pm; low season reduced hours. No flash photography. Avoid going 10am-1pm.)*

**TEMPLE OF ATHENA NIKE.** Currently undergoing renovation, this tiny temple was first raised during the Peace of Nikias (421-415 BC), a respite from the Peloponnesian War. Ringed by eight miniature Ionic columns, it housed a winged statue of Nike, the goddess of victory. Athenians, afraid Nike might abandon them, clipped the statue's wings. The remains of the 5m thick **Cyclopean wall** that once circled the Acropolis now lie below the temple.

**ERECHTHEION.** Completed in 406 BC, just before Sparta defeated Athens in the Peloponnesian War, the Erechtheion lies to the left of the Parthenon, supported by copies of the famous Caryatids in the museum. The building is named after a snake-bodied hero, whom Poseidon speared during in a dispute over the city's patronage. When Poseidon struck a truce with Athena, he was allowed to share her temple—the eastern half is devoted to the goddess of wisdom and the western part to the god of the sea. The eastern porch contained an olive-wood statue of Athena meant to contrast with the Parthenon's dignified Doric columns.

### OTHER SIGHTS

**AGORA.** The Agora served as Athens's marketplace, administrative center, and focus of daily life from the 6th century BC to the AD 6th century. Many of Athenian democracy's great debates were held here; Socrates, Aristotle, Demosthenes, Xenophon, and St. Paul all lectured in the Agora. The 415 BC ▨**Hephaesteion,** on a hill in the Agora's northwest corner, is Greece's best-preserved Classical temple, boasting friezes depicting Theseus's adventures. Built for Roman Emperor Agustus's son-in-law, the **Odeon of Agrippa** concert hall now stands in ruins on the left of the Agora. When the roof collapsed in AD 150, the Odeon was rebuilt to half its former size and served as a lecture hall. The **Stoa of Attalos,** an ancient shopping mall, was home to informal philosophers' gatherings. Reconstructed in the 1950s, it now houses the **Agora Museum.** *(Enter the Agora off Pl. Thission, from Adrianou, or as you descend from the Acropolis. ☎321 0185. Agora open daily 8am-7:30pm. Museum open Tu-Su 8am-7:20pm. €4, students and EU seniors €2, under 19 and with Acropolis ticket free.)*

**ROMAN AGORA.** Built between 19 and 11 BC with donations from Julius and Octavian Caesar, the Roman Agora was once a lively meeting place. The ruined columns of the two surviving *prophylae* (halls), a nearly intact entrance gate, and the **gate of Athena Archgetis** stand as testaments to what was once a lively meeting place. Also nearby are the *vespasianae* (public toilets), constructed in the AD first century, as well as a 1456 mosque. By far the most intriguing structure in the site is the well-preserved (and restored) **Tower of the Winds,** with reliefs of the eight winds on each side of the octagonal clock tower. A weathervane crowned the original stone structure, built in the first century BC by the astronomer Andronikos. Etched onto the walls are markings that allowed it to be used as a sundial from the outside and a water-clock from the inside. *(☎324 5220. Open daily 8am-7pm. €2; students €1; under 19, EU students, and with Acropolis ticket free.)*

**TEMPLE OF ZEUS AND HADRIAN'S ARCH.** On the edge of the National Gardens in Plaka, you can spot traces of the Temple of Zeus, the largest temple ever built in Greece. Shifts in power delayed the temple's complete until AD 131 under Roman emperor Hadrian, who added an arch to mark the boundary between the ancient city of Theseus and his new city. *(Vas. Olgas at Amalias. ☎922 6330. Open daily 8am-7pm. Temple €2, students €1, under 19 free. Arch free.)*

**PHILOPAPPOS HILL.** Southwest of the Acropolis, Philopappos Hill is a lush respite from park-deprived Athens. Abundant trails, sheltered picnic areas, and a postcard-perfect view of the Parthenon make this a great place for afternoon exploration. A marble road weaves past **Agios Dimitrious,** where you're likely to stumble upon a church service in progress. According to legend, Dimitrious persuaded God to smite 17th-century Turkish invaders with lightning before they could harm the worshippers in this small, icon-filled church. Just before Ag. Dimitrious, a narrow path veers off to the left, toward a stone cave with iron bars. This nondescript opening was once, as a sign indicates, **Socrates's Prison;** a series of rooms was carved into the cliff face and later used to house treasures from the Acropolis during World War II. Atop its peak, the marble **Monument of Philopappos,** erected between AD 114-116, has Athens's best view of the Acropolis. The angles and distance that render the view so beautiful also made the Acropolis an easy target for the Venetians in 1687; it was from this peak that they shot the disastrous volley, accidentally detonating the Parthenon's gunpowder stores.

**KERAMIKOS.** A large cemetery built around the **Sacred Way**—the road to Eleusis—is Keramikos's primary attraction. A wide boulevard ran from there to the sanctuary of **Akademes,** home of Plato's school. The **Oberlaender Museum** displays funerary stones, pottery, and sculptures. *(Northwest of the Agora. From Syndagma, walk 1km toward Monastiraki on Ermou. ☎346 3552. Open M 11am-7:30pm, Tu-Su 8am-7:30pm. €2; students and EU seniors €1; under 19, EU students, and with Acropolis ticket free.)*

**PANATHENAIC STADIUM.** Also known as *Kallimarmaro* ("Pretty Marble"), the horseshoe-shaped Panathenaic Stadium is wedged between the National Gardens and Pangrati. The site of the first modern Olympic Games in 1896, the

GREECE

## BELOVED BACKGAMMON

Walk down a Greek side street or past a cafe, and chances are you'll see people playing backgammon. Among the younger generation, it's usually a solitary activity, but with elderly men the game invokes good-natured ribbing and tense competition.

Although quite similar to its American cousin, Greece's unofficial national board game has a few differences. The patterned board is called the *tavli* and three variations of the game are played, often in succession: *portes*, *plakoto*, and *fevga*. Many Greeks learn all three games as children. Most like western backgammon, *portes* means "door" in Greek and represents a slight variation from American rules. Two checkers placed side-by-side form a "door" or wall that stops opposing markers from being played there. *Plakoto*—perhaps the original Greek variation—derives from the verb *plakono* (to stack). In this version, opponents can place checkers on top of other markers. Finally, in *fevga* (to run), players race to their home quarters.

One of the reasons for the game's popularity is that it has been played in Greece for thousands of years. Archaeological evidence of old *tavli* suggests ancient Greeks played backgammon, potentially learning it from Mesopotamian Persians. It is no wonder, then, that the game is a beloved pastime.

stadium seats over 60,000 and served as the finish line of the marathon and the venue for archery during the 2004 Summer Olympic Games. Be warned that visitors are no longer permitted to walk past the fence running along its open end. *(On Vas. Konstantinou. From Syndagma, walk down Amalias 10min. to Vas. Olgas, then follow it left. Or take trolley #2, 4, or 11 from Syndagma. Free.)*

**AROUND SYNDAGMA.** Be sure to catch the changing of the guard in front of the **Parliament** building. On the hour, the two Greek *evzones* (guardsmen) on duty synchronize a series of jerky marionette moves that lead them away from their posts. Athens's endangered species—greenery and shade—are preserved in the **National Gardens,** the closest to a wild forest that you can get in the metropolis, and a cool alternative to the beach for sunbathing.

**MOUNT LYCAVITTOS.** From the peak of Mt. Lycavittos, the tallest of Athens's seven hills, visitors can see the whole city. A **funicular** (2min., 2-6 per hr., round-trip €6) travels to the top. The **Chapel of Saint George,** with intricate religious murals adorning its wall, crowns the hill. *(A trail from the end of Loukianou in Kolonaki takes 15-20min. Travelers should not climb alone, especially at night.)*

## 🏛 MUSEUMS

**■ NATIONAL ARCHAEOLOGICAL MUSEUM.** Almost every artifact in this collection is a masterpiece. The museum's highlights include the so-called **Mask of Agamemnon,** excavated from the tomb of a king who lived at least three centuries before Agamemnon, as well as a female **Cycladic statue,** the largest, most intact such sculpture to have survived, topping 1.5m. *(Patission 44. Take trolley #2, 4, 5, 9, 11, 15, or 18 from the uphill side of Syndagma, or trolley #3 or 13 from the north side of Vas. Sofias. ☎821 7717. Open Apr.-Oct. Tu-Su 8:30am-3pm; Nov.-Mar. M 10:30am-5pm, Tu-Su 8:30am-3pm. €7, students and EU seniors €3, EU students and under 19 free. No flash photography.)*

**■ BENAKI MUSEUM AND BENAKI MUSEUM OF ISLAMIC ART.** Over the course of his travels, philanthropist Antoine Benaki assembled a formidable collection of artwork and artifacts now displayed in his former home. Its exhibits include Classical, Neolithic, and Roman sculptures, traditional Greek costumes, and re-created Byzantine rooms. *(Vas. Sofias and Koumbari 1 in Kolonaki. ☎367 1000. Open M, W, and F-Sa 9am-5pm, Th 9am-midnight, Su 9am-3pm. €6; seniors and adults with children €3; students, teachers, and journalists free.)* Built on ancient Athenian ruins, the **Benaki Museum of Islamic Art's** large glass windows, spotless marble staircases, and sparkling white walls showcase metalwork, tapestries, and tiles documenting the history of the Islamic world from the 12th to 18th centuries. The 17th-century inlaid-marble reception room transported from Cairo and the Kufic-inscribed pottery are must-sees. (*Ag. Asomaton 22, in Psiri. M: Thissou. ☎ 325 1311; www.benaki.gr. Open Tu and Th-Su 9am-3pm, W 9am-9pm. €5, students and seniors €2.50, W free.*)

**BYZANTINE AND CHRISTIAN MUSEUM.** Within its newly renovated interior, this well-organized museum documents the political, religious, and day-to-day aspects of life during the Byzantine Empire. Its collection of metalware, mosaics, sculpture, and painted icons presents Christianity in its earliest stages. (*Vas. Sofias 22. ☎ 721 1027. Open Tu-Su 8:30am-3pm. €4; students and seniors €2; EU students, under 18, disabled, families with 3 or more children, military, and classicists free.*)

**POPULAR MUSICAL INSTRUMENTS MUSEUM.** Showcasing instruments from the 18th, 19th, and 20th centuries, this interactive museum is no place for silent contemplation. Audio headsets reproduce the music of the *kementzes* (bottle-shaped lyres) and *tsambouras* (goatskin bagpipes) on display. (*Diogenous 1-2, in Plaka. ☎ 325 0198. Open Tu and Th-Su 10am-2pm, W noon-6pm. Free.*)

**GOULANDRIS MUSEUM OF CYCLADIC AND ANCIENT GREEK ART.** This 19-year-old museum houses a comprehensive collection of early Aegean art from 3000 BC to AD 300. The celebrated marble Cycladic figurines, one of them almost life-size, are prized possessions. A glass corridor leads visitors to the extension, a recently renovated Neoclassical house with further info and temporary exhibitions. (*Neophytou Douka 4. ☎ 722 8321. Open M and W-F 10am-4pm, Su 10am-3pm. €5, seniors €2.50, 18-26 €1, archaeologists and archaeology students free with university pass.*)

**NATIONAL GALLERY.** Also known as the "Alexander Soutzos Museum," the Gallery traces Cubism, Impressionism, Orientalism, and Symbolism in Greece from the 18th to the 21st centuries. The ground floor's 19th-century portraits memorialize Greece's War of Independence. The second floor displays contemporary works and temporary exhibits. (*Vas. Konstantinou 50, by the Hilton. ☎ 723 5857. Open M and W-Sa 9am-3pm, Su 10am-2pm. Temporary exhibits open M and W 9am-3pm and 6-9pm, Th-Sa 9am-3pm, Su 10am-2pm. €7, students and seniors €4, under 12 free.*)

## 🎵 🎭 ENTERTAINMENT AND NIGHTLIFE

The weekly *Athens News* (€1) lists cultural events, as well as news and ferry info. Summertime performances are staged in **Lycavittos Theater** as part of the **Athens Festival** (May-Aug.; www.greekfestival.gr). Chic Athenians head to the seaside clubs in **Glyfada**, enjoying the breezy night air. **Psiri** is the bar district, just across the main square in Monastiraki. Get started on **Miaouli,** where young crowds gather after dark. For traditional *ouzeries* and older patrons, head to **Plaka.** It's full of typical Greek places, although actually running into a local is rare. For an alternative to bar hopping, follow the guitar-playing local teens and couples that pack **Pavlou** at night. This serene promenade around the Acropolis is Athens's most romantic spot after sunset.

- 🍽 **Bretto's,** Kydatheneon 41 (☎232 2110), between Farmaki and Afroditis in Plaka. Prepare for a delicious sensuous assault when entering this high-ceilinged, century-old wooden distillery. Glass of wine from €3. Cup of *ouzo* €3. Open daily 10am-3am.

- **The Daily,** Xenokratous 47 (☎722 3430), under a covered trellis at the foot of Mt. Lycavittos. TVs show sports and locals mingle with the staff at this cozy cafe-bar. Outdoor seating in summer. Pints from €4. Mixed drinks €6-10. Open daily 8am-2am.

**Wunderbar,** Themistokleous 80 (☎381 8577), on Pl. Exarhia, plays pop and electronic music to relaxed martini-sippers. Late-night revelers lounge outside under large umbrellas. Beer €5-6. Mixed drinks €8-9. Open M-Th 9am-3am, F-Su 9am-sunrise.

**Flower,** Dorylaou 2, in Pl. Mavili, in Kolonaki. An intimate little dive, Flower offers drinks and snacks in a casual, mellow setting. Additional seating outside in the square. Shots €3. Mixed drinks €5. Open daily 7pm-late.

## ▨ DAYTRIPS FROM ATHENS

▨**CAPE OF SOUNION** Ακρωτήριο Σούνιο. On a windy cliff surrounded by sea, the ▨**Temple of Poseidon,** built in 600 BC, is possibly Attica's most enchanting destination. Despite drawing flocks of visitors, the 16 Doric columns—remnants of the 440 BC Periclean reconstruction—maintain their solitary charm. Hundreds of names are carved into the monumental structure, including Lord Byron's. *(Open daily 9:30am-sunset. Apr.-Oct. €4, students €2, EU students free; Nov.-Mar. free.)* Across the street and 500m below is the ill-preserved **Temple of Athena Sounias,** which is little more than a couple of rocks. *(☎22920 39 363. Closed Easter, May 1, and Dec. 25. Open daily 10am-sunset. €4, students and over 65 €2, EU students, under 18, and Nov.-Mar. Su free.)* KTEL **buses** leave Athens for Sounion from the stop at Mavromateon 14 (2hr., 1 per hr., €5). From Sounion, buses return to Athens (2 per hr., €5.) Athenians spend their free afternoons at **Vouliagmeni,** a crowded beach town on the coastal road to Sounion and about 50min. from Athens. Its warm, crystalline mineral lake is ideal for a relaxing—albeit costly—swim. From the center of town, walk 5min. in the direction of Sounion; the lake is on your left. *(Open daily until 7:30pm. €7.)*

**ELEUSIS.** The site of the enigmatic Eleusinian Mysteries, one of the ancient world's largest and most famous religious rituals, Eleusis was a center of worship from the Mycenaean Period until AD 400. The Mysteries honored the fertility goddess, Demeter. The expansive ruins include two triumphal **arches** and a small but fascinating **museum.** *(Open Tu-Su 8:30am-3pm. €3, students and seniors €2, EU students free.)* Take **bus** A16 or B16 from Pl. Eleftherias in Athens to the modern town of Elefsina (Ελευσίνα; 45-1hr., 3 per hr.), then follow the signs.

**GLYFADA.** Stretching along the sea from Faliro to Sounion, Glyfada has become synonymous with swanky clubs and crowded beaches. Both **tram** (6-7 per hr., €0.60) and **buses** (A2, A3, or B2; 30-40min., €0.90) hug the sea as they head from Vas. Amalias, at the upper right corner of Pl. Syndagma, in Athens to Glyfada, so you can scope out the free beaches, including popular **Batis** and party-crazed **Kalamaki.** Beyond Glyfada toward suburbs **Vouliagmeni** and **Varkiza,** more secluded, cleaner beaches charge entrance fees (€5-10) but provide bungalows and pools for their patrons. At the **Seaturtle Rescue Center,** on the Third Marina (toward the beach from tram stop Paleo Demarhio), visitors can walk around pools containing injured turtles rescued in Greece. Athens's only turtle hospital readily accepts volunteers. *(☎21089 82 600. Open daily 5-8pm. Free.)* Most daytime activity in Glyfada spreads along **Lazaraki** and **Metaxa,** both parallel to the nighttime strip running down the coast. Restaurants line **Konstantinopoleos.** After soaking up some daytime rays, join the heat at any of Glyfada's beachside clubs. Cover is usually €10-15, and clubwear (i.e., no shorts) is expected. Drinks typically range €6-12. A **taxi** (☎21096 05 600) to Glyfada can cost between €8 and €15.

# THE PELOPONNESE Πελοπόννησος

Stretching its fingers into the Mediterranean, the Peloponnese transports its visitors to another time and place. The achievements of ancient civilizations dot the peninsula's landscape, as most of Greece's significant archaeological sites—including Olympia, Mycenae, Messini, Corinth, Mystras, and Epida-vros—rest in this former home of King Pelops. Away from urban transportation hubs, serene villages welcome visitors to traditional Greece.

## NEW CORINTH Κόρινθος       ☎27410

New Corinth (pop. 37,000) is a modern town exploding with automobile and pedestrian traffic, reprising its ancient role as a transportation hub and gateway to the Peleponnese. In ancient times, the port controlled maritime activity on both sides of the nearby isthmus of the same name. Today, numerous shops and restaurants hint at the large crowds passing through town on their way to Athens and destinations all across Southwestern Greece. Those with a day to spare can take a **bus** to **Ancient Corinth,** where prosperous Greek merchants once mingled with *hetairai,* famously clever courtesans in the service of Aphrodite. (☎31 207. Open daily 8am-7:30pm. Site map €2.50. Guidebooks €6. Site and museum €6, students €3, EU students and under 18 free. Free Nov. 1-Mar. 31 Su; last weekends of Apr., May, June, and Sept.; major holidays.) Buses leave from outside the bakery on Koliatsou and Kolokotroni (20min., 2 per hr., 6:10am-9:10pm; return buses leave hourly at half past the hr. €1.20). The remains of the dead Roman city stand with the older Greek ruins at the base of the **Acrocorinth Fortress,** against a scenic mountain and ocean backdrop. Take a taxi there from the village of Ancient Corinth and walk to the top for a spellbinding panorama of Corinthia. Make sure you have the taxi wait for you, however, as no return bus exists (taxi €15 round-trip).

Recently renovated **Hotel Apollon ❹,** Damaskinou 2, located on the corner a block away from the in-town train station, offers small but comfortable rooms with TV and A/C. (☎25 920. Breakfast €7. Internet €1 per hr. Reservations recommended. Singles €35; doubles €45; triples €50. Low season reduced rates.) Cheaper, more basic lodging can also be found at the **Hotel Akti ❷,** Eth. Antistaseos 1, on the marina end of Ent. Antistaseos. (☎23 337. Singles €20; doubles €35. Cash only.) For the best restaurants and nightlife, head to **Kalamia Beach.** To reach Kalamia, walk down Ent. Antistaseos away from the marina until **Notara.** Make a right on Notara and follow it to the end; the beachside establishments will be on your left. Corinth's in-town **train station** (☎22 522) is on Dimokratias, off Damaskinou and services mainly the Peloponese's larger towns. **Trains** go to: Diakopto (1¼hr., 5 per day, €3; express 1hr., 2 per day, €5), Kyparissia (5hr., 1 per day, €7; express 4hr., 2 per day, €8), and Pirgos (4½hr., 1 per day, €5; express: 3½hr., 2 per day, €6). Corinth's in-town station offers connector trains to a second train station, off Argous Ave., about 2km away from town (6 per day, free). From there, trains travel to Athens (1hr., 9 per day, €6) and Athens International Airport (1¼hr., 8 per day, €8). **Buses** leave from three different stations, going to Athens (Station A, 1½hr., every 30min., 5am-9pm, €7) and Loutraki (Station C, 20min., 2 per hr., 5am-10pm, €2). The **tourist office** is at Ermou 51. (☎23 282. Open daily 8am-2pm.) **Postal Code:** 20100.

---

**TIP** **A FERRY HELPFUL HINT.** If the Greeks can't satiate your thirst for classical antiquity, hop on a Patras ferry bound for one of four Italian cities: Ancona (p. 712), Bari, Brindisi, or Venice (p. 669). Several ferries, all with different prices, make the trip, so check with multiple travel offices lining Othonoas Amalias to find the cheapest fares. **Superfast Ferries,** Oth. Amalias 12 (☎622 500; open daily 9am-9pm), accepts Eurail passes. Questions about departures from Patras should be directed to the Port Authority (☎341 002).

---

## PATRAS Πάτρας       ☎2610

Located on the Peloponnese's northwestern tip, Patras (pop. 350,000) operates as the region's fundamental transportation hub. Charter tourism often skips the city, favoring other nearby islands. During ◨**Carnival** (Jan. 17-Feb. 21; ☎222 157; www.carnivalpatras.gr), however, Patras becomes one gigantic dance floor of costumed, inebriated people consumed by pre-Lenten madness. The biggest European festival of its kind revives ancient celebrations in honor of Dionysus—god of debauchery. Follow the waterfront with the town to your left to reach **Agios Andreas**, which is entirely covered in colorful frescoes and Greece's largest Orthodox cathedral. (Dress modestly. Open daily 7am-9pm.) Sweet black grapes are made into Mavrodaphne wine at the ◨**Achaïa Clauss Winery.** Take bus #7 (dir: Seravali, 30min., €1.20) from the intersection of Kanakari and Gerokostopoulou. (☎368 276. Open daily 11am-3pm. English tours every hour. Free.) Built on the ruins of an ancient acropolis and continuously in use from the AD 6th century through WWII, Patras's **fortress** is up the steps from the central Nikolaou. (☎990 691. Open Tu-Su 8:30am-3pm. Free.) Visible from many beaches, the recently completed **Rio-Antirio Bridge** is the world's longest cable-anchored suspension bridge, connecting the Peloponnese region to the mainland. Centrally located ◨**Pension Nicos ❷**, Patreos 3, sparkles with marble and inlaid stone decor while offering affordable, pristine rooms. (☎623 757. Reception 3rd fl. Curfew 4am. Singles €20; doubles €30, with bath €35; triples €40/45. MC/V.) Lounge on the deck of ◨**Rooms to Let Spyros Vazouras ❸**, Tofalou 2, where roof-top ocean views complement brightly tiled rooms. (☎452 152. Singles €30; doubles €40; additional bed €10.) An old villa, **Patras Hostel ❶**, Polytechniou 62, across the street from the sea, has basic, crowded bunk-bed dorms. (☎427 278. Linens €0.50. Reception 24hr. Checkout 10:30am. Dorms €10. Cash only.) For more Patras accommodations and info, browse www.patrasrooms.gr. Serving large portions, enthusiastic Boston-raised Greeks run the laid-back, cafeteria-style ◨**Europa Center ❷**, on Amalias next to the tourist office. (Entrees €5-9. Internet €2 per hr. Open daily 7am-midnight. MC/V.) The hippest bar on the Ag. Nikolaou strip, **Cibo Cibo ❸**, on the right from the port, serves fresh, fancy Italian food during the day (entrees €9), and mixed drinks (from €6) during the night. (☎620 761. Open daily 7am-3am.)

  **Trains** (☎639 108) leave from Amalias 47, right across the port, for Athens (4¼hr., 8 per day, €10-13) and Kalamata (5½hr., 4 per day, €5-10) via Pirgos (2hr., €3-6), where you can catch a train to Olympia. KTEL **buses** (☎623 886; www.ktel.org) leave from farther down on Amalias for: Athens (3hr., 2 per hr., €17); Ioannina (4hr., 2 per day, €20); Kalamata (3½hr., 2 per day, €20); Thessaloniki (7½hr., 4 per day, €38). **Ferries** go to Corfu (7hr., M-W and F-Su midnight, €30-33), Vathy on Ithaka (2-3½hr.; Su-F 12:30, 8:30pm, Sat 12:30pm; €15), and Sami on Kephalonia (3hr.; Su-F 12:30, 8:30pm; €15). Six major ferry lines also travel to Italy: Ancona (21hr.); Bari (16hr.); Brindisi (14hr.); Venice (30hr.). The **tourist office** on Amalias, is 50m past the bus station. (☎461 740. Open daily 8am-10pm.) **Postal Code:** 26001.

# OLYMPIA Ολυμπία ☎26240

Every four years, ancient city-states would call a sacred truce and travel to Olympia for a pan-Hellenic assembly that showcased athletic ability and fostered peace and diplomacy. Modern Olympia, set among meadows and shaded by cypress and olive trees, is recognized as much for its pristine natural beauty as for its illustrious past. The ancient ◨**Olympic Site,** whose central sanctuary was called the **Altis,** draws hordes of tourists. Toward the entrance lie the ruins of the **Temple of Zeus.** Once home to master sculptor Phidias's awe-inspiring Statue of Zeus, one of the Seven Wonders of the Ancient World, the 27m sanctuary was the largest temple completed on the Greek mainland before the Parthenon. The **Temple of Hera**, dating from the 7th century BC, is better preserved than Zeus's Temple; it sits to the left facing the hill, past the temples of Metroön and the Nymphaeum. Today, the

**Olympic Flame** lighting ceremony takes place here before the symbol travels around the world to herald the Olympic Games' commencement. (Open June-Sept. daily 8am-7:30pm.) The **Archaeological Museum** has an impressive sculpture collection. (Open M 12:30-7:30pm, Tu-Su 8am-7:30pm. Temple and museum each €6, non-EU students €3, EU students free. Both €9/5/free.) The **Museum of the History of the Olympic Games** narrates Olympia's past through multilingual signs, supplemented with related artifacts from all over Greece. Next door, housed in the same small building as the bathrooms, is the **Museum of the History of Excavations,** with photographs documenting the site's recovery. (Both museums open M 12:30-7:30pm, Tu-Su 8am-7:30pm. Free.) Back in town, the **Museum of the Olympic Games** (also called the Sports Museum) on Angerinou, two blocks uphill from Kondili, houses a collection of Olympic paraphernalia. (☎22 544. Open Tu-Su 8am-3:30pm. €2.)

The centrally located **Youth Hostel ❶**, Kondili 18, across from the main square, is a cheap place to meet international backpackers and has bright, airy rooms with narrow balconies. (☎22 580. Linens €1. Hot showers only in early morning or late afternoon. Check-out 10am. Lockout 10am-12:30pm. Curfew 10:45pm. Open Feb.-Dec. Dorms €10; doubles €25. Cash only.) Mini-markets, bakeries, and fast food restaurants line **Kondili,** while a walk toward the railroad station or up the hill leads to inexpensive *tavernas*. A filling meal is as Greek as it gets at **Vasilakis Restaurant ❷**, on the corner of Karamanli and Spiliopoulou. Take a right off Kohili before the Youth Hostel walking towards the ruins. (☎22 104. *Souvlaki* pita €1.50. Chicken and fries €10. Open daily 11:30am-midnight.) **Wi-Fi** is available at **Epathlon Cafe,** 500m from the Old Stadium. (☎23 894; www.epathlon.blogspot.com. €2 per 30min.) **Trains** leave the station in the lower part of town for Pirgos (25min., 5 per day, €0.70), as do **buses** (45min., 15 per day, €1.90). The Town Hall **info center,** at the right end of Kondili, before the turn to the sights, serves as a tourist office. (☎22 549; aolympia@otenet.gr. Open M-F 8am-3pm.) **Postal Code:** 27065.

# SPARTA Σπάρτη ☎27310

Though the Spartans of antiquity purportedly threw babies off cliffs, they left little of their fierce legacy behind. Modern Spartans, no longer producing Greek hoplites, make olive oil. Barely worth exploring, a couple of stones and a grove of olive trees comprise the meager ruins at **Ancient Sparta,** a 1km walk north along Paleologou from the town center. Two blocks from the central *plateia* lies the city's **Archaeological Museum.** Opening into a garden of orange trees and headless statues, this museum displays fascinating votive masks, intricate mosaics, and lead figures resembling a toy army in addition to Grecian vases. (☎28 575. Open Tu-Su 8am-7:30pm. €2, students €1, EU students free.) Accommodations in Sparta rarely come cheap and few attractions exist to assuage an empty wallet.

**Hotel Cecil ❸**, Paleologou 125, on the corner of Thermopylon, has ordinary, spotless rooms with A/C, bath, phone, and TV in a recently renovated building. (☎24 980. Reserve ahead. Singles €25-35; doubles €45-55; triples €55-65.) **Diethnes ❷**, on Paleologou, a few blocks to the right of the main intersection with Lykergous facing the *plateia*, offers tasty Greek food in an intimate garden with orange trees, turtles, and cats. Though it has a few vegetarian options (€4.50), the restaurant specializes in €7 lamb entrees. (☎28 636. Entrees €5-8. Open 8am-midnight.) **Buses** from Sparta go to: Areopolis (1½hr., 4 per day, €6); Athens (3½hr., 10 per day, €17) via Tripoli (1hr., €5); Corinth (2½hr., €12); Monemvasia (2hr., 4 per day, €9). To reach the town center from the bus station, walk 10 blocks uphill on Lykourgou; the **tourist office** is on the third floor of the glass building in the *plateia*. (☎26 771. Open M-F 8am-2pm.) **Postal Code:** 23100.

GREECE

**⚡ DAYTRIP FROM SPARTA: MYSTRAS** ΜΥΣΤΡάς. Once all of Byzantium's religious center and the locus of Constantinople's rule over the Peloponnese, Mystras, 6km away from Sparta, is perhaps one of the best preserved medieval towns. Wildflowers, frescoed walls, and olive trees frame its chapels, churches, and monasteries. The Agia Sophia church, where the city's royalty lies buried, and the Agios Theodoros fresco contribute to Mystras's timelessness. Don't miss the Palace, with its pointed arches and stone walls dictating the region's history. Modest dress is required to visit the functioning convent and its beautifully decorated Pantanassa Church. The steep climb (10min.) to the fortified Kastro is breathtaking—literally and figuratively. The ruins can get very hot and the steps are slippery, so go early, bring water, and wear sturdy shoes. (☎83 377. Open daily Aug.-Sept. 8am-7:30pm; Oct.-July 8:30am-3pm. €5, students €3, EU students free.) Buses to Mystras leave from the station and from the corner of Lykourgou and Leonidou in Sparta for the ruins, returning 15min. later (20min., 4-9 per day, €2). Taxis go to Mystras from the corner of Paleologou and Lykourgou (€5).

## ⚓ MONEMVASIA Μονεμβασία ☎27320

On a monolithic rock that seems to spring from the sea, the island of Monemvasia is a Grecian treasure. No cars or bikes are allowed within the Old Town's walls, so wandering around the flowered balconies and picturesque corners gives the feeling that time stopped in the Middle Ages. On the top of the rock, uphill from the *plateia* is **Agia Sofia,** a 12th-century basilica. From Agia Sofia, paths continue uphill toward the old **citadel,** whose ruins are visible from the New Town. In the *plateia*, along the shop-lined main street, is the **Archaeological Museum.** (Open M noon-7:30pm, Tu-Su 8am-5pm. Free.) To get to the Old Town, cross the bridge from New Monemvasia and follow the road as it curves up the hill. It's an easy 20min. walk, but the heat and crowd both increase as the day wears on. It's better to go in the early morning or late evening, when the setting sun gives the panorama breathtaking shades. A bus also shuttles people up and down the road and leaves from the bridge at the foot of the hill (2min., 4 per hr. 8am-midnight, €1).

Waterfront *domatia* in the New Town are a budget traveler's best option. The rock walls and elegant interior of ⚓Hotel Belissis ❸, with lovely rooms, A/C, fridge, private bath, and TV, feel like they belong in the Old Town. From the bus station, walk along the main road, away from the bridge, for less than 5min. It's on the left, across the street from the ocean. (☎61 217. Singles and doubles €30-50; 4-person 2-fl. apartment with kitchenette and two baths €60-80. Cash only.) With a unique ambience, dining in the Old Town is beautiful but expensive. On the main road to the right, just before the Archaeological Museum, is **Restaurant Matoula ❸,** which offers terrace seating and unobstructed views of the waters below. (☎61 660. Entrees €8-14. *Moussaka* €8. Open daily noon-midnight. MC/V.) For those on a tight budget, there are many cheap Greek fast-food eateries and bakeries. Backpackers often picnic on the beach in New Town, soaking up the same beautiful views for free. **Buses** leave from Spartis for: Athens (1 per day, €26) and Sparta (2hr., €8.70). **Malvasia Travel Agency,** by the bus stop, provides **currency exchange,** charging 3% commission. (☎61 752. Open daily in high season 7am-3pm and 5-8pm; low season reduced hours.) **Postal Code:** 23070.

## NAFPLION Ναύφπλιο ☎27520

A tiny Venetian town surrounded on three sides by sky-blue waters, Nafplion is one of the Peloponnese's most beautiful—and most popular—tourist destinations. In July and August, the town plays host to more Americans and Italians than locals. After passing between the Venetians and the Ottomans, Nafplion became Greece's first capital in 1821. The town's dynamic history is quite evident today: in the **Old Town,** pl. Syndagma alone boasts a Venetian mansion, a Turkish mosque, and a Byzantine church, and the alleyways hold Ottoman fountains, monuments, and statues. The town's jewel is the 18th-century ▓**Palamidi fortress,** with spectacular views of the town and gulf. Walk up the 999 steps from across the central *plateia*, across from the bus station, or take a taxi up the 3km road. (Open 8am-7pm. €4, students €2, EU students and under 18 free.) A small, pebbly beach, **Arvanitia,** is farther along Polizoidhou, past the Palamidi steps; if it's too crowded, follow the footpath to private coves, or take a taxi (€5) to sandy **Karathona** beach.

To reach **Bouboulinas,** the waterfront promenade, go left from the bus station and follow Syngrou to the harbor; the Old Town is on your left. If you are coming from Arvanitia, you can also walk the short **path** around the promontory, keeping the sea to your left and the town's walls to your right. Accommodations in Old Town are often expensive, but ▓**Dimitris Bekas's Domatia ❷** is an excellent budget option. This small pension offers cozy rooms with a breathtaking roof deck view of Nafplion. The friendly manager steadfastly refuses to raise his prices during high season. From the bus station, walk right onto Fotomara until you reach the small Catholic church, then turn right onto Zygomala, and left up the first set of stairs. (☎24 256. Reserve ahead July-Aug. Singles €22; doubles €28, with bath €30.) Tucked into the mountainside, **Pension Marianna ❺,** Potamianou 9, has jaw-dropping views of the city. Expensive but worth it, this gem offers rooms with A/C, TV, and mini-bars. (☎24 256; www.pensionmarianna.gr. Breakfast €10-15. Singles €65; doubles €75; triples €85. MC/V.) Considering its central location, ▓**Ellas ❷,** in Pl. Syndagm, has inexpensive Greek and Italian food. The cheerful staff serves people-watching patrons on the outdoor *plateia*. (☎27 278. Entrees €5-7. Open daily noon-4pm and 7-11pm. MC/V.) **Breeze Games,** Bouboulinas 43, has a bar on the ground floor and **Internet** terminals upstairs. (☎26 141. Internet €2 per hr. Open daily 9am-3am.) Buy tickets on board for **buses** (☎27 323) leaving from Syngrou to: Athens (3hr., 1 per hr., €11.30); Epidavros (40min., 5 per day, €2.50); and Mycenae (45min., 3 per day, €2.50). The **tourist office** is at 25 Martiou, across from the bus station. (☎24 444. Open daily 9am-1pm and 4-8pm.) **Postal Code:** 21100.

## ▐ DAYTRIPS FROM NAFPLION

**EPIDAVROS** (Επίδαυρος). Like Olympia and Delphi, **Epidavros** was once both a town and a sanctuary—first to the ancient deity Maleatas and then to Apollo. Eventually, the sanctuary's energies were directed toward the demigod doctor Asclepius, Apollo's son who caught Zeus's wrath (and worse, his fatal thunderbolt) when he began to raise people from the dead. Under the patronage of Asclepius, Epidavros became famous across the ancient world as a center of medicine. Today, visitors can explore the **sanctuary,** which is undergoing heavy restoration, and visit an overcrowded and non-air-conditioned museum of ancient medical equipment and other artifacts. (*☎22 009. Sanctuary open daily June-Sept. 8am-7pm; Oct.-May 8am-5pm. Museum open June-Sept. M noon-7pm, Tu-Su 8am-7pm; Oct.-May M noon-5pm, Tu-Su 8am-5pm. Both open during festival F-Sa 8am-8pm. €6, students €3, EU students and under 19 free.*) The best-known structure at the site, however, is the splendidly preserved ▓**theater,** built in AD 2 and renowned for its extraordinary acoustics. When the theater is silent, you can hear a piece of paper being ripped on stage from any seat in the house, but the place is usually too packed to test it out. To the right of the path leading to the site, the **Festival Museum** is one of the town's most interesting and least-visited sights, displaying a fabulous collection of scene costumes and photos dedicated to the heroines and goddesses of ancient drama. (*Open daily 9am-9pm. Free.*) Fortunately for today's visitors, Greece's most famous ancient theater has come alive again after centuries of silence: during July and August it hosts the magical ◣**Epidavros Theater Festival,** with performances by international artists and modern interpretations of classical plays. The season program is available at the site as well as at the tourist info center in Athens. (☎ *210 3272 000; performances begin at 9pm, and tickets can be purchased at the site's box office; www.hellenicfestival.gr. €10-100.),* the Athens Festival Box Office (☎ 210 3221 459), or Nafplion's bus station. KTEL **buses** go to Nafplion (4 per day, €4) and make a special trip on performance nights (7:30pm, €4), returning spectators to Nafplion 20min. after the performance ends. Buses also go to Athens (2hr., 2 per day, €7). The **tourist office** is near the theater. *(☎ 22 026. Open June-Aug. M-Th 9am-7pm, F-Su 9am-10pm.)*

**MYCENAE** (Μυκήνες). The center of the Greek world from 1600 to 1100 BC, **Mycenae** was ruled by legendary Agamemnon, leader of the Greek forces in the Trojan War. Excavations of Mycenae have continued since 1876, turning the hillside ruins into one of Greece's most visited sites. Estimated to weigh 20 tons, the imposing **Lion's Gate** into the ancient city has two lions carved in relief above the lintel. On top, a line of stones marks the perimeter of what used to be one of the ancient world's most illustrious palaces. At the far end of the city, between the palace and the **postern gate,** is the **underground cistern,** which guaranteed water during sieges and is still open for exploration; watch your step and bring a flashlight. Across from the entrance, a **museum** details the history of the town and its excavations. Mycenae's most famous *tholos* (a beehive-shaped tomb built into the side of a hill) is the **Tomb of Agamemnon** (a.k.a. the Treasury of Atreus), 400m downhill toward the town. *(Open daily June-Oct. 8am-7:30pm; Nov.-May 8am-3pm. €8, students €4, EU students and children free. Keep your ticket for the museum and tholos or pay twice.)* From Mycenae, **buses** go to Nafplion (45min., 3 per day, €2.30) via Argos (30min., €2). For connections to Athens and Corinth, walk 3km downhill to Fihtio.

# NORTHERN AND CENTRAL GREECE

For travelers seeking distance from frenetic Athens and the tourist packed islands, northern and central Greece offer an idyllic escape, with fantastic hiking and Byzantine and Hellenistic heritage. Scattered across the region, traditional villages host diverse attractions: the depths of the Vikos Gorge, the heights of Mount Olympus, and the serenity of Meteora. The heartland of Greece also boasts some of the country's great cities, including Ioannina and Thessaloniki, the region's capital. Connected ethnically and historically to its Balkan neighbors, the north is where the modern, multicultural Greek state surfaces.

# THESSALONIKI Θεσσαλονίκη          ☎ 2310

Thessaloniki (a.k.a. Salonica; pop. 1,083,000), the Balkans' trade center, has historically been one of the most diverse cities in Greece, and is second in size only to Athens. The city is an energetic bazaar of cheap clothing shops and fashionable cafes, while its churches and mosques provide a material timeline of the region's restless past. Thessaloniki's current lack of tourism infrastructure and subway construction through 2012 may frustrate some travelers.

## ▐◣ TRANSPORTATION

**Flights: Macedonia Airport** (**SKG;** ☎985 000), 16km east of town. Take bus #78 from the KTEL station on Pl. Aristotelous (€0.60, 2 per hr.) or taxi (€15). **Olympic Airways,** Kountouriotou 3 (☎368 311; www.olympicairlines.com; open M-F 8am-4pm) and **Aegean Airlines,** 1 Nikis, off Venizelou, (☎239 225; www.aegeanair.com; open M-F

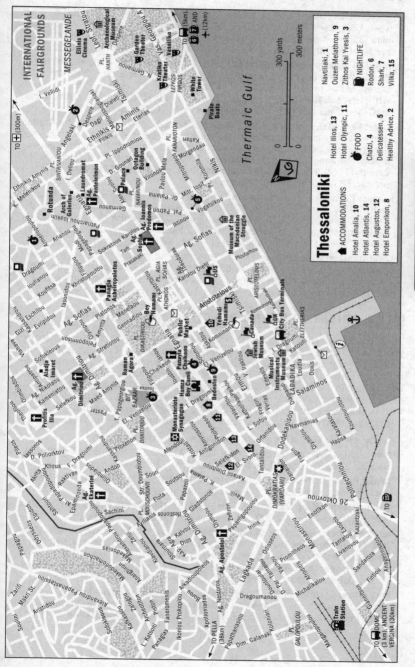

GREECE

**Thessaloniki**

▲ ACCOMMODATIONS

Hotel Amalia, 10
Hotel Atlantis, 14
Hotel Augustos, 12
Hotel Emporikon, 8

Hotel Ilios, 13
Hotel Olympic, 11

♦ FOOD

Chatzi, 4
Delicatessen, 5
Healthy Advice, 2

Navtiliaki, 1
Ouzeri Melathron, 9
Zithos Kai Yvesis, 3

NIGHTLIFE

Rodon, 6
Shark, 7
Vilka, 15

*Thermaic Gulf*

8am-3pm, Sa 8am-2pm) fly to: **Athens** (1hr., 24 per day, €80); **Chios** (50min., 4 per week, €60); **Corfu** (1hr., 5 per week, €65); **Hania** (1½hr., 4 per week, €130); **Ioannina** (35min., 4 per week, €55); **Iraklion** (1½hr., 1 per day, €115); **Lesvos** (1½hr., 1 per day, €93); **Rhodes** (2hr., 7 per week, €129); **Samos** (1½hr., 4 per week, €75).

**Trains:** To reach the **main terminal** (☎517 517), Monastiriou 28, in the western part of the city, take any bus down Egnatia (€0.60). Trains go to: **Athens** (7hr., 3 per day, €10; express 5hr., 4 per day, €25); **Xanthi** (4½hr., 3 per day, €7; express 3½hr., 4 per day, €19); **İstanbul, TUR** (14hr., 1 per day, €14); **Sofia, BUL** (7hr., 1 per day, €50); **Skopje, MAC** (4hr., 2 per day, €11). The **Travel Office** (☎ 11 10) has schedules.

**Buses:** Most **KTEL** buses leave from the central, dome-shaped **Macedonia Bus Station** 3km west of the city center (☎595 408). Bus #1 shuttles between the train and bus stations (6 per hr., €0.50). Bus #78 connects the bus station to the airport, passing through the waterfront corridor (2 per hr., €0.60). To: **Athens** (6hr., 8 per day, €24); **Corinth** (7½hr., 1 per day, €37); **Ioannina** (6½hr., 6 per day, €28); **Patras** (7½hr., 4 per day, €33). Schedules are subject to change.

**Ferries:** Buy tickets at **Karacharisis Travel and Shipping Agency,** Kountouriotou 8 (☎513 005). Open M-F 8:30am-8:30pm, Sa 8:30am-2:30pm. Ferries leave once per week for: **Chios** (20hr., €35) via **Limnos** (8½hr., €23); **Iraklion** (21-24hr., €38) via **Skiathos** (5½hr., €19); **Mykonos** (13½hr., €42); **Mytilini** (14 hr., €35); **Naxos** (14hr., €39) via **Syros** (12hr., €38); **Santorini** (17-18hr., €41).

**Local Transportation:** Local buses run often throughout the city. Buy tickets at *periptera* (newsstands; €0.50) or on board (€0.60). **Taxis** (☎551 525) run down Egnatia, Mitropoleos, and Tsimiski with stands at Ag. Sophia and the intersection of Mitropoleos and Aristotelous. Rides should not exceed €4, though phone orders cost an extra €1.50.

## ✴ 🗓 ORIENTATION AND PRACTICAL INFORMATION

Thessaloniki stretches along the Thermaic Gulf's northern shore from the iconic **White Tower** in the east to the prominent western **harbor.** Its rough grid layout makes it nearly impossible to get lost. Its most important arteries run parallel to the water. Closest to shore is **Nikis,** which goes from the harbor to the White Tower and is home to the city's main cafes. Farthest from shore is **Egnatia,** the city's busiest thoroughfare, a six-lane avenue; the Arch of Galerius stands at its intersection with D. Gounari. Farther inland from Egnatia are **Agios Dimitriou** and the **Old Town.** The city's center, Aristotelous has numerous banks, businesses, and restaurants.

**Tourist Offices: EOT,** at the airport, (www.eot.gr; open daily 9am-9pm).

**Banks:** Banks with currency exchange and 24hr. **ATMs** line Tsimiski, including **Citibank,** Tsimiski 21 (☎373 300). Open M-Th 8am-2:30pm, F 8am-2pm.

**Tourist Police:** Dodekanissou 4, 5th fl. (☎554 871). Open daily 7:30am-10pm. For the **local police,** call ☎553 800. Police booths also at the train station.

**Hospital: Acepa Hospital,** Kiriakidi 1 (☎993 111). **Hippokratio Public Hospital,** Costantinos Polius 49 (☎892 000). On weekends and at night call ☎ 1434.

**Internet Access:** Behind the shopping complex housing the American Consulate, **E-Global,** Vas. Irakliou 40 (☎252 780; www.e-global.gr), is 1 block to the right. €2.20 per hr.; min. €1. Open 24hr. Another location at Egnatia 17 (☎968 404), 1 block east of the Arch of Galerius. **Meganet,** Pl. Navarinou 5 (☎2 50 331; www.meganet.gr), in the square by the ruins of Galerius's palace. Noon-midnight €2 per hr., midnight-noon €1 per hr. Open 24hr.

**Post Office:** Aristotelous 26, just below Egnatia. Open M-F 7:30am-8pm, Sa 7:30am-2pm, Su 9am-1:30pm. Send parcels at the branch on Eth. Aminis near the White Tower (☎227 604). Open M-F 7am-8pm. Both offer *Poste Restante.* **Postal Code:** 54101.

# ACCOMMODATIONS

Budget options are available, but be prepared to get what you pay for. Thessaloniki's less expensive, slightly run-down hotels are along the western end of **Egnatia** between **Plateia Dimokratias** (500m east of the train station) and **Aristotelous.** Most face the chaotic road on one side and squalid back streets on the other. Hotels fill up quickly during Thessaloniki's high season, April through September.

**Hotel Olympic,** Egnatia 25 (☎566 870; fax 555 353). Simple, newly renovated rooms have A/C, bath, fridge, and TV. Eager English-speaking staff. Breakfast €5. Reception 24hr. Singles €40, doubles €50. Oct.-Aug. €10 Let's Go discount. AmEx/MC/V. ❸

**Hotel Emporikon,** Sygrou 14 (☎514 431), on Sygrou and Egnatia, between Aristotelous and Dimokratias Sq. Rooms with bright balconies have a 1970s feel. Tiled shared baths and hallway fridges. Singles €25; doubles €35, with bath €40; triples €45. ❷

**Hotel Augustos,** El. Svoronou 4 (☎522 955; www.augustos.gr). Better kept than most in the same price range. Comfortable rooms with frescoed ceilings and wooden floors. Singles €20, with A/C and bath €30; doubles €25/38; triples €50. Cash only. ❷

**Hotel Atlantis,** Egnatia 14 (☎540 131; atlalej@otenet.gr). Helpful English-speaking management offers rooms with sinks and tiny balconies. Some newly renovated rooms have A/C. Singles €20, with bath €25; doubles €25/40; triples €30/45. Cash only. ❷

**Hotel Ilios,** Egnatia 27 (☎512 620), on the western Egnatia budget strip, offers modern rooms with A/C, bath, fridge, phone, and TV. Singles €38; doubles €55; triples €67. ❸

**Hotel Amalia,** Ermou 33 (☎268 321). Amalia's green-, red-, and blue-themed rooms have A/C, large balcony, bath, radio, safe, and TV with double-paned windows. 1st fl. bar serves drinks (€4.50). Breakfast €6. Reception 24hr. Reserve at least 2 days ahead. Singles €55; doubles €73; triples €86. 10-20% student discount. MC/V. ❹

# FOOD

The old city overflows with *tavernas* and restaurants providing sweeping views of the gulf, while in and around the lovely **Bit Bazaar,** you will find characteristic *ouzeries.* Thessaloniki's restaurants have a delightful custom of giving patrons free watermelon or sweets after a meal, but if you crave anything from dried fruits to apple-sized cherries, head to the bustling public **market,** right off Aristotelous.

**Ouzeri Melathron,** Karypi 21-34 (☎275 016; www.ouzoumelathron.gr). Great prices and pub atmosphere make this a student favorite. The long, wittily subtitled menu features chicken, snails, lamb, octopus, and a variety of cheese tapas. Veal and mushrooms wrapped in cornbread €6. Entrees €4-14. Free round of drinks with ISIC. Open M-F 1:30pm-1:30am, Sa-Su 1:30pm-2am. D/MC/V. ❷

**Healthy Advice,** Alex Svolou 54 (☎283 255). This Canadian-run joint serves fresh, creative, and Western-style salads and sandwiches (€4-6). Salami straight from Italy, hard-to-find lean turkey and ham, and daily baked bread. Friendly staff speak fluent English, French, Arabic, and Greek. Open daily 11:30am-2am. ❷

**Delicatessen,** Kouskoura 7 (☎236 367). Hands down most popular among locals for *souvlaki* (€2). Waitstaff speaks little English. Open daily 11:30am-3am. ❶

**Chatzi,** El. Venizelou 50 (☎279 058; www.chatzis.gr), has served as Thessaloniki's Willy Wonka since 1908. For a less intense delight than pure sugar and honey Greek sweets, try their yogurt. The *kourkoumpinia* and *baklava* are orgasmic (€1.20 per 100g). Pastries €2-4. 4 branches in town. Open Su-F 7am-3am, Sa 7am-4am. MC/V. ❶

GREECE

**Navtiliaki,** Pl. Ag. Georgiou 8 (☎ 247 583), behind the Rotunda. This *ouzeri*, known for its excellent seafood, also has meat and vegetarian options in a relaxing, tree-lined setting. Entrees €8-10. Open daily 12:30pm-1am. Bar open daily 12:30pm-2am. ❷

**Zithos Kai Yvesis** (☎ 268 746), by the intersection of El. Venizelou and Filipou. Look for a sign reading "Venizelou 72." The restaurant serves Greek fare (€1.50-5.50) including *vlachiko* (pig's intestine stuffed with cheese and meat; €3). Open daily 6pm-2am. ❶

## 👁 SIGHTS

Reminders of Thessaloniki's Byzantine and Ottoman might pervade its streets. The **Roman Agora,** a 2nd-century odeon and covered market, still rests at the top of Aristotelous. Its lower square once held eight *caryatids*, sculptures of women believed to have been magically petrified. (Open daily 8am-8pm. Free) Originally a temple honoring Jupiter, the **Rotunda** (now **Agios Georgios**) was erected by the Roman Caesar Galerius at the end of the AD 3rd century. It later became a church honoring Christians martyred at the hands of Galerius and Diocletian, then a mosque under the Ottomans. (☎ 968 860. Open Tu-F 8am-7pm, Sa-Su 8:30am-3pm. Free.) At D. Gounari and Egnatia stands the striking ▨**Arch of Galerius,** known locally as just *Kamara* (Arch). Erected by Galerius to commemorate his victory over the Persians, it now serves as the main meeting spot for locals. Two blocks south of the arch in Pl. Navarino, a small section of the once 150 sq. km **Palace of Galerius** is open for viewing. The weathered mosaic floors and octagonal hall, believed to have housed Galerius's throne, are particularly notable. In keeping with its exalted position as second city of the Byzantine Empire, Thessaloniki uses its **Museum of Byzantine Culture,** Stratou 2, to tell a far-ranging secular tale. The museum exhibits the largest collection of early Christian wall paintings outside the Vatican. (Bus #12 or 39. ☎ 868 570; www.mbp.gr. Open M 10:30am-5pm, Tu-Su 8:30am-3pm; winter reduced hours. €6, students and seniors €3, EU students and children free.) Across the street, the ▨**Archaeological Museum** features some of the area's most prized artifacts, including the Derveni krater and sculptures of Greek goddesses. (☎ 830 538. Open in summer M 1-7:30pm, Tu-Su 8am-7pm; winter reduced hours. €6, students and seniors €3, EU students and children free.) Its gruesome executions earned the **White Tower** the nickname "Bloody Tower," all that remains of a 15th-century Ottoman seawall. A walk to the top of Thessaloniki's most prominent landmark no longer means inevitable death, instead offering a marvelous view of the city and its shoreline. (Bus #3, 5, 6, 33, or 39. ☎ 267 832. Open Tu-Su 8:30am-3pm. €2, students free.)

## 📢 NIGHTLIFE

Thessaloniki is a city that lives outside, with citizens leisurely patrolling its cafes, bars, and boardwalks. The **Ladadika** district, a two-by-three-block rectangle of *tavernas* behind the port, was the city's red-light strip until the 80s, but has since transformed into a sea of dance clubs. The heart of the city's social life during the winter, it shuts down almost entirely in summer, when everyone moves to the dance-till-you-drop open-air discos around the airport, popular with tourists as well. **Rodon,** east of the city along the main highway about 200m after the turn to the airport, and **Shark,** Themistokli Sofouli and Argonavton 2, are the city's most expensive clubs. (Rodon ☎ 476 720. Cover €10; includes 1 drink. Open 11pm-7:30am. Shark ☎ 416 855. Mixed drinks €10. Open 9pm-4am.) Located in an old factory, the **Vilka** complex, Andreou Georgiou 21, offers a variety of bars and clubs. Vilka's stage also hosts local rock legends. (☎ 515 006. Open daily midnight-8am.) As Thessaloniki's popular clubs change frequently, ask the locals for an update. The bustling waterfront cafes and the elegant **Aristotelous promenade** are always packed, as is the student-territory Bit Bazaar, a cobblestoned square of *ouzeries* and wine and tapas bars. For a unique experience, drink and dance to Greek, Latino disco, or reggae on one of the three ◼**pirate boats** that leave from behind the White Tower, touring the harbor for 30min.

# ◪ DAYTRIPS FROM THESSALONIKI

◼**ANCIENT VERGINA.** The tombs of Vergina (Βέργινα), final resting places of ancient Macedonian royalty, lie only 30km from Thessaloniki. The magnificent **museum** at Vergina, the area's principal sight, is designed to allow you to walk into the actual ◼**Great Tumulus,** a manmade burial mound 12m tall and 110m wide. Visitors enter this dimly-lit "Cave of Wonders" to see its ornate burial treasures, brilliant frescoes, and the tombs of royalty in their original 4th-century BC placement. The tombs' unparalleled splendor has convinced archaeologists that they hold the bones of **Philip II** and **Alexander IV,** respectively the murdered father and son of **Alexander the Great.** The museum's atmosphere will send shivers down your spine. *(Open in summer M noon-7:30pm, Tu-Su 8am-7:30pm; in winter Tu-Su 8:30am-3pm. €8, non-EU students €4, EU students free.)* **Buses** run from Thessaloniki to Veria (1hr., 1 per hr., €6.10), from which you can take the bus to Vergina's *plateia* (25-30min., 1 per hr., €1.30); follow the signs to reach the tombs.

**ANCIENT PELLA.** For more than a century, Pella was arguably the center of the world. Around 400 BC, **King Archelaus** moved the capital of his Macedonian state here from Vergina. The new capital, strategically situated on the Thermaic Gulf, achieved its greatest stature as Philip II's and **Alexander the Great's** home base; artists and intellectuals flocked here under their reign. After Alexander's death and his empire's dissolution, the city's power continued to wane until the Roman general **Aemilius Paulus** sacked it in 168 BC. Treasures in Paella's **museum** include gold-leaf jewelry and terracotta figurines. Exquisite mosaics line the museum and ruins. Across the street is Pella's vast **archaeological site,** with remains of the **agora,** the **House of Dionysus,** and the **House of the Abduction of Helen.** *(Open Apr.-Oct. M noon-7:30pm, Tu-Su 8am-7:30pm; Nov.-Mar. Tu-Su 8:30am-3pm. Site and museum €6, non-EU students €3, EU students and under 18 free.)* Ancient Pella is on the main Thessaloniki-Edessa highway, 38km west of Thessaloniki. **Buses** go to new Pella from Thessaloniki (1hr., every 40min., €2.60); ask the driver to be let off at the sights.

# MOUNT OLYMPUS Ολύμπος Όρος ☎ 23520

Erupting out of the Thermaic Gulf, the formidable slopes of Mt. Olympus, Greece's highest peak, mesmerized the ancient Greeks, who believed it to be their pantheon's divine dwelling place. Today, a network of well-maintained **hiking** trails makes the summit accessible to anyone with sturdy legs. Mt. Olympus has eight peaks: Ag. Andonios (2817m), Kalogeros (2701m), Mytikas (2918m), Profitis Ilias (2803m), Skala (2866m), Skolio (2911m), Stefani (the Throne of Zeus; 2907m), and Toumba (2801m). The region became Greece's first national park in 1938. All means for challenging Olympus originate from **Litochoro Town** (pop. 6000, 500m). The easiest and most popular trail begins at **Prionia** (1100m), 18km from the village, and ascends 4km through a sheltered, forested ravine to ◼**Zolotas** refuge, also known as Refuge A or—to the Greeks—as Spilios Agapitos. At the Zolotas refuge, you'll find reliable resources for all aspects of hiking: updates on weather and trail conditions, advice on routes, and reservations for any of the **Greek Alpine Club (EOS)** refuges. With years of experience, the staff is happy to dispense info over the phone in English. (☎81 800. Curfew 10pm. Open mid-May to Oct. Camping €5;

dorms €10.) After spending the night at Zolotas, you can ascend Olympus's summit the next day. Regrouping hikers may also stay the night in a mountaintop refuge, walking down to Diastavrosi (3-4hr.) the following morning. All trails are easy to follow, and most are marked with red and yellow blazes. Unless you're handy with crampons and an ice axe, make your ascent between May and October. Mytikas, the tallest peak, is accessible only with special equipment before June.

Litochoro Town, at the foot of the mountain, is a relaxed village, only a 5min. bus ride from the sea. On the last Sunday in June, the **Olympus Marathon** (www.olympus-marathon.com) gathers athletes and fans for a 44km run with the gods. The night before your hike, head to **Hotel Park ❷**, Ag. Nikolaou 23, at the bottom of the hill after the park. This simple hotel has mosaic floors and large rooms with A/C, bath, fridge, phone, TV, and a few balconies offering views of both snow-covered peaks and blue sea. (☎81 252; hotelpark_litochoro@yahoo.gr. Breakfast €5. Reception 24hr. Singles €25; doubles €35; triples €45. Cash only.) For a final feast before heading for the hills, try ▣**Gastrodromio En Olympo ❸**, just off the *plateia* by the church. Diners have a remarkable view of the mountain. (☎21 300; www.gastrodomio.gr. Entrees €8-14. Open daily 10am-midnight. MC/V.) Those wisely seeking water and trail snacks for the arduous hike up Olympus should stay away from the expensive supermarkets just above the *plateia* and head to **Arvanitides,** Perikliko Torba 14, at the end of Odos Ermi, which branches off Ag. Nikolaou opposite the *demotic* (public) school below the tourist office. (☎23520 21 195. Open 8am-9pm.) KTEL buses (☎81 271) leave from the Litochoro station, Ag. Nikolaou 20, opposite the tourist office, for Athens (5hr., 3 per day, €28), Plaka (15min., 1 per hr., €2), and Thessaloniki (1½hr., 16 per day, €8) via Katerini (30min., 1 per hr. €2). The **tourist office** is on Ag. Nikolaou by the park. (☎83 100. Open daily 7:30am-2:30pm.) **Postal Code:** 60200.

## IOANNINA Ιωάννινα ☎26510

The capital of Epirus, Ioannina (pop. 170,000) serves as the natural transportation hub for this region of northern Greece. The city reached its height of fame after its 1788 capture by **Ali Pasha,** an Albanian-born visionary leader and womanizer. Legend has it that when Ali Pasha wasn't able to get the girl he wanted, he strangled all of his other lovers and threw their bodies into Ioannina's lake. The city is also the site of the **Frourio,** a monumental fortress built in the 14th century, where many of Ioannina's residents still live today. The Frourio is one of the few ancient examples of cooperation among Jews, Muslims, and Christians, as all lived peacefully within its walls. To reach the **Itş Kale** (inner citadel) from the Frourio's main entrance, veer left, and follow the signs. To the immediate right along the wall are the remnants of Ali Pasha's **hamam** (baths). Catch a ferry from the waterfront (10min., 2 per hr. 7am-midnight, €2) for **Nisi** (the Island) to explore Byzantine monasteries and the **Ali Pasha Museum** (open daily 9am-9pm; €2).

**Hotel Tourist ❸**, Kolleti 18, on the right a few blocks up G. Averof from the *kastro*, offers simple rooms with A/C, baths, and phones. (☎25 070. Singles €30; doubles €45; triples €70.) Portions are huge and prices reasonable at **Limni ❷**, which also has a charming lakeside patio with views of the mountains and mosque. (☎78 988. Entrees €5-8.) **Buses,** Zossimadon 4, depart from the main terminal to: Athens (6hr., 7 per day, €34); Igoumenitsa (2hr., 8 per day, €9); Kalambaka (2hr., 2 per day, €11); Thessaloniki (5hr., 4 per day, €27). For info, call ☎26 286. To reach the **tourist office,** walk 500m down Dodonis; the office is on the left, immediately after the school. (☎46 662. Open M-F 7:30am-7:30pm.) **Postal Code:** 45110.

## ZAGOROHORIA Ζαγοροχώρια ☎26530

Between the Albanian border and the North Pindos mountain range, a string of 46 little hamlets (*horia*) show few signs of interference from modern society. Also home to **Vikos-Aoös National Park,** the region provides nature enthusiasts with plenty of hiking opportunities. Any trip should include a visit to the Zagori Information Center in the town of **Aspraggeli.** (☎22 241. Open daily 9am-6pm.) Though camera-laden hikers are now as common as goats and sheep in **Monodendri** (pop. 150), the tiny village retains its natural beauty; its location at the top of **Vikos Gorge**—the world's deepest canyon—and proximity to Ioannina (p. 524) lend to its irresistibility. North of Vikos Gorge, the two **Papingo** villages, **Megalo** (Μέγαλο; large) and **Mikro** (Μικρό; small), have recently become vacation destinations for wealthy Greeks and serve as the starting point for some beautiful hikes.

**⏚ TRANSPORTATION. Buses** go to Ioannina from Monodendri (1hr., 4 per week, €3) and from Papingo (1½hr., 2 per week, €5). Papingo visitors may consider hiking 3hr. to **Klidonia** to catch more frequent buses (1hr., 8 per day, €4). **Taxis** can take you to Ioannina or Konitsa (€35). The closest banks are in Kalpaki and Konitsa. It is a 5hr. walk from Vikos Village to Monodendri (9km) and 6hr. from the Papingos to Monodendri. The obliging owner of the Vikos Village taverna, **Foris,** in the *plateia*, provides rides (€30) to Monodendri. (☎42 170.)

**⏚ VIKOS GORGE** Φαράγγι Βίκου. Vikos Gorge, whose walls are 900m deep and only 110m apart, is the steepest on earth. In spring, the gorge's river rushes along the 15km stretch of canyon floor. By summer, all that is left is the occasional puddle in the dry riverbed. People have walked through the gorge's ravine since the 12th century BC, when early settlers took shelter in its caves. Today, hikers follow the well-marked **O3 domestic trail** (red diamonds on white square backgrounds) section of the Greek National E4 route through the gorge. The path stretches from the village of Kipi in the south to Megalo Papingo at its northernmost tip, winding through Zagorohoria's center. The gorge can be accessed from Kipi, Monodendri, the Papngo villages, and Vikos Village.

**⏚ MONODENDRI** Μονοδένδρι. To reach the must-see ◪**Oxia Point,** a natural overlook with breathtaking views of Vikos Gorge, follow the red-blazed trail beginning behind the Monodendri Hotel (1½hr.). Opposite the bus stop, **Monodendri Hotel ❸** has cozy rooms with colorful rugs and **exchanges currency** for guests and *Let's Go* readers. The owner's English-speaking son, Marios, picks up patrons from Vikos Village (€50) or Megalo Papingo (€40) after their hikes. (☎71 300; www.monodendrihotel.com. Breakfast €5. Bag lunch €4. Reception 8am-11pm. Singles €35; doubles €45; triples €60. MC/V.) The bus stop and most restaurants and hotels cluster on Monodendri's one paved road. Both the town kiosk and Monodendri Hotel have trail maps (€8). **Postal Code:** 44007.

**⏚ HIKING AROUND THE PAPINGOS** (Τα Πάπινγκα). The Papingos's increase in tourism has raised lodging prices. If pensions and domatia are full or high-season prices seem outrageous, backpackers may hike 3km to the EOS Refuge ❶, near Mt. Astraka. (☎26 553. 60-bed dorm €10.) Freelance camping is illegal. ◪Pension Koulis ❸, has rooms reminiscent of an alpine ski lodge. Facing the town from where the cobblestoned road starts, take the first left after the church. The pension is on the corner of the next crossroads to the left. (☎41 115. Breakfast included. Reception 24hr. Singles €35; doubles €50; triples €65. MC/V.) In Mikro Papingo, take the left fork off the main road to find Hotel Dias ❸, whose rooms will make you forget you're on a budget. (☎41 257. Breakfast included. Reception 8am-11pm. Singles €35; doubles €60; triples €75; quads €90.) At Tsoumanis Estiatorio ❷, outside town on the road to Mikro Papingo, two brothers serve lamb from their father's flock and vegetables from their gardens. (☎42 108. Entrees €5-9. Open 11am-1am.)

Zagorohoria's most spectacular hikes begin in **Mikro Papingo,** from where visitors can climb **Mount Astraka** (2436m). Most ascents take about 4hr. and are appropriate for intermediate-level hikers. More advanced hikers climb 4½hr. to the pristine ◪**Drakolimni** (Dragon Lake; 2000m), an alpine pool filled with spotted newts. Both hikes can be paired with a stay in the **EOS Refuge** (1900m), on a nearby ridge. From the refuge, a path (3km, 1¼hr.) descends into the blossom-dotted valley, passes **Xeroloutsa,** a shallow alpine lake, and ends at Drakolimni. Multi-day treks deep into the Pindos are possible, using the EOS hut as a starting point. For easier hikes, the family-friendly **Papingo Natural Pools** are a great option. When the road curves right before ascending to Mikro Papingo from Megalo on the main road, you'll see a small bridge and a parking lot. Opposite the parking lot, the white-rock trail begins. The pools become warmer and cleaner as you climb but beware taking a dip—snakes have been known to inhabit lower pools.

## METEORA Μετέωρα AND KALAMBAKA Καλαμπάκα ☎24320

The monastic community of Meteora lies atop a series of awe-inspiring pinnacles seeming to ascend into the sky. Believed to be inhabited by hermits as early as the 11th century, these summits were picked as the location of a series of 21 frescoed Byzantine monasteries in the 14th century. Six monasteries remain in use and open to the public. Don't expect a hidden treasure—tour buses and sweaty faces are as common in Meteora as Byzantine icons, and the traditionally dressed monks drive Jeeps and clip cell phones to their belts. For monastic silence and breathtaking sunset views of the valley, drive or walk up the complex after visiting hours. Though the museums are closed, Meteora's peace, impossible to experience during the day, settles in after hours. The largest, oldest, and most popular monastery, the ◪**Grand Meteora Monastery** houses a **folk museum** and the 16th-century **Church of the Transfiguration.** Its collection also includes early printed secular books by Aristotle and Plato and dozens of monks' skulls. The complex's second largest monastery, **Varlaam,** is 800m down the road. If you take the right fork, you'll reach **Roussanou,** visible from most of the valley, and one of the most spectacularly situated monasteries. Two wooden bridges lead to the monastery's entrance, which was accessible only by rope ladder until 1897. (Modest dress required. Hours vary by season and by monastery. Apr.-Sept. Grand Meteora open M and W-Su 9am-5pm; Varlaam open M-W and F-Su 9am-2pm and 3:15-5pm; Roussanou open M-Tu and Th-Su 9am-6pm. Each monastery €2.) Meteora is accessible from the Kalambaka central bus station (15min., 2 per day, €1) or visitors can walk 45min. up the hill along the footpath found at the end of Vlachava.

Meteora and Kalambaka's rocky landscapes create a **climber's** paradise; for info, equipment rental, guided excursions, and lessons, contact the local **Climbing Association.** (☎6972 567 582; kliolios@kalampaka.com.) Room owners may approach you at the bus station offering lower prices for decent rooms; be aware that picking up people from the station is illegal here. In the Old Town, at the base of Meteora, ◪**Alsos House ❸,** Kanari 5, has rooms with A/C, balcony, bath, and gorgeous views. From the Town Hall and *plateia,* walk along Vlachava until it ends, then follow the signs. The owner sometimes hires students in summer in exchange for food, accommodation, and tips. (☎24 097; www.alsoshouse.gr. Breakfast included. Free Internet and Wi-Fi. Free parking. Reserve ahead. Singles €30; doubles €40-50; triples €60; 2-room apartment with kitchen €70-80. 10% *Let's Go* or ISIC discount. AmEx/MC/V.) The next house up from Alsos, **Koka Roka ❷,** Kanari 21, rents large rooms and aims to satisfy a backpacker's every need, offering the town's best meat at its cheap *taverna.* (☎24 554; kokaroka@yahoo.com. Breakfast €2. Laundry €10. Internet €3 per hr. Reception 24hr. Singles €20; doubles €35-40; triples €50-60.) On the road up to Meteora, **Camping Vrachos Kastraki ❶** has 24hr. hot water, barbecues, a climbing wall, and free fridges and stoves, as well as a restaurant and mini-market. (☎23 134; www.campingmeteora.gr. €6; €3 per tent, €1 per car. MC/V.) Right in the center of town, ◪**Taverna Paramithy ❶**

(Fairy Tale), Dimitriou 14, has cheap, delicious traditional Greek cuisine cooked on a wood-burning grill. (☎24 441. Entrees €4-8. Open M-Su 11am-midnight. Cash only.) **Trains** leave Kalambaka for Athens (5hr., 2 per day, €21). **Buses** depart Kalambaka for: Athens (5hr., 7 per day, €24); Ioannina (3hr., 2 per day, €11); Patras (5hr.; Tu, F, Su 1 per day; €25); Thessaloniki (3½hr., 4 per day, €11). The **Office of Public Services,** at the beginning of Vlachava, is the closest thing to a tourist office. (☎77 900. Open M-F 8am-8pm, Sa 8am-2pm.) **Postal Code:** 42200.

# DELPHI Δελφοι
☎22650

Troubled denizens of the ancient world journeyed to the stunning mountain-top of the **Oracle of Delphi,** where the priestess of Apollo related the gods' cryptic prophecies. Leading up **Sacred Way** hillside are the remains of the legendary **Temple of Apollo,** followed by a perfectly preserved **theater** and a **stadium** that once hosted the holy **Delphic Games.** At the entrance to the site, the **archaeological museum** exhibits an extensive collection of artifacts found near the temple, including the **Sphinxes** (the oracle's guards). Head east from Delphi to reach the temple, but go early in the morning to avoid the nonstop flow of guided groups. (Temple open daily 7:30am-7:30pm. Museum open Tu-Su 7:30am-7:30pm. Each €6, both €9; students €3/5; EU students free.) For overnight stays, the recently renovated **Hotel Sibylla ❷,** Pavlou 9, offers wonderful views and private baths at the best prices in town. (☎82 335; www.sibylla-hotel.gr. No-commission currency exchange. Singles €20-24; doubles €26-30; triples €35-40. €2 *Let's Go* discount.) In July, Delphi springs to life with a series of musical and theatrical **performances** at its Cultural Center (☎210 331 2781; www.eccd.gr). From Delphi, **buses** go to Athens (3hr., 6 per day, €13). Delphi's **tourist office,** Pavlou 12 or Friderikis 11, is right up to the stairs next to the town hall. (☎82 900. Open M-F 8am-2:30pm.) **Postal Code:** 33054.

# ARAHOVA Αράχωβα
☎22670

The country's largest ski resort is 24km from nearby Parnassos's ski centers. **Pension Petrino ❸** (Πετρινο), down the first alley on the right after pl. Xenia, invites guests to unwind in cabin-style rooms with TV, private bath, and a second-story loft. (☎31 384. Singles €60-95; doubles €70-115. Low season singles €20-30; doubles €40. Discounts for longer stays. Prices lower for midweek stays during ski season.) The **bakeries** along the road to Delphi sell fresh bread and pastries (€0.50-2), and several small markets offer self-service options. **Buses** from Terminal B in Athens stop at Arahova's main *plateia* (2hr., 6 per day, €11) en route to Delphi. Getting from Arahova to Parnassos is easier during ski season, when a bus runs from the *plateia* (M-Th 8am, F-Su 3 per day 8:30am-2:30pm; €5) and returns daily at 3pm. In summer, hire a **taxi** (☎31 566; round-trip €30-40). When negotiating the price, arrange with the driver for a return pick-up. The **information office** is on the right before you enter town. (☎31 630. English spoken. Open M-F 9am-9pm, Sa-Su 9am-2pm and 5-8pm. Closed Su in summer.) **Postal Code:** 32004.

# ❚ DAYTRIPS FROM ARAHOVA

**MT. PARNASSOS** (Παρνασσός). Home to the best slopes in all Greece, **Mt. Parnassos** (2455m) comes alive from December 15 through May 1, when winter sport enthusiasts flock to the main ski centers, Kellaria and Fterolakka. Each center has lodges and equipment rental. (☎22340 22 373. Ski passes M-F €12 per day, Sa-Su €27 per day; €80 per week. Students €8 per day, children €5 per day. Family discounts available.) Because more goats than tourists frequent Parnassos in summer, it is a peaceful spot for **hiking** and **rock climbing.**

**OSIOS LOUKAS** (Όσιος Λουκάς). Gold-laden mosaics, vivid frescoes, and intricate brick- and stone-work adorn the famous Byzantine ■**monastery of Osios Loukas.** Founded by Saint Osios Loukas, the Church of the Panagia (Church of the Virgin Mary) was finished soon after his death in AD 953. Today it holds the shriveled body of the saint himself, in a glass coffin. The larger, more ornate **Katholikon of Osios Loukas,** built in 1011, is the site of his reliquary. In addition to the two churches, the monastery contains a crypt, monks' cells, and a museum. *(Open daily May-Sept. 8am-2pm and 4-6pm; Sept.-Apr. 8am-5pm. Dress modestly. €3, students €2.)* From Arahova take a **car** or **taxi** (☎31 566; round-trip €40) to the monastery. When negotiating the price, ask the driver to also bring you back to town. Most taxis will wait an hour for a higher fare.

# IONIAN ISLANDS Νησιά Του Ιόνιου

West of mainland Greece, the Ionian Islands entice travelers with their lush vegetation and turquoise waters. Never conquered by the Ottomans, the islands bear the marks of British, French, Russian, and Venetian occupants. Today, they are a favorite among Western Europeans and travelers seeking unconventional Greece.

## ■CORFU Κέρκυρα ☎26610

Ever since Homer's Odysseus washed ashore and raved about Corfu's lush beauty, the surrounding seas have brought a constant stream of conquerors, colonists, and tourists to the verdant island. Indeed, there is something for everyone in Corfu, with archaeological sights, traditional villages, beautiful beaches, and wild nightlife. **Corfu Town** (pop. 10,000) is a jumbled labyrinth of colorful Venetian buildings and clotheslines stretching from ornate iron balconies. Town events and cafe-bars center around the **Spianada,** an area that includes most of the important museums and a park with a cricket pitch; from there, follow the yellow roses and green-shuttered alleyways complementing the fortresses, museums, churches, and winding streets of the Old Town. Discover the pleasures of colonialism at the English-built ■**Mon Repos Estate,** which features lovely gardens and an exhibit depicting the island's archaeological treasures. (☎41 369. Estate open daily 8am-7pm. Museum open Tu-Su 8:30am-3pm. Estate free. Museum €3, EU students €2.) The **Palace of St. Michael and St. George,** another stately home, hosts a collection of Neoclassical sculpture and Asian artifacts. (☎30 443. Open Tu-Su 8:30am-7:30pm. €3, students and seniors €2, EU students free.) Farther south, the **Archaeological Museum** exhibits antiquities from all over Corfu. (☎30 680. Open Tu-Su 8:30am-3pm. €3, EU students free). The lovely beach of **Paleokastritsa,** with accessible caves perfect for exploring, lies west of Corfu Town; take a KTEL bus to Paleokastritsa (45min., 2-7 per day, €2). Traditional villages encircle ■**Mt. Pantokrator,** which offers a must-see sunset panorama and views into Albania and Italy.

Most visitors come to Corfu with all-inclusive packages or head to the campgrounds along the coast, so finding cheap accommodations in Corfu Town is virtually impossible. Plan to stay in a nearby village or book months ahead. The **Corfu Owners of Tourist Villas and Apartments Federation,** Polilas 2A, is more of a local service for hostel owners than a tourist office, but can be helpful in a crunch. (☎26 133; oitkcrf@otenet.gr. Open M-F 9am-3pm and 5-8pm.) KTEL **buses** run from Corfu Town to Ag. Gordios (45min., 3-6 per day, €1.90), home to an impressive beach and the backpacker's legend **Pink Palace Hotel ❷.** Famous among travelers, this 900-bed hostel hosts mainly American and Canadian backpackers. Patrons can partake in 24/7 bacchanalia: among the many excuses to drink and get naked at this quintessential party hostel are toga parties, the Booze Cruise (clothing optional), cliff diving (€15), and a kayak safari (€18). Lock up your valuables in the front desk's safety deposit box before enjoying any of the daily events. (☎53 103; www.thepinkpalace.com. Offers bus service to Athens; €49, round-trip €75. Scooter and kayak rentals €10 per day. 4-wheeler rental €15-30 per day. Bar open 24hr. Breakfast, cafeteria-style dinner, and ferry pickup included. Laundry €9. Internet €2 per 35min. Dorms from €18; private rooms €25-30.) For more mellow digs, take bus #11 to nearby Pelekas (20min., 7 per day, €1), where the friendly owners of the ◙Pension Tellis and Brigitte ❷, down the hill from the bus stop on the left side of the street, offer rooms with balconies and superb views. (☎94 326; martini@pelekas.com. Singles €20; doubles €30-40.)

Olympic and Aegean Airlines connect Corfu's small Ioannis Kapodistrias Airport (CFU or LGKR; ☎39 040) to Athens (1hr., 2-3 per day, €120-150) and Thessaloniki (1hr., 3 per week, €70-100). Ferries run from Corfu Town to: Bari, ITA (10hr., 4 per week); Brindisi, ITA (8hr., 1-2 per day); Igoumenitsa (1½hr., 1 per hr.); Patras (8hr., 5 per week); Paxi (4hr., 1-3 per day); Venice, ITA (24hr., 1 per day). Prices vary significantly. For more detailed info, try any of the travel agencies that line the road to the port. International Tours (☎39 007) and Ionian Cruises (☎31 649), both across the street from the old port on El. Venizelou, book international ferries. Buy your ticket at least a day ahead and ask if port tax is included. Green KTEL intercity buses depart from between I. Theotaki and the New Fortress for Athens (8hr., 3 per day, €38) and Thessaloniki (8hr., 2 per day, €36); prices include ferry. On the mainland, Igoumenitsa (☎30 627) has more frequent buses and better connections. Blue municipal buses leave from Pl. San Rocco (€0.70-1). The tourist office is in Pl. San Rocco in a green kiosk. (☎20 733. Open daily 9am-2pm and 6-9pm.) Postal Code: 49100.

# ◙KEPHALONIA Κεφαλόνια                ☎26710

With soaring mountains and subterranean lakes, Kephalonia (pop. 45,000) is a nature lover's paradise and deservedly popular. The bus schedules are erratic and the taxis very expensive, but armed with your own transportation, you can uncover picturesque villages on lush hillsides and cliff-cuddled beaches. Argostoli (pop. 8000), Kephalonia's capital, is a pastel-colored city that offers the easiest access to other points on the island. St. Gerassimos ❷, 6 Ag. Gerassimou Str., just off the waterfront road, is a family-run establishment offering seven rooms each equipped with A/C, balcony, private bath, and TV. (☎28 697. Open June-Sept. Rooms €20-45; prices negotiable.) People gravitate to La Gondola ❷, 21 Maiou, for its divine Italian dishes like *risotto sabbia d'oro* (€8.80) with pumpkin and shrimp. (Pizza €8.60-10. Pasta €5.60-11. Greek entrees €7-8.30. Wine from €8.50. Open daily 7pm-1am. MC/V.) Captain's Table Restaurant ❷, offers entrees for seafood lovers and vegetarians at two large locations: one on the waterfront at the corner of Metaxa and 21 Maiou, and one next to the *plateia* at Rizospaston 3. (☎27 170. Entrees €5.20-20. Open in summer daily 8:15am-2am.) The tourist office, near the ferry docks, opens irregularly. (☎23 364. Generally open July-Aug. daily 8am-2:30pm; Sept.-June M-F 8am-2:30pm.) Internet is available at B.B.'s Club, in the bottom right corner of the *plateia*, facing inland. (☎26 669. €2.50 per hr. Open daily 9am-2am) Ferries from Argostoli go to Kyllini on the Peloponnese (30min., 1 per day, €13) and Lixouri, Kephalonia (20min., 2 per hr. until 10:30pm, €2).

On the northeastern coast, 24km from Argostoli, the hushed town of Sami is a major port and a great base from which to explore many nearby beaches. Two and four kilometers west, the striking Melissani Lake and Drogarati Cave, are respectively an underground pool of cold crystalline water and a large stalactite- and stalagmite-filled cavern. (Lake ☎26740 22 997; cave 26740 23 302. Lake open daily 9:30am-sunset; €6. Cave open 8:30am-sunset; €4.) Fiskardo, on the island's northern tip and one of its most beautiful towns, has Venetian architecture that escaped the devastating 1953 earthquake. Nearby ◪**Myrtos Beach,** 4km from the main-road turn off, is possibly the single best spot on the island, with brilliant white pebbles and clear blue water lapping against sheer cliffs. This popular beach offers wonderful swims, but beware of the strong underwater currents and keep close to shore. Argostoli presents the best accommodation options for visitors looking to explore Sami and Fiskardo. **Buses** leave the Sami station on the left end of the waterfront for Argostoli (45min., 4 per day M-Sa, €4). From the Fiskardo parking lot next to the church, uphill from town, buses leave for Argostoli (1½hr., 2 per day, €5) and Sami (1½hr., 2 per day, €4). **Postal Codes:** 28100 (Argostoli) and 28080 (Sami).

## ◪ITHAKA Ιθάκη ☎26740

Discovering Ithaka means uncovering 6000 years of history and traversing the homeland of legendary Odysseus. Surprisingly not as touristy as its neighboring islands, Ithaka is relaxing beyond imagination and truly suspended in time. **Vathy,** Ithaka's alluring capital, wraps around a circular bay filled with fishing boats and yachts, with precipitous green hillsides nudging up against the water. Small enough for streets to have no names, Vathy is a cluster of authentic-looking island houses, competing for sea views as they rise up the steep hillside surrounding the pleasant stone *plateia*. Ithaka's largest town, Vathy hints at how deserted the island really is. Taxis to nearby villages are available but very expensive; it's best to rent a car or a scooter. ◪**Sholi Omirou** (Homer's School) is one of three sites contending for recognition as **Odysseus's Palace.** From the village of **Stavros,** accessible by bus from Vathy (1hr., 2 per day, €2), follow the signs to a dirt road, which ends about 500m later in a footpath leading to the site. The **Cave of the Nymphs** is 2km outside Vathy on the road uphill to Stavros, though the site appears poorly maintained and deserted. The enchanting **Monastery of Panagia Katharon** perches on Ithaka's highest mountain, ◪**Mt. Neritos,** and has views of the surrounding islands and sea; take a moped or taxi (€25 round-trip) toward the town of Anoghi and follow the signs up the curvy road for about 20min. The monks ask visitors to close the front door to keep goats from wandering in and expect women to cover their legs while in the church. (Open sunrise-sunset. Free.) On the stunning white pebble beaches of ◪**Filiatro** and **Sarakiniko,** 3.5 and 2.5km out, respectively, the water glows in the sun and rocky ridges steeply drop to the sea. From Vathy, walk to the end of town with the water on your left and turn uphill before the last houses. Another beautiful beach is by the tiny **Piso Aetos** port.

　Cheap **domatia** trump tempting but pricey hotels. Clean, convenient **Aktaion Domatia ❸**, across from the ferry dock on the right side of the waterfront (facing inland), has a pleasant view of the bay. Rooms include A/C, bath, minifridge, and TV. (☎32 387. Summer singles €30; doubles €56. Winter €25/40. Negotiate for low-season discounts. Cash only.) For a light snack, stop by **Drakouli ❶**, an old white mansion-turned-cafe, with an artificial lake in the palm garden and a pool table inside. Walk with the water to your left away from the Vathy *plateia* until you see the sea-fed pool. Try their signature sundae for €7. (☎33 435. Coffee €2-3.20. Ice cream €2 per scoop. Sandwiches €2-3.50. Open daily 9am-midnight. Cash only.) With specialties including *moussaka* (eggplant, onion, tomato, and lamb casserole; €6), calamari (€6), and *stifado* (veal braised in red wine; €8), **Niko's Taverna ❷**, down the road from the National Bank, satiates the carnivorous palette. (☎32 039. Open Apr.-Nov. daily 7pm-2am. MC/V.) **Ferries** depart from Piso Aetos to Sami, Kephalonia (45min., 2 per day, €2.50) or from Vathy to Sami, Kephanlonia (1hr., 2 per day, €6) and Patras (3¾hr., 2 per day, €15). **Postal Code:** 28300.

## ◪ZAKYNTHOS Ζάκυνθος ☎26950

Known as the greenest Ionian Island, Zakynthos is home to thousands of species of plants and flowers as well as a large *Caretta caretta* (loggerhead sea turtles) population. **Zakynthos Town** maintains a romantic, nostalgic air. Boats from Zakynthos Town go to many of the island's spectacular sights, including the glowing, stalactite-filled **Blue Caves** on the northeastern shore past Skinari. Southwest of the Blue Caves is ▓**Smuggler's Wreck.** A shipwrecked boat's remains has made the beach one of the most photographed in the world. **Keri Caves** and **Marathonisi,** also called Turtle Island because of its resemblance to a turtle, lay farther south. Agencies giving tours of Zakynthos advertise along Lomvardou; most excursions leave around 9:30am, return at 5:30pm, and cost €16-25. For a more intimate travel experience, skip the huge cruise ships and hire a small fishing boat from the docks in northern villages. In July and August, Zakynthos' long beaches draw as many tourists as its caves. **Laganas** is one of the most popular destinations; nauseatingly crowded bars, restaurants, and clubs line the shore. Paradoxically, a 10min. walk down the beach (with the water on your right) will take you to the beautifully deserted sands of ▓**Kalamaki,** a turtle nesting site and protected **National Marine Park** (www.nmp-zak.org). Some of the most picturesque beaches, like **Gerakas,** on the island's southeastern tip, are inhabited at night by the turtles.

> The loggerhead turtles that share Zakynthos's shores with beachgoers are an **endangered species,** and their nesting ground should be respected. Let's Go encourages readers to embrace the "Leave No Trace" ethic (p. 33) when visiting the island's more secluded beaches.

**Athina Marouda Rooms for Rent ❶,** on Tzoulati and Koutouzi, has simple, clean rooms with fans and large windows, communal baths, and backpacker-friendly prices. (☎45 194. June-Sept. singles €15; doubles €30. Oct.-May €10/20. Cash only.) Dining in the *plateias* and by the waterfront is a treat. The oddly named **Village Inn ❸,** Lomvardou 20, at the right end of the waterfront before Pl. Solomou, offers no rooms and feels more like a bayou lounge than small town eatery but has tables facing the water. (☎26 991. Entrees €6-15. Th night live Greek music. Open daily 8am-midnight. MC/V.) Getting around the island can be frustrating—taxis can be terribly overpriced and tour operators may seem like glorified tourist babysitters. Dozens of places in town rent **scooters** (€15 per day), but driver's license requirements are strictly enforced. **Buses** go from the station, located two blocks away from the water, to Laganas (20min., 15 per day, €1.20) and Kalamaki (20min., 12 per day, €1.20). Buses also board ferries to the mainland and continue to Athens (6hr., 5 per day, €23), Patras (3hr., 3 per day, €7), and Thessaloniki (10hr., Su-Th 1 per day, €43). **Postal Code:** 29100.

# CYCLADES Κυκλάδες

Sun-drenched, winding stone streets, and trellis-covered *tavernas* define the Cycladic islands, but subtle quirks make each distinct. Orange-and-black sands coat Santorini's shoreline of Santorini, and celebrated archaeological sites testify to Delos's mythical and historical significance. Naxos and Paros offer travelers peaceful mountains and villages, while notorious party spots Ios and Mykonos uncork some of the world's wildest nightlife.

## ▓ MYKONOS Μύκονος                    ☎22890

Coveted by 18th-century pirates, Mykonos still attracts revelers and gluttons. Although Mykonos is a fundamentally chic, sophisticates' playground, you don't have to break the bank to have a good time. Ambling down **Mykonos Town's** colorful alleyways at dawn or dusk, surrounded by tourist-friendly pelicans, is the cheap-

GREECE

THE LOCAL STORY

## PETROS: PELICAN OF MYSTERY

Every summer, tourist-paparazzi swarm Mykonos Town, attempting to get a photo of the area's biggest celebrity in action—taking a stroll by the windmills or enjoying a seafood dinner in Little Venice.

The town superstar is a pelican named "Petros." In his standard pose, the pink-and-white bird can be hard to pick out against the town's white buildings—at least until he blinks his beady black eyes and extends his heavy wings and slender neck. Though he is constantly surrounded by admirers, Petros's main concern is scoring free fish; if you feed him, be prepared to be followed and "asked" for more.

But Petros's obsessive fish habit, typical of most pelicans, is no mask for the fact that he's not really Petros after all. The first pelican known as "Petros" lived here for over 30 years after being stranded by a storm in the 1950s and adopted by locals. Since his death, any pelican in Mykonos gets the royal treatment; there are currently two to three regulars.

Petros (or possibly the Petroses) has been sighted all over the northwestern city. To catch a glimpse, wander around the Paraportiani churches and the surrounding tavernas. Some maintain Petros has a sweet tooth and hangs near Mykonos's bakery. Look for a crowd of tourists wielding cameras and one overindulged, puffed-up pelican.

est, most exhilarating way to experience the island. Drinking and sunbathing are Mykonos's main forms of entertainment. While the island's beaches are nude, bathers' degree of bareness varies; in most places, people prefer to show off their designer bathing suits rather than their birthday suits. **Platis Yialos** and **Super Paradise** appeal to more brazen nudists, while **Elia** beach attracts a tamer crowd. The superfamous **Paradise** beach is so crowded with hungover Italians and overpriced sun beds that you can barely see its gorgeous water. Buses run south from Mykonos Town to Platis Yialos and Paradise (20min., 2 per hr., €1.20-1.50) and to Elia (30min., 8 per day, €1.10). The **Skandinavian Bar,** inland from the waterfront towards Little Venice, is a two-building party complex. (☎22 669. Beer €4-6. Mixed drinks from €8. Open daily 9pm-5am.) After drinking the night away, usher in a new day at ☒**Cavo Paradiso,** on Paradise beach. Considered one of the world's top dance clubs, it hosts internationally renowned DJs and inebriated crowds. Take the bus to Paradise beach and follow the signs; it's a 10min. walk. (☎27 205. Drinks from €10. Cover €25, after 2am €40; includes 1 drink. Open daily 3-11am.)

Like everything else on Mykonos, accommodations are prohibitively expensive. Camping is the best budget option. The popular **Paradise Beach Camping ❶,** 6km from Mykonos Town, has decent facilities, plenty of services, and is just steps away from the beach. (☎22 129; www.paradisemykonos.com. Free pickup at port or airport. Safes available. Breakfast included. Internet €4.50 per hr. €5-10 per person, €2.50-4 per small tent, €4.50-7 per large tent; 1- to 2-person cabin €15-50. 3-person tent rental €8-18.) At **Hotel Philippi ❹,** Kalogera 25, in Mykonos Town, rooms with A/C, bath, and fridge center around a bright garden. (☎22 294. Open Apr.-Oct. Singles €55-85; doubles €70-110; triples €84-132. AmEx/MC/V.) ☒**Kalidonios ❸,** Dilou 1, off Kalogera, serves a range of Greek and Mediterranean dishes in a cozy, colorful interior. (☎27 606. Entrees €8-15. Open daily noon-12:30am. MC/V. ) For a cheap meal, head to **Pasta Fresca ❶,** on Georgouli, near the Skandinavian Bar. Its streetside take-out window is a good place to grab the best gyros (€2) and chicken pitas (€2) that Mykonos has to offer. (☎22 563. Open daily 4pm-late.) **Ferries** run from the New Port, west of town, to Naxos (3hr., 1 per week, €9.50), Paros (3hr., 1 per day, €8.40), and Piraeus (6hr., 1 per day, €26). The **tourist police** are at the ferry landing. (☎22 482. Open daily 8am-9pm.) **Windmills Travel,** on Xenias, around the corner from South Station, has GLBT resources. (☎26 555; www.windmillstravel.com. Open daily 8am-10pm.) **Postal Code:** 84600.

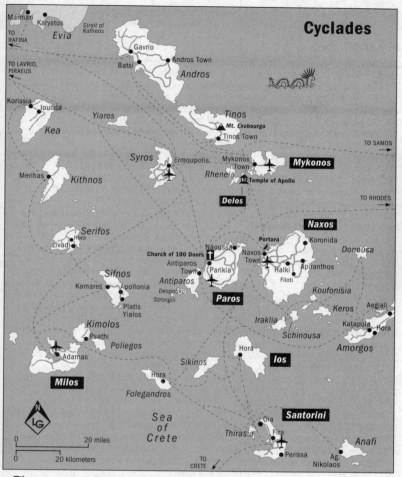

**Cyclades**

Marmari
Karystos
*Evia*
TO RAFINA
Strait of Kafireos
Gavrio
Andros Town
Batsi
*Andros*
TO LAVRIO, PIRAEUS
Korissia
Ioulida
*Yiaros*
*Tinos*
▲ Mt. Exobourgo
Tinos Town
TO SAMOS
*Kea*
Merihas
*Kithnos*
Syros
Ermoupolis
Mykonos Town
**Mykonos**
*Rheneia*
Ⅲ Temple of Apollo
**Delos**
TO RHODES
Serifos
Hora
Livadi
**Naxos**
Portara
Náoussa
Church of 100 Doors
Antiparos Town
Parikia
Naxos Town
Koronida
*Donoúsa*
Halki
Apiranthos
Filoti
Sifnos
Kamares
Apollonia
*Antiparos*
*Despotiko*
*Strongili*
**Paros**
*Koufonisia*
*Keros*
Aegiali
Platis Yialos
*Kimolos*
Psathi
*Iraklia*
Katapola
Hora
Schinousa
*Amorgos*
Adamas
*Poliegos*
*Sikinos*
Hora
**Ios**
**Milos**
Hora
*Folegandros*
N LG
0 ____ 20 miles
0 ____ 20 kilometers
*Sea of Crete*
Oia
**Santorini**
*Thirasia*
Fira
*Anafi*
Perissa
Ag. Nikolaos
TO CRETE

**GREECE**

◢ **DAYTRIP FROM MYKONOS:** ◤ **DELOS** ΔῆΛΟς. Delos was the ancient sacred center of the Cyclades. Though the island-wide archaeological site is expansive, its highlights can be seen in about 3hr. *(Open Tu-Su 8:30am-3pm. €5, students and EU seniors €3, EU students free.)* From the dock, head straight to the **Agora of the Competaliasts;** continue in the same direction and turn left onto the wide **Sacred Road** to reach the **Sanctuary of Apollo,** a group of temples that date from Mycenaean times to the 4th century BC. On the right is the biggest, most famous Delos structure, the **Temple of Apollo.** Continue 50m past the end of the Sacred Road to the beautiful **Terrace of the Lions.** The museum, next to the cafeteria, contains an assortment of archaeological finds. *(Open Tu-Su 8:30am-3pm. €5, students and seniors €3.)* From the museum, a path leads to the summit of **Mount Kythnos** (112m), from which Zeus supposedly watched Apollo's birth. Temples dedicated to Egyptian gods, including the **Temple of Isis,** line the descent. Excursion **boats** (30min.; 4 per day; round-trip €13, with tour €30) leave for Delos from Mykonos Town's Old Port, just past Little Venice. Buy tickets at Hellas or Blue Star Ferries on the waterfront.

# ◤ PAROS Πάρος ☎ 22840

A central transportation hub, Paros was once famed for its slabs of pure white marble, used for many of the great statues and buildings of the ancient world. Paros was a backpacker's haven in the 80s; currently, it's a favorite destination for families and older travelers, removed from the luxurious debauchery of Mykonos and the youth-filled streets of Ios. Behind the commercial surface of **Parikia,** Paros's port and largest city, flower-lined streets wind through archways to one of the world's most treasured Orthodox basilicas, the **Panagia Ekatontapiliani** (Church of Our Lady of 100 Doors). This white three-building complex is dedicated to St. Helen, mother of the Emperor Constantine, who reportedly had a vision of the True Cross here while traveling to the Holy Land. (Dress modestly. Open daily 7am-10pm. Mass M-Sa 7-7:30pm, Su 7-10am. Free.) About 8km north of town, **Naoussa** beach is the most popular and crowded destination on the island. On the opposite coast, **◩Aliki** beach is much quieter, but often windy.

Turn left at the dock and take a right after the cemetery ruins to reach the well-kept, cottage-like **Rena Rooms ❷.** (☎ 22 220; www.cycladesnet.gr/rena. Free pickup and luggage storage. Reserve ahead. Singles €15-35; doubles €20-40; triples €30-55. 20% *Let's Go* discount if paid in cash. MC/V.) The funky **◩Happy Green Cow ❸,** a block off the *plateia* behind the National Bank, serves delectable vegetarian dinners. (☎ 24 691. Entrees €12-15. Open Apr.-Nov. daily 7pm-midnight.) Touristy *tavernas* with Greek fare line the waterfront, but locals swear by family-run **Paros Taverna ❷,** 100m beyond *Panagia Ekatontapiliani,* which offers an affordable carnivore's feast. (☎ 24 397. Beef burgers €6.50. Grilled lamb chops €7. Vegetarian options. Open June-Sept. daily 1pm-1am.) At the far end of the Old Town's waterfront, 5min. past the port and bus station, Paros' nightlife pulses late into the night. A spacious central courtyard connects themed bar areas of **The Dubliner,** an Irish pub, **The Salsa Club,** a Latino bar, **The Scandi Bar,** complete with Scandinavian decor, and the **Paros Rock Cafe,** all decorated in bright colors and appropriate flags. This sweaty, pulsating party complex, which calls itself **The Parian Experience,** attempts to cater to every type of tourist. Follow the spotlight and crowds to the end of the harbor. (Beer €3-5. Mixed drinks €5-6. Cover €3; includes 1 drink.) **Ferries** go to: Folegandros (5hr., 3 per week, €9); Ios (3hr., 5 per week, €13); Mykonos (5hr., 5 per week, €7); Naxos (1hr., 2 per day, €7); Thessaloniki (19hr., 2 per week, €38). Ferry schedules fluctuate weekly; check with the budget-travel office **Polos Tours,** 50m to the right of the ferry dock gate, for departure times. (☎ 22 092; www.polostours.gr.) The **tourist police** are on the *plateia* behind the telephone office. (☎ 21 673. Open M-F 7am-2:30pm.) **Postal Code:** 84400.

# ◤ NAXOS Νάξος ☎ 22850

Ancient Greeks believed that Naxos (pop. 20,000), the largest of the Cyclades, was once home to Dionysus—the god of wine and revelry. Olive groves and wineries, small villages and chalky white ruins, silent monasteries and unadulterated hikes fill its interior, while sandy beaches line its shores. **Naxos Town,** its capital, is a dense collection of labyrinthine streets, bustling *tavernas,* and tiny museums, crowned by the **◩Kastro,** an inhabited Venetian fortress, tranquil despite the tourists. At the Kastro's entrance, the **Domus Della Rocca-Barozzi** (a.k.a. the Venetian Museum) exhibits photographs, books, and furniture belonging to a local aristocratic family still living there. The *domus* also features evening concerts with traditional Greek or classical music, dancing, and shadow theater, as well as complimentary tastings of local wines and spirits. (☎223 87; www.naxosisland.gr/ VenetianMuseum. Open daily in high season 10am-3pm and 7-11pm; low season 10am-3pm and 7-10pm. €5, students €3. Nightly summer concerts at 9:15pm. €10; reserve ahead at the museum reception.) The **Archaeological Museum** occupies the former Collège Français, where Nikos Kazantzakis, author of *The Last Temptation of Christ* and *Zorba the Greek*, studied. (Open Tu-Su 8am-5pm. €3, students €2.) The 6th-century BC ◪**Portara** archway, part of the **Temple of Apollo** complex, is visible from the waterfront, and is one of the few archaeological sites in Greece where children and travelers are allowed to climb on the ruins. (Open 24hr. Free.)

Accommodations in Naxos are available in private rooms and studios on the street between the town's center and the nearby Ag. Giorgios beach, or in campsites by the island's many beaches. Though most campgrounds vary little in price (generally €4-8 per person, €2-3 per tent), **Naxos Camping ❶** is the closest to Naxos Town (2km) and only 150m from **Ag. Giorgios** beach. (☎235 00. Prices vary seasonally.) To reach **Pension Irene II ❷**, in Naxos Town, take your first left after the police station on the road heading toward Ag. Giorgios and walk 100m. The recently renovated pension has A/C, a pool, and private verandas. (☎231 69; www.irenepension-naxos.com. Laundry €8. Singles €20; doubles €20-30; triples €25-35; 5-person apartments with kitchenettes €40-50.) Nearby **Heavens Cafe Bar ❷** serves scrumptious Belgian waffles with fresh fruit (€5) and offers an impressive selection of crepes with veggies and cheese for €4-5. (☎227 47. Internet €3 per hr.; free Wi-Fi. Open daily 8am-2am.) **Ferries** go from Naxos Town to: Crete (7hr., 1 per week, €21); Ios (1hr., 1 per day, €10); Mykonos (3hr., 1 per day, €9); Paros (1hr., 4 per day, €8); Piraeus (6hr., 4 per day, €28); Rhodes (13hr., 1 per week, €25); Santorini (3hr., 3 per day, €13). A bus goes from the port to the beaches of Ag. Giorgios, Ag. Prokopios, Ag. Anna, and Plaka (2 per hr. 7:30am-2am, €1.20). **Buses** (☎222 91) also run from Naxos Town to ◪**Apiranthos,** a beautiful village with narrow, marble paths (1hr., 5 per day, €2.30). To get to the **Tragea highland valley,** an enormous olive grove, take a bus from Naxos Town to Halki (30min., 7 per day, €1.20). The Naxos town **tourist office** is 300m up from the dock, next to the bus station. (☎229 93. Open daily 8am-11pm.) **Postal Code:** 84300.

# ◪IOS Ἴος                                               ☎22860

Despite recent concerted efforts to tone down its party-animal reputation, Ios remains the Greek debauchery heaven—or hell. Life on the island revolves around its insane and non-stop party scene: breakfast is served at 2pm, drinking begins at 3pm, people don't go out before midnight, and revelers dance madly in the streets until well after dawn. The **port** of Gialos is at one end of the island's sole paved road. The town of **Hora** sits above it on a hill, but most visitors spend their days at **Mylopotas beach,** a 25min. walk downhill from Hora or a short bus ride from town (3-6 per hr., €1.20). Establishments on the beach offer snorkeling, waterskiing, and windsurfing during the day (€9-45). Sunning is typically followed—or accompanied—by drinking; the afternoon bars are no less crowded than the nighttime ones. Head up from the *plateia* to reach the **Slammer Bar** for €3 tequila slammers. (☎91 019. Open daily 10pm-4:30am.) Next, stop by **Disco 69** for some dirty dancing. (☎91 064; www.disco69club.com. Beer €5. Cover €6 midnight-4am. Open daily 10pm-4am.) Get lost in the streetside **Red Bull** (☎91 019; beer €3; open daily 9pm-4:30am), dance on the tables at **Sweet Irish Dream** (beer €3; cover €5 2:30-4:30am; open 11am-4:30am), or grind to techno at **Scorpion Disco,** the island's largest club (cover €7 2-4:30am, includes a mixed drink and shot; open daily midnight-4:30am).

Most clubs close between 5 and 7am, when the drunkenness spills onto the streets. A few hours later, crowds begin to re-gather at the beach.

In addition to cheap dorms for hungover backpackers to crash in, ⊠**Francesco's** ❶ offers stunning sunset harbor views from its terrace. Take the steps up the hill to the left in the *plateia* and then the first left at the Diesel shop. (☎91 223; www.francescos.net. Breakfast 9am-2pm €2.50-5. Internet €1 per 15min. Reception 9am-2pm and 6-10pm. Check-out 11am. Dorms €11-18; 2- to 4-person rooms with A/C and bath €15-28 per person.) At the end of Mylopotas beach, **Far Out Beach Club and Camping** ❶ is a massive complex that has accommodations for any budget. In low season, the hotel rooms (€12) are a great value. (☎92 302; www.faroutclub.com. Laundry €3 per kg. Internet €1 per 15min. Check-out noon. Open Apr.-Oct. Tent sites €4-9, tent rental €1; cabins €5-12; 2- to 3-person bungalows €8-18; hotel rooms €12-35 per person.) Back in town, ⊠**Ali Baba's** ❷, next to Ios Gym, serves authentic Thai food. (☎91 558. Tempura €4-5. Entrees €6-12. Open Mar.-Oct. daily 6pm-1am.) Off the main church's *plateia*, **Old Byron's** ❸ is an intimate wine bar and bistro with creative renditions of Greek staples. (☎697 819 2212. Entrees €9-15. Reserve ahead. Open M-Sa 6-11:30pm, Su noon-11:30pm. MC/V.) Greek fast food and creperies pack the central *plateia*. **Ferries** go to: Naxos (1¾hr., 1-3 per day, €9); Paros (3hr., 1-3 per day, €10); Piraeus (8hr., 2-3 per day, €35); Santorini (1½hr., 3-5 per day, €7). **Postal Code:** 84001.

## ⊠ SANTORINI Σαντορίνη                                   ☎22860

Whitewashed towns sitting delicately on cliffs, black-sand beaches, and deeply scarred hills make Santorini's landscape nearly as dramatic as the volcanic cataclysm that created it. Despite the overabundance of expensive boutiques and glitzy souvenirs in touristy **Fira** (pop. 2500), the island's capital, nothing can ruin the pleasure of wandering the town's cobbled streets or browsing its craft shops. At Santorini's northern tip, the town of **Oia** (*EE-ah;* pop. 700) is the best place in Greece to watch the sunset, though its fame draws crowds hours in advance. To catch a glimpse of the sun, and not of someone taking a picture of it, walk down the hill from the village and settle alone near the many windmills and pebbled walls. To get to Oia, take a bus from Fira (25min., 23 per day, €1.20). Although every establishment in Oia makes you pay for the spectacular views, a romantic stroll along the gleaming paths should not be missed.

**Red Beach,** as well as the impressive archaeological excavation site of the Minoan city **Akrotiri**, entirely preserved by lava but currently closed for repairs, lie on Santorini's southwestern edge. Buses run to Akrotiri from Fira (30min., 15 per day, €1.60). Buses also leave Fira for the black-sand beaches of **Kamari** (20min., 32 per day, €1.20), **Perissa** (30min., 32 per day, €1.90), and **Perivolos** (20min., 21 per day, €1.90). The bus stops before Perissa in Pyrgos; from there, you can ⊠**hike** (2¼hr.) across a rocky mountain path to the ruins of **Ancient Thira**. Stop after 1hr. on a paved road at **Profitis Ilias Monastery**, whose lofty location provides an island panorama. (Open M and W 4-5pm, Sa 4:30-8:30pm. Dress modestly. Free.) Though frequent, Santorini's packed buses head only to the most popular destinations. With your own transportation, you can explore the many beautiful spots not serviced by bus. There are scooters, 4-wheelers, and car rentals seemingly every 20m, but all require a valid driver's license. (Scooters €12-15 per day; quads €18-20; cars €25-40.) Close to Perissa's beach, ⊠**Youth Hostel Anna** ❶ has colorful rooms and loads of backpackers hanging out on its streetside veranda. (☎82 182. Port pickup and drop-off included. Reception 9am-5pm and 7-10pm. Check-out 11:30am. Reserve ahead. June-Aug. 10-bed dorms €12; 4-bed dorms €15; doubles €50; triples €60. Sept.-May €6/8/22/30. MC/V.) Impeccable rooms, laundry service, and a roof-top bar with breakfast and a sunset Happy hour greet guests at the **Youth Hostel Oia** ❶.

(☎71 465. Breakfast included. Luggage storage and shower €1.50. Laundry €8 per 5kg. Reception 8am-10pm. Check-out 10am. Open May-Oct. Single-sex dorms €14-16.) Downhill from Fira, **Camping Santorini ❶** has hostel-like dorms. Look for the pink mini-bus when you get to the port. (Dorms €9.) At night, head to 🖤**Murphy's** in Fira, which claims to be Greece's first Irish pub. (Beer €5. Mixed drinks €6.50. Cover €5 after 10pm. Open Mar.-Oct. daily 11:30am-late.)

**Olympic Airways** (☎22 493) and **Aegean Airways** (☎28 500) fly from Fira's airport to Athens (50min., 4-7 per day, €85-120) and Thessaloniki (1¼hr., 1-2 per day, €125). **Ferries** depart from Fira to: Crete (4hr., 4 per week, €16); Ios (1hr., 1-3 per day, €7); Naxos (3hr., 1-2 per day, €16); Paros (4hr., 1-4 per day, €17); Piraeus (10hr., 2-3 per day, €33). Most ferries depart from Athinios Harbor. Frequent **buses** (25min., €1.70) with changing daily schedules connect to Fira, but most hostels and hotels offer shuttle service. Check bus and ferry schedules at any travel agency, and be aware that the self-proclaimed tourist offices at the port are actually for-profit agencies. **Postal Codes:** 84700 (Fira); 84702 (Oia).

## MILOS Μήλος                                                      ☎22870

Years of volcanic eruption, mineral deposits, and aquatic erosion have carved each Milonian beach into a small natural wonder. Dark, multicolored sand, cavernous rock formations, and steep, jutting cliffs characterize the island's unique coastline. Waders can navigate between the rocks at the canyon of 🖤**Papafragas,** near the Filokipi bus station, and marvel at years of graffiti engravings. Sunbathers lie near orange-and-red-striped sedimentary rock at **Provotas,** tiptoe across smooth, glacier-like rock at **Paleohori,** and stake out a spot at crowded **Hivadolimni.** Find hidden gems like **Tsigrados,** a glittering beach accessible only by private transport on tricky roads or on **kayak** excursions. **Buses** travel to most major shores (1 per 1-2hr., about €1). The tourist office and travel agencies arrange all-day **boat tours** (about €20; includes lunch stop in Kimolos). **Sea Kayak Milos** offers kayaking trips (☎21 365; www.seakayakgreece.com; trips €30-60), and **Milos Diving** (☎41 296; www.milosdiving.gr) provides a range of diving excursions for travelers. From **Adamas,** the port town, buses run to **Plaka** and **Trypiti** (15min., 1 per hr., €1.20), which has an **ancient theater,** the site where the Venus de Milo was found, and small, well-lit early Christian **catacombs** (☎21 625; open Tu-Su 8am-7pm; €1-2, Su free). **Camping Milos ❶** has a bar, pool, and cafeteria overlooking Hivadolimni beach, and a free shuttle to the port after the public bus stops running. (☎31 420. €5 per person, €4 per tent; 2-person bungalow with fridge and bath €50-70.) For an oceanside picnic or breakfast, grab some freshly baked goods and cheese at **Artemis Bakery ❶,** on the corner across from the Adamas's bus station. (Open daily 11am-6pm.) At dusk, the dozens of **waterfront tavernas** on Adamas's shoreline fill up with lively diners and the glow of hanging lanterns. **Ferries** from Adamas follow an ever-changing but, luckily, posted schedule. Sail to: Ios (1 per 1-2 days, €8); Naxos (1 per 1-2 days, from €8); Piraeus (7hr., 1 per day, €20); Santorini (1 per 1-2 days, €17); Serifos (2hr., 1 per day, €7); Sinfos (1hr., 1 per day, €6.30). The **tourist office** is across from the dock. (☎22 445; www.milos-island.gr. Free luggage storage. Open daily 10am-4pm and 6-11:30pm.) **Postal Code:** 84801.

# 🏔 CRETE Κρήτη

According to a Greek saying, a Cretan's first loyalty is to his island, his second to his country. Since 3000 BC, when Minoan civilization flourished on the island, Crete has maintained an identity distinct from the rest of Greece; pride in the island proves well-founded. Travelers will be drawn to Crete's warm hospitality, and enticing beaches, gorges, grottoes, monasteries, mosques, and villages.

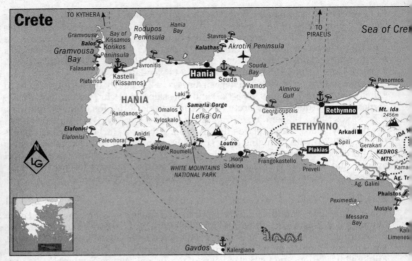

## IRAKLION Ηράκλειο ☎2810

Iraklion (pop. 130,000), Crete's capital and primary port, may not be particularly pretty but its importance as a transportation hub makes it a necessary stop on the way to Crete's more scenic destinations. **Olympic Airways** and **Aegean Airlines** fly domestically from the **Heraklion International Airport: Kazantzakis** (**HER;** ☎397 800; www.hcaa-eleng.gr/irak.htm) to Athens (50min., 5-6 per day, €75-115), Rhodes (1hr., 1-2 per week, €100-110), and Thessaloniki (1¾hr., 2 per day, €105-130). Budget airline **Wizz Air** also flies from Iraklion to Budapest, HUN (1¼-3hr., 1 per week, €270) and Katowice, POL (3¾hr., 1 per week, €280). From Terminal A, between the old city walls and the harbor, **buses** leave for Agios Nikolaos (1½hr., 23 per day, €6.20) and Hania (3hr., 16 per day, €12) via Rethymno (1½hr., €6.50). Buses leave across from Terminal B for Phaistos (1½hr., 10 per day, €5.10). **Ferries** also go to: Mykonos (8½hr., 2 per week, €25); Naxos (8hr., 3 per week, €22); Paros (7hr., 4 per week, €25); Santorini (4hr., 3 per week, €16). Check for travel delays online at **Netc@fé,** 1878 4. (€1.50 per hr. Open M-Sa 8:30am-8:30pm.)

Soothe away the burn of a missed flight with drinks or a borrowed book atop the quiet roof lounge at **Rent a Room Hellas ❶,** Handakos 24. Walk east along the waterfront and turn left on Handakos. (☎288 851. Free luggage storage. Checkout 11am. Dorms €11; doubles €25-31; triples €42.) The **open-air market** on 1866, near Pl. Venizelou, sells cheese, meat, and produce. (Open M-Sa 8am-9pm.) **Ouzeri Tou Terzaki ❷,** Loch. Marineli 17, in the center of town, serves fresh Greek meals with complimentary *raki* liquor and fruit. (☎221 444. Entrees €5-8. Open M-Sa noon-midnight. MC/V.) Those looking to kill time between connections should check out the **Tomb of Nikos Kazantzakis,** on top of the city walls. Even visitors unfamiliar with his most famous novel, *Zorba the Greek*, should make the climb to catch a spectacular sunset over Mt. Ida. **Postal Code:** 71001.

## KNOSSOS Κνωσός ☎2810

**Knossos,** Crete's most famous archaeological site, is a must-see. Excavations have revealed the remains of the largest and most complicated of Crete's **Minoan palaces.** It is difficult to differentiate between legend and fact at the palace of

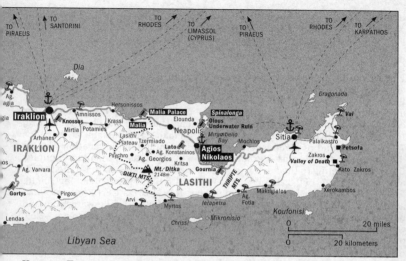

Knossos. Famous throughout history, the palace is the site of King Minos's machinations, the labyrinth with its monstrous son Minotaur, and the imprisonment—and winged escape—of Daedalus and Icarus. The first palace was built around 1700 BC, but was partially destroyed by fire around 1450 BC and subsequently forgotten. In the early 20th century, Sir Arthur Evans financed and supervised the excavations, restoring large parts of the palace. His work often crossed the line from preservation to tenuous interpretation, painting the palace's current form with controversy. Tourist crowds give the Minoan palace a Disneyland feel, but the sights are well worth navigating. Don't miss the **Queen's Bathroom,** where, over 3000 years ago, she took milk baths while gazing up at elaborate dolphin frescoes. Walking north from the royal quarters, you'll stumble across the grand **pithoi**—jars so big that, according to legend, Minos's son met a sticky demise by drowning in one filled with honey. (Open daily 8am-7:30pm. €6, students €3.) To reach Knossos from Iraklion, take **bus** #2 from Terminal A (20min., 2 per hr., €1.10).

## RETHYMNO Ρέθυμνο         ☎ 28310

Rich in history, Rethymno (pop. 20,000) today is brimming with tourists and locals navigating the city's many faces. Crete's numerous conquerors—Venetians, Ottomans, and even Nazis—have had a profound effect. Arabic inscriptions adorn the walls of the narrow streets, minarets highlight the skyline, and restless traffic marches through the Old Town's cobblestoned streets. The 16th-century ◼**Venetian Fortezza** looms over the harbor and the road running along the coast, and offers Rethymno's best views. Bring a picnic and walk along the fortress's sprawling white ruins. Replete with caves, chapels, and even a small outdoor amphitheater, the Fortezza provides hours of exploration. (Open daily 8am-8pm. €3.10, under 12 €2.60.) Walk east past Pl. Iroon (10min.) to reach **Ikarus Beach,** an unremarkable, but well-populated strip of fine sand and gentle waves. To get from the station to the **Rethymno Youth Hostel ❶,** Tombazi 41-45, walk down I. Gavriil and take the first left at Pl. Martiron; Tombazi is the second right. (☎ 22 848. Reception 8am-noon and 5-11pm. Dorms €9.) From the charming vine-draped entrance to the complimentary dessert of *raki* and honey-drizzled cheese pie, **Taverna Kyria Maria ❷,** Moskovitou 20, to the right down the small alley behind the Rimondi fountain, is one of the best bets in town. (☎29 078. Entrees €9. Open daily mid-Mar. to Oct. 10am-1am. MC/V.) **Buses** go to Hania (1hr., 17 per day, €6) and Iraklion (1½hr., 18 per day, €6.50). **Postal Code:** 74100.

## PLAKIAS Πλακιάς                                                    ☎28320

Plakias, on the hills south of Rethymno, exemplifies Crete's natural attractions: secluded beaches, steep gorges, and the southern coast's stunning hikes. **Plakias Beach,** with fine sand and large waves, starts about 100m east of the bus stop and stretches the rest of the length of the town; the sunbathers become less clothed as you move away from the bus station. (Umbrella and chair rental €5.) In a relaxing olive grove, the spectacular ▨**Plakias Youth Hostel ❶,** Mirthios 74060, is the kind of place where people come intending to vacation for two days but stay for months. Perhaps that's why, to date, six married couples trace their meeting to the hostel. (☎32 118; www.yhplakias.com. Kitchen available. Breakfast €1.50-3. Beer €1.15. Wine €1.50. Internet €0.60 per 10min. Reception 9am-noon and 5-8pm. Open Mar.-Nov. Dorms €8.) Find *souvlaki* and chips (€4.25) at **Nikos ❶,** off a street perpendicular to the waterfront and next to the post office. (☎31 921. Greek salad €2.75. Homemade ice cream €2.50. Open M and W-Su 5pm-midnight.) **Buses** drop off and pick up at the beach, and run to Preveli (30min., 1 per day, €1.50) and Rethymno (50min., 4 per day, €3.50). Rental **bikes** are available (€7-14) at **Easy Ride,** located behind Monza Travel (☎20 052. Open daily 9am-2pm and 6-10pm.) **Postal Code:** 74060.

## HANIA Χάνια                                                        ☎28210

Despite an avalanche of tourists, Hania (pop. 60,000), Crete's second largest city, still manages to remain low key. A day in Old Hania is easily spent people-watching from cafes or wandering along the waterfront. The **Venetian lighthouse** marks the entrance to the city's stunning architectural relic, the **Venetian Inner Harbor,** built by conquerors in the 13th century. From the fortress's ruins, sunset views over the open sea dazzle tourists. The inlet has retained its original breakwater and Venetian arsenal, though the Nazis destroyed much of it during WWII. Nestled away on the northwestern tip of Crete, the heavenly ▨**blue lagoon** of **Balos** is the island's uncontested best beach, where bright white sand, warm shallow water, and sky melt into one. The most popular excursion from Hania and Iraklion (p. 538) is the 5-6hr. hike down ▨**Samaria Gorge** (Φράγγι της Σαμαριάς), a spectacular 18km ravine extending through the White Mountains. Sculpted by 14 million years of rainwater, the gorge—Europe's longest—retains its beauty despite a somewhat disappointing manmade tourist attractions at its end and the overpriced boats and buses necessary to reach it (from Hania bus station 1hr., 4 per day, €6). Resting alongside the gorge's cold stream, watch golden eagles or endangered griffon vultures circle overhead while wild *agrimi* goats prance about. (Gorge open daily May to mid-Oct. 6am-3pm. €5, under 15 free.) For more info, call **Hania Forest Service** (☎92 287). The trail starts at **Xyloskalo;** take an early bus from Hania to Xyloskalo (1½hr., €6) for a day's worth of hiking. The 2pm bus from Hania will put you in **Omalos,** 5km from the gorge's entrance, where you can stay at one of two hotels, ready to set out hiking the next morning. The trail ends at **Agia Roumeli,** on the southern coast, where **boats** leave for Hora Sfakion (1hr., 4 per day, €5).

The only backpacker-friendly accommodation in Hania is central **Eftihis Rooms ❶,** 2 Tsouderon. From the bus station, walk toward the harbor on Halidon and turn right on Skrydlof, which becomes Tsouderon. (☎46 829. A/C. Singles €15; doubles €20; triples €30. Cash only.) Fresh food is available at the covered municipal **market,** connecting new and old Hania, while touristy *tavernas* also line the town. For Hania's best *bougatsa* (*mizithra*, or goat cheese, pastry; €2.40), check out ▧**Bougatsa Iorthanis ❶**, across from the municipal market at Apokronou 24. With Bougatsa, however, you snooze, you lose—specializing in one dish alone, the restaurant closes early. (☎88 855. Open Su-F 6am-2pm, Sa 6am-1pm.) Hania's nightlife buzzes along hopping **Sourmelis Street,** behind the mosque in the old harbor. **Ferries** arrive in the port of Souda, near Hania; buses connect from the port to Hania's municipal market (25min., €1). From Souda, ferries go to Piraeus (9½hr.; 2 per day; €30). **Buses** (☎93 052) leave from the corner of Kidonias and Kelaidi for the airport (25min., 3 per day), Iraklion (2½hr., 18 per day, €12), and Rethymno (1hr., 19 per day, €6). **Taxis** charge €16-18 to go to the airport. The **tourist office,** Kidonias 29, is next to the city hall. (☎36 155; www.chania.gr. Open M-F 8:30am-2:30pm; self-service M-F 8:30am-8pm, Sa 9am-2pm.) **Postal Code:** 73001.

## AGIOS NIKOLAOS Άγιος Νικόλαος     ☎28410

Catering to holiday-makers and hikers, Agios Nikolaos's harbor promenades, pedestrian streets, and open-air cafes provide a relaxing rest stop. A great hike runs through the cheerfully named **Valley of Death.** To get there, take the **bus** to Sitia (1½hr., 7 per day, €6) and then to the small village of Zakros (1hr., 3 per day, €3). To reach the unmarked ▧**Christodoulakis Pension ❷**, Stratigou Koraka 7, from the tourist office, turn away from the water, take a right up the stairs onto the street behind the taxi stand, and walk up the hill onto Stratigou Koraka. The friendly owners offer bright, airy rooms with a view of the harbor. (☎22 525. Singles €20; doubles €20-25; triples €30-40.) **Taverna Trata ❷**, on Akti Themistokleous, proves that not all waterfront property has to be expensive. Enjoy a hearty *stifado* (€6.50) and the sea breeze coming off of **Kitroplatia** beach without traumatizing your wallet. (☎22 028. Open daily 11:30am-midnight.) At night, ▧**Multiplace Peripou,** 28 Oktovriou 25, is a mellow, one-stop entertainment spot with a cafe, bar, Internet (€4 per hr.), and book- and music store for an international crowd. (Beer €3-5. Mixed drinks €5-7. Oct.-May Sa local artists and live music. Open daily 9:30am-2am.) **Ferries** sail to Rhodes (12hr., 1 per week, €26) and Piraeus (12hr., 2 per week, €34) via Milos (7hr., 2 per week, €21). To reach the **tourist office,** S. Koundourou 21A, cross the bridge at the harbor onto S. Koundourou. (☎22 357. Open Apr.-Nov. daily 8am-9:30pm.) **Postal Code:** 72100.

## ▶ DAYTRIPS FROM AGIOS NIKOLAOS

▧**SPINALONGA** (Σπιναλόγκα). This unassuming island houses some of the most intriguing history in Crete. Initially bought by the Venetians to host an impregnable fortress in 1204, it was surrendered in 1715 to Turkish invaders who later massacred the island's inhabitants. In 1903, the Cretans converted the island into a leper colony to frighten away Turkish settlers. It was Europe's last leper colony, finally closing in 1958. Enter through the grim **Dante's Tunnel,** formerly reserved for lepers, and explore the colony's **market street,** which ends at the **disinfecting room** where previous visitors to the island were required to sterilize all of their possessions before leaving for the mainland through a separate gate. Pay your respects to the saint of the sick at the **Church of Agios Pantalemonis,** where over 150 marriages took place during the island's stint as a leper colony, and spy the former eight-windowed **hospital,** located high on the hill to carry away the odor of rotting flesh. The far side of the island is barren, save for the **cemetery,** unmarked graves and the spare **Church of Agios Giorgios,** reserved for funerals. *(Open daily 9am-6pm. €2, EU students and children under 12 free.)* ▧**Nostos Tours** in Agios Nikolaos provides excellent guided boat and walking tours (1hr., €17),

GREECE

or catch a bus from Agios Nikolaos to Elounda (20min., 20 per day, €1.30) and then a ferry (Apr.-Oct. 1 per hr. 9:30am-4:30pm, €10) to Spinalonga.

**MALIA** (Μάλια). Malia's majestic ruins remind visitors that the town was once one of Minoan Crete's three great cities. Although Malia's **palace** lacks the breadth of Knossos and Phaistos, its importance as a center of Minoan power is undeniable. With six columns supporting its roof, the **Hall of Columns,** located on the northern side of the large central courtyard, is a must-see. The **Loggia,** a raised chamber on the western side, was used for state ceremonies; west of it are the palace's living quarters and archives. (☎28970 31 597. Open Tu-Su 8:30am-3pm. €4, students and seniors €2, under 19 and EU students free.) Follow the road from Agios Nikolaos toward Malia and turn right at the signs for the palace.

# EASTERN AEGEAN ISLANDS

Scattered along Turkey's coast, the islands of the **Dodecanese** are marked by a history of persistence in the face of countless invasions. The more isolated islands of the **Northeast Aegean** remain sheltered from creeping globalization. Cultural authenticity here is palpable—a traveler's welcome and reward.

## ◪RHODES Ρόδος ☎22410

Today, sun worshippers flock to Rhodes's welcoming shores, making the island the Dodecanese's undisputed capital. Rhodes's natural wonders dominate the island, with sandy beaches stretching along the east coast, jagged cliffs skirting the west, and green mountains dotted with villages filling the interior. The northern capital city of Rhodes, **Rhodes Town** amalgamates tourism and tradition. Constructed by the medieval Knights of St. John, Old Town's cobblestoned paths meander past souvenir shops and cater to sunburnt masses while clubs, bars, and beaches lie further to the north in the New Town. Rhodes is best known for a sight that no longer exists—the 33m **Colossus,** once one of the Seven Wonders of the Ancient World. At the top of the hill, a tall, square tower marks the entrance to the **Palace of the Grand Master,** which contains 300 rooms filled with intricate mosaic floorwork. (☎25 500. €6, students €3.) The beautiful halls and courtyards of the **Archaeological Museum,** which dominates the **Plateia Argiokastrou,** shelter the exquisite first century BC statue of Aphrodite Bathing. (☎25 500. Open Tu-Su 8:30am-3pm. €3, students €2.) On Rhodes's western shore, the ruins of **Kamiros** offer a glimpse of an ancient chessboard-patterned city. Daily **buses** run out of Rhodes Town. (☎40 037. €4, students €2.) North of Kamiros, **Petaloudes** (the Valley of Butterflies) attracts Jersey moths and nature-enthusiasts alike (☎81 801. Open Easter-Oct. €5.)

The vine-enclosed garden-bar of **Hotel Anastasia ❷,** 28 Oktovriou 46, complements bright pastel rooms. (☎28 007. Breakfast €4. Singles €35; doubles €50. V.) For cheap eateries, **Orfanidou** (popularly known as Bar St.) features venues with generic greasy food, while crepe stands (€2-5) line the streets of the Old Town. Nightlife in Rhodes's Old Town focuses around the street of **Militadou,** off Apelou. **Ferries** leave the eastern docks in Commercial Harbor, across from the Milon Gate into the Old Town. To: Halki (2½hr., 2 per week, €8); Kos (2½hr., 2 per day, €14); Patmos (7hr., daily, €22); Sitia, Crete (10hr., 2 per week, €25). The Rhodes Town **tourist office** is at the intersection of Makariou and Papagou. (☎44 333; www.ando.gr/eot. Open M-F 8am-2:45pm.) **Postal Code:** 8510.

## ◪KOS Κως ☎22420

Antiquity knew Kos as the sacred land of Asclepius, the god of healing, and the birthplace of Hippocrates, the father of modern medicine. Today a young crowd swarms **Kos Town,** exploring its umbrella-lined beaches and unkempt ruins during the day before hitting its energetic bar scene at night. More sedate travelers can escape to fields dotted by blue-roofed chapels or head to the ▨**Asclepeion,** 4km southwest of Kos Town—the location of Hippocrates's medical school, which opened in the 5th century BC. Summer trolleys run there from Kos Town. (Open Tu-Su 8am-7:30pm. €4, students €2.) The island's best **beaches**—all accessible by bus with stops made by request—stretch along southern Kos to Kardamena. For a steamy daytrip, hop on a ferry to the neighboring island of **Nisyros** (1½hr., 1 per week, €7.50) and trek into the sulphur-lined craters of ▨**Mandraki Volcano.** In Kos Town, take the first right off Megalou Alexandrou to get to **Pension Alexis ❷,** Irodotou 9, a beloved travel institution run by a mother and son eager to share insiders' tips on Kos. (☎28 798. Breakfast €5. Laundry €5. Singles €25; doubles €30-33; triples €39-45; quads €48-50.) Generous portions characterize **Taverna Hellas ❷,** Psaron 7, down the street from Pension Alexis at the corner of Amerikis. (☎30 322. Open daily 10am-3pm and 5pm-midnight.) Most bars radiate out from **Nafklirou (Bar Street),** circling **Place Iroön Politechniou** to continue along the beach. **Ferries** run to Kalymnos (1hr., 3 per week, €6), Piraeus (11-15hr., 1 per day, €44), and Rhodes (4hr., 1 per day, €14). The **tourist office** is at Vas. Georgiou B1. (☎24 460; www.hippocrates.gr. Open M-F 7:30am-3pm.) **Postal Code:** 85300.

## ▨ CHIOS Χίος ☎ 22710

With tree-speckled hills, Chios radiates natural charm. Traditional villages and sandy shores in the north give way to orange and lemon orchards in the south. The island's port city, **Chios Town** (pop. 30,000) has an electric pulse that doesn't pause for the wayward tourist. From mid-July through mid-September the open-air cinema in its public gardens shows nightly movies at 7 and 9pm. (Tickets €5; buy at cinema.) Take a green public **bus** from Chios Town south to **Mesta** (Μεστά; M-F 5 per day, €3.10). Founded in 1038, Mesta was designed to solve regional pirate problems. Residents constructed houses connected to one another, forming a fortification wall like that of a castle. Each house also had a ladder leading to the roof, enabling a quick escape and an incomplete staircase leading down, from which they could fend off raiders. Due to archaeological decree, all new houses must be built in the original style. On the same bus route from Chios Town (7 per day, €2.40), **Pyrgi** (Πυργί) is one of a string of villages (called *Mastichohoria*) that cultivate the lentisk trees responsible for Chios's famous resin used since antiquity in cosmetics, chewing gum, and medi-

## ON THE MENU

### THE IDIOT'S GUIDE TO DRINKING OUZO

When you go out for your first meal in Greece, don't be surprised, shocked, or flattered if your waiter rushes out before your entree arrives to present you with a shot glass of opaque liquor and the simple command, "Drink!" He's just assuming that you, like almost every Greek, want to cleanse your palate and ease your mind with some ouzo.

There's an art to enjoying the anise-flavored national drink, however, which is important to understand if you don't want to reveal yourself as a neophyte. First, don't go bottoms up. Good ouzo is around 40% alcohol by volume; it just isn't made to be chugged. It's invariably served with a glass of water for the purpose of mixing, which turns your shot milky-white. The key is to keep adding water as you drink to avoid dehydration and ill effects.

Second, snack on some *mezedes* while you take your ouzo. Nibbling on some cheese, a salad, or vegetables will temper the alcohol and prolong the experience. That's the point, after all: Greece's obsession with ouzo is not really focused on getting plastered on liquid licorice. Instead, it's about drinking lazily, relaxing in a *kafeneion,* and chatting with friends until the sun sets and dinner begins.

cines. For a haunting experience, head to **Anavatos** (Ανάβατος), an abandoned village built into the hillside. Anavatos's women and children threw themselves from its cliffs to protest the 1822 Turkish invasion. Most accommodations in Chios Town are on the waterfront, away from the from the ferry dock. Excellent harbor views make **Chios Rooms ❷**, Aigeou 110, a great place to stay. (☎20 198; www.chiosrooms.gr. Singles €25; doubles €35, with bath €40; triples with bath €45.) *Tavernas* can be found around **Pl. Vounakio.** *Ouzeri* **Paleo Petrino ❷**, Aigeou 80, on the waterfront, has traditional fare and local *ouzo*. (☎29 797. Entrees €5-7. Open daily noon-2am.) From Chios Airport (☎81 400), Olympic Airways **flies** to Athens (1hr., 2-5 per day, €65-83); Lesvos (30min., 2 per week, €40); Rhodes (1¾hr., 2 per week, €41); Thessaloniki (1-2hr., 4 per week, €60). **Ferries** sail to Athens (5-9hr., 1-2 per day €26-33) via Piraeus, Lesvos (1½-3hr., 1-2 per day, €14-19), and Thessaloniki (19hr., 1 per week, €31). The Chios Town **tourist office** is at Kanari 18. (☎44 344. Open May-Sept. M-F 7:30am-3pm and 6:30-9:30pm, Sa-Su 10am-1pm; Oct.-Apr. M-F 7:30am-2pm.) **Postal Code:** 82100.

## 🏛LESVOS Λέσβος                                                  ☎22510

Olive groves, remote monasteries, art colonies, and a petrified forest harmonize Lesvos, or Lesbos. Born on this island, the 7th-century lyrical poet Sappho collected a large female following. Due to her much-debated possible homosexuality, the word "lesbian"—once describing a native islander—developed its modern connotation. Visitors can gaze upon **Sappho's statue** at **Mytilini,** the island's capital and central port city, or walk on preserved mosaic floors excavated from the ancient villas in Ag. Kyriaki at the 🏛**Archaeological Museum,** 8 Noemvriou. (Open Tu-Su 8am-3pm. €3, students €2, EU students and under 18 free.) Only 4km south of Mytilini along El. Venizelou, the village of **Varia** is home to the **Musée Tériade,** which displays lithographs by Chagall, Matisse, Miró, and Picasso, and the **Theophilos Museum,** which features work by neo-Primitivist Theophilos Hadzimichali. (☎23 372. Musée Tériade open Tu-Su 9am-2pm and 5-8pm. Theophilos Museum open Tu-Su 10am-4pm. Each museum €2, students free.) **Local buses** (20min., 1 per hr.) leave Mytilini to Varia. Tell the driver you're going to the museums. **Molyvos,** a quintessential castle-crowned village, provides easy access to nearby **Eftalou's** hot springs and beaches. It can be reached by bus from Mytilini (2hr., 5 per day, €6). Farther south, the 20-million-year-old **petrified forest,** 18km from Sigri, is one of only two such forests worldwide. (Open daily May 15-Oct. 14 8am-8pm; Oct. 15-May 14 8am-4pm. €2.) Many of the petrified artifacts have been moved to Sigri at the 🏛**Natural History Museum of the Lesvos Petrified Forest.** (☎22530 54 434; www.petrifiedforest.gr. Open daily 8am-10pm. €5, students €2.50.) Doubles at Mytilini *domatia*—plentiful and well advertised—run €30-35 before July 15, and €35-50 during the high season. Enjoy *tabakas* (veal stewed with tomato, feta, and yogurt; €6) surrounded by canaries and hookahs outside at **Taverna Zoubouli ❷**, Vernardaki 2. (☎21 251. Entrees €4.50-7. Open daily noon-2am.) **Olympic and Aegean Airlines** fly out of the airport (☎61 590), 6km south of Mytilini, for: Athens (1hr., 6 per day, €50-150); Chios (25min., 2 per week, €31); Rhodes (1hr., 5 per week, €58); Samos (45min., 2 per week, €41). **Ferries** go from Mytilini to Chios (3hr., 1 per day, €14), Limnos (5hr., 3 per week, €17), and Thessaloniki (13hr., 1 per week, €35). **Zoumboulis Tours** (☎37 755) sells tickets. **Postal Code:** 81100.

## 🏛SAMOTHRAKI Σαμοθράκη                                          ☎22510

Samothraki (also called Samothrace) was once a pilgrimage site for Thracians who worshipped Anatolian gods. When the first colonists arrived in the 10th century BC, they saw the same vista still viewable from the ferry dock today: dry, grassy fields at the base of the Aegean's tallest peak, Fengari (1670m). **Kamariotissa,** Samothraki's port town, serves as a starting point for many excursions. From there, it is easy to get to the **Sanctuary of the Great Gods at Paleopolis,** where the famous *Winged Victory of Samothrace,* now a centerpiece in the Louvre, was found in 1863. (Open daily 8:30am-8:30pm. €3, students €2, EU students free.) Above the sanctuary rest the remains of the ancient Samothraki. **Therma,** a charming one-road village, has natural hot springs and hosts the trailhead for the 4hr. climb up Fengari. Unmarked waterfalls near Therma are also a worthwhile trip; check with the locals for hikes suiting your schedule and abilities. An easy but rewarding venture, **Fonias Waterfalls** has seven breathtaking cascades, the first three of which are reachable without a guide (2km, 1hr. to first waterfall). **Kaviros Hotel ❷,** to the left of the grocery store in Therma, has well-lit rooms with A/C, TV, and fridges. (☎98 277. Singles and doubles €30-40 depending on season.) **Sinatisi ❷,** a few doors down from the national bank in Kamariotissa, is a local favorite for fresh fish. (☎41 308. Open daily noon-5pm and 7pm-1am.) **Ferries** dock on the southern edge of Kamariotissa and run to: Alexandroupoli (3½hr.); Kavala (3½hr.); Lavrio via Psara (13hr.); Lesvos (7hr.); Limnos (3½hr.). **Postal Code:** 68002.

GREECE

# IRELAND

## REPUBLIC OF IRELAND

The green, rolling hills of Ireland, dotted with Celtic crosses, medieval monasteries, and Norman castles, have long inspired poets and musicians, from Yeats to U2. Today, the Emerald Isle's jagged coastal cliffs and untouched mountain ranges balance the country's thriving urban centers. Dublin pays tribute to the virtues of fine brews and the legacy of resisting British rule, while Galway offers a vibrant arts scene. In the past few decades, the computing and tourism industries have raised Ireland out of the economic doldrums, and current living standards are among the highest in Western Europe. Despite fears for the decline of traditional culture, the Irish language lives on in secluded areas known as the *gaeltacht*, and village pubs still echo with reels and jigs.

### 🌐 DISCOVER IRELAND: SUGGESTED ITINERARIES

**THREE DAYS.** Spend it all in **Dublin** (p. 557). Wander through **Trinity College,** admire the ancient **Book of Kells,** and sample the whiskey at the **Old Jameson Distillery.** Take a day to visit the **National Museums,** stopping to relax on **St. Stephen's Green,** and get smart at the **James Joyce Cultural Centre.** Work your pubbing potential by night in **Temple Bar** and on **Grafton Street.**

**ONE WEEK.** After visiting the sights and pubs of **Dublin** (3 days), enjoy the natural wonders of **Killarney** (1 day; p. 579) and the **Ring of Kerry** (1 day; p. 580). Return to the urban scene in the cultural center of **Galway** (2 days; p. 584).

**BEST OF IRELAND, THREE WEEKS.** Explore **Dublin** (4 days), then head to **Sligo** (3 days; p. 588) and visit the surrounding lakes and mountains. Continue on to **Galway** (3 days) and the **Aran Islands** (1 day; p. 587). After taking in the views from the **Cliffs of Moher** (1 day; p. 583), tour the scenic **Ring of Kerry** (2 days). Spend time in beautiful **Killarney** (2 days; p. 579) and the southernmost **Schull Peninsula** (1 day; p. 577) before hitting the big city of **Cork** (2 days; p. 573). On the way back to Dublin, stop by the beaches and crystal factory in Ireland's oldest city, **Waterford** (1 day, p. 571).

## LIFE AND TIMES

### HISTORY

**EARLY CHRISTIANS AND VIKINGS (AD 450-1200).** The pre-Christian inhabitants of Ireland left behind stone monuments such as **Newgrange,** the Neolithic tomb outside of present-day Dublin, and adopted the language and customs of **Celtic** groups from mainland Europe. Beginning with St. Patrick in the 5th century AD, a series of hopeful missionaries began piecemeal Christianization of the island. Vikings raided the Irish coast in the 9th century and established settlements and a ruling dynasty. After the **Dal Cais** clan defeated the Vikings in the epic **Battle of Clontarf** in 1014, Ireland was divided between competing chieftains **Rory O'Connor** and **Dermot MacMurrough**. MacMurrough unwisely sought the assistance

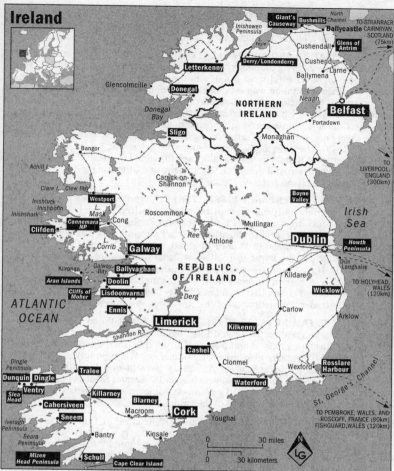

# Ireland

Giant's Causeway • Bushmills
North Channel
TO STRANRAER, CAIRNRYAN, SCOTLAND (75km)
Inishowen Peninsula
Ballycastle
Foyle
Cushendall • Glens of Antrim
Cushendun
Ballymena
Larne
Derry/Londonderry
Letterkenny
Glencolmcille •
Donegal
Donegal Bay
L. Neagh
Belfast
Portadown
NORTHERN IRELAND
Monaghan
Sligo
Bangor
Achill I.
Carrick-on-Shannon
Clare I. Clew Bay
Inishturk • Inishbofin • Inishshark
Westport
L. Mask
Cong
Connemara NP
Clifden
Roscommon
Boyne Valley
Irish Sea
L. Ree
Athlone
Mullingar
Dublin
Howth Peninsula
Galway
L. Corrib
REPUBLIC OF IRELAND
Dún Laoghaire
Galway Bay
Ballyvaghan
Kildare
Aran Islands
Kilronan
Doolin
Cliffs of Moher
Lisdoonvarna
L. Derg
Wicklow
TO HOLYHEAD, WALES (120km)
Ennis
Carlow
Arklow
ATLANTIC OCEAN
Limerick
Shannon R.
Kilkenny
Cashel
Clonmel
Wexford
Rosslare Harbour
St. George's Channel
Dingle Peninsula
Tralee
Dunquin • Dingle
Slea Head • Ventry
Killarney
Blarney
Macroom
Waterford
Youghal
Cahersiveen
Sneem
Cork
Iveragh Peninsula
Bantry
Kinsale
TO PEMBROKE, WALES, AND ROSCOFF, FRANCE (80km)
FISHGUARD, WALES (120km)
Beara Peninsula
Mizen Head Peninsula
Schull
Cape Clear Island

0    30 miles
0    30 kilometers

N

of the Norman earl, Richard de Clare, popularly known as **Strongbow,** who arrived from England in 1169 and cut a bloody swath through Leinster (eastern Ireland). After MacMurrough's death in 1171, Strongbow married MacMurrough's daughter Aoife and was ready to proclaim an independent Norman kingdom. Instead, the turncoat affirmed his loyalty to King Henry II and offered to govern Leinster on his behalf. Thus began English domination of Irish land.

**FEUDALISM (1200-1641).** The subsequent feudal period saw constant struggles between the English government, based in the area around Dublin known as the Pale, and the lords in other parts of the island who increasingly adopted Irish customs. When **Henry VIII** formed the Church of England in the 16th century, the Dublin Parliament passed the **Irish Supremacy Act** of 1537, which declared Henry VIII head of the Protestant Church of Ireland and effectively made the island property of the Crown. Ulster earl **Hugh O'Neill** raised an army of thousands in open rebellion during the **Nine Years War** of the late 1590s. His forces were demolished, and the rebels left Ireland in 1607 in what became known as the **Flight of the Earls,** leaving a power vacuum in the area.

**ULSTER PLANTATION AND CROMWELL (1641-1688).** The English embarked on a project of dispossessing Catholics of their land and "planting" Ulster with Protestants. The plan succeeded most notably in the province of Ulster in the north, where the **Ulster Plantation** was established. The landless Irish revolted in 1641, leading to the formation of the **Confederation of Kilkenny,** an uneasy alliance between lords of English and Irish descent who took power over two-thirds of Ireland. The Confederation entered into negotiations with England's King Charles I, but the talks ended when parliamentary forces ousted Charles in the **English Civil War** (1642-1649). The new English Commonwealth's despotic leader, **Oliver Cromwell,** led his army to Ireland in 1649 to take back the island from the Confederation. Cromwell's army destroyed everything in its path, and after the bloody conquest, the majority of Irish land fell to Protestant control.

**THE PROTESTANT ASCENDANCY (1688-1798).** Thirty years after the English Civil War, English political disruption again resulted in Irish bloodshed. Deposed Catholic monarch **James II,** driven from England by the **Glorious Revolution** of 1688, came to Ireland to gather military support. His war with **William of Orange,** the new Protestant king of England, ended with James's defeat and exile at the **Battle of the Boyne** in 1690. New **Penal Laws** enforced at the turn of the 18th century banned the practice of Catholicism in Ireland. The term "Ascendancy" was coined to describe the elite Anglicans who rose to prominence in Dublin and controlled Irish land. **Trinity College,** founded in 1592, came to be the quintessential institution of the Ascendancy Protestants.

**UNION AND THE FAMINE (1798-1870).** The 1800 **Act of Union** dissolved the Dublin Parliament, creating the United Kingdom of Great Britain and Ireland and the United Church of England and Ireland. During this time, the potato was the wonder-food of the rapidly growing Irish population. When potato blight wiped out the crop during the **Great Famine** (1845-1852), an estimated one million people died and a million more emigrated. Meanwhile, in 1858 **James Stephens** created the Irish Republican Brotherhood (IRB), commonly known as the **Fenians,** a secret society aimed at the violent removal of the British.

**CULTURAL NATIONALISM (1870-1914).** In 1870, Isaac Butt founded the **Irish Home Rule Party,** wanting to secure Ireland's autonomous rule. Meanwhile, various groups tried to revive a traditional Irish culture unpolluted by foreign influence. **Arthur Griffith** began the **Sinn Féin** (SHIN FAYN; translated as "ourselves alone") movement in 1905 advocating Irish abstention from British politics. Between 1910 and 1913, in opposition to this growing movement for independence, thousands of Protestants from the northern region joined a paramilitary organization named the **Ulster Volunteer Force (UVF).** Nationalists led by university professor **Eoin MacNeill** in Dublin responded by creating the **Irish Volunteers.**

**EASTER RISING (1914-1916).** In 1914, the British Parliament passed a **Home Rule Act** granting self-government to Ireland within the United Kingdom, but implementation was delayed as Britain fought **World War I.** Fenian leaders adopted the ideology of "blood sacrifice," believing that the deaths of martyrs would generate public support for Irish independence. Led by schoolteacher **Padraig (Patrick) Pearse,** the group planned to receive a shipment of German arms and use them in a nationwide revolt on Easter Sunday in 1916. The arms arrived too early and were never picked up, and Irish Volunteers leader MacNeill ordered his men to stay out of the revolt. Still, the operation was delayed only a day. On Monday, April 24, more than 1000 rebels seized the Dublin General Post Office on O'Connell St. (p. 561) and proclaimed an independent Irish Republic. This launched the **Easter Rising,** six days of fighting in which 450 people were killed. The British authorities put down the insurrection and executed 15 of the ringleaders, but the event swung public opinion in favor of the rebels and the anti-British movement.

**INDEPENDENCE AND CIVIL WAR (1917-1923).** Sinn Féin, incorrectly linked to the Easter Rising, rose to newfound fame in Ireland and won the 1918 elections under leader **Éamon de Valera.** The Irish Volunteers reorganized under Fenian bigwig **Michael Collins** and became known as the **Irish Republican Army (IRA),** Sinn Féin's military arm. De Valera proclaimed an Irish government and Parliament, and between 1919 and 1921 the IRA fought the guerilla-style **War of Independence** against the British. Hurried negotiations produced the **Anglo-Irish Treaty** in 1921, which created a 26-county **Irish Free State,** an independent republic whose members were required to take an oath of allegiance to the king. Sinn Féin, the IRA, and the population were split over whether to accept the Treaty. Although it also partitioned Northern Ireland, opposition to the treaty was focused on the oath. Collins said yes; de Valera disagreed. When the representative parliament voted in favor, de Valera resigned from the presidency and **Arthur Griffith** took office. In 1922, a portion of the IRA that opposed the Treaty, led by **General Rory O'Connor,** occupied the Four Courts (p. 566) in Dublin. The ensuing **civil war** lasted until the following year, when the pro-Treaty government emerged victorious.

**THE DE VALERA ERA (1923-1960).** In 1927, de Valera broke with Sinn Féin and the IRA and founded his own political party, **Fianna Fáil (Soldiers of Destiny).** The party won the 1932 election, and de Valera held power for much of the next 20 years. In 1937, voters approved the **Irish Constitution.** It declared the state's name to be **Éire** and established a government with a prime minister (Taoiseach; TISH-ek), a ceremonial president, and a two-chamber parliament. Ireland stayed neutral during **World War II,** known as **the Emergency** in Ireland, though many Irish citizens identified with the Allies and approximately 50,000 volunteered in the British army. In 1948, Taoiseach **John Costello** took the British by surprise when he declared to a reporter that the Irish Free State would leave the British Commonwealth and become the free **Republic of Ireland.** The UK recognized the Republic in 1949 but retains control over Northern Ireland, a region tied to the Crown since the settlement of Protestants in the Ulster Plantation.

**RECENT HISTORY (1960-2000).** Ireland's post-war boom didn't arrive until the early 1960s, and economic mismanagement and poor governmental policies kept it brief. In search of economic upturn, the Republic entered the European Economic Community (EEC), now the **European Union (EU),** in 1973. EEC funds were crucial in helping Ireland out of recession in the mid-80s and reducing its dependence on the UK. In 1990, the Republic broke social and political ground by electing its first female president, **Mary Robinson.** Social reform continued when the leftist **Labour Party** enjoyed unexpected success in the 1992 elections. The new Taoiseach, **Albert Reynolds,** declared that his priority was to stop violence in Northern Ireland. During the period known as **the Troubles** between the 1960s and 90s, periodic conflict broke out in Northern Ireland and the Republic between opposing paramilitary groups: the Catholic republican IRA and the Protestant loyalist UVF. In August 1994, Reynolds announced a cease-fire agreement between Nationalists and Unionists. In April 1998, the current Taoiseach **Bertie Ahern** helped to negotiate the **Belfast Agreement,** also known as the **Good Friday Accord,** under which the political parties would share power in the Northern Ireland Assembly. The following month, in the first island-wide election since 1918, 94% of voters in the Republic and 71% in Northern Ireland supported the enactment of the accord.

IRELAND

## TODAY

In 2001, the Irish populace voted against the **Nice Treaty,** an agreement that represented the first step in the process of adding Poland and 11 other eastern European nations to the EU. The result of the referendum caused quite a stir on the Continent. The government began a campaign to clarify the details of the treaty, as opinion polls found the Irish public pro-expansion but wary of the collapse of the union. The treaty eventually passed, and in May 2004, while Ireland held the presidency of the European Council, **Bertie Ahern** admitted the new countries.

In Northern Ireland, political squabbling at the negotiations table continued after the Good Friday Accord, punctuated by occasional violence in the streets. Britain suspended the Assembly in 2002 to take a more direct role in keeping the peace. After delayed elections finally took place in October 2003, the opposing parties began a series of meetings to discuss how to share power. On July 28, 2005, the IRA formally announced its **disarmament.** In May 2006, the Northern Ireland Assembly reconvened, but Ahern and British Prime Minister **Tony Blair** reserved the right to suspend the legislature again if parties did not participate peacefully in the government.

With EU funds, increased computer software development, and a thriving tourism industry, the Irish economy is flourishing. In the spring of 2006, Ireland had the highest per capita gross domestic product in the EU, and its educated workforce has lured foreign investment. The fast-growing nation has been nicknamed the **Celtic Tiger,** and its powerful roar has prompted the return of Irish expatriates and Irish-Americans from the US and the arrival of immigrants from Eastern Europe and other parts of the world.

## PEOPLE AND CULTURE

**CUSTOMS AND ETIQUETTE.** In Ireland, when the occasion warrants it, people form orderly lines, or queues, that are considered sacred. "Jumping the queue" will earn you disapproving stares and often verbal confrontations. Another easy way to anger the locals is to flip someone the **fingers.** Yes, fingers: the Irish flip both their middle finger and their index finger, forming a V shape. Flipping the birds is only insulting if your palm is facing inward. In addition, avoid jokes or references to leprechauns, Lucky Charms, pots of gold, and the "wee" people. Such comments will certainly not earn you friends at the local pub.

**LANGUAGE.** The English language came to Ireland with the Normans in the 12th century. Since then, it has become the island's primary language, but like many things British, the Irish have molded the language to make it their own. The Irish accent, or "lilt," differs throughout the country, but is particularly thick and guttural in the southern and western counties. In Dublin and in the North, expect clearer pronunciation and a sing-song style of conversing. Northern Irish accents also bear the mark of Scottish settlement.

Because English is overwhelmingly spoken in Ireland, the average traveler is often unaware of the strong legacy of the **Irish language.** The constitution of the Republic declares Irish the national language, and it is an official language of the EU. There are about 85,000 individuals who live in the Irish-speaking region, or **Gaeltacht** (GAYL-tacht), in the western part of the nation. Still, many households in this region no longer speak Irish fluently, and government studies suggest that the language may become extinct within several generations.

**RELIGION.** Over 92% of the population of the Republic of Ireland is Catholic, and the Church has been tightly woven into everyday life. Though divorce has been legal since 1995, the Republic remains solidly anti-abortion. Public schools have mandatory religion classes and Sunday Mass is a family event (often followed by a pint at the pub). Most of the nation's Protestants belong to the Anglican Church of Ireland; small Muslim, Jewish, and Buddhist populations can be found in the cities.

# THE ARTS

## LITERATURE

Irish bards (from the Irish *baird*), whose poetry told the stories of battles and kings, wrote the largest collection of European folklore. In the 17th century, wit and satire characterized the emerging modern Irish literature, especially in the biting works of **Jonathan Swift.** In addition to his masterpiece *Gulliver's Travels* (1726), Swift penned political essays decrying English cruelty to the Irish. While Dublin continued to breed talent over the following centuries, some gifted young writers like **Oscar Wilde** headed to London to make their names. Wilde wrote his best-known play, *The Importance of Being Earnest*, in 1895. Fellow playwright **George Bernard Shaw** also moved to London, where he became an active socialist and won the Nobel Prize for Literature in 1925.

Near the end of the 19th century, during the **Irish Literary Revival,** a crop of young Irish writers turned to their homeland for inspiration. The early poems of **William Butler Yeats** evoked the picturesque Ireland of a mythical past, earning him worldwide fame and a Nobel Prize in 1923. Other authors, including the nation's most famous expatriate, **James Joyce** (1882-1941), found Ireland too insular to suit their literary aspirations. Though Joyce spent most of his adult life in continental Europe, he still wrote about Ireland. In his first novel, *A Portrait of the Artist as a Young Man* (1916), protagonist Stephen Dedalus's experiences reflect Joyce's own youth in Dublin. Dedalus reappears in *Ulysses*, Joyce's revolutionary novel of 1922, loosely based on Homer's *Odyssey*. **Samuel Beckett's** world-famous plays from the mid-20th century, including *Waiting for Godot* and *Endgame*, convey a darkly comic, pessimistic vision. Beckett won the Nobel Prize in 1969 but refused to attend the ceremony because Joyce had never received the prize.

The grit of Ireland continues to provide fodder for new generations of writers. **Roddy Doyle** displays his trademark humor but also tackles serious themes in his works, including the *Barrytown* trilogy about family life in down-and-out Dublin and the Booker Prize-winning *Paddy Clarke Ha Ha Ha* (1993). **Frank McCourt** won the Pulitzer Prize in 1997 for *Angela's Ashes*, a memoir about his poverty-stricken childhood in Limerick, and continued his life story in *'Tis* (1999) and *Teacher Man* (2005). Not to be outdone, his brother **Malachy McCourt** published his own memoir, *A Monk Swimming* (1998). Dublin native **John Banville** has explored metaphysical themes in his award-winning novels such as *The Book of Evidence* (1989) and *The Sea* (2005). Other acclaimed modern Irish writers include **Dermot Healy, Patrick McCabe, John McGahern, Edna O'Brien,** and **William Trevor.** The most prominent living Irish poet, **Seamus Heaney,** grew up in rural County Derry in Northern Ireland and received the Nobel Prize in 1995. Heaney's works have directly addressed the violence in his homeland.

## MUSIC

Traditional Irish music, or **trad,** is an array of dance rhythms, cyclical melodies, and embellishments passed down through generations of musicians. Traditional musicians train by listening to and building on the work of others. A typical pub session will showcase a variety of styles, including reels, jigs, hornpipes, and slow airs. Beginning with the early recordings of the **Chieftains** and their mentor **Sean**

IRELAND

**O'Riada** in the 1960s, trad has been resurrected from near-extinction to become a national art form. In addition to the best-selling recording artists **Altan** and **De Danann**, some excellent trad groups include the **Bothy Band** and **Planxty** of the 1970s, and—more recently—**Nomos, Solas, Dervish,** and **Deanta.** For the best trad, head to a *fleadh* (FLAH), a festival at which musicians' scheduled sessions often spill over into nearby pubs. **Comhaltas Ceoltóirí Éireann** (☎ 01 280 0295; www.comhaltas.com), the national trad music association, organizes *fleadhs*.

Many of Ireland's most popular musical exports draw upon elements of traditional Irish music, including **Van Morrison, Sinéad O'Connor,** and **Enya.** The members of **U2** came together in Dublin in 1976 and have since catapulted to international superstardom. The band's 1983 song "Sunday Bloody Sunday" decried sectarian violence in Northern Ireland. Lead singer **Bono** has become a prominent advocate of humanitarian causes. Formed in 1984, **My Bloody Valentine** spearheaded "shoegazing" rock, a sound based on shimmery, textured guitar landscapes. Irish artists who achieved mainstream success in the 1990s include **The Corrs, The Cranberries,** and the teen groups **Boyzone** and **B*witched.**

### VISUAL ARTS

Hollywood discovered Ireland after John Ford's *The Quiet Man* (1952), giving an international audience their first view of the island's beauty through a stereotypical lens that Irish film has since struggled to change. Art-filmmakers like **Robert Flaherty,** who employed cinematic realism in his classic documentary *Man of Aran* (1934), have tried to capture a more accurate version of Ireland.

Beginning in the late 20th century, the government has encouraged a truly Irish film industry. Director **Jim Sheridan** helped kick off the cinematic renaissance with his universally acclaimed adaptation of Christy Brown's autobiography *My Left Foot* (1989). Sheridan also worked with Irish actor **Daniel Day-Lewis** in two films that compassionately examine the lives of Catholics and Protestants during the Troubles: *In the Name of the Father* (1993) and *The Boxer* (1997). Sheridan's more recent film *In America* (2002) is a personal tale of emigration and loss.

English director **John Boorman's** saga *The General* (1998) describes the rise and fall of notorious criminal Martin Cahill. The Ireland of fairy tales has been captured with exquisite cinematography in Mike Newell's *Into the West* (1992) and John Sayles's *The Secret of Roan Inish* (1994). Acclaimed Irish director **Neil Jordan** and actor **Liam Neeson** teamed up on *Michael Collins* (1996), chronicling the life of the Irish revolutionary, and *Breakfast on Pluto* (2005), based on Pat McCabe's novel about an Irish foster child. Dublin native **Colin Farrell,** who starred in the Irish gangster film *Ordinary Decent Criminal* (2000), has achieved Hollywood hunk status. The success of the darkly comic *I Went Down* (1997) demonstrates the growing overseas popularity of Irish independent film. *The Magdalene Sisters* (2002), which depicts three Irish women in a Catholic asylum, and *Adam and Paul* (2004), about Irish junkies, both won numerous awards at European film festivals. **Cillian Murphy** has captivated an international audience with his brooding characters in *28 Days Later* (2002), *Batman Begins* (2005), and *Redeye* (2005). He was recently praised for his role as an Irish revolutionary in Ken Loach's *The Wind that Shakes the Barley* (2006).

## HOLIDAYS AND FESTIVALS

**Holidays:** New Year's Day (Jan. 1); St. Patrick's Day (Mar. 17); Good Friday and Easter Monday (Mar. 21 and Mar. 24); and Christmas (Dec. 25). There are 4 bank holidays in the Republic and Northern Ireland, which will be observed on May 5, Jun. 2, Aug. 4, and Aug. 27 in 2008. Northern Ireland also observes Orangemen's Day (July 12).

**Festivals:** All of Ireland goes green for St. Patrick's Day (Mar. 17). On Bloomsday (June 16), Dublin celebrates James Joyce's *Ulysses*. In mid-July, the Galway Arts Festival offers theater, trad, rock, and film. Tralee crowns a lucky young lady "Rose of Tralee" at a festival in late August, and many return happy from the Lisdoonvarna Matchmaking Festival in the Burren in early September.

## ADDITIONAL RESOURCES

*A History of Ireland,* by Mike Cronin. Palgrave Macmillan (2001). Survey of Ireland's past that is brief enough for newcomers.

*Round Ireland With a Fridge,* by Tony Hawks. St. Martin's Press (2001). Recounts the comic adventures of a man who hitchhiked around Ireland with a kitchen appliance.

*Trinity,* by Leon Uris. Bantam (1977). Best-selling, readable historical fiction about Ireland's struggle for independence, from the 1840s to the Easter Rising.

# ESSENTIALS

### FACTS AND FIGURES

**Official Name:** Republic of Ireland.
**Capital:** Dublin.
**Major Cities:** Cork, Galway, Limerick.
**Population:** 4,109,000.

**Time Zone:** GMT.
**Languages:** English, Irish.
**Longest Place Name in Ireland:** Muckanaghederdauhaulia, in Galway County.

## WHEN TO GO

Ireland has a consistently cool, wet climate, with average temperatures ranging from around 4°C (39°F) in winter to 16°C (61°F) in summer. Travelers should bring raingear in any season. Don't be discouraged by cloudy, foggy mornings—the weather usually clears by noon. The southeastern coast is the driest and sunniest, while western Ireland is considerably wetter and cloudier. May and June offer the most sun; July and August are warmest. December and January have short, wet days, but temperatures rarely drop below freezing.

## DOCUMENTS AND FORMALITIES

**EMBASSIES AND CONSULATES.** Foreign embassies in Ireland are in Dublin (p. 557). Irish embassies abroad include: **Australia,** 20 Arkana St., Yarralumla, Canberra, ACT 2600 (☎06 273 3022; irishemb@cyberone.com.au); **Canada,** Ste. 1105, 130 Albert St., Ottawa, ON K1P 5G4 (☎613-233-6281; www.irishembassyottawa.com); **New Zealand,** Level 7, Citigroup Building, 23 Customs Street E., Auckland (☎09 977 2252; www.ireland.co.nz); **UK,** 17 Grosvenor Pl., London SW1X 7HR (☎020 72 35 21 71; www.ireland.embassyhomepage.com); **US,** 2234 Massachusetts Ave., NW, Washington, D.C., 20008 (☎202-462-3939; www.irelandemb.org).

**VISA AND ENTRY INFORMATION.** EU citizens do not need a visa. Citizens of Australia, Canada, New Zealand, and the US do not need a visa for stays of up to 90 days, beginning upon entry into any of the countries in the EU's freedom-of-movement zone. For more info, see p. 13. For stays longer than 90 days, non-EU citizens must register with the **Garda National Immigration Bureau,** 13-14 Burgh Quay, Dublin, 2 (☎01 666 9100; www.garda.ie/angarda/gnib.html).

IRELAND

# TOURIST SERVICES AND MONEY

| EMERGENCY | Ambulance, Fire, and Police: ☎999. Emergency: ☎112. |
|---|---|

**TOURIST OFFICES. Bord Fáilte** (Irish Tourist Board; ☎1850 23 03 30; www.ireland.ie) operates a nationwide network of offices. Most tourist offices book rooms for a small fee and a 10% deposit, but many hostels and B&Bs are not on the board's central list.

**MONEY.** The **euro (€)** has replaced the **Irish pound (£)** as the unit of currency in the Republic of Ireland. For more info, p. 16. Northern Ireland uses the **pound sterling (£).** For more info, see p. 135. As a general rule, it is cheaper to exchange money in Ireland than at home. If you stay in hostels and prepare your own food, expect to spend about €30 per person per day; a slightly more comfortable day (sleeping in B&Bs, eating one meal per day at a restaurant, going out at night) would cost €60. Most people working in restaurants do not expect a tip, unless the restaurant is targeted exclusively toward tourists. In that case, consider leaving 10-15%. Tipping is very uncommon for other services, such as taxis and hairdressers. In most cases, people are happy if you simply round up the bill to the nearest euro.

Ireland has a 21% **value added tax (VAT)**, a sales tax applied to most goods and services, excluding food, health services, and children's clothing. The prices listed in *Let's Go* include VAT. In the airport upon exiting the EU, non-EU citizens can claim a refund on the tax paid for goods purchased at participating stores. While there is no minimum purchase amount to qualify for a refund, purchases greater than €250 must be approved at the customs desk before the refund can be issued. For more info on qualifying for a VAT refund, see p. 18.

# TRANSPORTATION

**BY PLANE.** A popular carrier to Ireland is national airline **Aer Lingus** (☎081 836 5000, US 800-474-7424; www.aerlingus.com), with direct flights to London, Paris, and the US. **Ryanair** (☎081 830 3030; www.ryanair.com) offers low fares from Cork, Dublin, and Shannon to destinations across Europe. **British Airways** (Ireland ☎890 626 747, UK 0870 850 9850, US 800-247-9297; www.ba.com) flies into most major Irish airports daily.

**BY FERRY.** Ferries run between Britain and Ireland many times per day. Fares for adults generally range from €15 to 30, with additional fees for cars. **Irish Ferries** (Ireland ☎01 850 366 222, UK 8705 17 17 17, US 772-563-2856; www.irishferries.com) and **Stena Line** (☎01 204 7777; www.stenaline.com) typically offer discounts to students, seniors, families, and youth traveling alone. Ferries run from Dublin to Holyhead, BRI; from Cork to Roscoff, FRA (p. 570); and from Rosslare Harbour to Pembroke, Wales, Cherbourg, FRA, and Roscoff, FRA (p. 570).

**BY TRAIN. Iarnród Éireann** (Irish Rail; ☎01 850 366 222; www.irishrail.ie) is useful for travel to urban areas. The **Eurail Global pass** is accepted in the Republic but not in Northern Ireland. The **BritRail** pass does not cover travel in the Republic or in Northern Ireland, but the **BritRail+Ireland** pass (€345-550) offers five or 10 days of travel in a one-month period as well as ferry service between Britain and Ireland.

**BY BUS. Bus Éireann** (☎01 836 6111; www.buseireann.ie), Ireland's national bus company, operates Expressway buses that link larger cities as well as local buses that serve the countryside and smaller towns. One-way fares between cities generally range €5-25; student discounts are available. Bus Éireann offers the **Irish Rover** pass, which also covers the Ulsterbus service in Northern Ireland (3 of 8 consecutive days €73, under 16 €42; 8 of 15 days €165/90; 15 of 30 days €245/133). The **Emerald Card,** also available through Bus Éireann, offers unlimited travel on Expressway and other buses, Ulsterbus, Northern Ireland Railways, and local services (8 of 15 consecutive days €236, under 16 €118; 15 of 30 days €406/202).

Bus Éireann works in conjunction with ferry services and the bus company **Eurolines** (www.eurolines.com) to connect Ireland with Britain and the Continent. Eurolines passes for unlimited travel between major cities range €199-439. Discounts are available in the low season and for people under 26 or over 60. A major route runs between Dublin and Victoria Station in London; other stops include Birmingham, Bristol, Cardiff, Glasgow, and Liverpool, with services to Cork, Derry/Londonderry, Galway, Limerick, Tralee, and Waterford, among others.

**BY CAR.** Drivers in Ireland use the **left side** of the road. **Gasoline** (petrol) prices are high. Be particularly cautious at roundabouts—give way to traffic from the right. **Dan Dooley** (☎062 53103, UK 0800 282 189, US 800-331-9301; www.dandooley.com) and **Enterprise** (☎1 800 227 800, UK 0870 350 3000, US 800-261-7331; www.enterprise.com) will rent to drivers between 21 and 24, though such drivers must pay an additional daily surcharge. Fares are €85-200 per week (plus VAT), including insurance and unlimited mileage. If you plan to drive a car in Ireland for longer than 90 days, you must have an **International Driving Permit (IDP).** If you rent, lease, or borrow a car, you will need a **green card** or an **International Insurance Certificate** to certify that you have liability insurance that applies abroad. It is always significantly less expensive to reserve a car from the US than from within Europe.

**BY BIKE, FOOT, AND THUMB.** Ireland's countryside is well suited to **biking,** as many roads are not heavily traveled. Single-digit "N" roads are more trafficked and should be avoided. Ireland's mountains, fields, and hills make **walking** and **hiking** arduous joys. The **Wicklow Way,** a hiking trail in the mountains southeast of Dublin, has hostels within a day's walk of each other. Some locals caution against **hitchhiking** in County Dublin and the Midlands, where it is not very common. Let's Go does not recommend hitchhiking.

# KEEPING IN TOUCH

| PHONE CODES | **Country code: 353. International dialing prefix: 00.** For more info on how to place international calls, see **Inside Back Cover.** |
|---|---|

**EMAIL AND THE INTERNET.** Internet access is available in most cafes, hostels, and libraries. One hour of web time costs about €3-6, though discounts are often available with an ISIC. Find listings of Internet cafes at www.cybercafes.com.

**TELEPHONE.** Whenever possible, use a calling card for international phone calls, as long-distance rates for national phone services are often very high. Mobile phones are an increasingly popular and economical option, and carriers Vodafone and $O_2$ offer the best service. Direct-dial access numbers for calling out of Ireland include: **AT&T Direct** (☎800 550 000); **British Telecom** (☎800 550 144); **Canada Direct** (☎800 555 001); **MCI WorldPhone** (☎800 55 10 01); **Telecom New Zealand Direct** (☎800 55 00 64); **Telstra Australia** (☎800 55 00 61).

**MAIL.** Postcards and letters up to 50g cost €0.48 within Ireland and €0.75 to Europe and other international destinations. Airmail parcels take five to nine days between Ireland and North America. Dublin is the only place in the Republic with Postal Codes (p. 561). To receive mail in Ireland, have mail delivered **Poste Restante.** Mail will go to the main post office unless you specify a subsidiary by street address. Address mail to be held according to the following example: First name LAST NAME, *Poste Restante*, City, Ireland. Bring a passport to pick up your mail; there may be a small fee.

## ACCOMMODATIONS AND CAMPING

| IRELAND | ❶ | ❷ | ❸ | ❹ | ❺ |
|---|---|---|---|---|---|
| **ACCOMMODATIONS** | under €17 | €17-26 | €27-40 | €41-56 | over €56 |

A **hostel** bed will average €13-20. **An Óige** (an OYJ), the **HI** affiliate, operates 24 hostels countrywide. (☎ 01 830 4555; www.irelandyha.org. One-year membership €20, under 18 €10.) Many An Óige hostels are in remote areas or small villages and are designed to serve nature-seekers. They therefore do not offer the same social environment typical of other European hostels. Over 100 hostels in Ireland belong to **Independent Holiday Hostels** (**IHH**; ☎ 01 836 4700; www.hostels-ireland.com). Most IHH hostels have no lockout or curfew, accept all ages, require no membership card, and have a less institutional feel than their An Óige counterparts; all are Bord Fáilte-approved. In virtually every Irish town, **B&Bs** can provide a quiet, luxurious break from hostelling. Expect to pay €30-35 for singles and €45-60 for doubles. "Full Irish breakfasts" are often filling enough to last until dinner. **Camping** in Irish State Forests and National Parks is not allowed. Camping on public land is permissible only if there is no official campsite nearby. Sites cost €5-13. For more info, see www.camping-ireland.ie.

## FOOD AND DRINK

| IRELAND | ❶ | ❷ | ❸ | ❹ | ❺ |
|---|---|---|---|---|---|
| **FOOD** | under €6 | €6-10 | €11-15 | €16-20 | over €20 |

Food in Ireland can be expensive, but the basics are simple and filling. Find quick and greasy staples at **chippers** (fish and chips shops) and **takeaways.** Most pubs serve Irish stew, burgers, soup, and sandwiches. Cafes and restaurants have begun to offer more vegetarian options to complement the typical meat-based entrees. **Soda bread** is delicious, and Irish **cheddars** are addictive. **Guinness,** a rich, dark stout, is revered with a zeal usually reserved for the Holy Trinity. Known as "the dark stuff" or "the blonde in the black skirt," a proper pint has a head so thick that you can stand a match in it. **Irish whiskey,** which Queen Elizabeth once said was her only true Irish friend, is sweeter than its Scotch counterpart. "A big one" (a pint of Guinness) and "a small one" (a glass of whiskey) are often ordered alongside one another. Ordering at an Irish **pub** is not to be done willy-nilly. In a small group, one individual will usually approach the bar and buy a round of drinks for everyone. Once those drinks are downed, another individual will buy the next round. It's considered poor form to refuse someone's offer to buy you a drink. The legal age in Ireland to purchase alcohol is 18.

---

**TIP**

**ACT LIKE YOU OWN THE PLACE.** The Heritage Card, a VIP pass for anyone, provides admission year-round to 80 historical sites throughout the Republic. With individual admission costing up to €10, this card (€21, students €8) is well worth the investment, even if you only get to visit 2 or 3 sites. Cards can be purchased at most sites, all of which are managed by the Office for Public Works or the Department of the Environment, Heritage and Local Government. For more info, call ☎ 0164 76597, or visit www.heritageireland.ie.

# BEYOND TOURISM

To find opportunities that accommodate your interests and schedule, check with national agencies such as **Volunteering Ireland** (www.volunteeringireland.com). For more info on opportunities across Europe, see **Beyond Tourism**, p. 54.

**L'Arche Ireland,** "Seolta," Warrenhouse Rd., Baldoyle, Dublin, 13 (☎01 839 4356; www.larche.ie). Assistants can join residential communities in Cork, Dublin, or Kilkenny to live with, work with, and teach people with learning disabilities. Room, board, and small stipend provided. Commitment of 1-2yr. expected.

**Sustainable Land Use Company,** Doorian, Glenties, Co. Donegal (☎074 955 1286; www.donegalorganic.ie). Offers opportunities to assist with organic farming, forestry, habitat maintenance, and wildlife in the northern county of Donegal.

**Focus Ireland,** 9-12 High St., Dublin, 8 (☎01 881 5900; www.focusireland.ie). Advocacy and fundraising for the homeless in Dublin, Limerick, and Waterford.

# DUBLIN

☎01

In a country known for its rural landscapes, the international flavor and frenetic pace of Dublin stick out like the 120m spire in the city's heart. Ireland's capital since the Middle Ages, Dublin offers all the amenities of other world-class cities on a more manageable scale, with all buildings topping off at five stories. Prestigious Trinity College holds treasures of Ireland's past, while Temple Bar has become one of Europe's hottest nightspots. The city's musical, cultural, and drinkable attractions continue to draw droves of visitors.

## TRANSPORTATION

**Flights: Dublin Airport** (**DUB;** ☎814 1111; www.dublinairport.com). Dublin **buses** #41, 41B, and 41C run from the airport to Eden Quay in the city center (40-45min., 6 per hr., €1.80). **Airlink shuttle** (☎703 3139) runs nonstop to Busáras Central Bus Station and O'Connell St. (30-35min., 4 per hr., €6), and to Heuston Station (50min., €6). A **taxi** to the city center costs roughly €20-25.

**Trains: The Irish Rail Travel Centre,** 35 Lower Abbey St. (www.irishrail.ie), sells train tickets. Open M-F 9am-5pm. Info ☎836 6222 daily 8:30am-6pm.

**Pearse Station,** Pearse St. (☎286 000), is a departure point for **Dublin Area Rapid Transit (DART)** trains serving the suburbs and coast (4-6 per hr., €2-6.70).

**Connolly Station,** Amiens St. (☎703 2359), north of the Liffey and close to Busáras. Bus #20B heads south of the river, and the DART runs to Tara Station on the south quay. Trains to **Belfast** (2hr., 5-8 per day, €50) and **Sligo** (3hr., 3-4 per day, €34).

**Heuston Station** (☎703 3299), south of Victoria Quay and west of the city center (a 25min. walk from Trinity College). Buses #78 and 79 run to the city center. Trains to: **Cork** (3hr., 9 per day, €67); **Galway** (2¾hr., 8 per day, €67); **Limerick** (2½hr., 9 per day, €55); **Waterford** (2½hr., 4-5 per day, €30).

**Buses:** Intercity buses to Dublin arrive at **Busáras Central Bus Station,** Store St. (☎836 6111), next to Connolly Station. Buses to: **Belfast** (3hr., 6-7 per day, €20); **Derry/Londonderry** (4¼hr., 4-5 per day, €28); **Donegal** (4¼hr., 4-5 per day, €25); **Galway** (3½hr., 15 per day, €17); **Limerick** (3½hr., 13 per day, €21); **Rosslare** (3hr., 13 per day, €21); **Sligo** (4hr., 4-6 per day, €27); **Tralee** (6hr., 6 per day, €34). ISIC discount.

**Ferries:** Ferries depart for **Holyhead, BRI** at the **Dublin Port** (☎855 2296), and bus #53 runs from the port to Busáras station (1 per hr., €1.40). **Stena Line** ferries leave for Holyhead at the **Dún Laoghaire** ferry terminal (☎204 7777; www.stenaline.ie); from there DART trains run to the city center. Dublin Bus runs buses timed to fit the ferry schedules (€2.50).

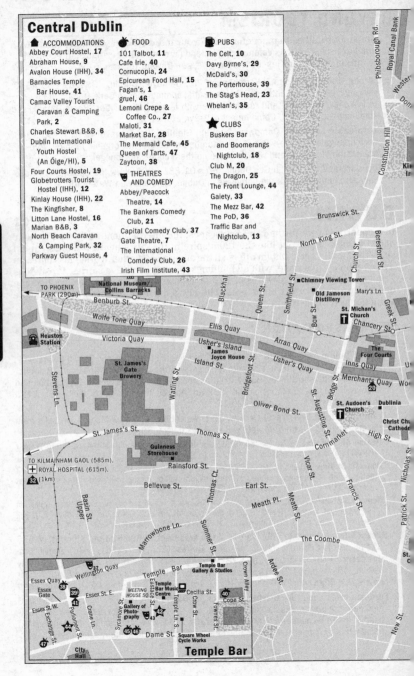

# Central Dublin

**ACCOMMODATIONS**
Abbey Court Hostel, **17**
Abraham House, **9**
Avalon House (IHH), **34**
Barnacles Temple
    Bar House, **41**
Camac Valley Tourist
    Caravan & Camping
    Park, **2**
Charles Stewart B&B, **6**
Dublin International
    Youth Hostel
    (An Óige/HI), **5**
Four Courts Hostel, **19**
Globetrotters Tourist
    Hostel (IHH), **12**
Kinlay House (IHH), **22**
The Kingfisher, **8**
Litton Lane Hostel, **16**
Marian B&B, **3**
North Beach Caravan
    & Camping Park, **32**
Parkway Guest House, **4**

**FOOD**
101 Talbot, **11**
Cafe Irie, **40**
Cornucopia, **24**
Epicurean Food Hall, **15**
Fagan's, **1**
gruel, **46**
Lemoni Crepe &
    Coffee Co., **27**
Maloti, **31**
Market Bar, **28**
The Mermaid Cafe, **45**
Queen of Tarts, **47**
Zaytoon, **38**

**THEATRES
AND COMEDY**
Abbey/Peacock
    Theatre, **14**
The Bankers Comedy
    Club, **21**
Capital Comedy Club, **37**
Gate Theatre, **7**
The International
    Comdedy Club, **26**
Irish Film Institute, **43**

**PUBS**
The Celt, **10**
Davy Byrne's, **29**
McDaid's, **30**
The Porterhouse, **39**
The Stag's Head, **23**
Whelan's, **35**

**CLUBS**
Buskers Bar
    and Boomerangs
    Nightclub, **18**
Club M, **20**
The Dragon, **25**
The Front Lounge, **44**
Gaiety, **33**
The Mezz Bar, **42**
The PoD, **36**
Traffic Bar and
    Nightclub, **13**

TO PHOENIX
PARK (290m)

National Museum/
Collins Barracks

Benburb St.

Wolfe Tone Quay

Victoria Quay

Heuston
Station

Stevens Ln.

St. James's
Gate
Brewery

Watling St.

St. James's St.

Guinness
Storehouse

Rainsford St.

TO KILMAINHAM GAOL (585m),
ROYAL HOSPITAL (615m),
**32** (1km)

Bellevue St.

Basin St.
Upper

Marrowbone Ln.

Thomas Ct.

Earl St.

Meath Pl.

Summer St.

Meath St.

Vicar St.

The Coombe

Francis St.

Blackhall

Queen St.

Smithfield

Ellis Quay

Usher's Island

James
Joyce House

Island St.

Bridgefoot St.

Oliver Bond St.

Thomas St.

Cornmarket

Bow St.

Arran Quay

Usher's Quay

St. Augustine St.

Bridg St.

Inns Quay

Merchants Quay

St. Audoen's
Church

High St.

Brunswick St.

North King St.

Church St.

Chimney Viewing Tower
Old Jameson
Distillery
Mary's Ln.
St. Michan's
Church
Chancery St.
Greek St.

Beresford St.

The
Four Courts

**20**

Dublinia

Christ Chu
Cathedra

Philsborough Rd.

Royal Canal Bank

Weste

Donn

Constitution Hill

Kil
In

Patrick St.

Nicholas St.

New St.

St.
C

Essex Quay
Wellington Quay
**37**
Essex Gate
Essex St. E.
Essex St.
**38**
**39**
**41**
Essex S.W.
Crane Ln.
Essex Exchange
Parliament St.
**44**
**47**
City
Hall
Sycamore St.
MEETING
HOUSE SQ.
Gallery of
Photo-
graphy
**45 46**
Temple Bar
Temple
Bar Music
Centre
Cecilia St.
Crow St.
Temple Ln. S.
**43 42**
Dame St.
Square Wheel
Cycle Works
Temple Bar
Gallery & Studios
Fownes St.
Cope St.
**40**
Crown Alley
Ardee St.

**Temple Bar**

IRELAND

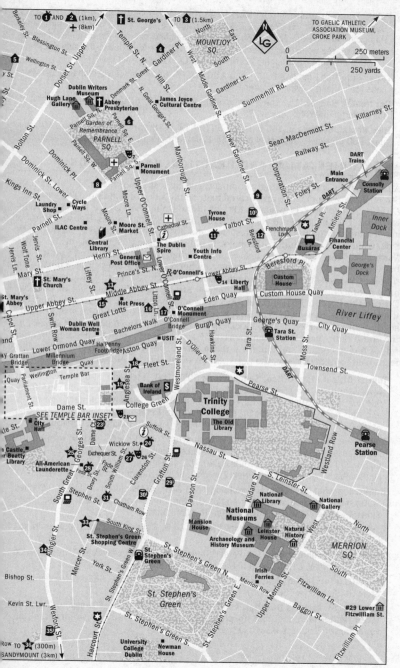

**Public Transportation:** Info on local bus service available at **Dublin Bus Office,** 59 Upper O'Connell St. (☎873 4222; www.dublinbus.ie). Open M 8:30am-5:30pm, Tu-F 9am-5:30pm, Sa 9am-2pm, Su 9:30am-2pm. **Rambler** passes offer unlimited rides for a day (€6) or a week (€21). Dublin Bus runs the **NiteLink** service to the suburbs (M-Th 12:30 and 2am, F-Sa 3 per hr. 12:30-4:30am; €4-6; passes not valid).

**Taxis: Blue Cabs** (☎802 2222) and **ABC** (☎285 5444) have wheelchair-accessible cabs (call ahead). Available 24hr.

**Car Rental: Budget,** 151 Lower Drumcondra Rd. (☎837 9611; www.budget.ie), and at the airport. From €40 per day. 23+.

**Bike Rental: Cycleways,** 185-6 Parnell St. (☎873 4748; www.cycleways.com). €20 per day, €80 per week. Open M-W and F-Sa 10am-6pm, Th 10am-8pm, Su 11am-5pm.

# ■ ⚡ ORIENTATION AND PRACTICAL INFORMATION

Although Dublin is refreshingly compact, getting lost is not much of a challenge. Street signs, when posted, are located high on the sides of buildings. The essential *Dublin Visitor Map* is available for free at the Dublin Bus Office and at the tourist office. The **Liffey River** divides Dublin's North and South Sides. Heuston Station and the more famous sights, posh stores, and upscale restaurants are on the **South Side,** while Connolly Station, the majority of hostels, and the bus station are on the **North Side.** The North Side is less expensive than the more touristed South Side, but it also has the reputation of being rougher, especially after dark. The streets running alongside the Liffey are called **quays** (pronounced "keys"); the name of the quay changes with every bridge. **O'Connell Street,** three blocks west of Busáras Central Bus Station, is the primary link between northern and southern Dublin. On the North Side, **Henry** and **Mary Streets** make up a pedestrian shopping zone, intersecting with O'Connell St. two blocks from the Liffey at the **General Post Office.** On the South Side, one block from the river, **Fleet Street** becomes **Temple Bar,** an area full of music centers and galleries. **Dame Street** runs parallel to Temple Bar and leads east to **Trinity College,** the nerve center of Dublin's cultural activity.

**Tourist Office: Main Office,** Suffolk St. (☎605 7700, international 0800 039 7000; www.visitdublin.com). Near Trinity College in a converted church. Open M-Sa 9am-5:30pm, Su 10:30am-3pm. July-Aug. open until 7pm. Reservation desks for buses and tour bookings close 30min. earlier. **Northern Ireland Tourist Board,** 16 Nassau St. (☎679 1977 or 1850 230 230). Open M-F 9:15am-5:30pm, Sa 10am-5pm.

**Embassies: Australia,** Fitzwilton House, Wilton Terr., 7th fl. (☎664 5300; www.australianembassy.ie); **Canada,** 65-68 St. Stephen's Green (☎417 4100); **UK,** 29 Merrion Rd. (☎205 3700; www.britishembassy.ie); **US,** 42 Elgin Rd. (☎668 8777; http://dublin.usembassy.gov). Citizens of **New Zealand** should contact their embassy in London.

**Banks:** Branches with **currency exchange** and 24hr. **ATMs** cluster on Lower O'Connell St. on the North Side of the river and on Grafton, Suffolk, and Dame St. on the South Side. Most open M-W and F 10am-4pm, Th 10am-5pm.

**Luggage Storage: Connolly Station.** Lockers €4-6. Open daily 7am-10pm. **Busáras.** Lockers €6-10. Open 24hr.

**Laundromat: Laundry Shop,** 191 Parnell St. (☎872 3541). Full service €10; self-service €8.80. Detergent €1.10. Open M-F 9am-7pm, Sa 9am-6pm.

**Police (Garda):** Dublin Metro Headquarters, Harcourt St. (☎666 6666; www.garda.ie); Store St. Station (☎666 8000); Fitzgibbon St. Station (☎666 8400).

**Hospitals: St. James's Hospital,** James's St. (☎410 3000; www.stjames.ie). Take bus #123. **Mater Misericordiae Hospital,** Eccles St. (☎803 2000; www.mater.ie), off Lower Dorset St. Buses #3, 10, 11, 16, 22, and 121.

# Experience Europe by Eurail!

It's not just the Best Way to See Europe, it's also the cleanest, greenest and smartest

*enjoy*

*experience*

*explore*

If you believe the journey's as important as the destination then rail's clearly the best way to experience the real Europe. Fast, sleek trains get you where you want to go when you want to go and - mile for mile - do less damage to the environment than cars or planes. Even better, you don't have to navigate unfamiliar roads, pay for gas (it's not cheap in Europe!) or find parking - leaving you more time and money to spend simply enjoying your travel.

Eurail has created a range of passes to suit every conceivable itinerary and budget. So whether you want to discover the whole continent, or focus on just one or two countries, you'll find Eurail the smartest way to do Europe, all around.

Welcome to Europe by Eurail!

*The best way to see Europe*

**Internet Access:** Free 50min. sessions and Wi-Fi are available to members at the **Central Library,** Henry and Moore St. (☎873 4333). Membership free with ID. **Global Internet Cafe,** 8 Lower O'Connell St. (☎878 0295; www.globalcafe.ie) and its partner **Central Cyber Cafe,** 6 Grafton St. (☎677 8298; www.centralcafe.ie), offer Internet. €3-4.50 per hr., students €2.70-4. Wi-Fi €2 per hr. or €10 for 8hr. in a 7-day period.

**Post Office: General Post Office,** O'Connell St. (☎705 7000). Open M-Sa 8am-8pm. Smaller post offices (Rathmines Post Office, 4 Upper Rathmines Rd.; Dun Laoghaire, Upper Georges St.) open M-Tu and Th-F 9am-6pm, W 9:30am-6pm. **Postal Codes:** The city is organized into regions numbered 1-18, 20, 22, and 24, with odd-numbered codes for areas north of the Liffey and even-numbered ones to the south. The numbers radiate out from the center of the city: North City Centre is 1, South City Centre 2. Dublin is the only city in the Republic with Postal Codes.

# ACCOMMODATIONS

Reserve at least a week ahead, especially in summer and on holidays. **Hostels** range €15-30 per night. Quality **B&Bs** are plentiful and charge €30-60 per person.

## HOSTELS

Some of Dublin's hostels tend toward the institutional. The beds south of the river fill up fast and tend to be expensive. Still, for travelers who plan to stay out late in Temple Bar, picking a hostel close by will make the stumble home much easier.

■ **Avalon House (IHH),** 55 Aungier St. (☎475 0001; www.avalon-house.ie). Turn off Dame St. onto S. Great Georges St. and walk 5min. An entertainment mecca with air hockey, foosball, ping-pong, and video games. Breakfast included. Lockers €1 per day. Laundry €5. Free Internet and Wi-Fi. Check-in 2pm. Check-out 10am. Dorms €14-27; singles €30-39; doubles €66-74. 10% discount for 1st night's stay with ISIC. AmEx/MC/V. ❶

■ **Globetrotters Tourist Hostel (IHH),** 46-7 Lower Gardiner St. (☎873 5893). Right near Busáras station and perfect for late-night arrivals. Finely decorated common areas and exceptionally clean rooms. Breakfast included. Towels €1, €5 deposit. Free Internet, luggage storage, and parking. Reserve at least 1 month ahead in summer. Dorms €20-23; singles €60-66; doubles €104-110; triples €114-126; quads €127. ❸

**Kinlay House (IHH),** 2-12 Lord Edward St. (☎679 6644). Great location a few blocks from Temple Bar. Well-run hostel with views of Christ Church Cathedral. Breakfast included. Lockers €1, deposit €5. Laundry €8. Free Internet. 16- to 24-bed dorms €17-20; 4- to 6-bed €24-29; singles €44-56; doubles €29-33; triples €27-33. ❷

**Abraham House,** 82-3 Lower Gardiner St. (☎855 0600). Take a left off Lower Abbey St. Staff is dependable for service, advice, and a laugh. Large dorms with bath. Comfortable private bedrooms sleep up to 4 and have TVs. Light breakfast included. Free luggage storage. Security box €1 per day, €5 deposit. Free Wi-Fi. 20- and 10-bed dorms €10-29; 8- and 6-bed €18-25; 4-bed €23-33; private rooms €80. ❷

**Barnacles Temple Bar House,** 19 Temple Ln. (☎671 6277; www.barnacles.ie). Unbeatable location near Temple Bar. Very clean. Kitchen and TV lounge. Continental breakfast included. Luggage storage available. Internet €1 per 15min. Reception 24hr. Check-out 10:30am. Dorms €16-26; doubles €68-82. MC/V. ❷

**Litton Lane Hostel,** 2-4 Litton Ln. (☎872 8389; www.littonlane.hostel.com), off Bachelor's Walk. Former studio for the likes of U2, Van Morrison, and Sinéad O'Connor. Free luggage storage. Free Wi-Fi. Key deposit €1. Dorms €20-22; doubles €80. ❷

**Abbey Court Hostel,** 29 Bachelor's Walk (☎878 0700; www.abbey-court.com), near O'Connell St. Clean, narrow rooms overlook the Liffey. Breakfast included. Free luggage storage; safe deposit box €1. Laundry €8. Internet €1 per 15min., €2 per 40min.

Check-in 2:30pm. Check-out 10:30am. Reserve 3 weeks ahead for weekends. Dorms €19-30; doubles €76-88. Discount for extended stays. MC/V. ❷

**Four Courts Hostel,** 15-17 Merchants Quay (☎672 5839), on the South Side, directly across from Four Courts. Bus #748 from the airport stops next door. Spacious, spotless rooms. Kitchen, pool table, TV room. Breakfast included. Free luggage storage. Safes and towels €1.50 each. Laundry €7.50. Internet €1 per 15min., €2 per 40min. Check-in 3:30pm. Check-out 10:30am. Dorms €17-27; doubles €62-70; triples €90. In winter, discounted weekly stays €99. MC/V. ❷

**An Óige (HI),** 61 Mountjoy St. (☎830 1766; www.anoige.ie). Take bus 16A or 41 from the airport to the Dorset St. stop. All rooms are large, bright, and single-sex. Kitchen and game room. Continental breakfast included; Irish breakfast €4. Lockers €1.25, bring your own lock. Laundry €2.50. Internet €1 per 15min. Check-in 11am. Check-out 10am. Dorms €19-22; singles €30-35; doubles €48-52; triples €72-78; quads €86-100. €2 HI discount. AmEx/MC/V. ❷

## BED AND BREAKFASTS

B&Bs with a green shamrock sign out front are registered and approved by Bord Fáilte. On the North Side, B&Bs cluster along Upper and Lower Gardiner St., on Sheriff St., and near Parnell Sq. All prices include a full Irish breakfast.

**Parkway Guest House,** 5 Gardiner Pl. (☎874 0469; www.parkway-guesthouse.com), 5min. walk from O'Connell St. Run by a cheery hurling veteran who offers advice on the city's restaurants and pubs. Singles €40; doubles €60-70, with bath €65-80. ❸

**Charles Stewart B&B,** 5-6 Parnell Sq. E (☎878 0350; www.charlesstewart.ie), close to the Dublin Writers' Museum. Dark wood furniture and large windows create an air of old-fashioned elegance. TV room with leather armchairs. Luggage storage. Check-in 2:30pm. Check-out 10:30am. Singles €57-63; doubles €75-99; triples €120-130. Discounts for online booking. ❺

**The Kingfisher,** 166 Parnell St. (☎872 8732; www.kingfisherdublin.com). Clean, modern rooms and attached restaurant. Check-in 1pm. Check-out noon. Rooms €35-60. 10% discount for stays longer than 5 days. AmEx/MC/V. ❸

**Marian B&B,** 21 Upper Gardiner St. (☎874 4129). The McElroys provide comfortable, well-decorated rooms near Mountjoy Sq. Reserve 2 weeks ahead in summer. Singles €35-45; doubles €70-90. MC/V. ❸

## CAMPING

Most official campsites are far away from the city center. While it may seem convenient, camping in **Phoenix Park** is both illegal and unsafe.

**North Beach Caravan and Camping Park** (☎843 7131; www.northbeach.ie), in Rush. Accessible by bus #33 from Eden Quay (45min., 25 per day), and by suburban rail. Open Apr.-Sept. €9 per person, €5 per child. Electricity €3. Showers €2. ❶

**Camac Valley Tourist Caravan and Camping Park,** Naas Rd. (☎464 0644; www.camacvalley.com), in Clondalkin near Corkagh Park. Take bus #69 (45min. from Aston Quay; dir.: Kingswood Cross) and ask to be let off at Camac. €10 per person, €22 per 2 people with car or camper, €26 per caravan. Electricity €4. Showers €1. ❶

## 🍴 FOOD

Fresh, cheap fixings are available at Dublin's many **open-air markets,** including the cozy market held on Sundays in Market Sq. in the heart of Temple Bar. On the North Side, Henry St., off O'Connell St., hosts a large market with fruit and flowers (M-Sa 7:30am-6pm). The **Epicurean Food Hall,** accessible from Lower Liffey St. and Middle Abbey St., offers fare from nearly every corner of the globe. (Most shops open M-W 9am-8pm, Th 9am-9pm, F-Su 9am-7pm.) The cheapest **supermarket** chain is **Tesco;** stores are located throughout the city.

☒ **Queen of Tarts,** Dame St. (☎670 7499), across from Dublin Castle. This little shop offers scrumptious homemade pastries, cakes, soups, and sandwiches. Go early for the apple crumble before it sells out. Breakfast €4-8. Flaky chocolate and raspberry scones with fresh cream €3. Open M-F 7:30am-6pm, Sa 9am-6pm, Su 9:30am-6pm. ❷

☒ **Market Bar,** Fade St. (613 9094; www.tapas.ie). Right off South Great Georges after Lower Stephen St. Old sausage factory now serves tasty tapas. Classy, high-ceilinged house usually packed to gills for fish pie. Small tapas €7.50. Large tapas €11. Food served M-W noon-9:30pm, Th noon-10pm, F-Sa noon-10:30pm, Su 3pm-9:30pm. ❸

**Cornucopia,** 19 Wicklow St. (☎677 7583). If there's space, sit down in this cozy, popular spot for a delicious and filling meal (€11-12) or a cheaper but equally tasty salad smorgasbord (€3-8 for choice of 2, 4, or 6 salads). Open M-W and F-Sa 8:30am-8pm, Th 8:30am-9pm, Su noon-7pm. ❷

**101 Talbot,** 101 Talbot St. (☎874 5011), between Marlborough and Gardiner St. Excellent Italian-Mediterranean food aimed at theater-goers. Large windows look onto busy Talbot St. below. Menu changes often but always has vegetarian specialties. Reserve ahead. Early bird 5-8pm €21. Entrees €14-20. Open Tu-Sa 5-11pm. ❹

**Fagan's,** Lower Drumcondra R. (836 9491), just before Botanic Ave. Attractive indoor and outdoor seating meets gorgeous food to produce beautiful evening in friendly pub. Worth the trek from the city or a must-stop for anyone staying in the north. Carvery €11. Entrees €10-15. Food served daily 12:30-3pm and 4-9pm. ❸

**Cafe Irie,** 11 Fownes St., off Temple Bar, on the left above the clothing store Sé Sí Progressive. Small, hidden eatery has bright Jamaican decorations and an impressive selection of heaping sandwiches (€5-6). Vegan- and vegetarian-friendly. Tomato, pesto, and mozzarella *panini* is especially good. Open daily 9am-9pm. Cash only. ❶

**Zaytoon,** 14-15 Parliament St. (☎677 3595). Coveted kebabs served into the wee hours. Excellent mixed *döner* meal (lamb and chicken) €9. Open daily noon-4am. ❷

**gruel,** 68 Dame St. (☎670 7119). Offers a selection of meat and organic vegetarian options, including the unique summer vegetable stew with goat cheese. Entrees €6-14. Open M-Sa 9am-8pm, Su 11:30am-8pm. Cash only. ❸

**The Mermaid Cafe,** 69-70 Dame St. (☎670 8236; www.mermaid.ie), near Great Georges St. Sophisticated entrees such as calf liver and duck breast €20-29. Open M-F 12:30-2:30pm and 6-10:30pm, Sa 12:30-2:30pm and 6-11pm, Su 12:30-3:30pm and 6-9pm. Reserve ahead on weekends. AmEx/MC/V. ❺

**Maloti,** 34-35 S. William St. (☎671 0428). Authentic Indian food with artistic style and presentation. Great lunch specials. 1-course €6, 2-course €8.50. Open M-Th noon-2:30pm and 5:30-11:30pm, F-Sa noon-2:30pm and 5:30-midnight, Su 1-11pm. ❶

**Lemon Crepe & Coffee Co.,** 66 S. William St. (☎672 9044). Squeeze into this tiny, trendy joint for crepes made on the spot. Chill at one of the streetside tables, or order take out. Savory and sweet crepes big enough to share €5-8. Vegetarian-friendly. Open M-W 8am-7:30pm, Th 8am-9pm, F-Sa 9am-7:30pm, Su 10am-6:30pm. ❶

# ⊙ SIGHTS

Most of Dublin's sights lie less than 2km from **O'Connell Bridge.** The two-hour **Historical Walking Tour,** led by Trinity College graduates, stops at many of them. Meet at the College's main gate. (Info 17 St. Mary's Pl., ☎087 688 9412; www.historicalinsights.ie. Tours May-Sept. daily 11am and 3pm; Apr. and Oct. daily 11am; Nov.-Mar. F-Su 11am. €12, students €10.) You can hop on and off **City Tour** buses that stop at major sights with guides that sing along the way (24hr. pass €14).

**TRINITY COLLEGE AND GRAFTON STREET.** The British built **Trinity College** in 1592 as a Protestant seminary that would "civilize the Irish and cure them of Popery." The Catholic Church still deemed it a cardinal sin to attend Trinity until the 1960s, so until then it served as an Oxbridge safety school. Today, Trinity is one of Ireland's most prestigious universities and a not-to-be-missed stop on a tour of Dublin. *(Between Westmoreland and Grafton St., on the South Side. The main entrance fronts the roundabout now called College Green. ☎608 1724; www.tcd.ie. Grounds always open. Free.)* Trinity's **Old Library** holds a collection of ancient manuscripts including the renowned **Book of Kells.** Upstairs, the **Long Room** contains Ireland's oldest harp—the **Brian Ború Harp,** pictured on Irish coins—and one of the few remaining copies of the original **1916 Proclamation** of the Republic of Ireland. *(On the south side of Library Sq. ☎608 2320; www.tcd.ie/library. Open May-Sept. M-Sa 9:30am-5pm, Su 9:30am-4:30pm; Oct.-Apr. M-Sa 9:30am-5pm, Su noon-4:30pm. €8, students €7.)* The blocks south of College Green are off-limits to cars, making the area a pedestrian playground. Performers on Grafton St. keep crowds entertained, while stores happily collect their money.

**KILDARE STREET.** Just southeast of Trinity College, the museums on Kildare St. offer scientific and artistic wonders. The ⚅**Natural History Museum** displays fascinating examples of taxidermy, including enormous Irish deer skeletons. Though the museum closed in 2007 for lengthy renovations, it is sure to regain its beloved status when it finally reopens in 2009. The **National Gallery's** extensive collection includes canvases by Brueghel, Caravaggio, Goya, Rembrandt, and Vermeer. *(Merrion Sq. W. Open M-W and F-Sa 9:30am-5:30pm, Th 9:30am-8:30pm, Su noon-5:30pm. Free.)* **Leinster House,** the former home of the Duke of Leinster, today provides chambers for the **Irish Parliament,** including the **Dáil** (DOIL) and the less powerful **Seanad** (SHAN-ad). The **National Museum of Archaeology and History,** Dublin's largest museum, has artifacts spanning the last two millennia, including the **Tara Brooch** and the bloody vest of nationalist **James Connolly.** *(Kildare St., next to Leinster House. ☎677 7444. Open Tu-Sa 10am-5pm, Su 2-5pm. Free.)*

**TEMPLE BAR.** West of Trinity College, between Dame St. and the Liffey, the narrow cobblestone streets and lively central square of Temple Bar contain cafes, hotels, and some of the best pubs and clubs in Dublin. But it's not just a place to throw back a pint; the government-sponsored Temple Bar Properties spent over €40 million to build a fleet of arts-related attractions. **The Irish Film Institute** screens specialty and art-house films. *(6 Eustace St. ☎679 5744; www.irishfilm.ie. Open M-F 10am-6pm.)* Ireland's **National Photographic Archive** includes extensive historical collections and holds special exhibitions. *(Meeting House Sq. ☎603 0374; www.nli.ie. Open M-F 10am-5pm and Sa 10am-2pm.)* The **Temple Bar Music Centre** hosts shows by local and international performers. *(Curved St. ☎670 9202; www.tbmc.ie.)*

**DAME STREET AND THE CATHEDRALS.** King John built **Dublin Castle** in 1204, and for the next 700 years it would be the seat of British rule in Ireland. Since 1938, each president of Ireland has been inaugurated here. *(Dame St., at the intersection of Parliament and Castle St. Open M-F 10am-4:45pm, Sa-Su 2-4:45pm. €4.50, students €3.50. Grounds free.)* At the **Chester Beatty Library,** behind Dublin Castle, visitors can see the treasures bequeathed to Ireland by American mining magnate Alfred Chester Beatty, including Asian art, illustrated Qur'an and Bible texts, and ancient Egyptian love poems on papyrus. *(☎407 0750; www.cbl.ie. Open May-Sept. M-F 10am-5pm, Sa 11am-5pm, Su 1-5pm; Oct.-Apr. closed M. Free.)* Across from the castle sits the historic **Christ Church Cathedral.** Sitric Silkenbeard, King of the Dublin Norsemen, built a wooden church on the site around 1038; Strongbow rebuilt it in stone in 1169. Fragments of the ancient pillars are now scattered about like bleached bones. *(At the end of Dame St. Take bus #50 from Eden Quay or 78A from Aston Quay. ☎677 8099. Open daily 9:45am-5pm, except during services. €5, students €2.50.)* Deriving its name from an ancient Latin term for Dublin, ▧**Dublinia** is an engaging three-story interactive exhibit recounting the city's history, with a focus on the Vikings and the medieval period. Try on ancient armor, smell spices, and see rune stones. *(Across from Christ Church Cathedral.* ☎ *679 4611; www.dublinia.ie. Open Apr.-Sept. daily 10am-5pm; Oct.-Mar. M-F 11am-4pm, Sa-Su 10am-4pm. Last entry 45min. before closing. €6.30, students €5.30.)* **St. Patrick's Cathedral,** Ireland's largest, dates to the 12th century, although Sir Benjamin Guinness remodeled much of it in 1864. Jonathan Swift spent his last years as Dean of St. Patrick's; his grave is marked on the floor of the south nave. *(Patrick St.* ☎ *475 4817; www.stpatrickscathedral.ie. Open Mar.-Oct. daily 9am-6pm; Nov.-Feb. Sa 9am-5pm, Su 10am-3pm. €5, students €4.)* **St. Audoen's Church,** Dublin's oldest parish church, is also worth a visit. *(High St.* ☎ *677 0088. Open June-Sept. daily 9:30am-4:45pm, except during Su services. €2.10, students €1.30.)* The 1215 **St. Audoen's Arch** is the only surviving gate from Dublin's medieval city walls.

**GUINNESS BREWERY AND KILMAINHAM.** Guinness brews its black magic at the St. James's Gate Brewery, right next door to the ▧**Guinness Storehouse.** Walk through the quirky seven-story atrium containing Arthur Guinness's 9000-year lease on the original brewery. Then drink, thirsty traveler, drink. *(St. James's Gate. From Christ Church Cathedral, follow High St. west through its name changes: Cornmarket, Thomas, and St. James. Or, take bus #51B or 78A from Aston Quay or #123 from O'Connell St. Open daily July-Aug. 9:30am-8pm; Sept.-June 9am-5pm. €14, students over 18 €9.50.)* Almost all the rebels who fought in Ireland's struggle for independence from 1792 to 1921 spent time at **Kilmainham Gaol,** located 600m west of the Guinness Storehouse. Guided tours of the jail wind through the eerie limestone corridors. *(Inchicore Rd. Take bus #51B, 51C, 78A, or 79 from Aston Quay.* ☎ *453 5984. Tours 2 per hr. Open Apr.-Sept. daily 9:30am-5pm; Oct.-Mar. M-F 9:30am-4pm, Su 10am-5pm. €5.30, students €2.10.)*

**O'CONNELL STREET AND PARNELL SQUARE.** Once Europe's widest street, O'Connell St. on the North Side now holds the less prestigious distinction of being Dublin's biggest shopping thoroughfare. Statues of Irish leaders **Daniel O'Connell, Charles Parnell,** and **James Larkin** adorn the traffic islands. The **General Post Office** on O'Connell St. was the center of the 1916 Easter Rising. Schoolteacher Padraig Pearse read the Proclamation of Irish Independence from its steps, and a number of bullet nicks are still visible today. *(☎ 705 7000. Open M-Sa 8am-8pm.)* Don't look too hard for **Nelson's Pillar**—this free-standing pillar commemorating Trafalgar was blown up by the IRA in 1966 on the 50th anniversary of the Easter Rising. The city's rich literary heritage comes to life at the **Dublin Writers' Museum,** which displays rare editions, manuscripts, and memorabilia of Beckett, Joyce, Wilde, Yeats, and other famous Irish writers. *(18 Parnell Sq. N.* ☎ *872 1302; www.writersmuseum.com. Open June-Aug. M-F 10am-6pm, Sa 10am-5pm, Su 11am-5pm; Sept.-May M-Sa 10am-5pm, Su 11am-5pm. €7, students €6.)* The **James Joyce Cultural Centre** features a wide range of Joyceana, including portraits of the individuals who inspired his characters. Call for info on lectures, Bloomsday events, and walking tours. *(35 N. Great Georges St.* ☎ *878 8547; www.jamesjoyce.ie. M-Sa 9:30am-5pm, Su 11am-5pm; Sept.-June M-Sa 9:30am-5pm, Su 12:30am-5pm. €5, students €4.)*

**ST. STEPHEN'S GREEN.** Once a private estate, **St. Stephen's Green** was later bequeathed to the city by the Guinness clan. The 27-acre park on the South Side, at the end of Grafton St., hosts musical and theatrical productions in the summer. *(Open M-Sa 8am-dusk, Su 10am-dusk.)* The restored **Newman House,** St. Stephen's Green South, was once the seat of **University College Dublin,** the Catholic answer to Trinity. Joyce's *A Portrait of the Artist as a Young Man* chronicles his time there. **Shaw's Birthplace** offers a glimpse at the childhood of author and playwright George Bernard Shaw. *(33 Synge St. Take bus #16, 19, or 122 from the city center. Open May-Sept. M-Tu and Th-F 10am-1pm and 2-5pm, Sa-Su 2-5pm. €7, students €6.)*

**IRELAND**

**ALONG THE QUAYS.** To see Dublin's greatest architectural triumph, visit the **Custom House,** east of O'Connell St. on Custom House Quay, designed by James Gandon. Carved heads along the frieze represent Ireland's rivers; Liffey is the sole woman. **Four Courts,** another Gandon masterpiece nearby, has an impressive facade. It was once seized by the IRA, sparking the Irish Civil War when members of the Free State Government attacked the garrison. The building now houses Ireland's highest national court. *(Inn's Quay. ☎888 6000. Open M-F 9am-4:30pm. Free.)* The dry air in the nave of ◪**St. Michan's Church** has preserved the corpses in the vaults; it was these seemingly living bodies that inspired Bram Stoker to write about the living dead in *Dracula.* The church, near Four Courts on Church St., boasts Dublin's earliest altar plates and an organ from 1723. *(☎872 4154. Open Mar. 18-Oct. M-F 10am-12:45pm and 2-4:30pm, Sa 10am-12:45pm; Nov.-Mar. 16 M-F 12:30-3:30pm, Sa 10am-12:45pm. Church of Ireland services Su 10am. Crypt tours €3.50, students €3.)*

> (deal) **THE REAL DEAL.** The Guinness Storehouse is a major tourist attraction and worth the trek, if only to work up a thirst in preparation for the free pint you'll receive in the penthouse Gravity Bar after your self-guided tour. The Old Jameson Distillery tour is very similar; it's best to pick whiskey or beer and visit only one of the factories. In the pub, however, there is no need to limit yourself.

**OTHER SIGHTS.** At the **Old Jameson Distillery,** learn how science, grain, and tradition come together to create world-famous Irish whiskey. Everyone gets a free glass of the "water of life" at the end of the 30min. tour. *(Bow St. From O'Connell Bridge, at the foot of O'Connell St., walk down the quays to Four Courts and take a right on Church St. Follow the signs to the Distillery, which is down a cobblestone street on the left. Buses #68, 69, and 79 run from the city center to Merchant's Quay. ☎807 2355; www.jamesonwhiskey.com. Tours daily 1-2 per hr. 9:30am-5:30pm. €9.80, students €8.)* Outside the city center, **Phoenix Park,** Europe's largest enclosed public park, is most infamous for the 1882 Phoenix Park murders. A nationalist splinter group stabbed the Chief Secretary of Ireland, Lord Cavendish, and his undersecretary just 180m from the **Phoenix Column.** The 1800-acre park now incorporates the President's residence *(Áras an Uachtaraín),* cricket pitches, polo grounds, and grazing deer. On nice days, hundreds of Dubliners can be found strolling, playing Gaelic football, or sunning themselves. The park also includes the **Dublin Zoo,** Europe's largest, which boasts 700 animals and the world's biggest egg. *(Take bus #10 from O'Connell St., or #25 or 26 from Middle Abbey St. ☎474 8900; www.dublinzoo.ie. Open M-Sa 9:30am-6pm, Su 10:30am-6pm. Last entry at 5pm. Zoo closes at dusk in winter. €14, students €12.)*

## ◪ ENTERTAINMENT

Whether you fancy poetry, punk, punchlines, or pubs, Dublin will entertain you. The free *Event Guide,* available at the tourist office and Temple Bar restaurants, offers comprehensive entertainment listings.

### THEATER

Dublin's curtains rise on a range of mainstream and experimental theater. There's no true theater district, but smaller theater companies thrive off Dame St. and Temple Bar. Call ahead for tickets. Showtime is generally around 8pm.

◪ **Abbey Theatre,** 23-26 Lower Abbey St. *(☎878 7222).* Ireland's national theater was founded in 1904 by Yeats and Lady Gregory to promote Irish culture and modernist theater. Box office open M-Sa 10:30am-7pm. Tickets €15-30; Sa 2:30pm matinee €18, students and seniors with ID €14.

**Peacock Theatre,** 26 Lower Abbey St. (☎878 7222). The Abbey's experimental studio theater downstairs offers evening shows in addition to occasional lunchtime plays, concerts, and poetry. Tickets €20; Sa 2:30pm matinee €12.

**Gate Theatre,** 1 Cavendish Row (☎874 4045; www.gate-theatre.ie). Another major Dublin theater, staging contemporary Irish and classic international dramas. Box office open M-Sa 10am-7:30pm. Tickets €18-30; M-Th students €10.

## COMEDY

There's nothing funny about how fast Dublin's comedy scene is growing. Popular festivals, such as **Bulmers International Comedy Festival** (www.bulmerscomedy.ie), are making their way onto the calendar. It's difficult to go wrong in any of the clubs, but *Event Guide* is helpful for weekly listings.

**The Capital Comedy Club,** Wellington Quay (☎677 0616; www.capitalcomedyclub.com.), upstairs from Ha' Penny Bridge Inn. Intimate and engaging setting sure to give you an ab workout. The MC, an up-and-coming stand-up, keeps the laughter rolling between big and small comedians. Cover €7; students €5. Doors open W and Su 9pm; show starts 9:30pm.

**The International Comedy Club,** 23 Wicklow St. (☎677 9250; www.theinternational-comedyclub.com). Popular club packs punchlines. Improv M. Cover €10; students €8. Doors open Th-Sa 8:45pm; show starts 9:15pm.

**The Bankers Comedy Club,** Trinity St. (☎6793697) Off Dame St. Showcases improv and stand-up two nights a week each to get you guffawing. Improv W and F; stand-up Th and Sa. Cover €10; students €8. Doors open 9pm.

## ◪ NIGHTLIFE

Begin your after-hours journey through Dublin's pubs and clubs at the gates of Trinity College, stumble onto Grafton St., teeter down Camden St., stagger onto South Great Georges St., and finally, crawl triumphantly into the Temple Bar area. Just don't expect to do any early sightseeing the next morning.

## PUBLIN

James Joyce once proposed that a "good puzzle would be to cross Dublin without passing a pub." A radio station later offered €125 to the first person to meet the challenge. The winner explained that you could take any route—you'd just have to visit them all on the way. Decades later, pubs still dominate Dublin's scene, and they quickly fill up at the end of every day of the week. Pubs normally close at 11:30pm Sunday through Wednesday and 12:30am Thursday through Saturday, but an increasing number of establishments are staying open later. Some of the best pubs in Temple Bar serve their brews until 2:30am.

**◪ The Stag's Head,** 1 Dame Ct. (☎679 3701), in Temple Bar. Victorian pub with stained-glass windows, marble-topped tables, and a gigantic moose head suspended above the bar. Additional bars upstairs and downstairs for busy nights. Excellent pub grub. Pints €4.10. Entrees €5-11. Live music W-Sa 9:30pm-midnight. Open M-Th 10:30am-11:30pm, F-Sa 10:30am-12:30am, Su 11:30am-11pm. Kitchen open M-Sa until 4pm.

**◪ The Porterhouse,** 16-18 Parliament St. (☎679 8847), in Temple Bar. A change in scenery and color; switch it up from the usual black stuff to this microbrewery's own popular Porterhouse Red. Live music every night. Pints €3.90. Open M-W 11:30am-11:30pm, Th-F 11:30am-2am, Sa 11:30am-2:30am, Su 11:30am-11pm. Pub grub until 9:30pm.

**The Celt,** 81-82 Talbot St. (☎878 8665), north of Trinity College. Tiny but mighty. Hosts some of the most energetic trad bands around and has cheaper pints than its southern counterparts. Pints €3.90. Trad M-Sa 9pm-close, Su 5-7pm and 9-11pm.

## WHISKEY BUSINESS

While Guinness is synonymous with Ireland the world over, Irish whiskey comes a close second as the unofficial national drink of the Emerald Isle. Indeed, seasoned Irish drinkers often chase a pint of Guinness ("a big one") with a glass of whiskey ("a small one"). Whiskey in Ireland was created by Medieval monks, who used the fiery tipple as an antidote to cold winters. In later years it was distilled at dangerous strengths in Irish homes, where the phrase "blind drunk" was sometimes quite literal. At the end of the 16th century, the English government cited spirits as the source of Irish unrest and declared martial law against all moonshiners, leading to the emergence of illegal establishments called *shabeens* selling extra-potent *poitín*.

*Poitín* is a 140-proof kick in the face. Culled from potatoes steeped in a mixture of apples, berries, and barley, then thrice-distilled in a gigantic copper worm, it is a clear liquid with a bouquet reminiscent of paint thinner. Because of its high alcohol content and risky mode of preparation, *poitín* is illegal. It is not served in pubs or brought out in polite company.

Most whiskey drinkers take their spirits neat, over ice, or with a bit of water. Other popular whiskey-based drinks are "hot Irish" (whiskey, lemon, cloves, brown sugar, and boiling water) and Irish coffee (black coffee, sugar, and whiskey, topped with cream).

Open M-Th 10:30am-11:30pm, F-Sa 10:30am-12:30am, Su 12:30-11pm.

**Whelan's,** 25 Wexford St. (☎478 0766), south of Temple Bar near St. Stephen's Green. Dark, busy pub with all-wood interior hosts big-name acts. The crowd depends on the music. Carvery lunch (starter, entree, dessert, and tea; €10) and entrees (€6-12) served noon-2pm. Live music nightly from 8:30pm; doors open 8pm. Cover €8-21. Open Su-W 10am-1:30am, Th-Sa 10:30am-2:30am.

**McDaid's,** 3 Harry St. (☎679 4395), off Grafton St. across from S. Anne St. Old books on high shelves recall McDaid's status as the center of the 1950s Irish literary scene. The din of the after-work, older crowd fills the pub. Pints €4.30. Open M-Th 10:30am-11:30pm, F-Sa 10:30am-12:30am, Su 12:30-11:30pm.

**Davy Byrne's,** 21 Duke St. (☎677 5217), off Grafton St. Lively, middle-aged crowd fills the pub where Joyce set the Cyclops chapter in *Ulysses*. Outdoor cafe; traditional Irish food (€8-11) served until 8:45pm. Pints €4.30. Trad Su-Tu 9-11pm. Open M-Th 11am-11:30pm, F-Sa 9am-12:30am, Su 12:30-11pm.

## CLUBLIN

As a general rule, clubs open at 10:30 or 11pm, but things don't really heat up until around midnight, after pubs start closing. Clubbing is an expensive way to end the night, as covers run €7-20 and mixed drinks cost €7-10. Some of the best clubs are run by their attached upstairs bars in the Temple Bar district. The gay nightclub scene is alive and well, with prominent spots clustered in the "pink triangle" zone of Parliament and S. Great Georges St. Keep up to date by checking out *In Dublin* for gay-friendly pubs, restaurants, and clubs, or call **Gay Switchboard Dublin** for event info and updates. (☎872 1055. Available M-F 7:30-9:30pm, Sa 3:30-6pm.)

⊠ **The PoD,** 35 Harcourt St. (☎478 0225; www.pod.ie), corner of Hatch St., in an old train station. A stylishly futuristic orange interior in a club that's serious about its music. Upstairs is **The Red Box** (☎478 0225), a huge, separate club with a warehouse atmosphere, brain-crushing music, and a crowd at the bar so deep it seems designed to winnow out the weak. The more mellow **Crawdaddy** hosts musical gigs, including some international stars. Cover €10-20; Th students €5. Open until 3am on weekends.

⊠ **Buskers Bar and Boomerang's Nightclub,** Fleet St. (☎612 9246), in Temple Bar. 3 bars, modern decor, and sizzling music attract a student crowd. Pints €4.70. 21+. Cover W-Th €5, F €10, Sa €15. Bar open M-Sa 11:30am-2am, Su noon-1am. Downstairs nightclub open W-Sa 9pm-2:30am.

**The Dragon**, 64-65 S. Great Georges St. (☎478 1590), south of Temple Bar, a few doors down from The George. Largest gay club in Dublin packs a happening crowd on weekends. Huge bar, lounge, dance floor, and high blue-lit ceilings with fuzzy lamps. Pints from €4.70. 18+. Open M and Th-Sa 5pm-2:30am, Tu-W 5-11:30pm, Su 5-11pm.

**The Front Lounge**, 33-34 Parliament St. (☎670 4112). The red velvet seats of this gay-friendly bar are filled nightly by a young, trendy, and mixed crowd. Pints €4.40. Mixed drinks €8.50. Open M-Th noon-midnight, F-Sa 3pm-3am, Su 3pm-midnight.

**Gaiety**, S. King St. (☎677 1717), at the end of Grafton St. opposite the shopping center. Elegant theater shows its late-night wild side F-Sa with jazz, Latin, salsa, swing, and soul bands. Cover F €12, Sa €15. Open F-Sa midnight-4am.

**Traffic Bar and Nightclub**, 54 Middle Abbey St. (☎873 4800), off O'Connell St. north of the Liffey. DJ spins hip-hop, house, or techno at the end of the long, mirrored bar as a twentysomething crowd gets down. 2 mixed drinks €10. 21+. Occasional cover €6-10. Open M-W noon-11:30pm, Th and Sa noon-2:30am, F 3pm-2:30am, Su noon-1:30am. Downstairs nightclub open Th-Sa 11pm-2:30am.

**Club M**, Blooms Hotel, Anglesea St. (☎671 5622; www.clubm.ie), in Temple Bar. One of Dublin's largest clubs, attracting a crowd of all ages and styles. 18+ keeps it on the young side. Avoid the cover; flyers along Temple Bar offer free admission on weeknights. Cover M-Th €5, F-Sa €12-15. Open M-Th 11pm-2:30am, F-Sa 10pm-2:30am.

**The Mezz Bar**, 21-25 Eustace St. (☎670 7655), in Temple Bar. Live bands rock every night. W reggae night. No cover. **The Hub** nightclub is in the basement. Cover €5-10.

# ▶ DAYTRIPS FROM DUBLIN

**BOYNE VALLEY.** The thinly populated Boyne Valley, 50km from Dublin, holds Ireland's greatest archaeological treasures. Between Slane and Drogheda lie no fewer than 40 Neolithic tombs from the fourth millennium BC. **Newgrange** is the most spectacular; a roof box over the entrance allows a solitary beam of sunlight to shine directly into the tomb for 17min. during winter solstice, a breathtaking sight that is simulated—though not as impressively—on the tour. Newgrange can only be entered with admission to **Brú na Bóinne Visitors Centre**, near Donore on the south side of the River Boyne, across from the tombs. *(By car, take the M1 motorway, exit at Donore, and continue 3km to the Visitors Centre. Or take a 1hr. bus to Drogheda and another to Brú na Bóinne. ☎041 988 0300. Open daily May and Sept. 9am-6:30pm; June-Aug. 9am-7pm; Mar.-Apr. and Oct. 9:30am-5:30pm; Nov.-Feb. 9:30am-5pm. Arrive early; tours sell out 1-2hr. in advance. Last tour 1¾hr. before closing. Centre and Newgrange tour €5.80, students €4.50.)* A group of enormous, well-preserved Norman castles—including **Trim Castle**, conquered by Mel Gibson in *Braveheart*—overlooks Trim proper on the River Boyne. *(By car, drive 40min. down Trim Rd. Buses run direct 4 per hr. from Busáras Central Bus Station to Trim. ☎046 943 8619. Open Easter-Sept. daily 10am-6pm; Oct. daily 10am-5:30pm; Nov.-Easter Sa-Su 10am-5pm. Grounds €1.60, students €1. Tour and grounds €3.70/1.30.)*

**HOWTH PENINSULA.** Only 30min. from Dublin, Howth (rhymes with "both") Peninsula is a popular destination for city-dwellers looking to escape life's hustle and bustle. A 4hr. ■ **cliff walk** circles the peninsula, passing fields of heather and thousands of seabird nests. To get to the trailhead from town, turn left from the DART station and follow Harbour Rd. past East Pier for about 20min. Just offshore is **Ireland's Eye**, a former monk sanctuary turned avian refuge. Seals flock to **Nicky's Plaice** on West Pier *(☎832 3557; www.nickysplaice.ie)* when a bell rings to announce feeding time daily at noon and 3pm. Don't miss the gorgeous **Rhododendron Gardens**, in bloom from April to June, beyond the private **Howth Castle**, a charming patchwork of architectural styles. To reach the castle, go right as you exit the

DART station and then left after 400m, at the entrance to the Deer Park Hotel. *(Northbound DART trains run to Howth. 30min., 4 per hr., €1.80.)*

**MALAHIDE.** An impressive cultural complex, housing several museums, **Malahide Castle** is more than just an 800-year-old blend of architectural styles surrounded by hectares of perfectly manicured parklands. The castle includes rooms full of 14th-through 19th-century furnishings and portraits; the paneled oak room and the great hall are magnificent. The audio tour is incredibly (sometimes overly) detailed. A live peacock welcomes those who discover the castle's best secret: the ⬛**Museum of Childhood,** a veritable Antiques Roadshow of 18th-century dollhouses and toys. This charity trust can't afford to advertise, so few are aware of the world's oldest known dollhouse, finished in 1700. Upstairs sits the spectacular Tara's Palace, a huge model mansion that fills an entire room. Beyond the main drag of clothing and craft boutiques, you'll find the gorgeous Malahide beach, as well as a beach-side walking path. Closer to neighboring Portmarnock (2km) is the even softer, more luxurious 2mi. stretch of beach known as the **Velvet Strand.** *(DART serves Malahide station; 20min., 2 per hr, roundtrip €3.40. From the DART station, turn right on Main St. and over the bridge, 15min., to get to the castle entrance gate. Castle ☎846 2184; www.malahidecastle.com. Open Jan.-Dec. M-Sa 10am-12:45pm and 2-5pm, Apr.-Sept. Su and bank holidays 10am-12:45pm and 2-6pm, Oct.-Mar. Su and bank holidays 11am-12:45pm and 2-5pm. Admission only by 35min. tour. €7, students €6. Museum open M-Sa 10am-1pm and 2-5pm, Su 2-6pm. €2. Gardens open May-Sept. 2-5pm. €4.)*

# SOUTHEASTERN IRELAND

Ireland's southeastern region is famous for its strawberries and oysters. Round towers, built by monks to defend against Viking attacks, litter the countryside from the medieval city of Kilkenny to the Rock of Cashel. The grassy fields and stunning mountain views provide a brilliant contrast to the trad and rock pumping through the pubs of Waterford, Kilkenny, and Wexford.

## ▐ TRANSPORTATION

**Rosslare Harbour** is a useful departure point for ferries to Wales or France. **Stena Line** (☎01 204 7777; www.stenaline.ie) and **Irish Ferries** (☎01 850 366 222; www.irishferries.com) bring passengers from Rosslare Harbour to Pembroke, BRI (3¾hr., 2 per day, €29) and to Roscoff and Cherbourg, FRA (18-19½hr., 1 per 2 days, €69-78). From Rosslare Harbour, **trains** run to Dublin and Limerick via Waterford, while **buses** go to: Dublin (3hr., 14 per day, €16); Galway via Waterford (6hr., 4 per day, €26); Limerick (4hr., 3-5 per day, €21); Tralee (2-4 per day, €26). Contact **Wexford Tourism** (☎053 912 3111) for more info.

## THE WICKLOW MOUNTAINS                                    ☎0404

Over 600m tall, carpeted in fragrant heather and pleated by sparkling rivers, the Wicklow summits provide a tranquil stop just outside Dublin. The **Wicklow Way,** a 125km hiking trail, winds past grazing sheep, scattered villages, and monastic ruins. The **National Park Information Office,** between the two lakes, is the best source for hiking advice. (☎45425. Open May-Aug. daily 10am-1pm and 2-6pm; Sept.-Apr. Sa-Su 10am-dusk.) When the office is closed, call the **ranger office** (☎45800) in nearby Trooperstown Wood. The valley of **Glendalough** is home to St. Kevin's sixth-century monastery. A particularly good hike in the area is the **Spinc and Glenealo Valley path** (3hr.), marked by white arrows. The trail ascends to a glorious lookout over Upper Lake, circles the valley where goats and deer wander, and passes old mining ruins before looping back. At the secluded 🏠**Glendalough International Hostel (HI) ❷,** 5min. up the road from the Glendalough Visitor Centre, guests won't hear rambunctious travelers, just chirping birds. (☎45342; www.anoige.ie. Breakfast €4-6.50; packed lunches €5.50; request the night before. Laundry €5. Single-sex dorms June-Oct. €23; Nov.-May €18. €2 HI discount. MC/V.) Just 1.5km up the road, tiny **Laragh** has food options and plenty of B&Bs. **St. Kevin's Bus Service** (☎01 281 8119; www.glendaloughbus.com) arrives at the Glendalough Visitor's Centre from the end of Dawson St. nearest to St. Stephen's Green in Dublin. (Buses run M-Sa 2 per day, €18.) Public transportation in the mountains is extremely limited; buses or taxis are your best bet. **Glendalough Cabs** (☎087 972 9452; www.glendaloughcabs.com) offers 24hr. service.

# KILKENNY                                                   ☎05677

Eight churches share the streets with 80 pubs in Kilkenny (pop. 30,000), Ireland's best-preserved medieval town. The 13th-century **Kilkenny Castle,** complete with well-maintained public grounds, housed the Earls of Ormonde until 1932. (☎21450. Open daily June-Aug. 9:30am-7pm; Sept. 10am-6:30pm; Oct.-Mar. 10:30am-12:45pm and 2-5pm; Apr.-May 10:30am-5pm. Required tour €5.30, students €2.10.) Don't miss the chance to grab a free pint at **Smithwicks Brewery,** Parliament St. (☎21014. Tours July-Aug. M-F 3pm. Pick up a free ticket in the morning at the security station on the right past the Watergate Theatre.) Climb the steep steps of the 30m tower of **St. Canice's Cathedral,** up the hill off Dean St., for a panoramic view. (☎64971. Open June-Aug. M-Sa 9am-6pm, Su 2-6pm; Apr.-May and Sept. M-Sa 10am-1pm and 2-5pm, Su 2-5pm; Oct.-Mar. M-Sa 10am-1pm and 2-4pm, Su 2-4pm. €4, students €3. Tower €3/2.50.)

Most B&Bs are on **Waterford Road.** Conveniently located near the pubs on High St., the welcoming **Kilkenny Tourist Hostel ❶,** 35 Parliament St., offers clean, spacious rooms. (☎63541. Laundry €5. Free Wi-Fi. Check-in 9am-11pm. Check-out 10am. Dorms €17; doubles €42; quads €76. Cash only.) **The Two Dames ❶,** 80 John St., serves creative sandwiches (€5) and stuffed baked potatoes (€5.50) that are as good as they smell. (Open M-F 8:30am-5pm, Sa 10am-4:30pm. Cash only.) Make a meal of free samples at the **SuperQuinn** grocery store in the Market Cross shopping center off High St. (☎52444. Open M-Tu 8am-8pm, W-F 8am-9pm, Sa 8am-7pm, Su 10am-7pm.) Start your pub crawl at the end of **Parliament Street,** then work your way to the wilder bars on **John Street,** which stay open later. The best *craic* is at the **Pump House** (☎63924), on Parliament St., **Tynan's Bridge House Bar** (☎21291), by the river, and **Ryan's** (☎62281), on Friary St. off High St.

**Trains** (☎22024) leave from Dublin Rd. for Dublin (2hr., €22-28) and Waterford (45min., €10-13). **Buses** (☎64933) depart from the same station for: Cork (3hr., 5 per day, €17); Dublin (2hr., 6 per day, €11); Galway (5hr., 5 per day, €21); Limerick (2½hr., 4 per day, €17); Rosslare Harbour (2hr., 2 per day, €17); Waterford (1½hr., 2 per day, €9). The **tourist office** is on Rose Inn St. (☎51500; www.southeastireland.com. Open May-Sept. M-F 9am-6:30pm, Sa 10am-6pm, Su 11am-5pm; Oct.-Apr. M-F 9:30am-5:30pm, Sa 10am-6pm.)

# WATERFORD                                                  ☎051

Waterford is Ireland's oldest city, founded in AD 914 by the grandson of Viking Ivor the Boneless. The small city, situated on a beautiful river, attracts travelers looking to shop, club, and relax on beaches. The city's real highlight, however, is the fully operational 🏠**Waterford Crystal Factory,** 3km away on N25. Tours allow you to watch experienced cutters transform grains of sand into molten glass and finally into sparkling crystal. The showroom contains the largest collection of Waterford crystal in the world. To get there, catch the City bus outside Dunnes on

Michael St. (10-15min., M-Sa 3-4 per hr., €1.40) and request to stop at the factory. (☎332 500; www.waterfordvisitorcentre.com. Open daily Mar.-Oct. 8:30am-6pm; Nov.-Feb. 9am-5pm. Free. 1hr. tours 3-4 per hr. in high season. €9, students €6.) **Waterford Treasures** at the granary has Viking artifacts and the only remaining item of Henry VIII's wardrobe, a velvet hat. (☎304 500; www.waterfordtreasures.com. Open Apr.-Sept. M-Sa 9:30am-6pm, Su 11am-6pm; Oct.-Mar. M-Sa 10am-5pm, Su 11am-6pm. €7, students €5.) Stellar tour guide Jack Burtchaell keeps audiences entertained on his ◫**Walking Tour of Historic Waterford.** (☎873 711. 1hr. tours depart from Waterford Treasures Mar.-Oct. daily 11:45am and 1:45pm. €7.)

Jane and Robert Hovenden provide clean, quiet accommodations at **Mayor's Walk B&B ❸**. From the bus station, walk down the quay to the clock tower and turn right. Head up the main street and turn right at the traffic lights. Mayor's Walk is the second road on the left up the hill. A bus for the Waterford Crystal Factory stops across the street. (☎855 427; www.mayorswalk.com. Shared bathrooms. Singles €28; doubles €50. Cash only.) **Cafe Sumatra ❷**, 53 John St., is a good option for lunch or dinner. (☎876 404. Sandwiches €7-8. Entrees €10-11. Open M-Th 8:30am-7pm, F-Sa 8:30am-11pm, Su 11am-9pm. MC/V.) The quay is full of pubs. **T&H Doolan's**, 31-32 George's St., has been serving drinks in its dark wooden interior for 300 years. (☎841 504. Trad nightly 9:30pm. Open M-Th 10:30am-11:30pm, F-Sa 10:30am-12:30am, Su 12:30-11pm. MC/V.) A younger crowd flocks to the "Golden Mile" of late bars at the intersection of **John, Manor,** and **Parnell Streets.** Try **Geoff's**, 8 John St. (☎874 787) or **Ruby Lounge** (☎858 130) on the corner.

**Trains** (☎873 401; www.irishrail.ie) leave from the quay across the bridge for: Dublin (2½hr., M-F 8 per day, €24); Kilkenny (50min., 3-5 per day, €10); Limerick (2½hr., 5 per day, €30). **Buses** depart for: Cork (2½hr.); Dublin (2¾hr.); Galway (5¾hr.); Limerick (2½hr.). The **tourist office** is across from the bus station. (☎875 823; www.southeastireland.com. Open in summer M-Sa 9am-6pm, Su 10am-6pm.)

# CASHEL ☎062

Cashel sits at the foot of the 90m ◫**Rock of Cashel** (also called **St. Patrick's Rock** or **Cashel of the Kings**), a limestone outcropping topped by medieval buildings. (☎61437. Open daily mid-June to mid-Sept. 9am-7pm; mid-Mar. to mid-June and mid-Sept. to mid-Oct. 9am-5:30pm; mid-Oct. to mid-Mar. 9am-4:30pm. Tours 1 per hr. €5.30, students €2.10.) Head down the cow path from the Rock to see the ruins of **Hore Abbey**, built by Cistercian monks and relatively free of tourist hordes. (Open 24hr. Free.) The internationally acclaimed **Brú Ború Heritage Centre**, at the base of the Rock, stages traditional music and dance performances. (☎61122; www.comhaltas.com. Mid-June to mid-Sept. Tu-Sa 9pm. €18, students €10.) The **Bolton Library**, on John St., houses rare manuscripts and what's reputed to be the world's smallest book. (☎61944. Open M-Th 10am-2:30pm.) Enjoy a view of the Rock from the homey rooms and campsite at ◫**O'Brien's Holiday Lodge ❷**, a 10min. walk out of town on Dundrum Rd. From the tourist office, walk down Main St. and turn right at the end. (☎61003; www.cashel-lodge.com. Laundry €12. Camping €9 per person. Dorms €18; doubles €65. MC/V.) **Spearman's ❶**, near the Friary St. end of Main St., has *panini* (€3.50-6) made from freshly baked bread. (☎61143. Open M-F 9am-5:45pm, Sa 9am-5pm. MC/V.) **Buses** (☎061 313 333) leave from Main St. near the tourist office for Cork (1½hr., 6 per day, €11) and Dublin (3hr., 6 per day, €10). Buy tickets in the SPAR grocery store. The **tourist office** is in City Hall on Main St. (☎62511; www.casheltouristoffice.com. Open daily 9:30am-5:30pm.)

# SOUTHWESTERN IRELAND

The dramatic landscape of Southwestern Ireland ranges from lakes and mountains to stark, ocean-battered cliffs. Rebels once hid among the coves and glens, but the region is now dominated by tourists taking in the stunning scenery of the Ring of Kerry and Cork's southern coast.

# CORK
☎ 021

Cork (pop. 150,000) hosts most of the cultural activities in the southwest. The county gained the nickname "Rebel Cork" from its residents' early opposition to the British Crown and 20th-century support for Irish independence. Today, Cork's river quays and pub-lined streets reveal architecture both grand and grimy, evidence of the city's legacy of resistance and reconstruction.

## TRANSPORTATION

**Trains: Kent Station,** Lower Glanmire Rd. (☎450 6766; www.irishrail.ie), across the North Channel from the city center. Open M-Sa 6am-8pm, Su 8am-8:50pm. To: **Dublin** (3hr., 10-15 per day, €55) via **Limerick** (1½hr., 9 per day, €23); **Killarney** (2hr., 6-9 per day, €23); **Tralee** (2½hr., 6-9 per day, €30).

**Buses:** Parnell Pl. (☎450 8188), on Merchant's Quay. Info desk open daily 9am-5:30pm. **Bus Éireann** to: **Dublin** (4½hr., M-Su 6 per day, €10); **Galway** (4hr., 12 per day, €15); **Killarney** (2hr., 11-14 per day, €14); **Limerick** (2hr., 14 per day, €11); **Rosslare Harbour** (4hr., 2-3 per day, €19); **Sligo** (7hr., 3 per day, €23); **Tralee** (2½hr., 11-14 per day, €16); **Waterford** (2¼hr., 2-3 per day, €15).

**Ferries: Brittany Ferries,** 42 Grand Parade, sails from Cork to Roscoff, FRA. (☎021 427 7801. 12hr., Sa only, from €108.)

**Public Transportation:** Downtown **buses** run 2-6 per hr. M-Sa 7:30am-11:15pm, with reduced service Su 10am-11:15pm. Fares from €1.30. Catch buses and pick up schedules along St. Patrick's St., across from the Father Matthew statue.

## ORIENTATION AND PRACTICAL INFORMATION

The center of Cork is compact and pedestrian-friendly, framed by the North and South Channels of the River Lee. From the bus station along the North Channel, **Merchant's Quay** leads west to **St. Patrick's Street,** which curves through the center of the city and becomes **Grand Parade.** On the other side of the North Channel, across St. Patrick's Bridge, **MacCurtain Street** runs east to **Lower Glanmire Road** and passes the train station before becoming the N8 to Dublin. Downtown shopping and nightlife concentrates on **Washington, Oliver Plunkett,** and St. Patrick's Streets.

**Tourist Office: Tourist House,** Grand Parade (☎425 5100; www.corkkerry.ie), near the corner of South Mall, books accommodations (€4) and provides a free city guide and map. Open June and Aug.-Sept. M-F 9am-6pm, Sa 9am-5pm; July M-F 9am-6pm, Sa 9am-5pm, Su 10am-5pm; Sept.-May M-Sa 9:15am-5pm.

**Banks: Ulster Bank Limited,** 88 St. Patrick's St. (☎427 0618; www.ulsterbank.ie). Open M 10am-5pm, Tu-F 10am-4pm. Most banks in Cork have 24hr. **ATMs.**

**Police (Garda):** Anglesea St. (☎452 2000).

**Pharmacies: Regional Late-Night Pharmacy,** Wilton Rd. (☎434 4575), opposite the hospital. Bus #8. Open M-F 9am-10pm, Sa-Su 10am-10pm. **Late Night,** 9 St. Patrick's St. (☎427 2511). Open M-F 8:30am-10pm, Sa 9am-10pm, Su 10am-10pm.

**Hospital: Cork University Hospital,** Wilton Rd. (☎454 6400). Bus #8.

**Internet Access:** ▨ **Wired To The World Internet Cafe,** 6 Thompson House, MacCurtain St., north of River Lee (www.wiredtotheworld.ie). Gaming, phone booths, and Wi-Fi. Internet €1 per hr. Open daily 8am-midnight. **Web Workhouse,** Winthrop St., (☎427

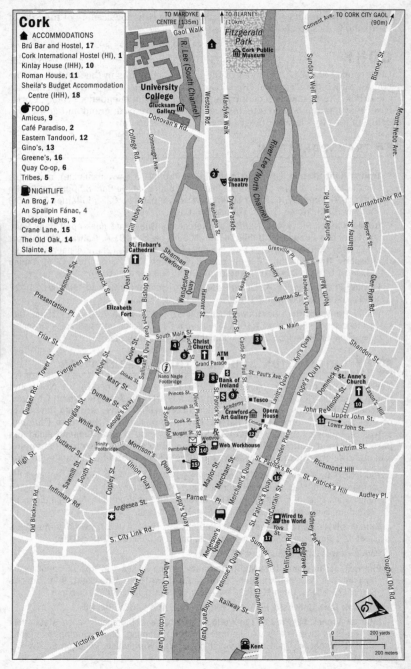

**Cork**

**▲ ACCOMMODATIONS**
Brú Bar and Hostel, 17
Cork International Hostel (HI), 1
Kinlay House (IHH), 10
Roman House, 11
Sheila's Budget Accommodation
Centre (IHH), 18

**● FOOD**
Amicus, 9
Café Paradiso, 2
Eastern Tandoori, 12
Gino's, 13
Greene's, 16
Quay Co-op, 6
Tribes, 5

**■ NIGHTLIFE**
An Brog, 7
An Spailpin Fánac, 4
Bodega Nights, 3
Crane Lane, 15
The Old Oak, 14
Slainte, 8

3090), between St. Patrick's St. and Oliver Plunkett St. in the city center. 8am-5pm €3 per hr., 5pm-3am €2.50 per hr., 3-8am €1.50 per hr.; Su €2.50 per hr. Open 24hr.

**Post Office:** Oliver Plunkett St. (☎485 1032). Open M-Sa 9am-5:30pm.

# ACCOMMODATIONS

Cork's fine array of busy hostels should put a smile on any budget traveler's face, but rooms go fast, so call ahead. For a full Irish breakfast and a little more privacy, head to one of the many B&Bs on **Western Road,** near the University.

■ **Sheila's Budget Accommodation Centre (IHH),** 4 Belgrave Pl. (☎450 5562; www.sheilashostel.ie). A perennial *Let's Go* favorite. Friendly and trustworthy staff take great pride in ensuring their guests feel safe and have fun. 24hr. reception desk doubles as general store. Free luggage storage. Free Internet. Breakfast €3. Laundry €6.50. Check-out 10:30am. Dorms €15-20; doubles €48-50. ❷

**Brú Bar and Hostel,** 57 MacCurtain St. (☎455 9667; www.bruhostel.com), north of the river. A lively place to stay up late and hang out at the attached bar (open 4pm-4am). Continental breakfast included. Towels €2. Laundry €5. Free Internet. Check-in 1pm. Check-out 10:30am. 6-bed dorms €17; 4-bed dorms €21-23; doubles €50. MC/V. ❷

**Kinlay House (IHH),** Bob and Joan's Walk (☎450 8966; www.kinlayhouse.ie), down the alley to the right of St. Anne's Church. Bright colors and warm atmosphere; some rooms have great views of the city. Plush lounge with TV and sunny Internet room. Continental breakfast included. Laundry €8. Internet €1 per 15min. Free parking. 8- to 15-bed dorms €15-18; doubles €46-54. Ensuite rooms available. AmEx/MC/V. ❷

**Roman House,** 3 St. John's Terr. (☎450 3606; www.romanhouse.info), across from Kinlay House. Colorful Roman House markets itself as a welcoming place for GLBT travelers. Full Irish breakfast included. Singles from €55; doubles from €75. ❹

**Cork International Hostel (An Óige/HI),** 1-2 Redclyffe, Western Rd. (☎454 3289), near University College and a 20min. walk from Grand Parade. Offers clean, spacious rooms with bath. Continental breakfast €4; Irish breakfast €6.50. Luggage storage available. Internet €1 per 15min. Reception 8am-midnight. Check-in 1pm. Check-out 10:30am. Dorms €17-19; doubles €42. €2 HI discount. ❶

# FOOD

Cork's famous international flavor is reflected in its countless great eateries. For more traditional Irish cuisine, hit the small towns, or make your own with local ingredients in the expansive **English Market,** accessible from Grand Parade, Patrick, and Oliver Plunkett St. Get groceries at **Tesco,** on Paul St. inside the Paul St. Shopping Centre. (☎427 0791. Open M-Sa 8am-10pm, Su 10am-8pm.)

■ **Eastern Tandoori,** 1-2 Emmett Pl., across from Opera House (☎427 2232). Delicious, authentic Indian fare served in a spacious, elegant dining room overlooking the water. 3-course early-bird special M-Th 5pm-7pm, F-Sa 5pm-6pm, Su 5pm-6:30pm, €15. Entrees €12-19. Open daily 5pm-11:30pm. AmEx/MC/V. ❹

**Ginos,** 7 Winthrop St. (☎427 4485). Heaping scoops of heavenly gelato flavors like honeycomb and hazelnut could be an entire meal. Small pizza €5. Ice cream €1.40 per scoop. Open daily 12pm-10pm. ❶

**Tribes,** 8 Tuckey St. (☎427 4446), off Oliver Plunkett St. Late-night, low-light java shop serves sandwiches, full meals and tea into the wee hours. Food served until 30min. before closing. Open Tu-Th 10:30am-midnight, F-Sa 10:30am-4am, Su 12pm-11pm. ❶

**Amicus,** St. Paul St., (☎427 6455), across from Tesco. Artistically presented dishes taste as good as they look. Lunch €8-12. Dinner €12-25. Open M-Sa 8am-10:30pm, Su 11:30am-10pm. MC/V. ❸

**Café Paradiso,** 16 Lancaster Quay (☎427 7939), near the University campus. Celebrated chefs make the most of what Mother Earth has to offer, serving up award-winning vegetarian meals. Menu changes often. Lunch €6-16. Dinner €11-23. Open Tu-Sa noon-3pm and 6:30-10:30pm. AmEx/MC/V. ❸

**Greene's,** 48 MacCurtain St. (☎455 2279), near Isaac's Hotel. Special occasions deserve the gorgeous waterfall and delicious gourmet cuisine found here. Entrees €20-29. Early-bird 3-course dinner 6-7pm, €26. Open M-Th 7-10am and 6-10pm, F 7-10am and 6-10:30pm, Sa 7-10:30am and 6-10:30pm, Su 7-10:30am and 6-9:30pm. ❺

# 🅖 SIGHTS

Cork's sights are concentrated in three areas: the old town, the Shandon neighborhood to the north, and the university to the west. All sights can be reached by foot, although the university and gaol are farther. Hop on and off the **Cork City Tour,** a 1hr. bus ride that leaves from the tourist office and stops at locations all over town. (July-Aug. 2 per hr., Apr. and Oct. 1 per hr.; €13, students and seniors €11.) Mike Collins also begins his **Historic Walking Tour,** loaded with insider's tidbits, at the tourist office. (☎085 100 7300. M-F 10am, noon, 2pm, 4pm.)

**THE OLD TOWN.** In a city lacking greenery, the area around **Christ Church** provides a quiet refuge and is packed with sunbathers in summer. The site suffered the Protestant torch three times between its 1270 inception and final renovation in 1729. *(Off Grand Parade just north of Bishop Lucy Park. Free.)* Across the South Channel, there's a decent view of Cork from Keyser Hill. At the top of the stairs leading up the hill, **Elizabeth Fort** stands as an ivy-covered remnant of English domination. *(Follow S. Main St. away from the city center, cross the South Gate Bridge, turn right on Proby's Quay, and turn left on Keyser Hill. Free.)* Looming over nearby Proby's Quay, **St. Finbarr's Cathedral** is a testament to the Victorian obsession with the neo-Gothic and a trademark of the city. The cathedral houses art exhibits in the summer. *(Bishop St. ☎963 387. Open M-F 10am-12:45pm and 2-5pm. €3, students €1.50.)*

**SHANDON AND EMMET PLACE.** Like Christ Church, **St. Anne's Church** was ravaged by 17th-century English armies; the current church was built in 1722. The steeple houses the **Bells of Shandon,** which you can ring before climbing to the top. Its four clock faces are notoriously out of sync, earning the church its nickname, "the four-faced liar." *(Walk up John Redmond St. and take a right at the Craft Centre; St. Anne's is on the right. ☎450 5906. Open M-Sa 10am-5:30pm. €6, students and seniors €5.)* Across the North Channel, the giant brick-and-glass **Opera House** was erected two decades ago after the older, more elegant opera house went down in flames. *(Emmet Pl., near Lavitt's Quay. ☎427 0022.)* The nearby **Crawford Art Gallery** has impressive collections of Greek and Roman sculpture casts and 19th-century Irish art. *(Emmet Pl., off Paul St. ☎490 7855. Open M-Sa 10am-5pm. Free.)*

**WESTERN CORK.** Built in 1845, 🅴**University College Cork's** campus is a collection of Gothic buildings, manicured lawns, and sculpture-studded grounds. The classic Stone Corridor is lined with Oghan stones, ancient gravestones marked with inscriptions representing an early example of pagan Irish language. The campus is also home to the architecturally striking **Lewis Glucksman Gallery,** which draws innovative, must-see exhibits. *(Main gate on Western Rd. ☎490 3000; www.ucc.ie. Gallery open Tu-W and F-Sa 10am-5pm, Th 10am-8pm, Su noon-5pm.)* 🅵**Fitzgerald Park** has beautiful rose gardens, a pond, and art exhibits courtesy of the **Cork Public Museum.** *(From the front gate of UCC, follow the signs across the street.* ☎ *427 0679. Open M-F 11am-1pm and 2:15-5pm, Su 3-5pm. Free.)* Don't miss the **Cork City Gaol** across the river from the park. Furnished cells, sound effects, and videos illustrate the experience of inmates at the 19th-century prison. *(☎ 430 5022; www.corkcitygaol.com. Open daily Mar.-Oct. 9:30am-6pm; Nov.-Feb. 10am-5pm. €6, students €5. 1hr. audio tour.)*

## 🔊 NIGHTLIFE

**Oliver Plunkett Street, Union Quay, Washington Street,** and **South Main Street** have pubs, clubs, and live music. Check out the free *WhazOn? Cork* pamphlet or the Thursday "Downtown" section in the *Evening Echo* newspaper.

▨ **The Old Oak,** 113 Oliver Plunkett St. (☎ 427 6165), across from the General Post Office. "Best Traditional Pub in Ireland" repeated winner. Huge, packed, and great for the early 20- and 30-something crowd. Pints €4. Varied live music Su-W from 10:30pm-close. Open M-Sa noon-1:45am, Su noon-1am. Kitchen open M-Sa noon-6pm. **Cyprus Avenue,** a music venue upstairs from the pub, is open nightly.

▨ **An Spailpín Fánac** (on spal-PEEN FAW-nuhk), 28 South Main St. (☎ 427 7949), across from Beamish Brewery. One of Cork's oldest (est. 1779) and favorite pubs. Visitors and locals come for live trad every night. Storytelling last Tu of every month.

**Slainte,** Market Lane, (☎ 427 4793) off Patrick St. Newer pub, far less sketchy than the name of its comedy club, **The Craichouse,** is quickly becoming known for hosting some of the area's best upcoming comedians on Su nights. W night Trad. F night jazz/rock or funk. Club cover €7, students €5.

**An Brog,** 72-73 Oliver Plunkett St. (☎ 427 1392), at the corner of Oliver Plunkett St. and Grand Parade. For those who crave good alternative rock and feel at home among students and eyebrow rings. Tends to get busy later. Pints €4. Open daily 2pm-2am.

**Crane Lane,** 1 Phoenix St. (☎ 427 8487). From Oliver Plunkett St., walk toward Parnell St., turn right onto Smith St., and right again onto Phoenix St. Live rock, trad and folk music 5-6 nights a week attracts locals and those lucky enough to find it. No cover.

**Bodega Nights,** 46-49 Corn Market St. (☎ 427 2878), north of Grand Parade, newly reinvented itself as a DJ friendly club with occasional live gigs. Large enough to house 5 bars including the "world's first organic bar."

## 🔊 DAYTRIP FROM CORK

**BLARNEY.** Those impressed by the Irish way of speaking should head to **Blarney Castle** and its legendary Blarney Stone. The legend goes that the Earl of Blarney cooed and cajoled his way out of giving up his abode to Queen Elizabeth I, and his smooth-talking skills were imparted to the stone, which when kissed passes on the "gift of Irish gab." After stealing a smooch, enjoy the views from the top and take a walk around the dreamlike **rock close** garden. *(Buses run from Cork to Blarney. 10-16 per day, round-trip €4.80. Open May-Aug. M-Sa 9am-7pm, Su 9:30am-5:30pm; Sept. M-Sa 9am-6:30pm, Su 9:30am-sunset; Oct.-Apr. M-Sa 9am-6pm, Su 9:30am-5:30pm. Last entry 30min. before closing. Castle and grounds €8, students €6.)*

## SCHULL AND THE MIZEN HEAD PENINSULA ☎ 028

The peaceful seaside hamlet of Schull (SKULL) is an ideal base for exploring Ireland's craggy southwestern tip. Although the town has only 700 residents in winter, its population increases to over 3000 in summer, offering numerous activites for warm weather. Sail with the world-renowned ⊠**Fastnet Marine Outdoor Education Centre,** or stargaze at the **Planetarium,** on Colla Rd. (Fastnet ☎28515; www.schullsailing.ie. Reserve ahead. 5-day sailing course €275. Planetarium ☎28552. 45min. shows June M, Th 8pm; July-Aug. M, Th 8pm, W, Sa 4pm.) The coastal road winds past **Barley Coast Beach** and continues on to **Mizen Head.** The Mizen becomes more scenic and less populated to the west of Schull, but it's mobbed in July and August, when vacationers hit the beach. **Betty Johnson's Bus Hire** offers 3hr. tours of the area. (☎28410, mobile 086 265 6078. Call ahead. €10 per person.) The quaint **Galley Cove House ❹,** a few kilometers before town on the Goleen Rd., is perfect for extended stays on the tiny village's shores. (☎35137; www.galleycovehouse.com. All rooms with bath and TV. Singles €45-55; doubles €152-180.) **Hillside B&B ❹,** up Cooryderrigan from Main St., is closer to Schull's sights and provides sea or mountain views depending on the room. (☎28248. Singles €40; doubles €64-68.) Many chippers claim to be Ireland's best, but **The Fish Shop ❷,** on the pier, may be right. (☎28599. Fish and chips €8. Wine €2. Open daily in summer noon-10pm.) The French chocolatier at **Gwen's Chocolates** romances shoppers with artisan delectables and ice cream. (☎27853. Open in summer daily 8am-6pm; winter F-Su 10am-5pm.) Schull has award-winning pubs to please the summer swarms. For a pint-sized pub crawl, head to Main St. for **Hackett's Bar** (☎28625), **Bunratty Inn** (☎28341), and **The Black Sheep** (☎28022), which all offer terrific food, *craic*, and music. **Back in Schull** (☎28278) runs **ferries** to Cape Clear Island (June-Sept. 2-3 per day, round-trip €13). **Buses** (☎021 450 8188; www.buseireann.ie) arrive in Schull from Cork (2-3 per day, €15) and Goleen (1-2 per day, €3.80). There is no other public transportation on the peninsula, though confident bicyclists can daytrip to Mizen Head (29km from Schull).

## CAPE CLEAR ISLAND (OILEÁN CHLÉIRE) ☎028

The beautiful island of Cape Clear is worth a daytrip from Schull or Baltimore. Its staggering cliffs make for steep walks, but once conquered, the heights reveal the land and sea's stunning scenery. A mere 129 people live year-round on Cape Clear, which is the historic seat of the O'Driscoll clan. The island provides asylum for gulls, petrels, and their attendant flocks of ornithologists at the **Cape Clear Bird Observatory** (☎39181) on North Harbour. The **Cape Clear Heritage Centre** has everything from a family tree of the ubiquitous O'Driscolls to a well-preserved chair from the *Lusitania.* (Open June-Aug. M-Sa noon-5pm, Su 2-5pm. €4, students €2.) On the road to the Heritage Centre, **Cléire Goats** (☎39126) sells all the goat-related products of your wildest dreams. Most popular is their goat's milk ice cream (€2.50) in chocolate, strawberry and vanilla. **Cape Clear Island Youth Hostel (HI) ❶** has simple but clean rooms and a fantastic location on the picturesque, secluded, and swimming-friendly South Harbour. It's a 10min. walk from the pier; turn right onto the main road past the pottery shop and stay to the left. (☎41968; www.anoige.fenlon.net. Internet €2 per 15min. Dorms €15.) The charming **Cluain Mara B&B ❷,** owned by Ciarán and Mary O'Driscoll, overlooks North Harbour. (☎39164. Rooms €30. MC/V.) To reach **Cuas an Uisce Campsite ❶,** follow directions to the hostel but bear right before Ciarán Danny Mike's; it's 400m up on the left. (☎39119. Open June-Sept. Tent sites €7 per person.) **Ciarán Danny Mike's Pub ❸** has the distinction of being Ireland's southernmost pub and serves food all day. (☎39153. Open noon-10pm.) Groceries, hot food (€6-16), and Wi-Fi are available at pier-side **An Siopa Beag.** (☎39099. Open June-Aug. daily 10am-8pm; Sept.-May M-Sa 11am-4pm.) **Ferries** go to Schull (☎28138; 45min., 3-4 per day, round-trip €14) and Baltimore (☎086 346 5110; www.islandtripper.com. 45min., 3-5 per day; €8, round-trip €14.) There is an **information office** in the pottery shop at the end of the pier. (☎39100. Open June-Sept. daily 11am-1pm and 3-6pm.)

# KILLARNEY AND KILLARNEY NATIONAL PARK ☎064

Killarney is just minutes from some of Ireland's most beautiful natural scenery. Outside of town, forested mountains rise from the famous three **Lakes of Killarney** in the 95 sq. km national park. It could take an entire day to explore ■**Muckross House,** 5km south of Killarney on Kenmare Rd., a 19th-century manor and garden. A path leads to the 20m **Torc Waterfall,** the starting point for several short trails along beautiful **Torc Mountain.** It's a 3.5km stroll in the opposite direction to the **Meeting of the Waters,** a quiet spot where channels come together. Away from the paved path, the more secluded dirt trail through **Yew Woods** is inaccessible to bikes. To get to the 14th-century **Ross Castle,** the last stronghold in Munster to fall to Cromwell's army, take a right on Ross Rd. off Muckross Rd. when leaving town. The castle is 3km from Killarney. For a more scenic route, take the footpaths from Knockreer, outside of town along New St. (☎35851. Open daily June-Aug. 9am-6:30pm; May and Sept. 10am-6pm; mid-Mar. to Apr. and Oct. 10am-5pm. €5.30, students €2.10.) The nicest outdoor activity in the area is the biking around the **Gap of Dunloe,** which borders **Macgillycuddy's Reeks,** Ireland's highest mountain range, or hop on a boat from Ross Castle to the head of the Gap (1½hr., €8; book at the tourist office). From **Lord Brandon's Cottage,** on the Gap trail, head left over the stone bridge, continue 3km to the church, and then turn right onto a winding road. Climb 2km and enjoy an 11km stroll downhill with gorgeous views. The 13km trip back to Killarney passes the ruins of **Dunloe Castle.** Bear right after Kate Kearney's Cottage, turn left on the road to Fossa, and turn right on Killorglin Rd.

■**Neptune's Hostel (IHH) ❶,** on Bishop's Ln. off New St., has a central location, clean dorms, and common spaces. The front desk books discounted tours of the Ring of Kerry and the Gap of Dunloe. (☎35255; www.neptuneshostel.com. Breakfast €2.50. Free bike storage. Laundry €7. Free Internet and Wi-Fi. Check-in 1-3pm. Check-out 10am. Dorms €13-16; doubles €37-42. 10% 1st night discount with student ID. MC/V.) The renovated **Fairview Guest House ❸,** College St., near the bus station, pampers guests with plush, sparkling suites, whirlpool tubs, and a range of breakfast options. (☎34164; www.fairviewkillarney.com. €53-105 per person; €35-54 for *Let's Go* readers.) For delectable meat, seafood, and vegetarian dishes, try **The Stonechat ❸,** 8 Fleming's Ln., the best restaurant in Killarney. (☎34295. Lunch €7-10. Dinner €13-20. Early-bird special 6-7:30pm, 4 courses for €22. Open M 6:30-10pm and Tu-Sa 12:30-3pm and 6:30-10pm.) Live music wafts down Killarney's streets on summer nights. A trendy twentysomething crowd gets down in the loungelike ■**McSorley's,** on College St., which starts the night with the usual trad, but switches it up with rock, and again with a late-night DJ. (☎39770. Pints €4. Cover F €7, Sa €10. Open M-Sa noon-2:30am, Su noon-1:30am. Nightclub upstairs open 11:30pm-2:30am.) **Scott's Bar,** also on College St., is a bit more relaxed and keeps it simple with trad. (☎31060. Pub food served daily noon-9pm.)

**Trains** (☎31067) leave from Killarney station, off E. Avenue Rd., for Cork (2hr., 7 per day, €20), Dublin (3½hr., 7 per day, €59), and Limerick (3hr., 7 per day, €22). Book ahead online for the best rates. **Buses** (☎30011) leave from Park Rd. for: Belfast, BRI (4 per day, €33); Cork (2hr., 10 per day, €15); Dublin (6hr., 6 per day, €22). **O'Sullivan's,** on Lower New St., rents **bikes.** (☎31282. Open daily 8:30am-6:30pm. €12 per day, €70 per week.) The **tourist office** is on Beech Rd. (☎31633; www.corkkerry.ie. Open July-Aug. M-Sa 9am-8pm, Su 10am-5:45pm; June and Sept. M-Sa 9am-6pm, Su 10am-5:45pm; Oct.-May M-Sa 9:15am-5pm.)

# RING OF KERRY

The Southwest's most celebrated peninsula offers picturesque villages, ancient forts, and rugged mountains. You'll have to brave congested roads hogged by tour buses, but rewards await those who take the time to explore on foot or by bike.

## ▐▛ TRANSPORTATION

The term "Ring of Kerry" usually describes the entire **Iveragh Peninsula,** though it technically refers to the ring of roads circumnavigating it. Hop on the circuit run by **Bus Éireann** (☎ 064 30011), based in Killarney (mid-June to Aug., 1 per day, departs 1:15pm, returns 5:30pm; entire ring in 1 day €21). Stops include Cahersiveen (2½hr. from Killarney, €12) and Caherdaniel (1hr. from Cahersiveen, €7.50). Or, book a bus tour with a private company; offices are scattered across town, and many accommodations will book a tour for you.

## CAHERSIVEEN                                    ☎066

Although best known as the birthplace of patriot Daniel O'Connell, Cahersiveen (CAH-her-sah-veen) also serves as a useful base for jaunts to Valentia Island, the Skelligs, and local archaeological sites. To see the ruins of **Ballycarbery Castle,** head past the barracks on Bridge St., turn left over the bridge, then left off the main road. About 200m past the castle turn-off stands a pair of Ireland's best-preserved stone forts, **Cahergall** and **Leacanabuaile Fort.** Enjoy views of the countryside and castle from the **Sive Hostel (IHH) ❶,** 15 East End, Church St. (☎947 2717. Laundry €8. Dorms €15; doubles €44. Camping €7 per person.) **O'Shea's B&B ❸,** next to the post office on Main St., has comfortable rooms and impressive views. (☎947 2402. Singles €35-40; doubles €66-70.) The pubs on **Main Street** still retain the authentic feel of their former proprietors' main businesses, including a general store, a smithy, and a leather shop. **The Harp** nightclub caters to local youth. (☎947 2436. 18+. Cover €7-9. Open F-Sa midnight-3am.) The Ring of Kerry **bus** stops in front of Banks Store on Main St. (mid-June to Aug., 2 per day) and continues on to Killarney (2½hr., €12) and Caherdaniel (1hr., €7.50). The **tourist office** is across from the bus stop. (☎947 2589. Open June to mid-Sept. M, W, F 9:15am-1pm and 2-5:15pm, Tu and Th 9:15am-1pm.)

Quiet, unspoiled **Valentia Island** makes a perfect daytrip, with roads ideal for biking or light hiking. Bridges on either end of the island connect it to the mainland, and a **ferry** runs from Reenard Point, 5km west of Cahersiveen (☎947 6141; Apr.-Sept. 7 per hr.; €2, cyclists €3). Another ferry sails to the **Skellig Rocks,** about 13km off the shore of the Iveragh Peninsula. From the boat, **Little Skellig** may appear snow-capped, but it's actually covered with white birds. Climb 630 steps to reach a **monastery** built by 6th-century Christian monks, whose dwellings remain intact. The hostel in Cahersiveen can arrange the ferry ride (about 1hr.) for €40.

## SNEEM                                        ☎064

Sneem is usually a quick stop for tour buses on the Ring of Kerry, but this tiny spot is worth more than a 20min. visit; in years past, it has won awards for being Ireland's tidiest and prettiest town. Its unique **Sculpture Park** provides just a taste of the town's charm. The two sides are connected by a stone bridge. The cheerful **Bank House B&B ❸,** in North Sq., has delicious breakfast options. (☎45226; the_bank_house@yahoo.ie. Singles €45; doubles €64-70.) **The Village Kitchen ❷,** in the center of town, serves fresh seafood and sandwiches made on homemade brown bread. (☎45281. Entrees €8-10. Open daily 9:30am-8:30pm.)

# DINGLE PENINSULA

For decades, the Ring of Kerry's undertouristed counterpart, the Dingle Peninsula, has maintained a healthy ancient-site-to-tour-bus ratio. Only recently has the Ring's tourist blitz begun to encroach upon the spectacular cliffs and sweeping beaches of this Irish-speaking peninsula.

## TRANSPORTATION

Dingle Town is most easily reached by **Bus Éireann** from Tralee (1¼hr., 2-6 per day, €9). The bus stop is behind the big SuperValu. There is no public transportation on the peninsula; many visitors chose to explore the area by **bike**.

## DINGLE TOWN ☎ 066

Dingle Town is the adopted home of **Fungi the Dolphin,** who has lived in the harbor for over two decades and is now a focus of the tourism industry. **Boat tours** leave from the pier daily 11am-6pm in summer; call ahead Sept.-June. (☎915 2626. 1hr. €16, 2-12 €8; free if Fungi gets the jitters and doesn't show.) **Sciúird Archaeology Tours** leave from the Dingle pier for bus tours of the area's ancient sites. (☎915 1606. 2½hr., 2 per day, €20.) **Moran's Tours** runs trips to Slea Head, passing through majestic scenery and stopping at historic sites. (☎915 1155. 2 per day, €20.) ◪**Ballintaggart Hostel (IHH) ❶,** a 25min. walk east of town on Tralee Rd. (N86), is supposedly haunted by the Earl of Cork's murdered wife. According to local legend, the Earl tried to kill her with poisonous mushrooms, but when that failed, he strangled her instead. (☎915 1454; info@dingleaccommodation.com. Quiet hours after 11pm. Laundry €8. Towels €1.50. Open Apr.-Oct. Dorms €13-19; doubles €55-70. Tent sites €8. MC/V.) The busy **Homely House Cafe ❷,** Green St., has a varied menu. (☎915 2431; www.homelyhouse.com. Entrees €4.50-11. Open July-Aug. M-Tu 11am-5pm, W-Sa 11am-5pm and 6-10pm; Sept.-June M-Sa 11am-5pm.) The **tourist office** is on Strand St. (☎915 1188. Open mid-June to mid-Sept. M-Sa 9am-7pm, Su 10am-1pm and 2:15-5pm; mid-Sept. to mid-June daily 9am-1pm and 2:15-5pm.)

## SLEA HEAD, VENTRY, AND DUNQUIN ☎ 066

The most rewarding way to see the cliffs and crashing waves of Dunquin and Slea Head is to **bike** along **Slea Head Drive.** Past Dingle Town toward Slea Head, the village of **Ventry** *(Ceann Trá)* is home to a **beach** and the **Celtic and Prehistoric Museum,** a collection that includes the largest intact woolly mammoth skull in the world. (☎915 9191; www.celticmuseum.com. Open Mar.-Nov. daily 10am-5:30pm; call ahead Dec.-Feb. €4.) Hop on one of seven free daily shuttles from Dingle Town to reach the **Ballybeag Hostel ❶** in Ventry. Its secluded yet convenient location makes it an ideal base for exploring the western end of the peninsula. (☎915 9876; www.iol.ie/~balybeag. Laundry €4. Dorms €17; doubles €48. Cash only.)

North of Slea Head and Ventry, the settlement of Dunquin *(Dún Chaoin)* consists of stone houses and little else. Past Dunquin on the road to Ballyferriter, the **Great Blasket Centre** has exhibits about the now-abandoned Blasket Islands. (☎915 6444. Open daily July-Aug. 10am-7pm; Easter-June and Sept.-Oct. 10am-6pm. Last entry 45min. before closing. €3.70, students €1.30.) At the **Dun Chaoin An Óige Hostel (HI) ❶** in Ballyferriter, on Dingle Way across from the turn-off to the Blasket Centre, each bunk has a panoramic ocean view. (☎915 6121; mailbox@anoige.ie. Breakfast €4. Reception 9-10am and 5-10pm. Lockout 10am-5pm. Open Feb.-Nov. Dorms €16-19; doubles €37. €2 HI discount. MC/V.) **Kruger's,** Europe's westernmost pub, has great views. (☎915 6127. Live music Tu, Th, Sa 9:30pm, Su 7:30pm. Open M-Th 11am-11:30pm, F-Sa 11am-12:30pm, Su 11am-11pm.)

## TRALEE                                                                ☎066

The economic and residential capital of Co. Kerry, Tralee (pop. 20,000) is a good base for exploring the Ring of Kerry or the Dingle Peninsula. The **Kerry County Museum,** in Ashe Memorial Hall on Denny St., colorfully illustrates the history of Ireland and Co. Kerry and takes visitors to an impressive lifelike reproduction of medieval Tralee. (☎712 7777; www.kerrymuseum.ie. Open June-Aug. daily 9:30am-5:30pm; Sept.-Dec. Tu-Sa 9:30am-5pm; Jan.-Mar. Tu-F 10am-4:30pm; Apr.-May Tu-Sa 9:30am-5:30pm. €8, students €6.50.) During the last week of August, Tralee hosts the nationally known **Rose of Tralee Festival,** at which lovely Irish lasses compete for the title of "Rose of Tralee."

Though most accommodations in the town center are either luxury hotels or grungy rooms above pubs, **Finnegan's Hostel ❷,** on Denny St., 100m from the museum, stands out as a beautiful home in the middle of the action. Gaze at the rose garden from rooms named after great Irish authors. (☎712 7610; www.finneganshostel.com. Breakfast included. Dorms €17; singles €30; doubles €40.) **Brat's Place ❷,** 18 Milk Market Ln., across the Mall from the eastern side of the square, serves superb vegetarian and vegan dishes made with organic ingredients. The hostess brings warm, spiced breads to those lucky enough to find a table. (Soup €3.50. Entrees €7-10. Open M-Sa 12:30-3pm.) **Trains** depart from the station on Oakpark Rd. for: Cork (2½hr., 3-5 per day, €23); Dublin (4hr., 3-6 per day, €31); Galway (5-6hr., 3 per day, €59); Killarney (40min., 4 per day, €8.20). **Buses** leave from the train station for: Cork (2½hr., 8 per day, €15); Galway (9 per day, €18); Killarney (40min., 10-14 per day, €5.90); Limerick (2¼hr., 10 per day, €14). To get from the station to the **tourist office** in Ashe Memorial Hall, head down Edward St., turn right on Castle St., and left on Denny St. (☎712 1288. Open July-Aug. M-Sa 9am-7pm, Su 10am-6pm; Sept.-May M-Sa 9am-6pm.)

# WESTERN IRELAND

Even Dubliners will say that the west is the "most Irish" part of Ireland; in remote areas you may hear Irish being spoken almost as often as English. The potato famine was most devastating in the west—entire villages emigrated or died—and the current population is still less than half of what it was in 1841.

## LIMERICK                                                              ☎061

Although the city's 18th-century Georgian streets and parks are regal and elegant, 20th-century industrial and commercial development cursed Limerick (pop. 80,000) with a featureless urban feel. The city gained a reputation for violence, and Frank McCourt's celebrated memoir *Angela's Ashes* revealed its squalor. But now, with help from the EU and a strong student presence, Limerick is a city on the rise. It is a fine place to stay en route to points west, but because of its lack of hostels, it's perhaps best seen in a single day. The **Hunt Museum,** in the Custom House on Rutland St., holds a gold crucifix that Mary, Queen of Scots gave to her executioner, as well as a coin reputed to be one of the infamous 30 pieces of silver paid to Judas by the Romans. (☎312 833; www.huntmuseum.com. Open M-Sa 10am-5pm, Su 2-5pm. €7.50, students €6.)

Limerick suffered from a series of hostel closures in 2002 and another smaller wave in 2005, but a number of B&Bs can be found on **O'Connell Street** or **Ennis Road.**

Sunny singles and a well-equipped kitchen make up for the distant location of **Courtbrack Accommodation ❸**, Dock Rd., 20min. from town. (☎302 500. Laundry €5. Free Wi-Fi. Singles €30; doubles €52. MC/V.) The lovely owner of **Glen Eagles B&B ❹**, 12 Vereker Gardens, off Ennis Rd. over the Sarsfield Bridge, has a soft spot for backpackers and a clean, quiet home close to the city center. (☎455 521; gleneaglesbandb@eircom.net. TV and coffee/tea facilities in all rooms. Breakfast included. Singles €40-45; doubles €60-70. MC/V.) **O'Grady's Cellar Restaurant ❷**, 118 O'Connell St., serves traditional favorites in a cozy underground spot. (☎418 286; www.ogradyscellarrestaurant.com. Entrees €8.50-14. Open daily 9am-10:30pm. MC/V.) Limerick's student population adds spice to the nightlife scene during termtime. The area where **Denmark Street** and **Cornmarket Row** intersect is a good place to quench your thirst or listen to live music. **Dolan's**, 3-4 Dock Rd., is a bit of a walk from the center of town, but hosts rambunctious local patrons and nightly trad in its dark interior. (☎314 483. Entrees €6-10. Lunch menu €3.50-8; served noon-7pm. Music nightly 9:30pm-close. Open M 7:30am-11:30pm, Tu-Th 9am-11:30pm, F-Sa 7:30am-2am, Su 10am-11pm. MC/V.)

**Trains** (☎315 555) leave for Cork (2½hr., 7-9 per day, €23) and Dublin (2½hr., 12-14 per day, €43). **Buses** (☎313 333; www.buseireann.ie) leave Colbert Station, off Parnell St., for Cork (2hr., 14 per day, €15), Dublin (3½hr., 1 per hr., €13), and Galway (2½hr., 1 per hr., €15). The **tourist office** is on Arthurs Quay. From the station, walk down Davis St., turn right on O'Connell St., and take a left at Arthurs Quay Mall. (☎317 522. Open June-Sept. M-Sa 9am-6pm, Su 9:30am-1pm and 2-5:30pm; Oct.-May M-F 9:30am-5:30pm, Sa 9:30am-1:30pm.)

# ⚑ LET'S GO TO WESTERN IRELAND: ENNIS     ☎065

Ennis's proximity to Shannon Airport and the Burren makes it a common stopover for tourists, though there is little to do in the town itself. **Trains** (☎684 0444; www.irishrail.ie) leave from Station Rd. for Dublin (7 per day, €43). **Buses** (☎682 4177) also leave from Station Rd. 1 per hour for: Cork (3hr., €14); Dublin (4hr., €17); Galway (1hr., €11); Limerick (40min., €8); Shannon Airport (40min., €6).

If you do care to explore Ennis, the friendly owners of **St. Jude's B&B ❸**, Greine Rd., are happy to provide info on the town. From the bus station, head down Station Rd. and make a left on Greine Rd. (☎684 2383. Doubles €60. Cash only.) The French chef serves up creative sandwiches (€5) and salads (€12-15) at **The Gourmet Store ❷**, 1 Barrack St. (☎684 3314. Open M-W 9:30am-7:30pm, Th-Sa 9:30am-9pm, Su noon-6pm. MC/V.) The **tourist office** is on Arthur's Row, off O'Connell Square. (☎682 8366; www.shannonregiontourism.ie. Open June-Aug. M-F 9:30am-5:30pm, Sa-Su 9:30am-1pm and 2-5:30pm; mid-Mar. to June and Sept.-Dec. M-Sa 9:30am-1pm and 2-5:30pm; Jan. to mid-Mar. M-F 9:30am-1pm and 2-5:30pm.)

# THE CLIFFS OF MOHER AND THE BURREN     ☎065

Plunging 213m straight down to the sea, the ▓**Cliffs of Moher** provide incredible views of the Kerry Mountains, the Twelve Bens mountains, and the Aran Islands. Be careful of extremely strong winds; they blow a few tourists off every year, though new barriers make it difficult to wander into danger. Let's Go strongly discourages straying from the established paths. The new **Visitors Centre** and **Atlantic Edge Exhibition** educate tourists on the cliffs. (☎708 6141; www.cliffsofmoher.ie. Open daily mid-July to mid-Aug. 9am-7:30pm; mid-Aug. to mid-July 9:30am-5:30pm. €4, students €3.50.) To reach the cliffs, head 5km south of Doolin on R478, or hop on the Galway-Cork **bus** (in summer 2-3 per day). From Liscannor, **Cliffs of Moher Cruises** (☎708 6060; www.mohercruises.com) sails under

### WILLY-NILLY LOVE

*An interview with Willie Daly, the Lisdoonvarna matchmaker.*

**LG:** How did the September matchmaking begin?

**A:** It started just before the turn of the century, and it started because Lisdoonvarna was a small market town. There was a doctor who lived there named Dr. Foster who found out there were sulphur and iron waters in the town, and he developed a health spa. The matchmaking started almost accidentally. The people who would come to the spa would be the more wealthy farmers. And they'd start matchmaking their children in conversation over breakfast, saying "now I have a John who is 28..." In the 30s and 40s the festival became popular, and they started having big bands and dances.

**LG:** What does it take to be a successful matchmaker these days?

**A:** Being a successful matchmaker is getting people together...there has to be an element of magic there, and today there has to be an element of love there, quickly. Irish men want a partner, someone to share their home, their life, to share their world with. There's a huge number of men in Ireland. In the past, most of the properties—restaurants, hotels, pubs, farms—would be left to a son. This would be done so that the family name would continue. And in hindsight, it's not good, because there are

the cliffs (1¾hr., 1 per day, €20). **Ferries** also run to the cliffs from Doolin (1hr., 2-3 per day, €20.)

The nearby **Burren** resembles an enchanted fairyland, with secluded coves, bright wildflowers, and 28 species of butterflies fluttering in the air. The old stone forts and isolated trees sprinkled around the countryside are supposedly home to leprechauns. The Burren town of **Lisdoonvarna** is known for its **Matchmaking Festival**, a six-week-long *craic*-and-snogging celebration that attracts over 10,000 singles each September. **Sleepzone Burren ❶**, past the smokehouse on Doolin Rd., is an elegant hotel-turned-hostel perfect for launching into the Burren wild. (☎707 4036. Breakfast included. Free Wi-Fi. Dorms €15-22; singles €30-45.) In the town of **Ballyvaughan**, guests at **O'Brien B&B ❸**, on Main St., enjoy the huge rooms and the fireplaces in the adjacent pub. The bus from Galway arrives in front of the B&B. (☎707 7003. Doubles from €60-70. MC/V.) **Monk's Pub and Restaurant ❷**, sits on the pier with a view across the bay to Galway city. Tourists crowd around the huge stone fireplace for trad, while locals gravitate toward the bar. (☎707 7059. Famous seafood chowder €6. Music 2 nights per week, usually Th and Sa.) There are **no ATMs** in Ballyvaughan. A **bus** (☎091 562 000) connects Galway to towns in the Burren a few times a day in summer but infrequently in winter.

# GALWAY ☎091

With its youthful, exuberant spirit, Galway (pop. 70,000) is one of the fastest growing cities in Europe. Performers dazzle crowds on the appropriately named Shop St., locals and tourists lounge in outdoor cafes, and hip crowds pack the pubs and clubs at night. In addition to its peaceful quay-side walks, Galway is only a short drive away from beautiful Connemara.

 **TRANSPORTATION. Trains** leave from Eyre Sq. (☎561 444) for Dublin (3hr., 5-6 per day, €30) via Portarlington (€24); transfer at Portarlington for all other lines. **Buses** also leave from Eyre Sq. (☎562 000) for: Belfast, BRI (7½hr., 3 per day, €30); Donegal (4hr., 5 per day, €19); and Dublin (4hr., 1 per hr., €14).

 **ORIENTATION AND PRACTICAL INFORMATION.** Galway's train and bus stations are on a hill to the northeast of **Eyre Square,** a recently renovated block of lawns and monuments. A string of small, cheap B&Bs are north of the square along **Prospect Hill.** The western corner of the square is the gateway to the pedestrian center, filled with shoppers seeking cups of coffee or pints of stout. From the square, ·**Shop Street** becomes **High Street,** which then becomes **Quay**

Street. The **Wolfe Tone Bridge** spans the River Corrib and connects the city center to the bohemian left bank. The **tourist office,** on Forster St. near the train and bus stations exchanges currency. (☎537 700. Open May-Sept. daily 9am-5:45pm; Oct.-June M-Sa 9am-5:45pm.) For **Internet,** head to **Runner Internet Cafe,** 4 Eyre Sq. (☎539 966. Noon-10pm €4 per hr., 9am-noon and 10pm-midnight €2 per hr. Open daily 9am-midnight.) The **post office** is at 3 Eglinton St. (☎534 720. Open M-Sa 9am-5:30pm.)

**▮▯ ACCOMMODATIONS AND FOOD.** The number of accommodations in Galway has recently skyrocketed, but reservations are necessary in summer. Most B&Bs are concentrated in Salthill or on College Rd. ▮**Barnacle's Quay Street House (IHH) ❶,** 10 Quay St., is the most conveniently located hostel in Galway. Its bright, spacious rooms are perfect for crashing after a night on the town. (☎568 644; www.barnacles.ie. Light breakfast included. Laundry €7. Towels €1. Free Wi-Fi. Single-sex dorms available. 4- to 12-bed dorms €17-24; doubles €56. Low season reduced rates. MC/V.) At **St. Martin's B&B ❸,** 2 Nun's Island Rd., on the west bank of the river at the end of O'Brien's Bridge, the gorgeous back garden features a waterfall cascading into the river. This friendly B&B caters to young travelers, and the owner greets every guest with coffee. (☎568 286; stmartins@gmail.com. Singles €35; doubles €70. Cash only.) **Sleepzone ❷,** Bóthar na mBán, Woodquay, up Prospect Hill, has large rooms and top-notch facilities. (☎566 999; www.sleepzone.ie. Breakfast included. Laundry €7. Free Wi-Fi. Single-sex dorms available. Dorms €20-25; singles €30-50; doubles €50-76. Weekend and low-season rates vary. MC/V.)

The cafes and pubs around Quay, High, and Shop Streets are good options for budget dining. On Saturdays, an **open-air market** on Market St. sells fruit and ethnic foods. (Open 8am-4pm.) At ▮**The Home Plate ❷,** on Mary St., diners enjoy large sandwiches and entrees (€6-10) on tiny wooden tables. (☎561 475. Open M-Th noon-8pm, F-Sa noon-9pm, Su noon-7pm. Cash only.) Cross Wolfe Tone Bridge and walk 3min. up Father Griffin Rd. to reach **Anton's ❷** and its homemade fare. The walls feature the work of local artists. (☎582 067; www.antonscafe.com. Sandwiches €5.50. Open M-F 8am-6pm. Cash only.) Take a left just before Shop St. for **Food For Thought ❶,** Lower Abbeygate St., a student hangout with wallet-friendly prices. (☎565 854. *Moussaka* €6.50. Open M-F 7:30am-6pm, Sa 8am-6pm, Su 11:30am-4pm. Cash only.) Artsy students flock to **Java's ❶,** 17 Upper Abbeygate St., for tapas (€5.75), New York-style bagels (€3.30), and everything in

too many men, and all the women have gone to Dublin, London, and New York. Irish men—the thing that they have that's so very rare in the world—they have a marvelous sense of humor, and a great aptitude for music, singing, dancing, and drinking, and a very relaxed lifestyle. It's this lifestyle that gives them so much time to make a woman feel cherished and loved. When a man from the West of Ireland finds a woman, he really adores her. He might look a bit rough and rugged, but he'll have a heart full of love, and his mind won't be confused, like so many people in towns and cities.

**LG:** What advice do you give your potential matches?

**A:** To someone from another country, I would say that some of the finest men in the world live in Ireland, and especially in the West of Ireland. They're so close to nature themselves; they are unspoiled, and that's important. A lot of women find themselves secure and okay in life, but not in love—I think in one life you owe it to yourself to try to find love, and to find happiness. If you die without that, you have lived life a little bit in vain.

*Willie and his daughter, Marie, can be found in the Matchmaker Bar on Th-Sa nights during the festival. They can also be contacted at: ☎707 1385 or williedaly@tinet.ie.*

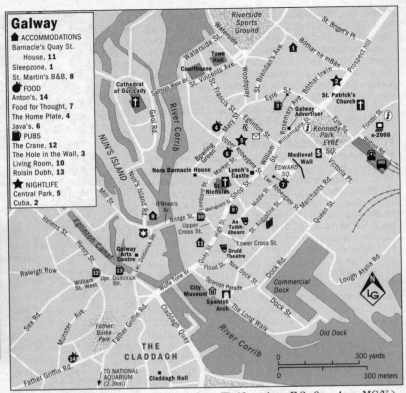

**Galway**

🏠 ACCOMMODATIONS
Barnacle's Quay St. House, **11**
Sleepzone, **1**
St. Martin's B&B, **8**

🍴 FOOD
Anton's, **14**
Food for Thought, **7**
The Home Plate, **4**
Java's, **6**

🍺 PUBS
The Crane, **12**
The Hole in the Wall, **3**
Living Room, **10**
Roisín Dubh, **13**

⭐ NIGHTLIFE
Central Park, **5**
Cuba, **2**

between. (☎532 890. Open Su-W 10am-3am, Th 10am-4am, F-Sa 8am-4am. MC/V.)

👁🎵 **SIGHTS AND ENTERTAINMENT.** The best *craic* in Galway is people-watching: Eyre Square and Shop St. are full of street performers, some unknowing. At the **Church of St. Nicholas** on Market St., a stone marks the spot where Columbus supposedly stopped to pray to the patron saint of travelers before sailing the ocean blue. (Open May-Sept. daily 8:30am-6:30pm. Free.) On Shop St., **Lynch's Castle** is a well-preserved 16th-century merchant's residence that now houses a bank. From Quay St., head across Wolfe Tone Bridge to the **Claddagh**, an area that was an Irish-speaking, thatch-roofed fishing village until the 1930s. The famous **Claddagh rings** are today's mass-produced reminders of yesteryear. The **Nora Barnacle House,** 8 Bowling Green, off Market St., has hardly changed since James Joyce's future wife Nora lived there with her family at the turn of the 20th century. Check out Joyce's love letters to his life-long companion. (www.norabarnacle.com. Open mid-May to mid-Sept. M-Sa 10am-1pm and 2-5pm, or by appointment. €2.50, students €2.) Satiate your aquatic cravings at the **National Aquarium of Ireland,** on the Salt Hill Promenade. (☎585 100; www.nationalaquarium.ie. Open Apr.-Sept. daily 9am-6pm; Oct.-Mar. M-F 9am-5pm, Sa-Su 9am-6pm. €9, students €6.50.) Event listings are published in the free *Galway Advertiser*, available at the tourist office and most accommodations. In mid-July, the **Galway Arts Festival** (☎566 577) attracts droves of filmmakers, rock groups, theater troupes, and trad musicians.

■ **NIGHTLIFE.** With approximately 650 pubs and 70,000 people, Galway maintains a low person-to-pub ratio. Pubs on Quay St., High St., and Eyre Sq. cater primarily to tourists, while locals stick to the more trad-oriented pubs on **Dominick Street** across the river. Fantastic trad fills two floors at ■**The Crane,** 2 Sea Rd. (☎587 419. Open M-Th 3-11:30pm, F-Sa 1pm-12:30am, Su 1-11pm. Cash only.) Nearby, at the **Roisín Dubh (The Black Rose),** on Dominick St., a bookshelved front hides some of Galway's hottest live music. (☎586 540; www.roisindubh.net. Pints €3.50. W stand-up comedy 9pm. Cover €5-25 most nights for music in the back room; front room and upstairs bar free. Open M-Tu 3-11:30pm, W-Su 3pm-2am.) At **Living Room,** Bridge St., weekend DJs keep the young crowd drinking and dancing at the red-lit bar. (☎563 804. Open M-W 10:30am-11:30pm, Th-Su 10:30am-2am.) **The Hole in the Wall,** Eyre St., is a student hangout with a beer garden. (☎565 593. DJ nightly 9:30pm. Open Su-Th 10:30am-11:30pm, F-Sa 10:30am-12:30am.)

Between 11:30pm and 12:30am, the pubs drain out, and the young and tireless go dancing. The crowd usually ends up at ■**Central Park,** 36 Upper Abbeygate St. With five bars and a huge dance floor, this is the place to be in Galway. (☎565 976; www.centralparkclub.com. Pints €4. Cover €5-10. Open Su-F 11pm-2am, Sa 10:45pm-2:30am.) **Cuba,** on Prospect Hill, past Eyre Sq., is second only to Central Park in popularity and features danceable live music on two floors. (☎565 991; www.cuba.ie. Su stand-up comedy 8:30pm; free admission to club afterward. Cover €6-10. Many hostels give out 50% discount cards. Open daily 11pm-2am.)

## ARAN ISLANDS (OILEÁIN ÁRANN)                    ☎099

The spectacular Aran Islands lie on the westernmost edge of Co. Galway, isolated by 32km of Atlantic Ocean. Churches, forts, ruins, and holy wells rise from the stony terrain of **Inishmore** (Inis Mór; pop. 900), the largest of the three islands. At the **Dún Aonghasa** ring fort, stones circle a sheer 100m drop. The **Inis Mór Way** is a mostly paved route that passes the majority of the island's sights. There are similar paths on **Inisheer** (Inis Oírr; pop. 260), the smallest island, and windswept **Inishmaan** (Inis Meáin; pop. 200). On Inishmore, the **Kilronan Hostel ❷,** next to the pier, offers free Internet and a TV room with DVD collection. (☎61255. Breakfast included. Single-sex dorms available. Dorms €20.) The **SPAR** supermarket in Kilronan has the island's only **ATM** (☎61203). **Aran Island Ferries** (☎091 561 767; www.aranislandferries.com) go from Rossaveal, west of Galway, to Inishmore (45min., 2-4 per day, round-trip €25) and Inisheer (2 per day). **Aran Direct** (☎566 535) also leaves from Rossaveal for Inishmore (45min., 3 per day, round-trip €25) and runs ferries. Both companies run **buses** to Rossaveal (€6), which leave from Kinlay House, on Merchant St. in Galway, 1½hr. before ferry departure. The **tourist office** on Inishmore stores luggage (€1) and helps find accommodations. (☎61263. Open daily June-Aug. 10am-7pm; Sept.-May 10am-5pm.)

# CONNEMARA

The Connemara region in northwest Co. Galway is an outdoorsman's dream, comprised of a lacy net of inlets and islands that provide stunning views of two major mountain ranges: the Twelve Bens and the Maumturks.

## CLIFDEN AND CONNEMARA NATIONAL PARK          ☎095

English-speaking **Clifden** attracts crowds of tourists. For the best scenery, bike along **Sky Road,** a 20km loop that overlooks the coastline, castles, and the towering Bens. **Bike** rental is available at **Mannion's,** on Bridge St. (☎21160. June-Aug. €15 per day, €70 per week; Sept.-May €10 per day. €10 deposit. Open daily 9:30am-7pm.) **The White Heather House B&B ❸,** on the square, offers panoramic views from most rooms with bath. (☎21655. Singles €35; doubles €60. MC/V.) Near the pubs,

**Clifden Town Hostel (IHH) ❶**, Market St., has a helpful owner and good facilities. (☎21076; www.clifdentownhostel.com. Open year-round, but call ahead Nov.-Feb. Dorms €15; doubles €36; triples €52; quads €65. AmEx.) **Shanaheever Campsite ❶** is 1.5km outside Clifden on Westport Rd. (☎22150; www.clifdencamping.com. Laundry €8. Tent or trailer sites €9 per person. Electricity €4. Free showers.) Most affordable restaurants in Clifden are attached to pubs. The family-run **Cullen's Bistro and Coffee Shop ❸**, Market St., cooks up hearty meals and delicious desserts. (☎21983. Irish stew €16. Open Apr.-Nov. daily noon-10pm.) **O'Connor's SuperValu,** on the square, sells groceries. (☎21182. Open M-Sa 8:30am-10pm, Su 9am-7pm.) Bus Éireann runs **buses** from the library on Market St. to Galway via Oughterard (1½hr.; 2-6 per day; €10, students €7.70) and to Westport via Leenane (1½hr., late June-Aug. M-Sa 1 per day, €11/9). Michael Nee (☎34682) buses leave across the street from the tourist office for Galway (1½hr.; 2 per day; €11, round-trip €14). The **tourist office** is on Galway Rd. (☎21163; www.irelandwest.ie. Open July-Aug. daily 10am-6pm; Mar.-June and Sept.-Oct. M-Sa 10am-5pm.)

**Connemara National Park** occupies 12.5 sq. km of mountainous countryside. Bogs, often covered by a thin screen of grass and flowers, constitute much of the park's terrain. The **Sruffaunboy Nature** and **Ellis Wood** trails are easy 20min. hikes. The newly constructed pathway up 🔲**Diamond Hill** is a more difficult journey, but it rewards climbers with views of the harbor and the spectacular Bens. Experienced hikers head for the **Twelve Bens** (Na Beanna Beola; also called the Twelve Pins), a rugged mountain range that reaches heights of 2200m. A tour of six peaks takes a full day. Trails are scarce, so consult the Clifden tourist office before jumping into the bog. **Biking** the 65km circle through Clifden, Letterfrack, and the Inagh Valley is truly captivating, but only appropriate for fit bikers. The **Visitors Centre** provides minimal help in planning hikes. (☎41054. Open daily June-Aug. 9:30am-6:30pm; Mar.-May and Sept. 10am-5:30pm.) Turn off from N59, 13km east of Clifden near Letterfrack, to reach the park.

# WESTPORT                                          ☎098

Natural attractions await just outside Westport's busy streets. Rising 650m over Clew Bay, **Croagh Patrick** has been revered as a holy site for thousands of years. According to legend, St. Patrick prayed on the mountain for 40 days and nights in AD 441 to banish all snakes from Ireland. Climbers start their journey up Croagh Patrick from the 15th-century **Murrisk Abbey,** west of town on R335 toward Louisburgh. **Buses** go to Murrisk via Louisburgh (2-3 per day); ask to be dropped off in Murrisk. Sheep rule **Clare Island,** a speck of land in the Atlantic. Hop on a bus to Roonagh Pier, 29km from Westport, and then take a ferry to the island. (Bus departs from Westport's tourist office July-Aug. 10am, returns by 6pm; €25 for bus and ferry combined.) B&Bs in Westport cluster on **Altamont Street** and **The Quay.** The extensive breakfast options at 🔲**The Altamont B&B ❸**, Altamont St., have kept travelers coming back for 44 years. (☎25226. Rooms €35-40.) Dine on **Bridge Street,** home to most of the town's restaurants and pubs, or grab groceries at the **SuperValu** market on Shop St. (☎27000. Open M-Sa 8am-10pm, Su 9am-9pm.) **Matt Molloy's,** owned by the flutist of the Chieftains, has nightly trad at 9:30pm. (☎26655. Pints €3.50. Open Su-Th 1pm-1am, F-Sa 1pm-2am.) **Trains** (☎25253) leave from the Altamont St. Station, a 10min. walk up the North Mall, to Dublin (3-4 per day, €32) via Athlone. **Buses** (☎71800) leave from Mill St. to Galway (2hr., 8 per day, €13). The **tourist office** is on James St. (☎25711. Open M-Sa 9am-5:45pm.)

# SLIGO                                             ☎071

Since the beginning of the 20th century, William Butler Yeats devotees have made literary pilgrimages to Sligo; the poet spent summers in town as a child and set many of his works around Sligo Bay. **Sligo Town** is the commercial center and an excellent base for daytrips to local nature adventures. **⬛Model Arts and Niland Gallery,** on the Mall, houses one of the country's finest collections of modern Irish art. (☎914 1405; www.modelart.ie. Open June-Oct. Tu-Sa 10am-5:30pm, Su 11am-4pm. Free.) The well-preserved former Dominican friary, **Sligo Abbey,** is on Abbey St. (Open Apr.-Dec. daily 10am-6pm, last entry 5:15pm; Jan.-Mar. reduced hours. €2.10, students €1.10.) Yeats is buried in **Drumcliffe Churchyard,** on the N15, 6.5km northwest of Sligo. To get there, catch a bus from Sligo to the Derry stop at Drumcliffe (10min., 7 per day, €5.50). At 500m, **Ben Bulben's Peak** dominates the skyline and offers a challenging hike. From N15, follow the signs to Ben Bulben Farm. A dirt road breaks off to mark the beginning of the journey.

Most **B&Bs** are near **Pearse Road.** Outside the center of town, **Eden Hill Holiday Hostel (IHH) ❶,** off Pearse Rd., offers mountain views and respite from the clamor of town. Follow Pearse Rd., go right at the Marymount sign and right again after one block. (☎914 3204; www.edenhillhostel.com. Bike rental €15 per day. Laundry €8. Dorms €11-15; doubles €40. 2-person tents €18. MC/V.) **Pepper Alley ❶,** Rockwood Parade by the river, serves sandwiches and pastries. (☎917 0720. Entrees €3.50-8. Open M-Sa 8am-5:30pm, Su 10am-4pm.) Grab groceries at the **Tesco** supermarket on O'Connell St. (☎916 2788. Open 24hr.) **The Left Bank,** 15-16 Stephen's St., across the river, is a popular destination for live music and dancing. (☎914 0100; www.leftbank.ie. Cover after 11pm W €5, F-Sa €6. Open M and W-Su noon-2:30am, Tu noon-12:30am.) Have a laugh with the locals in a comfortable atmosphere at **Foley's,** 14/15 Castle St. (☎914 2381. Pints €3.40. Open M-Sa 9:30am-11:30pm, Su 11am-11pm.)

**Trains** (☎1850 836 6222; www.irishrail.ie) leave from Lord Edward St. to Dublin (3hr., 6 per day, round-trip €26) via Carrick-on-Shannon and Mullingar. From the same station, **buses** (☎916 0066; www.buseireann.ie) head to: Belfast (4hr.; 3-4 per day; €24, students €18); Derry/Londonderry (3hr., 8-10 per day, €16/13); Donegal (1hr., 7-9 per day, €11/9); Dublin (3-4hr., 7 per day, €16/13); Galway (2½hr., 7 per day, €13/11). Turn left on Lord Edward St., then right on to Adelaide St., and head around the corner to Temple St. to reach the **tourist office.** (☎916 1201; www.irelandnorthwest.ie. Open July-Aug. M-F 9am-5pm, Sa 11am-3pm.)

# NORTHWESTERN IRELAND

A sliver of land connects the mountains, lakes, and ancient monuments of Co. Sligo to Co. Donegal. Among Ireland's counties, Donegal (DUN-ee-gahl) is second only to Cork in size. Its *gaeltacht* is the largest sanctuary of the living Irish language in Ireland, and its geographic isolation and natural beauty embrace travelers sick of the tourist hordes farther south.

## DONEGAL TOWN (DÚN NA NGALL)                     ☎074 97

A gateway for travelers heading to more isolated destinations in the north and northwest, the compact Donegal Town erupts with live music in pubs on weekends. The triangular center of town is called **the Diamond.** Six craftsmen open their studios to the public around the pleasant courtyard of the **⬛Donegal Craft Village,** 2km south of town on the Ballyshannon Rd. (☎22225. Open 10am-5pm, daily in summer, M-Sa spring and autumn, Tu-Sa winter.) The **Waterbus** shuttle provides aquatic tours of Donegal Bay, departing from the quay next to the tourist office. (☎23666. Departure times depend on tides; call ahead. €10.) For two weeks in July, the **Earagail Arts Festival** celebrates the county's art scene, while the **Donegal Bluestacks**

**Festival** features theater, arts, poetry, and music from late September to early October. (☎074 91 29186; www.donegalculture.com. Tickets range from free to €25.)

A 10min. walk from town, the family-run ◙**Donegal Town Independent Hostel (IHH/IHO) ❶**, Killybegs Rd., welcomes backpackers with murals on the ceilings of the dorms and a happy dog named Scooby. (☎22805. Dorms €16; doubles €36, with bath €40. Tent sites €9 per person. MC/V.) **The Blueberry Tea Room ❷**, Castle St., buzzes with patrons enjoying breakfast (€6) and daily specials (€10). Check email at their Internet cafe on the second floor. (☎22933. Internet €2 for 30min. Open M-Sa 8:30am-7:30pm.) For groceries, head to **SuperValu**, 2min. from the Diamond down Ballyshannon Rd. (☎22977. Open M-Sa 8:30am-9pm, Su 10am-7pm.) **The Reveller,** in the Diamond, caters to a young crowd with pool and loud music. (☎21201. Th-Su live music 10:30pm-close. Open M-Th 10:30am-11:30pm, F-Sa 10:30am-12:30am, Su noon-11pm.) At **The Reel Inn**, Bridge St. (☎086 25 12004; thereelinn@eircom.net), formerly Dunnion's Bar, the owners have established the center of Donegal Town's trad circuit. (Trad nightly, all year. Open M-Th 10:30am-11:30pm, F-Sa 10:30am-12:30am, Su noon-11pm.)

**Bus Éireann** (☎21101) leaves from the Abbey Hotel on the Diamond for Derry/Londonderry (1½hr.; M-Sa 7per day, Su 3 per day; €13) via Letterkenny (€6.40), Dublin (3½hr.; M-Th and Sa 6 per day, F and Su 7 per day; €17), and Galway (4hr.; M-Sa 6 per day, Su 4 per day; €12). To reach the very helpful **tourist office,** face away from the Abbey Hotel and turn right; the office is outside the Diamond on the Ballyshannon/Sligo Rd. (☎21148; www.donegaltown.ie. Open June-Aug. M-F 9am-6pm, Sa 10am-6pm, Su 11am-3pm; Sept-May M-F 9am-5pm.)

## LETTERKENNY                                   ☎074 91

Letterkenny is difficult to navigate, but it is a useful stop for making bus connections to the rest of Ireland and to Northern Ireland. Cool green rooms with bath sweep guests away from the outside traffic at the **Pearse Road Guesthouse ❸**. Walk down Pearse Rd. from the bus depot (7min.) and look for a large white house. (☎23002. Singles €40; doubles €70.) The town's only hostel is **The International Port Hostel (IHO) ❶**, Covehill Port Rd., behind the theater. (☎25315; www.porthostel.ie. Free Wi-Fi. Dorms Su-F €16, Sa €20; doubles Su-F €40, Sa €50. Reduced rates online and in winter. MC/V.) A **Tesco supermarket** is in the shopping center behind the bus station. (Open 24hr.) **Buses** leave from the station at the junction of Port (Derry) and Pearse Rd., in front of the shopping center. Bus Éireann (☎21309) runs to: Derry/Londonderry (35min., 3-8 per day, €7.50); Donegal Town (1hr., 4-6 per day, €8.40); Dublin (4½hr., 9 per day, €18); Galway (4½hr., 3-4 per day, €19); Sligo (2hr., 3-4 per day, €13). Lough Swilly (☎22863) buses run to Derry/Londonderry (M-F 9per day, Sa 4 per day) and the Inishowen Peninsula (M-Sa 2-3 per day). The **tourist office** (☎21160) is off the second roundabout at the intersection of Port (Derry) and Blaney Rd., 1.2km from town past the bus station.

# NORTHERN IRELAND

The calm tenor of everyday life in Northern Ireland has long been overshadowed by headlines about riots and bombs. While the violence has subdued, the divisions in civil society continue. Protestants and Catholics usually live in separate neighborhoods, attend separate schools, and patronize different stores and pubs. The 1998 Good Friday Accord (p. 549) began a slow march to peace, and all sides have renewed their efforts to make their country as peaceful as it is beautiful.

# BELFAST (BÉAL FEIRSTE)

☎ 028

The second-largest city on the island, Belfast (pop. 270,000) is the focus of Northern Ireland's cultural, commercial, and political activity. Queen's University testifies to the city's rich academic history—luminaries such as Nobel Laureate Seamus Heaney once roamed the halls of Queen's, and Samuel Beckett taught the young men of Campbell College. The Belfast pub scene ranks among the best in the world, combining the historical appeal of old-fashioned watering holes with more modern bars and clubs. While Belfast has suffered from the stigma of its violent past, it has rebuilt itself and now surprises most visitors with its neighborly, urbane feel. This is true for most of the city, with the exception of the still divided West Belfast area, home to separate communities of Protestants and Catholics.

## TRANSPORTATION

**Flights:** Belfast is served by 2 airports. **Belfast International Airport (BFS;** ☎9442 2448; www.belfastairport.com) in Aldergrove. **Aer Lingus** (☎0845 084 4444; www.aerlingus.com), **British Airways** (☎0845 850 9850; www.ba.com), **EasyJet** (☎0870 567 6676; www.easyjet.com), and many other airlines arrive from London and other European cities. **Translink Bus 300** (☎9066 6630; www.translink.co.uk) has 24hr. service from the airport to Europa bus station in the city center (1-6 per hr.; £6, round-trip £9). **Taxis** (☎9448 4353) make the trip for £25-30. **Belfast City Airport (BHD;** ☎9093 9093; www.belfastcityairport.com), at the harbor, has arrivals from regional carriers. To get from City Airport to Europa bus station, take **Translink Bus 600** (1-3 per hr.).

**Trains:** For train and bus info, contact **Translink.** (☎9066 6630; www.translink.co.uk. Inquiries daily 7am-8pm.) Trains leave Belfast's **Central Station,** E. Bridge St. to Derry/ Londonderry (2hr.; M-F 10 per day, Sa 9 per day, Su 5 per day; £10) and **Dublin** (2hr.; M-Sa 8 per day, Su 5 per day; £24). The **Metro** buses are free with rail tickets.

**Buses: Europa Bus Terminal,** off Great Victoria St., behind the Europa Hotel (☎9066 6630; ticket office open M-Sa 7:30am-6:30pm, Su 12:30-5:30pm). Buses to **Derry/ Londonderry** (1¾hr., 11-34 per day, £9) and **Dublin** (3hr.; M-Sa 17 per day, Su 1 per day, leaving from Glengall St. rather than Europa; £9.70). The Centrelink bus connects the station with the city center.

**Ferries: Norfolk Ferries** (www.norfolkline-ferries.co.uk) operates out of the SeaCat terminal and runs to **Liverpool, BRI** (8hr.; from £20, book online to avoid a £10 booking fee.) **Stena Line** (☎0870 570 7070; www.stenaline.com) has the quickest service to Scotland, docking in **Stranraer** (1¾hr.; fares seasonal, book online).

**Public Transportation:** Belfast has 2 bus services. Many local bus routes connect through Laganside Bus Station, Queen's Sq. Transport cards and tickets are available at the pink kiosks in Donegall Sq. W (open M-F 8am-6pm, Sa 9am-5:20pm) and around the city. **Metro buses** (☎9066 6630; www.translink.co.uk) gather in Donegall Sq. 12 main routes cover Belfast. **Ulsterbus** "blue buses" cover the suburbs. Travel within the city center £1, under 16 £0.50. **Nightlink Buses** travel from Donegall Sq. W. to towns outside Belfast. Sa 1 and 2am. £3.50.

**Taxis:** 24hr. metered cabs abound. **Value Cabs** (☎9080 9080); **City Cab** (☎9024 2000); **Fon a Cab** (☎9033 3333).

**Bike Rental: McConvey Cycles,** 183 Ormeau Rd. (☎9033 0322; www.mcconvey.com). M and F-Su £20; otherwise £10 per day, £40 per week. Locks supplied. Open M-W and F-Sa 9am-6pm, Th 9am-8pm. **Life Cycles,** 36-37 Smithfield Market (☎9043 9959; www.lifecycles.co.uk). £9 per day. Offers **bicycle city tours.**

IRELAND

**Belfast**

**⌂ ACCOMMODATIONS**
The Ark (HHH), **17**
Arnie's Backpackers (IHH), **19**
Avenue Guest House, **24**
Belfast Hostel (HINI), **11**
The Belfast Palace (Paddy's Place), **18**
Botanic Lodge, **16**
Camera Guesthouse, **22**
Windermere Guest House, **21**

**🍴 FOOD**
Archana Balti House and Little
India Vegetarian Restaurant, **10**
Benedict's, **12**
Blinkers, **6**
Bookfinders, **20**
Maggie May's Belfast Cafe, **13**
The Moghul, **14**
The Other Place, **15**
Tesco, **7**
Windsor Dairy, **8**

**🍸 NIGHTLIFE**
The Botanic Inn, **23**
The Duke of York, **3**
The John Hewitt, **4**
Katy Daly's Pub, **9**
The Kremlin, **1**
McHugh's, **5**
Mynt, **2**

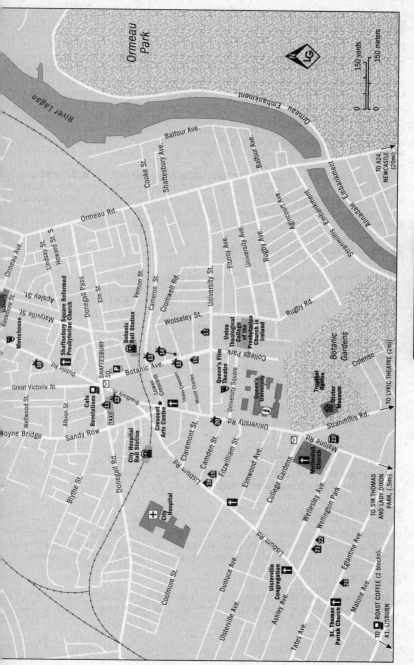

Ormeau Park

River Lagan

Ormeau Embankment

150 yards
150 meters

TO A24,
NEWCASTLE
(20mi)

IRELAND

Balfour Ave.
Cooke St.
Shaftesbury Ave.
Balfour Ave.

Annadale Embankment
Stranmillis Embankment
Agincourt Ave.

Ormeau Rd.

Ormeau Ave.
Lindsay St.
Howard St. S.
Apsley St.
Maryville St.
Bankmore St.
Gallery St.

Fitzroy Ave.
University Ave.
Rugby Ave.
Rugby Rd.

Vernon St.
Donegall Pass
Elm St.
Cameron St.
Cromwell Rd.
Wolseley St.
University St.

Moviehouse

Shaftesbury Square Reformed
Presbyterian Church

Dublin Rd.

Botanic
Rail Station

SHAFTESBURY
SQ.

Botanic Ave.

Union
Theological
College
of the
Presbyterian
Church in
Ireland

College Park

Botanic
Gardens

Colenso

TO LYRIC THEATRE (2mi)

Great Victoria St.

Cafe
Revelations

TAXI

Wellwood St.
Albion St.

Boyne Bridge

Sandy Row

Lower
Crescent
Upper Crescent
Mount Charles

Bradbury Pl.

Queen's Film
Theatre

University Square

Queen's
University

Tropical
Ravine

Ulster
Museum

Stranmillis Rd.

Crescent
Arts Centre

City Hospital
Rail Station

Donegall Rd.

Blythe St.

Lisburn Rd.
Claremont St.
Camden St.
Fitzwilliam St.

University Rd.

Elmwood Ave.

College Gardens

Malone Rd.

Methodist
Church

City
Hospital

Coolmore St.

Dunluce Ave.

Ulsterville Ave.

Ashley Ave.

Tates Ave.

Lisburn Rd.

Ulsterville
Congregation

St. Thomas
Parish Church

Wellesley Ave.
Wellington Park

Eglantine Ave.

TO SIR THOMAS
AND LADY DIXON
PARK, (.5mi)

TO ROAST COFFEE (2 blocks),
A1, LISBURN

## ✴ ORIENTATION

Buses arrive at the Europa Bus Station on **Great Victoria Street.** To the northeast is **City Hall** in **Donegall Square.** Donegall Pl. turns into **Royal Avenue** and runs from Donegall Sq. through the shopping area. To the east, in **Cornmarket,** pubs in narrow alleyways offer an escape. The stretch of Great Victoria St. between the bus station and Shaftesbury Sq. is known as the **Golden Mile** for its high-brow establishments and Victorian architecture. **Botanic Avenue** and **Bradbury Place** (which becomes **University Road**) extend south from Shaftesbury Sq. into **Queen's University** turf. While central Belfast is safer for tourists than most European cities, locals advise caution in the east and west. Westlink Motorway divides working-class **West Belfast,** more volatile than the city center, from the rest of Belfast. The Protestant district stretches along Shankill Rd., just north of the Catholic neighborhood, centered around Falls Rd. The **River Lagan** splits industrial **East Belfast** from Belfast proper. The shipyards and docks extend north on both sides of the river as it grows into **Belfast Lough.** During the week, the area north of City Hall is essentially deserted after 6pm. Although muggings are infrequent in Belfast, it's wise to use taxis after dark, particularly near clubs and pubs in the northeast.

## 🛈 PRACTICAL INFORMATION

**Tourist Information Centre: Belfast Welcome Centre,** 47 Donegall Pl. (☎9024 6609; www.gotobelfast.com). Offers helpful free booklet on Belfast and info on surrounding areas. Open June-Sept. M-Sa 9am-7pm, Su noon-5pm; Oct.-May M-Sa 9am-5pm.

**Banks:** Find 24hr. **ATMs** at **Bank of Ireland,** 54 Donegall Pl. (☎9023 4334) and **First Trust,** 92 Ann St. (☎9032 5599). Most banks open M-F 9am-4:30pm.

**Laundromat: Globe Drycleaners & Launderers,** 37-39 Botanic Ave. (☎9024 3956). £6.80 per load. Open M-F 8am-9pm, Sa 8am-6pm, Su noon-6pm.

**Police:** 6-18 Donegall Pass and 65 Knock Rd. (☎9065 0222).

**Hospitals: Belfast City Hospital,** 91 Lisburn Rd. (☎9032 9241). From Shaftesbury Sq., follow Bradbury Pl. and take a right at the fork. **Royal Victoria Hospital,** 12 Grosvenor Rd. (☎9024 0503). From Donegall Sq., take Howard St. west to Grosvenor Rd.

**Internet Access: Belfast Central Library,** 122 Royal Ave. (☎9050 9150). Open M and Th 9am-8pm, Tu-W and F 9am-5:30pm, Sa 9am-1pm. £1.50 per 30min. for nonmembers. **Belfast Welcome Centre,** 47 Donegall Pl., is the most central. £1.25 per 15min., students £1 per hr. Open M-Sa 9:30am-7pm, Su noon-5pm.

**Post Office: Central Post Office,** on the corner of High St. and Bridge St. (☎08457 223 344). Open M-Sa 10am-5:30pm. **Postal Code:** BT2 7FD.

## ⌂ ACCOMMODATIONS

Despite fluctuating tourism and rising rents, Belfast has a solid lineup of hostels. Almost all are near Queen's University, close to pubs and restaurants, and a short walk or bus to the city center. Lodgings fill up fast in summer, so reserve ahead.

### HOSTELS

▨ **Arnie's Backpackers (IHH),** 63 Fitzwilliam St. (☎9024 2867). Look for a cutout sign of a backpacker. Bunked beds in bright, clean rooms. Library of travel info includes bus and train timetables. Kitchen often has a small stack of free food. If you're looking to find work, check the bulletin board in the entryway. 8-bed dorms £9; 4-bed £11. ●

**The Belfast Palace (Paddy's Palace),** 68 Lisburn Rd. (☎9033 3367; www.paddyspalace.com), use the entrance at 70 Fitzwilliam St. Sociable new hostel offers free Internet (daily 8am-10:30pm), satellite TV, and videos in the lounge. Breakfast included. Reception M-Th and Su 8am-8pm, F-Sa 8am-10pm. Dorms from £10-17. ●

**The Ark (IHH),** 44 University St. (☎9032 9626). 10min. walk from Europa bus station. Spacious dorms and a well-stocked kitchen with free tea and coffee. Staff provides info on finding work and books tours of Belfast (£8) and Giant's Causeway (£16). Laundry £5. Internet £1 per 20min. Curfew 2am. Co-ed 4- to 6-bed dorms £11; doubles £36; long-term housing from £60 per week. ●

**Belfast Hostel (HINI),** 22 Donegall Rd. (☎9031 5435; www.hini.org.uk), off Shaftesbury Sq. A clean, inviting interior with a cafe (open daily 8-11am) and modern rooms. Books tours of Belfast and Giant's Causeway. Full breakfast £4. Laundry £3. Internet £0.05 per min.; Wi-Fi £3 per hr. Reception 24hr. M-Th and Su 4- to 6-bed dorms £8.50, F-Sa £9.50; ensuite upgrade £1. Triples £42-45. MC/V. ●

## BED AND BREAKFASTS

B&Bs cluster south of Queen's University between **Malone** and **Lisburn Roads.**

**Windermere Guest House,** 60 Wellington Park (☎9066 2693; www.windermereguesthouse.co.uk). Relatively cheap for a B&B. Leather couches provide comfy seating in the living room. Singles £28, with bath £40; doubles £52/55. Cash only. ●

**Camera Guesthouse,** 44 Wellington Park (☎9066 0026; malonedrumm@hotmail.com). Quiet, pristine Victorian house. Breakfast offers a selection of organic food and herbal teas. Singles £34, with bath £48; doubles £56/62. AmEx/MC/V. ●

**Avenue Guest House,** 23 Eglantine Ave. (☎9066 5904; www.avenueguesthouse.com). 4 large, airy rooms equipped with TV and Wi-Fi. Comfortable living room has DVDs and books. £25 per person. ●

**Botanic Lodge,** 87 Botanic Ave. (☎9032 7682), corner of Mt. Charles Ave. Larger B&B in the heart of the Queen's University area, surrounded by restaurants. All rooms with sink and TV. Singles £30; doubles £45, with bath £50. MC/V 5% surcharge. ●

## ♻ FOOD

Dublin Rd., Botanic Ave., and the Golden Mile around **Shaftesbury Square,** have the highest concentration of restaurants. The huge **Tesco Supermarket** is at 2 Royal Ave. (☎9032 3270. Open M-W and Sa 8am-7pm, Th 8am-9pm, F 8am-8pm, Su 1-5pm.)

**The Other Place,** 79 Botanic Ave. (☎9020 7200). Popular eatery serves fried breakfasts until 5pm (from £3), hearty specials, and ethnic entrees. Try the "bang bang chicken," with spicy soy, sweet chili, and crunchy peanut sauce. Open daily 8am-10pm. ●

**Bookfinders,** 47 University Rd. (☎9032 8269). 1 block from the University, on the corner of Camden St. and University Rd. Cluttered bookshelves and mismatched dishes. Soup and bread £2.50. Sandwiches £2.20. Open M-Sa 10am-5:30pm. ●

**Benedict's,** 7-21 Bradbury Pl. (☎9059 1999; www.benedictshotel.co.uk). Swanky hotel restaurant providing an upscale break from sandwiches and pizza. "Beat the Clock" meal deal offers fine meals daily 5-7:30pm for £7.50-10. Lunch £7.50-12. Dinner £12-16. Open M-Sa noon-2:30pm and 5:30-10:30pm, Su noon-3:30pm and 5:30-9pm. ●

**Archana,** 53 Dublin Rd. (☎9032 3713; www.archana.info). Cozy curry house. Dishes made with chicken, lamb, or vegetables. Features Handi dishes, complete with personal candlelit stove. Downstairs *Thali* lunch £2.50, dinner £7-9; upstairs from £5/8. Takeout available. Open M-Sa 11am-2pm and 5-11pm, Su 5-10pm. MC/V. ❸

**Windsor Dairy,** 4 College St. (☎9032 7157). Family-run bakery doles out piles of pastries (under £1), pies, and satisfying daily specials (£2-3). Come early before locals gobble up the best batches. Open M-Sa 7:30am-10:30pm. ❶

**Blinkers,** 1-5 Bridge St. (☎9024 3330). Inexpensive diner offers burgers (£1.80-3.65) and other greasy eats. Open M-W and F-Sa 9:30am-7pm, Th 11am-8pm. ❶

**The Moghul,** 62A Botanic Ave. (☎9032 6677). Enter around the corner on Cromwell Rd. Overlooks the street. Outstanding Indian Thali lunch M-Th noon-2pm (£3). Buffet F noon-2pm (£6). Take out available. Open for dinner Su-Th 5-11pm, F-Sa 5pm-midnight. ❷

**Maggie May's Belfast Cafe,** 50 Botanic Ave. (☎9032 2662). Grab a newspaper from the burlap sacks along the railing and relax in a booth with a thick cappuccino. Lots of vegetarian options. Breakfast served all day. Filled soda bread £3. Dinners £5. Open M-Sa 7:45am-11:15pm, Su 10am-11:15pm. ❷

## 📷 TOURS

■**BLACK CAB TOURS.** Black Cab tours provide commentary on the murals and sights on both sides of the Peace Line. Most drivers have been personally affected by the Troubles, but they take pains to avoid bias. Many hostels book tours with their favored **black cab** operators, usually for £8. **The Original Belfast Black Taxi Tours** give impassioned yet even-handed commentary, and one of the five Protestant and five Catholic drivers will answer any question. (☎0800 032 2003 or ☎077 5165 5359 *for Laurence, one of the owners. 1½hr. tour from £8 per person.)* Walter of **Backpackers Black Taxi Tours** (☎077 2106 7752) is the original of the bunch. Now in his 11th year, he still covers all the bases with his insight and wry humor.

**BAILEYS HISTORICAL PUB TOURS OF BELFAST.** A departure from recreational pubbing, this tour is a primer in Pint Studies. It guides visitors through seven or more of Belfast's oldest and best pubs with a little sightseeing and city history on the side. (☎9268 3665; www.belfastpubtours.com. *2hr. tour departs from Crown Dining Rooms, above the Crown Liquor Saloon, May-Oct. Th 7pm, Sa 4pm. Complimentary tumbler of Bailey's Irish Cream included. £6, £5 for groups of 10 or more; excludes drinks.)*

**BIKE TOURS.** In addition to bike rental, **Life Cycles** (see **Bike Rental,** p. 591) and **Irish Cycle Tours,** 27 Belvoir View Pk. (☎667 128 733; www.irishcycletours.com), offer tours of Belfast for £15 per day.

**BUS TOURS. Mini-Coach** (☎9031 5333) conducts tours of Belfast *(1hr.; departs M-F noon; £8, children £4)* and the Giant's Causeway *(M-Sa 9:40am-7pm, Su 9am-5:45pm; £15/10).* Tours depart from the Belfast International Youth Hostel. Tickets available at Belfast Welcome Centre.

## 👁 SIGHTS

**BELFAST CITY HALL.** The most dramatic, impressive piece of architecture in Belfast is also its administrative and geographic center. Dominating the grassy square that serves as the locus of downtown Belfast, its green copper dome is visible from nearly any point in the city. Inside, a grand staircase ascends to the second floor, where portraits of the city's Lord Mayors line the halls. The City Council's oak-paneled chambers, used only once per month, are deceptively austere, considering the Council's reputation for rowdy meetings (fists have been known to fly). The interior of City Hall is only accessible by guided tour. (☎9027 0456. 1hr. tours M-F 11am, 2, 3pm; Sa 2 and 3pm. Free.)

**QUEEN'S UNIVERSITY BELFAST.** Charles Lanyon designed the beautiful Tudor Gothic brick campus in 1849, modeling it after Magdalen College, Oxford. The **Visitors Centre,** in the Lanyon Room to the left of the main entrance, offers Queen's-related exhibits and merchandise, as well as a free pamphlet detailing a walking tour of the grounds. Upstairs, the **Naughton Gallery** displays rotating exhibits of contemporary art. (University Rd. Visitors Centre ☎9033 5252; www.qub.ac.uk/vcentre. Open May-Sept. M-Sa 10am-4pm; Oct.-Mar. M-F 10am-4pm. Gallery open M-Sa 11am-4pm. Free.) Join birds, bees, and Belfast's student population in the botanic gardens behind the university. The sunshine brings people to the park in droves. Inside the gardens lie two 19th-century greenhouses: the humid **Tropical Ravine,** and the more temperate, Lanyon-designed **Palm House,** which shelters an vast array of flowers. (☎9032 4902. Open daily 8am-dusk. Tropical Ravine and Palm House open Apr.-Sept. M-F 10am-noon and 1-5pm, Sa-Su 2-5pm; Oct.-Mar. M-F 10am-noon and 1-4pm, Sa-Su 2-4pm. Free.)

**ODYSSEY.** The posterchild of Belfast's riverfront revival, this attraction packs five distinct sights into one entertainment center. (2 Queen's Quay. ☎9045 1055; www.theodyssey.co.uk.) The **Odyssey Arena,** with 10,000 seats, is the largest indoor arena in Ireland. When the Belfast Giants ice hockey team isn't on the ice, big-name performers heat up the stage. (Performance box office ☎9073 9074; www.odysseyarena.com. Hockey ☎9059 1111; www.belfastgiants.com.) The **W5 Discovery Centre** (short for "whowhatwherewhenwhy?") is a playground for curious minds and hyperactive schoolchildren. Design your own racecar and rollercoaster, waltz up the musical stairs, or operate a replica of the Harland & Wolff cranes in a model of Port Belfast. (☎9046 7700; www.w5online.co.uk. Workshops run throughout summer. Wheelchair-accessible. Open M-Sa 10am-6pm, closes at 5pm when school is in session; Su noon-6pm. Last entry 1hr. before closing. £6.50, children £4.50. Family discounts available.) The **Sherbidan IMAX Cinema** plays both 2D and 3D films on its enormous 62 by 82 ft. screen, while **Warner Village Cinemas** shows Hollywood blockbusters on its 14 screens. (IMAX ☎9046 7014; www.belfastimax.com. £5; M-Th students £4.50, children £4. Multiplex ☎9073 9234. £6/4/3.80. M-F before 5pm £4.50.)

**GRAND OPERA HOUSE.** The opera house was repeatedly bombed by the IRA, restored to its original splendor at enormous cost, and bombed again. Visitors today enjoy the calm in high fashion, and tours offer a look behind the ornate facade. (☎9024 1919; www.goh.co.uk. Open M-F 8:30am-9pm. Tours W-Sa 11am. £3.)

**BELFAST CASTLE.** Constructed in 1870 by the Third Marquis of Donegall, the castle sits atop **Cave Hill,** long the seat of Ulster rulers, and offers the best panoramas of the Belfast port—on a clear day views extend as far as Scotland. The ancient King Matudan had his McArt's Fort here, where the United Irishmen plotted rebellion in 1795, although these days it sees more weddings than skirmishes. Marked trails lead north from the fort to five **caves.** Only the lowest is accessible to tourists. (☎9077 6925; www.belfastcastle.co.uk. Open M-Sa 9am-10pm, Su 9am-5:30pm. Free.)

**ST. ANNE'S CATHEDRAL.** This Church of Ireland cathedral was begun in 1899, but to keep from disturbing regular worship, it was built around a smaller church already on the site. Upon completion of the new exterior, builders extracted the earlier church brick by brick. Each of the cathedral's 10 interior pillars names one of Belfast's professional fields. In an enclave called the **Chapel of Unity,** visitors pray for understanding among Christians of all denominations. (Donegall St. Open M-Sa 10am-4pm, Su before and after services at 10, 11am, 3:30pm.)

IRELAND

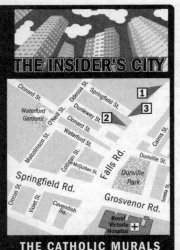

THE INSIDER'S CITY

## THE CATHOLIC MURALS

The murals of West Belfast are a powerful testament to the volatile past and fierce loyalties of the divided neighborhoods. Many of the most famous Catholic murals are on Falls Rd., an area that saw some of the worst of the Troubles.

**1** Illustrations of protestors during the **Hunger Strikes of 1981**, during which they fasted for the right to be considered political prisoners.

**2** Portrayal of **Bobby Sands,** the first hunger-striker to die, is located on the side of the Sinn Féin Office, Sevastopol St. Sands was elected as a member of the British Parliament under a "political prisoner" ticket during this time and is remembered as the North's most famous martyr.

**3** Formerly operating as Northern Ireland's **National RUC Headquarters,** the most bombed of any police station in England, the Republic, or the North. Its fortified, barbed wire facade is on Springfield St.

**SINCLAIR SEAMEN'S CHURCH.** Designed to accommodate the hordes of sinning sailors landing in Belfast port, this quirky church does things its own way—the minister delivers his sermons from a pulpit carved in the shape of a ship's prow, collections are taken in miniature lifeboats, and the choir uses an organ from a Guinness barge with port and starboard lights. (*Corporation St., down from the SeaCat terminal. ☎9071 5997. Open W 2-5pm; Su service at 11:30am and 7pm.*)

**SIR THOMAS AND LADY DIXON PARK.** The most stunning of the parks, visitors find it sitting pretty on Upper Malone Rd. 20,000 rose bushes of every variety imaginable bloom here each year. The gardens were founded in 1836 and include stud China roses, imported between 1792 and 1824. (*Open M-Sa 7:30am-dusk, Su 9am-dusk.*)

**BELFAST ZOO.** Set in the hills alongside Cave Hill Forest Park, the zoo's best attribute is its natural setting—catching sight of a lumbering elephant against the backdrop of Belfast lough can be a surreal experience. The recommended route highlights the standard lineup of tigers, giraffes, camels, zebras, and the acrobatic spider monkey. (*4 mi. north of the city on Antrim Rd. Take Metro bus #1. ☎9077 6277. Open daily Apr.-Sept. 10am-7pm; Oct.-Mar. 10am-4pm. Last entry 1hr. before closing. Apr.-Sept. £7.80, children £4.10; Oct.-Mar. £6.30/3.20. Seniors, under 4, and disabled free.*)

## WEST BELFAST AND THE MURALS

The neighborhoods of West Belfast have been at the heart of political tensions in the North; there were 1000 bomb explosions and over 400 murders in 1972 alone. The **Peace Line,** a 14m high wall, separates the Catholic and Protestant neighborhoods, centered on the **Falls Road** and the **Shankill** respectively. The Peace Line's grim, gray gates close at 5pm. West Belfast is not a tourist site in the traditional sense, though the walls and houses along the streets display political **murals,** the city's most striking and popular attraction. Those traveling to these sectarian neighborhoods often take **black taxis** (see p. 596). *Let's Go* offers two **neighborhood maps** of the Protestant (see right) and Catholic (see left) murals, allowing individuals to explore the murals for themselves.

**THE FALLS.** This Catholic and Republican neighborhood is larger than Shankill, following Castle St. west from the city center. As Castle St. continues across A12/Westlink, it becomes **Divis Street.** A highrise apartment building marks **Divis Tower,** an illfated housing development built by optimistic social planners in the 1960s. The project soon became an IRA stronghold and saw some of the worst of Belfast's Troubles in the 1970s.

> ❗ It's best to visit the Falls and Shankill during the day, when the neighborhoods are full of locals and, more importantly, the murals are visible. Do not visit the area during **Marching Season** (the weeks around July 12) when the parades are underscored by mutual antagonism that can lead to violence. Travelers are advised not to wander from one neighborhood to the other, but to return to the city center between visits to Shankill and the Falls.

Continuing west, Divis St. turns into **Falls Road.** The **Sinn Féin** office is easily spotted: one side of it is covered with an enormous portrait of Bobby Sands and an advertisement for the Sinn Féin newspaper, *An Phoblacht*. A number of murals line the side streets off Fall Rd. In the past, the Falls and the Shankill were home to paramilitaries; the murals reflected the tense times with depictions of the violent struggle. Today, both communities have focused on historical and cultural representations, even replacing older murals. The newest ones recall Celtic myths and legends, and depict events such as The Great Hunger.

Falls Rd. soon splits into **Andersonstown Road** and **Glen Road,** an urban area with a predominately Irish-speaking population. On the left are the Celtic crosses of **Milltown Cemetery,** the resting place of many fallen Republicans. Inside the entrance, you'll find a memorial to Republican casualties. Nearby, **Bombay Street** was the first street to be burned down during the Troubles. Another mile along Andersonstown Rd. lies a housing project that was formerly a wealthy Catholic neighborhood—and more murals. The Springfield Rd. Police Service of Northern Ireland station, previously named the RUC station, was the **most attacked police station in Ireland and the UK.** It was recently demolished. The **Andersonstown Barracks,** at the corner of Glen and Andersonstown Rd., are still heavily fortified.

**SHANKILL.** The Shankill Rd. begins at the Westlink and turns into Woodvale Rd. as it crosses Cambrai St. Woodvale Rd. intersects Crumlin Rd. at the Ardoyne roundabout and can be taken back into the city center. The Shankill Memorial Garden honors 10 people who died in a bomb attack on Fizzel's Fish Shop in October 1993; the garden is on the Shankill Rd., facing Berlin St. On the Shankill Rd., farther toward the city center, is a mural of James Buchanan, the 15th President of the United States (1857-1861), who was a descendant of Ulster Scots (known in the US as the "Scots-Irish"). Other cultural murals depict the 50th

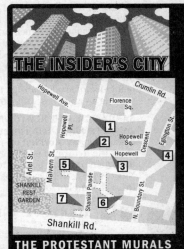

## THE PROTESTANT MURALS

Many of the Protestant murals, in the Shankill area of West Belfast, are overtly militant. Most are found near Hopewell St. and Hopewell Cr., to the north of Shankill Rd., or down Shankill Parade, and are accessed by traveling south from Crumlin Rd.

**1** Commemoration of the **Red Hand Commando,** a militant Loyalist group.

**2** Painting of a **Loyalist martyr,** killed in prison in 1997.

**3** Depiction of the **Grim Reaper,** with gun and British flag.

**4** A collage of Loyalist militant groups including the **UVF, UDU,** and **UDA.**

**5** Mural of the **Battle of the Boyne,** commemorating William of Orange's 1690 victory over James II.

**6** The **Marksman's** gun seems to follow you as you pass by.

**7** Portrait of the infamous **Top Gun,** a man responsible for the deaths of many high-ranking Republicans.

Jubilee of the coronation of Queen Elizabeth in 1952 and the death of the Queen Mother in 2002. These are at the beginning of the Shankill near the Rex Bar. Historical murals include a memorial to the UVF who fought at the Battle of the Somme in 1916 during WWI, also near the Rex Bar. In the Shankill Estate, some murals represent Cromwell suppressing the 1741 Rebellion against the Protestant plantation owners. The densely decorated **Orange Hall** sits on the left at Brookmount St. McClean's Wallpaper; on the right was where Fizzel's Fish Shop stood before being demolished. Through the estate, Crumlin Rd. heads back to the city center, passing an army base, the courthouse, and the jail.

**SANDY ROW AND NEWTOWNARDS ROAD.** This area's Protestant population is growing steadily, partly due to the redevelopment of the Sandy Row area, and also because many working-class residents are leaving the Shankill. Nearby murals show the Red Hand of Ulster, a bulldog, and William crossing the Boyne. Use **caution** when traveling in this area around Marching Season. A number of murals line Newtownards Rd. On the Ballymacart road, which runs parallel to Newtownards Rd., is a mural of local son C.S. Lewis's *The Lion, the Witch, and the Wardrobe.*

## 🍺 🎵 NIGHTLIFE AND PUBS

Pubs in Belfast are the place to experience the city's *craic* and meet its colorful characters. Pubs were targets for sectarian violence at the height of the Troubles, so most pubs in Belfast are new or restored, although many retain their historic charm. Those in the city center and university area are now relatively safe. For a full list of entertainment options, grab a free copy of *The Big List* or *Fate*, available in tourist centers, hostels, and certain restaurants and pubs.

■ **The Duke of York,** 7-11 Commercial Ct. (☎9024 1062). Old boxing venue turned Communist printing press, rebuilt after it was bombed by IRA in the 60s; now home to the city's largest selection of Irish whiskeys. Kitchen serves sandwiches and toasties daily until 2:30pm. Th trad at 10pm, F acoustic guitar, Sa disco with £5 cover. 18+. Open M 11:30am-11pm, Tu-F 11:30am-1am, Su 11:30am-2am.

■ **Katy Daly's Pub,** 17 Ormeau Ave. (☎9032 5942; www.the-limelight.co.uk). Go straight behind City Hall toward Queen's and make a left on Ormeau Ave. High-ceilinged, wood-paneled, antique pub is a true stalwart of the Belfast music scene. Lunch served M-F noon-2:30pm. Bar open M-Sa until 1am, Su until midnight.

**The Botanic Inn,** 23 Malone Rd. (☎9050 9740). Standing in as the unofficial student union, the hugely popular "Bot" is packed nightly. Upstairs disco features a DJ W-Sa (£5 cover), Su the DJ moves downstairs (no cover). 20+. Kitchen serves pub grub daily noon-8pm. Open M-Sa 11:30am-1am, Su noon-midnight.

**The John Hewitt,** 51 Lower Donegall St. (☎9023 3768; www.thejohnhewitt.com), around the corner from the Duke. Named after the late Ulster poet and run by the Unemployment Resource Centre. Half the profits go to the center, so drink up. 18+. Open M-F 11:30am-1am, Sa noon-1am, Su 6pm-1am.

**McHugh's,** 29-31 Queen's Sq. (☎9050 9999; www.mchughsbar.com), across from the Custom House, sells local Belfast Ale. Sleek wrought-iron banisters and a chess set featuring caricatures of political figures add to the allure of this historic pub, open since 1711. Th-F and Su live music. Sa DJ. Restaurant open M-Sa 5-10pm, Su noon-9pm. Open M and Su noon-midnight, Tu-Sa noon-1am.

**Mynt,** 2-16 Dunbar St. (☎9023 4520; www.myntbelfast.com). This spacious club is a bastion of the Belfast gay scene. Casual cafebar in front leads to 2 fl. of clubbing. F separate gay and lesbian parties. Sa karaoke downstairs and DJ upstairs. Cover £3-10. Open M-Tu noon-1am, W-F and Su noon-3am, Sa noon-6am.

**The Kremlin,** 96 Donegall St. (☎9031 6061; www.kremlin-belfast.com). Look for the statue of Lenin. A young crowd gathers in the downstairs Tsar Bar before spilling onto the dance floor. Cover varies, but free Su. Open Tu 9pm-2:30am, Th-Su 9pm-3am.

# ♫ ENTERTAINMENT

Belfast's cultural events and performances are covered in the monthly *Arts Council Artslink*, free at the Tourist Information Centre, while the bi-monthly *Arts Listings* covers arts and entertainment throughout Northern Ireland. **Fenderesky Gallery,** 2 University Rd., inside the Crescent Arts building, hosts contemporary shows and sells the work of local artists. (☎9023 5245. Open Tu-Sa 11:30am-5pm.) The **Old Museum Arts Centre,** 7 College Sq. N., is Belfast's largest venue for contemporary artwork. (☎9023 5053; www.oldmuseumartscentre.org. Open M-Sa 9:30am-5:30pm.) The **Grand Opera House,** 4 Great Victoria St., presents opera, ballet, musicals, and drama. Tickets for most shows can be purchased by phone until 9pm or in person at the box office. (☎9024 0411; www.goh.co.uk. Open M-F 8:30am-9pm. Tickets £9-27.) **The Lyric Theatre,** 55 Ridgeway St., presents a mix of classical and contemporary plays with an emphasis on Irish productions. (☎9038 1081; www.lyrictheatre.co.uk. Box office open M-Sa 10am-7pm. Tickets M-W £14, concessions £11; Th-Sa £17.) **Waterfront Hall,** 2 Lanyon Pl., one of Belfast's newest concert centers, hosts a variety of performances throughout the year. (☎9033 4400; www.waterfront.co.uk. Student discounts usually available.) The **Ulster Orchestra** plays concerts at Waterfront Hall and Ulster Hall. (☎9066 8798; www.ulster-orchestra.org.uk. Tickets £8-24.)

# ▓ DAYTRIP FROM BELFAST: ULSTER FOLK MUSEUM

*The Museum stretches across 170 acres in the town of Holywood. Take the Bangor road (A2) 7mi. east of Belfast. Buses and trains stop here on the way to Bangor. ☎9042 8428; www.uftm.org.uk. Open July-Sept. M-Sa 10am-6pm, Su 11am-6pm; Mar.-June M-F 10am-5pm, Sa 10am-6pm, Su 11am-6pm; Oct.-Feb. M-F 10am-4pm, Sa 10am-5pm, Su 11am-5pm. £5.50, students £3.50. Group discounts and season passes available.*

Established by an Act of Parliament in 1958, the ▓**Folk Museum** aims to preserve the way of life of Ulster's craftspeople, farmers, and weavers. The Museum contains over 30 buildings from the past three centuries divided into a town and rural area, the latter containing cottages from all nine Ulster counties, including the usually overlooked Monaghan, Cavan, and Donegal in the Republic. All but two of the buildings are transplanted originals. They have been artfully integrated into a landscape befitting their rural origins; the size of the property and the natural surroundings create an air of authenticity. Unobtrusive attendants in period costume stand nearby to answer questions. In Ballydugan Weaver's House, John the Weaver, a fourth-generation practitioner of his craft, operates the only working linen loom in Ireland. A fully functional printer's press still runs on Main St. Along with a cornmill and a sawmill from Fermanagh, the town is currently in the process of recreating a silent film house from Co. Down. The museum hosts special events, including trad sessions, dance performances and workshops, storytelling festivals, and textile exhibitions. Go on a sunny day and leave time to wander.

# DERRY/LONDONDERRY  ☎028

Modern Derry/Londonderry is trying to cast off the legacy of its political Troubles with much success. Although the landscape was razed by years of bombings, recent years have been relatively peaceful. Today's rebuilt city is beautiful and intimate with a cosmopolitan vibe.

# ▐▌ TRANSPORTATION AND PRACTICAL INFORMATION. Trains (☎7134 2228) arrive on Duke St., Waterside, from Belfast (2hr., 4-9 per day, £9.80). A free Rail-Link bus connects the **train station** and the **bus station,** on Foyle St., between the walled city and the river; it leaves the bus station 15min. before each train is due to depart. Ulsterbus **buses** (☎7126 2261) go to Belfast (1½-3hr., 10-36 per day,

> **WHAT'S IN A NAME?** Originally christened *Diore,* meaning "oak grove," the city's name was anglicized to Derry and finally to Londonderry. The city's label remains a source of contention, as the minority Protestant population uses the official title while many Republican Northerners and informal Protestants refer to the city as Derry. Even in the city center, some signs refer to Derry or Londonderry without any consistency.

£8.70). The **Tourist Information Centre,** 44 Foyle St., has free copies of the *Visitor's Guide to Derry.* (☎7126 7284; www.derryvisitor.com. Open July-Sept. M-F 9am-7pm, Sa 10am-6pm, Su 10am-5pm; low season reduced hours.) **Internet** is available at the central **library,** 35 Foyle St. (☎7127 2310. £3 per hr. Open M and Th 8:30am-8pm, Tu-W and F 8:30am-5:30pm, Sa 9:15am-5pm.) **Postal Code:** BT48 6AT.

**ACCOMMODATIONS AND FOOD.** Go down Strand Rd. and turn left up Great James St. to reach the social ◪**Derry City Independent Hostel ❶,** 44 Great James St. (☎7137 7989; www.derryhostel.com. Breakfast included. Free Internet. Dorms £10; doubles £28. MC/V.) **The Saddler's House (No. 36) ❸,** 36 Great James St., offers elegant rooms in a lovely Victorian home. (☎7126 9691; www.thesaddlershouse.com. TV and tea/coffee facilities in all rooms. Breakfast included. Singles £25-35; doubles £45-50. MC/V.) **The Ice Wharf/Lloyd's No. 1 Bar ❷,** 22-24 Strand Rd., has every type of food imaginable at incredibly low prices. Get two meals for the price of one all day long. (☎7127 6610; www.lloydsno1.co.uk. Open M-W, Su 10am-midnight, Th-Sa 10am-1am.) **The Sandwich Co. ❶,** The Diamond, is perfect for cheap sandwiches. (☎7137 2500. Sandwiches £2.60-4. Open M-F 8am-5pm, Sa 9am-5pm.) A **Tesco** supermarket is in the Quayside Shopping Centre, along Strand Rd. (☎7137 4400. Open M-Th 9am-9pm, F 8:30am-9pm, Sa 8:30am-8pm, Su 1-6pm.)

**SIGHTS AND NIGHTLIFE.** The **city walls,** 5.5m high and 6m thick, erected between 1614 and 1619, have never been breached—hence Derry's nickname "the Maiden City." The walls separate the commercial center of the city from the surrounding neighborhoods and bar-lined streets. The tower topping Derry's southeast wall past New Gate was built to protect **St. Columb's Cathedral,** on London St., the symbolic focus of the city's Protestant defenders. (☎7126 7313. Open M-Sa Easter-Oct. 9am-5pm; Nov.-Easter 9am-4pm. Tours £2.) The **Museum of Free Derry, 55 Glenfada Pk.,** covers the Catholic civil rights struggle in Northern Ireland up until Bloody Sunday, chronicling civil rights marches, the Battle of the Bogside, internment, and Free Derry in an eye-opening account. (☎7136 0880; www.museumoffreederry.org. Open June-Sept. M-F 9:30am-4:30pm, Sa-Su 1-4pm; Mar.-Sept. M-F 9:30am-4:30pm, Sa 1-4pm. £3, students £1.50.) West of the city walls, Derry's residential neighborhoods—both the Protestant **Waterside** and **Fountain Estate,** as well as the Catholic **Bogside**—display murals.

After dark, check out ◪**The Gweedore** or ◪**Peadar O'Donnell's,** 53-60 Waterloo St., where Celtic and Orangeman paraphernalia hang and rock bands bang at night. Peadar O'Donnell's has trad every night at 11pm, while The Gweedore has younger rock bands; both pubs are connected and owned by the same person, although they cater to different crowds. (☎7137 2318; www.peaderodonnells.com. Open daily 11am-1am.) **Sandino's Cafe Bar,** 1 Water St., is a good option for poetry readings or live music by local up-and-coming bands and international musicians. (☎7130 9297. M-Sa 11:30am-1am, Su 1pm-midnight.) A younger crowd chills out and enjoys live music on Tuesday and Thursday to Sunday at **Bound For Boston,** 27-31 Waterloo St. (☎7127 1315. Open M-Sa 1pm-1am, Su 12:15pm-1am.)

# ⚡ DAYTRIPS FROM DERRY/LONDONDERRY

## ▓ THE GIANT'S CAUSEWAY

*To get to the Giant's Causeway from Derry, take the free shuttle from the city bus station across the river to the train station (it leaves 15min. before the train departs), and catch a train to Coleraine. From Coleraine, catch bus #172 or 252 to the Causeway. Ulsterbuses #172, 252 (the Antrim Coaster), the Causeway Rambler, and the Bushmills Bus (you must catch the last 2 from Bushmills Distillery) drop visitors at the Giant's Causeway Visitors Centre. From the Centre, there is a minibus that runs to the most popular part of the Giant's Causeway (2min., 4 per hr., £1). ☎ 2073 1855; www.northantrim.com. Centre open daily July-Aug. 10am-6pm; Sept.-June 10am-5pm. The Causeway is free and always open.*

Geologists believe that the unique rock formations found at ▓**Giant's Causeway** were created some 60 million years ago by lava outpourings that left curiously shaped cracks in their wake. Although locals have different ideas, everyone agrees that the Causeway is an awesome sight to behold. Comprising over 40,000 symmetrical hexagonal basalt columns, it resembles a descending staircase leading from the cliffs to the ocean's floor. Several other formations stand within the Causeway: **the Giant's Organ, the Wishing Chair, the Granny, the Camel,** and **the Giant's Boot.** Advertised as the 8th natural wonder of the world, the Giant's Causeway is Northern Ireland's most famous natural sight, so expect large crowds, or visit early in the morning or after the center closes.

Once travelers reach the Visitors Centre, they have two trail options: the more popular low road, which directly swoops down to the Causeway (20min.), or the more rewarding high road, which takes visitors 4½ mi. up a sea cliff to the romantic Iron Age ruins of Dunseverick Castle. The trail is well-marked and easy to follow, but you can also consult the free map available at the Visitors Centre. The center also offers a 12min. film about the legend of Finn McCool and posits on the geological explanation for the formations.

## DUNLUCE CASTLE

*The castle is along the A2 between Bushmills and Portrush. The Causeway Rambler bus travels from Bushmills Distillery. Call ☎ 7032 5400 for the Coleraine bus station, or ☎ 9066 6630 for Rambler inquiries. Rambler runs daily 10:15am-5pm. All-day ticket £3.50. Castle open daily Oct.-Mar. 10am-5pm; Apr.-Sept. 10am-6pm. £2.*

This 16th-century castle is built so close to a cliff's edge that the kitchen fell into the sea during a grand banquet, resulting in the arrest of the host and the relocation of the lady of the house to a residence slightly farther inland. Beneath the castle, a hidden **sea cave** offers a quick escape route to Rathlin Island or Scotland. The most spectacular views of the cliffs above the Atlantic are afforded by stopping along the A2 motorway on the way to the castle.

## BUSHMILLS DISTILLERY

*At the intersection of the A2 and B17, 5km east of Portrush and 2 mi. west of the Causeway. On the Causeway Rambler bus route (see Dunluce Castle listing for Causeway Rambler info). ☎ 2073 1521; www.bushmills.com. Open Apr.-Oct. M-Sa 9:30am-5:30pm, Su noon-5:30pm; Nov.-Mar. daily 10am-4:30pm. 50min. tours £5, students and seniors £4.*

The town of Bushmills has been home to the Old Bushmills Distillery since 1608, when a nod from King James I established it as the first licensed whiskey producer in the world. Travelers have stopped here since ancient days, when the whiskey's strength was determined by gunpowder's ability to ignite when doused with the

▐ IRELAND

fiery liquid. When the plant is operating, the tour shows the various stages involved in the production of Irish whiskey, distilled three times rather than the two required for Scotch "whisky." During the three weeks in July when production halts for maintenance, the far less interesting experience is redeemed only by the free alcohol sample. Serious whiskey fans should shoulder their way to the front as the tour winds down for a chance to try five different whiskeys by volunteering when the guide makes his cryptic request for "help."

## GLENS OF ANTRIM                                                  ☎028

Glaciers left nine deep scars in the mountainous coastline of northeastern County Antrim. Over the years, water collected in these glens, fostering lush flora not usually found in Ireland. Today, the glens and their mountains and waterfalls provide some of Northern Ireland's best scenery. For more info about all glens, visit www.causewaycoastandglens.com. The broadest (and arguably most beautiful) glen is **Glenariff,** 6.5km south of Waterfoot along Glenariff Rd., in the large **Glenariff Forest Park.** Bus #150 stops at the park entrance (M-F 4-5 per day). The stunning 5km ◪**Waterfall Trail** follows the fern-lined Glenariff River from the park entrance to Manor Lodge. (☎2175 8769. Open daily 10am-5pm. £1.50 per pedestrian, £4 per car.) **Cushendall,** nicknamed the "Capital of the Glens" has goods, services, and pubs unavailable elsewhere in the region. The **Tourist Information Centre,** 25 Mill St., is near the bus stop at the northern end of town. (☎2177 1180. Open from mid-June to mid-Sept. M-F 10am-5pm, Sa 10am-1pm; mid-Sept. to mid-June Tu-Su 10am-1pm.) A warm welcome, huge rooms, and grazing cows await at ◪**Glendale B&B ❷,** 46 Coast Rd., south of Cushendall overlooking the sea. (☎2177 1495. Singles £25; doubles £40. MC/V.) In 1954, the National Trust bought the tiny village of **Cushendun,** a whitewashed and black-shuttered set of buildings. Travelers to the village fall in love with the vast beach and murky **caves** carved into red sea cliffs. **Mary McBride's ❷,** 2 Main St., used to be in the *Guinness Book of World Records* as the smallest bar in Europe. It has been expanded to create an upstairs restaurant and a lounge. (☎2176 1511. Bar food £6.50-7.50. Kitchen open daily 12:30-8:30pm. Bar open daily noon-1am.) The **Antrim Coaster** (#252) stops at every town on the road from Belfast to Coleraine (M-F and Su 2 per day; £4-9). Bus #150, from Belfast via Ballymena, stops in Glenariff (M-Sa 3-5 per day, £4.50).

# ITALY (ITALIA)

Innovation, elegance, and culture distinguish Italy and its beloved art, fashion, and food. Steep Alpine peaks in the north; hills, lush with olive trees, in the interior; and the aquamarine waters of the Riviera provide only a few of the country's breathtaking vistas. Civilizations evolved piecemeal throughout the country, bequeathing a culture whose people and traditions retain distinct regional characteristics. Ruins of the Roman empire contextualize the imposing sculptures and paintings of Renaissance masters and the couture creations of today's fashion designers. Indulging in daily siestas and frequently hosting leisurely feasts, Italians seem to possess a knowledge of and appreciation for life's pleasures, while their openness lets travelers ease into Italy's relaxed lifestyle.

## DISCOVER ITALY: SUGGESTED ITINERARIES

**THREE DAYS.** Spend it all in the Eternal City of **Rome** (p. 616). Go back in time at the **Ancient City**: be a gladiator in the **Colosseum**, explore the **Roman Forum**, and stand in the well-preserved **Pantheon**. Spend the next day admiring the fine art in the **Capitoline Museums** and the **Galleria Borghese**, then satiate your other senses in a disco. The next morning, redeem your debauched soul in **Vatican City**, gazing at the ceiling of the **Sistine Chapel**, gaping at **St. Peter's Cathedral**, and enjoying the **Vatican Museums**.

**ONE WEEK.** Spend 3 days taking in the sights in **Rome** before heading north to **Florence** (2 days; p. 691) to immerse yourself in Italy's amazing Renaissance art at the Uffizi Gallery. Move to **Venice** (2 days; p. 669) to float through the canals.

**BEST OF ITALY, 3 WEEKS.**
Begin by immersing yourself in the sights and history of **Rome** (3 days), seek out the medieval houses of **Siena** (1 day; p. 706), then move to **Florence** (3 days). Head up the coast to **Camogli** (1 day; p. 659), and the beautiful **Cinque Terre** (2 days; p. 660). Visit cosmopolitan **Milan** (2 days; p. 645) for shopping and **Lake Como** for hiking (1 day; p. 655). Find your Romeo or Juliet in **Verona** (1 day; p. 687). Be paddled through the winding canals in **Venice** (2 days) before flying south to **Naples** (2 days; p. 713), being sure to visit preserved, ancient **Pompeii** (1 day; p. 721). Then hike and swim along the **Amalfi Coast** (1 day; p. 723), and see the Grotto Azzura on the island of **Capri** (1 day; p. 722).

# LIFE AND TIMES

## HISTORY

**FROM INFANT TO EMPIRE (1200 BC-AD 476).** Although archaeological excavations at Isernia date the earliest inhabitants of Italy to the Paleolithic Era (100,000-70,000 BC), legendary **Aeneas** did not lead his tribe from the ruins of Troy to the Tiber valley to found the city of Alba Longa until 1200 BC. In 753 BC, two of Aeneas's descendants, **Remus** and **Romulus**, founded the city of Rome (p. 616) before their brotherly love deteriorated into fratricide, according to Roman tradition. The **Tarquin dynasty** ruled tyrannically for centuries until **Lucius Brutus** expelled the King, Sextus Tarquinius, after he raped the Roman Lucretia. Brutus then established the **Roman Republic** in 509 BC. A string of military victories

brought near total unification of the Italian peninsula in 474 BC, and victory in the **Punic Wars** made Rome the undisputed ruler of the Mediterranean, with control over all of Carthage's vast empire. The perceived corruption of the goals of the Republic set the stage for **Julius Caesar** to name himself dictator, a rule which lasted only one year before he was assassinated on the Ides of March (Mar. 15), 44 BC. Power eluded would-be successors Brutus and Marc Antony, and Octavian, Caesar's adopted heir, emerged victorious and took the name **Augustus** in 27 BC. His rule spread the *Pax Romana* (Roman Peace) throughout the Mediterranean, the republic morphed into an empire, and the era became known as the **Golden Age of Rome.** The Empire persecuted Christians until Constantine's **Edict of Milan** granted religious tolerance in AD 313. The symbolic end of the Roman Empire came with the sacking of Rome by the Visigoths in AD 410. While the East continued to thrive as the **Byzantine Empire** expanded and continued some of the Roman traditions, the West fell into the **Dark Ages.**

**OUT OF THE DARK (476-1500).** Rome's fall reverberated throughout the region for a millennium until artistic and literary culture was revived in the 14th century. Fueled by the rediscovery of Greek and Latin texts and art, the **Renaissance** sparked new interest in the Classical conception of humanistic education (rhetoric, grammar, and logic). As the medieval church's monopoly on knowledge gradually eroded, a new merchant middle class arose, epitomized by the exalted **Medici family** in Florence (p. 691). They rose from obscurity and eventually boasted three popes, a couple of cardinals, and a queen or two. Their power in Florence was consolidated under Cosimo and Lorenzo *(il Magnifico)*, who broadened the family's activities from banking and warring to patronizing the arts. Meanwhile, the **Borgia family,** Spanish in origin, brought new heights of corruption and decadence to the papacy, based in Rome since the Dark Ages.

**TO THE VICTOR GO THE SPOILS (1500-1815).** The 16th-18th centuries were difficult times for Italy: the peninsula was no longer able to support the economic demands placed upon it by the Holy Roman Empire. **Charles II,** the last Spanish **Habsburg** ruler, died in 1700, sparking the **War of the Spanish Succession.** Italy, weak and decentralized, became the booty in battles between the Austrian Habsburgs and the French and Spanish Bourbons. A century later, **Napoleon** decided to solve the booty battles by taking everything for himself; in doing so, he united much of northern Italy into the Italian Republic, conquered Naples, fostered national sovereignty, and declared himself monarch of the newly united **Kingdom of Italy** in 1804. After Napoleon's fall in 1815 at the **Battle of Waterloo,** the **Congress of Vienna** carved up Italy, granting considerable control to Austria.

**TOGETHER AGAIN (1815-1945).** Reaction against the arbitrary divisions of Italy catalyzed the establishment of the nationalist **Risorgimento** unification movement, led by **Giuseppe Mazzini, Giuseppe Garibaldi,** and **Camillo Cavour.** In 1861, Italy's first Parliament met in Turin. Once the elation of unification wore off, however, age-old provincial differences reasserted themselves. The North wanted to protect its money from the needs of the agrarian South, and cities were wary of surrendering power to a central administration. The Pope, who had lost power to the kingdom, threatened to excommunicate Catholics who participated in politics. Disillusionment increased as Italy became involved in **World War I.** The nationalism of war paved the way for the rise of fascism under the control of **Benito Mussolini,** *Il Duce,* who promised order and stability for the young nation. Mussolini established the world's first fascist regime in 1924, expelling all opposing parties from his government. As Mussolini initiated domestic development programs and an aggressive foreign policy, support for the fascist leader ran from intense loyalty to increasing discontent. In 1940, Italy entered **World War II** on the side of its Axis ally, Germany. Axis success was short-lived: the Allies landed in Sicily (p. 724) in 1943, pushing Mussolini from power. As a final indignity, he and his mistress were captured and executed by infuriated citizens, their naked bodies left hanging upside down in a public square. By the end of 1943, Italy had formally withdrawn its support from Germany. The Nazis responded promptly, invading their former ally. In 1945, Italy was freed from German domination, and was divided between those supporting the monarchy and those favoring a return to fascism.

**POST-WAR POLITICS AND RECOVERY (1945-1983).** The end of WWII highlighted the intense factionalism of Italy. The **Constitution,** adopted in 1948, established the **Republic;** instead of Caesar, Augustus, and warring lords, this modern republic had a prime minister, a bicameral parliament, and an independent judiciary. The **Christian Democratic Party (DC),** bolstered by Marshall Plan money and American military aid, soon overtook the **Socialist Party (PSI)** as the primary force in the government. More than 300 political parties, working in tenuous coalitions, composed the minority government, resulting in instability and nearly constant political change. Economic recovery, primarily in the North, began with 1950s industrialization. Despite the **Southern Development Fund** to build roads, construct schools, and finance industries, the South lagged behind. The 1969 *autunno caldo* (hot autumn), a season of strikes, demonstrations, and riots (mainly instigated by students and factory workers), ushered in the violence of the 1970s. The most shocking episode was the 1978 kidnapping and murder of former Prime Minister **Aldo Moro** by a group of left-wing militant terrorists. The horrors of the 1970s were offset by a few positive reforms, such as the legalization of divorce and the expansion of women's rights. In 1983, **Bettino Craxi** became Italy's first Socialist premier.

**CORRUPTION AND REFORM (1983-1999). Oscar Luigi Scalfaro,** elected in 1992, set out to reform Italy's corrupt government. Shortly thereafter, in the *Mani Pulite* (Clean Hands) campaign, Scalfaro and **Judge Antonio di Pietro** uncovered the *Tangentopoli* (Bribesville) scandal. This unprecedented political crisis implicated over 1200 politicians and businessmen. Reactions to the investigation included the May 1993 bombing of Florence's **Uffizi** (p. 700), the "suicides" of 10 indicted officials, and the murders of anti-Mafia investigators. The 1996 election brought the center-left coalition, the **l'Ulivo** (Olive Tree), to power, with **Romano Prodi,** a Bolognese professor and economist, as prime minister. For the first time in modern history, Italy was dominated by two stable coalitions: the center-left l'Ulivo and the center-right **Il Polo.** Prodi's coalition returned a vote of no confidence in October 1998; his government collapsed, and **Massimo D'Alema** became prime minister. D'Alema and **Carlo Ciampi** instituted fiscal reform that qualified Italy for entrance into the European Monetary Union (EMU) in January 1999.

# TODAY

Italy's tendency toward partisan schisms and quick government turnover was tempered, momentarily at least, by its faith in one individual: **Silvio Berlusconi.** The allure and nonstop drive of Italy's richest man secured his re-election as prime minister in May 2001, although he was widely criticized outside of Italy for alleged corruption. (He had served briefly as prime minister from 1994-1996.) Berlusconi led the longest serving government since WWII with his **Forza Italia** party, but resigned in May 2006 following the loss of his center-right coalition in the April elections to **Romano Prodi,** once again. The fragile government lived up to its reputation for instability when Prodi resigned in February 2007. After only a few days, Prodi returned to office upon the request of Italian president, **Giorgio Napolitano.**

# PEOPLE AND CULTURE

**LANGUAGE.** The **Italian** language evolved from Latin. As a result of Italy's fragmented history, variations in dialects are notable. The throaty **Neapolitan** is actually its own language, using different grammatical structures that make it difficult for a northerner to understand; **Ligurians** use a mix of Italian, Catalán, and French; **Sardo,** spoken in Sardinia, bears little resemblance to standard Italian; and many Tuscan dialects differ from Italian in pronunciation. Some in the northern border regions don't speak Italian at all: the population of Valle d'Aosta speaks mainly French, and Trentino-Alto Adige harbors a German-speaking minority. In the southern regions of Puglia, Calabria, and Sicily, entire villages speak a form of Albanian called **Arbresh.** To facilitate conversation, locals do their best to employ standard Italian when speaking with foreigners, although some may be shy or hesitant to do so at first. Many Italians, especially older people or those who live in rural towns, do not speak English, although many young people do.

# THE ARTS

## VISUAL ARTS

### ⚙ FEATURED ITINERARY: MASTERWORKS OF ITALY

Though many of the original details have faded from Leonardo da Vinci's *The Last Supper* in **Milan** (Chiesa di Santa Maria della Grazie, p. 650), its prestige has never diminished. Among **Venice's** masterworks is Veronese's *Rape of Europa.* (Palazzo Ducale, p. 681). Overflowing with artistic talent during the Renaissance, **Florence** is now home to Michelangelo's *David* (Accademia, p. 702), Botticelli's *Birth of Venus* (Uffizi, p. 700), and Donatello's *David* (Bargello, p. 701), the first nude since Antiquity. St. Francis may have given up his worldly possessions, but his namesake in **Assisi** retains a wealth of beauty; don't miss Giotto's

fresco cycle *The Life of St. Francis* (Basilica di San Francesco; p. 710). **Rome** played host to Renaissance man Michelangelo, whose paintings grace the ceiling of the Sistine Chapel (Vatican; p. 637), and whose sculpture *Pietá* resides in the St. Peter's Basilica (Vatican; p. 637). Along with the ruins scattered throughout the south, **Naples** contains both Titian's *Danae* and Bellini's *Transfiguration of Christ* (Museo and Gallerie di Capodimonte; p. 719). A short trip from Naples and Pompeii, **Herculaneum's** House of the Mosaic of Neptune and Anfitrite displays the breathtaking mosaic that gives the structure its name (p. 720).

**ARCHITECTURE.** The Greeks peppered southern Italy with **temples** and **theaters.** The best-preserved Greek temples in the world today are found not in Greece, but in Sicily (p. 724). Many ancient Roman houses incorporated **frescoes,** Greek-influenced paintings on plaster, and **mosaics,** designs formed from small pieces of ceramic set into a surface. The use of **arches** and the invention of **concrete** revolutionized the Roman practice of architecture, making possible monuments like the **Colosseum** (p. 633) and the **Pantheon** (p. 635), as well as public works like **aqueducts** and **thermal baths.** The **catacombs** (p. 638), built by early, persecuted Christians who had to flee underground, are among the most haunting and intriguing of Italian monuments. In the Renaissance, **Filippo Brunelleschi** studied math to perfect ancient Roman architectural forms. His engineering talent allowed him to raise the dome over **Santa Maria del Fiore** (p. 699). **Gianlorenzo Bernini** (1598-1680), a prolific High Baroque sculptor and architect, designed the colonnade of St. Peter's *piazza* and the *baldacchino* inside. Contemporary and rival, **Francesco Borromini** (1599-1667) was more adept at shaping the walls of his buildings into serpentine architectural masterpieces, like his **San Carlo alle Quattro Fontane** in Rome (p. 638).

**FILM.** In the early 20th century, Mussolini created the *Centro Sperimentale della Cinematografia*, a national film school that stifled artistic development. The fall of fascism coincided with the rise of **Neorealist cinema** (1943-1950), which rejected contrived sets and professional actors for a candid look at post-war Italy. This new style caught the world's attention and Rome soon became a hot spot for the international movie scene. The works of **Roberto Rossellini** and **Vittorio de Sica** best represent *Neorealismo;* de Sica's 1948 *Ladri di Biciclette* may be the period's most famous and successful film. In the 1960s, post-Neorealist directors like **Federico Fellini** emphasized visual effects and symbolism over plots and characters. Fellini's *La Dolce Vita* (1960), which was banned by the Pope, is an incisive film scrutinizing 1950s Rome. In a similar vein, **Pier Paolo Pasolini** delved into Italy's underworld in his *Accattone* (1961). Although Italian cinema has fallen into a recent slump, **Bernardo Bertolucci's** *The Last Emperor* (1987) and Oscar-winners **Giuseppe Tornatore** and **Gabriele Salvatore** have garnered the attention of international audiences. Sparkplug **Roberto Benigni** became one of Italy's leading cinematic figures when his *La Vita è Bella (Life is Beautiful)* gained international fame, receiving Best Actor and Best Foreign Film Oscars and a Best Picture Oscar nomination at the 1999 Academy Awards. More recently, Nanni Moretti snagged the Palm D'Or at Cannes in 2001 for *La Stanza del Figlio*, and Leonardo Pieraccioni released *Il Paradiso all'improvviso* to much acclaim in 2003.

**FINE ARTS. Donatello,** a sculptor, studied and practiced the realistic articulation of the human body in motion. The artistic torch was passed to three exceptional men: **Leonardo da Vinci, Michelangelo Buonarroti,** and **Raphael Santi.** Leonardo da Vinci was not only an artist but a scientist, architect, engineer, musician, and weapon designer. Michelangelo created the illusion of vaults on the flat ceiling of the Sistine Chapel (p. 637), which remains his greatest surviving achievement in painting. Deep down, however, sculpture was his true medium, and his deft hand was responsible for *David* (p. 702). Raphael's (1483-1520) frescoes in the papal apartments of the Vatican, including the *School of Athens* (p. 639), show his debt to classical standards and his technically perfect figuration. The Venetian school produced the prolific **Titian** (1488-1576), whose works are notable for their realistic facial expressions and rich Venetian colors. **Caravaggio** (1573-1610) relied on *chiaroscuro* and naturalism to create dramatically unsettling images. Italians in the 18th and 19th centuries experimented with rougher techniques. **Antonio Canova** explored the formal Neoclassical style, which professed a return to the rules of Classical antiquity, while the Macchiaioli group revolted with a unique technique of "blotting," a forerunner of the Impressionistic brushstroke. The Italian Futurist artists of the 1910s used machines to bring Italy back to the cutting edge, and **Amedeo Modigliani** painted figures famous for their long oval faces and empty eyes.

## LITERATURE

The poet **Virgil's** *Aeneid* (20 BC) set the divine origins of Rome to dactylic hexameter. It is primarily through **Ovid's** *Metamorphoses* (AD 8) that many classical Roman myths have been immortalized. He also wrote a treatise on romantic *amore* and some racy love poems. The Dark Ages put a stop to most literary musings, but some Tuscan writers breathed new life into the art form in the early 14th century. **Dante Alighieri** was one of the first Italian poets to write in the vernacular Italian instead of in Latin, as was the convention. In his enduring epic poem, *The Divine Comedy* (1308-1321), Dante explored the fiery levels of the afterlife. **Petrarch** mimicked ancient Roman writers, penning love sonnets to a married woman named Laura. **Giovanni Boccaccio,** a close friend of Petrarch, composed a collection of 100 bawdy stories in *The Decameron* (1348-1353). Paralleling the scientific exploration of the time, 15th- and 16th-century Italian authors entered new domains of human experience. **Alberti** and **Palladio** wrote treatises on architecture and art theory. **Niccolò Machiavelli's** *The Prince* (1513) gives a timeless, sophisticated assessment of seizing and maintaining political power. **Pellegrino Artusi's** 1891 cookbook, *Science in the Kitchen and the Art of Eating Well,* was the first attempt to assemble recipes from regional traditions into a unified Italian cuisine. Twentieth-century literature founded a new tradition in Italian literature as Nobel Prize-winning author and playwright **Luigi Pirandello** explored the relativity of truth in his *Six Characters in Search of an Author* (1921). Literary production slowed in the years preceding WWII, but the conflict's conclusion ignited an explosion in anti-fascist fiction in Italy. **Primo**

**Levi** wrote *If This Is a Man* (1947) about his experiences in Auschwitz. Mid-20th-century poets include Nobel Prize winners **Salvatore Quasimodo** and **Eugenio Montale**. Italo Calvino exemplified the postmodern era by creating new worlds in *The Baron in the Trees* (1957) and questioning the act of reading and writing in *If on a Winter's Night a Traveler* (1979). More recently, internationally known playwright and satirist **Dario Fo** claimed the 1997 Nobel Prize for literature.

## MUSIC

In the latter half of the 16th century, a circle of Florentine writers, noblemen, and musicians, known as the **Camerata**, came up with the idea of opera in an attempt to recreate ancient Greek drama. Their first tries were simply lengthy poems set to music. **Jacobo Peri** composed *Dafne*, the world's first complete opera, in 1597. The first successful opera composer, **Claudio Monteverdi**, drew freely from history, juxtaposing high drama and love scenes with bawdy humor. **Antonio Vivaldi** typified the Italian **Baroque** movement, composing over 400 concertos, culminating in *The Four Seasons* (1725). With convoluted plots and strong, dramatic music, 19th-century Italian opera continues to dominate modern stages. **Gioacchino Rossini** was the master of *bel canto*, which consists of long, fluid, melodic lines. **Giuseppe Verdi** remains the transcendent musical and operatic figure of 19th-century Italy. Verdi produced the touching, personal dramas of *Rigoletto* (1851), *La Traviata* (1853), *Il Trovatore* (1853), and the heroic conflicts of *Aida* (1871). At the turn of the 20th century, **Giacomo Puccini** released *La Bohème* (1896), *Tosca* (1900), and *Madame Butterfly* (1904), continuing the Italian operatic tradition. In 1958, Pulitzer Prize winner **Gian Carlo Menotti** founded the Spoleto Festival for the arts.

Since his introduction to the music industry in 1987, **Ligabue** has gained recognition as one of the most successful Italian rock stars. While his fame has been constrained primarily to Italy, contemporary **Andrea Bocelli** has reached a worldwide audience with his operatic tenor.

# HOLIDAYS AND FESTIVALS

**Holidays:** New Year's Day (Jan. 1); Epiphany (Jan. 6); Easter Sunday and Monday (Mar. 23-24); Liberation Day (Apr. 25); Labor Day (May 1); Ascension (May 1); Feast of the Assumption (Aug. 15); All Saints' Day (Nov. 1); Immaculate Conception (Dec. 8); Christmas (Dec. 25); Santo Stefano (Dec. 26).

**Festivals:** The most common reason for a local festival in Italy is the celebration of a religious event—everything from a patron saint's holy day to the commemoration of a special miracle counts. Carnevale, a country-wide celebration, is held during the 10 days leading up to Lent (Jan. 25-Feb. 5). In Venice, costumed Carnevale revelers fill the streets and canals. During Scoppio del Carro, held in Florence's P. del Duomo on Easter Sunday, Florentines set off a cart of explosives, remembering Pazziano dei Pazzi, who returned from the Crusades with a few splinters from the holy sepulcher, which he used to light a simple fireworks display. The Spoleto Festival (known as the Festival dei Due Mondi, or Festival of Two Worlds) is one of the world's most prestigious international arts events. Each June and July it features concerts, operas, ballets, film screenings, and modern art shows (www.spoletofestival.it). For more info on festivals in Italy, visit www.hostetler.net/italy/italy.cfm.

# ADDITIONAL RESOURCES

*A Concise History of Italy,* by Christopher Duggan. Cambridge University Press (1994). Considers the difficulties behind Italian unity throughout history.

ITALY

*Cosa Nostra: A History of the Sicilian Mafia,* by John Dickie. Palgrave Macmillan (2004). One of the best books on the mob, tracing it's roots back to the 1860s.

*Italy and Its Discontents: Family, Civil Society, State,* by Paul Ginsborg. Palgrave Macmillan (2006). Provides a detailed, straightforward description of Italian society and politics in the latter half of the 20th century.

# ESSENTIALS

### FACTS AND FIGURES

**Official Name:** Italian Republic.
**Capital:** Rome.
**Major Cities:** Florence, Milan, Naples, Venice.
**Population:** 58,148,000.
**Time Zone:** GMT +1.

**Language:** Italian; some German, French, and Slovene.
**Religion:** Roman Catholic (90%).
**Longest Salami:** Made by Rino Parenti in Zibello, displayed on Nov. 23, 2003; 486.8m in length.

## WHEN TO GO

Traveling to Italy in late May or early September, when the temperature averages a comfortable 77°F (25°C), will ensure a calmer, cooler vacation. When planning, keep in mind festival schedules and weather patterns in northern and southern areas. Tourism goes into overdrive in June, July, and August: hotels are booked solid and prices know no limits. In August, Italians flock to the coast for vacationing, but northern cities are infested with tourists.

## DOCUMENTS AND FORMALITIES

**EMBASSIES AND CONSULATES.** Foreign embassies in Italy are in Rome (p. 616). Italian embassies abroad include: **Australia,** 12 Grey St., Deakin, Canberra ACT 2600 (☎612 62 73 33 33; www.ambcanberra.esteri.it); **Canada,** 275 Slater St., 21st fl., Ottawa, ON K1P 5H9 (☎613-232-2401; www.ambottawa.esteri.it); **Ireland,** 63/65 Northumberland Rd., Dublin 4 (☎353 16 60 17 44; www.ambdublino.esteri.it); **New Zealand,** 34-38 Grant Rd., Wellington (☎644 473 5339; www.ambwellington.esteri.it); **UK,** 14 Three Kings Yard, London, W1K 4EH (☎020 73 12 22 00; www.embitaly.org.uk); **US,** 3000 Whitehaven St., Washington, D.C., 20008 (☎202-612-4400; www.ambwashingtondc.esteri.it).

**VISA AND ENTRY INFORMATION.** EU citizens do not need a visa. Citizens of Australia, Canada, New Zealand, and the US do not need a visa for stays of up to 90 days, beginning upon entry into any of the countries within the EU's freedom-of-movement zone. For more info, see p. 13. For stays longer than 90 days, all non-EU citizens need visas (around €60), available at Italian consulates. For more info on obtaining a visa visit www.esteri.it/visti/home_eng.asp.

## TOURIST SERVICES AND MONEY

### EMERGENCY

**Ambulance:** ☎118. **Fire:** ☎115. **Police:** ☎112.
**General Emergency:** ☎113.

**TOURIST OFFICES.** The **Italian State Tourist Board** (ENIT; www.enit.it) provides useful info about many aspects of the country, including the arts, history, nature, and leisure activities. The main office in Rome (☎06 49 71 11; sedecentrale@cert.enit.it) can help locate any local office that is not listed online.

**MONEY.** The **euro (€)** has replaced the **lira** as the unit of currency in Italy. For more info, see p. 16. At many Italian restaurants, a **service charge** *(servizio)* or **cover** *(coperto)* is included in the bill. Most locals do not tip, but it is appropriate for foreign visitors to leave an additional €1-2 at restaurants. Taxi drivers expect about a 10-15% tip. Bargaining is common in Italy, but use discretion. It is appropriate at markets, with vendors, and unmetered taxi fares (settle the price before getting in). Haggling over prices elsewhere is usually inappropriate.

Italy has a 20% **value added tax (VAT,** or **IVA** in Italy), a sales tax applied to most goods and services. The prices given in *Let's Go* include VAT. In the airport upon exiting the EU, non-EU citizens can claim a refund on the tax paid for goods purchased at participating stores. In order to qualify for a refund in a store, you must spend at least €150; make sure to ask for a refund form when you pay. For more info on qualifying for a VAT refund, see p. 18.

**BUSINESS HOURS.** Nearly everything closes around 1-3 or 4pm for *siesta*. Most museums are open 9am-1pm and 3-6pm; some are open through lunch, however. Monday is often a *giorno di chiusura* (day of closure).

# TRANSPORTATION

**BY PLANE.** Most international flights land at Rome's international airport, known as both **Fiumicino** and **Leonardo da Vinci** (FCO; ☎06 65 951; www.adr.it). Other hubs are Florence's **Amerigo Vespucci** airport (FLR) and Milan's **Malpensa** (MXP) and **Linate** (LIN) airports. **Alitalia** (☎800-223-5730; www.alitalia.com) is Italy's national airline. Budget airlines **Ryanair** (☎353 12 49 77 91; www.ryanair.com) and **EasyJet** (☎0871 244 2366; www.easyjet.com) offer inexpensive fares to cities throughout the country; reserve ahead, as the best deals are available weeks in advance.

**BY FERRY.** Sicily, Sardinia, Corsica, and smaller islands along the coast are connected to the mainland by **ferries** *(traghetti)* and **hydrofoils** *(aliscafi)*. Italy's largest private ferry service, **Tirrenia** (www.gruppotirrenia.it), runs ferries to Sardinia, Sicily, and Tunisia. Other lines, such as the **SNAV** (tickets and special offers available online at www.aferry.to/snav-ferry.htm), have hydrofoil services from major ports such as Ancona, Bari, Brindisi, Genoa, La Spezia, Livorno, Naples, and Trapani. Ferry service is also prevalent in the Lake Country. Reserve well ahead, especially in July and August.

**BY TRAIN.** The Italian State Railway **Ferrovie dello Stato,** or **FS** (national info line ☎848 88 80 88; www.trenitalia.com), offers inexpensive, efficient service and Trenitalia passes, the domestic equivalent of the Eurail Pass. There are several types of trains: the *locale* stops at every station on a line, the *diretto* makes fewer stops than the *locale*, and the *espresso* stops only at major stations. The air-conditioned *rapido*, an **InterCity (IC)** train, zips along but costs more. Tickets for the fast, pricey **Eurostar** trains require reservations. **Eurail Passes** are valid without a supplement on all trains except Eurostar. **Always validate** your ticket in the orange or yellow machine before boarding to avoid a €120 fine.

**BY BUS.** Intercity buses serve points inaccessible by train. For city buses, buy tickets in *tabaccherie* or kiosks. Validate your ticket immediately after boarding to avoid a €120 fine. Websites www.bus.it and www.italybus.it are helpful resources for trip planning.

**BY CAR.** To drive in Italy, you must be 18 or older and hold an **International Driving Permit (IDP)** or an EU license. There are four kinds of roads: *autostrada* (superhighways;

mostly tollroads; usually 130km per hr. speed limit); *strade statali* (state roads); *strade provinciali* (provincial); and *strade communali* (local). **Driving in Italy is frightening;** congested traffic is common in large cities and in the north. On three-lane roads, the center lane is for passing. **Mopeds** (€30-40 per day) can be a great way to see the more scenic areas but can be disastrous in the rain and on rough roads. Always exercise caution. Practice in empty streets and learn to keep up with traffic. Drivers in Italy—especially in the south—are notorious for ignoring traffic laws.

**BY BIKE AND BY THUMB.** While bicycling is a popular sport in Italy, bike trails are rare. Rent bikes where you see a *noleggio* sign. Let's Go does not recommend hitchhiking, which can be particularly unsafe in Italy, especially in the south.

# KEEPING IN TOUCH

| **PHONE CODES** | **Country code: 39. International dialing prefix:** 00. All 10-digit numbers listed in this chapter are mobile phones and do not require a city code. When calling within a city, dial 0 + city code + local number. For more info on how to place international calls, see **Inside Back Cover.** |
| --- | --- |

**EMAIL AND THE INTERNET. Internet** cafes in large cities swell with patrons, and rural areas and cities in the south are catching up. A new Italian law requires a passport or driver's license to use an Internet cafe. Rates are €1.50-6 per hr. For free Internet access, try local universities and libraries. While Italy initially lagged behind in jumping on the information superhighway, it's now playing catch-up impressively; however, easy laptop connection is still rare.

**TELEPHONE.** Almost all public phones require a prepaid card *(scheda),* sold at *tabaccherie,* Internet cafes, and post offices. Italy has no area codes, only regional prefixes that are incorporated into the number. Mobile phones are widely used in Italy; buying a prepaid SIM card for a GSM phone can be a good, inexpensive option. Of the service providers, **TIM** and **Vodafone** have the best networks. International direct dial numbers include: **AT&T Direct** (☎800 17 24 44); **British Telecom** (☎0800 17 24 41); **Canada Direct** (☎800 17 22 13); **Telecom New Zealand Direct** (☎800 17 26 41); **Telstra Australia** (☎800 17 26 10).

**MAIL.** Airmail letters sent from Australia, North America, or the UK to Italy take anywhere from four to 15 days to arrive. Since Italian mail is notoriously unreliable, it is usually safer and quicker to send mail priority *(prioritaria)* or registered *(raccomandata).* It costs €0.85 to send a letter worldwide. To receive mail in Italy, have mail delivered **Poste Restante.** Mail will go to the main post office unless you specify a subsidiary by street address. Address mail to be held according to the following example: First name LAST NAME, *Fermo Posta,* City, Italy. Bring a passport to pick up your mail; there may be a small fee.

# ACCOMMODATIONS AND CAMPING

| **ITALY** | ❶ | ❷ | ❸ | ❹ | ❺ |
| --- | --- | --- | --- | --- | --- |
| **ACCOMMODATIONS** | under €16 | €16-25 | €26-40 | €41-60 | over €60 |

**Associazione Italiana Alberghi per la Gioventù (AIG),** the Italian hostel federation, is a **Hostelling International (HI)** affiliate. A full list of AIG hostels is available online at www.ostellionline.org. Prices in Italy start at €8 per night for **dorms.** Hostels are the best option for solo travelers (single rooms are relatively scarce in hotels in the country), but curfews, lockouts, distant locations, and less-than-perfect security can detract from their appeal. Italian **hotel** rates are set by the state. A single room in a hotel *(camera singola)* usually starts at €25-50 per night, and a double *(camera doppia)* starts at €40-82 per room. A room with a private bath *(con bagno)* usually costs 30-50% more. Smaller **pensioni** are often cheaper than hotels. Be sure to confirm charges before checking in; Italian hotels are notorious for tacking on additional costs at check-out time. **Affittacamere** (rooms for rent in private houses) are an inexpensive option for longer stays. For more info, inquire at local tourist offices. There are over 1700 **campgrounds** in Italy; tent sites average €4.20. The **Federazione Italiana del Campeggio e del Caravaning** (www.federcampeggio.it) has a complete list of sites. The **Touring Club Italiano** (www.touringclub.it) publishes books and pamphlets on the outdoors.

# FOOD AND DRINK

| ITALY | ❶ | ❷ | ❸ | ❹ | ❺ |
|-------|-----|-----|-----|-----|-----|
| FOOD | under €7 | €7-15 | €16-20 | €21-25 | over €25 |

Breakfast is the simplest meal in Italy: at most, *colazione* consists of coffee and a *cornetto* or *brioche* (croissant). For *pranzo* (lunch), people grab *panini* (sandwiches) or salads at bars, or dine more calmly at an inexpensive *tavola calda* (cafeteria-style snack bar), *rosticceria* (grill), or *gastronomia* (snack bar with hot dishes for takeout). *Cena* (dinner) usually begins at 8pm or later. In Naples, it's not unusual to go for a midnight **pizza**. Traditionally, dinner is the longest meal of the day, usually lasting much of the evening and consisting of an *antipasto* (appetizer), a *primo piatto* (starch-based first course like pasta or risotto), a *secondo piatto* (meat or fish), and a *contorno* (vegetable side dish). Finally comes the *dolce* (dessert or fruit), then *caffè* **(espresso)**, and often an after-dinner liqueur.

However, lunch is usually the most important meal of the day in rural regions where daily work comes in two shifts and is separated by a long lunch and **siesta**. Many restaurants offer a fixed-price *menù turistico* including *primo*, *secondo*, bread, water, and wine. While food varies regionally—seafood in the South and the coast, heartier selections in the North, truffles in Piemonte, pesto in Liguria, gnocchi in Trentino-Alto Adige, parmesan and balsamic vinegar in Emilia-Romagna, and rustic stews in Tuscany—the importance of relaxing and having an extended meal does not. **La bella figura** (a good figure) is another social imperative, and the after-dinner **passeggiata** (walk) is as much a tradition as the meal itself. Dense **gelato** is a snack, a dessert, and even a budget meal in itself. **Coffee** and **wine** are their own institutions, each with their own devoted followers.

> **⛶TIP** **THE UGLY DUCKLING.** Before shelling out the euro for a *piccolo cono* (small cone), assess the quality of an establishment by looking at the banana *gelato*: if it's bright yellow, it's been made from a mix. If it's slightly gray, real bananas were used. *Gelati* in metal bins also tend to be homemade, whereas plastic tubs indicate mass-production.

# BEYOND TOURISM

From harvesting grapes on vineyards in Siena to restoring and protecting marine life in the Mediterranean, there are diverse options for working for a cause. Those in search of a more lucrative experience might consider working as an intern for the Italian press or teaching English in Italian schools. For more info on opportunities across Europe, see **Beyond Tourism,** p. 54.

**Associazione Culturale Linguista Educational (ACLE),** V. Roma 54, 18038 San Remo, Imperio (☎0184 50 60 70; www.acle.org). Non-profit association that works to bring theater, arts, and English language instruction to Italian children. Employees create theater programs in schools, teach English at summer camps, and have converted a medieval house in the village of Baiardio into a student art center.

**Carmelita's Cook Italy** (☎34 90 07 82 98; www.cookitaly.com). Region- or dish-specific cooking classes. Venues in Bologna, Lucca, and Sicily, among others. Courses run 3 days to 2 weeks. Program fee from €990 (including housing, meals, and recipes).

**Gruppi Archeologici d'Italia,** V. Baldo degli Ubaldi 168, 00165 Rome (☎06 638 5256; www.gruppiarcheologici.org). Organizes 2-week-long volunteer programs at archaeological digs throughout Italy. Offers links to various programs hoping to promote cultural awareness about archaeological preservation. Program fee €195-400.

# ROME (ROMA)                                                    ☎06

Rome (pop. 2.8 million), *La Città Eterna*, is a concentrated expression of Italian spirit. Whether flaunting the Italian 2006 World Cup victory or retelling the mythical story of the city's founding, Romans exude a fierce pride for the Rome that was and the Rome that will be. Crumbling pagan ruins form the backdrop for the center of Christianity's largest denomination, and hip clubs and bars border grand cathedrals. The aroma of homemade pasta, pop of opening wine bottles, and rumble of city buses will greet you at every turn on Rome's cobblestone streets.

# ✈ INTERCITY TRANSPORTATION

**Flights: Da Vinci International Airport** (**FCO;** ☎65 21 01), known as **Fiumicino,** handles most flights. The **Termini** line runs nonstop to Rome's main station, **Stazione Termini** (30min., 2 per hr., €11). After hours, take the blue COTRAL **bus** (☎80 01 50 008) to Tiburtina from outside the main doors after customs (4 per day, €5). From Tiburtina, take bus #175 or 492, or metro B to Termini. A few domestic and budget flights, including Ryanair, arrive at **Ciampino** (**CIA;** ☎79 49 41). To get to Rome, take the COTRAL bus (2 per hr., €1) to **Anagnina** station, or the **Terravision Shuttle** (www.terravision.it) to V. Marsala at the Hotel Royal Santina (40min., €8).

**Trains:** Trains leave Stazione Termini for: **Bologna** (2½-3½hr., €33-42); **Florence** (1½-3¾hr., €15-33); **Milan** (4½-8hr., €30-50); **Naples** (1¾-2½hr., €10-25); **Venice** (4½-5½hr., €33-50). Trains arriving in Rome between midnight and 5am arrive at **Stazione Tiburtina** or **Stazione Ostiense,** which are connected to Termini by the #175 bus.

# ✦ ORIENTATION

Because Rome's narrow, winding streets are difficult to navigate, it's helpful to orient yourself to major landmarks and main streets. The **Tiber River,** which snakes north-south through the city, is also a useful reference point. Most trains arrive at Stazione Termini east of Rome's historical center. **Termini** and neighboring **San Lorenzo** to the east are home to the city's largest university and most of its budget accommodations. **Via Nazionale** originates two blocks northwest of Termini Station in **Piazza della Repubblica** and leads to **Piazza Venezia,** the focal point of the city, recognizable by the immense white **Vittorio Emanuele II monument.** From P. Venezia,

Via dei Fori Imperiali runs southeast to the Ancient City, where the Colosseum and the Roman Forum attest to former glory. Via del Corso stretches north from P. Venezia to Piazza del Popolo, which has an obelisk in its center. The Trevi Fountain, Piazza Barberini, and the fashionable streets around Piazza di Spagna lie to the east of V. del Corso. Villa Borghese, with its impressive gardens and museums, is northeast of the Spanish Steps. West of V. del Corso is the centro storico, the tangle of streets around the Pantheon, Piazza Navona, Campo dei Fiori, and the old Jewish Ghetto. West of P. Venezia, Largo Argentina marks the start of Corso Vittorio Emanuele II, which runs through the *centro storico* to the Tiber River. Across the river to the north-west is Vatican City and the Borgo-Prati neighborhood. South of the Vatican is Trastevere and residential Testaccio. Be sure to pick up a free color map in English at the tourist office (Practical Information, p. 617).

# ⌐ LOCAL TRANSPORTATION

Public Transportation: The A and B Metropolitana subway lines (www.metroroma.it) meet at Termini and run 5:30am-11:30pm. ATAC buses (www.atac.roma.it) run 5am-midnight (with limited late-night routes); validate your ticket in the machine when you board. Buy tickets (€1) at *tabaccherie*, newsstands, and station machines; they're valid for 1 metro ride or unlimited bus travel within 1¼hr. of validation. BIG daily tickets (€4), 3-day tourist passes (€11), and CIS weekly tickets (€16) allow for unlimited public transport. Beware: pickpocketing is rampant on buses and trains.

Taxis: Radiotaxi (☎06 35 70). Taxis are expensive. Ride only in yellow or white taxis, and make sure your taxi has a meter (if not, negotiate the price before riding). Surcharges apply at night (€2.60), on Su (€1), and when heading to or from Fiumicino (€7.25) or Ciampino (€5.50). Fares run about €11 from Termini to Vatican City, around €35 between the city center and Fiumicino.

Bike and Moped Rental: Bikes generally cost €5 per hr. or €10 per day while scooters cost €35-55 per day. Try Bici & Baci, V. del Viminale 5 (☎48 28 443; www.bici-baci.com). 16+. Open daily 8am-7pm. AmEx/MC/V.

# ⌐ PRACTICAL INFORMATION

Tourist Office: ▨Enjoy Rome, V. Marghera 8/A (☎44 56 890; www.enjoyrome.com). From the middle concourse of Termini, exit right, with the trains behind you; cross V. Marsala and follow V. Marghera for 3 blocks. The helpful, English-speaking staff makes reservations at museums, shows, and accommodations. They also lead walking tours (€25, under 26 €20). Pick up their detailed map and a *When in Rome* booklet. Open Apr.-Oct. M-F 8:30am-7pm, Sa 8:30am-2pm; Nov.-Mar. M-F 9am-6pm, Sa 9am-2pm.

Embassies: Australia, V. Antonio Bosio 5 (☎85 27 21; www.italy.embassy.gov.au). Open M-F 9am-5pm. Canada, V. Zara 30 (☎85 44 41; www.canada.it). Open M-F 9am-5pm. Ireland, P. di Campitelli 3 (☎69 79 121). New Zealand, V. Zara 28 (☎44 17 171). Open M-F 8:30am-12:45pm and 1:45-5pm. UK, V. XX Settembre 80a (☎42 20 00 01). Consular section open M-F 9:15am-1:30pm. US, V. Vittorio Veneto 119/A (☎46 741; www.usembassy.it/mission). Open M-F 8:30am-5:30pm.

Currency Exchange: Banca di Roma and Banca Nazionale del Lavoro have good rates, but near-ubiquitous ATMs have the best. Open M-F 8:30am-1:30pm.

American Express: P. di Spagna 38 (☎67 641, lost cards 800 87 20 00). Open M-F 9am-5:30pm, Sa 9am-12:30pm.

Luggage Storage: In Termini, underneath track #24.

Lost Property: Oggetti Smarriti (☎58 16 040). On buses (☎58 16 040); Metro A (☎48 74 309), call M, W, F 9am-12:30pm; Metro B (☎57 53 22 65), call F 8am-6:30pm.

ITALY

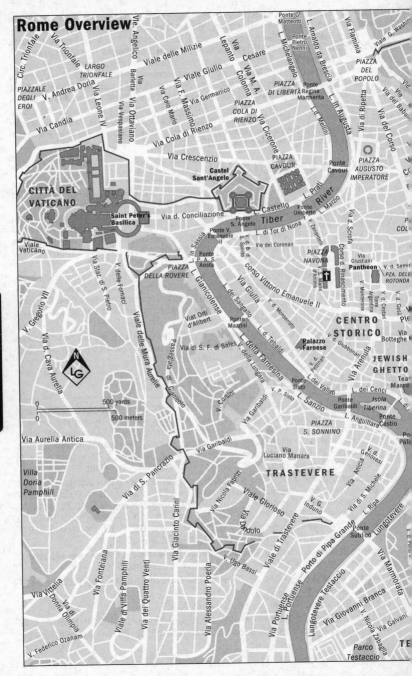

# Rome Overview

ITALY

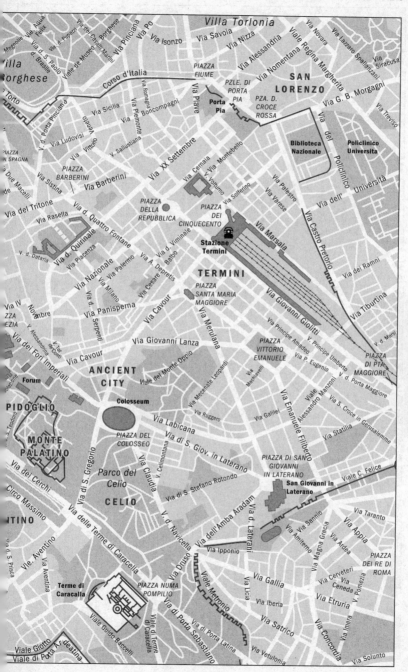

ITALY

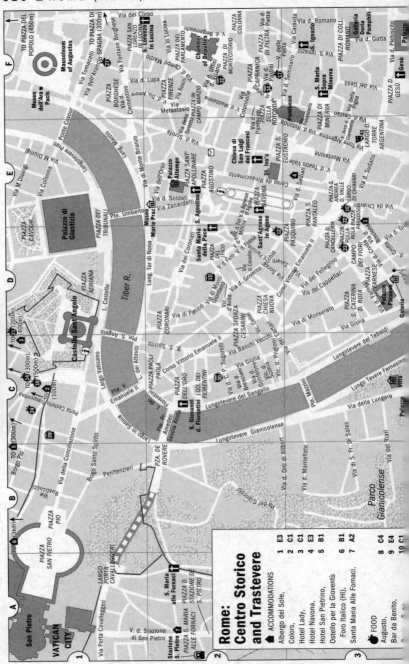

**Rome: Centro Storico and Trastevere**

| ▲ ACCOMMODATIONS | |
|---|---|
| Albergo del Sole, | E3 1 |
| Colors, | C1 2 |
| Hotel Lady, | C1 3 |
| Hotel Navona, | E3 4 |
| Hotel San Pietrino, | B1 5 |
| Ostello per la Gioventù Foro Italico (HI), | B1 6 |
| Santa Maria Alle Fornaci, | A2 7 |

| ● FOOD | |
|---|---|
| Augusto, | C4 8 |
| Bar da Benito, | E4 9 |
| | C1 10 |

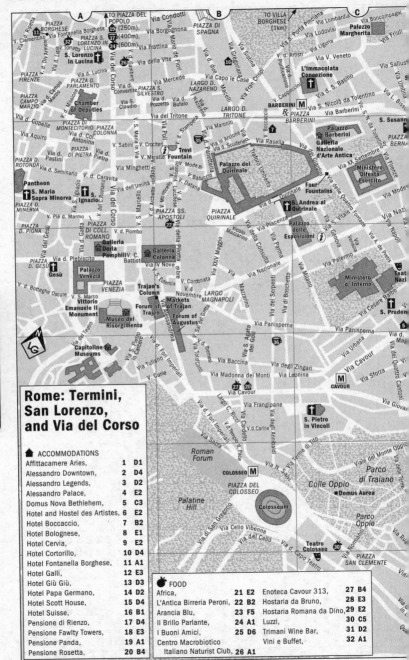

**ITALY**

# Rome: Termini, San Lorenzo, and Via del Corso

## ♠ ACCOMMODATIONS

## ♣ FOOD

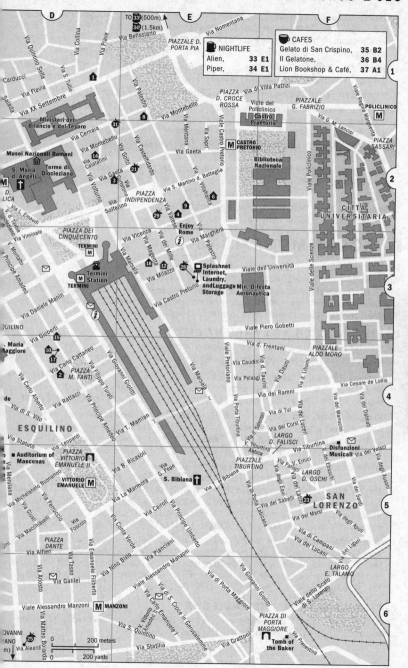

TO 33 (500m),
34 (1.5km)

PIAZZALE D.
PORTA PIA

| 🍴 NIGHTLIFE | | 🍨 CAFES | |
|---|---|---|---|
| Alien, | 33 E1 | Gelato di San Crispino, | 35 B2 |
| Piper, | 34 E1 | Il Gelatone, | 36 B4 |
| | | Lion Bookshop & Café, | 37 A1 |

Via Nomentana

Via Belisario

Via di Villa Patrizi

PIAZZA
D. CROCE
ROSSA

Viale del
Policlinico

PIAZZALE
G. FABRIZIO

Castro
Praetorio

Viale Regina Margherita

POLICLINICO Ⓜ

Via G. M. Lancisi

CASTRO
PRETORIO Ⓜ

Biblioteca
Nazionale

PIAZZA
SASSARI

Ministeri del
Bilancio e del Tesoro

Musei Nazionali Romani

Terme di
Diocleziano

S. Maria
d. Angeli ♱

D.
LICA

Viale Castro Pretorio

Viale Policlinico

CITTÀ
UNIVERSITARIA

Via L. Einaudi

PIAZZA
INDIPENDENZA

Via S. Martino d. Battaglia

PIAZZA DEI
CINQUECENTO

Enjoy
Rome ℹ

TERMINI Ⓜ

Via Viminale

Termini
Station

TERMINI

Splashnet
Internet,
Laundry,
and Luggage
Storage

Min. Difesa
Aeronautica

Viale dell'Università

Via delle Scienze

Via Daniele Manin

ℹ

QUILINO

Viale Piero Gobetti

. Maria
Maggiore

Via Gioberti

Via d. Frentani

PIAZZALE
ALDO MORO

Via Carlo Cattaneo

PIAZZA
M. FANTI

Via Caudini

Via d. Dauni

Via Pelasgi

Via d. Tauri

Via Cesare de Lollis

de

Via di S. Vito

Via dei Ramni

Via dei Dalmati

ESQUILINO

Via Porta Tiburtina

Via dei Corsi Luceri

Via dei Marrucini

Via Statuto

Via di Tizi

Via dei Luceri

LARGO
D. FALISCI

■ Auditorium of
Maecenas

PIAZZA
VITTORIO
EMANUELE II

V. Tiburtina
Antica

Via Tiburtina

■ Disfunzioni
Musicali ✉

Via degli Etruschi

Via degli Ausoni

Via dei Volsci

VITTORIO
EMANUELE Ⓜ

S. Bibiana ♱

PIAZZA
TIBURTINO

LARGO
D. OSCHI

Via dei Falisci

Via degli Equi

SAN
LORENZO

Via dei Sardi

Via di Porta Labicana

Via dei Marsi

Via degli Apuli

PIAZZA
DANTE

Via dei Sabelli

Via di Campani

Via dei Lucani

Via dei Liguri

Viale Alessandro Manzoni Ⓜ MANZONI

Via di Porta Maggiore

LARGO
E. TALAMO

GIOVANNI

Viale dello Scalo
di S. Lorenzo

PIAZZA DI
PORTA
MAGGIORE

Via Prenestina

Tomb of
the Baker

Via Statilia

0 ___ 200 meters
0 ___ 200 yards

**GLBT Resources: ARCI-GAY,** V. Goito 35/B (☎ 64 50 11 02; www.arcigayroma.it). Open M-F 4-8pm. **Circolo Mario Mieli di Cultura Omosessuale,** V. Efeso 2/A (☎ 54 13 985; www.mariomieli.org). **Libreria Babele,** V. d. Banchi Vecchi. (☎ 68 76 628; www.libreri-ababeleroma.it). Library focusing on gay literature. Open M-Sa 11am-7pm.

**Laundromat: BollaBlu,** V. Milazzo 20/B. (☎ 44 70 30 96). Laundry about €10. Open daily 8am-midnight. **OndaBlu** (info ☎ 800 86 13 46). 17 locations throughout the city.

**Pharmacies: Farmacia Piram,** V. Nazionale 228 (☎ 488 07 54). Open 24hr. MC/V.

**Hospitals: International Medical Center,** V. Firenze 47 (☎ 48 82 371; www.imc84.com). Call ahead. Referral service to English-speaking doctors. General visit €100. Open M-Sa 9am-8pm; on-call 24hr. **Rome-American Hospital,** V.E. Longoni 69 (24hr. service ☎ 22 551, appointments 22 55 290; www.rah.it). Visits average €100-200.

**Internet Access: Splashnet,** V. Varese 33 (☎ 49 38 04 50), near Termini. €1.50 per hr. Open daily in summer 8:30am-1am; in winter 8:30am-11pm. **Padma Internet Point,** V. Cavour 131 (☎ 48 93 03 80). 10 computers. Internet €2 per hr. Printing text €0.20 per page, graphics €0.75 per page. Open daily 8am-midnight.

**Post Office: Main Post Office (Posta Centrale),** P. San Silvestro 19. Open M-F 8am-7pm, Sa 8am-1:15pm. Branch at V. d. Terme di Diocleziano 30, near Termini.

# ▐ ACCOMMODATIONS

Rome swells with tourists around Easter, May through July, and in September. Prices vary widely with the seasons, and proprietors' willingness to negotiate depends on length of stays and group size. Termini swarms with hotel scouts. Many are legitimate and have IDs issued by tourist offices; however, be wary as some impostors with fake badges direct travelers to run-down locations charging exorbitant rates.

## CENTRO STORICO AND ANCIENT CITY

If being a bit closer to the sights is important to you, then choosing Rome's medieval center over the area near Termini may be worth the higher prices.

**Pensione Rosetta,** V. Cavour 295 (☎ 47 82 30 69; www.rosettahotel.com), a few blocks past the Fori Imperiali. 18 tidy rooms with bath, TV, and phone. A/C €10. Reserve 2 months ahead. Singles €60; doubles €85; triples €95; quads €110. AmEx/MC/V. ❹

**Albergo del Sole,** V. d. Biscione 76 (☎ 68 80 68 73; www.solealbiscione.it), off Campo dei Fiori. Comfortable, modern rooms with phone, TV, and antique furniture. Reception 24hr. Check-in and check-out 11am. Reserve 2 months ahead in high season. Singles €65, with bath €90; doubles €95-€150; triples €185; quads €220. Cash only. ❺

**Hotel Navona,** V. d. Sediari 8, 1st fl. (☎ 68 64 203; www.hotelnavona.com). Bus #64 to Corso Vittorio Emanuele II or #70 to Corso Rinascimento. Outdoor marking is very small. English-speaking owners have a nearby *residenza,* with apartments to rent for longer stays. Breakfast, TV, A/C, and bath included. Luggage storage. 24hr. reception. Check-out 10:30am. Singles €100-120; doubles €135-145; triples €180-210. Reservations with credit card and 1st-night deposit. 5% *Let's Go* discount. D/MC/V. ❺

**Hotel Fontanella Borghese,** Via Fontanella Borghese, 84., 2nd floor. (☎ 68 80 95 04; www.fontanellaborghese.com). Heading north from P. Venezia, take a left on Via Fontanella Borghese. Once owned by the Borghese Princes, this centrally located hotel now features 29 comfy rooms with A/C, minibar, phone, and satellite TV. Singles €130; doubles €205; triples €250; quads €265. AmEx/MC/V. ❺

## PIAZZA DI SPAGNA AND ENVIRONS

Though prices near P. di Spagna can be very steep, accommodations are often newer and closer to the metro than in the *centro storico.*

**Pensione Panda,** V. della Croce 35, 2nd fl. (☎67 80 179; www.hotelpanda.it). M: A-Spagna, between P. di Spagna and V. del Corso. 28 renovated rooms with faux marble statues and frescoed ceilings. English spoken. A/C €6. Free Wi-Fi. Reserve ahead. Singles €68, with bath €80; doubles €78/108; triples €140; quads €180. 5% *Let's Go* discount on cash payments. AmEx/MC/V. ❹

**Hotel Suisse,** V. Gregoriana 54, 3rd fl. (☎67 83 649; www.hotelsuisserome.com). M: A-Spagna. The antique furniture, huge rooms, and opulent sitting room make for a pleasant stay. Phone and bath in all rooms. Breakfast in bed included. Singles €100; doubles €165; triples €210; quads €230. Discounts on website. MC/V. ❺

**Hotel Boccaccio,** V. del Boccaccio 25, 1st fl. (☎48 85 962; www.hotelboccaccio.com). M: A-Barberini, near P. Barberini. 8 cozy, simply furnished rooms and a terrace. Singles €45; doubles €80, with bath €100; triples €108/135. AmEx/MC/V. ❸

## BORGO AND PRATI (NEAR VATICAN CITY)

*Pensioni* near the Vatican offer some of the best deals in Rome and the sobriety one would expect from a neighborhood with this kind of nun-to-tourist ratio.

**Colors,** V. Boezio 31 (☎68 74 030; www.colorshotel.com). M: A-Ottaviano. This colorful 3-fl. complex has 2 hostel areas and 1 pristine hotel. Breakfast included. Communal terraces and kitchens open 7:30am-10pm. Internet €2 per hr. Call by 9pm the night before to reserve dorms. Hostel dorms €27; singles €90, with bath €105; doubles €100/130; triples €120. Hotel singles €90; doubles €120; triples €140; quads €150. Cash only. ❸

**Hotel San Pietrino,** V. G. Bettolo 43, 3rd fl. (☎37 00 132; www.sanpietrino.it). M: A-Ottaviano. Spacious rooms are simple and clean with free A/C, DVD, and TV. Internet and communal fridge access. Bikes €5 per day. Laundry €6-8. Reserve 2-3 months ahead in high season. Singles €35-45; doubles €70-93; triples €120; family suite €135. 10% *Let's Go* discount. AmEx/MC/V. ❸

**Hotel Lady,** V. Germanico 198, 4th fl. (☎32 42 112; www.hoteladyroma.it). This cozy hotel's dimly lit hallways accentuate the ceiling's rich wooden beams. Rooms have antique furniture, sinks, desks, phones, and fans, but no A/C. High season singles €80; doubles €100, with bath €145; triples €130. Low-season rates vary. AmEx/MC/V. ❺

**Ostello Per La Gioventù Foro Italico (HI),** V. delle Olimpiadi 61 (☎32 36 267; bookingrome@tiscali.it). M: A-Ottaviano, then bus #32 from P. di Risorgimento to the 2nd "LGT Cadorna Ostello Gioventù" stop (10-15min.). The hostel is the white building behind the bushes

## TOP TEN PLACES TO SMOOCH IN ROMA

While you may be close enough to pucker up with strangers on the subway, save your saliva for these dreamy destinations.

**1.** Stroll through **Villa Borghese** (p. 636), find a secluded shade tree, and go in for the kill.

**2.** Bottle of red. Bottle of white. **Trevi Fountain** (p. 624) at night.

**3.** With the sun setting behind St. Peters and the swirling Tiber beneath you, **Ponte Sisto** is the perfect place to lay it on.

**4. St. Peter's Square** (p. 637). Just keep it PG with His Holiness watching.

**5.** Survey Circus Maximus from **Palatine Hill** (p. 633) and imagine 300,000 fans cheering you on.

**6.** The terrace of the **Vittorio Emanuele II monument** (p. 635). It's nicknamed the "wedding cake" for a reason.

**7.** Top of **the Spanish Steps** (p. 636). If you fail, you can always push the person down them.

**8.** Waiting for the **Metro.** You'd be surprised. It gets pretty steamy.

**9. Chiesa di Santa Maria in Cosmedin** (p. 635). Forget chocolates and roses, the skull and relics of St. Valentine are the key ingredient in any love potion.

**10.** Over a shared bowl of **spaghetti.** *Lady and the Tramp* style.

across the street. If you travel with 300 friends or feel nostalgic about college dorm life, this hostel is for you. A barrack-style marble building holds massive dorm rooms, bathrooms, a cafeteria, and a common area. Breakfast, showers, and linens included. Luggage storage €1 per day. Internet access with phone card. Reception 7am-11pm. Curfew 1-1:30am. Dorms €23. €5 HI discount. AmEx/MC/V. ❷

## SAN LORENZO AND EAST OF TERMINI

Welcome to budget traveler and backpacker central. While Termini is chock-full of traveler's services, use caution when walking in the area, especially at night, and keep a close eye on your pockets and/or purse.

▨ **Hotel and Hostel Des Artistes,** V. Villafranca 20, 5th fl. (☎44 54 365; www.hoteldesartistes.com). Des Artistes houses a hotel and a renovated hostel with large, pastel-colored rooms. Hostel towels €1, plus €10 deposit. 15min. free Internet. Reception 24hr. Check-out 10:30am. 4- to 10-bed dorms €20-26. Hostel cash only. Hotel AmEx/MC/V. ❷

**Pensione Fawlty Towers,** V. Magenta 39, 5th fl. (☎44 50 374; www.fawltytowers.org). Aside from the friendly, English-speaking staff, the best part of this hostel is its azalea-bedecked terrace, where guests hang out until 11pm. Common room with DVD, library, and TV. A/C in all rooms. Full kitchen and lockers available. Linens included; towels included only in private rooms. Check-out 9:30am. Call to reserve private rooms; no reservations for dorms. Dorms €18-25; singles €58, with shower €63; doubles €80/89; triples with shower €93, with full bath €99; quads €100. Cash only. ❷

**Hotel Galli,** V. Milazzo 20 (☎44 56 859; www.albergogalli.com). Turn right on V. Marsala and left on V. Milazzo. Reception on 2nd fl. 12 rooms have bath, minifridge, phone, TV, and safe. A/C €5. Check-in noon. Check-out 10am. Reserve by fax or email. Singles €65; doubles €95; triples €120; quads €140. AmEx/MC/V. ❹

**Hotel Cervia,** V. Palestro 55 (☎49 10 57; www.hotelcervia@wnt.it). Clean rooms with fans. Breakfast €3. Linens included. Reception 24hr. Check-out 11am. Reserve by email. In summer, 4- and 5-bed dorms €20; singles €40, with bath €70; doubles €70/90; triples €90/110; quads €100/135. 5% Let's Go discount if paid in cash. AmEx/MC/V. Same owners run quieter **Restivo** (5th fl. ☎44 62 172). ❷

## VIA XX SETTEMBRE AND NORTH OF TERMINI

Dominated by government ministries and private apartments, this area is less noisy and touristy than nearby Termini.

**Hotel Papa Germano,** V. Calatafimi 14/A (☎48 69 19; www.hotelpapagermano.com). Clean rooms with hair dryer, sink, and TV. Mini fridge in rooms with bath. A/C €5. Breakfast, linens, and towels included. Internet €2 per hr. Dorms €23-30; singles €35-45; doubles €60-100; triples €75-120; quads €100-140. AmEx/MC/V. ❷

**Hotel Bolognese,** V. Palestro 15, 2nd fl. (☎/fax 49 00 45; hbolognese@tiscalinet.it). The artist-owner's impressive paintings and private bath in every room set this otherwise standard hotel apart. Breakfast included. Check-out 11am. Singles €30-60; doubles €50-90; triples €90-120. AmEx/MC/V. ❸

**Alessandro Legends,** V. Curtatone 12 (☎44 70 32 17; www.hostelalessandrolegends.com). Pop in a DVD from the hostel's collection and enjoy a free cup of juice, coffee, or hot chocolate. All rooms have fans. Breakfast, pasta party (M-F 7pm), and linens included. Kitchen available. Reception 24hr. 10-bed dorms €21; 8-bed €20-25; 6-bed €29.50. AmEx/MC/V. ❷

**Affittacamere Aries,** V. XX Settembre 58/A (☎42 02 71 61; www.affittacamerearies.com). Comfortable, basic rooms with A/C, fridge, and TV. Breakfast €2.50. Singles €60; doubles €60-75; triples €105-135. MC/V. ❹

## ESQUILINO AND WEST OF TERMINI

Esquilino, south of Termini, has tons of cheap hotels close to major sights. The area west of Termini is more inviting than Esquilino, with busy, shop-lined streets.

**Alessandro Palace,** V. Vicenza 42 (☎44 61 958; www.hostelalessandropalace.com). Exit Termini from track #1. Turn left on V. Marsala, then right on V. Vicenza. Renovated dorms, all with bath and A/C. Fun, guests-only bar. Nightly pizza party at 8:30pm free with purchase of any drink. Breakfast included. Lockers available. Linens included. Towels €2 in dorms. Internet €2 per hr. Check-in 3pm. Check-out 10am. Dorms €25-30; doubles €90; triples €120; quads €140. AmEx/MC/V. ❷

**Alessandro Downtown,** V. C. Cattaneo 23 (☎44 34 01 47; www.hostelalessandrodowntown.com). Exit Termini by track #22, make a left on V. Giolitti, then a right onto V. C. Cattaneo. Fun, knowledgeable, English-speaking staff. Slightly quieter than the Palace, though guests can go to its bar. Kitchen, 2 common rooms, TV, and fans. Breakfast and pasta party (M-F 7pm) included. Lockers available. Towels €2. Internet €2 per hr. Dorms €24-25; doubles €70, with bath €90; quads €120/140. AmEx/MC/V. ❷

**Hotel Scott House,** V. Gioberti 30 (☎44 65 379; www.scotthouse.com). Colorful, modern rooms have A/C, bath, phone, and satellite TV. Breakfast included. Check-out 11am. Singles €35-68; doubles €68-98; triples €75-114; quads €88-129. AmEx/MC/V. €5 discount per night if paid in cash. ❸

**Hotel Giù Giù,** V. d. Viminale 8, 2nd fl. (☎48 27 734; www.hotelgiugiu.com). This elegant but fading *palazzo* filled with knick-knacks makes guests feel like they're at grandma's. Rooms with A/C; all but singles have baths. Check-out 10am. Singles €45; doubles €80; triples €120; quads €160. Cash only. ❸

**Hotel Cortorillo,** V. Principe Amedeo 79/A, 5th fl. (☎44 66 934; www.hotelcortorillo.it). This renovated hotel has A/C, bath, digital safe box, mini-fridge, and TV in all 14 spacious rooms. Breakfast included. Check-in noon. Check-out 10am. Singles €60; doubles €80; triples €95; quads €105. AmEx/MC/V. ❸

**Pensione di Rienzo,** V. Principe Amedeo 79/A, 2nd fl. (☎44 67 131; www.hoteldirienzo.it). A tranquil, family-run retreat. Fans and TVs. Check-out 10am. Singles €40, with bath €50-60; doubles €60/80; triples €90. MC/V. ❹

# ALTERNATIVE HOUSING

## RELIGIOUS HOUSING

Don't automatically think "Catholic" or even "inexpensive;" most are open to people of all religions, and single rooms can run to €155. Don't expect quaint rooms in cloisters: the rooms in religious housing have amenities similar to hotel rooms. Do, however, think sober: early curfews and/or chores are standard.

**Domus Nova Bethlehem,** V. Cavour 85/A (☎47 82 44 14). Take V. Cavour from Termini, past P. d. Esquilino. Religious icons abound. Rooms with A/C, bath, and TV. Huge terrace. Breakfast included. Internet with phonecard. Summer curfew 2am, winter 1am. Singles €78; doubles €114; triples €140; quads €150; quints €170. AmEx/MC/V. ❺

**Santa Maria Alle Fornaci,** P. S. Maria alle Fornaci 27 (☎39 36 76 32; www.trinitaridematha.it). Facing St. Peter's, turn left through a gate in the basilica onto P. del Uffizio. Take 3rd right onto V. d. Gasperi, which leads to P. S. Maria alle Fornaci. Go down the steps just to the church's left. Rooms have bath. Common room with Internet. Breakfast included. Reception 24hr. Singles €60; doubles €90; triples €125. AmEx/MC/V. ❹

## BED & BREAKFASTS

B&Bs in Rome can be guest rooms arranged in private homes, where the owners generally provide breakfast, or simply apartments with kitchens that clients can use. Both vary in quality and size. Pinpoint just how "centrally located" an apartment is before booking. The **Bed and Breakfast Association of Rome**, V. A. Pacinotti 73, sc. E, offers advice. (☎55 30 22 48; www.b-b.rm.it. M-F 9am-1pm and 3-7pm) **Your Flat in Rome/Byba Appartamenti**, Borgo Pio 160, rents spacious, short-term apartments in the Borgo area for as little as €25 per person per night. (☎338 95 60 061; www.yourflatinrome.com.) **Hotel Trastevere**, V. Luciano Manara 25 (☎06 58 14 713; www.hoteltrastevere.net), also has affordable short-term apartments available in the lively neighborhood.

# 🗋 FOOD

Traditional Roman cuisine includes *spaghetti alla carbonara* (egg and cream sauce with bacon), *spaghetti all'amatriciana* (thin tomato sauce with chiles and bacon), *carciofi alla giudia* (deep-fried artichokes, common in the Jewish Ghetto), and *fiori di zucca* (stuffed, fried zucchini flowers). Pizza is often a good and inexpensive option; like elsewhere in Italy, it is eaten with a fork and knife. Instead of the usually bland bread, try *pizza romana*, which is more like foccaccia: a flat bread with olive oil, sea salt, rosemary, and sometimes more toppings. Lunch is typically the main meal, though some Romans now enjoy *panini* on the go during the week. Restaurants tend to close between 3 and 6:30pm.

## RESTAURANTS

### ANCIENT CITY

The area around the Forum and the Colosseum is home to some of Italy's finest tourist traps. Avoid the main streets and head for the side streets.

☒ **I Buoni Amici,** V. Aleardo 4 (☎70 49 19 93). M: B-Colosseo. The owner's exceptional service complements the popular *linguine alle vongole* (with clams in the shell; €8) and the self-serve *antipasto* bar. *Primi* €7-8. *Secondi* €8-12. Wine €8-15. Homemade *dolci* €4. Cover €1. Open M-Sa 12:30-3pm and 7-11pm. AmEx/MC/V. ❷

☒ **Luzzi,** V. S. Giovanni in Laterano 88 (☎70 96 332), 3 blocks past the Colosseum coming from V. dei Fori Imperiali, yet always packed with locals. Cheap, traditional fare and house wine. The *penne con salmone* (€7) will leave you wanting more. *Primi* €5-7. *Secondi* €7-11. Open M-Tu and Th-Su noon-3pm and 7pm-midnight. AmEx/MC/V. ❷

**L'Antica Birreria Peroni,** V. San Marcello 19 (☎67 95 310). Ask for the *rosso*, 1 of 4 well-priced beers on tap. Fantastic *fiori di zucca* (€1). *Primi* €5-7. Cover €1.50. Open M-Sa noon-midnight. AmEx/MC/V. ❷

### CENTRO STORICO

The *centro storico* can be frightfully expensive and generic, especially near famous landmarks. For authentic Roman food, head to side streets, which have an abundance of affordable and delicious options. In the evenings, strolling pedestrians bring the area to life. The **Campo dei Fiori**, a daily food and clothing market, is surrounded by a labyrinth of crooked streets that can be frustrating to navigate.

☒ **Miscellanea,** V. della Paste 110A (☎67 80 983; www.miscellaneapub.it). A favorite of students and locals, just around the corner from the Pantheon. Priding itself on fresh food, gigantic portions, and low prices, Miscellanea exemplifies what a true *ristorante* should be. Salads (€6), *antipasti* (€6-7), and *panini* (€3) are the best values in town. Drinks (€2-4). Delicious desserts €2-3. Open daily 11am-2am. AmEx. ❶

**Pizza Art,** V. Arenula 76 (☎68 73 378). This place looks like a typical pizzeria but serves thick slices of foccaccia, priced per kg. Toppings include tomato, mozzarella, nutella, and goat cheese. Average slice €2.40. Open daily 12:30-11pm. Cash only. ❶

**Ristorante Grappolo d'Oro Zampanò,** P. della Cancelleria 80/84 (☎68 97 080), between C. Vittorio Emanuele II and Campo dei Fiori. This slightly upscale *osteria's* pastas are homemade. Decor is sleeker than that of the average *trattoria*. *Primi* €8-10. *Secondi* €14-15. Open M and W-F noon-4:30pm and 7:30-11pm, Sa noon-4:30pm and 7:30-11:30pm, Su noon-3pm and 7:30-11pm. MC/V. ❷

**L'Insalata Ricca,** Largo dei Chiavari 85-6 (☎68 80 36 56; www.linsalataricca.it), off C. V. Emanuele II near P. S. Andrea della Valle. 10 locations in Rome. Serves 45 kinds of salad (€7-8). *Primi* €6-8. *Secondi* €5.20-8.30. Open daily noon-4pm and 8pm-midnight. AmEx/MC/V. Also accepts US$. ❷

**Il Fico,** V. della Pace 36/A (☎68 65 205). Take V. d. Tor Millina off P. Navona, past V. del Pace. P. del Fico is on the right. Classic red and white checkered table cloths and a laid back atmosphere cater to a slightly older crowd. Try a bottle of the *vino della casa* for €8. *Primi* €6-11. *Secondi* €9-14. Open daily noon-midnight. D/MC/V. ❹

**La Pollarola,** P. Pollarola 25-27 (☎68 80 16 54), just behind Campo dei Fiori. Unreal renditions of *canelloni* (lasagna with meat), *spaghetti alle vongole* (with clams), and *penne all'arrabbiata* (with spicy tomato sauce; €7). Specials €8-12. Cover €1. Open M-Sa 12:30-3pm and 5:30-11pm. Reserve ahead. AmEx/D/MC/V. ❹

## JEWISH GHETTO

A 10min. walk south of the Campo, restaurants serve Roman specialties alongside traditional Jewish and kosher dishes. Many close on Saturdays.

**✠ Bar Da Benito,** V. d. Falegnami 14 (☎68 61 508). A rare combination—*secondi* for less than €5 and a place to sit and enjoy your food. Speedy service. *Primi* €4.50. *Secondi* €4.50-7.50. *Dolci* €2-3.50. Open Sept.-July M-Sa 6:30am-7pm. Cash only. ❷

**Trattoria da Giggetto,** V. d. Portico d'Ottavia 21-22 (☎68 61 105; www.giggettoalportico.com). Dark, large restaurant right next to the ruins of the Portico d'Ottavia. No animal parts go to waste here. In the Roman tradition, *fritto di cervello d'abbacchio* (brains with vegetables; €12) are served alongside delicacies like fried artichokes (€6). *Primi* €8.50-14. *Secondi* €9-20. Cover €1.50. Open Tu-Su 12:30-3:30pm and 7:30-11pm. Closed the last 2 weeks of July. Reserve ahead for dinner. AmEx/MC/V. ❸

**La Taverna del Ghetto,** V. d. Portico d'Ottavia 8 (☎68 80 97 71; www.latavernadelghetto.com). This lively kosher option offers homemade pasta and daily specials such as *lingua all'ebraica* (veal tongue). *Primi* €10.50. *Secondi* €13.50. Cover €1.50. Open M-Th and Sa-Su noon-3pm and 6:30-11pm, F noon-3pm. AmEx/MC/V. ❹

## PIAZZA DI SPAGNA

The P. di Spagna and Trevi Fountain area, though busy at night and closer to tourist destinations, offers few high quality options at low prices. Head off the main drags (V. del Corso and V. dei Condotti) for worthy eateries.

**Trattoria da Settimio all'Arancio,** V. dell'Arancio 50-52 (☎68 76 119). Take V. dei Condotti from P. di Spagna; bear right on V. Tomacelli after V. del Corso, then take the 1st left. It's the 2nd restaurant on the left (not the pizzeria). Portions are generous and dishes decadent. *Primi* from €8-15. *Secondi* from €8-20. Open M-Sa 12:30-3pm and 7:30-midnight. Reserve ahead. AmEx/MC/V. ❹

**Vini e Buffet,** V. della Torretta 60 (☎68 71 445), near P. di Spagna. A favorite of Romans with a penchant for regional wine, *pâtés* (€4-4.50), *crostini*, or *scamorze* (smoked mozzarella; €8-9). Salads €7.50-11. Wine €10-24. Open M-Sa 12:30-3pm and 7:30-11pm. Reservations recommended. Cash only. ❷

**Centro Macrobiotico Italiano Naturist Club,** V. della Vite 14, 4th fl. (☎67 92 509). This veggie haven has tuned traditional Roman cuisine to the pitch of organic vegan-vegetar-

ITALY

ian. Lunch *menù* €14, dinner *menù* €20-25. "Natural snacks" €8-10. Open M-F 12:30-3pm and 7:30-11pm, Sa 7:30-11pm. Dinner reservation required. AmEx/MC/V. ●

**Il Brillo Parlante,** V. della Fontanella 12 (☎32 43 334; www.ilbrilloparlante.com). The wood-burning oven turns out pizza (€7-10); handmade pasta and small plates, including *pecorino* cheese with honey and walnuts (€8.50), set this place apart. Open M 5pm-1am, Tu-Su 12:30-3:30pm lunch, 3:30-5pm pizza only, 5-7:30pm bar only, 7:30pm-1am dinner. Reserve ahead. MC/V. ●

## BORGO AND PRATI (NEAR VATICAN CITY)

The streets near the Vatican are paved with bars and pizzerias that serve mediocre sandwiches at inflated prices. For better, much cheaper food, venture down **Via Cola di Rienzo** several blocks toward P. Cavour and explore the side streets.

**Paninoteca da Guido e Patrizia,** Borgo Pio 13 (☎68 75 491), near Castel Sant'Angelo. Casual environment and homey decor make this place popular with lunching locals. Guido holds court behind a well-stocked *tavola calda* (snack bar). Full meal (*primo, secondo,* and beverage) runs around €11. Open M-Sa 8am-6pm. Cash only. ●

**Franchi,** V. Cola di Rienzo 200/204 (☎68 74 651; www.franchi.it). Benedetto Franchi ("Frankie") has been providing the citizens of Prati with luxurious picnic supplies for a half-century. Especially delicious *fritti misti* (deep-fried zucchini flowers, artichoke hearts, and zucchini) and the house ravioli. 2 people can stuff themselves for around €15. Open M-Sa 9am-8:30pm. AmEx/MC/V. ●

**Cacio e Pepe,** V. Giuseppe Avezzana 11 (☎32 17 268). From P. Mazzini, turn right on V. Settembrini, at P. dei Martiri di Belfiore, and again on V. G. Avezzana (a 20min. walk from P. di Risorgimento). Dine outside and enjoy the namesake pasta, piled high with olive oil, grated cheese, and freshly ground pepper (€6). Full lunch €5-10. Open M-F 12:30-3pm and 7:30-11pm, Sa 12:30-3pm. Cash only. ●

## TRASTEVERE

The waits are long and the street-side tables are always cramped, but you can't get more Roman than Trastevere. The tiny cobblestone side streets winding in and out of the *piazzas* are crowded with locals frequenting the cafes, stands, and restaurants. You won't miss the slick restaurant proprietors beckoning in English.

**⊠ Pizzeria San Callisto,** P. S. Callisto 9/A (☎58 18 256), off P. S. Maria. Simply the best pizza (€4-8) in Rome. Thin-crust pizzas so large they hang off the plates. Order takeout to avoid waits. Open Tu-Su 6:30pm-midnight. AmEx/MC/V. ❷

**Pizzeria San Marco,** V. Plinio 2 (☎32 35 398), off V. Cola d. Rienzo. 2nd best thin-crust pies. Over 25 white and red topping-heavy pizzas (€7-10). AmEx/MC/V. ❷

**Augusto,** P. de' Renzi 15 (☎58 03 798), before P. S. Maria when coming from the river. Daily specials (€5) appear almost as soon as you've ordered them. *Secondi* €5.50-8. Open Sept.-July M-F 12:30-3pm and 8-11pm, Sa 12:30-3pm. Cash only. ❶

**La Piazzetta,** V. Cardinale Merry del Val, 16B (☎58 06 241). Take V. Trastevere away from the Tiber and turn right on V. Cardinale Merry del Val. Eat outside under shady trees or inside under the discerning eyes of the dead fish on ice. Try the *fettucini con asparagi e porcini* (fettucini with asparagus and mushrooms). Cover €2. Primi €7-12. Salads €7-8. Pizzas €5-9. Open daily noon-midnight. AmEx/MC/V. ❷

## SAN LORENZO AND TERMINI

Tourist traps proliferate in the Termini area. There is a well-stocked **CONAD** supermarket on the lower floor of the Termini Station, just inside the V. Marsala entrance. (☎87 40 60 55. Open daily 8am-midnight.) In San Lorenzo, inexpensive food options with local character cater to budget-conscious students with discriminating palates. At night, map a route first and avoid walking alone.

■ **Hostaria Romana da Dino,** V. dei Mille, 10 (☎49 14 25). Exit Termini near track 1, take a left on V. Marsala, a right on V. Vicenza, and a left on V. dei Mille. Look for the vertical, blue Pizzeria sign. This humble choice provides ample seating and delicious dishes at low prices. Delectable pizzas (€5-7) and pastas (€4.50-5). Try the house wine for a mere €1.10 per 0.25L. Su-Tu and Th-Sa noon-3pm and 6:30-10:30pm. MC/V. ❶

**Africa,** V. Gaeta 26-28 (☎49 41 077), near P. Indipendenza. Decked out in orange, yellow, and black, Africa has been serving Eritrean and Ethiopian food for 32 years. The meat-filled *sambusas* (€3) are a flavorful starter. Vegetarian *secondi* €8-11. Cover €1. Open Tu-Su 8am-2am. MC/V. ❷

**Arancia Blu,** V. d. Latini 65 (☎44 54 105), off V. Tiburtina. This elegant and popular vegetarian restaurant has an inspired menu, affordable in spite of its fine ingredients and upscale style. Phenomenal warm pesto salad (€7.50). Extensive wine list €12-130 per bottle. Chocolate tasting *menù* (€15). Open daily 8:30pm-midnight. Cash only. ❷

**Hostaria da Bruno,** V. Varese 29 (☎49 04 03). From V. Marsala, take V. Milazzo and turn right on V. Varese. Italians who work in Termini lunch at this oasis amid tourist traps. Savor the *tortellini al sugo* (€7) or try the chocolate crepes (€4). Open M-F noon-3pm and 7-10pm, Sa 7-10pm. AmEx/MC/V. ❷

## TESTACCIO

■ **Il Volpetti Più,** V. Alessandro Volta 8 (☎57 44 306; www.volpetti.com). Turn left on V. A. Volta off V. Marmorata. This *tavola calda* serves lunch in large portions. Choose your food cafeteria-style, and battle the locals for a seat. Fresh salad, pasta, and pizza from €4. *Antipasti* €3-5. Open M-Sa 10:30am-3:30pm and 5:30-9:30pm. AmEx/MC/V. ❶

**Il Cantinone,** P. Testaccio 31/32 (☎57 46 253). M: B-Piramide. Go up V. Marmorata and turn left on V. G. B. Bodoni; P. Testaccio is after V. Luca della Robbia. With huge portions of pasta (*pappardelle* with boar sauce; €8), hearty meat dishes (€10-20), and terrific house wine (€6 per L), Il Cantinone gets the job done. Long tables cater to large parties. Open M and W-Su noon-3pm and 7pm-midnight. AmEx/D/MC/V. ❸

**Volpetti Salumeria-Gastronomia,** V. Marmorata 47 (☎57 42 352). Duck to avoid the meat hanging from the ceiling in this spiffy *gastronomia*. Il Volpetti Più's sister store has cheeses, homemade pastas, and breads. Be ready to fend off the locals at the counter. Items priced by the kg. Open M-Sa 8am-2pm and 5-10:15pm. AmEx/MC/V. ❷

# DESSERT

While *gelato* is everywhere in Rome, good *gelato* is not. Look for the signs of quality (See **The Ugly Duckling,** p. 615). But Rome's not just about *gelato;* bakeries sell a variety of cookies, pastries, and cakes, all priced by the *etto* (100g).

■ **Gelato di San Crispino,** V. della Panetteria 42, (☎67 93 924), 2nd left off V. del Lavatore. Forget Prince Charming—a scoop from San Crispino's, especially of the honey flavor, is worth wishing for at the Trevi fountain. Open Su-M and W-Th noon-12:30am, F-Sa noon-1:30am. Cash only.

■ **Biscottificio Artigiano Innocenti,** V. della Luce 21, Travestevere (☎57 03 926). From P. Sonnino, take V. Giulio Cesare Santina and turn left on V. della Luce. The shop sells divine cookies and biscuits at a counter in its no-nonsense stockroom. Try the hazelnut, chocolate, and jam cookies (€2.50 for 10 cookies).

**Pasticceria Ebraico Boccione,** V. del Portico d'Ottavia 1, Jewish Ghetto (☎68 78 637), on the corner of P. Costaguti under the white awning. This family-run bakery has a limited selection, including delicious challah twisted into croissants and filled with custard (€0.60). Su-Th 8am-7:30pm, F 8am-3:30pm. In summer closed Su 2-4pm.

**Il Gelatone,** V. dei Serpenti 28, Ancient City (☎48 20 187). From V. dei Fori Imperiali, take a left on V. Cavour, and another left onto V. dei Serpenti. Creamy, smooth, and vividly flavored. Their specialty is *Gelatone,* a blend of hazelnut, chocolate, and vanilla with chocolate chips. Also offers soy *gelato.* Cones €1.50-3. 4-flavor cone-bowls €4. Open daily 9:30am-midnight. Cash only.

**Giolitti,** V. degli Uffici del Vicario 40 (☎ 69 91 243; www.giolitti.it). Always crowded, this cafe serves *gelato* flavored with champagne, *limoncello,* and milk. Several flavors of *granite* (€2.50), the Italian version of a slushie, in summer. Pay at the register before stepping up to the counter. Open daily 7am-1am. AmEx/MC/V.

## COFFEE

Coffee is taken either standing up at the bar or sitting down at a table, with higher prices for the latter. In Rome, cafes are crammed with men in neat business suits starting around noon. In the summer, most cafes offer a delicious *granita di caffe con panna* (frozen coffee with fresh whipped cream).

▧ **The Lion Bookshop and Café,** V. dei Greci 33/36, P. di Spagna (☎ 32 65 40 07). This English-language bookstore has a cafe for thumbing through books while you sip espresso (€1.50-2.50) and listen to music from the conservatory across the street. Open M 3:30-7:30pm, Tu-Su 10am-7:30pm. AmEx/MC/V.

▧ **Bar Giulia (a.k.a. Cafe Peru),** V. Giulia 84, Ancient City (☎ 68 61 310), near P. V. Emanuele II. Serves possibly the cheapest and most *squisito* coffee in Rome (€0.60, at table €0.70) and adds your favorite liqueur free. Open M-Sa 5am-9:30pm. Cash only.

**Caffé Tazza d'Oro,** V. d. Orfani 84, Centro Storico (☎ 67 92 768). Facing away from the Pantheon's *portico,* look for the sign on the right. This famous coffee shop makes the highest-quality coffee in Rome, and has an extensive collection of tea. Espresso €0.80; cappuccino €1. Internet €1 per 15min. Open M-Sa 7am-8pm. AmEx/MC/V.

## ENOTECHE (WINE BARS)

The tinkling of crystal in intimate settings differentiates *enoteche* from more rough-and-tumble pubs. These wine bars usually serve small dishes, like cheese selections, smoked meats, *antipasti,* and salads, which make light, budget meals. Romans eat dinner around 9pm, so they either go to *enoteche* before dinner or sip and nibble their way through the entire night.

▧ **Enoteca Trastevere,** V. della Lungaretta, 86, Trastevere (☎ 58 85 659). A block off P. S. Maria. Staff helps pick a bottle from the high-caliber wine list. Make a meal of cured meats and cheeses (€9-12). Arrive after 10pm, as things pick up around midnight. Wine €3.50-5 per glass. Open M-Sa 6pm-2:30am, Su 6pm-1am.

**Trimani Wine Bar,** V. Cernaia 37/B (☎ 44 69 630), near Termini, perpendicular to V. Volturno. Look to the menu for suggested wines to complement mixed meat plates (€9-13.50) and the popular house special, chocolate mousse (€6.50). Wines from €3-15 a glass. Happy hour 11:30am-12:30pm and 5:30-7pm. Open M-Sa 11:30am-3pm and 5:30pm-12:30am. AmEx/MC/V.

**Cul de Sac,** P. Pasquino 73 (☎ 68 80 10 94), off P. Navona. One of Rome's first wine bars, Cul de Sac offers an extensive wine list (from €2 per glass) and divine dishes. Homemade *pâtés* such as boar and chocolate or pheasant with truffle (€6-7) are exquisite. Cheeses and meats €5-8. Open daily noon-4pm and 6pm-12:30am. MC/V.

**Enoteca Cavour 313,** V. Cavour 313, Ancient City (☎ 67 85 496). A short walk from M: B-Cavour. Sip wine from crystal glasses in this French wine bar. Try the *misto di formaggio* (mixed cheese plate; €8-10) and choose from the massive wine list (€3-8 per glass; €13-300 per bottle). Salads (€3-7) and desserts (€4-6) also available. Open Sept.-July M-Sa 12:30-2:30pm and 7:30pm-12:30am, Su 7:30pm-12:30am. AmEx/MC/V.

# ◎ SIGHTS

From ancient temples, medieval churches, and Renaissance basilicas to Baroque fountains and modern museums, *La Città Eterna* bursts with masterpieces. Dress modestly at churches and the Vatican. Travelers planning to visit many Roman monuments should consider the **Archeologica Card** (☎39 96 77 00; 7-day €22), valid at the Colosseum, Palatine Hill, and Baths of Caracalla, among others.

## ANCIENT CITY

**COLOSSEUM.** This enduring symbol of the Eternal City—a hollowed-out marble structure that dwarfs every other ruin in Rome—once held as many as 50,000 spectators. Within 100 days of its AD 80 opening, some 5000 wild beasts perished in the arena. The floor once covered a labyrinth of brick cells, ramps, and elevators used to transport wild animals from cages up to arena level. Not only animals were killed for sport: men were also pitted against each other. *(M: B-Colosseo. Open daily late Mar.-Aug. 8:30am-7:15pm; Sept. 9am-7pm; Oct. 9am-6:30pm; Nov. to mid-Feb. 9am-4:30pm; mid-Feb. to Mar. 9am-5pm. Combined ticket with Palatine Hill €11. English-language tours with archaeologist daily 1-2 per hr. 9:45am-1:45pm and 3-5:15pm. €3.50.)*

**IMBIBE THIS!** Remember that Rome's water is *potabile* (drinkable), and many fountains or spigots run throughout the city. Take a drink, or fill up your water bottle from these free sources of cold, refreshing *acqua naturale*.

**PALATINE HILL.** Legend has it that the Palatine Hill was home to the she-wolf who suckled brothers Romulus and Remus, mythical founders of Rome. The best way to attack the Palatine is from the stairs near the Forum's **Arch of Titus** (where ticket lines are shorter than at the Colosseum), which lead to gardens and lookouts. On the southwest side of the hill is an ancient village with the **Casa di Romulo**, alleged home of Romulus, and the podium of the **Temple of Cybele**. The stairs to the left lead to the **Casa di Livia**, home of Augustus's wife, which once connected to the **Casa Augusto** next door. Around the corner, the spooky **Cryptoporticus** tunnel ties Tiberius's palace to nearby buildings. **Domus Augustana** was once the emperors' private space; sprawling **Domus Flavia,** to its right, once held a gigantic octagonal fountain. Between them stands the **Stadium Palatinum**, or hippodrome, a sunken space once used as a riding school and now a museum with artifacts excavated from the hill. *(South of the Forum. Same hours and prices as Colosseum. Guided English-language tour daily 12:15pm. €3.50.)*

**ROMAN FORUM.** Etruscans and Greeks used the Forum as a marketplace, then early Romans founded a thatched-hut shanty town here in 753 BC. Enter through **Via Sacra**, Rome's oldest street, which leads to the **Arch of Titus**, passing the baths and the **Temple of Jupiter Stator** on the left. Off V. Sacra to the right is the **Curia** (Senate House). It was converted to a church in AD 630 and restored by Mussolini. The broad space in front of the Curia was the **Comitium**, where male citizens came to vote and representatives gathered for public discussion. Bordering the Comitium is the large brick **Rostra** (speaker's platform), erected by Julius Caesar in 44 BC. The hefty **Arch of Septimius Severus**, to the right of the *Rostra*, was dedicated in AD 203 to celebrate Septimus's victories in the Middle East. The **market square** holds a number of shrines and sacred precincts, including the *Lapis Niger* (Black Stone), where Romulus was supposedly murdered by Republican senators; below are the underground ruins of a 6th-century BC altar and the oldest

ITALY

## THE LIES OF MARCH

"Beware the Ides of March" ... more like, "beware the *lies* of March." After all, our dear friend Shakespeare did fictionalize the setting of the toga gang stabbing in his famous play, *Julius Caesar*. As a result, centuries of Roman travelers have mistakenly made pilgrimages to the Roman Forum's *curia* (senate house) instead of the Theater of Pompey. Shocker, huh?

On the Ides of March in 44 BC, Caesar was slated to address the senate near the Theater of Pompey. Despite bloody omens from a soothsayer and his wife, he was coerced into attending the meeting. Senator Casca made the first move and stabbed Caesar in the neck. The senatorial snake pit grew chaotic, and following a mass stabbing, Caesar looked into the eyes of his close aide, Brutus, and gasped "Et tu Brute?"

1600 years later, Shakespeare rewrote the event. History buffs who would like to see the actual site of Caesar's assassination should look no farther than the basements around Rome's Palazzo Pio, off Campo dei Fiori. While the theater is now ruined, remnants of the assassination site still exist underground. When visiting the Palazzo Pio area, be sure to check the cellars of nearby buildings. But beware the Ides of March— the 2000-year-old ghost of Julius Caesar might be lurking there.

known Latin inscription in Rome. In the square, the **Three Sacred Trees of Rome**—olive, fig, and grape—have been replanted. The most recent addition to the Forum is the **Column of Phocas**, erected in AD 608. The **Lower Forum** holds the eight-columned, 5th-century BC **Temple of Saturn**, next to the *Rostra*, which achieved mythological status during Rome's Golden Age, when it hosted Saturnalia, a raucous, anything-goes Roman winter party. Preserved column bases at the **Basilica Julia** give a vision of this courthouse's floorplan. At the end of Vicus Tuscus stands the **Temple of Castor and Pollux**, built to celebrate the 499 BC Roman defeat of the Etruscans. The vaguely curved wall uphill from the **Arch of Augustus** was once a circular building: the **Temple of Vesta**, where Vestal Virgins kept the city's sacred fire lit for more than 1000 years. Next to it lies the **House of the Vestal Virgins**, where the six virgins who officiated over Vesta's rites spent 30 secluded years beginning at the ripe old age of seven. Nearby, V. Sacra runs over the **Cloaca Maxima**, the ancient sewer that still drains water from the otherwise marsh-like valley. V. Sacra continues out of the Forum proper to the Velia and the gargantuan **Basilica of Maxentius**, which once contained a gigantic bronze and marble statue of Constantine. The remains are displayed at the Palazzo dei Conservatori on the Capitoline Hill (p. 635). V. Sacra leads to an exit from the Colosseum; the path that crosses before the Arch of Titus heads to the Palatine Hill. *(M: B-Colosseo, or bus to P. Venezia. Main entrance is on V. dei Fori Imperiali, at Largo C. Ricci. Open daily in summer 8:30am-7:15pm, last entry 6:15pm; in winter 9am-4:15pm, last entry 3:30pm. English-language guided tour 12:30pm. Audio tour €3.50.)*

**FORI IMPERIALI.** Closed indefinitely for excavations, the **Fori Imperiali,** across the street from the Ancient Forum, is a complex of temples, basilicas, and public squares constructed in the first and second centuries, still visible from the railing at V. dei Fori Imperiali. Built between AD 107 and 113, the **Forum of Trajan** included a colossal equestrian statue of Trajan and an immense triumphal arch. At one end of the now-destroyed Forum, 2500 carved legionnaires march their way up the almost perfectly preserved ■**Trajan's Column,** one of the greatest specimens of Roman relief-sculpture. The crowning statue is St. Peter, who replaced Trajan in 1588. The gray rock wall of the **Forum of Augustus** commemorates Augustus's victory over Caesar's murderers in 42 BC. The only remnant of **Vespasian's Forum** is the mosaic-filled **Chiesa della Santi Cosma e Damiano** across V. Cavour, near the Roman Forum. *(Visitors Center open daily 9am-6:30pm. Free.)*

**CAPITOLINE HILL.** Home to the original capitol, the **Monte Capitolino** still serves as the seat of the city government. Michelangelo designed its **Piazza di Campidoglio,** now home to the **Capitoline Museums** (p. 640). Stairs lead up to the rear of the 7th-century **Chiesa di Santa Maria in Aracoeli.** *(Santa Maria open daily 9am-12:30pm and 3-6:30pm. Donation requested.)* The gloomy **Mamertine Prison,** consecrated as the **Chiesa di San Pietro in Carcere,** lies down the hill from the back stairs of the Aracoeli. Imprisoned here, St. Peter baptized his captors with the waters that flooded his cell. *(Prison open daily in summer 9am-7pm; in winter 9am-12:30pm and 2-5pm. Donation requested.)* At the far end of the *piazza,* opposite the stairs, lies the turreted **Palazzo dei Senatori,** the home of Rome's mayor. *(Take any bus to P. Venezia. From P. Venezia, walk around to P. d'Aracoeli and take the stairs up the hill.)*

**VELABRUM.** The Velabrum area is in a Tiber flood plain, south of the Jewish Ghetto. At the bend of V. del Portico d'Ottavia, a shattered pediment and a few ivy-covered columns are all that remain of the once magnificent **Portico d'Ottavia.** The **Teatro di Marcello** next door was the model for the Colosseum's facade. One block south along V. Luigi Petroselli, the **Chiesa di Santa Maria in Cosmedin,** currently undergoing renovations, harbors the **Bocca della Verità,** a drain cover made famous by the film *Roman Holiday.* The river god's face on it will supposedly chomp any liar's hand. *(Chiesa open daily 9:30am-5:50pm.)*

**DOMUS AUREA.** Take a break from the relentless sun and enjoy the cacophony of birds chirping in the shady trees. Joggers, wild flowers, and ruins of a palatial estate now occupy Oppian Hill. This park houses a portion of Nero's "Golden House," which once covered a huge chunk of Rome. After deciding that he was a god, Nero had architects build a house worthy of his divinity. The Forum was reduced to a vestibule of the palace; Nero crowned it with the 35m *Colossus,* a huge statue of himself as the sun. *(Open daily 6:30am-9pm. Free.)*

# CENTRO STORICO

**VIA DEL CORSO AND PIAZZA VENEZIA.** Shopping street **Via del Corso,** which runs between P. del Popolo and busy P. Venezia, takes its name from its days as Rome's premier race course. **Palazzo Venezia** was one of the first Renaissance *palazzi* built in the city. Mussolini used it as an office and delivered his famous orations from its balcony, but today it's little more than a glorified roundabout dominated by the **Vittorio Emanuele II monument.** Off V. del Corso, the picturesque **Piazza Colonna** was named for the **Colonna di Marco Aurelio,** which imitated Trajan's column. Off the northwestern corner of the Piazza Colonoa is the **Piazza di Montecitorio,** dominated by Bernini's **Palazzo Montecitorio,** now the seat of the Chamber of Deputies.

**THE PANTHEON.** Architects still wonder how this 2000-year-old temple was erected. Its dome—a perfect half-sphere made of poured concrete without the support of vaults, arches, or ribs—is the largest of its kind. The light that enters the roof was used as a sundial and to indicate the dates of equinoxes and solstices. In AD 606, it was consecrated as the **Chiesa di Santa Maria ad Martyres.** *(In P. della Rotonda. Open M-Sa 8:30am-7:30pm, Su 9am-6pm. Free.)*

**PIAZZA NAVONA.** Originally an AD first-century stadium, the *piazza* hosted wrestling matches, track and field events, and mock naval battles in which the stadium was flooded and filled with fleets. Each of the river god statues in Bernini's **Fountain of the Four Rivers** represents one of the four continents of the globe (as known in 1651): Ganges for Asia, Danube for Europe, Nile for Africa, and Río de la Plata for the Americas. *(Open daily 9am-noon and 4-7pm.)* C. V. Emanuele II runs to **Il Gesu,** inside which Andrea Pozzo's **Chapel of S. Ignazio** and Bernini's **Monument to S. Bellarmino** are must-sees. *(Open daily 6:45am-12:45pm and 4-7:45pm.)*

**CAMPO DEI FIORI.** Across C. Vittorio Emanuele II from P. Navona, Campo dei Fiori is one of the last authentically Roman areas of the *centro storico*. Home to a bustling market Monday through Saturday mornings, it becomes a hot spot at night. The Renaissance **Palazzo Farnese,** built by Alessandro Farnese, the first Counter-Reformation pope, dominates P. Farnese, south of the Campo.

## THE JEWISH GHETTO

Rome's Jewish community is the oldest in Europe—Israelites came in 161 BC as ambassadors from Judas Maccabei, asking for help against invaders. The Ghetto, a tiny area to which Pope Paul IV confined the Jews in 1555, was dissolved in 1870 but is still the center of Rome's Jewish population. In the center are **Piazza Mattei** and the 16th-century **Fontana delle Tartarughe.** Nearby is the **Chiesa di Sant'Angelo in Pescheria** where Jews, forced to attend mass, resisted by stuffing wax in their ears. *(V. de Funari, after P. Campitelli. Church under restoration indefinitely.)* The **Sinagoga Ashkenazita,** on the Tiber near the Theater of Marcellus, was bombed in 1982; guards now search all visitors. Inside is the **Jewish Museum,** which has ancient Torahs and Holocaust artifacts. *(Synagogue open for services only. Museum open Oct.-May Su-Th 10am-10pm, F 10am-4pm; June-Sept. Su-Th 10am-7pm, F 9am-4pm. €7.50, students €3.)*

## PIAZZA DI SPAGNA AND ENVIRONS

■**FONTANA DI TREVI.** The bombastic **Fontana di Trevi** has enough presence to turn even the most jaded visitor into a romantic mush. Legend has it that a traveler who throws a coin into the fountain is ensured a speedy return to Rome; one who tosses two will fall in love there. Opposite is the Baroque **Chiesa dei Santi Vincenzo e Anastasio.** The crypt preserves the hearts and lungs of popes who served from 1590 to 1903. *(Open daily 7am-noon and 4-7pm.)*

**SCALINATA DI SPAGNA.** Designed by an Italian, paid for by the French, named for the Spaniards, occupied by the British, and currently featuring American greats like Ronald McDonald, the **Spanish Steps** exude worldliness. The pink house to the right is where John Keats died; it's now the **Keats-Shelley Memorial Museum.** *(Open M-F 9am-1pm and 3-6pm, Su 11am-2pm and 3-6pm. €3.50.)*

**PIAZZA DEL POPOLO.** In the center of the "people's square," once the venue for the execution of heretics, is the 3200-year-old **Obelisk of Pharaoh Ramses II** that Augustus brought back from Egypt in AD 10. The **Church of Santa Maria del Popolo** contains Renaissance and Baroque masterpieces. *(Open M-Sa 7am-noon and 4-7pm, Su 8am-1:30pm and 4:30-7:30pm.)* Two exquisite Caravaggios, *The Conversion of St. Paul* and *Crucifixion of St. Peter,* are in the **Cappella Cerasi,** which Raphael designed. *(Open M-Sa 7am-noon and 4-7pm, Su 7:30am-1:30pm and 4:30-7:30pm.)*

**VILLA BORGHESE.** To celebrate his purchase of a cardinalship, Scipione Borghese built the **Villa Borghese** north of P. di Spagna and V. V. Veneto. Its huge park houses three art museums: world-renowned **Galleria Borghese,** stark **Galleria Nazionale d'Arte Moderna,** and intriguing **Museo Nazionale Etrusco di Villa Giulia.** North of the Borghese are the **Santa Priscilla catacombs** and the **Villa Ada** gardens. *(M: A-Spagna and follow the signs. Open M-F 9:30am-6pm, Sa-Su 9:30am-7pm. €8.50.)*

## VATICAN CITY

Once the mightiest power in Europe, the foothold of the Roman Catholic Church now lies on 108½ autonomous acres within Rome. The Vatican has symbolically preserved its independence by minting coins (euros with the Pope's face), running a separate press and postal system, maintaining an army of Swiss Guards, and hoarding art in the **Musei Vaticani.** (M: A-Ottaviano. Or catch bus #64, 271, or 492 from Termini or Largo Argentina, #62 from P. Barberini, or #23 from Testaccio.)

**BASILICA DI SAN PIETRO (ST. PETER'S).** A colonnade by Bernini leads from **Piazza San Pietro** to the church. The **obelisk** in the *piazza*'s center is framed by two fountains; stand on the round discs set in the pavement and the quadruple rows of the colonnade will visually resolve into one perfectly aligned row. Above the colonnade are 140 statues of saints; those on the basilica represent Christ, John the Baptist, and the Apostles (except for Peter). The pope opens the **Porta Sancta** (Holy Door) every 25 years by knocking in the bricks with a silver hammer; on warm Wednesday mornings, he holds papal audiences on a platform in the *piazza.* The basilica itself rests on the reputed site of St. Peter's tomb. Inside, metal lines mark the lengths of other major world churches. To the right, Michelangelo's *Pietà* has been protected by bullet-proof glass since 1972, when an axe-wielding fiend smashed Christ's nose and broke Mary's hand. The climb to the top of the **dome** might very well be worth the heart attack it could cause. An elevator will take you up about 300 of the 350 stairs. (Modest dress required. Multilingual confession available. Church: Open daily Apr.-Sept. 7am-7pm; Oct.-Mar. 7am-6pm. Mass M-Sa 8:30, 10, 11am, noon, 5pm; Su 9, 10:30, 11:30am, 12:15, 1, 4, 5:30pm. Free. Dome: From inside the basilica, exit the building and re-enter the door to the far left. Open daily Apr.-Sept. 8am-5pm; Oct.-Mar. 8am-4pm. Stairs €4, elevator €7.)

> ⭐**TIP** **SISTINE SIGHTSEEING.** The Sistine Chapel is at the end of the standard route through the Vatican Museums (p. 639), and it's extremely crowded. Go straight to the Sistine Chapel to enjoy Michelangelo's masterpiece, and then backtrack. It's relatively empty early in the morning.

**SISTINE CHAPEL.** Since its completion in the 16th century, the Sistine Chapel (named for its founder, Pope Sixtus IV) has served as the chamber in which the College of Cardinals elects new popes. Michelangelo's ceiling, at the pinnacle of artistic creation, gleams post-restoration. The meticulous compositions hover above, each section depicting a story from Genesis, each scene framed by *ignudi* (young nude males). Michelangelo did not in fact paint flat on his back, but standing up craning backward, a position that irreparably strained his neck and eyes. *The Last Judgment* fills the altar wall; the figure of Christ, as judge, sits in the upper center surrounded by saints and Mary. Michelangelo painted himself as a flayed human skin hanging between heaven and hell. The cycle was completed by 1483 by artists under Perugino, including Botticelli, Ghirlandaio, Roselli, Pinturicchio, Signorelli, and della Gatta. The frescoes on the side walls predate Michelangelo's ceiling; on the right, scenes from the life of Moses parallel scenes of Christ's life on the left. (Admission included with Vatican Museums, p. 639.)

**CASTEL SANT'ANGELO.** Built by Hadrian (AD 117-138) as a mausoleum for himself and his family, this mass of brick and stone has been a fortress, prison, and palace. When the plague struck Rome, Pope Gregory the Great saw an angel at its top; the plague soon abated, and the edifice was rededicated to the angel. The fortress offers an incomparable view of Rome. (Walk along the river from St. Peter's toward Trastevere. Open in summer Tu-Su 9am-7:30pm; in winter daily 9am-7pm. €5. Audio tour €4.)

# TRASTEVERE

Right off the **Ponte Garibaldi** stands the statue of the famous dialect poet G. G. Belli. On V. di Santa Cecilia, through the gate and beyond the courtyard, is the **Basilica di Santa Cecilia in Trastevere.** Carlo Maderno's famous statue of Santa Cecilia lies under the altar. *(Open daily 9:30am-12:30pm and 4-6:30pm. Donation requested. Cloisters open M-F 10:15am-12:15pm, Sa-Su 11:15am-12:15pm. Cloisters €2.50. Crypt €2.50.)* From P. Sonnino, V. della Lungaretta leads west to P. S. Maria in Trastevere, home to stray dogs, expatriates, and the **Chiesa di Santa Maria in Trastevere,** built in the 4th century. *(Open M-Sa 9am-5:30pm, Su 8:30-10:30am and noon-5:30pm.)* North of the *piazza* are the Rococo **Galleria Corsini,** V. della Lungara 10, and the **Villa Farnesina** (p. 640), once home to Europe's wealthiest man. Atop the Gianicolo Hill is the **Chiesa di San Pietro in Montorio,** built on the spot believed to be the site of St. Peter's upside-down crucifixion. The church contains del Piombo's *Flagellation,* which uses Michelangelo's designs. Next door is Bramante's tiny ◼**Tempietto,** characterized by a combination of ancient and Renaissance architecture and commemorating Peter's martyrdom. Rome's **botanical gardens** have a rose garden that holds the bush from which all the world's roses are supposedly descended. *(Church and Tempietto open Tu-Su May-Oct. 9:30am-12:30pm and 4-6pm; Nov.-Apr. 9:30am-12:30pm and 2-4pm. Gardens open M-Sa Oct.-Mar. 9:30am-5:30pm; Apr.-Oct. 9:30am-6:30pm.)*

## NEAR TERMINI

◼**PIAZZA DEL QUIRINALE.** At the southeast end of V. del Quirinale, this *piazza* occupies the summit of one of Ancient Rome's seven hills. In its center, the enormous statues of Castor and Pollux stand on either side of an obelisk from the Mausoleum of Augustus. The President of the Republic resides in the imposing **Palazzo del Quirinale,** its Baroque architecture by Bernini, Maderno, and Fontana. Farther along the street lies the facade of Borromini's **Chiesa di San Carlo alle Quattro Fontane.** Bernini's ◼**Four Fountains** are built into the intersection of V. delle Quattro Fontane and V. del Quirinale. *(Palazzo closed to the public. San Carlo open M-F 10am-1pm and 3-6pm, Sa 10am-1pm.)*

**BASILICA OF SANTA MARIA MAGGIORE.** Crowning the Esquiline Hill, this is officially part of Vatican City. To the right of the altar, a marble slab marks **Bernini's tomb.** The 14th-century mosaics in the **loggia** *(open daily with guided tour at 1pm; €3)* depict the August snowfall that showed the pope where to build the church; the snowstorm is re-enacted each August with white flower petals. *(Modest dress required. Open daily 7am-7pm. Audio tour €4.)*

## SOUTHERN ROME

The area south of the center is a mix of wealthy and working-class neighborhoods and is home to the city's best nightlife as well as some of its grandest churches.

◼**APPIAN WAY.** The Appian Way was the most important thoroughfare of Ancient Rome. Early Christians secretly constructed maze-like catacombs under the ashes of their persecutors. Sundays, when the street is closed to traffic, take a break from the city to bike through the countryside. *(M: B-S. Giovanni to P. Appio; take bus #218 from P. di S. Giovanni to V. Appia Antica; get off at the info office.)* **San Callisto** is the largest catacomb in Rome. Its four levels once held 16 popes, St. Cecilia, and 500,000 other Christians. *(V. Appia Antica 126, entrance on road parallel to V. Appia. Open M-Tu and Th-Su 9am-noon and 2-5pm. €5.)* Catacomb **Santa Domitilla** houses an intact 3rd-century portrait of Christ and the Apostles. *(V. delle Sette Chiese 282. Facing V. Ardeatina from San Callisto exit, cross the street and walk right up V. Sette Chiese. Open Feb.-Dec. M and W-Su 9am-noon and 2-5pm. €5. Cash only.)*

**CAELIAN HILL.** Southeast of the Colosseum, the Caelian was the hill where elite Romans made their home in ancient times. The ◼**Chiesa di San Giovanni in Laterano**

was the seat of the papacy until the 14th century; founded by Constantine in AD 314, it is Rome's oldest Christian basilica. The two golden reliquaries over the altar contain the skulls of St. Peter and St. Paul. Outside to the left, **Scala Santa** has what are believed to be the 28 steps used by Jesus outside Pontius Pilate's home. *(Modest dress required. M: A-S. Giovanni or bus #16. Through the archway of the wall. Open daily 7am-6:30pm. €2, students €1.)* The **Chiesa di San Clemente** is split into three levels, each from a different era. A fresco cycle by Masolino dating from the 1420s graces its **Chapel of Santa Caterina.** *(M: B-Colosseo. Turn left down V. Labicana away from the Forum. Open M-Sa 9am-12:30pm and 3-6pm, Su 10am-12:30pm and 3-6pm. €5, students €3.50.)*

**AVENTINE HILL.** The **Roseto Comunale,** a public rose garden, is host to the annual Premio Roma, the worldwide competition for the best blossom. *(V. d. Valle Murcia, across the Circus Maximus from the Palatine Hill. Open May-June daily 8am-7:30pm.)* Just before the crest of the hill, stroll among orange trees at **Giardini degli Aranci.** *(Open daily dawn-dusk.)* The top left-hand panel of the wooden front doors at nearby **Chiesa di Santa Sabina** is one of the earliest-known representations of the Crucifixion. V. S. Sabina runs along the crest of the hill to **Piazza dei Cavalieri di Malta,** home of the crusading order of the Knights of Malta. Through the ▨**keyhole** in the cream-colored, arched gate is a perfectly framed view of the dome of St. Peter's Cathedral.

**EUR.** South of the city stands a residential area that remains as a memento of the second Roman Empire that never was. EUR (AY-oor) is the Italian acronym for Universal Exposition of Rome, the 1942 World's Fair that Mussolini intended to be a showcase of Fascist achievement, which was apparently the ability to build lots of identical square buildings. **Via Cristoforo Colombo,** EUR's main street, runs north from the metro station to **Piazza Guglielmo Marconi** and its 1959 **obelisk.** There is also a beautiful artificial lake surrounded by benches and jogging paths. The nearby hills are a popular lounging spot. *(Take bus #714 or M: B-EUR Palasport.)*

# 🏛 MUSEUMS

Etruscans, emperors, and popes have been busily stuffing Rome with artwork for several millennia, leaving behind a city teeming with collections. Museums are generally closed on Mondays, Sunday afternoons, and holidays.

**GALLERIA BORGHESE.** Upon entering, don't miss Mark Antonio's **ceiling,** depicting the Roman conquest of Gaul. **Room I,** on the right, houses Canova's sexy statue of **Paolina Borghese** portrayed as Venus triumphant with Paris's golden apple. The next rooms display the most famous sculptures by Bernini: a striking **David,** crouching with his slingshot; **Apollo and Daphne;** the weightless body in **Rape of Proserpina;** and weary-looking Aeneas in **Eneo e Anchise.** Paintings in the **Caravaggio Room** include *Self Portrait as Bacchus* and *David and Goliath.* The collection continues in the **pinacoteca** upstairs, accessible from the gardens around the back by a winding staircase. **Room IX** holds Raphael's ▨**Deposition** while Sodoma's *Pietà* graces **Room XII.** Look for del Conte's *Cleopatra and Lucrezia,* Rubens's *Pianto sul Cristo Morto,* and Titian's *Amor Sacro e Amor Profano. (Vle. del Museo Borghese. M: A-Spagna; take the Villa Borghese exit. Open Tu-Su 9am-7:30pm. Entrance every 2hr. Reserve ahead. Tickets €8.50. Audio tour €5.)*

**VATICAN MUSEUMS.** The Vatican Museums constitute one of the world's greatest art collections; plan to spend at least 4hr. exploring them. Ancient, Renaissance, and modern statues and paintings are rounded out with papal odds and ends. The **Museo Pio-Clementino** has the world's greatest collection of antique sculpture. Two Molossian hounds guard the entrance to the **Stanza degli Animali,** a marble menagerie. Other gems include the **Apollo Belvedere** and **Hercules.** From the last room, the Simonetti Stairway climbs to the **Museo Etrusco,** filled with artifacts from Tuscany and northern Lazio. Back on the landing of the Simonetti Staircase is the **Stanza della Biga** (ancient marble chariot room) and the **Galleria della Candelabra** (chandelier). The long trudge to the Sistine Chapel begins here, passing through the **Galleria degli Arazzi** (tapestries), the **Galleria delle Mappe** (maps), the **Apartamento di Pio V** (where there is a sneaky shortcut to *la Sistina*), the **Stanza Sobieski,** and the **Stanza della Immaculata Concezione.** A door leads into the first of the four ▓**Stanze di Rafaele,** apartments built for Pope Julius II in the 1510s. One *stanza* features Raphael's **School of Athens,** painted as a trial piece for Julius, who was so impressed that he fired his other painters and commissioned Raphael to decorate the entire suite. From here, there are two paths: a staircase leading to the brilliantly frescoed Borgia Apartments, which house the **Museum of Modern Religious Art,** and another route leading to the Sistine Chapel (p. 637). On the way out of the Sistine Chapel, take a look at the **Room of the Aldobrandini Marriage,** which contains a series of rare, ancient Roman frescoes. Finally, the Vatican's painting collection, the **pinacoteca,** spans eight centuries and is one of the best in Rome. It includes Perugino's *Madonna and Child*, Titian's *Madonna of San Nicoletta dei Frari*, and Raphael's *Transfiguration*. (*Walk north from P.S. Pietro along the wall of the Vatican City for 10 blocks.* ☎ *69 88 49 47; www.vatican.va. Open Mar.-Oct. M-F 10am-4:45pm, Sa 10am-2:45pm; Nov.-Feb. M-Sa 10am-1:45pm. Last entrance 1¼hr. before closing. €13, with ISIC €8. Open last Su of the month 9am-1:45pm. Free.*)

> ☀**TIP☀** **ARE WE THERE YET?** Lines for the Vatican Museums begin forming around 6:30am and become increasingly unbearable as the hours pass. It's not a bad idea to drag yourself out of your rock-hard hostel bed at an ungodly hour.

**MUSEI CAPITOLINI.** This collection of ancient sculpture is the world's first public museum of ancient art. Pope Clemente XII bought the *palazzo* in 1733 to exhibit Cardinal Alessandro Albani's ancient sculptures. The Palazzo dei Conservatori's courtyard contains fragments of the **Colossus of Constantine.** The original statue of **Marcus Aurelius,** Bernini's interesting **Head of Medusa,** and the famous **Capitoline Wolf**—a statue that has symbolized the city of Rome since antiquity—occupy the first floor. At the top of the stairs, the **pinacoteca's** masterpieces include Bellini's *Portrait of a Young Man*, Caravaggio's *St. John the Baptist* and *Gypsy Fortune-Teller*, Rubens's *Romulus and Remus Fed by the Wolf*, and Titian's *Baptism of Christ*. (*On Capitoline Hill behind the Vittorio Emanuele II monument.* ☎ *82 05 91 27. Open Tu-Su 9am-8pm. €6.50-8, students with ISIC €4.50-6.*)

**VILLA FARNESINA.** The villa was the sumptuous home of Europe's one-time wealthiest man, Agostino "il Magnifico" Chigi. To the right of the entrance lies the breathtaking **Sala of Galatea,** a vault displaying astrological signs and showing the stars as they were at 9:30pm on November 29, 1466, the moment of Agostino's birth. The room's masterpiece is Raphael's **Triumph of Galatea.** The ceiling of the **Loggia di Psiche** depicts the marriage of Cupid and Psiche. Returning to the entrance, a stucco-ceilinged stairway, with gorgeous perspective detail, ascends to Peruzzi's **Salone delle Prospettive,** which incorporates five different colored marbles in the floor design and offers views of Rome between columns. The adjacent bedroom, known as the **Stanza delle Nozze** (Marriage Room), is a highlight. A maze of stolen commissions between Raphael and Il Sodoma led to the latter's creating a masterful fresco of Alexander the Great's marriage to Roxane. (*V. della Lungara 230. Across from Palazzo Corsini on Lungotevere della Farnesina. Bus #23, 271, or 280; get off at Lungotevere della Farnesina or Ponte Sisto.* ☎ *68 02 72 67. Open M-Sa 9am-1pm; 1st Su of the month 9am-1pm. Last entry 12:40pm. €5.*)

**MUSEO NAZIONALE D'ARTE ANTICA.** This collection of 12th- through 18th-century art is split between Palazzo Barberini and Palazzo Corsini. **Palazzo Barberini** contains paintings from the medieval through Baroque periods, including works by Caravaggio, El Greco, and Raphael. *(V. Barberini 18. M: A-Barberini. Bus #492 or 62.* ☎ *48 14 591. Open Tu-Su 9am-7:30pm. €5.)* **Galleria Corsini** holds works by 17th- and 18th-century painters, from Rubens to Caravaggio. *(V. della Lungara 10. Opposite Villa Farnesina in Trastevere. Take bus #23 to between Ponte Mazzini and Ponte Sisto.* ☎ *22 58 24 93. Open Tu-Su; entrance from 9:30-9:45am, 11-11:15am, and 12:30-12:45pm. €4.)*

**GALLERIA SPADA.** Cardinal Bernardino Spada bought an imposing assortment of paintings and sculpture and commissioned an even more impressive set of rooms to house them. Time and good luck have left the palatial 17th-century apartments nearly intact; a visit to the gallery offers a glimpse of the luxury surrounding Baroque courtly life. In **Room 1,** the modest cardinal hung portraits of himself by Cerini, Guercino, and Reni. In **Room 2,** look for paintings by Venetians Tintoretto and Titian and a frieze by Vaga, originally intended for the Sistine Chapel. **Room 4** has three canvases by the father-daughter team of Orazio and Artemisia Gentileschi. *(P. Capo d. Ferro 13, in the Palazzo Spada. Bus #64.* ☎ *68 32 409. Open Tu-Su 8:30am-7:30pm. €5. Guided tour Su 10:45am from museum bookshop.)*

**MUSEI NAZIONALI ROMANI.** The fascinating **Museo Nazionale Romano Palazzo Massimo alle Terme** is devoted to the history of art during the Roman Empire, including the *Lancellotti Discus Thrower* and a rare Nero-era mosaic. *(Largo di V. Peretti 1, in P. dei Cinquecento. Open Tu-Su 9am-7:45pm. Combo ticket for Diocleziano, Crypta Balbi, and Palazzo Altemps €9.)* Nearby, the **Museo Nazionale Romano Terme di Diocleziano,** a beautifully renovated complex partly housed in the huge **Baths of Diocletian,** has exhibits on ancient epigraphy (writing) and a Michelangelo cloister. *(V. Enrico de Nicola 78. Open Tu-Su 9am-7:45pm.)* The **Aula Ottogonale** holds classical sculptures. *(V. Romita 8. Open daily 9am-1pm. Free.)* Across town, the **Museo Nazionale Romano Palazzo Altemps** displays sculpture, including the 5th-century *Ludovisi Throne.* *(P. Sant'Apollinare 44, just north of P. Navona. Open Tu-Su 9am-7:45pm. €5. Audio tour €4.)*

**OTHER COLLECTIONS.** The Doria **Pamphili** family, whose illustrious kin include Pope Innocent X, maintain a collection in their palatial home. A *trompe l'oeil* ceiling tops Raphael's *Double Portrait* and Velázquez's portrait of Pope Innocent X. *(P. del Collegio Romano 2. www.doriapamphilj.it. Open M-W and F-Su 10am-5pm. €8.)* **Museo Centrale Montemartini,** once a power plant, was converted to hold Classical sculpture and floor mosaics. *(V. Ostiense 106. M: B-Piramide. Open Tu-Su 9:30am-7pm. €4.20, with entrance to the Capitoline Museums €8.50.)* The eccentric **Museo Mario Praz** was the last home of Mario Praz, a small and eccentric professor of English literature and 18th- and 19th-century art collector. *(V. Zanardelli 1, top fl. Open M 2:30-6:30pm, Tu-Su 9am-1pm and 2:30-6:30pm. Free.)* Italy's art history is traced from Napoleon's time through to Futurism and Abstraction at the **Museo Nazionale d'Arte Moderna e Contemporanea,** which also attracts temporary traveling exhibits. *(Vle. delle Belle Arti 131, in Villa Borghese. Open Tu-Su 8:30am-7:30pm. €9.)*

# 🔳 ENTERTAINMENT

The weekly *Roma C'è* (with a section in English) and *Time Out*, both available at newsstands, have comprehensive and up-to-date club, movie, and event listings.

## THEATER AND CINEMA

The **Festival Roma-Europa** (www.romaeuropa.net) in late summer brings a number of world-class acts to Rome. For year-round performances of classic Italian theater, **Teatro Argentina,** Largo di Torre Argentina 52, is the matriarch of all Italian venues. (☎684 00 01 11. Box office open M-F 10am-2pm and 3-7pm, Sa 10am-2pm. Tickets €14-26, students €12-21. AmEx/D/MC/V.) **Teatro Colosseo,** V. Capo d'Africa 5/A, usually features work by foreign playwrights translated into Italian, but also hosts an English-language theater night. (☎70 04 932. M: B-Colosseo. Box office open Sept.-Apr. Tu-Sa 6-9:30pm. Tickets €10-20, students €8.)

Most English-language films are dubbed into Italian; for films in their original languages, check newspapers for listings with a **v.o.** or **l.o.** The theater of Italian director Nanni Moretti, **Nuovo Sacher,** Largo Ascianghi 1, shows independent films. (☎58 18 116. Films in the original language M-Tu. €7, matinee €4.50.)

## MUSIC

Founded by Palestrina in the 16th century, the **Accademia Nazionale di Santa Cecilia,** V. Vittoria 6, off V. del Corso (☎36 11 064 or 800 90 70 80; www.santacecilia.it) remains the best in classical music performance. Concerts are held at the **Parco della Musica,** V. Pietro di Coubertin 30, near P. del Popolo. (www.musicaper-roma.it. Tickets at Parco della Musica. Regular season runs Sept.-June. €15, students €8.) Known as one of Europe's best jazz clubs, ◩**Alexanderplatz Jazz Club,** V. Ostia 9, is decorated with messages left on its walls by old greats. The club moves outside to the Villa Celimontana during summer. (☎39 74 21 71; www.alexander-platz.it. M: A-Ottaviano. Required membership €10. Open daily Sept.-May 9pm-2am. Shows start at 10pm.) The **Cornetto Free Music Festival Roma Live** (www.cor-nettoalgida.it) has attracted the likes of Pink Floyd and the Black Eyed Peas; it takes place at various venues throughout the city during summer.

## SPECTATOR SPORTS

Though May brings tennis and equestrian events, sports revolve around *calcio*, or football. Rome has two teams in *Serie A*, Italy's prestigious league: **S.S. Lazio** and **A.S. Roma.** Matches are held at the **Stadio Olimpico,** in Foro Italico, almost every Sunday from September to June. Tickets (from €16) can be bought at team stores like **A.S. Roma,** P. Colonna 360 (☎67 86 514; www.asroma.it. Tickets sold daily 10am-6:30pm. AmEx/MC/V), and **Lazio Point,** V. Farini 34/36, near Termini. (☎48 26 688. Open daily 9am-7pm. AmEx/MC/V.) Tickets can also be obtained at the stadium before games, but beware of long lines and the possibility of tickets running out. If you're buying last minute, watch out for overpriced or fake tickets.

# ◪ SHOPPING

No trip to Italy is complete without a bit of shopping. There are four kinds of clothing shops in Rome. International chain stores like **Motivi, Mango, Stefanel, Intimissimi, Zara,** and the ubiquitous **United Colors of Benetton,** are supplemented by techno-blasting teen stores in the city center, boutiques like **Ethic** and **Havana** in the *centro storico* and throughout the city, and designer shrines like **Cavalli, Dolce & Gabbana,** and **Prada,** with their cardiac-arrest-inducing prices.

## SHOP LIKE A ROMAN

**Via del Corso,** the main street connecting P. del Popolo and P. Venezia, offers a mix of high- and low-end, leather goods, men's suits, and silk ties, but beware of high-priced tourist traps. For apparel, try **Stefanel** (1224/124, 295a), **United Colors of Benetton** (421/424), and **Zara** (201/204). **Etam** (170) and **Motivi** (318) are lower-priced Italian chains. **Calzedonia** (140, 190) and **Yammamay** (309, 139) are fabulous for cheap, colorful and fun tights, socks, and bikinis. Department store **La Rinascente**

(191) has a bit of everything. Add higher-end labels like **Diesel** (186/655), **Ferrari** (402), and **Puma** (403) to your wardrobe. Across the river from V. del Corso, **Via Cola di Rienzo** offers a more leisurely shopping approach—minus the tourists—with stores like Diesel, **Mandarina Duck, Mango,** Stefanel, and Benetton. **COIN** department store, V. Cola d. Rienzo 171/173, won't leave you penniless.

## BOUTIQUES

Unique boutiques and haute-couture designer stores cluster around the Spanish Steps and V. dei Condotti. Most of the upscale stores—**Armani, Bruno Magli, Dolce & Gabbana, Gianni Versace, Gucci, Prada, Salvatore Ferragamo**—can be found on **V. dei Condotti**. Italian favorite **Fendi** breaks the rule and is located on Largo Goldini, right off V. del Corso. For vintage clothing, furniture, and art stores, go to **Via dei Governo Vecchio,** near P. Navona.

## CHEAP AND CHIC

**Tezenis,** V. del Corso 148 (☎67 93 569; M-Sa 10am-8pm, Su 10:30am-8pm), offers women's, men's, and children's intimate apparel. The **General Store,** V. della Scala 62a (☎58 17 675), sells discounted Diesel, Adidas, and Nike. Authentic European clothing stores on **Via dei Giubbonari,** off Campo dei Fiori, will have you dressed to the nines before eight.

## OUTDOOR MARKETS

🔲 **Porta Portese,** in Trastevere. Tram #8 from Largo d. Torre Argentina. This gigantic flea market is a surreal experience, with booths selling lots of items you never knew you needed. Keep your friends close and your money closer. Open Su 5am-1:30pm.

**Campo dei Fiori,** in the *centro storico*. Tram #8 or bus #64. Transformed daily by stalls of fruit, vegetables, meat, poultry, and fish. Also find dried fruit, nuts, spices, fresh flowers, and the usual basic cotton tops, skirts, socks, and knock-off designer bags. Open M-Sa 7am until vendors decide their wares have run out (usually 1:30pm).

**Mercato delle Stampe,** Largo della Fontanella di Borghese. Bus #81, 116, 117, or 492. A bookworms' haven specializing in old books both used and antique, magazines, and other printed novelties. Open M-Sa 9:30am-6pm.

**Mercato Andrea Doria,** on V. Andrea Doria, northwest of the Vatican Museums. M: Ottaviano or bus #23 or 70. Caters mostly to the local population, so don't expect to find many English-speaking folks here. Fruits, vegetables, fish, groceries, clothes, and shoes sold in a huge open square. Open M-Sa 7am-1:30pm.

# 🔳 NIGHTLIFE

Romans find nighttime diversion at the pubs of San Lorenzo, the clubs of Testaccio, and everywhere in between. Check *Roma C'è* for the latest news on clubs. *Time Out* covers Rome's sparse but solid collection of gay nightlife listings, many of which require an ARCI-GAY pass (€10, see **GLBT Resources,** p. 624).

## PUBS

Though *enoteche* tend to be the primary destination for many locals, pubs are still a fun way to knock a few back without covers or sweaty polyester. Many are of the Irish variety, and the best are in Campo dei Fiori. Crowds of people flood P. Navona after bars close at 2am to continue the revelry.

■ **Caffé della Scala,** P. della Scala 4 (☎58 03 610), on V. della Scala before it intersects P. San Egidio. In nice weather, the filled tables at this casual cafe-bar line the neighboring street of V. della Scala day and night. The drinks menu uses unusual ingredients: Canadian whiskey, creme of cocoa, and cardamom pods in the potent "Christian Alexander." There's also a selection of equally distinct non-alcoholic drinks. Open daily 5:30pm-2am. Cash only.

**The Proud Lion Pub,** Borgo Pio 36 (☎68 32 841). A tiny pub in the Vatican area whose Roman location belies its Scottish atmosphere. Beer €4. Open daily noon-2am.

**Artu Café,** Largo Fumasoni Biondi 5 (☎58 80 398), in P. San Egidio, behind Santa Maria. Patrons swear this bar/lounge is the best in Trastevere. Beer €4.50. Wine €3-5.50 per glass. Exquisite martinis €6.50-7.50. Free snack buffet 7:30-9pm. Open Tu-Su 6pm-2am. MC/V.

## CLUBS

Italian discos are flashy and fun, but keep in mind that many clubs close during the summer in favor of more distant destinations like Fregene or Frascati. Testaccio is dependable through early August. Check *Roma C'è* or *Time Out* for updates.

**Distillerie Clandestine,** V. Libetta 13 (☎57 30 51 02). Speakeasy-like nightspot hosts a restaurant with live music and DJ. Cover F-Sa €20. Open Sept. to mid-June W-Sa 8:30pm-3am.

**Jungle,** V. di Monte Testaccio 95 (☎33 37 20 86 94; www.jungleclubroma.com). A rock feel pervades on F; it becomes a smoky bar full of Italian goths on Sa. Extravagant yet disorienting light effects. Cover €10. Open F-Sa midnight-4am.

**Gilda-Alien-Piper,** (www.gildabar.it). With steep covers and exclusive guest lists, this nightclub empire caters to the hipsters of Roman nightlife. In the summer, Piper and Alien move to Gilda on the Beach, located in Fregene near Fiumicino, 30km from Rome.

 **Alien,** V. Velletri 13-19 (☎84 12 212). One of the biggest discos in Rome. Attracts a well-dressed crowd. Cover €15, includes 1 drink; Sa €20. Open Tu-Su midnight-4:30am.

 **Piper,** V. Tagliamento 9 (☎85 55 398). North of Termini. From V. XX Settembre, take V. Piave (V. Salaria). Turn right on V. Po (V. Tagliamento). Or take bus #319 from Termini to Tagliamento. Caters to a more exclusive crowd, with international DJs spinning 70s, disco, house, rock, and underground. Cover €15-20, includes 1 drink. Open F-Sa 11pm-4:30am.

 **Gilda on the Beach,** Lungomare di Ponente 11 (☎66 56 06 49). Ultra-cool clientele make the pilgrimage to Gilda for 4 dance floors, a private beach, a pool, and a restaurant. Cover €20. Disco open daily 11pm-4am. Dinner served from 8:30pm. Open May-Sept. AmEx/MC/V.

## ▶ DAYTRIP FROM ROME: TIVOLI

*From M: B-Rebibbia, exit the station, turn right, and follow signs for Tivoli through an underpass to reach the other side of V. Tiburtina. Take the blue COTRAL bus to Tivoli. Tickets (€1.60) are sold in the metro station or in the bar next door. Once the bus reaches Tivoli (35-45min.), get off at Ple. delle Nazioni Unite. The return bus to Rome stops across the street from the tourist office, which offers maps and bus schedules. (☎0774 31 12 49. Open Tu-Su 10am-6pm.) There is also an information kiosk in Ple. delle Nazioni Unite with free maps.*

Tivoli is a beautifully preserved medieval town boasting villas once owned by Latin poets Horace, Catullus, and Propertius. The tourist office provides a **map** detailing sites such as a 15th-century castle, temple ruins, and Gothic-style houses, all within walking distance of the bus stop. **Villa d'Este,** a castle with a fountain-filled garden, was intended to recreate an ancient Roman *nymphaea* and pleasure palace. (☎0774 31 20 70; www.villadestetivoli.info. Open Tu-Su May-Aug. 8:30am-6:45pm; Sept. 8:30am-6:15pm; Oct. 8:30am-5:30pm; Nov.-Jan. 8:30am-4pm; Feb. 8:30am-4:30pm; Mar. 8:30am-5:15pm; Apr. 8:30am-6:30pm. €9. Audio tour €4.)
■ **Villa Gregoriana,** at the other end of town, is a park with hiking trails and views of Tivoli's well-preserved **Temple of Vesta.** (☎0639 96 77 61. Open Apr. to mid-Oct. 10am-6:30pm; mid-Oct. to Nov. and Mar. 10am-2:30pm; Dec.-Feb. by reservation

only. €4. Audio tour €4.) On the way back from Tivoli, visit the vast remains of **Villa Adriana,** the largest and most expensive villa built under the Roman Empire. Look for the *pecile*, built to recall the famous *Stoa Poikile* (Painted Porch) of Athens. (☎0774 38 27 33. Take bus #4 from P. Garibaldi's newsstand. Open daily 9am-7:30pm; last entry 6pm. €6.50. Archaeological tour €3.50, audio tour €4.)

# LOMBARDY (LOMBARDIA)

Part of the industrial triangle that drives Italy's economy, home to fashion mecca Milan, and producer of rice fields as lush as China's, Lombardy is one of the most prosperous regions of Italy. The Lombards who ruled the area after the fall of the Romans had close relations with the Franks and the Bavarians, and the region's modern culture has much in common with the traditions of its northern neighbors.

## MILAN (MILANO)                                                    ☎02

Unlike Rome, Venice, or Florence, which wrap themselves in veils of historic allure, Milan (pop. 1,400,000), once the capital of the western half of the Roman Empire, presents itself simply as it is: rushed, refined, and cosmopolitan. Home to Da Vinci's *Last Supper*, Milan owes much of its artistic heritage to the medieval Visconti and Sforza families, and its culture to Austrian, French, and Spanish occupiers. Now that Italians run the show, the city flourishes as the country's producer of cutting-edge style, hearty risotto, and die-hard football fans.

## ◰ TRANSPORTATION

**Flights: Malpensa Airport (MXP),** 48km from the city, handles intercontinental flights. **Malpensa Express** leaves from Stazione Nord for the airport. Accessible via Cadorna metro station (40min., €5). **Linate Airport (LIN),** 7km away, covers domestic and European flights. From there, take **Starfly buses** (20min., €2.50) to Stazione Centrale, which is quicker than bus #73 (€1) to San Babila Metro Station. Some budget airlines fly into **Orio al Serio Airport (BGY)** in Bergamo (p. 654).

**Trains: Stazione Centrale** (☎89 20 21; www.trenitalia.com), in P. Duca d'Aosta on M2. Trains run 1 per hr. to: **Bergamo** (1hr., €4.10); **Florence** (3½hr., €15-33); **Rome** (7hr., €52-73); **Turin** (2hr., €8.20); **Venice** (3hr., €27).

**Buses: Stazione Centrale.** Intercity buses tend to be less convenient and more expensive than trains. **Autostradale, SAL, SIA,** and other carriers leave from P. Castello (M1: Cairoli) and Porta Garibaldi for **Bergamo,** the **Lake Country, Trieste,** and **Turin.**

**Public Transportation:** The **Metro** (Metropolitana Milanese, or **M**) runs 6am-midnight. Line #1 (red) stretches from the *pensioni* district east of Stazione Centrale, through the center of town, and west to the youth hostel. Line #2 (green) connects Milan's 3 train stations. Use the **bus** system for trips outside the city proper. Metro tickets can be purchased at *tabaccherie,* ticket booths, and station machines. Single-fare tickets €1, 1-day pass €3, 2-day €5.50, 10 trips €9.20. White **taxis** are omnipresent.

## ✦ ❼ ORIENTATION AND PRACTICAL INFORMATION

Milan resembles a giant bull's-eye, defined by its ancient concentric city walls. In the outer rings lie suburbs built during the 50s and 60s to house southern immigrants. In the inner circle are four squares: **Piazza del Duomo,** where **Via Orefici, Via Mazzini,** and **Corso Vittorio Emanuele II** meet; **Piazza Castello** and the attached **Largo**

**Cairoli,** near the Castello Sforzesco; **Piazza Cordusio,** connected to Largo Cairoli by **Via Dante;** and **Piazza San Babila,** the entrance to the business and fashion district. The **duomo** and **Galleria Vittorio Emanuele** are roughly at the center of the circles. The **Giardini Pubblici** and the **Parco Sempione** radiate from the center. From the colossal **Stazione Centrale,** northeast of the city, take M3 to the *duomo.*

**Tourist Office: IAT,** P. Duomo 19A, Underground. (☎ 72 52 43 01; www.milanoinfotourist.com), in P. del Duomo. Pick up helpful *Hello Milano.* Open M-Sa 8:45am-1pm and 2-6pm, Su 9am-1pm and 2-5pm. **Branch** in Stazione Centrale (☎ 77 40 43 18) has shorter lines. Open M-Sa 9am-6pm, Su 9am-1pm and 2-5pm.

**American Express:** V. Larga 4 (☎ 72 10 41), on the corner of V. Larga and S. Clemente. Exchanges currency, handles wire transfers, and holds mail for up to 1 month for AmEx cardholders. Open M-F 9am-5:30pm.

**Lost Property: Ufficio Oggetti Smarriti Comune,** V. Fruili 30 (☎ 88 45 39 00).

**Hospital: Ospedale Maggiore di Milano,** V. Francesco Sforza 35 (☎ 55 031).

**24hr. Pharmacy:** (☎ 66 90 735). In Stazione Centrale's 2nd fl. *galleria.*

**Internet Access: Internet Enjoy,** Vle. Tunisia 11 (☎ 36 55 58 05). M1: Porta Venezia. €2-3 per hr. Open M-Sa 9am-midnight, Su 2pm-midnight.

**Post Office:** P. Cordusio 4 (☎ 72 48 21 26), near P. del Duomo. Currency exchange and ATM. Open M-F 8am-7pm, Sa 8:30am-noon. **Postal Code:** 20100.

# ACCOMMODATIONS

Every season is high season in expensive, fashionable Milan—except August, when many hotels close. Prices rise in September, November, March, and April due to theater season and business conventions. For the best deals, try the hostels on the city periphery or in the areas east of Stazione Centrale. Reserve well ahead.

## EAST OF STAZIONE CENTRALE

Unless otherwise noted, hotels are most accessible from M1/M2: Loreto or by tram #33 from Stazione Centrale. Women traveling alone should exercise caution.

**Hotel Malta,** V. Ricordi 20 (☎ 20 49 615; www.hotelmalta.it). Offers a respite from busy Milan. The 15 bright, quiet rooms have bath, fan, hair dryer, and TV; some have balconies over the rose garden. Reserve ahead. Singles €30-75; doubles €50-120. MC/V. ❹

**Hotel Cà Grande,** V. Porpora 87 (☎/fax 26 14 40 01; www.hotelcagrande.it). 7 blocks from P. Loreto, in a pleasant yellow house on the right. English-speaking owners will have you feeling right at home. All rooms have phone, sink, and TV. Breakfast included. Singles €40-60, with bath €45-85; doubles €55-85/60-110. AmEx/D/MC/V. ❹

**Albergo Villa Mira,** V. Sacchini 19 (☎ 29 52 56 18). 10 simple, clean rooms in a family-run hotel. Singles €26-35; doubles €45-62; triples €70. Cash only. ❸

## NEAR GIARDINI PUBBLICI

**Hotel San Tomaso,** Vle. Tunisia 6, 3rd fl. (☎ 29 51 47 47; www.hotelsantomaso.com). M1: Porta Venezia. Sparkling rooms with fan, phone, and TV. Singles €35-65; doubles €45-95, with bath €50-120; triples €75-135. AmEx/MC/V. ❸

**Hotel Aurora,** C. Buenos Aires 18 (☎ 20 47 960; www.hotelaurorasrl.com). M1: Porta Venezia. On the right side of C. Buenos Aires after V. F. Casati. Rooms with A/C and TV. Reserve ahead. Singles €50-80; doubles €80-125; triples €85-150. AmEx/MC/V. ❹

**Hotel Eva and Hotel Arno,** both at V. Lazzaretto 17, 4th fl. (☎ 67 06 093; www.hotelevamilano.com and www.hotelarno.com). M1: Porta Venezia. 18 large rooms with phone

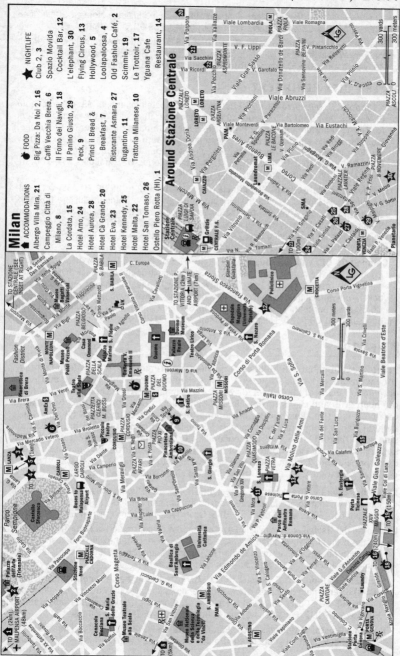

# Milan

**ACCOMMODATIONS**
Albergo Villa Mira, **21**
Campeggio Città di Milano, **8**
La Cordata, **15**
Hotel Arno, **24**
Hotel Aurora, **28**
Hotel Cà Grande, **20**
Hotel Eva, **23**
Hotel Kennedy, **25**
Hotel Malta, **22**
Hotel San Tomaso, **26**
Ostello Piero Rotta (HI), **1**

**FOOD**
Big Pizza: Da Noi 2, **16**
Caffè Vecchia Brera, **6**
Il Forno dei Navigli, **18**
Il Panino Giusto, **29**
Peck, **9**
Princi il Bread & Breakfast, **7**
Ristorante Asmara, **27**
Rugantino, **11**
Trattoria Milanese, **10**

★ **NIGHTLIFE**
Club 2, **3**
Spazio Movida Cocktail Bar, **12**
L'elephant, **30**
Flying Circus, **13**
Hollywood, **5**
Loolapaloosa, **4**
Old Fashion Café, **2**
Scimmie, **19**
Le Trottoir, **17**
Yguana Cafe Restaurant, **14**

## Around Stazione Centrale

**ITALY**

and TV. Ring bell to enter. Clean shared bathroom. Free luggage storage. 30min. free Internet. Singles €30-45; doubles €50-100; triples €65-90. AmEx/MC/V. ❸

**Hotel Kennedy,** Vle. Tunisia 6, 6th fl. (☎29 40 09 34; www.kennedyhotel.it). M1: Porta Venezia. Well-kept rooms with fan, phone, sink, and TV. Singles €36-75; doubles €55-80, with bath €70-120; triples €90-120; quads €100-160. AmEx/MC/V. ❸

## ON THE CITY PERIPHERY

🛏 **La Cordata,** V. Burigozzo 11 (☎58 31 46 75; www.ostellimilano.it. M3: Missori. From P. Missori, take tram #15 2 stops to Italia San Luca; then walk in the same direction for 1 block and turn right on V. Burigozzo. Entrance around the corner on V. Aurispa. Ideal for female and solo travelers. Common room with TV. Kitchen access. Laundry €3. Free Internet. Max. 7-night stay. Check-in 2-10pm. Check-out 11am. No curfew. Closed Aug. 10-20 and Dec. 23-Jan. 2. Single-sex dorms €21; doubles €70-100; triples €90-110; quads €100-120. Cash only. ❷

**Ostello per la Gioventù AIG Piero Rotta (HI),** V. M. Bassi 2 (☎39 26 70 95; www.ostellomilano.it. M1: QT8. Facing the church, turn right on V. Salmoiraghi; the hostel is 300m on the right. A bit far from the center, this hostel has 400 beds. Breakfast and linens included. Laundry €5.50. Max. 3-night stay. 24hr. reception. Check-out 10am. Lockout 10am-2pm. Closed Dec. 24-Jan. 12. Reserve ahead. 6-bed dorms €22; private rooms €25 per person. €3 HI discount. MC/V. ❷

**Campeggio Città di Milano,** V. G. Airaghi 61 (☎48 20 01 34; www.parcoaquatica.com). M1: De Angeli, then bus #72 to S. Romanello Togni. Backtrack 10m and turn right on V. Togni. Campsite is a 10min. walk straight ahead. Enter at Aquatica waterpark. Modern facilities. Laundry €5. Reserve ahead. Closed Dec.-Jan. €11 per person, €6.50-8.50 per tent, €6.50 per car. 2- to 6-person cabins €37-88; bungalows with bath and A/C €80-120. Electricity included. MC/V. ❶

# 🄵 FOOD

*Trattorie* still adhere to Milanese traditions by preparing *risotto alla Milanese* (rice with saffron), *cotoletta alla Milanese* (breaded veal cutlet with lemon), and *osso buco* (shank of lamb, beef, or veal). The Navigli district is home to all manner of cheap grub and the Saturday **Fiera di Sinigallia,** a food and clothing bargaining extravaganza (on Darsena Banks, a canal near V. d'Annunzio). The area's bars include Happy hour buffets of foccaccia, pasta, and risotto with drinks. The cuisine near Giardini Pubblici is influenced by the neighborhood's immigrants. A **PAM** supermarket is at Vle. Olona 1/3, outside the M2: S. Ambrogio stop. (Open M-Sa 8am-9pm, Su 9am-7:30pm.) **SMA Punto City** supermarket is at V. Felice Casati 8, just off V. A. Tadino near M1: Lima (open M-Sa 8:30am-1pm and 3:30-8pm).

🍴 **Princi il Bread & Breakfast,** V. Speronari 6, off P. del Duomo. Busy deli welcomes a lunch crowd that comes for its cheap takeout *primi* and *secondi* (€5). Fresh bread and pastries €1-4. *Panini* and pizza €3.50-5. Open M-Sa 7am-8pm. Cash only. ❶

🍴 **Il Forno dei Navigli,** V. A. Naviglio Pavese 2. At the corner of Ripa di Porta Ticinese. Out of "the oven of Navigli" come the most elaborate pastries in the city. The *cestini*, pear tarts with nutella, define decadence (€3). Pastries and breads €0.50-6. Open M-Sa 7am-2pm and 6pm-1am, Su 6pm-1am. Cash only. ❶

**Big Pizza: Da Noi 2,** V. G. Borsi 1 (☎83 96 77), takes its name seriously. Epic pizzas (€4-9) emerge from the stone oven, and beer flows liberally. The house pizza has pasta on top (€8.50). Cover €1. Open M-Sa 10am-2:30pm and 7pm-midnight. **Branches:** Ple. XXIV Maggio 7 (M2: Porta Genova) and V. Buonarroti 16 (M1: Buonarroti). ❷

**Il Panino Giusto,** V. Malpighi 3. M1: Porta Venezia. (☎29 40 92 97) If you believe sandwiches should contain goat cheese, truffled olive oil, veal *pâté,* or lard with honey and walnuts for under €8, welcome home. *Panini* €5-8. Beer €4-5. Open daily noon-1am. Branch on P. Beccaria near P. del Duomo. AmEx/MC/V. ❷

**Peck,** V. Spadari 9 (☎02 80 23 161; www.peck.it). Aromas from the ground floor spread throughout the wine cellar in the basement and the bar/restaurant above. *Primi* €9-18. *Secondi* €9-20. Open M 3-7:30pm, Tu-Sa 8:45am-7:30pm. AmEx/MC/V. ❷

**Caffè Vecchia Brera,** V. Dell'Orso 20 (☎86 46 16 95; www.vecchiabrera.it). M1: Cairoli. Take V. Cusani out of piazza Cairoli for 2 blocks. Sugar-topped, meat-filled, or liqueur-soaked crepes (€3.50-7). *Primi* €7.50-9. *Secondi* €12-14. Cover €1. Service 10%. Open daily 7am-2am. Happy hour 5-8:30pm; mixed drinks €5. AmEx/MC/V. ❸

**Rugantino,** V. Fabbri 1 (☎02 89 42 14 04), between the Chiesa d. San Lorenzo and the Roman pillars of C. Porta Ticinese. From M2: S. Ambrogio, walk down V. E. de Amicis. Savor oven-baked dishes in a candlelit wine bar. *Primi* and *secondi* €9-18. Pizza €7-10. Beer €4. Open daily 12:30-3pm and 7:30pm-midnight. AmEx/MC/V. ❸

**Ristorante Asmara,** V. L. Palazzi 5 (☎89 07 37 98). M1: Porta Venezia. Spicy Eritrean food includes a *zighini* platter (€11) with meat and veggie pieces served on *ingera* (flatbread). Vegetarian options available. *Antipasti* €4-5.50. Entrees €8-13. Cover €1.50. Open M-Tu and Th-Su 10am-4pm and 6pm-midnight. AmEx/MC/V. ❸

**Trattoria Milanese,** V. S. Marta 11 (☎86 45 19 91). M1/3: Duomo. From P. del Duomo, take V. Torino, turn right on V. Maurilio and again on V. S. Marta. Serves *cotoletta alla Milanese* (€17) and *mondeghili milanesi* (breaded meatballs; €12) in 2 rooms under brick arches. *Primi* €9-10. *Secondi* €10-22. Cover €2. Open M-F noon-3pm and 7-11:30pm. Closed last 2 weeks of July. AmEx/MC/V. ❹

# 👁 SIGHTS

## NEAR THE DUOMO AND IN THE GIARDINI PUBBLICI

▨**DUOMO.** The geographical and spiritual center of Milan and a good starting point for any walking tour of the city, the *duomo*—the third-largest church in the world—was begun in 1386 by **Gian Galeazzo Visconti,** who hoped to persuade the Virgin Mary to grant him a male heir. Work proceeded over the next centuries and was completed in 1809 at Napoleon's command. The marble tomb of **Giacomo de Médici** in the south transept was inspired by the work of Michelangelo. Climb (or ride) to the ▨**roof walkway** for prime views of the city and the Alps. *(M1/3: Duomo. Cathedral open daily 7am-7pm. Modest dress required. Free. Roof open daily mid-Feb. to mid-Nov. 9am-5:45pm; mid-Nov. to mid-Feb. 9am-4:15pm. €4, elevator €6.)* The **Museo del Duomo** displays artifacts relating to the cathedral's construction. *(P. del Duomo 14, to the right of the duomo. Open daily 10am-1:15pm and 3-6pm. €5, students €3.)*

▨**PINACOTECA AMBROSIANA.** The 23 palatial rooms of the Ambrosiana display exquisite works from the 14th through 19th centuries, including Botticelli's circular *Madonna of the Canopy,* Caravaggio's *Basket of Fruit* (the first Italian still-life), Raphael's wall-sized *School of Athens,* Titian's *Adoration of the Magi,* and da Vinci's *Portrait of a Musician.* The statue-filled courtyard is enchanting. *(P. Pio XI 2. M1/3: Duomo. Open Tu-Su 10am-5:30pm. €7.50, under 18 or over 65 €4.50.)*

**TEATRO ALLA SCALA.** Founded in 1778, La Scala has established Milan as the opera capital of the world. Its understated Neoclassical facade and lavish interior set the stage for premieres of works by Mascagni, Puccini, Rossini, and Verdi, performed by virtuosos like Maria Callas and Enrico Caruso. Visitors can soak up La Scala's historical glow at the **Museo Teatrale alla Scala.** *(Access through the Galleria Vittorio Emanuele from P. del Duomo. www.teatroallascala.org. Museum on left side of building. Open daily 9am-12:30pm and 1:30-5:30pm. €5, students €4.)*

ITALY

**MUSEO POLDI PEZZOLI.** Poldi Pezzoli, an 18th-century nobleman and art collector, bequeathed his house and its eclectic collection to the city in 1879. Today, the masterpieces hang in the Golden Room overlooking the garden. Smaller collections fill Pezzoli's former private chambers, where the decor reflects his fine taste. Particularly impressive is a tiny but interesting display of Italian military armaments. *(V. Manzoni 12. Open Tu-Su 10am-6pm. €7, students 5.)*

**GALLERIA VITTORIO EMANUELE II.** Light pours through a glass-and-metal cupola (48m) and into a five-story arcade of cafes, shops, and offices. Elegant mosaics on the floors and walls represent the continents besieged by the Romans. Spin on the mosaic bull three times for good luck. *(North of the duomo. Free.)*

**PALAZZO REALE.** This structure served as the town hall in 1138 before becoming the residence of Milanese royalty until the 19th century. Giuseppe Piermarini, architect of La Scala, designed its facade. Today, it displays temporary exhibits in the **Museo d'Arte Contemporanea.** *(South of the duomo. ☎ 02 88 451. Open only during exhibitions; call for more info. Wheelchair-accessible. Exhibits usually €8, students €6.)*

**GALLERIA D'ARTE MODERNA.** Napoleon lived here when Milan was the capital of the Napoleonic Kingdom of Italy (1805-1814). The gallery displays modern Lombard art and Impressionist works. Of note are Klee's *Wald Bau*, Modigliani's *Beatrice Hastings*, Morandi's *Natura Morta con Bottiglia*, and Picasso's *Testa*. *(V. Palestro 16, in the Villa Reale. M1/2: Palestro. Open Tu-Su 9am-1pm and 2-5:30pm. Free.)* The adjacent **Padiglione D'Arte Contemporanea (PAC)** has photographs, multimedia, and paintings. *(Open Tu-W and F 9:30am-5:30pm, Th 9:30am-9pm, Sa-Su 9:30am-7pm. Free)*

## CASTELLO SFORZESCO AND ENVIRONS

**⬛CASTELLO SFORZESCO.** The Castello Sforzesco was constructed in 1368 as a defense against Venice. Later, it was used as army barracks, a horse stall, and a storage house before da Vinci converted it into a studio. Restored after WWII bomb damage, the complex houses 10 **Musei Civici** (Civic Museums). The **Museum of Ancient Art** contains Michelangelo's unfinished *Pietà Rondanini* (1564), his last work, and the **Museum of Decorative Art** has ornate furnishings and Murano glass. The underground level has a small Egyptian collection. *(M1: Cairoli or M2: Lanza. Open Tu-Su 9am-5:30pm. Combined admission €3, students €1.50, F 2-5:30pm free.)*

**CHIESA DI SANTA MARIA DELLE GRAZIE.** The church's Gothic nave is dark and patterned with frescoes, in contrast to the airy Renaissance tribune Bramante added in 1497. To the left of the church entrance, in what was once the dining hall, is the **Cenacolo Vinciano** (Vinciano Refectory), home to one of the most important works of art in the world: Leonardo da Vinci's **⬛Last Supper.** Following a 20-year restoration effort, the painting was put back on display in 1999. Reserve ahead or risk missing it. *(P. di S. Maria della Grazie 2. M1: Conciliazione. From P. Conciliazione, take V. Boccaccio and then go right onto V. Ruffini for about 2 blocks. Church open M-Sa 7am-noon and 3-7pm, Su 7:30am-12:15pm and 3:30-9pm. Modest dress required. Refectory open Tu-Su 8:15am-6:45pm. €6.50. Reservations ☎ 89 42 11 46. Reservation fee €1.50.)*

**PINACOTECA DI BRERA.** The Brera Art Gallery presents a collection of 14th- to 20th-century paintings, with an emphasis on the Lombard School. Works include Bellini's *Pietà*, Mantegna's brilliant *Dead Christ*, and Raphael's *Marriage of the Virgin*. *(V. Brera 28. M2: Lanza. Wheelchair-accessible. Open Tu-Su 8:30am-7:15pm. €5.)*

**MUSEO NAZIONALE DELLA SCIENZA E DELLA TECNOLOGIA "DA VINCI".** This hands-on museum traces technological advances from da Vinci to today. The hall of computers features a piano converted to a typewriter. *(V. San Vittore 21, off V. G. Carducci. M2: S. Ambrogio. Open Tu-F 9:30am-5pm, Sa-Su 9:30am-6:30pm. €8, students €6.)*

**TRIENNALE DE MILAN (PALAZZO DELL'ARTE).** Situated in the historic Palace of Art, the Triennale organizes international exhibits on architecture, decorative arts, design, fashion, and urbanism. *(V. E. Alemagna 6, behind the castello. M2: Cairoli. www.triennale.it. Open daily 10:30am-8:30pm. Last entry 7:30. Exhibit admissions vary.)*

**BASILICA DI SANT'AMBROGIO.** A prototype for Lombard-Romanesque churches throughout Italy, Sant'Ambrogio is the most influential medieval building in Milan. St. Ambrose presided over this church from AD 379 to 386, and his skeletal remains rest beside martyr St. Protasio. The 4th-century **Cappella di San Vittore in Ciel D'oro,** with exquisite mosaics adorning its cupola, lies through the seventh chapel on the right. *(M2: S. Ambrogio. Walk up V. G. Carducci, and the church is on the right. Church open M-Sa 7:15am-noon and 2:30-7pm, Su 7:15am-1pm and 3-8pm. Free. Chapel open Tu-Su 9:30-11:45am and 2:30-6pm. €2, students €1.)*

## NAVIGLI AND CORSO DI PORTA TICINESE

**BASILICA DI SANT'EUSTORGIO.** Founded in the 4th century to house the bones of the Magi, the church lost its original function when the dead sages were spirited off to Cologne in 1164. A great masterpiece of early Renaissance art is the **Portinari Chapel,** to the left of the entrance. Frescoes below the rainbow dome illustrate the life of St. Peter. The chapel stands on a **Paleochristian cemetery;** pagan and early Christian tombs are down the steps before the chapel entrance. *(P. S. Eustorgio 3. M2: S. Ambrogio. Basilica open M and W-Su 8:30am-noon and 3:30-6pm. Cappella open Tu-Su 10am-6:30pm. Basilica free. Cappella €6, students and seniors €3.)*

**NAVIGLI DISTRICT.** Often called the Venice of Lombardy, the Navigli district, complete with canals, elevated footbridges, open-air markets, cafes, alleys, and trolleys, comes alive at night. The area was part of a medieval canal system that transported thousands of tons of marble to build the *duomo* and linked Milan to various northern cities and lakes. *(From M2: Porta Genova, take V. Vigevano.)*

**CHIESA DI SAN LORENZO MAGGIORE.** The oldest church in Milan, San Lorenzo Maggiore testifies to the city's 4th-century greatness. To its right lies the **Cappella di Sant'Aquilino.** Inside, a 5th-century mosaic of Christ among his apostles overlooks St. Aquilino's remains. *(M2: S. Ambrogio. V. E. de Amicis leads to P. Vetra and the church. Open daily 7am-12:30pm and 2:30-6:45pm. €2, students €1.)*

## 📷 🎵 SHOPPING AND ENTERTAINMENT

In a city where clothes really do make the man (or woman), fashionistas arrive in spring and summer to watch models dressed in the newest styles glide down the runway. When the music has faded and the designers have bowed, world-famous **saldi** (sales) in July and January usher the garb into the real world. The **Quadrilatero della Moda** (fashion district) has become a sanctuary in its own right. This posh land, where limos transport poodles dressed to impress and jean jackets can sell for €2000, is the block formed by Via Monte Napoleone, Borgospresso, Via della Spiga, and Via Gesu. On these streets, Giorgio and Donatella not only sell their styles, they live in the suites above their stores and nightclubs. Even though most stores close at 7:30pm, have no fear; you can shop around the clock at the touch screens outside the Ralph Lauren Store, so long as you don't mind waiting for delivery until the next morning. Designer creations are available to mere mortals at the trendy boutiques along **Corso di Porta Ticinese**. Small shops and affordable staples from brand names can be found on **Via Torino** near the *duomo* and on **Corso Buenos Aires** near M1: Porta Venezia. Those who don't mind being a season behind can purchase famous designer wear from *blochisti* (stocks or wholesale clothing outlets), such as the well-known **Il Salvagente**, V. Bronzetti 16, off C. XXII Marzo (M1: S. Babila), or **Gruppo Italia Grandi Firme**, V. Montegani #7/A (M2: Famagosta), which offers designer duds at 70% off. True bargain hunters cull the bazaars on **Via Faucé** (M2: Garibaldi; Tu and Sa) and **Viale Papinian** (M2: Agnostino; Sa mornings).

Milan's famed tradition and unparalleled audience enthusiasm make **La Scala** (see p. 649) one of the best places in the world to see an opera. La Scala also sponsors a **ballet** season run primarily out of **Teatro degli Arcimboldi**, north of the city. (Infotel Scala ☎72 00 37 44; www.teatroallascala.org. Opera season runs Jan.-July and Sept.-Nov. Central box office located in the Metro station beneath P. del Duomo. Open daily noon-6pm. Tickets €10-105.) The **Milan Symphony Orchestra** plays from September to May at the **Auditorium di Milano.** (☎83 38 92 01; www.orchestrasinfonica.milano.it. Tickets €13-50, students €10-25.) The football clubs **Inter Milan** and **AC Milan** face off at their shared three-tiered stadium. **Ticket One,** located in FNAC stores, sells tickets for both teams as well as for concerts and other events (☎39 22 61; www.ticketone.it). There are tours of the **stadium,** V. Piccolomini 5, on non-game days. (☎40 42 432. M2: Lotto. Entrance at Gate 21. Tours M-Sa 10am-6pm. €13, under 18 or over 65 €10.) Milan's increasingly popular **Carnevale,** during the days preceding Ash Wednesday, is the longest-lasting in Italy. One night each June, **La Notte Bianca** (White Night) keeps the Metro, theater, shops, and restaurants open all night (3pm-6am). The **Serate al Museo** celebrates music with free concerts (both classical and contemporary) throughout Milan's museum courtyards and great halls; find the schedule at the tourist office (☎88 46 23 45; www.comune.milano.it/museiemostre).

## 🎵 NIGHTLIFE

The nightlife in **Navigli** is popular with students and centers around V. Sforza. The **Brera** district invites tourists and Milanese to test their singing skills while sipping mixed drinks at one of its piano bars. **Corso di Porta Ticinese** is the sleek land of the all-night Happy-hour buffet, where the price of an mixed drink (€6-8) also buys dinner. A single block of **Corso Como** near **Stazione Garibaldi** is home to the most exclusive clubs. Bars and clubs cluster around **Largo Cairoli,** where summer brings Milan's hottest outdoor dance venues. Southeast of **Stazione Centrale** is home to an eclectic mix of bars and much of Milan's gay and lesbian scene.

▣ **Le Trottoir,** P. XXIV Maggio 1 (☎/fax 02 83 78 166; www.letrottoir.it) may be the loudest, most crowded bar and club in the Navagli. A young crowd comes nightly for underground music downstairs and jazz or a DJ upstairs. Pizza and sandwiches €8, available until 2am. Mixed drinks €6-9. Happy hour daily 6-8pm; beer €4, mixed drinks €6. Open daily 3pm-3am. Cover €8, includes 1 drink. AmEx/MC/V.

▣ **Old Fashion Café,** Vle. Alemagna 6 (☎80 56 231; www.oldfashion.it). M1/2: Cadorna F. N. Summer brings stylish clubgoers to couches encircling an outdoor dance floor with live music and DJ. Tu is the most popular night, with live music. F R&B. Cover M-Sa €20; W €10, students free. Open 11pm-4:30am.

**Scimmie,** V. A. Sforza 49 (☎89 40 28 74; www.scimmie.it). Legendary nightclub offers nightly performances. Talented underground musicians play blues, fusion, jazz, Italian swing, and reggae. Mixed drinks €4-9. Concerts 7:30-9:30pm and 10:30pm-1:30am. Schedule posted online. Open daily 7pm-2am. MC/V.

**Flying Circus,** P. Vetra 21 (☎58 31 35 77). A pair of cacti welcomes you to this glass-encased lounge. Mixed drinks and wine €6-8. Weekly themed calendar includes Tu "Re-Wine" (2nd wine free), W "Kill Beer" (€3 beer), Th "Chupa Chupitos" (€1 shots), and Sa "Try Flying" (3 cocktails for €15). Themes change in winter. Happy hour buffet daily 6:30-9:30pm. Open M-F 10am-2am, Sa 6:30pm-2am. AmEx/MC/V.

**Yguana Café Restaurant,** V. P. Gregorio XIV 16 (☎89 40 41 95), just off P. Vetra. Lounge outside or groove to DJs spinning house and hip hop. Mixed drinks €8-10. Happy hour buffet M-Sa 5:30-9:30pm, Su 5:30-10pm. Lunch M-F 12:30-3pm. Su brunch noon-4pm. Open for drinks daily 5:30pm-2am, F-Sa 5:30pm-3am. AmEx/MC/V.

**L'elephant,** V. Melzo 22 (☎29 51 87 68). M2: Porta Venezia. From C. Buenos Aires, go right on V. Melzo and continue about 5 blocks. A sultry feel makes the party at this gay-and-lesbian-friendly bar liable to overflow outside. Mixed drinks €7-9. Happy hour buffet 6:30-9:30pm. Open Tu-Su 6:30pm-2am. Cash only.

**Hollywood,** C. Como 15 (☎65 98 996). Slip into something stunning and pout for the bouncer: this disco selects its partiers with the utmost care. Tu hip hop, W house, Th-Sa music by resident DJs. Su tends to be invite-only for celebrities. Mixed drinks from €10. Cover €20. Open Tu-Su 11pm-5am. MC/V.

**Club 2,** V. Formentini 2 (☎86 46 48 07), down V. Madonnina from V. F. Chiari. Piano bar with restaurant upstairs, karaoke disco-pub downstairs. *Primi* and *secondi* €7-16. Beer €8. Mixed drinks €10. Open M-F 8:30pm-3am, Sa-Su 8pm-3am. AmEx/MC/V.

**Spazio Movida Cocktail Bar,** V. A. Sforza 41 (☎58 10 20 43; www.spaziomovida.it). Like its namesake Spanish cultural movement, Movida shakes up the scene by spilling Latin music out onto the street and serving drinks like "All Saints" (peach liqueur and sweet and sour). Extensive *panini* menu €4.50-5.50. Mixed drinks €6.50. Free Wi-Fi. Happy hour 6-9pm. Open daily 6pm-2am. MC/V.

**Loolapaloosa,** C. Como 15 (☎65 55 693), next to Hollywood. Bartenders entertain patrons by swinging lamps and ringing bells, while guests are invited to dance on the bar. Mixed drinks €10-15. Cover €6-20, includes 1 drink. Happy hour buffet 6:30-10:30pm. Open M-Sa noon-4am, Su 2pm-4am.

## TOP TEN MOST COMMON STREET NAMES IN ITALY

After only a day or two in Italy, it's apparent that just a few big names run Italy's streets.

**1.** In 1849 **Vittorio Emanuele II** became unified Italy's 1st king.

**2. Giuseppe Garibaldi,** a 19th-century military hero, is credited with making the unification of Italy possible.

**3. Count Camillo Benso di Cavour** designed the constitutional structure of the "Kingdom of Italy" in the 19th century.

**4. Guglielmo Marconi** sent three short beeps to Canada in 1901—the first transatlantic telegraph signals.

**5. XX Settembre** (1870) is the date of Italy's final unification.

**6.** Socialist **Giacomo Matteoti** wrote a book critical of fascism in 1924, but was murdered in response.

**7. Cesare Battisti,** a native of Trent, was a WWI martyr.

**8. Giuseppe Mazzini** tried to instigate popular uprisings to unify Italy, but failed time and again.

**9. Solferino** was a battle fought on June 24, 1859 for the the unification of Italy in the region between Milan and Verona. Italy along with French ally Napolean III defeated Austria.

**10. Umberto I,** reigned as King of Italy from 1878 until 1900 when he became and remains the only modern Italian head of state to be assassinated.

## ⚟ LET'S GO TO MILAN: BERGAMO ☎035

Home to the **Orio al Serio International Airport** (**BGY**; ☎32 63 23; www.sacbo.it), Bergamo (pop. 120,000) is a hub for budget airlines **Ryanair, SkyEurope,** and **Wizz Air. Trains** (☎24 79 50) run from Ple. Marconi to Milan (1hr., 1 per hr., €3.50). **Buses** run from the left of the train station to Como (6 per day, €4.40) and Milan (2 per hr., €4.40). **Airport buses** go to the train station in Bergamo (10min., €1.60) and Milan (1hr., 2 per hr., €6).

For overnight layovers or missed flights, head to the cheap rooms of **Ostello Città di Bergamo (HI) ❷,** V. G. Ferraris 1. From the airport, take bus 1C to Porta Nuova and change to bus #6; the hostel is at the next-to-last stop. (☎36 17 24; www.ostellodibergamo.it. 6- and 8-bed dorms €17; singles €27; doubles €40; 3-6 person rooms €18 per person. €3 HI discount.) Another option is the B&B **La Torretta Citta Alta ❹,** Via Rocca 2, in the high city. (☎23 17 71; www.latorrettabergamoalta.com. Singles €50-70; doubles €70-90; triples €90-110.) Dine at ⚟**Trattoria Casa Mia ❷,** V. S. Bernardino 20, which makes up for its out-of-the-way location with local flavor. From the station, walk along V. P. Giovanni to Largo Porta Nuova. Turn left on V. G. Tiraboschi, which becomes V. Zambonate, then turn left at the last intersection, onto V. S. Bernardino. (☎22 06 76. Lunch *menù* €9. Dinner *menù* €15. Open M-Sa noon-2pm and 7-10pm. Cash only.) Supermarket **Pellicano** is at Vle. V. Emanuele II 17; walk from the station past Ple. Repubblica. (Open M 8:30am-1:30pm, Tu-F 8:30am-1:30pm and 3:30-8pm, Sa 8:30am-8pm. MC/V.) **Postal Code:** 24122.

## MANTUA (MANTOVA) ☎0376

Though Mantua (pop. 47,000) did not become a dynamic cultural haven until the Renaissance, art and culture have shaped the city's history since the birth of the poet Virgil in 70 BC. Today, the huge international **Festivaletteratura** brings writers from John Grisham to Salman Rushdie to the city in early September. Mantua's grand *palazzi,* including the opulent **Palazzo Ducale,** P. Sordello 40, were built by the powerful Gonzaga family, who ascended to power in 1328, ruled for 400 years, and brought well-known artists to leave their marks on the town's mansions and churches. The **New Gallery** houses dozens of locally produced altarpieces from the 16th-18th centuries, removed from monasteries during the Habsburg and Napoleonic eras. (Open Tu-Su 8:45am-7:15pm. €6.50.) Music lovers first filled the balconies of the ⚟**Teatro Bibiena,** V. Accademia 4, when 14-year-old Mozart inaugurated the building in 1769. Inside, the rose and gray stone balconies create the illusion of a fairytale castle. (Open Tu-Su 9:30am-12:30pm and 3-6pm. €2.50, under 18 €1.20.) In the far south of the city, down V. P. Amedeo, which becomes V. Acrebi, through P. Veneto, and down Largo Parri, lies the **Palazzo del Te,** built by Giulio Romano in 1534 as a suburban retreat for Federico II Gonzaga. It is widely considered the finest building in the Mannerist style. The entirely frescoed ⚟ **Room of Giants** depicts the demise of the rebellious titans at the hands of Jupiter. The hidden garden and grotto at the far end are often overlooked. (Open M 1-6pm, Tu-Su 9am-6pm. €8, students €2.50.) Just south of P. Sordello is the 11th-century Romanesque **Piazza dell'Erbe.** Opposite the *piazza* is Leon Alberti's **Chiesa di Sant'Andrea,** Mantua's greatest contribution to the Italian Renaissance and one of the first great classical constructions since imperial Rome. (Open daily 8am-noon and 3-7pm. Free.)

Accommodations in Mantua are costly. **Hotel ABC ❹,** P. D. Leoni 25, across from the train station, is a modern hotel with comfortable rooms. (☎32 23 29; www.hotelabcmantova.it. Breakfast included. Reserve ahead. Singles €44-88; doubles €66-121; triples €77-160; quads €88-180.) **Ostello del Mincio ❷,** V. Porto 23/25, 10km from Mantua, is the only youth hostel in the area. (☎65 39 24; www.ostellodelmincio.org. Call for directions. Internet, TV, and phone. Dorms €15-20, with breakfast €17-22.) A friendly proprietor serves exquisite regional dishes at **Antica Osteria ai Ranari** ❸, V. Trieste 11, south of the canal. Try the *tortelli di zucca* or mint pesto. (☎32 84 31. *Primi* €6-7. *Secondi* €9-13. Wide variety of *salumi* €6-10. Cover €1. Open Tu-Su noon-3pm and 8pm-2am. Closed for 3 weeks in summer; call ahead. AmEx/MC/V.) A **market** is held every Thursday morning in P. d'Erbe. **Supermarket Sma,** V. Giustiziati 11, is behind the Rotonda di San Lorenzo on P. d'Erbe. (Open M-Sa 8:30am-7:30pm. AmEx/MC/V.)

**Trains** go from P. D. Leoni to Milan (2¼hr., 9 per day, €8.40) and Verona (40min., 20 per day, €2.30). From the train station, turn left on V. Solferino, then right on Via Bonomi to the main street, **Corso Vittorio Emanuele II.** Follow it to P. Cavallotti, across the river to C. Umberto I, which leads to P. Marconi, P. Mantegna, and the main *piazze,* **Piazza dell'Erbe** and **Piazza Sordello.** The **tourist office** is at P. Mantegna 6; follow V. Solferino until it becomes V. Fratelli Bandiera, then go right on V. Verdi. (☎32 82 53; www.aptmantova.it. Open daily 9am-7pm.) **Internet** access is available at **Bit and Phone,** V. Bertinelli 21. **Postal Code:** 46100.

# THE LAKE COUNTRY

When Italy's monuments start blurring together, escape to the clear waters and mountains of the northern Lake Country, partly in Piedmont, partly in Lombardy. Artistic visionaries like Liszt, Longfellow, and Wordsworth sought rest among the shores of the northern lakes. The mansion-spotted coast of Lake Como welcomes the rich and famous, palatial hotels dot Lake Maggiore's sleepy shores, and a young crowd descends upon Lake Garda for its watersports and bars.

## LAKE COMO (LAGO DI COMO)

As the numerous luxurious villas on the lake's shores attest, the well-to-do have been using Lake Como as a refuge since before the Roman Empire. Three lakes form the forked Lake Como, joined at the three central towns: Bellagio, Menaggio, and Varenna. These smaller towns offer a more relaxing stay than Como. For a taste of the Lake's true beauty, hop on a bus or ferry, and step off whenever a castle, villa, vineyard, or small town beckons.

▐ **TRANSPORTATION.** The only town on the lake accessible by **train** is Como. Trains go from Stazione San Giovanni (☎031 89 20 21) to Milan (1hr., 1-2 per hr., €4.90) and Zürich, SWI (4hr., 5 per day, €43). From P. Matteotti, **bus** C46 goes to Bergamo (2hr., 5 per day, €4.40), and C10 goes to Menaggio (1hr., 1 per hr., €3). From the train station, bus C30 goes to Bellagio (1hr., 16 per day, €2.60). Spend the day zipping between the boutiques, gardens, villas, and wineries of the lake by **ferry** (day pass €20), leaving from the piers at P. Cavour.

**COMO.** Situated on the southwestern tip of the lake, semi-industrial Como (pop. 86,000) is the lake's largest town. **Ostello Villa Olmo (HI)** ❷, V. Bellinzona 2, offers clean rooms and a friendly staff. From the train station, walk 20min. down V. Borgo Vico to V. Bellinzona. (☎031 57 38 00; ostellocomo@tin.it. Breakfast included. Reception 7-10am and 4pm-midnight. Lockout 10am-4pm. Strict curfew midnight. Open Mar.-Nov. Reserve ahead. Dorms €18. €3 HI discount. Cash only.) A **Gran Mercato** supermarket is at P. Matteotti 3. (Open Su-M 8:30am-1pm, Tu-F 8:30am-1:30pm and 3:30-7:30pm, Sa 8am-7:30pm.) The **tourist office** is at P. Cavour 17. From the station, go left on V. Fratelli Ricchi and right on Vle. Fratelli Rosselli, which turns into Lungo Lario Trento and leads to the *piazza.* (☎031 26 97 12. Open M-Sa 9am-1pm and 2:30-6pm, Su 9:30am-1pm.) **Postal Code:** 22100.

**MENAGGIO.** Halfway up Lake Como's western shore are the terra-cotta rooftops of Menaggio (pop. 3200). The town's beauty and excellent ferry connections make it the perfect base for exploring the lake. Daytrips by ferry to the gardens and villas of **Bellagio** and **Varenna** (both: 10-15min., 1-2 per hr., €3.40) are extremely popular. The **Rifugio Menaggio** mountain station is the starting point for a 2½hr. round-trip hike to **Monte Grona** (1736m) that offers views of the pre-Alps and the lakes; or a 2¼hr. hike to **Chiesa di San Amate** (1623m) that takes you over a mountain ridge to sneak a peak at alpine pasture. A number of shorter hikes start in Menaggio. To get to the laid-back **Ostello La Prinula (HI) ❶**, V. IV Novembre 86, head uphill from the ferry dock and turn left onto the main thoroughfare. The expert staff arranges outdoor activities. (☎ 034 43 23 56; www.menaggiohostel.com. Breakfast included. Reception 8-10am and 4pm-midnight. Lockout 10am-4pm. Curfew midnight. Reserve ahead. Open Mar.-Nov. Dorms €16; 4- to 6-bed suites with bath €18 per person. €3 HI discount. Cash only.) Just up the street from the ferry dock, **Super Cappa Market,** V. IV Novembre 107, stocks groceries and hiking supplies. (Open M 8-12:30pm, Tu-Sa 8am-12:30pm and 3-7pm.) In the *centro* at P. Garibaldi 4, the helpful **tourist office** has info and maps on lake excursions. **Postal Code:** 22017.

## LAKE MAGGIORE (LAGO MAGGIORE)

A translation of Stendhal reads: "If it should befall that you possess a heart and shirt, then sell the shirt and visit the shores of Lake Maggiore." Though writers have always been seduced by the lake's beauty, Lake Maggiore remains less touristed than its neighbors. **Stresa** is a perfect stepping-stone to the gorgeous **Borromean Islands.** Stay at the **Albergo Luina ❸**, V. Garibaldi 21, to the right past the ferry dock. (☎ 032 33 02 85. Breakfast €3.50. Reserve ahead in summer. Singles €35-52; doubles €55-80; triples €56-80. MC/V.) Daily excursion tickets allow you to travel between Stresa and the three islands. **Trains** run from Stresa to Milan (1¼hr., 2 per hr., €4.30). To reach the *centro* and the **IAT Tourist Office,** P. Marconi 16, from the ferry dock, exit the train station, turn right on V. P. d. Piemonte, take a left on Vle. D. d. Genova, and walk toward the water.

**◼ THE BORROMEAN ISLANDS.** On **Isola Bella,** the **Palazzo e Giardini Borromeo** showcases priceless tapestries and paintings. (Open Mar. 21-Oct. 21 daily 9am-5:30pm. €11.) From Isola Bella, ferries go to **Isola Superiore dei Pescatori,** which has a quaint fishing village with a rocky beach and ice-cold water. **Isola Madre** is the greenest island, most favored by the locals. The 16th-century **Villa Taranto** contains several puppet theaters, and its gardens hold exotic flowers. (Open daily 8:30am-6:30pm. €8.50. Combined ticket with the Palazzo e Giardini Borromeo €16.)

## LAKE GARDA (LAGO DI GARDA)

Garda has staggering mountains and breezy summers. **Desenzano,** the lake's southern transport hub, is only 1hr. from Milan and 2hr. from Venice. Sirmione and Limone are best explored as daytrips; accommodations are scant and pricey. Riva del Garda, at the lake's northern tip, has an affordable hostel to use as a base.

**SIRMIONE.** Exploring Sirmione's 13th-century castle and Roman ruins can fill a leisurely day or busy afternoon. Close to the end of the island by Grotte di Catullo, **Villa Paradiso ❸**, Via Arici 7, offers accommodations with panoramic views of the lake. (☎ 030 91 61 49. Doubles €66. Cash only.) **Buses** run to Verona (1hr., 1 per hr., €3.90). **Ferries** run to other lake cities until 8pm; check schedule at ferry docks. The **tourist office,** V. Guglilmo Marconi 6, is in the circular building 100m before the castle. (☎ 030 91 61 14; www.commune.sirmione.bs.it. Open Apr.-Oct. daily 9am-8pm; Nov.-Mar. M-F 9am-12:30pm and 3-6pm, Sa 9am-12:30pm.) **Postal Code:** 25019.

**LIMONE.** On the northwestern coast of Lake Garda, jagged mountainsides dive into the clear blue waters of the European home of lemons. In Limone, windsurfing, swimming, and eating all revolve around the unbelievable view of the lake as it winds through the mountains. Uphill from the center near the water, **La Limonaia del Castèl**, V. IV Novembre 25, transports tourists into the world of a functioning 18th-century citrus house that is spread over 1633 sq. yd. of terraces. This impressive structure grows clementines, grapefruits, lemons, and limes. (☎ 0365 95 40 08; www.limone-sulgarda.it. €1.) **Ferries** (☎ 030 91 49 511; www.navigazionelaghi.it) run to Desenzano (4 per day, €10-13), Riva (17 per day, €3.30-5.10), and Sirmione (8 per day, €10-13). The **tourist office**, V. IV Novembre 29, is across from the bus stop. (☎ 0365 91 89 87. Open daily 8:30am-9pm.) **Postal Code:** 25087.

**RIVA DEL GARDA.** Riva's calm and beautiful pebble beaches are Lake Garda's restitution for the budget traveler put off by steep local prices. Visitors swim, windsurf, hike, and climb near the most stunning portion of the lake, where cliffs crash into the sea. Sleep at backpacker hot spot **Ostello Benacus (HI) ❶**, P. Cavour 10. (☎ 0464 55 49 11. Breakfast included. Laundry €4. Internet €2 per hr. Reception 7-9am and 3-11pm. Reserve ahead. Dorms €14; private rooms €17 per person. AmEx/MC/V.) Riva is accessible by **bus** (☎ 0464 55 23 23) from Verona (2hr., 1 per hr., €5.20). **Ferries** (☎ 030 91 49 511) run to various southern lake cities constantly. Routes change throughout the day, so check the schedule. The **tourist office** is at Largo Medaglie d'Oro 5. (☎ 0464 55 44 44; www.gardatrentino.it. Open M-Sa 9am-noon and 3-6:30pm, Su 9am-noon and 3:30-6:30pm.) **Postal Code:** 38066.

# ITALIAN RIVIERA (LIGURIA)

The Italian Riviera stretches 350km along the Mediterranean between France and Tuscany, forming the most touristed area of the Italian coastline. Genoa anchors the luminescent Ligurian coastal strip between the **Riviera di Levante** (rising sun) to the east and the **Riviera di Ponente** (setting sun) to the west. The elegant coast is where Riviera glamor mixes with seaside relaxation, its lemon trees, almond blossoms, and turquoise seas greeting visitors. The **Cinque Terre** area (p. 660), just west of **La Spezia** (p. 662), is especially worth the journey.

## GENOA (GENOVA)                                    ☎ 010

Genoa (pop. 640,000), city of grit and grandeur, has little in common with its resort neighbors. As a Ligurian will tell you, "*si deve conoscerla per amarla*" (you have to know her to love her). Once home to Liguria's most noble families, Genoa's main streets are lined with *palazzi* and *piazze;* wander through medieval churches and maze-like pathways scented with pesto to discover this port city.

**🚉 TRANSPORTATION. Colombo Internazionale Airport (GOA;** ☎ 60 15 461), in Sesti Ponente, services European destinations. Volabus #100 runs to Stazione Brignole from the airport (3 per hr. 5:30am-10:30pm, €3). Most visitors arrive at one of Genoa's two train stations: **Stazione Principe**, in P. Acquaverde, or **Stazione Brignole**, in P. Verdi. **Trains** go to Rome (5-6hr., 12 per day, €33), Turin (2hr., 2-3 per hr., €8-12), and points along the Italian Riviera. AMT **buses** (☎ 55 82 414) run through the city (€1.20; day pass €3.50). **Ferries** to Olbia, Sardinia, and Palermo, Sicily depart from Terminal Traghetti in the Ponte Assereto section of the port.

**🔳🔳 ORIENTATION AND PRACTICAL INFORMATION.** From Stazione Principe, take V. Balbi to V. Cairoli, which becomes V. Garibaldi. Turn right on V. XXV

Aprile at P. delle Fontane Marose to get to **Piazza de Ferrari** in the center of town. From Stazione Brignole, turn right out of the station, then left on V. Fiume and right onto V. XX Settembre. Or, take bus #18, 19, or 30 from Stazione Principe, or bus #19 or 40 from Stazione Brignole. Travelers should avoid walking on **Via di Prè** and be cautious by **Via della Maddalena** and in the *centro* at night. The **tourist office,** GenovaInforma, has several locations, including a kiosk in P. Matteotti and one near the aquarium on Portico Antico. (☎86 87 452. Open daily 9am-1pm and 2-6pm.) **Internet** is available at **Number One Bar/Cafe,** P. Verdi 21R. (☎54 18 85. €4 per hr. Open M-Sa 7:30am-11:30pm.) **Postal Code:** 16121.

> **!** The shadowy streets of the *centro storico* are riddled with drug dealers and prostitutes, especially the area around Stazione Principe, as well as those around V. della Maddalena, V. Sottoripa, and V. di Prè. Avoid them when shops are closed and streets are empty.

**▢▢ ACCOMMODATIONS AND FOOD.** Delight in views of the city below at **Ostello per la Gioventù (HI) ❶,** V. Costanzi 120. From Stazione Principe, take bus #35 to V. Napoli and transfer to #40, which runs to the hostel. From Stazione Brignole, pick up bus #40 (last bus 12:50am) and take it all the way up the hill. (☎24 22 457; www.geocities.com/hostelge. Breakfast included. Dorms €16. HI members only.) The rooms at **Albergo Carola ❸,** V. Gropallo 4/12, are meticulously decorated. (☎83 91 340; albergocarola@libero.it. Singles €30; doubles €50, with bath €60; triples €80; quads €90. Cash only.) For camping, try **Genova Est ❶,** on V. Marcon Loc Cassa. Take the train from Stazione Brignole to Bogliasco (10min., 6 per day, €1). A van (5min., 1 per 2hr. 8:10am-6pm, free) runs from there to the cliffside camp-ground. (☎34 72 053; www.camping-genova-est.it. Laundry €3.50. €5.90 per person, €5.60-8.60 per tent. Electricity €2.20.) **◪Trattoria da Maria ❷,** V. Testa d'Oro 14R, off V. XXV Aprile, has authentic Genovese daily specials. (☎58 10 80. 2-course *menù* €9. Open M-Sa 11:45am-3pm. MC/V.) To sample Genoa's famous salami or pesto, stop by **Salvi Salumeria,** V. S. Lorenzo 2, near Porto Antico (MC/V).

**▣▢ SIGHTS AND ENTERTAINMENT.** Genoa's multitude of *palazzi* were built by its famous merchant families. Follow V. Balbi through P. della Nunziata and continue to L. Zecca, where V. Cairoli leads to **◪Via Garibaldi,** called "Via Aurea" (Golden Street) after the wealthy families who inhabited it. Rococo rooms bathed in gold and upholstered in red velvet fill the 17th-century **◪Palazzo Reale,** V. Balbi 10, west of V. Garibaldi. (Open Tu-W 9am-1:30pm, Th-Su 9am-7pm. €4, 18-25 €2.). The **Galleria di Palazzo Bianco,** V. Garibaldi 11, exhibits Dutch, Flemish, and Lig-urian paintings. Across the street, the 17th-century **Galleria Palazzo Rosso,** V. Garibaldi 18, has magnificent furnishings in a lavishly frescoed interior. (Both open Tu-F 9am-7pm, Sa-Su 10am-7pm. Each €5, both €7.) The **Villetta Di Negro,** on the hill farther down V. Garibaldi, contains grottoes, terraced gardens, and water-falls. From P. delle Fontane Marose, take Salita di S. Caterina to P. Corvetto. (Open daily 8am-dusk.) From P. de Ferrari, take V. Boetto to P. Matteotti for a glimpse of the ornate interior and Rubens paintings in **Chiesa di Gesù.** (Church open M-Sa 7am-4pm, Su 8am-5pm. Closed to tourists during Su Mass. Free.) Head past the church down V. di Porta Soprana to V. Ravecca to reach the twin-towered **Porta Soprana,** one of the four gates into the city, near the boyhood home of **Chris-topher Columbus.** (Porta and Columbus' home open daily 10am-6pm. Combo ticket €7.) **Centro storico,** the eerie and beautiful historical center bordered by Porto Antico, V. Garibaldi, and P. Ferrari, is a mass of winding streets. The area contains some of Genoa's most memorable sights, including the asymmetrical **San Lorenzo Duomo,** down V. San Lorenzo from P. Matteotti (open daily 9am-noon and 3-6pm;

free), and the medieval **Torre Embraici.** Go down V. S. Lorenzo toward the water, turn left on V. Chiabrera, and left on V. di Mascherona to reach the ◙**Chiesa Santa Maria di Castello,** in P. Caricamento, a labyrinth of chapels, courtyards, and crucifixes. (Open daily 9am-noon and 3:30-6:30pm. Closed to tourists during Su Mass. Free.) The ◙**aquarium** on Porto Antico is Europe's largest. (Open July-Aug. daily 9am-11pm; Mar.-June and Sept.-Oct. M-W and F 9am-7:30pm, Th 9am-10pm, Sa-Su 9am-8:30pm; Nov.-Feb. daily 9:30am-7:30pm. Last entry 1½hr. before closing. €15.)

**Corso Italia,** an upscale promenade, is home to much of Genoa's nightlife. Most people drive to get to clubs, as they are difficult to reach on foot and the city streets can be dangerous. Italian and international students flock to bars in **Piazza Erbe** and along **Via San Bernardo.** The swanky bar **Al Parador,** P. della Vittoria 49R, is easy and fairly safe to reach from Stazione Brignole. It's in the northeast corner of P. Vittoria, near the intersection of V. Cadorna and V. B. Liguria. (☎58 17 71. Mixed drinks €4.50. Open M-Sa 24hr. Cash only.)

# FINALE LIGURE                              ☎019

A beachside plaque proclaims Finale Ligure (pop. 12,000) the place for *"il riposo del popolo"* ("the people's rest"). From bodysurfing in choppy waves to browsing through chic boutiques to scaling the 15th-century ruins of **Castello di San Giovanni,** *riposo* takes many forms. The nearby towns **Borgio** and **Verezzi** are also worth exploring. Walk east along V. Aurelia to find a free **beach,** less populated than those closer to town. Enclosed by ancient walls, **Finalborgo,** Finale Ligure's historic center, is a 1km walk or 2min. ACTS bus ride up V. Bruneghi from the station.

With clean rooms and incomparable views, ◙**Castello Wuillerman (HI) ❶,** V. Generale Caviglia, is well worth the hike up its daunting steps. From the train station, cross the street and turn left onto V. Raimondo Pertica. After passing a church on the left, turn left onto V. Alonzo and climb the stairs to the *castello.* (☎69 05 15; www.hostelfinaleligure.com. Breakfast included. Reception 7-10am and 5-10pm. Curfew midnight. Dorms €14. HI members only. Cash only.) **Camping Del Mulino ❶,** on V. Castelli, has a restaurant and mini-market. Take the Calvisio bus from the station to the Boncardo Hotel, turn left at Piazza Oberdan, turn right on V. Porro, and follow the signs up the hill. (☎60 16 69; www.campingmulino.it. Reception 8am-8pm. Open Apr.-Sept. Tent sites €9.50-14. MC/V.) Cheap restaurants lie along **Via Rossi, Via Roma,** and **Via Garibaldi.** Fill up on huge portions of pasta at **Spaghetteria Il Posto ❷,** V. Porro 21. Bring a friend—each dish is made for two. (☎60 00 95. Entrees €7. Cover €1. Open Tu-Su 7-10:30pm. Closed for 2 weeks in Mar. Cash only.) Cafe and night spot **Pilade ❶,** V. Garibaldi 67, has live jazz on Fridays. (Beer from €3. Open daily 10am-2am. MC/V.) **Di per Di Express** supermarket is at V. Alonzo 10. (Open M-Sa 8:15am-1pm and 4:30-7:30pm, Su 9am-1pm. MC/V.)

**Trains** leave from P. V. Veneto for Genoa (1hr., 2 per hr., €4). SAR **buses** run from the train station to Borgo Verezzi (10min., 4 per hr., €1). The city is divided into **Finalpia** to the east, **Finalmarina** in the center, and **Finalborgo,** farther inland. The station and most sights are in Finalmarina. The IAT **tourist office** is at V.S. Pietro 14. (☎68 10 19; www.inforiviera.it. Open M-Sa 9am-1pm and 3:30-6:30pm, Su 9am-noon; low season M-Sa 9am-1pm and 3:30-6:30pm.) **Postal Code:** 17024.

# CAMOGLI                                    ☎0185

Postcard-perfect Camogli shimmers with color. Sun-faded peach houses crowd the hilltop, and red and turquoise boats bob in the water. Turn right out of the train station and keep walking until V. Repubblica turns into V. P. Schaffino to reach the handsomely furnished **Hotel Augusta ❸,** V.P. Schaffino 100. (☎77 05 92; www.htlaugusta.com. Buffet breakfast €10 per room. 15min. free Internet. Singles €35-65; doubles €68-98; triples €90-135. AmEx/MC/V.) The creamy *gelato* from ◙**Gelato e**

**Dintorni ❶**, V. Garibaldi 104/105, puts nationally ranked rivals to shame. (2 scoops €1.40. Open daily 11:30am-11pm. Cash only.) **Trains** run on the Genoa-La Spezia line to Genoa (40min., 38 per day, €1.60) and La Spezia (1½hr., 24 per day, €4). Golfo Paradiso **ferries**, V. Scalo 3 (☎77 20 91; www.golfoparadiso.it), near P. Colombo, go to Cinque Terre (round-trip €20) and Portofino (round-trip €13). Buy tickets on the dock; call ahead for the schedule. Turn right from the station to find the **tourist office**, V. XX Settembre 33. (☎77 10 66. Open M-Sa 9am-12:30pm and 3:30-7pm, Su 9am-12:30pm; low season reduced hours.) **Postal Code:** 16032.

## SANTA MARGHERITA LIGURE                                           ☎0185

Santa Margherita Ligure was a calm fishing village until the early 20th century, when it fell into favor with Hollywood stars. Today, glitz and glamor paint the shore, but the serenity of the town's early days still lingers. If you find gardens more enticing than beaches, take the paths off V. della Vittoria uphill to the pink-and-white ■**Villa Durazzo,** surrounded by flora and home to 16th-century paintings. Gardens open daily July-Aug. 9am-8pm; May-June and Sept. 9am-7pm; Apr. and Oct. 9am-6pm; Nov.-Dec. 9am-5pm. *Villa* open 9am-1pm and 2:30-6pm.) In Santa Margherita, there's no such thing as a long walk to the beach, but seaside accommodations come with a price. Cozy beds and private showers make ■ **Hotel Conte Verde ❹**, V. Zara 1, a good choice. From the train station, turn right on V. Trieste, which becomes V. Roma. (☎28 71 39; www.hotelconteverde.it. Breakfast included. Singles €40-120; doubles €65-150; triples €90-210; quads €100-230. AmEx/MC/V.) ■**Trattoria Da Pezzi ❷**, V. Cavour 21, is popular with the locals for its homestyle cuisine. (☎28 53 03. *Primi* €3.80-6.70. *Secondi* €4.80-15. Cover €0.80. Open Su-F 10am-2:15pm and 5-9:15pm. MC/V.) Come nightfall, youthful crowds head to **Sabot,** P. Martiri della Libertà 32, for drinks and dancing. (☎28 07 47. Beer €4-6. Mixed drinks €7. Open daily 4pm-4am. MC/V.) **Trains** along the Pisa-Genoa line go from P. Federico Raoul Nobili, at the top of V. Roma, to Genoa (50min., 2-4 per hr., €2.10) and La Spezia (1½hr., 1-2 per hr., €4). Tigullio **buses** (☎28 88 34) go from P. V. Veneto to Camogli (30min., 1-2 per hr., €1.10) and Portofino (20min., 3 per hr., €1). Tigullio **ferries**, V. Palestro 8/1B (☎28 46 70), run tours to Cinque Terre (early May-late Sept. 1 per day, round-trip €22) and Portofino (Sa-Su 1 per hr., €4.50). Turn right out of the train station, go right on C. Rainusso, and take the first left on V. Gimelli to find the **tourist office**, V. XXV Aprile 2/B. (☎28 74 85; iat.santamargher-italigure@provincia.genova.it. Open M-Sa 9:30am-12:30pm and 3-7:30pm, Su 9:30am-12:30pm and 4:30-7:30pm.) **Postal Code:** 16032.

## CINQUE TERRE                                                       ☎0187

Cinque Terre is an outdoorsman's paradise: strong hikers can cover all five villages—Corniglia, Manarola, Monterosso, Riomaggiore, and Vernazza—in about 5hr., and there are numerous opportunities for kayaking, cliff jumping, and horseback riding along the way. Rather than rushing, take the time to wander through the villages' tiny clusters of rainbow-colored houses amid hilly stretches of olive groves and vineyards. Though Cinque Terre was formerly a hidden treasure of the Ligurian coastline, increased publicity and word of mouth have made the towns fodder for a booming tourism industry.

■🛈 **TRANSPORTATION AND PRACTICAL INFORMATION. Trains** run along the Genoa-La Spezia (Pisa) line. A **Cinque Terre Card** (1-day €8, 3-day €19, 7-day €34) allows for unlimited train, bus, and path access among the five villages, La Spezia, and Levanto; it can be purchased at the train stations and Cinque Terre National Park. Monterosso is the most accessible village by train. From the station on V. Fegina, in the northern end of town, trains run to: Florence (3½hr., 1 per hr.,

€7.90); Genoa (1½hr., 1 per hr., €4.50); La Spezia (20min., 2 per hr., €1.60); Pisa (2½hr., 1 per hr., €4.70); Rome (7hr., 1 per 2hr., €17-27). **Ferries** run from La Spezia to Monterosso (2hr., 4 per day, €18). The five villages stretch along the shore between Levanto and La Spezia, connected by trains (5-20min., 1 per hr., €1.10), roads (although cars are not allowed inside the towns), and footpaths. **Monterosso** is the easternmost town and the largest, containing most of the services for the area, followed by higher-end **Vernazza**, cliffside **Corniglia**, swimming-cove-dotted **Manarola**, and affordable **Riomaggiore**. The Monterosso **park office** is at P. Garibaldi 20. (☎81 78 38. Open daily 8am-8pm.) The Pro Loco **tourist office,** V. Fegina 38, Monterosso, is below the train station. (☎/fax 81 75 06. Open daily 9:30am-6:30pm.) **Postal Codes:** 19016 (Monterosso); 19017 (Manarola and Riomaggiore); 19018 (Corniglia and Vernazza).

**▐▛▐ ACCOMMODATIONS AND FOOD.** Most hotels are in Monterosso, and they fill quickly in summer. The tourist office offers info on the plentiful *affittacamere* (private rooms). For help in Riomaggiore, call **Edi,** V. Colombo 111. (☎92 03 25; edi-vesigna@iol.it.) Popular with students, **▐Hotel Souvenir ❷,** V. Gioberti 30, Monterosso, has 47 beds and a friendly staff. (☎/fax 81 75 95. Doubles €50-80; triples €75-120. Cash only.) **▐Ostello Cinque Terre ❷,** V. B. Riccobaldi 21, in Manarola, is modern with a sweeping roof terrace. Turn right from the train station and continue up the hill. (☎92 02 15; www.hostel5terre.com. Bike, kayak, and snorkeling equipment rental. Breakfast €4. Laundry €6. Curfew 1am, midnight in winter. Dorms €22. MC/V.) All 23 rooms at **Hotel Gianni Franzi ❹,** P. Marconi 1, in Vernazza, have lovely antiques. (☎82 10 03; www.giannifranzi.it. Singles €42-65; doubles €60-85; triples €105. AmEx/MC/V.) **Mar-Mar ❷,** V. Malborghetto 4, in Riomaggiore, rents dorms and private rooms with bath. (☎92 09 32; www.5terre-marmar.com. Dorms €20; doubles €65-90. Cash only.)

Meals at **▐Il Ciliegio ❷,** Località Beo, in Monterosso, near P. Garibaldi, feature ingredients from the owner's garden. (☎81 78 29. *Primi* €6-10. *Secondi* €7-13. Open Tu-Su 12:30-2:30pm and 7:30-10:30pm. AmEx/MC/V.) **Focacceria Il Frantoio ❶,** V. Gioberti 1, in Monterosso, bakes mouth-watering focaccia (€1-3) stuffed with olives, herbs, and more. (☎81 83 33. Open M-W and F-Su 9am-2pm and 3:30-8pm. Cash only.) Vernazza's oldest *trattoria*, **Trattoria Gianni Franzi ❷,** P. Marconi 1, offers local specialties and is famed for its pesto. (☎82 10 03. *Primi* €4-12. *Secondi* €6-20. Open M-Tu and Th-Su noon-3pm and 7:30-9:30pm. AmEx/MC/V.) **Ripa del Sole ❸,**

**GIVING BACK**

## THE BEATEN PATH

Cinque Terre is doubtless a paradise for hikers, with trails connecting cliff-hugging towns along the mountainous shore of the Ligurian coast. Its beauty has even earned its inclusion on the UNESCO World Heritage List. The uniqueness of this land, however, is far from undiscovered, and the tourist stands that line the main streets of the towns offer proof of just that.

Even the picturesque trails, far into the brush, have been unable to escape tourism's impact. The shoes that have packed down the dirt trails have caused deterioration to the landscape, causing it to go (literally) downhill. In response, Cinque Terre was placed on the "World Monument Fund's List of 100 Sites at Risk," and workers at the Parco Nazionale delle Cinque Terre are committed to its restoration.

The Park's Landscape University organizes work camps to rebuild stone walls and stabilize trails. In exchange for your able hands, you will gain knowledge of the region's geography, customs, and specialized work techniques (hopefully perching on precarious cliffs doesn't faze you) and contribute to an effort that will ultimately enhance and preserve this vibrant patch of earth.

*For more info, contact the Parco Nazionale delle Cinque Terre (☎0187 76 00 00; info@parconazionale5terre.it).*

V. de Gasperi 282, in Riomaggiore, serves some of the area's best seafood. (☎92 07 43. *Primi* €9.50. *Secondi* €9-21. Open Tu-Su noon-2pm and 7-10pm. AmEx/MC/V.) Get groceries at **SuperCONAD Margherita**, P. Matteotti 9, Monterosso. (Open June-Sept. M-Sa 8am-1pm and 5-8pm, Su 8am-1pm. MC/V.)

**◪◧ OUTDOOR ACTIVITIES AND NIGHTLIFE.** The best sights in Cinque Terre are the five villages themselves, and the gorgeous paths that connect them. Monterosso has Cinque Terre's largest free **beach,** in front of the historic center, sheltered by a cliff cove. The hike between Monterosso and Vernazza (1½hr.) is considered the most difficult, with steep climbs winding past terraced vineyards and hillside cottages. From there, the trip to Corniglia (1½hr.) offers breathtaking views of the sea and olive groves, with scents of rosemary, lemon, and lavender. Near Corniglia, the secluded **Guvano Beach,** accessed through a tunnel, is popular with students and adventurous types willing to make the trek down the mountain. Take the stairs down to the station from V. della Stazione in Corniglia and turn left, following the path along the railroad tracks to the public beach; the hike to youthful Manarola (1hr.) begins just past the beach, and is easier, though less picturesque. The most famous Cinque Terre hike, the **Via dell'Amore,** from Manarola to Riomaggiore, the smallest of the five towns, is a 20min. slate-paved walk that features a stone tunnel of love decorated in graffiti with romantic scenes.

At night, the liveliest towns are Monterosso and Riomaggiore. In Monterosso, **Il Casello,** V. Lungo Fessario 70, lures backpackers with its beachside location. (Wine from €3. Mixed drinks from €6. Open daily noon-midnight. Cash only.) **Bar Centrale,** V. C. Colombo 144, Riomaggiore, caters to a young, international crowd. (Beer €2-4. Mixed drinks €4-6. Open daily 7:30am-1am. Cash only.)

## LA SPEZIA                                                                    ☎0187

Though the laid-back beach ambience of Cinque Terre is only a short ride away, La Spezia's fast-paced urban center seems like another world. The town is a great starting point for daytrips to the small fishing villages, beach resorts, and hidden coves in the area; it's also an unavoidable stopover to and from Cinque Terre. The unique collection of the **Museo Navale,** in P. Chiodo next to the **Arsenale Militare Marittimo** (Maritime Military Arsenal), features gargantuan iron anchors and tiny replicas of Egyptian, Roman, and European vessels. (☎78 30 16. Open M-Sa 8am-6:45pm, Su 8am-1pm. €1.60. Cash only.) **Albergo Il Sole ❷,** V. Cavallotti 3, offers spacious rooms. (☎73 51 64. Singles €25-35; doubles €45-55; triples €53-61; quads €80-92. MC/V.) Reasonably priced *trattorie* line V. del Prione. Groceries are available at **Supermercato Spesafacile,** V. Colombo 101. (Open M-Sa 8:30am-1pm and 4:15-8pm. MC/V.) La Spezia lies on the Genoa-Pisa train line, with frequent service to Cinque Terre. **Navigazione Golfo dei Poeti,** V. d. Minzoni 13 (☎73 29 87; www.navigazionegolfodeipoeti.it), runs **ferries** that stop in each of the five villages (€12, round-trip €21-23). The **tourist office,** V. Mazzini 45, is at the port. (☎25 43 11. Open M-Sa 9:30am-1pm and 3:30-7pm, Su 9:30am-1pm.) **Postal Code:** 19100.

# EMILIA-ROMAGNA

Go to Florence, Venice, and Rome to sightsee. Come to Emilia-Romagna to eat. Italy's wealthy wheat- and dairy-producing region covers the fertile plains of the Po River Valley, whose harvest weighs tables with some of the finest culinary traditions on the peninsula, freeing visitors from the binds of the elsewhere omni-present *menù turistico*. But Emilia-Romagna deserves more than just a quick stop-over for some *Bolognese*; combining a rich history with modern cities, it's an essential destination for any Italian traveler.

# BOLOGNA                                                           ☎ 051

Affectionately referred to as the *grassa* (fat) and *dotta* (learned) city, Bologna (pop. 369,955) has a legacy of excellent food, education, and art. Bologna's muse-ums and churches house priceless artistic treasures and its university is Europe's oldest. After experiencing the city's many free sights and student-friendly night-life, visitors leave Bologna satisfied, having tasted the Italian good life. Be as cau-tious in Bologna as in a big city; guard your wallet, and don't travel solo at night.

**TRANSPORTATION AND PRACTICAL INFORMATION. Trains** leave the northern tip of Bologna's walled city for: Florence (1½hr., 39 per day, €4.80); Milan (3hr., 46 per day, €19); Rome (3hr., 36 per day, €32); Venice (2hr., 29 per day, €8.20). **Buses** #25 and 30 run between the train station and the center at **Piazza Maggiore** (€1). Alternatively, head through P. XX Settembre to V. dell'Indipen-denza, which leads to P. del Nettuno and the nearby P. Maggiore. The **tourist office**, P. Maggiore 1, is in Palazzo del Podestà. (☎24 65 41; www.iperbole.bologna.it/bolognaturismo. Open daily 9:30am-7:30pm.) **Postal Code:** 40100.

**ACCOMMODATIONS AND FOOD.** Bologna's hotels, mostly located around V. Ugo Bassi and V. Marconi, are pricey; reserve ahead, especially in summer. Take V. Ugo Bassi from P. del Nettuno, then take the third left to reach **Albergo Panorama ❹**, V. Livraghi 1, 4th fl., where sunny rooms with high ceilings look out over V. Ugo Bassi and rooftop terraces. Three sparkling bathrooms serve all 10 rooms, which have sink and TV. (☎22 18 02; www.hotelpanoramabo-logna.it. Curfew 3am. Singles €50; doubles €60-70; triples €75-85; quads €85-95; quints €100. AmEx/MC/V.) Six kilometers northeast of the *centro*, **Ostello due Torre San Sisto (HI) ❷**, V. Viadagola 5, has a basketball court and a reading room with satellite TV. Take bus #93 (301 on Su) from V. Marconi 69 (M-Sa 2 per hr.); ask the driver for the San Sisto stop. The hostel is the yellow building on the right. (☎/fax 50 18 10. Lockout 10am-3:30pm. Dorms €18; doubles €36. €3 HI dis-count. AmEx/MC/V.) From V. Marconi, turning left on V. Riva di Reno and right on V. Morgani will take you to **Bed and Breakfast Baroni ❸**, V. Morgani 9, located in a quiet area of the *centro*. (☎340 29 41 752. Singles €45-65; doubles €65, with bath €80. MC/V.) Walk down V. Rizzoli and turn right into the gallery mall for **Garisenda ❹**, Galleria Leone 1, 3rd fl. whose small rooms with French doors are right near the *centro*. (☎22 43 69; fax 22 10 07. Breakfast included. Singles €45; doubles €65, with bath €85; triples €95/115. MC/V.)

Scout **Via Augusto Righi, Via Piella,** and **Via Saragozza** for traditional *trattorie* offering Bologna's signature *spaghetti alla Bolognese*. **Nuova Pizzeria Gianna ❶**, V. S. Stefano 76A, has some of the freshest pizza in Italy, made in front of your eyes. (☎22 25 16. Pizzas from €3.20, slices from €2. Open M-Sa 8:30am-11pm. Closed 2 weeks in Aug. 10% student discount. Cash only.) **Osteria dell'Orsa ❶**, V. Mentana 1/F, is a casual joint close to nightlife that caters to students with its fresh, simple dishes and social, communal seating. (☎23 15 76. *Piadini*, pitas €3.50-4.50. 0.5L of wine €4. Open daily noon-4pm and 7pm-midnight. Cash only.) Some of the best *gelato* in Italy is churned at **Il Gelatauro ❶**, V. S. Vitale 98B, where flavors like ginger and cinnamon squash are smoother than smooth. Also

## IF YOU CAN'T TAKE THE HEAT, GET OUT OF THE KITCHEN

To take a little of the "fat" city home with you, try a class at any of Bologna's short-term culinary schools. Consult the tourist office for a complete listing.

**La Vecchia Scuola Bolognese** (☎64 93 627; www.lavecchiascuola.com) is the mother of local cooking schools, offering a four-hour course topped off by a fabulous meal. Learn to make fresh pasta from a professional, English-speaking staff. When all is said and done, you'll get to eat your own pasta creations; if your attempts don't quite succeed, you'll still be served the school's own menu of typical Bolognese specialties.

**La Cucina di Petronilla,** V. San Vitale 53 (☎22 40 11), offers 8 classes or single one-on-one lessons upon request. The courses focus on wine pairing, table preparation, and regional dishes. The chef believes in healthy organic cuisine, but fear not: it's still typical, hearty Bolognese fare.

**La Cantina Bentivoglio** (☎26 54 16; www.affari.com/bentivoglio), a classy restaurant offering delicious local cuisine and live jazz, also has demonstrations (though not lessons) of the pasta-making process. The price and length of demonstrations vary, so call to create a custom demo with the restaurant.

sells wine, chocolate, and decadent pastries. (☎23 00 49. 2 scoops €2.60. Open M 8am-7pm, Tu-Su 8am-11pm. Closed Aug. Cash only.) A **PAM** supermarket, V. Marconi 26, is at the intersection with V. Riva di Reno. (Open M-Sa 7:45am-8pm. AmEx/MC/V.)

**◫ SIGHTS.** The ancient *palazzi* and expensive boutiques in ▨**Piazza Maggiore** are dwarfed by the Romanesque **Palazzo del Podestà,** designed by Aristotle Fioravanti, who also designed Moscow's Kremlin. The nearby **Basilica di San Petronio,** P. Maggiore 3, was meant to be larger than St. Peter's in Rome, but the jealous church leadership ordered that the funds instead be used to build the nearby **Palazzo Archiginnasio.** The basilica hosted both the Council of Trent (when it wasn't meeting in Trent) and the 1530 ceremony in which Pope Clement VII gave Italy to the German King Charles V. The world's largest zodiac sundial extends over the church floor from the base of the nave. (Basilica open daily 9:30am-12:30pm and 2:30-5:30pm. Free.) The Palazzo Archiginnasio, behind S. Petronio, was the first home of Bologna's modern university; the **Teatro Anatomico,** a wooden lecture hall, is above the central courtyard's arches. (V. Archiginnasio 1. Open M-F 9am-1pm. Free.) **Piazza del Nettuno** contains Giambologna's 16th-century fountain, **Neptune and Attendants.** Nearby, a series of portrait tiles commemorates the Bolognese resistance to Nazi occupation, while a plexiglass memorial recalls more recent victims of terrorism. Two towers rise from P. Porta Ravegana, at the end of V. Rizzoli; the **Torre degli Garisenda** leans violently to one side, but the nearly 98m **Torre degli Asinelli** is climbable. (Open daily 9am-6pm. €3.) From V. Rizzoli, follow V. S. Stefano to P. S. Stefano, where the Romanesque ▨**Chiesa Santo Stefano** stands on the remains of an Egyptian temple and contains the basin where Pontius Pilate absolved himself of responsibility for Christ's death. Bologna's patron saint, San Petronio, lies buried under the pulpit of the **Chiesa di San Sepolcro.** (☎22 32 56. Modest dress required. Open M-Sa 9am-noon and 3:30-6:45pm, Su 9am-12:45pm and 3:30-7pm. Free.) The **Pinacoteca Nazionale,** V. delle Belle Arti 56, off V. Zamboni, traces the history of Bolognese art. (☎42 09 411. Open Tu-Su 9am-7pm. €4, EU students €2.)

**▨ ♫ NIGHTLIFE AND ENTERTAINMENT.** Bologna's hip students account for the ample number of bars and clubs (and a disproportionate number of pubs) in the city and ensure raucous nighttime fun, especially around V. Zamboni. In June and July, clubs close and the party scene moves outdoors.

**Cluricaune,** V. Zamboni 18/B, a multi-level Irish pub, ropes in students with its beer selection. (☎26 34 19. Pints €3.10-4.20. Happy hour W 7-10:30pm; pints €2.50. Open daily noon-3am.) **Cassero,** located in a 17th-century salt warehouse in the Porta Saragozza, is popular with the gay community, but all are welcome. (☎64 94 416. Drinks €3-6. ARCI-GAY card, available at ARCI-GAY, V. Don Minzoni 18, required. Open M-F 10pm-2am, Sa-Su 10pm-5am.) Every year from mid-June to mid-September, the city commune sponsors a █**festival** of art, cinema, dance, music, and theater. Many events are free, and few cost much more than €5. Visitors to Bologna during the summer should contact the tourist office for a program. The **Teatro Comunale,** Largo Respighi 1, hosts world-class operas, symphonies, and ballet. (☎52 99 99; www.comunalebologna.it. Box office open Tu-Sa 11am-6:30pm. AmEx/MC/V.)

# PARMA                                                                      ☎ 0521

Though famous for its *parmigiano* cheese and *prosciutto*, Parma's (pop. 172,000) artistic excellence is not confined to the kitchen. Giuseppe Verdi composed some of his greatest works here, and native artists Parmigianino and Correggio cultivated Mannerist painting in the 16th century. The town centers around the 11th-century **duomo** where Correggio's *Virgin* ascends to a golden heaven, and the pink-and-white marble **baptistry** displays early Medieval frescoes of enthroned saints and apostles. From P. Garibaldi, follow Str. Cavour and take the third right on Str. al Duomo. (*Duomo* open daily 9am-12:30pm and 3-6:30pm. Baptistry open daily 9am-12:30pm and 3-6:30pm. Duomo free. Baptistry €4, students €3.) Built in 1521 to house a miraculous picture of the Virgin Mary, the **Chiesa Magistrale di Santa Maria della Steccata,** up V. Garibaldi from P. Garibaldi, features frescoes by Parmigianino on the arch above the presbytery. Ask the priest to see the **Crypt of the Garnese Dukes.** (Open daily 7:30am-noon and 3-6:30pm. Free.) From P. del Duomo, follow Str. al Duomo across Str. Cavour, walk one block down Str. Piscane, and cross P. della Pace to reach the 17th-century **Palazzo della Pilotta,** with the **Galleria Nazionale** and the wooden **Teatro Farnese.** (Both open Tu-Su 8:30am-1:45pm. Ticket office closes 1pm. Theater €2, students €1. Gallery €6, students €4.)

Take bus #2, 2N, or 13 from the bus station to the brand new █**Ostello della Gioventu (HI) ❷**, Via San Leonardo 86, and its young, English-speaking staff. (☎19 17 547; www.ostelloparma.it. Reception 24hr. Dorms €18; singles €21; doubles €40; triples €59; quads €76.) **Albergo Leon d'Oro ❸**, V. Fratti 4a, after intersection with Str. Garibaldi, has clean, basic rooms with shared bath. (☎77 31 82; www.leondoroparma.com. Singles €35-55; doubles €60-80. AmEx/MC/V.) Resist the urge to dine outside on one of Parma's many patios, and eat downstairs in the 14th-century stone building of **Ristorante Gallo d'Oro ❷**, Borgo della Salina 3. From P. Garibaldi, take Str. Farini and turn left. (☎20 88 46. *Primi* €6.50-9. *Secondi* €6.50-10. Cover €2. Open M-Sa noon-2:30pm and 7:30-11pm. AmEx/MC/V.) **K2,** Str. Cairoli 23, next to the Chiesa di San Giovanni Evangelista, tops each cone with creamy *gelato* in a flower shape. (*Gelato* from €1.50. Open M-Tu and Th-Su 11am-midnight. Cash only.) An **open-air market** comes to P. Ghiaia, off V. Marcotti near the intersection with Str. Mazzini, every Wednesday and Saturday morning 8am-1pm and Wednesday and Friday nights in summer. **Dimeglio** supermarket is at Str. Ventidue Luglio 27/c. (Open daily 8:30am-1:30pm and 4:30-8pm.) **Trains** go from P. Carlo Alberto della Chiesa to: Bologna (1hr., 3 per hr., €4.90); Florence (2hr., 3 per day, €9.20); Milan (1½hr., 3-5 per hr., €7.10). Walk left on V. Bottego from the station, turn right on Str. Garibaldi, then left on Str. Melloni to reach the **tourist office,** Str. Melloni 1/A. (☎21 88 89; www.turismo.comune.parma.it. Open M 9am-1pm and 3-7pm, Tu-Sa 9am-7pm, Su 9am-1pm.) **Postal Code:** 43100.

**ITALY**

# RAVENNA
☎0544

Ravenna (pop. 150,000) enjoyed its 15 minutes of fame 14 centuries ago, when Justinian and Theodora, rulers of the Byzantine Empire, made it the headquarters of their western campaign. They created a thriving artistic culture, evident today in the city's omnipresent mosaics. Take V. Argentario from V. Cavour to reach the 6th-century ▨Basilica di San Vitale, V. S. Vitale 17, whose thin windows let in enough light to make its mosaics glow. On either side, Byzantine mosaics depict Empress Theodora and Emperor Justinian. Across the courtyard is the tiny brick **Mausoleo di Galla Placidia,** where a single lamp illuminates 570 gold stars against a brilliant night sky. Around the sides are three stone sarcophagi. (☎21 62 92. Open daily Apr.-Sept. 9am-7pm; Mar. and Oct. 9am-5:30pm; Nov.-Feb. 10am-5pm.) To see the pastoral mosaics in the **Basilica di Sant'Apollinare,** take bus #4 or 44 across from the train station (€0.75) to Classe. (Basilica open M-Sa 8:30am-7:30pm, Su 9am-7pm. €3, under 18 free.) Ravenna's most popular monument is the unassuming, green-domed **Tomb of Dante Alighieri,** who was exiled from Florence in 1301 and died in Ravenna in 1321. The adjoining **Dante Museum** contains Wostry Carlo's illustrations of the poet's works, the fir chest that held Dante's bones, and 18,000 scholarly volumes on his works. From P. del Popolo, cut through P. Garibaldi to V. D. Alighieri. (☎33 667. Tomb open daily 9am-7pm. Free. Museum open Tu-Su Apr.-Sept. 9am-noon and 3:30-6pm; Oct.-Mar. 9am-noon. €2.)

From P. Farini, walk down Vle. Farini and make a left on V. Roma to get to a former orphanage that's now the luxurious ▨Ostello Galletti Abbiosi ❶, V. Roma 140. (☎/fax 31 313; www.galletti.ra.it. Breakfast included. Free Wi-Fi. Reception M-F 8am-6:30pm, Sa-Su 8am-6pm. Singles €55-60; doubles €80-100; triples €100-110; quads €120-130. AmEx/MC/V.) Take bus #70 or 80 from the train station (3-6 per hr., €1) to reach **Ostello Dante (HI) ❷,** V. Nicolodi 12, a basic hostel with a well-stocked common room. (☎42 11 64. Breakfast included. Laundry €2.50. Internet 1st 10min. free, €3 per hr. thereafter. Lockout 10am-3:30pm. Curfew 11:30pm; €1 key deposit. Dorms €17; family rooms €16 per person. €3 HI discount. MC/V.) **Piazza del Popolo** has a number of authentic restaurants and cafes. Feast on delicious thin-crust pizzas (€2-8) and local specialties like *cappaletti con ragu* (pasta with meat sauce; €6.50) at the small outdoor tables of **Babaleus ❷,** Vicolo Gabbani 7, on a quiet side street behind the *mercato coperto.* (☎21 64 64. *Primi* €6.50. *Secondi* €7-13. Open M-Tu, Th-Su noon-2:30pm and 7pm-midnight. AmEx/MC/V.) **Trains** run from P. Farini to Bologna (1hr., 1 per hr., €5) and Ferrara (1hr., 1 per hr., €4.50), with connections to Florence and Venice. Follow V. Farini from the station to V. Diaz and the central P. del Popolo to find the **tourist office,** V. Salara 8. (☎35 404; www.turismo.ravenna.it. Open Apr.-Sept. M-Sa 8:30am-7pm, Su 10am-6pm; Oct.-Mar. M-Sa 8:30am-6pm.) **Postal Code:** 48100.

# RIMINI
☎0541

The Ibiza of the Adriatic, Rimini is the party town of choice for young European fashionistas. Beaches, nightclubs, and boardwalks crammed with boutiques, fortune tellers, and artists characterize a city where it is perfectly acceptable—and admirable—to collapse into bed and bid the rising sun good night. Rimini's most treasured attraction is its remarkable **beach** with fine sand and mild Adriatic waves. Hotels reserve strips of beach with chairs and umbrellas for their guests, though non-guests can slip in for €3.50; there's also a public beach at the end of the shore. To reach the beach from the train station in **Piazzale Cesare Battisti,** turn right from the station, again into the tunnel at the yellow arrow indicating *"al mare,"* and follow Vle. Principe Amedeo. Rimini's nightlife heats up around the *lungomare* in southern Rimini and near the port. Bus #11 fills with rowdy partygoers as it traverses the strip of clubs. At █**Coconuts,** Lungomare Tintorin 5, a diverse crowd gathers until the wee hours for the tropical decor, two outdoor dance floors, and the platform dancers. (☎52 35; www.coconuts.it. Drinks €4-8. Open daily 6pm-5am.) From Coconuts, continue walking north along the *lungomare* to find **Rock Island by Black Jack,** at the farthest point from shore, on a pier. In the evening, the restaurant offers seafood specialties and classy beachside ambience. Later on, the lights of Rimini sparkle from the outdoor bar and dance floor. (☎50 178; www.rockislandrimini.com. Open Tu-Su. Dinner served 7:30pm-midnight; dancing until late. Reserve ahead for dinner.) **Spazi,** P. Cavour 5, a trendy bar right in the *centro,* caters to older crowds and those looking for a more relaxing night. (☎23 439. Wine from €3. Open M-Sa 5pm-2am. MC/V.)

**Hostel Jammin' Rimini (HI) ❷,** Vle. Derna 22, is at stop 13 of bus #11. Seconds from the beach, the brand-new hostel accommodates the Rimini partying lifestyle with a social bar, no lockout, and breakfast until 10:30am. (Breakfast and linens included. Open Feb.-Dec. Dorms €19. AmEx/MC/V.) After overspending on drinks, get groceries at the **STANDA** supermarket, V. Vespucci 13. (Open daily 8am-9pm. AmEx/MC/V.) **Trains** (☎89 20 21) run to Bologna (1½hr., 2 per hr., €6.70), Milan (3hr., 1 per hr., €28), and Ravenna (1hr., 1 per hr., €3). The **IAT tourist office** is at P. Fellini 3, stop 10 on bus #11. (Open in summer M-Sa 8:30am-7:30pm, Su 8:30am-2:30pm; winter M-Sa 9am-12:30pm and 3:30-6pm.) **Postal Code:** 47900.

# FERRARA                                                                    ☎ 0532

Rome has mopeds, Venice has gondolas, and Ferrara has *biciclette* (bicycles). In a city with 160,000 bicycles for 130,000 residents, bikers are a more common sight than pedestrians. Amid bike traffic, an imposing castle and *palazzi* fill the *centro*. Art from Ferrara's own school of painting hangs in the palaces and monuments. The **medieval wall** supports a 9km bike path with views of the city. The 14th-century █**Castello Estense** is surrounded by a fairytale moat. Inside, themed rooms, gardens, and dungeon tunnels wind through this former fortress. (☎29 92 33. Open Tu-Su 9:30am-5:30pm. €6, under 18 and over 65 €5. Audio tour €3.) From the *castello*, take C. Martiri della Libertà to P. Cattedrale and the rose-windowed **Duomo San Romano,** across V. S. Romano from the **Museo della Cattedrale,** home to the church's precious works. (*Duomo* open M-Sa 7:30am-noon and 3-6:30pm, Su 7:30am-12:30pm and 3:30-7:30pm. Museum open Tu-Su 9am-1pm and 3-6pm. €5, students €3.) From the *castello*, cross Largo Castello to C. Ercole I d'Este and walk to its intersection with C. Rossetti to reach the **Palazzo Diamanti,** whose facade is covered by white pyramid-shaped studs. Within, the **Pinacoteca Nazionale** holds works from the Ferrarese school and panels by El Greco. (Open Tu-W and F-Sa 9am-2pm, Th 9am-7pm, Su 9am-1pm. €4, students €2.) Follow C. Ercole I d'Este behind the *castello* to find the **Palazzo Massari,** C. Porta Mare 9, home to **Padiglione d'Arte Contemporanea, Museo d'Arte Moderna e Contemporanea Filippo de Pisis,** and tapestry-walled **Museo Ferrarese dell'Ottocentro/Museo Giovanni Boldini,** dedicated to the artist of its title. (All open Tu-Su 9am-1pm and 3-6pm. Filippo de Pisis €3, students €2. Ottocentro/Boldini €5/3. Combination ticket €8/3.)

█**Pensione Artisti ❷,** V. Vittoria 66, near P. Lampronti, offers free bike use and a shared kitchen. From C. Martiri d. Libertà, turn left at the cathedral, right on V. S. Romano, left on V. Ragno, then immediately left to reach the Pensione. (☎76 10 38. Singles €25; doubles €48, with bath €60. Cash only.) Regional fare graces plates in the 16th-century dining room at **Osteria Degli Angeli ❸,** V. delle Volte 4. From the *basilica*, take C. Porta Reno and turn left under the arch. (*Primi* €7-8. *Secondi* €7-15. Open daily 6-11pm; kitchen open 7-10pm. MC/V.) Italy's oldest *osteria*, **Osteria Al Brindisi ❸**, V. G. degli Adelardi 11, has wined and dined the likes of Titian and Pope John Paul II since 1435. (☎20 91 42. Cover €2. Open Tu-Su 9am-1am. MC/V.) For groceries, stop by **Supermercato Conad,** V. Garibaldi 53. (Open M-Sa 8:30am-8pm, Su 9:15am-1:15pm. MC/V.)

**Trains** go to: Bologna (30min., 3 per hr., €3); Padua (1hr., 2 per hr., €4.40); Ravenna (1hr., 1 per hr., €4.40); Rome (3-4hr., 12 per day, €23); Venice (1½hr., 1-2 per hr., €6.10). ACFT (☎59 94 92) and GGFP **buses** run from the train station to local beaches (1½hr., 12 per day, €4.30) and Bologna (1½hr., 15 per day, €3.40). Rent **bikes** at **Pirani e Bagni,** P. Stazione 2. (☎77 21 90. €2 per hr., €7 per day. Open M-F 7am-8pm, Sa 6am-2pm. Cash only.) To get to the *centro*, turn left out of the train station onto Viale Costituzione. This road becomes Viale Cavour and runs to the Castello Estense (1km). Or, take bus #2 to Castello (3 per hr., €0.90). The **tourist office** is in Castello Estense. (☎20 93 70. Open M-Sa 9am-1pm and 2-6pm, Su 9:30am-1pm and 2-5:30pm.) **Postal Code:** 44100

# TRENTINO-ALTO ADIGE

With its steep mountain trails and small towns largely free of tourist mobs, Trentino-Alto Adige appeals to outdoor enthusiasts. The near-impenetrable dolomitic rock has slowed major industrialization, preserving the jagged pink-purple cliffs of the Dolomites and evergreen forests that Le Corbusier once called "the most beautiful natural architecture in the world."

## TRENT (TRENTO)                                     ☎0461

Between the Dolomites and the Veneto, Trent (pop. 105,000) offers a sampling of northern Italian life with festivals, delicious food, and spectacular scenery. The **Piazza del Duomo,** Trent's epicenter, is anchored by the massive **Fontana del Nettuno** in the center of the *piazza*. Nearby is the **Cattedrale di San Vigilio,** where the Council of Trent first called for the Counter-Reformation. (Open daily 7am-noon and 2:30-6pm. Free.) Walk down V. Belenzani and head right on V. Roma to reach the historic **Castello del Buonconsiglio,** home to the execution site of famed Trentino martyrs Cesare Battisti, Damiano Chiesa, and Fabio Filzi. During WWI, the three men joined the Italian army, but because Trent was then a part of Austria-Hungry, they were identified as Austrian subjects and executed as traitors. (www.buonconsiglio.it. Open Tu-Su 9:30am-5pm. €6, students €3.) Check out the nearby **Museo Diocesano's** collection of restored tapestries, paintings, and manuscripts. (Open M and W-Su 9:30am-12:30pm and 2:30-6pm. €4, students €2.50.) From the station, turn right on V. Pozzo, then right on V. Torre Vanga to get to the tidy rooms of **Ostello Giovane Europa (HI) ❶,** V. Torre Vanga 11. (☎26 34 84. Breakfast included. Reception 7:30am-11pm. Ask for door code if returning after 11:30pm. Dorms €14; singles €25; doubles €40. AmEx/MC/V.) **Hotel Venezia ❹,** P. Duomo 45, offers rooms across from the *duomo*. (☎23 41 14. Singles €49; doubles €69. MC/V.) Head to the casual ⬛**Alla Grotta ❷,** Vico S. Marco 6, for huge pizzas piled high with toppings. (☎98 71 97. Pizza €4.10-7.20. *Primi* €5.60-7.20. Open noon-2:30pm and 6:30pm-midnight. MC/V.) For advice on local trails, festivals, and guided tours, head to the **tourist office,** V. Manci 2. Turn right from the train station and left on V. Roma, which becomes V. Manci. (☎21 60 00; www.apt.trento.it. Open daily 9am-7pm.) **Postal Code:** 38100.

## BOLZANO (BOZEN)                    ☎ 0471

German street names in Bolzano (pop. 100,000) alert visitors to the town's Italian-Austrian cultural fusion, while hikes among the snowy peaks and grassy rivers of the pre-Alps are its main draw. Gothic spires rise skyward from the Romanesque **duomo**, in P. Walther. (Open M-F 9:45am-noon and 2-5pm, Sa 9:45am-noon. Free.) At the **South Tyrol Museum of Archaeology**, V. Museo 43, near Ponte Talvera, tourists file by the freezer holding **Ötzi**, a 5000-year-old frozen Neanderthal. (Open Tu-W and F-Su 10am-5pm, Th 10am-7pm. €8, students €6.) The best hikes are accessible by the three *funivie* (funiculars) surrounding the town, especially **Funivia San Genesio.** Take a right from the train station and walk 5min. to reach the ▓**Youth Hostel Bolzano ❷,** V. Renon 22, where guests enjoy clean rooms and lots of amenities. (☎30 08 65. Breakfast included. Internet €2 per hr. Reception 8am-9pm. Dorms €21. €2 discount for longer stays. AmEx/MC/V.) The markets of **Piazza delle Erbe** and the **wurst stand** at the intersection of V. Museo and P. delle Erbe allow visitors to sample Bolzano's Austrian-influenced fare. (Market open M-F 7am-7pm, Sa 8am-1pm; wurst stand open M-Sa 8am-7pm). The **tourist office,** P. Walther 8, is near the *duomo.* (☎30 70 00; www.bolzano-bozen.it. Open M-F 9am-1pm and 2-7pm, Sa 9am-2pm.) **Postal Code:** 39100.

# THE VENETO

From the rocky foothills of the Dolomites to the fertile valleys of the Po River, the Veneto's geography is as diverse as its history. Once loosely united under the Venetian Empire, its towns have retained their cultural independence; in fact, visitors are more likely to hear regional dialects than standard Italian during neighborly exchanges. The tenacity of local culture and customs will come as a pleasant surprise for those expecting only mandolins and gondolas.

# VENICE (VENEZIA)                    ☎ 041

In Venice (pop. 60,000), palaces stand tall on a steadily sinking network of wood, and the waters of age-old canals creep up the mossy steps of abandoned homes. People flock year-round to peer into delicate blown-glass and gaze at the masterworks of Tintoretto and Titian. Though hordes of tourists and pigeons are inescapable, the city proves to be a unique source of wonder.

## ▟ TRANSPORTATION

The **train station** is on the northwest edge of the city; be sure to get off at **Santa Lucia,** not at Mestre on the mainland. Buses and boats arrive at **Piazzale Roma,** just across the Canal Grande from the train station. To get from either station to **Piazza San Marco,** take *vaporetto* (water bus) #82 or follow signs for a 40min. walk.

**Flights: Aeroporto Marco Polo (VCE;** ☎26 09 260; www.veniceairport.it), 10km north of the city. Take the **ATVO shuttlebus** (☎042 13 83 671) from the airport to Ple. Roma on the main island (30min., 1 per hr. 8am-midnight, €3).

**Trains: Stazione Santa Lucia.** Ticket windows open M-F 8:30am-7:30pm, Sa-Su 9am-1:30pm and 2-5:30pm. **Information office** (☎89 20 21) to the left as you exit the platforms. Open daily 7am-9pm. Trains go to: **Bologna** (2hr., 30 per day, €8.20); **Florence**

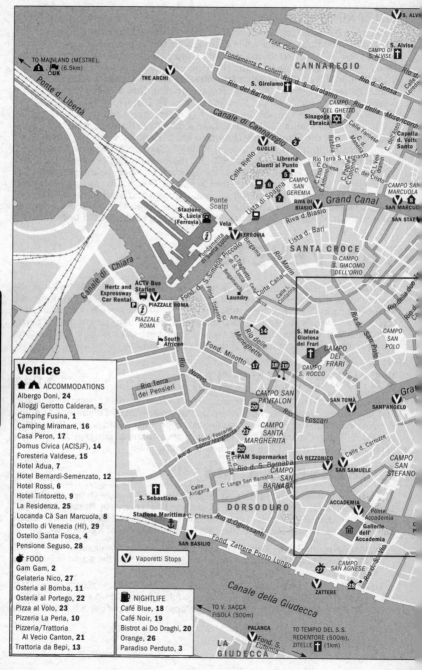

**ITALY**

TO MAINLAND (MESTRE),
OUK (6.5km)

Ponte d. Libertà

TRE ARCHI

CANNAREGIO

S. ALVI
S. Alvise
CAMPO DI
S. ALVISE
Fond. Contarini
Rio d.
Rio d. Sensa

Fondamenta C. Colletti Rio d. S. Girolamo
S. Girolamo
Rio del Battello

Canale di Cannaregio

CAMPO
DEL GHETTO
Rio della
Sinagoga
Ebraica

Rio della Misericordia
Capella
d. Volto
Santo

GUGLIE

Libreria
Giunti al Punto

Calle Riello

Rio Terra S. Leonardo

CAMPO
SAN
MARCUOLA
SAN MARCUO

SAN STAE

Lista di Spagna

CAMPO
SAN
GEREMIA

RIVA DI
BIASIO
Riva d.Biasio

Grand Canal

Ponte
Scalzi

Lista di Bari

Stazione
S. Lucia
(Ferrovia)

Ponte d. Libertà

Vela

FERROVIA

SANTA CROCE

CAMPO
S. GIACOMO
DELL'ORIO

Canale di Chiara

Fondamenta
di Simeon Piccolo

Rio Marin

Bergamo

Corte Canal

Laundry

Rio della

CAMPO
SAN
POLO

ACTV Bus
Station
PIAZZALE ROMA

Hertz and
Expressway
Car Rental

PIAZZALE
ROMA

South
African

Laundry

C. Amai

Rio delle
Muneghette

S. Maria
Gloriosa
dei Frari

CAMPO
DEI
FRARI

Rio di San Polo

Fond. d. Tolentini

14

18 19

CAMPO
S. ROCCO

Rio della

Fond. Minotto

Rio Nuovo

Rio Terra
dei Pensieri

17

CAMPO SAN
PANTALON

20

Rio
Foscari

SAN TOMÀ

SANT'ANGELO

Gra

CAMPO
SAN
STEFANO

CAMPO
SANTA
MARGHERITA

23

Fond. Foscarini
Rio d. Santa Margherita

26

PAM Supermarket

CÀ REZZONICO

Calle d. Carrozze

CAMPO
SAN
SAMUELE

S. Sebastiano

Rio d. S. Barnaba
CAMPO
SAN
BARNABA

Calle
Avogaria

C. Lunga San Barnaba

DORSODURO

ACCADEMIA

Stazione Marittima
C. Chiesa
Rio d'Ognissanti

Ponte
Accademia

Gallerie
dell'
Accademia

SAN BASILIO

Fond. Zattere Ponto Lungo

CAMPO
SAN AGNESE

27

28

ZATTERE

Canale della Giudecca

TO V. SACCA
FISOLA (500m)

PALANCA

Fond. S.
Eufemia

LA
GIUDECCA

TO TEMPIO DEL S.S.
REDENTORE (500m),
ZITELLE (1km)

## Venice

### 🏠 ⛺ ACCOMMODATIONS
Albergo Doni, **24**
Alloggi Gerotto Calderan, **5**
Camping Fusina, **1**
Camping Miramare, **16**
Casa Peron, **17**
Domus Civica (ACISJF), **14**
Foresteria Valdese, **15**
Hotel Adua, **7**
Hotel Bernardi-Semenzato, **12**
Hotel Rossi, **6**
Hotel Tintoretto, **9**
La Residenza, **25**
Locanda Cà San Marcuola, **8**
Ostello di Venezia (HI), **29**
Ostello Santa Fosca, **4**
Pensione Seguso, **28**

### 🍴 FOOD
Gam Gam, **2**
Gelateria Nico, **27**
Osteria al Bomba, **11**
Osteria al Portego, **22**
Pizza al Volo, **23**
Pizzeria La Perla, **10**
Pizzeria/Trattoria
  Al Vecio Canton, **21**
Trattoria da Bepi, **13**

🅥 Vaporetti Stops

### 🌙 NIGHTLIFE
Café Blue, **18**
Café Noir, **19**
Bistrot ai Do Draghi, **20**
Orange, **26**
Paradiso Perduto, **3**

TO MURANO (1.5km), ↗ CIMITERO 🚤
TORCELLO (4km), BURANO (7km),
AEROPORTO MARCO POLO ✈ (10km),

ORTO 🚤

Chiesa della
Madonna dell'Orto †

Sacca
della
Misericordia

Isola di San
Michele

Canale delle Fondamente Nuove

S. Maria
Valverde †

Madonna dell'Orto

Rio Tarmatin

3⃝

S. Fosca †

9⃝

Calle Loredan

Rio di Noale

Chiesa
dei Gesuiti †

CAMPO
DEL GESUITI

Calle Larga
dei Botteri

FONDAMENTE NUOVE 🚤

Fondamente Nuove

Calle Lunga Santa Caterina

Calle delle Vele

Ruga Due Pozzi

C. del Fumo

OSPEDALE 🚤

Billa
Supermarket

Strada Nuova

11⃝

12⃝

13⃝ 10⃝

Rio dei Santi Apostoli

Campo
S.S.
APOSTOLI

Ospedale
Civile ✚

Cà d'Oro

CÀ D'ORO 🚤

Rio d. San Marina

S.S. Giovanni
e Paolo †

Barbaria delle Tole

C. d. Cappuccine

CELESTIA 🚤

0    200 meters

0    200 yards.

N

AN POLO

Ponte
di Rialto

Riva del Vin

SILVESTRO
🚤
RIALTO 🚤

al

Riva del Carbon

Rio di S. Salvador

Calle d. Mandola

Calle dei Fabbri

S. Luca

CAMPO
MANIN

ANGELO

N MARCO

Frezzaria

Rio di San
Mois

Rio della
Ostreghe

GIGLIO 🚤

eim

CAMPO S.
BARTOLOMEO

CAMPO
S. MARIA
FORMOSA

Sal. di S. Lio

Ruga Giuffa

Ponte
Rosso
Fava

15⃝

B. Lorenzo
C. Castello

CAMPO SAN
S LORENZO

Scuola Dalmata
San Giorgio
degli Schiavoni

S. Francesco
della Vigna †

CAMPO D.
CELESTIA

TO 16⃝
(10km)

Rio di S. Giorgio

Calle Lion  C. d. Furlani

CAMPO
BANDIERA
E MORO

Rio d. Gorne

S. Maria
Formosa †

CASTELLO

C. Corfona

S.S. 21⃝ 22⃝
Provolo

Fond.
Osmarin

S. Zaccaria †

24⃝  C. del Vin

CAMPO
S. ZACCARIA

C. d.
Madonna

Calle della Pietà

C. Pietà

25⃝ C. Crosera

C. del
Dose

C. del
Forno

TO ARSENALE
(150m)

Rio dell'Arsenale

SALUTE 🚤

S. Maria
della Salute †

PIAZZA
SAN MARCO

San
Marco †

Palazzo
Ducale

i

i

SAN MARCO 🚤

Riva   degli   Schiavoni

S. ZACCARIA 🚤

ARSENALE 🚤

TO GIARDINI
PUBLICI (250m)

**SEE CENTRAL VENICE MAP, P. 672**

Canale di San Marco

SAN GIORGIO 🚤

S. Giorgio
Maggiore †

Isola di
S. Giorgio
Maggiore

TO LIDO (2km)

ZITELLE 🚤 ← TO 29⃝ (100m)

Fond. delle Zitelle

Zattere ai Saloni

Rio di Fornace

ITALY

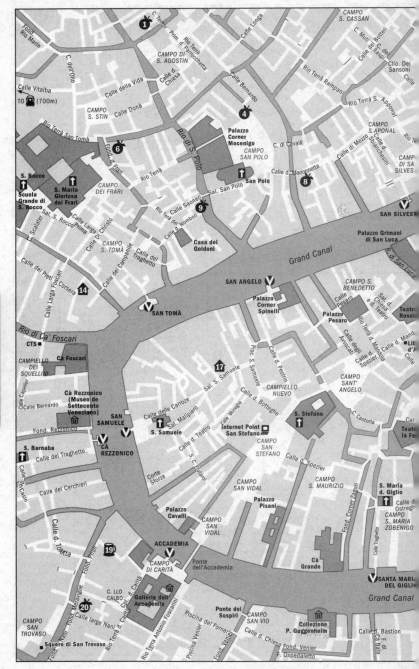

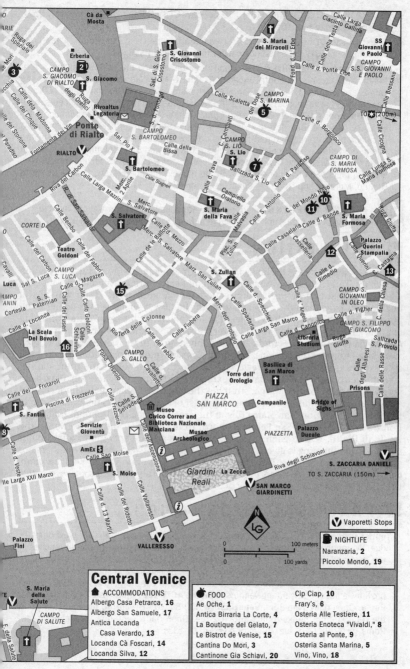

**Central Venice**

⌂ ACCOMMODATIONS
Albergo Casa Petrarca, **16**
Albergo San Samuele, **17**
Antica Locanda
  Casa Verardo, **13**
Locanda Cà Foscari, **14**
Locanda Silva, **12**

🍴 FOOD
Ae Oche, **1**
Antica Birraria La Corte, **4**
La Boutique del Gelato, **7**
Le Bistrot de Venise, **15**
Cantina Do Mori, **3**
Cantinone Gia Schiavi, **20**

Cip Ciap, **10**
Frary's, **6**
Osteria Alle Testiere, **11**
Osteria Enoteca "Vivaldi," **8**
Osteria al Ponte, **9**
Osteria Santa Marina, **5**
Vino, Vino, **18**

Ⓥ Vaporetti Stops

🌙 NIGHTLIFE
Naranzaria, **2**
Piccolo Mondo, **19**

(3hr., 8 per day, €30); **Milan** (3hr., 19 per day, €13); **Rome** (4½hr., 7 per day, €57). **Luggage storage** by track #14.

**Buses:** Local **ACTV** buses (☎24 24; www.hellovenezia.it), in Ple. Roma. Open daily 7:30am-8pm. **ACTV long-distance carrier** runs buses to **Padua** (1hr., 2 per hr., €4).

**Public Transportation:** The **Canal Grande** can be crossed on foot only at the Scalzi, Rialto, and Accademia *ponti* (bridges). **Traghetti** (gondola ferry boats) traverse the canals at 7 locations, including Ferrovia, San Marculola, Cà d'Oro, and Rialto (€0.50). **Vaporetti** (V; water buses) provide 24hr. service around the city, with reduced service midnight-5am (single-ride €3.50, the Canal Grande €5; 24hr. *biglietto turistico* pass €12, 3-day €25). Buy tickets at *vaporetti* stops. Stock up on tickets by asking for a pass *non timbrato* (unvalidated), then validate before boarding by inserting tickets into one of the yellow boxes at each stop. **Lines #1** (slow) and **82** (fast) run from the station down Canal Grande and Canale della Giudecca; lines **#41** and **51** circumnavigate Venice from the station to Lido; **#42** and **52** do the reverse; line **LN** runs from F. Nuove to Burano, Murano, and Lido, and connects to Torcello.

---

 **ISLAND HOPPING.** *Vaporetto* ticket prices border on extortion. Buy the 24hr. *vaporetto* pass for €12, then leap from 1 island to the next in 1 day.

---

# ◪ ORIENTATION

Venice is composed of 118 islands in a lagoon, connected to the mainland by a thin causeway. The city is a veritable labyrinth and can confuse even natives, most of whom simply set off in a general direction and patiently weave their way. If you unglue your eyes from the map and go with the flow, you'll discover some of the unexpected surprises. Yellow signs all over the city point toward the following landmarks: **Ponte di Rialto** (in the center), **Piazza San Marco** (central south), **Ponte Accademia** (southwest), **Ferrovia** (or the train station, in the northwest), and **Piazzale Roma** (south of the station). The **Canal Grande** winds through the city, creating six *sestieri* (sections): **Cannaregio** is in the north and includes the train station, Jewish ghetto, and Cà d'Oro; **Castello** extends east toward the Arsenale; **Dorsoduro**, across the bridge from S. Marco, stretches the length of Canale della Giudecca and up to Campo S. Pantalon; **Santa Croce** lies west of S. Polo, across the Canal Grande from the train station; **San Marco** fills in the area between the Ponte di Rialto and Ponte Accademia; and **San Polo** runs north from Chiesa S. Maria dei Frari to the Ponte di Rialto. Within each *sestiere*, addresses are not specific to a particular street—every building is given a number, and jumps between address numbers are completely unpredictable. If *sestiere* boundaries prove too vague, Venice's **parrochie** (parishes) provide a more defined idea of where you are; *parrochia* signs, like *sestiere* signs, are on the sides of buildings.

# ◪ PRACTICAL INFORMATION

**Tourist Office: APT,** Cal. della Ascensione, S. Marco 71/F (☎52 98 740; www.doge.it), directly opposite the basilica. Open daily 9am-3:30pm. Avoid the mobbed branches at the train and bus stations. The **Rolling Venice Card** (€4) offers discounts on transportation and at over 200 restaurants, cafes, hotels, museums, and shops for ages 14-29. Cards are valid for 1 year from date of purchase and can be purchased at APT, which provides a list of participating vendors, or at the **ACTV VeLa** office (☎27 47 650) in Ple. Roma. Open daily 7am-8pm. **VeneziaSi** (☎800 84 30 06), next to the tourist office in the train station, books rooms for a €2 fee. Open daily 8am-9pm. Branches in Ple. Roma (☎52 28 640) and the airport (☎54 15 133).

**Budget Travel: CTS,** F. Tagliapietra, Dorsoduro 3252 (☎52 05 660; www.cts.it). From Campo S. Barnaba, cross the bridge closest to church and follow the road through the *piazza*. Turn left at the foot of the large bridge. Sells discounted student plane tickets and issues ISICs. English spoken. Open M-F 9:30am-1:30pm and 2:30-6pm. MC/V.

**Pharmacy: Farmacia Italo-Inglese,** Cal. della Mandola, S. Marco 3717 (☎52 24 837). Follow Cal. Cortesia out of Campo Manin. Open Apr.-Nov. M-F 9am-1:30pm and 2:30-7:30pm, Sa 3:30-7:30pm; Dec.-Mar. M-F 9am-12:30pm and 3:45-7:30pm, Sa 3:30-7:30pm. MC/V. Pharmacies rotate staying open late-night and weekends; check the list posted in the window of any pharmacy.

**Hospital: Ospedale Civile,** Campo S. S. Giovanni e Paolo, Castello (☎52 94 111).

**Internet Access: ABColor,** Lista di Spagna, Cannaregio 220 (☎52 44 380). Look for the "@" symbol on a yellow sign, left off the main street heading from the train station. €6 per hr., students €4. Printing €0.15 per page. Open M-Sa 10am-8pm. **Internet Station,** Cannaregio 5640. Just over the bridge toward S. Marco from C. Apostoli. €4 per 30min., €7 per hr. 20% student discount with ID. Open M-Sa 10am-1pm and 3-8pm.

**Post Office: Poste Venezia Centrale,** Salizzada Fontego dei Tedeschi, S. Marco 5554 (☎27 17 111), off Campo S. Bartolomeo. Open M-Sa 8:30am-6:30pm. **Postal Codes:** 30121 (Cannaregio); 30122 (Castello); 30123 (Dorsoduro); 30135 (S. Croce); 30124 (S. Marco); 30125 (S. Polo).

# 🏠🏕 ACCOMMODATIONS AND CAMPING

Hotels in Venice are often more expensive than those elsewhere in Italy, but savvy travelers can find cheap rooms if they sniff out options early in summer. Agree on a price before booking, and reserve one month ahead. **VeneziaSi** (see **Tourist Offices,** p. 674) finds rooms on the same day, but not cheap ones. If you're looking for a miracle, try religious institutions, which often offer rooms in summer for €25-110. Options include: **Casa Murialdo,** F. Madonna dell'Orto, Cannaregio 3512 (☎71 99 33); **Domus Cavanis,** Dorsoduro 896 (☎52 87 374), near the Ponte Accademia; **Istituto Canossiano,** F. delle Romite, Dorsoduro 1323 (☎24 09 713); **Istituto Ciliota,** Cal. Muneghe S. Stefano, San Marco 2976 (☎52 04 888); **Patronato Salesiano Leone XIII,** Cal. S. Domenico, Castello 1281 (☎52 87 299). For camping, plan on a 20min. boat ride from Venice. In addition to camping options listed here, Litorale del Cavallino, on the Lido's Adriatic side, has multiple beach campgrounds.

## CANNAREGIO AND SANTA CROCE

The station area, around the Lista di Spagna, has some of Venice's best budget accommodations. Although a bit far away from some sights, the area is busy with students at night and offers easy *vaporetto* access from F. Nuove.

🏨 **Alloggi Gerotto Calderan,** Campo S. Geremia 283 (☎71 55 62; www.casagerottocalderan.com). Half hostel, half hotel, all good. Location makes it the best deal in Venice. Check-in 2pm. Check-out 10am. Curfew 12:30am. Reserve at least 15 days ahead. Dorms €25; singles €40-50; doubles €50-90; triples €75-105. 10% Rolling Venice discount; reduced prices for extended stays. Cash only. ❷

🏨 **Hotel Bernardi-Semenzato,** Cal. dell'Oca, Cannaregio 4366 (☎52 27 257; www.hotel-bernardi.com). From V: Cà d'Oro, turn right on Str. Nuova, left on Cal. del Duca, and then right. Squeaky clean, elegantly furnished rooms, all with A/C and TV. Check-out 11am. Singles €30-40; doubles €70-75, with bath €60-90; triples €95; quads €120-130. 10% Rolling Venice discount on larger rooms. AmEx/MC/V. ❸

**Locanda Cà San Marcuola,** Campo S. Marcuola, Cannaregio 1763 (☎71 60 48; www.casanmarcuola.com). From the Lista di Spagna, follow signs for S. Marcuola. 2 stone lions guard the entrance to the plush red velvet and gold-trimmed lobby. Large rooms have A/C, bath, refrigerator, and TV. Wheelchair-accessible. Breakfast included. Free Internet. Reception 24hr. Singles €70-90; doubles €120-140; triples €140-170; quads €170-200. Discount with cash payments. AmEx/MC/V. ❺

**Ostello Santa Fosca,** F. Canal, Cannaregio 2372 (☎/fax 71 57 33). From Lista di Spagna, turn into Campo S. Fosca. Cross 1st bridge and turn left on F. Canal. A brick-enclosed walkway leads to this social hostel in a series of crumbling courtyards of questionable romanticism. Internet available. Curfew July-Sept. 12:30am. Dorms €19; doubles €44. €2 ISIC or Rolling Venice discount. MC/V. ❷

**Hotel Rossi,** Lista di Spagna, Cannaregio 262 (☎71 51 64; www.hotelrossi.ve.it). Friendly owner keeps 14 spacious rooms down an alley by Lista di Spagna. A/C and small bookshelf with multilingual selection. Breakfast included. Reception 24hr. June-Sept. reserve ahead. Singles €44-53, with bath €54-69; doubles €64-92; triples €92-112; quads €107-132. 10% Rolling Venice discount. MC/V. ❹

**Hotel Adua,** Lista di Spagna, Cannaregio 233/A (☎71 61 84; www.aduahotel.com). Decor and mosaic lights create a serene feel in large rooms with A/C and TV. Singles €70, with bath €90; doubles €110/140; triples €170. AmEx/MC/V. ❺

**Hotel Tintoretto,** Campo S. Fosca 2316 (☎72 15 22; www.hoteltintoretto.com). Head down Lista di Spagna from the station and follow the signs. Rooms have A/C, bath, and TV. Breakfast included. Reception 24hr. Singles €41-140; doubles €74-195. Extra bed €37. Prices vary seasonally. AmEx/MC/V. ❹

## SAN MARCO AND SAN POLO

Surrounded by designer boutiques, souvenir stands, scores of restaurants, near-domesticated pigeons, and many of Venice's most popular sights, these accommodations are pricey options for those in search of Venice's showy side.

**Albergo Casa Petrarca,** Cal. Schiavine, San Marco 4386 (☎52 00 430). From Campo S. Luca, follow Cal. Fuseri, take the 2nd left, and then a right. Cheerful proprietors run a tiny hotel with 7 upbeat rooms, most with bath and A/C. Breakfast included. Singles €80-90; doubles €125, with canal view €155. Extra bed €35. Cash only. ❺

**Albergo San Samuele,** Salizzada S. Samuele, San Marco 3358 (☎52 28 045; www.albergosansamuele.it). Follow Cal. delle Botteghe from Campo S. Stefano and turn left on Salizzada S. Samuele. Small but well-kept rooms, with welcoming staff and great location. Reserve 1-2 months ahead. Singles €55; doubles €75-90, with bath €100-120; triples €110-130. Cash only. ❹

**Domus Civica (ACISJF),** Campiello Chiovere Frari, San Polo 3082 (☎72 11 03). From the station, cross Ponte Scalzi and turn right. Turn left on F. dei Tolentini and left through the courtyard onto Corte Amai. The hostel's rounded facade is after the bridge. Spartan white rooms with shared TV, piano, and bath. Free Internet. Reception 7am-12:30am. Strict curfew 12:30am. Open June-Sept. 25. Singles €31; doubles €54; triples €81. 15% Rolling Venice discount; 20% ISIC discount. AmEx/MC/V. ❸

**Casa Peron,** Salizzada S. Pantalon, Santa Croce 84 (☎71 00 21; www.casaperon.com). From station, cross Ponte Scalzi and turn right. Turn left just before the bridge and continue down Fond. Minotto until Casa Peron appears on the left. Small lobby decorated with lace and glass gives way to basic, white rooms, some with A/C, all with shower. Breakfast included. Singles €50; doubles €80, with bath €95; triples €100/120. V. ❸

## CASTELLO

Castello, the *sestiere* where most Venetians live, is arguably the prettiest part of Venice. A second- or third-floor room with a view of the sculpted skyline is worth getting lost in the dead ends and barricaded alleys of some of the narrowest, most tightly clustered streets in the city.

**Foresteria Valdese,** Castello 5170 (☎52 86 797; www.diaconiavaldese.org/venezia). From Campo S. Maria Formosa, take Cal. Lunga S. Maria Formosa; it's over the 1st bridge. A crumbling but grand 18th-century guest house run by Venice's largest Protestant church, 2min. from major sights. Breakfast and linens included. Internet €5 per hr. Reception 9am-1pm and 6-8pm. Lockout 10am-1pm. Reservations required. Dorms €21-23; doubles with TV €60-64, with bath and TV €76-80; quads with bath and TV €110-118; quints with bath €127-137; apartments (no breakfast) €104. Min. 2-night stay for private rooms. €1 Rolling Venice discount. MC/V. ❷

**Albergo Doni,** Cal. del Vin, Castello 4656 (☎52 24 267; www.albergodoni.it). From P. San Marco, turn left immediately after the 2nd bridge on Cal. del Vin and take the left fork when the street splits. Friendly staff and proximity to P. San Marco make this hotel an amazing deal. Rooms with phone, TV, and fan or A/C. Breakfast included. Reception 24hr. Singles €40-65; doubles €60-95, with bath €80-120; triples €80-125, with bath 120-160; quads €140-200. €5 discount with cash payment. MC/V. ❸

**Antica Locanda Casa Verardo,** Castello 4765 (☎52 86 127; www.casaverardo.it). From the basilica, take Cal. Canonica, turn right before bridge, and left over the bridge on Ruga Giuffa into Campo S. Filippo e Giacomo. Follow Cal. della Chiesa left out of the *campo* until reaching a bridge. A historic treasure with the original mosaic floors and heavy drapes of a 16th-century palace. All rooms with A/C and TV, most with tub or shower. Terrace breakfast and Internet included. Singles €60-150; doubles €90-298. Discounts for web reservations or cash payment. AmEx/MC/V. ❺

**La Residenza,** Campo Bandiera e Moro, Castello 3608 (☎52 85 315; www.venicelaresidenza.com). From V: Arsenal, turn left on Riva degli Schiavoni and right on Cal. del Dose into the *campo*. This sumptuously decorated 15th-century palace looks out onto a courtyard. Great location 5min. from San Marco. All rooms recently renovated with A/C, bath, minibar, safe, and TV. Breakfast included. Reception 24hr. Singles €50-100; doubles €80-180. MC/V. ❹

**Locanda Silva,** F. del Rimedio, Castello 4423 (☎52 27 643; www.locandasilva.it). From P. S. Marco, walk under the clock tower, turn right on Cal. Larga S. Marco, then left on Cal. d. Angelo before the bridge. Head right on Cal. d. Rimedio and follow it to the end. Rooms have exposed beams, and the breakfast room overlooks the canal. Breakfast included. Reception 24hr. Open Feb.-Nov. Singles €35-50, with bath €50-70; doubles €60-80/70-110; triples with bath €110-140; quads with bath €130-160. MC/V. ❹

## DORSODURO

Between Chiesa dei Frari and Ponte Accademia, hotels here tend to be pricey.

**Pensione Seguso,** F. Zattere ai Saloni, Dorsoduro 779 (☎52 86 858; www.pensioneseguso.it). From V: Zattere, walk to the right. Views of the Giudecca Canal and antique decor. Breakfast included. Singles €80-110, with bath €100-120; doubles €120-158/180-190; triples with bath €180-230. AmEx/MC/V. ❺

**Locanda Cà Foscari,** Cal. della Frescada, Dorsoduro 3887/B (☎07 10 401; www.locandacafoscari.com). From V: San Tomà, turn left at the dead end, cross the bridge, turn right, then left at the alley. *Carnevale* masks embellish this tidy hotel, which offers basic rooms in a quiet neighborhood. Breakfast included. Reception 24hr. Reserve 2-3 months ahead. Singles €57, with bath €62; doubles €78/98; triples €110/130; quads €130. MC/V. ❹

## ON THE CITY PERIPHERY

▨ **Ostello di Venezia (HI),** F. Zitelle, Giudecca 87 (☎52 38 211). From V: Zitelle, turn right along canal; the hostel is a 3min. walk to the left. This efficiently managed hostel has sparkling baths and sweeping views of the city. 250 beds on single-sex floors. Breakfast and linens included. Dinner €9.50. Reception 7-9:30am and 1:30pm-midnight. Lockout 9:30am-1:30pm. Curfew 11:30pm. Reserve online at www.hostelbooking.com. Dorms €20. €3 HI discount. MC/V. ❷

**Camping Miramare,** Lungomare Dante Alighieri 29 (☎96 61 50; www.camping-miramare.it). A 1hr. ride on V #LN from P. S. Marco to Punta Sabbioni. Campground is 700m along the beach on the right. Min. 2-night stay in high season. Open Apr.-Oct. €4.70-7 per person; cabins €27-60 plus per-person charge. MC/V. ❶

**Camping Fusina,** V. Moranzani 93 (☎54 70 055; www.camping-fusina.com), in Malcontenta. From Mestre, take bus #11. ATM, Internet, laundromat, restaurant, and TV onsite. Free hot showers. Call ahead to reserve cabins. €8-9 per person, €8.50 per tent. Cabin singles €25; doubles €30. AmEx/MC/V. ❷

# 🍴 FOOD

With few exceptions, the best restaurants lie in alleyways, not along the canals around San Marco that advertise a *menù turistico*. Venetian cuisine is dominated by fish, like *sarde in saor* (sardines in vinegar and onions), available only in Venice and sampled cheaply at most bars with other types of *cicchetti* (tidbits of seafood, rice, and meat; €1-3). **Wines** of the Veneto and Friuli regions include the whites *Prosecco della Marca, bianco di Custoza,* and dry *Tocai,* as well as the red *Valpolicella.* Venice's renowned Rialto **markets** spread between the Canal Grande and the San Polo foot of the Rialto every Monday through Saturday morning. A **BILLA supermarket,** Str. Nuova, Cannaregio 5660, is near Campo S. Fosca. (Open M-Sa 8:30am-8:30pm, Su 9am-8:30pm. AmEx/MC/V.)

## CANNAREGIO

**Trattoria da Bepi,** Cannaregio 4550. From Campo S. S. Apostoli, turn left on Salizzada del Pistor. This traditional Venetian *trattoria* attracts tourists and locals who come for the expertly prepared cuisine. *Primi* €7-11. *Secondi* from €10. Cover €1.50. Reserve ahead for outdoor seating. Open M-W and F-Su noon-3pm and 7-10pm. MC/V. ❸

**Pizzeria La Perla,** Rio Terra dei Franceschi, Cannaregio 4615. From Str. Nuova, turn left on Salizzada del Pistor in Campo S. S. Apostoli. Follow to the end, then follow signs for the F. Nuove. Satisfied diners savor over 40 varieties of sizable pizzas. Pizza €4.70-9. Pasta €6.10-8.20. Cover €1.10. Service 10%. Open M-Tu and Th-Su noon-3pm and 6:30-10:30pm; daily in Aug. AmEx/MC/V. ❷

**Gam Gam,** Canale di Cannaregio, Cannaregio 1122 (☎71 52 84). From Campo S. Geremia, cross the bridge and turn left. Israeli appetizers with falafel €9.50. Main courses €9-15. 10% discount with *Let's Go.* Open Su-Th noon-10pm, F noon-4pm. Cash only. ❷

**Osteria al Bomba,** Cannaregio 4297/98 (☎52 05 175). From Hotel Bernardi-Semenzato, exit right onto Str. Nuova, then turn right into the next alleyway. Seat yourself at the long communal table for a meal, or enjoy your *prosecco* (€1) and *cicchetti* (€1 for a skewer; €15 for a mixture) on the patio. *Primi* €10-15. *Secondi* €12.50-19. Cover €2. Open daily 11am-3pm and 6-11pm. MC/V. ❸

## CASTELLO

▨ **Cip Ciap,** Cal. del Mondo Novo 5799/A (☎52 36 621). From Campo S. Maria Formosa, follow Cal. del Mondo Novo. Tiny pizzeria uses fresh ingredients and sells pizza by the gram (€2-2.50 per kg). Cheap, filling calzones (€2.50). There's no seating, so find a bench in the nearby *campo*. Open M and W-Su 9am-9pm. Cash only. ❶

**Osteria al Portego,** Cal. Malvasia 6015. Heading south on Salizzada S. Lio, turn left onto Cal. Malvasia, and left again toward Cte. Perina. This hidden *osteria*, filled with barrels of wine, is a favorite of students and locals. Dizzying array of *cicchetti* and wine. Open M-Sa 10:30am-3pm and 5:30-10pm. Cash only. ❶

**La Boutique del Gelato,** Salizzada S. Lio, Castello 5727 (☎52 23 283). From Campo Bartolomeo, go under Sottoportego de la Bissa, cross the bridge into Campo S. Lio, and follow Salizzada S. Lio. Doles out big portions of *gelato*. 1 scoop €1, 2 scoops €1.70. Open daily July-Aug. 10:30am-10:30pm; Sept.-June 10:30am-8:30pm. Cash only. ❶

**Pizzeria/Trattoria Al Vecio Canton,** Castello 4738/A (☎52 85 176). From Campo S. Maria Formosa, with church on right, cross the bridge and follow Ruga Giuffa. Turn right at the end. A crowded neighborhood favorite with over 50 pizza varieties (€4.50-10) and other *primi* (€6-18). Try the *menù Veneziano*—a plate overflowing with spaghetti, clams, and calamari (€14). *Secondi* €12-20. Cover €2. Open M and W-Su 9am-3pm and 6pm-midnight. Cash only. ❸

**Osteria Alle Testiere,** Cal. del Mondo Novo, Castello 5801 (☎/fax 52 27 220). From Campo S. Maria Formosa, take Cal. del Mondo Novo. This tiny restaurant specializes in modern, light cooking with fruits and vegetables. *Primi* €16. *Secondi* €24-28. Open Sept.-July Tu-Sa noon-3pm and 7pm-midnight. Reserve ahead. MC/V. ❺

**Osteria Santa Marina,** Campo S. Marina, Castello 5911 (☎52 85 239). From Cal. Lio, take Cal. Carminati to the end, turn right, follow to the end, and turn left. Fresh, seasonal menu served in an upscale, intimate setting. *Primi* €14-18. *Secondi* €24-30. Cover €3. Open M 7:30-10pm, Tu-Sa 12:30-2:30pm and 7:30-10pm. MC/V. ❹

# SAN MARCO

🔲 **Le Bistrot de Venise,** Cal. dei Fabbri, San Marco 4685 (☎52 36 651). From P. S. Marco, go through 2nd Sottoportego dei Dai under the awning. Follow road over a bridge and turn right. Delicious dishes, true to medieval and Renaissance recipes. *Enoteca: cichetti* €3-4, meat and cheese plates €12-24. Restaurant: *primi* €12-22, *secondi* €29-32. Wine from €5 per glass. Service 12%. Open daily 10am-1am. MC/V. ❺

**Vino, Vino,** Ponte delle Veste, San Marco 2007/A. From Cal. Larga XXII Marzo, turn on Cal. delle Veste. Jazz plays quietly in this bar, which offers over 350 kinds of wine, plus traditional *sarde in saor* and pasta from a daily *menù*. *Primi* €9-10. *Secondi* €10-17. Cover €2. Open daily 11:30am-11:30pm. 10% Rolling Venice discount. Cash only. ❸

# DORSODURO

🔲 **Cantinone Gia Schiavi,** F. Meraviglie, Dorsoduro 992 (☎52 30 034). From the Frari, follow signs for Ponte Accademia. Just before Ponte Meraviglie, turn right toward the church of S. Trovaso and cross the 1st bridge. Take your pick from hundreds of bottles (from €3.50), or enjoy a glass canal-side with some tasty *cicchetti* (€1-4). Open M-Sa 8:30am-2:30pm and 3:15-8:30pm. Cash only. ❶

🔲 **Gelateria Nico,** F. Zattere, Dorsoduro 922 (☎52 25 293). Near V: Zattere, with a great view of the Giudecca Canal. Try the sinful Venetian *gianduiotto de passeggio*, a brick of dense chocolate-hazelnut ice cream dropped into a cup of whipped cream (€2.50). *Gelato* €1, 2 scoops €1.70, 3 scoops €2.10. Prices higher for sit-down. Open M-W and F-Su 6:45am-10pm. Cash only. ❶

**Pizza al Volo,** Campo S. Margherita, Dorsoduro 2944 (☎52 25 430). This tiny pizzeria and its young, hip staff serve delicious thin-crust pizza to the student-dominated local crowd. Giant slices from €1.50. Pizzas from €3.50. Open daily 11:30am-4pm and 5pm-1:30am. Cash only. ❶

## SAN POLO AND SANTA CROCE

**Antica Birraria La Corte,** Campo S. Polo, San Polo 2168 (☎27 50 570). Large restaurant and bar with outside tables. Pizza €5-9. *Primi* €9-11. *Secondi* €11-19. Cover €2. Open mid-Aug. to mid-July daily 12:30-3pm and 7-10:30pm; mid-July to mid-Aug. M-F 12:30-3pm and 7-10:30pm, Sa-Su 12:30-3pm. AmEx/MC/V. ❸

**Frary's,** F. dei Frari, San Polo 2559 (☎72 00 50). Across from the entrance to S. Maria Gloriosa dei Frari. Tasty Greek and Arabic dishes served in a colorful dining room. Satisfying lunch *menù* (€10) with antipasto and main course. Entrees €8-13. Cover €1.50. Open M and W-Su noon-3:15pm and 6-10:30pm. ❸

**Ae Oche,** Santa Croce 1552A/B (☎52 41 161). From Campo S. Giacomo, take Cal. del Trentor. American advertisements from the 1960s painted onto unfinished wooden walls make strange bedfellows with the cartoonish duck logo, but the overall effect is charming. Pizza €4.50-9. *Primi* €5.50-7. *Secondi* €8-15. Cover €1.50. Service 12%. Open daily noon-3:30pm and 7-11:30pm. MC/V. ❷

**Osteria al Ponte,** Cal. Saoneri, San Polo 2741/A (☎52 37 238). From Campo S. Polo, follow signs to Accademia; it's immediately across the 1st bridge. Hungry locals devour a sampling of seafood dishes. Try the black *spaghetti al nero di seppia* (spaghetti cooked in squid ink) or one of the weekly specials. *Primi* €7-12. *Secondi* €9-16. Cover €2. Open Tu-Su 10am-2:30pm and 6-10pm. AmEx/MC/V. ❸

**Osteria Enoteca "Vivaldi,"** San Polo 1457 (☎52 38 185). From the Campo. S. Polo, opposite the church, cross the bridge to Cal. della Madonnetta. Tiny neighborhood restaurant has classical instruments mounted on its walls, but its draw is hearty Venetian cuisine. *Primi* €8-13. *Secondi* €12-22. Cover €1.50. Service 10%. Open M-Tu and Th-Su 11am-3pm and 6pm-midnight. AmEx/MC/V. ❸

**Cantina Do Mori,** Cal. dei Do Mori, San Polo 401 (☎52 25 401). From the Rialto, take a left onto Ruga Veccio, then the 1st right, and then left. Brass pots dangle in the dark interior of Venice's oldest wine bar. If you're going to try *sarde in saor* (€1.40), do so here. Limited seating. Open M-Sa 8:30am-8pm. ❶

# ◙ SIGHTS

Venice's layout makes sightseeing a disorienting affair. Most sights center around the **Piazza San Marco,** but getting lost can be better than being found in its tourist crowds. Museum passes (€18, students €12), sold at participating museums, grant one-time admission to each of 10 museums over the course of three months. The Foundation for the Churches of Venice sells the **Chorus Pass** (☎27 50 462; www.chorusvenezia.org), which provides admission to all of Venice's churches. A yearly pass (€8, students €5) is available at most participating churches.

## AROUND PIAZZA SAN MARCO

Venice's only official *piazza,* **Piazza San Marco,** is an un-Venetian expanse of light, space, and architectural harmony. Enclosing the *piazza* are rows of cafes and expensive shops along the Renaissance **Procuratie Vecchie.** The 96m brick **campanile** (bell tower; open daily 9am-9pm, €6), built on a Roman base, provides one of the best views of the city; on clear days, the panorama spans Croatia and Slovenia.

■**BASILICA DI SAN MARCO.** The symmetrical arches and incomparable mosaics of Venice's crown jewel grace Piazza San Marco. The city's premier tourist attraction, the Basilica di San Marco also has the longest lines. To avoid them, visit early in the morning; still, late afternoon visits profit from the best natural light. Begun in the 9th century to house the remains of St. Mark, which had been stolen from Alexandria by Venetian merchants, 13th-century Byzantine and 16th-century Renaissance mosaics now make the interior sparkle. Behind the altar, the **Pala d'Oro** relief frames a parade of saints in gem-encrusted gold. The golden, rose-adorned tomb of St. Mark rests at the altar. The **tesoro** (treasury) contains gold and relics from the Fourth Crusade. Steep stairs in the atrium lead to the **Galleria della Basilica,** which has views of tiny golden tiles in the basilica's vast ceiling mosaics and the original bronze **Cavalli di San Marco** (Horses of St. Mark). A balcony overlooks the piazza. *(Basilica open M-Sa 9:45am-5pm, Su 2-4pm. Modest dress required. Free. Pala d'Oro open M-Sa 9:45am-5:30pm, Su 2-4pm. €1.50. Treasury open M-Sa 9:45am-7pm, Su 2-4:30pm; €2. Galleria open M-F 9:45am-4:15pm, Sa-Su 9:45am-4:45pm. €3.)*

■ **PALAZZO DUCALE (DOGE'S PALACE).** Once the home of Venice's *doge* (mayor), the Palazzo Ducale is now a museum. Veronese's *Rape of Europa* is among its spectacular works. In the courtyard, Sansovino's enormous sculptures, *Mars* and *Neptune,* flank the **Scala dei Giganti** (Stairs of the Giants), upon which new *doges* were crowned. The Council of Ten, the *doge*'s administrators, would drop the names of suspected criminals into the **Bocca di Leone** (Lion's Mouth), on the balcony. The *doge*'s apartments and the Republic's state rooms contain a great deal of ornate wooden carving, thick gold leaf, and oil canvases. Climb the **Scala d'Oro** (Golden Staircase) to the **Sala delle Quattro Porte** (Room of the Four Doors), whose ceiling depicts biblical judgements, and the **Sala dell'Anticollegio** (Antechamber of the Senate), whose decorations are myths about Venice. Courtrooms of the much-feared Council of Ten and the even-more-feared Council of Three lead to the **Sala del Maggior Consiglio** (Great Council Room). It is dominated by Tintoretto's *Paradise,* the largest oil painting in the world. Near the end, thick stone lattices line the **Ponte dei Sospiri** (Bridge of Sighs), named after the mournful groans of prisoners who walked it on their way to the prison's damp cells. *(Wheelchair-accessible. Open daily Apr.-Oct. 9am-7pm; Nov.-Mar. 9am-5pm. €12, students €6.50.)*

■ **CHIESA DI SAN ZACCARIA.** Designed in the late 1400s by Coducci and others, and dedicated to John the Baptist's father, this Gothic-Renaissance church holds S. Zaccaria's corpse in an elevated sarcophagus along the nave's right wall. Nearby is Bellini's *Virgin and Child Enthroned with Four Saints,* a Renaissance masterpiece. *(S. Marco. V: S. Zaccaria. Open daily 10am-noon and 4-6pm. Free.)*

# AROUND THE PONTE RIALTO

■ **THE GRAND CANAL.** The Grand Canal is Venice's "main street." Over 3km long and nearly 50m wide, it loops through the city and passes under three bridges: the **Ponte Scalzi, Rialto,** and **Accademia.** The *bricole,* candy-cane posts used for mooring boats on the canal, are painted with the colors of the family whose *palazzo* adjoins them. *(For great facade views, ride V. #1, 4 or 82 from the train station to P. S. Marco. The facades are lit at night and produce dazzling reflections.)*

■ **RIVOALTUS LEGATORIA.** Step into the book-lined Rivoaltus shop on any given day and hear Wanda Scarpa greet you from the attic, where she has been sewing leatherbound, antique-style ■journals for an international cadre of customers and faithful locals for more than three decades. Though Venice is now littered with shops selling journals, Rivoaltus was the first and remains the best. *(Ponte di Rialto 11. Notebooks €18-31. Photo albums €31-78. Open daily 10am-7:30pm.)*

**PONTE RIALTO.** This architectural structure is named after Rivo Alto, the first colony built in Venice. The original wood bridge collapsed in the 1500s; the stone replacement is strong enough to support the plethora of shops that line it today.

## SAN POLO

The second-largest *campo* in Venice, **Campo San Polo** once hosted bloody bull-baiting matches during *Carnevale*. Today, the *campo* is dotted with elderly women and trees, and blood is no longer spilled—only *gelato*.

**BASILICA DI SANTA MARIA GLORIOSA DEI FRARI.** Titian's corpse and two of his paintings reside within this Gothic church, known as *I Frari* and begun by Franciscans in 1340. ✪**Assumption** (1516-18), on the high altar, marks the height of the Venetian Renaissance. The golden Florentine chapel, to the right of the high altar, frames Donatello's gaunt wooden sculpture, **St. John the Baptist.** Titian's tomb is an elaborate lion-topped triumphal arch with bas-relief scenes of Paradise. (*S. Polo. V: S. Tomà. Open M-Sa 9am-6pm, Su 1-6pm. €2.50.*)

**CHIESA DI SAN GIACOMO DI RIALTO.** Between the Rialto and nearby markets stands Venice's first church, diminutively called "San Giacometto." An ornate clock-face adorns its *campanile*. Across the *piazza*, a statue called *Il Gobbo* (The Hunchback) supports the steps, once used for announcements. At the foot of the statue, convicted thieves would collapse after being forced to run naked from P. S. Marco. (*V: Rialto. Cross bridge and turn right. Church open daily 9:30am-noon and 4-6pm. Free.*)

**SCUOLA GRANDE DI SAN ROCCO.** The most illustrious of Venice's *scuole* (schools) commemorates Jacopo Tintoretto, who left Venice only once in his 76 years, and who sought to combine "the color of Titian with the drawing of Michelangelo." The school commissioned Tintoretto to complete all the paintings in the building, which took 23 years. The *Crucifixion* in the last room upstairs is the collection's crowning glory. (*Behind Basilica dei Frari in Campo S. Rocco. Open daily Mar. 28-Nov. 2 9am-5:30pm; Nov. 3-Mar. 27 10am-4pm. €7, students and Rolling Venice €5.*)

## DORSODURO

**■COLLEZIONE PEGGY GUGGENHEIM.** Guggenheim's Palazzo Venier dei Leoni displays works by Dalí, Duchamp, Ernst, Kandinsky, Klee, Magritte, Picasso, and Pollock. The Marini sculpture *Angel in the City*, in front of the palazzo, was designed with a detachable penis so that Ms. Guggenheim could avoid offending her more prudish guests. (*F. Venier dei Leoni, Dorsoduro 701. V: Accademia. Turn left and follow the yellow signs. Open M and W-Su 10am-6pm. €10; students and Rolling Venice €5.*)

**■GALLERIE DELL'ACCADEMIA.** The Accademia houses the world's most extensive collection of Venetian art. Among the enormous altarpieces in **Room II,** Giovanni Bellini's *Madonna Enthroned with Child, Saints, and Angels* stands out with its soothing serenity. **Rooms IV** and **V** have more Bellinis plus Giorgione's enigmatic *La Tempesta*. In **Room VI,** three paintings by Tintoretto, *The Creation of the Animals, The Temptation of Adam and Eve,* and *Cain and Abel,* grow progressively darker. **Room X** displays Titian's last painting, a *Pietà* intended for his tomb. In **Room XX,** works by Bellini and Carpaccio depict Venetian processions and cityscapes so accurately that scholars use them as "photos" of Venice's past. (*V: Accademia. Open M 8:15am-2pm, Tu-Su 8:15am-7:15pm. €6.50. English tours Tu-Su 11am €7.*)

**CHIESA DI SANTA MARIA DELLA SALUTE.** The *salute* (Italian for "health") is a hallmark of the Venetian skyline: perched on Dorsoduro's peninsula just southwest of San Marco, the church and its domes are visible from everywhere in the city. In 1631, the city had **Baldassarre Longhena** build the church for the Virgin, who they believed would end the current plague. Next to the *salute* stands the *dogana*, the customs house, where ships sailing into Venice were required to pay duties.

*(Dorsoduro. V: Salute. ☎522 55 58. Open daily 9am-noon and 2:30-5:30pm. Free. Entrance to sacristy with donation. The inside of the dogana is closed to the public.)*

**CÀ REZZONICO.** Longhena's great 18th-century Venetian *palazzo* houses the newly restored **Museo del Settecento Veneziano** (Museum of 18th-Century Venice). Known as the "Temple of Venetian Settecento," this grand palace features a regal, fresco-ceilinged ballroom, elaborate Venetian Rococo decor, and two extensive portrait galleries. *(V: Cà Rezzonico. ☎24 10 100. Open M and W-Su Apr.-Oct. 10am-6pm; Nov.-Mar. 10am-5pm. €6.50, students and Rolling Venice €4.50.)*

**CHIESA DI SAN SEBASTIANO.** This church is devoted to Renaissance painter **Veronese**, who took refuge in this white-marble and brown-stucco, 16th-century church when he fled Verona in 1555 after allegedly killing a man. By 1565 he had filled the church with a series of paintings and frescoes. His breathtaking *Stories of Queen Esther* covers the ceiling, while the artist's body rests by the organ. *(Dorsoduro. V: S. Basilio. Open M-Sa 10am-5pm, Su 1-5pm. €2.50.)*

# CASTELLO

**CHIESA DI SANTISSIMI GIOVANNI E PAOLO.** This brick structure, also called San Zanipolo, is built primarily in the Gothic style but has a Renaissance portal and an arch supported by columns of Greek marble. Inside, monumental walls and ceilings enclose the tombs and monuments of the *doges*. An altarpiece by Bellini depicts St. Christopher, St. Sebastian, and St. Vincent Ferrer. The equestrian statue of local mercenary Bartolomeo Colleoni stands on a marble pedestal outside; he left Venice his inheritance on the condition that his monument stand in San Marco, but the city chose this more modest spot. *(Castello. V: Fond. Nuove. Turn left, then right on Fond. dei Mendicanti. ☎52 35 913. Open M-Sa 9:30am-6pm, Su 1-6pm. €2.50, students €1.25.)*

**CHIESA DI SANTA MARIA DEI MIRACOLI.** The Lombardi family designed this small Renaissance jewel in the late 1400s. Inside the tiny pink-, white-, and blue-marble exterior sits a fully functional parish with a dark golden ceiling and pastel walls interrupted only by the vibrant blue-and-yellow window above the apse. *(Cross the bridge directly in front of S. Giovanni e Paolo, and continue down Cal. Larga Gallina over 2 bridges. Open July-Aug. M-Sa 10am-5pm; Sept.-June M-Sa 10am-5pm, Su 1-5pm. €2.50.)*

**SCUOLA DALMATA SAN GIORGIO DEGLI SCHIAVONI.** Carpaccio's finest artwork, visual tales of St. George, Jerome, and Tryfon, hang in the early 16th-century building. *(Castello 3259/A. V: S. Zaccaria. Modest dress required. Open Tu-Sa 9:15am-1pm, 2:45-6pm, M, Su 9:15am-1pm. €3, Rolling Venice €2.)*

**GIARDINI PUBLICI AND SANT'ELENA.** For a short commune with nature, walk through the shady lanes of Napoleon's bench-lined public gardens or bring a picnic lunch to the lawns of Sant'Elena. *(V: Giardini or S. Elena. Free.)*

# CANNAREGIO

**JEWISH GHETTO.** In 1516 the *doge* forced Venice's Jewish population into the old cannon-foundry area, creating the first Jewish ghetto in Europe and coining the word "ghetto," the Venetian word for foundry. In the Campo del Ghetto Nuovo, the **Schola Grande Tedesca** (German Synagogue), the area's oldest synagogue, and the **Museo Ebraica di Venezia** (Hebrew Museum of Venice) now share a building. *(Cannaregio 2899/B. V: S. Marcuola. Museum open Su-F June-Sept. 10am-7pm; Oct.-May 10am-4:30pm. Enter synagogue by 40min. tour every hr. daily June-Sept. 10:30am-5:30pm; Oct.-May 10:30am-4:30pm. Museum €3, students €2. Museum and tour €8.50/7.)*

ITALY

**CHIESA DELLA MADONNA DELL'ORTO.** Tintoretto's brick 14th-century parish church, the final resting place of the painter and his children, contains 10 of his largest paintings, as well as some works by Titian. Look for Tintoretto's *Last Judgment* and *The Sacrifice of the Golden Calf* near the high altar. There is a light switch for illuminating the works at the far corners. *(V: Madonna dell'Orto. Open M-Sa 10am-5pm. €2.50. Audio tour €0.50.)*

**CHIESA DEI GESUITI.** Soaring exterior columns open onto a sea of green-and-white marble that stretches from the floor to the stone curtain in the pulpit. The church, founded in the 12th century and reconstructed in the 18th, also features a dizzying ceiling with gilt-rimmed stucco around painted portals to heaven. Titian's *Martyrdom of Saint Lawrence* hangs in the altar, to the left at the entrance. *(Cannaregio 4885. V: F. Nuove. Open daily 10am-noon and 4-6pm. Free.)*

**CÀ D'ORO.** Delicate spires and interlocking arches make the Cà d'Oro's facade the most spectacular on the Canal Grande. Built between 1425 and 1440, it now houses the **Galleria Giorgio Franchetti.** For the best view of the palace, take a *traghetto* (ferry) across the canal to the Rialto Markets. *(V: Cà d'Oro. Open M 8:15am-2pm, Tu-Su 8:15am-7:15pm. €5, EU students and under 35 €2.50. Audio tour €4.)*

# ■ ISLANDS OF THE LAGOON

■ **LIDO.** The breezy resort island of Lido provided the setting for Thomas Mann's haunting novella, *Death in Venice*. Visonti's film version was also shot here at the Hotel des Bains, Lungomare Marconi 17. Today, people flock to Lido to enjoy the surf at the popular public beach. An impressive shipwreck looms at one end, and a casino, horseback riding, and the fine Alberoni Golf Club add to the island's charm. *(V #1 and 82: Lido. Beach open daily 9am-8pm. Free.)*

■ **MURANO.** Famous since 1292 for its glass (Venice's artisans were forced off Venice proper because their kilns started fires), the six-island cluster of Murano affords visitors the opportunity to witness resident artisans blowing crystalline creations for free. Quiet streets are lined with shops and boutiques with jewelry, vases, and delicate figurines for a variety of prices; for demonstrations, look for signs directing to the *fornace*, concentrated around the Colona, Faro, and Navagero *vaporetto* stops. The collection at the **Museo Vetrario** (Glass Museum) ranges from first-century funereal urns to a cartoonish, sea-green octopus presumably designed by Carlo Scarpa in 1930. *(V #DM, LN, 5, 13, 41, 42: Faro from either S. Zaccaria or F. Nuove. Museo Vetrario, F. Giustian 8. Open M-Tu and Th-Su Apr.-Oct. 10am-5pm; Nov.-Mar. 10am-4pm. €4, students and Rolling Venice €2.50. Combined ticket with Burano Lace Museum €6, students and Rolling Venice €4. Basilica open daily 8am-7pm. Modest dress required. Free.)*

**BURANO.** Postcard-pretty Burano is a traditional fishing village where hand-tatted lace has become a community art. The small and somewhat dull **Scuola di Merletti di Burano** (Lace Museum), once the home of the island's professional lace-making school, features strips from the 16th century and yellowing lace-maker diplomas. From October to June, ask about seeing the lace-makers at work. *(40min. by boat from Venice. V #LN: Burano from F. Nuove. Museum in P. Galuppi. Open M and W-Su Apr.-Sept. 10am-5pm; Oct.-Mar. 10am-4:30pm. €4, students and Rolling Venice €2.50.)*

**TORCELLO.** Torcello, a safe haven for early fishermen fleeing barbarians on the mainland, was the most powerful island in the lagoon before Venice usurped its inhabitants and its glory. The island's cathedral, **Santa Maria Assunta,** contains *Psychosis*, a mosaic in the nave, which depicts both a peaceful heaven and a scorching snake- and skull-filled hell. The *campanile* affords splendid views of the outer lagoon. *(45min. by* *boat from Venice. V #T: Torcello from Burano. Cathedral open daily 10:30am-6pm, ticket office closes at 5:30. Modest dress required. €3; church, campanile, and museum €8.)*

**ISOLA DI SAN MICHELE.** You'll face only small crowds on Venice's cemetery island, San Michele, home to Coducci's tiny **Chiesa di San Michele in Isola** (1469), the first Renaissance church in Venice. Enter the grounds through the church's right-hand portal and look up to see a relief depicting St. Michael slaying the dragon. Poet and fascist sympathizer Ezra Pound is buried in the Protestant cemetery, while Russian composer Igor Stravinsky and choreographer Sergei Diaghilev are entombed in the Orthodox graveyard. *(V: Cimitero from F. Nuove. Church and cemetery open daily Apr.-Sept. 7:30am-6pm; Oct.-Mar. 7:30am-4pm. Free.)*

# 🎵 🌸 ENTERTAINMENT AND FESTIVALS

Admire Venetian houses and *palazzi* via their original canal pathways. **Gondola** rides are most romantic about 50min. before sunset and most affordable if shared by six people. The rate that a gondolier quotes is negotiable, but expect to pay €80-100 for a 40min. ride. The most price-flexible gondoliers are those standing by themselves rather than those in groups at the "taxi-stands" throughout the city.

  **Teatro Goldoni,** Cal. del Teatro, S. Marco 4650/B (☎24 02 011), near the Ponte di Rialto, showcases live productions with seasonal themes. Check with the theater for more info. The **Mostra Internazionale di Cinema** (Venice International Film Festival), held annually from late August to early September, draws established names and rising stars from around the world. Movies are shown in their original language. (☎52 18 878. Tickets sold throughout the city, €20. Some late-night outdoor showings free.) The famed **Biennale di Venezia** (☎52 11 898; www.labiennale.org), a contemporary exhibit of provocative art (odd-numbered years) or architecture (even-numbered), takes over the Giardini Pubblici and the Arsenal. The weekly *A Guest in Venice*, free at hotels and tourist offices or online (www.unospitedivenezia.it), lists current festivals, concerts, and art exhibits.

  Be wary of **shopping** in the heavily touristed P. S. Marco or around the Rialto (excluding Rivoaltus). Shops outside these areas often have better quality products and a greater selection for about half the price. Interesting clothing, glass, and mask boutiques line the streets leading from the Rialto to Campo S. Polo and Str. Nuova and from the Rialto toward the station. The map accompanying the Rolling Venice card lists many shops that offer discounts for cardholders. The most concentrated and varied selections of Venetian glass and lace require trips to the nearby islands of Murano and Burano, respectively.

  Banned by the church for several centuries, Venice's famous **Carnevale** was successfully reinstated in the early 1970s. During the 10 days preceding Ash Wednesday, masked figures jam the streets while outdoor performances spring up all over. For **Mardi Gras** (Feb. 5, 2008), the population doubles. Contact the tourist office for details, and make lodging arrangements well ahead. Venice's second-most colorful festival is the **Festa del Redentore** (3rd Su in July), originally held to celebrate the end of the 16th-century plague. It kicks off with a magnificent fireworks display at 11:30pm the Saturday before. On Sunday, craftsmen build a pontoon bridge across the Giudecca Canal, connecting **Il Redentore** to the **Zattere.**

# 🔒 NIGHTLIFE

Most residents would rather spend an evening sipping wine or beer in a *piazza* than bumping and grinding in a disco. Establishments come and go with some regularity, though student nightlife is consistently concentrated around **Campo Santa Margherita,** in Dorsoduro, while that of tourists centers around the **Lista di Spagna.**

▨ **Café Blue,** Dorsoduro 3778 (☎71 02 27). From S. Maria Frari, take Cal. Scalater and turn right at the end. Grab a glass of wine (from €1.50) and a stool to watch the day-time coffee crowd turn into a chill and laid-back set as night falls. Free Wi-Fi and 1 computer for Internet. DJ W, live music in winter F. Open daily 8am-2am. MC/V.

**Naranzaria,** Sottoportego del Banco, San Polo 130 (☎72 41 035). At the canal-side corner of C. S. Giacomo. Up-close views of the Grand Canal and Rialto complement the wine, *cicchetti* (including sushi), and trendy vibe. Open Tu-Su noon-2am. MC/V.

**Bistrot ai Do Draghi,** Campo S. Margherita 3665 (☎52 89 731). The crowd at this tiny bistro is not as fierce as the name ("dragon") implies. Its wine selection has won accolades. Wine from €1.20 per glass. Open daily 7am-1am.

**Paradiso Perduto,** F. della Misericordia, Cannaregio 2540 (☎09 94 540). From Str. Nuova, cross Campo S. Fosca and the bridge, and continue in the same direction, crossing 2 more bridges. Students flood this unassuming bar, which also serves *cicchetti* (mixed plate €11-15). Live jazz F. Open daily 11am-3pm and 6pm-1am.

**Piccolo Mondo,** Accademia, Dorsoduro 1056/A (☎52 00 371). Facing toward the Accademia, turn right. Ring bell to enter. Disco, hip hop, and vodka with Red Bull (€10) keep a full house at this small, popular *discoteca,* which heats up late behind its heavy, locked doors. Drinks from €7. Open daily 11pm-4am. AmEx/MC/V.

**Orange,** Dorsoduro 3054/A (☎52 34 740). Across from Duchamp in Campo S. Margherita. The bar looks like it's on fire at this funky modern spot; gather there with your drink, or outside on the *campo.* Sip €6 tequila sunrises to match the color scheme. Beer from €2. Mixed drinks €3.50-7. Open daily 9am-2am. AmEx/MC/V.

**Cafe Noir,** Dorsoduro 3805 (☎71 09 25). Faded images of Marilyn Monroe cover the walls of Cafe Noir, where no-nonsense decor augments the artistic feel. Open M-Sa 7am-2am, Su 9am-2am. Cash only.

# PADUA (PADOVA) ☎049

The oldest institutions in Padua (pop. 210,000) are the ones that still draw visitors: St Anthony's tomb, the looping Prato della Valle, and the university, founded in 1222. It once hosted such luminaries as Copernicus, Donatello, Galileo, and Giotto, and now keeps an energetic population buzzing in the streets well past dusk. The starry blue ceiling of the ▨**Cappella degli Scrovegni,** P. Eremitani 8, overlooks Giotto's epic 38-panel fresco cycle depicting Mary, Jesus, St. Anne, and St. Joachim in *Last Judgment.* Buy tickets at the attached **Musei Civici Eremitani,** whose art collection includes Giotto's beautiful crucifix, which once adorned the Scrovegni Chapel. (☎20 10 020; www.cappelladegliscrovegni.it. Entrance to chapel only with museum. Open daily Feb.-Oct. 9am-7pm; Nov.-Jan. 9am-6pm. Reserve ahead. Museum €10, with chapel €12, students €8. AmEx/MC/V.) Pilgrims flock to see St. Anthony's jawbone, tongue, and tomb displayed at the **Basilica di Sant'Antonio,** in P. del Santo. (☎82 42 811. Modest dress required. Open daily Apr.-Sept. 6:15am-7:45pm; Nov.-Mar. 6:15am-7pm. Free.) The university centers around the two interior courtyards of **Palazzo Bò,** as does the student-heavy nightlife. The chair of Galileo is preserved in the **Sala dei Quaranta,** where he once lectured. Across the street, **Caffè Pedrocchi** served as the headquarters for 19th-century liberals who supported Risorgimento leader Giuseppe Mazzini. Next to the **duomo,** in P. Duomo, sits the tiny **Battistero,** with a domed interior coated with New Testament frescoes. (*Duomo* open M-Sa 7:20am-noon and 4-7:30pm, Su 8am-1pm and 4-8:30pm. Free. *Battistero* open daily 10am-6pm. €2.50, students €1.50.)

The stone artwork in the lobby of **Hotel Al Santo ❹**, V. del Santo 147, near the basilica, leads to large, wood-floored rooms. (☎87 52 131. Breakfast included. Reception 24hr. Singles €65; doubles €80-100; triples €120. AmEx/MC/V.) Go to V. Aleardi and turn left; walk to the end of the block and **Ostello Città di Padova (HI) ❷**, V. Aleardi 30, and its no-frills, six-bed dorms will be on your left. (☎87 52 219; pdyhtl@tin.it. Wheelchair-accessible. Internet €5 per hr. Lockout 9:30am-3:30pm. Curfew midnight. Reserve ahead. Dorms €17. MC/V.) The place to go for Paduan cuisine is **Antica Trattoria Paccagnella ❷**, V. del Santo 113. (☎/fax 87 50 549. *Primi* €7-11. *Secondi* €7-15. Cover €2.50. Open M-Sa 8am-4pm and 6:30pm-midnight. AmEx/MC/V.) Morning **markets** are held in P. delle Erbe and P. della Frutta. **Fly**, Galleria Tito Livio 4/6, between V. Roma and Riviera Tito Livio, is a pedestrian cafe by day and a swinging hot spot by night. The nearby V. Roma and strong student presence make this bar a great choice anytime. (☎87 52 892. Wine €2-3.50; mixed drinks €3.50-4.50. Open M-Sa 9am-midnight.) **Trains** run from P. Stazione to: Bologna (1½hr., 34 per day, €6); Milan (2½hr., 25 per day, €12); Venice (30min., 82 per day, €2.70); Verona (1hr., 44 per day, €4.80). **SITA Buses** (☎82 06 834) leave from P. Boschetti for Venice (45min., 32 per day, €3.05). The **tourist office** is in the train station. (☎87 52 077. Open M-Sa 9am-7pm, Su 9am-12:30pm.) To reach the *centro* from the station, take Corso del Popolo south from the train station, continuing as it becomes Corso Garibaldi. **Postal Code:** 35100.

# VERONA

☎045

In Verona (pop. 245,000), bright gardens and life-like sculptures delight the hopeless romantics who wander into its walls, seeking Romeo or Juliet, whose drama Shakespeare set here. But there's more to Verona than star-cross'd lovers: its rich wines, local cuisine, and world renowned opera are affordable even for students.

**🖥🔃 TRANSPORTATION AND PRACTICAL INFORMATION. Trains** (☎89 20 21) go from P. XXV Aprile to: **Bologna** (2hr., 22 per day, €6); **Milan** (2hr., 34 per day, €7); **Trent** (1hr., 25 per day, €4.70); **Venice** (1½hr., 41 per day, €8). From the station walk 20min. up **Corso Porta Nuova** or take bus #11, 12, 13, 51, 72, or 73 (Sa-Su take #91, 92, or 93) to Verona's center, the **Arena** in **Piazza Brà**. The **tourist office** is next to the *piazza* at V. d. Alpini 9. (☎806 86 80. Open M-Sa 9am-7pm, Su 9am-3pm.) Check email at **Internet Train**, V. Roma 17/A. (☎801 33 94. €5 per hr. Open M-F 10am-10pm, Sa-Su 2-8pm. MC/V.) **Postal Code:** 37100.

**🖥🔲 ACCOMMODATIONS AND FOOD.** Reserve hotel rooms ahead, especially during opera season (June-Sept.). The **Ostello della Gioventù (HI) ❶**, Villa Francescatti, Salita Fontana del Ferro 15, is in a renovated 16th-century villa with handsome gardens and antique frescoes. From the station, take bus #73 or night bus #90 to P. Isolo, turn right, and follow the yellow signs uphill. (☎59 03 60. Breakfast included; dinner €8. Lockout 9am-5pm. Curfew 11:30pm; flexible for opera-goers. Dorms €15; family rooms €19. HI members only. Cash only.) To get to the romantic, central **Bed and Breakfast Anfiteatro ❹**, V. Alberto Mario 5, follow V. Mazzini toward P. Brà until it branches to the right to become V. Alberto Mario. (☎347 24 88 462; www.anfiteatro-bedandbreakfast.com. TV and private bath. Breakfast included. Singles €60-90; Doubles €80-130.) ◙**Osteria al Duomo ❷**, V. Duomo 7/a, on the way to the *duomo*, offers a small menu, but serves authentic, simple cuisine like *tagliatelle* with shrimp and zucchini. (☎80 04 505. *Primi* €6-6.30; *secondi* €8-12. Cover €1. Open Tu-Sa noon-2:30pm and 7-10pm. Cash only.) A **PAM** supermarket is at V. dei Mutilati 3. (Open M-Sa 8am-8:30pm, Su 9am-8pm.)

ITALY

◨ ◧ **SIGHTS AND ENTERTAINMENT.** The heart of Verona is the tiered first-century **Arena** in P. Brà. (☎80 03 204. Open M 1:30-7:30pm, Tu-Su 8:30am-7:30pm. Closes 4:30pm on opera night. Ticket office closes 1hr. before Arena. €4, students €3. Cash only.) From late June to early September, tourists and singers from around the world descend on the Arena for the city's annual ◧**Opera Festival.** *Aida*, *Nabucco*, and *Carmen* are among the 2008 highlights. (☎80 05 151; www.arena.it. Box office open on opera night 10am-9pm, non-performance days 10am-5:45pm. General admission Su-Th €17-25, F-Sa €19-27. AmEx/MC/V.) From P. Brà, V. Mazzini leads to the markets and stunning architecture of **Piazza delle Erbe.** The 83m ◧**Torre dei Lambertini,** in P. dei Signori, offers a perfect view of Verona. (Open Su-Th 9:30am-8:30pm, F-Sa 9:30am-10pm. Elevator €4, students €3; stairs €3. Cash only.) The **Giardino Giusti,** V. Giardino Giusti 2, is a 16th-century garden with a thigh-high floral labyrinth, whose cypress-lined avenue gradually winds up to porticoes and curving balconies with stunning views of Verona. (☎80 34 029. Open daily Apr.-Sept. 9am-8pm; Oct.-Mar. 9am-7pm. €4.50.) The della Scala family fortress, **Castelvecchio,** down V. Roma from P. Brà, now has an art collection that includes Pisanello's *Madonna della Quaglia*. (☎80 62 611. Open M 1:30-7:30pm, Tu-Su 8:30am-7:30pm. €4, students €3. Cash only.) The balcony at **Casa di Giulietta** (Juliet's House), V. Cappello 23, overlooks a courtyard of tourists waiting to rub the statue of Juliet and lovers adding their vows to graffitied walls. The Capulets never lived here, so save your money for another scoop of *gelato*. (☎80 34 303. Open M 1:30-7:30pm, Tu-Su 8:30am-7:30pm. €4, students €3. Courtyard free.)

# FRIULI-VENEZIA GIULIA

Bounded by the Veneto to the west and Slovenia to the east is the kaleidoscope that is Friuli-Venezia Giulia. Regional control has changed hands multiple times, resulting in a potpourri of cuisines, styles, and architecture, appealing to writers and musicians: James Joyce began *Ulysses* in Trieste coffeehouses; Ernest Hemingway envisioned the plot of *A Farewell to Arms* in the region's Carso cliffs; and Franz Liszt, Sigmund Freud, and Rainer Maria Rilke all worked in Friuli.

## TRIESTE (TRIEST) ☎040

After being volleyed among Italian, Austrian, and Slavic powers for hundreds of years, Trieste (pop. 241,000) celebrated its 50th anniversary as an Italian city in 2004. Subtle reminders of Trieste's Eastern European past are manifest in its churches, cuisine, and portraits of smirking Habsburg rulers in museums. The fast-paced center swarms with motorcycles and people on the move, but the Carsoian hillside and Adriatic Sea temper the city with natural beauty. The gridded streets of the Città Nuova, all lined with majestic Neoclassical palaces, center around the Canale Grande. Facing the canal from the south is the blue-domed Serbian Orthodox **Chiesa di San Spiridione.** (Open Tu-Sa 9am-noon and 5-8pm, Su 9am-noon. Modest dress required.) The ornate **Municipio** (Town Hall) is in the **P. dell'Unità d'Italia,** the largest waterfront *piazza* in Italy. P. della Cattedrale overlooks the town center. In the mid-19th century, Archduke Maximilian of Austria commissioned the lavish ◧**Castello Miramare,** where each room is carefully preserved. Legend holds that visitors can still hear the wailing of Carlotta, Maximilian's wife, who went crazy after his murder. Take bus #36 (15min.; €0.90) to Ostello Tergeste and walk along the water for 15min. (Open M-Sa 9am-7pm, Su 8:30am-7pm. Ticket office open daily 9am-6:30pm. €4, 18-25 €2.) The ◧**Museo Revoltella,** V. Diaz 21, showcases modern art. (☎67 54 350; www.museorevoltella.it. Open Sept.-July M and W-Su 9am-1:30pm and 4-7pm; Aug. M 9am-1:30pm and 4-7pm, W-Sa 9am-1:30pm and 4pm-midnight, Su 10am-7pm. €6, students €4.)

Centrally located 🏠**Nuovo Albergo Centro** ❸, V. Roma 13, has spacious rooms. (☎34 78 790; www.hotelcentrotrieste.it. Breakfast included. Internet €4 per hr. Singles €35, with bath €48; doubles €50/68. 10% *Let's Go* discount. AmEx/MC/V.) Catch bus #36 (€0.90; runs until 9pm) from the V. Miramare side of the train station to reach **Ostello Tergeste (HI)** ❶, V. Miramare 331. Ask for the Ostello stop. From there, walk along the Barcola until you see a yellow villa with a terrace on your right. (☎22 41 02. Breakfast included. Reception 8-10am and 3:30pm-midnight. Dorms €14-18. HI members only. Cash only.) On a shaded *piazza*, family-run 🏠**Buffet da Siora Rosa** ❷, P. Hortis 3, serves Triestini favorites, like bread *gnocchi* (€6.20) and *prosciutto panini* (€1.20-4) doused in mustard and horseradish. (☎30 14 60. *Primi* €4-7. *Secondi* €5-10. Cover €1. Reserve ahead for outdoor seating. Open daily 8am-4pm and 6:30-9:30pm. MC/V.) The covered market at V. Carducci 36/D has tables piled high with fruits and cheese. (Open M 8am-2pm, Tu-Sa 8am-5pm.) Find groceries at the giant **PAM** supermarket, V. Miramare 1, across from the train station. (Open M-Sa 8am-8pm and Su 9am-7pm.) At night, trendsetters frequent **Via Roma Quattro**, whose name is also its address. (☎634 633. Open M-Sa 7:30am-11:30pm.) **Trains** leave P. della Libertà 8, down C. Cavour from the quay for Udine (1½hr., 28 per day, €6.60) and Venice (2hr., 20 per day, €8). The APT **tourist office** is at P. dell'Unità d'Italia 4/E, near the harbor. (☎34 78 312. Open daily 9:30am-7pm.) **Postal Code:** 34100.

# PIEDMONT (PIEMONTE)

More than just the source of the Po River, Piedmont rose to prominence when the Savoys briefly named Turin capital of their reunited Italy in 1861. Today, European tourists escape Turin's whirlwind pace on the banks of Lake Maggiore, while hikers and skiers conquer Alpine mountaintops. Piedmont is renowned for its high standard of living and modern, well-organized infrastructure.

## TURIN (TORINO)                                                   ☎011

A century and a half before Turin (pop. 910,000) was selected to host the 2006 Winter Olympics, it served as the first capital of a unified Italy. Renowned for chocolate and its cafe culture, Turin also lays claim to numerous parks and contemporary art pieces, as well as some of the country's best social and nightlife offerings, all while avoiding the pollution and crime problems of a big city.

🖹🚆 **TRANSPORTATION AND PRACTICAL INFORMATION. Trains** (☎66 53 098) run from **Porta Nuova,** in the center of the city, on C. V. Emanuele II to: Genoa (2hr., 1 per hr., €8.20); Milan (2hr., 1 per hr., €8.20); Rome (6-7hr., 26 per day, from €44); Venice (5hr., 20 per day, €35). A new **metro line** was recently installed and Turin's transportation system will continue to change in the next few years. Eventually, Porta Susa will be the main train station; for now, it is a departure point for trains to Paris via Lyon, FRA (5-6hr., 4 per day). Contact the **Turismo Torino,** P. Solferino, for brochures with art, literary, and walking tours. (☎53 51 81; www.turismotorino.org. Open M-Sa 9:30am-7pm, Su 9:30am-3pm.) Unlike in other Italian cities, streets in Turin meet at right angles, so it's relatively easy to navigate. V. Roma is the major north-south thoroughfare. It runs to P. Castello, from which V. Pietro Micca extends southwest to the Olympic Atrium. **Postal Code:** 10100.

## EAT. SHOP. LEARN.

n January 2007, a new restau-ant opened in Turin. Actually, 10 of them did, all under one oof. More than just a food court, Eataly (right) is a culinary amusement park.

Each of Eataly's restaurants specialize in a different food group and prepare your meal in front of you. Including the €1 cover, dishes generally cost €8-5 at each station, a bargain for heir high quality. Splitting meals s highly recommended in order to aste from more stations. The daily menus of cheese, meat, pasta, pizza, seafood, and vegetables are only the beginning. A coffee shop and *gelato* stand are also on the ground floor, while the basement showcases meat and cheese cellars. The basement also has two more restaurants, one dedicated to wine and one to beer. The bottled wine selection is overwhelming but, if you are the mood for something simple, you can fill up your own liter from the tap for €1.30-4 per L.

You can take the cooking into your own hands at the expansive organic food store or at the learning center, which offers varied and valuable cooking lessons from world-famous guest chefs €20-100). While the calendar of classes is in Italian, many of the cooking lessons are also available in English for groups. (*V. Nizza 224. Take bus #1, 18, or 35 o the Biglieri stop. Reservations 011 19 50 68; www.eataly.com.*)

**▞▚ ACCOMMODATIONS AND FOOD.** Turin's budget options are scattered around the city, though a few cluster near Stazione Porta Nuova. Family-run bed and breakfasts offer some of the best deals, though many close in summer. The new **◪Open 011 ❷**, C. Venezia 11, near the V. Chiesa della Salute stop on bus #11, has a bar, library, restaurant, TV, and Wi-Fi. (☎51 62 038; www.openzero11.it. Dorms €17; singles €30; doubles €42.) To get to comfortable **Ostello Torino (HI) ❶**, V. Alby 1, take bus #52 (#64 on Su) from Porta Nuova. After crossing the river, get off at the Lanza stop at V. Crimea and follow the "Ostello" signs to C. G. Lanza, before turning left at V. L. Gatti. (☎66 02 939; www.ostellotorino.it. Breakfast and linens included. Laundry €4. Reception M-Sa 7am-12:30pm and 3-11pm, Su 7-10am and 3-11pm. Lockout 10am-3pm. Curfew 11pm; ask for key if going out. Closed Dec. 21-Jan. 14. Single-sex or co-ed 3- to 8-bed dorms €15; doubles €31-38; triples €51; quads €68. MC/V.) The **Albergo Azalea ❸**, V. Mercanti 16, 3th floor, has cozy rooms and a great location. Exit Porta Nuova on the right and take #58 or 72 to V. Garibaldi. Turn left on V. Garibaldi, then left on V. Mercanti. (☎53 81 15; albergo.azalea@virgilio.it. Singles €35, with bath €45; doubles €55-65. MC/V.)

Spend the day at **◪Eataly,** via Nizza 224, Turin's new 10,000 sq. ft. culinary amusement park. Tastings of wine and beer are just the beginning: classrooms feature cooking classes by famous guest chefs, meat and cheese lockers are on display, and museum-quality exhibits demonstrate various food preparation techniques. Rotate around the restaurant counters dedicated to beer, *gelato*, meat, pasta, pizza, and wine, each with its own daily menu. Take bus #1, 18 or 35 to the Biglieri stop, near the Lingotto Expo Center. (☎19 50 68 11; www.eataly.it. Reserve ahead for classes and wine tasting. Open daily 10am-10:30pm.) Chocolate has been the city's glory ever since Turin nobles began taking an evening cup of it in 1678. *Gianduiotto* (hazelnut chocolate) turns up in candies and *gelato*. Sample *bicerin* (Turin's hot coffee-chocolate-cream drink; €4), craved by Nietzsche and Dumas, at **Caffè Cioccolateria al Bicerin ❶**, Piazza della Consolata, 5. (☎43 69 325. Open M-Tu and Th-F 8:30am-7:30pm, Sa-Su 8:30am-1pm and 3:30-7:30pm.) If Eataly doesn't have everything you need, head to **Porta Palazzo,** P. della Repubblica, perhaps Europe's largest open-air market. (M-F 7:30am-2pm, Sa 7:30am-sunset.)

**◪▚ SIGHTS AND NIGHTLIFE.** The **Torino Card** (48hr. €18; 72hr. €20) is the best deal in the city: it provides entrance to more than 140 castles, monuments, museums, and royal residences in Turin, many of which are worth a visit. Once the largest structure in the world built using traditional masonry, the ■**Mole Antonelliana,** V. Montebello 20, a few blocks east of P. Castello, was originally a synagogue. It's home to the eccentric **Museo Nazionale del Cinema,** which plays hundreds of movie clips. (Museum open Tu-F and Su 9am-8pm, Sa 9am-11pm. €5.20, students €4.20.) The city possesses one of the more famous relics of Christianity: the **Holy Shroud of Turin,** said to be Jesus' burial cloth, is housed in the **Cattedrale di San Giovanni,** behind the **Palazzo Reale.** With rare exception, a photograph of the shroud is as close as visitors will get. (Open daily 8am-noon and 3-6pm. Free.) The **Museo Egizio,** in the **Palazzo dell'Accademia delle Scienze,** V. dell'Accademia delle Scienze 6, has a world-class collection of Egyptian artifacts. (Open Tu-Su 8:30am-7:30pm. €6.50, ages 18-25 €3.) The same building houses the **Galleria Sabauda,** which features a large collection of Renaissance paintings, including works by Rembrandt and van Dyck. (Open Nov.-May Tu and F-Su 8:30am-2pm, W 2-7:30pm, Th 10am-7:30pm; June-Oct. Tu and F-Su 8:30am-2pm, W-Th 2-7:30pm. €4, ages 18-25 €2.) Many exhibits at the sleek modern and contemporary art venue, **Castello di Rivoli Museo D'Arte Contemporanea,** P. Mafalda di Savoia, were designed for its cavernous spaces. (☎95 65 222. In Rivoli. Take bus #36 or 66; ask at bus station about shuttles. Open Tu-Th 10am-5pm, F-Su 1am-9pm. €6.50, students €3.50.)

■**I Murazzi** is the center of Turin's social scene and consists of two stretches of boardwalk, one between Ponte V. Emanuele I and Ponte Umberto, and another smaller stretch downstream. Most people show up between 7:30-9:30pm and spend the next 5hr. sipping drinks, maneuvering among crowds at the waterfront, or dancing in the clubs. **The Beach,** V. Murazzi del Po 18-22, has the best dance floor in Turin. By 1am, this large, modern club fills with the young and the trendy, dancing to electronica music. (☎88 87 77. Mixed drinks €6. Open Tu-W 10pm-2am and Th-Sa noon-4am.) **Quadrilatero Romano,** the recently renovated buildings between P. della Repubblica and V. Garibaldi, attracts those who would rather sit, drink, and chat until 4am than dance to techno music. **Arancia di Mezzanotte,** P. E. Filiberto 11/I, is a popular place for an *aperitivo*. (Open daily 6pm-4am. MC/V.) Across the *piazza*, **Shore,** P. E. Filiberto 10/G, serves large mixed drinks until the early morning to a score of chill-out music. (Open daily 6:30pm-2:30am.)

# TUSCANY (TOSCANA)

Recently, popular culture has glorified Tuscany as a sun-soaked sanctuary of art, nature, and civilization, and this time pop culture has gotten it right. Every town claims a Renaissance master, every highway offers scenic vistas, every celebration culminates in parades, festivals, and galas, and every year brings more tourists to the already beaten Tuscan path.

# FLORENCE (FIRENZE)                    ☎055

Florence (pop. 400,000) is the city of the Renaissance. By the 14th century, it had already become one of the most influential cities in Europe. In the 15th century, Florence overflowed with artistic excellence as the Medici family amassed a peerless collection, supporting masters like Botticelli, Brunelleschi, Donatello, and Michelangelo. These days, the tourists who flood the streets are captivated by Florence's distinctive character, creative spirit, and timeless beauty.

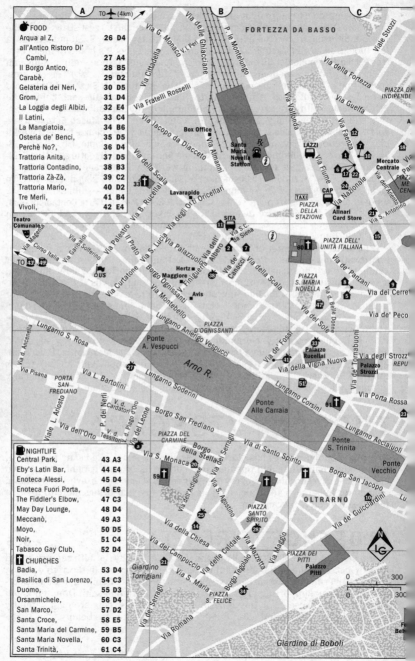

**FOOD**

| | |
|---|---|
| Arqua al Z, | **26 D4** |
| all'Antico Ristoro Di' | |
| Cambi, | **27 A4** |
| Il Borgo Antico, | **28 B5** |
| Carabè, | **29 D2** |
| Gelateria dei Neri, | **30 D5** |
| Grom, | **31 D4** |
| La Loggia degli Albizi, | **32 E4** |
| Il Latini, | **33 C4** |
| La Mangiatoia, | **34 B6** |
| Osteria de' Benci, | **35 D5** |
| Perchè No?, | **36 D4** |
| Trattoria Anita, | **37 D5** |
| Trattoria Contadino, | **38 B3** |
| Trattoria Zà-Zà, | **39 C2** |
| Trattoria Mario, | **40 D2** |
| Tre Merli, | **41 B4** |
| Vivoli, | **42 E4** |

**NIGHTLIFE**

| | |
|---|---|
| Central Park, | **43 A3** |
| Eby's Latin Bar, | **44 E4** |
| Enoteca Alessi, | **45 D4** |
| Enoteca Fuori Porta, | **46 E6** |
| The Fiddler's Elbow, | **47 C3** |
| May Day Lounge, | **48 D4** |
| Meccanò, | **49 A3** |
| Moyo, | **50 D5** |
| Noir, | **51 C4** |
| Tabasco Gay Club, | **52 D4** |

**CHURCHES**

| | |
|---|---|
| Badia, | **53 D4** |
| Basilica di San Lorenzo, | **54 C3** |
| Duomo, | **55 D3** |
| Orsanmichele, | **56 D4** |
| San Marco, | **57 D2** |
| Santa Croce, | **58 E5** |
| Santa Maria del Carmine, | **59 B5** |
| Santa Maria Novella, | **60 C3** |
| Santa Trinità, | **61 C4** |

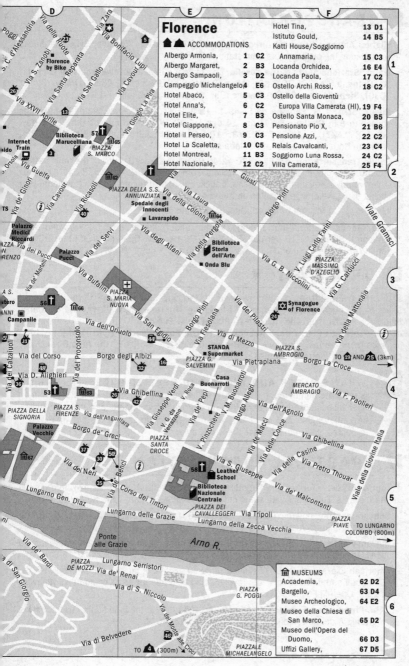

### Florence

🏠🏠 ACCOMMODATIONS

| | |
|---|---|
| Albergo Armonia, | 1 C2 |
| Albergo Margaret, | 2 B3 |
| Albergo Sampaoli, | 3 D2 |
| Campeggio Michelangelo | 4 E6 |
| Hotel Abaco, | 5 C3 |
| Hotel Anna's, | 6 C2 |
| Hotel Elite, | 7 B3 |
| Hotel Giappone, | 8 C3 |
| Hotel il Perseo, | 9 C3 |
| Hotel La Scaletta, | 10 C5 |
| Hotel Montreal, | 11 B3 |
| Hotel Nazionale, | 12 C2 |
| Hotel Tina, | 13 D1 |
| Istituto Gould, | 14 B5 |
| Katti House/Soggiorno Annamaria, | 15 C3 |
| Locanda Orchidea, | 16 E4 |
| Locanda Paola, | 17 C2 |
| Ostello Archi Rossi, | 18 C2 |
| Ostello della Gioventù Europa Villa Camerata (HI), | 19 F4 |
| Ostello Santa Monaca, | 20 B5 |
| Pensionato Pio X, | 21 B6 |
| Pensione Azzi, | 22 C2 |
| Relais Cavalcanti, | 23 C4 |
| Soggiorno Luna Rossa, | 24 C2 |
| Villa Camerata, | 25 F4 |

🏛 MUSEUMS

| | |
|---|---|
| Accademia, | 62 D2 |
| Bargello, | 63 D4 |
| Museo Archeologico, | 64 E2 |
| Museo della Chiesa di San Marco, | 65 D2 |
| Museo dell'Opera del Duomo, | 66 D3 |
| Uffizi Gallery, | 67 D5 |

ITALY

# ⊫ TRANSPORTATION

**Flights: Amerigo Vespucci Airport** (**FLR;** ☎30 61 300), in Peretola. **SITA** runs buses connecting the airport to the train station (€4.50).

**Trains: Stazione Santa Maria Novella,** across from S. Maria Novella. Trains run 1 per hr. to: **Bologna** (1hr., €4.70-6.80); **Milan** (3½hr., €29); **Pisa** (1hr., €5.20); **Rome** (3½hr., €30); **Siena** (1½hr., €5.70); **Venice** (3hr., €16). For more info visit www.trenitalia.it.

**Buses: SITA,** V. S. Caterina da Siena 17 (☎800 37 37 60; www.sita-on-line.it), runs buses to **San Gimignano** (1½hr., 14 per day, €5.90) and **Siena** (1½hr., 2 per day, €6.50). **LAZZI,** P. Adua 1-4R (☎35 10 61; www.lazzi.it), runs to **Pisa** (1 per hr., €6.10). Both offices are near S. Maria Novella.

**Public Transportation: ATAF** (☎800 42 45 00; www.ataf.net), outside the train station, runs orange city buses 6am-1am. Tickets 70min. €1.20; 24hr. €5; 3-day €12. Buy them at any newsstand, *tabaccheria,* or ticket dispenser before boarding. Validate your ticket using the orange machine on board or risk a €50 fine.

**Taxis:** ☎43 90, 47 98, or 42 42. Outside the train station.

**Bike/Moped Rental: Alinari Noleggi,** V. San Zanobi, 38r (☎28 05 00; www.alinarirental.com). Bikes €12-16 per day. Scooters €30 per day. Open M-Sa 9:30am-1:30pm and 2:45-7:30pm, Su and holidays 10am-1pm and 3-6pm. MC/V.

# ⊁ ORIENTATION

From the train station, a short walk on V. Panzani and a left on V. dei Cerretani leads to the **duomo,** in the center of Florence. The bustling walkway **Via dei Calzaiuoli** runs south from the *duomo* to **Piazza della Signoria.** V. Roma leads from the *duomo* through **Piazza della Repubblica** to the **Ponte Vecchio** (Old Bridge), which crosses from central Florence to **Oltrarno,** the district south of the **Arno River.** Note that most streets change names unpredictably.

**WHAT'S BLACK AND WHITE AND RED ALL OVER?** Florence's streets are numbered in red and black sequences. Red numbers indicate commercial establishments, and black (or blue) numbers denote residences (including most sights and hotels). If you reach an address and it's not what you expected, you probably have the wrong color.

# ▮ PRACTICAL INFORMATION

**Tourist Office: Informazione Turistica,** P. della Stazione 4 (☎21 22 45). Info on cultural events. Free maps with street index. Open M-Sa 8:30am-7pm, Su 8:30am-2pm.

**Consulates: UK,** Lungarno Corsini 2 (☎28 41 33). Open M-F 9am-1pm and 2-5pm. **US,** Lungarno Amerigo Vespucci 38 (☎26 69 51). Open M-F 9am-12:30pm.

**Currency Exchange:** Local banks have the best rates; beware of independent exchange services with high fees. Most banks are open M-F 8:20am-1:20pm and 2:45-3:45pm.

**American Express:** V. Dante Alighieri 22R (☎50 98). From the *duomo,* walk down V. dei Calzaiuoli and turn left on V. dei Tavolini. Mail held free for AmEx customers, otherwise €1.55. Open M-F 9am-5:30pm.

**24hr. Pharmacies: Farmacia Comunale** (☎28 94 35), at the train station by track #16. **Molteni,** V. dei Calzaiuoli 7R (☎28 94 90). AmEx/MC/V.

**Internet Access:** Walk down almost any busy street and you'll find an Internet cafe. **Internet Train,** V. Guelfa 54/56R, has 15 locations in the city listed on www.internettrain.it. €4.30 per hr., students €3.20. Most branches open M-F 9am-midnight, Sa 10am-8pm, Su noon-9pm. AmEx/MC/V.

**Post Office:** V. Pellicceria (☎27 36 480), off P. della Repubblica. Poste Restante available. Open M-Sa 8:15am-7pm. **Postal Code:** 50100.

# ▐ ACCOMMODATIONS

Lodging in Florence doesn't come cheap. **Consorzio ITA,** in the train station by track #16, can find rooms for a €3-8.50 fee. (☎066 99 10 00. Open M-Sa 8am-8pm, Su 10am-7pm.) It is best to make a *prenotazioni* (reservation) ahead, especially if you plan to visit during Easter or summer. If you have any complaints, first talk to the proprietor and then to the **Tourist Rights Protection Desk,** V. Cavour 1R (☎29 08 32 33), or **Servizio Turismo,** V. Manzoni 16 (☎27 60 552; uff.turismo@provincia.fi.it).

## HOSTELS AND CAMPING

▨ **Ostello Archi Rossi,** V. Faenza 94R (☎29 08 04; www.hostelarchirossi.com), near S. Maria Novella station. Outdoor patio is packed with students after dark. Home-cooked breakfast included. Laundry €6. Free Internet. Lockout 11am-2:30pm. Curfew 2am. Reserve online 1 week ahead, especially in summer. Dorms €21-26. MC/V. ❷

**Istituto Gould,** V. dei Serragli 49 (☎21 25 76; www.istitutogould.it), in the Oltrarno. Take bus #36 or 37 from the train station to the 2nd stop across the river. Spotless rooms. Reception M-F 8:45am-1pm and 3-7:30pm, Sa 9am-1:30pm. Dorms €21; singles €36, with bath €42; doubles €52-62. MC/V. ❷

**Ostello Santa Monaca,** V. S. Monaca 6 (☎26 83 38; www.ostello.it). Follow the directions to the Istituto Gould, but turn left off V. dei Serragli onto V. S. Monaca. Breakfast €2.70-3.80. Laundry €6.50 per 5kg. Internet €3 per hr. June-Sept. max. stay 7 nights. Curfew 1am. Reserve ahead. 10-bed dorms €18. AmEx/MC/V. ❷

**Ostello della Gioventù Europa Villa Camerata (HI),** V. Augusto Righi 2-4 (☎60 14 51), northeast of town. Take bus #17 from the train station (near track #5); ask for Salviatino. From the entrance, walk 10min. up a driveway past a vineyard. Tidy and crowded, in a beautiful villa. Breakfast included. Laundry €5.20. Max. stay 3 nights. Lockout 10am-2pm. Strict midnight curfew. Dorms €21. €3 HI discount. MC/V. ❷

**Pensionato Pio X,** V. dei Serragli 106 (☎/fax 22 50 44), in the Oltrarno. Rooms, while not fancy, are clean and quiet. Check-out 9am. Curfew 1am. Dorms €17. Cash only. ❷

**Campeggio Michelangelo,** V. Michelangelo 80 (☎68 11 977; www.ecvacanze.it), beneath P. Michelangelo. Bus #13 from the bus station (15min.; last bus 11:25pm). Reception 7am-11pm. €11 per person, €16 per tent site. MC/V; min. €100. ❶

**Villa Camerata,** V. A. Righi 2-4 (☎60 03 15; fax 61 03 00). Take bus #17 outside the train station (near track #5); ask for Salviatino stop. Walk down driveway. Same entrance and reception as HI hostel (p. 695). Breakfast €2. Reception 7am-12:30pm and 1pm-midnight. Max. stay 6 nights. €8 per person, €7 per tent site. MC/V. ❶

## HOTELS

### OLD CITY (NEAR THE DUOMO)

▨ **Locanda Orchidea,** Borgo degli Albizi 11 (☎24 80 346; hotelorchidea@yahoo.it). Dante's wife was born in this 12th-century *palazzo*, built around a still-intact tower. Carefully decorated rooms with marble floors; some open onto a garden. Singles €55; doubles €75; triples with shower €100; quads with shower €120. Cash only. ❹

**Hotel Il Perseo,** V. de Cerretani 1 (☎21 25 04; www.hotelperseo.it). 20 spotless rooms with fans, satellite TVs, and free Internet. Breakfast included. Singles €85-95; doubles €110-140; triples €135-170; quads €160-210. AmEx/MC/V; min. 2 nights. ❺

**Relais Cavalcanti,** V. Pellicceria 2 (☎21 09 62). Unbeatable location just steps from P. della Repubblica. Ring bell to enter. Beautiful gold-trimmed rooms with antique wardrobes. Singles €100; doubles €125; triples €155. 10% *Let's Go* discount. MC/V. ❺

## PIAZZA SANTA MARIA NOVELLA AND ENVIRONS

🏨 **Soggiorno Luna Rossa,** V. Nazionale 7 (☎23 02 185). 3rd fl. Airy rooms have fan, TV, and colorful stained-glass windows. Small shared baths. Breakfast included. Dorms €22. Singles €35; doubles €85; triples €100; quads €140. Cash only. ❷

**Hotel Abaco,** V. dei Banchi 1 (☎23 81 919; www.abaco-hotel.it). Extravagant rooms, each one named after a Renaissance master. Breakfast and A/C included when paying in cash. Laundry €7. Limited Internet access free at reception. Doubles €75, with bath €90; triples €110; quads €135. 10% *Let's Go* discount Nov.-Mar. MC/V. ❺

**Hotel Elite,** V. della Scala 12 (☎21 53 95). Brass bedposts shine in lovely rooms. Breakfast €6. Singles €50; doubles €75-90; triples €110; quads €130. MC/V. ❹

**Hotel Giappone,** V. dei Banchi 1 (☎21 00 90; www.hotelgiappone.com). 10 clean rooms in centrally located hotel have A/C, Internet jack, phone, and TV. Singles €50, with bath €55; doubles €75-110; triples €95. MC/V. ❹

**Albergo Margaret,** V. della Scala 25 (☎21 01 38; www.dormireintoscana.it/margaret). 7 rooms decked in red linens and puffy orange quilts, with TVs and A/C. Curfew midnight. Singles €40-60; doubles €60-90. Cash only. ❹

**Hotel Montreal,** V. della Scala 43 (☎23 82 331; www.hotelmontreal.com). Wood-furnished rooms, all with TV and A/C. Breakfast included July-Aug., low season €5. Curfew 2am. Singles €60, with bath €130; doubles €100/150; triples €150/200; quads with bath €250. Cash only. ❹

## AROUND PIAZZA SAN MARCO

🏨 **Albergo Sampaoli,** V. S. Gallo 14 (☎28 48 34; www.hotelsampaoli.it). Helpful staff and a large common area with fridge access. All rooms with fans, some with balcony. Singles €30-40, with bath €60-65; doubles €65/75; triples €70/80. MC/V. ❹

**Hotel Tina,** V. S. Gallo 31 (☎48 35 19; www.hoteltina.it). *Pensione* with new furniture, and amiable owners. Singles €30-50; doubles €46-65; extra bed €25. MC/V. ❹

## AROUND VIA NAZIONALE

🏨 **Katti House/Soggiorno Annamaria,** V. Faenza 21/24 (☎21 34 10). Lovingly kept lodgings with 400-year-old antiques and an attentive staff. Large, recently renovated rooms with A/C, bath, and TV. Singles €60-75; doubles €75-120; triples €90; quads €120. Nov.-Mar. reduced rates. MC/V. ❹

**Hotel Nazionale,** V. Nazionale 22 (☎23 82 203; www.nazionalehotel.it). 9 sunny rooms with comfy beds and A/C. Breakfast brought to your room 8-9:30am (€6). Singles €60-70; doubles €85-115; triples €115-145. MC/V. ❺

**Via Faenza 56** houses 4 *pensioni* that are among the best deals in the area. From the train station, exit left onto V. Nazionale, walk 1 block, and turn left on V. Faenza.

**Pensione Azzi** (☎21 38 06; www.hotelazzi.com) has large rooms and a terrace. Styled as an artists' inn. Breakfast included. Singles €55-70; doubles €80-110. AmEx/MC/V. ❹

**Hotel Anna's** (☎23 02 714; www.hotelannas.com), on the 2nd fl. Rooms with TV, bath, phone, and A/C. Breakfast €5. Singles €60-80; doubles €80-100; triples €75-130. AmEx/MC/V. ❹

**Locanda Paola** (☎21 36 82) has doubles with views of the surrounding hills. Breakfast included. Internet access. Flexible 2am curfew. Dorms €25. MC/V. ❸

**Albergo Armonia** (☎21 11 46). Rooms have high ceilings. Singles €42; doubles €65; triples €75. Extra bed €25. Low season reduced rates. Cash only. ❸

## OLTRARNO

▓ **Hotel La Scaletta,** V. Guicciardini 13B (☎28 30 28; www.hotellascaletta.it). Turn right onto V. Roma from the *duomo,* cross Ponte Vecchio, and take V. Guicciardini. Breakfast included. Reception until midnight. Singles €55-100; doubles €70-140; triples €85-160; quads €100-180. €10 *Let's Go* discount on cash payment. MC/V. ❺

# ◖ FOOD

Florentine specialties include *bruschetta* (grilled bread soaked in oil and garlic and topped with tomatoes, basil, and anchovy or liver paste) and *bistecca alla Fiorentina* (thick sirloin). The best local cheese is pecorino, made from sheep's milk. A liter of house wine usually costs €3.50-6 in a *trattoria,* but stores sell bottles of chianti for as little as €2.50. The local dessert is *cantuccini di prato* (almond cookies) dipped in *vinsanto* (a rich dessert wine). Florence's own Buontalenti family supposedly invented *gelato;* extensive sampling is a must. For lunch, visit a *rosticceria gastronomia,* peruse the city's pushcarts, or pick up fresh produce and meats at the **Mercato Centrale,** between V. Nazionale and S. Lorenzo. (Open June-Sept. M-Sa 7:30am-2pm; Oct.-May M-F 7am-2pm, Sa 7am-2pm and 4-8pm.) To get to **STANDA** supermarket, V. Pietrapiana 1R, turn right on V. del Proconsolo, take the first left on Borgo degli Albizi, and continue straight through P. G. Salvemini. (Open M-Sa 8am-9pm, Su 9am-9pm. MC/V.)

## RESTAURANTS

### OLD CITY (NEAR THE DUOMO)

▓ **Osteria de' Benci,** V. de' Benci 13R (☎23 44 923), on the corner of V. dei Neri. Join locals for classics like *carpaccio* (thinly sliced beef; €14). *Primi* €9. *Secondi* €9-14. Cover €3.30. Reserve ahead. Open M-Sa 1-2:45pm and 7:30-11:45pm. AmEx/MC/V. ❹

▓ **Acqua al 2,** V. Vigna Vecchia 40R (☎28 41 70), behind the Bargello. Popular with young Italians and tourists. Serves Florentine specialties, including an excellent *filetto al mirtillo* (steak in a blueberry sauce; €15). *Primi* €7. *Secondi* €8-19. Cover €1. Service 10%. Reserve ahead. Open daily 7pm-1am. AmEx/MC/V. ❸

**Trattoria Anita,** V. del Parlascio 2R (☎21 86 98), behind the Bargello. Dine by candlelight, surrounded by shelves of expensive wine. Traditional Tuscan fare, including pasta, roast chicken, and steak. *Primi* €5. *Secondi* from €6. Lunch *menù* €6. Cover €1. Open M-Sa noon-2:30pm and 7-10pm. AmEx/MC/V. ❷

**La Loggia degli Albizi,** Borgo degli Albizi 39R (☎24 79 574). From behind the *duomo,* go right on V. del Proconsolo and take the 1st left onto Borgo degli Albizi. Head 2 blocks down and look right. A hidden treasure, this bakery/cafe offers an escape from the tourist hordes. Pastries and coffee from €0.80, more at tables. Open M-Sa 7am-8pm. ❶

### PIAZZA SANTA MARIA NOVELLA AND ENVIRONS

▓ **Il Latini,** V. dei Palchetti 6R (☎21 09 16). Crowds line up nightly; prepare to wait for your *arrosto misto* (platter of roast meats). Waiters keep the wine flowing. *Primi* €6-8. *Secondi* €10-18. Reserve ahead. Open Tu-Su 12:30-2:30pm and 7:30-10:30pm. Closed 2 weeks in Aug. AmEx/MC/V. ❸

ITALY

**Trattoria Contadino,** V. Palazzuolo 71R (☎23 82 673). Filling, homestyle, fixed-price *menù* (€10-11) includes *primo, secondo,* bread, water, and 0.25L of wine. Open Sept.-May daily 11am-2:30pm and 6-9:30pm. June-July closed Sa-Su. AmEx/MC/V. ❷

**Tre Merli,** entrances on V. del Moro 11R and V. dei Fossi 12R (☎28 70 62). In a dining room close to the river, soft red light accents sumptuous dishes like *spaghettino all'Imperiale* (with mussels, clams, and shrimp; €14). *Primi* €7.50-14. *Secondi* €12-19. Lunch *menù* €12. Cover €2. Open daily 11am-11pm. 10% discount and free glass of wine with *Let's Go.* AmEx/MC/V. ❹

## THE STATION AND UNIVERSITY QUARTER

◪ **Trattoria Zà-Zà,** P. del Mercato Centrale 26R (☎21 54 11). Wooden-beam ceilings and brick archways inside, lively patio outside. Try the *tris* (mixed bean and vegetable soup; €7) or the *tagliata di manzo* (cut of beef; €14-19). Cover €2. Reserve ahead. Open daily 11am-11pm. AmEx/MC/V. ❸

**Trattoria Mario,** V. Rosina 2R (☎21 85 50), around the corner from P. del Mercato Centrale. Informal lunch establishment with incredible pasta, a stellar rendition of *bistecca alla Fiorentina,* and a loyal local following. *Secondi* €3.10-11. Cover €0.50. Open M-Sa noon-3:30pm. Closed Aug. Cash only. ❷

## OLTRARNO

◪ **all'Antico Ristoro Di' Cambi,** V. S. Onofrio 1R (☎21 71 34). Near Ponte Vespucci. Prosciutto hangs from the restored 5th-century ceiling. 3rd-generation owner Stefano serves up Florentine speciality *bistecca alla Fiorentina* (€4 per 100g). The *sorbetto limone* (€4) is the ideal finish. *Primi* €6-8. *Secondi* €7-16. Cover €1. Open M-Sa noon-3pm and 7:30pm-midnight. Closed 2 weeks in mid-Aug. AmEx/MC/V. ❹

◪ **Il Borgo Antico,** P. S. Spirito 6R (☎21 04 37). Trendy spot with young staff and student-heavy clientele. Memorable pastas, pizzas, and salads (€7). *Primi* €7. *Secondi* €10-20. Cover €2. Reserve ahead. Open daily June-Sept. 11am-midnight; Oct.-May 12:45-2:30pm and 7:45pm-1am. AmEx/MC/V. ❸

**La Mangiatoia,** P. S. Felice 8R (☎22 40 60). Continue straight on V. Guicciardini from Ponte Vecchio. Quality Tuscan fare and an extensive takeout menu. *Primi* €4-6. *Secondi* €5-9. Cover €1.50. Open Tu-Su 11am-3pm and 6:30-10pm. AmEx/MC/V. ❷

# GELATERIE

Florence's *gelaterie* get crowded, and to avoid making salespeople cranky, follow protocol when ordering: first, pay at the register for the size you request, then—receipt in hand—choose a flavor. Most *gelaterie* also serve *granite,* flavored ices that are easier on the waistline.

◪ **Grom,** Via del Campanile (☎21 61 58). The kind of *gelato* you'll be talking about in 50 years. As fresh as it gets. Sublimely balanced texture. Cups start at €2. Open daily Apr.-Sept. 10:30am-midnight; Oct.-Mar. 10:30am-11pm.

◪ **Vivoli,** V. Isole della Stinche 7 (☎29 23 34), behind the Bargello. A renowned *gelateria* and long-time contender for the distinction of the best ice cream in Florence. Cups from €1.60. Open Tu-Sa 7:30am-1am, Su 9:30am-1am.

**Gelateria dei Neri,** V. dei Neri 20-22R (☎21 00 34). Stand outside and watch through the window as dozens of delicious flavors are mixed right before your eyes. Try *crema giotto* (coconut, almond, and hazelnut). Cones and cups from €1.40.

**Perchè No?,** V. Tavolini 19R (☎23 98 969), off V. dei Calzaiuoli. This centrally located, crowded parlor serves mouth-watering chocolate and chunky *nocciolosa*. Cones from €1.80. Open M and W-Su 11am-1am.

**Carabè,** V. Ricasoli 60R (☎28 94 76). Lemons shipped from Sicily elevate fruit flavors. Cups from €2. Open daily May-Sept. 10am-midnight; Mar.-Apr. and Oct. noon-midnight.

## ENOTECHE (WINE BARS)

Check out an *enoteca* to sample Italy's fine wines. A meal can often be made out of complementary side dishes (cheeses, olives, toast and spreads, and salami).

**Enoteca Alessi,** V. della Oche 27/29R (☎21 49 66), 1 block from the *duomo*. Among Florence's finest wine bars, with a cavernous interior that stocks over 1000 wines. Doubles as a candy store. Open M-F 9am-1pm and 3:30-7:30pm. AmEx/MC/V.

**Enoteca Fuori Porta,** V. Monte alle Croci 10R (☎23 42 483), near S. Miniato. This casual *enoteca,* popular with young Italians, serves an extensive selection of *bruschetta* (€1-2.50) and *crostini* (€4.50-7.50). Cover €1.50. Open daily noon-4pm and 7-10pm. Closed Su in Aug. MC/V.

# ◉ SIGHTS

For a full list of museum openings, check out www.firenzeturismo.it. For museum reservations, call **Firenze Musei** (☎29 48 83; www.firenzemusei.it). There are **no student discounts** at museums and admission can be expensive. Choose destinations carefully and plan to spend a few hours at each landmark.

## PIAZZA DEL DUOMO

**▨ DUOMO (CATTEDRALE DI SANTA MARIA DEL FIORE).** In 1296, the city fathers commissioned Arnolfo di Cambio to erect a cathedral so magnificent that it would be "impossible to make it either better or more beautiful with the industry and power of man." Di Cambio succeeded, designing a massive nave with the confidence that by the time it was completed (1418), technology would have advanced enough to provide a solution to erect a dome. **Filippo Brunelleschi** was called in to add a dome: after studying long-neglected classical methods, he came up with his double-shelled, interlocking-brick construction. The *duomo* claims the world's third longest nave, trailing only St. Peter's in Rome and St. Paul's in London. *(Open M-W and F 10am-5pm, Th 10am-4:30pm, Sa 10am-4:45pm, Su 1:30-4:45pm. Mass daily 7am, 12:30, 5-7pm. Free.)* Climb the 463 steps inside the dome to **Michelangelo's lantern,** which offers an expansive view of the city from the 100m high external gallery. *(Open M-F 8:30am-7pm, Sa 8:30am-5:40pm. €6.)* The climb up the 82m **campanile** next to the duomo, also called "Giotto's Tower," reveals views of the *duomo,* the city, and the **battistero** (baptistry), whose bronze doors, forged by Ghiberti, are known as the **▨Gates of Paradise.** Byzantine-style mosaics inside the baptistry inspired details of the *Inferno* by Dante, who was christened here. *(Campanile open daily 8:30am-7:30pm. €6. Baptistry open M-Sa noon-7pm, Su 8:30am-2pm. €3.)* Most of the *duomo*'s art resides behind the cathedral in the **Museo dell'Opera del Duomo.** Up the first flight of stairs is a late *Pietà* by Michelangelo; according to legend, he broke Christ's left arm in a fit of frustration. *(P. del Duomo 9, behind the duomo. ☎23 02 885. Open M-Sa 9am-7:30pm, Su 9am-1:40pm. €6.)*

**▨ ORSANMICHELE.** Built in 1337 as a granary, the Orsanmichele became a church after a fire convinced officials to move grain operations outside the city. The ancient grain chutes are still visible outside. Within, tenacious visi-

ITALY

tors will discover Ghiberti's *St. John the Baptist* and *St. Stephen*, Donatello's *St. Peter* and *St. Mark*, and Giambologna's *St. Luke. (V. Arte della Lana, between the* duomo *and P. della Signoria. Open Tu-Su 10am-5pm. Free.)*

## PIAZZA DELLA SIGNORIA AND ENVIRONS

From P. del Duomo, **Via dei Calzaiuoli,** one of the city's oldest streets, runs south past crowds, street vendors, *gelaterie,* and chic shops to **Piazza della Signoria,** the 13th-century *piazza* bordered by the Palazzo Vecchio and the Uffizi. With the construction of the Palazzo Vecchio in 1299, the square became Florence's civic and political center. In 1497, religious zealot Girolamo Savonarola lit the **Bonfire of the Vanities** here, barbecuing some of Florence's best art. Today P. della Signoria fills daily with photo-snapping tourists who later return for drinks and dessert in its upscale cafes. Monumental sculptures bunch in front of the *palazzo* and inside the 14th-century **Loggia dei Lanzi.** *(Free.)*

■ **THE UFFIZI.** Giorgio Vasari designed this palace in 1554 for the offices *(uffizi)* of Duke Cosimo's administration; today, the gallery holds one of the world's finest art collections. Beautiful statues overlook the walkway from niches in the columns; play "spot the Renaissance man" and try to find Leonardo, Machiavelli, Petrarch, and Vespucci among them. Botticelli, Caravaggio, Cimabue, Fra Angelico, della Francesca, Giotto, Michelangelo, Raphael, del Sarto, Titian, da Vinci, even Dürer, Rembrandt, Rubens—you name it, it's here. Be sure to visit the **Cabinet of Drawings and Prints** on the first floor before confining yourself to the U-shaped corridor of the second floor. A few rooms are usually closed each day, and some works may be on loan. A sign at the ticket office lists the rooms that are closed; ask when they will reopen. *(From P. B. S. Giovanni, take V. Roma past P. della Repubblica, where the street turns into V. Calimala. Continue until V. Vaccereccia and turn left.* ☎ *23 88 651. Open Tu-Su 8:15am-6:50pm. €6.50. Reserve ahead for €3 fee. Audio tour €4.70.)*

■ **PALAZZO VECCHIO.** Arnolfo del Cambio designed this fortress-like *palazzo* in the late 13th century to be the seat of government. It included apartments which served as living quarters for members of the city council while they served two-month terms. After the *palazzo* became the Medici's home in 1470, Michelozzo decorated the courtyard. The **Monumental Apartments,** which house the *palazzo*'s extensive art collections, are now an art and history museum. The worthwhile **Activities Tour** includes the "Secret Routes," which reveal hidden stairwells and chambers tucked behind exquisite oil paintings. The ceiling of the **Salone del Cinquecento,** where the Grand Council of the Republic met, is so elaborately decorated that the walls can hardly support its weight. The tiny **Studio di Francesco I** is a treasure trove of Mannerist art. *(*☎*27 68 224. Open M-W and F-Sa 9am-7pm, Su 9am-1pm. Palazzo and Monumental Apartments each €6, ages 18-25 €4.50. Activities tour €8/5.50. Courtyard free. Reserve ahead for tours.)*

**PONTE VECCHIO.** From the Uffizi, follow V. Georgofili left and turn right along the river to reach the Ponte Vecchio, Florence's oldest bridge, built in 1345. In the 1500s, the Medici gentrified: they kicked out the butchers and tanneries and installed goldsmiths and diamond-carvers in their place. Today, the medieval-looking boutiques of the shop owners' descendants make the bridge glitter with chic necklaces, brooches, and charms; tourists and street performers make up the bulk of its traffic. Don't miss the ■**sunset view** from neighboring **Ponte alle Grazie.**

# THE BARGELLO AND ENVIRONS

■ **BARGELLO.** The heart of medieval Florence is in this 13th-century fortress, once the residence of the chief magistrate and later a brutal prison with public executions in its courtyard. It was restored in the 19th century and now houses the sculpture-filled, largely untouristed **Museo Nazionale.** Donatello's bronze *David*, the first free-standing nude since antiquity, stands opposite the two bronze panels of the *Sacrifice of Isaac*, submitted by Ghiberti and Brunelleschi in the baptistry door competition. Michelangelo's early works, including *Bacchus*, *Brutus*, and *Apollo*, are on the ground floor. *(V. del Proconsolo 4, between the duomo and P. della Signoria.* ☎ *23 88 606. Open daily 8:15am-6pm. Closed 2nd and 4th M of each month. €4.)*

**BADIA.** The site of medieval Florence's richest monastery, the Badia church is now buried in the interior of a residential block. Filippino Lippi's *Apparition of the Virgin to St. Bernard*, one of the most famous paintings of the 15th century, hangs in eerie gloom to the left of the church. Be sure to glance up at the intricately carved dark wood ceiling. Some say Dante may have first glimpsed his beloved Beatrice here. Visitors are asked to walk silently among the prostrate, white-robed worshippers. *(Entrance on V. Dante Alighieri, off V. Proconsolo.* ☎ *26 44 02. Open to tourists M 3-6pm, but respectful visitors can walk through at any time.)*

**MUSEO DI STORIA DELLA SCIENZA.** The telescopes, astrological models, clock workings, and anatomical figures of this collection date from the Renaissance. **Room 4** displays Galileo's tools, including the lens through which he first saw Jupiter's satellites. *(P. dei Giudici 1, behind Palazzo Vecchio and the Uffizi.* ☎ *26 53 11. Open M and W-F 9:30am-5pm, Tu and Sa 9:30am-1pm. €6.50, under 18 €4.)*

**CASA DI DANTE.** The Casa di Dante is reputedly identical to the house Dante inhabited. Those with interest in Dante will enjoy the displays, which trace the poet's life from youth to exile to the artistic creation that immortalized him. Nearby is a replica of the abandoned little church where Beatrice, Dante's unrequited love and spiritual guide in *Paradiso*, attended mass. *(Corner of V. Dante Alighieri and V. S. Margherita, 1 block from the Bargello.* ☎ *21 94 16. Ring bell to enter. Open Tu-Sa 10am-5pm, Su 10am-1pm. 1st Su of each month 10am-4. Closed last Su of each month. €4.)*

# PIAZZA DELLA REPUBBLICA AND FARTHER WEST

The largest open space in Florence, the P. della Repubblica teems with crowds, overpriced cafes, restaurants, and *gelaterie*. In 1890, it replaced the Mercato Vecchio as the site of the city market, but has since traded stalls for more fashionable vendors. The inscription *"antico centro della città, da secolare squalore, a vita nuova restituito"* ("ancient center of the city, squalid for centuries, restored to new life") makes a derogatory reference to the *piazza*'s location in the old Jewish ghetto. The area around Mercato Nuovo and V. Tornabuoni was Florence's financial capital in the 1400s. Now it's residential, but still touristy.

■ **CHIESA DI SANTA MARIA NOVELLA.** This church houses the chapels of the wealthiest 13th- and 14th-century merchants. Santa Maria Novella was home to an order of Dominicans, or *Domini canes* (Hounds of the Lord), who took a bite out of sin and corruption. The facade of the *chiesa* is made of Florentine marble and is considered one of the great masterpieces of early Renaissance architecture. The Medicis commissioned Vasari to paint new frescoes over the 13th-century ones on the walls, but the painter spared Masaccio's ■**Trinity,** the first painting to use geometric perspective. In the **Gondi Chapel** is Brunelleschi's *Crucifix*, designed in response to Donatello's, in Santa Croce, which Brunelleschi found too full of "vigorous naturalism." Donatello was supposedly so impressed by his rival's creation that he dropped the bag of eggs he was carrying. *(Open M-Th and Sa 9am-5pm. €2.70.)*

**CHIESA DI SANTA TRINITÀ.** Hoping to spend eternity in elite company, the most fashionable *palazzo* owners commissioned family chapels in this church. The facade, designed by Bernardo Buontalenti in the 16th century, is almost Baroque in its elaborate ornamentation. Scenes from Ghirlandaio's *Life of St. Francis* decorate the **Sassetti Chapel** in the right arm of the transept. The famous altarpiece, Ghirlandaio's *Adoration of the Shepherds*, resides in the Uffizi—this one is a copy. *(In P. S. Trinità. Open M-Sa 7am-noon and 4-7pm, Su 7-noon. Free.)*

**MERCATO NUOVO.** The *loggie* (guilds) of the New Market have housed gold and silk traders since 1547. Today, imitation designer gear dominates vendors' wares. Rubbing the snout of Pietro Tacca's plump statue, *Il Porcellino* (The Little Pig) is reputed to bring luck, but don't wait for that purse you covet to become real leather. *(Off V. Calimala, between P. della Repubblica and the Ponte Vecchio. Open dawn-dusk.)*

**PALAZZO DAVANZATI.** Built to show off Florence's 15th-century boom economy, this cavern-like *palazzo* is now the **Museo della Casa Fiorentina Antica.** The interior is closed, but the courtyard has restored frescoes, ornaments, and original furniture, which recreate a 15th-century merchant's life of luxury. *(V. Porta Rossa 13. Open daily 8:30am-1:50pm. Closed 1st, 3rd, and 5th M, 2nd and 4th Su of each month. Free.)*

# SAN LORENZO AND FARTHER NORTH

▨ **ACCADEMIA.** It doesn't matter how many pictures of him you've seen—when you come around the corner to see Michelangelo's triumphant ▨**David** towering in self-assured perfection under the rotunda designed just for him, you will be blown away. The statue's base was struck by lightning in 1512, the figure was damaged by anti-Medici riots in 1527, and David's left wrist was broken by a stone, after which he was moved here from P. della Signoria in 1873. In the hallway leading to *David* are Michelangelo's four **Slaves** and a *Pietà*. The master purposely left these statues unfinished, staying true to his theory of "releasing" figures from the living stone. Botticelli's Madonna paintings and Uccello's works are worth seeing. *(V. Ricasoli 60, between the churches of S. Marco and S. S. Annunziata. ☎ 23 88 609. Open Tu-Su 8:15am-6:50pm. Reserve ahead. May-Sept. €10; Oct.-Apr. €7.)*

**BASILICA DI SAN LORENZO.** Because the Medicis lent the funds to build this church, they retained artistic control over its construction and decided to add Cosimo dei Medici's grave to Brunelleschi's spacious basilica. They cunningly placed it in front of the high altar to make the entire church his personal mausoleum. Michelangelo began the exterior, but, disgusted by Florentine politics, he abandoned the project, which accounts for the plain facade. *(Open M-Sa 10am-5pm. Mar.-Oct. open M-Sa 10am-5pm, Su 1:30-5pm. €2.50.)* While the **Cappelle dei Medici** (Medici Chapels) offer a rare glimpse of the Baroque in Florence, the **Cappella dei Principi** (Princes' Chapel) emulates the baptistry in P. del Duomo. Michelangelo sculpted the **Sacrestia Nuova** (New Sacristy) to hold two Medici tombs. On the tomb of Lorenzo he placed the female Night and the muscular male Day; on Giuliano's sit the more androgynous Dawn and Dusk. *(Walk around to the back entrance in P. Madonna degli Aldobrandini. Open daily 8:15am-5pm. Closed 1st and 3rd M and 2nd and 4th Su. €6.)* The adjacent **Laurentian Library** houses one of the world's most valuable manuscript collections. Michelangelo's *pietra serena* sandstone staircase at its entrance is one of his most innovative architectural designs. *(Open daily 8:30am-1:30pm. Free with entrance to San Lorenzo.)*

**MUSEO DELLA CHIESA DI SAN MARCO.** Remarkable works by Fra Angelico adorn this museum, once part of a convent complex and one of the most peaceful places in Florence. A large room to the right of the courtyard houses some of the painter's major works, including the church's altarpiece. The second floor displays Angelico's *Annunciation*. Every cell in the convent has its own Angelico fresco. To the right of the stairwell, Michelozzo's library, modeled on Michelangelo's work in S. Lorenzo, is designed for reflection. In cells 17 and 22, underground artwork, excavated from the medieval period, peeks through a glass floor. Toward the exit, the two rooms of the **Museo di Firenze Antica** show Florence's ancient roots. Be sure to peek into the church itself, next to the museum, to admire the elaborate altar and vaulted ceiling. *(Enter at P.S. Marco 3. Open M-F 8:15am-1:50pm, Sa 8:15am-6:50pm, Su 8:15am-7pm. Closed 2nd and 4th M and 1st and 3rd Su of each month. €4.)*

## PIAZZA SANTA CROCE AND ENVIRONS

**⧫CHIESA DI SANTA CROCE.** The Franciscans built this church as far as possible from their Dominican rivals at S. Maria Novella; construction began in 1294 and finished in 1442. Ironically, the ascetic Franciscans produced what is arguably the most splendid church in the city, distinguished by an Egyptian cross layout and marble sculptures on the tomb. Luminaries buried here include Galileo, Machiavelli, Michelangelo (whose tomb was designed by Vasari), and humanist Leonardo Bruni, shown holding his beloved *History of Florence.* Check out Donatello's *Crucifix,* so irksome to Brunelleschi, in the Vernio Chapel, and his gilded *Annunciation,* by Bruni's tomb. At the end of the cloister next to the church is the ⧫**Cappella Pazzi,** whose proportions are perfect and whose decorations include Luca della Robbia's *tondi* of the apostles and Brunelleschi's moldings of the evangelists. *(Open M-Sa 9:30am-5:30pm, Su 1-5:30pm. €5.)*

**SYNAGOGUE OF FLORENCE.** This synagogue, also known as the **Museo del Tempio Israelitico,** is resplendent with Sephardic domes, arches, and patterns. David Levi, a wealthy Florentine Jewish businessman, donated his fortune in 1870 to build "a monumental temple worthy of Florence," recognizing the Jews' new freedom to live and worship outside the old Jewish ghetto. *(V. Farini 4, at V. Pilastri. ☎ 24 52 52. Free tours 1 per hr.; reserve ahead. Open Su-Th 10am-6pm, F 10am-2pm. €4.)*

**CASA BUONARROTI.** This little museum houses Michelangelo memorabilia and two of his most crucial early works, *The Madonna of the Steps* and *The Battle of the Centaurs*, both completed when he was 16 and indicative of his growth from bas-relief to sculpture. *(V. Ghibellina 70. ☎ 25 17 52. From P. S. Croce, follow V. dei Pepi and turn right on V. Ghibellina. Open M and W-Su 9:30am-2pm. €6.50, students €4.)*

## THE OLTRARNO

Historically disdained by downtown Florentines, the far side of the Arno remains an animated and unpretentious quarter, filled with students and relatively few tourists. Head back on Ponte S. Trinità after dallying in P. San Spirito.

**⧫ PALAZZO PITTI.** Luca Pitti, a 15th-century banker, built his *palazzo* east of P. S. Spirito against the Boboli hill. The Medicis acquired the *palazzo* and the hill in 1550 and expanded it in every way possible. Today, it houses six museums, including the ⧫**Galleria Palatina.** Florence's most important art collection after the Uffizi, the gallery has works by Caravaggio, Raphael, Rubens, and Titian. Other museums display Medici family costumes, porcelain, carriages, and **Royal Apartments**—lavish reminders of the time when the *palazzo* was the living quarters of the royal House of Savoy. The **Galleria d'Arte Moderna** hides one of Italian art history's big surprises, the proto-Impressionist works of the Macchiaioli group. *(Open Tu-Su 8:15am-6:50pm. Ticket for Palatine Gallery, Royal Apartments, and Modern Art Gallery €8.50.)*

**BOBOLI GARDENS.** With geometrically sculpted hedges, contrasting groves of holly and cypress trees, and bubbling fountains, the elaborate gardens are an exquisite example of stylized Renaissance landscaping. A large oval lawn is just up the hill from the back of the Palazzo Pitti, with an Egyptian obelisk in the middle and marble statues dotting the perimeter. Spend an afternoon wandering through the grounds and the small on-site museums. *(Open daily June-Aug. 8:15am-7:30pm; Apr.-May and Sept.-Oct. 8:15am-6:30pm; Nov.-Mar. reduced hours. €6.)*

## SAN MINIATO AL MONTE AND ENVIRONS

■ **SAN MINIATO AL MONTE.** An inlaid marble facade and 13th-century mosaics provide a prelude to the floor inside, patterned with doves, lions, and astrological signs. Visit at 5:40pm to hear the monks chanting. *(Take bus #13 from the station or climb the stairs from Piazzale Michelangelo. ☎23 42 731. Open daily Mar.-Nov. 8am-7pm; Dec.-Feb. 8am-1pm and 2:30-6pm. Free.)*

**PIAZZALE MICHELANGELO.** A visit to Piazzale Michelangelo is a must. At sunset, waning light casts a warm glow over the city. Views from here are even better (and certainly cheaper) than those from the top of the *duomo*. Make the challenging uphill trek at around 8:30pm during the summer to arrive at the *piazza* in time for sunset. Unfortunately, the *piazza* doubles as a large parking lot, and is home to hordes of tour buses during summer days. *(Cross the Ponte Vecchio to the Oltrarno and turn left, walk through the piazza, and turn right up V. de Bardi. Follow it uphill as it becomes V. del Monte alle Croci, where a staircase to the left heads to the piazza.)*

## 🎵 ENTERTAINMENT

May starts the summer music festival season with the classical **Maggio Musicale.** The **Festa del Grillo** (Festival of the Cricket) is held on the first Sunday after Ascension Day, when crickets in tiny wooden cages are sold in the Cascine park to be released into the grass—Florentines believe the song of a cricket is good luck. In June, the *quartieri* of Florence turn out in costume to play their own medieval version of football, known as **calcio storico,** in which two teams face off over a wooden ball in one of the city's *piazze*, their games so often ending in riots that the festival was actually cancelled in 2007. The **Festival of San Giovanni Battista,** on June 24, features a tremendous fireworks display visible all along the Arno, beginning around 10pm. The **Estate Fiesolana** (June-Aug.) fills the Roman theater in nearby Fiesole with concerts, opera, theater, ballet, and film events (☎800 41 42 40; www.estatefiesolana.com). In summer, the **Europa dei Sensi** program hosts **Rime Rampanti** (☎348 58 04 812; www.firenzenotte.it), nightly cultural shows with music, poetry, and food from a chosen European country.

## 🛍 SHOPPING

For both the budget shopper and the big spender who's looking to make the splurge of a lifetime, Florence offers too many options and temptations. *Saldi* (sales) take over in January and July, even in V. Tornabuoni's swanky boutiques.

The city's artisanal traditions thrive at its open markets. **San Lorenzo,** the largest, cheapest, and most touristed, sprawls for several blocks around P. S. Lorenzo. In front of the leather shops, vendors sell all kinds of goods—bags, clothes, food, toys, and flags. High prices are rare, but quality and honesty can be too. (Open daily 9am-twilight.) For everything from pot-holders to parakeets, shop at the market in **Parco delle Cascine,** which begins four bridges west of the Ponte Vecchio at P. V. Veneto and stretches along the Arno River each Tuesday morning. *Carta fiorentina,* paper covered in intricate floral designs, adorns books, journals, and paper goods, at **Alinari,** L. Alinari 15. (☎23 951. Open M 2:30-6:30pm, Tu-F 9am-1pm and 2:30-6:30pm, Sa 9am-1pm and 3-7pm. Closed 2 weeks in Aug. AmEx/MC/V.) Florentine **leatherwork** is affordable and renowned for its quality. Some of the best leather artisans in the city work around P. S. Croce and V. Porta S. Maria. The **Santa Croce Leather School,** in Chiesa di Santa Croce, offers first-rate products at reasonable prices. (☎24 45 34; www.leatherschool.it. Open Mar. 15-Nov. 15 daily 9:30am-6pm; Nov. 16-Mar. 14 M-Sa 10am-12:30pm and 3-6pm. AmEx/MC/V.)

# ▣ NIGHTLIFE

For reliable info, consult the city's entertainment monthly, *Firenze Spettacolo* (€2). **Piazza Santo Spirito** in Oltrarno has live music in summer. To go to clubs or bars that are far from the *centro*, keep in mind that the last bus may leave before the fun winds down, and taxis are rare in the area with the most popular discos.

## BARS

**Moyo,** V. dei Banchi 23R (☎24 79 738), near P. Santa Croce. Thriving lunch spot by day, hip bar by night, always crowded with young Italians. Lunch options from €7. Evening cocktails include free, self-serve snacks. Open daily 8am-3am. AmEx/MC/V.

**Noir,** Lungarno Corsini 12R (☎21 07 51). This bar mixes mojitos (€7) and other refreshing cocktails for locals. After paying, take your drink outside by the Arno. Mixed drinks €5-6.50. Beer from €3.50. Open 11am-1am. Closed 2 weeks in Aug. MC/V.

**May Day Lounge,** V. Dante Alighieri 16R. Aspiring artists display their work on the walls of this eclectic lounge that fills with offbeat Italians. Play Pong on the early 80s gaming system or sip mixed drinks (€4.50-6.50) to the beat of the background funk. Beer €4.50. Happy hour 8-10pm. Open daily 8pm-2am. Closed most of Aug. AmEx/MC/V.

**The Fiddler's Elbow,** P. S. Maria Novella 7R (☎21 50 56). Irish pub where expat bartenders serve cider and Guinness (pints €4.50) to crowds of foreigners. Open daily 11am-1am. MC/V.

**Eby's Latin Bar,** V. dell'Oriuolo 5R (☎338 65 08 959). Eby's blends fresh mixed drinks from seasonal fruit. Great nachos and sangria, a raucous young crowd, and salsa music. Beer €3.50. Mixed drinks €5.50-7. Happy hour 6-9pm. Open M-Sa noon-3pm and 6pm-3am. Closed 1st 2 weeks in Aug.

## DISCOS

**Central Park,** in Parco della Cascinè (☎35 35 05). Open-air dance floor pulses with hip-hop, reggae, and rock. Favored by Florentine and foreign teens and college students. Mixed drinks €8. Cover €20; no cover for foreign students before 12:30am. Open M-Tu and Th-Sa 11pm-late, W 9pm-late. AmEx/MC/V.

**Meccano',** V. degli Olmi 1 (☎33 13 71), near Parco della Cascinè. One of the most popular discos, catering to a slightly older crowd. Open-air dance floors make for wild nights. Drinks €7. Cover €16, includes 1 drink. Open Tu-Sa 11pm-4am. AmEx/MC/V.

**Tabasco Gay Club,** P. S. Cecilia 3R, near Palazzo Vecchio. Smoke machines and strobe lights on the dance floor. Florence's most popular and classiest gay disco caters primarily to men. 18+. Cover €13, includes 1 drink. Open Tu-Su 10pm-4am. AmEx/MC/V.

# SIENA ☎ 0577

Many travelers rush from Rome to Florence, ignoring medieval Siena (pop. 50,000) despite its rich artistic, political, and economic history. *Il Palio*, Siena's intoxicating series of bareback horse races, is a party and a spectacle.

🖪🛛 **TRANSPORTATION AND PRACTICAL INFORMATION. Trains** run from P. Rosselli to Florence (1¾hr., 16 per day, €5.70) and Rome (3hr., 20 per day, €13) via Chiusi. TRA-IN/SITA **buses** (☎ 20 42 46) run from P. Gramsci and the train station to Florence (1 per hr., €6.50) and San Gimignano (31 per day, €5.20). Across from the train station, take TRA-IN buses #3, 4, 7-10, 17, or 77 (€0.90) to **Piazza del Sale** or **Piazza Gramsci**, then follow signs to **Piazza del Campo,** Siena's *centro storico*, also known as **Il Campo.** The central APT **tourist office** is at P. del Campo 56. (☎28 05; www.terresiena.it. Open mid-Mar. to mid-Nov. daily 9:30am-1pm and 2:30-6pm; mid-Nov. to mid-Mar. M-Sa 8:30am-1pm and 3-7pm, Su 9am-1pm.) Check email at **Cafe Internet,** Galleria Cecco Angiolieri 16. (€1.80 per hr. Open M-Sa 8:30am-11pm, Su 9am-11pm.) **Postal Code:** 53100.

🖫🖸 **ACCOMMODATIONS AND FOOD.** Finding a room in Siena can be difficult between Easter and October. Reserve at least a month ahead for *Il Palio*. **Prenotazioni Alberghi e Ristoranti,** in P. S. Domenico, finds rooms for a €2 fee. (☎94 08 09. Open M-Sa 9am-7pm, Su 9am-noon.) 🖫**Casa Laura ❸,** V. Roma 3, is in the less touristy university area; ring the doorbell, labeled "Bencini Valentini." (☎22 60 61; fax 22 52 40. Kitchen available. Doubles €65-67; triples €70; quads €75. MC/V.) Bus #10 and 15 from P. Gramsci stop at the spotless **Ostello della Gioventù "Guidoriccio" (HI) ❶,** V. Fiorentina 89, in Località Lo Stellino. (☎52 212. Curfew midnight. Dorms €14. Cash only.) To **camp** at **Colleverde ❶,** Str. di Scacciapensieri 47, take bus #3 or 8 from P. del Sale; confirm destination with driver. (☎28 00 44; www.terresiena.it. Open late Mar. to mid-Nov. €7.80 per person, €3.50 per tent site. MC/V.)

Sienese bakeries prepare *panforte*, a confection of honey, almonds, and citron, sold at **Bar/Pasticceria Nannini ❶,** V. Banchi di Sopra 22-24, the oldest *pasticceria* in Siena (€2.10 per 100g). At **Il Cantiere del Gusto ❸,** V. Calzoleria 12, behind the curve of P. del Campo off V. Banchi d. Sotto, classics like *tagliatelle al ragù di coniglio* (pasta with rabbit sauce; €6.50) are delivered by friendly waitstaff. (☎28 90 10. *Primi* €5-6. *Secondi* €8-20. Cover €1. Service 10%. Open M 12:30-2:30pm, Tu-Sa 12:30-2:30pm and 7-10pm. MC/V.) **Osteria La Chiacchera ❷,** Costa di S. Antonio 4, serves delicious, cheap pasta. (☎28 06 31. *Primi* €5-6. *Secondi* €8-12. Open M and W-Su noon-3:30pm and 7pm-midnight. AmEx/MC/V.) A **CONAD** supermarket is in P. Matteoti. (Open M-Sa 8:30am-8:30pm, Su 9am-1pm and 4-8pm.)

🖬🎵 **SIGHTS AND ENTERTAINMENT.** Siena radiates from 🖫**Piazza del Campo (Il Campo),** a shell-shaped brick square designed for civic events. At the top of the slope by Il Campo is the **Fonte Gaia,** a marble fountain that has refreshed Siena since the 1300s. At the bottom, the **Torre del Mangia** bell tower looms over the graceful **Palazzo Pubblico.** Inside the *palazzo*, the **Museo Civico** is best appreciated for its late medieval and early Renaissance collection of Sienese style painting. (*Palazzo*, museum, and tower open daily Mar.-Oct. 10am-6:15pm; Nov.-Feb. 10am-5:30pm. Museum €7, students €4.50. Tower €6. Combo €10.) From the *palazzo* facing Il Campo, take the left stairs and cross V. di Città to get to Siena's hilltop 🖫**duomo.** To prevent the apse from being left hanging in mid-air, the lavish **baptistry** was constructed below. (Open June-Aug. M-Sa 10:30am-8pm, Su 1:30-6pm; Mar.-May and Sept.-Oct. M-Sa 10:30am-7:30pm, Su 1:30-6pm; Nov.-Feb. M-Sa 10:30am-6:30pm, Su 1:30-5:30pm. €3-5.50.) The decorated underground rooms of the *cripta* (crypt) were used by pilgrims about to enter the *duomo*. (Check hours at the *duomo*. €6, students €5.) The **Museo dell'Opera della Metropolitana,** to the right of the *duomo*, houses its overflow art. Particularly impressive are the works of Sienese mater Duccio. (Open mid-Mar. to Sept. daily 9am-7:30pm; Oct. to mid-Mar. reduced hours. €6.) Veer into the university area along V. Pantaneto for untouristed and inexpensive cafes. Every year on July 2 and August 16, ▓**Il Palio** morphs the mellow Campo into a chaotic arena as horses speed around its edge. Arrive three days early to watch the trial runs and to pick a favorite *contrada* (team).

▓ **DAYTRIP FROM SIENA: SAN GIMIGNANO.** The hilltop village of San Gimignano (pop. 7000) looks like an illustration from a medieval manuscript with prototypical churches, palaces, and towers looming above the city walls. San Gimignano's 14 famous towers, all that remain of the original 72, attract many daytrippers due to their massive presence in the tiny town. The **Museo Civico,** on the second floor of **Palazzo Comunale,** has a collection of Sienese and Florentine artwork. Within the museum is the entrance to the ▓**Torre Grossa,** the *palazzo*'s tallest remaining tower; climb its 218 steps for a view of Tuscany's harmonious hills. *(Open daily Mar.-Oct. 9:30am-7pm; Nov.-Feb. 10am-5:30pm. €5, students €4.)* **Piazza della Cisterna** is the center of life in San Gimignano and adjoins **Piazza del Duomo,** site of the impressive tower of the **Palazzo del Podestà.** The famous **Vernaccia di San Gimignano,** a light, sweet white wine, is sold at **La Buca,** V. S. Giovanni 16, as are sausages and meats from the store's own farm. *(Open daily Apr.-Oct. 9am-8pm; Nov.-Mar. 10am-6pm. AmEx/MC/V.)* **Buses** leave P. Montemaggio for Florence (1½hr., 1 per hr., €6) via Poggibonsi, and Siena (1½hr., 1 per 1-2hr., €5.20). To reach the *centro*, pass through Porta San Matteo and follow V. San Giovanni to P. della Cisterna, which merges with P. del Duomo on the left. **Postal Code:** 53037.

# LUCCA
☎ **0583**

Lucca ("LOO-ka"; pop. 9000) dabbles successfully in every area of tourist enjoyment: bikers rattle along the tree-lined promenade atop the town's medieval walls, fashionistas shop at trendy boutiques, and art lovers admire the architecture of the *centro*. No tour of the city is complete without seeing the perfectly intact city walls, or ▓**baluardi** (battlements). The 4km path along the walls, closed to cars, is perfect for an afternoon picnic or for a sunset view. The **Duomo di San Martino** was begun in the 6th century and finished in the 15th century. Nearby, the **Museo della Cattedrale** houses religious objects from the *duomo*. (*Duomo* open M-F 9:30am-5:45pm, Sa 9:30am-6:45pm, Su between masses. Free. *Museo* open Apr.-Oct. daily 10am-6pm; Nov.-Mar. M-F 10am-2pm, Sa-Su 10am-5pm. €4.) Climb the 227 stairs of the narrow **Torre Guinigi,** V. Sant'Andrea 41, for a view of the city and the hills beyond. (☎31 68 46. Open daily June-Sept. 9am-11pm; Oct.-Jan. 9am-7pm; Feb.-May 9am-5pm. €5, students €3.) For some more exercise, climb the 207 steps of the **Torre delle Ore** (Clock Towers), V. Fillungo 24., where you can watch the inner workings of the city's tallest timepiece. (Open daily in summer 10:30am-7pm; in winter 10:30am-5pm. €4, students €2.50. Combined ticket for both towers €6/4.) The **Basilica di San Frediano** was originally built in the 6th century with the facade facing west, but was rebuilt in the 12th century with an eastward orientation. (Open daily in summer 9am-noon and 3-6pm; in winter 9am-noon and 3-5pm. Free.) In the evening, *Lucchese* pack the **Piazza Anfiteatro and** the **Piazza Napoleone.**

Hospitality is the middle name of the family that runs ▓**Bed and Breakfast La Torre ❸,** V. del Carmine 11, which offers large, bright rooms. (☎/fax 95 70 44; www.roomslatorre.com. Breakfast included. Free Internet. Singles €35, with bath

## LUCCAN LORE

The Luccan tale of Lucida Mansi breathes serious morals into Italian primping practices. Lucida was a drop-dead gorgeous woman who knew exactly how to seduce men and get what she wanted. An active lover, she even killed her husband to indulge in such revelry. In vanity, she covered the rooms of her *palazzo* (Palazzo Mansi, still in Lucca today) with mirrors.

Eventually Lucida began to age—wrinkles won out on her flawless skin. To thwart these unsightly signs of age, Lucida did the only thing she could think of: she contacted the Devil. The Devil gave her 30 years of youth in exchange for her soul.

Lucida continued her hedonistic life of fashion, passion, and great wine. At the end of her 30 years, the punctual Devil returned, and the two fell into an abyss. In the *palazzo*'s Camera degli Sposi, there is a ring believed to have been their entrance to Hell.

Though there is no evidence of her existence, Lucida is one of Tuscany's most famous ghosts. Luccans say that along the town's walls, and over the pond in the Botanical Gardens, her seductive ghost appears at night, riding wild and nude on a blazing chariot. Some even say you can see the reflection of her face in the pond's water.

€50; doubles €50/80. MC/V.) From P. Napoleone, take V. Beccheria, then turn right on V. Roma and left on V. Fillungo. After six blocks, turn left into P. San Frediano and right on V. della Cavallerizza to reach the **Ostello per la Gioventù San Frediano (HI) ❶**, V. della Cavallerizza 12. (☎46 99 57; www.ostellolucca.it. Breakfast €2.50. Linens included. Towels €1.50. Laundry available. Reception 7:30-10am and 3:30pm-midnight. Lockout 10am-3:30pm. Dorms €18; 2- to 6-person rooms with bath €48-138. €3 HI discount. Cash only.) **Ristorante da Francesco ❷**, Corte Portici 13, off V. Calderia between P. San Salvatore and P. San Michele, offers patio seating and well-prepared dishes. (☎41 80 49. *Primi* €6. *Secondi* €8-12. 1L wine €7.20. Cover €1.50. Open Tu-Su noon-2:30pm and 8-10:30pm. MC/V.) Pizza *al taglio* (by the slice) flies over the countertop into hungry hands at **Pizzeria da Felice ❶**, V. Buia 12. (☎49 49 86. Slices from €1.40. Open daily 10am-8:30pm.) Offering interesting *gelato* flavors and swanky seating, **Gelateria Veneta**, V. V. Veneto 74, is the place to see and be seen on Saturday nights. (☎46 70 37. Cones €1.80-3.50. Open M-F and Su 10am-1am, Sa 10am-2am.)

**Trains** (☎89 20 21) run hourly from Ple. Ricasoli to Florence (1½hr., €4.80), Pisa (30min., €2.20), and Viareggio (20min., €2.20). **Buses** (☎46 49 63) leave hourly from Ple. Verdi, next to the tourist office, for Florence (1½hr., €4.70) and Pisa (50min., €2.50). The **tourist office** is in Ple. San Donato. (☎58 31 50. Open daily 9am-7pm.) Rent bikes at **Cicli Bizzari**, P. Santa Maria 32. (☎49 60 31. €2.50 per hr., €13 per day. Open daily 9am-7:30pm. Cash only.) **Postal Code:** 55100.

# PISA ☎050

Millions of tourists arrive in Pisa (pop. 95,000) each year to marvel at the famous "Leaning Tower," forming a *gelato*-slurping, photo-snapping mire. Commanding a beautiful stretch of the Arno River, Pisa has a diverse array of cultural and artistic diversions, as well as a top-notch university. The **Piazza del Duomo,** also known as the **Campo dei Miracoli** (Field of Miracles), is a grassy expanse that contrasts with the white stone of the tower, *duomo*, baptistry, and surrounding museums. Begun in 1173, the famous ⬛**Leaning Tower** began to tilt when the soil beneath it suddenly shifted. The tilt intensified after WWII, and thanks to the tourists who climb its steps daily, the tower slips 1-2m each year, though it's currently considered stable. Tours of 30 visitors are permitted to ascend the 294 steps once every 30min. (Tours depart daily June-Aug. 8:30am-11pm; Sept.-May 8:30am-7:30pm. Assemble next to info office 10min. before tour. €15.) Also on the Campo, the dazzling **duomo** has a collection of splendid art, including a mosaic by Cimabue, and is considered one of the finest Romanesque cathedrals in the world. (Open Apr.-Sept. M-Sa 10am-8pm; Mar. and Oct. M-Sa 10am-7pm, Su 1-5:45pm; Nov.-Feb. M-F 10am-5pm. €2.) Next door is the 🖼Battistero (Baptistry), whose precise acoustics allow an unamplified choir to be heard 2km away. An acoustic demonstration by the guard on duty occurs every 30min. (Open daily Apr.-Sept. 8am-7:30pm; Mar. and Oct. 9am-5:30pm; Nov.-Feb. 9am-4:30pm. €6, includes admission to one other monument on the combined ticket list.) The **Camposanto,** a cloistered cemetery, is filled with Roman sarcophagi and covered with earth that Crusaders brought from Golgotha, the site of Jesus's crucifixion (same hours as *Battistero*). Occasional concerts take place in the adjacent *duomo;* call **Opera della Primaziale Pisana,** P. Duomo 17 (☎38 72 210; www.opapisa.it). An **all-inclusive ticket** to the Campo's sights—excluding the tower—costs €10 and is available at the two *biglietterie* (ticket booths) on the Campo (at the Museo del Duomo and next to the tourist office behind the tower).

Two minutes from the *duomo*, the **Albergo Helvetia ❸**, V. Don Gaefano Boschi 31, off P. Archivescovado, has large, clean rooms, a multilingual staff, and a welcoming bar downstairs. (☎55 30 84. Reception 8am-midnight. Reserve ahead. Singles €35, with bath €50; doubles €45-62. Cash only.) **Centro Turistico Madonna dell'Acqua ❶**, V. Pietrasantina 15, is 2km from the tower, next to a creek and an old church. Take bus marked LAM ROSSA (red line) from the station (4 per hr., last bus 9:45pm; ask the driver to stop at *ostello*. (☎89 06 22. Linens €1. Reception 6-9pm. Dorms €15. MC/V.) Steer clear of the countless touristy pizzerias near the tower and head for the river, where the restaurants offer a more authentic ambience and consistently high quality. Try the heavenly risotto at 🖼Il Paiolo ❶, V. Curtatone e Montanara 9, near the university. (*Menù* €5-8. Open M-F 12:30-3pm and 8pm-1am, Sa-Su 8pm-2am. MC/V.) Get groceries at **Pam,** V. Giovanni Pascoli 8, just off C. Italia. (Open M-Sa 7:30am-8:30pm, Su 9am-1pm. Cash only.) **Trains** (☎89 20 21) run from P. della Stazione, in the southern end of town, to Florence (1hr., 1 per hr., €5.20), Genoa (2½hr., 1 per hr., €7.90), and Rome (3hr., 12 per day, €23-29). To reach the **tourist office,** walk straight out of the train station and go left in P. Vittorio Emanuele. (☎422 91; www.turismo.toscana.it. Open M-F 9am-7pm, Sa 9am-1:30pm.) Take bus marked LAM ROSSA (€0.85) from the station to the Campo. **Postal Code:** 56100.

# UMBRIA

Umbria is known as the "green heart of Italy" due to its wild woods, fertile plains, craggy gorges, and gentle hills. Cobblestone streets and active international universities give the region a lively character rooted in tradition and history. Umbria holds Giotto's greatest masterpieces and was home to medieval master painters Perugino and Pinturicchio. Today, Umbria's artistic spirit lives on in the Spoleto and Umbria Jazz Festivals.

## PERUGIA ☎075

In Perugia (pop. 160,000), visitors can experience the city's renowned jazz festival, digest its decadent chocolate, and meander through its two universities. The city's most popular sights frame **Piazza IV Novembre,** the heart of Perugia's social life. At its center, the **Fontana Maggiore** is adorned with sculptures and bas-reliefs by Nicolà and Giovanni Pisano. At the end of the *piazza* is the rugged, unfinished exterior of the Gothic **Cattedrale di San Lorenzo,** also known as the *duomo*, which houses the purported wedding ring of the Virgin Mary. (Open M-Sa 8am-12:45pm and 4-5:15pm, Su 4-5:45pm. Free.) The 13th-century **Palazzo dei Priori,** on the left when looking at the fountain, contains the impressive **Galleria Nazionale dell'Umbria,** C. Vannucci 19,

ITALY

which displays magnificent 13th- and 14th-century religious works. (Open Tu-Su 8:30am-7:30pm. €6.50.) From behind the *duomo*, medieval V. Rocchi, the city's oldest street, winds through the northern city and straight underneath the **Arco di Etrusco,** a perfectly preserved Roman arch built on Etruscan pedestals. Past Porta S. Pietro at the end of town, the **Basilica di San Pietro,** on V. Borgo XX Giugno, has a beautiful medieval garden. The lower half (through the stone archway) opens to a postcard-perfect view of the Umbrian countryside. The basilica's interior is covered with frescoes. (Open daily 8am-noon and 3-6:30pm.)

🖼**Ostello della Gioventù/Centro Internazionale di Accoglienza per la Gioventù ❶,** V. Bontempi 13, is a welcoming and well-located hostel, with frescoed ceilings in the lobby, kitchen access, a reading room, and a terrace. From P. IV Novembre, keep to the right past the *duomo* and P. Danti into P. Piccinino, and onto V. Bontempi. (☎57 22 880; www.ostello.perugia.it. Linens €2. Lockout 9:30am-4pm. Curfew 1am, midnight in winter. Closed mid-Dec. to mid-Jan. Dorms €15. AmEx/MC/V.) On the corner of P. B. Ferri and C. Vannucci, **Albergo Anna ❸,** V. dei Priori 48, has antique furnishings in large rooms that match the character of the medieval street outside. (☎57 36 304. Breakfast €2. Singles €30; doubles €58. AmEx/MC/V.) Locals flock to 🖼**Trattoria Dal Mi Cocco ❷,** C. Garibaldi 12, for its generous *menù* which includes an appetizer, two courses, and dessert. (*Menù* €13. Reserve ahead. Open Tu-Su 1-2pm and 8:30-10pm. MC/V.) **Pizzeria Mediterranea ❶,** P. Piccinino 11/12, offers an extensive selection at a good value. (Pizza €4-12. Cover €1.10. Open daily 12:30-2:30pm and 7:30-11pm. MC/V.) No trip to Perugia would be complete without a visit to its famous chocolate store, **Perugina,** C. Vannucci 101. (Open M 2:30-8pm, Tu-Sa 9:30am-7:45pm, Su 10:30am-1:30pm and 3-8pm.) *Torta di formaggio* (cheese bread) and *mele al cartoccio* (apple pie) are area specialities available at **Ceccarani,** P. Matteotti 16. (☎57 21 960. Open M-Sa 7:30am-8pm, Su 9am-1:30pm.) Pick up groceries at **Coop,** P. Matteotti 15. (Open M-Sa 9am-8pm. MC/V.) Be sure to visit Perugia in mid-July, during the **Umbria Jazz Festival** (www.umbriajazz.com) or in mid-October for **Eurochocolate,** a festival that pays tribute to the cacoa bean (☎50 25 880; www.eurochocolate.com).

**Trains** leave Perugia FS in P. Vittorio Veneto, Fontiveggio, for: Assisi (25min., 1 per hr., €1.80); Florence (2hr., 6 per day, from €8); Orvieto (1¾hr., 11 per day, €11); Rome (2½hr., 7 per day, €11) via Terontola or Foligno. From the station, take **bus** #6, 7, 9, 11, 13D, or 15 to the central P. Italia (€1); then walk down C. Vannucci, the main shopping street, to P. IV Novembre and the *duomo*. V. Baglioni is one block east of P. IV Novembre and leads to P. Matteotti and the **tourist office,** P. Matteotti 18. Be sure to grab a **Perugia Little Blue,** a guide written in English with a student's perspective. (☎57 36 458. Open M-Sa 8:30am-1:30pm and 3:30-6:30pm, Su 9am-1pm.) **Postal Code:** 06100.

# ASSISI                                                                    ☎075

Assisi's atmosphere emanates tranquility, owing its character to the legacy of St. Francis, patron saint of Italy and the town's favorite son. The undeniable jewel of Assisi (pop. 25,000) is the 13th-century 🖼**Basilica di San Francesco.** The subdued art of the lower church celebrates St. Francis's modest lifestyle and houses his tomb, while Giotto's renowned fresco cycle, the *Life of St. Francis*, adorns the walls of the upper church, paying tribute to the saint's consecration. (Lower basilica open daily 6am-6:45pm. Upper basilica open daily 8:30am-6:45pm. Modest dress required. Free.) Hike up to the looming fortress **Rocca Maggiore** for panoramic views of the countryside. From P. del Comune, follow V. S. Rufino to P. S. Rufino. Continue up V. Porta Perlici and take the first left up a narrow staircase. (Open daily 9am-8pm. €3.50, students €2.50.) The pink-and-white **Basilica di Santa Chiara** houses the crucifix that is said to have spoken to St. Francis. It is surrounded by a dazzling courtyard, with a fountain and spectacular views of Umbrian scenery. (Open daily 6:30am-noon and 2-7pm.) ◼Camere Martini ❷, V. S. Gregorio 6, has sunny rooms surrounding a central courtyard and a familial atmosphere. (☎81 35 36; cameremartini@libero.it. Singles €25-27; doubles €40; triples €55; quads €65. Cash only.) Ostello della Pace (HI) ❶, V. d. Valecchi 177, offers bright rooms with two or three bunk beds and shared baths. From the train station, take the bus to P. Unità d'Italia; then walk downhill on V. Marconi, turn left at the sign, and walk for 500m. (☎81 67 67; www.assisihostel.com. Breakfast included. Dinner €9.50. Laundry €3.50. Reception 7-9:30am and 3:30-11:30pm. Lockout 9:30am-3:30pm. Curfew 11pm. Reserve ahead. Dorms €15, with bath €17. HI card required; buy at hostel. MC/V.) Grab a personal pizza (€5-7) at Pizzeria Otello ❶, V. San Antonio 1. (Open daily noon-3pm and 7-10:30pm. AmEx/MC/V.)

From the station near the Basilica Santa Maria degli Angeli, **trains** go to Florence (2½hr., 7 per day, €9), Perugia (30min., 1-2 per hr., €1.80), and Rome (2½hr., 7 per day, €9). From P. Matteotti, follow V. del Torrione to P. S. Rufino, where the downhill left leads to V. S. Rufino, **Piazza del Comune,** the city center, and the **tourist office.** (☎81 25 34. Open M-Sa 8am-2pm and 3-6pm, Su 9am-1pm.) **Postal Code:** 06081.

# ORVIETO                                      ☎0763

A city upon a city, Orvieto (pop. 21,000) was built in layers: medieval structures stand over ancient subterranean tunnels that Etruscans began burrowing into the hillside in the 7th century BC. **Underground City Excursions** offers the most complete tour of the city's twisted bowels. (☎34 48 91. English-language tours leave the tourist office daily 11:15am and 4:15pm. €5.50, students €3.50.) It took 600 years, 152 sculptors, 68 painters, 90 mosaic artisans, and 33 architects to construct Orvieto's ◼duomo. The **Capella della Madonna di San Brizio,** off the right transept, houses the dramatic apocalypse frescoes of Luca Signorelli. Opposite it, the ◼Cappella Corporale holds the gold-encrusted chalice-cloth, soaked with the blood of Christ. (Open M-Sa 7:30am-12:45pm and 2:30-7pm, Su 2:30-6:45pm. Modest dress required. *Duomo* free. *Capella* €5.) Two blocks down from the *duomo*, V. della Piazza del Popolo leads to the luxurious **Grand Hotel Reale ❸,** P. del Popolo 25. The deal is unparalleled. (Breakfast €8. Singles €35, with bath €66; doubles €55/88. V.) **Nonnamelia ❸,** V. del Duomo 25, cooks fresh ingredients into creative dishes. (☎34 24 02. *Primi* €5.50-10. *Secondi* €7.50-13. Open

## ON THE MENU

## SLOW FOOD SPREADS FAST

The Slow Food movement sprung in 1986 when Carlo Petrini of Bra, Italy decided enough was enough with grab-n-go fast-food chains. In a mere 22 years, his movement has grown to 80,000 members from all points of the globe, who are attempting to counteract consumers' dwindling interest in the food they eat. Where is it from? What does it taste like? Sometimes we eat too fast to even remember.

Slow Food's requirements are three fold: the food must be good, clean, and fair. In other words, it must taste good, not harm the environment, and food producers must receive fair compensation for their work. Ultimately, their view is that when you lift your fork to swirl that first bite of *linguine*, you are not a consumer, but an informed co-producer.

Keep an eye out for Slow Food's snail symbol on the doors of many restaurants in Italy for assured quality. They've even opened a University of Gastronomical Sciences in 2004, offering Bachelor's and Master's degrees, along with many cultural seminars.

So before you grab that panini *"da portare via"* ("to go"), take a moment to step back and remember where your food is coming from. Even a little acknowledgment is a start.

*For more info, visit www.slow-food.com.*

daily noon-3pm and 7-11pm. Cash only.) For a free tasting of Orvieto Classico and other wines, try **Cantina Freddano,** C. Cavour 5. (☎30 82 48. Bottles from €3.50. Open M-F 9:30am-1pm and 3-8pm, Sa-Su 10am-8pm.) **Trains** run hourly to Florence (2½hr., €11) and Rome (1½hr., €7.10). The funicular travels up the hill from the train station to the center, **Piazza Cahen,** and a shuttle goes to the **tourist office,** P. del Duomo 24. (☎34 17 72. Open M-F 8:15am-1:50pm and 4-7pm, Sa-Su 10am-1pm and 3-6pm.) **Postal Code:** 05018.

# THE MARCHES (LE MARCHE)

In the Marches, green foothills separate the gray shores of the Adriatic from Apennine peaks, and umbrella-dotted beaches from traditional hill towns. Inland villages, easily accessible by train, rely on agriculture and preserve the region's historical legacy in the architectural remains of the Gauls and Romans.

## URBINO ☎0722

The birthplace of Raphael, Urbino (pop. 15,500) charms visitors with stone dwellings scattered along its steep streets. Most remarkable is the Renaissance **Palazzo Ducale,** in P. Rinascimento, a turreted palace that ornaments the skyline. Inside, a stairway leads to the **Galleria Nazionale delle Marche,** in the former residence of Duke Frederico da Montefeltro. Watch for Raphael's *Portrait of a Lady,* and don't miss the subterranean servants' tunnels. (☎32 26 25. Open M 8:30am-2pm, Tu-Su 8:30am-7:15pm. Ticket office closes 1hr. before museum. €4, students 18-25 €2.) Walk back across P. della Repubblica onto V. Raffaello to the site of Raphael's 1483 birth, the **Casa Natale di Raffaello,** V. Raffaello 57, now a museum of period furniture, works by local masters, and the *Madonna col Bambino,* attributed to Raphael himself. (☎32 01 05. Open Mar.-Oct. M-Sa 9am-1pm and 3-7pm, Su 10am-1pm; Nov.-Feb. M-Sa 9am-2pm, Su 10am-1pm. €3. Cash only.)

Just doors down from Raphael's home, **Pensione Fosca ❷,** V. Raffaello 67, is a great value. (☎32 96 22. Call ahead to arrange check-in. Singles €21; doubles €35; triples €45. Cash only.) **Piero della Francesca ❸,** V. Comandino 53, has modern rooms with balconies, bath, phone, and TV. (☎32 84 28. Singles €31; doubles €52; triples €68. AmEx/MC/V.) At **Pizzeria Le Tre Piante ❷,** V. Voltaccia della Vecchia 1, a cheery staff serves pizzas (€2.50-8) on a terrace overlooking the Apennines. (☎48 63. *Primi* from €6.30. *Secondi* from €8. Reserve ahead F-Sa. Open Tu-Su noon-3pm and 7-11:30pm. Cash only.) **Supermarket Margherita** is on V. Raffaello 37. (Open M-Sa 7:30am-2pm and 4:30-8pm. MC/V.) **Bucci buses** (☎0721 32 401) run from Borgo Mercatale to Rome (4½hr., 2 per day, €25). V. Mazzini leads from Borgo Mercatale to P. della Repubblica, the city's hub. From there, V. Vittorio Veneto leads to P. Rinascimento, the *palazzo,* and the **tourist office,** V. Puccinotti 35. (☎26 13. Open M and Sa 9am-1pm, Tu-F 9am-1pm and 3-6pm.)

## ANCONA ☎071

Ancona (pop. 102,000) is the center of transportation for those heading to Croatia, Greece, and Slovenia. The P. del Duomo, atop Monte Guasco, a vigorous hike up a series of stairways, offers a view of the red rooftops and sapphire port below. Across the *piazza* is the **Cattedrale di San Ciriaco,** a Romanesque church with its namesake saint shrouded in velvet in the crypt. (☎52 688. Open in summer M-Sa 8am-noon and 3-7pm; winter M-Sa 8am-noon and 3-6pm. Free.) **Pasetto Beach** seems far from the port's industrial clutter, though its "beach" is concrete. From the train station, cross the *piazza*, turn left, take the first right, then make a sharp right behind the newsstand to reach the **Ostello della Gioventù (HI) ❶**, V. Lamaticci 7. (☎42 257. Lockout 11am-4:30pm. Dorms €16. AmEx/MC/V.) Decent hotels surround the station; try **Hotel Italia ❸**, P. Rosselli 9, with clean, simple rooms. (☎42 607; www.italia51.supereva.it. Singles €27, with bath €38; doubles with bath €65. MC/V.) **La Cantineta ❷**, V. Gramsci, offers specialties like *stoccafisso* (stockfish) at reasonable prices. (☎20 11 07. *Primi* €4-12. *Secondi* €5-15. Cover €1.50. Open Tu-Su noon-2:45pm and 7:30-10:45pm. AmEx/MC/V.) **Di per Di** supermarket is at V. Matteotti 115. (Open M-W and F 8:15am-1:30pm and 5-7:35pm, Th 8:15am-1:30pm, Sa 8:15am-1pm and 5-7:40pm. Cash only.) **Ferries** leave Stazione Marittima for Croatia, Greece, and northern Italy. Jadrolinija (☎20 43 05; www.jadrolinija.hr) runs to Split, CRO (9hr., €37-47). ANEK (☎20 72 346; www.anekitalia.com) ferries go to Patras, GCE (22hr., €50-70). Schedules and tickets are available at the Stazione Marittima. Get up-to-date info at www.doricaportservices.it. **Trains** leave P. Rosselli for: Bologna (2½hr., 1-2 per hr., €11); Milan (4-5hr., 16 per day, €34); Rome (3-4hr., 11 per day, €14); Venice (5hr., 1 per hr., €28). The train station is a 25min. walk from Stazione Marittima. **Buses** #1, 1/3, and 1/4 (€0.90) head up C. Stamira to P. Cavour, the city center. The **tourist office** is across from Stazione Marittima. (☎20 79 029. Open daily Apr.-Sept. 9:30am-2pm and 3-7:30pm; Oct.-Dec. 10am-1:30pm and 2:30-6pm.) **Postal Code:** 60100.

# CAMPANIA

Sprung from the shadow of Mt. Vesuvius, Campania thrives in defiance of natural disasters. The submerged city at Baia, the relics at Pompeii, and the ruins at Cumae all attest to a land resigned to harsh natural outbursts. While the vibrant city of Naples and the emerald waters of the Amalfi Coast reel in tourists, Campania is one of Italy's poorest regions, often overshadowed by the prosperous North.

# NAPLES (NAPOLI)                                    ☎081

Italy's third largest city, Naples (pop. 1 million), is also its most chaotic—Naples moves a million miles per minute. Neapolitans spend their waking moments out on the town, eating, drinking, shouting, laughing, and pausing in the middle of busy streets to finish conversations. The birthplace of pizza and the modern-day home of tantalizing seafood, Neapolitan cuisine is unbeatable. Once you submit to the rapid pulse of Naples, everywhere else will just seem slow.

## ▐ TRANSPORTATION

**Flights: Aeroporto Capodichino**, V. Umberto Maddalena (**NAP**; ☎78 96 259; www.gesac.it), northeast of the city. Connects to major Italian and European cities. **Alibus** (☎53 11 706) goes to P. Municipio and P. Garibaldi (20min., 6am-11:30pm, €3).

**Trains: Trenitalia** (www.trenitalia.it) goes from Stazione Centrale in P. Garibaldi to **Milan** (9hr., 13 per day, €50) and **Rome** (2hr., 40 per day, €11). **Circumvesuviana** (☎800 05 39 39) runs to **Herculaneum** (€1.70) and **Pompeii** (€2.30).

**Ferries:** Depart from **Stazione Marittima**, on Molo Angioino, and **Molo Beverello**, at the base of P. Municipio. From P. Garibaldi, take the R2, 152, 3S, or the Alibus to P. Muni-

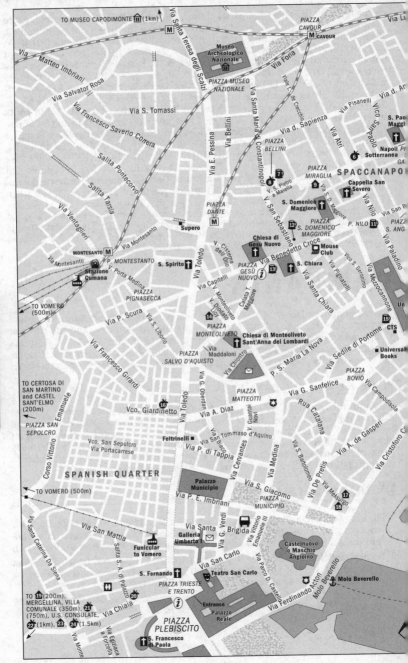

TO MUSEO CAPODIMONTE 🏛 (1km)

Via Santa Teresa degli Scalzi

PIAZZA
CAVOUR

Ⓜ CAVOUR

Via Lu

Via d. An

Via Matteo Imbriani

Museo
Archeologico
Nazionale 🏛

PIAZZA MUSEO
NAZIONALE

Via Foria

Viale L. de Crecchio

Via Salvator Rosa

Via S. Tomassi

Via Francesco Saverio Correra

Via S. Pessina

Via Bellini

Via Santa Maria di Constantinopoli

Via d. Sapienza

Via Pisanelli

Via Atri

S. Paol
Maggi

Salita Pontecorvo

PIAZZA
BELLINI

PIAZZA
MIRAGLIA

SPACCANAPO

🔟6 Napoli PI
Sotterranea

Salita Tarsia

Via Ventaglieri

PIAZZA
DANTE

Ⓜ

🔟7
🔟8 V. S. Pietro
a Maiella

🔟9

V. S. D. Maggiore

S. Domenico
Maggiore 🕇

Cappella San
Severo 🕇

GA

Via Nilo

Via San B

Via Montesanto

Supero

V. San Sebastiano

PIAZZA
S. DOMENICO
MAGGIORE

P. NILO

🔟11

PIAZZ
S. ANG

MONTESANTO Ⓜ

P. MONTESANTO

Via Montesanto

Stazione
Cumana

Porta Medina

S. Spirito 🕇

Via Toledo

V. Cisterna
dell'Olio

Chiesa di
Gesù Nuovo 🕇

🔟12

Mouse
Club

S. Chiara 🕇

Via Benedetto Croce

Vico S. Geronimo

Via Mezzocannone

Via Paladino

PIAZZA
PIGNASECCA

Via Capitelli

Via Diodato
Lioy

Via Montesanto

PIAZZA
GESÙ
NUOVO ⓘ

🔟13

Via Santa Chiara

Via Pignatelli

Un

TO VOMERO
(500m)

Via P. Scura

Via S. Liborio

🔟14

PIAZZA
MONTEOLIVETO

Chiesa di Monteoliveto
Sant'Anna dei Lombardi 🕇

Calata T.
Maggiore

Via Chiostro

🔟15
CTS

Via Francesco Girardi

PIAZZA
SALVO D'AQUISTO

Via
Maddaloni

P. S. Maria La Nova

Via Sedile di Portome

Universal
Books

TO CERTOSA DI
SAN MARTINO
and CASTEL
SANT'ELMO
(200m)

Corso Vittorio Emanuele

Vco. Giardinetto

🔟16

Via Toledo

Via G. Oberdan

Via A. Diaz

PIAZZA
MATTEOTTI

✚

PIAZZA
BOVIO

Via G. Sanfelice

Rua Catalana

Via A. de Gasperi

Via Campodisola

Via Cristoforo C

PIAZZA SAN
SEPOLCRO

Vco. San Sepulcro

Via Portacarrese

Feltrinelli ■

Via S. Baisco

Via Tommaso d'Aquino

V. Guantai
Novi

Via Cervantes

Via P. di Tappia

Via S. Bartolomeo

Via Medina

Via De Pretis

Via Melsurgo

🔟17

🔟18

SPANISH QUARTER

Via Santa Caterina Da Siena

TO VOMERO (500m)

Via San Mattia

Salita S. A. di Palazzo

Palazzo
Municipio

Via S. Giacomo

Via P. E. Imbriani

PIAZZA
MUNICIPIO

Castelnuovo
o Maschio
Angioino

Via Ferdinando Acton

Molo Beverello

Molo Beverello

Funicular
to Vomero

🅷

🔟20

S. Fernando 🕇

Via Santa
Brigida

Galleria
Umberto I ✉

Via G. Verdi

Via San Carlo

Teatro San Carlo ▥

Via Vittorio Emanuele III

Via Parco di Castello

✚

TO 🔟19 (200m),
MERGELLINA, VILLA
COMUNALE (350m),
(750m), U.S. CONSULATE,
🔟22 (1km), 🔟23 🔟24 (1.5km)

🔟21

Via Chiaia

Via Eglaca a Forcella

Via Montes

PIAZZA TRIESTE
E TRENTO

ⓘ

Entrance
Palazzo
Reale

PIAZZA
PLEBISCITO

S. Francesco
di Paola 🕇

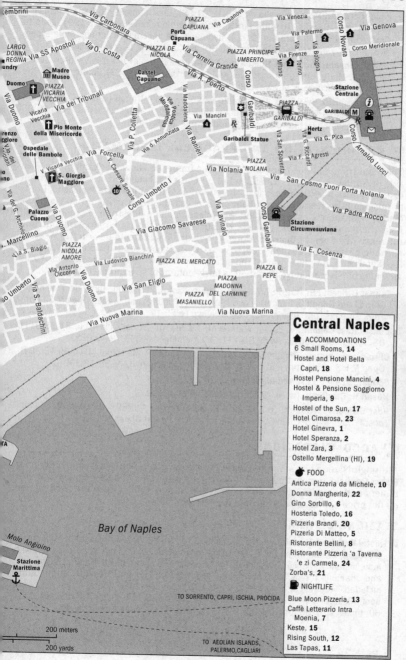

**Central Naples**

🏠 ACCOMMODATIONS

6 Small Rooms, **14**
Hostel and Hotel Bella
  Capri, **18**
Hostel Pensione Mancini, **4**
Hostel & Pensione Soggiorno
  Imperia, **9**
Hostel of the Sun, **17**
Hotel Cimarosa, **23**
Hotel Ginevra, **1**
Hotel Speranza, **2**
Hotel Zara, **3**
Ostello Mergellina (HI), **19**

🍖 FOOD

Antica Pizzeria da Michele, **10**
Donna Margherita, **22**
Gino Sorbillo, **6**
Hosteria Toledo, **16**
Pizzeria Brandi, **20**
Pizzeria Di Matteo, **5**
Ristorante Bellini, **8**
Ristorante Pizzeria 'a Taverna
  'e zi Carmela, **24**
Zorba's, **21**

🍷 NIGHTLIFE

Blue Moon Pizzeria, **13**
Caffè Letterario Intra
  Moenia, **7**
Keste, **15**
Rising South, **12**
Las Tapas, **11**

ITALY

cipio. **Caremar,** Molo Beverello (☎199 12 31 99), runs frequently to **Capri** and **Ischia** (both 1½hr., €4.80). **Tirrenia Lines,** Molo Angioino (☎199 12 31 199), goes to **Cagliari** (16hr.) and **Palermo** (11hr.). Hydrofoils are generally faster and more expensive. The daily newspaper *Il Mattino* (€0.90) lists up-to-date ferry schedules.

**Public Transportation:** One **UnicoNapoli** (www.napolipass.it) ticket is valid on buses, funicular, Metro, and train in Naples (€1 per 1½hr., full-day €3). Route info for the Metro and funiculars is at www.metro.na.it.

**Taxis: Consortaxi** (☎55 25 252); **Radio** (☎55 15 151); **Napoli** (☎55 64 444). Only take metered taxis, and always ask about prices up front. Meter starts at €2.60; €0.05 per 70m thereafter. €2.10 surcharge added from 10pm-7am.

## ✦ 🗲 ORIENTATION AND PRACTICAL INFORMATION

The main train and bus terminals are in the immense **Piazza Garibaldi** on the east side of Naples. From P. Garibaldi, a left on **Corso Garibaldi** leads to the waterfront district; **Piazza Guglielmo Pepe** is at the end of C. Garibaldi. **Piazza Plebiscito,** home to upscale little restaurants and shops, is accessible by walking down **Via Nuova Marina** with the water on your left. **Via Toledo,** a chic pedestrian shopping street, links the waterfront to the Plebiscito district, where the well-to-do hang out, and the maze-like **Spanish Quarter.** Along V. Toledo, **Piazza Dante** lies on the western extreme of the **Spaccanapoli** *(centro storico)* neighborhood. Walking away from the waterfront, a right at any of the streets will lead to the historic district. While violent crime is rare in Naples, theft is fairly common, so exercise caution.

**Tourist Offices: EPT** (☎26 87 79; www.eptnapoli.info), at Stazione Centrale. Free maps. Grab 📖 **Qui Napoli,** a bimonthly publication full of listings and events. Open M-Sa 9am-7pm, Su 9am-1pm. **Branch** at P. Gesù Nuovo (☎55 12 701).

**Consulates: Canada,** V. Carducci 29 (☎40 13 38). **UK,** V. dei Mille 40 (☎42 38 911). **US,** P. della Repubblica (☎58 38 111, 24hr. emergency 033 79 45 083).

**Currency Exchange: Thomas Cook,** at the airport and in P. Municipio 70 (☎55 18 399). Open M-F 9:30am-1pm and 3-7pm. **Branch:** P. Municipio 70 (☎55 18 399).

**Police:** ☎79 41 111. **Ambulance:** ☎75 28 282.

**Hospital: Cardarelli** (☎74 72 859), on the R4 or OF line.

**Post Office:** P. Matteotti (☎552 42 33), at V. Diaz on the R2 line. Unreliable *fermo-posta.* Open M-F 8:15am-6pm, Sa 8:15am-noon. **Postal Code:** 80100.

## 🏠 ACCOMMODATIONS

Although Naples has some fantastic bargain accommodations, especially near **Piazza Garibaldi,** be cautious when choosing a room. Avoid hotels that solicit customers at the station, never give your passport until you've seen the room, agree on the price before unpacking, and be alert for hidden costs.

### STAZIONE CENTRALE

📷 **Hostel Pensione Mancini,** V. P. S. Mancini, 33 (☎55 36 731; www.hostelpensioneman-cini.com), off the far end of P. Garibaldi from station, 2nd fl.; not to be confused with more distant V. Mancini. Owners share their extensive knowledge of Naples. Bright, tidy, and spacious rooms, with new common room and kitchen. Breakfast and Internet included. Free luggage storage and lockers. Reception 24hr. Check-in and check-out noon. Reserve 1 week ahead. Dorms €20; singles €35, with bath €45; doubles €55/60; triples €75/80; quads €90/100. 10% *Let's Go* discount. Cash only. ❷

**Hotel Zara,** V. Firenze 81 (☎28 71 25; www.hotelzara.it). Quiet, large, renovated rooms, all with TV, A/C, and bath; some with Internet. Breakfast €4. Internet €4 per hr. Reserve ahead. Singles €35; doubles €45, with bath €65; triples €80; quads €100. 5% *Let's Go* discount. AmEx/MC/V. ❸

**Hotel Ginevra,** V. Genova 116, 2nd fl. (☎/fax 28 32 10; www.hotelginevra.it). Exit P. Garibaldi on C. Novara; turn right on V. Genova. A short walk from the train station. Comfortable and convenient for late-night arrivals. Internet €4 per hr. Reserve ahead. Singles €35, with bath €55; doubles €55/65; doubles with A/C, bath, minibar, and TV €80; triples €100. 10% *Let's Go* discount with cash payment. AmEx/MC/V. ❸

**Hotel Speranza,** V. Palermo, 30/31 (☎26 92 86) by Piazza Garibaldi. Spacious rooms with nice views of the city include A/C, bath, phone, and TV. Breakfast included. Singles €40; doubles €60; triples €80. ❸

## WATERFRONT

▩ **Hostel and Hotel Bella Capri,** V. Melisurgo 4 (☎55 29 494; www.bellacapri.it). Take the R2 bus from station, exit at V. De Pretis. Top-notch hostel offers kitchen and clean rooms with A/C and TV. Breakfast included. Free luggage storage, lockers, and Internet. Reception 24hr. Dorms €20; singles €45-50, with bath €60-70; doubles €55-60/70; triples €80-84/90-100; quads €90-100/100-110. 10% *Let's Go* discount. AmEx/MC/V. ❸

▩ **Hostel of the Sun,** V. Melisurgo 15 (☎42 06 393; www.hostelnapoli.com). Take the R2 bus from station, exit at V. De Pretis. Buzz #51. Take the elevator (€0.05) during business hours. Large, colorful common room has satellite TV, DVDs, and small library. Dorms and private rooms are spacious, clean, and equipped with free lockers. Kitchen available. Breakfast included. Laundry €3, free load with 3-day stay. Free Internet. Reserve ahead in summer. Dorms €20; singles €45, with bath €50; doubles €55/70; triples €80/90; quads €90/100. 10% *Let's Go* discount. MC/V. ❷

**Ostello Mergellina (HI),** V. Salita della Grotta 23 (☎76 12 346; fax 76 12 391). M: Mergellina. Make 2 sharp rights after Metro stop. After overpass, turn right onto driveway, which is unlit at night. Laundry €6. Lockout 9am-3pm. Curfew 12:30am. Reserve ahead July-Aug. Dorms €14; doubles €36; family rooms €16 per person. MC/V. ❶

## SPACCANAPOLI (CENTRO STORICO) AND VOMERO

▩ **Hotel Cimarosa,** V. D. Cimarosa 29, 5th fl. (☎55 67 044; www.hotelcimarosa.it). Take the funicular from near P. Plebiscito, exit at the station. Go around the corner to the right. Buzz to enter (in the same building as the Centrale funicular station). Over 30 beautiful rooms share spotless baths. A bit out of the way, it feels far from the bustle of Naples. Great views of the harbor. Check-out 11am. Curfew 1am. Singles €40; doubles €70; triples €95. With private bath, prices nearly double. MC/V. ❹

**6 Small Rooms,** V. Diodato Lioy 18 (☎79 01 378; www.6smallrooms.com). No sign; look for the call button. Friendly Australian owner and larger rooms than the name suggests. Kitchen available. Free lockers. Key (€5 deposit) for returning after midnight curfew. Call for dorm beds after 10pm the night before arrival. Dorms €18; singles with bath €35; doubles €55, with bath €65. Cash only. ❷

**Hostel and Pensione Soggiorno Imperia,** P. Miraglia 386 (☎45 93 47; www.soggiornoimperia.it). Take the R2 from station, walk up V. Mezzocannone through P. S. Domenico Maggiore, and enter the 1st set of doors to the left. 9 clean rooms in a peaceful 16th-century *palazzo*. Reserve ahead. Dorms €20; singles €30; doubles €50, with bath 65; triples €65/90; quads €90/100. AmEx/MC/V. ❸

## ◨ FOOD

### PIZZERIE

If you ever doubted that Neapolitans invented pizza, Naples's *pizzerie* will take that doubt, knead it into a ball, throw it in the air, spin it on their collective finger, punch it down, cover it with sauce and mozzarella, and serve it *alla margherita*.

▨ **Gino Sorbillo,** V. dei Tribunali 32 (☎44 66 43; www.accademiadellapizza.it). The pizzeria's owners claim links to a forbearer who invented the *ripieno al forno* (calzone) and has 21 pizza-makers in this generation. The kitchen has the original brick oven. *Margherita* €3. Service 10%. Open M-Sa noon-3:30pm and 7-11:30pm. MC/V. ❶

▨ **Pizzeria Di Matteo,** V. dei Tribunali 94 (☎45 52 62), near V. Duomo. Former President Clinton ate here during the G-7 Conference in 1994. Pies, like the *marinara* (€2), burst with flavor, while the building bursts with pizza aficionados—put your name on the list and expect a short wait. Pizza €2.50-6. Open M-Sa 9am-midnight. Cash only. ❶

**Antica Pizzeria da Michele,** V. Cesare Sersale 1/3 (☎55 39 204). Huge line advertises the quality inside. Watch sweltering chefs toss pies from pizza-board to flame-licked oven and finally onto plates with superhuman grace and dexterity. *Margherita* and *marinara* pizzas €3.50-4.50. Open M-Sa 10am-11pm. Cash only. ❶

**Pizzeria Brandi,** Salita S. Anna di Palazzo 1 (☎41 69 28; www.brandi.it), off V. Chiaia. In 1889, Raffaele Esposito invented the *margherita* in Brandi's ancient oven to symbolize Italy's flag—green basil, white mozzarella, red tomatoes. The famous story keeps customers lining up. Cover €1.80. Service charge 12%. Reserve ahead Sa-Su. Open M and W-Su 12:30-3pm and 7:30pm-12:30am. AmEx/MC/V. ❷

### RESTAURANTS AND TRATTORIE

For a culinary change of pace from the plethora of pizza, the **waterfront** offers traditional Neapolitan seafood. In the *centro storico*, small restaurants can be found on side streets, away from the more expensive *trattorie*. Some of the cheapest, most authentic options lie along **Via dei Tribunali** in the heart of Spaccanapoli.

▨ **Hosteria Toledo,** Vicolo Giardinetto 78A (☎42 12 57), in the Spanish Quarter. Prepare yourself for courses of Neapolitan comfort food. The *gnocchi* (€6) is hearty enough to be a meal on its own. If you're feeling adventurous or indecisive, try the chef's surprise. *Primi* €6-12. *Secondi* €5-10. Open daily 8pm-midnight. MC/V. ❷

**Donna Margherita,** Vico II Alabardieri 4/5/6 (☎40 01 29). This place offers high quality food in a location close to city nightlife. Beautiful decoration inside displays the elegance and simplicity of the Neapolitan lifestyle. Pizzas €3.50-7. *Primi* €6-15. Open daily noon-3pm and 7pm-midnight. ❷

**Zorba's,** V. Martucci 5 (☎66 75 72). M: Mergellina. Greek fare is a delightful change of pace. Try the *satanas* (spicy mini-sausages; €7). Fresh baklava €3. Open Tu-F and Su 8:30pm-1am, Sa 8:30pm-3am. Cash only. ❷

**Ristorante Bellini,** V. Santa Maria di Constantinopoli 79-80, off P. Bellini. Come for an evening *al fresco*, surrounded by flowers. Try the *linguine al cartoccio* (€11) or anything from the *pesce* menu. *Primi* €6.50-11. *Secondi* from €8.50. Open daily 9am-4pm and 7pm-midnight. Closed Su evening in summer. MC/V. ❸

**Ristorante Pizzeria 'a Taverna 'e zi Carmela,** V. Niccolò Tommaseo 11-12 (☎76 43 35 81), on the corner of V. Partenope. Locals arrive at this waterfront restaurant for its excellent seafood, especially the *polpo* (octopus). Try the *rigatoni al sappori di mare* (€7) or ask waiters to recommend the freshest catch. *Primi* €3.50-12. *Secondi* €5-12. Open in summer daily 11:15am-1:30pm and 7:30pm-1am. Cash only. ❷

# SIGHTS

**MUSEO ARCHEOLOGICO NAZIONALE.** Situated in a 16th-century *palazzo* and former military barracks, one of the world's oldest archaeological museums contains treasures from Pompeii, Herculaneum, and the personal collection of Charles Bourbon. Unreliable labeling makes a guidebook, tour, or audio tour a good investment. The mezzanine has a mosaic room, with one design featuring a fearless Alexander the Great routing the Persian army. Check out the Farnese Bull, the largest extant ancient statue. The *Gabinetto Segreto* (secret cabinet) of Aphrodite grants glimpses into the goddess's life. *(M: P. Cavour. Turn right from the station and walk 2 blocks. ☎44 01 66. Open M and W-Su 9am-7:30pm. €6.50, EU students €3.30. Audio tour in English, French, or Italian €4.)*

**MUSEO AND GALLERIE DI CAPODIMONTE.** Housed in another 16th-century *palazzo*, the museum resides inside a park often filled with locals. A plush royal apartment and the Italian National Picture Gallery are within the palace. Among its impressive works are Bellini's *Transfiguration*, Masaccio's *Crucifixion*, and Titian's *Danae*. *(Take bus #24, 110, M4, or M5 from the Archaeological Museum and exit at the gate to the park, on the right. 2 entrances: Porta Piccola and Porta Grande. ☎74 99 111. Open M-Tu and Th-Su 8:30am-7:30pm. €7.50, after 2pm €3.80.)*

**PALAZZO REALE AND MASCHIO ANGIONO.** The 17th-century Palazzo Reale contains opulent royal apartments, the **Museo di Palazzo Reale,** and a view from the terrace of the **Royal Chapel.** *(P. Plebescito 1. Take the R2 bus from P. Garibaldi to P. Trieste e Trento and walk around the palazzo to the entrance on P. Plebiscito. ☎40 05 47; www.pierreci.it. Open M-Tu and Th-Su 9am-7pm. €4, EU students and under 18 free.)* The **Biblioteca Nazionale** stores 1.5 million volumes, including the scrolls from the **Villa dei Papiri** in Herculaneum. *(☎78 19 231. Open M-F 10am-1pm with reservation.)* The **Teatro San Carlo's** acoustics are reputed to top those of Milan's La Scala. *(Theater entrance on P. Trieste e Trento. ☎66 45 45; www.teatrosancarlo.it. Open daily 9am-7pm.)* It's impossible to miss **Maschio Angiono,** whose five turrets shadow the Bay of Naples. Built in 1286 by Charles II of Anjou as his royal residence, the fortress's most stunning feature is its entrance, where reliefs depict the arrival of Alphonse I of Aragon in 1443. The castle also holds the magnificent **Hall of the Barons,** where King Ferdinand once trapped rebellious barons. Bullet holes from WWII are visible on the northern wall. *(P. Municipio. Take the R2 bus from P. Garibaldi. ☎42 01 241. Open M-Sa 9am-7pm. €5.)*

## TRASH TALK

The beautiful *centro storico* in Naples is being overshadowed by a new kind of monument: 10ft. trash piles.

Over 3000 tons of uncollected trash—along with rats and other pests attracted to the filth—started piling up on the streets when safety violations caused the government to close all four city dumps in May 2007. As a city whose trash collection is largely controlled by Camorra (the Neapolitan mafia), Naples is no stranger to garbage problems.

In 2004, internal problems in Camorra—whose waste-removal profits are an estimated €22 million per year—caused collectors to stop collecting. It is rumored that the mafia is also involved in the 2007 garbage crisis, and that the organizations is pocketing a lot of the money that would otherwise go towards waste collection. When the trash started piling up, citizens began setting fire to uncollected heaps of waste—up to 150 fires a day—and wearing masks to avoid toxic fumes. With schools closures due to rat infestations, a threat of infectious diseases, and a suspected link between the chronic waste problem and increases in cancer and genetic defects, Naples knows it must act quickly to avoid a smellier version of Pompeii's destruction by burial.

**VIRGIL'S TOMB.** The celebrated Latin poet's resting place is at V. Salita della Grotta. Below the tomb is the entrance to the closed Crypta Neapolitana, built during the reign of Augustus, which connected ancient Neapolis to Pozzuoli and Baia. Call ahead for a translator to explain the inscriptions, or just come for the view. *(M: Mergellina. From the station, take 2 quick rights. Entrance between overpass and tunnel. ☎ 66 93 90. Guided tours upon request. Open daily 9am-1hr. before sunset. Free.)*

**NAPOLI SOTTERRANEA (CATACOMBS AND THE UNDERGROUND).** The catacombs of S. Gennaro, S. Gaudioso, and S. Severo all date back to the early centuries AD. Tours of the subterranean alleys beneath the city are fascinating: they involve crawling through narrow underground passageways, spotting Mussolini-era graffiti, and exploring Roman aqueducts. Napoli Sotterranea runs below the historic center. *(P. S. Gaetano 68. Take V. dei Tribunali and turn left right before S. Paolo Maggiore. ☎ 29 69 44. Tours 1 per 2hr. M-F noon-4pm, Sa-Su 10am-6pm. €9.30, students €8.)*

**DUOMO.** Begun in 1315 by Robert of Anjou, the *duomo* has been redone over the centuries. Its main attraction is the **Capella del Tesoro di San Gennaro,** decorated with Baroque paintings. A beautiful 17th-century bronze grille protects the high altar, which houses the saint's head and two vials of his coagulated blood. According to legend, disaster will strike the city if the blood does not liquefy on the celebration of his *festa* (3 times a year). Behind the main altar lies the saint's crypt. Visitors can also view the newly opened underground **excavation site,** a tangle of Greek and Roman roads. *(Walk 3 blocks up V. Duomo from C. Umberto I or take bus #42 from P. Garibaldi. ☎ 44 90 97. Open M-Sa 8:30am-noon and 4:30-6pm. Free. Excavation site €3.)*

# ▓ NIGHTLIFE

Content to groove at small clubs and discos during the winter, Neapolitans take to the streets and *piazze* in summer. **Piazza Vanvitelli** is accessible by the funicular from V. Toledo or the bus C28 from P. Vittoria. **Via Santa Maria La Nova** is another hot spot. Outdoor bars and cafes are a popular choice in **Piazza Bellini,** near P. Dante. **ARCI-GAY/Lesbica** (☎ 55 28 815) has info on gay and lesbian club nights.

■ **Rising South,** V. S. Sebastiano 19, nearby P. Gesu Nuovo. *Enoteca*, bar, cinema—this club does it all. Plush oriental carpets, vintage chandeliers, and a sound-proof main hall carved from rock set the scene for a students' hot spot. Drinks €3-6. Bar open daily Sept.-May 10pm-3am, with special events in summer. Cash only.

**Keste,** Largo San Giovanni Maggiore (☎ 15 51 39 84), in *Centro Storico* in front of L'Istituto Orientale. Underground, alternative feel attracts all strata of Neapolitan society. Sit outside by the garden or dance to music inside. Beer €3. Open daily 9pm-2am.

**Caffè Letterario Intra Moenia,** P. Bellini 70. Appeals to intellectuals by keeping books amid the wicker furniture. Outside, vines grow up the walls, and the remains of an excavated Roman building lie on the ground. Open daily 10am-2am. Cash only.

**Blue Moon Pizzeria,** V. T. de Amicis 4, right in P. Gesu Nuovo. Supplier of large €1.50 bottles of Peroni beer for the masses, as well as all the food needed for a night of socializing in the *piazza*. Open daily 7pm-late. Cash only.

**Las Tapas,** V. Paladino 56. A low-key favorite of university students, close to the bustling nightlife of P.S. Domenico Maggiore. Outdoor seating down V. Nilo from V. dei Tribunali. Sangria €2.50 per glass, €12 per liter. Service 10%. Open daily Sept.-July 7pm-2am.

# ▓ DAYTRIPS FROM NAPLES

■ **HERCULANEUM.** Buried deeper than Pompeii, Herculaneum is less excavated than its neighbor, and a modern city sits on its remains. Don't miss the **House of**

**Deer.** *(Open daily 8:30am-7:30pm. €10.)* As its name suggests, the **House of the Mosaic of Neptune and Amphitrite** is famous for its mosaics. The city is 500m downhill from the Ercolano Scavi stop on the Circumvesuviana train from Naples (dir.: Sorrento; 20min.). The **tourist office** (☎78 81 243) is at V. IV Novembre 84.

**POMPEII.** On the morning of August 24, AD 79, a deadly cloud of volcanic ash from Mt. Vesuvius settled over the Roman city of Pompeii, catching the 12,000 prosperous residents by surprise and engulfing the city in suffocating black clouds. Mere hours after the eruption, stately buildings, works of art, and human bodies were sealed in hardened casts of ash. These natural tombs would remain undisturbed until 1748, when excavations began to unearth a stunningly well-preserved picture of daily Roman life. Walk down V. della Marina to reach the colonnaded **Forum,** which was once the civic and religious center of the city. Exit the Forum through the upper end by the cafeteria and head right on V. della Fortuna to reach the **House of the Faun,** where a bronze dancing faun and the spectacular Alexander Mosaic (today in the Museo Archeologico Nazionale) were found. Continue on V. della Fortuna and turn left on V. dei Vettii to reach the **House of the Vettii** and the most vivid frescoes in Pompeii. Backtrack on V. dei Vettii, cross V. della Fortuna to V. Storto, turn left on V. degli Augustali, and take a quick right to reach a small frescoed **brothel** (the *Lupenare*). V. dei Teatri, across the street, leads to the oldest standing **amphitheater** in the world (80 BC), which once held up to 20,000 spectators. To get to the ◪**Villa of the Mysteries,** the ancient city's best-preserved villa, head west on V. della Fortuna, right on V. Consolare, and all the way up Porta Ercolano and V. della Tombe. *(Archaeological site open daily Apr.-Oct. 8:30am-7:30pm; Nov.-Mar. 8:30am-5pm. €10.)* The **tourist office** is at V. Sacra 1. *(Open M-F 8am-3:30pm, Sa 8am-2pm.)* Take the Circumvesuviana **train** (☎77 22 444) from Naples to the Pompeii Scavi stop *(dir.: Sorrento; 40min., 2 per hr., round-trip €2.30.)*

**MOUNT VESUVIUS.** Peer into the only active volcano in mainland Europe at Mt. Vesuvius. It hasn't erupted since March 31, 1944 (scientists estimate the volcano becomes active, on average, every 30 years), and experts claim the trip up the mountain is relatively safe. Great views of the **Bay of Naples** can be enjoyed from the top. *(No wheelchair access. Vesuvio Express buses, ☎73 93 666, run from Herculaneum to the crater of Vesuvius. 3 per hr., or as soon as the van is filled. Round-trip €10.)*

**CASERTA.** Few palaces, no matter how opulent, can hold a candle to Caserta's glorious ◪**La Reggia,** often referred to as "The Versailles of Naples." A world apart from the stark brutality of Pompeii, the palace and grounds resonate with a passion for art and beauty. When King Charles III commissioned the palace in 1751, he intended it to rival Louis XIV's spectacular abode. The vast expanse of lawns filled with fountains and sculptures culminates in a 75m manmade waterfall—the setting for the final scene of *Star Wars* (1977). To the right are the **English Gardens,** with fake ruins inspired by Pompeii and Paestum. The **palazzo** boasts 1200 rooms, 1742 windows, 34 staircases, and grandiose furnishings. *(Open M and W-Su 9am-7:30pm. Palazzo and gardens €6. Trains go to Naples from Caserta; 40min.; 35 per day.)*

# BAY OF NAPLES

## SORRENTO
☎ 081

The most touristed town on the peninsula, cliffside Sorrento makes a convenient base for daytrips around the Bay of Naples. **Ostello Le Sirene ❷,** V. degli Aranci 160, is located near the train station. (☎80 72 925. Dorms €18-25; doubles €60.) Wooded seaside campground **Santa Fortunata Campogaio ❶,** V. del Capo 39, has a private beach. (☎80 73 579. Tent sites €16-25. Dorms €19.) Try the *gnocchi* (€5) or the *linguini al cartoccio* (linguini with mixed seafood; €7) at **Ristorante e Pizzeria Giardiniello ❷**, V. dell'Accademia 7. (☎87 84 616. Cover €1. Open Apr.-Nov. daily 11am-midnight; Dec.-Mar. M-W and F-Su 11am-midnight. AmEx/MC/V.) After dark, a crowd gathers for drinks on the rooftop above **The English Inn**, C. Italia 57. (Open daily 9am-1am.) **Ferries** and **hydrofoils** depart for the Bay of Naples islands. **Linee Marittime Partenopee** (☎80 71 812) runs ferries (40min., 5 per day, €7.50) and hydrofoils (20min., 19 per day, €11) to Capri. The **tourist office**, L. de Maio 35, is off P. Tasso, in the C. dei Forestieri compound. (☎80 74 033. Open M-Sa Apr.-Sept. 8:30am-6:30pm; Oct.-Mar. 8:30am-2pm and 4-6:15pm.) **Postal Code:** 80067.

# 🄰CAPRI                                                                  ☎081

Augustus fell in love with Capri in 29 BC, and since then, the "pearl of the Mediterranean" has been a hot spot for the rich and famous. There are two towns on the island—**Capri** proper, near the ports, and **Anacapri**, high on the hills. The best times to visit are in late spring and early fall, as crowds and prices increase in summer. Visitors flock to the **Blue Grotto**, a sea cave where the water shimmers a vivid neon blue. (Short boat ride from Marina Grande €10. Tickets at Grotta Azzurra Travel Office, V. Roma 53. Tours until 5pm.) Buses departing from V. Roma make the trip up the mountain to Anacapri every 15min. until 1:40am; buses leave Anacapri for most tourist attractions. Away from the throngs of pricey Capri, Anacapri is home to less expensive hotels, lovely vistas, and quiet mountain paths. Upstairs from P. Vittoria in Anacapri, **Villa San Michele** has lush gardens, ancient sculptures, and summer concerts. (Open daily 9am-6pm. €6.) Take the chairlift up 🄼**Monte Solaro** from P. Vittoria for great views. (Chairlift open Mar.-Oct. daily 9:30am-4:45pm. Round-trip €7.) For those who prefer cliff to coastline, the **Faraglioni**, three massive rocks, are accessible by a 1hr. walk, and there's a steep 1½hr. hike to the ruins of Emperor Tiberius's **Villa Jovis**. The view from the **Cappella di Santa Maria del Soccorso**, built onto the villa, is unrivaled. (Open daily 9am-6pm. €2.)

🄱**Bussola di Hermes ❸**, V. Traversa La Vigna 14, in Anacapri, is the best accommodation deal on the island. Call from P. Vittoria in Anacapri for pickup. (☎83 82 010; www.bussolahermes.com. Reserve ahead. Dorms €27-30; doubles €70-110. MC/V.) For convenient access to the beach and Capri's center, stay at **Vuotto Antonio ❹**, V. Campo di Teste 2. Take V. V. Emanuele out of P. Umberto, a left onto V. Camerelle, a right onto V. Cerio, and left onto V. Campo di Teste. Housed in "Villa Margherita," simple, elegant rooms are nicely decorated. (☎83 70 230. Doubles €55-95. Cash only.) 🄱**Ristorante Il Cucciolo ❷**, V. La Fabbrica 52, in Anacapri, has fresh food at low prices. (☎83 71 917. *Primi* and *secondi* €6-9 with *Let's Go* discount.) The **supermarket**, V.G. Orlandi 299, in Anacapri, is well-stocked. (Open M-Sa 8:30am-1:30pm and 5-8:30pm, Su 8:30am-noon.) At night Italians dressed to kill come out for Capri's bars near **Piazza Umberto**, open late; younger crowds head to Anacapri.

Caremar (☎83 70 700) **ferries** run from Marina Grande to Naples (1¼hr., 3 per day, €7). LineaJet (☎83 70 819) runs **hydrofoils** to Naples (40-50min., 11 per day, €12) and Sorrento (25min., 15 per day, €10). Boats to other destinations run less frequently; check at Marina Grande for more info. The Capri **tourist office** sits at the end of Marina Grande. (☎83 70 634; www.capritourism.com. Open June-Sept. daily 9am-1pm and 3:30-6:45pm; Oct.-May reduced hours.) In Anacapri, it's at V. Orlandi 59; turn right when leaving the bus stop. (☎83 71 524. Open M-Sa 9am-3pm; Oct.-May reduced hours.) **Postal Codes:** 80073 (Capri); 80021 (Anacapri).

# 🄸ISCHIA                                                                 ☎081

Travelers have sought out Ischia since ancient times; both *The Iliad* and *The Aeneid* mention the island. Ischia (pop. 60,000) was once an active volcano, but now lemon groves, hot springs, and ruins keep travelers coming back. SEPSA **buses** CS, CD, and #1, and 2 (2-4 per hr.) depart from the intersection on V. Iasolino and V. B. Cossa, stopping at: **Ischia Porto,** the major port town and site of the island's most active nightlife, **Casamicciola Terme** and **Lacco Ameno,** homes of legendary thermal waters, and **Forio,** the island's largest town. The **Ring Hostel ❷,** V. Gaetano Morgera 66, in Forio, is in a 19th-century convent. (☎98 75 46; www.ringhostel.com. 12-bed dorms €17; singles €30.) Take bus #13 from Ischia Porto to reach **Eurocamping dei Pini ❶,** V. delle Ginestre, 34. Ideal for budget travelers, this campsite offers clean areas, friendly services, and a restaurant. (☎98 20 69. €7-10 per person, €6-10 per tent. Bungalows €13-25 per person.) **Castillo de Aragona ❷,** Ischia Ponte (☎98 31 53), right next to the entrance of the Castello Aragonese, offers amazing views and inexpensive cuisine. (*Primi* €7-10. Open daily 10am-3am.) Caremar **ferries** (☎98 48 18; www.caremar.it) head to Naples (1½hr., 8 per day, €11). Alilauro (☎99 18 88) runs **hydrofoils** to Capri (1 per day, €13) and Sorrento (1 per day, €15). The **tourist office** is on V. Iasolino. (☎50 74 231. Open M-Sa 9am-2pm and 3-8pm.) **Postal Code:** 80077.

# THE AMALFI COAST ☎089

It happens almost imperceptibly: after the exhausting tumult of Naples and the compact grit of Sorrento, the highway narrows to a two-lane, coastal road, and the horizon becomes illuminated with lemon groves and bright village pastels. Though the coastal towns combine simplicity and sophistication, the region's ultimate appeal rests in the tenuous balance it strikes between man and nature.

**■ TRANSPORTATION. Trains** run to Salerno from Naples (45min., 40 per day, €5-10) and Rome (2½-3hr., 22 per day, €21-33). **SITA buses** (☎26 66 04) connect Salerno to Amalfi (1¼hr., 20 per day, €1.80). From Amalfi, buses also go to Positano (40min., 25 per day, €1.30) and Sorrento (1¼hr., 1 per hr., €2.40). Travelmar (☎87 29 50) runs **hydrofoils** from Amalfi to Positano (25min., 7 per day, €5) and Salerno (35min., 6 per day, €4), and from Salerno to Positano (1¼hr., 6 per day, €6).

**AMALFI AND ATRANI.** Jagged rocks of the Sorrentine Peninsula, azure waters of the Tyrrhenian, and bright lemons define Amalfi. Visitors crowd P. del Duomo to admire the elegant 9th-century **Duomo di Sant'Andrea** and the nearby **Fontana di Sant'Andrea.**

**TOP TEN MUST-EATS IN CAMPANIA**

**1. Limoncello:** Don't fall for the tourist-trap, fluorescent-yellow fakers; the authentic, syrupy sweet liqueur is made in small family-owned restaurants, using generations-old recipes passed down from *nonna* to *mamma*.

**2. Pizza alla Margherita:** the signature dish of Napoli, with fresh tomato, delicious mozzarella, and aromatic basil.

**3. Granita:** Remember that Italian ice you used to get at junior league baseball games? This is it, but better. Think fresh lemons.

**4. Peperone:** Find the hot, red peppers hanging from roadside stands all along the Amalfi Coast. Not to be confused with pepperoni sausage—very different.

**5. Gnocchi alla Sorrentina:** Typical of Sorrento, the *gnocchi* are smothered with crimson tomatoes and melted mozzarella.

**6. Sfogliatelle:** A soft, flaky ricotta-filled pastry, invented in Naples in 1785. Best served warm.

**7. Pasta ai frutti di mare:** Literally, "fruit of the sea," featuring octopus, mussels, and shrimp.

**8. Scialatelli:** A Neapolitan pasta painstakingly made by hand from egg and semolina grain.

**9. Insalata caprese:** A beautiful combo of tomatoes, basil, and mozzarella, drizzled with olive oil.

**10. Mozzarella di bufala:** Moist and creamy, this mozzarella made from buffalo milk is abundant in dishes throughout the region.

The hostel **A'Scalinatella ❶**, P. Umberto 6, runs dorms, private rooms, and camping all over Amalfi and Atrani. (☎87 19 30; www.hostelscalinatella.com. Tent sites €5 per person. Dorms €21; doubles €50-60, with bath €73-83. Cash only.) Amalfi's many *paninoteche* (sandwich shops) are perfect for a tight budget. The **AAST Tourist Office** is at C. Repubbliche Marinare 27. On the same street, a tunnel leads to beach town Atrani, 750m down the coast. The 4hr. **Path of the Gods** follows the coast from **Bomerano** to **Positano,** with great views along the way. The hike from **Atrani** to **Ravello** (1½-2hr.) runs through gently bending lemon groves, up secluded stairways, and down into green valleys. **Postal Code:** 84011.

**RAVELLO.** Perched atop cliffs, Ravello has been claimed by artists and intellectuals, its natural beauty seeping into their works. The Moorish cloister and gardens of **Villa Rufolo,** off P. del Duomo, inspired Boccaccio's *Decameron* and Wagner's *Parsifal.* (Open daily 9am-8pm. €5.) The villa puts on a **summer concert series** in the gardens; tickets are sold at the Ravello Festival box office, V. Roma 10-12 (☎85 84 22; www.ravellofestival.com). Don't miss Ravello's **duomo** and its bronze doors; follow V. S. Francesco out of P. Duomo to the impressive **Villa Cimbrone,** whose floral walkways and gardens hide temples, grottoes, and magnificent views. (Open daily 9am-sunset. €5.) **Palazzo della Marra ❸,** V. della Marra 3, offers immaculate rooms with terraces and kitchen access. (☎85 83 02. Breakfast included. Reserve ahead. Doubles €60-80. MC/V.) **Postal Code:** 84010.

**POSITANO.** Today, Positano's most frequent visitors are the wealthy few who can afford its high prices, but the town still has its charms for the budget traveler. To see the large *pertusione* (hole) in the mountain **Montepertuso,** hike 45min. uphill or take the bus from P. dei Mulini. The three **Isole dei Galli,** islands off Positano's coast, were allegedly home to Homer's mythical Sirens. The beach at **Fornillo** is a serene alternative to **Spiaggia Grande,** the area's main beach. **Ostello Brikette ❷,** V. Marconi 358, with two large terraces and free Wi-Fi, is accessible by the orange Interno bus or SITA bus; exit at the Chiesa Nuova stop and walk 100m to the left of Bar Internazionale. (☎87 58 57. Dorms €22-25; doubles €65-100. MC/V.) The *pasta alla norma* (pasta in tomato sauce with eggplant; €8) at ▓**Da Gabrisa ❷,** Vle. Pasitea 219, is a treat. (☎81 14 98. *Primi* and *secondi* €6-15. Open daily 6-11pm. MC/V.) The four small bars on the beach at Fornillo serve simple, fresh food. The **tourist office,** V. del Saraceno 4, is below the *duomo.* (☎87 50 67. Open M-Sa 8am-2pm and 3-8pm; low season reduced hours.) **Postal Code:** 84017.

**SALERNO.** While industrial Salerno is best used as a base for daytrips to **Paestum,** the town is home to most of the peninsula's nightlife. Paestum is the site of preserved ▓**Doric temples,** including the **Temples of Ceres** and **Poseidon,** as well as a **museum** of artifacts taken from the sites. (Train from Salerno 30min., €5.40. Temples open daily 9am-7:30pm. Museum open daily 9am-6:30pm. Both closed 1st and 3rd M of each month; low season reduced hours. Combined ticket €6.50.) To reach ▓**Ostello Ave Gratia Plena ❶,** V. Canali, take C. V. Emanuele to V. dei Mercanti, and head right onto V. Canali. (☎23 47 76; www.ostellodisalerno.it. Curfew 2am. Dorms €14; doubles €45. AmEx/MC/V.) At night, younger crowds gather on the seaside promenade near **Bar/Gelateria Nettuno,** Lungomare Trieste 136-138. (☎22 83 75. Open daily 7am-2am.) **Postal Code:** 84100.

# SICILY (SICILIA)

An island of contradictions, Sicily owes its cultural complexity to Phoenicians, Greeks, Romans, Arabs, and Normans, all of whom invaded and left their mark.

Ancient Greeks lauded the golden island as the second home of the gods. Now, tourists seek it as the home of *The Godfather*. While the Mafia's presence lingers in Sicily, its power is waning. Active volcano Mt. Etna ominously shadows chic resorts, archaeological treasures, and fast-paced cities.

## ▐ TRANSPORTATION

From southern Italy, take a train to Reggio di Calabria, then a Trenitalia **hydrofoil** (25min., 7-14 per day, €2.80) to Messina, Sicily's transport hub. **Buses** (☎ 090 77 19 14) serve destinations throughout the island and also make the long trek to mainland cities. **Trains** head to Messina directly (via ferry) from Rome (9hr., 6 per day, €43), then connect to Palermo (3½hr., 22 per day, €11), Syracuse (3½hr., 16 per day, €8.75), and Taormina (40min., 27 per day, €15).

## PALERMO
☎091

In gritty Palermo (pop. 680,000), the shrinking shadow of organized crime hovers over the twisting streets lined with ruins. While poverty, bombings, and centuries of neglect have taken their toll on much of the city, Palermo is currently experiencing a revival. Operas and ballets are performed year-round at the Neoclassical ▓**Teatro Massimo,** where the climactic opera scene of *The Godfather: Part III* was filmed. Walk up V. Maqueda from Quattro Canti; it's on P. Verdi. (Tu-Su 10am-3pm. Tours 25min., 2 per hr., €3.) From Quattro Canti, take a left on V. Vittorio Emanuele and another one just before P. Indipendenza to get to the ▓**Cappella Palatina,** full of incredible golden mosaics, in **Palazzo dei Normanni.** (Open M-Sa 8:30am-5pm, Su 8:30am-12:30pm. Tu-Th €4; M and F-Su €6.) At the haunting **Cappuccini Catacombs,** P. Cappuccini 1, 8000 corpses in various states of decay line the underground tunnels. Take bus #109 from Stazione Centrale to P. Indipendenza, then transfer to bus #327. (Open daily 9am-noon and 3-5:30pm. €1.50.) Just 8km outside town, the **Duomo of Monreale** offers a stunning interior, peaceful cloisters, and vistas of all Palermo. Take bus #389 from P. Indipendenza. (Cathedral open M-Sa 8am-6:30pm, Su 8am-1pm and 3:30-7pm; closed Nov.-Apr. 12:30-2:30pm. Free. Balcony open daily 9am-5:30pm. €1.50. Modest dress required. Cloister open daily 9am-6:30pm. €6.)

For the sake of comfort and safety, plan to spend a bit more on accommodations in Palermo. Homey **Hotel Regina ❷,** C. Vittorio Emanuele 316, is near the intersection of V. Maqueda and C. V. Emanuele. Be sure to double-check your reservation before arriving. (☎61 14 216. Singles €25; doubles €44, with bath €54; triples €66/75. AmEx/MC/V.) The best restaurants in town are between Teatro Massimo and the Politeama. Markets **Ballarò,** behind V. Maqueda and C. V. Emanuele, **Capo,** behind Teatro Massimo, and **Vucciria,** between V. V. Emanuele and P. S. Domenico, are open Monday through Saturday. **Trains** leave Stazione Centrale in P. Giulio Cesare at the southern end of V. Roma and V. Maqueda, for Rome (12hr.; 6 per day; €45, with bunk €70). All **bus** lines run from V. Balsamo, next to the train station. After buying tickets, ask the ticket agent for the exact departure point. Pick up a combined metro and bus map from an **AMAT** or **metro** info booth. Buses #101 and 102 (€1 for 2hr.) circle the large downtown area. To reach the **tourist office,** P. Castelnuovo 34, at the west end of the *piazza*, take a bus from the station to P. Politeama, at the end of V. Maqueda. (☎60 58 351; www.palermotourism.com. Open M-F 8:30am-2pm and 2:30-6pm.) **Postal Code:** 90100.

## SYRACUSE (SIRACUSA)
☎0931

With the glory of its Grecian golden days behind it, the city of Syracuse (pop. 125,000) takes pride in its extraordinary ruins and in the architectural beauty of its offshore island, Ortigia. Syracuse's role as a Mediterranean superpower is still evident in the **Archaeological Park,** on the northern side of town. Aeschylus premiered his *Persians* before 15,000 spectators in the park's enormous **Greek theater.** (Open daily 9am until 2hr. before sunset; low season 9am-3pm. €6.) Across from the tourist office on V. S. Giovanni is the ▧**Catacomba di San Giovanni,** 20,000 now-empty tombs carved into the remains of a Greek aqueduct. (Open Tu-Su 9:30am-12:30pm and 2:30-5:30pm. Mandatory guided tour 3-4 per hr. €5.) More ruins lie over the Ponte Umbertino on **Ortigia,** the serene island where the attacking Greeks first landed. The ruined **Temple of Apollo** has a few columns still standing, but those of the **Temple of Athena** inside the *duomo* are much more impressive. For those who prefer tans to temples, take bus #21 or 22 to **Fontane Bianche,** a glitzy beach with plenty of discos. Recently opened **lolhostel ❷,** V. Francesco Crispi 92/96, is becoming a true Syracuse gem as the city's first youth hostel. (☎46 50 88; www.lolhostel.com. Kitchen available. A/C. Internet €3 per hr. Dorms €17-20; singles €33-40; doubles €50-65. Cash only.) ▧**Ristorante Porta Marina ❸,** V. dei Candelai 35, offers a great selection of seafood in a sleek modern setting under an ancient stone archway. (☎44 61 58. *Primi* €6.50-14. *Secondi* €7-14. AmEx/MC/V.) Get the best deals around the station and Archaeological Park, or at Ortigia's **open-air market,** V. Trento, off P. Pancali. (Open M-Sa 8am-1pm.) On the mainland, C. Umberto links Ponte Umbertino to the train station, passing through P. Marconi, from which C. Gelone extends through town to the Archaeological Park. **Trains** leave V. Francesco Crispi for Messina (3hr., 19 per day, €8.75) and Rome (10-13hr., 6 per day, €38). To get from the train station to the **tourist office,** V. S. Sebastiano 45, take V. F. Crispi to C. Gelone, turn right on V. Teocrito, then left on V. S. Sebastiano. (☎48 12 32. Open M-F 8:30am-1:30pm and 3:30-6:30pm, Sa 9am-1pm and 3:30-6:30pm, Su 9am-1pm; low season reduced hours.) **Postal Code:** 96100.

## TAORMINA                                              ☎0942

Legend has it that Neptune wrecked a Greek boat off the eastern coast of Sicily in the 8th century BC, and the sole survivor, inspired by the scenery on shore, founded Taormina. As historians tell it, the Carthaginians founded Tauromenium at the turn of the 4th century BC only to have it wrested away by the Greek tyrant Dionysius. Taormina's Greek roots are apparent in its best-preserved treasure, the **Greek theater.** (Open daily 9am until 1hr. before sunset. €6.) The 5000-seat theater offers unrivaled views of Mt. Etna and hosts the annual ▧**Taormina Arte** summer concert, theater, and dance series. (www.taormina-arte.com. Box office in P. V. Emanuele.) The 13th-century **duomo** was rebuilt during the Renaissance. (Hours vary; inquire at Museo Sacra next door.) ▧**Taormina's Odyssey Youth Hostel ❷,** Traversa A. d. V. G. Martino 2, offers clean rooms and a social environment that make it worth the hike. Take V. C. Patrizio to V. Cappuccini; when it forks, turn right onto V. Fontana Vecchia and follow signs to the hostel. (☎24 533. Breakfast included. Dorms €18; doubles €60. Cash only.) Off C. Umberto, **La Cisterna del Moro ❶,** V. Bonifacio 1, serves pizza on its terrace. (☎23 001. Pizza €5-8.50. Open daily noon-3pm and 7pm-midnight. AmEx/MC/V.) An **SMA** supermarket is at V. Apollo Arcageta 21, at the end of C. Umberto, near the post office. (Open M-Sa 8:30am-9:30pm, Su 8:30am-12:30pm.) **Trains** run to Messina (1hr., 1 per hr., €3) and Syracuse (2hr., 11 per day, €10). The **tourist office** is in the courtyard of Palazzo Corvaja, off C. Umberto across from P. V. Emanuele. (☎23 243; www.gate2taormina.com. Open daily 9am-2pm and 4-7pm.) **Postal Code:** 98039.

# AEOLIAN ISLANDS (ISOLE EOLIE)          ☎090

Homer believed these islands to be a home of the gods, while residents consider them *Le Perle del Mare* (Pearls of the Sea). The rugged shores, pristine landscapes, ruins, volcanoes, and mud baths might as well be divinely inspired. However, living among the gods isn't cheap and prices rise steeply in summer.

**TRANSPORTATION.** The archipelago lies off the Sicilian coast, north of **Milazzo,** the principal and least expensive departure point. Trains run from Milazzo to Messina (30min., 1 per hr., €3) and Palermo (3hr., 13 per day, €10). An orange AST **bus** runs from Milazzo's train station to the port (10min., 2 per hr., €0.90). Ustica (☎92 87 821), Siremar (☎92 83 242), and Navigazione Generale Italiana (NGI; ☎92 84 091) **ferries** depart for Lipari (2hr., 3 per day, €6.60) and Vulcano (1½hr., 3 per day, €6.30). **Hydrofoils** run twice as fast as ferries and more frequently, but for twice the price. Ticket offices are on V. dei Mille in Milazzo.

>  **SITTIN' ON THE DOCK OF THE BAY.** Give yourself extra time when planning travel in the Aeolian islands as ferry schedules change daily and are only on time about 30% of the time.

**LIPARI.** Lipari, the largest and most developed of the islands, is renowned for its beaches, which summer visitors ravage just as pirates did centuries ago. To reach the beaches of the **Spiaggia Bianca** and **Porticello,** take the Lipari-Cavedi **bus** to **Canneto.** Lipari's best sights—aside from its beaches—are all in the hilltop *castello,* where a **fortress** with ancient Greek foundations dwarfs the surrounding town. Nearby is the ■**Museo Archeological Eoliano,** whose collection includes Greek and Sicilian pottery. (Open daily May-Oct. 9am-1pm and 3-7pm; Nov.-Apr. reduced hours. €4.) *Affittacamere* (private rooms) may be the best deals, but ask to see the room before accepting and get a price in writing. Relax on your private terrace away from the bustle of the main drag in one of the eight rooms with bath and A/C at **Villa Rosa ②,** V. Francesco Crispi 134. To reach it from the port, turn right away from the city center and walk until you reach a gas station. (☎98 80 280; www.liparivillarosa.it. Doubles €30-90.) Camp at **Baia Unci ①,** V. Marina Garibaldi 2, at the entrance to the hamlet of Canneto, 2km from Lipari. (☎98 11 909. Open mid-Mar. to mid-Oct. Tent sites €8-14. Cash only.) ■**Da Gilberto e Vera ①,** V. Marina Garibaldi 22-24, is renowned for its sandwiches. (☎98 12 756. *Panini* €4.50. Open daily Mar.-Oct. 7am-4am; Nov.-Feb. 7am-2am. AmEx/MC/V.) Shop at **UPIM** supermarket, C. V. Emanuele 212. (Open M-Sa 8am-9:30pm, Su 8am-2pm. AmEx/MC/V.) The **tourist office,** C. V. Emanuele 202, is near the dock. (☎98 80 095; www.aasteolie.191.it. Open July-Aug. M-F 8am-2pm and 4:30-9:30pm, Sa 8am-2pm and 4-9pm; Sept.-June M-F 8am-2pm and 4:30-9:30pm.) **Postal Code:** 98050.

**VULCANO.** Black beaches, bubbling seas, and sulfuric mud spas attract international visitors to Vulcano. A steep 1hr. **hike** (€3) to the inactive ■**Gran Cratere** (Grand Crater), at the summit of Fossa di Volcane, snakes between the volcano's *fumaroli* (emissions of yellow, noxious smoke). On a clear day, you can see all the other islands from the top. The allegedly therapeutic **Laghetto di Fanghi** (volcanic mud pool) is just up V. Provinciale to the right from the port (€2). This spa's pungent odor is impossible to miss. If you prefer not to bathe in reeking mud, you can step into the scalding waters of the **acquacalda,** where underwater volcanic outlets make the shoreline bubble like a hot tub, or visit the nearby black sands and clear waters of **Sabbie Nere** (follow the signs off V. Ponente). To get to Vulcano, take the **hydrofoil** from the port at Lipari (10min., 17 per day, €5.50). Ferries and hydrofoils dock at **Porto di Levante,** on the eastern side of **Vulcanello,** the youngest volcano. V. Provinciale heads toward Fossa di Vulcane from the port. V. Porto Levante goes up a small hill, then forks at the statue of Aeolus; the *acquacalda* and Laghetto di Fanghi are on the right. Straight ahead, the path leads to Sabbie Nere. For more info, check the **tourist office,** V. Provinciale 41. (☎98 52 028. Open Aug. daily 8am-1:30pm and 3-5pm) or get info from **Sprint da Luigi** (☎98 52 208), a scooter rental shop on V. Provinciale. **Postal Code:** 98050.

**STROMBOLI.** If you find hot springs a bit tame, a visit to Stromboli's active ■**volcano,** which spews cascades of orange lava and molten rock about every

ITALY

10min., might quench your thirst for adventure. Hiking the volcano on your own is illegal and dangerous, but **Magmatrek,** on V. V. Emanuele, offers **tours,** which also should be taken at your own risk. Don't wear contact lenses, as the wind sweeps ash and dust everywhere. (☎/fax 98 65 768. Helmets provided. Reserve 2-3 days ahead. €25.) From the main road, walk uphill to P. S. Vincenzo and then follow the small side street next to the church to reach ⊠**Casa del Sole ❶,** on V. Cincotta. The large rooms face a shared terrace. (☎/fax 98 60 17. Open Mar.-Oct. Dorms €13-27; doubles €30-70. Cash only.) From July to September, you won't find a room without a reservation; your best bet may be an *affittacamera*. Siremar (☎98 60 16) and Ustica (☎98 60 03) run **ferries** and **hydrofoils** between Stromboli and the other Aeolian Islands, Milazzo, and mainland Reggio Calabria. **Postal Code:** 98050.

# SARDINIA (SARDEGNA)

An old Sardinian legend says that when God finished making the world, He had a handful of dirt left over, which He took, threw into the Mediterranean, stepped on, and—behold—created the island of Sardinia. African, Spanish, and Italian influences have shaped its architecture, language, and cuisine.

## ◪ TRANSPORTATION

Alitalia **flights** link Alghero, Cagliari, and Olbia to major Italian cities, and recently Ryanair and easyJet have started to serve Sardinia's airports as well. Tirrenia **ferries** (☎89 21 23; www.tirrenia.it) run to Olbia from Civitavecchia, just north of Rome (5-7hr., 2 per day, €22-91), and Genoa (13hr., 6 per week, from €23-50), and to Cagliari from Civitavecchia (14½hr., 1 per day, €29-44), Naples (16hr., 1 per week, €29-44), and Palermo (13½hr., 1 per week, €28-42). **Trains** run from Cagliari to Olbia (4hr., 1 per day, €15), Oristano (1hr., 17 per day, €5.20), and Sassari (4hr., 4 per day, €14). From Sassari, trains run to Alghero (35min., 11 per day, €2.20). **Buses** connect Cagliari to Oristano (1½hr., 2 per day, €6.50) and run from Olbia to Palau (12 per day, €2.50), where ferries access the beaches of La Maddalena.

## CAGLIARI
☎070

Cagliari's Roman ruins and cobblestones contrast with the sweeping beaches just minutes away. Climb Largo Carlo Felice to reach the city's **duomo,** P. Palazzo 4. Gold mosaics top each of its entrances. (Open M-F 8am-12:30pm and 4:30-8pm, Su 8am-1pm and 4-8pm.) The **Roman amphitheater** comes alive with concerts, operas, and plays during the **arts festival** in July and August. For sun, take city bus P, PF, or PQ to **Il Poetto beach** (20min., €1). Unfortunately, its pure, white sand has been covered by an erosion-preventing brown variety, but the crystal clear waters are beautiful regardless. Cross V. Roma from the train station or ARST station and turn right to get to ⊠**B&B Vittoria ❸,** V. Roma 75. Its spacious rooms all have A/C, bath, phone, and radio. (☎64 04 026; www.bbvittoria.com. Singles €48; doubles €78. 10% *Let's Go* discount. Cash only.) The B&B's owners also run **Hotel aer Bundes Jack ❹,** in the same unassuming building. One of Cagliari's loveliest accommodations since 1938, the hotel offers 20 rooms with the same amenities as the B&B. (☎/fax 66 79 70; hotel.aerbundesjack@libero.it. Breakfast €6. Check-in on 2nd fl. Reserve ahead. Singles €54; doubles €82-86; triples €114. Cash only.) The **tourist office** is in P. Matteotti. (☎66 92 55. Open M-F 8:30am-1:30pm and 2-8pm; Sa-Su 8am-8pm; low season reduced hours.) **Postal Code:** 09100.

## ALGHERO
☎079

Vineyards, ruins, and horseback rides are just a short trip away from Alghero's parks and palms. Between massive white cliffs, 654 steps plunge downward at

**Grotte di Nettuno,** 70-million-year-old, stalactite-filled caverns in Capo Caccia. Take the **bus** (50min., 3 per day; round-trip €3.50) or a **boat** (1¼hr.; 3-8 per day; round-trip €13, includes tour but not cave entrance. Cave open daily Apr.-Sept. 9am-7pm; Oct. 9am-5pm; Nov.-Mar. 9am-4pm. €10.) Outside of Alghero proper, **Hostal de l'Alguer ❶,** V. Parenzo 79, is the cheapest option in the area. A fun-loving staff offers 100 beds, bike rental, and maps. From the port, take bus AF to Fertilia; turn right, and walk down the street. (☎/fax 93 20 39. Breakfast included. Large dorms €17; 4- to 6-bed dorms €18-20; doubles €21-25. €3 HI discount.) Toward Fertilia, 2km from Alghero, **La Mariposa ❶** campground, V. Lido 22, has a bar, beach access, bikes, diving excursions, and a restaurant. (☎95 03 60; www.lamariposa.it. Hot showers €0.50. Mar.-Oct. €8-11 per person, €4-13 per tent; 4-person bungalows €45-75. Apr.-June no charge for tents and cars. AmEx/MC/V.) The **tourist office,** P. Porta Terra 9, is to the right of the bus stop. (☎97 905. Open Apr.-Oct. M-Sa 8am-8pm, Su 10am-1pm; Nov.-Mar. M-Sa 8am-8pm.) **Postal Code:** 07041.

## ORISTANO AND THE SINIS PENINSULA ☎0783

The town of Oristano is an excellent base for excursions to the nearby Sinis Peninsula. From the train station, follow V. Vittorio Veneto straight to P. Mariano, then take V. Mazzini to P. Roma to reach the town center. Rent a **moped** or **car** to explore the beaches, white cliffs, and ruins on the mystical Sinis Peninsula. At its tip, 17km west of Oristano, lie the ruins of the ancient Phoenician port of **Tharros** (open daily in summer 9am-8pm, €5). To get there, take the ARST bus to San Giovanni di Sinis (dir.: Is Arutas; 40min.; 5 per day, last return 7:45pm; round-trip €3). The secluded white quartz sands of **Spiaggia Arutas** are well worth the trip. Along the coastal San Giovanni-Oristano road, glimpse pink flamingoes at **Laguna di Mistras,** in the Gulf of Oristano. The **Eleonora B&B ❸,** P. Eleonora 12 (☎70 435; www.eleonora-bed-and-breakfast.com), right in Oristano's center, retains its 12th-century brick and stone walls and has rooms with A/C, bath, and TV. (Singles €35-40; doubles €65-70. Cash only.) The **tourist office** is at V. Ciutadella de Minorca 8. (☎70 621. Open daily 9am-1pm and 4-8pm.) **Postal Code:** 09170.

## ◪ THE MADDALENA ARCHIPELAGO ☎0789

Maddalena was once part of a massive land bridge connecting Corsica and Sardinia. Its white-sand beaches are now protected by its incorporation in a national park. Nearby island **Razzoli** has magnificent swimming holes and small islands, such as **Santa Maria** and **Spargi,** accessible by boat. **Marinella IV** (☎33 92 30 28 42; www.marinellagite.it) runs tour boats from Palau, on Sardinia's northern coast. They make two or three 2hr. stops at beaches and normally serve lunch on the way. (€35; boats leave at 10 or 11am and return 5-6pm. Purchase tickets 1 day ahead.) La Maddalena's **Panoramica Dei Comi** is a paved road circling the island—bike or motor along it for sea views, making stops for sunbathing. **Buses** (9 per day 9am-7pm, €1) run to the pristine aquamarine beaches of **Cala Spalmatore, Porto Massimo,** and **Bassa Trinita;** the longer you ride, the less crowded the beaches you reach will be. **Hotel Arcipelago ❹,** V. Indipendenza 2, is a good deal but a 20min. walk from the *centro.* From P. Umberto, follow V. Mirabello along the water until the intersection with the stoplight, turn left, then take your first right on V. Indipendenza. Take the first left on a branch of the main road; the hotel is around the corner from the grocery store. (☎72 73 28. Breakfast included. Reservation required July-Aug. Singles €45-55; doubles €60-85. V.) A **Despar** supermarket is at V. Amendola 6, at the intersection with V. Italia. (Open daily 8am-1:30pm and 5:30-8:30pm.) EneRmaR and Saremar run **ferries** from Palau (15min., 2 per hr., round-trip €10). Though there is no tourist office on the archipelago, Palau's tourist office usually has paper handouts featuring La Maddalena's major attractions, so check with them before boarding the ferry. **Postal Code:** 07024.

ITALY

# LIECHTENSTEIN

 Every year on Assumption Day (Aug. 15), Prince Hans-Adam II invites all of Liechtenstein's citizens to celebrate with him at his Vaduz palace. Lucky for his chefs and his wallet, only 35,000 people reside in the 160 sq. km nation. Despite its miniscule size and population, Europe's only absolute monarchy boasts unspoiled mountains with great biking, hiking, and skiing.

## DISCOVER LIECHTENSTEIN: SUGGESTED ITINERARY

**8AM.** Wake-up. Shower.

**8:15AM.** Breakfast. Brush your teeth!

**9AM.** Spy on the royal family outside **Schloß Vaduz** (p. 732).

**9:25AM.** Debate the best hiking routes (p. 732) with the tourist office staff.

**9:55AM.** 5min. bathroom break.

**10AM.** Stampede the **Postmuseum.**

**11AM.** Lose track of time at the **Liechtensteinisches Landesmuseum** (p. 732).

**NOON.** Devour a pizza at **Brasserie Burg.**

**12:30PM.** Leave for Malbun.

**1:15PM.** Ride the chairlift and marvel at views of the **Silberhorn** and **Sareiserjoch.**

**2PM.** Become king of two mountains; trek the **Fürstin-Gina-Weg.**

**3:22PM.** 10min. hiking break. Eat trail mix and have a drink—water, preferably.

**6:45PM.** Shed your clothes (but don a swimsuit) for a refreshing dip in the **Alpenhotel** pool.

**7:45PM.** If hiking smell persists, shower.

**8PM.** Dinner and bed. You're done!

## HISTORY

Turbulent take-overs characterize Liechtenstein's past. **Romans** invaded in 15 BC, and the area fell under the control of a German duke in the 4th century. In 1719, **Prince Johann Adam Andreas** bought the land and created the Principality of Liechtenstein. Napoleon accepted Liechtenstein into the **Rhine Confederation** in 1806, permitting the state to retain its sovereignty. Following Napoleon's Waterloo defeat, Liechtenstein joined the 1815 **German Confederacy.** The confederation's 1866 dissolution permitted Liechtenstein to reclaim full autonomy. In 1938, **Prince Franz Josef II** ascended the throne and began transforming his country into one of the world's wealthiest nations. Liechtenstein joined the UN in 1990 and the European Economic Area in 1995. In 2003, Liechtensteiners granted Head of State Prince Hans-Adam II—who threatened to quit if a constitutional referendum failed—absolute power to dismiss parliament in exchange for more sway in enacting national amendments. Although still nominally in charge, Prince Hans-Adams II bestowed day-to-day responsibilities on his son, Crown Prince Alois, in August 2004.

## ESSENTIALS

**DOCUMENTS AND FORMALITIES.** Citizens of Australia, Canada, New Zealand, the UK, and the US do not need a visa for stays of up to 90 days.

**TRANSPORTATION.** Catch a **bus** from Feldkirch in Austria (30min., 1 per hr., 3.80CHF), or from Buchs (25min., 4-5 per hr., 3.60CHF) or Sargans (30-40min. 4 per hr., 5.80CHF), across the border in Switzerland. Liechtenstein has no rail sys-

## FACTS AND FIGURES

**Official Name:** Principality of Liechtenstein.

**Capital:** Vaduz.

**Major Towns:** Schaan, Triesen.

**Population:** 35,000.

**Land Area:** 160 sq. km.

**Coastline:** 0km. The only other doubly landlocked country besides Uzbekistan.

**Time Zone:** GMT +1

**Language:** German (see p. 1054).

**Religions:** Roman Catholic (76%), Protestant (7%).

**Form of Government:** Constitutional hereditary monarchy.

**Major Exports:** Machinery, Dental Products, Stamps.

tem. Its cheap, efficient **PostBus** (www.sbb.ch) system links all 11 towns. A **one-week bus ticket** (19CHF) covers the entire principality and buses to Swiss and Austrian border towns. You can buy all tickets and passes on board. The SwissPass (p. 935) and Swiss Youth Pass are valid in Liechtenstein.

**MONEY.** The Liechtenstein unit of currency is the **Swiss franc (CHF),** plural Swiss francs. One Swiss franc is equal to 100 centimes, with standard denominations of 5, 10, 20, and 50 centimes and 1, 2, and 5CHF in coins, and 10, 20, 50, 100, 200, 500, and 1000CHF in notes. AmEx/MC/V are widely accepted. As restaurant checks generally include a small service charge, most patrons round up their bill rather than leave an additional tip. Go to Switzerland to exchange currency at reasonable rates. Conversion rates for the Swiss franc are listed on p. 934.

Liechtenstein has a 7.6% **value added tax (VAT),** a sales tax applied to national deliveries and services made in return for payments, in-house consumption, importing services and objects. The prices given in *Let's Go* include VAT. In the airport upon exiting Liechtenstein and the EU, non-EU citizens can claim a refund on VAT paid for goods purchased at participating stores. In order to qualify for a refund, you must spend at least 400CHF; make sure to ask for a refund form when you pay. For more info on qualifying for a VAT refund, see p. 18.

**BEYOND TOURISM. European Voluntary Service** programs (http://europa.eu.int/comm/youth/program/guide/action2_en.html) enable EU citizens to spend a fully funded year doing service in another European nation. Non-EU residents may visit local tourist offices to see about regional positions available. The **Special Olympics** (www.specialolympics.li) also provides travelers with volunteer opportunities. For more info on opportunities across Europe, see **Beyond Tourism,** p. 54.

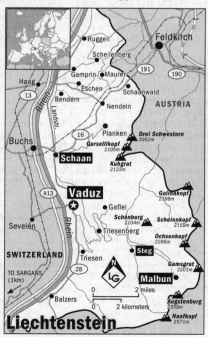

## VADUZ AND LOWER LIECHTENSTEIN      ☎ 00423

As the capital, **Vaduz** (pop. 5000) attracts the most visitors of any village in Liechtenstein. Home to the ruling Prince, the 12th-century **Schloß Vaduz** (Vaduz Castle) is the principality's most recognizable icon. Its interior is off-limits, but visitors can hike to the castle for a closer look. The 20min. trail begins down the street from the tourist office. Diagonally across from the tourist office at Städtle 32 is a cube-shaped building, the **Kunstmuseum Liechtenstein.** The collection is split between Neoclassical art owned by the royal family and rotating exhibits of contemporary art. The curators are happy to assist in interpreting some of the more peculiar modern art pieces. (☎ 235 0300; www.kunstmuseum.li. Open Tu-W and F-Su 10am-5pm, Th 10am-8pm. 8CHF, students 5CHF.) The **Liechtensteinisches Landesmuseum,** Städtle 43, chronicles the principality's history, beginning with its first inhabitants 8000 years ago. (☎ 239 6820; www.landesmuseum.li. Open Tu and Th-Su 10am-5pm, W 10am-8pm.) Above the tourist office, the **Postmuseum** showcases almost every stamp the country has printed and bursts with other philatelic paraphernalia. (☎ 239 6846. Open daily 10am-noon and 1-5pm. Free.)

In between Vaduz and the village of **Schaan** sits Liechtenstein's sole **Jugendherberge (HI) ❷,** Untere Rüttig. 6. From Vaduz, take bus #11, 12, or 14 to Mühleholz, walk to the intersection, turn left on Marianumstr., and follow the signs. (☎ 232 5022; www.youthhostel.ch/schaan. Breakfast included. Laundry 6CHF. Internet 1CHF per 5min. Reception 7:30-10am and 5-10pm. Open Mar.-Oct. Dorms 37CHF; singles 62CHF; doubles 94CHF. 6CHF HI discount. AmEx/MC/V.) Finding cheap food in Liechtenstein may turn into a never-ending quest. Cut your losses and head to **Brasserie Burg ❸,** Städtle 15, in the center of Vaduz, for sandwiches and burgers for 10-15CHF. (☎ 232 2131. Salad buffet 18 CHF. Pizza 16-23CHF. Open M-F 8:30am-11pm, Sa 9am-midnight, Su 9:30am-11pm. AmEx/MC/V.) Pick up a **hiking map** (16CHF) at Liechtenstein's **tourist office,** Städtle 37, up the hill from the Vaduz bus stop. (☎ 239 6300; www.tourismus.li. Open M-F 9am-noon and 1:30-5pm.)

## UPPER LIECHTENSTEIN      ☎ 00423

Full of winding roads and hiking trails, the villages in Upper Liechtenstein are where the country's real beauty lies. In the principality's southeastern corner, **Malbun** sits in an Alpine valley accessible by bus #21 (30min., 1 per hr.). A popular hiking trail (4-5hr.) starts at the **chairlift** base at the Malbun Zentrum bus stop and follows **Fürstin-Gina-Weg** along two mountain crests. Be careful on the ridges above Malbun: the paths are narrow and often edge very close to cliffs. (Chairlift open July to mid-Oct. daily 8am-12:15pm and 1:15-4:50pm. 9CHF, students 7CHF; round-trip 13/10CHF.) In winter, skiers take to the slopes on the **Sareiserjoch** and the **Silberhorn.** (Chairlift open mid-Dec. to mid-Apr. 9am-4pm. ½-day passes 46CHF, students 35CHF; 1 day 68/55CHF; 2 days 123/98CHF.) **Hotel Steg ❶,** in the village of Steg, has the country's cheapest lodging. Take bus #21 to Steg Hotel. (☎ 263 2146. Breakfast included. Linens included for private rooms. 10-bed dorms 25CHF; singles 45CHF; doubles 80CHF. MC/V.) **Alpenhotel Malbun ❸,** opposite the Malbun Jörabaoda bus stop, has an indoor pool. (☎ 263 1181; www.alpenhotel.li. Reception 8am-10pm. Open mid-May to Oct. and mid-Dec. to Apr. Singles 40-70CHF, with bath 70-110CHF; doubles 80-130/120-180CHF. AmEx/MC/V.) The **Schädler-Shop,** between the chairlift and the tourist office, has groceries. (Open M-F 8am-12:30pm and 1:30-5pm, Sa-Su 8am-6pm.) The **tourist office** is down the street from the Malbun Zentrum bus stop. (☎ 263 6577; www.malbun.li. Open June-Oct. and mid-Dec. to mid-Apr. M-F 8am-6pm, Sa 9am-5pm, Su 8am-5pm.)

# LUXEMBOURG

Tiny Luxembourg is often overlooked by travelers smitten with Dutch windmills or hungry for Belgian waffles. However, its castles rival those of the Rhineland, its villages are uncrowded and perfect for easy hikes, and Luxembourg City is a European financial powerhouse. It might be a stretch to call Luxembourg the "lux" of the Benelux countries, but the world's last grand duchy has considerable draw.

## DISCOVER LUXEMBOURG: SUGGESTED ITINERARY

Budget two days for **Luxembourg City** (p. 736), where you can explore the capital's maze of well-fortified tunnels by day and its lively nightlife after hours. The towns of **Echternach** (p. 742) and **Vianden** (p. 742) are notable stops, the former for its historic basilica and the latter for its hilltop château. From there, proceed west to the village of **Esch-sur-Sûre** (p. 743) for scenic hiking through wooded river valleys.

# LIFE AND TIMES

## HISTORY

The Grand Duchy of Luxembourg has a long history of occupation and domination by its larger European neighbors. Luxembourg was once inhabited by Belgic tribes and controlled by Romans. In the early Middle Ages, the territory was annexed by the Franks, then claimed by **Charlemagne.** It became an independent region in AD 963 under the control of **Siegfried, Count d'Ardennes.** The region became a duchy in 1354 by edict of **Emperor Charles IV,** but in 1443, the Duchess of Luxembourg was forced to abdicate when the Dukes of Burgundy asserted control over most of the Low Countries. Luxembourg passed into the hands of the **Habsburgs** in the early 16th century, only to be conquered by France after the devastating **Thirty Years' War** (1618-1648). After the fall of Napoleon at Waterloo, the **Congress of Vienna** of 1815 made Luxembourg a grand duchy and gave it to **William I** of the Netherlands. After Belgium's 1830 revolt against William, part of Luxembourg was ceded to the Belgians, and the remainder became a sovereign

and independent state. The 1867 **Treaty of London** reaffirmed Luxembourg's autonomy and asserted its neutrality, although 20th-century Luxembourg was occupied
by Germany during both WWI and WWII. After liberation by the **Allied Powers** in
1944, Luxembourg became a member of the **Benelux Economic Union,** along with
Belgium and the Netherlands. It relinquished its neutral status in 1948 in order to
join various international economic, military, and political institutions, including
**NATO** and the **United Nations.** It was also one of the six founding members of the
**European Economic Community,** which later became the **European Union.**

## TODAY

Luxembourg's economy once revolved around the production of steel, but after
diversifying, their GDP is one of the highest per capita in the world. More than 30%
of the country's population are citizens of other nations, although Luxembourg
natives retain strong national and regional identities. The country is governed by a
**constitutional monarchy** in which **Grand Duke Henri** holds formal authority. Executive and legislative power is vested in the Chamber of Deputies, a unicameral legislature elected by popular vote, as well as the prime minister, **Jean-Claude Juncker.**
Juncker, a champion of the EU since his election in 1995, is nicknamed "Mr. Euro."
A new **coalition government** between Juncker's center-right Christian Social People's Party (CSV) and the center-left Socialist Workers' Party (LSAP) is working to
liberalize the country's **asylum policy,** while continuing to attract immigrants.

## HOLIDAYS AND FESTIVALS

**Holidays:** New Year's Day (Jan. 1); Maundy Thursday (Mar. 20); Easter (Mar. 23-24);
Labor Day (May 1); Ascension (May 1); May Day (May 1); Whit Sunday and Monday
(May 11-12); Corpus Christi (May 22); National Day (June 23); Assumption (Aug. 15);
All Saints' Day (Nov. 1); Christmas (Dec. 25); St. Stephen's Day (Dec. 26).

**Festivals:** The weeks leading up to Lent bring parades and masked balls under the
guise of Carnival. Echternach hosts the International Music Festival in May and June,
while Riesling Open wine festivals kick off in Wormeldange, Ahn, and Ehnen during
the 3rd weekend of September.

## ESSENTIALS

### FACTS AND FIGURES

**Official Name:** Grand Duchy of Luxembourg.

**Capital:** Luxembourg City.

**Population:** 480,000.

**Land Area:** 2,600 sq. km.

**Time Zone:** GMT+1.

**Languages:** Luxembourgish, French, and
German. English is widely spoken.

**Religion:** Roman Catholic 87%.

**No. of Cars per 1000 People:** Approx.
650, one of the highest rates in the world.

## WHEN TO GO

The sea winds that routinely douse Belgium with rain have usually shed their
moisture by the time they reach Luxembourg; good weather prevails from May
through October, although travelers leery of crowds may want to avoid July and
August. Temperatures average 17°C (64°F) in summer, and 1°C (34°F) in winter.

# DOCUMENTS AND FORMALITIES

**EMBASSIES AND CONSULATES.** Foreign embassies and consulates are in Luxembourg City. Luxembourgian embassies and consulates abroad include: **Australia**, Level 4, Quay West, 111 Harrington St., Sydney, NSW, 2000 (☎02 9253 4708); **UK**, 27 Wilton Cres., London, SW1X 8SD (☎020 72 35 69 61); **US**, 2200 Massachusetts Ave., NW, Washington, D.C., 20008 (☎202-265-4171; www.luxembourg-usa.org). **Canadians** should visit the Luxembourg embassy in Washington, D.C.; **Irish** citizens should go to the embassy in London.

**VISA AND ENTRY INFORMATION.** EU citizens do not need a visa. Citizens of Australia, Canada, New Zealand, and the US do not need a visa for stays of up to 90 days, beginning upon entry into any of the countries in the EU's freedom-of-movement zone. For more info, see p. 13.

# TOURIST SERVICES AND MONEY

| EMERGENCY | Ambulance: ☎112. Fire: ☎112. Police: ☎113. |
|---|---|

**TOURIST OFFICES.** For general info, contact the **Luxembourg National Tourist Office,** Gare Centrale, P.O. Box 1001, L-1010 Luxembourg (☎42 82 821; www.visitluxembourg.lu).

**MONEY.** The **euro (€)** has replaced the **Luxembourg franc** as the unit of currency in Luxembourg. For more info, see p. 15. The cost of living in Luxembourg City is quite high, although the countryside is more reasonable. Restaurant bills usually include a service charge, although an extra 5-10% tip is a classy gesture. Tip taxi drivers 10%. Luxembourg has a 15% **value added tax (VAT),** a sales tax applied to most purchased goods. The prices given in *Let's Go* include VAT. In an airport upon exiting the EU, non-EU citizens can claim a refund on the tax paid for goods purchased at participating stores. In order to qualify for a refund in a store, you must spend at least €100; make sure to ask for a refund form when you pay. For more info on qualifying for a VAT refund, see p. 18.

# TRANSPORTATION

**BY PLANE.** The national airline, **Luxair** (☎2456 4242; www.luxair.lu), and a slew of other European airlines fly to the Luxembourg City airport (LUX). Cheap last-minute flights on Luxair are often available online.

**BY TRAIN AND BUS.** A **Benelux Tourrail Pass** (€94 second class, under 26 €71) allows five days of unlimited train travel in a one-month period in Belgium, Luxembourg, and the Netherlands. Within Luxembourg, the **Billet Réseau** (€5, book of 5 €20) is good for one day of unlimited bus and train travel. The **Luxembourg Card** (€10-24) includes one to three days of unlimited transportation along with free or discounted admisoion to 50+ sights around the country.

**BY BIKE AND THUMB.** A 575km network of **cycling paths** already snakes its way through Luxembourg, and plans are in place to add another 325km to the network in the near future. Bikes aren't permitted on buses, but domestic trains will transport them for a small fee (€1.20). While Let's Go does not recommend hitchhiking as a safe means of transport, service areas in Luxembourg are popular places to hitch rides into Belgium, France, and the Netherlands, as many motorists stop to take advantage of relatively low fuel prices.

LUXEMBOURG

# KEEPING IN TOUCH

| PHONE CODES | Country code: 352. International dialing prefix: 00. Luxembourg has no city codes. For more info on how to place international calls, see **Inside Back Cover.** |
|---|---|

**TELEPHONES.** There are no city codes in Luxembourg; from outside the country, dial 352 plus the local number. Public phones can only be operated with a phone card, available at post offices, train stations, and newspaper stands. Internet cafes are not abundant. **Mobile phones** are an increasingly popular and economical alternative (p. 27). International direct dial numbers include: **AT&T** (☎8002 0111); **British Telecom** (☎8002 0044); **Canada Direct** (☎8002 0119); **MCI** (☎8002 0112); **Sprint** (☎8002 0115); **Telecom New Zealand** (☎8002 0064); **Telstra Australia** (☎8002 0061).

**LANGUAGE.** The three official languages of Luxembourg are Luxembourgish, French, and German. While Luxembourgish, a West Germanic language, is used primarily in daily conversation, official documents are written in French, and the press is in German. English is often spoken as a second, third, or fourth language.

# ACCOMMODATIONS AND CAMPING

| LUXEMBOURG | ❶ | ❷ | ❸ | ❹ | ❺ |
|---|---|---|---|---|---|
| **ACCOMMODATIONS** | under €18 | €18-24 | €25-34 | €35-55 | over €55 |

Luxembourg's nine **HI youth hostels** (*Auberges de Jeunesse*) are often booked solid during summer, and it's wise to reserve ahead. About half of the hostels close for several weeks in December. Beds are approximately €17-20. Contact **Centrale des Auberges de Jeunesse Luxembourgeoises** (☎26 27 66 40; www.youthhostels.lu) for more info. **Hotels** are expensive, costing upwards of €40 per night in the capital. Luxembourg is a camper's paradise, and most towns have nearby campsites. Contact **Camprilux** (www.camping.lu/gb/gbstart.htm) for more info.

# FOOD AND DRINK

| LUXEMBOURG | ❶ | ❷ | ❸ | ❹ | ❺ |
|---|---|---|---|---|---|
| **FOOD** | under €5 | €5-9 | €10-14 | €15-22 | over €22 |

Luxembourgish cuisine combines elements of French and German cooking. Specialties include *Judd mat Gaardenbou'nen* (smoked pork with beans), *Friture de la Moselle* (fried fish), and *Quetscheflued* (plum tart). Riesling wines, which show up most Chardonnays, are produced in the Moselle Valley.

# LUXEMBOURG CITY

As an international banking hot spot, Luxembourg City (pop. 76,000) has become one of the wealthiest cities in the world. Though small, the metropolis has a lot to offer, from the relics of its military history to the boons of its thriving economy.

## ▛ TRANSPORTATION

**Flights: Findel International Airport** (LUX; www.aeroport.public.lu), 6km from the city. Bus #16 (€1.50, 2-4 per hr.) runs to the train station. Taxis are €17-25 (more on Su) to the city center.

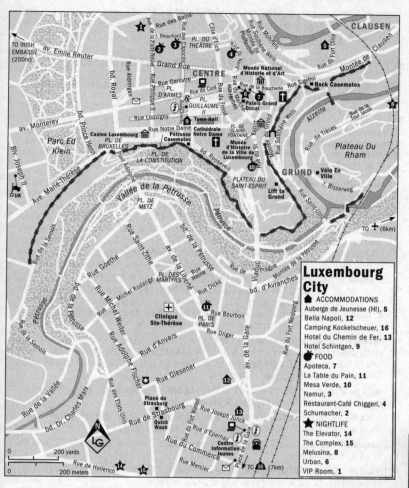

## Luxembourg City

**🏠 ACCOMMODATIONS**
Auberge de Jeunesse (HI), **5**
Bella Napoli, **12**
Camping Kockelscheuer, **16**
Hotel du Chemin de Fer, **13**
Hotel Schintgen, **9**
**🍎 FOOD**
Apoteca, **7**
La Table du Pain, **11**
Mesa Verde, **10**
Namur, **3**
Restaurant-Café Chiggeri, **4**
Schumacher, **2**
**★ NIGHTLIFE**
The Elevator, **14**
The Complex, **15**
Melusina, **8**
Urban, **6**
VIP Room, **1**

**Trains: Gare CFL**, pl. de la Gare (☎ 24 89 24 89; www.cfl.lu), a 15min. walk south of the city center. To: **Amsterdam, NTH** (6hr.; 1 per hr.; €52, under 26 €36); **Brussels, BEL** (2¾hr., 1 per hr., €30/16); **Ettelbrück** (25min., 3 per hr., €5); **Frankfurt, GER** (3½hr., 1 per hr., €52); **Paris, FRA** (2½-4hr., 1 per 2hr., €25-84).

**Buses:** For travel within the city, buy a **billet courte distance** (short-distance ticket; €1.50, book of 10 €10), valid for 1hr. A **billet réseau** (network pass; €5, book of 5 €20), also accepted on trains, allows for unlimited travel throughout the entire country for 1 day and is the most economical option for intercity travel. Most buses run until midnight. The **free night bus** (☎ 47 96 29 75) runs F-Sa 10pm-3:30am.

**Taxis:** €2.40 per km. 10% more 10pm-6am; 25% more on Su. **Colux Taxis:** ☎ 48 22 33.

**Bikes:** Rent from **Vélo en Ville,** 8 r. Bisserwé (☎47 96 23 83), in the Grund. Open Apr.-Oct. M-Sa 10am-noon and 1-8pm. €5 per hr., €13 per half-day, €20 per day, €38 per weekend, €75 per week. Under 26 20% discount for full day and longer. MC/V.

## ■✚ 🛈 ORIENTATION AND PRACTICAL INFORMATION

Five minutes by bus and 15min. by foot from the train station, Luxembourg City's historic center revolves around the **Place d'Armes.** From the train station, follow av. de la Gare or av. de la Liberté, then watch for signs with directions to the city's main sights. From the pl. d'Armes, walk down r. de Chimay; you will see the **Pétrusse Valley** in front of you, the **Place de la Constitution** on your right, and the **Pétrusse Casemates** to your left. Once there, the city's lower areas, the **Grund** and the **Clausen,** will be located diagonally to your right and left, 10min. and 15min. on foot, respectively. Halfway between these areas are the **Bock Casemates.**

**Tourist Offices: Grand Duchy National Tourist Office** (☎42 82 82 20; www.ont.lu), in the train station. Open daily June-Sept. 8:30am-6:30pm; Oct.-May 9:15am-12:30pm and 1:45-6pm. **Luxembourg City Tourist Office,** pl. Guillaume II (☎22 28 09; www.lcto.lu). Open Oct.-Mar. M-Sa 9am-6pm, Su 10am-6pm; Apr.-Sept. M-Sa 9am-7pm, Su 10am-6pm. In summer, look for the helpful **"Ask Me"** representatives around the city. **Centre Information Jeunes,** 26 pl. de la Gare (☎26 29 32 00; www.visitluxembourg.lu), across from the station inside Galerie Kons, provides young travelers with everything from tourist info to help on finding jobs in the area. Open M-F 10am-6pm.

**Embassies: Ireland,** 28 rte. d'Arlon (☎45 06 10). Open M-F 9:30am-12:30pm. **UK,** 5 bd. Joseph II (☎22 98 64; www.britain.lu). Open M-F 9:30am-12:30pm. **US,** 22 bd. Emmanuel Servais (☎46 01 23; luxembourg.usembassy.gov). Open M-F 8:30am-5:30pm. **Australians, Canadians,** and **New Zealanders** should contact their embassies in France or Belgium.

**Currency Exchange:** Banks are the only option for changing money or cashing traveler's checks. Most are open M-F 8:30am-4 or 4:30pm. Only the banks at the airport and at the train station are opened on weekends. Expect to pay commissions of €5 for cash and €8 for traveler's checks.

**Luggage Storage:** (☎49 90 55 74), in the train station. €3 per bag. 1-day storage during opening hours. Open daily 6am-9:30pm.

**Laundromat: Quick Wash,** 31 pl. de Strasbourg (☎26 19 65 42), near the station. Wash and dry €10. Open M-F 8:30am-6:30pm, Sa 8am-6pm.

**Pharmacy:** Pharmacies are marked by green crosses. Call ☎90 07 12 34 32 for a list of 24hr. pharmacies.

**Hospital: Clinique St-Thérèse,** 36 r. Ste-Zithe (☎49 77 61 or 49 77 65; www.zitha.lu). Call ☎90 07 12 34 32 for a schedule of 24hr. hospitals.

**Internet Access: Centre Information Jeunes** (see above) has limited free Internet for students. **Cyberbeach,** 3 r. du Curé, (☎26 47 80 70; www.cyber-beach.lu), by pl. d'Armes. From €1 per hr. Open M-F 10am-10pm, Sa 2-8pm.

**Post Office:** 38 pl. de la Gare, across the street and to the left of the station. Open M-F 6am-7pm, Sa 6am-noon. Address mail to be held according to the following example: First name LAST NAME, *Poste Restante,* L-1009 Luxembourg G-I Gare, LUXEMBOURG. Branch at 25 r. Aldringen, near pl. d'Armes. Open M-Sa 7am-7pm, Su 7am-5pm.

## 🏠 🏕 ACCOMMODATIONS AND CAMPING

Aside from camping, the city hostel is the only budget option in Luxembourg City. Hotels are cheaper near the train station than in the city center.

▩ **Auberge de Jeunesse (HI),** 2 r. du Fort Olisy (☎22 68 89 20; www.youthhostels.lu). Take bus #9 (dir.: Neudorf) and ask to get off at the hostel. From bus stop, take the steep pathway down alongside bridge. This new hostel has river views and a restaurant. Bike rentals €8 per half-day, €15 per day. Breakfast and linens included. In-room lockers; bring or rent a lock. Laundry €7.50. Internet €2.50 per 30min. Reception 24hr. Call ahead to reserve shuttles straight from airport (€3) or train station (€2), M-F 9am-5pm. Dorms €23; singles €35; doubles €55. €3 HI discount. AmEx/MC/V. ❷

**Bella Napoli,** 4 r. de Strasbourg (☎49 33 67). Hotel located above a pizza joint. Simple rooms with hardwood floors and full bath. Breakfast included. Reception 8am-midnight. Singles €41; doubles €48; triples €60. AmEx/MC/V. ❹

**Hotel Schintgen,** 6 r. Notre Dame (☎22 28 44). One of the cheaper options in the Old Center, though loud. Breakfast included. Private shower and bath. Reception 7am-11pm. Singles €70; doubles €85; triples €90; quads €95. AmEx/MC/V. ❺

**Hotel Du Chemin De Fer,** 4 r. Joseph Junck (☎49 35 28). Ordinary, clean rooms right across from the train station. Singles €45; doubles €65; triples €80. MC/V. ❸

**Camping Kockelscheuer,** 22 rte. de Bettembourg (☎47 18 15), 5km outside Luxembourg City. Take bus #5 from the station or city center to Kockelscheuer-Camping. Tennis courts, mini golf, hot water. Showers included. Laundry €5. Open Easter-Oct. Reception 7am-noon and 2-10:30pm; cars must arrive when reception is open. Tent sites €4.50, each additional adult €3.75. Cash only. ❶

## ▣ FOOD

Although the area around the pl. d'Armes teems with a strange mix of fast-food joints and upscale restaurants, there are a few affordable and appealing alternatives. Stock up on groceries at **Supermarché Boon,** in Galerie Kons across from the train station. (Open M-F 8am-8pm, Sa 8am-6pm, Su 8am-noon.)

▩ **Apoteca,** 12 r. de la Boucherie (☎26 73 77 77; www.apoteca.lu). Offers an innovative menu that changes weekly. Downstairs bar offers a less expensive, but limited menu. Entrees €16-29. Restaurant open Tu-Sa noon-2pm and 7:30-10pm; bar open Tu-Sa 5pm-1am. AmEx/MC/V. ❹

▩ **Restaurant-Café Chiggeri,** 15 r. du Nord (☎22 82 36). Serves traditional French food amid shimmering, night-sky decor. Wine list offers 2300 vintages. Dine more affordably at the cafe downstairs. Entrees €17-24. Open daily 11am-midnight. AmEx/MC/V. ❹

**Mesa Verde,** 11 r. du St-Esprit (☎46 41 26), down the street from the pl. de Clairefontaine. A local favorite, this bright vegetarian restaurant features an ever-changing array of hand-painted murals and billowing fabrics decorating the walls. Entrees €19-25. Open Tu-Sa 6:30-11:30pm. Open for lunch W-F noon-2pm. MC/V. ❹

**Namur,** 27 r. des Capucins (☎22 34 08), down the street from pl. d'Armes. Marble floors, outdoor seating, and elegant ambience make the selection of pastries, chocolates, and sundaes (€5-6) even sweeter. Open M 2-6pm, Tu-Sa 8:30am-6pm. MC/V. ❷

**La Table du Pain,** 37 av. de la Liberté (☎29 56 63). Serves sandwiches (€5-7), salads (€10-14), and baked goods on wooden tables. Open M-F 7am-6pm. Cash only. ❷

**Schumacher,** 18 av. de la Porte-Neuve (☎22 90 09). Get takeout for picnics in the Pétrusse Valley. Sandwiches €3-5. Open M-Sa 7am-6pm. AmEx/MC/V. ❶

## ◉ SIGHTS

Luxembourg City is compact enough to be explored on foot. The most spectacular views of the city are from **Place de la Constitution** and from the bridge closest to the **Bock Casemates.** For guidance on your stroll, follow the signs pointing out the **Wen-**

**zel Walk.** It leads visitors through 1000 years of history as it winds around the old city, from the **Chemin de la Corniche** down into the casemates.

**FORTRESSES AND THE OLD CITY.** The city's first fortress, built in AD 963, saw its network of fortifications expand so far over the years that the city earned the nickname "Gibraltar of the North." The fortress contains the ◪**casemates,** an intricate 17km network of tunnels through the fortress walls. First built to fortify the city's defenses, the casemates were partially dismantled when Luxembourg was declared a neutral state in 1867. Start at the **Bock Casemates** fortress, part of Luxembourg's original castle; the fortress looms over the Alzette River Valley and offers a fantastic view of the **Grund** and the **Clausen.** A useful brochure allows visitors to tour this system of casements on their own. (Entrance on r. Sigefroi, just past the bridge leading to the hostel. ☎ 22 28 09 or 22 67 53. Open Mar.-Oct. daily 10am-5pm. €1.75, students €1.50.) A visit to the ◪**Pétrusse Casemates,** built by the Spanish in the 1600s, takes explorers down 250 steps into historic chambers while providing views of the Pétrusse Valley. A tour is required, but it's interesting, short (30min.), and cheap. (Pl. de la Constitution. English-language tours 1 per hr., July-Aug. 11am-4pm; intermittently in June. €1.75, students €1.50.) The peaceful paths of the green **Pétrusse Valley** beckon for a stroll or an afternoon picnic in the shadow of the fortress walls. More sedentary visitors can catch one of the **Pétrusse Express tourist trains** that depart from pl. de la Constitution and meander through the city and into the valley. (Mid-Mar. to Oct. 2 per hr. 10am-12:30pm and 1:30-6pm. Trip lasts 50-60min. €8. Purchase tickets at pl. de la Constitution.) Double-decker **tourist buses** allow you to "hop on" and "hop off" at will; recordings play commentary in multiple languages. (Info for train and buses ☎ 26 65 11; www.sightseeing.lu. 3 per hr. 9:40am-5:20 or 6:20pm from marked stops throughout the city. €12, students €10. Ticket valid for 24hr. Wheelchair-accessible.)

**MUSEUMS.** The **Luxembourg Card** covers entrance to 55 museums and tourist attractions throughout the country. (www.luxembourgcard.lu. Available at tourist offices and youth hostels. 1-day card €10, 2-day €17, 3-day €24.) The collection at the ◪**Musée National d'Histoire et d'Art** includes both modern and ancient art and a chronicle of the conquering powers' influences on Luxembourg's art. (Marché-aux-Poissons, at r. Boucherie and Sigefroi. ☎ 47 93 30 214; www.mnha.lu. Open Tu-Su 10am-5pm. €5, students free.) There's no gambling at **Casino Luxembourg,** only contemporary art exhibits. (41 r. Notre Dame, near pl. de la Constitution. ☎ 22 50 45; www.casino-luxembourg.lu. Open M, W, F 11am-7pm, Th 11am-8pm, Sa-Su 11am-6pm. €4, under 26 €3, under 18 free.) The **Musée d'Histoire de la Ville de Luxembourg** narrates the history of the city with interactive displays. Most exhibits are in French and German. (14 r. du St-Esprit, near pl. de Clairefontaine. ☎ 47 96 45 00. Open Tu-W and F-Su 10am-6pm, Th 10am-8pm. €5, students €3.70.)

**OTHER SIGHTS.** The **Palais Grand Ducal** was originally a town hall, burned down in 1554 and was rebuilt with a Spanish Renaissance facade, becoming the official residence of the Grand Duke in 1890. It's open to the public each summer while the Duke vacations. (Reservations ☎ 22 28 09. Tickets sold at the Luxembourg City tourist office. Tours mid-July to early Sept. M-Tu and Th-Su 10am-5pm. €6.) Nearby is the 17th-century **Cathédrale Notre Dame.** (Entrance at bd. Roosevelt. Open M-F 9:15am-6:15pm, Sa 9:15am-6:30pm, Su 9-10:30am and noon-6pm. Su mass. Crypt open daily until 5:30pm. Free.)

## 🎵 🎭 ENTERTAINMENT AND NIGHTLIFE

There is no central location for nightlife in Luxembourg City, so an evening of bar-hopping also involves hopping on and off the city's night bus until bars close at 2am. In summer, the **Place d'Armes** comes to life with free concerts (www.summerinthecity.lu) and stand-up comedy. Pick up a copy of *UP FRONT* at the tourist office for a list of nightlife action and events.

**Melusina,** 145 r. de la Tour Jacob (☎43 59 22). Eat at the classy restaurant or dance all night on weekends. Cover €8. 1 free drink 11pm-midnight. Restaurant open M-Sa noon-2pm and 7-11pm. Club open F-Sa 11pm-3am. Restaurant MC/V; club cash only.

**Urban,** at the corner of r. de la Boucherie and r. du Marché-aux-Herbes (☎26 47 85 78). A friendly, crowded bar in the heart of downtown. Beer €2-4. Mixed drinks €6. Open daily noon-1am. AmEx/MC/V.

**The Complex,** 42-44 r. de Hollerich, is a cluster of bars in the south of the city. Take bus #1 or 22, or walk on av. de la Gare away from the center. **Marx** caters to the 25+ crowd. DJs W and F-Sa. (☎48 84 26. Beer €2.20. Mixed drinks €6.50. Open M-F and Su 5pm-1am, Sa 6pm-1am. MC/V.) Next door, **Chocolate Elvis** features party music and beer (€2.20), the **Bronx** high decibels. (☎29 79 46. Mixed drinks €6-6.50. Open M-F 5pm-1am, Sa-Su 6pm-1am.)

**VIP Room,** 19 r. des Bains (☎26 18 78 67), near the pl. du Théatre. Glitzy and exclusive, this club has an atmosphere modeled after VIP clubs in Paris and St-Tropez. Open before 7pm for dinner. Club open Tu 7pm-midnight, W-Sa 7pm-late. AmEx/MC/V.

**The Elevator,** 48 r. de Hollerich (☎29 41 64), down the road from The Complex. A local favorite, with electronic music that's never mainstream. Shots €2.50. Wine €2-3. Beer €3-4. W Happy hour 5-8pm with half-price drinks. Open M-F 5pm-1am, Sa 7pm-1am.

# THE ARDENNES

In 1944, one of the bloodiest battles of World War II, the Battle of the Bulge, took place in these hills. Now quiet towns, imposing castles, and stunning scenery make the Ardennes an ideal tourist attraction. Carry raingear, as the humidity here often breaks into short storms. Check transportation schedules thoroughly and budget extra time for waiting; the system is geared toward locals, not tourists.

**ETTELBRÜCK.** The main railway linking Luxembourg City to Liège, BEL, runs through Ettelbrück (pop. 7500), making the town the transportation hub for the Ardennes. Little else draws tourists to Ettelbrück, although history buffs waiting out a layover might investigate the **General Patton Memorial Museum,** 5 r. Dr. Klein, which commemorates Luxembourg's liberation during WWII. Take a right from the station, a left on r. de la Gare, a left on ave. J. F. Kennedy, and a right on r. Dr. Klein. (☎81 03 22. Open June-Sept. 15 daily 10am-5pm; Sept. 16-May 30 Su 2-5pm. €2.50.) Near the train station is the **Hotel Herckmans ❹,** 3 pl. de la Résistance, a

## NO WORK, ALL PLAY

### MAKE A WISH, YOUR HIGHNESS

Luxembourg's diminutive size doesn't stop it from throwing one hell of a royal birthday party. The circumstances of the June 23 bash are a little puzzling, since Grand Duke Henri, the head of Luxembourg's constitutional monarchy, was born on April 16, 1955. Henri inherited the date, changing from his grandmother, Grand Duchess Charlotte, born on January 23, 1896. When he court realized that mid-winter doesn't lend itself to open-air bashes, they pushed celebrations back five months. Reluctant to further confuse their subjects, both Henri and his father Jean took June 23 as their own.

A procession through the old city starts things off on the evening of June 22. At 11pm, fireworks rip through the air, putting the city's bridges into sharp relief. In a flash, the narrow streets are transformed into impromptu all ages bars and dance floors; alcohol flows like water, spirits are high, and it takes the rising sun to finally break up the party. The disheveled partygoers pour into the Place d'Armes for breakfast before staggering home to sleep. June 23 is a public holiday, so once the city wakes around noon, everyone heads downtown to see Henri strolling through the streets. With his aged parents in tow and royal security out of sight, the duke restores calm and a sense of routine to a city unaccustomed to such glorious commotion.

small hotel above Stone's Steakhouse. The modest rooms offer the most budget-friendly option in town. (☎81 74 28. Breakfast included. Singles €35-40; doubles €45-60; triples €80. AmEx/MC/V.) From the train station, turn left on Prince Henry, turn right when the road ends, and then take the first left onto the pedestrian-only Grande Rue, where much of commercial Ettelbrück is located. Grab a quick meal at **Bakes ②**, 55 Grande Rue. (☎81 13 33. Sandwiches €2.65-4.20. Pastas €8.65. Open daily 7am-5:30pm. AmEx/MC/V.) **Trains** go to Clervaux (30min., 1 per hr., €5) and Luxembourg City (25min., 3 per hr., €4.50). The station at Ettelbrück (open 5:50am-8:30pm) is the hub for buses throughout the Ardennes. Buy the €5 day pass for unlimited bus and train use for one day; validate the pass yourself at the orange booth on the platform. To reach the **tourist office,** walk to the end of Grande Rue and turn right onto r. de Bastogne. (☎81 20 68; www.sit-e.lu. Open Tu-Sa 9am-noon and 1:30-5pm.)

**ECHTERNACH.** In the heart of the Little Switzerland region, Echternach (pop. 5200) is a charming tourist village and a paradise for the **hikers** and **bikers** who venture out into the surrounding woodlands. The turrets of the 15th-century **town hall** share the skyline with the towering **Basilica of St. Willibrord,** less interesting inside than out. To get there, go down r. de la Gare and take a left at pl. du Marché. (Open M-Sa 9am-6pm, Su noon-6pm. Free.) St. Willibrord draws thousands of pilgrims every Whit Tuesday (Pentecost) for the **Dancing Procession.** The basilica and the intimate Église Saints Pierre-et-Paul host Echternach's renowned **International Music Festival** from May to July. (☎72 83 47; www.echternachfestival.lu. Tickets free to €47.) The remains of a **Roman villa,** 47a r. des Romains, can be found near the lake, a 25min. walk from the station; take r. de la Gare and make a right from pl. du Marché onto rte. de Luxembourg, then a left on r. C.M. Spoo, which will become r. des Romains, and follow signs. The museum and open-air exhibit cast light on the area's 2000-year history (☎26 72 09 74; www.villa-echternach.lu. Open Tu-Sa from the Su before Easter-June 30 11am-1pm and 2-5pm; July-Aug. 11am-6pm; Oct.-Nov. 1 11am-1pm and 2-5pm. €3.)

The lakeside ■**Auberge de Jeunesse (HI) ②**, 1 chemin vert Roudenhaff, is a 30min. walk from the station, and is equipped with a sports hall and an indoor climbing wall. Walk past the Roman villa to get there. (☎72 01 58; www.youthhostels.lu. Wheelchair-accessible. Breakfast and linens included. Reception 8am-10pm. Check-in 2-10pm. Bike rental €2.50 per hr., €8 per half-day, €16 per day. Reserve ahead in summer. Dorms €21; singles €33; doubles €26. €3 HI discount. MC/V.) **Camping Officiel ①**, 5 rte. de Diekirch, is a 5min. walk from the bus station. (☎72 02 72; www.camping-echternach.lu. Laundry €2.50. Bring your own toilet paper. Open 9am-7pm. Tent sites €5, extra person €5. AmEx/MC/V.) Pick up groceries at **Match,** near pl. du Marché. (Open M-F 8am-7pm, Sa 8am-1pm.) **Buses** run to Ettelbrück (#500; 50min., 1 per hr.) and Luxembourg City (#111 or 110; 45min.-1hr., 2 per hr.). Rent **bikes** at **Trisport,** 31 rte. de Luxembourg. (☎72 00 86. €2.50 per hr., €15 per day. Open Tu-Sa 9am-noon and 2-6pm.) The **tourist office,** 9 parvis de la Basilique, is in front of the Basilica. (☎72 02 30; www.echternach-tourist.lu. Open July-Aug. daily 9:30am-5:30pm; June and Sept. M-Sa 10am-noon and 2-5pm; Oct.-May M-F 9am-noon and 2-4pm.)

**VIANDEN.** The village of Vianden (pop. 2000) is home to one of the most impressive castles in Western Europe. A patchwork of Carolingian, Gothic, and Renaissance architecture, the ■**Château de Vianden** holds displays of armor, furniture, and tapestries. Captions are mainly in German, but the main attraction is the view from the top of the hill, where you can look down at the castle towers and countryside. (☎84 92 91; www.castle-vianden.lu. Open daily Apr.-Sept. 10am-6pm; Oct. and Mar. 10am-5pm; Nov.-Feb. 10am-4pm. €5.50, students €4.50.) The **Maison Victor Hugo,** 37 r. de la Gare, housed the author during his exile from France. (☎26 87

40 88; www.victor-hugo.lu. Open Tu-Su 11am-5pm. €4, students €3.50.) Take the **Chairlift** from 3 r. du Sanatorium up the mountain for thrilling views. (☎83 43 23. €3, round-trip €4.50. Open Easter-Oct. M-Sa 10am-5pm, Su 10am-6pm.) Vianden has hiking trails, and bike rides go to Diekirch (22km) and Echternach (30km). Rent **bikes** at the bus station. (Open mid-July to Aug. M-Sa 8am-noon and 1-5pm. €10 per half-day, €14 per day.) Modern, clean rooms await at the **🌑Auberge de Jeunesse (HI) ❷**, 3 Montée du Château, near the foot of the castle. To get there, climb Grande Rue up the hill and toward the castle. The road will change to Montée du Château, and the hostel is behind Hotel Oranienburg. (☎83 41 77. Breakfast included. Reception 8-10am and 5-9pm. Dorms €19; singles €31. €3 HI discount.) **Hotel Petry's Restaurant ❹**, 15 r. de la Gare, serves filling dishes in a cozy atmosphere. (☎83 41 22. Meat entrees €6-19. Open May-Aug. daily 8am-9:30pm.) **Buses** head to Ettelbrück (#570; 30min., 2 per hr.) and Clervaux (#663; 40min., M-Sa 4 per day, Su 2 per day.) From the bus station, take r. de la Gare to the center of town; the **tourist office,** 1 r. du Vieux Marché, is over the bridge on the right. (☎83 42 571; www.tourist-info-vianden.lu. Internet €2 per hr. Open mid-July to Aug. M-F 8am-6pm, Sa-Su 10am-2pm; Sept.-June M-F 8am-noon and 1-5pm, Sa-Su 10am-2pm.)

**CLERVAUX.** You are likely to find more faces in Clervaux's **château** than in the tiny town (pop. 2000); the castle is now home to what has been dubbed the greatest photographic exhibit of all times, Edward Steichen's **🌑Family of Man.** (☎92 96 57. Open Tu-Su 10am-6pm. €4.50, students €2.50.) To get to the château, turn left out of the train station onto r. de la Gare, which becomes Grande Rue, and walk until the road splits into three. Take the street farthest to the right up the hill to the castle. From the city, the red roof of the **Benedictine Abbey** can be seen above the treeline on the hill behind the château; reach it from the castle by walking down Montée du Château and taking the first left onto r. Schloff. Take the path on either side of the church up the hill. (Open M-F 8:30-10:15am, 11:30am-12:30pm, 1:45-5:45pm, 6:45-7:20pm; Sa-Su 1:45-4:45pm and 5:45-7:20pm. Free.) Head back to Ettelbrück or Vianden for accommodations. Walk down Montée du Château and take the first right onto Grande Rue. There, as soon as the street turns right, you will see on your left the Hôtel International, and next to it, **Le Rhinocerus ❸**, 10 Grande Rue, which serves up satisfying local dishes. (☎92 93 91. Entrees around €8. Open daily 7am-9:30pm. AmEx/MC/V.) **Trains** run to: Brussels, BEL (3hr., 1 per 2hr.), Ettelbrück (25min.), and Luxembourg City (50min.). The station has **lockers** available. The **tourist office** in the castle offers **Internet** for €2 per hr. (☎92 00 72; www.tourisme-clervaux.lu. Open July-Aug. daily 10am-noon and 2-6pm; Sept.-Oct. M-Sa 2-6pm; Mar.-Apr. and Nov.-Dec. W-Sa 10am-noon.)

**ESCH-SUR-SÛRE.** Cradled by the green Ardennes mountains and encircled by the ruins of Luxembourg's oldest castle, this village (pop. 320) is an ideal base for exploring the **Haute-Sûre Nature Reserve,** 15 rte. de Lultzhausen (☎89 93 311), or the area's 700km of nature trails. (Reserve open Mar.-Oct. M-Tu and Th-F 10am-noon and 2-6pm, Sa-Su 2-6pm; Nov.-Apr. closes 5pm.) **Hotel de la Sûre ❸**, 1 r. du Pont, the village's unofficial tourist office, is the best bet for lodgings. From the bus stop, walk up r. de l'Église (the street on the right closest to the tunnel) past the church. (☎83 91 10; www.hotel-de-la-sure.lu. Bike rental €5 per hr., €19-22 per day. Breakfast included. Free Internet. Reception 7am-midnight. Singles M-Th €27-70, F-Su €30-77. Discounts for longer stays. AmEx/MC/V.) **Camping im Aal ❶**, r. du Moulin, a 10min. walk from the bus drop-off point, is next to the Sûre river. To get there, cross the bridge and turn right past the playgrounds. (☎83 95 14; www.esch-sure.lu. Wash €3.50, dry €2.50. Open Feb.-Dec. Reception 8am-noon and 1-5pm. Tent sites €5 per person. Cash only.) **Buses** to Ettelbrück leave every hour, except on Sundays when they leave every two to four hours (#535; 25min.).

# THE NETHERLANDS (NEDERLAND)

 The Dutch take great pride in their country, in part because they created vast stretches of it, claiming land from the ocean using dikes and canals. With most of their country's land area below sea level, the task of keeping their iconic tulips and windmills on dry ground has become something of a national pastime. Over the centuries, planners built dikes higher and higher to hold back the sea, culminating in a new "flexible coast" policy that depends on spillways and reservoirs to contain potentially disastrous floods. For a people whose land constantly threatens to become ocean, the staunch Dutch have a deeply grounded culture and a down-to-earth friendliness. Time-tested art, ambitious architecture, and dynamic nightlife make the Netherlands one of the most popular destinations in Western Europe.

## DISCOVER THE NETHERLANDS: SUGGESTED ITINERARIES

**THREE DAYS.** Go no farther than the canals and coffee shops of **Amsterdam** (p. 752). **Museumplein** is home to some of the finest art collections in Europe, while the houses of ill repute in the **Red Light District** are shockingly lurid.

**ONE WEEK.** Begin in the capital city of **Amsterdam** (4 days). Take time to recover among the stately monuments of **The Hague** (2 days; p. 780). End the week in youthful, hyper-modern **Rotterdam** (1 day; p. 782).

**TWO WEEKS.** You can't go wrong starting off in **Amsterdam** (5 days), especially if you detour to the flower trading in **Aalsmeer** (1 day; p. 777) and the beaches of **Texel** (1 day; p. 788) The history of **Haarlem** (1 day; p. 778) is next, then on to **The Hague** (2 days) and **Rotterdam** (1 day). Explore the museums in the college town of **Utrecht** (1 day; p. 784). The paths of **De Hoge Veluwe National Park** (1 day; p. 786) and **Maastricht** (1 day; p. 787) mark the end of the trail.

## LIFE AND TIMES

### HISTORY

**FROM ROMANS TO HABSBURGS (100 BC TO AD 1579).** Romans under **Julius Caesar** invaded the region in the 1st century BC, displacing justifiably disgruntled Celtic and Germanic tribes. The native Germanic tribes had the last laugh in the AD 4th century as their retaliating forces swept through Roman lands in the Low Countries, the Netherlands, Belgium, and Luxembourg. Freedom was short-lived: the **Franks** supplanted the Romans from the 5th to the 8th century. During this period, towns rose as powerful, independent centers. The **House of Burgundy** infiltrated the region in the 14th century to establish a more centralized albeit truncated monarchy. By the 15th century, the Austrian **Habsburgs** had seized the Dutch crown by marriage. When **Philip I** of the Habsburgs married into the Spanish royal family, the Netherlands was subjected to yet another foreign power.

**UTRECHT AND THE START OF THE GOLDEN AGE (1579-1651).** The Netherlands was officially founded in 1579 under the **Union of Utrecht**, which aimed to form an independent group of provinces and cities led by a **States-General**. Under

# The Netherlands

Prince **William of Orange,** the Dutch declared independence from Spain in 1580. This sparked a prolonged struggle and religious debate between the Protestant Netherlands and Catholic Spain. The conflict was settled in 1609 by the **Twelve Years' Truce,** which recognized the Netherlands' sovereignty. But the feisty Spanish kept fighting until Dutchman **Frederick Henry** defeated them on land, while the Dutch navy near Cuba and along the English coast stopped them at sea. An embarrassed Spain offered the **Peace of Westphalia** (1648), which acknowledged Dutch independence and pushed for an alliance against the growing French state.

During the 17th century **Age of Exploration,** also known as the **Dutch Golden Age,** Dutch conquerors fanned out over the globe and gained control of all the major trade routes across Europe. This generated incredible prosperity for the Dutch— the **Dutch East India Company** was responsible for much of this economic surge— but also trod on the toes of the British, who resented invasion of their commercial spheres. To protect trade routes, the company colonized the **Cape of Good Hope** and other strategic posts. Meanwhile, the **Dutch West India Company** explored the New World, creating colonies such as **New Amsterdam** (now New York). This global activity further spurred the growth of Dutch wealth, culture, and trade.

## WAR GAMES AND POWER STRUGGLES (1651-1780). Neighboring European

powers resented the domestic and foreign success of the Dutch. England sought recompense by passing **Navigation Acts** in 1651 and 1660 aimed at limiting Dutch incursions on English trade, then by attacking the Dutch navy. The vastly stronger Brits prevailed, forced peace, and secretly drafted the **Act of Seclusion,** forever banning the independence-seeking Prince of Orange from Dutch politics. Grand Pensionary **Johan de Witt** managed to rebuild the Netherlands' military and economy, but bitterness between English and the Dutch remained. With the restoration of **King Charles II** of England in 1660, the Dutch negotiated an alliance with the French and sabotaged the English fleet in 1667 in the **Raid on the Medway.**

In 1667, France reneged and invaded the Netherlands, threatening the interests of both the English and the Dutch, who in turn formed an unlikely coalition. Betrayed, King **Louis XIV** of France proposed an alliance with the English, subsidized by the French. When England accepted in 1672, the Netherlands found itself in an impossible situation, at war against both countries. Against all odds, under the leadership of **William III,** the country repeatedly managed to defeat the Franco-English fleets. However, the glory of winning was quickly undermined by a strategic marriage: William wed his first cousin **Mary,** daughter of English king **James II,** and ascended the throne in England with the 1688 **Glorious Revolution,** subjecting the Netherlands to England. The Dutch entered a period of decline, with international trade dwindling in the 18th century as that of neighboring countries grew.

**FRENCH RULE AND INDEPENDENCE (1780-1914).** The Netherlands was the second country, after France, to recognize the American Revolution—sparking English anger, another attack, and yet another war. In 1795, French forces under **Napoleon Bonaparte** invaded, conquering a Netherlands weakened by war and perhaps overly sympathetic to the French Revolution. After Napoleon's defeat at Waterloo, the **Treaty of Vienna** (1815) established the **Kingdom of the Netherlands,** which included Belgium and Luxembourg. Although this new union did not last, with Belgium revolting and gaining independence in 1839, King **William I of Orange** still managed to rebuild the economy and trade routes. Under William, the Dutch created a constitution establishing the Netherlands as a **constitutional monarchy** in which parliament held most of the power, leading to the formation of modern political parties. **Queen Wilhelmina** succeeded to the throne in 1890, breaking the tradition of male ascendancy.

**THE WORLD WARS (1914-1945).** When **World War I** broke out, the Dutch remained neutral, focusing on trade and economy. Surrounded by combatting nations, their country suffered deprivation as intense as that of WWI's active participants. **World War II** again breached Dutch neutrality: the Nazis invaded in May 1940 and occupied the nation for five years. The Dutch suffered horribly. All acts of resistance were punished severely, and the population nearly starved. Jews, including **Anne Frank** and her family, were sent to concentration camps. Frank's diary is now a quintessential account of life under Nazi rule and her home was made into a museum in Amsterdam (p. 769).

**THE POST-WAR ERA (1945-1990).** After the war, Wilhelmina supported sweeping democratic changes for the nation, creating proportional representation in government. The nation also abandoned its policy of neutrality, joining **NATO** and creating the **Benelux** economic union with Belgium and Luxembourg. To recover from the devestation of WWII, the government started an economic policy that focused on industrial and commercial expansion.

While the nation experienced relative peace throughout the 1950s, the economic and political problems of the 1960s brought rioting students and workers. In the 1980s, Dutch politics saw the disintegration of old parties and alliances. The recent rise of the **Christian Democratic Appeal (CDA)** has provided a new outlet for major Christian factions. Though centrist, the CDA supports limiting drug legality, prostitution, and abortion. The center-left **Labour Party (PvdA)** has managed to avoid ties with extreme groups and allied with the CDA in 1989. The **Liberal Party (VVD)** supports private business and hands-off economic policy.

## TODAY

The Netherlands is an integral member of the **European Union (EU).** The government is a parliamentary democracy with a constitutional monarchy: parliament has all legislative power while **Queen Beatrix,** who has been queen since 1980, holds a symbolic role. Immigration has become a central issue in politics. On both the right and the left, people fear the influx of conservative newcomers who might threaten their open Dutch society. In 2002 elections, populist politician **Pim Fortuyn** and his new **Lijst Pim Fortuyn (LPF)** party, which advanced a platform with many anti-immigration tenets, seemed on their way to a victory. Fortuyn was dramatically assassinated just before the parliamentary election. The CDA won the election, attracting many who might have supported Fortuyn. Although the party was leaderless, the LPF still gained seats in parliament. **Jan Peter Balkenende,** the leader of the CDA, has been prime minister since 2002 and is currently at the head of a coalition, formed following the 2006 elections, between the CDA, the PvdA, and the **Christian Union (CU)** party.

Long-known for its relaxed drug policies, the Netherlands has been trying to crack down, especially in order to diminish its role as European entry point for cocaine and ecstasy. The Netherlands continues to play a disproportionately large role in global politics, having taken on the role of international arbiter. The **International Court of Justice,** housed in the Vredespaleis (Peace Palace) in **The Hague** (p. 780), oversees disputes between sovereign nations.

## THE ARTS

### LITERATURE

Dutch literature dates back to the 10th-century **Wachtendonck Psalm Fragments,** the work of an anonymous translator who rendered the Latin psalms, line by line, into Old Dutch. Additional influential works emerged during the 17th-century Golden Age, as the Dutch returned from world travels with stories to tell and new ideas to ponder. The epoch's primary author was **Henric Laurenszoon Spieghel,** whose *Heart-Mirror* (1614) was the first philosophical work written in Dutch. The Reformed Church commissioned the *States Bible* (1620), the first Dutch translation of the Bible, further standardizing and legitimizing the language. Poet and dramatist **Joost van den Vondel** firmly established the Netherlands in the literary world, satirizing the church and government. *Lucifer* (1654), his masterpiece, depicts an imagined conflict between the angels and God, and is said to have influenced John Milton's *Paradise Lost*. In the 19th century, **Nicolaas Beets** translated Lord Byron into Dutch and published his own *Camera Obscura* (1839), popular humorous stories of everyday life. During WWI and WWII, literature focused on social and philosophical questions. **Willem Frederik Hermans** examined the wartime Netherlands in *The Dark Room of Damocles* (1958), while **Anne Frank** recorded her days hiding from the Nazis in *The Diary of Anne Frank*.

### VISUAL ARTS

The Netherlands has trained and displayed some of the West's best artists and canvases from the 17th century onwards. The monumental genius of **Rembrandt van Rijn,** draftsman and painter, raised him above the other portraitists of the 1620s. Using **chiaroscuro**—the technique of painting in high contrast between light and dark—and rich, luxuriant color and sensual brushwork in such paintings as *Judas Returning the Thirty Pieces of Silver* (1629), he distinguished himself early and left a legacy. Later in the 17th century, **Johannes Vermeer** explored bold perspectives and aspects of light in detailed, compelling portraits of people and everyday life, including *Girl with a Pearl Earring*. In the 19th century, **Vincent van Gogh,** swept thick brushstrokes of bright, vibrantly contrasting colors across canvases. Many of his works are on display in the extensive **van Gogh Museum** (p. 770) in Amsterdam. **Piet Mondrian,** founder of the influential *De Stijl* magazine, formulated the theory of **neoplasticism,** which held that art should not attempt to recreate real life but should instead express universal absolutes. His signature works are characterized by black grids over primary-color blocks.

## HOLIDAYS AND FESTIVALS

**Holidays:** New Year's Day (Jan. 1); Epiphany (Jan. 6); Good Friday (Mar. 21); Easter (Mar. 23-24); Queen's Day (Apr. 30); Ascension (May 1); WWII Remembrance Day (May 4); Liberation Day (May 5); Pentecost (May 11-12); Corpus Christi (May 22); Assumption (Aug. 15); All Saints' Day (Nov. 1); Saint Nicholas' Eve (December 5); Christmas (Dec. 25); Boxing Day (Dec. 26).

**Festivals:** Koninginnedag (Queen's Day; Apr. 30) turns the country into a huge carnival. The Holland Festival (June; www.hollandfestival.nl) has been celebrating performing arts in Amsterdam since 1948. In the Bloemencorso (Flower Parade; early Sept.), flower-covered floats crawl from Aalsmeer to Amsterdam. Historic canal houses and windmills are open to the public for National Monument Day (Sept. 13-14). The High Times Cannabis Cup (late Nov.) celebrates pot.

## ESSENTIALS

### FACTS AND FIGURES

**Official Name:** Kingdom of the Netherlands.

**Capital:** Amsterdam; The Hague is the seat of government.

**Major Cities:** The Hague, Rotterdam, Utrecht.

**Population:** 16,571,000.

**Land Area:** 41,500 sq. km.

**Time Zone:** GMT +1.

**Language:** Dutch; English is spoken almost universally.

**Religions:** Catholic (31%), Protestant (20%), Muslim (6%).

**Land below sea level:** One third of the country, kept dry by an extensive network of dikes 1500 miles (2400km) long.

## WHEN TO GO

July and August are lovely for travel in the Netherlands, as the crowded hostels and lengthy lines during those months will confirm. If you fancy a bit more elbow room, you may prefer April, May, and early June, as tulips and fruit trees furiously bloom and temperatures hover around 12-20°C (53-68°F). The Netherlands is famously drizzly year-round, so travelers should bring raingear.

## DOCUMENTS AND FORMALITIES

**EMBASSIES AND CONSULATES.** Foreign embassies and consulates are in The Hague (p. 780). Both the UK and the US have consulates in Amsterdam (p. 752). Dutch embassies abroad include: **Australia,** 120 Empire Circuit, Yarralumla Canberra, ACT, 2600 (☎262 20 94 00; www.netherlands.org.au); **Canada,** 350 Albert St., Ste. 2020, Ottawa, ON, K1R 1A4 (☎613-237-5030; www.netherlandsembassy.ca); **Ireland,** 160 Merrion Rd., Dublin, 4 (☎12 69 34 44; www.netherlandsembassy.ie);

**New Zealand,** P.O. Box 840, at Ballance and Featherston St., Wellington (☎044 71 63 90; www.netherlandsembassy.co.nz); **UK,** 38 Hyde Park Gate, London, SW7 5DP (☎20 75 90 32 00; www.netherlands-embassy.org.uk); **US,** 4200 Linnean Ave., NW, Washington, D.C., 20008 (☎202-244-5300; www.netherlands-embassy.org).

**VISA AND ENTRY INFORMATION.** EU citizens do not need a visa. Citizens of Australia, Canada, New Zealand, and the US do not need a visa for stays of up to 90 days, beginning upon entry into any of the countries in the EU's freedom of movement zone. For more info, see p. 13. For stays longer than 90 days, all non-EU citizens need visas (around US$80), available at Dutch embassies and consulates or online at www.minbuza.nl/en/home, the website for the Dutch Ministry of Foreign Affairs. It will take about two weeks after application submission to receive a visa.

# TOURIST SERVICES AND MONEY

| EMERGENCY | Ambulance, Fire, and Police: ☎112. |
| --- | --- |

**TOURIST OFFICES. VVV** (vay-vay-vay) tourist offices are marked by triangular blue signs. The website www.visitholland.com is also a useful resource. The **Holland Pass** (www.hollandpass.com, €25) grants free admission to five museums or sites of your choice and also provides discounts at restaurants and attractions.

**MONEY.** The **euro (€)** has replaced the **guilder** as the unit of currency in the Netherlands. For more info, see p. 16. As a general rule, it's cheaper to exchange money in the Netherlands than at home. A bare-bones day in the Netherlands will cost €35-40; a slightly more comfortable day will run €50-60. Hotels and restaurants include a service charge in the bill; additional tips are appreciated but not necessary. Taxi drivers are generally tipped 10% of the fare.

The Netherlands has a 19% **value added tax (VAT),** a sales tax applied to retail goods. The prices given in *Let's Go* include VAT. In the airport upon exiting the EU, non-EU citizens who have stayed in the EU fewer than 180 days can claim a refund on the tax paid for purchases at participating stores. In order to qualify for a refund in a store, you must spend at least €130; make sure to ask for a refund form when you pay. For more info on qualifying for a VAT refund, see p. 18.

# TRANSPORTATION

**BY PLANE.** Most international flights land at **Schiphol Airport** in Amsterdam (**AMS;** ☎800 72 44 74 65, info ☎900 724 4746; www.schiphol.nl). Budget airlines, like **Ryanair** and **easyJet,** fly out of **Eindhoven Airport** (**EIN;** ☎314 02 91 98 18; www.eindhovenairport.com), 10min. away from Eindhoven, and Amsterdam's Schiphol Airport, to locations around Europe. The Dutch national airline, **KLM** (☎020 474 7747, US ☎800-447-4747, UK ☎08705 074 074; www.klm.com), offers student discounts. For more info on traveling by plane around Europe, see p. 44.

**BY TRAIN.** The national rail company is the efficient **Nederlandse Spoorwegen (NS;** Netherlands Railways; www.ns.nl). **Sneltreinen** are the fastest, while **stoptreinen** make many local stops. One-way tickets are called *enkele reis.* Same-day, round-trip tickets *(dagretour)* are valid only on the day of purchase, but are roughly 15% cheaper than normal round-trip tickets. **Weekendretour** tickets are not quite as cheap, but are valid from 7pm Friday through 4pm Monday. A day pass *(dagkaart)* allows unlimited travel throughout the country for one day, for the price equivalent to the most expensive one-way fare across the country. **Eurail** and **InterRail** have passes that are valid in the Netherlands. The **Holland Rail pass** is good for three or five travel days in any one-month period. Although available in the US, the

Holland Rail pass is cheaper in the Netherlands at DER Travel Service or RailEurope offices. Overall, train service tends to be faster than bus service. For more info on traveling by train around Europe, see p. 45

 **ALL ABOARD.** Nederlandse Spoorwegen is the Dutch national rail company, operating the country's intercity train service. Their website, www.ns.nl, has a user-friendly English-language section with train times, prices, and door-to-door directions for all stops in the Netherlands.

**BY BUS.** With transportation largely covered by the extensive rail system, bus lines are limited to short trips and travel to areas without rail lines. A nationalized fare system covers city buses, trams, and long-distance buses. The country is divided into zones: a trip between destinations in the same zone costs two strips on a *strippenkaart* (strip card); a trip in two zones will set you back three strips. On buses, tell the driver your destination and he or she will cancel the correct number of strips; on trams and subways, stamp your own in either a yellow box at the back of the tram or in the subway station. Drivers sell cards with two, three, and eight strips, but it's cheaper to buy 15-strip or 45-strip cards at tourist offices, post offices, and some newsstands. Day passes *(dagkaarten)* are valid for travel throughout the country and are discounted as special summer tickets *(zomerzwerfkaarten)* June through August. Riding without a ticket can result in a fine.

**BY CAR.** Normally, tourists with a driver's license valid in their home country can drive in the Netherlands for fewer than 185 days. The country has well-maintained roadways, although drivers may cringe at high fuel prices, traffic, and scarce parking near Amsterdam, The Hague, and Rotterdam. The yellow cars of the **Royal Dutch Touring Club** (**ANWB;** toll-free ☎ 08 00 08 88) patrol many major roads, and will offer prompt roadside assistance in the case of a breakdown.

**BY BIKE AND BY THUMB. Cycling** is the way to go in the Netherlands—distances between cities are short, the countryside is absolutely flat, and most streets have separate bike lanes. Bike rentals run €6-10 per day and €30-40 per week. For a database of bike rental shops and other cycling tips and information, visit www.holland.com/global/discover/active/cycling. **Hitchhiking** is illegal on motorways but common elsewhere. Droves of hitchhikers can be found along roads leading out of Amsterdam. Those choosing this mode of transport often try their luck close to a town. Let's Go does not recommend hitchhiking.

# KEEPING IN TOUCH

**EMAIL AND THE INTERNET.** Email is easily accessible within the Netherlands. Travelers with Wi-Fi-enabled computers may be able to take advantage of an increasing number of hot spots, which offer Wi-Fi for free or for a small fee. Websites like www.jiwire.com, www.wi-fihotspotlist.com, and www.locfinder.net can help locate hot spots.

 **PHONE CODES** **Country code: 31. International dialing prefix: 00.** For more info on how to place international calls, see **Inside Back Cover.**

**TELEPHONE.** Some pay phones still accept coins, but phone cards are the rule. KPT and Telfort are the most widely accepted varieties, the former available at post offices and the latter at train stations (from €5). Whenever possible, use a calling card for international phone calls, as long-distance rates for national phone services are often very high. Mobile phones are an increasingly popular and economical option. Major mobile carriers include **Vodafone, KPN, T-Mobile,** and **Telfort.** For directory assistance, dial ☎09 00 80 08, for collect calls ☎08 00 01 01. Direct-dial access numbers for calling out of the Netherlands include: **AT&T Direct** (☎0800 022 9111); **British Telecom** (☎0800 022 0444); **Canada Direct** (☎0800 022 9116); **Telecom New Zealand** (☎0800 022 4464); **Telstra Australia** (☎0800 022 0061). For more info on calling home from Europe, see p. 26.

**MAIL.** Post offices are generally open Monday through Friday 9am-5pm, Thursday or Friday nights, and Saturday mornings in some larger towns. Amsterdam and Rotterdam have 24hr. post offices. Mailing a postcard or letter within the EU costs €0.69 and up to €0.85 outside of Europe. To receive mail in the Netherlands, have mail delivered **Poste Restante.** Mail will go to the main post office unless you specify a subsidiary by street address. Address mail to be held according to the following example: First Name, Last Name, Poste Restante, followed by the address of the post office. Bring a passport to pick up your mail; there may be a small fee.

## ACCOMMODATIONS AND CAMPING

| NETHERLANDS | ❶ | ❷ | ❸ | ❹ | ❺ |
|---|---|---|---|---|---|
| **ACCOMMODATIONS** | under €36 | €36-55 | €56-77 | €78-100 | over €100 |

VVV offices around the country supply travelers with accommodation listings and can almost always reserve rooms for a €2-5 fee. **Private rooms** cost about two-thirds the price of a hotel, but are harder to find; check with the VVV. During July and August, many cities add a tourist tax (€1-2) to the price of all rooms. The country's 30 **Hostelling International (HI) youth hostels** are run by **Stayokay** (www.stayokay.com) and are dependably clean and modern. There is **camping** across the country, although sites tend to be crowded during the summer months; **CityCamps Holland** has a network of 17 well-maintained sites. The website www.strandheem.nl has camping information.

## FOOD AND DRINK

| NETHERLANDS | ❶ | ❷ | ❸ | ❹ | ❺ |
|---|---|---|---|---|---|
| **FOOD** | under €8 | €8-12 | €13-17 | €18-22 | over €22 |

Traditional Dutch cuisine is hearty, heavy, and meaty. Expect bread for breakfast and lunch, topped with melting **hagelslag** (flaked chocolate topping) in the morning and cheese later in the day. Generous portions of meat and fish make up dinner, traditionally the only hot meal of the day. **Seafood,** from various grilled fish and shellfish to fish stews and raw herring, is popular. For a truly authentic Dutch meal (most commonly available in May and June), ask for **spargel** (white asparagus), served with potatoes, ham, and eggs. Light snacks include **tostis** (hot grilled-cheese sandwiches, sometimes with ham) and **broodjes** (light, cold sandwiches). The Dutch colonial legacy has brought Surinamese and Indonesian cuisine to the Netherlands, bestowing cheaper and lighter dining options and a wealth of falafel stands in cities. Wash down meals with brimming glasses of Heineken or Amstel.

# BEYOND TOURISM

Volunteer and work opportunities often revolve around international politics or programs resulting from liberal social attitudes. Studying in the Netherlands can entail in-depth looks at sex and drugs. For more info on opportunities across Europe, see **Beyond Tourism,** p. 54.

THE NETHERLANDS

**COC Amsterdam,** Rozenstr. 14, Amsterdam (☎626 3087; www.cocamsterdam.nl). The world's oldest organization dedicated to the support of homosexuals and their families. Contact for involvement in support groups, gay pride activities, and publications.

**University of Amsterdam,** Spui 21, Amsterdam (☎525 8080 or 525 3333; www.uva.nl/english). Amsterdam's largest university offers a full range of degree programs in Dutch. Open to college and graduate students. The Summer Institute on Sexuality, Culture, and Society (www.ishss.uva.nl/summerinstitute), set in the heart of one of the world's most tolerant cities, examines sexuality in various cultures. Tuition €1445-10,000 per year, depending on the program. Discounts offered for EU citizens.

# AMSTERDAM ☎020

Amsterdam's reputation precedes it—and what a reputation it is. Born out of a murky bog and cobbled together over eight centuries, the "Dam on the River Amstel" (pop. 743,000) coaxes visitors with an alluring blend of grandeur and decadence. Thick clouds of marijuana smoke waft from subdued coffee shops, and countless bicycles zip past blooming tulip markets. Yet there is much more to Amsterdam than stereotypes. Against the legacy of Vincent van Gogh's thick swirls and Johannes Vermeer's luminous figures, gritty street artists spray graffiti in protest. Squatters sharpen the city's defiant edge, while professional politicians push the boundaries of progressive reform. GLBT citizens blend seamlessly into a social landscape that defines tolerance but also faces difficult questions as the 21st century unfolds. With Muslim integration into Dutch secularism, the limits of liberalism in an interdependent world, and the endless fight to fend off the encroaching seas, this city has its work cut out for it.

# ▶ TRANSPORTATION

**Flights: Schiphol Airport (AMS;** ☎0800 72 44 74 65, flight info 0900 724 4746). **Sneltrainen** connect the airport to Centraal Station (15-20min., €3.60).

**Trains: Centraal Station,** Stationspl. 1 (☎0900 9292, €0.50 per min.; www.ns.nl). To: **Brussels, BEL** (2½-3hr.; 5 per day; €32, under 26 €24); **Groningen** (3hr., 2 per hr., €27); **Haarlem** (20min., 6 per hr., €3.60); **The Hague** (50min., 1-6 per hr., €9.60); **Rotterdam** (1¼hr., 1-5 per hr., €13); **Utrecht** (30min., 3-6 per hr., €6.40).

**Buses:** Trains are quicker, but the **GVB** (below) will direct you to a bus stop for domestic destinations not on a rail line. **Muiderpoort** (2 blocks east of Oosterpark) sends buses east; **Marnixstation** (at the corner of Marnixstr. and Kinkerstr.) west; and the **Stationsplein** depot north and south.

**Public Transportation: GVB** (☎460 6060; www.gvb.nl), on Stationspl. in front of Centraal Station. Open M-F 7am-9pm, Sa-Su 10am-6pm. **Tram, metro,** and **bus** lines radiate from Centraal Station. Trams are most convenient for center-city travel; the metro leads to outlying neighborhoods. Runs daily 6am-12:15am. **Night buses** traverse the city 12:30-7am; pick up a schedule and map at the GVB (€3 per trip). 2 strips (€1.60) get you to almost all sights within the city center and include unlimited transfers for 1hr.

**Bike Rental:** ◼ **Frédéric Rent a Bike,** Brouwersgr. 78 (☎624 5509; www.frederic.nl), in the Scheepvaartbuurt. Bikes €10 per day, €40 per week. Lock and theft insurance included. Maps and advice liberally dispensed. Open daily 9am-6pm. Cash only. **Bike City,** Bloemgr. 68-70 (☎626 3721; www.bikecity.nl). €10 per 24hr. €45 per 5 days. Bring a government-issued ID. Deposit €25. Open daily 9am-6pm.

# ✴ ORIENTATION

Let the canals guide you through Amsterdam's cozy but confusing neighborhoods. In the city center, water runs in concentric half-circles, beginning at Centraal Sta-

> TIP **BIKE THE DIKES.** The best way to get around Amsterdam is by bike. Get a single-speed bike that has lights in the front and back—you can be ticketed for not using both at night. Get 2 locks—one for each wheel—and secure your bike to something sturdy. You'll inevitably see people biking down the wrong side of a street, running red lights, and playing chicken with trucks, but that doesn't mean you should join in the fun. Always bike perpendicular to tram rails (so your wheels don't get caught in them) and, finally, use hand signals.

tion. The **Singel** runs around the **Centrum,** which includes the **Oude Zijd** (Old Side), the infamous **Red Light District,** and the **Nieuwe Zijd** (New Side), which, oddly enough, is older than the Oude Zijd. Barely a kilometer in diameter, the Centrum overflows with bars, brothels, clubs, and tourists wading through wafts of marijuana smoke. The next three canals—the **Herengracht,** the **Keizersgracht,** and the **Prinsengracht**—constitute the **Canal Ring.** Nearby **Rembrandtplein** and **Leidseplein** sport classy nightlife that spans flashy bars and traditional *bruin cafes.* Just over the **Singelgracht, Museumplein** is home to the city's most renowned art museums as well as the verdant, sprawling **Vondelpark.** Farther out lie the more residential Amsterdam neighborhoods: to the north and west, the **Scheepvaartbuurt, Jordaan, Westerpark,** and **Oud-West;** to the south and east, **Jodenbuurt, Plantage, De Pijp,** and far-flung **Greater Amsterdam.** Though these districts are populated by dense housing, they still boast excellent eateries and brilliant museums.

## PRACTICAL INFORMATION

**Tourist Office: VVV,** Stationspl. 10 (☎0900 400 4040, €0.40 per min.; www.amsterdamtourist.nl), opposite Centraal Station. Books rooms and sells maps for €2. Open daily 9am-5pm. Branches at Stadhouderskade 1, Schiphol Airport, and inside Centraal.

**Consulates:** All foreign embassies are in **The Hague** (p. 780). **UK Consulate,** Koningslaan 44 (☎676 4343). Open M-F 8:30am-1:30pm. **US Consulate,** Museumpl. 19 (☎575 5309; http://amsterdam.usconsulate.gov). Open M-F 8:30-11:30am. Closed last W of every month.

**Currency Exchange: American Express,** Damrak 66 (☎504 8777), offers the best rates, no commission on American Express Travellers Cheques, and a €4 flat fee for all non-euro cash and non-AmEx traveler's checks. Open M-F 9am-5pm, Sa 9am-noon.

**Library: Openbare Bibliotheek Amsterdam,** Prinsengr. 587 (☎523 0900). Reserve free Internet access for 30min. at the information desk. Adequate English selection. Open M 1-9pm, Tu-Th 10am-9pm, F-Sa 10am-5pm; Oct.-Mar. also Su 1-5pm.

**GLBT Resources: Pink Point** (☎428 1070; www.pinkpoint.org), a kiosk in front of the Westerkerk, provides info on GLBT life in Amsterdam. Open daily noon-6pm. **Gay and Lesbian Switchboard** (☎623 6565; www.switchboard.nl) takes calls M-F noon-10pm, Sa-Su 4pm-8pm.

**Laundromat: Rozengracht Wasserette,** Rozengr. 59 (☎638 5975), in the Jordaan. You can do it yourself (wash €6, with dry €7 per 5kg load) or have it done for you (€8 for 5kg). Open daily 9am-9pm. Cash only.

**Police:** Headquarters at Elandsgr. 117 (☎559 9111). The national non-emergency line, ☎0900 8844, connects you to the nearest station or the rape crisis department.

**Crisis Lines:** General counseling at Telephone Helpline (☎675 7575). Open 24hr. Rape crisis hotline (☎612 0245) staffed M-F 10:30am-11pm, Sa-Su 3:30-11pm. Drug counseling at the Jellinek Clinic (☎570 2378). Open M-F 9am-5pm.

**24hr. Pharmacy:** A hotline (☎694 8709) will direct you to the nearest 24hr. pharmacy.

**Medical Services:** For hospital care, **Academisch Medisch Centrum,** Meibergdreef 9 (☎566 9111), is easily accessible on subway #50 or 54 (dir.: Gein; stop: Holendrecht). **Tourist Medical Service** (☎592 3355) offers 24hr. referrals for visitors.

SCHEEPVAARTBUURT

SEE "NIEUWE ZIJD, OUDE ZIJD, AND
THE RED LIGHT DISTRICT," p. 756

Frederik
Hendrik
Plantsoen

VAN
OLDENBARNE
VELDTPLEIN

HEREN-
MARKT

Electric
Ladyland

Anne
Frank
Huis

Koninklijk
Paleis

RED
LIGHT
DISTRICT

Westerkerk

JORDAAN

NIEUWE
ZIJD

Driekoningen

CANAL
RING
WEST

OUD
ZIJ

DA COSTA-
PLEIN

Amsterdam
Historisch
Museum

Marnixstr.
Terminal

Begijn-
hof

Bijbels
Museum

Centrale
Bibliotheek

KONINGS-
PLEIN

MUNT-
PLEIN

REMBRANDTPLEIN

REMBRA

OUD-
WEST

De Appel

Foam
Photography
Museum

Museum
Van Loon

CENTRAL
CANAL
RING

Laund

LEIDSEPLEIN

MacBike

Rijksmuseum

Filmmuseum

Vondelpark

Van Gogh
Museum

Wetering
Plantsden

Den Texstr.

MUSEUMPLEIN
AND VONDELPARK

MUSEUM-
PLEIN

Heineken
Experience

DE PIJP

Concertgebouw

TO
(300m)

TO
(30m)

THE NETHERLANDS

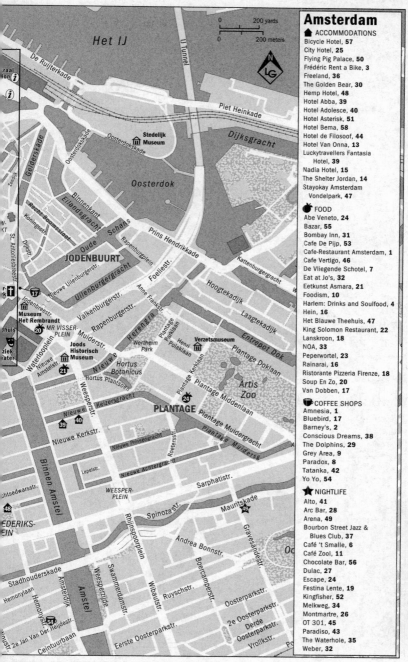

# Amsterdam

**ACCOMMODATIONS**
Bicycle Hotel, **57**
City Hotel, **25**
Flying Pig Palace, **50**
Frédéric Rent a Bike, **3**
Freeland, **36**
The Golden Bear, **30**
Hemp Hotel, **48**
Hotel Abba, **39**
Hotel Adolesce, **40**
Hotel Asterisk, **51**
Hotel Bema, **58**
Hotel de Filosoof, **44**
Hotel Van Onna, **13**
Luckytravellers Fantasia
    Hotel, **39**
Nadia Hotel, **15**
The Shelter Jordan, **14**
Stayokay Amsterdam
    Vondelpark, **47**

**FOOD**
Abe Veneto, **24**
Bazar, **55**
Bombay Inn, **31**
Cafe De Pijp, **53**
Cafe-Restaurant Amsterdam, **1**
Cafe Vertigo, **46**
De Vliegende Schotel, **7**
Eat at Jo's, **32**
Eetkunst Asmara, **21**
Foodism, **10**
Harlem: Drinks and Soulfood, **4**
Hein, **16**
Het Blauwe Theehuis, **47**
King Solomon Restaurant, **22**
Lanskroon, **18**
NOA, **33**
Peperwortel, **23**
Rainarai, **16**
Ristorante Pizzeria Firenze, **18**
Soup En Zo, **20**
Van Dobben, **17**

**COFFEE SHOPS**
Amnesia, **1**
Bluebird, **17**
Barney's, **2**
Conscious Dreams, **38**
The Dolphins, **29**
Grey Area, **9**
Paradox, **8**
Tatanka, **42**
Yo Yo, **54**

**NIGHTLIFE**
Alto, **41**
Arc Bar, **28**
Arena, **49**
Bourbon Street Jazz &
    Blues Club, **37**
Café 't Smalle, **6**
Café Zool, **11**
Chocolate Bar, **56**
Dulac, **27**
Escape, **24**
Festina Lente, **19**
Kingfisher, **52**
Melkweg, **34**
Montmartre, **26**
OT 301, **45**
Paradiso, **43**
The Waterhole, **35**
Weber, **32**

THE NETHERLANDS

Nieuwe Zijd, Oude Zijd, and Red Light District

**Internet Access:** Many coffee shops and hostels offer Internet access for customers and guests. ▓**easyInternetcafé,** Damrak 33 (☎320 8082). €1 per 22min., €6 for 24hr., €10 per 1 week, €22 per 20 days. Open daily 9am-10pm.

**Post Office:** Main post office, Singel 250, at Raadhuisstr. Open M-W and F 9am-6pm, Th 9am-8pm, Sa 10am-1:30pm.

# ACCOMMODATIONS

The chaos of the **Red Light District** prompts accommodations in the **Centrum** to enforce strong security measures, while hostels and hotels in the **Canal Ring** and across the Singelgr. are more laissez-faire. Accommodations in the Red Light District are often bars with beds over them. Before signing up for a bunk, consider just how much noise and drug use you can tolerate from your neighbors. Amsterdam's canal-side hotels and hostels offer affordable accommodations with beautiful views, although they are often criticized for their tight quarters.

## CENTRUM

▓**Flying Pig Downtown,** Nieuwendijk 100 (☎420 6822; www.flyingpig.nl). Knockout location and stylish decor. A perennial favorite among party-hardy backpackers. Breakfast included. Key deposit, including locker, €10. Linens included. Free Internet. 16- to 22-bed dorms €21; 8- to 10-bed dorms €24; 4- to 6-bed dorms €27; singles €76. ISIC holders get a free beer in summer and a 5% discount in winter. AmEx/MC/V. ❶

**Stayokay Amsterdam Stadsdoelen,** Kloveniersburgwal 97 (☎624 6832; www.stayokay.com/stadsdoelen). This branch of the chain sleeps 158 and provides clean, drug-free lodgings in (relatively) quiet environs. Breakfast, lockers, and linens included. Locker deposit €20 or passport. Internet access €5 per hr. Reception 24hr. Co-ed or single-sex 8- to 20-bed dorms €25-27. €2.50 HI discount. MC/V. ❶

**Hotel Brouwer,** Singel 83 (☎624 6358; www.hotelbrouwer.nl). 8 gorgeously restored rooms, each with private bath and canal view. Elevator. Breakfast included. Singles €55; doubles €90; triples €115. Cash or traveler's checks only. ❷

**Hotel Royal Taste,** Oudezijds Achterburgwal 47 (☎623 2478; www.hotelroyaltaste.nl). Clean, comfortable, almost fancy accommodations at reasonable prices. Breakfast €7.50. Singles with sink €50, with bath €60; doubles with bath €100-110, with canal view €120; triples €150-165; quads €190. Cash only. ❷

**Aivergo Youth Hostel,** Spuistr. 6 (☎421 3670). An Arabian Nights theme permeates huge, perfectly clean dorm rooms decorated co-ed dorms. Free lockers and Internet access. Dorms €25-40; 1 double €60. Cash only. ❶

**Hotel The Crown,** Oudezijds Voorburgwal 21 (☎626 9664; www.hotelthe-crown.com). Handsome digs in a fun, if at times rowdy, environment. Loads of British tourists stay here for its convenience to the action. Beds €40-55 per person in rooms that sleep 1-3 people; rooms with hall showers €10 less. AmEx/MC/V. ❷

**Bob's Youth Hostel,** Nieuwezijds Voorburgwal 92 (☎623 0063). Provides bare-bones necessities to its backpack-toting clientele. Free luggage storage. Breakfast (eggs, toast, and jam) included. Lockers included with a €10 deposit. Linens included, but bring a towel. Key deposit €10. Min. 2-night weekend stay; max. 7-night stay. Reception 8am-3am. No reservations. Dorms €21; doubles with shared bath €70; triples with private bath and shared kitchen €90. ❶

**Durty Nelly's Hostel,** Warmoesstr. 115-117 (☎638 0125; www.xs4all.nl/~nellys). Clean, cozy hostel above its own Irish pub. Popular with young travelers. Breakfast and linens included. Locker deposit €10. Reception 24hr. at bar, where guests can drink after hours. Internet reservations only. Dorms €25-45. AmEx/MC/V. ❶

## CANAL RING AND REMBRANDTPLEIN

**Hemp Hotel,** Frederikspl. 15 (☎625 4425; www.hemp-hotel.com). Each room is designed and decorated according to a different cultural theme. Revel in all things hemp. Breakfast—featuring yummy hemp bread—included 11am-noon. 1 single €50; doubles €65-80. MC/V; 5% surcharge. ❷

**Nadia Hotel,** Raadhuisstr. 51 (☎620 1550; www.nadia.nl). Each well-kept, cozy room includes fridge, safe, and TV. Breakfast included. Wi-Fi. Weekday high-season singles €75; doubles €115; triples €150. Higher prices for balcony or rooms with canal views and on weekends. AmEx/MC/V. ❸

**City Hotel,** Utrechtsestr. 2 (☎627 2323; www.city-hotel.nl). Classy, spacious accommodations above a pub on Rembrandtpl. Popular with young travelers. Rooms and baths all immaculately kept. Breakfast included in a spacious dining room with great views. Reception 24hr. 2- to 8-bed rooms €45 per person. AmEx/MC/V. ❷

**Hotel Asterisk,** Den Texstr. 16 (☎626 2396 or 624 1768; www.asteriskhotel.nl). Beautiful hotel with friendly, professional staff. Pristine rooms with phone, safe, and TV. High-season singles €45-59, with shower or toilet €49-64; doubles €59-79, with bath €84-129; triples €99-144; quads €119-165. MC/V; 4% surcharge. ❷

**The Golden Bear,** Kerkstr. 37 (☎624 4785; www.goldenbear.nl). Amsterdam's oldest openly gay hotel. Rooms with phone, safe, TV, VCR, and DVD. Continental breakfast included 8:30am-noon. Singles from €60, with bath €105; doubles €62-132. ❸

## WEST OF TOWN

🛡 **Frédéric Rent a Bike,** Brouwersgr. 78 (☎624 5509; www.frederic.nl). 3 lived-in, homey, and cheerful rooms in the back of a bike shop—each named after a different painter. Another cheap option is to stay with Frédéric's parents in 1 of 2 rooms in their home. Reception 9am-6pm. *Chez* Frédéric's parents €35; singles €40-50; doubles €60-100; houseboats for 2-4 people €100-160. Apartments available for short-term stays from €140 for 2 people to €225 for 6. Cash only; AmEx/MC/V required for reservation. ❶

**Hotel Abba,** Overtoom 122 (☎618 3058; www.abbabudgethotel.com). Close to Leidsepl. Breakfast included 8-9:30am. Reception until 11pm. Credit card needed for reservation. Singles €35-50; twins €65-80; family-style quints €175. Cash only. ❶

**Hotel de Filosoof,** Anna Vondelstr. 6 (☎683 3013; www.hotelfilosoof.nl). Each room in this lovely hotel is dedicated to a different philosopher. Pretty garden out back and an even prettier garden (Vondelpark) just steps away. All rooms with cable TV, phone, and bath. Breakfast included. Singles €125; small doubles €108, larger doubles €175. ❺

**Hotel Van Onna,** Bloemgr. 104 (☎626 5801; www.vanonna.nl). Friendly, knowledgeable owner. Cozy rooms all have private bath. Breakfast included. Reception 8am-11pm. Singles €45; doubles €90; triples €135; quads €180. Cash only. ❷

**The Shelter Jordan,** Bloemstr. 179 (☎624 4717; www.shelter.nl). Well-run Christian hostel. No obligation to participate in any of the hostel's religious activities. Best suited for those under 35. No drugs or alcohol. Breakfast included 8-10:30am. Lockers with €5 key deposit and free storage for larger bags and packs. Linens €2. Cafe with Internet access (€0.50 per 20min.) and a piano. Max. 1-month stay. 14- to 20-bed single-sex dorms Sept.-May €18; June-Aug. €20. MC/V; 5% surcharge. ❶

# LEIDSEPLEIN AND MUSEUMPLEIN

*— clean but dumpy*

🏠 **Stayokay Amsterdam Vondelpark,** Zandpad 5 (☎589 8996; www.stayokay.com/vondelpark). Palatial, spotless hostel. Breakfast and linens included; towels €3. Internet €0.50 per min. Reception 7:30am-midnight. 12- to 14-bed dorms in high season €24; 6- or 8-bed dorms €26; doubles €80; quads €116. €2.50 HI discount. MC/V. ❶

🏠 **Freeland,** Marnixstr. 386 (☎622 7511; www.hotelfreeland.com). Happy, fresh, and well-run establishment. All rooms with DVD player and private bath; most with A/C. Breakfast included. Free Internet in lobby; Wi-Fi throughout the hotel. Singles €65-80; doubles €90-110; triples €115-130. Book early. AmEx/MC/V. ❸

**Hotel Bema,** Concertgebouw 19B (☎679 1396; www.bemahotel.com). Winning 7-room hotel with airy accommodations, a friendly staff, and a funky style. Breakfast included. Reception 8am-midnight. Singles €35-45; doubles and twins €65, with shower €90; triples €85/100; quads with shower €100-115. AmEx/MC/V; 5% surcharge. ❶

**Flying Pig Palace,** Vossiusstr. 46-47 (☎400 4187; www.flyingpig.nl). Communal, friendly attitude in a tranquil setting. Ample breakfast included. Free Internet. Reception 8:30am-9:30pm. High-season 14-bed dorms €24; 10-bed dorms €27; 8-bed dorms €29; 4-bed dorms €32; double with bath €36. For long-term stays, ask about working in exchange for rent. AmEx/MC/V. ❶

# DE PIJP, JODENBUURT, AND PLANTAGE

🏠 **Bicycle Hotel,** Van Ostadestr. 123 (☎679 3452; www.bicyclehotel.com). Clean digs and spotless bathrooms, plus a large, airy common room and leafy garden. Free parking in its bike garage and maps of recommended bike trips. Bike rental €7.50 per day. Sink and TV in all rooms. Breakfast included (served 8-10am). Free Internet and safe. Min. 3-night weekend stay. Singles €65, with bath €95; doubles €80-115; triples €95-130. 4-person canal house in the Plantage €130. AmEx/MC/V; 4% surcharge. ❸

**Luckytravellers Fantasia Hotel,** Nieuwe Keizersgr. 16 (☎623 8259; www.fantasia-hotel.com). Younger, more laid-back feel than most hotels in the neighborhood. Rooms have an eclectic, homemade design. Facilities include radios, phones, coffeemakers, and safe. Breakfast included. Singles €65-75; doubles €85-95; triples €120-130; quads and family rooms €150. AmEx/MC/V; 3% surcharge. ❸

**Hotel Adolesce,** Nieuwe Keizersgr. 26 (☎626 3959; www.adolesce.nl). Pristine, quiet, completely angst-free 10-room hotel in an old canal house. Drug-free. All rooms with sink, TV, and phone; many have sofa and desk. Breakfast included; served all day. Reception 8:30am-1am. Singles €65-75; doubles €85-95; triples €125. MC/V. ❸

# ▣ MUNCHIES

Cheap restaurants cluster around Leidseplein, Rembrandtplein, and De Pijp. Cafes, especially in the Jordaan, serve inexpensive sandwiches (€2-5) and good Dutch fare (€6-10). Bakeries line **Utrechtsestraat,** south of Prinsengr. Fruit, cheese, flowers, and even live chickens are sold at markets on **Albert Cuypstraat** in De Pijp. (Open M-Sa 9am-5pm.) **Albert Heijn** supermarkets are plentiful. Two of the most popular can be found in Dam Sq. and underneath Museumpl.

## CENTRUM

🏠 **Cafe Latei,** Zeedijk 143 (☎625 7485; www.latei.net). At this unique cafe and curiosity shop, nearly everything is for sale—even your plate. Sandwiches around €3. All-day continental breakfast €6.40. Fresh juices €2-4. Th couscous nights; call for other special events. Open M-F 8am-6pm, Sa 9am-6pm, Su 11am-6pm. ❶

## BICYCLE BUILT FOR YOU

Even if you've experienced the Red Light District or clouded yourself in smoke at all of Amsterdam's coffeeshops, you can't say you've truly done this city unless you've ridden a bike here. The red bike lanes and special bike lights, as well as the multitude of cheap and convenient rental companies, permit tourists to whiz around as if they were locals. If you're bent on remaining a tourist, you can pay for a guided bike tour or a map with one laid out, but if you're keen on blending in, you can simply pedal your way to destinations you'd planned on seeing anyway. A horseshoe-shaped path along any of the canals of the Central Canal Ring—Prinsengracht is prettiest—passes near the Anne Frank Huis, the Rijksmuseum, the van Gogh Museum, and the Heineken Brewery.

Of course you might as well take advantage of your increased mobility to explore places your tootsies wouldn't take you. Leave Amsterdam to ride along the Amstel River, glimpsing windmills, houseboats, and quintessentially Dutch rolling hills. Cycle east along green trails to the seaside town of Spaarndam (20-25km). Or, use the canals as racetracks, leaving mellow locals in the dust.

*MacBike (p. 752), Weteringsschans 2 (☎528 76 88; www.macbike.nl), in Leidseplein, rents bikes and sells reliable bike-tour maps.*

**In de Waag,** Nieuwmarkt 4 (☎452 7772; www.indewaag.nl). A high-class restaurant with stone walls and long wood tables in a weigh-house from 1488. Lunch sandwiches €5-10. Dinner entrees around €20. Open daily 10am-midnight. ❹

**Pannenkoekenhuis Upstairs,** Grimburgwal 2 (☎626 5603). Adorned with vintage photos of Dutch royalty and only 4 tables. Traditional pancakes said to be among the best in Amsterdam (€9). Open M and F noon-7pm, Sa noon-6pm, Su noon-5pm. ❷

**Ristorante Caprese,** Spuistr. 259-261 (☎620 0059). Authentic Italian food and relaxed jazz by comforting candlelight. Main pasta dishes €10-11. Meat and fish dishes €18-22. Open daily 5pm-1am. Kitchen closes at 11:45pm. ❸

**Aneka Rasa,** Warmoesstr. 25-29 (☎626 1560). Clean, relaxed Indonesian joint with very friendly staff. Popular *rijsttafel* €17-18 per person. Other main dishes €12-13. Vegetarian plates €7.50-8.40. Open daily 5-10:30pm. AmEx/MC/V. ❷

**Taste of Culture,** Zeedijk 109 (☎638 1466). All you can eat Chinese in 1hr. for only €8.50. All about the buffet, on your right as you walk in. Drinks €1.50. Plenty of vegetarian options. Open daily noon-11pm. Cash only. ❷

**Green Planet,** Spuistr. 122 (☎625 8280; www.greenplanet.nl). Diehard vegetarian restaurant with tasty Asian stir-fry (€16). Salads from €5.50; extra ingredients €2.50-4.50 each. Lots of vegan options. Open M-Sa 5:30pm-midnight. ❸

## CANAL RING AND REMBRANDTPLEIN

**Lanskroon,** Singel 385 (☎623 7743). Traditional Dutch pastries like *stroopwafels* (honey-filled cookies; €1.50), fresh fruit pies (€2.50), and exotically flavored sorbets, made on-site. Open Tu-F 8am-5:30pm, Sa 9am-6pm, Su 10am-6pm. Cash only. ❶

**NOA,** Leidsegr. 84 (☎626 0802; www.withnoa.com). Artsy, elegant restaurant that serves up a diverse menu of pan-Asian dishes. Everything on the menu €6-17. Mixed drinks €7-9. Open Tu-Th and Su noon-midnight; F-Sa noon-1am. AmEx/MC/V. ❸

**Ristorante Pizzeria Firenze,** Halvemaanstg. 9-11 (☎627 3360). Delightful little Italian restaurant and pizzeria, complete with murals of the Italian countryside, friendly service, and simply unbeatable prices. 25 types of pizza (€4.60-8) and pasta (€5.30-8). Lasagna €8.50. Glass of house wine €2.30. Open daily 1-11pm. MC/V. ❶

**Foodism,** Oude Leliestr. 8 (☎427 5103). Bright green walls, red tables, and a cozy, alternative air surround a friendly staff serving vegetarian and pasta platters (€10-13). Breakfast all day (€9.50). Open M-Sa 11:30am-10pm, Su 1-10pm. Cash only. ❷

**Hein,** Berenstr. 20 (☎623 1048). Watch fresh food prepared in the open kitchen from of the seating area. The menu changes daily, subject to the owner's tastes. Entrees average €10. Open M-Sa 8:30am-4pm, Su 9am-4pm. Reservations accepted. Cash only. ❷

**Van Dobben,** Korte Reguliersdwarsstr. 5-9 (☎624 4200). No-frills food on the go. Choose from the large selection of sandwiches under €3, including roast beef and ham. Open M-Th 9:30am-1am, F-Sa 9:30am-2am, Su 11:30am-8pm. Cash only. ❶

## WEST OF TOWN

▨ **Cafe-Restaurant Amsterdam,** Watertorenpl. 6 (☎682 2667; www.cradam.nl). Surprisingly casual and child-friendly, with a continental menu of meat, fish, and vegetable choices (€10-20) that changes seasonally. Open M-Th 10:30am-midnight, F-Sa 10:30am-1am. Kitchen open M-Th until 10:30pm, F-Sa until 11:30pm. AmEx/MC/V. ❸

**Harlem: Drinks and Soulfood,** Haarlemmerstr. 77 (☎330 1498). American Southern soul food infused with Cajun and Caribbean flavors. Dinner entrees €11-17. Open M-Th 10am-1am, F-Sa 10am-3am, Su 11am-1am. Kitchen closes 10pm. MC/V. ❸

**De Vliegende Schotel,** Nieuwe Leliestr. 162-168 (☎625 2041; www.vliegendeschotel.com). Simple, organic vegetarian food. Soups and starters from €2.50. Entrees from €9.40. Open daily 5-11:30pm. Kitchen closes at 10:15pm. AmEx/MC/V. ❷

**Peperwortel,** Overtoom 140 (☎685 1053; www.peperwortel.nl). Deli-slash-restaurant and a foodie's paradise. Rotating menu of entrees (around €9.50) like Indonesian beef or couscous and ratatouille. Open M-F 4-9pm, Sa-Su 3-9pm. Cash only. ❷

**Rainarai,** Prinsengr. 252 (☎624 9791; www.rainarai.nl). Small but special Algerian restaurant, market, and deli serves absolutely delicious food. 7 daily dishes made with fresh ingredients like quail, tomatoes, or sole. Open daily 10am-10pm. Cash only. ❶

## LEIDSEPLEIN AND MUSEUMPLEIN

▨ **Eat at Jo's,** Marnixstr. 409 (☎624 1777; www.melkweg.nl). Multiethnic, freshly prepared menu that changes daily earns rave reviews. Bands often grab a bite to eat after a performance at Melkweg. Open W-Su noon-9pm. Cash only. ❸

**Bombay Inn,** Lange Leidsedwarsstr. 46 (☎624 1784). Stands out for delicately spiced dishes at excellent value. Generous "tourist menu" includes 3 courses (chicken menu €8.50; lamb menu €9.50). Veggie sides come cheap as well (€5.50). Rice (€2.30) and other extras not included. Open daily 5-11pm. AmEx/MC/V. ❷

**Cafe Vertigo,** Vondelpark 3 (☎612 3021; www.vertigo.nl). Forgo the cafe's pricier dinner menu in favor of the filling lunch sandwiches (BLTC—C is for chicken—€5.50) and tasty snacks (spring rolls €3.50). You'd have to be psycho to skip Vertigo. Sept.-Mar. Sa disco nights. Lunch until 5pm, soups and salads available 5-6pm, and dinner 6-10pm. Open daily 10am-1am. MC/V. ❶

## DE PIJP, JODENBUURT, AND PLANTAGE

▨ **Cafe De Pijp,** Ferdinand Bolstr. 17-19 (☎670 4161). Hip and sociable restaurant in the heart of De Pijp. Good Mediterranean-influenced food is complemented by even better company. Popular tapas starter for 2 €15. Entrees €13-15. Mixed drinks €5. Open M-Th 3:30pm-1am, F 3:30pm-3am, Sa noon-2am, Su noon-1am. Cash only. ❸

**Abe Veneto,** Plantage Kerklaan 2 (☎639 2364). Dizzying selection of more than 45 freshly made pizzas (€5-9.50), pastas (€7-9.50), and salads (under €5). Wine by the bottle or the carafe (½-carafe €6.50). Takeout and delivery available to nearby hotels. Open daily noon-midnight. Cash only. ❷

**Bazar,** Albert Cuypstr. 182 (☎664 7173). Massive, high-ceilinged wonder housed in the open space of a former church. Menu features inexpensive cuisine from North Africa,

Lebanon, and Turkey. Lunch special €10 per person (min. 2 people). Breakfast (think Algerian pancakes and Turkish yogurt) and lunch start at €3.50. Reserve ahead for dinner. Open M-Th 9am-1am, F-Sa 9am-2am, Su 9am-midnight. ❷

**Eetkunst Asmara,** Jonas Daniel Meijerpl. 8 (☎627 1002). Enjoy personally prepared East African specialties (beef with assortment of mild herbs; €9) served on *injera*, a spongy bread. Vegetarian options available. Open daily 6-11pm. Cash only. ❷

**Soup En Zo,** Jodenbreestr. 94A (☎422 2243). Let your nose guide you to the amazing broth at this tiny soupery. Several soups and sizes (€2.70-6) with free bread and delicious toppings (coriander, dill, cheese, nuts). Small selection of salads under €6. The restaurant is only a takeout counter. Open M-F 11am-8pm, Sa-Su noon-7pm. ❶

# ◎ SIGHTS

Amsterdam is not a city of traditional sights—if you want to join the sweating masses in endless lines to catch a glimpse of a postcard monument, you've come to the wrong place. But don't be fooled: this city—as a collection of nearly 100 interlocking islands—is a sight in itself. Amsterdam is fairly compact, so tourists can easily explore the city on foot. For those not inclined toward pedestrian navigation, the tram system will get you to any of the city's major sights within minutes. For a peaceful view of the city from the water, the Saint Nicolaas Boat Club (www.amsterdamboatclub.com) organizes canal tours.

## CENTRUM

▨ **NIEUWMARKT.** Nieuwmarkt is one of Amsterdam's most beloved squares, lined with cafes, restaurants, markets, and coffee shops. On warm summer days, crowds pack the forum's endless terraces. Be sure to stop and to take a look at the **Waag** (the giant fortress in the center; it's hard to miss), Amsterdam's largest surviving medieval building. Dating from the 15th century, the Waag came into existence as one of Amsterdam's fortified city gates (at the time known as Sint Antoniespoort). As Amsterdam expanded, the gate became obsolete, and it was converted into a house for public weights and measures. At the end of the 17th century, the Surgeon's Guild built an amphitheater at the top of the central tower to house public dissections as well as private anatomy lessons—famously depicted by **Rembrandt van Rijn's** *The Anatomy Lesson of Dr. Tulp*. The Waag has also housed a number of other sites, including the Jewish Historical Museum and the Amsterdam Historical Museum. *(Metro to Nieuwmarkt.)*

▨ **BEGIJNHOF.** You don't have to take vows to enter this secluded courtyard in the 14th-century home of the Beguines—a sect of free-thinking and religiously devoted laywomen. The casual visitor will be rewarded with access to one of the area's more attractive sights. The peaceful Begijnhof's rosy gardens, beautifully manicured lawns, gabled houses, and tree-lined walkways afford a much-needed respite from the excesses of the Nieuwe Zijd. While there, visit the court's two churches, the **Engelsekerk** and the **Begijnhofkapel.** *(From Dam, take Nieuwezijds Voorburgwal south 5min. to Spui, turn left, and then go left again on Gedempte Begijnensloot; the gardens are on the left. Alternatively, follow signs to Begijnhof from Spui. No guided tours, bikes, or pets. Open daily 9am-5pm. Free.)* One of the oldest houses in Amsterdam, **Het Houten Huys** (The Wooden House), is located on the premises. *(☎623 5554. Open M-F 10am-4pm.)*

**RED LIGHT DISTRICT.** No trip to Amsterdam would be complete without witnessing the notorious spectacle that is the Red Light District. After dark, the area actually glows red—sex theaters throw open their doors, and the streets are thick with people gawking at lingerie-clad prostitutes pressing themselves against windows. Wall-to-wall brothels crowd **Warmoesstraat** and **Oudezijds Achterburgwal.** There are also **sex shows,** in which actors perform strictly choreographed fantasies on stage; the most famous takes place at **Casa Rosso.** *(Oudezijds Achterburgwal 106-108. ☎627 8954; www.janot.com. Open M-Th 8pm-2am, F-Sa 8pm-3am. €35, with 4 drinks €45.)*

 **FLESH PHOTOGRAPHY.** As tempting as it may be, do not take pictures in the Red Light District, especially of prostitutes. Taking pictures is considered incredibly rude and can land the photographer in trouble.

**OUDE KERK.** Located smack in the middle of the otherwise lurid Red Light District, the Old Church may be the only church in the world completely bounded by prostitution sites. Erected in 1306, the Oude Kerk was the earliest parish church built in Amsterdam, but it is now a center for cultural activities, hosting photography and modern art exhibits. At the head of the church is the massive **Vater-Müller organ,** which was built in 1724 and is still played for public concerts. The Gothic church has seen hard times, having been stripped of its artwork and religious artifacts during the Alteration. The Protestant church has since served a number of functions: a home for vagrants, a theater, a market, and a space for fishermen to mend broken sails. Today, there is still an empty, spare feeling inside the building, but the church is nevertheless one of the most impressive and prominent structures in the city. *(Oudekerkspl. 23. ☎625 8284; www.oudekerk.nl. Open M-Sa 11am-5pm, Su 1-5pm. €4.50, students and over 65 €3.50, under 12 free. Additional charge for exhibits.)*

**SINT NICOLAASKERK.** A burst of color emanates from the stained-glass windows over the impressive columned altar of this relatively new Roman Catholic church. Completed in 1887 to honor the patron saint of sailors, it replaced a number of Amsterdam's secret Catholic churches from the era of the Alteration. T The walls of the church are art themselves, lined with magnificent murals depicting the life and story of St. Nicolaas. Take time to admire its massive 2300-pipe organ. *(Prins Hendrikkade 73. ☎624 8749. Daily service 12:30pm; Su mass 10:30am Dutch, 1pm Spanish. Organ festival July-Sept. Sa 8:15pm. Contemporary and classical organ concerts occasionally Sa 3pm—call ahead. Open M 1-4pm, Tu-F 11am-4pm, Sa noon-3pm. Organ festival €6.)*

**DAM SQUARE AND KONINKLIJK PALEIS.** Next to the Nieuwe Kerk on Dam Sq. is the Koninklijk Paleis, one of Amsterdam's most impressive architectural feats. The palace is closed for renovations until 2009, but even the edifice's exterior bursts with architecture and history. The building was opened in 1655 and fully completed 10 years later. It originally served as the town hall, but it was no ordinary municipal building. In a city at the center of a burgeoning worldwide trade and governed by a group of magistrates, the town hall became the most important government building in the city. Its architect, Jacob van Campen, aimed to replace the entrenched Amsterdam Renaissance style with a more Classicist one. Across Dam Sq. is the Dutch **Nationaal Monument,** unveiled on May 4, 1956, to honor Dutch victims of WWII. Inside the 22m white stone obelisk is soil from all 12 of the Netherlands's provinces and the Dutch East Indies. Along the back of the monument, you'll find the provinces' crests bordered by the years 1940 and 1945. In addition to this reminder of Dutch suffering during the war, the monument is one of Amsterdam's central meeting and people-watching spots. *(Tram #5, 13, 17, or 20 to Dam.)*

**SPUI.** Pronounced "spow," this tree-lined, cobblestone square—perfect for quiet lounging on summer afternoons—is home to an art market on Sundays, hosts a book market on Fridays, and is surrounded by bookstores. Look out for **Het Lievertje** (The Little Urchin), a small bronze statue by Carel Kneulman that became a symbol for the Provos, a Dutch counter-culture movement, and was the site of many meetings and riots in the 1960s. *(Tram #1, 2, 4, 5, 9, 14, 16, 24, or 25 to Spui.)*

# CANAL RING AND REMBRANDTPLEIN

**WESTERKERK.** This stunning Protestant church was designed by Roman Catholic architect Hendrick de Keyser and completed in 1631. The blue and yellow imperial crown of Maximilian of Austria—the Habsburg ruler of the Holy Roman Empire in the late 15th century—rests atop the 85m tower, which has become a patriotic symbol for the citizens of Amsterdam. Rembrandt is believed to be buried here, but no one knows exactly where, so watch your step. In contrast to the decorative exterior, the Protestant church remains properly sober and plain inside; it is still used by a Presbyterian congregation. Make sure to climb the **Westerkerkstoren** as part of a 30min. guided tour for an awe-inspiring view of the city. *(Prinsengr. 281. ☎ 624 7766. Open Apr.-Sept. M-F 11am-3pm; July-Aug. M-Sa 11am-3pm. Tower closed Oct.-Mar. Tower tours Apr.-Sept. every 30min. 10am-5:30pm. €5.)*

**HOMOMONUMENT.** Since 1987, the Homomonument has marked Amsterdam as a testament to the strength and resilience of the homosexual community. Conceived by Karin Daan, its pale pink granite triangles allude to the symbols homosexuals were required to wear in Nazi concentration camps. The raised triangle points to the **COC,** the oldest gay rights organization in the world; the ground-level triangle points to the **Anne Frank Huis;** and the triangle with steps into the canal points to the **Nationaal Monument** on the Dam, a reminder that homosexuals were among those sent to concentration camps. On Queen's Day (Apr. 30) and Liberation Day (May 5), massive celebrations surround the monument. *(Next to Westerkerk.)*

**CENTRAL CANAL RING.** You haven't seen Amsterdam until you've spent some time wandering in the Central Canal Ring, the city's highest rent district and arguably its most beautiful. The **Prinsengracht** (Prince's Canal), **Keizersgracht** (Emperor's Canal), and **Herengracht** (Gentleman's Canal) are collectively known as the *grachtengordel* (canal girdle). In the 17th century, residents of Amsterdam were taxed according to the width of their homes, and houses could not be more than one plot (a few meters) wide. To encourage investment in construction, the city government allowed its elite to build homes that were twice as wide on a stretch now known as the **Golden Bend,** on Herengr. between Leidsegr. and Vijzelstr. Across the Amstel is the **Magere Brug** (Skinny Bridge), which sways precariously above the water. It is the oldest of the city's many pedestrian drawbridges and the only one still operated by hand.

**REMBRANDTPLEIN.** Rembrandtpl. proper is a grass rectangle surrounded by scattered flower beds, criss-crossed by pedestrian paths, and populated with half-dressed locals lazing about (when weather permits, of course). A bronze likeness of the famed master **Rembrandt van Rijn** and a 3D version of his famous painting *Night Watch* overlook the scene. By night, Rembrandtpl. competes with Leidsepl. for Amsterdam's hippest nightlife and partygoers, with a particularly rich concentration of GLBT hot spots in the area. South and west of the square lies **Reguliersdwarsstraat,** dubbed by locals as "the gayest street in Amsterdam." *(In the northeast corner of the Canal Ring, just south of the Amstel.)*

## LEIDSEPLEIN AND MUSEUMPLEIN

■**VONDELPARK.** With meandering walkways, green meadows, and several ponds, this leafy park—the largest within the city center—is a lovely meeting place. In addition to a few good outdoor cafes, Vondelpark has an open-air theater where visitors can enjoy free music and dance concerts Thursday through Sunday during the summer. Every Friday, you can meet up with about 350-600 in-line skaters at 8pm by the Filmmuseum for a group skate through Amsterdam. For the less daring, try wandering around the hexagonally shaped, beautifully maintained rose gardens. There's also a special children's play area toward the center of the grounds. *(In the southwestern corner of the city, outside the Singelgr. www.vondelpark.org. Theater ☎ 673 1499; www.openluchttheater.nl.)*

**LEIDSEPLEIN.** Leidsepl. is a crush of cacophonous street musicians, blaring neon lights, and clanging trams. Daytime finds the square packed with countless shoppers, smokers, and drinkers lining the busy sidewalks. When night falls, tourists flock to the square. A slight respite from the hordes is available just east of Leidsepl. along Weteringschans at **Max Euweplein.** The square sports an enormous chess board with oversized pieces. One of Amsterdam's more bizarre public spaces, it is notable both for the tiny park across the street (where bronze iguanas provide amusement) and for the motto inscribed above its pillars: *Homo sapiens non urinat in ventum* ("a wise man does not pee into the wind").

## DE PIJP, JODENBUURT, AND PLANTAGE

■**HORTUS BOTANICUS.** With over 4000 species of plants, this outstanding botanical garden is a terrific place to get lost. Visitors can wander past lush palms, flowering cacti, and working beehives or stroll through simulated ecosystems, a rock garden, a rosarium, an herb garden, a three-climate greenhouse, and a butterfly room. Many of its more exceptional specimens, including a smuggled Ethiopian coffee plant whose clippings spawned the Brazilian coffee empire, were gathered during the 17th and 18th centuries by members of the Dutch East India Company. *(Plantage Middenlaan 2A. ☎ 638 1670; www.dehortus.nl. Open Feb.-June and Sept.-Nov. M-F 9am-5pm, Sa-Su 10am-5pm; July-Aug. M-F 9am-9pm, Sa-Su 10am-9pm; Dec.-Jan. M-F 9am-4pm, Sa-Su 10am-4pm. Guided tours in English Su 2pm €1. €6, ages 5-14 and seniors €3. Cafe open M-F 10am-5pm, Sa-Su 11am-5pm; in summer also daily 6-9pm.)*

**HEINEKEN EXPERIENCE.** Heineken stopped producing here in 1988 and has turned the place into a corporate altar devoted to their green-bottled beer. Visitors guide themselves past holograms, virtual reality machines, and other multimedia treats that inform you of more than you ever needed to know about the Heineken corporation and beer production. Some of the attractions can get absurd, but you'll eventually go along with it and have fun—after a few drinks. A visit includes three beers or soft drinks and a souvenir, all of which is in itself well worth the price of admission. To avoid the crowds, come before 11am and take your alcohol before noon like the real fans do. *(☎ 523 9666; www.heinekenexperience.com. Open in*

**TIME:** Most of the day, but you won't notice.

**SEASON:** Year-round.

Amsterdam's army of coffee shops can be overwhelming to even the most experienced toker. Here is a tour offering a sampling of the city's best coffee shops, munchies, and psychedelic sights. By the end of the tour, you're guaranteed to be stoned and even a bit more cultured—but mostly just stoned.

**1. BARNEY'S.** Wake and bake, sunshine! Stoners can start the day with Barney's—they have a long trek ahead—and tuck into a hearty breakfast of bacon, eggs, sausages, and toast while smoking their favorite weed. Barney's has received the Cannabis Cup (an award for best weed strain) numerous times (p. 774).

**2. ELECTRIC LADYLAND.** On the left side of the street, this "First Museum of Fluorescent Art" will befuddle the already-boggled mind. Hippie soulmate/owner Nick Padalino will guide visitors through this collection of fluorescent sculptures, minerals, and everyday objects (p. 770).

**3. ABRAXAS.** The so-inclined can top off their breakfast with a refreshing hash smoothie. Mellow mood lighting and mosaics make this an enjoyable place to rest. The drink will fortify the venturer for the long, perplexing walk ahead.

**4. VONDELPARK.** Fatigued tokers can take a break and relish the park's soft greenery with other locals who come here to relax—or else marvel at the hilarious street performers (p. 765).

**5. VAN GOGH MUSEUM.** The stoned will stare at the swirling textures of Van Gogh's masterpieces and chill out in this breezy, bright space. Be warned, though! The sunflowers may look a little strange, and the birds in *Wheatfield with Crows* may seem a bit sinister (p. 770).

**6. BOAT TOUR.** Tour boats will take customers on a relaxing, immobile, delightfully touristy journey through the Jordaan's winding canals and eventually deposit them at the departure point on Singelgracht outside the Rijksmuseum. With one ticket, you can access tour boats for the entire day without another charge.

**7. DAMPKRING.** Those looking for a high may enjoy this coffee shop, one of the city's classiest. Users choose from 10 pre-rolled joints and relax in a deep blue and golden orange space. Those whose brains have been addled by the day can ask the expert staff for help (p. 773).

**8. CANNABIS COLLEGE.** Stoners learn everything they've ever wanted to know about the stuff they're smoking—including effects, medicinal uses, and political dimensions—in the company of some hard-core cannabis lovers. Best of all, it's free (p. 769).

**9. TASTE OF CULTURE.** Munchies starting to kick in? You may be ready for this restaurant's hearty challenge: all you can eat in 1hr. for only €8.50. Greasy Chinese food in all its glory will level diners out for the stumble to the last coffee shop stop (p. 760).

**10. GREY AREA.** Your last smoke of the day! This tiny shop has a big following. Grey Area has sold great stuff for years—they have received more than 20 awards at the Cannabis Cup since 1996 (p. 773). Those ready to pass out by now can trip on home to their comfy beds; otherwise, this tour leaves its attendees near some of the city's best nightlife. Only minutes away, **Club NL** plays trance music that matches your heightened state (p. 775). Farther out, in the Jordaan, **Café 't Smalle** is ideal for a mellow night of drinks (p. 776).

**STONER'S TOUR OF AMSTERDAM**

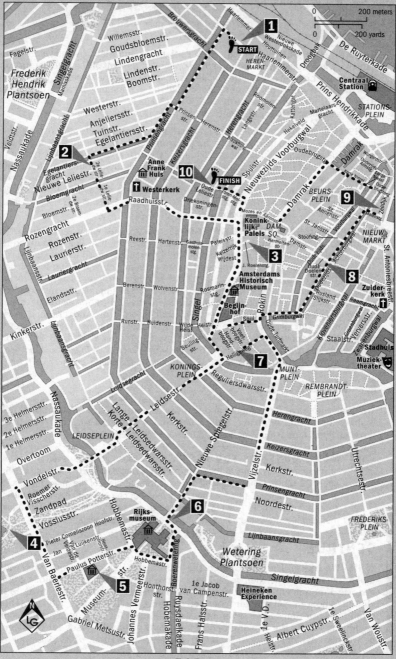

*summer daily 10am-7pm, last entry at 5:45pm; otherwise Tu-Su 10am-6pm, last entry at 5pm. Under 18 must be accompanied by a parent. €11. MC/V.)*

**HOLLANDSCHE SCHOUWBURG.** Now a poignant memorial to Amsterdam's Holocaust victims, Hollandsche Schouwburg opened at the end of the 19th century as a Dutch theater on the edge of the old Jewish quarter. A stone monument now occupies the space where the theater's stage used to be. A memorial room reminds visitors of the extraordinary toll of WWII. *(Plantage Middenlaan 24. ☎531 0430; www.hollandscheschouwburg.nl. Open daily 11am-4pm; closed on Yom Kippur. Free.)*

**ARTIS ZOO.** Artis is the oldest zoo and park in the Netherlands; it is also a zoological museum, a museum of geology, an aquarium, and a planetarium. A day of good weather is enough to make the Artis complex worth a visit. The zoo's got all the big guns: a polar bear, several massive gorillas, elephants, giraffes, a whole building full of scary bugs, and hundreds of free-roaming schoolchildren—be careful not to trip over any as you stroll the grounds. *(Plantage Kerklaan 38-40. ☎523 3400; www.artis.nl. Open daily 9am-5pm, during daylight saving time 9am-6pm. €18, ages 3-9 €14, seniors €17, under 3 free. Guidebooks €2.50. AmEx/MC/V.)*

**PORTUGEES-ISRAELIETISCHE SYNAGOGE.** Amsterdam's early Sephardic Jewish community, mainly refugees fleeing religious persecution in Spain, founded this large synagogue, known as the Esnoga (the Portuguese word for synagogue), in 1675. One of the few tangible remnants of Amsterdam's once-thriving Jewish community, the synagogue features a plain but beautiful *chuppah* (a Jewish wedding canopy). The large worship hall is free to walk through and features massive brass candelabras and an architectural style similar to the arches of Amsterdam's canal houses. A video presentation gives some background on Amsterdam's Jewish community as an introduction to your visit. Just after you leave, take a look at **The Dockworker,** a bronze statue just behind the synagogue. *(Mr. Visserpl. 1-3. ☎624 5351; www.esnoga.com. Open Apr.-Oct. M-F and Su 10am-4pm; Nov.-Mar. M-Th and Su 10am-4pm, F 10am-3pm. €6.50, students, seniors, and Museumjaarkaart holders €5, under 17 €4.)*

# 🏛 MUSEUMS

Whether you crave Rembrandts and van Goghs, cutting-edge photography, WWII history, or sexual oddities, Amsterdam has a museum for you. The useful www.amsterdammuseums.nl has info for easy planning.

> **TIP** **MORE MUSEUMS FOR LESS.** Visitors planning to see even a handful of museums may want to invest in a ▨ **Museumjaarkaart.** The pass (€35, under 25 €20) entitles the holder to admission at most of the major museums in the Netherlands. Cards are good for a year, but can be worth it even for those staying one week. To buy the pass, bring a passport photo to a participating museum. For more info, check the Dutch-only www.museumjaarkaart.nl.

## CENTRUM

▨ **NIEUWE KERK.** The New Church, the extravagant 15th-century brick-red cathedral at the heart of the Nieuwe Zijd, now serves a triple role as a religious edifice, historical monument, and art museum. **Commemorative windows** are given to the church to honor royal inaugurations and other events. The church, which has been rebuilt several times after several fires, is still used for royal inaugurations and weddings. Check the website before you go; the church closes for two weeks between art exhibits. *(Adjacent to Dam Sq., beside Koninklijk Paleis. ☎638 6909; www.nieu-*

*wekerk.nl. Open daily 10am-5pm. Organ recitals June-Sept. Th 12:30pm, Su 8pm. Call ahead for exact times. €8, 6-15 and seniors €6.)*

■ **AMSTERDAMS HISTORISCH MUSEUM.** Even though nothing beats a walk around the city itself, this archival museum offers an eclectic introduction to Amsterdam's historical development by way of ancient archaeological findings, medieval manuscripts, Baroque paintings, and multimedia displays. The section of the museum that features artistic accounts of gory Golden Age anatomy lessons is particularly interesting. Catch one of the Historical Museum's hidden surprises: in the covered passageway between the museum and the Begijnhof, there is an extensive collection of large 17th-century paintings of Amsterdam's civic guards. *(Kalverstr. 92 and Nieuwezijds Voorburgwal 357. ☎ 523 1822; www.ahm.nl. Open M-F 10am-5pm, Sa-Su 11am-5pm; closed Queen's Day. €7, 6-16 €3.50, seniors €5.30.)*

■ **MUSEUM AMSTELKRING "ONS' LIEVE HEER OP SOLDER".** The continued persecution of Catholics after the Alteration led Jan Hartmann, a wealthy Dutch merchant, to build this secret church in 1663. The chapel is housed in the attics of three separate canal houses and includes a fantastic 18th-century Baroque altar. The large antique organ, designed especially for this secret church's unique situation in 1794, is equally impressive. Small exhibitions and period rooms re-create life during the Dutch Reformation, embellished by the museum's collection of Dutch painting and antique silver. The church is still active, holding mass six times per year and performing marriages on request; check the website for information on either. *(Oudezijds Voorburgwal 40, at Heintje Hoeksstg. ☎ 624 6604; www.opsolder.nl. Open M-Sa 10am-5pm, Su and holidays 1-5pm. €7, students €5, 5-18 €1, under 5 free.)*

■ **CANNABIS COLLEGE.** If weed piques your interest, your best bet is this staggeringly informative non-academic think tank. The staff of volunteers is unbelievably friendly, knowledgeable, and eager to answer any questions. If you think you're enough of an expert and want to spread your reefer know-how, don't be afraid to ask about lending a hand. *(Oudezijds Achterburgwal 124. ☎ 423 4420; www.cannabiscollege.com. Open daily 11am-7pm. Free.)*

**AMSTERDAM SEX MUSEUM.** This almost requisite museum will disappoint only those looking for a sophisticated examination of sexuality. The first of four floors features some amusing life-size mannequins of pimps, prostitutes, and even a flasher. The museum features such ancient artifacts as a stone phallus from the Roman age, but the exhibits are hardly informative; the majority is composed of photograph after photograph of sexual acts, some more familiar than others. The gallery of fetishes is not for the weak of stomach. *(Damrak 18. ☎ 622 8376; www.sexmuseumamsterdam.nl. Open daily 10am-11:30pm. €3.)*

# CANAL RING AND WEST OF TOWN

■ **ANNE FRANK HUIS.** In 1942, the Nazis began deporting all Jews to ghettos and concentration camps, forcing Anne Frank's family and four other Dutch Jews to hide in the *achterhuis*, or annex, of this warehouse on the Prinsengracht. All eight refugees lived in this secret annex for two years, during which time Anne penned her diary. Displays of various household objects, text panels mounted with pages from the diary, and video footage of the rooms as they looked during WWII give some sense of life in that tumultuous time. The original bookcase used to hide the entrance to the secret annex remains, cracked open for visitors to pass through. The endless line stretching around the corner attests to the popularity of the Anne Frank Huis, but it is not as long before 10am and after 7pm. *(Prinsengr. 267. ☎ 556 7100; www.annefrank.nl. Open daily Apr.-Aug. 9am-9pm; Sept.-Mar. 9am-7pm; closed on Yom Kippur. Last entry 30min. before closing. €6.50, 10-17 €3, under 10 free.)*

**MUSEUM VAN LOON.** The Museum Van Loon provides an exciting look at the history of Amsterdam. Built in 1672, the house eventually fell into the hands of the Van Loon family. Their portraits, along with the family crest commemorating their connection with the East Indies, adorn the walls of this exquisite residence. Numerous other heirlooms and antique furniture decorate each room. *(Keizersgr. 672, between Vijzelstr. and Reguliersgr. ☎624 5255; www.museumvanloon.nl. Open Sept.-June F-M 11am-5pm; July-Aug. daily 11am-5pm. €5, students €4, under 12 free.)*

**FOAM PHOTOGRAPHY MUSEUM.** Housed in a traditional canal house, the Foam Photography Museum fearlessly explores every aspect of modern photography. All genres of the photographed image are welcome here, regardless of message or content. The museum hosts as many as 20 exhibits per year. *(Keizersgr. 609. ☎551 6500; www.foam.nl. Open daily 10am-5pm. €6, students with ID €5.)*

**BIJBELS MUSEUM.** Inside two canal houses, this museum presents information on both the contents and history of the Bible and the cultural context in which it was written. Opened in 1851 with a display of the ancient Israeli Tabernacle, it includes the first Bible ever printed in the Netherlands. The house is a monument in itself, containing artistic designs that demonstrate the Bible's influence on culture and society. *(Herengr. 366-368. ☎624 2436; www.bijbelsmuseum.nl. Open M-Sa 10am-5pm, Su 11am-5pm. €6, students and children 13-18 €3, under 13 free.)*

**DE APPEL.** Anything goes at De Appel, which showcases and develops contemporary art from around the world. The first museum to show video art in the Netherlands, De Appel is now a testing ground for the newest, most daring multimedia installations. *(Nieuwe Spiegelstr. 10. ☎622 5215; www.deappel.nl. Open Tu-Su 11am-6pm. €4. Tu programs 8pm €5.)*

**ELECTRIC LADYLAND: THE FIRST MUSEUM OF FLUORESCENT ART.** Knowledgeable owner Nick Padalino has collected a singularly impressive assortment of fluorescent objects from the mines of New Jersey to the heights of the Himalayas. A visit to the museum is essentially a private tour with the endearingly eccentric and passionate owner. *(2e Leliedwarsstr. 5, off Prinsengr. between Bloemgr. and Egelantiersgr. ☎420 3776; www.electric-lady-land.com. Open Tu-Sa 1-6pm. €5, under 12 free.)*

## MUSEUMPLEIN

**▓VAN GOGH MUSEUM.** For better or for worse, the van Gogh Museum is one of Amsterdam's biggest cultural tourist attractions. You'll find the shortest wait if you show up around 10:30am or after 4pm. You'll find the permanent collection, including the meat of the museum, the van Gogh masterpieces, on the first floor. The second floor is home to a study area with web consoles and a small library, while the third floor houses a substantial collection of important 19th-century art by Impressionist, post-Impressionist, Realist, and Symbolist painters and sculptors. The partially subterranean exhibition wing is the venue for the museum's top-notch traveling exhibitions. *(Paulus Potterstr. 7. ☎570 5252; www.vangoghmuseum.nl. Open Sa-Th 10am-6pm, F 10am-10pm. €10, 13-17 €2.50, under 12 free. Audio tours €4. AmEx/MC/V; min. €25.)*

---

**TIP** **TGIF.** The Rijksmuseum and the van Gogh Museum are open until 10pm on Fridays, but the tourist hordes seem to spend that time somewhere else. Take advantage for some personal moments with the world's greatest painters.

---

**▓RIJKSMUSEUM AMSTERDAM.** Even though the main building of the museum is closed for renovations, the Rijksmuseum is still a mandatory Amsterdam excursion. Originally opened in 1800, the Rijks—or "state"—museum settled into its current monumental quarters, designed by the architect of Centraal Station, in 1885. As the national museum of art and history, it houses masterpieces by Rembrandt van Rijn, Johannes Vermeer, Frans Hals, and Jan Steen. Of this tour-de-force collection, **Rembrandt's** gargantuan militia portrait *Night Watch* is a crowning, and deservedly famous, achievement. Equally astounding is the museum's collection of paintings by **Vermeer,** including *The Milkmaid. (Stadhouderskade 42. Visitors must enter instead through the Philips Wing, around the corner at the intersection of Hobbemastr. and Jan Luijkenstr. ☎674 7000; www.rijksmuseum.nl. Open Su-Th and Sa 10am-5pm, F 10am-10pm. Maps available at the ticket counters. €10, under 18 free. Audio tour €4.)*

**FILMMUSEUM.** As the national center for cinema in the Netherlands, the Filmmuseum's collection of films and books on film claims 35,000 titles stretching back to 1898. In addition to screening several films per day, they have occasional exhibits (€2) and maintain an information center at Vondelstr. 69. *(Vondelpark 3. ☎589 1400; www.filmmuseum.nl.)*

# JODENBUURT AND PLANTAGE

■**STEDELIJK MUSEUM FOR MODERN AND CONTEMPORARY ART.** As the Stedelijk's building on Museumpl. undergoes extensive renovations, its home until 2009 is a drab 11-story building to the east of Centraal Station. The museum has integrated its mission into the space admirably, filling two cavernous floors with exhibits of contemporary art that rotate every three months. These pieces, none of which predate 1968, are sometimes interspersed with masterpieces from the museum's extensive permanent collection of avant-garde and contemporary art. *(Oosterdokskade 5. ☎573 2745, recorded info 573 2911; www.stedelijk.nl. Open daily 11am-6pm. €9; 7-16, over 65, and groups of 15+ €4.50; under 7 free; families €23.)*

**JOODS HISTORISCH MUSEUM.** In the heart of Amsterdam's traditional Jewish neighborhood, the Jewish Historical Museum links four different 17th- and 18th-century Ashkenazi synagogues with glass and steel connections. Through exhibits by Jewish artists and galleries of historically significant Judaica, the museum presents the Netherlands's most comprehensive picture of Jewish life. *(Jonas Daniel Meijerpl. 2-4. ☎531 0310; www.jhm.nl. Open F-W 11am-5pm, Th 11am-9pm; closed on Yom Kippur. Free audio tour. €7.50, seniors and ISIC holders €4.50, ages 13-17 €3, under 13 free.)*

**MUSEUM HET REMBRANDT.** Dutch master Rembrandt van Rijn's house at Waterloopl. has become the happy home of the artist's impressive collection of 250 etchings. In the upstairs studio, Rembrandt produced some of his most important works. On display are some of his tools and plates, including an original pot he used to mix paint. *(Jodenbreestr. 4, at the corner of Oude Schans. ☎520 0400; www.rembrandthuis.nl. Open daily 10am-5pm. €8, students €5.50, ages 6-15 €1.50, under 6 free.)*

**VERZETSMUSEUM.** The Resistance Museum uses a wide variety of media and presentations to illustrate life under the Nazi occupation and the steps the Dutch took to oppose the German forces. Displays allow visitors to track the occupation and resistance chronologically, ending with an enlightening exhibit on post-war Dutch regeneration. *(Plantage Kerklaan 61. ☎620 2535; www.verzetsmuseum.org. Open Sa-M noon-5pm, Tu-F 10am-5pm, public holidays noon-5pm. €5.50, ages 7-15 €3, under 7 free. Tour of neighborhood available by phone or email appointment; €9 per person.)*

# GREATER AMSTERDAM

■**COBRA MUSEUM.** This museum pays tribute to the 20th-century CoBrA art movement: the name is an abbreviation of the capital cities of the group's founding members (Copenhagen, Brussels, and Amsterdam). The beautiful, modern museum effectively presents a range of the movement's work from Karel Appel's experimentation with sculpture to Corneille's developing interest in color and non-Western worlds. (*Sandbergpl. 1-3, south of Amsterdam in Amstelveen. Tram #5 or bus #170, 171, or 172. The tram stop is a 10min. walk from the museum; after a 15min. ride, the bus will drop you off across the street.* ☎ *547 5050, tour reservations 547 5045; www.cobra-museum.nl. Open Tu-Su 11am-5pm. €7, students and seniors €4, 6-18 €3. AmEx/MC/V.*)

# ☕ COFFEE SHOPS AND SMART SHOPS

Soft drugs, including marijuana and mushrooms, are tolerated in the Netherlands. **Let's Go does not recommend drug use in any form.** Those who decide to partake should use common sense and remember that any experience with drugs can be dangerous. If you do choose to indulge in drug tourism, you must follow basic ground rules and take careful safety precautions. Never buy drugs from street dealers. If a friend is tripping, it is important never to leave his or her side. If there is a medical emergency, call ☎ **112 for an ambulance.**

> **KNOW THE LAW.** On July 1, 2008, Amsterdam will ban smoking indoors. At coffee shops, this means that you can only puff your stuff in designated smoking rooms. Add that to the list of already-mandated regulations: no advertising that a shop sells marijuana; no one under age 18 permitted; no hard drugs; no alcohol; and no aggression or disruptive behavior. Shops cannot store more than 500g of cannabis and cannot sell more than 5g to a person per day. Tokers should also know that they are personally allowed to possess up to 30g.

## COFFEE SHOPS

Amsterdam's coffee shops aren't there for the coffee. Places calling themselves coffee shops sell hashish, marijuana, and "space" goodies. As a general rule, the farther you travel from the touristed spots, the better value and higher quality the establishments you'll find. Look for the green-and-white **BCD** sticker that certifies a shop's credibility. When you move from one coffee shop to another, it is obligatory to buy a drink in the next shop even if you already have weed. While it's all right to smoke on the outdoor patio of a coffee shop, don't go walking down the street smoking a joint: it's simply not done. Not only is this an easy way for pickpockets and con artists to pick out a tourist, but locals also consider it offensive.

Coffee-shop menus have more variety than you might think. **Hashish** comes in three varieties: blonde (Moroccan), black (Indian), and Dutch (Ice-o-Lator), all of which can cost €4-35 per g. Typically, cost is proportional to quality and strength. Black hash hits harder than blonde, and Ice-o-Lator can send even a seasoned smoker off his or her head. What separates hash from weed is that, while weed is the flower, hash is the extracted resin crystals, which give a different kind of high.

**Marijuana** is a dried, cured flower whose Dutch variety is incredibly strong. Take it easy so you don't pass out. The Dutch tend to mix tobacco with their pot as well, so joints are harsher on your lungs and throat if you're not a cigarette smoker. Pre-rolled joints are always rolled with tobacco; most coffee shops also offer pure joints at up to twice the cost. A coffee shop's staff is accustomed to explaining the different kinds of pot on the menu to tourists. It is recommended that you buy only a gram at a time. Most places will supply rolling papers and filter tips—Europeans smoke only joints. When pipes or bongs are provided, they are usually for tourists. Another popular way of getting high in Amsterdam is to use a vaporizer. These devices heat up cannabis products until the hallucinogenic substances like THC become gaseous, extracting more out of the product than regular burning via cigarettes. Beware that vaporizers are very strong, and those with copper piping may release nasty (and potentially carcinogenic) copper particles.

**Space cakes**, brownies, and all members of the baked-goods family are made with hash or weed, but the drugs take longer to affect a person, producing a "body stone" that can take up to two hours or longer to start. Start off with half a serving and see how you feel after an hour or two. It's always easier to eat more later than to wait out a higher dose than you can handle. The amount of pot or hash in baked goods cannot be standardized, and it is impossible to know what grade of drugs is in them. This makes ingesting this form of cannabis much more dangerous than smoking, with which you can monitor your intake more closely.

**Amnesia,** Herengr. 133 (☎ 638 3003). Slightly larger and significantly more elegant than other coffee shops. Wide selection of drinks, shakes, or snacks. Buy 5 joints (€3-5 each) and get 1 free. For an extra treat, try the Amnesia Haze (€11 per g), a 2004 Cannabis Cup winner. Open daily 9:30am-1am.

**Kadinsky,** Rosmarijnstg. 9 (☎ 624 7023; www.kadinsky.nl). One of the city's friendliest, hippest, and most comfortable stoneries. Joints €3.40-4. Weed €7-11 per g. 20% off 5g purchases. Open daily 9:30am-1am.

**Dampkring,** Handboogstr. 29 (☎ 638 0705). Scenes from the film *Ocean's Twelve* were shot in this shop. Extremely detailed cannabis menu with 10 choices of pre-rolled joints €3.50-8. Salad Bowl weed €5 per g. NYC Diesel €8.50 per g. Open M-F 10am-1am.

**Yo Yo,** 2e Jan van der Heijdenstr. 79 (☎ 664 7173). One of the few coffee shops where neighborhood non-smokers can relax. Apple pie (€1.80), *tostis*, soup, and (normal) brownies served. All weed is organic and sold in bags for €5 or €10, with a monthly €3.50 special. Joints €2.50. Open M-Sa noon-7pm.

**Rusland,** Rusland 16 (☎ 627 9468). More than just a drug store: choose from over 40 varieties of herbal tea or refreshing yogurt shakes (€2.40). Admire the selection of handblown pipes while relaxing on the pillowed benches for an afternoon smoke. Pre-rolled joints €2.50-4.50. Especially tasty Afghan bud €7 per g. Space muffins €5. Open Su-Th 10am-midnight, F-Sa 10am-1am. Cash only.

**Grey Area,** Oude Leliestr. 2 (☎ 420 4301; www.greyarea.nl). Borrow a glass bong to smoke, or hit one of Amsterdam's cheapest pure marijuana joints (€3.50). Juice (€1.50) is also available. Open Tu-Su noon-8pm.

**Siberië,** Brouwersgr. 11 (☎ 623 5909; www.siberie.nl). Extensive menu of snacks, including *tostis*, different types of yogurt (€2-2.50), and an assortment of teas. Pre-rolled joints (€4) are especially popular. Experienced smokers can try the strong White Widow Mighty Whitey (€6.50 per g). Open M-F 11am-11pm, Sa-Su 11am-midnight.

**Bluebird,** Sint Antoniesbreestr. 71 (☎ 622 5232, www.coffeeshopbluebird.nl). At this companionable spot, the vast menu is presented in 2 thick scrapbooks that include real samples of each variety of hash and marijuana for inspection. High-quality house blend 1.4g for €13. Volcano vaporizer and bongs available. Open daily 9:30am-1am.

**Hill Street Blues,** Warmoesstr. 52 (www.hill-street-blues.nl). It's all about leisurely comfort at this busy but mellow coffee shop. Space cakes and cookies €3-5. Pot and hash €4.50-12 per g. Pre-rolled joints €3. Open Su-Th 9am-1am, F-Sa 9am-3am.

**The Dolphins,** Kerkstr. 39 (☎ 625 9162). Smoke with the fishes at this underwater-themed coffee shop. Pre-rolled joints €7. Try the White Dolphin reefer (€10 per g; pure joint €5.50) for an uplifting high. Open Su-Th 10am-1am, F-Sa 10am-3am.

**Paradox,** 1e Bloemdwarsstr. 2 (☎ 623 5639; www.paradoxamsterdam.demon.nl). More of a gallery or cafe feel than a typical coffee shop. Weed from €3.80 per g, hash from €6.50 per g. Bongs for borrowing. Beginning smokers or those looking to unwind can try a "bluff," a light joint (€2). Open daily 10am-8pm.

THE NETHERLANDS

**Barney's,** Haarlemmerstr. 102 (☎ 625 9761; www.barneys.biz). So popular that you might find yourself waiting for a table. Impressive collection of Cannabis Cup trophies behind the counter. Busiest in the mornings, when you can get big breakfasts (omelettes €8, pancakes €6.50). Pot €8-15 per g. Hash €7-13 per g. Pre-rolled joints €4-6. 2 vaporizers free of charge. Open daily 7am-8pm; food served until noon.

## SMART SHOPS

Smart shops are scattered throughout Amsterdam and peddle a variety of "herbal enhancers" and hallucinogens like **magic mushrooms ('shrooms).** Beginners usually use **Mexican** and **Thai:** they are the least potent and give a laughy, colorful, speedy high with some visual hallucination. **Philosophers' stones** and **Hawaiians** are significantly more intense and should be taken only by experienced users. A mild high is a dose of about 10-15g of fresh 'shrooms; a weak trip has 15-30g; a strong trip has 30-50g. Be sure to ask the salesperson exactly how many grams there are in your purchase. 'Shrooms will start to work around 30-50min. after ingestion, and the effects will last anywhere from three to eight hours, depending on the amount of the dose. Do not take more than one dose at a time—many first-time users take too much because they don't feel anything immediately. A bad trip will occur if you mix hallucinogens with each other, marijuana, or alcohol. Be sure that you take 'shrooms in a safe surrounding with people you know, preferably outside and during daytime hours. Don't be ashamed to tell someone if you have a bad trip. You won't be arrested, and locals have seen it all before.

■ **Conscious Dreams,** Kerkstr. 119 (☎ 626 6907; www.consciousdreams.nl). Variety of mushrooms, herbs, vitamins, "dream extracts," and herbal ecstasies. Don't hesitate to ask the staff for help. Mushrooms €12-15. Herbal ecstasy €12 for 2 servings. Open daily 11am-10pm. AmEx/MC/V for purchases over €25.

**Conscious Dreams Kokopelli,** Warmoesstr. 12 (☎ 421 7000). Perhaps the best place to begin with psychedelic experimentation. Books, gifts, pipes, and lava lamps available with an overwhelming selection of 'shrooms, oxygen drinks, fertility elixirs, vitamins, and herbs. A staff with background in neurobiology and botany on hand. Herbal XTC €12-14. Mushrooms €13-18 for a colorful variety of effects. Discuss all drugs' intensity and safety with the staff first. Open daily 11am-10pm.

**Magic Valley,** Spuistr. 60 (☎ 320 3001). Small, colorful shop also vends sex stimulants. Potent Hawaiian 'shrooms €18. Mexican (€13) and Thai (€14) less potent but still pack a punch. Ask for help from the well-versed staff. Small back section that sells bongs and souvenirs. Open Su-Th 11am-10pm, F-Sa 10am-10pm. AmEx/MC/V.

**Tatanka,** Korte Leidsedwarsstr. 151A (☎ 771 6916). Sells 'shrooms (Mexican and Thai €12; The Philosopher €15), smart drugs, grow-your-own kits, and hats and T-shirts. A selection of intricate, handmade glass pipes (€18) and glass bongs (€20). Internet access €3 per hr. Buy 4 packs of mushrooms, get 1 free. Open daily 10am-10pm.

# ♫ ENTERTAINMENT

The **Amsterdams Uit Buro (AUB),** Leidsepl. 26, is stuffed with free monthly magazines, pamphlets, and tips to help you sift through seasonal offerings. It also sells tickets and makes reservations for just about any cultural event in the city for a commission. One of the best deals you'll find in Amsterdam is the half-off tickets at the **Last Minute Ticket Shop,** part of the AUB. Visit the office for a list of same-day performances at 50% off. (☎ 0900 0191; www.amsterdamsuitburo.nl or www.lastminuteticketshop.nl. AUB open M-Sa 10am-7:30pm, Su noon-7:30pm. Last Minute Ticket Shop begins selling tickets daily at noon.) The theater desk at the **VVV,** Stationspl. 10, can also make reservations for cultural events. (☎ 0900 400 4040, €0.40 per min.; www.amsterdamtourist.nl. Open F-Sa 9am-8pm.)

**Filmmuseum,** Vondelpark 3 (☎589 1400; www.filmmuseum.nl). At least 4 screenings per day, many of them older classics or organized around a special theme. Also houses an extensive information center, with 1900 periodicals and over 30,000 books on film theory, history, and screenplays. Box office open 9am-10:15pm.

**Boom Chicago,** Leidsepl. 12 (☎423 0101; www.boomchicago.nl). English improv comedy show Su-Th 8:15pm (€20) and 2 shows per day F-Sa (€24) after a 2-course meal (appetizers from €5, entrees around €15). Open Su-Th 10am-1am, F-Sa 10am-3am.

**Concertgebouw,** Concertgebouwpl. 2-6 (☎671 8345; www.concertgebouw.nl). Gorgeous concert hall and home to the **Royal Concertgebouw Orchestra.** Hosts 650 events per year. Su morning concerts with guided tours before the performance are cheaper options (€12; tours 9:30am, €3.50). Rush tickets for persons age 26 and under from €7.50. Additional free lunchtime concerts during fall, winter and spring W 12:30pm-no tickets necessary. Ticket office open daily 10am-7pm; until 8:15pm for same-day ticketing. Telephone reservations until 5pm. AmEx/MC/V.

**Stadhuis-Het Muziektheater,** Waterloopl. (☎625 5455; www.hetmuziektheater.nl). Also known as the "Stopera," this gargantuan complex is home to the Dutch National Ballet (☎551 8225; www.het-nationale-ballet.nl), the Holland Symfonia (☎551 8823; www.hollandsymfonia.com), and the Netherlands Opera (☎625 5455; www.dno.nl). Tickets can be bought through either the box office or the AUB. Box office open M-Sa 10am-6pm, Su and holidays 11:30am-2:30pm, or until curtain (usually 8pm) on performance days. Opera tickets start at €20; ballet tickets from €15. AmEx/MC/V.

# ▓ NIGHTLIFE

**Leidseplein** and **Rembrandtplein** remain the busiest areas for nightlife, with coffeeshops, loud bars, and tacky clubs galore. Amsterdam's most traditional joints are the old, dark, wood-paneled *bruin cafes* (brown cafes). The concept of a completely "straight" versus "gay" nightlife does not really apply; most establishments are gay-friendly and attract a mixed crowd. Rembrandtpl. is the hub for gay bars almost exclusively for men.

## CENTRUM

**Café de Jaren,** Nieuwe Doelenstr. 20-22 (☎625 5771). This fabulous 2-floor cafe's air of sophistication doesn't quite mesh with its budget-friendly prices. Popular with students and staff from the nearby University of Amsterdam. 2 impressive bars serve mixed drinks and beer (€1.80-3.10). Open Su-Th 10am-1am, F-Sa 10am-2am. Kitchen closes Su-Th at 10:30pm, F-Sa midnight. MC/V.

**Club NL,** Nieuwezijds Voorburgwal 169 (☎622 7510; www.clubnl.nl). Dress to impress at this upscale club, where the beautiful flock to sip designer mixed drinks and groove to the happy house tunes of nightly DJs. Cover F-Su €5. Mandatory €1 coat check. Open Su-Th 10pm-3am, F-Sa 10pm-4am. AmEx/MC/V.

**Absinthe,** Nieuwezijds Voorburgwal 171 (☎320 6780). Whitewashed stone walls and cushioned niches are bathed in light from several disco balls. 17 varieties of absinthe available (€5-18). Open Su-Th 10pm-3am, F-Sa 10pm-4am. Cash only.

**Club Winston,** Warmoesstr. 129 (☎625 3912; www.winston.nl). Eclectic little club with a packed crowd and deceptively large dance floor. Cover varies nightly, but usually €3-7. Opening time varies, but usually daily 9pm-3am.

**Cockring,** Warmoesstr. 96 (☎623 9604; www.clubcockring.com). "Amsterdam's Premier Gay Disco." Straddles the line between a dance venue and a sex club. Live strip shows Th-Su from 1am. Special "SafeSex" parties 1st and 3rd Su of the month (€7.50, with free condoms; dress code "shoes only" or naked; 3-7pm). Men only. Cover M-W €2.50, Th-F and Su €3.50, Sa €5. Open Su-Th 11pm-4am, F-Sa 11pm-5am.

**HARD SELL.** In the Red Light District, it is not uncommon to be approached by drug pushers selling hard drugs such as cocaine and ecstasy. Remember, however, that **all hard drugs are illegal** in the Netherlands.

## CANAL RING AND REMBRANDTPLEIN

■ **Café Zool,** Oude Leliestr. 9 (☎ 065 131 8542; www.cafezool.nl). Neighborhood bar with a friendly clientele and a wonderful feel. Ask for Tim or Bas, great sources for information about Amsterdam. Open Su-Th 4pm-1am, F 4pm-3am, Sa noon-3am. Cash only.

**Arc Bar,** Reguliersdwarsstr. 44 (☎ 689 7070; www.bararc.com).Young, trendy crowd that overtakes the bar weekend nights. Mixed drinks €7.50-9. DJs spin nightly and dancing begins 6pm on the weekends. Open Su-Th 4pm-1am, F-Sa 4pm-3am. AmEx/MC/V.

**Montmartre,** Halvemaanstg. 17 (☎ 620 7622). Voted best gay bar by local gay mag *Gay Krant* 7 years in a row, but definitely straight-friendly. Popular with transgendered folks. Open Su-Th 5pm-1am, F-Sa 5pm-3am. Cash only.

**Escape,** Rembrandtpl. 11 (☎ 622 1111; www.escape.nl). One of Amsterdam's hottest clubs, with 6 bars, a breezy upstairs lounge, and a cafe on the 1st fl. Lines grow long through 2am. Beer €2.30. Mixed drinks €7.50. Cover Th-Sa €10-16, students Th €6. Club open Th 11pm-4am, F-Sa 11pm-5am, Su 11pm-4:30am. Cash only.

## WEST OF TOWN

■ **Dulac,** Haarlemmerstr. 118 (☎ 624 4265). Attracts Amsterdammers and university exchange students with its dimly lit interior, pool table, and ample nooks and booths. Entrees are priced from €7.50-17 and are half-price for student ID holders. Pint €3.50. Mixed drinks €7. DJ spins F-Sa 10pm-3am. Open Su-Th 4pm-1am, F-Sa 4pm-3am. Kitchen open daily until 10:30pm. AmEx/MC/V.

**OT301,** Overtoom 301 (www.squat.net/ot301). Frequent weekend club nights fill the basement with young, open-minded people ready to dance and have fun. Cover never more than €5. Beer €2. Check the website in advance for events and opening hours.

**Festina Lente,** Looiersgr. 40 (☎ 638 1412; www.cafefestinalente.nl). Super-charming bar and cafe that attracts a young, fashionable, and friendly crowd. Multi-level indoor space filled with books. Wine and beer from €2.50. Open M 2pm-1am, Tu-Th 10:30am-1am, F 10:30am-3am, Sa 11am-3am, Su noon-1am. Cash only.

**Café 't Smalle,** Egelantiersgr. 12 (☎ 623 9617). A bar rich with its own history. A good place in the afternoon as well as in the evening. Rightfully one of the west's most popular cafes. Wieckse Witte beer €2.50. Open Su-Th 10am-1am, F-Sa 10am-2am.

## LEIDSEPLEIN

■ **Alto,** Korte Leidsedwarsstr. 115. Vibe is subdued but the jazz is sizzling. Show up early to get a table up front or listen from the bar. Free nightly jazz (and occasionally blues) Su-Th 10pm-2am, F-Sa 10pm-3am. Open Su-Th 9pm-3am, F-Sa 9pm-4am. Cash only.

**The Waterhole,** Korte Leidsedwarsstr. 49 (☎ 620 8904; www.waterhole.nl). Shoot a round of pool with the locals over a lager (€4.20) in this eclectic live-music bar. Music varies by night, with performances ranging from reggae to classic rock. Su-W are jam nights, and Th-Sa mostly feature local bands. Music starts nightly around 8:30pm. Open Su-Th 4pm-3am, F-Sa 4pm-4am.

**Bourbon Street Jazz & Blues Club,** Leidsekruisstr. 6-8 (☎ 623 3440; www.bourbon-street.nl). A slightly older tourist crowd dances with abandon to blues, funk, rock, and soul bands. Beer €2.50. Cover Th and Su €3, F-Sa €5. Music Su-Th 10:30pm-3am, F-Sa 11pm-4am. Open Su-Th 10pm-4am, F-Sa 10pm-5am. AmEx/MC/V.

**Paradiso,** Weteringschans 6-8 (☎ 626 4521; www.paradiso.nl). In the summer, this popular concert hall hosts a full lineup of big-name rock, punk, New Wave, hip-hop, and reggae acts. After concerts, it becomes a nightclub with multiple dance halls for a variety of music styles. Concert tickets €5-25; additional mandatory monthly membership fee €2.50. M-Th nightclub cover €6, F-Su €13. Open until 2am.

**Melkweg,** Lijnbaansgr. 234A (☎ 531 8181; www.melkweg.nl). 1-stop shopping for forward-looking live music, food, film, and dance parties. Concert tickets €9.50-22 plus €2.50 monthly membership. Box office open M-F 1-5pm, Sa-Su 4-6pm, show days also 7:30pm to end of show. Check website for details.

**Weber,** Marnixstr. 397 (☎ 622 9910). Friendly bar hosts crowds of both pre-club tourists and locals. Popular spot for local musicians and artists; can get very crowded on the weekends. Beer €2.10. Open Su-Th 8pm-3am, F-Sa 8pm-4am. Cash only.

## DE PIJP, JODENBUURT, AND PLANTAGE

**▨ Kingfisher,** Ferdinand Bolstr. 24 (☎ 671 2395). Low-key and unpretentious but hipper and more stylish than its neighbors. Global beer selections €2-4. Great food, too. Mixed drinks €6. Frozen fruit smoothies €2. Club sandwiches €4.50. Open M-Th 11am-1am, F-Sa 11am-3am, Su noon-1am. Cash only.

**Chocolate Bar,** 1e Van Der Helststr. 62A (☎ 675 7672). In summer, 20-somethings lounge on sofas on the terrace, heading indoors to enjoy DJs spinning lounge music on the weekends. Mixed drinks €6-7. Open Su-Th 10am-1am, F-Sa 10am-3am. MC/V.

**Arena,** 's-Gravesandestr. 51-53 (☎ 850 2400). Club bizarrely housed in the chapel of a former Catholic orphanage. More than enough enthusiasm for someone looking for a big night out. Different theme parties every night. Cover €10-25. Open F-Su 11pm-4am.

# ▶ DAYTRIPS FROM AMSTERDAM

## AALSMEER

*Take bus #172 across from the Victoria Hotel near Centraal Station to the flower auction (Bloemenveiling Aalsmeer) and then on to the town of Aalsmeer. The first bus leaves at 5:12am. (45min.; every 15min.; 6 strips to the flower auction, 2 more to the town.)*

Really the only reason to visit Aalsmeer is the ▨**Bloemenveiling Aalsmeer** (Aalsmeer flower auction), Legmeerdijk 313. This massive warehouse and trading floor hosts thousands of traders every day representing some of the world's largest flower-export companies. Nineteen million flowers and over two million plants are bought and sold daily, with an annual turnover of almost US$2 billion. All of the flowers, often flown overnight from across the globe, go through Aalsmeer's massive trading floor, making it the largest commercial trading space in the world. Since the flowers have to make it to their final destination by the end of the day, almost all the trading is finished by 11am. To see the most action, go between 7 and 9am. The trading floor is visible to tourists via a large catwalk along the ceiling. This self-guided tour takes approximately an hour to complete. (☎ 739 2185; www.aalsmeer.com. Open M-F 7-11am. €5, ages 6-11 €3, €4 per person for groups of 15+. Guides available to hire for €75.)

## ZAANSE SCHANS

*From Centraal, take the stoptrein toward Alkmaar and get off at Koog Zaandijk (20min., €2.80). From there, follow the signs to Zaanse Schans, a 12min. walk across a bridge.*

Feel free to fumble clumsily with an oversized map while fiddling with your fanny pack, since Zaanse Schans embraces and encourages a tourist's curiosity. Most attractions in Zaanse Schans are open daily 10am-5pm in summer but only on weekends in winter. The highlights are inarguably the ☒**working windmills** at Kalverringdijk 29 and 31. For a little context, visit the lovely **Museum Zaans,** Schansend 7. (☎616 2862; www.museumzaans.nl. Open daily 9am-5pm. €5.40, ages 4-12 and over 65 €2.70, under 4 free.) Craftsmen mold blocks of wood into attractive but sadly impractical clogs at **Klompenmakerij de Zaanse Schans,** Kraaienest 4, and then sell them in the gift shop. (☎617 7121. Open daily 8am-6pm.) Follow your nose to the **Cheesefarm Catharina Hoeve,** Zeilenmakerspad 5, a replica of the original cheese farm. (☎621 5820. Open daily 8am-6pm. Free.)

# HAARLEM                                                    ☎023

Haarlem's (pop. 150,000) narrow cobblestone streets, rippling canals, and fields of tulips in spring make for a great escape from the urban frenzy of Amsterdam, but the city also beats with a relaxed energy that befits its size.

**▣❼ TRANSPORTATION AND PRACTICAL INFORMATION. Trains** depart for Amsterdam every few minutes (20min., €3.60). The **VVV,** Stationspl. 1, sells maps (€2) and finds accommodations for a €5 fee. It also sells discounted passes to museums. (☎0900 616 1600, €0.50 per min.; www.vvvzk.nl. Open Oct.-Mar. M-F 9:30am-5pm, Sa 10am-3pm; Apr.-Sept. M-F 9am-5:30pm, Sa 10am-4pm.)

**▐▐▐▌ ACCOMMODATIONS AND FOOD.** The best place to stay in Haarlem is the **Stayokay Haarlem ❶,** Jan Gijzenpad 3, 3km from the train station. Rooms are spare but cheery and clean with bath. (☎537 3793; www.stayokay.com/haarlem. Breakfast included. Dorms in high season €29; doubles €102. €2.50 HI discount. AmEx/MC/V.) Ideally located right in the town square is **Hotel Carillon ❷,** Grote Markt 27. Bright, clean rooms all have TV, shower, and phone. (☎531 0591; www.hotelcarillon.com. Breakfast included. Reception and bar daily in summer 7:30am-1am; in winter 7:30am-midnight. Singles €40, with bath €60; doubles €65/80; triples €102; quads €110. MC/V.) The Indonesian ☒**Toko Nina ❷,** Koningstr. 48, has delicious prepared foods behind the deli counter. (☎531 7819; www.tokonina.nl. Combo meals €5.80-8.80. Open M 11am-7pm, Tu-F 9:30am-7pm, Sa 9:30am-6pm, Su 1-6pm. Cash only.) **Fortuyn ❸,** Grote Markt 23, is one of the smaller *grandcafes* in Grote Markt, so the service is a little more personal. Sandwiches (€5-8) and snacks are served until 5pm, dinner (€18-23) until 10pm. (☎542 1899; www.grandcafefortuyn.nl. Open Su-W 10am-midnight, Th-Sa 10am-1am. Cash only.)

**◪ SIGHTS.** The action in Haarlem centers on Grote Markt, its vibrant main square. Its main attraction is the ☒**Grote Kerk,** whose interior glows with light from the enormous stained-glass windows and houses the splendid, mammoth Müller organ, once played by both Handel and Mozart. Also known as St. Bavo's, it holds many historical artifacts and the graves of Jacob van Ruisdael, Pieter Saenredam, and Frans Hals. (☎553 2040; www.bavo.nl. Open Nov.-Feb. M-Sa 10am-4pm, Mar.-Oct. Tu-Sa 10am-4pm. €2, children €1.30. Guided tours by appointment €0.50. Organ concerts Tu 8:15pm, June-Sept. also Th 3pm; www.organfestival.nl. €2.50.) These painters' masterpieces can be found in the ☒**Frans Hals Museum,** Groot Heiligland 62. Spread through recreated period rooms, the paintings are displayed as they might have been in the Golden Age. Hals's work reveals breezy casual brush strokes that are now understood as an initial move toward Impressionism. (☎511 5775; www.franshalsmuseum.com. Wheelchair-accessible. Open Tu-Sa 11am-5pm, Su noon-5pm. €7, under 19 free, groups €5.30 per person.) The ☒**Corrie ten Boomhuis,** Barteljorisstr. 19, despite its location on one of the city's most traveled thoroughfares, served as a secret headquarters for the Dutch Resistance in WWII. It is estimated that Corrie ten Boom saved the lives of over 800 people by arranging to have them hidden in houses, including her own. The mandatory one-hour tour through the house provides a glance at her moving life, but the most extraordinary sight is undoubtedly the famed hiding spot. (☎ 531 0823; www.corri-etenboom.com. Open daily Apr.-Oct. 10am-4pm (last tour 3:30pm); Nov.-Mar. 11am-3pm (last tour 2:30pm). Tours every 30min., alternating between Dutch and English; call or check the clock outside for times. Free, but donations accepted.) The **Teylers Museum,** Spaarne 16, is the oldest in the Netherlands. It feels like an oversized cabinet of curiosities, with a mammoth skull and an elephant bird egg, among others. (☎ 531 9010; www.teylersmuseum.nl. Wheelchair-accessible. Open Tu-Sa 10am-5pm, Su noon-5pm. €7, ages 6-17 €2, groups €5 per person.)

## ▣ DAYTRIP FROM HAARLEM: ZANDVOORT AND BLOEMENDAAL AAN ZEE.

A mere 11km from Haarlem, the seaside town of **Zandvoort aan Zee** draws sun-starved Dutch and Germans to its miles of sandy beaches. You can stake out a spot on the sand for free, but most locals catch their rays through the comfort of **beach clubs,** wood pavilions that run along the shore with enclosed restaurants and out-door patios. These clubs open early each morning, close at midnight, and are only in service during the summer. Nearby **Bloemendaal aan Zee** does not even qualify as a town; instead, it's a purely hedonistic collection of fashionable and fabulous beach clubs. Local club **Woodstock 69** is the granddaddy of them all, clocking in at almost 15 years old. There is a distinct hippie feel here; there are hammocks, tiki torches, a small stage, and lots of loose clothing. (☎ 573 8084.) **Bloomingdale** tends to be the favorite of most locals. (☎ 573 7580; www.bloomingdaleaanzee.com. Open daily 10am-midnight.) From Zandvoort, take a **train** to Amsterdam (30min., 3 per hr., €4.70) or Haarlem (10min., round-trip €3.20). Bloemendaal is a 30min. walk north of Zandvoort. You can also take **bus** #81 to Haarlem from both. Zandvoort's **VVV,** Schoolpl. 1, is about eight minutes from the beach and the train station. The friendly staff can provide a guide to the beaches and accommodations, a map of hiking and biking trails in nearby Kennemerland National Park, and lots of infor-mation on the city. (☎ 571 7947; www.vvzk.nl. Open Oct.-Mar. M-F 9am-12:30pm and 1:30-4:30pm, Sa 10am-2pm; Apr.-Sept. M-F 9am-12:30pm and 1:30-4:30pm, Sa 10am-4pm.)

# LEIDEN

☎ 070

Home to one of the oldest and most prestigious universities in Europe, Leiden (pop. 120,000) brims with bookstores, canals, windmills, gated gardens, antique churches, hidden walkways, and some truly outstanding museums. The ▣**Rijksmu-seum voor Volkenkunde,** Steenstr. 1, displays Incan sculptures, Chinese paintings, African bronzes, and Indonesian artifacts. In all, the collection holds more than 200,000 artifacts depicting the dress, customs, and artwork of myriad indigenous cultures. (☎ 516 8800; www.volkenkunde.nl. Open Tu-Su 10am-5pm. €7.50, ages 4-12 and over 65 €4.) The prize ▣**Museum Naturalis,** Darwinweg 2, brings natural his-tory to life through stunning exhibits of animals, plants, minerals, rocks, and fos-sils—all brilliantly explained on English and Dutch panels. (☎ 568 7600; www.naturalis.nl. Open July-Aug. daily 10am-6pm; Sept.-June Tu-F 10am-5pm, Sa-Su 10am-6pm. €9, ages 4-17 €5, under 3 free.) The ▣**Rijksmuseum van Oudheden,** Rapenburg 28, focuses on the cultures of Ancient Egypt, Greece, and Rome as well as the ancient beginnings of the Netherlands, showcasing everything from mum-mies and sarcophagi from North Africa and Europe to outstanding Dutch artifacts from the Roman Empire. (☎ 516 3163; www.rmo.nl. Open Tu-F 10am-5pm, Sa-Su noon-5pm. €8.50, 4-17 €5.50, over 65 €7.50.) ▣**Stedelijk Museum De Lakenhal Leiden,** Oude Singel 28-32, smaller than the local national museums, is housed in the former cloth hall that was vital to Leiden's economic development as one of Europe's textile centers. It provides a glimpse into the history and development of the city through masterpieces by Rembrandt van Rijn, Lucas van Leyden, and Jan Steen. (☎516 5360. Open Tu-F 10am-5pm, Sa-Su noon-5pm. €4, under 18 free.) Scale steep staircases to inspect a functioning windmill at the **Molenmuseum "De Valk,"** 2e Binnenvestgr. 1. The living quarters on the mill's ground floor have been preserved to depict the life of a 19th-century miller. A climb to the top grants visitors a sweeping view of Leiden's green expanses. (☎516 5353; http://home.wanadoo.nl/molenmuseum. Open Tu-Sa 10am-5pm, Su 1-5pm. €2.50.)

Your best bet for a bed is ◼**Hotel Pension Witte Singel** ❷, Witte Singel 80. The 7-room guesthouse the friendly owners share with their guests is elegant and clean. A series of large, well-appointed, and immaculate rooms have an excellent view overlooking Leiden's gorgeous gardens and canals. (☎512 4592; www.pension-ws.demon.nl. Breakfast included. Free Wi-Fi. Singles €44-50; doubles €64-85. MC/V; 2% surcharge.) The restaurant and cafe **Annie's Verjaardag** ❷, Hoogstr. 1A, is a favorite with locals and students. During the day, choose from a selection of salads and sandwiches (€3-9). In the evening, pick one of the reasonably priced entrees (€13-16) or just stop by for a drink and enjoy the surroundings. (☎512 5737. Open Su-Th noon-1am, F noon-2am, Sa 11am-2am. MC/V.)

**Trains** haul out of Leiden's slick, translucent Centraal Station from Amsterdam (35min., 8 per hr., €7.60) and The Hague (20min., 4 per hr., €3.10). To get to the **VV**, Stationsweg 2D, walk for five minutes on Stationsweg from the train station's south exit toward the city center. The office sells maps and brochures (€2-5) and can help find hotel rooms (€2.30 fee for 1 person, €1.80 for each additional person). Be sure to ask about Leiden's walking tours, which cover various aspects of Leiden's past. (☎516 1211; www.hollandrijnland.nl. Open M 11am-5:30pm, Tu-F 9:30am-5:30pm, Sa 10am-4:30pm; Apr.-Aug. also Su 11am-3pm.)

# THE HAGUE (DEN HAAG)                    ☎070

Whereas Amsterdam is the cultural and commercial center of the Netherlands, The Hague (pop. 480,000) is without a doubt the political nucleus. All of the Netherlands's important governmental institutions find their homes in The Hague. It's best known, however, as the world's epicenter for international law. World-class art museums (the stunning Mauritshuis in particular), a happening city center, high-class shopping, and more parks per sq. km than almost any other Dutch city combine to make the Netherlands's political hub anything but boring.

**▐▊ ▐▋ TRANSPORTATION AND PRACTICAL INFORMATION. Trains** run to Amsterdam (50min., 1-6 per hr., €9.60) and Rotterdam (30min., 1-6 per hr., €4.20) to both of The Hague's major stations, Den Haag Centraal and Holland Spoor. The **VV**, Hofweg 1, has lots of city guides, bicycle maps, and guidebooks for sale in their shop, and the desk can arrange canal, carriage, and city tours. (☎361 8888; www.denhaag.com. Open M-F 10am-6pm, Sa 10am-5pm, Su noon-5pm.)

**▐▊ ▐▍ ACCOMMODATIONS AND FOOD.** Stay OK at the ◼**Stayokay City Hostel Den Haag** ❶, Scheepmakerstr. 27, near Holland Spoor. One of the best hostels in the Netherlands, it has sparkling rooms with private baths and lots of space in which to lounge around. (☎315 7888; www.stayokay.com/denhaag. Breakfast buffet included 7:30-9:30am. Locker rental €2 per 24hr. Internet €5 per hr. Reception 7:30am-10:30pm. Special night keycard and deposit required to stay out past 1am. 4- to 8-bed dorms €26; singles €56; doubles €61-66; triples €94; quads €113. €2.50 HI discount. €2.50 weekend surcharge. MC/V.) **Hotel 't Centrum** ❶, Veenkade 5-6, has lovely rooms. (☎346 3657. Breakfast €10. Singles €35, with bath €60; doubles with bath €70; 1-person apartments €70; 2-person €85; 3-person €100. AmEx/MC/V.) ◼**HNM Café** ❶, Molenstr. 21A, has floor-to-ceiling windows, brightly colored chairs and walls, and a big bowl of Thai noodle soup

(€7) on the menu. (☎365 6553. Open M-W noon-midnight, Th-Sa noon-1am, Su noon-6pm. Cash only.) The excellent **Tapaskeuken Sally ❷**, Oude Mol-str. 61, is one of The Hague's best-kept secrets, with great tapas (€2.50-7) accompanied on Monday nights by live music. (☎345 1623. Open W-Sa 5:30-10:30pm. Cash only.)

🔲 🎵 **SIGHTS AND ENTERTAINMENT.** The opu-lent home of the International Court of Justice and the Permanent Court of Arbitration, the ◼**Peace Pal-ace,** Carnegiepl. 2, has served as the site of interna-tional arbitrations, peace-treaty negotiations, and high-profile conflict resolutions. Although the Per-manent Court of Arbitration is closed to the public, hearings of the International Court of Justice are free to attend. (☎302 4242, guided tours 302 4137; www.vredespaleis.nl. Tours M-F 10, 11am, 2, 3pm. Book 1 week ahead. No tours when the court is in session. €5, under 13 €3. Cash only.) With only two modest stories, the ◼**Mauritshuis,** Korte Vijverberg 8, is one of the most beautiful small museums any-where, with a near-perfect collection of Dutch Golden Age art. Not counting the precious selection of paintings by Peter Paul Rubens, Jacob van Ruis-dael, and Jan Steen, the museum has several excel-lent Rembrandts, including his famous *The Anatomy Lesson of Dr. Tulp.* The showstopping pieces are *Girl with a Pearl Earring* and *View of Delft,* both by Johannes Vermeer. (☎302 3435; www.mauritshuis.nl. Open Tu-Sa 10am-5pm, Su 11am-5pm. Free audio tour. €9.50, under 18 free.) Show up at the **Binnenhof,** Binnenhof 8A, for a guided tour that covers both the historic **Ridderzaal** (Hall of Knights) and the **Second Chamber of the States-General,** the Netherlands's main legislative body. Tours don't run when Parliament is in ses-sion, but if you show up early you can sit in on the proceedings. The Binnenhof's courtyard is one of The Hague's most photogenic sights. (☎364 6144; www.eerstekamer.nl or www.tweedekamer.nl. Open M-Sa 10am-4pm. Last tour 3:45pm. Parliament is often in session Tu-Th, and you can enter the Second Chamber only if you show up with a passport or driver's license. Entrance to courtyard free. Tours €5, seniors and children €4.30. Cash only.) The best reason to visit the **Gemeentemuseum,** Stadhouders-laan 41, is for the world's collection of paintings by Piet Mondrian, 280 in all, but it would be a shame not to glance at the other highlights of the collec-tion, including works by Wassily Kandinsky, Karel Appel, and Pablo Picasso. (☎338 1111; www.gemeen-temuseum.nl. Open Tu-Su 11am-5pm. €8.50, seniors €6.50, Museumjaarkaart holders free.)

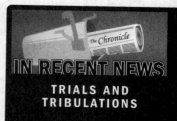

## IN RECENT NEWS

### TRIALS AND TRIBULATIONS

Charles Taylor, warlord and former president of Liberia, is set to go on trial in The Hague. He is accused of supporting rebels who committed atrocities in neighbor-ing Sierra Leone and of trafficking in guns and diamonds. The judges who will preside over Tay-lor's trial wished for the trial to occur in a more neutral place than Sierra Leone, where it could instigate instability; in The Hague, his supporters would be unable to disrupt decorum.

The Hague is the rational-choice for the trial, since it has an established practice for hosting infamous war-crimes suspects, gaining visas for involved parties, and consolidating international agencies as it is in the former president's case: Taylor will be tried under the auspices of the Special Court of Sierra Leone, held in the Netherlands, and jailed, if found guilty, in Britain.

The International Court of Jus-tice is housed in the neo-Baroque Peace Palace, which was endowed by Andrew Carnegie in the 1900s, mostly designed by French architect Louis Cordon-nier, and completed in 1913. The city itself was put on the map in 1899, when the young Nicholas II, czar of Russia, planned a disar-mament conference here. Since then, The Hague has held interna-tional courts and weapons confer-ences, and has ushered in a tradition of world leaders assem-bling in support of peace.

In late June, The Hague hosts what the Dutch hail as the largest free public pop concert in Europe, **Parkpop**, on 3 big stages in Zuiderpark. (☎ 523 9064; www.parkpop.nl.) At other times, experimental theater, opera, jazz and blues, world-class classical ensembles, indie music, and modern dance all find a home at the **Theater aan het Spui**, Spui 187. (Ticket office ☎ 880 0333, main office 880 0300; www.theateraanhetspui.nl. Closed late June-Aug. Ticket office open Tu-Sa 11am-6pm.) For a cozy, pleasant bar, ■**De Paas**, Dunne Bierkade 16A, has 11 unusually good beers on tap, 170 or so more available in bottles, and about as many friendly faces around the bar. (☎ 360 0019; www.depaas.nl. Beer from €1.70. Open Su-Th 3pm-1am; F-Sa 3pm-1:30am. Cash only.)

■ **DAYTRIP FROM THE HAGUE: DELFT.** Lilied canals and stone footbridges still line the streets of picturesque Delft (pop. 100,000). Delft is famously the birthplace of the 17th-century Dutch painter **Johannes Vermeer** and the home of the famous blue-and-white ceramic pottery known as ■**Delftware.** The best of the three factories that produce it is **De Candelaer**, Kerkstr. 13. This smallest and most centrally located Delftware factory makes the stuff from scratch, and visitors can listen to a free explanation of the process. (☎ 213 1848; www.candelaer.nl. Open daily 9am-6pm. Will ship to the US. AmEx/MC/V.) William of Orange, father of the Netherlands, used ■**Het Prinsenhof,** St. Agathapl. 1, as his headquarters during the Dutch resistance to Spain in the 16th century. In 1584, an assassin killed William on this spot. The gorgeous old building now houses a museum chronicling his life as well as a collection of paintings, Delftware, and other artifacts from the Dutch Golden Age. (☎ 260 2358; www.prinsenhof-delft.nl. Open Tu-Sa 10am-5pm, Su 1-5pm. €5, 12-16 €4, under 12 free.) Admire the 27 stained-glass windows at the ■**Oude Kerk,** Heilige Geestkerkhof 25. The three antique organs are worth an examination, and the church is also Vermeer's final resting place. Its tower is approximately 75m high and leans a staggering—and slightly unnerving—1.96m out of line. (☎ 212 3015; www.oudekerk-delft.nl. Open Apr.-Oct. M-Sa 9am-6pm; Nov.-Mar. M-F 11am-4pm, Sa 10am-5pm. Entrance to both Nieuwe Kerk and Oude Kerk €3, 3-12 €1.50, seniors €2.) You can catch the **train** to either of the two train stations in The Hague (8min., €2) or to Amsterdam (1hr., €9). The **Tourist Information Point,** Hippolytusbuurt 4, has free **Internet** terminals as well as free maps and information on sights and events. (☎ 215 4015; www.delft.nl. Open Su-M 10am-4pm, Tu-F 9am-6pm, Sa 9am-5pm.)

# ROTTERDAM ☎ 010

Marked by a razor-sharp skyline, countless steamships, and darting high-speed trains, Rotterdam (pop. 590,000) is the busiest port in Europe. It's also the country's most exciting multicultural capital, with the largest traditional immigrant population in the Netherlands. Festivals, art galleries, and extremely dynamic nightlife make Rotterdam a busy center of cultural activity and the hippest, most up-and-coming city in the Netherlands.

■■ **TRANSPORTATION AND PRACTICAL INFORMATION. Trains** roll out of Rotterdam Centraal to Amsterdam (1¼hr., 1-5 per hr., €13) and The Hague (30min., 1-4 per hr., €4.20). Rotterdam has a network of buses, trams, and two Metro lines (**Calandlijn** and **Erasmuslijn**) that intersect in the center of the city at Beurs station. Metro tickets are equivalent to two strips and are valid for two hours. The **VVV,** Coolsingel 5, has free maps of public transportation as well as maps of the city. (☎ 0900 271 0120, €0.40 per min.; from abroad 414 0000; www.vvvrotterdam.nl. Open M-Th 9:30am-6pm, F 9:30am-9pm, Sa 9:30am-5pm.) Also stop by the student-oriented ■**Use-it Rotterdam,** Conradstr. 2. (☎ 240 9158; www.use-it.nl.)

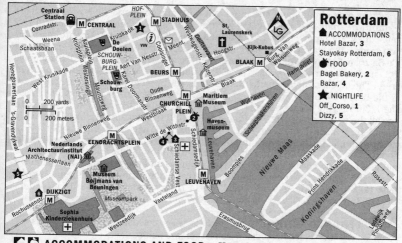

## ACCOMMODATIONS AND FOOD.

Knowledgeable staff and clean, comfortable rooms help create a pleasant and relaxed air at the **Stayokay Rotterdam ❶**, Rochussenstr. 107-109. In April 2008, this location will shut its doors but will reopen in a series of the famed cube houses, at Overblaak 85-87, taking its comfort and convenience into the trendiest of Rotterdam's architectural attractions. (☎436 5763; www.stayokay.com/rotterdam. Internet €5 per hr. Reception 24hr. Dorms €23; singles €40-45; doubles €56-65. €2.50 HI discount. AmEx/MC/V.) If you're tired of Europe, you can escape to the Middle East, Africa, or South America at the **Hotel Bazar ❸**, Witte de Withstr. 16. Each of the 27 hip, well-decorated rooms has a bath and TV. (☎206 5151; www.hotelbazar.nl. Breakfast included. Check-in M-Sa 8am-11pm, Su 9am-11pm, or until the restaurant closes. Singles €60-100; doubles €75-120. Extra bed €30. AmEx/MC/V.) Its restaurant, **Bazar ❷**, attracts nightly crowds with glittering colored lights, bright blue tables, and satisfying Middle Eastern fusion cuisine. (Sandwiches €4. Special of the day dinner entree €8. Breakfast and lunch are served all day. Reservations recommended for dinner. Open M-Th 8am-1am, F 8am-2am, Sa 10am-2am, Su 10am-midnight. AmEx/MC/V.) **Bagel Bakery ❷**, Schilderstr. 57A-59A, is a popular stop for students, with artfully topped bagels in a well-lit and hip environment. In the evening it becomes more formal, with a wide range of dinner entrees. Whatever you do, don't leave without trying their delicious freshly baked *liefdesbrood*, "true love bread." (☎412 1560. Open Tu-Th 9am-9pm, F-Sa 9am-10pm, Su 10am-9pm. Cash only.) On Witte de Withstr., you can easily grab Chinese or Shawarma for under €5.

## SIGHTS AND ENTERTAINMENT.

Only the extremely ambitious should attempt to see all of the **Museum Boijmans van Beuningen**, Museumpark 18-20, in one day. On the ground floor, you'll find post-war work by artists like Andy Warhol. The second floor is home to a large selection of Surrealist paintings as well as Expressionist pieces, plus several Claude Monets and an impressive collection of Dutch and Flemish art by the likes of Hans Memling, Anthony van Dyck, Jan Steen, Frans Hals, and Rembrandt van Rijn. (☎441 9400; www.boijmans.nl. Open Tu-Sa 10am-5pm, Su 11am-5pm. €9, seniors €3.50, under 18 and Museumjaarkaart holders free. Library open M-F 10am-4pm; free with entrance ticket.) The **Nederlands Architectuurinstituut (NAI)**, Museumpark 25, boasts one of the most extraordinary designs in all of Rotterdam. The multi-leveled glass and steel construction—which traverses a manmade pool and looks out onto Museumpark—is home to several exhibition spaces, a world-class archive, and 39,500 books. Entrance to the museum grants free access to the 🏠**Sonnenveld House,** a former private mansion restored to the way it would have looked in 1933. (☎440 1200; www.nai.nl. Open Tu-Sa 10am-5pm, Su 11am-5pm. Library and reading room open Tu-Sa 10am-5pm. €8, students and seniors €5, 4-12 €1, under 15 and Museumjaarkaart holders free.) The tallest structure in the Netherlands, the popular **Euromast,** Parkhaven 20, is the best way to take in a panoramic view of Rotterdam's jagged skyline. From the 112m viewing deck, you can take an elevator to the 185m mark, where you can see all the way to Delft and The Hague. (☎436 4811; www.euromast.nl. Open daily Apr.-Sept. 9:30am-11pm; Oct.-Mar. 10am-11pm. €8, ages 4-11 €5.20.) For a dramatic example of Rotterdam's urban design, check out the unusual **Cube Houses,** Overblaak 70, on the old harbor. The tilted, yellow, cube-shaped abodes are mounted on one corner on tall concrete columns and are designed to resemble a forest. Though they've been inhabited as private homes for over 20 years, a **Show Cube (Kijk-Kubus)** is open to the public. (☎414 2285; www.cubehouse.nl. Open Mar.-Dec. daily 11am-5pm; Jan.-Feb. Sa-Su 11am-5pm. €2, 4-12 and seniors €1.50.)

---

**TIP**

**LEARNED DRINKING.** Student travelers: don't forget to ask bartenders if there is a student discount. It's almost always worth a shot.

---

The **Rotterdamse Schouwburg,** Schouwburgpl. 25, is Rotterdam's main theater venue, with over 200 performances of opera, musical theater, modern dance, classical ballet, theater, and family performances. (☎411 8110; www.rotterdamse-schouwburg.nl.) **De Doelen,** Doelen Schouwburgpl. 50, the biggest concert hall in the Netherlands, is home to the **Rotterdam Philharmonic Orchestra.** (☎217 1717; www.dedoelen.nl. Philharmonic ☎217 1707; www.rpho.nl.) Coffee shops line **Oude** and **Nieuwe Binnenweg.** At **Off_Corso,** Kruiskade 22, art exhibitions share the bill with regular dance parties. (☎280 7359; www.offcorso.nl). 🏠**Dizzy,** 's-Gravendijkwal 127, Rotterdam's premier jazz cafe for 25 years, Dizzy hosts frequent jam sessions. (☎477 3014; www.dizzy.nl. Beer €1.80. Whiskey €5.20. Open M-Th noon-1am, F-Sa noon-2am, Su noon-midnight. AmEx/MC/V.)

# UTRECHT ☎030

Smack-dab in the center of the Netherlands lies Utrecht (pop. 290,000), a mecca for both history buffs and student partiers. The swarms of fraternity boys that fill the city's outdoor cafes are a visible testament to Utrecht's status as the Netherlands's largest university town, with a student population pushing 60,000. Utrecht is also a cultural hub: visitors come here for action-packed festivals, museums, nightlife, and winding, tree-lined canals. The **Museumkwartier** boasts no fewer than seven museums in one area, rendering it a perfect choice for an afternoon walk.

**TRANSPORTATION AND PRACTICAL INFORMATION.** Take the **train** to Amsterdam (30min., 3-6 per hr., €6.40). The **VVV,** Dompl. 9, is in a building called the **RonDom,** a Visitors Center for cultural history, across from the Domkerk. Pick up a free map of the city and a complete listing of museums and sights. (☎0900 128 8732, €0.50 per min.; www.utrechtyourway.nl. Open Apr.-Sept. M-Sa 10am-5pm, Su noon-5pm; Oct.-Mar. Su-F noon-5pm, Sa 10am-5pm.)

**ACCOMMODATIONS AND FOOD.** 🏠**Strowis Hostel** ❶, Boothstr. 8, has a laid-back staff, convenient location, and unbeatable prices. This former squat feels more like a homey country villa. Rooms and bathrooms are kept very clean. (☎238

0280; www.strowis.nl. Breakfast €5. Linens and blanket €1.30. Free Internet access. Free lockers. Max. 2-week stay. Curfew M-F 2am, Sa-Su 3am. 14-bed dorms €15; 8-bed €16; 6-bed €17; 4-bed €18; doubles €58; triples €69.) The three-story **B&B Utrecht City Centre ❶**, Lucasbolwerk 4, feels like a utopian commune. For a flat fee, you get a dorm bed, 24hr. fridge access, a music corner full of instruments, and a home video system. (☎ 065 043 4884; www.hostelutrecht.nl. Linens €2.50. Free Wi-Fi. Bike rental €5 per day. Dorms €17; singles €55; doubles €65; triples €90; quads €120. MC/V.) Utrecht lacks extensive budget dining options, but cheap eats in the form of pizzerias, pubs, and sandwich shops, are on **Nobelstraat**. ◨**Het Nachtrestaurant ❷**, Oudegr. 158, has a decadent, pillow-lined cellar dining room, while the flashier clientele crowds the canal-side terrace. (☎ 230 3036. Tapas €3-6. Open M-Sa 6-11pm or later. Becomes a nightclub Sa 11pm. AmEx/MC/V.)

◨◨ **SIGHTS AND NIGHTLIFE.** Utrecht's **Domtoren**, Achter de Dom 1, is impossible to ignore: the city's most beloved landmark is also the highest church tower in the Netherlands. The 112m tower presides over the province with magnificent spires and 26,000kg of bronze bells. The brick-red **Domkerk** was attached to the tower until an errant tornado blew away the nave in 1674. During the tour, you'll learn about the history of the church and get a glimpse of the church's bells. (☎ 231 0403. Open Oct.-Apr. M-F 11am-4pm, Sa 11am-3:30pm, Su 2-4pm; May-Sept. M-F 10am-5pm, Sa 10am-3:30pm, Su 2-4pm. Free concert every Sa 3:30pm. Domtoren accessible only through 1hr. tours daily Oct.-Mar. M-F noon, 2, 4pm, Sa 1 per hr. 10am-5pm, Su 1 per hr. noon-5pm. Apr.-Sept. M-Sa 1 per hr. 10am-5pm, Su 1 per hr. noon-5pm. Domkerk free. Domtoren €7.50, ages 4-12 €4.50.) At the **Centraal Museum**, Nicolaaskerkhof 10, visitors enter a labyrinth of pavilions to experience Dutch art from Roman and medieval archaeological finds to old masterpieces to modern art. The museum oversees the world's largest collection of work by *De Stijl* designer Gerrit Rietveld, but many of these objects have been transferred to the avant-garde **Rietveld Schroderhuis**, a UNESCO World Heritage Site. It is accessible only by guided tour through the Centraal Museum, so call ahead for reservations. (☎ 236 2362 or 236 2310 for Rietveld Schroderhuis; www.centraalmuseum.nl. Open Tu-Th and Sa-Su noon-5pm, F noon-9pm. Audio tour free. €8, students €3, under 12 free.) In honor of Utrecht's religious history, the **Museum Catharijneconvent**, Lange Nieuwstr. 38, a converted 16th-century monastery, has assembled a survey of Dutch Christianity through works of visual art by artists like Rembrandt van Rijn and Frans Hals. Items from the permanent collection juxtapose with modern renditions of similar Christian themes. (☎ 231 3835; www.catharijneconvent.nl. Open Tu-F 10am-5pm, Sa-Su 11am-5pm. €8.50, seniors and students €7.50, ages 6-17 €4.50, under 5 free; families €23. AmEx/MC/V.)

The Netherlands's largest college town has nightlife to match. At ◨**'t Oude Pothuys**, Oudegr. 279, uninhibited patrons have been known to jump off the bar's terrace into the canal after a long night of festivities. (☎ 231 8970. Live music nightly 11pm. Beer €2. Open Su-W 3pm-2am, Th-Sa 3pm-3am. AmEx/MC.) A former squat turned political/cultural center, ◨**ACU Politiek Cultureel Centrum**, Voorstr. 71, hosts live music (W and F; cover €5-6), a political discussion group (M 8pm-2am), and a Sunday movie night. (☎ 231 4590; www.acu.nl. Beer €1.70. Open Su-M 8pm-2am, Tu-W 6pm-2am, Th 6pm-3am, F-Sa 9pm-4am. Cash only.) Utrecht's theater school, ◨**Hofman**, Janskerkhof 17A, is packed with students and twentysomethings throughout the week. Take advantage of student-friendly events like a free Argentine Tango night (Tu 9pm), a cocktail night with a new mixed drink every week (Th 9pm), and live music nights. (☎ 230 2470; www.hofman-cafe.nl. Beer €2. Open Su-Th 11am-2am, F-Sa 11am-3:30am. Cash only.)

THE NETHERLANDS

## DE HOGE VELUWE NATIONAL PARK ☎ 0318

At 13,565 acres, De Hoge Veluwe is the largest nature reserve in the Netherlands. Exploration through the park reveals wooded areas, moors, grassy plains, diverse wildlife, and—extraordinarily—sand dunes. The park's 36km of biking trails are its main attraction, and 1700 white bikes are available free of charge at five convenient spots in the park. (Grounds open daily Apr. 8am-8pm; May and Aug. 8am-9pm; June-July 8am-10pm; Sept. 9am-8pm; Oct. 9am-7pm; Nov.-Mar. 9am-6pm. €7, ages 6-12 €3; 50% discount May-Sept. after 5pm. Cars €6. V.) Begin by picking up a map (€2.50) at any of the park entrances or at the De Hoge Veluwe Visitors Center, known as the **Bezoekerscentrum**. (☎ 59 16 27; www.hogeveluwe.nl. Open daily Apr.-Oct. 9:30am-6pm, Nov.-Mar. 9:30am-5pm.) The world-class ◪**Kröller-Müller Museum** is tucked deep within the park's expanses, boasting an astounding 87 paintings and 180 drawings by **Vincent van Gogh**. The sprawling complex is also home to work by other early Modernist masters. The museum and its grounds—both worthy of hyperbole—should not be missed. (☎ 59 12 41; www.kmm.nl. Open Tu-Su 10am-5pm; sculpture garden closes 4:30pm. €7, ages 6-12 €3.50, under 6 free.)

**Arnhem** is a good base for exploring the park. From its rail station, trains go to Amsterdam (1¼hr., 4 per hr., €14). From Arnhem, take bus #105 to Otterloo and transfer to bus #106, a shuttle bus, into De Hoge Veluwe. (M-F 10 per day 8:03am-4:02pm, Sa 9 per day 8:03am-4:02pm, Su 7 per day 10:03am-4:02pm; €4.80 or 6 strips). Your best bet for accommodations is the **Stayokay Arnhem ❶**, Diepenbrocklaan 27, whose exceptionally clean rooms appeal to a slightly older crowd. (☎ 442 0114; www.stayokay.com/arnhem. Breakfast included. Laundry €3.50; dryer €2. Reception 8am-11pm. 6-bed dorms €23-32; 4-bed €25-35; doubles €63-90. €2.50 HI discount. AmEx/MC/V.) For food, the elegant and inviting ◪**Zilli & Zilli ❸**, Marienburgstr. 1, is one of the most popular spots in Arnhem. (☎ 442 0288; www.zillizilli.nl. Sandwiches €4.50-8.50; salads €7-12. Pasta entrees €7.50-14. Meat entrees €16-22. Lunch served 11:30am-4:30pm. Dinner served after 5pm. Open Su-Th 11:30am-1am, F-Sa 11:30am-2am. AmEx/MC/V.)

## GRONINGEN ☎ 050

Groningen (pop. 185,000), easily the most happening city in the northern Netherlands, pulses with rejuvenated spirit. Heavily bombed in WWII, Groningen rebuilt itself completely, yet unlike some other Dutch cities, Groningen managed to retain its Old World feel alongside its bland 1950s architecture. More than half of the city's inhabitants are under 35, due in no small part to its universities. As a result, Groningen is known throughout the Netherlands as a party city. **Vera**, Oosterstr. 44, bills itself as the "club for the international pop underground." This center for live music and cinema of all stripes is a not-to-be-missed party nearly every night. (☎ 313 4681; www.vera-groningen.nl. Events from €4-11. Open daily 10pm-3am, sometimes later.) **Jazzcafe de Spieghel**, Peperstr. 11, is an intimate, candlelit cafe with two bars and a large stage for live jazz, funk, or blues nightly at 11pm or later. The Monday open jazz session (10:30pm) is a tradition, and big names in jazz have been known to stop by and play impromptu sets. (☎ 312 6300. Wine €2.20 per glass. Open daily 8pm-4am.) **Dee's Cafe**, Papengang 3, has a neon-blue light scheme, rock music, and foosball and pool tables (both €0.50). Its weed and hash are grown and cut without chemicals or other additives. (www.cafedees.nl. Weed sold in €5 and €12 denominations. Space cakes €2.70. Internet access €1 per 30min. Open M-W 11am-midnight, Th 11am-1am, F-Sa noon-3am.) For higher culture, the ◪**Groninger Museum**, Museumeiland 1, presents modern art, traditional paintings, and ancient artifacts in steel-trimmed pavilions for a futuristic laboratory vibe. There are some Golden Age paintings detailing the early history of Groningen, but the point here is revolutionary design and contemporary art.

(☎366 6555; www.groninger-museum.nl. Open Sept.-June Tu-Su 10am-5pm; July-Aug. M 1-5pm, Tu-Su 10am-5pm. €8, seniors €7, children €4.)

**☒Simplon Jongerenhotel ❶**, Boterdiep 73-2, pulls in fun, young residents with its clean lodgings, rock-bottom prices, and homey feel. (☎313 5221; www.simplon-jongerenhotel.nl. Breakfast and linens included with private rooms. Free lockers with €10 deposit. Laundry €4. Reception 24hr. Lockout noon-3pm. Bike rental €6. Large dorm €13; small dorm €18; singles €33-39; doubles €50-55; triples €70; quads €100; quints €120; 6-person room €132. Cash only.) **Ben'z ❸**, Peperstr. 17, serves dishes from North Africa, Europe, and the Middle East. (☎313 7917; www.restaurantbenz.nl. Appetizers €3-4. Entrees €10-17. 5-course menu €33. Open daily 4:30pm-midnight. Kitchen open until 10pm. Cash only.)

The **train** to Amsterdam is one of the longer trips you can take in the Netherlands, and you must transfer in Amersfoort (2½hr., with an additional 30min. between trains; 2 per hr.; €27). The **VVV**, Grote Markt 25, has a friendly and enthusiastic staff that gives guided walking tours throughout the year; reserve in advance. (☎900 202 3050, €0.50 per min.; www.vvvgroningen.nl. Open M-W 9am-6pm, Sa 10am-5pm; July-Aug. also Su 11am-3pm.)

# MAASTRICHT                                                       ☎043

In a little pocket of land surrounded by Belgium and Germany, Maastricht's (pop. 120,000) strategic location has made it a hotbed of military conquest. As one of the oldest and richest cities in the Netherlands, Maastricht has a pleasingly sedate, Old World feel. The manmade **☒Caves of Mt. St. Pieter** began life as a Roman limestone quarry; over centuries, the Dutch expanded it into the world's second largest underground complex with more than 20,000 passages totaling 200km. Capable of sheltering up to 40,000 people at a time, this enormous underground labyrinth was used repeatedly as a defensive hideaway during the many sieges of Maastricht. Graffiti, carvings, and charcoal drawings from as early as Roman times cover the miles and miles of limestone. The caves average a temperature of 9°C—wear a coat or sweater. There are two entrances to the vast system of caves; the most convenient starting point is Grotten Noord, Luikerweg 71. (☎325 2121; www.pietersberg.nl. €4.30, under 12 €3.30; combination with entrance to Fort St. Pieter €5.50/3.50. 1hr. English-language tours, Apr.-June and Sept.-Oct. Sa-Su 2pm, depending on demand.) The Zonneberg Caves, Slavante 1, are more difficult to reach. (English-language tours June-Aug. daily 1:55pm—plan to arrive at the docks at 1pm. Prices same as Grotten Noord; combination boat trip and visit €10.50, children €7.20. V.) The official seat of government for the Dutch province of Limburg, the sleek **☒Province House**, Limburglaan 10, has an impressive collection of modern artwork mostly by local artists, including paintings, sculptures, and tapestries. Most famously, on February 7, 1992, the leaders of 12 European nations met to sign the **Maastricht Treaty** at the small table in the center of the Council Chamber. The historic treaty established the modern European Union, leading to a common European currency and countless internal squabbles. There is a small plaque on the table commemorating the mammoth event. (☎389 9999; www.limburg.nl. Open M-F 8am-5pm.)

The brand-new **Stayokay Maastricht ❶**, Maasblvd. 101, is your best bet for budget digs. It boasts a waterside terrace, clean rooms with bath, a small bar, and a restaurant. (☎750 1790; www.stayokay.com/maastricht. Breakfast and linens included. Towels €1.30. Internet access €5 per hr. Bike rental €11.50 per day. 6-bed dorms €21-30; 4-bed dorms €23-33; 2-bed dorms €28-40. €2.50 HI discount. AmEx/MC/V.) Enjoy a night and morning over the River Maas at the **Botel ❶**, Maasblvd. 95. This boat's tiny cabins adjoining a cozy deck room lounge are solid budget digs in this town. (☎321 9023. Breakfast €4. Reception 24hr. Singles €27, with bath €31; doubles €42/46; quads €92; 6-person room €138. Cash only.) **☒New City**

❶, Hoenderstr. 11, is the best deal in town. Scarf down hot, fresh Indonesian and Chinese dishes prepared in the kitchen right next to the seating area. (☎326 1031. All-you-can-eat buffet €7. Open daily noon-10pm. Cash only.)

A steady stream of visitors from nearby Belgium, Germany, and France endow Maastricht with a relatively high number of coffee shops. ◙**Heaven 69,** Brusselsestr. 146, doubles as a serious restaurant. (☎325 3493; www.heaven69.nl. 3 types of marijuana and 4 types of hash €7-10 per g. Pre-rolled joints €4-5. Open daily 9am-midnight. Kitchen closes at 10pm.) **Cool Runnings,** is cheery upstairs while the basement is darker, with loud music and graffiti covering literally every surface. Happy Brother weed (€13 per g), the specialty, is some of the strongest pot in Maastricht. (Jasmina pre-rolled joints €4. Pizza and hot dogs €2. Milkshakes €2.80. Open M-Th 10am-midnight, F-Sa 10am-2am, Su 2pm-midnight. Cash only.) The best bars in town are run by fraternities at the University of Maastricht: **De Uni,** Brusselsestr. 31, has evolved into an unbeatable local spot. (www.deuni.nl. Beer €1. Shots €1-1.50. Mixed drinks €2. €5 or €10 cards buy 5 or 10 beers. Open W-Th 9:30pm-2am, F-Sa 9:30pm-3am. Closed mid-July to mid-Aug. Cash only.)

**Trains** to Amsterdam (2½hr., 2 per hr., €27) leave from the station on the quiet east side of Maastricht. The **VVV,** Kleine Staat 1, sells maps (€1.30) of the city center and hefty €2.20 tourist booklets. (☎325 2121; www.vvvmaastricht.nl. Open May-Oct. M-Sa 9am-6pm, Su 11am-3pm; Nov.-Apr. M-Th 9am-6pm, Sa 9am-5pm.)

# TEXEL                                                                 ☎0222

Tucked away off the northwestern coast of the Netherlands, the Wadden Islands are an unassuming vacation destination. The islands offer excellent beaches where the sun-warmed shallows of the Waddenzee make for temperate swimming. Texel is the most touristed island, offering all the amenities of the mainland in a remote-feeling setting. The diversity of landscape here is dazzling, and its dunes, woods, heaths, salt marshes, and mud flats are all entirely bikeable. The isle's stretch of sand runs up the western coast and is divided into strands, called *paals*, which run in ascending numerical order from south to north. The most popular strands lie near De Koog, including **paal 20.** All beaches are open to the public, and the water becomes friendly to swimmers when it warms in July and August. No need to worry if the sun fails to shine, though; Texel boasts five fine museums. The **Ecomare Museum and Aquarium,** Ruijslaan 92, aims to spread the word about Texel's ecology. A seal refuge at the center houses around 30 seals per year; they are fed (to the delight of huge crowds) at 11am and 3pm. (☎31 77 41; www.ecomare.nl. Open daily 9am-5pm. €8, 4-13 €5, under 4 free.) The **Schipbreuk- en Juttersmuseum Flora,** Pontweg 141, is a wonderful showcase of almost 70 years of beachcombing. (☎32 12 30. €4, under 16 €2.50. Open M-Sa 10am-5pm. Cash only.) On the other side of the island is the quaint burg of Oudeschild, where a windmill marks the site of the **Maritiem en Jutters Museum,** Barentzstr. 21. Visitors can climb into the windmill or stroll across a constructed canal to peer into life-size replicas of smiths' and fishermen's houses from turn-of-the-century Oudeschild. Indoor displays include hundreds of letters found in bottles washed up on the Texel shores. (☎31 49 56; www.texelsmaritiem.nl. Open Sept.-June Tu-Sa 10am-5pm; July-Aug. M-Sa 10am-5pm. €5, under 14 €3.50.)

The massive **Stayokay Texel ❶,** Haffelderweg 29, is the island's cheapest and most reliable accommodations option. In addition to immaculately kept dorms and private rooms, the hostel boasts a small playground, a football pitch, a large restaurant and bar, and a lounge area filled with giant beanbags. (☎31 54 41. Breakfast and linens included. Internet access €1 per 30min. Reception 8am-8pm. Bar open 5pm-midnight. 4- to 6-bed dorms €30; 2-bed dorms from €35.) **Campgrounds** are an inexpensive and adventurous way to commune with the island's nature. Ask the tourist office about reservations. For a sit-down meal in Den Burg, walk anywhere in the center to find a bite; fresh seafood is served in most restaurants. The pub **De 12 Balcken Tavern ❶**, Weverstr. 20, in Den Burg, has a cozy *bruin cafe* feel and serves heavenly marinated or grilled spare ribs with salad and a heaping bowl of french fries (€13-14; feeds 2). Sample a shot of *'t Juttertje*, the island's popular licorice-flavored schnapps (€2.20). Weekends are busy, so reserve ahead. (☎31 26 81. Open M-Sa 10am-3am.) In De Koog, venture down Dorpsstr. for all manner of beach bars, cafes, Shawarma huts, and ice cream stands. De Koog caters more to tourists and less to locals, and food can be pricey to match. After the sun sets, the young and sunburned masses migrate to shore-side De Koog for its sprightly nightlife. **Le Berry,** Dorpsstr. 3, has the air of a pub and caters to a slightly older crowd. There is dancing most nights, though, especially on weekends in the summer. (☎31 71 14; www.leberry.nl. DJ W-Su nights. Open noon-4am. Dancing from 11pm.) To the right of Le Berry is **De Blauwe Piste,** a nightclub offering two rooms: a wintery dance floor (complete with snow machine) and a beach bar. (☎20 06 00. Dance floor open daily 10pm-4am. Beach bar open daily 5pm-4am.)

Take the **train** to Amsterdam from Den Helder (1½hr., €11), but first you must take a **Teso ferry** there from Het Horntje, the southernmost town on Texel (20min.; 1 per hr. 6:30am-9:30pm; round-trip €3, under 12 €1.50, additional €2.50 for bikes). **Buses** depart from the ferry dock to various locales throughout the island; purchase a **Texel Ticket,** which allows unlimited one-day travel on the island-wide bus system (runs mid-June to mid-Sept., €4.50). The **VVV,** Emmalaan 66, is located just outside Den Burg about 300m south of the main bus stop. (☎31 47 41; www.texel.net. Open M-F 9am-5:30pm, Sa 9am-5pm.)

# PORTUGAL

While Portugal is small, its imposing forests and mountains, scenic vineyards, and almost 2000km of coastline rival the attractions of Spain. Portugal's capital, Lisbon, offers marvelous museums, castles, and churches. The country experienced international glory and fabulous wealth 400 hundred years ago during the Golden Age of Vasco da Gama. Despite suffering under the dictatorship of Salazar for 30 years in the 20th century, Portugal has reemerged as a European cultural center with a growing economy. Extremes of fortune have contributed to the unique Portuguese concept of *saudade*, a yearning for the glories of the past and a dignified resignation to the fact that the future can never compete. Visitors may experience *saudade* through a *fado* singer's song or over a glass of port, but Portugal's attractions are more likely to inspire delight than nostalgia.

##  DISCOVER PORTUGAL: SUGGESTED ITINERARIES

**THREE DAYS.** Make your way through **Lisbon** (1 day; p. 799); venture through its famous Moorish district, the Alfama, Castelo de São Jorge, and the Parque das Nações. By night, listen to *fado* and hit the clubs in Bairro Alto. Daytrip to **Sintra's** fairytale castles (1 day; p. 812), then sip wine in **Porto** (1 day; p. 813).

**ONE WEEK.** After wandering the streets of **Lisbon** (2 days) and **Sintra** (1 day), lounge on the beaches of **Lagos** (1 day; p. 821) and admire the cliffs of **Sagres** (1 day; p. 823). Move on to the university town of **Coimbra** (1 day; p. 819) before ending your week in **Porto** (1 day).

**BEST OF PORTUGAL, TWO WEEKS.**
After taking in the sights, sounds, and cafes of **Lisbon** (3 days), daytrip to enchanting **Sintra** (1 day). Head down to the infamous beaches and bars of **Lagos** (2 days), where hordes of visitors dance the night away. Take an afternoon in **Sagres** (1 day), once considered the edge of the world. Check out the macabre bone chapel in **Évora** (1 day; p. 818) and the impressive monastery in **Batalha** (1 day; p. 820). Head north to vibrant **Coimbra** (2 days) and **Porto** (2 days), then finish your tour in the impressive squares of **Viana do Castelo** (1 day; p. 815).

# LIFE AND TIMES

## HISTORY

**EARLY HISTORY (UNTIL AD 1139).** Settlement of Portugal began around 8000 BC when neolithic hunters and fishermen arrived from Andalucía. Several tribes, including the Celts, Phoenicians, Greeks, and Carthaginians, began to populate the Iberian Peninsula in the first millennium BC. After their victory over Carthage in the Second Punic War (218-201 BC) and their defeat of the Celts in 140 BC, the Romans gained control of central and southern Portugal. Six centuries of Roman rule Latinized Portugal's language and customs.

The decline of the Roman Empire in the third and fourth centuries permitted the ascendance of the **Visigoths,** a nomadic Germanic tribe who arrived in AD 469 and dominated the Peninsula for the next two centuries. In AD 711, however, the **Moors** invaded Iberia, toppling the Visigoth monarchy. They established Muslim communities called *al-Gharb* (Algarve) along the southern coast. After nearly four centuries of rule, the Moors left a legacy of agricultural advances, architectural landmarks, and linguistic and cultural customs.

## THE CHRISTIAN RECONQUISTA AND THE BIRTH OF PORTUGAL (1139-1385).

The **Reconquista** picked up steam in the 11th century when **Fernando I** united Castilla and León, thereby providing a base from which to reclaim territory for Christendom from the Moors. In 1139, **Dom Afonso Henriques** (Afonso I), a noble from the territory around Porto, declared independence from Castilla and León. Soon thereafter, he named himself the first king of Portugal. The division between Spain and Portugal is the oldest established border in Europe. With the help of Christian military groups like the **Knights Templar,** the new monarchy battled Muslim forces, capturing Lisbon in 1147. By 1249, the Reconquista under **Afonso III** defeated the remnants of Muslim power through successful cam-

paigns in the Alentejo and the Algarve. The Christian kings, led by **Dinis I** (1279-1325), promoted the Portuguese language over Spanish, and, with the **Treaty of Alcañices** (1297), settled border disputes with neighboring Castilla. Portugal's identity as Europe's first unified, independent nation was confirmed.

## THE AGE OF DISCOVERY (1385-1580).

The reign of **João I** (1385-1433), the first king of the **House of Avis,** ushered in a period of unity and prosperity. João increased the power of the crown, establishing a strong base for future Portuguese expansion and economic success. Under the leadership of João's son, **Prince Henry the Navigator,** Portugal also established itself as a world leader in maritime science and exploration. Portuguese adventurers captured the Moroccan city of Ceuta in 1415, discovered Madeira in 1419, happened upon the uninhabited Açores in 1427, and began to plunder the African coast for slaves and riches. Lagos became Europe's first slave market in 1441.

The Portuguese monarchs, while refusing to sponsor Christopher Columbus's expedition, did fund a number of momentous voyages. **Bartolomeu Dias** rounded Africa's Cape of Storms (later renamed the Cape of Good Hope) in 1488, opening the route to the East and paving the way for Portuguese entrance into the spice trade. In 1497, the royal family supported **Vasco da Gama,** who led the first European naval expedition to India. Three years later, **Pedro Álvares Cabral** claimed Brazil for Portugal. Portugal's international power peaked during the reign of **Manuel I** (1495-1521), the "King of Gold," who controlled a spectacular commercial empire. During his rule, Fernão de Magalhães, known as **Magellan,** completed the first circumnavigation of the globe in 1521. Concurrently, other European powers began developing their own routes to the East, and Portuguese dominance of trade waned by the end of the 16th century.

**BRING ON THE BRAGANÇA (1580-1807).** In 1580, Habsburg King **Felipe II** of Spain forcibly claimed the Portuguese throne, and the Iberian Peninsula was briefly ruled by one monarch. Over the next 60 years, the Habsburgs dragged Portugal into several ill-fated battles, including the failed **Spanish-Portuguese Armada** in 1588. By the end of Habsburg rule, Portugal had lost much of its once-vast empire. In 1640, the **House of Bragança** engineered a nationalist rebellion against the **King Felipe IV.** After a brief struggle, they assumed control, asserting Portuguese independence from Spain. To secure sovereignty, the Bragança dynasty re-established ties with England, beginning to restore prosperity to Portugal. However, the momentous **earthquake of 1755** devastated far more than the economies of Lisbon and southern Portugal; as many as 60,000 people died in the quake and during the subsequent tsunami and fire. A mass grave containing the bodies of 3000 Portuguese who died in the tragedy was recently found in the cloisters of a Franciscan convent. Despite the damage, dictatorial minister **Marquês de Pombal** rebuilt Lisbon and instituted national economic reform.

**NAPOLEON MAKES IT PERSONAL (1807-1910).** Napoleon took control of France in 1799 and soon set his sights on the rest of Europe. When he reached Portugal in 1807, his army met with little resistance. Rather than risk death, the Portuguese royal family fled to Brazil. The **Constitution of 1822,** drawn up during their absence, severely limited the power of the monarchy, and soon the ultimate sibling rivalry exploded into the **War of the Two Brothers** (1826-1834). Constitutionalists supported Pedro, the new king of Brazil, and monarchists supported Miguel, Pedro's brother. Continued tensions between the constitutionalists and the monarchists marked the next 75 years.

**FROM THE "FIRST REPUBLIC" TO SALAZAR (1910-1970).** Portugal spent the first decade of the 20th century trying to recover from the political discord of the 19th century. On October 5, 1910, 20-year-old **King Manuel II** fled to England seeking amnesty from civil unrest. Portugal's new government, the **First Republic,** received worldwide disapproval for its expulsion of the Jesuits and other religious orders. Conflict between the government and labor movements heightened tensions. Portugal's decision to enter **World War I** on the side of the Allies proved economically draining and internally divisive, despite eventual victory. The weak republic wobbled and eventually fell in a 1926 military coup. The provisional military government that took control named **General António Óscar de Fragoso Carmona** its leader, and appointed **António de Oliveira Salazar,** a prominent economics professor, minister of finance. In 1932, Salazar became prime minister, the position soon devolving into a dictatorship. His **Estado Novo** (New State) granted suffrage to women but did little else to end the country's authoritarian tradition. While Portugal's international economic standing improved, the regime laid the cost of progress squarely on the shoulders of the working class, the peasantry, and colonial subjects in Africa. A terrifying secret police **(PIDE)** crushed domestic opposition to Salazar's rule, and African rebellions were subdued in bloody battles that drained the nation's economy.

**FROM IMPERIALISM TO SOCIALISM (1970-1999).** The slightly more liberal **Marcelo Caetano** dragged on the unpopular African wars after Salazar's death in 1970, but international disapproval of Portuguese imperialism and the army's dissatisfaction with colonial entanglements led **General António Spinola** to call for decolonization. On April 25, 1974, a left-wing military coalition calling itself the **Armed Forces Movement** overthrew Caetano in a coup. The **Revolution of the Carna-**

**tions** sent citizens dancing into the streets; today, every town in Portugal seems to have its own Rua 25 de Abril. When the new government took over, Marxist-dominated armed forces established civil and political liberties; Portugal also withdrew its claims on African colonies by 1975, resulting in a deluge of refugees. In 1976, the country's first elections brought Socialist prime minister **Mario Soares** to power. Soares raised Portugal out of economic crisis, and in 1986 the country entered the European Economic Community (now the **European Union**).

# TODAY

The European Union declared Portugal a full member in 1999, the same year that Portugal ceded Macau, its last overseas territory, to the Chinese. Portugal has also agreed to aid the Indonesian government in the reconstruction of East Timor, its former colony.

In the Portuguese Republic, the president represents the nation, serves as commander of the armed forces, and appoints the prime minister in accordance with the results of parliamentary elections. **President Jorge Sampaio,** of the center-left Socialist Party, won a second term in January 2001. Prime Minister **Jose Manuel Durão Barroso,** of the Social Democratic Party, resigned in 2004 to become president of the European Commission (the executive body of the EU). **Pedro Santana Lopes** served as prime minister for less than a year. President Sampaio appointed **José Sócrates** to take his place after the Socialist Party's landslide victory in March 2005.

Prime Minister Sócrates was also one of the organizers of the **2004 European Football Championship** in Portugal, in which Greece took an unexpected victory over the host team. In preparation for the tournament, Portuguese local transportation and national rail lines were vastly improved. In 2005, a severe drought hit the Algarve region, hampering agricultural projects and tourism. Because these industries account for more than 60% of Portugal's active workforce, the drought's impact was devastating. In March 2007, Sócrates came under fire when his degree in civil engineering was called into question after the school from which he received his diploma, the **Universidade Independente,** was investigated and shut down for "irregularities." Although Sócrates did earn his degree, he is not eligible to call himself an engineer because he is not licensed to practice engineering by the state.

# PEOPLE AND CULTURE

### CUSTOMS AND ETIQUETTE

Wearing shorts and flip-flops may be seen as disrespectful in some public establishments and rural areas, even on hot days. Though dress in Portugal is more casual during the summer than in winter, strapless tops on women and collarless t-shirts on men are generally unacceptable. Skimpy clothes are always taboo in churches, as are tourist visits during masses or services. Do not assume that the Portuguese will understand the Spanish language. While many Portuguese do speak Spanish, one of the best ways to offend a local is to tacitly suggest that Portugal is part of Spain.

Politeness is foremost among Portuguese values. Be sure to address locals either as *senhor* (Mr.), *senhora* (Ms.), or *senhora dona* (Mrs.) followed by first name. It is a good idea to be as formal as possible upon first meeting.

### LANGUAGE

**Portuguese,** a Romance language and the world's sixth most widely spoken, is the official language of Portugal. Although many residents, especially in heavily touristed areas, speak English, Spanish, or French, the Portuguese appreciate it when travelers try to speak at least a few phrases of their language. As your mother always told you, please *(por favor)* and thank you *(obrigado/a)* are especially important. Be aware that the sounds of Brazilian and continental Portuguese are quite different, due to variations in pronunciation and vocabulary. For a glossary of Portuguese phrases, see **Phrasebook: Portuguese,** p. 1056.

In 1999, as part of a movement to preserve Europe's dying dialects, **Mirandese** was made an official language of Portugal. Mirandese remains the first language of many Portuguese dwelling in the county of Miranda do Douro, a small region on the Spanish border. In the Middle Ages, Latin diverged into three distinct linguistic varieties on the Iberian Peninsula—one the origin of Portuguese, one of Spanish, and the last of Mirandese, a Austurian-Leonese tongue.

## RELIGION

Roughly 85% of the Portuguese population is **Roman Catholic.** A major force in shaping Portugal's history, the Catholic Church is a respected and powerful influence in modern-day Portugal as well; attendance is high at Sunday masses, and festivals honoring *romarias* (patron saints) are celebrated everywhere. There are also many Protestants, Jehovah's Witnesses, and Mormons in Portugal, along with 35,000 Muslims and some 700 Jews.

# THE ARTS

## ARCHITECTURE

Portugal's signature **Manueline** style celebrates the prosperity and imperial expansion of Manuel I's reign. Manueline pieces routinely combine Christian images and maritime motifs. Their rich and lavish ornaments reflect a hybrid of northern Gothic, Spanish Plateresque, and Moorish influences. The style found its most elaborate expression in the church and tower at Belém (p. 808), built to honor Vasco da Gama; the **Abadia de Santa Maria de Vitória** in Batalha features a combination of Gothic and Manueline styles.

Although few Moorish structures survived the Christian Reconquista, their style influenced later Portuguese architecture. One beautiful tradition is the painted ceramic *azulejo* tiling that graces walls and ceilings all over Portugal. First carved in relief by the Moors, these tiles later took on Italian and Flemish designs. Many are blue, but their name doesn't come from their color—rather from the Arabic word *azulayj*, meaning "little stone."

## LITERATURE

In the 12th century, poet-king **Dinis I** declared Portuguese the region's official language, jump-starting Portuguese literature. **Gil Vicente,** actor, director, playwright, and part of the royal court of King João II, is considered to be the father of Portuguese theater. During the Renaissance, **Luís de Camões** celebrated Vasco da Gama's sea voyages to India in Portugal's greatest epic, *Os Lusíadas* (*The Lusiads;* 1572), modeled on Virgil's *Aeneid.*

Spanish hegemony, intermittent warfare, and imperial decline combined to make the literary themes of the 17th and 18th centuries less ambitious than those of past eras. The 19th century, however, saw a dramatic rebirth of literature with the romantic poetry of **João Baptista de Almeida Garrett** and the histories of **Alexandre Herculano,** both writers exiled because of their liberal politics.

Modernist poet **Fernando Pessoa** wrote in English and Portuguese under four different pen names, each associated with a different writing style. **José Saramago,** winner of the 1998 Nobel Prize for Literature, is Portugal's most important living writer. His work, written in the style of magical realism, has achieved new acclaim in the post-Salazar era.

## MUSIC

**Fado** (FAH-doe), literally translated as "fate," is a musical tradition unique to Portugal. Characterized by a sense of *saudade* (yearning or longing), *fado* is known for its tragic, romantic lyrics, and mournful melodies. These solo ballads, accompanied by the acoustic *guitarra* (a flat-backed guitar resembling a mandolin), show the romantic side of Portuguese culture. *Fado's* true origin remains a mystery; some suggest that the musical style evolved from Moorish songs sung during the occupation of the Algarve, while others hold that it is descended from African slave songs. Still others believe that fishermen's wives yearning for their husbands away at sea first sung these bittersweet ballads.

## PAINTING

**The Age of Discovery** (1415-1580) was an era of cross-cultural exchange. Flemish masters such as **Jan van Eyck** brought their talent to Portugal, and many Portuguese artists polished their skills in Antwerp, Belgium. Manuel I's favorite High Renaissance artist, **Jorge Afonso**, was a master of the realistic portrayal of human anatomy.

The **Baroque** era featured more diverse styles and themes, including the elaborate woodcarvings of sculptor **Joachim Machado** and numerous historical, religious, and allegorical works by **Domingos António de Sequeira,** whose technique would later inspire French Impressionists. In the 20th century, Cubism, Expressionism, and Futurism trickled into Portugal despite Salazar's censorship. More recently, **Maria Helena Vieira da Silva** won international recognition for her abstract work, and **Carlos Botelho** (1899-1982) became world-renowned for his comic vignettes of Lisbon life.

# HOLIDAYS AND FESTIVALS

**Holidays:** New Year's Day (Jan. 1); Epiphany (Jan. 6); Good Friday (Mar. 21); Easter (Mar. 23-24); Liberation Day (Apr. 25); Ascension (May 1); Labor Day (May 1); Corpus Christi (May 22); Portugal Day (June 10); Assumption (Aug. 15); Republic Day (Oct. 5); All Saints' Day (Nov. 1); Restoration of Independence Day (Dec. 1); Immaculate Conception (Dec. 8); Christmas (Dec. 25); New Year's Eve (Dec. 31).

**Festivals:** All of Portugal celebrates *Carnaval* (Feb. 5) and Holy Week (Apr. 1-8). Coimbra holds the *Queima das Fitas* (Burning of the Ribbons) festival in early May, celebrating the end of the university school year. In June, Batalha holds a *Feira International* celebrating the food, wine, and traditional handicrafts of the region, and Lisbon hosts the *Festas da Cidade,* honoring the birth of St. Anthony with music, games, parades, and street fairs. For more information on Portuguese festivals, see www.portugal.org.

# ADDITIONAL RESOURCES

*Culture Shock! Portugal,* by Volker Poelzl. Marshall Cavendish Inc. (2007). Comprehensive coverage of Portuguese history, customs, etiquette, and bureaucracy.

*Prince Henry 'the Navigator:' a Life,* by Peter Russell. Yale University Press (2001). Peter Russell debunks the myth of Prince Henry as a brave explorer with a modern mindset.

*Blindness,* by José Saramago. Harcourt Books (1999). This mystical novel about epidemic of blindness won Portuguese author Saramago the Nobel Prize for Literature.

# ESSENTIALS

## WHEN TO GO

Summer is high season, but the southern coast draws tourists between March and November. In the low season, many hostels slash their prices, and reservations are seldom necessary. While Lisbon and some of the larger towns (especially the university town of Coimbra) burst with vitality year-round, many smaller towns virtually shut down in winter, and sights reduce their hours.

PORTUGAL

# DOCUMENTS AND FORMALITIES

**EMBASSIES AND CONSULATES.** Foreign embassies in Portugal are in Lisbon. Portuguese embassies abroad include: **Australia,** 23 Culgoa Circuit, O'Malley, Canberra, ACT 2606 (☎612 6290 1733); **Canada,** 645 Island Park Dr., Ottawa, ON K1Y 0B8 (☎613-729-2270); **Ireland,** Knocksinna Mews, 7 Willow Park, Foxrock, Dublin, 18 (☎353 289 4416); **UK,** 11 Belgrave Sq., London, SW1X 8PP (☎020 7235 5331); **US,** 2012 Massachusetts Ave. NW, Washington, D.C., 20036 (☎202-350-5400). **New Zealand** citizens should contact the embassy in Australia.

**VISA AND ENTRY INFORMATION.** EU citizens do not need a visa. Citizens of Australia, Canada, New Zealand, the UK, and the US do not need a visa for stays up to 90 days, beginning upon entry into any of the countries within the EU's freedom-of-movement zone. For more info, see p. 13. For stays longer than 90 days, all non-EU citizens need visas (around $100), available at Portuguese consulates.

# TOURIST SERVICES AND MONEY

**EMERGENCY** | **General Emergency:** ☎112.

**TOURIST OFFICES.** For general info, contact the **Portuguese Tourism Board,** Av. Antonio Augusto de Aguiar 86, 1004 Lisbon (☎808 78 12 12; www.portugal.org/index.shtml). When in Portugal, stop by municipal and provincial tourist offices, listed in the **Practical Information** section of each city and town.

**MONEY.** The **euro (€)** has replaced the **escudo** as the unit of currency in Portugal. For more info on the euro, see p. 15. Generally, it's cheaper to exchange money in Portugal than at home. **ATMs** have the best exchange rates. Credit cards also offer good rates and may sometimes be required to reserve hotel rooms or rental cars; **MasterCard** (known in Portugal as **Eurocard**) and **Visa** are the most frequently accepted. **Tips** of 5-10% are customary only in fancy restaurants or hotels. Some cheaper restaurants include a 10% service charge; if they don't and you'd like to leave a tip, round up to the nearest euro and leave the change. Taxi drivers do not expect tips except for especially long trips. **Bargaining** is not customary in shops, but you can give it a shot at the local market *(mercado)* or when looking for a private room *(quarto)*. Portugal has a 21% **value added tax (VAT),** a sales tax applied to retail goods. The prices given in *Let's Go* include VAT. In the airport upon exiting the EU, non-EU citizens can claim a refund on the tax paid for goods purchased at participating stores. In order to qualify for a refund in a store, you must spend at least €50-100, depending on the shopkeeper; make sure to ask for a refund form when you pay. For more info on qualifying for a VAT refund, see p. 18.

**BUSINESS HOURS.** Shops are open M-F from 9am to 6pm, although many close for a few hours in the afternoon. Restaurants serve lunch from noon to 3pm and dinner from 7 to 10pm—or later. Museums are often closed on Monday, and many shops are closed over the weekend. Banks usually open around 9am M-F and close in the afternoon.

# TRANSPORTATION

**BY PLANE.** Most international flights land at **Portela Airport** in Lisbon (**LIS**; ☎218 41 35 00); some also land at **Faro** (**FAO**; ☎289 80 08 00) or **Porto** (**OPO**; 229 43 24 00). **TAP Air Portugal** (Canada and the US ☎800-221-7370, Portugal ☎707 20 57 00, UK ☎845 601 0932; www.tap.pt) is Portugal's national airline, serving domestic and international locations. **Portugália** (☎218 93 80 70; www.flypga.pt) is smaller and flies between Faro, Lisbon, Porto, major Spanish cities, and other Western European destinations. For more information on European air travel, see p. 41.

**BY TRAIN.** **Caminhos de Ferro Portugueses** (☎213 18 59 90; www.cp.pt) is Portugal's national railway. Lines run to domestic destinations, Madrid, and Paris. For travel outside of the Braga-Porto-Coimbra-Lisbon line, buses are better. Lisbon, where local trains are fast and efficient, is the exception. Trains often leave at irregular hours, and posted schedules *(horários)* aren't always accurate; check ticket booths upon arrival. Fines for riding without a ticket *(sem bilhete)* are high. Those under 12 or over 65 get half-price tickets. **Youth discounts** are only available to Portuguese citizens. Train passes are usually not worth buying, as tickets are inexpensive. For more information on getting to Portugal, see p. 45.

**BY BUS.** Buses are cheap, frequent, and connect to just about every town in Portugal. **Rodoviária** (☎212 94 71 00), formerly the national bus company, has recently been privatized. Each company name corresponds to a particular region of the country, such as Rodoviária Alentejo or Minho e Douro, with a few exceptions such as **EVA** in the Algarve. Private regional companies, including **AVIC, Cabanelas,** and **Mafrense,** also operate buses. Beware of non-express buses in small regions like Estremadura and Alentejo, which stop every few minutes. Express service *(expressos)* between major cities is good, and inexpensive city buses often run to nearby villages. Portugal's main **Euroline** (p. 48) affiliates are Internorte, Intercentro, and Intersul. **Busabout** coaches stop in Portugal at Lisbon, Lagos, and Porto. Every coach has a guide on board to answer questions and to make travel arrangements en route.

**BY CAR.** A **driver's license** from one's home country is required to rent a car; no International Driving Permit is necessary. Portugal has the **highest automobile accident rate** per capita in Western Europe. The highway system *(itinerarios principais)* is easily accessible, but off the main arteries, the narrow roads are difficult to negotiate. Speed limits are ignored, recklessness is common, and lighting and road surfaces are often inadequate. Parking space in cities is nonexistent. In short, buses are safer. The national automobile association, the **Automóvel Clube de Portugal (ACP),** (☎800 50 25 02; www.acp.pt), has breakdown and towing service, as well as first aid.

**BY THUMB.** In Portugal, **hitchhiking** is rare. Beach-bound locals occasionally hitchhike in summer, but more commonly stick to the inexpensive bus system. Rides are easiest to come by between smaller towns and at gas stations near highways and rest stops. Let's Go does not recommend hitchhiking.

# KEEPING IN TOUCH

| **PHONE CODES** | **Country code: 351. International dialing prefix: 00.** Within Portugal, dial city code + local number. For more info on placing international calls, see **Inside Back Cover.** |
|---|---|

**EMAIL AND THE INTERNET.** Internet cafes in cities and most towns charge around €1.20-4 per hr. for Internet access. When in doubt, try the library, where there is often at least one computer equipped for Internet access.

**TELEPHONE.** Whenever possible, use a calling card for international phone calls, as long-distance rates for national phone services are often very high. Mobile

PORTUGAL

phones are an increasingly popular and economical option. Major mobile carriers include: **TMN, Optimus Telecom SA,** and **Vodafone.** Direct-dial access numbers for calling out of Portugal include: **AT&T Direct** (☎800 80 01 28); **British Telecom** (☎800 80 04 40); **Canada Direct** (☎800 80 01 22); **Telecom New Zealand Direct** (☎800 80 06 40); **Telstra Australia** (☎800 80 06 10). For more info on calling home from Europe, see p. 26.

**MAIL.** Mail in Portugal is somewhat inefficient. **Airmail** *(via aerea)* takes one to two weeks to reach Canada or the US, and more to get to Australia and New Zealand. **Surface mail** *(superficie),* for packages only, takes up to two months. **Registered** or **blue mail** takes five to eight business days for roughly three times the price of airmail. **EMS** or **Express Mail** will most likely arrive overseas in three to four days, though it costs more than double the blue mail price. To receive mail in Portugal, have mail delivered **Poste Restante.** Mail will go to the main post office unless you specify a subsidiary by street address. Address mail to be held according to the following example: Last Name, First Name, Posta Restante, Postal code City, PORTUGAL; AIRMAIL.

# ACCOMMODATIONS AND CAMPING

| PORTUGAL | ❶ | ❷ | ❸ | ❹ | ❺ |
|---|---|---|---|---|---|
| ACCOMMODATIONS | under €16 | €16-20 | €21-30 | €31-40 | over €40 |

**Movijovem,** R. Lúcio de Azevedo 27, 1600-146 Lisbon (☎707 20 30 30; www.pousadasjuventude.pt), the Portuguese Hostelling International affiliate, oversees the country's **HI hostels.** All bookings can be made through them. A bed in a *pousada da juventude* costs €9-15 per night, including breakfast and linens, slightly less in the low season. Though often the cheapest option, hostels may lie far from the town center. To reserve rooms in the high season, get an **International Booking Voucher** from Movijovem (or your country's HI affiliate) and send it to the desired hostel four to eight weeks in advance. In the low season (Oct.-Apr.), double-check to see if the hostel is open. **Hotels** in Portugal tend to be pricey. Rates typically include breakfast and showers, and most rooms without bath or shower have a sink. When business is slow, try bargaining in advance—the "official price" is just the maximum. **Pensões,** also called **residencias,** are a budget traveler's mainstay, cheaper than hotels and only slightly more expensive (and much more common) than crowded youth hostels. Like hostels, *pensões* generally provide linens and towels. Many do not take reservations in high season; for those that do, book a week ahead. **Quartos** are rooms in private residences, similar to Spain's *casas particulares.* These may be the the cheapest option in cities and the only option in town; tourist offices can help find one. Prices are flexible and bargaining expected. Portugal has 150 **official campgrounds** *(parques de campismo),* often beach-accessible and equipped with grocery stores and cafes. Urban and coastal parks may require reservations. Police are cracking down on illegal camping, so don't try it. Tourist offices stock *Portugal: Camping and Caravan Sites,* a free guide to official campgrounds.

# FOOD AND DRINK

| PORTUGAL | ❶ | ❷ | ❸ | ❹ | ❺ |
|---|---|---|---|---|---|
| FOOD | under €6 | €6-10 | €11-15 | €16-20 | over €20 |

Portuguese dishes are seasoned with olive oil, garlic, herbs, and sea salt, but few spices. The fish selection includes *choco grelhado* (grilled cuttlefish), *linguado grelhado* (grilled sole), and *peixe espada* (swordfish). Portugal's renowned *queijos* (cheeses) are made from cow, goat, and sheep milk. For dessert, try *pudim flan* (egg custard). A hearty *almoço* (lunch) is eaten between noon and

2pm; *jantar* (dinner) is served between 8pm and midnight. *Meia dose* (half-portions) cost more than half-price but are often more than adequate. The *prato do dia* (special of the day) and the set *menú* of appetizer, bread, entree, and dessert, are also filling choices. Cheap, high-quality Portuguese *vinho* (wine) is astounding. Its delicious relative, *vinho do porto* (port), is a dessert in itself. Coffees include *bica* (black espresso), *galão* (with milk, in a glass), and *café com leite* (with milk, in a cup). **Mini-Preço** and **Pingo Doce** have cheap groceries.

> **TIP** **NO SUCH THING AS A FREE LUNCH.** Waiters in Portugal will put an assortment of snacks, ranging from simple bread and butter to sardine paste, cured ham, or herbed olives, on your table before the appetizer is served. But check the menu for the prices before you dig in: you nibble it, you buy it.

# BEYOND TOURISM

As a **volunteer** in Portugal, you can contribute to efforts concerning environmental protection, social welfare, or political activism. While not many students think of **studying** abroad in Portugal, most Portuguese universities open their gates to foreign students. Being an au pair and teaching English are popular options for longterm **work,** though many people choose to seek more casual—and often illegal—jobs in resort areas. Let's Go does not recommend any type of illegal employment. For more info on opportunities across Europe, see **Beyond Tourism,** p. 54.

**Canadian Alliance for Development Initiatives and Projects** (www.cadip.org/volunteer-in-portugal.htm). Posts opportunities to volunteer for development projects in Granja do Ulmeiro, Coimbra.

**Teach Abroad** (www.teachabroad.com). Brings you to listings around the world for paid or stipend positions teaching English.

**Universidade de Lisboa,** Rectorate Al. da Universidade, Cidade Universitária, 1649-004 Lisbon, POR (☎217 96 76 24; www.ul.pt). Allows foreign students to enroll directly.

**Volunteer Abroad** (www.volunteer-abroad.com/Portugal.cfm). Offers opportunities to volunteer with conservation efforts around Portugal.

# LISBON (LISBOA) ☎21

In 1755, a terrible earthquake destroyed much of Lisbon—a tragedy kept fresh by the nostalgic ballads of *fado* singers. But today, Portugal's seaside capital thrives as a center of architecture, art, and nightlife. Romans and Arabs once called Lisbon home, and the city remains one of the most multicultural in Europe.

# ◄ TRANSPORTATION

**Flights: Aeroporto de Lisboa (LIS;** ☎841 3500). From the terminal, turn right and follow the path to the bus stop. Take the express **AeroBus** #91 (15min., 3 per hr., €1.50) to Pr. dos Restauradores, in front of the tourist office, or take bus #44 or 45 to the same location (15-20min., every 12-15min., €1.50). A **taxi** from downtown costs about €10 plus a €1.60 baggage fee. Ask at the tourist office (☎845 0660) inside the airport about buying prepaid vouchers for taxi rides from the airport. (M-F €15, Sa-Su €18. Open daily 7am-midnight.) Major airlines have offices at Pr. Marquês do Pombal and along Av. da Liberdade.

**Trains: Caminhos de Ferro Portugueses** (☎808 20 82 08; www.cp.pt). 5 main stations, each serving different destinations. Trains in Portugal—slow, inconsistent, and

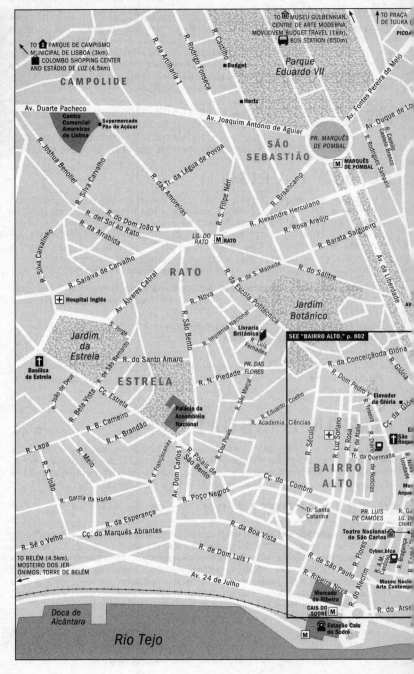

TO 🏠 PARQUE DE CAMPISMO
MUNICIPAL DE LISBOA (3km),
COLOMBO SHOPPING CENTER
AND ESTÁDIO DE LUZ (4.5km)

TO 🏛 MUSEU GULBENKIAN,
CENTRE DE ARTE MODERNA,
MOVIJOVEM BUDGET TRAVEL (1km),
🚌 BUS STATION (650m)

TO PRAÇA
DE TOURA (
PICOA

Parque
Eduardo VII

CAMPOLIDE

■ Budget

■ Hertz

Av. Duarte Pacheco

Centro
Comercial
Amoreiras
de Lisboa

■ Supermercado
Pão de Açúcar

Av. Joaquim António de Aguiar

SÃO
SEBASTIÃO

PR. MARQUÊS
DE POMBAL

Ⓜ MARQUÊS
DE POMBAL

R. da Artilharia 1

R. Rodrigo Fonseca

R. Castilho

Av. Fontes Pereira de Melo

Av. Duque de Lo

R. Camilo
Castelo Branco

R. Rodrigues Sampaio

R. Joshua Benoliel

R. Silva Carvalho

R. da Tr. da Légua de Povoa

R. das Amoreiras

R. do Dom João V

R. del Sol ao Rato

R. da Arrabida

R. S. Filipe Néri

R. Braancamp

R. Alexandre Herculano

R. Rosa Araújo

R. Barata Salgueiro

LG. DO
RATO

Ⓜ RATO

RATO

R. de S. Mamede

R. do Salitre

Av. da Liberdade

AV

R. Silva Carvalinho

R. Saraiva de Carvalho

Av. Álvares Cabral

R. Nova

R. da Escola Politécnica

Jardim
Botánico

✚ Hospital Inglês

S. Jorge

R. São Bento

R. Imprensa Nacional

Livraria
Britânica

SEE "BAIRRO ALTO." p. 802

Jardim
da
Estrela

✝ Basílica
da Estrela

R. João de Deus

R. Bela Vista

Cç. Estrela

R. de São Bernardo

R. do Santo Amaro

R. Luis
Fernades

PR. DAS
FLORES

R. N. Piedade

R. São Marçal

R. da Conceiçãoda Glória

R. Dom Pedro V

Elevador
da Glória

R. Teixeira

Cç. da Glo

R. Século

R. Luz Soriano

R. Rosa

R. da Atalia

R. Diário

R. No
Trindade

Mus
Arque

R. Lapa

R. B. Carneiro

R. A. Brandão

R. d Franciscanas

R. Polais de
São Bento

Cuz Polais

R. Eduardo
Coelho

R. Academia Ciências

✚

Tr. da Queimada

BAIRRO
ALTO

✚ São
Roque

R. Meio

R. Garcia da Horta

Av. Dom Carlos I

R. Poço Negros

Cç. do
Combro

R. de Noticias

R. S. João

Tr. Santa
Catarina

PR. LUIS
DE CAMÕES

LG. D
CHIA

R. Ga

Palácio da
Assembléia
Nacional

ESTRELA

R. Sé o Velho

R. da Esperança

Cç. do Marqués Abrantes

R. da Boa Vista

R. de Dom Luís I

Teatro Nacional
de São Carlos

R. de Flores

Cyber.blca

R.A.M.
Cardoso

R. Bra

Bragança

TO BELÉM (4.5km),
MOSTEIRO DOS JER-
ÓNIMOS, TORRE DE BELÉM

R. de São Paulo

R. Ribeira Nova

R. do Alecrim

Museu Nacio
Arte Contemp

Av. 24 de Julho

Mercado
da Ribeira

CAIS DO
SODRÉ Ⓜ

R. do Arse

Doca de
Alcântara

Estação Cais
do Sodré

Ⓜ

Rio Tejo

PORTUGAL

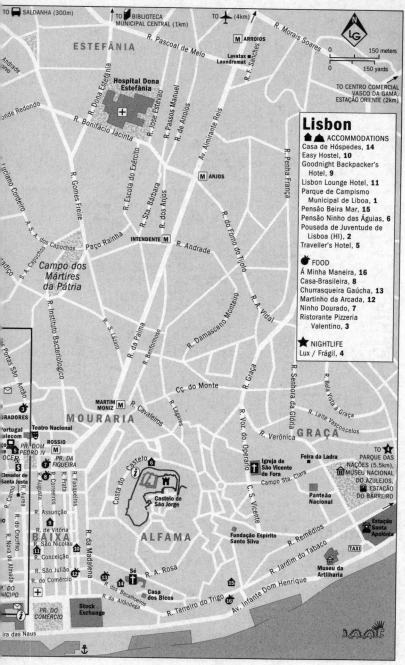

TO 🚇 SALDANHA (300m)

TO 📖 BIBLIOTECA
MUNICIPAL CENTRAL (1km)

TO ✈ (4km)

R. Morais Soares

Ⓜ ARROIOS

R. Pascoal de Melo

ESTEFÂNIA

R. F. Sanches

Lavatax ■
Laundromat

Andrade nno

R. Dona Estefânia

0        150 meters

onde Redondo

Hospital Dona
Estefânia

R. José Estêvão

R. Passos Manuel

R. de Arroios

0        150 yards

TO CENTRO COMERCIAL
VASCO DA GAMA,
ESTAÇÃO ORIENTE (2km)

R. Bonifácio Jácinta

Luciano Cordeiro

R. Gomes Freire

R. Escola do Exército

R. Sta. Bárbara

R. dos Anjos

Av. Almirante Reis

Ⓜ ANJOS

R. Penha França

S. A. S A. dos Capuchos

adiço

Paço Rainha

INTENDENTE Ⓜ

R. Andrade

R. do Forno do Tijolo

R. A. Vidal

### Lisbon

🏠🏔 ACCOMMODATIONS
Casa de Hóspedes, **14**
Easy Hostel, **10**
Goodnight Backpacker's
 Hotel, **9**
Lisbon Lounge Hotel, **11**
Parque de Campismo
 Municipal de Liboa, **1**
Pensão Beira Mar, **15**
Pensão Ninho das Águias, **6**
Pousada de Juventude de
 Lisboa (HI), **2**
Traveller's Hotel, **5**

🍎 FOOD
Á Minha Maneira, **16**
Casa-Brasileira, **8**
Churrasqueira Gaúcha, **13**
Martinho da Arcada, **12**
Ninho Dourado, **7**
Ristorante Pizzeria
 Valentino, **3**

⭐ NIGHTLIFE
Lux / Frágil, **4**

Campo dos
Mártires
da Pátria

R. Instituto Bacteriológico

R. S. Lázaro

R. da Palma

R. Benformoso

R. Damasceno Monteiro

R. Graça

R. Senhora da Glória

R. Bela Vista à Graça

Cç. do Monte

Portas São Antão

RADORES

ortugal elecom

PR. DOM
PEDRO IV

OCER

MARTIM
MONIZ Ⓜ

R. Cavaleiros

R. Jagães

R. Voz. do Operário

R. Leite Vasconcelos

R. Verónica

GRAÇA

MOURARIA

Teatro Nacional

ROSSIO Ⓜ

PR. DA
FIGUEIRA

Elevador de
Santa Justa

R. Augusta

R. Prata

R. Faisqueiros

R. Correeiros

Costa do Castelo

Castelo de
São Jorge

Igreja de
São Vicente
de Fora

Feira da Ladra

Campo Sta. Clara

C. S. Vicente

TO ⭐
PARQUE DAS
NAÇÕES (5.5km),
MUSEU NACIONAL
DO AZULEJOS,
ESTAÇÃO
DO BÁRREIRO

R. Aurea

R. Assunção

R. de Vitória

BAIXA

R. São Nicolau

R. Conceição

R. da Madalena

Panteão
Nacional

R. São Julião

R. do Comércio

Sé

R. A. Rosa

ALFAMA

Fundação Espírito
Santo Silva

R. Remédios

Estação
Santa
Apolónia

R. do Crucifixo

R. Nova do Almada

DO NICIPO

PR. DO
COMÉRCIO

Stock
Exchange

R. dos Bacalhoeiros

R. da Alfândega

Casa
dos Bicos

R. Terreiro do Trigo

R. Jardim do Tabaco

TAXI

Museu da
Artilharia

Av. Infante Dom Henrique

ira das Naus

N
LG

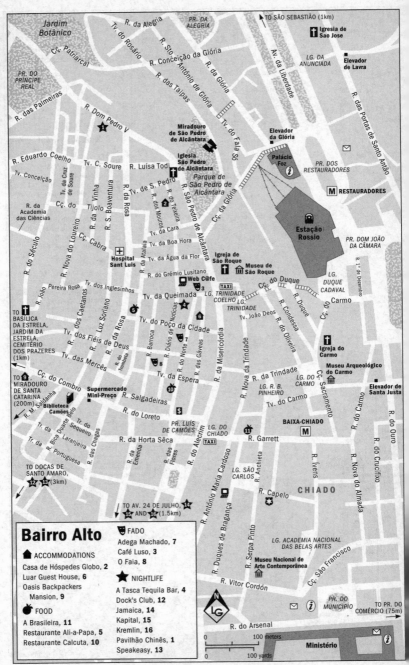

**Bairro Alto**

**⌂ ACCOMMODATIONS**
Casa de Hóspedes Globo, **2**
Luar Guest House, **6**
Oasis Backpackers
  Mansion, **9**

**🍓 FOOD**
A Brasileira, **11**
Restaurante Ali-a-Papa, **5**
Restaurante Calcuta, **10**

**🍷 FADO**
Adega Machado, **7**
Café Luso, **3**
O Faia, **8**

**★ NIGHTLIFE**
A Tasca Tequila Bar, **4**
Dock's Club, **12**
Jamaica, **14**
Kapital, **15**
Kremlin, **16**
Pavilhão Chinês, **1**
Speakeasy, **13**

confusing—are the bane of every traveler's existence; buses, though more expensive and lacking toilets, are faster and more comfortable.

**Estação do Barreiro** (☎347 2930), across the Rio Tejo. Travels south. Accessible by ferry from the Terreiro do Paço dock off Pr. do Comércio (30min., 2 per hr., €2). To get to **Évora** and **Lagos,** take a train to **Pinhal Novo** station and transfer. From Pinhal Novo, trains go to: **Lagos** (3½hr., 5 per day 9:04am-8:04pm, €12-17) and **Évora** (1½hr., 2 per day, €7).

**Estação Cais do Sodré** (☎347 0181), just beyond R. do Alecrim, near Baixa. M: Cais do Sodré. Take the metro or bus #36, 45, or 91 from Pr. dos Restauradores or tram #28 from Estação Santa Apolónia. To: the monastery in **Belém** (10min., 4 per hr., €1.20), **Cascais** and **Estoril** (30min., 2 per hr., €1.60), and the youth hostel in **Oeiras** (20min., 2 per hr., €1.30).

**Estação Rossio** (☎346 5022). M: Rossio or Restauradores. Travels west.

**Estação Santa Apolónia** (☎888 4025), Av. Infante Dom Henrique, runs the international, northern, and eastern lines. All trains to Santa Apolónia also stop at **Estação Oriente** (M: Oriente) by the Parque das Nações. The international terminal has currency exchange and an info desk. To reach downtown, take bus #9, 46, or 59 to Pr. dos Restauradores. To: **Aveiro** (3-3½hr., 20 per day, €16-24); **Braga** (5hr., 3 per day, €2-30); **Coimbra** (2½hr., 24 per day, €16-23); **Madrid, SPA** (10hr., 10:05pm, €60); **Porto** (3-4½hr., 20 per day, €19-30).

**Buses:** M: Jardim Zoológico. In the metro station, follow exit signs to Av. C. Bordalo Pinheiro, cross the street, and follow the path up the stairs. Look for *autocarros* signs.

**Rede Expressos** buses (☎707 22 33 44; www.rede-expressos.pt) go to: **Braga** (5hr., 13 per day, €17); **Coimbra** (2½hr., 25 per day, €12); **Évora** (2hr., 20 per day, €11); **Faro** (4hr., 16 per day, €17); **Lagos** (4-5hr., 16 per day, €17); **Porto** (3½-4hr., 19 per day, €16) via **Leiria** (2hr., €9).

**Public Transportation: CARRIS** (☎361 3000; www.carris.pt) runs **buses, trams,** and **funiculars.** If you plan to stay in Lisbon for any length of time, consider a *passe turístico,* good for unlimited travel on all CARRIS transports. 1- and 5-day passes are sold in CARRIS booths in most train stations and busier metro stations. (€3.40/13.50.) The 4 lines of the **metro** (☎350 0100; www.metrolisboa.pt) cover downtown and the modern business district. Single ride €0.80; unlimited daily-use ticket €3.40; book of 10 tickets €11. Trains run daily 6:30am-1am; some stations close earlier.

**Taxis: Rádio Táxis de Lisboa** (☎811 9000), **Autocoope** (☎793 2756), and **Teletáxis** (☎811 1100). Along Av. da Liberdade and Rossio. Luggage €1.60.

# ■ ORIENTATION

The city center is made up of three neighborhoods: **Baixa** (low district), **Bairro Alto** (high district), and hilly **Alfama.** The suburbs extending in both directions along the river represent some of the fastest-growing sections of the city. Several kilometers from downtown, **Belém** is a walk into Portugal's past. **Alcântara** is home to much of Lisbon's party scene as well as the **Parque das Nações,** site of the 1998 World Expo. Baixa's grid of mostly pedestrian streets is bordered to the north by **Rossio** (a.k.a. Praça Dom Pedro IV) and to the south by **Praça do Comércio,** on the Rio Tejo (River Tagus). East of Baixa is Alfama, Lisbon's oldest, labyrinthine district, and west of Baixa is Bairro Alto. Bairro Alto's upscale shopping district, the **Chiado,** is crossed by R. do Carmo and R. Garrett. **Avenida da Liberdade** runs north, uphill from Pr. dos Restauradores.

# ■ PRACTICAL INFORMATION

**Tourist Office: Palácio da Foz,** Pr. dos Restauradores (☎346 3314). M: Restauradores. Open daily 9am-8pm. The **Welcome Center,** Pr. do Comércio (☎031 2810), the city's main office, sells the Lisbon Card, which includes transportation and entrance to most sights (1-day €15, 2-day €26, 3-day €31). English spoken. Open daily 9am-8pm. Kiosks at Santa Apolónia, Belém, and other locations provide tourist info.

**Embassies and Consulates: Australia,** Av. da Liberdade 200 (☎310 1500; www.portugal.embassy.gov.au); **Canada,** Av. Liberdade 196 (☎444 3301; geo.international.gc.ca/canada-europa/portugal); **Ireland,** R. da Imprensa a Estrela 1-4 (☎392 9440). **New Zealand,** R. da Vista Alegre 10 (☎370 5787); **UK,** R. de São Bernardo 33 (☎392 4000; www.britishembassy.gov.uk/portugal); **US,** Av. das Forças Armadas (☎727-3300; www.american-embassy.pt).

**Currency Exchange: Banks** are open M-F 8:30am-3pm. **Cota Câmbios,** Pr. Dom Pedro IV 41 (☎322 0480), exchanges currency. Open daily 9am-8pm. The main post office, most banks, and travel agencies also change money. Exchanges line the streets of Baixa, but fees can be high.

**Police:** R. Capelo 13 (☎346 6141 or 342 1634). English spoken.

**Late-Night Pharmacy:** ☎118 (directory assistance). Look for the green cross at intersections, or try **Farmácia Azevedos,** Pr. Dom Pedro IV 31 (☎343 0482), at the base of Rossio in front of the metro.

**Hospital: Hospital de Saint Louis,** R. Luz Soriano 182 (☎321 6500), Bairro Alto. Open daily 9am-6pm.

**Internet Access: Web C@fé,** R. Diário de Notícias 126 (☎342 1181). €0.75 per 15min. Open daily 4pm-2am. **Cyber.bica,** R. Duques de Bragança 7 (☎322 5004), in Bairro Alto. €0.75 per 15min. Open M-Sa 11am-midnight.

**Post Office: Main office,** Ctt. Correios, Pr. dos Restauradores (☎323 8700). Open M-F 8am-10pm, Sa-Su 9am-7pm. Often crowded. Branch at Pr. do Comércio (☎322 0920). Open M-F 8:30am-6:30pm. Cash only. Central Lisbon **Postal Code:** 1100.

# ACCOMMODATIONS AND CAMPING

Hotels cluster on **Avenida da Liberdade,** while many convenient hostels are in Baixa along the Rossio and on **Rua da Prata, Rua dos Correeiros,** and **Rua do Ouro.** Most youth hostels are in Bairro Alto and around Santa Catarina. Lodgings near the Castelo de São Jorge are quiet and close to the sights. At night, be careful in Baixa, Bairro Alto, and especially Graça—many streets are isolated and poorly lit.

## BAIRRO ALTO

**Oasis Backpackers Mansion,** R. de Santa Catarina 24 (☎347 8044; www.oasislisboa.com). M: Baixa-Chiado, exit Largo do Chiado. The Oasis is a backpacker's dream, located in a gorgeous building with a spacious living room. Enjoy an incredible dinner M-Sa for €5 and complimentary Portuguese lessons. Breakfast included. Laundry €6. Free Internet. Co-ed dorms €20. Cash only. ❷

**Luar Guest House,** R. das Gáveas 101 (☎346 0949; www.pensaoluar.com). Follow the beautiful *azulejo* and wood staircase to brightly decorated rooms. Laundry €10 per 6kg. Singles €15, with shower €20; doubles €30; triples €45; quads €60. Cash only. ❷

**Casa de Hóspedes Globo,** R. Teixeira 37 (☎346 2279; www.pensaoglobo.com). Popular for its location near nightlife. Rooms with phone, TV, and often bath. English spoken. Laundry €10 per 6kg. Internet €2 per hr. Singles €35; doubles €40; triples with bath €45; quads with bath €60. Low season €10-15 discount. Cash only. ❷

## BAIXA

**Lisbon Lounge Hostel,** R. de São Nicolau 41, 2nd fl. (☎346 2061). M: Rossio or Baixa-Chiado. The hostel with the look of a sleek resort features a living room, in addition to a lounge area on each floor. Perks include free Internet, Wi-Fi, and lockers. Breakfast included; dinner €6. Dorms €20; doubles with bath €54. Cash only. ❸

🏨 **Easy Hostel,** R. de São Nicolau 13, 4th fl. (☎886 4280). This recently opened hostel in the middle of Baixa offers spacious rooms, Internet, and free breakfast with fresh-baked bread. Laundry is cheap, and there is a living room for hanging out with fellow travelers. An elevator makes life at Easy so much easier. Dorms €18. Cash only. ❷

**Traveller's House,** R. Augusta 89 (☎210 11 59 22) M: Baixa-Chiado. Wooden bunk beds and 4 common areas give this well-located hostel a warm and inviting ambiance. Free Internet, Wi-Fi, and breakfast. Lunch or dinner €5-6. Co-ed dorms €20. Cash only.

**Goodnight Backpacker's Hostel,** R. dos Correeiros 113, 3rd fl. (☎343 0139). M: Rossio. To get to this brand-new hostel, walk through the storefront, go through the mirrored doors, and climb up the *azulejo*-lined staircase. Bright colors splashed on the walls and whimsical Andy Warhol art give Goodnight a cheerful atmosphere. 2 common rooms, free Internet and Wi-Fi, and a smoke-free environment, as well as free lockers. Breakfast included. 8-bed dorms €19, 4-bed €20. Cash only.

## ALFAMA

🏨 **Pensão Ninho das Águias,** Costa do Castelo 74 (☎885 4070). Climb the spiral staircase on the terrace to reach the reception desk. Among the best views Lisbon has to offer, especially from rooms 5, 6, and 12-14. English and French spoken. Reserve ahead in summer. May-Aug. singles €30; doubles €45, with bath €50; triples €60. Sept.-Apr. prices €5 lower. Cash only. ❸

**Pensão Beira Mar,** Lg. Terreiro do Trigo 16 (☎886 9933; beira@iol.pt), near the Sta. Apolonia train station. Close to the water, the Beira Mar is a calm getaway for budget travelers. Brightly decorated rooms include a shower, television, and sink. Breakfast included. Free Internet and snacks. Living room and kitchen available. Reservations by email only. June-Aug. singles €20-35; doubles €30-40; triples €45; quads €60. Oct.-May prices €5 lower. Cash only. ❷

**Casa de Hóspedes,** R. da Padaria 38 (☎886 7710). Located near many of the district's sights. June-Aug. doubles €30; triples €45. Cash only. ❶

## OTHER AREAS

**Pousada de Juventude de Lisboa (HI),** R. Andrade Corvo 46 (☎353 2696). M: Picoas. Spacious, recently renovated rooms with a bar and reading room. Breakfast included. Reserve ahead. Dorms €16; doubles with bath €43. HI members only. MC/V. ❶

**Parque de Campismo Municipal de Lisboa** (☎762 3100), on the road to Benfica. Take bus #14 to Parque Florestal Monsanto; campsite is at entrance to park. Pool and supermarket nearby. €5 per person, €5-6 per tent, €3.50 per car. Low season discounts. ❶

# 🍴 FOOD

Lisbon offers some of Europe's best wine and cheapest restaurants. Dinner costs €7-12 per person; the *prato do dia* (daily special) is often only €5. Head to **Rua dos Bacalhoeiros** and **Rua dos Correeiros** to find smaller and usually less expensive restaurants. The city's culinary specialties include *creme de mariscos* (seafood chowder with tomatoes) and *bacalhau cozido com grão e batatas* (cod with chickpeas and boiled potatoes). For cheap groceries, look for any **Mini-Preço** or **Pingo Doce** supermarket. (Most open M-Sa 8:30am-9pm.)

## BAIRRO ALTO

**A Brasileira,** R. Garrett 120-122 (☎346 9541). M: Baixa-Chiado. A former stomping ground of early 20th-century poets and intellectuals. Sandwiches and croissants €2-5. Entrees €6-13. Open daily 8am-2am. AmEx/MC/V. ❷

**Restaurante Calcuta,** R. do Norte 17 (☎342 8295; www.calcuta1.com), near Lg. Camões. Listen to soothing Indian music while you enjoy Calcutta favorites like the prawn masala (€9.50). Offers a wide selection of vegetarian options (€6.50-7.50). Open M-F noon-3pm and 6-11pm, Sa-Su 6-11pm. AmEx/MC/V. ❷

**Restaurante Ali-a-Papa,** R. da Atalaia 95 (☎347 4143). Serves generous helpings of Moroccan food in a peaceful space; dishes include couscous and tangine. Vegetarian-friendly. Entrees €9-15. Open M and W-Sa 7pm-12:30am. AmEx/MC/V. ❸

## BAIXA AND ALFAMA

■ **À Minha Maneira,** Lg. do Terreiro do Trigo 1 (☎886 1112; www.a-minha-maneira.pt). A former bank vault has been revamped as a wine closet. Menu consists of various meat and fish dishes. Free Internet and printing. Entrees €8-15. Open daily 11am-11pm. Cash only. ❷

**Churrasqueira Gaúcha,** R. dos Bacalhoeiros 26C-D (☎887 0609). Affordable Portuguese food cooked to perfection in a comfortable, cavernous setting. The best restaurant on a street already packed with great deals. Fresh meat, poultry, and fish. Open M-Sa 10am-midnight. AmEx/MC/V. ❷

**Ristorante-Pizzeria Valentino,** R. Jardim do Regedor 37-45 (☎346 1727), in the Pr. do Restauradores. Watch the chefs prepare a variety of pizzas and pastas in an open kitchen. Try the popular pizza hawaii (€8) or the pasta dish *tagliatelle mare e monti* (€8). Pizzas €4-10. Entrees €7-19. Open daily noon-midnight. AmEx/MC/V. ❷

**Martinho da Arcada,** Pr. do Comércio 3 (☎887 9259). Founded in 1782, this is the oldest restaurant in Lisbon and a former haunt of poet Fernando Pessoa. The entrees (€17-35) are somewhat overpriced, but the ambience is one of a kind. Outdoor seating available. Open M-Sa noon-3pm and 7-10:30pm. AmEx/MC/V. ❸

**Casa-Brasileira,** R. Augusta 267-269 (☎346 9713). A great place to grab a quick bite while sightseeing in Baixa, Casa-Brasileira offers cheap sandwiches (€4), pizza (€2-4), and a variety of fresh fruit smoothies (€1.30-2). Open 10am-midnight. ❶

# ◙ SIGHTS

## BAIXA

Though Baixa has few historic sights, the neighborhood's happening mood and dramatic history make it a monument in its own right.

**AROUND THE ROSSIO.** The **Rossio** (Pr. Dom Pedro IV) was once a cattle market, the site of public executions, a bullring, and carnival ground. Now, the *praça* is the domain of ruthless local motorists who circle a statue of Dom Pedro IV. A statue of Gil Vicente, Portugal's first great dramatist (p. 794), sits at the top of the **Teatro Nacional de Dona Maria II** at one end of the *praça*. Adjoining the Rossio is the elegant **Praça da Figueira,** on the border of Alfama.

**AROUND PRAÇA DOS RESTAURADORES.** Just past the Rossio train station, an obelisk and a bronze sculpture of the "Spirit of Independence" commemorate Portugal's break from Spain in 1640. Numerous shops line the *praça* and C. da Glória, the hill that leads to Bairro Alto. Pr. dos Restauradores also begins **Avenida da Liberdade,** Lisbon's most elegant promenade. Modeled after the wide boulevards of 19th-century Paris, this shady thoroughfare ends at **Praça do Marquês de Pombal,** where an 18th-century statue of the Marquês himself overlooks the city.

**AROUND PRAÇA DO COMÉRCIO.** Pr. do Comércio's grid of pedestrian streets is perfect for wandering. After the 1755 earthquake leveled this area, the Marquês de Pombal designed the streets as a conduit for goods from the Rio Tejo to the city center. Streets are designated for specific trades: *sapateiros* (shoemakers), *douradores* (gold workers), and *bacalhoeiros* (cod merchants) each have their own avenue.

# BAIRRO ALTO

Intellectuals mix with teens and university students in the Bairro Alto. **Praça Luís de Camões,** in the neighborhood's center, is a good place to rest while sightseeing.

**■ MUSEU ARQUEOLÓGICO DO CARMO.** Located under the skeletal arches of an old church destroyed in the 1755 earthquake, this partially outdoor museum allows visitors to get very close to historical relics like mummies and a coat of arms. *(Lg. do Carmo. Open M-Sa 10am-8pm. €2.50, students €1.50, under 14 free.)*

**BASÍLICA DA ESTRELA.** Directly across from the Jardim da Estrela, the Basílica da Estrela dates back to 1796 and casts an imposing presence over the *praça*. Its dome, poised behind a pair of tall belfries, towers over surrounding buildings in the Lisbon skyline. Half-mad Dona Maria I promised God anything for a son. When she finally gave birth to a baby boy, she built this church in thanks. Ask to see the 10th-century nativity. *(Pr. da Estrela. Accessible by metro or tram #28 from Pr. do Comércio. ☎ 396 0915. Open daily 7:45am-8pm. Free.)*

**IGREJA DE SÃO ROQUE.** When pesky rodents and their epidemic-inducing germs miraculously disappeared upon the arrival of Sr. Roque's bones to Lisbon, he was made a *são* (saint), and a Jesuit church with all the bells and whistles was quickly built. Inside, the **Capela de São João Baptista** blazes with agate, lapis lazuli, and precious metals. The ceiling is covered entirely by a magnificent painting portraying scenes from the life of Jesus. *(Lg. Trinidade Coelho. ☎ 323 5383. Open daily 8:30am-5pm, Catholic holidays 8:30am-1pm.)*

**ELEVADOR DE SANTA JUSTA.** The Elevador de Santa Justa, a historic elevator built in 1902 inside a Gothic wrought iron tower, once served as transportation up to Bairro Alto, but now just carries tourists 45m up to the top. *(Open daily 10am-1pm and 2-6pm. €1.40, €2.60 roundtrip.)*

# ALFAMA

Alfama, Lisbon's medieval quarter, was the only neighborhood to survive the infamous 1755 earthquake. The area descends in tiers from the **Castelo de São Jorge** facing the Rio Tejo. Between Alfama and Baixa is the **Mouraria** (Moorish quarter), ironically established following the expulsion of the Moors in 1147. This labyrinth of *becos* (alleys), *escandinhas* (small stairways), and unmarked streets is a challenge to navigate, so be careful after nightfall.

**■ CASTELO DE SÃO JORGE.** Built in the 5th century by the Visigoths and enlarged 400 years later by the Moors, this castle was again improved and converted into the royal family's playground between the 14th and 16th centuries. Today the Castelo consists of little more than stone ramparts, but the towers provide spectacular views of Lisbon. Wander around the ruins, explore the ponds, or gawk at exotic birds in the gardens. *(☎ 880 0620; www.egeac.pt. Open daily Mar.-Oct. 9am-9pm; Nov.-Feb. 9am-6pm. €5, students €2.50, under 10 and over 65 free.)*

**LOWER ALFAMA.** The small **Igreja de Santo António** was built in 1812 over the beloved saint's alleged birthplace. The construction was funded with money collected by the city's children, who fashioned miniature altars bearing saintly images to place on doorsteps—a custom reenacted annually on June 13, the saint's feast day and Lisbon's biggest holiday. *(Veer right when you see Igreja da Madalena in Lg. da Madalena on the right. Take R. de Santo António da Sé and follow the tram tracks. ☎ 886 9145. Open daily 8am-7pm. Mass daily 11am, 5, 7pm.)* In the square beyond the church is the

12th-century ■**Sé de Lisboa.** Although the cathedral's interior lacks the ornamentation of the city's other churches, its age and treasury make for an intriguing visit. The cloister includes an archaeological dig with ruins from the Iron Age, the Roman Empire, and the Muslim and Medieval Ages in Lisbon. (☎886 6752. *Open daily 9am-7pm except during Mass, held Tu-Sa 6:30pm and Su 11:30am and 7pm. Free. Treasury open M-Sa 10am-5pm. €2.50, students €1.50. Cloister open daily May-Sept. 2-7pm; Oct.-Apr. M-Sa 10am-6pm, Su 2-6pm. €2.50, students €1.30.*)

# GRAÇA

Graça is one of Lisbon's oldest neighborhoods. In addition to views of the city and river, it offers impressive historical sights that keep tourists trekking up its hilly streets. Graça is mainly a residential area, accessible by tram (#28; €1.30).

■**PANTEÃO NACIONAL.** The massive building that is now the Panteão Nacional (National Pantheon) was originally meant to be the Igreja da Santa Engrácia. The citizens of Graça started building the church in 1680 to honor their patron saint, but their ambitions soon outstripped their finances. Salazar's military regime eventually took over construction, completing the project and dedicating it in 1966 as the Panteão Nacional, a burial ground for important statesmen. When democracy was restored in 1975, the new government relocated the remains of prominent anti-fascist opponents to this building. The building also houses the honorary tombs of explorers like Vasco da Gama and Pedro Cabral, as well as the remains of Portuguese artists. (*Take tram #28 from R. do Loreto or R. Garrett.* ☎885 4820. *Open Tu-Su 10am-5pm. €2, seniors €1.*)

**IGREJA DE SÃO VICENTE DE FORA.** The church, built between 1582 and 1692, is dedicated to Lisbon's patron saint. Ask to see the *sacristia* (chapel) with its inlaid walls of Sintra marble. (*Open daily 10am-6pm except for Mass, Tu and F-Sa 9:30am, Su 10:00am. Free. Chapel open Tu-Su 10am-5pm. €2.*)

# SÃO SEBASTIÃO

Located north of Baixa, São Sebastião features busy avenues, department stores, and scores of strip malls. The area also houses two of the finest art museums in Portugal, legacies of oil tycoon Calouste Gulbenkian.

■**MUSEU CALOUSTE GULBENKIAN.** When British citizen Calouste Gulbenkian died in 1955, he left his extensive art collection to Portugal, the country he chose to call home. The formidable collection includes Egyptian, European, Greek, Islamic, Mesopotamian, Oriental and Roman art from the 15th to 20th centuries. Highlights include works by Dégas, Manet, Monet, Rembrandt, Renoir, and Rodin. (*Av. Berna 45. M: São Sebastião.* ☎782 3000; www.gulbenkian.pt. *Open Tu-Su 10am-5:45pm. €3; students, teachers, and seniors free; Su free.*)

**CENTRO DE ARTE MODERNO.** The Centro de Arte Moderno showcases Portuguese talent from the late 19th century to the present. The museum also has art from Portugal's former colonies. (*R. Dr. Nicolau Bettencourt. M: São Sebastião.* ☎782 3474. *Open Tu-Su 10am-5:45pm. €3; students, teachers, and seniors free; Su free.*)

# BELÉM

The concentration of monuments and museums in Belém, a suburb of Lisbon, makes it a crucial stop on any tour of the capital. To reach Belém, take tram #15 from Pr. do Comércio (15min.) and get off at the Mosteiro dos Jerónimos stop, one stop beyond the regular Belém stop. Alternatively, take the train from Estação Cais do Sodré. Exit the station by the the overpass near the Padrão dos Descobrimentos. To reach the Mosteiro dos Jerónimos, exit the overpass to the right, then go through the public gardens to R. de Belém.

■ **MOSTEIRO DOS JERÓNIMOS.** Established in 1502 to commemorate Vasco da Gama's expedition to India, the Mosteiro dos Jerónimos was granted UNESCO World Heritage status in the 1980s. The country's most refined celebration of the Age of Discovery, the monastery showcases Portugal's native Manueline style, combining Gothic forms with minute Renaissance detail. Note the anachronism on the main church door: Prince Henry the Navigator mingles with the Twelve Apostles on both sides of the central column. The symbolic tombs of Luís de Camões and navigator Vasco da Gama lie in opposing transepts. (☎ 362 0034. Open Tu-Su May-Sept. 10am-6:30pm; Oct.-Apr. 10am-5:30pm. Church free. Cloister €4.50.)

**TORRE DE BELÉM.** The best-known tower in Portugal and a UNESCO World Heritage site, the Torre de Belém rises from the north bank of the Rio Tejo and is surrounded by the ocean on three sides. This icon of Portuguese grandeur offers panoramic views of Belém and the Atlantic. Built under Manuel I from 1515 to 1520 as a military stronghold, the Torre has since served several functions, including a stint as Portugal's most famous political prison. (Open Tu-Su May-Sept. 10am-6:30pm; Oct.-Apr. 10am-5:30pm. €3, under 25 and seniors €1.50.)

**PADRÃO DOS DESCOBRIMENTOS.** Directly across from the Mosteiro is the 52m Monument to the Discoveries, built in 1960 to commemorate the 500-year anniversary of Prince Henry the Navigator's death. The white monument is shaped like a narrow cross and depicts Henry and his celebrated compatriots, Vasco da Gama and Diogo Cão. (Across the highway from the Mosteiro. ☎ 303 1950. Open May-Sept. Tu-Su 10am-6:30pm; Oct.-Apr. 10am-5:30pm. €3, students and seniors €1.50.)

## ■ PARQUE DAS NAÇÕES

The Parque das Nações (Park of Nations) inhabits the former Expo '98 grounds. Until the mid-1990s, the area was a muddy wasteland with a few run-down factories and warehouses along the banks of the Tejo. However, the government transformed it to prepare for the World Exposition and afterward spent millions converting the grounds into a park. The entrance leads through the Centro Vasco da Gama **shopping mall** (open daily 10am-midnight) to the center of the grounds, where kiosks provide maps. (M: Oriente. Park ☎ 891 9393; www.parquedasnacoes.pt.)

■ **OCEANÁRIO.** The park's biggest attraction, this enormous oceanarium has interactive sections recreating the four major oceans down to their sounds, smells, and climates. A main tank has over 470 different species of fish, sharks, and other sea creatures. Visitors can get within arm's length of playful sea otters and penguins. (☎ 891 7002; www.oceanario.pt. Open daily Apr.-Oct. 10am-7pm; Nov.-Mar. 10am-6pm. €11, over 65 €5.80, under 12 €5.30, families €25.)

**PAVILIONS.** The numerous pavilions scattered around the park appeal to a variety of interests. The **Pavilhão do Conhecimento** (Pavilion of Knowledge) is an interactive science museum. (☎ 891 7100; www.pavconhecimento.pt. Open Tu-F 10am-6pm, Sa-Su 11am-7pm. €6, under 17 and over 65 €3.) The rides of the **Virtual Reality Pavilion** challenge the senses. The **Atlantic Pavilion** hosts many of Lisbon's concerts, and the **International Fairgrounds** accommodate rotating exhibits.

# ♫ ENTERTAINMENT

*Agenda Cultural* and *Follow Me Lisboa*, free at the tourist office and at kiosks in the Rossio on R. Portas de Santo Antão, have information on concerts, *fado*, movies, plays, and bullfights. They also have lists of museums, gardens, and libraries.

## FADO

Lisbon's trademark is **fado** (p. 795), an art combining singing and narrative poetry that expresses *saudade* (nostalgia). Numerous *fado* houses lie in the small streets of **Bairro Alto** and near R. de São João da Praça in **Alfama**. Some also offer folk-dancing performances. Popular *fado* houses have high minimum consumption requirements (normally €10-20). To avoid breaking the bank, explore nearby streets where various bars and small venues offer free shows with less notable performers. Arrive early if you don't have a reservation.

■ **Café Luso,** Tv. da Queimada 10 (☎342 2281; www.cafeluso.pt). Pass below the club's yellow sign to reach *fado* nirvana. Lisbon's premier *fado* club combines the best of Portuguese music, cuisine, and atmosphere. *Fado* and folk dance, 5 singers per night. Set menu €25. Entrees €22-29. Min. consumption €20, for late night show €15. *Fado* 9-10:30pm and 11pm-2am. Open M-Sa 8pm-2am. F-Su reserve ahead. AmEx/MC/V. ●

**O Faia,** R. Barroca 56 (☎342 6742). Performances by famous fadistas like Anita Guerreiro and Lenita Gentil and some of the finest Portuguese cuisine available make O Faia worth your time and money. 4 singers. Entrees €23-30. Min. consumption €18; includes 2 drinks. Fado 9:30, 11:30pm. Open M-Sa 8pm-2am. AmEx/MC/V. ●

**Adega Machado,** R. do Norte 91 (☎322 4640; fax 46 75 07). One of the larger *fado* restaurants, Machado features some of the best-known *cantadeiras* and guitarists. Numerous portraits and wall decorations make this cavernous bar feel warm and inviting. Min. consumption €16. *Fado* 9:15pm. Open Tu-Su 8pm-3am. AmEx/MC/V. ●

## BULLFIGHTING

Portuguese bullfighting differs from its Spanish counterpart in that the bull is not killed in the ring, a tradition that dates back to the 18th century. These spectacles take place most Thursdays from late June to late September at ■**Praça de Touros de Lisboa,** Campo Pequeno. (☎793 2143. Open daily 10pm-2am.) The newly renovated *praça* is a shopping center during the day and a venue for the distinctly Portuguese *toureio equestre* (horseback bullfighting) at night.

## ▓ FESTIVALS

In June, the people of Lisbon spill into the city for a summer's worth of revelry. Open-air *feiras* (fairs)—smorgasbords of food, drink, live music, and dance—fill the streets. On the night of June 12, the streets explode in song and dance during the **Festa de Santo António.** Banners are strung between streetlights, confetti coats Av. da Liberdade, crowds pack the streets of Alfama, and grilled *sardinhas* (sardines) and *ginginha* (wild cherry liqueur) are sold everywhere. Lisbon also has a number of commercial *feiras*. From late May to early June, bookworms burrow for three weeks in the outdoor **Feira do Livro** in the Parque Eduardo VII behind Pr. Marquês do Pombal. The **Feira Internacional de Lisboa** occurs every few months in the Parque das Nações, while in July and August the **Feira de Mar de Cascais** and the **Feira de Artesania de Estoril,** celebrating famous Portuguese pottery, take place near the casino. Year-round *feiras* include the **Feira de Oeiras** (antiques), on the fourth Sunday of every month, and the **Feira de Carcanelos** (clothes) in Rato (Th 8am-2pm). Packrats will enjoy the **Feira da Ladra** (flea market; literally "thieves' fair"), held behind the Igreja de São Vicente de Fora in Graça (Tu 7am-1pm, Sa 7am-3pm). To get there, take tram #28 (€1.30).

## ▓ NIGHTLIFE

**Bairro Alto,** where small bars and clubs fill side streets, is the premier destination for nightlife in Lisbon. **Rua do Norte, Rua do Diário Notícias,** and **Rua da Atalaia** have many small clubs packed into three short blocks. Several gay and lesbian clubs are between **Praça de Camões** and **Travessa da Queimada,** as well as in the **Rato** area near the edge of Bairro Alto. The **Docas de Santo Amaro** hosts waterfront clubs and bars, while **Avenida 24 de Julho** and **Rua das Janelas Verdes** in the Santos area have the most popular clubs and discos. Another hot spot is the area along the river opposite the **Santa Apolónia** train station. Jeans, sandals, and sneakers are generally not allowed. At clubs, beer runs are €3-5. Crowds flow in around 2am and stay until dawn. The easiest option to reach most clubs is to take a taxi.

**■ A Tasca Tequila Bar**, Tr. da Queimada 13-15 (☎ 919 40 79 14). This always-full Mexican bar is a great place to go on a slow week night. Bartenders at the T-shaped counter serve potent beverages. Mixed drinks €5. Open M-Sa 6pm-2am.

**Pavilhão Chinês**, Dom Pedro V 89 (☎ 342 4729). Ring the doorbell and a red-vested waiter will let you in. Despite the thousands of collection pieces hanging from the ceiling and covering the walls, this famous bar manages to look classy. The place to chill or play pool. Open daily 6pm-2am.

**Dock's Club**, R. da Cintura do Porto de Lisboa 226 (☎395 0856). This huge club plays hip hop, Latin, and house music and has an outdoor bar where you can cool down (or dry off). Famous Tu ladies nights, where the women get in free and receive 4 free drinks. Open Tu-Sa 11pm-6am.

**Jamaica**, R. Nova do Carvalho 6 (☎342 1859). M: Cais do Sodre. This small club is famous for playing 80s music. Packed until the early morning. Women get in free, but men pay a €6 cover (includes 3 beers). Be careful when leaving the club; it's not the safest neighborhood late at night. Open Tu-Sa 10:30pm-6am.

**Lux/Frágil**, Av. Infante D. Henrique A, Cais da Pedra a Sta. Apolonia (☎882 0890). Described by many of its fans as the perfect nightclub, Lux has a high-tech lighting system and an amazing view of the water from its roof. Min. consumption is usually €15. Open Tu-Sa 10pm-6am. AmEx/MC/V.

**Kapital**, Av. 24 de Julho 68 (☎395 7101). The classiest club in Lisbon has a ruthless door policy that makes admission a competitive sport. 3 floors, with a terrace on top level. Mixed drinks €5-8. Cover €10-20. Open M-Sa 11pm-6am. AmEx/MC/V.

**Kremlin**, Escandinhas da Praia 5 (☎395 7101), off Av. 24 de Julho. Run by the same management as Kapital, but a more mixed crowd, including Kapital rejects. Rave music and vibe. Cover women €7, men €12. Open W-Th midnight-7am, F-Sa midnight-9am.

**Speakeasy**, Docas de Santo Amaro (☎390 9166), between the Santos and Alcântara stops, near the river. More of a concert with waiters and beer than a bar, this is a premier jazz and blues center. Older crowd. Beer €3. Live shows nightly. Jazz M. Open M-Sa 9pm-4am. Restaurant 8-11pm. Cash only.

# ▶ DAYTRIPS FROM LISBON

## CASCAIS

*Trains from Lisbon's Estação Cais do Sodré (☎213 42 48 93; M: Cais do Sodré) head to Cascais (30min., 3 per hr., €1.60). Take the "SAAP"; it has fewer stops. ScottURB has a bus terminal in downtown Cascais, underground next to the blue glass tower of the shopping center by the train station. Buses #417 (40min., 1 per hr.) and the more scenic #403 (1½hr., 1 per hr.) go from Cascais to Sintra for €3.20.*

Cascais (*"CASH-kise"*) is a beautiful beach town, serene during the low season but full of vacationers in summer. **Praia da Ribeira, Praia da Rainha,** and **Praia da Conceição** are especially popular with sunbathers. To reach Praia da Ribeira, take a right upon leaving the tourist office and walk down Av. dos Combatantes de Grande Guerra until you see the water. Facing the water, Praia da Rainha and Praia da Conceição are to your left. Those in search of less crowded beaches should take advantage of the ■**free bike rentals** offered at two kiosks in Cascais. One is in front of the train station; the other is in the parking lot of the Cidadela fortress, up Av. dos Carlos I. Bring your passport or driver's license and hotel information to use the bikes from 8am to 6:30pm. Ride along the coast (to your right when facing the water) to reach the ▓Boca de Inferno (Mouth of Hell), so named because the cleft carved in the rock by the Atlantic surf creates a haunting sound as waves pummel the cliffs. This natural wonder is 1km outside Cascais.

When the sun sets, nightlife picks up on **Largo Luís de Camões,** the main pedestrian square. There are good restaurants on Av. dos Combatantes de Grande Guerra, between the tourist office and the ocean. The best is **Restaurante Dom Manolo ❷,** which serves big portions of chicken, mussels, and salmon. (☎214 83 11 26. Entrees €5-11. Open daily 10am-midnight.) To get to the **tourist office,** Av. dos Combatantes de Grande Guerra 25, exit the train station through the ticket office. To the right of McDonald's is Av. Valbom; the office is the yellow building at the end of the street. (☎214 86 82 04. Open in summer M-Sa 9am-8pm, Su 10am-6pm; in winter M-Sa 9am-7pm, Su 10am-6pm.)

# SINTRA                                                                      ☎219

*Trains (☎219 23 26 05) arrive at Av. Dr. Miguel Bombarda from Lisbon's Estação Sete Rios (35min., 6 per hr., €1.50). ScottURB buses (☎214 69 91 00; www.scotturb.com) leave from Av. Dr. Miguel Bombarda for Cascais (#417 or 403; 40min., 1 per hr., €3.25) and Estoril (#418; 40min., 1 per hr., €3.25). Down the street, Mafrense buses go to Ericeira (50min., 1 per hr., €1.80).*

For centuries, monarchs and the wealthiest of noblemen were drawn by the hypnotic beauty of Sintra (pop. 20,000). They left a trail of opulence and grandeur behind them. The town's must-see is the UNESCO World Heritage Site ▓Quinta da Regaleira, a stunning palace whose backyard was turned into a fantasy land by its eccentric millionaire owner at the turn of the 20th century. Statues, fountains, and ponds blanket the small park, which is surrounded by lush green trees and beautiful gardens. The *Poço Iniciático* (Initiatory Well) was inspired by secret Knights Templar rituals; bring a flashlight for exploring the "Dantesque" caves lurking beneath the main sights. To get to the palace, turn right out of the tourist office and follow R. Consiglieri Pedroso out of town as it turns into R.M.E.F. Navarro. (☎10 66 50. Open daily Apr.-Sept. 10am-8pm; Oct. and Feb.-Apr. 10am-6:30pm; Nov.-Jan. 10am-5:30pm. €5, students €4. Tours €10; 10:30am, 11am, noon, 2:30, 3:30pm.) Equally embellished is the **Palácio de Pena,** a colorful Bavarian palace resting atop a dark green mountain that features a lavish ballroom, fresco-covered "Arab Room," and fantastic terrace view. (ScottURB bus #434 goes to the palace; €4. ☎10 53 40; www.parquesdesintra.pt. Open Tu-Su June-Sept. 10am-5:30pm; Oct.-May 10am-4pm. €8, children and seniors €4. Tours €4.50.) Other Sintra highlights include the **Palácio Nacional de Sintra,** a palace built in many architectural styles in the center of town, and the 8th-century **Castelo dos Mouros,** down the hill from the Palácio de Pena.

Restaurants crowd the end of **Rua João de Deus** and **Avenida Heliodoro Salgado.** ▓Restaurante Apeadeiro ❷, Av. Miguel Bombarda 3A, serves authentic Portuguese cuisine, including delicious meat and fish, for the cheapest prices in town (€7-13). **Tourist offices** are located in Pr. da República 23 (☎23 11 57) and in the train station (☎24 16 23. Both open daily June-Sept. 9am-8pm; Oct.-May 9am-7pm.)

# ERICEIRA                                                                    ☎261

*Mafrense buses run from Lisboa's Campo Grande; the bus for Ericeira leaves from the leftmost part of the waiting area (1½hr., 1 per hr., €4.70). Get off at the bus station. Buses run from Ericeira to Lisboa (1½hr., 1 per hr., €4.40), via Mafra (25min., €1.60), and to Sintra (50min., €1.80).*

Ericeira is a pleasant fishing village whose shores are inundated by surfers. The town more or less maintains its traditional way of life despite the visitors frolicking in the waves of its internationally renowned beaches—favorites include nearby **Praia do Norte,** a long beach to the right of the port, and **Praia do Sul** to the left. Though the waves close to town are great for novices, experienced surfers head beyond Praia do Norte to pristine **Praia de São Sebastião, Praia da Ribeira d'Ilhas,** 3km away, or **Praia dos Coxos** (Crippled Beach), just past Ribeira d'Ilhas. Seafood restaurants and several bars can be found along **Rua Dr. Eduardo Burnay,** which runs from Pr. da República. If you decide to stay, see the **tourist office,** R. Dr. Eduardo Burnay 46, for a list of accommodations. From the bus station, cross the street, turn left, and walk uphill. Take a right onto R. Prudêncio Franco da Trinidade and go straight until Pr. da República; the office is at the end of the square. (☎863 122. Multilingual staff. Open M-F 10am-1pm and 2:30-6:30pm, Sa 10am-1pm and 3-10pm, Su 10am-1pm and 3-7pm.)

# NORTHERN PORTUGAL

The unspoiled Costa da Prata (Silver Coast), plush greenery of the interior, and rugged peaks of the Serra Estrela compose the Three Beiras region. To the north, port flows freely and *azulejo*-lined houses grace charming streets.

## PORTO (OPORTO)                    ☎22

Porto (pop. 263,000) is famous for its namesake product—a strong, sugary wine developed by English merchants in the early 18th century. The port industry is at the root of the city's successful economy, but Porto has more to offer than fine alcohol. The city retains traditional charm with granite church towers, orange-tiled houses, and graceful bridges.

**🖪🔃 TRANSPORTATION AND PRACTICAL INFORMATION.** Airlines including **TAP Air Portugal** (☎608 0231), Pr. Mouzinho de Albuquerque 105, fly to major European cities from **Aeroporto Francisco de Sá Carneiro (OPO;** ☎943 2400), 13km from downtown. The recently completed metro E (violet line) goes to the airport (25min., €1.35). The **aerobus** (☎225 07 10 54) runs from Av. dos Aliados near Pr. da Liberdade to OPO (40min., 2 per hr., €4). **Taxis** to Lisbon are €18-20 (15-20min.). Most **trains** (☎808 20 82 08; www.cp.pt) pass through Porto's main station, **Estação de Campanhã,** on R. da Estação. Trains run to: Aveiro (1hr., 47 per day, €2-13); Braga (1hr., 26 per day, €2-13); Coimbra (1½-2hr., 24 per day, €12-16); Lisbon (3½-4½hr., 18 per day, €16-29); Viana do Castelo (1½-2hr., 11 per day, €4-7); Madrid, SPA via Entroncamento (11-12hr., 1 per day, €64). **Estação São Bento,** Pr. Almeida Garrett, has local and regional trains. Internorte (☎605 2420), Pr. Galiza 96, sends **buses** to Madrid, SPA (10hr., 1-2 per day, €43) and other international hubs. Rede Expressos buses (☎200 6954; www.redeexpresso.pt), R. Alexandre Herculano 366, travel to: Braga (1¼hr., 10 per day, €5); Coimbra (1½hr., 11 per day, €10); Lisbon (4hr., 11 per day, €16); Viana do Castelo (1¾hr., 4 per day, €6.40). Renex (☎200 3395), Campo Mártires da Pátria, has express service to Lagos (8½hr., 6 per day, €23) via Lisbon (3½hr., 12 per day, €16). Buy tickets for local buses and **trams** at kiosks or at the **STCP** office, Pr. Almeida Garrett 27, across from Estação São Bento (€1.60 for 2 trips, day-pass €4). The city's main **tourist office,** R. Clube dos Fenianos 25, is off Pr. da Liberdade. (☎339 3470; www.porto-turismo.pt. Open M-F 9am-6:30pm, Sa-Su 9:30am-6:30pm.) **OnWeb,** Pr. Gen. Humberto Delgado 291, has **Internet** access. (Open M-Sa 10am-2am, Su 3pm-2am. Min. 1hr. €1.20 per hr., Wi-Fi €0.60 per hr.) The **post office** is in Pr. Gen. Humberto Delgado. (☎340 0200. Open M-F 8:30am-7:30pm, Sa 9:30am-3pm.) **Postal Code: 4000.**

## I EAT MY FEELINGS

You've probably found yourself ogling the glass display case of Portugal's many *pastelarias* wondering which tempting treat to pick. Wonder no more—here's a guide to heaven:

**Altreia.** A sweet and simple treat from Northern Portugal made of pasta cooked with eggs and sugar topped with cinnamon.

**Arroz-doce.** Sweet rice. There are many variations of this rice pudding, so try it in different places.

**Bolinhos.** Little balls of cake filled with cream and/or dried fruit .

**Bolinhos de Jerimu.** Pumpkin, egg, and Port fried to sweet perfection. Yum.

**Dolce de Ovos.** Aveiro's small sweets made of egg yolks and sugar.

**Pão-de-ló.** The Portuguese version of sponge cake.

**Pastel de Natas.** Petit pastries filled with cinnamon cream, also known as *pastel de Belém*.

**Pastel de Santa Clara.** Star shaped puffs filled with almond flavored cream from the North east.

**Rabanadas.** Thick slices of bread soaked in milk or wine, tossed in sugar, and fried.

**Pão de Deus.** Sweet bread topped with a pineapple and coconut concoction. Add butter and the bread melts in your mouth while the shredded coconut gives a slight crunch. God's bread indeed.

**ACCOMMODATIONS AND FOOD.** For good deals, look on **Praça Filipa de Lancastre** or near the *mercado* on **Rua Fernandes Tomás** and **Rua Formosa,** perpendicular to Av. dos Aliados. The **☒Pensão Duas Nações ❶,** Pr. Guilherme Gomes Fernandes 59, has the best combination of low price and high comfort. (☎208 1616. Reserve ahead or arrive well before noon. Laundry €7. Internet €1 per 30min. Singles €14, with bath €23-25; doubles €23-25; triples €36; quads €46. Cash only.) For a hip hostel option, head up a few blocks from the S. Bento train station toward the tower. **Oporto Poets Hostel ❷,** Tv. da Ferraz 13, is just around the corner, with clean, bright rooms. (☎332 4209. Dorms €20; doubles €44. Low season €18/40. Cash only.)

Quality budget meals can be found near Pr. da Batalha on **Rua Cimo de Vila** and **Rua do Cativo.** Places selling *bifanas* (small pork sandwiches) line R. Bomjardim. **Ribeira** is the place to go for a high-quality, affordable dinner. The **Café Majestic ❷,** R. de Santa Catarina 112, is a snapshot of 19th-century bourgeois opulence. (☎200 3887. Entrees €9-16. Open M-Sa 9:30am-midnight. AmEx/MC/V.) At the **Confeitaria Império ❶,** R. de Santa Catarina 149-151, choose from a huge selection of pastries and inexpensive lunch specials. (☎200 5595. Open M-Sa 7:30am-8:30pm.) The sprawling **☒Mercado de Bolhão** has a wide range of fresh food. Produce is on the upper level. (Open M-F 8am-5pm, Sa 7am-1pm.)

**WINERIES.** No visit to Porto is complete without one of the city's famous wine tasting tours. They are cheap (€1-3) if not free, and take about 30min. Wine tasting is most prevalent across the river, in Vila Nova de Gaia, where there are 17 large port lodges. Tours often include visits to the wine cellars below. To get there, walk across the Ponte de D. Luiz I in Ribeira. Find unbeatable deals at **☒Vinhos de Quinta,** a non-profit wine shop. (☎208 9257. Open daily Tu-Su 11am-7pm.)

> **THE REAL DEAL.** To find the cheapest prices on port, avoid retail stores and check out the wineries and non-profit stores scattered around the city. If you are looking for a particular label, be sure to call before heading out.

**SIGHTS AND ENTERTAINMENT.** Your first brush with Porto's rich stock of fine artwork may be the celebrated collection of *azulejos* (painted tiles) in the **São Bento train station.** From the station, follow signs downhill on R. Mouzinho da Silveira to R. Ferreira Borges and the **☒Palácio da Bolsa** (Stock

Exchange), the epitome of 19th-century Portuguese elegance. The most striking room of the *Palácio* is the extravagant **Sala Árabe** (Arabian Hall). Its gold and silver walls are covered with the juxtaposed inscriptions "Glory to Allah" and "Glory to Doña Maria II." (☎339 9000. Open daily Apr.-Oct. 9am-7pm; Nov.-Mar. 9am-1pm and 2-6pm. €5, students €3. Multilingual tours 2 per hr.) Nearby on R. Infante Dom Henrique, the Gothic **Igreja de São Francisco** glitters with an elaborately gilded wood interior. The neighboring museum houses religious art and artifacts; in the basement lies the *Ossário*, a labyrinth of cavernous catacombs with mass graves. (☎206 2100. Open daily in summer 9am-8pm; winter 9am-5pm. €3, students €2.50.) On R. dos Clérigos rises the **Torre dos Clérigos** (Tower of Clerics), adjacent to the 18th-century **Igreja dos Clérigos.** (☎200 1729. Tower open daily Apr.-Oct. 9:30am-1pm and 2:30-7pm; Nov.-Mar. 10am-noon and 2-5pm. Church open M-Sa 8:45am-12:30pm and 3:30-7:30pm, Su 10am-1pm and 8:30-10:30pm. Tower €2, church free.) From there, head up R. da Restauração, turn right on R. Alberto Gouveia, and go left on R. Dom Manuel II to reach the **Museu Nacional de Soares dos Reis,** R. Dom Manuel II 44. This former royal residence houses a collection of 19th-century Portuguese art. (☎339 3770. Open Tu 2-6pm, W-Su 10am-6pm. €3, students and seniors €1.50. Su before 2pm free.) Porto is not a party city after hours—most people congregate around the bar-restaurants of Ribeira, where fiery Brazilian music plays until 2am.

# BRAGA

☎253

The beautiful gardens, plazas, museums, and markets of Braga (pop. 166,000) have earned it the nickname "Portuguese Rome." The treasury of the **Sé,** Portugal's oldest cathedral, showcases the archdiocese's most precious paintings and relics, including a collection of *cofres cranianos* (brain boxes), one of which contains the 6th-century cortex of Braga's first bishop. (☎26 33 17. Open Tu-Su 9am-noon and 2-5:30pm. Mass daily 5:30pm. Cathedral free. Treasury and chapels €2.) Braga's most famous landmark, **Igreja do Bom Jesús,** is 5km outside of town. This 18th-century church was built in an effort to recreate Jerusalem in Braga, providing Iberian Christians with a pilgrimage site closer to home. Take the bus labeled "#02 Bom Jesús" at 10- or 40min. past the hour in front of Farmácia Cristal, Av. da Liberdade 571 (€1.30). At the site, either go on a 285m ride on the funicular (8am-8pm, 2 per hr., €1) or walk up the granite-paved pathway that leads to a 326-step zig-zagging staircase (20-25min.).

Take a taxi (€5 from the train station) to ⚑**Pousada da Juventude de Braga (HI) ●,** R. Santa Margarida 6, which has a convenient location. (☎61 61 63. Reception 8am-noon and 6pm-midnight. Lockout noon-6pm. Dorms €9; doubles with bath €22.) Cafes on **Praça da República** are perfect for people-watching. Be sure to try *pudim do Abade de Priscos*, a pudding flavored with caramel and port wine. The **market** is in Pr. do Comércio. (Open M-Sa 7am-3pm.) A supermarket, **Pingo Doce,** is in the basement of the Braga shopping mall. (Open daily 10am-11pm.) **Trains** (☎808 20 82 08) pull into Estação da Braga, 1km from Pr. da República. Take R. do Souto and pass through the town gate; the station is 400m down on the left. Trains run to Lisbon (4-5½hr., 3 per day, €22-30) via Porto (1hr., 26 per day, €2-13). **Buses** leave Central de Camionagem (☎20 94 00) for: Coimbra (3hr., 6 per day, €12); Faro (12-15hr., 3-6 per day, €25); Lisbon (5¼hr., 10-11 per day, €17); Porto (1¼hr., 25 per day, €5). The **tourist office** is at Av. da Liberdade 1. (☎26 25 50. Open June-Sept. M-F 9am-7pm, Sa-Su 9am-12:30pm and 2-5:30pm; Oct.-May M-Sa 9am-12:30pm and 2-6:30pm.) **Postal Code:** 4700.

# VIANA DO CASTELO

☎258

Situated in the northwest corner of the country, Viana do Castelo (pop. 37,000) is one of the loveliest coastal cities in Portugal. Though visited mainly for its beaches, Viana also has a historical district centered around the stately **Praça da República.**

Here, the **Museu de Traje** provides a glimpse into the region's distinctive clothing. (☎80 01 71. Open June-Sept Tu-Sa 10am-1pm and 3-7pm; Oct-May Tu-Sa 10am-1pm and 3-6pm. €2, students €1.) Across the plaza, granite columns support the flowery facade of the **Igreja da Misericórdia,** known for its *azulejo* (painted tile) interior. (Open Su 11:30am-noon and some summer weekdays; see tourist office for info. Free.) The **Monte de Santa Luzia,** overlooking the city, is guarded by the **Templo de Santa Luzia.** The early 20th-century church isn't much to look at, but the view from the hill is fantastic. Either brave the hundreds of stairs (30min.) or take a taxi (€5) to the top. (Open daily June-Aug. 8am-7pm; Sept.-May 8am-5pm. Mass Sa 4pm, Su 11am and 4pm. Free.) Sunbathers, swimmers, and windsurfers fill the beautiful if chilly beaches of Viana do Castelo and its neighboring towns. **Praia Norte,** at the end of Av. do Atlântico at the west edge of town, is an easy 15min. walk from the town center and has two natural swimming pools.

■**Pousada de Juventude de Viana do Castelo (HI) ❶,** R. de Límia, on the marina off R. da Argaçosa and Pr. da Galiza, has a bar, ping-pong tables, and rooms with balconies. (☎80 02 60. Breakfast included. Laundry €2.50. Internet €15 per hr. Reception 8am-midnight. Check-out noon. Dorms €11-13; doubles €30-32, with bath €36-38.) Devour *bolos de berlim* (cream-filled pastries; €0.75) at **Pastelaria Zé Natário ❶,** R. Manuel Espregueira 37. (☎82 68 56. Open M and W-Su 7am-10pm.) Get groceries at **Modelo Bonjour Supermercado,** in the mall next to the train station. (☎10 05 40. Open daily 9am-11pm.) A **market** is held Fridays off Av. Campo do Castelo. **Trains** (☎82 13 15) run from Av. dos Combatentes da Grande Guerra to Porto (2hr., 11-14 per day, €7). **Buses** (☎82 50 47) run from the mall next to the train station to Braga (1½hr., 8 per day, €3.70), Lisbon (5½hr., 1-2 per day, €15), and Porto (2hr., 4-6 per day, €4.60). The **tourist office** is on R. Hospital Velho. From the train station, take the fourth left on R. da Picota and then a right. (☎82 26 20; turismo.viana@rtam.pt. Open Aug. M-F 9:30am-7pm, Sa 9:30am-1pm and 2:30-6pm, Su 9:30am-1pm; May-July and Sept. M-F 9:30am-1pm and 2-6pm, Sa 9:30am-1pm and 2:30-6pm, Su 9:30am-1pm; Oct.-Apr. M-F 9:30am-1pm and 2-5:30pm, Sa 9:30am-1pm and 2:30-5:30pm, Su 9:30am-1pm.) **Postal Code:** 4900.

# COIMBRA                                                    ☎239

For centuries, the Universidade de Coimbra was the only institute of higher education in Portugal, attracting young men from the country's elite. Today, tourists of all ages are drawn to the the historic university district, but it is the many students who dominate youthful Coimbra (pop. 200,000).

■◪ **TRANSPORTATION AND PRACTICAL INFORMATION.** Regional **trains** (☎808 20 82 08; www.cp.pt) stop at both Estação Coimbra-B (Velha) and Estação Coimbra-A (Nova), just two short blocks from the town center of Coimbra, while long-distance trains stop only at Coimbra-B station. A local train connects the two stations, departing after regional trains arrive (4min.; €1, free if transferring from another train). Trains run to Lisbon (2-3hr., 17 per day, €12-30) and Porto (1-2hr., 28 per day, €7-20). **Buses** (☎23 87 69) go from the end of Av. Fernão de Magalhães, 15min. past Coimbra-A, to Lisbon (2½hr., 18 per day, €12) and Porto (1-2hr., 14 per day, €11). From the bus station, turn right, follow the avenue to Coimbra-A, then walk to Lg. da Portagem to reach the **tourist office.** (☎85 59 30; www.turismo-centro.pt. Open June 16-Sept. 14 daily 9am-7pm; Sept. 15-June 15 M-F 9:30am-5:30pm, Sa-Su 10am-1pm and 2:30-5:30pm.) **Espaço Internet,** Pr. 8 de Maio, has free **Internet,** but you may have to wait in line. (Passport or driver's license required. Open M-Sa 10am-midnight, Su 2pm-midnight.) **Postal Code:** 3000.

**🏠📷 ACCOMMODATIONS AND FOOD. Residencial Vitória ❷**, R. da Sota 11-19, has spacious, newly renovated rooms with bath, phone, cable TV, and A/C. Older rooms are cheaper, and still roomy and quiet. (☎82 40 49. Breakfast €2.50. In summer, singles €15-30; doubles €25-45; triples €60. Winter €15-25/25-40/50. AmEx/MC/V.) It is an uphill hike to get to **Pousada da Juventude de Coimbra ❶**, R. Henrique Seco 14, but the hostel has a kitchen, a TV room with foosball and a pool table, and clean bathrooms. (☎82 01 14. Dorms €11; doubles €26, with bath €28. AmEx/MC/V.) 📷**Restaurante Adega Paço do Conde ❶**, R. do Paço do Conde, is a local favorite. A budget oasis surrounded by tourist traps, the restaurant offers a variety of fish and meat options for only €5 and has outdoor seating. (☎82 56 05. Open M-Sa 11:30am-3pm and 7-10:30pm. MC/V.) Even cheaper fare can be found at the **UC Cantinas ❶**, the university student cafeterias, where full meals run under €2. One is on the right side of R. Oliveiro Matos, and the other is up the stairs in Lg. Dom Dinis. (ISIC required. Open daily for lunch at noon, dinner at 7pm.) The supermarket **Pingo Doce**, R. João de Ruão 14, is 3min. up R. da Sofia from Pr. 8 de Maio. (☎85 29 30. Open daily 8:30am-9pm.)

**📷🎵 SIGHTS AND ENTERTAINMENT.** Take in the sights of the **cidade velha** (Old Town) by following the narrow stone steps from the river up to the university. Begin your ascent at the **Arco de Almedina**, a remnant of the Moorish town wall, one block uphill from Lg. da Portagem. The looming 12th-century Romanesque **Sé Velha** (Old Cathedral) is at the top. (Open M-Th and Sa 10am-6pm, F 10am-1pm. Cloister €1, students €0.80.) Follow signs to the Jesuit-built **Sé Nova** (New Cathedral), with its blinding gold altar. (Open Tu-Sa 9am-noon and 2-6:30pm. Free.) Just a few blocks uphill is the 16th-century **Universidade de Coimbra**. Enter through the **Porta Férrea** (Iron Gate), off R. São Pedro, to the **Pátio das Escolas**, through which an excellent view of the rural outskirts of Coimbra stretches out to the horizon. The stairs to the right lead to the **Sala dos Capelos** (Graduates' Hall), which houses portraits of Portugal's kings, six of whom were born in Coimbra. The 📷**Capela de São Miguel**, the university chapel, is adorned with magnificent *talha dourada* (gilded wood) carvings. The 18th-century **Biblioteca Joanina** (university library) lies past the Baroque clock tower. Tickets to all university sights can be purchased outside the Porta Férrea, in the Biblioteca General. (☎85 98 00. Open daily Mar. 13-Oct. 9am-7:20pm; Nov.-Mar. 12 10am-5:30pm. Chapel and library €3.50, students and seniors €2.50; combined ticket €6/4.20.)

## LOCAL LEGEND

### THE REAL CORPSE BRIDE

When Prince Dom Pedro took one look at his wife's lady-in-waiting, Inês de Castro, it was (forbidden) love at first sight. Upon discovering this illicit amor, Dom Pedro's father, King Alfonso, condemned the affair and had Inês exiled to a convent in Coimbra. The prince's wife soon died in childbirth, however, and Pedro and Inês continued their affair for the next decade. The prince's plans for a wedding were cut short: his father had Inês killed for fear that her and Pedro's children would eventually claim the throne. Dom Pedro, in retaliation, waged war against the king until his mother convinced him to put the civil strife to an end.

Two years later, Dom Pedro took the throne; he had his lover's assassins tracked down and brought to the public courtyard. There, he watched as their hearts were torn from their living bodies. He then set about making his children rightful heirs to the throne. In a shocking announcement, Dom Pedro ordered a posthumous matrimonial ceremony to take place. Five years after her death, Inês was removed from her grave and dressed like a queen. Dom Pedro forced the court to kneel before her corpse and kiss her rotting hand. He had his own tomb built opposite hers, and on it reads *"Até ao fim do mundo"* (until the end of the world).

Coimbra's nightlife is best from October to July, when students are in town. ■A **Capela,** R. Corpo de Deus, a former chapel converted into a small late-night cafe, is the best place to hear Coimbra-style *fado*, which is performed by both students and professionals. (☎83 39 85. Mixed drinks €4-5. *Fado* at 9:30, 10:30, 11:30pm. Cover €10; includes 1 drink. Open daily 1pm-3am.) **Quebra Club,** Parque Verde do Mondego, blasts jazz and funk by the river. (☎83 60 36. Beer €1-3. Mixed drinks €4-5. Open Su-Th noon-2am, F-Sa noon-4am. AmEx/MC/V.) Students run wild during the **Queima das Fitas** (Burning of the Ribbons), Coimbra's week-long festival in the second week of May. The festivities commence when graduates burn the narrow ribbons they got as first-years and receive wide ribbons in return.

## AVEIRO                                                            ☎234

A network of canals, from which traditional *moliceiros* (seaweed-coated fishing boats) drift out to sea, runs through the old center of the "Venice of Portugal." The main attraction of Aveiro (pop. 80,000) is the ■Museu de Aveiro, on Av. Sta. Joana Princesa, which tells the life story of King Afonso's daughter, Infanta Joana, who decided to become a nun despite her father's objections. (☎42 32 97. Open Tu-Su 10am-5:30pm. €2, students and seniors €1, under 14 and Su 10am-2pm free.) Some of the beaches near Aveiro have beautiful dunes worth a daytrip; most are easily accessible by ferry. The beaches **Barra** and **Costa Nova** can be reached by bus from the *canal central* or train station stops (20min., 21 per day, €1.60).

Inexpensive hostels line the streets of the old town, north of Pr. Humberto Delgado and on the side of the canal with the tourist office; look for *quartos* or *dormidas* signs. The newly renovated rooms of **Residencial Palmeira ❸,** R. de Palmeira 7-11, have cable TV and baths. (☎42 25 21. Breakfast included. Free Internet. June-Sept. singles €30; doubles €40; 1 triple €50. Oct.-May €20/30/40. MC/V.) Seafood restaurants cluster around the fish market off Pr. do Peixe. The **fisherman's market** (open daily 7am-noon) is a sight to behold. Aveiro's specialty, *ovos moles* (sweetened egg yolks), can be sampled at most of the *pastelarias* along Av. Dr. Lourenço Peixinho. Supermarket **Pingo Doce,** R. Batalhão Caçadores 10, is across the canal from the tourist office. (☎38 60 42. Open daily 9am-10pm.)

**Trains** (☎38 16 32) run from Lg. Estação, at the end of Av. Dr. Lourenço Peixinho, to Coimbra (1hr., 32 per day, €5-14), Lisbon (5hr., 19 per day, €13-25), and Porto (45min., 47 per day, €2). To reach the **tourist office,** R. João Mendonça 8, from the train station, walk straight up Av. Dr. Lourenço Peixinho until the bridge; the office is on the next block. (☎42 07 60. Open daily 9am-8pm.) **Postal Codes:** 3800 (north of the canal); 3810 (south of the canal).

# CENTRAL PORTUGAL

Jagged cliffs and whitewashed fishing villages line the Costa de Prata of Estremadura, which has beaches that rival even those of the Algarve. Lush greenery surrounds historic sights in the fertile region on the banks of the Rio Tejo.

## ÉVORA                                                            ☎266

Évora (pop. 55,000) is the capital and largest city of the Alentejo region. Moorish arches line the streets of its historic center, which boasts a Roman temple, an imposing cathedral, and a 16th-century university. Attached to the **Igreja Real de São Francisco** in Pr. 1 de Mayo, the eerie ■Capela dos Ossos (Chapel of Bones) was built by three Franciscan monks out of the bones of 5000 people as a hallowed space to reflect on the profundity of life and death. From Pr. do Giraldo, follow R. República; the church is on the right and the chapel is to the right of the main entrance. (☎70 45 21. Open daily May-Sept. 9am-12:50pm and 2:30-5:45pm; Oct.-Apr. 9am-1pm and 2:30-5:15pm. €1.50; photos €0.50.) The 2nd-century **Templo Romano,** on Lg. Conde do Vila Flor, was built for the goddess Diana. Its large and well-preserved columns look spectacular at night. Facing the temple is the **Convento dos Loíos,** whose chapel interior is covered with dazzling *azulejos*. The actual monastery is now a luxury hotel. (Open Tu-Su 10am-12:30pm and 2-6pm. €3.) Around the corner is the colossal 12th-century **Basílica Catedral;** the 12 apostles on the doorway are masterpieces of medieval Portuguese sculpture. Climb the stairs of the cloister for an excellent view of the city. The **Museu de Arte Sacra,** above the nave, houses religious artifacts, including the sacred jewel-encrusted *Relicário do Santo Lenho,* a relic made from a piece of the cross on which Jesus was crucified. (Cathedral open daily in summer 9am-4:45pm; in winter 9am-12:30pm and 2-4:30pm. Cloisters open daily 9am-noon and 2-4:30pm. Museum open Tu-Su in summer 9am-4:30pm; in winter 9am-12:30pm and 2-4:30pm. Cathedral €1. Cloisters and museum €3, students €2.50.)

*Pensões* cluster around **Praça do Giraldo.** From the tourist office, turn right onto R. Bernardo Matos to get to cozy **Casa Palma ❷,** R. Bernardo Matos 29A. (☎70 35 60. Singles €15-25; doubles €30-35. Cash only.) Budget restaurants can be found near the streets off Pr. do Giraldo, particularly **Rua Mercadores.** Intimate 🖾**Restaurante Burgo Velho ❷,** R. de Burgos 10, serves *alentejano* cuisine. (☎22 58 58. Entrees €5-9. Open M-Sa noon-3pm and 7-10pm. AmEx/MC/V.) After sunset, head to **Praxis,** R. Valdevinos, the only club in town. From Pr. do Giraldo, take R. 5 de Outubro; the club will be on the right. (☎933 35 57 82. Beer €1.50. Mixed drinks €4-6. Min. consumption for men €7, for women €5. Open daily 11pm-4am.) **Trains** (☎70 21 25; www.cp.pt) run from Av. dos Combatentes de Grande Guerra to Faro (5hr., 2 per day, €13-20) and Lisbon (2½hr., 4-6 per day, €11). **Buses** (☎76 94 10; www.rede-expressos.pt) go from Av. São Sebastião to: Braga (8-10hr., 8 per day, €20) via Porto (6-8½hr., 10 per day, €19); Faro (4hr., 3 per day, €14); Lisbon (2hr., 20 per day, €11). The **tourist office** is at Pr. do Giraldo 73. (☎77 70 71. Open daily May-Oct. 9am-7pm; Nov.-Apr. 9am-6pm.) **Postal Code:** 7999.

# LEIRIA                                                                                  ☎244

A large transportation hub with accommodations that are among Portugal's best in quality and price, Leiria (pop. 120,000) makes a good base for exploring the surrounding region. The city is a mix of old and new, exemplified by an ancient castle near a new football stadium. The **Castelo de Leiria,** a granite fort that Dom Afonso Henriques built atop the crest of a volcanic hill after he captured the town from the Moors, is the city's most notable sight. The passing centuries have left the remains in an adventurous state of disrepair. (☎81 39 82. Open Apr.-Sept. M-F 9am-6:30pm, Sa-Su 10am-6:30pm; Oct.-Mar. M-F 9am-5:30pm, Sa-Su 10am-5:30pm. €2.50, students €1.30.) **Pousada da Juventude de Leiria (HI) ❶,** Cândido dos Reis 7, has an elegant courtyard and small book-swap. (☎83 18 68. Lockout noon-6pm. Dorms €11; doubles €26-28. HI card required. AmEx/MC/V.) **Residencial Dom Dinis ❷,** Tr. Tomar 2, offers 25 neatly decorated rooms with phone, TV, and private baths. (July-Aug. singles €25; doubles €38; triples €50. Sept.-June €23/34/45. AmEx/MC/V.) **Trains** (☎88 20 27) run from 3km outside town to Coimbra (2hr., 6 per day, €4.50-7) and Lisbon (1¾hr., 6 per day, €5-11). **Buses** (☎81 57 17) depart from the station off Pr. Paulo VI, near the tourist office, to: Batalha (20min., 13 per day, €2-3); Coimbra (1hr., 11 per day, €8); Lisbon (2hr., 13 per day, €8.70); Porto (3½hr., 10 per day, €12); Tomar (1hr., 2 per day, €3). The **tourist office,** in the Jardim Luís de Camões, has maps and a precise **model** of Batalha's monastery made entirely of egg whites, sugar, and water. (☎84 87 70. Open daily May-Sept. 10am-1pm and 3-7pm; Oct.-Apr. 10am-1pm and 2-6pm.) **Postal Code:** 2400.

## GIVING BACK

### STATELY STORKS

A hollow clatter fills the air. Guarding your eyes from Faro's afternoon sun, you see a winged silhouette sporting what appears to be a beard. Meet the white stork, a migratory bird native to Europe, the Middle East, South Africa, and west-central Asia.

Year after year, the storks come to Faro to construct enormous nests, sometimes more than 2m in diameter. Some nests, built on medieval structures, have been used for centuries.

But increased pollution, pesticide use, and wetland drainage have endangered the storks' eating and breeding grounds, leading to population decline, especially in Western Europe. Catch-and-release efforts have yielded semi-domesticated storks that forgo migration in order to to feast on the abundant fish and shellfish in Faro's marina and beaches. Locals welcome these prehistoric-looking neighbors, but the birds' habit of nesting on power lines led to the electrocution of a stork and the subsequent blackout of all of southern Portugal in 2000. **The Sociedade Portuguesa para o Estudo das Aves (SPEA)** has initiated volunteer groups to monitor and help move nests located on or near power lines.

E-mail spea@spea.pt or call ☎213 22 04 30 to get involved.

## ◨ DAYTRIPS FROM LEIRIA

### BATALHA ☎244

The centerpiece of Batalha (pop. 75,000) is the gigantic ◨**Mosteiro de Santa Maria da Vitória.** Built in 1386, the Gothic and Manueline monastery remains one of Portugal's greatest monuments. *(Open daily Apr.-Sept. 9am-6pm; Oct.-Mar. 9am-5pm. €4.50, 15-25 and seniors €2.25, under 14 and Su before 2pm free.)* Take a taxi (€30-40 round-trip) outside town to a series of spectacular underground *grutas* (caves) in Estremadura's natural park. The **Grutas de Mira de Aire,** with a river 110m below ground level, are the deepest and largest caves in Portugal. Leaving across from the monastery, **buses** run to Leiria (20min., 16 per day, €1.60). For more info on the caves, check with the **tourist office,** Pr. Mouzinho de Albuquerque. *(☎76 51 80. Open daily May-Sept. 10am-1pm and 3-7pm; Oct.-Apr. 10am-1pm and 2-6pm.)* **Postal Code:** 2440.

### TOMAR ☎249

For centuries, the Knights Templar plotted crusades from a convent-fortress high above the small town of Tomar (pop. 20,000). The ◨**Convento de Cristo** complex, built in 1160, is an architectural treasure filled with peaceful cloisters, stunning domes, and winding staircases. *(☎31 34 81. Open daily June-Sept. 9am-6pm; Oct.-May 9am-5pm. €4.50, under 25 and seniors €2.25.)* **Trains** (☎808 20 82 08; www.cp.pt) run from Av. dos Combatentes da Grande Guerra to Coimbra (2½hr., 12 per day, €8.20) and Lisbon (2hr., 16 per day, €8.20). **Buses** (☎968 94 35 50) leave from near the train station for Leiria (1hr., 1-2 per day, €3.10). The **tourist office** is on Av. Cândido Madureira. *(☎32 24 27; www.tomartourism.com. Open daily 10am-1pm and 2-6pm.)* **Postal Code:** 2300.

# ALGARVE

The Algarve, a desert on the sea, is a popular vacation spot, largely due to the nearly 3000 hours of sunshine it receives every year. In July and August, tourists mob the resorts and beaches, packing bars and clubs from sunset until long after sunrise. In low season, the resorts become pleasantly depopulated.

### FARO ☎289

Many Europeans begin their holidays in Faro (pop. 58,000), the Algarve's capital city. The **Vila Adentro** (Old Town)—a medley of museums, handicraft shops, and churches—begins at the **Arco da Vila,** a stone passageway. On Lg. do Carmo stands the **Igreja de Nossa Senhora do Carmo** and its chilling **Capela dos Ossos** (Chapel of Bones), built from the remains of monks buried in the church's cemetery. More than 1245 skulls and many other bones are arrayed in geometric designs on the walls and ceiling. (☎82 44 90. Open May-Sept. M-F 10am-1pm and 3-6pm; Oct.-Apr. M-F 10am-1pm and 3-5pm, Sa 10am-1pm. Su Mass 8:30am. Church free. Chapel €1.) To get to the sunny beach **Praia de Faro,** take bus #16 from the bus station or from the front of the tourist office (5-10min.; 5 per day, return 9 per day; €1). **Pousada da Juventude (HI)** ❶, R. Polícia de Segurança Pública, near the police station, is a bargain. (☎82 65 21; faro@movijovem.pt. Breakfast included. July-Aug. dorms €13; doubles €28, with bath €36. Sept.-June €9/22/25. AmEx/MC/V.) Enjoy coffee and local marzipan at cafes along **Rua Conselheiro Bívar** and **Praça Dom Francisco Gomes.** A selection of fresh pastries and Portugal's famed port wines is available at **Supermercado Garrafeira Rui** on Praça Ferreira de Almeida. (☎82 15 86. Open 10am-1pm, 3pm-7pm.) **Trains** (☎82 64 72) run from Lg. da Estação to Évora (4½-6hr., 3-4 per day, €13) and Lagos (1½hr., 9 per day, €17). EVA **buses** (☎89 97 00) go from Av. da República to Lagos (2hr., 8 per day, €4.30). Renex (☎81 29 80), across the street, sends buses to Porto (7½hr., 6-13 per day, €22) via Lisbon (4hr., 9 per day, €15). Turn left past the garden on Av. República to reach the **tourist office,** R. da Misericórdia 8. (☎80 36 04. Open daily May-Sept. 9:30am-12:30pm and 2-7pm; Oct.-Apr. 9:30am-12:30pm and 2-5:30pm.) **Postal Code:** 8000.

## LAGOS ☎282

Lagos resembles an exotic fraternity at night, swarming with surfers and college-aged students spilling out of bars into the stone streets. The city keeps you soaking in the ocean views, the sun on the beach, and the drinks at the bars.

**TRANSPORTATION AND PRACTICAL INFORMATION.** **Trains** (☎76 29 87) run from behind the marina to Évora (5-5½hr., €14-€22) and Lisbon (4hr., 7 per day, €16). The bus station (☎76 29 44), off **Avenida dos Descobrimentos,** is across the channel from the train station and marina. **Buses** run to Faro (2½hr., 6 per day 7am-5:15pm, €4), Lisbon (5hr., 6 per day, €15), and Sagres (1hr., 16 per day, €3.05). Running along the channel, Av. dos Descobrimentos is the main road carrying traffic to and from Lagos. From the train station, walk through the marina and cross the pedestrian suspension bridge, then turn left onto Av. dos Descobrimentos. From the bus station, walk straight until you reach Av. dos Descobrimentos and turn right; after 15min., take another right onto R. Porta de Portugal to reach **Praça Gil Eanes,** the center of the Old Town. Praça Gil Eanes extends into Lg. Marquêz de Pombal, where the **tourist office** is located. (☎76 41 11. Open M-Sa 10am-6pm.) Check email and the inferior weather back home at **Snack Bar Ganha Pouco,** first right after the footbridge coming from the bus station. (Internet €2.50 per hr.; €0.50 per fax. Open M-Sa 10am-7pm.) **Postal Code:** 8600.

**ACCOMMODATIONS AND FOOD.** In summer, budget accommodations fill up quickly; reserve at least two weeks ahead. Some accommodations, such as the Rising Cock, reserve a limited number of last-minute rooms to maintain a diverse vibe. Locals renting rooms in their homes will greet you at the station. Though these rooms are often inconveniently located, they are frequently the best deals (€10-15 per person). Never agree to a room without first seeing it. The personable staff and social lodgers at **Pousada da Juventude de Lagos (HI)** ❶, R. Lançarote de Freitas 50, congregate in the TV room with billiards, foosball, and a guitar. (☎76 19 70. In summer, book through the central Movijovem office ☎217 23 21 00. Breakfast included. Mid-June to mid-Sept. dorms €16;

doubles with bath €43. Mid-Sept. to mid-June €11/30. Cash only.) It's hard not to have a good time at the ▨**Rising Cock ❷,** Tv. do Forno 14. The hostel is a short walk from most of Lagos's bars and keeps up the city's famous party-town reputation with two patios, a common room, and a DVD library. (☎ 969 41 11 31; www.risingcock.com. Free Internet. High season dorms €20, low season €15; prices may vary. Cash only.) Follow Av. dos Descobrimentos in the direction of Sagres to find **Camping Trindade ❶,** just outside town. (☎ 289 76 38 93. €4 per tent site, €3.10 per person, €4.30 per car.)

Peruse multilingual tourist menus around **Praça Gil Eanes** and **Rua 25 de Abril.** A dedicated following goes to **Casa Rosa ❶,** R. do Ferrador 22, which offers diners many vegetarian options and provides free Internet. (☎ 18 02 38. All-you-can-eat spaghetti or vegetarian bolognaise €7. Open daily 5-11pm.) **Mediterraneo ❷,** R. Senhora da Graça 2, has the most options for vegetarians with an extensive menu of Mediterranean and Thai cuisine. (☎ 76 84 76. Entrees €9-17. Open Tu-Sa 6-10:30pm.) Locals and expats both swear by **A Forja ❷,** R. dos Ferreiros 17, which serves traditional Algarvian seafood. (☎ 76 85 88. Entrees €5-15. Open daily noon-3pm and 6:30-10pm. AmEx/MC/V.) **Nah Nah Bah ❶,** Travessa do Forno 11, serves innovative, Portuguese-inspired dishes for low prices. (Entrees €6.50-8. Open 7pm-2am.) The indoor **market,** outside Pr. Gil Eanes on Av. dos Descobrimentos, has cheap, fresh food on Saturday. **Supermercado São Roque** is on R. da Porta de Portugal 61. (☎ 76 28 55. Open July-Sept. M-F 9am-8pm, Sa 9am-7pm; Oct.-June M-F 9am-7:30pm, Sa 9am-7pm. AmEx/MC/V.)

**◩◪ SIGHTS AND BEACHES.** The few historic sights of Lagos can all be seen in under two hours on an afternoon walk back from the beach. The **Fortaleza da Ponta da Bandeira,** a 17th-century fortress with maritime exhibits and a tiled chapel, overlooks the marina. (☎ 76 14 10. Open Tu-Su 9:30am-12:30pm and 2-5pm. €2, students €1, under 13 free.) Also near the waterfront is the old **Mercado dos Escravos,** the site of the first sale of African slaves in Portugal in 1441. Opposite the Mercado dos Escravos is the gilded **Igreja de Santo António,** which houses a museum filled with artifacts from Lagos's past rulers. (Church and museum open Tu-Su 9:30am-12:30pm and 2-5pm. Church free. Museum €2.20, students and seniors €2.10.) The waterfront and marina offer jet ski rentals, scuba diving lessons, sailboat and dolphin-sighting trips, and motorboat tours of the ▨**coastal rocks and grottoes.** For a lazier day, head to one of Lagos's many beaches. A 4km blanket of sand marks **Meia Praia,** across the river from town. Take a 20min. walk over the footbridge or hop on the quick ferry near Pr. Infante Dom Henrique (€0.50). For a less crowded beach, follow Av. dos Descobrimentos toward Sagres to **Praia de Pinhão** (20min.). A bit farther down the coast, **Praia Dona Ana** features the sculpted cliffs and grottoes that grace many Algarve postcards.

If you're up for more than lounging, Lagos offers a wide variety of water sports, from scuba diving to surfing to (booze) cruising. Companies that offer tours of the grottoes line Av. dos Descobrimentos and the marina. **Surf Experience,** R. dos Ferreiros 21, offers one- to two-week surfing trips including lessons, transportation, and accommodations in Lagos. (☎ 76 19 43; www.surf-experience.com. Apr.-Nov. 1-week €525, 2-week €881; Dec.-Mar. €473/836.) The **Booze Cruise** is a 4hr., all-you-can-drink afternoon boat ride around Lagos's coast. (☎ 969 41 11 31; €35.) **Algarve Dolphins,** Marina de Lagos 10, organizes 1½hr. dolphin-watching tours in high-speed rescue boats. (☎ 08 75 87; www.algarve-dolphins.com. €30.)

**▨ NIGHTLIFE.** As the sun sets, beachgoers head en masse to bars and cafes between **Praça Gil Eanes** and **Praça Luís de Camões.** For late-night establishments, try **Rua Cândido dos Reis** and **Rua do Ferrador,** as well as the intersection of **Rua 25 de Abril, Rua Silva Lopes,** and **Rua Soeiro da Costa.** Brits and Aussies flood **The Red**

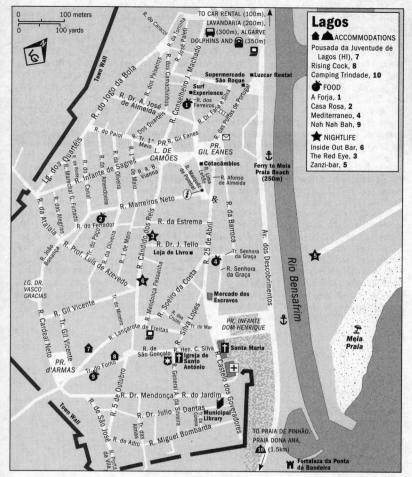

**Lagos**

🏠🏠 ACCOMMODATIONS
Pousada da Juventude de
  Lagos (HI), **7**
Rising Cock, **8**
Camping Trindade, **10**

🍴 FOOD
A Forja, **1**
Casa Rosa, **2**
Mediterraneo, **4**
Nah Nah Bah, **9**

⭐ NIGHTLIFE
Inside Out Bar, **6**
The Red Eye, **3**
Zanzi-bar, **5**

**Eye,** R. Cândido dos Reis 63, in search of classic rock, cheap liquor, and games of pool. (Beer €2-3. Mixed drinks €3.50-5. Shots €2.50. Free shot with 1st drink. Happy hour 8-10pm. Open daily 8pm-2am.) **Inside Out Bar,** R. Cândido dos Reis 119, serves a house specialty—the Fishbowl, made with an entire bottle of vodka. (Beer €3. Shots €1-3. Fishbowl €25. Open daily 8pm-4am.) **Zanzi-bar,** R. 25 de Abril 93, is frequented by locals. (Shots €2.50-3. Beer €2-3. Open daily 8pm-4am.)

# SAGRES                    ☎282

Marooned atop a windy plateau at the southwesternmost point in Europe, desolate Sagres (pop. 2500) and its cape were once believed to be the edge of the world. Near the town stands the 🏛**Fortaleza de Sagres,** former home to Prince Henry the Navigator and his famous school of navigation. The pentagonal 15th-century fortress and its surrounding paths yield striking views of the cliffs and sea. (Open daily May-Sept. 9:30am-8pm; Oct.-Apr. 9:30am-5:30pm. €3, under 25 €1.50.) Six kilometers west lies the dramatic **Cabo de São Vicente,** where the second most powerful lighthouse in Europe shines over 100km out to sea. Take the bus from R. Comandante Matoso near the tourist office (10min., 2 per day, €1) or embark on a scenic hour-long walk. The most well-known beach in the area is windy **Mareta,** at the bottom of the road away from **Praia da Baleeira.** Striking rock formations can be found at **Praia da Belixe,** 3km outside of town on the way to Cabo de São Vicente. The nearby coves of **Salema** and **Luz** are intimate and picturesque.

Finding a bed in Sagres is not hard—windows everywhere display multilingual signs for rooms, many in converted one-story houses run by Sagres residents and families. Haggle with owners and be sure to check out a room before you agree; prices range €15-30 for singles and doubles, €25-40 for triples, with rates lower in winter. Otherwise, follow R. Comandante Matoso toward the tourist office and take a left on R. Patrão António Faustino to reach █**Atalaia Apartamentos ❷,** on R. da Atalaia, which features beautiful, fully furnished rooms with baths, refrigerators, and TVs. Apartments for rent have a bath, kitchen, living room, and terrace. (☎62 46 81. July-Sept. doubles €40; 2-person apartments €60; 3- to 4-person apartments €80-90. Apr.-June €30/40/50-60. Oct.-Mar. €30/30/40-50.) At night, a surfer crowd fills **Água Salgada,** on R. Comandante Matoso. (☎62 42 97. Beer from €1.50. Mixed drinks €3.50-4.50. Open daily June-Aug. 10am-4am; Sept.-May M and W-Su 10am-4am. AmEx/MC/V.) Next door is **O Dromedário,** where a DJ keeps the party bumping. (☎62 42 97. Beer €1-2. Mixed drinks €3.50-5. Crepes €2.20-4. Open in summer daily 10am-3am; low season Su-Th 10am-2am, F-Sa 10am-4am. AmEx/MC/V.) **EVA buses** (☎76 29 44) run to Lagos (1hr., 14 per day, €3.10). From July to September, buses also run to Lisbon (1 per day, €15). The **tourist office,** on R. Comandante Matoso, is up the street from the bus stop. (☎62 48 73; www.visitalgarve.pt. Open Tu-Sa 9:30am-12:30pm and 1:30-5:30pm.) **Postal Code:** 8650.

# SPAIN (ESPAÑA)

The fiery spirit of flamenco; the energy of artistic genius; the explosive merging of urban style and archaic tradition—this is Spain. Here, dry golden plains give way to rugged coastline, and modern architectural feats rise from ancient plazas. Explore winding medieval alleyways that lead to bustling city centers, or watch from a sidewalk cafe as curiously hair-styled youth pass by. In Spain, there is always a reason to stay up late, and there is always time for an afternoon *siesta*.

 **DISCOVER SPAIN: SUGGESTED ITINERARIES**

# LIFE AND TIMES

## HISTORY

**RULE HISPANIA (PRE-HISTORY TO AD 711).** Spain played host to a succession of civilizations—**Basque, Celtiberian, Phoenician,** and **Greek**—before the **Romans** arrived in the 3rd century BC. Over the next seven centuries, the Romans drastically altered the face and character of Spain, introducing their language, architecture, and agricultural techniques for the cultivation of grapes, olives, and wheat. A slew of Germanic tribes swept through the region in the early AD 5th century, and the **Visigoths**—newly converted Christians—emerged victorious. In AD 419, they established court at Barcelona and ruled Spain for the next 300 years.

**PLEASE, SIR, MAY I HAVE SOME MOORS? (711-1469).** Following Muslim unification, a small force of **Arabs, Berbers,** and **Syrians** invaded Spain in 711. The Moors encountered little resistance from the divided Visigoths, and the peninsula soon fell to the caliph of Damascus, the spiritual leader of Islam. The Moors made **Córdoba** (p. 865) their Iberian capital, which in the 10th century became the largest city in Europe. Ruler **Al Mansur** snuffed out all opposition within his court and

**Spain**

Bay of Biscay

COSTA VERDE

La Coruña  Oviedo  Cangas de Onís

**Guernica**  **San Sebastián**  FRANCE

**Santiago de Compostela**  CORDILLERA CANTÁBRICA  **Bilbao**  PYRENEES  ANDORRA

Astorga  León  Burgos  Pamplona  **Jaca**  **Vielha**  **Figueres**  Cadaqués

RÍAS BAJAS  Miño  Sierra de la ....  **Torla**  Montserrat  **Girona**  COSTA BRAVA

**Zamora**  Valladolid  Duero  Zaragoza  **Sitges**  **Barcelona**

CORDILLERA IBÉRICA  Ebro  COSTA DORADA

**Salamanca**  **Segovia**  Sigüenza  *Menorca*

Béjar  Ávila  **El Escorial**  Tajo  Ciudadela  Mahón

PORTUGAL  ☆ **Madrid**  TO MENORCA →

CORDILLERA CENTRAL  Balearic

**Cáceres**  **Trujillo**  **Toledo**  **Cuenca**  Golfo de  Sea  ● Palma

Aranjuez  Valencia  *Mallorca*

Badajoz  Guadiana  Buñol  **Valencia**  *Ibiza*  ISLAS BALEARES

Mérida  Júcar  *Eivissa*

Zafra  COSTA DEL AZAHAR  *Formentera*

SIERRA  MORENA  **Alicante**

Guadalquivir  SIERRA DE SEGURA  COSTA BLANCA

**Córdoba**  *Mediterranean Sea*

**Seville**  **Granada**

Golfo de  **Ronda**

Cádiz  Jerez de la Frontera  **Málaga**  ALGERIA

COSTA DE LA LUZ  **Cádiz**  Arcos de la Frontera  **Marbella**  COSTA DE ALMERÍA

Algeciras  **Gibraltar**  COSTA DEL SOL

ATLANTIC OCEAN  **Tarifa**  Cueta

Strait of Gibraltar

MOROCCO  0  100 miles

0  100 kilometers

undertook a series of military campaigns that climaxed with the destruction of **Santiago de Compostela** (p. 924) in 997 and the kidnapping of its bells. It took the Christians 240 years—until **Fernando III** took Córdoba in 1236—to retrieve them.

The death of Al Mansur and the subsequent power vacuum in Córdoba marked a turning point in Muslim-Christian relations. The Moorish holdings shattered into petty states called *taifas*, and with power less centralized, Christians were able to gain the upper hand. Fortunately, the Christians were usually tolerant of Muslims and Jews, fostering unique cultural and artistic interactions. During the Middle Ages, however, countless Moorish structures were destroyed in the **Reconquista,** and many mosques were converted into churches.

**EXPLORATION AND INQUISITION (1469-1516).** In 1469, the marriage of **Fernando de Aragón** and **Isabel de Castilla,** the ultimate power couple, marked the union of Iberia's mightiest Christian kingdoms. In 1478, aiming to strengthen the church and unify Spain, the Catholic monarchs began executing and exiling heretics, Jews, and Muslims during the infamous **Inquisition.** In 1492, Fernando and Isabel captured **Granada** (p. 878), the last Moorish stronghold, and sent **Christopher Columbus** to find a new route to Asia. During their approximately 50 years of rule, the pair established Spain as an economic, political, and cultural powerhouse that continued to flourish with the aid of lucrative conquests in the Americas.

**ENTER THE HABSBURGS (1516-1713).** The daughter of Fernando and Isabel, **Juana la Loca** (the Mad), married **Felipe el Hermoso** (the Fair) of the powerful Habsburg dynasty. When Felipe died in a game of *jai alai*, La Loca took the news badly, dragging his corpse through the streets screaming (see p. 883). Juana and Felipe had secured their legacy with the birth of **Carlos I**, better known as Holy Roman Emperor Charles V. He eventually retired to a monastery, leaving **Felipe II** a handful of rebellious territories in the Protestant Netherlands. The 1554 marriage of Felipe II to Mary Tudor, Queen of England, created an international Catholic alliance; Felipe believed his life's purpose was to create a Catholic empire. In 1581, the Dutch declared their independence from Spain, starting a war and spurring antagonism with England's new Protestant Queen, Elizabeth I. The conflict with the British heralded Spain's downfall; **Sir Francis Drake** decimated Spain's "invincible" **Armada** in 1588. With much of his empire lost and his wealth from the Americas depleted, Felipe retreated to **El Escorial** (p. 855), sulking in its monastery until his death. In 1609, **Felipe III** (r. 1598-1621) expelled nearly 300,000 of Spain's remaining Moors. After him, **Felipe IV** (r. 1621-1665) painstakingly held the country together through a long, tumultuous reign, while fostering the arts (painter **Diego Velázquez** graced his court). Defending Catholicism began to drain Spain's resources after the outbreak of the **Thirty Years' War** (1618-1648), which ended in the marriage of Felipe IV's daughter María Teresa to **Louis XIV** of France. However, their son was not fit to succeed to the throne. **Carlos II el Hechizado** (the Bewitched; r. 1665-1700), the product of generations of inbreeding, was known to fly into fits of rage and suffered from seizures. From then on, little went right: Carlos II died without heirs, Spain fell into economic depression, and cultural bankruptcy ensued. Rulers battled for the crown in the **War of the Spanish Succession** (1701-1714).

**THE REIGN IN SPAIN (1713-1931).** The 1713 **Peace of Utrecht** ended the ordeal and seated **Felipe V,** a Bourbon grandson of Louis XIV, on the Spanish throne. Though the new king cultivated a flamboyant, debaucherous court, he administered the empire competently, reining in the Spanish-American trade. As part of his bid for world domination, **Napoleon** invaded Spain in 1808, inaugurating an occupation as short as the general himself. The victory of the Protestant Brits over the Corsican's troops at **Waterloo** (1814) led to the restoration of **Fernando VII** (1814-1833), who sought to revoke the repressive constitution of 1812. Spurred to action by Fernando's ineptitude and inspired by liberal ideas, most of Spain's Latin American empire threw off the colonial yoke and declared independence.

Parliamentary liberalism was restored in 1833 upon the death of Fernando VII, and the monarchy was so weakened after the first **Carlist War** (1833-1840) that the first **Spanish Republic** was proclaimed. Despite the ensuing political anarchy, the last two decades of the 19th century were marked by rapid industrialization. However, any remaining dreams of colonial wealth were crushed with the Spanish loss in the **Spanish-American War** of 1898. Other embarrassing military defeats threw the country into political and social chaos. Spain remained neutral in WWI, occupied by internal conflict. In 1923, **General Miguel Primo de Rivera** brought order to the situation in the form of Spain's first dictatorship. However, seven years later, having lost the support of his own army, he resigned.

**REPUBLIC AND REBELLION (1931-1939).** In April 1931, King **Alfonso XIII** (1902-1931), disgraced by his support for Rivera, abdicated the throne, thus giving rise to the **Second Republic** (1931-1936). Republican Liberals and Socialists established safeguards for farmers and industrial workers, granted women's suffrage, assured religious tolerance, and chipped away at traditional military dominance in politics. The cohesion of nationalist euphoria, however, faded fast. The 1933 elections split the Republican-Socialist coalition, increasing the power of right-wing and Catholic parties in parliament. By 1936, left-wing and centrist parties had formed a **Popular Front** to win the elections, though their victory was short-lived. **Generalísimo Francisco Franco** snatched control of the Spanish army, military uprisings ensued, and the nation was plunged into war. The **Spanish Civil War** (1936-1939) ignited ideological passions worldwide, a symbolic but quite real battle between liberalism and fascism. Germany and Italy dropped troops, supplies, and weapons into Franco's lap, while the US and war-weary European states hid behind a policy of non-intervention. The Soviet Union organized the **International Brigades**—a coalition of leftist volunteers—to battle Franco's fascism, but aid waned as Stalin moved toward an alliance with Hitler. Without international aid, Republican forces were cut off from supplies. Bombings, executions, combat, starvation, and disease took nearly 600,000 lives. In 1939, Franco's forces marched into Madrid and ended the war. Franco maintained Spain's neutrality throughout WWII, although he considered aiding Hitler until the tide of the combat turned.

**FRANCO AND THE NATIONAL TRAGEDY (1939-1975).** As scientists, artists, intellectuals, and sympathizers emigrated or faced imprisonment and execution, dissatisfied workers and students took to the streets, encouraging regional discontent and international isolation. Groups like the Basque nationalist **ETA** resisted the dictatorship throughout Franco's reign, often through terrorist acts. In his old age, Franco tried to smooth international relations by joining NATO, courting the Pope, and encouraging tourism, but the **national tragedy** (as it was later called) did not officially end until Franco's death in 1975. King **Juan Carlos I** (1975-), nominally a Franco protégé, carefully set out to undo Franco's damage.

**TRANSITION TO DEMOCRACY (1975-2000).** In 1978, under centrist prime minister **Adolfo Suárez,** Spain adopted a new constitution that led to the restoration of parliamentary government and regional autonomy. Suárez's resignation in early 1981 left the country ripe for the attempted coup on February 23 of that year, when a group of rebels took over parliament in an effort to impose a military-backed government. King Juan Carlos I used his personal influence to convince the rebels to stand down, paving the way for charismatic **Felipe González** to lead the **Spanish Socialist Workers' Party (PSOE)** to victory in the 1982 elections. González oversaw Spain's integration into the European Economic Community (now the **European Union**) four years later, and despite unpopular economic stands, he was re-elected in 1986 to continue a program of massive public investment in order to rejuvenate Spain's economy. By 1994, however, recession and large-scale corruption led to a resounding Socialist defeat at the hands of the **Popular Party (PP)** in the parliamentary elections. The PP's leader, **José María Aznar,** managed to maintain a fragile coalition with the support of the Catalonia and Canary Islands regional parties.

# TODAY

Though Aznar won an absolute majority in 2000, his successor lost to **José Luis Rodríguez Zapatero** of the PSOE in the March 2004 elections. Many attribute this to voters' loss in faith in the PP after its attempts to shirk responsibility for the terrorist attacks (see below) that had occurred in Madrid days before the vote.

Despite government crackdowns, Basque separatists in northwestern Spain pressed on in their effort to establish an autonomous state. The movement's militant wing, the **Euskadi Ta Askatasuna** (ETA; Basque Homeland and Freedom), is known for its terrorist activities. Over 800 people have been killed since 1968 by their arson and murders, which commonly target PP and PSOE members, journalists, and army officers. The ETA claimed responsibility for a series of car bombings in Madrid in February and May 2005. On March 22, 2006, ETA declared a permanent ceasefire and urged the Spanish government to respond positively to this new development. On June 5, 2007, the ETA revoked its "permanent" ceasefire, claiming that the Spanish government had not cooperated enough in negotiations—considering that the ETA claimed responsibility for a December 2006 bombing in a Madrid carpark, the ceasefire seems to have had little effect on stemming the violence.

On **March 11, 2004,** Madrid suffered the worst terrorist attack in modern Spanish history, often referred as **11-M** *(el once eme).* Ten bombs exploded on four commuter trains as they entered the city, killing 191 passengers and injuring more than

1800. Spain was rattled to its core, and the day became a signal of the growing threat of terrorism on a global scale. Although Spanish authorities initially speculated that the ETA was responsible for the attacks, they were later attributed to al-Qaeda.

Spain became the third country to legalize gay marriage in 2005. As the country is predominantly Catholic, the decision was a controversial one.

# PEOPLE AND CULTURE

**RELIGION.** The **Roman Catholic Church** has dominated everyday life in Spain since the Battle of Granada, but there are still remnants of the nation's strong **Jewish** and **Muslim** heritages. Many towns still celebrate their patron saint's feast day as they have for hundreds of years. Churches should be treated with the utmost respect, as most Spaniards are deeply religious and expect visitors to behave properly in places of worship.

**LANGUAGE.** *Castellano* (Castilian) Spanish is the official language of the Kingdom of Spain, but many region have their own specific language which, in addition to Castilian, is official in that region. Under Franco's dictatorship, local languages were repressed, but today, protected under the Spanish constitution, local languages are again a source of great regional pride and identity. Most Spaniards are at least bilingual, speaking Castilian in addition to their regional language. The languages with the highest number of speakers are Catalan (spoken in Catalonia), Euskera (spoken in Basque Country), and Galician (spoken in Galicia). However, there are many other region-specific languages, all of which are protected. It would be incorrect to label these languages "dialects"; while many sound similar to Castilian, they are still linguistically distinct. For a Castilian Spanish phrasebook and pronunciation guide, see the **Phrasebook: Spanish,** p. 1058.

**BULLFIGHTING.** The national spectacle that is **la corrida** (bullfighting) dates, in its modern form, from the early 1700s. A bullfight is divided into three principal stages. In the first, **picadores** (lancers on horseback) pierce the bull's neck. Next, assistants on foot thrust **banderillas** (decorated darts) into his back. Finally, the **torero** (bullfighter or matador) performs the kill. If a torero has shown special skill and daring, the audience waves white **pañuelos** (handkerchiefs), imploring the bullfight's president to award him the coveted ears (and, very rarely, the tail) of the bull. Bullfighting has always had its critics—in the 18th century, the Catholic Church felt that the associated risks made it equivalent to suicide. More recently, the challenge comes from animal rights activists who object to the gruesome and drawn-out slaughter.

# THE ARTS

## ARCHITECTURE

Scattered **Roman ruins**, notably the **aqueduct** in Segovia (p. 859), testify to six centuries of colonization. After their AD 711 invasion, the **Moors** built mosques and palaces throughout southern Spain. Because the Qur'an forbids images of humans and animals, Moorish architects adorned their buildings with geometric designs, horseshoe arches, and ornate tiles. The spectacular 14th-century **Alhambra** in Granada (p. 881) and the **Mezquita** in Córdoba (p. 865) epitomize the Moorish style.

Long periods of peaceful coexistence between Islam and Christianity inspired the unique **mudéjar** architectural movement. Seville's **Alcázar** (p. 873) is an exquisite example of this tradition. The **Spanish Gothic** style, introduced in 1221, experimented with pointed arches, flying buttresses, and stained-glass windows. Next, New World riches inspired the **Plateresque** (silversmith) style, a flashy Gothic fashion used in wealthier parts of Spain. Intricate stonework and extravagant use of gold and silver splashed 15th- and 16th-century buildings, most notably in **Salamanca** (p. 860), where the university drips with ornamentation.

In the late 16th century, Italian innovations in perspective and symmetry toned down the Plateresque style and influenced **Juan de Herrera's** design for **El Escorial**

(p. 855), Felipe II's immense palace-cum-monastery. Opulence took center stage in 17th- and 18th-century **Baroque** Spain when three brothers pioneered the **Churrigueresque** style, whose elaborate ornamentation with lavish sculptural detail gave buildings a rich exuberance, most resonant in Salamanca's **Plaza Mayor** (p. 860).

In the late 19th and early 20th centuries, Catalonia's **Modernistas** burst onto the scene in Barcelona, led by the eccentric genius of **Antoni Gaudí** and **Luís Domènech i Montaner.** *Modernista* structures defied previous standards with their voluptuous curves and unusual textures. Gaudí's unfinished **La Sagrada Família** (p. 902) and **Casa Milà** (p. 903) stand as some of the finest examples of Catalan *Modernisme*. In the mid-20th century, Catalan architect **Josep Luís Sert** helped introduce European Modernism with his stark concrete buildings. Spain's outstanding architectural tradition continues to this day with current stars like **Rafael Moneo** and **Santiago Calatrava,** who has become a sensation with his elegant steel-and-crystal buildings in Valencia (p. 889) and his unmistakable bridges in Seville, Mérida, and Bilbao. Spain has also acquired several new landmarks from foreign architects, including Frank Gehry's stunning **Guggenheim Museum** in Bilbao (p. 921).

## FILM

During Franco's regime (1939-1975), censors stifled most creative tendencies and left the public with nothing to watch but cheap westerns and bland spy flicks. As censorship waned in the early 1970s, Spanish cinema showed signs of life, led by **Carlos Saura's** dark, subversive hits like *El jardín de las delicias* (1970) and *Cria cuervos* (1976). In the wake of Franco's death, domestic censorship laws were completely revoked, and depictions of the exuberant excess of a liberated Spain found increasing international attention. Basque director **Eloy de la Iglesia's** *El diputado* (1979) explored the risqué themes on which contemporary Spanish cinema often focuses. Equally radical are the films of Spain's most highly acclaimed director, **Pedro Almodóvar.** His *Todo sobre mi madre* (1999) won the Oscar for Best Foreign Film in 2000, and his recent film *Volver* (2006) won Best Screenplay at the Cannes Film Festival. Other influential Spanish directors of the past and present include **Icíar Bollaín, Luis Buñuel,** and **Bigas Luna.** Although written directed by Mexican **Guillermo del Toro,** the Oscar-winning 2006 film *El laberinto del fauno* (Pan's Labyrinth) is a grim fairy tale set during the Spanish Civil War.

## LITERATURE

Spain's literary tradition first blossomed in the late Middle Ages (1000-1500), but literature, poetry, and drama truly thrived during Spain's **Siglo de Oro** (Golden Age; 16th and 17th centuries). It was in this era that **Tirso de Molina's** famed *El Burlador de Sevilla* (1630) introduced Don Juan into the national psyche and **Miguel de Cervantes** brought the nobly misguided *Don Quixote de la Mancha* (1605-1615) into the world.

The 18th century brought a belated Enlightenment, while the 19th century inspired **Rosalía del Castro's** innovative lyrical verse and the naturalistic novels of **Leopoldo Alas** (a.k.a. Clarín). Essayist and philosopher **Miguel de Unamuno** and critic **José Ortega y Gasset** led the **Generación de 1898,** along with novelist **Pío Baroja,** playwright **Ramón del Valle Inclán,** and poets **Antonio Machado** and **Juan Ramón Jiménez.** Reacting to Spain's defeat in the Spanish-American War (1898), these nationalistic authors argued that each individual must attain peace spiritually before society can do the same. These men influenced the **Generación de 1927,** a group of experimental lyric poets like **Federico García Lorca** and **Rafael Alberti.** In the 20th century, the Nobel Committee honored playwright and essayist **Jacinto Benavente y Martínez** (1922), poets **Juan Ramón Jiménez** (1956) and **Vicente Aleixandre** (1977), and novelist **Camilo José Cela** (1989). **Ana Rossetti** and **Juana Castro** lasciviously led a new generation of erotic poets into the 1980s, placing women at the forefront of Spanish literature for the first time. As Spanish artists migrate to

Madrid, just as they did in the early part of the century, an avant-garde spirit—known as *La Movida*—is being reborn in the capital.

## MUSIC

**Flamenco,** one of Spain's most famous—and most clichéd—traditions, combines melodramatic song, guitar, and dance. True flamenco artists are said to perform with *duende*, the soul or spirit behind a passionate performance. The music originated among Andalusian gypsies and continues to hypnotize audiences around the world. **Andrés Segovia** was instrumental in endowing the flamenco guitar with the same renown as the violin and the cello.

**Pau Casals,** a Catalan cellist, conductor, composer, pianist, and humanitarian, was one of the most influential classical musicians of the 20th century and promoted world peace through music. **Enrique Granados** contributed the opera *Goyescas* (1991), based on paintings by Goya, and his own personal takes on the **zarzuela,** a form of light opera particular to Madrid. Arguably the greatest Spanish composer of the century, Cádiz native **Manuel de Falla** wrote the popular opera *El sombrero de tres picos* (The Three-Cornered Hat), which premiered in London in 1919 with stage design by Picasso. Barcelona-born **José Carreras** and **Plácido Domingo** are generally recognized as two of the world's finest operatic tenors.

## PAINTING

It was not until Spain's imperial ascendance in the 16th century that painting reached its **Siglo de Oro** (Golden Age; roughly 1492-1650). Felipe II imported foreign art and artists to jump-start native production and embellish his palace, El Escorial. Although he supposedly came to Spain seeking a royal commission, **El Greco** was rejected because of his shocking and intensely personal style. However, his dramatic, haunting figures, such as those gracing Toledo's (p. 855) Iglesia de Santo Tomé, have since received due appreciation. Felipe IV's court painter, **Diego Velázquez,** captured light with virtually photographic precision, whether depicting the royal family, court jesters, or dwarves. Nearly half of the artist's works reside in the **Prado** (p. 850) in Madrid, including his *Las Meninas* (1656)—consistently ranked among the top paintings in the world by art historians. **Francisco de Goya** (1746-1828), official court painter of Carlos IV, ushered European art into the modern age. His depictions of royalty are like caricatures, and the works of his later years are nightmarish, fantastic visions that inspired expressionist and surrealist artists of the following century.

Perhaps no artist influenced 20th-century painting as profoundly as Málaga-born **Pablo Picasso** (1881-1973). Moving between Barcelona and Paris, the artist progressed through several stylistic phases before founding **Cubism,** a method of geometric abstraction. Catalan painter and sculptor **Joan Miró** (1893-1983) worked with simple shapes and bright primary colors. His whimsical creations became a statement against the authoritarianism of fascist Spain. In contrast, fellow Catalan **Salvador Dalí** (1904-1989) scandalized society and leftist intellectuals in France and Spain by claiming to support the Fascists. Dalí's name is now synonymous with **Surrealism,** the artistic expression of the liberated imagination. An odd character and self-congratulatory fellow, the artist founded the **Teatro-Museu Dalí** in Figueres (p. 910).

Since Franco's death in 1975, a new generation of artists, including unorthodox collage artist **Antoni Tápies** and hyperrealist painter **Antonio López García,** has thrived. With new museums in Madrid, Barcelona, Valencia, Seville, and Bilbao, Spanish artists once again have a national forum for their work.

# HOLIDAYS AND FESTIVALS

**Holidays:** New Year's Day (Jan. 1); Epiphany (Jan. 6); Maundy Thursday (Mar. 20); Good Friday (Mar. 21); Easter (Mar. 23-24); Labor Day (May 1); Assumption (Aug. 15); National Day (Oct. 12); All Saints' Day (Nov. 1); Constitution Day (Dec. 6); Feast of the Immaculate Conception (Dec. 8); Christmas (Dec. 25); New Year's Eve (Dec. 31).

SPAIN

**Festivals:** Almost every town in Spain has several festivals. In total, there are more than 3000. Nearly everything closes during festivals. All of Spain celebrates *Carnaval* the week before Ash Wednesday (Feb. 6); the biggest parties are in Catalonia and Cádiz. During the annual festival of *Las Fallas* in mid-Mar., Valencia honors St. Joseph with parades, fireworks, and the burning of effigies. The entire country honors the Holy Week, or *Semana Santa* (Mar. 16-22). Seville's *Feria de Abril* has events showcasing many different Andalusian traditions, including bullfighting and flamenco (Apr. 8-13). *San Fermín* (The Running of the Bulls) takes over Pamplona July 6-14 (see p. 915). for more info, see www.tourspain.es or www.gospain.org/fiestas.

# ADDITIONAL RESOURCES

*The Broadsheet,* web edition at www.tbs.com.es. A monthly magazine published for English speakers in Spain.

*Contemporary Spain: A Handbook,* by Christopher Ross. Arnold Publishers (2002). A broad and informative discussion of Spanish politics, culture, society, and travel.

*The Sun Also Rises,* by Ernest Hemingway. Scribner (1995). The bullfighting of Pamplona was immortalized in this classic about expatriates, impotence, and love.

# ESSENTIALS

### FACTS AND FIGURES

**Official Name:** Kingdom of Spain.

**Capital:** Madrid.

**Government:** Parliamentary monarchy.

**Major Cities:** Barcelona, Granada, Seville, Valencia.

**Population:** 40,448,000.

**Land Area:** 500,500 sq. km.

**Time Zone:** GMT +1.

**Languages:** Spanish (Castilian), Basque, Catalan, Galician.

**Religion:** Roman Catholic (94%).

**Largest Paella Ever Made:** 20m in diameter, this paella fed 100,000 people in 1992.

# WHEN TO GO

Summer is high season in Spain, though in many parts of the country, *Semana Santa* and other festival days are particularly busy. Tourism peaks in August, when the coastal regions overflow while inland cities empty out. Winter travel has the advantage of lighter crowds and lower prices, but sights reduce their hours.

# DOCUMENTS AND FORMALITIES

**EMBASSIES.** Foreign embassies in Spain are in Madrid. Spanish embassies abroad include: **Australia** and **New Zealand,** 15 Arkana St., Yarralumla, ACT, 2600 (☎6273 35 55; www.mae.es/embajadas/canberra/es/home); **Canada,** 74 Stanley Ave., Ottawa, ON, K1M 1P4 (☎613-747-2252; www.embaspain.ca); **Ireland,** 17 Merlyn Park, Ballsbridge, Dublin, 4 (☎353 126 08 066; www.mae.es/embajadas/dublin); **UK,** 39 Chesham Pl., London, SW1X 8SB (☎020 72 35 55 55); **US,** 2375 Pennsylvania Ave., NW, Washington, D.C., 20037 (☎202-728-2340; www.mae.es/embajadas/washington/es/home). All countries listed have consulates in Barcelona. Australia, the UK, and the US also have consulates in Seville.

**VISA AND ENTRY INFORMATION.** EU citizens do not need a visa. Citizens of Australia, Canada, New Zealand, the US, and many Latin American countries do not need a visa for stays of up to 90 days, beginning upon entry into the EU's freedom-of-movement zone. For more info, see p. 13. For stays longer than 90 days, all non-EU citizens need visas, available at Spanish consulates (€100).

# TOURIST SERVICES AND MONEY

| EMERGENCY | Ambulance: ☎061. Fire: ☎080. Local Police: ☎092. National Police: ☎091. General Emergency: ☎112. |
| --- | --- |

**TOURIST OFFICES.** For general info, contact the **Instituto de Turismo de España**, Jose Lazaro Galdiano 6, 28071 Madrid (☎913 433 500; www.tourspain.es).

**MONEY.** The **euro (€)** has replaced the **peseta** as the unit of currency in Spain. For more info, see p. 15. As a general rule, it's cheaper to exchange money in Spain than at home. **ATMs** usually have good exchange rates. In restaurants, all prices include a service charge. Satisfied customers occasionally toss in some spare change—usually no more than 5%—and while it is purely optional, **tipping** is becoming increasingly widespread in restaurants and other places that cater to tourists. Many people give train, airport, and hotel porters €1 per bag, while taxi drivers sometimes get 5-10%. **Bargaining** is only common at flea markets and with street vendors.

Spain has a 7% **value added tax (VAT**; in Spain, **IVA)** on restaurant meals and accommodations and a 16% VAT on retail goods. The prices listed in *Let's Go* include VAT. In an airport upon exiting the EU, non-EU citizens can claim a refund on the tax paid for goods purchased at participating stores. In order to qualify for a refund in a store, you must spend at least €50-100, depending on the shop; make sure to ask for a refund form when you pay. For more info on qualifying for a VAT refund, see p. 18.

**BUSINESS HOURS.** Almost all museums, shops, and churches close from 2-4pm or longer for an afternoon **siesta**. Most Spaniards eat lunch during their *siesta* (as well as nap), so restaurants open in the late afternoon. Shops and sights reopen at 3pm, and some may stay open until 8pm. Most restaurants will start serving dinner by 9pm, although eating close to midnight is very common in Spain. After midnight, the clubhopping commences. Increasingly, some large chains and offices are open all day, in large part due to an effort by the Spanish government to encourage a stronger economy and more "normal" business hours. It's still a safe bet that nearly every store will be closed on Sundays.

# TRANSPORTATION

**BY PLANE.** Flights land mainly at **Barajas Airport** in Madrid (**MAD**; ☎913 93 60 00) and the **Barcelona International Airport** (**BCN**; ☎932 98 39 25). Contact AENA (☎902 40 47 04; www.aena.es) for info on flight times at most airports. See p. 41 for info on flying to Spain.

**BY FERRY.** Spain's islands are accessible by ferry; see the **Balearic Islands** (p. 926). Ferries are the least expensive way of traveling between Spain and **Tangier** or the Spanish enclave of **Ceuta** in Morocco. See p. 52.

**BY TRAIN.** Direct trains are available to Madrid and Barcelona from several European cities, including Geneva, SWI; Lisbon, POR; and Paris, FRA. Spanish trains are clean, relatively punctual, and reasonably priced. However, most train routes do tend to bypass small towns. Spain's national railway is **RENFE** (☎902 24 02 02; www.renfe.es). When possible, avoid *transvía, semidirecto,* or *correo* trains, as they are very slow. *Estrellas* are slow night trains with bunks and showers. *Cercanías* (commuter trains) go from cities to suburbs and nearby towns. There is no reason to buy a Eurail Pass if you plan to travel only within Spain. Trains are cheap, so a pass saves little money; moreover, buses are the most efficient means of traveling around Spain. Several Rail Europe passes cover travel within Spain. See www.raileurope.com for more info on the following passes. The **Spain Flexipass** ($155) offers three days of unlimited travel in a two-month period. The **Spain Rail 'n' Drive Pass** ($307) is good for three days of unlimited first-class train travel and two days of unlimited mileage in a rental car. The **Spain-Portugal Pass** offers three days or more of unlimited first-class travel in Spain and Portugal over a two-month period (from $289). For more info, see p. 45.

**JUST SAY NO.** If you are planning on traveling only within Spain (and Portugal), do not buy a **Eurail Pass.** Bus travel is usually the best option, and trains are less expensive than in the rest of Europe. A Eurail Pass makes sense only for those planning to travel in other European countries as well.

**BY BUS.** In Spain, buses are cheaper and have far more comprehensive routes than trains. Buses provide the only public transportation to many isolated areas. For those traveling primarily within one region, **buses are the best method of transportation.** Spain has numerous private companies and the lack of a centralized bus company may make itinerary planning difficult. Companies' routes rarely overlap, so it is unlikely that more than one will serve your intended destination. **Alsa/Enatcar** (☎913 27 05 40; www.alsa.es) serves Asturias, Castilla and León, Galicia, and Madrid, as well as international destinations including France, Germany, Italy, and Portugal. **Auto-Res/Cunisa, S.A.** (☎902 02 09 99; www.auto-res.net) serves Castilla y León, Extremadura, Galicia, Valencia, and Portugal.

**BY CAR.** Spain's highway system connects major cities by four-lane *autopistas*. **Speeders beware:** police can "photograph" the speed and license plate of your car and issue a ticket without pulling you over. If you are pulled over, fines must be paid on the spot. **Gas** prices, €0.80-1.10 per liter, are lower than in many European countries but high by North American standards. **Renting** a car is cheaper than elsewhere in Europe. Spain accepts Canadian, EU, and US driver's licenses; otherwise, an International Driving Permit (IDP) is required. Try **Atesa** (Spain ☎902 10 01 01, elsewhere 10 05 15; www.atesa.es), Spain's largest rental agency. The automobile association is **Real Automóvil Club de España** (**RACE**; ☎902 40 45 45; www.race.es). For more on renting and driving a car, see p. 48.

**BY THUMB.** Hitchhikers report that Castilla and Andalucía are long, hot waits, and hitchhiking out of Madrid is virtually impossible. The Mediterranean coast and the islands are more promising; remote areas in the Balearics, Catalonia, or Galicia may be best accessible by hitchhiking. Although approaching people for rides at gas stations near highways and rest stops purportedly gets results, Let's Go does not recommend hitchhiking.

## KEEPING IN TOUCH

|  **PHONE CODES** | **Country code: 34. International dialing prefix:** 00. Within Spain, dial city code + local number, even when dialing inside the city. For more info on how to place international calls, see **Inside Back Cover.** |
| --- | --- |

**EMAIL AND THE INTERNET.** Email is easily accessible within Spain. Internet cafes are listed in most towns and all cities, and generally charge as little as €2 per hr. In small towns, if Internet is not listed, check the library or the tourist office, which may have public Internet access. For a list of internet cafes in Spain, consult www.cybercafes.com.

**TELEPHONE.** Whenever possible, use a prepaid phone card for international phone calls, as long-distance rates for national phone service are often very high. Find them at tobacconists. However, some public phones will only accept change. Mobile phones are an increasingly popular and economical option, costing as little as €30 (not including minutes). Major mobile carriers include **Movistar** and **Vodafone.** Direct-dial access numbers for calling out of Spain include: **AT&T Direct** (☎900 990 011); **British Telecom** (☎900 990 044); **Canada Direct** (☎900 990 015); **Telecom New Zealand Direct** (☎900 990 064); **Telstra Australia** (☎900 990 061).

**MAIL.** Airmail *(por avión)* takes five to eight business days to reach Canada or the US; service is faster to the UK and Ireland and slower to Australia and New Zealand. Standard postage is €0.78 to North America. Surface mail *(por barco)* can take over a month, and packages take two to three months. Certified mail *(certificado)* is the most reliable way to send a letter or parcel and takes four to seven business days. Spain's overnight mail is not actually overnight, and is thus not worth the expense. To receive mail in Spain, have it delivered **Poste Restante.** Mail will go to the main post office unless you specify a subsidiary by street address. Address mail to be held according to the following example: Last Name, First Name; *Lista de Correos;* City; Postal Code; SPAIN; AIRMAIL.

# ACCOMMODATIONS AND CAMPING

| SPAIN | ❶ | ❷ | ❸ | ❹ | ❺ |
|---|---|---|---|---|---|
| ACCOMMODATIONS | under €15 | €15-24 | €25-34 | €35-40 | over €40 |

The cheapest and most basic options are *refugios, casas de huéspedes,* and *hospedajes,* while *pensiones* and *fondas* tend to be a bit nicer. All are essentially boarding houses with basic rooms, shared bath, and no A/C. Higher up the ladder but not necessarily more expensive, *hostales* generally have sinks in bedrooms and provide linens and lockers, while *hostal-residencias* are similar to hotels in overall quality. The government rates *hostales* on a two-star system; even establishments receiving one star are typically quite comfortable. The system also fixes *hostal* prices, posted in the lounge or main entrance. Prices invariably dip below the official rates in the low season (Sept.-May), so bargain away. **Red Española de Albergues Juveniles** (REAJ), the Spanish **Hostelling International** (HI) affiliate (Madrid ☎915 22 70 07; www.reaj.com), runs more than 200 hostels year-round. Prices depend on season, location, and services offered, but are generally €9-15 for guests under 26 and higher for those 26 and over. Breakfast is usually included; lunch and dinner are occasionally offered at an additional charge. Hostels usually have lockouts around 11am and have curfews between midnight and 3am. As a rule, don't expect much privacy—rooms typically have 4-20 beds in them. To reserve a bed in the high season (July-Aug. and during festivals), call at least a few weeks in advance. **Campgrounds** are generally the cheapest choice for two or more people. Most charge separate fees per person, per tent, and per car; others charge for a *parcela* (a small plot of land), plus per-person fees. Tourist offices can provide more info, including the *Guía de Campings.*

# FOOD AND DRINK

| SPAIN | ❶ | ❷ | ❸ | ❹ | ❺ |
|---|---|---|---|---|---|
| FOOD | under €6 | €6-10 | €11-15 | €16-20 | over €20 |

Fresh, local ingredients are still an integral part of Spanish cuisine, varying according to each region's climate, geography, and history. The old Spanish saying holds true: *"Que comer es muy importante, porque de la panza, ¡nace la danza!"* (Eating is very important, because from the belly, dance is born!)

Spaniards start the day with a light breakfast *(desayuno)* of coffee or thick, hot chocolate, and a pastry. The main meal of the day *(comida)* consists of several courses and is typically eaten around 2 or 3pm. Dinner at home *(cena)* tends to be light. Dining out begins anywhere between 8pm and midnight. Bar-hopping for tapas is an integral part of the Spanish lifestyle. Some restaurants are "open" from 8am until 1 or 2am, but most serve meals only from 1 or 2 to 4pm and 8pm to midnight. Many restaurants offer a *plato combinado* (main course, side dish, bread, and sometimes a beverage) or a *menú del día* (two or three set dishes, bread, beverage, and dessert) for roughly €5-9. If you ask for a *menú,* this is what you may receive; *carta* is the word for menu.

**Tapas** (small dishes of savory meats and vegetables cooked according to local recipes) are quite tasty, and in most regions they are paired with beer or wine.

*Raciones* are large tapas served as entrees; *bocadillos* are sandwiches. Spanish specialties include *tortilla de patata* (potato omelet), *jamón serrano* (smoked ham), *calamares fritos* (fried squid), *arroz* (rice), *chorizo* (spicy sausage), *gambas* (shrimp), *lomo de cerdo* (pork loin), *paella* (steamed saffron rice with seafood, chicken, and vegetables), and *gazpacho* (cold tomato-based soup). Vegetarians should learn the phrase *"yo soy vegetariano"* (I am a vegetarian) and specify this means no *jamón* (ham) or *atún* (tuna). A normal-sized draft beer is a *caña de cerveza;* a *tubo* is a little bigger. A *calimocho* is a mix of Coca-Cola and red wine, while *sangria* is a drink of red wine, sugar, brandy, and fruit. *Tinto de verano* is a lighter version of sangria: red wine and Fanta. *Café solo* means black coffee; add a touch of milk for a *nube;* a little more and it's a *café cortado;* half milk and half coffee makes a *café con leche.*

# BEYOND TOURISM

Spain offers volunteer opportunities from protecting dolphins on the Costa del Sol to fighting for immigrants' rights. Universities in major cities host thousands of foreign students every year, and language schools are a good alternative to university **study** if you desire a deeper focus on language or a slightly less rigorous courseload. Those seeking **long-term work** in Spain should consider teaching English. Short-term jobs are widely available in the restaurant, hotel, and tourism industries, and are typically held by those without permits. For more info on opportunities across Europe, see **Beyond Tourism**, p. 54.

**Don Quijote,** Placentinos 2, 37008 Salamanca (☎923 26 88 60; www.don-quijote.org). A nationwide language school offering Spanish courses for all levels throughout the country. Very social atmosphere. 2-week intensive courses start at €338. €95 enrollment fee. Discounts for longer sessions.

**Ecoforest,** Apdo, Correos 29, 29100 Coin, Málaga (☎661 07 99 50; www.ecoforest.org). Fruit farm and vegan community in southern Spain that uses ecoforest education to help participants develop a sustainable lifestyle.

**Escuela de Cocina Luis Irizar,** C. Mari 5 Bajo, 20003 San Sebastián (☎943 43 15 40; www.escuelairizar.com). Learn how to cook Basque cuisine at this culinary institute. Programs range from week-long summer courses to comprehensive 2-year apprenticeships. Some summer courses may be taught in English.

# MADRID                                                    ☎91

After Franco's death in 1975, young *Madrileños* celebrated their liberation from totalitarian repression with raging all-night parties across the city. This revelry became so widespread that it defined an era, and *la Movida* (the Movement) is now recognized as a world-famous nightlife renaissance. The newest generation has kept the spirit of *la Movida* alive—other claimants aside, Madrid is truly the city that never sleeps. While neither as funky as Barcelona nor as charming as Seville, Madrid is the political, intellectual, and cultural capital of Spain.

# ▉ TRANSPORTATION

**Flights:** All flights land at **Aeropuerto Internacional de Barajas** (**MAD;** ☎902 40 47 04), 20min. northeast of Madrid. The **Barajas metro line** connects the airport to all of Madrid (€1). Another option is the **Bus-Aeropuerto #200** (look for "EMT" signs), which runs to the city center. (☎902 50 78 50. 4-6 per hr., €1.) The bus stops in the metro station **Avenida de América.**

**Trains:** 2 *largo recorrido* (long distance) **RENFE** stations, **Atocha** and **Chamartín,** connect Madrid to the rest of Europe. Call RENFE (☎902 24 02 02; www.renfe.es) for info.

  **Estación de Atocha** (☎506 6137). M: Atocha Renfe. Domestic service only. AVE (☎506 6137) has high-speed service to southern Spain, including **Seville** (2½hr., 22 per day, €63-70) via **Córdoba** (1¾hr., €40-52). Grandes Líneas trains leave for **Barcelona** (4½-5hr., 9 per day, €36-63).

**Estación Chamartín** (☎300 6969). M: Chamartín. Bus #5 runs to and from Puerta del Sol (45min.). Alternatively, take a red Cercanías train (15min., 6 per hr., €1.05) from M: Atocha Renfe. Chamartín services both international and domestic destinations in the northeast and south. Major destinations include: **Barcelona** (9hr., 2 per day, €35-42); **Bilbao** (6½hr., 2 per day, €32-40); **Lisbon, POR** (9¼hr., 10:45pm, €54); **Paris, FRA** (13½hr., 7pm, €112-129). Chamartín offers services, including a **tourist office**, Vestíbulo, Puerta 14 (☎315 9976; open M-Sa 8am-8pm, Su 8am-2pm), **accommodations service, car rental, currency exchange, luggage storage** (consignas; €2.40-4.50; open daily 7am-11pm), **police**, and **post office**.

**Buses:** Many private companies, each with its own station and set of destinations, serve Madrid. Most pass through the Estación Sur de Autobuses and Estación Auto-Res.

**Estación Auto-Res:** C. Fernández Shaw 1 (☎902 02 09 99; www.auto-res.net). M: Conde de Casal. Info booth open daily 6:30am-1am. To **Cuenca** (2½hr., 6-10 per day, €10-14), **Salamanca** (3hr., 9 per day, €11-16), and **Valencia** (5hr., 10-11 per day, €29).

**Estación La Sepulvedana:** C. Palos de la Frontera 16 (☎559 5955; www.lasepulvedana.es). M: Príncipe Pío (via extension from M: Ópera). To **Segovia** (1½hr., 2 per hr., €6).

**Estación Sur de Autobuses:** C. Méndez Álvaro (☎468 4200; www.estaciondeautobuses.com). M: Méndez Álvaro. Info booth open daily 6am-1am. **ATMs** and **luggage storage** (€1.25 per bag per day) available. Destinations include **Alicante, Santiago de Compostela**, and **Toledo**.

**Local Transportation:** Madrid's **metro** is safe, speedy, and spotless (☎902 44 44 03; www.metromadrid.es). Metro tickets cost €1; a metrobus (ticket of 10 rides valid for the metro and bus) is €6.40. Buy them at machines in any metro stop, estanco (tobacco shop), or newsstand. Also available are 1-, 2-, 3-, 5-, and 7-day unlimited ride tickets (abono turístico; €4-40). Hold onto your ticket until you leave the metro or face a fine. Spanish-language **bus** info ☎406 8810. Buses run 6am-11pm. Bus fares are the same as metro fares and tickets are interchangeable. Búho (owl), the **night bus** service, runs 2 buses per hr. midnight-3am, 1 per hr. 3-6am. Look for buses N1-N24.

**Taxis:** Call **Radio Taxi** (☎405 5500), **Radio-Taxi Independiente** (☎405 1213), or **Teletaxi** (☎371 3711). A libre sign in the window or a green light indicates availability. Base fare is €1.85 (€2.90 after 10pm), plus €0.87-1 per km from 6am-10pm and €1-1.10 from 10pm-6am. **Teletaxi** charges a flat rate of €1 per km.

# ✈ ORIENTATION

Marking the epicenter of both Madrid and Spain, **Kilómetro 0** in **Puerta del Sol** ("Sol" for short) is within walking distance of most sights. To the west are the **Plaza Mayor,** the **Palacio Real,** and the **Ópera** district. East of Sol lies **Huertas,** the heart of cafe, museum, and theater life. The area north of Sol is bordered by **Gran Vía,** which runs northwest to Plaza de España. North of Gran Vía are three club- and bar-hopping districts, linked by Calle de Fuencarral: **Malasaña, Bilbao,** and **Chueca.** Modern Madrid is beyond Gran Vía and east of Malasaña and Chueca. East of Sol, the tree-lined thoroughfares **Paseo de la Castellana, Paseo de Recoletos,** and **Paseo del Prado** split Madrid in two, running from **Atocha** in the south to **Plaza Castilla** in the north, passing the Prado, the fountains of **Plaza de Cibeles,** and **Plaza de Colón.** Madrid is safer than many European cities, but Sol, Pl. de España, Pl. Chueca, and Pl. Dos de Mayo are still intimidating at night. Travel in groups, avoid the parks and quiet streets after dark, and watch for thieves and pickpockets in crowds.

# ⏹ PRACTICAL INFORMATION

**Tourist Offices: Madrid Tourism Centre,** Pl. Mayor 27 (☎588 1636; www.esmadrid.com). M: Sol. **Branches** at Estación Chamartín, Estación de Atocha, and the airport. English and French usually spoken. All open daily 9:30am-8pm. Regional Office of the **Comunidad de Madrid,** C. del Duque de Medinaceli 2 (☎429 4951; www.madrid.org). M: Banco de España. Open M-Sa 8am-8pm, Su 9am-2pm. Pick up the Guía del Ocio (€1) or In Madrid for info on city events and establishments.

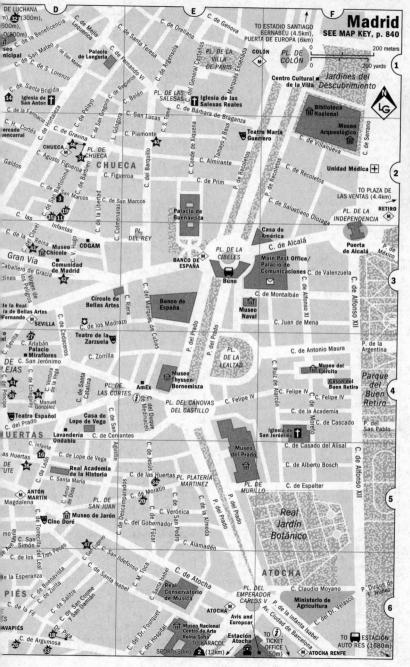

# Madrid
SEE MAP, pp. 838

 ACCOMMODATIONS

| | | |
|---|---|---|
| Albergue Juvenil Santa Cruz de Marcenado (HI), | 1 | B1 |
| Camping Alpha, | 2 | E6 |
| Casa Chueca, | 3 | D2 |
| Cat's Hostel, | 4 | C5 |
| Hostal A. Nebrija, | 5 | A2 |
| Hostal Betanzos, | 6 | C5 |
| Hostal Esparteros, | 7 | C4 |
| Hostal Oriente, | 8 | B3 |
| Hostal Paz, | 9 | B3 |
| Hostal Plaza D'Ort, | 10 | C5 |
| Hostal Rio Miño, | 11 | D2 |
| Hostal Santillan, | 12 | B2 |
| Hostal Valencia, | 13 | A3 |
| Hostal-Residencia Domínguez, | 14 | D1 |
| Hostal-Residencia Luz, | 15 | B4 |
| La Posada de Huertas, | 16 | D5 |
| Mad Hostel, | 17 | C5 |

🍗 FOOD

| | | |
|---|---|---|
| Achuri, | 18 | D6 |
| Al-Jaima, Cocina del Diserto, | 19 | D2 |
| Arrocería Gala, | 20 | E5 |
| Café Comercial, | 21 | D1 |
| Café de Oriente, | 22 | A3 |
| Casa Alberto, | 23 | D5 |
| Cervecería 100 Montaditos, | 24 | B4 |
| El Estragón Vegetariano, | 25 | A5 |
| Eucalipto, | 26 | D6 |
| La Finca de Susana, | 27 | D4 |
| Heladería Giuseppe Ricci, | 28 | D5 |
| Inshala, | 29 | A4 |
| Museo del Jamón, | 30 | B4 |
| Restaurante Casa Granada, | 31 | C5 |
| Rey de Tallarines, | 32 | D1 |
| Taberna "Er 77," | 33 | D6 |
| Taberna Maceira, | 34 | E5 |
| El Tigre, | 35 | D2 |
| La Trucha, | 36 | D4 |

⭐ NIGHTLIFE

| | | |
|---|---|---|
| Acuarela, | 37 | D2 |
| Café Jazz Populart, | 38 | D5 |
| Cardamomo, | 39 | D4 |
| El Clandestino, | 40 | E2 |
| Cuevas de Sésamo, | 41 | D4 |
| De Las Letras Restaurante, | 42 | D3 |
| Del Diego, | 43 | D3 |
| La Ida, | 44 | C1 |
| Ocho y Medio Club, | 45 | C3 |
| Palacio Gaviria, | 46 | B4 |
| Taberna Vinocola Mentridana, | 47 | D5 |
| El Truco, | 48 | D2 |
| Tupperware, | 49 | C1 |
| Via Láctea, | 50 | C1 |

**General Information Line:** ☎901 30 06 00 or 010. Info on anything about Madrid, from police locations to zoo hours. Ask for *inglés* for an English-speaking operator.

**Embassies: Australia,** Pl. del Descubridor Diego de Ordás 3, 2nd fl. (☎353 6600; www.spain.embassy.gov.au). **Canada,** Núñez de Balboa 35 (☎423 3250; www.canada-es.org). **Ireland,** Po. Castellana 46, 4th fl. (☎436 4093). **New Zealand,** Pl. de la Lealtad 2, 3rd fl. (☎523 0226). **UK,** Po. de Recoletos 7-9 (☎524 9700; www.ukinspain.com). **US,** C. Serrano 75 (☎587 2200; www.embusa.es).

**Currency Exchange:** In general, credit and ATM cards offer the best exchange rates. Avoid changing money at airport and train station counters; they tend to charge exorbitant commissions. **Banco Santander Central Hispano** charges no commission on AmEx **Travellers Cheques** up to €300. Main branch, Po. Castellana 7 (☎558 1111). M: Sol. Follow C. San Jerónimo to Pl. Canalejas. Open Apr.-Sept. M-F 8:30am-2pm; Oct.-Mar. M-F 8:30am-2pm, Sa 8:30am-1pm. **Banks** usually charge 1-2% commission (min. charge €3). Booths in Sol and Gran Vía are not a good deal.

**Luggage Storage:** At the airport and bus and train stations (€2.75 per bag per day).

**GLBT Resources:** Most establishments in Chueca carry a free guide to gay nightlife in Spain called **Shanguide**. The **Colectivo de Gais y Lesbianas de Madrid (COGAM),** C. de las Infantas 40, 1st fl. (☎522 4517; www.cogam.org), M: Gran Vía, provides a wide range of services and activities. Reception M-Sa 5-10pm.

**Laundromat: Lavandería Ondablu,** C. León, 3 (☎913 69 50 71). M: Antón Martín, Sol, or Sevilla. Wash €3.50, dry €1. Also available in most hostels for €5 wash and dry. (**Internet** access available.) Open M-F 9:30am-10pm, Sa 10:30am-7pm. Also at C. Hortaleza, 84 (☎915 31 28 73). M: Chueca. Same hours and prices.

**Police:** C. de los Madrazos 9 (☎322 1160). M: Sevilla. From C. de Alcalá, take a right onto C. Cedacneros and a left onto C. de los Madrazos. Open daily 9am-2pm. To report crimes committed in the **metro,** go to the office in the Sol station.

**Medical Services:** In a medical emergency, dial ☎061 or 112. **Hospital de Madrid,** Pl. del Conde del Valle Suchil 16 (☎447 6600; www.hospitaldemadrid.com). **Hospital Ramón y Cajal,** Ctra. Colmenar Viejo, km 9100 (☎336 8000). Bus #135 from Pl. de Castilla. For non-emergencies, go to **Unidad Médica,** C. del Conde de Aranda 1, 1st fl. (☎435 1823; www.unidadmedica.com). M: Serrano or Retiro. Regular personnel on duty M-F 9am-8pm, Sa 10am-1pm. Initial visit €110, students €75. AmEx/MC/V. Embassies and consulates keep lists of English-speaking doctors.

**Internet Access:** Internet cafes are everywhere. While the average is €2 per hr., small shops in apartments charge even less; keep a lookout. Internet in hostels is often free. ▨**SATS XXI,** C. San Jerónimo (☎/fax 532 0970), has fast connections, printing, fax, disks, and CDs. €1.85 per hr. Open daily 10am-midnight.

**Post Office: Palacio de Comunicaciones,** C. Alcalá 51, on Pl. de Cibeles (☎902 19 71 97; www.correos.es). M: Banco de España. Fax and **Lista de Correos.** Windows open M-Sa 8:30am-9:30pm, Su 8:30am-2pm for stamp purchases. **Postal Code:** 28080.

# ACCOMMODATIONS

Make reservations for summer visits. Expect to pay €15-50 per person, depending on location, amenities, and season. While prices are high in El Centro, the triangle between Puerta del Sol, Ópera, and Pl. Mayor, the location is as good as it gets, especially for those planning to brave the legendary nightlife. The cultural hotbed of **Huertas,** framed by Ctra. de San Jerónimo, C. de las Huertas, and C. de Atocha, is almost as central and more fun. Trendy and eclectic Malasaña and Chueca, bisected by C. Fuencarral, boast cheap rooms in the heart of the action, but the sleep-deprived should beware; the party never stops. *Hostales,* like temptations, are everywhere among Gran Vía's sex shops and scam artists.

## EL CENTRO: SOL, ÓPERA, AND PLAZA MAYOR

▨ **Hostal-Residencia Luz,** C. de las Fuentes 10, 3rd fl. (☎542 0759; www.hostalluz.com). M: Ópera. Redecorated rooms are clean and comfortable. A/C and TV. Free Wi-Fi. Laundry €5. Singles €36; doubles €72; triples €108. Discounts for longer stays. MC/V. ❷

▨ **Hostal Paz,** C. Flora 4, 1st and 4th fl. (☎547 3047). M: Ópera. Spotless rooms with A/C and satellite TV. Laundry €10. Singles €30; doubles €36-38, with shower €42; triples with shower €54; quad €68. Monthly rentals available; reserve ahead. MC/V. ❸

**Hostal Esparteros,** C. de Esparteros 12, 4th fl. (☎521 0903). M: Sol. Unbeatable location and sparkling rooms with balconies or large windows; some have private bath, fans, and TV. Laundry €9-10. Singles €25; doubles €35; triples €45. Cash only. ❷

**Hostal Oriente,** C. Arenal 23, 1st fl. (☎548 0314; www.hostaloriente.com). M: Ópera. Classy, hotel-quality hostel with chandeliers, tiled floors, and friendly owners. 17 rooms with A/C, bath, phone, and TV. Singles €40; doubles €60; triples €80. MC/V. ❸

**Hostal Valencia,** Pl. del Oriente 2, 3rd fl. (☎559 8450; www.hostalvalencia.tk). M: Ópera. An elevator lifts you to 7 elegant rooms with fan, TV, and Old World flair. Ask for a room overlooking the Pl. del Oriente. TV and fan. Reserve ahead. Singles €45; doubles €75-95; master suite €110. MC/V. ❹

## HUERTAS

▨ **La Posada de Huertas,** C. Huertas, 21 (☎429 5526; www.posadadehuertas.com). M: Antón Martín or Sol. Small rooms of 4 or 8 are clean, well-kept, and equipped with comfortable beds. Bathrooms are spotless. Breakfast, kitchen, and Wi-Fi included. Laundry €5. Luggage storage available. Beds from €18. MC/V. ❷

**Cat's Hostel,** C. Cañizares 6 (☎369 2807; www.catshostel.com). M: Antón Martín. This renovated 18th-century palace features dorms with up to 16 beds, small doubles with private baths, an authentic *mudéjar* patio area, a bar, and a cafe. Cheap beer (€2-3). Bathrooms are not the cleanest. Breakfast, luggage storage, and Internet included. Laundry €5. Dorms €20; doubles €22. MC/V. ❷

**Hostal Plaza D'Ort,** Pl. del Angel 13 (☎429 9041; www.plazadort.com). M: Antón Martín. Conveniently located outside Pl. Santa Ana. Beautiful rooms are comfortable and a good deal. All have A/C, phone and TV. Internet and in-room movies €11. Singles €30, with bath €40; doubles €50/60; triples €75-85; suite €110. MC/V. ❸

**Mad Hostel,** C. Cabeza 24 (☎506 4840; www.madhostel.com) M: Tirso de Molina. A relaxed and brand-new hostel with high-tech flair. Dorms are sparking. A bar area with pool table, gym, kitchen, and rooftop terrace. Breakfast included. Free Wi-Fi. Laundry €5. Reserve ahead. Dorms €20-22. MC/V. ❷

**Hostal Betanzos,** C. Luis de Guevera 8, 3rd fl. (☎369 1440). M: Antón Martín. Climb the fantastic but ancient double staircase to classic rooms with sinks and wooden furniture. Singles €15; doubles €25. Cash only. ❷

## GRAN VÍA

**Hostal Santillan,** Gran Vía 64, 8th fl. (☎548 2328; www.hostalsantillan.com). M: Pl. de España. Take the elevator to the top of this gorgeous building. Leaf-patterned curtains and wooden furniture give rooms a homey feel. All with fan, shower, sink, and TV. Doubles €50-55; triples €66. MC/V. ❸

**Hostal A. Nebrija,** Gran Vía 67, 8th fl., elevator A (☎547 7319). M: Pl. de España. Management is friendly and most rooms have great views of the city. Rooms have fans, high ceilings, and TV. No smoking. Singles €28; doubles €36; triples €54. AmEx/MC/V. ❸

## MALASAÑA AND CHUECA

**Hostal-Residencia Domínguez,** C. de Santa Brígida 1. (☎532 1547). M: Tribunal. A modern look and low prices. Brand new, immaculate doubles on the 2nd and 3rd fl. are immaculate and brand new. Hospitable young owner provides tips on local nightlife. Singles €39; doubles with A/C and bath €49; triples €59. Cash only. ❸

**Casa Chueca,** C. de San Bartolomé 4, 2nd fl. (☎523 8127; www.casachueca.com). M: Chueca. Rooms have A/C, free Internet, and satellite TV. "Mini-breakfast" included. Reservations required. Singles €40; doubles €55; triples €70. MC/V. ❹

**Hostal Rio Miño,** C. de Barbieri 3, 1st fl. (☎522 1417). M: Chueca. Simple rooms are cheap and of decent quality. All have A/C. Common baths are very clean. Reserve 2 weeks ahead. Singles €20; doubles €28, €40 with bath; triples €54. Cash only. ❷

## ELSEWHERE AND CAMPING

Budget lodgings are rare near the **Chamartín** train station. There are a handful of hostels near the **Atocha** train station. Tourist offices have info on the 22 campsites surrounding Madrid. For further camping info, contact the **Consejería de Educación** (☎901 51 06 10).

**Albergue Juvenil Santa Cruz de Marcenado (HI),** C. de Santa Cruz de Marcenado 28 (☎547 4532). M: Argüelles. From the metro, walk 1 block down C. de Alberto Aguilera away from C. de la Princesa, turn right on C. de Serrano Jóver, then left on C. de Santa Cruz de Marcenado. Single-sex floors. Breakfast included. Max. stay 6 nights. Reception 9am-10pm. Quiet hours after midnight. Curfew 1:30am. Reserve ahead. Dorms €17, under 26 €12. €3.50 HI discount. ❶

**Camping Alpha** (☎695 8069; www.campingalpha.com), on a tree-lined site 12.4km down Ctra. de Andalucía in Getafe. M: Legazpi. From the metro, walk down Vado Santa Catalina, cross the bridge, and bear right. Take the green bus #447, which stops across from the Museo de Jamón (10min., 1-2 per hr., €1.25). Ask for the Camp Alpha stop. Cross the footbridge and walk 1.5km back toward Madrid along the busy highway; signs lead the way. Amenities include laundry, paved roads, pool, tennis courts, and showers. €6.50 per person, €6.70 per tent or per car. Singles €36; doubles €45; bungalows 1-2 people €62, 3-4 people €92. IVA not included. ❶

## ▣ FOOD

In Madrid, it's not hard to fork it down without forking over too much. Most restaurants offer a *menú del día* (€9-11), which includes bread, one drink, and a choice of appetizer, main course, and dessert. Many small eateries cluster on **Calles Echegaray, Ventura de la Vega,** and **Manuel Fernández González** in Huertas. Chueca is filled with bars *de cañas* (small beer from the tap), which serve complimentary tapas. The streets west of **Calle Fuencarral** in Gran Vía are lined with cheap restaurants, while **Bilbao** has affordable ethnic cuisine. Linger in Madrid's cafes to absorb the sights of the city; you won't be bothered with the check until you ask. Keep in mind the following words for quick, cheap *madrileño* fare: *bocadillo* (a sandwich on half a baguette; €2-3); *ración* (a large tapa served with bread; €3-6); and *empanada* (a puff pastry with meat fillings; €1.30-2). The *Guía del Ocio* has a complete listing of Madrid's vegetarian options under the section *"Otras Cocinas."* **%Día** and **Champion** are the cheapest supermarket chains; smaller markets are open later but are more expensive.

**▨ La Finca de Susana,** C. Arlabán 4 (☎369 3557). M: Sevilla. Of the lesser-known restaurateur philosophy that quality should not come with a high price, this fine-dining establishment is packed every day for lunch—come early to avoid the ever-present line. *Menú* M-F €8.40. Open daily 1-3:45pm and 8:30-11:45pm. AmEx/MC/V. ❷

**▨ El Estragón Vegetariano,** Pl. de la Paja 10 (☎365 8982; www.guiadelocio.com/estragonvegetariano). M: La Latina. Among the best medium-priced restaurants in Madrid, with vegetarian delights that tempt even the most die-hard carnivores to switch teams. *Menú* (M-F €10, Sa-Su and evenings €25). Open daily 1:30-4pm and 8pm-midnight. AmEx/MC/V. ❸

**Taberna "Er 77",** C. Argumosa 8. M: Lavapiés. The small kitchen of this local find produces some of the area's most creative dishes. Try the asparagus with raw salmon (€7). Entrees €5-11. Open Tu-Th 6pm-midnight, F-Sa 1pm-1am, Su 1pm-6pm. Cash only. ❷

## ON THE MENU

### TAPAS A TO Z

Food on toothpicks and in small bowls? The restaurant isn't being stingy, and your food isn't shrinking; you're merely experiencing an integral part of the Spanish lifestyle. The tapas tradition is one of the oldest in Spain. These tasty little dishes are Spain's answer to hors d'oeuvres, but have more taste, less pretension, and are eaten instead of meals.

To the untrained tourist, tapas menus are often indecipherable, if the bar has even bothered to print any. In order to avoid awkward encounters with tentacles or parts of the horse you rode in on, keep the following things in mind before *tapeando* (eating tapas).

Servings come in three sizes: *pinchos* (eaten with toothpicks), *tapas* (small plate), and *raciónes* (meal portion). On any basic menu you'll find: *Aceitunas* (olives), *albóndigas* (meatballs), *callos* (tripe), *chorizo* (sausage), *gambas* (shrimp), *jamón* (ham), *patatas bravas* (fried potatoes with spicy sauce), *pimientos* (peppers), *pulpo* (octopus), and *tortilla española* (onion and potato omelette). The more adventurous should try *morcilla* (blood sausage), or *sesos* (cow's brains). Often, bartenders will offer tastes of tapas with your drink and strike up a conversation. Ask for a *caña* (glass) of the house *cerveza* (beer) to guarantee the full respect of the establishment.

**Heladería Giuseppe Ricci (Gelato & Cafe),** C. de las Huertas 9 (☎687 98 96 12; www.heladeriaricci.com). M: Antón Martín. Forget tapas and *jamón*—this *gelato* provides the best relief from a hot Madrid day. Small cones €2, large €3. Open M-Th and Su 10am-10pm, F-Sa 10am-10:30pm. ❶

**Al-Jaima, Cocina del Desierto,** C. de Barbieri 1 (☎523 1142). M: Gran Vía or Chueca. Egyptian, Lebanese, and Moroccan food served to patrons seated on pillows on the floor. Specialties include kebabs and *tajine* (appetizer €4, main courses €8). Try *pollo con higos y miel* (chicken with figs and honey; €6.10). Open daily 1:30-4pm and 9pm-midnight. Reserve ahead. MC/V. ❷

**Taberna Maceira,** C. de Jesús 7 (☎914 29 15 84). M: Antón Martín. Branch at C. Huertas 66 (☎429 5818). This funky tavern has fantastic seafood and great prices. 2 people can feast for under €25. Open M 8pm-12:45am, Tu-F 1-4:15pm and 8:30pm-12:45am, Sa-Su 1-4:45pm and 8:30pm-1:30am. Cash only. ❸

**Inshala,** C. de la Amnistía 10 (☎548 2632). M: Ópera. Eclectic selection of delicious Italian, Japanese, Mexican, Moroccan, and Spanish dishes. Weekday lunch *menú* €9. Dinner €10-26. Reserve ahead. Open in summer M-Th noon-5pm and 8pm-1am, F-Sa noon-5pm and 8pm-2am; in winter M-Sa noon-2am. MC/V. ❸

**Arrocería Gala,** C. de Moratín 22 (☎429 2562; www.paellas-gala.com). M: Antón Martín. Decor is as colorful as the specialty, paella. *Menú* (€14) includes dessert, paella, salad, and wine. Excellent sangria. Lush, vine-covered interior garden. Reserve ahead F-Sa. Open Tu-Su 1-5pm and 9pm-1:30am. Cash only. ❸

**Rey de Tallarines,** C. Cardenal Cisneros 33 (☎447 6828). Huge portions of Beijing cuisine and tiny prices. *Menú* €8.30. Noodle dishes €3-8. Open daily noon-midnight. ❷

**Achuri,** C. Argumosa 21 (☎468 7856). M: Lavapiés. A cheap, mostly vegetarian restaurant with a young clientele. *Bocadillos* €2.70. *Raciones* €4.80. Wine €0.80-2.20 per glass. Open Su-Th 1:30pm-2am, F-Sa 1:30pm-2:30am. Cash only. ❶

**Café de Oriente,** Pl. del Oriente 2 (☎547 9831). M: Ópera. A traditional cafe catering to a ritzy, older crowd and hungry tourists strolling by the Palacio. Specialty coffees (€4-7). Open Su-Th 8:30am-1:30am, F-Sa 8:30am-12:30am. AmEx/D/MC/V. ❶

**Café Comercial,** Glorieta de Bilbao 7 (☎521 5655). M: Bilbao. Founded in 1887, Madrid's oldest cafe boasts cushioned chairs, high ceilings, and huge mirrors perfect for people-watching. Coffee at the bar €1.20, at a table €1.90. Internet €1 per 50min. Open M-Th 7:30am-1am, F 7:30am-2am, Sa 8:30am-2am, Su 10am-1am. ❶

**Museo del Jamón,** C. San Jerónimo 6 (☎521 0346). M: Sol. 10 other branches in Madrid, including C. Mayor 7 (☎531 4550). A vegetarian's nightmare and pork-lover's dream. Hooves and shanks hang around the bar; the restaurant upstairs serves the chef's specialties (€3.75-7). *Menú* €7.30. Open daily 8am-12:30am, restaurant 1-11:30pm. *Menú* served 1-5pm and 8-11pm. MC/V. ❶

**Eucalipto,** C. Argumosa 4, south of Huertas (☎629 33 49 98). M: Lavapiés. Offers refreshing *zumos tropicales* (fresh juice; €2.60-3.50). Try the Brazilian Lulo berry or *batidos* (€3-3.50). Spike the night with a daiquiri (€4.50-4.80), or enjoy a huge fruit salad (€7). Sidewalk seating. Open daily 5pm-2am. ❶

# TAPAS

Not long ago, bartenders in Madrid covered *(tapar)* drinks with saucers to keep away the flies. Later, servers began putting little sandwiches on top of the saucers, which became known as "tapas." Hopping from bar to bar gobbling tapas is an alternative to a full sit-down meal. Most tapas bars *(tascas* or *tabernas)* are open noon-4pm and 8pm-midnight; many are on **Plaza Santa Ana** and **Plaza Mayor** as well as north of Gran Vía in **Chueca.** Bars pack **Calle Cuchilleros** and **Calle de la Cruz.**

▨ **Restaurante Casa Granada,** C. Doctor Cortezo 17, 6th fl. (☎420 0825). Enter in an unmarked door on the left side of C. Doctor Cortezo as you head downhill. Come around 8pm and stay for the sunset. Place your name on the outdoor seating list when you arrive. *Cañas* of beer (small glass; €2.20) come with tapas. *Raciones* €5.50-8. Open M-Sa noon-midnight, Su noon-9pm. MC/V. ❶

▨ **El Tigre,** C. Infantas 30 (☎532 0072), is the most happening *cañas* spot in Chueca. Tapas free with drink. Young and inviting crowd. Beer €1.50. *Raciones* €4-7. Open M-F 12:30pm-1:30am, Sa-Su 1pm-2am. Cash only. ❶

**Casa Alberto,** C. de las Huertas 18 (☎429 9356; www.casaalberto.es). M: Antón Martín. A classic tapas bar founded in 1827. Sweet vermouth (€1.50) is served with original house tapas. Try the delicious *gambas al ajillo* (shrimp with garlic; €11) or the *canapés* (€2.25-3). Open Tu-Sa noon-5:30pm and 8pm-1:30am. MC/V. ❷

**Cervecería 100 Montaditos,** C. Mayor 22 (☎902 19 74 94; www.cerveceria100montaditos.es). M: Sol. This little cafe with many branches in the city serves 100 varieties of creative *bocadillos* (€1.20). Perfect for a snack or light lunch. Open M-Th 10am-12:30am, F-Sa 10am-2am. ❶

**La Trucha,** C. Manuel Fernández González 3 (☎429 5833). M: Sol. Branch at C. Núñez de Arce 6 (☎532 0890). Impressive selection of seasonal veggies (€5-9) and daily specials. Try the *rabo de toro* (bull's tail with potatoes; €12). Entrees €12-15. Open daily 12:30-4pm and 7:30pm-midnight. AmEx/MC/V. ❸

# 👁 SIGHTS

Madrid, large as it may seem, is a walking city. Its public transportation should only be used for longer distances or between the day's starting and ending points; you don't want to miss the sights above ground. Although the word *paseo* refers to a major avenue (such as Paseo de la Castellana or Paseo del Prado), the word means "a stroll." Do just that from Sol to Cibeles and from Pl. Mayor to the Palacio Real. Madrid also offers excellent places to relax. Whether soothing tired feet after perusing the **Avenida del Arte** or seeking shelter from summer's sweltering heat, there's nothing better than a shaded sidewalk cafe or a romantic park.

## EL CENTRO

The area known as El Centro, spreading out from Puerta del Sol (Gate of the Sun), is the gateway to historical Madrid. Although several rulers carved the winding streets, the Habsburgs and the Bourbons built El Centro's most celebrated monuments. As a result, the easily navigable area is divided into two major sections: Habsburg Madrid and Bourbon Madrid. Unless otherwise specified, Habsburg directions are given from Puerta del Sol and Bourbon directions from Ópera. Kilómetro 0, the origin of six national highways, marks the center of the city in the most chaotic of Madrid's plazas. Puerta del Sol bustles day and night with taxis, performers, and locals trying to evade luggage-laden tourists. Both *Madrileños* and visitors converge upon **El oso y el madroño,** a bronze statue of the bear and berry tree that grace the city's heraldic coat of arms *(M: Sol).*

### HABSBURG MADRID

Densely packed with monuments and tourists, "Old Madrid" is the city's central neighborhood. When Felipe II moved the seat of Castilla to Madrid in 1561, he commissioned court architects to update the city's buildings in the latest styles.

**PLAZA MAYOR.** Juan de Herrera, the architect of El Escorial (p. 855), also designed this plaza. Its elegant arcades, spindly towers, and open verandas, built for Felipe III in 1620, are defining elements of the "Madrid-style," which inspired architects nationwide. Toward evening, Pl. Mayor awakens as *Madrileños* resur-

**START:** M: Estación Atocha
**FINISH:** M:Pl. de Castellana
**DISTANCE:** 7km
**DURATION:** From 3hr. to 3 days

Madrid's *paseos* are a great starting point for walking tours, since most major sights are located on these main avenues. Trees in the the grassy medians offer shade and provide a nice buffer from the zooming traffic. You may be tempted to head to El Retiro after the Museo del Prado, or venture to Puerta del Sol once you have reached Pl. de Cibeles. Regardless of the path chosen, the *paseos* are a simple way to acquaint yourself with the city and organize a daily itinerary.

**1. REINA SOFÍA.** Directly across from Estación Atocha, the **Museo Nacional Centro de Arte Reina Sofía** (p. 851), home to Picasso's *Guernica,* presides over Pl. del Emperador Carlos V. Its glass elevators hint at the impressive collection of modern art within.

**2. MUSEO DEL PRADO.** Walking up Po. del Prado, you'll pass the **Real Jardín Botánico** on the right. Next to the garden is the world-renowned **Museo del Prado** (p. 850); behind it, on C. Ruíz de Alarcón, stands the **Iglesia de San Jerónimo,** Madrid's royal church. Built by Hieronymite monks, the church has witnessed the coronation of Fernando and Isabel and the marriage of King Alfonso XII. These days, only Madrid's social elite wed in the church. *(Open daily 10am-1pm and 5-8:30pm.)*

**3. PLAZA DE LA LEALTAD.** Back on Po. del Prado, to the north in Pl. de la Lealtad, stands the **Obelisco a los Mártires del 2 de Mayo,** filled with the ashes of those who died in the 1808 uprising against Napoleon. Its four statues represent constancy, virtue, valor, and patriotism. Behind the memorial sits the colonnaded classical **Bolsa de Comerico** (Madrid's Stock Exchange). Ventura Rodríguez's **Fuente de Neptuno,** in Pl. Cánovas de Castillo, is one of three aquatic masterpieces along the avenue, famous enough to have earned him a Metro stop. Crossing the plaza brings you to another great museum, the **Museo Thyssen-Bornemisza** (p. 851).

**4. PLAZA DE CIBELES.** The arts of the Po. del Prado transition into the Po. de Recoletos at the flower-encircled **Plaza de Cibeles.** From the plaza, the small **Museo Naval** is to the right *(Entrance on C. Juan de Mena, 1. ☎913 79 52 99; www.museonavalmadrid.com. Open Tu-Su 10am-2pm. Closed Aug. Free.)* In the southeast corner of the plaza sits the spectacular **Palacio de Comunicaciones** (p. 841), designed by Antonio Palacios and Julián Otamendi of Otto Wagner's Vienna School in 1920, which functions as Madrid's central post office. On the corner opposite the Palacio lies the equally impressive **Banco de España.**

**5. CASA DE AMÉRICA.** Looking to the right up C. Alcalá from the Palacio de Comunicaciones is Sabatini's **Puerta de Alcalá,** the 18th-century emblematic gateway and court symbol. On the northeastern corner of the plaza roundabout (behind black gates) is the former **Palacio de Linares,** a 19th-century townhouse built for Madrid nobility. Proven by a team of "scientists" to be inhabited by ghosts, it is now the **Casa de América** with a library and lecture halls for the study of Latin American culture and politics. It also sponsors art exhibits and guest lectures. *(Pl. de las Cibeles, 2. M: Banco de España. ☎915 95 48 00; www.casamerica.es. Open M-F 11am-2pm and 5-8pm.)*

**6. BARRIO DE SALAMANCA.** Continuing north toward the brown **Torres de Colón** (Towers of Columbus), you'll pass the **Biblioteca Nacional** (National Library), which often hosts temporary exhibitions and celebrations in the summer. *(Entrance at P. de Recoletos, 20-22. ☎915 80 78 23; www.bne.es. Open M-F 9am-9pm, Sa 9am-2pm. Free.)* Behind the library is the massive **Museo Arqueológico Nacional.** Madrid's display of the history of the Western world, including a 4th-century urn, Felipe II's astrolabe, and a 16th-century porcelain clock, settled in this huge museum in 1895 after countless moves. *(C. Serrano, 13. M: Serrano. ☎915 77 79 12; www.man.mcu.es. Open in summer Tu-Sa 9:30am-8:00pm, Su 9:30am-3pm. €3.01, Sa after 2:30pm and Su free.)* The museum entrance is on C. Serrano, an avenue lined with pricey boutiques in the posh **Barrio de Salamanca.**

**7. PLAZA DE COLÓN.** The museum and library huddle just before the modern **Plaza de Colón** *(M: Colón)* and the **Jardines del Descubrimiento** (Gardens of Discovery). On one side loom huge

clay boulders, inscribed with trivia about the New World, including Seneca's prediction of its discovery, the names of the mariners onboard the caravels, and passages from Columbus's diary. A neo-Gothic spire honoring Columbus rises opposite a thundering fountain in the center of the plaza. An inlaid map detailing Columbus's journey covers the wall behind the waterfall. Concerts, lectures, ballets, and plays are held in the **Centro Cultural de la Villa** (☎914 80 03 00; www.esmadrid.com/ccvilla/jsp/index.jsp. Box office open Tu-Su 11am-1:30pm and 5-7pm or check on www.telentrada.com), the municipal art center beneath the statue.

**8. PASEO DE LA CASTELLANA.** Nineteenth- and early 20th-century aristocrats dislodged themselves from Old Madrid to settle along Po. de la Castellana. During the Civil War, Republican forces used the mansions as barracks, but they weren't so effective, and in 1939, Franco marched his army down the Castellana. Most of the mansions were torn down in the 1960s when banks and insurance companies commissioned more innovative structures. Some notables include: Rafael Moneo's **Bankinter,** #29, the first to integrate rather than demolish a townhouse; the Sevillian-tiled **Edificio ABC,** #34, formerly the office of the pro-monarchy newspaper and now a shopping center; **Banco Urquijo,** known as "the coffeepot"; the pink **Edificio Bankunion,** #46; **Banca Catalana Occidente,** #50, which looks like an ice cube on a cracker; and the famous chandelier-like **Edificio La Caixa,** #61.

**9. PLAZA DE LIMA.** Just south of the **American Embassy,** between Pl. de Colón and Glorieta de Emilio Castelar, is a very small **open-air sculpture garden** with works by Joan Miró and Eduardo Chillida. Smaller museums, including the **Museo Lázaro Galdiano** (p. 851), are just off the Paseo. At **Plaza de Lima** is the 110,000-seat **Estadio Santiago Bernabéu** (M: Lima), home to the beloved **Real Madrid** soccer club, which won its 9th European Championship in 2002 and its 30th Spanish La Liga Championship in 2007. Considerably farther north is the **Puerta de Europa,** with its two 27-story leaning towers connected by a tunnel (M: Pl. de Castilla).

THE PASEOS

847

face, tourists multiply, and cafes. Live flamenco performances are a common treat. While the cafes are a nice spot for a drink, food is overpriced; have dinner elsewhere. (*M: Sol. Walk down C. Mayor. The plaza is on the left.*)

**CATEDRAL DE SAN ISIDRO.** Though Isidro, patron saint of crops, farmers, and Madrid, was humble, his final resting place is anything but. Designed in the Jesuit Baroque style at the beginning of the 17th century, the cathedral received San Isidro's remains in 1769. During the Spanish Civil War, rioters damaged much of the cathedral, burning its exterior—the main chapel, a 17th-century banner, and the mummified remains of San Isidro and his wife were all that survived. (*M: Latina. From Pta. del Sol, take C. Mayor to Pl. Mayor, cross the plaza, and exit on C. de Toledo. Open daily in summer 7:30am-1:30pm and 5:30-9pm; in winter 7:30am-1pm and 5:30-8:30pm. Free.*)

**PLAZA DE LA VILLA.** Plaza de la Villa marks the heart of what was once Old Madrid. The horseshoe-shaped door on C. Codo is one of the few examples of the Gothic-*mudéjar* style left in Madrid, and the 15th-century *Torre de los Lujanes* was once the prison of French king Francisco I. Across the plaza is the 17th-century **Ayuntamiento,** designed in 1640 by Juan Gómez de Mora as both the mayor's home and the city jail. Inside is Goya's *Allegory of the City of Madrid.* (*M: Sol. Go down C. Mayor and past Pl. Mayor.*)

## BOURBON MADRID

Weakened by plagues and political losses, the Habsburg era in Spain ended with the death of Carlos II in 1700. Felipe V, the first of Spain's Bourbon monarchs, ascended the throne in 1714. Bankruptcy, industrial stagnation, and widespread disillusionment compelled Felipe V to embark on a crusade of urban renewal. The lavish churches, palaces, and parks that resulted are the most touristed in Madrid.

**PALACIO REAL.** The luxurious Palacio Real lies at the western tip of central Madrid, overlooking the Río Manzanares. Felipe V commissioned Giovanni Sachetti to replace the Alcázar, which burned down in 1734, with a palace that would dwarf all others—he succeeded. Today, King Juan Carlos and Queen Sofía use the palace only on special occasions. Its most impressive rooms are decorated in the Rococo style. The **Salón del Trono** (Throne Room) contains the two magnificent Spanish thrones, supported by golden lions. According to tradition, the thrones are never actually used during state visits; the king and queen stand in front of them. The room also features a ceiling fresco painted by Tiepolo, outlining the qualities of the ideal ruler. The **Salón de Gasparini,** site of the king's ceremonial dressing before the court, houses Goya's portrait of Carlos IV. Perhaps most beautiful is the **Chinese Room,** whose walls swirl with green tendril patterns. The **Real Oficina de Farmacia** (Royal Pharmacy) has crystal and china receptacles used to hold royal medicine. Also open to the public is the **Real Armería** (Armory), which has an entire floor devoted to knights' armor. (*From Pl. de Isabel II, head toward the Teatro Real. M: Ópera. ☎ 454 8788. Open Apr.-Sept. M-Sa 9am-6pm, Su 9am-3pm; Oct.-Mar. M-Sa 9:30am-5pm, Su 9am-2pm. €8, students €3.50; with tour €6/10. Under 5 free. W EU citizens free.*)

**PLAZA DE ORIENTE.** Royal paranoia was responsible for this sculpture park. Most of the statues were designed for the palace roof, but due to the queen's nightmare about the roof collapsing under their weight, they were placed in this shady plaza instead. Treat yourself to an expensive coffee on one of the elegant *terrazas* that ring the plaza. The **Jardines de Sabatini,** to the right as you face the palace, is the romantic's park of choice. (*M: Ópera. From Pl. de Isabel II, walk past Teatro Real. Across the street from the Palacio Real.*)

## HUERTAS

The area east of Sol is a wedge bounded by C. de Alcalá to the north, C. de Atocha to the south, and Po. del Prado to the east. Huertas's sights, from authors' houses to famous cafes, reflect its artistic focus. Home to Calderón, Cervantes, Góngora, Moratín, and Quevedo during the *Siglo de Oro* (Golden Age; 1500-1700), Huertas enjoyed a fleeting return to literary prominence when Hemingway dropped by to drink in the 1920s. **Plaza Santa Ana** and its *terrazas* are the center of this old literary haunt. **Casa de Lope de Vega** is the home where the prolific playwright and poet spent the last 25 years of his life and wrote over two-thirds of his plays. Highlights include the simple garden described in his works and the library filled with crumbling books. *(C. de Cervantes 11. With your back to Pl. de Santa Ana, turn left onto C. del Prado, right onto C. León, and left onto C. de Cervantes. ☎ 429 9216. Open Tu-F 9:30am-2pm, Sa 10am-2pm. Entrance and tour €2, students €1. Free on Sa.)*

## GRAN VÍA

Urban planners paved the Gran Vía in 1910 to link C. Princesa with Pl. de Cibeles. Madrid gained wealth as a neutral supplier during WWI, and then funneled much of its earnings into making the Gran Vía one of the world's great thoroughfares. Actual sights are few and far between; the best way to experience Gran Vía is to throw yourself into the throngs on the sidewalk and keep up the pace. At the top of Gran Vía in **Plaza del Callao** (M: Callao), Postigo San Martín splits southward, where you'll find the famed **Convento de las Descalzas Reales.** Westward from Pl. del Callao, the Gran Vía descends toward **Plaza de España** (M: Pl. de España).

## MALASAÑA AND CHUECA

Devoid of the numerous historical monuments and palaces that characterize most of Madrid, the labyrinthine streets of Malasaña and Chueca house many undocumented "sights," from platform-shoe stores to spontaneous street performances. These streets are a funky, ultra-modern relief for travelers weary of crucifixes and brush strokes. Chueca in particular remains an ideal area for people-watching and shopping. While the area between **Calle de Fuencarral** and **Calle de San Bernardo** contains some of Madrid's most avant-garde architecture and contemporary art exhibits, street drawings, and residents are its main attractions.

## ARGÜELLES

The area known as Argüelles and the zone surrounding C. de San Bernardo form a cluttered mixture of elegant middle-class houses, student apartments, and bohemian hangouts. Unlike the majority of Madrid, it is easily navigable due to its grid-like organization. Heavily bombarded during the Civil War, Argüelles inspired Chilean poet Pablo Neruda, then a resident, to write *España en el corazón*. By day, families and joggers roam the city's largest park, **Casa del Campo.** The park is unsafe by night. The **Parque de la Montaña** is home to the ▣**Templo de Debod,** built by King Adijalamani of Meröe in the 2nd century BC; it is the only Egyptian temple in Spain. The Egyptian government shipped the temple stone by stone to Spain in appreciation of Spanish archaeologists who helped to rescue the Abu Simbel temples from the floods of the Aswan Dam. *(M: Pl. de España or Ventura Rodríguez. Buses #1 and 74. From the metro, walk down C. Ventura Rodríguez to Parque de la Montaña; the temple is on the right. ☎ 366 7415; www.munimadrid.es/templodebod. Guided tours available. Open Apr.-Sept. Tu-F 10am-2pm and 6-8pm, Sa-Su 10am-2pm; Oct.-Mar. Tu-F 9:45am-1:45pm and 4:15-6:15pm, Sa-Su 10am-2pm. Free.)* Although out of the way, the **Ermita de San Antonio de la Florida** contains Goya's pantheon, a frescoed dome that arches above his grave. Goya's skull, apparently stolen by a phrenologist, was missing when the corpse arrived from France. *(M: Príncipe Pío. Go right onto Po. de la Florida and walk to the first traffic circle. Open Tu-F 9:30am-8pm, Sa-Su 10am-2pm. Free.)*

## OTHER SIGHTS

**■ PARQUE DEL BUEN RETIRO.** Join an array of vendors, palm-readers, football players, and sunbathers in the area Felipe IV converted from a hunting ground into a *buen retiro* (nice retreat). The 300-acre park is centered around a magnificent monument to King Alfonso XII and a rectangular lake, the **Estanque Grande.** Rowboats for four people are available for €5 per 45min. Sundays from 5pm to midnight, over 100 percussionists gather for an intense ■drum circle by the monument on the Estanque; hypnotic rhythms and hash smoke fill the air. The **Palacio de Velázquez** exhibits frequently changing contemporary and experimental works. *(From the Estanque, walk straight to Pl. de Honduras and turn left onto Po. Venezuela. The palace will be on your right.* ☎ *573 6245. Open Apr.-Sept. M-Sa 11am-8pm, Su 11am-6pm; Oct.-Mar. M-Sa 10am-6pm, Su 10am-4pm. Free.)* Built by Ricardo Velázquez to exhibit Filipino flowers, the steel-and-glass **Palacio de Cristal** now hosts art shows. *(From Palacio de Velázquez, head out the main door until you reach the lake and the palace.* ☎ *574 6614. Open Apr.-Sept. M-Sa 11am-8pm, Su 11am-6pm; Oct.-Mar. M-Sa 10am-6pm, Su 10am-4pm. Free.)*

**EL PARDO.** Built as a hunting lodge for Carlos I in 1547, El Pardo was enlarged by generations of Habsburgs and Bourbons. It gained attention in 1940 when Franco made the country palace his home, residing there until his death in 1975. El Pardo is renowned for its collection of tapestries, several of which were designed by Goya. The palace also holds paintings by Velázquez and Ribera. *(Take bus #601 from the stop above M: Moncloa; 4 per hr., €1.* ☎ *376 1500. Open Apr.-Sept. M-Sa 10:30am-6pm, Su 9:25am-1:40pm; Oct.-Mar. M-Sa 10:30am-5pm, Su 9:55am-1:40pm. Mandatory 45min. Spanish-language tour. €4, over 65 and students €2.70, W free for EU citizens.)*

## 🏛 MUSEUMS

Considered individually to be among the world's best art galleries, the Museo del Prado, Museo de Thyssen-Bornemisza, and the Museo Nacional Centro de Arte Reina Sofía together form the impressive "Avenida del Arte."

**■ MUSEO DEL PRADO.** One of Europe's finest centers for 12th- to 17th-century art, the Prado is Spain's most prestigious museum and home to the world's greatest collection of Spanish paintings. Its 7000 pieces from the 12th to the 17th centuries are the result of hundreds of years of Habsburg and Bourbon art-collecting. The museum provides an indispensable guide for each room. English-language audio tours are available for €3. The sheer quantity of paintings means you'll have to be selective—walk past the rooms of imitation Rubens and Rococo cherubs and into the realms of the masters. On the first floor, keep an eye out for the unforgiving realism of **Diego Velázquez** (1599-1660). His technique of "illusionism" is on display in the magnificent ■**Las Meninas,** considered by many art historians to be the best painting ever made. Court portraitist **Francisco de Goya y Lucientes** (1746-1828) created the stark *2 de Mayo* and *Fusilamientas de 3 de Mayo*, which depict the terrors of the 1808 Napoleonic invasion. Deaf and alone, Goya painted the *Pinturas Negras (Black Paintings)*, so named for the darkness of both their color and their subject matter. The Prado also displays many of **El Greco's** religious paintings, characterized by luminous colors, elongated figures, and mystical subjects. On the second floor are works by other Spanish artists, including **Murillo** and **Ribera.**

The Prado also has a formidable collection of Italian works, including pieces by **Botticelli, Raphael, Tintoretto,** and **Titian.** As a result of the Spanish Habsburgs' control of the Netherlands, the Flemish holdings are also top-notch. Works by **van Dyck** and **Albrecht Durer** are here, as well as **Peter Bruegel the Elder's** *The Triumph of Death*, in which Death drives a carriage of skulls on a decaying horse. **Hieronymus Bosch's** *The Garden of Earthly Delights* depicts hedonists and the destiny that awaits them. A large extension to the Prado with an auditorium and new space for temporary exhibitions is planned to open at the end of 2007. (*Po. del Prado at Pl. Cánovas del Castillo. M: Banco de España or Atocha. ☎330 2800; www.museoprado.es. Open Tu-Su 9am-8pm. €6, students €3, under 18 and over 65 free, Su free.*)

### ■ MUSEO NACIONAL CENTRO DE ARTE REINA SOFÍA.

Since Juan Carlos I decreed this renovated hospital a national museum in 1988, the Reina Sofía's collection of **twentieth-century art** has grown steadily. The building itself is a work of art, and is much easier to navigate than the Prado. Rooms dedicated to **Salvador Dalí, Juan Gris,** and **Joan Miró** display Spain's vital contributions to the Surrealist movement. Picasso's masterpiece, ■**Guernica,** is the highlight of the Reina Sofía's permanent collection. It depicts the Basque town (p. 924) bombed by the Germans at Franco's request during the Spanish Civil War. Picasso denounced the bloodshed in a huge, colorless work of agonized figures. When asked by Nazi officials if he was responsible for this work, Picasso answered, "No, you are." He lent the canvas to New York's Museum of Modern Art on condition that it be returned to Spain when democracy was restored. Delivered to the Prado in 1981, its subsequent transfer to the Reina Sofía sparked an international controversy—Picasso's other stipulation was that the painting hang only in the Prado. (*Pl. Santa Isabel 52. ☎774 1000; www.museoreinasofia.es. M: Atocha. Open M and W-Sa 10am-9pm, Su 10am-2:30pm. €3, students €1.50. Sa after 2:30pm, Su, holidays, under 18, over 65 free.*)

### ■ MUSEO THYSSEN-BORNEMISZA.

Unlike the Prado and the Reina Sofía, the Thyssen-Bornemisza covers many periods and media, with exhibits ranging from 14th-century paintings to 20th-century sculptures. Baron Heinrich Thyssen-Bornemisza donated his collection in 1993. Today, the museum's pieces constitute the world's most extensive private showcase. To view the collection in chronological order and observe the evolution of styles and themes, begin on the top floor and work your way down. The top floor is dedicated to the **Old Masters** collection, which includes such notables as Hans Holbein's austere *Portrait of Henry VIII* and El Greco's *Annunciation.* The Thyssen-Bornemisza's **Baroque** collection, with pieces by Caravaggio, Claude Lorraine, and Ribera, rivals the Prado's. The **Impressionist** and **Post-Impressionist** collections explode with texture and color—look for works by Cézanne, Degas, van Gogh, Manet, Matisse, Monet, and Renoir. The highlight of the museum is the **twentieth-century** collection on the first floor. The showcased artists include Chagall, Dalí, Hopper, O'Keeffe, Picasso, Pollock, and Rothko. (*On the corner of Po. del Prado and C. Manuel González. M: Banco de España or Atocha. ☎369 0151; www.museothyssen.org. Open Tu-Su 10am-7pm. Last entry 6:30pm. €6, students with ISIC and seniors €4, under 12 free. Audio guides €3.*)

### MUSEO DE AMÉRICA.

This under-appreciated museum documents the cultures of America's pre-Hispanic civilizations and the legacy of the Spanish conquest. Especially fascinating are paintings depicting interracial families and the ethnic identities assigned to their offspring, revealing the colonial mindset and stereotypes. (*Av. de los Reyes Católicos 6, next to the Faro de Moncloa. ☎549 2641; www.museodeamerica.mcu.es. M: Moncloa. Open Tu-Sa 9:30am-3pm, Su 10am-3pm. €3, under 18 and over 65 free. Sa after 2:30pm and Su free.*)

### MUSEO LÁZARO GALDIANO.

This small palace, once owned by 19th-century financier Lázaro Galdiano, displays a private collection of Italian Renaissance bronzes and Celtic and Visigoth brasses. Paintings include *Young Christ,* unofficially attributed to Leonard da Vinci, and Hieronymus Bosch's *Ecce Homo,* along with the Spanish trifecta: El Greco, Goya, and Velázquez. (*C. Serrano, 122. M: Gregorio Marañón. Turn right off Po. de la Castellana onto C. María de Molina. ☎561 6084; www.flg.es. Open M and W-Su 10am-4:30pm. €4, students €3, W free for EU citizens.*)

# ♫ ENTERTAINMENT

### ⊠ EL RASTRO (FLEA MARKET)

*El Rastro* has been a Sunday morning tradition in Madrid for hundreds of years. The market begins in La Latina at Pl. Cascorro off C. de Toledo and ends at the bottom of C. Ribera de Cortidores. Although the calls of street vendors and pushing about of patrons mean the market can be somewhat overwhelming at first, make like a child in a candy shop and dive into the mayhem with gusto. Seek out that zebra hide, antique tool, or pet bird you've been dying for since your first day in Madrid and haggle for it until you're blue in the face. As crazy as the market seems, it is actually thematically organized. The main street is a labyrinth of clothing, cheap jewelry, leather goods, incense, and sunglasses, branching out into side streets, each with its own concert of vendors and wares. Antique-sellers contribute their peculiar mustiness to C. del Prado, and in their own shops in small plazas off C. Ribera de Cortidores. Fantastic collections of old books and LPs are sold in Pl. del Campillo del Mundo, at the bottom of C. de Carlos Arnides. Tapas bars and small restaurants line the streets and provide an cool respite for market-weary bargainers. The flea market is a pickpocket's paradise, so leave the camera in your room, bust out the money belt, and turn that backpack into a frontpack. Fortunately, police are ubiquitous. *(Open Su and holidays 9am-3pm.)*

## MUSIC AND FLAMENCO

Madrid's principal performance venue is the prestigious **Teatro Real,** Pl. de Oriente, which features the city's best ballet and opera. (☎ 516 0606. M: Ópera. Tickets sold M-Sa 10am-1:30pm and 5:30-8pm.) Check the *Guía del Ocio* for info on city-sponsored concerts, movies, and plays. Flamenco in Madrid is tourist-oriented and expensive. A few nightlife spots are authentic but pricey. **Las Tablas,** Pl. de España 9, on the corner of C. Bailén and Cuesta San Vicente, has lower prices than most other flamenco clubs (€22). Shows start nightly at 10:30pm. *(M: Pl. de España. ☎ 542 0520; www.lastablasmadrid.com.)* **Casa Patas,** C. Cañizares 10, has excellent shows and offers intensive courses in flamenco. *(M: Antón Martín. ☎ 369 0496; www.casapatas.com. Shows €25-30; M-Th 10:30pm, F-Sa 8pm and midnight. Course €65.)*

## FÚTBOL

Spanish sports fans go ballistic for *fútbol* (football). Every Sunday and some Saturdays from September to June, one of the two local teams plays at home. **Real Madrid** plays at Estadio Santiago Bernabéu. *(Av. Cochina Espina 1. M: Santiago Bernabéu. ☎ 457 1112.)* **Atlético de Madrid** plays at Estadio Vicente Calderón. *(Po. de la Virgen del Puerto 67. M: Pirámides or Marqués de Vadillos. ☎ 364 2234. Tickets €22-50.)*

## BULLFIGHTS

Controversial bullfights are a Spanish tradition, and locals joke that they are the only events in Spain to ever start on time. Hemingway-toting Americans and true fans of the contorted struggle between man and beast clog Pl. de las Ventas for the heart-pounding, albeit gruesome, events. From early May to early June, the **Fiestas de San Isidro** stage a daily *corrida* (bullfight) with the top *matadores* and the fiercest bulls. Advance tickets are recommended; those without a seat crowd into bars to watch the televised festival. There are bullfights every Sunday from March to October and less frequently during the rest of the year. Look for posters in bars and cafes for upcoming *corridas* (especially on C. Victoria, off C. San Jerónimo). **Plaza de las Ventas,** C. de Alcalá 237, is the biggest ring in Spain. *(M: Ventas. ☎ 356 2200; www.las-ventas.com. Seats €2-115. Tickets available at booth F-Su.)* **Plaza de Toros Palacio de Vistalegre** also hosts bullfights and cultural events. *(M: Vista Alegre. ☎ 422*

*0780.)* To watch amateurs, head to the **bullfighting school,** which has its own *corridas. (M: Batán. ☎470 1990. Tickets €7, children €3.50. Open M-F 10am-2pm.)*

# ▓ FESTIVALS

The brochure *Madrid en Fiestas*, available at tourist offices, contains comprehensive details on Spain's festivals. Madrid bursts with dancing and processions during **Carnaval** in February, culminating on Ash Wednesday (Feb. 6, 2008) with the beginning of Lent and the *Entierro de la Sardina* (Burial of the Sardine), commemorating the arrival and prompt burial of a shipload of rotting sardines to the city during the reign of Carlos III. Madrid celebrates its struggle against the French invasion of 1808 during the **Fiestas del Dos de Mayo** (May 2). Starting May 15, the week-long **Fiestas de San Isidro** honor Madrid's patron saint with concerts, parades, and Spain's best bullfights. Late June or early July, Madrid goes crazy with ▓**Orgullo Gay** (Gay Pride). An outrageous parade shuts down traffic between El Retiro and Puerta del Sol on the festival's first Saturday. The festivities continue with bar crawls in the streets of Chueca and free concerts in Pl. Chueca. Throughout the summer, the city sponsors the **Veranos de la Villa,** an outstanding set of cultural activities, including a film festival, opera, *zarzuela* (Spanish light opera), ballet, and sports. The **Festivales de Otoño** (Autumn Festivals), from September to November, also bring an impressive array of music, theater, and film. In November, an **International Jazz Festival** entices great musicians to Madrid.

# ▓ NIGHTLIFE

Spaniards average one hour less sleep per night than other Europeans, and *Madrileños* claim to need even less than that. Proud of their nocturnal offerings, they'll say with a straight face that Paris or New York bored them and won't retire until they've "killed the night" and a good part of the morning. *Madrileños* start in the tapas bars of Huertas, move to the youthful scene in Malasaña, and end at the wild parties of Chueca or late-night clubs of Gran Vía. Students fill the streets of Bilbao and Moncloa, where *terrazas* and *chiringuitos* (outdoor cafebars) line the sidewalks. Madrid's fantastic gay scene centers on **Plaza Chueca.** Most clubs don't heat up until around 2am; don't be surprised by lines at 5:30am. The *entrada* (cover) can be as high as €18 but usually includes a drink. Bouncers on power trips love to make examples; dress well to avoid being overcharged or denied. Women may not be charged at all.

## EL CENTRO: SOL, ÓPERA, AND PLAZA MAYOR

In the middle of Madrid and at the heart of the action are the grandiose, spectacular clubs of El Centro. With multiple floors, swinging lights, cages, and disco balls, they meet even the wildest clubber's expectations. This extravagance comes at a price, however; a night of fun here is the most expensive in the city.

▓ **Taberna Vinocola Mentridana,** C. San Eugenio 9 (☎527 8760), 1 block from M: Antón Martín off C. Atocha. A popular local tapas bar by day, this place revs up at night when locals get thirsty for a glass of wine or a vermouth (€2.50-7). The crowd is sophisticated and somewhat philosophical, so don't forget your thinking cap. MC/V.

▓ **Palacio Gaviria,** C. Arenal 9 (☎526 6069; www.palaciogaviria.com). M: Sol or Ópera. Party like royalty in 3 ballrooms of this palace-turned-disco, but don't spill Red Bull and vodka on the high art. Mixed drinks €10. Cover €15; includes 1 drink. Open Tu-W and Su 11pm-3:30am, Th 10:30pm-4:30am, F-Sa 11pm-6am.

**De Las Letras Restaurante,** C. Gran Vía 11 (☎523 7980; www.hoteldelasletras.com). Situated on the border between El Centro, Chueca, and Gran Vía, this beautiful terrace atop the hotel of the same name is a great place to start the night. Drinks are pricey but the view is impressive. Open Su-Th 7:30pm-midnight, F-Sa 7:30pm-12:30am. MC/V.

## HUERTAS

Though quieter than El Centro, Malasaña, and Chueca, Pl. Santa Ana, **Calle del Príncipe,** and **Calle de Echegaray** are alive with jazz bars and busy terraces.

🏅 **Cuevas de Sésamo,** C. del Príncipe 7 (☎429 6524). M: Antón Martín. "Descend into these caves like Dante!" (Antonio Machado) is the first of many literary tidbits that welcome you to this underground gem. Cheap pitchers of sangria (small €6.50, large €10) and live jazz piano draw hipsters of all ages. Open daily 7pm-2am.

**Cardamomo,** C. de Echegaray 15 (☎369 0757; www.cardamomo.net). M: Sevilla. Flamenco and Latin music spin all night. Those who prefer to relax retreat to the lounge area. Beer €4. W live music midnight-late. Open daily 9pm-3:30am.

**Café Jazz Populart,** C. Huertas 22 (☎429 8407; www.populart.es). M: Sevilla or Antón Martín. This intimate cafe hosts local and foreign talent. Live blues, jazz, and reggae. Shows daily 11pm and 12:30am. No cover. Open daily 6pm-3am.

## GRAN VÍA

Subtlety has never been the strong suit of the flashy clubs of Gran Vía. The area is not known for its safety: exercise caution at night.

**Ocho y Medio Club,** C. Mesonero Romanos 13 (☎541 3500; www.tripfamily.com). Where cool kids go for their late-night *discoteca* fix; the line will probably be long, but the wait is worth it. Locals dance to electronica remixes of their favorite tunes. F new DJ or live performance. Sa "Dark Hole," a gothic extravaganza. Check website for schedule. Drinks €7. Cover €8; includes 1 drink. Open F-Sa 1-6am.

**Del Diego,** C. de la Reina 12 (☎523 3106). M: Gran Vía. A classy refuge for the after-business crowd. Frosted glass windows hide a modern bar. Beer €4. Mixed drinks €8. Open Sept.-July M-Sa 7pm-3am.

## MALASAÑA AND CHUECA

Wild, trendy Malasaña and Chueca come to life in the early evening, especially in Pl. Chueca and **Plaza Dos de Mayo.** Gay nightlife thrives and alcohol flows freely; the area is ideal for bar-hopping until 2 or 3am, when it's time to hit the clubs near Sol, Centro, and Gran Vía.

🏅 **La Ida,** C. Colón 11 (☎522 9107), a few blocks from Pl. Chueca towards Malasaña. Young locals fill this colorful bar. Bartenders make tourists feel at home. Mojitos €6. Open daily 1pm-2am. MC/V.

**Acuarela,** C. de Gravina 10 (☎522 2143). M: Chueca. A welcome alternative to the club scene. Candles surround antique furniture and conversation flows. Coffees and teas €1.80-4.50. Liquors €3.20-5. Open daily 11pm-2am.

**El Clandestino,** C. del Barquillo 34 (☎521 5563). M: Chueca. A chill 20-something crowd drinks and debates at the bar upstairs, then heads down to the caves to dance to funk, fusion, and acid jazz. Beer €3. Mixed drinks €6. Live music most Th-Sa at 11:30pm. Open M-Sa 6:30pm-3am.

**El Truco,** C. de Gravina 10 (☎532 8921). M: Chueca. This gay- and lesbian-friendly club blasts pop far into the night. The line gets very long and the club gets very packed; luckily, there is outdoor seating. Same owners also run the popular **Escape,** nearby on the plaza. Cover €1. Open Th 10pm-late, F-Sa midnight-late.

**Tupperware,** Corredera Alta de San Pablo 26 (☎925 52 35 61; http://plan-x.tupperware-club.com). M: Tribunal. Where latte sippers go for liquor. The mural of hipsters on the wall is a reflection of the local crowd—soul patches and horizontal stripes galore. DJ plays a great mix of rock and pop. Mixed drinks €4.50-5. Open daily 9pm-3am.

**Vía Láctea,** C. de Velarde 18 (☎446 7581). M: Tribunal. Dive into the Brit punk rock scene nightly 9-11pm, when soft drinks and beer on tap are €2-3.50. After midnight, a late 20s crowd gets groovy between the pink walls. Th funk and *afrodisia,* with 3 DJs spinning new mixes. Open M-Th 9pm-2:45am, F-Su 9pm-3:15am.

▶ **DAYTRIP FROM MADRID: EL ESCORIAL.** This enormous complex was described by Felipe II as "majesty without ostentation." The **Monasterio de San Lorenzo del Escorial** was a gift from Felipe II to God, the people, and himself, commemorating his victory over the French at the battle of San Quintín in 1557. Near the town of San Lorenzo, El Escorial is filled with artistic treasures, a church, a magnificent library, two palaces, and two pantheons. To avoid crowds, enter via the gate on C. Floridablanca, on the western side. The adjacent **Museo de Arquitectura y Pintura** has an exhibit comparing El Escorial's construction to that of similar structures. The **Palacio Real,** lined with 16th-century *azulejo* tiles, includes the majestic **Salón del Trono** (Throne Room), Felipe II's spartan 16th-century apartments, and the luxurious 18th-century rooms of Carlos III and Carlos IV. *(Autocares Herranz buses run between El Escorial and Moncloa Metro.; 50min., 2-6 per hr., €3.20. Complex ☎918 90 59 03. Open Tu-Su Apr.-Sept. 10am-7pm; Oct.-Mar. 10am-6pm. Last entry 1hr. before closing. Monastery €7, with guide €9; students and seniors €3.50.)*

# CENTRAL SPAIN

Medieval cities and olive groves fill Castilla La Mancha, the land south and east of Madrid. Castilla y León's dramatic cathedrals are testaments to its storied history. Farther west, bordering Portugal, stark Extremadura was the birthplace of world-famous explorers such as Hernán Cortés and Francisco Pizarro.

## CASTILLA LA MANCHA

Land of austere plains and miles of empty landscapes, Castilla La Mancha has played host to bloody conflicts and epic heroes both real and imaginary. The region is one of Spain's least developed and provokes the imagination with its solitary crags, gloomy medieval fortresses, and whirling windmills.

## TOLEDO
☎925

Cervantes called Toledo (pop. 66,000) "the glory of Spain and light of her cities." The city is a former capital of the Holy Roman, Visigoth, and Muslim Empires, and its churches, synagogues, and mosques share twisting alleyways. Toledo is known as the "City of Three Cultures," symbol of a time when Spain's three religions coexisted peacefully, although locals will tell you the history is a bit romanticized.

**◼ ▶ TRANSPORTATION AND PRACTICAL INFORMATION.** From the station on Po. de la Rosa, just over Puente de Azarquiel, **trains** (RENFE info ☎902 24 02 02) run to Madrid (30min., 9-11 per day, €9). **Buses** run from Av. Castilla La Mancha (☎21 58 50), 5min. from **Puerta de Bisagra** (the city gate), to Madrid (1½hr., 2 per hr., €4.40) and Valencia (5½hr., 1 per day, €24). Within the city, buses #5 and

SPAIN

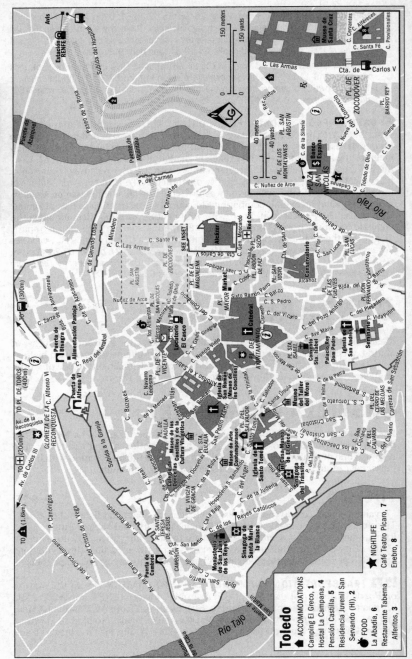

**Toledo**

**▲ ACCOMMODATIONS**
Camping El Greco, **1**
Hostal La Campana, **4**
Pensión Castilla, **5**
Residencia Juvenil San
Servando (HI), **2**

**● FOOD**
La Abadía, **6**
Restaurante Taberna
Alfileritos, **3**

**★ NIGHTLIFE**
Café Teatro Pícaro, **7**
Enebro, **8**

6 serve the bus and train stations and the central **Plaza de Zocodóver**. Buses (€1; at night €1.30) stop to the right of the train station, underneath and across the street from the bus station. Though Toledo's streets are well-labeled, it's easy to get lost; pick up a map at the **tourist office**, at Pta. de Bisagra. (☎22 08 43. Open July-Sept. M-F 9am-7pm, Sa 10am-6pm, Su 10am-2pm; Oct.-June M-F 9am-6pm, Sa 10am-6pm, Su 10am-2pm.) **Postal Code:** 45070.

**┏╻┗╏ ACCOMMODATIONS AND FOOD.** Toledo is full of accommodations, but finding a bed in summer can be a hassle, especially on weekends. Reservations are strongly recommended. ■**Hostal La Campana ❹**, C. de la Campana 10-12, has monuments at its doorstep and quintessential Toledo hospitality. Rooms are quaint and clean, and all have A/C, bath, phone, TV, and Wi-Fi. (☎22 16 59 or 22 16 62; www.hostalcampana.com. Breakfast included. Singles €36; doubles €60. MC/V.) Spacious rooms among suits of armor await at the **Residencia Juvenil San Servando (HI) ❶**, Castillo San Servando, uphill on Subida del Hospital from the train station, in a 14th-century castle with a pool, TV room, and Internet. (☎22 45 54. Dorms €11, with breakfast €15; under 30 €9.20/11. MC/V.) To reach **Pensión Castilla ❷**, C. Recoletos 6, go down C. Las Armas from Pl. de Zocodóver and turn left on C. Recoletos. The *pensión* has a great price and location. (☎22 45 54; reservations 22 16 78. Midnight curfew. Reserve ahead. Singles €18; doubles €26, with bath €29. Cash only. ) Take bus #7 from Pl. de Zocodóver to get to **Camping El Greco ❶**, 1.5km from town on Ctra. CM-4000. The shady, wooded site features a bar, pool, restaurant, and supermarket. (☎22 00 90. €4.90 per person, per tent, and per car. VAT not included. MC/V.)

*Pastelería* windows beckon with *mazapán* (marzipan) of every shape and size. For the widest array, stop by the **market** in Pl. Mayor, behind the cathedral. (Open M-Sa 9am-8pm.) To reach **La Abadía ❷**, Pl. de San Nicolás 3, bear left when C. de la Sillería splits; Pl. de San Nicolás is on the right. Dine on the regional lunch *menú* (€10) in a maze of underground rooms. (☎25 11 40. Open daily 8am-midnight. AmEx/MC/V.) The postmodern decor of **Restaurante Taberna Alferitos ❸**, C. Alferitos 24, contrasts with its medieval architecture. The ground floor is a popular tapas stop (€5-8), while the three stories above seat a classy dining crowd. (Entrees €12-15. Open daily 8pm-midnight. MC/V.)

**◙╏ SIGHTS AND NIGHTLIFE.** Within the fortified walls, Toledo's attractions form a belt around its middle. Most sights are closed Mondays. At Arco de Palacio, up C. del Comercio from Pl. de Zocodóver, Toledo's ■**cathedral** boasts five naves, delicate stained glass, and unapologetic ostentation. Beneath the dome is the **Capilla Mozárabe**, the only place where the ancient ■**Visigoth mass** (in Mozarabic) is still held. The **sacristía** holds 18 El Grecos (including *El Espolio*), as well as paintings by other notable Spanish and European masters. (☎22 22 41. Open M-Sa 10am-6:30pm, Su 2-6:30pm. €8, students €6. Audio tour €3. Dress modestly.) Greek painter Doménikos Theotokópoulos, better known as El Greco, spent most of his life in Toledo. Though the majority of his masterpieces have been carted off to the Prado (p. 850), some are still displayed throughout town. The best place to start is the **Casa Museo de El Greco**, on C. Samuel Leví 2, which contains 19 of his works. (☎22 44 05. Open in summer Tu-Sa 10am-2pm and 4-9pm, Su 10am-2pm; in winter Tu-Sa 10am-2pm and 4-6pm, Su 10am-2pm. €2.40; students, under 18, Sa afternoon, and Su free. Closed for renovations until mid-2008.) On the same street as the Museo El Greco is the **Sinagoga del Tránsito,** one of two remaining synagogues in Toledo's *judería* (Jewish quarter). Inside, the **Museo Sefardí** documents early Jewish history in Spain. Look up at the Hebrew letters carved into the *mudéjar* plasterwork and a stunning *artesonado* (coffered) wood ceiling. (☎711 35 52 30; www.museosefardi.net. Open Mar.-Nov. Tu-Sa 10am-2pm and 4-9pm, Su 10am-2pm; Dec.-Feb. Tu-Sa

10am-2pm and 4-6pm, Su 10am-2pm. €2.40, students, seniors, and under 18 free. Sa after 4pm and Su free.) At the western edge of the city stands the **Monasterio de San Juan de los Reyes,** a Franciscan monastery commissioned by Fernando and Isabel to commemorate their 1476 victory over the Portuguese in the Battle of Toro. (☎22 38 02. Open daily Apr.-Sept. 10am-7pm; Oct.-Mar. 10am-6pm. €1.90.)

For nightlife, head through the arch and to the left from Pl. de Zocodóver to **Calle Santa Fé,** which brims with beer and local youth. **Enebro,** Pl. Santiago de los Caballeros 4, off C. Cervantes, serves free tapas with every drink in the evenings. (Beer €1.50. Open daily 10am-1am.) For upscale bars and clubs, try **Calle de la Sillería** and **Calle los Alfileritos,** west of Pl. de Zocodóver. To escape from the raucous noise, check out the chill **Café Teatro Pícaro,** C. Cadenas 6, where lights bounce off abstract art and it's just as cool to be sipping on a *batido* (milkshake; €3) as a beer. (☎22 13 01; www.picarocafeteatro.com. Beer €1.50-2.50. Mixed drinks €4. Open M-F 4pm-3am, Sa-Su 4pm-5am.)

## CUENCA                                                            ☎969

Cuenca (pop. 50,000) is a quiet hilltop retreat that owes its fame to the geological foundations upon which it stands. The city is flanked by two rivers and the stunning rock formations they have carved. The enchanting **Old Town** includes the famed ▓**casas colgadas** (hanging houses), which sit precariously on cliffs above the Río Huécar. Walk across the San Pablo Bridge at sunrise for a spectacular view of the *casas* and cliffs. The **Museo de Arte Abstracto Español,** in Pl. Ciudad de Ronda, is in the only *casa* open to the public. (☎21 29 83. Open July-Sept. Tu-F 11am-2pm and 5-7pm, Sa 11am-2pm and 4-9pm, Su 11am-2:30pm; Oct.-June Tu-F 11am-2pm and 4-6pm, Sa 11am-2pm and 4-8pm, Su 11am-2:30pm.) The **Catedral de Cuenca** is the centerpiece of the **Plaza Major.** A perfect square, it is the only Anglo-Norman Gothic cathedral in Spain. (Open July-Sept. M-F 10am-2pm and 4-7pm, Sa 10am-7pm, Su 10am-6:30pm; Oct.-Apr. daily 10:30am-1:30pm and 4-6pm; May-June Sa 10:30am-2pm and 4-6pm, Su 10:30am-2pm and 4-6:30pm. €2.80.)

It's worth spending a little extra to stay in the quaint Old Town with its stunning views of the gorge. ▓**Posada de San José ❷,** C. Julián Romero 4, a block from the cathedral, has bright rooms with gorgeous vistas and a **restaurant** on its terrace. (☎21 13 00. Breakfast €8. Entrees €7-11. Restaurant open Tu-Su 8-11am and 6-10:30pm. Singles €25, with bath €50; doubles €38/75; triples with bath €83; quads with bath €128. *Semana Santa* increased prices; Su-Th and low season reduced prices. AmEx/MC/V.) Budget dining spots line **Calle Cervantes** and **Avenida de la República Argentina;** the cafes off **Calle Fray Luis de León** are even cheaper. **Trains** (☎902 24 02 02) run from C. Mariano Catalina 10 to Madrid (2½-3hr., 5-6 per day, €11) and Valencia (3-4hr., 3-4 per day, €12). **Buses** (☎22 70 87) depart from C. Fermín Caballero 20 to Barcelona (9hr., 1 per day, €35), Madrid (2½hr., 8-9 per day, €10-11), and Toledo (2¼hr., 1-2 per day, €11-13). To get to Pl. Mayor from either station, turn left onto C. Fermín Caballero, following it as it becomes C. Cervantes and C. José Cobo, and then bearing left through Pl. Hispanidad as the street becomes C. Carretería. The **tourist office** is at Pl. Mayor 1. (☎24 10 51; www.cuenca.org. Open daily July-Sept. 9am-9pm; Oct.-June M-Sa 9am-2pm and 4-6:30pm, Su 9am-2pm.) **Postal Code:** 16002.

# CASTILLA Y LEÓN

Well before Fernando of Aragón and Isabel of Castilla were joined in world-shaking matrimony, Castilla was the political and military powerhouse of Spain. *Castellano* became the dominant language of the nation in the High Middle Ages. The aqueduct of Segovia, the Gothic cathedrals of León, and the sandstone of Salamanca continue to stand out as national images. Castilla's comrade in arms, León, though chagrined to be lumped with Castilla in a 1970s provincial reorganization, shares many cultural similarities with its co-province.

# SEGOVIA

☎ 921

Legend has it that the devil built Segovia's (pop. 56,000) famed aqueduct in an effort to win the soul of a Segovian water-seller named Juanilla. With or without Lucifer's help, Segovia's attractions draw their share of eager tourists.

**TRANSPORTATION AND PRACTICAL INFORMATION. Trains** (RENFE ☎ 902 24 02 02) run from Po. Obispo Quesada, rather far from town, to Madrid (2hr., 7-9 per day, €5.60). La Sepulvedana **buses** (☎ 42 77 07) run from Estación Municipal de Autobuses, Po. Ezequiel González 12, to Madrid (1½hr., 2 per hr., €6.30) and Salamanca (3hr., 2 per day, €9.30). From the train station, bus #8 stops near the **Plaza Mayor,** the city's historical center and site of the regional **tourist office.** Segovia is impossible to navigate without a map, so pick one up. (☎ 46 03 34. Open July-Sept. 15 Su-Th 9am-8pm, F-Sa 9am-9pm; Sept. 16-June 9am-2pm and 5-8pm.) Access the **Internet** for free at the **public library,** C. Juan Bravo 11. (☎ 46 35 33. Passport required. Limit 30min. Open Sept.-June M-F 9am-9pm, Sa 9am-2pm; July-Aug. M-F 9am-3pm, Sa 9am-2pm.) **Postal Code:** 40001.

**ACCOMMODATIONS AND FOOD.** Reservations are a must for any of Segovia's hotels, especially those near major plazas. Arrive early to ensure space and expect to pay €21 or more for a single. *Pensiones* are significantly cheaper, with basic rooms and shared bathrooms. **Natura La Hosteria ④,** C. Colón 5 and 7, is located just outside the Plaza Mayor with big and beautiful—though pricey—rooms. (☎ 46 67 10; www.naturadesegovia.com. Free Wi-Fi. Prices vary, so call ahead. Generally, singles €35-40; doubles €70-80. MC/V.) **Hospedaje El Gato ②,** Pl. del Salvador 10, offers a bar as well as rooms with A/C, comfortable beds, private baths, and satellite TV. To reach El Gato, follow the aqueduct up the hill, turning left on C. Ochoa Ondategui; it meets San Alfonso Rodríguez, which leads into Pl. del Salvador. (☎ 42 32 44. Singles €23; doubles €38; triples €52. MC/V.) **Camping Acueducto ①,** C. Borbón 49/Highway CN-601, km 112, is 2km toward La Granja. Take the Autobús Urbano #5 (€0.80) from Pl. del Azoguejo to *Nueva Segovia* and cross the highway. (☎ 42 50 00; www.campingacueducto.com. *Semana Santa* and July-Aug. €5 per person, car, or tent site; Apr.-June and Sept. €4.50 each.)

Sample Segovia's famed lamb, *cochinillo asado* (roast suckling pig), or *sopa castellana* (soup with bread, eggs, and garlic), but steer clear of expensive Pl. Mayor and Pl. del Azoguejo. For eclectic and scrumptious dishes (€4-11), try **Restaurante La Almuzara ②,** C. Marqués del Arco 3, past the cathedral. (☎ 46 06 22. Salads €4-11. Soups €6.50-9. Lunch *menú* €10. Open Tu 8-11:30pm, W-Su 12:45-4pm and 8-11:30pm. MC/V.) Follow locals to **Las Tres BBB ①,** Pl. Mayor 13, for cheap seafood. (☎ 46 21 25. *Bocadillos* €2.10-3.20. Entrees €2.40-10. Bar open daily 8am-1:30am. Kitchen open 1-4pm and 8-11pm. MC/V.) At the casual but classy **Bar-Mesón Cueva de San Estéban ③,** C. Vadeláguila 15, off Pl. Esteban and C. Escuderos, the owner knows his wines and the food is excellent. (☎ 46 09 82. Lunch *menú* M-F €9, Sa-Su €10. Entrees €7-18. Open daily 11am-midnight. MC/V.) Buy groceries at **%Día,** C. Gobernador Fernández Jiménez, 3, off Av. de Fernández Ladreda. (Open M-Th 9:30am-2pm and 5:30-8:30pm, F-Sa 9am-9pm.)

**SIGHTS AND ENTERTAINMENT.** The serpentine **Roman aqueduct,** built in 50 BC and spanning 813m, commands the entrance to the Old Town. Some 20,000 blocks of granite were used in the construction—without a drop of mortar. This spectacular feat of engineering, restored by the monarchy in the 15th century, can transport 30L of water per second and was used until the late 1940s. With its spiraling towers and smooth, pointed turrets, Segovia's ▨**Alcázar,** a late-medieval castle and site of Isabel's coronation in 1474, would be at home in a fairy tale—it was reportedly a model for the castle in Disney's *Cinderella*. In the **Sala de Solio** (throne room), an inscription reads: *Tanto monta, monta tanto* ("she mounts, as does he"). Get your mind out of the gutter—it signifies that Fernando and Isabel had equal authority as sovereigns. The **Torre de Juan II** (80m), 140 steps up a nausea-inducing spiral staircase, provides a view of Segovia and the surrounding plains. (Pl. de la Reina Victoria Eugenia. ☎ 46 07 59. *Alcázar* open daily Apr.-Sept. 10am-7pm; Oct.-Mar. 10am-6pm. Tower closed Tu. Palace €4, seniors and students €2.50. Tower €2. English-language audio tour €3.) The 23 chapels of the **cathedral,** towering over Pl. Mayor, earned it the nickname "The Lady of all Cathedrals." The interior may look less impressive than the facade, but its enormity will make you feel truly small. (☎ 46 22 05. Open daily Apr.-Oct. 9am-6:30pm; Nov.-Mar. 9:30am-5:30pm. Mass M-Sa 10am, Su 11am and 12:30pm. €3, under 14 free.)

Though the city isn't particularly known for its sleepless nights, *segovianos* know how to party. Packed with bars and cafes, the **Plaza Mayor** is the center of it all. Head for **Calle Infanta Isabel,** appropriately nicknamed *calle de los bares* (street of the bars). Find drinks and plastic tchotchkes in the fun techno club **Toys,** C. Infanta Isabel 13. (☎ 609 65 41 42. Beer €1. Mixed drinks €4.50-5.50. Open daily 10pm-4am.) An older crowd frequents **Bar Santana,** C. Infanta Isabel 18. (☎ 46 35 64. Beer €1.10. Mixed drinks €4.50. Open daily 10:30pm-3:30am.) From June 23 to 29, Segovia holds a **fiesta** in honor of San Juan and San Pedro, with free open-air concerts on Pl. del Azoguejo and dances and fireworks on June 29.

▨ **DAYTRIP FROM SEGOVIA: LA GRANJA DE SAN ILDEFONSO.** The royal palace of **La Granja,** 9km southeast of Segovia, is the most extravagant of Spain's four royal summer retreats. Nostalgic for Versailles, where he spent his childhood, Felipe V chose the site for its hunting and gardening potential. Crystal chandeliers and a collection of Flemish tapestries fill the palace, while carefully manicured gardens surround it. Don't miss the ▨**Cascadas Nuevas,** a beautiful ensemble of illuminated fountains, pools, and pavilions representing the continents and seasons. Buses run to La Granja from Segovia (20min., 12-14 per day, round-trip €3). From the bus stop, walk uphill through the gates and follow the signs. (☎ 921 47 00 19. *Gardens open daily 10am-9pm. Palace open daily June 17-Aug. 10am-9pm; May-June 16 and Sept. 10am-8pm; Apr. 10am-7pm; Mar. and Oct. 10am-6:30pm; Nov.-Feb. 10am-6pm. €5, with Spanish-language tour €5.50; students and under 16 €3.)*

# SALAMANCA ☎ 923

Salamanca *"la blanca"* (pop. 363,000), city of royals, saints, and scholars, glows with the yellow stones of Spanish Plateresque architecture by day and a vivacious club scene by night. The prestigious Universidad de Salamanca, grouped in medieval times with Bologna, Oxford, and Paris as one of the "four leading lights of the world," continues to add the energy of thousands of students to the city.

▣▨ **TRANSPORTATION AND PRACTICAL INFORMATION. Trains** go from Po. de la Estación (☎ 12 02 02) to Madrid (2½hr., 6-7 per day, €15) and Lisbon, POR (6hr., 1 per day, €47). **Buses** leave from the station (☎ 23 67 17) on Av. Filiberto Villalobos 71-85 for: Barcelona (11hr., 2 per day, €45); León (2½hr., 4-6 per day, €13); Madrid (2½hr., 16 per day, €12-17); Segovia (2¾hr., 2 per day, €10). Majestic **Plaza Mayor** is the center of Salamanca. From the train station, catch bus #1 (€0.80) to Gran Vía and ask to be let off at Pl. San Julián, a block from Pl. Mayor. The **tourist**

**office** is at Pl. Mayor 32. (☎21 83 42. Open June-Sept. M-F 9am-2pm and 4:30-8pm, Sa 10am-8pm, Su 10am-2pm; Oct.-May M-F 9am-2pm and 4:30-6:30pm, Sa 10am–6:30pm, Su 10am-2pm.) *DGratis*, a free weekly newspaper about events in Salamanca, is available from newsstands, tourist offices, and around Pl. Mayor. Free **Internet** is available at the **public library**, C. Compañía 2, in Casa de las Conchas. (☎26 93 17. Limit 30min. Open July to mid-Sept. M-F 9am-3pm, Sa 9am-2pm; mid-Sept. to June M-F 9am-9pm, Sa 9am-2pm.) **Postal Code:** 37080.

**ACCOMMODATIONS AND FOOD.** Reasonably priced *hostales* and *pensiones* cater to the floods of student visitors, especially off Pl. Mayor and C. Meléndez. **Hostal Las Vegas Centro ❷**, C. Meléndez 13, 1st fl., has friendly owners and spotless rooms with terrace and TV. (☎21 87 49; www.lasvegascentro.com. Singles €20, with bath €24; doubles €30/36. MC/V.) At nearby **Pensión Barez ❶**, C. Meléndez 19, 1st fl., clean rooms overlook the street. (☎21 74 95. Rooms €13. Cash only.) **Pensión Los Ángeles ❷**, Pl. Mayor 10, 2nd-3rd fl., has spectacular views, but rooms are not the cleanest. (☎21 81 66; www.pensionlosangeles.com. Breakfast €4. Rooms €22, with bath €25. MC/V.) **Camping Regio ❶**, which offers first-class campsites with hot showers, is 4km toward Madrid on Ctra. Salamanca. (Salamantino buses run from Gran Vía; 2 per hr., €0.80. ☎13 88 88; www.campingregio.com. Laundry €3. €3.20 per person, €2.80 per tent, car, or for electricity. MC/V.)

Many cafes and restaurants are in Pl. Mayor. Pork is the city's speciality, with dishes ranging from *chorizo* (spicy sausage) to *cochinillo* (suckling pig). Funky **Restaurante Delicatessen Café ❷**, C. Meléndez 25, serves a wide variety of *platos combinados* (€9.50-10) and a lunch *menú* (€11) in a colorful solarium. (☎28 03 09. Open daily 1:30-4pm and 9pm-midnight. MC/V.) *Salamantinos* crowd **El Patio Chico ❷**, C. Meléndez 13, but the hefty portions are worth the wait. (☎26 51 03. Entrees €5-10. *Menú* €14. Open daily 1-4pm and 8pm-midnight. MC/V.) At **El Ave Café ❷**, C. Libreros 24, enjoy your lunch (*menú* €11) on the terrace or relax inside among colorful cubist murals. (☎26 45 11. Open daily 8am-midnight. MC/V.) **Champion**, C. Toro 82, is a central supermarket. (☎21 22 08. Open M-Sa 9am-9:30pm.)

**SIGHTS AND NIGHTLIFE.** From Pl. Mayor, follow R. Mayor, veer right onto T. Antigua, and left onto C. Libreros to reach ▨**La Universidad de Salamanca** (est. 1218), the city's focal point. Hidden in the delicate Plateresque filigree of the entryway is a tiny frog perched on a skull. According to legend, those who can spot him without assistance will be blessed with good luck. The old lecture halls inside are open to the public. The 15th-century classroom **Aula Fray Luis de León** has been left in more or less its original state. Located on the second floor atop a Plateresque staircase is the **Biblioteca Antigua,** one of Europe's oldest libraries. The staircase is thought to represent the ascent of the scholar through careless youth, love, and adventure on the perilous path to true knowledge. Don't miss the 800-year-old scrawlings on the walls of the **Capilla del Estudiante.** Across the street and through the hall on the left corner of the patio is the **University Museum.** The reconstructed **Cielo de Salamanca**, the library's famous 15th-century ceiling fresco of the zodiac, is preserved here. (University ☎29 44 00, museum ☎29 12 25. University open M-F 9:30am-1:30pm and 4-7:30pm, Sa 9:30am-1:30pm and 4-7pm, Su 10am-1:30pm. €4, students and seniors €2. Museum open Tu-Sa noon-2pm and 6-9pm, Su 10am-2pm.) It's not surprising it took 220 years to build the stunning **Catedral Nueva,** in Pl. de Anaya. Be sure to climb the tower to get a spectacular ▨**view** from above. The route through the tower connects the old and new cathedrals. Admission includes an exhibit contrasting the architecture of the two structures. Architects of modern renovations have also left their marks; look for an astronaut

S P A I N

and a ◪**dragon** eating an ice cream cone on the left side of the main door. (Open daily Apr.-Sept. 9am-8pm; Oct.-Mar. 9am-1pm and 4-6pm. Tower open daily 10am-8pm, last entry 7:45pm. Cathedral free. Tower €3.) The smaller **Catedral Vieja** was built in the Romanesque style in AD 1140. The **cupola,** assembled from intricately carved miniature pieces, is one of the most detailed in Spain. Students and tourists congregate on the **Patio Chico** for a view of both cathedrals. (Enter through the Catedral Nueva. ☎21 74 76. Open daily Oct.-Mar. 10am-1:30pm and 4-7:30pm; Apr.-Sept. 10am-7:30pm. €4, students €3.25, children €2.50.)

According to *salamantinos,* Salamanca is the best place in Spain to party. It is said that there is one bar for every 100 people living in the city. There are *chupiterías* (shot bars), *bares,* and *discotecas* on nearly every street. Nightlife centers on **Plaza Mayor,** where troubadours serenade women, then spreads out to **Gran Vía, Calle Bordadores,** and side streets. **Calle Prior** and **Rúa Mayor** are also full of bars, while intense partying occurs off **Calle Varillas.** After a few shots (€1-2) at ◪**Bar La Chupitería,** Pl. de Monterrey, wander from club to club on C. Prior and C. Compañía, where tipsy Americans mingle with tireless *salamantinos.* Once you get past the bouncers, **Niebla,** C. Bordadores 14 (☎26 86 04), **Gatsby,** C. Bordadores 16 (☎21 73 62), **Camelot,** C. Bordadores 3 (☎21 21 82), and **Cum Laude,** C. Prior 5-7 (☎26 75 77) all offer a party that doesn't peak until 2:30-3:30am and stays strong for another 2hr. (Dress to impress. All clubs have no cover and are cash only.)

**🔼 DAYTRIP FROM SALAMANCA: ZAMORA.** Located atop a rocky cliff over the Río Duero, Zamora (pop. 70,000) is a mix of modern and medieval where 15th-century palaces harbor Internet cafes. Hooded mannequins guard elaborately sculpted floats used during the *romería* processions of *Semana Santa* (Mar. 16-22, 2008) at the ◪**Museo de Semana Santa,** Pl. Santa María la Nueva 9. The crypt-like setting makes the museum an eerie yet worthwhile stop. *(☎980 53 22 95. Open Tu-Sa 10am-2pm and 5-8pm, Su 10am-2pm. €3, under 12 €1.)* Twelve **Romanesque churches** remain within the walls of the old city. Almost all were built in the 11th and 12th centuries, though their ornate altars were not added until the 15th and 16th centuries. *(All open Mar.-Sept. Tu-Sa 10am-1pm and 5-8pm; Oct.-Jan. 6 10am-2pm and 4:30-6:30pm. Free.)* Zamora's foremost attraction, its Romanesque **cathedral,** features intricately carved choir stalls and a main altar made of marble, gold, and silver. Inside the cloister, the **Museo de la Catedral** features the 15th-century Black Tapestries, which tell the story of Achilles's defeat during the Trojan War. *(☎980 53 06 44. Cathedral and museum open Tu-Su 10am-2pm and 5-8pm. Mass M-F 10am, Sa 10am and 6pm, Su 10am and 1pm. Cathedral free. Museum €3, students €1.50.)* For great views of the surrounding area, walk along the grounds of the **castle,** located behind the cathedral. Alongside Zamora's medieval architecture sits the **Museo Etnográfico** (Ethnographic Museum), C. Sacramento, with a collection of over 1000 works depicting the last several centuries of life in Castilla y León. *(☎980 53 17 08. Open Mar.-Sept. Tu-Su 10am-2pm and 5-8pm; Oct.-Dec. Tu-Sa 10am-2pm and 4:30-6:30pm. €3, students €1.)* The best way to reach Zamora is by bus. **Buses** run from Salamanca to the station on Av. Alfonso Peña. *(☎980 52 12 81. 1hr., 6-15 per day, €4.)* More info can be found at the **tourist office,** Av. Princípe de Asturias 1. *(☎980 53 18 45; www.ayto-zamora.org. Open July to mid-Sept. Su-Th 9am-8pm, F-Sa 9am-9pm; mid-Sept. to June daily 9am-2pm and 5-8pm.)*

# LEÓN ☎987

Formerly the center of Christian Spain, León (pop. 165,000) is best known today for its 13th-century Gothic ◪**cathedral,** in Pl. Regla, arguably the most beautiful in Spain. Its spectacular 1800 meters of stained glass have earned León the nickname "La Ciudad Azul" (The Blue City). The cathedral's **museum** displays gruesome wonders, including a sculpture depicting the skinning of a saint. (☎87 57 70; www.catedraldeleon.org. Cathedral open July-Sept. M-Sa 8:30am-1:30pm and 4-8pm; Oct.-June 8:30am-1:30pm and 4-7pm. Museum open June-Sept. M-F 9:30am-1:30pm and 4-6:30pm, Sa 9:30am-1pm; Oct.-May M-F 9:30am-1pm and 4-6pm. Cathedral free. Museum €4, cloisters €1. Required tour of museum in Spanish.) The **Basílica San Isidoro,** Pl. San Isidoro, houses the remains of royals in the frescoed Panteón Real. From Pl. Santo Domingo, walk up C. Ramón y Cajal; the basilica is up the stairs on the right. (Open July-Aug. M-Sa 9am-8pm, Su 9am-2pm; Sept.-June M-Sa 10am-1:30pm and 4-6:30pm, Su 10am-1:30pm. €3, Th afternoon free.)

Most accommodations are on **Avenida de Roma, Avenida de Ordoño II,** and **Avenida República Argentina,** which lead into the old town from Pl. Glorieta Guzmán el Bueno. **Hostal Bayón ①,** C. Alcázar de Toledo 6, 2nd fl., has peaceful, sun-drenched rooms with hardwood floors. The shared bathrooms are very clean. (☎23 14 46. Singles €15, with shower €25; doubles €28/35. Cash only.) Inexpensive eateries fill the area near the cathedral and the small streets off C. Ancha; also check **Plaza de San Martín,** near Plaza Mayor. The **Eroski Center Supermercado,** Av. de Ordoño II 16, sells groceries. (☎25 60 53. Open daily 9:30am-9:30pm. AmEx/MC/V.) For bars, head to the *barrio húmedo* (drinker's neighborhood) around **Plaza de San Martín** and **Plaza Mayor.** RENFE **trains** (☎902 24 02 02) run from Av. de Astorga 2 to Barcelona (9½hr., 2-3 per day, €44-57), Bilbao (5½hr., 1 per day, €23), and Madrid (4½hr., 7 per day, €21-37). **Buses** (☎21 00 00) leave from Po. del Ingeniero Sáenz de Miera for Madrid (4½hr., 9-13 per day, €20-30) and Salamanca (2½hr., 3-6 per day, €12). The **tourist office** is at Pl. Regla 3. (☎23 70 82; www.turismocastillayleon.com. Open M-F 9am-2pm and 5-7pm, Sa-Su 10am-2pm and 5-8pm. July and Aug. open M-F 9am-7pm and Sa-Su 10am-8pm.) **Postal Code:** 24004.

**⬛ DAYTRIP FROM LEÓN: ASTORGA.** Astorga's fanciful ■**Palacio Episcopal,** designed by Gaudí in the late 19th century, now houses the **Museo de los Caminos.** (☎987 61 88 82. Open July-Sept. Tu-Sa 10am-2pm and 4-8pm, Su 10am-2pm; Oct.-June Tu-Sa 11am-2pm and 4-6pm, Su 11am-2pm. €2.50.) Opposite the palace are Astorga's **cathedral,** built in a mix of Baroque, Gothic, and Neoclassical styles, and its relic-filled museum. (☎987 61 58 20. Cathedral open daily 9am-noon and 5-6:30pm. Museum open daily 10am-2pm and 4-8pm. Cathedral free. Museum €2.50, joint ticket with the Museo de los Caminos €4.) The sweet-toothed should not miss the **Museo de Chocolate,** C. José María Goy 5. From the Palacio Episcopal, walk up C. los Sitios to Pl. Obispo Alcolea and veer right on C. Lorenzo Segura. C. José María Goy is on the right. Visitors receive free samples of locally made chocolate in this delectable museum, which details the history of chocolate production. (☎987 61 62 20. Open Tu-Sa 10:30am-2pm and 4:30-7pm, Su 10:30am-2pm. €2.) Astorga is accessible by **train** from the RENFE station on Av. de Astorga 2, in Leon León (40min., 8 per day 3:02am-11:48pm, €3.05). **Postal Code:** 24700.

# EXTREMADURA

Arid plains bake under the intense summer sun, relieved only by scattered patches of golden sunflowers. This land of harsh beauty and cruel extremes hardened New World conquistadors such as Hernán Cortés and Francisco Pizarro. The region is only now beginning to draw tourists looking for the "classic" Spanish countryside.

## CÁCERES                                                               ☎927

Built between the 14th and 16th centuries by rival noble families in an architectural war for prestige and political control, Cáceres's **ciudad monumental** (Old Town) is comprised of miniature palaces once used to show off each family's power and wealth. From the bus or train station, the best way to get to the center of Cáceres (pop. 90,000) is via bus #1 (€0.75 per ride, 10 rides for €5.50). From the station, walk out the exit opposite the buses, turn left uphill, then turn right at the intersection. The *ciudad monumental* is a melting pot of architectural influences: wealthy Spanish families incorporated Arabic, Gothic, Incan, Renaissance, and Roman influences into their palaces. The main attraction is the neighborhood itself, since most buildings don't let tourists in beyond a peek into the patio from an open door. From the Pl. Mayor, take the stairs from the left of the tourist office to the Arco de la Estrella, the entrance to the walled city. The 16th-century **Casa del Sol** is the most famous of Cáceres's numerous mansions; its crest is the city's emblem. The **Palacio Y Torre de Carvajal,** on the corner of C. Amargura, is one of the few *palacios* in the city open to the public. (Open M-F 8am-8pm, Sa-Su 10am-2pm. Free.) Inside the Casa de los Caballos, the **Museo de Cáceres** is a must-see, housing a tiny but brilliant Who's Who of Spanish art—El Greco, Miró, Picasso, and recent abstractionist stars. The neighboring **Casa de las Veletas** (House of Weathervanes), on Pl. de las Veletas, displays Celtiberian stone animals, Visigothic tombstones, and an astonishing ▓**Muslim cistern.** (☎01 08 77. Open Apr.-Sept. Tu-Sa 9am-2:30pm and 5-8:15pm, Su 10:15am-2:30pm. Oct.-Apr. Tu-Sa 9am-2:30pm and 4-7:15pm, Su 10:15am-2:30pm. €1.20; students, seniors, and EU citizens free.)

Hostels are scattered throughout the new city and line Pl. Mayor in the Old Town. Reserve ahead on summer weekends. **Pensión Carretero ❷,** Pl. Mayor 22, has spacious rooms with painted tile floors. (☎24 74 82; pens_carretero@yahoo.es. June-Aug. singles €25; doubles €30; triples €40; Sept.-May €15/20/35. AmEx/MC/ V.) **Plaza Mayor** overflows with restaurants and cafes serving up *bocadillos*, *raciones*, and *extremeño* specialties. Take in the stork-covered walls of the *ciudad monumental* while the friendly staff of **Cafetería El Pato ❸,** in the Pl. Mayor, dishes out everything from ham and eggs to ewe's milk cheese sandwiches. (☎24 67 36. Entrees €6.60-15. *Menú* €10-13. Open Tu-Sa noon-4pm and 8pm-midnight. AmEx/MC/V.) **Hiper Tambo,** C. Alfonso IX 25, has wine, groceries, and a deli counter (☎21 17 71. Open M-Sa 9:30am-9pm. AmEx/MC/V).

Nightlife centers in Pl. Mayor and along **Calle Pizarro,** which is lined with bars showcasing live music. ▓**La Traviata,** C. Sergio Sánchez, 8, blasts a mix of lounge, pop, and techno, and hosts one-man shows on Thursdays at 10:30pm. (☎21 13 74. Giant espresso €1. Beer €2.50. Mixed drinks €2-4.50. Open Su-Th 4pm-3am, F-Sa 4pm-3:30am. Cash only.) Later, the party migrates to **La Madrila,** an area near Pl. del Albatros in the new city. RENFE **trains** (☎23 37 61), run from on Av. de Alemania, 3km from the Old Town, to Lisbon, POR (6hr., 2 per day, €35), Madrid (4hr., 6 per day, €16-35), and Seville (4hr., 1 per day, €15). **Buses** (☎23 25 50) go from Av. de la Hispanidad to Madrid (4-5hr., 7-9 per day, €19), Salamanca (4hr., 7-28 per day, €13), and Seville (4hr., 8-14 per day, €16). The **tourist office** is on Pl. Mayor 9-10 (☎01 08 34; otcaceres@eco.juntaex.es), in the outer wall of the *ciudad monumental.* (Open July-Sept. M-F 8am-3pm, Sa-Su 10am-2pm; Oct.-June M-F 9am-2pm, Sa-Su 9:45am-2pm.) The **post office** is on Av. Miguel Primo de Rivera. (☎62 66 81. Open M-F 8:30am-8:30pm, Sa 9:30am-2pm.) **Postal Code:** 10071.

▶ **DAYTRIP FROM CÁCERES: TRUJILLO.** Scattered with medieval palaces, Roman ruins, Arabic fortresses, and churches of all eras, hilltop Trujillo (pop. 9200) is often called the "Cradle of Conquistadors" because the city produced over 600 explorers of the New World. Crowning the hill are the ruins of a 10th-century **Moorish castle.** *(Open daily June-Sept. 10am-2pm and 5-8:30pm; Oct.-May 9:30am-2pm and 4:30-8:30pm. €1.40.)* Trujillo's **Plaza Mayor** was the inspiration for the Plaza de Armas in Cuzco, Perú. To reach the Gothic **Iglesia de Santa María la Mayor,** take C. de las Cambroneras from the plaza in front of the Iglesia de San Martín and turn right on C. de Sta. María. The steps leading to the top of the Romanesque church tower are exhausting, but the ▓**360° view** is worth the effort. *(Open daily May-Oct.*

*10am-2pm and 4:30-8:30pm; Nov.-Apr. 10am-2pm and 4-6:30pm. €1.25. Su mass 11am.)* At the bottom of the hill lies the **Museo del Queso y el Vino,** which offers advice on how to enjoy wine and cheese. *(☎32 30 31. Open daily May-Sept. 11am-3pm and 6-8pm; Oct.-Apr. 11am-3pm and 5:30-7:30pm. Tickets €1.30, with tasting €2.40.)* Don't be deceived by the looks of the little metal shack at the bottom of the hill leading to Pl. Mayor. It happens to be **Churrería El Paseo ❶,** purveyor of the best *churros* in Extremadura. *(☎32 21 67. Open daily 8am-noon. Cash only.)* **Buses** *(☎927 32 12 02)* run from the corner of C. de las Cruces and C. del M. de Albayada to Cáceres (45min., 1-4 per day, €3). The **tourist office** is in Pl. Mayor, on the left when facing Pizarro's statue. Tours (€6.75) leave from the front of the office at 11am and 5pm. *(☎32 26 77. Open daily June-Sept. 10am-2pm and 4:30-7:30pm; Oct.-May 9:30am-2pm and 4-7pm.)*

# SOUTHERN SPAIN

Southern Spain (Andalucía) is all that you expect of Spanish culture—flamenco, bullfighting, tall pitchers of sangria, and streets lined with orange trees. The Moors arrived in AD 711 and bequeathed to the region far more than flamenco music and gypsy ballads—they sparked the European Renaissance by reintroducing the wisdom of Classical Greece and the Near East. The cities of Seville and Granada reached the pinnacle of Islamic arts, while Córdoba matured into the most culturally influential city in medieval Islam. Despite (or perhaps because of) modern-day poverty and high unemployment, Andalusians maintain a passionate, unshakable dedication to living the good life. Their never-ending *festivales, ferias,* and *carnavales* are world-famous for their extravagance.

## CÓRDOBA ☎957

Captivating Córdoba (pop. 310,000), located on the south bank of the Río Guadalquivir, was Western Europe's largest city in the 10th century. Remnants of the city's heyday survive in its well-preserved Roman, Jewish, Islamic, and Catholic monuments. Today, lively festivals and nonstop nightlife make Córdoba one of Spain's most beloved cities.

**▐ TRANSPORTATION.** RENFE **trains** (☎40 02 02; www.renfe.es) run from Pl. de las Tres Culturas, off Av. de América, to: Barcelona (10-11hr., 4 per day, €50-76); Cádiz (2½hr., 5 per day, €24); Madrid (2-4hr., 21-33 per day, €47); Málaga (2-3hr., 5 per day, €12-22); Seville (45min., 4-8 per day, €8-15). **Buses** (☎40 40 40) leave from Estación de Autobuses, on Glorieta de las Tres Culturas across from the train station. Alsina Graells Sur (☎27 81 00) sends buses to Cádiz (4-5hr., 1-2 per day, €20), Granada (3-4hr., 9-11 per day, €12), and Málaga (3-3½hr., 5 per day, €12). Bacoma (☎902 42 22 42) runs to Barcelona (10hr., 3 per day, €63). Secorbus (☎902 22 92 92) has cheap buses to Madrid (4½hr., 3-6 per day, €14).

**▟▐ ORIENTATION AND PRACTICAL INFORMATION.** Córdoba is split into two parts: the old city and the new city. The modern and commercial northern half extends from the train station on Av. de América down to **Plaza de las Tendillas,** the city center. The old section in the south includes a medieval maze known as the **Judería** (Jewish quarter). The easiest way to reach the old city from the train station is to walk (20min.). Exit left from the station, cross the parking plaza and take a right onto Av. de los Mozárabes. Walk through the **Jardines de la Victoria** in the middle of the boulevard. When the gardens end and the boulevard turns back into one avenue, **Puerta Almodóvar,** an entrance to la Judería, will be on your left.

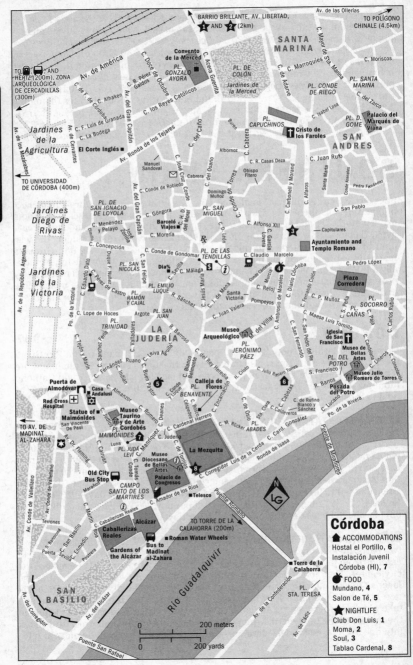

**Córdoba**

🏠 ACCOMMODATIONS
Hostal el Portillo, 6
Instalación Juvenil
Córdoba (HI), 7

🍴 FOOD
Mundano, 4
Salon de Té, 5

⭐ NIGHTLIFE
Club Don Luis, 1
Moma, 2
Soul, 3
Tablao Cardenal, 8

To get to the **tourist office**, C. Torrijos 10, from the train station, take bus #3 along the river to the Puente Romano. Walk under the stone arch and the office will be on your left. (☎35 51 79. Open July-Aug. M-F 9:30am-7:30pm, Sa 10am-7:30pm, Su 10am-2pm; Sept.-June M-Sa 9am-7:30pm, Su 10am-2pm.) **Banks** and **ATMs** can be found on the streets around the Mezquita and Pl. de las Tendillas. **Tele-Click**, C. Eduardo Dato 9, has **Internet**. (☎94 06 15. €1.80 per hr. Open M-F 10am-3pm and 5:30-10:30pm, Sa-Su noon-11pm.) The **post office** is at C. José Cruz Conde 15. (☎47 97 96. Open M-F 8:30am-8:30pm, Sa-Su 9:30am-2pm.) **Postal Code:** 14070.

**⌂⌂ ACCOMMODATIONS AND FOOD.** Most accommodations can be found around the whitewashed walls of the Judería and in Old Córdoba, a more residential area between the Mezquita and C. de San Fernando. Reserve ahead during *Semana Santa* and May through June. Popular ⬛**Instalación Juvenil Córdoba (HI) ❷**, Pl. Judá Leví, is a former mental asylum converted into a backpacker's paradise. The large rooms all have A/C and bath. (☎29 01 66. Wheelchair-accessible. Breakfast included; dinner €5.50. Linens €1.20. Laundry €4. Reception 24hr. Private rooms available. Mar.-Oct. dorms €20, under 26 €19; Nov.-Feb. €18/17. €3.50 HI discount. MC/V.) **Hostal el Portillo ❷**, C. Cabezas 2, is a traditional yet unexpectedly decorated Andalusian house in the quiet area. Rooms are spacious and equipped with bath and A/C. (☎47 20 91. Singles €18-20; doubles €30-35. MC/V.) **Hostal-Residencia Séneca ❷**, C. Conde y Luque 7, has a beautiful patio and large rooms with fans or A/C. (☎/fax 47 32 34. Breakfast included. Singles €19-25, with bath €32-37; doubles €35-43/42-50; triples and 1 quad €89. MC/V.)

*Córdobeses* converge on the outdoor *terrazas* between **Calle Doctor Severo Ochoa** and **Calle Doctor Jiménez Díaz** for drinks and tapas before dinner. Cheap restaurants are farther away from the Judería in **Barrio Cruz Conde** and around **Avenida Menéndez Pidal** and **Plaza de las Tendillas**. Regional specialties include *salmorejo* (cream soup) and *rabo de toro* (bull's tail simmered in tomato sauce). ⬛**Mundano ❶**, C. Conde de Cárdenas 3, combines delicious home-style food—including many vegetarian options—with a funky style and art shows. (☎47 37 85. Entrees €3-5. Tapas €1-3. Open M-F 10am-5pm and 10pm-2am, Sa noon-6pm and 10pm-2am. Cash only.) For a taste of the old Moorish Córdoba, head to **Salon de Té ❶**, C. Buen Pastor 13, a recreated 12th-century teahouse with a huge variety of Arab pastries, juices, and teas. (☎48 79 84. Beverages €2-4. Pastries €1.50-3. Open daily 11am-10:30pm. Cash only.) A mainstay since 1872, **Taberna Sociedad de Plateros ❶**, C. San Francisco 6, is known for its generous portions of tapas. (☎47 00 42. Tapas €1-3. *Raciones* €5-15. Open M-F 8am-4pm and 8pm-midnight, Sa 8am-4pm and 7:30pm-midnight. AmEx/MC/V.) Find groceries at **El Corte Inglés**, Av. Ronda de los Tejares 30. (Open M-Sa 10am-10pm. AmEx/MC/V.)

**◙ SIGHTS.** Built in AD 784, Córdoba's ⬛**La Mezquita** mosque is considered the most important Islamic monument in the Western world. Visitors enter through the **Patio de los Naranjos**, a courtyard featuring carefully spaced orange trees and fountains. Inside, 850 granite and marble columns support hundreds of striped arches. At the far end of the Mezquita lies the **Capilla Villaviciosa**, the first Christian chapel to be built in the mosque. In the center, pink-and-blue marble Byzantine mosaics shimmer across the arches of the **Mihrab** (prayer niche), which is covered in Kufic inscriptions of the 99 names of Allah. Although the town rallied violently against the proposed construction of a **cathedral** in the center of the mosque, the towering *crucero* (transept) and *coro* (choir dome) were built after the Crusaders conquered Córdoba in 1236. (☎47 91 70. Strict silence enforced. Wheelchair-accessible. Open Mar.-Oct. M-Sa 8:30am-7pm, Su 8:30-10:30am and 2-7pm. €8, 10-14 €4, under 10 free. Admission free during mass M-Sa 8:30-10am, Su 11am and 1pm.)

Along the river on the left of the Mezquita is the ⬛**Alcázar,** built for Catholic monarchs in 1328 during the *Reconquista*. Fernando and Isabel bade Columbus *adiós* here; the building later served as Inquisition headquarters. The gardens have ponds and beautiful greenery. (☎42 01 51. Open Tu-Sa 8:30am-2:30pm and 4:30-6:30pm, Su and holidays 9:30am-2:30pm. Gardens open summer 8pm-midnight. Alcázar €4, gardens €2; F free.) The **Judería** is the historic area northwest of the Mezquita. Just past the statue of Maimonides, the small **Sinagoga,** C. Judíos 20, is one of few Spanish synagogues to survive the Inquisition; it is a solemn reminder of the 1492 expulsion of the Jews. (☎20 29 28. Open Tu-Sa 9:30am-2pm and 3:30-5:30pm, Su 9:30am-1:30pm. €0.30, EU citizens free.) The **Museo Taurino y de Arte Cordobés,** on Pl. Maimónides, highlights the history of bullfighting. The museum is currently undergoing renovation but is slated to reopen in 2008. (☎20 10 56. Open Tu-Sa 10:30am-2pm and 5:30-7:30pm, Su 9:30am-2pm. €3, students €1.50, F free.) The **Museo Julio Romero** displays Romero's sensual portraits of Cordoban women. (☎49 19 09. Open Tu-Sa 8:30am-2:30pm, Su and holidays 9:30am-2:30pm. €4.)

🔲🔲 **ENTERTAINMENT AND NIGHTLIFE.** For the latest cultural events, pick up a free copy of the *Guía del Ocio* at the tourist office. Flamenco is not cheap in Córdoba, but the shows are high quality and a bargain compared to similar shows in Seville and Madrid. Hordes of tourists flock to see the prize-winning dancers at the **Tablao Cardenal,** C. Torrijos 10. (☎48 33 20. €18, includes 1 drink. Shows M-Sa 10:30pm.) **Soul,** C. Alfonso XIII 3, is a hip bar with an older crowd and deafening bass. (☎49 15 80; www.bar-soul.com. Beer €2.10. Mixed drinks €4.50. Open Sept.-June daily 9am-4am.) Starting in June, the **Barrio Brillante,** uphill from Av. de América, is packed with young, well-dressed *córdobeses* hopping between dance clubs and outdoor bars. Bus #10 goes to Brillante from the train station until about 11pm, but the bars don't pick up until around 1am (most are open until 4am); a lift from **Radio Taxi** (☎76 44 44) costs €4-6. To walk, head up Av. Brillante; it is a 45min. uphill hike from the Judería. A string of popular nightclubs runs along **Avenida Brillante,** such as **Club Don Luis** (open Th-Sa midnight-4:30am; cash only). Pubs with crowded *terrazas* line ⬛**Avenida Libertad,** including chic, African-influenced **Moma.** (☎76 84 77. Beer €2-2.50. Mixed drinks from €5. Open Su-W 9am-3am, Th-Sa 9am-5am; AmEx/MC/V) An alternative to partying is a nighttime stroll along the ⬛**walk-through fountains** and falling sheets of water that line Av. de América directly between Pl. de Colón and the train station.

Of Córdoba's festivals, floats, and parades, **Semana Santa** (Holy Week; Mar. 16-22, 2008) is the most extravagant. The first few days of May are dedicated to the **Festival de las Cruces,** during which residents make crosses decorated with flowers. In the first two weeks of May during the **Festival de los Patios,** the city erupts with classical music concerts, flamenco, and a city-wide patio-decorating contest. Late May brings the **Feria de Nuestra Señora de Salud** (*La Feria de Córdoba*), a week of colorful garb, dancing, music, and wine-drinking. Every July, Córdoba hosts a **guitar festival,** attracting talented strummers from all over the world.

# SEVILLE (SEVILLA) ☎954

Site of a Roman acropolis, capital of the Moorish empire, focal point of the Spanish Renaissance, and guardian of traditional Andalusian culture, romantic Seville (pop. 700,000) is a conglomeration of cultures. Bullfighting, flamenco, and tapas are at their best here, and Seville's cathedral is among the most impressive in Spain. The city offers more than historical sights: its *Semana Santa* and *Feria de Abril* celebrations are among the most elaborate in Europe.

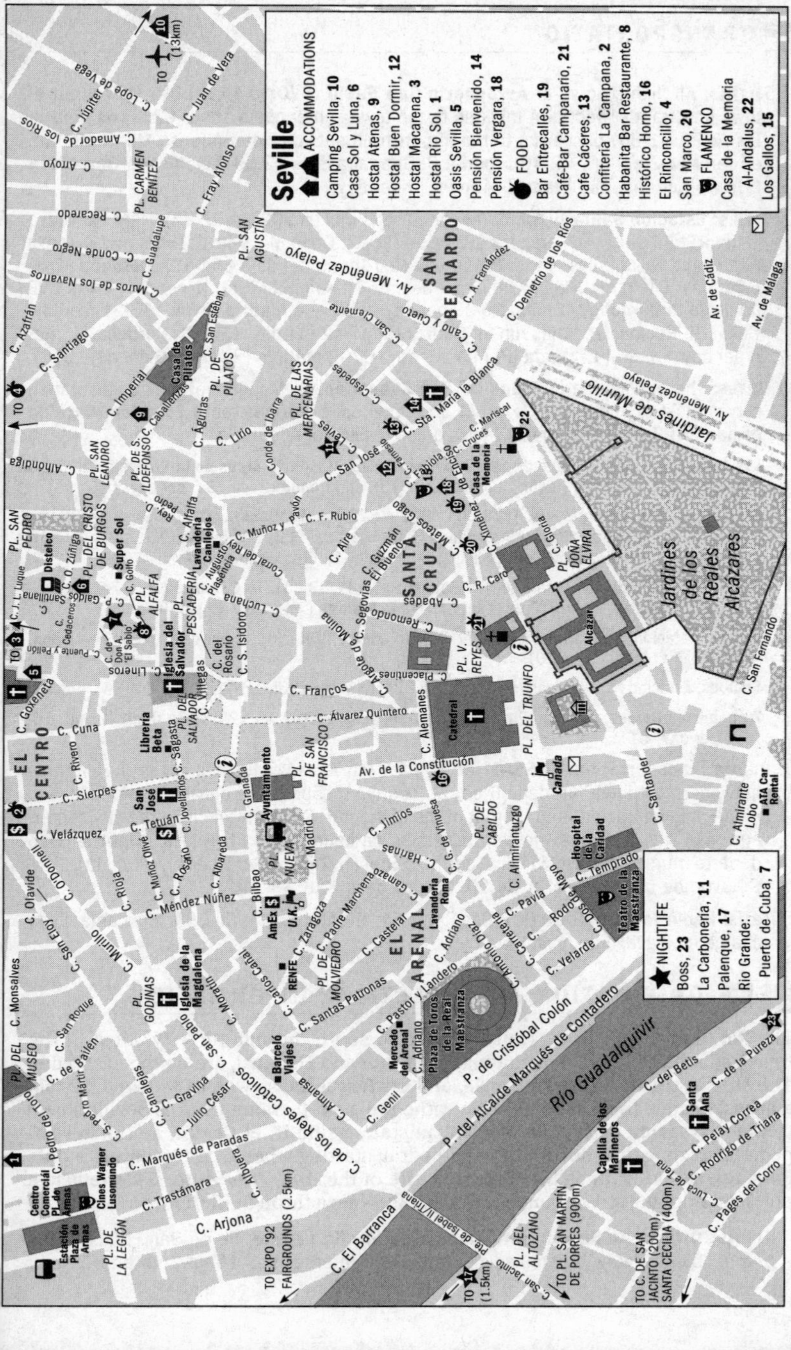
Seville
ACCOMMODATIONS
Camping Sevilla, 10
Casa Sol y Luna, 6
Hostal Atenas, 9
Hostal Buen Dormir, 12
Hostal Macarena, 3
Hostal Río Sol, 1
Oasis Sevilla, 5
Pensión Bienvenido, 14
Pensión Vergara, 18
FOOD
Bar Entrecalles, 19
Café-Bar Campanario, 21
Cafe Cáceres, 13
Confitería La Campana, 2
Habanita Bar Restaurante, 8
Histórico Horno, 16
El Rinconcillo, 4
San Marco, 20
FLAMENCO
Casa de la Memoria
Al-Andalus, 22
Los Gallos, 15
NIGHTLIFE
Boss, 23
La Carbonería, 11
Palenque, 17
Río Grande:
Puerto de Cuba, 7
EL CENTRO
SANTA CRUZ
SAN BERNARDO
EL ARENAL
Río Guadalquivir
Jardines de los Reales Alcázares
Jardines de Murillo
Alcázar
Catedral
Ayuntamiento
Casa de Pilatos
Plaza de Toros de la Real Maestranza
Hospital de la Caridad
Teatro de la Maestranza
Iglesia del Salvador
Iglesia de la Magdalena
Capilla de los Marineros
Santa Ana
San José
Estación Plaza de Armas
Centro Comercial Pl. de Armas
Cines Warner Lusomundo
Mercado del Arenal
Barceló Viajes
Librería Beta
Lavandería Canllejos
Lavandería Roma
Super Sol
Distelco
AmEx
U.K.
RENFE
Canada
ATA Car Rental
Av. de la Constitución
Av. Menéndez Pelayo
P. de Cristóbal Colón
P. del Alcalde Marqués de Contadero
C. de los Reyes Católicos
C. Sierpes
C. Tetuán
C. Velázquez
C. San Fernando
Av. de Cádiz
Av. de Málaga
C. Arjona
C. El Barranca
Pte. de Isabel II/Triana
TO EXPO '92 FAIRGROUNDS (2.5km)
TO (13km)
TO PL. SAN MARTÍN DE PORRES (900m)
TO C. DE SAN JACINTO (200m), SANTA CECILIA (400m)

SPAIN

# TRANSPORTATION

**Flights:** All flights arrive at **Aeropuerto San Pablo (SVQ; ☎**44 90 00), 12km out of town on Ctra. de Madrid. A taxi ride to the town center costs about €25. **Los Amarillos** (☎98 91 84) buses run to the airport from outside Hotel Alfonso XIII at the Pta. de Jerez (1-2 per hr., €2.40). **Iberia,** C. Guadaira 8 (☎22 89 01), flies to **Barcelona** (1hr., 6 per day) and **Madrid** (45min., 6 per day).

**Trains: Estación Santa Justa,** on Av. de Kansas City (☎902 24 02 02). Near Pl. Nueva is the **RENFE** office, C. Zaragoza 29. (☎54 02 02. Open M-F 9am-1:15pm and 4-7pm.) Altaria and Talgo trains run to: **Barcelona** (9-13hr., 3 per day, €54-88); **Córdoba** (1hr., 6 per day, €13); **Madrid** (3½hr., 2 per day, €53); **Valencia** (9hr., 1 per day, €44). AVE trains go to **Córdoba** (45min., 15-20 per day, €22) and **Madrid** (2½hr., 15-21 per day, €64-70). *Regionales* trains run to: **Cádiz** (2hr., 7-12 per day, €9.10); **Córdoba** (1½hr., 6 per day, €7.60); **Granada** (3hr., 4 per day, €20); **Málaga** (2½hr., 5-6 per day, €16).

**Buses:** The bus station at **Prado de San Sebastián,** C. Manuel Vázquez Sagastizabal, serves most of Andalucía. (☎41 71 11. Open daily 5:30am-1am.) **Estación Plaza de Armas** (☎90 80 40) primarily serves areas outside of Andalucía.

**Los Amarillos,** Estación Prado de San Sebastián (☎98 91 84). To **Arcos de la Frontera** (2hr., 2-3 per day, €7), **Marbella** (3½hr., 2-3 per day, €15), and **Ronda** (2½hr., 3-5 per day, €10).

**Alsa,** Estación Pl. de Armas (☎90 78 00 or 902 42 22 42). To: **Cáceres** (4¼hr., 9 per day, €15); **León** (11hr., 3 per day, €38); **Salamanca** (8hr., 5 per day, €27); **Valencia** (9-11hr., 4 per day, €44-51). Under 26 and seniors 10% discount, under 12 50% discount. MC/V.

**Alsina Graells,** Estación Prado de San Sebastián (☎41 88 11). To **Córdoba** (2hr., 7-9 per day, €9.50), **Granada** (3½hr., 10 per day, €18), and **Málaga** (2½hr., 10-12 per day, €14).

**Damas,** Estación Pl. de Armas (☎90 77 37). To **Lagos, POR** (7hr., 4 per day, €18) and **Lisbon, POR** (6¼hr., 3 per day, €29).

**Socibus,** Estación Pl. de Armas (☎902 22 92 92). To **Madrid** (6hr., 14 per day, €19). V.

**Transportes Comes,** Estación Prado de San Sebastián (☎902 19 92 08). To **Cádiz** (1½hr., 10-12 per day, €11).

**Public Transportation: TUSSAM** (☎900 71 01 71; www.tussam.es) is the city bus network. Most lines run daily 6 per hr. (6am-11:15pm) and converge on Pl. Nueva, Pl. de la Encarnación, and in front of the cathedral. C-3 and C-4 circle the city center, and #34 hits the youth hostel, university, cathedral, and Pl. Nueva. **Night service** departs from Pl. Nueva (Su-Th 1 per hr. midnight-2am, F-Sa 1 per hr. all night). Fare €1, 10-ride *bonobús* ticket €4.50, 30-day pass €26.

**Taxis: Radio Taxi** (☎58 00 00). Base rate €1, €0.40 per km, Su 25% surcharge. Extra charge for luggage and night taxis.

# ORIENTATION AND PRACTICAL INFORMATION

The **Río Guadalquivir** flows roughly north to south through the city. Most of the touristed areas of Seville, including **Santa Cruz** and **El Arenal,** are on the east bank. The *barrios* of **Triana, Santa Cecilia,** and **Los Remedios,** as well as the **Expo '92 fairgrounds,** occupy the west bank. The cathedral, next to Santa Cruz, is Seville's centerpiece. **Avenida de la Constitución** runs alongside it. **El Centro,** a commercial pedestrian zone, lies north of the cathedral, starting where Av. Constitución hits **Plaza Nueva** and **Plaza de San Francisco,** site of the *Ayuntamiento.* **Calle Tetuán,** a popular shopping street, runs north from Pl. Nueva through El Centro.

**Tourist Offices: Centro de Información de Sevilla Laredo,** Pl. de San Francisco 19 (☎59 52 88; www.turismo.sevilla.org). Free Internet M-F 10am-2pm and 5-8pm;

max. 1hr. Open M-F 8am-3pm. **Turismo Andaluz,** Av. de la Constitución 21B (☎22 14 04; fax 22 97 53). Info on all of Andalucía. English spoken. Open M-F 9am-7pm, Sa 10am-2pm and 3-7pm, Su 10am-2pm.

**Luggage Storage:** Estación Prado de San Sebastián (€1 per bag per day; open 6:30am-10pm), Estación Plaza de Armas (€3 per day), and the train station (€3 per day).

**Laundromat: Lavandería y Tintorería Roma,** C. Castelar 2C (☎21 05 35). Wash, dry, and fold €6 per load. Open M-F 9:30am-2pm and 5:30-8:30pm, Sa 9am-2pm.

**24hr. Pharmacy:** Check list posted at any pharmacy for those open 24hr.

**Medical Services:** Red Cross (☎913 35 45 45). **Ambulatorio Esperanza Macarena** (☎42 01 05). **Hospital Virgen Macarena,** Av. Dr. Fedriani 56 (☎955 00 80 00).

**Internet Access: Post Office,** Av. de la Constitución 32. €1.50 per hr. Open M-F 8:30am-10pm, Sa 9:30am-10pm, Su noon-10pm. **Distelco,** C. Ortiz Zuñiga 3 (☎22 99 66). €2 per hr. Open M-F 10:30am-11pm, Sa-Su 6-11pm.

**Post Office:** Av. de la Constitución 32 (☎21 64 76), opposite the cathedral. **Lista de Correos** and fax. Open M-F 8:30am-8:30pm, Sa 9:30am-2pm. **Postal Code:** 41080.

## ■▀ ▀ ACCOMMODATIONS AND CAMPING

Rooms vanish and prices soar during *Semana Santa* and the *Feria de Abril;* reserve several months ahead. In Santa Cruz, the streets around **Calle Santa María la Blanca** are full of cheap, centrally located hostels. Hostels by the **Plaza de Armas** bus station are convenient for visits to **El Centro** and **Calle del Betis** across the river.

▨ **Hostal Atenas,** C. Caballerizas 1 (☎21 80 47), near Pl. Pilatos. Slightly pricier than other options but with good reason—everything about this hostel is appealing, from ivy arches leading to an old-fashioned indoor patio to cheerful rooms. All rooms with A/C and bath. Singles €35; doubles €58; triples €70. MC/V. ❸

▨ **Casa Sol y Luna,** C. Pérez Galdós 1A (☎21 06 82). Beautiful hostel with marble staircase, antique mirrors, and themed rooms. Laundry €10. Min. 2-night stay. Singles €22; doubles €38, with bath €45; triples €60; quads €80. Cash only. ❷

**Oasis Sevilla,** reception at Pl. Encarnación, 29 1/2, rooms above reception and at C. Alonso el Sabio 1A (☎429 3777; www.hostelsoasis.com). The place to be for travelers looking for hotel amenities such as a pool. Dorms on Pl. Encarnación are crowded but centrally located; doubles and 4-bed dorms on C. Alonso are more quieter. Breakfast included. Free Internet. Reserve ahead. Dorms €18; doubles €40. MC/V. ❷

**Pensión Vergara,** C. Ximénez de Enciso 11, 2nd fl. (☎21 56 68), above the souvenir shop at C. Mesón del Moro. Quirky, antique decor and perfect location. Most rooms have fans and a few have A/C. Towels provided upon request. Singles €20; doubles €40; triples €60; quads €80. Cash only. ❷

**Pensión Bienvenido,** C. Archeros 14 (☎41 36 55). 5 simple but comfortable (and cheap) rooftop rooms surround a social patio in the heart of Santa Cruz; downstairs rooms overlook an inner atrium. All have A/C. Singles €20; doubles €38, with bath €50; triples and quads €60-64. MC/V. ❷

**Hostal Buen Dormir,** C. Farnesio 8 (☎21 74 92). A central location on a tiny pedestrian street makes "Good Sleep" one of the best deals in town. Rooftop terrace. Singles have fans; doubles and triples have A/C. Singles €20; doubles €30, with shower €35, with bath €40; triples with shower €50, with bath €55. Cash only. ❷

**Hostal Macarena,** C. San Luis 91 (☎37 01 41). Soft citrus-colored rooms in a quiet neighborhood make for a relaxing stay. All rooms with A/C. Singles €20; doubles €30, with bath €40; triples €45/50. MC/V. ❷

**Hostal Rio Sol,** C. Marqués de Paradas 25 (☎22 90 38). Across the street from the bus station, this hostel is perfect for those exhausted upon arrival. Rooms vary in size, but with tiled walls and private baths, all are a good value. Singles €20; doubles €45; triples €55. AmEx/MC/V. ❷

**Camping Sevilla,** Ctra. Madrid-Cádiz km 534 (☎51 43 79), near the airport. From Pr. San Sebastián, take bus #70 (stops 800m away at Parque Alcosa). Hot showers, supermarket, and pool. €3.80 per tent, €3.30 per car. MC/V. ❶

## 🍴 FOOD

Seville, which claims to be the birthplace of tapas, keeps its cuisine light. Tapas bars cluster around **Plaza San Martín** and along **Calle San Jacinto.** Popular venues for *el tapeo* (tapas barhopping) include **Barrio de Santa Cruz** and **El Arenal.** Find produce at **Mercado de la Encarnación,** near the bullring in Pl. de la Encarnación. (Open M-Sa 9am-2pm.) There is a supermarket in the basement of **El Corte Inglés,** in Pl. del Duque de la Victoria. (☎27 93 97. Open M-Sa 9am-10pm. AmEx/MC/V.)

🏛 **Habanita Bar Restaurant,** C. Golfo 3 (☎606 71 64 56; www.andalunet.com/habanita), on a tiny street off C. Pérez Galdós, next to Pl. Alfalfa. Exquisite Cuban fare, including *yucca* (yam) and *ropa vieja* ("old clothes"; shredded beef and rice). Entrees €7-15. Open M-Sa 12:30-4:30pm and 8pm-12:30am, Su 12:30-4:30pm. MC/V. ❷

**Bar Entrecalles,** C. Ximenez de Enciso 14 (☎617 86 77 52). Situated at the center of the tourist buzz, but retains a local following. Tapas €2. Generous portions of delicious gazpacho (€2). Open daily 1pm-2am. Cash only. ❶

**San Marco,** C. Mesón del Moro 6 (☎56 43 90), in Santa Cruz's *casco antiguo*. Pizza, pasta, and dessert in an 18th-century house with 17th-century Arab baths. Other San Marco locations around town are in equally impressive settings. Entrees €5-10; salads €4-9. Open daily 1:15-4:30pm and 8:15pm-12:30am. AmEx/MC/V. ❷

**El Rinconcillo,** C. Gerona 40 (☎22 31 83). This hangout teems with gray-haired men deep in conversation and locals coming in for a quick glass of wine. Tapas €1.70-2.50. *Raciones* (small dishes) €5-14.50. Open daily 1:30pm-1:30pm. AmEx/MC/V. ❷

**Café Cáceres,** C. San José 24 (☎21 54 26). Choose from a huge spread of cheeses, cereals, jams, yogurts, fresh orange juice, and omelettes. *Desayuno de la casa* (€6) includes coffee, ham, eggs, and toast. Open in summer M-F 7:30am-5pm, Sa 8am-2pm; in winter Sa-Su 7:30am-7:30pm. MC/V. ❶

**Histórico Horno, SA,** Av. de la Constitución 16 (☎22 18 19). Renowned for its delicious desserts as well as its gourmet *jamón* (ham). Enjoy your delicacy inside or have it *para llevar* (to go). Open M-Sa 8am-11pm, Su 9am-11pm. AmEx/D/MC/V. ❷

**Café-Bar Campanario,** C. Mateos Gago 8 (☎56 41 89). This clean-cut, modern cafe-bar is more vegetarian-friendly than most tapas bars. Gaze at the cathedral as you sip some of the strongest sangria in town (0.5L €12, 1L €15). Tapas €2.20-3.10. *Raciones* €8.80-13. Open daily 11am-midnight. AmEx/MC/V. ❷

**Confitería La Campana,** C. Sierpes 1 and 3. Seville's most famous cafe and dessert stop, founded in 1885, serves *granizadas de limón*, ice cream, and homemade pastries (€1.40-2.50). Sit outside and watch shoppers pass by or choose a few desserts to go. Open daily 8am-11pm. AmEx/MC/V. ❶

## 👁 SIGHTS

🏛 **CATEDRAL.** Legend has it that 15th-century *reconquistadores* wished to demonstrate their religious fervor by constructing a church so great that "those who come after us will take us for madmen." With 44 chapels, the cathedral of Seville is the third largest in the world (after St. Peter's Basilica in Rome and St. Paul's Cathedral in London) and the biggest Gothic edifice ever constructed. The cathedral took more than a century to complete. In the center, the **Capilla Real** stands opposite **choir stalls** made of mahogany recycled from a 19th-century Austrian railway. The **retablo mayor,** one of the largest in the world, is a golden wall of intricately wrought saints and disciples. Nearby is the **Sepulcro de Cristóbal Colón** (Columbus's tomb), which supposedly holds the explorer's remains, brought back from Havana after Cuba's independence in 1902. The black-and-gold pallbearers represent the monarchs of Castilla, León, Aragón, and Navarra. Farther on stands the **Sacristía Mayor** (treasury), which holds Juan de Arefe's gilded panels of Alfonso X el Sabio, works by Ribera and Murillo, and a glittering Corpus Christi icon, **La Custodia Processional.** In 1401, a 12th-century Almohad mosque was destroyed to clear space for the massive cathedral. All that remains of it is the **Patio de Los Naranjos,** where the faithful would wash before prayer, the **Puerta del Perdón** entryway on C. Alemanes, and **La Giralda,** a minaret with 35 ramps leading to the top. A small, disembodied head of John the Baptist eyes visitors as they enter the gift shop. (☎ 21 49 71. *Entrance by the Pl. de la Virgen de los Reyes. Open M-Sa 9:30am-4pm, Su 2:30-6pm. €7.50, seniors and students €2, under 16 free. Audio tour €3. Mass in the Capilla Real M-Sa 8:30, 10am, noon, 5pm; Su 8:30, 10, 11am, noon, 1, 5, 6pm.*)

**◼ ALCÁZAR.** The oldest European palace still used as a private residence for royals, Seville's Alcázar epitomizes extravagance. Though the Alhambra in Granada gets more press, the Alcázar features equally impressive architecture. Built by the Moors in the 7th century, the palace was embellished greatly during the 17th century. It now displays an interesting mix of Moorish, Gothic, Renaissance, and Baroque architecture, most prominently on display in the *mudéjar* style of many of the arches, tiles, and ceilings. Catholic monarchs Fernando and Isabel are the palace's most well-known former residents; their grandson Carlos V also lived here and married his cousin, Isabel of Portugal, in the **Salón Carlos V.** Visitors enter through the **Patio de la Montería,** across from the Almohad facade of the Moorish palace. Through the archway lie the Arabic residences, including the **Patio del Yeso** (Patio of Mortar) and the **Patio de las Muñecas** (Patio of the Dolls), so named because of the miniature faces carved into the bottom of one of the room's pillars. Of the Christian additions, the most notable is the **Patio de las Doncellas** (Patio of the Maids). Court life in the Alcázar revolved around this columned quadrangle. The golden-domed **Salón de los Embajadores** (Ambassadors' Room) is allegedly the site where Fernando and Isabel welcomed Columbus back from the New World.

**LOCAL LEGEND**

### SEVILLE'S TRAGIC TALE

Among its many legacies, the *Judería* left Seville one of its most tragic legends: that of Susona, La Hermosa Hembra (vulgar for "beautiful woman"). During the 15th century, even as relations between Seville's Christian and Jewish populations were increasingly tense, Susona, the daughter of a Jewish merchant, fell in love with a Christian knight. Every night, she would sneak out the window, meet her lover by the army barracks, and make it back home before dawn unnoticed. One night, however, she overheard her father plotting a rebellion against the Christian government and, fearing that she would lose her lover forever, Susona warned him of the plot. The Christian army's retaliation was swift and merciless—Susona's entire family was slaughtered, and their bodies were left to scavengers. Susona's street thereafter bore the name C. Muerte.

Deeply remorseful, Susona confessed in Seville's Cathedral, received baptism, and retreated into a convent. When she died, she asked that her head be placed above her doorway as a symbol of redemption for all and, strangely, nobody touched it for over one-hundred years. While Susona's skull no longer can be seen on what is now C. Susona, a plaque still bears testimony to her tragic story.

The upstairs **private residences,** the official home of the king and queen of Spain, have been renovated and redecorated throughout the centuries; most of the furniture today dates from the 18th and 19th centuries. These residences are accessible only by 25min. tours. **Gardens** adorned with fountains and exotic flowers stretch in all directions from the residential quarters. (*Pl. del Triunfo 7. ☎50 23 23. Open Tu-Sa 9:30am-7pm, Su 9:30am-5pm. Tours of the upper palace living quarters 2 per hr. Aug.-May 10am-1:30pm and 3:30-5:30pm; June-July 10am-1:30pm; max. 15 people per tour. Buy tickets in advance. €7; disabled, students, under 16, and over 65 free. Tours €4. Audio tours €3.*)

**CASA DE PILATOS.** Inhabited continuously by Spanish aristocrats since the 15th century, this large private residence combines all the virtues of Andalusian architecture and art. It has only recently been opened to the public, and sections are still used as a private home. On the ground floor, Roman artifacts and tropical gardens coexist in *mudéjar* patios. The second floor features rooms decorated with oil portraits, sculptures, and tapestries. (*Pl. de Pilatos 1. ☎22 52 98. Open daily 9am-7pm. Tours 2 per hr. Ground level only €5, with 2nd fl. €8; EU citizens free Tu 1-5pm.*)

**MUSEO PROVINCIAL DE BELLAS ARTES.** Cobbled together from the treasures of decommissioned convents in the mid-1800s, this museum contains Spain's finest collection of works by painters of the *Sevillana* School, notably Murillo, Valdés Leal, and Zurbarán, as well as El Greco and Dutch master Jan Brueghel. The art is heavily biased toward religious themes, but later works include landscape paintings and portraits of Seville, its environs, and its residents. The building itself is a work of art; take time to sit in one of its tiny courtyards. (*Pl. del Museo 9. ☎78 65 00; www.museosdeandalucia.es. Open Tu 2:30-8:30pm, W-Sa 9am-8:30pm, Su 9am-2:30pm. €1.50, students and EU citizens free.*)

**PLAZA DE TOROS DE LA REAL MAESTRANZA.** Home to one of the two great bullfighting schools (the other is in **Ronda**, p. 877), Plaza de Toros de la Real Maestranza fills to capacity (13,800) for weekly fights and the 13 *corridas* of the *Feria de Abril.* Visitors must follow the multilingual tours through the small **Museo Taurino de la Real Maestranza;** tours also go behind the ring to the chapel where *matadores* pray before fights and to the medical emergency room, used when their prayers go unanswered. (*☎22 45 77; www.realmaestranza.com. Open May-Oct. 9:30am-8pm; Nov.-Apr. 9:30am-7pm. Tours 3 per hr. €5; seniors 20% discount.*)

**BARRIO DE SANTA CRUZ.** King Fernando III forced Jews exiled from Toledo to live in the Barrio de Santa Cruz, a neighborhood of winding alleys and courtyards. A turn down C. Gloria leads to the 17th-century **Hospital de los Venerables,** a hospital-church adorned with art from the *Sevillana* School. (*☎56 26 96. Open daily for tours 10am-2pm and 4-8pm. €4.75, students €2.40. Su free.*) Beyond C. Lope de Rueda, off C. Ximénez de Enciso, is the **Plaza de Santa Cruz.** South of the plaza are the shady **Jardines de Murillo.** Pl. de Santa Cruz's church houses the grave of the artist Bartoloméo Murillo, who died after falling from a scaffold while painting ceiling frescoes in a Cádiz church. Nearby, **Iglesia de Santa María la Blanca,** built in 1391 on the foundation of a synagogue, contains Murillo's *Last Supper.* (*C. Santa María la Blanca. Open M-Sa 10-11am and 6:30-8pm, Su 9:30am-2pm and 6:30-8pm. Free.*)

**LA MACARENA.** This area northwest of El Centro is named for the Virgin of Seville. The **Convento de Santa Paula,** Pl. Santa Paula 11, includes a church with Gothic, *mudéjar,* and Renaissance elements, a magnificent ceiling, and Montañés's sculptures. Nuns sell scrumptious ▓homemade marmalade and pastries. (*☎53 63 30. Open Tu-Su 10am-1pm. €2.*) A stretch of 12th-century **murallas** (walls) runs between the Pta. Macarena and the Pta. Córdoba on Ronda de Capuchinos. At the western end is the **Basílica de la Macarena,** whose venerated image of *La Virgen de la Macarena* is paraded through the streets during *Semana Santa.*

*(C. Bécquer 1. ☎90 18 00. Open daily 9:30am-2pm and 5-8pm. €3, students €1.50. Mass M-F 9, 11:30am, 8, and 8:30pm; Sa 9am and 8pm; Su 10:30am, 12:30, and 8pm.)* At the **Iglesia de San Lorenzo y Jesús del Gran Poder,** which houses Montañés's sculpture *El Cristo del Gran Poder*, worshippers kiss Jesus's ankle through an opening in the bulletproof glass. *(Pl. San Lorenzo. ☎91 56 72. Open M-Th 8am-1:30pm and 6-9pm, F 7am-2pm and 5-10pm, Sa-Su 8am-1:30pm and 6-9pm. Free.)*

## 🎵 ENTERTAINMENT

The tourist office distributes *El Giraldillo* (also online, www.elgiraldillo.es), a free magazine with listings of music, art exhibits, theater, dance, fairs, and film.

### FLAMENCO

Flamenco—traditionally consisting of dance, guitar, and song, and originally brought to Spain by gypsies—is at its best in Seville. Rhythmic clapping, intricate fretwork on the guitar, throaty wailing, and rapid foot-tapping form a mesmerizing backdrop for the swirling dancers. Flamenco can be seen either in highly touristed *tablaos*, where skilled professional dancers perform, or in *tabernas*, bars where locals merrily dance *sevillanas*. Both have merit, but the *tabernas* tend to be free. The tourist office has a complete list of *tablaos* and *tabernas;* ask about student discounts. **Los Gallos,** Pl. de Santa Cruz 11, is arguably the best tourist show in Seville. Buy tickets ahead and arrive early. (☎21 69 81; www.tablaolosgallos.com. Shows nightly 8 and 10:30pm. €27, includes 1 drink.) A less expensive alternative is the impressive 1hr. show at the cultural center ⬛**Casa de la Memoria Al-Andalus,** C. Ximénez de Enciso 28, in the middle of Santa Cruz. Ask at their ticket office for a schedule of performances. (☎/fax 56 06 70. Shows daily in summer 9 and 10:30pm. Limited seating; buy tickets ahead. €13, students €11, under 10 €6.)

### BULLFIGHTING

Seville's bullring, one of the most beautiful in Spain, hosts bullfights from *Semana Santa* through October. The cheapest place to buy tickets is at the ring on Po. Alcalde Marqués de Contadero. When there's a good *cartel* (line-up), the booths on C. Sierpes, C. Velázquez, and Pl. de Toros might be the only source of advance tickets. Ticket prices can run from €20 for a *grada de sol* (nosebleed seat in the sun) to €75 for a *barrera de sombra* (front-row seat in the shade); scalpers usually add 20%. *Corridas de toros* (bullfights) and *novilladas* (fights with apprentice bullfighters and younger bulls) are held on the 13 days around the *Feria de Abril* and into May, on Sundays April through June and September through October, more often during Corpus Cristi in June and early July, and during the *Feria de San Miguel* near the end of September. During July and August, *corridas* occasionally occur on Thursday at 9pm; check posters around town. For current info and ticket sales, call the Plaza de Toros ticket office at ☎50 13 82.

## 🎆 FESTIVALS

Seville swells with tourists during its fiestas, and with good reason. If you're in Spain during any of the major festivals, head straight to Seville. Reserve a room a few months in advance, and expect to pay two or three times the normal rate. Seville's world-famous ⬛**Semana Santa** lasts from Palm Sunday to Easter Sunday (Mar. 16-22, 2008). Thousands of penitents in hooded cassocks guide *pasos* (lavishly decorated floats) through the streets, illuminated by hundreds of candles. On Good Friday, the entire city turns out for the procession along the bridges and through the oldest neighborhoods. The city rewards itself for its Lenten piety with the ⬛**Feria de Abril** (Apr. 12-17, 2008). Begun as part of a 19th-century revolt against foreign influence, the *Feria* has grown into a massive celebration of all things Andalusian, with circuses, bullfights, and flamenco shows. At the fairgrounds at the southern end of Los Remedios, an array of flowers and lanterns decorates over 1000 kiosks, tents, and pavilions, collectively called *casetas*. Each has a small kitchen, bar, and dance floor. Most *casetas* are privately owned, so the only way to get invited is by making friends with the locals. Luckily, there are a few large public *casetas*. People-watching from the sidelines can be almost as exciting, as costumed girls dance *sevillanas* and men parade on horseback. The city holds bullfights daily during the festival; buy tickets in advance.

## 🎵 NIGHTLIFE

Seville's reputation for hoopla is tried and true—most clubs don't get going until well after midnight, and the real fun often starts only after 3am. A typical night of *la marcha* (bar-hopping) begins with visits to several bars for tapas and mixed drinks, continues with dancing at *discotecas*, and culminates with an early morning breakfast of *churros con chocolate*. Popular bars can be found around **Calle Mateos Gago** near the cathedral, **Calle Adriano** by the bullring, and **Calle del Betis** across the river in Triana. Many gay clubs are around **Plaza de Armas**.

- **La Carbonería**, C. Levies 18 (☎22 99 45), off C. Santa María La Blanca. Guitar-strumming Romeos abound on the massive outdoor stage and the sea of picnic tables. Tapas €1.50-2. Beer €1.50. *Agua de Sevilla* (champage, cream, 4 liquors, and pineapples) €15-20. Sangria pitchers €8. Th free live flamenco. Open daily 8pm-3am. Cash only.

- **Boss**, C. del Betis, knows how to get a crowd fired up. Irresistible beats and a hip atmosphere make this a wildly popular destination. Beer €3.50. Mixed drinks €6. Open fall-spring daily 9pm-5am. MC/V.

- **Palenque**, Av. Blas Pascal (☎46 74 08). Cross Pte. de la Barqueta, turn left, and follow C. Materático Rey Pastor to the first big intersection. Turn left again and look for the entrance on the right. Gigantic dance club, complete with 2 dance floors and a small ice skating rink (€3; includes skate rental; closes at 4am). During the summer, the crowd consists largely of teenagers. Beer €3. Mixed drinks €5. Cover Th free, F-Sa €7. Dress to impress. Open June-Sept. Th-Sa midnight-7am. MC/V.

- **Alfonso**, Av. la Palmera (☎23 37 35), adjacent to Po. de las Delicias. Avoid the longer lines elsewhere and shake it to the DJ's crazy beats in this spacious outdoor club. Palm trees and mini-bars are scattered around the dance floor. Beer €1.50-2.50. Mixed drinks €4.50-6. Open Su-Th 10pm-5am, F-Sa 10pm-7am. AmEx/MC/V.

- **Río Grande: Puerto de Cuba**, on the right as you cross into Triana on the San Telmo bridge. Wicker couches and pillow-strewn dingies provide a unique and intimate club setting on the riverbank. Drinks from €6. Open in summer daily 11pm-4:30am.

- **Terraza Chile**, Po. de las Delicias. Loud salsa and pop keep this small, breezy dance club packed and pounding through the early morning hours. Young *sevillano* professionals mingle with Euro-chic American exchange students. Beer €2. Mixed drinks €5. Open June-Sept. daily 9am-6am; Oct.-May Th-Sa 8pm-5am. MC/V.

## 📅 DAYTRIPS FROM SEVILLE

### CÁDIZ

*RENFE trains (☎956 25 43 01) run from Pl. de Sevilla to: Barcelona (12hr., 2 per day, €73); Córdoba (3hr., 2 per day, €16); Madrid (5hr., 1 per day, €55-85); Seville (2hr., 7-12 per day, €8-20). Transportes Generales Comes buses (☎956 22 78 11) arrive at Pl. de la Hispanidad 1 from Seville (2hr., 10-12 per day, €10).*

Thought to be the oldest continuously inhabited city in Europe, Cádiz (pop. 155,000) is renowned for its extravagant *Carnaval*, the only festival of its size and kind not suppressed during Franco's regime. One of Spain's most dazzling parties, *Carnaval* (Feb. 5, 2008) makes Cádiz an essential winter stop. Year-round, the city's golden **beaches** put its pebbly eastern neighbors to shame. **Playa de la Caleta** is the most convenient beach near the Old Town, but better sand awaits in the new city. Take bus #1 from Pl. España to Pl. Glorieta Ingeniero (€0.90), or walk along the *paseo* by the water (20-30min. from behind the cathedral) to reach ◼**Playa de la Victoria,** whose clean expanse of sand has made it a local favorite and earned it an EU *bandera azul* ("blue flag"; award of excellence). In town, the gold-domed, 18th-century **cathedral,** Pl. de la Catedral, is considered the last great cathedral built by colonial riches. The nearby museum has treasures and art. (☎956 28 61 54. Cathedral and museum open Tu-F 10am-1:30pm and 4:30-6:30pm, Sa 10am-12:30pm. €4, students €3. Tu-F 7-8pm and Su 11am-1pm free.) From the train station, walk two blocks past the fountain with the port on your right to reach **Plaza San Juan de Dios,** the town center. To get to the **tourist office** from the bus station, walk along the water with the port on your left to Paseo de Canalejas. (☎956 24 10 01. Open M-F in summer 9am-2pm and 5-8pm; in winter 9am-2pm and 4-7pm.)

## ARCOS DE LA FRONTERA

*Los Amarillos buses (☎956 32 93 47) run from C. Corregidores to Seville (2hr., 2 per day, €6.30). Transportes Generales buses go to Cádiz (1½hr., 6 per day, €4.80), Costa del Sol (3-4hr., 1 per day, €10-13), and Ronda (1¾hr., 4 per day, €6).*

Peaceful and romantic, Arcos (pop. 33,000) is the best of Spain's *pueblos blancos* (white towns). In town square is the **Basílica de Santa María de la Asunción,** a hodgepodge of Baroque, Gothic, and Renaissance styles under renovations through 2008. (Open M-F 10am-1pm and 3:30-6:30pm, Sa 10am-2pm. €1.50.) Wander through the **cuarto viejo** (Old Quarter) and marvel at the view from ◼**Plaza del Cabildo.** The Gothic **Iglesia de San Pedro** stands on the site of an Arab fortress. (Open daily 10am-1:30pm. €1.) To reach the *cuarto viejo* from the bus station, exit left, follow the road, turn left again, and continue uphill on C. Josefa Moreno Seguro. Take a right on C. Muñoz Vásquez; upon reaching Pl. de España, veer left onto C. Debajo del Coral, which becomes C. Corredera. Manolo Blanco **buses** run every 30min. from the bus station to C. Corredera (€1). Cheap cafes and restaurants cluster at the bottom end of **Calle Corredera,** while tapas nirvana can be achieved in the *cuarto viejo.* Enjoy delicious *pollo a la blancha* (grilled chicken; €6.40) at **Mesón Los Murales ❷,** Pl. Boticas 1 (☎956 70 06 07. *Menú* €9. Entrees €7.50-11.50. Open M-Th and Sa-Su 9am-midnight. MC/V.) The **tourist office** is on Pl. del Cabildo. (☎956 70 22 64. Open mid-Mar. to mid-Oct. M-Sa 10am-2pm and 4-8pm, Su 10am-2pm; mid-Oct. to mid-Mar. M-Sa 10am-2pm and 3:30-7:30pm, Su 10am-2pm.)

## RONDA

*Trains (☎952 87 16 73) depart from Av. Alferez Provisional for Granada (3hr., 3 per day, €12), Madrid (4½hr., 2 per day, €62), and Málaga (2hr., 1 per day, €8). Buses (☎952 18 70 61) go from Pl. Concepción García Redondo 2 to Cádiz (4hr., 2-3 per day, €13), Málaga (2½hr., 8-11 per day, €9), and Seville (2½hr., 3-5 per day, €10).*

Ancient bridges, old dungeons, and a famed bullring attract many visitors to picturesque Ronda (pop. 350,000), which has all the charm of a small, medieval town with the amenities and culture of a thriving city. A precipitous 100m gorge, carved by the Río Guadalevín, drops below the **Puente Nuevo,** opposite Pl. España. The ◼**views** from the **Puente Nuevo, Puente Viejo,** and **Puente San Miguel** are unparalleled. Take the first left after crossing the Puente Nuevo to Cuesta de Santo Domingo, and descend the steep stairs of the **Casa Del Rey Moro** into the 14th-century water mine for an otherworldly view of the ravine. (☎952 18 72 00. Open daily 10am-7pm. €4, children €2.) Bullfighting aficionados charge to Ronda's **Plaza de Toros**, Spain's oldest bullring (est. 1785) as well as the cradle of the modern *corrida*. In early September, the Pl. de Toros hosts *corridas goyescas* (bullfights in traditional costumes) as part of the **Feria de Ronda**. The small but comprehensive **Museo Taurino** traces the history of bullfighting. (☎952 87 15 39; www.rmcr.org. Bullring and museum open daily mid-Apr. to Oct. 10am-8pm; Nov.-Feb. 10am-6pm; Mar. to mid-Apr. 10am-7pm. €6.) For a selection of 50 kinds of *montaditos* (small but substantial sandwiches; €1.20), head to **Case Ke No ❶**, C. Molino 6B. (Open Tu-Su noon-4pm and 7pm-midnight. Cash only.) The town fills to capacity during the festival; reserve rooms months in advance if you plan to spend the night. The **tourist office** is at Po. Blas Infante, across from the bullring. (☎952 18 71 19. English spoken. Open June-Aug. M-F 9:30am-7:30pm, Sa-Su 10am-2pm and 3:30-6:30pm; Sept.-May M-F 9:30am-6:30pm, Sa-Su 10am-2pm and 3:30-6:30pm.)

# GRANADA  ☎958

The splendors of the Alhambra, the magnificent palace which crowns the highest point of Granada (pop. 238,000), have fascinated both prince and pauper for centuries. Legend has it that in 1492, when the Moorish ruler Boabdil fled the city, the last Muslim stronghold in Spain, his mother berated him for casting a longing look back at the Alhambra. "You do well to weep as a woman," she told him, "for what you could not defend as a man." The Albaicín, an enchanting maze of Moorish houses, is Spain's best-preserved Arab quarter. Granada has grown into a university city infused with the energy of students, backpackers, and Andalusian youth.

## ☐ TRANSPORTATION

**Trains: RENFE Station,** Av. Andaluces (☎902 24 02 02; www.renfe.es). To **Barcelona** (12-13hr., 2 per day, €54), **Madrid** (5-6hr., 2 per day, €32-36), and **Seville** (4-5hr., 4 per day, €21).

**Buses:** The bus station (☎18 54 80) is on the outskirts of Granada on Ctra. de Madrid, near C. Arzobispo Pedro de Castro. **ALSA** (☎15 75 57) goes to **Alicante** (6hr., 11 per day, €26), **Barcelona** (14hr., 6 per day, €62), and **Valencia** (9hr., 9 per day, €38). **Alsina Graells** (☎18 54 80) runs to: **Cádiz** (5½hr., 4 per day, €26); **Córdoba** (3hr., 9-10 per day, €11); **Madrid** (5-6hr., 18 per day, €15); **Málaga** (2hr., 17-18 per day, €8.30); **Marbella** (2hr., 6 per day, €14); **Seville** (3hr., 10 per day, €17).

**Public Transportation:** Pick up a free bus map at the tourist office. Important buses include: Alhambra bus **#30** from Gran Vía de Cólon or Pl. Nueva; **#31** from Gran Vía or Pl. Nueva to the Albaicín; **#10** from the bus station to C. de Ronda, C. Recogidas, and C. Acera de Darro; **#3** from the bus station to Av. de la Constitución, Gran Vía, and Pl. Isabel la Católica. Rides €1, *bonobus* (10 rides) €5.20.

## ◩ ◪ ORIENTATION AND PRACTICAL INFORMATION

The center of Granada is the small **Plaza Isabel la Católica,** at the intersection of the city's two main arteries, **Calle de los Reyes Católicos** and **Gran Vía de Colón.** The **cathedral** is on Gran Vía. Two blocks uphill on C. de los Reyes Católicos sits **Plaza Nueva.** Downhill on C. de los Reyes Católicos lies **Plaza Carmen**, site of the **Ayuntamiento** and **Puerta Real.** The **Alhambra** commands the steep hill above **Plaza Nueva.**

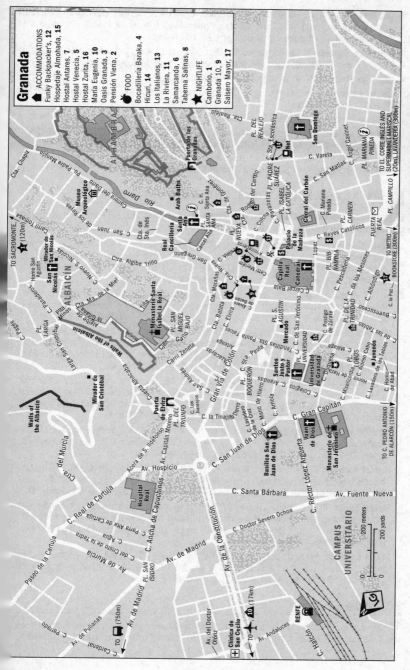

## Granada

**ACCOMMODATIONS**
Funky Backpacker's, **12**
Hospedaje Almohada, **15**
Hostal Antares, **7**
Hostal Venecia, **5**
Hostal Zurita, **16**
Maria Eugenia, **10**
Oasis Granada, **3**
Pensión Viena, **2**

**FOOD**
Bocadillería Baraka, **4**
Hicuri, **14**
Los Italianos, **13**
La Riviera, **11**
Samarcanda, **6**
Taberna Salinas, **8**

**NIGHTLIFE**
Camborio, **1**
Granada 10, **9**
Salsero Mayor, **17**

**Tourist Offices: Junta de Andalucía,** C. Santa Ana 2 (☎22 59 90). Open M-F 9am-8pm, Sa 10am-8pm, Su 10am-2pm. **Oficina Provincial,** Pl. Mariana Pineda 10 (☎24 71 28). Open M-F 9am-8pm, Sa 10am-7pm, Su 10am-4pm.

**American Express:** C. de los Reyes Católicos 31 (☎22 45 12), between Pl. Isabel la Católica and Pta. Real. Open M-F 9am-10pm, Sa 11am-3pm, Su 4-9pm.

**Luggage Storage:** 24hr. storage at the train station (€3).

**Laundromat:** C. de la Paz 19. Wash €6, dry €1 per 10min. Detergent included. Open M-F 10am-2pm and 5-8pm.

**Medical Services: Clínica de San Cecilio,** C. Dr. Olóriz 16 (☎28 02 00), toward Jaén.

**Internet Access: Net,** Pl. de los Girones 3 (☎22 69 19). €1 per hr. With *Bono* card €8 per 10hr. Open M-F 10am-2:30pm and 5-10pm, Sa-Su 5-10pm.

**Post Office:** Pta. Real (☎22 48 35). **Lista de Correos** and **fax** service. Open M-F 8:30am-8:30pm, Sa 9:30am-2pm. **Postal Code:** 18009.

## ACCOMMODATIONS AND CAMPING

Hostels line **Cuesta de Gomérez, Plaza Trinidad,** and **Gran Vía.** Be sure to call ahead during *Semana Santa* (Mar. 16-22, 2008).

▨ **Funky Backpacker's,** Cuesta de Rodrigo del Campo 13 (☎22 14 62). Take in an incredible view of the Alhambra while drinking a cold one at the bar. The friendly staff hangs out with travelers. Dorms are unusually large with A/C and lockers. Breakfast included. Laundry €7. Free Internet. Dorms €17; doubles €38. MC/V. ❶

▨ **Hostal Venecia,** Cuesta de Gomérez 2, 3rd fl. (☎22 39 87). Eccentrically decorated, this small hostel has the most character per square foot of any in Granada. Complimentary tea. Dorms and singles €18; doubles €32; triples €45; quads €60. MC/V. ❷

**Hospedaje Almohada,** C. Postigo de Zarate 4 (☎20 74 46). Red doors with hand-shaped knockers open to a staircase lined with boldly-colored rooms. Lounge in the TV area, listen to the stereo, use the fridge, and cook your own pasta. Laundry €5 per 8kg. Dorms €15; singles €19; doubles €35; triples €50. Cash only. ❶

**Oasis Granada,** Placeta Correo Viejo 3 (☎21 58 48; free from inside Spain 900 162 747; www.hostelsoasis.com). Weekly parties and daily activities like tapas tours and pub crawls around Granada. 3-course dinner €3.50. Breakfast included. Free Internet. Reserve ahead or arrive early. Dorms €15; doubles €36. MC/V. ❶

**Pensión Viena,** C. Hospital Santa Ana 2 (☎/fax 22 18 59; www.hostalviena.com). Bare rooms with A/C and a view of Pl. Nueva. Singles €25, with bath €35; doubles €37/45; triples €50/60; quads €57/70; quints €60/90. MC/V. ❷

**Hostal Antares,** C. Cetti Meriém 10 (☎22 83 13; www.hostalantares.com). The motley color schemes seem influenced by the owner's idol, Jimi Hendrix. Rooms with A/C and TV. Su-Th singles €18; doubles €28, with bath €38; F-Sa €20/30/40. Cash only. ❷

**Hostal Zurita,** Pl. Trinidad 7 (☎/fax 27 50 20; www.pensionzurita.com). Sound-proof balcony doors allow you to escape the noise of the busy student neighborhood. Rooms are small but adequate; all have TV and A/C. Singles €20; doubles €32, with bath €40; triples €48/60. MC/V. ❷

**María Eugenia,** Av. Andalucía (☎20 06 06; fax 20 94 10), at km 436 on the road to Málaga. Take the Santa Fé or Chauchina bus from the train station (2 per hr.). Open year-round. €4.50 per person, €3.50 per child. ❶

## FOOD

The best way to eat on a budget is to order a few beers and then take advantage of the free tapas. Cheap North African cuisine can be found around the Albaicín, while more typical *menús* await in Pl. Nueva and Pl. Trinidad. The adventurous eat well in Granada—try *tortilla sacromonte* (omelette with calf brains, bull testicles, ham, shrimp, and veggies). Picnickers can gather fresh fruit, vegetables, and meat at the large indoor **market** on Pl. San Agustín. (Open M-Sa 9am-3pm.)

🟦 **Bocadillería Baraka,** C. Elvira 20 (☎ 22 97 60). The cheapest and tastiest of Granada's Middle Eastern eateries, Baraka serves delicious pitas (€2.50-3) and homemade lemonade infused with *hierbabuena* (€1). Open daily 1pm-2am. Cash only. ❶

🟦 **Hicuri,** C. Santa Escolástica 12 (☎ 22 12 82), on the corner of Pl. de los Girones. This popular restaurant has a huge selection of vegetarian and vegan dishes. Entrees €5-6. Menú €11. Open daily 8:30am-4:30pm. ❷

**La Riviera,** C. Cetti Meriem 7 (☎ 22 79 69). Serves traditional, generously-sized tapas. Drinks €1.50-2. Open daily 12:30-4pm and 8pm-midnight.

**Los Italianos,** Gran Vía 4 (☎ 22 40 34). Great ice cream at extremely low prices. Cups and cones from €0.50. Open daily 9am-2am. Cash only. ❶

**Samarcanda,** C. Calderería Vieja 3 (☎ 21 00 04). Delicious Lebanese food. Entrees €6-10. Open M-Tu and Th-Su 1-4:30pm and 7:30pm-midnight. MC/V. ❷

**Taberna Salinas,** C. Elvira 13 (☎ 22 14 11). Rustic tavern serves light, authentic Spanish dishes. Entrees €8-20. Open daily 12:30pm-2am. MC/V. ❸

## 👁 SIGHTS

### 🟦 THE ALHAMBRA

*Walk up Cuesta de Gomérez from Pl. Nueva (20min.), or take the quick Alhambra minibus from Pl. Nueva (12 per hr., €1). ☎ 57 51 26, reservations 902 22 44 60; online reservations www.alhambratickets.com. Open daily Apr.-Sept. 8:30am-8pm; Oct.-Mar. M-Sa 8:30am-6pm. Nighttime visits June-Sept. Tu-Sa 10-11:30pm; Oct.-May Sa 8-9:30pm. €10. Worthwhile English-language audio tour €3. Admission is limited, so arrive early or reserve tickets in advance online. Enter the Palace of the Nasrids (Alcázar) during the 30min. time slot specified on your ticket, but stay as long as you wish.*

From the streets of Granada, the Alhambra, meaning "the red one" in Arabic, appears blocky and practical—a military base planted in the foothills of the Sierra Nevada. But up close, the Alhambra is an elaborate and detailed work of architecture, one that unites water, light, wood, stucco, and ceramics to create a fortress-palace of aesthetic grandeur. Celebrated by poets and artists throughout the ages, the Alhambra continues to inspire those who come to admire its timeless beauty. The age-old saying holds true: *"Si mueres sin ver la Alhambra, no has vivido."* (If you die without seeing the Alhambra, you have not lived.)

🟦 **THE ALCÁZAR.** Follow signs to the *Palacio Nazaries* to see the Alcázar, a 14th-century royal palace full of stalactite archways, multi-colored tiles, and sculpted fountains. The entrance leads into the **Mexuar,** a pillared council chamber. Attached to the Mexuar is a small prayer hall with an intricately decorated *mihrab* marking the direction to Mecca. The magnificently carved walls of the **Patio del Cuarto Dorado** (Patio of the Gilded Hall) are topped by the shielded windows of the harem, designed so that the women could see out but no one could see in. Off the far side of the patio, horseshoe archways of diminishing width open onto the **Cuarto Dorado,** whose carved wooden ceiling is inlaid with ivory and mother-of-pearl. The **Patio de los Arrayanes** (Courtyard of Myrtles) features an emerald pond filled with goldfish. Stand at the top of the patio for a glimpse of the 14th-century **Fachada de Serallo,** the palace's intricately carved facade. In the elaborate **Sala de los Embajadores** (Hall of Ambassadors), Granada was formally surrendered to the Catholic Monarchs; it was also here that Fernando and Columbus discussed finding a new route to India. The Mozárabe dome, carved of more than 8000 pieces of wood and inlaid with cedar, forms its own system of constellations. A fountain, currently under reconstruction to restore the 12 marble lions that support it, babbles in the center of the **Patio de los Leones**. The **Sala de los Abencerrajes** is where Boabdil had the throats of 16 sons of the Abencerrajes family slit after one of them allegedly had amorous encounters with his sultana Zorahayda. Through stalactite archways at the far end of the *Patio de los Leones* is the **Sala de los Reyes** (Hall of Kings). Across the courtyard, the resplendent **Sala de las Dos Hermanas** (Chamber of the Two Sisters) gets its name from the two huge matching slabs of marble that compose most of the floor.

**EL GENERALIFE.** Over a bridge, across the **Callejón de los Cipreses** and the **Callejón de las Adelfas**, are the vibrant blossoms, towering cypresses, and streaming waterways of El Generalife, vacation retreat of the sultans. In 1313, Arab engineers changed the Darro River's flow by 18km and employed dams and channels to prepare the soil for Aben Walid Ismail's design of El Generalife. Over the centuries, the estate passed through private hands until it was finally repatriated in 1931. The two buildings of El Generalife, the **Palacio** and the **Sala Regia**, connect across the **Patio de la Acequia**, embellished with a narrow pool fed by fountains whose falling water forms an archway. Honeysuckle vines scale the back wall, and shady benches invite long rests. A dead cypress tree stands at the place where the sultana Zorahayda had her liasons with a nobleman from the Abencerrajes family.

**THE ALCAZABA.** The Christians drove the first Nasrid King Alhamar from the Albaicín to this more strategic hill, where he built the series of rust-colored brick towers which form the *Alcazaba* (fortress). A dark, spiraling staircase leads to the **Torre de la Vela** (watchtower), where visitors have a 360° view of Granada and the surrounding mountains. The tower's bells were rung to warn of impending danger and to coordinate the Moorish irrigation system. Every New Year, during the commemoration of the Christian conquest of Granada, local girls scramble up the tower stairs. Legend holds that any girl who rings the bell before the new year begins will receive a marriage proposal within 365 days. Purely utilitarian, the Alcazaba is the least impressive part of the Alhambra. Exit through the **Puerta del Vino**, the original entrance to the *medina* (city), where inhabitants of the Alhambra once bought tax-free wine (alas, no more).

**PALACIO DE CARLOS V.** After the *Reconquista* drove the Moors from Spain, Fernando and Isabel restored the *Alcázar*. Only two generations later, Emperor Carlos V demolished part of it to make way for his *Palacio*, a Renaissance masterpiece by Pedro Machuca, a disciple of Michelangelo. Although it is incongruous with the surrounding Moorish splendor, scholars concede that the palace is one of the most beautiful Renaissance buildings in Spain. The palace, a square building with a circular inner courtyard wrapped in two stories of Doric colonnades, is Machuca's only surviving design. Inside, the small but impressive **Museo de la Alhambra** contains the only original furnishings remaining from the Alhambra. (☎02 79 00. Open Tu-Sa 9am-2pm. Free.) Upstairs, the **Museo de Bellas Artes,** displaying religious sculptures and paintings of the Granada school, is currently undergoing renovations.

## ▨ THE ALBAICÍN

*Although generally safe, the Albaicín is disorienting and should be approached with caution at night. Bus #12 runs from beside the cathedral to C. Pagés at the top of the Albaicín. Buses #30 and 31 go from Gran Vía and Pl. Nueva to the neighborhood.*

A labyrinth of steep, narrow alleys, the Albaicín was the only Moorish neighborhood to escape the torches of the *Reconquista*. After the fall of the Alhambra, a small Muslim population remained here until their expulsion in the 17th century.

Today, with North African cuisine, outdoor bazaars blasting Arabic music, teahouses, and the mosque near Pl. San Nicolás, the Albaicín attests to the persistence of Islamic culture in Andalucía. Spectacular sunsets over the surrounding mountains can be seen from C. Cruz de Quirós, above C. Elvira. The best way to explore this maze is to proceed along Carrera del Darro off Pl. Santa Ana, climb the Cuesta del Chapiz on the left, then wander through the Muslim ramparts, cisterns, and gates. On Pl. Santa Ana, the 16th-century **Real Cancillería**, with its arcaded patio and stalactite ceiling, was the Christians' *Ayuntamiento* (city hall). Farther uphill are the 11th-century **Arab baths**. *(Carrera del Darro 31.* ☎ *02 78 00. Open Tu-Sa 10am-2pm. Free.)* The **Museo Arqueológico** showcases funerary urns, classical sculpture, Carthaginian vases, Muslim lamps, and ceramics. *(Carrera del Darro 41.* ☎ *22 56 40. Open Tu 2:30-8:30pm, W-Sa 9am-8:30pm, Su 9am-2:30pm. €1.50, EU citizens free.)* The ■**mirador** adjacent to **Iglesia de San Nicolás** affords the city's best view of the Alhambra, especially in winter when snow adorns the Sierra Nevada behind it.

**CAPILLA REAL AND CATHEDRAL.** Downhill from the Alhambra, the **Capilla Real** (Royal Chapel), Fernando and Isabel's private chapel, exemplifies Christian Granada. During their prosperous reign, the Catholic Monarchs funneled almost a quarter of the royal income into the chapel's construction (1504-1521) to build a proper burial place. Their efforts did not go unrewarded; intricate Gothic masonry and meticulously rendered figurines, as well as **La Reja,** the gilded iron grille of Maestro Bartolomé, grace the couple's resting place. Behind La Reja lie the lifelike marble figures of the royals themselves. Facing the altar, Fernando and Isabel are on the right. Beside them rest their daughter Juana la Loca (the Mad) and her husband Felipe el Hermoso (the Fair). Much to the horror of the rest of the royal family, Juana insisted on keeping the body of her husband with her for an unpleasantly long time after he died. The lead caskets where all four monarchs were laid to rest lie directly below the marble sarcophagi in a crypt down a small stairway on the left. The smaller, fifth coffin belongs to the hastily buried child-king of Portugal, Miguel, whose death allowed Carlos V to ascend the throne. The adjacent **Sacristía** houses Isabel's private **art collection,** which favors 15th-century Flemish and German artists. In the middle of the sacristy shine the **royal jewels,** including the queen's golden crown and the king's sword. *(The Capilla is on C. Oficios through the Pta. Real off Gran Vía.* ☎ *22 92 39. Capilla and Sacristía open M-Sa 10:30am-1pm and 4-7pm, Su 11am-1pm and 4-7pm. Both sights €3.)* Behind the Capilla Real and the Sacristía is Granada's **cathedral.** After the *Reconquista,* construction of the cathedral began upon the smoldering embers of Granada's largest mosque and was not completed until 1704. *(*☎ *22 29 59. Open Apr.-Sept. M-Sa 10:45am-1:30pm and 4-8pm, Su 4-8pm; Oct.-Mar. M-Sa 10:30am-1:30pm and 3:30-6:30pm, Su 11am-1:30pm and 3:30-6:30pm. €3.)*

# ☒ NIGHTLIFE

Granada's policy of free tapas with a drink lures students and tourists to its many pubs and bars. Great tapas bars can be found off the side streets near Pl. Nueva. The most boisterous nightspots belong to **Calle Pedro Antonio de Alarcón,** between Pl. Albert Einstein and Ancha de Gracia, while hip new bars and clubs line **Calle Elvira** from Cárcel to C. Cedrán. Gay bars are around **Carrera del Darro.** The *Guía del Ocio,* sold at newsstands (€1), lists clubs, pubs, and cafes.

**Camborio,** Camino del Sacromonte 48 (☎22 12 15), a 20min. walk uphill from Pl. Nueva. Night bus #31 runs until 2am. Pop music spun by DJs echoes through dance floors to the rooftop patio. Striking view of the Alhambra. Beer €1.80-3. Mixed drinks €5-6. Cover F-Sa €7. Open Tu-Sa 11pm-dawn. Cash only.

**Salsero Mayor,** C. la Paz 20 (www.salseromayorgranada.com). Locals and tourists flock here for crowded nights of *bachata*, merengue, and salsa. Beer €2-3. Mixed drinks €5. Open Su-Th 10pm-3am, F and Sa 1pm-4am. Cash only.

**Granada 10,** C. Cárcel Baja 3 (☎22 40 01). Movie theater by evening (shows Sept.-June at 8 and 10pm), raging dance club by night. Flashy and opulent. Strict dress code. Open Su-Th 12:30am-4am, F-Sa 12:30am-5am. MC/V.

# COSTA DEL SOL

The Costa del Sol combines rocky beaches with chic promenades and swank hotels. While some spots are over-developed and can be hard on the wallet, elsewhere the coast's stunning landscape has been left untouched. Summer brings swarms of tourists, but nothing takes away from the main attraction: eight months of spring and four months of summer.

## MÁLAGA                                                                    ☎952

Málaga (pop. 550,000) is the transportation hub of the coast, and while its beaches are known more for bars than for natural beauty, the city has much to offer. Towering high above the city, the medieval **Alcazaba** is Málaga's most imposing sight. At the east end of Po. del Parque, the 11th-century structure was originally used as both a military fortress and royal palace for Moorish kings. (Open June-Aug. Tu-Su 9:30am-8pm; Sept.-May Tu-Sa 8:30am-7pm. €2, students and seniors €0.60. Free Su after 2pm.) Málaga's breathtaking **cathedral,** C. Molina Lario 4, is nicknamed *La Manquita* (One-Armed Lady) because one of its two towers was never completed. (☎22 03 45. Open M-F 10am-6pm, Sa 10am-5pm. Mass daily 9am. €3.50, includes audio tour.) Picasso's birthplace, Pl. de la Merced 15, is now home to the **Casa Natal y Fundación Picasso,** which organizes concerts, exhibits, and lectures. Upstairs is a permanent collection of Picasso's drawings, photographs, and pottery. (☎06 02 15; www.fundacionpicasso.es. Open daily 9:30am-8pm. €1; students, seniors, and under 17 free.)

One of few spots in Málaga just for backpackers, friendly ▣**Picasso's Corner ❷,** C. San Juan de Letrán 9, off Pl. de la Merced, offers free Internet and top-notch bathrooms. (☎21 22 87; www.picassoscorner.com. Dorms €18-19; doubles €45. MC/V.) Sit outside and indulge in a mojito (€2.50 glass, €6 pitcher) and any of the couscous or combo dishes (€1.80-8.20) at ▣**Mediterráneo ❶,** C. Santiago 4, offering Arabic cuisine with a Greek spin. (☎21 64 38. Open Tu-Su 8pm-12am.) RENFE **trains** (☎902 24 02 02) leave from Explanada de la Estación for: Barcelona (13hr., 2 per day, €55); Córdoba (2hr., 9 per day, €16); Madrid (5hr., 7 per day, €35); Seville (3hr., 5-6 per day, €17). **Buses** run from Po. de los Tilos (☎35 00 61), one block from the RENFE station along C. Roger de Flor, to: Cádiz (5hr., 3-6 per day, €21); Córdoba (3hr., 7 per day, €12); Granada (2hr., 17-19 per day, €9); Madrid (7hr., 8-12 per day, €20); Marbella (1½hr., 1 per hr., €5); Ronda (3hr., 4-12 per day, €10); Seville (3hr., 11-12 per day, €14). To get to the city center from the bus station, take bus #3, 4, or 21 (€1) or exit right onto Callejones del Perchel, walk through the intersection with Av. de la Aurora, turn right on Av. de Andalucía, and cross Puente de Tetuán. Alameda Principal leads into Pl. de la Marina and the **tourist office.** (☎12 20 20. Open M-F 9am-7pm.) **Postal Code:** 29080.

## MARBELLA                                                                  ☎952

While much of Spain draws visitors looking to engage in the country's history and culture, people come to Marbella (pop. 115,000) looking for something quite different: a tan. The city was once a key merchant town occupied by the Phoenicians,

Greeks, Romans, and Arabs. The influence of these groups is still evident in the structures of the *casco antiguo* (Old Town), though ancient buildings now house upscale restaurants and swimwear shops. Buses #6, 7, and 26 (dir.: San Pedro or Hipercor; €1), running along Av. Ricardo Soriano, bring you to the chic port. Marbella has over 20km of beaches. Shores to the east of the port are popular with British backpackers; those to the west attract a more posh crowd.

The town's popularity has dwindled in recent years, making beds much easier to find last-minute. **Hostal de Pilar ❷**, C. Mesoncillo 4, has a bar, fireplace, and pool table, and accommodates backpackers on the roof when dorms are full. (☎82 99 36; www.hostel-marbella.com. July-Aug. roof €15; dorms €18; doubles €30-35; triples €53. Sept.-June dorms €15; doubles €25; triples €36. Discounts for longer stays in winter. Cash only.) **El Gallo ❷**, C. Lobatas 44, is one of the few truly local restaurants in the area. The €8 *menú* offers the most food for the least money, but the rabbit in garlic sauce (€8) steals the show. (☎82 79 98. Open M-W and F-Su 9am-4:30pm and 7-11:30pm. MC/V.) The nightlife routine in Marbella consists of hitting up bars in the *casco antiguo* at midnight or 1am, then proceeding to clubbing capital **Puerto Banús**, 7km west (€10 by taxi), around 3am. **O'Brien's Irish Pub**, Pl. de los Olivos, is one of the most popular bars in the *casco antiguo*, mixing traditional Celtic music with modern beats. (☎76 46 95. Beer €2.50. Mixed drinks €5. Open M-Th 6pm-3am, F-Sa 6pm-4am, Su 3pm-3am. Cash only.) From the station on Ctra. del Trapiche (☎76 44 00), **buses** go to: Cádiz (2¾hr., 6 per day, €16); Granada (3½hr., 7 per day, €14); Málaga (1½hr., 22-27 per day, €5); Seville (4hr., 2-3 per day, €16). The **tourist office** is in Pl. de los Naranjos. (☎82 35 50. Open M-F 9am-9pm, Sa 10am-2pm.) **Postal Code:** 29600.

# TARIFA
☎956

Prepare for wind-blown hair—when the breezes pick up in the southernmost city of continental Europe, it becomes clear why Tarifa (pop. 15,000) is known as the Hawaii of Spain. World-renowned winds combined with kilometers of white beaches attracts some of the best kite and windsurfers from around the world, while the tropical, relaxed environment beckons to the less adventurous. Directly across the Strait of Gibraltar from Tangier, Morocco, Tarifa boasts incomparable views of Africa, the Atlantic, and the Mediterranean. Next to the port and just outside the Old Town are the facade and ruins of the **Castillo de Guzmán el Bueno**. (Open Tu-Su Apr.-Oct. 11am-2pm and 6-8pm; Nov.-May 11am-2pm and 4-6pm. €1.80.) Those with something less historical in mind can head 200m south to **Playa de los Lances** for 5km of the finest sand on the Atlantic coast. Bathers should be aware of the occasional high winds and strong undertow. Adjacent to Playa de los Lances is **Playa Chica**, which is tiny but sheltered from the winds. **Tarifa Spin Out Surfbase**, 9km up the road toward Cádiz, rents **windsurfing** and **kitesurfing** boards and instructs all levels. (☎23 63 52; www.tarifaspinout.com. Book ahead. Windsurf rental €25 per hr., €56 per day; 2hr. lesson including equipment €50. Kite and board rental €28 per hr., €58 per day; 1½hr. lesson with all equipment €99.)

The cheapest accommodations line **Calle Batalla del Salado** and its side streets. Prices rise significantly in summer; those visiting in August and on weekends from June to September should call ahead and arrive early. Comfortable **Hostal Villanueva ❷**, Av. de Andalucía, 11, has a restaurant and rooftop terrace with an ocean view. Spotless rooms all have bath and TV. (☎68 41 49. Breakfast €2.25. Singles €20-25; doubles €35-45. Cash only.) **Hostal Facundo I and II ❶**, C. Batalla del Salado, 47, with its "Welcome backpackers" slogan, draws a young, budget crowd. (☎68 42 98; www.hostalfacundo.com. Dorms €10-22; singles €25; doubles €22-45, with bath €26-55. Cash only.) Hard-core windsurfers often stay at one of the several **campgrounds** along the beach several kilometers from town; all have full bath and shower facilities, bars, and mini-markets. Guests must bring their own tents. Although Cádiz-bound buses will drop you off if you ask, flagging one down to get back to town is next to impossible; surfers call for taxis or befriend fellow surfers with cars. For cheap sandwiches (€1.50-3), try any one of the many *bagueterías* around C. Sancho IV el Bravo. Alternatively, C. San Francisco offers a variety of affordable, appetizing options. Take off your shoes and lounge on eclectic, pillow-covered couches in the open-air seating area of ▇Bamboo ❷, across from the castle. The lounge becomes a bar at night. (☎62 73 04. Teas €1.60-2. Fresh juices €2.50-3. Panini €2.80-3.50. Full breakfast €4. F-Sa Live DJ. Open Su-Th 10am-2pm, F-Sa 10am-3am. MC/V.) **Pizzería Horno de Leña** ❷ inside the **Tarifa EcoCenter**, C. San Sebastián, 6, uses only organic local ingredients in its pizzas, staying true to its "Don't panic, it's organic" mantra. (☎62 72 20. Pizzas €4.50-9. Open Tu-Sa 9am-2am, Su-M 9am-1:30pm. Cash only.)

At night, sunburnt travelers mellow out in the Old Town's many bars, which range from jazz to psychedelic to Irish. **Moskito**, C. San Francisco 11, is a combination bar-club with a Caribbean motif, dance music, and tropical cocktails. (Free salsa lessons W night 10:30pm. Beer €2.50. Mixed drinks €4.50-6. Open in summer daily 11pm-3am; in winter Th-Sa 11pm-late.) **La Tribu**, C. Nuestra Señora de la Luz 7, a favorite among kite surfers, makes some of the most creative mixed drinks in town (€4-7). Trance and techno pump energy into this otherwise mellow nightspot. (Beer €2-3. Shots €1.50. Open daily 8pm-2am.)

From the bus station on C. Batalla del Salado 19 (☎68 40 38), **buses** run to Cádiz (2¼hr., 7 per day, €7.50) and Seville (3hr., 4 per day, €15). FRS **ferries** (☎68 18 30; www.frs.com) run to Tangier, MOR (35min., 1 per 2hr., €29). For a **taxi**, call **Parada Taxi** (☎68 42 41). The **tourist office**, in Parque de la Alameda, has info on adventure sports. (☎68 09 93; www.tarifaweb.com. Open in summer M-F 10:30am-2pm and 6-8pm, Sa-Su 9am-2pm; in winter M-F 10am-2pm and 4-6pm, Sa-Su 9:30am-3pm.) The **post office**, C. Coronel Moscardó, 9, is near Pl. San Matéo. (☎68 42 37. Open M-F 8:30am-2:30pm, Sa 9:30am-1pm.) **Postal Code:** 11380.

# GIBRALTAR

The craggy face of the Rock of Gibraltar emerges imposingly from the mist just off the southern shore of Spain. Ancient seafarers called "Gib" one of the Pillars of Hercules, believing that it marked the end of the world. Among history's most contested plots of land, Gibraltar today is officially a self-governing British colony, though Spain continues to campaign for its sovereignty. Gibraltar has a culture all its own—a curious mixture of not-quite-British, definitely-not-Spanish that makes it a sight worth visiting, despite the fact that it is something of a tourist trap.

**PHONE CODES** ☎350 from the UK or the US. ☎9567 from Spain.

▇▇ **TRANSPORTATION AND PRACTICAL INFORMATION. Buses** run from the Spanish border town of La Línea to: Cádiz (3hr., 4 per day, €13); Granada (5hr., 2 per day, €20); Madrid (7hr., 2 per day, €26); Seville (6hr., 4 per day, €20). Turner & Co., 65/67 Irish Town St. (☎783 05; fax 720 06), runs **ferries** to Tangier, MOR (1¼hr.; 1 per day; £18/€32, under 12 £9/€17). British Airways (☎793 00) **flights** leave from **Gibraltar Airport** (**GIB**; ☎730 26) for London, BRI (2½hr., 2 per day, £168/€233). You must have a valid passport to enter Gibraltar or you'll be turned away at the border. From the bus station in La Línea, walk toward the Rock; the border is 5min. away. Once through customs and passport control, catch bus #9 or 10 or walk across the airport tarmac into town (20min.). Stay left on Av. Winston Churchill when the road forks. The **tourist office** is at Duke of Kent House, Cathedral Sq. (☎450 00. Open M-F 9am-4:30pm, Sa 10am-1pm.)

**(dea) THE REAL DEAL.** Although the euro is accepted almost everywhere (except in pay phones and post offices), the **pound sterling (£)** is the preferred method of payment in Gibraltar. ATMs dispense money in pounds. Merchants and sights sometimes charge a higher price in the euro than in the pound's exchange equivalent. However, unless stated otherwise, assume an establishment will accept the euro, although change is often given in British currency. The exchange rate fluctuates around £1 to €1.50. As of press time, **1£ = €1.47.**

**▛▟ ACCOMMODATIONS AND FOOD.** Gibraltar is best done as a daytrip. The few accommodations in the area are relatively pricey and often full, especially in summer, and camping is illegal. Spending the night in La Línea across the border is cheaper. In Gib, **Emile Youth Hostel Gibraltar ❷,** on Montague Bastian, has bunks in cheerful, painted rooms with clean communal baths. (☎511 06; www.emilehostel.com. Breakfast included. Lockout 10:30am-4:30pm. £1 for luggage storage and towels. Dorms £15/€25; doubles £34/€51. Cash only.) International restaurants are easy to find, but you may choke on the prices. Sample the treats of Gibraltar's thriving Hindu community at **Mumtaz ❶,** 20 Cornwalls Ln., where authentic tastes come at low prices. (☎442 57. Entrees £2.50-6.75, with ample vegetarian selection. Takeout available. Open daily 11am-3pm and 6pm-12:30am. Cash only.) **Marks & Spencer** on Main St. has decent prepackaged food and fresh breads. (Open M-F 9am-7pm, Sa 9:30am-5pm. AmEx/MC/V.)

**◀ SIGHTS.** See the titanic ◪**Rock of Gibraltar,** even if just to say that you've seen it. About halfway up is the infamous **Apes' Den,** where Barbary Macaques cavort on the sides of rocks, the tops of taxis, and the heads of tourists. At the northern tip of the Rock, facing Spain, are the **Great Siege Tunnels.** Originally used to fend off a Franco-Spanish siege in the 18th century, the underground tunnels were expanded to span 53km during WWII. Thousands of years of water erosion formed the eerie chambers of **St. Michael's Cave,** 500m from the siege tunnels. At the southern tip of Gibraltar, **Europa Point** commands a view of the straits; its lighthouse can be seen from 27km away at sea. The top of the Rock is accessible by car or cable car, or for the truly adventurous and athletic, by foot. (Cable car daily 6 per hr. Round-trip £8/€13.50. Combined ticket to all sights, including one-way cable car ride, £16/€21.50.)

# EASTERN SPAIN

Its rich soil and famous orange groves, fed by Moorish irrigation systems, have earned Eastern Spain the nickname *Huerta de España* (Spain's Orchard). Dunes, jagged promontories, and lagoons mark the coastline, while fountains and pools grace landscaped public gardens in Valencian cities. The region has made a rapid transition from traditional to commercial, and continues to modernize.

# ALICANTE (ALICANT)                    ☎965

Alicante (pop. 320,000) is a city with verve. Though its wild bars, crowded beaches, and busy streets seem decidedly modern, the looming castle-topped crag, 14th-century churches, and marble esplanades declare otherwise. Alicante, once the Roman city Lucentum, is also home to the remains of a 5th-century Iberian settlement.

## NO WORK, ALL PLAY

### SEEING RED

On the last Wednesday of every August, tens of thousands of tourists descend upon the small town of Buñol, a town in Valencia, to participate in the world's largest food fight: La Tomatina. A tradition since 1944, this tomato battle serves as the culmination of a week-long festival. Although the sloppy free-for-all is followed by a celebration of the town's patron saints, the tomato fight has no significance beyond the primal desire to get dirty and throw food.

Festivities begin when an overgrown ham is placed on a greased pole in the center of town. Locals and tourists scramble up the slippery pole, climbing on top of one another to be the captor of the prized ham. Once a winner is announced, a cannon starts the marinara blood bath.

Throngs of tourists wearing clothes destined for the dumpster crowd around the open-bed trucks that haul 240,000 lb. of tomatoes into the plaza. Over the next 2hr., Buñol becomes an every-man-for-himself battle of oozy carnage. Revelers pelt one another with tomatoes until the entire crowd is covered in tomato guts.

The origins of this food fight are unclear: some say it began as a fight between friends, while others say the original tomatoes were directed at unsatisfactory civil dignitaries. Today, no one is safe from the wrath of tomatoes hurled at friends and foreigners alike.

**TRANSPORTATION AND PRACTICAL INFORMATION.** RENFE **trains** (☎902 24 02 02) run from Estación Término on Av. Salamanca to Barcelona (4½-6hr., 5-6 per day, €45), Madrid (4hr., 4-9 per day, €42-73), and Valencia (1½hr., 10 per day, €10-24). **Buses** (☎13 07 00) leave C. Portugal 17 for: Barcelona (9hr., 2 per day, €38); Granada (6hr., 10 per day, €26-32); Madrid (5hr., 15 per day, €24-32); Málaga (8hr., 6 per day, €35-43); Seville (10hr., daily, €45); Valencia (3hr., 14-21 per day, €16-18). The **tourist office** is by the bus station. (☎92 98 02; www.alicanteturismo.com. Open M-F 9am-2pm and 5-8pm, Sa 10am-2pm.) **Internet** is available at **Fundación BanCaja,** Rbla. Méndez Nuñez 4, 2nd fl. (1hr. free with ISIC. Open M-F 9am-2pm and 4-9pm, Sa 9am-2pm.) **Postal Code:** 03002.

**ACCOMMODATIONS AND FOOD.** Hostels are plentiful but the nicest, in the **casco antigua,** close to the port, must be booked in advance. For simple, airy rooms with A/C and views of the town's oldest church, try ⬥**Hostal-Pension La Milagrosa** ❶, C. Villa Vieja, which has a rooftop terrace for socializing and admiring the incredible castle view. (☎21 69 18. Laundry €2. Internet €1 per hr. Dorms €15. MC/V.) **Hostal Les Monges Palace** ❸, corner of C. san Agustin and C. Monjas, is in a palatial building with beautiful rooms. (☎21 50 46; www.lesmonges.net. Singles €29.) ⬥**Kebap** ❶, Av. Dr. Gadea 5, has the best Middle Eastern food in Alicante. (☎22 92 35. Entrees €6-7. Open Su-Th 1-4pm and 8pm-midnight, F-Sa 1pm-midnight. MC/V.) For a more local taste, try the family-run restaurants in the *casco antiguo.* Buy groceries at **Supermarket Mercadona,** C. Alvarez Sereix 5, off Av. Federico Soto. (☎21 58 94. Open M-Sa 9am-9pm.)

**SIGHTS AND NIGHTLIFE.** The **Castell de Santa Barbara** keeps imposing guard over Alicante's shores. The 166m high Carthaginian monument exhibits 9th- to 17th-century artifacts and offers a spectacular panorama of the city. (☎26 31 31. Open daily Apr.-Sept. 10am-7:30pm; Oct.-Mar. 9am-6:30pm. Elevator €2.40 on C. Jovellanos near the beach.) The *casco antigua* offers an architectural window into the city's past, from the Gothic-styled **Iglesia de Santa Maria** to the Baroque **Concatedral de San Nicolas de Bari** to the twisted columns of the **Ayuntamiento.** The **Museu Arqueológico Provincial de Alicante,** Pl. Dr. Gomez Ulls, imaginatively showcases finds dating to prehistoric times and includes a hall dedicated to historical Alicante. (☎14 90 00; www.marqalicante.com. Open Tu-Sa 10am-7pm, Su 10am-2pm. €3, students €1.50.) Alicante's **Playa del Postiguet,** blocks from the *casco antigua,* attracts beach-lovers, as do nearby **Playa de San Juan** (TAM bus #21, 22, or 31) and **Playa del Mutxavista** (TAM bus #21). Buses (€0.95) depart every 15-25min.

Nightlife in Alicante is unrelenting and unpredictable. Delightfully bizarre bars in the *casco antiguo* are the best place to start the night. ■**Astrónomo,** C. Virgen de Belén, at C. Padre Maltés (☎965 14 35 22), plays traditional and modern Spanish tunes. When the dance floor gets hot, retreat to a gated outdoor terrace. (Beer €3. Mixed drinks from €5. Happy hour midnight-2am. Open Th-Sa 11pm-4am.) Don't miss **El Coscorrón,** C. Tarifa 3, named for the bump on the head you might receive from the four-foot doorframe. Open since 1936, it claims to be the oldest bar in Alicante. (Beer €2.50. Mojito €2.50. Mixed drinks €4-6. Open Su-W 10:30pm-2:30am, Th-Sa 7pm-4am.) The bars that overlook the water in the **main port** and the discos on **Puerto Nuevo** tend to fill up after 2:30am. Night owls can test their stamina on the **Tramsnochador** night train, which careens from Estación Marina to disco gardens in Benidorm that stay packed until 6am. (July-Aug. 1 per hr. 9pm-5am. Check tourist office for prices.) The **Fogueres de Sant Joan** (Bonfire of Saint John; June 19-24, 2008) sets Alicante aflame for a week, celebrating the summer solstice with revelry from morning until night. *Fogueras* (giant papier-mâché structures) are erected and then burned in the street during *la Cremà*. Afterward, firefighters soak everyone during *la Banyà* and the party continues until dawn.

# VALENCIA ☎963

Valencia's white beaches, palm-lined avenues, and architectural treasures are noticeably less crowded than those of Spain's other major cities. Yet Valencia (pop. 807,000) possesses the energy of Madrid, the off-beat sophistication of Barcelona, and the warmth of Seville. Explore the life aquatic at L'Oceanogràfic or fulfill a quest for the Holy Grail at the Catedral de Santa María.

**◨◪ TRANSPORTATION AND PRACTICAL INFORMATION. Trains** arrive at Estación del Norte, C. Xàtiva 24 (☎52 02 02) and a slick new metro line runs from the **Airport of Valencia** to C. Colon. **RENFE** (☎902 24 02 02) runs to: Alicante (2-3hr., 12 per day, €10-24); Barcelona (3hr., 8-16 per day, €29-37); Madrid (3½hr., 12 per day, €20-39); Seville (8½hr., 11:20am, €44). **Buses** (☎46 62 66) go from Av. Menéndez Pidal 13 to: Alicante via the Costa Blanca (4½hr., 10-30 per day, €16-18); Barcelona (4½hr., 19 per day, €21); Granada (8hr., 9 per day, €36-43); Madrid (4hr., 13 per day, €21-26); Málaga (11hr., 9 per day, €44-53); Seville (11hr., 3-4 per day, €43-50). Trasmediterránea **ferries,** Muelle de Poniente (☎902 45 46 45; www.trasmediterranea.es), sail to the Balearic Islands (p. 924). Take bus #1 or 2 from the bus station. The huge **tourist office,** C. de la Paz 48, has branches at the train station and at Pl. de la Reina. (☎98 64 22; www.valencia.es. Open M-F 9am-2:30pm and 4:30-8pm.) **Ono,** C. San Vicente Mártir 22, provides daily **Internet** until 1am. (☎28 19 02. €1-4 per hr.) The **post office** is at Pl. del Ajuntament 24. (☎51 23 70. Open M-F 8:30am-8:30pm, Sa 9:30am-2pm.) **Postal Code:** divided into zones, 46000-46025.

**◪◩ ACCOMMODATIONS AND FOOD.** For the best deals and proximity to restaurants, nightlife, and architectural marvels, try hostels around Plaça del Ajuntament, Plaça del Mercat, and Plaça de la Reina. From Pl. de la Reina, turn right on C. de la Paz to reach the chic and hopping ■Red Nest Youth Hostel 2, C. de la Paz 36, a great location for clubgoers. The hostel is spotless and smoothly operated, with an avant-garde decor. (☎42 71 68; www.nest-hostelsvalencia.net. Kitchen, dining area, and vending machines. Free luggage storage. Linens included. Internet €1 per hr. 4-12 person dorms €18-20; doubles €41/47. AmEx/MC/V.) The Home Youth Hostel 1, C. Lonja 4, is across from the Mercado Central on a side street off Pl. Dr. Collado. A couch-laden lounge and relaxed atmosphere make this funky 20-room complex the area's most social hostel. (☎91 62 29; www.likeathome.net. Fully equipped kitchen. Linens included. Internet €0.50 per 15min. Singles €23; doubles €40. MC/V.)

Valencia is renowned for its paella, served in mammoth skillets all over town. Stuff yourself with huge portions of *paella valenciana* in the intimate courtyard outside **El Rall ❸,** by the old Gothic silk exchange monument on C. Tundidores 2. (☎92 20 90. Paella €10-21 per person, min. 2 people. Open daily 1:30-4pm and 9-11:30pm. Reserve ahead. MC/V.) **Zumeria Naturalia ❶,** C. Del Mar 12, by the Pl. de la Reina, is a sherbert-hued gem offering over 100 fruit drinks (half without alcohol) and crepes made quick. (Open M-W 5pm-midnight, Th 5pm-1am, F-Sa 5pm-2am, Su 5-10:30pm.) For groceries, stop by the booths of the **Mercado Central,** where fresh fish, meat, and fruit (including Valencia's famous oranges) are sold.

**◪ SIGHTS.** Most sights line the Río Turia or cluster near Pl. de la Reina, Pl. del Mercado, and Pl. de la Virgin. EMT bus #5 is the only public bus that passes by most of Valencia's historical sites; for a guided tour, try the **Bus Turistico** from Pl. de la Reina (☎15 85 15; €12). The 13th-century ◪**Catedral de Santa María** in Pl. de la Reina, which holds a chalice said to be the Holy Grail, is an impressive mix of Romanesque, Gothic, and Baroque architecture. Catch incredible views of Valencia's skyline atop the **Miguelete,** the cathedral tower. (☎91 01 89. Cathedral open daily 7:30am-1pm and 4:30-8:30pm. Closes earlier in winter. Tower open daily 10am-1pm and 4:30-7pm. Cathedral free. Tower €2.) Be sure to pass around back through the marbled **plaza de la Virgin** and the **Basilica de la Virgin. El Palacio de los Marqueses de Dos Aguas,** C. Porta Querol 2, off C. de la Paz, is an architecturally stunning 14th-century building that recreates the home of a noble Valencian family, with a ceramics museum on upper floors. (☎51 63 92. Open Tu-Sa 10am-2pm and 4-8pm. Tu-F €2.40.) Many museums are across the fortified bridges of what was once the Río Turia—today, the riverbed is a lush green park perfect for bike rides, picnics, or walks. The blue-domed **Museu Provincial de Belles Artes,** C. Sant Pío V, displays stunning 14th- to 16th-century Valencian art and is home to El Greco's *San Juan Bautista,* Velázquez's self-portrait, and a number of works by Goya. (☎60 57 93. Open Tu-Sa 10am-8pm. Free.) Next door, pass through the eclectic **Jardines del Real.** Take bus #35 from Pl. del Ajuntament to reach the mini-city that is the ◪**Ciutat de les Arts i de les Ciències.** The complex is divided into five large spaces, including the eye-shaped **L'Hemisfèric** (with an IMAX theater and planetarium) and the **Museu de les Ciències Príncipe Felipe,** an interactive science playground. The **Palau de les Arts** houses performances and **L'Oceanogràfic,** an enormous aquarium, recreates nine aquatic environments. (☎902 10 00 31; www.cac.es. Hourly shows at L'Hemisfèric IMAX and planetarium. Open M-Th 11am-7pm, F-Sa 11am-9pm. Museum open mid-June to mid-Sept. daily 10am-8pm; Mar. to mid-June and mid-Sept. to Jan. Su-F 10am-6pm and Sa 10am-8pm. L'Oceanogràfic open Aug. daily 10am-midnight; mid-June to Aug. daily 10am-8pm; Sept. to mid-June Su-F 10am-6pm, Sa 10am-8pm. Combination tickets for the entire complex €30.50.)

**◪◪ ENTERTAINMENT AND NIGHTLIFE.** To reach Valencia's two most popular beaches, **Las Arenas** and **Malvarrosa,** bike along Av. de la Puerta or take bus #20, 21, 22, or 23. If you have time to spare, take an **Autocares Herca** bus from the corner of Gran Vía de Germanias and C. Sueca (☎49 12 50. 30min., 1 per hr. 7am-9pm, €1-1.10) to the pristine beach of **Salér.** On Pl. de la Virgin along C. Caballeros, bars and pubs kick into action around midnight. Most dance clubs here do not have a cover. Discos dominate the university area, while the gay and lesbian scene centers further along C. Caballeros on **Calle Quart.** Sip *agua de Valencia* (orange juice, champagne, and vodka) at the outdoor terraces in Pl. Tossal. There you will find ◪**Bolsería Café,** C. Bolsería 41, a cafe-style club packed every night with the very beautiful and the very chic. (☎91 89 03. Beer €3. Mixed drinks €6. Funk W, house music Sa-Su. Open daily 7:30pm-3:30am. Cash only.) **Radio City,** C. Sta. Teresa 19, along C. Caballeros past Bolseria, offers a relaxed bar and wild dance floor. (☎91 41 51; www.radiocityvalencia.com. Beer €3.50. Mixed drinks from €6. Flamenco Tu 11pm. Open daily 7:30pm-3:30am. Cash only.) For more info, consult the entertainment supplement *La Cartelera* (€0.50), or the free *24/7 Valencia*, available at hostels and cafes. The most famous festival in Valencia is **Las Fallas** (Mar. 12-19), in which hundreds of colossal papier-mâché puppets are paraded down the street and burned at the end of the week in celebration of spring. The nearby town of **Buñol** hosts the world's largest food fight (Aug. 27, 2008; see p. 888).

# NORTHERN SPAIN

Northern Spain encompasses the country's most fiercely regionalistic areas. From rocky Costa Brava to chic Barcelona, prosperous Catalonia *(Cataluña)* is graced with the nation's richest resources. However, Catalonia isn't the only reason to head northeast. The area is also home to the parties of the Balearic Islands, the coasts of the Basque Country, and the beauty of Galicia and the Pyrenees.

# BARCELONA                                       ☎93

Home to expats from the US, South America, and a host of other countries, Barcelona is a city in which there are no outsiders. In the 16 years since it hosted the Olympics, travelers have been drawn to its beaches, clubs, and first-rate restaurants. The city has a strong art scene, which continues the tradition of the whimsical and daring *Modernisme* architectural movement and Barcelonese painter Pablo Picasso. Barcelona is a gateway, not only to Catalan art and culture, but also to the Mediterranean and the Pyrenees.

## ◤ INTERCITY TRANSPORTATION

**Flights: Aeroport El Prat de Llobregat** (BCN; ☎902 40 47 04; www.aena.es and choose Airport: Barcelona from the dropdown on the left), 13km southwest of Barcelona. To get to Pl. Catalunya, take **RENFE train** L10 (20-25min., 2 per hr., €2.40) or the **Aerobus** (☎415 6020; 30min., 4-10 per hr., €4).

**Trains:** Barcelona has 2 main train stations. **Estació Barcelona-Sants,** in Pl. Països Catalans (M: Sants-Estació), is the main terminal for domestic and international traffic. **Estació de França,** on Av. Marquès de l'Argentera (M: Barceloneta), serves regional destinations and some international arrivals. RENFE (Spain ☎902 24 02 02, international 902 24 34 02; www.renfe.es) **trains** go to: **Bilbao** (9-10hr., 12:30 and 10pm, €38-50); **Madrid** (5-9hr., 10 per day, €37-66); **Seville** (10-12hr., 3 per day, €33-85); **Valencia** (3-5hr., 12-15 per day, €21-38). 20% discount on round-trip tickets.

**Buses:** Most buses arrive at the **Barcelona Nord Estació d'Autobusos,** C. Alí-bei 80 (☎902 26 06 06; www.barcelonanord.com). M: Arc de Triomf or #54 bus. Buses also depart from Estació Barcelona-Sants and the airport. **Sarfa** (☎902 30 20 25; www.sarfa.es) goes to **Cadaqués** (2½hr., 3 per day, €19). **Eurolines** (☎367 4400; www.eurolines.es) travels to **Paris, FRA** (15hr., M-Sa 8:30pm, €84) and **Naples, ITA** (24hr; M, W, F 5:30pm; €120). **ALSA/Enatcar** (☎902 42 22 42; www.alsa.es) goes to: **Alicante** (8-9hr., 11 per day, €37-42); **Madrid** (8hr., 3 per day, €26-34); **Seville** (14-16hr., 2 per day, €71-83); **Valencia** (4-5hr., 14 per day, €23-28).

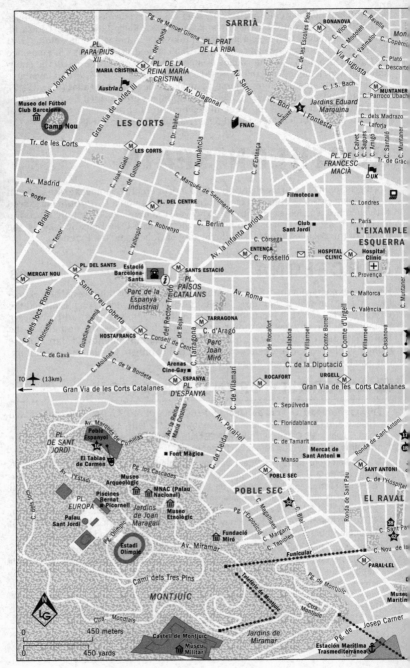

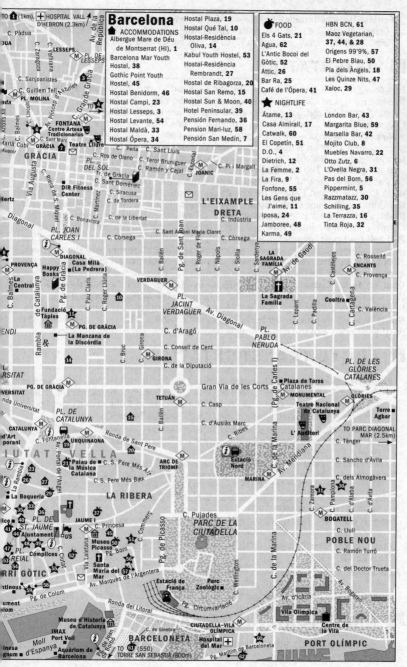

**Barcelona**

**ACCOMMODATIONS**
Albergue Mare de Déu
  de Montserrat (HI), 1
Barcelona Mar Youth
  Hostel, 38
Gothic Point Youth
  Hostel, 45
Hostal Benidorm, 46
Hostal Campi, 23
Hostal Lesseps, 3
Hostal Levante, 54
Hostal Maldà, 33
Hostal Ópera, 34

Hostal Plaza, 19
Hostal Qué Tal, 10
Hostal-Residència
  Oliva, 14
Kabul Youth Hostel, 53
Hostal-Residència
  Rembrandt, 27
Hostal de Ribagorza, 20
Hostal San Remo, 15
Hostal Sun & Moon, 40
Hotel Peninsular, 39
Pensión Fernando, 36
Pensión Mari-luz, 58
Pensión San Medín, 7

**FOOD**
Els 4 Gats, 21
Agua, 62
L'Antic Bocoi del
  Gòtic, 52
Attic, 26
Bar Ra, 25
Café de l'Ópera, 41

**NIGHTLIFE**
Átame, 13
Casa Almirall, 17
Catwalk, 60
El Copetín, 51
D.O., 4
Dietrich, 12
La Femme, 2
La Fira, 9
Fonfone, 55
Les Gens que
  J'aime, 11
iposa, 24
Jamboree, 48
Karma, 49

HBN BCN, 61
Maoz Vegetarian,
  37, 44, & 28
Origens 99'9%, 57
El Pebre Blau, 50
Pla dels Àngels, 18
Les Quinze Nits, 47
Xaloc, 29

London Bar, 43
Margarita Blue, 59
Marsella Bar, 42
Mojito Club, 8
Otto Zutz, 6
L'Ovella Negra, 31
Pas del Born, 56
Pippermint, 5
Razzmatazz, 30
Schilling, 35
La Terrazza, 16
Tinta Roja, 32

SPAIN

**Ferries: Trasmediterránea** (☎902 45 46 45; www.transmediterranea.es), in Terminal Drassanes, Moll Sant Bertran. Ferries go to **Ibiza** (5-9hr., 1 per day, €50), **Mahón** (3½-9hr., 1 per day, €50), and **Palma** (3½-7hr., 2-3 per day, €70).

# ⚜ ORIENTATION

Imagine yourself perched on Columbus's head at the **Monument a Colom** (on Passeig de Colom, along the shore), viewing the city with the sea at your back. From the harbor, the city slopes upward to the mountains. From the Monument a Colom, **La Rambla**, a pedestrian thoroughfare, runs from the harbor to **Plaça de Catalunya** (M: Catalunya), the city center. *Let's Go* uses "Las Ramblas" to refer to the general area and "La Rambla" in address listings. The **Ciutat Vella** (Old City) centers around Las Ramblas and includes the neighborhoods of Barri Gòtic, La Ribera, and El Raval. The **Barri Gòtic** is east of Las Ramblas, enclosed on the other side by **Vía Laietana.** East of V. Laietana lies the maze-like **La Ribera,** bordered by Parc de la Ciutadella and Estació de França. Beyond La Ribera—farther east, outside the Ciutat Vella—are **Poble Nou** and **Port Olímpic.** To the west of Las Ramblas is **El Raval.** Farther west rises **Montjuïc,** with sprawling gardens, museums, the 1992 Olympic grounds, and a fortress. Directly behind the Monument a Colom is the **Port Vell** (old port) development, where a wavy bridge leads across to the ultramodern shopping and entertainment complexes **Moll d'Espanya** and **Maremàgnum.** North of the Ciutat Vella is **l'Eixample,** a gridded neighborhood created during the expansion of the 1860s, which sprawls from Pl. Catalunya toward the mountains. **Gran Vía de les Corts Catalanes** defines its lower edge, and the **Passeig de Gràcia,** l'Eixample's main avenue, bisects the neighborhood. **Avinguda Diagonal** marks the border between l'Eixample and the **Zona Alta** (uptown), which includes **Pedralbes, Gràcia,** and other older neighborhoods in the foothills. The peak of **Tibidabo,** the northwest border of the city, offers the most comprehensive view of Barcelona.

# ▐ LOCAL TRANSPORTATION

**Public Transportation:** ☎010. Passes *(abonos)* work for the Metro, bus, urban lines of FGC commuter trains, RENFE *cercanías*, Trams, and Nitbus. A *sencillo* ticket (1 ride) costs €1.20. A **T-10 pass** (€6.90) is valid for 10 rides; a **T-Día pass** entitles you to unlimited bus and Metro travel for 1 day (€5.25) and the **T-mes** (€45) for 1 month.

**Metro:** ☎298 70 00; www.tmb.net. Vending machines and ticket windows sell passes. Hold on to your ticket until you exit or risk a €40 fine. Trains run M-Th 5am-midnight, F-Sa 5am-2am, Su and holidays 6am-midnight. €1.25.

**Ferrocarrils de la Generalitat de Catalunya (FGC):** ☎205 1515; www.fgc.es. Commuter trains to local destinations; main stations at Pl. de Catalunya and Pl. d'Espanya. After Tibidabo, rates increase by zone. Info office at the Pl. de Catalunya station open M-F 7am-9pm. €1.25.

**Buses:** Go just about anywhere, usually 5am-10pm. Most stops have maps posted. Buses run 4-6 per hr. in central locations. €1.25.

**Nitbus:** ☎901 511 151. 18 different lines run every 20-30min. 10:30pm-4:30am. Buses depart from Pl. de Catalunya, stop by most club complexes, and go through Ciutat Vella and Zona Alta.

**Taxis:** Try **RadioTaxi033** (☎303 3033; www.radiotaxi033.com; AmEx/MC/V) or **Servi-Taxi** (☎330 0300).

**Car Rental: Avis,** C. Corcega 293-295 (☎237 5680; www.avis.com). Also at airport (☎298 3600. Open M-Sa 7am-12:30am, Su 7am-midnight) and Estació Barcelona-Sants, Pl. dels Països Catalans. (☎330 4193. Open M-F 7:30am-10:30pm, Sa 8am-7pm, Su 9am-7pm.)

# ▐ PRACTICAL INFORMATION

**Tourist Offices:** ☎907 30 12 82; www.barcelonaturisme.com. In addition to several tourist offices, Barcelona has numerous mobile information kiosks.

**Aeroport El Prat de Llobregat,** terminals A and B (☎ 478 0565). Info and last-minute accommodation booking. Open daily 9am-9pm.

**Estació Barcelona-Sants,** Pl. Països Catalans. M: Sants-Estació. Info and last-minute accommodation booking. Open in summer daily 8am-8pm; winter M-F 8am-8pm, Sa-Su 8am-2pm.

**Oficina de Turisme de Catalunya,** Pg. de Gràcia 107 (☎ 238 4000; www.gencat.es/probert). M: Diagonal. Open M-Sa 10am-7pm, Su 10am-2pm.

**Plaça de Catalunya,** Pl. de Catalunya 17S. M: Catalunya. The biggest, best, and busiest tourist office. Free maps, brochures on sights and public transportation, booking service for last-minute accommodations, gift shop, currency exchange, and box office. Open daily 9am-9pm.

**Plaça de Sant Jaume,** C. Ciutat 2. M: Jaume I. Open M-F 9am-8pm, Sa 10am-8pm, Su and holidays 10am-2pm.

**Currency Exchange: ATMs** give the best rates; the next-best rates are available at banks. General banking hours are M-F 8:30am-2pm. Las Ramblas has many exchange stations open late, but the rates are not as good and a commission will be taken.

**Luggage Storage: Estació Barcelona-Sants.** €3-4.50 per day. Open daily 5:30am-11pm. **Estació de França.** €3 per day. Open daily 7am-10pm.

**Library: Biblioteca Sant Pau,** C. de l'Hospital 56 (☎ 302 0797). M: Liceu. Walk to the far end of the courtyard; the library is on the left. Do not confuse it with the Catalan library, which you'll see first and requires permission to enter. Free Internet. Open mid-Sept. to June M-Tu and F 3:30-8:30pm, W-Th and Sa 10am-2pm.

**Laundromat: Tintorería Ferrán,** C. Ferran 11 (☎ 301 8730). M: Liceu. Wash, dry, and fold €15. Open M-F 9am-2pm and 4-8pm. **Lavomatic,** Pl. Joaquim Xirau (☎ 268 4768). Wash €4.75, dry €0.85 per 5min. Both open M-Sa 9am-9pm

**Tourist Police:** La Rambla 43 (☎ 344 1300). M: Liceu. Multilingual officers. Open 24hr.

**Late-Night Pharmacy:** Rotates; check any pharmacy window for the nearest on duty.

**Medical Services: Medical Emergency:** ☎ 061. **Hospital Clínic i Provincal,** C. Villarroel 170 (☎ 227 5400). M: Hospital Clínic. Main entrance at the intersection of C. Roselló and C. Casanova.

**Internet Access:**

▨ **Easy Internet Café,** La Rambla 31 (☎ 301 7507). M: Liceu. Reasonable prices and over 200 terminals in a bright, modern center make this Internet heaven. Digital camera, CD burning, faxing, copying, and scanning services. €2.20 per hr., 1-day pass €7, 1-week €15, 1-month €30. Open daily 8am-2:30am. **Branch** at Ronda Universitat 35. M: Catalunya. €2 per hr., 1-day pass €3, 1-week €7, 1-month €15. Open daily 8am-2am.

**Navegaweb,** La Rambla 88-94 (☎ 317 9026). M: Liceu. Good rates on international calls. Internet €1.60 per hr. Open Su-Th 9am-midnight, F 9am-1am, Sa 9am-2am.

**Bcnet (Internet Gallery Café),** C. Barra de Ferro 3 (☎ 932 68 15 07.) M: Jaume I. €2.90 per hr.; 10hr. ticket €19. Open M-F 10am-11pm, Sa-Su noon-11pm.

**Post Office:** Pl. d'Antoni López (☎ 902 19 71 97). M: Jaume I or Barceloneta. Fax and **Lista de Correos.** Open M-F 8:30am-10pm, Su noon-10pm. **Postal Code:** 08003.

# ACCOMMODATIONS

While there are plenty of accommodations in Barcelona, finding an affordable room can be difficult. To crash in touristy **Barri Gòtic** or **Las Ramblas** during the busier months (June-Sept. and Dec.), make reservations weeks, even months, ahead. Consider staying outside the tourist hub of Ciutat Vella; there are many nice hostels in **l'Eixample** and **Gràcia** that tend to have more vacancies. Travelers should not assume that rooms have A/C, phone, or TV unless specified. A handful of campgrounds lie on the outskirts of the city, accessible by intercity buses (20-45min., €1.50). The **Associació de Càmpings i C.V. de Barcelona,** Gran Via de les Corts Catalanes 608 (☎ 412 5955; www.campingsbcn.com) has more info.

## LOWER BARRI GÒTIC

Backpackers flock to these hostels to be close to happening Las Ramblas.

■ **Hostal Levante,** Baixada de San Miquel 2 (☎317 9565; www.hostallevante.com). M: Liceu. This hostel has a TV lounge and large, tastefully decorated rooms with light wood furnishings and fans. Ask for a newly renovated room; some have balconies. 4- to 8-person apartments have kitchen, living room, and laundry machine. Singles €33-43; doubles €56-65; apartments €30 per person. MC/V. ❸

■ **Pensión Fernando,** C. Ferran 31 (☎301 7993; www.hfernando.com). M: Liceu. This clean hostel is conveniently located. Dorms with A/C and lockers. Common kitchen with dining room and TV on 3rd fl. Towels €2. Dorms €16-21; singles €30-36, with bath €40-45; doubles with bath €52-64; triples with bath €58-70. MC/V. ❷

**Hostal Benidorm,** La Rambla 37 (☎302 2054; www.hostalbenidorm.com). M: Drassanes or Liceu. One of the best values on La Rambla, with phone, bath, A/C, and balconies overlooking the street. Vending machines in lobby. Internet €1 per 15min. Singles €36; doubles €56; triples €76; quads €90; quints €105. MC/V. ❸

**Pensión Mari-luz,** C. del Palau 4 (☎317 3463; www.pensionmariluz.com), up 3 flights. M: Liceu or Jaume I. Recent renovations turned this hostel into a modern and sunny space around a historic courtyard. Free Wi-Fi. Dorms €20, with bath €21; singles €30/38, doubles €35/50, triples €42/63, quads €56-80/70-84. Hostel also offers nearby short-term apartments. MC/V. ❷

**Kabul Youth Hostel,** Pl. Reial 17 (☎318 5190; www.kabul.es). M: Liceu. Legendary among backpackers, this hostel squeezes in up to 200 travelers in rooms of 4-20. Lounge with pool table and terrace. Breakfast included. Laundry €2.50. Key deposit €15. Check-out 11am. Reservations only on website with credit card, especially during the summer. Dorms €18-24. MC/V. ❷

## UPPER BARRI GÒTIC

Between C. Fontanella and C. Ferran. Accommodations here are pricier but more serene than in the lower Barri Gòtic. Early reservations are essential in summer.

■ **Hostal-Residència Rembrandt,** C. de la Portaferrissa 23 (☎318 1011; www.hostalrembrandt.com). M: Liceu. This fantastic hostel has rooms superior to others in the area; all are unique, some with large bath, patio, sitting area, and TV. Restaurant-quality dining area for breakfast (€5). Fans available. Reception 9am-11pm. Reservations require credit card. Singles €28; doubles €45/55; triples €70-80. MC/V. ❸

■ **Hostal Maldà,** C. Pi 5 (☎317 3002). M: Liceu. Enter inside the shopping center. The friendly owner keeps this hostel's great, affordable rooms occupied. No reservations; claim your space 9-11am. Doubles €30; triples with shower €45. Cash only. ❸

**Hostal Plaza,** C. Fontanella 18 (☎301 0139; www.plazahostal.com). Cheery rooms decorated with colorful art, many with A/C. Free Internet and great location. Singles €45-50, with bath €60-70; doubles €40-55/60-75; triples €75-90. AmEx/MC/V. ❺

**Hostal Campi,** C. Canuda 4 (☎301 3545; www.hostalcampi.com). A centrally located bargain with good service. Most rooms have balconies. Prices vary, but generally singles €27; doubles €50, with bath €58; triples €69-78. MC/V. ❷

## LA RIBERA AND EL RAVAL

Be careful in the areas near the port and farther from Las Ramblas at night.

■ **Gothic Point Youth Hostel,** C. Vigatans 5 (☎268 7808; www.gothicpoint.com). M: Jaume I. Hostel offers colorfully painted lounge area with TV, rooftop terrace, weekly craft fair, and jungle-gym rooms with A/C. Breakfast included. Free Wi-Fi. Lockers €1.50 per day. Linens €2, towels €2. Refrigerator access. High season dorms €22; mid-season €19; low season €17. AmEx/MC/V; €2 fee. ❷

**Hotel Peninsular**, C. de Sant Pau 34 (☎302 3138; www.hotelpeninsular.net). M: Liceu. 80 beautiful rooms with phone and A/C around a 4-story interior courtyard. Breakfast included. Singles €30, with bath €52; doubles with bath €75. MC/V. ❸

**Barcelona Mar Youth Hostel**, C. de Sant Pau 80 (☎324 8530; www.barcelonamar.es). M: Parallel. This hostel squeezes 120 dorm-style beds into rooms with A/C. Breakfast included. Free Internet. All beds come with locker. Linens €2.50, towels €2.50, both €3.50. Self-serve laundry €4.50; laundry service available. Dorms in summer €22-23; in winter €16-19. Double beds Su-Tu €5, F-Sa €6.50 AmEx/MC/V. ❷

**Hostal de Ribagorza**, C. Trafalgar 39 (☎319 1968; www.hostalribagorza.com). M: Urquinaona. Stay in a *Modernisme* building complete with marble staircase and tile floors. TV and fan. Doubles €45-60; triples €60-70. Prices lower in winter. MC/V. ❸

**Hostal Ópera**, C. de Sant Pau 20 (☎318 8201; www.hostalopera.com). M: Liceu. Renovated rooms feel new; all have A/C, bath, and phone. Cafe downstairs. Free Internet. Singles €46; doubles €66. MC/V. ❹

## L'EIXAMPLE

Although L'Eixample may be far from the sights of Las Ramblas and the Barri Gòtic, it is home to Barcelona's most beautiful architecture. Accommodations here tend to be much nicer than those in Ciutat Vella.

**Hostal Residència Oliva**, Pg. de Gràcia 32, 4th fl. (☎488 0162; www.lasguias.com/hostaloliva). M: Pg. de Gràcia. Elegant wooden bureaus, mirrors, and a marble floor give this hostel a classy character. 5 of the 16 rooms look onto Pg. de Gràcia or neighboring streets, and all have high ceilings, TVs, and fans. Singles €36; doubles €60, with bath €75; triples with bath €84. Cash only. ❸

**Hostal Qué Tal**, C. Mallorca 290 (☎459 2366; www.quetalbarcelona.com), near C. Bruc. M: Pg. de Gràcia or Verdaguer. This high-quality gay- and lesbian-friendly hostel has one of the best interiors in the city, with murals, a plant-filled terrace, and snazzy decor in all 13 rooms. Singles €45; doubles €65, with bath €84. Cash only. ❹

**Hostal San Remo**, Ausiàs Marc 19 (☎302 1989; www.hostalsanremo.com). M: Urquinaona. 8 spacious rooms have TV, A/C, and windows; 4 have terraces. Free Internet. Reserve ahead. Singles €20, with bath €36; doubles €50/60; triples €60/72. Nov. and Jan.-Feb. reduced prices. MC/V. ❸

## ZONA ALTA: GRÀCIA AND OUTER BARRIS

Gràcia is Barcelona's "undiscovered" quarter, so last-minute arrivals may find vacancies here, even though options are few. The most visited part of Zona Alta is Gràcia, incorporated into Barcelona in 1897 despite the protests of many of its residents. Calls for Gràcian independence continue even today.

**Albergue Mare de Déu de Montserrat (HI)**, Pg. Mare de Déu del Coll 41-45 (☎210 5151; www.xanascat.net). M: Vallcarca. Take the 92 or 28 bus from the station, to the right when facing the mountain. Once home to a wealthy Catalan family, this palatial turn-of-the-century building is a dazzling alternative to hostels in the Ciutat Vella. Breakfast included. Max. stay 5 days. Dorms €20-24, under 25 €16-20. MC/V. ❷

**Hostal Lesseps**, C. Gran de Gràcia 239 (☎218 4434; www.hostallesseps.com). M: Lesseps. The 16 spacious rooms have TV and bath; 4 have A/C (€5 extra). Rooms facing the street are a bit noisy. Cats and dogs allowed. Free Internet access and Wi-Fi. Singles €45; doubles €75; triples €80; quads €90. MC/V. ❹

**Pensión San Medín**, C. Gran de Gràcia 125 (☎217 3068; www.sanmedin.com). M: Fontana. Embroidered curtains and ornate tiling adorn this family-run pension's 12 rooms, 4 with balcony and all with TV. Reception open 8am-midnight. Singles €32, with bath €42; doubles €62. MC/V. ❸

SPAIN

# ◘ FOOD

**Port Vell** and **Port Olímpic** are known for seafood. The restaurants on **Carrer Aragó** by Pg. de Gràcia have great lunchtime *menús*, and the **Passeig de Gràcia** has beautiful outdoor dining. Gràcia's **Plaça Sol** and La Ribera's **Santa Maria del Mar** are the best tapas (or cheap, laid-back dinner) spots. For fruit, cheese, and wine, head to ◙**La Boqueria (Mercat de Sant Josep)**, off La Rambla outside M: Liceu. (Open M-Sa 6am-8pm.) Buy groceries at **Champion**, La Rambla 13. (M: Liceu. Open M-Sa 9am-10pm.)

## BARRI GÒTIC

◙ **Les Quinze Nits,** Pl. Reial 6 (☎317 3075). M: Liceu. Popular restaurant with nightly lines halfway through the plaza; arrive early to have dinner in this beautiful setting. Catalan entrees at shockingly low prices. Pasta and rice €4-7. Fish €7-9. Meat €6-10. Open daily 1-3:45pm and 8:30-11:30pm. MC/V. ❶

◙ **L'Antic Bocoi del Gòtic,** Baixada de Viladecols 3 (☎310 5067). M: Jaume I. Bounded by an ancient Roman wall, this restaurant is tiny and romantic. Excellent salads (€6.50-7.50), exquisite pâtés (€9-12), and fine cheese platters (€11.50-16) feature *jamón iberico* (ham). Reserve early. Open M-Sa 8:30pm-midnight. AmEx/V. ❷

**Els 4 Gats,** C. Montsió 3 (☎302 4140; www.4gats.com). M: Catalunya. Picasso's old *Modernista* hangout with plenty of bohemian character. Cuisine includes Mediterranean salad (€9.50) and Iberian pork with apples (€18). Entrees €12-26. The M-F lunch *menú* (€12) is the best deal and comes with epic desserts; try the *crema catalana*. Live piano 9pm-1am. Open daily 1pm-1am. AmEx/MC/V. ❹

**Attic,** La Rambla 120 (☎302 4866; www.angrup.com). M: Liceu. This chic, modern restaurant has surprisingly reasonable prices for touristy La Rambla. Mediterranean fusion cuisine, including fish (€9-13), meat (€6-14), and rice (€6-9) dishes. Open daily 1-4:30pm and 7pm-midnight. AmEx/MC/V. ❸

**Maoz Vegetarian,** 3 locations: at C. Ferran 13; La Rambla 95; and C. Jaume I 7 (www.maozvegetarian.com). A vegetarian chain and city institution with only 1 menu option—falafel, with or without hummus—and an array of fresh vegetable toppings. Falafel €2.90-4.70. Open M-Th and Su 11am-2:30am, F-Sa 11am-3am. MC/V. ❶

**Café de l'Ópera,** La Rambla 74 (☎317 7585; www.cafeoperabcn.com). M: Liceu. This antique mirror-covered cafe was once a post-opera tradition of the bourgeoisie; now, it's beloved for its breakfast. The hot chocolate (€1.80) is as thick as a melted candy bar. *Churros* €1.30. Tapas €3-6. Salads €3-8. Open daily 8am. Cash only. ❶

**Xaloc,** C. de la Palla 13-17 (☎301 1990). M: Liceu. This large, classy delicatessen popular with locals features a many different meat and poultry sandwiches—hot and cold—on baguettes or Catalan bread (€4-12). Lunch *menú* €11. Open M-F 9am-midnight, Sa-Su 10am-midnight. AmEx/MC/V. ❷

## ELSEWHERE IN BARCELONA

◙ **Orígens 99'9%,** C. Enric Granados 9 (☎453 1120; www.origen99.com), C. Vidrieria 6-8 (☎310 7531), Pg. de Born 4 (☎295 6690), and C. Ramón y Cajal 12 (☎213 6031). Delectable entrees such as the beef-stuffed onion (€4.85) and the rabbit with almonds (€5) are made with 99.9% local ingredients. Small soups and vegetarian and meat dishes €5-6. Open 12:30pm-1am. AmEx/MC/V. ❶

◙ **Bar Ra,** Pl. de la Garduña (☎615 95 98 32; www.ratown.com). M: Liceu. Lots of vegetarian options. Enjoy creative cuisine like grilled tuna with avocado (€12) on the shady terrace with a view of La Boqueria. Entrees €9-15. Obligatory lunch *menú* €11. Dinner *menú* €12.50. Reservations required. Open daily 9:30am-1:30am. Kitchen open 1:30-4pm and 9:30pm-midnight. AmEx/MC/V. ❷

**HBN BCN,** C. Escar 1 (☎225 0263; www.habanabarcelona.com), right on Platja San Sebastián in Barceloneta, at the end of Pg. Joan de Borbó on the right. M: Barceloneta. Try the combined plate of Cuban tapas (plantains, yucca, avocado, shredded beef, rice, and beans; €8). Lunch *menú* €9. Dinner reservations recommended. Kitchen open 1pm-midnight. Th Salsa lessons; €30. MC/V. ❸

**Pla dels Àngels,** C. Ferlandina 23 (☎349 4047). M: Universitat. The decor of this inexpensive eatery is fitting for its proximity to the contemporary art museum. Healthy dishes, including a large vegetarian selection, are served on a terrace. Entrees €7-15. Open M-Sa 1:30-4pm and 9-11:30pm. MC/V. ❷

**Agua,** Pg. Marítim de la Barceloneta 30 (☎225 1272; www.grupotragaluz.com), the last building on the ocean side of Pg. Marítim before Barceloneta, near the giant copper fish. Enjoy seafood and rice dishes from the terrace on the beach. Vegetarian options. Entrees €7-16. Wheelchair-accessible. Open daily 1-3:45pm and 8-11:30pm, later on weekends. Reserve ahead. AmEx/MC/V. ❸

**El Pebre Blau,** C. Banys Vells 21 (☎319 1308). M: Jaume I. This *nouveau* gourmet restaurant serves dishes that fuse Mediterranean and Middle Eastern flavors. Salads €9-17. Reserve ahead. Kitchen open 9-11:30pm. MC/V. ❹

# ◉ SIGHTS

The **Ruta del Modernisme** pass is the cheapest and most flexible option for those with an interest in seeing Barcelona's major sights. Passes (free with the purchase of a €12 guidebook, €5 per additional adult, under 18 free) give holders a 25-30% discount on attractions including Palau de la Música Catalana, the Museu de Zoología, tours of Hospital de la Santa Creu i Sant Pau, and the facades of La Manzana de la Discòrdia. Purchase passes at the Pl. Catalunya tourist office or at the Modernisme Centre at Hospital Santa Creu i Sant Pau, C. Sant Antoni Maria Claret 167. (☎933 17 76 52; www.rutadelmodernisme.com.)

## LAS RAMBLAS

This pedestrian-only strip (roughly 1km long) is a cornucopia of street performers, fortune-tellers, human statues, pet and flower stands, and artists. The wide, tree-lined street, known in Catalan as *Les Rambles*, is actually six *ramblas* (promenades) that form one boulevard from the Pl. de Catalunya and the **Font de Canaletes**. According to legend, visitors who sample the water will return to Barcelona. Pass the **Mirador de Colom** on your way out to Rambla del Mar for a beautiful view of the Mediterranean.

**▧ GRAN TEATRE DEL LICEU.** After burning down for the second time in 1994, the Liceu was rebuilt and expanded; a tour of the building includes not just the original 1847 Sala de Espejos (Hall of Mirrors), but also the 1999 Foyer (a curvaceous bar/lecture hall/small theater). The five-level, 2292-seat theater is considered one of Europe's top stages, adorned with palatial ornamentation, gold facades, and sculptures. *(La Rambla 51-59, by C. Sant Pau. M: Liceu. ☎485 9913, tours 85 99 14; www.liceubarcelona.com. Box office open M-F 2-8:30pm, Sa 1hr. before show. 20min. guided visits daily 10am-1pm; €4. 1¼hr. tours 10am by reservation only, call 9am-2pm; €8.50.)*

**CENTRE D'ART DE SANTA MÓNICA.** One can only imagine what the nuns of this former convent would have thought of the edgy art installations that now rotate through this large modern gallery. *(La Rambla 7. M: Drassanes. ☎316 2810. Open Tu-Sa 11am-8pm, Su 11am-3pm. Free.)*

**LA BOQUERIA (MERCAT DE SANT JOSEP).** Just the place to pick up that hard-to-find animal part you've been looking for, La Boqueria is a traditional Catalan market located in a giant, all-steel *Modernista* structure. Specialized vendors sell produce, fish, and meat from a seemingly infinite number of independent stands. (*La Rambla 89. M: Liceu. Open M-Sa 6am-8pm.*)

**MONUMENT A COLOM.** Ruis i Taulet's monument to Columbus towers at the port end of Las Ramblas. Nineteenth-century *Renaixença* enthusiasts convinced themselves that Columbus was Catalan, but historians agree that he was Italian. Mysteriously, the explorer proudly points toward Libya, not the Americas. Take the elevator to the top for a stunning view. (*Portal de la Pau. M: Drassanes. Elevator runs daily June-Sept. 9am-8:30pm; Oct.-May 10am-6:30pm. €2.30, children and seniors €1.50.*)

**MUSEU DE L'ERÒTICA.** Barcelona's most intrepid tourists flock to this museum, which houses an odd assortment of pictures and figurines that span human history and depict seemingly impossible sexual acrobatics. (*La Rambla 96b. M: Liceu. ☎ 318 98 65; www.erotica-museum.com. Open 10am-10pm. €7.50, students €6.50.*)

**PALAU DE LA VIRREINA.** Once the residence of a Peruvian viceroy, this 18th-century palace houses the Institute of Culture and displays rotating contemporary photography, music, and graphic art exhibits. (*La Rambla 99. M: Liceu. ☎ 316 10 00. Open Tu-Sa 11am-8:30pm; Su 11am-3pm. Ground fl. free, exhibits from €3.*)

# BARRI GÒTIC

Brimming with cathedrals, palaces, and unabashed tourism, Barcelona's oldest zone masks its old age with unflagging energy. Today, the neighborhood is the political center of the city, with a split personality that is alternately quaint and overwhelming. Catalan commercialism persists in all its glory with store-lined streets and fine restaurants.

■ **MUSEU D'HISTÒRIA DE LA CIUTAT.** Buried some 20m below a seemingly innocuous old plaza lies one of the two components to the Museu d'Història de la Ciutat: the subterranean excavations of the Roman city of Barcino. This 4000-square-meter **archaeological exhibit** displays incredibly well-preserved 1st- to 6th-century ruins. Built on top of those 4th-century walls, the second part, **Palau Reial Major,** served as the residence of the Catalan-Aragonese monarchs. When restoration on the building began, the Gothic **Saló de Tinell** (Throne Room) was discovered; it is supposedly the place where Fernando and Isabel received Columbus after his journey to America. (*Pl. del Rei. M: Jaume I. ☎ 315 1111; www.museuhistoria.bcn.es. Wheelchair-accessible. Open June-Sept. Tu-Sa 10am-8pm, Su 10am-3pm; Oct.-May Tu-Sa 10am-2pm and 4-8pm, Su 10am-3pm. Palace €4, students €2.50. Archaeological exhibit €1.50/1. Combination ticket €4.50/3.50.*)

■ **ESGLÉSIA CATEDRAL DE LA SANTA CREU.** This cathedral is one of Barcelona's most recognizable monuments. The altar holds a cross designed by Frederic Marès in 1976 and beneath lies the Crypt of Santa Eulàlia. The museum in La Sala Capitular holds Bartolomé Bermejo's *Pietà*. (*M: Jaume I. In Pl. Seu, up C. Bisbe from Pl. St. Jaume. Cathedral open daily 8am-12:45pm and 5:15-7:30pm. Cloister open daily 9am-12:30pm and 5:15-7pm. Elevator to the roof open M-Sa 10:30am-6pm; €2. Choir area open M-F 9am-12:30pm and 5:15-7pm, Sa-Su 9am-12:30pm; €1. Guided tours daily 1-5pm; €4.*)

**PLAÇA DE SANT JAUME.** Pl. de Sant Jaume has been Barcelona's political center since Roman times. Two of Catalonia's most important buildings have dominated the square since 1823: the **Palau de la Generalitat,** headquarters of Catalonia's government, and the **Ajuntament,** or city hall. (*Generalitat open 2nd and 4th Su of the month 10:30am-1:30pm. Closed Aug. Mandatory tours in Catalan, English, and Spanish 2 per hr. starting at 10:30am. Free. Ajuntament open 2nd and 4th Su 10am-1:30pm. Free.*)

**PLAÇA REIAL.** This is the most crowded, happening *plaça* in the Barri Gòtic. Tourists and locals congregate here to eat and drink at night and to buy and sell at the Sunday morning flea market. Near the fountain in the center of the square are two street lamps designed by Antoni Gaudí. *(M: Liceu or Drassanes.)*

# LA RIBERA

This neighborhood has recently evolved into a bohemian nucleus, with art galleries, chic eateries, and exclusive bars. La Ribera's streets are even closer together than those in the Barri Gòtic, but the atmosphere is far less congested.

■ **PALAU DE LA MÚSICA CATALANA.** In 1891, the Orfeó Català Choir Society commissioned *Modernista* master Luis Domènech i Montaner to design this must-see concert venue. By day, the music hall is illuminated by tall stained-glass windows and an ornate stained-glass skylight, which gleam again after dark by electric light. Sculptures of wild horses and busts of the seven muses run on the walls flanking the stage. The **Sala de Luis Millet** has an up close view of the intricate "trencadis" pillars. *(C. Sant Francesc de Paula 2. ☎ 295 7200; www.palaumusica.org. M: Jaume I. Mandatory 50min. tours in English; 1 per hr. Open daily July-Sept. 10am-7pm, but call ahead for hours; Oct.-June 10am-3:30pm. €9, students and seniors €8, with Barcelona Card €6.40. Check the Guía del Ocio for concert listings. Concert tickets €6-330. MC/V.)*

■ **MUSEU PICASSO.** Barcelona's most-visited museum traces Picasso's artistic development with the world's most comprehensive collection of work from his formative Barcelona period. Picasso donated 1700 of the museum's 3600 works. *(C. Montcada 15-23. ☎ 319 6310; www.museupicasso.bcn.es. M: Jaume I. Open Tu-Su 10am-8pm. Last entrance 30min. before closing. €6, students and seniors €4, temporary exhibits €2.50/1. Under 16 and 1st Su of the month free.)*

**PARC DE LA CIUTADELLA.** Host of the 1888 World's Fair, the park harbors several museums, well-labeled horticulture, the Cascada fountains, a pond, and a zoo. The sprawling lawns are filled with strolling families, students smoking and playing instruments, and affectionate couples. Buildings of note include Domènech i Montaner's *Modernista* **Castell dels Tres Dracs** (now the **Museu de Zoología**) and and Josep Amergós's **Hivernacle**. The **Parc Zoològic** is home to several threatened and endangered species, including the Iberian wolf and the Sumatran tiger. *(M: Ciutadella or Marina. Park open daily 8am-9pm. Zoo open daily June-Sept. 10am-7pm; low season 10am-5pm. Park €15, children 3-12 €9, over 65 €8.)*

**MUSEU DE LA XOCOLATA (CHOCOLATE MUSEUM).** The museum presents gobs of information about the history, production, and ingestion of this sensuous sweet. Chocolate sculptures include La Sagrada Família and football star Ronaldo. The cafe offers tasting and baking workshops. *(Pl. Pons i Clerch, by C. Comerç. ☎ 268 7878; www.museudelaxocolata.com. M: Jaume I. Open M and W-Sa 10am-7pm, Su 10am-3pm. Workshops for kids from €6.50; reservations required. €4, students and seniors €3.50, under 7 free.)*

**ESGLÉSIA DE SANTA MARIA DEL MAR.** This 14th-century architectural wonder was built in only 55 years. The high ceiling's supporting columns are set 13m apart—farther than in any other medieval building in the world. *(Pl. Santa María, 1. M: Jaume I. Open M-Sa 9am-1:30pm and 4:30-8pm, Su 10am-1:30pm and 4:30-8pm. Free.)*

# EL RAVAL

Located next to La Rambla and the Barri Gòtic, the northern part of El Raval is a favorite among Barcelona's natives rather than its tourists. The southern portion of the area is home to many Indian and Middle Eastern immigrants. This diverse and mostly working-class neighborhood has a special charm, with quirky shops and eateries, welcoming bars, and hidden historical attractions. In the late 19th and early 20th centuries, overcrowding here led to an urban nightmare of rampant crime, prostitution, and drug use. Revitalization efforts, especially since the 1992 Olympic Games, have cleaned up the neighborhood.

■ **PALAU GÜELL.** Gaudí's 1886 Palau Güell, the Modernist residence built for patron Eusebi Güell, has one of Barcelona's most spectacular interiors. Güell spared no expense on this house, considered to be the first example of Gaudí's revolutionary style. The *palau* is closed for renovations until an undetermined date. (*C. Nou de La Rambla 3-5. M: Liceu. ☎317 3974. Mandatory tour every 15min. Open Mar.-Oct. M-Sa 10am-8pm, Su 10am-2pm; Nov.-Dec. M-Sa 10am-6pm. €3, students €1.50.*)

**MUSEU D'ART CONTEMPORANI (MACBA).** The MACBA has received worldwide acclaim for its focus on post-avant-garde art and contemporary works. Its main attractions are its innovative three-month rotating exhibitions and the "Nits MACBA," which keep the museum open until midnight—and let you in cheap. (*Pl. dels Àngels, 1. M: Catalunya. ☎412 0810; www.macba.es. Open M, W 11am-7:30pm, Th-F 11am-midnight, Sa 10am-8pm, Su 10am-3pm. English language tours M 6pm. €7.50, students €6, under 14 free; exhibits €4/3. W €3.50 for everything. Nits MACBA Th-F, €3 after 8pm.*)

**CENTRE DE CULTURA CONTEMPORÀNIA DE BARCELONA (CCCB).** The center stands out for its mixture of architectural styles, incorporating an early 20th-century theater with a 1994 sleek wing of black glass. CCCB has a bookstore, cafe, gallery space, and screening room. It's also the main daytime venue for the **Sonar Music Festival;** check the *Guía del Ocio* for scheduled events. (*Casa de Caritat. C. Montalegre, 5. M: Catalunya or Universitat. ☎306 4100; www.cccb.org. Open Tu-Su 11am-8pm. €6.60, students €4.40, under 16 and 1st W of the month free.*)

# L'EIXAMPLE

The Catalan Renaissance and Barcelona's 19th-century growth pushed the city past its medieval walls and into modernity. **Ildefons Cerdà** drew up a plan for a new neighborhood where people of all social classes could live side by side; however, l'Eixample (luh-SHOMP-luh) did not thrive as a utopian community but became a playground for the bourgeoisie. Despite gentrification, L'Eixample remains an innovative neighborhood full of *Modernista* oddities.

■ **LA SAGRADA FAMÍLIA.** Antoni Gaudí's masterpiece is far from finished, which makes La Sagrada Família the world's most visited construction site. Only 8 of the 18 planned towers have been completed and the church still lacks an "interior," yet millions of people make the touristic pilgrimage to witness its work-in-progress majesty. Of the three facades, only the **Nativity Facade** was finished under Gaudí. A new team of architects led by Jordi Bonet hopes to lay the last stone by 2026 (the 100th anniversary of Gaudí's death). The affiliated museum displays plans and computer models of the fully realized structure. (*C. Mallorca 401. ☎207 3031; www.sagradafamilia.org. M: Sagrada Família. Open daily Apr.-Sept. 9am-8pm; Oct.-Mar. 9am-5:45pm. Elevator open Apr.-Sept. 9am-7:45pm; Oct.-Mar. 9am-5:45pm. Entrance €8, with ISIC €5. Combined ticket with Casa-Museu Gaudí €9. Elevator €2. English-language tours in summer 11am, 1pm, 3pm, 5pm; winter 11am and 1pm. €3.*)

■ **LA MANZANA DE LA DISCÒRDIA.** A short walk from Pl. de Catalunya, the odd-numbered side of Pg. de Gràcia between C. Aragó and C. Consell de Cent has been leaving passersby scratching their heads for a century. The Spanish nickname, which translates to the "block of discord," comes from the stylistic clashing of its three most extravagant buildings. Sprouting flowers, stained glass, and legendary doorway sculptures adorn **Casa Lleó i Morera,** #35, by Domènech i Montaner, on the far left corner of the block. Two buildings down is

Puig i Cadafalch's geometric, Moorish-influenced facade makes **Casa Amatller,** #41, perhaps the most beautiful building on the block. The real discord comes next door at **Casa Batlló,** #43, popularly believed to represent Catalonia's patron Sant Jordi (St. Jordi) slaying a dragon. The chimney plays the lance, the scaly roof is the dragon's back, and the bony balconies are the remains of his victims. The house was built using shapes from nature, especially from the ocean—the balconies ripple like the ocean. (☎ 488 0666; www.casabatllo.es. Open daily 9am-8pm. €16.50, students €13.20. Call for group discounts. Free multilingual audio tour.)

**CASA MILÀ (LA PEDRERA).** From the outside, this Gaudí creation looks like the sea—the undulating walls seem like waves and the iron balconies are reminiscent of seaweed. Chimneys resembling armored soldiers have views of every corner of Barcelona. The entrance fee entitles visitors to tour one well-equipped apartment, the roof, and the winding brick attic, now functioning as the **Espai Gaudí,** a multimedia presentation of Gaudí's life and works. The summer concert series transforms the roof into a jazz cabaret on weekend nights. (Pg. de Gràcia 92. ☎ 902 40 09 73. Open daily in summer 9am-8pm, last admission 7:30pm, Nov.-Feb. 9am-6:30pm. €8, €4.50 students and seniors. Free audio tour. Concerts F-Sa last weekend of June through July, 9pm-midnight. €12, drink included. Tickets only through Tel Entrada.)

**HOSPITAL DE LA SANTA CREU I SANT PAU.** Designated a UNESCO monument in 1997, this is Europe's second-oldest functioning hospital and Domènech i Montaner's lifetime *Modernista* masterpiece. The entire complex covers nine l'Eixample blocks with whimsically decorated pavilions resembling gingerbread houses and Taj Mahals. (Sant Antoni M. Claret 167. ☎ 291 9000; www.santpau.es. M: Hospital de St. Pau, L5. Open 24hr. Guided tours 10:15am-1:15pm; €5. Info desk open daily 10am-2pm.)

**FUNDACIÓ ANTONI TÀPIES.** Less than 20 years old, this museum has a floor devoted to **Antoni Tàpies,** a Barcelonese sculptor and painter. But the real attractions are the rotating exhibitions on the two lower floors, which feature some of the world's best modern photography and video art as well as film screenings and lectures. In summer, DJ nights on the terrace have free drinks and after-hours gallery access. (C. Aragó 255. ☎ 487 0315. M: Pg. de Gràcia. Open Tu-Su 10am-8pm. Guided tours by arrangement only. €6, students and seniors €4. Temporary exhibitions Oct.-June.)

# MONTJUÏC

Historically, whoever controlled Montjuïc (mon-joo-EEK; "Hill of the Jews") controlled the city. Dozens of rulers have occupied and modified the **Castell de Montjuïc,** a fortress built atop an ancient Jewish cemetery. Franco made it one of his "interrogation" headquarters. Today, the area is a peaceful park by day and a debaucherous playground by night.

**FUNDACIÓ MIRÓ.** An large collection of sculptures, drawings, and paintings from Miró's career, ranging from sketches to wall-sized canvases, engages visitors with the work of this Barcelona-born artist. His best-known pieces here include *El Carnival de Arlequín, La Masia,* and *L'or de l'Azuz.* The gallery also displays experimental work by young artists and a few other famous contributors, including Alexander Calder. (☎ 443 9470; www.bcn.fjmiro.es. Funicular from M: Parallel or Park Montjuïc bus from Pl. Espanya. Open July-Sept. Tu-W and F-Sa 10am-8pm; Oct.-June Tu-W and F-Sa 10am-7pm; all year Th 10am-9:30pm, Su and holidays 10am-2:30pm. Last entry 15min. before closing. €7.50, students and seniors €5, under 14 free. Temporary exhibitions €4/3.)

**MUSEU NACIONAL D'ART DE CATALUNYA (PALAU NACIONAL).** Designed by Enric Català and Pedro Cendoya for the 1929 International Exposition, the beautiful Palau Nacional has housed the Museu Nacional d'Art de Catalunya (MNAC) since 1934. Its main hall is a public event space, while the wings are home to the world's finest collection of Catalan Romanesque art and a wide variety of Gothic pieces. Highlights include Miró's *Gorg Bleu* stained glass, a gallery of Romanesque cathedral apses, and works by Joaquím Mir, a modernist painter known for color-saturated landscapes. The museum recently acquired the entire holdings of the Museu d'Art Modern, formerly located in the Parc de la Ciutadella, and is now the principal art museum of Catalonia. The **Fonts Luminoses** and the central **Font Màgica** are lit up by weekend laser shows. (☎ 622 0376; www.mnac.es. *From M: Espanya, walk up Av. Reina María Cristina away from the twin brick towers. Open Tu-Sa 10am-7pm, Su and holidays 10am-2:30pm. Temporary exhibits €3-5; 2 temporary exhibits €6; all exhibits €8.50. 30% discount for students and seniors; under 14 and first Su of the month free. Audio tour included.*)

**CASTELL DE MONTJUÏC.** This historic fortress and its **Museu Militar** sit high on the hill, and from the scenic outlook, guests can enjoy a multitude of panoramic jaw-droppers and photo-ops. The *teleféric* (funicular) to and from the castle is usually half the fun. (☎ 329 8613. *From M: Parallel, take the funicular to Av. Miramar and then the cable car to the castle. Funicular open M-Sa 10am-9pm, low season 10am-7pm. €5.50, round-trip €7.50. Parc de Montjuïc bus runs up the slope from in front of the teleféric. Open daily 9am-10pm. Museum open Tu-Sa Mar.-Nov. 9:30am-8pm; Dec.-Feb. 9:30am-5pm. €3 for museum, fortress, Plaza de Armas, and outlook; €1 without museum.*)

# WATERFRONT

■ **MUSEU D'HISTÒRIA DE CATALUNYA.** The last gasp of the Old City before entering the tourist trap of Barceloneta, the Museu provides an exhaustive and patriotic introduction to Catalan history, politics, and culture. There is a particularly good section devoted to Franco. Recreations of a 1930s Spanish bar and an 8th-century Islamic prayer tent make the museum a full sensory experience. (*Pl. Pau Vila 3. Near the entrance to the Moll d'Espanya; to the left as you walk out toward Barceloneta.* ☎ 225 4700; mhc.cultura@gencat.net. *Open Tu and Th-Sa 10am-7pm, W 10am-8pm, Su 10am-2:30pm. €3; students €2.10, EU students free; under 7 and over 65 free.*)

**TORRE SAN SEBASTIÀ.** One of the best ways to view the city is from the cable cars spaning the Port Vell, which connect beachy Barceloneta with mountainous Montjuïc. The full ride, which takes about 10min. each way and makes an intermediate stop at the Jaume I Tower near Colom, gives a bird's-eye view of the city. (*Pg. Joan de Borbó. M: Barceloneta. In Port Vell, as you walk down Joan de Borbó and see the beaches to the left, stay right and look for the high tower. Open daily 11am-8pm. To Montjuïc one-way €9, round-trip €12.50; elevator to the top €4.*)

**L'AQUÀRIUM DE BARCELONA.** This kid-friendly aquarium features sharks, exhibits on marine creatures, and a cafeteria. Its highlight is a life-size model of a sperm whale. (*Moll d'Espanya. M: Drassanes or Barceloneta.* ☎ 221 7474; www.aquariumbcn.com. *Open daily July-Aug. 9:30am-10pm; Oct.-May 9:30am-9:30pm; June and Sept. 9:30am-9pm. €16, students with ISIC €14, under 12 and seniors €12.50. AmEx/MC/V.*)

**VILA OLÍMPICA.** The Vila Olímpica, beyond the east side of the zoo, was built to house 15,000 athletes and entertain millions of tourists for the 1992 Summer Olympics. It's home to several public parks, a shopping center, and offices. In nearby **Barceloneta,** beaches stretch out from the old port. (*M: Ciutadella or Vila Olímpica. Walk along the water on Ronda Litoral toward the 2 towers.*)

# ZONA ALTA

Zona Alta (Uptown) is the section of Barcelona that lies at the top of most maps: past l'Eixample, in and around the Collserola Mountains, and away from the low-lying waterfront districts. The most visited part of Zona Alta is Gràcia, incorporated into Barcelona in 1897 despite the protests of many of its residents. The area has always had a political streak, and calls for Gràcian independence crop up sporadically. Gràcia packs a surprising number of *Modernista* buildings and parks, international cuisine, and chic shops into a relatively small area.

**▨ PARC GÜELL.** This fantastical park was designed entirely by Gaudí but, in typical Gaudí fashion, was not completed until after his death. Gaudí intended Parc Güell to be a garden city, and its buildings and ceramic-mosaic stairways were designed to house the city's elite. However, only one house, now know as the **Casa-Museu Gaudí,** was built. Two staircases flank the park, leading to a towering *Modernista* pavilion originally designed as an open-air market but now occasionally used as a stage by street musicians. The longest park bench in the world, a multi-colored serpentine wonder made of tile shards, decorates the top of the pavilion. *(Bus #24 from Pl. Catalunya stops at the upper entrance. Park open daily 10am-dusk. Museum open daily Apr.-Sept. 10am-8pm; Oct.-Mar. 10am-6pm. Park free. Museum €4, with ISIC €3.)*

**MUSEU DEL FÚTBOL CLUB BARCELONA.** A close second to the Picasso Museum as Barcelona's most-visited museum, the FCB merits all the attention it gets from football fanatics. Fans will appreciate the storied history of the team. The high point is entering the stadium and taking in the 100,000-seat **Camp Nou.** *(Next to the stadium. ☎496 3608. M: Collblanc. Enter through access gate 7 or 9. Open M-Sa 10am-6:15pm, Su and holidays 10am-2pm. €7, students and seniors €5.60. Museum and tour €11/8.80.)*

# ♫ ENTERTAINMENT

For tips on entertainment, nightlife, and food, pick up the *Guía del Ocio* (www.guiadelociobcn.es; €1) at any newsstand. The best shopping in the city is in the **Barri Gòtic,** but if you feel like dropping some extra cash, check out the posh **Passeig de Gràcia** in l'Eixample. Grab face paint to join fans of **F.C. Barcelona (Barça)** at the Camp Nou stadium for **fútbol.** (Box office C. Arístedes Maillol 12-18. ☎902 18 99 00. Tickets €30-60.) **Barceloneta** and **Poble Nou** feature sand for topless tanning and many places to rent sailboats and water-sports equipment. Head up to Montjuïc to take advantage of the **Olympic Facilities,** which are now open for public use, including **Piscines Bernat Picornell,** a gorgeous pool complex. (Av. de l'Estadi 30-40. ☎423 4041. Open M-F 6:45am-midnight, Sa 7am-9pm, Su 6am-4pm.)

# ❀ FESTIVALS

Check sight and museum hours during festival times, as well as during the Christmas season and *Semana Santa* (Holy Week). The **Festa de Sant Jordi** (St. George; Apr. 23, 2008) celebrates Catalonia's patron saint with a feast. Men give women roses, and women give men books. In the last two weeks of August, city folk jam at Gràcia's **Festa Mayor;** lights blaze in *plaças* and music plays all night. The three-day **Sónar** music festival comes to town in mid-June, attracting renowned DJs and electronica enthusiasts from all over the world. Other major music festivals include **Summercase** (indie and pop) and **Jazzaldia.** Check www.mondosonoro.com or pick up the *Mondo Sonoro* festival guide for more info. In July and August, the **Grec Festival** hosts dance performances, concerts, and film screenings. The **Festa Nacional de Catalunya** (Sept. 11) brings traditional costumes and dancing. **Festa de Sant Joan** takes place the night of June 23; ceaseless fireworks will prevent any attempts to sleep. The largest celebration in Barcelona is the **Festa de Mercè,** the weeks before and after September 24. To honor the patron saint of the city, *Barceloneses* revel with fireworks, *sardana* dancing, and concerts.

#  NIGHTLIFE

Barcelona's wild, varied nightlife treads the line between slick and kitschy. In many ways, the city is clubbing heaven—things don't get going until late (don't bother showing up at a club before 1am), and they continue until dawn. Yet for every full-blown dance club, there are 100 more relaxed bars, from Irish pubs to absinthe dens. Check the *Guía del Ocio* (www.guiadelocio.com) for the address and phone number of that place your hip Barcelonese friend just told you about.

> **TIP** **DON'T FEAR FLYERS.** Many clubs hand out flyers, particularly in La Ribera. They are far from a tourist trap—travelers can save lots of money with free admission and drink passes.

## BARRI GÒTIC

Main streets such as C. Ferran have *cervecerías* and *bar-restaurantes* every five steps. C. Escudellers is the location for post-bar dancing, while Pl. Reial remains packed until the early morning. Las Ramblas, while lively, becomes a bit questionable late at night, as prostitutes emerge where families roamed in the daylight.

**Jamboree,** Pl. Reial 17 (☎319 1789; www.masimas.com). M: Liceu. A maze of stone arches and lights thumps with hip-hop; 2nd fl. plays 80s and 90s music. Cover M €3, Tu-Su €10; look for flyers with discounts. Drinks €8-10. Open daily 8pm-5am. Jazz 9-11pm, €3-10. Upstairs, **Tarantos** hosts flamenco shows (€5). Open M-Sa 8-11pm.

**Fonfone,** C. Escudellers 24 (☎317 1424; www.fonfone.com). M: Liceu or Drassanes. Trippy orange and red bubbles protruding from the wall combined with funky music draw crowds 1-3am. Different DJs nightly from around the world; check the website. Beer €3. Mixed drinks €6-8. Open daily 10pm-2:30 or 3am.

**Schilling,** C. Ferran 23 (☎317 6787). M: Liceu. One of the more laid-back and spacious wine bars in the area, with dim lighting and velvet seat cushions. Excellent sangria (pitcher €17). Wine €2-3, bottle from €13. Serves breakfast and sandwiches (€3-6) during the day. Though officially affiliated with neither group, Schilling often attracts British and gay crowds. Open M-W 10am-2:30am, Th-Sa 10am-3am, Su noon-3am.

**Karma,** Pl. Reial 10 (☎302 5680; www.karmadisco.com). M: Liceu. Quite a change from the dive upstairs and the airy terrace outside, this multicolored tunnel of a club, and its bar with a fountain view, keeps a Pl. Reial crowd dancing and drinking. Beer (€3) and mixed drinks (€4-6) are less expensive than at other clubs. Bar open Tu-Su 6pm-2:30am; club (cover €8-10) midnight-5am.

**Margarita Blue,** C. Josep Anselm Clavé 6 (☎317 7176; www.margaritablue.com). M: Drassanes. Popular with locals, this Mexican-themed bar draws an earlier dinner crowd and a later bar crowd with mojitos and Mexican food. Entrees €6-12. Margaritas €3.50. W and Su magic shows 11:30pm. W-Su DJ 10pm-1am. Open M-W and Su 7pm-2am, Th 7pm-2:30am, F-Sa 7pm-3am. AmEx/MC/V.

## LA RIBERA AND EL RAVAL

La Ribera has recently evolved into a hip, artsy district, attracting young locals and a few tourists in the know. The streets of El Raval hold a place for every variety of bar-hopper—Irish pubbers, American backpackers, absinthe aficionados, lounge lizards, and foosball maniacs will find themselves at home.

**El Copetín,** Pg. del Born 19. (607 2021 76) M: Jaume I. Cuban rhythm pervades this casual, dimly lit nightspot with a crowd of variable age. Copetín's headstart on many other bars (it's full before some places open) makes it a good place to start the night. Awe-inspiring mojitos €7. Open M-Th and Su 7pm-2:30am, F-Sa 7pm-3am. Cash only.

**Marsella Bar,** C. de Sant Pau 65. M: Liceu. Religious figurines grace the walls of Barcelona's oldest bar, first opened in 1820; perhaps they're praying for the *absenta* (absinthe; €3.30) drinkers. Beer €3.20. Mixed drinks €4-6. Open M-Sa 10pm-2am.

**Casa Almirall,** C. Joaquín Costa 33. M: Universitat. Cavernous space with weathered couches, dim lights, and equally laid-back clientele. It's house policy to stop you after your 3rd absinthe (€5-8), but the staff is fond of saying that you won't make it there anyway. Beer €2-4. Mixed drinks €5-7. Open M-Th and Su 5pm-2:30am, F-Sa 7pm-3am, Su 7pm-2am. Cash only.

**London Bar,** C. Nou de la Rambla 34 (☎318 5261). M: Liceu. Don't let the name fool you: this tavern is for locals and expats alike. Live music (usually rock or blues) nightly at 11:30pm. Beer, wine, and absinthe €2-3. Mixed drinks €6-7. Open Tu-Sa 8:30am-3:15am. AmEx/MC/V.

**iposa,** C. Floristes de la Rambla. With cheap beer (€1.60) and mixed drinks (€3-5), iposa (short for "butterfly") attracts a young international crowd. During the day, tea is served on the terrace. Open daily 1pm-3am. Cash only.

**Muebles Navarro (El Café que Pone),** C. la Riera Alta 4 (442 3966). Enjoy the mellow ambience and watch your friends get friendlier as they sink into the comfy couches. Beer and wine €2-3. Mixed drinks €5-6. Open Tu-Th 6pm-1am, F-Su 6pm-3am.

**Pas del Born,** C. Calders 8. M: Barceloneta or Jaume I. This bar's bright pink exterior is indicative of the stylish yet unpretentious clientele and interior decoration. Weekends find a couple of trapeze artists swinging, to music, through Pas's modest balcony. Open M-Th 7pm-2am, F-Sa 7pm-3am. Cash only.

## L'EIXAMPLE

Home to some of Europe's best gay nightlife, L'Eixample is dotted with upscale bars. Get to know the **NitBus** schedule or bring money for a taxi to return from far-flung clubs.

**Mojito Club,** C. Rosselló 217 (☎237 6528; www.mojitobcn.com). M: Diagonal. This club lures a fun-loving crowd with Latin beats. W free samba lessons 11pm; F-Sa salsa 11pm-1:30am; 10-week courses available. W Brazilian party with live salsa. Th and Su free drink with entry. F-Sa cover €10 cash after 2:30am; includes 1 drink. Open daily 11pm-4:30am. V.

**Dietrich,** C. Consell de Cent 255 (☎451 7707; www.dietrichcafe.com). M: Pg. de Gràcia. A caricature of a semi-nude Marlene Dietrich greets patrons at this inclusive gay bar. Beer €5. Mixed drinks €6-8. Nightly trapeze show 1:30am, drag shows some weekends. Open M-Sa 11pm-2:30am. MC/V.

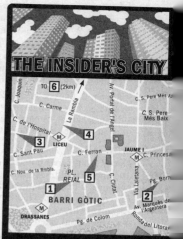

THE INSIDER'S CITY

## BARHOPPING IN BARÇA

To aid you on your late-night adventures, here are our favorite places to bar-hop in Barcelona:

**1** **Plaça Reial.** The center of the Barri Gòtic, you can begin your evening here with dinner and stay until the clubs get out the next morning.

**2** **Passeig del Born.** The Ribera's main drag is a relaxed good time from dusk to dawn. Every kind of bar draws a young crowd.

**3** **C. Gran de Gràcia.** From this short stretch in L'Eixample, turn off onto a sidestreet and enjoy the best dancing in Barcelona.

**4** **Rambla del Raval.** This neighborhood offers terraces and tea during the day and laid-back bars at night.

**5** **La Boqueria.** Once the pesky market crowd has gone home, you'll find colorful bars that serve elaborate mixed drinks.

**6** **C. Ferran.** This often gritty offshoot of La Rambla features Irish bars, late-night falafel, and everything in between.

**La Fira,** C. Provença 171 (☎ 650 85 53 84). M: Hospital Clínic or FGC: Provença. A hip crowd is surrounded by carousel swings, mirrors, and a fortune teller. F dance show and class 2, 3, 4am. Open W-Th 11pm-2:30am, F-Sa 11pm-5am. Cash only.

**Les Gents que J'aime,** C. València 286, downstairs (☎ 215 6879). M: Pg. de Gràcia. Background soul, funk, and jazz soothe patrons enjoying drinks like *Les Gents* (kiwi, lime, and pineapple juice) while lounging in the red velvet armchairs. Beer €3.50. Half-bottles of wine €12. Open daily 7pm-2:30am, F-Sa later.

**Átame,** C. Consell de Cent 257 (☎ 454 9273). M: Pg. de Gràcia. Next door to Dietrich, with an industrial gray interior, this bar is frequented mainly by gay men. It's not as scandalous as its name ("tie me up") might imply. Beer €3. Mixed drinks €4-6. Happy hour with free tapas Tu 7-10pm. Open daily 7pm-2:30am. Cash only.

## MONTJUÏC

Lower Montjuïc is home to **Poble Espanyol,** Av. Marqués de Comillas, a re-creation of famous buildings and sights from all regions of Spain. At night the complex becomes a disco theme park that offers the craziest clubbing experience in all of Barcelona. (☎ 508 6300; www.poble-espanyol.com. M: Espanya.) When Poble Espanyol closes, buses take the most serious party animals to "los afters"—clubs open 6am-7pm, such as the popular **Merci** and **Souvenir.**

■ **Tinta Roja,** C. Creus dels Molers 17 (☎ 443 3243; www.tintaroja.net), is the best combination bar and dance floor in the city. It often has tango music after midnight. Open Th 9pm-1:30am, F-Sa 9pm-2:30am, Su 7pm-midnight. Cash only.

**La Terrazza,** Avda. Marquès de Comillas, s/n (☎ 934 23 12 85). An outdoor madhouse and the undisputed king of Poble Espanyol nightlife. Cover €10; €3 with flyer. Open June-Oct. Th-Sa midnight-6am.

## WATERFRONT

Once mostly a wasteland of old factories and warehouses, **Poble Nou** and **Port Olímpic** today are home to docked sailboats, restaurants, and a long strip of nightclubs that draws crowds long into the night. The entire waterfront area, which stretches all the way from **Maremàgnum** to **Port Vell,** may be as hedonistic and touristy as Barcelona gets. Come nightfall, Maremàgnum, the city's biggest mall, turns into a tri-level maze of clubs packed with crowds even on weeknights. There is no cover; clubs make their money by charging exorbitant drink prices (beer €5; mixed drinks €8-10). Catching a cab home can be difficult.

**L'Ovella Negra (Megataverna del Poble Nou),** C. Zamora 78 (☎ 309 5938; www.ovellanegra.net). M: Bogatell or Marina. On the corner with C. Pallars. What was once a warehouse is now the place to come for the first few beers of the night. Large beers €2, 2L pitchers €8.50. Mixed drinks €4-5. Open Th 10pm-2:30am, F-Sa 5pm-3am, Su 7pm-1am. Kitchen open all night. Cash only.

**Razzmatazz,** C. Pamplona 88 and Almogàvers 122, around the corner (☎ 272 0910; www.salarazzmatazz.com). M: Marina. A huge warehouse houses 5 clubs: Pop, The Loft, Razz Club, Lo*Li*Ta, and Rex Room, each with its own live music specialty. Concert prices vary; call ahead or check website. Beer €3.50. Mixed drinks €7. Cover €12-15; includes access to all 5 clubs. Open F-Sa and holidays 1-5am. AmEx/MC/V.

**Catwalk,** C. Ramón Trias Fargas 2-4 (☎ 224 0740). M: Port Olímpic. A sleek interior and a crowd dressed to the nines make this one of the hottest places in town. 1st fl. house music, 2nd fl. R&B. Cover €18. Open W-Su midnight-6am. MC/V.

## ZONA ALTA

The area around C. de Marià Cubí has great nightlife undiscovered by tourists. Take a taxi or the NitBus. For more accessible fun in Gràcia, head to **Plaça del Sol.**

■ **Otto Zutz,** C. Lincoln 15 (☎238 0722). FGC: Pl. Molina or M: Fontana. One of Barcelona's most famous clubs, with three dance floors. Beer €6. Mixed drinks €6-12. Cover €10-15, includes 1 drink. Open Tu-Sa midnight-6am. AmEx/MC/V.

**D.O.,** C. Verdi 36 (☎218 9673). Offers late-night tapas (€3-7). Extensive wine list. Mixed drinks €3-8. Open M and W-Sa 6pm-2am. Cash only.

**La Femme,** C. Plató 13 (☎201 6207), on the corner with Muntaner. FCG: Muntaner. Caters to lesbians of all ages. Beer €5. Mixed drinks €7. Open F 11pm-3am, Sa 11:30pm-last customer. Cash only.

**Pippermint,** C. Bori i Fontestà 20 (☎208 0000), has perhaps the largest drinks you'll ever see—6L *cuba libre* (€38) and 13L beer (€70). Normal-sized 1L drinks are available for tamer groups (€10-12). Open daily 4pm-last customer. MC/V.

## ⚑ LET'S GO TO BARCELONA: GIRONA ☎972

Girona (pop. 92,000) is home to the **Aeropuerto de Girona-Costa Brava (GRO;** ☎18 66 00), served by budget airline **Ryanair** (☎47 36 50; www.ryanair.com). While Girona is not without worthwhile sights—it was once the home of the *cabalistas de Girona*, who spread the teachings of Kabbalah (mystical Judaism) in the West—many tourists simply fly into GRO and head straight out to Barcelona or other cities. **Barcelona Bus** (☎902 36 15 50; www.barcelonabus.com) runs express shuttles from GRO to Barcelona (1¼hr., 23-28 per day, €11) and Figueres (1hr., 3-6 per day, €4-5). RENFE **trains** (☎902 24 02 02) run from Pl. de Espanya in Girona to Barcelona (1½hr., 25 per day, €6-7), Figueres (30-40min., 13 per day, €2.40-2.70), and Madrid (10½hr., 1 per day, €42).

Those interested in sightseeing should head to the *barrio antiguo*, across the **Riu Onyar** from the train station. The remnants of the Middle Ages Jewish community **El Call** are around the corner from the imposing Gothic **Cathedral de Girona.** Inside, the **Tresor Capitular** contains some of Girona's most valuable art. (☎21 44 26; www.lacatedraldegirona.com. Open daily Apr.-Oct. 10am-8pm; Nov.-Mar. 10am-7pm. Cathedral €1. *Tresor* and cloister €3, students and seniors €2, 7-16 €0.90, under 7 free.) A must for movie buffs, the ◨**Museu del Cinema,** C. Sèquia 1, chronicles the rise of cinema from the mid-17th to 20th centuries. (☎41 27 77; www.museudelcinema.org. Open May-Sept. Tu-Su 10am-8pm; Oct.-Apr. Tu-F 10am-6pm, Sa 10am-8pm, Su 11am-3pm. €4, students and seniors €2, under 16 free. AmEx/MC/V.)

Quality budget accommodations can be found in the *barrio antiguo.* Plain **Alberg de Joventut Cerverí de Girona (HI) ❶,** C. dels Ciutadans 9, is affordable and well-located. Sitting rooms have board games, ping-pong, TV, and videos. (☎21 80 03; www.xanascat.net. Breakfast included. Lockers available. Linens included. Wash €2, dry €1.50. Internet €1 per day. Reception 8:30am-2:30pm, 3:30-9:30pm, 10-11pm. Check-in 24hr. Dorms July-Sept. €24, under 25 €21; Oct.-June €20/17. €2 HI discount. AmEx/MC/V.) **Carrer Cort-Reial** is the best place to find good, cheap food, while cafes on **Plaza de la Independencia** offer outdoor seating. Pick up groceries at **Caprabo,** C. Sèquia 10, a block off Gran Via de Jaume I. (☎902 11 60 60. Open M-Sa July-Aug. 9am-9pm; Sept.-June 9am-2pm and 5-9pm. MC/V.) Girona's major nightlife destination in summer is **Las Carpas,** an outdoor circus of dance floors, bars, and lights in the middle of the Parc de la Devesa. (Drinks from €3. Open Apr.-Sept. 15 M-Th and Su 11pm-3:30am, F-Sa 11pm-4am.) The **tourist office,** Rbla. de la Libertat 1, is by Pont de Pedra on the old bank. (☎22 65 75; www.ajuntament.gi. Open M-Sa 8am-8pm, Su 9am-2pm.) **Postal Code:** 17007.

# ▶ DAYTRIPS FROM BARCELONA

## MONTSERRAT

*FGC trains (☎932 05 15 15) to Montserrat leave from M: Espanya, line R5, in Barcelona (1hr., 1 per hr., round-trip including cable car €13); get off at Montserrat-Aeri, not Olesa de Montserrat. From the base of the mountain, the Aeri cable car runs up to the monastery. (July-Aug. daily; 4 per hr. Schedules change frequently; call ☎938 77 77 01. €8, included in FGC fare.) Alternatively, take the FGC's Cremallera de Montserrat train. (☎902 31 20 20; www.cremalleradedmontserrat.com.) Purchase a combined R5 train plus Cremallera ticket instead of the cable car. (Cremallera €6.30, seniors €5.70, children €3.50; combo ticket, including train from Pl. Espanya, €13/12/11.) Get off at Monistrol de Montserrat and take the railway up (1-2 per hr.).*

A 1235m peak sharply protruding from the Río Llobregat Valley with a colorful blend of limestone, quartz, and slate, Montserrat's name appropriately translates to "Sawed Mountain." In the 9th century, a wandering mountaineer had a vision of the Virgin Mary here; as the story spread, pilgrims flocked to the mountain. In the 11th century, a **monastery** was founded to worship the Virgin. During the Catalan *Renaixença* (Renaissance) of the 19th century, politicians and artists turned to Montserrat as a source of Catalan legend and tradition. Under Franco, it became a center for political resistance. The site remains a major pilgrimage center. The monastery's ornate **basílica** is above Pl. Creu and looks onto Pl. Santa Noría. To the right of the main chapel, a route through side chapels leads to the 12th-century Romanesque **La Moreneta** (the black Virgin Mary), Montserrat's venerated icon. (Walkway open in summer M-F 8-10:30am and noon-6:30pm, Sa-Su 8-10:30am, noon-6:30pm, and 7:30-8:15pm; low season daily 8-10:30am and noon-6:30pm.) In Pl. Santa María, the small **Museu de Montserrat** exhibits a variety of art, from an Egyptian mummy to Dalí's *El Mariner* and Picasso's *Old Fisherman*. (Open daily June 26 to Sept. 15 10am-7pm; Sept. 16 to June 25 10am-5:45pm. €6.50, students and over 65 €5.50, 6-12 €3.50, under 8 free.) The steep **Santa Cova funicular** descends from Pl. Creu to paths that wind along the face of the mountain past religious sculptures, culminating at the ancient hermitage **Santa Cova**, where the Virgin Mary sighting took place. (Funicular 3 per hr. 10am-1pm and 2-5:30pm. Round-trip €2.60, students and over 65 €2.40, 3-14 €1.40. Santa Cova open Apr.-Oct. daily 10:30am-5:15pm; Nov.-Mar. M-F 11:30am-4:15pm, Sa-Su 10:30am-4:30pm.) Take the **St. Joan funicular** up the hill for truly inspirational views. (Apr.-Oct. daily; 3 per hr. 10am-6:40pm; Nov.-Mar. M-F 11am-5pm, Sa-Su 10am-5pm. Round-trip €6.10; combo ticket with the Sta. Cova funicular €7, students €6.20.) The dilapidated **St. Joan monastery** and **shrine** are only 20min. from the highest station. There are amazing views from the peak of **St. Jerónim.** The hike up is about 1½hr. from Pl. Creu or 1hr. from the terminus of the St. Joan funicular. The **info booth** in Pl. Creu provides free maps, schedules of religious services, and gives advice on mountain navigation. (☎938 77 77 77. Open Apr.-Sept. daily 9am-7:50pm; Oct.-Mar. M-F 9am-5:30pm, Sa-Su 9am-7pm.) **Postal Code:** 08199.

## THE COSTA BRAVA: FIGUERES AND CADAQUÉS

*From Figueres, trains (☎902 24 02 02) leave Pl. de l'Estació for Barcelona (2hr., 14-22 per day, €8-10) and Girona (30min., 14-22 per day, €3). Buses (☎972 67 33 54) run from Pl. de l'Estació to Barcelona (2¼hr., 2-5 per day, €15), Cadaqués (1hr., 6-7 per day, €4.30), and Girona (1hr., 2-5 per day, €4). Buses from Cadaqués go to Barcelona (2½hr., 3-5 per day, €19), Figueres (1hr., 3-7 per day, €4.30), and Girona (2hr., 1-2 per day, €8).*

The Costa Brava's jagged cliffs cut into the Mediterranean Sea from Barcelona to the France. Visitors here are demanding super-vacationers, which keeps the food world-class and the beaches pristine. In 1974, Salvador Dalí chose his native, beachless **Figueres** (pop. 35,000) as the site to build a museum to house his works, catapulting the city to international fame. His personal tribute is a Surrealist masterpiece, the second-most popular museum in Spain, and a prime example of ego run delightfully amok. The ■**Teatre-Museu Dalí** is at Pl. Gala i Salvador Dalí 5. From La Rambla, take C. Girona, which becomes C. Jonquera, and climb the steps to the left. The museum contains the artist's nightmarish landscapes and bizarre installations, as well as his tomb. (☎972 67 75 00; www.salvador-dali.org. Open daily Aug. 9am-7:15pm and 10pm-12:30am; July and Sept. 9am-7:45pm; Oct.-June Tu-Su 10:30am-5:45pm. Aug. €11, Sept.-July €10, students and seniors €7.) The **tourist office** is in Pl. Sol. (☎972 50 31 55; www.figueresciutat.com. Open July-Sept. M-Sa 8am-8pm, Su 10am-3pm; Apr.-June and Oct. M-F 8:30am-3pm and 4:30-8pm, Sa 9:30am-1:30pm and 3:30-6:30pm; Nov.-Mar. M-F 8am-3pm.) **Postal Code:** 17600.

The whitewashed houses and small bay of **Cadaqués** (pop. 2900) have attracted artists, writers, and musicians ever since Dalí built his summer home in nearby Port Lligat. Take C. Miranda away from the ocean and follow the signs to Port Lligat and the Casa de Dalí (20min.). Alternatively, take a trolley to Port Lligat (1hr., 6 per day, €7) from Pl. Frederic Rahola. ◙**Casa-Museu Salvador Dalí** was the home of Dalí and his wife until her death in 1982. Though two of Dalí's unfinished original paintings remain in the house, the wild decorations—including a lip-shaped sofa and a Pop-Art miniature Alhambra—are the best part. (☎972 25 10 15. Open mid-June to mid-Sept. daily 10:30am-9pm; mid-Sept. to Jan. and mid-Mar. to mid-June Tu-Su 10:30am-6pm. Tour required; make reservations 5 days ahead. €10; students, seniors, and children €8.) **Nightlife** centers on C. Miguel Rosset. With your back to the bus station, walk right along Av. Caritat Serinyana to get to Plaça Frederic Rahola. The **tourist office**, C. Cotxe 2, is to the right of the *plaça*, opposite the beach. (☎972 25 83 15. Open July-Aug. M-Sa 9am-2pm and 3-9pm, Su 10:30am-1pm; Sept.-June M-Sa 9am-2pm and 4-7pm.) **Postal Code:** 17488.

## THE COSTA DORADA: SITGES

*Cercanías trains (☎934 90 02 02) run from Barcelona to Sitges (30-40min., 2-4 per hr., €2.50). Mon Bus (☎938 93 70 60) runs late-night buses between Pg. de Villagranca in Sitges and Rbla. de Catalunya in Barcelona midnight-4am (€2.90).*

A gay nightlife mecca, Sitges makes a wild adventure any time of the day. The town's beaches, less crowded than neighboring ones, leave you plenty of space to tan. ◙**Calle Primer de Maig,** which runs directly from the beach and Pg. de la Ribera, and **Calle Marquès Montroig,** off C. de les Parellades, are the centers of Sitges nightlife. Bars and clubs welcoming a mixed crowd blast pop from 10pm to 3am. Beer generally costs €3, and mixed drinks €6. Find a crazy party at the "disco-beach" **Atlàntida,** in Platja les Coves (☎934 53 05 82; Th "foam party"), or at legendary **Pachá,** on Pg. de Sant Didac in nearby Vallpineda (☎938 94 22 98). Buses run all night on weekends to the two discos from C. Primer de Maig. Other popular night-spots are on **Calle Bonaire** and **Calle Sant Pau;** most are open only on weekends. Gay clubs include **Trailer,** C. Àngel Vidal 36 (☎600 55 94 40; cover €20-25; open daily June-Sept. 1-6am, Oct.-May Sa and holidays 1-6am; MC/V), which hosts infamous foam parties on Wednesdays and Sundays, and **Bar Perfil,** C. Espalter 7 (☎656 37 67 91; open daily 10:30pm-3am). For more info on nightlife, pick up *Sitges Daily, Guía del Ocio,* or *Gay Map Sitges* from the **tourist office,** C. Sinia Morera 1. (☎902 94 50 04; www.sitgestur.com. Open July-Sept. daily 9am-8pm; Oct.-June M-F 9am-2pm and 4-6:30pm.) **Postal Code:** 08870.

# THE PYRENEES

The dramatic mountain scenery, Romanesque architecture, and cultural diversity of Spain's Pyrenees mountain range draw numerous explorers, hikers, and skiers searching for outdoor adventure. The Pyrenees are best reached by car, as public transportation is as common as the area's endangered bears.

## VAL D'ARAN ☎973

Some of the most dazzling peaks of the Catalan Pyrenees cluster around the Val d'Aran, in the northwest corner of Catalonia, best known for its chic ski resorts. The Spanish royal family's favorite slopes are those of **Baquiera-Beret.** Nearby, Salardú's 13th-century **Església de Sant Andreu** houses beautifully restored 16th-century murals. For skiing info and reservations, contact the **Oficeria de Baquiera-Beret.** (☎63 90 00; www.baquiera.es. €39 for day pass.) The **Auberja Era Garona (HI) ❶**, Ctra. de Vielha, is a five-minute walk up the highway from Salardú towards Baquiera. The enormous Auberja has plenty of dorm rooms, and boasts a gigantic patio and a game room/*discoteca*. Front door locked at midnight, and only opened every hour on the hour. (☎64 52 71; www.eragarona.com. Breakfast included; lunch and dinner available for additional price. Private bath €3. Bike and ski rentals available. Linens €3. Laundry €3.70. Internet €3.50 per hr. Reception 8am-11:30pm. Dorms €20-24, under 25 €16-20. MC/V.)

The capital of the valley, **Vielha** (pop. 4,500) welcomes hikers and skiers and offers many services for the adventure-seeker. Several inexpensive *pensiones* cluster at the end of C. Reiau, off Pg. Libertat (which intersects Av. Casteiro at Pl. Sant Antoni). **Pensión Casa Vicenta ❷**, C. Reiau 3, is a good value with quiet rooms (several with skylights), private baths, and a comfy common area. (☎64 08 19; casavincenta@teleline.es. Closed parts of May, June, Oct.-Nov. Singles €20; doubles €27. Cash only.) **Eth Breç ❶**, Av. Castièro 5, beneath Hotel d'Aran along the main road, serves delicious pastries (€1-3), teas, and has free Internet access. (☎64 00 50. Open daily 8:30am-1:30pm and 4-8:30pm. MC/V.) Alsina Graells (☎27 14 70) runs **buses** from Vielha to Barcelona (6hr., 2-3 per day, €28-33). Consult the **tourist office,** C. Sarriulèra 10, for an updated schedule of buses within Val D'Aran. For a **taxi,** call ☎64 01 95. **Postal Code:** 25530.

## PARQUE NACIONAL DE ORDESA Y MONTE PERDIDO ☎974

Well-maintained trails cut across forests, escarpments, and snow-covered peaks in the Parque Nacional de Ordesa y Monte Perdido. The main trail, running up the **Río Arazas** to the foot of Monte Perdido with views of three spectacular waterfalls, is the most rewarding, albeit crowded, hike. Several companies offer expeditions and adventure sports. For more info, visit www.ordesa.net. Within the park, the only accommodation is ▓**Refugio Góriz,** a 5hr. hike on the main trail. With a stunning location right up against the highest peaks in the area, it is well worth the walk. (☎34 12 01, www.goriz.com. Basic kitchen available. Breakfast €4.80. Lunch or dinner €14. Reserve ahead. Dorms €12.) Another option is the quirky **Refugio L'Atalaya ❶**, C. Ruata 45, one block away from the bus stop in **Torla.** (☎48 60 22. Kitchen access. Open *Semana Santa*-Oct. Dorms €9 per person. Restaurant and bar open daily. MC/V.) Pick up food at **Supermercado Torla,** near the bus station. (☎48 61 63. Open daily 9am-2pm and 5-8:30pm. MC/V.)

To reach the park, travel to Torla and take the shuttle to Ordesa (July-Sept. 15min., 4 per hr., €2.40). In low season, drive to a parking lot, hike the 8km to the park entrance, or catch a Jeep **taxi** (☎630 41 89 18; €15). The same company also offers van tours for up to eight people. Alosa (☎48 00 45, www.alosa.es) runs **buses** from Jaca to Sabiñánigo (20min., 8 per day, €1.40), and all **trains** on the Zaragoza-Huesca-Jaca line stop at Sabiñánigo. From Sabiñánigo, buses run to Torla (55min., 2 per day, €2.80). The park **Visitors Center** is 1.8km beyond the park entrance and has campsite info. (Open daily Mar.-Dec. 9am-2pm and 4-7pm.) There is a small Visitors Center in Torla, across the street from the bus stop station. (☎48 64 72. Open July-Sept. M-F 8am-3pm, Sa-Su 9am-2pm and 4:30-7pm; Oct.-June M-F 8am-3pm.) **Postal Code:** 22376.

# JACA

☎974

Many centuries ago, the town of Jaca (pop. 14,000) served as a refuge for weary pilgrims crossing the Pyrenees on the **Camino de Santiago.** Today, it is traversed by those with both pious and vertical aspirations: it serves as a perfect base for excursions to the Pyrenees in summer and to the nearby ski resorts in winter. The western side of the city is dominated by the enormous, pentagonal **Ciudadela,** a military fortification from the 16th century complete with moat, arrow slits, and cannon. Jaca's hostels and *pensiones* cluster around C. Mayor and the cathedral. The funky █**La Casa del Arco ❷,** C. San Nicolás 7, provides imaginatively decorated rooms in an old stone house. Look for the yellow building off Pl. de Ripa, adjacent to Pl. de Biscos, just across the plaza from the bus station. (☎36 44 48. Breakfast €4. Reserve ahead. Singles €18-20; doubles with bath €50. Cash only.) *Bocadillos* (sandwiches) dominate the menus on **Avenida Primer Viernes de Mayo.** Locals fill the many cafes on **Plaza de la Catedral.** Find groceries at **Supermercado ALVI,** C. Correos 9. (Open M-Sa 9:30am-2pm and 5:30-8:30pm. V.) Alosa **buses** (☎902 21 07 00, www.alosa.es) run to Pamplona (2¼hr., 2 per day, €7). The **tourist office** is at Pl. de San Pedro 11-13. (☎36 00 98; www.jaca.es. Open July-Aug. M-Sa 9am-9pm, Su 9am-3pm; Sept.-June 9am-1:30pm and 4:30-7:30pm.) **Postal Code:** 22700.

# NAVARRA

From the unfathomable mayhem of Pamplona and the Running of the Bulls to the many hiking trails that wind up the peaks of the Pyrenees, there is seldom a dull moment in Navarra. Bordered by Basque Country and Aragón, the region is a mix of overlapping cultures and traditions.

# PAMPLONA (IRUÑA)

☎948

*El encierro, la Fiesta de San Fermín,* the Running of the Bulls, utter debauchery: call it what you will, the outrageous festival of the city's patron saint is the principal reason tourists come to Pamplona (pop. 200,000). Since the city's immortalization in Ernest Hemingway's *The Sun Also Rises,* hordes of travelers have flocked to Pamplona for a week each July to witness the daily *corridas* and ensuing chaos. The city's monuments, museums, and parks merit exploration as well.

> **!** Although Pamplona is usually safe, crime skyrockets during *San Fermín.* Beware of assaults and muggings and do not walk alone at night during the festival.

**▣◪ TRANSPORTATION AND PRACTICAL INFORMATION. Trains** (☎902 24 02 02) run from Estación RENFE, Av. de San Jorge, to Barcelona (6-8hr., 3 per day, from €33), Madrid (3¾hr., 4 per day, €50), and San Sebastián (1½hr., 2-3 per day, €19). **Buses** leave from the corner of C. Conde Oliveto and C. Yangüas y Miranda for Barcelona (6-8hr., 4 per day, €24), Bilbao (2hr., 5-6 per day, €13), and Madrid (5hr., 6-10 per day, €26). From Pl. del Castillo, take C. San Nicolás, turn right on C. San Miguel, and walk through Pl. San Francisco to reach the **tourist office,** C. Hilarión Eslava. (☎42 04 20; www.turismo.navarra.es. Open during *San Fermín* daily 8am-8pm; July-Aug. M-Sa 9am-8pm, Su 10am-2pm; Sept.-June M-Sa 10am-2pm and 4-7pm, Su 10am-2pm.) **Luggage storage** is at the Escuelas de San Francisco in Pl. San Francisco during *San Fermín.* (€2 per day. Open from July 4 at 8am to July 16 at 2pm.) The **biblioteca** has free **Internet.** (Open Sept.-June M-F 8:30am-8:45pm, Sa 8:30am-1:45pm, July-Aug. M-F 8:30am-2:45pm.) **Postal Code:** 31001.

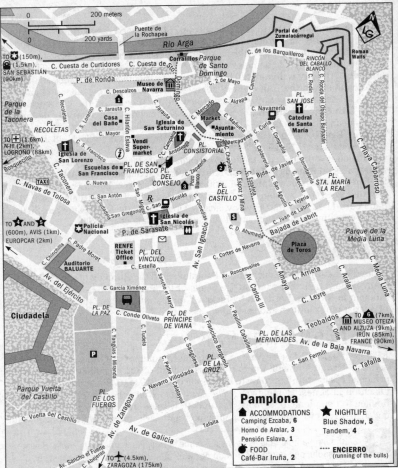

**Pamplona**

🛏 ACCOMMODATIONS
Camping Ezcaba, **6**
Horno de Aralar, **3**
Pensión Eslava, **1**

★ NIGHTLIFE
Blue Shadow, **5**
Tandem, **4**

🍴 FOOD
Café-Bar Iruña, **2**

---- ENCIERRO
(running of the bulls)

🛏🍴 **ACCOMMODATIONS AND FOOD.** Smart *San Ferministas* book their rooms up to a year ahead; without a reservation, it's nearly impossible to find a room. Expect to pay rates up to four times the normal price. Check the newspaper *Diario de Navarra* for *casas particulares* (private homes that rent rooms). Be aware, though, that some owners prefer Spanish guests. Many roomless backpackers are forced to fluff up their sweatshirts and sleep on Pl. de los Fueros, Pl. del Castillo, the lawns of the Ciudadela, along the banks of the river, or not at all. Be careful—stay in large groups, and if you can't store your backpack, sleep on top of it. During the rest of the year, finding a room in Pamplona is no problem. Budget accommodations line **Calle San Gregorio** and **Calle San Nicolás** off Pl. del Castillo. Deep within the *casco antiguo* (Old Town), **Pensión Eslava ❶**, C. Hilarión Eslava 13, 2nd fl., is quieter and less crowded than other *pensiones*. Older rooms have a balcony and shared bath. (☎22 15 58. Singles €10-15; doubles €20-30, during *San Fermín* €100. Cash only.) Small **Horno de Aralar ❸**, C. San Nicolás 12, above the restaurant, has five spotless rooms with bath and TV. (☎22 11 16. Singles €35; doubles €45; during *San Fermín* all rooms €200. MC/V.) To get to **Camping Ezcaba ❶**, 7km from the city in Eusa, take city bus line 4-V (4 per day, 26 per day during *San Fermín*) from Pl. de las Merindades. (☎33 03 15. €4.50 per person, €4.80 per tent, €4.30 per car. *San Fermín* €9 per person, €8 per tent. MC/V.)

Look for hearty *menús* at the cafe-bars above **Plaza de San Francisco** and around **Paseo de Ronda.** Thoroughfares **Calle Navarrería** and **Paseo de Sarasate** are home to good *bocadillo* bars. **Café-Bar Iruña ❸**, Pl. del Castillo, the former casino made famous in Hemingway's *The Sun Also Rises*, is notable for its storied past and elegant interior. The *menú* (€12) is required if eating at a table, but the restaurant serves drinks and sandwiches at the bar or terrace. (☎22 20 64. Open M-Th 8am-11pm, F 8am-2am, Sa 9am-2am, Su 9am-11pm. MC/V.) Get groceries at **Vendi Supermarket,** C. Hilarión Eslava and C. Mayor. (☎22 15 55. Open M-F 9am-2pm and 5:30-7:30pm, Sa 9am-2pm; *San Fermín* M-Sa 9am-2pm. MC/V.)

**◨◧ SIGHTS AND NIGHTLIFE.** Pamplona's rich architectural legacy is reason enough to visit during the 51 other weeks of the year. The restored 14th-century Gothic **Catedral de Santa María,** at the end of C. Navarrería is one of only four cathedrals of its kind in Europe. (☎22 29 90. Open M-F 10am-2pm and 4-7pm, Sa 10am-2pm. Free.) The walls of the pentagonal ◨**Ciudadela** enclose free art exhibits, various summer concerts, and an amazing *San Fermín* fireworks display. Follow Po. de Sarasate to its end and go right on C. Navas de Tolosa, then take the next left onto C. Chinchilla and follow it to its end. (☎22 82 37. Open M-Sa 7:30am-9:30pm, Su 9am-9:30pm. Closed for *San Fermín*. Free.)

Central **Plaza del Castillo,** with outdoor seating galore, is the heart of Pamplona's social scene. A young crowd parties in the *casco antiguo*, particularly along the bar-studded **Calle San Nicolás, Calle Jarauta,** and **Calle San Gregorio.** The small plaza **Travesía de Bayona,** 600m past the Ciudela on Av. del Ejército just off Av. de Bayona, has bars and *discotecas*. **Blue Shadow** (☎948 27 51 09) and **Tandem,** Tr. de Bayona 3 and 4, both have good dancing and big crowds. (Beer €3.50. Mixed drinks €6. Blue Shadow open Th-Sa 9pm-3:30am. Tandem open Th-Sa 6pm-6am.)

**▧FIESTA DE SAN FERMÍN (JULY 6-14, 2008).** Visitors overcrowd the city as it delivers an eight-day frenzy of bullfights, concerts, dancing, fireworks, parades, parties, and wine in what is perhaps Europe's premier party. Pamplonese, clad in white

The Chronicle

# IN RECENT NEWS

## SAN FERMÍN EXPOSED

A mass of flesh running through the streets of Pamplona may sound like old news, but for the past five years, the bare hides have not belonged only to the bulls. Since 2002, the international organization People for the Ethical Treatment of Animals, or PETA, has annually held the "Running of the Nudes," a clothes-free march through the streets of Pamplona to protest the treatment of the bulls throughout San Fermín.

Exactly 24hr. before the official San Fermín festivities start, the marchers gather near the lower corrals where the bulls are kept. Due to controversy, the authorities in Pamplona have permitted the mock run to proceed only under the condition that the marchers are not fully exposed. These are no meek tree-huggers, however; the participants have since made an art form of stripping down as much as possible.

Carrying anti-bullfighting signs in multiple languages and shouting slogans such as *"Fiesta Sí Corrida no!"* (Yes to the party! No to Bullfights!) or *"La cultura no es tortura"* (Culture isn't torture), the participants walk through the center of Pamplona, passing by masses of curious spectators. The march quickly becomes an all-out party in the spirit of the *fiesta*.

*Full video highlights, complete with a sexiest runner spotlight and details about PETA's campaign can be found at www.runningofthe nudes.com.*

**TIP**

**RUNNING SCARED.** So, you're going to run, and nobody's going to stop you. Because nobody—except the angry, angry bulls—wants to see you get seriously injured, here are a few words of *San Fermín* wisdom:

1. Research the *encierro* before you run; the tourist office has a pamphlet that outlines the route and offers tips for the inexperienced. Running the entire 850m course is highly inadvisable; it would mean 2-8min. of evading 6 bulls moving at 24kph (15mph). Instead, pick a 50m stretch.

2. Don't stay up all night drinking and carousing. Experienced runners get lots of sleep the night before and arrive at the course around 6:30am.

3. Take a fashion tip from the locals: wear the traditonal white-and-red outfit with closed-toe shoes. Ditch the baggy clothes, backpacks, and cameras.

4. Give up on getting near the bulls and concentrate on getting to the bullring in one piece. Though some whack the bulls with rolled newspapers, runners should never distract or touch the animals.

5. Never stop in doorways, alleys, or corners; you can be trapped and killed.

6. Run in a straight line; if you cut someone off, they can easily fall.

7. Be particularly wary of isolated bulls—they seek company in the crowds. In 2007, 13 runners were seriously injured by a bull who separated from the pack.

8. If you fall, stay down. Curl up into a fetal position, lock your hands behind your head, and do not get up until the clatter of hooves has passed.

with red sashes and bandanas, throw themselves into the merry-making, displaying obscene levels of both physical stamina and alcohol tolerance. *El encierro*, or "The Running of the Bulls," is the highlight of *San Fermines;* the first *encierro* takes place on July 7 at 8am and is repeated at 8am every day for the next seven days. Hundreds of bleary-eyed, hungover, hyper-adrenalized runners flee from large bulls as bystanders cheer from balconies, barricades, doorways, and windows. Both the bulls and the mob are dangerous; terrified runners react without concern for those around them. To participate in the bullring excitement without the risk of the *encierro*, onlookers should arrive at 6:45am. Tickets for the *grada* section of the ring are available at 7am in the bullring box office (July 7, 8 and 14 €5.50, July 9-13 €4.50). You can watch for free, but the free section is overcrowded, making it hard to see and breathe. To watch a **bullfight**, wait in the line that forms at the bullring around 7:30pm. As one fight ends, the next day's tickets go on sale. (Tickets from €10; check www.feriadeltoro.com for details.) Tickets are incredibly hard to get at face value, as over 90% belong to season holders. Once the running ends, insanity spills into the streets and builds until nightfall, when it explodes with singing in bars, dancing in alleyways, spontaneous parades, and a no-holds-barred party in **Plaza del Castillo.**

# BASQUE COUNTRY (PAÍS VASCO)

The varied landscape of Spain's Basque Country combines energetic cities, lush hills, industrial wastelands, and fishing villages. Many believe that the strongly nationalistic Basques are the native people of Iberia, as their culture and language cannot be traced to any known source.

## SAN SEBASTIÁN (DONOSTIA)                    ☎943

Glittering on the shores of the Cantabrian Sea, coolly elegant San Sebastián (pop. 185,000) is known for its world-famous bars, beaches, and scenery. Locals and

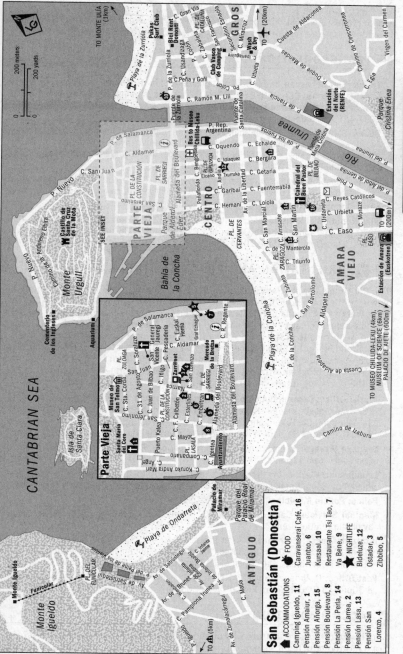

travelers consume *pintxos* (tapas) and drinks in the *parte vieja* (Old Town), which claims the most bars per square meter in the world. Residents and posters provide a constant reminder: you're not in Spain, you're in Basque Country.

## ■ TRANSPORTATION

**Trains:** San Sebastián has 2 train stations. **Estación de Amara** runs trains to **Bilbao** (2½hr., 1 per hr., €6). **RENFE** (☎902 24 02 02) sends trains from **Estación del Norte,** Po. de Francia, to **Barcelona** (8½hr., 1-2 per day, €37-47), **Madrid** (8hr., 2 per day, €37-48), and **Salamanca** (6½hr., 2 per day, €31).

**Buses:** San Sebastián has no actual bus station, only a platform and a series of ticket windows at Av. de Sancho el Sabio 31-33 and Po. de Vizcaya 16. Buses run to: **Barcelona** (7hr., 3 per day, €28); **Bilbao** (1¼hr., 1-2 per hr., €9); **Madrid** (6hr., 7-9 per day, €29); **Pamplona** (1hr., 6-10 per day, €6.20).

**Public Transportation:** Local **buses** (☎00 02 00). €1. Map and schedule available at tourist office. Bus #16 runs from Alameda del Boulevard to campground and beaches.

**Taxis: Donostia** (☎46 46 46) and **Vallina** (☎40 40 40).

**Bike Rental: Bici Rent Donosti,** Pte. de la Zurriola 22 (☎72 44 58). Bikes €12 per 4hr., €20 per day. Tandem bikes €6 per hr., €20 per 4hr., €36 per day. Open daily July-Sept. 10am-9pm; Oct.-June 10am-2pm and 4-8:30pm.

## ■ ⑦ ORIENTATION AND PRACTICAL INFORMATION

The **Río Urumea** splits San Sebastián down the middle, with the **parte vieja** (Old Town) to the east and **El Centro** (the new downtown) to the west, separated by the wide walkway **Alameda del Boulevard.** The city center, most monuments, and the popular beaches **Playa de la Concha** and **Playa de Ondarreta** also line the peninsula on the western side of the river. At the tip of the peninsula rises **Monte Urgull.** The **bus platform** is south of the city center on Pl. Pío XII. To get to the *parte vieja* from the train station, cross the Puente María Cristina and turn right at the fountain. Continue four blocks north to Av. de la Libertad, then turn left and follow it to the port; the *parte vieja* fans out to the right and Playa de la Concha sits to the left.

**Tourist Office: Centro Municipal de Atracción y Turismo,** C. Reina Regente 3 (☎48 11 66; www.sansebastianturismo.com), on the edge of the *parte vieja*. Open July-Aug. M-Sa 9am-8pm, Su 10am-2pm and 3:30-7pm; June 15-Aug. M-Sa 9am-8pm, Su 10am-2pm; Oct.-May M-Sa 9am-1:30pm and 3:30-7pm, Su 10am-2pm.

**Luggage Storage:** At Estación del Norte. €3 per day. Buy tokens at the ticket counter. Open daily 7am-11pm.

**Laundromat: Wash & Dry,** Iparragirre 6 (☎29 31 50), on the east side of the river, over Puente de Santa Catalina. €6 wash, €6 dry, €0.50 detergent. Open daily 8am-10pm.

**Police: Policia Municipal,** C. Easo 41 (☎092).

**Medical Services: Casa de Socorro,** C. Bengoetxea 4 (☎44 06 33). Services only available to EU citizens.

**Internet Access: Zarr@net,** C. San Lorenzo 6 (☎43 33 81). €2 per hr. Open M-Sa 10am-10pm, Su 4-10pm. **Biblioteca Central,** Pl. Ajuntamiento, facing the Casa Consistorial. Free; 45min. max. Open M-F 10am-8:30pm, Sa 10am-2pm and 4:30-8pm.

**Post Office:** C. Urdaneta (☎902 19 71 97), behind the cathedral. Open M-F 8:30am-8:30pm, Sa 9:30am-2pm. **Postal Code:** 20006.

## ■ ACCOMMODATIONS

Small *pensiones* are scattered throughout the streets of the noisy *parte vieja*. For a more restful night's sleep, look for hostels and *pensiones* on the outskirts of

El Centro. Backpackers scramble for rooms in July and August, particularly during *San Fermín* and *Semana Grande;* September's film festival is just as booked. Many *pensiones* don't take reservations in summer; come early in the day and be prepared to shop around. Single rooms are particularly hard to find.

**Pensión Amaiur,** C. 31 de Agosto 44, 2nd fl. (☎42 96 54; www.pensionamaiur.com). To the right of the Iglesia Santa María. English-speaking owner offers lovely rooms in an historic house. Internet €1 per 18min. Singles €24-42; doubles €35-60; triples €54-80; quads €65-95. 10% *Let's Go* discount. AmEx/MC/V. ❷

**Pensión San Lorenzo,** C. San Lorenzo 2 (☎42 55 16; www.pensionsanlorenzo.com), off C. San Juan. Sunny rooms with fridge and private bath. Internet €1.50 per hr.; free Wi-Fi. Singles available Oct.-May €20; doubles year-round €28-50. Cash only. ❷

**Pensión La Perla,** C. Loiola 10, 2nd fl. (☎42 81 23; www.pensionlaperla.com), on the pedestrian street in front of the cathedral. Balcony, private bath, and hardwood floors in each room. Singles €25-35; doubles €35-55. Cash only. ❸

**Pensión Boulevard,** Alameda del Boulevard 24, 2nd fl. (☎42 94 05; www.pensionboulevard.com). All rooms in this luxurious *pensión* have balcony, bath, mini-fridge, and TV. Doubles €45-75. Cash only. ❷

**Pensión Larrea,** C. Narrica, 21, 2nd fl. (☎342 2694; www.pensionlarrea.com). Every room has a small balcony. Microwave and fridge access. Internet €1 per 18min. July-Aug. singles €28; doubles €50; triples €70; Sept.-June €20/38/48. Cash only. ❸

**Pensión Añorga,** C. Easo, 12 (☎346 7945; www.pensionanorga.es). Quiet *pensión* for travelers in search of a peaceful night's sleep. Spacious, spotless rooms have wood floors and comfy beds. Some rooms have fridges. Free Wi-Fi. Singles €24-42; doubles with private bath €38-66. Cash only. ❹

**Pensión Lasa,** C. Bergara 15, 2nd fl. (☎42 30 52), 5-10min. walk from the beach and Old Town. With a high max. capacity, this *pensión* is a good option for backpackers without a reservation in high season. Big, plain rooms; most have terraces. Singles €37; doubles €48-53. MC/V. ❷

**Camping Igueldo** (☎321 4502; www.campingigueldo.com), 5km west of town atop Monte Igueldo. Bus #16 ("Barrio de Igueldo-Camping") runs between the site and Alameda del Boulevard (1 per hr. 7:30am-10pm, €1). Min. 5-night stay. *Parcelas* (spot for 2 people with room for car and tent) June 16-Sept. 15 and *Semana Santa* €28.20, Sept. 16-June 15 €19-25. €4.40 per person. Fully equipped family-size bungalows €60-85. Electricity €3.50. MC/V. ❷

## ❏ FOOD

*Pintxos* (tapas), washed down with the fizzy regional white wine *txakoli*, are a religion in San Sebastián. Find groceries at the **Mercado de la Bretxa,** in an underground shopping center. (Open M-Sa 8am-9pm.)

**Juantxo,** C. Esterlines (☎42 74 05). Selection of *bocadillos* (sandwiches; €3-3.50), *pintxos* (€1.20-2), and *raciones* (small dishes; €3-5). Excellent *filete* with onions, cheese, and peppers (€3). Open M-Th 9am-11:30pm, F-Su 9am-1:45am. Cash only. ❶

**Kursaal,** Po. de la Zurriola 1 (☎00 31 62; www.restaurantekursaal.com), across the river from the *parte vieja*. Treat yourself to a gourmet lunch on Kursaal's breezy patio. The chef is legendary. M-F lunch cafeteria *menú* from €19. Entrees €20-30. Open Sept.-July W-Sa 1:30-3:30pm and 8:30-10:30pm, Tu and Su 1:30-3:30pm; Aug. Tu-Sa 1:30-3:30pm and 8:30-10:30pm, Su 1:30-3:30pm. AmEx/MC/V. ❹

**Restaurante Tsi Tao,** Po. de Salamanca 1 (☎42 42 05; www.tsitao.com). This super-stylish restaurant serves filling Asian cuisine. Lunch *menú* €13. Try the green tea flan for dessert. Reserve ahead. Open daily 1-3:30pm and 8:30-11pm. AmEx/MC/V. ❸

**Caravanseraí Café,** Pl. del Buen Pastor (☎ 47 54 18), near the cathedral. Chic and artsy, without pretentious prices. Fabulous vegetarian appetizers and entrees (€4-10). Open M-Th 8am-midnight, Sa-Su 10:30am-11:30pm. AmEx/MC/V. ❷

**Va Bene,** Alameda del Boulevard 14 (☎ 42 24 16). Frequented by tourists and locals alike. The place to go for high-quality, low-price hamburgers and hot dogs served in the tradition of American diners. Burgers €2.80-4.80. Open daily 11am-1am. Cash only. ❶

## 👁 🏔 SIGHTS AND OUTDOOR ACTIVITIES

**▧ MUSEO CHILLIDA-LEKU.** The Museo Chillida-Leku houses a large collection of the works of Eduardo Chillida, San Sebastián's contemporary art guru. His stone and steel sculptures are spread throughout a peaceful, spacious outdoor garden. The 16th-century farmhouse, a spectacular construction of interlaced wood and arching stone, displays some of the artist's earliest works. (*Bo. Jauregui 66. 15min. from the city center. Autobuses Garayar, line G2, leave from C. Oquendo 2 per hr., €1.20. ☎ 33 60 06; www.museochillidaleku.com. Open July-Aug. M-Sa 10:30am-8pm, Su 10:30am-3pm; Sept.-June M, W-Su 10:30am-3pm. Walking tours and 45min. audio tours in 5 languages included in admission. €8, students and seniors €6.*)

**▧ MONTE IGUELDO.** Though the views from both of San Sebastián's mountains are spectacular, those from Monte Igueldo are superior. By night, **Isla de Santa Clara** seems to float in a halo of reflected moonlight. The sidewalk from the city ends just before the base of Monte Igueldo at Eduardo Chillida's sculpture *El Peine de los Vientos* (Comb of the Winds). The road leading to the top is a favorite local spot for romantic picnics at sunset. A **funicular** (€1.20, 4 per hr.) runs to the summit. (*☎ 21 02 11. Open July-Sept. daily 10am-10pm; Oct. and Jan.-May M-F 11am-6pm, Sa-Su 11am-8pm; Apr.-June M-F 11am-8pm, Sa 11am-10pm, Su 10am-10pm.*)

**MONTE URGULL.** Across the bay from Monte Igueldo, the gravel paths on Monte Urgull wind through shady woods and past stunning vistas. The **Castillo de Santa Cruz de la Mota,** atop the summit, has 12 cannons, a chapel, and a statue of the *Sagrado Corazón de Jesús* blessing the city. (*Several paths lead to the summit from Po. Nuevo; the official Subido al Castillo starts at the end of Pl. de Kaimingaintxo, past the Iglesia de Santa María toward Santa Clara. Castillo open daily 8am-1:30pm and 5-8pm. Free.*)

**PALACES.** Fancy buildings sprang up like wildflowers after Queen Isabel II began vacationing in San Sebastián in the mid-19th century. The **Palacio de Miramar** has passed through the hands of the Spanish court, Napoleon III, and Bismarck; it is now managed by the *Ayuntamiento* (local municipality), but you can stroll through the adjacent **Parque de Miramar.** The other royal residence, **Palacio de Aiete,** is also closed to the public, but its garden is not. (*Head up Cuesta de Aldapeta or take bus #19 or 31. Grounds open daily June-Sept. 8am-9pm, Oct.-May 8am-7pm. Free.*)

**BEACHES AND WATER SPORTS.** The gorgeous **Playa de la Concha** curves from the port to the **Pico del Loro,** the promontory home of the Palacio de Miramar. The flat beach disappears during high tide. Sunbathers crowd onto the smaller and steeper **Playa de Ondarreta,** beyond Palacio de Miramar, while surfers flock to **Playa de la Zurriola,** across the river from Monte Urgull. The Isla de Santa Clara, in the bay, is a good picnic spot. A motorboat ferry (*5min., 2 per hr., round-trip €3.30*) runs June through September from docks behind *Ayuntamiento.* Several companies offer sporting activities and lessons. **Pukas Surf Club,** Av. de la Zurriola 24, has surfing lessons and rentals. (*☎ 32 00 68. Fins €3 per hr. Surfboards €25 per day. Wetsuits €20 per 2 days. Lessons €37 per hr. Open M-Sa 9:30am-8pm. MC/V.*)

## 🎵 🎭 ENTERTAINMENT AND NIGHTLIFE

The *parte vieja* pulls out all the stops in the months of July and August, particularly on **Calle Fermín Calbetón**, three blocks away from Alameda del Boulevard. During the year, when students outnumber backpackers, nightlife moves beyond the *parte vieja*. **Ostadar,** C. Fermín Calbetón 13, attracts locals and tourists with its cheap beer and hip decor. (☎42 62 78. Beer €2. Mixed drinks €5. Open daily 5pm-3am. Cash only.) **Zibbibo,** Pl. de Sarriegi 8, is perhaps San Sebastián's most popular dance club among young backpackers. (☎42 53 34. 2-pint Heineken €5. Happy hour daily 7-9pm and 10-11:30pm. Open M-W 4pm-2:30am, Th-Sa 4pm-3:30am. MC/V.) At **Bideluze,** Pl. Gipuzkoa 14, sip on coffee (€1.50) and enjoy the chill music while lounging in plush red chairs. (☎42 28 80. *Bocadillos* €4-7. Open M-F 8am-1am, Sa 9am-2am, Su 11am-1am. Cash only.)

# BILBAO (BILBO)                    ☎944

Bilbao (pop. 354,000) is a city transformed. What was once a gritty industrial town is now a modern city with wide boulevards, grand buildings, expansive parks, and an efficient subway system. The shining Guggenheim Museum has been the most visible contribution to Bilbao's rise to international prominence, but there is more to Bilbao than its oddly shaped claim to fame.

📠 **TRANSPORTATION.** To reach the **airport (BIO;** ☎86 96 64), 25km from Bilbao, take the Bizkai bus (☎902 22 22 65) marked *Aeropuerto* from the Termibús terminal or Pl. Moyúa (line A-3247; 25min., 2 per hr., €1.10). RENFE **trains** (☎902 24 02 02) leave from Estación de Abando, Pl. Circular 2, for Barcelona (9-10hr., 2 per day, €38-49), Madrid (6hr., 2 per day, €37-42), and Salamanca (5hr., 2pm, €27). Trains run between Bilboa's Estación de Atxuri and San Sebastián (2¾hr., 17-18 per day). Most **bus** companies leave from Termibús, C. Gurtubay 1 (☎39 52 05; M: San Mamés), for: Barcelona (7¼hr., 4 per day, €39); Madrid (4-5hr., 10-18 per day, €25); Pamplona (2hr., 4-6 per day, €12); San Sebastián (1¼hr., 1-2 per hr., €8.70).

📑 🚻 **ORIENTATION AND PRACTICAL INFORMATION.** The **Ría de Bilbao** runs through the city and separates the historic **casco viejo** from the newer parts of town. The train stations are directly across the river from the *casco viejo* on the west bank. The city's major thoroughfare, **Gran Vía de Don Diego López de Haro** connects three of Bilbao's main plazas. Heading east from Pl. de Sagrado Corazón, Gran Vía continues through the central Pl. Moyúa and ends at Pl. Circular. Past Pl. Circular, cross the Río de Bilbao on **Puente del Arenal** to arrive in **Plaza de Arriaga,** the entrance to the *casco viejo* and **Plaza Nueva.** The **tourist office** is at Pl. Ensanche 11. (☎79 57 60; www.bilbao.net/bilbaoturismo. Open M-F 9am-2pm and 4-7:30pm.) **Net House,** C. Villariás 6, has **Internet.** (☎23 71 53. €1.50 per 1st 30min., €0.05 per min. thereafter. Open daily 9am-11pm.) **Postal Code:** 48008.

🛏 🍴 **ACCOMMODATIONS AND FOOD. Plaza Arriaga** and **Calle Arenal** have many budget accommodations, while upscale hotels are in the new city off **Gran Vía.** Rates climb during *Semana Grande*. **Iturrienea Ostatua ❸,** C. Santa Maria 14 (☎16 15 00; www.iturrieneaostatua.com) is in the heart of the *casco viejo*. (All rooms with private bath and TV, some with balcony. Breakfast €8. Singles €50; doubles €60-66; triples €80. MC/V.) **Pensión Méndez ❷,** C. Sta. María 13, 4th fl., offers cheery rooms with spacious balconies. (☎16 03 64. Singles €25; doubles

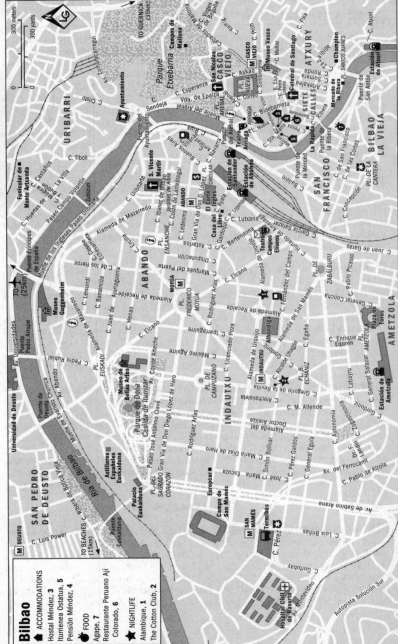

**Bilbao**

**♦ ACCOMMODATIONS**
Hostal Méndez, 3
Iturrienea Ostatua, 5
Pensión Méndez, 4

**● FOOD**
Agape, 6
Restaurante Peruano Ají
Colorado, 6

**★ NIGHTLIFE**
Alambique, 1
The Cotton Club, 2

€35; triples €50. MC/V.) **Hostal Méndez ❸,** on the first floor of the same building, is even more comfortable; rooms all have large windows, full bath, and TV. (☎ 16 03 64. Singles €40; doubles €50-55; triples €65-70. MC/V.) Restaurants and bars in the *casco viejo* offer a wide selection of local dishes, *pintxos* (tapas), and *bocadillos*. The new city has even more variety. **■Restaurante Peruano Ají Colorado ❸,** C. Barrenkale 5, specializes in traditional Andean *ceviche* (marinated raw fish; €10-13), and also serves Peruvian mountain dishes. (☎ 15 22 09. M-F lunch *menú* €12. Open Tu-Sa 1:30-4pm and 9-11pm, Su 1:30-4pm. MC/V.) **Agape ❷,** C. Hernani 13, has creative modern Spanish cuisine. During lunchtime, it fills with locals eager to try out the specials on the daily €9.50 *menú*. (☎ 16 05 06. Open W-Sa 1-4pm and 8-11pm, Tu 1-4pm. MC/V.) **Mercado de la Ribera,** on the riverbank by C. Pelota, is the biggest indoor market in Spain. (Open M-Th and Sa 8am-2pm, F 8am-2:30pm and 4:30-7:30pm.) Pick up groceries at **Champion,** Pl. Santos Juanes, past Mercado de la Ribera. (Open M-Sa 9am-9:30pm. AmEx/MC/V.)

**⬛ SIGHTS.** Frank Gehry's **■Museo Guggenheim Bilbao,** Av. Abandoibarra 2, is awe-inspiring. Lauded in the international press with every superlative imaginable, it has catapulted Bilbao straight into cultural stardom. Sheathed in titanium, limestone, and fluid glass, the €95 million building is said to resemble either an iridescent fish or a blossoming flower. The dramatic, spacious interior features a towering atrium and a series of unconventional exhibition spaces. The museum hosts rotating exhibits drawn from the Guggenheim Foundation's often eccentric collection; don't be surprised if you are asked to take your shoes off, lie on the floor, or even sing throughout your visit. (☎ 35 90 80; www.guggenheim-bilbao.es. Wheelchair-accessible. Admission includes English-language guided tours Tu-Su 11am, 12:30, 4:30, 6:30pm; sign up 30min. before tour at the info desk. Open July-Aug. daily 10am-8pm; Sept.-June Tu-Su 10am-8pm. €13, students €7.50, under 12 free.) Although the **■Museo de Bellas Artes,** Pl. del Museo 2, can't boast the name recognition of the Guggenheim, it wins the favor of locals. Holding artistic riches behind an unassuming facade, the museum has an impressive collection of 12th- to 20th-century art, including excellent 15th- to 17th-century Flemish paintings, canvases by Basque artists, and works by Mary Cassatt, El Greco, Gauguin, Goya, and Velázquez. Take C. Elcano to Pl. del Museo or bus #10 from Pte. del Arenal. (☎ 39 60 60, guided tours 39 61 37. Open Tu-Sa 10am-8pm, Su 10am-2pm. €5, students and seniors €4, under 12 and W free.) The best view of Bilbao's landscape is from atop **Monte Artxanda,** between the *casco viejo* and the Guggenheim. (Funicular 3min.; 4 per hr. M-F, June-Sept. also Sa; €0.80. Wheelchair-accessible lift €0.30.)

**🎵🎭 ENTERTAINMENT AND NIGHTLIFE.** Bilbao has a thriving bar scene. In the *casco viejo*, locals spill out into the streets to sip their *txikitos* (chee-KEE-tos; small glasses of wine), especially on **Calle Barrenkale,** one of Bilbao's seven original streets. A young crowd fill **Calle Licenciado Poza** on the west side of town, especially between C. General Concha and Alameda de Recalde, where a covered alleyway connecting C. Licenciado Poza and Alameda de Urquijo teems with bars. Mellow **Alambique,** Alda. Urquijo 37, provides elegant seating and chance for conversation under chandeliers and photos of old Bilbao. (☎ 43 41 88. Beer €2-3. Open M-Th 8am-2am, F-Sa 8am-3am, Su 5pm-3am.) **The Cotton Club,** C. Gregorio de la Revilla 25 (entrance on C. Simón Bolívar around the corner from the metro stop), decorated with over 30,000 beer bottle caps and featuring over 100 whiskeys, draws a huge crowd on Friday and Saturday nights, while the rest of the week is a little more low-key. (☎ 10 49 51. Beer €3. Mixed drinks €6. Rum €6. Open M-Th 5pm-3:30am, F-Sa 5pm-6am, Su 6:30pm-3:30am.) The massive *fiesta* in honor of *Nuestra Señora de Begoña* (Our Lady of Begoña)—complete with bullfighting, concerts, fireworks, and theater—occurs during **Semana Grande** (Aug. 17-25, 2008). Pick up a *Bilbao Guide* from the tourist office for event listings.

## THE LOCAL STORY

### THE TRAGEDY OF GUERNICA

Billing itself today as a "City of Peace," Guernica was once the site of one of the most horrifying displays of absolute warfare. The historic Basque town was almost entirely wiped out on April 26, 1937, as bomb after bomb was dropped on the town for more than 3hr., until over 100,000 lb. of explosives had been unloaded on the battered buildings.

The bombardment was carried out at the behest of Generalissimo Francisco Franco by the German Condor Legion, eager to test out its new strategy of carpet-bombing civilian populations to achieve quick military victories. The Spanish leader-to-be wanted to make an example of Guernica and to nip any potential Basque uprising in the bud. While the town itself had no real strategic military significance, both Franco and the Germans had something to gain from the utterly demoralizing blow it delivered.

Survivors from that Monday, a market day, recall being chased in the fields and forced into their homes by machine-gun fire, only to have the buildings above them torn apart by the bombs moments later. One woman recalled fires burning in the town for three days after the bombardment. When it was all over, over three-quarters of the town had been destroyed, leaving only the Casa de Juntas (the Biscayan assembly chamber), the church of Santa Maria, and the symbolic oak tree of Guernica untouched. Hun-

**⚑ DAYTRIP FROM BILBAO: GUERNICA.**
Founded in 1366, Guernica (Gernika; pop. 16,000) long served as the ceremonial seat of the Basque Country. On April 26, 1937, at the behest of General Franco, the Nazi "Condor Legion" dropped 29,000kg of explosives on Guernica, obliterating 70% of the city in three hours. The atrocity, which killed nearly 2000 people, is immortalized in Pablo Picasso's masterpiece, **Guernica** (p. 851). The thought-provoking ▨**Guernica Peace Museum**, Pl. Foru 1, features a variety of multimedia exhibits. From the train station, walk two blocks up C. Adolfo Urioste and turn right on C. Artekalea. (☎946 27 02 13. Open July-Aug. Tu-Sa 10am-8pm, Su 10am-2pm; Sept.-June Tu-Sa 10am-2pm and 4-7pm, Su 10am-2pm. English-language tours noon and 5pm. €4, students and seniors €2.) ▨**El Árbol,** a 300-year-old oak trunk encased in stone columns, marks the former political center of the *País Vasco*. **Trains** (☎902 54 32 10; www.euskotren.es) head to Bilbao (45min., 1-2 per hr., €2.25). Bizkai Bus (☎902 22 22 65) runs frequent, convenient **buses** between Guernica and Bilbao's Estación Abando; buses leave from Hdo. Amezaga in front of the Bilbao RENFE station. (Lines A-3514 and A-3515; 45min., 2-4 per hr., €2.20.) To reach the **tourist office,** C. Artekale 8, from the train station, walk three blocks up C. Adolfo Urioste, turn right on C. Barrenkale, go left at the alleyway, and look for the signs. (☎946 25 58 92; www.gernika-lumo.net. Open July-Aug. M-Sa 10am-7pm, Su 10am-2pm; Sept.-June M-Sa 10am-2pm and 4-7pm, Su 10am-2pm.)

# GALICIA (GALIZA)

If, as the Galician saying goes, "rain is art," then there is no gallery more beautiful than the Northwest's misty skies. Often veiled in silvery drizzle, it is a province of fern-laden eucalyptus woods, slate-roofed fishing villages, and endless white beaches. Locals speak *Gallego*, a linguistic hybrid of Castilian and Portuguese.

## SANTIAGO DE COMPOSTELA          ☎981

Santiago (pop. 94,000) is a city of song; its plazas are filled with roving *guita* players and outdoor operas. However, as the terminus of the ancient **Camino de Santiago** (Way of St. James), Santiago is also a city of pilgrimage. Each of the four facades of Santiago's ▨**cathedral** is a masterpiece of a different era, with entrances opening to four different plazas: Inmaculada, Obradoiro, Praterías, and Quintana. The **Obradoiro** is considered one of the most beautiful squares

in the world. (☎58 35 48. Open daily 7am-9pm. Free.)
Entrance to the cathedral **museums** includes a visit to
the archaeology rooms, archives, chapter house,
cloister, library, relics, tapestry room, and treasury.
(☎58 11 55. Open June-Sept. M-Sa 10am-2pm and 4-
8pm, Su and holidays 10am-2pm; Oct.-May M-Sa
10am-1:30pm and 4-6:30pm, Su and holidays 10am-
1:30pm. €5, students €3.) The **Museo das Peregri-
nacións**, R. de San Miguel 4, details the history of the
Camino de Santiago. (☎58 15 58; www.mdperegrina-
cions.com. Open Tu-F 10am-8pm, Sa 10:30am-1:30pm
and 5-8pm, Su 10:30am-1:30pm. €2.40; children, students, and seniors €1.20; pilgrims free. Free during
special expositions and most of the summer.)

Nearly every street in the *ciudad vieja* (Old
Town) has at least one *pensión*. ◪**Hospedaje Ramos
❷**, R. da Raíña 18, 2nd fl., has well-lit rooms with
shining floors, noise proof windows, and private
baths. Reserve two weeks ahead in summer. (☎58 18
59. Singles €22; doubles €35. Cash only.) The sunny
rooms of **Hospedaje Fonseca ❶**, R. de Fonseca 1, 2nd
fl., are popular with students. (☎57 24 79. July-Aug.
singles €20; doubles €30. Sept. 16-June singles €15;
doubles €30; triples €45. Cash only.) Most restaurants are on R. do Vilar, R. do Franco, R. Nova, and R.
da Raíña. ◪**A Tulla ❷**, R. de Entrerúas 1, is a small
family restaurant serving fresh seafood, accessible
only through an alley between R. do Vilar and R.
Nova. The *menús* (€9-12) are a superb value. (☎58
08 89. Entrees €6.50-8.50. Open M-Sa 1-4pm and
8:30pm-midnight. MC/V.) Santiago's **mercado** (market) is located between Pl. San Felix and Convento
de Santo Agustín. (Open M-Sa 8am-2pm.) At night,
take R. Montero Ríos to the bars and clubs off **Praza
Roxa** to party with local students. ◪**Casa das Crechas**,
Vía Sacra 3, is a cavernous, witchcraft-themed drinking hole, renowned for live jazz and Galician folk
concerts. (☎56 07 51. Beer €2. Open daily in summer
noon-4am; winter 4pm-3am.)

**Trains** (☎902 24 02 02) run from R. do Hórreo to Bilbao (10¾hr., 1 per day, €41) via León (6½hr., €29)
and Madrid (8hr., 2 per day, €43-67). To reach the
city, take bus #6 to Pr. de Galicia or walk up the stairs
across the parking lot from the main entrance, bear
right onto R. do Hórreo, and continue uphill for
about 10min. **Buses** (☎54 24 16) run from R. de
Rodríguez to Madrid (8-9hr.; 4-6 per day; €39-56) and
San Sebastián (13½hr., 2 per day, €54-102) via Bilbao
(11¼hr., 2 per day, €45). To get to the Old Town from
the bus station, walk 20min. or take bus #5 or 10 to
Pr. de Galicia. The **tourist office** is at R. do Vilar 63.
(☎55 51 29; www.santiagoturismo.com. Multilingual

dreds had been killed in the attack
and many thousands more injured.
In just a few hours, Guernica had
been transformed into a smoldering
shell of its former self.

Guernica was rebuilt over the following five years, but it has remained
a symbol of the atrocities of warfare
and indiscriminate killing. Many pictures, sketches, and paintings have
attempted to capture this nightmarish
day. In a painting now at the Guernica Peace Museum (p. 924), Sofía
Gandarias women holding dead children underneath the words "*y del
cielo llovía sangre*" (and from the sky
rained blood). Picasso's famous masterpiece, Guernica, which now hangs
in Madrid's Reina Sofia (p. 851), captured the horror of that day, and
brought Guernica's tragedy lasting
widespread international recognition.
When asked by a German ambassa-
dor, "Did you do this?" Picasso
answered simply, "No, you did."

Today, however, Guernica is looking to move beyond its devastating
past and become a herald of peace
and reconciliation throughout the
world. In 1989, the town received a
public apology from the president of
Germany for his country's role in the
attack, and it has since adopted the
motto "*renunciar a olvidar, renunciar a la venganza*" (renounce for-
getfulness, renounce vengeance).
Once the setting for some of humanity's darkest moments, Guernica is
now looking to light the way for the
rest of the world.

staff. Open daily June-Sept. 9am-9pm; Oct.-May 9am-2pm and 4-7pm.) **Internet** is available at **CyberNova 50,** R. Nova 50. (☎57 51 88. €1.20 per hr. Open M-Sa 9am-midnight, Su 10am-midnight.) **Postal Code:** 15703.

# BALEARIC ISLANDS ☎971

While all of the *Islas Baleares* are famous for their beautiful beaches and landscapes, each island has its own character. Mallorca absorbs the bulk of moneyed, package-tour invaders, Ibiza has perhaps the best nightlife in Europe, and quieter Menorca offers tranquil white beaches, hidden coves, and Bronze Age megaliths.

## ▐ TRANSPORTATION

**Flying** is the easiest way to reach the islands. Students with an ISIC can often get discounts from **Iberia** (☎902 40 05 00; www.iberia.com), which flies to Ibiza and Palma de Mallorca from Barcelona (40min., €80) and Madrid (1hr., €50). **Air Europa** (☎902 40 15 01; www.air-europa.com), **Spanair** (☎902 92 91 91; www.spanair.com), and **Vueling** (☎902 33 39 33; www.vueling.com) offer budget flights to and between the islands (€20-50). Another option is a **charter flight,** which may include a week's stay in a hotel; some companies, called *mayoristas,* sell left-over spots on package-tour flights as "seat-only" (find them through travel agencies).

Ferries to the islands are less popular and take longer. **Trasmediterránea** (☎902 45 46 45; www.trasmediterranea.com) departs from Barcelona's Estació Marítima Moll and Valencia's Estació Marítima for Ibiza, Mallorca, and Menorca (€69-110). Fares between the islands run €28-82. **Buquebus** (☎902 41 42 42) has fast catamaran service between Barcelona and Palma de Mallorca (4hr., 2 per day, €11-150). The three major islands have extensive **bus** systems with fares ranging €1.20-7, though transportation comes to a halt on Sundays in most locations; check schedules. **Car** rental costs about €40 per day, **mopeds** €30, and **bikes** €6-15.

## ▐ MALLORCA

A favorite of Spain's royal family, Mallorca has long attracted the rich and famous. Lemon groves and olive trees adorn the jagged cliffs of the northern coast, while lazy beaches sink into calm bays to the east. The capital of the Balearics, **Palma** (pop. 375,000) is filled with Brits and Germans, but still retains genuine local flavor. In many of its cafes and traditional tapas bars, the native dialect of *mallorquí* is the only language heard. The tourist office distributes a list of over 40 nearby **beaches**. Popular choices are **El Arenal** (bus #15), 11km southeast of town toward the airport, **Cala Major** (bus #3) and **Illetes** (bus #3).

Budget accommodations are scarce and must be reserved weeks ahead. **Hostal Ritzi ❸**, C. Apuntadors 6, stands a block away from Pl. de la Reina. Located in the culinary heart of the *casco antiguo*, this hostel with old-fashioned rooms is flanked by the area's best bars and eateries. (☎71 46 10. Breakfast included. Laundry €7. Singles €30; doubles €45, with shower €48, with bath €52. Cash only.) Palma's many round-the-clock ethnic restaurants are paradise for those sick of tapas. Budget travelers head to the crooked streets between Pl. de la Reina and Pl. Llotja. Try the *frito mallorquín* (fried lamb liver with potato, peppers, and herbs) at ◪**Sa Premsa ❶**, Pl. Obispo, a cavernous restaurant that serves local cuisine. (☎72 35 29; www.cellersapremsa.com. ½-portions €3.70-6.40. Entrees €3.75-8.50. Open M-Sa noon-4pm and 7:30-11:30pm. MC/V.) **AProp**, on C. Felip Bauzá, sells groceries. (☎900 70 30 70. Open M-F 8:30am-8:30pm, Sa 9am-2pm.)

A law requiring downtown bars to close by 1am during the week and 3am on weekends has shifted the late-night action to the waterfront. ◪**The Soho**, Av. Argentina 5), is a hip bar that plays 80s hits, classic rock, and techno. (Beer €1-2.50. Open daily 8pm-2am. MC/V, min. €5.) Nearby, the swanky **Costa Galana**, Av. Argentina 45, mixes surfing videos with electronica. (Beer €1.80-2.50. Mixed drinks €5-6. Open M-Th and Su 8am-2am, F-Sa 8am-4am. MC/V.) For great live blues and jazz music, head to **Blues Ville Cafe Bar**, C. Ma d'es Moro 3. With rollicking music every night and no cover, this club packs in locals. (Beer €1-2. Mixed drinks €3-5. Open daily 10:30pm-4am. Cash only.) Palma's clubbers start their night in the *bares-musicales* lining the **Passeig Marítim/Avinguda Gabriel Roca** strip, then move on to the *discotecas* around 3am. **Tito's**, in a gorgeous Art Deco palace on Pg. Marítim, is the city's coolest club, sporting fountains, a glass elevator, a view of the water, and beautiful people. (Beer €3. Mixed drinks €5. Cover €15-18, includes 1 drink. Open daily 11pm-6:30am. MC/V.) The **tourist office** is in Pl. d'Espanya (bus #1; 15min. 3 per hr. €1.10). There is also a branch at Pg. del Born 27, in the bookshop at Casa Solleric. (☎22 59 00; www.a-palma.es. Open daily 9am-8pm.) **Postal Code:** 07003.

# ◪IBIZA

Nowhere on Earth are decadence, opulence, and hedonism celebrated as religiously as on the glamor-

## THE LOCAL STORY

### ROCKCREATION

Mallorca's terrain is a dramatic mosaic of azure coastline, smooth limestone, vaulting hillsides, and sharp cliffs. While sun-seeking tourists flock to the island's beaches during the summer, packs of gung-ho daredevils come in cooler seasons for an island adventure beyond the disco strips of Palma: a chance to conquer the world-famous rock climbing routes of Mallorca.

Mallorca's efficient bus routes and network of cliffsides make climbing an easy getaway. The island's climbing terrain includes more than 900 routes and over 20 crags. Difficulty ranges from grades 4 to 8c, accommodating everyone from family groups to intrepid individual climbers.

The eastern part of the island has the easiest routes. Many travelers looking for routes with a range of difficulty take to the vintage train to Soller, where many climbs and hikes are available.

One of the most popular climbing areas is Sa Gubia, a gorge with more routes and variation than anywhere else on the island. Cala Magraner is also a popular destination for climbers with children. Its beachside locale, caves, and long walls are well-suited for neophytes.

*For more information on rock climbing on Mallorca, check out www.rockandsun.com, www.mondaventura.com, or www.tramuntana-pursuits.com.*

## IBIZA'S FLOWER POWER

The hundreds of hippies that flocked to Ibiza in the 1960s and 70s brought with them free love, rock star groupies, and copious amounts of psychedelic drugs. To the shock of locals, the formerly tranquil island was suddenly invaded by droves of nudist peace-lovers.

Famous rock stars, including Mick Jagger and Jim Morrison, ran rampant in this bohemian playground during the 60s and 70s. Bob Dylan set up house in a windmill and Nico, frequent collaborator with The Velvet Underground, intently frequented the island's party scene and eventually died here. The island became notorious for its free-wheeling Saturday afternoon jam sessions, when famous rock 'n' rollers would indulge listeners with impromptu concerts while the free spirits in the audience passed joints and marinated in good vibes.

Ibiza still retains bohemian charm. Hippie markets selling organic produce and macramé trinkets dot the island, and John Lennon Street graces Ibiza's urban center. Bob Dylan's windmill, which later appeared on a Pink Floyd album cover, is now a popular pilgrimage for latter-day hippies. The 60s are over, but travelers can still "turn on, tune in, and drop out" on this island of peace, love, and rock 'n' roll.

ous island of Ibiza (pop. 84,000). A hippie enclave in the 1960s, Ibiza has entered a new age of debauchery and extravagance. Disco-goers, fashion gurus, movie stars, and party-hungry backpackers arrive to immerse themselves in the island's outrageous clubs and gorgeous beaches. Only one of Ibiza's beaches, **Figueretes,** is within walking distance of **Eivissa** (Ibiza City), but most, including bar-lined **Platja d'en Bossa,** are a bike or bus ride away. The best beach near the city is **Playa de ses Salinas,** where you can groove to the music of DJs warming up for club gigs. (Bus #11 runs to Salinas from Av. d'Isidor Macabich.)

Cheap *hostales* in town are rare, especially in summer; reserve well ahead. Rooms to rent in private homes (*casa de huéspedes;* look for the letters "CH" in doorways) are a much better deal, although they still run above €30. **CH La Peña ❷,** C. La Virgen 76, is nestled into a cobblestoned alley right off the port. This house offers great, clean rooms at low prices. (☎19 02 40. Open June-Sept. Singles €23; doubles €32; triples €48. MC/V.) **La Bodeguita Del Medio ❶,** C. St. Cruz 15, has outdoor tables ideal for consuming beer (€3) and plates of paella, *tortillas* (€6.40), and tapas. (☎39 92 90. Cash only.) The **Mercat Vell,** at the end of the bridge leading to D'alt Villa, sells meat and produce. (Open M-Sa 7am-7pm.)

The crowds return from the beaches by nightfall. The bar scene centers around **Carrer de Barcelona,** while **Carrer de la Verge** is the nexus of gay nightlife. The island's giant **discos** are world-famous—and outrageously expensive. Always be on the lookout for publicity flyers, which list the week or night's events and often double as a coupon for a discounts. Club promoters are everywhere, and they are good sources of information and deals. Don't be afraid to bargain—you might even score a free pass. The **Discobus** runs to major hot spots (leaves Eivissa from Av. d'Isidor Macabich; 1 per hr. 12:30-6:30am, €1.75). **Amnesia,** on the road to the city of San Antoni, has a phenomenal sound system and psychedelic lights. (☎19 80 41. W drag performances. Cover €20-50. Open daily midnight-8am.) World-famous **Pachá,** on Pg. Perimitral, is a 15min. walk or a 2min. cab ride from the port. (☎31 36 00; www.pacha.com. M "Release Yourself" night with up-and-coming DJs. Cover €45-60. Open daily midnight-7:30am.) Cap off your night in **Space,** on Platja d'en Bossa, which starts hopping around 8am, peaks mid-afternoon, and doesn't wind down until 5pm. (☎39 67 93; www.space-ibiza.es. Cover €30-60.) The **tourist office,** Pl. d'Antoni Riquer 2, is across from the Estació Marítima, with booths on Pg. Vara del Rey and at the airport. (☎30 19 00. Open June-Nov. M-F 9am-9pm, Sa 9:30am-7:30pm; Dec.-May M-F 8:30am-3pm, Sa 10:30am-1pm.) **Postal Code:** 07800.

# 🐟 MENORCA

Menorca's (pop. 75,000) fantastic 200km of coastline, rustic landscapes, and picturesque towns draw ecologists, photographers, and sun-worshippers. Atop a steep bluff, **Mahón** (Maó; pop. 21,000) is the gateway to the island. Although generally quiet during the day, the town becomes considerably more crowded when cruise ships stop in the harbor. The popular **beaches** outside Mahón are accessible by **bus.** Transportes Menorca buses leave from the bus station, up C. Vasallo at the far end of Pl. de s'Esplanada, for **Platges de Son Bou** (30min., 7 per day, €1.90), the island's largest beach, which spreads out into 4km of gorgeous but jam-packed sand on the southern shore. Autobuses Fornells **buses** leave Mahón for the breathtaking **Arenal d'en Castell** (30min., 2-5 per day, €1.90), while TMSA buses go to the heavily touristed **Cala'n Porter** (7 per day, €1.20). While there, don't miss the 🏝Covas d'en Xoroi, an amazing network of caves in the cliffs high above the sea. Naturally air-conditioned, the caves house several bars during the day (cover €3.50-9, includes 1 drink; open Apr.-Oct. daily 11am-11pm) and a crowded ambient disco at night. (☎37 72 36. Beer €3. Mixed drinks €5-8. Th foam parties. Cover €17-21. Open Apr.-Oct. daily 11pm-late.)

To get to the splashy rooms of **Posada Orsi ❷**, C. de la Infanta 19, from Pl. de s'Esplanada, take C. Moreres, which becomes C. Hannover; turn right at Pl. Constitució and follow C. Nou through Pl. Real. (☎36 47 51. Fans available on request. Singles €20-25; doubles €30-40, with shower €40-50. Cash only.) 🏝Elefant ❷, Moll. de Llevant 106, is a bohemian niche with sunset views and deliciously creative lunches. (☎676 89 24 23. Tapas €3.80-5. Entrees €8-14. Open M and W-Su noon-4pm and 7pm-midnight. Cash only.) The Mahón **tourist office,** Moll. de Llevant 2, at the port, also has a branch at the airport open 24hr. (☎35 59 52; www.e-menorca.org. Open M-F 8am-8:30pm, Sa 8am-1pm.) **Postal Code:** 07700.

# SWITZERLAND

## (SCHWEIZ, SUISSE, SVIZZERA)

While the stereotype of Switzerland as a country of bankers, choco-latiers, and watchmakers still holds partly true, an energetic youth culture and a growing adventure sports industry belies its staid repu-tation. The country's gorgeous lakes and formidable peaks entice out-door enthusiasts from around the globe. Mountains dominate three-fifths of the country: the Jura cover the northwest region, the Alps stretch across the lower half, and the eastern Rhaetian Alps border Austria. Only in Switzerland can you indulge in chocolate and in three cultures at once.

---

### ▶ DISCOVER SWITZERLAND: SUGGESTED ITINERARIES

**THREE DAYS.** Experience the great out-doors at **Interlaken** (1 day; p. 941). Head to **Luzern** (1 day; p. 951) for the perfect combination of city culture and natural splendor before jetting to interna-tional **Geneva** (1 day; p. 961).

**ONE WEEK.** Begin in **Luzern** (1 day), which will fulfill your visions of a charm-ing Swiss city. Then head to the capital, **Bern** (1 day; p. 937), before getting your adventure thrills in **Interlaken** (1 day). Get a taste of Italian Switzerland in **Locarno** (1 day; p. 970), then traverse northern Italy to reach **Zermatt** and the

**Matterhorn** (1 day; p. 959). End your trip in cosmopolitan **Geneva** (2 days).

**TWO WEEKS.** Start in **Geneva** (2 days), then check out **Lausanne** (1 day; p. 966) and **Montreux** (1 day; p. 967). Tackle the Matterhorn in **Zermatt** (1 day) and keep hiking above **Interlaken** (1 day). Bask in **Locarno's** sun (1 day), then explore the **Swiss National Park** (1 day; p. 958). Head to **Luzern** (1 day) and **Zürich** (2 days; p. 944). Unwind in tiny **Stein am Rhein** (1 day; p. 954) and visit the abbey of **St. Gallen** (1 day; p. 953). Return to civilization via the capital, **Bern** (1 day).

---

# LIFE AND TIMES

## HISTORY

**AGAINST THE EMPIRE (1032-1520).** Switzerland was a loose union of relatively united cantons as part of the **Holy Roman Empire** until 1032. But when Emperor **Rudolf of Hapsburg** tried to assert control over the region in the late 13th century, the Swiss rebelled. Three Alemanni communities (the Forest Cantons) signed an **Everlasting Alliance** in 1291, agreeing to defend each other from outside attack—which they did in a series of sporadic territorial struggles with the Habsburg empire over the next 350 years. The Swiss consider the alliance to be the begin-ning of the **Swiss Confederation.** However, the union of culturally distinct states made for uneasy cooperation. The **Swabian War** (1499-1500) against the empire brought the alliance virtual independence from the Habsburgs, but internal strug-gles over cultural and religious differences continued.

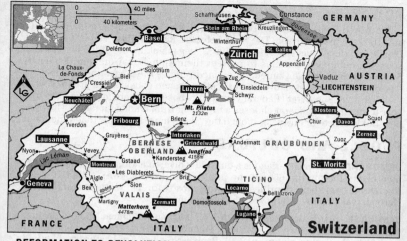

Switzerland

**REFORMATION TO REVOLUTION (1520-1800).** With no strong central government to settle religious quibbles among cantons, Switzerland was divided by the **Protestant Reformation.** Zürich's **Ulrich Zwingli** and Geneva's **John Calvin** instituted Protestant reforms, but the rural cantons remained loyal to the Catholic Church. When religious differences between the urban Protestant and the rural Catholic cantons escalated into full-fledged battle in the mid-16th century, the Confederation intervened, granting Protestants freedom but prohibiting them from imposing their faith on others. The Swiss remained neutral during the **Thirty Years' War,** escaping the devastation wrought on the rest of Europe. The **Peace of Westphalia,** which ended the war in 1648, officially granted the neutral Confederation independence from the Habsburg empire—which it had, at that point, been enjoying for 150 years. Swiss independence was fairly short-lived: **Napoleon Bonaparte** invaded in 1798 and established the **Helvetic Republic.** After Napoleon's defeat at Waterloo in 1815, Swiss neutrality was again officially recognized in the **Treaty of Vienna.**

**NEUTRALITY AND DIPLOMACY (1815-2002).** With neutrality established, Switzerland turned its attention to domestic issues. Industrial growth brought prosperity, but religious differences continued to fuel tension. A civil war broke out in 1847, lasting only 25 days. The Protestants were victorious, and the country wrote a new constitution modeled on that of the United States. Once it stabilized, Switzerland established a reputation for resolving international conflicts. The **Geneva Convention** of 1864 established international laws for conduct during war, and Geneva became the headquarters for the **International Red Cross** (p. 965).

The country's neutrality was tested in **World War I** when French- and German-speaking Switzerland claimed different cultural loyalties. In 1920, the Allies chose Geneva as the headquarters of the **League of Nations,** solidifying Switzerland's reputation as a center for international mediation. During World War II, both sides viewed Switzerland (and its banks) as neutral territory. As the rest of Europe cleared the rubble of two global wars, Switzerland nurtured its already robust economy: Zürich emerged as a banking and insurance center, while Geneva solidified its position as the world's diplomatic headquarters. Despite joining the United Nations in 2002, Switzerland remains isolationist, declining membership in the North Atlantic Treaty Organization and the European Union.

## TODAY

Since WWII, Switzerland has become increasingly wealthy and liberal, and is still fiercely independent. The Swiss elected **Ruth Dreifuss** as both their first female and first Jewish president in 1998. They maintain one of the world's most stringent ecological policies to protect their Alpine environment. Under the Swiss constitution, the Confederation incorporates the 26 cantons and its legislature, the Federal Assembly. The executive branch consists of a group of seven members, the **Bundesrat** (Federal Council), whose members are elected to four-year terms. The Bundesrat chooses a president from among its ranks. The president holds office for one year, though the post is more symbolic than functional.

## PEOPLE AND CULTURE

**DEMOGRAPHICS.** Switzerland is a culturally diverse nation, with people of German origin making up 65% of the population, French 18%, Italian 10%, and Romansch 1%. Other minorities, including mostly foreign workers from Eastern Europe, make up the other 6% of the population.

**LANGUAGE.** Switzerland has three official languages: **German,** spoken throughout central and eastern Switzerland; **French,** spoken in the west; and **Italian,** spoken in the Ticino region (p. 969). **Romansch,** a form of bastardized Latin, is used in the isolated valleys of Graubünden (p. 957). German speakers beware: *Schwyzerdütsch* (Swiss German) is unlike any other German or Austrian dialect and is nearly unintelligible to a speaker of *Hochdeutsch* (High German). If you want to pick it up, start with the basic practical terms that are nearly the same in all dialects, such as the days of the week. The Swiss will appreciate any effort you make to speak their language, so take a breath and practice saying *"Grüezi"* (hello). See **Phrasebook: French** (p. 1052), **Phrasebook: German** (p. 1054), **and Phrasebook: Italian** (p. 1055).

**CUSTOMS AND ETIQUETTE.** The Swiss are punctual and mind their manners. Say hello and goodbye to shopkeepers and proprietors of bars and cafés, and always shake hands when being introduced. At mealtimes, keep both hands above the table, but elbows off. In general, the Swiss cut soft food, including salads, potatoes and fruit, with a fork instead of a knife. When done, put the silverware in the lower right-hand corner of the plate, pointing towards the center. The Swiss consider chewing gum or cleaning your nails in public impolite.

## THE ARTS

### LITERATURE

**Jean-Jacques Rousseau,** born in Geneva in 1712, is today best known for his *Social Contract* (1762), which helped inspire the 1789 French Revolution. He was proud of his Swiss background, despite the fact that he spent most of his life in France and despite the burning of his books by offended Protestants in Geneva. **J. J. Bodmer** (1698-1783) and **J. J. Breitinger** (1701-1776) advocated writing literature in the Swiss-German language. **Conrad Ferdinand Meyer** (1825-1898) was an influential poet whose writings united Romanticism and Realism. **Carl Jung,** whose psychiatric practice in Zürich informed his famous *Psychology of the Unconscious* (1912), is considered to be the founder of analytical psychology. Switzerland has also produced several respected modern playwrights: critics laud **Max Frisch** for his exploration of the space between the narrator and the audience and his thoughtful treatment of Nazi Germany in works such as *Andorra* (1961). In the same year, **Friedrich Dürrenmatt** won renown for his tragicomic portrayal of human corruptibility in *The Physicists*.

## VISUAL ARTS

Switzerland has long been a prime center of artistic experimentation. **Paul Klee** (1879-1940), one of Switzerland's most famous painters, helped shape abstraction. In 1916, Zürich became the birthplace of the **Dada** movement, which rejected traditional aesthetic ideals and attempted to make people reconsider their social values. For a glimpse into Switzerland's lively modern art scene, visit Zürich's **Kunsthaus** (p. 949).

# HOLIDAYS AND FESTIVALS

**Holidays:** New Year's Day (Jan. 1); Epiphany (Jan. 6); Good Friday (Mar. 21); Easter (Mar. 23-24); Ascension (May 1); Labor Day (May 1); Pentecost (May 12); Whit Monday (May 13); Corpus Christi (May 22); Swiss National Day (Aug. 1); All Saints' Day (Nov. 1); Christmas (Dec. 25-26).

**Festivals:** Two raucous festivals are the *Fasnacht* (Feb. 11-13, 2008; www.fasnacht.ch.) in Basel and the *Escalade*, celebrating the invading Duke of Savoy's 1602 defeat by Geneva (Dec. 12-14, 2008; www.compagniede1602.ch/home_page.htm). Music festivals occur throughout the summer, including Open-Air St. Gallen (Late June; ☎0900 500 700; www.openairsg.ch) and the Montreux Jazz Festival (July; ☎963 8282; www.montreux.ch/mjf).

# ADDITIONAL RESOURCES

*Switzerland: A Village History,* by David Birmingham. Swallow Press (2004). Follows one Alpine village from the Napoleonic invasion onward.

*Living and Working in Switzerland: A Survival Handbook,* by David Hampshire. Survival Books, Ltd. (2003). Perfect for appetites whetted by the silverware advice in **Customs and Etiquette** (p. 932).

# ESSENTIALS

**FACTS AND FIGURES**

**Official Name:** Swiss Confederation.
**Capital:** Bern.
**Major Cities:** Basel, Geneva, Zürich.
**Population:** 7,555,000.
**Land Area:** 41,300 sq. km.
**Time Zone:** GMT+1.

**Languages:** German (64%), French (19%), Italian (8%), Romansch (1%).
**Religions:** Roman Catholic (48%), Protestant (44%), other (8%).
**Avg. Chocolate Consumed:** 23 lb. per person annually (twice as much as an American citizen).

## WHEN TO GO

During ski season (Nov.-Mar.) prices double in eastern Switzerland and travelers must make reservations months ahead. The situation reverses in the summer, especially July and August, when the flatter, western half of Switzerland fills with vacationers and hikers enjoying low humidity and temperatures rarely exceeding 26°C (80°F). A good budget option is to travel during the shoulder season: May-June and September-October, when tourism lulls and the daytime temperature ranges from -2-7°C (46-59°F). Many mountain towns throughout Switzerland shut down completely in May and June, however, so call ahead.

## DOCUMENTS AND FORMALITIES

**EMBASSIES.** Most foreign embassies in Switzerland are in Bern (p. 937). Swiss embassies abroad include: **Australia,** 7 Melbourne Ave., Forrest, Canberra, ACT, 2603 (☎02 6162 8400; www.eda.admin.ch/australia); **Canada,** 5 Marlborough Ave.,

Ottawa, ON, K1N 8E6 (☎613-235-1837; www.eda.admin.ch/canada); **Ireland,** 6 Ailesbury Rd., Ballsbridge, Dublin, 4 (☎353 12 18 63 82; www.eda.admin.ch/dublin); **New Zealand,** 22 Panama St., Wellington (☎04 472 15 93; www.eda.admin.ch/wellington); **UK,** 16-18 Montagu Pl., London, W1H 2BQ (☎020 76 16 60 00; www.eda.admin.ch/london); **US,** 2900 Cathedral Ave., NW, Washington, D.C., 20008 (☎202-745-7900; www.eda.admin.ch/washington).

**VISA AND ENTRY INFORMATION.** EU citizens do not need a visa. Citizens of Australia, Canada, New Zealand, and the US do not need a visa for stays of up to 90 days. For stays longer than 90 days, all visitors need visas (around US$44), available at Swiss consulates. Travelers should anticipate a processing time of about six to eight weeks.

# TOURIST SERVICES AND MONEY

| EMERGENCY | Ambulance: ☎ 144. Fire: ☎ 118. Police: ☎ 117. |
|---|---|

**TOURIST OFFICES.** Branches of the **Swiss National Tourist Office,** marked by a standard blue "i" sign, are present in nearly every town in Switzerland; most agents speak English. The official tourism website for Switzerland is www.myswitzerland.com.

**THE REAL DEAL.** If you're planning on spending a long time in Switzerland, consider the **Museum Pass** (30CHF). Available at some tourist offices and participating venues, it lets you into most major Swiss museums.

**MONEY.** The Swiss unit of currency is the **Swiss franc (CHF),** plural Swiss francs. One Swiss franc is equal to 100 centimes (called *Rappen* in German Switzerland), with standard denominations of 5, 10, 20, and 50 centimes and 1, 2, and 5CHF in coins, and 10, 20, 50, 100, 200, 500, and 1000CHF in notes. Widely accepted credit cards include American Express, MasterCard, and Visa. **Euros** (€) are also accepted at many museums and restaurants. Switzerland is not cheap; if you stay in hostels and prepare most of your own food, expect to spend 55-80CHF per day. Generally, it's less expensive to exchange money at home than in Switzerland. **ATMs** offer the best exchange rates. Although restaurant bills already include a 15% service charge, an additional **tip** of 1-2CHF for a modest meal or 5-10CHF for a more upscale dinner is expected. Give hotel porter and doormen about 1CHF per bag and airport porters 5CHF per bag.

Switzerland has a 7.6% **value added tax (VAT),** a sales tax applied to goods and services. The prices given in *Let's Go* include VAT. In the airport upon exiting Switzerland, non-Swiss citizens can claim a refund on the tax paid for goods purchased at participating stores. In order to qualify for a refund in a store, you must spend at least 500CHF; make sure to ask for a refund form when you pay. For more info on qualifying for a VAT refund, see p. 18.

| SWISS FRANC (CHF) | | |
|---|---|---|
| AUS$1 = 0.99CHF | 1CHF = AUS$1.01 | |
| CDN$1 = 1.15CHF | 1CHF = CDN$0.87 | |
| EUR€1 = 1.64CHF | 1CHF = EUR€0.61 | |
| NZ$1 = 0.86CHF | 1CHF = NZ$1.16 | |
| UK£1 = 2.42CHF | 1CHF = UK£0.41 | |
| US$1 = 1.21CHF | 1CHF = US$0.83 | |

# TRANSPORTATION

**BY PLANE.** Major international airports are in **Bern** (BRN; ☎031 960 21 11; www.alpar.ch), **Geneva** (GVA; ☎022 717 71 11; www.gva.ch), and **Zürich** (ZRH; ☎043 816 86 00; www.zurich-airport.com). From London, **easyJet** (☎0871 244 23 66; www.easyjet.com) has flights to Geneva and Zürich. **Aer Lingus** (Ireland ☎0818 365 000, Switzerland 422 86 99 33, UK 0870 876 5000; www.aerlingus.com) sells tickets from Dublin, IRE to Geneva. For more info on flying to Switzerland from other locations, see p. 44.

**BY TRAIN.** Federal (**SBB, CFF**) and private railways connect most towns with frequent trains. For times and prices, check online (www.sbb.ch). **Eurail, Europass,** and **Inter Rail** are all valid on federal trains. The **Swiss Pass,** sold worldwide, offers four, eight, 15, 22, or 30 consecutive days of unlimited rail travel. It also doubles as a **Swiss Museum Pass,** allowing free entry to 400 museums. (2nd-class 4-day pass US$194, 8-day US$276, 15-day US$336, 21-day US$390, 1mo. US$434.)

**BY BUS. PTT Post Buses,** a barrage of government-run yellow coaches, connect rural villages and towns that trains don't service. **Swiss Passes** are valid on many buses; **Eurail** passes are not. Even with the SwissPass, you might have to pay 5-10CHF extra if you're riding certain buses.

**BY CAR.** Roads, generally in good condition, may become dangerous at higher altitudes in the winter. The speed limit is 50kph in cities, 80kph on open roads, and 120kph on highways. Many small towns forbid cars; some require special permits or restrict driving hours. US and British citizens 18 and older with a valid driver's license may drive in Switzerland for up to one year following their arrival; for stays longer than one year, drivers should contact the **Service des automobiles et de la navigation** (SAN; ☎022 388 30 30; www.geneve.ch/san) about acquiring a Swiss permit. Custom posts sell windshield stickers (US$33) required for driving on Swiss roads. Call ☎140 for roadside assistance.

**BY BIKE.** Cycling is a splendid way to see the country. Find bikes to rent at large train stations. The **Touring Club Suisse,** with locations throughout Switzerland (☎022 417 22 20; www.tcs.ch), is a good source for maps and route descriptions.

# KEEPING IN TOUCH

| **PHONE CODES** | **Country code: 41. International dialing prefix:** 00. For more information on how to place international calls, see **Inside Back Cover.** |
| --- | --- |

**EMAIL AND THE INTERNET.** Most Swiss cities, as well as a number of smaller towns, have at least one Internet cafe with web access available for about 12-24CHF per hour. Hostels and restaurants frequently offer Internet access as well, but it seldom comes for free: rates can climb as high as 12CHF per hour.

**TELEPHONE.** Whenever possible, use a calling card for international phone calls, as long-distance rates are often exorbitant for national phone services. For info about using mobile phones abroad, see p. 27. Most pay phones in Switzerland accept only prepaid taxcards, which are available at kiosks, post offices, and train stations. Direct access numbers include: **AT&T Direct** (☎800 89 00 11); **Canada Direct** (☎800 55 83 30); **MCI WorldPhone** (☎800 444 41 41); **Sprint** (☎800 877 46 46); **Telecom New Zealand** (☎800 55 64 11).

**MAIL.** Airmail from Switzerland averages three to 15 days to North America, although times are unpredictable from smaller towns. Domestic letters take one to three days. Bright yellow logos outside buildings mark Swiss national post offices, referred to as **Die Post** in German or **La Poste** in French. Letters from Switzerland weighing less than 20g cost 1.40CHF to mail to the US, 1.30CHF to mail to the UK, and 0.85CHF mailed nationally. To receive mail in Switzerland, have mail delivered **Poste Restante.** Mail will go to the main post office unless you specify a subsidiary by street address. Address mail to be held according to the following example: LAST NAME, First Name, *Postlagernde Briefe*, Postal Code, City, SWITZERLAND. Bring a passport to pick up your mail; there may be a small fee.

# ACCOMMODATIONS AND CAMPING

| SWITZERLAND | ❶ | ❷ | ❸ | ❹ | ❺ |
|---|---|---|---|---|---|
| **ACCOMMODATIONS** | under 30CHF | 30-42CHF | 43-65CHF | 66-125CHF | over 125CHF |

There are **hostels** (*Jugendherbergen* in German, *Auberges de Jeunesse* in French, *Ostelli* in Italian) in all cities in Switzerland as well as in most towns. **Schweizer Jugendherbergen** (SJH; www.youthhostel.ch) runs HI hostels throughout Switzerland. Non-HI members can stay in any HI hostel, where beds are usually 30-44CHF; members typically receive a 6CHF discount. The more informal **Swiss Backpackers (SB)** organization (☎062 892 2675; www.backpacker.ch) lists over 25 hostels aimed at young, foreign travelers interested in socializing. Most Swiss **campgrounds** are not idyllic refuges but large plots glutted with RVs. Prices average 12-20CHF per tent site and 6-9CHF per extra person. **Hotels** and **pensions** tend to charge at least 65-80CHF for a single room and 80-120CHF for a double. The cheapest have *Gasthof*, *Gästehaus*, or *Hotel-Garni* in the name. **Privatzimmer** (rooms in a family home) run about 30-60CHF per person. Breakfast is included at most hotels, pensions, and *Privatzimmer*.

**HIKING AND SKIING.** Nearly every town has **hiking trails:** Interlaken (p. 941), Grindelwald (p. 943), Luzern (p. 951), and Zermatt (p. 959) offer particularly good hiking opportunities. Trails are marked with either red-white-red markers (only sturdy boots and hiking poles needed) or blue-white-blue markers (mountaineering equipment needed). **Skiing** in Switzerland is less expensive than in North America, provided you avoid pricey resorts. **Ski passes** run 40-70CHF per day, 100-300CHF per week; a week of lift tickets, equipment rental, lessons, lodging, and *demi-pension* (breakfast plus one other meal) averages 475CHF. **Summer skiing** is available in a few towns such as Zermatt.

# FOOD AND DRINK

| SWITZERLAND | ❶ | ❷ | ❸ | ❹ | ❺ |
|---|---|---|---|---|---|
| **FOOD** | under 9CHF | 9-23CHF | 24-32CHF | 33-52CHF | over 52CHF |

Switzerland is not for the lactose intolerant. The Swiss are serious about dairy products, from rich and varied **cheeses** to decadent **milk chocolate**—even the major Swiss soft drink, **Rivella,** contains dairy. Swiss dishes vary from region to region. Bernese **rösti,** a plateful of hash-brown potatoes (sometimes flavored with bacon or cheese), is prevalent in the German regions; cheese or meat **fondue** is popular in the French regions. Try Valaisian **raclette,** made by melting cheese over a fire, scraping it onto a baked potato, and garnishing it with meat or vegetables. Supermarkets **Migros** and **Co-op** double as cafeterias; stop in for a cheap meal and groceries. Water from the fountains that adorn cities and large towns is usually safe; filling your bottle with it will save you money. *Kein Trinkwasser* or *Eau non potable* signs indicate unclean water. Each canton has its own local beer, which is often cheaper than soda.

## BEYOND TOURISM

Although Switzerland's volunteer opportunities are limited, a number of ecotourism and rural development organizations allow you to give back to the country. Your best bet is to go through a placement service. Look for opportunities for short-term work on websites like www.emploi.ch. For more info on opportunities across Europe, see **Beyond Tourism**, see p. 54.

**Bergwald Projekt/Mountain Forest Project,** Hauptstr. 24, 7014 Trin (☎081 630 41 45; www.bergwaldprojekt.ch). Organizes week-long conservation projects in Austria, Germany, and Switzerland.

**Workcamp Switzerland,** Komturei Tobel, Postfach 7, 9555 Tobel (☎071 917 24 86; www.workcamp.ch). Offers 2-3 week sessions during which volunteers live in a group environment and work on a common community service project.

# GERMAN SWITZERLAND

German Switzerland encompasses 65% of the country. While the region's intoxicating brews and industrious cities will remind visitors of Germany, the natural beauty at every turn is uniquely Swiss. Different forms of Swiss German, a dialect distinct from High German, are spoken (see p. 932).

# BERNESE OBERLAND

The peaks of the Bernese Oberland shelter a pristine wilderness best seen on hikes up the mountains and around the twin lakes, the Thunersee and Brienzersee. Not surprisingly, the area's opportunities for paragliding, mountaineering, and whitewater rafting are unparalleled. North of the mountains lies the relaxed city of Bern, Switzerland's capital and the heartbeat of the region.

## BERN

☎031

Bern (pop. 127,000) has been Switzerland's capital since 1848, but don't expect power politics or men in suits—the Bernese prefer to focus on the more leisurely things in life, strolling through the arcades of the *Altstadt* or along the banks of the serpentine Aare River.

**⌂ ⁊ TRANSPORTATION AND PRACTICAL INFORMATION.** Bern's small **airport** (BRN; ☎960 2111) is 20min. from the city. A **bus** runs from the train station 50min. before each flight (10min., 14CHF). **Trains** run from the station at Bahnhofpl. to: Geneva (2hr., 2 per hr., 45CHF); Luzern (1½hr., 2 per hr., 34CHF); St. Gallen (2¼hr., 1 per hr., 63CHF); Zürich (1¼hr., 4 per day, 45CHF); Berlin, GER (12hr., 1-2 per hr., 95CHF); Paris, FRA (6hr., 4-5 per day, 115CHF). Local Bernmobil **buses** (departing from the left of the train station) and **trams** (departing from the front of the station) run 5:45am-midnight. (☎321 86 41; www.bernmobil.ch. Single ride 3.20CHF, day pass 12CHF.) **Buses** depart from the back of the station and post

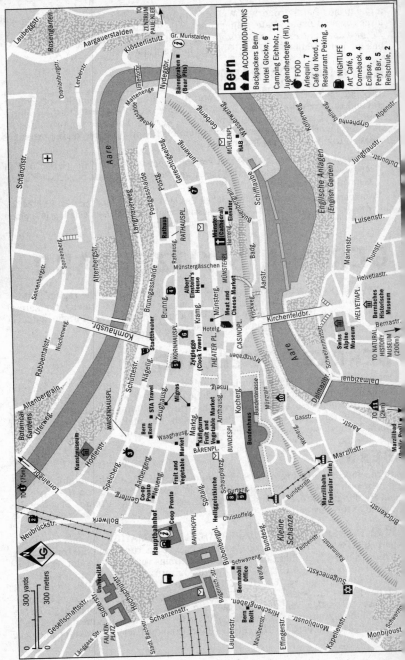

**Bern**

▲ ACCOMMODATIONS
Backpackers Bern/
Hotel Glocke, 6
Camping Eichholz, 11
Jugendherberge (HI), 10

● FOOD
Arlequin, 7
Café du Nord, 1
Restaurant Peking, 3

■ NIGHTLIFE
Art' Café, 9
Comeback, 4
Eclipse, 8
Pery Bar, 5
Reitschule, 2

SWITZERLAND

office. **Free bikes** are available from **Bern Rollt** at two locations, on Hirscheng. near the train station and on Zeugausg. near Waisenhauspl. (☎079 277 2857; www.bernrollt.ch. Passport and 20CHF deposit. Open May-Oct. daily 7:30am-9:30pm.)

Most of old Bern lies to your left as you leave the train station, along the Aare River. Bern's main train station is an often confusing tangle of essential services and extraneous shops. Take extra caution in the parks around the Parliament (Bundeshaus), especially at night. The **tourist office** is on the street level of the station. (☎328 1212; www.berninfo.ch. Open June-Sept. daily 9am-8:30pm; Oct.-May M-Sa 9am-6:30pm, Su 10am-5pm.) The **post office,** Schanzenpost 1, is one block to the right from the train station. (Open M-F 7:30am-9pm, Sa 8am-4pm, Su 4-9pm.) **Postal Codes:** CH-3000 to CH-3030.

Embassies in Bern include: **Canada,** Kirchenfeldstr. 88 (☎357 3200; www.geo.international.gc.ca/canada-europa/switzerland); **Ireland,** Kirchenfeldstr. 68 (☎352 1442); **UK,** Thunstr. 50 (☎359 7700; www.britishembassy.gov.uk/switzerland); **US,** Jubilaumsstr. 93 (☎357 7011; bern.usembassy.gov). The **Australian** consulate is in Geneva (p. 963). **New Zealanders** should contact their embassy in Berlin, GER (p. 397).

**▐▐ ACCOMMODATIONS AND FOOD.** If Bern's cheaper hostels are full, check the tourist office for a list of private rooms. **Backpackers Bern/Hotel Glocke ❷,** Rathausg. 75, in the middle of the *Altstadt*, has friendly owners and a large common room. From the train station, cross the tram lines and turn left on Spitalg., continuing onto Marktg. Turn left at Kornhauspl., then right on Rathausg. (☎311 3771; www.bernbackpackers.ch. Internet 1CHF per 10min. Reception 8am-11am and 3-10pm. Dorms 31CHF; singles 65CHF; doubles 78-140CHF, with bath 160CHF; quads 114CHF. AmEx/MC/V.) At **Jugendherberge (HI) ❷,** Weiherg. 4 near the river, guests receive free access to a public swimming pool. From the station, go down Christoffelg.; take the stairs to the left of the park gates, go down the slope, and turn left on Weiherg. (☎311 6316; www.youthhostel.ch/bern. Breakfast included. Internet 6CHF per hr. Reception June to mid-Sept. 7-10am and 2pm-midnight; mid-Sept. to May 7-10am and 5pm-midnight. Closed 2nd and 3rd weeks of Jan. Dorms 34CHF; singles 55CHF; doubles 84-98CHF.; quads 148CHF. 1.30CHF visitor's fee; 6CHF HI discount. AmEx/MC/V.) Take tram #9 to Wabern, backtrack 50m, and walk downhill at the first right to reach **Camping Eichholz ❶,** Strandweg 49, near to a beach on the Aare. (☎961 2602; www.campingeichholz.ch. Showers 1.50CHF per 5min. Laundry 5CHF. Internet 2.50CHF per 15min. Reception 7am-10pm. Open late Apr.-Sept. 8CHF per person, 15-17CHF per tent; students 14-16CHF/7CHF. Bungalow doubles 35CHF; triples 60CHF; quads 100CHF. MC/V.)

**Markets** sell produce daily at Weinhauspl. and every Tuesday and Saturday on Bundespl. from May through October. A friendly couple owns **Arlequin ❷,** Gerechtigkeitsg. 51, an 80s-inspired restaurant. (☎311 3946. Sandwiches 6-12CHF. Meat fondue 35CHF. Open Tu-W 11am-11:30pm, Th-F 11am-1:30am, Sa 11am-11pm. AmEx/MC/V; min. 20CHF). A diverse crowd gathers under stage lights on the terrace at **Café du Nord ❸,** Lorrainestr. 2. (☎332 2328. Pasta 18-25CHF. Meat entrees 22-32CHF. Open M-W 8am-11:30pm, Th-F 8am-1:30am, Sa 9am-1:30am, Su 4pm-11:30pm. Kitchen open M-Sa 11:30am-2pm and 6:30-10pm, Su 4:30-11:30pm. MC/V.) **Restaurant Peking ❷,** Speicherg. 27, off Waisenhauspl., has Chinese takeout. (☎312 1528. Take out 10-12CHF. Eat in 12-15CHF. Open M-Sa 11am-2:30pm and 6-11:30pm. AmEx/MC/V.) For groceries, head to **Migros,** Marktg. 46. (Open M 9am-6:30pm, Tu 8am-6:30pm, W-F 8am-9pm, Sa 7am-4pm.)

**◪ SIGHTS.** Bern's historic center (*Altstadt*), one of the best-preserved in Switzerland, is a UNESCO World Heritage sight. Covered arcades allow for wandering and window shopping, while the wide cobblestone streets are dotted by medieval wells topped with Renaissance statues. The Swiss national parliament meets in the massive **Bundeshaus,** which rises high over the Aare; water tumbles from fountains in front of the entrance. (www.parlament.ch. Under renovation; no tours until mid-2008. 1 45min. tour per hr. M-Sa 9-11am and 2-4pm. English-language tour usually 2pm. Free.) From the Bundeshaus, Kocherg. and Herreng. lead to the 15th-century Protestant **Münster** (Cathedral); above the main entrance, a golden sculpture depicts the torments of hell. For a fantastic view of the city, climb the Münster's 100m spire. (Cathedral open Easter-Oct. Tu-Sa 10am-5pm, Su. 11:30am-5pm; Nov.-Easter Tu-Sa 10am-noon, Su 11:30am-2pm. Free. Tower open Easter-Oct. M-Sa 10am-4:30pm, Su 11:30am-4:30pm; Nov.-Mar. M-F 2pm-3pm, Sa 2pm-5pm, Su 11:30am-1pm. 4CHF.) For some early medieval flair, check out the **Zytglogge,** a 12th-century clock tower on Kramg. that once marked the city's western boundary. Down the road is **Albert Einstein's house,** Kramg. 49, where he conceived the theory of general relativity in 1915. His home is now filled with photos, letters, and video exhibits. (☎312 0091; www.einstein-bern.ch. Open Apr.-Sept. daily 10am-5pm; Feb.-Mar. Tu-F 10am-5pm, Sa 10am-4pm. 6CHF, students 4.50CHF.) Several steep walkways lead from the Bundeshaus to the **Aare River.** On hot days, locals dive from the banks and the bridges to ride the river's currents, but only experienced swimmers should join. To participate in this river-jumping, walk upstream from the free public swimming pool, **Marzilibad.** Monbijoubrücke is the best spot from which to jump. While swimming downstream, be careful to exit at or before the Marzilibad landings, as that's the last place to get out before the waterfalls after the high Kirchenfeldbrücke.

A recent addition to Bern's many museums is the ◨**Zentrum Paul Klee,** Monument im Fruchtland 3, which houses the world's largest Klee collection in a ripple-shaped building built into a hillside. (☎359 0101; www.zpk.org. Take bus #12 to Zentrum Paul Klee. Open Tu-Su 10am-5pm, Th 10am-9pm. 16CHF, students 14CHF.) Near Lorrainebrücke, the **Kunstmuseum,** Hodlerstr. 8-12, has paintings from the Middle Ages to the contemporary era and features a smattering of big 20th-century names: Giacometti, Kandinsky, Kirchner, Picasso, and Pollock. (☎328 0944; www.kunstmuseumbern.ch. Open Tu 10am-9pm, W-Su 10am-5pm. 7CHF, students 5CHF. Special exhibits up to 18CHF.) At the east side of the river, across the Nydeggbrücke, lie the **Bärengraben** (Bear Pits), where gawking crowds amuse themselves by tossing fruit (3CHF) into the cement abodes of three European brown bears. (Open daily June-Sept. 9:30am-5pm; Oct.-May 10am-4pm.) The path up the hill to the left leads to the ◨**Rosengarten** (Rose Garden), which provides visitors with a memorable view of Bern's *Altstadt.* Anything and everything relating to Bern's long history, from technological innovations to religious art, is on display in the jam-packed **Bernisches Historische Museum,** Helvetiapl. 5. (☎350 7711; www.bhm.ch. Open Tu-Su 10am-5pm. 13CHF, students 8CHF.)

🎭🎵 **ENTERTAINMENT AND NIGHTLIFE.** Check out *Bewegungsmelder,* available at the tourist office, for events. July's **Gurten Festival** (www.gurtenfestival.ch) draws young and energetic crowds and has attracted such luminaries as Bob Dylan and Elvis Costello while jazz-lovers arrive in early May for the **International Jazz Festival** (www.jazzfestivalbern.ch). Bern's traditional folk festival is the **Onion Market,** which brings 50 tons of onions to the city (Nov. 24, 2008). The orange grove at **Stadtgärtnerei Elfenau** (tram #19, dir.: Elfenau, to Luternauweg) has free Sunday concerts in summer. From mid-July to mid-August, **OrangeCinema** (☎0800 07 80 78; www.orangecinema.ch) screens recent films outdoors; tickets are available from the tourist office in the train station.

Find new DJs at ◨**Art' Café,** Gurteng. 6, a cafe and club with huge windows overlooking the street. (☎318 2070; www.artcafe.ch. Open M-W 7am-1:30am, Th-F 7am-3:30am, Sa 8am-3:30am, Su 10am-3:30am. Cash only.) The Art' Café crowd wanders next door to **Eclipse,** which has the same owners. (☎882 0888; www.eclipse-bar.ch. Open M-W 7am-1:30am, Th-F 7am-3am, Sa 9am-3am. The candlelit **Pery Bar,** Schmiedenpl. 3, provides a romantic setting for early-evening drinks. (☎311 5908. Beer 5.50CHF. Wine 7CHF. DJs W-Sa. Open M-W 5pm-1:30am, Th 5pm-2:30am, F 5pm-3:30am, Sa 4pm-3:30am. AmEx/MC/V.) To escape the fashionable folk that gather in the *Altstadt* at night, head to the **Reitschule,** Neubrückestr. 8, a graffiti-covered center for Bern's counterculture. (Open daily 8pm-late.) **Comeback,** Rathausg. 42, a gay and lesbian basement bar, caters to thirtysomethings. (☎311 7713. Beer 5CHF. Open Su-M 6pm-12:30am, Tu-Th 6pm-2:30am, F-Sa 6pm-3:30am. AmEx/MC/V.)

# JUNGFRAU REGION

The most famous region of the Bernese Oberland, Jungfrau draws tourists with its splendid hiking trails, glacier lakes, and snow-capped peaks. From Interlaken, the valley splits at the foot of the Jungfrau Mountain. The eastern valley contains Grindelwald, with easy access to two glaciers, while the western valley harbors many smaller towns. The two valleys are divided by an easily hikeable ridge.

# INTERLAKEN
☎033

Interlaken (pop. 21,000) lies between the Thunersee and the Brienzersee at the foot of the largest mountains in Switzerland. Countless hiking trails, raging rivers, and peaceful lakes have turned the town into one of Switzerland's prime tourist attractions and its top adventure-sport destination.

**🖪🔂 TRANSPORTATION AND PRACTICAL INFORMATION.** Westbahnhof (☎826 4750) and Ostbahnhof (☎828 7319) have **trains** to: Basel (2-3hr., 1-2 per hr., 53CHF); Bern (1hr., 1-2 per hr., 25CHF); Geneva (3hr., 1-2 per hr., 61CHF); Zürich (2hr., 1 per 2hr., 61CHF). Ostbahnhof also sends trains to Grindelwald (1-2 per hr., 10CHF) and Luzern (2hr., 1-2 per hr., 30CHF).

The **tourist office,** Höheweg 37, in Hotel Metropole, gives out maps and books hotel rooms for free. (☎826 5300; www.interlaken.ch. Open May-Oct. M-F 8am-7pm, Sa 8am-5pm, Su 10am-noon and 5pm-7pm; Nov.-Apr. M-F 8am-noon and 1:30-6pm, Sa 9am-noon.) Both train stations rent **bikes.** (31CHF per day. Open M-F 6am-8pm, Sa-Su 8am-8pm.) For **weather info,** call ☎828 7931. The **post office** is at Marktg. 1. (Open M-F 8am-noon and 1:45-6:30pm, Sa 8:30am-4pm.) **Postal Code:** CH-3800.

**🏠⛽ ACCOMMODATIONS AND FOOD.** Interlaken is a backpacking hot spot, especially in summer months, so hostels tend to fill up quickly; reserve more than a month ahead. Diagonally across the Höhenmatte from the tourist office, the friendly, low-key 🔳**Backpackers Villa Sonnenhof ❷,** Alpenstr. 16, includes admission to a nearby spa for the duration of your stay, minigolf, and free use of local buses. (☎826 7171; www.villa.ch. Breakfast included. Laundry 10CHF. Internet 1CHF per 8min. Free Wi-Fi. Reception 7:30-11am and 4-10pm. Mid-Apr. to mid-Sept. and mid-Dec. to mid-Jan. dorms 35CHF; doubles 98CHF; triples 135CHF; quads 156CHF. Mid-Sept. to mid.-Dec. and mid-Jan. to mid-Apr. dorms 33-37CHF; doubles 90CHF; triples 123CHF. AmEx/MC/V.) In contrast, 🔳**Balmer's Herberge ❶,** Hauptstr. 23, Switzerland's oldest private hostel (est. 1945), is a place to party, not to relax. Services include mountain bike rental (35CHF per day), nightly movies, free sleds, and an extremely popular bar. (☎822 1961. Breakfast included. Laundry 4CHF. Internet 10CHF per hr. Reception in summer 7am-9pm, in winter 6:30-10am and 4:30-10pm. Dorms 27-29CHF; doubles 74-78CHF; triples 99-105CHF; quads 99-105CHF. AmEx/MC/V.) **Funny Farm ❶,** just off Hauptstr., attracts partiers with bonfires, a climbing wall, a swimming pool, and crazy Saturday night beach volleyball.

## A SAINTLY BREED

n AD 1050, the Archdeacon Bernard de Menthon founded a hospice in a mountain pass in the ungfrau region and brought with him a breed of large, furry dogs of Gallic origin. In addition to providing shelter for passing merchants, Bernard and the monks working under him would venture into blizzards in search of stranded travelers. Though it is uncertain whether the dogs accompanied he monks on their rescue missions—early accounts relate that dogs were used to run an exercise wheel that turned a cooking spit— by the time of Bernard's canonization, dogs bearing his name had become famous and regularly patrolled the pass (now also named after Bernard).

Gifted with a fine sense of smell, a thick coat, an amiable manner, and a neck just made to tie a barrel of brandy to, the St. Bernards made a name for themselves by saving over 2000 lives over several hundred years. In the 810s, a single dog named Barry saved 40 lost travelers. Today, ew St. Bernards still work as rescue dogs—smaller, lighter breeds ess liable to sink in the snow have taken their place. The St. Bernard is now a popular household pet, as well as the star of popular films like Cujo and the Beethoven movies. But it will always have dignity as the Alpine ixture it once was.

(☎079 652 6127; www.funny-farm.ch. Laundry 10CHF. Internet 5CHF per 25min. Reception 24hr. Dorms 20-28CHF, with bath 30-39CHF. MC/V.) To camp at **Sackgut ❶**, Brienzstr. 24, turn right from the Ostbanhof, cross the bridge, go right, then turn right again. (☎822 4434; www.campingtcs.ch. Open Apr.-Oct. Reception 9-11:30am and 4-6pm. 8CHF per person, 15CHF per tent site. Cash only.)

**My Little Thai ❷**, Hauptstr. 19 (right next to Balmer's Herberge), fills with hungry backpackers in the evening. (☎821 1017. Pad thai 14-21CHF. Vegetarian options available. Internet 8CHF per hr. Open daily 11:30am-10pm. AmEx/MC/V.) **El Azteca ❷**, Jungfraustr. 30, serves cactus salad (16CHF), fajitas (28-38CHF), and other Mexican fare. (☎822 7131. Open daily 7:30am-2pm and 6:30pm-11:30pm. AmEx/MC/V.) There are **Migros** and **Coop** supermarkets by both train stations. (Open M-Th 8am-6:30pm, F 8am-9pm, Sa 7:30am-5pm.)

🏔 **OUTDOOR ACTIVITIES.** With the incredible surrounding Alpine scenery, it's no wonder that many of Interlaken's tourists seem compelled to try otherwise unthinkable adventure sports. ⛷**Alpin Raft**, Hauptstr. 7 (☎823 4100; www.alpinraft.ch), the most established company in Interlaken, has qualified, entertaining guides and offers a wide range of activities, including paragliding (150CHF), river rafting (99-110CHF), skydiving (380CHF), and hanggliding (185CHF). They also offer two different types of **bungee jumping**. At the 85m Glacier Bungee Jump (125CHF), thrill-seekers leap off a ledge above the Lutschine River. At the Alpin Rush Jump (165CHF), jumpers attached to one of the longest bungee cords in the world leap out of a gondola 134m above a lake, surrounded by the green peaks of the Simmental Valley and herds of grazing cattle. One of the most popular adventure activities at Alpin Raft is **canyoning** (110-175CHF), which involves rappelling down a series of gorge faces, jumping off cliffs into pools of churning water, and swinging—Tarzan-style—from ropes and zip cords through the canyon. All prices include transportation to and from any hostel in Interlaken, and usually a beer upon completion. ⛷**Skywings Adventures** has witty professionals and a wide range of activities from paragliding (150-220CHF) to river rafting (99CHF); their booth is across the street from the tourist office (☎079 266 8282; www.skywings.ch). **Outdoor Interlaken**, Hauptstr. 15 (☎826 7719; www.outdoor-interlaken.ch), offers many of the same activities as Alpin Raft at similar prices, as well as rock-climbing lessons (½-day 89CHF) and whitewater **kayaking** tours (½-day 155CHF). At **Sky-**

**dive Xdream,** you can skydive with one of the best in the world; the owner, Stefan Heuser, was on the Swiss skydiving team for 12 years and won three world championship medals. Skydivers can make their ascent over gorges and glaciers in a glass-walled helicopter, then jump from a standing position—an exhilarating option that's very different from the usual sitting take-off that skydivers make from planes. (☎079 759 3483; www.justjump.ch. 380CHF per tandem plane jump; 430CHF per tandem helicopter jump. Open Apr.-Oct. Pick-ups 9am and 1pm, Sa-Su also 4pm. Call for winter availability.) **Swiss Alpine Guide** offers **ice climbing,** running full-day trips to a nearby glacier and providing all the equipment needed to scale vertical glacier walls and rappel into icy crevasses. (☎822 6000; www.swissalpineguides.ch. Trips May-Nov. daily, weather permitting. 160CHF.)

> ▼ Interlaken's adventure sports industry is thrilling, but **accidents do happen.** On July 27, 1999, 21 tourists were killed by a sudden flash flood while canyoning. Be aware that you participate in all adventure sports at your own risk.

Interlaken's most traversed trail climbs Harder Kulm (1310m). From the Ostbahnhof, head toward town, take the first road bridge right across the river, and follow the yellow signs that give way to white-red-white rock markings. From the top, signs lead back down to the Westbahnhof. The hike should be about 2½hr. up and 1½hr. down. In summer, the Harderbahn funicular runs from the trailhead to the top. (Open daily May to Oct. 15CHF, round-trip 25CHF. 25% Eurail and 50% SwissPass discount.) For a flatter trail, turn left from the train station and left before the bridge, then follow the canal over to the nature reserve on the shore of the Thunersee. The 3hr. trail winds along the Lombach River, through pastures at the base of Harder Kulm, and back toward town.

# GRINDELWALD                                            ☎033

Interlaken is frenetic center for adventure sports; Grindelwald (pop. 4500) is its more serene counterpart, with more opportunities for hiking and skiing. Tucked between the Eiger and the Jungfraujoch, the village is the launching point for the only glaciers accessible by foot in the Bernese Oberland. The **Bergführerbüro** (Mountain Guide's Office), in the sports center near the tourist office, sells hiking maps and coordinates glacier walks, ice climbing, and mountaineering. (☎853 1200. Open June-Oct. M-F 9am-noon and 2-5pm.) The **Untere Grindelwaldgletscher** (Lower Glacier) hike is moderately steep (5hr.). To reach the trailhead, walk away from the station on the main street and follow the signs downhill to Pfinstegg. Hikers can either walk the first forested section of the trail (1hr.) or take a funicular (July to mid-Sept. 8am-7pm; mid-Sept. to June 9am-5:30pm; 12CHF, SwissPass 9CHF). From there, signs lead up the glacier-filled valley to **Stieregaße,** which sells food. Grindelwald is also the largest ski resort in the Jungfrau, with 220 km of slopes; the **Sportpass Jungfrau** gives you access to the entire region (2 days 123CHF, 3 days 169CHF, 6 days 295CHF). Grindelwald has countless **toboggan** courses, including ⬛**Europe's longest run**—during the winter, hike to Faulhorn peak (3hr.), then glide a thrilling 15km back to the village on the "Big Pintenfritz." Pet goats greet guests at the ⬛**Jugendherberge (HI) ❷,** whose rooms have terraces that offer spectacular views. To reach the lodge, head left out of the train station for 400m, then cut uphill to the right and follow the steep trail all the way up the hill for 20 minutes. (☎853 1009; www.youthhostel.ch/grindelwald. Breakfast included. Reception 7:30-10am and 3-10pm. Summer dorms 29-37CHF; doubles 76-106CHF. Winter dorms 31-38CHF; doubles 78-106CHF. 6CHF HI discount. AmEx/MC/V.) **Downtown Lodge ❶** is conveniently located 200m past the tourist office, to the right of the train station. It offers great views of the mountains, as well as free entrance to the public swimming pool. (☎ 853 0825; www.downtown-lodge.ch. Breakfast included. Dorms 25-35CHF; doubles 70-90CHF. AmEx/MC/V.) **Hotel Eiger,** on Hauptstr. near the tourist office, houses a bar and two restaurants, **Memory ❷** and the slightly more upscale **Barry's ❸.** (☎ 854 3131. Memory open daily 8:30am-midnight, meals 10-30CHF; Barry's open daily 6pm-midnight, meals 12-40CHF; bar open daily 5pm-1am. AmEx/MC/V.) A **Coop** supermarket is on Hauptstr., across from the tourist office. (Open M-F 8am-6:30pm, Sa 8am-6pm.) The **Jungfraubahn train** runs to Grindelwald from Interlaken's Ostbahnhof (35min., 2 per hr., 10CHF). The **tourist office,** in the Sport-Zentrum 200m to the right of the station, provides chairlift information and a list of free guided excursions. (☎ 854 1212. Open July-Aug. M-F 8am-noon and 1:30-6pm, Sa 8am-noon and 1:30-5pm; Sept.-June M-F 9am-noon and 2-5pm, Sa 2-5pm.) **Postal Code:** CH-3818.

**▣ DAYTRIP FROM GRINDELWALD: JUNGFRAUJOCH.** It's a splurge to reach "the top of Europe," but the Jungfrau mountaintop, with Europe's highest train station, remains one of Switzerland's most popular destinations. While the journey is the most famous part of the trip up the mountain, the peak offers more than just a pretty view of the **Aletschgletscher,** the longest glacier in the Alps. Since the completion of the **Jungfrau Railway** in 1912, the building at the summit has evolved from a wood and aluminum Tourist Lodge to the present **five-story complex,** which includes three restaurants, two outdoor lookout points, an Ice Palace, and an exhibition room. The **adventure center** is a fun stop, with free sleds (5CHF deposit), a Flying Fox zipline (20CHF), a hole-in-one golf tee (10CHF), and an all-day summer ski pass (33CHF, all equipment and clothing included). Follow the signs toward the Aletschgletscher. The **Jungfraubahn** runs from Grindelwald to the peak. *(Open June to mid.-Sept. First train leaves Grindelwald at around 8am; last train leaves Jungfraujoch around 6pm. 1½ hr., 2 per hr., 154CHF. Good Morning ticket 134CHF; departs Grindelwald 7:15am, returns to Jungraujoch 12:45pm.)*

# CENTRAL SWITZERLAND

In contrast to the unspoiled scenic vistas of the mountainous southern cantons, Central Switzerland seems to overflow with people and culture. Unique museums, majestic cathedrals, and lovely *Altstädte* (Old Towns) in Zürich and other cities are the main attractions of this vibrant region.

# ZÜRICH ☎ 044

Battalions of briefcase-toting executives charge daily through Zürich, Switzerland's largest city (pop. 360,000) and the world's fourth-largest stock exchange—bringing with them enough money to keep upper-crust boutiques thriving. But only footsteps away from the flashy Bahnhofstr. shopping district is the city's student quarter, home to an energetic counter-culture that has inspired generations of Swiss philosophers and artists.

## ▐ TRANSPORTATION

**Flights: Zürich-Kloten Airport (ZRH;** ☎ 816 2211; www.zurich-airport.com) is a major hub for Swiss International Airlines (☎ 084 885 2000; www.swiss.com). Daily connections to: **Frankfurt, GER; London, BRI; Paris, FRA.** Trains connect the airport to the *Hauptbahnhof* in the city center. 3-6 per hr., 6CHF. Eurail and SwissPass valid.)

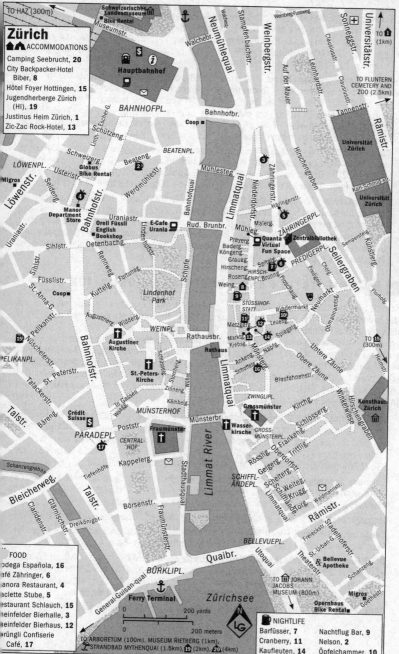

SWITZERLAND

**Zürich**

▲ ♠ ACCOMMODATIONS

Camping Seebrucht, **20**
City Backpacker-Hotel
Biber, **8**
Hôtel Foyer Hottingen, **15**
Jugendherberge Zürich
(HI), **19**
Justinus Heim Zürich, **1**
Zic-Zac Rock-Hotel, **13**

FOOD
Bodega Española, **16**
Café Zähringer, **6**
Manora Restaurant, **4**
Raclette Stube, **5**
Restaurant Schlauch, **15**
Rheinfelder Bierhalle, **3**
Rheinfelder Bierhaus, **12**
Sprüngli Confiserie
Café, **17**

♫ NIGHTLIFE
Barfüsser, **7**          Nachtflug Bar, **9**
Cranberry, **11**        Nelson, **2**
Kaufleuten, **14**       Öpfelchammer, **10**

**Trains:** Run to: **Basel** (1¼hr., 2-3 per hr., 30CHF); **Bern** (1¼hr., 3-4 per hr., 45CHF); **Geneva** (3hr., 1-2 per hr., 77CHF); **Luzern** (1hr., 1-2 per hr., 22CHF); **St. Gallen** (½hr.; 2-3 per hr.; 27CHF); **Locarno** (2hr.; 1 per 2hr.; 55CHF); **Milan, ITA** (4hr., 1 per 2hr., 72-87CHF); **Munich, GER** (5hr., 4-5 per day, 90CHF); **Paris, FRA** (5hr., 4 per day, 112-140CHF, under 26 86CHF).

**Public Transportation: Trams** criss-cross the city, originating at the *Hauptbahnhof.* Tickets valid for 1hr. cost 4CHF (press the blue button on automatic ticket machines); tickets for shorter rides (valid for 30min.) cost 2.40CHF (yellow button). Police fine riders without tickets 60CHF. If you plan to ride several times, buy a 24hr. **Tageskarte** (7.60CHF; green button), valid on trams, buses, and ferries. **Night buses** (5CHF ticket valid all night) run from the city center to outlying areas (F-Su).

**Car Rental:** The tourist office offers a 20% discount and free upgrade deal with **Europcar** (☎804 4646; www.europcar.ch). Prices from 155CHF per day for 1-2 days with unlimited mileage. 20+. Branches at the airport (☎043 255 5656), Josefstr. 53 (☎271 5656), and Lindenstr. 33 (☎383 1747). Rent in the city; a 40% tax is added at the airport.

**Bike Rental:** Bike loans from **Züri Rollt** (☎043 288 3400; www.zuerirollt.ch) are free for 6hr. during business hours, otherwise 5CHF per day, 20CHF per night. Pick up a bike from **Globus City,** the green hut on the edge of the garden between Bahnhofstr. and Löwenstr.; **Opernhaus,** by the opera house past Bellevuepl.; **Velogate,** across from *Hauptbahnhof's* tracks next to the Landesmuseum castle. Bikes must be returned to original rental station. Passport and 20CHF deposit. Open May-Oct. 7:30am-9:30pm.

## ✈ 🔃 ORIENTATION AND PRACTICAL INFORMATION

Zürich is in north-central Switzerland, close to the German border and on some of the lowest land in the country. The **Limmat River** splits the city down the middle on its way to the **Zürichsee** (Lake Zürich). The **Hauptbahnhof** (train station) lies on the western bank and marks the beginning of **Bahnhofstraße,** the city's main shopping street. Two-thirds of the way down Bahnhofstr. lies **Paradeplatz,** the banking center of Zürich, which marks the beginning of the last stretch of the shopping street (reserved for those with trust funds). The eastern bank of the river is dominated by the university district, which stretches above the narrow **Niederdorfstraße** and pulses with bars, clubs, and restaurants.

**Tourist Office:** In the **Hauptbahnhof** (☎215 40 00; www.zuerich.com). An electronic hotel reservation board is at the front of the station. Also sells the **ZürichCARD,** which is good for unlimited public transportation, free museum admission, and discounts on sights and tours (1-day pass 17CHF, 3-day 34CHF). Open May-Oct. M-Sa 8am-8:30pm, Su 8:30am-6:30pm; Nov.-Apr. M-Sa 8:30am-7pm, Su 9am-6:30pm.

**Currency Exchange:** On the main floor of the train station. Cash advances for MC/V with photo ID; min. 200CHF, max. 1000CHF. Open daily 6:30am-9:30pm. **Crédit Suisse,** at Paradepl. 5CHF commission. Open M-F 8:15am-5pm.

**Luggage Storage:** Middle level of *Hauptbahnhof.* 5-8CHF. Open daily 4:15am-1:30am.

**Bookstore: The Orell Füssli Bookshop,** Bahnhofstr. 70, has an extensive selection of English books. (☎211 0444. Open M-F 9am-8pm, Sa 9am-5pm. AmEx/MC/V.)

**GLBT Resources: Homosexuelle Arbeitsgruppe Zürich (HAZ),** on the 3rd fl. of Sihlquai 67 (☎271 22 50; www.haz.ch), has a library, meetings, and the newsletter *InfoSchwül.* Open W 2-6pm. **Frauenzentrum Zürich,** Matteng. 27 (☎272 0504; http://frauenzentrum.fembit.ch), provides resources for lesbians. Open Tu and Th 6-8pm.

**24hr. Pharmacy: Bellevue Apotheke,** Theaterstr. 14, on Bellevuepl. (☎266 6222).

**Internet Access: Quanta Virtual Fun Space** (☎260 7266), at the corner of Mühleg. and Niederdorfstr. 3CHF per 15min. Open daily 9am-midnight. **E-Cafe Urania,** Uraniastr. 3 (☎210 33 11), next to the parking garage at the bridge. 0.25CHF per min. Open M-F 7am-11pm, Sa 8am-11pm, Su 10am-10pm.

**Post Office: Sihlpost,** Kasernestr. 95-97, behind the station. Open M-F 6:30am-10:30pm, Sa 6:30am-8pm, Su 10am-10:30pm. Branches throughout the city. **Postal Code:** CH-8021.

# ACCOMMODATIONS AND CAMPING

Zürich's few budget accommodations are easily accessible by foot or public transportation. Reserve ahead, especially in summer.

**Justinus Heim Zürich,** Freudenbergstr. 146 (☎362 2980; justinuszh@bluewin.ch). Take tram #9 or 10 (dir.: Bahnhof Oerlikon) to Seilbahn Rigiblick, then take the funicular to the top (open daily 5:20am-12:40am). This hillside hostel, which hosts students during the term period, is removed from the downtown bustle but is easily accessible. Beautiful view of the city. Breakfast included. Reception 8am-noon and 5-9pm. Singles 50CHF, with shower 65CHF; doubles 90-110CHF. Rates higher in July and Aug. V. ❸

**The City Backpacker-Hotel Biber,** Niederdorfstr. 5 (☎251 9015; www.city-back-packer.ch). From the Hauptbanhof, cross the bridge and Limmatquai, turn right onto Niederdorfstr., and walk for 5min. The beds are somewhat uncomfortable and the street noise constant—but with Niederdorfstr. nightlife right outside, you may not need your bunk bed. Kitchens and showers on each floor. Linens and towels each 3CHF, blanket provided. Next-day laundry service 10CHF. Internet 6CHF per hr. Reception 8-11am and 3-10pm. Check-out 10am. Dorms 33CHF; singles 69CHF; doubles 98CHF; triples 135CHF; quads 176CHF. MC/V. ❷

**Hôtel Foyer Hottingen,** Hottingenstr. 31 (☎256 1919; www.foyer-hottingen.ch). Take tram #3 (dir.: Kluspl.) to Hottingerpl. Families and student backpackers fill this newly renovated house a block from the Kunsthaus. Women-only dorms. Breakfast included. Reception 7am-11pm. Partitioned dorms 38CHF; singles 85-95CHF, with bath 120-135CHF; doubles 120/160-170CHF; triples 145/190CHF; quads 180CHF. MC/V. ❷

**Jugendherberge Zürich (HI),** Mutschellenstr. 114 (☎399 7800; www.youthhostel.ch/zuerich). From the station, take tram #7 (dir.: Wollishofen) to Morgental, then backtrack 20m and head down Mutschellenstr. 24hr. snack bar with beer on tap. Breakfast included. Internet 1CHF per 4min. Reception 24hr. Dorms 44CHF; singles with shower 105CHF; doubles with shower 123CHF; triples 141CHF, with shower 156CHF; quads 178CHF; quints 194CHF. Rates rise July-Aug. HI discount 6CHF. MC/V. ❸

**Zic-Zac Rock-Hotel,** Marktg. 17 (☎261 2181; www.ziczac.ch). Hotel is 1min. down the road past City Backpacker. Each room is named after a band and decorated with funky paintings. Rooms have TV, phone, and sink. Internet 1CHF per 4min. Reception 24hr. Singles 83CHF, with shower 94CHF; doubles 133/147CHF; triples 173/180CHF; quads with shower 280CHF. AmEx/MC/V. ❹

**Camping Seebrucht,** Seestr. 559 (☎482 1612), by the lake. Take tram #11 to Bürklipl., then bus #161 or 165 to Stadtgrenze. Reception 8am-noon and 3-9pm. Check-out 11:30am. 8CHF per person, 20CHF per tent. Showers 2CHF. MC/V. ❶

# FOOD

Zürich's more than 1300 restaurants offer a bite of everything. The cheapest meals are available at *Würstli* (sausage) stands for 5CHF. The **farmer's markets** at Bürklipl. (Tu and F 6-11am) and Rosenhof (Th 10am-8pm, Sa 10am-5pm) sell produce and flowers. Head to **Niederdorfstraße** for a variety of snack bars and cheaper restaurants interspersed among fancier establishments.

**Café Zähringer,** Zähringerpl. 11 (☎ 252 0500; www.cafe-zaehringer.ch). Enjoy mainly vegetarian and vegan fare in this colorful, student-friendly cafe. Try their *Kefirwasser*, a purple, fizzy drink made from dates and mushrooms fed with sugar (4CHF). Order at the front. Salads 7-13CHF. Pasta 4-14CHF. Stir-fry 16-27CHF. Open M 6pm-midnight, Tu-Th, Su 8am-midnight, F-Sa 8am-12:30am. Cash only. ❷

**Restaurant Schlauch,** Münstergasse 20. Enjoy the billiard tables at this affordable downtown eatery. Soups 5-8.50CHF. Salads 7-17CHF. Entrees 8-20CHF. Open Tu-Sa 11:30am-2pm and 6-9pm. AmEx/MC/V. ❷

**Bodega Española,** Münster. 15 (☎ 251 2310). Has been serving Catalán delights since 1874. Egg-and-potato tortilla dishes 16-18CHF. Tapas 4.80CHF. Open daily 10am-midnight. Kitchen open noon-2pm and 6-10pm. AmEx/MC/V. ❷

**Sprüngli Confiserie Café,** Paradepl. (☎ 224 4711), a Zürich landmark, was founded by one of the original Lindt chocolate makers. Pick up a handful of the bite-size *Luxemburgerli* (8.40CHF per 100g) or eat a full meal (19-28CHF). Open M-F 7am-8pm, Sa 8am-7pm, Su 10am-6pm. Branches at Stadelhoferpl. near the lake (open M-F 7am-6:30pm, Sa 8am-4pm) and in the Hauptbahnof (open M-F 6:45am-9pm, Sa 6:45am-8pm, Su 8:45am-5pm). AmEx/MC/V. ❷

**Rheinfelder Bierhalle,** Niederdorfst. 72. This restaurant and bar near the Hauptbahnof attracts boisterous patrons looking for hearty meals and plentiful liquor. Soups 3-6CHF. Würste 6-15CHF. Entrees 10-20CHF. Open daily 9am-midnight. MC/V. ❷

**Manora Restaurant,** Banhofst. 75. Mingle with bankers at this fast-paced self-serve restaurant on the 5th fl. of the Manor department store. Sandwiches 3-6CHF. Salads 4-11CHF. Entrees 6-15CHF. Open M-F 9am-8pm, Sa 9am-5pm. AmEx/MC/V. ❶

**Rheinfelder Bierhaus,** Marktg. 19. Night crowds fill the outdoor seating at this bright, very Swiss downtown restaurant (not to be confused with Rheinfelder Bierhalle down the street). Entrees 12-21CHF. Vegetarian dishes 12-16CHF. Open daily 8:30am-midnight. Kitchen open daily 11am-11pm. AmEx/MC/V. ❷

**Raclette Stube,** Zähringerstr. 16 (☎ 251 4130). Family-style restaurant has all-you-can-eat *raclette* (round cheese; 33CHF). Fondues 25-35CHF. Open daily 6-10pm. MC/V. ❹

# 🔍 SIGHTS

**Bahnhofstraße** leads into the city from the train station. The street is filled with shoppers during the day but falls dead quiet after 6pm and on weekends. At the Zürichsee end of Bahnhofstr., **Bürkliplatz** is a good place to begin walking along the lake shore. The *platz* itself hosts a Saturday **flea market** *(May-Oct. 6am-3pm)*. On the other side of the Limmat River, the pedestrian zone continues on Niederdorfstr. and Münsterg., where shops run from ritzy to erotic and crowds keep busy until well after midnight. Off Niederdorfstr., **Spiegelgasse** was once home to Goethe and Lenin. **Fraumünster, Grossmünster,** and **St. Peters Kirche** straddle the Limmat River. For a view of Zürich from the water, as well as a chance to see some of the towns on the banks of the Zürichsee, **boat tours** costing a fraction of those in other Swiss cities leave from the ferry terminal at Bürklipl. The shortest tour, **A Kleine Rundfahrten,** lasts 1½hr. *(May-Sept. daily 11am-6:30pm., 7.80CHF.)*

**FRAUMÜNSTER.** Marc Chagall's stained glass windows depicting Biblical scenes add vibrancy to this otherwise austere 13th-century Gothic cathedral. A mural decorating the courtyard's archway depicts Felix and Regula (the decapitated patron saints of Zürich) with their heads in their hands. *(Off Paradepl. Open May-Nov. M-Sa 10am-6pm, Su 11:30am-6pm; Dec.-Apr. M-Sa 10am-4pm, Su 11:30am-4pm. Free.)*

**GROSSMÜNSTER.** Ulrich Zwingli kickstarted the Swiss German Reformation at Grossmünster in the 16th century. Today, the cathedral is Zürich's main landmark. Its defining twin towers are best viewed on the bridge near the Fraumünster. *(Towers open daily Mar.-Oct. 9:15am-5pm; Nov.-Feb. 10:15am-4:30pm. 2CHF.)* One of Zwingli's Bibles lies in a case near his pulpit. Downstairs in the cavernous 12th-century crypt is a menacing statue of Charlemagne and his 2m sword. *(Church open daily mid-Mar. to Oct. 9am-6pm; Nov. to mid-Mar. 10am-5pm. Free.)*

**ZOO ZÜRICH.** Far from downtown's bustle, this hillside zoo holds around 2,000 animals of 250 different species, along with a few million children. Explore tropical rainforests and their inhabitants at the enormous Masoala biosphere. *(Take tram #6 (dir.: Zoo) to the last stop, then walk up Zürichbergst. to your left. Open daily Mar.-Oct. 9am-6pm, Nov.-Mar. 9am-5pm. 22CHF, 16-25 16CHF. AmEx/MC/V.)*

**BEACHES.** When the weather heats up, a visit to the beaches along the Zürichsee offers respite. The city has numerous free swimming spots, which are labeled on a map distributed by the tourist office. The convenient and popular **Arboretum** is about 100m down from the Quaibrücke. *(Tram #5 to Rentenanstalt and head to the water.)* Across the lake, **Zürichhorn** draws crowds with its peaceful gardens and a famous statue by Jean Tinguely. *(Tram #2 or 4 to Frolichst., then walk towards the lake.)* **Strandbad Mythenquai,** along the western shore, offers diving towers and a water trampoline. *(Tram #7 to Brunaustr. and walk 2min. in the same direction until you see a set of stairs. Look for signs. ☎ 201 0000. Check out www.sportamt.ch for info on water quality and other bathing locations. Open daily May to early Sept. 9am-8pm. 6CHF, 16-20 4.50CHF.)*

**GARDENS AND PARKS.** For views of the city and river, climb up to **Lindenhof,** once a checkpoint for Roman settlement; walk uphill on Strehlg., Rennweg, or Glockeng. The lush **Rieter-Park,** overlooking the city, creates a romantic back-drop for the **Museum Rietberg.** *(Tram #7 to Museum Rietberg. Turn right onto Sternenstr. and follow the signs uphill to the museum. Free.)* The **Stadtgärtnerei's** aviary attracts botanists and ornithologists alike—17 species of tropical birds swoop overhead. *(Sackzelg. 25-27. Tram #3 to Hubertus; head down Gutstr. ☎ 492 1423; www.stadtgaertnerei.ch. Open daily 9-11:30am and 1:30-4:30pm. Free.)*

# 🏛 MUSEUMS

**▨ MUSEUM RIETBERG.** Rietberg presents an outstanding collection of Asian, African, and other non-European art, housed in three structures spread around the Rieter-Park. The basement of the new **Emerald building** houses masterpieces from Asia and Africa; highlights include Chinese boddhisatvas and Japanese Noh masks. **Villa Wesendonck** (where Wagner wrote Tristan and Isolde) holds works from South Asia, Central America, and Oceania, while **Park-Villa Rieter** includes a small collection of Near Eastern art. *(Gablerstr. 15. Tram #7 to Museum Rietberg. ☎ 206 3131; www.rietberg.ch. All buildings open Apr.-Sept. Tu, F-Su 10am-5pm, W-Th 10am-8pm. 12CHF, students 10CHF, under 16 free. MC/V; buy tickets in the Emerald building.)*

**▨ KUNSTHAUS ZÜRICH.** The Kunsthaus, Europe's largest privately funded museum, houses a vast collection ranging from religious works by the Old Masters to 21st-century American Pop Art. Compositions by Chagall, Dalí, Gauguin, van Gogh, Munch, Picasso, Rembrandt, Renoir, and Rubens stretch from wall to wall in a patchwork of rich color. *(Heimpl. 1. Take tram #3, 5, 8, or 9 to*

*Kunsthaus.* ☎ 253 8484; www.kunsthaus.ch. English-language audio tour and brochure. Open Tu-Th 10am-9pm, F-Su 10am-5pm. 16CHF, students 10CHF. AmEx/MC/V.)

**SCHWEIZERISCHES LANDESMUSEUM.** In the cement imitation-castle next to the *Hauptbahnhof*, this museum of Swiss history and culture displays centuries-old artifacts. Highlights include 16th-century astrological tools, Ulrich Zwingli's weapons from the 1531 Battle of Kappel, and a tiny jeweled clock with a golden skeleton indicating the hour. *(Museumstr. 2.* ☎ 218 6511; www.musee-suisse.com. Open Tu-Su 10am-5pm. 5CHF, students 3CHF.)

**JOHANN JACOBS MUSEUM.** Exhibits on the cultural history of coffee are best viewed while sipping a free cup. *(Seefldquai 17. Take tram #2, 4, 5, 8, 9, 11, or 15 to Bellevue, then walk along the lake and turn onto Seefeldquai.* ☎ 388 6151; www.johann-jacobs-museum.ch. Open F 2-7pm, Sa 2-5pm, Su 10am-5pm. 5CHF, students 3CHF.)

## ♫ 🎭 ENTERTAINMENT AND NIGHTLIFE

Most movies in Zürich are screened in English with French and German subtitles (marked "E/D/F"). Films generally cost 15CHF and up, but less on Mondays. From mid-July to mid-August, the **OrangeCinema,** an open-air cinema at Zürich-horn (tram #2 or 4 to Fröhlichstr.), attracts huge crowds to its lakefront screenings. Every August, the **Street Parade** (mid-Aug.) brings together ravers from all over for the world's biggest techno party.

>  **THAT EXPLAINS THE TASSELS.** Beware the deceptive and common title of "night club"—it's really just a euphemism for "strip club."

For information on after-dark happenings, check **ZüriTipp** (www.zueritipp.ch) or pick up a free copy of *ZürichGuide* or *ZürichEvents* from the tourist office. On **Niederdorfstraße,** the epicenter of Zürich's *Altstadt* nightlife, bars are packed to the brim almost every night. **Kreis 5,** once the industrial area of Zürich, has recently developed into party central, with ubiquitous clubs, bars, and lounges taking over former factories; this is where the city's young, hip, and in-the-know come to play after the sun goes down. Kreis 5 lies northwest of the *Hauptbahnhof*, with Hard-str. as its axis. To get there, take tram #4 (dir.: Werdholzi) or #13 (dir.: Albisgütli) to Escher-Wyss-Pl. and follow the crowds. Closer to the Old Town, **Langstraße,** reached by walking away from the river on the city's western side, is the reputed red-light district, with a number of cheap bars and clubs (some sleazier than others). Beer in Zürich is pricey (from 6CHF), but a number of cheap bars have established themselves on Niederdorfstr. near Mühleg.

■ **Kaufleuten,** Pelikanstr. 18 (☎ 225 3322; www.kaufleuten.ch). A former theater, this trendy club—still decked out in red velvet—attracts the who's who of Zürich by throwing nightly themed parties. Madonna and Prince have both paid visits. Check website to see what's going on any given evening. Cover 10-30CHF. Hours vary, but generally open Su-Th 11pm-2am, F-Sa 11pm-4am. MC/V.

**Nelson,** Beateng. 11 (☎ 212 6016). Locals, backpackers, and businessmen chug beer (9CHF per pint) at this large Irish pub. 20+. Open M-W 11:30am-2am, Th 11:30am-3am, F 11:30am-4:30am, Sa 3pm-4:30am, Su 3pm-2am. MC/V.

**Barfüsser,** Spitalg. 14 (☎ 251 4064), off Zähringerpl. Freely flowing mixed drinks (14-17CHF) and wine (6-9CHF) accompany delicious sushi at this gay bar. Open M-Th noon-1am, F-Sa noon-2am, Su 5pm-1am. AmEx/MC/V.

**Nachtflug Bar, Café, and Lounge,** Stüssihofstatt 4 (☎ 261 9966; www.n8flug.ch). Sleek bar with outdoor seating. Wine from 6CHF. Beer from 4.90CHF. Open M-Th 9am-midnight, F 9am-1:30am, Sa 11am-1:30am, Su 11am-midnight. Outdoor bar open M-W 9am-midnight, Th-F 9am-10pm, Sa-Su 11am-10pm. AmEx/MC/V.

**Öpfelchammer,** Rindermarkt 12 (☎251 2336). This wine bar (8-10CHF per glass) has low ceilings and wooden crossbeams covered with initials and messages from 200 years of merry-making. Those who can hang upside from the beams while drinking a complimentary glass of wine get to engrave their names on the wall—it's harder than it looks. Open mid-Aug. to mid-July Tu-Sa 11am-12:30am. AmEx/MC/V.

**Cranberry,** Metzgerg. 3 (☎261 2772; www.cranberry.ch), attracts a primarily gay, sociable clientele with funky lights, peppy music, and a wide selection of mixed drinks (around 13CHF). Happy hour 5-7pm; drinks are double-sized. Open Su-W 5pm-12:30am, Th 5pm-1am, F-Sa 5pm-2am. AmEx/MC/V.

# LUZERN (LUCERNE)                                    ☎041

Luzern (pop. 60,000) welcomes busloads of tourists each day in the summer, and with good reason. The streets of the *Altstadt* lead down to the placid Vierwaldstättersee (Lake Lucerne), the covered bridges over the river are among the most photographed sights in Switzerland, and the sunrise over the famous Mt. Pilatus has hypnotized artists—including Goethe, Twain, and Wagner—for centuries.

**TRANSPORTATION AND PRACTICAL INFORMATION. Trains** leave the large Bahnhof for: Basel (1hr., 2 per hr., 30CHF); Bern via Olten (1½hr., 2 per hr., 34CHF); Geneva (3½hr., 1-2 per hr., 70CHF); Zürich (1hr., 2 per hr., 22CHF). VBL **buses** depart in front of the train station and provide extensive coverage of Luzern. **Boats** leave from across the road to destinations all over Lake Luzern; some offer themed cruises (☎612 9090; www.lakelucerne.ch. Cruises 15-60CHF). Route maps are available at the station **tourist office,** Bahnhofstr. 3, which reserves rooms for free, and holds daily guided tours at 9:45 am. (☎227 1717; www.luzern.org. Open May-Oct. M-F 8:30am-6:30pm, Sa 9am-6:30pm; Nov.-Apr. M-F 8:30am-5:30pm, Sa 9am-1pm.) There are two **post offices** by the train station; the older building by the bridge is the main one.

**ACCOMMODATIONS AND FOOD.** Inexpensive beds are limited, so call ahead. To reach **Backpackers Lucerne ❷,** Alpenquai 42, turn right from the station onto Inseliquai and follow it for 20min. until it turns into Alpenquai. The hostel's distance from the center of town may be inconvenient, but it has a fun, communal vibe. (☎360 0420; www.backpackerslucerne.ch. Laundry 9CHF. Internet 10CHF per hr. Reception 7:30-10am and 4-11pm. Dorms 29CHF; doubles 66-70CHF. Bike rental 18CHF per day. Cash only.) Overlooking the river from the *Altstadt* is the **Tourist Hotel ❷,** St. Karliquai 12, which offers plain rooms and a prime location. From the station, walk along Bahnhofstr., cross the river at the second covered bridge, and make a left onto St. Karliquai. (☎410 2474; www.touristhotel.ch. Breakfast included. Summer dorms 38-43CHF; doubles 98-112CHF; triples 129-138CHF; quads 172-180CHF. Winter dorms 38-40CHF; doubles 88-98CHF; triples 111-129CHF; quads 152-172CHF. AmEx/MC/V.) Watch trains roll by while gorging on delicious Middle Eastern fare at **Erdem Kebab ❶,** down Zentralstr. from the Banhof. (Falafel 8CHF. Kebab 8-12CHF. Open M-Th 10am-midnight, Fri-Sa 11am-8pm. Cash only.) **Markets** along the river sell cheap, fresh food on Tuesday and Saturday mornings. There's also a **Coop** supermarket at the train station. (Open M-Sa 6:30am-9pm, Su 8am-9pm.)

**SIGHTS AND ENTERTAINMENT.** The *Altstadt*, across the river from the station, is famous for its frescoed houses; the best examples are those on Hirschenpl. and Weinmarkt. The 14th-century **Kapellbrücke,** a wooden-roofed bridge, runs from left of the train station to the *Altstadt* and is decorated with Swiss histor-

## LOCAL LEGEND

### HI-YO, SWISS INDEPENDENCE!

Everyone knows some element of the William Tell story, whether it be the famous apple-shooting scene or the ubiquitous overture from Rossini's opera (later appropriated, of course, as the theme song of *The Lone Ranger*). But few would guess that this tale of martial defiance originated in neutral Switzerland.

According to legend, Wilhelm Tell lived in the 14th century in the canton of Uri, just south of Zürich. The Hapsburg emperors installed an Austrian "protector," Hermann Gessler, to further their attempts to dominate the region. Gessler demanded that all citizens of Altdorf bow before a pole with his hat on it, but the stubborn Tell refused. The protector ordered Tell to shoot an apple off his son's head, or else both would be executed.

Tell, an expert marksman, had no problem with his crossbow. He then declared that if he had hit his son, he would have immediately attacked Gessler. None too happy, Gessler ordered Tell brought to his castle on the Vierwaldstättersee. Tell escaped his captors in a storm, waited for the Austrian in the castle, and promptly dispatched him at first sight—with a crossbow, of course. The act sparked a wave of defiance that led to the formation of the Swiss Confederation.

ical scenes. Farther down the river, the **Spreuerbrücke** is adorned by Kaspar Meglinger's eerie *Totentanz* (Dance of Death) paintings. On the hills above the river, the **Museggmauer** and its towers are all that remain of the medieval city's ramparts. Three of the towers are accessible to visitors and provide panoramic views of the city; one, the **Zyt**, features the inner workings of Luzern's oldest clock, a 16th-century doozy that chimes one minute before all other city clocks. From Mühlenpl., walk up Brugglig., then head uphill to the right on Museggstr. and follow the castle signs. (Open in summer daily 8am-7pm.) To the east is the magnificent **Löwendenkmal,** the dying lion of Luzern, carved into a cliff on Denkmalstr. to honor the Swiss soldiers who died defending King Louis XVI of France during the invasion of the Tuileries in 1792. Right next to it is the **Gletschergarten** (Glacier Garden), which showcases an odd but interesting collection including Ice Age formations, a 19th-century Swiss house, and a hall of mirrors. (☎410 4340; www.gletschergarten.ch. Open daily Apr.-Oct. 9am-6pm, Nov.-Mar. 10am-5pm. 12CHF.)

Europe's largest transportation museum, the ■**Verkehrshaus der Schweiz** (Swiss Transport Museum), Lidostr. 5, has interactive displays on everything from early flying machines to cars, but the highlight is its train warehouse. Take bus #6, 8, or 24 to Verkehrshaus. (☎370 4444; www.verkehrshaus.ch. Open daily Apr.-Oct. 10am-6pm; Nov.-Mar. 10am-5pm. 24CHF, students 22CHF, with Eurail Pass 14CHF.) The **Picasso Museum,** Am Rhyn Haus, Furreng. 21, displays a some of Picasso's sketches and a large collection of photographs from the artist's later years. From Schwanenpl., take Rathausquai to Furreng. (☎410 3533. Open daily Apr.-Oct. 10am-6pm; Nov.-Mar. 11am-1pm and 2pm-4pm. 8CHF, students 5CHF.)

Although Luzern's nightlife is more about chilling than club-hopping, there are still many options. **The Loft,** Haldenstr. 21, hosts special DJs and theme nights. (Beer 9-11CHF. Open W 9pm-2am, Th-Su 10am-4am.) The mellow **Jazzkantine** club, Grabenstr. 8, is affiliated with the renowned **Luerne School of Music.** (Sandwiches 6-8CHF. Open mid-Aug. to mid-July M-Sa 7am-1:30am, Su 4pm-1:30am. MC/V.) Luzern attracts big names for its two jazz festivals: **Blue Balls Festival** (last week of July) and **Blues Festival** (2nd week of Nov.).

▶ **DAYTRIP FROM LUZERN: MT. PILATUS.** The view of the Alps from the top of Mt. Pilatus (2132m) is phenomenal. It is also crowded, with two hotels and a restaurant just 20min. from the summit. For the most memorable trip, catch a boat from Luzern to Alpnachstad (1½hr.), ascend by the world's steepest

**cogwheel train,** then descend by cable car to Kriens and take bus #1 back to Luzern (entire trip 82CHF). For less money and more exercise, take a train to Alpnachstad and hike to the top of Mt. Pilatus (4hr.) before descending by cable car (29CHF, with SwissPass 15CHF). Embark on the summer **Rodelbahn** (toboggan) run from Fräkmüntegg; for 8CHF, you can whiz down the hillside past grazing cows at surprising speed. For info on all of Mt. Pilatus' attractions, visit www.pilatus.ch.

# ST. GALLEN                                         ☎071

Though called "the metropolis of eastern Switzerland," St. Gallen (pop. 75,000) is anything but imposing. Founded as a religious center by the Irish monk Gallus in the 7th century, the city has retained an intimate feel—especially in the historic center, where you can get enjoyably lost in a maze of narrow, winding streets lined with shops, restaurants, bars, and the occasional open-air market.

**■⁊ TRANSPORTATION AND PRACTICAL INFORMATION. Trains** leave from the *Hauptbanhof* for: Luzern (2hr., 2 per hr., 45CHF); Zürich (1¼hr., 1-2 per hr., 25CHF); Bern (1½hr., 1 per hr., 63CHF.); Geneva (4hr., 1 per hr., 95CHF); Lausanne (3½hr., 2 per hr., 81CHF). The **tourist office,** in front of the station, books rooms for free (May-Oct. M-F 9am-6pm, Sa 10am-3pm; Nov.-Apr. M-F 9am-3pm, Sa 10am-1pm). The post office is opposite the train station. **Postal Code:** CH-9000.

**▮▯ ACCOMMODATIONS AND FOOD. Jugendherberge (HI) ❷,** 25 Jüchstr., has clean rooms and scenic views of the hillside; take the orange Trogenerbahn tram (dir: Trogen) from the right of the train station to the Schuleraus stop, then walk up the hill for 5min. and turn left. (☎245 4777. Breakfast included. Reception 7:30-10am, 5-10:30pm. Laundry 6CHF. Internet 12CHF per hr. Dorms 30-36CHF; singles 50-52CHF; doubles 39-42CHF.) There's no shortage of restaurants; for low prices and friendly surroundings seek out **Isabel's Imbisshöck ❷,** tucked away in a quiet corner at the end of Engelgaße. (Meals 6-14CHF. Mixed drinks 3-9CHF. Wines 20-22CHF. Open M-Th 11am-2pm and 5-10pm, F-Sa 11am-2pm and 5pm-12:30am. Cash only.) If pious St. Gallen moves you to gluttony, indulge with two floors of glorious Swiss cocoa at the **Chocolaterie Maestrani ❶,** next to the Abbey Precinct. (Open Tu-W 9am-9pm, Th-F 9am-6:30pm, Sa 9am-5pm, Su 9:30am-4pm.)

**◪ ♫ SIGHTS AND ENTERTAINMENT.** The **▨Abbey Precinct** is a grouping of remarkable Benedictine structures—some dating back to the 1400s—with UNESCO World Heritage Landmark status. The soaring towers of the Baroque **cathedral,** constructed from 1755 to 1767, dominate the scene; the ornate interior, with its majestic painted ceiling, is no less dramatic. (Open M-Tu and Th-F 9am-6pm, W 10am-6pm, Sa 9am-3:45pm, Su 12:15am-5:30pm.) The **Abbey Library** has a world-famous collection of over 140,000 valuable books and manuscripts, all housed in a fittingly grand Rococo hall. (Open Jan. 2-Feb. 25; Mar. 3-Nov. 11; Dec. 3-Dec. 31; M-Sa 10am-5pm, Su 10am-4pm. 7CHF.) The **Lapidarium** holds ancient artifacts from the 8th century onwards. (Open M-Sa 10am-5pm, Su 10am-4pm. 3CHF.) Religious egalitarians shouldn't miss the neighboring **Church of St. Laurence,** once the hotbed of Reformation in St. Gallen; visitors who make the long trek up to the church's viewing platform (mind those immense, oft-ringing bells) will find divine views of the city and surrounding countryside. (Church open M 9:30-11:30am and 2-4pm, Tu-F 9:30am-6pm, Sa 9:30am-4pm. Viewing platform open M-Sa 9:30-11:30am and 2-4pm. 2CHF.)

St. Gallen isn't all worship. Museumstr., next to the **City Park (Stadtpark),** is lined by all manner of cultural institutions. Indulge a love of dinosaurs at the **National History Museum (Naturmuseum).** The **Museum of Art (Kunstmuseum),** housed in the same building, features a collection of contemporary sculpture—as you might infer from the giant fly out front. (Both museums open Tu, Th-Su 10am-5pm; W 10am-8pm). The **Museum of History and Ethnology (Historisches und Völkerkundemuseum)** offers exhibits on nearly every part of the world. There's a section for the *Kinder*, too. (☎242 0642; www.hmsg.ch. Open Tu-Su 10am-5pm.) The **St. Gallen Theatre** is famous for its mix of musicals, drama, and dance, while the **Tonhalle,** across the street, is home to the St. Gallen Symphony Orchestra and renowned guest soloists. (Theater: www.theatresg.ch; Tonhalle: www.sinfonieorchestersg.ch. Box office for both: ☎242 0606. Open M-Su 10am-12:30pm.) St. Gallen rocks out with its **Open Air Festival,** held annually at the end of June and featuring some of the world's biggest acts (in 2007, the Arctic Monkeys and Arcade Fire).

## STEIN AM RHEIN                                                  ☎052

The tiny, medieval *Altstadt* of Stein am Rhein (pop. 3190) is postcard-perfect, with traditional Swiss architecture framed by hills and the Rhine River. To reach the Old Town, walk down Bahnhofstr. from the station, turn right onto Wagenhauserstr., then go downhill and over the bridge. The buildings on the main square, the **Rathausplatz,** date back to the 15th century and feature remarkable facade paintings depicting the animal or scene for which each house is named. Ground level floors are occupied by small (and pricey) shops and restaurants. The stately **Rathaus** (town council building) is to the right upon reaching the square. Heading away from the Rathauspl., the **Understadt,** the main road running through the village, leads to the **Museum Lindwurm,** a 19th-century house restored to its bourgeois glory, roosters and all. (Open Mar.-Oct. M and W-Su 10am-5pm. 5CHF, students 3CHF.) For a look at a completely different facet of village life, visit Stein am Rhein's oldest claim to fame, the 12th-century **Kloster St. Georgen.** You can reach the tucked-away entrance to this Benedictine monastery by going through the arch across from the tourist office, behind and to the left of the Rathaus. Explore monks' dormitories, a scriptorium, preserved wall drawings, and the gorgeous ▧**Festsaal,** a room where feet may not touch the red-green tiled floor and the sun is the only source of lighting. (☎741 2142. Open Apr.-Oct. Tu-Su 10am-5pm. 4CHF, students 3CHF.) The picturesque castle **Burg Hohenklingen** sits atop a hill overlooking the village; the view of the Rhine and the villages from its grounds is worth the hike. From the Rathauspl., take Brodlauberg. 30min. away from the river.

The clean, family-oriented **Jugendherberge (HI) ❷,** Hemishoferstr. 87, is a 20min. walk from the train station; cross the Rhein and walk left out of the Old Town along the main road or take bus #7349 (dir.: Singen), which runs once per hour from Untertor station, to Strandbad and walk 5min. farther in the same direction. (☎741 1255; www.youthhostel.ch/stein. Breakfast included. Dinner 13CHF. Internet 1CHF per 10min. Reception 8-10am and 5-9pm. Open Mar.-Oct. Dorms 32-36CHF; singles 46CHF; doubles 80CHF. 6CHF HI discount. AmEx/MC/V.) The **Weinstube zum Rother Ochsen ❷,** Rathauspl. 9, built in 1466, is the oldest public house in the town. Though full meals are not available, their regional soups (8.50CHF), appetizers (8-20CHF), and wines (4-14CHF) are filling. (☎741 2328. Open Tu-Sa 10am-11pm, Su 10am-6pm. Kitchen open 11:30am-2pm and 6-10pm.) **Volg market** is located at Rathauspl. 17. (Open M-F 8:15am-6:30pm, Sa 8am-8pm.)

**Trains** connect Stein am Rhein to Constance, GER (40min., 1 per hr., 10CHF) via Kreuzlingen, and to Zürich (1hr., 1-2 per hr., 21CHF) via Winterthur or Schaffhausen. **Boats** (☎634 0888; www.urh.ch) depart for Bodensee towns, including Constance (2¼hr., 4-6 per day, 27CHF), and Schaffhausen (1¼hr., 4-6 per day, 21CHF), which is within an hour's walk of the Rhine Falls, Europe's biggest waterfall. Those who want to tour the area by land can rent **bikes** from **River Bike,** Rathauspl. 15. (☎741 5541; www.riverbike.ch. 15-20CHF per 2hr., 18-28CHF per half day, 29-35CHF per day. Open M 1:30-6:30pm, Tu-F 9am-6:30pm, Sa 9am-4pm, Su 11am-5pm.) The **tourist office,** Oberstadt. 3, on the other side of the Rathaus, has free maps for visitors, and also books rooms for free. (☎42 20 90; www.stein-amrhein.ch. Open July-Aug. M-Sa 9:30am-noon and 1:30-4pm; Sept.-June M-F 9:30am-noon and 1:30-4pm.) **Postal Code:** CH-8260.

# NORTHWESTERN SWITZERLAND

Though at the junction of the French and German borders, this peaceful region remains defiantly Swiss; locals speak Swiss-German and welcome visitors with distinctive hospitality. The best part of Northwestern Switzerland is youthful Basel, Switzerland's preeminent university town.

## BASEL (BÂLE)                    ☎061

Basel bills itself as Switzerland's "cultural capital," and though nearby Zürich might beg to differ, it's hard to argue with the city's lively medieval quarter and many museums. Basel is home to one of the oldest universities in Europe—former professors include Erasmus and Nietzsche.

**TRANSPORTATION AND PRACTICAL INFORMATION.** Basel has three train stations: the **French (SNCF)** and **Swiss (SBB)** stations on Centralbahnpl., near the *Altstadt*, and the **German (DB)** station across the Rhine (take tram #2 from the other train stations or connect directly from the SBB). **Trains** leave from the SBB to: Bern (1¼hr., 1-2 per hr., 36CHF); Geneva (3hr., 1 per hr., 67CHF); Lausanne (2½hr., 1 per hr., 57CHF); Zürich (1hr., every 15-30min., 30CHF). The main **tourist office** is on Steinenbergstr., in the Stadt Casino building (from the SBB station, take #6, 8, 14, 16, or 17 to Barfüsserpl.). There is also a branch in the SBB station. (Both offices: ☎268 6868; www.baseltourismus.ch. Open M-F 8:30am-6:30pm, Sa 9am-5pm, Su 10am-4pm.) For info on **GLBT** establishments, stop by the bookstore **Arcados,** Rheing. 69. (☎681 3132; www.arcados.com. Open Tu-F 1-7pm, Sa noon-4pm.) To reach the **post office,** Rüdeng. 1, take tram #1 or 8 to Marktpl. and back-track away from the river. (Open M-F 7:30am-9pm, Sa 8am-5pm, Su 2-7pm.)

**ACCOMMODATIONS AND FOOD.** The **Jugendherberge (HI) ❷,** St. Alban-Kirchrain 10, is located near the Rhine in a beautiful 19th-century building. To get there, take tram #2 or 15 to Kunstmuseum, turn right on St. Alban-Vorstadt, then follow the signs. (☎272 0572; www.youthhostel.ch/basel. Breakfast included. Laundry 7CHF. Internet 6CHF per hr. Reception Mar.-Oct. 7-10am and 2pm-midnight; Nov.-Feb. 7-10am and 2-11pm. Dorms 37-39CHF; doubles 112CHF; quads 168CHF. HI discount 6CHF. AmEx/MC/V.) **Basel Back Pack ❷,** Dornacherstr. 192, is far from the *Altstadt,* but the hostel provides free tickets for all trams and buses. To reach it, walk out the back entrance of the SBB station, turn left on Güterst., then turn right onto Brudenholzst. at Tellpl. The hostel is in the complex on your left after a block. (☎333 0037; www.baselbackpack.ch. Breakfast 7CHF. Laundry 6CHF. Internet 1CHF per 5min. Reception 8-11:30am, 2-6pm, and 8-10:30pm. Dorms 31CHF; singles 80CHF; doubles 96CHF; triples 123CHF; quads 144CHF; quints 180CHF. AmEx/MC/V; min. 60CHF.)

SWITZERLAND

**Barfüsserplatz** and **Marktplatz** are full of satisfying restaurants. ◪**Restaurant Hirscheneck ❷**, Lindenberg 23 in Klein-Basel, is popular with students, vegetarians, and Basel's alternative crowd. (Take tram #2 or 15 to Wettsteinpl., then walk back towards the river and turn right on Kartausg. ☎ 692 7333; www.hirscheneck.ch. Daily menu 12-24CHF. Smaller portions 9-15CHF. Su brunch 10am-4pm. Open M 2pm-midnight, Tu-Th 11am-1am, Sa 2pm-1am, Su 10am-midnight. Cash only.) On the other bank of the Rhine off Barfüsserpl., **Café Barfi ❸**, Leonhardsberg 4, belies its name with tasty, affordable Italian meals. (☎ 261 7038. Pizza 18-21CHF. Pasta 15-20CHF. Open M-Sa 11am-11pm). **Brauerei Fischerstube ❹**, Rheing. 45, serves intoxicating dishes such as beer soup. (☎ 692 6635. Beer 4.30CHF. Full dinner menu 42CHF; served from 6pm. Open M-Th 10am-12:30am, F-Sa 10am-1:30am, Su 5pm-midnight. AmEx/MC/V.) Groceries are available at the **Migros** in the SBB station. (Open M-F 6am-10pm, Sa-Su 7:30am-10pm.)

**◨ SIGHTS.** The Rhine separates Groß-Basel (Greater Basel) and the SBB/SNCF train stations from the Klein-Basel (Lesser Basel). Behind the Marktpl., the nearly 800-year-old **Mittlere Rheinbrücke** (Middle Rhine Bridge) connects the two halves of the city. To get to the Old Town from the train station, take tram #16. The very red **Rathaus** (City Hall) brightens the lively **Marktplatz** with its blinding facade and striking gold-and-green statues. Behind Marktpl. stands the red sandstone **Münster** (Cathedral), where you can see the tomb of Erasmus or climb the tower for a spectacular view of the city. (Church open Easter to mid-Oct. M-F 10am-5pm, Sa 10am-4pm, Su 11:30am-5pm; mid-Oct. to Easter M-Sa 11am-4pm, Su 11:30am-4pm. Tower closes 30min. before the church. Church free. Tower 3CHF.) Get off at the Theater stop to see the spectacular ◪**Jean Tinguely Fountain,** also known as the **Fasnachtsbrunnen.** The fountain's various moving metal parts spray water in all directions. From Marktpl., walk up to the **University Quarter.** Nearby looms the huge **Spalentor,** a remnant of the medieval city's fortifications.

**▥ MUSEUMS.** Basel has over 30 museums; pick up a comprehensive guide at the tourist office. The **Basel Card,** also available at the tourist office, provides admission to most museums, free sightseeing tours, and other discounts. (1-day pass 20CHF, 2-day 27CHF, 3-day 35CHF.) The must-see ◪**Kunstmuseum** (Museum of Fine Arts), St. Alban-Graben 16, houses what may be Switzerland's greatest collections of new and old masters. Admission also gives access to the **Museum für Gegenwartskunst** (Museum of Modern Art), St. Alban-Rheinweg 60, which has changing exhibitions of contemporary work. (Kunstmuseum open Tu and Th-Su 10am-5pm, W 10am-7pm. Gegenwartskunst open Tu-Su 11am-5pm. Each museum 12CHF, students 5CHF. Free daily 4-5pm and 1st Su of each month.) At **Museum Tinguely,** Paul-Sacher-Anlage 1, everything rattles in homage to the sculptor's vision of metal and movement. Take tram #2 or 15 to Wettsteinpl., then bus #31 or 36 to Museum Tinguely. (☎ 681 9320. Open Tu-Su 11am-7pm. 10CHF, students 7CHF.) The **Fondation Beyeler,** Baselstr. 101, has one of Europe's finest private art collections. Take tram #6 to Fondation Beyeler. (☎ 645 9700. Open M-Tu and Th-Su 10am-6pm, W 10am-8pm. 23CHF, students 12CHF.)

**EURO CUP 2008.** The **2008 European Football Championship** (June 7-29) will be held in Austria and Switzerland. Basel, Bern, Geneva, and Zürich will host matches. Expect crowds and unrestrained merrymaking. Visit www.uefa.com for more info. For venues in Austria, see p. 85.

**▦ ◨ FESTIVALS AND NIGHTLIFE.** Basel's **Fasnacht** (Feb. 11-13, 2008) commences the week after Lent with the *Morgestraich*, a three-day parade with a centuries-old goal—to scare away winter. Head to **Barfüsserplatz** and the adjoining **Steinenvorstadt** for an evening of bar-hopping. **Atlantis,** Klosterberg 13, is a multi-level, sophisticated bar that plays reggae, jazz, and funk. (☎228 9696. Summer drink special 12CHF. Cover 10-15CHF; students with ID 5CHF discount; July-Sept. no cover F. Open M 11:30am-2pm, Tu-Th 11:30am-2pm and 6pm-midnight, F 11:30am-2pm and 6pm-4am, Sa 6pm-4am. AmEx/MC/V.)

# GRAUBÜNDEN

Graubünden's rugged gorges, fir forests, and eddying rivers give the region a wildness seldom found in comfortably settled Switzerland. Visitors should plan their trips carefully, especially during ski season when reservations are absolutely required, and in May and June, when nearly everything shuts down.

## DAVOS ☎081

Davos (pop. 13,000) sprawls along the valley floor under mountains criss-crossed with chairlifts and cable cars. Originally a health resort, the city catered to such *fin-de-siècle* giants as Robert Louis Stevenson and Thomas Mann. The influx of tourists and political conferences has given the city a somewhat artificial feel, but the thrill of carving down the famed, wickedly steep ski slopes or exploring the 700km of hiking paths may make up for it. Davos provides direct access to two mountains—**Parsenn** and **Jakobshorn**—and four skiing areas. Parsenn, with long runs and fearsome vertical drops, is the mountain around which Davos built its reputation. (Day pass 60CHF.) Jakobshorn has found a niche with the younger crowd since opening a snowboarding park with two half-pipes (day pass 55CHF). Cross-country trails cover 75km, and one is lit at night. In the summer, ski lifts (½-price after 3pm) connect to **hiking trails,** such as the **Panoramaweg** (2hr.). Europe's largest natural **ice rink** (18,000 sq. m) allows for curling, figure skating, hockey, ice dancing, and speed skating. (☎41 53 04. Open July-Aug. and Dec. 15-Feb., 10am-4:30pm. 5CHF; M and Th evening free evening skating. Skate rental 6.50CHF.)

Davos has high prices; staying in nearby Klosters is a more economical option. But avid skiers and snowboarders will appreciate **Snowboardhotel Bolgenschanze** ❸, Skistr. 1. Dorms are sold as a package with lift passes. (☎414 9020; www.davosklosters.ch. 18+. Open mid-Dec. to mid-Mar. 1-night, 2-day ski pass 195-405CHF; 6-night, 7-day pass 650-865CHF. AmEx/MC/V.) Davos is accessible by **train** from Klosters (25min., 2 per hr., 9.20CHF). The town is divided into two areas, Davos-Platz and Davos-Dorf, each with a train station. Platz has the post office and the main **tourist office,** Promenade 67, which is up the hill and to the right on Promenade from the station. (☎415 2121; www.davos.ch. Free Internet. Open Dec. to mid-Apr. and mid-June to mid-Oct. M-F 8:30am-6:30pm, Sa 9am-5pm, Su 10am-noon and 3-5:30pm; mid-Oct. to Nov. and mid-Apr. to mid-June M-F 8:30am-noon and 1:45pm-6pm, Sa 9am-noon.) **Postal Code:** CH-7260.

## KLOSTERS ☎081

Though Klosters (pop. 3000) is not far from Davos, it's a world away in atmosphere. Davos aspires to be cosmopolitan, while Klosters, despite receiving international attention as a favorite ski resort of the British royals, capitalizes on its natural serenity and cozy chalets. **Ski passes** for the Klosters-Davos region run 121CHF per two days and 282CHF per six days, including public transportation. The **Grotschnabahn,** right behind the train station, gives access to Parsenn and Strela in Davos and Madrisa in Klosters (1-day pass 60CHF; 6-day pass 324CHF). The **Madrisabahn** leaves from Klosters-Dorf on the other side of town (1-day pass;

47CHF). **Ski rental** is also available at **Sport Gotschna**, Alte Bahnhofstr. 5, across from the tourist office. (☎422 1197. Skis and snowboards 28-50CHF per day plus 10% insurance. Open mid-June to late April M-F 8am-6:30pm, Sa-Su 8am-6pm. AmEx/MC/V.) In summer, Klosters has access to fantastic **biking trails.** On the lush valley floor, hikers can make a large loop from Klosters's Protestant church on Monbielstr. to Monbiel. The route continues to an elevation of 1488m and turns left, passing through Bödmerwald, Fraschmardintobel, and Monbieler Wald before climbing to its highest elevation of 1634m and returning to Klosters via Pardels. There are fourteen other local routes available, from the genteel to the exhausting. Several adventure companies offer **river rafting, canoeing, horseback riding, paragliding,** and **glacier trekking.** Summer cable car passes (valid on Grotschnabahn and Madrisabahn) are also available (4-day pass 80CHF).

To get to **Jugendherberge Soldanella (HI)** ❷, Talstr. 73, from the station, go left

**THE REAL DEAL.** Staying in Klosters but skiing in both Klosters and Davos is the most affordable and pleasant option for the budget traveler. Many ski packages include mountains from both towns, and Kloster's main lift, the **Grotschnabahn,** leads to a mountain pass accessing both.

uphill past Hotel Alpina to the church, then cross the street and head up the alleyway to the right of the Kirchpl. bus station sign. Walk 10min. along the path. This massive, renovated chalet has a comfortable reading room, a flagstone terrace, and friendly, English-speaking owners. (☎422 1316; www.youthhostel.ch/klosters. Breakfast included. Reception 8-10am and 5-9pm. Open mid-Dec. to mid-Apr. and late June to mid-Oct. Dorms 35CHF; singles 46CHF; doubles 88CHF; family rooms 44CHF per person. HI discount 6CHF. AmEx/MC/V.) Turn right from the train station to reach the **Coop** supermarket, Bahnhofstr. 10. (Open M-F 8am-12:30pm and 2-6:30pm. Sa 8am-5pm.) Trains run to Davos (25min., 2 per hr., 9.20CHF) and Zürich via Landquart (2hr., 1 per hr., 45CHF). The main **tourist office,** reached by turning right from the station and taking another right on Alte Banhofstr., has Internet (5CHF per 30min.) as well as free hiking and biking maps of the area. (☎410 2020; www.klosters.ch. Open May-Nov. M-F 9am-5pm; Dec.-Apr. M-F 8:30am-6pm, Sat-Su 8:30am-5pm.) **Postal code:** CH-7250.

# SWISS NATIONAL PARK                                    ☎081

One of the world's best-kept nature preserves, the Swiss National Park showcases some of the Graubünden region's abundant wildlife and most stunning views. A network of 20 hiking trails, mostly concentrated in the center, runs throughout the park. Few trails are level; most involve a lot of climbing, often into snow-covered areas. All trails are clearly marked, and it is against park rules to wander off the designated trails. Trails that require no mountaineering gear are marked with white-red-white markers. Keep in mind that every route can be tricky.

**Zernez** is the main gateway to the park and home to its headquarters, the **National Parkhouse.** The staff provides helpful trail maps as well as information on which trails are navigable. (☎856 1378; www.nationalpark.ch. Open June-Oct. daily 8:30am-6pm.) To reach the park itself, take a post **bus** (1 per hr., 4.60CHF) from the front of the train station to one of several destinations within the wilderness. Trains and buses also run to other towns in the area, including **Scuol, Samedan,** and **S-chanf.** Despite its location in ski-happy Graubünden, the park, closed November through May, is not a site for winter sports. It is one of the most strictly regulated nature reserves in the world; camping and campfires are prohibited, as is collect-

## THE SCRAPED DISH

Though fondue is Switzerland's main culinary claim to fame, visitors to the western, French-speaking part of the country will notice another item popping up on menus: *raclette*. Not surprisingly, it also involves cheese.

*Raclette* dates from the medieval era, when peasants would heat cheese made from their cows' milk next to evening fires. When the cheese had reached the right consistency and softness, the farmers would scrape it off the plate onto some bread—hence the name (the French *racler* means "to scrape"). The German equivalent was termed *Bratchas*, or "roasted cheese."

Today, the dish has left the Alpine pastures and advanced into the resorts that dot the region, especially the Valais (home of the Matterhorn). The cheese is still heated and scraped, though in many cases fires have given way to stovetops. Traditional embellishments include bell peppers, tomatoes, pickles, and potatoes. *Raclette* is accompanied by warm beverages or white wine; the combination of a chilled drink and hot cheese is thought to cause indigestion.

So do your best to ignore the parade of expensive lodges and tourists around you; enjoy some roasted, scraped cheese in the tradition of Swiss mountain herders. Partaking on steep Alpine slopes may lend a certain authenticity to the experience—just don't forget the wine.

forecasts, and info on guided climbing. (www.alpin-center-zermatt.ch. Open daily July-Sept. 8:30am-noon and 3-7pm; late Dec. to mid-May 4-7pm.) The Bergführerbüro is also the only company to lead formal expeditions above Zermatt. Groups scale Breithorn (4164m, 2hr., 155CHF), Castor (4228m, 5-6hr., 319CHF), and Pollux (4091m, 5-6hr., 302CHF) daily in summer. Prices do not include equipment, insurance, sleeping huts, or lifts to departure points. **Rental prices** for skis and snowboards are standard in Zermatt (28-50CHF per day). For a new perspective on the Matterhorn, try a tandem flight with **Paraglide Zermatt** (☎967 6744; www.paragliding-zermatt.ch. 150-190CHF.) For those who prefer to stay on the ground, the Gornergrat Bahn rack railway, departing from just across the train station, brings spectators 3089m above sea level to a viewing platform and Europe's highest hotel (☎921 4711; www.gornergrat.ch; 36CHF, 72CHF round trip).

**Hotel Bahnhof ❷**, on Bahnhofpl. 54, to the left of the station, provides hotel housing at hostel rates. Though small, it has a central location and mountain views. (☎967 2406; www.hotelbahnhof.com. Open mid-June to Oct. and mid-Dec. to mid-May. Reception 8am-8pm. Dorms 35CHF; singles 68CHF, with shower 78CHF; doubles 92-108CHF; quads 184CHF. MC/V.) A wide variety of traditional Swiss fare is available at **Walliserkanne ❷**, Bahnhofstr. 32, next to the post office. (☎966 4610. *Raclette* 8CHF. Pasta 17-25CHF. Cheese fondues 23-25CHF. Open daily 8am-midnight. Kitchen closes 11pm. AmEx/MC/V.) Get groceries at the **Coop Center,** opposite the station. (Open M-Sa 8:15am-6:30pm.) **The Pipe Surfer's Cantina ❸**, on Kirchstr., specializes in Mexican-Thai-Indian fusion cuisine and caramel vodka (6CHF), and by night throws the craziest "beach parties" in the Alps. (☎079 213 3807; www.gozermatt.com/thepipe. Salads 23-27CHF. Entrees 28-32CHF. Happy hour 6-7pm, in winter 4-5pm. Open daily 4pm-midnight. MC/V.) Just down the street from The Pipe, heading away from Bahnhofstr., is the **Papperla Pub,** Steinmattstr. 34. The club in their basement, **Schneewittchen,** hosts some of the winter's wildest ragers. (☎967 4040; www.apresski.ch. Free Internet. Pub open daily May-Nov. 11am-2am; Dec.-Apr. 2pm-2am. Schneewittchen open May-Nov. Tu-Sa 10:30pm-3:30am; Dec.-Apr. daily 10:30pm-3:30am. MC/V.)

To preserve the alpine air, cars and buses are banned in Zermatt; the only way in is the hourly **BVZ** (Brig-Visp-Zermatt) rail line, which connects to Lausanne (3hr., 71CHF) and Bern (3hr., 78CHF) via Brig. Buy hiking maps (26CHF) at the **tourist office,** in the station. (☎966 8100; www.zermatt.ch. Open mid-June to Sept. M-Sa 8:30am-6pm, Su 8:30am-noon and 1:30-6pm; Oct. to mid-June M-Sa 8:30am-noon and 1:30-6pm, Su 9:30am-noon and 4-6pm. **Postal Code:** CH-3920.

## THE SCRAPED DISH

Though fondue is Switzerland's main culinary claim to fame, visitors to the western, French-speaking part of the country will notice another item popping up on menus: *raclette*. Not surprisingly, it also involves cheese.

*Raclette* dates from the medieval era, when peasants would heat cheese made from their cows' milk next to evening fires. When the cheese had reached the right consistency and softness, the farmers would scrape it off the plate onto some bread—hence the name (the French *racler* means "to scrape"). The German equivalent was termed *Bratchas*, or "roasted cheese."

Today, the dish has left the Alpine pastures and advanced into the resorts that dot the region, especially the Valais (home of the Matterhorn). The cheese is still heated and scraped, though in many cases fires have given way to stovetops. Traditional embellishments include bell peppers, tomatoes, pickles, and potatoes. *Raclette* is accompanied by warm beverages or white wine; the combination of a chilled drink and hot cheese is thought to cause indigestion.

So do your best to ignore the parade of expensive lodges and tourists around you; enjoy some roasted, scraped cheese in the tradition of Swiss mountain herders. Partaking on steep Alpine slopes may lend a certain authenticity to the experience—just don't forget the wine.

forecasts, and info on guided climbing. (www.alpincenter-zermatt.ch. Open daily July-Sept. 8:30am-noon and 3-7pm; late Dec. to mid-May 4-7pm.) The Bergführerbüro is also the only company to lead formal expeditions above Zermatt. Groups scale Breithorn (4164m, 2hr., 155CHF), Castor (4228m, 5-6hr., 319CHF), and Pollux (4091m, 5-6hr., 302CHF) daily in summer. Prices do not include equipment, insurance, sleeping huts, or lifts to departure points. **Rental prices** for skis and snowboards are standard in Zermatt (28-50CHF per day). For a new perspective on the Matterhorn, try a tandem flight with **Paraglide Zermatt** (☎967 6744; www.paragliding-zermatt.ch. 150-190CHF.) For those who prefer to stay on the ground, the Gornergrat Bahn rack railway, departing from just across the train station, brings spectators 3089m above sea level to a viewing platform and Europe's highest hotel (☎921 4711; www.gornergrat.ch; 36CHF, 72CHF round trip).

**Hotel Bahnhof ❷**, on Bahnhofpl. 54, to the left of the station, provides hotel housing at hostel rates. Though small, it has a central location and mountain views. (☎967 2406; www.hotelbahnhof.com. Open mid-June to Oct. and mid-Dec. to mid-May. Reception 8am-8pm. Dorms 35CHF; singles 68CHF, with shower 78CHF; doubles 92-108CHF; quads 184CHF. MC/V.) A wide variety of traditional Swiss fare is available at **Walliserkanne ❷**, Bahnhofstr. 32, next to the post office. (☎966 4610. *Raclette* 8CHF. Pasta 17-25CHF. Cheese fondues 23-25CHF. Open daily 8am-midnight. Kitchen closes 11pm. AmEx/MC/V.) Get groceries at the **Coop Center,** opposite the station. (Open M-Sa 8:15am-6:30pm.) **The Pipe Surfer's Cantina ❸,** on Kirchstr., specializes in Mexican-Thai-Indian fusion cuisine and caramel vodka (6CHF), and by night throws the craziest "beach parties" in the Alps. (☎079 213 3807; www.gozermatt.com/thepipe. Salads 23-27CHF. Entrees 28-32CHF. Happy hour 6-7pm, in winter 4-5pm. Open daily 4pm-midnight. MC/V.) Just down the street from The Pipe, heading away from Bahnhofstr., is the **Papperla Pub,** Steinmattstr. 34. The club in their basement, **Schneewittchen,** hosts some of the winter's wildest ragers. (☎967 4040; www.apresski.ch. Free Internet. Pub open daily May-Nov. 11am-2am; Dec.-Apr. 2pm-2am. Schneewittchen open May-Nov. Tu-Sa 10:30pm-3:30am; Dec.-Apr. daily 10:30pm-3:30am. MC/V.)

To preserve the alpine air, cars and buses are banned in Zermatt; the only way in is the hourly **BVZ** (Brig-Visp-Zermatt) rail line, which connects to Lausanne (3hr., 71CHF) and Bern (3hr., 78CHF) via Brig. Buy hiking maps (26CHF) at the **tourist office,** in the station. (☎966 8100; www.zermatt.ch. Open mid-June to Sept. M-Sa 8:30am-6pm, Su 8:30am-noon and 1:30-6pm; Oct. to mid-June M-Sa 8:30am-noon and 1:30-6pm, Su 9:30am-noon and 4-6pm. **Postal Code:** CH-3920.

# FRENCH SWITZERLAND

The picturesque scenery and refined cities of French Switzerland have attracted herds of tourists for centuries, and there's no denying that the area's charm often comes at a steep price. But the best experiences in French Switzerland are free: strolling down tree-lined avenues, soaking up endearing *vieilles villes* (Old Towns), and taking in the mountain vistas from across Lac Léman (Lake Geneva) and Lac Neuchâtel.

## GENEVA (GENÈVE)                                     ☎022

Geneva (pop. 183,000) began with a tomb, blossomed into a religious center, became the "Protestant Rome," and ultimately emerged as a center for world diplomacy. Today, thanks to the presence of dozens of multinational organizations, including the United Nations and the Red Cross, the city is easily the most worldly in Switzerland. But Geneva's heritage lingers; you can sense it in the street names paying homage to Genevese patriots of old and the ubiquitous presence of the cherished cuckoo clock.

SWITZERLAND

## ◩ TRANSPORTATION

**Flights:** Cointrin Airport (GVA; ☎717 7111, flight info 799 3111 or 717 7105) is a hub for **Swiss International Airlines** (☎0848 85 20 00) and also serves **Air France** (☎827 8787) and **British Airways** (☎0848 80 10 10). Several direct flights per day to **Amsterdam, NTH; London, BRI; New York, USA; Paris, FRA;** and **Rome, ITA.** Bus #10 runs to the Gare Cornavin (15min., 6-12 per hr., 3CHF), but the train trip is shorter (6min., 6 per hr., 3CHF).

**Trains:** Trains run 4:30am-1am. **Gare Cornavin,** pl. Cornavin, is the main station. To: **Basel** (2¾hr., 1 per 2 hr., 67CHF); **Bern** (2hr., 2 per hr., 45CHF); **Lausanne** (40min., 3-4 per hr., 20CHF); **Zürich** (3½hr., 1-2 per hr., 77CHF); **St. Gallen** (4 hr., 1-2 per hr., 95CHF). Ticket counter open M-F 5:15am-9:30pm, Sa-Su 5:30am-9:30pm. **Gare des Eaux-Vives** (☎736 1620), on av. de la Gare des Eaux-Vives (tram #12 to Amandoliers SNCF), connects to France's regional rail through **Annecy, FRA** (1½hr., 6 per day, 15CHF) or **Chamonix, FRA** (2½hr., 4 per day, 25CHF).

**Public Transportation:** Geneva has an efficient bus and tram network (www.tpg.ch). Single tickets valid for 1hr. within the "orange" city zone, which includes the airport, are 3CHF, rides of 3 stops or less 2CHF. **Day passes** (10CHF) and a **9hr. pass** (7CHF) are available for the canton of Geneva. Day passes for the whole region 18CHF. Stamp multi-use tickets before boarding at machines in the station. Buses run 5am-12:30am; **Noctambus** (F-Sa 12:30-3:45am, 3CHF) offers night service.

**Taxis:** Taxi-Phone (☎331 4133). 6.80CHF plus 2.90CHF per km. 30CHF from airport.

**Bike Rental:** Geneva has well-marked bike paths and special traffic signals. Behind the station, **Genève Roule,** pl. Montbrillant 17 (☎740 1343), has ◪ **free bikes** (passport and 50CHF deposit; fines run upward of 300CHF if bike is lost or stolen). Slightly nicer bikes from 10CHF per day. Other locations at Bains des Pâquis and pl. du Rhône. Arrive before 9am, as bikes go quickly. Free bike maps available. Open daily May-Oct. 7:30am-9:30pm; Nov.-Apr. 8am-6pm. Cash only.

**Hitchhiking:** Let's Go does not recommend hitchhiking. Those headed to Germany or northern Switzerland take bus #4 to Jardin Botanique, where they try to catch a ride. Those headed to France take bus #4 to Palettes, then line D to St. Julien.

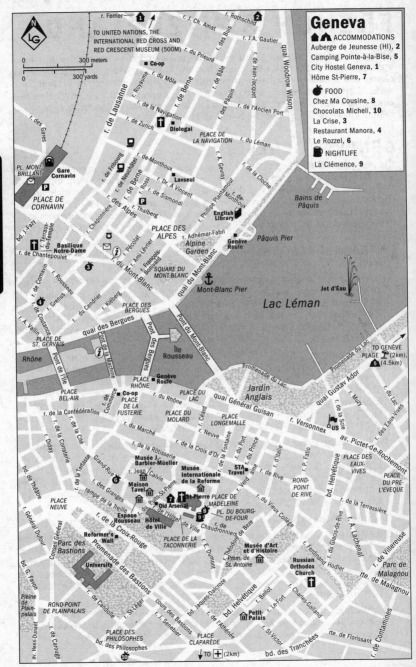

r. Ferrier

TO UNITED NATIONS, THE
INTERNATIONAL RED CROSS AND
RED CRESCENT MUSEUM (500M)

N
LG

0          300 meters
0          300 yards

## Geneva

**ACCOMMODATIONS**
Auberge de Jeunesse (HI), **2**
Camping Pointe-à-la-Bise, **5**
City Hostel Geneva, **1**
Hôme St-Pierre, **7**

**FOOD**
Chez Ma Cousine, **8**
Chocolats Micheli, **10**
La Crise, **3**
Restaurant Manora, **4**
Le Rozzel, **6**

**NIGHTLIFE**
La Clémence, **9**

r. J. Ch. Amat
r. Rothschild
r. des Buis
r. J.A. Gautier
r. du Prieuré
r. de Bâle
r. de Jean-Jacquet
r. de l'Ancien Port
quai Woodrow Wilson

● Co-op

r. Royaume
r. du Môle
r. de Berne
r. des Pâquis

r. de Lausanne
r. de la Navigation
r. de Zurich

† Diolognal
PLACE DE
LA NAVIGATION
r. du Léman

r. de Fribourg
r. de Monthoux
r. de Berne
r. de Neuchâtel

Gare Cornavin
PL. MONT BRILLANT
PLACE DE CORNAVIN

r. des Gares

r. du Rossi
r. de Sismondi
● Lavseul
r. Dr A Vincent

r. des Alpes
† Thalberg

r. de l'Ancien Port
r. de la Cloche

Bains de Pâquis

bd. J-Fazy
r. Terraux-du-Temple
Basilique Notre-Dame †
r. de Chantepoulet

r. Chaponnière
✉
i
r. Pécolat
r. Ami-Lévrier
r. François Bonivard

PLACE DES ALPES
r. Adhémar-Fabri
Alpine Garden
Genève Roule
English Library

r. de Cornavin
Rousseau
r. Grenus
r. du Cendrier
Kléberg

r. A. Vallin
r. de Coutance
PLACE DES BERGUES

PLACE DE ST. GERVAIS

Rhône

quai des Bergues
Pont de la Machine
Pont des Bergues
Île Rousseau

Pont du Mont-Blanc

Square du Mont-Blanc
quai du Mont-Blanc
⚓
Mont-Blanc Pier

Pâquis Pier

Lac Léman

Jet d'Eau

Promenade du Lac
TO GENÈVE PLAGE (2km),
(4.5km)

PLACE BEL-AIR
Genève Roule
PLACE RHÔNE
● Co-op
PLACE DE LA FUSTERIE

r. de la Confédération
r. de Commerce
r. du Rhône
PLACE DU LAC
Jardin Anglais
quai Général Guisan
quai Gustav Ador

PLACE DU MOLARD
PLACE LONGEMALLE
Versonnex
US
r. de la Scie
r. des Eaux-Vives

r. de la Cité
r. du Marché
r. de la Rôtisserie
r. Neuve
r. de la Croix-d'Or
r. de la Fontaine
r. du Port
r. du Prince
r. d'Italie
r. de Rive
P. Fatio
PLACE DES EAUX-VIVES
PLACE DU PRE L'EVEQUE

r. du Diday
bd. de Théâtre
Grand-Rue
r. de la Terrasse
r. des Granges
rampe de la Treille
r. Jean Calvin
r. Puits-St-Pierre

Musée J. Barbier-Mueller
Maison Tavel
Musée Internationale de la Reforme
STA Travel
Vend aine
r. du Vieux Collège
ROND-POINT DE RIVE
bd. Helvétique

PLACE NEUVE
r. Général Dufour
Conseil Général
Espace Rousseau
r. de la Croix-Rouge
St-Pierre †
Old Arsenal
Hôtel de Ville
PLACE DE MADELEINE
PL. DU BOURG-DE-FOUR
r. de Chaudronniers
Théodore de Bèze

PLACE DE LA TACONNERIE
E. Dumont
Prom. de St. Antoine
Musée d'Art et d'Histoire
Russian Orthodox Church †

r. du Glacis-de-Rive
r. Ferdinand Hodler
r. A. Lachenal
Parc de Malagnou
rte. de Malagnou
r. de Villereuse

Reformer's Wall
University
Promenade des Bastions
Parc des Bastions

bd. G. Favon
Pleine de Plain-palais
ROND-POINT DE PLAINPALAIS

r. de Candolle
r. St-Léger
r. J. Senebier
cours des Bastions
bd. Jaques-Dalcroze
bd. Helvétique
Petit-Palais
r. Bellot
r. Le-Fort
Charles-Galland
r. de la Terrassière

av. Henri-Dunant
r. de Carouge
PLACE DES PHILOSOPHES
bd. des Philosophes
PLACE CLAPARÈDE
TO ✚ (2km)
bd. des Tranchées
St-Victor
rte. de Florissant
r. de Contamines

SWITZERLAND

## ⚡🛈 ORIENTATION AND PRACTICAL INFORMATION

The twisting, cobbled streets and quiet squares of the historic *vieille ville* (Old Town), centered on **Cathédrale de St-Pierre**, make up the heart of Geneva. Across the **Rhône River** to the north, five-star hotels give way to lakeside promenades, **International Hill**, and rolling parks. Across the **Arve River** to the south lies the village of **Carouge**, home to student bars and clubs (take tram #12 or 13 to pl. du Marché).

**Tourist Office:** r. du Mont-Blanc 18 (☎909 7000; www.geneva-tourism.ch), in the Central Post Office Building. From Cornavin, walk 5min. toward the Pont du Mont-Blanc. Staff books hotel rooms for 5CHF, leads English-language walking tours, and offers free city maps. Open M 10am-6pm, Tu-Su 9am-6pm.

**Consulates: Australia,** chemin des Fins 2 (☎799 9100). **Canada,** av. de l'Ariana 5 (☎919 9200). **New Zealand,** chemin des Fins 2 (☎929 0350). **UK,** r. de Vermont 37 (☎918 2400). **US,** r. Versonnex 7 (☎840 5160, recorded info 840 5161).

**Currency Exchange:** ATMs have the best rates. The currency exchange inside the **Gare Cornavin** has good rates with no commission on traveler's checks, makes cash advances on credit cards (min. 200CHF), and arranges **Western Union** transfers. Open M-Sa 7am-8pm, Su 8am-5:50pm.

**GLBT Resources: Dialogai,** r. de la Navigation 11-13, entrance Rue d. Levant 5 (☎906 4040). From Gare Cornavin, turn left, walk 5min. down r. de Lausanne, and turn right onto r. de la Navigation. Offers brochures and maps on GBLT nightlife; doubles as a cafe and nighttime hot spot. Mostly male, but women welcome. Open M 9am-10pm, Tu-Th 9am-6pm, F 9am-5pm.

**Laundromat: Lavseul,** r. de Monthoux 29 (☎735 9051). Wash 5CHF, dry 1CHF per 9min. Open daily 7am-midnight.

**Police:** R. de Berne 6 (☎117). Open M-F 9am-noon and 3-6:30pm, Sa 9am-noon.

**Hospital: Hôpital Cantonal,** r. Micheli-du-Crest 24 (☎372 3311; www.hug-ge.ch). Bus #1 or 5 or tram #12. Door #2 is for emergency care; door #3 is for consultations. For info on walk-in clinics, contact the **Association des Médecins** (☎320 8420).

**Internet Access: Charly's Multimedia Check Point,** r. de Fribourg 7 (☎901 1313; www.charlys.com). 1CHF per 10min., 6CHF per hr. Open M-Sa 9am-midnight, Su 1-11pm. **12Mix,** r. de-Monthoux 58 (☎731 6747; www.12mix.com). 3CHF per 30min., 5CHF per hr. Open daily 10am-midnight.

**Post Office: Poste Centrale,** r. du Mont-Blanc 18, 1 block from Gare Cornavin. Open M-F 7:30am-6pm, Sa 9am-4pm. **Postal Code:** CH-1200.

## 🏠🏕 ACCOMMODATIONS AND CAMPING

The indispensable *Info Jeunes* lists about 30 budget options, and the tourist office publishes *Budget Hotels*, which stretches the definition of budget to 120CHF per person. Cheap beds are relatively scarce, so be sure to reserve ahead.

**Hôme St-Pierre,** Cour St-Pierre 4 (☎310 3707; info@homestpierre.ch). Take bus #5 to pl. Neuve, then walk up Rampe de la Treille, turn left onto R. Puits-St.-Pierre, then right on R. du Solil Levant. The hostel will be on your left. This 150-year-old "home" has comfortable beds and a great location beside the cathedral. It acts primarily as a dorm for women, so backpackers (especially men) may be cramped. Church bells ring at all hours of the night. Breakfast M-Sa 7CHF. Wi-Fi available. Reception M-Sa 9am-noon and 4-8pm, Su 9am-noon. Dorms 27CHF; singles 40CHF; doubles 60CHF. MC/V. ❶

**City Hostel Geneva,** r. Ferrier 2 (☎901 1500; www.cityhostel.ch). From the train station, head down r. de Lausanne. Take the 1st left on r. du Prieuré, which becomes r. Ferrier.

Spotless, cozy rooms. Kitchens on each floor. Linens 3.50CHF. Internet 5CHF per hr. Reception 7:30am-noon and 1pm-midnight. Single-sex dorms (3-4 beds) 31CHF; singles 59-63CHF; doubles 72-86CHF. Reserve ahead in summer. MC/V. ❷

**Auberge de Jeunesse (HI),** r. Rothschild 30 (☎732 6260; www.youthhostel.ch/geneva). Standard rooms, some of which have lakeviews. Breakfast included. Laundry 8CHF. Internet 4CHF per hr. Max. 6-night stay. Reception 6:30-10am and 2pm-midnight. Dorms 34CHF; doubles 92CHF, with shower 102CHF; quads 154CHF. 6CHF HI discount. AmEx/MC/V. ❷

**Camping Pointe-à-la-Bise,** chemin de la Bise (☎752 1296). Take bus #8 or tram #16 to Rive, then bus E north to Bise. Reception July-Aug. 8am-noon and 2-9pm; Apr.-June and Sept. 8am-noon and 4-8pm. Open Apr.-Sept. Reserve ahead. 7CHF per person, 18 CHF per tent, 4-person bungalows 98CHF. AmEx/MC/V. ❶

## 🍴 FOOD

Geneva has it all, from sushi to paella, but you may need a banker's salary to foot the bill. Pick up basics at *boulangeries*, *pâtisseries*, or supermarkets, which often have attached cafeterias. Try the **Coop** on the corner of r. du Commerce and r. du Rhône, in the Centre Rhône Fusterie, or the **Migros** in the basement of the Places des Cygnes shopping center on r. de Lausanne, down the street from the station. A variety of relatively cheap ethnic eateries center in the **Les Pâquis** area, bordered by r. de Lausanne and Gare Cornavin on one side and the quais Mont-Blanc and Wilson on the other. Around **place du Cirque** and **plaine de Plainpalais** are student-oriented tea rooms. To the south, the neighborhood of **Carouge** is known for its cozy pizzerias and funky *brasseries*.

🍴 **Le Rozzel,** Grand-Rue 18 (☎312 4272). Take bus #5 to pl. Neuve, then walk up the hill on r. Jean-Calvin to Grand-Rue. Pleasant outdoor seating on a winding street in the *vieille ville*. Sweet crepes 7-12CHF; savory crepes 14-18CHF. Open M, W, F 7:30am-8:30pm, Tu and Th 7:30am-7pm, Sa 7:30am-6pm. MC/V. ❷

🍴 **La Crise,** r. de Chantepoulet 13 (☎738 0264). Every morning, the vegetables for the soup of the day (3.50CHF) are prepared in front of customers at this small but popular snack bar. *Plat du jour* 15CHF; 11CHF for a smaller portion. Open M-F 6am-3pm and 6-8pm, Sa 6am-3pm. Lunch served after noon. Cash only. ❷

**Chocolats Micheli,** r. Micheli-du-Crest 1 (☎329 9006). Take tram #13 to Plainpalais and walk up bd. des Philosophes until it intersects with r. Micheli-du-Crest. Confectionary masterpieces (1-3CHF) abound in this Victorian cafe. Purists should try the "100% chocolate." Coffee 3.40CHF. Open M-F 8am-6:45pm, Sa 8am-5pm. MC/V. ❶

**Chez Ma Cousine,** pl. du Bourg-de-Four 6 (☎310 9696), down the stairs behind the cathedral. This cheery cafe has perfected *poulet*, offering only 3 chicken dishes (all 14CHF), as well as chicken salads (14-15CHF). Open M-Sa 11am-11:30pm, Su 11am-10:30pm. AmEx/MC/V. ❷

**Restaurant Manora,** r. de Cornavin 4 (☎909 490), on the top floor of the Manor department store. Varied selection and free water (a rarity in Switzerland). The sign might say "no picnics allowed," but the occasional birds flying overhead upstairs make it feel like the great outdoors. Entrees 5-12CHF. Open M-W 9am-7pm, Th 9am-9pm, Fri 9am-7:30pm, Sa 8:30am-6pm. AmEx/MC/V. ❶

## 👁 SIGHTS

The city's most interesting historical sites are located within walking distance from the **vieille ville** (Old Town). The tourist office has 2hr. English-language walking tours. (Mid-June to Sept. M, W, F-Sa 10am, Tu and Th at 6:30pm; Oct. to mid-June Sa 10am. 15CHF, students 10CHF.)

**VIEILLE VILLE.** From 1536 to 1564, Calvin preached at the **Cathédrale de St-Pierre,** which looms over the *vieille ville* from its hilltop location. Climb the **north tower** if the stairs around the cathedral aren't enough of a workout. *(Cathedral open June-Sept. daily 9am-7pm; Oct.-May M-Sa 10am-12pm and 2-5pm, Su 11am-12:30pm and 1:30-5pm. Tower open June-Sept. M-F 9am-6pm, Sa 9am-4:30pm. Cathedral free; tower 4CHF.)* Ruins, including a Roman sanctuary and an AD 4th-century basilica, rest in an ▨**archaeological site** below the cathedral; you can even see the tomb around which the city was built. *(Open Tu-Su 10am-5pm; Oct.-May Tu-F 2-5pm, Sa-Su 1:30-5:30pm. 8CHF, students 4CHF.)* For a dense presentation of Reformation 101 and an informative look at Geneva's history, visit the **Musée International de la Réforme,** 4 r. du Cloître, housed on the site of the city's official acceptance of Protestantism in 1536. *(☎310 2431; www.musee-reforme.ch. Open Tu-Su 10am-5pm. 10CHF, students 7CHF.)* At the western end of the *vieille ville* sits the 12th-century **Maison Tavel,** which now houses a museum showcasing Geneva's history. *(Open Tu-Su 10am-5pm. Free.)* Across the street is the **Hôtel de Ville** (Town Hall), where world leaders met on August 22, 1864 for the first Geneva Convention. The **Grand-Rue,** beginning at the Hôtel de Ville, is lined with medieval workshops and 18th-century mansions. Plaques commemorate famous residents like Jean-Jacques Rousseau, who was born at #40. Visit the ▨**Espace Rousseau** there for a short but informative audiovisual presentation of his life and work. *(☎310 1028; www.espace-rousseau.ch. Open Tu-Su 11am-5:30pm. 5CHF, students 3CHF.)* Below the cathedral, along r. de la Croix-Rouge, the **Parc des Bastions** stretches from pl. Neuve to pl. des Philosophes and includes **Le Mur des Réformateurs** (The Reformers' Wall), a sprawling collection of bas-relief figures depicting Protestant Reformers. The hulking **Musée d'Art et d'Histoire,** R. Charles-Galland 2, offers everything from prehistoric relics to contemporary art. *(☎418 2600, mah.ville-ge.ch. Open Tu-Su 10am-5pm. Free.)*

**WATERFRONT.** As you descend from the cathedral to the lake, medieval lanes give way to wide streets and chic boutiques. Down quai Gustave Ardor, the **Jet d'Eau,** Europe's highest fountain and Geneva's city symbol, spews a seven-ton plume of water 134m into the air. The **floral clock** in the **Jardin Anglais** pays homage to Geneva's watch industry. Possibly the city's most overrated attraction, it was once its most hazardous—the clock had to be cut back because tourists, intent on taking the perfect photograph, repeatedly backed into oncoming traffic. For a day on the waterfront, head up the south shore of the lake to **Genève Plage,** where there is a water slide and an enormous pool. *(☎736 2482; www.geneve-plage.ch. Open mid-May to mid-Sept. daily 10am-8pm. 7CHF, students 4.50CHF.)*

**INTERNATIONAL HILL.** North of the train station, the International Red Cross building contains the impressive ▨**International Red Cross and Red Crescent Museum,** av. de la Paix 17. *(Bus #8, F, V or Z to Appia ☎748 9511. www.micr.org. Open M and W-Su 10am-5pm. 10CHF, students 5CHF. English-language audio tour 3CHF.)* Across the street, the European headquarters of the **United Nations,** av. de la Paix 14, is in the same building that once held the League of Nations. The constant traffic of international diplomats is entertainment in itself. *(☎917 4896. Open July-Aug. daily 10am-5pm; Apr.-June and Sept.-Oct. daily 10am-noon and 2-4pm; Nov.-Mar. M-F 10am-noon and 2-4pm. 10CHF, students 8CHF.)*

# ♫ ▨ ENTERTAINMENT AND NIGHTLIFE

*Genève Agenda*, available at the tourist office, features event listings from major festivals to movies. In late June, the **Fête de la Musique** fills the city with nearly 500 free concerts of all styles. Parc de la Grange has free **jazz concerts.** Geneva hosts the biggest celebration of **American Independence Day** outside the US (July 4), and the **Fêtes de Genève** in early August fill the city with international music and fireworks. **L'Escalade** (Dec. 12-14, 2008) commemorates the repulsion of invading Savoyard troops.

Nightlife in Geneva is divided by neighborhood. **Place Bourg-de-Four,** below the cathedral in the *vieille ville,* attracts students to its charming terraces. **Place du Molard** has loud, somewhat upscale bars and clubs. For something more frenetic, head to **Les Pâquis,** near Gare Cornavin and pl. de la Navigation. The city's red-light district, it has a wide array of rowdy, low-lit bars and some nightclubs. This neighborhood is also home to many of the city's gay bars. **Carouge,** across the Arve River, is a student-friendly locus of nightlife activity. In the *vieille ville,* generations of students have had their share of drinks at the intimate bar of **La Clémence,** pl. du Bourg-de-Four 20. You can count on it to be open even when the rest of the city has shut down. Try the local Calvinus beer (7CHF) to do your part for Protestantism. (Open M-Th 7am-12:30am, F-Sa 7am-1:30am.)

# LAUSANNE                                                                    ☎021

The unique museums, medieval *vieille ville,* and lazy Lac Léman waterfront of Lausanne (pop. 125,000) make it well worth a visit. The centerpiece of the *vieille ville* is the Gothic **Cathédrale,** which features an extremely detailed rose window and several old tombs. (Open May to mid-Sept. M-F 7am-7pm, Sa-Su 8am-7pm; mid-Sept. to Apr. M-F 7am-5:30pm, Sa-Su 8am-5:30pm.) Below the cathedral is the city hall, **Hôtel de Ville,** on pl. de la Palud, the meeting point for **guided tours** of the town. (☎321 7766; www.lausanne.ch/visites. Tours May-Sept. M-Sa 10am and 3pm. 10CHF, students free.) The ◪**Musée Olympique,** quai d'Ouchy 1, is to Lausanne what the EU headquarters is to Brussels; the International Olympic Committee was founded here by Pierre de Coubertin in 1894. The museum is a high-tech shrine to modern Olympians; best of all is the extensive video collection, allowing visitors to relive almost any moment of the games. Take bus #2 to Ouchy, bus #8 to Musée Olympique, or bus #4 to Montchoisi. (☎621 6511; www.olympic.org. Open Apr.-Oct. daily 9am-6pm; Nov.-Mar. Tu-Su 9am-6pm. 15CHF, students 10CHF.) The fascinating **Collection de l'Art Brut,** av. Bergières 11, is filled with unusual sculptures, drawings, and paintings by fringe artists—schizophrenics, peasants, and criminals. Take bus #2 to Jomini or 3 to Beaulieu. The museum is behind the trees across from the Congress Center. (☎315 2570; www.artbrut.ch. Open July-Aug. daily 11am-6pm; Sept.-June Tu-Su 11am-10pm. 8CHF, students 5CHF.) The inhabitants of the city descend to the lake on weekends and after work, making it one of the liveliest places in the city. In Ouchy, Lausanne's port, several booths along quai de Belgique rent **pedal boats** (13CHF per 30min., 20CHF per hr.) and offer **water skiing** or **wake boarding** (35CHF per 15min.) on Lac Léman. **Lausanne Roule** loans **free bikes** beside pl. de la Riponne on R. du Tennel (☎076 441 8378. www.lausanneroule.ch. ID and 20CHF deposit. Open late Apr. to late Oct. daily 7:30am-9:30pm.)

◪**Lausanne Guesthouse and Backpacker** ❷, chemin des Epinettes 4, at the train tracks, manages to keep the noise out and makes the most of its location with lakeviews, an equipped kitchen, a cozy living room, and a rose garden with grills. Head left and downhill out of the station on W. Fraisse; take the first right on chemin des Epinettes. (☎601 8000; www.lausanne-guesthouse.ch. Bike rental 20CHF per day. Linens 5CHF. Internet 8CHF per hr. Reception daily 7:30am-noon and 3-10pm. Dorms 32CHF; singles 85CHF, with bath 94CHF; doubles 90/110CHF. 5% ISIC discount. MC/V.) Sleep by Roman ruins on the lake at **Camping de Vidy** ❶, right down the road from Hotel Jeunotel at Ch. du Camping 3. (☎622 5000. www.clv.ch. 10-18 per tent, 7CHF per person, bungalows 56CHF for 1-2 people, 88CHF for 3-4 people. AmEx/MC/V.) Restaurants center around **Place St-François** and the *vieille ville,* while *boulangeries* sell sandwiches on practically every street. **Le Barbare ❶**, Escaliers du Marché 27, near the cathedral, has sandwiches (5.50CHF) and omelettes (7.50-16CHF) for cheap. (☎312 2132. Open M-Sa 8:30am-midnight. AmEx/MC/V.) Bar-hop in the area just south of the cathedral between r. Centrale, av. B. Constant, and r. Caroline. **Trains** leave for: Basel (2½hr., 1 per 2 hr., 57CHF); Geneva (50min., 3-4 per hr., 20CHF); Montreux (20min., 3-4 per hr., 10CHF); Zürich (2½hr., 1-2 per hr., 65CHF); Paris, FRA (4hr., 4 per day, 104CHF). **Tourist offices** in the train station and by the Ouchy lakefront reserve rooms for 4CHF. (☎613 7373. Open daily 9am-7pm.) **Postal Code:** CH-1000.

# MONTREUX
☎021

Although Montreux (pop. 23,000) is a gaudy resort at heart, its views of snow-capped peaks and Lac Léman are free. Though long past its Jazz Age heyday, the city still swings during the annual ▓**Montreux Jazz Festival,** which erupts for 15 days starting the first Friday in July (July 4, 2008). World-famous for discovering and drawing exceptional talent, the festival has hosted icons like Bob Dylan and and Miles Davis. (www.montreuxjazz.com. Tickets 59-189CHF.) If you can't get tickets, come anyway for **Montreux Jazz Under the Sky,** 500 hours of free, open-air concerts on three stages. The area has long drawn artists and celebrities; for a unique tour, try **The Poet's Ramble,** a 10km walk through town punctuated by "talking benches" with recordings of excerpts from the likes of Rousseau, Tolstoy, and Hemingway (maps at tourist office). The ▓**Château de Chillon,** a medieval fortress on a nearby island, features all the comforts of home: prison cells, a torture chamber, and a weapons room. Don't miss Lord Byron's etched autograph in Bonivard's cell. Take bus #1 (3CHF) to Chillon. (☎966 8910; www.chillon.ch. Open daily Apr.-Sept. 9am-6pm; Mar. and Oct. 9:30am-5pm; Nov.-Feb. 10am-4pm. 12CHF, students 10CHF. Tours in summer daily 11:30am and 3:30pm. 6CHF.)

Cheap rooms in Montreux are scarce year-round and nonexistent during the Jazz Festival, so reserve ahead. ▓**Riviera Lodge ❷**, pl. du Marché 5, in the neighboring town of Vevey, is worth the commute for its friendly staff and water views. Guests receive a pass including free bus transportation and discounts on museums and attractions. Take the train or bus #1 to Vevey (15min., 6 per hr., 2.80CHF). Head to the left away from the train station on the main road and follow the brown signs to the lodge, located in the main square on the water. (☎923 8040; www.rivieralodge.ch. Breakfast 8CHF. Linens 5CHF. Laundry 6CHF. Internet 7CHF per hr. Reception 8am-noon and 4-8pm. Call ahead if arriving late. Dorms 32CHF; doubles 88CHF. Prices 4-7CHF higher during festival. MC/V.) The **Auberge de Jeunesse (HI) ❷**, Passage de l'Auberge 8, has colorful, festival-themed décor and a prime location on the lake, though a railway bridge passes right above it. Take bus #1 to L'Eaudine (stop on request), then head back and turn left on R. de l'Auberge, continuing down the stairs. (☎963 4934; www.youthhostel.ch/montreux. Breakfast included. Internet 6CHF per hr. Reception open daily 7:30-9am and 5-10pm. Dorms 38CHF; doubles 102CHF; quads 164CHF. AmEx/MC/V). **Babette's ❷**, Grand-Rue 60, downstairs from the station and to the left, serves crepes (6-15CHF) for lunch and dessert. (☎963 7796. Open daily 7am-7pm. MC/V.) Grand-Rue and av. de Casino have inexpensive markets. There is a **Coop Pronto** supermarket to the right of the train station. (Open daily 6am-10pm.) **Trains** leave for Geneva (1hr., 2-3 per hr., 27CHF), and Lausanne (20min., 4-6 per hr., 9.80CHF). The **tourist office** is on Grand-Rue, downstairs and left from the station. (☎962 8484; www.montreux-vevey.com. Open May to mid-Sept. M-F 9am-6pm, Sa-Su 9:30am-5pm; mid-Sept. to Apr. M-F 9am-noon and 1-5:30pm, Sa-Su 10am-2pm.) **Postal Code:** CH-1820.

**SWITZERLAND**

# NEUCHÂTEL ☎032

Alexandre Dumas once said that the town of Neuchâtel (pop. 30,000) appeared to be carved out of butter; visitors gazing down street after street filled with yellow stone architecture will immediately see why. The *vieille ville* centers around **place des Halles**, a block from **place Pury**, the hub of every bus line. From pl. des Halles, turn left on r. de Château and climb the stairs on the right to reach the **Collégiale Church** and the **château** that gives the town its name. (Church open daily Apr.-Sept. 9am-8pm; Oct.-Mar. 9am-6:30pm.) Entrance to the château is available only through a free tour. (1 per hr. Apr.-Sept. M 2-4pm, Tu-F 10am-4pm, Sa-Su 2-4pm.) The nearby **Tour des Prisons** (Prison Tower), on r. Jeanne-Hochberg, has old prison cells, models of the town in centuries past, and a prime view of the city, lake, and countryside. (Open Apr.-Sept. daily 8am-6pm. 1CHF.) The **Musée d'Histoire Naturelle**, Av. Léopold-Robert 63, has a great collection of just about every stuffed creature imaginable. Turn right from pl. des Halles onto Croix du Marché, which becomes r. de l'Hôpital, then turn left onto R. des Terraux. (☎967 6071. Open Tu-Su 10am-6pm. 6CHF, students 4CHF. W free.) The **Musée d'Arts et d'Histoire**, esplanade Léopold-Robert 1, houses an collection of paintings, weapons, textiles, and teacups. Exit the tram station and head to the right along the promenade for about 100m. (Open Tu-Su 11am-6pm. 8CHF, students 4CHF. W free.) At the edge of the waterside square by the tourist office, **Neuchâtel Roule** lends free bikes. (☎717 5091; www.neuchatelroule.ch. Passport and 20CHF deposit. Open Apr.-Sept. daily 7:30am-9:30pm.; Oct. 8:30am-8:30pm.) For the best views of the area, ride your bike or take bus #7 to La Coudre, where you can hop on the **funicular** that rises up through the forest to the village of Chaumont. (1 per hr. 9am-7pm. 4.60CHF.) The "Watch Valley" area in between Lac de Neuchâtel and the French border offers great **hiking** opportunities, with nearly 20 long-distance trails of varying difficulty; pick up a free map at the tourist office. **Pedal boats** (24-35CHF per hr., 70-100CHF per day) and **motor boats** (50-70CHF per hr., 200-250CHF per ½-day, 350-450CHF per day) can be rented in the Town Harbor behind the tourist office.

The 🏠**Auberg'inn**, Rue Fleury 1, offers themed rooms in the middle of the *vieille ville*. From Place des Halles, walk up R. du Trésor until you reach Croix-du-Marché; the hostel is in the small square on your left. (☎078 615 8421; www.auberginn.com. Reception open M 7:30am-9pm, Tu-W 7:30am-10pm, Th 7:30am-1pm, F-Sa 7:30am-2pm, Su 7:30am-9pm. Dorms 35CHF; singles 80CHF; doubles 120CHF; triples 135CHF; quads 160CHF; quints 175CHF. MC/V.) **Wodey-Suchard ❶**, r. de Trésor 5, serves omelettes (6-8CHF) and salads (4-13CHF)—don't miss the *chocolaterie* in back, which has been going strong ever since Philippe Suchard first brought chocolate to Neuchâtel in 1825. (Open M 11am-6:30pm, Tu-F 6:30am-6:30pm, Sa 6:30am-5pm. Cash only.) **Migros**, r. de l'Hôpital 12, sells groceries. (Open M-W 8am-6:30pm, Th 8am-10pm, F 7:30am-6:30pm, Sa 7:30am-7pm.) **Trains** run to: Basel (1¾hr., 1 per hr., 34CHF); Bern (45min., 1 per hr., 18CHF); Zürich (1½hr., 1 per hr., 44CHF); Geneva (1½hr., 1 per hr., 37CHF). A **tram** (1CHF) runs from the station to the shore. Head to the right after disembarking and walk 5min. along the lake to the **tourist office**, which books rooms for free. (☎889 6890; www.neuchateltourisme.ch. Open July-Aug. M-F 9am-6:30pm, Sa 9am-4pm, Su 10am-2pm; Sept.-June M-F 9am-noon and 1:30-5:30pm, Sa 9am-noon.) **Postal Code:** CH-2001.

# FRIBOURG (FREIBURG) ☎026

Encircled by a gorge and nestled into a bend in the Sarine River, Fribourg (pop. 33,000) boasts beautiful churches, monasteries, and towers. To reach the *vieille ville* from the station, head down r. de Romont, past pl. Georges Python, and along

r. de Lausanne, which empties into pl. de Nova-Fribourg, a busy intersection with a fine view of the **Hôtel de Ville** (Town Hall). Follow Grand-Rue downhill until it reaches pl. du Petit-St-Jean, the heart of the *vieille ville*, or walk down Bl. de Pérolles from the station and turn left on the Ritter Path. The path leads through a forest, follows the river, and passes several medieval monasteries and churches before reaching the *vieille ville*. The bell tower of the **Cathédrale St-Nicolas** in pl. Notre Dame shoots above the Fribourg skyline; climb its 368 steps for a spectacular view. (Cathedral open M-Sa 7:30am-7pm, Su 8:30am-9:30pm; tower open Mar.-Oct. M-F 10am-noon and 2-5pm, Su 2-5pm. Cathedral free; tower 3.50CHF, students 2.50CHF.) The **Musée d'Art et d'Histoire**, r. de Morat 12, is a 16th-century mansion-turned-museum featuring mostly local work, some of it dating back to the Middle Ages. (☎305 5140. Open Tu-W and F-Su 11am-6pm, Th 11am-8pm. 6-10CHF, depending on exhibits; students 4-7CHF.)

For the standard **Auberge de Jeunesse (HI) ❷**, r. de l'Hôpital 2, head left out of the train station on av. de la Gare, which becomes r. de Romont; turn left onto r. de l'Hôpital. (☎323 1916; www.youthhostel.ch/fribourg. Breakfast included. Reception 7:30-10am and 5-10pm. Open Mar.-Oct. Dorms 36-39CHF; singles 61CHF; doubles 96CHF; quads 146CHF. 1.75CHF resort tax. 6CHF HI discount. AmEx/MC/V.) For a relaxed evening, try ▇**Café Belvedere ❷**, Grand-Rue 36, with its terrace view of the gorge at the end of the Old Town. (☎323 4407. Cafe open M-Tu 2-11:30pm, W-Th 2pm-1:30am, F 2pm-2am, Sa 11am-2pm, Su 2pm-midnight; restaurant open Tu-Su 12-2:30pm and 7-11pm. AmEx/MC/V.) The **Manor** department store to the left of the train station, R. de Romont 30, has a supermarket (☎350 6690. Open M-W and F 8am-7pm, Th 8am-9pm, Sa 8am-4pm). **Trains** run to: Bern (25min., 2 per hr., 13CHF); Lausanne (50min., 1 per hr., 22CHF); Geneva (1½hr., 2 per hr., 37CHF); Zürich (2 hr., 1 per hr., 51CHF). The **tourist office,** av. de la Gare 1, is 100m to the right of the station. (☎350 1111; www.fribourgtourisme.ch. Open May-Sept. M-Sa 9am-3pm; Oct.-May M-Sa 9am-12:30pm.) **Postal Code:** CH-1700.

# ITALIAN SWITZERLAND

Ever since Switzerland won Ticino, the only Italian-speaking Swiss canton, from Italy in 1512, the region has been renowned for its mix of Swiss efficiency and Italian *dolce vita*. It's no wonder the rest of Switzerland vacations here among jasmine-laced villas painted in the muted pastels of gelato.

## LUGANO
☎091

Set in a valley between sloping green mountains, Lugano (pop. 52,000) draws plenty of visitors with its mix of artistic flair and historical religious sites. The frescoes inside the 16th-century **Cattedrale San Lorenzo**, just down the ramp from the train station, are still vivid. The most spectacular fresco in town is the gargantuan crucifix in the **Chiesa Santa Maria degli Angiuli**, 200m to the right as you leave the tourist office. Armed with topographic maps and trail guides (sold at the tourist office), hikers can tackle the rewarding 5hr. **hike** to the top of **Monte Boglia** (1516m). Tamer souls can turn around after 2hr. at the peak of **Monte Bré** (923m), which is also accessible by **funicular.** (V. Ceresio 36; take bus #1,11, or 12 to the Cassarate M. Bré stop, then walk foward for several minutes and turn left on Via Pico. ☎971 3171; www.montebre.ch. Open Apr.-Oct. daily 9am-7pm. 14CHF, round-trip 20CHF. Cash only.) Those who simply want to stroll can head for the **Parco Civico**, right in the center of town, which provides lakeside views of the city and surrounding hillsides. In early July, the **Estival Jazz** fills Lugano's colorful, crowded streets and main *piazza* with free jazz performances.

Surrounded by palm trees, the pink 19th-century villa of **Hotel and Hostel Montarina ❶**, V. Montarina 1, has a swimming pool, a terrace, and a convenient location next to the train station, though backpackers will find themselves in cramped ground floor rooms. At the end of the station parking lot, cross the tracks, and walk up the hill to the right until you reach the gate on your left. (☎966 7272; www.montarina.ch. Breakfast 12CHF. Linens 4CHF. Laundry 5CHF. Reception 8am-10:30pm. Open Mar.-Oct. Dorms 25CHF; singles 70CHF, with bath 80CHF; doubles 100/120CHF. AmEx/MC/V.) Groceries are available at **Piccobello** at the train station. (Open daily 6am-10pm.) The **Coop City** supermarket, V. Nassa 22, has a food court on the top floor. (Open M-W and F 8am-6:30pm, Th 8am-9pm, Sa 8am-5pm.) **Trains** leave P. della Stazione on the hill above the city for Locarno via Giubiasco (1hr., 2 per hr., 16.20CHF), Milan, ITA (1½hr., 1 per hr., 25CHF), and Zürich (3hr., 11 per day, 57CHF). The **tourist office,** across from the ferry station at the corner of P. Rezzonico, reserves rooms for 4CHF and has answers to all your adventure sports questions. Free guided walks of the city are on Monday at 9am. (☎913 3232; www.lugano-tourism.ch. Open Apr.-Oct. M-F 9am-7pm, Sa 9am-6pm, Su 10am-6pm; Nov.-Mar. M-F 9am-noon and 2-5pm.) **Postal Code:** CH-6900.

# LOCARNO                                                                    ☎091

A Swiss vacation spot on the shores of Lago Maggiore, Locarno (pop. 30,000) gets over 2200 hours of sunlight per year—more than anywhere else in Switzerland. The sunshine is enjoyed in different ways: some vacationers enjoy lazy waterfront promenades, while the adrenaline-hungry partake in heart-stopping adventure sports. For centuries, visitors have journeyed here to see the orange-yellow church of **Madonna del Sasso** (Madonna of the Rock), founded in 1487. Take the funicular (4 per hr.; 4.50CHF, round-trip 6.60CHF), or walk for 20min. up the smooth stones of the Via Crucis (open 6:30am-6pm) to the top, passing wooden niche reliefs depicting the Stations of the Cross along the way. Hundreds of heart-shaped medallions on the interior church walls commemorate acts of Mary's intervention in the lives of worshippers who have journeyed here. (Grounds open daily 6:30am-6:45pm.) For view of all of Locarno, take the **Cardada gondola** from the top funicular station to a lookout point high in the mountains. (Open daily June-Sept. 8am-10pm; Mar.-May and Oct.-Nov. M-Th 9am-9pm, F-Su 8am-10pm. 23CHF, round-trip 27CHF.) For ten days at the beginning of August, Locarno swells with pilgrims of a different sort and prices soar when its world-famous open-air **film festival** draws over 150,000 to the Piazza Grande.

For **Pensione Città Vecchia ❷**, V. Toretta 15, turn right onto V. Toretta from P. Grande. (☎751 4554. Breakfast included. Dorms 37CHF; doubles 120CHF; triples 150CHF. Cash only.) For **Palagiovani (HI) ❷**, V. Varenna 18, take bus #36 (dir.: Zandone) to 5 Vie, walk to the stoplights, and turn right on V. Varenna. (☎756 1500. Breakfast included. Laundry 8CHF. Internet 3CHF per 15min. July to mid-Aug. dorms 48CHF; doubles 96CHF. Jan.-June 45SF/90CHF. 6CHF HI discount. AmEx/MC/V.) **Ristorante Manora ❶**, V. della Stazione 1, offers self-service dining. (Salad bar 4.50-11CHF. Pasta buffet 6-13CHF. Entrees 11-19CHF. Gelato 2.90CHF. Open Apr.-Oct. M-Sa 7:30am-10pm, Su 8am-10pm; Nov.-Mar. M-Sa 7:30am-9pm, Su 8am-9pm.) Find groceries at the **Migros** in the station. (Open daily 6am-10pm.) **Trains** run from P. Stazione to Lugano (1hr., 2 per hr., 16CHF) via Giubiasco, Luzern (2½hr., 1 per 2hr., 51CHF), and Milan, ITA (2hr., 2 per hr., 37CHF) via Bellinzona. The **tourist office,** on P. Grande in the *Kursaal* (casino), makes hotel reservations. From the station, go left down V. della Stazione until you reach P. Grande. (☎791 0091; www.maggiore.ch. Open Apr.-Oct. M-F 9am-6pm, Sa 10am-6pm, Su 10am-1:30pm and 2:30-5pm; Nov.-Mar. M-F 9am-6pm, Sa 10am-6pm.) **Postal Code:** CH-6600.

# HEADING NORTH

The nations of Finland, Iceland, Norway, and Sweden have a strong cultural affinity for Western Europe, with Denmark historically serving as the link between the two regions. The Öresund Bridge, built in 1995, connected Copenhagen to the Swedish port of Malmö opened up the first land route to the Scandinavian peninsula since the last Ice Age. Geographical isolation kept the Nordic countries ethnically homogeneous and sparsely populated, but now their capital cities have emerged as energetic cultural centers. It's mostly outside of these metropolitan areas that the Nordic nations radically distinguish themselves from the rest of the continent. Hiking through the Lappland wilderness of northern Scandinavia is enough to make anyone reevaluate what it means to see Europe "off the beaten path." In this chapter, you'll find a smattering of what Scandinavia has to offer. To learn more, check out a copy of *Let's Go: Europe 2008.*

971

# FINLAND (SUOMI)

## ESSENTIALS

**EMBASSIES AND CONSULATES.** Foreign embassies in Finland are in Helsinki (p. 972). Finnish embassies abroad include: **Australia** and **New Zealand,** 12 Darwin Ave., Yarralumla, ACT, 2600 (☎26 273 38 00; www.finland.org.au); **Canada,** 55 Metcalfe St., Ste. 850, Ottawa, ON, K1P 6L5 (☎613-288-2233; www.finland.ca/en); **Ireland,** Russell House, Stokes Pl., St. Stephen's Green, Dublin, 2 (☎01 478 1344; www.finland.ie/en); **UK,** 38 Chesham Pl., London, SW1X 8HW (☎020 78 38 62 00; www.finemb.org.uk/en); **US,** 3301 Massachusetts Ave., NW, Washington, D.C., 20008 (☎202-298-5800; www.finland.org).

**VISA AND ENTRY INFORMATION.** EU citizens do not need a visa. Citizens of Australia, Canada, New Zealand, and the US do not need a visa for stays of up to 90 days, beginning upon entry into any of the countries in the EU's freedom-of-movement zone. For more info, see p. 13. For stays longer than 90 days, all non-EU citizens need Schengen visas (around US$41), available at Finnish embassies and online at www.finland.org/en. Application processing takes about two weeks.

**MONEY.** In 2002, the **euro (€)** replaced the markka as the unit of currency in Finland. For more info, see p. 16. Banks exchange currency for a €2-5 commission, though **Forex** offices and **ATMs** offer the best exchange rates. Food from grocery stores runs €10-17 per day; meals cost around €8 for lunch and €12 for dinner. Although restaurant bills include a service charge, leaving small change for particularly good service is becoming more common. For other services, tips are not expected. Finland has a 22% **value added tax (VAT),** a sales tax applied to services and imports. The nation has a reduced VAT of 17% for food products and 8% for public transportation, books, and medicines. The prices given in *Let's Go* include VAT. In the airport upon exiting the EU, non-EU citizens can claim a refund on the tax paid for goods purchased at participating stores. In order to qualify for a refund, you must spend at least €40 in a store; make sure to ask for a refund form when you pay. For more info on qualifying for a VAT refund, see p. 18.

| FINLAND | ❶ | ❷ | ❸ | ❹ | ❺ |
|---|---|---|---|---|---|
| **ACCOMMODATIONS** | under €15 | €15-28 | €29-50 | €51-75 | over €75 |
| **FOOD** | under €8 | €8-15 | €16-20 | €21-30 | over €30 |

# HELSINKI (HELSINGFORS) ☎09

With all the appeal of a big city but none of the grime, Helsinki's (pop. 560,000) broad avenues, grand architecture, and parks make it a showcase Northern Europe. A hub of the design world, the city also distinguishes itself with multicultural flair and youthful energy mingling with old-world charm.

## ▌ TRANSPORTATION

**Flights: Helsinki-Vantaa Airport (HEL;** ☎0200 146 36; www.ilmailulaitos.fi). **Bus** #615 runs from airport Platform 1B and the train station. (40min., 1-6 per hr.; from the airport M-F 5:30am-1am, Sa-Su 6am-1am; to the airport M-F 4:50am-1:20am, Sa-Su 5:20am-1:20am. €3.60. Cash only.) A **Finnair bus** runs from airport Platform 1A and the Finnair

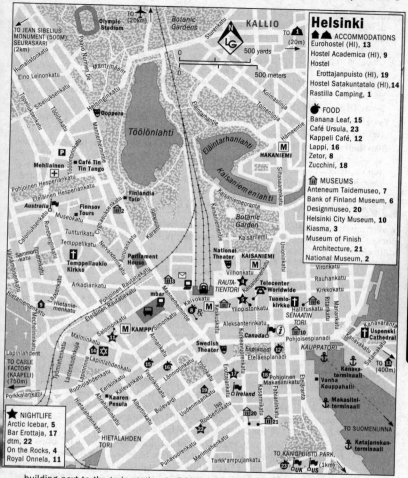

**Helsinki**

▲▲ ACCOMMODATIONS
Eurohostel (HI), **13**
Hostel Academica (HI), **9**
Hostel
Erottajanpuisto (HI), **19**
Hostel Satakuntatalo (HI),**14**
Rastilla Camping, **1**

🍴 FOOD
Banana Leaf, **15**
Café Ursula, **23**
Kappeli Café, **12**
Lappi, **16**
Zetor, **8**
Zucchini, **18**

🏛 MUSEUMS
Anteneum Taidemuseo, **7**
Bank of Finland Museum, **6**
Designmuseo, **20**
Helsinki City Museum, **10**
Kiasma, **3**
Museum of Finish
Architecture, **21**
National Museum, **2**

★ NIGHTLIFE
Arctic Icebar, **5**
Bar Erottaja, **17**
dtm, **22**
On the Rocks, **4**
Royal Onnela, **11**

HEADING NORTH

building next to the train station (☎0600 140 140; www.finnair.com. 35min., 1-3 per hr.; from the airport 6am-1am; to the airport 5am-midnight. €5.20. AmEx/MC/V.)

**Trains:** (☎English-language 231 999 02; www.vr.fi.) To: **Rovaniemi** (10-13hr., 5-8 per day, €76), **Tampere** (2hr., 8-12 per day, €26), and **Turku** (2hr., 12 per day, €23-34).

**Buses:** Leave from the Kamppi shopping center, Narinkka 3 (☎0200 4000; www.mat-kahuolto.fi). From the train station, take Postik. past the statue of Mannerheim. Cross Mannerheimintie onto Salomonk. Station will be on your left. To **Lahti** (1½-3hr., 1-6 per hr., €19), **Tampere** (2½hr., 1 per hr., €22), and **Turku** (2½hr., 2 per hr., €25).

**Ferries: Viking Line,** Lönnrotink. 2 (☎12 351; www.vikingline.fi), sails to **Stockholm, SWE** (16hr., 5:30pm, from €48) and **Tallinn, EST** (4hr., 12:30pm, €21). Tram #2 or bus #13 to Katajanokka terminal. **Tallinksilja,** Erottajank. 19 (☎228 311; www.tallink-silja.com), sails to **Tallinn, EST** (2-3½hr.; May to mid-Aug. 6-7 per day, mid-Aug. to Apr. 3-5 per day; from €22). Take bus #15 to West terminal.

**Local Transportation:** (☎310 1071; www.hkl.fi). **Buses, trams,** and the **metro** run 5:30am-11pm; major bus and tram lines, including tram #3T, run until 1:30am. **Night buses,** marked with "N," run F-Sa after 2am (€3.50). Single-fare tram €1.80; with 1hr. transfers to buses, trams, and the metro €2.20. **HKL Palvelupiste** (City Transport Office) is in the Rautatientori metro, below the train station. Open mid-June to July M-Th 7:30am-6pm, F 7:30am-5pm, Sa 10am-3pm; Aug. to mid-June M-Th 7:30am-7pm, F 7:30am-5pm, Sa 10am-3pm. Sells the **tourist ticket** (as does the tourist office), a good investment for unlimited access to buses, trams, the metro, and trains. 1-day €6, 3-day €12, 5-day €18. AmEx/MC/V.

**Taxis: Taxi Centre Helsinki** (☎0100 0700). Special airport fares with **Yellow Line** (☎0600 555 555). 30-55min. Reserve 1 day ahead, before 6pm. €22. AmEx/MC/V.

**Bike Rental:** From mid-June to Aug., the city provides over 300 ⬛ **free, lime-green bikes** at major destinations throughout the city; it can be tricky to track one down, but when you do, deposit a €2 coin in the lock and then retrieve your deposit upon "returning" the bike to any location. Free cycling maps of the city are available at the tourist office.

## ■ ⚡ 🛈 ORIENTATION AND PRACTICAL INFORMATION

Water surrounds Helsinki in every direction, with many beaches and lakeside parks. The city's main street, **Mannerheimintie,** passes between the bus and train stations on its way south to the city center, ending at the **Esplanadi.** This tree-lined promenade leads east to **Kauppatori** (Market Square) and the beautiful South Harbor. Northeast of the city center lies **Kallio,** the bohemian district. Both Finnish and Swedish are used on all street signs and maps; *Let's Go* uses the Finnish names.

**Tourist Offices:** Pohjoisesplanadi 19 (☎3101 3300; www.visithelsinki.fi). From the train station, walk 2 blocks down Keskusk. and turn left on Pohjoisesplanadi. Free **Internet** and **Wi-Fi.** Open May-Sept. M-F 9am-8pm, Sa-Su 9am-6pm; Oct.-Apr. M-F 9am-6pm, Sa-Su 10am-4pm. Representatives in green vests patrol the city center in summer to distribute maps and answer questions. **Helsinki Card,** sold at the **Tour Shop** in the tourist office, provides unlimited local transportation and free or discounted guided tours and museum admission, although cardholders have to keep up a blistering pace to make their purchase worthwhile. 1-day €33, 2-day €43, 3-day €53. The shop also books various amenities for a fee. (☎2288 1500; www.helsinkiexpert.fi. Open June-Aug. M-F 9am-7pm, Sa-Su 9am-5pm; Sept.-May M-F 9am-5pm, Sa 10am-4pm. AmEx/MC/V.) **Finnsov Tours,** Museok. 15 (☎436 6961; www.finnsov.info) arranges trips to Russia and expedites the visa process. Open M-F 8:30am-5pm. AmEx/MC/V.

**Embassies: Canada,** Pohjoisesplanadi 25B (☎228 530; www.canada.fi). Open June-Aug. M-Th 8am-noon and 1-4:30pm, F 8am-1:30pm; Sept.-May M-F 8:30am-noon and 1-4:30pm. **Ireland,** Erottajank. 7A (☎646 006; helsinki@dfa.ie). Open M-F 9am-5pm. **UK,** Itäinen Puistotie 17 (☎2286 5100; www.britishembassy.gov.uk/finland). Open late June-late Aug. M-F 8:30am-3pm; late Aug. to late June M-F 9am-5pm. Citizens of **Australia** and **New Zealand** should contact the UK embassy. **US,** Itäinen Puistotie 14A (☎616 250; www.usembassy.fi). Open M-F 8:30am-5pm.

**Currency Exchange: Forex** (☎020 751 2510) has 4 locations and the best rates in the city. Hours vary; the branch in the train station is open M-F 8am-9pm, Sa-Su 9am-7pm.

**Luggage Storage:** Lockers in the train station €2-3 per day. The Kiasma museum (p. 977) provides free same day storage even if you don't pay admission.

**GBLT Resources: Seta Ry,** Mannerheimintie 170A 4, 5th fl. (☎681 2580; www.seta.fi). Tram #10. A national organization with info on gay services in the country and a trans support center. Copies of *Gay Guide Helsinki* are at the tourist office.

**Laundromat: Café Tin Tin Tango,** Töölöntorink. 7 (☎2709 0972; www.tintintango.info), a combination bar, cafe, laundromat, and sauna. Wash €3.50, dry €1.80, detergent €1. Sandwiches €5-8. Open M-Th 7am-midnight, F 7am-2am, Sa 9am-2am, Su 10am-2am. AmEx/MC/V. For a traditional laundromat, try **Kaaren Pesula,** Kalevank. 45 (☎679 789). Wash €5 per 5kg, dry €4 per 5kg, detergent €1. Open M-Th 10am-8pm, F 10am-6pm, Sa 10am-4pm. Cash only.

**Police:** ☎100 22. **24hr. Medical Hotline:** ☎100 23.

**24hr. Pharmacy: Yliopiston Apteekki,** Mannerheimintie 96. (☎0203 202 00).

**Hospital:** 24hr. clinic **Mehiläinen,** Pohjoinen Hesperiankatu 17. (☎010 414 4444).

**Telephone: Telecenter Worldwide,** Vuorik. 8 (☎670 612; www.woodgong.com), offers reasonable rates to call most countries. Open M-F 10am-9pm, Sa 11am-7pm, Su noon-7pm. Australia €0.16 per min., UK €0.20, US €0.21. MC/V.

**Internet Access: Library 10,** Elielinaukio 2G (☎3108 5000), upstairs in the main post office building. Free Wi-Fi, free 30min. slots of Internet, up to 2hr. with reservation. Open M-Th 10am-8pm, F-Su noon-6pm. **mbar,** Mannerheimintie 22-24 (☎6124 5420; www.mbar.fi), offers free Wi-Fi and 11 terminals. €5 per hr. Open M-Tu 9am-midnight, W-Th 9am-2am, F-Sa 9am-3am, Su noon-midnight. AmEx/MC/V. Many cafes provide free Internet and Wi-Fi. Visit www.hel.fi/en/wlan or check the tourist office for locations.

**Post Office:** Elielinaukio 2F (☎2007 1000). Open M-F 7am-9pm, Sa-Su 10am-6pm. **Postal Code:** 00100. Address mail to be held in the following format: First name LAST NAME, *Poste Restante,* post office address, Helsinki, FINLAND.

## ACCOMMODATIONS AND CAMPING

**Hostel Erottajanpuisto (HI),** Uudenmaank. 9 (☎642 169; www.erottajanpuisto.com). Well-kept rooms in a central location. Breakfast €5. Lockers €1. Laundry €7. Free Internet and Wi-Fi. Reception 24hr. High season dorms €24; singles €46; doubles €63. Low season singles €48; doubles €64. €2.50 HI discount. AmEx/MC/V. ❷

**Hostel Satakuntatalo (HI),** Lapinrinne 1A (☎6958 5232; www.sodexho.fi/satakunta). M: Kamppi. Spacious, well-equipped rooms near the city center. Breakfast, sauna, and towels included. Lockers €2. Linens €5. Laundry €5.50. Free Internet and Wi-Fi; cables not included. Reception 24hr. Open June-Aug. Dorms €20; singles from €36; doubles from €54; triples from €75; quads from €86. €2.50 HI discount. AmEx/MC/V. ❷

**Hostel Academica (HI),** Hietaniemenk. 14 (☎1311 4334; www.hostelacademica.fi). M: Kamppi. Turn right onto Runebergink. and left after crossing the bridge. University housing becomes a hostel in summer. Rooms have kitchenettes and private bath. Morning sauna, swim, linens, and towels included. Internet €2 per 30min.; Wi-Fi €2 per hr., €5 per day. Reception 24hr. Open June-Aug. Dorms €22; singles €40-53; doubles €60-67. €2.50 HI discount. AmEx/MC/V. ❷

**Eurohostel (HI),** Linnank. 9 (☎622 0470; www.eurohostel.fi), near Katajanokka ferry terminal. Bright rooms, cafe, and free morning sauna. Breakfast €6.50. Linens and towels included. Laundry €1. Internet €2 per 15min. Wi-Fi €5 per day. Reception 24hr. Singles €39-43; doubles €47-54; triples €70-80. €2.50 HI discount. AmEx/MC/V. ❸

**Rastila Camping,** Karavaanik. 4 (☎3107 8517; www.hel.fi/rastila). M: Rastila. Change trains at Itäkeskus. A large campground 12km from the city next to a public beach. Kitchen, showers, and electricity each €4.50-7. Reception mid-May to mid-Sept. 24hr.; mid-Sept. to mid-May daily 8am-10pm. €5 per person; €10 per tent site in summer, €6 in winter; cabins €38-64. Hostel (HI) open mid-June to July. Dorms €19. MC/V. ❶

## FOOD

Restaurants and cafes are easy to find on Esplanadi and the streets branching off **Mannerheimintie** and **Uudenmaankatu.** Cheaper options surround the **Hietalahti** flea market at the southern end of Bulevardi. A large **supermarket** is under the train station. (Open M-Sa 7am-10pm, Su 10am-10pm.) Helsinki has many budget restaurants that serve all manner of ethnic food. Get lunch at the open-air market **Kauppatori,** where stalls sell freshly cooked fish and local produce; a meal from one of the cafes will cost about €5-8. (Open June-Aug. M-Sa 6:30am-6pm; Sept.-May M-F 7am-5pm.)

**Zetor,** Mannerheimintie 3-5 (☎666 966; www.zetor.net), in the mall opposite the train station. Cheeky menu, cheekier farm-inspired decor, a trademark tractor, and ridiculously good Finnish food. Homemade beer €5. Entrees €12-28. Attached bar 22+. Open Su-M 3pm-1am, Tu 3pm-3am, W-F 3pm-4am, Sa 11am-4am. AmEx/MC/V. ❷

**Kappeli Café,** Eteläesplanadi 1 (☎766 3880; www.kappeli.fi). This cafe has served the bohemian and the elite since 1867. Salads and sandwiches €8-9. Open May to mid-Sept. M-Th 9am-midnight, F-Sa 9am-2am, Su 9am-11pm; mid-Sept. to Apr. M-Sa 10am-midnight, Su 10am-11pm. Kitchen closes 1hr. before closing. AmEx/MC/V. ❶

**Café Ursula,** Ehrenströmintie 3 (☎652 817; www.ursula.fi). This upscale cafe also has delicious budget options and an idyllic setting on the Baltic Sea. Sandwiches €5-6. Salad bar €11. Entrees €9-18. Open daily in summer 9am-midnight; spring and fall 9am-10pm; winter 9am-8pm. AmEx/MC/V. ❷

**Zucchini,** Fabianink. 4 (☎622 2907), south of the tourist office. Popular vegetarian and vegan fare with organic produce. Open M-F 11am-4pm. Closed July. AmEx/MC/V. ❷

**Banana Leaf,** Fredrikink. 49 (☎605 167; www.malesia.net/bananaleaf). Delicious Malaysian and Thai food in a serene setting. Ask the server to add some spice to your dish—Finns take their Asian food bland. Lunch buffet €8. Entrees €9-20. Open M-F 11am-11pm, Sa-Su noon-3pm. AmEx/MC/V. ❷

**Lappi,** Annank. 22 (☎645 550; www.lappires.com). Tourists splurge on specialties like reindeer, lingonberries, and Arctic char amid smoky smells, wood, and fur. Entrees from €16. Reserve ahead. Open in summer daily 5-10:30pm; winter M-F noon-10:30pm, Sa-Su 1-10:30pm. AmEx/MC/V. ❸

## SIGHTS

Helsinki's Neoclassical buildings and new forms reflect Finnish architect Alvar Aalto's joke: "Architecture is our form of expression because our language is so impossible." Helsinki's Art Nouveau *(Jugendstil)* and Modernist structures are home to a dynamic design community. Much of the layout and architecture of the old center, however, is the brainchild of German Carl Engel, who modeled his design after St. Petersburg. Older buildings are adorned with humorous statues, so keep an eye out. Most sights are in the city's compact center, making it ideal for walking tours; pick up *See Helsinki on Foot* from the tourist office for routes. Trams #3B and 3T loop around the major sights in 1hr., providing a cheap alternative to tour buses. Helsinki has many parks, including **Kaivopuisto** in the south, **Töölönlahti** in the north, and **Esplanadi** and **Tähtitorninvuori** in the center of town.

**SUOMENLINNA.** This 18th-century military fortification, spanning five islands, was built by Sweden to stave off Russia. The fortress's dark passageways are an adventure to explore. The **Suomenlinna Museum** details the history of the fortress and its accompanying fleet. (☎4050 9691; www.suomenlinna.fi. *Museum open daily May-*

*Aug. 10am-6pm; Sept.-Apr. 11am-4pm. €5, students €4. 30min. film 2 per hr. AmEx/MC/V.)* The islands also feature the world's only combination church and **lighthouse** and Finland's only remaining WWII **submarine**, the *Vesikko*. *(Church ☎ 709 2665. Usually open May-Aug. W-F noon-4pm. Submarine ☎ 1814 6238. Open mid-May to Aug. 11am-6pm. €4, students €2. Cash only. Fortress tours leave from the museum June-Aug. daily 11am and 2pm; Sept.-May Sa-Su 1:30pm. Summer €6, winter €6.50, including admission to the Ehrensvard Museum, the Commander's residence. AmEx/MC/V.)*

**SENAATIN TORI (SENATE SQUARE).** The square and its gleaming white ◼**Tuomi-okirkko** (Dome Church) showcase Carl Engel's architecture and exemplify the splendor of Finland's 19th-century Russian period. The church's stunning marble reliefs house an interior so elegantly simple that every gilded detail becomes magnified. *(Unioninkatu 29. ☎ 2340 6120. Free organ recitals W noon in July. Church open June-Aug. M-Sa 9am-6pm, Su noon-6pm; Sept.-May M-Sa 9am-6pm, Su noon-6pm.)* The red-brick ◼**Uspenski Orthodox Cathedral** (Uspenskinkatedraadi), the largest Orthodox church in Northern and Western Europe, evokes images of Russia with its ornate interior and 13 golden cupolas. *(☎ 634 267. Open M and W-F 9:30am-4pm, Tu 9:30am-6pm, Sa 9:30am-2pm, Su noon-3pm. Closed M in winter.)*

**ESPLANADI AND MANNERHEIMINTIE.** A boulevard dotted with statues and fountains, Esplanadi is a great place to people-watch. The **Designmuseo** presents the work of designers like Aalto and Eliel Saarinen alongside creations by young artists and first-rate temporary exhibits. *(Korkeavuorenk. 23. ☎ 622 0540; www.designmuseum.fi. Open June-Aug. daily 11am-6pm; Sept.-May Tu 11am-8pm, W-Su 11am-6pm. €7, students €3. AmEx/MC/V.)* At the end of Esplanadi, turn right onto Mannerheimintie and right again onto Kaivok. past the train station for the **Ateneum Art Museum** (Ateneum Taidemuseo), Finland's largest, with comprehensive exhibits on Finnish art. *(Kaivok. 2, opposite the train station. ☎ 1733 6401; www.ateneum.fi. Open Tu and F 9am-6pm, W-Th 9am-8pm, Sa-Su 11am-5pm. €6, students €4; €8/6.50 during temporary exhibits, W free 5-8pm. AmEx/MC/V.)* Continue on Mannerheimintie to ◼**Kiasma** (Museum of Contemporary Art), a warehouse that features top-flight modern art and calibrates the width of its doors to Fibonacci's golden ratio. The first floor and outdoor exhibits are often free. *(Mannerheiminaukio 2. ☎ 1733 6501; www.kiasma.fi. Open Tu 9am-5pm, W-Su 10am-8:30pm. €6, students €4, F free 5-8:30pm. AmEx/MC/V.)* From Kiasma, head down Arkadiank. away from the city center and turn right on Fredrikink. to reach the heavily touristed **Temppeliaukio Kirkko**. This striking church is hewn out of a hill of rock with only the domed roof visible from the outside. *(Lutherink. 3. ☎ 494 698. English-language services Su 2pm. Usually open M-Tu and Th 10am-8pm, W and F 10am-6pm, Sa 10am-noon, Su 11:45am-1:45pm and 3:30-6pm; winter M-Th 10am-5pm.)*

**OTHER SIGHTS.** The University of Helsinki's **Botanic Garden** is north of Senate Sq. along Unionink. *(Unionink. 44. Take trams #3B/3T or 6 to Kaisaniemi. ☎ 1912 4455. Garden open M-F 7am-8pm, Sa-Su 9am-8pm. Free. Greenhouses open Apr.-Sept. Tu-Su 10am-5pm; Oct.-Mar. 10am-3pm. €4.20, students €2.20. MC/V.)* West of downtown, the **Cable Factory** *(Kaapeli)* houses three museums, dozens of studios and galleries, and various performance areas. The **Finnish Museum of Photography** (www.fmp.fi) has provocative displays, the **Hotel and Restaurant Museum** (www.hotellijaravintolamuseo.fi) offers a history of menus and minibars, and the **Theater Museum** (www.teatterimuseo.fi) contains set models and costume designs from the National Theater. *(Tallbergink. 1. M: Ruoholahti. After exiting, walk 5 blocks down Itämerenk. Museums are in the G entrance. ☎ 020 796 1670; www.kaapelitehdas.fi. Open Tu-Su 11am-6pm. Theater Museum closed in July. Photography Museum €6, students €4; Hotel and Restaurant Museum €2/1; Theater Museum €5.50/2.50. MC/V.)* Near the Western Harbor, the

## ETERNAL GLORY

Looking for a way to sate your competitive appetite? You have come to the right place. Finland has world championships in:

**Wife Carrying:** Inspired by the 19th century practice of stealing wives from neighboring villages. Brave the 253.5m obstacle course, but be careful: a wife dropping infraction leads to a 15sec. penalty (and likely a night on the couch). Prize: Wife's weight in beer. (www.sonkajarvi.fi. July 5, 2008. Sonkajärvi)

**Sauna Endurance:** Compete on the cusp of death or injury. The temperature starts at a mild 110°C (230°F) and rises every 30sec. The winner is the last person sitting upright who can walk out unassisted. Prize: A one week vacation to a different type of sauna: Morocco. (www.saunaheinola.com. Aug., 2008. Heinola)

**Mobile Phone Throwing:** Finland has the most cell phones per capita in the world. Might as well throw some. Prize: A new phone. (www.savonlinnafestivals.com. Aug. 2008, Savonlinna)

**Mosquito-Killing:** Henri Pellonpää is the world record holder, with 21 kills in 5min. in 1995. The government worries that the event will disrupt the balance of nature, but it doesn't seem like a scarcity of mosquitos will ever be possible in Finland. Squash away. Prize: Mosquitoes will fear you. (Summer 2008. Pelkosenniemi)

crowded **Jean Sibelius Monument** pays homage to one of the 20th century's great composers. (On Mechelinink. in Sibelius Park. Take bus #24, dir.: Seurasaari to Rasjasaarentie; the monument will be behind you.)

## 🎵 ENTERTAINMENT

Helsinki's parks are always animated. A **concert series** enlivens the Esplanadi park all summer Monday through Friday at 4pm. Highlights of the program are **Jazz Espa** in July, and **Ethno Espa** showcasing international music (www.kulttuuri.hel.fi/espanlava). In fall and winter, the Espa stage is used as an exhibition for young artists. Late June's **Helsinki Pride** (www.helsinkipride.fi) is Finland's largest GLBT event. The **Helsinki Festival** (www.helsinkifestival.fi), toward the end of August, wraps up the summer with cultural events ranging from music and theater to film and visual arts. At the end of September, **Helsinki Design Week** (www.helsinkidesignweek.fi) reinforces the city's image as a style capital, while the **Love and Anarchy Film Festival** (www.hiff.fi) features works from across the globe. Throughout summer, concerts rock **Kaivopuisto** (on the corner of Puistok. and Ehrenstromintie, in the southern part of town) and **Hietaniemi Beach** (down Hesperiank. on the western shore). The free English-language papers *Helsinki This Week*, *Helsinki Your Way*, and *City* list popular cafes, nightspots, and events; get them at the tourist office or your hostel. Also check out the ◼Nordic Oddity pamphlet series, with insider advice on sights, bars, and activities. For high culture, try the Helsinki Philharmonic and Radio Symphony Orchestra, the National Opera, or the National Theater. **Lippupiste** and **Lippupalvelu**, Aleksanterink. 52 (☎0600 900 900), in the Stockmann department store, sell tickets for most big venues (AmEx/MC/V).

## 🎶 NIGHTLIFE

Bars and beer terraces fill up in late afternoon; most clubs don't get going until midnight and stay crazy until 4am. Bars and clubs line **Mannerheimintie, Uudenmaankatu,** and **Iso Roobertinkatu.** East of the train station, nightlife centers around **Yliopistonkatu** and **Kaisaniemenkatu,** while in bohemian Kallio, the bars around **Fleminginkatu** have some of the cheapest beer in the city. A popular night activity is heavy-metal karaoke; check out Wednesday and Sunday at **Hevimesta,** Hallitusk. 3.

**Royal Onnela,** Fredrikink. 46 (☎020 7759 460; www.ravintolaonnela.fi). The biggest nightclub in Scandinavia has a room for most music tastes, from Finnish pop to disco and 80s/90s hits. Beer €4.50, €1 W, Th, Su. Mixed drinks €7. M-Sa 22+, Su 20+. Cover F-Sa €7. Club open M and W-Su 10pm-3:30am. Lapland Poro Bar M and W-Su 6pm-4am. Karaoke bar M and W-Su 8pm-2:30am, Tu 8pm-3:30am. AmEx/MC/V.

**On the Rocks,** Mikonk. 15 (☎612 2030; www.ontherocks.fi). This legendary rock bar and club offers Finnish bands for cheap. Beer €4.80. Tu-Th live music. 23+. Cover Tu-Th free-€12, F-Sa €7. Open daily in summer noon-4am; winter 4pm-4am. AmEx/D/MC/V.

**Bar Erottaja,** Erottajank. 13-17 (☎611 196). This art-student hangout is usually packed with people engaged in conversation over music. Beer €4.50. F-Sa DJ. 22+ after 6pm. Open M 2pm-1am, Tu 2pm-2am, W-Sa 2pm-3am, Su 6pm-3am. AmEx/D/MC/V.

**dtm,** Iso Roobertink. 28 (☎676 314; www.dtm.fi). This popular gay club draws a mixed crowd to 2 stories of everything from foam parties to drag shows. Beer €4.60. Occasional F or Sa lesbian nights. 22+ after 10pm. Cover Sa €5, special events €5-10. Happy hour M-Sa 9am-4pm. Open M-Sa 9am-4am, Su noon-4am. AmEx/MC/V.

**Arctic Icebar,** Yliopistonk. 5 (☎278 1855; www.labodega.fi). Not affiliated with the other Icebars around the globe, this one sets itself apart by being the smallest (with a capacity of 12) and coldest (-10°C). The €10 cover gets you a thermal parka, gloves, boots, and a vodka-based drink—the only kind that won't crack the glasses. Additional drinks €10 each. 18+. Open daily 4-11:30pm. AmEx/MC/V.

## 🏞 OUTDOOR ACTIVITIES

Just north of the train station lie the two city lakes, **Töölönlahti** and **Eläintarhanlahti.** Take an afternoon walk on the winding paths around them. Northwest of the Sibelius Monument across a bridge, the island of **Seurasaari** offers retreat from the city. It is also home to an **open-air museum** of farmsteads and churches transplanted from around Finland. On Midsummer's Eve, tall *kokko* (bonfires) are set ablaze during a drunken party. *(Take bus #24 from Erottaja to the last stop. The island is always open for hiking. Museum ☎4050 9660. Open June-Aug. M-Tu and Th-Su 11am-5pm, W 11am-7pm; late May and early Sept. M-F 9am-3pm, Sa-Su 11am-5pm. Tours June 15 to Aug. 15 daily 3pm. €5, students €4. MC/V.)* Many islands south of the city feature **public beaches** that are accessible by ferry, including a nude beach on Pihlajasaari Island. Beyond Espoo to the west is the **Nuuksio National Park,** where flying squirrels are more common than anywhere else in Finland. *(☎0205 64 4790; www.outdoors.fi/nuuksionp. Take the train to Espoo station and bus #85 from there to Nuuksionpää.)* For a real trek that doesn't actually involve Helsinki but is simply too glorious to pass up, head to the northern Finnish town of **Rovaniemi,** where Santa Claus holds office hours at his **village** and runs an empire of gift shops. It's unclear why Santa lives in a gift shop in northern Finland and who maintains the North Pole workshop while he hangs out here. (☎356 2096; www.santaclausvillage.info. Open daily May-Aug. 9am-6pm; Sept.-Nov. and Jan.-Apr. 9am-5pm; Dec. 9am-7pm. Closed for "Santa naptime" 11am-noon and 3-4pm.) **Trains** run from Helsinki to Rovaniemi (10hr., 4-5 per day, €78) via Oulu (2½hr., €30) and Kuopio (8hr., 3-4 per day, from €55).

# ICELAND (ÍSLAND)

## ESSENTIALS

**EMBASSIES AND CONSULATES.** Foreign embassies in Iceland are in Reykjavík. Icelandic embassies and consulates abroad include: **Australia,** 16 Hann St., Griffith,

Canberra (☎262 95 68 19; benefitfarm@bigpond.com.au); **Canada,** 360 Albert St., Ste. 710, Ottawa, ON, K1R 7X7 (☎613-482-1944; www.iceland.org/ca); **Ireland,** Cavendish House, Smithfield, Dublin (☎1 872 9299; jgg@goregrimes.ie); **New Zealand,** Sanford Ltd., 22 Jellicoe St., Auckland (☎9 379 4720); **UK,** 2A Hans St., London, SW1X 0JE (☎020 72 59 39 99; www.iceland.org/uk); **US,** 1156 15th St. NW, Ste. 1200, Washington, D.C., 20005 (☎202-265-6653; www.iceland.org/us).

**VISA AND ENTRY INFORMATION.** EU citizens do not need a visa. Citizens of Australia, Canada, New Zealand, and the US do not need a visa for stays of up to 90 days, beginning upon entry into any of the countries in the EU's freedom-of-movement zone. For more info, see p. 16. For stays longer than 90 days, all non-EU citizens need visas, available at embassies abroad; check www.utl.is/english/visas/apply to find the nearest to you.

| ICELANDIC KRÓNUR (ISK) | | |
|---|---|---|
| AUS$1 = 54.36ISK | | 100ISK = AUS$1.84 |
| CDN$1 = 64.31ISK | | 100ISK = CDN$1.56 |
| EUR€1 = 91.84ISK | | 100ISK = EUR€1.09 |
| NZ$1 = 47.42ISK | | 100ISK = NZ$2.11 |
| UK£1 = 135.01ISK | | 100ISK = UK£0.74 |
| US$1 = 68.16ISK | | 100ISK = US$1.47 |

**MONEY.** Iceland's unit of currency is the **króna (ISK),** plural krónur. One króna is equal to 100 aurars, with standard denominations of 1, 5, 10, 50, and 100kr in coins, and 500, 1000, and 5000kr in notes. For currency exchange, **ATMs** are located throughout the larger cities. Banks are usually open M-F 9:15am-4pm. Major Icelandic banks, such as Landsbankinn, do not have sister banks in other countries that allow lower exchange fees. In general, there's no way around the high costs in Iceland. On average, a night in a hostel will cost 1700ISK, a guesthouse 3000-4000ISK, and a meal's worth of groceries 700-1200ISK. Restaurants include a service charge on the bill. **Tipping** further is unnecessary and even discouraged.

Iceland has a 24.5% **value added tax (VAT),** a sales tax on goods and services purchased within the European Economic Area (EEA: the EU plus Iceland, Liechtenstein, and Norway). The prices given in *Let's Go* include VAT. In the airport upon exiting the EEA, non-EEA citizens can claim a refund on the tax paid for goods at participating stores. In order to qualify for a refund in a store, you must spend at least 4000ISK; make sure to ask for a refund form when you pay. For more info on qualifying for a VAT refund, see p. 18.

| ICELAND | ❶ | ❷ | ❸ | ❹ | ❺ |
|---|---|---|---|---|---|
| **ACCOMMODATIONS** | under 2000ISK | 2000-3000ISK | 3001-5000ISK | 5001-10,000ISK | over 10,000ISK |
| **FOOD** | under 500ISK | 500-1000ISK | 1001-1400ISK | 1401-2000ISK | over 2000ISK |

# REYKJAVÍK

Home to three-fifths of Icelanders, Reykjavík (pop. 190,000) is a modestly sized capital with an international clubbing reputation. Bold, modern architecture juts out above the blue waters of the Faxaflói Bay, and the city's refreshingly clear air complements the clean streets and well-kept gardens. The spring rain and the endless winter night force social life indoors, where many locals sip espresso while arguing over environmental policy in this hub of renewable energy.

# ▐ TRANSPORTATION

**Flights:** International flights arrive at **Keflavík Airport (KEF),** 55km from Reykjavík. From the main exit, catch a **Flybus** (☎562 1011; www.flybus.is) to BSÍ Bus Terminal (40-50min.; 1200ISK, round-trip 2100ISK). Flybus also offers free minivan transport from the bus terminal to many hostels and hotels; check website for more info. A public bus to the city center runs from Gamla-Hringbraut stop across the street from the bus terminal (M-F 7am-midnight, Sa-Su 10am-midnight; 275ISK). Flybus service to the airport departs from BSÍ; most hostels and hotels can also arrange trips. Nearby **Reykjavík Airport (RKV)** is the departure point for domestic flights. Take bus #15 or Flybus from BSÍ.

**Buses: Umferðarmiðstöð BSÍ** (BSÍ Bus Terminal), Vatnsmýrarveg. 10 (☎562 1011; www.bsi.is), off Gamla-Hringbraut. Walk 15-20min. south along Tjörnin from the city center or take bus #14, 15, S1, or S3-S6 (2-3 per hr., 275ISK). Open daily May-Oct. 24hr.; Nov.-Apr. 5am-10pm.

**Public Transportation:** Bus service can be infrequent and roundabout; walking is often a speedier option. **Strætó** (☎540 2700; www.bus.is) operates yellow city buses (275ISK). **Lækjartorg,** on Lækjarg., is the main bus station for the city center. **Hlemmur,** 1km east of Lækjartorg where Hverfisg. meets Laugavegur, is another major terminal with more connections than Lækjartorg (open M-Sa 7am-11:30pm, Su 10am-11:30pm). Pick up a schedule at the terminal. Don't feel bad asking for navigational help at hostels and information desks—recent changes in the bus routes have confused even some drivers. Buy packages of 10 adult fares (2000ISK) or pay fare with coins; drivers do not give change. Ticket packages are sold at the terminal and at swimming pools. If you need to change buses, ask the driver of the first bus for *skiptimiði* (a free transfer ticket), valid for 1hr. after the fare has been paid. Most buses 2-3 per hr. M-Sa 7am-midnight, Su 10am-midnight.

**Taxis:** BSR (☎561 0000). 24hr. service. **Hreyfill** (☎588 5522; www.hreyfill.is/english). Also offers private tours for groups of 1-8 people, 7900-44,000ISK.

**Car Rental: Berg,** Bíldshöfða 10 (☎577 6050; www.bergcar.is). Under 100km from 4900ISK per day, unlimited km from 8850ISK per day; low season reduced rates. Pickup available at Keflavík and Reykjavík Airports (2000ISK). **Hertz** (☎505 0600; www.hertz.is), at the Reykjavík Airport. From 6110ISK per day. Pickup available at Keflavík Airport (2300ISK). **Avis** (☎591 4000; www.avis.is) and **Budget** (☎562 6060; www.budget.is) have locations in Reykjavík. Fuel costs around 3000ISK per day.

**Bike Rental: Reykjavík Youth Hostel** campground (p. 983). 1700ISK per 6hr., 2000ISK per day. Helmet included. **Borgarhjól,** Hverfisgata 50, is closer to the city center, down the road from Culture House. (☎551 5653. Call for prices; fees change frequently.)

**Hitchhiking:** Many foreigners hitchhike outside of Reykjavík because of confusing bus routes, but it is never completely safe. Let's Go does not recommend hitchhiking.

# ▟ ▐ ORIENTATION AND PRACTICAL INFORMATION

**Lækjartorg** is Reykjavík's main square and a good base for navigation. **Lækjargata,** a main street, leads southwest from Lækjartorg and becomes **Fríkirkjuvegur** when it reaches **Lake Tjörnin** (the Pond), the southern limit of the city center. Reykjavík's most prominent thoroughfare extends eastward from Lækjartorg, changing names from **Austurstræti** to **Bankastræti** and then to **Laugavegur,** as it is most

## SURVIVING ICELAND

You might have the sixth sense—and no, not the one involving Bruce Willis and dead people. The Icelandic sixth sense allows you to see *huldufolk* (hidden people), magical creatures that 80% of Icelanders believe exist. Some *huldufolk* are friendly, upstanding citizens. Others are up to no damn good. To help you get through your trip to Iceland, Let's Go offers a brief survival guide:

**Elves:** Apparently, some look like humans, which makes picking them out a total crapshoot. **Strategy:** No cause for alarm. They're harmless and live in their Westman Islands village.

**Faeries:** A deceptive bunch. The beautiful faeries are known to lure you with soft, plaintive music. Then, BOOM—they'll carry you off. **Strategy:** Earplugs, or just run if you hear soft, plaintive music.

**Gnomes:** Small and subterranean. **Strategy:** Nothing to fear. Icelandic roads are often built around their settlements. They're that respected.

**Trolls:** Bad news if you run into one of these nocturnal beasts. Some live in Dimmuborgir, near Mývatn. **Strategy:** Although they're ugly, trolls fuss over hygiene. Get them dirty, mess with their hair, etc. The Reykjavík power plant at Nesjavelliri, for example, maintains a shower for the trolls to enjoy so they don't meddle with the water supply. An A+ tactic.

commonly known. Helpful publications, including *What's On in Reykjavík*, *Reykjavík City Guide*, and *The Reykjavík Grapevine*, are available for free at tourist offices. The *Grapevine*, published by American expatriates, includes opinionated local news coverage and comprehensive listings of current music and arts events.

**Tourist Offices: Upplýsingamiðstöð Ferðamanna í Reykjavík,** Aðalstr. 2 (☎590 1550; www.visitreykjavik.is). Open June-Aug. daily 8:30am-7pm; Sept.-May M-Sa 9am-6pm, Su 10am-2pm. Sells the **Reykjavík Card** (1-day 1200ISK, 2-day 1700ISK, 3-day 2200ISK), which allows unlimited public transportation, free entry to some sights and thermal pools (p. 985), and limited Internet access at the tourist center. Several discount coupon books are also available at the center. **Kleif Tourist Information Center,** Bankastræti 2 (☎510 5700; www.kleif.is). Open June-Aug. daily 8am-9pm; Sept.-May. M-F 8am-6pm, Sa-Su 8am-4pm. **City Hall Information Center,** Vonarstræti 3 (☎563 2005), in the lobby of City Hall. Open M-F 8:20am-6:15pm, Sa-Su noon-4pm. Visit www.reykjavik.com for general info on sights around the city.

**Embassies: Canada,** Túng. 14 (☎575 6500). Open M-F 9am-noon. **UK,** Lauf. 31 (☎550 5100). Open M-F 9am-noon. **US,** Lauf. 21 (☎562 9100). Open M-F 9am-5pm.

**Luggage Storage:** At BSÍ Bus Terminal (☎580 5462), next to the ticket window. 400ISK for the 1st day, 200ISK per day thereafter. Open daily 7:30am-7pm.

**GLBT Resources: Gay Community Center,** Laugavegur 3, 4th fl. (☎552 7878; www.samtokin78.is). Open M and Th 1-5pm and 8-11pm, Tu-W and F 1-5pm; cafe open M and Th 8-11:30pm; library open M and Th 8-11pm. More info at www.gayice.is.

**Police:** Hverfisg. 113 (☎444 1000).

**24hr. Pharmacy: Lyfja Lágmúla,** Lágmúla 5 (☎533 2300).

**Hospital: National Hospital,** on Hringbraut (☎543 1000), has 24hr. emergency services. Take bus #14, S1, or S3-S6 southeast from the city center.

**Internet Access: Reykjavík Public Library,** Tryggvag. 15 (☎563 1705), is the cheapest option. 200ISK per hr. Open M-Th 10am-7pm, F-Su 1-5pm. Cash only. **Snarrót,** Laugavegur 21 (☎551 8927). In the basement of Kaffi Hljómalind (p. 984), Snarrót is also a hub for local student activism. 300ISK per hr. Open M-F 9am-11pm, Sa-Su 10am-11pm. MC/V. **Ground Zero,** Vallarstr. 4 (☎562 7776). 300ISK per 30min., 500ISK per hr. Open M-F 11am-1am, Sa-Su noon-1am. AmEx/MC/V.

**Post Office: Íslandspóstur,** Pósthússtr. 5 (☎580 1121), at the intersection with Austurstr. Open M-F 9am-6:00pm. Address mail to be held in the following format: First name LAST NAME, **Poste Restante,** ÍSLANDSPÓSTUR, Pósthússtr. 5, 101 Reykjavík, ICELAND.

# ▌ ACCOMMODATIONS AND CAMPING

*Gistiheimili* (guesthouses) offer accommodations starting from 2500ISK (bed and pillow in a small room; add 300-600ISK for linens). Hotels cost at least 5500ISK. Call ahead for reservations, especially in summer.

▨ **Reykjavík Youth Hostel (HI),** Sundlaugarveg. 34 (☎553 8110). Bus #14 from Lækjarg. This popular, eco-friendly hostel is east of the city center, but it's adjacent to Reykjavík's largest thermal pool and has excellent facilities. The staff gives tips for exploring the city's less touristy sights. Breakfast 800ISK. Linens 600ISK. Laundry 350ISK. Internet 300ISK per 30min, 500ISK per hr. Reception 8am-midnight; ring bell after hours. Dorms 2050ISK, with HI discount 1700ISK; doubles 4100/3500ISK. ❷

**Salvation Army Guesthouse,** Kirkjustr. 2 (☎561 3203; www.guesthouse.is). Located near City Hall in the heart of Reykjavík, this bright yellow hostel is cozy with modest, but neat, accommodations. Its prime location makes it ideal for exploring Reykjavík's nightlife. Breakfast 700ISK. Laundry 800ISK. Sleeping-bag accommodations 2500ISK; singles 5500ISK; doubles 8000ISK. AmEx/MC/V. ❷

**Domus Guesthouse,** Hverfisgt. 45 (☎561 1200). Take bus #13, S1, or S3-S6 and get off across from the Regnboginn movie theater on Hverfisgötu. Close to the city center, the guesthouse offers spacious rooms with TV and couches. All sleeping-bag accommodations are located across the street in a large room partitioned by curtains. Breakfast included with private rooms. Sleeping-bag accommodations 3900ISK; singles 9500ISK; doubles 11,300ISK. Reduced prices Oct.-Apr. MC/V. ❸

**Flóki Inn,** Flókag. 1 (☎552 1155; www.innsoficeland.is), a 15min. walk from the city center. A relaxing, intimate guesthouse with kettle, fridge, and TV in every room. Breakfast included. Reception 24hr. Check-in 2pm. Check-out 11am. Singles 8300ISK; doubles 10,900ISK. Extra bed 3700ISK. Reduced prices Oct.-May. AmEx/MC/V. ❹

**Reykjavík Youth Hostel Campsite** (☎568 6944), next to the hostel. Helpful staff and a sociable character make this a good alternative to indoor facilities. Luggage storage 300ISK. Reception 24hr. Open mid-May to mid-Sept. Tent sites 800ISK. 4-person cabins 4500ISK. Showers. Electricity 400ISK. MC/V. ❶

# ▐ FOOD

An authentic Icelandic meal featuring *hákarl* (shark meat that has been allowed to rot underground), lamb, or puffin costs upwards of 1500ISK, but it's worth the splurge at least once. To maintain a leaner budget, head to the stands west of Lækjartorg, which hawk *pylsur* (lamb meat hot dogs) for around 200ISK. Ask for "the works," including *remoulade* (a spicy mayonnaise-based sauce). Pick up groceries at **Bónus,** Laugavegur 59. (☎562 8200. Open M-F noon-6:30pm, Sa 10am-8pm.) Other branches are located on Austurstræti and Hverfisgata.

▨ **Á Næstu Grösum,** Laugavegur 20B (☎552 8410), entrance off Klapparstígur. The first all-vegetarian restaurant in Iceland uses only fresh, seasonal ingredients in creative ways. The airy dining room showcases the work of up-and-coming local artists. Soup (700ISK) comes with free refills. Small plate 550ISK; medium 850ISK; large 1250ISK. Open M-F 11:30am-10pm, Sa 1-10pm, Su 5-10pm. MC/V. ❷

⬛ **Babalú Coffeehouse,** Skólavörðustigur 22A (☎552 2278). A perfect place to relax. Serves savory crepes (920ISK) and smaller, sweet crepes (500ISK). Enjoy a coffee (280ISK) on the patio. Free Wi-Fi. Open daily 11am-10pm. AmEx/MC/V. ❷

**Kaffi Hljómalind,** Laugavegur 21 (☎517 1980), east of the city center. Organic, vegetarian-friendly cafe serves big portions of soup, with free refill and bread (700ISK). Free Wi-Fi, vocal patrons, a box of toys, and large windows make this a great place for people-watching or passing the time before nightlife kicks into high gear. Live music (500ISK) or poetry reading W-F 8pm. Open M-Sa 9am-11pm, Su 11am-6pm. MC/V. ❷

**Nonnabiti,** Hafnarstr. 9 (☎551 2312), west of Lækjartorg. toward the main tourist office. This no-frills sandwich shop is good for cheap, satisfying meals. Burgers 440ISK. Hot sandwiches 610ISK. 100ISK discount on subs M-F 9:30am-1:30pm. Open Su-Th 9:30am-2am, F-Sa 8:30am-6:00am. MC/V. ❶

**Bæjarins Beztu,** corner of Tryggvag. and Pósthússtr. This tiny stand on the harbor serves the Icelandic hot dog (210ISK) by which all others are measured. The owner proudly displays a picture of Bill Clinton eating one of her franks. Weekend crowds head here to satisfy late-night cravings, often singing while they wait. Open until 12:30am, or until crowds dissipate—sometimes past 6am. MC/V. ❶

# 👁 SIGHTS

**CITY CENTER.** Reykjavík's **City Hall,** on the northern shore of **Lake Tjörnin,** houses an impressive three-dimensional model of Iceland that vividly renders the country's striking topography. *(Open in summer M-F 8am-7pm, Sa-Su 10-6pm; winter M-F 8am-7pm, Sa-Su noon-6pm. Free.)* Just beyond City Hall lies **Aðalstræti,** the oldest street in the city. The recently opened **871 +/- 2 Settlement Museum,** 16 Aðalstræti, features the preserved foundation of a Viking longhouse, with interactive displays and artifacts. By dating surrounding volcanic deposits, archaeologists theorize that the structure was built around AD 869-873. *(☎411 6370. Open daily 10am-5pm. 600ISK. AmEx/MC/V.)* The **Hafnarhús** (Harbor House) is the most eclectic of the three wings of the **Reykjavík Art Museum.** The museum, a renovated warehouse, holds a collection of paintings by Erro, Iceland's preeminent contemporary artist. *(Tryggvag. 17, off Aðalstr. ☎590 1201; www.listasafnreykjavikur.is. Open daily high season 10am-5pm; low season 1-4pm. 500ISK. Th free.)* Follow Tryggvag. to the intersection of Lækjarg. and Hverfisg. to see the **statue of Ingólfur Arnason,** Iceland's first settler, and enjoy the mountain views to the north. The ⬛**Culture House** has a detailed exhibit on Iceland's ancient history and mythology, including carefully preserved vellum manuscripts of the Eddas and Sagas. *(Hverfisg. 15. ☎545 1400. Open daily 11am-5pm. Free.)*

East of Lake Tjörnin, the **National Gallery of Iceland** presents highlights of contemporary Icelandic art. The toys and cushions on the bottom floor aren't part of an ultramodern exhibit; they're for the restless children of patrons. *(Fríkirkjuveg. 7. ☎515 9600. Open Tu-Su 11am-5pm. Free.)* Continue eastward to the landmark **Hallgrímskirkja** church on Skólavörðustígur, designed by Guðjón Samúelsson to look like it formed from a volcanic eruption. *(☎510 1000. Open daily 9am-5pm. Elevator to the top 350ISK.)* Across from the church, the **Einar Jónsson Museum** on Njarðarg. exhibits 300 of the sculptor's imposing, allegorical works inspired by Iceland's Christian and pagan heritage. Don't miss the free sculpture garden in the back. *(☎561 3797; www.skulptur.is. Open June to mid-Sept. Tu-Su 2-5pm; mid-Sept.-May Sa-Su 2-5pm. 400ISK.)*

**LAUGARDALUR.** Sights cluster around Laugardalur, a large park east of the city center. The white dome of the **Ásmundarsafn** (Ásmundur Sveinsson Sculpture Museum), on Sigtún, houses works spanning Sveinsson's career in a building the

**DON'T GET FLEECED.** Visiting Reykjavík isn't cheap. For deals on clothes, music, and jewelry, check out the **Sirkus** (flea market) on Laugavegur next to Kaffi Hljómalind (June-Aug. F-Sa). Cap it off with a discounted brew.

artist designed and lived in. The free sculpture garden around the museum features larger works, some of which are interactive pieces ideal for climbing. (Take bus #14 to the Laugardalslaug thermal pools, turn left and walk down Reykjavegur to Sigtún. ☎553 2155. Open daily May-Sept. 10am-4pm; Oct.-Apr. 1-4pm. 500ISK, includes admission to Harbor House. Th free.) Walking out of the museum, continue straight down Sigtún until it becomes Engjaveg. and proceed to the **Reykjavík Botanic Garden,** one of the few forested areas in Iceland. (Skúlatún 2. ☎553 8870. Garden open 24hr. Greenhouse and pavilion open daily Apr.-Sept. 10am-10pm; Oct.-Mar. 10am-5pm. Free.) Just outside the garden, opposite the pavilion and greenhouse, a free outdoor exhibit outlines the history of the **Washing Springs,** Reykjavík's geothermal square, where the women of the city once came to do their cooking and laundry. The city's largest thermal swimming pool, **Laugardalslaug** (see **Thermal Pools,** below), is also in the area.

**OTHER SIGHTS.** The renovated ◼**National Museum** has a comprehensive overview of Iceland's past with audio/visuals and interactive exhibits that let you try on Icelandic garb. (Suðurgt. 41. Bus #14, S1, or S3-S6 from Hlemmur station. ☎530 2200; www.natmus.is. Open May-Sept. 15 daily 10am-5pm; Sept 16-Apr. Tu-Su 11am-5pm. 600ISK, students 300ISK. W free.) From the National Museum, take bus #12 to **Árbæjarsafn,** an open-air museum chronicling the lives and architecture of past Icelanders. Check www.reykjavikmuseum.is for summer weekend special events, like folk dances and Viking games. (Kistuhylur 4. ☎577 1111. Open June-Aug. M 11am-4pm, Tu-F 10am-5pm, Sa-Su 10am-6pm. 600ISK. Low season tours M, W, F 1pm; call ahead.) The **Saga Museum** rivals London's Madame Tussauds with its depiction of Icelandic history using life-size wax models. One figure shows a woman exposing her breast, an event that supposedly caused the entire army of Norway to retreat during a bygone battle. We don't get it either. (Bus #18 south to Perlan. ☎511 1517; www.sagamuseum.is. Open Mar.-Oct. 10am-6pm; Nov.-Feb. noon-5pm. 800ISK, students 600ISK.)

## ◨ THERMAL POOLS

Reykjavík's thermal pools are all equipped with a hot pot (naturally occurring hot tub) and steam room or sauna, although each pool maintains a distinct character. Freeloaders should seek out the city beach and its free hot pot at Nauthólsvik. All pools listed below charge 350ISK admission, with 10 visits for 3000ISK.

**Laugardalslaug,** Laugardalslaug-Sundlaugarveg. 105 (☎411 5100). Take bus #14 from the city center; entrance is on the right, facing the parking lot. The city's largest thermal pool features indoor and outdoor facilities, a water slide, a children's slide, 4 hot pots, and a sauna. Swimsuit or towel rental 350ISK. Open Apr.-Sept. M-F 6:30am-10:30pm, Sa-Su 8am-10pm; Oct.-Mar. M-F 6:30am-10:30pm, Sa-Su 8am-8pm. MC/V.

**Sundhöll Reykjavíkur,** Barónsstígur 101 (☎551 4059). Take bus #14, 15 or 16. This centrally located pool has a smaller outdoor area than other pools, but is the only one with diving boards. Open M-F 6:30am-9:30pm, Sa-Su 8am-7pm. AmEx/MC/V.

**Sundlaug Seltjarness,** Suðurströnd 170 (☎561 1551). Take bus #11 from Hlemmur station to Sundlaug stop and follow the signs. Recently renovated, this is the only pool that offers saltwater hot pots. Facilities include a water slide, 2 hot pots, and a sauna. Swimsuit or towel rental 300ISK. Open M-F 7am-9pm, Sa-Su 8am-7pm. AmEx/MC/V.

HEADING NORTH

**Ylströndin Nauthólsvík.** Take bus #16 south until the last stop, or take bus #18 to Perlan and hike down Öskuhlíð. Though the locals don't consider this a classic thermal pool, this remote city beach is worth the hard trek to soak in the hot pot in the midst of sea water and take in the view of Reykjavík's smaller fjords. Lockers 200ISK. Swimming free. Open May-Sept. daily 10am-8pm. Closed in rainy weather.

## 🏔 HIKING

Reykjavík has a range of hikes for different experience levels. Check the weather before scaling heights—conditions on hilltops can be very different compared to weather at sea level. For easier hikes, take bus #18 to the Perlan stop by the Saga Museum to reach trails on the forested hill around Perlan, one of which features a working model of the Strokkur Geyser (see **Gullfoss and Geysir,** p. 987). At the southwest corner of the park is **Nauthólsvík** beach (see **Thermal Pools,** above) and a scenic trail around the airport that leads back to the city. If you get tired, catch bus #12 on Skeljanes back to the center. Pick up maps at the tourist office. If basking in the midnight sun on a black lava beach is what you've always dreamed of, visit the bird reserve 🏔**Grótta** on the western tip of the peninsula. Take bus #11 out to Hofgarður and walk 15min. along the sea on Byggarðstangi. Although the Grótta itself is closed during nesting season (May-June), the bird-filled sky is still an amazing sight. Check out the lighthouse at the edge of the peninsula: high tides make it a temporary island. South of the city lies the **Heiðmörk Reserve,** a large park with picnic spots and beginner to intermediate hiking trails. Take bus S1 or S2 from Hlemmur to Hamraborg and transfer to bus #28. Ask the driver to let you off at Lake Elliðavatn; from there, walk 3-4km south to the reserve.

> **TIP**
>
> **DOOR-TO-DOOR.** Legs aching after a long hike? The BSÍ bus drivers will generally let you off anywhere along the route upon request. You can also flag buses down like taxis and they will often stop to pick you up.

## 🎵 NIGHTLIFE

Despite being unnervingly quiet on weeknights, Reykjavík asserts its status as a wild party town each weekend. The city's thriving independent music scene centers at 🏔**12 Tónar,** Skólavörðustígur 12, and **Bad Taste Records,** Laugavegur 59, in the basement of the Bónus supermarket. After taking in the concerts, Icelanders hit the bars and clubs until the wee hours. Most bars do not have cover charges, but bouncers tend to regulate who enters after 2am. Clubs have steep drink prices, so many locals drink at home or head to the *vínbuð* (liquor store) before going out. Don't bother showing up before 12:30am and plan to be partying until 4 or 5am. Boisterous crowds tend to bar-hop around **Austurstræti, Tryggvagata,** and **Laugavegur.** The establishments listed below are 20+, unless otherwise noted.

🏔 **Barinn,** Laugavegur 22 (☎578 7800). With 3 floors, this bar and club has a DJ every night playing a mix of 80s, classic R&B, and contemporary Icelandic beats for dancing. The top floor is the conversation room for those literally above it all. Beer 500ISK. Mixed drinks 700ISK. Open Su-Th 10am-1am, F-Sa 10am-5:30am. AmEx/MC/V.

**Sirkus,** Klapparstíg. 30 (☎551 1999). A plant-filled, well-lit patio and upstairs bungalow room contribute to a deliciously out-of-place atmosphere at this venue frequented by local underground artists. Beer 500ISK. Open Su-Th 2pm-1am, F-Sa 2pm-5am.

**Sólon,** Bankastr. 7A (☎562 3232). This trendy cafe morphs at night into a posh club bouncing with hip hop, pop, and electronica. Cafe downstairs, large dance floor and bar upstairs. Try their famous drink, the Black Death, used to stave off the dark, cold winters (550ISK). Beer 500ISK. Th live music. Open M-Th 11am-1am, F-Sa 11am-5:00am.

**Café Cozy,** Austurstræti 3 (☎511 1033; cafecozy@simnet.is), near the tourist center. This quiet cafe serves traditional Icelandic fare (such as lamb soup) during the day, but at night it's one of the wildest clubs in Reykjavík. Gay-friendly. Attracts a mixed, energetic crowd. Expect to see dancing on the tables by 3am. Beer 600ISK. Mixed drinks 800ISK. F-Sa live DJ. Open Su-Th 11am-1am, F-Sa 10am-6am. AmEx/MC/V.

**Vegamót,** Vegamótarstíg. 4 (☎511 3040), off Laugavegur. Students and well-dressed urban professionals head to this posh bar to flaunt it and see others do the same. Beer 500ISK. Th-Sa live DJ. Open M-Th 11:30am-1am, F-Sa 11:30am-5am. MC/V.

## ▶️ DAYTRIPS FROM REYKJAVÍK

Iceland's main attractions are its natural wonders. **Iceland Excursions** runs the popular "Golden Circle Classic" tour, which stops at Hveragerði, Kerið, Skálholt, Geysir, Gullfoss, and Þingvellir National Park. (☎540 1313; www.grayline.is. 9-10hr., 6600ISK.) **Highlanders** offers exciting, but pricey, off-road tours in jeeps that can traverse rivers, crags, and glaciers. (☎568 3030; www.hl.is. 10,600-17,500ISK.)

**GULLFOSS AND GEYSIR.** The glacial river Hvita plunges down 32m to create **Gullfoss** (Golden Falls). A dirt path passes along the falls, where many get soaked in the mist. The adjacent hill houses a small cafeteria and gift shop and affords a stunning view of the surrounding mountains, plains, and cliffs. On the horizon you can see the tip of Longjökull, a glacier the size of Hong Kong. The **Geysir** area, 10km down the road, is a teeming bed of hot springs in a barren landscape. The **Strokkur Geyser** (the Churn) erupts every 5min., spewing sulfurous water at heights up to 35m. Exercise caution around the thermal pools—more than one tourist has fallen into the nearby **Blesi pool** and been badly scalded. The excellent **museum** at the visitors center offers a multimedia show on the science behind these natural phenomena. The top portion of the museum is dedicated to Aðalbjörg Egilsdottur, who donated her collection of early 19th-century Icelandic artifacts, including a spinning wheel, stove, and saddle. (*Museum 500ISK, students 400ISK. BSÍ runs a round-trip bus to Gullfoss and Geysir with Iceland Excursions, departing from the BSÍ Terminal in Reykjavík June-Aug. daily 1pm; 6hr., round-trip 5200ISK.*)

**BLUE LAGOON.** The southwest corner of the Reykjanes peninsula harbors an oasis in the middle of a lava field: a vast pool of geothermally heated water. The lagoon has become a tourist magnet, but it's still worth braving the crowds. The cloudy blue waters, rich in silica, minerals, and algae, are famous for their healing powers. Bathers who have their fill of wading through the 36-39°C (97-102°F) waters can indulge in a steam bath, a silica facial, or an in-water massage (1600ISK per 10min.). Stand under the waterfall for a free, all-natural shoulder massage. (*Buses run from BSÍ Bus Terminal in Reykjavík. 1hr., 6 per day 8:30am-8pm; round-trip 2200ISK, 3800 ISK with Blue Lagoon admission. ☎420 8800; www.bluelagoon.com. Open daily mid-May to Aug. 9am-9pm; Sept. to mid-May 10am-8pm. Towel rental 350ISK. Bathing suit rental 400ISK. Admission and locker 1800ISK, over 67 1200ISK, 12-15 900ISK, under 11 free. AmEx/MC/V.*)

HEADING NORTH

# NORWAY

## ESSENTIALS

**EMBASSIES AND CONSULATES.** Foreign embassies in Norway are in Oslo. Norwegian embassies abroad include: **Australia,** 17 Hunter St., Yarralumla, ACT, 2600 (☎262 73 34 44; www.norway.org.au); **Canada,** 90 Sparks St., Ste. 532, Ottawa, ON, K1P 5B4 (☎613-238-6571; www.emb-norway.ca); **Ireland,** 34 Molesworth St., Dublin 2 (☎16 62 18 00; www.norway.ie); **UK,** 25 Belgrave Sq., London, SW1X 8QD (☎20 75 91 55 00; www.norway.org.uk); **US,** 2720 34th St., NW, Washington, D.C., 20008 (☎202-333-6000; www.norway.org).

**VISA AND ENTRY INFORMATION.** EU citizens do not need a visa. Citizens of Australia, Canada, New Zealand, and the US do not need a visa for stays of up to 90 days, beginning upon entry into any of the countries within the EU's freedom of movement zone. For more info, see p. 13. For stays longer than 90 days, all non-EU citizens need visas (around US$80; fee is waived for students and teachers traveling for educational purposes), available at Norwegian consulates. For more info on obtaining a visa go to www.norway.org/visas.

| NORWEGIAN KRONER (KR) | | |
|---|---|---|
| AUS$1 = 4.74KR | 10KR = AUS$2.11 |
| CDN$1 = 5.61KR | 10KR = CDN$1.78 |
| EUR€1 =8.01KR | 10KR = EUR€1.25 |
| NZ$1 = 4.14KR | 10KR = NZ$2.41 |
| UK£1 = 11.78KR | 10KR = UK£0.85 |
| US$1 = 5.95KR | 10KR = US$1.68 |

**MONEY.** The Norwegian unit of currency is the **krone (kr),** plural **kroner.** One krone is equal to 100 **øre.** Banks and large post offices change money, usually for a small commission. It's generally cheaper to exchange money in Norway than at home. **Tipping** is not expected, but an extra 5-10% is always welcome for good restaurant service. It is customary to leave coins on the counter or table rather than putting the tip on a credit card. Hotel bills often include a 15% service charge.

Norway has a 25% **value added tax (VAT),** a sales tax applied to goods and services. The prices given in *Let's Go* include VAT. In the airport upon exiting the EU, non-EU citizens can claim a refund on the tax paid for goods purchased at participating stores. In order to qualify for a refund in a store, you must spend at least 315kr in a single store; be sure to ask for a refund form when you pay. For more info on qualifying for a VAT refund, see p. 18.

| NORWAY | ❶ | ❷ | ❸ | ❹ | ❺ |
|---|---|---|---|---|---|
| **ACCOMMODATIONS** | under 160kr | 160-260kr | 261-400kr | 401-550kr | over 550kr |
| **FOOD** | under 60kr | 60-100kr | 101-150kr | 151-250kr | over 250kr |

# OSLO ☎21, 22, 23

Scandinavian capitals consent to being urban without renouncing the landscape around them, and Oslo (pop. 550,000) is no exception. The Nordmarka forest to the north and Oslofjord to the south bracket the city's cultural institutions, busy cafes, and expensive boutiques. While most of Norway remains homogeneous,

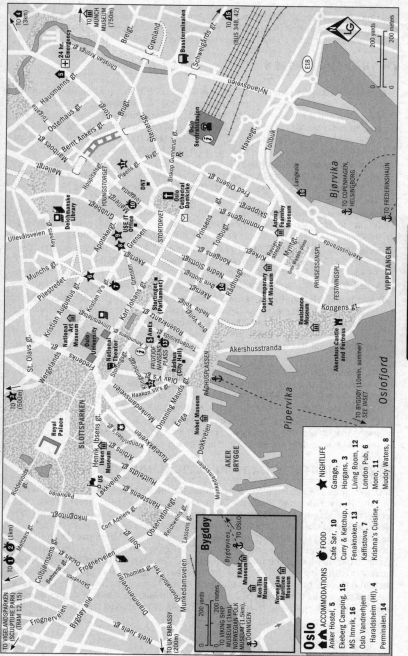

HEADING NORTH

TO VIGELANDSPARKEN
(SCULPTURE PARK)
(TRAM 12, 15)

TO 1 2 (1km)

TO 3 (500m)

TO 4 (3km)

TO MUNCH MUSEUM (750m)

24 hr. Emergency

Busterminalen

(Schweigaards gt.)

Oslo Sentralstasjon

Bjørvika
TO COPENHAGEN, HELSINGBORG

TO FREDERIKSHAVN

Oslofjord

Pipervika

Akershus Castle and Fortress

VIPPETANGEN

TO BYGDØY (10min, summer)
SEE INSET

Royal Palace

SLOTTSPARKEN

National Art Museum

Oslo University

National Theater

Stortinget (Parliament)

Rådhus (City Hall)

Oslo Cathedral Domkirke

Deichmanske Library

USE IT Office

DNT

Contemporary Art Museum

Astrup Fearnley Museum

Resistance Museum

Nobel Museum

RÅDHUSPLASSEN

Akershusstranda

Henrik Ibsen Museum

US

TO UK EMBASSY
(200m)

**Bygdøy**

Bygdøynes
TO OSLO

TO VIKING SHIP MUSEUM (1km),
NORWEGIAN FOLK MUSEUM (1.5km),
DRØNNINGEN

FRAM Museum

Kon-Tiki Museum

Norwegian Maritime Museum

## Oslo

**ACCOMMODATIONS**
Anker Hostel, 5
Ekeberg Camping, 15
MS Innvik, 16
Oslo Vandrerhjem
Haraldsheim (HI), 4
Perminalen, 14

**FOOD**
Cafe Sør, 10
Curry & Ketchup, 1
Fenaknoken, 13
Kaffistova, 7
Krishna's Cuisine, 2

**NIGHTLIFE**
Garage, 9
Horgans, 3
Living Room, 12
London Pub, 6
Mono, 11
Muddy Waters, 8

Oslo has a small multi-ethnic immigrant community in its eastern and northern sections. Even with globalization, Norwegian history and folk traditions still shape Oslo, a somewhat pricey city but an essential stop on any trip to Scandinavia.

## ▄ TRANSPORTATION

**Flights: Oslo Airport Gardermoen (OSL;** ☎81 55 02 50; www.osl.no), 45km north of the center. The high-speed **FlyToget train** (☎815 0777; www.flytoget.no) runs between the airport and downtown (20min.; 3-6 per hr.; 160kr, students 80kr). White SAS **Flybussen** run a similar route. (☎22 80 49 71; www.flybussen.no. 40min.; 2-3 per hr.; 120kr, students 60kr; round-trip 220/110kr.) See **Let's Go to Oslo** (p. 996) for info on Sadefjord Airport Torp, a major budget airline hub for the region.

**Trains: Oslo Sentralstasjon (Oslo S)**, Jernbanetorget 1 (☎81 50 08 88). To: **Bergen** (6-8hr., 4-5 per day, 716kr); **Trondheim** (6-8hr., 2-5 per day, 797kr); **Copenhagen, DEN** via **Gothenburg, SWE** (7-8hr., 2 per day, from 717kr); **Stockholm, SWE** (4¾hr., 3 per day, from 650kr). Mandatory seat reservations for domestic trains 41-71kr.

**Buses: Nor-way Bussekspress,** Schweigårds gt. 8 (☎81 54 44 44; www.nor-way.no). Follow the signs from the train station through the Oslo Galleri Mall to the Bussterminalen Galleriet. Schedules available at the info office. 25-50% ISIC discount.

**Ferries: Color Line** (☎81 00 08 11; www.colorline.com). To **Frederikshavn, DEN** (12½hr.; 7:30pm; 250-490kr, in winter students 95kr-230kr) and **Kiel, GER** (19½hr.; 2pm; 780-3690kr/390-1845kr). **DFDS Seaways** (☎21 62 13 40; www.dfdsseaways.com). To **Copenhagen, DEN** (16hr.) and **Helsingborg, SWE** (14½hr.) daily at 5pm (both 810-1010kr).

**Public Transportation:** Buses, ferries, subways, and **trams** cost 30kr per ride or 20kr in advance. Tickets include 1hr. of unlimited transfers. If you are caught traveling without a valid ticket, you can be fined 700-900kr. **Trafikanten** (☎ 177; www.trafikanten.no), in front of Oslo S, sells the **Dagskort** (day pass; 60kr), **Flexicard** (8 trips; 160kr), and **7-day Card** (210kr). Open M-F 7am-8pm, Sa-Su 8am-6pm. Tickets also at Narvesen kiosks and Automat machines in the metro.

**Bike Rental:** The city's bike-share system allows visitors to borrow one of the 1000+ bikes available at racks throughout the city center. Both the main tourist office and the Oslo S branch sell system enrollment cards (70kr per day). Note that bikes must be returned to a rack every 3hr., a means of keeping track of them.

**Hitchhiking:** Hitchhiking is not common in this area of Norway because of the extensive transportation network. Some travelers report hitching rides to major cities at truck terminals. Let's Go does not recommend hitchhiking.

## ▄ ▐ ORIENTATION AND PRACTICAL INFORMATION

In Oslo center, the garden plaza **Slottsparken (Castle Park)** lies beside **Oslo University** and the **Nationaltheatret (National Theater)** and surrounds the **Royal Palace.** The city's main street, **Karl Johans gate,** runs through the heart of town from Slottsparken to the train station **Oslo Sentralstasjon (Oslo S)** at the eastern end. Ferries depart from the harbor, southwest of Oslo S near Akershus Castle. Many museums and beaches are southwest on the **Bygdøy** peninsula. Ferries to Bygdøy depart from the dock behind **Rådhus (City Hall).** Massive construction projects are currently reshaping the harbor, a project marked by a new opera house. Parks are scattered throughout Oslo, especially north of the Nationaltheatret. Of note is **Saint Hanshaugen,** a hilly park north of the city center up **Akersgata** as it becomes **Ullevålsveien.** A network of public trams, buses, and subways makes transit through the outskirts quick and easy. **Grünerløkka** to the north and **Grønland** to the east, largely home to Oslo's immigrant population, are often cheaper than the city's other neighborhoods, and their boutiques, cafes, and parks showcase the latest urban trends. While some believe this area is less safe, crime is generally low.

**Tourist Offices:** Fridtjof Nansenspl. 5 (☎81 53 05 55; www.visitoslo.com). Sells the **Oslo Pass,** offering unlimited public transport and admission to most museums. 1-day pass 250kr, 2-day 300kr, 3-day 390kr. Open June-Aug. daily 9am-7pm; Sept. and Apr.-May M-Sa 9am-5pm; Oct.-Mar. M-F 9am-4pm. **Oslo Central Station Tourist Info,** Jernbanetorget 1, outside Oslo S. Open M-F 7am-8pm, Sa-Su 8am-8pm. ◙**Use-It,** Møllergt. 3 (☎24 14 98 20; www.unginfo.oslo.no/useit), targets students and backpackers but welcomes all travelers. Helps find beds for no fee, offers free Internet and baggage storage, and publishes the invaluable *Streetwise Budget Guide to Oslo.* Open July-Aug. M-F 9am-6pm; Sept.-June M-F 11am-5pm.

**TIP** **A HAPPENING PLACE.** Use-It organizes summer events and "happenings" for youth and foreign travelers in Oslo. Check at the office for details.

**Embassies and Consulates: Australia:** contact the embassy in Denmark (p. 238). **Canada,** Wergelandsv. 7, 4th fl. (☎22 99 53 00; www.canada.no). Open June-Aug. M-F 8am-4pm; Sept.-May M-F 8:30am-4:30pm. **Ireland,** Haakon VII's gt. 1 (☎22 01 72 00; osloembassy@dfa.ie). Open M-F 8:30am-4:30pm. **UK,** Thomas Heftyes gt. 8 (☎23 13 27 00; www.britian.no). Open in summer M-F 8:30am-4pm; in winter M-F 9am-4pm. **US,** Henrik Ibsens gt. 48 (☎22 44 85 50; www.usa.no). Open M-F 7:30am-5pm.

**Currency Exchange:** At any major bank: **Christiania, Den Norske, Landsbanker** and **Forebu Oslo. Forex,** Fridtjof Nansens pl. 6 (☎22 41 30 60), offers the best rates.

**Luggage Storage:** Lockers at Oslo S and at the Nationaltheatret station. 20-45kr per 24hr. Max. 7 days. Available 4:30am-1:10am. Office open M-F 9am-3pm. You can leave bags in the Use-It office (p. 991) for an afternoon or night.

**Library and Internet Access:** Free terminals at the **Deichmanske Library,** Arne Garborgs pl. 4. Sign up for 1hr. drop in for 15-30min. Open Sept.-May M-F 10am-7pm, Sa 11am-2pm; June-Aug. M-F 10am-6pm, Sa 11am-2pm.

**GLBT Resources: Landsforeningen for Lesbisk og Homofil fri gjøring (LLH),** Kongensgt. 12 (☎23 10 39 39; www.llh.no). Tourist office also has GLBT resources.

**Laundromat:** Look for the word *"myntvaskeri."* **Selva AS,** Ullevålsveien 15 (☎41 64 08 33). Wash 40kr, dry 30kr. Open M-F 8am-9pm, Sa 10am-3pm.

**Police:** ☎02800 to bypass dispatch and connect directly.

**24hr. Pharmacy: Jernbanetorvets Apotek** (☎23 35 81 00), opposite Oslo S.

**Hospital: Oslo Kommunale Legevakt,** Storgt. 40 (☎22 93 22 93).

**Post Office:** Main branch at Kirkegt. 20 (☎23 35 86 90). Address mail to be held in the following format: First name, LAST NAME, *Poste Restante,* Oslo Central Post Office, N-0101 Oslo, NORWAY. Open M-F 9am-6pm, Sa 10am-3pm. The post office at Oslo S is open M-F 9am-8pm. **Postal Code:** 51060.

## ACCOMMODATIONS AND CAMPING

Hostels in Oslo fill up in summer. Reservations are essential. The **private rooms** available through **Use-It** (p. 991) are good deals, starting from 140kr. **Pensjonater** (pensions) are centrally located but can be more expensive. Check with the tourist office for last-minute accommodation deals. Travelers can **camp** for free in the forest north of town; try the end of the Sognsvann line #3. Young Norwegians often drink at home before heading out because of high bar prices, but most hostels, including HI, prohibit alcohol consumption on their premises.

■ **Perminalen,** Øvre Slottsgt. 2 (☎23 09 30 81; www.perminalen.no). 15min. walk from Oslo S or tram #12 to Christianian Torv. Backpackers looking for the full package head to this central hotel/hostel. Spacious rooms equipped with A/C and cable TV. Breakfast included. Internet 15kr per 15min. Reception 24hr. Dorms 335kr; singles 499kr; doubles 720kr. AmEx/D/MC/V. ❸

**Anker Hostel,** Storgt. 55 (☎22 99 72 00, booking 22 99 72 10; www.ankerhostel.no). Walk 10min. north from Oslo S or take tram #11, 12, 13, or 17 to Hausmanns gt. Renovated rooms with kitchenettes and bath. Breakfast 75kr. Linens 50kr. Internet 10kr per 15min. Reception in summer 24hr. Dorms 200kr; doubles 500kr. AmEx/D/MC/V. ❷

**Oslo Vandrerhjem Haraldsheim (HI),** Haraldsheimvn. 4 (☎22 22 29 65; www.haraldsheim.oslo.no). Take tram #17 from Stortorvet for 15min. to Sinsenkrysset and walk up the hill through the park. Standard bunk dorms in a quiet, residential neighborhood. Breakfast included. Linens 50kr. Reception 24hr. Dorms 220kr, with bath 245kr; singles 320/425kr; doubles 495/575kr. 15% HI discount. MC/V. ❷

**MS Innvik,** Langkaia 49 (☎22 41 95 00; www.msinnvik.no). From Oslo S, cross the highway E18 overpass and head right along the harbor. This artsy, boat-borne B&B is on Bjørvika Bay. Don't worry—the boat is very stable and seasickness is a non-issue. Compact cabins come with bath. Breakfast included. Reception 24hr. Check-in 5pm. Check-out noon. Singles 425kr; doubles 750kr. MC/V. ❹

**Ekeberg Camping,** Ekebergveien 65 (☎22 19 85 68; www.ekebergcamping.no), 3km from town. Bus #34A or 46. 24hr. security. Grocery store open daily 8am-10pm. Showers 10kr per 6min. Laundry 40kr. Reception 7:30am-11pm. Open June-Aug. 2-person tent sites 150kr, 4-person 245kr; 55kr per extra person. AmEx/D/MC/V. ❶

##  FOOD

Visitors can choose between hearty, often bland Norwegian fare and a variety of ethnic dishes. Either way, they usually feel robbed blind once the check arrives. Smart backpackers stock up at the city's grocery stores. Look for the chains **ICA, Kiwi,** and **Rema 1000** (generally open M-F 9am-9pm, Sa-Su 9am-6pm), or pick up fresh produce at the Youngstorget **open-air market** (M-Sa 7am-2pm). In the budget-friendly **Grønland** district, east of Oslo S, vendors hawk **kebabs** and **falafel** (around 40kr), while *halal* butchers can provide travelers with cooking meat.

> **DINING FOR POCKET CHANGE.** Oslo's sky-high food prices can bring travelers to tears. For a bite on the cheap, head east beyond Karl Johans gate to the Grønland neighborhood, home to low cost ethnic eateries.

**Cafe Sør,** Torggata 11 (☎41 46 30 47). This artsy, relaxing cafe attracts a young crowd with an array of teas and coffees (26-31kr) and free Wi-Fi. Sandwiches 87kr. Beer 36-53kr. Open M-Th 11am-1:30am, F-Sa 11am-3am, Su 2pm-1:30am. MC/V. ❷

**Kaffistova,** Rosenkrantz gt. 8 (☎23 21 41 00). Posh, airy eatery with modest portions of Norwegian fish, meat, and porridges. Vegetarian options. Lunch from 64kr. Dinner 150-169kr. Open M-F 10am-9pm, Sa-Su 11am-7pm. AmEx/D/MC/V. ❸

**Krishna's Cuisine,** Kirkeveien 59B (☎22 60 62 50), on the 2nd fl. Large plates of inexpensive Indian food. Exclusively vegetarian fare prepared with fresh seasonal ingredients. Lunch served all day 65kr. Entrees 60-90kr. Open M-F noon-8pm. Cash only. ❷

**Curry and Ketchup,** Kirkeveien 51 (☎22 69 05 22). A neighbor of Krishna's, this restaurant has a relaxed, sit-down feel. Generous helpings of Indian mainstays. Entrees 69-99kr. Open daily 2-10:30pm. Cash only. ❷

**Fenaknoken,** Matkultur i Tordenskidsgt. 7 (☎22 42 34 57). Gourmet Norwegian food store with seafood and free samples of delicacies like smoked elk or reindeer sausage. Fresh snack rolls 25kr. Open M-F 10am-5pm, Sa 10am-2pm. AmEx/MC/V. ❷

## 👁 SIGHTS

**▨ VIGELANDSPARKEN.** Sculptor Gustav Vigeland (1869-1943) designed this 80-acre expanse west of the city center. The park is home to over 200 of his mammoth works, each depicting a stage of the human life cycle. His controversial, puzzling art is worth deciphering. *Monolith* is a towering granite column of intertwining bodies in the middle of the park. *(Entrance on Kirkeveien. Take bus #20 or tram #12 or 15 to Vigelandsparken. Open 24hr. Free.)* While wandering through the park, stop at the **Oslo Bymuseum** (Oslo City Museum) for art and photocopy collections, displays on the city's history, and restored pavilions. *(☎23 28 41 70; www.oslobymuseum.no. Open June-Aug. Tu-Su 11am-5pm; Sept.-May Tu-Su noon-4pm. Free.)* Next to the park, the **Vigelandmuseet** (Vigeland Museum) traces the artist's development from his early works to the monumental pieces of his later years. The museum is housed in the building Vigeland used as his apartment and studio. *(Nobelsgt. 32. ☎23 49 37 00. Open June-Aug. Tu-Su 10am-5pm; Sept.-May Tu-Su noon-4pm. 45kr, students 25kr. Oct.-Mar free. MC/V.)*

**ART MUSEUMS.** Recent renovations at **Munchmuseet** (Munch Museum) improved its security system after a 2004 theft of two paintings, including a version of *The Scream*, Munch's most famous work. The paintings have been recovered, albeit with some damage. The museum has a collection of Munch's other abstract works along with temporary Impressionist exhibits. *(Tøyengt. 53. Take the subway to Tøyen or bus #20 to Munchmuseet. ☎23 49 35 00; www.munch.museum.no. Open June-Aug. daily 10am-6pm; Sept.-May Tu-F 10am-4pm, Sa-Su 11am-5pm. 65kr, students 35kr; free with Oslo Pass. AmEx/D/MC/V.)* The definitive version of *The Scream* is at the **Nasjonalmuseet** (National Art Museum), which also has a collection of works by Cézanne, Gauguin, van

**THE LOCAL STORY**

## UP FOR SOME KUBB?

A funny thing might happen walking through Oslo's parks. Out o nowhere, you may stumble upon people throwing wooden sticks a figurines. What's going on here Are they vandalizing those poor defenseless figurines?

Closer inspection reveals a whole world of fun you never knew existed—Kubb. No, not the obscure British band of the same name. Kubb is a game, nicknamed "Viking Chess," that combines bowling, chess, and horseshoes. The objective is to knock down your opponent's ten kubbs, rectangular wooden blocks. After taking these down you move on to eliminate the king kubb, marked by a carved crown design, for the win.

Kubb dates back to AD 1000 and was likely played by Vikings It spread throughout Europe during the Norman conquests. Morbidly, some maintain that the Vikings played with the skulls and bones of their victims rather than wooden blocks. When rampant plundering and using your victims for games went out of fashion, the transition to wooden blocks began. Others believe that wooden blocks have always been used. They are common in Scandinavia, after all, and it would be unfortunate to postpone a game of kubb due to lack of skulls. Talk about a gathering gone wrong. The game involves a surprising amount of strategy. Try your luck but don't bet your life savings.

Gogh, Matisse, Picasso, and Sohlberg. *(Universitetsgt. 13.* ☎ *21 98 20 00; www.nasjonalmuseet.no. Open Tu-W and F 10am-6pm, Th 10am-8pm, Sa-Su 10am-5pm. Free.)* Next door at Oslo University's **Aulaen** (Assembly Hall), several of Munch's dreamy, idealistic murals show his interest in bringing art to the masses. *(Enter through the door by the ionic columns off Karl Johans gt. Open June 27-Aug 3 M-F 10am-4pm. Free.)*

The **Museet for Samtidskunst** (Contemporary Art Museum) displays works by Norwegian artists and rotates its collection frequently. If you can find it, check out *Inner Space V,* a steel staircase leading to a mysterious corridor with a true "light at the end of the tunnel." *(Bankplassen 4. Take bus #60 or tram #10, 12, 13, or 19 to Kongens gt.* ☎ *22 86 22 10. Open Tu-W and F 10am-6pm, Th 10am-8pm, Sa-Su 10am-5pm. Free.)* Nearby, the private **Astrup Fearnly Museum of Modern Art** has a more international collection, with some striking installations and video pieces. *(Dronningens gt. 4.* ☎ *22 93 60 60; www.afmuseet.no. Open Tu-W and F 11am-5pm, Th 11am-7pm, Sa-Su noon-5pm. Free.)*

**AKERSHUS CASTLE AND FORTRESS.** Originally constructed in 1299, this waterfront complex was rebuilt as a Renaissance palace after Oslo burned in 1624. Norway's infamous traitor, Vidkun Quisling, was imprisoned here prior to his execution for aiding the 1940 Nazi invasion. *(Tram #10 or 12 to Rådhusplassen.* ☎ *23 09 39 17. Complex open daily 6am-9pm. Castle open May-Aug. M-Sa 10am-4pm, Su 12:30-4pm. Sept.-Oct. admission for guided tours only. English- and Norwegian-language guided tours mid-June to early Aug. M-Sa 11am, 1, 2, 3pm; Su 1, 3pm; in winter English-language Th 1pm. Grounds free. Castle 50kr, students 35kr; free with Oslo Pass. Cash only.)* The castle grounds include the powerful **Resistance Museum,** which documents Norway's campaign against the Nazi occupation. *(*☎ *23 09 31 38. Open June-Aug. M-Sa 10am-5pm, Su 11am-5pm; Sept.-Apr. Tu-F 11am-4pm, Sa-Su 11am-5pm. 30kr, students 15kr. Cash only.)*

**BYGDØY.** Bygdøy peninsula, across the inlet from central Oslo, is mainly residential, but its beaches and museums are worth a visit. In summer, a public **ferry** leaves from Pier 3, Råhusbrygges, in front of City Hall. *(*☎ *23 35 68 90; www.boatsightseeing.com. 10min.; Apr.-Sept. and late May to mid-Aug. 2-3 per hr.; 20kr, 30kr on board. Or take bus #30 from Oslo S to Folkemuseet or Bygdøynes.)* The open-air ■**Norsk Folkemuseum,** near the ferry's first stop at Dronningen, recreates the lifestyle of medieval Norway with restored thatch huts, actors in period costume, and performances. *(Walk uphill from the dock and follow signs to the right for 10min., or take bus #30 from Nationaltheatret.* ☎ *22 12 37 00; www.norskfolkemuseum.no. Open mid-May to mid-Sept. daily 10am-6pm; mid-Sept. to mid-May M-F 11am-3pm, Sa-Su 11am-4pm. In summer 90kr, students 60kr; in winter 70/45kr. MC/V.)* Down the road (5min.), the **Vikingskipshuset** (Viking Ship Museum) showcases the stunning remains of three well-preserved burial vessels. *(*☎ *22 13 52 80; www.khm.uio.no. Open daily May-Sept. 9am-6pm; Oct.-Apr. 11am-4pm. 50kr, students 25kr; free with Oslo Pass. MC/V.)* At Bygdøynes, the ferry's second stop, the ■**Kon-Tiki Museet,** named after a displayed balsa wood raft used on a journey from Lima, Peru to the Polynesian Islands, depicts Oscar-winning documentarian Thor Heyerdahl's globe-trotting adventures. *(Bygdøynesveien 36.* ☎ *23 08 67 67; www.kon-tiki.no. Open daily June-Aug. 9:30am-5:30pm; Apr.-May and Sept. 10am-5pm; Oct.-Mar. 10:30am-4pm. 45kr, students 30kr; free with Oslo Pass. Guidebook 50kr. D/MC/V.)* Next door, the **Norsk Sjøfartsmuseum** (Norwegian Maritime Museum) is home to Norway's oldest boat. Learn about the nation's seafaring history, from log canoes to cruise ships, and enjoy the view of Oslofjord. *(Bygdøynesveien 37.* ☎ *24 11 41 50. Open mid-May to Aug. daily 10am-6pm; Sept. to mid-May M-W and Sa-Su 10:30am-4pm, Th 10:30am-6pm. 40kr, students 25kr. Audio tour 30kr. D/MC/V.)* The Arctic exploration vessel **FRAM,** adjacent to the museum, was used on three expeditions in the early 20th century and has advanced farther north and south than any other vessel in history. Visitors can roam through the well-preserved interior. *(Bygdøynesveien 36. ☎23 28 29 50. Open daily mid-June to Aug. 9am-6:45pm; May to mid-June 10am-5:45pm; Sept. 10am-4:45pm; Oct.-Apr. 10am-3:45pm. 40kr, students 20kr. MC/V.)* The southwestern side of Bygdøy is home to two popular beaches: **Huk** appeals to a younger crowd, while **Paradisbukta** is more family-oriented. The shore between them is a nude beach. *(Take bus #30 or walk south for 25min. left along the shore from the Bygdøynes ferry stop.)*

**OTHER SIGHTS.** The **Royal Palace**, in Slottsparken, is open for guided tours, although tickets sell out well ahead. Watch the daily changing of the guard for free at 1:30pm in front of the palace. *(Tram #12, 15, 19, or bus #30-32 or 45 to Slottsparken. Open late June to mid-Aug. English-language tours M, Th, Sa noon, 2, 2:20pm; F and Su 2 and 2:20pm. Buy tickets at post and tourist offices. 80kr, students 70kr.)* The nearby **Ibsenmuseet** (Henrik Ibsen Museum) documents the notoriously private playwright's life with a dramatic exhibition space and guided tours of his apartment. *(Henrik Ibsens gt. 26. ☎22 12 35 50; www.ibsen.net/ibsen-museum. Open mid-May to mid-Sept. Tu-Su 11am-6pm; mid-Sept. to mid-May Tu-Su 11am-3pm. English- and Norwegian-language tours 7 per day; in winter 3 per day. 35kr; with tour 70kr, students 45kr. AmEx/D/MC/V.)* The **Domkirke,** next to Stortorvet in the city center, is hard to miss. The Lutheran cathedral has a colorful ceiling with biblical motifs. *(Karl Johans gt. 11. ☎23 31 46 00; www.oslodomkirke.no. Open M-Th 10am-4pm, F 10am-4pm and 10pm-midnight, Sa 10am-4pm and 9-11pm. Free.)* The **Nobel Museum,** by the harbor, features profiles on all 112 laureates. *(Brynjulf Bulls Plass 1. Tram #12 to Aker Brygge. ☎23 31 46 00; www.nobelpeace.org. Open June-Aug. daily 10am-6pm; Jan.-May and Sept.-Dec. W and F 10am-4pm, Th 10am-6pm, Sa-Su 11am-5pm; 80kr, students 55kr.)* Climb the Holmenkollen ski jump, after an elevator ride halfway up, for views of the city and an exploration of 4000 years of skiing history at the world's oldest **Ski Museum,** founded in 1923. A simulator recreates a leap off a ski jump and a blisteringly swift downhill run. *(Kongeveien 5. Take subway #1 on the Frognerseteren line to Holmenkollen and follow the signs 10min. ☎22 92 32 64; www.skiforeningen.no. Open daily June-Aug. 9am-8pm; Sept. and May 10am-5pm; Oct.-Apr. 10am-4pm. Museum 70kr, students 60kr; free with Oslo Pass. Simulator 50kr, with Oslo Pass 40kr. AmEx/D/MC/V.)*

🎵 🎭 **ENTERTAINMENT AND NIGHTLIFE**

The monthly *What's On in Oslo*, free at tourist offices, follows the latest in opera, symphony, and theater. **Filmens Hus,** Dronningens gt. 16, is the center of Oslo's indie film scene. *(☎22 47 45 00. Open Tu-W and F noon-5pm, Th noon-7pm, Sa noon-4pm. 70kr per movie, members 45kr; registration 100kr.)* Jazz enthusiasts head to town for the **Oslo Jazz Festival** in mid-August. *(☎22 42 91 20; www.oslojazz.no).* Countless bars along **Karl Johans gate** and in the **Aker Brygge** harbor complex attract a hard-partying crowd, while a mellow mood prevails at the cafe-by-day, bar-by-night lounges along **Thorvald Meyers gate** in Grüner Løkka. Alcohol tends to be expensive out on the town, so young Norwegians have taken to the custom of the *Vorspiel*—gathering at private homes to sip comparatively cheap, store-bought liquor before staggering out to the streets.

   **Mono,** Pløens gt. 4 *(☎22 41 41 66).* Jam to classic rock at this popular, funky club. Backyard area for drinks during the day. Beer 52kr. Su-Th 20+, F-Sa 22+. Cover for concerts 50-70kr. Open M-Sa 3pm-3:30am, Su 6pm-3:30am. MC/V.

   **Garage,** Grensen 9 *(☎22 42 37 44; www.garageoslo.no).* A venue M-Th for live music from across the globe. A bouncing club F-Su with rock beats. Beer 52kr at night, 42kr during the day. Su-Th 20+, F-Sa 22+. Cover for concerts 50-180kr. Open M-Sa 2pm-3:30am, Su 6pm-3:30am. MC/V.

**Muddy Waters,** Grensen 13 (☎22 40 33 70; www.muddywaters.no). Lives up to its billing as one of Europe's top blues clubs. Attracts an older crowd. Beer 56kr. 20+. Cover F-Sa around 90kr. Open daily 2pm-3am. AmEx/D/MC/V.

**Living Room,** Olav V's gt. 1 (☎22 83 63 54; www.living-room.no). Popular lounge morphs into dance floor on weekends. Fairly strict dress code. Beer 61kr. 24+. Cover F-Sa 100kr. Open W-Su 11pm-3am. AmEx/D/MC/V.

**Horgans,** Hegdehaugsv. 24 (☎22 60 87 87). Boisterous sports bar with plenty of TVs showing the latest games, especially football matches. Also a club on weekends. Beer 54kr. Th student night. F-Sa club. 22+. Cover Sa 50kr. Open M-Tu 5pm-midnight, W-Th and Su 5pm-1:30am, F-Sa 5pm-3am. AmEx/D/MC/V.

**London Pub,** C.J. Hambros pl. (☎22 70 87 00; www.londonpub.no). Entrance on Rosenkrantz gt. Oslo's "gay headquarters" since 1979. Large upstairs dance floor plays a mix of beats. Basement pool tables and bars. Beer 36-52kr. 21+. Cover F-Sa 40kr. Open daily 3pm-4am. AmEx/D/MC/V.

### ⚑ LET'S GO TO OSLO: SANDEFJORD                    ☎33

**Sandefjord Airport Torp** (TRF; ☎42 70 00; www.torp.no), 120km south of Oslo, is a budget airline hub for **Ryanair, Widerøe,** and **Wizz Air. Trains** (☎81 50 08 88) run to Oslo (1¾hr.; 1 per hr.; 222kr, students 167kr). Buses (2 per hr.) and taxis shuttle between the train station and airport. **Buses** also go to Oslo (1-2 per hr., 140kr) and coordinate with Ryanair arrivals and departures.

# THE FJORDS AND WEST NORWAY

No trip to Norway is complete without seeing the Western Fjords. The region boasts a dramatic grandeur, from the depths of Sognefjord to the peaks of Jotunheimen National Park. Tourists come to Sogndal and Stryn to walk on the Jostedalsbreen glacier, continental Europe's largest, and visit fjord towns like Balestrand and Geiranger. On the Atlantic coast, Bergen is the region's major port city.

> **?** **WHAT THE FJUCK IS A FJORD?** Fjords are long, narrow, U-shaped valleys flooded by the sea. Norway's formed from deep grooves cut into the ground by glacial erosion during the last Ice Age.

## 🚍 TRANSPORTATION

Transportation around the Western Fjords can be tricky and often involves lengthy rides, but scenery-gazing is half the fun. Trains go to **Åndalsnes** in the north and **Bergen** in the south. Buses and boats run to locales in between these cities, including the main fjords and national parks. From Strandkaiterminalen in Bergen, **HSD express boats** (☎55 23 87 80; www.hsd.no) run to Stavanger and points south of the city, while **Fylkesbaatane** (☎55 90 70 710; www.fjord1.no/fylkesbaatane) sails north into Nordfjord, Sognefjord, and Sunnfjord. Almost all destinations connect via **bus** to Bergen; check www.nor-way.no for schedules and fares. **Fjord1** (www.fjord1.no), a consortium of boat, bus, and ferry, companies, is an invaluable resource for planning regional trips. Schedules vary daily; call ☎177 for transportation info. Tourist offices, boat terminals, and bus stations can also help with itineraries. Plan your trip at least 2-3 days ahead.

# SOGNEFJORD

The slender fingers of Sognefjord, Europe's longest and the world's second longest fjord, reach the foot of the Jotunheimen Mountains in central Norway. **Jostedalsbreen** glacier, the largest in mainland Europe, lies just north of the region. The town of Sogndal is the main gateway for glacier trips, while Balestrand and Fjærland are more charming villages ideal for sightseeing and exploring the fjord. Due to uncertain road conditions and limited bus routes, regional overland transportation is often more confusing than it's worth. For an alternative way to explore the area, try Fylkesbaatane **boats** (☎55 90 70 70; www.fylkesbaatane.no), which leave from Bergen on tours of Sognefjord and the Flåm valley.

**BALESTRAND.** Balestrand (pop. 1400) is known as a community for artists, who first flocked to the area in the 1800s, lured by the scenery. This legacy continues with the town's many free galleries. ◪**Golden House,** in the same building as the tourist office, features a town history museum, Scandinavian art displays, and works and greeting cards by local artists. (☎91 56 28 42. Open daily May-Sept 10am-10pm. Free.) In front of Balestrand's docks, **Sognefjord Akvarium** showcases the rarely seen marine life of the fjords. The aquarium also has **Cafe Fløyfisken ❷.** Try some fish soup (70kr) or the grilled ham and cheese (35kr) while enjoying the dockside views. (☎57 69 13 03. Open daily late June to mid-Aug. 9am-11:30pm; May-late June and mid-Aug. to early Sept. 10am-6pm. 70kr. 50% discount for Kringsjå Hostel guests. AmEx/D/MC/V.) To reach the well-marked **hiking trails** from the harbor, head uphill to the right, take the second left, and walk along the main road next to the youth hostel for 10min.; turn right on Sygna and follow the signs. **Moreld** leads 3hr. **kayak** tours (390kr) and day excursions (600kr, with lunch 700kr) on Sognefjord. They also rent kayaks. (☎40 46 71 00; www.moreld.net. Single kayaks 350kr per day, double 525kr per day. Branch in Sogndal.) Walk up the hill past the tourist office, follow the curve right and take the next left to reach ◪**Kringsjå Hotel and Youth Hostel (HI) ❷.** The top-floor dorms have excellent fjord views. (☎57 69 13 03; www.kringsja.no. Breakfast included. Linens 60kr. Laundry 30kr. Open July to mid-Aug. Dorms 210kr; singles 450kr; doubles 620kr; triples 750kr. 15% HI discount. MC/V.) **Sjøtun Camping ❶** is past the brown church on the coastal road. (☎57 69 12 23; www.sjotun.com. Showers free. Reception 9-9:30am, 6-6:30pm, and 9-9:30pm; call for other arrival times. Open June-early Sept. Tent sites 60kr. 4- to 6-person cabins 235-330krkr. Cash only.) **Buses** run to: Bergen (4½hr., 1-2 per day), Oslo (8-8½hr., 3-4 per day), and Sogndal (1¼hr., 2-3 per day). Fylkesbaatane **express boats** run to Balestrand (4hr.; M-Sa 2 per day; 433kr, students 215kr) and Flåm (1½hr.). The **tourist office,** across from the aquarium and just off the ship landing, rents **scooters** (300kr per day) and **bikes.** (☎57 69 12 55; www.sognefjord.no. Bikes 75kr per 6hr., 140kr per day. Internet 15kr per 15min. Open mid-June to mid-Aug. M-Sa 7:30am-6pm, Sa-Su 10am-5pm; May to mid-June and mid-Aug. to Sept. M-F 10am-5pm, Sa-Su 10am-3pm; Oct.-Apr. M-F 8:30am-3:30pm.)

**FJÆRLAND AND FJÆRLANDSFJORD.** ◪**Fjærlandsfjord** branches off Sognefjord in a thin northward line past Balestrand to the town of Fjærland (pop. 300) at the base of Jostedalsbreen glacier. The town's preserved houses have largely been converted into secondhand bookstores set against stellar scenery. ◪**Norwegian Book Town,** a network of 15 secondhand shops, holds over 250,000 volumes and sells novels for as little as 10kr. (☎57 69 22 10; www.bokbyen.no. Open May-Sept. daily 10am-6pm. MC/V.) The **Norsk Bremuseum** (Glacier

Museum), 3km outside town on the only road, is famous for its eccentric geometric architecture. (☎57 69 32 88; www.bre.museum.no. Open daily June-Aug. 9am-7pm; Apr.-May and Sept.-Oct. 10am-4pm. 85kr, students 40kr. AmEx/D/MC/V.) Fjærland does not offer many winter activities because of inadequate bus transportation, but summer thaws out a dozen well-marked **trails**. One of the longer hikes runs up **Flatbreen** (2-3hr.), an arm of Jostedalsbreen glacier, to the Flatbrehytta self-service **cabin**. The hike begins 5km northeast from the Norsk Bremuseum at the Øygard parking lot. (☎57 69 32 29. Limited availability June-Aug. Reserve ahead and bring a sleeping bag.) **Ferries** run to Balestrand (1¼hr.; 2 per day; 175kr, students 84kr). The **Glacier Bus** provides a guided **tour** of the area and shuttles passengers from Mundal (Fjærland's ferry dock) to the Norsk Bremuseum, two Jostedalsbreen outcroppings, and then back to the harbor. (2 per day; 124-135kr; transportation back from glacier museum to Mundal 24kr). From behind the Norsk Bremuseum, **buses** run to Ålesund (6hr.; 4 per day; 349kr, students 277kr), Sogndal (30min.; M-Sa 2-5 per day; 99kr, students 65kr), and Stryn (2¼hr., 1 per day, 250kr). Pick up groceries at the **Joker** across from the tourist office (open M-F 9am-5pm). The **tourist office,** near the harbor, rents **bikes** (30kr per hr., 140kr per day) and provides hiking info. (☎57 69 32 33; www.fjaerland.org. Open daily May-Sept. 10am-6pm.)

**SOGNDAL.** East of Balestrand along the fjord, Sogndal (pop. 6700) is a less charming town. While Balestrand is the superior base for fjord exploration and sightseeing, Sogndal is an essential stop for trips to Jostedalsbreen glacier and a key transportation hub. Adventure companies like the **Jostedalen Breførarlag** (☎57 68 31 11; www.bfl.no) run easy glacier walks (from 150kr) and offer courses in rock climbing (from 2050kr, not including equipment). **Icetroll** (☎57 68 32 50; www.icetroll.com) runs kayaking trips Jostedalsbreen's glacial lakes, some combined with hiking (from 750kr); in summer, huge boulders of ice splinter off the glacier into the water. Most adventure tours depart from Gaupne or Jostedal, two small towns north of Sogndal. **Buses** run to Gaupne (45min.) and Jostedal (2-2½hr.) fairly often; visit the tourist office for more info or check www.fjord1.no and www.nor-way.no. **Sogndal Vandrerhjem (HI)** ❷, Helgheimsvegen 9, has some of the town's more affordable rooms. (☎57 62 75 75. Breakfast included. Linens 105kr. Open mid-June to mid-Aug. Dorms 200kr; singles 280kr; doubles 450-610kr. 15% HI discount.) **Buses** run from the west end of Gravensteinsgata in the town center to: Balestrand (1¼hr., 2-3 per day); Bergen (4½-5hr., 3-4 per day, 389kr); Fjærland (30min.; M-Sa 2-5 per day; 99kr, students 65kr); Oslo (7hr., 3-4 per day, 505kr); Stryn via Skei (2¾hr., 1 per day, 270kr). Fylkesbaatane **express boats** run to Bergen (4½hr.; M-Sa 2 per day; 500kr, students 250kr) and stop at several destinations along Sognefjord. The **tourist office,** Hovevegen 2, is near the bus station. (☎57 67 30 83; www.sognefjord.no. Open late June to late Aug. M-F 9am-8pm, Sa 9am-5pm, Su 3-8pm; Sept. to late June M-F 9am-4pm.)

# GEIRANGERFJORD

The 16km long Geirangerfjord, a UNESCO World Heritage Site, is lined with cliffs and waterfalls that make it one of Norway's most spectacular—and heavily touristed—destinations. While cruising through the icy blue water, watch for the Seven Sisters waterfalls and, across from them, the wooing Suitor waterfall. The suitor was soundly rejected by all seven sisters and took to the bottle, explaining why the shape of a beer bottle is visible through the roaring water. So the story goes. Geirangerfjord can be reached from the north via the Trollstigen road from Åndalsnes, or by bus from Ålesund or Stryn via ferry from Hellesylt.

**GEIRANGER.** Geiranger (pop. 300), at the eastern end of Geirangerfjord, is a tourist mecca at the final point of the Trollstigen road. In summer, thousands overrun the town to take in the stunning views of the fjord. The surrounding, well-marked **trails** offer stunning views and some escape from the crowds, although hikers are unlikely to be alone. Nearby natural attractions include **Flydalsjuvet Cliff** (round-trip 2hr.), **Storseter Waterfall** (2½hr.), and views of the Seven Sisters waterfalls from **Skageflå Farm** (5hr.), which was abandoned in 1916. At **Lanfvaten,** hikers can climb into cloud cover that shrouds the top of **Dalsnibba Mountain Plateau,** 1476m in the sky. To get there, take a bus from opposite the ferry docks (1hr., 2 per day, 160kr). The **Geiranger Fjordsenter,** a 15min. walk from the tourist office on Rte. 63, explores the history and the people of the region. Concerts and traditional Norwegian music and folklore performances are held throughout summer. (☎70 26 30 07; www.geirangerfjord.no. Open daily July 9am-10pm; June and Aug. 9am-6pm; May and Sept. 9am-4pm; 85kr. Concerts M and Th 9pm, 50kr.) For free summer **concerts,** check out the white **Geiranger Kyrkje** church overlooking the town every Wednesday at 9pm. 🏕**Geiranger Camping ❶,** 100m from the town center by the water, is set at the mouth of the fjord. **Kayak** rentals (150kr per hr., 225kr per 2hr., 1000kr per 2 days) are also available. (☎70 26 31 20. Showers 5kr per 5min. Laundry 80kr. Reception 8am-10pm. Open mid-May to early Sept. 20kr per person, 85kr per tent site. MC/V.) For the tentless, **Villa Utsikten Hotel & Restaurant ❸,** 3½km from the town center, has affordable room options. (☎70 26 96 60; www.villautsikten.no. Open May-Sept. Rooms from 300kr.) **Buses** run to Ålesund (3hr., 2-4 per day, 182kr). There is no bus station; buy tickets on board. **Ferries** depart for Hellesylt (1hr., 4-6 per day, 100kr). For info on hiking, rental **bikes** (50kr per hr., 150kr per day), and **boats,** visit the excellent **tourist office,** up the path from the ferry landing. (☎70 26 30 99; www.visitgeirangerfjorden.com. Open daily mid-June to Aug. 9am-7pm; mid-May to mid-June and Sept. 9am-5pm.)

**HELLESYLT.** West of Geiranger at the intersection of Geirangerfjord and **Sunnylvsfjord,** Hellesylt (pop. 600), a base for seven well-marked **hikes,** is quieter than Geiranger. **Skaret** (2-3hr.) has a mountainside outlook with views of the town and fjord. From there, you can continue to **Steimnebba,** a nearby peak that adds an extra uphill climb to the trip (4-6hr.). The **Peer Gynt Gallery,** behind the tourist office, features ten life-size wood carvings depicting the epic story of Norwegian playwright Henrik Ibsen's famous protagonist. (☎70 26 38 80. Open June-Aug. daily 11am-7pm; Sept. Sa-Su 11am-7pm. 50kr.) The **Stadheimfossen Campground ❶** has tent sites and cabins for groups. (☎70 26 50 79; www.stadheimfossen.no. Open Jan.-Sept. 50kr per tent site, 350kr per 4-person cabin.) **Hellesylt Vandrerhjem (HI) ❷,** in a white building above **Hellesyltfossen waterfall,** is a funky, 60s-style lodge. (☎70 26 51 28. Breakfast 55kr. Linens and towels 30kr. Free Internet. Open June-early Sept. Dorms 160kr; singles 290kr; doubles 400kr. 15% HI discount.) When hunger strikes after mountain excursions, head to one of two grocery stores in town, **Spar** and **Coop.** They also offer sporting equipment. **Buses** go to Ålesund (3 per day, 350kr) and Styrn (2-3 per day, 150kr). **Ferries** depart for Geiranger (1hr., 4-6 per day, 100kr). The **tourist office,** by the docks, stores luggage for free. (☎70 26 50 52. Open June-Aug. daily 9am-5:30pm.)

HEADING NORTH

# SWEDEN

## ESSENTIALS

**EMBASSIES AND CONSULATES.** Foreign embassies in Sweden are in Stockholm (p. 1004). Swedish embassies and consulates abroad include: **Australia,** 5 Turrana St., Yarralumla, Canberra, ACT, 2600 (☎2 62 70 27 00; www.sweden-abroad.com/canberra); **Canada,** 377 Dalhousie St., Ottawa, ON, K1N 9N8 (☎613-241-8553; www.swedenabroad.com/ottawa); **Ireland,** 13-17 Dawson St., Dublin 2 (☎1 474 44 00; www.swedenabroad.com/dublin); **New Zealand,** Vogel Building, Level 13, Aitken St., Wellington (☎4 499 9895; www.sweden-abroad.com/canberra); **UK,** 11 Montagu Pl., London, W1H 2AL (☎020 79 17 64 00; www.swedenabroad.com/london); **US,** 901 30th St., NW, Washington, D.C., 20007 (☎202-467-2600; www.swedenabroad.com/washington).

**VISA AND ENTRY INFORMATION.** EU citizens do not need a visa. Citizens of Australia, Canada, New Zealand, and the US do not need a visa for stays of up to 90 days, beginning upon entry into any of the countries in the EU's freedom-of-movement zone. For more info, see p. 13. For stays longer than 90 days, all non-EU citizens need visas (around US$75), available at Swedish consulates or online at www.swedenabroad.com. For US citizens, visas are usually issued a few weeks after application submission.

| SWEDISH KRONOR (KR) | |
|---|---|
| AUS$1 = 5.53KR | 10KR = AUS$1.81 |
| CDN$1 = 6.53KR | 10KR = CDN$1.53 |
| EUR€1 = 9.35KR | 10KR = EUR€1.07 |
| NZ$1 = 4.82KR | 10KR = NZ$2.07 |
| UK£1= 13.74KR | 10KR = UK£0.73 |
| US$1 = 6.93KR | 10KR = US$1.44 |

**MONEY.** Swedish voters rejected the adoption of the euro as the country's currency in September 2003. The Swedish unit of currency remains the **krona (kr),** plural kronor. One krona is equal to 100 öre, with standard denominations of 50 öre, 1kr, 5kr, and 10kr in coins, and 20kr, 50kr, 100kr, 500kr, and 1000kr in notes. Many **ATMs** do not accept non-Swedish debit cards. Banks and post offices exchange currency; expect a 20-35kr commission for cash, and 5-15kr for traveler's checks. **Forex** generally offers the best exchange rates, and has ATMs that accept foreign debit cards. Note that many Swedish ATMs do not accept PINs longer than four digits; if your PIN is longer than this, entering the first four digits of your PIN should work. Although a service charge is usually added to the bill at restaurants, **tipping** is becoming more common and a 7-10% tip is now considered standard. Tip taxi drivers 5-10%. For more info on money in Europe, see p. 15. Sweden has a whopping 25% **value added tax (VAT),** a sales tax applied to most goods and services. The prices given in *Let's Go* include VAT. In the airport upon exiting the EU, non-EU citizens can claim a refund on the tax paid for goods purchased at participating stores. Some stores may have minimum expenditure requirements for refunds; make sure to ask for a refund form when you pay. For more info on qualifying for a VAT refund, see p. 18.

| SWEDEN | ❶ | ❷ | ❸ | ❹ | ❺ |
|---|---|---|---|---|---|
| **ACCOMMODATIONS** | under 160kr | 160-230kr | 231-350kr | 351-500kr | over 500kr |
| **FOOD** | under 50kr | 50-75kr | 76-100kr | 101-160kr | over 160kr |

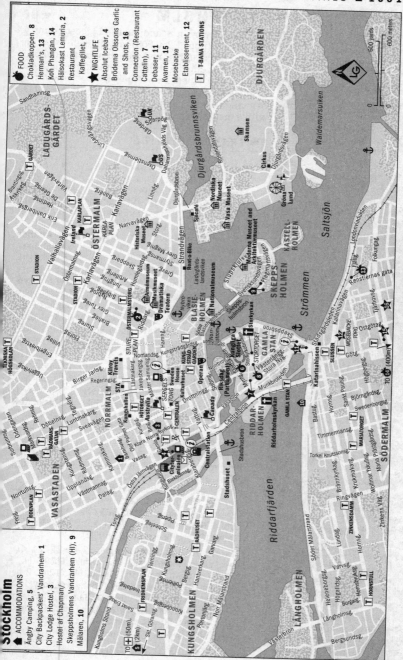

# Stockholm

**ACCOMMODATIONS**
Ängby Camping, 5
City Backpackers' Vandrarhem, 1
City Lodge Hostel, 3
Hostel af Chapman/
Skeppsholmens Vandrarhem (HI), 9
Mälaren, 10

**FOOD**
Chokladkoppen, 8
Herman's, 13
Koh Phangan, 14
Hälsokast Lemuria, 2
Restaurant
Kaffegillet, 6

**★ NIGHTLIFE**
Absolut Icebar, 4
Bröderna Olssons Garlic
and Shots, 16
Connection (Restaurant
Cattelin), 7
Debaser, 11
Kvarnen, 15
Mosebacke
Etablissement, 12

**T T-BANA STATIONS**

**HEADING NORTH**

### GOAT ROAST!

Gävle, 170 km north of Stockholm, had a problem. In 1966, the town center wasn't attracting many tourists. Naturally, the solution was to build a gigantic straw Yule Goat. At 13m high, 7m long, and 3 tons, it became an epic draw for the region. The dividends for Gävle have been astounding.

Just not in the way they expected. When the clock struck midnight on January 1st, 1967, the new year came in with a bang—the goat exploded in flames, the victim of vandalism. The first Gävle goat had perished, but surely it was a mere fluke. Better luck next year.

The goat survived the 1967 and 1968 holidays, but disaster struck again in a 1969 inferno, again lit by vandals. This ushered in four decades of carnage in which 50% of the goats were destroyed, be it by fireworks, flames, or rampaging cars.

It isn't easy being a goat in Gävle. As the troubles have continued, the goat has received protection worthy of a king, with fences, fireproofing, military, and webcams. Tourism has increased as people from around the world head to Sweden to have a crack at burning the goat to the ground, or just watch it happen. Of course, first degree straw goatslaughter is a crime, but no one can deny that it has spurred holiday crowds in the town center, realizing the 1966 goal. Over the years, only four assailants have been caught. Let's Go does not recommend burning straw goats.

# STOCKHOLM    ☎ 08

The largest city in Scandinavia's biggest country, Stockholm (pop. 1,250,000) is aptly self-titled the "capital of the north" and a focal point for culture, design, and cuisine. Built on an archipelago, the elegant city exists by virtue of a latticework of bridges connecting its islands and peninsulas, bringing together individual neighborhoods each with a distinct character.

## ⌐ TRANSPORTATION

**Flights: Arlanda Airport (ARN; ☎797 6000; www.arlanda.com)**, 42km north of the city. **Flygbussarna** shuttles (☎600 1000; www.flygbussarna.se) run between Arlanda and Centralstationen in Stockholm (40min.; every 15min. Station to airport 4am-10pm, airport to station 4:50am-12:30am; 95kr, students, children, and seniors 65kr; MC/V), as do **Arlanda Express** trains (☎0202 222 24; www.arlandaexpress.com. 20min.; every 15min. 5am-midnight; 200kr, students 100kr). **Bus #583** runs to the T-bana stop Märsta (10min., 20kr); take the T-bana to T-Centralen in downtown Stockholm (40min., 20kr). Flygbussarna also operates shuttles to **Västerås Airport (VST;** ☎218 056 00) coordinating with Ryanair departures (1½hr., 100kr). See **Let's Go to Stockholm** (p. 1009) for info on Skavsta Airport, a major budget airline hub for the region.

**Trains: Centralstationen** (☎762 2580). T-bana: T-Centralen. To: **Copenhagen, DEN** (5½hr.; 7-14 per day; 1099kr, under 26 948kr), **Gothenburg** (3-5hr.; every 1-2hr.; 512-1110kr, under 26 437-955kr), and **Oslo, NOR** (6-8hr.; 1-5 per day; 672kr, under 26 572kr). Book up to 90 days in advance for lower fares. Fewer trains on Sa.

**Buses: Cityterminalen**, upstairs on the north end of Centralstationen. **Terminal Service** (☎762 5997) goes to the airport (95kr, 65kr students) and Gotland ferries (70kr). **Biljettservice** (☎762 5979) makes reservations with Sweden's bus companies for longer routes. **Swebus** (☎7712 182 18; www.swebusexpress.se), one of the largest, runs to **Copenhagen, DEN** (9hr., 2per day, 400-500kr), **Gothenburg** (7hr., 7 per day, 250-300kr), and **Malmö** (8½hr., 3 per day, 400-500kr).

**Ferries: Tallinksilja**, Kungsg. 2 (☎22 21 40; www.tallinksilja.com), sails to: **Helsinki, FIN** (17hr., 1 per day at 5pm, from 75kr); **Turku, FIN** (12hr., 2 per day, from 150kr); **Tallinn, EST** (16hr., 1 per day, from 470kr, low season 260kr). T-bana: Gärdet, follow signs to Värtahamnen, or take the Tallinksilja bus (20kr) from Cityterminalen. 50% Scanrail discount on select fares. **Viking Line** (☎452 4000; www.vikingline.fi) sails to:

**Helsinki, FIN** (17hr.; 1 per day; mid-June to mid-Aug. from 430kr, low season 300kr);
**Turku, FIN** (12hr.; 2 per day; mid-June to mid-Aug. from 230kr, low season 130kr).
Office in Cityterminalen (open M-Th 8am-7pm, F 7:30am-6:30pm, Sa 8am-5pm).

**Public Transportation: T-bana** (Tunnelbana, Stockholm's subway; stations marked
with white circular sign with blue "T") runs Su-Th 5am-12:30am, F-Sa 5am-3am.
**Night buses** run 12:30am-5:30am. Tickets 20kr; 10 rides 180kr, sold at Pressbyrån
news agents; 1hr. unlimited transfer. The **SL Tourist Card** (Turistkort) is valid on all
public transportation. 1-day 90kr; 3-day 190kr. Office in Centralstationen (☎600
1000). T-bana: T-Centralen. Open M-Sa 6:30am-11:15pm, Su 7am-11:15pm. MC/V.

**Taxis:** Many cabs have fixed prices to certain destinations; ask when you enter the cab. Expect
to pay 440-475kr from Arlanda to Centralstationen. Major companies include **Taxi 020** (☎33
66 99), **Taxi Kurir** (☎30 00 00; www.taxikurir.se), and **Taxi Stockholm** (☎15 00 00;
www.taxistockholm.com).

**Bike Rental: Rent-a-Bike,** Strandvägen, Kajplats 24 (☎0762 26 76 83). From 200kr
per day. Open daily May-Sept. 10am-6pm. MC/V. **Djurgårdsbrons Sjöcafé,** Galärvarvs-
vägen 2 (☎660 5757). Bikes 250kr per day, canoes 300kr per day, in-line skates
200kr per day, kayaks 500kr per day. Open daily June-Aug. 9am-9pm. AmEx/MC/V.

# ⬛🛈 ORIENTATION AND PRACTICAL INFORMATION

Stockholm spans a number of small islands (linked by bridges and the T-bana) at the
junction of **Lake Mälaren** to the west and the **Baltic Sea** to the east. The large northern
island is divided into two sections: **Norrmalm,** home to Centralstationen and the
crowded shopping district around Drottningg., and **Östermalm,** which boasts the
**Strandvägen** waterfront and upscale nightlife fanning out from **Stureplan.** The mainly
residential western island, **Kungsholmen,** features beaches, waterside promenades,
and the *Stadhuset* (city hall) on its eastern tip. The southern island of **Södermalm**
retains a traditional feel in the midst of a budding cafe culture and club scene. Nearby
**Långholmen** houses a nature preserve and a prison-turned-hotel and museum, while
the similarly woodsy eastern island **Djurgården** exhibits several popular museums on
its western side. At the center of these five islands is **Gamla Stan** (Old Town). Gamla
Stan's less-trafficked neighbor (via Norrmalm) is **Skeppsholmen,** home to many of the
city's art museums. Each of Stockholm's streets begins with number "1" at the end
closest to the Kungliga Slottet (p. 1006) in Gamla Stan; the lower the numbers, the
closer you are to Old Town. Street signs also contain that block's address numbers.

**⚡TIP** **PEDESTRIAN TACTICS 101.** Stockholm lends itself to exploration on
foot, but the network of elevated streets and footbridges can be confusing. To
get from **Centralstationen** to **Sergels Torg,** turn left out of the station on
Vasag., take the stairs up to Klarag., and head straight. To get to the **Stadhuset,**
turn right out of the station and walk to Vasabron, then walk down the steps to
the water just before the bridge, and follow the quay under Centralbron. There
are different ways to navigate the cloverleaf bridge from Gamla Stan to Södermalm, depending on your destination. To reach **Södermalmstorg** or the cliffs,
stay on the bridge to the left. To reach **Södermalärstrand,** stay as far to the right
as possible and then take the ramp down to the water.

**Tourist Offices: Sweden House** (Sverigehuset), Hamng. 27 (☎508 285 08; www.stock-
holmtown.com), entrance off Kungsträdgården. From Centralstationen, walk up Klarabergsg. to Sergels Torg (look for the glass obelisk), bear right on Hamng., and turn right
at the park. Agents sell the **SL card** and **Stockholm Card** (Stockholmskortet), which
includes public transportation and admission to 75 museums and attractions. 1-day

HEADING NORTH

290kr; 2-day 420kr; 3-day 540kr. Internet 1kr per min. Open M-F 9am-7pm, Sa 10am-5pm, Su 10am-4pm. AmEx/MC/V.

**Budget Travel: Kilroy Travels,** Kungsg. 4 (☎0771 54 57 69; www.kilroytravels.se). Open M-F 10am-6pm. **STA Travel,** Kungsg. 30 (☎0771 61 10 10; www.statravel.se). Open M-F 10am-6pm. AmEx/MC/V.

**Embassies: Australia,** Sergels Torg 12, 11th fl. (☎613 2900; www.sweden.embassy.gov.au). Open M-F 8:30am-4:30pm. **Canada,** Tegelbacken 4, 7th fl. (☎453 3000; www.canadaemb.se). Open 8:30am-noon and 1-5pm. **Ireland,** Östermalmsg. 97 (☎661 8005). Open M-F 10am-noon and 2:30-4pm. **UK,** Skarpög. 6-8 (☎671 3000; www.britishembassy.se). Open M-F 9am-5pm. **US,** Daghammarskjölds väg 31 (☎783 5300; www.usemb.se). Open M-Th 9-11am and 1-3pm, F 9-11am.

**Currency Exchange: Forex,** Centralstationen (☎411 6734; open daily 7am-9pm) and Cityterminalen (☎21 42 80; open M-F 7am-8pm, Sa 8am-5pm). 25kr commission.

**Luggage Storage:** Lockers are available at Centralstationen and Cityterminalen (30-80kr per day). Cash only.

**GLBT Resources:** The Queer Extra (QX) and the QueerMap give info about Stockholm's GLBT hot spots. Swedish-language version available at the Sweden House tourist office or online at www.qx.se. For an English-language version, visit www.qx.se/english. Website updated daily.

**24hr. Pharmacy:** Look for green-and-white Apoteket signs. **Apoteket C. W. Scheele,** Klarabergsg. 64 (☎454 8130), at the overpass over Vasag. T-bana: T-Centralen.

**Hospitals: Karolinska** (☎517 740 93), north of Norrmalm near Solnavägen. T-Bana: Skt. Eriksplan. **Sankt Göran** (☎587 010 00), on Kungsholmen. T-Bana: Fridhemsplan.

**Medical Services:** 24hr. hotline ☎32 01 00.

**Telephones:** Almost all public phones require **Telia** phone cards; buy them at Pressbyrån newsstands in increments of 50 (50kr) or 120 (100kr) units.

**Internet Access: Stadsbiblioteket** (library), Odeng. 53, in the annex. T-bana: Odenplan. Sign up for 2 free 30min. slots daily or drop in for 15min., but bring your passport. Open M-Th 9am-9pm, F 9am-7pm, Sa-Su noon-4pm. **Dome House,** Sveavg. 108, has almost 80 terminals. 19kr per hr. Open 24hr. **Sidewalk Express** Internet stations are located inside malls and 7-Elevens throughout the city. 19kr per hr., 149kr monthly pass. Open 24hr. MC/V.

**Post Office:** 84 Klarabergsg. (☎23 22 20). Open M-F 7am-7pm. Address mail to be held as follows: First name, Last Name, **Poste Restante,** Postal Code, City, SWEDEN. Stamps also available at press stands and souvenir shops.

# ACCOMMODATIONS AND CAMPING

Reservations are indispensable in summer. In high season, many HI hostels limit stays to five nights. If you haven't booked ahead, arrive around 8am. Some non-HI hostels are hotel-hostel combinations. Specify that you want to stay in a dorm-style hostel, or risk paying hotel rates. Stockholm's **botels** (boat-hotels) often make for camaraderie, but they can be cramped—request a room with harbor views. There are also various **B&B booking services,** including the **Bed and Breakfast Agency.** (☎643 8028; www.bba.nu. Open M 10am-noon and 1-5pm, Tu-W 9am-12pm and 1-5pm.) The **Sweden House** tourist office can also help book rooms (5kr hostel booking fee, 75kr hotel booking fee). An SL or Stockholm Card is the cheapest way for campers to reach some of the more remote **campgrounds.** The right of public access does not apply within the city limits.

■ **Hostel af Chapman/Skeppsholmens Vandrarhem (HI),** Flaggmansväg. 8 (☎463 2266; www.stfchapman.com). T-bana: Kungsträdgården. Bus #65 from Centralstation.

This modern, roomy hostel is accompanied by a newly renovated 19th-century schooner botel. Breakfast 70kr. Linens 65kr. Laundry 35kr. Internet 1kr per min. Reception 24hr. Lockout 11am-3pm. Dorms 215kr; 3-6 person dorm 260kr; doubles 590kr. 5-10kr HI discount for meals, linens, and laundry. 50kr HI discount for rooms. AmEx/MC/V. ❷

**City Backpackers' Vandrarhem,** Upplandsg. 2A (☎20 69 20; www.citybackpackers.se). T-bana: T-centralen. Just north of the city center, this hostel features friendly service, free pasta, coffee, and tea. Linens 50kr. Laundry 50kr. Sauna 20kr, late-afternoon free. Free Internet and Wi-Fi. Reception 8am-2pm. Low season dorms from 190kr, 210kr high season; doubles 560kr. MC/V. ❷

**City Lodge Hostel,** Klara Norra Kyrkog. 15 (☎22 66 30; www.citylodge.se). T-bana: T-centralen. Newly renovated, tidy rooms, and a can't-beat location make this a great place to rest. Breakfast 50kr. Linens 50kr. Towels 10kr. Laundry 50kr. Free Internet. Reception June-Aug. 8:30am-11pm, Sept.-May 8:30am-10pm. 16-bed dorms 185kr, 6-bed 250kr; doubles from 590kr. MC/V. ❷

**Mälaren,** Södermälarstrand, Kajplats 6 (☎644 4385; www.theredboat.com). T-bana: Gamla Stan. This bright red steamer botel has a great location just south of Gamla Stan. Breakfast 60kr. Towels 20kr. Reception 8am-11pm. Internet 10kr per 15min. Dorms 210kr; singles 430kr; doubles 530kr; triples 720kr; quads 960kr. MC/V. ❷

**Ängby Camping,** Blackebergsv. 24 (☎37 04 20; www.angbycamping.se), on Lake Mälaren. T-bana: Ängbyplan. Wooded campsite with swimming area. Cable TV 10kr. Stockholm Card vendor. Reception June-Aug. 8am-10pm; Sept.-May 5-8pm. 2-person tent sites 135kr; cabins 475-725kr. Electricity from 35kr. AmEx/MC/V. ❶

# 🔲 FOOD

**Götgatan** and **Folkunggatan** in Södermalm offer affordable cuisine from around the world, while pizza and kebabs are plentiful on Vasastaden's **Odengatan**. The **SoFo** (south of Folkunggatan) neighborhood offers many trendy cafe options. Grocery stores are easy to find around any T-bana station. Head to the outdoor fruit market at **Hötorget** for your Vitamin C fix (open M-Sa 7am-6pm), or to the **Kungshallen** food hall, Kungsg. 44, for a meal from one of the international food stands. (www.kungshallen.com. Open M-F 9am-11pm, Sa 11am-11pm, Su noon-11pm.) The **Östermalms Saluhall,** Nybrog. 31 (T-bana: Östermalmstorg), is a more traditional indoor market with fish, meat, cheese, fruit, and pastry stands, as well as more expensive restaurants serving Swedish dishes. (www.ostermalmshallen.se. Open M-Th 9:30am-6pm, F 9:30am-6:30pm, Sa 9:30am-4pm.) Take advantage of low lunch prices and track down *dagens rätt* (lunch specials; 50-80kr) to save money.

**Herman's,** Fjällg. 23A (☎643 9480). T-bana: Slussen. Hearty, well-seasoned vegetarian fare, served buffet-style with a view of the water. Lunch (78-118kr) and dinner (118-168kr) include dessert and drink combos. Open daily June-Aug. 11am-11pm, arrive by 9:30pm for full buffet; Sept.-May 11am-10pm. MC/V. ❹

**Restaurant Kaffegillet,** Trangsund 4 (☎21 39 95). T-bana: Gamla Stan. Excellent place to try Swedish cuisine, highlighted by 14th-century arches. The reindeer roast (215kr) and the popular marinated herring with sour cream (135kr) are popular choices. Small dishes 95-105kr. Swedish Kitchen 135-345kr. Desserts 65-95kr. Salad and bread included. Open daily May-Sept 9am-11pm; Oct-Apr 9am-6pm. AmEx/MC/V. ❹

**Koh Phangan,** Skåneg. 57 (☎642 5040). T-Bana: Skanstull. Dine on Thai food in this stellar restaurant made to look like a jungle tree house. Vegetarian entrees 135-155kr. Meat entrees 150-200kr. Seafood 180-265kr. Open M-Th 11am-11pm, F 11am-11:45pm, Sa 2-11:45pm, Su 2-11pm. AmEx/MC/V. ❺

HEADING NORTH

**Chokladkoppen,** Stortorg. 18 (☎20 31 70). T-bana: Gamla Stan. Caters to a younger crowd with light meals (39-80kr) and generous desserts (23-48kr). The outdoor seating is a top people-watching spot on Stortorget. Open in summer Su-Th 9am-11pm, F-Sa 9am-midnight; low season Su-Th 9am-10pm, F 9am-midnight. Cash only. ❷

**Hälsokust Lemuria,** Nybrog. 26 (☎660 0221). T-bana: Östermalmstorg. Near the Öster-malms Saluhall. Serves nicely balanced gluten- and lactose-free vegetarian and vegan lunches (55kr). Open M-F 11am-3pm. AmEx/MC/V. ❶

## 🔵 SIGHTS

With over 75 museums, visitors to Stockholm never lack places to see. Break up your tour of the city's inner neighborhoods with T-bana rides to more remote locations to get a sense of the capital's scope. The T-bana, spanning 110km, has been called the world's longest art exhibit—over the past 50 years, the city has commissioned more than 140 artists to decorate its stations. The blue line's art is particularly notable, while the murals and sculptures of T-Centralen remain the best-recognized example of T-bana artistry.

**GAMLA STAN (OLD TOWN).** The Baltic trading port of Stockholm was once con-fined to the small island of Staden. Today, the island is the center of the city. The main pedestrian street is **Västerlånggatan,** but its maze of small side streets that preserves the area's historic feel. *(Tours of the island are available June-Aug. M and W-Th 7:30pm. Meet at the obelisk in front of Storkyrkan. 60kr. Cash only.)* Gamla Stan is domi-nated by the magnificent 1754 ◼**Kungliga Slottet** (Royal Palace), one of the largest palaces in Europe and the winter home of the Swedish royal family. The **Royal Apartments** and the adjacent **Rikssalen** (State Hall) and **Slottskyrkan** (Royal Chapel, open W-F) are all lavishly decorated in blue and gold, the colors of the Swedish flag. The **Skattkammaren** (Royal Treasury) houses a small collection of jewel-encrusted crowns, scepters, and other regal accoutrements. The statues in the **Gustav III Antikmuseum** are forgettable, while the **Museum Tre Konor** offers an inter-esting look at the foundation of a 13th-century castle that once stood on the same site. Expect lines in summer. *(Main ticket office and info area at the rear of the complex, near the Storkyrkan. ☎402 6130; www.royalcourt.se. Open Feb. to mid-May Tu-Su noon-4pm; mid-May to June 1st daily 10am-4pm; June 1st-Aug. daily 10am-5pm; Sept. 1st to mid-Sept. daily 10am-4pm; mid-Sept. to mid-May Tu-Su noon-3pm. Each attraction 90kr, stu-dents 35kr. Combination ticket 130/65kr. Guided tours every hour. AmEx/MC/V.)* Across the street from the palace ticket office is the gilded **Storkyrkan** church, where recip-ients of the Nobel Peace Prize speak after accepting their awards. Don't miss the statue of St. George slaying the dragon. *(☎723 3016. Open M-Sa June-Aug. 9am-6pm; Sept.-May 9am-4pm. Church 25kr. 3 tower tours per day in summer. Cash only.)* Around the corner on **Stortorget,** the main square, the small **Nobelmuseet** traces the story of the Nobel Prize and its laureates. *(☎534 818 00; www.nobelprize.org/nobelmuseum. Open mid-May to mid-Sept. Tu 10am-8pm, M and W-Su 10am-5pm; mid-Sept. to mid-May Tu 11am-8pm, W-Su 11am-5pm. 60kr, students 40kr. Guided English-language tours: M-F 11:15am and 3pm, Sa-Su 11:15am and 4pm. AmEx/MC/V.)*

**KUNGSHOLMEN.** The **Stadshuset** (City Hall) has been the seat of local government since the early 20th century. The required tour of the interior takes you through the council room and the enormous Blue Hall, where a 10,000-pipe organ greets Nobel Prize banquet attendees. In the stunning **Gold Room,** 18 million shimmering tiles make up a gold Art Deco mosaic. The **tower** provides the best panoramic view of the city center. *(Hantverkarg. 1. T-bana: T-Centralen. ☎508 290 58; www.stockholm.se/*

*stadshuset. Open daily May-Sept. 9am-4pm. Call the day of your visit to make sure the building will not be closed for a banquet or reception. 20kr. Tours daily June-Aug. 1 per hr. 10am-4pm; Sept. 10am, noon, 2pm; Oct.-May 10am, noon. 60kr, students 50kr. AmEx/MC/V.)*

**SKEPPSHOLMEN AND BLASIEHOLMEN.** The collection of ▨**Moderna Museet,** on the island of Skeppsholmen (SHEPS-hole-men), contains canvases by Dalí, Matisse, Munch, Picasso, Pollock, and Warhol. *(T-Bana: Kungsträdgården. Bus #65. ☎519 552 00; www.modernamuseet.se. 80kr, students 60kr, under 19 free. Open Tu 10am-8pm, W-Su 10am-6pm. MC/V.)* In the same building, the **Arkitekturmuseet** displays the history of Swedish architecture and design using 3D models. *(T-Bana: Kungsträdgården. Bus #65. ☎587 270 00. Open Tu 10am-8pm, W-Su 10am-6pm. 50kr, F free. Combination ticket for both museums 110kr, students 90kr. MC/V.)* Across the bridge on Blasieholmen peninsula, the **Nationalmuseum,** Sweden's largest art museum, features pieces by Cézanne, El Greco, Monet, and Rembrandt. *(T-bana: Kungsträdgården. Bus #65. ☎519 544 10; www.nationalmuseum.se. Open Sept.-May Tu and Th 11am-8pm, W and F-Su 11am-5pm; June-Aug. Tu 11am-8pm, W-Su 11am-5pm. 80kr, students 60kr, under 19 free. AmEx/MC/V.)*

**ÖSTERMALM.** Among the houses of this quiet area are a number of small, quirky museums—the **Musikmuseet** is both. Try an array of instruments or visit the room dedicated to 1970s Swedish pop group ABBA. *(Sibylleg. 2. T-bana: Östermalmstorg, exit Sibylleg. ☎519 554 90; www.stockholm.music.museum. Open Tu-Su July-Aug. 10am-5pm; Sept.-June noon-5pm. 40kr, students 20kr, under 19 free.)* Less than a block away, the **Armému-seum** chronicles Swedish military history. All signs are in Swedish, so be sure to pick up a language guide at the ticket desk. *(Riddarg. 13. T-bana: Östermalmstorg, exit Sibylleg. ☎519 563 00; www.armemuseum.se. Open late June-Aug. Tu 10am-8pm, M and W-Su 10am-5pm. Sept.-June W-Sa 11am-5pm. 40kr, under 20 free.)* For a more complete account of Sweden's history, head to the **Historiska Museet,** which plays host to famous collections of both Viking and ecclesiastical memorabilia. *(Narvav. 13-17. T-bana: Karlaplan. ☎519 556 00; www.historiska.se. Open May-Sept. daily 10am-5pm; Oct.-Apr. Tu-W and F-Su 11am-5pm, Th 11am-8pm. 50kr, students and seniors 40kr, under 19 free.)*

**DJURGÅRDEN.** This national park is a perfect summer picnic spot. The main attraction is the haunting ▨**Vasa Museet,** home to a massive warship that sank in Stockholm's harbor during its maiden voyage in 1628 and was salvaged, fantastically preserved, three centuries later. *(From the Galärvarvet bus stop, take bus #44, 47, or 69. ☎519 548 00; www.vasamuseet.se. Open June-Aug. daily 8:30am-6pm; Sept.-May W 10am-8pm, M-Tu and Th-Su 10am-5pm. 80kr, students 40kr. AmEx/MC/V.)* Next door, the **Nordiska Museet** explores Swedish cultural history from the 1500s to the present day. *(☎519 546 00; www.nordiskamuseet.se. Open June-Aug. daily 10am-5pm; Sept.-Aug. M-F 10am-4pm, Sa-Su 11am-5pm. 60kr, special exhibits 60kr. AmEx/MC/V.)* The **Gröna Lund** amusement park features a handful of exciting rides, including roller coasters. *(☎587 502 00; www.gronalund.se. Open daily late Apr. to late Aug., usually 11am-11pm; check website for detailed schedule. 60kr, rides 20-60kr each.)*

# 🎵 🌺 ENTERTAINMENT AND FESTIVALS

Stockholm's smaller performance venues are featured in the *What's On* pamphlet, available at the Sweden House tourist office. There are also a number of larger, more widely known performance spots. The stages of the national theater, **Dramatiska Teatern,** Nybroplan (☎667 0680; www.dramaten.se), feature performances of works by August Strindberg and others (60-300kr). Arrive an hour early to snatch up a 35% discount on last minute tickets. A smaller affiliated stage behind the theater focuses on experimental material. The **Kulturhuset at Sergels Torg** (☎508 315

08; www.kulturhuset.se) houses art galleries, performance spaces, and a variety of cultural venues often free to the public. It also hosts **Lava** (☎508 314 44; www.lava-land.se. Closed in July), a popular hangout with a stage, library, and cafe that lend themselves to poetry readings and other events geared toward a younger crowd. The **Operan**, Jakobs Torg 2, stages operas and ballets from late August through mid-June. (☎791 4400. Tickets 265-590kr. Student rush tickets available. AmEx/MC/V.) Call **BiljettDirect** (☎0771 707 070; www.ticnet.se) for tickets. The world-class ◪**Stockholm Jazz Festival** arrives in mid- to late July. (☎556 924 40; www.stockholmjazz.com.) Other festivals include the GLBT **Stockholm Pride** (early Aug.; ☎33 59 55; www.stockholmpride.org), the November **Stockholm Film Festival**, eleven days of cinematic bliss (☎677 5000; www.filmfestival.se), and late August's **Strindberg Festival**, a celebration of Sweden's most famous morose playwright.

## ◗ NIGHTLIFE

For a city with lasting summer sunlight, Stockholm knows a thing or two about nightlife. The scene varies by neighborhood, with particular social codes prevailing in different areas. The posh **Stureplan** area in Östermalm (T-bana: Östermalmtorg) and **Kungsgatan** (T-bana: Hötorget) are where beautiful people party until 5am. Expect long lines and note that many clubs honor strict guest lists. Across the river, **Södermalm's** (T-bana: Mariatorget) nightlife is less glitzy but more accessible and just as popular, with a diverse mix of bars and clubs along Götg. and around Medborgarpl. In the northern part of town, nightlife options line **Sveavägen** and the **Vasastaden** area (T-bana: Odenplan or Rådmansg.). Many bars and clubs set age limits as high as 25 to avoid crowds of drunk teenagers, but showing up early may get you in. Stockholm is compact enough to walk among all the islands, although night buses cover most of the city. The T-bana is generally safe until closing. Pick up *Queer Extra (QX)* and the *QueerMap* for gay nightlife tips.

◪ **Absolut Icebar,** Vasaplan 2-4 (☎505 631 24; www.absoluticebar.com), in the Nordic Sea Hotel. T-bana: T-Centralen. Provided jacket and gloves keep you warm in the -5°C temperature of this bar, made completely out of natural ice—from the walls to the furniture and glasses. Make reservations at least 3 days in advance. Drop in usually requires waiting in line. Cover 160kr with alcoholic drink; 105kr with non-alcoholic drink; under 18 60kr. Refills 85kr. Open June-Aug.M-W 12:45pm-midnight, Th-Sa 12:45pm-1am, Su 12:45pm-10pm; check website for details on Sept.-May hours. AmEx/MC/V.

**Mosebacke Etablissement,** Mosebacke Torg 3 (☎556 098 90). T-bana: Slussen. Take the Katarina lift (10kr) to Söder Heights. Usually a large crowd inside at the bar and on the dance floor. Outside terrace is more relaxed with 3 bars, a great view, and ample seating. Beer 46kr. Mixed drinks 74kr. 20+. Cover 50-150kr. Open F-Sa 5pm-2am, Su-Th 5pm-1am. Terrace open in summer daily 11am-1am. AmEx/MC/V.

**Kvarnen,** Tjärhovsg. 4 (☎643 0380; www.kvarnen.com). T-bana: Medborgarpl. Look for the red windmill. The mod cocktail lounge **H2O,** the energetic **Eld** dance club, and a 200-year-old beer hall coexist under the same roof. Beer 29-42kr. Su-Th 21+, F-Sa 23+. Open M-F 11am-3am, Sa noon-3am, Su 5pm-3am. MC/V.

**Connection,** Storkyrkobrinken 9 (☎20 18 18; www.clubconnection.nu). Inside Restaurant Cattelin. T-bana: Gamla Stan, or bus #3 or 53. This spacious gay bar fills up quickly with a diverse clientele that drinks and dances to disco and Madonna. Beer 48kr, mixed drinks 86-108kr. Mixed crowd W and Sa, mostly men F. W 18+, F-Sa 23+. Open W and F-Sa 10pm-3am. AmEx/MC/V.

**Debaser,** Karl Johans Torg 1 (☎462 9860; www.debaser.nu). T-bana: Slussen. This popular rock club draws crowds with live music. 18+. Cover 60-100kr. Bar open daily 5pm-3am. Club open daily June-Aug. 10pm-3am; Sept.-May 8pm-3am. AmEx/MC/V.

**Bröderna Olssons Garlic and Shots,** Folkungag. 84 (☎640 8446; www.garlicand-shots.com). T-bana: Medborgarpl. Follow your nose 3 blocks up Folkungag. This laid-back, 2-floor rocker-style locale serves up garlic beer (39kr) and a repertoire of 130 shots (39kr). 23+. Open daily 5pm-1am. AmEx/MC/V.

## ⚑ LET'S GO TO STOCKHOLM: NYKÖPING ☎155

**Stockholm Skavsta Airport (NYO;** ☎28 04 00; www.skavsta.se) is 100km south of Stockholm in the town of Nyköping. Skavsta is a budget airline hub for Ryanair and Wizz Air. Flygbussarna (☎08 600 1000; www.flygbussarna.se) operates fre-quent **buses** from Stockholm (1¼hr., 100-200kr) coordinated with Ryanair arriv-als and departures. SJ **trains** (☎0771 75 75 75; www.sj.se/english) also run from Stockholm (1hr., 1-2 per hr., 90-160kr). Taxis (200kr) and local buses (20kr) run to the airport from Nyköping station.

## ▶ DAYTRIP FROM STOCKHOLM: THE ARCHIPELAGO

The wooded islands of the Stockholm archipelago become less developed as the chain of 24,000 islands coils its way out into the Baltic Sea. **Vaxholm** is the defacto capital of the archipelago and its most touristed island. Its pristine **beaches,** Eriksö and Tenö in particular, and 16th-century **fortress** have spawned pricey waterside cafes, but the rest of the streets still maintain their charm. Vaxholm is accessible by ferry (1hr., late June-late Aug. 2 per hr., 65kr) or bus #670 from T-bana: Tekniska Hogskolan (45min., 1-4 per hr., 20kr). The **tourist office** is on Torget 1 (☎541 314 80; www.vaxholm.se). Three hours from Stock-holm, **Sandhamn** is a bit quieter, although the white sands of Trouville Beach have plenty of devotees. The island, with its active nightlife scene, is especially popular among a younger crowd. Hikers can escape from the masses by exploring coastal trails on the **Finnhamn** group and **Tjockö** to the north. Ask at Sweden House about **hostels.** They are usually booked up months in advance, but there are alternatives—the islands are a promising place to exercise the right of public access. Waxholmsbolaget runs **ferries** to even the tiniest islands year-round. All ferries depart from Vaxholm. (☎679 5830; www.waxholmsbolaget.se. June-Aug. 1 per hr.; Sept.-May 1 per 2hr. 65kr, ages 7-19 40kr, under 7 free. AmEx/MC/V.) Swe-den House sells the **Båtluffarkort card,** good for unlimited Waxholmsbolaget rides. The pass pays for itself after a few long trips. (5-day 300kr; 30-day 700kr.)

# HEADING EAST

The term "Eastern Europe" is a largely political and arbitrary designation: Prague is located farther west than Vienna, Greece is separated from the "West" by hundreds of miles of "East," and most of Russia is, quite frankly, in Asia. With that in mind, it seems unsurprising that many countries that once lived on the same Bloc now have little in common and, in some cases, little to do with each other. Since the fall of the Iron Curtain, the region has undergone an astounding political and cultural transformation, but the shift has been far from uniform. Perhaps all that can be said of the region as a whole is that the countries here are changing—and that the resulting aura of uncertainty, potential, and adventure makes the area a haven for budget travelers. Untouristed cities, pristine national parks, empty hostel beds, and absurdly cheap beer abound. Prague and Budapest have exploded onto the scene as destinations rivaling the great capitals of Western Europe, as-yet uncrowded Bratislava is on its way to joining them, and the Dalmatian Coast attracts travelers with azure waters and medieval towns.

Eastern European bureaucracies can be infuriating and, in some cases, amenities that Westerners take for granted may be hard to find. Should the absurdity of the post-Soviet world ever get you down, take comfort in knowing that for every stoic border guard and badgering *babushka*, there are countless locals willing to give you a bed, a shot of homemade liquor, and a ride to the next town. No, Eastern Europe's not easy, but like a tracksuit-clad mafioso on a Moscow street corner, it has what you need. Geographically varied, historically rich, and culturally dynamic—with enough fog-draped bridges, white nights, and haunted landscapes to inspire any would-be author—it is a region untamed, with both heavily backpacked cities and, vitally, wondrously, yet-to-be-discovered terrain.

# CROATIA (HRVATSKA)

## ESSENTIALS

### FACTS AND FIGURES

**Official Name:** Republic of Croatia.
**Capital:** Zagreb.
**Major Cities:** Dubrovnik, Split.
**Population:** 4,493,000.

**Time Zone:** GMT + 1.
**Language:** Croatian.
**Country Code:** ☎385.
**Population Growth Rate:** -0.035%.

**EMBASSIES AND CONSULATES.** Embassies abroad include: **Australia,** 14 Jindalee Crescent, O'Malley ACT 2606, Canberra (☎262 866 988; croemb@dynamite.com.au); **Canada,** 229 Chapel Street, Ottawa, ON K1N 7Y6 (☎613-562-7820; www.croatiaemb.net); **Ireland,** Adelaide Chambers, Peter St., Dublin, 8 (☎01 476 7181; croatianembassy@eircom.net); **New Zealand,** 291 Lincoln Rd., Henderson (☎9 836 5581; cro-consulate@xtra.co.nz), mail to: P.O. Box 83-200, Edmonton, Auckland; **UK,** 21 Conway Street, London, W1P 5HL. (☎020 7387 2022; http://croatia.embassyhomepage.com); **US,** 2343 Massachusetts Ave., NW, Washington, D.C. 20008 (☎202-588-5899; http://www.croatiaemb.org)

**VISA AND ENTRY INFORMATION.** Citizens of the EU, Australia, Canada, New Zealand, and the US do not need a visa for stays of up to 90 days. Visas cost US$26 (single-entry), US$33 (double-entry), and US$52 (multiple-entry). Apply for a visa at your nearest Croatian embassy or consulate at least one month before planned arrival. All visitors must **register with the police** within 48hr. of arrival—hotels, campsites, and accommodation agencies should automatically register you, but those staying with friends or in private rooms must do so themselves to avoid fines or expulsion. Police may check foreigners' passports at any time and place. There is no entry fee. The easiest way of entering or exiting Croatia is by bus or train between Zagreb and a neighboring capital.

| CROATIA | ❶ | ❷ | ❸ | ❹ | ❺ |
|---|---|---|---|---|---|
| ACCOMMODATIONS | under 150kn | 151-250kn | 251-350kn | 351-450kn | over 450kn |
| FOOD | under 30kn | 31-60kn | 61-90kn | 91-150kn | over 150kn |

| CROATIAN KUNA (KN) | | |
|---|---|---|
| AUS$1 = 4.44KN | | 1KN = AUS$0.23 |
| CDN$1 = 5.07KN | | 1KN = CDN$0.20 |
| EUR€1 = 7.39KN | | 1KN = EUR€0.14 |
| NZ$1 = 3.89KN | | 1KN = NZ$0.26 |
| UK£1 = 10.94KN | | 1KN = UK£0.09 |
| US$1 = 5.91KN | | 1KN = US$0.17 |

# DALMATIAN COAST

Touted as the new French Riviera, the Dalmatian Coast offers a stunning seascape of unfathomable beauty set against a backdrop of dramatic mountains. With more than 1100 islands, Dalmatia not only is Croatia's largest archipelago, but it also has the cleanest and clearest waters in the Mediterranean.

## ZADAR

☎ 023

Zadar (pop. 77,000), crushed in both WWII and the recent Balkan war, is now beautifully rejuvenated. Though its modern neighborhoods might not impress

**Croatia**

those entering the city, in the *Stari Grad* (Old Town) time seems to have stopped long before both conflicts. With the extraordinary Kornati Islands just a boat ride away, a history so well preserved that Roman ruins serve as city benches, and plenty of boutiques and cafes, Zadar is the quintessential Dalmatian city. On the southern dock of the Old Town, concrete steps into the water are actually part of a 70m long 🎵**Sea Organ,** which plays notes at random as the seawater rushes in, resulting in continual melody. In the ancient Forum in the center of the peninsula, the Byzantine **St. Donat's Church** (Crkva Sv. Donata), a rare circular church, sits atop the ruins of an ancient Roman temple. (Open daily 9am-7:30pm. 10kn.)

At the entrance to the Old Town, coming from Obala Kralja Tomislava, **Miatours** ❷, on Vrata Sv. Krševana, books private rooms and transportation to nearby islands. (☎25 44 00; www.miatours.hr. Open July-Aug. 8am-8pm; Sept.-June 8am-2:30pm. Doubles 200-300kn. AmEx/MC/V.) 🍴**Trattoria Canzona** ❷, Stomorica 8, is always packed with young Zadarians, as are many of the similar restaurants in this rocking corner of town. (☎21 20 81. Entrees 30-70kn. Open M-Sa 10am-11pm, Su noon-11pm. Cash only.) There is also a small **supermarket** between Borelli and Madijevaca. (Open M-Sa 6:30am-9pm, Su 7am-noon.)

**Buses** (☎21 15 55) run from Ante Starevica 1 to: Dubrovnik (8hr., 8 per day, 157-220kn); Pula (7hr., 3 per day, 190kn); Rijeka (4½hr., 12 per day, 125-160kn); Split (3¼hr., 2 per hr., 90-110kn); Zagreb (3½hr., 2 per hr., 105-130kn); Trieste, ITA (7hr.,

2 per day, 170kn). **Luggage storage** is available at the bus station. (1.20kn per hr. Open 6am-10pm.) Both the train and bus stations are a 20min. walk from town, but trains are less convenient. To get to the Old Town, go through the pedestrian underpass and on to Zrinsko-Frankopanska to the water and turn left. At the **Kopnena Vrata** (Main Gate) of the Old Town, turn on Široka, the main street. The **tourist office**, M. Klaića bb, in the far corner of Narodni trg, has free maps and an English-speaking staff. (☎31 61 66; tzg-zadar@zd.tel.hr. Open daily 8am-midnight; low season 8am-8pm.) There is **Internet** on Varoska 3. (☎31 12 65. 30kn per hr. Open daily 10am-11pm.) **Postal Code:** 23000.

## PAKLENICA NATIONAL PARK

The 400m high cliffs of Paklenica, near Zadar, make the national park a favorite stop for climbers, who compete annually in the **Big Wall Speed Climbing** competition on May 1. But while Paklenica is best known for climbing, it's only one feature of the amazing topography of the park. Chalky karsts jump out of tall forests, and abundant fauna—over 80 species of butterfly, along with peregrine falcons and sparrowhawks—make the deep gorges and meadows of Paklenica worth a visit. **Mala** and **Vela Paklenica** are popular cliffs to climb, while underground explorers prefer the half-submerged caves, the largest of which, **Manića Paklenica**, runs for 200m inside the mountain range. **Anića Kuk** (712m) is the most popular peak for hikers and climbers. All climbing routes are outfitted with spits and petons, except the "Psycho Killer" route. For a panoramic view out to the islands, try **Velika Golić** (1285m); passing through limestone ridges and farms bordered by drystone walls, the walk itself is a hard but rewarding 4-5hr. ascent.

Two campsites are available in the park. **Camping Paklenica ❶**, Dr. Franje Tudjman, is on the beach and has excellent facilities. (☎320 9062. Open Apr.-Oct. 54kn per adult, 80kn per site.) The cheaper **National Park Camping ❶**, Dr. Franje Tudjman, is also beach-accessible but does not accept reservations. (☎36 91 55. Open Apr.-Oct. 30kn per adult, 35kn per site.) Outside of camping, private rooms are undoubtedly the cheapest option. The **Stari Grad Tourist Office** (☎36 92 55) helps book rooms (150-300kn). There are several **huts** along the ridges, but be sure to book ahead in summer. There's a **supermarket** near the park entry; otherwise, head to the **Lugarnica ❶** hut for a range of grilled options. (Open daily in the summer.)

To reach Paklenica, take the Rijeka-Zadar **bus.** Facing **Hotel Alan,** walk to your right for 300m up the dirt road to the park entrance. The **Park Office** provides a

## GIVING BACK

### DEFENDING THE DOLPHINS

Human tourists aren't the only ones who flock to the Adriatic waters off Veli Losinj; in recent years, a large pod of around 120 bottlenose dolphins have become permanent residents. Fortunately, you won't find the Losinj harbors teeming with tour boats offering travelers a chance to swim with these sleek creatures.

Instead, Blue World, a marine research and conservation organization has established itself in the port, and has made protecting the dolphins' natural habitat its primary mission.

Co-operating with local excursion companies to avoid interference with ongoing research, Blue World's workers have been given a unique dolphin-watching opportunity. These opportunities are in turn open to anyone who wishes to join a minimum 12-day volunteer course in Rovenska Bay. Volunteers help with collecting and logging data and doing preliminary analysis. When the weather prevents researchers from taking to the waters, volunteers get to listen to lectures by experts in the field of marine biology.

*For those who wish to aid Blue World but cannot volunteer for the minimum period, the organization accepts donations as part of its adopt-a-dolphin program. All funds go directly towards the organization's non profit activities. Check out the website www.blue-world.com for more details.*

map with the entrance fee (30kn per day, 60kn per 3 days, 90kn per 5 days). For serious hikes, fork out the 15-25kn for a more detailed map. (☎36 92 02; www.paklenica.hr. Open Apr.-Oct. M-F 8am-3pm.)

# SPLIT ☎021

With many activities and nightlife, this city by the sea is more a cultural center than a beach resort. The *Stari Grad* (Old Town), wedged between a mountain range and a palm-lined waterfront, sprawls inside and around a luxurious open-air **palace,** where the Roman Emperor Diocletian used to summer when not persecuting Christians. Here, centuries of history have left their trace, making the city a fascinating labyrinth of perfectly preserved Roman monuments, medieval streets with laundry hanging from the windows, and modern bars with huge TV screens showing football matches. The city's **cellars** are near the palace entrance, at the beginning of pedestrian street Obala hrvatskog narodnog preporoda; lose your way in this haunting maze of imperial statues, modern art exhibits, and the cool relief of underground Split. (Open M-F 9am-9pm, Sa-Su 9am-6pm. 8kn.)

Through the cellars and up the stairs is the open-air **peristyle,** a roofless, round building that leads to the Catholic **cathedral,** the world's oldest. Ironically, it was once Diocletian's mausoleum and is now opulently decorated in an elaborate combination of styles. The treasury inside is replete with gold and silver. The view from the adjoining ◪**Bell Tower of St. Dominus** (Zvonik sv. Duje; 60m) is incredible, but watch your head when climbing up. (Cathedral and tower open daily 7am-noon and 5-7pm. 5kn each.) A 25min. walk along the waterfront, the ◪**Mestrović Gallery** (Galerija Ivana Meštrovića), Šetaliste Ivana Meštrovića 46, houses the splendid bronze, stone, and wood works of Croatia's most celebrated sculptor in a gorgeous villa facing the sea. To get there from the center of town, walk right facing the water, pass the marina, and follow the road up the hill; the gallery is right after the Archaeological Museum. (☎34 08 00. Open May-Sept. Tu-Sa 9am-9pm; Su noon-9pm; Oct.-Apr. Tu-Sa 9am-4pm, Su 10am-3pm. 20kn, students 10kn.) At night, locals swim at the hip **Bacvice beach,** near a strip of waterfront bars.

The small **Daluma Travel Agency,** Obala kneza domagoja 1, near the train station, books private rooms, exchanges currency, and organizes excursions. (☎33 84 84; www.daluma.hr. Open July-Aug. M-F 8am-9pm, Sa 8am-8pm, Su 8am-1pm; Sept.-June M-F 8am-8pm, Sa 8am-1pm.) **Al's Place ❶,** Kruziceva 10, is the first hostel in Split, outside the right corner of the palace. There are only 12 beds, which are usually full; reserve ahead. (☎09 89 18 29 23; www.hostel-split.com. June-Aug. 150kn; Sept.-May 100kn. Cash only.) In the Old Town there are plenty of snack bars and restaurants, as well as kiosks with filling pizzas (slices 6-8kn) and *bureks* (10kn); you can also stock up on fruit and vegetables at the crowded **market** on the road between **Obala Riva** and the bus and ferry terminal. The best cafes are on palm-lined Obala Riva, and at night they turn into popular bars. ◪**St. Riva,** right in the center, has side-street swing-couches and a narrow balcony packed with partying youth. Hidden on a narrow line of steps, ◪**Puls** is a great bar with low tables, cushions directly on the pavement, and occasional live jazz. To get there from Obala Riva, enter Trg brace Radic, turn right at the corner snack bar, and continue straight. (Open M-F 7am-midnight, Sa 7am-1am, Su 4pm-midnight.)

**Buses** (☎32 73 27; www.ak-split.hr) run to: Dubrovnik (4¼hr.; 19 per day; 90-130kn, round-trip 160-195kn); Rijeka (7½hr., 13 per day, 270kn); Zadar (3¼hr., 2 per hr., 100kn); Zagreb (5hr., 2 per hr., 185kn); Ljubljana, SLV (11hr., 1 per day, 280kn). **Ferries** (☎33 83 33) depart from the dock right across from the bus station to: Supetar, Brač Island (45min., 10-14 per day, 28kn) and *Stari Grad,*

Hvar Island (1hr., 3 per day, 38kn). Ferries also leave the international harbor to Ancona, ITA (10hr., 4 per week, 330kn) and Bari, ITA (25hr., 3 per week, 330kn). Deciphering the ferry schedules distributed at the **Jadrolinija** office can be a bit nerve-wracking, so ask for help from the busy assistants. (Open daily 4:15am-8:30pm.) The **tourist office** is at Obala HNP 12. (☎34 72 71; www.turist-biro-split.hr. Open July-Aug. M-F 8am-9pm, Sa 8am-10pm, Su 8am-1pm; Sept.-June M-F 8am-9pm, Sa 8am-10pm.) Those who stay in town for more than three days are entitled to a free **SplitCard** that gets big discounts for sightseeing, shopping, and sleeping. Bring a hostel receipt to any tourist office to prove your stay; otherwise purchase one for 60kn. **Postal Code:** 21000.

# HVAR ISLAND
☎021

The thin, 88km Hvar Island (pop. 11,000) grants its visitors mind-blowing views of mainland mountains and nearby islands from its own rugged, lavender-covered hills. Hvar is a prime destination for classy tourists, with an increasing number of wealthy Americans and a consequent rise in prices. **Hvar Town** maintains its easy-going village feel, even as the latest American pop hits play from buses' radios and souvenir shops. Many other destinations reachable by car or a rented boat remain virtually untouched by tourists. The island is packed in July and August. From mid-May to mid-October, the **Hvar Summer Festival** brings outdoor classical music and drama performances to the island's Franciscan monastery. **Trg Sv. Stjepana**, directly below the bus station by the waterfront, is the main square. From there, facing the sea, take a left to reach the **tourist office** and ferry terminal. To the right, stairs lead to the 13th-century Venetian ◪**Fortica**. The climb up is short (20min.) but steep; avoid climbing in the heat and bring water. Once there, you can relax at the restaurant, count the islands in front of Hvar, or—legend has it—watch the fairies that dance here at night. Nearby, the **Hellish Islands** (Pakleni Otoci), which include **Palmižana** beach, with sparse sand, and **Jerolim**, with nude sunbathers, provide relief from the crowds. (Taxi boats 2 per hr. 10am-6:30pm; 30-40kn.)

Lodging rates in Hvar are not backpacker-friendly; for the cheapest rooms, try haggling with the owners of the *sobes* (private rooms). Expect to pay 100-150kn. The **Green Lizard Hostel ❶**, Lučića bb, offers spotless dorms as well as private doubles for reasonable rates. Reserve ahead. (☎74 25 60; www.greenlizard.hr. July-Aug. dorms 135-150kn.) At the end of Riva past the Jadrolinija office, waterfront ◪**Carpe Diem** has low sofas, a hip crowd, and live DJs playing from inside the Roman stone walls. (☎74 23 69; www.carpe-diem-hvar.com. Juices and shakes 28-38kn. Sandwiches 48kn. Mixed drinks 55-68kn. Open daily 9am-2am.) **Luna ❷**, on a side street up the steps to the fortress, has a gorgeous "moon" terrace. (☎74 86 95. Entrees 50-120kn. Cover 8kn. Open daily noon-3pm and 6pm-midnight.)

**Ferries** run to Split (2hr., 3-7 per day, 38kn) and Vela Luka, Korčula (3hr., 1 per day, 22kn). Faster private **catamarans** go directly to Korčula Town (2hr., 1 per day, 33kn) and Split (1 per day, 32kn) from Hvar Town. **Buses** connect Old Town to Hvar Town (25min., 7 per day, 17kn); from the marina, walk through Trg Sv. Stjepana, bearing left of the church. **Jadrolinija**, Riva bb, on the left tip of the waterfront, sells ferry tickets for *Stari Grad*. (☎74 11 32. Open M-Sa 5:30am-1pm and 3-8pm; Su 8-9am, noon-1pm, and 3-4pm.) The **tourist office**, Trg Sv. Stjepana 16, has island maps (20kn) and bus schedules. (☎74 10 59; www.tzhvar.hr. Open July-Aug. M-Sa 8am-1pm and 5-9pm, Su 9am-noon; Sept.-June 8am-2pm. **Postal Code:** 21450.

# BRAČ ISLAND
☎021

Central Dalmatia's largest island, Brač (pop. 13,000) is an ocean-lover's paradise. Most visitors come here for **Zlatni rat,** a beautiful and crowded peninsula of white-pebble beach surrounded by emerald waters, and big waves. If you prefer the "deserted island" environment, head for the less explored, calmer beaches to the east of town. Bol is also pleasant, small enough to cross in 10min., and equipped with its fair share of ice-cream parlors, exchange offices, and plenty of tiny chapels. The 1475 **Dominican Monastery**, on the eastern tip of Bol, displays Tintoretto's altar painting *Madonna with Child*. (Open daily 10am-noon and 5-7pm. 10kn.) There are five **campsites** around Bol; most of them lie on the road into the western part of town. The largest is **Kito ❶**, Bračka cesta bb.(☎63 55 51; kamp_kito@inet.hr. Open May-Sept. 60kn per person, tent and tax included.)

The **ferry** from Split docks at Supetar (1hr., 12-16 per day, 25kn), the island's largest town. (Open daily 4:15am-8:30pm and 12:45-1:30am. AmEx/MC/V.) From there, take a **bus** to Bol (1hr.; 9 per day, last bus M-Sa 7pm, Su 6pm; 24kn). The hourly buses don't always coordinate with the ferries' arrivals; if you don't want to wait, you can take a slightly overpriced **taxi van** to Bol. (35min., 400kn, max. 7 people). Otherwise, kill the wait at the beach across the street. With your back to the water from the bus station in Bol, walk right to reach the **tourist office**, Porad bolskich pomorca bb, on the far side of the marina. (☎63 56 38; www.bol.hr. Open M-Sa 8:30am-2pm and 5-9pm, Su 9am-1pm.) **Postal Code:** 21420.

## KORČULA

Within sight of the mainland, the slender cypresses of the town of Korčula mark Marco Polo's birthplace, where sacred monuments date back to the time of the Apostles. **Marko Polo's house** is in the Old Town, in a tower with views of the sea. (Open daily 9:30am-1:30pm and 4:30-8pm. 10kn.) Though now a biweekly tourist attraction, the **Festival of Sword Dances** is a millennia-old tradition in which dancers reproduce the story of the White Prince and Black Prince fighting over a kidnapped princess. The sword fight is spectacular; go on July 29 for the real (not touristy) thing. (www.moreska.hr. 90kn; tickets available at travel agencies.)

▧**Marko Polo ❷**, Biline 5, is a helpful travel agency who books rooms. (☎71 54 00; www.korcula.com. Reserve ahead. Open daily 8am-9pm.) ▧**The Happy House (Korčula Backpacker) ❶**, Hrvatske Bratske Zajednice 6, is a colorful party hostel, with clean, comfortable co-ed rooms. The common room turns into pub at night, with music, cheap beer, and international snacks for 20kn. (☎09 89 97 63 53; booking@korculabackpacker.com. Shuttle service to Dubrovnik 90kn. Mountain biking and fishing daytrips 300kn. Ages 18-35 only. Dorms 90kn. Cash only.) Camping is available at **Autocamp Kalac ❶**, with a sandy beach and nice views of the mainland across the water. A bus (10min., 1 per hr., 13kn) runs to the camp from the station. (☎71 11 82. Reception daily 7am-10pm. 40kn per person, 35kn per tent. Tourist tax 7.50kn.) ▧**Fresh ❶**, right next to the bus station, specializes in healthy wraps (22-25kn) and smoothies. Find some beach reading from their English-language book exchange (☎09 18 96 75 09; www.igotfresh.com. Open daily 9am-2am. Cash only.) The eatery **Adio Mare ❷**, Marka Pola 2, serves authentic local fare. (☎71 12 53. Entrees 40-90kn. Open M-Sa 5:30pm-midnight, Su 6pm-midnight.)

**Buses** (Obala Korčulanskih Brodograditelja) board ferries to the mainland and head to Dubrovnik (3½hr., 1 per day, 85kn) and Zagreb (11-13hr., 1 per day, 210kn). On the island, they run to Lumbarda (9 per day, 13kn), Pupnat (8 per day, 40kn), and Vela Luka (5 per day, 30kn). Ticket and info office is open Monday through Saturday 6am-8pm and Sunday 2-8pm. The **Jadrolinija** office sells ferry tickets. (☎71 54 10. Open M-F 5:30am-7pm, Sa-Su 7:30am-7:30pm. AmEx/MC/V.) Ferries run to Dubrovnik (3½hr., 5 per week, 79kn) from both sides of Korčula Town; make sure to check where yours leaves. **Postal Code:** 20260.

## DUBROVNIK

Lord Byron considered Dubrovnik (du-BROV-nik; pop. 43,800) "the pearl of the Adriatic," and George Bernard Shaw knew it as "Paradise on Earth." Although it's

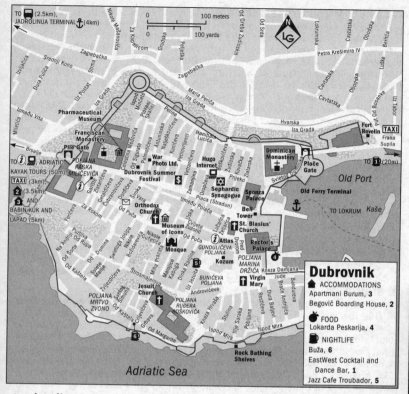

**Dubrovnik**

▲ ACCOMMODATIONS
Apartmani Burum, **3**
Begović Boarding House, **2**

🍴 FOOD
Lokarda Peskarija, **4**

🍸 NIGHTLIFE
Buža, **6**
EastWest Cocktail and
Dance Bar, **1**
Jazz Cafe Troubador, **5**

tough to live up to such adulation, a stroll through the torch-lit winding lanes of the *Stari Grad* (Old Town) and look into the sea at sunset from the city walls certainly justify Dubrovnik's reputation as one of Croatia's best destinations.

**🖢🕿 TRANSPORTATION AND PRACTICAL INFORMATION.** Jadrolinija **ferries** (☎41 80 00; www.jadrolinija.hr) depart opposite Obala S. Radica 40 for Korčula (3½hr., 5 per week, 79kn); Rijeka (22hr., 2 per week, 233kn); Split (8hr., 4 per day, 115kn); and Bari, ITA (9hr., 5 per week, 97kn). The **Jadrolinija** office is across the dock. (Open M-Tu and Th 8am-8pm, W and F 8am-8pm and 9-11pm, Sa 8am-2pm and 7-8pm, Su 8-10am and 7-8:30pm.) **Buses** (☎35 70 88) run from Vukovarska, behind the new port, to: Rijeka (12hr., 4 per day, 415kn); Split (4½hr., 1 per hr., 132kn); Zagreb (11hr., 8 per day, 234kn); and Trieste, ITA (15hr., 1 per day, 370kn). There's **luggage storage** at the station (open daily 5am-10:30pm; 15kn per bag) and also a gigantic **Konzum** supermarket (open M-Sa 8am-9pm, Su 8am-2pm). To reach the Old Town, face away from the station and turn left on Ante Starčevića; follow it 25min. uphill to the **Pile Gate.** All local buses except #5, 7, and 8 go to the Pile Gate (8kn at kiosks, 10kn on board).

Walk 50m away from the Old Town's entrance to reach the **tourist office,** Ante Starčevića 7, for free maps and cheap **Internet.** (☎42 75 91. Internet 8am-10pm 10kn per 15min. Office open daily 8am-9pm.) The **post office,** Široka 8, in the *Stari Grad,* has **ATMs,** public telephones, and offers Western Union services. (☎32 34 27. Open M-F 7:30am-9pm, Sa 10am-5pm.) **Postal Code:** 20108.

**▐▌▐▌ ACCOMMODATIONS AND FOOD.** A private room tends to be the cheapest and most comfortable option for two; arrange one through any of the indistinguishable agencies or bargain with locals at the station (doubles should go for 100-150kn per person). Take bus #6 from *Stari Grad* or #7 from the ferry and bus terminal, get off two stops past the Lapad post office, cross the street, climb the steps uphill on Mostarska, and turn left at Dubravkina to reach ▨**Apartmani Burum ❶**, Dubravkina 16, in Babin Kuk. This popular guesthouse is comfortable, and the owner is known to drive guests around town for a small fee. (☎43 54 67; www.burum-accommodation.com. Kitchen available. Pickup available. 100-150kn per person. Cash only.) **Begović Boarding House ❶**, Primorska 17, offers spacious doubles and apartments in a cozy villa with satellite TVs, a social terrace shaded by fig trees, and a pleasant family feel. Call ahead and the owner will pick you up. (☎43 51 91; bega_dbk@yahoo.com. Reserve ahead July-Aug. Singles 150-200kn; doubles 200-240kn; triples 180-300kn. Cash only.) ▨**Lokarda Peskarija ❷**, Na Ponti bb, has excellent and affordable seafood. From the bell tower, take a right out on Pred Dvorum and the first left out of the city walls. (☎32 47 50. Seafood 35-60kn. Open daily 8am-3am.) Exchange books, savor smoothies, and nosh on wraps at **Fresh ❷**, on Vetranićeva. (Wraps 25kn. Smoothies 20kn. Open daily 8am-2am.)

> **!** Make sure to ask for a receipt when you pay for a private room. No receipt means that your stay won't be registered and that the accommodation is illegal.

**◪ SIGHTS.** The Old Town is packed with churches, museums, monasteries, palaces, and fortresses. The entrance to the 2km limestone ▨**city wall** *(gradske zidine)* lies just inside the Pile Gate, on the left, with a second entrance at the other end town. Go at dusk to be dazzled by the sunset. (Open daily 8am-7:30pm. 50kn, students 20kn. Audio tour 40kn.) The 14th-century **Franciscan Monastery** (Franjevački samostan), next to the city wall entrance on Placa, houses the oldest pharmacy in Europe (est. 1317) and an elegant courtyard. (Open daily 9am-6pm. 20kn, students 13kn.) The **Cathedral of the Assumption of the Virgin Mary** (Riznica Katedrale), Kneza Damjana Jude 1, is built on the site of a Romanesque cathedral and a 7th-century Byzantine cathedral. Its treasury houses the "Diapers of Jesus," along with a host of glittering golden reliquaries. (Cathedral open daily 6:30am-8pm. Free. Treasury open daily 8am-8pm. 10kn.) The 19th-century **Serbian Orthodox Church** (Pravoslavna Crkva) and its **Museum of Icons** (Muzej Ikona), Od Puča 8, stand as a symbol of Dubrovnik's tolerance with the small, but intricate **synagogue** and **mosque**. (Museum open M-Sa 10am-2pm; 10kn. Synagogue open May-Oct. M-F 9am-8pm; 15kn. Mosque open daily 10am-1pm and 8-9pm. Free.) Classical performances are held in summer in many of the Old Town's churches.

**◪ BEACHES.** Outside the fortifications of the Old Town are a number of **rock shelves** for sunning and swimming. To reach a pristine but overcrowded **pebble beach** from the Placa's end, turn left on Svetog Dominika, bear right after the footbridge, and continue on Frana Supila. Descend the stairs by the post office. For a surreal seaside swim, take a dip in the cove at the foot of the old ▨**Hotel Libertas**. Once Dubrovnik's most luxurious hotel, the building was damaged during WWII and then abandoned; new construction, though, has taken away from its post-apocalyptic appeal. Local kids carelessly dive into the sea from 6 ft. rocks,

> **!** As tempting as it may be to stroll through the hills above Dubrovnik or wander the unpaved paths on Lopud, both may still be laced with **landmines**. Stick to paved paths and beaches.

but this isn't the smartest idea: the water often is much shallower than it looks. Ferries run daily from the Old Port (20min., 2 per hr., round-trip 35kn) to the nearby island of **Lokrum,** which has a nude beach with great cliff jumping. More modest travelers can stroll (fully clothed) through the **nature preserve** to a smaller section of rock shelves on the other side of the island.

**FESTIVALS AND NIGHTLIFE.** Dubrovnik becomes a party scene and cultural mecca from mid-July to mid-August during the **Dubrovnik Summer Festival** (Dubrovački Ljetni Festival). The **festival office** on Placa has schedules and tickets. (☎42 88 64; www.dubrovnik-festival.hr. Open daily during the festival 8:30am-9pm, tickets 9am-2pm and 3-7pm. 50-300kn.) By night Dubrovnik's crowds gravitate to bars in *Stari Grad* and cafes on Buničeva Poljana, where live bands and street performers turn up in summer. From the open-air market, climb the stairs toward the monastery, veer left, and follow the signs marked "Cool Drinks and (truly) the Most Beautiful View" along Od Margarite to **Buža,** Crijevićeva 9. Above the bright blue Adriatic, this laid-back watering hole on the city's rocks is the best place to enjoy spectacular sunsets and a midnight swim. (Beer 17-22kn. Mixed drinks 30kn. Open daily 9am-2am.) Enjoy occasional belly dancing at the classy but unpretentious **Jazz Cafe Troubador,** Buničeva 2. (Beer 18-40kn. Wine 20-40kn. Open daily 9am-2am.) At **EastWest Cocktail and Dance Bar,** Frana Supila bb, a dressed-to-impress clientele reclines on white leather sofas and plush beds on the beach. (Beer 12-30kn. Mixed drinks 40-100kn. Thai massage 200kn for 30min., 300kn for 1hr. Open daily 8am-4am.)

**DAYTRIP FROM DUBROVNIK: LOPUD ISLAND.** A short walk along Lopud's shore leads to an abandoned **monastery;** check it out, but beware of crumbling floors. The island's highlight is its beach, **Plaža Šunj.** Arguably the best in Croatia, this cove has one thing that most of the Dalmatian Coast lacks: sand. Facing the water, walk turn left on the road between the high wall and the palm park; look for the Konoba Barbara sign and continue over the hill, and then keep right when the path forks. Ferries run regularly from Gruz harbor (1hr., round-trip 120kn).

# CZECH REPUBLIC (ČESKÁ REPUBLIKA)

## ESSENTIALS

### FACTS AND FIGURES

**Official Name:** Czech Republic.
**Capital:** Prague.
**Major Cities:** Brno, Olomouc, Plzeň.
**Population:** 10,229,000.
**Time Zone:** GMT +1.

**Language:** Czech.
**Country Code:** ☎420.
**Annual Beer Consumption Per Capita:** 161L (the largest in the world).

**EMBASSIES AND CONSULATES.** Czech consulates and embassies abroad include: **Australia,** 8 Culoga Circuit, O'Malley, Canberra, ACT 2606 (☎02 62 90 13 86; www.mzv.cz/canberra); **Canada,** 251 Cooper St., Ottawa, ON K2P 0G2 (☎613-562-3875; www.embassy.mzv.cz/Ottawa); **Ireland,** 57 Northumberland Rd., Balls-

HEADING EAST

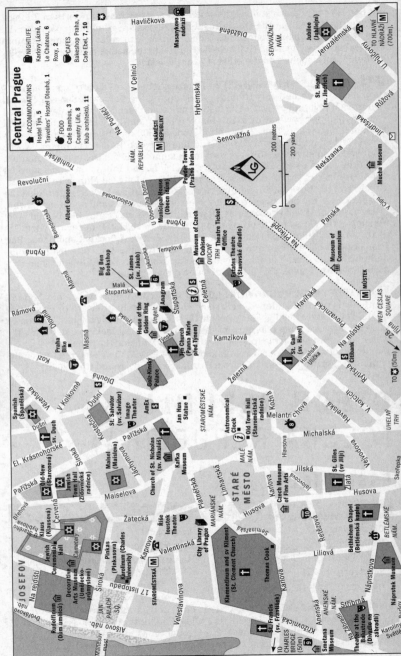

**Central Prague**

**■ ACCOMMODATIONS**
Hostel Týn, 5
Travellers' Hostel Dlouhá, 1

**● FOOD**
Cafe Bambus, 3
Country Life, 8
Klub architektů, 11

**◆ NIGHTLIFE**
Karlovy Lázné, 9
Le Chateau, 6
Roxy, 2

**☕ CAFES**
Bakeshop Praha, 4
Cafe Ebel, 7, 10

200 meters

200 yards

bridge, Dublin 4 (☎016 681 135; www.embassy.msz.cz/Dublin); **New Zealand,** Level 3, BMW Mini Centre, 11-15 Great South Road and corner of Margot Street, Newmarket, Auckland (☎9 522 8736; auckland@honorary.mvz.cz); **UK,** 6-30 Kensington Palace Gardens, Kensington, London W8 4QY (☎020 72 43 11 15; www.mzv.cz/london); **US,** 3900 Spring of Freedom St., NW, Washington, D.C. 20008 (☎202-274-9100; www.mzv.cz/washington).

**VISA AND ENTRY INFORMATION.** Citizens of Australia, Canada, New Zealand and the US do not need a visa for stays of up to 90 days; UK citizens do not need visas for stays of up to 180 days. Visas for extended stays are available at embassies or consulates. One cannot obtain a Czech visa at the border. Processing takes 14 days when visa is submitted by mail, seven when submitted in person.

| CZECH REPUBLIC | ❶ | ❷ | ❸ | ❹ | ❺ |
|---|---|---|---|---|---|
| **ACCOMMODATIONS** | under 320Kč | 320-500Kč | 501-800Kč | 801-1200Kč | over 1200Kč |
| **FOOD** | under 80Kč | 80-110Kč | 111-150Kč | 151-200Kč | over 200Kč |

| CZECH KORUNY (Kč) | | |
|---|---|---|
| AUS$1 = 16.34Kč | 10Kč = AUS$0.61 | |
| CDN$1 = 19.33Kč | 10Kč = CDN$0.52 | |
| EUR€1 = 27.33Kč | 10Kč = EUR€0.36 | |
| NZ$1 = 14.26Kč | 10Kč = NZ$0.70 | |
| UK£1 = 40.74Kč | 10Kč = UK£0.25 | |
| US$1 = 20.56Kč | 10Kč = US$0.49 | |

# PRAGUE (PRAHA)

Home to stately Prague Castle and Old Town Square's pastel facades, Prague (pop. 1,200,000) retains a small-town charm despite its size. In the 14th century, King of Bohemia and Holy Roman Emperor Charles IV added to the city's decadence, refurbishing it with stone bridges and lavish palaces still visible today. Since the lifting of the Iron Curtain in 1989, hordes of outsiders have flooded the Czech capital. In summer, most locals leave for the countryside when foreigner-to-resident ratio soars above nine-to-one. Despite rising prices and a hyper-touristed *Staré Město* (Old Town), Prague still commands begrudging awe from its visitors.

# ⊏ INTERCITY TRANSPORTATION

**Flights: Ruzyně Airport (PRG;** ☎220 111 111), 20km northwest of the city. Take bus #119 to Metro A: Dejvická (12Kč, luggage 6Kč per bag); buy tickets from kiosks or machines. **Airport buses** run by **Cedaz** (☎220 114 296; 20-45min., 2 per hr.) collect travelers from nám. Republiky (120Kč) and Dejvická Metro stops (90Kč). **Taxis** to the airport are expensive (700-900Kč); try to settle on a price before departing.

**Trains:** (☎221 111 122, international 224 615 249; www.vlak.cz). Prague has 4 main terminals. **Hlavní nádraží** (☎224 615 786; Metro C: Hlavní nádraží) and **Nádraží Holešovice** (☎224 624 632; Metro C: Nádraží Holešovice) are the largest and cover most international service. Domestic trains leave **Masarykovo nádraží** (☎840 112 113; Metro B: nám. Republiky) and from **Smíchovské nádraží** (☎972 226 150; Metro B: Smíchovské nádraží). International trains run to: **Berlin, GER** (5hr., 6 per day, 1400Kč); **Bratislava, SLK** (4½-5½hr., 6 per day, 600Kč); **Budapest, HUN** (7-9hr., 5 per day, 1400Kč); **Kraków, POL** (7-8hr., 3 per day, 900Kč); **Moscow, RUS** (31hr., 1 per day, 3000Kč); **Munich, GER** (7hr., 3 per day, 1650Kč); **Vienna, AUT** (4½hr., 7 per day, 1000Kč); **Warsaw, POL** (9½hr., 2 per day, 1290Kč).

**Buses:** (☎900 144 444; www.vlak-bus.cz.) State-run **ČSAD** (☎257 319 016) has several terminals. The biggest is **Florenc**, Křižíkova 4 (☎900 149 044; Metro B or C: Florenc). Info office open daily 6am-9pm. Buy tickets ahead. To: **Berlin, GER** (7hr., 2 per day, 900Kč); **Budapest, HUN** (8hr., 3 per day, 1600Kč); **Paris, FRA** (15hr., 2 per day, 2200Kč); **Sofia, BUL** (24hr., 2 per day, 1600Kč); **Vienna, AUT** (5hr., 1 per day, 600Kč). 10% ISIC discount. The **Tourbus** office (☎224 218 680; www.eurolines.cz), at the terminal, sells **Eurolines** and airport bus tickets. Open M-F 7am-7pm, Sa 8am-7pm, Su 9am-7pm.

# ⚒ ORIENTATION

Shouldering the river **Vltava,** greater Prague is a mess of suburbs and maze-like streets. All destinations of interest to travelers are in the compact downtown. The Vltava runs south to north through central Prague, separating **Staré Město** (Old Town) and **Nové Město** (New Town) from **Malá Strana** (Lesser Side). On the right bank, **Staroměstské náměstí** (Old Town Square) is Prague's focal point. From the square, the elegant **Pařížská ulice** (Paris Street) leads north into **Josefov,** the old Jewish quarter. South of *Staré Město,* the more modern **Nové Město** houses **Václavské náměstí** (Wenceslas Square), the city's commercial core. West of Staroměstské nám., **Karlův Most** (Charles Bridge) spans the Vltava, connecting Staré Město with **Malostranské náměstí** (Lesser Town Square). **Pražský Hrad** (Prague Castle) overlooks Malostranské nám. from **Hradčany** hill. The Hlavní nádraží train station and Florenc bus station lie northeast of Václavské nám. All train and bus terminals are on or near the Metro. To reach Staroměstské nám., take Metro A line to Staroměstská and follow Kaprova away from the river.

# ▐ LOCAL TRANSPORTATION

**Public Transportation:** Buy interchangeable tickets for the **bus, Metro,** and **tram** at newsstands, *tabák* kiosks, machines in stations, or the DP (*Dopravní podnik;* transport authority) kiosks. Validate tickets in machines above escalators to avoid fines issued by plainclothes inspectors who roam transport lines. 3 **Metro** lines run daily 5am-midnight: A is green on maps, B yellow, C red. **Night trams** #51-58 and **buses** #502-514 and 601 run after the last Metro and cover the same areas as day trams and buses (2 per hr. 12:30am-4:30am); look for dark blue signs with white letters at bus stops. 8Kč tickets are good for a 15min. ride or 4 stops. 12Kč tickets are valid for 1hr., with transfers, for all travel in the same direction. Large bags and baby carriages 6Kč. DP office (☎296 191 817; www.dpp.cz; open daily 7am-9pm), in the Muzeum stop on Metro A and C lines, sells **multi-day passes** (1-day 80Kč, 3-day 220Kč, 1-week 280Kč).

**Taxis:** City Taxi (☎257 257 257) and **AAA** (☎140 14). 30Kč base, 22Kč per km, 4Kč per min. waiting. Hail a cab anywhere but call ahead to avoid getting ripped off.

---

**⬙TIP** **GOING THE DISTANCE.** To avoid taxi scams, always ask in advance for a receipt *(Prosím, dejte mi paragon)* with distance traveled and price paid.

---

# ▟ PRACTICAL INFORMATION

**Tourist Offices:** Green "i"s mark tourist offices. **Pražská Informační Služba** (PIS; Prague Information Service; ☎12 444; www.pis.cz) is in the Staroměstské Radnice (Old Town Hall). Open Apr.-Oct. M 11am-6pm, Tu-Su 9am-6pm; Nov.-Mar. M 11am-5pm, Tu-Su

9am-5pm. Branches at Na příkopě 20 and Hlavní nádraží. Open in summer M-F 9am-7pm, Sa-Su 9am-5pm; winter M-F 9am-6pm, Sa 9am-3pm. Branch in the tower by the Malá Strana side of the Charles Bridge. Open Apr.-Oct. daily 10am-6pm.

**Budget Travel: CKM,** Mánesova 77 (☎222 721 595; www.ckm-praha.cz). Metro A: Jiřího z Poděbrad. Sells budget airline tickets to those under 26. Also books accommodations in Prague from 300Kč. Open M-Th 10am-6pm, F 10am-4pm. **GTS,** Ve smečkách 27 (☎222 119 700; www.gtsint.cz). Metro A or C: Muzeum. Offers student discounts on airline tickets (225-2500Kč in Europe). Open M-F 8am-10pm, Sa 10am-4pm.

**Embassies and Consulates: Australia,** Klimentská 10, 6th fl. (☎296 578 350; www.embassy.gov.au/cz.html; open M-Th 8:30am-5pm, F 8:30am-2pm) and **New Zealand,** Dykova 19 (☎222 514 672) have consulates, but citizens should contact the UK embassy in an emergency. **Canada,** Muchova 6 (☎272 101 800; www.canada.cz). Open M-F 8:30am-12:30pm and 1:30-4:30pm. Consular section open only in the morning. **Ireland,** Tržiště 13 (☎257 530 061; irishembassy@iol.cz). Metro A: Malostranská. Open M-F 9:30am-12:30pm and 2:30-4:30pm. **UK,** Thunovská 14 (☎257 402 111; prague@fco.gov.uk). Metro A: Malostranská. Open M-Th 9am-noon. **US,** Tržiště 15 (☎257 530 663, after-hours 257 022 000; www.usembassy.cz). Metro A: Malostranská. Open M-F 8am-4:30pm. Consular section open M-F 8:30-11:30am.

**Currency Exchange:** Exchange counters are everywhere but rates vary wildly. The counters in the train station have high rates. Never change money on the street. **Cheque points** are plentiful and open late but can charge large commissions. **Komerční banka,** Na příkopě 33 (☎222 432 111), buys notes and checks for 2% commission. Open M-W 9am-6pm, Th-F 9am-5pm. **ATMs** are scarce and most often attached to banks. A 24hr. **Citibank** is at Rytířska 24 near Wenceslas Square.

**American Express/Interchange:** Václavské nám. 56 (☎222 800 224). Metro A or C: Muzeum. AmEx **ATM** outside. **Western Union** services available. MC/V **cash advances** (3% commission). Western Union services available. Open daily 9am-7pm.

**Luggage Storage:** Lockers in train and bus stations take 2 5Kč coins. For storage over 24hr., use the luggage offices to the left in the basement of Hlavní nádraží. 20Kč per day, bags over 15kg 40Kč. Fine for forgotten lock code 30Kč. Open 24hr. with breaks 5:30-6am, 11-11:30am, and 5:30-6pm.

**English-Language Bookstore:** ◙**The Globe Bookstore,** Pštrossova 6 (☎224 934 203; www.globebookstore.cz). Metro B: Národní třída. Exit Metro left on Spálená, take the 1st right on Ostrovní, then the 3rd left on Pštrossova. Wide variety of new and used books and periodicals. Internet 1.50Kč per min. Open daily 9:30am-midnight.

**Laundromat: Laundry Kings,** Dejvická 16 (☎233 343 743; www.laundry.czweb.org). Metro A: Hradčanská. Trams #1, 8, 18, 25, 26. Exit Metro to Dejvická, cross the street, and turn left. Wash 40Kč per 8min., dry from 90Kč; detergent 10-20Kč. Open M-F 6am-10pm, Sa-Su 8am-10pm. Last wash 9:30pm.

**Medical Services: Na Homolce** (Hospital for Foreigners), Roentgenova 2 (☎257 271 111, after hours 257 272 146; www.homolka.cz). Bus #167. Open 24hr. **Canadian Medical Center,** Velesavínská 1 (☎235 360 133, after hours 724 300 301; www.cmc.praha.cz). Open M, W, F 8am-6pm, Tu and Th 8am-8pm.

**24hr. Pharmacy: U Lékárna Anděla,** Štefánikova 6 (☎257 320 918, after hours 257 324 686). Metro B: Anděl. With your back to the train station, turn left and follow Nádražní, which becomes Štefánikova. For after-hours service, press the button marked "Pohotovost" to the left of the main door.

**Telephones:** Phone cards sold at kiosks, post offices, and some exchange establishments for 200Kč and 300Kč. Coins also accepted (local calls from 4Kč per min.).

**Internet Access:** ◙ **Bohemia Bagel,** Masná 2 (☎224 812 560; www.bohemiabagel.cz), Metro A: Staroměstská. 2Kč per min. Open daily 7am-midnight,

**Post Office:** Jindřišská 14 (☎221 131 445). Metro A or B: Můstek. Internet 1Kč per min. Open daily 2am-midnight. Tellers close 7pm. **Postal Code:** 11000.

# ACCOMMODATIONS AND CAMPING

Hotel prices are through the roof in Prague, and hostel rates are on the rise. Reservations are a must at hotels and even at the nicer hostels in summer. A growing number of Prague residents rent affordable rooms.

## HOSTELS

If you tote a backpack in Hlavní nádraží or Holešovice stations, you will likely be approached by hostel runners offering cheap beds. Many of these are university dorms vacated June to August, and they often provide free transportation, convenient for late-night arrivals. However, more personal, well-appointed options can be had at similar prices. Staff at hostels typically speak English.

### STARÉ MĚSTO

**Travellers' Hostel,** Dlouhá 33 (☎224 826 662; www.travellers.cz). Metro B: nám. Republiky. Branches at Husova 3, Josefská, Střelecký Ostrov, and U Lanové Dráhy 3. Social atmosphere. Smallish dorms. Same building as the Roxy (p. 1032). Breakfast and linens included. Laundry 150Kč. Internet 1Kč per min. Reserve ahead in summer. 10-bed dorm 380Kč; 6-bed dorms 450Kč; singles 1120Kč, with bath 1300Kč; doubles 650/750Kč; apartments 2400-3500Kč. 40Kč ISIC discount. AmEx/D/MC/V. ❷

**Hostel Týn,** Týnská 19 (☎224 828 519; www.hostel-tyn.web2001.cz). Metro A: Staroměstská. From Staroměstské nám., head down Dlouhá, bear right on Masná, and turn right again on Týnská. Hostel is through the gate to the right. In the heart of Staré Město, Hostel Týn skillfully avoids the extremes of overcrowding and boredom: dorms are small, but the crowd is young and social. Soft beds. Clean, orderly facilities. In-room lockers. Check-out 10am. 5-bed dorms 400Kč; doubles 1100Kč. 200Kč deposit. ❷

### NOVÉ MĚSTO AND VINOHRADY

🏆**Czech Inn,** Francouzská 76 (☎267 267 600; www.czech-inn.com). Metro A: nám. Míru. From the Metro, take tram #4, 22, or 23 to Krymská and walk uphill. This ultra-modern, fashionable hostel sets sky-high standards for budget accommodations. Crisp white linens and designer bathrooms. Breakfast 120Kč. Internet 50Kč per hr. Reserve 2 weeks ahead. Dorms 390-450Kč; singles 1200Kč; doubles 1400Kč. Private room prices increase 200Kč on weekends. AmEx/MC/V. ❷

**Miss Sophie's,** Melounová 3 (☎296 303 532; www.missophies.com). Metro C: IP Pavlova. Take 1st left from subway platform, then follow Katerinská to 1st right onto Melounová. For the stylish budget traveler, a brick cellar lounge and artistic dorm decor make up for the bathroom shortage. Free Internet. Reception 24hr. High-season dorms 400-490Kč; singles 1590Kč; doubles 1790Kč; triples 2100Kč; apartments 1990-3390Kč. Low-season 350/1200/1500/1700/1400-1900Kč. AmEx/MC/V. ❷

**Hostel Elf,** Husitská 11 (☎222 540 963; www.hostelelf.com). Metro B: Florenc. From the Metro, take bus #207 to U Památníku; the hostel is through the wooden gate. Despite noisy train tracks nearby, this graffiti-covered hostel is always packed. The party continues past dawn in the downstairs lounge. Breakfast included. Free Internet. 9-bed dorms 340Kč; singles 800Kč, with baths 1000Kč; doubles 900/1200Kč. ❷

**Pension Unitas Art Prison Hostel,** Bartolomějská 9 (☎224 221 802; www.unitas.cz). Metro B: Národní třída. Cross Národní třída, head up Na Perštýně, and turn left on Bartolomějská. This former 🔱Communist prison is now a clean and colorful hostel, with small spotless rooms. Superb breakfast buffet included. Reception 24hr. Check-out 10am. Apr.-Oct. dorms

440Kč; singles 1350Kč; doubles 1700Kč; triples 2100Kč; quads 2360Kč. Nov.-Mar. 350/890/980/1380/1700Kč. 7th night free. MC/V. ❷

**Hostel U Melounu,** Ke Karlovu 7 (☎224 918 322; www.hostelumelounu.cz). Metro C: I.P. Pavlova. Follow Sokolská and go right on Na Bojišt, then left onto Ke Karlovu. Historic building with bar and private garden. Breakfast included. Check-out 10am. Dorms 390Kč; singles 750Kč; doubles 1000Kč. 30Kč ISIC discount. AmEx/MC/V. ❷

## OUTSIDE THE CENTER

▨ **Sir Toby's,** Dělnická 24 (☎283 870 635; www.sirtobys.com). Metro C: Nádraží Holešovice. From the Metro, take the tram to Dělnická, walk to the corner of Dělnická, and turn left. Beautiful, classy hostel with a huge, fully equipped kitchen. Free Wi-Fi. Dorms 350-420Kč; singles 1000Kč; doubles 2900Kč. MC/V. ❷

▨ **Hostel Boathouse,** Lodnická 1 (☎241 770 051; www.hostelboathouse.com). Take tram #3, 17,or 52 from Karlovo nám. south toward Sídliště. Get off at Černý Kůň (20min.), go down the ramp to the left, and follow the yellow signs. Social atmosphere, caring staff, and home-cooked meals. Breakfast included. Dorms from 420Kč. ❶

**Welcome Hostel at Strahov Complex,** Vaníčkova 7 (☎224 320 202; www.bed.cz). Take bus #149 or 217 from Metro A: Dejvická to Koleje Strahov (15min.) and cross the street to reach the hostel reception, located in Block 3. Right by an enormous stadium, Strahov is 10 concrete blocks of bright blue high-rise dormitories. Rooms are basic but clean and only 10min. by foot from Prague Castle. Not luxurious but sufficient. Open July-Sept. Singles 400Kč; doubles 500Kč. 10% ISIC discount. ❶

# HOTELS AND PENSIONS

Budget hotels are scarce, and generally the better hostel options offer more bang for your buck. Lower rates at hotels are often available if you call ahead.

**Dům U Krále Jiřího** (Hotel King George), Liliová 10 (☎222 220 925; www.kinggeorge.cz). Metro A: Staroměstská. Elegant rooms with private bath. Breakfast included. Reception 7am-11pm. Singles 2250Kč; doubles 3550Kč; triples 4950Kč; apartments 3550-7500Kč. Prices fall by 500-900Kč Nov.-Feb. ❺

**Pension Museum,** Mezibranská 15 (☎296 325 186; www.pension-museum.cz). Metro C: Muzeum. From the Metro, go right on Mezibranská and walk uphill; it's on the right. This ultra-modern B&B near Wenceslas Sq. is well worth the splurge. Beautiful court-

## THE LOCAL STORY

### BREW HA-HA

Tourists befuddled by visiting the Czech factory of the allegedly all-American Budweiser aren't alone in their confusion. In fact, they've stumbled upon one of the world's longest standing legal battles: who has the right to use the Budweiser name on their product.

The American version, first bottled under the name in 1876, reminded its brewer, Adolphus Busch, of the lagers from his German homeland; he therefore gave his beer a distinctly German name. While the Czech version received the name in 1895, the beer had been brewed in Budějovice since the 14th century. Initially, the identically titled beers did not compete with one another. But the increasing popularity of both products has led to heated court battles across the globe. The Czech version, banned in the United States by a 1939 agreement, has won out in much of the rest of the world. In Germany, Budweiser Budvar has rights to the name and Anheuser-Busch must sell its products under a different name. In the U.K., both companies have been permitted to hawk their products under the Budweiser name, leading to quite a bit of confusion. Needless to say, while in the Czech Republic, there is nary an American Budweiser in the land—and asking for it will not endear you to Czechs.

yard leads to elegant rooms with TVs and spacious baths. Reserve 1-2 months ahead. Apr.-Dec. singles 2460Kč; doubles 2920Kč; apartments 3000-6000Kč. Jan.-Mar. 1580/1970/2000-5000Kč. AmEx/MC/V. ❺

## CAMPING

Campgrounds can be found on the Vltava Islands as well as on the outskirts of Prague. Bungalows must be reserved ahead, but tent sites are generally available without prior notice. Tourist offices sell a guide to sites near the city (20Kč).

**Camp Sokol Troja**, Trojská 171 (☎233 542 908), north of the center in the Troja district. From Metro C: Nádraží Holešovice, take bus #112 and ask for Kazanka. Similar places line the road. Clean facilities. July-Aug. and Dec. tent sites 120Kč per person, 90-150Kč per tent site. Singles 330Kč; doubles 660Kč. Low season reduced rates. ❶

# 🍴 FOOD

The nearer you are to the city center, the more you'll pay. You will be charged for everything the waiter brings to the table; check your bill carefully. **Tesco**, Národní třída 26, has groceries. (Open M-F 7am-10pm, Sa 8am-8pm, Su 9am-8pm.) Look for the **daily market** in *Staré Město*. After a night out, grab a *párek v rohlíku* (hot dog) or a *smažený sýr* (fried cheese sandwich) from a Václavské nám. vendor.

## RESTAURANTS

### STARÉ MĚSTO

🏅 **Klub architektů,** Betlémské nám. 169/5A (☎224 401 214). Metro B: Národní třída. A 12th-century cellar with 21st-century ambience. Veggie options 70-150Kč. Meat entrees 160-320Kč. Open daily 11:30am-midnight. AmEx/MC/V. ❸

**Lehká Hlava (Clear Head),** Boršov 2 (☎222 220 665; www.lehkahlava.cz). Metro A: Staroměstská. Follow Křížovnická south past the Charles Bridge, bear left onto Karoliny Světle and turn left onto Boršov. Cooks up vegetarian and vegan cuisine that even devout carnivores will enjoy. Try the savory eggplant and cheese quesadilla with fresh guacamole (110Kč) and wash it down with a pint of fresh lemonade with mint (50Kč). Entrees 80-160Kč. Open M-F 11:30am-11:30pm, Sa-Su noon-11:30pm. Kitchen closed 2:30pm-5pm. Only cold food after 10pm. Cash only. ❷

**Country Life,** Melantrichova 15 (☎224 213 366; www.countrylife.cz). Metro A: Staroměstská. 3 fresh vegetarian buffets—hot, cold, and salad bar—are a welcome respite from meat-heavy Czech cuisine. Buffet 20-50Kč per 100g. Soup 20Kč. Juices from 20Kč. Open M-Th 9am-8:30pm, F 8:30am-5pm, Su 11am-8:30pm. Cash only. ❷

**Yami Restaurant,** Masná 3 (☎222 312 756) Metro A: Staroměstská. Some of the best and most reasonably priced sushi in Prague, Yami dishes up a wide variety of Japanese dishes in a Zen dining room. The courtyard holds 4 coveted tables behind a bamboo screen where diners devour Yami's creative fusion rolls (196-320Kč per 8pc.). Entrees 120-260Kč. Sushi 55-320Kč. Open daily noon-11pm. MC/V. ❸

**Cafe Bambus,** Benediktská 12 (☎224 828 110; www.cafebambus.com). Metro B: nám. Republiky. Patrons nosh on Thai and Indian dishes (around 130Kč) and Czech *palančinky* (crepes; 55-75Kč*)*. Beer from 42Kč. Good variety of alcoholic and non-alcoholic drinks. Open M-F 9am-2am, Sa 11am-2am, Su 11am-midnight. AmEx/MC/V. ❷

### NOVÉ MĚSTO

🏅 **Radost FX,** Bělehradská 120 (☎224 254 776; www.radostfx.cz). Metro C: I.P. Pavlova. A stylish dance club and late-night cafe with an imaginative menu and great vegetarian food. Entrees 120-195Kč. Brunch Sa-Su 50-200Kč. Open daily 9am-late. ❸

**Universal,** V. jirchářích 6 (☎224 934 416). Metro B: Národní třída. Asian, French, and Mediterranean cuisines served in an eclectically decorated dining room. Huge, fresh salads 131-195Kč. Entrees 150-300Kč. Su brunch buffet 185-205Kč. Open M-Sa 11:30am-1am, Su 11am-midnight. MC/V; min. 500Kč. ❸

**Ultramarin Grill,** Ostrovní 32 (☎224 932 249; www.ultramarin.cz). Metro B: Národní třída. With your back to the Metro, turn left and then immediately right on narrow Ostrovní. Classy decor without the prices to match. Many American dishes as well as Thai-inspired steak, duck, and lamb entrees 130-350Kč. Salads 100-180Kč. Open daily 10am-11pm. AmEx/MC/V. ❸

**Velryba** (The Whale), Opatovická 24. Metro B: Národní třída. Cross the tram tracks and follow Ostrovní, then go left onto Opatovická. Relaxed Italian/Czech restaurant with art gallery downstairs. Entrees 62-145Kč. Open daily 11am-midnight. MC/V. ❷

## MALÁ STRANA

**Bar bar,** Všehrdova 17 (☎257 313 246; www.barbar.cz). Metro A: Malostranská. From Malostranské nám., go down Karmelitská and left on Všehrdova. Reggae-inspired basement cafe with affordable international menu. Lunch noon-2pm 100Kč. Entrees 98-175Kč. Beer from 28Kč. Open Su-Th noon-midnight, F-Sa noon-2am. MC/V. ❷

**U Tří Černých Ruží,** Zámecká 5 (☎257 530 019; www.u3c.com). Metro A: Malostranská. At the foot of the New Castle steps. A small, quirky restaurant and bar that serves large portions and pours endless pints at low prices. Entrees 80-250Kč. Beer 25Kč. Open daily 11am-midnight. ❷

## CAFES AND TEAHOUSES

▧ **Cafe Rybka,** Opatovická 7. Metro B: Národní třída. Congenial corner cafe with a sea motif, fantastic coffee, and a tiny bookstore. Espresso 25Kč. Tea 22Kč. Open daily 9:15am-10pm. Cash only.

▧ **Cafe Ebel,** Řetězová 9 (☎603 441 434; www.ebelcoffee.cz). Metro A or B: Staroměstská. Ebel's espresso (40-50Kč) is blended in-house by people who clearly know what they're doing. Small selection of sandwiches and pastries. English spoken. Branch at Týnská 2. Both open M-F 8am-8pm, Sa-Su 8:30am-8pm. AmEx/MC/V.

**Kavárna Medúza,** Belgická 17. Metro A: nám. Míru. Walk down Rumunská and turn left at Belgická. Local clientele by day, hipsters by night. Coffee 19-30Kč. Crepes 52-70Kč. Open M-F 10am-1am, Sa-Su noon-1am. MC/V.

**U zeleného čaje,** Nerudova 19 (☎225 730 027). Metro A: Malostranská. From Malostranské nám., go down Nerudova. This adorable shop at the foot of Prague Castle takes tea to new heights. Serves up several alcohol-infused teas. Tea 35-75Kč. Open daily 11am-10pm. Cash only.

**Bakeshop Praha,** Kozí 1. Metro A: Staroměstská. From Staroměstské nám., follow Dlouhá to the intersection with Kozí. Mouth-watering pastries, salads, sandwiches, and quiches at incredibly reasonable prices. Branch at Lázenska 19. 10% extra to sit down. Open daily 7am-7pm.

# 👁 SIGHTS

Escape the crowds that flock to Prague's downtown sights by venturing away from **Staroměstské náměstí,** the **Charles Bridge,** and **Václavské náměstí.** There are plenty of attractions for visitors hidden in the old Jewish quarter of **Josefov,** the hills of **Vyšehrad,** and the streets of **Malá Strana.**

## STARÉ MĚSTO (OLD TOWN)

At midday, navigating the 1000-year-old **Staré Město** (Old Town)—a jumble of narrow streets and alleys—can be difficult. Once the sun sets, the ancient labyrinth comes alive with the city's youth, who enliven its many bars and jazz clubs.

**CHARLES BRIDGE.** Thronged with tourists and the hawkers who feed on them, the Charles Bridge (Karlův Most) is one of Prague's most treasured landmarks. The defense towers on each side offer splendid views. Five stars and a cross mark the spot where, according to legend, St. Jan Nepomuck was tossed over the side of the bridge for concealing the queen's extramarital secrets from a suspicious King Wenceslas IV in the 14th century. *(Metro A: Malostranská or Staroměstská.)*

**OLD TOWN SQUARE.** **Staroměstské náměstí** (Old Town Square) is the heart of Staré Město, surrounded by eight magnificent towers. *(Metro A: Staroměstská; Metro A or B: Můstek.)* Composed of several different architectural styles, the **Staroměstské Radnice** (Old Town Hall) has been missing a piece of its front facade since the Nazis partially demolished it in the final days of WWII. Crowds gather on the hour to watch the **astronomical clock** chime as skeletal Death empties his hourglass and a procession of apostles marches by. *(Exhibition hall open in summer M 10am-7pm, Tu-F 9am-7pm, Sa-Su 9am-6pm. Clock tower open daily 10am-6pm; enter through 3rd fl. of Old Town Hall. Exhibition hall 20Kč, students 10Kč. Clock tower 60/40Kč.)* The spires of **Týn Church** (Chrám Matky Boží před Týnem) rise above a mass of baroque homes. Buried inside is astronomer Tycho Brahe, whose overindulgence at Emperor Rudolf's lavish dinner party in 1601 may have cost him his life. Since it was deemed improper to leave the table unless the emperor himself did so, Tycho had to remain in his chair until his bladder burst. He died 11 days later, though scholars believe mercury poisoning may have been the culprit. *(Open M-F 9am-noon and 1-2pm. Mass July-Aug. W-F 6pm, Sa 8am, Su 11am, 12:30 and 9pm; Sept.-June W-F 6pm, Sa 8am, Su 11am and 9pm. Free.)* The bronze statue of 15th-century theologian **Jan Hus,** the country's most famous martyr, stands in the middle of the square. Barely a surface in **St. James's Church** (kostel sv. Jakuba) remains un-figured, un-marbleized, or unpainted. But keep your hands to yourself—legend has it that 500 years ago a thief tried to pilfer a gem from the Virgin Mary of Suffering, whereupon the figure sprang to life and yanked off his arm. *(Metro B: Staroměstská. On Malá Štupartská, behind Týn Church. Open M-Sa 10am-noon and 2–3:45pm. Mass Su 8, 9, and 10:30am.)*

# NOVÉ MĚSTO (NEW TOWN)

Established in 1348 by Charles IV, Nové Město has become Prague's commercial center. The Franciscan Gardens offer a calm oasis from the bustling businesses.

**WENCESLAS SQUARE.** More a commercial boulevard than a square, **Václavské náměstí** (Wenceslas Square) owes its name to the statue of 10th-century Czech ruler and patron **Saint Wenceslas** (Václav) that stands in front of the National Museum. At his feet in solemn prayer kneel smaller statues of the country's other patron saints: St. Agnes, St. Adalbert (Vojtěch), St. Ludmila, and St. Prokop. The sculptor, Josef Václav Myslbek, took 25 years to complete the statue. The inscription under St. Wenceslas reads, "Do not let us and our descendants perish." *(Metro A or B: Můstek or Metro A or C: Muzeum.)*

**FRANCISCAN GARDEN AND VELVET REVOLUTION MEMORIAL.** Franciscan monks somehow manage to preserve this serene **rose garden** in the heart of Prague's commercial district. *(Metro A or B: Můstek. Enter through the arch to the left of Jungmannova and Národní, behind the statue. Open daily mid-Apr. to mid-Sept. 7am-10pm; mid-Sept. to mid-Oct. 7am-8pm; mid-Oct. to mid-Apr. 8am-7pm. Free.)* Down the street on Národní, a **plaque** under the arcades and across from the Black Theatre memorializes the hundreds of citizens beaten by police in a 1989 protest. A subsequent wave of protests led to the collapse of communism in Czechoslovakia during the Velvet Revolution.

**DANCING HOUSE.** American architect Frank Gehry (of Guggenheim-Bilbao fame) built the gently swaying **Tančící dům** (Dancing House) at the corner of Resslova and Rašínovo nábřeží. Since its 1996 unveiling, it has been called an eyesore by some and a shining example of postmodern design by others. *(Metro B: Karlovo nám. As you walk down Resslova toward the river, the building is on the left.)*

## JOSEFOV

Josefov, Central Europe's oldest Jewish settlement, lies north of Staroměstské nám., along Maiselova. In 1180, Prague's citizens built a 4m wall around the area. The closed neighborhood bred exotic tales, many of which centered around **Rabbi Loew ben Bezalel** (1512-1609) and his legendary *golem*—a mud creature that supposedly came to life to protect Prague's Jews. The city's Jews remained clustered in Josefov until WWII, when the Nazis sent the residents to death camps. Ironically, Hitler's decision to create a "museum of an extinct race" sparked the preservation of Josefov's cemetery and synagogues.

**SYNAGOGUES.** The **Maiselova synagoga** (Maisel Synagogue) displays artifacts from the Jewish Museum's collections, only returned to the community in 1994. *(On Maiselova, between Široká and Jáchymova.)* Turn left on Široká to reach the **Pinkasova** (Pinkas Synagogue). Drawings by children interred at the Terezín camp are upstairs. Some 80,000 names line the walls downstairs, a sobering requiem for Czech Jews persecuted in the Holocaust. Backtrack along Široká and go left on Maiselova to reach Europe's oldest operating synagogue, the 700-year-old **Staronová** (Old-New Synagogue), still the religious center of Prague's Jewish community. Up Široká at Dušní, the **Španělská** (Spanish Synagogue) has an ornate Moorish interior and was first in adopting the 1830s Reform movement. *(Metro A: Staroměstská. Men must cover their heads; kippot free. Synagogues open M-F and Su Apr.-Oct. 9am-6pm; Nov.-Mar. 9am-4:30pm. Closed Jewish holidays. Admission to all synagogues except Staronová 290Kč, students 190Kč. Staronová 200/140Kč.)*

**OLD JEWISH CEMETERY.** Filled with thousands of broken headstones, the Old Jewish Cemetery (Starý židovský hřbitov) stretches between the Pinkas Synagogue and the Ceremonial Hall. Between the 14th and 18th centuries, the graves were dug in layers. The clustering tombstones visible today formed as older stones rose from beneath newer graves. Rabbi Loew is buried by the wall opposite the entrance. *(At the corner of Široká and Žatecká.)*

## MALÁ STRANA

Criminals and counter-revolutionaries' hangout for nearly a century, the cobblestone streets of Malá Strana have become prized real estate. In **Malostranské Náměstí,** the towering dome of the Baroque **St. Nicholas's Cathedral** (Chrám sv. Mikuláše) is one of Prague's most prominent landmarks. Mozart played the organ here when he visited Prague, and the cathedral now hosts nightly classical music concerts. *(Metro A: Malostranská. Follow Letenská to Malostranské nám. ☎ 257 534 215. Open daily 8:30am-4:45pm. 50Kč, students 25Kč. Concerts 390Kč/290Kč.)* Along Letenská, a wooden gate opens into the **Wallenstein Garden** (Valdštejnská zahrada). With a beautifully tended stretch of green and a bronze Venus fountain, this is one of the city's best-kept secrets. *(Letenská 10. Metro A: Malostranská. Open Apr.-Oct. daily 10am-6pm. Free.)* The **Church of Our Lady Victorious** (Kostel Panny Marie Vítězné) contains the famous wax statue of the **Infant Jesus of Prague,** said to bestow miracles on the faithful. *(Follow Letecká through Malostranské nám. and continue onto Karmelitská. ☎ 257 533 646. Open daily 8:30am-7pm. Catholic mass Su noon. Free.)* ▨ **Petřín Gardens and View Tower,** on the hill beside Malá Strana, provide a tranquil retreat with spectacular views. Climb the steep, serene footpath, or take the funicular from above the intersection of Vítězná and Újezd. *(Look for Lanovka Dráha signs. Funicular 4-6 per hr. 9am-11pm, 20Kč. Tower open daily 10am-10pm. Tower 50Kč, students 40Kč.)*

# PRAGUE CASTLE (PRAŽSKÝ HRAD)

Prague Castle, one of the world's biggest castles, has been the seat of the Czech government for over 1000 years. Since the first Bohemian royal family established their residence here in the 9th century, the castle has housed Holy Roman Emperors, the Communist Czechoslovak government, and now the Czech Republic's president. In the **Royal Gardens** (Královská zahrada), the **Singing Fountain** spouts its harp-like tune before the **Royal Summer Palace.** *(Trams #22 or 23 to Pražský Hrad and go down U Prašného Mostu. ☎ 224 373 368; www.hrad.cz. Castle open daily Apr.-Oct. 9am-5pm; Nov.-Mar. 9am-4pm. Royal Garden open Apr.-Oct. 24hr. Ticket office opposite St. Vitus's Cathedral, inside castle walls. Tickets valid for 2 days at all sites. 350Kč, students 175Kč.)*

**ST. VITUS'S CATHEDRAL.** Inside the castle walls stands the beautiful Gothic St. Vitus's Cathedral (Katedrála sv. Víta), which was completed in 1929, after 600 years of construction. To the right of the high altar stands the silver **tomb of St. Jan Nepomuck.** In the main church, precious stones and paintings telling the saint's story line the walls of **St. Wenceslas's Chapel** (Svatováclavská kaple). Climb the 287 steps of the **Great South Tower** for an excellent view, or descend underground to the **Royal Crypt** (Královská hrobka), which holds the tomb of Charles IV.

**OLD ROYAL PALACE.** The Old Royal Palace (Starý královský palác), to the right of the cathedral, is one of the Czech's few castles where visitors can wander largely unattended. The lengthy **Vladislav Hall** once hosted jousting competitions. Upstairs in the **Chancellery of Bohemia,** a Protestant assembly found two Catholic governor guilty of religious persecution and threw them out the window during the 1618 Second Defenestration of Prague. The men landed in a pile of manure and survived, but the event contributed to the beginning of the Thirty Years' War.

**ST. GEORGE'S BASILICA AND ENVIRONS.** Across the courtyard from the Old Royal Palace stands St. George's Basilica (Bazilika sv. Jiří), where the skeleton of St. Ludmila is on display. The convent next door houses the **National Gallery of Bohemian Art,** which displays pieces ranging from Gothic to Baroque. *(Open Tu-Su 10am-6pm. 100Kč, students 50Kč.)* To the right of the Basilica, follow Jiřská halfway down and take a right on tiny **Golden Lane** (Zlatá ulička), where alchemists once tried to perfect their art. Franz Kafka had his workspace at #22.

# OUTER PRAGUE

In the beautiful neighborhood of Troja, French architect J. B. Mathey's 17th-century **château** overlooks the Vltava. The building has a terraced garden, oval staircase, and a collection of 19th-century Czech artwork. *(Metro C: Nádraží Holešovice, take bus #112 to Zoologická Zahrada. Open Apr.-Oct. Tu-Su 10am-6pm; Nov.-Mar. Sa-Su 10am-5pm. 100Kč, students 50Kč.)* For wilder pursuits, venture next door to the **Prague Zoo.** *(Open daily 9am-7pm. Apr.-Sept. 80Kč, students 50Kč; Oct.-Mar. 50/30Kč.)* Guided by a divine dream to build a monastery atop a bubbling stream, King Boleslav II and St. Adalbert founded **Břevnov Monastery,** Bohemia's oldest, in AD 993. To the right of **St. Margaret's Church** (Bazilika sv. Markéty), the stream leads to a pond. *(Metro A: Malostranská. Take tram #22 to Břevnovský klášter. Church open for mass M-Sa 7am and 6pm, Su 7:30, 9am, and 6pm. Tours Sa-Su 10am, 2, 4pm. 50Kč, students 30Kč.)*

# 🏛 MUSEUMS

▓**MUCHA MUSEUM.** The museum is devoted to the work of Alfons Mucha, the Czech's most celebrated artist. Mucha, an Art Nouveau pioneer, gained fame for his poster series of "la divine" Sarah Bernhardt. *(Panská 7. Metro A or B: Můstek. Walk up Václavské nám. toward the St. Wenceslas statue. Go left on Jindřišská and left again on Panská. ☎ 221 451 333; www.mucha.cz. Open daily 10am-6pm. 120Kč, students 60Kč.)*

HEADING EAST

**⬛FRANZ KAFKA MUSEUM.** This fantastic multimedia exhibit of Kafka memorabilia uses photographs and original letters to bring visitors back to 19th-century Prague, as experienced by the renowned author. *(Cihelná 2b. Metro A: Malostranská. Go down Klárov toward the river, turn right on U. Luzické Semináré and left on Cilhená. ☎ 221 451 333; www.kafkamuseum.cz. Open daily 10am-6pm. 120Kč, students 60Kč.)*

**CITY GALLERY PRAGUE.** With seven locations throughout greater Prague, the City Gallery (Galerie Hlavního Města Prahy) offers a variety of permanent and rotating collections. The **House of the Golden Ring** has an especially massive permanent collection of 19th- and 20th-century Czech art. *(Týnská 6. Metro A: Staroměstská. Behind and to the left of Týn Church. ☎ 222 327 677; www.citygalleryprague.cz. Open Tu-Su 10am-6pm. Museum 70Kč; top 3 fl. 60Kč, students 30Kč; 1st Tu of each month free.)*

**MUSEUM OF ⬛COMMUNISM.** This gallery tries to expose the flaws of the Communist system that oppressed the Czech people from 1948 to 1989. Nowhere will you find more pitchforks or propaganda. *(Na Příkopě 10. Metro A: Můstek. ☎ 224 212 966; www.museumofcommunism.com. Open daily 8am-9pm. 180Kč, students 140Kč.)*

# 🎵 ENTERTAINMENT

To find info on Prague's concerts and performances, consult *The Prague Post*, *Threshold*, *Do města-Downtown*, or *The Pill* (all free at many cafes and restaurants). Most performances start at 7pm and offer standby tickets 30min. before curtain. Between mid-May and early June, the **Prague Spring Festival** (May 7-15, 2008) draws musicians from around the world. June brings all things avant-garde with the **Prague Fringe Festival** (☎224 935 183; www.praguefringe.com), featuring dancers, comedians, performance artists, and—everyone's favorite—mimes. For tickets to the city's shows, try **Bohemia Ticket International,** Malé nám. 13, next to Čedok. (☎224 227 832; www.ticketsbti.cz. Open M-F 9am-5pm, Sa 9am-1pm.)

**HIGH CULTURE, LOW BUDGET.** Prague's state-run theaters often hold a group of seats in the higher balconies until the day of the performance before selling them at reduced prices. By visiting your venue of choice the morning of a performance, you can often score tickets for as little as 50Kč.

The majority of Prague's theaters close in July and August, but the selection is extensive during the rest of the year. The **National Theater** (Národní divadlo), Národní 2/4, stages ballet, drama, and opera. (☎224 901 487; www.narodni-divadlo.cz. Metro B: Národní třída. Box office open Sept.-June daily 10am-8pm and 45min. before performances. Tickets 30-1000Kč.) Every performance at the **Image Theatre,** Pařížská 4, is silent, conveying the message through dance, pantomime, and creative use of black light. (☎222 314 448; www.blacktheatreprague.cz. Performances daily 8pm. Box office open daily 9am-8pm.) The **Marionette Theater** (Říše loutek), Žatecká 1, stages a hilarious version of *Don Giovanni*, now in its 15th season. (☎224 819 322. Metro A: Staroměstská. Performances June-July M-Tu and Th-Su 8pm. Box office open daily 10am-8pm. 490-600Kč, students 390-590Kč.)

# 🔊 NIGHTLIFE

With some of the world's best beer on tap, it's no surprise that pubs and beer halls are Prague's most popular nighttime hangouts. Tourists have overrun the city center, so authentic pub experiences are largely restricted to the suburbs and outlying Metro stops. Although clubs are everywhere, Prague isn't a prime dancing town—locals prefer the many jazz and rock hangouts scattered throughout the city.

## BARS

🔲 **Vinárna U Sudu,** Vodičkova 10 (☎222 237 207). Metro A or B: Můstek. Cross Václavské nám. to Vodičkova and follow the curve left. An infinite labyrinth of cavernous cellars. 1L red wine 125Kč. Open M-Th 8am-3am, F-Sa 8am-4am, Su 8am-2am. MC/V.

**Vinárna Vinečko,** Lodynská 135/2 (☎222 511 035). Metro A: Nám. Miru. Head west on Rumunská and turn left on Lodynská. A classy-feeling wine bar in the heart of the Vino-hrady district brimming with thirsty locals and expats. 0.2L wine 26-34Kč, bottle 64-92Kč. Open M-F 11am-midnight, Sa-Su 2pm-midnight. MC/V.

**Le Chateau,** Jakubská 2 (☎222 316 328). From Metro B: nám. Republiky, walk through the Powder Tower to Celetná, then take a right on Templová. Seductive red walls and a youthful clientele keep this place overflowing onto the street until dawn. Open M-Th noon-3am, F noon-6am, Sa 4pm-6am, Su 4pm-2am.

**Jo's Bar and Garáž,** Malostranské nám. 7. Metro A: Malostranská. Foosball, darts, card games, and a dance floor downstairs and American bar food upstairs—burgers, burritos, nachos, and steaks (60-295Kč). Beer from 31Kč. Long Island iced tea 115Kč. Open M-Th 11am-8pm, Sa-Su 11am-2am. AmEx/MC/V.

## CLUBS AND DISCOS

🔲 **Radost FX,** Bělehradská 120 (☎224 254 776; www.radostfx.cz). Metro C: IP Pavlova. Radost is the best of Prague nightlife, playing only the hippest music from internation-ally renowned DJs. The spacious, ventilated chill-out room is perfect for taking a break from the dance floor. Creative drinks (Frozen Sex with an Alien 140Kč) will expand your clubbing horizons. Cover from 100Kč. Open M-Sa 10pm-5am.

**Karlovy Lázně,** Novotného lávka 1, next to the Charles Bridge. Popularly known as "Five Floors," this tourist magnet boasts 5 levels of sweaty, themed dance floors. Cover 120Kč, 50Kč before 10pm and after 4am. Open daily 9pm-5am.

**Roxy,** Dlouhá 33. Metro B: nám. Republiky. Same building as the Travellers' Hostel (p. 1024). Hip, youthful studio and club with experimental DJs and theme nights. Beer 35Kč. Cover Tu and Th-Sa 100-350Kč. Open daily 10pm-late.

**Mecca,** U Průhonu 3 (☎283 870 522; www.mecca.cz). Metro C: Nádraží Holešovice. The place for Prague's beautiful celebrities to gather until the wee hours, Mecca offers a tastefully packed house, with industrial-chic decoration lit by every color of neon imag-inable. House music dominates with some techno. Live DJs nightly. Open 9pm-late.

**U Malého Glena II,** Karmelitská 23 (☎257 531 717; www.malyglen.cz), near Prague Castle. Basement bar with nightly live music including blues, jazz, and salsa. Call ahead for weekend tables. Beer 35Kč. Entrees 95-130Kč. Shows at 9:30pm, F-Sa 10pm-1:30am. Cover 100-150Kč. Open daily 8pm-2am. AmEx/MC/V.

## GLBT NIGHTLIFE

All of the places below distribute *Amigo* (90Kč; www.amigo.cz), the most thor-ough English-language guide to gay life in the Czech Republic. Check www.pra-guegayguide.net or www.praguesaints.cz for a list of attractions and resources.

**The Saints,** Polská 32 (☎332 250 326; www.praguesaints.cz). Metro A: Jiřího z Poděbrad. This small, comfy club welcomes GLBT visitors and organizes the GLBT com-munity. Foreign and local crowd. Free Wi-Fi. Beer from 22Kč. Open daily 7pm-4am.

**Friends,** Bartolomejská 11 (☎224 236 272; www.friends-prague.cz). Metro B: Národní třída. From the station, turn right, head down Na Perštýně, and take a left on Bartolom-ejská. Rotating schedule features music videos, parties, and theme nights. Women and straight customers welcome, but rare. Beer from 30Kč. Open daily 6pm-5am.

**Valentino,** Vinohradská ul. 40 (☎222 513 491; www.club-valentino.cz). Metro A or C: Muzeum. The Czech Republic's largest gay club draws crowds to its 4 bars and 3 levels. House music dominates the packed and sweaty dance floors, although rotating DJs spice it up. Chill downstairs or at the outside tables. No cover. Open daily 11am-late.

# ■ DAYTRIPS FROM PRAGUE

**TEREZÍN (THERESIENSTADT).** In 1941, when the Nazis opened a concentration camp at Terezín, their propaganda films touted the area as a resort. In reality, over 30,000 Jews died there, while another 85,000 were transported to camps farther east. The **Ghetto Museum,** left of the bus stop, places Terezín in the wider context of WWII. Across the river, the **Small Fortress** was used as a Gestapo prison. *(Bus from Prague's Florenc station to the Terezín LT stop. 1hr., 70Kč. Museum and barracks open daily Apr.-Oct. 9am-6pm; Nov.-Mar. 9am-5:30pm. Fortress open daily Apr.-Oct. 8am-6pm; Nov.-Mar. 8am-4:30pm. Tour included in admission price for groups larger than 10; reserve ahead. Museum, barracks, and fortress 180Kč, students 140Kč.)* Outside the walls lie the incredibly moving **cemetery** and **crematorium.** Men should cover their heads before entering. *(Open Su-F Apr.-Sept. 10am-5pm; Nov.-Mar. 10am-4pm. Free.)* Since WWII, Terezín has been repopulated to about half its former size. Families live in the former barracks, and supermarkets occupy old Nazi offices. The **tourist office,** nám. ČSA 179, is near the bus stop. *(☎416 782 616; www.terezin.cz. Open M-Th 8am-5pm, F 8am-1:30pm, Su 9am-3pm.)*

**KARLŠTEJN.** Charles IV built Karlštejn fortress in the 14th century. To reach it, turn right from the train station and go left over the bridge; turn right and walk through the village for 25min. *(Train from Hlavní nádraží 55min., 4 per day, 50Kč. ☎311 681 617; www.hradkarlstejn.cz. Open Tu-Su July-Aug. 9am–noon and 12:30-6pm; May-June and Sept. 9am–noon and 12:30-5pm; Apr. and Oct. 9am–noon and 1-4pm; Jan.-Mar. 9am–noon and 1-3pm. Mandatory English-language tours 7-8 per day, 220Kč, children 150Kč.)* The **Chapel of the Holy Cross** houses the castle's precious jewels and holy relics. *(☎274 008 154; rezervace@stc.npu.cz. Chapel tours July-Oct. by reservation only. 300Kč, children 150Kč. MC/V.)*

**ČESKÝ RÁJ NATIONAL PRESERVE.** The sandstone pillars and gorges of **Prachovské skály** (Prachovské rocks) offer climbs and hikes with stunning views. Highlights include the **Pelíšek** rock pond and the ruins of the 14th-century **Pařez** castle. A network of **trails** cross the 588 acres of the park; green, blue, and yellow signs guide hikers to sights, while triangles indicate scenic vistas. Red signs mark the "Golden Trail," which connects Prachovské skály to **Hrubá Skála** (Rough Rock), a rock town surrounding a castle. From the castle, the trail leads up to the remains of **Valdštejnský Hrad** (Wallenstein Castle). The red and blue trails are open to cyclists, but only the blue trail is suited for biking. *(Buses run from Prague's Florenc station to Jičín. From there, buses go to Prachovské skály and other spots in Český Ráj. Buses can be unpredictable; you can walk along a 6km trail from Motel Rumcajs, Konwva 331, to the Preserve.)*

# HUNGARY

## ESSENTIALS

**EMBASSIES AND CONSULATES.** Foreign embassies to Hungary are in Budapest (see p. 1037). Hungary's embassies and consulates abroad include: **Australia,** 17 Beale Crescent, Deakin, ACT 2600 (☎62 82 32 26; www.mata.com.au/~hungemb);

## FACTS AND FIGURES

**Official Name:** Hungary.
**Capital:** Budapest.
**Major Cities:** Debrecen, Miskolc, Szeged.
**Population:** 9,957,000.

**Time Zone:** GMT + 1.
**Language:** Hungarian.
**Country code:** ☎36.
**Number of McDonald's Restaurants:** 76.

**Canada,** 299 Waverley St., Ottawa, ON K2P 0V9 (☎613-230-2717; www.docuweb.ca/Hungary); **Ireland,** 2 Fitzwilliam Pl., Dublin 2 (☎661 2902; www.kum.hu/dublin); **New Zealand,** Consulate-General, 37 Abbott St., Wellington 6004 (☎973 7507; www.hungarianconsulate.co.nz); **UK,** 35 Eaton Pl., London SW1X 8BY (☎20 72 35 52 18; www.huemblon.org.uk); **US,** 3910 Shoemaker St., NW, Washington, D.C. 20008 (☎202-362-6730; www.hungaryembwas.org)

| HUNGARY | ❶ | ❷ | ❸ | ❹ | ❺ |
|---|---|---|---|---|---|
| **ACCOMMODATIONS** | under 2500Ft | 2500-4000Ft | 4001-7000Ft | 7001-12,000Ft | over 12,000Ft |
| **FOOD** | under 600Ft | 600-1200Ft | 1201-2000Ft | 2001-3200Ft | over 3200Ft |

**HUNGARIAN FORINTS (FT)**

| | |
|---|---|
| AUS$1 = 155.96FT | 1000FT = AUS$6.41 |
| CDN$1 = 173.71FT | 1000FT = CDN$5.76 |
| EUR€1 = 250.43FT | 1000FT = EUR€3.99 |
| NZ$1 = 138.24FT | 1000FT = NZ$7.23 |
| UK£1 = 371.214FT | 1000FT = UK£2.69 |
| US$1 = 182.99FT | 1000FT = US$5.46 |

**VISA AND ENTRY INFORMATION.** Citizens of Australia, Canada, Ireland, New Zealand, and the US can visit Hungary without visas for up to 90 days; UK citizens for up to 180 days. Consult your embassy for longer stays. Passports must be valid for six months after the end of the trip. There is no fee for crossing a Hungarian border. In general, border officials are efficient; plan on 30min. crossing time.

# BUDAPEST                                                         ☎01

While other parts of Hungary maintain a slow pace of life, Budapest (pop. 1.9 million) has seized upon cosmopolitan chic with a vengeance without giving up its old-time charms. Unlike in toyland Prague, the sights of Budapest spread throughout the energetic city, giving it a life independent of the growing crowds of tourists; Turkish thermal baths and Roman ruins mix seamlessly with modern buildings and a legendary night scene. The area now considered Budapest was once two entities: the pasture-ruled city of Pest and viticulture hills of Buda. In 1873, the two areas separated by the Danube were unified by a Habsburg initiative. Although the city was ravaged by WWII, Hungarians rebuilt it, and then weathered a Soviet invasion and 40 years of Communism. That resilient spirit resonates through the streets as the city reassumes its place as a major European capital.

## ◨ TRANSPORTATION

**Flights: Ferihegy Airport (BUD;** ☎296 9696). **Malév** (Hungarian Airlines; reservations ☎235 3888) flies to major cities. To the center, take **bus** #93 (20min., every 15min. 4:55am-11:20pm, 260Ft), then M3 to Kőbánya-Kispest (15min. to Deák tér, in downtown Budapest). **Airport Minibus** (☎296 8555) goes to hotels or hostels (2300Ft).

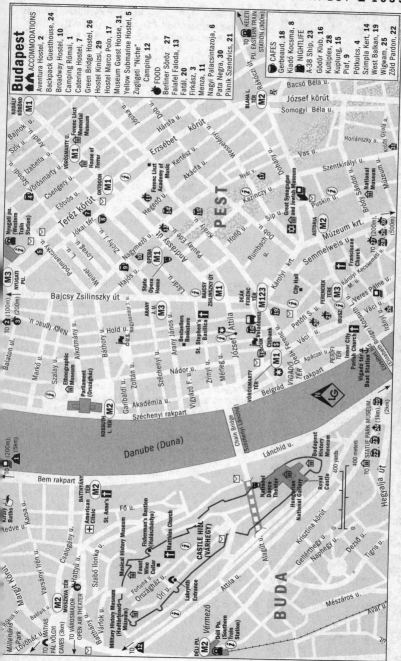

### Budapest

**ACCOMMODATIONS**
Aventura Hostel, 2
Backpack Guesthouse, 24
Broadway Hostel, 10
Camping Római, 1
Caterina Hostel, 7
Green Bridge Hostel, 26
Hostel Kinizsi, 29
Hostel Marco Polo, 17
Museum Guest House, 31
Yellow Submarine Hostel, 5
Zugligeti "Niche" Camping, 12

**FOOD**
Berliner Söröz, 27
Falafel Faloda, 13
Fatál, 20
Firkász, 3
Menza, 11
Nagyi Palacsintazója, 6
Pata Negra, 30
Piknik Szendvics, 21

**CAFES**
Gerbeaud, 18
Kiadó Kocsma, 8

**NIGHTLIFE**
A-38 Ship, 23
Gödör Klub, 16
Kultiplex, 28
Kuplung, 15
Piaf, 9
Pótkulcs, 4
Szimpla Kert, 14
West Balkan, 19
Wigwam, 25
Zöld Pardon, 22

## REVISITING THE GYPSY FOLKTALE

Eastern Europe is home to an estimated seven to nine million gypsies, or Roma, making them the region's largest minority group. In Hungary, they account for 9-11% of the population. Roma are believed to have migrated from India, and they have been living in Europe for centuries, particularly in the Balkans. The scarf-clad gypsies have long been a staple character in Eastern European folk tales, stereotypically cast as colorful roving musician-types.

In reality, the Roma story is not so rosy—they have long been victims of extreme discrimination, with inadequate access to housing, jobs, public education, and healthcare. At its most extreme, this discrimination has taken the form of forced sterilization or racially motivated murders.

The plight of the Roma is beginning to generate a worldwide outcry. The first large-scale conference to address the situation was held in Budapest in 2003. Delegates from eight Eastern European countries and international NGOs joined forces to launch the "Decade of Roma Inclusion," beginning in 2005. It aims to "change the lives of Roma" across the region and reduce poverty and illiteracy. Recent news updates suggest that the Roma are slowly on the path to an improved socioeconomic status. (*See www.romadecade.com for info.*)

**Trains:** Major stations are **Keleti Pályaudvar, Nyugati Pályaudvar,** and **Déli Pályaudvar.** (International and domestic information ☎40 49 49 49.) Most international trains arrive at Keleti pu., but some from Prague go to Nyugati pu. For schedules, check www.elvira.hu. To: **Berlin, GER** (12-15hr.; 2 per day; 28,305Ft, reservation 765Ft); **Bucharest, ROM** (14hr., 5 per day, 19,482Ft); **Prague, CZR** (8hr., 4 per day, 11,700Ft); **Vienna, AUT** (3hr.; 17 per day; 3315Ft); **Warsaw, POL** (11hr.; 2 per day; 18,411Ft). The daily **Orient Express** stops on its way from **Paris, FRA** to **Istanbul, TUR.** Trains run to most major destinations in Hungary. Purchase tickets at an **International Ticket Office** (Keleti pu. open daily 8am-7pm; Nyugati pu. open M-Sa 5am-9pm; info desk 24hr.). Or try **MÁV Hungarian Railways,** VI, Andrássy út 35, with branches at all stations. (☎461 5500. Open Apr.-Sept. M-F 9am-6pm, Oct.-Mar. M-F 9am-5pm. Say *"diák"* for student or under-26 discounts.) The HÉV **commuter railway** station is at Batthyány tér, opposite Parliament. Trains head to **Szentendre** (45min., every 15min. 5am-9pm, 460Ft). Purchase tickets at the station for transport beyond the city limits.

**Buses:** Buses to international and some domestic destinations leave from the **Népliget** station, X, Ulloi u. 131. (M3: Népliget. ☎382 0888. Ticket window open M-F 6am-9pm, Sa-Su 6am-4pm.) To **Berlin, GER** (14½hr., 6 per week, 17,010Ft); **Prague, CZR** (8hr., 6 per week, 9810Ft); **Vienna, AUT** (3-3½hr., 5 per day, 2950Ft). Catch buses to destinations east of Budapest at the **Népstadion** station, XIV, Hungária körút 46-48. (M2: Népstadion. ☎252 4498. Open M-F 6am-6pm, Sa-Su 6am-4pm.) Buses to the Danube Bend and parts of the Uplands depart outside **Árpád híd** metro station on the M3 line. (☎329 1450. Cashier open 6am-8pm.) Check www.volanbusz.hu for schedules.

**Public Transportation: Subways, buses,** and **trams** are cheap and convenient. The **metro** has 3 lines: M1 (yellow), M2 (red), and M3 (blue). Night transit (É) buses run midnight-5am along major routes: #7É and 78É follow the M2 route; #6É follows the 4/6 tram line; #14É and 50É follow the M3 route. **Single-fare tickets** for public transport (one-way on 1 line; 230Ft, trams 160Ft) are sold in metro stations, in *Trafik* shops, and by sidewalk vendors. Punch them in the orange boxes at the gate of the metro or on buses and trams; punch a new ticket when you change lines, or face fines. One-way tickets are cheaper in blocks of 10 or 20. Day pass 1350Ft, 3-day 3100Ft, 1-week 3600Ft, 2-week 4800Ft, 1-month 7350Ft.

**Taxis:** Beware of scams; check for a yellow license plate and running meter. **Budataxi** (☎222 4444) charges less for rides requested by phone. Also reliable are **Főtaxi** (☎222 2222), **6x6 Taxi** (☎466 6666), and **Tele 5 Taxi** (☎355 5555). Prices should not exceed: base fare 300Ft, 350Ft per km, 70Ft per min. waiting.

## ⚡ ORIENTATION

Buda and Pest are separated by the **Danube River** (Duna), and the modern city preserves the distinctive character of each side. On the west bank, **Buda** has winding streets, beautiful vistas, a hilltop citadel, and the Castle District. Down the north slope of **Várhegy** (Castle Hill) is **Moszkva tér**, Buda's tram and local bus hub. On the east bank, **Pest**, the commercial center, is home to shopping boulevards, theaters, Parliament (Országház), and the Opera House. Metro lines converge in Pest at **Deák tér**, next to the main international bus terminal at **Erzsébet tér**. Two blocks west toward the river lies **Vörösmarty tér** and the pedestrian shopping zone **Váci utca**. Three main bridges join Budapest's halves: **Széchenyi Lánchíd** (Chain Bridge), **Erzsébet híd** (Elizabeth Bridge), and **Szabadság híd** (Freedom Bridge).

Budapest addresses begin with a Roman numeral representing one of the city's 23 **districts**. Central Buda is I; central Pest is V. A **map** is essential for navigating Budapest's confusing streets; pick one up at any tourist office or hostel.

## 🛈 PRACTICAL INFORMATION

**Tourist Offices:** All offices sell the **Budapest Card** (Budapest Kártya), which provides discounts, unlimited public transportation, and admission to most museums (2-day card 6450Ft, 3-day 7950Ft.). A great deal, except on M when museums are closed. An excellent 1st stop in the city is **Tourinform**, V, Sütő u. 2 (☎438 8080; www.hungary.com). M1, 2, or 3: Deák tér. Off Deák tér behind McDonald's. Open daily 8am-8pm. **Vista Travel Center**, Andrássy út 1 (☎429 9751; incoming@vista.hu), arranges tours and accommodations. Open M-F 9am-6:30pm, Sa 9am-2:30pm. ▣ **Budapest in Your Pocket** (www.inyourpocket.com) is an up-to-date city guide.

**Embassies and Consulates: Australia**, XII, Királyhágó tér 8/9 (☎457 9777; www.australia.hu). M2: Déli pu., then bus #21 or tram #59 to Királyhágó tér. Open M-F 9amnoon. **Canada**, XII, Ganz u. 12-14 (☎392 3360). Open M-Th 8:30-10:30am and 2-3:30pm. **Ireland**, V, Szabadság tér 7 (☎302 9600), in Bank Center. M3: Arany János. Walk down Bank u. toward the river. Open M-F 9:30am-12:30pm and 2:30-4:30pm. **New Zealand**, VI, Nagymezo u. 50 (☎302 2484). M3: Nyugati pu. Open M-F 11am-4pm by appointment only. **UK**, V, Harmincad u. 6 (☎266 2888; www.britemb.hu), near the intersection with Vörösmarty tér. M1: Vörösmarty tér. Open M-F 9:30am-12:30pm and 2:30-4:30pm. **US**, V, Szabadság tér 12 (☎475 4164, after hours 475 4703; www.usembassy.hu). M2: Kossuth tér. Walk 2 blocks on Akadémia and turn on Zoltán. Open M-Th 1-4pm, F 9am-noon and 1-4pm.

**Currency Exchange:** Banks have the best rates. **Citibank**, V, Vörösmarty tér 4 (☎374 5000). M1: Vörösmarty tér. Cashes traveler's checks for no commission and provides MC/V cash advances. Bring your passport. Open M-Th 9am-5pm, F 9am-4pm.

**Luggage Storage: Lockers** at all 3 train stations. 150-600Ft.

**English-Language Bookstore: Libri Könyvpalota**, VII, Rákóczi u. 12 (☎267 4843). M2: Astoria. The best choice in the city; a multilevel bookstore, it has 1 fl. of up-to-date English titles. Open M-F 10am-7:30pm, Sa 10am-3pm. MC/V.

**GLBT Hotline: GayGuide.net Budapest** (☎06 30 93 23 334; www.budapest.gayguide.net). Posts an online guide and runs a hotline (daily 4-8pm) with info and reservations at GLBT-friendly lodgings.

**Tourist Police:** V, Sütő u. 2 (☎438 8080). M1, 2, or 3: Deák tér. Inside the Tourin-form office. Open 24hr. Beware of people on the street pretending to be Tourist Police and demanding to see your passport.

**Pharmacies:** Look for green-and-white signs labeled *Apotheke, Gyógyszertár,* or *Pharmacie.* Minimal after-hours service fees apply. **II,** Frankel Leó út 22 (☎212 4406). AmEx/MC/V. **VI,** Teréz krt. 41 (☎311 4439). Open M-F 8am-8pm, Sa 8am-2pm. **VII,** Rákóczi út 39 (☎314 3695). Open M-F 7:30am-9pm, Sa 7:30am-2pm; no after-hours service.

**Medical Services: Falck (SOS) KFT,** II, Kapy út 49/b (☎275 1535). Ambulance service US$120. **American Clinic,** I, Hattyú u. 14 (☎224 9090; www.americanclinics.com). Open M 8:30am-7pm, Tu-W 10am-6pm, Th 11:30am-6pm, F 10am-6pm. 24hr. emergency ☎224 9090. The US embassy also maintains a list of English-speaking doctors.

**Telephones: Phone cards** are sold at kiosks and metro stations. 50-unit card 800Ft, 120-unit card 1800Ft. Domestic operator and info ☎198; international operator 190, info 199.

**Internet Access:** Internet cafes are everywhere, but they can be expensive and long waits are common. **Ami Internet Coffee,** V, Váci u. 40 (☎267 1644; www.amicoffee.hu). M3: Ferenciek tér. 200Ft per 15min., 700Ft per hr. Open daily 9am-2am.

**Post Office:** V, Városház u. 18 (☎318 4811). **Poste Restante** (Postán Mar) in office around the right side of the building. Open M-F 8am-8pm, Sa 8am-2pm. Branches at Nyugati pu.; VI, Teréz krt. 105/107; Keleti pu.; VIII, Baross tér 11/c; and elsewhere. Open M-F 7am-8pm, Sa 8am-2pm. **Postal Code:** Depends on the district—postal codes are 1XX2, where XX is the district number (1052 for post office listed above).

## ACCOMMODATIONS AND CAMPING

Budapest's hostels are centers for the backpacker social scene, and their common rooms can be as exciting as most bars and clubs. Many hostels are run by the **Hungarian Youth Hostels Association (HI),** which operates from an office in Keleti pu. Representatives wearing Hostelling International shirts—and legions of competitors—accost travelers as they get off the train. Beware that they may provide inaccurate descriptions of other accommodations in order to sell their own. Private rooms are more expensive than hostels, but they do offer peace, quiet, and private showers. Arrive early, bring cash, and haggle. ▨**Best Hotel Service,** V, Sütő u. 2, arranges apartment, hostel, and hotel reservations (6000Ft and up). Take M1, 2, or 3 to Deák tér. (☎318 4848; www.besthotelservice.hu. Open daily 8am-8pm.)

▨ **Backpack Guesthouse,** XI, Takács Menyhért u. 33 (☎385 8946; www.backpackers.hu), 12min. from central Pest. Common room stocked with movies and a slew of hammocks in an inner garden make this neighborhood house a quiet, earthy hideaway from the traffic of the city. The 49E night bus runs here after trams stop. Laundry 1500Ft. Free Internet. Reception 24hr. Mattress in gazebo 2500Ft; 7- to 11-bed dorms 3000Ft, 4- to 5-bed dorms 3500Ft; doubles 9000Ft. MC/V. ❷

▨ **Aventura Hostel,** XIII, Visegrádi u. 12 (☎703 102 003; www.aventurahostel.com), in Pest. M3: Nyugati tér. Tasteful interior design and clean bathrooms. Provides info on special event and party listings around town. Breakfast included. Laundry 1500Ft. Free Internet. Reception 24hr. Dorms 3500-4500Ft; doubles 12,500Ft. Cash only. ❸

**Yellow Submarine Hostel,** VI, Podmaniczky u. 27, 1st floor (☎331 9896, www.yellow-submarinehostel.com). It's known as a party hostel, and rowdy crowds hang out in the common room. Large dorms with bunk beds and lockers. Doubles and triples in nearby apartments. Breakfast included for dorms. Laundry 1700 Ft. Internet 10Ft per min. Check-out 10am. Dorms 3000Ft; singles 8000Ft; doubles 9600Ft; triples 11,100Ft; quads 14,800Ft. 10% HI discount. MC/V. ❷

**Green Bridge Hostel,** V, Molnár u. 22-24 (☎266 6922; greenbridge@freemail.hu), in Pest's central district. Unbeatable location, friendly staff, and free snacks. Free Internet. Reception 24hr. Reserve ahead. Dorms 3750-4500Ft. Cash only. ❸

**Museum Guest House,** VIII, Mikszáth Kálmán tér 4, 1st fl. (☎318 9508; museumgh@freemail.c3.hu), in Pest. M3: Kálvin tér. Convenient location, colorful rooms, and loft beds. English spoken. Free Internet. Reception 24hr. Check-out 11am. Reserve ahead. Dorms 3200Ft. Cash only. ❸

**Broadway Hostel,** VI, Ó u. 24-26 (☎688 1662; www.broadwayhostel.hu), in Pest's theater district. M1: Opera. A new, luxurious alternative to the backpacking scene, with curtain partitions, fluffy comforters, and lockable closets. Inner courtyard with hammocks provides a laid-back hangout. Internet 250Ft per 30min. Reception 24hr. Check-out 10:30am. Dorms 3200-3300Ft; singles 5500Ft; doubles 9500Ft. Cash only. ❷

**Red Bus Hostel,** V, Semmelweis u. 14 (☎266 0136; www.redbusbudapest.hu). Newly renovated hardwood-floor rooms on a quiet street near the action of downtown Pest. A large common room provides a hangout for travelers. Kitchen available. Breakfast included. Free luggage storage. Laundry 1300Ft. Internet 10Ft per min. Reception 24hr. Check-out 10am. Dorms 3600Ft; singles and doubles 9500Ft; triples 11,350Ft. V. ❷

**Caterina Hostel,** III, Teréz krt. 30, apt. #28, ring code: #48 (☎269 5990; www.caterinahostel.hu). M1: Oktogon, or trams #4 or 6. Rooms open to an inner courtyard on the 3rd fl. of an apartment building. Fresh linens and in-room TVs. Transport to airport 2000Ft. English spoken. Laundry 1400Ft. Free Internet. Reception 24hr. Check-out 10am. Lockout 10am-1pm. Dorms 2500-3000Ft; private rooms 6800Ft. Cash only. ❷

**Hostel Marco Polo,** VII, Nyár u. 6 (☎413 2555; www.marcopolohostel.com). M2: Astoria or Blaha Lujza tér. Hotelesque and more private than other hostels, as dorm bunks are in separate compartments blocked off by curtains. Courtyard patio and basement restaurant with bar open 24hr. Laundry 600Ft. Internet 250 per 30min. Reception 24hr. Reserve ahead July-Aug. Dorms 4400Ft; singles 15,400Ft; doubles 19,200Ft; triples 21,000Ft; quads 25,400Ft. 400Ft ISIC discount. Cash only. ❸

**Hostel Kinizsi,** IX, Kinizsi u. 2-6 (☎933 0660, www.kinizsi.uni-corvinus.hu). In an artsy district, a block from the Museum of Applied Arts, this university dorm is across the street from the Danube and 2 tram stops from the Palace of Arts. Large common room and adjoining cafe open late draw many backpackers out of their rooms to chat and mingle. 5500Ft shuttle service to airport. Check-out 10am. 5-bed dorm 3200Ft; triples 3400Ft; doubles 3600Ft. Open July-Aug. Cash only. ❶

**Camping Római,** III, Szentendrei út. 189 (☎388 7167). M2: Batthyány tér. Take HÉV to Római fürdő; walk 100m toward river. If you're looking to get away from the buzz of the city, this campground offers a huge complex with swimming pool, park, and nearby grocery store and restaurants. Laundry 800Ft. Tent sites 4400Ft per person; bungalows 3000Ft per person. Cars 4710Ft. Electricity included. 3% tourist tax. 10% HI discount. Reserve far ahead as campsites fill up quickly in the summer. ❸

**Zugligeti "Niche" Camping,** XII, Zugligeti út 101 (☎/fax 200 8346; www.campingniche.hu). Take bus #158 from above Moszkva tér to Laszállóhely, the last stop. Communal showers. 1400Ft per person, 990Ft per tent, 1400Ft per large tent, 1050Ft per car, 2550Ft per caravan. Cash only. ❶

# ⬧ HUNGARY?

Cafeterias with *"Önkiszolgáló Étterem"* signs serve cheap food (entrees 300-500Ft), and a neighborhood *kifőzés* (kiosk) or *vendéglő* (family-style restaurant) offers a real taste of Hungary. Corner markets, many with 24hr. windows, stock the basics. The ■**Grand Market Hall,** IX, Fövam tér 1/3, next to Szabadság híd (M3: Kálvin tér), has two and a half acres of stalls, making it an attraction in itself. Ethnic restaurants inhabit the upper floors of **Mammut Plaza,** just outside the Moszkva tér metro in Buda, and **West End Plaza,** near the Nyugati metro in Pest.

## RESTAURANTS

■ **Fatál,** V, Váci u. 67 (☎266 2607), in Pest. M3: Ferenciek tér. Enormous portions of down-home, delicious Hungarian cuisine in a cool underground setting, off hustling Váci u. Entrees 590-2500Ft. Open daily 11:30am-2am. MC/V. ❷

■ **Nagyi Palacsintazoja,** II, Hattyu u. 16 (☎201 5321), in Buda. M2: Moszkva tér. Tiny, mirror-covered eatery dishes out sweet and savory crepes (118-298Ft) piled with toppings like cheese, fruit, or chocolate sauce. Open 24hr. ❶

**Berliner Söröző,** IX, Ráday u. 5 (☎217 6757; www.berliner.hu). Mix of old-school Hungarian flavors and smooth Belgian drafts. Lively patio lets you enjoy summer nights. Beer 400Ft. Open M-Sa noon-1am. Cash only. ❸

**Firkász,** XIII, Tátra u. 18 (☎450 1118; www.firkaszetterem.hu). The most traditional Hungarian restaurant in the city, from its paprika-infused dishes to its white, delicately embroidered table cloths. Try stuffed cabbage (1200Ft). Entrees 800Ft-3000Ft. Open daily noon-midnight. Cash only. ❸

**Pata Negra,** IX, Kávin tér 8 (www.patanegra.hu). This Spanish restaurant stands at the center of Kávin tér. Tapas (300Ft-580Ft) on a patio that gives guests subtle glimpses of the Freedom Bridge in the distance. Entrees (300Ft-1900Ft) are dirt cheap and daringly Latin. Open M-Th and Su 11am-midnight, F-Sa noon-midnight. Cash only. ❶

**Menza,** Liszt Ferenc tér 2 (☎413 1482; www.menza.co.hu). Reminiscent of Communist-era *menza*, or canteens, this elegant eatery's decor offers a mix of 70s camp and modern chic. Menu boards list all manner of excellent Hungarian and international dishes on offer. Entrees 650-1790Ft. Open daily 10am-1am. AmEx/MC/V. ❷

**Falafel Faloda,** VI. Paulay Ede u. 53 (☎351 1243), in Pest. M1: Opera. Vegetarians come in droves for on-the-go falafel (20Ft) and the city's best salad bar. Salads 280-420Ft. Smoothies 290-350Ft and a wide selection of teas 180-220Ft. Open M-F 10am-8pm, Sa 10am-6pm. Cash only. ❶

**Piknik Szendvics,** V, Haris Köz 1 (☎318 3334; www.piknik-szendvics.hu), in Pest. M3: Ferenciek tér. Create a meal from inexpensive appetizer-sized open-faced sandwiches (120-290Ft). Open M-F 9am-6pm, Sa 9am-2pm. Cash only. ❶

## CAFES

Once the haunts of the literary, intellectual, and cultural elite—as well as political dissidents—Budapest's cafes boast mysterious histories and delicious pastries.

**Kiadó Kocsma,** VI, Jókai tér 3 (☎331 1955), in Pest, next to Cafe Alhambra. M1: Oktogon. Irresistibly playful atmosphere and tranquil, shady terrace, perfect for coffee (250Ft), tea (200Ft), or spirits (550-700Ft) as well as light, Hungarian-style snacks (390-590Ft) or crazy twists on Hungarian entrees try the salami and mushroom *gnocchi* with mascarpone sauce (2490Ft). Open daily 5pm-2am. MC/V.

**Gerbeaud,** V, Vörösmarty tér 7 (☎429 9020; www.gerbeaud.hu). M1: Vörösmarty tér. Hungary's most famous cafe and dessert shop has served delicious, homemade layer cakes (680Ft) and ice cream (260Ft) since 1858. Large terrace. Go for the tradition, but beware that sweets here cost at least double the price of any other dessert shop, and you'll be surrounded by twice the tourists. Open daily 9am-9pm. AmEx/MC/V.

HEADING EAST

# ☉ SIGHTS

In 1896, Hungary's millennial birthday bash prompted the construction of what are today Budapest's most prominent sights. Among the works commissioned by the Habsburgs were **Hősök tér** (Heroes' Square), **Szabadság híd** (Liberty Bridge), **Vajdahunyad Vár** (Vajdahunyad Castle), and continental Europe's first **metro** system. Slightly grayer for wear, war, and occupation, these monuments attest to the optimism of a capital on the verge of its Golden Age. See the sights, find your way around, and meet other travelers with **Absolute Walking and Biking Tours.** (☎211 8861; www.absolutetours.com. 3½hr. tours 4000Ft, students 3500ft. Specialized tours 4000-7000Ft.) **Boat tours** leave from Vigadó tér piers 6-7, near Elizabeth Bridge in Pest. The evening *Danube Legend* costs 4200Ft; its daytime counterpart, the *Duna Bella*, costs 3800Ft for 2hr.

## BUDA

On the east bank of the Danube, Buda sprawls between the base of **Várhegy** (Castle Hill) and southern **Gellérthegy** and leads into the city's main residential areas. Older and more peaceful than Pest, Buda is filled with parks and lush hills.

**CASTLE DISTRICT.** Towering above the Danube on Várhegy, the Castle District has been razed three times in its 800-year history, most recently in 1945. With its winding, statue-filled streets, impressive views, and hodgepodge of architectural styles, the UNESCO-protected district now appears much as it did under the Habsburg reign. The reconstructed **Buda Castle** (Vár) houses fine museums (p. 1043). Bullet holes in the facade recall the 1956 uprising. *(M1, 2, or 3: Deák tér. From the metro, take bus #16 across the Danube. Or, from M2: Moszkva tér, walk up to the hill on Várfok u. "Becsi kapu" marks the castle entrance.)* Beneath Buda Castle, the ◪**Castle Labyrinths** (Budvári Labirinths) provide a spooky glimpse of the subterranean city. *(Úri u. 9. ☎212 0207; www.labirintus.com. Open daily 9:30am-7:30pm. 1500Ft, students 1200Ft.)*

**MATTHIAS CHURCH.** The colorful roof of Matthias Church (Mátyás templom) on Castle Hill is one of Budapest's most photographed sights. The church was converted into a mosque in 1541, then renovated again 145 years later when the Habsburgs defeated the Turks. Ascend the spiral steps to view the exhibits of the **Museum of Ecclesiastical Art.** *(I, Szentháromság tér 2. Open M-F 9am-5pm, Sa 9am-1:45pm, Su 1-5pm. High mass daily 7, 8:30am, 6pm; Su and holidays also 10am and noon. Church and museum 650Ft, students 450Ft.)*

**GELLÉRT HILL.** After the coronation of King Stephen, the first Christian Hungarian monarch, in AD 1001, the Pope sent Bishop Gellért to convert the Magyars. After those unconvinced by the bishop's message hurled him to his death from the summit of Budapest's principal hill, it was named Gellérthegy in his honor. The **Liberation Monument** (Szabadság Szobor), on the hilltop, honors Soviet soldiers who died ridding Hungary of Nazis. The adjoining **Citadel** was built as a symbol of Habsburg power after the foiled 1848 revolution; the view from there is especially stunning at night. At the base of the hill is **Gellért** (p. 1044), Budapest's most famous Turkish bath. *(XI. Take tram #18 or 19 or bus #7 to Hotel Gellért; follow Szabó Verjték u. to Jubileumi Park, continuing on marked paths to the summit. Citadel 1200Ft.)*

## PEST

Constructed in the 19th century, the winding streets of Pest now link cafes, corporations, and monuments. The crowded **Belváros** (Inner City) is based around **Vörösmarty tér** and the swarming pedestrian boulevard **Váci utca**.

HEADING EAST

**PARLIAMENT.** The palatial Gothic Parliament (Országház) stands 96m tall, a number that symbolizes the date of Hungary's millennial anniversary. The building was modeled after the UK's, right down to the facade and the riverside location. The **crown jewels** were moved from Hungary's National Museum to the Cupola Room here in 1999. *(M2: Kossuth tér. ☎ 441 4000. English-language tours M-F 10am, noon, 2, 2:30pm; Sa-Su 10am; arrive early. Min. 5 people. Ticket office at Gate X opens at 8am. Entrance with mandatory tour 2300Ft, students 1150Ft, free with EU passport.)*

**GREAT SYNAGOGUE.** The largest synagogue in Europe and the second-largest in the world, Pest's Great Synagogue (Zsinagóga) was designed to hold 3000 worshippers. The enormous metal **Tree of Life**, a Holocaust memorial, sits in the garden above a mass grave for thousands of Jews killed near the end of the war. The Hebrew inscription reads: "Whose pain can be greater than mine?" and the Hungarian beneath pledges: "Let us remember." Each leaf bears the name of a family that perished. Next door, the **Jewish Museum** (Zsidó Múzeum) documents the storied past of Hungary's Jews. *(VII. At the corner of Dohány u. and Wesselényi u. M2: Astoria. Open May-Oct. M-Th 10am-5pm; F and Su 10am-2pm; Nov.-Apr. M-Th 10am-3pm; F and Su 10am-1pm. Services F 6pm. Admissions often start at 10:30am. Covered shoulders required. Tours M-Th 10:30am-3:30pm on the half-hour, F and Su 10:30, 11:30am, 12:30pm. Admission 1400Ft, students 750Ft. Tours 1900/1600Ft.)*

**ST. STEPHEN'S BASILICA (SZ. ISTVÁN BAZILIKA).** Though seriously damaged in WWII, the neo-Renaissance facade of the city's largest church has been mostly restored. The **Panorama Tower** offers an amazing 360° view of the city. A curious attraction is St. Stephen's mummified right hand, one of Hungary's most revered religious relics; a 100Ft donation dropped in the box will illuminate it for 2min. *(V. M1, 2, or 3: Deák tér. Open May-Oct. M-Sa 9am-5pm; Nov.-Apr. M-Sa 10am-4pm. Mass M-Sa 7, 8am, 6pm; Su 8:30, 10am, noon, 6pm. Free. Tower open daily June-Aug. 9:30am-6pm; Sept.-Oct. 10am-5:30pm; Apr.-May 10am-4:30pm. 500Ft, students 400Ft.)*

**ANDRÁSSY ÚT AND HEROES' SQUARE.** Hungary's grandest boulevard, Andrássy út extends from Erzsébet tér northeast to Heroes' Square (Hősök tér). The **State Opera House** (Magyar Állami Operaház) is a vivid reminder of Budapest's Golden Age; its gilded interior glows on performance nights. Take a tour if you can't see an opera. *(Andrássy út 22. M1: Opera. ☎ 332 8197. 1hr. English-language tours daily 3 and 4pm. 2500Ft, students 1300Ft.)* At the Heroes' Sq. end of Andrássy út, the **Millennium Monument** (Millenniumi emlékmű) commemorates the nation's most prominent leaders.

**CITY PARK (VÁROSLIGET).** Budapest's park, located northeast of Heroes' Sq., is home to a zoo, a circus, an aging amusement park, and the lakeside **Vajdahunyad Castle.** The castle's collage of Baroque, Gothic, and Romanesque styles chronicles the history of Hungarian design. Outside the castle is the hooded statue of King Béla IV's **anonymous scribe,** who left the major record of medieval Hungary. Rent a **rowboat** or **ice skates** on the lake next to the castle. The park's main road is closed to automobiles on weekends. *(XIV. M1: Széchényi Fürdő. Zoo ☎ 343 3710. Open May-Aug. M-Th 9am-6:30pm, F-Su 9am-7pm; Mar. and Oct. M-Th 9am-5pm, F-Su 9am-5:30pm; Apr. and Sept. M-Th 9am-5:30pm, F-Su 9am-6pm; Nov.-Jan. daily. 9am-4pm. 1700Ft, students 1200Ft. Park ☎ 363 8310. Open July-Aug. daily 10am-8pm; May-June M-F 11am-7pm, Sa-Su 10am-8pm. M-F 3100Ft, children 2100Ft; Sa-Su 3500Ft/2500Ft.)*

# ▥ MUSEUMS

**MUSEUM OF APPLIED ARTS (IPARMŰVÉSZETI MÚZEUM).** This collection of handcrafted pieces—including ceramics, furniture, metalwork, and Tiffany glass—deserves careful examination. Excellent temporary exhibits highlight specific crafts. Built for the 1896 millennium, the tiled Art Nouveau edifice is as intricate as the pieces within. *(IX. Üllői út 33-37. M3: Ferenc krt. ☎456 5100. Open Tu-Su 10am-6pm. Prices vary; usually around 1600Ft, students 800Ft. Tours usually 2300/1150Ft.)*

■ **HOUSE OF TERROR.** Both the Nazi and Soviet regimes housed prisoners in the basement of this building near Heroes' Sq. An acclaimed museum opened here in 2002 to document life under the two reigns of terror and memorialize the victims who were tortured and killed. *(VI. Andrássy Út 60. M1: Vörösmarty u. ☎374 2600; www.terrorhaza.hu. Open Tu-F 10am-6pm, Sa-Su 10am-7:30pm. 1500Ft, students 750Ft.)*

**LUDWIG MUSEUM (LUDVIG MÚZEUM).** Located on the outskirts of the city, the Ludwig Museum ("LuMu") displays cutting-edge Hungarian painting and sculpture. *(IX. Komor Marcell u. 1. Take tram #4 or 6 to Boráros tér, then take the HÉV commuter rail 1 stop to Lagymanyosi híd. ☎555 3444; www.ludwigmuseum.hu. Open Tu-Su 10am-8pm, last Sa of the month 10am-10pm. Temporary exhibit 1200Ft, students 600Ft.)*

**MUSEUM OF FINE ARTS (SZÉPMŰVÉSZETI MÚZEUM).** A spectacular collection of European art is housed in this museum near Heroes' Sq. The El Greco room is not to be missed. *(M1: Hősök tér. ☎496 7100. Open Tu-Su 10am-6pm, ticket booth until 5pm. 2400Ft, students 1200Ft.)*

**NATIONAL MUSEUM (NEMZETI MÚZEUM).** An extensive exhibit on the second floor chronicles the history of Hungary from the founding of the state through the 20th century; the first floor is reserved for temporary exhibits. *(VIII. Múzeum krt. 14/16. M3: Kálvin tér. ☎338 2122; www.mng.hu. Open Tu-Su 10am-6pm. 600Ft.)*

**STATUE PARK MUSEUM.** After the collapse of Soviet rule, the open-air Statue Park Museum (Szoborpark Múzeum) was created in Buda, south of Gellérthegy, to display Soviet statues removed from Budapest's parks and squares. The indispensable English-language guidebook (1000Ft) explains the statues' histories. *(XXII. On the corner of Balatoni út and Szabadkai út. Take express bus #7 from Keleti pu. to Étele tér, then take the yellow Volán bus from terminal #7 bound for Diósd 15min., every 15 min., and get off at the Szoborpark stop. ☎424 7500; www.szoborpark.hu. BudapestCards and 2-week passes for intercity transportation not taken. Open daily 10am-dusk. 600Ft, students 400Ft.)*

**BUDA CASTLE.** Buda Castle (p. 1041) houses several museums. **Wings B-D** hold the huge **Hungarian National Gallery** (Magyar Nemzeti Galéria), a definitive collection of Hungarian painting and sculpture. Its treasures include works by Realist Mihály Munkácsy and Impressionist Paál Lászlo, and medieval gold altarpieces. *(☎375 7533. Open Tu-Su 10am-6pm. Free. Special exhibits 800Ft, students 400Ft.)* In **Wing E,** the **Budapest History Museum** (Budapesti Történeti Múzeum) displays a collection of recently unearthed medieval artifacts. *(I. Szent György tér 2. ☎225 7815. Open daily May-Sept. 10am-6pm; Nov.-Feb. 10am-4pm. 900Ft, students 450Ft.)*

## ✺ ♫ FESTIVALS AND ENTERTAINMENT

The **Budapest Spring Festival** (www.fesztivalvaros.hu), March 14-30 in 2008, showcases Hungary's premier musicians and actors. In August, Óbudai Island hosts the week-long **Sziget Festival** (www.sziget.hu), an open-air rock festival. *Budapest Program, Budapest Panorama, Pesti Est,* and *Budapest in Your Pocket* are the best English-language entertainment guides, available at tourist offices and hotels. The "Style" section of the *Budapest Sun* (www.budapestsun.com; 300Ft) has film reviews and a 10-day calendar. Prices are reasonable; check **Ticket Express Hungary,** Andrássy u. 18. (☎312 0000; www.tex.hu. Open M-F 9:30am-6:30pm.)

The ■**State Opera House** (Magyar Állami Operaház), VI, Andrássy út 22, is one of Europe's leading performance centers. (M1: Opera. Box office ☎353 0170; www.opera.hu. Tickets 800-8700Ft. Box office open M-Sa 11am-7pm, Su 11am-

## STAYIN' A-LAVA

A bustling town by day, Eger seems suspiciously quiet at night. That's because the real scene is underground—literally—as Eger continues to offer festive diversions in the form of clubs built into a series of lava tunnels.

Unknown to most visitors, an elaborate labyrinth lies below Eger, the carved remnants of the 120km bed of lava upon which the city was founded. Locals have converted three sections into nightclubs, invisible to the world above except for small, barely marked entrances.

One of the most popular is **Club Amazon,** on Pyrter 3, alongside Kossuth L. u, under the Eger Cathedral, where youths dance the night away in the jungle-like disco. Guest DJs give the place a dynamic vibe. *(☎596 3848. Open W 10pm-5am, Cover 500Ft, Sa 10pm-5am, Cover 800Ft. Every 2nd F 10pm-5am, select W in June students 400Ft.)*

Another popular spot is the Liget Dance Cafe, on Erksekkert, under Excalibur Restaurant in the Archbishop's Gardens. *(☎427 7547. Cover (cash only) 800Ft. Open F-Sa 10pm-5am. AmEx/MC/V.)* Clearly marked by spotlights, the club draws a younger crowd. **Hippolit Club and Restaurant,** Katona ter 2, is classier and more subdued with a secluded, candle-lit second-floor patio. *(☎411 031. Open Tu-Th 9pm-3am, F-Sa 9pm-5am.)*

1pm and 4-7pm. Closes at 5pm on non-performance days.) The **National Dance Theater** (Nemzetí Táncszínház), Szinház u. 1-3, on Castle Hill, hosts a variety of shows, but Hungarian folklore is the most popular. (☎201 4407, box office 375 8649; www.nemzetitancszinhaz.hu. Most shows 7pm. Tickets 1200-4000Ft. Box office open M-Th 10am-6pm, F 10am-5pm.) The lovely **Városmajor Open-Air Theater,** XII, Városmajor, in Buda, hosts musicals, operas, and ballets. (M1: Moszkva tér. ☎375 5922; www.szabadter.hu. Open June 27-Aug. 18. Box office open daily 2-6pm.)

Both travelers and locals head to Budapest's **thermal baths** to soak away the urban grime. In operation since 1565, the baths offer services from mud baths to massages. ▧**Széchenyi,** XIV, Állatkerti u. 11/14, is one of Europe's largest bath complexes. (M1: Hősök tér. ☎363 3210. Open May-Sept. daily 6am-7pm; Oct.-Apr. M-F 6am-7pm, Sa-Su 6am-5pm. 2400Ft; 400Ft returned if you leave within 2hr., 200Ft within 3hr.; **keep your receipt.** 15min. massage 2000Ft. Cash only.) The elegant **Gellért,** XI, Kelenhegyi út 4/6, has a rooftop sundeck and an outdoor wave pool. Take bus #7 or tram #47 or 49 to Hotel Gellért, at the base of Gellérthegy. (Open May-Sept. daily 6am-7pm; Oct.-Apr. M-F 6am-7pm, Sa-Su 6am-5pm. 3100Ft, with scaled refund. 15min. massage 2500Ft. MC/V.)

## ▧ NIGHTLIFE

Relaxing garden cafe-clubs, elegant after-hours scenes, and nightly "freakin'" fests make up Budapest's nightlife scene. Pubs and bars stay busy until at least 4am and more club-like venues are alive past 5am. Upscale cafes near Pest's **Ferencz Liszt tér** (M2: Oktogon) attract Budapest's hip residents in their 20s and 30s, while less apparent, side streets house a more relaxed setting.

▧ **West Balkan,** VIII, Futó u. 46 (☎371 1807; www.westbalkan.com), in Pest. M3: Ferenc körút. 3 bars, indoor dance floor, and a whimsical outdoor garden keep Budapest's alternative scene grooving. Beer 450Ft. Open daily 4pm-4am.

▧ **Szimpla Kert,** VII, Kazinczy u. 14 (www.szimpla.hu). Graffiti designs on the walls, unique and personal furniture and colorful lighting give this garden-cafe-bar with movie screen and concert stage the most balanced and down-to-earth atmosphere in the city. Fresh crepes (100Ft) and a changing menu satisfy late-night hunger. Booze is plentiful and cheap. Beer 250Ft. Open 10am-2am. Cash only.

**Kultiplex,** IX, Kinizsi u. 28 (☎219 0706; www.kulti.hu), in Pest. M3: Kálvin tér. With 2 bars, a cinema, a concert hall, and a courtyard, this hangout serves inexpensive beer (250Ft) and screens movies (250-500Ft). Cover usually 200Ft. Open daily 11am-5am.

**A-38 Ship,** XI (☎464 3940; www.a38.hu), anchored on the Buda side of the Danube, south of Petőfi Bridge. DJs spin on the decks of this revamped Ukrainian freighter. Beer 300Ft. Cover varies. Restaurant open daily 11am-midnight. DJ nights open 11am-4am.

**Zöld Pardon,** XI (www.zp.hu), on the Buda side of Petőfi Bridge. This giant open-air summer festival features a pool and 5 bars; 3 large screens project the crowd on the dance floor. Beer 250-400Ft. Cover 100Ft. Open Apr. 20-Sept. 16 daily 9am-6am.

> **! NIGHTLIFE SCAM.** There have been reports of a scam involving English-speaking Hungarian women who ask foreign men to buy them drinks. When the bill comes, accompanied by imposing men, it can be US$1000 per round. If victims claim to have no money, they are directed to an ATM in the bar. For a list of questionable establishments, check the US Embassy website at http://budapest.usembassy.gov/tourist_advisory.html. If you are taken in, call the police. You'll probably still have to pay, but get a receipt to file a complaint.

**Piaf,** VI, Nagymező u. 25, in Pest. M1: Opera. Knock on the inconspicuous door at this popular lounge near the bus station. Cover 800Ft; includes 1 beer. Open Su-Th 10pm-6am, F-Sa 10pm-7am.

**Pótkulcs,** VII, Csengery u. 65/b. (☎269 1050; www.potkulcs.hu). No sign at the entrance, but look for the house number. Huge selection of drinks (try Honey Palinka; 450Ft) at this outdoor garden that serves Hungarian food until midnight—try the popular beef stew (1290Ft). Tu live Hungarian folk music. Open daily 5pm-2am. Cash only.

**Kuplung,** VI, Király u. 46 (www.kuplung.net). An old warehouse provides a huge, open hall with distinctive, one-of-a-kind furniture. Mixed crowd of locals in their late teens to 30s come to drink and listen to free concerts (3 per week). Check online for schedules of local bands. Open 6pm-late. Cash only.

**Gödör Klub,** V, Erzsébet tér. (☎201 3868; www.godorklub.hu). Outside setting right at the middle of Elizabeth square makes you the center of attention at this nightclub that hosts jazz and rock concerts and other special events every night, beginning around 9pm. Check website for schedules. Shots 300Ft. Beer 400Ft. Open M-Sa 5pm-4am.

**WigWam,** XI, Fehérvári u. 202 (☎ 208 5569; www.wigwamrockclub.hu). Tram #47 from Moricz Zsigmond. Crowded with young locals and adventure-seeking travelers, this club is host to rock-music weekends, karaoke, erotic shows, singing competitions, and wild foam parties. Cover varies. Open daily 9pm-5am. Cash only.

**⚑ DAYTRIP FROM BUDAPEST: SZENTENDRE.** The cobblestone streets of Szentendre (pop. 23,000) brim with upscale galleries and restaurants. Head up **Templomdomb** (Church Hill) in Fő tér for an amazing view from the 13th-century church. The **Czóbel Museum,** Templom tér 1, exhibits work by post-Impressionist artist Béla Czóbel, including his bikini-clad *Venus of Szentendre. (Open Tu-Su 10am-6pm. 500Ft, students 300Ft.)* The popular **Kovács Margit Museum,** Vastagh György u. 1, off Görög u., displays whimsical ceramics by the 20th-century Hungarian artist. *(Open daily Oct.-Feb. 9am-7pm; Mar.-Sept. 9am-5pm. 700Ft.)* The real "thriller" at the ⬛**Szamos Marzipan Museum and Confectionery,** Dumtsa Jenő u. 12, is an 80kg white-chocolate statue of Michael Jackson. *(www.szamosmarcipan.hu. Open daily May-Oct. 10am-7pm; Nov.-Apr. 10am-6pm. 350Ft.)* The **Nemzeti Bormúzeum** (National Wine Museum), Bogdányi u. 10, exhibits wines from across Hungary. *(www.bor-kor.hu. Open daily 10am-10pm. Exhibit 200Ft, tasting and English-language tour 1800Ft.)*

HÉV **trains** go to Szentendre (45min., 3 per hr., 480Ft) from Budapest's Batthyány tér station. **Buses** run from Szentendre to Budapest's Árpád híd metro station (30min., 1-3 per hr., 280Ft), Esztergom (1½hr., 1 per hr., 660Ft), and Visegrád (45min., 1 per hr., 359Ft). The train and bus stations are 10min. from Fő tér; descend the stairs past the HÉV tracks and head through the underpass up Kossuth u. At the fork, bear right onto Dumtsa Jenő u. **Tourinform,** Dumtsa Jenő u. 22, is between the center and the stations. (☎026 31 79 65. *Open mid-Mar. to Oct. daily 9:30am-1pm and 1:30-4:30pm; Nov. to mid-Mar. M-F 9:30am-1pm and 1:30-4:30pm.*)

# SLOVAKIA (SLOVENSKO)

## ESSENTIALS

### FACTS AND FIGURES

**Official Name:** Slovak Republic.

**Major Cities:** Bratislava.

**Population:** 5,448,000.

**Time Zone:** GMT +2.

**Languages:** Slovak (84%), Hungarian (11%).

**Phone Code:** ☎385.

**Known Mammal Species:** 85.

**EMBASSIES AND CONSULATES.** Foreign embassies to Slovakia are in Bratislava. Slovak embassies abroad include: **Australia,** 47 Culgoa Circuit, O'Malley, Canberra, ACT 2606 (☎262 901 516; www.slovakemb-aust.org); **Canada,** 50 Rideau Ter., Ottawa, ON K1M 2A1 (☎613-749-4442; www.ottawa.mfa.sk); **Ireland,** 20 Clyde Rd., Ballsbridge, Dublin 4 (☎33 56 66 00 12; fax 660 0014); **UK,** 25 Kensington Palace Gardens, London W8 4QY (☎020 73 1364 70; www.slovakembassy.co.uk); **US,** 3523 International Ct., NW, Washington, D.C. 20008 (☎202-237-1054; www.slovakembassy-us.org).

**VISA AND ENTRY INFORMATION.** Citizens of Australia, Canada, Ireland, New Zealand, the UK, and the US can travel to Slovakia without a visa for up to 90 days. Those traveling for business, employment, or study must obtain a temporary residence permit. There are many kinds of visas, including single- and multiple-entry, as well as long-term, and they range in price from US$37-154.

| SLOVAKIA | ❶ | ❷ | ❸ | ❹ | ❺ |
|---|---|---|---|---|---|
| **ACCOMMODATIONS** | under 250Sk | 251-500Sk | 501-800Sk | 801-1000Sk | over 1000Sk |
| **FOOD** | under 120Sk | 120-190Sk | 191-270Sk | 271-330Sk | over 330Sk |

| **SLOVAKIAN KORUNY (SK)** | | |
|---|---|---|
| AUS$1 = 22.26SK | 10SK = AUS$0.45 | |
| CDN$1 = 27.00SK | 10SK = CDN$0.37 | |
| EUR€1 = 38.07SK | 10SK = EUR€0.26 | |
| NZ$1 = 18.73SK | 10SK = NZ$0.53 | |
| UK£1 = 55.77SK | 10SK = UK£0.18 | |
| US$1 = 30.15SK | 10SK = US$0.33 | |

## BRATISLAVA                                                     ☎02

Often eclipsed by its famous neighboring capitals, sophisticated Bratislava (pop. 450,000) is finally stepping into the limelight. Every night of the week, the city's artfully lit streets buzz with activity. During the day, both locals and visitors can be found sipping coffee at the hundreds of chic cafes dotting the cobblestoned *Staré Mesto* (Old Town), sauntering along the Danube River, or exploring the well-kept castle that shines over the city.

# ▐ TRANSPORTATION

**Flights: M.R. Štefánik International Airport** (BTS; ☎ 48 57 11 11; www.letiskobratislava.sk), 9km northeast of town. Often used as a hub to reach Vienna, AUT (see **Let's Go to Vienna,** p. 85). To reach the center of Bratislava, take bus #61 (1hr.) to the train station and then take tram #1 to Poštová on nám. SNP.

**Trains: Bratislava Hlavná Stanica,** at the end of Predstaničné nám., off Šancová. **Železnice Slovenskej republiky** (☎ 20 29 11 11; www.zsr.sk) posts schedules on its website. To: **Košice** (5-6hr., 10 per day, 518Sk), **Prague, CZR** (4½-5½hr., 3 per day, 400Sk), and **Vienna, AUT** (1hr., 1 per hr., round-trip 283Sk). Make sure to get off at **Hlavná Stanica,** the main train station. To reach the center from the **train station,** take tram #2 to the 6th stop or walk downhill, take a right, then an immediate left, and walk down Stefanikova (15-20min.).

**Buses:** Mlynské nivy 31 (☎ 55 42 16 67, info 09 84 22 22 22). Bus #210 runs between the train and bus stations. Check your ticket for the bus number (č. aut.), as several depart from the same stand. **Eurolines** has a 10% discount for under 26. To: **Banská Bystrica** (3-4½hr., 2-3 per hr., 290-450Sk); **Budapest, HUN** (4hr., 2 per day, 610Sk); **Prague, CZR** (4¾hr., 5 per day, 520Sk); **Vienna, AUT** (1½hr., 1 per hr., 400Sk). From the station, take trolley #202, or turn right on Mlynské nivy and walk to Dunajská, which leads to **Kamenné námestie** (Stone Sq.) and the center of town (15-20min.).

**Local Transportation: Tram** and **bus** tickets (10min. 14Sk, 30min. 18Sk, 1hr. 22Sk) are sold at kiosks and at the orange *automaty* in bus stations. Use an *automat* only if its light is on. Stamp your ticket when you board; the fine for riding ticketless is 1200Sk. Trams and buses run 4am-11pm. **Night buses,** marked with blue and yellow numbers with an "N" in front of them, run midnight-4am. Some kiosks and ticket machines sell **passes** (1-day 90Sk, 2-day 170Sk, 3-day 210Sk).

**Taxis: BP** (☎ 169 99); **FunTaxi** (☎ 167 77); **Profi Taxi** (☎ 162 22).

# ▐ ORIENTATION AND PRACTICAL INFORMATION

The **Dunaj** (Danube) flows eastward across Bratislava. Four bridges span the river; the main **Nový Most** (New Bridge) connects Bratislava's center, **Staromestská** (Old Town), in the north, to the commercial and entertainment district on the river's southern bank. **Bratislavský Hrad** (Bratislava Castle) towers on a hill to the west, while the city center sits between the river and **námestie Slovenského Národného Povstania** (nám. SNP; Slovak National Uprising Square).

**Tourist Office: Bratislava Culture and Information Center (BKIS),** Klobúčnicka 2 (☎ 161 86; www.bkis.sk). Books **private rooms** and hotels (800-3000Sk plus 50Sk fee); sells **maps** (free-80Sk) and books **tours** (1200Sk per hr.; max. 19 people). Open June-Oct. 15 M-F 8:30am-7pm, Sa 9am-6pm, Su 9:30am-6pm; Nov.-May M-F 8am-6pm, Sa 9am-4pm, Su 10am-3pm. **Branch** in train station annex open M-F 8am-2pm and 2:30-7pm, Sa-Su 8am-2pm and 2:30-5pm.

**Embassies:** Citizens of **Australia** and **New Zealand** should contact the UK embassy in an emergency. **Canada,** Mostová 2 (☎ 59 20 40 31). Open M-F 8:30am-noon and 1:30pm-4:30pm. **Ireland,** Mostová 2 (☎ 59 30 96 11; bratislava@dfa.ie). Open M-F 9am-12:30pm. **UK,** Panská 16 (☎ 59 98 20 00; www.britishembassy.sk). Open M-F 8:30-11am. **US,** Hviezdoslavovo nám. 5 (☎ 54 43 08 61, emergency 09 03 70 36 66; www.usembassy.sk). Open M-F 8am-noon and 2pm-3:30pm.

**Currency Exchange: Ľudová Banka,** nám. SNP 15 (☎ 59 21 17 63, ext. 760; www.luba.sk) cashes American Express **Traveler's Cheques** for 1% commission and offers MC/V **cash advances.** Open M-F 8am-8pm.

**Luggage Storage:** At train station 30-40Sk. Open daily 5:30am-midnight.

**Ambulance and General Emergency:** ☎ 112. **Fire:** ☎ 150. **Police:** ☎ 158.

HEADING EAST

**Internet:** There are Internet cafes all over central Bratislava, especially along Michalská and Obchodná. **Megainet,** Šancová 25. 1Sk per min. Open daily 9am-10pm.

**Post Office:** Nám. SNP 34 (☎59 39 31 11). Offers **fax** service. **Poste Restante** and phone cards at counters #2-4. Poste restante M-F 7am-8pm, Sa 7am-2pm. Open M-F 7am-8pm, Sa 7am-6pm, Su 9am-2pm. **Postal Code:** 81000 Bratislava 1.

# ▌ ACCOMMODATIONS

In July and August, several **university dorms** open as hostels (from 150Sk). Pensions and private rooms are inexpensive and comfy alternatives. Most places add a 30Sk tourist tax. **BKIS** (p. 1047) has more info.

▨ **Patio Hostel,** Špitálska 35 (☎529 257 97; www.patiohostel.com), near the bus station. From the train station, take tram #13 to the arch. The entrance is tucked behind a dimly lit, run-down archway, but the hostel itself is clean and comfortable, with sunny rooms, a friendly staff, and a colorful common area. Free Internet. Check-in 1pm. Check-out 10pm. 2- to 12-bed dorms 600-800Sk. MC/V. ❸

**Downtown Backpacker's Hostel,** Panenská 31 (☎546 411 91; www.backpackers.sk). From the train station, turn left on Stefánikova and right on Panenská, or take bus #81, 91, or 93 for 2 stops. Swanky, centrally located 19th-century building, with backpackers relaxing under a bust of Lenin and enjoying beers from the downstairs bar. Laundry 200Sk. Reception 24hr. Check-out noon. Reserve ahead. Dorms 500-600Sk; doubles 1000Sk. 60-100Sk HI discount. 30Sk Tourist tax. MC/V. ❸

**Družba,** Botanická 25 (☎654 200 65; www.hotel-druzba.sk). Take bus #32 (dir.: Pri Kríži) or tram #1 or 5 to Botanická Záhrada. Cross the pedestrian overpass and go to the 2nd of the 2 concrete buildings. The combination university dorm and hotel is far from the Old Town, but its dorms are brightly painted and remarkably cheap. Dorms open early July-late Aug. Reception 24hr. Dorms 170Sk. Hotel open year-round. Reception M-Th 7am-3:30pm, F 7am-1pm. Singles 790Sk; doubles 1966Sk. MC/V. ❶

**Slovenská Zdravotnicka Univerzita,** Limbová 12 (☎593 701 00; www.szu.sk). From the train station, take bus #32 or tram #204 for 5 stops to Nemocnica Kramárel. Clean, comfortable rooms in a green concrete tower located far from the city center. Reception 24hr. Check-out 10am. 760Sk per person. Cash only. ❸

# ▐ FOOD

Buy groceries at **Tesco Potraviny,** Kamenné nám. 1. (Open M-F 8am-10pm, Sa 8am-8pm, Su 9am-8pm.) Or, try the nearby indoor **fruit market** at Stará Trznícá, Kamenné nám. (Open M-F 7am-6pm, Sa 7am-1pm.)

▨ **1 Slovak Pub,** Obchodná 62 (☎905 35 32 30; www.slovakpub.sk). Join the student crowd at one of Bratislava's largest and cheapest traditional Slovakian restaurants. Each of the rooms has a theme, including "country cottage" and "Room of Poets." Lunch until 5pm; 35-89Sk. Dinner entrees 79-250Sk. 10% discount for Patio Hostel guests. Open M-Th 10am-midnight, F-Sa 10am-2pm, Su noon-midnight. Cash only. ❷

**Govinda,** Obchodná 30 (☎529 623 66). The veggie fare is heavenly. Combination plate 95/150Sk. Open M-F 11am-8pm, Sa 11:30am-7:30pm. Cash only. ❶

**Elixir 14,** Stefánikova 14 (☎524 998 49; www.elixir.sk). The menu is a treasure trove of creative vegetarian dishes. Vegan and meat options available. Daily lunch special 99Sk. Entrees 115-235Sk. Open M-W 10am-10pm, Th-F 10am-midnight, Sa 11am-midnight, Su 11am-10pm. MC/V. ❷

HEADING EAST

**Prašná Bašta,** Zámočnícka 11 (☎544 349 57; www.prasnabasta.sk). Hidden away from the Old Town bustle, this eatery's counter-culture vibe draws 20-somethings for generous portions of Slovak cuisine. Sit outside on the leafy terrace or downstairs amid sculptures and artful decor. Entrees 85-325Sk. Open daily 11am-11pm. MC/V. ❸

**Bagetka,** Zelená 8 (☎544 194 36). This sandwich bar is a fast, cheap, and satisfying option. Entrees 50-90Sk. Open M-Sa 9:30am-9pm, Su 2-9pm. Cash only. ❶

**Chez David,** Zámocká 13 (☎544 138 24). Located in a quarter steeped in Jewish culture. Elegant, excellent dishes (57-397Sk). Open daily 7am-10pm. AmEx/MC/V. ❸

# 👁 SIGHTS

**NÁMESTIE SNP AND ENVIRONS.** Most of the city's major attractions are in the Staré Mesto (Old Town). From Nám. SNP, which commemorates the bloody 1944 Slovak National Uprising, walk down Uršulínska to the pink-and-gold ▧**Primate's Palace** (Primaciálny Palác), built in the 1700s for Hungary's religious leaders and now home to Bratislava's mayor. In the Hall of Mirrors (Zrkadlová Sieň), Napoleon and Austrian Emperor Franz I signed the 1805 Peace of Pressburg. *(Primaciálné nám. 1. Buy tickets on 2nd fl. Open Tu-Su 10am-5pm. 40Sk, students free.)* Established in September 2000, the contemporary ▧**Danubiana-Meulensteen Art Museum** is a piece of modern art in itself. On a small peninsula near the Hungarian border, the museum is surrounded by a small sculpture park. The remote location prevents crowding, so you can admire cutting-edge exhibits at your leisure. *(Take bus #91 from beneath Nový Most to the last stop, Cunovo; 35min., 20Sk. Follow the signs 3.5km to the museum. ☎09 03 60 55 05; www.danubiana.sk. Open Tu-Su May-Sept. 10am-8pm; Oct.-Apr. 10am-6pm. 80Sk, students 40Sk. MC/V.)* **Hviezdoslavovo námestie** is home to the gorgeous 1886 **Slovak National Theater** (Slovenské Národné Divadlo). With the Danube on your left, walk along the waterfront to the gaudy, neon-lit **Nový Most** (New Bridge), designed by the Communist government in the 70s. Its space-age design was intended to balance the antiquated presence of Bratislava Castle. The top, or UFO as it is known, contains a viewing deck and a restaurant. *(☎62 53 03 00; www.u-f-o.sk. Deck open daily 10am-10pm. 50Sk, free with restaurant reservations. Restaurant open M-F and Su 10am-1am, Sa 10am-10pm.)* The **Museum of Jewish Culture** preserves artifacts from Slovak Jews. *(Židovská 17. ☎54 41 85 07; www.slovak-jewish-heritage.org. Open M-F and Su 11am-5pm; last entry 4:30pm. 200Sk, students 60Sk.)*

**CASTLES.** On an imposing cliff 9km west of the center, the stunning **Devín Castle** (Hrad Devín) ruins overlook the confluence of the mighty Danube and Morava rivers. With the advent of communism, Devín became a functioning symbol of totalitarianism: sharpshooters hid in the ruins with orders to open fire on anyone who tried to cross this area—the barbed-wire fence beside the Morava. Today, visitors can walk along the rocks and ruins. A museum details the castle's history. *(Bus #29 from Nový Most to the last stop. ☎65 73 01 05. English-language info 35Sk. Open July-Aug. Tu-F 10am-5pm, Sa-Su 10am-7pm; May-June and Sept.-Oct. Tu-Su 10am-5pm; last entry 30min. before closing. Museum 90Sk, students 40Sk.)* Visible from Danube Banks, the four-towered **Bratislava Castle** (Bratislavský Hrad) is Bratislava's defining landmark. Ruined by a fire in 1811 and finished off by WWII bombings, the castle's current stark form is largely a Communist-era restoration that doesn't quite capture its 18th-century glory. The spectacular view from the Crown Tower (Korunná Veža) is a highlight. *(Castle open daily Apr.-Sept. 9am-8pm; Oct.-Mar. 9am-6pm. Free. Museum ☎54 41 14 44; www.snm-hm.sk. Open Tu-Su 9am-5pm; last entry 4:15pm. 100Sk, students 70Sk.)*

HEADING EAST

## ENTERTAINMENT AND NIGHTLIFE

The weekly English newspaper, *Slovak Spectator*, also has current events info. **Slovenské Národné Divadlo** (Slovak National Theater), Hviezdoslavovo nám. 1, puts on ballets and operas. (☎54 43 30 83; www.snd.sk. Box office open M-F 8am-5:30pm, Sa 9am-1pm. Closed July-Aug. 100-200Sk.) The **Slovenská Filharmónia** (Slovak Philharmonic), Medená 3, has two to three performances per week in fall and winter. The **box office**, Palackého 2, is around the corner. (☎54 43 33 51; www.filharm.sk. Open M-Tu and Th-F 1-7pm, W 8am-2pm. 100-200Sk.)

By night, The Old Town is filled with young people priming for a night out. Nightlife in Bratislava is relatively subdued, but there is no shortage of places to party. For info on **GLBT nightlife,** pick up a copy of *Atribut* at any kiosk. At the packed hotspot ◨**Klub Laverna,** Laurinská 19, a slide transports drunken clubbers from the upper level to the floor. (☎54 43 31 65; www.laverna.sk, entrance on SNP street. Mixed drinks 75-230Sk. Cover F-Sa 100Sk. Open daily 9pm-6am.) For a less crazed evening, head to **Medusa Cocktail Bar,** Michalská 33, which defines chic with its posh decor and huge selection of mixed drinks. (Open M-Th 11am-1am, Sa 11am-3am, Su 11am-midnight. AmEx/MC/V.)

# APPENDIX

## LANGUAGE PHRASEBOOK

### CZECH

| ENGLISH | CZECH | PRONOUNCE | ENGLISH | CZECH | PRONOUNCE |
|---|---|---|---|---|---|
| Yes/No | Ano/Ne | AH-no/neh | Train/Bus | Vlak/Autobus | vlahk/OW-toh-boos |
| Please | Prosím | PROH-seem | Station | Nádraží | NA-drah-zhee |
| Thank you | Děkuji | DYEH-koo-yee | Airport | Letiště | LEH-teesh-tyeh |
| Hello | Dobrý den | DOH-bree den | Ticket | Lístek | LIS-tek |
| Goodbye | Nashledanou | NAS-kleh-dah-noh | Taxi | Taxi | TEHK-see |
| Sorry/ Excuse me | Promiňte | PROH-meen-teh | Hotel | Hotel | HOH-tel |
| Help! | Pomoc! | POH-mots | Bathroom | WC | VEE-TSEE |
| I'm lost. (m/f) | Zabloudil(a) jsem. | ZAH-bloh-dyeel-(ah) sem | Open/Closed | Otevřeno/ Zavřeno | O-te-zheno/ZAV-rzhen-o |
| Police | Policie | POH-leets-ee-yeh | Left/Right | Vlevo/Vpravo | VLE-voh/VPRAH-voh |
| Embassy | Velvyslanectví | VEHL-vee-slah-nehts-vee | Bank | Banka | BAN-ka |
| Passport | Cestovní pas | TSEH-stohv-nee pahs | Exchange | Směnárna | smyeh-NAR-na |
| Doctor | Lékař | LEH-karzh | Grocery | Potraviny | PO-tra-vee-nee |

| ENGLISH | CZECH | PRONOUNCE |
|---|---|---|
| Where is...? | Kde je...? | gdeh yeh |
| How much does this cost? | Kolik to stojí? | KOH-lihk STOH-yee |
| When is the next...? | Kdy jede příští...? | gdi YEH-deh przh-EESH-tyee |
| Do you have (a vacant room)? | Máte (volný pokoj)? | MAA-teh (VOHL-nee POH-koy) |
| I would like... | Prosím... | PROH-seem |
| I do not eat... | Nejím maso... | NEH-yeem MAH-soh |
| Do you speak English? | Mluvíte anglicky? | MLOO-vit-eh ahng-GLEET-skee |

### DANISH

| ENGLISH | DANISH | PRONOUNCE | ENGLISH | DANISH | PRONOUNCE |
|---|---|---|---|---|---|
| Yes/No | Ja/ne | yah/ney | Ticket | Billet | bih-LEHD |
| Please | Vær så venlig | vair soh VEN-lee | Train/Bus | Tog/Bus | too/boos |
| Thank you | Tak | tahk | Airport | Lufthavn | LOFD-haown |
| Hello | Hallo | HAH-lo | Departure | Afgang | OW-gahng |
| Goodbye | Farvel | fah-VEL | Market | Marked | MAH-gehth |
| Sorry/ Excuse me | undskyld | OHN-scoolt | City center | Centrum | SEHN-trum |

| ENGLISH | DANISH | PRONOUNCE | ENGLISH | DANISH | PRONOUNCE |
|---------|--------|-----------|---------|--------|-----------|
| Help! | Hjælp! | yailp | Hotel/Hostel | Hotel/Van-drerhjem | ho-TEL/VAN-druh-yem |
| Police | Politiet | poh-lee-TEE-ehht | Pharmacy | Apotek | ah-poh-TEYG |
| Embassy | Ambassade | ahm-bah-SAH-theh | Toilet | Toilet | toe-ah-LEHD |

| ENGLISH | DANISH | PRONOUNCE |
|---------|--------|-----------|
| Where is...? | Hvor er...? | voa air |
| How do I get to...? | Hvordan kommer jeg til...? | vo-DAN KOM-ah yey tee |
| How much does this cost? | Hvad koster det? | vah KOS-ter day |
| I'd like a... | Jeg vil gerne have en... | yay vee GEHR-neh hah en |
| Do you speak English? | Taler du engelsk? | TAY-luh doo ENG-elsk |

# DUTCH

Most Dutch consonants, with a few exceptions, share their sounds with English, sometimes rendering Dutch into a phonetic version of English with a foreign accent. Vowels are a different story. The combinations "e," "ee," "i," and "ij" are occasionally pronounced "er" as in "mother."

| ENGLISH | DUTCH | PRONOUNCE | ENGLISH | DUTCH | PRONOUNCE |
|---------|-------|-----------|---------|-------|-----------|
| Yes/No | Ja/Nee | yah/nay | Ticket | Kaartje | KAHR-chuh |
| Please/ You're welcome | Alstublieft | Als-too-BLEEFT. | Train/Bus | Trein/Bus | train/boos |
| Thank you | Dank u wel | DAHNK oo vell | Station | Station | stah-SHON |
| Hello | Dag/Hallo | Dakh/Hallo | Taxi | Taxi | TAHK-see |
| Goodbye | Tot ziens | Tot zeens | Grocery | Kruidenier | kraow-duh-NEER |
| Excuse me | Neem me niet kwalijk | neym muh neet KWAH-lek | Tourist office | VVV | fay-fay-fay |
| Help! | Help! | helup | City center | Centrum | SEHN-trum |
| Police | Politie | po-LEET-see | Shop | winkel | VIN-kerl |
| Embassy | Ambassade | ahm-bah-SAH-duh | Toilet | Toilet | twah-LEYT |
| Pharmacy | Apotheek | ah-po-TEYK | Wooden shoes | Klompen | KLOM-pern |

| ENGLISH | DUTCH | PRONOUNCE |
|---------|-------|-----------|
| Where is...? | Waar is...? | VAHR ihss |
| I'm lost. | Ik ben verdwaald | Ik ben fer-VAHLDT |
| How much does this cost? | Wat kost het? | wat KOST et |
| Do you have...? | Heeft u...? | HEYFT oo |
| Do you speak English? | Sprekt u Engels? | SPREYKT oo ENG-els |

# FRENCH

*Le* is the masculine singular definite article (the), *la* the feminine; both are abbreviated to *l'* before a vowel, while *les* is the plural definite article for both genders.

*Un* is the masculine singular indefinite article (a or an), *une* the feminine, while *des* is the plural indefinite article for both genders ("some").

| ENGLISH | FRENCH | PRONOUNCE | ENGLISH | FRENCH | PRONOUNCE |
|---------|--------|-----------|---------|--------|-----------|
| Hello | Bonjour | bohn-zhoor | Exchange | L'échange | ley-shanzh |
| Please | S'il vous plaît | see voo pley | Grocery | L'épicerie | ley-pees-ree |
| Thank you | Merci | mehr-see | Market | Le marché | leuh marzh-chay |
| Excuse me | Excusez-moi | ex-ku-zeh mwah | Police | La police | la poh-lees |
| Yes/No | Oui/Non | wee/nohn | Embassy | L'ambassade | lahm-ba-sahd |
| Goodbye | Au revoir | oh ruh-vwahr | Passport | Le passeport | leuh pass-por |
| Help! | Au secours! | oh seh-coor | Post Office | La poste | la pohst |
| I'm lost. | Je suis perdu. | zhe swee pehr-doo | One-way | Le billet simple | leuh bee-ay samp |
| Train/Bus | Le train/Le bus | leuh tran/leuh boos | Round-trip | Le billet aller-retour | leuh bee-ay a-lay-re-toor |
| Station | La gare | la gahr | Ticket | Le billet | leuh bee-ay |
| Airport | L'aéroport | la-ehr-o-por | Single room | Une chambre simple | oon shahm-br samp |
| Hotel | L'hôtel | lo-tel | Double room | Une chambre pour deux | oon shahm-br poor deuh |
| Hostel | L'auberge | lo-berzhe | With shower | Avec une douche | a-vec une doosh |
| Bathroom | La salle de bain | la sal de bahn | Taxi | Le taxi | leuh tax-ee |
| Open/Closed | Ouvert/Fermé | oo-ver/fer-meh | Ferry | Le bac | leuh bak |
| Doctor | Le médecin | leuh mehd-sen | Tourist office | Le bureau de tourisme | leuh byur-oh de toor-eesm |
| Hospital | L'hôpital | loh-pee-tal | Town hall | L'hôtel de ville | lo-tel de veel |
| Pharmacy | La pharmacie | la far-ma-see | Vegetarian | Végétarien | vay-zhey-tah-ree-ehn |
| Left/Right | À gauche/À droite | a gohsh/a dwat | Kosher/Halal | Kascher/Halal | ka-shey/ha-lal |
| Straight | Tout droit | too dwa | Newsstand | Le tabac | leuh ta-bac |
| Turn | Tournez | toor-neh | Cigarette | La cigarette | la see-ga-ret |

| ENGLISH | FRENCH | PRONOUNCE |
|---------|--------|-----------|
| Do you speak English? | Parlez-vous anglais? | par-lay voo ahn-glay |
| Where is...? | Où se trouve...? | oo seh-trhoov |
| When is the next...? | À quelle heure part le prochain...? | ah kel ur par leuh pro-chan |
| How much does this cost? | Ça fait combien? | sah fay com-bee-en? |
| Do you have rooms available? | Avez-vous des chambres disponibles? | av-ay voo day shahm-br dees-pon-eeb-bl? |
| I would like... | Je voudrais... | zhe voo-dray |
| I don't speak French. | Je ne parle pas Français. | zhe neuh parl pah frawn-say |
| I'm allergic to... | Je suis allergique à... | zhe swee al-ehr-zheek a |
| I love you. | Je t'aime. | zhe tem |

# GERMAN

In German, every letter in the word is pronounced. Consonants are pronounced exactly as they are in English, with the following exceptions: "j" is pronounced as "y"; "qu" is pronounced "kv"; a single "s" is pronounced "z"; "v" is pronounced "f"; "w" is pronounced "v"; and "z" is pronounced "ts." "Sch" is "sh," "st" is "sht," and "sp" is "shp." The "ch" sound, as in "ich" ("I") and "nicht" ("not"), is tricky; you can substitute a "sh." The letter ß (ess-tset) represents a double "s"; pronounce it "ss."

| ENGLISH | GERMAN | PRONOUNCE | ENGLISH | GERMAN | PRONOUNCE |
|---|---|---|---|---|---|
| Yes/No | Ja/Nein | yah/nein | Train/Bus | Zug/Bus | tsoog/boos |
| Please | Bitte | BIH-tuh | Station | Bahnhof | BAHN-hohf |
| Thank you | Danke | DAHNG-kuh | Airport | Flughafen | FLOOG-hah-fen |
| Hello | Hallo | HAH-lo | Taxi | Taxi | TAHK-see |
| Goodbye | Auf Wiedersehen | owf VEE-der-zayn | Ticket | Fahrkarte | FAR-kar-tuh |
| Excuse me | Entschuldigung | ent-SHOOL-dih-gung | Departure | Abfahrt | AHB-fart |
| Help! | Hilfe! | HIL-fuh | One-way | Einfache | AYHN-fah-kuh |
| I'm lost. | Ich habe mich verlaufen. | eesh HAH-buh meesh fer-LAU-fun | Round-trip | Hin und zurück | hin oond tsuh-RYOOK |
| Police | Polizei | poh-lee-TSAI | Reservation | Reservierung | reh-zer-VEER-ung |
| Embassy | Botschaft | BOAT-shahft | Ferry | Fährschiff | FAYHR-shiff |
| Passport | Reisepass | RYE-zeh-pahss | Bank | Bank | bahnk |
| Doctor/Hospital | Arzt/Krankenhaus | ahrtst/KRANK-en-house | Exchange | Wechseln | VEHK-zeln |
| Pharmacy | Apotheke | AH-po-TEY-kuh | Grocery | Lebensmittelgeschäft | LEY-bens-miht-tel-guh-SHEFT |
| Hotel/Hostel | Hotel/Jugendherberge | ho-TEL/YOO-gend-air-BAIR-guh | Tourist office | Touristbüro | TU-reest-byur-oh |
| Single room | Einzellzimmer | EIN-tsel-tsihm-meh | Post Office | Postamt | POST-ahmt |
| Double room | Doppelzimmer | DOP-pel-tsihm-meh | Old town/City center | Altstadt | AHLT-shtat |
| Dorm | Schlafsaal | SHLAF-zahl | Vegetarian | Vegetarier | Feh-geh-TEHR-ee-er |
| With shower | Mit dusche | mitt DOO-shuh | Vegan | Veganer | FAY-gan-er |
| Bathroom | Badezimmer | BAH-deh-tsihm-meh | Kosher/Halal | Koscher/Halaal | KOH-sheyr/hah-LAAL |
| Open/Closed | Geöffnet/Geschlossen | geh-UHF-net/geh-SHLOS-sen | Nuts/Milk | Nüsse/Milch | NYOO-seh/mihlsh |
| Left/Right | Links/Rechts | lihnks/rekhts | Bridge | Brücke | BRUKE-eh |
| Straight | Geradeaus | geh-RAH-de-OWS | Castle | Schloß | shloss |

| ENGLISH | GERMAN | PRONOUNCE |
|---|---|---|
| Where is...? | Wo ist...? | vo ihst |
| How do I get to...? | Wie komme ich nach...? | vee KOM-muh eesh NAHKH |
| How much does that cost? | Wieviel kostet das? | VEE-feel KOS-tet das |
| Do you have...? | Haben Sie...? | HOB-en zee |
| I would like... | Ich möchte... | eesh MERSH-teh |
| I'm allergic to... | Ich bin zu...allergisch. | eesh bihn tsoo...ah-LEHR-gish |

| ENGLISH | GERMAN | PRONOUNCE |
|---------|--------|-----------|
| Do you speak English? | Sprechen sie Englisch? | SHPREK-en zee EHNG-lish |

# GREEK

| ENGLISH | GREEK | PRONOUNCE | ENGLISH | GREEK | PRONOUNCE |
|---------|-------|-----------|---------|-------|-----------|
| Yes/No | Ναι/Όχι | neh/OH-hee | Train/Bus | Τραίνο/Λεωφορείο | TREH-no/leh-o-fo-REE-o |
| Please | Παρακαλώ | pah-rah-kah-LO | Ferry | Πλοίο | PLEE-o |
| Thank you | Ευχαριστώ | ef-hah-ree-STO | Station | Σταθμός | stath-MOS |
| Hello/Goodbye | Γειά σας | YAH-sas | Airport | Αεροδρόμιο | ah-e-ro-DHRO-mee-o |
| Sorry/Excuse me | Συγνόμη | sig-NO-mee | Taxi | Ταξί | tahk-SEE |
| Help! | Βοήθειά! | vo-EE-thee-ah | Hotel/Hostel | Ξενοδοχείο | kse-no-dho-HEE-o |
| I'm lost. | Έχω χαθεί. | EH-o ha-THEE | Rooms to let | Δωμάτια | do-MA-tee-ah |
| Police | Αστυνομία | as-tee-no-MEE-a | Bathroom | Τουαλέττα | tou-ah-LET-ta |
| Embassy | Πρεσβεία | prez-VEE-ah | Open/Closed | Ανοικτό/Κλειστό | ah-nee-KTO/klee-STO |
| Passport | Διαβατήριο | dhee-ah-vah-TEE-ree-o | Left/Right | Αριστερά/Δεξία | aris-teh-RA/de-XIA |
| Doctor | Γιατρός | yah-TROSE | Bank | Τράπεζα | TRAH-peh-zah |
| Pharmacy | Φαρμακείο | fahr-mah-KEE-o | Exchange | Ανταλλάσσω | an-da-LAS-so |
| Post Office | Ταχυδρομείο | ta-hi-dhro-MEE-o | Market | Αγορά | ah-go-RAH |

| ENGLISH | GREEK | PRONOUNCE |
|---------|-------|-----------|
| Where is...? | Που είναι...? | poo-EE-neh |
| How much does this cost? | Πόσο κάνει? | PO-so KAH-nee |
| Do you have (a vacant room)? | Μηπώς έχετε (ελέυθερα δωμάτια)? | mee-POSE EK-he-teh (e-LEF-the-ra dho-MA-tee-a) |
| I would like... | Θα ήθελα... | thah EE-the-lah |
| Do you speak English? | Μιλατε αγγλικά? | mee-LAH-teh ahn-glee-KAH |
| I don't speak Greek. | Δεν μιλαώ ελληνικά. | dthen mee-LOW el-lee-nee-KAH |

# ITALIAN

In many Italian words, stress falls on the next-to-last syllable. When stress falls on the last syllable, accents indicate where stress falls: *città* (cheet-TAH) or *perchè* (pair-KAY). Stress can fall on the first syllable, but this occurs less often.

| ENGLISH | ITALIAN | PRONOUNCE | ENGLISH | ITALIAN | PRONOUNCE |
|---------|---------|-----------|---------|---------|-----------|
| Yes/No | Sì/No | see/no | Departure | La partenza | lah par-TEN-zuh |
| Please | Per favore/Per piacere | pehr fah-VOH-reh/pehr pyah-CHAY-reh | One-way | Solo andata | SO-lo ahn-DAH-tah |
| Thank you | Grazie | GRAHT-see-yeh | Round-trip | Andata e ritorno | ahn-DAH-tah eh ree-TOHR-noh |
| Hello (informal/formal) | Ciao/Buongiorno | chow/bwohn-JOHR-noh | Reservation | La prenotazione | lah pray-no-taht-see-YOH-neh |

| ENGLISH | ITALIAN | PRONOUNCE | ENGLISH | ITALIAN | PRONOUNCE |
|---------|---------|-----------|---------|---------|-----------|
| Goodbye | Arrivederci/ Arrivederla | ah-ree-veh-DEHR-chee/ah-ree-veh-DAIR-lah | Ticket | Il biglietto | eel beel-YEHT-toh |
| Sorry/ Excuse me | Mi dispiace/ Scusi | mee dees-PYAH-cheh/SKOO-zee | Train/Bus | Il treno/l'auto-bus | eel TRAY-no/aow-toh-BOOS |
| Help! | Aiuto! | ah-YOO-toh | Station | La stazione | lah staht-see-YOH-neh |
| Police | La Polizia | lah po-leet-ZEE-ah | Airport | L'aeroporto | LAYR-o-PORT-o |
| Embassy | L'Ambasciata | lahm-bah-shee-AH-tah | Taxi | Il tassì | eel tahs-SEE |
| Passport | Il passaporto | eel pahs-sah-POHR-toh | Ferry | Il traghetto | eel tra-GHEHT-toh |
| Hotel/Hostel | L'albergo | lal-BEHR-go | Bank | La banca | lah bahn-KAH |
| Single room | Una camera singola | OO-nah CAH-meh-rah SEEN-goh-lah | Exchange | Il cambio | eel CAHM-bee-oh |
| Double room | Una camera doppia | OO-nah CAH-meh-rah DOH-pee-yah | Grocery | Gli alimentari | lee ah-lee-mehn-TA-ree |
| With shower | Con doccia | kohn DOH-cha | Pharmacy | La farmacia | lah far-mah-SEE-ah |
| Bathroom | Un gabinetto/ Un bagno | oon gah-bee-NEHT-toh/oon BAHN-yoh | Tourist office | L'Azienda Pro-mozione Turis-tica | lah-tzee-EHN-da pro-mo-tzee-O-nay tur-EES-tee-kah |
| Open/Closed | Aperto/Chiuso | ah-PAIR-toh/ KYOO-zoh | Doctor | Il Medico | eel MEH-dee-koh |
| Left/Right | La sinistra/La destra | lah see-NEE-strah/DEH-strah | Vegetarian | Vegetariano | ve-ge-tar-ee-AN-o |
| Straight | Sempre diritto | SEHM-pray DREET-toh | Kosher/Halal | Kasher/Halal | KA-sher/HA-lal |
| Turn | Gira a | JEE-rah ah | Nuts/Milk | La noce/Il latte | lah NO-cheh/eel LA-teh |

| ENGLISH | ITALIAN | PRONOUNCE |
|---------|---------|-----------|
| Where is...? | Dov'è...? | doh-VEH |
| How do I get to...? | Come si arriva a...? | KOH-meh see ahr-REE-vah ah |
| How much does this cost? | Quanto costa? | KWAN-toh CO-stah |
| Do you have...? | Hai...? | hi |
| Do you speak English? | Parla inglese? | PAHR-lah een-GLEH-zeh |
| I'd like... | Vorrei... | VOH-ray |
| I'm allergic to... | Ho delle allergie... | oh DEHL-leh ahl-lair-JEE-eh |

# PORTUGUESE

Vowels with a *til* (ã, õ, etc.) or before "m" or "n" are pronounced with a nasal twang. At the end of a word, "o" is pronounced "oo" as in "room," and "e" is sometimes silent. "S" is pronounced "sh" or "zh" when it occurs before another consonant. "Ch" and "x" are pronounced "sh"; "j" and "g" (before e or i) are pronounced "zh." The combinations "nh" and "lh" are pronounced "ny" and "ly" respectively.

| ENGLISH | PORTUGUESE | PRONOUNCE | ENGLISH | PORTUGUESE | PRONOUNCE |
|---|---|---|---|---|---|
| Hello | Olá/Oi | oh-LAH/oy | Hotel | Pousada | poh-ZAH-dah |
| Please | Por favor | pohr fah-VOHR | Bathroom | Banheiro | bahn-yey-roo |
| Thank you (m/f) | Obrigado/Obrigada | oh-bree-GAH-doo/dah | Open/Closed | Aberto/Fechado | ah-BEHR-toh/feh-CHAH-do |
| Sorry/Excuse me | Desculpe | dish-KOOL-peh | Doctor | Médico | MEH-dee-koo |
| Yes/No | Sim/Não | seem/now | Pharmacy | Farmácia | far-MAH-see-ah |
| Goodbye | Adeus | ah-DAY-oosh | Left/Right | Esquerda/Direita | esh-KER-dah/dee-REH-tah |
| Help! | Socorro! | soh-KOO-roh | Bank | Banco | BAHN-koh |
| I'm lost. (m/f) | Estou perdido/perdida. | ish-TOW per-DEE-doo/dah | Exchange | Câmbio | CAHM-bee-yoo |
| Ticket | Bilhete | beel-YEHT | Market | Mercado | mer-KAH-doo |
| Train/Bus | Comboio/Autocarro | kom-BOY-yoo/OW-to-KAH-roo | Police | Polícia | po-LEE-see-ah |
| Station | Estação | eh-stah-SAO | Embassy | Embaixada | ehm-bai-SHAH-dah |
| Airport | Aeroporto | aye-ro-POR-too | Post Office | Correio | coh-REH-yoh |

| ENGLISH | PORTUGUESE | PRONOUNCE |
|---|---|---|
| Do you speak English? | Fala inglês? | FAH-lah een-GLEYSH |
| Where is...? | Onde é...? | OHN-deh eh |
| How much does this cost? | Quanto custa? | KWAHN-too KOOSH-tah |
| Do you have rooms available? | Tem quartos disponíveis? | teng KWAHR-toosh dish-po-NEE-veysh |
| I want/would like... | Eu quero/gostaria de... | eh-oo KER-oh/gost-ar-EE-ah day |
| I don't speak Portuguese. | Não falo Português | now FAH-loo por-too-GEZH |
| I cannot eat... | Não posso comer... | now POH-soo coh-MEHR |
| Another round, please. | Mais uma rodada, por favor. | maish OO-mah roh-DAH-dah pohr fah-VOHR |

# SPANISH

| ENGLISH | SPANISH | PRONOUNCE | ENGLISH | SPANISH | PRONOUNCE |
|---|---|---|---|---|---|
| Hello | Hola | O-lah | Hotel/Hostel | Hotel/Hostal | oh-TEL/ohs-TAHL |
| Please | Por favor | pohr fah-VOHR | Bathroom | Baño | BAHN-yoh |
| Thank you | Gracias | GRAH-see-ahs | Open/Closed | Abierto(a)/Cerrado(a) | ah-bee-EHR-toh/sehr-RAH-doh |
| Sorry/Excuse me | Perdón | pehr-DOHN | Doctor | Médico | MEH-dee-koh |
| Yes/No | Sí/No | see/no | Pharmacy | Farmacia | far-MAH-see-ah |
| Goodbye | Adiós | ah-DYOYS | Left/Right | Izquierda/Derecha | ihz-kee-EHR-da/deh-REH-chah |
| Help! | ¡Ayuda! | ay-YOOH-dah | Bank | Banco | BAHN-koh |
| I'm lost. | Estoy perdido (a). | ess-TOY pehr-DEE-doh (dah) | Exchange | Cambio | CAHM-bee-oh |
| Ticket | Boleto | boh-LEH-toh | Grocery | Supermercado | soo-pehr-mer-KAH-doh |
| Train/Bus | Tren/Autobús | trehn/ow-toh-BOOS | Police | Policía | poh-lee-SEE-ah |
| Station | Estación | es-tah-SYOHN | Embassy | Embajada | em-bah-HA-dah |
| Airport | Aeropuerto | ay-roh-PWER-toh | Post Office | Oficina de correos | oh-fee-SEE-nah deh coh-REH-ohs |

APPENDIX

| ENGLISH | SPANISH | PRONOUNCE |
|---|---|---|
| Do you speak English? | ¿Habla inglés? | AH-blah een-GLEHS? |
| Where is...? | ¿Dónde está...? | DOHN-deh eh-STA? |
| How much does this cost? | ¿Cuánto cuesta...? | KWAN-toh KWEHS-tah...? |
| Do you have rooms available? | ¿Tiene habitaciones libres? | tee-YEH-neh ah-bee-tah-see-YOH-nehs LEE-brehs? |
| I want/ would like... | Quiero/Me gustaría... | kee-YEH-roh/meh goos-tah-REE-ah |
| I don't speak Spanish. | No hablo español. | no AH-bloh ehs-pahn-YOHL |
| I cannot eat... | No puedo comer... | no PWEH-doh coh-MEHR... |

# WEATHER

| City | JANUARY | | | APRIL | | | JULY | | | OCTOBER | | |
|---|---|---|---|---|---|---|---|---|---|---|---|---|
| | High (F/C) | Low (F/C) | Rain (in.) | High (F/C) | Low (F/C) | Rain (in.) | High (F/C) | Low (F/C) | Rain (in.) | High (F/C) | Low (F/C) | Rain (in.) |
| Amsterdam | 40/4 | 31/-1 | 2.7 | 55/13 | 38/3 | 2.1 | 71/22 | 53/12 | 3 | 58/14 | 44/7 | 2.9 |
| Athens | 56/13 | 44/7 | 1.8 | 66/19 | 53/12 | 1.0 | 88/31 | 73/23 | 0.2 | 73/22 | 59/15 | 1.9 |
| Berlin | 35/2 | 26/-3 | 1.7 | 55/13 | 39/4 | 1.7 | 73/23 | 55/13 | 2.1 | 55/13 | 42/6 | 1.4 |
| Copenhagen | 37/2 | 30/-1 | 1.7 | 49/9 | 36/2 | 1.6 | 69/20 | 55/12 | 2.6 | 53/11 | 44/6 | 2.1 |
| Dublin | 46/8 | 37/3 | 2.7 | 53/12 | 40/4 | 2.0 | 66/19 | 53/12 | 2.0 | 57/14 | 46/8 | 2.8 |
| London | 44/7 | 32/0 | 3.1 | 54/12 | 38/3 | 2.1 | 71/22 | 52/11 | 1.8 | 59/15 | 43/6 | 2.9 |
| Madrid | 51/10 | 32/0 | 1.8 | 63/17 | 42/5 | 1.8 | 90/32 | 61/16 | 0.4 | 68/20 | 47/8 | 1.8 |
| Paris | 43/6 | 34/1 | 2.2 | 57/13 | 42/5 | 1.7 | 75/23 | 58/14 | 2.3 | 59/15 | 46/7 | 2.0 |
| Rome | 55/13 | 38/3 | 3.2 | 64/18 | 46/8 | 2.2 | 83/28 | 64/18 | 0.6 | 71/22 | 53/12 | 3.7 |
| Vienna | 36/2 | 27/-3 | 1.5 | 57/14 | 41/5 | 2.0 | 77/25 | 59/15 | 2.5 | 57/14 | 43/6 | 1.6 |

# INDEX

## A

Aachen, GER 441
Aalborg, DEN 253
Aalsmeer, NTH 777
Aberfoyle, BRI 225
accommodations
  bed & breakfasts 30
  camping 33
  guesthouses 30
  home exchange 32
  hostels 29
  hotels 30
  long-term 32
  private rooms 30
  university dorms 30
Aeolian Islands, ITA 726
Ærø, DEN 251
Agios Nikolaos, GCE 541
airplane travel 41
Aix-en-Provence, FRA 357
Ajaccio, FRA 374
alcohol 20
Alfonso XIII 846
Algarve, POR 820–821
Alghero, ITA 728
Alicante, SPA 887
Allinge, DEN 249
Alsace-Lorraine, FRA 317–324
Amalfi Coast, ITA 723
Amalfi, ITA 723
Ambleside, BRI 200
Amboise, FRA 300
American Red Cross 23
Amsterdam, NTH 752–777
Ancona, ITA 712
Andalucía, SPA 865–887
Andechs Monastery and Brewery, GER 472
Angers, FRA 302
Annecy, FRA 334
Antibes, FRA 371
Antwerp, BEL 119, 120
apartment rental. See long-term accommodations.
**Appendix** 1051–1058
  language phrasebook 1051

weather 1058
Aquitaine, FRA 340–343
Arahova, GCE 527
Aran Islands, IRE 587
Arcos de la Frontera, SPA 877
The Ardennes, LUX 741
Århus, DEN 251
Arles, FRA 360
Arnhem, NTH 786
Assisi, ITA 710
Astorga, SPA 863
Athens, GCE 501–512
ATMs 15
Atrani, ITA 723
au pair work 59
**Austria** 62–101
  Dachstein Ice Caves 92
  Euro Cup 2008 85
  Franz-Josefs-Höhe 95
  Graz 100
  Hallstatt 91
  Heiligenblut 94
  Hohe Tauern National Park 94
  Innsbruck 95
  Kitzbühel 99
  Krimml 94
  Salzburg 85
  Salzburger Land and Hohe Tauern Region 85
  Schloß Ambras 98
  Styria 100
  Tyrol 95
  Vienna 70
  Zell am See 92
Avebury, BRI 171
Aveiro, POR 818
Avignon, FRA 358
Azay-le-Rideau, FRA 301

## B

Bacharach, GER 451
backpacks 34
Bakewell, BRI 192
Balearic Islands, SPA 926–929
Balestrand, NOR 997
Barcelona, SPA 891–909
bargaining 18

Basel, SWI 955
Basque Country, SPA 916–924
Bastia, FRA 376
Batalha, POR 820
Bath, BRI 172
Bavaria, GER 460–479
Bay of Naples, ITA 721
Bayeux, FRA 309
Bayonne, FRA 342
Beaune, FRA 316
Belfast, BRI 591–601
**Belgium** 102–125
  Antwerp 119
  Bruges 115
  Brussels 108
  Dinant 124
  Flanders 115
  Ghent 120
  Han-sur-Lesse 125
  Liège 123
  Mechelen 114
  Namur 124
  Rochefort 125
  Tournai 123
  Wallonie 123
  Ypres 122
Ben Nevis, BRI 227
Berchtesgaden National Park, GER 472
Berchtesgaden, GER 472
Bergamo, ITA 654
Berlin, GER 390–421
Bern, SWI 937
Bernese Oberland, SWI 937–941
Besançon, FRA 322
**Beyond Tourism** 54–60
  au pair work 59
  community development 55
  conservation 55
  humanitarian and social services 56
  language schools 57
  long-term work 58
  short-term work 60
  studying abroad 56
  teaching English 59
  volunteering 54
Biarritz, FRA 341
Bilbao, SPA 921

INDEX

# GET CONNECTED & SAVE WITH THE HI CARD

An HI card gives you access to friendly and affordable accommodations at over 4,000 hostels in over 60 countries, including across Europe. Members also receive complementary travel insurance, members-only airfare deals, and thousands of discounts on everything from tours and dining to shopping, communications and transportation.

Join millions of HI members worldwide who save money and have more fun every time they travel.

**Hostelling International USA**

# MAP INDEX

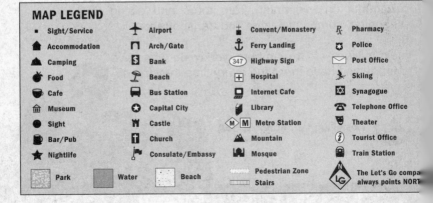

## MAP LEGEND

| | | | |
|---|---|---|---|
| ■ Sight/Service | ✈ Airport | ♱ Convent/Monastery | ℞ Pharmacy |
| 🏠 Accommodation | ⊓ Arch/Gate | ⚓ Ferry Landing | ✚ Police |
| ▲ Camping | $ Bank | (347) Highway Sign | ✉ Post Office |
| 🍴 Food | 🏖 Beach | ✚ Hospital | 🎿 Skiing |
| ☕ Cafe | 🚌 Bus Station | 💻 Internet Cafe | ✡ Synagogue |
| 🏛 Museum | ★ Capital City | 📖 Library | ☎ Telephone Office |
| ● Sight | ♜ Castle | Ⓜ Ⓜ Metro Station | 🎭 Theater |
| 🍺 Bar/Pub | ✝ Church | ⛰ Mountain | ⓘ Tourist Office |
| ★ Nightlife | 🚩 Consulate/Embassy | 🕌 Mosque | 🚂 Train Station |
| Park | Water | Beach | Pedestrian Zone |
| | | | Stairs |
| | | | The Let's Go compa[ss] always points NORT[H] |